Glencoe Earth Science
Contents in Brief

Teacher Wraparound Edition

Student Edition

W9-CHU-678

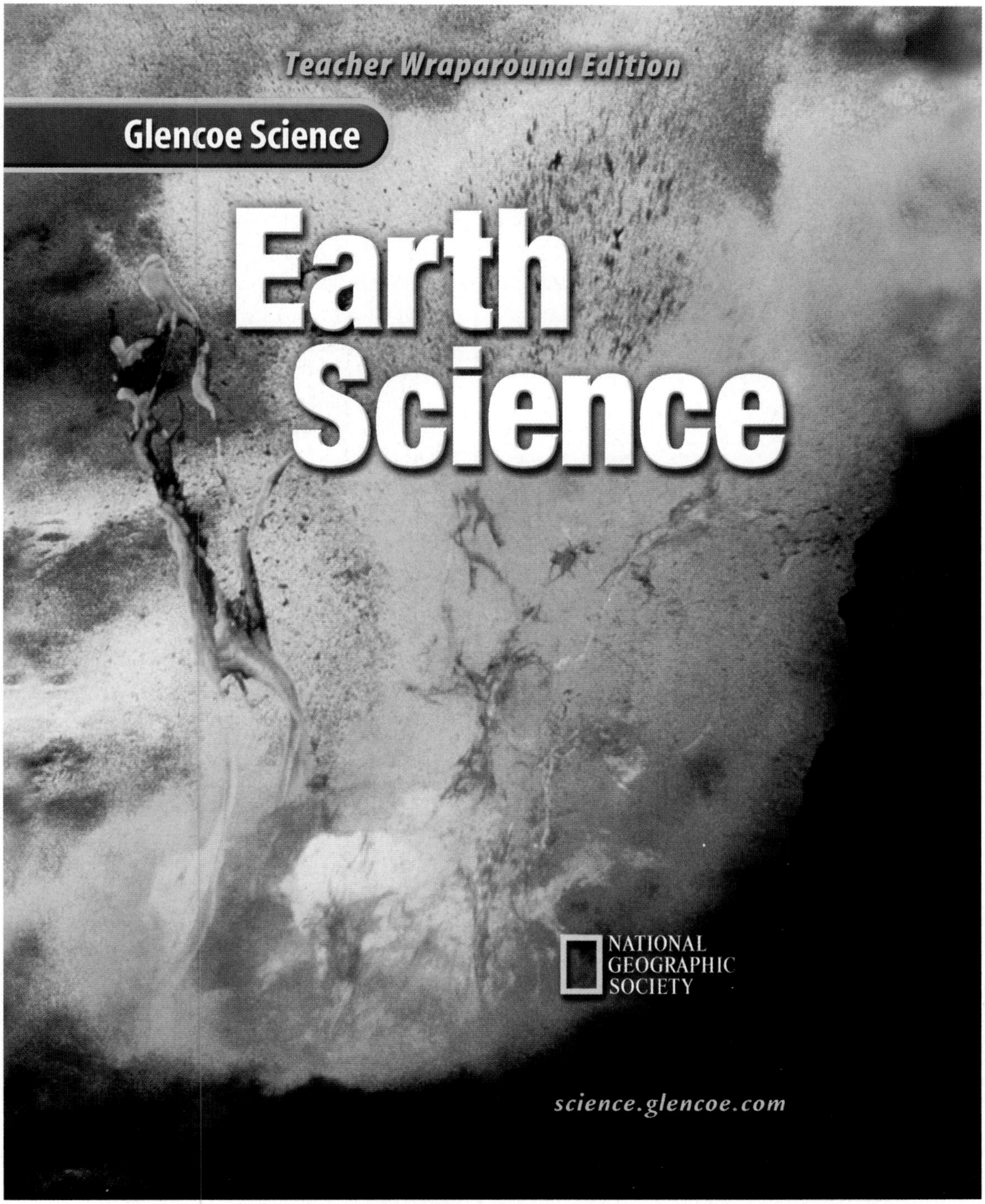

Teacher Wraparound Edition

Glencoe Science

Earth Science

NATIONAL
GEOGRAPHIC
SOCIETY

science.glencoe.com

Glencoe
McGraw-Hill

New York, New York   Columbus, Ohio   Woodland Hills, California   Peoria, Illinois

GLENCOE EARTH SCIENCE

Student Edition
Teacher Wraparound Edition
Interactive Teacher Edition CD-ROM
Interactive Lesson Planner CD-ROM
Lesson Plans
Content Outline for Teaching
    Directed Reading for Content Mastery
    Foldables: Reading and Study Skills
Assessment
    Chapter Review
    Chapter Tests
    ExamView Pro Test Bank Software
    Assessment Transparencies
    Performance Assessment in the Science Classroom
    The Princeton Review Test Practice Booklet
Spanish Directed Reading for Content Mastery
Spanish Resources
Reinforcement
Enrichment

Activity Worksheets
Section Focus Transparencies
Teaching Transparencies
Laboratory Activities
Science Inquiry Labs
Critical Thinking/Problem Solving
Reading and Writing Skill Activities
Mathematics Skill Activities
Cultural Diversity
Laboratory Management and Safety
Mindjogger Videoquizzes and Teacher Guide
Interactive Explorations and Quizzes CD-ROM
    with Presentation Builder
Vocabulary Puzzlemaker Software
Cooperative Learning
Environmental Issues in the Science Classroom
Home and Community Involvement
Using the Internet in the Science Classroom
Dinah Zike's Teaching Science with Foldables

THE PRINCETON REVIEW

"Test-Taking Tip," "Study Tip," and Test practice features in this book were written by The Princeton Review, the nation's leader in test preparation. Through its association with McGraw-Hill, The Princeton Review offers the best way to help students excel on standardized assessments.

The Princeton Review is not affiliated with Princeton University or Educational Testing Service.

Glencoe/McGraw-Hill

A Division of The McGraw·Hill Companies

Send all inquiries to:

    Glencoe/McGraw-Hill
    8787 Orion Place
    Columbus, OH 43420

ISBN 0-07-823719-X

Printed in the United States of America

1 2 3 4 5 6 7 8 9 10 071/043 10 09 08 07 06 05 04 03 02 01

Authors, Reviewers, and Consultants

for the *Teacher Wraparound Edition*

Authors

Ralph M. Feather Jr., PhD
Science Department Chair
Earth Science Teacher
Derry Area School District
Derry, Pennsylvania

Susan Leach Snyder
Earth Science Teacher, Consultant
Jones Middle School
Upper Arlington, Ohio

Dinah Zike
Educational Consultant
Dinah-Might Activities, Inc.
San Antonio, Texas

Reviewer

Gilbert Naizer, PhD
Assistant Professor of Elementary Education
Texas A&M University
Commerce, Texas

Cultural Diversity Consultants

Nedaro Bellamy
Associate Director,
    Rice Model Science Laboratory
Lanier Middle School, Houston ISD
Houston, Texas

Joyce Hilliard-Clark, PhD
Director, Imhotep Academy
North Carolina State University
Raleigh, North Carolina

Inclusion Strategies Consultant

Barry Barto
Special Education Teacher
John F. Kennedy Elementary School
Manistee, Michigan

National Science Education Standards

About the Standards

This book, published by the National Research Council, represents the contributions of thousands of educators and scientists, and offers a comprehensive vision of a scientifically literate society. The standards describe what all students should know at the end of grades 4, 8, and 12, and offer guidelines for science teaching and assessment.

How *Glencoe Earth Science* Aligns with *The National Science Education Standards*

Content Standards
The correlations that follow show the close alignment between *Glencoe Earth Science* and the grade-appropriate standards. *Glencoe Earth Science* allows students to discover concepts within each of the content standards and gives students opportunities to make connections among the science disciplines. Hands-on activities and inquiry-based lessons reinforce the science processes emphasized in the standards.

Teaching Standards
Glencoe Earth Science provides activities and discussions that allow students to discover science concepts through inquiry and to apply the knowledge they've constructed to their own lives. The *Teacher Wraparound Edition* supports this endeavor with an abundance of effective strategies for guiding students of different ability levels and interests as they explore science.

Assessment Standards
Glencoe Earth Science provides many opportunities in many different formats to assess students' understanding of important concepts. Ideas for portfolios, performance activities, and written assessments accompany every section. Glencoe's Professional Series booklet *Performance Assessment in the Science Classroom* contains rubrics and Performance Task Assessment Lists. This booklet also contains information about evaluating cooperative work. Learning outcomes improve for students of all ability levels in a cooperative learning environment.

Correlation to **National Science Education Standards**

The following chart illustrates how *Glencoe Earth Science* addresses the
National Science Education Standards.

Content Standard	Chapter and Section
(UCP) Unifying Concepts and Processes	
1. Systems, order, and organization	2-1, 2-3, 3-1, 4-1, 4-2, 4-3, 4-4, 9-1, 9-2, 9-3, 16-1, 16-2, 16-3, 17-3, 19-1, 19-3, 24-2, 24-3, 24-4, 25-3
2. Evidence, models, and explanation	1-1, 1-2, 5-1, 6-3, 8-1, 8-2, 8-3, 10-1, 10-2, 10-3, 11-1, 11-2, 11-3, 13-1, 13-2, 14-1, 14-2, 14-3, 15-1, 16-3, 17-3, 18-2, 19-2, 22-1, 22-2, 22-3, 23-1, 23-2, 23-3, 24-1, 25-1, 25-4
3. Change, constancy, and measurement	1-1, 1-2, 2-2, 4-1, 5-2, 5-3, 6-2, 10-1, 10-2, 10-3, 12-1, 12-2, 12-3, 13-3, 14-1, 14-2, 14-3, 15-2, 15-3, 16-2, 17-1, 17-3, 18-3, 20-1, 20-2, 20-3, 21-1, 21-2
4. Evolution and equilibrium	7-1, 7-2, 7-3, 14-1, 14-2, 14-3, 17-2, 18-1, 25-3
5. Form and function	3-2, 3-3, 4-1, 6-1, 25-2
(A) Science as Inquiry	
1. Abilities necessary to do scientific inquiry	1-1, 1-2, 2-1, 2-2, 2-3, 3-1, 3-2, 3-3, 4-1, 4-2, 4-3, 4-4, 5-1, 5-3, 6-1, 6-2, 6-3, 7-1, 7-2, 7-3, 8-1, 8-2, 8-3, 9-1, 9-2, 9-3, 10-1, 10-2, 10-3, 11-2, 11-3, 12-1, 12-2, 12-3, 13-1, 13-2, 13-3, 14-2, 14-3, 15-1, 15-2, 15-3, 16-1, 16-3, 17-1, 17-3, 18-2, 18-3, 19-1, 19-2, 19-3, 20-2, 20-3, 21-1, 21-2, 22-1, 22-2, 22-3, 23-1, 23-2, 23-3, 24-1, 24-2, 24-3, 24-4, 25-1, 25-3, 25-4
2. Understandings about scientific inquiry	1-1, 1-2, 10-1, 10-3, 14-1, 16-3, 17-3
(B) Physical Science	
1. Properties and changes of properties in matter	2-1, 2-2, 12-2, 12-3, 13-3, 18-2, 18-3, 25-3
2. Motions and forces	5-1, 5-2, 11-1, 11-2, 11-3, 15-3, 18-2, 18-3, 24-2
3. Transfer of energy	2-3, 11-1, 11-2, 11-3, 15-2, 25-2
(C) Life Science	
1. Structure and function in living systems	17-2, 19-2
2. Reproduction and heredity	14-1
3. Regulation and behavior	19-2
4. Populations and ecosystems	17-4, 19-2, 21-1, 21-2
5. Diversity and adaptations of organisms	13-1, 14-1, 14-2, 14-3, 17-5, 19-2, 20-1, 20-2, 20-3
(D) Earth and Space Science	
1. Structure of the Earth system	3-1, 3-2, 3-3, 4-1, 4-2, 4-3, 4-4, 5-1, 5-2, 5-3, 6-1, 6-2, 6-3, 7-1, 7-2, 7-3, 8-1, 8-2, 8-3, 9-1, 9-2, 9-3, 10-1, 10-2, 10-3, 11-1, 11-2, 11-3, 12-1, 12-2, 12-3, 15-1, 15-2, 15-3, 17-1, 17-2, 17-3, 18-1, 18-2, 18-3, 19-1, 19-3
2. Earth's history	8-2, 10-1, 10-2, 10-3, 13-1, 13-2, 13-3, 14-1, 14-2, 14-3, 16-1, 16-2, 16-3, 18-1
3. Earth in the solar system	15-1, 18-3, 22-1, 22-2, 22-3, 23-1, 23-2, 23-3, 24-1, 24-2, 24-3, 24-4, 25-1, 25-2, 25-3, 25-4
(E) Science and Technology	
1. Abilities of technological design	1-1, 1-2, 5-1, 5-2, 16-3, 23-3
2. Understandings about science and technology	1-1, 1-2, 5-1, 5-2, 6-3, 7-3, 8-1, 16-1, 16-3, 18-3
(F) Science in Personal and Social Perspectives	
1. Personal Health	5-1, 9-2, 11-3, 21-1
2. Populations, resources, and environments	3-3, 5-2, 5-3, 7-3, 19-1, 19-3, 20-1, 20-2, 20-3, 21-1, 21-2
3. Natural hazards	8-1, 11-3, 12-1, 12-2, 16-1, 16-2, 21-2
4. Risks and benefits	5-1, 5-2, 5-3, 8-3, 19-3, 21-1, 21-2
5. Science and technology in society	1-1, 1-2, 3-3, 4-4, 5-1, 5-2, 5-3, 6-2, 6-3, 9-3, 11-3, 16-3, 19-3, 20-3, 21-1, 21-2, 22-2, 22-3
(G) History and Nature of Science	
1. Science as a human endeavor	1-1, 1-2, 5-3, 7-3, 10-1, 10-2, 10-3, 13-3, 15-3, 16-3, 18-3, 19-3, 21-2, 22-2, 23-3
2. Nature of science	1-1, 1-2, 2-3, 5-3, 11-3, 12-3, 13-3, 19-3, 24-4
3. History of science	1-1, 1-2, 3-3, 6-3, 10-1, 10-2, 10-3, 14-1, 17-3, 18-3, 21-2, 23-3

National Council of Teachers of Mathematics
Principles and Standards for School Mathematics

Students often make personal, educational, and career choices on their own that can influence the rest of their lives. Throughout their school years, they acquire skills that help them make these decisions. The development of keen mathematical skills can ensure that students have a wide variety of life options.

Principles and Standards for School Mathematics of the National Council of Teachers of Mathematics describes the foundation of mathematical concepts and applications that can provide students with the necessary mathematical skills to help achieve their life goals.

The ten categories of mathematical concepts and applications, as shown in the table below, include a broad range of topics that build on previous knowledge. They also allow students to increase their abilities to visualize, describe, and analyze situations in mathematical terms.

In *Glencoe Earth Science,* each Math Skill Activity and Problem-Solving Activity provides students with the opportunity to practice and apply some of the mathematical concepts and applications described in the Standards. These activities serve to reinforce mathematical skills in real-life situations, thus, preparing students to meet their needs in an ever-changing world.

Correlation of
Glencoe Earth Science to NCTM Standards Grades 6–8

Standard	Page
1. Number and Operations	47, 70, 108, 140, 171, 194, 253, 321, 350, 386, 417, 438, 465, 494, 530, 552, 612, 712, 738
2. Algebra	47, 108, 194, 253, 321, 350, 386, 417, 465, 530, 552, 612, 712
3. Geometry	648
4. Measurement	47, 530
5. Data Analysis and Probability	21, 70, 140, 194, 225, 438, 494, 552, 591, 612, 738
6. Problem Solving	21, 70, 108, 140, 171, 194, 225, 253, 286, 350, 386, 438, 465, 494, 530, 591, 612, 685, 738
7. Reasoning and Proof	21, 140, 225, 286, 350, 685
8. Communication	21, 70, 140, 171, 225, 286, 350, 386, 417, 438, 494, 591, 685, 738
9. Connections	21, 47, 70, 108, 140, 171, 194, 225, 253, 286, 321, 350, 386, 417, 438, 465, 494, 530, 552, 591, 612, 648, 685, 712, 738
10. Representation	21, 70, 140, 171, 194, 225, 286, 438, 648, 738

Benchmarks for Science Literacy

Benchmarks for Science Literacy is a publication by the American Association for the Advancement of Science that describes how students should progress toward science literacy. People who are science literate are "equipped with knowledge and skills they need to make sense of how the world works, to think critically and independently, and to lead interesting, responsible, and productive lives in a culture increasingly shaped by science and technology."

Benchmarks was the culmination of Project 2061, the work of scientists, mathematicians, engineers, and educators to develop benchmarks, or statements, of what *all* students should know or be able to do in science, mathematics, and technology by the end of grades 2, 5, 8, and 12.

Glencoe Earth Science is aligned with *Benchmarks* in the following ways:

- Concepts are presented in ways that help students understand the how and why of science, not just requiring them to learn facts that they commit to short-term memory.

- Science concepts are related to students' daily experiences.

- Teachers are provided strategies for encouraging students in independent work and for addressing the needs of students of varied abilities.

- Specific strategies are provided for identifying and addressing student misconceptions.

IDENTIFYING Misconceptions

Educators are becoming increasingly aware of the importance of identifying and addressing misconceptions—prescientific or naïve ideas—that students may hold about science. Students often develop these from their experiences as a way to make sense of the world.

A one-page feature, Identifying Misconceptions, is found on the F interleaf pages preceding selected chapters in the *Teacher Wraparound Edition*. This feature provides specific teaching strategies to find out what students think about a particular concept, to help them understand the concept, and to assess the accuracy of their understanding after learning the concept.

Correlation to **Benchmarks**

Glencoe Earth Science addresses many of the Benchmarks for Science Literacy.

Benchmark	Chapter(s)
4 The Physical Setting	
4A. The Universe	22, 23, 24, 25
4B. The Earth	2, 3, 4, 5, 6, 10, 11, 12, 15, 16, 17, 18, 19
4C. Processes That Shape the Earth	4, 7, 8, 9, 10, 11, 12, 16, 18, 20, 21
4D. Structure of Matter	2, 3, 4, 5
4E. Energy Transformation	5, 10, 15, 25
4F. Motion	10, 11, 12, 15, 24
4G. Forces of Nature	10, 11, 12, 24
5 The Living Environment	
5A. Diversity of Life	13, 14, 19
5D. Interdependence of Life	13, 14, 19
5E. Flow of Matter and Energy	13, 14, 19
5F. Evolution of Life	13, 14
8 The Designed World	
8C. Energy Sources and Use	5, 20, 21
9 The Mathematical World	
9A. Numbers	All Math Skills and Problem-Solving Activities
9B. Symbolic Relationships	All Math Skills and Problem-Solving Activities
9E. Reasoning	All Math Skills and Problem-Solving Activities
10 Historical Perspectives	
10A. Displacing the Earth from the Center of the Universe	22, 23, 24, 25
10B. Uniting the Heavens and Earth	10, 13, 23, 24, 25
10E. Moving the Continents	10, 13, 14
12 Habits of Mind	
12A. Values and Attitudes	1, All "Oops, Accidents in Science!," "Science and History," and "Science and Language Arts" features.
12B. Computation and Estimation	All Chapters 1–25
12D. Communication Skills	All Activities and Skill Builders

Planning Your Course

Glencoe Earth Science is a flexible program that allows you to decide the pace at which you cover the content and which topics to present, based on the needs of your students and on district requirements. The *Glencoe Interactive Lesson Planner* integrates the *Teacher Classroom Resources* with an electronic lesson planner to make your job easier.

Pacing Options

Two approaches to covering all content are provided in the Planning Guide.

- A **traditional, full-year** course comprises 180 periods of approximately 45 minutes each.
- A **block scheduling** approach involves covering the same information in fewer days but in longer class periods.

Chapter Organizers

A two-page organizer (A–B pages) precedes every chapter in the teacher edition. These organizers include:

- pacing information and objectives.
- correlations to standards.
- lists of activities and the materials needed.
- lists of reproducible resources, assessments, and technologies with page or booklet references.

Interactive Lesson Planner

This easy-to-use CD-ROM allows you to:

- plan daily, weekly, monthly, or yearlong lessons in a versatile calendar format.
- select or customize a built-in plan, or make a new plan.
- print lesson plans.
- access all print components of the *Teacher Classroom Resources* through a convenient pop-up menu.

- print student pages and answer keys from the resource list or from the lesson plan.

Unit	Chapter	Single-Class (180 days*)	Block (90 days*)
1	**Earth Materials**		
	1 The Nature of Science	5	2.5
	2 Matter	7	3.5
	3 Minerals	6	3
	4 Rocks	9	4.5
	5 Earth's Energy and Mineral Resources	6	3
2	**The Changing Surface of Earth**		
	6 Views of Earth	7	3.5
	7 Weathering and Soil	6	3
	8 Erosional Forces	6	3
	9 Water Erosion and Deposition	7	3.5
3	**Earth's Internal Processes**		
	10 Plate Tectonics	8	4
	11 Earthquakes	7	3.5
	12 Volcanoes	7	3.5
4	**Change and Earth's History**		
	13 Clues to Earth's Past	7	3.5
	14 Geologic Time	8	4
5	**Earth's Air and Water**		
	15 Atmosphere	7	3.5
	16 Weather	7	3.5
	17 Climate	8	4
	18 Ocean Motion	7	3.5
	19 Oceanography	8	4
6	**You and the Environment**		
	20 Our Impact on Land	7	3.5
	21 Our Impact on Water and Air	7	3.5
7	**Astronomy**		
	22 Exploring Space	7	3.5
	23 The Sun-Earth-Moon System	8	4
	24 The Solar System	9	4.5
	25 Stars and Galaxies	9	4.5

The suggested number of days are the recommended maximum number of days needed to thoroughly cover a chapter. Individual planning will vary.

Student Edition Features

This table will help you choose from many options that will help you teach the chapter.

Program Resources

Feature	Location and Suggestions For Use
Design Your Own Experiment	• Find near end of chapter where concept is taught. • Promote inquiry learning through open-ended activities. • Reinforce understanding of scientific methods.
Use the Internet	• Find near end of chapter where concept is taught. • Strengthen skills in collecting, organizing, and sharing data. • Integrate the Internet into your class easily.
Model and Invent	• Find near end of chapter where concept is taught. • Reinforce the use of models to represent relationships or abstract ideas, and to predict outcomes. • Strengthen investigative skills.
Other Full-Length Activities	• Find near end of chapter where concept is taught. • Strengthen lab skills. • Reinforce understanding of science process.
Mini LAB / **TRY AT HOME Mini LAB**	• Find in every chapter. • Do as a demonstration. • Involve parents in the student's learning. • Reinforce that science is not restricted to the classroom.
EXPLORE ACTIVITY	• Find at beginning of each chapter. • Stimulate curiosity for the topic and focus students' attention.
Problem-Solving Skills / **Math Skills Activity**	• Find one in every chapter at the point where the concept is taught. • Use after reading or other work to strengthen critical thinking and math skills.
SCIENCE Online	• Find in every chapter. • Focus students' Internet time with predetermined links.

Feature	Location and Suggestions For Use
Skill Builders	• Find at the end of every Section Assessment. • Assign as homework or class work.
FOLDABLES Reading & Study Skills	• Find on every Chapter Opener and Chapter Study Guide. • Provide a purpose for reading with these fun, simple, hands-on activities. • Encourage students to use as a study tool for review of chapter content.
Interdisciplinary Connections **Oops! Accidents in Science** **Science and Language Arts** **ScienceStats** **TIME** **Science & History** **TIME** **Science & Society**	• Find one of these five features in every chapter. • Stimulate students' interest by studying science-related events that are out of the ordinary. • Advance reading and writing skills through literature connected to science. • Show students the fun side of mathematics and how it is an integral part of science. • Illustrate how scientific phenomena, discoveries, and inventions shape history. • Connect science to people's everyday lives.
NATIONAL GEOGRAPHIC **Visualizing**	• Find in every chapter. • Use the discussion and activities to teach science content.
Career Connection	• Find in every Science & Language Arts feature. • Point out that people of all ages, ethnicities, and training work in science.
Field GUIDE	• Find in the back of the student text. • Promote interest and independent study. • Teach students how to use a classification key.
Science, Technology, and Math Skill Handbooks	• Find at the back of the student and teacher editions. • Use to teach students scientific processes. • Use to teach students how to organize information. • Refer students to handbooks for assistance.

Teacher Wraparound Edition Features

This table will help you locate features of the *Teacher Wraparound Edition* that will help you develop your lesson plans.

Component	Where and How Many	What It Provides
Teacher to Teacher	Every Unit Opener	Teaching tip that relates to teaching unit content or activities.
Chapter Organizer	A and B pages preceding every chapter	• Objectives • Occurrence of activities and other features within each section • List of materials needed for each activity • List of materials from the *Teachers Classroom Resources* box • List of technology resources
Science Content Background	In every chapter on E page and F page where an Identifying Misconceptions feature does not appear	• Helps you prepare for the lesson by giving you more information about each section • Assists you with questions the students might ask
IDENTIFYING Misconceptions	F page of some chapters	Strategies to • determine misconceptions students may hold • promote understanding of concept • assess understanding
Key to Teaching Strategies	B page preceding every chapter	Coding to assist in planning for individual needs
Three-Step Teaching Cycle 1 Motivate 2 Teach 3 Assess	Every chapter	• Help for a first-year teacher • Help for experienced teacher in the first year in a new program
Resource Manager	C and D pages of every chapter Every two pages throughout each chapter	**C and D pages:** • List of transparencies • List of chapter teacher resources **Throughout chapter:** • List of reproducible resources • List of technology resources
Activity	Throughout all chapters in side wrap	Reinforces science concepts

Program Resources

Component	Where and How Many	What It Provides
Quick Demo	Throughout all chapters in side wrap	Idea to illustrate a concept; performed in a short amount of time, using available materials
LAB DEMONSTRATION	Throughout all chapters in bottom wrap	Teacher-performed activity, more complex than Quick Demo, often involving students
Extension	Throughout all chapters in side wrap	An activity idea for: • more advanced students • students who finish their work early • students who want to learn more about the topic
Teacher FYI	Throughout all chapters in side wrap	Additional information about a concept
Visual Learning	Throughout all chapters in side and bottom wrap	Idea for discussion or activity related to a graphic
Fun Fact	Throughout all chapters in side and bottom wrap	Interesting science content to share with students
Make a Model	Throughout all chapters in side wrap	Idea for model that students can make to clarify or illustrate abstract concepts
Use an Analogy	Throughout all chapters in side wrap	Way to make abstract concepts more concrete
Curriculum Connection	Throughout all chapters in bottom wrap	Way that science ties in with other curricular areas
Cultural Diversity	Throughout all chapters in bottom wrap	Current or historical background on a custom or belief associated with a science concept
Use Science Words	Throughout all chapters in side wrap	Strategies for students to learn word origins, meanings, and uses
Active Reading Strategies	Throughout all chapters in bottom wrap	Strategies to help students read and understand content
Science Journal	Throughout all chapters in bottom wrap	Writing exercises that promote writing and critical thinking skills
✔ *Assessment*		
Section Assessment	First page of every section	• Location of Portfolio, Performance, and Content Assessments in the section
Chapter Assessment	Chapter Assessment page	• Ideas for Portfolio and Performance Assessments
Assessment Resources	Chapter Assessment page	• List of Reproducible Masters, CD-ROMs, and other technologies for assessment

Technology Resources

Online Science

The Glencoe Science Web site is an invaluable resource for all teachers and students.

Teachers can:

- share ideas on Teacher Bulletin Board.
- access current scientific information on your textbooks updates.

Students can:

- access previewed web links.
- record information on printable Internet log worksheets.
- review chapter content with the Interactive Tutor.
- prepare for tests using Interactive Quizzes.
- share data with students worldwide using our exclusive Internet Activities.

Interactive Explorations, Quizzes, and Presentation CD-ROM Program

Provides students the opportunity to:

- develop hypotheses.
- manipulate variables.
- build presentations.
- review content.
- think critically.

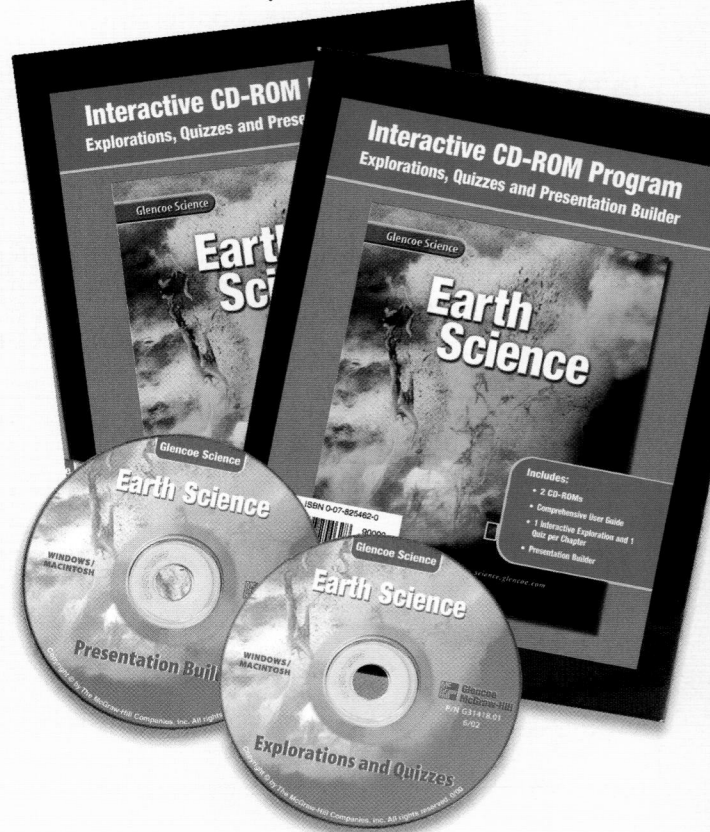

ExamView Pro Computer TestMaker Software

You can design and create your own test instruments in minutes, using Glencoe Earth Science ExamView Pro Testmaker software. This versatile program allows you to create paper tests as well as tests that can be used on your school LAN system, or posted on your class Web site. Choose and edit questions from a question bank, or write your own.

Interactive Lesson Planner

Need help planning your lessons and organizing you resources? Glencoe's Interactive Lesson Planner is the perfect solution. All you need to do is to identify your length of course and number of class days and the program automatically places all the materials available for each day for each chapter into the calendar. Every page of your Teacher Classroom Resources are available to you at the click of a mouse.

Guided Reading Audio Program
English/Spanish

MindJogger
Videoquizzes

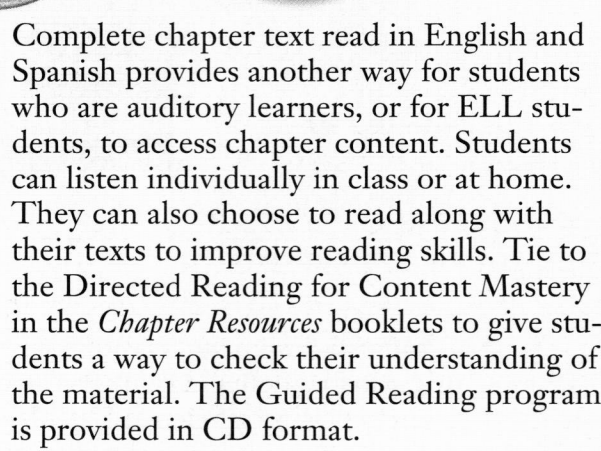

Complete chapter text read in English and Spanish provides another way for students who are auditory learners, or for ELL students, to access chapter content. Students can listen individually in class or at home. They can also choose to read along with their texts to improve reading skills. Tie to the Directed Reading for Content Mastery in the *Chapter Resources* booklets to give students a way to check their understanding of the material. The Guided Reading program is provided in CD format.

The interactive quiz-show format of the Glencoe Earth Science Mindjogger Videoquizzes provides fun for your students while reviewing key concepts for every chapter. The three levels of increasing difficulty add to the drama and excitement of the game, and help you assess your students' understanding of the concepts.

Interactive **Teacher Edition**

Imagine having your entire Teacher Edition and all your Teacher Classroom Resources available to you on one CD-ROM. That is what the Interactive Teacher Edition provides for you. The program allows you to view all teacher material and the student text on your computer screen. You can export all worksheet masters to your own word processor for editing.

Vocabulary **PuzzleMaker** Software

This software program allows you to create crossword puzzles, jumble puzzles, or word searches in minutes to review chapter vocabulary. The puzzles can be printed or played on the computer screen.

Teacher Classroom Resources

Chapter Resources—An Easy Way to Stay Organized!

We've organized all of the materials you need for each chapter into convenient chapter-based booklets!

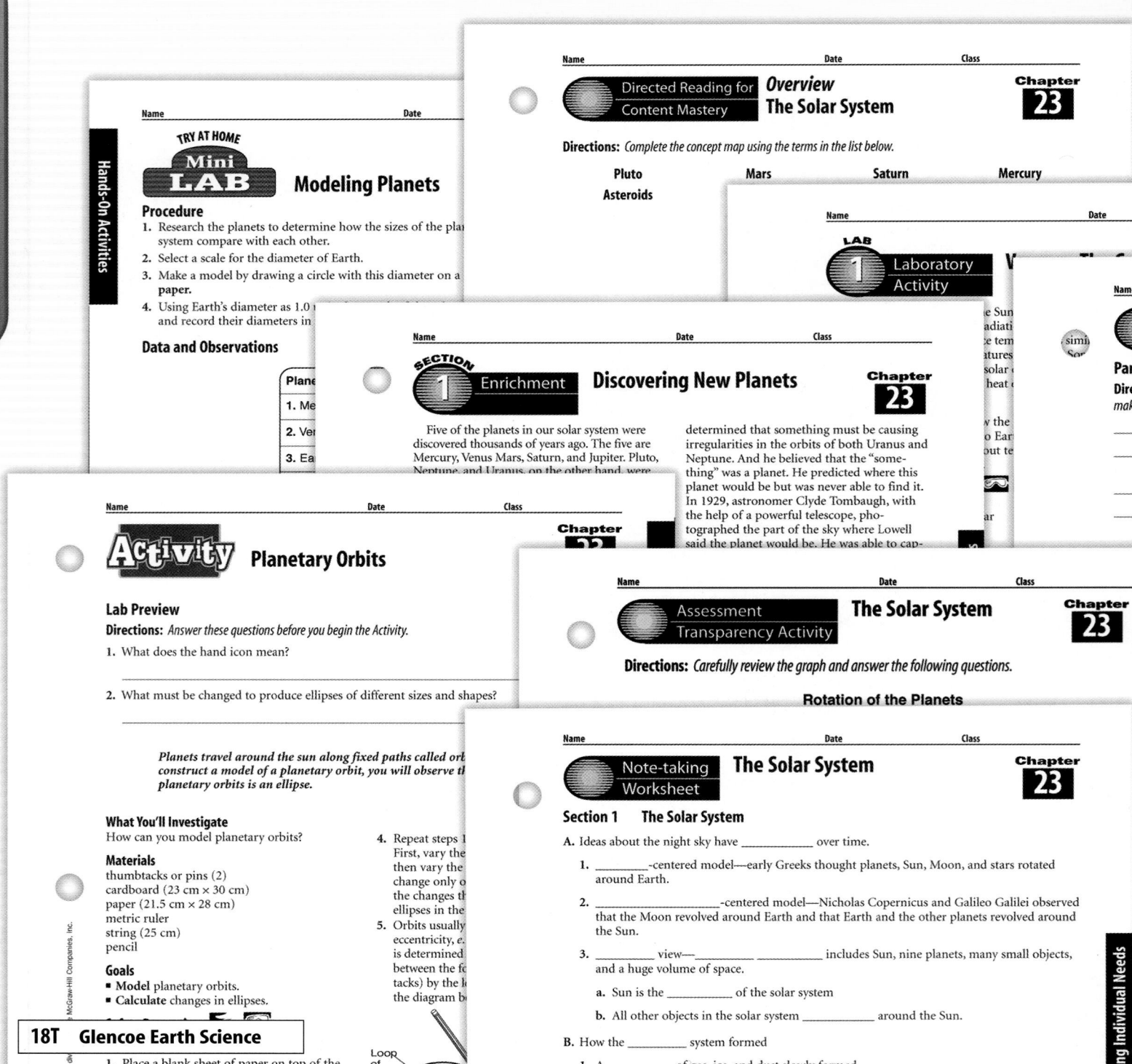

Program Resources

Hands-On Activities

Name _____ **Date** _____

TRY AT HOME
Mini LAB Modeling Planets

Procedure
1. Research the planets to determine how the sizes of the pla[nets in the solar] system compare with each other.
2. Select a scale for the diameter of Earth.
3. Make a model by drawing a circle with this diameter on a [sheet of] paper.
4. Using Earth's diameter as 1.0 [unit] and record their diameters in [the table.]

Data and Observations

Plane[t]
1. Me[rcury]
2. Ver[us]
3. Ea[rth]

Name _____ **Date** _____ **Class** _____

Directed Reading for Content Mastery **Overview The Solar System** **Chapter 23**

Directions: Complete the concept map using the terms in the list below.

Pluto	Mars	Saturn	Mercury
Asteroids			

Name _____ **Date** _____

LAB 1 Laboratory Activity

[...the Sun]
[...r]adiati[on]
[...c]e tem[per-]
[...]atures
[...]solar [...]
[...]heat [...]

Part [A]

Direct[ions]
make [...]

[simil...]
Sol...

Name _____ **Date** _____ **Class** _____

SECTION 1 Enrichment **Discovering New Planets** **Chapter 23**

Five of the planets in our solar system were discovered thousands of years ago. The five are Mercury, Venus Mars, Saturn, and Jupiter. Pluto, Neptune, and Uranus, on the other hand, were [...] determined that something must be causing irregularities in the orbits of both Uranus and Neptune. And he believed that the "something" was a planet. He predicted where this planet would be but was never able to find it. In 1929, astronomer Clyde Tombaugh, with the help of a powerful telescope, photographed the part of the sky where Lowell said the planet would be. He was able to cap-

Name _____ **Date** _____ **Class** _____

Activity **Planetary Orbits** **Chapter** 2[3]

Lab Preview
Directions: Answer these questions before you begin the Activity.

1. What does the hand icon mean?
_____

2. What must be changed to produce ellipses of different sizes and shapes?
_____

Planets travel around the sun along fixed paths called orb[its.] construct a model of a planetary orbit, you will observe th[at planetary orbits is an ellipse.

What You'll Investigate
How can you model planetary orbits?

Materials
thumbtacks or pins (2)
cardboard (23 cm × 30 cm)
paper (21.5 cm × 28 cm)
metric ruler
string (25 cm)
pencil

Goals
■ **Model** planetary orbits.
■ **Calculate** changes in ellipses.

4. Repeat steps [...] First, vary the [...] then vary the [...] change only o[...] the changes th[...] ellipses in the [...]
5. Orbits usually [...] eccentricity, e. [...] is determined [...] between the fo[...] tacks) by the l[...] the diagram b[...]

Name _____ **Date** _____ **Class** _____

Assessment Transparency Activity **The Solar System** **Chapter 23**

Directions: Carefully review the graph and answer the following questions.

Rotation of the Planets

Name _____ **Date** _____ **Class** _____

Note-taking Worksheet **The Solar System** **Chapter 23**

Section 1 The Solar System

A. Ideas about the night sky have _____ over time.
   1. _____-centered model—early Greeks thought planets, Sun, Moon, and stars rotated around Earth.
   2. _____-centered model—Nicholas Copernicus and Galileo Galilei observed that the Moon revolved around Earth and that Earth and the other planets revolved around the Sun.
   3. _____ view—_____ _____ includes Sun, nine planets, many small objects, and a huge volume of space.
      a. Sun is the _____ of the solar system
      b. All other objects in the solar system _____ around the Sun.

B. How the _____ system formed
   1. A _____ of gas, ice, and dust slowly formed

Meeting Individual Needs

© [Glencoe/]McGraw-Hill Companies, Inc.

a div[ision of The McGraw-Hill Companies, Inc.]

1. Place a blank sheet of paper on top of the

Loop of

Each **Chapter Resources** booklet contains:

Reproducible Student Pages

Assessment
- Chapter Review
- Chapter Test

Hands-On Activities
- Activity Worksheets for each activity in the *Student Edition*
- Two additional laboratory activities
- Foldables: Reading and Study Skills

Meeting Individual Needs
- Extension and Intervention
- Directed Reading for Content Mastery
- Directed Reading for Content Mastery *in Spanish*
- Reinforcement
- Enrichment
- Note-taking Worksheets

Transparency Activities
- Section Focus Activity
- Teaching Transparency Activity
- Assessment Transparency Activity

Teacher Support and Planning
- Content Outline for Teaching
- Spanish Resources
- Teacher Guide and Answers

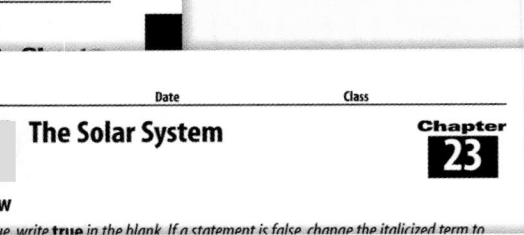

Date	Class

The Solar System

Chapter 23

iew

*true, write **true** in the blank. If a statement is false, change the italicized term to*

Name | Date | Class

FOLDABLES
Reading & Study
Skills

The Solar System

Chapter 23

Hands-On Activities

Directions: *Use this page to label your Foldable in the **Before You Read** at the beginning of the chapter.*

Compare & Contrast

Inner Planets

Outer Plar

Mars

Saturn

Earth

Venus

Neptune

Uranus

Pluto

Jupiter

Mercury

small, rocky plar

made mostly of

made mostly of

four planets clos

five planets fartl

most of these pl

most have man

Name | Date | Class

Chapter Test

The Solar System

Chapter 23

I. Testing Concepts
Directions: *For each of the following, write the letter of the term or phrase that best completes the sentence.*

_____ 1. The planet with the lowest density and hundreds of thin rings is _____.
  a. Jupiter   b. Uranus   c. Saturn   d. Neptune

_____ 2. Johannes Kepler discovered that the orbits of planets are _____.
  a. parabolic   b. circular   c. elliptical   d. spherical

_____ 3. A planet that is very hot and has sulfuric acid in its clouds is _____
  a. Mars   b. Venus   c. Mercury   d. Earth

_____ 4. The closest moon to Jupiter, _____, is volcanically active.
  a. Io   b. Callisto   c. Ganymede   d. Europa

_____ 5. _____ axis of rotation is nearly parallel to the plane of its orbit.
  a. Mars'   b. Uranus'   c. Mercury's   d. Earth's

_____ 6. Two planets with similar mass and size are _____.
  a. Mercury and Jupiter   c. Earth and Pluto
  b. Saturn and Uranus   d. Venus and Earth

_____ 7. The planet that averages 150 million km, or one AU, from the Sun is _____.
  a. Mars   b. Jupiter   c. Mercury   d. Earth

_____ 8. _____ is the largest moon in the solar system.

Additional Resources

These resources are available as stand-alone booklets to give you the flexibility to decide when to use them.

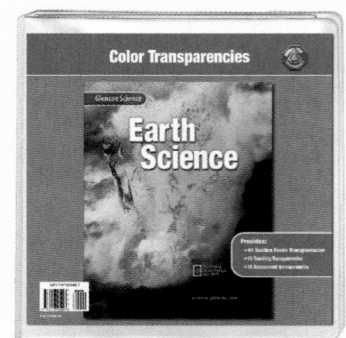

Transparencies
Section Focus Transparencies
Teaching Transparencies
Assessment Transparencies

Content Outline for Teaching

Lesson Plans

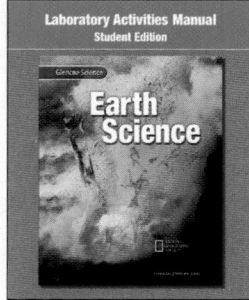

Laboratory Activities *SE*

Math Skills Activities *(SE and TE)*

Reading and Writing Skills Activities *(SE and TE)*

Science Inquiry Labs *(SE and TE)*

Standardized Test Practice *(SE and TE)*

Critical Thinking/ Problem Solving

Earth Science

Home and
Community
Involvement

Laboratory
Management
and Safety

Dinah Zike's
Teaching
Science
with
Foldables

Guide to
Using the
Internet
in the
Science
Classroom

Cooperative Learning

Cultural Diversity

Performance Assessment
in the Science Classroom

Meeting Individual Needs

Each student brings his or her unique set of abilities, perceptions, and needs into the classroom. *Glencoe Earth Science Teacher Wraparound Edition* offers you a variety of strategies so that your students can learn science concepts through many different methods.

Strategy	Designation
Ability Levels Activities are provided that accommodate students of all ability levels.	L1 Basic activities that reinforce the concepts for lower-ability students L2 Application activities that give all students an opportunity for practical application of concepts L3 Challenging activities that allow students to expand their perspectives on the basic concepts
English-Language Learners These strategies focus on overcoming a language barrier. It is important not to confuse ability in speaking/reading English with academic ability or "intelligence."	ELL These activities reinforce content and aid in the development of science vocabulary.
Learning Styles A variety of instructional strategies help students to learn science concepts through their preferred learning styles. Students generally display more than one of these styles. You may want to assign activities to students that accommodate their strongest learning styles, but assign other activities that help to develop their weaker styles.	LS Look for these bold-faced designations wherever you see this logo: • **Kinesthetic** learners learn through touch, movement, and manipulating objects. • **Visual-Spatial** learners think in terms of images, illustrations, and models. • **Logical-Mathematical** learners understand numbers easily and have highly-developed reasoning skills. • **Linguistic** learners write clearly and easily understand the written word. • **Auditory-Musical** learners remember spoken words and can create rhythms and melodies. • **Interpersonal** learners understand and work well with other people. • **Intrapersonal** learners can analyze their own strengths and weaknesses and may prefer to work on their own.

Support for All Learners

Strategy	Designation
Inclusion Strategies Inclusion strategies provide you with additional support for helping students with special needs.	Look for these bold-faced designations and strategies wherever you see the **Inclusion** Strategies • **Learning Disabled**—ideas for additional concept review • **Behaviorally Disordered**—activities for helping to keep students on task • **Physically Challenged**—tips for adjusting activities to accommodate students who have less mobility or dexterity than others • **Visually Impaired** or **Hearing Impaired**—ideas for aiding these students in grasping concepts • **Gifted**—challenging activities and research projects that extend chapter concepts
Cooperative Learning In cooperative learning, students work together in small groups to learn content and interpersonal skills. Group members learn that each is responsible for accomplishing an assigned group task as well as for learning the material. Cooperative learning fosters academic, personal, and social success for all students.	COOP LEARN Strategies with this designation are suitable for group work that will help students to: • develop positive attitudes toward science and school; • build respect for others, regardless of race, ethnic origin, or gender; and • increase their sensitivity to and tolerance of diverse perspectives.
Cultural Diversity Classrooms in the United States reflect the rich and diverse cultural heritage of the American people. Students come from different ethnic backgrounds and different cultural experiences into a common classroom that must assist all of them in learning.	**Cultural Diversity** The Cultural Diversity features provide insights into unique ways in which different people have approached science or adapted to their environments. The intent of these features is to build awareness and appreciation for the global community in which we live.
Misconceptions Students have had many experiences outside the science classroom that have shaped their understandings of the natural world. Unfortunately, interpretations based on casual observation are not always accurate. For example, based on their observations, some students might think that the Sun moves around Earth. As a science teacher, you need strategies to help replace these naive conceptions with scientific facts.	IDENTIFYING Misconceptions This one-page feature provides ideas about the types of misconceptions your students may have. It provides you with teaching strategies to uncover misconceptions and to help students understand concepts. You can find these preceding many chapters on the F interleaf pages of the Teacher Wraparound Edition. In addition, you will find several misconceptions stated, followed by the correct information, in the teacher wrap throughout each chapter.

Support for All Learners

Reading and Writing in the Content Area

Glencoe Earth Science is designed to increase science literacy through improving reading comprehension and deepening students' understanding of ideas and concepts. The reading strategies are active, constructive, and engaging.

In the Student Edition

Pre-Reading Activities on each Unit Opener prepare students to read by helping them focus on important content before reading and studying the chapter. Previewing the chapters' visuals, questions, vocabulary, and captions will set a purpose for reading the material for all students.

> ### Pre-Reading Activity
> Have students read the objectives for each section, and search for charts and pictures that relate to each objective.

Reading Checks throughout each chapter stimulate quick recall to keep students focused on main ideas and important details.

> ### ✔ Reading Check
> *Why do surface waves damage buildings?*

The Before You Read and After You Read Activities in every chapter set a purpose for reading and help students to construct a graphic organizer to use for learning content and as a study aide.

Skill Builder Activities in each Section Assessment often include questions that directly address reading and writing skills. Students are referred to the *Science Skill Handbook* for help.

> **Communicating** Many planets have more than one moon. In your Science Journal, write a description of what tides might be like if Earth had two moons. **For more help, refer to the** Science Skill Handbook.

Caption Questions throughout each chapter help students to comprehend what they have read through interpreting the visual. This is especially useful for less proficient readers.

> **Figure 18**
> A tsunami begins over the earthquake focus. *What might happen to towns located near the shore?*

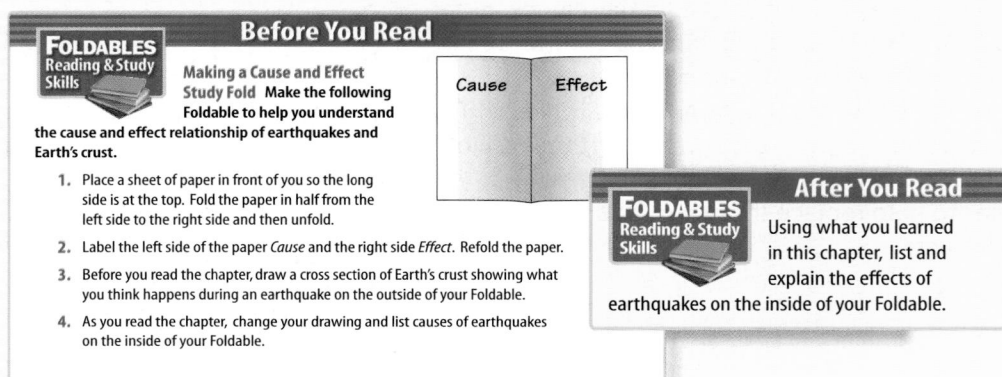

Before You Read

FOLDABLES Reading & Study Skills

Making a Cause and Effect Study Fold Make the following Foldable to help you understand the cause and effect relationship of earthquakes and Earth's crust.

Cause	Effect

1. Place a sheet of paper in front of you so the long side is at the top. Fold the paper in half from the left side to the right side and then unfold.
2. Label the left side of the paper *Cause* and the right side *Effect*. Refold the paper.
3. Before you read the chapter, draw a cross section of Earth's crust showing what you think happens during an earthquake on the outside of your Foldable.
4. As you read the chapter, change your drawing and list causes of earthquakes on the inside of your Foldable.

After You Read

FOLDABLES Reading & Study Skills

Using what you learned in this chapter, list and explain the effects of earthquakes on the inside of your Foldable.

Print and Technology Resources to Promote Reading and Writing in the Content Area

Ancillaries

Chapter Resources

- Directed Reading for Content Mastery pages *(in English and Spanish)*
- Foldables: Reading and Study Skills Worksheets
- Note-taking Worksheets

Dinah Zike's Teaching Science with Foldables

Reading and Writing Skill Activities

Technology

Guided Reading Audio Program (English and Spanish)

MindJogger VideoQuizzes

Interactive CD-ROM

Vocabulary PuzzleMaker

Glencoe Science Online

Support for All Learners

Foldables: Improving Reading and Study Skills

Students love Foldables because they're fun. Teachers love them because they're effective.

What is a Foldable?

Foldables are three-dimensional, interactive graphic organizers. As students fold paper, cut tabs, write, and manipulate what they have made, they are kinesthetically involved in learning. These unique, hands-on tools for studying and reviewing were created exclusively for Glencoe Science by teaching specialist Dinah Zike.

Foldables are Useful!

Reading in the Content Area

Foldables help students develop ways of organizing information that are fun and creative. These useful activities help students practice basic writing skills, find and report main ideas, organize information, review key vocabulary terms, and much more!

Every chapter begins with a Foldable activity. Students make the physical structure of a Foldable that incorporates one of many prereading strategies. Then, as students read through the chapter and do the activities, students record information as they learn it in the appropriate part of the foldable. In the Chapter Study Guide, the After You Read feature gives students a strategy for using the fold they made to help them review the chapter concepts.

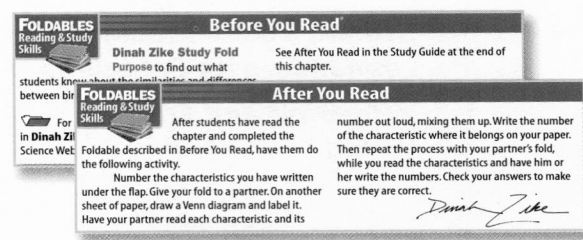

Review One advantage of Foldables is that they result in an organized study guide. The Foldables then can be used not only while preparing for the chapter test, but they can also be used for reviewing for unit tests, end of course exams, and even standardized tests.

Assessment Foldables present an ideal opportunity for you to probe the depth of your students' knowledge. You'll get detailed feedback on exactly what they know and what misconceptions they may have.

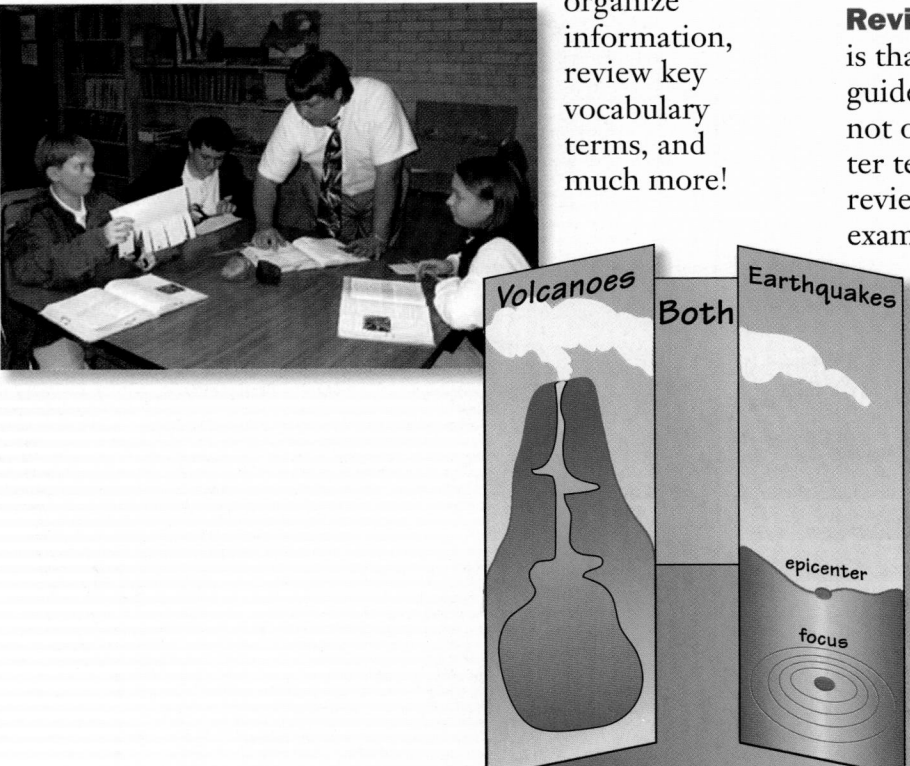

Support for All Learners

Foldables are Easy!

Anyone who has paper, scissors, and maybe a stapler or some glue can implement Foldables in the classroom. Glencoe's Foldables have been tested with teachers and middle school students to make sure the directions are easy for both students and teachers. After doing a couple of them, your class will quickly become seasoned experts. Don't be surprised if you find them inventing their own for use in projects and reports in all of their classes!

A message from **the creator of Foldables,** Dinah Zike

You might not know my name or me, but I bet you have seen at least one of my graphic organizers or folds used in supplemental programs or teacher workshops. Today, my graphic organizers and manipulatives are used internationally. I present workshops and keynote presentations to over 50,000 teachers a year, sharing the manipulatives I began inventing, designing, and adapting over thirty years ago. Around the world, students of all ages are using them as daily work, note-taking activities, student-directed projects, forms of alternative assessment, science lab journals, quantitative and qualitative observation books, graphs, tables, and more. But through all my years of teaching, designing, and publishing, my materials had never been featured in a middle school textbook. When Glencoe/McGraw-Hill approached me to share some of my three-dimensional, manipulative graphic organizers with you in this new and innovative science series, I was thrilled.

Working with Glencoe, we all had the vision that Foldables should be an integral part of the curriculum, not simply tacked on. What we ended up with was a strategy that will help students read and learn science concepts. One of the advantages of using the same manipulative repeatedly is that students are immersed in what they are learning. It is not out of sight and out of mind. How long is your average student actively involved with a duplicated activity sheet? Ten minutes? Fifteen? Students will use the Foldable at the beginning of each chapter, before reading the chapter, during reading, and after reading. That's a lot of immersion!

Dinah Zike

Reading and Writing in the Content Area

In the **Teacher Edition**

Science & Language Arts

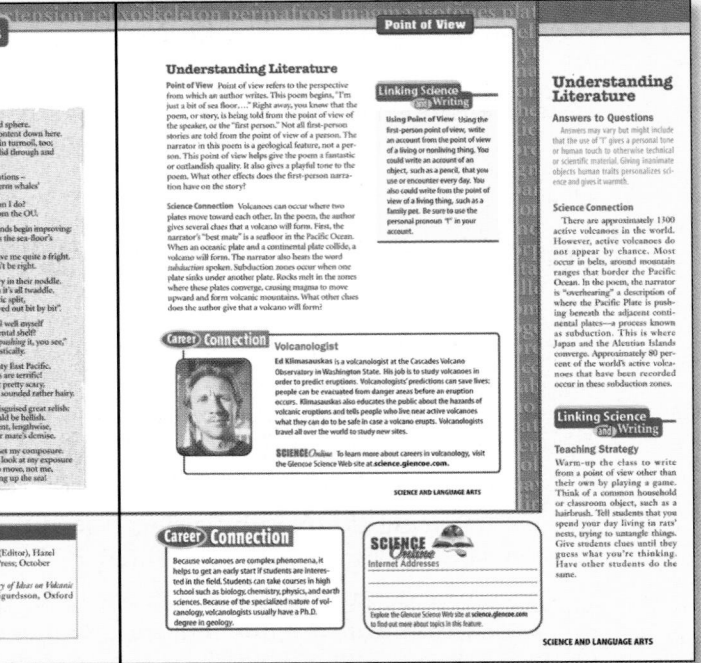

Pre-Reading Activity helps students draw upon their personal experience and sets a purpose for reading.

Respond to the Reading provides active reading strategies that provide a variety of ways for students to respond to the feature through listening, speaking, and writing activities. It also provides students with an opportunity to make connections to the theme.

Linking Science and Writing provides options that all students can use to respond in writing to the feature.

Use Science Words

Word Usage In 1802, Luke Howard classified clouds using the Latin terms *cirrus, cumulus, stratus,* and *nimbus.* Have students use a dictionary and other reference sources to find how the meanings of these words relate to cloud descriptions. *Cirrus* comes from a word meaning "hair"; *cumulus* from "heap"; *stratus* from "layer"; and *nimbus* from "rain."

Use Science Words appears throughout each chapter and provides three types of reading strategies. Students structurally analyze root words (Word Origin), develop vocabulary (Word Meaning), or apply their knowledge of science terms (Word Usage).

Science Journal

Animal Behavior Some animals react to changes in air pressure and humidity. Before a storm, birds and bats fly lower and frogs croak more frequently. Have students research and write short reports on other ways that animals react to weather changes. L2 IS **Linguistic**

Science Journals throughout each chapter provide opportunities for students to write responses to questions that require critical thinking; to conduct research and write about it; or to practice creative writing skills.

Active Reading Strategies

A variety of active reading strategies are provided throughout the *Teacher Wraparound Edition*. These strategies utilize a variety of learning styles, and encourage cooperative learning and intrapersonal reflection on chapter content.

☑ Active Reading

Think-Pair Share This strategy encourages students to think first before discussing their ideas or thoughts about a topic. Ask students to respond to a question by writing a response. After thinking for a few minutes, partners share responses to the question. Finally, ask the students to share responses with the class. Have students become involved in a Think-Pair Share about cathode rays.

Making Concept Maps and Charts

Bubble Map Students brainstorm and organize words in clusters to describe concepts.

Double-Bubble Map Students compare concepts using two bubble maps.

Flow Chart Students logically analyze and draw a sequence of events.

Cause and Effect Chart Students visually represent the causes and effects of an event or process.

Supporting Idea Chart Students make a concept map to analyze the relationship between a whole and its parts.

Using the Science Journal

Double Entry Journal Students read and record ideas, then reflect on the text and respond to the ideas.

Metacognition Students analyze what and how they have learned.

Learning Journal Students write and reflect on notes about content.

Problem-Solution Journal Students analyze problems and suggest workable solutions.

Speculation About Effects/ Prediction Journal Students examine events and speculate about their possible long-term effects.

Synthesis Journal Students reflect on a project, a paper, or a performance task and plan how to apply what they have learned to their own lives.

Reflective Journal Students identify what they learned in an activity and record responses.

Quickwrites Students use spontaneous writing to discover what they already know.

Collaborative Learning Strategies

Pair of Pairs Partners respond to a question and compare their response to that of other pairs and to the class.

Write-Draw-Discuss Students write about and draw a picture of a concept, then share it with the class.

Four-Corner Discussion The class works in four groups to debate a complex issue.

Jigsaw Students work in groups to become experts on a portion of text and share their expertise with their "home" group.

Buddy Interviews Students interview one another to find out what helps them to understand what they are reading.

Reciprocal Teaching Students take turns reading the text and retelling it in their own words, then asking one another questions.

News Summary Students are given several minutes to summarize, retell, or analyze an activity for a "TV" audience.

ReQuest The teacher reads aloud an article or story. Student pairs then construct discussion questions and review the content.

Support for All Learners

Concept Maps

Helping students understand concepts through visuals

Concept maps are visual representations or graphic organizers of relationships among particular concepts. Concept maps can be generated by individual students, small groups, or an entire class. Four types of concept maps that are most applicable to studying science are developed and reinforced in this program. Students can learn how to construct each of these types of concept maps by referring to the Skill Handbook in the ***Student Edition.***

Concept maps can be used to increase understanding of science concepts, to strengthen reading skills, to promote cooperative learning, and to assess learning. When evaluating concept maps, look for the conceptual strength of student responses, not absolute accuracy.

- **Science Concepts** Concept mapping helps students to understand science concepts through analyzing relationships among ideas and reinforcing those relationships by visualizing them.

- **Reading Skills** Concept maps can help students preview a chapter's content by visually relating the concepts to be learned and aiding students to read with purpose. Students learn key science terms by choosing the terms to use, supplying connecting words, or by placing terms and connecting words when provided by the teacher. To further develop concept mapping skills, the *Chapter Resources* booklet for each chapter contains concept maps in the reproducible student pages Directed Reading for Content Mastery.

- **Cooperative Learning** Construction of concept maps using cooperative learning strategies allows students to practice interpersonal skills as they work together to build the map.

- **Review and Assessment** As a review, constructing concept maps reinforces main ideas and clarifies their relationships. As an assessment tool, concept maps can be constructed by students or students can fill in the terms. Look for concept mapping assessment in the Chapter Assessment section of every chapter.

Support for All Learners

Network Tree
- Order information from general to specific.
- Show a hierarchy.
- Use branching procedures.
- Explain relationships with connecting terms.

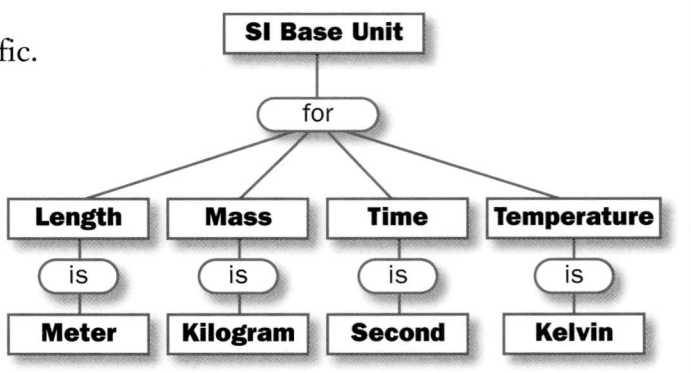

Events Chain

- Describe the stages of a process.
- Order the steps in a linear procedure.

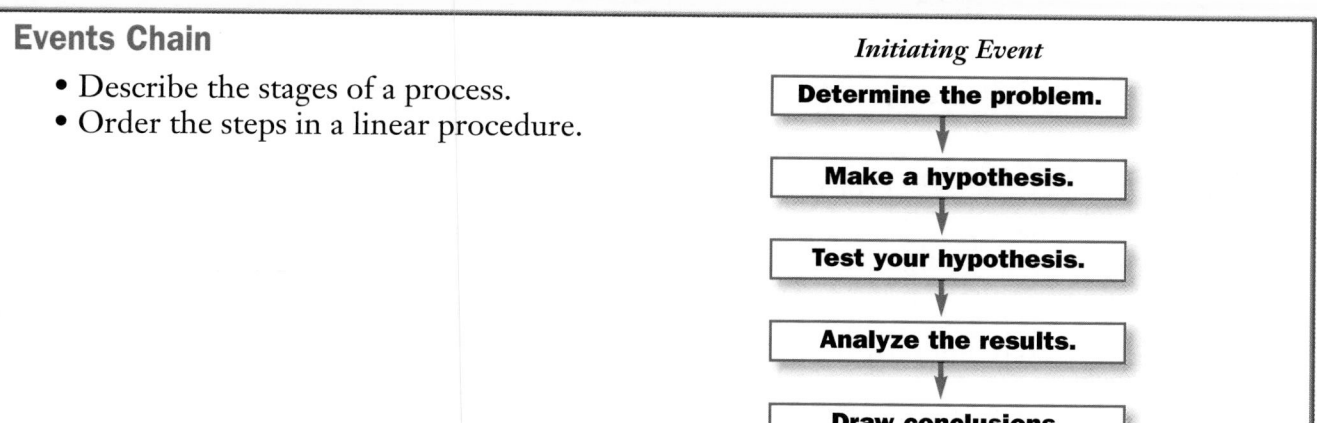

Initiating Event

| Determine the problem. |

↓

| Make a hypothesis. |

↓

| Test your hypothesis. |

↓

| Analyze the results. |

↓

| Draw conclusions. |

Cycle Concept Map

- Show how a series of events interact.
- Depict how the last event relates to the initiating event.

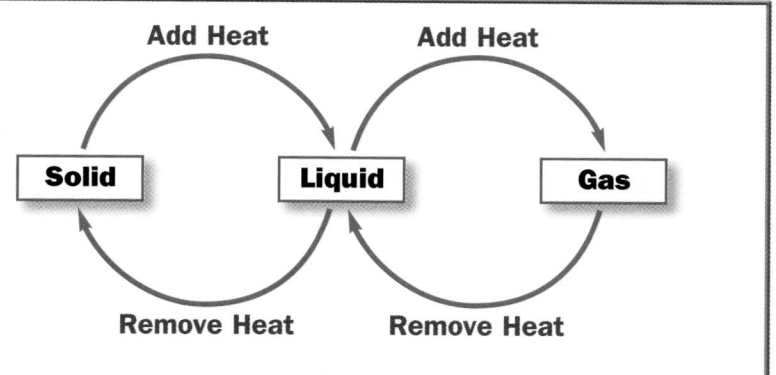

Add Heat   Add Heat

Solid   **Liquid**   **Gas**

Remove Heat   Remove Heat

Spider Concept Map

- Use for brainstorming.
- Separate and group unrelated terms.
- Show relationship of nonrelated terms to a central idea.

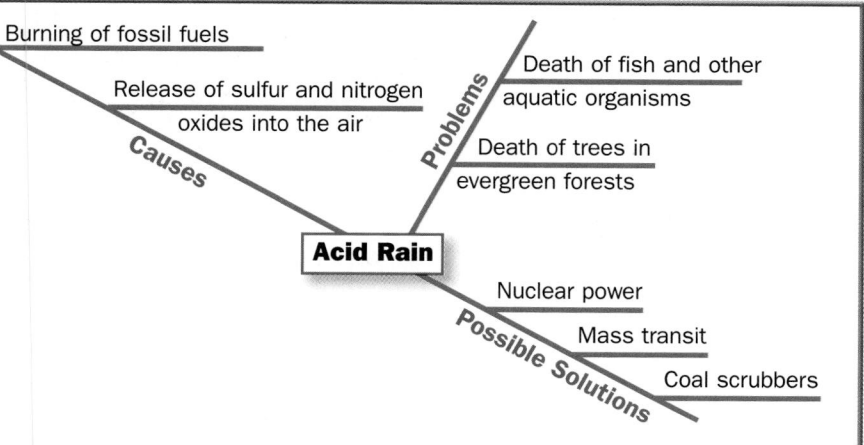

Burning of fossil fuels

Release of sulfur and nitrogen oxides into the air

Causes

Problems

Death of fish and other aquatic organisms

Death of trees in evergreen forests

Acid Rain

Possible Solutions

Nuclear power

Mass transit

Coal scrubbers

Assessment Support

Glencoe Earth Science offers the Glencoe Assessment Advantage, a system of assessment options designed to give you the flexibility and tools to conduct standardized test preparation, and content and performance assessment.

Glencoe has partnered with *The Princeton Review*, a nationally renowned company that helps students prepare for state and national tests. This partnership has resulted in the Study Tips and Test Practice questions at the end of each Chapter Assessment in the *Student Edition*. Test practice booklets help prepare students for success on standardized tests.

Content Assessment

- **Section Assessment** questions and **Skill Builder Activities** appear in every chapter of the *Student Edition*.

- A **Study Guide** at the end of each chapter in the *Student Edition* allows you to determine whether reteaching is needed.

- The **Chapter Assessment** questions in the *Student Edition* help you evaluate students' knowledge and ability to apply science concepts.

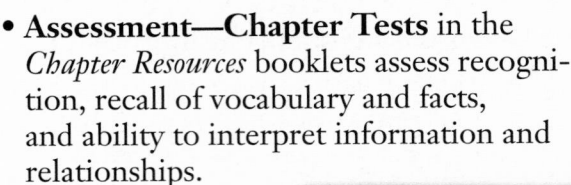

- **Assessment—Chapter Tests** in the *Chapter Resources* booklets assess recognition, recall of vocabulary and facts, and ability to interpret information and relationships.

- **MindJogger Videoquizzes** offer interactive videos that provide a fun way for your students to review chapter concepts.

- The **Interactive CD-ROM/DVD** provides quizzes that can be used as a whole-class presentation or as a review for individual students. These materials also are available on the Glencoe Science Web site.

- **ExamView Pro Test Bank Software (English/Spanish)** Software for Macintosh and Windows provides an easy way to make, edit, and print tests. You can add your own questions and graphics.

Support for All Learners

Performance Assessment

Performance Assessment refers to the strategies used to assess students' level of science literacy. Performance Assessment is based on judging the quality of a student's response to a performance task. A performance task is constructed to require the use of important concepts with supporting information, work habits important to science, and one or more of the elements of scientific literacy.

Performance Task Assessment Lists

Performance Assessments accompany **Activities** and **Chapter Assessments** in the ***Glencoe Earth Science Student Edition***. Task Assessment Lists are provided in Glencoe's *Performance Assessment in the Science Classroom*. Both the teacher and the student assess the work and assign points based on the well-defined categories and possible points for each category. These task lists were developed for the summative performance tasks included in the booklet.

Assessing Student Work with Rubrics

A rubric is a set of descriptions of the quality of a process and a product. The set of descriptions includes a continuum of quality from excellent to poor. Rubrics for various types of assessment products are provided in the Glencoe Professional Development Series booklet *Performance Assessment in the Science Classroom*. In addition to sample rubrics, blank rubric forms allow teachers to customize assessment methods. The booklet also

provides a step-by step model showing teachers how to use the materials most effectively.

Portfolios

Portfolio suggestions are featured throughout each chapter in the ***Glencoe Earth Science Teacher Wraparound Edition***. The Portfolio should help the student see the big picture of how he or she is performing in gaining knowledge and skills and how effective his or her work habits are. The performance portfolio is not a complete collection of all worksheets and other assignments but rather a collection that reflects the student's growth in concept attainment and skill development. Writings and drawings from the student's **Science Journal**, featured in the ***Student Edition*** and the ***Teacher Wraparound Edition***, often are suggested to include in portfolios.

Group Assessment

All students benefit from a cooperative learning environment. Research has shown that student-learning outcomes improve for students of all ability levels. An example, along with information about evaluating cooperative work, is provided in the booklet *Performance Assessment in the Science Classroom*.

Lab Safety

The activities in *Glencoe Earth Science* have been tested in the laboratory and have been reviewed by safety consultants. Even so, there are no guarantees against accidents. For additional help, refer to the *Laboratory Management and Safety* booklet, which contains safety guidelines and masters to test students' lab and safety skills.

General Guidelines

- Post safety guidelines, fire escape routes, and a list of emergency procedures in the classroom. Make sure students understand these procedures. Remind them at the beginning of *every* lab session.

  - Understand and make note of the Safety Symbols used in each activity.

  - Have students fill out a safety contract. Students should pledge to follow the rules, to wear safety attire, and to conduct themselves in a responsible manner.

- Know where emergency equipment is stored and how to use it.

- Supervise students at all times. Check assembly of all setups.

- Perform all activities before you allow students to do so.

- Instruct students to follow directions carefully.

- Make sure that all students are wearing proper safety attire: goggles and aprons when using chemicals, a heat source, or a hammer. They should secure long hair and loose clothing. Do not permit wearing contact lenses, even with safety glasses; splashing chemicals could infuse under a lens and cause eye damage.

Handling Chemicals

- Handle chemicals carefully at all times. Always wear safety goggles, gloves, and an apron when handling chemicals. Treat all chemicals as potentially dangerous.

- Never ingest chemicals. Use proper techniques to smell solutions.

- Use a fume hood when handling chemicals that are poisonous or corrosive or that give off a vapor.

- *Always add acids to water, never the reverse.*

- Prepare solutions by adding the solid to a small amount of distilled water and then diluting with water to the volume listed. If you use a hydrate that is different from the one specified in a particular preparation, you will need to adjust the amount of hydrate to obtain the correct concentration.

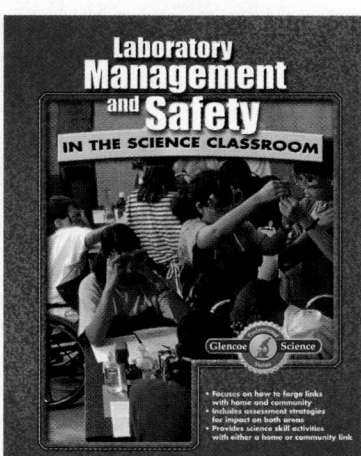

- Consider purchasing premixed solutions from a scientific supply house to reduce the amount of chemicals on hand.

- Maintain appropriate MSDS (Materials Safety Data Sheets) in the laboratory.

Classroom Activities and Materials

Chemical Storage and Disposal

The following are some commonly used guidelines for chemical storage and disposal, but your school or local government may have additional requirements for handling chemicals. It is your responsibility to be informed of the rules governing chemical storage and disposal in your area.

- Use wood shelving rather than metal. All shelving should be firmly attached to the wall and have antiroll edges.

- Store only those chemicals you intend to use. Do not store chemicals above eye level.

- Store chemicals in labeled containers that indicate the contents, concentration, source, date purchased (or prepared), safety precautions for handling, and expiration date.

- Separate chemicals by reaction type. Store acids in one place and bases in another. Oxidants should be stored away from easily oxidized materials, for example.

- Dispose of outdated or waste chemicals properly.

- Follow regulations for storing hazardous chemicals.

Disposal of Chemicals

Local, state, and federal laws regulate the disposal of chemicals. Consult these laws before attempting to dispose of any chemicals. The following resource provides some general guidelines for handling and disposing of chemicals: *Prudent Practices in the Laboratory: Handling and Disposal of Chemicals.* Washington, DC: National Academy Press, 1995. Current laws in your area supersede the information in this book.

Disclaimer

Glencoe/McGraw-Hill makes no claims to the completeness of this discussion of laboratory safety and chemical storage. The material presented is not all-inclusive, nor does it address all of the hazards associated with handling, storage, and disposal of chemicals, or with laboratory management.

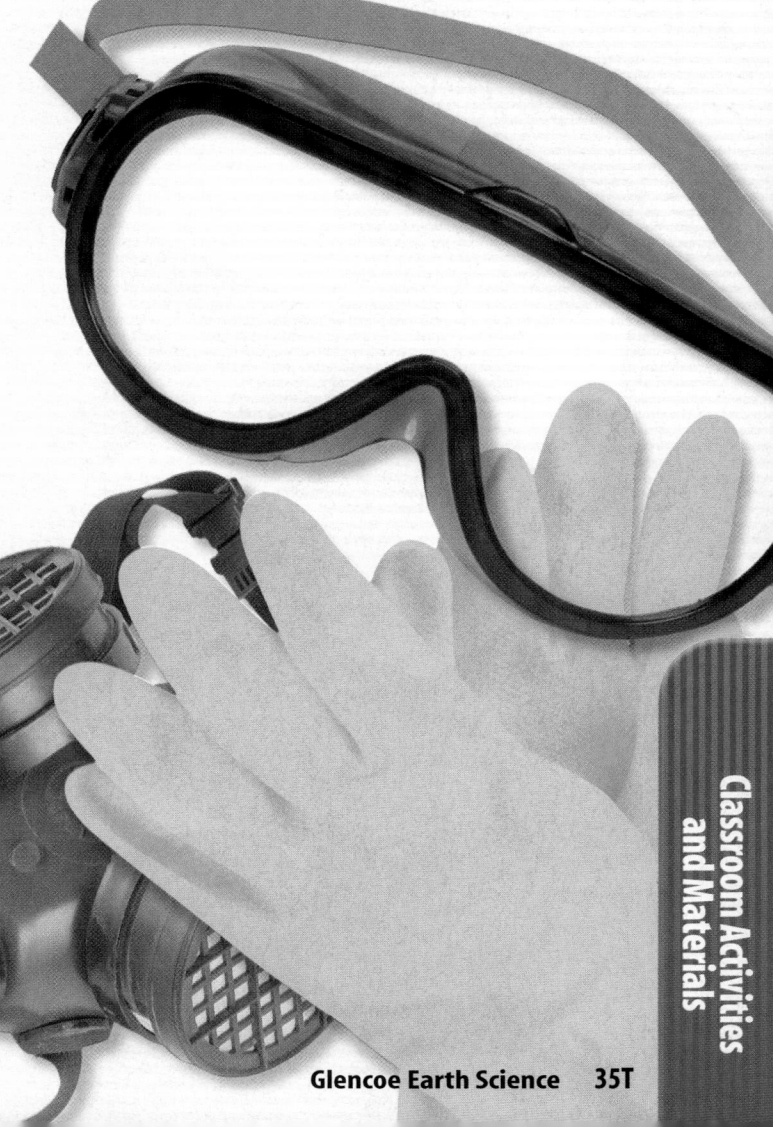

Classroom Activities and Materials

Activity Materials

Glencoe Earth Science makes it easy for you to plan and facilitate activities in your classroom.

- You'll find a variety of hands-on activities, from short to long, from directed to open-ended.
- Many activities use common, inexpensive materials.
- Activities are easy to manage, with clearly numbered steps and illustrations.
- All MiniLABS have been teacher tested.

All laboratory activities have been thoroughly reviewed by a safety expert.

All full-length labs were bench tested by Science Kit to ensure quality and safety.

It's Quick and Easy to Order

Glencoe and Science Kit, Inc., have teamed up to make materials for *Glencoe Earth Science* easier with an activity-materials folder. This folder contains two convenient ways to order materials and equipment for the program—the **Activity Plan Checklist** and the **Activity Materials List** master. Call Science Kit at 1-800-828-7777 to get your folder.

Materials Support Provided by

Science Kit® & Boreal®
Laboratories
Your Classroom Resource
777 East Park Drive
Tonawanda, NY 14151-5003
Phone: 800-828-7777
Fax 800-828-3299
www.sciencekit.com

Classroom Activities and Materials

List of Activity Materials

It is assumed that goggles, laboratory aprons, tap water, textbooks, paper, calculators, pencils, and pens are available for all activities.

Non-Consumables

Item	EXPLORE ACTIVITY Page	Mini LAB Page	Activity Chapter/Section
3-Speed electric fan			18-1
Aluminum pie pan	239		
Aquarium gravel		213	
Baking pan		213	
Baking trays			20-1
Balance		439	2-1, 2-2, 3-2, 18-2
Ball		439	
Beaker(s)	33, 521		2-2, 3-1, 6-1, 7-1, 9-2, 21-1
Bolts	701		
Bowl	367		8-2, 18-2
Box, small			12-2
Bricks		213	
Building blocks		322	
Can(s), large			17-2
Casserole dish, clear, colorless		289	
Clamp for tubing			12-2
Clock	33		18-1, 20-2
Clothespin	735		
Clothing made of artificial material			20-1
Clothing made of natural fibers			20-1
Coffee can		479	
Coffee can with lid	183		
Computer probe			7-2
Container, clear-plastic		139, 252, 621	
Cup		139	
Dish(es)		188	5-1
Dissecting probe		104	
Dowel			2-1
Dropper	119, 239, 521	338, 561	3-2, 4-2
Electric meter		127	
Fertilizer, plant			21-1
File, steel			3-2
Flashlight		493, 689	
Funnel		249	
Glass	433	139, 529	
Glass, drinking		249	
Gooseneck lamp			5-1, 18-1, 23-2
Graduated beaker		252	
Graduated cylinder			2-1, 2-2, 3-2, 7-1, 7-2, 18-2
Gravel	211	252	7-1, 8-2
Hairdryer			8-2
Hand lens	61	63, 104, 192, 226, 623	3-1, 3-2, 4-1, 4-2, 7-1, 9-1, 16-1
Hose		653	
Hot plate	33, 461	289	3-1, 7-2
Jar(s)	367, 609		17-1
Knife		278, 589	
Light bulb	639		23-2
Light source, unshaded			23-1
Magnet			9-1
Magnifying lenses			22-1
Marble(s)	701		

Activity Materials

Item	**EXPLORE ACTIVITY** Page	**Mini LAB** Page	**Activity** Chapter/Section
Metal block			2-2
Metal cake pan	701		
Metal can		464	
Metal nuts	701		
Metal pans	461		
Metal tray, large			8-1
Metal washers (5)			1-2
Microscope			21-2
Microscope slide		561	
Microscope, light		561	
Mirror, curved			22-1
Mirror, flat			22-1
Nail, iron			3-2
Overhead light source with reflector			8-1, 15-2
Paint roller pan			9-2
Pan	119	501	2-2, 3-1, 7-1, 8-2, 21-2
Paper clip(s)		278	1-2, 3-1
Pavement		679	
Ph computer probe		621	
Pins			24-1
Plastic boxes, clear (2)			15-2
Plastic lids (4)			21-2
Plastic model of a landform			6-1
Plastic storage box		529, 533	6-1, 18-1
Plastic tray, large			8-1
Plate		674	
Plate, glass			3-2
Plate, streak			3-2
Protractor		344	1-2, 3-2
Psychrometer			17-2
Rain gauge, plastic		249	
Reference-atlas	155		
Reference-classroom map	491		
Reference-globe	155, 491	418, 493	2-1, 11-1, 23-1
Reference-map of the United States		158	
Reference-Moh's scale of hardness			3-2
Reference-U.S. Geological Survey maps			6-2
Reference-world atlas	491		
Reference-world map	155	163, 418	10-2, 20-2
Ring stand			5-1, 15-2
Rock/Mineral-calcite		72	
Rock/Mineral-cobbles and pebbles	183		
Rock/Mineral-copper			3-2
Rock/Mineral-gabbro			4-1
Rock/Mineral-general samples			3-2
Rock/Mineral-granite	61		4-1
Rock/Mineral-gypsum	61	72	
Rock/Mineral-halite		72	
Rock/Mineral-mica	61		
Rock/Mineral-muscovite mica		72	
Rock/Mineral-obsidian			4-1

Non-Consumables *continued*

Item	EXPLORE ACTIVITY Page	Mini LAB Page	Activity Chapter/Section
Rock/Mineral-pumice			4-1
Rock/Mineral-quartz	61		2-2
Rock/Mineral-rhyolite			4-1
Rock/Mineral-rock			2-2
Rock/Mineral-rock fragments	89		
Rock/Mineral-rock sample			2-1
Rock/Mineral-rock, large, flat		213	
Rock/Mineral-sandstone	61, 119		
Rock/Mineral-schist	61		
Rock/Mineral-sediment samples		104	4-2
Rock/Mineral-shale	119		
Rock/Mineral-vesicular basalt			4-1
Sand	211	252, 344	6-2, 7-1, 8-1, 8-2, 9-1, 9-2
Sandpaper, medium-grained	303		
Scissors	275, 397	19	7-1, 12-2, 13-2, 16-2, 20-1, 24-2, 25-1
Screen			9-2
Sewing needle		674	
Shells	367	278	
Shoe box		19	
Shoe box lid	211		
Sink		213, 249	
Sod		226	
Soil	239	192	5-1, 7-1, 15-2, 20-1
Soup can		445, 479	
Spoon		529, 533	3-1, 21-1
Spray bottle			6-2, 20-1
Spring	549		
Sprinkling can		249	8-2
Steel nuts		653	
Steel wool		188	
Stick			2-1
Stick, flat wooden			3-1
Stiring rod		464	
Stopwatch	549		9-2
Stream table			8-1
Tape	33, 303	479, 533, 674	6-1, 8-2, 12-2, 15-2, 20-1, 23-2, 25-2
Teaspoon			18-2
Telescope, refracting			25-1
Thermal cup holder		139	
Thermal mitt(s)		289	3-1
Thermometer(s)		464	2-1, 5-1, 15-2, 17-1, 17-2, 23-2
Thermos bottle		139	
Thumbtack(s)			7-1, 24-1
Tray tables (2)		553	
Tripod, small			25-1
Tweezers	397	104	
Wallpaper trays, disposable			9-2
Watch	33		7-1, 18-1, 20-2, 23-2
Watch with second hand			1-2, 5-1
Watering can		213	
Wind sock			17-2
Wire			13-2
Wood block(s)			2-2, 8-1, 9-2

Activity Materials

Consumables *continued*

Item	EXPLORE ACTIVITY Page	Mini LAB Page	ACTIVITY Chapter/Section
Aluminum foil			5-2
Balloon	639, 735		12-2
Cardboard	433, 644		3-1, 5-2, 8-2, 13-2, 24-1, 25-1
Chalk		679	7-2, 11-1
Cheesecloth			7-1
Chenille Stems			13-2
Clay		278	2-2, 7-1, 13-2
Confetti			16-2
Construction paper	397, 445		13-2
Cork		533	2-2
Deck of playing cards			14-1
Food coloring	521, 609	289, 529	6-1
Food-apple		589	
Food-colored powdered drink mix	701		
Food-cooking oil	119		
Food-dried bread			20-2
Food-flour			12-2
Food-gelatin powder		213	
Food-jelly beans		384	
Food-olive oil		338	
Food-popcorn kernels			20-2
Food-potato, small, uncooked			18-2
Food-salt	61	63, 529	3-1, 18-2
Food-sugar		344	3-1
Food-vinegar			4-2
Food-white flour	701		
Food-white vinegar			7-2
Gelatin, plain			21-2
Glue		91	5-2, 13-2
Graph paper			5-1, 11-2, 19-1
Grass clippings			16-2
Ice	461, 521	139, 464	8-1
Modeling clay		278, 689	
Newspaper			12-2
Paper	367, 583	158, 408, 716	5-2, 12-1, 12-2, 16-2, 24-1
Paper cup, large		91	
Paper plate(s)		344	
Paper towel(s)		464, 553	4-2, 6-2
pH indicator paper		621	
Photographs from discarded magazines	275		
Plaster of Paris	367	344	13-2
Plastic coffee can lids (3)			7-1
Plastic cups		338	7-1
Plastic foam cup		674	
Plastic sheets	639		
Polystyrene ball			23-1
Polystyrene cups, large			7-1
Precipitation sample		621	
Rubber band(s)	303	322	7-1
Rubber stopper		653	
Rubber tubing (20 cm)			9-2
Sponge			2-2
String	735	653, 679	1-2, 2-1, 3-1, 11-1, 24-1, 24-2
Sunscreen, several different brands			15-1

Consumables *continued*

Item	EXPLORE ACTIVITY Page	Mini LAB Page	Activity Chapter/Section
Toothpick(s)			13-2, 20-1
Tubing, plastic			12-2
Water	33, 139, 239, 367, 433, 461, 521, 561, 609	139, 188, 213, 249, 252, 289, 338, 445, 464, 5-1, 529, 533	2-1, 2-2, 4-2, 6-1, 6-2, 7-1, 7-2, 8-2, 9-2, 18-1, 18-2, 20-1
White cloth		623	
Yarn	397		

Chemical Supplies

Item	EXPLORE ACTIVITY Page	Mini LAB Page	Activity Chapter/Section
5% hydrochloric acid			3-1, 4-2

Suppliers

Scientific Suppliers

Carolina Biological Supply Company
2700 York Road
Burlington, NC 27215
800-334-5551
www.carolina.com

Fisher Scientific Educational
485 South Frontage Road
Burr Ridge, IL 60521
800-955-1177
www.fisheredu.com

Fisher Scientific Company
4500 Turnberry Drive
Hanover Park, IL 60103
800-766-7000
www.fishersci.com

Flinn Scientific
P.O. Box 219
770 N. Raddant Road
Batavia, IL 60510
800-452-1261
www.flinnsci.com

Frey Scientific
100 Paragon Road
Mansfield, OH 44903
800-225-3739
www.freyscientific.com

Sargent-Welch/Cenco
P.O. Box 5229
911 Commerce Court
Buffalo Grove, IL 60089
800-727-4368
www.sargentwelch.com

Science Kit & Boreal Laboratories
777 East Park Drive
Tonawanda, NY 14150
800-828-7777
www.sciencekit.com

Ward's Natural Science Establishment, Inc.
P.O. Box 92912
5100 Henrietta Road
Rochester, NY 14692
800-962-2660
www.wardsci.com

Software Distributors

(AIT) Agency for Instructional Technology
Box A
Bloomington, IN 47402-0120
800-457-4509
www.ait.net

Educational Activities, Inc.
1937 Grand Avenue
Baldwin, NY 11510
800-645-3739
www.edact.com

IBM Educational Systems
Department PC
4111 Northside Parkway
Atlanta, GA 30327
800-426-4968
www.IBM.com

Microphys
12 Bridal Way
Sparta, NJ 07871
800-832-6591
www.microphys.com

Queue, Inc.
338 Commerce Drive
Fairfield, CT 06432
800-335-0906
www.queueinc.com

School Division of The Learning Company
6160 Summit Drive
Minneapolis, MN 55430
www.learningcompanyschool.com

Ventura Educational Systems
P.O. Box 425
Grover Beach, CA 93483
2782 Sevada
Arroyo, CA 93420
800-336-1022
www.venturaES.com

Audiovisual Distributors

Aims Multimedia
9710 Desoto Avenue
Chatsworth, CA 91311-4409
800-367-2467
www.amismultimedia.com

BFA Educational Media
2349 Chaffee Drive
St. Louis, MO 63146
800-221-1274
www.phoenixcoronet.com

CRM Films
2215 Faraday Avenue
Carlsbad, CA 92008
800-421-0833
www.crmfilms.com

Encyclopedia Britannica Educational Corp (EBEC)
310 S. Michigan Avenue
Chicago, IL 60604
800-554-9862 ext. 7007
www.ebec.com

Hawkill Associates, Inc.
125 E. Gilman Street
Madison, WI 53703
800-422-4295
www.hawkill.com

Lumivision
877 Federal Boulevard.
Denver, CO 80204
303-446-0400
www.lumivision.com

National Geographic School Publishing
P.O. Box 10579
De Moines, IA 50340
17th and "M" Streets, NW
Washington, DC 20009
800-368-2728
www.nationalgeographic.com\education

Time-Life Education
P.O. Box 8502
Richmond, VA 23285
800-449-2010
www.timelifeedu.com

Video Discovery
Suite 600
1700 Westlake Avenue, N
Seattle, WA 98109
800-548-3472
www.videodiscovery.com

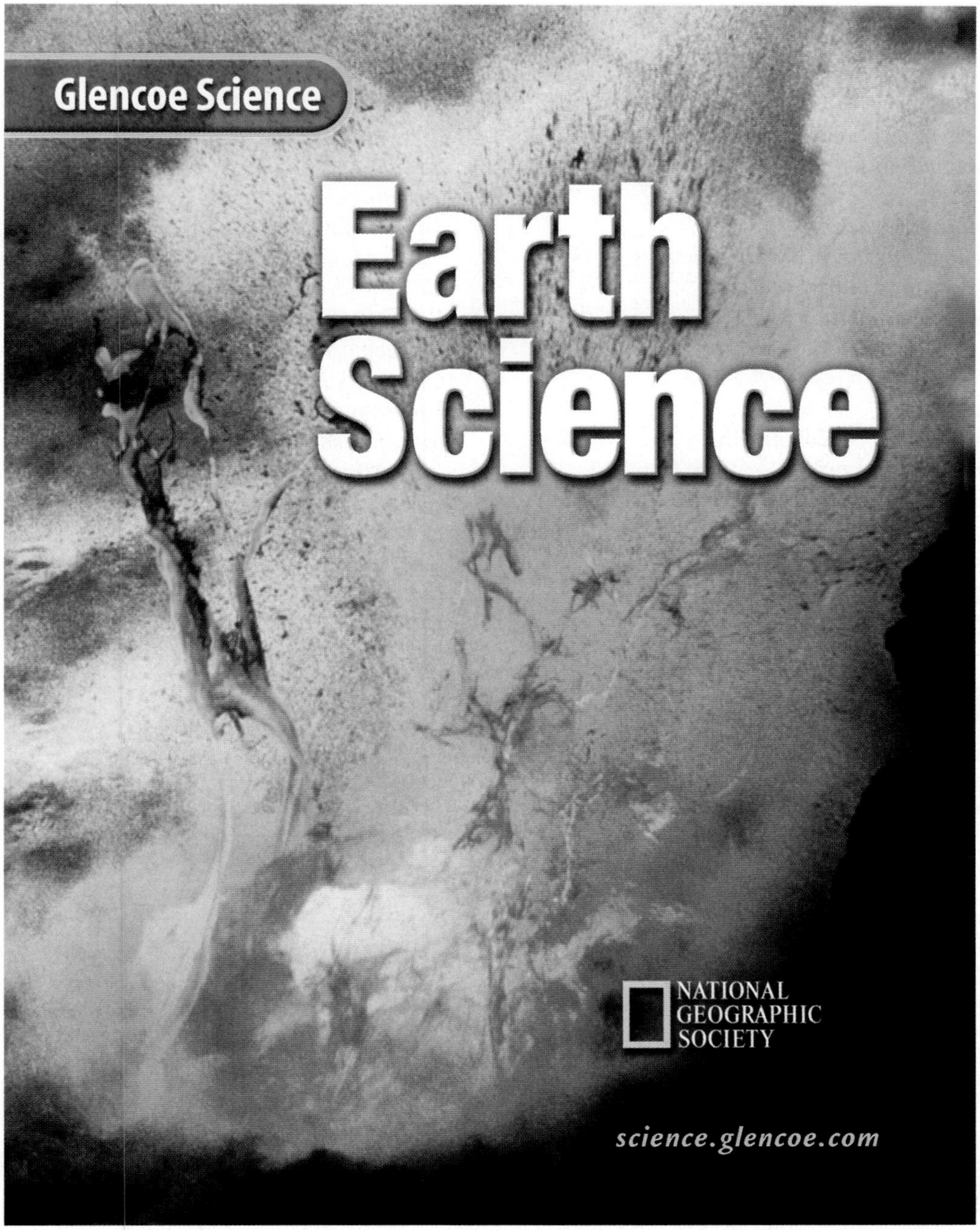

Glencoe Science

Earth Science

NATIONAL
GEOGRAPHIC
SOCIETY

science.glencoe.com

Glencoe
McGraw-Hill

New York, New York   Columbus, Ohio   Woodland Hills, California   Peoria, Illinois

Glencoe Science

Glencoe Earth Science

Student Edition
Teacher Wraparound Edition
Interactive Teacher Edition CD-ROM
Interactive Lesson Planner CD-ROM
Lesson Plans
Content Outline for Teaching
Dinah Zike's Teaching Science with Foldables
Directed Reading for Content Mastery
Foldables: Reading and Study Skills
Assessment
    Chapter Review
    Chapter Tests
    ExamView Pro Test Bank Software
    Assessment Transparencies
    Performance Assessment in the Science Classroom
    The Princeton Review Standardized Test Practice Booklet
Directed Reading for Content Mastery in Spanish
Spanish Resources
English/Spanish Audiocassettes
Guided Reading Audio Program

Reinforcement
Enrichment
Activity Worksheets
Section Focus Transparencies
Teaching Transparencies
Laboratory Activities
Science Inquiry Labs
Critical Thinking/Problem Solving
Reading and Writing Skill Activities
Mathematics Skill Activities
Cultural Diversity
Laboratory Management and Safety in the Science Classroom
Mindjogger Videoquizzes and Teacher Guide
Interactive Explorations and Quizzes CD-ROM with
    Presentation Builder
Puzzlemaker Software
Cooperative Learning in the Science Classroom
Environmental Issues in the Science Classroom
Home and Community Involvement
Using the Internet in the Science Classroom

"Study Tip," "Test-Taking Tip," and the "Test Practice" features in this book were written by The Princeton Review, the nation's leader in test preparation. Through its association with McGraw-Hill, The Princeton Review offers the best way to help students excel on standardized assessments.

The Princeton Review is not affiliated with Princeton University or Educational Testing Service.

Glencoe/McGraw-Hill

A Division of The **McGraw·Hill** Companies

Cover Images: Highly fluid lava erupting from a volcanic vent.

Send all inquires to:
Glencoe/McGraw-Hill
8787 Orion Place
Columbus, OH 43240

ISBN 0-07-823718-1
Printed in the United States of America.
1 2 3 4 5 6 7 8 9 10 027/043 06 05 04 03 02 01

Authors

Ralph M. Feather Jr., PhD
Science Department Chair
Derry Area School District
Derry, Pennsylvania

Susan Leach Snyder
Earth Science Teacher, Consultant
Jones Middle School
Upper Arlington, Ohio

Dinah Zike
Educational Consultant
Dinah-Might Activities, Inc.
San Antonio, Texas

Reading Consultants

Carol A. Senf, PhD
Associate Professor of English
Georgia Institute of Technology
Atlanta, Georgia

Nancy Woodson, PhD
Professor of English
Otterbein College
Westerville, Ohio

Math Consultants

Michael Hopper, DEng
Manager of Aircraft Certification
Raytheon Company
Greenville, Texas

Teri Willard, EdD
Department of Mathematics
Montana State University
Belgrade, Montana

Safety Consultants

Aileen Duc, PhD
Science II Teacher
Hendrick Middle School
Plano, Texas

Sandra West, PhD
Associate Professor of Biology
Southwest Texas State University
San Marcos, Texas

Reviewers

William Blair
J. Marshall Middle School
Billerica, Massachusetts

Connie Cook Fontenot
Bethune Academy
Houston, Texas

Lois Burdette
Green Bank Elementary/Middle School
Green Bank, West Virginia

Annette Garcia
Kearney Middle School
Commerce City, Colorado

Marcia Chackan
Pine Crest School
Boca Raton, Florida

Nerma Coats Henderson
Pickerington Jr. High School
Pickerington, Ohio

Anthony DiSipio
Octorana Middle School
Atglen, Pennsylvania

Michael Mansour
John Page Middle School
Madison Heights, Michigan

Mary Ferneau
Westview Middle School
Goose Creek, South Carolina

Sharon Mitchell
William D. Slider Middle School
El Paso, Texas

Joanne Stickney
Monticello Middle School
Monticello, New York

CONTENTS IN BRIEF

UNIT 1 Earth Materials—2

CONTENTS

CONTENTS

CONTENTS

Geologic Time—396

UNIT **5** Earth's Air and Water—430

Atmosphere—432

CONTENTS

Contents

CHAPTER
19

Oceanography—548

UNIT

6 You and the Environment—580

CHAPTER
20

Our Impact on Land—582

CONTENTS

UNIT 7 Astronomy—636

CONTENTS

Interdisciplinary Connections

NATIONAL GEOGRAPHIC Unit Openers

NATIONAL GEOGRAPHIC VISUALIZING

Feature Contents

Interdisciplinary Connections

Science Stats

Full Period Labs

Activities

Mini LAB

Feature Contents

Feature Contents

Activities

Feature Contents

Math Skills Activities

Skill Builder Activities

Science

Classifying: 51, 66, 135, 141, 625
Collecting and Organizing Data: 599
Communicating: 14, 44, 93, 141, 172, 201, 279, 339, 375, 405, 441, 480, 499, 538, 569, 625, 661, 686, 713, 725, 744, 757
Comparing and Contrasting: 14, 38, 44, 79, 216, 250, 256, 279, 347, 353, 451, 495, 538, 555, 645, 751, 757
Concept Mapping: 93, 102, 161, 189, 196, 260, 282, 339, 375, 446, 469, 480, 525, 569, 691, 706
Drawing Conclusions: 22, 72, 256
Forming Hypotheses: 307, 323, 499, 594, 725
Identifying and Manipulating Variables and Controls: 564
Interpreting Data: 381, 713
Interpreting Scientific Illustrations: 97, 165, 441, 744
Making Models: 172
Making and Using Graphs: 97, 469, 587

Science Connections

Math

Technology

Science INTEGRATION

SCIENCE Online

THE
PRINCETON
REVIEW

Feature Contents

UNIT 1

Unit Contents

Pre-Reading Activity

Have students search through the chapters and identify any minerals, rocks, and resources with which they are familiar.

UNIT 1 **Earth Materials**

How Are Rocks & Fluorescent Lights Connected?

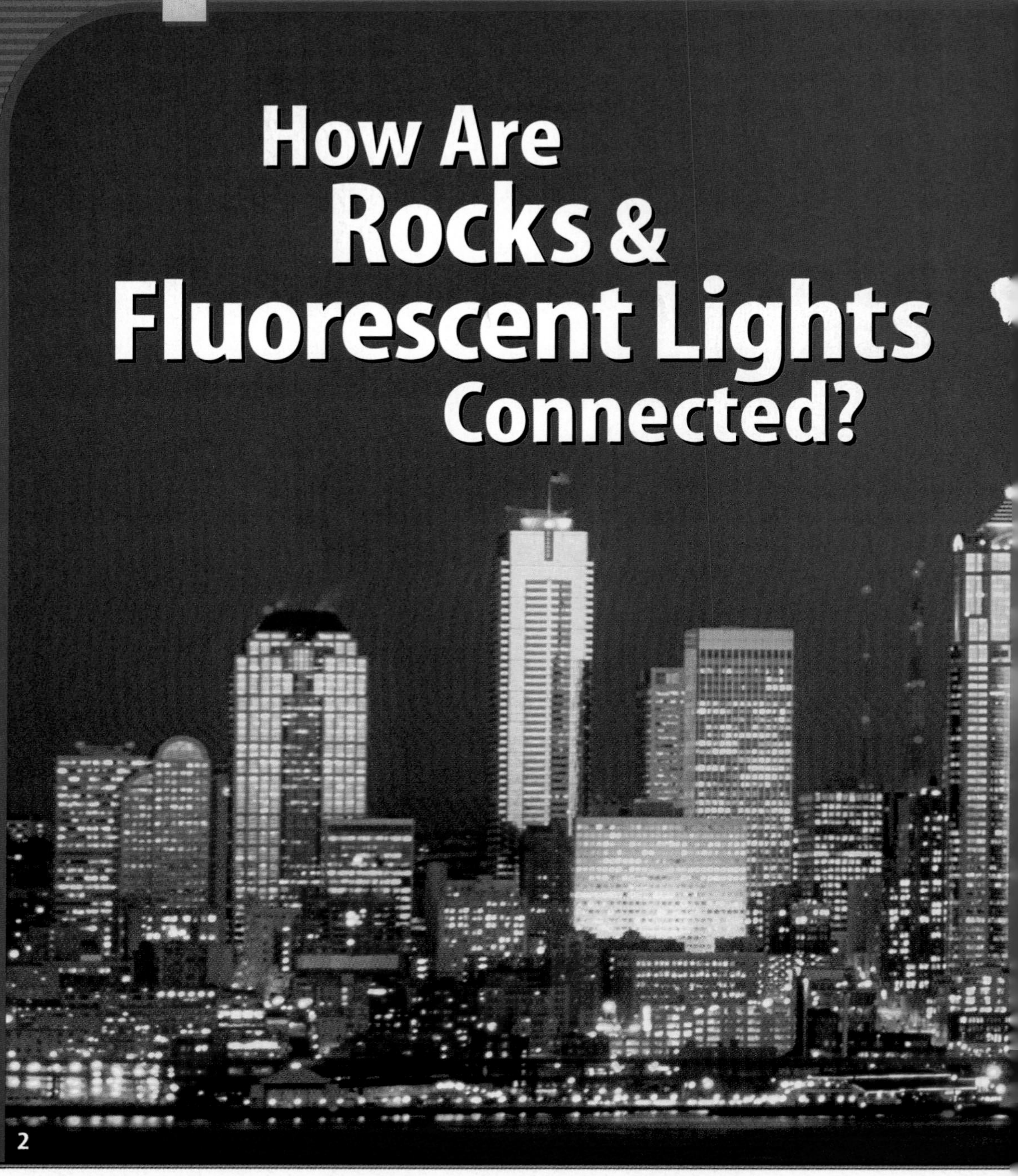

2

Teacher to Teacher

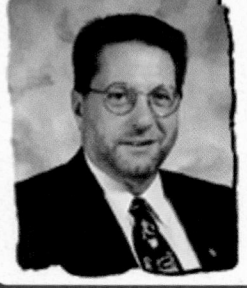

"To help students think about how important Earth resources are to them, I ask them to compile a list of eight items from the classroom, their lockers, or their homes that are made from Earth resources. Next to each item, I have them write the Earth resource from which the product is produced."

Ralph M. Feather, Jr., Teacher
Derry Area High School
Derry, PA

NATIONAL GEOGRAPHIC

A round 1600, an Italian cobbler found a rock that contained a mineral that could be made to glow in the dark. The discovery led other people to seek materials with similar properties. Eventually, scientists identified many fluorescent and phosphorescent (fahs fuh RE sunt) substances—substances that react to certain forms of energy by giving off their own light. As seen above, a fluorescent mineral may look one way in ordinary light (front), but may give off a strange glow (back) when exposed to ultraviolet light. In the 1850s, a scientist wondered whether the fluorescent properties of a substance could be harnessed to create a new type of lighting. The scientist put a fluorescent material inside a glass tube and sent an electric charge through the tube, creating the first fluorescent lamp. Today, fluorescent light bulbs are widely used in office buildings, schools, and factories.

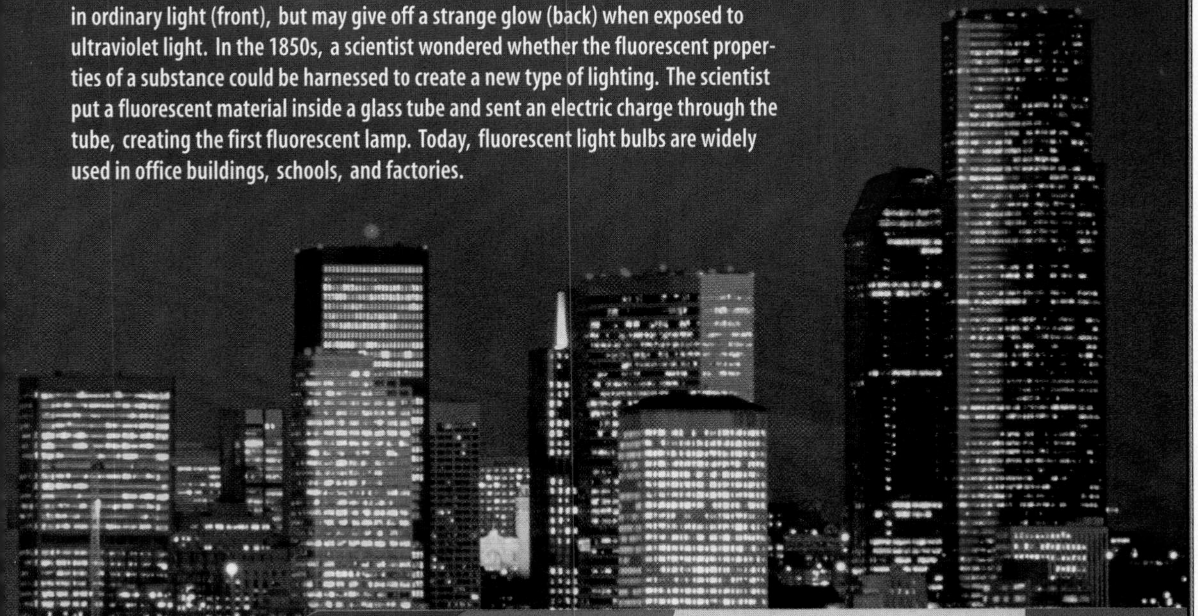

SCIENCE CONNECTION

FLUORESCENT MINERALS Some minerals fluoresce—give off visible light in various colors—when exposed to invisible ultraviolet (UV) light. Using library resources or the Glencoe Science Web site at **science.glencoe.com**, find out more about fluorescence in minerals. Write a paragraph that answers the following questions: Would observing specimens under UV light be a reliable way for a geologist to identify minerals? Why or why not?

SCIENCE CONNECTION
Activity
When ultraviolet light strikes certain materials, it causes them to fluoresce. Because the spectrum of fluorescent light is characteristic of a material's composition, it can be used for screening minerals.

SCIENCE Online
Internet Addresses

_____

_____

_____

Explore the Glencoe Science Web site at **science.glencoe.com** to find out more about topics in this unit.

NATIONAL GEOGRAPHIC

Introducing the Unit

How Are Rocks & Fluorescent Lights Connected?

The emission of light by matter (luminescence) has always been known to exist. Lightning, the aurora borealis, and light emission by bacteria or in decaying matter are common natural phenomena.

There are many types of luminescence. Bioluminescence is luminescence produced by living organisms, such as glowworms, fireflies, microscopic organisms living in the sea, and various fungi and bacteria found on rotting wood or decomposing flesh. Chemiluminescence is produced by certain chemical reactions. Electroluminescence is produced by electric discharges, which may appear when silk or fur is stroked or when adhesive surfaces are separated. Fluorescence, or luminescence emitted from a substance under stimulation by light, had been observed in rocks and certain other substances for hundreds of years.

Scientific investigation of luminescence didn't begin until 1603, when Vincenzo Casciarolo, a Balognian shoemaker and alchemist, accidentally prepared an artificial phosphor that glowed on its own after exposure to light. For the next three centuries scientists studied phosphorescence, and in 1911 the first fluorescent lighting was developed.

Section/Objectives	Standards		Activities/Features
Chapter Opener	**National**	**State/Local**	**Explore Activity:** Measure in SI, p. 5 **Before You Read,** p. 5
	See p. 5T for a Key to Standards.		
Section 1 Science All Around 🕐 2 sessions 📦 1 block 1. **Describe** scientific methods. 2. **Define** science and Earth science. 3. **Distinguish** among independent variables, dependent variables, constants, and controls.	National Content Standards: UCP2, UCP3, A1, A2, E1, E2, F5, G1, G2, G3		**Science Online,** p. 9 **Life Science Integration,** p. 10 **MiniLAB:** Designing an Experiment, p. 11 **Visualizing the History of Earth Science Technology,** p. 13
Section 2 Scientific Enterprise 🕐 3 sessions 📦 1.5 blocks 1. **Explain** why science is always changing. 2. **Compare and contrast** scientific theories and scientific laws. 3. **Discuss** the limits of science.	National Content Standards: UCP2, UCP3, A1, A2, E1, E2, F5, G1, G2, G3		**Science Online,** p. 17 **MiniLAB:** Observing a Scientific Law, p. 19 **Health Integration,** p. 20 **Problem-Solving Activity:** How can bias affect your observations?, p. 21 **Activity:** Understanding Science Articles, p. 23 **Activity:** Testing Variables of a Pendulum, pp. 24–25 **Science and Language Arts:** The Microscope, pp. 26–27

Activity Materials	Reproducible Resources	Section Assessment	Technology
Explore Activity: metric ruler, textbook	**Chapter Resources Booklet** Foldables Worksheet, p. 15 Directed Reading Overview, p. 17 Note-taking Worksheets, pp. 29–30	*GLENCOE'S* **ASSESSMENT** *ADVANTAGE*	
MiniLAB: no materials needed *Need materials?* Contact Science Kit at 1-800-828-7777 or www.sciencekit.com on the Internet.	**Chapter Resources Booklet** Transparency Activity, p. 40 MiniLAB, p. 3 Lab Activity, pp. 9–10 Enrichment, p. 27 Reinforcement, p. 25 Directed Reading, p. 18 Transparency Activity, pp. 43–44 **Reading and Writing Skill Activities,** pp. 9, 49 **Earth Science Critical Thinking/ Problem Solving,** p. 5	**Portfolio** Science Journal, p. 12 Challenge, p. 14 **Performance** MiniLAB, p. 11 Skill Builder Activities, p. 14 **Content** Section Assessment, p. 14	Section Focus Transparency Teaching Transparency Interactive CD-ROM/DVD Guided Reading Audio Program
MiniLAB: shoe box, scissors, rubber ball **Activity:** magazine articles about Earth science topics **Activity:** string, 5 metal washers, watch with a secondhand, metric ruler, paper clip, protractor	**Chapter Resources Booklet** Transparency Activity, p. 41 MiniLAB, p. 4 Lab Activity, pp. 11–13 Enrichment, p. 28 Reinforcement, p. 26 Directed Reading, pp. 19, 20 Activity Worksheets, pp. 5–6, 7–8 **Cultural Diversity,** pp. 27, 29 **Science Inquiry Labs,** p. 29 **Lab Management and Safety,** p. 63	**Portfolio** Cultural Diversity, p. 16 Active Reading, p. 17 **Performance** MiniLAB, p. 19 Problem-Solving Activity, p. 21 Skill Builder Activities, p. 22 **Content** Section Assessment, p. 22	Section Focus Transparency Interactive CD-ROM/DVD Guided Reading Audio Program

GLENCOE'S **ASSESSMENT** *ADVANTAGE*

End of Chapter Assessment

Blackline Masters	Technology	Professional Series
Chapter Resources Booklet Chapter Review, pp. 33–34 Chapter Tests, pp. 35–38 **Standardized Test Practice by The Princeton Review,** pp. 11–14	MindJogger Videoquiz CD-ROM Explorations and Quizzes Vocabulary Puzzle Makers ExamView Pro Test Bank Interactive Lesson Planner Interactive Teacher's Edition	Performance Assessment in the Science Classroom (PASC)

Transparencies

Section Focus

Section 1 Transparency — An Investigation Amply Rewarded

The methods of science can be applied to unravel mysteries, both modern and ancient. After years of research and exhaustive, methodical excavation, Howard Carter discovered the tomb of the Egyptian pharaoh Tutankhamen in 1922. The only royal Egyptian tomb ever found intact, Tutankhamen's tomb is one of the most famous archaeological discoveries.

1. How did Howard Carter make use of the scientific method?
2. What are the advantages of following a series of well-designed steps?
3. How do fieldwork and laboratory work complement each other?

L2

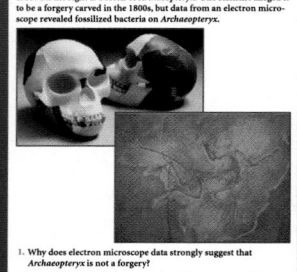

Section 2 Transparency — Hoax or Not

On the left is a skull found in 1912 that many scientists accepted as a genuine fossil. Named Piltdown Man, it was proven to be a hoax in 1953. On the right is a fossil of *Archaeopteryx*. One scientist alleged it to be a forgery carved in the 1800s, but data from an electron microscope revealed fossilized bacteria on *Archaeopteryx*.

1. Why does electron microscope data strongly suggest that *Archaeopteryx* is not a forgery?
2. How might the desire to prove a theory have encouraged the acceptance of Piltdown Man as a genuine fossil?
3. What aspects of the scientific method help scientists correct for misconceptions and omissions?

L2

This is a representation of key blackline masters available in the Teacher Classroom Resources. See Resource Manager boxes within the chapter for additional information.

Assessment

Assessment Transparency — The Nature of Science

Directions: Carefully review the table and answer the following questions.

Steps in the Scientific Method	
Steps	**Procedures**
Identify a problem	Pick a question to be tested
Researching the problem	Collect information
Forming a hypothesis	Make an informed guess about the results
Testing the hypothesis	Do an experiment and collect data to see if the hypothesis is correct
Analyzing the results	Look at the data to see how it answers the original question
Conclusion	Compare the data to the hypothesis for a final answer

1. According to the table, looking up information on the computer about different types of soil is an example of ___.
   A identifying a problem   C analyzing results
   B researching   D hypothesis testing
2. According to the table, which step does not involve data collected in an experiment?
   F identifying a problem   H analyzing results
   G hypothesis testing   J conclusion
3. Which step of the Scientific Method shows the results of your guess?
   A identifying a problem   C hypothesis testing
   B researching   D conclusion

L2

Teaching

Section 1 Teaching Transparency — Scientific Method

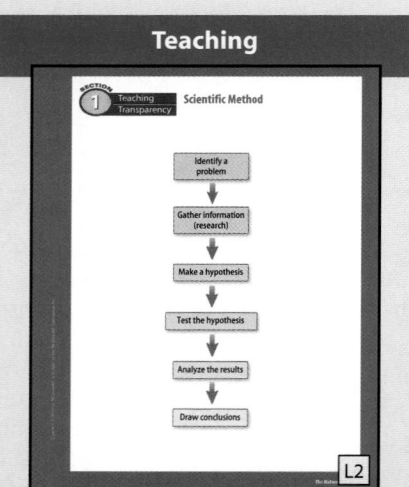

Identify a problem
↓
Gather information (research)
↓
Make a hypothesis
↓
Test the hypothesis
↓
Analyze the results
↓
Draw conclusions

L2

Key to Teaching Strategies

The following designations will help you decide which activities are appropriate for your students.

L1 Level 1 activities should be appropriate for students with learning difficulties.

L2 Level 2 activities should be within the ability range of all students.

L3 Level 3 activities are designed for above-average students.

ELL ELL activities should be within the ability range of English Language Learners.

COOP LEARN Cooperative Learning activities are designed for small group work.

LS Multiple Learning Styles logos, as described on page 22T, are used throughout to indicate strategies that address different learning styles.

P These strategies represent student products that can be placed into a best-work portfolio.

Hands-on Activities

Activity Worksheets

Activity — Understanding Science Articles

Lab Preview
Directions: Answer these questions before you begin the Activity.
1. What will you be reading to discover in this activity?

2. Would you expect to find the names of scientists in the articles you will be reading? Explain.

You know that scientists conduct investigations to learn things about our world. It is important for researchers to share what they learn so other researchers can repeat and expand upon their results. One important way that scientific results are shared is by publishing them in journals and magazines. How can you learn about recent work by scientists? How do you interpret information that you read?

What You'll Investigate
What information about Earth science and scientific methods can you learn by reading an appropriate magazine article?

Materials
magazines about Earth science topics

Goals
• **Obtain** a recent magazine article concerning a research topic in Earth science.
• **Identify** aspects of science and scientific methods in the article

Procedure
1. Locate a recent magazine article about a topic in Earth science research.
2. Read the article paying attention to details that are related to science, research, and scientific methods.
3. What branch of Earth science does the article discuss?
4. **Describe** what the article is about. Does it describe a particular event or discuss more general research?
5. Are the names of any scientists mentioned? If so, what was the role of each in the research being discussed?
6. Are particular hypotheses being tested? If so, is the research project complete or is it still continuing?
7. **Describe** how the research is conducted. What is being measured? What observations are being recorded?

L2

Laboratory Activities

Lab 1 Laboratory Activity — Problem Solving and a Scientific Method

Think back to the last problem you had to solve. No matter how you solved the problem, you probably used some or all of the steps of a "Scientific Method." A scientific method is a logical approach to solving problems. There are many methods used by scientists to solve problems. However, most scientists recognize four basic steps: (1) determining the problem, (2) testing, (3) analyzing the results, and (4) drawing conclusions.

Strategy
You will use the scientific method to determine the density of an ice cube.

Materials
ice cubes   alcohol
graduated beaker   stirring rods
metric ruler   balance
forceps or tongs   water
graduated cylinder
CAUTION: *Do not ingest alcohol or breathe fumes. Some alcohol is poisonous. Liquid and vapor are extremely flammable.*

Procedure
1. In order to solve the problem, you must first determine what it is you need to know. Place an ice cube on the tabletop and make some observations. It is best to organize your initial observations into a data table for easy review. Now fill out Table 1 below.

2. What other information is helpful that cannot be gained from initial observation? A little research might be helpful at this time. Your closest source of information is your textbook.
   A. Define the unknown terms:
   Density _____

   Mass _____

   Volume _____

3. Design a test (in this case a procedure) that will enable you to determine the density of an ice cube.

Ice cube	Observation
A. View on tabletop for 5 minutes	
B. Shape	
C. Size	
D. In water	
E. In alcohol	

First Trial Procedure
A. _____
B. _____
C. _____
D. _____
E. _____

L2

Meeting Different Ability Levels

Content Outline

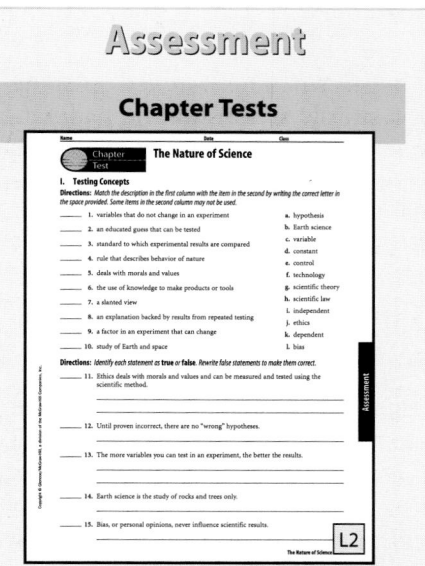

Chapter Outline — Matter

Section 1 Atoms

A. Matter—anything that has _____ and takes up space
  1. Matter is made up of tiny particles called _____.
  2. Substances that contain only one type of atom are _____.
B. Three basic particles make up an atom: _____, _____, and _____

  1. Protons and neutrons make up the _____ of an atom.
    a. Protons—particles that have _____ electric charge
    b. Neutrons—particles that have _____ electrical charge
    c. The nucleus has a _____ charge.
  2. Electrons—_____ charged particles that move around the nucleus
  3. Atomic number—the number of _____ in an atom's nucleus
    a. All atoms of a specific element have the same _____ in an atom's nucleus
    b. This number also equals the number of _____ in the atom's electron cloud.
  4. Mass number—the number of _____ and _____ making up an atom's nucleus
C. Isotopes—atoms of the same element that have different numbers of _____
Section 2 Combinations of Atoms
A. When atoms of more than one element combine, they form a _____.
B. _____—describes a change that occurs when one substance reacts with another substance
C. _____—the force that holds atoms in compounds together
  1. _____ bonds form by sharing electrons.
  2. Atoms that become positively or negatively charged form _____ bonds.
    a. Electrically charged atoms are called _____.

L2

Reinforcement

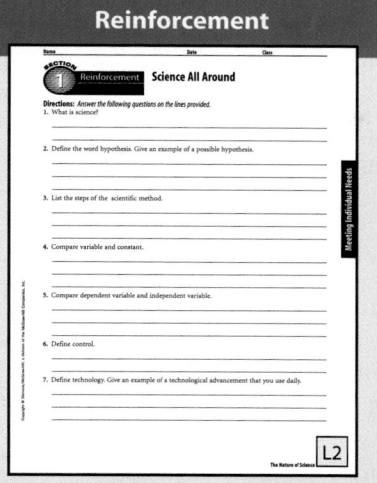

Reinforcement — Science All Around

Directions: Answer the following questions on the lines provided.
1. What is science?

2. Define the word hypothesis. Give an example of a possible hypothesis.

3. List the steps of the scientific method.

4. Compare variable and constant.

5. Compare dependent variable and independent variable.

6. Define control.

7. Define technology. Give an example of a technological advancement that you use daily.

L2

Directed Reading

Directed Reading for Content Mastery — Overview The Nature of Science

Directions: Complete the concept map by using the words below.

scientific theory   constants   technology   hypothesis
dependent variables   experiments   dependent variables

One scientific method for problem-solving
involves developing a
  which can be the basis of a new   that can be tested by designing   which can lead to
  2.   3.   4.
or the use of science for practical purposes   composed of variables such as   or scientific explanations
  5.   6.   7.
  that change   that do not change   that are measured

Directions: Circle the terms in parentheses that best complete the sentence.
8. Problems that deal with ethics (can, cannot) be solved using scientific methods.
9. Ethics deals with (moral values, scientific facts).
10. There (are, are no) limits to what science can explain.

L1

Assessment

Chapter Tests

Chapter Test — The Nature of Science

I. Testing Concepts
Directions: Match the description in the first column with the item in the second by writing the correct letter in the space provided. Some items in the second column may not be used.

____ 1. variables that do not change in an experiment   a. hypothesis
____ 2. an educated guess that can be tested   b. Earth science
____ 3. standard to which experimental results are compared   c. variable
____ 4. rule that describes behavior of nature   d. constant
____ 5. deals with morals and values   e. control
____ 6. the use of knowledge to make products or tools   f. technology
____ 7. a slanted view   g. scientific theory
____ 8. an explanation backed by results from repeated testing   h. scientific law
____ 9. a factor in an experiment that can change   i. independent
____ 10. study of Earth and land   j. ethics
  k. dependent
  l. bias

Directions: Identify each statement as true or false. Rewrite false statements to make them correct.
____ 11. Ethics deals with morals and values and can be measured and tested using the scientific method.

____ 12. Until proven incorrect, there are no "wrong" hypotheses.

____ 13. The more variables you can test in an experiment, the better the results.

____ 14. Earth science is the study of rocks and trees only.

____ 15. Bias, or personal opinions, never influence scientific results.

L2

Enrichment

Enrichment — Saving the Ozone Layer

There is no doubt that chlorofluorocarbons (CFCs) in the atmosphere are depleting Earth's ozone layer. Why does this matter? Atmospheric ozone, most of which is concentrated in the stratosphere about 15–30 kilometers above Earth's surface, absorbs the most dangerous ultraviolet light (UV-B) from the Sun. UV-B is known to cause skin cancer and to damage eyes. It also harms various crops and forms of marine life. Without the ozone, Earth would be a much more dangerous place to live.

CFCs
The CFCs, which were manufactured for use as refrigerants, solvents, and other applications, can eventually be carried by winds high into the stratosphere. Normally they are very stable, but in the stratosphere they break down and release atomic chlorine. It takes only one chlorine atom to destroy 100,000 ozone molecules.

Early Experiments
This knowledge came about because of experiments begun in the 1880s when scientists began to find ways of detecting and measuring the various gases present in the atmosphere. One experiment lead to another as new hypotheses were tested and either discarded or proven true. It was at this time that ozone was shown to be the substance protecting Earth from UVB radiation.
In 1970 a British scientist was able to detect CFCs carried by winds to many parts of the globe. This is not surprising, at that time nearly 1 billion kilograms of CFCs were being manufactured yearly. No one yet knew the danger they posed.

Rowland-Molina Hypothesis
Two scientists, Sherwood Rowland and Mario Molina, decided to find out what happened to all the CFCs. Basing their studies on work previously done by many other scientists, they asserted that CFC chlorine atoms were combining with and destroying ozone molecules in the stratosphere. Not all scientists agreed. Some advanced the hypothesis that chlorine from volcanic eruptions and other natural sources might be depleting the ozone. Two years later the Rowland-Molina hypothesis was confirmed by the National Academy of Sciences.

Hole Over Antarctica
In 1984, a hole in the ozone layer was discovered over Antarctica. This was verified the following year by a NASA satellite. The danger was now real. More than 160 countries agreed to reduce the amount of CFCs released into the atmosphere. Deadlines have been set for their complete elimination. In the meantime, there has been a new hypothesis regarding the effect of global warming on ozone depletion, and new experiments will have to be conducted.
It will be many years before the ozone layer once again fully protects Earth from UV-B radiation. Had it not been for the curiosity of scientists like Rowland and Molina and their painstaking approach to the scientific testing, it might not have been discovered until it was too late.

1. Why didn't scientists know before the 1880s the role that ozone plays in the atmosphere?

2. What is it in CFCs that destroys ozone?

3. Why were nearly 1 billion kilograms of dangerous CFCs being manufactured in 1970?

L3

Spanish Directed Reading

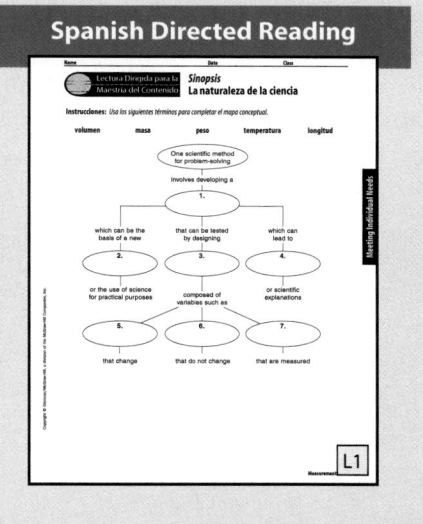

Lectura Dirigida para la Maestría del Contenido — Sinopsis La naturaleza de la ciencia

Instrucciones: Usa los siguientes términos para completar el mapa conceptual.

volumen   masa   peso   temperatura   longitud

One scientific method for problem-solving
involves developing a
  1.
which can be the basis of a new   that can be tested by designing   which can lead to
  2.   3.   4.
or the use of science for practical purposes   composed of variables such as   or scientific explanations
  5.   6.   7.
  that change   that do not change   that are measured

L1

Test Practice Workbook

Standardized Test Practice
Teacher Edition

Glencoe Science

Earth Science

• Correlates to TEKS
• Prepares students for TAKS II
• Written by Kaplan

L2

Chapter Review

Chapter Review — Air Pollution

Part A. Vocabulary Review
Directions: Write the correct term in the spaces beside each definition. The boxed letters should spell the words that describe the most important scientific tool.
1. a prediction or statement that can be tested
2. use of knowledge to make products or tools
3. a factor in an experiment that can change
4. a standard to which experimental results can be compared
5. variable being measured
6. variable that changes
7. problem-solving by following steps to draw a conclusion
8. used to measure scientific phenomena
9. The boxed letters spell:

Part B. Concept Review
Directions: Number these steps for doing an experiment in the correct order in the blanks provided.
____ 1. Draw conclusions.
____ 2. Form a hypothesis.
____ 3. Communicate results.
____ 4. Test your hypothesis.
____ 5. Recognize the problem.
____ 6. Analyze your data.

L2

Science Content Background

Science All Around

Repeating Experiments

The importance of being able to repeat experiments was brought to light in 1989 when a pair of scientists from the University of Utah claimed to have achieved cold fusion. Cold fusion is the fusion of two nuclei at or very near room temperature, without the use of a particle accelerator. Achieving this kind of nuclear fusion would be a phenomenon that would be unable to be explained by any existing scientific law or theory. In the wake of the groundbreaking news that cold fusion had been successfully achieved, other physicists went to work attempting to replicate the experiment. The results of the original experiment were not obtained by other members of the scientific community. Because the results of the experiment could not be replicated consistently, the phenomenon of cold fusion was dismissed by most scientists. Many scientists think that there is no evidence to support the claim that a nuclear reaction took place during the 1989 experiment, and that the results of the experiment were misinterpreted by the scientists.

AFP/Corbis

Most of the time in science, discoveries are the result of careful observation, data collection, and thoughtful interpretation of results. However, sometimes things are discovered completely by accident. It is said that Newton's determination of the Law of Gravity began when he watched an apple fall from a tree, a simple action that he had witnessed and taken for granted a thousand times before. It was not until he questioned why the apple always falls straight down that he began to postulate on the force of gravity. Other accidents in science include the discovery of Teflon, X rays, and artificial sweeteners.

Fun Fact

"Red sky at night, sailor's delight. Red sky at morning, sailor take warning."

This weather proverb, more than two thousand years old, has valid meteorological roots. When the humidity is low, usually an indication of fair weather, dry dust particles are present in the air. Red or pink skies at dusk can occur when light is scattered as it passes through air holding these particles.

Using Technology

Satellites are being used today by NASA and other scientists to record a host of important data about Earth. A new program at NASA involves using satellites to monitor large fires occurring around the world. A new instrument on NASA's Earth Observing System Terra satellite is able to measure the intensity of fires. The instrument can also collect data on the amount of smoke and aerosols being released from a fire. All of this assists in the management and control of wild fires and gives scientists the ability to further access damage to or impact on the environment.

Other scientists are using satellites to more precisely map flood plain areas. Many people do not even realize that their property is on a 50- or 100-year flood plain. In many cases it is a lack of accurate records that accounts for this oversight. By analyzing satellite images, scientists are able to identify areas that have once been inundated by large floods. When a flood plain area is located, detailed images of that area are studied and the area is mapped precisely.

The information is then logged into a database that is available for public use.

Some scientists are using satellite images to help them find fossils. By searching images of deserts for areas that have the kind of rock in which particular fossils often are found, researchers can go directly to the site and begin digging. This method is often less expensive and time consuming than exploring a desert region using more conventional methods.

SECTION 2

Scientific Enterprise

Measuring Humidity

A hygrometer is used to measure humidity. A simple hygrometer usually contains a human hair attached to a pointer. As humidity increases, the amount of water vapor in the air increases. The hair absorbs this moisture and lengthens. As the length of the hair becomes shorter or longer with changes in humidity, the pointer records the data on a graph. The results from a simple hygrometer are considered to be approximate, rather than scientifically accurate. Blonde hair is purported to be the best type for this exercise, as it has the fastest response time.

Gathering Weather Data

Weather balloons are equipped with an instrument called a radiosonde, which transmits data back to a meteorological station. Radiosonde weather balloons make measurements of wind strength and direction, temperature, pressure, and humidity in the atmosphere. Radiosonde balloons can operate as high as 30,000 m. Other research balloons can go as high as 50,000 m.

Ethics

One example of a fraud in the scientific community was the so-called discovery of the Piltdown man. It was claimed that the bones found near Piltdown, England in 1912 were those of a previously unknown species of primate, one that was proposed to be closely related to humans. In 1953, fluorine-dating tests revealed

Yogi, Inc./Corbis

that the bones were the skull of a modern human (from the Middle Ages) and the jaw of an orangutan.

SCIENCE *Online*

For additional content background on this topic, go to the Glencoe Science Web site at science.glencoe.com.

The Nature of Science

Chapter Vocabulary

hypothesis
scientific methods
science
Earth science
variable
independent variable
constant
dependent variable
control
technology
scientific theory
scientific law
ethics
bias

What do you think?

Science Journal The photographs show fossil dinosaur eggs. Scientists use fossils such as these to make inferences about dinosaurs, including their appearance during life, whether they were warm-blooded, and whether they nurtured their young.

The Nature of Science

Inside the chest of a small dinosaur nicknamed Willo is something amazing—what appears to be a heart preserved as stone. An X-ray scan of this 66-million-year-old skeleton shows possible heart structures inside the stone. Scientists still are debating whether this clump of stone is a preserved heart, and more research will be necessary. But that's the nature of science.

What do you think?

Science Journal Look at the photo below. Discuss what you think this might be. Here's a hint: *The one Willo came from may have looked a lot like these.* Write your answer or best guess in your Science Journal.

4

Theme Connection

Systems and Interactions Science is a system of knowledge based on observations. Science involves trying to solve problems and answer questions about the universe by observing how things interact.

EXPLORE
ACTIVITY

H ow big is big? How small is small? Big and small are words people use a lot. But, the meaning of these words depends on your experiences and what you are describing. Your description could be confusing to another person who hasn't had the same experiences you've had. Early in human history, people developed ways to measure things. In the following activity, try some of these measuring devices.

Measure in SI

1. Using only your hands and fingers as measuring devices, measure the length and width of the cover of this book.
2. Compare your measurements with those of other students.
3. Using a metric ruler, repeat the measurement process.
4. Again, compare your measurements with the measurements of other students in the classroom.

Observe

In your Science Journal, infer and describe several advantages of using standardized measuring devices.

Purpose Use the Explore Activity to introduce students to the reason people use standardized measuring devices. [L2] [ELL] [COOP LEARN] **Interpersonal and Logical-Mathematical**
Materials textbook, metric ruler
Teaching Strategies

- Direct students to measure the length of the book from top to bottom and the width from side to side.
- Demonstrate the use of the hands and fingers as measuring devices.
- Encourage students to be as precise with their measurements as possible.

Observe

By using standardized measuring devices, people can make measurements that are accurate and consistent.

✔Assessment

Performance Have students list as many standardized measuring devices as they can. Next to each device, have them list its units of measurement. For example, a metric ruler measures millimeters and centimeters. Use **Performance Assessment in the Science Classroom,** p. 109.

Before You Read

FOLDABLES
Reading & Study Skills

Making a Vocabulary Study Fold Knowing the definition of vocabulary words is a good way to ensure you understand the content of the chapter.

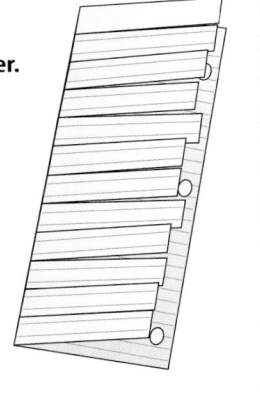

1. Place a sheet of notebook paper in front of you so the short side is at the top and the holes are on the right side. Fold the paper in half from the left side to the right side.
2. Through the top thickness of paper, cut along every third line from the outside edge to the centerfold, forming tabs.
3. Before you read the chapter, write vocabulary words from each section in this chapter on the front of the tabs. Under each tab, write what you think the word means.
4. As you read the chapter, add to and correct your definitions.

5

Before You Read

FOLDABLES
Reading & Study Skills

Dinah Zike Study Fold
Purpose Use this activity to expose students to the chapter's content and vocabulary before they read, and to encourage a search for terms and definitions as they read. The resulting Foldable can be used as an assessment tool and study guide before, during, and after reading.

📁 For additional help, see Foldables Worksheet, p. 15 in **Chapter Resources Booklet,** or go to the Glencoe Science Web site at **science.glencoe.com.** See After You Read in the Study Guide at the end of this chapter.

SECTION

Science All Around

1 Motivate

Bellringer Transparency

Display the Section Focus Transparency for Section 1. Use the accompanying Transparency Activity Master. L2

ELL

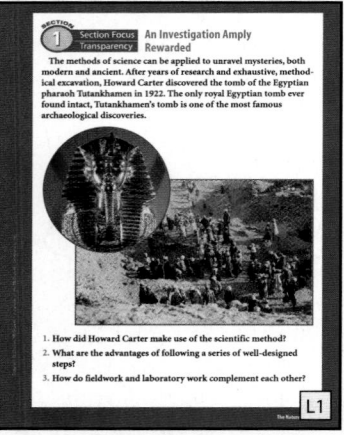

Tie to Prior Knowledge

Students have observed and interpreted information about their surroundings since they were infants. Explain that these same processes are used in science. In this section, students will learn more about scientific methods.

As You Read

What You'll Learn

- **Describe** scientific methods.
- **Define** science and Earth science.
- **Distinguish** among independent variables, dependent variables, constants, and controls.

Vocabulary

hypothesis	constant
scientific methods	dependent
science	variable
Earth science	control
variable	technology
independent variable	

Why It's Important

Scientific methods are used every day when you solve problems.

Figure 1
Along the Cascadia subduction zone, the Juan de Fuca Plate is sinking under the North American Plate.

Mysteries and Problems

Scientists are often much like detectives trying to solve a mystery. One such mystery occurred in 1996 when Japanese scientists were looking through historical records. They reported finding accounts of a tsunami that had smashed the coast of Honshu Island on January 27, 1700. That lead to the question: What had triggered theses huge ocean waves?

The Search for Answers The scientists suspected that an earthquake along the coast of North America was to blame. From the coast of British Columbia to northern California is an area called the Cascadia subduction zone, shown in **Figure 1.** A subduction zone is where one section of Earth's outer, rigid layer, called a plate, is sinking beneath another plate. In areas like this, earthquakes are common. However, one problem remained. Based on the size of the tsunami, the earthquake had to have been an extremely powerful one, sending waves rolling all the way across the Pacific Ocean. That would be a much stronger earthquake than any known to have occurred in the area. Could evidence be found for such a large earthquake?

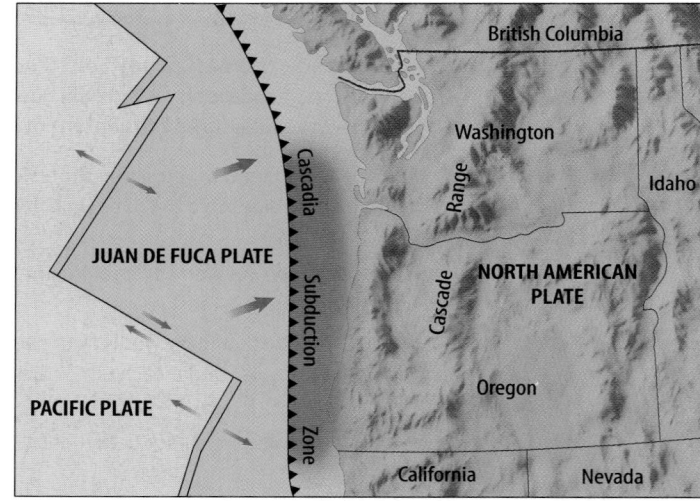

Section ✓*Assessment* Planner

PORTFOLIO
Science Journal, p. 12
Challenge, p. 14
PERFORMANCE ASSESSMENT
Try at Home MiniLAB, p. 11
Skill Builder Activities, p. 14
See page 30 for more options.

CONTENT ASSESSMENT
Section, p. 14
Challenge, p. 14
Chapter, pp. 30–31

Gathering Evidence Evidence of a large earthquake in the distant past did seem to exist along the coasts of Washington and Oregon. Much of the coast in that area had sunk, submerging coastal forests and killing thousands of trees. However, dating the earthquake to a specific year would be difficult.

A Possible Solution One scientist, whose field of study was tree rings, thought he knew how the earthquake could be dated. He made an educated guess, called a **hypothesis,** that tree rings in the drowned trees could be used to determine when the earthquake occurred.

☑ **Reading Check** *What is a hypothesis?*

The hypothesis was based on what scientists know about tree growth. Each year, a living tree makes a new ring of tissue in its trunk, called an annual growth ring. You can see the annual rings in the cross section of a tree trunk shown in **Figure 2.** Two groups of scientists analyzed the rings in drowned trees, like the remains of cedar trees shown in **Figure 3.** Their data showed that the trees had died or were damaged after August 1699 but before the spring growing season of 1700. That evidence put the date of the earthquake in the same time period as the tsunami on Honshu island.

Importance of Solving the Mystery In addition to solving the mystery of what caused the tsunami, the tree rings also provided a warning for people living in the Pacific Northwest. Earthquakes much stronger than any that have occurred in modern times are possible. Scientists warn that it's only a matter of time until another huge quake occurs.

Figure 2
You can see the growth rings in this tree trunk. *How much time does each ring represent?*

Figure 3
Growth rings from these and other trees linked a huge earthquake along the coast of Washington to a tsunami in Japan that occurred more than 300 years ago.

Teacher FYI

Dendrochronology is the science of dating events and climatic changes by observing growth rings in trees. If growth rings are close together, the tree grew slowly. This indicates that the growing conditions were not optimal. The climate might have been cold or dry or both. If growth rings are far apart, the climate might have been warm or moist or both.

Resource Manager

Chapter Resources Booklet
   Transparency Activity, p. 40
   Directed Reading for Content Mastery, pp. 17, 18
Life Science Critical Thinking/Problem Solving, p. 4

② Teach

Mysteries and Problems

Use Science Words
Word Meaning *Tsunami* is a Japanese word. It means "wave in the harbor." Some people call a tsunami a tidal wave. Have students explain why tidal wave isn't a good synonym for tsunami. A tsunami has nothing to do with tides. Instead, it is caused by submarine Earth movement. L2 IS **Linguistic**

☑ **Reading Check**

Answer an educated guess

Caption Answer
Figure 2 one year

Activity
Obtain several cross sections of tree trunks. On each sample, use a pencil and ruler to draw a straight line from the center of the wood to the outer edge. Have students determine the ages of the trees by counting the annual growth rings that intersect the pencil lines. L2 IS **Visual-Spatial and Kinesthetic**

Extension
Have students prepare a bulletin board display of current topics in science. Discuss several of these with students. L1 IS **Visual-Spatial**

Activity
Ask the school librarian to arrange a session during which the use of science books, reference books, magazines, and Internet sources is explained. L2

Scientific Methods

Visual Learning

Figure 4 Why should you gather information before developing a hypothesis? By learning about what is already known, you are better prepared to write a hypothesis that makes sense. Having a good understanding of a topic will also help in designing an effective way to test the hypothesis.

Science

Reading Check

Answer process of observing, studying, and thinking about things in the world to gain knowledge

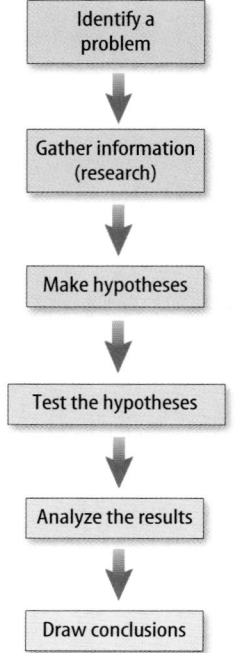

Identify a problem
↓
Gather information (research)
↓
Make hypotheses
↓
Test the hypotheses
↓
Analyze the results
↓
Draw conclusions

Figure 4
By using scientific methods, you can solve many problems.

Figure 5
The columns in Devils Postpile rise between 12 m and 18 m from the valley floor. This unusual formation was created when hot lava cooled and cracked.

Scientific Methods

When scientists try to solve a mystery like what caused the tsunami in Japan in 1700, they perform problem-solving procedures called **scientific methods.** As shown in **Figure 4,** some of the scientific methods they use include, identifying a problem, gathering information (researching), developing hypotheses, testing the hypotheses, analyzing the results, and drawing conclusions. When you use methods like these, you are solving problems in a scientific way.

Science

Science means "having knowledge." **Science** is a process of observing, studying, and thinking about things in your world to gain knowledge. Many observations can't be explained easily. When people can't explain things, they ask questions. For example, you might observe that the sky appears to be blue during the day but often appears to be red at sunset and sunrise. You might ask yourself why this happens. You might visit or see a picture of Devils Postpile in California, shown in **Figure 5,** and notice that the dark rock is divided into long, thin, six-sided columns. Many fallen columns lie at the base of this mass of rock. You might wonder how and when this strange-looking rock formed. You also might wonder why rocks can be smooth or rough, shiny or dull, and can be so many different colors. Science involves trying to answer questions and solve problems to better understand the world. Every time you attempt to find out how and why things look and behave the way they do, you are performing science.

Reading Check *What is science?*

Figure 6
Earth science includes the study of climate, volcanoes, space, and much more. *Which Earth science topics are represented here?*

Caption Answer
Figure 6 oceans, mountains, weather

Reading Check
Answer Possible answers: rocks, volcanoes, earthquakes, maps, fossils, mountains, land use, storm patterns, climates, weather, freshwater, ocean water, objects in space

Earth Science Science is divided into different areas of study. The kind of science you will learn about this year is Earth science. **Earth science** is the study of Earth and space. Some Earth science topics include rocks, minerals, soil, volcanoes, earthquakes, maps, fossils, mountains, climates, weather, ocean water, and objects in space. Some of these topics are represented in **Figure 6.** Much of the information you'll learn about has been discovered over the ages by people who conducted scientific tests or investigations. However, many unanswered questions remain and much more is waiting to be discovered.

✔ **Reading Check** *What topics do Earth scientists study?*

Working in the Lab

Testing, or experimenting, is an important part of science, and if you really want to learn from an investigation, it must be carefully designed. Suppose after listening to advertisements for several dishwashing liquids, you want to know which brand of dishwashing liquid really cleans dishes the best. To find the answer, you would need to do some library or Internet research on dishwashing liquids. After researching, several thoughts might go through your mind. For example, you might hypothesize that brand X will clean dishes better than any other brand. You also might consider that there would be no difference in how well the different liquids clean.

Next, you would design an experiment that tests the validity of your hypotheses. You would need to think about which dishwashing liquids you would test, the amount of each dishwashing liquid you would use, the temperature of the water, the number of dishes you would wash, the kind and amount of grease you would put on the dishes, and the brand of paper towels you would use. All these factors can affect the outcome.

Research Visit the Glencoe Science Web site at **science.glencoe.com** for information about the different areas of Earth science. Prepare a collage that illustrates what you learn.

Working in the Lab

Extension

Have students interview scientists and talk with them about their careers and how they use scientific methods in their work. Have students make poster presentations of their interviews. L2 IS **Linguistic and Visual-Spatial**

SCIENCE Online
Internet Addresses
_____
_____
_____
_____

Explore the Glencoe Science Web site at **science.glencoe.com** to find out more about topics in this section.

Inclusion Strategies

Gifted Have these students choose Earth science topics to research. Have them list the tools, equipment, and instruments used by scientists to study these topics. L3

Resource Manager

Chapter Resources Booklet
    Transparency Activity, pp. 43–44
    Note-taking Worksheets, pp. 29–30
Physical Science Critical Thinking/Problem Solving, pp. 1, 4

Quick Demo

Tell students you are going to test whether a tennis ball or a golf ball bounces higher. Drop the tennis ball from 1 m and the golf ball from 10 cm. The tennis ball will bounce higher. Students should protest that you were testing two variables at the same time: ball type and height of the drop. **Why should you test only one variable at a time?** By testing one variable at a time, you can better determine cause-and-effect relationships.

Life Science
INTEGRATION

The independent variable is the kind of soil. Constants include the type, size, and health of cactus plants at the beginning of the experiment; the temperature and amount of water each plant gets; the size of the pots; the amount of soil in each pot; and the exposure of each plant to sunlight. The dependent variable is the size and health of the cactus plants at the end of the experiment.

Use Science Words

Word Meaning Have students explain why the variable being measured is called a *dependent* variable. Its value is affected by another variable (the independent variable). L2 IN **Linguistic**

✔ Reading Check

Answer It's a standard to which results can be compared.

Caption Answer
Figure 7 Doing so is a constant in the experiment; if this weren't done, the cleanest dish couldn't really be determined.

Figure 7
Wiping each dish in the same manner with a different paper towel is an important constant. *Why?*

Life Science
INTEGRATION

Suppose you wanted to design an experiment to find out what kind of soil is best for growing cactus plants. What would be your variables and constants in the experiment?

Variables and Constants The different factors that can change in an experiment are **variables.** However, you want to design your experiment so you test only one variable at a time. The variable you want to test is the brand of dishwashing liquid. This is called the **independent variable**—the variable that changes. **Constants** are the variables that do not change in an experiment. Constants in this experiment would be the amount of dishwashing liquid used, the amount of water, the water temperature, the number of dishes, the kind and amount of grease applied to each dish, the brand of paper towels that were used, and the manner in which each dish was wiped. For example, you might use 20 equally greasy dishes that are identical in size, soaked in 20 L of hot water (30°C) to which 10 mL of dishwashing liquid have been added. You might rub each dish with a different dry paper towel of the same brand after it has soaked for 20 min and air-dried, as the student in **Figure 7** is doing. If grease does not appear on the towel, you would consider the dish to be clean. The amount of grease on the towel is a measure of how clean each dish is and is called the dependent variable. A **dependent variable** is the variable being measured.

Controls Many experiments also need a control. A **control** is a standard to which your results can be compared. The control in your experiment is the same number of greasy dishes, placed in 20 L of hot water except that no dishwashing liquid is added to the water. These dishes also are allowed to soak for 20 min and air-dry. Then they are wiped with paper towels in the same manner as the other dishes were wiped.

✔ Reading Check   *Why is a control used in an experiment?*

10   CHAPTER 1   The Nature of Science

Visual Learning

Figure 7 Why should each dish be wiped with the same brand of paper towel? Different brands of paper towels have different textures. This variable might affect your ability to determine how clean each dish is.

Repeating Experiments For your results to be valid or reliable, your tests should be repeated many times to see whether you can confirm your original results. For example, you might design your experiment so you repeat the procedures five times for each different dishwashing liquid and control. Also, the number of samples being tested should be large. That is why 20 plates would be chosen for each test of each dishwashing liquid. The control group also would have 20 plates. By repeating an experiment five times, you can be more confident that your conclusions are accurate because your total sample for each dishwashing liquid would be 100 plates. If something in an experiment occurs just once, you can't base a scientific conclusion on it. However, if you can show that brand X cleans best 100 times under the same conditions, then you have a conclusion you can feel confident about.

Testing After you have decided how you will conduct an experiment, you can begin testing. During the experiment, you should observe what happens and carefully record your data in a table like the one in **Figure 8.** Your final step is to draw your conclusions. You analyze your results and try to understand what they mean.

When you are making and recording observations, be sure to include any unexpected results. Many discoveries have been made when experiments produced unexpected results.

SECTION 1 Science All Around **11**

TRY AT HOME
Mini LAB

Designing an Experiment

Procedure
1. Design an experiment to test the question: *Which flashlight battery lasts the longest?*
2. In your design, be sure to include detailed steps of your experiment.
3. Identify the independent variable, constants, dependent variable, and control.

Analysis
1. List the equipment you would need to do your experiment.
2. Explain why you should repeat the experiment.

Figure 8
Arranging your data in a table makes the information easier to understand and analyze.

TRY AT HOME
Mini LAB

Purpose Students design an experiment to test a question. They will identify variables, constants, and a control.
L2 ELL COOP LEARN
LS Logical-Mathematical

Teaching Strategies
- The independent variable is the brand of battery. Constants include identical new flashlights, new batteries, and the same timing device. The dependent variable is how long the lights shine. The control could be a brand of battery the student has seen advertised on TV.
- If time permits and materials are available, have students perform the experiment in class.

Analysis
1. two or more flashlights, two or more different brands of batteries, timing device
2. By repeating the experiment, students can be more confident that their conclusions are valid.

✓ Assessment

Oral Have students explain why used flashlights and batteries should not be used in the experiment. Use **Performance Assessment in the Science Classroom,** p. 89.

Curriculum Connection

Health It takes a new drug many years to reach pharmacies in the United States. After being developed, a drug must be tested for safety, dosage, and effectiveness. Testing is done in test tubes, on laboratory animals, and in clinical trials on humans. If found safe, the drug is approved. **Is all of this testing really necessary?** Yes; it helps ensure that drugs will be safe and effective for all users. L2

Resource Manager

Chapter Resources Booklet
    MiniLAB, p. 3
    Lab Activity, pp. 9–10
Cultural Diversity, pp. 47, 59

Technology

Use an Analogy

Music notes are to symphonies as the sciences are to technologies. By combining notes into melodies, symphonies are created. By using science discoveries, new technologies are developed.

Discussion

Ask students what our knowledge of space would be if we did not have telescopes, computers, and other instruments. We would know only what we can see. Explain that it is because of technology that we have instruments with which to study our universe.

Caption Answers

- **Figure 9** We live in homes, attend schools, visit malls, ride in motorized vehicles, and use many devices.
- **Figure 9B** There would be no electricity, paved roads, mass transit, high-rise buildings, or computerized traffic lights.
- **Figure 9C** Possible answers: electric lights, range and hood, materials used in the cabinets and furnishings

Technology

Science doesn't just add to the understanding of your natural surroundings, it also allows people to make discoveries that help others. Science makes the discoveries, and technology puts the discoveries to use. **Technology** is the use of scientific discoveries for practical purposes.

When people first picked up stones to use as tools or weapons, the age of technology had started. The discovery of fire and its ability to change clay into pottery or rocks into metals made the world you live in possible. Think back to the Explore Activity at the beginning of this chapter. Measuring devices like the metric ruler you used are examples of technology.

Everywhere you look, you can see ways that science and technology have shaped your world. Look at **Figure 9** to see how many examples of technology you can identify in each of the pictures. **Figure 10** shows a time line of some important examples of technology used in Earth science. Notice how different cultures have added to discoveries and inventions of the centuries.

Figure 9
Examples of technology are all around you. *What are some ways these examples affect your life?*

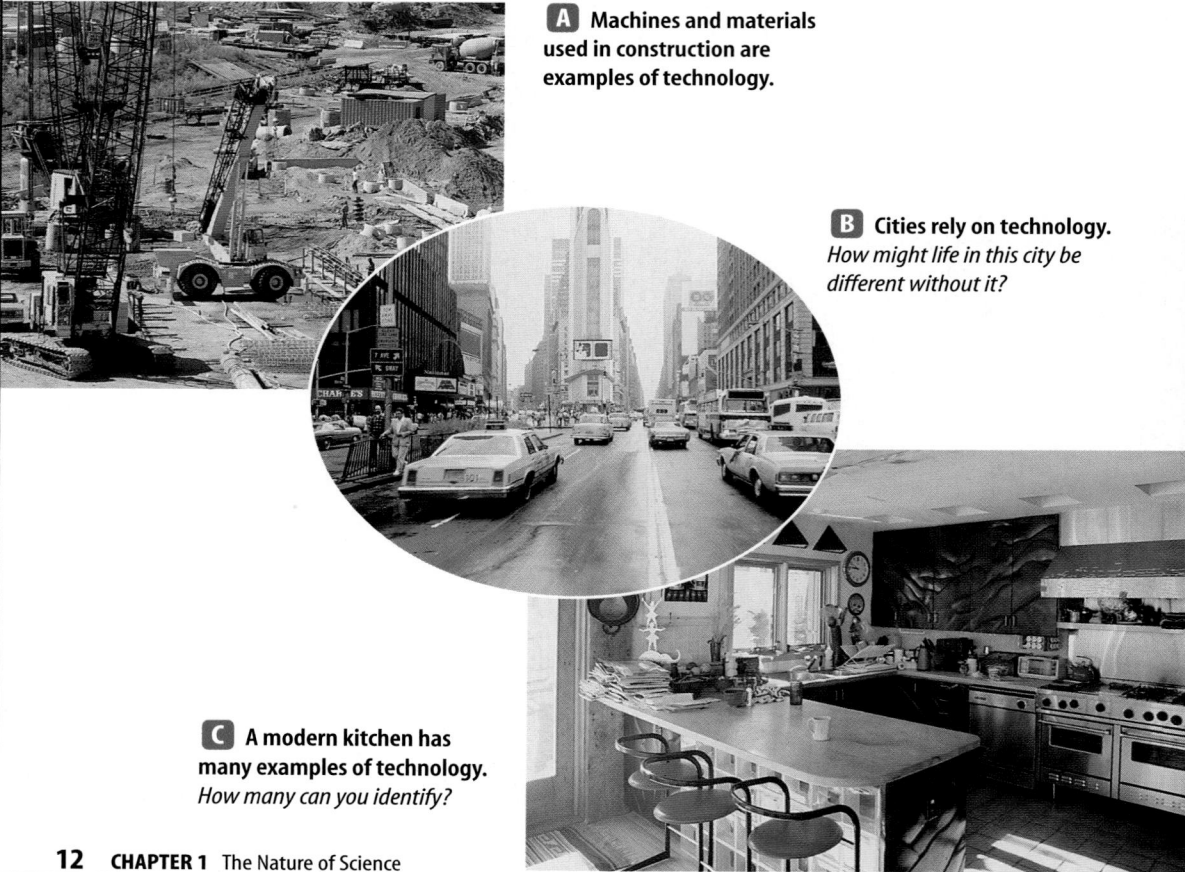

A Machines and materials used in construction are examples of technology.

B Cities rely on technology. *How might life in this city be different without it?*

C A modern kitchen has many examples of technology. *How many can you identify?*

Science Journal

Technology at Work Have students write in their Science Journals essays that describe how they use technology to do their homework. Students might describe how the following are used: writing implements, paper, ruler, stapler, hole punch, paper clips, scissors, calculator, computer, and electricity. L2 ELL
Linguistic P

Inclusion Strategies

Behaviorally Disordered Scientists from all over the world have made new technologies. Johann Vaaler, born in 1866 in Norway, invented the first paper clip in 1899. There is a saying, "Necessity is the mother of invention." Paper clips were made to attach papers to one another. Give students paper clips and have them find and demonstrate a new use for them. L2 ELL
Logical-Mathematical

Figure 10

For thousands of years, discoveries made by people of many cultures have advanced the study of Earth. This time line shows milestones and inventions that have shaped the development of Earth science technology and led to a greater understanding of the planet and its place in the universe.

10,000 B.C.: First pottery (Japan)

7000 B.C.: Copper metalworking (Turkey)

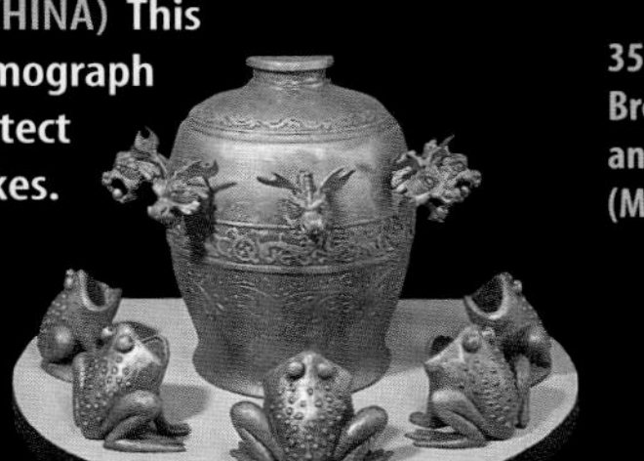

A.D. 132 (CHINA) This early seismograph helped detect earthquakes.

3500 B.C.: Bronze tools and weapons (Mesopotamia)

900: Terraced field for soil conservation (Peru)

650: Windmill (Persia)

A.D. 100

1000 B.C.

80 B.C.: Astronomical calendar (Greece)

1942 (FRANCE) Breathing from tanks of compressed air lets divers move underwater without being tethered to an air source at the surface.

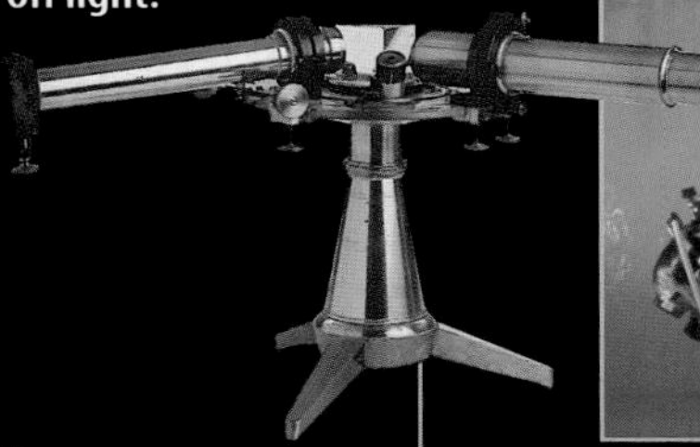

1814 (GERMANY) A spectroscope allowed scientists to determine which elements are present in an object or substance that is giving off light.

1090: Magnetic compass (Arabia, China)

Streamer holes

1000 (NORWAY) Streamers tied through holes in Viking wind vanes indicated wind direction and strength.

1880: Modern seismograph (England)

1538: Diving bell (Spain)

1592: Thermometer (Italy)

1957: Space satellite (former U.S.S.R.)

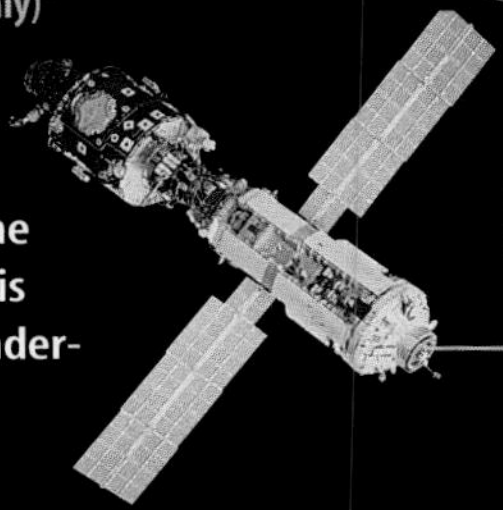

1998–2006: *INTERNATIONAL SPACE STATION* With participants from 16 countries, the *International Space Station* is helping scientists better understand Earth and beyond.

1926: Liquid-fuel rocket (United States)

2000

SECTION 1   Science All Around   **13**

Resource Manager

Chapter Resources Booklet
    Enrichment, p. 27
    Reinforcement, p. 25
Science Inquiry Labs, p. 37

Visualizing the History of Earth Science Technology

Have students examine the pictures and read the captions. Then ask the following questions.

Which of the developments on the timeline seem as if they were made specifically for the study of science? The seismographs (both ancient and modern), the diving bell, the spectroscope, the space station, space satellite, and liquid-fuel rocket. The others solved practical problems.

How might the pottery, copper, and bronze shown at the beginning of the timeline have advanced the study of Earth? These inventions moved humans out of the Stone Age and into the realm of technology. They allowed for development of sophisticated tools, and ultimately to the invention of scientific instruments.

Activity

Make copies of a simple world map and have students mark the approximate location of each development listed on the timeline. Have them research to find several more developments important to Earth science and to plot those on their maps. Encourage them to find inventions from areas of the world not represented on the timeline.

Extension

Challenge students to choose one development on the timeline and find out how it contributed to society at that particular place and time. Have them draw conclusions about how scientific technology contributes to human survival.

Caption Answer

Figure 11 Tiny radio transmitters attached to endangered animals can be monitored by satellites; knowing where the animals are enables wildlife experts to offer better protection.

③ Assess

Reteach

As a class, have students develop a hypothesis to answer the question, "How is paint affected by temperature change?" Have students explain how they could test their hypothesis. Students should include details about the independent and dependent variables, the constants, and the control. L2 LS **Linguistic**

Challenge

Have students look through newspapers and magazines to find examples of technology. Ask each student to make a poster presentation of their articles to share with classmates. L2 LS **Visual-Spatial** P

✓Assessment

Oral Of all the technologies that have ever been created, which do you think is the most important? Why? Use **Performance Assessment in the Science Classroom,** p. 89.

Figure 11
Weather satellites help forecasters predict future storms. *How might this same technology be used to protect endangered species?*

Using Technology Most people immediately think of huge and exotic inventions when the word technology is mentioned. However, the use of scientific knowledge has resulted in such common yet important things as paper, can openers, buckets, aspirin, rubber boots, locks and keys, microfiber clothing, ironing boards, bandages, and scissors. It also has resulted in robots that check underwater oil rigs for leaks and others that manufacture cars. Technology also includes calculators and computers that process information.

Transferable Technology Technology is a natural outcome of using scientific knowledge to solve problems and make people's lives easier and better. The wonderful thing about technology is that it is transferable. That means that it can be applied to new situations. For example, many types of technology that are now common were originally developed for use in outer space.

Scientists developed robotic parts, new fibers, and microminiaturized instruments for spacecraft and satellites. After these materials were developed, many were modified for use here on Earth. Technology that once was developed by the military, such as radar and sonar, has applications in the study of space, weather, Earth's structures, and medicine.

Earth scientists rely on information from weather satellites like the one in **Figure 11** to gather weather data. But biologists also use satellites to track animals. A tiny radio transmitter attached to an animal sends signals up to a satellite. The satellite then sends data on the animal's location to a ground station. Some researchers use the data to track bird migration.

Section ① Assessment

1. What is a hypothesis? Why must hypotheses be testable?
2. What is Earth science?
3. Explain why it is important that scientists perform an experiment more than one time.
4. Explain why it is important to use constants in an experiment.
5. **Think Critically** Name an example of technology you use every day and, as best you can, describe the science behind the technology.

Skill Builder Activities

6. **Comparing and Contrasting** Compare and contrast an independent variable and a dependent variable. **For more help, refer to the** Science Skill Handbook.

7. **Communicating** In your Science Journal, write a paragraph about how you would try to describe a modern device such as a TV, microwave oven, or computer to someone living in 1800. **For more help, refer to the** Science Skill Handbook.

Answers to Section Assessment

1. An educated guess; if it can't be tested, the answer to the question or problem cannot be determined.
2. study of Earth and space
3. Repeating an experiment confirms whether results are consistent and valid.
4. By using constants, only one variable is tested at a time.
5. Possible answer: A pencil is made of graphite, wood, paint, rubber, and metal. Sciences include studies of minerals and metals, the mechanics of making saws to cut wood and machines to place graphite into the wood, and the chemistry of paint and rubber.
6. independent variable: variable being tested; dependent variable: variable measured to see the effects of independent variable
7. Students should include what the modern device does and as much as they can about how it works. They might also include information about how the technology affects their lives.

A Work in Progress

Throughout time, people have been frightened by and curious about their surroundings all at the same time. Storms, erupting volcanoes, comets, seasonal changes, and other natural phenomena fascinated people thousands of years ago, and they fascinate people today. As shown in **Figure 12,** early people relied on mythology to explain what they observed. They believed that mythological gods were responsible for creating storms, causing volcanoes to erupt, causing earthquakes, bringing the seasons, and making comets appear in the sky.

Recording Observations Some early civilizations went so far as to record what they saw. They developed calendars that described natural recurring phenomena. Six thousand years ago, Egyptian farmers observed that the Nile River flooded their lands every summer. Their crops had to be planted at the right time in order to make use of this water. The farmers noticed that shortly before flood time, the brightest star in the sky, Sirius, appeared at dawn in the east. The Egyptians developed a calendar based on the appearance of this star, which occurred about every 365 days.

Later, civilizations created instruments to measure things. As you saw in the Explore Activity, instruments allow for precise measurements. As instruments got better, accuracy of observations got better. While observations were being made, people tried to reason why things happened the way they did. They made inferences, or conclusions, to help explain things. Some people developed hypotheses that they tested. Their experimental conclusions allowed them to learn even more.

As You Read

What You'll Learn

- **Explain** why science is always changing.
- **Compare and contrast** scientific theories and scientific laws.
- **Discuss** the limits of science.

Vocabulary

scientific theory   ethics
scientific law   bias

Why It's Important

Science helps you understand the world around you.

Figure 12
Early Scandinavian and Germanic peoples believed that a god named Thor controlled the weather. In this drawing, Thor is creating a storm. Lightning flashed whenever he threw his heavy hammer.

SECTION 2 Scientific Enterprise **15**

Section ✓*Assessment* Planner

---

1 Motivate

Bellringer Transparency

Display the Section Focus Transparency for Section 2. Use the accompanying Transparency Activity Master. [L2] [ELL]

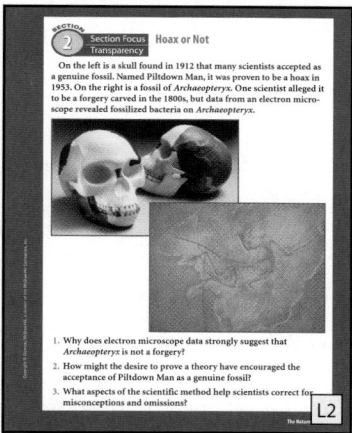

Section Focus Transparency — Hoax or Not

On the left is a skull found in 1912 that many scientists accepted as a genuine fossil. Named Piltdown Man, it was proven to be a hoax in 1953. On the right is a fossil of *Archaeopteryx*. One scientist alleged it to be a forgery carved in the 1800s, but data from an electron microscope revealed fossilized bacteria on *Archaeopteryx*.

1. Why does electron microscope data strongly suggest that *Archaeopteryx* is not a forgery?
2. How might the desire to prove a theory have encouraged the acceptance of Piltdown Man as a genuine fossil?
3. What aspects of the scientific method help scientists correct for misconceptions and omissions?

[L2]

Tie to Prior Knowledge

Students are familiar with daily TV weather reports, but they may never have thought about how humans learned so much about weather. This section presents a history of human understanding of weather as an example that all scientific knowledge is a work in progress.

Resource Manager

Chapter Resources Booklet
Transparency Activity, p. 41

A Work in Progress

Discussion

Suppose you want to learn more about meteorology. **The Internet is a good place to start your research, but why can't you believe everything you read on the Internet?** Anyone can post information. **How can you know if a particular source is reliable?** Check the credentials of the author of the article. Reliable sources include government agencies, universities, professional organizations, and professional journals.

The History of Meteorology

Visual Learning

Figure 13 Glass thermometers with an alcohol column are still used today. As the alcohol grows warmer, it expands and rises in the glass tube. Red dye is added so you can see the alcohol. Mercury or alcohol are used in thermometers because they have a higher boiling point and a lower freezing point than temperatures normally found on Earth. **Why isn't water used as the liquid in thermometers?** The freezing point of water is a temperature normally found on Earth. Water would freeze and break the glass tube at 0°C. L2

Visual-Spatial and Linguistic

✔ Reading Check

Answer barometer, thermometer, hygrometer, anemometer

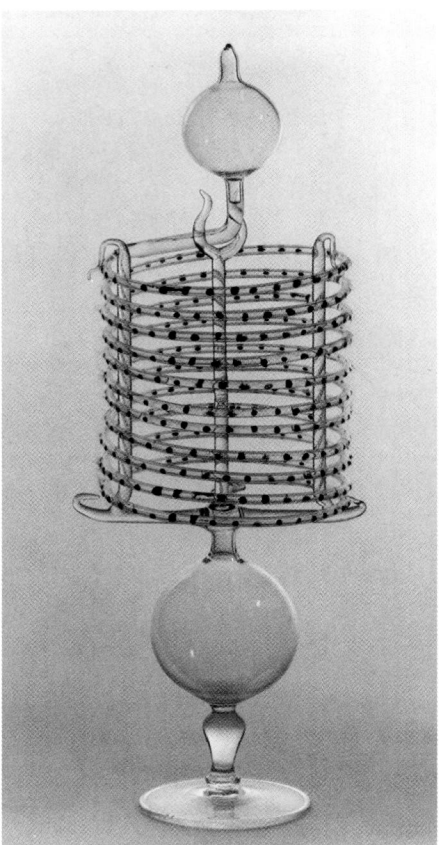

Figure 13
This photo shows a replica of a 1660 Italian alcohol thermometer.

The History of Meteorology

Today, scientists know what they know because of all the knowledge that has been collected over time. The history of meteorology, which is the study of weather, illustrates how an understanding of one area of Earth science has developed over time.

Weather Instruments As you have read, ancient peoples believed that their gods controlled weather. However, even early civilizations observed and recorded some weather information. The rain gauge was probably the first weather instrument. The earliest reference to the use of a rain gauge to record the amount of rainfall appears in a book by the ruler of India from 321 B.C. to 296 B.C.

It wasn't until the 1600s that scientists in Italy began to develop other instruments to study weather. These instruments included the barometer—to measure air pressure; the thermometer—to measure temperature, shown in **Figure 13;** the hygrometer—to measure water vapor in the air; and the anemometer—to measure wind speed. With these instruments, the scientists set up weather stations across Italy.

✔ Reading Check
What instruments were developed in the 1600s to study weather?

Weather Prediction in the United States Benjamin Franklin was the first American to suggest that weather could be predicted. Franklin read newpaper accounts of storms from newspapers across the country. From these articles, Franklin concluded that severe storms generally move across the country from west to east. He also concluded that observers could monitor a storm and notify those ahead of its path that it was coming. Franklin's ideas were finally put to practical use shortly after the telegraph was invented in 1837.

By 1849, an organized system of weather observation sites was set up and weather reports from volunteer weather observers were sent by telegraph to the Smithsonian Institution. In 1850, Joseph Henry, secretary of the Smithsonian Institution in the United States, began drawing maps from the weather data he received. A large weather map was displayed at the Institution and a weather report was sent to the *Washington Evening Post* to be published in the newspaper.

16   CHAPTER 1 The Nature of Science

Cultural Diversity

Saving the Netherlands Storm surges and rising sea levels are real threats for people in the Netherlands. Much of the country's coastal region is below sea level. At one time, the only thing the Dutch could do during a bad storm was use sandbags and hope their specially made dikes would keep out the water. In 1953, storm waves plunged over the dikes, killing 1,850 people. Then, the Dutch designed a better way to keep out the water. In 1997, they completed a ten-year project to construct two gigantic steel walls that can be closed to block storm waves entering the Rhine River. The walls can be opened when seas are calm to allow for ship traffic. The gates are controlled by computers. Have students research and write a report about other ways people use technology to protect their coastlines. L2 **Linguistic** P

National Weather Service By the late 1800s, the United States Weather Bureau was functioning with more than 350 observing sites across the country. By 1923, weather forecasts were being carried by 140 radio stations across the United States. Finally in 1970, the Bureau name was changed to the National Weather Service and it became part of the National Oceanic and Atmospheric Administration (NOAA).

Today's weather is forecast using orbiting satellites, weather balloons, radar, and other sophisticated technology. Each day about 60,000 reports from weather stations, ships, aircraft, and radar transmitters are gathered and filed. **Figure 14** shows instruments used to gather data at a weather station. All the information gathered is compiled into a report that is distributed to radio stations, television networks, and other news media.

Today, if you want to know about the weather anywhere in the world—at any time of day or night—you could watch a television weather channel, listen to a radio news station, or check an internet site. If you live in an area that has tornadoes, hurricanes, or other severe weather conditions, you know it is important to have weather watches and warnings available to your community.

SCIENCE *Online*

Research Visit the Glencoe Science Web site at **science.glencoe.com** for more information about weather forecasting. Communicate to your class what you learn.

Make a Model
Have students make models of weather instruments. Set aside an area of the classroom to display the models. [L2] [IS] **Kinesthetic**

Teacher FYI
The United States Weather Research Program (USWRP) fosters collaboration among four government agencies: NOAA, NASA, the National Science Foundation, and the United States Navy. USWRP coordinates scientific research to improve short-term weather forecasts that significantly impact society. A short-term forecast is made one hour to 14 days in advance of a weather event. The USWRP's highest priority is to improve hurricane forecasting.

SCIENCE *Online*
Internet Addresses
_____
_____
_____
_____
Explore the Glencoe Science Web site at **science.glencoe.com** to find out more about topics in this section.

Figure 14
Some weather stations are operated by meteorologists, but many are now automated. Data from automated stations is transmitted to a central office where they are studied.

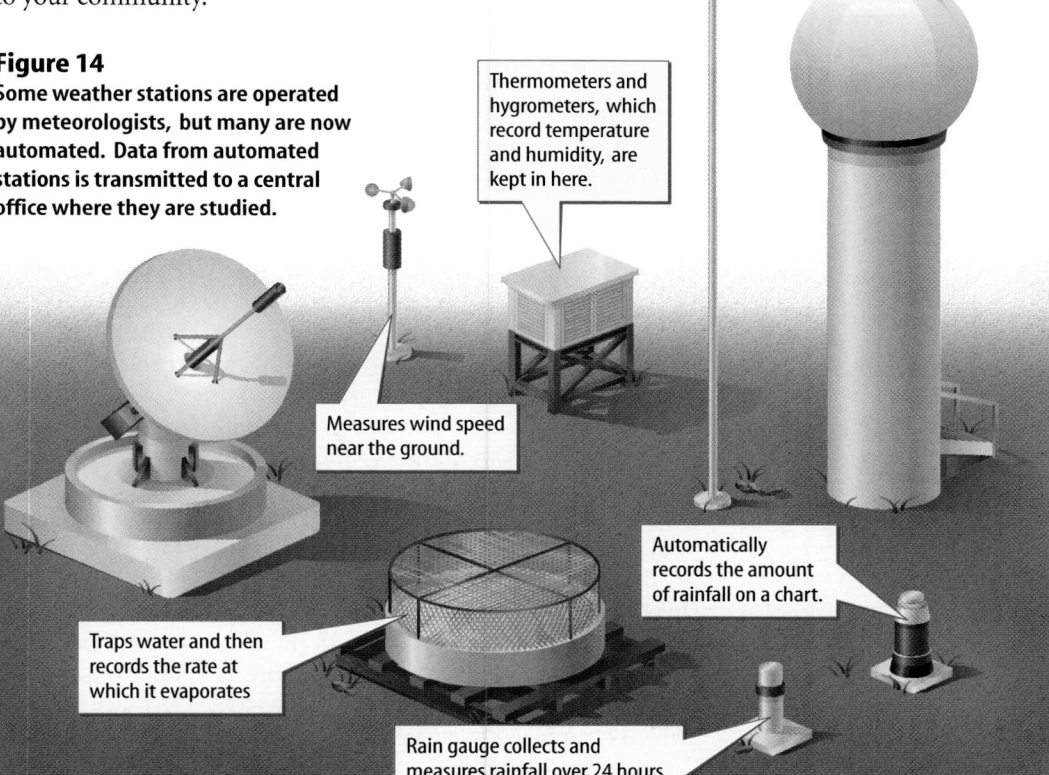

Thermometers and hygrometers, which record temperature and humidity, are kept in here.

Measures wind speed near the ground.

Traps water and then records the rate at which it evaporates

Automatically records the amount of rainfall on a chart.

Rain gauge collects and measures rainfall over 24 hours.

✓ Active Reading

Flow Chart A flow chart helps students logically sequence events. Have students write *The History of Meteorology*, *Weather Prediction in the United States*, and *The National Weather Service* in a sequence of large rectangles. Underneath each of these major heads, have students write, in chronological order, the events discussed in the text. [IS] **Logical-Mathematical** [P]

Resource Manager

Chapter Resources Booklet
  Directed Reading for Content Mastery, pp. 19, 20
Reading and Writing Skill Activities, p. 43

Figure 15
The Global Positioning System (GPS) can pinpoint a person's location on Earth. A radio receiver gets signals from several orbiting *Navstar* satellites like this one. By comparing how far the receiver is from each satellite, the receiver's position can be determined and displayed.

Continuing Research

Scientific knowledge continues to change as scientists develop better instruments and testing procedures. As it changes, scientists have a greater understanding of nature. As you saw in **Figure 14,** scientists use a variety of technologies to study weather. Scientists have similar technologies to study Earth's interior, the oceans, environmental problems, and space. How could the technology shown in **Figure 15** be used by Earth scientists?

It is impossible to predict the types of instruments scientists will have in the future. But it is easy to predict that as research continues and instruments improve, knowledge will grow. Perhaps one day you will make a scientific breakthrough that changes people's understanding of the world.

Scientific Theories As you learned earlier, scientists test hypotheses. If data gathered over a long period of time support a hypothesis, scientists become convinced that the hypothesis is useful. They use results from many scientists' work to develop a scientific theory. A **scientific theory** is an explanation or model backed by results obtained from many tests or experiments.

✔ Reading Check

How can a scientific hypothesis become a scientific theory?

Examine how one hypothesis became a theory. Comets once were believed to be the forecasters of disaster. People often were terrified yet fascinated by the ghostly balls appearing in the sky. Slowly over the years, comets lost much of their mystery. However, from the 1800s until 1949 most scientists hypothesized that comets were made of many particles of different kinds of materials swarming in a cluster. Based on this hypothesis, a comet was described as a swirling cloud of dust.

In 1949, American astronomer Fred L. Whipple, proposed a hypothesis that a comet was more like a dirty snowball—that the nucleus of a comet contains practically all of a comet's mass and consists of ices and dust. If a comet's orbit brings it close to the Sun, the heat vaporizes some of the ices, releasing dust and gas which form the comet's tail. Dr. Whipple's hypothesis was published in the March 1950 *Astrophysical Journal.*

Hypothesis Supported Before it became an accepted theory, Dr. Whipple's hypothesis was subjected to many years of tests and observations. Some of the most important were the 1986 observations of Halley's comet, shown in **Figure 16.** A group of astronomers from the University of Arizona, headed by Dr. Susan Wyckoff, studied the composition of the comet. Dr. Wyckoff observed the comet many times, using giant telescopes in Arizona and Chile in South America. At other times, she studied the observations of other astronomers, including those who studied data collected by the *Giotto* and other spacecrafts. All these observations and data supported Dr. Whipple's original hypothesis. With so much support, Dr. Whipple's hypothesis has become an accepted scientific theory.

Scientific Laws A **scientific law** is a rule that describes the behavior of something in nature. Usually, a scientific law describes what will happen in a given situation but doesn't explain why it happens. An example of a scientific law is Newton's first law of motion. According to this law, an object, such as a marble or a spacecraft, will continue in motion or remain at rest until it's acted upon by an outside force. According to Newton's second law of motion, when a force acts on an object, the object will change speed, direction, or both. Finally, according to Newton's third law, for every action, there is an equal and opposite reaction. This law explains how rockets that are used to launch space probes to study Halley's comet and other objects in space work. When the burning gases are forced out of the back of a rocket, a force of equal strength but opposite direction pushes the rocket forward.

Figure 16
The view of Halley's comet from the *Giotto* spacecraft allowed scientists to determine the size of the icy nucleus, and that the nucleus was covered by a black crust of dust. Jets of gas blasted out from holes in the crust to form the comet's tail.

Mini LAB

Observing a Scientific Law

Procedure
1. Cut one end from a **shoe box.**
2. Put the box on the floor. Place a **rubber ball** in the closed end of the box.
3. Pushing on the closed end of the box, move the box rapidly across the floor. Then suddenly stop pushing.

Analysis
1. What happened when the box stopped?
2. How does Newton's first law of motion explain this?

Mini LAB

Purpose Students observe Newton's first law of motion.
L2 **Kinesthetic and Visual-Spatial**

Materials shoe box, scissors, rubber ball

Teaching Strategy The ball will roll rapidly out of the box. Suggest students move the box in a direction so that the ball moves toward a wall, not the center of the room.

Safety Precaution Caution students to use care when cutting the box.

Analysis
1. The ball rolled out of the box and across the floor.
2. The ball was in motion as the box was being pushed. When the box was stopped, the ball had nothing to stop its movement and it continued until it hit something or until friction with the floor slowed it down.

✔ Assessment

Performance Have students design an experiment that demonstrates Newton's second law of motion. Use **Performance Assessment in the Science Classroom,** p. 95.

Teacher FYI

Sir Isaac Newton (1642–1727) wrote the laws of motion in his work titled *Philosophiae Naturalis Principia Mathematica*, published in 1687. The information in his book helped Edmund Halley make his predictions of the orbital motion of comets.

Resource Manager

Chapter Resources Booklet
  MiniLAB, p. 4
Home and Community Involvement, p. 33

Activity

Have students think about observations they have made throughout the day. Then have them each write two questions about what they saw. One should be an ethical question; the other, a question that could be tested using scientific methods. Have students share their questions orally. L2 COOP LEARN
 **Interpersonal**

Health
INTEGRATION

Since it is wrong to harm humans and other animals, their health and well-being should be considered when planning an experiment. Some procedures have the potential for doing harm to test subjects, whereas other procedures do not. The ethically correct choice is to use procedures that do not harm test subjects.

✔ Reading Check

Answer Ethical issues do not have variables that can be observed, measured, and tested.

Doing Science Right

Teacher FYI

Several professional science organizations have developed codes of ethics. For example, the American Chemical Society has "The Chemist's Code of Conduct." Members are expected to adhere to the highest ethical standards in dealing with the public, the science of chemistry, the profession, employers, employees, students, associates, clients, and the environment.

Figure 17
Ethical questions can't be solved by using scientific methods.

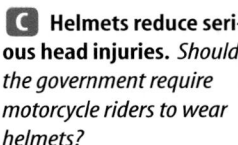

B Disease-carrying mosquitoes live in this swamp. *Should swamps be drained, even if other species lose their habitat?*

A These animals live on the African plains. *Should they be hunted as trophies?*

C Helmets reduce serious head injuries. *Should the government require motorcycle riders to wear helmets?*

Health
INTEGRATION

When doing science projects, you must treat animals and human subjects responsibly and safely. You should not hurt animals, subject them to any kind of stress, or embarrass or put people at any kind of physical or emotional risk. Why is the health of your subjects an important ethical concern?

Limits of Science

Will science always provide answers to all your questions? No, science doesn't have answers to all the questions and problems in the universe. Science is limited in what it can explain. For a question or problem to be scientifically studied, there must be variables that can be observed, measured, and tested. Problems that deal with ethics and belief systems cannot be answered using these methods. **Ethics** deals with moral values about what is good or bad. Belief systems deal with religious and/or other beliefs. Examples of ethical and belief-system questions that science cannot answer are: Do humans have more value on Earth than other life-forms?, Should the federal government regulate car emissions?, and Should animals be used in medical experiments? Look at **Figure 17.** What's your opinion?

✔ Reading Check
Why can't science be used to answer ethical questions?

Doing Science Right

Although ethical questions cannot be answered by science, there are ethical ways of doing science. The correct approach to doing science is to perform experiments in a way that honestly tests hypotheses and draws conclusions in an unbiased way.

Resource Manager

Chapter Resources Booklet
 Enrichment, p. 28
 Reinforcement, p. 26
Mathematics Skill Activities, p. 51

Science Journal

Honest Testing Have students write a short essay explaining why it is important to perform experiments in a way that honestly tests a hypothesis. Students should note that if the experiment does not have the correct constants and controls for testing a particular hypothesis, wrong conclusions likely will be made. L2  **Linguistic**

Being Objective When you do scientific experiments, be sure that you design your experiments in a way that you objectively test your hypotheses. If you don't, your **bias**, or personal opinion, can affect your observations. For example, in the 1940s, Soviet scientist Trofim Lysenko believed that individuals of the same species would not compete with one another. His ideas were based on the political beliefs held in the Soviet Union at that time. Based on his personal opinion, Lysenko ordered 300,000 tree seedlings planted in groups in a reforestation project. He believed that the trees in each group would aid one another in competing against other plant species. However, the area where the trees were planted was extremely dry and swept by constant winds. Without enough water and nutrients, most of the trees died and Lysenko's personal opinion was proven wrong. It turned out to be a costly experiment for the Soviet government.

Suppose you wanted to grow as many plants as possible in a single flowerpot. Would you assume that all of the plants in the pot shown in **Figure 18** could survive, or would you set up an experiment to objectively test this hypothesis? Unless you test various numbers of plants in pots under the same conditions, you could not make a valid conclusion.

Figure 18
These seedlings are crowded into a single pot. *How many do you think could survive?*

Discussion

Suppose you want to know whether boys or girls have a better short-term memory. You hypothesize that boys do. You ask your male and female friends to participate in your study, and you make up a list of things that you will ask them to remember. Most of the items on the list are statistics for your favorite baseball team that you and your male friends are always talking about. **What are the problems with your experiment?** The boys may know a lot of the statistics before the experiment and may score higher on your test than the girls. As a result, your test may not be a good test of the boys' short-term memories.

Problem-Solving Activity

How can bias affect your observations?

Do you think bias can affect a person's observations? With the help of her classmates, Sharon performed an experiment to find out.

Identifying the Problem

Sharon showed ten friends a photograph of an uncut amethyst and asked them to rank the quality of color from 1 to 10. She then wrote the words "prize amethyst" on top of the photo and asked ten more friends to rank the quality of color.

Solving the Problem

1. Examine the tables. Do you think the hint affected the way Sharon's classmates

Rankings Without Hint		Rankings With Hint	
5	7	7	8
4	5	8	9
6	4	9	8
5	6	10	8
5	3	7	9
Average: 5.0		**Average: 8.3**	

rated the amethyst? What effect did the hint have on them?

2. Do you think bias could affect the results of a scientific experiment? Explain. How could this bias be prevented?

SECTION 2 Scientific Enterprise **21**

Curriculum Connection

Social Studies Science is often used in solving criminal cases. Suppose a truck runs a stop light, hits a car, and injures several people. Police arrive at the scene and see skid marks and crushed vehicles but don't make any measurements. A traffic investigator is asked to conduct acceleration tests to determine the maximum speed the truck could have been going when it hit the car. Because the truck was crushed in the accident, a motorcycle is tested instead. Its maximum speed is reported to city officials. Have students explain why this scientific investigation would not have been performed properly. In order to be fair, a truck must be used in the acceleration tests. A motorcycle will give different results. L2 IS **Logical-Mathematical**

Doing Science Right, continued

Caption Answer

Figure 19 You will have a detailed record of what you did; others will know precisely how the experiment was performed; the experiment will be reproducible.

③ Assess

Reteach

Have students look again at **Figure 10,** and ask them to describe what this time line would look like if scientists had worked in isolation and had not shared scientific knowledge. Students should realize that most of the technologies shown in this time line would not exist. `L2` `LS` **Visual-Spatial**

Challenge

Compare a scientist who falsifies his or her data to a student who cheats on a test. Both are dishonest. Both are representing their work in an untruthful manner.

✓Assessment

Process Have students read the following statement; classify it as a hypothesis, theory, or law; and defend their answers: All things fall to the ground because of gravity. It's a law because it is a rule that describes the behavior of something in nature. Use **Performance Assessment in the Science Classroom,** p. 91.

Figure 19
Scientists take detailed notes of procedures and observations when they do science experiments. *Why should you do the same thing?*

Being Ethical and Open People who perform science in ethical and unbiased ways, keep detailed notes of their procedures like the scientists shown in **Figure 19.** Their conclusions are based on precise measurements and tests. They communicate their discoveries by publishing their research in journals or presenting reports at scientific meetings. This allows other scientists to examine and evaluate their work. Scientific knowledge advances when people work together. Much of the science you know today has come about because of the collaboration of investigations done by many different people over many years.

The opposite of ethical behavior in science is fraud. Scientific fraud involves dishonest acts or statements. Fraud could include such things as making up data, changing the results of experiments, or taking credit for work done by others.

Section ② Assessment

1. Why is science always changing?
2. How can a hypothesis be supported?
3. What is the difference between a scientific theory and a scientific law?
4. What kinds of questions can't be answered by science?
5. **Think Critically** When reading science articles in newspapers, magazines, or on the Internet, why should you look for the authors' biases?

Skill Builder Activities

6. **Drawing Conclusions** Describe what would have happened if the 1986 observations of Halley's comet had not supported Dr. Whipple's original hypothesis. **For more help, refer to the** Science Skill Handbook.

7. **Using a Word Processor** Use a computer to write a paragraph explaining how fraud could damage science. **For more help, refer to the** Technology Skill Handbook.

22   CHAPTER 1 The Nature of Science

Answers to Section Assessment

1. Scientific knowledge changes as scientists develop better instruments and better testing procedures.
2. Repeated testing by many scientists can support a hypothesis.
3. A scientific theory is an explanation backed by results from repeated testing. A scientific law is a rule that describes the behavior of something in nature.
4. Questions that lack variables that can be observed, measured, and tested cannot be answered by science.
5. If the author is biased, the information in the article might be slanted and might not reflect what is factual.
6. His hypothesis would have been revised or rejected.
7. Possible answer: Fraud is misrepresenting results. This may cause people harm if technologies are developed from false data.

Understanding Science Articles

You know that scientists conduct investigations to learn things about our world. It is important for researchers to share what they learn so other researchers can repeat and expand upon their results. One important way that scientific results are shared is by publishing them in journals and magazines. How can you learn about recent work by scientists? How do you interpret information that you read?

What You'll Investigate
What information about Earth science and scientific methods can you learn by reading an appropriate magazine article?

Materials
magazine articles about Earth science topics

Goals
- **Obtain** a recent magazine article concerning a research topic in Earth science.
- **Identify** aspects of science and scientific methods in the article.

Procedure

1. Locate a recent magazine article about a topic in Earth science research.
2. Read the article paying attention to details that are related to science, research, and scientific methods.
3. What branch of Earth science does the article discuss?
4. **Describe** what the article is about. Does it describe a particular event or discuss more general research?
5. Are the names of any scientists mentioned? If so, what was the role of each in the research being discussed?

6. Are particular hypotheses being tested? If so, is the research project complete or is it still continuing?
7. **Describe** how the research is conducted. What is being measured? What observations are recorded?

Conclude and Apply

1. Are data available that do or do not support any hypotheses? Explain.
2. What do other scientists think about the research?
3. Are references provided that tell you where you can find more information about this particular research or the more general topic? If not, what are some sources where you might locate more information?

Communicating Your Data
Prepare an oral report on the article you read. Present your report to the class. **For more help, refer to the** Science Skill Handbook.

ACTIVITY 23

Resource Manager

Chapter Resources Booklet
  Activity Worksheets, pp. 5–6, 7–8
  Lab Activity, pp. 11–13
Lab Management and Safety, p. 63

Communicating Your Data
When students present their oral reports to the class, encourage other students to ask questions about the scientific methods and other details of the research.

Purpose Students will learn about real-life scientific research methods by reading an article concerning a topic in Earth science. L2 IS **Linguistic**
Process Skills observing and inferring, communicating
Time Required 45 minutes
Teaching Strategies
- Students may find articles in either printed magazines or on the Internet.
- Allow students to work in groups of two or three to discuss the articles.

Troubleshooting Preview articles to be sure they are not too advanced. Some articles may not clearly identify the research methods, views of scientists, or hypotheses.

Answers to Questions
1. Answers will depend on the article the student reviews.
2. Answers should describe various opinions by other scientists that may be mentioned in the article.
3. Students should mention references given either in the body or at the end of the article. If no references are given, students should describe other sources of information such as other magazines or books.

Assessment

Portfolio Have students write a summary of the article they reviewed. They should describe why they think the research is useful and give their opinion of the methods used for the research. Use **PASC,** p. 159.

Activity

BENCH TESTED

What You'll Investigate

Purpose

Students observe how variables affect the swing of a pendulum.

L2 COOP LEARN IS **Kinesthetic and Interpersonal**

Process Skills

identifying and manipulating variables, observing and inferring, measuring in SI, using numbers, recording, interpreting data, predicting

Time Required

40 minutes

Materials

Each team of students will need 60 cm of string, a metric ruler, a paper clip, 5 metal washers, a protractor, and a watch with a second hand.

Safety Precautions

Advise students to be careful when swinging the pendulums so that they do not hit each other or other objects in the room. Have students wear goggles.

Procedure

Teaching Strategies

- The student holding the pendulum should hold his or her hand still while the pendulum is moving.
- The pendulum should swing freely without touching anything in its path.
- A complete swing is from the point where the pendulum is released to the highest point where it returns.

Activity

Testing Variables of a Pendulum

A pendulum is an old, but accurate timekeeping device. It works because of two natural phenomena—gravity and inertia—that are important in the study of Earth science. Gravity makes all objects fall toward Earth's surface. Inertia makes matter remain at rest or in motion unless acted upon by an external force. In the following activity, you will test some variables that might affect the swing of a pendulum.

What You'll Investigate

How do the length of a pendulum, the attached mass, and the angle of the release of the mass affect the swing of a pendulum?

Materials

string (60 cm)
metal washers (5)
watch with a second hand
metric ruler
paper clip
protractor

Goals

- **Manipulate** variables of a pendulum.
- **Draw** conclusions from experimentation with pendulums.

Safety Precautions

Table 1 Length of the Pendulum

Length of String (cm)	Swings Per Minute		
	Trial 1	Trial 2	Average
10			
20			
30			
40			
50			

Table 2 Amount of Mass on the Pendulum

Units of Mass	Swings Per Minute		
	Trial 1	Trial 2	Average
1			
2			
3			
4			
5			

Table 3 Angle of the Release of the Mass

Angle of Release	Swings Per Minute		
	Trial 1	Trial 2	Average
90°			
80°			
70°			
60°			
50°			
40°			

24 CHAPTER 1 The Nature of Science

Inclusion Strategies

Physically Challenged Have students who have difficulty doing the testing make sure their partner is doing the procedures with precision.
COOP LEARN IS **Interpersonal**

Discussion

Why does the pendulum eventually stop moving? Newton's first law of motion explains that an object will continue in motion until it is acted upon by an outside force. In this experiment, as the pendulum moves, it encounters air molecules and is acted upon by gravity. The outside forces that stop its motion are friction and gravity.

Procedure

1. Copy the three data tables into your Science Journal.
2. Bend the paper clip into an S-shape and tie it to one end of the string.
3. Hang one washer from the paper clip.
4. **Measure** 10 cm of string from the washer and hold the string at that distance with one hand.
5. Use your other hand to pull back the end of the pendulum with the washer so it is parallel with the ground. Let go of the washer.
6. Count the number of complete swings the pendulum makes in 1 min. Record this number in **Table 1**.
7. Repeat step 5 and record the number of swings in **Table 1** under "Trial 2".
8. Average the results of steps 5 and 6

and record the average swings per minute in **Table 1**.

9. Repeat Steps 4 through 7, using string lengths of 20 cm, 30 cm, 40 cm, and 50 cm. Record your data in **Table 1**.
10. Copy the data with the string length of 50 cm in **Table 2**.
11. Repeat Steps 5 and 6 using 2, 3, 4, and 5 washers. Record these data in **Table 2**.
12. Use 50 cm of string and one washer for the third set of tests.
13. Use the protractor to measure a 90° drop of the mass. Repeat this procedure, calculate the average, and record the data in Table 3.
14. Repeat procedures 12 and 13, using angles of 80°, 70°, 60°, 50°, and 40°.

Conclude and Apply

1. When you tested the effect of the angle of the drop of the pendulum on the swings per minute, which variables did you keep constant?
2. **Infer** which of the variables you tested affects the swing of a pendulum.
3. Suppose you have a pendulum clock that indicates an earlier time than it really is. (This means it has too few swings per minute.) What could you do to the clock to make it keep better time?

Communicating Your Data

Graph the data from your tables. Title and label the graphs. Use different colored pencils for each graph. **Compare** your graphs with the graphs of other members of your class. **For more help, refer to the** Science Skill Handbook.

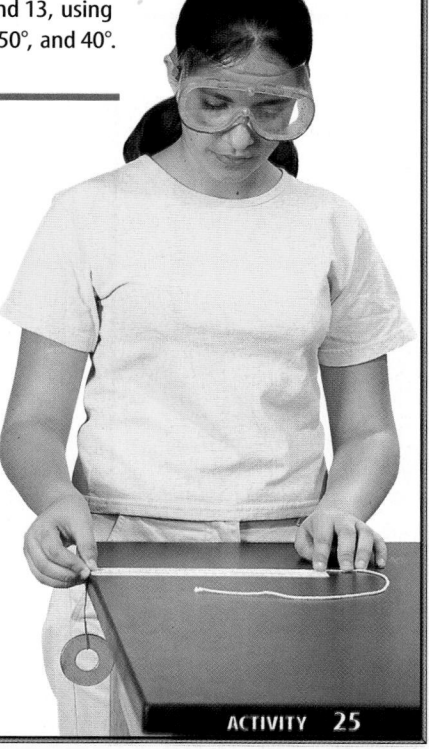

ACTIVITY 25

Expected Outcome
The mass and the angle of the drop do not affect the number of swings per minute of the pendulum. The length of string does. The longer the string, the fewer the number of swings per minute.

Conclude and Apply
1. The length of string and the mass were kept constant.
2. length of the string
3. Shorten the length of the string.

Error Analysis
Ask students whether their observations make sense. Have them explain why they did or didn't expect their results and how their own biases might have affected their results. Have students work with their partners to brainstorm possible errors that might have occurred in their experiments. Errors might include miscounting the number of swings and not keeping some variables constant.

Assessment

Oral According to Newton's first law of motion, an object will continue in motion or remain at rest until it is acted upon by an outside force. **Infer what forces caused the pendulum to swing and eventually stop.** Tension on the string pulls on the mass while gravity pulls it down. Friction with air also slows the pendulum. Use **Performance Assessment in the Science Classroom,** p. 89.

Communicating Your Data

Graphs should be correctly titled and labeled; the y-axis labeled with the dependent variable *Swings Per Minute;* and the x-axis labeled with the independent variables *Length of String in Centimeters, Number of Masses,* and *Angle of the Drop in Degrees.* Students may use electronic spreadsheet software to make their feature.

"The Microscope"
by Maxine Kumin

Science and Language Arts

☑ Pre-Reading Activity

Tell students that in the passage they are about to read, a scientist discovers that simply looking at an object does not reveal everything about the object. Ask students to write in their science journals about a time when they discovered that things aren't always what they appear to be.

Respond to the Reading

Active Reading Strategies

Listen Read the poem aloud. Notice the rhyme scheme. Which part of each line in the poem rhymes?

Reflect Think about times when your peers considered you different. How did that make you feel?

Analyze What do you think the attitude of the author is toward Anton? Does the author think Anton is crazy or does she admire him?

Question Consider why Anton examined the objects he did under a microscope. Might there be a reason for his choices?

Answers to Questions

1. No; he made a living selling cloth and other sewing materials.
2. microscopic organisms not visible to the human eye
3. because he claimed to see things that were not visible to the human eye

Respond to the Reading

1. Do you think Anton was a scientist by trade? Why or why not?
2. What did Anton find inside a water drop?
3. What are some possible explanations for why some people thought Anton was crazy?

Maxine Kumin

Anton Leeuwenhoek was Dutch.
He sold pincushions, cloth, and such.
The waiting townsfolk fumed and fussed
As Anton's dry goods gathered dust.

He worked, instead of tending store,
At grinding special lenses for
A microscope. Some of the things
He looked at were: mosquitoes' wings,
the hairs of sheep, the legs of lice,
the skin of people, dogs, and mice;
ox eyes, spiders' spinning gear,
fishes' scales, a little smear
of his own blood, and best of all,
the unknown, busy, very small
bugs that wim and bump and hop
inside a simple water drop.

Impossible! Most Dutchmen said.
This Anton's crazy in the head!
We ought to ship him off to Spain.
He says he's seen a housefly's brain.
He says the water that we drink
Is full of bugs. He's mad, we think!

They called him *dumkopf*, which means "dope".
That's how we got the microscope.

Reading Further

Other works on this topic include:

The Beginner's Guide to Scientific Method by Stephen S. Carey, Wadsworth Publishing Company, June 1997.

How Do You Know It's True?: Discovering the Difference Between Science and Superstition by Hyman Ruchlis, Hyman Ruchlis, Prometheus Books, August 1991.

Understanding Literature

Rhyming Couplets A couplet is a poetic convention in which every two lines rhyme. The poem you just read rhymes in couplets. Some of the most famous poems that use rhyming couplets describe heroic deeds and often are epic tales. An epic tale is a long story that describes a journey of exploration. You might have heard of Homer, a famous Greek poet who wrote epic tales of adventure such as *The Illiad* and *The Odyssey*. Why do you think the poet used rhyming couplets in the poem you just read?

Science Connection In this chapter, you learned about different scientific instuments that increase our scientific knowledge. For example, microscopes have changed the scale at which humans can make observations. Electron microscopes allow observers to obtain images at magnifications ranging from about $10,000\times$ to $1,000,000\times$. In a microscope with a magnification of $10,000\times$, a 0.001-mm object will appear as a 1-cm image.

Microscopes are used in Earth science to observe the arrangement and composition of minerals in rocks. These observations give clues about the conditions that formed the rock.

Linking Science and Writing

Write a heroic poem Write a heroic verse or poem that rhymes. Pick a scientific method or discovery from your textbook. If necessary, research the discovery to find out its origin. Use rhyming words that describe the discovery and the person or people who made it. If possible, try using couplet rhyming, where every two lines of the poem rhyme.

Career Connection

Mineralogist

Julie Sheets Dr. Sheets and other geologists use light and electron microscopes to observe tiny defects in rock such as holes, fractures, and mistakes in the arrangement of atoms which allow gas and fluid to move through solid rock. These features influence the physical properties of rock, like how they deform when Earth's plates collide, or how they lose or gain chemical elements. She and other scientists hypothesize that defects in crystal and rock influence how fast minerals weather, or degrade, when exposed to water. This type of research is also important for determining the age of some rocks because elements used to date them may be lost to weathering.

SCIENCE *Online* To learn more about careers in mineralogy, visit the Glencoe Science Web site at **science.glencoe.com.**

Career Connection

Mineralogy focuses on chemical and physical properties of minerals and mineral origins. Interested students should take courses in the Earth sciences, chemistry, and physics. Because mineralogy deals with sophisticated research methods, a student must complete advanced graduate work in order to become a mineralogist.

SCIENCE *Online*
Internet Addresses

_____

_____

_____

_____

Explore the Glencoe Science Web site at **science.glencoe.com** to find out more about topics in this feature.

Understanding Literature

Answers to Questions

The author used rhyming couplets similar to the great heroic epics of our time because she believes that Anton is a scientific hero. Tales about scientific discoveries are like heroic tales in that they tell of journeys of exploration.

Science Connection

Anton van Leeuwenhoek was the first to observe bacteria and protozoa. This discovery was important both in the history of biological sciences, particularly bacteriology, and in the implications of microscopy that were later applied to all the sciences, including the Earth sciences.

The type of microscope he used has become the most common: the optical, or light, microscope, in which lenses are used to form the image. Optical microscopes can consist of a single lens or compound lenses. The magnifying power of a microscope is an expression of the number of times the object being examined appears to be enlarged. The resolution, usually expressed in millimeters, is the size of the smallest detail that can be observed. Single lens microscopes may have magnifying powers of from 1 to 10 magnitudes, with resolutions to about 0.01-millimeter (mm) possible.

Linking Science and Writing

Teaching Strategies

Ask students to do a quick write recalling discoveries in the Earth sciences that they have read about or seen on television.

Chapter **1** Study Guide

Reviewing Main Ideas

Preview

Students can answer the questions in their Science Journals. Discuss the answers as you go through the chapter. **IS Linguistic**

Review

Students can write their answers, then compare them with those of other students. **IS Interpersonal**

Reteach

Students can look at the illustrations and describe details that support the main ideas of the chapter. **IS Visual-Spatial**

Answers to Chapter Review

SECTION 1

4. volcanoes

SECTION 2

1. Earth-based optical telescopes are much more precise and are used to see objects at a greater distance than could be seen with Galileo's telescope. The Hubble Space Telescope collects images that are not affected by the atmosphere. Other telescopes and instruments measure radiowaves, X rays, and other wavelengths of energy coming from space. Space probes, space shuttles, satellites, and computers collect and analyze data.

Reviewing Main Ideas

Section 1 Science All Around

1. Scientific methods are used to solve problems or answer questions.

2. Scientific methods include identifying a problem or question, gathering information, developing hypotheses, designing an experiment to test the hypotheses, performing the experiment, collecting and analyzing data, and forming conclusions.

3. Science experiments should be repeated to see whether results are consistent. The results of an experiment often allow conclusions to be made and usually lead to additional questions.

4. Science is a process of observing and studying the world. *What do you think the scientist shown here is studying?*

5. In an experiment, the independent variable is the variable being tested. Constants are variables that do not change. The variable being measured is the dependent variable. A control is a standard to which things can be compared.

6. Technology is the use of scientific discoveries. Technology has changed as new scientific discoveries were made.

Section 2 Scientific Enterprise

1. Today, everything known in science results from knowledge that has been collected over time. Science has changed and will continue to change because of continuing research and improvements in instruments and testing procedures. *How have instruments used to study space changed since Galileo used a telescope like the one shown here to study Jupiter's moons?*

2. Scientific theories are explanations or models that are supported by repeated experimentation. If data gathered over a long period of time support a hypothesis, it can become a scientific theory.

3. Scientific laws are rules that describe the behavior of something in nature. Laws are used to predict natural events but usually do not explain them.

4. There are limits to the kinds of questions and problems science can be used to answer and solve. Problems that deal with ethics and belief systems cannot be answered using scientific methods.

FOLDABLES
Reading & Study Skills

After You Read

Exchange your Vocabulary Study Fold with a classmate and quiz each other to see how many vocabulary words you can define without looking under the tabs.

FOLDABLES
Reading & Study Skills

After You Read

After students have read the chapter and completed the Foldable described in Before You Read, have them do the activity on the student page.

Dinah Zike

Visualizing Main Ideas

Complete the following concept map about variables, constants, and controls.

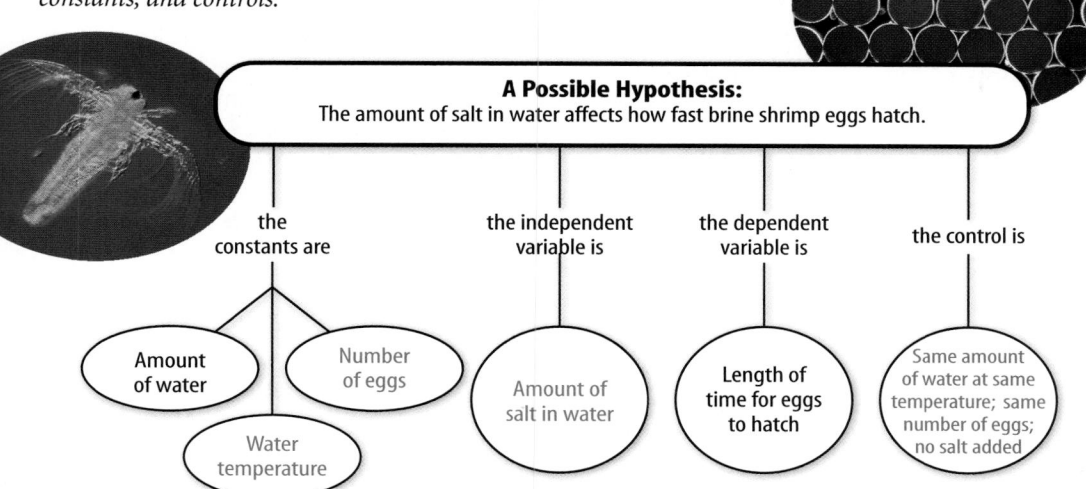

A Possible Hypothesis:
The amount of salt in water affects how fast brine shrimp eggs hatch.

the constants are	the independent variable is	the dependent variable is	the control is
Amount of water / Number of eggs / Water temperature	Amount of salt in water	Length of time for eggs to hatch	Same amount of water at same temperature; same number of eggs; no salt added

Vocabulary Review

Vocabulary Words

a. bias
b. constant
c. control
d. dependent variable
e. Earth science
f. ethics
g. hypothesis
h. independent variable
i. science
j. scientific law
k. scientific methods
l. scientific theory
m. technology
n. variable

THE PRINCETON REVIEW   Study Tip

Use acronyms to help you remember sequences. For example, the acronym TSMTE helps you remember that the layers of the atmosphere extending from Earth's surface are the troposphere, stratosphere, mesosphere, thermosphere, and exosphere.

Using Vocabulary

Use what you know about the vocabulary words to explain the differences in the following sets of words. Then explain how the words are related.

1. constant, control
2. dependent variable, independent variable
3. scientific law, scientific theory
4. science, technology
5. hypothesis, scientific theory
6. science, Earth science
7. independent variable, constant
8. variable, control
9. Earth science, technology
10. ethics, bias

See student page.

Using Vocabulary

1. Constant: a variable that doesn't change; control: standard to which results are compared; both are used in experiments.
2. A dependent variable is a measured change caused by an independent variable (variable being tested).
3. Scientific law: rule describing behavior of something; scientific theory: explanation backed by experimental results; both explain observations.
4. Science makes the discoveries and technology puts the discoveries to use.
5. Hypothesis: an educated guess; scientific theory: explanation backed by repeated tests; a hypothesis can become theory.
6. Science: process of observing and studying things; Earth science focuses on Earth and space.
7. Independent variable: changes in an experiment; constant: does not change; both are variables.
8. Variable: factor that can change; control: standard to which results are compared; both are used in experiments.
9. Earth science: study of Earth and space; technology: use of scientific discoveries for practical purposes; Earth science discoveries help technology, and vice versa.
10. Ethics deals with moral values; bias is a personal opinion; to practice ethical science, bias should be avoided.

Chapter 1 Assessment

Checking Concepts

1. A
2. C
3. D
4. B
5. D
6. C
7. A
8. C
9. B
10. D

Thinking Critically

11. Gather information about cactus plants. Make a hypothesis. Plan a way to test the hypothesis by identifying the independent variable, constants, and control. Test the hypothesis, analyze the results, and draw conclusions. If the hypothesis is not supported by data, revise it and retest.

12. Some technologies have resulted in air, water, and soil pollution; soil erosion; and habitat destruction. Other technologies have made the environment cleaner. Today, people are using technology to study and monitor the environment to reverse damages and protect it from further harm.

13. It means that technology can be applied to new situations.

14. A theory is developed only when many scientists' work supports a hypothesis.

15. Possible answer: make observations and identify problems, gather information, develop hypotheses, collect and analyze information, draw conclusions

Checking Concepts

Choose the word or phrase that best answers the question.

1. Which of these best describes science?
   A) have knowledge
   C) study
   B) observe
   D) solve

2. Which word is the standard used for comparison in an experiment?
   A) variable
   C) control
   B) theory
   D) law

3. Which of the following is the first step in using scientific methods?
   A) develop hypotheses
   B) make conclusions
   C) test hypotheses
   D) identify a problem

4. Which word means an educated guess?
   A) theory
   C) variable
   B) hypothesis
   D) law

5. The idea that a comet is like a dirty snowball is which of the following?
   A) hypothesis
   C) law
   B) variable
   D) theory

6. The statement that an object at rest will remain at rest unless acted upon by a force is an example of which of the following?
   A) hypothesis
   C) law
   B) variable
   D) theory

7. Which of the following questions could NOT be answered using scientific methods?
   A) Is being an honest person a good trait?
   B) Does sulfur affect the growth of grass?
   C) How do waves cause erosion?
   D) Does land heat up faster than water?

8. Which of the following describes variables that stay the same in an experiment?
   A) dependent variables
   C) constants
   B) independent variables
   D) controls

9. Which of the following is a variable that is being tested in a science experiment?
   A) dependent variable
   C) constant
   B) independent variable
   D) control

10. What should you do if your data are different from what you expected?
   A) Conclude you made a mistake in the way you collected the data.
   B) Change your data to be consistent with your expectation.
   C) Conclude that you made a mistake when you recorded your data.
   D) Conclude that your expectation might have been wrong.

Thinking Critically

11. Suppose you had two plants— a cactus and a palm. You planted them in potting soil and watered them daily. After two weeks, the cactus was dead. What scientific methods could you use to find out why the cactus died?

12. How have advances in technology affected society?

13. What is meant by the statement, *Technology is transferable?*

14. Why don't all hypotheses become theories?

15. What are some scientific methods you use every day to answer questions or solve problems?

Developing Skills

16. **Identifying and Manipulating Variables and Controls** How would you set up a simple experiment to test whether salt-crystal growth is affected by temperature?

Chapter ✓*Assessment* Planner

Portfolio Encourage students to place in their portfolios one or two items of what they consider to be their best work. Examples include:
• Science Journal, p. 12
• Challenge, p. 14
• Cultural Diversity, p. 16
• Active Reading, p. 17

Performance Additional performance assessments, Performance Task Assessment Lists, and rubrics for evaluating these activities can be found in Glencoe's **Performance Assessment in the Science Classroom.**

17. Forming Hypotheses You observe two beakers containing clear liquid and ice cubes. In the first beaker, the ice cubes are floating. In the second, the ice cubes are on the bottom of the beaker. Write a hypothesis to explain the difference in your observations about the two beakers.

18. Recognizing Cause and Effect Explain why scientific methods cannot be used to answer ethical questions.

19. Interpreting Data A friend tells you that dark colors absorb more heat than light colors do. You conduct an experiment to determine which color of fabric absorbs the most heat. Analyze your data below. Was your friend correct? Explain.

Color and Heat Absorption		
Color	Beginning Temperature (°C)	Temperature (°C) after 10 minutes
Red	24°	26°
Black	24°	28°
Blue	24°	27°
White	24°	25°
Green	24°	27°

Performance Assessment

20. Poster Research an example of Earth science technology that is not shown in **Figure 10.** Create a poster that explains the contribution this technology made to the understanding of Earth science.

TECHNOLOGY

Go to the Glencoe Science Web site at **science.glencoe.com** or use the **Glencoe Science CD-ROM** for additional chapter assessment.

THE PRINCETON REVIEW **Test Practice**

Scientists must use different tools to measure amounts and distances during experiments. Some measuring equipment is divided into two groups in the boxes below.

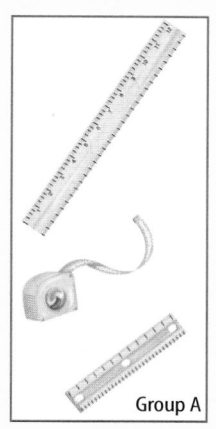 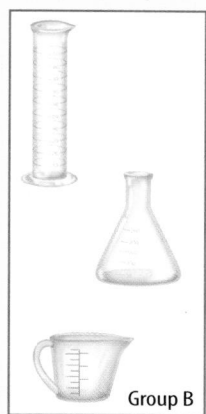

Group A   Group B

Study the pictures and answer the following questions.

1. The pieces of equipment in Group A are different from the equipment in Group B because only the equipment in Group A can be used to measure _____ .
  A) distance
  B) volume
  C) weight
  D) mass

2. Which of the following belongs with Group B above?
  F) a bathroom scale
  G) a soda can
  H) a beaker
  J) a stopwatch

THE PRINCETON REVIEW **Test Practice**

The Test-Taking Tip was written by The Princeton Review, the nation's leader in test preparation.
1. A
2. H

Developing Skills

16. Research salt crystals and make a hypothesis. Then add 10 g of salt to a 250-mL beaker containing 200 mL of ice water. Mix well. Tie one end of a 12-cm piece of string around the center of a pencil. Place the pencil across the top of the beaker, and let the string fall into the bottom of the beaker. Repeat these procedures with a beaker of warm water. Place the cold beaker in a cold place like a refrigerator, and place the warm beaker in a warm place like on top of a heating pad, turned to low. Observe crystal growth for one week, analyze observations, and conclude whether the hypothesis is correct.

17. The liquid in which the ice cubes float is more dense than the liquid in which the ice cubes sank.

18. Ethical questions do not have variables that can be observed, measured, and tested.

19. Yes; black (the darkest color) absorbed the most heat; white (the lightest color) absorbed the least heat.

Performance Assessment

20. Posters should be accurate and colorful. Display the posters throughout the classroom. Use **PASC,** p. 145.

✔*Assessment* **Resources**

📁 **Reproducible Masters**
Chapter Resources Booklet
Chapter Review, pp. 33–34
Chapter Tests, pp. 35–38
Assessment Transparency Activity, p. 45
Glencoe Science Web site
Interactive Tutor
Chapter Quizzes

Glencoe Technology
🖥 Assessment Transparency
💿 Interactive CD-ROM Chapter Quizzes
💿 ExamView Pro Test Bank
💿 Vocabulary PuzzleMaker Software
📼 MindJogger Videoquiz DVD/VHS

Section/Objectives	Standards		Activities/Features
Chapter Opener	**National**	**State/Local**	**Explore Activity:** Change the state of water, p. 33
	See p. 5T for a Key to Standards.		**Before You Read,** p. 33
Section 1 Atoms ⏲ 2 sessions ▦ 1 block 1. **Identify** the states of matter. 2. **Describe** the internal structure of an atom. 3. **Compare** isotopes of an element.	National Content Standards: UCP1, A1, B1		**MiniLAB:** Searching for Elements, p. 35 **Health Integration,** p. 37
Section 2 Combinations of Atoms ⏲ 2 sessions ▦ 1 block 1. **Describe** several ways atoms combine to form compounds. 2. **List** differences between compounds and mixtures	National Content Standards: UCP3, A1, B1		**Science Online,** p. 40 **MiniLAB:** Classifying Forms of Matter, p. 43 **Chemistry Integration,** p. 44 **Activity:** Scales of Measurement, p. 45
Section 3 Properties of Matter ⏲ 3 sessions ▦ 1.5 blocks 1. **Distinguish** between chemical and physical properties. 2. **List** the four states of matter.	National Content Standards: UCP1, A1, B2, G2		**Math Skills Activity:** Calculating Density, p. 47 **Visualizing States of Matter,** p. 49 **Activity:** Determining Density, p. 52 **Science Stats:** Amazing Atoms, p. 54

Activity Materials	Reproducible Resources	Section Assessment	Technology
Explore Activity: 1,000-mL glass beaker, water, tape, hot plate, clock or watch	**Chapter Resources Booklet** Foldables Worksheet, p. 13 Directed Reading Overview, p. 15 Note-taking Worksheets, pp. 29–31	*GLENCOE'S* **ASSESSMENT** *ADVANTAGE*	
MiniLAB: Periodic Table of the Elements, highlighter *Need materials?* Contact Science Kit at 1-800-828-7777 or www.sciencekit.com on the Internet.	**Chapter Resources Booklet** Transparency Activity, p. 40 MiniLAB, p. 3 Enrichment, p. 26 Reinforcement, p. 23 Directed Reading, p. 16 **Cultural Diversity,** p. 55	**Portfolio** Science Journal, p. 35 **Performance** MiniLAB, p. 35 Skill Builder Activities, p. 38 **Content** Section Assessment, p. 38	🔋 Section Focus Transparency 💿 Interactive CD-ROM/DVD 🎧 Guided Reading Audio Program
MiniLAB: none **Activity:** triple-beam balance, 100-mL graduated cylinder, 2 metersticks, 3 non-mercury thermometers, stick or dowel, rock sample, string, globe, water	**Chapter Resources Booklet** Transparency Activity, p. 41 MiniLAB, p. 4 Lab Activity, pp. 9–10 Enrichment, p. 27 Reinforcement, p. 24 Directed Reading, p. 16 Activity Worksheet, pp. 5–6 Transparency Activity, pp. 43–44 **Science Inquiry Labs,** p. 51	**Portfolio** Cultural diversity, p. 41 **Performance** MiniLAB, p. 43 Skill Builder Activities, p. 44 **Content** Section Assessment, p. 44	🔋 Section Focus Transparency 🔋 Teaching Transparency 💿 Interactive CD-ROM/DVD 🎧 Guided Reading Audio Program
Activity: pan, triple-beam balance, 100-mL beaker, 250-mL graduated cylinder, water, sponge, piece of quartz, piece of clay, small wooden block, small metal block, small cork, rock, ruler	**Chapter Resources Booklet** Transparency Activity, p. 42 Lab Activity, pp. 11–12 Enrichment, p. 28 Reinforcement, p. 25 Directed Reading, pp. 17, 18 Activity Worksheet, pp. 7–8 **Mathematics Skill Activities,** p. 9	**Portfolio** Extension, p. 49 **Performance** Math Skills Activity, p. 47 Skill Builder Activities, p. 51 **Content** Section Assessment, p. 51	🔋 Section Focus Transparency 💿 Interactive CD-ROM/DVD 🎧 Guided Reading Audio Program

End of Chapter Assessment

GLENCOE'S **ASSESSMENT** *ADVANTAGE*

Blackline Masters	Technology	Professional Series
Chapter Resources Booklet Chapter Review, pp. 33–34 Chapter Tests, pp. 35–38 **Standardized Test Practice by The Princeton Review,** pp. 15–18	📼 MindJogger Videoquiz 💿 CD-ROM Explorations and Quizzes 💿 Vocabulary Puzzle Makers 💿 ExamView Pro Test Bank 💿 Interactive Lesson Planner 💿 Interactive Teacher's Edition	Performance Assessment in the Science Classroom (PASC)

Transparencies

Section Focus

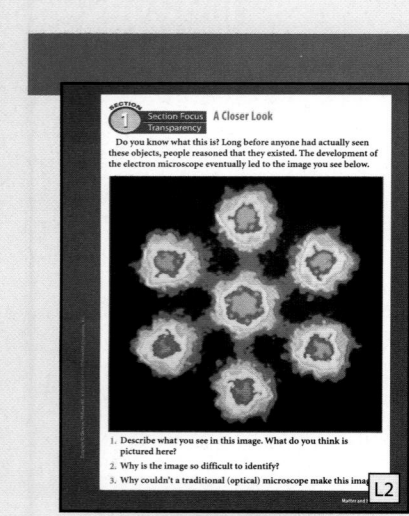

SECTION 1 Section Focus Transparency **A Closer Look**

Do you know what this is? Long before anyone had actually seen these objects, people reasoned that they existed. The development of the electron microscope eventually led to the image you see below.

1. Describe what you see in this image. What do you think is pictured here?
2. Why is the image so difficult to identify?
3. Why couldn't a traditional (optical) microscope make this image? **L2**

SECTION 2 Section Focus Transparency **Oxygen-Oxygen**

All matter, including everything in this scene, is composed of atoms in different combinations. Oxygen is an atom that is very important to living things. As you look at this scene, try to figure out what oxygen has to do with it all.

1. What kind of substance is oxygen?
2. Why is oxygen important to everything in the picture?
3. How do plants and animals exchange oxygen? **L2**

SECTION 3 Section Focus Transparency **Water doesn't look tense.**

You've probably drunk, bathed, and swum in water without thinking about its very interesting properties. Surface tension, for example, is a property of liquids that describes their tendency to form a thin, film-like barrier at the surface.

1. Why is surface tension a physical property?
2. How is the insect able to walk on the water's surface?
3. How is this different from floating? **L2**

This is a representation of key blackline masters available in the Teacher Classroom Resources. See Resource Manager boxes within the chapter for additional information.

Key to Teaching Strategies

The following designations will help you decide which activities are appropriate for your students.

L1 Level 1 activities should be appropriate for students with learning difficulties.

L2 Level 2 activities should be within the ability range of all students.

L3 Level 3 activities are designed for above-average students.

ELL ELL activities should be within the ability range of English Language Learners.

COOP LEARN Cooperative Learning activities are designed for small group work.

LS Multiple Learning Styles logos, as described on page 22T, are used throughout to indicate strategies that address different learning styles.

P These strategies represent student products that can be placed into a best-work portfolio.

Assessment

Assessment Transparency **Matter and Its Changes**

Directions: *Carefully review the graph and answer the following questions.*

Changes in Water Density

1. According to the graph which statement best describes what happens to the density of water as it is heated from minus 10 degrees C to 110 degrees C?
A Density decreases and then increases
B Density increases and then decreases
C Density increases and then remains the same
D Density decreases and then remains the same
2. If the temperature is 110 degrees C and is decreased by 75 degrees, the water will eventually return to a _____.
F liquid   G solid   H vapor   J mix of all three
3. According to this information, in which state will the water molecules be the farthest apart?
A Solid   C Vapor
B Liquid   D Always the same distance **L2**

Teaching

SECTION 2 Teaching Transparency **Covalent and Ionic Bonds**

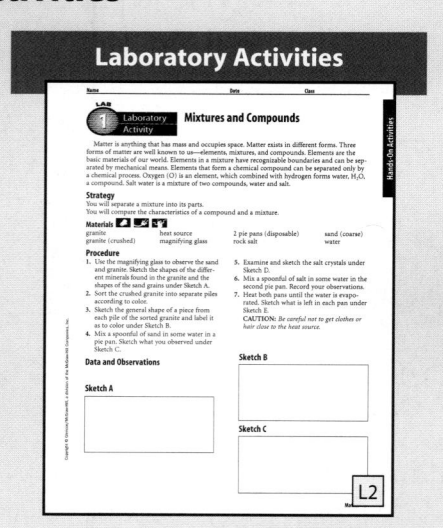

Na — : Ċi:
Sodium   Chlorine **L2**

Hands-on Activities

Activity Worksheets

Activity **Scales of Measurement**

Lab Preview
Directions: *Answer these questions before you begin the Activity.*
1. What physical properties are you measuring in this activity?

2. Why is the sharp safety symbol shown?

How would you describe some of the objects in your classroom? Perhaps your desktop is about one-half the size of a door. Measuring physical properties in a laboratory experiment will help you make better observations.

What You'll Investigate
How are physical properties of objects measured?

Materials
triple beam balance   non-mercury thermometers (3)   string
100-mL graduated cylinder   stick or dowel   globe
metersticks (2)   rock sample   water

Goals
• Measure various physical properties in SI.
• Determine sources of error.

Safety Precautions
CAUTION: Do not "shake down" lab thermometers.

Procedure
1. Go to every station and determine the measurement required. Record your observations in the data table on the next page and list sources of error.
   a. Use a balance to determine the mass, to the nearest 0.1g, of the rock sample.
   b. Use a graduated cylinder to measure the water volume, to the nearest 0.5 mL.
   c. Use three thermometers to determine the average temperature, to the nearest 0.5°C, at a selected location in the room.
   d. Use a meterstick to measure the length, to the nearest 0.1 cm, of the stick or dowel.
   e. Use a meterstick and string to measure the circumference of the globe. Be accurate to the nearest 0.1 cm. **L2**

Laboratory Activities

LAB 1 Laboratory Activity **Mixtures and Compounds**

Matter is anything that has mass and occupies space. Matter exists in different forms. Three forms of matter are well known to us—elements, mixtures, and compounds. Elements are the basic materials of our world. Elements in a mixture have recognizable boundaries and can be separated by mechanical means. Elements that form a chemical compound can be separated only by a chemical process. Oxygen (O) is an element, which combined with hydrogen forms water, H_2O, a compound. Salt water is a mixture of two compounds, water and salt.

Strategy
You will separate a mixture into its parts.
You will compare the characteristics of a compound and a mixture.

Materials
granite   heat source   2 pie pans (disposable)   sand (coarse)
granite (crushed)   magnifying glass   rock salt   water

Procedure
1. Use the magnifying glass to observe the sand and granite. Sketch the shapes of the different minerals found in the granite and the shapes of the sand grains under Sketch A.
2. Sort the crushed granite into separate piles according to color.
3. Sketch the general shape of a piece from each pile of the sorted granite and label it as to color under Sketch B.
4. Mix a spoonful of sand in some water in a pie pan. Sketch what you observed under Sketch C.
5. Examine and sketch the salt crystals under Sketch D.
6. Mix a spoonful of salt in some water in the second pie pan. Record your observations.
7. Heat both pans until the water is evaporated. Sketch what is left in each pan under Sketch E.
CAUTION: *Be careful not to get clothes or hair close to the heat source.*

Data and Observations

Sketch A

Sketch B

Sketch C

L2

Meeting Different Ability Levels

Content Outline

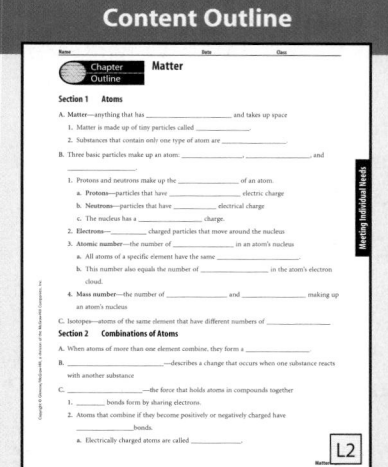

L2

Reinforcement

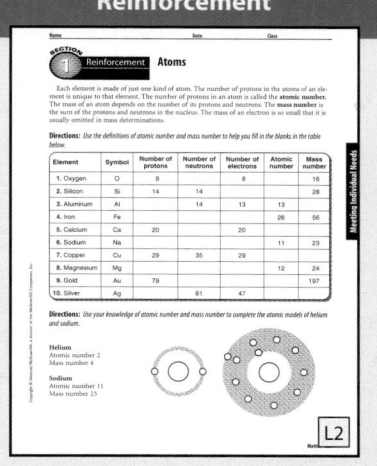

L2

Directed Reading

Overview Matter

L1

Assessment

Chapter Tests

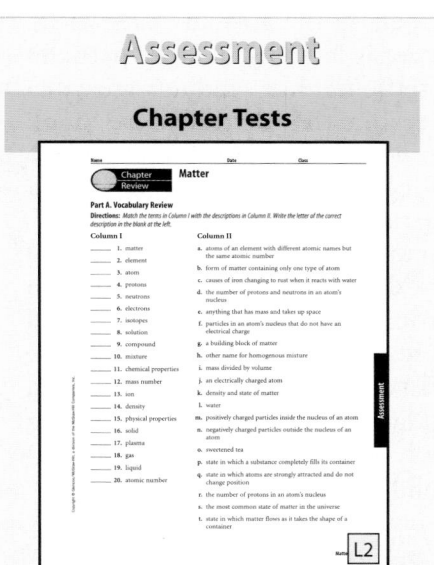

L2

Enrichment

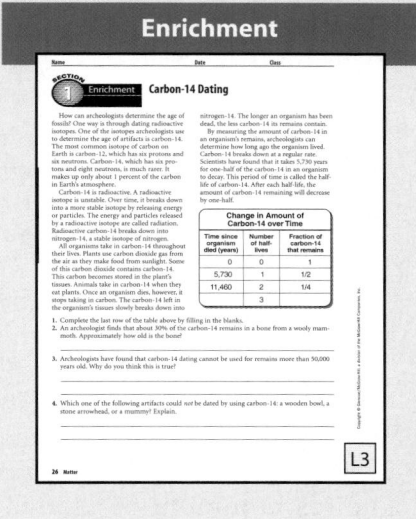

Carbon-14 Dating

L3

Spanish Directed Reading

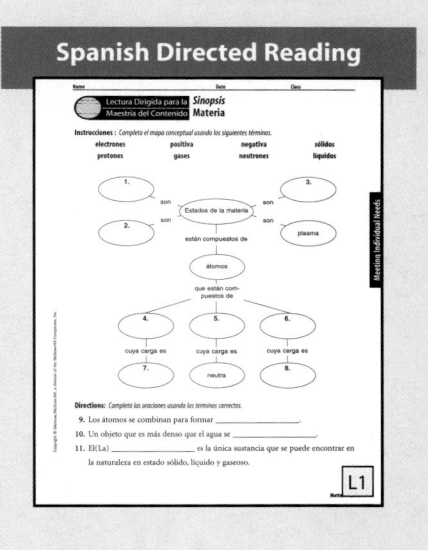

Sinopsis Materia

L1

Test Practice Workbook

Standardized Test Practice
Teacher Edition

Glencoe Science

Earth Science

NATIONAL GEOGRAPHIC SOCIETY

science.glencoe.com

L2

Chapter Review

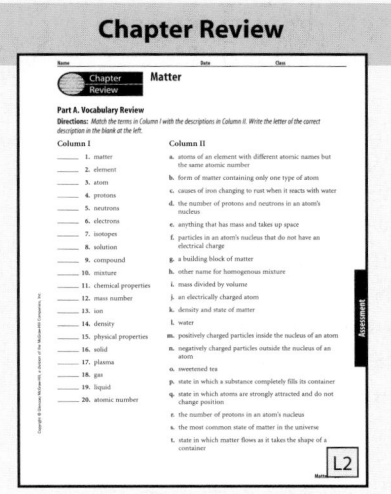

Matter

L2

Science Content Background

Atoms

Uses of Isotopes

Radon gas (R-222) exists naturally in the environment. It is one of several isotopes produced as radioactive uranium decays into lead. The radon itself decays, and during this process it gives off particles. Continued exposure to radon gas and its harmful particles can result in tissue damage and lung cancer in humans. In the open air, radon gas is not threatening because it exists in such small amounts. It can, however, leak from the ground into buildings and homes and accumulate to dangerously high levels. The same sequence of uranium-to-lead decay that yields the potentially deadly radon gas is one of the most common and accurate methods that scientists use to determine the age of rocks.

Fun Fact

Dry ice, which is carbon dioxide in a solid state at −78°C, changes to a gas without first being a liquid. This is the process of sublimation, where matter goes directly from a solid to a gas, skipping the liquid phase.

Combinations of Atoms

Hydrogen Bonds

Hydrogen bonds commonly occur between hydrogen and oxygen atoms. They also occur between hydrogen and nitrogen atoms and hydrogen and fluorine atoms. Although the attractions between atoms formed by hydrogen bonds are not strong enough to bond them into molecules (hydrogen bonds are only five percent of the strength of covalent bonds), hydrogen bonds do contribute to the strength and stability of a molecule. They also influence the three-dimensional structure of some larger molecules in the human body, such as proteins and DNA. Hydrogen bonds help form the "rungs" of the ladder in the double helix model of a DNA molecule. The bonds are formed because hydrogen atoms of one base pair are attracted to the nitrogen or oxygen atoms of the nearby base.

Mixtures

A colloid or a colloidal dispersion differs from solutions and heterogeneous mixtures because of the size of the particles. A homogeneous mixture, or a solution, has the smallest particles, all of which are dissolved in the solution and do not settle out. A heterogeneous mixture has the largest particles. When a heterogeneous mixture is in a liquid form the particles will remain suspended as the mixture is stirred. When the mixture is left to stand, the particles will eventually settle out like sand in water. In a colloidal dispersion the particles are small enough to remain suspended; however, unlike a solution, a colloid will scatter light passing through the mixture. Colloids can exist in several forms. Some types of colloids consist of liquids that are dispersed into a gas. Fog, in which water droplets are suspended in air, and aerosol sprays are examples. Paint is an example of a colloidal dispersion where a solid has been dispersed into a liquid medium. In colloids such as marshmallows and Styrofoam a gas is dispersed into a solid medium.

Properties of Matter

Plasma

The electrons of an atom can be completely separated from the atom itself under conditions of extremely high energy, such as those produced at temperatures of more than 2,000°C. When electrons are separated from an atom, plasma—a gaseous mixture of positive ions and electrons—is formed. Besides the Sun and other stars, other familiar examples of plasma include neon signs, fluorescent lamps, and auroras. Auroras occur at high latitudes near Earth's poles. Aurora borealis, "northern lights," occurs in the northern hemisphere and Aurora austalis, "southern lights," occurs in the southern hemisphere. Auroras are created when charged particles from solar wind, which is plasma from the Sun's surface that travels through the solar system at rates of up to 800 km/sec, come in contact with Earth's magnetic field. Once the particles enter the magnetic field, they begin to travel toward Earth's north and south magnetic poles. As the charged particles move closer to Earth, they interact with gases high in the atmosphere. The continued interaction between the charged particles and the gases generates the celestial light known as an aurora. The main colors of auroras are green and red.

Changes in Physical Properties

One of the unique properties of water is that the solid phase, ice, is less dense than the liquid phase. Fresh water has its highest density at 4°C. This property accounts for the fact that there is overturn in lakes in the fall and spring. As surface water cools to 4°C in the fall, it becomes more dense than the water below it and therefore sinks. This process brings oxygen to the bottom waters of lakes and returns nutrients to the surface. As the surface water continues to cool below 4°C, it becomes less dense than the water below it. It does not sink; it forms ice if the temperature drops to 0°C. The ice acts as an insulator for the deeper water, enabling aquatic life to survive the winter. In the spring as the surface water warms up to 4°C, it reaches its maximum density and sinks, thus beginning the spring overturn.

SCIENCE *Online*

For additional content background on this topic, go to the Glencoe Science Web site at **science.glencoe.com**.

Mike Macri/Masterfile

Matter

Chapter Vocabulary

matter
atom
element
proton
neutron
nucleus
electron
atomic number
mass number
isotope
compound
ion
mixture
heterogeneous mixture
homogeneous mixture
density

What do you think?

Science Journal The photograph is of silicon atoms.

Matter

What is most striking about this picture—water, ice, or steam? What do these things have in common? How are they different? In this chapter, you will find the answers to these questions. You also will learn about the matter that makes up your surroundings and makes up your body.

What do you think?

Science Journal Look at the picture below with a classmate. Discuss what you think these might be. Here's a hint: *They could be part of the landscape of a far-off planet or something in your desk.* Write your answer in your Science Journal.

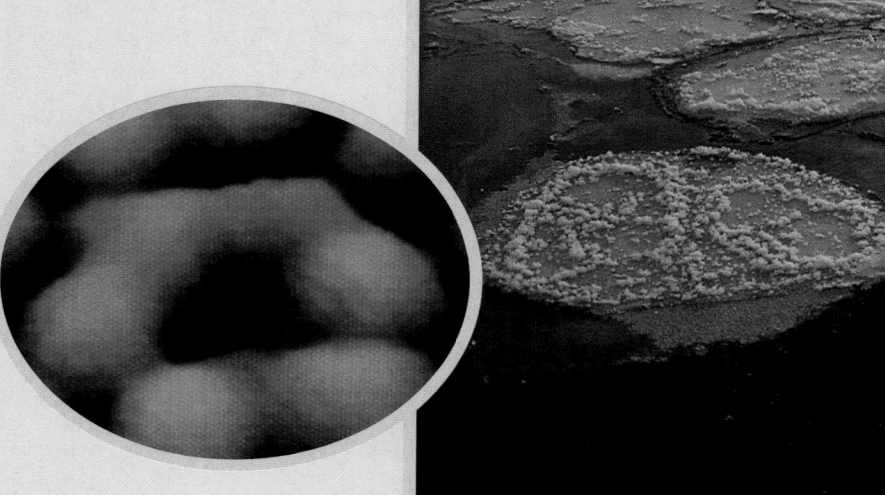

32

Theme Connection

Scale and Structure The theme of scale and structure is highlighted through the use of large-scale models that illustrate the internal structure of atoms and molecules. This theme is also developed through the discussion of the properties of matter, which are determined by the structure of atoms and molecules.

On Earth water is unique because it is found as a solid, liquid, or gas. On a cool autumn morning, you might see gaseous water condensing into fog over a lake or a river whose surface soon will be solid ice. The following activity will help you visualize how matter can change states.

Change the state of water

Safety Precautions

1. Pour 500 mL of water into a 1,000-mL glass beaker.
2. Mark the level of water in the beaker with the bottom edge of a piece of tape.
3. Place the beaker on a hot plate.
4. With the help of an adult, heat the water until it boils for 5 min. Let the water cool.
5. With the help of an adult, compare the level of the water to the bottom edge of the tape.

Observe

What came out of the beaker as the water boiled? Did the amount of water that you started with change? In your Science Journal, explain what happened to the water.

Before You Read

Making a Vocabulary Study Fold
Knowing the definition of vocabulary words is a good way to ensure that you understand the content of the chapter.

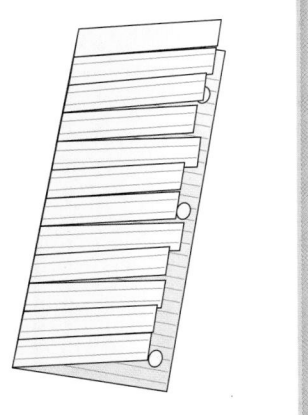

1. Place a sheet of notebook paper in front of you so the short side is at the top and the holes are on the right side. Fold the paper in half from the left side to the right side.
2. Through the top thickness of paper, cut along every third line from the outside edge to the center fold, forming tabs.
3. Before you read, write vocabulary words from each section in this chapter on the front of the tabs. Under each tab, write what you think the word means.
4. As you read the chapter, add to and correct your definitions.

33

Purpose Use the Explore Activity to introduce students to the different states of matter. Inform students that water is found in its solid, liquid, and gaseous states on Earth's surface. L1 IS **Visual-Spatial**

Preparation Several days before beginning this chapter, obtain a hot plate and a 1,000-mL glass beaker.

Materials hot plate, 1,000-mL glass beaker, water

Teaching Strategies

- Have students compare their results with those of other students. Discuss differences and similarities.
- Students must use permanent markers for marking the glass beaker.

Safety Precautions Provide adult supervision as students heat the water, making certain no one touches hot surfaces.

Observe

Steam moved out of the beaker as the water was heated to boiling. Some of the water was changed to the gaseous state when the water boiled. This water escaped from the beaker as steam. As a result, the amount of liquid water that remained was less than the original amount.

✓ Assessment

Oral Ask students to discuss their results in groups. Have one representative from each group explain to the class the group's conclusions. Use **Performance Assessment in the Science Classroom,** p. 89.

FOLDABLES
Reading & Study Skills

Before You Read

Dinah Zike Study Fold
Purpose Students will be exposed to the chapter's content and vocabulary before they read, and will be encouraged to search for terms and definitions as they read. The resulting Foldable can be used as an assessment tool and study guide before, during, and after reading.

For additional help, see Foldables Worksheet, p. 13 in **Chapter Resources Booklet,** or go to the Glencoe Science Web site at **science.glencoe.com.** See After You Read in the Study Guide at the end of this chapter.

SECTION

1

Atoms

1 Motivate

Bellringer Transparency

 Display the Section Focus Transparency for Section 1. Use the accompanying Transparency Activity Master. L2

ELL

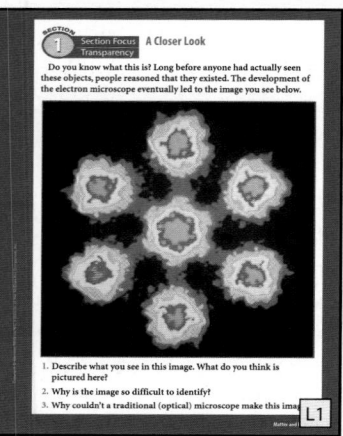

SECTION
1 Section Focus Transparency A Closer Look

Do you know what this is? Long before anyone had actually seen these objects, people reasoned that they existed. The development of the electron microscope eventually led to the image you see below.

1. Describe what you see in this image. What do you think is pictured here?
2. Why is the image so difficult to identify?
3. Why couldn't a traditional (optical) microscope make this ima... L1

Tie to Prior Knowledge

Help students recall that most soft drink cans are made from the lightweight element aluminum. Ask them to list other objects made of aluminum. Possible answer: lawn chairs and chalkboard borders

---

SECTION

1 Atoms

As You Read

What You'll Learn

- **Identify** the states of matter.
- **Describe** the internal structure of an atom.
- **Compare** isotopes of an element.

Vocabulary

matter	electron
atom	atomic number
element	mass number
proton	isotope
neutron	

Why It's Important

Nearly everything around you—air, water, food, and clothes—is made of atoms.

The Building Blocks of Matter

What do the objects you see, the air you breathe, and the food you eat have in common? They are matter. **Matter** is anything that has mass and takes up space. Heat and light are not matter, because they have no mass and do not take up space. Glance around the room. If all the objects you see are matter, why do they look so different from one another?

Atoms Matter, in its various forms, surrounds you. You can't see all matter as clearly as you see water, which is a transparent liquid, or rocks, which are colorful solids. You can't see air, for example, because air is a colorless gas. The forms or properties of one type of matter differ from the properties of another, because matter is made up of tiny particles called **atoms.** The structures of different types of atoms and how they join together determine all the properties of matter that you can observe. **Figure 1** illustrates how small objects, like atoms, can be put together in different ways.

Figure 1
Like atoms, the same few blocks can combine in many ways. *How could this model help explain the variety of matter?*

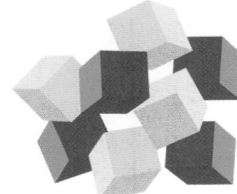

Section ✓*Assessment* Planner

PORTFOLIO
Science Journal, p. 35
PERFORMANCE ASSESSMENT
Try at Home MiniLAB, p. 35
Skill Builder Activities, p. 38
See page 58 for more options.

CONTENT ASSESSMENT
Section, p. 38
Challenge, p. 38
Chapter, pp. 58–59

The Structure of Matter Matter is joined together much like the blocks shown in **Figure 1.** The building blocks of matter are atoms. The types of atoms in matter and how they attach to each other give matter its properties.

Elements When atoms combine, they form many different types of matter. Your body contains several types of atoms combined in different ways. These atoms form the proteins, DNA, tissues, and other matter that make you the person you are. Most other objects that you see also are made of several different types of atoms. However, some substances are made of only one type of atom. **Elements** are substances that are made of only one type of atom and cannot be broken down by normal chemical or physical means.

Elements are useful for making a variety of items you depend on every day. They also combine to make up the minerals that compose Earth's crust. Some minerals, however, are made up of only one element. These minerals, which include copper and silver, are called native elements. **Table 1** shows some common elements and their uses. A table of the elements, called the periodic table of the elements, is included on the inside back cover of this book.

TRY AT HOME
Mini LAB

Searching for Elements
Procedure
1. Obtain a copy of the **periodic table of the elements** and familiarize yourself with the elements.
2. Search your house for items made of various elements.
3. Use a **highlighter** to highlight the elements you discovered on your copy of the periodic table.

Analysis
1. Were certain types of elements more common?
2. Infer why you did not find many of the elements.

Table 1 Some Common Uses of Elements

Element	Sulfur	Silver	Copper	Carbon
Native State of the Element	Sulfur	Silver	Copper	Graphite
Uses of the Element	Fertilizer	Tableware	Wire	Ski wax

Science Journal

Electrical Wire Have students research why electrical wire is often made of copper. Then have them write a report in their Science Journals identifying the traits of copper that make it suited for electrical wire. Copper is a good conductor of electricity. L1 P

Resource Manager

Chapter Resources Booklet
Transparency Activity, p. 40
Directed Reading for Content Mastery, pp. 15, 16
Note-taking Worksheets, pp. 29–31
MiniLAB, p. 3

---

② Teach

The Building Blocks of Matter

Caption Answer
Figure 1 Both atoms and blocks can be combined in a variety of ways to form many different substances and structures.

Mini LAB

Purpose Students identify everyday materials that are made of only one element. L2
ELL IS **Visual-Spatial**
Materials Periodic Table of the Elements, highlighter
Teaching Strategies
• Obtain copies of the Periodic Table that students can highlight and write on.
• Help students begin by explaining that some gems, such as diamonds, are made of only one element.
Analysis
1. Possible answer: Metallic elements, such as iron, copper, and gold, were more common.
2. Most elements are found in compounds with other elements. For example salt is a compound of sodium and chlorine.

 **Assessment**

Content To further assess students' understanding, have them work in groups of three to identify items in the classroom made of only one element. Possible answers: oxygen in the air, copper wire, aluminum containers Use **PASC**, p. 91.

Section 1 Atoms **35**

Modeling the Atom

Activity

Display the elements noted in **Table 1** as well as other common elements. Ask students to identify the mass and state of matter of each element. Have them relate the properties of each element to its position in the periodic table.

Quick Demo

Use interlocking plastic blocks to demonstrate how atoms are the building blocks of matter.

Fun Fact

If an atom were the size of a football stadium, the nucleus of the atom would be the size of a tennis ball located in the center of the stadium.

Figure 2
This model airplane is a small-scale version of a large object.

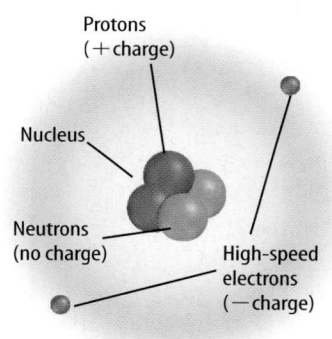

Protons (+charge)

Nucleus

Neutrons (no charge)

High-speed electrons (—charge)

Figure 3
This model of a helium atom shows two protons and two neutrons in the nucleus, and two electrons in the electron cloud.

Modeling the Atom

How can you study things that are too small to be seen with the unaided eye? When something is too large or too small to observe directly, models can be used. The model airplane, shown in **Figure 2,** is a small version of a larger object. A model also can describe tiny objects, such as atoms, that otherwise are difficult or impossible to see.

The History of the Atomic Model The current model of the atom is based on the work of many scientists over hundreds of years. The idea that matter is composed of atoms dates back more than 2,300 years when the Greek philosopher Democritus (dih MAH krih tuhs) proposed that matter is composed of small particles. He called these particles atoms and said that different types of matter were composed of different types of atoms. More than 2,000 years later, John Dalton expanded on these ideas. He theorized that all atoms of an element contain the same type of atom.

Protons and Neutrons In the early 1900s, additional work led to the development of the current model of the atom, shown in **Figure 3.** Three basic particles make up an atom—protons, neutrons (NOO trahnz), and electrons. **Protons** are particles that have a positive electric charge. **Neutrons** have no electric charge. Both particles are located in the nucleus—the center of an atom. With no negative charge to balance the positive charge of the protons, the charge of the nucleus is positive.

Electrons Particles with a negative charge are called **electrons,** and they exist outside of the nucleus. In 1913, Niels Bohr, a Danish scientist, proposed that an atom's electrons travel in orbitlike paths around the nucleus. He also proposed that electrons in an atom have energy that depends on their distance from the nucleus. Electrons in paths that are closer to the nucleus have lower energy, and electrons further from the nucleus have higher energy.

The Current Atomic Model Over the next several decades, research showed that although electrons do have specific amounts of energy, they do not travel in orbitlike paths. Instead, electrons move in an electron cloud surrounding the nucleus. Electrons can be anywhere within the cloud, but evidence suggests that they are located near the nucleus most of the time. To understand how this might work, imagine a beehive. The hive represents the nucleus of an atom. The bees swarming around the hive are like electrons moving around the nucleus. As they swarm, you can't predict their exact location, but they usually stay close to the hive.

Curriculum Connection

Archaeology Have students research how archaeologists use isotopes to determine the age of artifacts such as clothing, wood, bones, and structures. Possible answer: Over time, an isotope changes form. By comparing the amounts of each isotope present in the artifact, the age of the specimen is determined.

Visual Learning

Figure 3 The model in this figure shows an atom of helium with two electrons, two protons, and two neutrons. Ask students to identify the electrical charge of a proton, neutron, and electron. A proton is positive, a neutron has no charge, and an electron is negative. Have students determine the overall charge of the atom's nucleus and of the atom as a whole. +2, no charge

Counting Atomic Particles

You now know where protons, neutrons, and electrons are located, but how many of each are in an atom? The number of protons in an atom depends on the element. All atoms of the same element have the same number of protons. For example, all iron atoms—whether in train tracks or breakfast cereal—contain 26 protons, and all atoms with 26 protons are iron atoms. The number of protons in an atom is equal to the **atomic number** of the element. This number can be found above the element symbol on the periodic table. Notice that as you go from left to right on the periodic table, the atomic number of the element increases by one.

 **Reading Check** *How many protons are in an atom of gold, which has an atomic number of 79?*

How many electrons? In a neutral atom, the number of protons is equal to the number of electrons. This makes the overall charge of the atom zero. Therefore, for a neutral atom:

Atomic number = number of protons = number of electrons

Atoms of an element can lose or gain electrons and still be the same element. When this happens, the atom is no longer neutral. Atoms with fewer electrons than protons have a positive charge, and atoms with more electrons than protons have a negative charge.

How many neutrons? Unlike protons, atoms of the same element can have different numbers of neutrons. The number of neutrons in an atom isn't found on the periodic table. Instead, you need to know the atom's mass number. The **mass number** of an atom is equal to the number of protons plus the number of neutrons. The number of neutrons is determined by subtracting the atomic number from the mass number. In **Figure 4,** the number of neutrons can be determined by counting the blue spheres and the number of protons by counting orange spheres. Atoms of the same element that have different numbers of neutrons are called **isotopes.** **Table 2** lists useful isotopes of some elements.

 **Reading Check** *How are isotopes of the same element different?*

 **Health**
INTEGRATION

Some isotopes of elements are radioactive. Physicians can introduce these isotopes into a patient's circulatory system. The low-level radiation they emit allows the isotopes to be tracked as they move throughout the patient's body. Explain how this would be helpful in diagnosing a disease.

Figure 4
This atom is common in organic material. *Use the periodic table to determine which element it is.*

Reteach

Have students use common materials to construct atomic models of the hydrogen-1, hydrogen-2, and carbon-12 isotopes. L2 IS **Kinesthetic**

Challenge

Have students select three different elements from the periodic table and list the information identified on the table for each element. Ask students to describe what each symbol or number represents. Have them share their information in a visual such as a chart or diagram. Possible answer: Fe, iron; atomic number, 26 = number of protons or electrons; mass number, 56 = number of protons and neutrons in the atom's nucleus

Assessment

Performance Have groups of students create and share unique representations of the structure of matter. Use **Performance Assessment in the Science Classroom,** p. 123.

Table 2 Some Useful Isotopes

Isotope	Number of Protons	Number of Neutrons	Number of Electrons	Atomic Number	Mass Number
Hydrogen-1	1	0	1	1	1
Hydrogen-2	1	1	1	1	2
Hydrogen-3	1	2	1	1	3
Carbon-12	6	6	6	6	12
Carbon-14	6	8	6	6	14
Uranium-234	92	142	92	92	234
Uranium-235	92	143	92	92	235
Uranium-238	92	146	92	92	238

Uses of Isotopes Scientists have found uses for isotopes that benefit humans. For example, medical doctors use radioactive isotopes to treat certain types of cancer, such as prostate cancer. Geologists use isotopes to determine the ages of some rocks and fossils.

As you continue to investigate matter in this chapter, you will explore how atoms of different elements combine to form the materials around you.

Section ① Assessment

1. How does the air you breathe fit the definition of matter?
2. What are the basic particles found in the nucleus of an atom?
3. How do isotopes of an element differ from one another?
4. What is an element?
5. **Think Critically** Oxygen-16 and oxygen-17 are isotopes of oxygen. The numbers 16 and 17 represent their mass numbers, respectively. If the element oxygen has an atomic number of 8, how many protons and neutrons are in these two isotopes?

Skill Builder Activities

6. **Comparing and Contrasting** Review the material in Section 1. How do atoms and elements differ? How are they the same? **For more help, refer to the** Science Skill Handbook.

7. **Solving One-Step Equations** The mass number of nitrogen is 14. Find its atomic number in the periodic table shown on the inside back cover. Then determine the number of neutrons in its nucleus by subtracting the atomic number from the mass number. Write this equation. **For more help, refer to the** Math Skill Handbook.

Answers to Section Assessment

1. Air has mass and takes up space.
2. protons (p+) and neutrons (n⁰)
3. Different isotopes of the same element contain different numbers of neutrons.
4. An element is a substance that is made of only one type of atom and cannot be broken down by normal chemical or physical means.
5. Oxygen-16 has eight protons and eight neutrons; oxygen-17 has eight protons and nine neutrons.
6. Atoms, the building blocks of all matter, are composed of three kinds of particles. Atoms are the basic units that compose all matter. An element is matter made of only one type of atom. Both atoms and elements are forms of matter.
7. 7; mass number (14) − atomic number (7) = 7 neutrons

Combinations of Atoms

Interactions of Atoms

When you take a shower, eat your lunch, or do your homework on the computer, you probably don't think about elements. But everything you touch, eat, or use is made from them. Elements are all around you and in you.

There are 90 naturally occurring elements on Earth. When you think about the variety of matter in the universe, you might find it difficult to believe that most of it consists of combinations of these same elements. How could so few elements produce so many different things? This happens because elements can combine in countless ways. For example, the same oxygen atoms that you breathe also can be found in many other objects, as shown in **Figure 5.** As you can see, each combination of atoms is unique. How do these combinations form and what holds them together?

As You Read

What You'll Learn
- **Describe** several ways atoms combine to form compounds.
- **List** differences between compounds and mixtures.

Vocabulary
compound
ion
mixture
heterogeneous mixture
homogeneous mixture
solution

Why It's Important
On Earth, most matter exists as compounds or mixtures.

A Solid limestone has oxygen within its structure.

Figure 5
Oxygen is a common element found in many different solids, liquids, and gases. *How can the same element, made from the same type of atoms, be found in so many different materials?*

B Oxygen also is present in the juices of these apples.

C This canister contains pure oxygen gas.

SECTION 2 Combinations of Atoms **39**

Combinations of Atoms

1 Motivate

Bellringer Transparency
Display the Section Focus Transparency for Section 2. Use the accompanying Transparency Activity Master. L2
ELL

Tie to Prior Knowledge

Remind students that electrons are located outside the nucleus in the electron cloud. Ask students which electrons, those closer to the nucleus or those farther from the nucleus, would most likely react to form compounds. those farther from the nucleus

---

Section ✓Assessment Planner

PORTFOLIO
Cultural Diversity, p. 41
PERFORMANCE ASSESSMENT
MiniLAB, p. 43
Skill Builder Activities, p. 44
See page 58 for more options.

CONTENT ASSESSMENT
Section, p. 44
Challenge, p. 44
Chapter, pp. 58–59

Resource Manager

Chapter Resources Booklet
Transparency Activity, p. 41
Directed Reading for
Content Mastery, p. 16

Interactions of Atoms

Discussion

Explain to students that table salt is a compound of sodium and chlorine (NaCl). Have them use the Periodic Table in the appendix to hypothesize and discuss which elements might replace sodium in this compound. Elements above or below sodium on the chart will replace it in compounds. HCl is hydrochloric acid, KCl is the mineral sylvite, which is also a salt.

✔ Reading Check

Answer three; two hydrogen atoms and one oxygen atom

Bonding

Quick Demo

Soak steel wool in vinegar to remove the soap or any other coating on the wool. Rinse the steel wool and place it in a shallow dish. Leave the uncovered dish on a windowsill. Have students observe any changes that occur. Have them explain the cause of the changes. The steel wool will become covered in a red-brown coating. Iron in the steel wool reacted with oxygen in the air in the presence of water to form the compound iron oxide (rust). LS **Visual-Spatial**

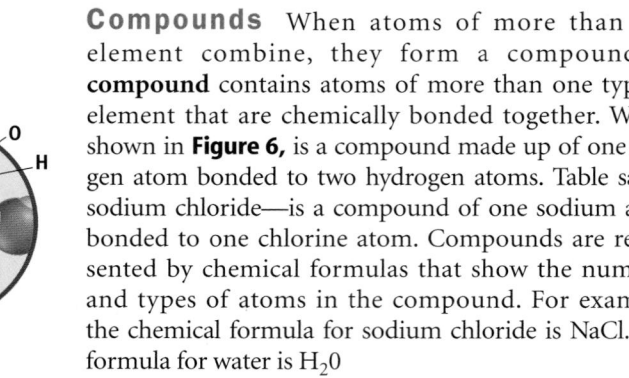

Figure 6
The water you drink is a compound consisting of hydrogen and oxygen atoms.

Compounds When atoms of more than one element combine, they form a compound. A **compound** contains atoms of more than one type of element that are chemically bonded together. Water, shown in **Figure 6,** is a compound made up of one oxygen atom bonded to two hydrogen atoms. Table salt—sodium chloride—is a compound of one sodium atom bonded to one chlorine atom. Compounds are represented by chemical formulas that show the numbers and types of atoms in the compound. For example, the chemical formula for sodium chloride is NaCl. The formula for water is H_2O

✔ Reading Check
How many atoms does a water molecule have?

The properties of compounds often are very different from the properties of the elements that combine to form them. Sodium is a soft, silvery metal, and chlorine is a greenish, poisonous gas, but the compound they form is the white, crystalline table salt you use to season food. Under normal conditions on Earth, the hydrogen and oxygen that form water are gases. Water can be solid ice, liquid water, or gaseous vapor. Which state do you think is most common for water at Earth's south pole?

Chemical Properties A property that describes a change that occurs when one substance reacts with another is called a chemical property. For example, one chemical property of water is that it changes to hydrogen and oxygen gas when an electric current passes through it. The chemical properties of a substance depend on what elements are in that substance and how they are arranged. Iron atoms in the mineral biotite will react with water and oxygen to form iron oxide, or rust, but iron mixed with chromium and nickel in stainless steel resists rusting.

Bonding

The forces that hold the atoms in compounds together are called chemical bonds. Some atoms are reactive and form bonds easily. Other atoms are much less reactive. For example, atoms that have eight electrons in the outermost portion of their electron cloud are not likely to combine with other atoms. If an atom has fewer than eight electrons in the outermost portion of its electron cloud, it is unstable and is more likely to combine with other atoms. One exception to this rule is the element helium, with only two electrons in its electron cloud. This atom is stable and does not react easily.

Covalent Bonds Atoms can combine to form compounds in two different ways. One way is by sharing the electrons in the outer portion of their electron clouds. The type of bond that forms by sharing outer electrons is a covalent bond. A group of atoms connected by covalent bonds is called a molecule. For example, two atoms of hydrogen can share outer electrons with one atom of oxygen to form a molecule of water, as shown in **Figure 7.** Each of the hydrogen atoms has one outer electron and the oxygen has six outer electrons. This arrangement causes hydrogen and oxygen atoms to bond together. Each of the hydrogen atoms becomes stable by sharing one electron with the oxygen atom, and the oxygen atom becomes stable by sharing two electrons with the two hydrogen atoms.

Ionic Bonds In addition to sharing electrons, atoms also combine if they become positively or negatively charged. This type of bond is called an ionic bond. Atoms can be neutral, or under certain conditions, atoms can lose or gain electrons. When an atom loses electrons, it has more protons than electrons, so the atom is positively charged. When an atom gains electrons, it has more electrons than protons, so the atom is negatively charged. Electrically charged atoms are called **ions.**

Ions are attracted to each other when they have opposite charges. This is similar to the way magnets behave. If the ends of a pair of magnets have the same type of pole, they repel each other. Conversely, if the ends have opposite poles, they attract one another. Ions form electrically neutral compounds when they join. The mineral halite, commonly used as table salt, forms in this way. A sodium (Na) atom loses an outer electron and ecomes a positively charged ion. As shown in **Figure 8,** if the sodium ion comes close to a negatively charged chlorine (Cl) ion, they attract each other and form the salt you use on french fries or popcorn.

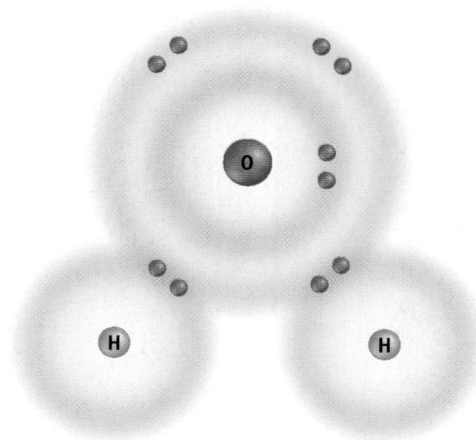

Figure 7
A molecule of water consists of two atoms of hydrogen that share outer electrons with one atom of oxygen.

Figure 8
Table salt forms when a sodium ion and a chlorine ion are attracted to one another. *What kind of bond holds ions together?*

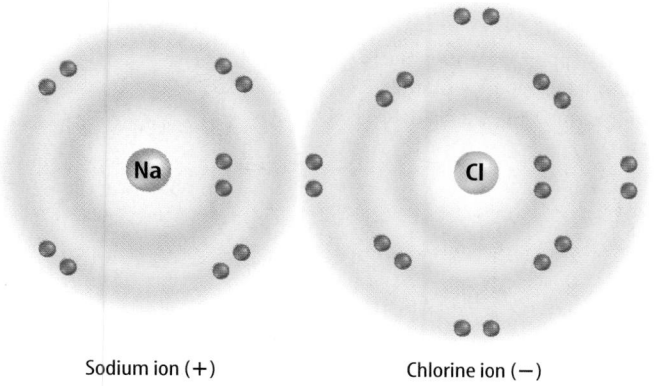

Sodium ion (+)   Chlorine ion (−)

SECTION 2 Combinations of Atoms **41**

Figure 9
Electrons move freely between the copper atoms in this wire.
What type of bond holds copper atoms together?

Metallic Bonds Metallic bonds are found in metals such as copper, gold, aluminum, and silver. In this type of bond, electrons are free to move from one positively charged ion to another. This free movement of electrons is responsible for key characteristics of metals. The movement of electrons, or conductivity, allows metals like copper, shown in **Figure 9,** to pass an electric current easily.

Hydrogen Bonds Some types of bonds, such as hydrogen bonds, can form without the interactions of electrons. The arrangement of hydrogen and oxygen atoms in water molecules causes them to be polar molecules. A polar molecule has a positive end and a negative end. This happens because the atoms do not share electrons equally. When hydrogen and oxygen atoms form a molecule with covalent bonds, the hydrogen atoms produce an area of partial positive charge and the oxygen atom produces an area of partial negative charge. The positive end of one molecule is attracted to the negative end of another molecule, as shown in **Figure 10,** and a weak hydrogen bond is formed. The different parts of the water molecule are slightly charged, but as a whole, the molecule has no charge. This type of bond is easily broken, indicating that the charges are weak.

Hydrogen bonds are responsible for several properties of water, some of which are unique. Cohesion is the attraction between water molecules that allows them to form raindrops and to form beads on flat surfaces. Hydrogen bonds cause water to exist as a liquid, rather than a gas, at room temperature. As water freezes, hydrogen bonds force water molecules apart, into a structure that is less dense than liquid water.

Figure 10
The ends of polar molecules, such as water, have opposite charges. This allows molecules to be held together by hydrogen bonds.

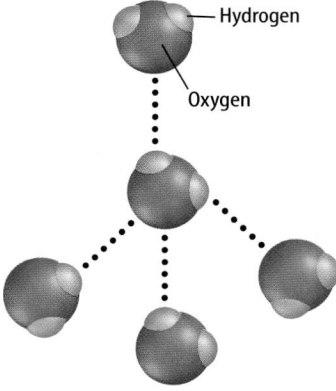

— Hydrogen

Oxygen

42 CHAPTER 2 Matter

Figure 11
This rock contains a variety of minerals that together form a mixture.

Mixtures

Sometimes compounds and elements mix together but do not combine chemically. A **mixture** is composed of two or more substances that are not chemically combined. There are two different types of mixtures—heterogeneous and homogeneous. The components of a **heterogeneous mixture** are not mixed evenly and each component retains its own properties. Maybe you've seen a rock like the one in **Figure 11.** Several different minerals are mixed together, but if you were to examine the minerals separately, you would find that they have the same properties and appearance as they have in the rock.

The components of a **homogeneous mixture** are evenly mixed throughout. You can't see the individual components. Another name for a homogeneous mixture is a **solution.** The properties of the components of this type of mixture often are different from the properties of the mixture. Ocean water is an example of a liquid solution that consists of salts mixed with liquid water.

Reading Check *What is a solution?*

Separating Mixtures and Compounds

The components of a mixture can be separated by physical means. For example, you can sit at your desk and pick out the separate items in your backpack, or you can let the water evaporate from a saltwater mixture and the salt will remain.

Separating the components of a mixture is a relatively easy task compared to separating those of a compound. The substances in a compound must be separated by chemical means. This means that an existing compound can be changed to one or more new substances by chemically breaking down the original compound. For example, a drop of dilute hydrochloric acid (HCl) can be placed on calcium carbonate ($CaCO_3$) and carbon dioxide (CO_2) is released. To break down most compounds, several steps usually are required.

SECTION 2 Combinations of Atoms **43**

Assessment

Oral To further assess students' understanding of different forms of matter, have them classify various materials found in the classroom. Use **Performance Assessment in the Science Classroom,** p. 89.

Mini LAB

Classifying Forms of Matter

Procedure
1. Make a chart with columns titled Mixtures, Compounds, and Elements.
2. Classify each of these items into the proper column on your chart: **air, sand, hydrogen, muddy water, sugar, ice, sugar water, water, salt, oxygen, copper.**
3. Make a solution using two or more of the items listed above.

Analysis
1. How does a solution differ from other types of mixtures?
2. How does an element differ from a compound?

Mixtures

Mini LAB

Purpose Students will determine the differences between mixtures, compounds, and elements. L1 IS **Kinesthetic Teaching Strategy** Students can make a solution by mixing salt or sugar into a beaker of water. Students' charts should resemble the one below.

Mixtures	Compounds	Elements
air	water	gold
muddy water	ice	oxygen
water	sugar	hydrogen
salt water	salt	copper
sand		

Analysis
1. One substance is thoroughly and evenly mixed in another substance.
2. Compounds are chemical combinations of two or more elements that cannot be separated physically.

Reading Check

Answer a homogeneous mixture where the component are evenly mixed throughout

Separating Mixtures and Compounds

Make a Model

Ask students to make molecular models of compounds using common classroom items. Have them place the completed models in a large box to represent a mixture. Ask students how they would separate the mixture and then the compounds. To separate the mixture just separate the molecules; to separate the compounds you must break the bonds holding them together.

Exploring Matter

Since its chemical properties have not changed, salt can be tasted in the water. Physical properties such as crystal size have changed. As the salt dissolves, ions of sodium and chlorine dissociate from the crystal and form a solution with the water.

③ Assess

Reteach

Carefully burn a small piece of paper to form ash to demonstrate how the properties of substances change when they combine to form a compound. Then mix salt and pepper together to show how the components of a mixture retain their properties.

Challenge

Ask students to identify the similarities and differences between covalent and ionic bonds. Similarity: Both are ways that compounds form. Differences: In covalent bonds, atoms share their outermost electrons. In ionic bonds, ions are held together by the strong attraction of the opposite charges.

✔Assessment

Oral Ask students to explain how hydrogen bonds are responsible for the cohesion of water molecules. Water molecules are polar molecules. The positive side of one molecule attracts the negative side of another. Water droplets form because of cohesive attraction. Use **Performance Assessment in the Science Classroom,** p. 89.

Figure 12
The ocean is a mixture of many different forms of matter. The ocean water itself is a solution.

Chemistry
INTEGRATION

When one substance dissolves in another, some of the properties of the dissolving substance change. When salt dissolves in water, decide whether its chemical or physical properties change.

Exploring Matter

Air, sweetened tea, salt water, and the contents of your backpack are examples of mixtures. The combination of rocks, fish, and coral shown in **Figure 12** also is a mixture. In each case, the materials within the mixture are not chemically combined. The individual components are made of compounds, or elements. The atoms that make up these components lost their individual properties when they combined. Even though atoms are known as the building blocks of matter, they are composed of protons, neutrons, and electrons, which are even smaller. As you continue to explore matter, apply what you've learned about atoms, elements, compounds, mixtures, and solutions to your studies.

Section ② Assessment

1. How do atoms or ions combine to form compounds?
2. Why is sweetened tea considered to be a solution rather than a compound?
3. Describe the chemical property of iron that results in rust.
4. Explain what makes a solution different from a heterogeneous mixture.
5. **Think Critically** How can you determine whether salt water is a solution or a compound?

Skill Builder Activities

6. **Comparing and Contrasting** How are solutions and compounds similar? How are they different? **For more help, refer to the** Science Skill Handbook.
7. **Communicating** Design an investigation that would show whether sugar water is a mixture or a compound. Discuss your design with your teacher. Perform the investigation and write the results in your Science Journal. **For more help, refer to the** Science Skill Handbook.

Answers to Section Assessment

1. Atoms share electrons to form molecules of a compound. They can also lose or gain electrons to form ions. Ions attract each other and combine to form compounds.
2. The chemical properties of the sugar and the tea have not changed. They can be separated by evaporation.
3. Iron will combine with oxygen to form iron oxide.
4. One substance is thoroughly and evenly mixed in another substance in a solution. In a heterogeneous solution they are unevenly mixed.
5. by determining whether the salt and water will separate by evaporation
6. In both two or more substances are combined. The components of a solution retain their properties; the properties of components of a compound change.
7. Let sugar water evaporate. Sugar will be left behind. Sugar water is a mixture.

Scales of Measurement

How would you describe some of the objects in your classroom? Perhaps your desktop is about one-half the size of a door. Measuring physical properties in a laboratory experiment will help you make better observations.

What You'll Investigate
How are physical properties of objects measured?

Materials
triple beam balance   rock sample
100-mL graduated cylinder   string
metersticks (2)   globe
non-mercury thermometers (3) water
stick or dowel

Goals
- ■ **Measure** various physical properties in SI.
- ■ **Determine** sources of error.

Safety Precautions

Procedure
Do not "shake down" lab thermometers.

1. Go to every station and determine the measurement requested. Record your observations in a data table and list sources of error.
   a. Use a balance to determine the mass, to the nearest 0.1 g, of the rock sample.
   b. Use a graduated cylinder to measure the water volume to the nearest 0.5 mL.
   c. Use three thermometers to determine the average temperature, to the nearest 0.5°C, at a selected location in the room.
   d. Use a meterstick to measure the length, to the nearest 0.1 cm, of the stick or dowel.
   e. Use a meterstick and string to measure the circumference of the globe. Be accurate to the nearest 0.1 cm.

Measurement and Error		
Sample at Station	Value of Measurement	Causes of Error
a. rock	mass = _____ g	possible answers include:
b. water	volume = _____ mL	
c. (location)	average temp. = _____ °C	human error
d. stick or dowel	length = _____ cm	instrument error
e. globe	circumference = _____ cm	rounding error

Conclude and Apply

1. **Compare** your results with those of other students who measured the same objects. Review the values provided by your teacher. How do the values you obtained compare with those provided by your teacher and other students?

2. **Calculate** your percentage of error in each case. Use this formula.

   $$\text{your value} - \text{teacher's value} \times 100 = \text{\% of error}$$

3. Decide what percentage of error will be acceptable. Generally, being within five percent to seven percent of the correct value is considered good. If your values exceed ten percent error, what could you do to improve your results and reduce error? What was the most common source of error?

*C*ommunicating Your Data

Compare your conclusions with those of other students in your class. **For more help, refer to the** Science Skill Handbook.

BENCH TESTED

Purpose Students will demonstrate safety, accuracy, and precision in using simple laboratory equipment to determine some of the physical properties of sample objects. L1

LS **Kinesthetic**

Process Skills measuring in SI, communicating, using numbers, interpreting data, forming operational definitions

Time Required 40 minutes

Safety Precautions Caution students to handle equipment and materials with care.

Teaching Strategy Set up stations in advance for each of the five tasks.

Troubleshooting Each sample should be identified with a letter or number to avoid confusion.

Answers to Questions
1. Answers will vary depending on the samples used and students' results.
2. Answers will vary depending on the samples used and students' results.
3. Taking several measurements of the same property should decrease error. A common source of error is improper measuring methods.

✔ *Assessment*

Oral To further assess students' understanding of the physical properties of objects, have them measure various objects in the classroom. Use **PASC**, p. 91.

Resource Manager

Chapter Resources Booklet
Reinforcement, p. 24
Activity Worksheet, pp. 5–6

Physical Science Critical Thinking/Problem Solving, p. 10

*C*ommunicating Your Data

Have students discuss sources of error. For example, balance not preset at 0 g, sliding indicator not set in slot; incorrect reading of liquid level in graduated cylinder; inaccurate thermometers, misreading of temperature scale; not starting measurement at 0 cm on meterstick; and other improper methods.

SECTION

③ Properties of Matter

① Motivate

Bellringer Transparency

Display the Section Focus Transparency for Section 3. Use the accompanying Transparency Activity Master. L2
ELL

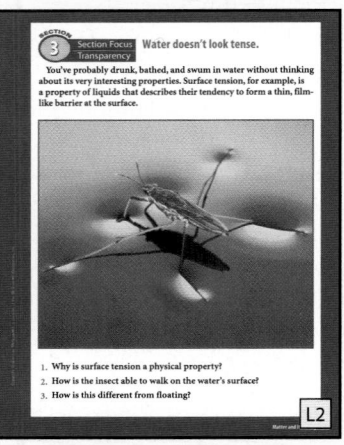

As You Read

What You'll Learn

- **Distinguish** between chemical and physical properties.
- **List** the four states of matter.

Vocabulary
density

Why It's Important
You can recognize many substances by their physical properties.

Tie to Prior Knowledge

Ask a volunteer to name the physical properties of an item in the classroom. Have listeners use the information to name the item. Guide students in recognizing that the properties of an item are unique.

Physical Properties of Matter

In addition to the chemical properties of matter that you have already investigated in this chapter, matter also has other properties that can be described. You might describe a pair of blue jeans as soft, blue, and about 80 cm long. A sandwich could have two slices of bread, lettuce, tomato, cheese, and turkey. These descriptions can be made without altering the sandwich or the blue jeans in any way. The properties that you can observe without changing a substance into a new substance are physical properties.

One physical property that you will use to describe matter is density. **Density** is a measure of the mass of an object divided by its volume. Generally, this measurement is given in grams per cubic centimeter (g/cm^3). For example, the average density of liquid water is about 1 g/cm^3. So 1 cm^3 of pure water has a mass of about 1 g.

An object that's more dense than water will sink in water. On the other hand, an object that's not as dense as water will float in water. When oil spills occur on the ocean, as shown in **Figure 13,** the oil floats on the surface of the water and washes up on beaches. Because the oil floats, even a small spill can spread out and cover large areas.

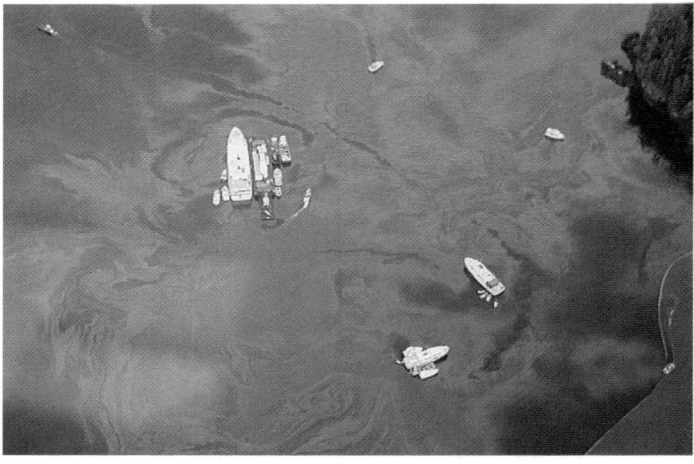

Figure 13
Oil spills on the ocean spread across the surface of the water.
How does the density of oil compare to the density of water?

46   CHAPTER 2 Matter

Section ✓ *Assessment* Planner

PORTFOLIO
Extension, p. 49
PERFORMANCE ASSESSMENT
Math Skills Activity, p. 47
Skill Builder Activities, p. 51
See page 58 for more options.

CONTENT ASSESSMENT
Section, p. 51
Challenge, p. 51
Chapter, pp. 58–59

States of Matter

On Earth, matter occurs in four physical states. These four states are solid, liquid, gas, and plasma. You might have had solid toast and liquid milk or juice for breakfast this morning. You breathe air, which is a gas. A lightning bolt during a storm is an example of matter in its plasma state. What are the differences among these four states of matter?

Solids The reason some matter is solid is that its particles are in fixed positions relative to each other. The individual particles vibrate, but they don't switch positions with each other. Solids have a definite shape and take up a definite volume.

Suppose you have a puzzle that is completely assembled. The pieces are connected so one piece cannot switch positions with another piece. However, the pieces can move a little. For example, you can push on one end of the puzzle and move each individual puzzle piece, but the pieces of the puzzle stay attached to one another. The puzzle pieces in this model represent particles of a substance in a solid state. Such particles are strongly attracted to each other and resist being separated.

Math Skills Activity

Calculating Density

You want to find the density of a small cube of an unknown material. It measures 1 cm × 1 cm × 2 cm. It has a mass of 8 g.

Solution

1 *This is what you know:*   mass: $m = 8$ g
volume: $v = 1 \text{ cm} \times 1 \text{ cm} \times 2 \text{ cm} = 2 \text{ cm}^3$

2 *This is what you need to find:*   density: d

3 *This is the equation you need to use:* $d = m/v$

4 *Substitute the known values:* $d = 8 \text{ g}/2 \text{ cm}^3$
$d = 4 \text{ g/cm}^3$

Check your answer by multiplying by the volume. Do you calculate the same mass that was given? Explain.

Practice Problem

Your aunt brings you a souvenir gold bar from her visit to Fort Knox. It measures 10 cm × 5 cm × 2 cm. It has a mass of 1,544 g. Find the density of gold.

For more help refer to the Math Skill Handbook.

Resource Manager

Chapter Resources Booklet
Transparency Activity, p. 42
Directed Reading for Content Mastery, pp. 17, 18

Mathematics Skill Activities, p. 9

---

② Teach

Physical Properties of Matter

Caption Answer
Figure 13 Because oil floats on top of water, it must be less dense than the water.

Discussion
Display several items with a wide variety of physical properties. Have students work in groups to identify the physical properties of each item. [L2]
IS Interpersonal

States of Matter

Extension
Have students make a Venn diagram comparing the processes of evaporation and boiling. Both involve a change in state from liquid to gas. Evaporation occurs at the liquid's surface; boiling occurs throughout the liquid. **IS Visual-Spatial**

Math Skills Activity

National Math Standards
Correlation to Mathematics Objectives
1, 2, 4, 9

Answer to Practice Problem
mass: $m = 1544$ g
volume: $v = 10 \text{ cm} \times 5 \text{ cm} \times 2 \text{ cm}$
   $= 100 \text{ cm}^3$
   $d = m/v$
   $d = 1544 \text{ g}/100 \text{ cm}^3$
   $d = 15.44 \text{ g/cm}^3$

If students compare this value with the density of gold listed, they will find that the souvenir is not really gold.

IDENTIFYING Misconceptions

Students may not realize that matter can change from a solid to a gas without going through the liquid phase. This process is called sublimation.

Quick Demo

Obtain a piece of dry ice (carbon dioxide in a frozen, solid state). Place the dry ice on a plate in view of students. The dry ice will quickly change into carbon dioxide gas via sublimation. Students should note that it doesn't pass through a liquid state. **CAUTION:** *Do not touch the dry ice. Always use a thermal mitt and tongs to manipulate the ice. Perform the demonstration in a well-ventilated area.*

✔ Reading Check

Answer Air fresheners release molecules of a gas that spread out and fill the room.

SCIENCE *Online*

Research Visit the Glencoe Science Web site at **science. glencoe.com** for information about the four states of matter. Communicate to your class what you learn.

Figure 14
The Sun is an example of a plasma.

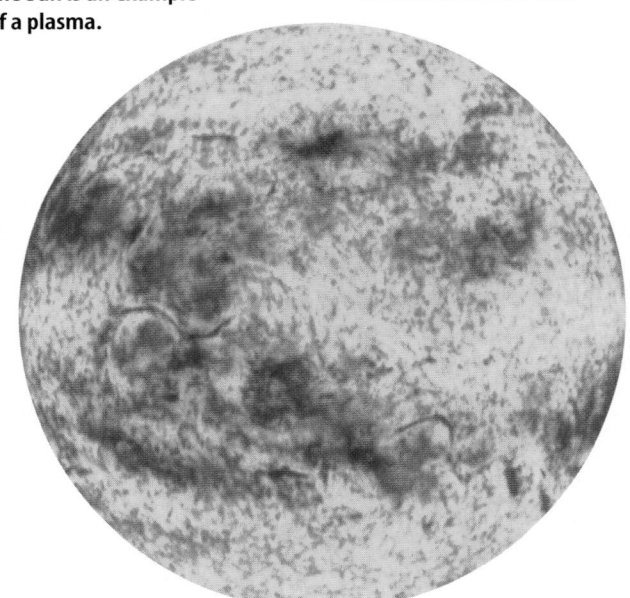

Liquids Particles in a liquid are attracted to each other, but not as strongly as they are in the solid shown in **Figure 15A.** This is because liquid particles have more energy than solid particles. This energy allows them to move around and change positions with each other.

When you eat breakfast, you might have several liquids at the table such as syrup, juice, and milk. These are substances in the liquid state, even though one flows more freely than the others at room temperature. The particles in a liquid can change positions to fit the shape of the container they are held in. You can pour any liquid into any container, and it will flow until it matches the shape of its new container.

Gases The particles that make up gases have almost no attractive force on each other. This allows them to move freely and independently. Unlike liquids and solids, gases spread out and fill the container in which they are placed. Air fresheners work because of this property. If an air freshener is placed in a corner, it isn't long before the particles from the air freshener have spread throughout the room. Look at the hot-air balloon shown in **Figure 15C.** The particles in the balloon move apart until they're evenly spaced throughout the balloon. The balloon floats in the sky, because the hot air inside the balloon is less dense than the colder air around it.

✔ Reading Check *Why do air fresheners work?*

Plasma The most common state of matter in the universe is plasma. This state is associated with high temperatures. Can you name something that is in the plasma state? Stars like the Sun, shown in **Figure 14,** are composed of matter in the plasma state. Plasma also exists in Jupiter's magnetic field. On Earth, plasma is found in lightning bolts, as shown in **Figure 15D.** Plasma is composed of ions and electrons. It forms when high temperatures cause some of the electrons normally found in an atom's electron cloud to escape and move outside of the electron cloud.

48 CHAPTER 2 Matter

🔬 LAB DEMONSTRATION

Purpose to see that molecular attraction affects how a liquid flows
Materials syrup, milk, two 250-mL beakers
Preparation Set out containers of syrup and milk so that both will be at room temperature for the demonstration.

Procedure Instruct students to observe as you pour syrup and milk into two separate containers. Ask students to contrast the rates at which the two liquids flow.
Expected Outcome Students will note that the two liquids flowed at different rates and that the syrup was thicker.

✔ Assessment

Why does the syrup move more slowly than the milk? The syrup flows more slowly because it is thicker. This is caused by a stronger attraction between molecules in the syrup than in the milk.

Figure 15

Matter on Earth exists naturally in four different states—solid, liquid, gas, and plasma—as shown here. The state of a sample of matter depends upon the amount of energy its atoms or molecules possess. The more energy that matter contains, the more freely its atoms or molecules move, because they are able to overcome the attractive forces that tend to hold them together.

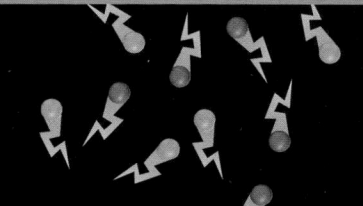

D **PLASMA** Electrically charged particles in lightning are free moving.

A **SOLID** In a solid such as galena, the tightly packed atoms or molecules lack the energy to move out of position.

B **LIQUID** The atoms or molecules in a liquid such as water have enough energy to overcome some attractive forces and move over and around one another.

C **GAS** In air and other gases, atoms or molecules have sufficient energy to separate from each other completely and move in all directions.

49

Visualizing States of Matter

Have students examine the pictures and read the captions. Then ask the following questions.

How are the properties of shape and volume used to distinguish among a solid, a liquid, and a gas? A solid has a definite shape and volume. A liquid has a definite volume, but takes the shape of its container. A gas takes up the total volume available and has no shape other than the container that encloses it.

How would the arrangement of water molecules differ in liquid water and ice? The molecules in ice are closer together and lack the energy to move out of position, while the molecules in water are able to move over and around one another.

Activity

Organize the class into several groups. Call out a letter of the alphabet. Give the groups 30 seconds to write as many examples as they can for each of the three states of matter that begins with that letter; for example, *A:* gas—air, liquid—alcohol, solid—aluminum. Then ask a group member to read the list. Repeat with other letters. Discuss which state of matter they found easiest to identify examples.

Extension

Have students investigate plasmas that occur in everyday objects such as fluorescent lamps, neon signs, and sodium vapor streetlights. Ask students to make a poster describing how one of these devices works. [L2] **LS Visual-Spatial** [P]

Inclusion Strategies

Behaviorally Disordered Hide an open bottle of vinegar or clove oil in the classroom. Have students raise their hands when they detect the odor. Ask students to describe the direction of the flow of molecules of the gas from the bottle through the air.

Resource Manager

Chapter Resources Booklet
   Lab Activity, pp. 11–12
   Enrichment, p. 28
Science Inquiry Labs, p. 43

Changing the State of Matter

Caption Answer
Figure 16 The heat energy causes molecules to spread farther apart and move around each other.

Activity

Put 100 mL of water and five ice cubes in a 600-mL beaker. Record the temperature of the water. Slowly heat the beaker, and record the water temperature at one-minute intervals. Note when the ice melts and when the water begins to boil. Measure and record the temperature as the water boils for five minutes. Have students graph the temperature of the water as a function of time. L3

- **What was the maximum temperature reached when ice was still in the water?** $0°C$
- **What was the maximum temperature reached?** $100°C$
- **What do the horizontal portions of your graph represent?** changes of state

Changes in Physical Properties

Caption Answer
Figure 17 Ice would enclose the fish and they would die.

Visual Learning

Figure 17 Have students hypothesize why ice is less dense than liquid water. Molecules move farther apart as water freezes.

✔ Reading Check

Answer Ice is less dense than water.

Figure 16
A solid metal can be changed to a liquid by adding thermal energy to its molecules. *What is happening to the molecules during this change?*

Figure 17
If ice were more dense than water, lakes would freeze solid from the bottom up. *What effect might this have on the fish?*

Changing the State of Matter

Matter is changed from a liquid to a solid at its freezing point and from a liquid to a gas at its boiling point. Water is the only substance that occurs naturally on Earth as a solid, liquid, and gas, because its freezing and boiling points are within the range of temperatures found on Earth. Water does not exist as plasma on Earth. Other substances don't exist naturally in three states on Earth, because their boiling and freezing points are above or below the typical temperatures experienced on Earth. Temperatures and conditions needed for matter to exist naturally as plasma are even less common on Earth.

The attraction between particles of a substance and their rate of movement are factors that determine the state of matter. When thermal energy is added to ice, the rate of movement of its molecules increases. This allows the molecules to move more freely and causes the ice to melt. As **Figure 16** shows, even solid metal can be converted into liquid when enough thermal energy is added.

Changes in state also occur because of increases or decreases in pressure. You can demonstrate this with an ice cube. When subjected to pressure, the ice will change to liquid water when no thermal energy is added. This occurs because the melting temperature of the ice is lowered as more pressure is added. This might explain how the base of a glacier can move around some rock obstacles. It is thought that the pressure of the glacier on the rock melts the ice, creating a thin layer of water. The water then flows around the obstacle and refreezes on the other side.

Changes in Physical Properties

Chemical properties of matter don't change when the matter changes state, but some of its physical properties change. For example, the density of water changes as water changes state. Ice floats in liquid water, as seen in **Figure 17,** because it is less dense than liquid water. This is unique, because most materials are denser in their solid state than in their liquid state.

✔ **Reading Check** *Why does ice float in water?*

Some physical properties of substances don't change when they change state. For example, water is colorless and transparent in each of its states.

Resource Manager

Chapter Resources Booklet
  Reinforcement, p. 25
  Activity Worksheet, pp. 7–8
Home and Community Involvement, p. 30

Inclusion Strategies

Visually Impaired Help students recognize the different states of matter by having them use other senses to detect each state of matter. Have them touch a wood block and the liquid in a cup of water. Have them sense a gas by having them smell an open bottle of vanilla. As an alternative, place a cup of ice near the students so they can feel the change from the solid to the liquid state of water.

Changing Mars's Matter

Matter in one state often can be changed to another state by adding or removing thermal energy. Changes in thermal energy might explain why Mars appears to have had considerable water on its surface in the past but now has little or no water on its surface. Recent images of Mars reveal that there might still be some groundwater that occasionally reaches the surface, as shown in **Figure 18,** but nothing could explain the huge water-carved channels formed long ago. Much of the liquid water on Mars is thought to have changed state as the planet cooled to its current temperature. Scientists believe that some of Mars's liquid water soaked into the ground and froze, forming permafrost. Some of the water might have frozen to form the polar ice caps. Even more of the water might have evaporated into the atmosphere and escaped to space.

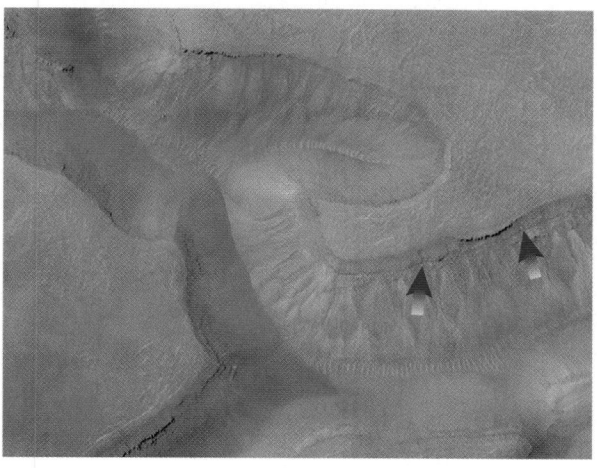

Figure 18
Groundwater might reach the surface of Mars along the edge of this large channel.

Section 3 Assessment

1. List the four states of matter in order from lowest to highest in terms of amount of particle movement.

2. Compare and contrast the movement of water molecules when water is in a solid, liquid, and gaseous state. How is the movement of water molecules dependent upon temperature?

3. As water freezes, what happens to the water molecules that causes ice to float? Why is this unique?

4. What type of properties of a substance can be observed without changing it into a new substance?

5. **Think Critically** Suppose you blow up a balloon and then place it in a freezer. Later, you find that the balloon has shrunk and has drops of frozen liquid in it. Explain what has happened.

Skill Builder Activities

6. **Classifying** Classify the following items into the four types of matter: *groundwater, lightning, lava, snow, textbook, ice cap, notebook, apple juice, eraser, glass, cotton, helium, iron oxide, lake, limestone,* and *water vapor.* Compare and contrast their characteristics. **For more help, refer to the** Science Skill Handbook.

7. **Using Graphics Software** Research the melting and boiling points in degrees Celsius of several compounds, including water. Use your computer to make a line graph showing the temperatures at which these several compounds change state from solid to liquid to gas. Rearrange your data in order of increasing melting and boiling points. **For more help, refer to the** Technology Skill Handbook.

Activity

Recognize the Problem

Purpose

Students will design and carry out an experiment to measure the volume and mass of various objects and to determine their densities. L1 IS **Interpersonal**

Process Skills

measuring in SI, using numbers, interpreting data, inferring, communicating, making and using tables, forming a hypothesis, designing an experiment, separating and controlling variables

Time Required

two class periods: one class period for students to devise a method of measuring the volume of objects and to complete the measurements; one class period for students to calculate the density of the objects and to discuss the procedure and outcome

Form a Hypothesis

Possible Hypotheses

- The volume of an object can be determined by submerging it in water and measuring the volume of water displaced.
- The volume of an object can be determined by measuring its length, width, and height.
- The density of an object is determined by dividing its mass by its volume.

Activity *Design Your Own Experiment*

Determining Density

Which has a greater density—a rock or a sponge? Is cork more dense than clay? Density is the ratio of an object's mass to its volume.

Recognize the Problem

How can you determine the densities of several objects in your classroom?

Form a Hypothesis

State a hypothesis about what process you can use to measure and compare the densities of several materials.

Possible Materials

pan
triple-beam balance
100-mL beaker
250-mL graduated cylinder
water
sponge
piece of quartz
piece of clay
small wooden block
small metal block
small cork
rock
ruler

Goals

- **List** some ways that the density of an object can be measured.
- **Design** an experiment that compares the densities of several materials.

Safety Precautions

WARNING: *Be wary of sharp edges on some of the materials and take care not to break the beaker or graduated cylinder. Wash hands thoroughly with soap and water when finished.*

52

Test Your Hypothesis

Possible Procedures

- Most students will realize that the volume and mass of each object must be determined in order to calculate the density. However, students may have difficulty devising a method for measuring volume.

- Measuring the volume of water displaced by an object will provide the volume of the object.
- The volume of objects with straight sides can be obtained by measuring their width, length, and height.
- The mass of an object can be obtained by using the pan balance.

Test Your Hypothesis

Plan

1. As a group, agree upon and write the hypothesis statement.
2. As a group, list the steps that you need to take to test your hypothesis. Be specific, describing exactly what you will do at each step. List your materials.
3. While working as a group, use this equation: density = mass/volume. Devise a method of determining the mass and volume of each material to be tested.
4. **Design** a data table in your Science Journal so that it is ready to use as your group collects data.

Check the Plan

1. Read over your entire experiment to make sure that all steps are in a logical order.
2. Should you run the process more than once for any of the materials?
3. **Identify** any constants, variables, and controls of the experiment.
4. Make sure your teacher approves your plan before you start.

Do

1. Carry out the experiment as planned.
2. While the experiment is going on, write any observations that you make and complete the data table in your Science Journal.

Analyze Your Data

1. Do you observe anything about the way objects with greater density feel compared with objects of lower density?

2. Which of the objects you tested would float in water? Which would sink?

Draw Conclusions

1. Based on your results, would you hypothesize that a cork is more dense, the same density, or less dense than water?

2. Without measuring the density of an object that floats, conclude how you know that it has a density of less than 1.0 g/cm³.

3. Would the density of the clay be affected if you were to break it into smaller pieces?

Communicating Your Data

Write an informational pamphlet on different methods for determining the density of objects. Include equations and a step-by-step procedure.

Teaching Strategies

Tie to Prior Knowledge Have students recall that density can be compared by attempting to float one material within another.

Troubleshooting Use oil-based clay that is not water-soluble. Since the wood block may absorb water, it should not be left in water for any extended length of time.

Expected Outcome

Students should be able to measure the volume and mass of each object and calculate densities within a 10 percent error.

Analyze Your Data

1. Denser objects feel heavier than less dense objects of the same size. Objects like these are said to have greater heft.
2. Cork, sponge, wooden block float in water. Other objects sink.

Error Analysis

Ask students why comparing the heft of two different-sized objects would not be as useful.

Draw Conclusions

1. The cork is less dense than water.
2. Water has a density of 1 g/cm³. Any object that floats in water must have a density less than 1 g/cm³.
3. As long as the same sample is used, the density of the clay is not affected by the size of the piece.

✓*Assessment*

Performance To further assess students' understanding of density and measuring physical properties, have them repeat the above experiment using different samples of the materials they tested. Have them list possible causes of any differences observed. Use **Performance Assessment in the Science Classroom,** p. 89.

Communicating Your Data

Use a computer spreadsheet to make a data table for your results. Table column headings should be *object, length, width, height, volume, mass,* and *density*. Table row headings, under object, should be *sponge, quartz, clay, wood block, metal block, cork,* and *rock.*

Content Background

Aside from being the heaviest of the natural elements, uranium was also the first element discovered to be radioactive. Today uranium is found naturally in many minerals and is used as fuel for nuclear reactors.

Discussion

Have students recall what the mass number of an atom represents. Possible answer: The mass number of an atom is equal to the number of protons plus the number of neutrons. **What are isotopes of atoms and how are they represented symbolically?** Possible answer: Isotopes are atoms of the same element that have a different number of neutrons and therefore a different mass number than the parent atom. In print, they are indicated by the name of the atom or its symbol followed by the mass number; for example, uranium-234.

Activity

Organize students into groups. Each group can research information on one of the eight groups on the Periodic Table. Have students include which elements are in the group, information on the properties of those elements, some common uses of those elements, and possibly some fun facts about the elements. Students can present their results in a show-and-tell format using visual aids they have made. Encourage students to be creative with the format of their presentations. For example, for the element sodium, students can bring in salt as an example of a common use.

Science Stats

Amazing Atoms

Did you know . . .

. . . The diameter of an atom is about 100,000 times as great as the diameter of its nucleus. Suppose that when you sit in a chair, you represent the nucleus of an atom. The nearest electron in your atom would be about 120 km away—nearly half the distance across the Florida peninsula.

. . . Uranium has the greatest mass of the natural elements. One atom of uranium has a mass number that is more than 235 times greater than the mass number of one hydrogen atom, the element with the least mass. However, the diameter of a uranium atom is only about three times the size of a hydrogen atom, similar to the difference between a baseball and a volleyball.

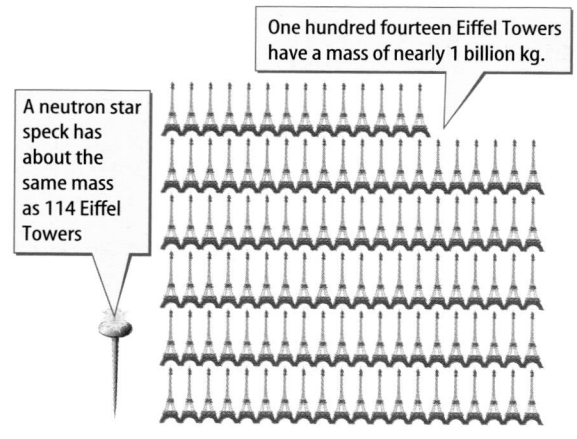

A neutron star speck has about the same mass as 114 Eiffel Towers

One hundred fourteen Eiffel Towers have a mass of nearly 1 billion kg.

. . . The densest material in the universe is found in a neutron star. The core of this type of star is made only of neutrons. Although neutron stars are small, measuring about 10 km to 20 km in diameter, they have a greater mass than the Sun. One tiny pinhead-sized speck of a neutron star would have the same mass as about 114 Eiffel Towers.

54 CHAPTER 2 Matter

Curriculum Connection

Math Have students make a circle graph that represents the percentage of the different elements that compose air. **How do the percentages in the graph compare with the elements found in the Earth's crust?** Both graphs show the 2 elements—nitrogen and oxygen in air, and oxygen and silicon in Earth's crust—have the largest percentages. Air and Earth's crust have about 1% other elements and Earth's crust contains small percentages of 6 other elements. Earth's crust contains more oxygen than air does.

... The melting point of Cesium is 28.4°C. It would melt in your hand if you held it. You would not want to hold cesium, though, because it would react strongly with your skin. In fact, the metal might even catch fire.

... An atomic fountain clock is the world's most accurate timepiece. This timepiece is called an atomic fountain clock because it uses a fountainlike movement of atoms to record time. The atoms are cooled to an extremely low temperature and tossed into a vacuum chamber. The natural vibrations of the atoms are measured. Atomic fountain clocks gain or lose only 1 s in more than 20 million years.

... Ninety elements occur naturally. However, about 98% of Earth's crust consists of only the eight elements shown here.

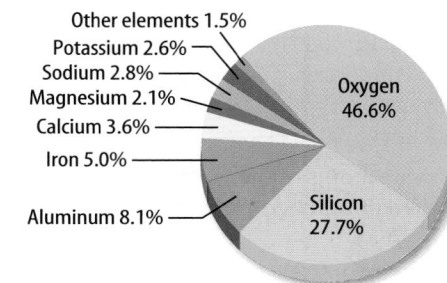

Other elements 1.5%
Potassium 2.6%
Sodium 2.8%
Magnesium 2.1%
Calcium 3.6%
Iron 5.0%
Aluminum 8.1%
Oxygen 46.6%
Silicon 27.7%

Do the Math

1. Looking at the circle graph, which is the third most abundant element in Earth's crust?
2. How much lower is the melting point of cesium than the average human body temperature of 37°C?
3. The diameter of the Sun is 1,392,000 km. How many neutron stars, each measuring 15 km in diameter, would fit along the Sun's diameter when placed side to side?

Go Further

Do research on the Glencoe Science Web site at **science.glencoe.com** to find out more about atoms and isotopes. What is a radioactive isotope of an element? How are isotopes used in science?

SCIENCE STATS **55**

Do the Math

Teaching Strategies

Have students review how to read a pie chart.

Answers

1. Aluminum at 8.1 percent
2. 8.6°C
3. 92,800 neutron stars

Go Further

Have students present their results in a simple chart with the headings: "Isotope" and "Scientific Use." Have students choose one example of radioactive decay, such as uranium-238, and illustrate the entire sequence on a poster. Information on the half-life of the isotopes can be included as well.

SCIENCE *Online*
Internet Addresses

_____
_____
_____
_____

Explore the Glencoe Science Web site at **science.glencoe.com** to find out more about topics in this feature.

Reviewing Main Ideas

Preview

Students can answer the questions in their Science Journals. Discuss the answers as you go through the chapter. **LS** **Linguistic**

Review

Students can write their answers, then compare them with those of other students. **LS** **Interpersonal**

Reteach

Students can look at the illustrations and describe details that support the main ideas of the chapter. **LS** **Visual-Spatial**

Answers to Chapter Review

SECTION 1

1. Atoms can combine in different ways to form different forms of matter, just as a few blocks can combine in many different ways.

SECTION 2

2. Each item in the book bag retains its own physical properties.

SECTION 3

2. Plasma is composed of ions and electrons where many of the electrons are outside of the ion's electron cloud.
4. Liquid water is more dense.

Reviewing Main Ideas

Section 1 Atoms

1. Matter is anything that has mass and takes up space. *How is matter similar to the snap-together blocks shown below?*

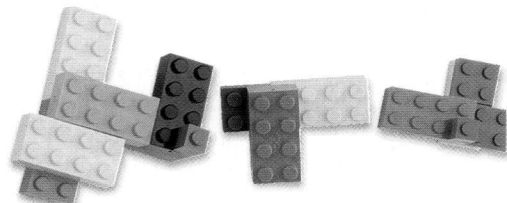

2. Protons and neutrons make up the nucleus of an atom. Protons have a positive charge, and neutrons have no charge. Electrons have a negative charge and surround the nucleus, forming an electron cloud.

3. Isotopes are atoms of the same element that have different numbers of neutrons.

Section 2 Combinations of Atoms

1. Atoms join to form compounds and molecules. A compound is a substance made of two or more elements. The properties of a compound differ from the chemical and physical properties of the elements of which it is composed.

2. A mixture is a substance in which each of the components are not chemically combined. *Why are the contents of the book bag, shown to the right, considered to be a mixture and not a compound?*

Section 3 Properties of Matter

1. Physical properties can be observed and measured without causing a chemical change in a substance. Chemical properties can be observed only when one substance reacts with another substance.

2. Atoms or molecules in a solid are in fixed positions relative to one another. In a liquid, the atoms or molecules are close together but are freer to change positions. Atoms or molecules in a gas have almost no attractive force on one another. *What makes up plasma, such as the lightning to the right?*

3. Water is the only substance on Earth that occurs naturally as a solid, liquid, and gas because its freezing and boiling points are within the range of temperatures found on Earth.

4. One physical property that is used to describe matter is density. Density is a ratio of the mass of an object to its volume. A material that is less dense will float in a material that is more dense. *Ice floats in liquid water, so which state of water is more dense?*

FOLDABLES Reading & Study Skills — **After You Read**

Use each vocabulary word on your Vocabulary Study Fold in a sentence about matter and write it next to the definition of the word.

FOLDABLES Reading & Study Skills — **After You Read**

After students have read the chapter and completed the Foldable described in Before You Read, have them do the activity on the student page.

Dinah Zike

Visualizing Main Ideas

Complete the following concept map on matter. Use the following terms: liquids, plasma, matter, *and* solids.

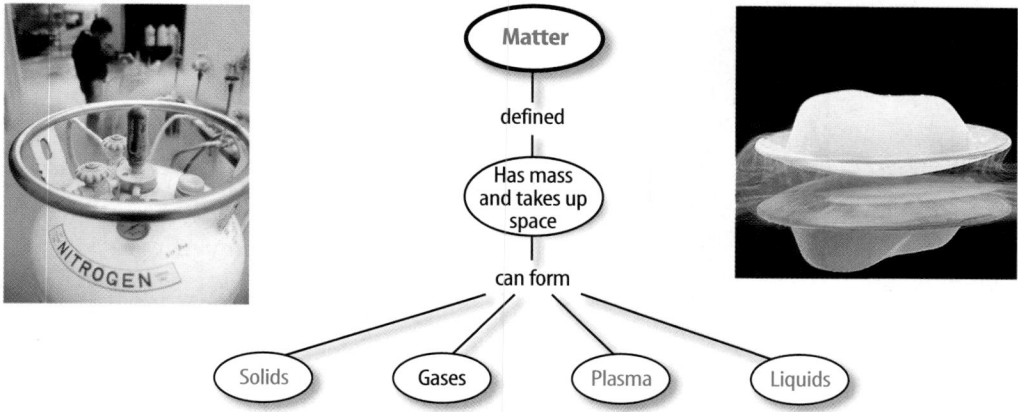

Visualizing Main Ideas

See student page.

Vocabulary Review

Vocabulary Words

a. atom
b. atomic number
c. compound
d. density
e. electron
f. element
g. ion
h. isotope
i. heterogeneous mixture
j. homogeneous mixture
k. mass number
l. matter
m. mixture
n. neutron
o. proton
p. solution

Study Tip

Take good notes, even during lab. Lab experiments reinforce key concepts, and looking back on these notes can help you better understand what happened and why.

Using Vocabulary

Explain the difference between the vocabulary words in each of the following sets.

1. atom, element
2. mass number, atomic number
3. solution, heterogeneous mixture
4. matter, compound, element
5. heterogenous mixture, homogeneous mixture
6. proton, neutron, electron
7. isotope, atom
8. atom, ion
9. mixture, compound
10. neutron, mass number

Vocabulary Review

Using Vocabulary

1. Atoms are composed of protons, neutrons, and electrons. Elements are substances that contain only one type of atom.
2. Atomic number is the number of protons in an atom's nucleus. Mass number is the number of protons and neutrons an atom's nucleus.
3. A solution is a mixture in which one substance is thoroughly and evenly mixed in another substance. In a heterogeneous mixture, the substances are not mixed evenly.
4. Matter can be in the form of a compound (two or more elements) or an element (one type of atom).
5. In a homogeneous mixture, one substance is thoroughly and evenly mixed in another substance. In a heterogeneous mixture, the substances are not mixed evenly.
6. Protons and neutrons are in the nucleus of an atom; electrons are outside the nucleus. A proton has a positive charge. A neutron has no charge. An electron has a negative charge.
7. Atoms are the basic particles of matter. Isotopes are atoms of the same element that have different numbers of neutrons in their nuclei.
8. An atom has a neutral charge. An ion is an atom that has lost or gained electrons and therefore has a charge.
9. Compounds are composed of molecules containing atoms of two or more elements. Mixtures are composed of two or more substances that are not chemically combined.
10. A neutron is an uncharged particle in the nucleus of an atom. The mass number of an element is the total number of protons and neutrons found in the nucleus of its atoms.

Checking Concepts

1. C
2. B
3. A
4. A
5. B
6. A
7. D
8. D
9. B
10. D

Thinking Critically

11. The number of protons in the nucleus of the atom is equal to the number of electrons in the electron cloud.
12. carbon-14 (8)
13. Yes; isotopes differ in the number of neutrons.
14. They will combine to form a compound. Lithium has only one electron in the outermost portion of its electron cloud. Chlorine has seven. Both atoms will "seek" to have a total of eight electrons in the outermost portion of their electron clouds; therefore, they will readily combine.
15. The oil and water is a mixture. It is not a solution because neither the water nor the oil is evenly spread throughout the other.

Chapter (2) Assessment

Checking Concepts

Choose the word or phrase that best answers the question.

1. Which of the following contains only one type of atom?
   A) plasma   C) element
   B) mixture   D) solid

2. Which of the following has a positive electric charge?
   A) electron   C) neutron
   B) proton   D) plasma

3. In an atom, what forms a cloud around the nucleus?
   A) electrons   C) neutrons
   B) protons   D) positively charged particles

4. A carbon atom has a mass number of 12. How many protons and how many neutrons does it have?
   A) 6, 6   C) 6, 12
   B) 12, 12   D) 12, 6

5. On Earth, oxygen usually exists as which of the following?
   A) solid   C) liquid
   B) gas   D) plasma

6. Which of the following isotopes has seven neutrons?
   A) boron-12   C) carbon-14
   B) nitrogen-12   D) hydrogen-2

7. Which type of bond occurs because of the polar molecules of water?
   A) ionic   C) metallic
   B) covalent   D) hydrogen

8. Which of the following are electrically charged?
   A) molecule   C) isotope
   B) solution   D) ion

9. What type of property is the color of your clothes?
   A) chemical property
   B) physical property
   C) isotopic property
   D) molecular property

10. Which of the following is not a physical property of water?
    A) transparent
    B) colorless
    C) higher density than ice
    D) changes to hydrogen and oxygen when electricity passes through it

Thinking Critically

11. If an atom has no electric charge, what can be said about the number of protons and electrons it contains?

12. Carbon has six protons and nitrogen has seven protons. Which has the greatest number of neutrons—carbon-13, carbon-14, or nitrogen-14?

13. Would isotopes of the same element have the same number of electrons? Explain.

14. A chlorine atom comes in contact with a lithium atom. Do they combine to form a compound? Why or why not?

15. You pour cooking oil into a glass of water. You briefly stir the materials in the glass. Does the glass contain a mixture? Does it contain a solution? Explain.

Chapter ✔*Assessment* Planner

Portfolio Encourage students to place in their portfolios one or two items of what they consider to be their best work. Examples include:
• Science Journal, p. 35
• Cultural Diversity, p. 41
• Extension, p. 49

Performance Additional performance assessments, Performance Task Assessment Lists, and rubrics for evaluating these activities can be found in Glencoe's **Performance Assessment in the Science Classroom.**

Developing Skills

16. Classifying Use the periodic table of the elements, located on the inside back cover, to classify the following substances as elements or compounds: iron, aluminum, carbon dioxide, gold, water, and sugar.

17. Making and Using Graphs Use the following data to make a line graph. For each isotope, plot the mass number along the y-axis and the atomic number along the x-axis. What is the relationship between mass number and atomic number?

Atomic Number versus Mass Number

Element	Atomic Number	Mass Number
Fluorine	9	19
Lithium	3	7
Carbon-12	6	12
Nitrogen	7	14
Beryllium	4	9
Boron	5	11
Oxygen-16	8	16
Neon	10	20

Performance Assessment

18. Song with Lyrics Create a song about how matter changes state by changing the words to a song you know. Include in your song as many states of matter as possible.

TECHNOLOGY

Go to the Glencoe Science Web site at **science.glencoe.com** or use the **Glencoe Science CD-ROM** for additional chapter assessment.

THE PRINCETON REVIEW — Test Practice

Marlena was instructed by her teacher to find examples of elements and their isotopes. The examples she found are presented in the table below.

Element	Number of Protons	Number of Neutrons
Hydrogen-1	1	0
Hydrogen-2	1	1
Hydrogen-3	1	2
Carbon-12	6	6
Carbon-14	6	8
Oxygen-16	8	8
Oxygen-18	8	10

Study the table and answer the following questions.

1. The hydrogen atom listed first is different from the hydrogen-2 and hydrogen-3 isotopes, because the first hydrogen isotope has _____ .
   A) only one neutron
   B) fewer neutrons
   C) more electrons
   D) more neutrons

2. The mass number of an atom is equal to the number of protons and neutrons in its nucleus. According to this definition, which of these has the highest mass number?
   F) hydrogen-3
   G) carbon-14
   H) oxygen-18
   J) oxygen-16

THE PRINCETON REVIEW — Test Practice

The Test-Taking Tip was written by The Princeton Review, the nation's leader in test preparation.

1. D
2. H

Developing Skills

16. iron—element, aluminum—element, carbon dioxide—compound, gold—element, water—compound, sugar—compound

17. The mass number increases as the atomic number increases at a ratio of approximately 2:1.

Performance Assessment

18. Songs may be simple as long as the lyrics describe changes in the state of matter. Use **Performance Assessment in the Science Classroom**, p. 151.

✓Assessment Resources

 Reproducible Masters

Chapter Resources Booklet
Chapter Review, pp. 33–34
Chapter Tests, pp. 35–38
Assessment Transparency Activity, p. 45

Glencoe Science Web site
Interactive Tutor
Chapter Quizzes

Glencoe Technology
Assessment Transparency
Interactive CD-ROM Chapter Quizzes
ExamView Pro Test Bank
Vocabulary PuzzleMaker Software
MindJogger Videoquiz DVD/VHS

Section/Objectives	Standards		Activities/Features
Chapter Opener	**National**	**State/Local**	**Explore Activity:** Distinguishing rocks from minerals, p. 61 **Before You Read,** p. 61
	See p. 5T for a Key to Standards.		
Section 1 Minerals 🕐 2 sessions 📦 1 block 1. **Describe** characteristics that all minerals share. 2. **Explain** how minerals form.	National Content Standards: UCP1, A1, D1		**MiniLAB:** Inferring Salt's Crystal System, p. 63 **Visualizing Crystal Systems,** p. 64 **Physics Integration,** p. 65 **Activity:** Crystal Formation, p. 67
Section 2 Mineral Identification 🕐 2 sessions 📦 1 block 1. **Describe** physical properties used to identify minerals. 2. **Identify** minerals using physical properties such as hardness and streak.	National Content Standards: UCP5, A1, D1		**Problem-Solving Activity:** Identifying Minerals, p. 70 **MiniLAB:** Observing Mineral Properties, p. 72
Section 3 Uses of Minerals 🕐 2 sessions 📦 1 block 1. **Describe** characteristics of gems that make them more valuable than other minerals. 2. **Identify** useful elements that are contained in minerals.	National Content Standards: UCP5, A1, D1, F2, F5, G3		**Science Online,** p. 76 **Chemistry Integration,** p. 77 **Science Online,** p. 78 **Activity:** Mineral Identification, pp. 80–81 **Science and History:** Dr. Dorothy Crowfoot Hodgkin, pp. 82–83

NATIONAL GEOGRAPHIC

Teacher's Corner

PRODUCTS AVAILABLE FROM GLENCOE
To order call 1-800-334-7344:
CD-ROM
NGS PictureShow: Geology
Curriculum Kit
GeoKit: Rocks and Minerals

Transparency Set
NGS PicturePack: Rocks and Minerals

INDEX TO NATIONAL GEOGRAPHIC SOCIETY
The following articles may be used for research relating to this chapter:
"Physical World," by Joel L. Swerdlow, May 1998.

"Life Grows Up," by Richard Monastersky, April 1998.
"The Rise of Life on Earth," by Richard Monastersky, March 1998.
"Under Our Skin: Hot Theories on the Center of the Earth," by Keay Davidson, January 1996.

Activity Materials	Reproducible Resources	Section Assessment	Technology
Explore Activity: hand lens, quartz crystal, table salt, samples of sandstone, granite, gypsum, mica, schist	**Chapter Resources Booklet** Foldables Worksheet, p. 13 Directed Reading Overview, p. 15 Note-taking Worksheets, pp. 29, 30	GLENCOE'S ASSESSMENT ADVANTAGE	
MiniLAB: hand lens, table salt **Activity:** 250-mL beakers (2), cardboard, large paper clip, table salt, flat wooden stick, granulated sugar, cotton string, hot plate, hand lens, thermal mitt, shallow pan, spoon	**Chapter Resources Booklet** Transparency Activity, p. 40 MiniLAB, p. 3 Enrichment, p. 26 Reinforcement, p. 23 Directed Reading, p. 16 Activity Worksheet, pp. 5–6 Lab Activity, pp. 9–10 **Cultural Diversity,** p. 37 **Mathematics Skill Activities,** p. 47	**Portfolio** Science Journal, p. 65 **Performance** MiniLAB, p. 63 Skill Builder Activities, p. 66 **Content** Section Assessment, p. 66	Section Focus Transparency Interactive CD-ROM/DVD Guided Reading Audio Program
MiniLAB: samples of clear minerals such as gypsum, muscovite mica, halite, and calcite *Need materials?* Contact Science Kit at 1-800-828-7777 or www.sciencekit.com on the Internet.	**Chapter Resources Booklet** Transparency Activity, p. 41 MiniLAB, p. 4 Enrichment, p. 27 Reinforcement, p. 24 Directed Reading, p. 17 Transparency Activity, pp. 43–44	**Portfolio** Activity, p. 69 **Performance** Problem-Solving Activity, p. 70 MiniLAB, p. 72 Skill Builder Activities, p. 72 **Content** Section Assessment, p. 72	Section Focus Transparency Teaching Transparency Interactive CD-ROM/DVD Guided Reading Audio Program
Activity: mineral samples, hand lens, pan balance, graduated cylinder, water, piece of copper, glass plate, mall iron nail, steel file, streak plate 5% HCl with dropper, Mohs scale of hardness, Appendix F, safety goggles	**Chapter Resources Booklet** Transparency Activity, p. 42 Enrichment, p. 28 Reinforcement, p. 25 Directed Reading, pp. 17, 18 Activity Worksheet, pp. 7–8 Lab Activity, pp. 11–12 **Lab Management and Safety,** pp. 54–57 **Home and Community Involvement,** p. 34 **Cultural Diversity,** p. 35	**Portfolio** Use Science Words, p. 74 Extension, p. 76 **Performance** Skill Builder Activities, p. 79 **Content** Section Assessment, p. 79	Section Focus Transparency Interactive CD-ROM/DVD Guided Reading Audio Program

End of Chapter Assessment

GLENCOE'S ASSESSMENT ADVANTAGE

Blackline Masters	Technology	Professional Series
Chapter Resources Booklet Chapter Review, pp. 33–34 Chapter Tests, pp. 35–38 **Standardized Test Practice by The Princeton Review,** pp. 19–22	MindJogger Videoquiz CD-ROM Explorations and Quizzes Vocabulary Puzzle Makers ExamView Pro Test Bank Interactive Lesson Planner Interactive Teacher's Edition	Performance Assessment in the Science Classroom (PASC)

Transparencies

Section Focus

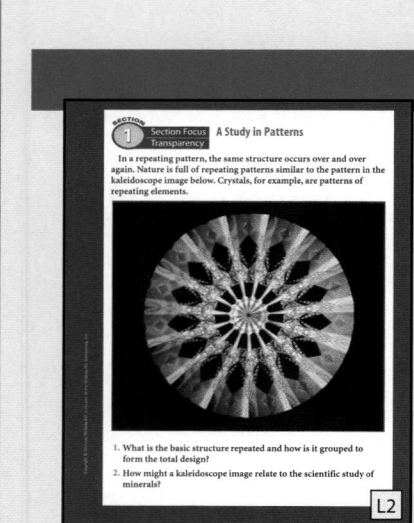

Section Focus Transparency ① A Study in Patterns

In a repeating pattern, the same structure occurs over and over again. Nature is full of repeating patterns similar to the pattern in the kaleidoscope image below. Crystals, for example, are patterns of repeating elements.

1. What is the basic structure repeated and how is it grouped to form the total design?
2. How might a kaleidoscope image relate to the scientific study of minerals?

L2

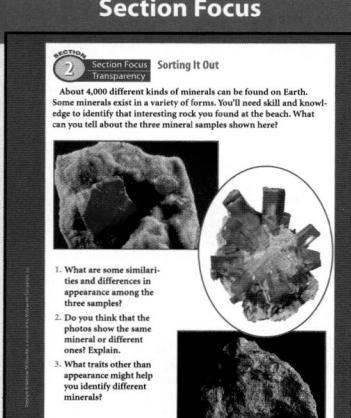

Section Focus Transparency ② Sorting It Out

About 4,000 different kinds of minerals can be found on Earth. Some minerals exist in a variety of forms. You'll need skill and knowledge to identify that interesting rock you found at the beach. What can you tell about the three mineral samples shown here?

1. What are some similarities and differences in appearance among the three samples?
2. Do you think that the photos show the same mineral or different ones? Explain.
3. What traits other than appearance might help you identify different minerals?

L2

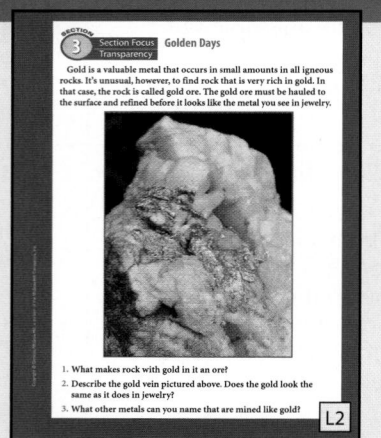

Section Focus Transparency ③ Golden Days

Gold is a valuable metal that occurs in small amounts in all igneous rocks. It's unusual, however, to find rock that is very rich in gold. In that case, the rock is called gold ore. The gold ore must be hauled to the surface and refined before it looks like the metal you see in jewelry.

1. What makes rock with gold in it an ore?
2. Describe the gold vein pictured above. Does the gold look the same as it does in jewelry?
3. What other metals can you name that are mined like gold?

L2

This is a representation of key blackline masters available in the Teacher Classroom Resources. See Resource Manager boxes within the chapter for additional information.

Key to Teaching Strategies

The following designations will help you decide which activities are appropriate for your students.

L1 Level 1 activities should be appropriate for students with learning difficulties.

L2 Level 2 activities should be within the ability range of all students.

L3 Level 3 activities are designed for above-average students.

ELL ELL activities should be within the ability range of English Language Learners.

COOP LEARN Cooperative Learning activities are designed for small group work.

LS Multiple Learning Styles logos, as described on page 22T, are used throughout to indicate strategies that address different learning styles.

P These strategies represent student products that can be placed into a best-work portfolio.

Assessment

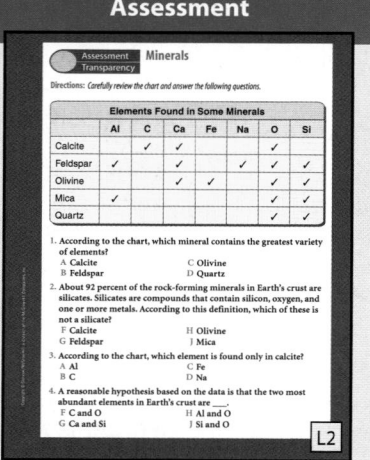

Assessment Transparency Minerals

Directions: Carefully review the chart and answer the following questions.

Elements Found in Some Minerals							
	Al	C	Ca	Fe	Na	O	Si
Calcite		✓	✓			✓	
Feldspar	✓		✓		✓	✓	✓
Olivine			✓	✓		✓	✓
Mica	✓					✓	✓
Quartz						✓	✓

1. According to the chart, which mineral contains the greatest variety of elements?
   A Calcite   C Olivine
   B Feldspar   D Quartz
2. About 92 percent of the rock-forming minerals in Earth's crust are silicates. Silicates are compounds that contain silicon, oxygen, and one or more metals. According to this definition, which of these is not a silicate?
   F Calcite   H Olivine
   G Feldspar   J Mica
3. According to the chart, which element is found only in calcite?
   A Al   C Fe
   B C   D Na
4. A reasonable hypothesis based on the data is that the two most abundant elements in Earth's crust are ____.
   F C and O   H Al and O
   G Ca and Si   J Si and O

L2

Teaching

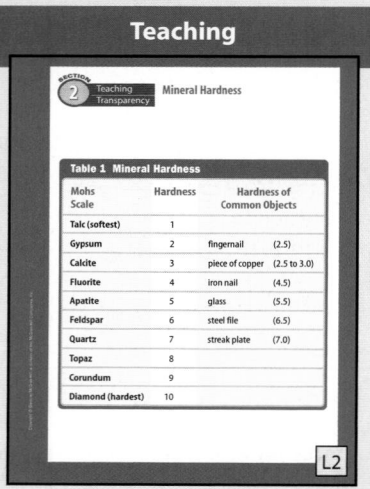

Teaching Transparency ② Mineral Hardness

Table 1 Mineral Hardness		
Mohs Scale	Hardness	Hardness of Common Objects
Talc (softest)	1	
Gypsum	2	fingernail (2.5)
Calcite	3	piece of copper (2.5 to 3.0)
Fluorite	4	iron nail (4.5)
Apatite	5	glass (5.5)
Feldspar	6	steel file (6.5)
Quartz	7	streak plate (7.0)
Topaz	8	
Corundum	9	
Diamond (hardest)	10	

L2

Hands-on Activities

Activity Worksheets

Laboratory Activities

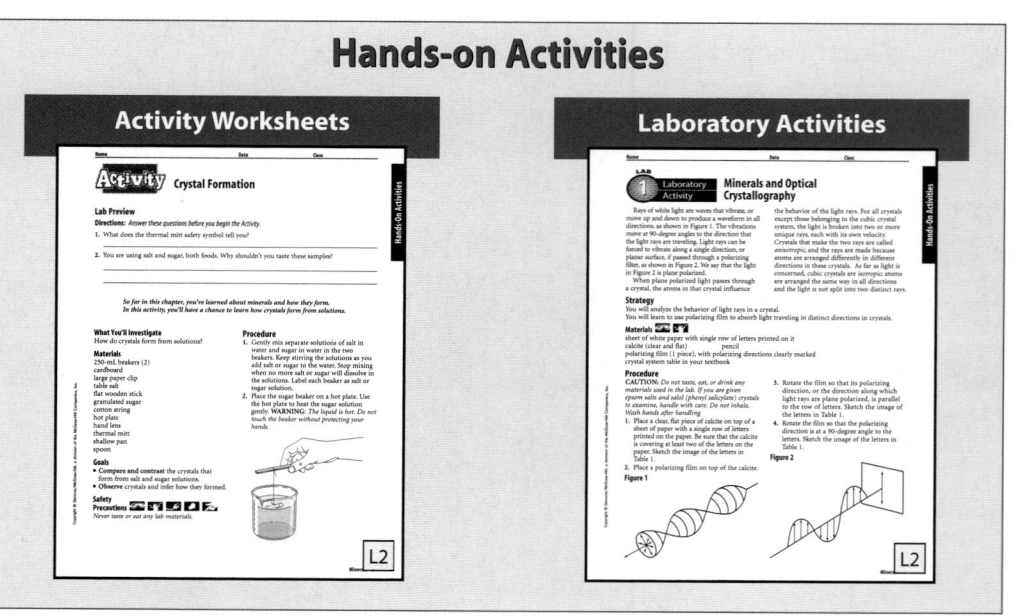

Activity Crystal Formation

Lab Preview

Directions: Answer these questions before you begin the Activity.

1. What does the thermal mitt safety symbol tell you?

2. You are using salt and sugar, both foods. Why shouldn't you taste these samples?

So far in this chapter, you've learned about minerals and how they form. In this activity, you'll have a chance to learn how crystals form from solutions.

What You'll Investigate
How do crystals form from solutions?

Materials
250-mL beakers (2)
cardboard
large paper clip
table salt
flat wooden stick
granulated sugar
cotton string
hot plate
hand lens
thermal mitt
shallow pan
spoon

Goals
- Compare and contrast the crystals that form from salt and sugar solutions.
- Observe crystals and infer how they formed.

Safety Precautions
Never taste or eat any lab materials.

Procedure

1. Gently mix separate solutions of salt in water and sugar in water in the two beakers. Keep stirring the solutions as you add salt or sugar to the water. Stop mixing when no more salt or sugar will dissolve in the solutions. Label each beaker as salt or sugar solution.
2. Place the sugar beaker on a hot plate. Use the hot plate to heat the sugar solution gently. **WARNING:** The liquid is hot. Do not touch the beaker without protecting your hands.

Figure 1

L2

Laboratory Activity ① Minerals and Optical Crystallography

Rays of white light are waves that vibrate, or move up and down to produce a waveform in all directions, as shown in Figure 1. The vibrations move at 90-degree angles to the direction that the light rays are traveling. Light rays can be forced to vibrate along a single direction, or planar surface, if passed through a polarizing filter, as shown in Figure 2. We say that the light in Figure 2 is plane polarized.

When plane polarized light passes through a crystal, the atoms in that crystal influence the behavior of the light rays. For all crystals except those belonging to the cubic crystal system, the light is broken into two or more unique rays, each with its own velocity. Crystals that make the two rays are called anisotropic, and the rays are made because atoms are arranged differently in different directions in these crystals. As far as light is concerned, cubic crystals are isotropic: atoms are arranged the same way in all directions and the light is not split into two distinct rays.

Strategy
You will analyze the behavior of light rays in a crystal.
You will learn to use polarizing film to absorb light traveling in distinct directions in crystals.

Materials
sheet of white paper with single row of letters printed on it
calcite (clear and flat)   pencil
polarizing film (1 piece), with polarizing directions clearly marked
crystal system table in your textbook

Procedure
CAUTION: Do not taste, eat, or drink any materials used in the lab. If you are given epsom salts and salol (phenyl salicylate) crystals to examine, handle with care. Do not inhale. Wash hands after handling.

1. Place a clear, flat piece of calcite on top of a sheet of paper with a single row of letters printed on the paper. Be sure that the calcite is covering at least two of the letters on the paper. Sketch the image of the letters in Table 1.
2. Place a polarizing film on top of the calcite.

3. Rotate the film so that its polarizing direction, or the direction along which light rays are plane polarized, is parallel to the row of letters. Sketch the image of the letters in Table 1.
4. Rotate the film so that the polarizing direction is at a 90-degree angle to the letters. Sketch the image of the letters in Table 1.

Figure 2

L2

Meeting Different Ability Levels

Content Outline

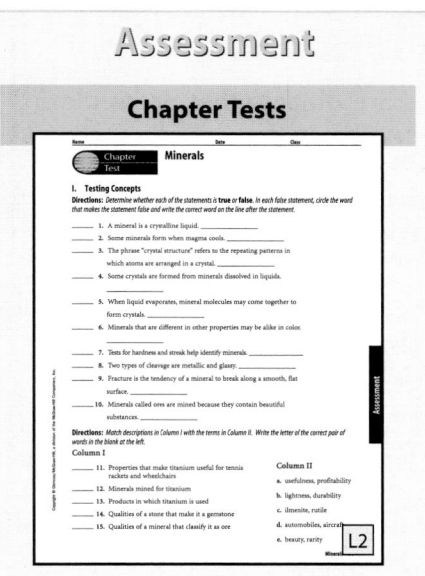

Reinforcement

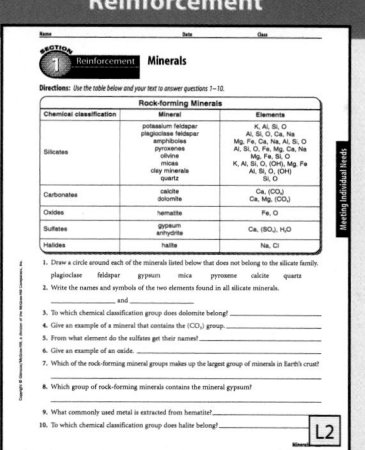

Directed Reading

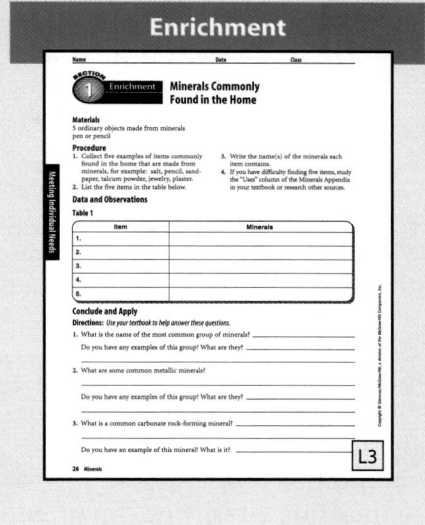

Assessment

Chapter Tests

Enrichment

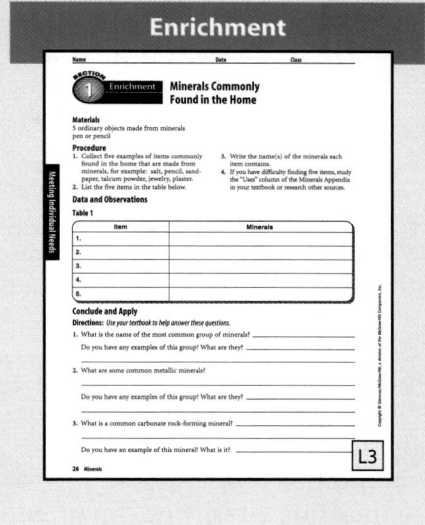

Spanish Directed Reading

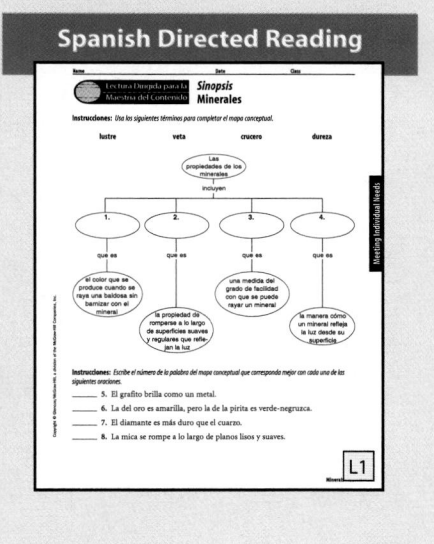

Test Practice Workbook

Chapter Review

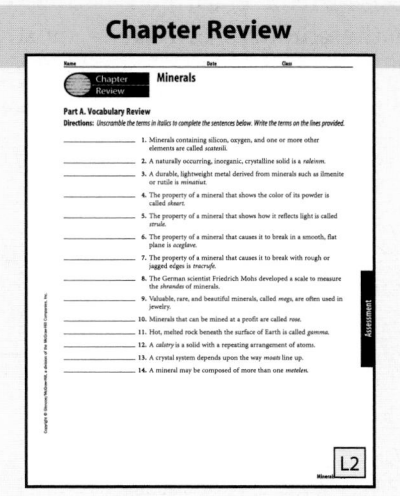

Science Content Background

SECTION **1**

Minerals
General Characteristics

Between 40 and 50 new minerals are identified each year. Only eight elements comprise the majority of minerals. The 24 or so minerals that make up most rocks are called the rock forming minerals. Coal, which fits many of the characteristics of minerals, is not a mineral because it comes from once-living material.

Graphite is the softest mineral, and diamond is the hardest mineral. Both of these minerals are composed of carbon. The type of bond between the atoms of carbon causes the differences in the properties of these minerals. Because of this difference in bonding, the two minerals have widely different uses. Diamonds are used in jewelry, as abrasives, and in cutting tools. Graphite is used as a lubricant and in pencil lead. Minerals that have identical composition but different properties are called polymorphs.

Mineral Composition

Although each type of mineral has a unique composition, the composition of individual mineral specimens can vary within limits. For example, the chemical composition of olivine ranges from Fe_2SiO_4 to Mg_2SiO_4. For this reason, the composition of olivine is often written $(Fe,Mg)_2SiO_4$. A more precise chemical formula can be written when the amounts of iron and magnesium are known, for example $(Fe_{.77}Mg_{.23})_2SiO_4$.

Mineral Identification
Hardness

Most silicate minerals do not leave a streak because they have a hardness greater than 6 on the Mohs scale. The hardness of a mineral is related to its crystal structure and to the type of atomic bonds in the mineral. The difference between the hardness of diamond (Mohs 10) and corundum (Mohs 9) is far greater than the difference in hardness between corundum and the softest mineral, talc. This means that the Mohs scale is nonlinear.

Student Misconception

Minerals are rare objects that are seldom used in everyday materials.

Refer to the facing page for teaching strategies to address this misconception. Refer to pages 77–79 for content related to this topic.

Uses of Minerals
Valuing Diamonds

The value of diamonds varies depending on whether they are tinted. The most common diamonds of gem quality have yellow or brown tints. These diamonds are less valuable than those with no tint. Diamonds with blue or pink tints are the most valuable.

SCIENCE *Online*

For additional content background on this topic, go to the Glencoe Science Web site at science.glencoe.com.

Barry L. Runk/Grant Heilman Photography, Inc.

Misconceptions

Find Out What Students Think

Students may think that . . .

- **Minerals are rare objects that are seldom used in everyday materials.**

Students are often asked to observe and classify minerals. However, some students fail to understand that these materials are part of their everyday lives.

Discussion
Ask students to raise their hands if they used minerals before coming to school this morning.

Then ask how many brushed their teeth using toothpaste. Explain that when one uses toothpaste, one is using minerals. Phosphate materials, aluminum oxide, and the mineral silica are used as abrasives in toothpaste. Fluoride comes from the mineral fluorite. Stannous fluoride (or tin fluorite) is also found in toothpaste. The sparkle in toothpaste comes from the mineral mica.

Have students handle and observe the minerals that furnish the ingredients for toothpaste.

Promote Understanding

Discussion
Reproduce the information shown below, which lists the amount of minerals the average

person uses in a lifetime. Have students discuss the different ways in which minerals impact their lives.

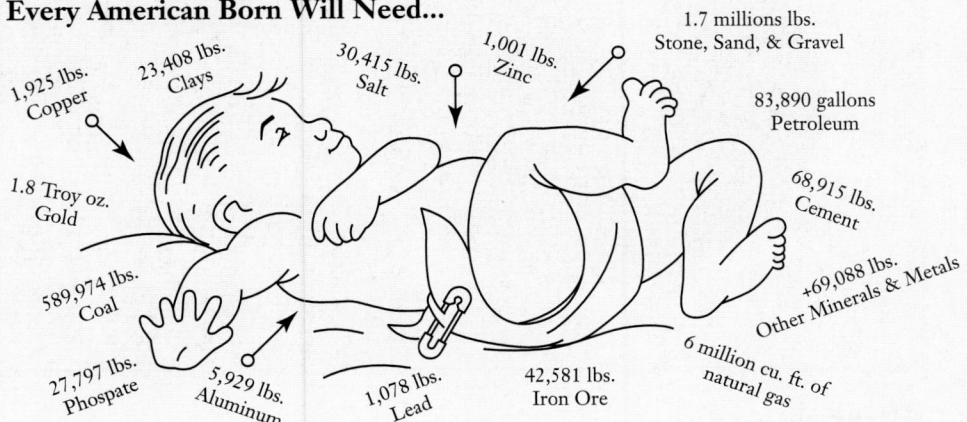

Every American Born Will Need...

1,925 lbs. Copper

23,408 lbs. Clays

30,415 lbs. Salt

1,001 lbs. Zinc

1.7 millions lbs. Stone, Sand, & Gravel

83,890 gallons Petroleum

1.8 Troy oz. Gold

68,915 lbs. Cement

589,974 lbs. Coal

+69,088 lbs. Other Minerals & Metals

27,797 lbs. Phospate

5,929 lbs. Aluminum

1,078 lbs. Lead

42,581 lbs. Iron Ore

6 million cu. ft. of natural gas

3³/4 million pounds of minerals, metals, and fuels in a lifetime

© 2000 Mineral Information Institute Golden, Colorado

Assess

After completing the chapter, see *Identifying Misconceptions* in the Study Guide.

Minerals

Chapter Vocabulary

mineral
crystal
magma
silicate
hardness
luster
streak
cleavage
fracture
gem

What do you think?

Science Journal The photograph shows a geode. These hollow bodies consist of an outer chalcedony layer that surrounds a lining of crystals. Geodes form as bubbles in volcanic rock, or as mud balls in sedimentary rock. When cracked open, geodes reveal crystals of agate, jasper, chalcedony, quartz, calcite, or amethyst.

Minerals

Caveat emptor—let the buyer beware. One of the gems in this photograph was produced in a laboratory. A trained jeweler could tell which is the imposter, but if you try, don't be fooled by shape, size, or color. Diamonds can be yellow, brown, black, green, blue, purple, pink, red, or perfectly clear. As you'll soon learn, a requirement for being a mineral is that it must be naturally occurring, which increases its rarity—and its price. In this chapter, you'll learn about minerals and gems and how to identify and differentiate between them.

What do you think?

Science Journal Look at the picture below with a classmate. Discuss what this might be. Here's a hint: *This "egg" was laid by a volcano.* Write your answer or best guess in your Science Journal.

60

Theme Connection

Scale and Structure The structure of minerals is discussed. On the atomic scale, minerals have definite crystal structure, that is, a regularly repeated pattern of atomic arrangement. Emphasizing the relationship between the internal structure of a mineral and its properties and uses will help clarify the uniqueness of these solids that make up Earth's rocks.

W hat's the difference between a rock and a mineral? Just as a building is made of many different materials such as concrete, wood, plaster, and iron, rocks are made of many different types of minerals. Some minerals are made of only one or two elements but others are a complicated mixture of elements. However, when it is viewed with a magnifying glass, a mineral looks the same throughout. When examining a rock, you see different types of minerals. Can you tell a rock from a mineral?

Distinguish rocks from minerals

1. Use a magnifying glass to examine a quartz crystal, salt grains, and samples of: sandstone, granite, calcite, mica, and schist (SHIHST).

2. Determine which samples are made of one type of material and should be classified as minerals.

3. Determine which samples are made of more than one type of material and should be classified as rocks.

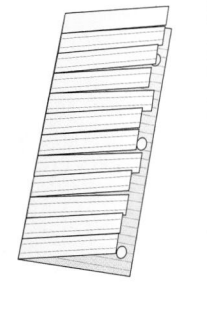

Observe

In your Science Journal, compile a list of descriptions for the minerals you examined and a second list of descriptions for the rocks. Compare and contrast your observations of minerals and rocks.

Before You Read

FOLDABLES
Reading & Study Skills

Making a Question Study Fold Asking yourself questions helps you stay focused and better understand minerals when you are reading the chapter.

1. Place a sheet of notebook paper in front of you so the short side is at the top and the holes are on the right side. Fold the paper in half from the left side to the right side.

2. Through the top thickness of paper, cut along every third line from the outside edge to the centerfold, forming tabs as shown.

3. Before you read the chapter, write questions you have about minerals on the front of the tabs. As you read the chapter, add more questions and write answers under the tabs.

61

Purpose Use this Explore Activity to introduce students to the differences between rocks and minerals.

Preparation Place one sample of each type of rock and mineral in a container. Each group will receive one container of samples.

Materials magnifying lens, quartz crystal, salt grains, sample of sandstone, sample of granite, sample of gypsum, sample of mica, sample of schist per group

Teaching Strategy To be certain all group members observe all the samples, have each student write a list of the samples and check off each sample as it is observed.

Observe

• Minerals: quartz, salt, gypsum, mica.

• Rocks: granite, sandstone, schist.

• minerals are homogeneous, rocks are heterogeneous

Content Ask students to collect a dozen rock or mineral samples from around the school or their homes and to classify each sample as either a rock or a mineral. Use **Performance Assessment in the Science Classroom,** p. 212.

Before You Read

FOLDABLES
Reading & Study Skills

Dinah Zike Study Fold

Purpose Get students thinking about minerals before they read the chapter by asking them to pose questions that guide their reading. Have students record answers to their questions in a Foldable, which becomes a study guide.

For additional help, see Foldables Worksheet, p. 13 in **Chapter Resources Booklet,** or go to the Glencoe Science Web site at **science.glencoe.com.** See After You Read in the Study Guide at the end of this chapter.

SECTION

1

Minerals

1 Motivate

Bellringer Transparency

 Display the Section Focus Transparency for Section 1. Use the accompanying Transparency Activity Master. L2

ELL

Tie to Prior Knowledge

Help students recall that atoms are the building blocks of matter and that atoms can combine to form molecules. The structure of a mineral is determined by the repeating pattern of atoms in the mineral.

SECTION

1

Minerals

As You Read

What You'll Learn

- **Describe** characteristics that all minerals share.
- **Explain** how minerals form.

Vocabulary
mineral
crystal
magma
silicate

Why It's Important
You use minerals every day.

Figure 1
You probably use minerals or materials made from minerals every day without thinking about it. *How many objects in this picture might be made from minerals?*

What is a mineral?

How important are minerals to you? Very important? You actually own or encounter many things made from minerals every day. Ceramic, metallic, and even some paper items are examples of products that are derived from or include minerals. **Figure 1** shows just a few of these things. Metal lockers, bookshelves, and the glass in windows would not exist if it weren't for minerals. A **mineral** is a naturally occurring, inorganic solid with a definite chemical composition and an orderly arrangement of atoms. About 4,000 different minerals are found on Earth, but they all share these four characteristics.

Mineral Characteristics First, all minerals are formed by natural processes. These are processes that occur on or inside Earth with no input from humans. For example, salt formed by the natural evaporation of seawater is the mineral halite, but salt formed by evaporation of saltwater solutions in laboratories is not a mineral. Second, minerals are inorganic. This means that they aren't made by life processes. Third, every mineral is an element or compound with a definite chemical composition. For example, halite's composition, NaCl, gives it a distinctive taste that adds flavor to many foods. Fourth, minerals are crystalline solids. All solids have a definite volume and shape. Gases and liquids like air and water have no definite shape, and they aren't crystalline. Only a solid can be a mineral, but not all solids are minerals.

Atom Patterns The word *crystalline* means that atoms are arranged in a pattern that is repeated over and over again. For example, graphite's atoms are arranged in layers. Opal, on the other hand, is not a mineral in the strictest sense because its atoms are not all arranged in a definite, repeating pattern, even though it is a naturally occuring, inorganic solid.

Section ✓ Assessment Planner

PORTFOLIO
Science Journal, p. 65
PERFORMANCE ASSESSMENT
Try at Home MiniLAB, p. 63
Skill Builder Activities, p. 66
See page 86 for more options.

CONTENT ASSESSMENT
Section, p. 66
Challenge, p. 66
Chapter, pp. 86–87

Figure 2
More than 200 years ago, the smooth, flat surfaces on crystals led scientists to infer that minerals had an orderly, internal structure inside.

A The well-formed crystal shapes exhibited by these clear quartz crystals suggest an orderly structure. **B** Even though this rose quartz looks uneven on the outside, its atoms have an orderly arrangement on the inside.

The Structure of Minerals

Do you have a favorite mineral sample or gemstone? If so, perhaps it contains well-formed crystals. A **crystal** is a solid in which the atoms are arranged in orderly, repeating patterns. You can see evidence for this orderly arrangement of atoms when you observe the smooth, flat outside surfaces of crystals. A crystal system is a group of crystals that have similar atomic arrangements and therefore similar external crystal shapes.

✓ Reading Check *What is a crystal?*

Crystals Not all mineral crystals have smooth surfaces and regular shapes like the clear quartz crystals in **Figure 2A.** The rose quartz in **Figure 2B** has atoms arranged in repeating patterns, but you can't see the crystal shape on the outside of the mineral. This is because the rose quartz crystals developed in a tight space, while the clear quartz crystals developed freely in an open space. The six-sided, or hexagonal crystal shape of the quartz crystals in **Figure 2A,** and other forms of quartz can be seen in some samples of the mineral. **Figure 3** illustrates the six major crystal systems, which classify minerals according to their crystal structures. The hexagonal system to which quartz belongs is one example of a crystal system.

Crystals form by many processes. Next, you'll learn about two of these processes—crystals that form from magma and crystals that form from solutions of salts.

TRY AT HOME
Mini LAB

Inferring Salt's Crystal System

Procedure
1. Use a **magnifying glass** and a **dissecting probe** to observe grains of common **table salt.** Sketch the shape of a salt grain. **WARNING:** *Do not taste or eat mineral samples. Keep hands away from your face.*
2. Compare the shapes of the salt crystals with the shapes of crystals shown in **Figure 3.**

Analysis
1. Which characteristics do all the grains have in common?
2. Research another mineral with the same crystal system as salt. What is this crystal system called?

✓ Active Reading

Metacognition Journal In this strategy, each student analyzes his or her own thought processes. Have students divide a sheet of paper in half. On the left, have them record what they have learned about a topic. On the right, have them record the reason they learned it. Have students write a Metacognition Journal about a concept about minerals, for example, crystal structures.

② Teach

What is a mineral?

Caption Answer
Figure 1 Students might list parts of the building, such as cement and glass. They should not list living items such as trees.

The Structure of Minerals

Visual Learning

Figure 2 Both of these mineral samples are quartz. **What crystal shape do you think the sample shown in Figure 2A might have?** hexagonal

✓ Reading Check

Answer a solid in which the atoms are arranged in orderly, repeating patterns

---

TRY AT HOME
Mini LAB

Purpose Students will observe cubic crystals of table salt. L2
IS Visual-Spatial
Materials hand lens, table salt
Teaching Strategy Tell students to observe crystals against a dark background.
Analysis
1. All the salt grains are cubes.
2. Other minerals of the isometric (cubic) system include fluorite, galena, and pyrite.

✓ Assessment

Oral Have students classify samples of crystals that you provide. Use **Performance Assessment in the Science Classroom,** p. 121.

Visualizing Crystal Systems

Have students examine the pictures and read the captions. Then ask the following questions.

How do tetragonal crystals compare to hexagonal crystals?
Tetragonal crystals are four-sided while hexagonal crystals are six-sided. Both include a third dimension longer or shorter than the other two.

Which of the crystal systems includes the least right angles?
Triclinic crystals have no right angles; all angles where the crystal surfaces meet are oblique.

Activity

Have groups of students compete to brainstorm the greatest number of ordinary, non-mineral, objects that conform to the described crystal systems. Examples might include a skyscraper, tissue box, and unsharpened colored pencil. Offer a special bonus to any group that can describe an object conforming to the triclinic system.

Extension

Challenge students to search through mineral guides and find one mineral conforming to each of the crystal systems. Have them describe the physical properties of each mineral. After comparing notes with their classmates, ask them to describe ways in which minerals with similar crystal systems are also similar in physical properties.

Figure 3

A crystal's shape depends on how its atoms are arranged. Crystal shapes can be organized into groups known as crystal systems—shown here in 3-D with geometric models (in blue). Knowing a mineral's crystal system helps researchers understand its atomic structure and physical properties.

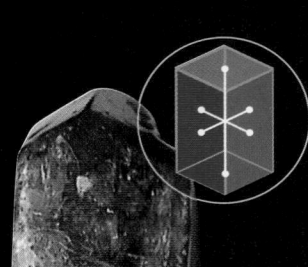

► CUBIC Fluorite is an example of a mineral that forms cubic crystals. Minerals in the cubic crystal system are equal in size along all three principal dimensions.

▲ HEXAGONAL (hek SA guh nul) In hexagonal crystals, two dimensions are equal and form 60° or 120° angles where crystal surfaces intersect. The third dimension is longer or shorter than the other two. For example, a lengthwise cross section of quartz would be a hexagon.

◄ TETRAGONAL (te TRA guh nul) Zircon crystals are tetragonal. Tetragonal crystals are much like cubic crystals, except that one of the principal dimensions is longer or shorter than the other two dimensions.

▲ ORTHORHOMBIC (awr thuh RAHM bihk) Minerals with orthorhombic structure, such as barite, have dimensions that are unequal in length, resulting in crystals with a brick-like shape.

▲ MONOCLINIC (mah nuh KLIH nihk) Minerals in the monoclinic system, such as orthoclase, also exhibit unequal dimensions in their crystal structure. Only one right angle forms where crystal surfaces meet. The other angles are oblique, which means they don't form 90° angles where they intersect.

▲ TRICLINIC (tri KLIH nihk) The triclinic crystal system includes minerals exhibiting the least symmetry. Triclinic crystals, such as rhodonite (ROH dun ite), are unequal in all dimensions, and all angles where crystal surfaces meet are oblique.

64

Teacher FYI

The hexagonal crystal system possesses one axis of six-fold or three-fold symmetry perpendicular to, and not equal in length to, three equal axes intersecting at 120°. Crystals with six-fold symmetry are classified as hexagonal—apatite and graphite are examples. Crystals with three-fold symmetry are classified as trigonal—calcite and some varieties of quartz are examples.

Figure 4
Minerals form by many natural processes.

A This rock formed as magma cooled slowly, allowing large mineral grains to form.

Labradorite

Crystals from Magma Natural processes form minerals in many ways. For example, hot melted rock, called **magma,** cools as it rises toward Earth's surface, or even if it's trapped below the surface. As magma cools, its atoms lose heat energy, move closer together, and begin to combine into compounds. Molecules of the different compounds then arrange themselves into orderly, repeating patterns. The type and amount of elements present in a magma partly determine which minerals will form. Also, the size of the crystals that form depends partly on how rapidly the magma cools.

When magma cools slowly, the crystals that form are generally large enough to see with the unaided eye, as shown in **Figure 4A.** This is because the atoms have enough time to move together and form into larger crystals. When magma cools rapidly, the crystals that form will be small. In such cases, you can't easily see individual mineral crystals.

Crystals from Solution Crystals also can form from minerals dissolved in water. When water evaporates, as in a dry climate, ions that are left behind can come together to form crystals like those in **Figure 4B.** Or, if too much of a substance is dissolved in water, ions can come together and crystals of that substance can begin to form in the solution. Minerals can come out of a solution in this way without the need for evaporation.

B Some minerals form when salt water evaporates, such as these white crystals of halite in Death Valley, California.

Physics
INTEGRATION

Evaporites commonly form in dry climates. Research a change in state of matter that takes place when a saline lake or shallow sea evaporates to form halite or gypsum.

IDENTIFYING
Misconceptions
Students may think that all minerals are as beautiful as cut diamonds and other gems. Show students a piece of jewelry containing a gemstone. Also obtain some samples of minerals without well-formed crystals. Have students contrast the minerals. Show students pictures of gem-stones before and after they have been cut and polished. Have students contrast the photographs. L2
 Visual-Spatial

Fun Fact

Polymorphs are minerals that are composed of the same elements but have different arrangements of atoms in their structures. The minerals diamond and graphite are an example.

Physics
INTEGRATION

Evaporite minerals form when a saline lake or shallow saltwater sea evaporates. During this process, liquid water changes to a gas and solids that are dissolved in the water precipitate out to form layers of evaporite minerals, such as halite (rock salt), gypsum, and sylvite. The order of precipitation, from least to most soluble, is gypsum, halite, and sylvite.

Resource Manager

Chapter Resources Booklet
Enrichment, p. 26
Directed Reading for Content Mastery, pp. 15, 16
Lab Activity, pp. 9–10

Science
Journal

Describing Minerals In their Science Journals, have students write descriptions of seven objects around the room. Encourage them to select any items they wish. Their descriptions must provide distinguishing evidence that the objects are or are not minerals. L2 **Linguistic** P

Mineral Compositions and Groups

Extension

Have students research and describe what examples of each of the following mineral groups have in common; silicates, oxides, carbonates, sulfides, sulfates, and native elements. silicates, silicon and oxygen; oxides, oxygen combined with another element; carbonates, CO_3 group; sulfides, sulfur combined with another element; sulfates, SO_4 group; native elements, made of only one element

3 Assess

Reteach

Hold up several items in front of the class. Ask students whether each item is a mineral.

Challenge

Provide crystals with obvious crystal shapes. Have students make large-scale line drawings of them. Then ask students to identify the crystal systems of their sample crystals using their drawings and **Figure 3.** L2 ELL

✓ Assessment

Process Have students make a Venn diagram that compares and contrasts crystals formed from magma with crystal formed from solutions. Use **PASC,** p. 167.

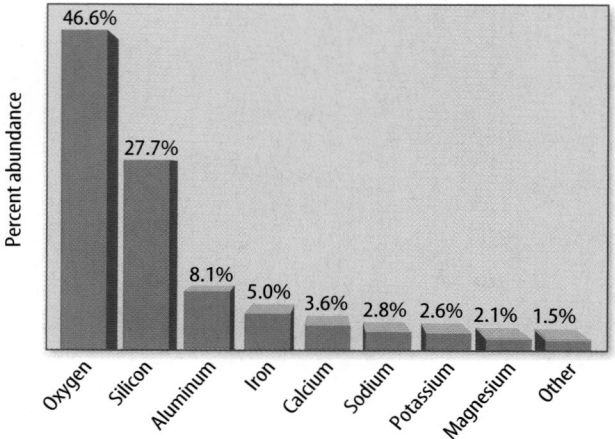

Elements in Earth's Crust

Percent abundance

46.6% Oxygen
27.7% Silicon
8.1% Aluminum
5.0% Iron
3.6% Calcium
2.8% Sodium
2.6% Potassium
2.1% Magnesium
1.5% Other

Figure 5
Most of Earth's crust is composed of these eight elements.

Mineral Compositions and Groups

Ninety elements occur naturally in Earth's crust. Approximately 98 percent (by weight) of the crust is made of only eight of these elements, as in **Figure 5.** Of the thousands of known minerals, only a few dozen are common, and these are mostly composed of the eight common elements in Earth's crust.

Most of the common rock-forming minerals belong to a group called the silicates. **Silicates** (SIH luh kayts) are minerals that contain silicon (Si) and oxygen (O) and usually one or more other elements. Silicon and oxygen are the two most abundant elements in Earth's crust. These two elements alone combine to form the basic building blocks of most of the minerals in Earth's crust and mantle. Feldspar and quartz, which are silicates, and calcite, which is a carbonate, are examples of common, rock-forming minerals. Other mineral groups also are defined according to their compositions.

Section 1 Assessment

1. What four characteristics must a substance have to be a mineral?
2. Describe two processes involving solutions that form minerals.
3. Diamonds can be made in the laboratory by subjecting starting materials containing carbon to high pressure. Are these diamonds minerals? Explain.
4. How are crystals of minerals classified?
5. **Think Critically** The mineral dolomite, a rock-forming mineral, contains oxygen, carbon, magnesium, and calcium. Is dolomite a silicate? In your Science Journal, compare and contrast rock-forming minerals and silicates.

Skill Builder Activities

6. **Classifying** Discover some items in your home or classroom that are made from minerals. How many items are metals? How many are non-metals? **For more help, refer to the** Science Skill Handbook.
7. **Using an Electronic Spreadsheet** Use spreadsheet software to make a graph of your own design that shows the relative percentages of the eight most common elements in Earth's crust. Of these eight elements only, what percentage of the crust is made up of iron and aluminum? Use the spreadsheet to perform this calculation. **For more help, refer to the** Technology Skill Handbook.

66   CHAPTER 3 Minerals

Answers to Section Assessment

1. A mineral must be a naturally occurring, inorganic, crystalline solid and have a definite composition.
2. Minerals can precipitate out of a solution where too much of a substance is dissolved, or form as a solution evaporates.
3. No; since the diamonds are made in the lab, they are not naturally occurring.

4. Crystals are classified by the shapes produced by the internal arrangement of their atoms.
5. No; this rock-forming mineral is a carbonate. Silicate rock-forming minerals contain silicon and oxygen. Both are very common. Silicates are one of a type of rock-forming mineral.

6. Possible answers: aluminum soft drink can, pencil lead (graphite), magnets, glass beaker; aluminum and magnets are metals, glass and graphite are nonmetals.
7. Student's graphs should include the information from **Figure 5.** They can be bar graphs, shaded-block graphs, or circle graphs; 13.7 percent.

Crystal Formation

So far in this chapter, you've learned about minerals and how they form. In this activity, you'll have a chance to learn how crystals form from solutions.

What You'll Investigate
How do crystals form from solution?

Materials
250-mL beakers (2)	cotton string
cardboard	hot plate
large paper clip	hand lens
table salt	thermal mitt
flat wooden stick	shallow pan
granulated sugar	spoon

Goals
■ **Compare and contrast** the crystals that form from salt and sugar solutions.
■ **Observe** crystals and infer how they formed.

Safety Precautions

WARNING: *Never taste or eat any lab materials.*

Procedure

1. Gently mix separate solutions of salt in water and sugar in water in the two beakers. Keep stirring the solutions as you add salt or sugar to the water. Stop mixing when no more salt or sugar will dissolve in the solutions. Label each beaker as a salt or sugar solution.

2. Place the sugar beaker on a hot plate. Use the hot plate to heat the sugar solution gently. **WARNING:** *The liquid is hot. Do not touch the beaker without protecting your hands.*

3. Tie one end of the thread to the middle of the wooden stick. Tie a large paper clip to the free end of the string for weight. Place the

stick across the opening of the sugar beaker so the thread dangles in the sugar solution.

4. Cover the beaker with a piece of cardboard. Place it in a location where it won't be disturbed.

5. Pour a thin layer of the salt solution into the shallow pan.

6. Leave the beaker and the shallow pan undisturbed for at least one week.

7. After one week, examine each solution with a hand lens to see whether crystals have formed.

Conclude and Apply

1. **Compare and contrast** the crystals that formed from the salt and the sugar solutions. How do they compare with samples of table salt and sugar?

2. **Describe** what happened to the saltwater solution in the shallow pan.

3. Did this same process occur in the sugar solution? Explain.

*C*ommunicating
Your Data

Make a poster that describes your methods of growing salt and sugar crystals. Present your results to your class.

Resource Manager

Chapter Resources Booklet
  Activity Worksheet, pp. 5, 6
  Reinforcement, p. 23
Cultural Diversity, p. 37

*C*ommunicating
Your Data

Have students draw illustrations of the different crystals produced in this activity.

BENCH TESTED

Purpose Students demonstrate and describe two methods of growing crystals. L2 ELL COOP LEARN LS **Visual-Spatial**

Process Skills observing and inferring, communicating, experimenting, classifying, comparing and contrasting

Time Required 20 minutes on each of two days

Safety Precautions Caution students not to handle beakers without protecting their hands. Also, caution students to wear safety goggles and not to touch the hot plate.

Teaching Strategy The beakers should need to remain undisturbed for at least a week. The more gradually the solution is cooled, the larger the crystals tend to grow.

Troubleshooting Add seed crystals on the thread to help precipitation.

Answers to Questions

1. salt crystals—cubic; sugar crystals—orthorhombic; sample crystals—same structure, probably smaller

2. The water evaporated, leaving the salt behind.

3. No; the liquid in the beaker cooled, and sugar crystals precipitated from a supersaturated solution.

Assessment

Content Encourage students to write a story that explains what happens to the atoms of a material to allow them to gradually form crystals. Have them work in groups of four to complete their stories. Use **Performance Assessment in the Science Classroom,** p. 159.

Mineral Identification

Mineral Identification

Mineral Identification

1 Motivate

Bellringer Transparency

Display the Section Focus Transparency for Section 2. Use the accompanying Transparency Activity Master. L2
ELL

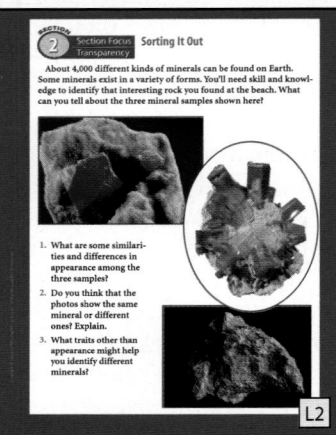

Tie to Prior Knowledge

Remind students that the physical properties of a substance can be helpful for identifying the substance. Show students two or three different minerals, and have them list several physical properties of each. L2

IS Visual-Spatial

As You Read

What You'll Learn
- **Describe** physical properties used to identify minerals.
- **Identify** minerals using physical properties such as hardness and streak.

Vocabulary
hardness   cleavage
luster   fracture
streak

Why It's Important
Identifying minerals helps you recognize valuable mineral resources.

Physical Properties

Why can you recognize a classmate when you see him or her in a crowd away from school? A person's height or the shape of his or her face helps you tell that person from the rest of your class. Height and facial shape are two properties unique to individuals. Individual minerals also have unique properties that distinguish them.

Mineral Appearance Just like height and facial characteristics help you recognize someone, mineral properties can help you recognize and distinguish minerals. Color and appearance are two obvious clues that can be used to identify minerals.

However, these clues alone aren't enough to recognize most minerals. The minerals pyrite and gold are gold in color and can appear similar, as shown in **Figure 6.** As a matter of fact, pyrite often is called fool's gold. Gold is worth a lot of money, whereas pyrite has little value. You need to look at other properties of minerals to tell them apart. Some other properties to study include how hard a mineral is, how it breaks, and its color when crushed into a powder. Every property you observe in a mineral is a clue to its identity.

Figure 6
The general appearance of a mineral often is not enough to identify it.

Gold

Pyrite

A Using only color, observers can be fooled when trying to distinguish between pyrite and gold.

B The mineral azurite is identified readily by its striking blue color.

Section ✔ *Assessment* Planner

PORTFOLIO
Activity, p. 69
PERFORMANCE ASSESSMENT
Problem-Solving Activity, p. 70
MiniLAB, p. 72
Skill Builder Activities, p. 72
See page 86 for more options.

CONTENT ASSESSMENT
Section, p. 72
Challenge, p. 72
Chapter, pp. 86–87

Hardness A measure of how easily a mineral can be scratched is its **hardness.** The mineral talc is so soft you can scratch it loose with your fingernail. Talcum powder is made from this soft mineral. Diamonds, on the other hand, are the hardest mineral. Some diamonds are used as cutting tools, as shown in **Figure 7.** A diamond can be scratched only by another diamond. Diamonds can be broken, however.

 **Reading Check** *Why is hardness sometimes referred to as scratchability?*

Sometimes the concept of hardness is confused with whether or not a mineral will break. It is important to understand that even though a diamond is extremely hard, it can shatter if given a hard enough blow in the right direction along the crystal.

Mohs Scale In 1824, the Austrian scientist Friedrich Mohs developed a list of common minerals to compare their hardnesses. This list is called Mohs scale of hardness, as seen in **Table 1.** The scale lists the hardness of ten minerals. Talc, the softest mineral, has a hardness value of one, and diamond, the hardest mineral, has a value of ten.

Here's how the scale works. Imagine that you have a clear or whitish-colored mineral that you know is either fluorite or quartz. You try to scratch it with your fingernail and then with an iron nail. You can't scratch it with your fingernail but you can scratch it with the iron nail. Because the hardness of your fingernail is 2.5 and that of the iron nail is 4.5, you can determine the unknown mineral's hardness to be somewhere around 3 or 4. Because it is known that quartz has a hardness of 7 and fluorite has a hardness of 4, the mystery mineral must be fluorite.

Some minerals have a hardness range rather than a single hardness value. This is because atoms can be arranged in different directions in a mineral's crystal structure.

Figure 7
Some saw blades have diamonds embedded in them to help slice through materials, such as this limestone. Blades are kept cool by running water over them.

Table 1 Mineral Hardness

Mohs Scale	Hardness	Hardness of Common Objects	
Talc (softest)	1		
Gypsum	2	fingernail	(2.5)
Calcite	3	piece of copper	(2.5 to 3.0)
Fluorite	4	iron nail	(4.5)
Apatite	5	glass	(5.5)
Feldspar	6	steel file	(6.5)
Quartz	7	streak plate	(7.0)
Topaz	8		
Corundum	9		
Diamond (hardest)	10		

---

2 Teach

Physical Properties

Activity

Diamonds that are used in cutting tools can be made synthetically. Have students research how synthetic diamonds are produced. Have them write a one-page report on their findings. Synthetic diamonds can be made by heating graphite at high pressure. L2 IS **Linguistic** P

✔ Reading Check

Answer Hardness is a measure of how easily a mineral can be scratched. It is tested by attempting to scratch one mineral with a common object or another mineral of known hardness.

Activity

Have students work in pairs to test for hardness and streak of samples of quartz, gypsum, calcite, galena, and pyrite. Relative hardness can be determined by scratching each of the minerals against the others. Hardness can be determined by using a hardness kit. Streak is observed by rubbing each mineral against a piece of unglazed porcelain tile or streak plate. L2 ELL COOP LEARN IS **Interpersonal**

Curriculum Connection

Auto Mechanics Some motor oil is dark gray in color. This is caused by the presence of graphite in the oil. Have students find out why graphite is added to motor oil. Because of its softness and atomic arrangement, graphite can be used to lubricate the moving parts of a motor. Graphite can also be used to lubricate moving parts in door hinges and locks. L2

Physical Properties, continued

Visual Learning

Figure 8 The two minerals shown have metallic and glassy lusters. Have students relate the way that light reflects off of different minerals to the way it reflects off a piece of chrome, a stainless-steel butter knife, brushed aluminum framing a chalkboard, and a piece of plastic. The lusters of the pieces of metal are all metallic. However, some are shiny and others are not. The luster of the plastic is shiny, but not metallic. L2

ELL LS **Visual-Spatial**

Problem-Solving Activity

Answers

1. Hardness test: Hematite would scratch a penny; copper would not scratch a penny.
2. streak test; unglazed porcelain tile
3. Apply other tests; observe luster, specific gravity, etc.

Graphite

Fluorite

Figure 8
Luster is an important physical property that is used to distinguish minerals. Graphite has a metallic luster. Fluorite has a nonmetallic, glassy luster.

Luster Luster is the way a mineral reflects light. Luster can be metallic or nonmetallic. Minerals with a metallic luster, like the graphite shown in **Figure 8,** shine like metal. Metallic luster can be compared to the shine of a metal belt buckle, the shiny chrome trim on some cars, or the shine of metallic cooking utensils. When a mineral does not shine like metal, its luster is nonmetallic. Examples of terms for nonmetallic luster include *dull, pearly, silky,* and *glassy.* Common examples of minerals with glassy luster are quartz, calcite, halite, and fluorite.

Specific Gravity Minerals also can be distinguished by comparing their heft. The **specific gravity** of a mineral is the ratio of its weight compared with the weight of an equal volume of water. Like hardness, specific gravity is expressed as a number. If you were to research the specific gravities of gold and pyrite, you'd find that gold's specific gravity is about 17, and pyrite's is 5. This means that gold is about 17 times heavier than water and pyrite is 5 times heavier than water. You could experience this by comparing equal-sized samples of gold and pyrite in your hands—the pyrite would feel much lighter.

Problem-Solving Activity

Identifying Minerals

Properties of Minerals		
Mineral	**Hardness**	**Streak**
Copper	2.5–3	copper-red
Galena	2.5–3	dark gray
Gold	2.5–3	yellow
Hematite	6.5	red to brown
Magnetite	6–6.5	black
Silver	2.5–3	silver-white

You have learned that minerals are identified by their physical properties, such as streak, hardness, cleavage, and color. Use your knowledge of mineral properties and your ability to read a table to solve the following problems.

Identifying the Problem
The table includes hardnesses and streak colors for several minerals. How can you use these data to distinguish minerals?

Solving the Problem
1. What test would you perform to distinguish hematite from copper? How would you carry out this test?
2. How could you distinguish copper from galena? What tool would you use?
3. What would you do if two minerals had both the same hardness and the same streak color?

LAB DEMONSTRATION

Purpose to show that minerals can be identified by unique physical properties
Materials sulfur, calcite, magnetite
Preparation Wear safety goggles and an apron.
Procedure Show students the bright yellow color of sulfur. Drop dilute HCl on calcite to show its fizzing reaction. Show the magnetic property of magnetite by using it to pick up some iron filings.

Expected Outcome Students see that color can help identify certain minerals. They will see that unique properties might be the only clue needed to identify certain minerals.

✓Assessment

What would happen if HCl were dropped on other minerals in the same group as calcite? The minerals would probably fizz (although not all carbonates will readily react to acid).

Streak **Streak** is the color of a mineral when it is in a powdered form. The streak test works only for minerals that are softer than the streak plate. When a mineral is rubbed across a piece of unglazed porcelain tile, as in **Figure 9,** a streak of powdered mineral is left behind. Gold and pyrite can be distinguished by a streak test. Gold has a yellow streak and pyrite has a greenish-black or brownish-black streak.

Some soft minerals will leave a streak even on paper. The last time you used a pencil to write on paper, you left a streak of the mineral graphite. One reason that graphite is used in pencil lead is because it is soft enough to leave a streak on paper.

✔ **Reading Check** *Why do gold and pyrite leave a streak, but quartz does not?*

Cleavage and Fracture The way a mineral breaks is another clue to its identity. Minerals that break along smooth, flat surfaces have **cleavage** (KLEE vihj). Cleavage, like hardness, is determined by the arrangement of the mineral's atoms. Mica is a mineral that has one perfect cleavage. You can see in **Figure 10** how it breaks along smooth, flat planes. If you were to take a layer cake and separate its layers, you would show that the cake has cleavage. Not all minerals have cleavage. Minerals that break with uneven, rough, or jagged surfaces have **fracture.** Quartz is a mineral with fracture. If you were to grab a chunk out of the side of that cake, it would be like breaking a mineral that has fracture.

Figure 9
Color is not always useful for mineral identification. Hematite, for example, can be dark red, gray, or silver in color. However, its streak is always dark reddish-brown.

Mica

Halite

Figure 10
Weak bonds within the structures of mica and halite allow them to be broken along smooth, flat cleavage planes. *If you broke quartz, would it look the same?*

Answer Both gold and pyrite are softer than the streak plate; quartz is harder than the streak plate.

Use an Analogy

Explain that some minerals show perfect cleavage, breaking into thin sheets that can be compared to sheets of paper. In fact, relatively large samples of muscovite or biotite are called "books." This is so because the individual sheets of mica can be separated along one cleavage plane, similar to separating the pages of a book.

Teacher FYI

Sheets of white mica were once used to make the "isinglass" heatproof windows of stoves and ranges. It was also used in Russia for window panes and became known as "Muscovy glass." This later became "muscovite," the current name for white mica.

Caption Answer
Figure 10 No; quartz breaks with uneven, jagged surfaces.

Resource Manager

Chapter Resources Booklet
   MiniLAB, p. 4
   Reinforcement, p. 24
   Transparency Activity, pp. 43–44

Physical Properties, continued

Purpose to observe how properties can be used to identify minerals [IS] **Visual-Spatial**

Teaching Strategy Place a clear calcite cleavage fragment over a dot on an overhead projector transparency. Rotate the calcite so that one dot revolves around the other.

Analysis
1. calcite
2. double refraction

✓ Assessment

Oral Have students describe the double image of a dot through different thicknesses of calcite. *The greater the distance between cleavage planes, the farther apart the dots appear.* Use **PASC,** p. 89.

③ Assess

Reteach

Obtain samples of magnetite. Have students determine its properties. *magnetic, has a metallic luster, hardness greater than glass, black in color and streak, exhibits uneven fracture*

Challenge

Have students hypothesize whether mineral samples contain iron. *Iron content will make a mineral feel heavy, give it a dark color, and possibly make it magnetic.*

✓ Assessment

Performance Have students make a table classifying familiar minerals according to types of cleavage. Use **PASC,** p. 109.

72   CHAPTER 3 Minerals

Mini LAB

Observing Mineral Properties

Procedure
1. Obtain samples of some of the following clear minerals: **gypsum, muscovite mica, halite,** and **calcite.**
2. Place each sample over the print on this page and observe the letters.

Analysis
1. Which mineral can be identified by observing the print's double image?
2. What other special property is used to identify this mineral?

Figure 11
Some minerals are natural magnets, such as this lodestone, which is a variety of magnetite.

Other Properties Some minerals have unique properties. Magnetite, as you can guess by its name, is attracted to magnets. Lodestone, a form of magnetite, will pick up iron filings like a magnet, as shown in **Figure 11.** Light forms two separate rays when it passes through some calcite specimens, causing you to see a double image. Calcite also can be identified because it fizzes when hydrochloric acid is put on it.

Now you know that you sometimes need more information than color and appearance to identify a mineral. You also might need to test its streak, hardness, luster, and cleavage or fracture. Although the overall appearance of a mineral can be different from sample to sample, its physical properties remain the same.

Section ② Assessment

1. What is the difference between a mineral that has cleavage and one that has fracture?
2. How can an unglazed porcelain tile be used to identify a mineral?
3. Why is streak often more useful for mineral identification than color?
4. What hardness does a mineral have if it does not scratch glass but it scratches an iron nail?
5. **Think Critically** What does the presence of cleavage planes within a mineral tell you about the chemical bonds that hold the mineral together?

Skill Builder Activities

6. **Drawing Conclusions** A large piece of the mineral halite (salt) is broken repeatedly into several perfect cubes. How can this be explained? **For more help, refer to the** Science Skill Handbook.
7. **Making and Using Tables** In your Science Journal, make a list of three minerals. Next to each mineral, write another mineral that is similar in appearance. In a third column, list one physical property that can be used to distinguish the pair of similar-looking minerals. **For more help, refer to the** Science Skill Handbook.

72   CHAPTER 3 Minerals

Answers to Section Assessment

1. A mineral with cleavage breaks along smooth, flat planes. One that fractures breaks with uneven or jagged surfaces.
2. A mineral softer than an unglazed porcelain tile will leave a powdered streak on the tile. The streak color can help identify the mineral.
3. Several different samples of one mineral may have different colors, but they usually will have the same streak.
4. between 4.5 and 5.5
5. Cleavage planes occur where weak bonds exist within the mineral's structure.
6. Halite has three directions of cleavage oriented at 90° to each other.
7. Possible answer: Calcite-quartz: calcite fizzes with HCl. Pyrite-gold: has a greenish-black streak. Magnetite-galena: magnetite is magnetic.

Uses of Minerals

Gems

Walking past the window of a jewelry store, you notice a large selection of beautiful jewelry—a watch sparkling with diamonds, a necklace holding a brilliant red ruby, and a gold ring. For thousands of years, people have worn and prized minerals in their jewelry. What makes some minerals special? What unusual properties do they have that make them so valuable?

Properties of Gems **Gems** or gemstones, like the ones shown in **Figure 12,** are highly prized minerals because they are rare and beautiful. Most gems are special varieties of a particular mineral. They are clearer, brighter, or more colorful than common samples of that mineral. The difference between a gem and the common form of the same mineral can be slight. Amethyst is a gem form of quartz that contains just traces of iron in its structure. This small amount of iron gives amethyst a desirable purple color. Sometimes a gem has a crystal structure that allows it to be cut and polished to a higher quality than that of a non-gem mineral. **Table 2** lists popular gems and some locations where they have been collected.

As You Read

What You'll Learn
- **Describe** characteristics of gems that make them more valuable than other minerals.
- **Identify** useful elements that are contained in minerals.

Vocabulary
gem

Why It's Important
Minerals are necessary materials for decorative items and many manufactured products.

Figure 12
It is easy to see why gems are prized for their beauty and rarity. Shown here is The Imperial State Crown, made for Queen Victoria of England in 1838. It contains thousands of jewels, including diamonds, rubies, sapphires, and emeralds.

SECTION 3 Uses of Minerals **73**

Uses of Minerals

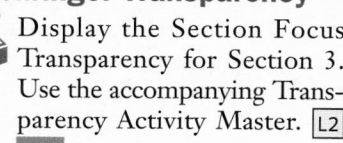
1 Motivate

Bellringer Transparency
Display the Section Focus Transparency for Section 3. Use the accompanying Transparency Activity Master. L2
ELL

Tie to Prior Knowledge
Have students recall the last time they saw jewelry in a jewelry store or a department store. Have students describe the jewelry. Most will say it was shiny, colorful, or looked brilliant under the lights in the store. Explain that jewelry is one common use of minerals. L2 IS **Visual-Spatial**

Section ✔*Assessment* Planner

PORTFOLIO
Use Science Words, p. 74
Extension, p. 76
PERFORMANCE ASSESSMENT
Skill Builder Activities, p. 79
See page 86 for more options.

CONTENT ASSESSMENT
Section, p. 79
Challenge, p. 79
Chapter, pp. 86–87

Resource Manager

Chapter Resources Booklet
Transparency Activity, p. 42
Enrichment, p. 28

2 Teach

Gems

Use Science Words

Word Usage Have students read advertisements and use **Table 2** to discover what gems are commonly used in jewelry. Ask them also to find out what minerals the gems are set in. They also could discover where the minerals were found. Have them write their findings in their Science Journals. Possible answer: gems used in jewelry—emeralds, rubies, tanzanite, topaz, peridot, almandine, pyrope, amethyst, sapphires, diamonds; gem settings—gold, silver, platinum; where minerals found—quartz veins and placer deposits, among others L2 ELL
IS **Visual-Spatial and Linguistic** P

Make a Model

Have students research the crystal systems of the gemstones listed in **Table 2**. Once the crystal system has been identified, have students construct models of each crystal system. Students should use **Figure 3** and a book on mineralogy to assist in planning their models. Student models should include the following crystal systems: cubic—spinel and garnet; hexagonal—beryl, quartz, and corundum; orthorhombic—zoisite, topaz, and olivine. L2 ELL IS **Kinesthetic**

Table 2 Minerals and Their Gems

Fun Facts	Mineral	Gem Example	Some Important Locations
Beryl is named for containing the element beryllium. Some crystals reach several meters in length.	Beryl	Emerald	Colombia, Brazil, South Africa, North Carolina
One red spinel weighs 352 carats and is part of the British crown jewels. One carat weighs 0.2 grams.	Spinel	Ruby spinel	Sri Lanka, Thailand, Myanmar (Burma)
Purplish-blue examples of zoisite were discovered in 1967 near Arusha, Tanzania.	Zoisite	Tanzanite	Tanzania
The most valuable examples are yellow, pink, and blue varieties.	Topaz (uncut)	Topaz (gem)	Siberia, Germany, Japan, Mexico, Brazil, Colorado, Utah, Texas, California, Maine, Virginia, South Carolina

74 CHAPTER 3 Minerals

Cultural Diversity

Quartz The mineral quartz has been recognized for its hardness and utility since prehistoric times. Quartz tools that are more than 350,000 years old have been found at sites such as Zhoukoudianzhen, China. Quartz has also been esteemed by many cultures for its beauty. The Japanese and Chinese carved clear rock quartz into art objects and spheres, as did the Greeks. Large transparent crystals are found in Madagascar, Japan, Burma, and Brazil. Quartz occurs in many colors and has been used for ornamentation. Purple amethyst comes from Mexico and Brazil. Cairngorm, a brown quartz, was named after the Cairngorm Mountains of Scotland. It also can be found in Switzerland, Japan, and Colorado. Have students research modern uses of quartz. Possible answer: timepieces and jewelry

Fun Facts	Mineral	Gem Example	Some Important Locations
Olivine composes a large part of Earth's upper mantle. It also is present in moon rocks.	Olivine	Peridot	Myanmar (Burma), Zebirget (Saint John's Island, located in the Red Sea), Arizona, New Mexico
Garnet is a common mineral found in a wide variety of rock types. The red color of the variety almandine is caused by iron in its crystal structure.	Garnet	Almandine	Ural Mountains, Italy, Madagascar, Czechoslovakia, India, Sri Lanka, Brazil, North Carolina, Arizona, New Mexico
Quartz makes up about 30 percent of Earth's continental crust.	Quartz	Amethyst	Colorless varieties in Hot Springs, Arkansas; Amethyst in Brazil, Uruguay, Madagascar, Montana, North Carolina, California, Maine
The blue color of sapphire is caused by iron or titanium in corundum.	Corundum	Blue sapphire	Thailand, Cambodia, Sri Lanka, Kashmir

Resource Manager

Chapter Resources Booklet
Directed Reading for Content Mastery, pp. 17, 18
Activity Worksheet, pp. 7–8

Activity

Have students suppose that they have a liquid that has a density of 4.0 g/cm³. Ask students to design an experiment that would enable them to separate several gems into two piles; one of diamonds and the other of cubic zirconium crystals. Possible answer: The density of diamond is 3.52 g/cm³ and the density of cubic zirconium is 4.7 g/cm³. Place the gems in the liquid. The diamonds will float and the cubic zirconium crystals will sink.
L3 **Logical-Mathematical**

Extension

Have students research the method used to make diamond-edged surgical scalpels, razor blades, dental drills, and diamond-coated computer parts. Possible answer: Microwaves are used to strip the hydrogen atoms away from the methane molecule. The carbon atoms then link together on the surface of the instrument being coated, forming tiny rows of diamonds.

Discussion

Ruby and sapphire are varieties of the mineral corundum. Why are rubies red and some sapphires blue? Blue sapphire is colored by iron and titanium impurities, while the red color of ruby is caused by the presence of minor chromium.

Gems, continued

Extension

Students can investigate the areas of the world that produce most of the world's gems. Have them make a collage of what they discover. Their collages could include images of the gems and the places where they are found. L2 [IS] **Visual-Spatial** P

Visual Learning

Figure 13 Two famous and very valuable diamonds are shown here. But what makes a diamond valuable? The value of diamonds varies depending on whether or not they are tinted. The most common diamonds of gem quality have yellow or brown tints and are less valuable that diamonds with no tints. Diamonds with blue or pink tints are more valuable than those with no tints. **Why might these stones be more valuable?** Possible answer: They are more rare.

Figure 13
These gems are among the most famous examples of precious stones.

A The Great Star of Africa is part of a sceptre in the collection of British crown jewels.

Important Gems All gems are prized, but some are truly spectacular and have played an important role in history. For example, the Cullinan diamond, found in South Africa in 1905, was the largest uncut diamond ever discovered. It weighed a total of 3,106.75 carats (about 621 g). The Cullinan diamond was cut into 9 main stones and 96 smaller ones. The largest of these is called the Cullinan 1 or Great Star of Africa. It weighs 530.20 carats (about 106 g) and is now part of the British monarchy's crown jewels, shown in **Figure 13A.**

Another well-known diamond is the Blue Hope diamond, shown in **Figure 13B.** This is perhaps the most notorious of all diamonds. It was purchased by Henry Philip Hope around 1830, after whom it is named. Because his entire family as well as a later owner suffered misfortune, the Hope diamond has gained a reputation for bringing its owner bad luck. The Hope diamond weighs 45.52 carats (about 9 g) and currently is displayed in the Smithsonian Institution in Washington.

Useful Gems In addition to their beauty, some gems serve useful purposes. You learned earlier that diamonds have a hardness of 10 on Mohs scale. They can scratch almost any material—a property that makes them useful as industrial abrasives and cutting tools. Other useful gems include rubies, which are used to produce specific types of laser light. Quartz crystals are used in electronics and as timepieces. When pressurized, quartz vibrates steadily, which helps control frequencies in electronic devices and allows for accurate timekeeping.

Most industrial diamonds and other gems are synthetic, which means that humans make them. However, the study of natural gems led to their synthesis, allowing the synthetic varieties to be used by humans readily.

B Beginning in 1668, the Hope Diamond was part of the French crown jewels. Then known as the French Blue, it was stolen in 1792, and later surfaced in London, England in 1812.

Curriculum Connection

Art Ask the art teacher to bring jewelry-making supplies to class. Materials might include copper, brass, and silver, as well as precut and polished stones. Students could even make jewelry from stones they find near their homes. Have samples of the mineral ores that copper and other materials come from available for students to observe. L3 ELL [IS] **Visual-Spatial**

Science Journal

Fake Diamonds Tell students that someone has placed an ad in the newspaper that reads, "Real gems for sale! We'll prove these are genuine diamonds by cutting glass with them before your very eyes!" Have students describe why cutting glass wouldn't prove the stones were diamonds. Possible answer: Many minerals other than diamonds cut glass. L2 [IS] **Linguistic**

Bauxite

Useful Elements in Minerals

Gemstones are perhaps the best-known use of minerals, but they are not the most important. Look around your home. How many things made from minerals can you name? Can you find anything made from iron?

Ores Iron, used in everything from frying pans to ships, is obtained from its ore, hematite. A mineral or rock is an ore if it contains a useful substance that can be mined at a profit. Magnetite is another mineral that contains iron.

 *When is a mineral also an ore?*

Extracting Elements Aluminum sometimes is refined, or purified, from the ore bauxite, shown in **Figure 14.** In the process of refining aluminum, aluminum oxide powder is separated from unwanted materials that are present in the original bauxite. After this, the aluminum oxide powder is converted to molten aluminum by a process called smelting.

During smelting, a substance is melted to separate it from any unwanted materials that may remain. Aluminum can be made into useful products like bicycles, soft-drink cans, foil, and lightweight parts for airplanes and cars. The plane flown by the Wright brothers during the first flight at Kitty Hawk had an engine made partly of aluminum.

Chemistry INTEGRATION

In 1886, Charles Martin Hall discovered an important process that led to modern aluminum refinement. Research the Hall process. Describe what you learn in your Science Journal.

SECTION 3 Uses of Minerals **77**

Extension

Provide students with a sample or photograph of limestone with a vein calcite deposit. Ask students which of the processes of mineral formation might have caused the deposit of calcite to form. Ask them to hypothesize whether the vein formed from magma, by evaporation, or by precipitation from solution. Possible answer: As a fluid solution flowed through cracks in the limestone; conditions changed calcite and precipitated out of solution.

✔ Reading Check

Answer Fluids travel through weaknesses in rocks, such as natural fractures or cracks, faults, and surfaces between rock layers.

IDENTIFYING Misconceptions

Many students think that minerals are rare objects that are seldom used in everyday materials. Refer to page 60F for teaching strategies that address this misconception.

Figure 15
The mineral sphalerite (arrow) is an important source of zinc. Iron often is coated with zinc to prevent rust in a process called galvanization.

SCIENCE Online

Research Visit the Glencoe Science Web site at **science.glencoe.com** for recent news or magazine articles on uses of titanium. Communicate to your class what you learn.

Figure 16
Rutile and ilmenite are common ore minerals of the element titanium.

Vein Minerals Under certain conditions, metallic elements can dissolve in fluids. These fluids then travel through weaknesses in rocks and form mineral deposits. Weaknesses in rocks include natural fractures or cracks, faults, and surfaces between layered rock formations. Mineral deposits left behind that fill in the open spaces created by the weaknesses are called vein mineral deposits.

✔ Reading Check   *How do fluids move through rocks?*

Sometimes, vein mineral deposits fill in the empty spaces after rocks collapse. An example of a mineral that can form in this way is shown in **Figure 15.** This is the shiny mineral sphalerite, a source of the element zinc, which is used in batteries. Sphalerite sometimes fills spaces in collapsed limestone.

Minerals Containing Titanium You might own golf clubs with titanium shafts or a racing bicycle containing titanium. Perhaps you know someone who has a titanium hip or knee replacement. Titanium is a durable, non-toxic, lightweight, metallic element derived from minerals that contain this metal in their atomic structures. Two minerals that are sources of the element titanium are ilmenite (IHL muh nite) and rutile (rew TEEL), shown in **Figure 16.** Ilmenite and rutile are common in rocks that form when magma cools and solidifies. They also occur as vein mineral deposits and in beach sands.

SCIENCE Online
Internet Addresses
_____
_____
_____

Explore the Glencoe Science Web site at **science.glencoe.com** to find out more about topics in this section.

Resource Manager

Home and Community Involvement, p. 34

Uses for Titanium Titanium is used in automobile body parts, such as connecting rods, valves, and suspension springs. It is used in the manufacture of aircraft and eyeglass frames. Low density and durability make titanium valuable in the production of these goods and of sports equipment such as tennis rackets and bicycles. Wheelchairs used by people who want to race or play basketball often are made from titanium, as shown in **Figure 17.** Titanium is one of many examples of useful materials that come from minerals and that enrich humans' lives.

Figure 17
Wheelchairs used for racing and playing basketball often have parts made from titanium.

3 Assess

Reteach
Have students to explain why titanium is used to make sports-equipment. Titanium is light-weight and wears well. L2

Challenge
Have students research the property of copper that makes it useful in electrical wires. Ask them to determine what types of chemical elements have this property. Possible answer: The electrical conductivity of copper makes it useful in electrical wires. Usually, metals are the types of chemical elements that conduct electricity well.

✓ Assessment

Content What must be true for a mineral or rock to be classified as an ore? It must contain a useful substance that can be mined at a profit. Use **Performance Assessment in the Science Classroom,** p. 89.

Section ③ Assessment

1. Why is the Cullinan diamond considered to be important?

2. What do rubies and sapphires have in common?

3. Describe how vein minerals form.

4. Why is bauxite considered to be a useful rock?

5. **Think Critically** Titanium is a nontoxic metal. Why is this an important characteristic in the manufacture of artificial body parts?

Skill Builder Activities

6. **Comparing and Contrasting** Compare and contrast gem-quality amethyst with regular quartz. **For more help, refer to the** Science Skill Handbook.

7. **Using Percentages** On average, Earth's continental crust contains 5 percent iron and 0.007 percent zinc. How many times more iron than zinc is present in the average continental crust? **For more help, refer to the** Math Skill Handbook.

Answers to Section Assessment

1. It was the largest uncut diamond ever found. Part of it is now part of the British Monarchy's crown jewels.
2. Both are forms of corundum.
3. Vein minerals form when minerals precipitate from fluids moving along faults or fractures.
4. Bauxite is an ore of aluminum.

5. Body parts manufactured from titanium are less likely to damage body tissues.
6. Gem-quality amethyst is a variety of quartz that contains impurities that color it. This makes the amethyst rare and beautiful. Pure quartz is colorless.

7. $0.05/0.00007 = 714$; average continental crust contains about 714 times more iron than zinc.

ACTIVITY

Recognize the Problem

Purpose
Students design and carry out an investigation to identify unknown mineral samples. L2
IS Interpersonal

Process Skills
comparing and contrasting, forming a hypothesis, interpreting data, observing and inferring, designing an experiment

Time Required
60-80 minutes

Safety Precautions
Review precautions on student page.

Form a Hypothesis

Possible Hypothesis
Begin by determining the hardness of each mineral and use this property to attempt mineral identification. Lay out all minerals, study their appearance and hefts (specific gravity), and decide which property would be most helpful in identifying each mineral.

Test Your Hypothesis

Possible Procedure
Lay out all minerals, and study their appearances and hefts (specific gravity). Determine hardness and streak, and use the results to identify each mineral.

ACTIVITY Design Your Own Experiment

Mineral Identification

Some mineral properties can be more useful than others when testing a particular mineral. Although certain minerals can be identified observing only one property, others require testing several properties to identify them.

Recognize the Problem
How can you identify unknown minerals?

Form a Hypothesis
Make a hypothesis about which properties you think will be most useful in identifying particular minerals.

Goals
■ **Determine** which properties of a mineral you will use for identification purposes.
■ **Design** an experiment that tests these properties to help identify minerals.

Possible Materials
mineral samples	streak plate
hand lens	5% hydrochloric
pan balance	acid (HCI) with
graduated cylinder	dropper
water	*vinegar
piece of copper	Mohs scale
*copper penny	Reference
glass plate	Handbook,
small iron nail	Minerals
steel file	*Alternate materials

Safety Precautions

Use care when handling acids. Be careful when handling materials with sharp edges. **WARNING:** *HCl can cause burns. If spillage occurs, notify your teacher and rinse with a generous flow of cool water until you are told to stop. Do not taste, eat, or drink any lab materials. Never hold a glass plate in your hands while testing hardness because the plate could break.*

Resource Manager

Chapter Resources Booklet
   Reinforcement, p. 25
Lab Management and Safety, pp. 54–57

Inclusion Strategies

Learning Disabled After students have completed the activity, have them play a game based on 20 Questions. One student can think of a mineral while others try to narrow the choice by asking five *yes* or *no* questions related to luster, hardness, cleavage or fracture, and so on. This will encourage students to use good questioning strategies and classification and memory skills.
L1 ELL **IS** Interpersonal

Test Your Hypothesis

Plan

1. As a group, agree upon and write your hypothesis statement.

2. As a group, list the steps you will need to take to test your hypothesis. Be specific, describing exactly what you will do at each step.

3. **List** the materials you will need to complete your experiment.

4. **List** the various properties of minerals that you will test.

5. **Predict** any special properties you expect to observe or test.

6. Reread your experiment to make sure that steps are in a logical order.

7. Should you test the properties of the minerals more than once?

8. How will you summarize your data?

9. **Identify** all constants, variables, and controls of the experiment.

Do

1. Make sure your teacher approves your plan before you start.

2. Carry out the experiment as planned.

3. While doing the experiment, write any observations that you or other members of your group make. Summarize your data in your Science Journal.

Analyze Your Data

1. Which properties were most useful in identifying your samples? Which properties were least useful?

2. **Compare** the properties that worked best for you with those that worked best for other students.

Draw Conclusions

1. For five minerals, discuss reasons why certain properties are useful and others are not.

2. **Determine** two properties that distinguish clear, transparent quartz from clear, transparent calcite. Explain your choice of properties.

*C*ommunicating Your Data

For three minerals, **list** physical properties in the order of their increasing importance in identification. **For more help, refer to the Science Skill Handbook.**

Teaching Strategies

• Label the minerals and use a key so you can distinguish them.

• Encourage students to test mineral properties several times and to average the results in order to achieve the best result.

Expected Outcome

Students will discover that whichever property they choose, it will not be enough to identify all minerals. They will discover that using a combination of properties is best when identifying unknown mineral samples.

Analyze Your Data

1. Although answer will vary, hardness and streak will generally be the properties most commonly cited as most useful. Color is usually the least helpful property.

2. Comparisons among groups will vary but should lead to discussions about different ways to test minerals.

Error Analysis

Have students compare their results and their hypotheses and explain why any differences occurred. Ask students whether their hypotheses were too limited for this study.

Draw Conclusions

1. Discussion among groups will vary, but, color will most likely prove to be unreliable. Hardness and streak are very useful because these properties tend to be the same for all samples of the same mineral.

2. Students could choose hardness, cleavage/fracture, reaction to acid, or double refraction.

✓*Assessment*

Performance To further assess mineral identification, ask students to bring mineral samples from home or supply students with additional mineral samples. Have them repeat this activity to identify the additional samples. Use **Performance Assessment in the Science Classroom,** p. 121.

*C*ommunicating Your Data

Have students compare conclusions by asking each group to prepare and deliver a five-minute presentation. Have each group use their data table as a visual aid for the presentation.

Content Background

In 1895 Wilhelm Conrad Roentgen discovered a type of non-visible radiation, which he termed X rays because their nature was unknown. Within a few months X ray tubes were being used all over Europe for research, medical diagnosis and entertainment.

In 1912 Max von Laue showed that X rays were part of the electromagnetic spectrum and, like visible light, could be diffracted, absorbed, and polarized. Two years later William and Lawrence Bragg developed the means to analyze the patterns created by the diffraction of X rays in crystalline structure.

Applying this knowledge to biochemistry, Dorothy Hodgkin was able to describe the atomic structure of insulin and vitamin B12. Her work led to a better understanding of how organic chemicals function and the development of synthetic versions of the same compounds.

Unlike a medical X ray that records the absorption of the radiation as it passes though an object, X ray crystallography uses a high-power emitter with its beam narrowly focused on a single point. The result is not a picture of the substance but a pattern produced by the bending of the beam. The pattern will indicate the density, atomic number, and thickness variations of static solid objects. A number of images must be made and correlated to positively identify any particular substance. Hodgkin, von Laue, and the Braggs all received Nobel Prizes.

Dr. Dorothy

Like X rays, electrons are diffracted by crystalline substances, revealing information about their internal structures and symmetry. This electron diffraction pattern of titanium was obtained with an electron beam focused along a specific direction in the crystal.

What contributions did Dorothy Crowfoot Hodgkin make to science?

Dr. Hodgkin used a method called X-ray crystallography (kris tuh LAH gruh fee) to figure out the structures of crystalline substances, including vitamin B12, vitamin D, penicillin, and insulin. Her studies showed how the atoms in these molecules are organized.

What's X-ray crystallography?

Using X rays, scientists are able to figure out the shapes and the atomic structures of crystalline substances.

As X rays travel through a crystal, the crystal diffracts or scatters the X rays into a regular pattern. Like an individual's fingerprints, each crystalline substance has a unique diffraction pattern.

Crystallography has applications in the life, Earth, and physical sciences. For example, geologists use X-ray crystallography to study minerals found in Earth's rocks. Minerals like diamonds and graphite have the same chemical makeup, but different atomic structures. Because the atomic structure of a mineral is unique, X-ray crystallography helps geologists know exactly which substance they are examining.

82

Resources for Teachers and Students

Women in Chemistry and Physics, a Bibliographic Sourcebook, edited by L.S. Grinstein, R. K. Rose, M.H Rafailovich, Westport, CT: Greenwood Press, 1993.

The X ray Century, Madison, WI: Medical Physics Corp, 1996.

X-rays: the First Hundred years, edited by Alan Michette and Slawka Pfauntsch Chichester; New York, John Wiley & Sons, 1996.

"She will be remembered as a great chemist, a saintly, gentle, and tolerant lover of people, and a devoted protagonist on peace."

—Max F. Perutz, Recipient of the 1962 Nobel Prize, Chemistry

Crowfoot Hodgkin

Trailblazing scientist and humanitarian

How does Hodgkin's research help people today?

Dr. Hodgkin's discovery of the structure of insulin helped scientists learn how to control diabetes, a disease that affects over 15 million Americans. Diabetics' bodies are unable to process sugar efficiently. Diabetes can be fatal. Fortunately, Dr. Hodgkin's research with insulin has saved many lives.

What were some obstacles Hodgkin overcame?

Dorothy Hodgkin was born in 1910. When she was four, she and her sisters were left in England while their parents traveled to Egypt.

Dr. Hodgkin always said that this helped encourage her independent spirit. During the 1930s, there were few women scientists. It was a man's world. Hodgkin was not even allowed to attend meetings of the chemistry faculty where she taught because she was a woman. Eventually, she won over her stubborn colleagues with her intelligence and tenacity. Hodgkin died in 1994.

What else did she do?

Dr. Hodgkin was involved in world peace, nuclear disarmament, and aiding poorer nations. She also helped make it a bit easier for women scientists to be accepted by men.

Discussion

Why is the knowledge of atomic structure important? Possible answers: Knowing the atomic structure of substances with similar chemical composition but different characteristics helps chemists make those substances artificially and manufacture new products and medicines based on them.

What problems might Dr. Hodgkin have faced as a result of being excluded from her colleagues' meetings because she was a woman? Possible answers: She would not have been in a position to easily communicate the results of her work or gain the necessary support from her colleagues to acquire funding.

Historic Significance

The discovery of X rays and their many uses has enabled the development of diagnostic tools in almost every branch of science. Have students research the various uses of X rays and prepare a wall chart cataloguing scientific and industrial advances that would not have been possible without them. Arrange their findings in the style of a family tree beginning with Roentgen and ending with the present.

CONNECTIONS Research Look in reference books or go to the Glencoe Science Web site for information on how X-ray crystallography is used to study minerals. Write your findings and share them with your class.

SCIENCE *Online*
For more information, visit
science.glencoe.com

CONNECTIONS Debate Have students research electromagnetism and detail the properties of the various levels of radiation. The results can be presented as a bulletin board using the colors of the visible spectrum as a graph displayed vertically with red at the bottom and violet on top. The nonvisible portions should be placed in order of frequency above and below the visible light.

SCIENCE *Online*

Internet Addresses

_____
_____
_____

Explore the Glencoe Science Web site at **science.glencoe.com** to find out more about topics in this feature.

Reviewing Main Ideas

Preview

Students can answer the questions in their Science Journals. Discuss the answers as you go through the chapter. **IS Linguistic**

Review

Students can write their answers and then compare them with those of other students. **IS Interpersonal**

Reteach

Students can look at the illustrations and describe details that support the main ideas of the chapter. **IS Visual-Spatial**

Answers to Chapter Review

SECTION 1

2. The crystals grew freely in the open space of the cavity.

SECTION 2

2. metallic

SECTION 3

2. Diamond has a hardness of 10.

Reviewing Main Ideas

Section 1 Minerals

1. You use minerals every day of your life. The pencil "lead" you write with is the mineral graphite. The pretzels you eat for a snack are sprinkled with halite. Gold, silver, gems, and semiprecious stones are used in jewelry. Much of what you use each day is made at least in some part from minerals.

2. All minerals are formed by natural processes and are inorganic solids with definite chemical compositions and orderly internal atomic structures. *Why do minerals in geodes like the one shown here have nicely formed crystal faces?*

3. Minerals have crystal structures in one of six major crystal systems.

Section 2 Mineral Identification

1. Hardness is a measure of how easily a mineral can be scratched.

2. Luster describes how light reflects from a mineral's surface. *What type of luster does this cube-shaped mineral have?*

3. Streak is the color of the powder left by a mineral on an unglazed porcelain tile.

4. Minerals that break along smooth, flat surfaces have cleavage. When minerals break with rough or jagged surfaces, these surfaces are called fracture.

5. Some minerals have special properties that aid in identifying them. For example, clear crystals of calcite display a double image when placed over type on a page. The mineral magnetite is identified readily by its attraction to a magnet.

Section 3 Uses of Minerals

1. Gems are minerals that are more rare and beautiful than common minerals.

2. Minerals are useful for their physical properties and for the elements they contain. Titanium is a useful element that is derived from the minerals ilmenite and rutile. Rocks containing ilmenite and rutile are ores of titanium, provided that they can be mined at a profit. *What physical property of diamond makes it useful as an industrial tool as well as a beautiful gem?*

FOLDABLES
Reading & Study Skills

After You Read

Exchange Foldables with a classmate and quiz each other to see if you know the answers to your mineral questions.

FOLDABLES
Reading & Study Skills

After students have read the chapter and completed the Foldable described in Before You Read, have them do the activity on the student page.

Dinah Zike

Chapter ③
Study Guide

Visualizing Main Ideas

Complete the following concept map about minerals. Use the following words and phrases: the way a mineral breaks, the way a mineral reflects light, ore, a rare and beautiful mineral, how easily a mineral is scratched, streak, *and* a useful substance mined for profit.

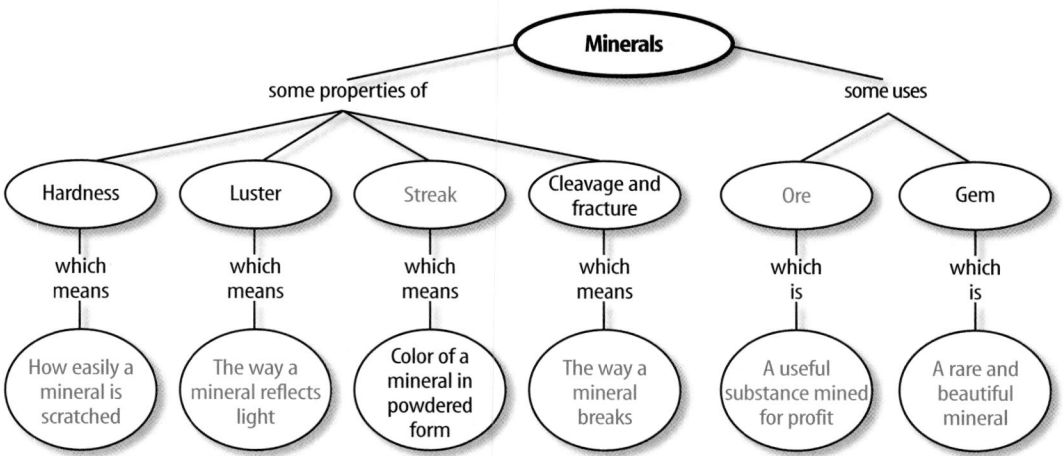

Vocabulary Review

Vocabulary Words

a. cleavage
b. crystal
c. fracture
d. gem
e. hardness
f. luster
g. magma
h. mineral
i. silicate
j. specific gravity
k. streak

Using Vocabulary

Explain the difference between the vocabulary words in each of the following sets.

1. cleavage, fracture
2. crystal, mineral
3. luster, streak
4. magma, crystal
5. hardness, specific gravity
6. magma, mineral
7. crystal, luster
8. mineral, silicate
9. gem, crystal
10. streak, specific gravity

CHAPTER STUDY GUIDE 85

Visualizing Main Ideas

See student page.

Vocabulary Review

Using Vocabulary

1. Cleavage is when minerals break along a flat surface. Fractures are when a mineral breaks along a jagged or smooth curved surface.
2. A crystal forms from the regular pattern of atoms in a mineral or other crystalline solid. A mineral is a naturally-occurring, inorganic crystalline solid.
3. luster—how light reflects from a mineral; streak—color of the powdered mineral
4. Magma is molten rock. Crystals form in the rock as it cools and hardens.
5. hardness—how easily a mineral can be scratched; specific gravity—weight of a mineral relative to an equal volume of water
6. Magma is molten rock. Rock is made of minerals.
7. luster—the way a mineral reflects light; crystal—solid with an orderly internal arrangement of atoms
8. Minerals make up rocks. Silicate is a mineral that contains silicon and oxygen.
9. A gem is a rare and beautiful crystal. A crystal is the regular arrangement of atoms found in all minerals.
10. streak—color of the powdered form of a mineral; specific gravity—weight of a mineral relative to an equal volume of water

---

◆IDENTIFYING Misconceptions

Assess

Use the assessment as follow-up to page 60F after students have completed the chapter.

Materials mineral samples that correspond to minerals found in vitamin tablets, such as calcium, copper fluoride, iron, and zinc.

Procedure Provide each small group of students with a mineral sample and the matching mineral found in vitamins. Samples could include the mineral halite from salt or the mineral calcite and the supplement calcium.

Expected Outcome Students will realize that they use minerals every day, even as part of the essential parts of the foods they eat.

Checking Concepts

1. D
2. B
3. A
4. C
5. B
6. D
7. B
8. C
9. C
10. D

Thinking Critically

11. On Earth, water can exist as a solid, a liquid, or a gas. Water is a mineral only when it is a solid that has formed naturally such as glacial ice.
12. Each perfect cubic salt crystal has six sides.
13. No; sugar, although it is a solid formed in nature with a definite composition and internal structure, is not a mineral because it is an organic compound.
14. No; a diamond is harder than a streak plate and will scratch the plate.
15. Using common objects and the minerals on the Mohs hardness scale allows you to determine the relative hardness of any mineral. Minerals are harder than other minerals or objects they scratch and softer than minerals or objects that scratch them. Minerals and objects that scratch each other are the same hardness.

Chapter 3 Assessment

Checking Concepts

Choose the word or phrase that best answers the question.

1. Which is a characteristic of a mineral?
   A) It can be a liquid.
   B) It is organic.
   C) It has no crystal structure.
   D) It is inorganic.

2. What must all silicates contain?
   A) magnesium
   B) silicon and oxygen
   C) silicon and aluminum
   D) oxygen and carbon

3. What is hot, melted rock material called?
   A) magma
   B) quartz
   C) salt water
   D) gypsum

4. Which mineral group does quartz belong to?
   A) oxides
   B) carbonates
   C) silicates
   D) sulfides

5. What is the measure of how easily a mineral can be scratched?
   A) luster
   B) hardness
   C) cleavage
   D) fracture

6. What is the color of a powdered mineral formed when rubbing it against an unglazed porcelain tile?
   A) luster
   B) density
   C) hardness
   D) streak

7. In what way does quartz break?
   A) cleavage
   B) fracture
   C) luster
   D) flat planes

8. Which of the following must crystalline solids have?
   A) carbonates
   B) cubic structures
   C) ordered atoms
   D) cleavage

9. Which is hardest on Mohs scale?
   A) talc
   B) quartz
   C) diamond
   D) feldspar

10. Which crystal system do halite crystals belong to?
    A) triclinic
    B) hexagonal
    C) monoclinic
    D) cubic

Thinking Critically

11. Water is a nonliving substance that is formed by natural processes on Earth. It has a unique composition. Sometimes water is a mineral and other times it is not. Explain.

12. How many sides does a perfect salt crystal have?

13. Suppose you let a sugar solution evaporate, leaving sugar crystals behind. Are these crystals minerals? Explain.

14. Will diamond leave a streak on a streak plate? Explain.

15. Explain how you would use **Table 1** to determine the hardness of any mineral.

Developing Skills

16. **Drawing Conclusions** Suppose you found a white mineral with a glassy, nonmetallic luster that was harder than calcite. You identify the sample as quartz. What are your observations? What is your conclusion?

17. **Interpreting Data** Using **Table 1,** identify a mineral with these properties: pink color, nonmetallic and glassy luster, softer than topaz and quartz, scratches apatite, harder than fluorite, has cleavage, and is scratched by a steel file.

18. **Collecting Data** Make an outline of how at least seven physical properties can be used to identify unknown materials.

Chapter ✓Assessment Planner

Portfolio Encourage students to place in their portfolios one or two items of what they consider to be their best work. Examples include:
• Science Journal, p. 65
• Activity, p. 69
• Use Science Words, p. 74
• Extension, p. 76

Performance Additional performance assessments, Performance Task Assessment Lists, and rubrics for evaluating these activities can be found in Glencoe's **Performance Assessment in the Science Classroom.**

19. Measuring in SI The volume of water in a graduated cylinder is 107.5 mL. A specimen of quartz, tied to a piece of string, is immersed in the water. The new water level reads 186 mL. What is the volume of the piece of quartz?

20. Concept Mapping Make a network tree concept map showing two crystal systems and two examples from each group. Use the following words and phrases: *hexagonal, corundum, halite, fluorite,* and *quartz.*

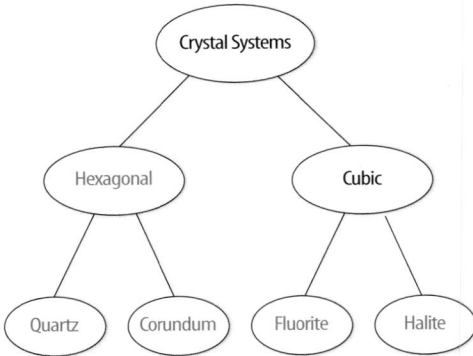

Performance Assessment

21. Poster Make a poster that shows the six crystal systems of minerals. Research the crystal systems of minerals and give three examples for each crystal system. Are any of the minerals found in your state? Do any of the minerals have an important use? Display your poster for the class.

TECHNOLOGY

Go to the Glencoe Science Web site at **science.glencoe.com** or use the **Glencoe Science CD-ROM** for additional chapter assessment.

Test Practice

Stacey's science teacher gave her nine different mineral samples that are on the Mohs Hardness Scale (see chart below). Her task was to identify each sample using hardness tests.

Mohs Hardness Scale		Approximate Hardness of Common Objects	
Talc	1	Fingernail	(2.5)
Gypsum	2		
Calcite	3	Copper penny	(3.5)
Fluorite	4		
Apatite	5	Iron nail	(4.5)
Feldspar	6		
Quartz	7	Glass	(5.5)
Topaz	8		
Corundum	9	Steel file	(6.5)
Diamond	10	Streak plate	(7.0)

Study the diagram and answer the following questions.

1. One of Stacey's mineral samples can scratch glass but is scratched by a steel file. According to the chart, which mineral is it?

A) calcite   **C)** feldspar
B) apatite   **D)** quartz

2. Which of the following is a method that will distinguish samples of topaz and corundum?

F) scratching both samples with glass
G) scratching both samples with a steel file
H) scratching both samples with a streak plate
J) scratching the samples on each other

Test Practice

The Test-Taking Tip was written by The Princeton Review, the nation's leader in test preparation.

1. C
2. J

Developing Skills

16. The observations include the white color, the glassy luster, and the fact that hardness of the mineral was greater than calcite. The conclusion is that the mineral is quartz.
17. feldspar
18. Answers should include at least the following terms from **Section 2:** hardness, luster, color, streak, cleavage and fracture, magnetism, and reaction to acid
19. 186 mL − 107.5 mL = 78.5 mL = 78.5 cm^3
20. See student page.

Performance Assessment

21. Posters should correctly show the six crystal systems with three examples listed for each one. Be sure students answer the two questions concerning their minerals. Use **Performance Assessment in the Science Classroom,** p. 145.

✓Assessment Resources

 Reproducible Masters
Chapter Resources Booklet
    Chapter Review, pp. 33–34
    Chapter Tests, pp. 35–38
    Assessment Transparency Activity, p. 45

Glencoe Science Web site
    Interactive Tutor
    Chapter Quizzes

Glencoe Technology
    Assessment Transparency
    Interactive CD-ROM Chapter Quizzes
    ExamView Pro Test Bank
    Vocabulary PuzzleMaker Software
    MindJogger Videoquiz DVD/VHS

Section/Objectives	Standards		Activities/Features
	National	**State/Local**	
Chapter Opener	See p. 5T for a Key to Standards.		**Explore Activity:** Determine what rocks are made of, p. 89 **Before You Read,** p. 89
Section 1 The Rock Cycle ⏱ 2 sessions 🎴 1 block 1. **Distinguish** between a rock and a mineral. 2. **Describe** the rock cycle and some changes that a rock could undergo.	National Content Standards: UCP1, UCP3, UCP4, A1, D1		**MiniLAB:** Modeling Rock, p. 91 **Visualizing the Rock Cycle,** p. 92
Section 2 Igneous Rocks ⏱ 2 sessions 🎴 1 block 1. **Recognize** magma and lava as the materials that cool to form igneous rocks. 2. **Contrast** the formation of intrusive and extrusive igneous rocks. 3. **Contrast** granitic and basaltic igneous rocks.	National Content Standards: UCP1, A1, D1		**Chemistry Integration,** p. 97 **Activity:** Igneous Rock Clues, p. 98
Section 3 Metamorphic Rocks ⏱ 2 sessions 🎴 1 block 1. **Describe** the conditions in Earth that cause metamorphic rocks to form. 2. **Classify** metamorphic rocks as foliated or nonfoliated.	National Content Standards: UCP1, A1, D1		**Science Online,** p. 100
Section 4 Sedimentary Rocks ⏱ 3 sessions 🎴 1.5 blocks 1. **Explain** how sedimentary rocks form from sediments. 2. **Classify** sedimentary rocks as detrital, chemical, or organic in origin.	National Content Standards: UCP1, A1, D1, F5		**MiniLAB:** Classifying Sediments, p. 104 **Chemistry Integration,** p. 106 **Math Skills Activity,** p. 108 **Activity:** Sedimentary Rocks pp. 110–111 **Science and Society:** Australia's Controversial Rock, pp. 112–113

NATIONAL GEOGRAPHIC

Teacher's Corner

PRODUCTS AVAILABLE FROM GLENCOE
To order call 1-800-334-7344:
CD-ROM
NGS PictureShow: Geology

Curriculum Kit
GeoKit: Rocks and Minerals
Transparency Set
NGS PicturePack: Rocks and Minerals

Activity Materials	Reproducible Resources	Section Assessment	Technology
Explore Activity: 3–4 different rock fragments	**Chapter Resources Booklet** Foldables Worksheet, p. 13 Directed Reading Overview, p. 15 Note-taking Worksheets, pp. 31–33	GLENCOE'S ASSESSMENT ADVANTAGE	
MiniLAB: white glue (125 mL), sand (62.5 mL), large paper cup	**Chapter Resources Booklet** Transparency Activity, p. 42 MiniLAB, p. 3 Enrichment, p. 27 Reinforcement, p. 23 Directed Reading, p. 16 Lab Activity, pp. 9–10 Transparency Activity, pp. 47–49	**Portfolio** Curriculum Connection, p. 92 **Performance** MiniLAB, p. 91 Skill Builder Activities, p. 93 **Content** Section Assessment, p. 93	♨ Section Focus Transparency ♨ Teaching Transparency ◉ Interactive CD-ROM/DVD ⌒ Guided Reading Audio Program
Activity: rhyolite, basalt, vesicular basalt, pumice, granite, obsidian, gabbro, hand lens	**Chapter Resources Booklet** Transparency Activity, p. 43 Activity Worksheet, pp. 5–6 Enrichment, p. 28 Reinforcement, p. 24 Directed Reading, p. 16 **Reading and Writing Skill Activities, p. 27**	**Portfolio** Chemistry Integration, p. 97 **Performance** Skill Builder Activities, p. 97 **Content** Section Assessment, p. 97	♨ Section Focus Transparency ◉ Interactive CD-ROM/DVD ⌒ Guided Reading Audio Program
Need materials? **Contact Science Kit at 1-800-828-7777 or www.sciencekit.com on the Internet.**	**Chapter Resources Booklet** Transparency Activity, p. 44 Enrichment, p. 29 Reinforcement, p. 25 Directed Reading, p. 17 Lab Activity, pp. 11–12	**Portfolio** Science Journal, p. 101 **Performance** Skill Builder Activities, p. 102 **Content** Section Assessment, p. 102	♨ Section Focus Transparency ◉ Interactive CD-ROM/DVD ⌒ Guided Reading Audio Program
MiniLAB: different samples of sediment, tweezers or a dissecting probe, hand lens **Activity:** unknown sedimentary rock samples, marking pen, 5 % hydrochloric acid (HCl) or vinegar, dropper, paper towels, water, hand lens, metric ruler	**Chapter Resources Booklet** Transparency Activity, p. 45 MiniLAB, p. 4 Enrichment, p. 30 Reinforcement, p. 26 Directed Reading, pp. 17, 18 Activity Worksheet, pp. 7–8 **Lab Management and Safety, p. 70**	**Portfolio** Science Journal, p. 105 **Performance** MiniLAB, p. 104 Skill Builder Activities, p. 109 **Content** Section Assessment, p. 109	♨ Section Focus Transparency ◉ Interactive CD-ROM/DVD ⌒ Guided Reading Audio Program

End of Chapter Assessment

GLENCOE'S ASSESSMENT ADVANTAGE

Blackline Masters	Technology	Professional Series
Chapter Resources Booklet Chapter Review, pp. 35–36 Chapter Tests, pp. 37–40 **Standardized Test Practice by The Princeton Review, pp. 23–26**	▭ MindJogger Videoquiz ◉ CD-ROM Explorations and Quizzes ◉ Vocabulary Puzzle Makers ◉ ExamView Pro Test Bank ◉ Interactive Lesson Planner ◉ Interactive Teacher's Edition	Performance Assessment in the Science Classroom (PASC)

Transparencies

Section Focus

Section 1 Focus Transparency — A Cone Cave Place To Live

Have you ever thought about living in a rock? This is an area in Turkey called Cappadocia. People have carved their homes into the giant rock cones at Cappadocia for at least 2,000 years.

1. What properties of these cones make them useful for carving homes?
2. Do you think the processes that formed the cones continue? Explain.
3. What processes can change rock?

L2

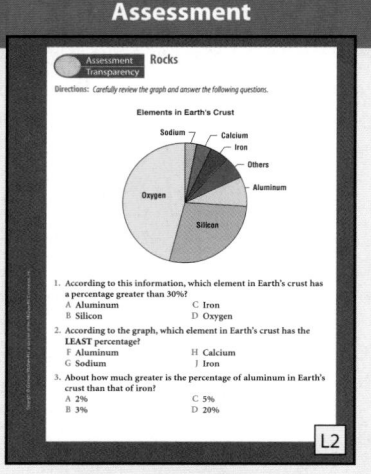

Section 2 Focus Transparency — Bad For Pompeii, Good For Archaeology

The ancient city of Pompeii in Italy was buried by the eruption of Mt. Vesuvius in 79 A.D. The ruins were discovered in the late 1500s, but excavations were not systematized until the Italian archaeologist Guiseppe Fiorelli became director of the site in 1860.

1. How did the volcano preserve the artifacts in Pompeii?
2. Where on the rock cycle do you think most rocks from the excavation of Pompeii belong?

L2

Section 3 Focus Transparency — Pressured to Change

Marble, a highly valued stone used in buildings and art, must be carefully cut from quarries. Marble, however, doesn't start out as marble. It is formed when limestone and mineral deposits come together to form a new substance.

1. What forces beneath the surface of Earth cause limestone and minerals to combine?
2. Marble comes in different colors and with varying internal striations. Why is there so much variation?
3. Why is marble so valued by sculptors?

L2

This is a representation of key blackline masters available in the Teacher Classroom Resources. See Resource Manager boxes within the chapter for additional information.

Key to Teaching Strategies

The following designations will help you decide which activities are appropriate for your students.

L1 Level 1 activities should be appropriate for students with learning difficulties.

L2 Level 2 activities should be within the ability range of all students.

L3 Level 3 activities are designed for above-average students.

ELL ELL activities should be within the ability range of English Language Learners.

COOP LEARN Cooperative Learning activities are designed for small group work.

LS Multiple Learning Styles logos, as described on page 22T, are used throughout to indicate strategies that address different learning styles.

P These strategies represent student products that can be placed into a best-work portfolio.

Assessment

Assessment Transparency — Rocks

Directions: Carefully review the graph and answer the following questions.

Elements in Earth's Crust

(pie chart: Sodium, Calcium, Iron, Others, Aluminum, Silicon, Oxygen)

1. According to this information, which element in Earth's crust has a percentage greater than 30%?
   A Aluminum   C Iron
   B Silicon   D Oxygen
2. According to the graph, which element in Earth's crust has the LEAST percentage?
   F Aluminum   H Calcium
   G Sodium   J Iron
3. About how much greater is the percentage of aluminum in Earth's crust than that of iron?
   A 2%   C 5%
   B 3%   D 20%

L2

Teaching

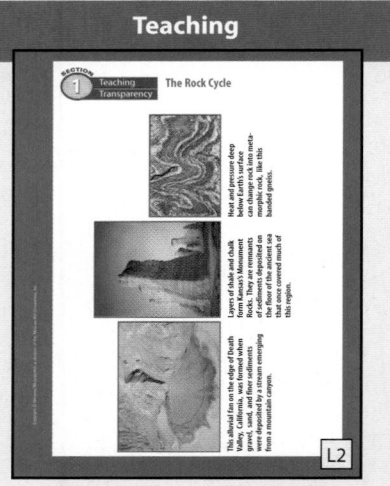

Section 1 Teaching Transparency — The Rock Cycle

L2

Hands-on Activities

Activity Worksheets

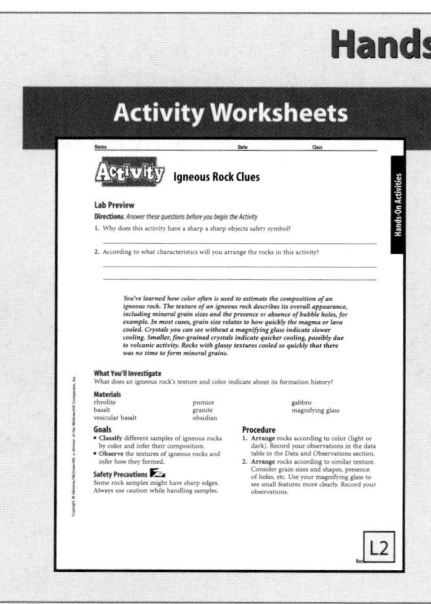

Activity — Igneous Rock Clues

Lab Preview
Directions: Answer these questions before you begin the Activity.
1. Why does this activity have a sharp objects safety symbol?

2. According to what characteristics will you arrange the rocks in this activity?

You've learned how color often is used to estimate the composition of an igneous rock. The texture of an igneous rock describes its overall appearance, including mineral grain sizes and the presence or absence of bubble holes, for example. In most cases, grain size relates to how quickly the magma or lava cooled. Crystals you can see without a magnifying glass indicate slower cooling. Smaller, fine-grained crystals indicate quicker cooling, possibly due to volcanic activity. Rocks with glassy textures cooled so quickly that there was no time to form mineral grains.

What You'll Investigate
What does an igneous rock's texture and color indicate about its formation history?

Materials
rhyolite   pumice   gabbro
basalt   granite   magnifying glass
vesicular basalt   obsidian

Goals
• Classify different samples of igneous rocks by color and infer their composition.
• Observe the textures of igneous rocks and infer how they formed.

Safety Precautions
Some rock samples might have sharp edges. Always use caution while handling samples.

Procedure
1. Arrange rocks according to color (light or dark). Record your observations in the data table in the Data and Observations section.
2. Arrange rocks according to similar texture. Consider grain size and shapes, presence of holes, etc. Use your magnifying glass to see small features more clearly. Record your observations.

L2

Laboratory Activities

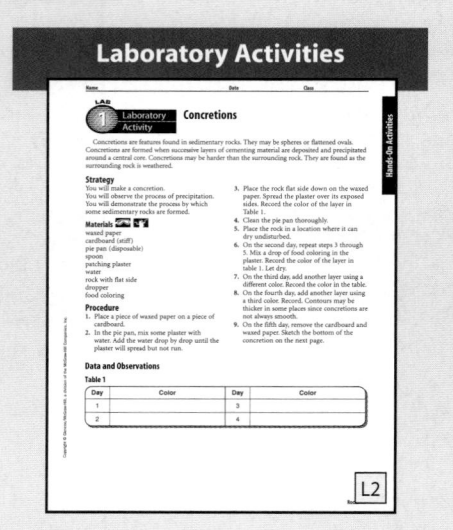

Laboratory Activity 1 — Concretions

Concretions are features found in sedimentary rocks. They may be spheres or flattened ovals. Concretions are formed when successive layers of cementing materials are deposited and precipitated around a central core. Concretions may be harder than the surrounding rock. They are found as the surrounding rock is weathered.

Strategy
You will make a concretion.
You will observe the process of precipitation.
You will demonstrate the process by which some sedimentary rocks are formed.

Materials
waxed paper
cardboard (stiff)
pie pan (disposable)
spoon
patching plaster
water
rock with flat side
dropper
food coloring

Procedure
1. Place a piece of waxed paper on a piece of cardboard.
2. In the pie pan, mix some plaster with water. Add the water drop by drop until the plaster will spread but not run.

3. Place the rock flat side down on the waxed paper. Spread the plaster over its exposed sides. Record the color of the layer in Table 1.
4. Clean the pie pan thoroughly.
5. Place the rock in a location where it can dry undisturbed.
6. On the second day, repeat steps 3 through 5. Mix a drop of food coloring in the plaster. Record the color of the layer in table 1. Let dry.
7. On the third day, add another layer using a different color. Record the color in the table.
8. On the fourth day, add another layer using a third color. Record. Contours may be thicker in some places since concretions are not always smooth.
9. On the fifth day, remove the cardboard and waxed paper. Sketch the bottom of the concretion on the next page.

Data and Observations
Table 1

Day	Color	Day	Color
1		3	
2		4	

L2

RESOURCE MANAGER

Meeting Different Ability Levels

Content Outline

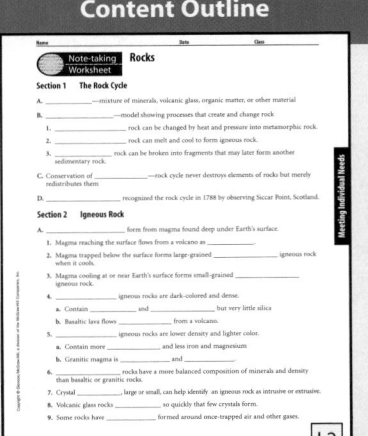

Reinforcement

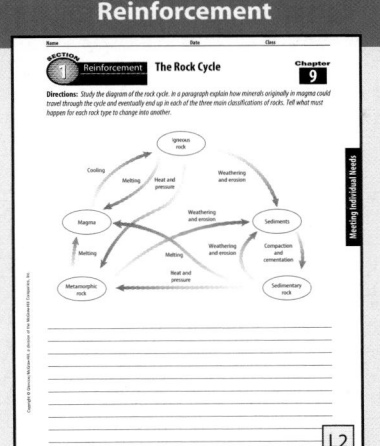

Directed Reading

Assessment

Chapter Tests

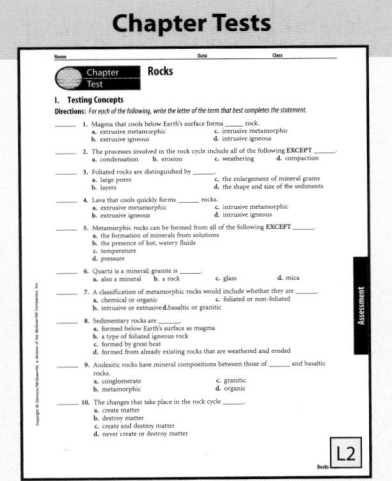

Enrichment

Spanish Directed Reading

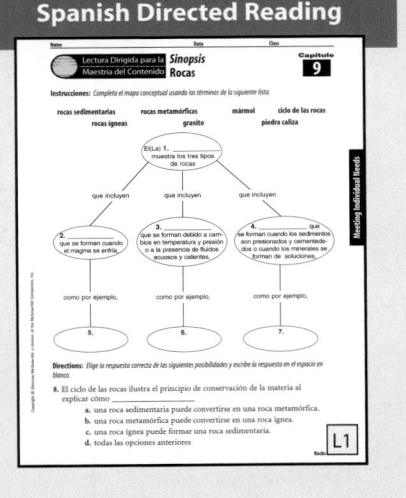

Test Practice Workbook

Chapter Review

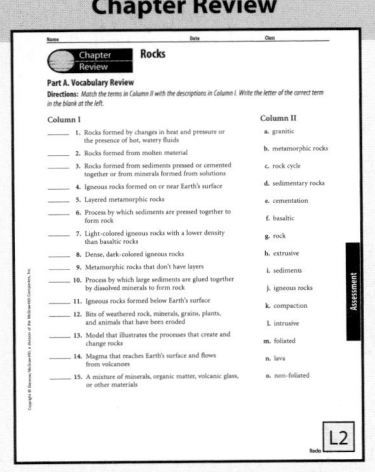

Science Content Background

SECTION 1

The Rock Cycle

Many Paths

There is no set path through the rock cycle. A rock from any of the three groups of rocks can be changed into a rock belonging to another group, or it can be changed into a rock belonging to its original group. A study of the rock cycle reveals the relationships among the three groups of rocks.

SECTION 2

Igneous Rocks

Texture and Grain Size

The size and arrangement of mineral grains determine igneous rock textures. Some rocks are coarse grained, and individual grains can be seen with the unaided eye. Other rocks are fine grained, and individual minerals are not visible with the unaided eye. In rocks with glassy textures, few or no mineral crystals are visible. The sizes of mineral grains in an igneous rock are determined by cooling rates. The faster the magma or lava cooled during an igneous rock's formation, the smaller the grain size is.

Magma

As magma cools, different minerals will crystallize at different temperatures. This relationship is known as Bowen's reaction series. The first silicate minerals to crystallize from magma are lower in silica and higher in iron and magnesium. As crystallization progresses, minerals higher in silica and lower in iron and magnesium form.

Fun Fact

Sedimentary rocks start to form at a depth of 1–3 km, metamorphic rocks form at a depth of 10–30 km, and magma forms at a depth greater than 30 km.

D. Cavagnaro/DRK Photo

Olivine is one of the first minerals to crystallize. Next, pyroxenes such as augite form, which have a different composition and structure. This reaction continues through amphiboles such as hornblende and boitite mica. One of the last minerals to crystallize is potassium feldspar. Quartz (SiO_2) crystallizes when most of the remaining melt consists of silicon and oxygen.

This continuous evolution of minerals produces igneous rocks of different composition, from ultramafic through mafic (basaltic) and intermediate (andesitic) to felsic (granitic).

SECTION 3 Metamorphic Rocks

How Rocks Change

The overall chemical compositions of metamorphic rocks can be similar to the compositions of the rocks from which they form. However, new minerals may form in response to changes in temperature, pressure, and fluid activity.

Fun Fact

Hexagonal diamonds sometimes found in meteorites are formed directly from graphite at the moment of impact. The high temperatures and pressures of about 1,056,000 kg/cm² needed to form these diamonds occur for a few millionths of a second upon impact.

Heat, Pressure, and Fluids

Changes in temperature, pressure, and fluids can have several causes. One common cause is mountain building. Processes of mountain building cause metamorphism of rock over a large area. This type of metamorphism, called regional metamorphism, is responsible for producing large amounts of metamorphic rock. Another type of metamorphism, called contact metamorphism, occurs when magma comes in contact with surrounding rocks. A zone of metamorphic rock called an aureole forms around the magma. No melting occurs to form this metamorphic aureole, but fluids from the magma do pass into and react with the surrounding rock.

SECTION 4 Sedimentary Rocks

Formation

Understanding the processes by which sedimentary rocks form allows one to discern the history of the rock: the source of the sediment, the means by which the sediment was transported, and the environment that existed where the sediment was deposited.

Sedimentary rocks form under two main sets of conditions. These are referred to as environments of deposition and are either marine (in the sea) or terrestrial (on continents). Rocks that form in a shore zone are considered to form under conditions that are transitional between the marine and terrestrial environments.

Sedimentary Rock Layers

Three of the most important principles used by geologists to interpret sedimentary rock layers were formulated by Nicholas Steno in 1669 and are referred to as Steno's principles. The principle of superposition states that the oldest rock layers lie at the bottom of an undisturbed sequence of sedimentary rock. The principle of original horizontality states that sedimentary rock layers must have been disturbed after they were deposited. The principle of original lateral continuity states that sedimentary rock layers originally extended until they thinned to zero thickness or butted into the edge of the area in which they were deposited. This last principle allow geologists to conclude that a rock layer now cut by a canyon was once continuous across it.

SCIENCE Online

For additional content background on this topic, go to the Glencoe Science Web site at **science.glencoe.com**.

Rocks

Chapter Vocabulary

rock
rock cycle
igneous rock
lava
intrusive
extrusive
basaltic
granitic
metamorphic rock
foliated
nonfoliated
sediment
sedimentary rock
compaction
cementation

What do you think?

Science Journal The rock shown is a form of limestone called chalk. Chalk is composed largely of the remains of once-living marine organisms that were deposited on the ocean bottom millions of years ago.

Rocks

Have you ever seen a rock and wondered where it might have come from or how old it is? Whether it is a small pebble found by the side of the road or a mountain of solid rock, every rock is like a history book that tells how and where it was formed. In this chapter, you will learn about how rocks form. You'll learn about the three different groups of rocks—igneous, sedimentary, and metamorphic. You also will learn about the cycle that describes how rocks change from one type to another.

What do you think?

Science Journal Look at the picture below with a classmate. Discuss what you think this might be. Here's a hint: *Your teacher sometimes uses this to announce an assignment.* Write your answer or best guess in your Science Journal.

88

Theme Connection

Systems and Interactions The interactions of heat and pressure inside Earth and weathering and erosion on its surface cause rocks to undergo changes through a process known as the rock cycle.

El Capitan rises straight up from the valley floor in Yosemite National Park, California. The hard rock that attracts rock climbers and sightseers from around the world is made of small mineral grains that lock together like pieces of a puzzle. Other rocks form from grains of sand tightly held together or from lava flowing from a volcano. If you examine rocks closely, you sometimes can tell what they are made of.

Safety Precautions 🧤 🥽 🧪

Determine what rocks are made of

1. Collect three or four different rock fragments near your home or school.

2. Draw a picture of the details you see in each rock.

3. Look for different types of materials within the same rock. If these different materials could be separated by physical means, then the rock would be considered a mixture.

Observe

Describe the characteristics of each rock. Are your rocks mixtures? If so, what might these mixtures contain? Write your observations in your Science Journal.

Before You Read

Making an Organizational Study Fold **Make the following Foldable to help you organize your thoughts into clear categories about types of rock.**

1. Stack two sheets of paper in front of you so the short side of both sheets is at the top.

2. Slide the top sheet up so about four centimeters of the bottom sheet show.

3. Fold both sheets top to bottom to form four tabs and staple along the topfold as shown.

4. Title the top flap *Three Types of Rocks.* Label each flap *Igneous, Metamorphic,* and *Sedimentary*.

5. As you read the chapter, record what you learn about the three types of rocks on the flaps.

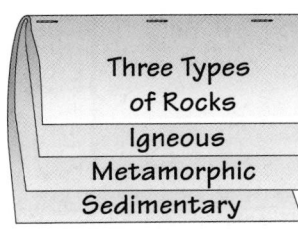

Purpose Use the Explore Activity to introduce students to the composition of different rocks. L2 ELL COOP LEARN **Visual-Spatial**

Preparation Have each student bring in several rocks.

Materials hand lens, rocks

Teaching Strategy Have each group appoint one student to report the group's observations to the rest of the class.

Observe

Students might notice what looks like grains of materials of different colors or textures that are part of the rock. Rocks are mixtures of minerals, rock fragments, glass and organic matter. These materials are present in a wide variety of proportions in natural samples.

✓*Assessment*

Performance Have groups exchange rocks and repeat the activity. Have them compare and contrast observations. Use **Performance Assessment in the Science Classroom,** p. 89.

FOLDABLES
Reading & Study Skills

Before You Read

Dinah Zike Study Fold

Purpose Use this activity to determine what students know about the three types of rocks before they read the chapter. Have students make a Foldable for recording and organizing notes on igneous, metamorphic, and sedimentary rocks.

📁 For additional help, see Foldables Worksheet, p. 13 in **Chapter Resources Booklet,** or go to the Glencoe Science Web site at **science.glencoe.com.** See After You Read in the Study Guide at the end of this chapter.

① Motivate

Bellringer Transparency

Display the Section Focus Transparency for Section 1. Use the accompanying Transparency Activity Master. L2
ELL

Tie to Prior Knowledge

Ask students to recall rocks they have seen. **Do all rocks look the same?** no **What differences can you recall?** Possible answers: color, texture, density, luster, or shininess Tell students that the way rocks form dictates their composition and the way they look. Let students know that they will find out in this section how rocks form and change.

The Rock Cycle

As You Read

***What* You'll Learn**

- **Distinguish** between a rock and a mineral.
- **Describe** the rock cycle and some changes that a rock could undergo.

Vocabulary
rock
rock cycle

***Why* It's Important**
Rocks are everywhere around you—near your school, your home, and even in the sidewalks you walk on.

What is a rock?

Imagine it's the top of the sixth inning. With the sweltering Sun at your back, you scrape your shoe along the infield, waiting for the pitch. Among all the sand and dull-looking, gray stones, your eye catches a glint from a piece of rock that has shiny crystals in it. You quickly snatch it up and put it in your pocket for further examination after the game.

Common Rocks The next time you walk past a large building or monument, stop and take a close look at it. Chances are that it is made out of common rock. In fact, most rock used for building stone contains one or more common minerals, called rock-forming minerals, such as quartz, feldspar, mica, or calcite. When you look closely, the sparkles you see are individual crystals of minerals. A **rock** is a mixture of such minerals, volcanic glass, organic matter, or other materials. **Figure 1** shows minerals mixed together to form the rock granite. You might even find granite on your baseball field.

feldspar

quartz

mica

hornblende

Figure 1
Mount Rushmore, in South Dakota, is made of granite. Granite is a mixture of feldspar, quartz, mica, hornblende, and other minerals.

Section ✓ *Assessment* Planner

PORTFOLIO Curriculum Connection, p. 92 **PERFORMANCE ASSESSMENT** Try at Home MiniLAB, p. 91 Skill Builder Activities, p. 93 See page 116 for more options.	**CONTENT ASSESSMENT** Section, p. 93 Challenge, p. 93 Chapter, pp. 116–117

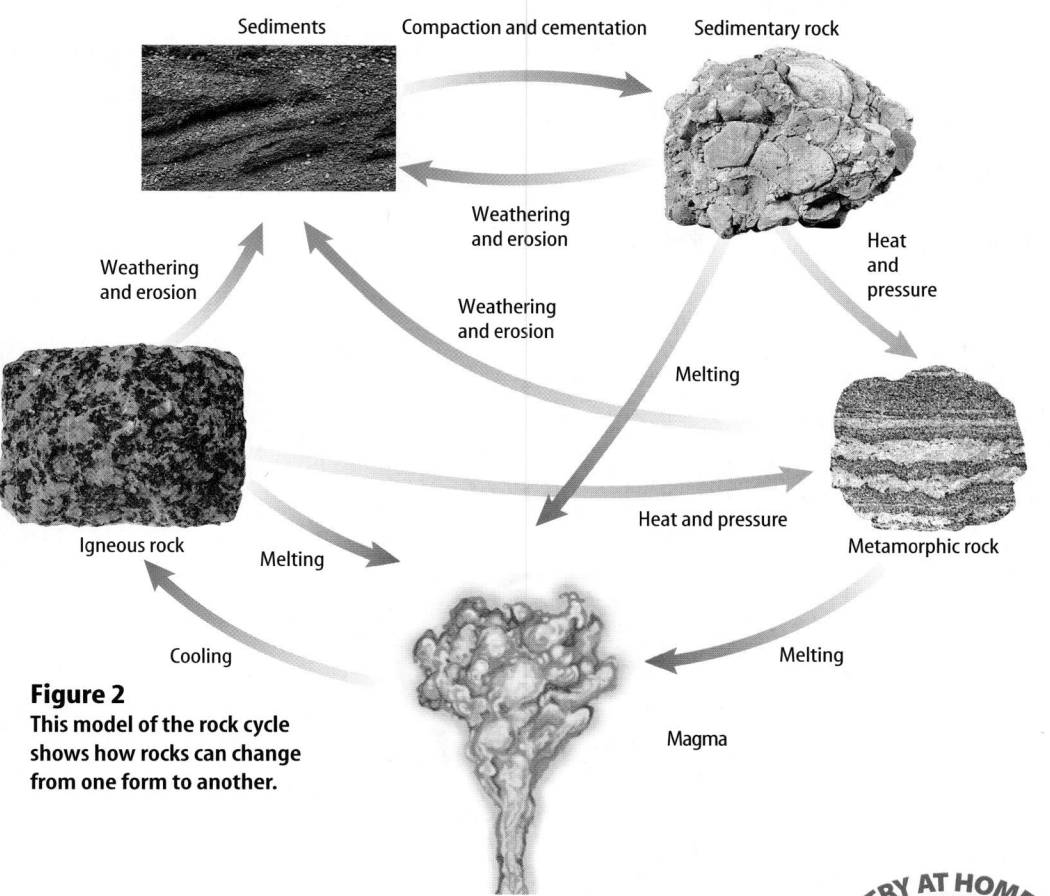

Sediments — Compaction and cementation — Sedimentary rock

Weathering and erosion

Weathering and erosion

Weathering and erosion

Weathering and erosion

Heat and pressure

Melting

Heat and pressure

Metamorphic rock

Igneous rock

Melting

Melting

Cooling

Melting

Magma

Figure 2
This model of the rock cycle shows how rocks can change from one form to another.

The Rock Cycle To show how rocks slowly change through time, scientists have created a model called the **rock cycle,** shown in **Figure 2.** It illustrates the processes that create and change rocks. The rock cycle shows the three types of rock—igneous, metamorphic, and sedimentary—and the processes that form them. Look at the rock cycle and notice that rocks change by many processes. For example, a sedimentary rock can change by heat and pressure to form a metamorphic rock. The metamorphic rock then can melt and later cool to form an igneous rock. The igneous rock then could be broken into fragments by weathering and erode away. The fragments might later compact and cement together to form another sedimentary rock. Any given rock can change into any of the three major rock types. A rock even can transform into another rock of the same type. How many paths can you see through the rock cycle?

 **Reading Check**   *What is illustrated by the rock cycle?*

TRY AT HOME
Mini LAB

Modeling Rock
Procedure 👓 🧤
1. Mix 125 mL of **white glue** with 62.5 mL of **sand** in a **large paper cup.**
2. Stir the mixture and then allow it to harden overnight.
3. Tear away the paper cup carefully from your mixture.

Analysis
1. Which rock type is similar to your hardened mixture?
2. Which part of the rock cycle did you model?

What is a rock?

Visual Learning

Figure 2 What are the processes by which rocks can change from one form to another? melting, cooling, weathering and erosion, compaction and cementation, and heat and pressure

TRY AT HOME
Mini LAB

Purpose Students will create sedimentary rock. L2 ELL
IS Kinesthetic
Materials glue, sand, water, paper cups
Teaching Strategy Explain to students that sedimentary rock form under natural circumstances requires millions of years.
Analysis
1. Sedimentary rock.
2. The compacting and cementing of rock fragments into sedimentary rock.

✓Assessment

Process Ask students to model sedimentary rock using a variety of different materials such as gravel, ground up shells, and different colored sand. Make a display of student rock models in the classroom. Use **Performance Assessment in the Science Classroom,** p. 123.

Resource Manager

Chapter Resources Booklet
  Transparency Activity, p. 42
  Directed Reading for Content Mastery, pp. 15, 16
  MiniLAB, p. 3
  Lab Activity, pp. 9–10

Inclusion Strategies

Learning Disabled Place large, labeled samples of basalt, granite, gneiss, slate, shale, sandstone, and limestone in a science center. Ask students in groups of three to study the samples and to take turns selecting a rock and telling its type and the processes that formed it. L1 COOP LEARN
IS Logical-Mathematical and Naturalist

✓ **Reading Check**

Answer the three types of rocks, how they form, and the processes that change one type into another

Visualizing the Rock Cycle

Have students examine the pictures and read the captions. Then ask the following questions.

What are some possible ways the black beach sand could become rock? It could be compacted and cemented to become sedimentary rock; it could be melted and cooled to once again form igneous rock.

What processes formed Kansas's Monument Rocks? Layers of sediments that formed on the ancient sea floor were compacted and/or cemented to form the sedimentary rocks.

Activity

Assign small groups a rock structure, such Garden of the Gods in Colorado, the Palisades in New York, the White Cliffs of Dover in England, the Cathedral Spires of South Dakota's Black Hills, or Devil's Postpile in California. Ask each group to prepare a travel brochure that shows a map of the feature's location and a description of how it was formed. L2 ELL
L̄S̄ Visual-Spatial and Linguistic

Extension

Ask students to imagine they are going to build a house that uses three different rocks. Have them write a paragraph describing which rocks they would use, where they would use them, and why they chose the rocks they did for those purposes. L2
L̄S̄ Linguistic and Logical-Mathematical

NATIONAL GEOGRAPHIC VISUALIZING THE ROCK CYCLE

Figure 3

Rocks continuously form and transform in a process that geologists call the rock cycle. For example, molten rock—from volcanoes such as Washington's Mount Rainier, background—cools and solidifies to form igneous rock. It slowly breaks down when exposed to air and water to form sediments. These sediments are compacted or cemented into sedimentary rock. Heat and pressure might transform sedimentary rock into metamorphic rock. When metamorphic rock melts and hardens, igneous rock forms again. There is no distinct beginning, nor is there an end, to the rock cycle.

▲ The black sand beach of this Polynesian island is sediment weathered and eroded from the igneous rock of a volcano nearby.

▲ This alluvial fan on the edge of Death Valley, California, was formed when gravel, sand, and finer sediments were deposited by a stream emerging from a mountain canyon.

▲ Layers of shale and chalk form Kansas's Monument Rocks. They are remnants of sediments deposited on the floor of the ancient sea that once covered much of this region.

▲ Heat and pressure deep below Earth's surface can change rock into metamorphic rock, like this banded gneiss.

92 CHAPTER 4

Resource Manager

Chapter Resources Booklet

Enrichment, p. 27

Reinforcement, p. 23

Transparency Activity, pp. 47–49

Note-taking Worksheets, pp. 31–33

Curriculum Connection

Language Arts The word igneous comes from the Latin word *ignis*, which means "fire." Ask students to write a paragraph describing where the words *metamorphic* and *sedimentary* come from. *Metamorphic,* which means "change of form," comes from the Greet roots *meta,* meaning "after" and *morphe,* meaning "form." *Sedimentary* comes from the word "sediment." L2 P

Matter and the Rock Cycle The rock cycle, illustrated in **Figure 3,** shows how rock can be weathered to small rock and mineral grains. This material then can be eroded and carried away by wind, water, or ice. When you think of erosion, it might seem that the material is somehow destroyed and lost from the cycle, but this is not the case. The chemical elements that make up minerals and rocks are not destroyed. This fact illustrates the principle of conservation of matter. The changes that take place in the rock cycle never destroy or create matter. The elements are just redistributed in other forms.

Figure 4
The rock formations at Siccar Point, Scotland show that rocks undergo constant change.

Reading Check *What is the principle of conservation of matter?*

Discovering the Rock Cycle James Hutton, a Scottish physician and naturalist, first recognized in 1788 that rocks undergo profound changes. Hutton noticed, among other things, that some layers of solid rock in Siccar Point, shown in **Figure 4,** had been altered since they formed. Instead of showing a continuous pattern of horizontal layering, some of the rock layers at Siccar Point are tilted and partly eroded. However, the younger rocks above them are nearly horizontal.

Hutton published these and other observations, which proved that rocks are subject to constant change. Hutton's early recognition of the rock cycle continues to influence geologists—even after over 200 years have passed.

Section 1 Assessment

1. What materials are rocks made of?
2. What are the three basic types of rock?
3. Describe the major processes of the rock cycle.
4. Describe one way that the rock cycle can illustrate the principle of conservation of matter.
5. **Think Critically** Look at the model of the rock cycle. How would you define magma based on the illustration in **Figure 2?** How would you define sediment and sedimentary rock?

Skill Builder Activities

6. **Concept Mapping** Using a computer, make a concept map explaining how igneous rocks can become sedimentary, then metamorphic, and finally, other igneous rocks. **For more help, refer to the** Science Skill Handbook.

7. **Communicating** Review the model of the rock cycle in **Figure 2.** In your Science Journal, write a story or poem that explains what can happen to a sedimentary rock as it changes through the rock cycle. **For more help, refer to the** Science Skill Handbook.

SECTION 1 The Rock Cycle **93**

What is a rock?
continued

Teacher FYI
The rock cycle did not happen to form the rocks that exist today and then stop. It is always occurring as various processes in different parts of the crust on Earth's surface.

Reading Check

Answer Matter is neither created nor destroyed.

③ Assess

Reteach
Demonstrate that rocks are mixtures by showing a sample of granite. Point out to students that granite is a mixture of the minerals feldspar, quartz, hornblende, and mica. L1

Challenge
Have students write a list of possible paths that a crystal in granite bedrock might take through the rock cycle. L2
IS Interpersonal

Assessment

Content Have students research the word *cycle* and then write a short paragraph explaining why the rock cycle is truly a cycle. Use **Performance Assessment in the Science Classroom,** p. 159.

Answers to Section Assessment

1. minerals, rock fragments, volcanic glass, organic matter, and other materials
2. igneous, metamorphic, sedimentary
3. Weathering and erosion break down rock; erosion and deposition transport and deposit the sediment, which is compacted and cemented into new rock; pressure and heat inside Earth change rock from one form to another. Formation of magma from preexisting rock solidifies to form igneous rock.
4. The changes never destroy or create matter. For example, weathering and erosion of existing rock produces sediment that is deposited to form new rock. Accept any reasonable answers.
5. Magma is melted rock material. Sediments are eroded rock fragments. Sedimentary rock is formed from compacted and cemented sediment.
6. Concept map should resemble **Figure 2.**
7. Stories or poems can include any reasonable pathways through the rock cycle, as long as the processes forming the new rock are logical.

Section 1 The Rock Cycle **93**

SECTION

2

Igneous Rocks

Igneous Rocks

1 Motivate

Bellringer Transparency

Display the Section Focus Transparency for Section 2. Use the accompanying Transparency Activity Master. L2 ELL

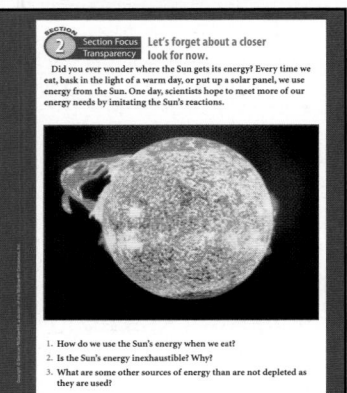

Tie to Prior Knowledge

Have students recall a volcanic eruption they've seen in person or on television. **What comes out of erupting volcanoes?** lava, ash, rock, steam **Describe lava.** They might describe it as soft material that flows out of a volcano. Inform students that lava is the basic ingredient for a certain type of rock and that in this section they will learn how lava becomes rock.

As You Read

What You'll Learn

- **Recognize** magma and lava as the materials that cool to form igneous rocks.
- **Contrast** the formation of intrusive and extrusive igneous rocks.
- **Contrast** granitic and basaltic igneous rocks.

Vocabulary

igneous rock   extrusive
lava   basaltic
intrusive   granitic

Why It's Important

Igneous rocks are the most abundant kind of rock in Earth's crust. They contain many valuable resources.

Figure 5
Some lava is fluid and free-flowing, as shown by this spectacular lava fall in Volcano National Park, East Rift, Kilauea, Hawaii.

Formation of Igneous Rocks

Perhaps you've heard of recent volcanic eruptions in the news. When some volcanoes erupt, they eject a flow of molten rock material, as shown in **Figure 5.** Molten rock material, called magma, flows when it is hot and becomes solid when it cools. When hot magma cools and hardens, it forms **igneous** (IHG nee us) **rocks.** Why do volcanoes erupt, and where does the molten material come from?

Magma In certain places within Earth, the temperature and pressure are just right to melt rocks and form magma. Most magmas come from deep below Earth's surface. Magma is located at depths ranging from near the surface to about 150 km below the surface. Temperatures of magmas range from about 650°C to 1,200°C, depending on their chemical compositions and pressures exerted on them.

The heat that melts rocks comes from sources within Earth's interior. One source is the decay of radioactive elements within Earth. Some heat is left over from the formation of the planet which originally was molten. Radioactive decay of elements contained in rocks balances some heat loss as Earth continues to cool.

Because magma is less dense than surrounding solid rock, it rises toward the surface, as shown in **Figure 6.** When magma reaches Earth's surface and flows from volcanoes, it is called **lava.**

Section ✓ *Assessment* Planner

PORTFOLIO
Chemistry Integration, p. 97
PERFORMANCE ASSESSMENT
Skill Builder Activities, p. 97
See page 116 for more options.

CONTENT ASSESSMENT
Section, p. 97
Challenge, p. 97
Chapter, pp. 116–117

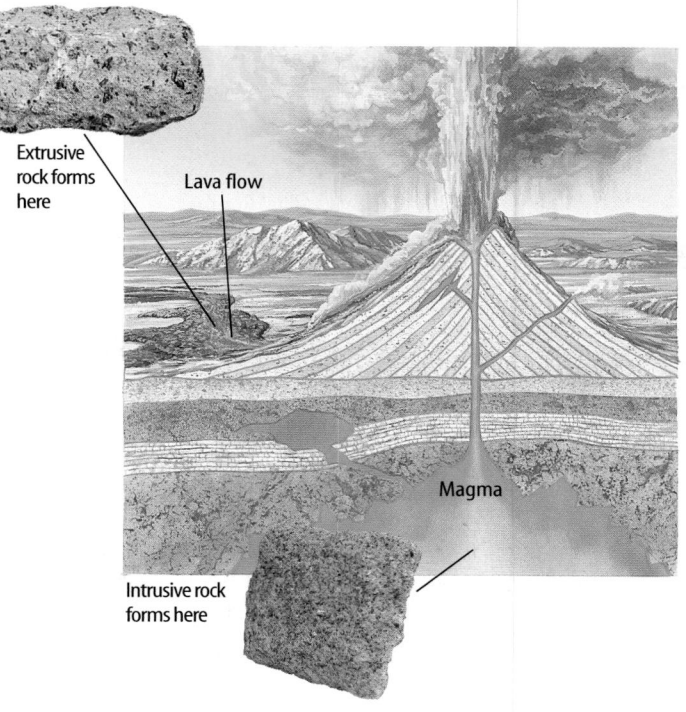

Extrusive rock forms here

Lava flow

Intrusive rock forms here

Figure 6
Intrusive rocks form from magma trapped below Earth's surface. Extrusive rocks form from lava flowing at or near the surface.

Magma

Intrusive Rocks Magma is made up of atoms and molecules of melted minerals. As magma cools, the atoms and molecules rearrange themselves into new crystals called mineral grains. Rocks form as these mineral grains grow together. Rocks that form from magma below the surface illustrated in **Figure 6,** are called **intrusive** igneous rocks. Intrusive rocks are found at the surface only after the layers of rock and soil that once covered them have been removed by erosion. Erosion occurs when the rocks are pushed up by forces within Earth. Because intrusive rocks form at depth and they are surrounded by other rocks, it takes a long time for them to cool. Slowly-cooled magma produces individual mineral grains that are large enough to be observed with the unaided eye.

Extrusive Rocks **Extrusive** igneous rocks are formed as lava cools on or near the surface of Earth. When lava flows on the surface, as illustrated in **Figure 6,** it is exposed to air and moisture. Lava, such as the basaltic lava shown in **Figure 5,** cools quickly under these conditions. The quick cooling rate keeps mineral grains from growing large, because the atoms and molecules don't have the time to arrange into large crystals. Therefore, extrusive igneous rocks are fine grained.

✔️ **Reading Check** *What controls the grain size of an igneous rock?*

Field GUIDE

Are there any igneous rocks used as building stones in your area? To find out more about rocks used in construction, see the **Building Stones Field Guide** at the back of the book.

SECTION 2 Igneous Rocks **95**

Science Journal

Floating Rocks Have students determine why pumice floats on water and scoria does not. Ask them to write a short explanation in their Science Journals. Pumice floats because of its composition of lighter elements and gases that were trapped in the lava as it cooled. Scoria forms from basaltic lava, which contains heavier elements that make it more dense. [L2] [IS] **Naturalist and Linguistic**

②Teach

Formation of Igneous Rocks

Visual Learning

Figure 6 Ask students to contrast the size of the grains in the intrusive and extrusive rocks shown here. Students should notice that the intrusive rocks have larger grains.

Use Science Words

Word Origin Have students use dictionaries to compare the origins of the words *intrusive* and *extrusive* with the origins of *interior* and *exterior*. [L2] [IS] **Linguistic**

Fun Fact

Pumice is an extrusive igneous rock that forms as bubble-filled, frothy lava cools and hardens. Because it is filled with holes, pumice is very light—so light that it floats.

✔️ **Reading Check**

Answer the rate at which magma or lava cools

Section 2 Igneous Rocks **95**

Formation of Igneous Rocks, continued

Extension

Invite interested students to collect rocks from various parts of your community and then use a rock and mineral guide to identify any igneous rocks they find among them. Have students label the rocks and display them in class. Invite other students to do the same with sedimentary and metamorphic rocks in upcoming sections. L2 ELL COOP LEARN IS **Visual-Spatial and Naturalist**

Classifying Igneous Rocks

✔ Reading Check

Answer whether they form above or below the ground, and the type of magma from which they form

SCIENCE *Online*
Internet Addresses

_____

_____

_____

Explore the Glencoe Science Web site at **science.glencoe.com** to find out more about topics in this section.

Table 1 Common Igneous Rocks

Magma Type	Basaltic		Andesitic	Granitic		
Intrusive	Gabbro		Diorite	Granite		
Extrusive	Basalt	Scoria	Andesite	Rhyolite	Pumice	Obsidian

SCIENCE *Online*

Research Visit the Glencoe Science Web site at **science.glencoe.com** for more information about intrusive and extrusive rocks. Summarize new information you learn in your Science Journal

Volcanic Glass Pumice, obsidian, and scoria are examples of volcanic glass. These rocks cooled so quickly that few or no visible mineral grains formed. Most of the atoms in these rocks are not arranged in orderly patterns, and few crystals are present.

In the case of pumice and scoria, air and other gases become trapped in the gooey molten material as it cools. These gases eventually escape, but holes are left behind where the rock formed around the pockets of gas.

Classifying Igneous Rocks

Igneous rocks are intrusive or extrusive depending on how they are formed. A way to further classify these rocks is by the magma from which they form. As shown in **Table 1,** an igneous rock can form from basaltic, andesitic, or granitic magma. The type of magma that cools to form an igneous rock determines important chemical and physical properties of that rock. These include mineral composition, density, color, and melting temperature.

✔ Reading Check   *Name two ways igneous rocks are classified.*

✔ Active Reading

Buddy Interviews Have students interview one another to find out what helps them to understand what they are reading, how they find answers, and how they assimilate new vocabulary terms. Have students use Buddy Interviews to help them master the differences among igneous rocks.

Resource Manager

Chapter Resources Booklet
　Directed Reading for Content Mastery, p. 16
　Reinforcement, p. 24
Reading and Writing Skill Activities, p. 27

Basaltic Rocks **Basaltic** (buh SAWL tihk) igneous rocks are dense, dark-colored rocks. They form from magma that is rich in iron and magnesium and poor in silica, which is the compound SiO_2. The presence of iron and magnesium in minerals in basalt gives basalt its dark color. Basaltic lava is fluid and flows freely from volcanoes in Hawaii, such as Kilauea. How does this explain the black beach sand common in Hawaii?

Granitic Rocks **Granitic** igneous rocks are light-colored rocks of a lower density than basaltic rocks. Granitic magma is thick and stiff and contains lots of silica but lesser amounts of iron and magnesium. Because granitic magma is stiff, it can build up a great deal of gas pressure, which is released explosively during violent volcanic eruptions.

Andesitic Rocks **Andesitic** igneous rocks have mineral compositions between those of granitic and basaltic rocks. Many volcanoes around the rim of the Pacific Ocean formed from intermediate magma compositions. Like volcanoes formed from granitic magma, these volcanoes also can erupt violently.

Take another look at **Table 1.** Basalt forms at or near the surface of Earth because it is an extrusive rock. Granite forms below Earth's surface from magma with a high concentration of silica. When you identify an igneous rock, you can infer how it formed and the type of magma that it formed from.

Chemistry
INTEGRATION

As heat increases inside Earth, materials contained in rocks begin to melt. In your Science Journal, describe what is happening to the atoms and molecules to cause this change of state.

Section ② Assessment

1. Why do some types of magma form igneous rocks that are dark colored and dense?

2. How do intrusive and extrusive igneous rocks differ?

3. What property of magma causes it to rise toward Earth's surface?

4. The texture of obsidian is best described as glassy. Why does obsidian contain few or no mineral grains?

5. **Think Critically** Study the photographs of granite and rhyolite in **Table 1.** How are granite and rhyolite similar? How are these rocks different?

Skill Builder Activities

6. **Interpreting Scientific Illustrations** Suppose you are given a photograph of two igneous rocks. You are told one is an intrusive rock and one is extrusive. How could you tell which is which? **For more help, refer to the** Science Skill Handbook.

7. **Making and Using Graphs** Four elements make up most of the rocks in Earth's crust. They are: *oxygen—46.6 percent, aluminum—8.1 percent, silicon—27.7 percent,* and *iron—5.0 percent.* Make a graph of these data. What might you infer from the low amount of iron? **For more help, refer to the** Science Skill Handbook.

Classifying Igneous Rocks, continued

Chemistry
INTEGRATION

As thermal energy increases, atoms move faster, and the material changes from solid to liquid.

③ Assess

Reteach

Ask students to make a concept map that shows basaltic, andesitic, and granitic magmas and the rocks that form from them. L2 [IS] **Visual-Spatial**

Challenge

Have students compare granitic and basaltic rocks of similar size. Have one student close his or her eyes while another student places the rocks in the first student's hands. Have students hypothesize which rocks are basaltic and which are granitic based on the heft of the rock. L2 [IS] **Kinesthetic**

Oral Have students write questions on the material in the section and then take turns quizzing each other aloud. Use **Performance Assessment in the Science Classroom,** p. 91.

Answers to Section Assessment

1. The magma or lava is rich in iron and magnesium, which are contained in relatively dark and dense minerals.
2. intrusive—form under the surface and have relatively large mineral grains; extrusive—form above the surface and have smaller mineral grains
3. Magma is less dense than surrounding rocks and is forced upward.
4. Obsidian solidifies so quickly that there is no time for mineral grains to form.
5. Granite and rhyolite both are granitic igneous rocks composed of the same minerals. Granite is intrusive and rhyolite is extrusive.
6. Texture is used to help classify igneous rocks. Intrusive rocks have large mineral grains; extrusive rocks are fine-grained.
7. Students' bar graphs should be drawn to scale and properly labeled. On average, crustal rocks contain a fairly low concentration of iron as compared to oxygen, silicon, and aluminum.

Activity

Purpose Students observe the texture and color of igneous rocks to determine how they formed. L2 ELL LS **Kinesthetic**

Process Skills observing, classifying, recording data, making and using tables, analyzing, inferring

Time Required 45–50 minutes

Materials Supply hand lenses that students can use to observe the rocks.

Teaching Strategy Have students work in pairs. If rock samples are in short supply, allow students to take turns using the same samples.

Answers to Questions

1. rocks that are light in color
2. Rocks with smaller grains; quick cooling does not allow large grains (crystals) to form.
3. Pumice and vesicular basalt; holes in rock suggest that gas was escaping as it cooled.
4. Obsidian and pumice; they cool so quickly that individual grains (crystals) do not have the chance to form.
5. Answers will vary depending on samples observed. The presence of grains that are all visible to the unaided eye indicate rocks are not volcanic.

Assessment

Process Encourage students to use a word processing program to make a table that lists and classifies the rocks used in the activity. Use **PASC**, p. 109.

Activity

Igneous Rock Clues

You've learned how color often is used to estimate the composition of an igneous rock. The texture of an igneous rock describes its overall appearance, including mineral grain sizes and the presence or absence of bubble holes, for example. In most cases, grain size relates to how quickly the magma or lava cooled. Crystals you 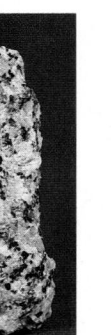 can see without a magnifying glass indicate slower cooling. Smaller, fine-grained crystals indicate quicker cooling, possibly due to volcanic activity. Rocks with glassy textures cooled so quickly that there was no time to form mineral grains.

What You'll Investigate
What does an igneous rock's texture and color indicate about its formation history?

Materials
rhyolite   granite
basalt   obsidian
vesicular basalt   gabbro
pumice   magnifying glass

Goals
■ **Classify** different samples of igneous rocks by color and infer their composition.
■ **Observe** the textures of igneous rocks and infer how they formed.

Safety Precautions
Some rock samples might have sharp edges. Always use caution while handling samples.

Procedure

1. **Arrange** rocks according to color (light or dark). Record your observations in your Science Journal.
2. **Arrange** rocks according to similar texture. Consider grain sizes and shapes, presence of holes, etc. Use your magnifying glass to see small features more clearly. Record your observations.

Conclude and Apply

1. Infer which rocks are granitic based on color.
2. Infer which rocks cooled quickly. What observations led you to this inference?
3. Identify any samples that suggest gases were escaping from them as they cooled.
4. Which samples have a glassy appearance? How did these rocks form?
5. **Infer** which samples are not volcanic. Explain your choices.

Communicating Your Data

Research the compositions of each of your samples. Did the colors of any samples lead you to infer the wrong compositions? Communicate to your class what you learned.

Resource Manager

Chapter Resources Booklet
   Activity Worksheet, pp. 5–6

Communicating Your Data

Students can present a written report to the class. They should show pictures they have located in print or through the Glencoe Science Web site to support their conclusions.

③ Metamorphic Rocks

Formation of Metamorphic Rocks

Have you ever packed your lunch in the morning and not been able to recognize it at lunchtime? You might have packed a sandwich, banana, and a large bottle of water. You know you didn't smash your lunch on the way to school. However, you didn't think about how the heavy water bottle would damage your food if the bottle was allowed to rest on the food all day. The heat in your locker and the pressure from the heavy water bottle have changed the form of your sandwich. Like your lunch, rocks can be affected by temperature changes and pressure.

Metamorphic Rocks Rocks that have changed because of changes in temperature and pressure or the presence of hot, watery fluids are called **metamorphic rocks.** Changes that occur can be in the form of the rock, shown in **Figure 7,** the composition of the rock, or both. Metamorphic rocks can form from igneous, sedimentary, or other metamorphic rocks. What Earth processes can change these rocks?

As You Read

What You'll Learn
- **Describe** the conditions in Earth that cause metamorphic rocks to form.
- **Classify** metamorphic rocks as foliated or non-foliated.

Vocabulary
metamorphic rock
foliated
nonfoliated

Why It's Important
Metamorphic rocks are useful because of their unique properties.

+ pressure →

Figure 7
Ⓐ The mineral grains in granite are flattened and aligned when pressure is applied to them. Ⓑ As a result, gneiss is formed.
What other conditions can cause metamorphic rocks to form?

SECTION 3 Metamorphic Rocks **99**

Section ✓Assessment Planner

PORTFOLIO
Science Journal, p. 101
PERFORMANCE ASSESSMENT
Skill Builder Activities, p. 102
See page 116 for more options.

CONTENT ASSESSMENT
Section, p. 102
Challenge, p. 102
Chapter, pp. 116–117

---

③ Metamorphic Rocks

① Motivate

Bellringer Transparency
Display the Section Focus Transparency for Section 3. Use the accompanying Transparency Activity Master. [L2] [ELL]

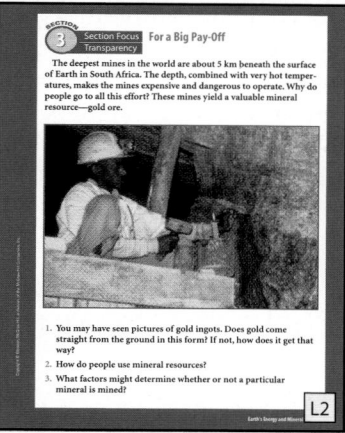

Section Focus For a Big Pay-Off

The deepest mines in the world are about 5 km beneath the surface of Earth in South Africa. The depth, combined with very hot temperatures, makes the mines expensive and dangerous to operate. Why do people go to all this effort? These mines yield a valuable mineral resource—gold ore.

1. You may have seen pictures of gold ingots. Does gold come straight from the ground in this form? If not, how does it get that way?
2. How do people use mineral resources?
3. What factors might determine whether or not a particular mineral is mined?

[L2]

Tie to Prior Knowledge
Help students recall the meaning of the word *metamorphosis.* Have them use this knowledge to speculate about the nature of metamorphic rocks.

Text Question Answer
heat and pressure deep inside Earth

Caption Answer
Figure 7 increased heat

Section 3 Metamorphic Rocks **99**

Formation of Metamorphic Rocks

Use an Analogy

Use this analogy to explain how heat generated from hot magma can cause an adjacent area of rock to change. Remind students what happens to beef as it is seared in a pan. The outside of the meat is cooked as it comes in contact with the pan. If removed from the heat soon enough, the inside of the meat remains unchanged. Hot magma changes rock in contact with its surface, leaving the areas within the rock unchanged. If the cooking continues, the center of the meat will eventually change. The same thing happens with metamorphism. If it continues long enough, eventually the entire rock body in contact with the magma will be changed.
[LS] Visual-Spatial

✔ Reading Check

Answer Different types of metamorphic rock form depending on the temperature, pressure, and fluid conditions.

Visual Learning

Figure 8 What is the source of the heat in the fluids? The heat source is the melted rock, or magma.

SCIENCE Online
Internet Addresses
_____
_____
_____
_____
Explore the Glencoe Science Web site at **science.glencoe.com** to find out more about topics in this section.

SCIENCE Online

Research Visit the Glencoe Science Web site at **science. glencoe.com** for more information on the metamorphism of shale. Communicate to your class what you learn.

Figure 8
In the presence of hot, water-rich fluids, solid rock can change in mineral composition without having to melt.

Heat and Pressure Rocks beneath Earth's surface are under great pressure from rock layers above them. Temperature also increases with depth in Earth. In some places, the heat and pressure are just right to cause rocks to melt and magma to form. In other areas where melting doesn't occur, some mineral grains can become flattened like the sandwich in the lunch bag. Sometimes, under these conditions, minerals exchange atoms with surrounding minerals and new, bigger minerals form.

Depending upon the amount of pressure and temperature applied, one type of rock can change into several different metamorphic rocks, and each type of metamorphic rock can come from several kinds of parent rocks. For example, the sedimentary rock shale will change into slate. As increasing pressure and temperature are applied, the slate can change into phyllite, then schist, and eventually gneiss. Schist also can form when basalt is metamorphosed, or changed, and gneiss can come from granite.

✔ Reading Check *How can one type of rock change into several different metamorphic rocks?*

Hot Fluids Did you know that fluids can move through solid rock? These fluids, which are mostly water with dissolved particles of elements, can react chemically with a rock and change its composition, especially when the fluids are hot. That's what happens when rock surrounding a hot magma body reacts with hot fluids from the magma, as shown in **Figure 8.** Most fluids that transform rocks during metamorphic processes are hot and mainly are comprised of water and carbon dioxide.

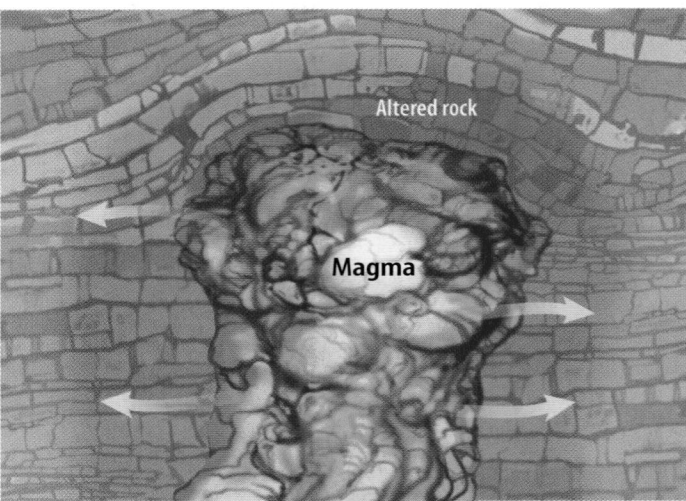

Altered rock

Magma

✔ Active Reading

Jigsaw In this collaborative learning strategy, individuals become experts on a portion of a text and share their expertise with their "home" group. Everyone shares responsibility for learning the assigned reading. Assign each person in each home group an "expert" number (1 through 5, for example). Have students gather into the expert groups that correspond to the number they were assigned. There, have them read, discuss, and master chapter concepts and determine how best to teach them to their home groups. Have students return to home groups and share the content they learned in their expert groups. Have students use the Jigsaw strategy to learn about igneous, metamorphic, and sedimentary rocks.

Classifying Metamorphic Rocks

Metamorphic rocks form from igneous, sedimentary, or other metamorphic rocks. Heat, pressure, and hot fluids trigger the changes. Each resulting rock can be classified according to its composition and texture.

Foliated Rocks When mineral grains flatten and line up in parallel layers, the metamorphic rock is said to have a **foliated** or banded texture. Two examples of foliated rocks are slate and gneiss. Slate forms from the sedimentary rock shale. The minerals in shale arrange into layers when they are exposed to heat and pressure. As **Figure 9** shows, slate separates easily along these foliation layers.

The minerals in slate are pressed together so tightly that water can't pass between them easily. Because it's watertight, slate is ideal for paving around pools and patios. The naturally flat nature of slate and the fact that it splits easily make it useful for roofing and tiling many surfaces.

Gneiss (NISE), another foliated rock, forms when granite and other rocks are changed. Quartz, feldspar, mica (MI kuh), and other minerals that make up granite aren't changed much, but they arrange into alternating bands of light and dark minerals.

✔ Reading Check *What type of metamorphic rock is composed of layers of mineral grains?*

Figure 9
Slate often is used as a building or landscaping material. *What property makes slate so useful for these purposes?*

Classifying Metamorphic Rocks

Activity

Obtain samples of slate, schist, and gneiss. Using **Figure 7**, have students determine where pressure was applied to change each rock. Possible answer: Pressure would have been applied perpendicular to the alignment of mineral grains. L2
🅛🅢 **Visual-Spatial**

✔ Reading Check

Answer foliated metamorphic rocks

Caption Answer

Figure 9 Slate is watertight and easily split into layers.

Science Journal

Rock Uses Ask students to observe the area near their homes for uses of metamorphic rock. Examples include marble in statues and slate as roof tile or patio stones. Have students write in their Science Journals about the many uses of metamorphic rocks. L2 🅛🅢 **Linguistic** P

Classifying Metamorphic Rocks,
continued

Reteach

Have students take turns brainstorming facts they now know about metamorphic rocks. Write their contributions on the board. Use this information to stimulate discussion about the origins and classification of metamorphic rocks. [L1]
LS Interpersonal

Challenge

Have students sketch foliated and nonfoliated metamorphic rocks. Call on individual students to describe what their sketches show. Encourage students to obtain samples of the rocks they have sketched. [L2]
LS Visual-Spatial

✔ *Assessment*

Performance Provide students with a variety of metamorphic rocks. Have them classify each rock according to its texture. Use **Performance Assessment in the Science Classroom,** p. 121.

Figure 10
This exhibit in Vermont shows the beauty of carved marble.

Nonfoliated Rocks In some metamorphic rocks, layering does not occur. The mineral grains grow and rearrange, but they don't form layers. This process produces a **nonfoliated** texture.

Sandstone is a sedimentary rock that's often composed mostly of quartz grains. When sandstone is heated under a lot of pressure, the grains of quartz grow in size and become interlocking, like the pieces of a jigsaw puzzle. The resulting rock is called quartzite.

Marble is another nonfoliated metamorphic rock. Marble forms from the sedimentary rock limestone, which is composed of the mineral calcite. Usually, marble contains several other minerals besides calcite. For example, hornblende and serpentine give marble a black or greenish tone, whereas hematite makes it red. As **Figure 10** shows, marble is an attractive, popular material for artists to sculpt, because it is not hard.

So far, you've investigated only a portion of the rock cycle. You still haven't observed how sedimentary rocks are formed and how igneous and metamorphic rocks evolve from them. The next section will complete your investigation of the rock cycle.

Section **3** Assessment

1. How is the formation of metamorphic rocks different from that of igneous, or sedimentary, rocks?
2. What role do fluids play in rock metamorphism?
3. How are metamorphic rocks classified? What are the characteristics of rocks in each of these classifications?
4. Give an example of a foliated and nonfoliated metamorphic rock. Name one of its possible parent rocks.
5. **Think Critically** Marble is a common material used to make sculptures, but not just because it's a beautiful stone. What properties of marble make it useful for this purpose?

Skill Builder Activities

6. **Concept Mapping** Put the following events in an events-chain concept map that explains how a metamorphic rock might form from an igneous rock. Here's a hint: *Start with "igneous rock forms."* Use each event just once. **For more help, refer to the** Science Skill Handbook.

Events: *sedimentary rock forms, weathering occurs, heat and pressure are applied, igneous rock forms, metamorphic rock forms, erosion occurs, sediments are formed, deposition occurs*

7. **Using Graphics Software** Use a graphics program to illustrate how metamorphic rocks form. Be sure to show how directed pressure causes alignment of mineral grains. **For more help, refer to the** Technology Skill Handbook.

Chapter Resources Booklet
Lab Activity, pp. 11–12
Reinforcement, p. 25
Cultural Diversity, p. 27

Answers to Section Assessment

1. Metamorphic rocks form under changing conditions of pressure and/or temperature. The temperatures involved are high enough for metamorphism to proceed, but too low for melting to occur.
2. Hot fluids chemically react with rocks with which they are in contact, changing their compositions.

3. Foliated or nonfoliated; foliated rocks have layers of mineral grains; nonfoliated rocks have little or no layering.
4. foliated: slate; parent rock: shale; nonfoliated: marble; parent rock: limestone
5. It is also relatively easy to shape because it is not very hard.

6. Igneous rock forms. Weathering occurs. Sediments are formed. Erosion occurs. Deposition occurs. Sedimentary rock forms. Heat and pressure are applied. Metamorphic rock forms.
7. Illustrations should include change that results from heat as well as pressure.

SECTION 4

Sedimentary Rocks

Formation of Sedimentary Rocks

Igneous rocks are the most common rocks on Earth, but because most of them exist below the surface, you might not have seen too many of them. That's because 75 percent of the rocks exposed at the surface are sedimentary rocks.

Sediments are loose materials such as rock fragments, mineral grains, and bits of plant and animal remains that have been moved by wind, water, ice, or gravity. If you look at the model of the rock cycle, you will see that sediments come from already-existing rocks that are weathered and eroded. **Sedimentary rocks** form when sediments are pressed and cemented together, or when minerals form from solutions.

Stacked Rocks Sedimentary rocks often form as layers. The older layers are on the bottom because they were deposited first. Sedimentary rock layers are a lot like the books and papers in your locker. Last week's homework is on the bottom, and today's notes will be deposited on top of the stack. However, if you disturb the stack, the order in which the books and papers are stacked will change, as shown in **Figure 11.** Sometimes, forces within Earth overturn layers of rock, and the oldest are no longer on the bottom.

As You Read

What You'll Learn
- **Explain** how sedimentary rocks form from sediments.
- **Classify** sedimentary rocks as detrital, chemical, or organic in origin.

Vocabulary

sediment
sedimentary rock
compaction
cementation

Why It's Important
Some sedimentary rocks, like coal, are important sources of energy.

Figure 11
Like sedimentary rock layers, the oldest paper is at the bottom of the stack. If the stack is disturbed, then it is no longer in order.

SECTION 4 Sedimentary Rocks **103**

Section ✓Assessment Planner

PORTFOLIO
Science Journal, p. 105
PERFORMANCE ASSESSMENT
MiniLAB, p. 104
Math Skills Activity, p. 108
Skill Builder Activities, p. 109
See page 116 for more options.

CONTENT ASSESSMENT
Section, p. 109
Challenge, p. 109
Chapter, pp. 116–117

SECTION 4

Sedimentary Rocks

1 Motivate

Bellringer Transparency
Display the Section Focus Transparency for Section 4. Use the accompanying Transparency Activity Master. L2
ELL

Tie to Prior Knowledge
Have students describe what happens when sugar is stirred into a glass of cold water. **What happened?** Some grains dissolve, others drop to the bottom of the glass. Explain that some rocks form from sediment that drops to the bottom of water bodies. Others form from chemicals dissolved in water. Tell students they will learn in this section how this happens.

Classifying Sedimentary Rocks

Purpose Students classify sediments according to grain size.

L2 ELL COOP LEARN

LS **Kinesthetic**

Materials paper, samples of silt, sand, and gravel-sized sediment grains (with both rounded and sharp edges), tweezers or dissecting probe

Teaching Strategy Review with students the appearance of rounded grains as opposed to grains with sharp edges. For example, grains need not be spherical in shape to be considered well-rounded.

Safety Precautions Caution students to handle sharp instruments with care and to wear goggles while handling samples.

Analysis

1. Students should describe grains by size and the smoothness or angularity of their edges.
2. Conglomerate from rounded gravel, breccia from angular gravel; If other sediments are used: shale from clay, siltstone from silt, sandstone from sand.

Assessment

Performance Have students paste silt, sand, and gravel-sized sediment onto a note card. Then use the cards to determine the grain sizes of several sedimentary rock samples. Use **PASC,** p. 121.

Mini LAB

Classifying Sediments

Procedure 🔬 〰️ ✋

WARNING: *Use care when handling sharp objects.*

1. Collect different samples of **sediment.**
2. Spread them on a sheet of **paper.**
3. Use **Table 2** to determine the size range of gravel-sized sediment.
4. Use **tweezers or a dissecting probe** and a **magnifying lens** to separate the gravel-sized sediments.
5. Separate the gravel into piles—rounded or angular.

Analysis

1. Describe the grains in both piles.
2. Use **Table 2** to determine what rock probably would be made from each type of sediment you have.

Figure 12
During compaction, pore space between sediments decreases, causing them to become packed together more tightly.

Reading Check

Answer As layers of sediment build up, pressure from upper layers on lower layers compacts lower layers into rock.

Classifying Sedimentary Rocks

Sedimentary rocks can be made of just about any material found in nature. Sediments come from weathered and eroded igneous, metamorphic, and sedimentary rocks. Sediments also come from the remains of plants and animals. The composition of a sedimentary rock depends upon the composition of the sediments from which it formed.

Like igneous and metamorphic rocks, sedimentary rocks are classified by their composition and by the manner in which they formed. Sedimentary rocks usually are classified as detrital, chemical, or organic.

Detrital Sedimentary Rocks

The word *detrital* (Dih TRY tul) comes from the Latin word *detritus,* which means "to wear away." Detrital sedimentary rocks, such as those shown in **Table 2,** are made from the broken fragments of other rocks. These loose sediments are compacted and cemented together to form solid rock.

Weathering and Erosion When rock is exposed to air, water, or ice, it is unstable and breaks down chemically and mechanically. This process, which breaks rocks into smaller pieces, is called weathering. **Table 2** shows how these pieces are classified by size. The movement of weathered material is called erosion.

Compaction Erosion moves sediments to a new location, where they then are deposited. Here, layer upon layer of sediment builds up. Pressure from the upper layers pushes down on the lower layers. If the sediments are small, they can stick together and form solid rock. This process, shown in **Figure 12,** is called **compaction.**

Reading Check   *How do rocks form through compaction?*

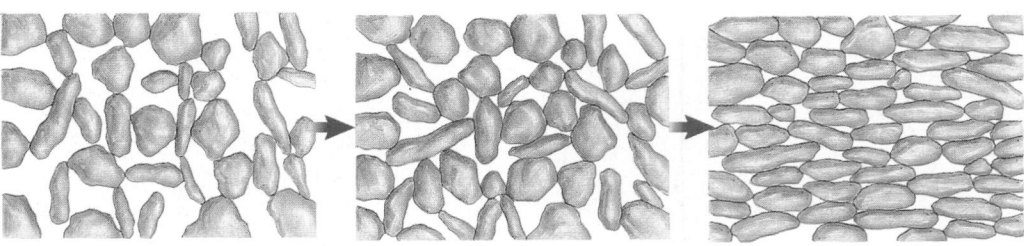

Inclusion Strategies

Visually Impaired Provide students with samples of rounded and angular gravel that they can feel to determine the size and shape of grains. Also provide samples of conglomerate and breccia in which the students can feel the embedded sediments.

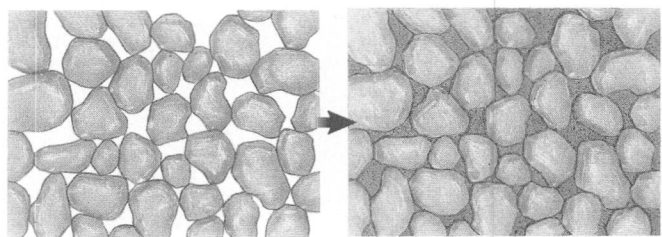

Figure 13
Sediments are cemented together as minerals crystallize between grains.

Cementation If sediments are large, like sand and pebbles, pressure alone can't make them stick together. Large sediments have to be cemented together. **Cementation,** which is shown in **Figure 13,** occurs when water soaks through soil and rock. As water moves through soil and rock, it picks up atoms and molecules released from minerals during weathering. The resulting solution of water and dissolved materials moves through open spaces between sediments. Minerals such as quartz, calcite, hematite, and limonite are deposited between the pieces of sediment. These minerals, acting as natural cements, hold the sediment together like glue, making a detrital sedimentary rock.

Shape and Size of Sediments Detrital rocks have granular textures much like granulated sugar. They are named according to the shapes and sizes of the sediments that form them. For example, conglomerate and breccia both form from large sediments, as shown in **Table 2.** If the sediments are well rounded, the rock is called conglomerate. If the sediments have sharp angles, the rock is called breccia. The roundness of sediment particles is controlled by the distance that the particles travel.

Table 2 Sediment Sizes and Detrital Rocks

Sediment	Clay	Silt	Sand	Gravel
Size Range	<0.004 mm	0.004–0.063 mm	0.063–2 mm	>2 mm
Example	Shale	Siltstone	Sandstone	Conglomerate (shown) or Breccia

SECTION 4 Sedimentary Rocks **105**

Detrital Sedimentary Rocks

Visual Learning

Figure 13 Why is a cementing material needed to hold coarse-grained sedimentary rocks together? Pressure alone can't make large grains stick together. They need a cementing material to act as glue to hold them together.

Discussion

Have students imagine a swiftly-flowing river that empties into a quiet bay.

- **Where in the bay would you expect to find the coarsest sediments being deposited? Explain.** The coarsest sediments would be deposited nearest the mouth of the river. This is where the water loses velocity and drops the largest sediments in its load.

- **Where would you expect to find the finest sediments being deposited? Explain.** The finest sediments would be deposited farther from the mouth of the river. Because these sediments are lighter, they stay suspended longer, even when the velocity of the water slows.

- Have students use **Table 2** to answer this question. **If these sediments became cemented together, what type of rock would form in each location?** Sandstone or conglomerate would form near the mouth of the river. Shale or siltstone would form farther out in the bay.

Observing Rock Exhibit a piece of sandstone. Have students examine the rock and write a brief geologic history that explains how the sandstone could have formed. Then have students hypothesize what might happen to the rock if it were exposed to weathering and erosion, or to heat and pressure. L2 IS **Logical-Mathematical** P

Activity

Form groups of three students. Supply each group with containers of clay, silt, fine sand, coarse sand, and rounded and angular gravel. Make samples of shale, siltstone, sandstone, conglomerate, and breccia available to each group. Have students use a hand lens to match sediment type with the appropriate rock sample. One student in each group should present a report containing the conclusions drawn by the group. [L2] COOP LEARN [IS] **Interpersonal**

Chemical Sedimentary Rocks

Chemistry INTEGRATION

Water that seeps below the surface contains carbon dioxide. The carbon dioxide combines with the water to form a weak acid (carbonic acid) that dissolves the limestone.

✔ Reading Check

Answer They form when dissolved minerals come out of solution or when liquid evaporates.

Conglomerate

Figure 14
Although concrete strongly resembles conglomerate, concrete is not a rock because it does not occur in nature.

Chemistry INTEGRATION

You may know of large caves or caverns that have formed underground in limestone deposits. Research the chemical reactions that form caves in Carlsbad Caverns, New Mexico, or Mammoth Cave, Kentucky.

Materials Found in Sedimentary Rocks The gravel-sized sediments in conglomerate and breccia can consist of any type of rock or mineral. Often, they are composed of chunks of the minerals quartz and feldspar. They also can be pieces of rocks such as gneiss, granite, or limestone. The cement that holds the sediments together usually is made of quartz or calcite.

Have you ever looked at the concrete in sidewalks, driveways, and stepping stones? The concrete in **Figure 14** is made of gravel and sand grains that have been cemented together. Although the structure is similar to that of naturally occurring conglomerate, it cannot be considered a rock.

Sandstone is formed from smaller particles than conglomerates and breccias. Its sand-sized sediments can be just about any mineral, but they are usually grains of the minerals quartz and feldspar that are compacted and cemented together. Siltstone is similar to sandstone except it is made of smaller, silt-sized particles. Shale is a detrital sedimentary rock that is made mainly of clay-sized particles. Clay-sized sediments are compacted together by pressure from overlying layers.

Chemical Sedimentary Rocks

Chemical sedimentary rocks form when dissolved minerals come out of solution. You can show that salt is deposited in the bottom of a glass or pan when saltwater solution evaporates. In a similar way, minerals collect when seas or lakes evaporate. The deposits of minerals that come out of solution form sediments and rocks. For example, the sediment making up New Mexico's White Sands desert is a chemical sedimentary rock called rock gypsum. Chemical sedimentary rocks are different because they are not made from pieces of other rocks.

✔ Reading Check   *How do chemical sedimentary rocks form?*

Cultural Diversity

Rock Art Native Americans used flint to make arrowheads, axes, and other tools that need a sharp edge. Flint is an extremely fine-grained, dense, glossy sedimentary rock made of quartz. It often is found embedded in deposits of chalk or limestone. Flint is an even-grained rock that breaks easily into smooth, curved flakes with sharp edges. This makes it ideal for the manufacture of cutting tools. Today people learn the art of flint napping as a craft. *Napping* is the method of striking a flint rock in such a way that a sharp-edged flake results. Have students find out what archaeologists have learned about the flint tools used by ancient Americans. Then have them make a classroom bulletin board showing the locations, types, and appearances of the flint artifacts.

Limestone Calcium carbonate is carried in solution in ocean water. When calcium carbonate comes out of solution as calcite and its many crystals grow together, limestone forms. Limestone also can contain other minerals and sediments, but it must be at least 50 percent calcite. Limestone usually is deposited on the bottom of lakes or shallow seas. Large areas of the central United States have limestone bedrock because seas covered much of the country for millions of years. It is hard to imagine Kansas being covered by ocean water, but it has happened several times throughout geological history.

Rock Salt When water that is rich in dissolved salt evaporates, it often deposits the mineral halite. Halite forms rock salt, shown in **Figure 15**. Rock salt deposits can range in thickness from a few meters to more than 400 m. Companies mine these deposits because rock salt is an important resource. It's used in the manufacturing of glass, paper, soap, and dairy products. The halite in rock salt is used as table salt.

Figure 15
Rock salt is extracted from this mine in Germany. The same salt can be processed and used to season your favorite foods.

Organic Sedimentary Rocks

Rocks made of the remains of once-living things are called organic sedimentary rocks. One of the most common organic sedimentary rocks is fossil-rich limestone. Like chemical limestone, fossil-rich limestone is made of the mineral calcite ($CaCO_3$). However, fossil-rich limestone mostly contains remains of once-living ocean organisms instead of only calcite that has come out of ocean water.

Animals such as mussels, clams, corals, and snails make their shells from $CaCO_3$ that eventually becomes calcite. When they die, their shells accumulate on the ocean floor. When these shells are cemented together, fossil-rich limestone forms. If a rock is made completely of shell fragments that you can see, the rock is called coquina (koh KEE nuh).

Chalk Chalk is another organic sedimentary rock that is made of microscopic shells. When you write with naturally occurring chalk, you're crushing and smearing the calcite-shell remains of once-living ocean organisms.

IDENTIFYING Misconceptions

Some students may think that most salt is used as a food seasoning. About 50% of the salt sold in the United States is used as a winter deicer. About 15% is used in conditioning water, 15% is used by the chemical industry, 10% is used in agriculture, and about 10% is used as a food seasoning.

Quick Demo

Show students what happens to salt water that is left to evaporate. Place a thin layer of salt water in the bottom of a pie pan and leave overnight. Explain to students that as the water evaporated, crystals of salt formed.

Organic Sedimentary Rocks

Discussion

Explain that the limestone caves of Carlsbad Caverns are located in the dry southern part of New Mexico. **What does that tell you about how the environment of southern New Mexico was once different than it is today?** A sea that formed the limestone once covered the area.

SECTION 4 Sedimentary Rocks **107**

Resource Manager

Chapter Resources Booklet
    Enrichment, p. 30
Reading and Writing Skill Activities, p. 21
Mathematics Skill Activities, p. 29

Teacher FYI

Many deposits of chalk formed during the Cretaceous Period, between 145 and 66 million years ago. The word *cretaceous* comes from the Latin word for chalk, which is *creta*.

Organic Sedimentary Rocks, continued

Quick Demo

Display samples of peat, lignite, and bituminous and anthracite coal. Have students observe the peat to see that it is made of plant material. Demonstrate the relative ease with which you can break the lignite and the bituminous coal as opposed to the harder anthracite. **Infer what happens to the hardness of coal as it changes from peat to lignite, bituminous, and anthracite.** The coal becomes harder.

Math Skills Activity

National Math Standards

Correlation to Mathematics Objectives

1, 2, 6, 9

Answer to Practice Problem

What you know:
original thickness of plant matter = 0.9 m; original coal thickness = 0.3 m; new coal thickness = 0.6 m

What you need to know:
thickness of plant matter needed to form 0.6 m of coal

Equation to use:
(thickness of plant matter)/ (new coal thickness) = (original thickness of plant matter) / original coal thickness

Substitute known values:
? m plant matter/0.6 m coal = 0.9 m plant matter/0.3 m coal

Solve the equation:
? m plant matter = (0.9 m plant matter)(0.6 m coal)/0.3 m = 1.8 m

---

Coal Another useful organic sedimentary rock is coal, shown in **Figure 16.** Coal forms when pieces of dead plants are buried under other sediments in swamps. These plant materials are chemically changed by microorganisms. The resulting sediments are compacted over millions of years to form coal, an important source of energy. Much of the coal in North America and Europe formed during a period of geologic time that is so named because of this important reason. The Carboniferous Period, which spans from approximately 360 to 286 million years ago, was named in Europe. So much coal formed during this interval of time that coal's composition—primarily carbon—was the basis for naming a geologic period.

Math Skills Activity

Calculating Thickness

Example Problem

It took 300 million years for a layer of plant matter about 0.9m thick to produce a bed of bituminous coal 0.3m thick. Estimate the thickness of plant matter that produced a bed of coal 0.15m thick.

Solution

1 *This is what you know:*
original thickness of plant matter = 0.9m
original coal thickness = 0.3m
new coal thickness = 0.15m

2 *This is what you need to know:*
thickness of plant matter needed to form 0.15m of coal

3 *This is the equation you need to use:*
(thickness of plant matter) / (new coal thickness) = (original thickness of plant matter) / original coal thickness

4 *Substitute the known values:*
(?m plant matter) / (0.15m coal) = (0.9m plant matter) / (0.3m coal)

5 *Solve the equation:*
(?m plant matter) = (0.9m plant matter) (0.15m coal) / (0.3m coal) = 0.45m

Multiply your answer by the original coal thickness. Divide by original plant matter thickness. Do you get the new coal thickness that was given?

Practice Problem

Estimate the thickness of plant matter that produced a bed of coal 0.6m thick.

For more help, refer to the Math Skill Handbook.

 ## LAB DEMONSTRATION

Purpose to observe that some sedimentary rocks react with hydrochloric acid (HCl)

Materials samples of calcite, limestone, and marble; dilute HCl

Procedure Place a few drops of dilute HCl on each sample. **CAUTION:** Wear goggles and protect clothing and work surfaces.

Expected Outcome Students will observe that all samples fizz.

Assessment

Why do all three samples react to acid?
Students should infer that all the samples contain a substance that reacts with HCl. Limestone and marble contain calcite.

Figure 16
This coal layer in Alaska is easily identified by its jet-black color, as compared with other sedimentary layers.

Another Look at the Rock Cycle

You have seen that the rock cycle has no beginning and no end. Rocks change continually from one form to another. Sediments come from rocks and minerals that have been broken apart. Even the magma that forms igneous rocks comes from the melting of rocks that already exist.

All of the rocks that you've learned about in this chapter formed through some process within the rock cycle. All of the rocks around you, including those used to build houses and monuments, are part of the rock cycle. Slowly, they are all changing, because the rock cycle is a continuous, dynamic process.

Section 4 Assessment

1. Where do sediments come from?
2. Explain how compaction and cementation are important in forming sedimentary rocks.
3. Explain the difference between detrital and chemical sedimentary rock.
4. List chemical sedimentary rocks that are essential to your health or that are used to make life more convenient. How is each used?
5. **Think Critically** Use the rock cycle to explain how pieces of granite and slate could be found in the same piece of conglomerate.

Skill Builder Activities

6. **Making and Using Tables** You are told to identify several rocks based on their compositions and other physical properties. What physical properties would you consider? How would you organize these properties so the rocks could be identified easily? **For more help, refer to the** Science Skill Handbook.

7. **Calculating Ratios** Sediment sizes of different sedimentary rock types are presented in **Table 2.** Estimate how many times larger the largest grains of silt and sand are compared to clay grains. **For more help, refer to the** Math Skill Handbook.

Make a Model

Have students make a model of the rock cycle. Encourage them to be creative and to present their models in class.

Assess

Reteach

Have students construct a table that summarizes the characteristics of detrital, chemical, and organic sedimentary rocks. L2

Challenge

Have students explain which is older: detrital sedimentary rock or the sediments it contains. Have them explain their answer. The sediments are older.

Assessment

Performance Assess students' abilities to sequence events by having them make an events chain for the process of changing a metamorphic rock to a sedimentary rock. Use **PASC,** p. 163.

Answers to Section Assessment

1. weathered and eroded rock
2. Compaction squeezes sediments together. Cementation glues sediments together.
3. Detrital rocks are made from the pieces of weathered rocks; chemical rocks form as dissolved minerals come out of solution or as liquid evaporates.

4. Possible answers: salt: preservation, seasoning, manufacture of glass, paper, and soap; limestone: material for buildings and statues
5. If granite and slate were weathered and eroded, they could be deposited as sediments that form conglomerate.

6. Samples can be organized by grain size, texture, or how they were formed. Accept any reasonable classification scheme.
7. The largest grains of silt are about 16 times larger than clay, and the largest grains of sand are about 500 times larger than clay.

Resource Manager

Chapter Resources Booklet
Reinforcement, p. 26
Activity Worksheet, pp. 7–8

Lab Management and Safety, p. 70

Activity

What You'll Investigate

Purpose

Students use various characteristics to classify sedimentary rocks. L2 ELL COOP LEARN

IS Interpersonal

Process Skills

observing and inferring, communicating, classifying, forming operational definitions, interpreting qualitative data, comparing and contrasting

Time Required

50 minutes

Materials

Suitable rocks include: fossil-rich limestone, rock salt, shale, siltstone, sandstone, and conglomerate. HCl can be made by mixing 1 part muriatic acid with 19 parts tap water.

Safety Precautions

Have students wear goggles, aprons, and rubber gloves when handling acid in the lab.

Procedure

Teaching Strategy

Make several rock and mineral identification books available in class. The books should identify the characteristics of rocks that students encounter in class.

Activity

Sedimentary Rocks

Sedimentary rocks are formed by compaction and cementation of sediment. Because sediment is found in all shapes and sizes, do you think these characteristics could be used to classify detrital sedimentary rocks? Sedimentary rocks also can be classified as chemical or organic.

What You'll Investigate

How are rock characteristics used to classify sedimentary rocks as detrital, chemical, or organic?

Goals

- **Observe** sedimentary rock characteristics.
- **Compare and contrast** sedimentary rock textures.
- **Classify** sedimentary rocks as detrital, chemical, or organic.

Materials

unknown sedimentary rock samples
marking pen
5 percent hydrochloric acid (HCl)
*vinegar
dropper
paper towels
  water
  magnifying lens
  metric ruler
  Alternate materials

Safety Precautions

WARNING: *Use care when handling sharp objects.*

Science Journal

Emphasizing Safety In preparation for this lab exercise, demonstrate how to check samples for reaction with HCl. Be sure to wear goggles and an apron. Ask students to write a description of the reaction in their Science Journals. Also, have students explain the need for wearing goggles and an apron while performing this activity. L2 ELL **IS Linguistic**

Sedimentary Rock Samples

Sample	Observations	Minerals or Fossils Present	Sediment Size	Detrital, Chemical, or Organic	Rock Name
A	fizzes in acid	calcite, fossils	varies	organic	fossil-rich limestone
B	feels gritty	quartz, feldspar	sand	detrital	sandstone
C	breaks in layers	kaolinite, quartz	clay	detrital	shale
D	sediment easily seen	pebbles of any rock or mineral	pebble and sand	detrital	conglomerate
E	soft	halite	not grainy	chemical	rock salt

Expected Outcome

Students will identify the rock samples based on characteristics such as hardness, texture, layering, size and feel of grains, and reaction to acid. They also will classify them as detrital, chemical, or organic.

Conclude and Apply

1. to determine whether calcite was present; carbonates
2. Rocks of both textures form from sedimentary processes. Rocks with a granular texture are made of pieces of other rocks, minerals, and/or shells. Rocks with a nongranular texture are formed by chemical or organic means.

Error Analysis

Rocks could be misclassified if students were not able to correctly identify grain size or the relative hardness of samples, or if they had trouble getting the samples to react in the presence of acid.

Procedure

1. Make a Sedimentary Rock Samples chart similar to the one shown above in your Science Journal.

2. **Determine** the sizes of sediments in each sample, using a magnifying lens and a metric ruler. Using **Table 2,** classify any grains of sediment in the rocks as gravel, sand, silt, or clay. In general, the sediment is silt if it is gritty and just barely visible, and clay if it is smooth and if individual grains are not visible.

3. Place a few drops of HCl or vinegar on each rock sample. Bubbling on a rock indicates the presence of calcite. **WARNING:** *HCl is an acid and can cause burns. Wear goggles and a lab apron. Rinse spills with water and wash hands afterwards.*

4. **Examine** each sample for fossils and describe any that are present.

5. **Determine** whether each sample has a granular or nongranular texture.

6. **Classify** your samples as detrital, chemical, or organic. Identify each rock sample.

Conclude and Apply

1. Explain why you tested the rocks with acid. What minerals react with acid?

2. **Compare and contrast** sedimentary rocks that have a granular texture with sedimentary rocks that have a nongranular texture.

Communicating Your Data

Compare your conclusions with those of other students in your class. **For more help, refer to the** Science Skill Handbook.

Assessment

Performance Provide students with large samples of unidentified rocks. Ask them to determine whether the rocks are sedimentary, and if so, whether they are detrital, chemical, or organic. Use **Performance Assessment in the Science Classroom,** p. 99.

Communicating Your Data

Encourage students to use a spreadsheet program to display the characteristics of sedimentary rock samples used in this activity.

Content Background

According to Anangu, Earth's surface was once featureless. Places like Uluru did not exist until ancestral beings—in the form of people, plants, and animals—started to travel across the land. As they traveled from one area to another, these ancestral beings formed the features of the landscape. The travels and activities of the ancestral beings linked places throughout the country by iwara (paths or tracks). Iwara are not immediately visible to visitors unless interpreted and shown by Anangu people. Iwara link places often separated by hundreds of kilometers. Uluru represents one meeting point in a network of such ancestral tracks.

Anangu knowledge of their land is based on Tjukurpa (Dream Time.) They pass on this knowledge through ceremony, song, dance, and art. The four major elements of the Tjukurpa for Uluru are Kuniya (woma python), Liru (poisonous snake), Kurpany (monster dog-like creature), and Mala (hare-wallaby). These beings and the stories associated with them connect Anangu with the land around them. For example, Mala Puta Cave, formed by erosion of Uluru, represents the pouch of the female hare-wallaby. The oldest exposed rocks at Uluru split off from the underlying rock during the development of topographic joints. To the Anangu, the huge grooves in these rocks were made by Kuniya as she came and went on her search for food.

Australia's controversial rock star

One of the most famous rocks in the world is causing serious problems for Australians

Uluru (yew LEW rew) is one of the most popular tourist destinations in Australia. This sandstone skyscraper is more than 8 km around, over 300 m high, and extends as much as 4.8 km below the surface. One writer describes it as an iceberg in the desert. Geologists believe that the mighty Uluru rock began forming 550 million years ago in the Precambrian Eon. That's when large mountain ranges started to form in Central Australia. About 300 million years later, sediment from these ranges settled on the Amadeus Basin. The sandy material hardened into rock. Faults in Earth weakened the rock. Erosion eventually cut away this weakened surrounding rock to expose the massive sandstone structure called Ayers Rock. Today, erosion continues to slowly cut away at the rock.

For more than 25,000 years, this geological wonder has played an important role in the lives of the Aboriginal peoples, the Anangu (a NA noo). These native Australians are the original owners of the rock, and have spiritual explanations for its many caves, holes, and scars.

In 1873, the rock was named in honor of Sir Henry Ayers, an Australian government official. Few people in the early 1900s visited it. But as transportation technology improved, so did the rock's tourist appeal. In 1958, the Australian government made Ayers Rock part of a national park. In the 1980s, 100,000 tourists visited it. In 2000, the rock attracted about 400,000 tourists.

112

Resources for Teachers and Students

"Into the Red Center," by Diana Somerville, *Earth*, January 1994.

Australia, by April Pulley Sayre, Twenty-First Century Books, 1998.

A Natural History of Australia, by Tim M. Berra, Academic Press, 1998.

Australia: Land of Natural Wonders, by Alberto Ruiz de Larramendi, Childrens Press, 1994.

Australian Dreaming: 40,000 Years of Aboriginal History, edited by Jennifer Isaacs, Lansdowne Press, 1980.

Tourists Take Over

This increase in tourism is causing serious problems. The Anangu take offense at the climbing of their sacred rock, a holy site. However, if climbing the rock were outlawed, tourism would be seriously hurt. And that would mean less income for Australians. One Australian marketing director sums up the apparent threat to tourism: Going to Uluru and not climbing is like going to the Great Barrier Reef and not diving.

Some steps have been taken to respect the native people's wishes. In 1985, the government returned Ayers rock to the Anangu, and agreed to call it by its traditional name. As part of this arrangement, the Anangu leased back the rock to the Australian government until the year 2084, when management of Uluru and the surrounding park goes back to the Anangu. Until then, the Anangu will collect 25 percent of the money people pay to visit the rock.

The Aboriginal people encourage tourists to respect their beliefs. They offer a walking tour around the rock, and they show videos about Aboriginal traditions. The Anangu sell T-shirts that say "I *didn't* climb Uluru." They hope visitors to Uluru will wear the T-shirt with pride and respect.

Athlete Nova Benis-Kneebone had the honor of receiving the Olympic torch near the sacred Uluru and carried it partway to the Olympic stadium.

Discussion

What are the advantages and disadvantages to the Anangu of having tourists visit Uluru? Possible answer: advantages—financial rewards, opportunity to explain their beliefs to tourists; disadvantages—tourists climbing their sacred rock; tourists not respecting their beliefs and traditions.

Activity

Have small groups of students design a travel brochure for Uluru that explains the geology of the formation and that also encourages visitors to respect the sacred nature of the formation to the Anangu.

Investigate the Issue

Place students into groups to research examples of landmarks or land or water formations in the United States that Native Americans consider sacred. Have them find out about any conflicts between Native Americans and local or federal government over the management of these places. Have students record the information they find and answer the question "How are people working together to solve problems related to tourism, while respecting the beliefs of native peoples?"

CONNECTIONS Write Research a natural landmark or large natural land or water formation in your area. What is the geology behind it? When was it formed? How was it formed? Write a folktale that explains its formation. Share your folktale with the class.

SCIENCE *Online*
For more information, visit science.glencoe.com

CONNECTIONS Have students examine physical maps of your state to locate natural landforms and water formations. After a site is selected, have students research the geology of the formation to answer the questions in the student text before writing their folktales. Before sharing their folktales, have students explain the formation's geologic history to the class.

SCIENCE *Online*

Internet Addresses
_____
_____
_____
_____

Explore the Glencoe Science Web site at **science.glencoe.com** to find out more about topics in this feature.

Reviewing Main Ideas

Preview

Students can answer the questions in their Science Journals. Discuss the answers as you go through the chapter. **IS** **Linguistic**

Review

Students can write their answers, then compare them with those of other students. **IS** **Interpersonal**

Reteach

Students can look at the illustrations and describe details that support the main ideas of the chapter. **IS** **Visual-Spatial**

Answers to Chapter Review

SECTION 1

2. Igneous rock can be weathered and eroded. The weathered pieces can collect as sediment and then become compacted and cemented, forming a sedimentary rock.

SECTION 2

3. basalt

SECTION 3

2. Foliated metamorphic rocks have a distinctly layered appearance, while nonfoliated metamorphic rocks are more uniform in mineral content and orientation of grains.

SECTION 4

3. shells of marine organisms

Reviewing Main Ideas

Section 1 The Rock Cycle

1. A rock is a mixture of one or more minerals, rock fragments, organic matter, or volcanic glass.

2. The rock cycle includes all processes by which rocks form. *How could an igneous rock change to a sedimentary rock?*

Section 2 Igneous Rocks

1. Magma and lava are molten materials that harden to form igneous rocks.

2. Intrusive igneous rocks form when magma cools slowly below the surface. Extrusive igneous rocks form when lava cools rapidly at or near the surface.

3. Basalt is dense and dark colored. Granite is light colored and less dense than basalt. Andesite has intermediate density and color, somewhere between basalt and granite. *What kind of rock is shown below?*

Section 3 Metamorphic Rocks

1. Heat, pressure, and fluids can cause metamorphic rocks to form. Metamorphic rocks can have foliated textures or nonfoliated textures.

2. Slate and gneiss are examples of foliated metamorphic rocks. Quartzite and marble are examples of non-foliated metamorphic rocks. *How are these rocks different?*

Section 4 Sedimentary Rocks

1. Detrital sedimentary rocks form when fragments of rocks and minerals are compacted and cemented together. Detrital rocks always have a granular texture.

2. Chemical sedimentary rocks come out of solution or are left behind by evaporation. Chemical rocks generally have a non-granular texture.

3. Organic sedimentary rocks are made mostly of the remains of once-living organisms. *What kinds of remains make up the rock to the right?*

FOLDABLES Reading & Study Skills — **After You Read**
Using the information in your Foldable for help, write examples of each type of rock under the flaps of your Foldable.

FOLDABLES Reading & Study Skills — **After You Read**

After students have read the chapter and completed the Foldable described in Before You Read, have them do the activity on the student page.

Dinah Zike

Visualizing Main Ideas

Complete the following concept map on rocks. Use the following terms:
organic, metamorphic, foliated, extrusive, igneous, *and* chemical.

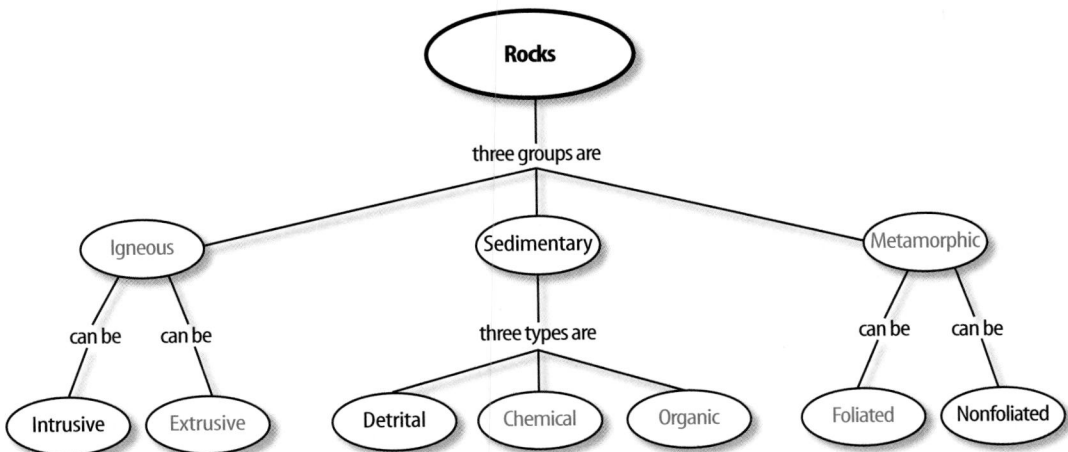

Vocabulary Review

Vocabulary Words

a. basaltic
b. cementation
c. compaction
d. extrusive
e. foliated
f. granitic
g. igneous rock
h. intrusive

i. lava
j. metamorphic rock
k. nonfoliated
l. rock
m. rock cycle
n. sediment
o. sedimentary rock

THE PRINCETON REVIEW **Study Tip**

If you're not sure of the relationship between terms in a question, try making a concept map of the terms to see how they fit together. Ask your teacher if the relationships you drew are correct.

Using Vocabulary

Explain the difference between the vocabulary words in each of the following sets.

1. foliated, nonfoliated

2. cementation, compaction

3. sediment, lava

4. extrusive, intrusive

5. rock, rock cycle

6. metamorphic rock, igneous rock, sedimentary rock

7. sediment, sedimentary rock

8. lava, igneous rock

9. rock, sediment

10. basaltic, granitic

CHAPTER STUDY GUIDE **115**

Visualizing Main Ideas

See student page.

Vocabulary Review

Using Vocabulary

1. Foliated metamorphic rocks contain layered minerals; nonfoliated metamorphic rocks do not.
2. Compaction is the pressing of mineral grains together during the formation of sedimentary rock; cementation is the gluing of the grains together by dissolved mineral matter coming out of solution.
3. Sediment is weathered pieces of solid Earth materials; lava is hot, molten rock that reaches Earth's surface through volcanic eruptions.
4. Extrusive rocks form at or near Earth's surface; intrusive rocks form below Earth's surface.
5. A rock is a mixture of minerals, volcanic glass, organic matter, or other materials; the rock cycle describes how one type of rock can change into another.
6. Igneous rock forms when magma or lava solidifies; sedimentary rock forms from the deposition, compaction, and cementation of sediment or when minerals form from solution; metamorphic rock forms when one of the other types of rock is changed by heat and pressure and fluids inside Earth.
7. Sediment consists of grains of weathered and eroded rock; sedimentary rock is formed by the compaction and cementation of sediment or when minerals form from solution.
8. Lava is molten rock that has reached Earth's surface; extrusive igneous rocks form from lava that has cooled and solidified.
9. Sediment is composed of weathered pieces of rock and other Earth materials.
10. Basaltic magma is low in silica and high in magnesium and iron compared to granitic magma.

Checking Concepts

1. D
2. D
3. A
4. D
5. B
6. B
7. C
8. D
9. B
10. A

Thinking Critically

11. Because granite is an intrusive rock. Pumice and scoria form above ground where the molten rock can quickly expand, forming air bubbles.
12. Marble is metamorphic. The processes that form it often destroy organic remains.
13. It is made of shell fragments from living organisms, so it is organic. The shell fragments give the rock a granular texture.
14. Sandstone; quartz grains in sandstone are held together by cement, whereas quartz grains in quartzite have grown in size and have become interlocking.
15. Most granitic rocks are lighter in color than basaltic rocks because they contain fewer minerals that are strongly colored. Transition metal elements, such as iron, are more abundant in strongly colored minerals.

Chapter 4 Assessment

Checking Concepts

Choose the word or phrase that best answers the question.

1. Why does magma tend to rise toward Earth's surface?
   A) It is more dense than surrounding rocks.
   B) It is more massive than surrounding rocks.
   C) It is cooler than surrounding rocks.
   D) It is less dense than surrounding rocks.

2. During metamorphism of granite into gneiss, what happens to minerals?
   A) They partly melt.
   B) They become new sediments.
   C) They grow smaller.
   D) They align into layers.

3. Which rock has large mineral grains?
   A) intrusive   C) obsidian
   B) extrusive   D) pumice

4. What do igneous rocks form from?
   A) sediments   C) gravel
   B) mud   D) magma

5. What kind of rock is marble?
   A) foliated   C) intrusive
   B) non-foliated   D) extrusive

6. What sedimentary rock is made of large, angular pieces of sediments?
   A) conglomerate   C) limestone
   B) breccia   D) chalk

7. Which of the following is an example of a detrital sedimentary rock?
   A) limestone   C) breccia
   B) evaporite   D) chalk

8. During what process are sediments pressed together?
   A) cooling   C) melting
   B) weathering   D) compaction

9. What is molten material at Earth's surface called?
   A) limestone   C) breccia
   B) lava   D) granite

10. Which of these is an organic sedimentary rock?
    A) coquina   C) rock salt
    B) sandstone   D) conglomerate

Thinking Critically

11. Granite, pumice, and scoria are igneous rocks. Why doesn't granite have airholes like the other two?

12. Why does marble rarely contain fossils?

13. Why is coquina classified as an organic rock with a granular texture?

14. Would you expect a quartzite or a sandstone to break more easily? Explain your answer.

15. Why are granitic igneous rocks lighter in color than basaltic rocks?

Developing Skills

16. **Comparing and Contrasting** Compare and contrast basaltic and granitic magmas.

17. **Forming Hypotheses**
    A geologist found a sequence of rocks in which 200-million-year-old shales were on top of 100-million-year-old sandstones. *Hypothesize how this could happen.*

18. **Recognizing Cause and Effect** Explain the effects of pressure and temperature on shale.

Chapter ✓Assessment Planner

Portfolio Encourage students to place in their portfolios one or two items of what they consider to be their best work. Examples include:
- Curriculum Connection, p. 92
- Chemistry Integration, p. 97
- Science Journal, p. 101
- Science Journal, p. 105

Performance Additional performance assessments, Performance Task Assessment Lists, and rubrics for evaluating these activities can be found in Glencoe's **Performance Assessment in the Science Classroom.**

19. Measuring in SI Assume that the conglomerate shown on the first page of the 2-page Activity is one half of its actual size. Determine the average length of the gravel in the rock.

20. Concept Mapping Copy and complete the concept map shown below. Use the following terms and phrases: *magma, sediments, igneous rock, sedimentary rock, metamorphic rock*. Add and label any missing arrows.

Performance Assessment

21. Poster Collect a group of small rocks. Make a poster that shows the classifications of rocks, and glue your rocks to the poster under the proper headings. Display your poster to the class. Describe your rocks and explain where you found them.

TECHNOLOGY

Go to the Glencoe Science Web site at **science.glencoe.com** or use the **Glencoe Science CD-ROM** for additional chapter assessment.

THE PRINCETON REVIEW — Test Practice

Ellen did research on some common rocks. The information she gathered is listed in the table below.

Rock Properties and Uses

Rocks	Properties	Uses
Granite	Hard; resistant to attack by air and natural waters	Building stones and monuments
Pumice	Lightweight and porous	Polishing mixtures and cleansers
Limestone	Soft; weathers in presence of natural waters	Gravel, concrete
Slate	Nonporous and splits into thin sheets	Roofing, paving, chalkboards

Study the table and answer the following questions.

1. According to the table, which rock would be a good choice to use as a grave marker in a cemetery?
A) granite
B) pumice
C) sandstone
D) slate

2. According to the information given, which rock would most likely be used in toothpaste?
F) granite
G) pumice
H) sandstone
J) slate

THE PRINCETON REVIEW — Test Practice

The Test-Taking Tip was written by The Princeton Review, the nation's leader in test preparation.
1. A
2. G

Developing Skills

16. Both are molten materials that form deep within Earth. Basaltic magma is fluid and is rich in iron and magnesium. Granitic magma is more viscous and contains large amounts of silica.

17. Movement of rock inside Earth because of tectonic or other forces caused the older layer to be thrust over the younger layer.

18. Over time, increasing pressure and temperature turn shale into slate, then phyllite, then schist, then gneiss.

19. approximately 15 mm

20. See student page.

Performance Assessment

21. Posters should classify rocks as igneous, sedimentary, or metamorphic, and list their names. Use the **Performance Task Assessment List for Posters** in PASC, p. 145.

✓Assessment Resources

Reproducible Masters

Chapter Resources Booklet
Chapter Review, pp. 35–36
Chapter Tests, pp. 37–40
Assessment Transparency Activity, p. 49

Glencoe Science Web site
Interactive Tutor
Chapter Quizzes

Glencoe Technology

Assessment Transparency
Interactive CD-ROM Chapter Quizzes
ExamView Pro Test Bank
Vocabulary PuzzleMaker Software
MindJogger Videoquiz DVD/VHS

Section/Objectives	Standards		Activities/Features
	National	**State/Local**	
Chapter Opener	See p. 5T for a Key to Standards.		**Explore Activity:** Compare Rock Porosity, p. 119 **Before You Read,** p. 119
Section 1 Nonrenewable Energy Resources 🕐 2 sessions 📦 1 block 1. **Identify** examples of nonrenewable energy resources. 2. **Describe** the advantages and disadvantages of using fossil fuels. 3. **Explain** the advantages and disadvantages of using nuclear energy.	National Content Standards: UCP2, A1, B3, D1, E1, E2, F1, F2, F4, F5		**Life Science Integration,** p. 121 **Science Online,** p. 125 **Visualizing Methane Hydrates,** p. 8 **MiniLAB:** Practicing Energy Conservation, p. 127
Section 2 Inexhaustible and Renewable Energy Resources 🕐 1 session 📦 0.5 block 1. **Compare and contrast** inexhaustible and renewable energy resources. 2. **Explain** why inexhaustible and renewable resources are used less than nonrenewable resources.	National Content Standards: UCP3, B3, D1, E1, E2, F2, F4, F5		**Physics Integration** p. 131 **Science Online,** p. 133 **Activity:** Soaking up Solar Energy, p. 136
Section 3 Mineral Resources 🕐 3 sessions 📦 1.5 blocks 1. **Explain** the conditions needed for a mineral to be classified as an ore. 2. **Describe** how market conditions can cause a mineral to lose its value as an ore. 3. **Compare and contrast** metallic and nonmetallic mineral resources.	National Content Standards: UCP3, A1, D1, F2, F4, F5, G1, G2		**MiniLAB:** Observing the Effects of Insulation, p. 139 **Problem-Solving Activity:** Why should we recycle?, p. 140 **Activity:** Home Sweet Home, pp. 142–143 **Oops! Accidents in Science:** Oil's Well that Ends Well, pp. 144–145

 **NATIONAL GEOGRAPHIC**

Teacher's Corner

PRODUCTS AVAILABLE FROM GLENCOE
To order call 1-800-334-7344:
CD-ROM
NGS PictureShow: Geology
Curriculum Kit
GeoKit: Rocks and Minerals

Transparency Set
NGS PicturePack: Rocks and Minerals
INDEX TO NATIONAL GEOGRAPHIC SOCIETY
The following articles may be used for research relating to this chapter:
"Physical World," by Joel L. Swerdlow, May 1998.

"Life Grows Up," by Richard Monastersky, April 1998.
"The Rise of Life on Earth," by Richard Monastersky, March 1998.
"Under Our Skin: Hot Theories on the Center of the Earth," by Keay Davidson, January 1996.

Activity Materials	Reproducible Resources	Section Assessment	Technology
Explore Activity: sandstone, shale, shallow baking pan, dropper, cooking oil, timer	**Chapter Resources Booklet** Foldables Worksheet, p. 17 Directed Reading Overview, p. 19 Note-taking Worksheets, pp. 33–35	GLENCOE'S **ASSESSMENT** ADVANTAGE	
MiniLAB: electric meter *Need materials?* Contact Science Kit at 1-800-828-7777 or www.sciencekit.com on the Internet.	**Chapter Resources Booklet** Transparency Activity, p. 44 MiniLAB, p. 3 Enrichment, p. 30 Reinforcement, p. 27 Transparency Activity, pp. 47–48 Lab Activity, pp. 9–12 Directed Reading, p. 20 **Cultural Diversity,** pp. 45, 49	**Portfolio** Cultural Diversity, p. 122 Curriculum Connection, p. 125 **Performance** MiniLAB, p. 127 Skill Builder Activities, p. 129 **Content** Section Assessment, p. 129	Section Focus Transparency Teaching Transparency Interactive CD-ROM/DVD Guided Reading Audio Program
Activity: dry black, brown, and sandy white soils; 3 thermometers, ring stand, graph paper, 3 colored pencils, metric ruler, 3 clear glass or plastic dishes, 200-watt gooseneck lamp, watch or clock with second hand	**Chapter Resources Booklet** Transparency Activity, p. 45 Enrichment, p. 31 Reinforcement, p. 28 Directed Reading, p. 20 Lab Activity, pp. 13–16 Activity Worksheet, pp. 5–6 **Earth Science Critical Thinking/ Problem Solving,** pp. 10, 17	**Portfolio** Extension, p. 132 **Performance** Skill Builder Activities, p. 135 **Content** Section Assessment, p. 135	Section Focus Transparency Interactive CD-ROM/DVD Guided Reading Audio Program
MiniLAB: warm and cold water, Thermos bottle, ice, glass, thermal cup holder, cup, glass container **Activity:** paper, ruler, pencils, cardboard, glue, aluminum foil	**Chapter Resources Booklet** Transparency Activity, p. 46 MiniLAB, p. 4 Enrichment, p. 32 Reinforcement, p. 29 Directed Reading, pp. 21, 22 Activity Worksheet, pp. 7–8 **Lab Management and Safety,** p. 71	**Portfolio** Challenge, p. 141 **Performance** MiniLAB, p. 139 Problem-Solving Activity, p. 140 Skill Builder Activities, p. 141 **Content** Section Assessment, p. 141	Section Focus Transparency Interactive CD-ROM/DVD Guided Reading Audio Program

GLENCOE'S **ASSESSMENT** ADVANTAGE

End of Chapter Assessment

Blackline Masters	Technology	Professional Series
Chapter Resources Booklet Chapter Review, pp. 37–38 Chapter Tests, pp. 39–42 **Standardized Test Practice by The Princeton Review,** pp. 27–30	MindJogger Videoquiz CD-ROM Explorations and Quizzes Vocabulary Puzzle Makers ExamView Pro Test Bank Interactive Lesson Planner Interactive Teacher's Edition	Performance Assessment in the Science Classroom (PASC)

Transparencies

Section Focus

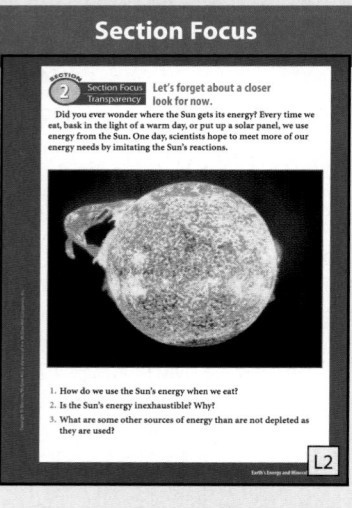

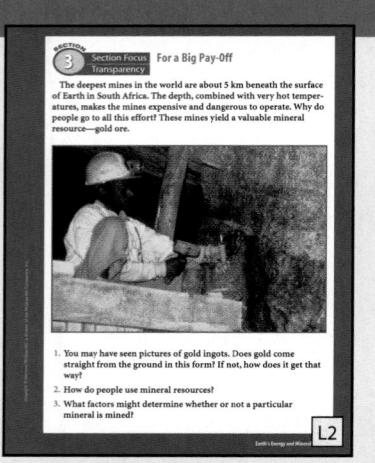

This is a representation of key blackline masters available in the Teacher Classroom Resources. See Resource Manager boxes within the chapter for additional information.

Assessment

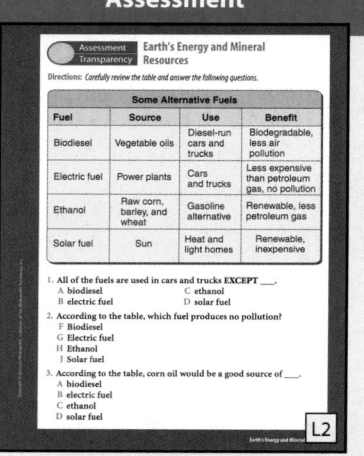

Teaching

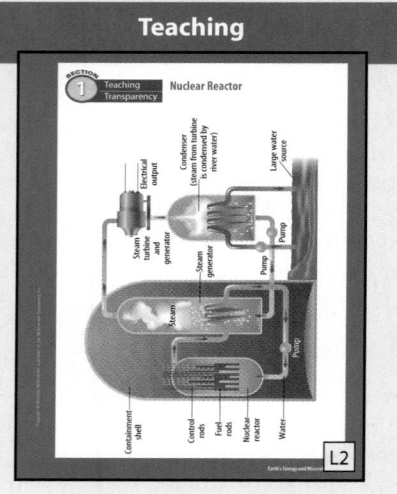

Key to Teaching Strategies

The following designations will help you decide which activities are appropriate for your students.

L1 Level 1 activities should be appropriate for students with learning difficulties.

L2 Level 2 activities should be within the ability range of all students.

L3 Level 3 activities are designed for above-average students.

ELL ELL activities should be within the ability range of English Language Learners.

COOP LEARN Cooperative Learning activities are designed for small group work.

LS Multiple Learning Styles logos, as described on page 22T, are used throughout to indicate strategies that address different learning styles.

P These strategies represent student products that can be placed into a best-work portfolio.

Hands-on Activities

Activity Worksheets

Laboratory Activities

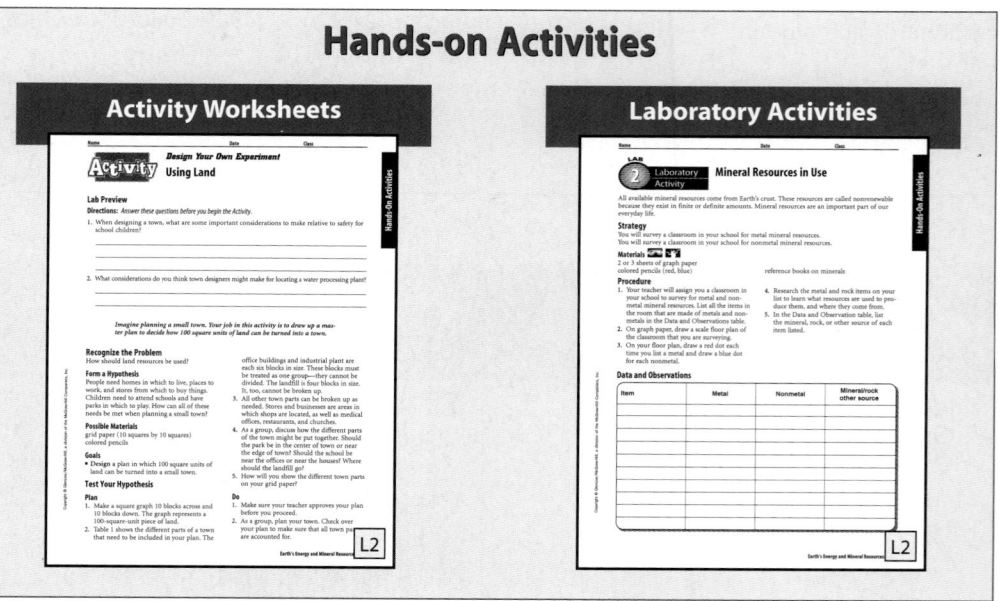

Meeting Different Ability Levels

Content Outline

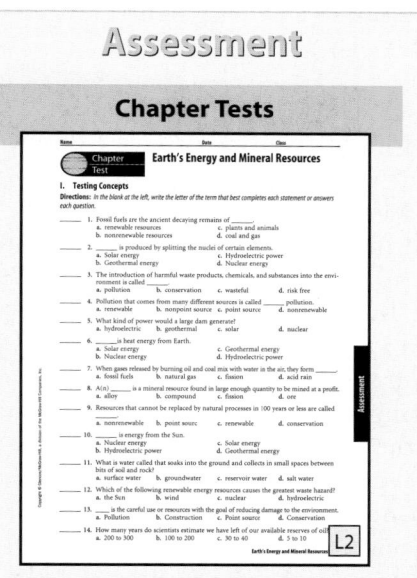

Energy Resources

L2

Reinforcement

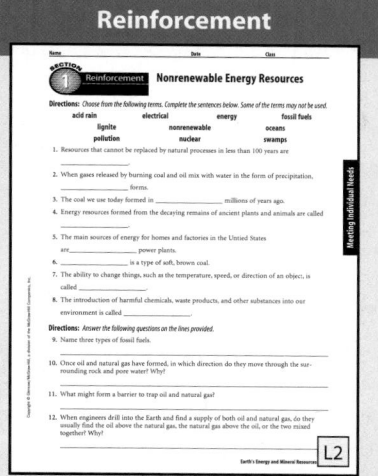

Nonrenewable Energy Resources

L2

Enrichment

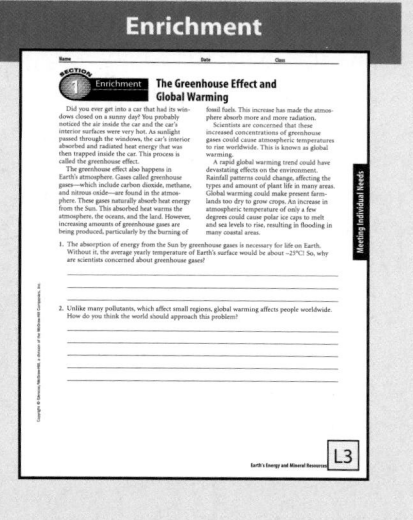

The Greenhouse Effect and Global Warming

L3

Directed Reading

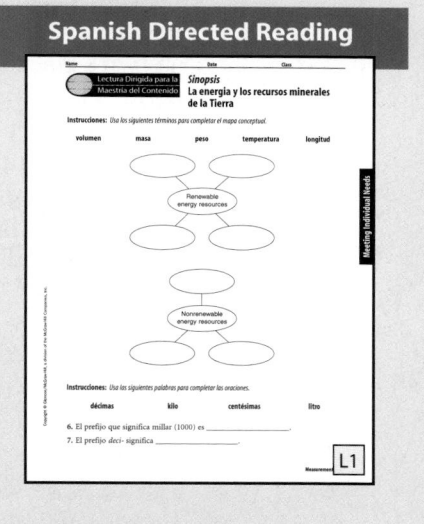

Overview
Earth's Energy and Mineral Resources

L1

Spanish Directed Reading

Lectura Dirigida para la Maestría del Contenido

Sinopsis
La energía y los recursos minerales de la Tierra

L1

Assessment

Chapter Tests

Chapter Test

Earth's Energy and Mineral Resources

L2

Test Practice Workbook

Standardized Test Practice
Teacher Edition

Glencoe Science

Earth Science

L2

Chapter Review

Chapter Review

Earth's Energy and Mineral Resources

L2

Science Content Background

SECTION 1

Nonrenewable Energy Resources

Synthetic Fuels

Coal is gasified when steam and oxygen are introduced under heat and pressure. The end product is a gas that can be burned as fuel consisting of carbon monoxide, hydrogen, and methane. This process can be done below ground without extracting the coal. There are several different methods that can be utilized in the liquification of coal. One method begins with the gasification of coal. The carbon monoxide and hydrogen produced from this step are then recovered from the gaseous mixture. The union of the carbon monoxide and hydrogen forms a liquid fuel. Another method takes place under high pressure as hydrogen gas is added to solid coal. Next, a chemical reaction between the hydrogen and the coal takes place under high heat. As the product cools, it forms a liquid fuel.

Methane Hydrates

The name of the group of compounds in which methane hydrates are classified, the *clathrates*, gives an apt description of its structure in nature. The word clathrate is derived from the Latin word *clathratus* which means "furnished with a lattice." The structure of a methane hydrate is just that—molecule of methane trapped within a lattice of water molecules, frozen into a formation closely resembling ice. Methane hydrates were first studied by French scientists in the late 1800s. In the 1930s they were found forming in and blocking gas pipelines in colder areas. Methane hydrates were not discovered in nature until the 1960s. At that time, Russian scientists found methane hydrates in the permafrost of Siberia while drilling for natural gas. A decade later, methane hydrates were discovered in marine sediments. Today, methane hydrates have been found worldwide on continental margins.

SECTION 2

Inexhaustible and Renewable Energy Resources

Energy from Earth

The use of geothermal energy can be divided into three categories depending on the amount of technology involved. The use geothermal energy without first changing it to electricity is called direct use. Another way to use geothermal energy is through heat pumps. Heat pumps are used to heat and cool buildings with the help of a heat exchanger. Power plants use the heat from Earth's interior as an energy source to generate electricity.

Direct use is the simplest application. Evidence suggests that humans have been using hot springs for thousands of years. In North America, hot springs were used for cooking, bathing, and relaxing. In some areas of the world, such as New Guinea, hot springs still are used to boil potatoes and eggs. The Japanese macaque, a monkey that lives in the mountainous areas of Japan and China, sits for hours in the hot springs of those regions, taking refuge from the cold during winter. Aside from recreation, other direct-use applications include heating homes, greenhouses and fish farms and using the water as a source of heat to dehydrate fruits and vegetables and to pasteurize milk.

Fun Fact

In some coastal areas where the difference between high tide and low tide is significant, power plants have been built near shore in order to produce electricity using the energy of raising and ebbing tides.

Alcohol—A Form of Energy from the Sun

Alcohol was used as a source of fuel to run internal combustion engines in the late 1800s. Although alcohol does not contain as much energy as gasoline, gasoline-alcohol blends have been used as fuel for cars in Europe during times of oil shortages. Brazil produces large amounts of ethanol by fermenting sugar cane. The ethanol is used either directly as fuel for automobiles, or it is mixed with gasoline in a 20:80 ratio and the resulting gasohol is used as fuel.

SECTION 3 — Mineral Resources

Ores

Although aluminum is one of the most abundant elements in Earth's crust, it is not easily retrievable in a pure state. Bauxite is the main source of commercial aluminum. When rocks containing large stores of aluminum are weathered in tropical regions, bauxite is produced. Large bauxite deposits are found in France, West Africa, Jamaica, and Brazil. In the United States bauxite deposits are found in Arkansas, Alabama, and Georgia, areas that had a tropical climate millions of years ago.

Iron is another element that is abundant in Earth's crust. However, iron is not found in a pure state. Hematite, which is a combination of iron and oxygen, is a commonly mined iron ore. In the United States, hematite is found in Minnesota, Wisconsin, and Michigan, as well as in the Appalachian Mountains.

Building Materials

Limestone is a sedimentary rock made of calcium carbonate. Limestone can be formed from large deposits of dead marine organisms whose shells or *tests*, were composed of calcium carbonate or aragonite. In some areas of the world, such as Bermuda, a type of limestone called *coquina*, which is composed of broken shells held together by calcium carbonate, is used to build homes.

Fun Fact

The source of almost 33 percent of the world's supply of garnet is the rocks of the Adirondack Mountains.

SCIENCE Online

For additional content background on this topic, go to the Glencoe Science Web site at science.glencoe.com.

Jeremy Woodhouse/DRK Photo

Chapter Vocabulary

fossil fuel
coal
oil
natural gas
reserve
nuclear energy
solar energy
wind farm
hydroelectric energy
geothermal energy
biomass energy
mineral resource
ore
recycling

What do you think?

Science Journal The photo shows a drill bit that is used on the end of the string of pipe that is lowered down to drill for oil.

Earth's Energy and Mineral Resources

Oil fields in Texas, like the one shown here, harbor some of the world's richest reserves of energy resources. In this chapter, you'll learn about many different types of resources that humans derive from Earth. You also will appreciate the importance of conserving these resources—especially those that are extracted faster than nature can produce them.

What do you think?

Science Journal Look at the picture below with a classmate. Discuss what this might be. Here's a hint: *It's on the cutting edge of oil exploration.* Write your answer in your Science Journal.

118

Theme Connection

Energy The theme is developed throughout the chapter in an exploration of Earth's renewable (biomass, geothermal), inexhaustible (solar, wind), and nonrenewable (fossil fuels, nuclear) energy resources.

The physical properties of Earth materials determine how easily liquids and gases move through them. Geologists use these properties, in part, to predict where reserves of energy resources like petroleum or natural gas can be found.

Compare rock permeability

1. Obtain a sample of sandstone and a sample of shale from your teacher.
2. Make sure that your samples can be placed on a tabletop so that the sides facing up are reasonably flat and horizontal.
3. Place the two samples side by side in a shallow baking pan.
4. Using a dropper, place three drops of cooking oil on each sample.
5. For ten minutes, observe what happens to the oil on the samples.

Observe

Write your observations in your Science Journal. Infer which rock type might be a good reservoir for petroleum.

Purpose Students compare the permeability of sandstone and shale. L2 IS **Kinesthetic**

Preparation Be sure the rock samples can be placed so that the upper side is reasonably flat.

Materials small samples of sandstone and shale, small amount of cooking oil, dropper, baking pan, timer

Teaching Strategy Students may need to place the rocks on a small amount of modeling clay to make sure that a flat side is horizontal.

Observe

Sandstone is porous, so oil seeps through it easily. Oil pools on top of shale. Sandstone is a good reservoir for petroleum because it absorbs petroleum like a sponge.

Portfolio Have students make posters showing how petroleum might be trapped in sandstone sandwiched between layers of shale. Use **Performance Assessment in the Science Classroom**, p. 145.

Before You Read

FOLDABLES
Reading & Study Skills

Making a Main Ideas Study Fold Make the following Foldable to help you identify the major topics about energy and mineral resources.

1. Place a sheet of paper in front of you so the long side is at the top. Fold the paper in half from the left side to the right side and then unfold.
2. Fold each side in to the centerfold line to divide the paper into fourths. Fold the paper in half from top to bottom and unfold.
3. Through the top thickness of paper, cut along both of the middle fold lines to form four tabs. Label the tabs *Nonrenewable Energy Resources, Inexhaustible Energy Resources, Renewable Energy Resources,* and *Mineral Resources.*
4. As you read the chapter, list examples on the front of the tabs and write about each type of resource under the tabs.

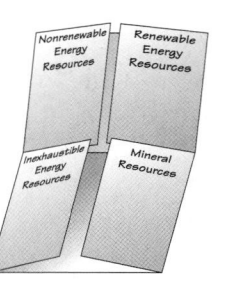

Before You Read

FOLDABLES
Reading & Study Skills

Dinah Zike Study Fold
Purpose Before reading the chapter, have students determine what they know about Earth's mineral and energy resources. Have students make a Foldable for recording and organizing notes on renewable, nonrenewable, inexhaustible, and mineral resources as they read.

📁 For additional help, see Foldables Worksheet, p. 17 in **Chapter Resources Booklet,** or go to the Glencoe Science Web site at **science.glencoe.com.** See After You Read in the Study Guide at the end of this chapter.

Nonrenewable Energy Resources

Nonrenewable Energy Resources

1 Motivate

Bellringer Transparency

Display the Section Focus Transparency for Section 1. Use the accompanying Transparency Activity Master. L2

ELL

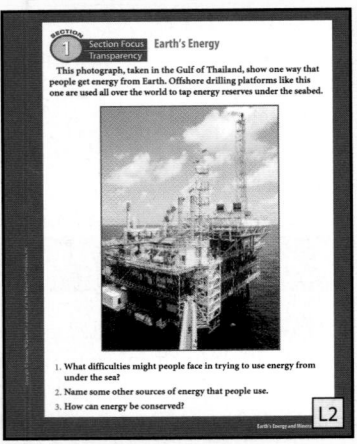

Tie to Prior Knowledge

Ask students to think of ways they use fossil fuels (coal, oil, natural gas) in their everyday lives. Possible answers: heating with oil or natural gas, gasoline fuel for cars made from petroleum, coal or oil burned in power plants to make electricity, petroleum made into plastic Tell students they will learn more about nonrenewable energy resources in this section.

As You Read

What You'll Learn

■ **Identify** examples of nonrenewable energy resources.
■ **Describe** the advantages and disadvantages of using fossil fuels.
■ **Explain** the advantages and disadvantages of using nuclear energy.

Vocabulary

fossil fuel   natural gas
coal   reserve
oil   nuclear energy

Why It's Important

Nonrenewable resources should be conserved to ensure their presence for future generations.

Energy

The world's population relies on energy of all kinds. Energy is the ability to cause change. Some energy resources on Earth are being used faster than natural Earth processes can replace them. These resources are referred to as nonrenewable energy resources. Most of the energy resources used to generate electricity are nonrenewable.

Fossil Fuels

Nonrenewable energy resources include fossil fuels. **Fossil fuels** are fuels such as coal, oil, and natural gas that form from the remains of plants and other organisms that were buried and altered over millions of years. Coal is a sedimentary rock formed from the compacted and transformed remains of ancient plant matter. Oil is a liquid hydrocarbon that often is referred to as petroleum. Hydrocarbons are compounds that contain hydrogen and carbon atoms. Other naturally occurring hydrocarbons occur in the gas or semisolid states. Fossil fuels are processed to make gasoline for cars, to heat homes, and for many other uses, as shown in **Table 1.**

Table 1 Uses of Fossil Fuels

Coal	■ To generate electricity
Oil	■ To produce gasoline and other fuels ■ As lubricants ■ To make plastics, home shingles, and other products
Natural Gas	■ To heat buildings ■ As a source of sulfur

Section ✓Assessment Planner

PORTFOLIO
Cultural Diversity, p. 122
Curriculum Connection, p. 125
PERFORMANCE ASSESSMENT
Try at Home MiniLAB, p. 127
Skill Builder Activities, p. 129
See page 148 for more options.

CONTENT ASSESSMENT
Section, p. 129
Challenge, p. 129
Chapter, pp. 148–149

Figure 1
This coal layer is located in Castle Gate, Utah. *Using the map and legend below, can you determine what type of coal it is?*

Legend:
- Anthracite
- Bituminous
- Lignite

Coal The most abundant fossil fuel in the world is coal, shown in **Figure 1.** If the consumption of coal continues at the current usage rate, it is estimated that the coal supply will last for about another 250 years.

Coal is a rock that contains at least 50 percent plant remains. Coal begins to form when plants die in a swampy area. The dead plants are covered by more plants, water, and sediment, preventing atmospheric oxygen from coming into contact with the plant matter. The lack of atmospheric oxygen prevents the plant matter from decaying rapidly. Bacterial growth within the plant material causes a gradual breakdown of molecules in the plant tissue, leaving carbon and some impurities behind. This is the material that eventually will become coal after millions of years. Bacteria also cause the release of methane gas as the original plant matter breaks down. You can smell methane gas in swamps today. The scent is somewhat like that of rotten eggs.

✔ **Reading Check** *What happens to begin the formation of coal?*

Synthetic Fuels Unlike gasoline, which is refined from petroleum, other fuels called synthetic fuels are extracted from solid organic material. Synthetic fuels can be created from coal—a sedimentary rock containing hydrocarbons. The hydrocarbons are extracted from coal to form liquid and gaseous synthetic fuels. Liquid fuels can be processed to produce gasoline for automobiles and fuel oil for home heating. Gaseous synthetic fuels can be used to generate electircity and heat buildings.

Life Science
INTEGRATION

The coal found in the eastern and midwestern United States formed from plants that lived in great swamps about 300 million years ago during the Carboniferous period of geologic time. Research the Carboniferous period to find out what types of plants lived in these swamps. Describe the plants in your Science Journal.

SECTION 1 Nonrenewable Energy Resources **121**

Energy

Use Science Words
Word Usage Have students use the term *nonrenewable energy resources* in a sentence describing their characteristics. Possible answer: Nonrenewable energy resources are those that require great amounts of time for Earth's natural processes to make.

Fossil Fuels

Teacher FYI
Much of the coal burned today formed from plants that lived during the Mississippian and Pennsylvanian Periods of the Paleozoic Era.

Life Science
INTEGRATION

There were many cone-bearing plants. The world *carboniferous* means "cone-bearing." In addition there were many ferns, fern-like trees, and mosses that grew in the "coal swamps."

✔ **Reading Check**

Answer Plants die in a swampy area.

Caption Answer
Figure 1 Lignite

Resource Manager

Chapter Resources Booklet
Directed Reading for Content Mastery, pp. 19, 20
Transparency Activity, p. 44

Inclusion Strategies

Gifted Have students find the heat value of each type of coal in BTU/pound. Ask them to decide which type of coal provides the most heat per pound. BTU stands for British Thermal Unit, a unit of heat. Peat—3,000 to 5,000; lignite coal—7,000; bituminous coal—12,000; anthracite coal—14,000; anthracite provides the most heat per pound. L3 IS **Logical-Mathematical**

Visual Learning

Figure 2 Ask students to compare the appearance of peat and anthracite in the photos. **How has the appearance of coal changed between its first stage of development, peat, and its last stage of development, anthracite?** Peat looks soft and brownish, and the plant material from which it forms is visible. Anthracite is black and dense like a rock.

Activity

Have student groups examine samples of peat, lignite coal, bituminous coal, and anthracite coal, but do not tell them what the samples are. Have them contrast the color, texture, and hardness of each sample. Explain that the specimens represent the four different stages in the formation of coal. Have students arrange the samples from least to most changed. L2
COOP LEARN IS **Visual-Spatial**

Discussion

Why are bacteria need to produce coal? Bacteria break down plant matter in the first stage of coal formation.

Extension

Have students investigate world production of coal and graph their findings. Possible answer: top ten producers: China—33.9%, United States—28.4%, India—6.8%, Australia—6.5%, Russia—6.0%, South Africa—5.6%, Poland—4.5%, Germany—3.9%, Kazakhstan—2.2%, Ukraine—2.2%
L2 IS **Logical-Mathematical**

Stages of Coal Formation As decaying plant material loses gas and moisture, the concentration of carbon increases. The first step in this process, shown in **Figure 2**, results in the formation of peat. Peat is a layer of organic sediment. When peat burns, it releases large amounts of smoke because it has a high concentration of water and impurities.

As peat is buried under more sediment, it changes into lignite, which is a soft, brown coal with much less moisture. Heat and pressure produced by burial force water out of peat and concentrate carbon in the lignite. Lignite releases more energy and less smoke than peat when it is burned.

As the layers are buried deeper, bituminous coal, or soft coal, forms. Bituminous coal is compact, black, and brittle. It provides lots of heat energy when burned. Bituminous coal contains various levels of sulfur, which can pollute the environment.

If enough heat and pressure are applied to buried layers of bituminous coal, anthracite coal forms. Anthracite coal contains the highest amount of carbon of all forms of coal. Therefore, anthracite coal is the cleanest burning of all coals.

Figure 2
Coal is formed in four basic stages.

A Plant material accumulates in swamps and eventually forms a layer of peat.

B Over time, heat and pressure cause the peat to change into lignite coal.

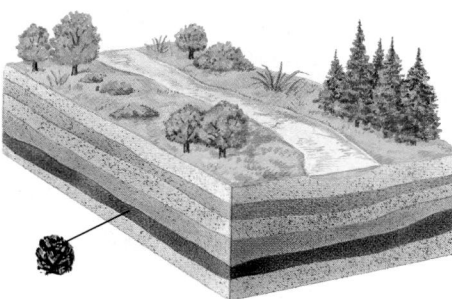

C As the lignite coal becomes buried by more sediments, heat and pressure change it into bituminous coal.

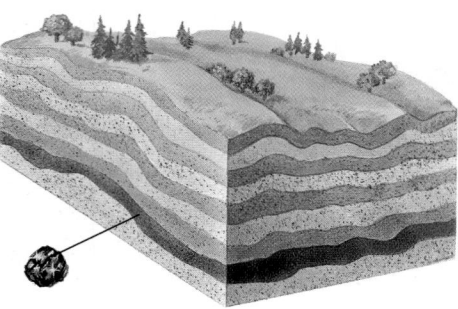

D When bituminous coal is heated and squeezed during metamorphism, anthracite coal forms.

122 **CHAPTER 5** Earth's Energy and Mineral Resources

Cultural Diversity

Limiting Technology The Amish are a religious group with communities in the United States and Canada. Amish principles involve separation from worldly things, including most technology. As a result, the energy crisis that affects most other Americans who use electricity and drive cars is not a concern for them. Restrictions on the use of electricity are universal among the Old Order Amish. Most Amish farm the land, relying extensively on human and animal power. Fossil fuel use is limited. Kerosene is used for lamps, and gasoline-driven motors may be used for some farm equipment. But machinery must move via horse-drawn wagons. Have students research to find out more about how the Amish use (or avoid) modern energy resources. Have them write a report on their findings. P

Oil and Natural Gas Coal isn't the only fossil fuel used to obtain energy. Two other fossil fuels that provide large quantities of the energy used today are oil and natural gas. **Oil** is a thick, black liquid formed from the buried remains of microscopic marine organisms. **Natural gas** forms under similar conditions and often with oil, but it forms in a gaseous state. Oil and natural gas are hydrocarbons. However, natural gas is composed of hydrocarbon molecules that are lighter than those in oil.

Residents of the United States burn vast quantities of oil and natural gas for daily energy requirements. As shown in **Figure 3,** Americans obtain most of their energy from these sources. Natural gas is used mostly for heating and cooking. Oil is used in many ways, including as heating oil, gasoline, lubricants, and in the manufacture of plastics and other important compounds.

Formation of Oil and Natural Gas Most geologists agree that petroleum forms over millions of years from the remains of tiny marine organisms in ocean sediment. The process begins when marine organisms called plankton die and fall to the seafloor. Similar to the way that coal is buried, sediment is deposited over them. The temperature rises with depth in Earth, and increased heat eventually causes the dead plankton to change to oil and gas after they have been buried deeply by sediment.

Oil and natural gas often are found in layers of rock that have become tilted or folded. Because they are less dense than water, oil and natural gas are forced upward. Rock layers that are impermeable, such as shale, stop this upward movement. When this happens, a folded shale layer can trap the oil and natural gas below it. Such a trap for oil and gas is shown in **Figure 4.** The rock layer beneath the shale in which the petroleum and natural gas accumulate is called a reservoir rock.

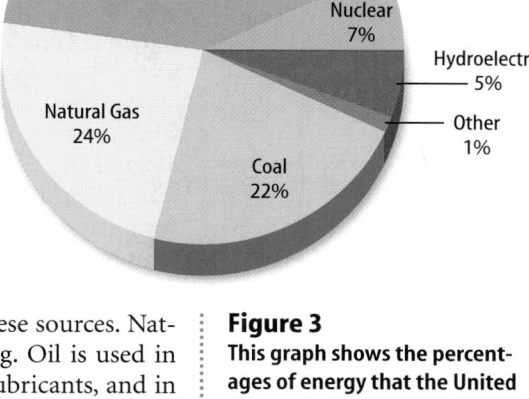

Figure 3
This graph shows the percentages of energy that the United States derives form various energy resources.

Figure 4
Oil and natural gas are fossil fuels formed by the burial of marine organisms. These fuels can be trapped and accumulate beneath Earth's surface.

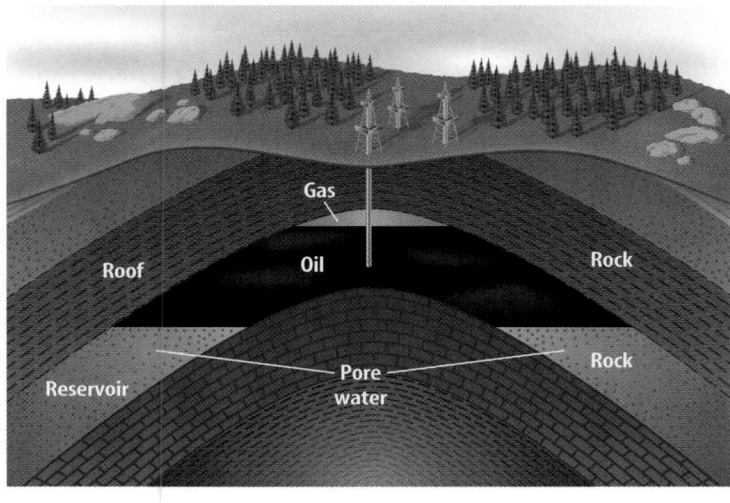

Fossil Fuels, continued

Make a Model

Have students use clay, small gravel, and pieces of wet, balled-up paper towels (representing oil deposits) to model layers of oil-bearing rock, such as in **Figure 4.** Models should show the layers and trapped oil in cross section. Instruct students to use this model to show where oil and natural gas would collect in the porous layer between two nonporous clay layers. The models should show that oil and natural gas have moved up through the porous rock and have collected at the highest location under the nonporous clay. L2 IS **Kinesthetic**

Extension

Have students draw maps of the United States that show the location of coal, oil, and natural gas reserves. Discuss with students where each type of resource is generally located. coal: Appalachian and Rocky Mountains as well as parts of the Midwest and Great Plains; petroleum: mid-Appalachians, Texas, Oklahoma and parts of the Great Plains, southwestern California; natural gas: northern Appalachians, Gulf Coast, Great Plains, California's Central Valley L3 IS **Visual-Spatial**

Resource Manager

Chapter Resources Booklet
   Note-taking Worksheets, pp. 33–35
Earth Science Critical Thinking/Problem Solving, p. 2

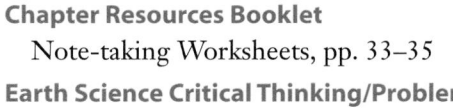

Fossil Fuels Have students make a table in their Science Journals that lists the advantages and disadvantages of using fossil fuels. Possible advantages: produce energy inexpensively compared to some other sources, presently available; possible disadvantages: pollutes the environment, nonrenewable

Removing Fossil Fuels from the Ground

Visual Learning

Figure 5A Why might open-pit mining be of concern to those who are trying to protect endangered species? Open-pit mining disturbs Earth's surface in a way that would destroy animal habitats.

Use an Analogy

Use the following analogy to help students understand the two basic ways to remove coal from the ground. Ask students how they would go about looking for an object that their dog has buried behind a stone wall. Some students might dig a hole behind the wall and remove the object from the hole. Other students might remove stones from the wall and dig a tunnel into the ground behind the wall, hoping to find the object. Small pieces of wood could be used to support the top and sides of the tunnel. The first example is analogous to an open-pit mine, and the second example is analogous to an underground mine.

Removing Fossil Fuels from the Ground

Coal is removed from the ground using one of several methods of excavation. The two most common methods are strip mining, also called open-pit mining, and underground mining, shown in **Figure 5.** Oil and natural gas are removed by pumping them out of the ground.

Coal Mining During strip mining, shown in **Figure 5A,** layers of soil and rock above coal are removed and piled to one side. The exposed coal then is removed and loaded into trucks or trains and transported elsewhere. After the coal has been removed, mining companies often return the soil and rock to the open pit and cover it with topsoil. Trees and grass are planted in a process called land reclamation. If possible, animals native to the area are reintroduced. Strip mining is used only when the coal deposits are close to the surface.

In one method of underground coal mining, tunnels are dug and pillars of rock are left to support the rocks surrounding the tunnels. Two other types of coal mines are drift mines and slope mines. Drift mining, shown in **Figure 5B,** is the removal of coal that is not close to Earth's surface through a horizontal opening in the side of a hill or mountain. In slope mining, an angled opening and air shaft are made in the side of a mountain to remove coal.

Figure 5
Coal is a fossil fuel that can be removed from Earth in many different ways.

A During open-pit mining, coal is accessed by removing the soil and rock above it.

B During underground coal mining, tunnels are made into the earth. *How do you think the coal is removed from these tunnels?*

124   CHAPTER 5 Earth's Energy and Mineral Resources

LAB DEMONSTRATION

Purpose to contrast auto emissions from new and old cars that burn gasoline for fuel
Materials three white socks
Preparation Select a fairly new car and an old, poorly running car. Place a sock over the tailpipe of each car. Keep the third sock clean. Start and run each car for two minutes.

Procedure Show students the three socks, and explain how the material on each sock was obtained.

Expected Outcome Students should see that the old car deposits more particulates on the sock than the new car.

✓ Assessment

Ask students to predict whether an old car that needs maintenance or a new car that is well maintained will have a more negative impact on air quality. The older car that needs maintenance will have a more negative impact on air quality.

Drilling for Oil and Gas Oil and natural gas are fossil fuels that can be pumped from underground deposits. Geologists and engineers drill wells through rocks where these resources might be trapped, as shown in **Figure 6.** As the well is being drilled, it is lined with pipe to prevent it from caving in. Because oil and natural gas are fluids that are under pressure, when they are reached, they sometimes can travel easily up the narrow pipe to Earth's surface. These gushing wells then must be capped. The oil and gas then are pumped from them in a controlled manner.

 **Reading Check** *How are oil and natural gas brought to Earth's surface?*

Fossil Fuel Reserves

The amount of a fossil fuel that can be extracted at a profit using current technology is known as a **reserve.** This is not the same as a fossil fuel resource. A fossil fuel resource has fossil fuels that are concentrated enough that they can be extracted from Earth in a useful amount. However, a resource is not classified as a reserve unless the fuel can be extracted economically. What might cause a known fossil fuel resource to become classified as a reserve?

Methane Hydrates You have learned that current reserves of coal will last about 250 years. Enough natural gas is located in the United States to last about 60 more years. However, recent studies indicate that a new source of methane, which is the main component of natural gas, might be located beneath the seafloor. Icelike substances known as methane hydrates could provide tremendous reserves of methane.

Methane hydrates are stable molecules found hundreds of meters below sea level in ocean floor sediment. They form under conditions of relatively low temperatures and high pressures. The hydrocarbons are trapped within the cagelike structure of ice, as described in **Figure 7.** Scientists estimate that more carbon is contained in methane hydrates than in all current fossil fuel deposits combined. Large accumulations of methane hydrates are estimated to exist off the eastern coast of the United States. Can you imagine what it would mean to the world's energy supply if relatively clean-burning methane could be extracted economically from methane hydrates?

Figure 6
Oil and natural gas are recovered from Earth by drilling deep wells.

 **SCIENCE** *Online*

Research Visit the Glencoe Science Web site at **science.glencoe.com** for more information about methane hydrates. Communicate to your class what you learn.

Curriculum Connection

Geography Have students research the world's five leading oil producers in terms of barrels per day. Tell them to make a bar graph that displays the data. Saudi Arabia—8,885,000; United States—8,290,000; Russia—6,200,000; Iran—3,705,000; Mexico—3,065,000 P LS **Logical-Mathematical**

✔ **Reading Check**

Answer They are pumped to Earth's surface through wells.

Fossil Fuel Reserves

 **SCIENCE** *Online*
Internet Addresses
_____
_____
_____
_____

Explore the Glencoe Science Web site at **science.glencoe.com** to find out more about topics in this section.

Text Question Answer
   an increase in the price of the resource that would make it profitable to extract; a change in technology that would make a resource previously too difficult or expensive to extract easier to extract and therefore profitable

IDENTIFYING Misconceptions

Because Saudi Arabia is the leading producer of oil, students may also think Saudi Arabia is the leading producer of natural gas and coal. Inform students that Russia and the United States are the top two producers of natural gas and that China and the United States are the leading producers of coal.

Visualizing Methane Hydrates

Have students examine the pictures and read the captions. Then ask the following questions.

Why is it important that methane hydrates are flammable? They represent an enormous source of potential energy.

What environmental problems could be associated with harvesting methane hydrates? Possible answers: Both permafrost and oceans are environmentally sensitive areas. Mining ocean sediments and digging in permafrost implies the need for equipment and manpower—both bringing wastes, as well as the disruption of habitat for resident organisms.

Activity

Have students make posters depicting an imaginary mining site for methane hydrates. Encourage them to include information on necessary equipment, types of professionals, and the environments in which methane hydrates are likely to to be found. **LS Visual-Spatial**

Extension

Have students research the hitory of discoveries and encounters with methane hydrates. French scientists studied them in the 1890s. In the 1930s, natural gas pipelines in cold climates would get plugged with them. In the 1960s, "frozen natural gas" was discovered in Russia. In 1981 the *Glomar Challenger* bored into a methane hydrate desposit.

NATIONAL GEOGRAPHIC VISUALIZING METHANE HYDRATES

Figure 7

Reserves of fossil fuels—such as oil, coal, and natural gas—are limited and will one day be used up. Methane hydrates could be an alternative energy source. This icelike substance, background, has been discovered in ocean floor sediments and in permafrost regions worldwide. If scientists can harness this energy, the world's gas supply could be met for years to come.

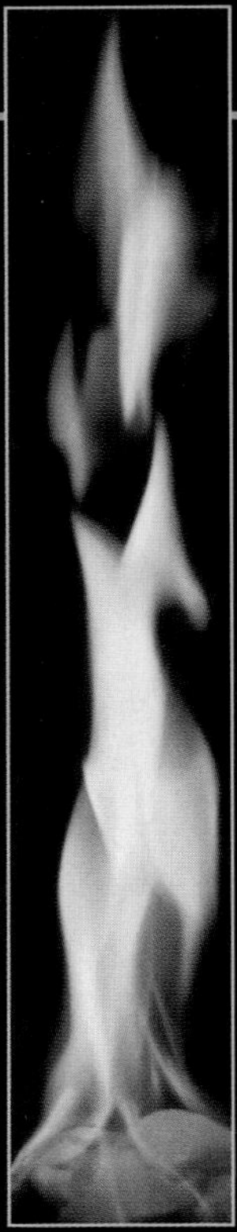

Methane hydrates are highly flammable compounds made up of methane—the main component of natural gas—trapped in a cage of frozen water. Methane hydrates represent an enormous source of potential energy. However, they contain a greenhouse gas that might intensify global warming. More research is needed to determine how to safely extract them from the seafloor.

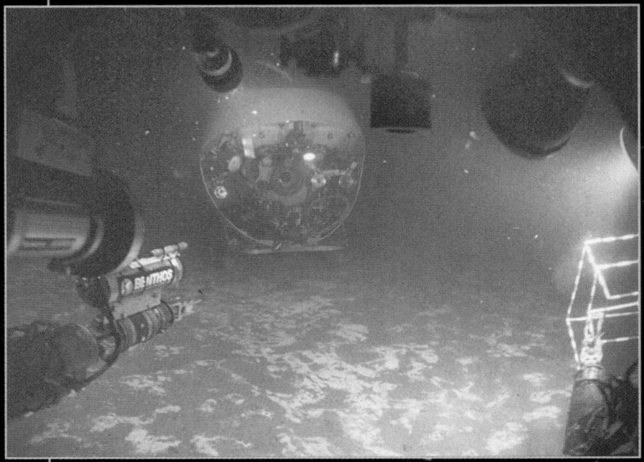

In the photo above, a Russian submersible explores a site in the North Atlantic that contains methane hydrate deposits.

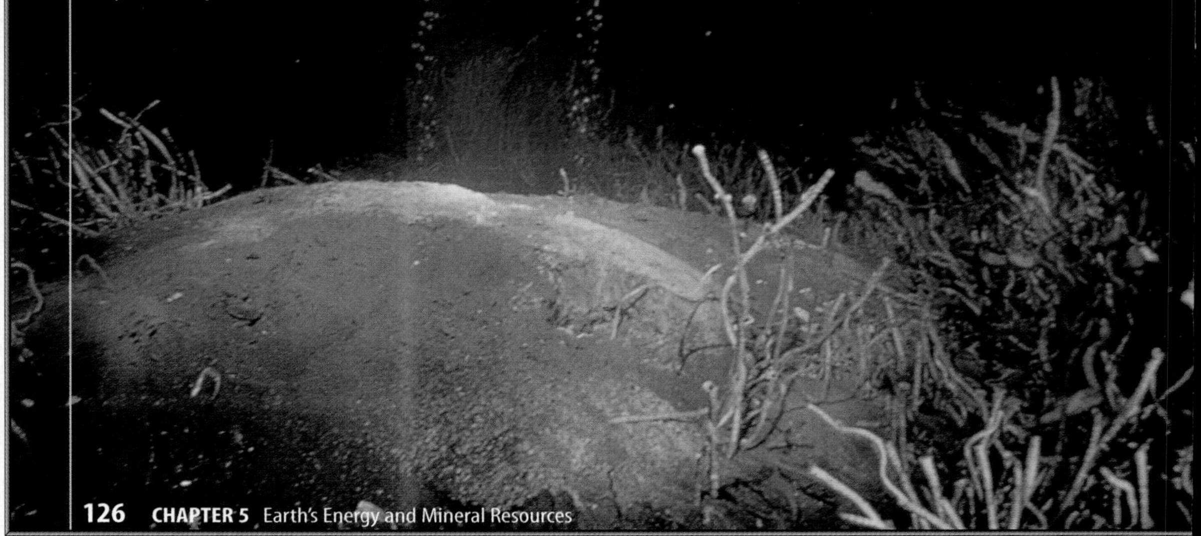

Resource Manager

Chapter Resources Booklet
MiniLAB, p. 3
Lab Activity, pp. 9–12
Science Inquiry Labs, p. 33

Conserving Fossil Fuels Do you sometimes forget to turn off the lights when you walk out of a room? Wasteful habits might mean that electricity to run homes and industries will not always be as plentiful and cheap as it is today. Fossil fuels take millions of years to form and are used much faster than Earth processes can replenish them.

Today, coal provides about 25 percent of the energy that is used worldwide and 22 percent of the energy used in the United States. Oil and natural gas provide almost 61 percent of the world's energy and about 65 percent of the U.S. energy supply. At the rate these fuels are being used, they could run out someday. How can this be avoided?

By remembering to turn off lights and appliances, you can avoid wasting fossil fuels. Another way to conserve fossil fuels is to make sure doors and windows are shut tightly during cold weather so heat doesn't leak out of your home. If you have air-conditioning, run it as little as possible. Ask the adults you live with if more insulation could be added to your home or if an insulated jacket could be put on the water heater.

Energy from Atoms

Most electricity in the United States is generated in power plants that use fossil fuels. However, alternate sources of energy exist. **Nuclear energy** is an alternate energy source produced from atomic reactions. When the nucleus of a heavy element is split, lighter elements form and energy is released. This energy can be used to light a home or power the submarine shown in **Figure 8.**

The splitting of heavy elements to produce energy is called nuclear fission. Nuclear fission is carried out in nuclear power plants using a type of uranium as fuel.

TRY AT HOME Mini LAB

Practicing Energy Conservation

Procedure
1. Have an adult help you find the **electric meter** for your home and record the reading in your **Science Journal.**
2. Do this for several days, taking your meter readings at about the same time each day.
3. List things you and your family can do to reduce your electricity use.
4. Encourage your family to try some of the listed ideas for several days.

Analysis
1. Keep taking meter readings and infer whether the change makes any difference.
2. Have you and your family helped conserve energy?

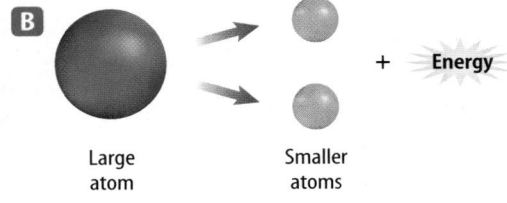

A

Figure 8
Atoms can be a source of energy.
A These submarines are powered by nuclear fission. **B** Energy is given off when a larger atom, like uranium, splits into smaller atoms.

B

Large atom → Smaller atoms + Energy

Fossil Fuel Reserves, continued

Text Question Answer
Conservation could make the resources last longer.

TRY AT HOME Mini LAB

Purpose Students will observe the results of conserving energy. [L2]
IS Logical-Mathematical

Teaching Strategy Students should practice taking meter readings before doing the activity. You might contact the local electric utility for a publication that shows how to read meters.

Analysis
1. Students should note a reduction in electricity use after the household tries conservation measures.
2. If students are successful, the family should have conserved energy and saved money on the electric bill.

✓ Assessment

Performance Have students come up with a list of conservation measures that could be used at school. Encourage them to get permission to put their measures into effect. Use **Performance Assessment in the Science Classroom,** p. 89.

Energy from Atoms

Fun Fact
The most commonly used fuel in fission power plants is uranium-235.

✔ Active Reading

Speculation About Effects/Prediction Journal This strategy allows students to examine events and speculate about their possible long-term effects. Have students divide sheets of paper in half. On the left side they should record "what happened." On the right, have them write "What might/should happen as a result of this." Have students write a Speculation About Effects/Prediction Journal as they study the use of energy sources and the consequences, both good and bad, of using the different types of energy.

Energy from Atoms,
continued

Use Science Words
Word Meaning Have students find out why the current process of producing energy from nuclear reactions is called *fission*. The term fission means "splitting apart," which is what happens to the atoms.

Discussion
Would you want to live next to a nuclear power plant? Why or why not? Accept all opinions as a basis for discussion. Some students would be concerned because of possible danger from radiation leakage. Others might feel that safety procedures would keep the area around the plant safe.

✔ Reading Check

Answer Heat is released as atoms split. The heat is used to boil water, which gives off steam. The steam drives a turbine, which turns a generator, producing electricity.

Teacher FYI
Nuclear reactors have several different systems that control their reactions. One system consists of control rods made of materials that absorb neutrons. If the reactions speed up too much, the control rods are lowered between the fuel rods, slowing or stopping the reactions. A reactor's temperature also is controlled by a water-cooling system.

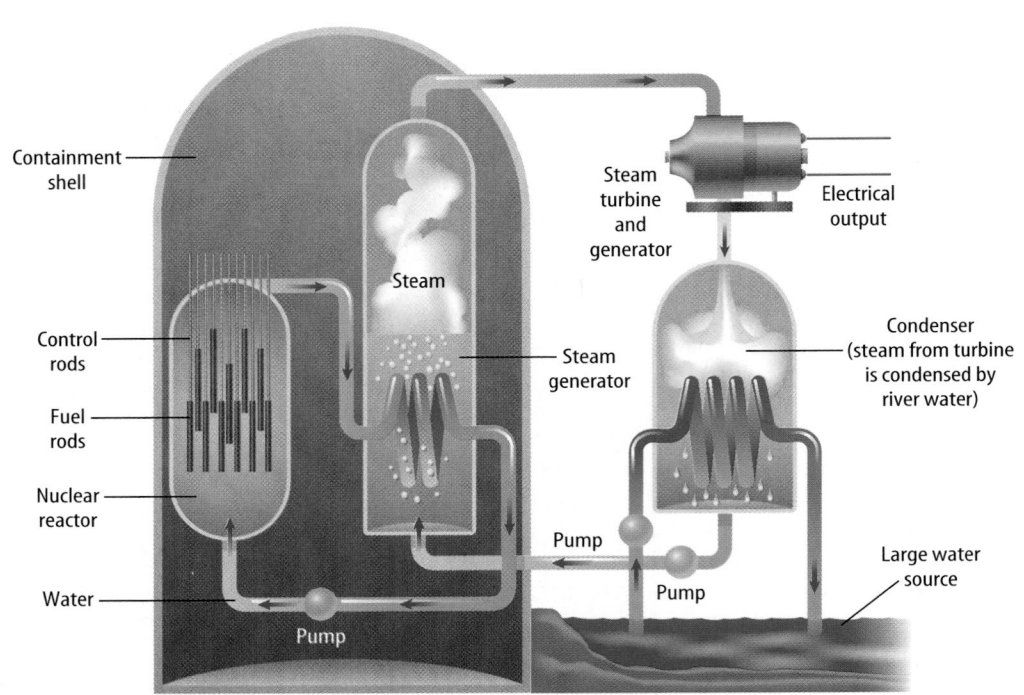

Figure 9
Heat released in nuclear reactors produces steam, which in turn is used to produce electricity. This is an example of transforming nuclear energy into electrical energy.

Electricity from Nuclear Energy A nuclear power plant, shown in **Figure 9,** has a large chamber called a nuclear reactor. Within the nuclear reactor, uranium fuel rods sit in a pool of cooling water. Neutrons are fired into the fuel rods. When the uranium-235 atoms are hit, they break apart and fire out neutrons that hit other atoms, beginning a chain reaction. As each atom splits, it not only fires neutrons but also releases heat that is used to boil water to make steam. The steam drives a turbine, which turns a generator that produces electricity.

✔ Reading Check
How is nuclear energy used to produce electricity?

Nuclear energy from fission is considered to be a nonrenewable energy resource because it uses uranium-235 as fuel. A limited amount of uranium-235 is available for use. Another problem with nuclear energy is the waste material that it produces. Nuclear waste from power plants consists of highly radioactive elements formed by the fission process. Some of this waste will remain radioactive for thousands of years. The Environmental Protection Agency (EPA) has determined that nuclear waste must be stored safely and contained for at least 10,000 years before reentering the environment.

128 CHAPTER 5 Earth's Energy and Mineral Resources

Resource Manager

Chapter Resources Booklet
  Enrichment, p. 30
Physical Science Critical Thinking/Problem Solving, pp. 14, 20

Fusion Environmental problems related to nuclear power could be eliminated if usable energy could be obtained from fusion. The Sun is a natural fusion power plant that provides energy for Earth and the solar system. Someday fusion also might provide energy for your home.

As shown in **Figure 10,** during fusion, materials of low mass are fused together to form a substance of higher mass. No fuel problem exists if the low-mass material is a commonly occurring substance. Also, if the end product is not radioactive, storing nuclear waste is not a problem. In fact, fusion of hydrogen into helium would satisfy both of these conditions. However, technologies do not currently exist to enable humans to fuse hydrogen into helium at reasonably low temperatures in a controlled manner. If this is accomplished, nuclear energy could be considered an inexhaustible fuel resource. You will learn the importance of inexhaustible and renewable energy resources in the next section.

Figure 10
Lasers are used in research facilities to help understand and control fusion.

Reteach

Ask students to hypothesize how their lives might change if the supply of fossil fuels ended or were drastically reduced. Possible answers: Travel might be restricted because of shortages of gasoline; home heating would be dependent on other energy sources, such as wood; materials made of plastic would be less plentiful.
L2 IS **Logical-Mathematical**

Challenge

Challenge students to find out how long the American supply of the resources of fossil fuels we use most (oil, natural gas, coal) will last. Have students write reports and draw graphs that explain the data they find. Use the results of the research as the basis for a class discussion of the need for Americans to conserve energy resources. P
L3 IS **Logical-Mathematical**

Assessment

Performance Have students use the graph they make in Question 6 to compare the energy consumption of nonrenewable fuels with the amount that of inexhaustible and renewable energy resources. Energy consumption from nonrenewable fuels is 92 percent. Inexhaustible and renewable fuel sources total about 8 percent. Use **Performance Assessment in the Science Classroom,** p. 109.

Section ① Assessment

1. Why are coal, oil, and natural gas considered to be fossil fuels?
2. Why are fossil fuels considered to be nonrenewable energy resources?
3. Describe similarities and differences among peat, lignite, bituminous coal, and anthracite coal.
4. How is nuclear energy obtained? What are two disadvantages of nuclear energy?
5. **Think Critically** Fossil fuels form in specific geologic environments. Why are you likely to find natural gas and oil deposits in the same location, but less likely to find coal and petroleum deposits at the same location?

Skill Builder Activities

6. **Making and Using Tables** Current energy consumption by source in the United States is as follows: *petroleum, 38 percent; natural gas, 24 percent; coal, 22 percent; nuclear energy, eight percent;* and *inexhaustible and renewable resources, eight percent.* Make a bar graph of these data. **For more help, refer to the** Science Skill Handbook.

7. **Using Percentages** Using the data from question 6, what total percent of energy in the United States comes from petroleum and natural gas? How many times more energy is obtained from these sources than from coal? **For more help, refer to the** Math Skill Handbook.

Answers to Section Assessment

1. They form from the remains of plants and animals that lived millions of years ago and were buried in soil and rock.
2. It takes fossil fuels millions of years to form. Once we use up the present supply, they are gone.

3. All four form from plant remains. Lignite is brown, while bituminous and anthracite coals are black. As you move from peat to anthracite, the percentage of carbon and the amount of heat produced per unit increase. Anthracite is the cleanest-burning type of coal.

4. Nuclear fission releases energy that is used to produce electricity. Possible answer: Nuclear energy is nonrenewable and can produce radioactive waste.
5. Petroleum and natural gas form from the decay of buried marine organisms; coal forms from the

decay of buried plants that grew on land.
6. Student graphs should have five bars: Petroleum, Natural Gas, Coal, Nuclear energy, Inexhaustible and Renewable energy Resources.
7. 62 percent; 3 times

1 Motivate

Bellringer Transparency

Display the Section Focus Transparency for Section 2. Use the accompanying Transparency Activity Master. L2

ELL

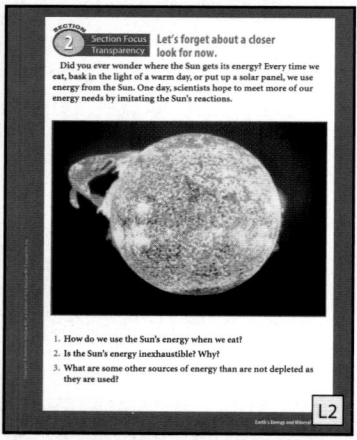

Tie to Prior Knowledge

Ask students whether they've ever seen a windmill. Ask them what they think it was used for. Tell students that some windmills were used long ago to grind grain, but now they are sometimes used for making electricity. Tell students they will find out in this section how wind, the Sun, and heat from Earth can produce electric power.

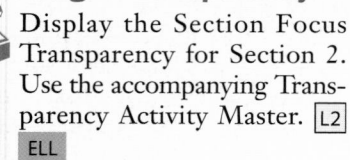

SECTION 2

Inexhaustible and Renewable Energy Resources

As You Read

What You'll Learn

- **Compare and contrast** inexhaustible and renewable energy resources.
- **Explain** why inexhaustible and renewable resources are used less than nonrenewable resources.

Vocabulary

solar energy
wind farm
hydroelectric energy
geothermal energy
biomass energy

Why It's Important

As fossil fuel reserves continue to diminish, alternate energy resources will be needed.

Inexhaustible Energy Resources

How soon the world runs out of fossil fuels depends on how they are used and conserved. Fortunately, there are inexhaustible energy resources. These sources of energy are constant and will not run out in the future as fossil fuels will. Inexhaustible energy resources include the Sun, wind, water, and geothermal energy.

Energy from the Sun When you sit in the Sun, walk into the wind, or sail against an ocean current, you are experiencing the power of solar energy. **Solar energy** is energy from the Sun. You already know that the Sun's energy heats Earth, and it also causes Earth's atmosphere and oceans to circulate. Ocean currents and global winds are examples of nature's use of solar energy. Thus, solar energy is used indirectly when the wind and some types of moving water are used to do work.

People can use solar energy in a passive way or in an active way. South-facing windows on buildings act as passive solar collectors, warming exposed rooms. Solar cells actively collect energy from the Sun and transform it into electricity. Solar cells were invented to generate electricity for satellites. Now they also are used to power calculators, streetlights, and experimental cars. Some people have installed solar energy cells on their roofs, as shown in **Figure 11.**

Figure 11
Solar panels, such as on this home in Laguna Niguel, California, can be used to collect inexhaustible solar energy to power appliances and heat water.

130   CHAPTER 5 Earth's Energy and Mineral Resources

Section ✓*Assessment* Planner

PORTFOLIO
Extension, p. 132
PERFORMANCE ASSESSMENT
Skill Builder Activities, p. 135
See page 148 for more options.

CONTENT ASSESSMENT
Section, p. 135
Challenge, p. 135
Chapter, pp. 148–149

Wind farms are used to produce electricity.

Disadvantages of Solar Energy Solar energy is clean and inexhaustible, but it does have some disadvantages. Solar cells work less efficiently on cloudy days and cannot work at all at night. Some systems use batteries to store solar energy for use at night or on cloudy days, but it is difficult to store large amounts of energy in batteries. Worn out batteries also must be discarded. This can pollute the environment if not done properly.

Energy from Wind What is better to do on a warm, windy day than fly a kite? A strong wind can lift a kite high in the sky and whip it around. The pull of the wind is so great that you wonder if it will whip the kite right out of your hands. Wind is a source of energy. It was and still is used to power sailing ships. Windmills have used wind energy to grind corn and pump water. Today, windmills can be used to generate electricity. When a large number of windmills are placed in one area for the purpose of generating electricity, the area is called a **wind farm,** as shown in **Figure 12.**

Wind energy has advantages and disadvantages. Wind is nonpolluting and free. It does little harm to the environment and produces no waste. However, only a few regions of the world have winds strong enough to generate electricity. Also, wind isn't steady. Sometimes it blows too hard and at other times it is too weak or stops entirely. For an area to use wind energy consistently, the area must have a persistent wind that blows at an appropriate speed.

 **Reading Check** *Why are some regions better suited for wind farms than others?*

 **Physics INTEGRATION**

Wind is an inexhaustible energy resource that is used by windmills to produce energy. As the blades rotate, turbines are turned to produce electricity. Find out which areas utilize wind farms and report in your Science Journal how much electricity is produced and what it is used for.

Inexhaustible Energy Resources

Quick Demo

Use a hand lens, a foil pie pan, and a ball of tissue paper to demonstrate the potential of focused sunlight. Place the ball of tissue paper in the pie pan. Hold the hand lens in the sunlight to focus the rays on the paper. Within a few minutes, the paper should begin to burn. Discuss the reason the paper burns. Have students consider how solar panels focus and collect solar energy for use in heating buildings. **CAUTION:** *Warn students NOT to repeat this demo on their own.* L2
LS Visual-Spatial

Physics INTEGRATION

Student reports should include the wind farms in California, but also may mention those in Scotland, Tasmania, and the American Midwest.

Reading Check

Answer These areas have fairly strong and constant wind.

Chapter Resources Booklet
Transparency Activity, p. 45
Directed Reading for Content Mastery, p. 20

Teacher FYI

Some energy experts project that wind power could provide more than 20 percent of the world's electricity, and 10 to 25 percent of the electricity generated in the United States, by the middle of the twenty-first century.

Inexhaustible Energy Resources, continued

Make a Model

Have student groups make models that demonstrate how energy from wind or water can be used. There are several possibilities, including: a pinwheel toy, a model sailboat, a model water wheel, or a model dam with water flowing over a wheel that models a turbine. Have groups explain their models in short classroom presentations.
[S] Kinesthetic

Extension

Have students draw a map of the United States that locates the areas where geothermal energy is predominant. Ask them to research how that energy is used and write a brief report on their findings. [L2]
[S] Linguistic [P]

Visual Learning

Figure 13 **How was the area behind the dam probably different before the dam was built?** The huge lake behind the dam was not there, and the land that is under the lake was dry, exposed ground. A river (the one that still flows downstream from the dam) flowed through a now-drowned river valley behind the dam.

Figure 13
Hydroelectric power is important in many regions of the United States. **[A]** Hoover Dam was built on the Colorado River to supply electricity for a large area.
[B] The power of running water is converted to usable energy in a hydroelectric power plant.

132

Energy from Water For a long time, waterwheels steadily spun next to streams and rivers. The energy in the flowing water powered the wheels that ground grain or cut lumber. More than a pretty picture, using a waterwheel in this way is an example of microhydropower. Microhydropower has been used throughout the world to do work.

Today energy from running water is used to generate electricity. Electricity produced by waterpower is called **hydroelectric energy.** To generate electricity from water running in a river, a large concrete dam is built to retain water, as illustrated in **Figure 13.** A lake forms behind the dam. As water is released, its force turns turbines at the base of the dam. The turbines then turn generators that make electricity.

At first it might appear that hydroelectric energy doesn't create any environmental problems and that the water is used with little additional cost. However, when dams are built, upstream lakes fill with sediment and downstream erosion increases. Land above the dam is flooded, and wildlife habitats are damaged.

Energy from Earth Erupting volcanoes and geysers like Old Faithful are examples of geothermal energy in action. The energy that causes volcanoes to erupt or water to shoot up as a geyser also can be used to generate electricity. Energy obtained by using hot magma or hot, dry rocks inside Earth is called **geothermal energy.**

When using magma, water is pumped into rock near magma bodies. The magma's heat turns the water into steam. In a newer method, water becomes steam when it is pumped through broken, hot, dry rocks. The steam then is used to turn turbines that run generators to make electricity. The advantage of using hot, dry rocks is that they are found just about everywhere. Geothermal energy presently is being used in Hawaii and in parts of the western United States. A geothermal energy plant is illustrated in **Figure 14.**

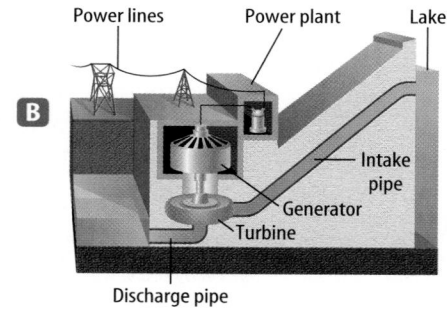

Figure 14
Geothermal energy is used to supply electricity to industries and homes.

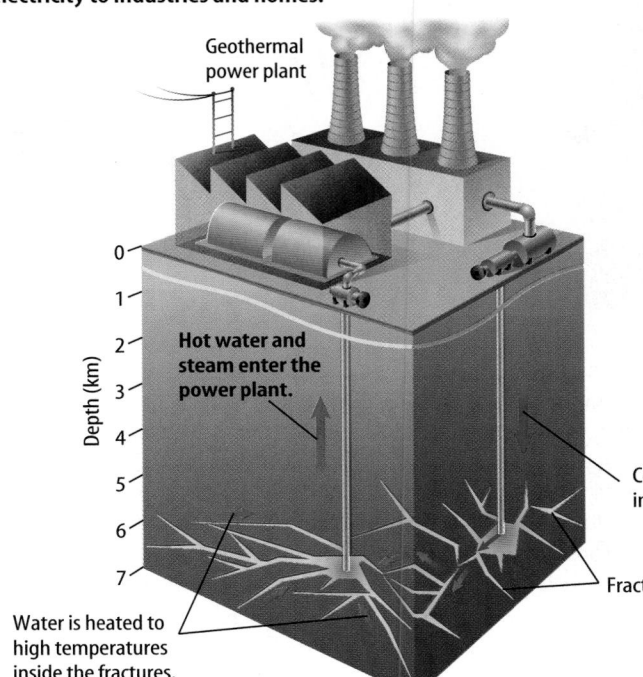

Geothermal power plant

Depth (km)

Hot water and steam enter the power plant.

Cold water is pumped into fractured hot rock.

Fractures

Water is heated to high temperatures inside the fractures.

Geothermal plant in California

Renewable Energy Resources

Energy resources that can be replaced in nature or by humans within a relatively short period of time are referred to as renewable energy resources. This short period of time is defined generally as being within a human life span. For example, trees can be considered a renewable energy resource. As one tree is cut down, another can be planted in its place. The new tree might be left untouched or harvested.

You have learned that most energy used in the United States—about 90 percent—comes from fossil fuels, which are nonrenewable energy resources. Next, you'll look at some renewable energy resources and how they might fit into the world's total energy needs now and in the future.

Biomass Energy

A major renewable energy resource is biomass materials. **Biomass energy** is energy derived from burning organic material such as wood, alcohol, and garbage. The term *biomass* is derived from the words *biological* and *mass*.

SCIENCE Online

Research Visit the Glencoe Science Web site at **science.glencoe.com** for more information about biomass energy. Communicate to your class what you learn.

Renewable Energy Resources

Activity

Have students draw a plan for a town in which all of the energy needs are met by inexhaustible and renewable energy sources. Have them show the main energy utility (if there is one) and how it works, as well as individual initiatives such as solar panels on roofs, passive solar heating, waterwheels, or private windmills. Have students share their plans with the class. Discuss whether any of these ideas could be used in your community. L3 LS **Visual-Spatial**

Biomass Energy

SCIENCE Online

Internet Addresses

Explore the Glencoe Science Web site at **science.glencoe.com** to find out more about topics in this section.

Resource Manager

Chapter Resources Booklet
Enrichment, p. 31
Reinforcement, p. 28
Cultural Diversity, p. 41

Inclusion Strategies

Learning Disabled Ask students how many of them have ever sat in front of a wood-burning stove or fireplace. Emphasize that the wood is biomass. Ask students to explain why wood is considered a biomass fuel. It comes from trees, which are organic.

Biomass Energy, continued

Visual Learning

Figure 15 What else, in addition to energy for cooking and light, is the wood providing for the campers? It is providing heat energy to keep the campers warm.

Discussion

Would it make sense for Americans to switch from a dependence on fossil fuels to a dependence on biomass? Have students explain their answers. Some students will think it is a good idea because biomass is renewable, especially if trees or crops are planted for use as fuel. Other students will think that biomass is not a good solution because it could require cutting forests (wood) or using a larger amount of fossil fuel energy to distill the fuel (ethanol) than would be produced burning it.

Teacher FYI

About 14 percent of the energy used worldwide to cook food and provide heat comes from burning wood and manure. In the United States and Canada, only 4 to 5 percent of energy used for those purposes comes from wood and manure.

✔ Reading Check

Answer Air pollution; producing liquid biomass fuels takes more energy than is produced.

Figure 15
These campers are using wood, a renewable energy resource, to produce heat and light.

Energy from Wood If you've ever sat around a campfire, like the campers shown in **Figure 15,** or close to a wood-burning fireplace to keep warm, you have used energy from wood. The burning wood is releasing stored solar energy as heat energy. Humans have long used wood as an energy resource. Much of the world still cooks with wood. In fact, firewood is used more widely today than any other type of biomass fuel.

Using wood as a biomass fuel has its problems. Gases and small particles are released when wood is burned. These materials can pollute the air. When trees are cut down for firewood, natural habitats are destroyed. However, if proper conservation methods are employed or if tree farms are maintained specifically for use as fuel, energy from wood can be a part of future energy resources.

Energy from Alcohol Biomass fuel can be burned directly, such as when wood or peat is used for heating and cooking. However, it also can be transformed into other materials that might provide cleaner, more efficient fuels.

For example, during distillation, biomass fuel, such as corn, is changed to an alcohol such as ethanol. Ethanol then can be mixed with another fuel. When the other fuel is gasoline, the mixture is called gasohol. Gasohol can be used in the same way as gasoline, as shown in **Figure 16,** but it cuts down on the amount of fossil fuel needed to produce gasoline. Fluid biomass fuels are more efficient and have more uses than solid biomass fuels do.

The problem with this process is that presently, growing the corn and distilling the ethanol often uses more energy from burning fossil fuels than the amount of energy that is derived from burning ethanol. At present, biomass fuel is best used locally.

Figure 16
Gasohol sometimes is used to reduce dependence on fossil fuels.

✔ Reading Check

What are the drawbacks of biomass fuels?

134 CHAPTER 5 Earth's Energy and Mineral Resources

Resource Manager

Chapter Resources Booklet
  Activity Worksheet, p. 5–6
  Lab Activity, pp. 13–16
Physical Science Critical Thinking/Problem Solving, p. 17

Energy from Garbage Every day humans throw away a tremendous amount of burnable garbage. As much as two thirds of what is thrown away could be burned. If more garbage were used for fuel, as shown in **Figure 17,** human dependence on fossil fuels would decrease. Burning garbage is a cheap source of energy and also helps reduce the amount of material that must be dumped into landfills.

Compared to other nations, the United States lags in the use of municipal waste as a renewable energy resource. For example, in some countries in Western Europe, as much as half of the waste generated is used for biomass fuel. When the garbage is burned, heat is produced, which turns water to steam. The steam turns turbines that run generators to produce electricity.

Unfortunately, some problems can be associated with using energy from garbage. Burning municipal waste can produce toxic ash residue and air pollution. Substances such as heavy metals could find their way into the smoke from garbage and thus into the atmosphere.

Figure 17
Garbage can be burned to produce electricity at trash-burning power plants such as this one in Virginia.

Section 2 Assessment

1. What are some advantages and disadvantages of using solar energy, wind energy, and hydroelectric energy?

2. What is the difference between inexhaustible and renewable energy resources? Give specific examples of each.

3. How is geothermal energy used to create electricity?

4. Why are nonrenewable resources used more than inexhaustible and renewable resources?

5. **Think Critically** How could nuclear energy, which normally is classified as a nonrenewable energy resource, be reclassified as an inexhaustible energy resource?

Skill Builder Activities

6. **Classifying** Classify the following energy resources as inexhaustible or renewable: *wood, solar energy, hydroelectric energy, geothermal energy, ethanol, garbage,* and *wind energy.* **For more help, refer to the** Science Skill Handbook.

7. **Using an Electronic Spreadsheet** Using the spreadsheet capabilities of a computer, make a table of energy resources. Include an example of how each resource could be used. Then write a description in your Science Journal about how you could reduce the use of energy resources at home. **For more help, refer to the** Technology Skill Handbook.

Reteach

Ask students why garbage is considered a renewable energy resource and wind is considered inexhaustible. Garbage is renewable because people will always generate more. Wind is inexhaustible because the winds will never stop blowing. The only problem is finding a place where wind is strong and steady. L2

Challenge

Have students research the production and use of methanol gas, another biomass fuel. Methanol is an alcohol fuel produced mostly from natural gas, but which can also be produced from wood, garbage, coal, and farm waste such as corncobs. When used as a vehicle fuel, methanol produces less total air pollution than many other fuels. Making it can be expensive, however, and there are increased emissions of toxic formaldehyde.

Content Ask students to classify the following fuels as nonrenewable, renewable, or inexhaustible: wind, natural gas, ethanol, biomass, solar, nuclear, coal. nonrenewable: natural gas, nuclear, coal; renewable: ethanol, biomass; inexhaustible: wind, solar Use **Performance Assessment in the Science Classroom,** p. 89.

Answers to Section Assessment

1. solar: advantages—nonpolluting, disadvantages—sunshine needed; wind: advantages—nonpolluting, disadvantages—need steady, strong wind; hydroelectric: advantages—no pollution, disadvantages—upstream lakes fill with sediment, animal habitat is destroyed

2. Inexhaustible energy resources (solar, wind, water, geothermal) will never run out; renewable energy resources (wood, alcohol, garbage) can be replenished in a short period of time.

3. Heat from magma or hot dry rocks changes water to steam that is then used to run turbines that generate electricity.

4. Possible answer: The technology for using nonrenewwable resources is more common and widespread.

5. Fusion would be virtually inexhaustible.

6. inexhaustible: geothermal, solar, hydroelectric, wind; renewable: wood, ethanol, garbage

7. Table should include energy sources discussed in text and give an example of how each resource could be used.

Activity

BENCH TESTED

Purpose Students observe how color affects energy absorption.

L2 LS **Kinesthetic**

Process Skills using variables, constants, and controls; collecting and organizing data; observing; making and using tables; making and using graphs; analyzing data; inferring

Time Required 40–45 minutes

Alternate Materials 200-watt lamp with reflector and clamp, stopwatch

Safety Precautions Tell students to use thermal mitts when handling the light source.

Teaching Strategy Have students predict what will happen and then check their predictions after the activity.

Answers to Questions

1. black soil; white sandy soil
2. At a certain point, the soils had absorbed the maximum amount of energy they were capable of absorbing.
3. The black plates absorb the most solar energy.
4. The darker the color, the greater its ability to absorb energy.
5. Darker clothing absorbs more energy, keeping people warmer in cold weather.

Activity

Soaking up Solar Energy

Winter clothing tends to be darker in color than summer clothing. The color of the material used in the clothing affects its ability to absorb energy. In this activity, you will use different colors of soil to study this effect.

What You'll Investigate
How does color affect the absorption of energy?

Time and Temperature			
Time (min)	Temperature Dish A (°C)	Temperature Dish B (°C)	Temperature Dish C (°C)
0.0	22	22	22
0.5	26	23	25
1.0	29	24	27
1.5	32	25	29

Materials
dry, black soil   clear glass or plastic dishes (3)
dry, brown soil   200-watt gooseneck lamp
dry, sandy,   *200-watt lamp with
    white soil   reflector and clamp
thermometers (3)   watch or clock
ring stand   with second hand
graph paper   *stopwatch
colored pencils (3)   *Alternate materials
metric ruler

Safety Precautions
◎ ⌇ ◢ ⬱

WARNING: *Handle glass with care so as not to break it. Wear thermal mitts when handling the light source.*

Goals
- **Determine** whether color has an effect on the absorption of solar energy.
- **Relate** the concept of whether color affects absorption to other applications.

Procedure
1. Fill each plastic dish with a different color of soil to a depth of 2.5 cm.

2. Arrange the dishes close together on your desk and place a thermometer in each dish. Be sure to cover the thermometer bulb in each dish completely with the soil.

3. Position the lamp over all three dishes.

4. **Design** a data table for your observations similar to the sample table above. You will need to read the temperature of each dish every 30 s for 20 min after the light is turned on.

5. Turn on the light and begin your experiment.

6. Use the data to construct a graph. Time should be plotted on the horizontal axis and temperature on the vertical axis. Use a different colored pencil to plot the data for each type of soil, or use a computer to design a graph that illustrates your data.

Conclude and Apply
1. Which soil had the greatest temperature change? The least?
2. Why do the curves on the graph flatten?
3. Why do flat-plate solar collectors have black plates behind the water pipes?
4. How does the color of a material affect its ability to absorb energy?
5. Why is most winter clothing darker in color than summer clothing?

✓ Assessment

Performance To further assess how color affects the ability of substances to absorb energy, have students place thermometers under three different-colored pieces of cloth. Have students compare the results. Use **Performance Assessment in the Science Classroom,** p. 97.

Communicating

Your Data

Encourage students to use an electronic spreadsheet program to help them design a data table.

Mineral Resources

Metallic Mineral Resources

If your room at home is anything like the one shown in **Figure 18,** you will find many metal items. Metals are obtained from Earth materials called metallic mineral resources. A **mineral resource** is a deposit of useful minerals. See how many metals you can find. Is there anything in your room that contains iron? What about the metal in the frame of your bed? Is it made of iron? If so, the iron might have come from the mineral hematite. What about the framing around the windows in your classroom? Is it aluminum? Aluminum, like that in a soft-drink can, comes from a mixture of minerals known as bauxite. Many minerals contain these and other useful elements. Which minerals are mined as sources for the materials you use every day?

Ores Deposits in which a mineral or minerals exist in large enough amounts to be mined at a profit are called **ores.** Generally, the term *ore* is used for metallic deposits, but this is not always the case. The hematite that was mentioned earlier as an iron ore and the bauxite that was mentioned earlier as an aluminum ore are metallic ores.

✔ **Reading Check** *What is an ore?*

As You Read

***What* You'll Learn**
- **Explain** the conditions needed for a mineral to be classified as an ore.
- **Describe** how market conditions can cause a mineral to lose its value as an ore.
- **Compare and contrast** metallic and nonmetallic mineral resources.

Vocabulary
mineral resource
ore
recycling

***Why* It's Important**
Many products you use are made from mineral resources.

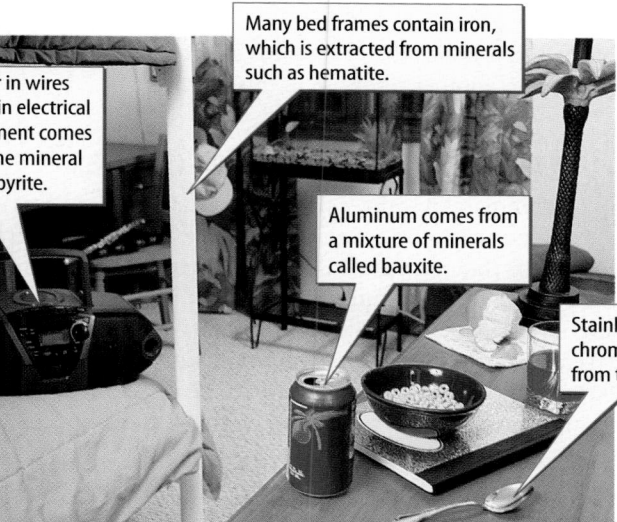

Copper in wires found in electrical equipment comes from the mineral chalcopyrite.

Many bed frames contain iron, which is extracted from minerals such as hematite.

Aluminum comes from a mixture of minerals called bauxite.

Stainless steel contains chromium, which comes from the mineral chromite.

Figure 18
Many items in your home are made from metals obtained from metallic mineral resources.

Section ✔️*Assessment* Planner

PORTFOLIO
Challenge, p. 141
PERFORMANCE ASSESSMENT
MiniLAB, p. 139
Problem-Solving Activity, p. 140
Skill Builder Activities, p. 141
See page 148 for more options.

CONTENT ASSESSMENT
Section, p. 141
Challenge, p. 141
Chapter, pp. 148–149

Mineral Resources

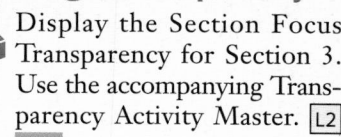

Bellringer Transparency

📖 Display the Section Focus Transparency for Section 3. Use the accompanying Transparency Activity Master. L2
ELL

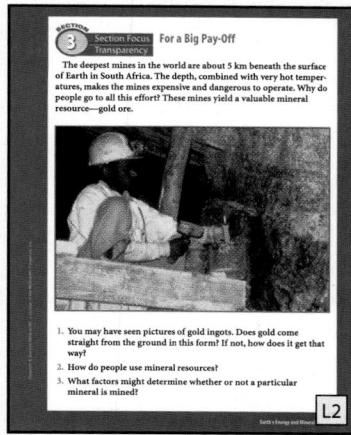

Section Focus Transparency For a Big Pay-Off

The deepest mines in the world are about 5 km beneath the surface of Earth in South Africa. The depth, combined with very hot temperatures, makes the mines expensive and dangerous to operate. Why do people go to all this effort? These mines yield a valuable mineral resource—gold ore.

1. You may have seen pictures of gold ingots. Does gold come straight from the ground in this form? If not, how does it get that way?
2. How do people use mineral resources?
3. What factors might determine whether or not a particular mineral is mined?

L2

Tie to Prior Knowledge

Ask students to brainstorm materials or products they use that are made from minerals. possible answers: gold or silver jewelry, metal coins, iron or steel cars or appliances, salt [halite] for food Tell students they will learn about the many minerals they use each day in this section.

Resource Manager

Chapter Resources Booklet
Transparency Activity, p. 46

Metallic Mineral Resources

Text Question Answer

Possible answer: Hematite (iron) and bauxite (aluminum) are among the minerals mined.

✔ Reading Check

Answer a deposit in which a mineral or minerals exist in amounts large enough to be mined at a profit

Caption Answer

Figure 19 part of the frame of your bed, part of your school desk, or any product made from iron or steel

Activity

List the following metals on the chalkboard: copper, bronze, gold, tin, steel, and silver. Have students find out which metals are minerals, and which mineral ore each metal comes from. Copper, gold, tin, and silver are minerals. Copper comes from chalcopyrite and native copper; gold comes from native gold; tin comes from cassiterite and native tin; silver comes from argentite and native silver; iron in steel comes from hematite; bronze is an alloy of copper and tin.

Nonmetallic Mineral Resources

Fun Fact

The world's main source of phosphate is the mineral apatite. The main source of potassium is the mineral sylvite.

Figure 19
Iron ores are smelted to produce nearly pure iron. *What could this iron be used for?*

Economic Effects When is a mineral deposit considered an ore? The mineral in question must be in demand. Enough of it must be present in the deposit to make it worth removing. Some mining operations are profitable only if a large amount of the mineral is needed. It also must be fairly easy to separate the mineral from the material in which it is found. If any one of these conditions isn't met, the deposit might not be considered an ore.

Supply and demand is an important part of life. You might have noticed that when the supply of fresh fruit is down, the price you pay for it at the store goes up. Economic factors largely determine what an ore is.

Refining Ore The process of extracting a useful substance from an ore involves two operations—concentrating and refining. After a metallic ore is mined from Earth's crust, it is crushed and the waste rock is removed. The waste rock that must be removed before a mineral can be used is called gangue (GANG).

Refining produces a pure or nearly pure substance from ore. For example, iron can be concentrated from the ore hematite, which is composed of iron oxide. The concentrated ore then is refined to be as close to pure iron as possible. One method of refining is smelting, illustrated in **Figure 19.** Smelting is a chemical process that removes unwanted elements from the metal that is being processed. During one smelting process, a concentrated ore of iron is heated with a specific chemical. The chemical combines with oxygen in the iron oxide, resulting in pure iron. Note that one resource, fossil fuel, is burned to produce the heat that is needed to obtain the finished product of another resource, in this case iron.

Nonmetallic Mineral Resources

Any mineral resources not used as fuels or as sources of metals are nonmetallic mineral resources. These resources are mined for the nonmetallic elements contained in them and for the specific physical and chemical properties they have. Generally, nonmetallic mineral resources can be divided into two different groups—industrial minerals and building materials. Some materials, such as limestone, belong to both groups of nonmetallic mineral resources, and others are specific to one group or the other.

138 CHAPTER 5 Earth's Energy and Mineral Resources

Curriculum Connection

Geography Have students list the top five countries for the production of copper, gold, and silver. Tell them to place symbols for each metal on a world map. copper: Chile, U.S., Canada, Russia, Indonesia; gold: South Africa, U.S., Australia, China, Russia; silver: Mexico, Peru, U.S., Canada, Chile

Teacher FYI

The consumption of minerals in the United States has been calculated to be about 18,000 pounds per person annually. This includes metals such as steel, iron, aluminum, copper, and zinc, as well as nonmetals such as salt, cement, sand, and stone.

Industrial Minerals Many useful chemicals are obtained from industrial minerals. Sandstone is a source of silica (SiO_2), which is a compound that is used to make glass. Some industrial minerals are processed to make fertilizers for farms and gardens. For example, sylvite, a mineral that forms when seawater evaporates, is used to make potassium fertilizer.

Many people enjoy a little sprinkle of salt on french fries and pretzels. Table salt is a product derived from halite, a nonmetallic mineral resource. Halite also is used to help melt ice on roads and sidewalks during winter and to help soften water.

Other industrial minerals are useful because of their characteristic physical properties. For example, abrasives are made from deposits of corundum and garnet. Both of these minerals are hard and able to scratch most other materials they come into contact with. Small particles of garnet can be glued onto a sheet of heavy paper to make abrasive sandpaper. **Figure 20** illustrates just a few ways in which nonmetallic mineral resources help make your life more convenient.

Figure 20
You benefit from the use of industrial minerals every day.

A Road salt melts ice on streets.

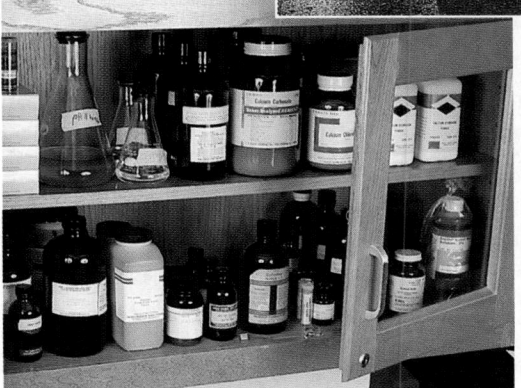

B Many important chemicals are made from industrial minerals.

C An industrial mineral called trona is important for making glass.

Procedure
1. Pour **warm water** into a **thermos bottle.** Cap it and set it aside.
2. Pour **cold water** with **ice** into a **glass** surrounded by a **thermal cup holder.**
3. Pour **warm water**—the same temperature as in step #1—into an **uncovered cup.** Pour cold water with ice into a glass container that is not surrounded by a thermal cup holder.
4. After 2 h, measure the temperature of each of the liquids.

Analysis
1. Infer how the insulation affected the temperatures of each liquid.
2. Relate the usefulness of insulation in a thermos bottle to the usefulness of fiberglass insulation in a home.

Mini LAB

Purpose Students will observe the benefits of insulation. L2

IS Kinesthetic

Materials thermos bottle, thermal cup holder, two glasses, cup, 4 thermometers, water

Teaching Strategy Review the reading of thermometers before beginning the activity.

Safety Precautions Students should use care when handling glass equipment.

Analysis
1. The thermos bottle kept the water in it warmer than the water in the open cup. The water in the cup with the thermal cup holder stayed colder than the water in the glass without one.
2. Home insulation helps keep heat from a furnace or heater inside a home, the way insulation in a thermos holds in the heat of warm liquids.

☑ Assessment

Performance Have students repeat the experiment with the warm water. Tell them to measure the temperature of the water in the thermos bottle and the water in the open cup periodically until both have reached a temperature you determine. Have them determine how much longer the thermos bottle kept the warm water warm. Use **Performance Assessment in the Science Classroom,** p. 97.

Resource Manager

Chapter Resources Booklet
MiniLAB, p. 4
Directed Reading for Content Mastery, pp. 21, 22

Inclusion Strategies

Visually Impaired Have these students dip one hand into the cold water from the glass in the thermal cup holder and the other hand into the cold water from the glass without the holder. Have students determine which water was kept colder.

Reading Check

Answer sandstone, limestone, sylvite, halite, corundum, garnet, aggregate, gypsum

Teaching Strategies

Discuss science and technology, the price for each, the "good" and "bad" of each, and the decisions that are made, what they are based on, and the effects of the decisions made.

What stones are used in buildings where you live? To find out more about building stones, see the **Building Stones Field Guide** at the back of the book.

Building Materials One of the most important nonmetallic mineral resources is aggregate. Aggregate is composed of crushed stone or a mixture of gravel and sand and has many uses in the building industry. For example, aggregates can be mixed with cement and water to form concrete. Quality concrete is vital to the building industry. Limestone also has industrial uses. It is used as paving stone and as part of concrete mixtures. Have you ever seen the crushed rock in a walking path or driveway? The individual pieces might be crushed limestone. Gypsum, a mineral that forms when seawater evaporates, is soft and lightweight and is used in the production of plaster and wallboard. If you handle a piece of broken plaster or wallboard, note its appearance which is similar to the mineral gypsum.

Rock also is used as building stone. You might know of buildings in your region that are made from granite, limestone, or sandstone. These rocks and others are quarried and cut into blocks and sheets. The pieces then can be used to construct buildings. Some rock also is used to sculpt statues and other pieces of art.

 **Reading Check** *What are some important nonmetallic mineral resources?*

Problem-Solving Activity

Why should you recycle?

Recycling in the United States has become a way of life. In 2000, 88 percent of Americans participated in recycling. Recycling is important because it saves precious raw materials and energy. Recycling aluminum saves 95 percent of the energy required to obtain it from its ore. Recycling steel saves up to 74 percent in energy costs, and recycling glass saves up to 22 percent.

Recycling Rates in the United States			
Material	**1995 (%)**	**1997 (%)**	**2000 (%) (estimated)**
Glass	24.5	24.3	29–33
Steel	36.5	38.4	41–46
Aluminum	34.6	31.2	37–39
Plastics	5.3	5.2	6–7

Identifying the Problem

The following table includes materials that currently are being recycled and rates of recycling for the years 1995, 1997, and 2000. Examine the table to determine materials for which recycling increased or decreased between 1995 and 2000.

Solving the problem

1. Has the recycling of materials increased or decreased over time? Which materials are recycled most? Which materials are recycled least? Suggest reasons why some materials might be recycled more than others are.
2. How can recycling benefit society? Explain your answer.

140 CHAPTER 5 Earth's Energy and Mineral Resources

Resource Manager

Chapter Resources Booklet
Enrichment, p. 32
Reinforcement, p. 29

Teacher FYI

Aggregate is used in the building industry. When concrete is mixed, aggregate is added to provide it with strength, and cement is added as a binder to make it hard as a rock. More than 85 metric tons of aggregate is used to build every two kilometers of a four-lane highway.

Recycling Mineral Resources

Mineral resources are nonrenewable. You've learned that nonrenewable resources are those that Earth processes cannot replace within an average human's lifetime. Most mineral resources take millions of years to form. Have you ever thrown away an empty soft-drink can? Many people do. These cans become solid waste. Wouldn't it be better if these cans and other items made from mineral resources were recycled into new items?

Recycling is using old materials to make new ones. Recycling has many advantages. It reduces the demand for new mineral resources. The recycling process often uses less energy than it takes to obtain new material. Because supplies of some minerals might become limited in the future, recycling could be required to meet needs for certain materials, as shown in **Figure 21.**

Recycling also can be a profitable experience. Some companies purchase scrap metal and empty soft-drink cans for the aluminum and tin content. The seller receives a small amount of money for turning in the material. Schools and other groups earn money by recycling soft-drink cans.

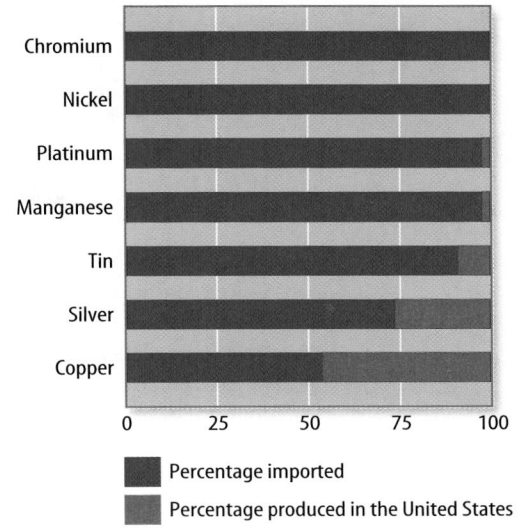

Figure 21
The United States produces only a small percentage of the metallic resources it consumes.

Section 3 Assessment

1. How are metals obtained from metallic mineral resources used in your home and school? Which of these products could be recycled easily?

2. What characteristics define a mineral deposit as an ore?

3. List two industrial uses for nonmetallic mineral resources.

4. How can supply and demand of a material cause a mineral to become an ore?

5. **Think Critically** Gangue is waste rock remaining after a mineral ore is removed. Why is gangue sometimes reprocessed?

Skill Builder Activities

6. **Classifying** Classify the following mineral resources as metallic or nonmetallic: *hematite, limestone, bauxite, sandstone, garnet,* and *chalcopyrite.* Explain why you classified each one as you did. **For more help, refer to the** Science Skill Handbook.

7. **Communicating** Research the element titanium and its uses. Write a description in your Science Journal explaining the importance of this element and the mineral resource it comes from. Explain why this element is used in the ways that you found. **For more help, refer to the** Science Skill Handbook.

Reteach

Take a brief mineral identification walk through the neighborhood near the school with students. Point out buildings or objects as you walk, and ask students to identify the minerals that could have gone into building or producing the object in question. Have students take notes and write a paragraph summing up what they have discovered.

Challenge

Challenge students to do research using print resources and the Internet to make a mineral resource map of the United States, showing the locations of major minerals with symbols they design. Students can work in groups of two or three. Display the maps in class. L2 COOP LEARN P

Assessment

Content Have students work in groups of three to write a poem using the terms *mineral resource* and *ore* in a way that shows their meaning. Use **Performance Assessment in the Science Classroom,** p. 151.

Answers to Section Assessment

1. Answers will vary; desks, bedframes, kitchen utensils, soft drink cans, window or chalkboard casings. Soft drink cans can be recycled easily.
2. when there is enough of the mineral present for it to be mined at a profit
3. manufacture of chemicals, abrasives
4. A material that can be mined at a profit is an ore. If there is no demand,

there is no profit. If there is a high demand, there is a profit.
5. If the price of the metal goes up or technology improves, the amount of metal still in the gangue might be removed at a profit.
6. Metallic: hematite, bauxite, chalcopyrite; nonmetallic: limestone, sandstone, garnet; metals are derived

from hematite, bauxite, and chalcopyrite but not from the others.
7. Titanium is a durable, lightweight metal derived from ilmenite and rutile. Its properties make it valuable in the production of sports equipment, wheelchairs, and artificial limbs.

Activity

BENCH TESTED

Recognize the Problem

Purpose
Students will design and build a model of an energy-efficient home. **L2** **IS** **Logical-Mathematical**

Process Skills
observing and inferring, recognizing cause and effect, making models, communicating

Time Required
two weeks

Thinking Critically

Discussion Ask students to list the desirable characteristics of an energy-efficient home.

Possible Materials
Be sure the cardboard used in the construction of the model homes is sturdy. If using poster board, students may need to reinforce it or use a double layer.

Alternate Materials
Instead of cardboard, students may use corrugated cardboard from packing boxes.

Planning the Model

Teaching Strategies
- Allow students to work in small groups when designing and building their models.
- Encourage communication between groups. Ask selected students to research different aspects of the topic of energy-efficient homes and present their findings to the class.

Activity *Model and Invent*

Home Sweet Home

As fossil fuel supplies continue to be depleted, an increasing U.S. population has recognized the need for alternative energy sources. United States residents might be forced to consider using renewable and inexhaustible energy resources to meet some of their energy needs. The need for energy-efficient housing is more relevant now than ever before. A designer of energy-efficient homes considers proper design and structure, a well chosen building site with wise material selection, and selection of efficient energy generation systems to power the home. Energy-efficient housing uses less energy and produces fewer pollutants.

Recognize the Problem

What does the floor plan, building plan, or a model of an energy efficient home look like?

Thinking Critically

How and where should your house be designed and built to use the alternative energy resources you've chosen efficiently?

Goals
- **Research** various renewable and inexhaustible energy resources available to use in the home.
- **Design** blueprints for an energy-efficient home and/or design and build a model of an energy-efficient home.

Possible Materials
paper
ruler
pencils
cardboard
glue
aluminum foil

Data Source
SCIENCE*Online* Go to the Glencoe Science Web site at **science.glencoe.com** for more information about designing an energy-efficient home.

FOR SALE
AWARD WINNING
PASSIVE SOLAR HOUSE

Resource Manager

Chapter Resources Booklet
   Activity Worksheet, pp. 7–8
Lab Management and Safety, p. 71

SCIENCE *Online*
Internet Addresses
_____
_____
_____

Explore the Glencoe Science Web site at **science.glencoe.com** to find out more about topics in this activity.

Planning the Model

Plan

1. **Research** current information about energy-efficient homes.

2. **Research** inexhaustible energy resources such as wind, hydroelectric power, or solar power, as well as energy conservation. Decide which energy resources are most efficient for your home design.

3. Decide where your house should be built to use energy efficiently.

4. Decide how your house will be laid out and draw mock blueprints for your home. Highlight energy issues such as where solar panels can be placed.

5. Build a model of your energy-efficient home.

Do

1. Ask your peers for input on your home. As you research, become an expert in one area of alternative energy generation and share your information with your classmates.

2. **Compare** your home's design to energy-efficient homes you learn about through your research.

Making the Model

1. Think about how most of the energy in a home is used. Remember as you plan your home that energy-efficient homes not only generate energy—they also use it more efficiently.

2. Carefully consider where your home should be built. For instance, if you plan to use wind power, will your house be built in an area that receives adequate wind?

3. Be sure to plan for backup energy generation. For instance, if you plan to use mostly solar energy, what will you do if it's a cloudy day?

Analyzing and Applying Results

1. Devise a budget for building your home. Could your energy-efficient home be built at a reasonable price? Could anyone afford to build it?

2. Create a list of pro and con statements about the use of energy-efficient homes. Why aren't inexhaustible and renewable energy sources widely used in homes today?

Present your model to the class. **Explain** which energy resources you chose to use in your home and why. Have an open house. Take prospective home owners/classmates on a tour of your home and sell it.

Tie to Prior Knowledge

Have students name and describe the benefits of energy-efficient designs in their homes, such as double-paned windows and storm doors.

Troubleshooting Encourage students to think about energy losses through the roof, ceiling, doors, and windows, as well as the home's location and source of energy.

Making the Model

Expected Outcome

Students will learn about the many ways a home can be made energy efficient.

Analyzing and Applying Results

1. Budgets should list major supplies needed as well as their costs. Students should realize that some energy-efficient designs are prohibitively expensive, but many methods for improving energy efficiency are affordable.

2. Possible answer: Energy-efficient homes conserve Earth's natural resources and reduce environmental damage, but they are often expensive. Readily available and affordable renewable energy sources yet to be developed.

Assessment

Oral After completing the project, have students discuss the different energy-efficient technologies they investigated, describing the benefits and disadvantages of each technology. Use **PASC**, p. 89.

Inclusion Strategies

Learning Disabled Working in small groups will allow students to work off each other's ideas as they design and build the model homes. Allow class time for them to discuss the project. Provide students with suggestions as needed to help them develop their ideas.

Have students use computer graphics software to prepare a half-page advertisement for their home. The advertisement should describe details of the energy-efficient design of the home. These pages can be available to prospective buyers during the open-house tour of their home.

Content Background

Petroleum from ground seepages, often in the form of asphalt or tar, has been used since ancient times for boat sealing, as a medicine, and for lighting purposes. Before the 1850s, lamp oil was derived from whales. However, whales were overhunted and lamp oil became more expensive, leading to the search for substitutes. Oil began to be dug from surface seeps and refined by heating into kerosene, which was used as a lamp oil.

After water and food, petroleum may be the most important substance used in modern society. It provides the raw materials for products ranging from plastics and many other synthetics to those used in medicine and agricultural, as well as fuel for heating, industry, and transportation.

Discussion

What are some ways that oil has played a part in your preparation for school today?
Possible answers: some homes are heated by fuel oil; some clothing is made from raw materials that come from oil; vehicles powered by gasoline or other petroleum-based fuel transported some of them to school.

Oil's Well That

What if you went out to your backyard, started digging a hole, and all of a sudden oil spurted out of the ground? Dollar signs might flash before your eyes.

It wasn't quite that exciting for Charles Tripp. Tripp, a Canadian, is credited with being the first person to strike oil. And he wasn't even looking for what has become known as "black gold."

In 1851, Tripp built a factory in Ontario, Canada, not far from Lake Erie. He used a natural, black, thick, sticky substance that could be found nearby to make asphalt for paving roads and to erect buildings. He also sold the product to waterproof boats.

The Titusville, Pennsylvania, oil well drilled by Edwin Drake. This photo was taken in 1864.

144

Resources for Teachers and Students

"World Oil Reserves—Which Number to Believe?" by Jean Laherrere, *OPEC Bulletin*, February 1995, pp. 9–13.

Business Builders in Oil, by Nathan Aaseng, Oliver Press, 2000.

The Spindletop Gusher, by Carmen Bredeson, Millbrook Press, 1996.

Where Does Oil Come From? By C. Vance Cast, Barron's, 1993.

In 1855, Tripp dug a well looking for fresh water for his factory. After digging just 2 m or so, he unexpectedly came upon liquid. It wasn't clear, clean, and delicious; it was smelly, thick, and black. You guessed it—oil! Tripp didn't understand the importance of his find and how it might help his business. Nor did he realize that it might make him rich someday. So, two years after his accidental discovery, Tripp sold his company to James Williams.

In 1858, Williams continued to search for water for the factory, but, as luck would have it, diggers kept finding oil. So workers barreled up the oil and sold it as liquid grease for the train industry. By 1861, 1.5 million L of crude oil had been barreled and shipped. The finds also led to a short boom in oil production in the area.

Some people argue that the first oil well in North America was in Titusville, Pennsylvania, when Edwin Drake hit oil in 1859. However, most historians agree that Williams was first in 1858. But they also agree that it was Edwin Drake's discovery that led to the growth of the oil industry. So, Drake and Williams can share the credit!

Ends

Some people used TNT to search for oil. This photo was taken in 1943.

The accidental discovery of a gloppy black substance helped change the planet

Well

Today, many oil companies are drilling beneath the sea for oil.

SCIENCE
Online

For more information, visit science.glencoe.com

CONNECTIONS Make a Graph Research the leading oil-producing nations and make a bar graph of the top five producers. Go further and research how rising and falling prices of crude oil can affect the U.S. and world economies. Share your findings with your class.

Activity

Organize the class into five groups. Assign each of the groups one of the following areas: agriculture and food; housing; clothing; medicine; and transportation. Have each group research the different products in their area that are made from petroleum. Have each group make a poster illustrating what they find. Then have them present their poster to the class.

Analyze the Event

Ask students to brainstorm how their lives might be different today if people hadn't realized the importance of the discovery of oil. Possible answers: Most forms of transportation use fuels derived from petroleum—gasoline, diesel fuel, and jet fuel—so transportation would be different and probably difficult. Many power plants use oil to generate electricity, so electricity would not be as readily available and would probably be more expensive. Homes and businesses would not be able to use fuel oil for heating. Many products, such as plastics, synthetic fibers, and Plexiglas, which come from petrochemicals, wouldn't exist.

CONNECTIONS Students should find that the world's major producers of oil are Saudi Arabia, United States, Russia, Iran, and China. However, Saudi Arabia, Russia, Iran, Iraq, Venezuela, Kuwait, United Arab Emirates, Mexico, and China all have more proven oil reserves than the United States. Oil is a major factor in the world's economic condition. During the Arab oil embargo of the 1970s, the United States gross national product declined and unemployment doubled. In 1990, in response to a threat to Middle East oil supplies, the Gulf War was fought.

SCIENCE
Online

Internet Addresses

_____

_____

_____

Explore the Glencoe Science Web site at **science.glencoe.com** to find out more about topics in this feature.

Reviewing Main Ideas

Preview

Students can answer the questions in their Science Journals. Discuss the answers as you go through the chapter. **IS** **Linguistic**

Review

Students can write their answers, then compare them with those of other students. **IS** **Interpersonal**

Reteach

Students can look at the illustrations and describe details that support the main ideas of the chapter. **IS** **Visual-Spatial**

Answers to Chapter Review

SECTION 1

2. heating homes, schools, or businesses; producing electric power

SECTION 2

1. low cost once they are installed, nonpolluting, inexhaustible energy source, reduces the need for other energy resources

SECTION 3

4. Aggregate is a building material.

Reviewing Main Ideas

Section 1 Nonrenewable Energy Resources

1. Fossil fuels are considered to be nonrenewable energy resources.

2. The higher the concentration of carbon in coal is, the cleaner it burns. *What might the coal in this truck be used for?*

3. Oil and natural gas form from altered and buried marine organisms and often are found near one another.

4. Nuclear energy is obtained from the fission of heavy isotopes.

Section 2 Inexhaustible and Renewable Energy Resources

1. Inexhaustible energy resources—solar energy, wind energy, water energy, and geothermal energy—are constant and will not run out. *What are some advantages of using solar panels to produce electricity?*

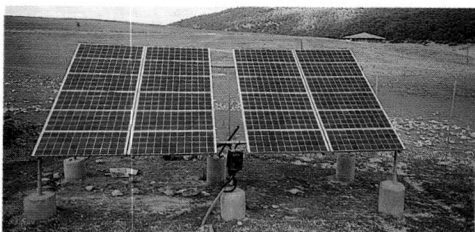

2. Renewable energy resources are replaced within a relatively short period of time.

3. Biomass energy is derived from burning organic material.

Section 3 Mineral Resources

1. Metallic mineral resources provide metals when they are processed.

2. Ores are mineral resources that contain a usable substance that can be mined at a profit.

3. Smelting is a chemical process that removes unwanted elements from a metal that is being processed.

4. Nonmetallic mineral resources are classified as industrial minerals or building materials. *Is the aggregate that is being produced here an industrial mineral or a building material?*

FOLDABLES
Reading & Study Skills

After You Read

Circle the resources you think are the most valuable on your Foldable. Explain why and write about similarities and differences among the resources.

FOLDABLES
Reading & Study Skills

After You Read

After students have read the chapter and completed the Foldable described in Before You Read, have them do the activity on the student page.

Dinah Zike

Visualizing Main Ideas

Fill in the following table that lists advantages and disadvantages of different energy resources.

Energy Resources		
Resource	**Advantages**	**Disadvantages**
Fossil Fuels	economical, works with current technology	nonrenewable
Nuclear Energy	alternate source as fossil fuels are depleted	Fission produces radioactive waste.
Solar Energy	inexhaustible	not always sunny
Wind Energy	inexhaustible	not always windy
Geothermal Energy	inexhaustible	not available everywhere
Biomass Fuel	readily available in different forms	can produce air pollution

Visualizing Main Ideas

See student page.

Vocabulary Review

Vocabulary Words

a. biomass energy
b. coal
c. fossil fuel
d. geothermal energy
e. hydroelectric energy
f. mineral resource
g. natural gas
h. nuclear energy
i. oil
j. ore
k. recycling
l. reserve
m. solar energy
n. wind farm

THE PRINCETON REVIEW **Study Tip**

To understand the information that a graph is trying to communicate, write a sentence that describes the relationship between the axes.

Using Vocabulary

Each phrase below describes a vocabulary word from the list. Write the word that matches the phrase describing it.

1. mineral resource that can be mined at a profit

2. fuel that is composed mainly of the remains of dead plants

3. method of conservation in which items are processed to be used again

4. inexhaustible energy resource that is used to power the *Hubble Space Telescope*

5. energy resource that is based on the fission of atoms

6. liquid from remains of marine organisms

Vocabulary Review

Using Vocabulary

1. ore
2. fossil fuel
3. recycling
4. solar energy
5. nuclear energy
6. oil

Chapter 5 Assessment

Chapter 5 Assessment

Checking Concepts

1. D
2. A
3. C
4. C
5. A
6. C
7. A
8. A
9. D
10. D

Thinking Critically

11. Plants use energy from the Sun to make food through photosynthesis. Fossil fuels were formed from dead and decayed plant matter. When the fuels are burned, they release the energy that was stored as food in plant tissues long ago.

12. the possibility of uncontrolled reactions, thermal pollution, storage and disposal of radioactive wastes

13. Winds will always blow, so wind energy will never run out.

14. Biomass fuels are made from organic material. They include wood, alcohols made from plants, and certain types of garbage.

15. If the price of a metal being mined increases, or new technology makes it easier and cheaper to mine, it might become profitable to remove the metal in the gangue.

Checking Concepts

Choose the word or phrase that best answers the question.

1. Which of the following has the highest content of carbon?
   - A) peat
   - B) lignite
   - C) bituminous coal
   - D) anthracite coal

2. Which of the following is the first step in the evolution of coal?
   - A) formation of peat
   - B) formation of lignite
   - C) formation of bituminous coal
   - D) formation of anthracite coal

3. Which of the following is an example of a fossil fuel?
   - A) wind
   - B) water
   - C) natural gas
   - D) uranium-235

4. What is the waste material that must be separated from an ore?
   - A) smelter
   - B) mineral resource
   - C) gangue
   - D) petroleum

5. What common rock structure can trap oil and natural gas under it?
   - A) folded rock
   - B) sandstone rock
   - C) porous rock
   - D) unconsolidated rock

6. Which type of energy resource uses large dams in a river?
   - A) wind
   - B) nuclear
   - C) hydroelectric
   - D) solar

7. What is a region where many windmills are located in one place in order to generate electricity from wind called?
   - A) wind farm
   - B) hydroelectric dam
   - C) oil well
   - D) steam-driven turbine

8. Which of the following is a deposit of hematite that can be mined at a profit?
   - A) ore
   - B) anthracite
   - C) gangue
   - D) energy resource

9. What is an important use of petroleum?
   - A) making plaster
   - B) making glass
   - C) as abrasives
   - D) making gasoline

10. Which of the following is a nonrenewable energy resource?
    - A) water
    - B) wind
    - C) geothermal
    - D) petroleum

Thinking Critically

11. Explain how solar energy becomes stored in plants and other organisms and is released later when fossil fuels are burned.

12. Describe the major problems associated with generating electricity using nuclear power plants.

13. Why is wind considered to be an inexhaustible energy resource?

14. Which type of energy resources are considered to be biomass fuels?

15. What conditions could occur to cause gangue to be reclassified as an ore?

Developing Skills

16. **Predicting** If a well were drilled into a rock layer containing petroleum, natural gas, and water, which substance would be encountered first? Explain.

17. **Comparing and Contrasting** Create a table comparing and contrasting solar energy and wind energy.

Chapter ✓Assessment Planner

Portfolio Encourage students to place in their portfolios one or two items of what they consider to be their best work. Examples include:
- Cultural Diversity, p. 122
- Curriculum Connection, p. 125
- Extension, p. 132
- Challenge, p. 141

Performance Additional performance assessments, Performance Task Assessment Lists, and rubrics for evaluating these activities can be found in Glencoe's **Performance Assessment in the Science Classroom.**

18. Concept Mapping Complete the following concept map about mineral resources.

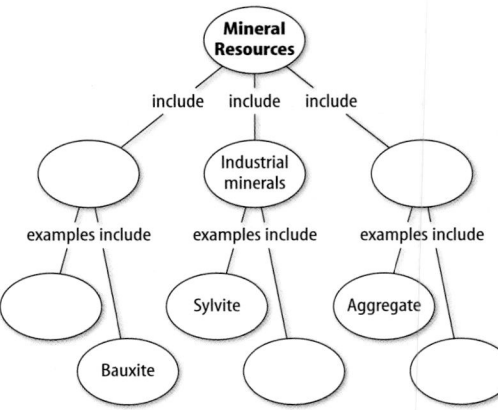

19. Making Models Make a model of a house that has been built to use passive solar energy.

Performance Assessment

20. Oral Presentation Research the latest information on inexhaustible energy resources. Develop a presentation that tries to persuade consumers to reduce their use of fossil fuels and to use inexhaustible energy resources instead.

21. Letter Write a letter to the Department of Energy asking how usable energy might be obtained from methane hydrates in the future. Also inquire about methods to extract methane hydrates.

TECHNOLOGY

Go to the Glencoe Science Web site at **science.glencoe.com** or use the **Glencoe Science CD-ROM** for additional chapter assessment.

THE PRINCETON REVIEW — Test Practice

The graph below shows the average abundance of some important metals in Earth's crust.

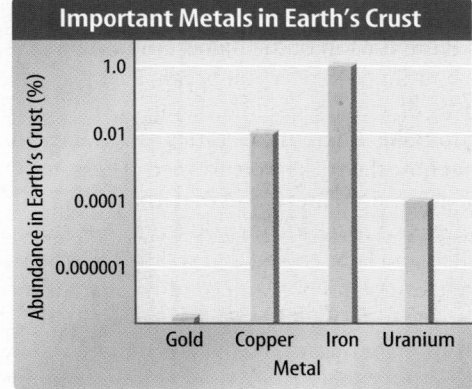

Study the bar graph and answer the following questions.

1. After examining this graph, you should conclude that these important metals _____ .
A) are concentrated in Earth's crust
B) are valuable for jewelery
C) are mined out
D) are generally rare in Earth's crust

2. Which of the following best explains the occurrence of rich ores of these metals?
F) The metals are concentrated in some places by Earth processes.
G) Metal-rich meteorites frequently strike Earth.
H) Some metals are more abundant in Earth's core.
J) Percentages often are misleading.

THE PRINCETON REVIEW — Test Practice

The Test-Taking Tip was written by The Princeton Review, the nation's leader in test preparation.
1. D
2. F

Developing Skills

16. The densest substance would be at the bottom, with the least dense substance at the top; from top to bottom: natural gas, petroleum, water.
17. Tables should show that both are low-cost fuels, nonpolluting, inexhaustible, and limited by weather and geographic location. Unlike wind, which can be used at any time of day or night, solar energy is limited to daylight hours when the Sun shines.
18. See student page.
19. The house plans should include large windows facing the Sun.

Performance Assessment

20. Presentations should list the benefits of inexhaustible energy resources and the problems with fossil fuels, including the fact that they will run out someday. Use **PASC**, p. 143.
21. Letters should refer to gas hydrate deposits. Students can search the Internet for an address at the Department of Energy web site. Use **PASC**, p. 139.

✔Assessment Resources

📁 **Reproducible Masters**

Chapter Resources Booklet
Chapter Review, pp. 37–38
Chapter Tests, pp. 39–42
Assessment Transparency Activity, p. 49

Glencoe Science Web site
Interactive Tutor
Chapter Quizzes

Glencoe Technology
🖌 Assessment Transparency
💿 Interactive CD-ROM Chapter Quizzes
💿 ExamView Pro Test Bank
💿 Vocabulary PuzzleMaker Software
📼 MindJogger Videoquiz DVD/VHS

Standardized Test Practice

QUESTION 1: B

Students need to use clues from the passage, such as *causes the rock to melt*. This identifies that the best meaning of the word *molten* is choice B.

QUESTION 2: F

Students should refer to first paragraph of the passage in order to locate the information about the three categories of rocks.

QUESTION 3: D

Students need to reread the passage and look for the phrases used in the choices.

- **Choice A** No; burial and cementing form sedimentary rock.
- **Choice B** No; heat and pressure form metamorphic rock.
- **Choice C** No; weathering and erosion form sediments.
- **Choice D** Yes; melting and solidification form igneous rock.

THE PRINCETON REVIEW   All questions written and validated by The Princeton Review.

Read the passage. Then read each question that follows the passage. Decide which is the best answer to each question.

Obsidian Uses

From the top of the highest mountain to the bottom of the deepest ocean, Earth is made mostly of rock. Geologists classify rocks according to three different categories depending upon how the rocks were formed. These are igneous, sedimentary, and metamorphic.

Igneous rocks are formed from rock that melted and later cooled and solidified. When temperature and pressure conditions are just right, often deep within Earth, rocks will melt. This <u>molten</u> rock, called magma, moves up toward the surface of Earth over time or might even reach the surface quickly in a volcanic eruption. When magma erupts at Earth's surface, it is called lava. When lava cools quickly, small mineral crystals will form. If it cools even more quickly, volcanic glass can form.

Obsidian is a type of volcanic rock. It is often referred to as volcanic glass because it has a smooth surface. It was a prized material among prehistoric cultures because it fractures with sharp edges and can be used as a weapon or tool. Knives, arrowheads, and spear points were made from obsidian. Prehistoric people also used obsidian as mirrors. In modern times, obsidian has been used for surgical scalpel blades.

The beauty and mystery of igneous rocks have inspired many artists. Some artists care-

Test-Taking Tip   As you read the passage, write a one-sentence summary for each paragraph.

This is obsidian, a type of volcanic glass.

fully sculpt already cooled volcanic rock into beautiful, one-of-a-kind pieces of art.

1. In this passage, the word <u>molten</u> means
   A) deep
   B) melted
   C) igneous
   D) cooled

2. According to the passage, the three categories, or groups, of rocks are _____.
   F) igneous, metamorphic, and sedimentary
   G) volcanic, glassy, and irregular
   H) chemical, organic, and detrital
   J) residual, original, and primitive

3. Which conclusion is best supported by information given in the passage?
   A) When magma cools rapidly, it produces rocks with many large crystals.
   B) Igneous rocks can be made into tools and pieces of art.
   C) Obsidian was used by prehistoric cultures to build stone houses.
   D) Igneous rock forms when rocks melt, cool, and then solidify.

Reasoning and Skills

Read each question and choose the best answer.

Igneous Rocks

Formed	Light-colored	Dark-colored
Below Earth's Surface	granite	gabbro
At Earth's Surface	rhyolite	basalt

1. According to the chart, lava that flows onto the surface from a volcano should cool to form the dark-colored rock _____.

A) granite   **C)** rhyolite
B) gabbro   **D)** basalt

Test-Taking Tip   Reread the question and think about the color of the rock and where the rock was formed.

2. Earth's crust is estimated to be composed of about 46% oxygen, 28% silicon, 8% aluminum, and 18% other elements. Which area of the graph represents aluminum?

F) Q
G) R
H) S
J) T

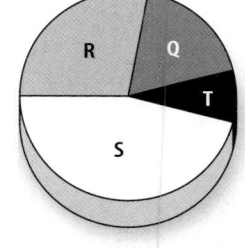

Test-Taking Tip   Think about the quantities of the element the question refers to compared to the sizes of each portion of the graph.

Selected Rock Data

Volume of Sample (cm^3)	Mass of Sample (g)
1	3
2	6
3	9
4	12
5	?

3. These data were collected after determining the mass and volume of three different samples of the same rock. If everything remains the same, what will be the mass of a fifth sample whose volume is 5 cm^3?

A) 9 g   **C)** 15 g
B) 10 g   **D)** 20 g

Test-Taking Tip   If you know the mass of a 1 cm^3 sample of the rock, you can use math to calculate the mass of a 5-cm^3 sample.

Consider this question carefully before writing your answer on a separate sheet of paper.

4. Many igneous rocks contain crystals. Geologists have observed that igneous rocks containing large crystals formed slowly, while those containing small crystals formed rapidly. Design an experiment, using sugar and water, to show that the rate at which crystals form affects their size.

Test-Taking Tip   You can use a super-saturated solution and seed crystals to speed up the rate at which the sugar crystals form.

QUESTION 1: D

Students need to read the question carefully and then refer to the table. Key words in the question are *onto the surface* and *dark-colored rock*. Only choice D, basalt, formed at the surface and is dark-colored.

QUESTION 2: J

Students need to retrieve information from the chart in order to identify the correct answer. Aluminum is the smallest percentage in the graph, and choice J is the smallest slice of the pie chart.

QUESTION 3: C

Students need to retrieve information from the table in order to identify the correct answer. Students need to extrapolate by spotting the trend in the data. The mass is always 3× the volume. Thus, for a sample whose volume is 5 mL, the mass must be choice C.

QUESTION 4: Answers will vary.

Students' experiments should provide for two setups: one in which the salt water is heated to speed up evaporation and another in which the salt water is allowed to evaporate slowly, for example, overnight.

UNIT 2

Unit Contents

Pre-Reading Activity

Have students read the captions for several figures in the unit and briefly describe what they see in each photograph or illustration.

UNIT 2 The Changing Surface of Earth

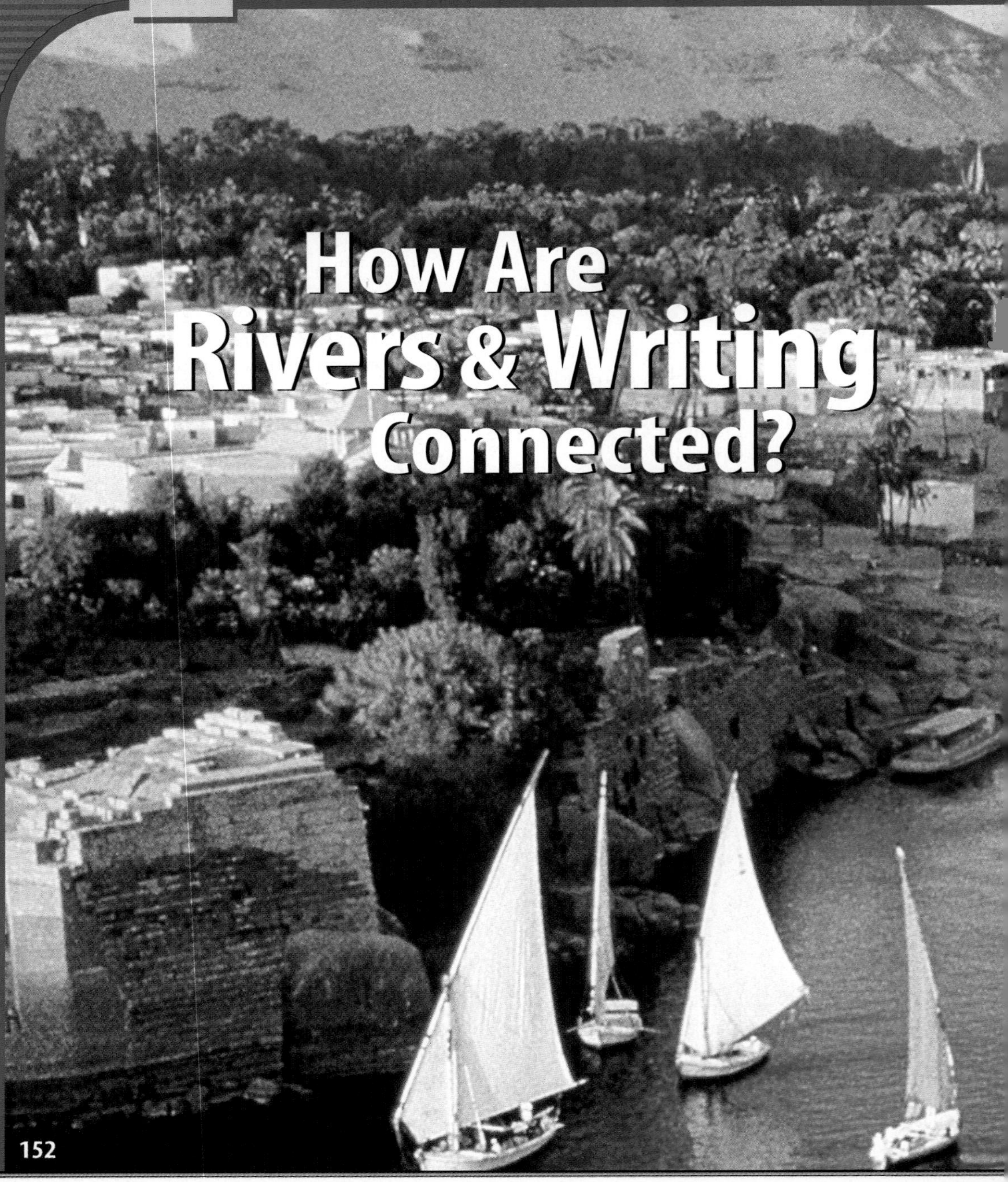
How Are
Rivers & Writing
Connected?
152

Teacher to Teacher

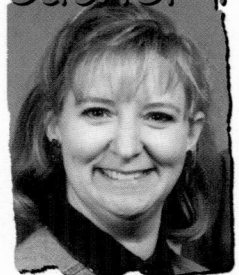

"To learn new vocabulary, students can identify terms, write key words from the text that describe the new vocabulary, and confirm or modify the information using the glossary. Then they can write a complete sentence using their key facts and create an illustration for their definition."

Patricia M. Horton, Mentor Teacher
Summit Intermediate School
Etiwanda, CA

Introducing the Unit

How Are Rivers & Writing Connected?

An important factor in the history of civilization was the development of agriculture. The ability to cultivate and harvest crops allowed the development of sedentary, and much larger, populations capable of almost unlimited growth. An agricultural life required an understanding of the processes of nature by which the Earth's surface is continuously modified. The growth of the human population, however, has begun to influence these same processes. Certain agricultural practices have led to an increased rate of topsoil erosion, which can in turn result in decreased harvests and food shortages. The water requirements of large urban centers have necessitated the damming of rivers and streams to produce large reservoirs. The long-term effects of this practice on local climate conditions are still unclear.

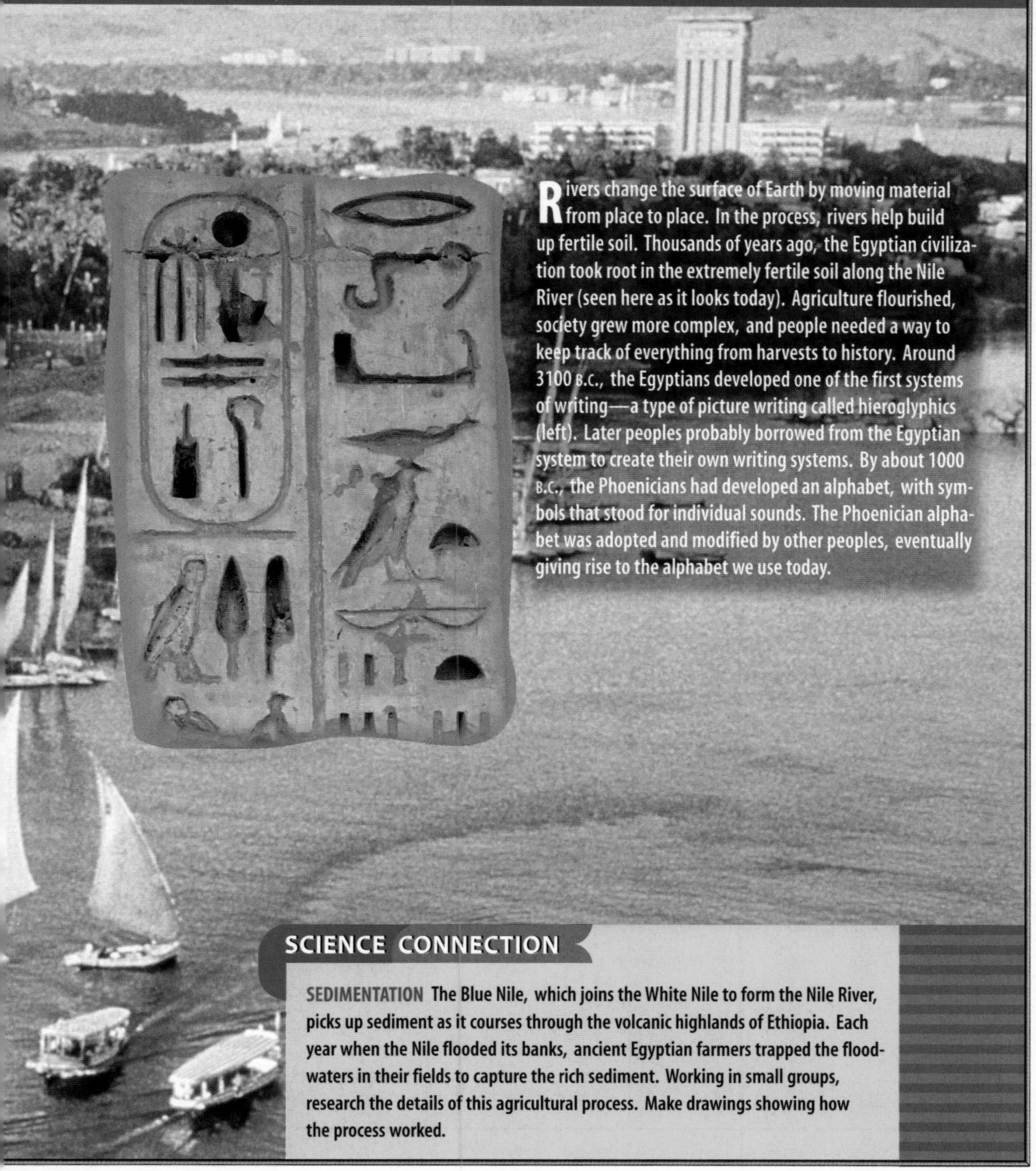

R ivers change the surface of Earth by moving material from place to place. In the process, rivers help build up fertile soil. Thousands of years ago, the Egyptian civilization took root in the extremely fertile soil along the Nile River (seen here as it looks today). Agriculture flourished, society grew more complex, and people needed a way to keep track of everything from harvests to history. Around 3100 B.C., the Egyptians developed one of the first systems of writing—a type of picture writing called hieroglyphics (left). Later peoples probably borrowed from the Egyptian system to create their own writing systems. By about 1000 B.C., the Phoenicians had developed an alphabet, with symbols that stood for individual sounds. The Phoenician alphabet was adopted and modified by other peoples, eventually giving rise to the alphabet we use today.

SCIENCE CONNECTION

SEDIMENTATION The Blue Nile, which joins the White Nile to form the Nile River, picks up sediment as it courses through the volcanic highlands of Ethiopia. Each year when the Nile flooded its banks, ancient Egyptian farmers trapped the floodwaters in their fields to capture the rich sediment. Working in small groups, research the details of this agricultural process. Make drawings showing how the process worked.

SCIENCE Online
Internet Addresses
_____
_____
_____
_____
_____

Explore the Glencoe Science Web site at **science.glencoe.com** to find out more about topics in this unit.

SCIENCE CONNECTION

Activity

Earth's surface changes continuously. Erosion by water and wind are not the only agents of change. Ask students to identify other features of Earth's surface and their natural causes. Possible answers: Many island chains, like the Hawaiian Islands, were formed and are continually changing because of undersea volcanic activity. Mountain ranges and elevated plateaus arise as the continental plates collide and push against one another. Shorelines of continents change as ocean levels rise and fall in response to increasing and decreasing global temperature.

Section/Objectives	Standards		Activities/Features
Chapter Opener	**National**	**State/Local**	**Explore Activity:** Describe landforms, p. 155 **Before You Read,** p. 155
	See p. 5T for a Key to Standards.		
Section 1 Landforms 🕐 2 sessions 📦 1 block 1. **Discuss** differences between plains and plateaus. 2. **Describe** folded, upwarped, fault-blocked and volcanic mountains.	National Content Standards: UCP5, A1, D1		**MiniLAB:** Profiling the United States, p. 158 **Physical Science Integration,** p. 159 **Science Online,** p. 159
Section 2 Viewpoints 🕐 2 sessions 📦 1 block 1. **Define** latitude and longitude. 2. **Explain** how latitude and longitude are used to identify locations on Earth. 3. **Determine** the time and date in different time zones.	National Content Standards: UCP3, A1, D1, F5		**MiniLAB:** Interpreting Latitude and Longitude, p. 163 **Life Science Integration,** p. 164
Section 3 Maps 🕐 3 sessions 📦 1.5 blocks 1. **Explain** the differences among Mercator, Robinson, and conic projections. 2. **Describe** features of topographic maps, geologic maps, and satellite maps.	National Content Standards: UCP2, A1, D1, E2, F5, G3		**Physics Integration,** p. 168 **Visualizing Topographic Maps,** p. 169 **Science Online,** p. 170 **Problem-Solving Activity:** How can you create a cross section from a geologic map?, p. 171 **Activity:** Making Topographic Map, p. 173 **Activity:** Constructing Landforms, pp. 174–175 **Science and History:** Location, Location, pp. 176–177

NATIONAL GEOGRAPHIC

Teacher's Corner

PRODUCTS AVAILABLE FROM NATIONAL GEOGRAPHIC SOCIETY
To order call 1-800-368-2728:
Books
Exploring Your World: the Adventure of Geography
National Geographic Satellite Atlas for

Young Explorers
National Geographic World Atlas for Young Explorers
Maps and Globe
Explorer Globe; Physical Earth
World Satellite
World Physical/Ocean Floor

Videos
Latitude and Longitude
Mapping Your World
Physical Geography of the Continent Series (6 videos)
When We Learn About Earth from Space

Activity Materials	Reproducible Resources	Section Assessment	Technology
Explore Activity: globe, atlas, or world map	**Chapter Resources Booklet** Foldables Worksheet, p. 15 Directed Reading Overview, p. 17 Note-taking Worksheets, pp. 31–32	GLENCOE'S **ASSESSMENT** ADVANTAGE	
MiniLAB: piece of paper, pencil, map of the United States	**Chapter Resources Booklet** Transparency Activity, p. 42 MiniLAB, p. 3 Enrichment, p. 28 Reinforcement, p. 25 Directed Reading, p. 18 Transparency Activity, pp. 45–46 **Cultural Diversity,** p. 33	**Portfolio** Cultural diversity, p. 158 **Performance** MiniLAB, p. 158 Skill Builder Activities, p. 161 **Content** Section Assessment, p. 161	Section Focus Transparency Teaching Transparency Interactive CD-ROM/DVD Guided Reading Audio Program
MiniLAB: world map *Need materials?* Contact Science Kit at 1-800-828-7777 or www.sciencekit.com on the Internet.	**Chapter Resources Booklet** Transparency Activity, p. 43 MiniLAB, p. 4 Lab Activities, pp. 9–11, 13–14 Enrichment, p. 29 Reinforcement, p. 26 Directed Reading, p. 19	**Portfolio** Challenge, p. 165 **Performance** MiniLAB, p. 163 Skill Builder Activities, p. 165 **Content** Section Assessment, p. 165	Section Focus Transparency Interactive CD-ROM/DVD Guided Reading Audio Program
Activity: plastic model of a landform, water tinted with food coloring, transparency, transparency marker, clear plastic storage box with lid, beaker, metric ruler, tape **Activity:** U.S. Geological Survey 7.5 minute quadrangle maps, sandbox sand, rolls of brown paper towels, spray bottle filled with water, ruler	**Chapter Resources Booklet** Transparency Activity, p. 44 Enrichment, p. 30 Reinforcement, p. 27 Directed Reading, pp. 19, 20 Activity Worksheets, pp. 5–6, 7–8 **Earth Science Critical Thinking/ Problem Solving,** p. 5 **Cultural Diversity,** pp. 27, 49 **Reading and Writing Skill Activities,** p. 21 **Lab Management and Safety,** p. 66	**Portfolio** Extension, p. 169 **Performance** Problem-Solving Activity, p. 171 Skill Builder Activities, p. 172 **Content** Section Assessment, p. 172	Section Focus Transparency Interactive CD-ROM/DVD Guided Reading Audio Program

GLENCOE'S
ASSESSMENT
ADVANTAGE

End of Chapter Assessment

Blackline Masters	Technology	Professional Series
Chapter Resources Booklet Chapter Review, pp. 35–36 Chapter Tests, pp. 37–40 **Standardized Test Practice by The Princeton Review,** pp. 31–34	MindJogger Videoquiz CD-ROM Explorations and Quizzes Vocabulary Puzzle Makers ExamView Pro Test Bank Interactive Lesson Planner Interactive Teacher's Edition	Performance Assessment in the Science Classroom (PASC)

Transparencies

Section Focus

Section Focus Transparency 1 — Sacred Heights

Mount Fuji, or Fujiyama, is Japan's highest mountain at 3,776 m (12,388 feet) high. Mount Fuji is a sacred mountain, and its name means "everlasting life."

1. What might Mount Fuji's shape tell you about the process by which it was formed?
2. How might wind and precipitation change the shape of a mountain?
3. Name some other mountain-forming processes.

L2

Section Focus Transparency 2 — A Lovely Planet

This is an image of Earth made from space. Even on this flat photo, you can tell Earth is a sphere. Notice the way light from the Sun changes over the surface of Earth.

1. Which parts of Earth does this image show?
2. If you were standing on one of the landmasses shown, how would you describe your location to a friend calling from North America?
3. How might a grid overlaying Earth help to indicate exact locations?

L2

Section Focus Transparency 3 — A Map of the Times

This is a map of the world that was made in Europe in 1617. Cartography, or map making, dates to prehistoric times when maps were used to show hunting and fishing grounds. Today, cartographers can use images from satellites to help them make better maps.

1. Judging from this map, what parts of the world did Europeans know well in 1617? What parts of the world are mapped inaccurately?
2. How do you explorers affected cartography?
3. Think about different maps of your state that you have seen. Do all maps provide the same information? How many different kinds of maps can you name?

L2

This is a representation of key blackline masters available in the Teacher Classroom Resources. See Resource Manager boxes within the chapter for additional information.

Assessment

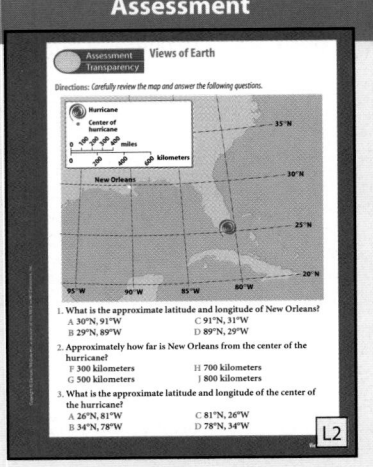

Assessment Transparency — Views of Earth

Directions: Carefully review the map and answer the following questions.

1. What is the approximate latitude and longitude of New Orleans?
   A 30°N, 91°W   C 91°N, 31°W
   B 29°N, 89°W   D 89°N, 29°W
2. Approximately how far is New Orleans from the center of the hurricane?
   F 300 kilometers   H 700 kilometers
   G 500 kilometers   I 800 kilometers
3. What is the approximate latitude and longitude of the center of the hurricane?
   A 26°N, 81°W   C 81°N, 26°W
   B 34°N, 78°W   D 78°N, 34°W

L2

Teaching

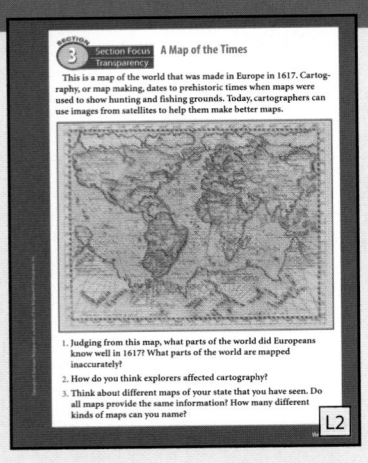

Teaching Transparency 2 — Latitude and Longitude

North Pole (90° North Latitude)
80°N
40°N
20°N
0° Equator
20°S
40°S
60°S
80°S
South Pole (90° South Latitude)

L2

Key to Teaching Strategies

The following designations will help you decide which activities are appropriate for your students.

L1 Level 1 activities should be appropriate for students with learning difficulties.

L2 Level 2 activities should be within the ability range of all students.

L3 Level 3 activities are designed for above-average students.

ELL ELL activities should be within the ability range of English Language Learners.

COOP LEARN Cooperative Learning activities are designed for small group work.

LS Multiple Learning Styles logos, as described on page 22T, are used throughout to indicate strategies that address different learning styles.

P These strategies represent student products that can be placed into a best-work portfolio.

Hands-on Activities

Activity Worksheets

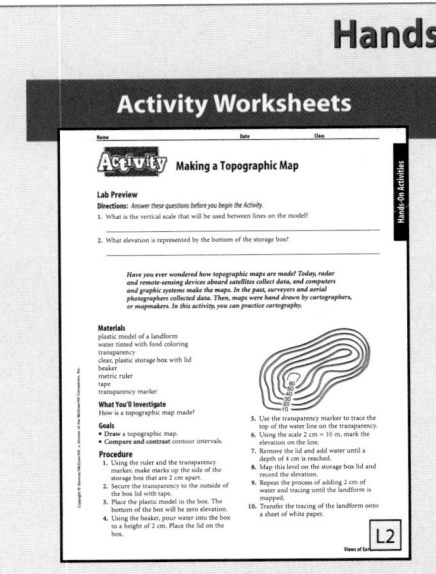

Activity — Making a Topographic Map

Lab Preview
Directions: Answer these questions before you begin the Activity.
1. What is the vertical scale that will be used between lines on the model?
2. What elevation is represented by the bottom of the storage box?

Have you ever wondered how topographic maps are made? Today, radar and remote-sensing devices aboard satellites collect data, and computers and graphic systems make the maps. In the past, surveyors and aerial photographers collected data. Then, maps were hand drawn by cartographers, or mapmakers. In this activity, you can practice cartography.

Materials
plastic model of a landform
water tinted with food coloring
transparency
clear, plastic storage box with lid
beaker
metric ruler
tape
transparency marker

What You'll Investigate
How is a topographic map made?

Goals
• Draw a topographic map.
• Compare and contrast contour intervals.

Procedure
1. Using the ruler and the transparency marker, make marks up the side of the storage box that are 2 cm apart.
2. Secure the transparency to the outside of the box lid with tape.
3. Place the plastic model in the box. The bottom of the box will be zero elevation.
4. Using the beaker, pour water into the box to a height of 2 cm. Place the lid on the box.
5. Use the transparency marker to trace the top of the water line on the transparency.
6. Using the scale 2 cm = 10 m, mark the elevation on the line.
7. Remove the lid and add water until a depth of 4 cm is reached.
8. Map this level on the storage box lid and record the elevation.
9. Repeat the process of adding 2 cm of water and tracing until the landform is mapped.
10. Transfer the tracing of the landform onto a sheet of white paper.

L2

Laboratory Activities

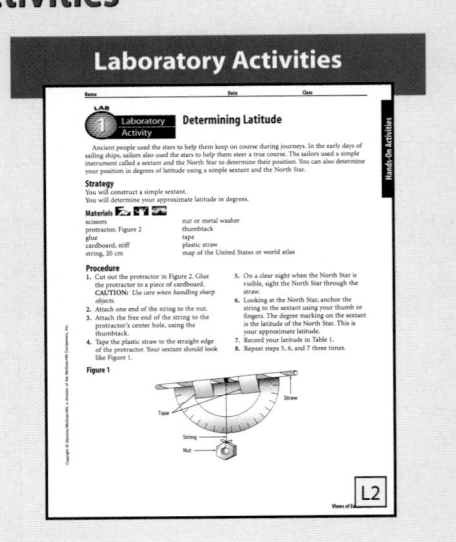

Laboratory Activity — Determining Latitude

Ancient people used the stars to help them keep on course during journeys. In the early days of sailing ships, sailors also used the stars to help them steer a true course. The sailors used a simple instrument called a sextant and the North Star to determine their position. You can also determine your position in degrees of latitude using a simple sextant and the North Star.

Strategy
You will construct a simple sextant.
You will determine your approximate latitude in degrees.

Materials
scissors
protractor, Figure 2
glue
cardboard, stiff
string, 20 cm
nut or metal washer
thumbtack
tape
plastic straw
map of the United States or world atlas

Procedure
1. Cut out the protractor in Figure 2. Glue the protractor to a piece of cardboard. CAUTION: Use care when handling sharp objects.
2. Attach one end of the string to the nut.
3. Attach the free end of the string to the protractor's center hole, using the thumbtack.
4. Tape the plastic straw to the straight edge of the protractor. Your sextant should look like Figure 1.

5. On a clear night when the North Star is visible, sight the North Star through the straw.
6. Looking at the North Star, anchor the string to the sextant using your thumb or fingers. The degree marking on the sextant is the latitude of the North Star. This is your approximate latitude.
7. Record your latitude in Table 1.
8. Repeat steps 5, 6, and 7 three times.

Figure 1

L2

Meeting Different Ability Levels

Content Outline

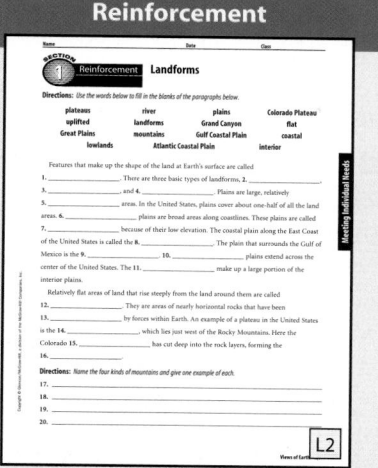

L2

Reinforcement

L2

Directed Reading

L1

Assessment

Chapter Tests

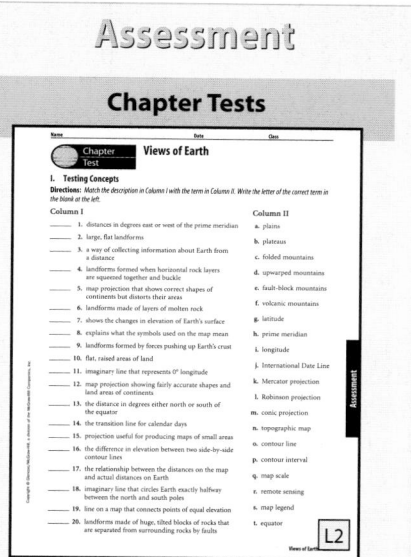

L2

Enrichment

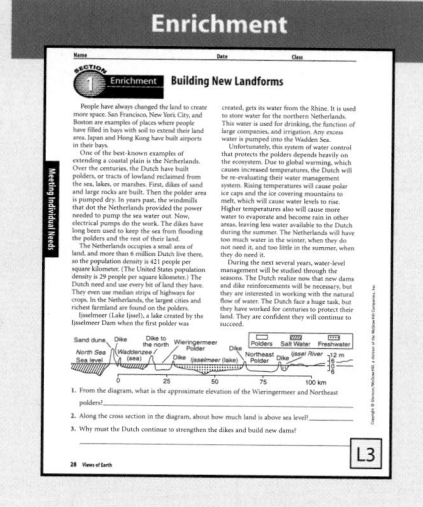

L3

Spanish Directed Reading

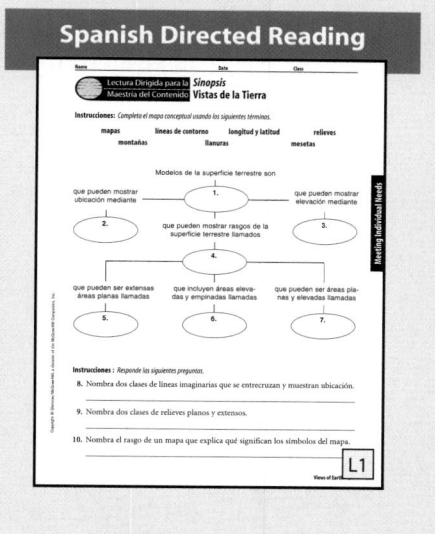

L1

Test Practice Workbook

L2

Chapter Review

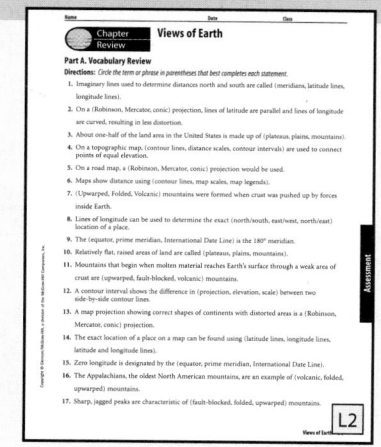

L2

Science Content Background

SECTION 1

Landforms
Plains and Mountains

Plains form in a variety of ways. Some are formed by the weathering and erosion of plateaus and mountains. Others are formed by the deposition of sediments into valleys or other depressions. Mountains are classified according to their most dominant characteristics. These characteristics are caused by the processes involved in mountain building, such as folding, faulting, upwarping, and igneous and metamorphic activities.

Earth Satellite Corporation/Science Photo Library/Photo Researchers, Inc.

SECTION 2

Viewpoints
Latitude and Longitude

Latitude is defined as the angle formed between the point in the sky directly above an observer (zenith) and the plane of Earth's equator. Each degree of latitude circles 111 km. Lines of latitude form imaginary circles around Earth that are parallel to the equator. The diameter of these circles decrease with distance from the equator. At the poles, the circles are mere points.

> ### Student Misconception
>
> Earth is not a sphere, but is flat.
>
> **Refer to the facing page for teaching strategies to address this misconception. Refer to pages 162–165 for content related to this topic.**

Longitude lines are not parallel to one another. Rather, they are vertical lines that circle Earth. The length of one degree of longitude varies with distance from the equator. At the poles, the length of degree of longitude is 0 km.

SECTION 3

Maps
Map Projections

A map projection is made by transferring data about Earth onto paper. Because Earth is round and paper is flat, some distortion is always present in map projections. The larger the area covered by the map, the greater the distortion. Gerhardus Mercator developed the projection named for him in 1569. In a Mercator projection, the size of Greenland is exaggerated 1,500 percent. When Arthur Robinson created his projection in 1963, he visualized how each country should look like on a map, then used mathematics and computers to draw their shapes. The Robinson projection has a 60 percent exaggeration of the size of Greenland.

SCIENCE *Online*

For additional content background on this topic, go to the Glencoe Science Web site at science.glencoe.com.

IDENTIFYING ▷ Misconceptions

Find Out What Students Think

Students may think that . . .

• Earth is not a sphere, but is flat.
This misconception is a result of students' common experience—from the ground, Earth's surface looks flat. In addition, many students have yet to grasp the idea of gravity pulling all parts of Earth, and the people and other objects on its surface, toward its center. Thus students think that if Earth were a sphere, people on the bottom would "fall off."

Demonstration
Evidence, both direct and indirect, needs to be provided to students to help them understand that Earth is spherical and that it rotates. Evidence could include

• satellite photos of Earth.

S. Nielsen/DRK Photo

• photographs showing Earth's curved shadow on the Moon during a lunar eclipse.

Promote Understanding

Activity
Provide each pair of students with construction paper, scissors, tape, and a basketball or other sports ball.

• Have students make a small representation of a sail boat using the construction paper and tape. Instruct them to tape the boat onto the basketball.

• Have students stand about 3 m from their partners. Direct the partner to hold the basketball in front of his or her body, with the boat toward them. Then have them slowly rotate the ball so the boat appears to move up and over the top of the ball.

• As the ship appears, have the watching partner closely observe which parts of the boat appear first. Then have students switch roles.

Discussion
After all students have observed the approach of the boat, bring the class together and discuss their observations. Bring out the idea that as a ship disappears over the horizon the last part that one observes is the mast. As it approaches, the first thing one sees is the mast. If Earth were flat, one would see the entire boat either appear or disappear.

Assess
After completing the chapter, see *Identifying Misconceptions* in the Study Guide.

Chapter Vocabulary

plain
plateau
folded mountain
upwarped mountain
fault-block mountain
volcanic mountain
equator
latitude
prime meridian
longitude
conic projection
topographic map
contour line
map scale
map legend

What do you think?

Science Journal A hand-held receiver for a global positioning system (GPS) is shown. The GPS is a system of 24 satellites in orbit around Earth. A person holding a GPS receiver can pinpoint his or her exact location on Earth's surface by receiving signals from those satellites. This is especially useful for hiking in the woods, boating in the ocean, driving in an unfamiliar city, or flying a small airplane over unfamiliar terrain.

Viewing Earth from satellites, often called remote sensing, is a powerful way to learn about Earth's landforms, weather, and vegetation. This colorful image shows the metropolitan area of New York City and surrounding regions. Vegetation shows up as green, uncovered land is red, water is blue, and human-made structures appear gray. In this chapter, you will learn about studying Earth from space. You'll learn about Earth's major landforms, and you'll learn how to locate places on Earth's surface.

What do you think?

Science Journal Look at the picture below with a classmate. Discuss what you think this might be. Here's a hint: *It can keep you from getting lost on land or at sea.* Write your answer or best guess in your Science Journal.

154

Theme Connection

Scale and Structure The structural differences among major landforms are examined. Students also focus on understanding the scale and structure of maps.

EXPLORE ACTIVITY

Pictures of Earth from space are acquired by instruments attached to satellites. Scientists use these images to make maps because they show features of Earth's surface, such as mountains and rivers. In the activity below, use a map or a globe to explore Earth's surface.

Describe landforms

Using a globe, atlas, or a world map, locate the following features and describe their positions on Earth relative to other major features. Provide any other details that would help someone else find them.

1. Andes mountains
2. Amazon, Ganges, and Mississippi Rivers
3. Indian Ocean, the Sea of Japan, and the Baltic Sea
4. Australia, South America, and North America

Observe

Choose one country on the globe or map and describe its major physical features in your Science Journal.

Before You Read

FOLDABLES
Reading & Study Skills

Making a Main Ideas Study Fold Make the following Foldable to help you identify the major topics about landforms.

1. Stack two sheets of paper in front of you so the short side of both sheets is at the top.
2. Slide the top sheet up so about 4 cm of the bottom sheet show.
3. Fold both sheets top to bottom to form four tabs and staple along the fold. Turn the Foldable so the staples are at the bottom. Cut mountain shapes on the top tab.
4. Label the tabs *Main Landform Types, Plains, Plateaus,* and *Mountains.* Before you read the chapter, write what you know about each landform under the tabs.
5. As you read the chapter, add to and correct what you have written.

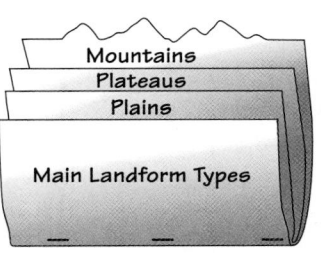

155

EXPLORE ACTIVITY

Purpose Students reinforce map skills by using a world map or globe to observe and record the relative positions of Earth's landforms. [L2] [ELL] [LS] **Visual-Spatial**

Preparation Be sure the maps and globes you use have the listed features clearly labeled.

Materials globe or world map for every three students

Teaching Strategy Have students practice describing landform locations before they begin the activity. For example, have them describe the location of the Rocky Mountains. north-south mountain range in western North America

Observe
Answers will vary depending on the country chosen.

✓Assessment

Performance Ask students to describe in writing how mountains and rivers are indicated on the globe or world map they used. Use **Performance Assessment in the Science Classroom,** p. 159.

Before You Read

FOLDABLES
Reading & Study Skills

Dinah Zike Study Fold
Purpose Determine what students know about the three main landform types before reading the chapter. Provide a Foldable for recording and organizing notes on plains, plateaus, and mountains as they read.

📁 For additional help, see Foldables Worksheet, p. 15 in **Chapter Resources Booklet,** or go to the Glencoe Science Web site at **science.glencoe.com.** See After You Read in the Study Guide at the end of this chapter.

SECTION

Landforms

Bellringer Transparency

Display the Section Focus Transparency for Section 1. Use the accompanying Transparency Activity Master. L2

ELL

Tie to Prior Knowledge

Have students brainstorm the names of prominent landforms in or near your community. List them on the board. Tell students they will learn about several types of landforms in this section.

As You Read

What You'll Learn

- **Discuss** differences between plains and plateaus.
- **Describe** folded, upwarped, fault-block, and volcanic mountains.

Vocabulary

plain
plateau
folded mountain
upwarped mountain
fault-block mountain
volcanic mountain

Why It's Important

Landforms influence how people can use land.

Figure 1
Three basic types of landforms are plains, plateaus, and mountains.

Plains

Earth offers abundant variety—from tropics to tundras, deserts to rain forests, and freshwater mountain streams to salt-water tidal marshes. Some of Earth's most stunning features are its landforms, which can provide beautiful vistas, such as vast, flat, fertile plains; deep gorges that cut through steep walls of rock; and towering, snowcapped peaks. **Figure 1** shows the three basic types of landforms—plains, plateaus, and mountains.

Even if you haven't ever visited mountains, you might have seen hundreds of pictures of them in your lifetime. Plains are more common than mountains, but they are more difficult to visualize. **Plains** are large, flat areas, often found in the interior regions of continents. The flat land of plains is ideal for agriculture. Plains often have thick, fertile soils and abundant, grassy meadows suitable for grazing animals. Plains also are home to a variety of wildlife, including foxes, ground squirrels, and snakes. When plains are found near the ocean, they're called coastal plains. Together, interior plains and coastal plains make up half of all the land in the United States.

Mountains

Plateau

Section ✓ *Assessment* Planner

PORTFOLIO
Cultural Diversity, p. 158

PERFORMANCE ASSESSMENT
Try at Home MiniLAB, p. 158
Skill Builder Activities, p. 161
See page 180 for more options.

CONTENT ASSESSMENT
Section, p. 161
Challenge, p. 161
Chapter, pp. 180–181

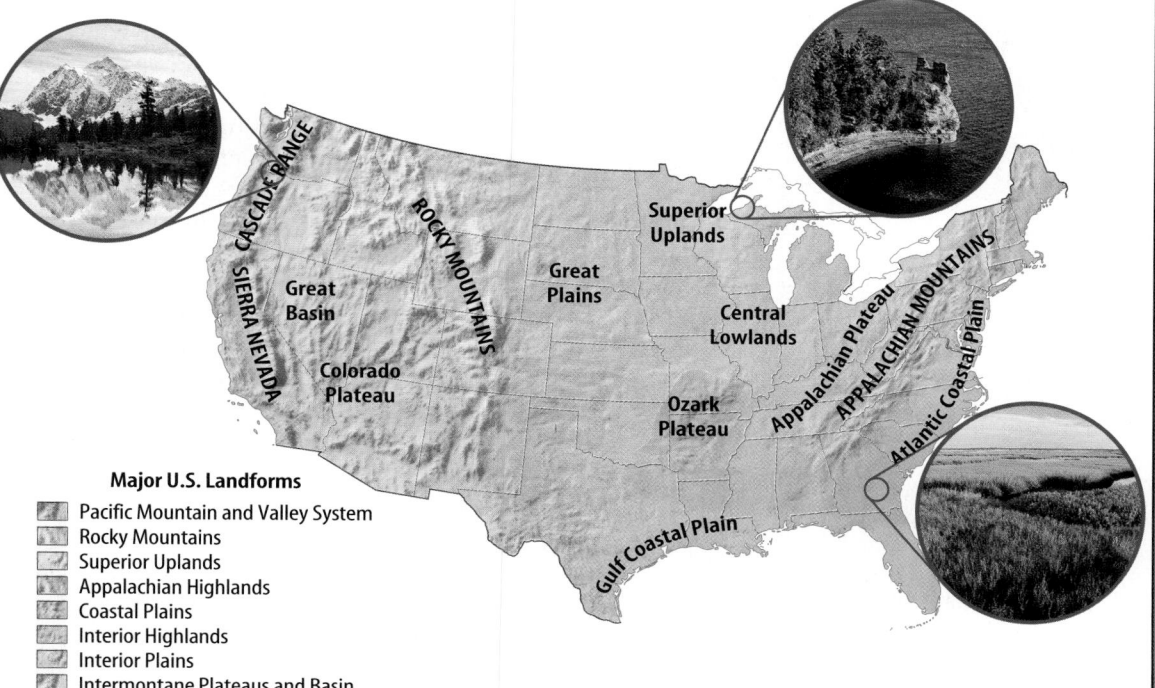

Major U.S. Landforms

- Pacific Mountain and Valley System
- Rocky Mountains
- Superior Uplands
- Appalachian Highlands
- Coastal Plains
- Interior Highlands
- Interior Plains
- Intermontane Plateaus and Basin

Coastal Plains A coastal plain often is called a lowland because it is lower in elevation, or distance above sea level, than the land around it. You can think of the coastal plains as being the exposed portion of a continental shelf. The continental shelf is the part of a continent that extends into the ocean. The Atlantic Coastal Plain is a good example of this type of landform. It stretches along the east coast of the United States from New Jersey to Florida. This area has low rolling hills, swamps, and marshes. A marsh is a grassy wetland that usually is flooded with water.

The Atlantic Coastal Plain, shown in **Figure 2,** began forming about 70 million years ago as sediment began accumulating on the ocean floor. Sea level eventually dropped, and the seafloor was exposed. As a result, the coastal plain was born. The size of the coastal plain varies over time. That's because sea level rises and falls. During the last ice age, the coastal plain was larger than it is now because so much of Earth's water was contained in glaciers.

The Gulf Coastal Plain includes the lowlands in the southern United States that surround the Gulf of Mexico. Much of this plain was formed from sediment deposited in deltas by the many rivers that enter the Gulf of Mexico.

✔ **Reading Check** *How are coastal plains formed?*

Figure 2
The United States has eight major landform regions, which include plains, mountains, and plateaus. After looking at this map, describe the region that you live in.

Section 1 Landforms **157**

---

2 Teach

Plains

Activity

Display a relief map of North America. Have students compare and contrast the different landforms. L2 IS **Visual-Spatial**

IDENTIFYING Misconceptions

Students may think that because plains are flat, they are always found at much lower elevations than mountains. Explain that plains can be found at any elevation. For example, Denver, Colorado, is at the western edge of the Great Plains at an elevation of 1624.5 m. In comparison, the average elevation of the Appalachian Mountains is less than 2,000 m above sea level.

Extension

Encourage several students to interview a city or county engineer to find out why he or she needs to know about local landforms when planning new roads and other projects. Have students share this information with their classmates. L2 IS **Interpersonal**

✔ **Reading Check**

Answer from sediment deposited in deltas by rivers

Curriculum Connection

Social Studies More than half the world's population lives on plains. Have students research possible explanations for this fact. Students should discover that plains are often fertile farmlands. L2

IS **Logical-Mathematical**

Resource Manager

Chapter Resources Booklet
Transparency Activity, p. 42
Directed Reading for Content Mastery, pp. 17, 18
Note-taking Worksheets, pp. 31–32

Plains, continued

TRY AT HOME
Mini LAB

Purpose Students make a profile that shows the major landforms of the United States. L2

IS Visual-Spatial

Materials **Figure 2,** metric ruler, pencil, physical map of the United States.

Teaching Strategy If possible, project a transparency of **Figure 2.** With a clear transparency as an overlay, use a marking pen to show students how to make the profile.

Analysis
1. Profiles progress from mountains near the west coast, to a narrow interior lowland, and then to a wide set of steep mountains representing the Rockies. A wide plain should stretch from these mountains through much of the central area of the country. A range of lower mountains lies between the central plain and the coastal plain.
2. Many landforms run north-south in the United States, thus these profiles would not show as much change in elevation.

✔ Assessment

Performance Have students write a travelogue describing the landforms they would see along the route shown in their profiles. Use **PASC,** p. 159.

TRY AT HOME
Mini LAB

Profiling the United States

Procedure
1. Place the bottom edge of a piece of **paper** across the middle of **Figure 2,** extending from the west coast to the east coast.
2. Mark where different landforms are located along this edge.
3. Use a **map of the United States** and the **descriptions of the landforms in Section 1** to help you draw a profile, or side view, of the United States. Use steep, jagged lines to represent mountains. Low, flat lines can represent plains.

Analysis
1. Describe how your profile changed shape as you moved from west to east.
2. Describe how the shape of your profile would be different if you oriented your paper north to south.

Interior Plains The central portion of the United States is comprised largely of interior plains. Shown in **Figure 3,** you'll find them between the Rocky Mountains, the Appalachian Mountains, and the Gulf Coastal Plain. They include the Central Lowlands around the Missouri and Mississippi Rivers and the rolling hills of the Great Lakes area.

A large part of the interior plains is known as the Great Plains. This area lies between the Mississippi River and the Rocky Mountains. It is a flat, grassy, dry area with few trees. The Great Plains also are referred to as the high plains because of their elevation, which ranges from 350 m above sea level at the eastern border to 1,500 m in the west. The Great Plains consist of nearly horizontal layers of sedimentary rocks.

Plateaus

At somewhat higher elevations, you will find plateaus (pla TOHZ). **Plateaus** are flat, raised areas of land made up of nearly horizontal rocks that have been uplifted by forces within Earth. They are different from plains in that their edges rise steeply from the land around them. Because of this uplifting, it is common for plateaus, such as the Colorado Plateau, to be cut through by deep river valleys and canyons. The Colorado River, as shown in **Figure 3,** has cut deeply into the rock layers of the plateau, forming the Grand Canyon. Because the Colorado Plateau is located mostly in what is now a dry region, only a few rivers have developed on its surface. If you hiked around on this plateau, you would encounter a high, rugged environment.

Figure 3
Plains and plateaus are fairly flat, but plateaus have higher elevation. **A** This short-grass prairie in Kansas is part of an interior plain. **B** The Colorado River has carved the Grand Canyon into the Colorado Plateau.

👥 Cultural Diversity

Landforms and Ancient Builders Among the mountains and canyons of northwestern New Mexico is Pueblo Bonito, a three-acre stone and mortar structure built by many generations of Anasazi Indian masons. The builders used the sandstone to fashion rectangular blocks for the walls of the structure. Mud and water mortar knits the blocks together. Pueblo Bonito contains more than 600 rooms. Like many Anasazi structures, it was abandoned about 900 years ago when a prolonged drought made living in this dry area difficult. Many of the structures are still partially standing. Have students use the Internet to research the ruins of Chaco Canyon, including Pueblo Bonito. Have them write short reports on what they find. L2 **IS** Linguistic P

Mountains

Mountains with snowcapped peaks often are shrouded in clouds and tower high above the surrounding land. If you climb them, the views are spectacular. The world's highest mountain peak is Mount Everest in the Himalaya—more than 8,800 m above sea level. By contrast, the highest mountain peaks in the United States reach just over 6,000 m. Mountains also vary in how they are formed. The four main types of mountains are folded, upwarped, fault-block, and volcanic.

 **Reading Check** *What is the highest mountain peak on Earth?*

Folded Mountains The Appalachian Mountains and the Rocky Mountains in Canada, shown in **Figure 4,** are comprised of folded rock layers. In **folded mountains,** the rock layers are folded like a rug that has been pushed up against a wall.

Physics INTEGRATION To form folded mountains, tremendous forces inside Earth squeeze horizontal rock layers, causing them to buckle and fold. The Appalachian Mountains formed 250 million to 350 million years ago and are among the oldest and longest mountain ranges in North America. The Appalachians once were higher than the Rocky Mountains, but weathering and erosion have worn them down. They now are less than 2,000 m above sea level. The Ouachita (WAH shuh tah) Mountains of Arkansas are extensions of the same mountain range.

Research Visit the Glencoe Science Web site at **science.glencoe.com** to learn how landforms can affect economic development.

Figure 4
Folded mountains form when rock layers are squeezed from opposite sides. These mountains in Banff National Park, Canada, consist of folded rock layers.

Reading Check

Answer Mount Everest

Use Science Words

Word Usage Obtain photographs of the three basic kinds of landforms: plains, plateaus, and mountains. Have students write a sentence using each term. L2
IS **Linguistic**

Fun Fact

The Colorado Plateau has been rising approximately 0.3 cm every year for the last 10 million years. It is presently 2 km higher than the area that surrounds it.

Quick Demo

Demonstrate the formation of folded mountains by laying a sheet of paper on a flat surface. Have a student place a hand on one end. Have another student place a hand on the other end. Tell the students to slide the ends of the paper toward the center. Have the class note the high folded loop that forms. L1 ELL
COOP LEARN IS **Visual-Spatial**

Internet Addresses
_____
_____
_____
_____

Explore the Glencoe Science Web site at **science.glencoe.com** to find out more about topics in this section.

Teacher FYI

The highest mountain peak in the United States is Mount McKinley, which rises 6,194 m in the Alaska Range. The mountain was named for President William McKinley. The Athabaskan Indians of the area called the peak Denali, which means "The Great One." The preserve surrounding the mountain now bears the Indian name, as Denali National Park.

Resource Manager

Chapter Resources Booklet
  MiniLAB, p. 3
  Enrichment, p. 28
Reading and Writing Skill Activities, p. 3

Mountains, continued

Make a Model

Have students use clay to make models of the different kinds of mountains discussed in this section. L1 ELL
IS Kinesthetic

Discussion

Tell students that the Ridge and Valley area of Pennsylvania is composed of parallel lines of rounded ridges with lowlands between them. **Is this area more likely to be composed of folded or fault-block mountains?** Folded mountains; fault-block mountains have high peaks and steep slopes, unlike the more rounded peaks of folded mountains. Some students may recognize that the mountains of Pennsylvania are part of the Appalachians, which are identified as folded mountains in the text.

Caption Answer

Figure 6 majestic peaks and steep slopes

Activity

Have students use a world map to locate major volcanic mountain chains. Have them write a statement in their Science Journals about where most of these mountains occur. L2
IS Visual-Spatial and Linguistic

Figure 5
The southern Rocky Mountains are upwarped mountains that formed when crust was pushed up by forces inside Earth.

Upwarped Mountains The Adirondack Mountains in New York, the southern Rocky Mountains in Colorado and New Mexico, and the Black Hills in South Dakota are upwarped mountains. **Figure 5** shows a mountain range in Colorado. Notice the high peaks and sharp ridges that are common to this type of mountain. **Upwarped mountains** form when blocks of Earth's crust are pushed up by forces inside Earth. Over time, the soil and sedimentary rocks at the top of Earth's crust erode, exposing the hard, crystalline rock underneath. As these rocks erode, they form the peaks and ridges.

Fault-Block Mountains **Fault-block mountains** are made of huge, tilted blocks of rock that are separated from surrounding rock by faults. These faults are large fractures in rock along which mostly vertical movement has occurred. The Grand Tetons of Wyoming, shown in **Figure 6,** and the Sierra Nevada in California are examples of fault-block mountains. As **Figure 6** shows, when these mountains formed, one block was tilted and pushed up, while the adjacent block dropped down. This mountain-building process produces majestic peaks and steep slopes.

Figure 6
Fault-block mountains such as the Grand Tetons are formed when faults occur. Some rock blocks move up, and others move down. *How are fault-block mountains different from upwarped mountains?*

160 CHAPTER 6 Views of Earth

Resource Manager

Chapter Resources Booklet
   Reinforcement, p. 25
   Transparency Activity, pp. 45–46
Cultural Diversity, p. 33

Science Journal

Young Rocks Tell students that the Himalayas are still growing. Have students locate these mountains on a map and describe in their Science Journals why these mountains are still growing. Students should discover that the Himalayas are being pushed up as the Indian plate converges with the Asian plate. L2

Figure 7
Mount Shasta is a volcanic mountain made up of layers of lava and ash.

Volcanic Mountains **Volcanic mountains,** like the one shown in **Figure 7,** begin to form when molten material reaches the surface through a weak area of the crust. The deposited materials pile up, layer upon layer, until a cone-shaped structure forms. Two volcanic mountains in the United States are Mount St. Helens in Washington and Mount Shasta in California. The Hawaiian Islands are the peaks of huge volcanoes that sit on the ocean floor. Measured from the base, Mauna Loa in Hawaii would be higher than Mount Everest.

Plains, plateaus, and mountains offer different kinds of landforms to explore. They range from low, coastal plains and high, desert plateaus to mountain ranges thousands of meters high.

Section 1 Assessment

1. Describe the eight major landform regions in the United States that are mentioned in this chapter.
2. How do plains and plateaus differ?
3. Why are some mountains folded and others upwarped?
4. How are volcanic mountains different from other mountains?
5. **Think Critically** If you wanted to know whether a particular mountain was formed by movement along a fault, what would you look for?

Skill Builder Activities

6. **Concept Mapping** Make an events-chain concept map to explain how upwarped mountains form. **For more help,** refer to the Science Skill Handbook.
7. **Using an Electronic Spreadsheet** Design a spreadsheet that compares the origin and features of the following: *folded, upwarped, fault-block,* and *volcanic mountains.* Then, explain an advantage of using a spreadsheet to compare different types of mountains. **For more help, refer to the** Technology Skill Handbook.

Mountains, continued

Visual Learning

Figure 7 What visual clues tell you that Mount St. Helens is a volcanic mountain rather than a folded mountain? Mount St. Helens has a cone shape, rather than the gentler rounded shape of folded peaks. Part of the top has been blown away by an eruption.

3 Assess

Reteach

Use wooden blocks or rectangular sponges cut at various angles to demonstrate the formation of fault-block mountains. L1 ELL IS **Visual-Spatial**

Challenge

Challenge partners to do research to compare and contrast the processes that formed the Appalachian Mountains with those that formed the Black Hills. Encourage students to use labeled diagrams to illustrate the processes. Students should find that lateral forces formed the Appalachians and vertical forces formed the Black Hills. L3 IS **Interpersonal**

✓ Assessment

Process Have students make a concept map that shows how volcanic mountains form. Use **PASC,** p. 161.

Answers to Section Assessment

1. Atlantic Coastal Plain: lowland along the east coast; Gulf Coastal Plain: lowland along the Gulf of Mexico; Rockies: west-central mountains; Appalachians: eastern folded mountains; Central Lowlands: lowlands around Great Lakes and Mississippi and Missouri Rivers; Great Plains: flat area between the Mississippi and Rockies; Colorado Plateau: raised, flat region in the Southwest; Hawaiian islands: volcanic islands
2. Plateau edges rise steeply from the land around them; the edges of plains do not.
3. Folded: rock layers are squeezed from opposite sides; upwarped: crust is thrust upward by pressure.
4. Other mountains form when crust is squeezed or pushed upward. Volcanoes form when molten material is deposited on Earth's surface.
5. nearby faults and blocky-looking mountains
6. crust blocks pushed up → soil erodes → hard rocks exposed forming sharp peaks
7. Check students' work. Spreadsheets organize material in a way that makes comparisons easy to see.

SECTION

2

Viewpoints

1 Motivate

Bellringer Transparency

Display the Section Focus Transparency for Section 2. Use the accompanying Transparency Activity Master. L2

ELL

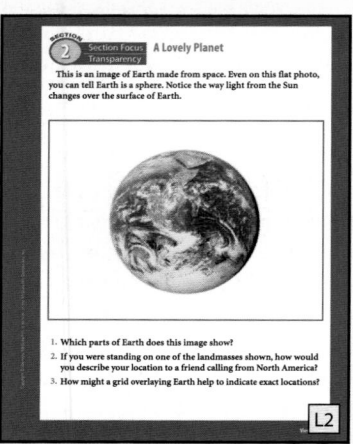

Tie to Prior Knowledge

Have students recall the appearance of maps and globes, and the straight lines that form a grid on these maps. Explain that in this section, they will learn how these lines help pinpoint locations on Earth's surface.

IDENTIFYING Misconceptions

Some students may think that Earth is not a sphere, but flat. See page 154F for strategies that address this misconception.

As You Read

What You'll Learn

- **Define** latitude and longitude.
- **Explain** how latitude and longitude are used to identify locations on Earth.
- **Determine** the time and date in different time zones.

Vocabulary

equator   prime meridian
latitude   longitude

Why It's Important

Latitude and longitude allow you to locate places on Earth.

Figure 8

Latitude and longitude are measurements that are used to indicate locations on Earth's surface.

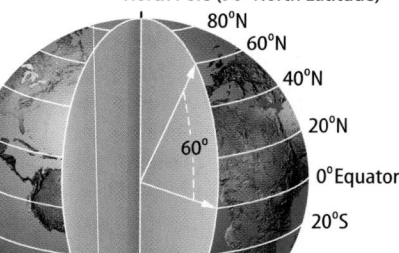

80°N
60°N
40°N
20°N
60°
0°Equator
20°S
40°S
60°S
80°S
South Pole (90° South Latitude)

Prime Meridian
30°W   90°
0°   60°   60°E

A Latitude is the measurement of the imaginary angle created by the equator, the center of Earth, and a location on Earth.

B Longitude is the measurement of the angle along the equator, between the prime meridian, the center of Earth, and a meridian on Earth.

Latitude and Longitude

During hurricane season, meteorologists track storms as they form in the Atlantic Ocean. To identify the exact location of a storm, latitude and longitude lines are used. These lines form an imaginary grid system that allows people to locate any place on Earth accurately.

Latitude Look at **Figure 8.** The **equator** is an imaginary line that wraps around Earth exactly halfway between the north and south poles, separating Earth into two equal halves, called the northern hemisphere and the southern hemisphere. Lines running parallel to the equator are called lines of **latitude,** or parallels. Latitude is the distance, measured in degrees, either north or south of the equator. Because they are parallel, lines of latitude do not intersect, or cross, one another.

The equator is at 0° latitude, and the poles are each at 90° latitude. Locations north and south of the equator are referred to by degrees north latitude and degrees south latitude, respectively. Each degree is further divided into segments called minutes and seconds. There are 60 minutes in one degree and 60 seconds in one minute.

Section ✓*Assessment* Planner

PORTFOLIO
Challenge, p. 165
PERFORMANCE ASSESSMENT
MiniLAB, p. 163
Skill Builder Activities, p. 165
See page 180 for more options.

CONTENT ASSESSMENT
Section, p. 165
Challenge, p. 165
Chapter, pp. 180–181

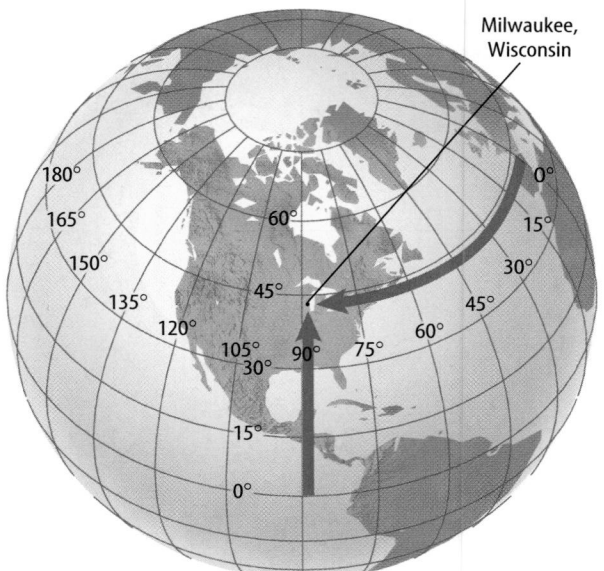

Milwaukee, Wisconsin

Figure 9
The city of Milwaukee, Wisconsin is located at about 43°N, 88°W. *How is latitude different from longitude?*

Longitude The vertical lines, seen in **Figure 8B,** have two names—meridians and lines of longitude. Longitude lines are different from latitude lines in many important ways. Just as the equator is used as a reference point for lines of latitude, there's a reference point for lines of longitude—the **prime meridian.** This imaginary line represents 0° longitude. In 1884, astronomers decided the prime meridian should go through the Greenwich (GREN ihtch) Observatory near London, England. The prime meridian had to be agreed upon, because no natural point of reference exists.

Longitude refers to distances in degrees east or west of the prime meridian. Points west of the prime meridian have west longitude measured from 0° to 180°, and points east of the prime meridian have east longitude, measured similarly.

Prime Meridian The prime meridian does not circle Earth as the equator does. Rather, it runs from the north pole through Greenwich, England, to the south pole. The line of longitude on the opposite side of Earth from the prime meridian is the 180° meridian. East lines of longitude meet west lines of longitude at the 180° meridian. You can locate places accurately using latitude and longitude as shown in **Figure 9.** Note that latitude position always comes first when a location is given.

✔️ **Reading Check** *What line of longitude is found opposite the prime meridian?*

Mini LAB

Interpreting Latitude and Longitude

Procedure
1. Find the equator and prime meridian on a **world map.**
2. Move your finger to latitudes north of the equator, then south of the equator. Move your finger to longitudes west of the prime meridian, then east of the prime meridian.

Analysis
1. Identify the cities that have the following coordinates:
   a. 56°N, 38°E
   b. 34°S, 18°E
   c. 23°N, 82°W
2. Determine the latitude and longitude of the following cities:
   a. London, England
   b. Melbourne, Australia
   c. Buenos Aires, Argentina

SECTION 2 Viewpoints **163**

Resource Manager

Chapter Resources Booklet
   Transparency Activity, p. 43
   Directed Reading for Content Mastery, p. 19
   MiniLAB, p. 4

---

2 Teach

Latitude and Longitude

Mini LAB

Purpose Students learn to use latitude and longitude to locate places on Earth's surface. L2 ELL COOP LEARN
LS **Visual-Spatial**

Materials world map, pencil, paper

Teaching Strategy Have students work in pairs. Encourage partners to compare their answers with those of other pairs.

Analysis
   Allow a couple of degrees leeway in each answer, as students will be estimating in areas between marked longitude and latitude lines.
1. a) Moscow, Russia
    b) Cape Town, South Africa
    c) Havana, Cuba
2. a) 51°N, 1°W
    b) 38°S, 145°E
    c) 36°S, 62°W

✓ **Assessment**

Performance Have students use a map to determine the latitude and longitude of their hometown. Use **PASC,** p. 99.

✔️ **Reading Check**

Answer 180° meridian

Visual Learning

Figure 10 What time is it where we live when it is 7:00 a.m. in Atlanta? Answers will vary depending on your location.

Caption Answer

Figure 10B 6:00 P.M.

Quick Demo

Demonstrate the concept of Earth time using a bright light to represent the Sun and a rotating globe. Point out that noon, midnight, 6 P.M., and 6 A.M. remain stationary with regard to the Sun, while positions on Earth's surface rotate toward or away from a specific time.

Discussion

Why do you think each time zone is about 15° of longitude wide? If students need a hint, remind them that Earth's circumference equals 360°. 360° divided by 24 hours is 15° per hour.

Life Science
INTEGRATION

Have students discuss what it felt like, how long it took to recover, and whether they took any special action to get over jet lag, such as drinking fruit juices, eating special foods, or taking vitamins.

✔ Reading Check

Answer Each day has 24 hours.

Figure 10
The United States has six time zones.

B But students in Seattle, Washington, which lies in the Pacific time zone, are eating dinner. *What time would it be in Seattle when the students in Washington, D.C., are sleeping at 9:00 P.M.?*

Life Science
INTEGRATION

If you travel east or west across three or more time zones, you could suffer from jet lag. Jet lag occurs when your internal time clock does not match the new time zone. Jet lag can disrupt the daily rhythms of sleeping and eating. Have you or any of your classmates ever suffered from jet lag?

A Washington, D.C., lies in the eastern time zone. Students there would be going to sleep at 9:00 P.M.

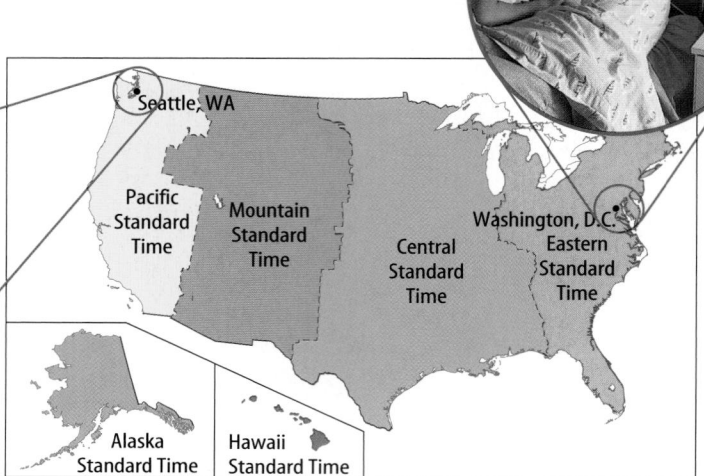

Seattle, WA

Pacific Standard Time

Mountain Standard Time

Central Standard Time

Washington, D.C. Eastern Standard Time

Alaska Standard Time

Hawaii Standard Time

Time Zones

What time it is depends on where you are on Earth. Time is measured by tracking Earth's movement in relation to the Sun. Each day has 24 h, so Earth is divided into 24 time zones. Each time zone is about 15° of longitude wide and is 1 h different from the zones on each side of it. The United States has six different time zones. As you can see in **Figure 10,** people in different parts of the country don't experience dusk simultaneously. Because Earth rotates, the eastern states end a day while the western states are still in sunlight.

✔ Reading Check   *What is the basis for dividing Earth into 24 time zones?*

Time zones do not follow lines of longitude strictly. Time zone boundaries are adjusted in local areas. For example, if a city were split by a time zone boundary, the results would be confusing. In such a situation, the time zone boundary is moved outside of the city.

Calendar Dates

In each time zone, one day ends and the next day begins at midnight. If it is 11:59 P.M. Tuesday, then 2 min later it will be 12:01 A.M. Wednesday in that particular time zone.

Resource Manager

Chapter Resources Booklet
Lab Activity, pp. 9–11, 13–14
Enrichment, p. 29
Reinforcement, p. 26

Teacher FYI

In 1884, an international committee agreed upon our current system of 24 time zones, 15° apart, starting with the Prime Meridian through Greenwich, England. Daylight saving time was instituted during World War I to conserve fuel for the war effort by extending evening daylight hours.

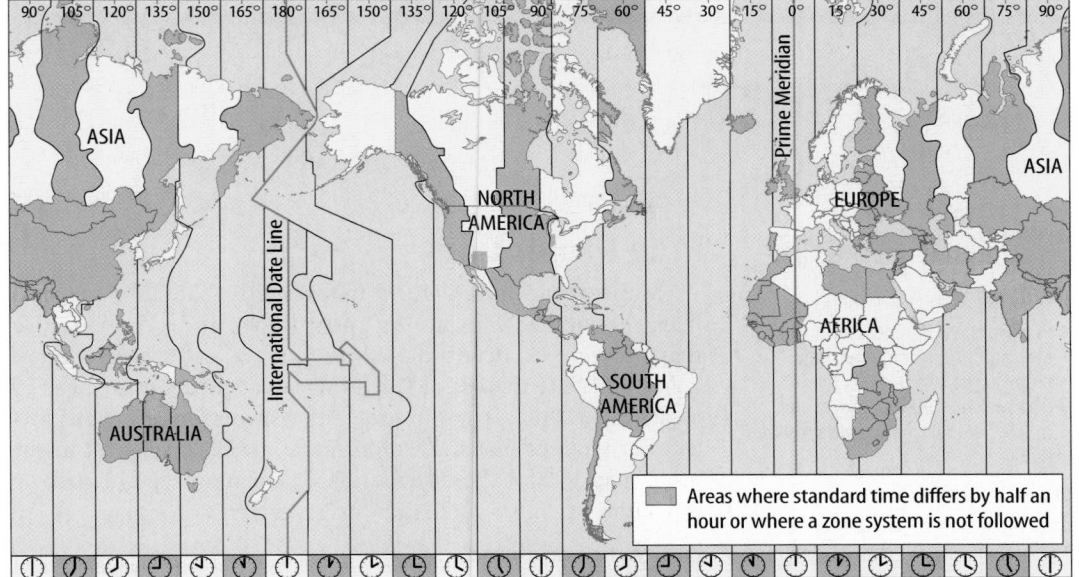

Figure 11
Lines of longitude roughly determine the locations of time zone boundaries. These boundaries are adjusted locally to avoid splitting cities and other political subdivisions, such as counties, into different time zones.

Areas where standard time differs by half an hour or where a zone system is not followed

International Date Line You gain or lose time when you enter a new time zone. If you travel far enough, you can gain or lose a whole day. The International Date Line, shown on **Figure 11,** is the transition line for calendar days. If you were traveling west across the International Date Line, located at the 180° meridian, you would move your calendar forward one day. If you were traveling east when you crossed it, you would move your calendar back one day.

Section 2 Assessment

1. What are latitude and longitude?
2. How do lines of latitude and longitude help people find locations on Earth?
3. What are the latitude and longitude of New Orleans, Louisiana?
4. If it were 7:00 P.M. in New York City, what time would it be in Los Angeles?
5. **Think Critically** How could you leave home on Monday to go sailing on the ocean, sail for 1 h on Sunday, and return home on Monday?

Skill Builder Activities

6. **Interpreting Scientific Illustrations** Use a world map to find the latitude and longitude of the following locations: Sri Lanka; Tokyo, Japan; and the Falkland Islands. **For more help, refer to the** Science Skill Handbook.
7. **Using Fractions** If you started at the prime meridian and traveled east one fourth of the way around Earth, what line of longitude would you reach? **For more help, refer to the** Math Skill Handbook.

Calendar Dates

Discussion

Tell students that on Monday, September 25, 2000, people living in Ohio could watch live coverage of the Olympic games occurring on Tuesday, September 26 in Australia. **Can you explain why that was possible?** The time difference between Ohio and Australia is large enough to make Australia one day ahead of Ohio.

3 Assess

Reteach

Obtain a globe that shows time zones. Using the current time in your area, have students determine the corresponding time in Quito, Equador; Paris, France; Beijing, China; and Cairo, Egypt.

Challenge

Challenge students to explain in writing how the spacing between lines of longitude and lines of latitude differs. Lines of latitude are always parallel. Lines of longitude are far apart at the equator, but become closer together as they near the poles. Lines of longitude eventually meet at the poles. P

Assessment

Process Assess students' abilities to interpret scientific illustrations by asking them to name the continent located between 11° and 39° south latitude and 116° and 153° east longitude. Australia Use **Performance Assessment in the Science Classroom,** p. 91.

Answers to Section Assessment

1. latitude: distance in degrees north or south of the equator; longitude: distance in degrees east or west of the prime meridian
2. They form an imaginary grid system that helps pinpoint locations.
3. About 30°N, 90°W

4. 4:00 P.M.
5. It's possible if you sail in waters through which the International Date Line passes. If you started west of the line on Monday, then sailed east, it would be Sunday. If you then sailed west over the line again, it would again be Monday.

6. Sri Lanka: 8°N, 82°E; Tokyo: 35°N, 139°E; Falkland Islands: 50°S, 61°W
7. 270°

SECTION

3

Maps

1 Motivate

Bellringer Transparency

 Display the Section Focus Transparency for Section 3. Use the accompanying Transparency Activity Master. [L2]

ELL

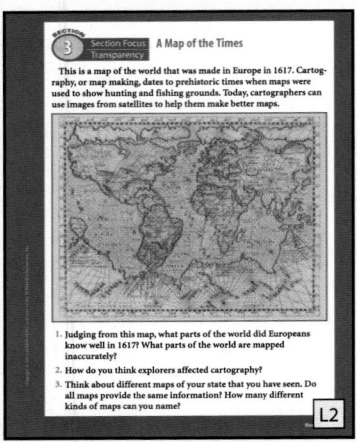

SECTION
3 Section Focus Transparency
A Map of the Times

This is a map of the world that was made in Europe in 1617. Cartography, or map making, dates to prehistoric times when maps were used to show hunting and fishing grounds. Today, cartographers can use images from satellites to help them make better maps.

1. Judging from this map, what parts of the world did Europeans know well in 1617? What parts of the world are mapped inaccurately?
2. How do you think explorers affected cartography?
3. Think about different maps of your state that you have seen. Do all maps provide the same information? How many different kinds of maps can you name?

[L2]

Tie to Prior Knowledge

Ask students if they've ever noticed that maps of the same place on Earth often look very different. To illustrate, show students two maps of the United States made with two different map projections. Have students observe how the maps differ.

As You Read

What You'll Learn

- **Explain** the differences among Mercator, Robinson, and conic projections.
- **Describe** features of topographic maps, geologic maps, and satellite maps.

Vocabulary

conic projection
topographic map
contour line
map scale
map legend

Why It's Important

Maps help people navigate and understand Earth.

Figure 12
Lines of longitude are drawn parallel to one another in Mercator projections. *What happens near the poles in Mercator projections?*

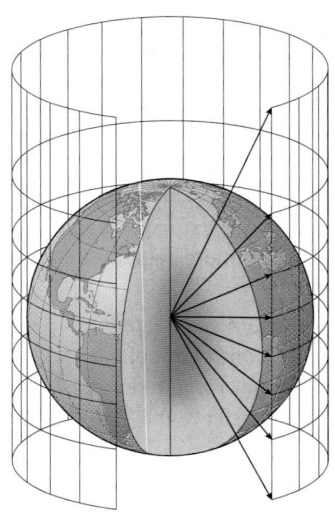

Map Projections

Maps—road maps, world maps, maps that show physical features such as mountains and valleys, and even treasure maps—help you determine where you are and where you are going. They are models of Earth's surface. Scientists use maps to locate various places and to show the distribution of various features or types of material. For example, an Earth scientist might use a map to plot the distribution of a certain type of rock or soil. Other scientists could draw ocean currents on a map.

Reading Check *What are possible uses a scientist would have for maps?*

Many maps are made as projections. A map projection is made when points and lines on a globe's surface are transferred onto paper, as shown in **Figure 12.** Map projections can be made in several different ways, but all types of projections distort the shapes of landmasses or their areas. Antarctica, for instance, might look smaller or larger than it is as a result of the projection that is used for a particular map.

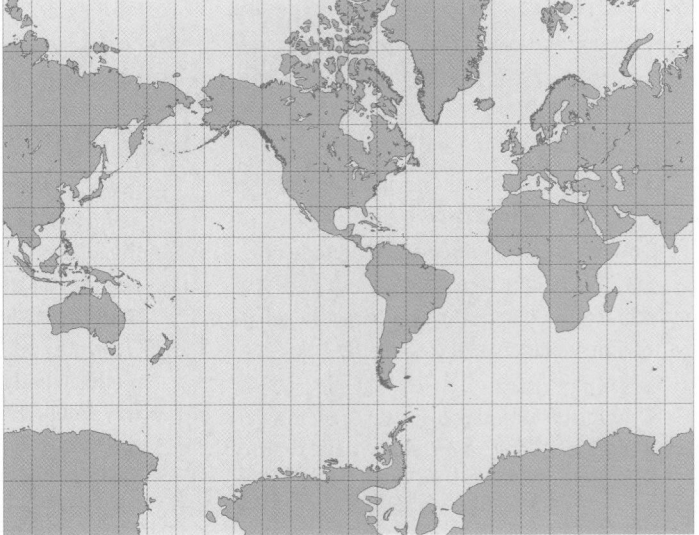

166 CHAPTER 6 Views of Earth

Section ✓ *Assessment* Planner

PORTFOLIO
Extension, p. 169
PERFORMANCE ASSESSMENT
Problem-Solving Activity, p. 171
Skill Builder Activities, p. 172
See page 180 for more options.

CONTENT ASSESSMENT
Section, p. 172
Challenge, p. 172
Chapter, pp. 180–181

Figure 13
Robinson projections show little distortion in continent shapes and sizes.

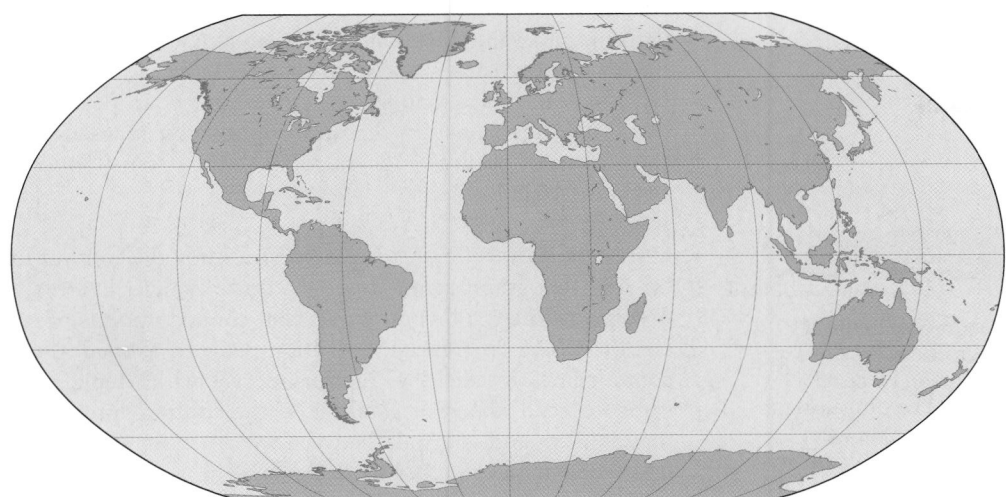

Mercator Projection Mercator (mer KAY ter) projections are used mainly on ships. They project correct shapes of continents, but the areas are distorted. Lines of longitude are projected onto the map parallel to each other. As you learned earlier, only latitude lines are parallel. Longitude lines meet at the poles. When longitude lines are projected as parallel, areas near the poles appear bigger than they are. Greenland, in the Mercator projection in **Figure 12,** appears to be larger than South America, but Greenland is actually smaller.

Robinson Projection A Robinson projection shows accurate continent shapes and more accurate land areas. As shown in **Figure 13,** lines of latitude remain parallel, and lines of longitude are curved as they are on a globe. This results in less distortion near the poles.

Conic Projection When you look at a road map or a weather map, you are using a conic (KAH nihk) projection. Conic projections, like the one shown in **Figure 14,** often are used to produce maps of small areas. These maps are well suited for middle latitude regions but are not as useful for mapping polar or equatorial regions. **Conic projections** are made by projecting points and lines from a globe onto a cone.

✔ Reading Check *How are conic projections made?*

Figure 14
Small areas are mapped accurately using conic projections.

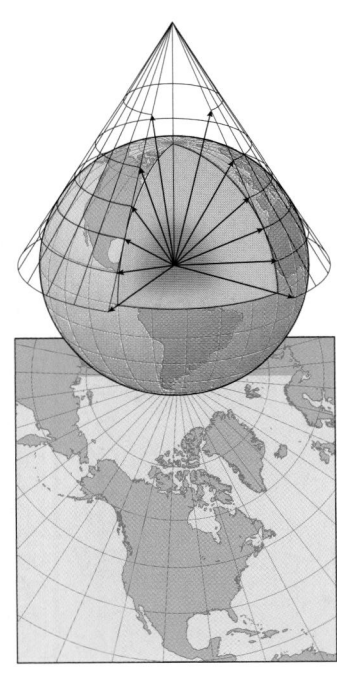

SECTION 3 Maps **167**

Section 3 Maps **167**

---

2 Teach

Map Projections

✔ Reading Check

Answer to locate various places and to show the distribution of various features or types of material

Caption Answer
Figure 12 Size is exaggerated.

Quick Demo
Illustrate a different map projection by drawing a rough world map on a grapefruit. Then slice the grapefruit into eight identical wedges. Remove the fruit and press the wedges down side by side on a flat surface as they were on the fruit. Have students observe the way this "projection" shows the world. Discuss the pros and cons of such a projection. Pros: It doesn't distort the size of land areas. Cons: The features are interrupted, making the map hard to use.
LS Visual-Spatial

✔ Reading Check

Answer by projecting points and lines from a globe onto a cone

---

LAB DEMONSTRATION

Purpose to make a Mercator projection grid
Materials globe, large sheet of tracing paper, marking pen, meterstick
Procedure Form a paper cylinder around the globe as shown in **Figure 12.** Trace latitude lines by bending the paper so that it is touching the globe. Mark where longitude lines intersect the equator. Remove the paper from the globe and use a meterstick to draw the longitude lines perpendicular to the equator.

Expected Outcome A Mercator projection grid is created.

✔ Assessment

Where is the greatest distortion on the projection? near the poles **Which area has the least distortion?** areas near the equator

Topographic Maps

Text Question Answer

It avoids having contour lines too close together or too far apart. If a small interval were used for a mountainous area, the closely-spaced contours would be impossible to read. If a large contour interval were used for a flat area, the lines would be so widely spaced that it would be difficult to interpret elevation.

Activity

Obtain two topographic maps of your area, one up-to-date and the other as old as possible. Have students compare and contrast the two maps. Students may find that one map contains features such as buildings or roads not found on the other map. Have students use their observations of these maps to explain why maps should be regularly updated. L2

ELL IS **Visual-Spatial**

Physics
INTEGRATION

The data collected by these probes provides scientists information on elevation at various points on the surface. Contour maps of the planets' surfaces can be made using these data.

Physics
INTEGRATION

Topographic maps of Venus and Mars have been made by space probes. The probes send a radar beam or laser pulses to the surface and measure how long it takes for the beam or pulses to return to the probe.

Topographic Maps

For nature hiking, a conic map projection can be helpful by directing you to the location where you will start your hike. On your hike, however, you would need a detailed map identifying the hills and valleys of that specific area. A **topographic map,** shown in **Figure 15,** models the changes in elevation of Earth's surface. With such a map, you can determine your location relative to identifiable natural features. Topographic maps also indicate cultural features such as roads, cities, dams, and other structures built by people.

Contour Lines Before your hike, you study the contour lines on your topographic map to see the trail's changes in elevation. A **contour line** is a line on a map that connects points of equal elevation. The difference in elevation between two side-by-side contour lines is called the contour interval, which remains constant for each map. For example, if the contour interval on a map is 10 m and you walk between two lines anywhere on that map, you will have walked up or down 10 m.

In mountainous areas, the contour lines are close together. This situation models a steep slope. However, if the change in elevation is slight, the contour lines will be far apart. Often large contour intervals are used for mountainous terrain, and small contour intervals are used for fairly flat areas. Why? **Table 1** gives additional tips for examining contour lines.

Index Contours Some contour lines, called index contours, are marked with their elevation. If the contour interval is 5 m, you can determine the elevation of other lines around the index contour by adding or subtracting 5 m from the elevation shown on the index contour.

Table 1 Contour Rules

1. **Contour lines close around hills and basins.** To decide whether you're looking at a hill or basin, you can read the elevation numbers or look for hachures (ha SHOORZ). These are short lines drawn at right angles to the contour line. They show depressions by pointing toward lower elevations.

2. **Contour lines never cross.** If they did, it would mean that the spot where they cross would have two different elevations.

3. **Contour lines form Vs that point upstream when they cross streams.** This is because streams flow in depressions that are beneath the elevation of the surrounding land surface. When the contour lines cross the depression, they appear as Vs pointing upstream on the map.

Inclusion Strategies

Gifted Have students interview a cartographer, and then write a report detailing the steps involved in the map-making process, from obtaining raw data to making the actual map. Encourage students to illustrate each step. L3
IS **Interpersonal**

✔ Active Reading

Buddy Interviews This strategy helps students understand and clarify the reading. Have students interview one another to find out what helps them understand what they are reading, how they find answers, and how they assimilate new vocabulary terms. Have students use Buddy Interviews to help them master the concept of topographic maps.

Figure 15

Planning a hike? A topographic map will show you changes in elevation. With such a map, you can see at a glance how steep a mountain trail is, as well as its location relative to rivers, lakes, roads, and cities nearby. The steps in creating a topographic map are shown here.

A To create a topographic map of Old Rag Mountain in Shenandoah National Park, Virginia, mapmakers first measure the elevation of the mountain at various points.

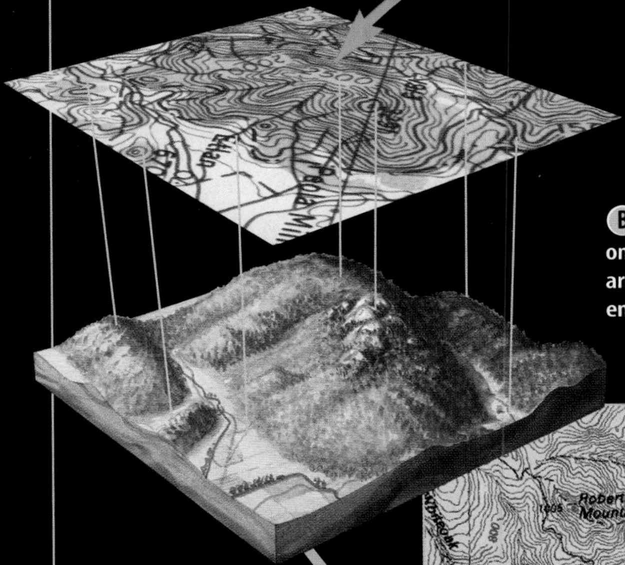

B These points are then projected onto paper. Points at the same elevation are connected, forming contour lines that encircle the mountain.

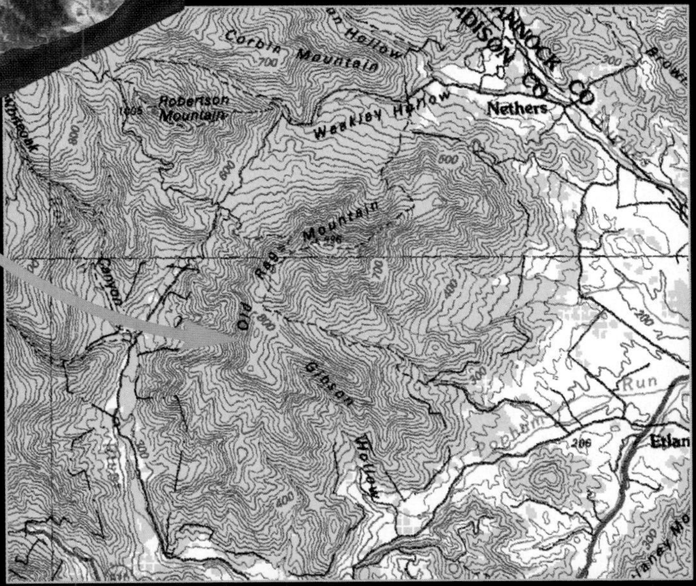

C Where contour lines on a topographic map are close together, elevation is changing rapidly—and the trail is very steep!

SECTION 3 Maps **169**

Visualizing Topographic Maps

Have students examine the pictures and read the captions. Then ask the following questions.

Besides hiking, what are some other reasons people would use a topographic map? Possible answers: For planning highways, bridges, and tunnels

How would a topographic map help someone planning to build a house? These maps could be used to show the differences in elevation, the steepness of slopes, the location of streams, and the proximity to roads.

Activity

Take students to an area near school where they can observe a prominent landscape feature. Take along a topographic map and have students explain how the feature compares to its representation on the map.

Extension

Have students prepare brief written reports on the sport of orienteering. L2 IN **Linguistic** P

Resource Manager

Earth Science Critical Thinking/Problem Solving, p. 5

Cultural Diversity, p. 27

Reading and Writing Skill Activities, p. 21

Explore the Glencoe Science Web site at **science.glencoe.com** to find out more about topics in this section.

Discussion

What is the contour interval of a map if two side-by-side contour lines represent elevations of 200 m and 300 m? 100 m Suppose a student draws a map using the scale 1 cm: 100 miles. **Is this a proper scale? Explain.** No; units of measurement on each side of the ratio must be the same.

Geologic Maps

Extension

Tell students to find a geologic map of the area in which you live. Have them write a paragraph that describes the geology of the area as portrayed by the map. L2 **ELL** COOP LEARN **Visual-Spatial**

Text Question Answer

Drill into rock or soil to get core samples or other evidence.

SCIENCE Online
Data Update Visit the Glencoe Science Web site at **science.glencoe.com** for recent news or magazine articles about map technology.

Figure 16
Geologists use block diagrams to understand Earth's subsurface. The different colors represent different rock layers.

Map Scale When planning your hike, you'll want to determine the distance to your destination before you leave. Because maps are small models of Earth's surface, distances and sizes of things shown on a map are proportional to the real thing on Earth. Therefore, real distances can be found by using a scale.

The **map scale** is the relationship between the distances on the map and distances on Earth's surface. Scale often is represented as a ratio. For example, a topographic map of the Grand Canyon might have a scale that reads 1:80,000. This means that one unit on the map represents 80,000 units on land. If the unit you wanted to use was a centimeter, then 1 cm on the map would equal 80,000 cm on land. The unit of distance could be feet or millimeters or any other measure of distance. However, the units of measure on each side of the ratio must always be the same. A map scale also can be shown in the form of a small bar that is divided into sections and scaled down to match real distances on Earth.

Map Legend Topographic maps and most other maps have a legend. A **map legend** explains what the symbols used on the map mean. Some frequently used symbols for topographic maps are shown in the appendix at the back of the book.

Map Series Topographic maps are made to cover different amounts of Earth's surface. A map series includes maps that have the same dimensions of latitude and longitude. For example, one map series includes maps that are 7.5 minutes of latitude by 7.5 minutes of longitude. Other map series include maps covering larger areas of Earth's surface.

Geologic Maps

One of the more important tools to Earth scientists is the geologic map. Geologic maps show the arrangement of rocks at Earth's surface. Using geologic maps and data collected from rock exposures, a geologist can infer how rock layers might look below Earth's surface. The block diagram in **Figure 16** is a 3-D model that illustrates a solid section of Earth. The top surface of the block is the geologic map. Side views of the block are called cross sections, which are derived from the surface map. Developing block diagrams and cross sections is extremely important for the exploration and extraction of natural resources. What can a scientist do to determine whether a cross section accurately represents the underground features?

Inclusion Strategies

Learning Disabled Draw a contour map with five concentric contours, each 2 cm apart. Draw a straight reference line from the center of the map to any point along the outermost contour. Give students a copy of the map. Have them cut along the outermost contour line, then trace the circular pattern on a piece of cardboard. Have them place an X where the reference line meets the cardboard. Direct students to cut out the cardboard along the traced line. Have them repeat this process with each of the other four contours, moving inward. Be sure students place an X where the reference line meets the cardboard for each cut. When all the contours have been cut out, have students paste the cardboard cutouts together, one on top of the other, lining up the X's. The stair-step result is a model of a hill. **Kinesthetic**

Three-Dimensional Maps Topographic maps and geologic maps are two-dimensional models that are used to study features of Earth's surface. To visualize Earth three dimensionally, scientists often rely on computers. Using computers, information is digitized to create a three-dimensional view of features such as rock layers or river systems. Digitizing is a process by which points are plotted on a coordinate grid.

Map Uses As you have learned, Earth can be viewed in many different ways. Maps are chosen depending upon the situation. If you wanted to determine New Zealand's location relative to Canada and you didn't have a globe, you probably would examine a Mercator projection. In your search, you would use lines of latitude and longitude, and a map scale. If you wanted to travel across the country, you would rely on a road map, or conic projection. You also would use a map legend to help locate features along the way. To scale the highest peak in your region, you would take along a topographic map.

Problem-Solving Activity

How can you create a cross section from a geologic map?

Earth scientists are interested in knowing the types of rocks and their configurations underground. To help them visualize this, they use geologic maps. Geologic maps offer a two-dimensional view of the three-dimensional situation found under Earth's surface. You don't have to be a professional geologist to understand a geologic map. Use your ability to create graphs to interpret this geologic map.

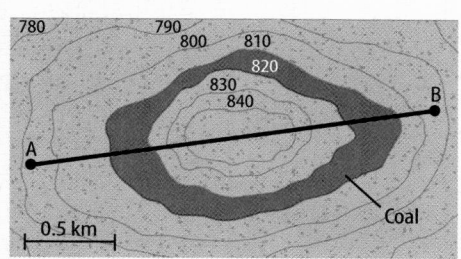

Identifying the Problem

At the right is a simple geologic map showing where a coal seam is found on Earth's surface. Place a straight edge of paper along the line marked A–B and mark the points where it meets a contour. Make a different color mark where it meets the exposure of coal. Make a graph on which the various elevations are marked on the *y*-axis. Lay your marked edge of paper along the *x*-axis and transfer the points directly above onto the proper elevation line. Now connect the dots to draw in the land's surface and connect the marks you made for the coal seam separately.

Solving the Problem
1. What type of topography does the map represent?
2. At what elevation is the coal seam?
3. Does this seam tilt, or is it horizontal? Explain how you know.

Geologic Maps,
continued

Use Science Words
Word Origin Have students use dictionaries to find the meaning and origin of the word *cartography*. Students will discover that cartography is the science of making maps. The word has two roots: *carte* comes from the French word meaning "card" or "map"; *-ography* comes from the Latin *-graphia*, meaning "writing." Ask students the technical name for a mapmaker. cartographer

---

Problem-Solving Activity

National Math Standards
Correlation to Mathematics Objectives
1, 6, 8–10

Answers
1. a hill
2. 820 m
3. Horizontal; only one elevation is given for the seam.

Teacher FYI
Two common types of maps are thematic maps and inventory maps. A thematic map shows the distribution of a particular feature over a certain area, for example, the difference in population density or amount of rainfall over a state or country. An inventory map shows the location of a certain type of item over an area, for example, the location of nuclear power plants in state.

Resource Manager
Chapter Resources Booklet
Enrichment, p. 30
Reinforcement, p. 27
Cultural Diversity, p. 49

Remote Sensing

Reteach

Have pairs of students prepare one type of map that gives the reader information about your community. The map can be a topographic map of a neighborhood, a road map, an inventory map showing the location of schools, or some other type. Have students present their maps to the class and explain how they were made. L2 COOP LEARN
Interpersonal

Challenge

Challenge students to find out how Landsat images can be obtained. (These images can be obtained on the Internet.) Have students obtain imagery for your area, and write a short paragraph that explains how the images are interpreted. Discuss in class what the image shows.
Visual-Spatial

Assessment

Process Have students prepare charts that compare and contrast topographic and geologic maps. Use **Performance Assessment in the Science Classroom,** p. 109.

Figure 17
Sensors on *Landsat 7* detect light reflected off landforms on Earth.

Remote Sensing

Scientists use remote-sensing techniques to collect much of the data used for making maps. Remote sensing is a way of collecting information about Earth from a distance, often using satellites.

Landsat One way that Earth's surface has been studied is with data collected from Landsat satellites, as shown in **Figure 17.** These satellites take pictures of Earth's surface using different wavelengths of light. The images can be used to make maps of snow cover over the United States or to evaluate the impact of forest fires, such as those that occurred in the western United States during the summer of 2000. The newest Landsat satellite is *Landsat 7,* which was launched in April of 1999. It can acquire the most detailed Landsat images yet.

Global Positioning System The Global Positioning System, or GPS, is a satellite-based, radio-navigation system that allows users to determine their exact position anywhere on Earth. Twenty-four satellites orbit 20,200 km above the planet. Each satellite sends a position signal and a time signal. The satellites are arranged in their orbits so that signals from at least six can be picked up at any given moment by someone using a GPS receiver. By processing the signals, the receiver calculates the user's exact location. GPS technology is used to navigate, to create detailed maps, and to track wildlife.

Section 3 Assessment

1. How do Mercator, Robinson, and conic projections differ?
2. Why does Greenland appear to be larger on a Mercator projection than it does on a Robinson projection?
3. Why can't contour lines ever cross?
4. What is a geologic map?
5. **Think Critically** Would a map that covers a large area have the same map scale as a map that covers a small region? How would the scales differ?

Skill Builder Activities

6. **Making Models** Architects make detailed maps called scale drawings to help them plan their work. Make a scale drawing of your classroom. **For more help, refer to the** Science Skill Handbook.
7. **Communicating** Draw a map in your Science Journal that your friends could use to get from school to your home. Include a map legend and a map scale. **For more help, refer to the** Science Skill Handbook.

Answers to Section Assessment

1. Areas of distortion differ, so they are best for different purposes. Mercator has great distortion in polar areas. Robinson has less distortion at the poles. Conic projections are accurate for relatively small areas of Earth's surface.

2. Lines of longitude and latitude are parallel on a Mercator, stretching any landmasses in polar areas. There is less distortion in polar areas on a Robinson projection, so Greenland isn't as stretched out.

3. One location cannot have two different elevations.
4. a map that shows the arrangement of rocks at Earth's surface
5. No; the ratio for the scale would be much bigger on a map that shows a larger area.

6. Encourage students to start by making a grid system for the class and determining a scale, such as 1 cm = 1 m.
7. Maps should show a route with streets and symbols for landmarks.

Activity

Making a Topographic Map

Have you ever wondered how topographic maps are made? Today, radar and remote-sensing devices aboard satellites collect data, and computers and graphic systems make the maps. In the past, surveyors and aerial photographers collected data. Then, maps were hand drawn by cartographers, or mapmakers. In this activity, you can practice cartography.

Materials
plastic model of a landform
water tinted with food coloring
transparency
clear, plastic storage box with lid
beaker
metric ruler
tape
transparency marker

What You'll Investigate
How is a topographic map made?

Goals
- **Draw** a topographic map.
- **Compare and contrast** contour intervals.

Procedure

1. Using the ruler and the transparency marker, make marks up the side of the storage box that are 2 cm apart.
2. Secure the transparency to the outside of the box lid with tape.
3. Place the plastic model in the box. The bottom of the box will be zero elevation.
4. Using the beaker, pour water into the box to a height of 2 cm. Place the lid on the box.
5. Use the transparency marker to trace the top of the water line on the transparency.

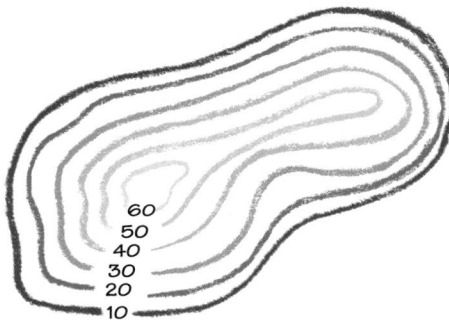

6. Using the scale 2 cm = 10 m, mark the elevation on the line.
7. Remove the lid and add water until a depth of 4 cm is reached.
8. Map this level on the storage box lid and record the elevation.
9. Repeat the process of adding 2 cm of water and tracing until the landform is mapped.
10. Transfer the tracing of the landform onto a sheet of white paper.

Conclude and Apply

1. What is the contour interval of this topographic map?
2. How does the distance between contour lines on the map show the steepness of the slope on the landform model?
3. **Determine** the total elevation of the landform you have selected.
4. How was elevation represented on your map?
5. How are elevations shown on topographic maps?
6. Must all topographic maps have a contour line that represents 0 m of elevation? Explain.

ACTIVITY 173

Resource Manager

Chapter Resources Booklet
   Activity Worksheets, pp. 5–6, 7–8
Lab Management and Safety, p. 66

Communicating
Your Data
Have students compare the topographic maps and landforms produced by other groups with their own.

Activity

BENCH TESTED

Purpose Students make a topographic map from a landform model. L2 ELL COOP LEARN
IS Kinesthetic
Process Skills measuring in SI, making models, interpreting data, comparing and contrasting
Time Required 45–50 minutes
Teaching Strategy Suggest that students stand directly over the model with one eye closed to make each tracing, so that each will be done from the same position.
Troubleshooting Some students may need extra help in understanding the scale to be used.

Answers to Questions
1. 10 m
2. The closer the contour lines, the steeper the slope.
3. Answers will vary, but they should equal the height of the model in centimeters multiplied by 500. (2 cm = 10 m; therefore 1 cm = 5 m or 500 cm)
4. lines drawn on the transparency
5. contour lines
6. No, the 0-m contour line is only on maps with elevations at sea level.

✓Assessment

Performance To further assess students' understanding of making topographic maps from landform models, have them repeat the activity using a second landform model. Have them compare and contrast their two completed topographic maps. Use **Performance Assessment in the Science Classroom,** p. 123.

Activity

Recognize the Problem

Purpose

Students will show the relationship between topographic maps and landforms by making a 3-D model from a topographic map.

L2 ELL COOP LEARN

Kinesthetic P

Process Skills

interpreting scientific illustrations, making models, using numbers, observing and inferring

Time Required

45 minutes

Thinking Critically

Discussion

Ask students to discuss how they would walk across a sloping field while keeping their eyes level. Students will walk on a line of equal elevation, similar to a contour line on a topographic map. Mention to students that steep slopes are shown on a topographic map as areas where contour lines are very close.

Possible Materials

Obtain 7.5 minute quadrangle maps from the U.S. Geological Survey and the book, *100 Topographic Maps*, by Richard Debruin, available from Hubbard. Obtain sandbox sand from a local hardware store. Ask maintenance for rolls of brown paper towels and empty spray bottles.

Activity *Model and Invent*

Constructing Landforms

Most maps perform well in helping you get from place to place. A road map, for example, will allow you to choose the shortest route from one place to another. If you are hiking, though, distance might not be so important. You might want to choose a route that avoids steep terrain. In this case you need a map that shows the highs and lows of Earth's surface, called relief. Topographic maps use contour lines to show the landscape in three dimensions. Among their many uses, such maps allow hikers to choose routes that maximize the scenery and minimize the physical exertion.

Recognize the Problem

What does a landscape depicted on a two-dimensional topographic map look like in three dimensions?

Thinking Critically

How can you model a landscape?

Goals

- **Research** how contour lines show relief on a topographic map.
- **Determine** what scale you can best use to model a landscape of your choice.

- Working cooperatively with your classmates, model a landscape in three dimensions from the information given on a topographic map.

Possible Materials

U.S. Geological Survey 7.5 minute quadrangle maps
sandbox sand
rolls of brown paper towels
spray bottle filled with water
ruler

Data Source

SCIENCE *Online* Go to the Glencoe Science Web site at **science.glencoe.com** for more information about topographic maps.

Inclusion Strategies

Physically Challenged Place your physically challenged students with other students who will help them make their models. Provide a large flat board on which lab groups can work on their models. This will enable them to move the project from place to place, making it easier for physically challenged students to participate.

SCIENCE *Online*
Internet Addresses

_____
_____
_____

Explore the Glencoe Science Web site at **science.glencoe.com** to find out more about topics in this section.

Planning the Model

1. **Choose** a topographic map showing a landscape easily modeled using sand. Check to see what contour interval is used on the map. Use the index contours to find the difference between the lowest and the highest elevations shown on the landscape. Check the distance scale to determine how much area the landscape covers.

2. **Determine** the scale you will use to convert the elevations shown on your map to heights on your model. Make sure the scale is proportional to the distances on your map.

3. **Plan** a model of the landscape in sand by sketching the main features and their scaled heights onto paper. Note the degree of steepness found on all sides of the features.

Check the Model Plans

1. **Prepare** a document that shows the scale you plan to use for your model and the calculations you used to derive that scale. Remember to use the same scale for distance as you use for height. If your landscape is fairly flat, you can exaggerate the vertical scale by a factor of two or three. Be sure your paper is neat, is easy to follow, and includes all units. Present the document to your teacher for approval.

2. **Research** how the U.S. Geological Survey creates topographic maps and find out how it decides upon a contour interval for each map. This information can be obtained from the Glencoe Science Web site.

Making the Model

1. Using the sand, spray bottle, and ruler, create a scale model of your landscape on the brown paper towels.

2. **Check** your topographic map to be sure your model includes the landscape features at their proper heights and proper degrees of steepness.

Analyzing and Applying Results

1. Did your model accurately represent the landscape depicted on your topographic map? Discuss the strengths and weaknesses of your model.

2. Why was it important to use the same scale for height and distance? If you exaggerated the height, why was it important to indicate the exaggeration on your model?

3. Why did the mapmakers choose the contour interval used on your topographic map?

4. **Predict** the contour intervals mapmakers might choose for topographic maps of the world's tallest mountains—the Himalayas, and for topographic maps of Kansas, which is fairly flat.

ACTIVITY 175

Planning the Model

Teaching Strategies

- Have students use a topographic map that has a feature on which at least four contour lines have been drawn.
- Some students will need help in making their sand models of the topographic map. They should begin with the highest and lowest elevations and shape the sand in between to the proper contours.

Making the Model

Expected Outcome

The model will look like a hill, a slope, or a valley as presented on the topographic map. The model should show a gradual increase in elevation from one contour line to the next.

Analyzing and Applying Results

1. Students should note that their models approximate the shape of landforms on their maps. One strength is the fact that the sand models actual land features. One weakness is that it is difficult to keep the sand from shifting.

2. If the same scale is not used, the shape of the landform will be distorted. Indicating how the model was exaggerated will help explain distortions in the model.

3. The contour interval is based on how great the change in elevation is on the map.

4. 100 meters; 5 meters

✔Assessment

Performance To further assess students' understanding of making a 3-D landform model from a topographic map, have them make a model using the topographic map they made in the activity. Have them compare their completed model with the plastic model used in that activity. Use **Performance Assessment in the Science Classroom**, p. 123.

Communicating
Your Data

Students can prepare an oral report that is given to the class. In their reports, students should explain how their models are similar to the actual landforms and the method used to make the model. Students should also explain any exaggerations used in the making of the model.

Content Background

Cultural geography is the study of the relationship between people and their environment. A major focus of cultural geographers is how culture and the surrounding environment fit together.

The environment includes landforms, climate, and natural resources such as water, soil, and vegetation. Culture is a way of life developed by a population for getting along with each other and their environment. It consists of beliefs, philosophies, knowledge, arts, science, technologies, and economies.

When studying the interactions between these people and their environment, geographers try to answer certain questions. How did the people living in an area get there? What aspects of the environment enticed people to settle in the area? How has the environment influenced the people's livelihood? How have the people influenced their environment? If culture or the environment changes, will the people be able to keep up with the changes?

The general consensus among geographers is that the environment does not solely determine culture nor does culture control the environ. Rather they interact and influence each other, thus shaping the lives of the people living in an area.

TIME
SCIENCE AND HISTORY
SCIENCE CAN CHANGE THE COURSE OF HISTORY!

LOCATION,

New York Harbor in 1849

Rich Midwest farmland

Georgia peaches

Why is New York City at the mouth of the Hudson River and not 300 km inland? Why are there more farms in Iowa than in Alaska? What's the reason for growing lots of peaches in Georgia but not in California's Death Valley? It's all about location. The landforms, climate, soil, and resources in an area determine where cities and farms grow and what people connected with them do.

Landforms Are Key

When many American cities were founded hundreds of years ago, waterways were the best means of transportation. Old cities such as New York City and Boston are located on deep harbors where ships could land with people and goods. Rivers also were major highways centuries ago. They still are. A city such as New Orleans, located at the mouth of the Mississippi River, receives goods from the entire river valley.

It then ships the goods from its port to places far away.

Topography and soil also play a role in where activities such as farming take root. States such as Iowa and Illinois have many farms because they have lots of flat land and fertile soil. Growing crops is more difficult in mountainous areas or where soil is stony and poor.

Climate and Soil

Climate limits the locations of cities and farms, as well. The fertile soil and warm, moist climate of Georgia make it a perfect place to grow peaches. California's Death Valley can't support such crops because it's a hot desert. Deserts are too dry to grow much of anything without irrigation. Deserts also don't have large population centers unless water is brought in from far away. Los Angeles and Las Vegas are both desert cities that are huge only because they pipe in water from hundreds of miles away.

176

Resources for Teachers and Students

Cultural Geography: A Critical Introduction, by Don Mitchell. Blackwell Publishers, Malden, MA, 2000.

People, Land and Time, by Peter Atkins, Ian Simmons, and Brian Roberts. John Wiley & Sons, New York, 1998.

Explorations in the Understanding of Landscape: A Cultural Geography, by William Norton. Greenwood Press, New York, 1989.

Resources Rule

The location of an important natural resource can change the rules. A gold deposit or an oil field can cause a town to grow in a place where the topography, soil, and climate are not favorable. For example, thousands of people now live in parts of Alaska only because of the great supply of oil there. People settled in rugged areas of the Rocky Mountains to mine gold and silver. Maine has a harsh climate and poor soil. But people settled along its coast because they could catch lobsters and fish in the nearby North Atlantic.

LOCATION

Alaska pipeline

Maine fishing and lobster industry

The rules that govern where towns grow and where people live are a bit different now than they used to be. Often information, not goods, moves from place to place on computers that can be anywhere. But as long as people farm, use minerals, and transport goods from place to place, the natural environment and natural resources will always help determine where people are and what they do.

Cities, farms, and industries grow in logical places

CONNECTIONS Research Why was your community built where it is? Research its history. What types of economic activity were important when it was founded? Did topography, climate, or resources determine its location? Are they important today? Report to the class.

SCIENCE *Online*

For more information, visit science.glencoe.com

SCIENCE *Online*

Internet Addresses

_____

_____

_____

Explore the Glencoe Science Web site at **science.glencoe.com** to find out more about topics in this feature.

Discussion

Facilitate a brainstorming session in which students list the factors that might affect where people settle. Have students discuss how each factor might affect the establishment and success of a community. Possible answers might include landforms, climate, soil conditions, and resources of various types. Landforms such as mountains might make transportation and settlement difficult, but might provide needed resources such as minerals and water. Desert settlements have to address the need for water and good soil. Settling near waterways presents numerous advantages including rich soil for agriculture, transportation, and commerce.

Historical Significance

Throughout history civilizations have established themselves in areas that supported their daily needs. Early hunters and gatherers gave way to village life, as agriculture became the main source of food. Trade routes opened villages to resources that were unavailable locally. In general, populations flourished in areas of mild climate were the terrain was level and the soil was fertile. Additionally, settlements were established where other natural resources, fresh water, and minerals also were abundant.

These conditions were found along waterways and coastal areas. Over time, populations began expanding into the interior regions. These inland areas tend to be drier and lacking in natural resources. As a result, new challenges had to be met in order for populations to succeed.

Chapter ⑥ Study Guide

Reviewing Main Ideas

Preview

Students can answer the questions in their Science Journals. Discuss the answers as you go through the chapter. **IS Linguistic**

Review

Students can write their answers, then compare them with those of other students. **IS Interpersonal**

Reteach

Students can look at the illustrations and describe details that support the main ideas of the chapter. **IS Visual-Spatial**

Answers to Chapter Review

SECTION 1

2. mountains

SECTION 2

4. six (Eastern, Central, Mountain, Pacific, Alaska, Hawaii-Aleutian)

SECTION 3

2. a geologic map

Reviewing Main Ideas

Section 1 Landforms

1. The three main types of landforms are plains, plateaus, and mountains.

2. Plains are large, flat areas. Plateaus are relatively flat, raised areas of land made up of nearly horizontal rocks that have been uplifted. Mountains rise high above the surrounding land. *Which type of landform is shown in the photograph below?*

Section 2 Viewpoints

1. Latitude and longitude form an imaginary grid system that enables points on Earth to be located exactly.

2. Latitude is the distance in degrees north or south of the equator. Longitude is the distance in degrees east or west of the prime meridian.

3. Reference lines have been established for measuring latitude and longitude. Latitude is measured from Earth's equator, an imaginary line halfway between Earth's poles. Longitude is measured from the prime meridian. The prime meridian runs from pole to pole through Greenwich, England.

4. Earth is divided into 24 time zones. Each time zone represents a 1-h difference. The International Date Line

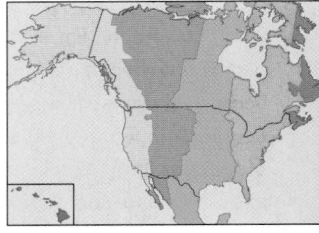

separates different calendar days. *How many time zones are in the United States?*

Section 3 Maps

1. Mercator, Robinson, and conic projections are made by transferring points and lines on a globe's surface onto paper.

2. Topographic maps show the elevation of Earth's surface. Geologic maps show the types of rocks that make up Earth's surface. *What type of map is shown here?*

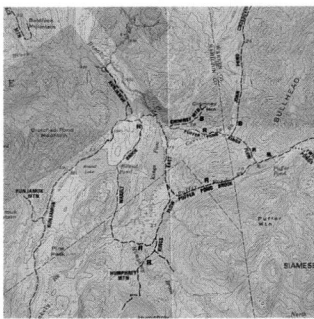

3. Remote sensing is a way of collecting information about Earth from a distance. Satellites are important remote-sensing devices.

FOLDABLES Reading & Study Skills

After You Read

To help you review the three main landform types, use the Foldable you made at the beginning of this chapter.

FOLDABLES Reading & Study Skills

After You Read

After students have read the chapter and completed the Foldable described in Before You Read, have them do the activity on the student page.

Dinah Zike

Visualizing Main Ideas

Complete the following concept map on landforms.

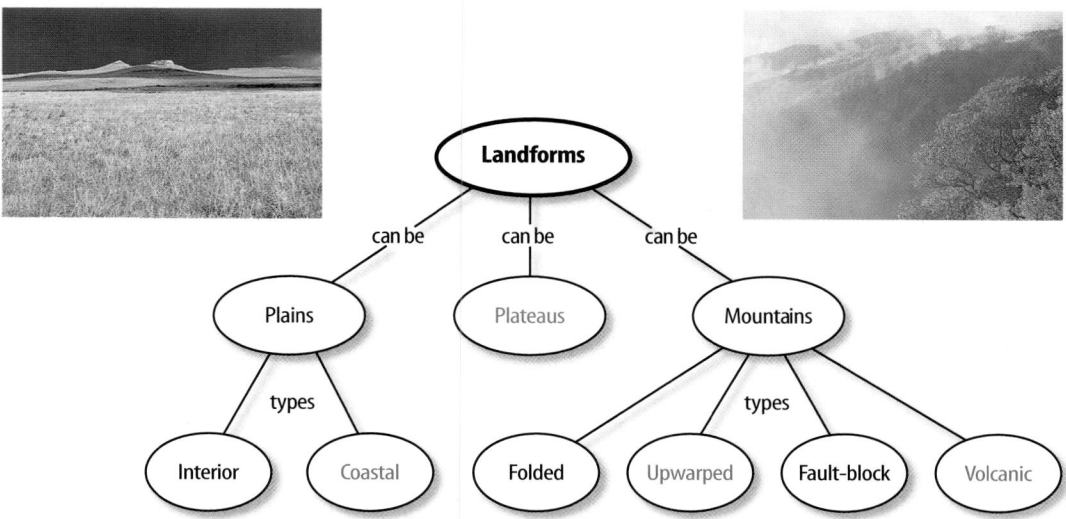

Visualizing Main Ideas

See student page.

Vocabulary Review

Using Vocabulary

1. The equator is not a type of mountain.
2. The prime meridian is not a landform.
3. A volcanic mountain is not part of a topographic map.
4. A folded mountain is not a reference point on a map grid.
5. A plateau is not a type of mountain.
6. A map scale is not part of a grid system for maps.

Vocabulary Review

Vocabulary Words

a. conic projection
b. contour line
c. equator
d. fault-block mountain
e. folded mountain
f. latitude
g. longitude
h. map legend
i. map scale
j. plain
k. plateau
l. prime meridian
m. topographic map
n. upwarped mountain
o. volcanic mountain

Using Vocabulary

For each set of terms below, choose the one term that does not belong and explain why it does not belong.

1. upwarped mountain, equator, volcanic mountain
2. plain, plateau, prime meridian
3. topographic map, contour line, volcanic mountain
4. prime meridian, equator, folded mountain
5. fault-block mountain, upwarped mountain, plateau
6. prime meridian, map scale, contour line

Study Tip

Make a plan! Before you start your homework, write a checklist of what you need to do for each subject. As you finish each item, check it off.

IDENTIFYING Misconceptions

Assess

Use the assessment as follow-up to page 154F after students have completed the chapter.

Activity Organize the class into small groups. Challenge each group to devise a skit that they can perform for the class. The skit should illustrate what might happen if Earth were flat. For example, they might act out a ship sailing off the edge of the world or Earth's shadow on the Moon as having a straight edge. After each group acts out its skit, have the class explain what actually happens on Earth, since it is a sphere.

Expected Outcome Students should understand by this point that Earth is a sphere, not flat.

Chapter 6 Assessment

Checking Concepts

1. B
2. D
3. B
4. A
5. C
6. D
7. B
8. B
9. C
10. B

Thinking Critically

11. The map of the Atlantic Coastal Plain would show little change in elevation, and the contour interval would be small. The map of the Rockies would show many closed contours indicating mountain peaks, and the contour interval would be large.
12. Tuesday
13. 160°
14. Anchorage, San Francisco, Denver, Houston, Bangor
15. The map with a scale of 1:50,000 would show less detail than the map with a scale of 1:24,000.

Checking Concepts

Choose the word or phrase that best answers the question.

1. What makes up about 50 percent of all land areas in the United States?
   - **A)** plateaus
   - **B)** plains
   - **C)** mountains
   - **D)** volcanoes

2. Where is the north pole located?
   - **A)** 0°N
   - **B)** 180°N
   - **C)** 50°N
   - **D)** 90°N

3. What kind of mountains are the Hawaiian Islands?
   - **A)** fault-block
   - **B)** volcanic
   - **C)** upwarped
   - **D)** folded

4. What are lines that are parallel to the equator called?
   - **A)** lines of latitude
   - **B)** prime meridians
   - **C)** lines of longitude
   - **D)** contour lines

5. How many degrees apart are the 24 time zones?
   - **A)** 10
   - **B)** 34
   - **C)** 15
   - **D)** 25

6. Which type of map is distorted at the poles?
   - **A)** conic
   - **B)** topographic
   - **C)** Robinson
   - **D)** Mercator

7. Which type of map shows changes in elevation at Earth's surface?
   - **A)** conic
   - **B)** topographic
   - **C)** Robinson
   - **D)** Mercator

8. What is measured with respect to sea level?
   - **A)** contour interval
   - **B)** elevation
   - **C)** conic projection
   - **D)** sonar

9. What kind of map shows rock types making up Earth's surface?
   - **A)** topographic
   - **B)** Robinson
   - **C)** geologic
   - **D)** Mercator

10. Which major U.S. landform includes the Grand Canyon?
    - **A)** Great Plains
    - **B)** Colorado Plateau
    - **C)** Gulf Coastal Plain
    - **D)** Appalachian Mountains

Thinking Critically

11. How would a topographic map of the Atlantic Coastal Plain differ from a topographic map of the Rocky Mountains?

12. If you left Korea early Wednesday morning and flew to Hawaii, on what day of the week would you arrive?

13. If you were flying directly south from the north pole and reached 70° north latitude, how many more degrees of latitude would you pass over before reaching the south pole?

14. Using a map, arrange these cities in order from the city with the earliest time to the one with the latest time on a given day: Anchorage, Alaska; San Francisco, California; Bangor, Maine; Denver, Colorado; Houston, Texas.

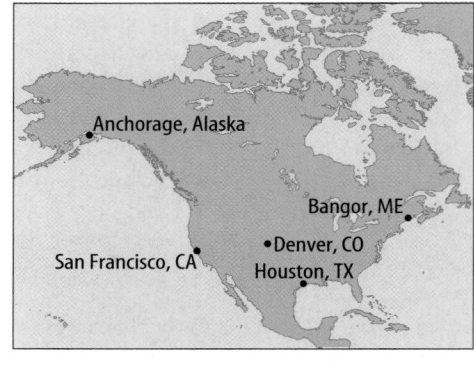

15. How is a map with a scale of 1:50,000 different from a map with a scale of 1:24,000?

Chapter ✓ Assessment Planner

Portfolio Encourage students to place in their portfolios one or two items of what they consider to be their best work. Examples include:
- Cultural Diversity, p. 158
- Challenge, p. 165
- Extension, p. 169

Performance Additional performance assessments, Performance Task Assessment Lists, and rubrics for evaluating these activities can be found in Glencoe's **Performance Assessment in the Science Classroom.**

Developing Skills

16. Comparing and Contrasting Compare and contrast Mercator, Robinson, and conic map projections.

17. Forming Hypotheses You are visiting a mountain in the northwest part of the United States. The mountain has steep sides and is not part of a mountain range. A crater can be seen at the top of the mountain. Hypothesize about what type of mountain you are visiting.

18. Concept Mapping Complete the following concept map about parts of a topographic map.

```
        Topographic Maps
              |
           include
        /    |    |    \
Contour lines  Scale  Symbols  Legend
```

Performance Assessment

19. Poem Create a poem about the different types of landforms. Include characteristics of each landform in your poem. Display your poem with those of your classmates.

20. Poster Create a poster showing how satellites can be used for remote sensing.

TECHNOLOGY

Go to the Glencoe Science Web site at **science.glencoe.com** or use the **Glencoe Science CD-ROM** for additional chapter assessment.

THE PRINCETON REVIEW — Test Practice

Alicia was looking at a map of the United States because her science teacher suggested that she learn about the land-form regions in the United States.

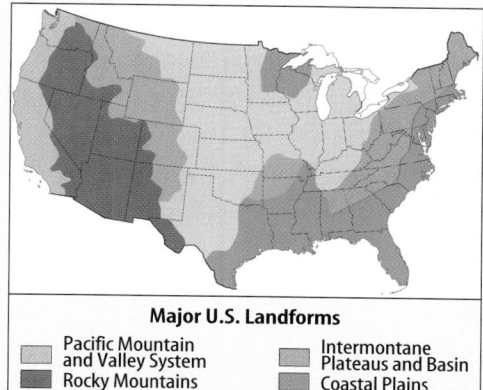

Major U.S. Landforms

- Pacific Mountain and Valley System
- Rocky Mountains
- Superior Uplands
- Appalachian Highlands
- Intermontane Plateaus and Basin
- Coastal Plains
- Interior Highlands
- Interior Plains

Study the diagram and answer the following questions.

1. Which technological development would have had the greatest impact on the accuracy of Alicia's map?
- **A)** radio communications
- **B)** measurement with lasers
- **C)** computer-assisted design
- **D)** satellite imaging

2. Which of the following landform regions would contain high, rugged mountains?
- **F)** Coastal Plains
- **G)** Interior Plains
- **H)** Appalachian Highlands
- **J)** Rocky Mountains

CHAPTER ASSESSMENT 181

THE PRINCETON REVIEW — Test Practice

The Test-Taking Tip was written by The Princeton Review, the nation's leader in test preparation.
1. D
2. J

Developing Skills

16. Each depicts a round Earth on a flat surface. Mercator projections exaggerate the areas near the poles and are used mainly for navigation. Robinson projections are good for depicting accurate continent shapes and have less distortion near the poles. Conic projections are good for mapping small areas and are used for road maps.

17. volcanic mountain

18. See student page.

Performance Assessment

19. Poems may be simple as long they describe different types of landforms. Encourage students to be creative. Use **PASC**, p. 151.

20. Posters should correctly show how satellites can be used for remote sensing. Use **PASC**, p. 145.

✓Assessment Resources

📁 Reproducible Masters

Chapter Resources Booklet
Chapter Review, pp. 35–36
Chapter Tests, pp. 37–40
Assessment Transparency Activity, p. 47

Glencoe Science Web site
Interactive Tutor
Chapter Quizzes

Glencoe Technology
- Assessment Transparency
- Interactive CD-ROM Chapter Quizzes
- ExamView Pro Test Bank
- Vocabulary PuzzleMaker Software
- MindJogger Videoquiz DVD/VHS

Section/Objectives	Standards		Activities/Features
Chapter Opener	**National**	**State/Local**	**Explore Activity:** Model weathering, p. 183 **Before You Read,** p. 183
	See p. 5T for a Key to Standards.		
Section 1 Weathering 🕐 1 sessions 📦 0.5 block 1. **Describe** the difference between mechanical weathering and chemical weathering. 2. **Explain** the effects of climate on weathering.	National Content Standards: UCP4, A1, D1		**Science Online,** p. 187 **MiniLAB:** Observing the Formation of Rust, p. 188
Section 2 The Nature of Soil 🕐 2 sessions 📦 1 block 1. **Explain** how soil develops from rock. 2. **Describe** soil by comparing soil horizons. 3. **Describe** factors that affect the development of soils.	National Content Standards: UCP4, A1, D1		**Visualizing Formation of Soil,** p. 191 **MiniLAB:** Comparing Components of Soil, p. 192 **Life Science Integration,** p. 193 **Math Skills Activity:** Calculating Percentages of Soil Particles, p. 194 **Activity:** Soil Characteristics, p. 197
Section 3 Soil Erosion 🕐 3 sessions 📦 1.5 blocks 1. **Explain** why soil is important. 2. **Identify** human activities that lead to soil loss. 3. **Describe** ways to reduce soil loss.	National Content Standards: UCP4, A1, D1, E2, F2, G1		**Physics Integration,** p. 199 **Science Online,** p. 199 **Activity:** Weathering Chalk, pp. 202–203 **Science and Language Arts:** Landscape, History, and the Pueblo Imagination, pp. 204–205

NATIONAL GEOGRAPHIC

Teacher's Corner

PRODUCTS AVAILABLE FROM GLENCOE
To order call 1-800-334-7344:
CD-ROM
NGS PictureShow: Dynamic Earth
NGS PictureShow: Geology
Curriculum Kit
GeoKit: Dynamic Earth

Transparency Sets
NGS PicturePack: Dynamic Earth
NGS PicturePack: Geology
PRODUCTS AVAILABLE FROM NATIONAL GEOGRAPHIC SOCIETY
To order call 1-800-368-2728:

Videos
Our Dynamic Earth

INDEX TO NATIONAL GEOGRAPHIC SOCIETY
The following articles may be used for research relating to this chapter:
"Acid Rain: How Great a Menace?"
Anne La Bastille, November 1981.

Activity Materials	Reproducible Resources	Section Assessment	Technology
Explore Activity: coffee can with lid, cobbles and pebbles	**Chapter Resources Booklet** Foldables Worksheet, p. 13 Directed Reading Overview, p. 15 Note-taking Worksheets, pp. 29–31	GLENCOE'S **ASSESSMENT** ADVANTAGE	
MiniLAB: steel wool, shallow glass dish, water *Need materials?* Contact Science Kit at 1-800-828-7777 or www.sciencekit.com on the Internet.	**Chapter Resources Booklet** Transparency Activity, p. 40 MiniLAB, p. 3 Enrichment, p. 26 Reinforcement, p. 23 Directed Reading, p. 16 Lab Activity, pp. 9–10 **Earth Science Critical Thinking/ Problem Solving,** p. 4 **Physical Science Critical Thinking/ Problem Solving,** p. 16	Portfolio Science Journal, p. 185 Curriculum Connection, p. 188 Performance MiniLAB, p. 188 Skill Builder Activities, p. 189 Content Section Assessment, p. 189	Section Focus Transparency Interactive CD-ROM/DVD Guided Reading Audio Program
MiniLAB: soil sample, hand lens **Activity:** soil sample, cheese-cloth squares, sand, 100-mL graduated cylinder, gravel, plastic coffee-can lids (3), clay, rubber bands (3), water, 250-mL beakers (3), watch, large polystyrene or plastic cups (3), pie pans, hand lens, scissors, thumbtack	**Chapter Resources Booklet** Transparency Activity, p. 41 MiniLAB, p. 4 Enrichment, p. 27 Reinforcement, p. 24 Transparency Activity, pp. 43–45 Directed Reading, p. 17 Activity Worksheet, pp. 5–6 Lab Activity, pp. 11–12 **Life Science Critical Thinking/ Problem Solving,** p. 22 **Performance Assessment in the Science Classroom,** p. 44	Portfolio Science Journal, p. 192 Performance MiniLAB, p. 192 Math Skills Activity, p. 194 Skill Builder Activities, p. 196 Content Section Assessment, p. 196	Section Focus Transparency Teaching Transparency Interactive CD-ROM/DVD Guided Reading Audio Program
Activity: equal-sized pieces of chalk (6), small beakers (2), metric ruler, water, white vinegar (100 mL), hot plate, 250-mL graduated cylinder, computer probe for temperature	**Chapter Resources Booklet** Transparency Activity, p. 42 Enrichment, p. 28 Reinforcement, p. 25 Directed Reading, pp. 17, 18 Activity Worksheet, pp. 7–8 **Lab Management and Safety,** p. 65	Portfolio Activity Assessment, p. 197 Performance Skill Builder Activities, p. 201 Content Section Assessment, p. 201	Section Focus Transparency Interactive CD-ROM/DVD Guided Reading Audio Program

End of Chapter Assessment

GLENCOE'S **ASSESSMENT** ADVANTAGE

Blackline Masters	Technology	Professional Series
Chapter Resources Booklet Chapter Review, pp. 33–34 Chapter Tests, pp. 35–38 **Standardized Test Practice by The Princeton Review,** pp. 35–38	MindJogger Videoquiz CD-ROM Explorations and Quizzes Vocabulary Puzzle Makers ExamView Pro Test Bank Interactive Lesson Planner Interactive Teacher's Edition	Performance Assessment in the Science Classroom (PASC)

Transparencies

Section Focus

Section Focus Transparency 1 — Going, Going . . .

Can you read this inscription? The effects of weathering have greatly reduced your chances of doing so. This stone is in Kempton Cemetery in Columbus, Ohio.

1. How did weathering wear away the writing on this stone?
2. What steps might be taken to preserve the writing that remains?

L2

Section Focus Transparency 2 — More Than Just Dirt

You probably see the material shown here every day, but you may not even notice it. You may only think about it when it makes your room or clothes dirty, but soil is also a valuable resource.

1. What components of soil can you identify in this picture?
2. How does the worm interact with the soil?
3. Why isn't soil the same everywhere?

L2

Section Focus Transparency 3 — Blowing in the Wind

During the 1930s, poor soil conservation led to catastrophic "black blizzards" experienced in many states of the southern Great Plains. One storm carried over 300 million tons of dirt all the way to the east coast. Today people are increasingly conscious of soil conservation.

1. What is occurring in this picture?
2. Why is the loss of topsoil harmful?
3. How could poor soil conservation have caused something so devastating?

L2

This is a representation of key blackline masters available in the Teacher Classroom Resources. See Resource Manager boxes within the chapter for additional information.

Key to Teaching Strategies

The following designations will help you decide which activities are appropriate for your students.

L1 Level 1 activities should be appropriate for students with learning difficulties.

L2 Level 2 activities should be within the ability range of all students.

L3 Level 3 activities are designed for above-average students.

ELL ELL activities should be within the ability range of English Language Learners.

COOP LEARN Cooperative Learning activities are designed for small group work.

LS Multiple Learning Styles logos, as described on page 22T, are used throughout to indicate strategies that address different learning styles.

P These strategies represent student products that can be placed into a best-work portfolio.

Assessment

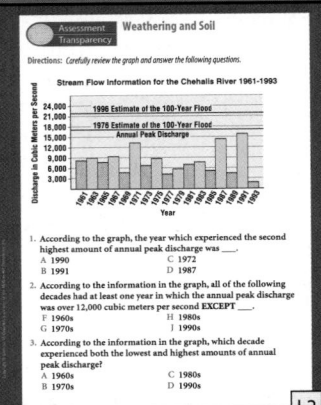

Assessment Transparency — Weathering and Soil

Directions: Carefully review the graph and answer the following questions.

Stream Flow Information for the Chehalis River 1961-1993

1. According to the graph, the year which experienced the second highest amount of annual peak discharge was ___.
   A 1990   C 1972
   B 1991   D 1987
2. According to the information in the graph, all of the following decades had at least one year in which the annual peak discharge was over 12,000 cubic meters per second EXCEPT ___.
   F 1960s   H 1980s
   G 1970s   J 1990s
3. According to the information in the graph, which decade experienced both the lowest and highest amounts of annual peak discharge?
   A 1960s   C 1980s
   B 1970s   D 1990s

L2

Teaching

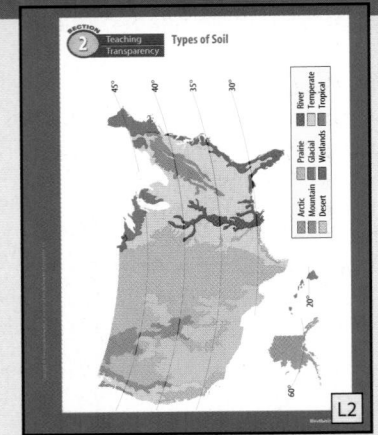

Teaching Transparency 2 — Types of Soil

L2

Hands-on Activities

Activity Worksheets

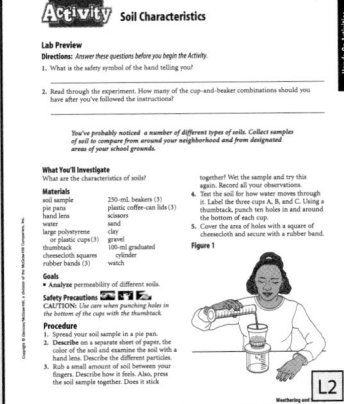

Activity — Soil Characteristics

Lab Preview
Directions: Answer these questions before you begin the Activity.
1. What is the safety symbol of the hand telling you?

2. Read through the experiment. How many of the cup-and-beaker combinations should you have after you've followed the instructions?

You've probably noticed a number of different types of soils. Collect samples of soil to compare from around your neighborhood and from designated areas of your school grounds.

What You'll Investigate
What are the characteristics of soils?

Materials
soil sample
pie pans
hand lens
water
large polystyrene or plastic cups(3)
thumbtack
cheesecloth square
rubber bands (3)
250-mL beakers (3)
plastic coffee-can lids(3)
scissors
sand
clay
gravel
100-mL graduated cylinder
watch

Goals
• Analyze permeability of different soils.

Safety Precautions
CAUTION: Use care when punching holes in the bottom of the cups with the thumbtack.

Procedure
1. Spread your soil sample in a pie pan.
2. Describe on a separate sheet of paper, the color of the soil and examine the soil with a hand lens. Describe the different particles.
3. Rub a small amount of soil between your fingers. Describe how it feels. Also, press the soil sample together. Does it stick

together well? Wet the sample and try this again. Record all your observations.
4. Test the soil for how water moves through it. Label the three cups A, B, and C. Using a thumbtack, punch ten holes in and around the bottom of each cup.
5. Cover the area of holes with a square of cheesecloth and secure with a rubber band.

Figure 1

L2

Laboratory Activities

Laboratory Activity 1 — Chemical Weathering

Rocks are mixtures of minerals that are either elements or chemical compounds. Chemical weathering is the chemical reaction of these minerals with carbon dioxide, water, oxygen, or other substances at Earth's surface. For example, in minerals containing iron, the iron reacts with oxygen in the air to form rust. Rotted plant material combines with water to form humic acid, that causes chemical weathering.

Strategy
You will cause a chemical reaction between a copper strip and combined salt and vinegar at room temperature.
You will observe a chemical reaction between iron and atmospheric oxygen.

Materials
copper strip (dirty)
pie pan (disposable)
graduated cylinder
salt
vinegar (white)
iron (II) sulfate, $FeSO_4$
water
beaker
apron
goggles

Procedure
1. For the first activity, place a copper strip in the pie pan and place 5 mL salt on the strip.
2. Carefully pour 30 mL of vinegar over the copper. Record your observations in Table 1.
3. Wash the salt and vinegar off the copper. CAUTION: The material formed is an acid. Avoid contact with skin and clothing.
4. For a separate activity, mix 5 g of iron (II) sulfate in 50 mL of water.

CAUTION: Iron(II) sulfate is poisonous. Avoid contact with skin. Record the color of the solution and any other observations in Table 1.
5. Let both the beaker and the copper strip stand undisturbed overnight.
6. Next day, observe the beaker and the copper. Record your observations in Table 1.

Data and Observations

Table 1

	Start	Next day
1. Copper strip		
2. Beaker $FeSO_4$		

L2

Meeting Different Ability Levels

Content Outline

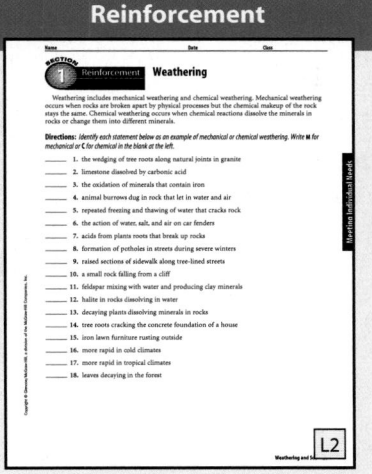

L2

Reinforcement

L2

Directed Reading

L1

Assessment

Chapter Tests

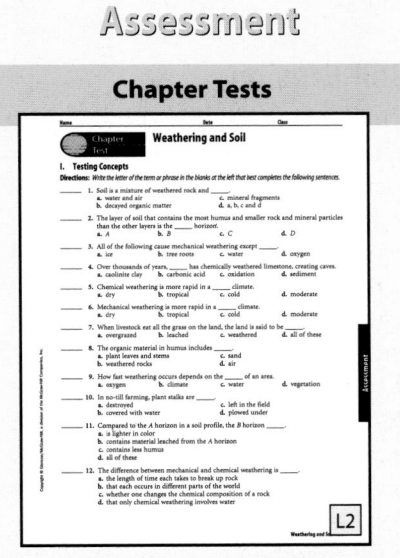

L2

Enrichment

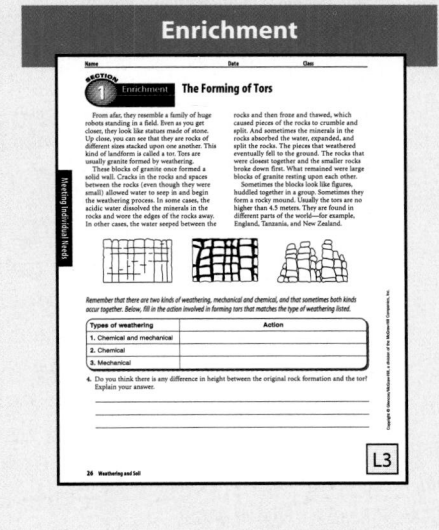

L3

Spanish Directed Reading

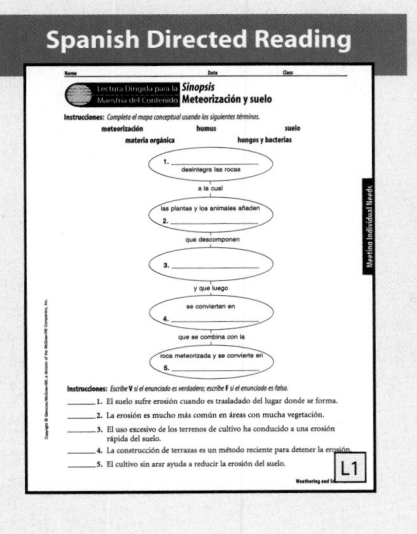

L1

Test Practice Workbook

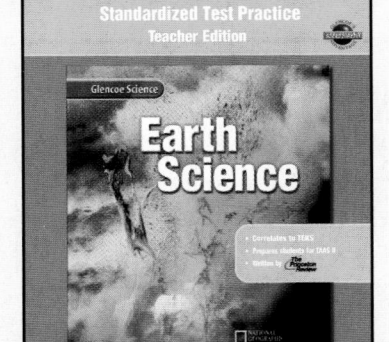

L2

Chapter Review

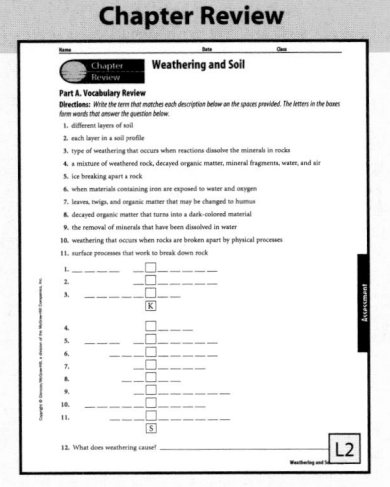

L2

Science Content Background

Weathering

Evidence of Weathering

Potholes and sidewalk cracks, crumbling rocks, discolored paint, rusted automobiles, and eroded statues all show evidence of different types of weathering.

Chemical Weathering

When oxygen, water, and/or carbon dioxide combine with chemicals in rocks, new compounds are formed. These processes of chemical weathering are called oxidation, hydration, and carbonation, depending upon which chemical compounds or elements are involved.

Nitrogen oxide and sulfur dioxide, two compounds released into the atmosphere when fossil fuels are burned, also can cause chemical weathering. When mixed with water, these chemicals form acid rain, which can dissolve rocks, statues, and buildings.

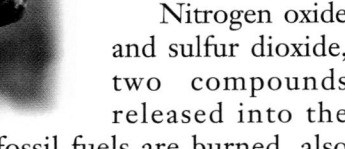
Runk/Schoenberger/Grant Heilman Photography, Inc.

The Nature of Soil

Formation of Soil

Residual soils are those that form by the gradual weathering of bedrock and remain in place once they are formed. Transported soils have been carried from their sources by gravity, wind, water, or glaciers and deposited in a new location.

Soil Profiles

Leaching and redeposition of minerals typically result in a unique soil profile that extends from the topsoil to the other layers in the horizon and finally to the bedrock. Because residual soils have the same composition as the bedrock under them, the horizons are usually poorly defined or absent, and there is a sharp discontinuity between the soil and the bedrock.

Student Misconception

Climate does not affect weathering.

Refer to the facing page for teaching strategies to address this misconception. Refer to pages 187–188 for content related to this topic.

Soil Erosion

Preventing Soil Erosion

Methods of reducing soil loss include planting shelter belts of trees to break the force of the wind and covering of exposed soils with decaying plants to hold soil in place. Water erosion can be reduced by terracing steep slopes or removing these slopes from cultivation. On gentle slopes, plowing along the natural contours of the land and planting crops in strips help reduce erosion by water. In strip cropping, a crop that covers the ground is alternated with a crop such as corn that exposes a considerable amount of soil. In recent years, many farmers have begun no-till farming, in which new plants are grown among the stalks of last year's crop.

SCIENCE Online

For additional content background on this topic, go to the Glencoe Science Web site at science.glencoe.com.

IDENTIFYING ▶ **Misconceptions**

Find Out What Students Think

Students may think that . . .

• Climate does not affect weathering.

Students often think that mechanical and chemical weathering occur at the same rate regardless of climate. Students develop this misconception because they incorrectly infer that what can be experienced and observed locally applies globally.

Discussion

Organize the class into small groups. Have students in each group use a globe to identify the locations of a variety of different climates on Earth. Then have them discuss which agents might have the greatest effect on weathering in each different area. Some examples are listed below.

- Tundra (arctic areas and ice caps): mechanical weathering caused by freezing and thawing

- Rain forests (tropical or temperate): a combination of mechanical and chemical weathering, as water and plant roots mechanically weather rocks and plant acids chemically weather rocks

As an extension, have students identify which areas would have relatively slow weathering rates (desert and polar regions) and which would have relatively fast weathering rates (tropical regions). Have students make a Venn diagram comparing and contrasting the climates in these different areas.

Promote Understanding

Activity

Again, organize the class into small groups. Have each group plan and carry out an experiment showing how weathering is affected by climate. Suggest that students use stream tables in their experiments. Caution students to wear goggles when blowing sand or soil and to keep dryer cords well away from water sources. Some ideas for different climates are listed below.

- For a desert environment, have students use sand in the stream table and add very few plants to the soil. Suggest that they use a hair dryer set on low to simulate wind erosion and a sprinkling can to simulate a rainstorm.

- For a temperate or tropical environment, have students use potting soil mixed with a small amount of sand. They can add a variety of plants to the soil and use the hair dryer and sprinkling can to simulate wind and rain.

- In a polar (or winter) climate, suggest that students devise a way to show how ice wedging can mechanically weather rocks. They might soak porous rocks in water and then freeze them to show that frozen water can shatter rock.

Assess

After completing the chapter, see *Identifying Misconceptions* in the Study Guide.

CHAPTER 7

Weathering and Soil

Chapter Vocabulary

weathering
mechanical weathering
ice wedging
chemical weathering
oxidation
climate
soil
humus
horizon
soil profile
litter
leaching
terracing

What do you think?

Science Journal This photograph shows tree roots growing in a rock. A tree seed landed in a crack in the rock. There was enough soil in the crack for the seedling to grow. As the roots grew, they wedged the rock apart.

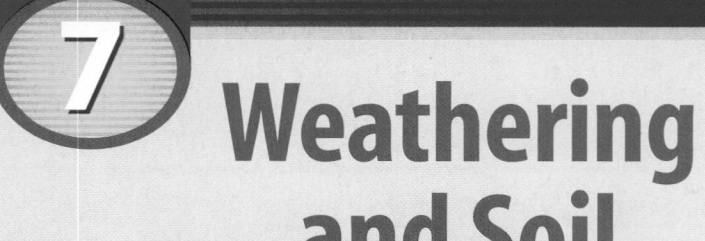

CHAPTER 7

Weathering and Soil

Can you imagine how these balanced rocks were formed? For millions of years, nature has been working on them, wearing away softer materials and leaving behind more resistant rock. In this chapter, you'll read about how rocks are weathered into small fragments such as sand and clay. You also will learn how soil forms, how it erodes, and how to prevent soil erosion.

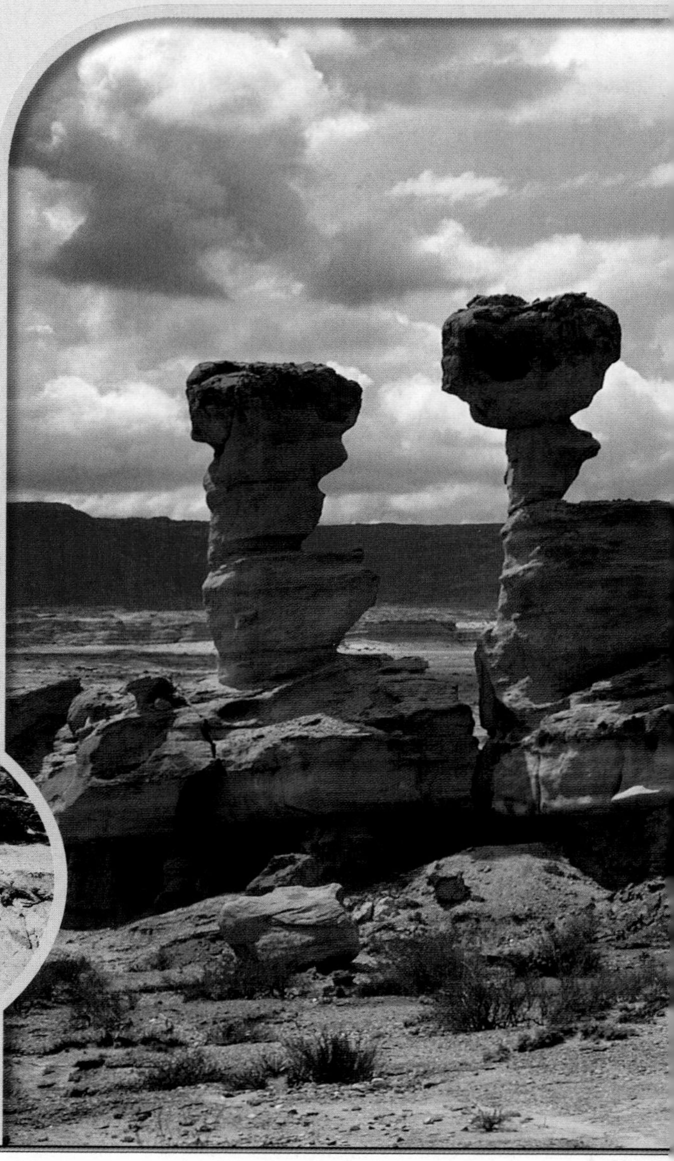

What do you think?

Science Journal Examine the picture below with a classmate. Discuss what you think this might be or what is happening. Here's a hint: *It's a strange place to grow.* Write your answer or best guess in your Science Journal.

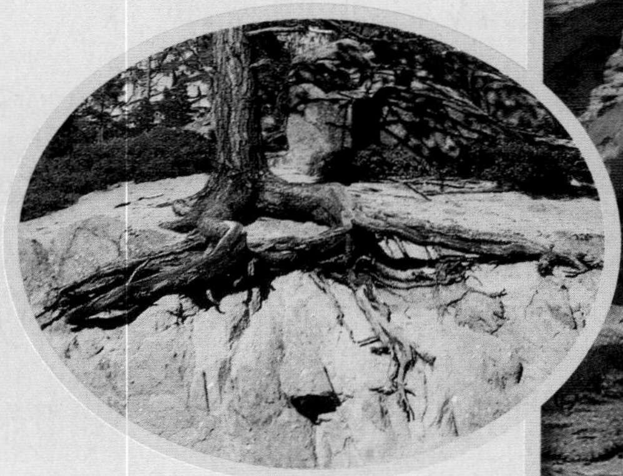

182

Theme Connection

Stability and Change This theme is developed in the discussion of how soils develop over long periods of time from weathered rock and organic matter, and how soil erosion changes Earth's surface.

EXPLORE ACTIVITY

Weathering breaks apart rock by exposing it to natural elements such as water and ice. Do you think you can simulate weathering on Earth's surface?

Model weathering

1. Form groups of four or five students as instructed by your teacher.
2. Fill a coffee can one third of the way full with small cobbles and pebbles obtained from your school yard.
3. Observe the cobbles and pebbles that you collected. Sketch their shapes in your Science Journal.
4. Put the lid on the coffee can and take turns shaking the can vigorously from side to side for several minutes.
5. Remove the lid and examine the rocks.

Observe

Describe in your Science Journal what happened to the rocks. How is this similar to weathering?

Before You Read

FOLDABLES
Reading & Study Skills

Making a Vocabulary Study Fold To help you study this chapter, make the following vocabulary Foldable. Knowing the definition of vocabulary words in a chapter is a good way to ensure you have understood the content.

1. Place a sheet of notebook paper in front of you so the short side is at the top and the holes are on the right side. Fold the paper in half from the left side to the right side.
2. Through the top thickness of paper, cut along every third line from the outside edge to the center fold, forming tabs as shown.
3. On the front of each tab, write a vocabulary word listed on the first page of each section in this chapter. On the back of each tab, define the word.
4. As you read the chapter, write a sentence using the vocabulary words.

183

EXPLORE ACTIVITY

Purpose Use this Explore Activity to introduce your students to the processes of mechanical weathering. Explain that they will be learning about several different types of weathering in this chapter.

Preparation Ask students in advance to save and bring in coffee cans from home.

Materials coffee can with lid, cobbles and pebbles

Safety Precautions Students should wear safety goggles and apron.

Teaching Strategies After the activity, be sure materials are disposed of properly.

Observe

After shaking in the can, pebbles that had weaknesses, such as fractures, before shaking should break apart. This produces more and smaller individual stones. Note that better results will be obtained from pebbles and cobbles collected from soil. Samples in soil are more likely to have sustained more weathering.

✓ Assessment

Process Ask students to infer how environment might increase the rate of mechanical weathering of stone. Possible answer: Windy or rainy climates can cause abrasion that weathers the stone. Use **Performance Assessment in the Science Classroom,** p. 89.

Before You Read

FOLDABLES
Reading & Study Skills

Dinah Zike Study Fold

Purpose Expose students to the chapter's content and vocabulary before reading. Encourage them to search for terms and definitions during reading and to write them in their Foldables. This will provide a Foldable study guide for review after reading.

📁 For additional help, see Foldables Worksheet, p. 13 in **Chapter Resources Booklet,** or go to the Glencoe Science Web site at **science.glencoe.com.** See After You Read in the Study Guide at the end of this chapter.

SECTION

1

Weathering

1 Motivate

Bellringer Transparency

Display the Section Focus Transparency for Section 1. Use the accompanying Transparency Activity Master. L2
ELL

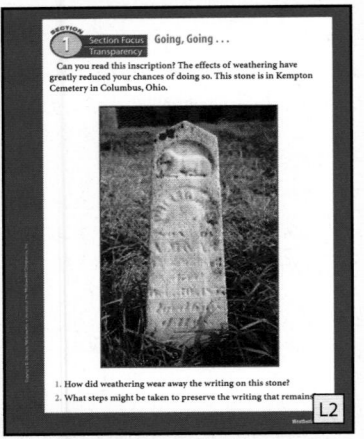

Tie to Prior Knowledge

Explain that in this section, students will learn about weathering—the breaking down of rock into smaller pieces in nature. **Where have you seen small pieces of rock that could have been broken down by weathering?** Possible answers: boulders, large pebbles, or sand on beaches; pebbles on roads or in parking lots; rocks in streams, soil

SECTION

1 # Weathering

As You Read

What You'll Learn

- **Describe** the difference between mechanical weathering and chemical weathering.
- **Explain** the effects of climate on weathering.

Vocabulary
weathering
mechanical weathering
ice wedging
chemical weathering
oxidation
climate

Why It's Important
Weathering causes rocks to crumble and shapes many landforms.

Weathering and Its Effects

Can you believe that tiny moss plants, a burrowing vole shrew, and even oxygen in the air can affect solid rock? These things and many more weaken and break apart rock at Earth's surface. Together, surface processes that work to break down rock are called **weathering.**

Weathering breaks rock into smaller and smaller pieces, such as sand, silt, and clay. These smaller, loose pieces are called sediment. The terms sand, silt, and clay are used to describe specific sizes of sediment. Sediment then changes gradually into soil. The formation of soil depends upon the amount of weathering that occurs in a specific place.

Over millions of years, weathering has changed Earth's surface. The process continues today. Weathering wears mountains down to hills as shown in **Figure 1.** Rocks at the top of mountains are broken down by weathering and then carried downhill by gravity, water, and ice. Weathering also produces strange rock formations like those shown at the beginning of this chapter. Two different types of weathering—mechanical weathering and chemical weathering—work together to shape Earth's surface.

Figure 1
Over long periods of time, weathering wears mountains down to rolling hills.

Section ✓ Assessment Planner

PORTFOLIO
Science Journal, p. 185
Curriculum Connection, p. 188

PERFORMANCE ASSESSMENT
Try at Home MiniLAB, p. 188
Skill Builder Activities, p. 189
See page 208 for more options.

CONTENT ASSESSMENT
Section, p. 189
Challenge, p. 189
Chapter, pp. 208–209

Figure 2
Growing tree roots can be agents of mechanical weathering.

A Tree roots can grow beneath a sidewalk, cracking the concrete and pushing it up.

B Tree roots also can grow into cracks in rock, breaking it apart.

Mechanical Weathering

Mechanical weathering occurs when rocks are broken apart by physical processes. This means that the chemical makeup of the rock stays the same. Each fragment keeps the same characteristics as the original rock. Growing plants, burrowing animals, and expanding ice are some of the things that can mechanically weather rock. These physical processes produce enough force to break rocks into smaller pieces.

✔ **Reading Check** *What can cause mechanical weathering?*

Plants and Animals Water and nutrients that collect in the cracks of rocks result in conditions in which plants can grow. As the roots grow, they wedge rock apart. You've seen this kind of mechanical weathering if you've ever tripped on a crack in a sidewalk near a tree, as shown in **Figure 2A.** Sometimes the roots will wedge rock apart, as shown in **Figure 2B.**

Burrowing animals also cause mechanical weathering as shown in **Figure 3.** As these animals burrow, they loosen sediments and push them to the surface. Once the sediments are brought to the surface, other weathering processes can act on them.

Figure 3
Small animals mechanically weather rock when they burrow by breaking apart sediment and moving it to the surface.

SECTION 1 Weathering **185**

Visual Learning

Figure 4 How might this cliff look several hundred years from now? Possible answer: Because of weathering, the face of the cliff would be farther back, more talus (rocks and sediment) would be at its base, and the cliff would have a gentler slope.

Quick Demo

Model the way frost action breaks pieces off rock. Display a clay brick. Soak it in a bucket of water overnight. The next day, place the brick in a freezer. On the third day, remove the brick from the freezer. Students should observe broken pieces.

Discussion

Why is ice wedging more likely to occur at higher elevations than at lower elevations? Temperatures are more extreme at higher elevations. Nighttime temperatures often are below freezing, while daytime temperatures are above freezing. This freezing and thawing cycle is most likely to cause ice wedging.

Fun Fact

According to the Federal Highway Administration, $20–$25 billion is spent each year on pothole repair for streets and highways, some of which is caused by ice wedging. This adds up to about $14,000 per mile.

Use Science Words

Word Origin Have students research ways the Latin word *speleum* is used in cave terminology. Speleum means cave. People who explore caves for a hobby are called spelunkers. The scientific study of caves is called speleology; scientists who study caves are speleologists. Speleothems are cave formations.

Figure 4
When water enters cracks in rock and freezes, it expands, causing the cracks to enlarge and the rock to break apart.

Figure 5
As rock is broken apart by mechanical weathering, the amount of rock surface exposed to air and water increases. The background squares show the total number of surfaces exposed.

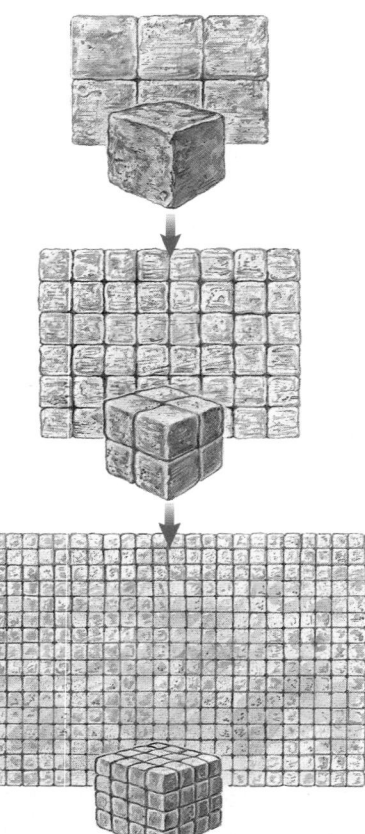

Ice Wedging The mechanical weathering process known as ice wedging is illustrated in **Figure 4. Ice wedging** occurs in temperate and cold climates where water enters cracks in rocks and freezes. Because water expands when it turns to ice, pressure builds up in the cracks. This pressure can extend the cracks and break apart rock. The ice then melts, allowing more water to enter the crack, where it freezes and breaks the rock even more. Ice wedging is most noticeable in the mountains, where warm days and cold nights are common. It is one process that wears down mountain peaks. This cycle of freezing and thawing not only breaks up rocks, but also can break up roads and highways. When water enters cracks in road pavement and freezes, it forces the pavement apart. This causes potholes to form in roads.

Surface Area Mechanical weathering by plants, animals, and ice wedging reduces rocks to smaller pieces. These small pieces have more surface area than the original rock body, as shown in **Figure 5.** As the amount of surface area increases, more rock is exposed to water and oxygen. This results in a different type of weathering called chemical weathering.

Inclusion Strategies

Learning Disabled Have students collect and display photographs of objects that are being weathered. Pictures might include cracks in rocks, sidewalks, buildings, or cliffs. L1 ELL IS **Visual-Spatial**

Curriculum Connection

Art Direct students to draw a diagram, with labels, that illustrates one type of mechanical weathering. Students can choose from among growing plants, burrowing animals, or ice wedging. L2 ELL IS **Visual-Spatial**

Chemical Weathering

Chemistry INTEGRATION

The second type of weathering, **chemical weathering,** occurs when chemical reactions dissolve the minerals in rocks or change them into different minerals. This type of weathering changes the chemical composition of the rock, which can weaken the rock. Next, you will see how chemical weathering happens.

Natural Acids Naturally formed acids can weather rocks chemically. When water mixes with carbon dioxide gas in the air or soil, a weak acid, called carbonic acid, forms. This is the same weak acid that makes soft drinks fizzy, especially when shaken. Carbonic acid reacts with minerals such as calcite, which is the main mineral that makes up limestone. This reaction causes the calcite to dissolve. Over many thousands of years, carbonic acid has weathered so much limestone that caves, such as the one shown in **Figure 6,** have formed.

Chemical weathering also occurs when naturally formed acids come in contact with other rocks. Over a long period of time, the mineral feldspar, which is found in granite, some types of sandstone, and other rocks, is broken down into a clay mineral called kaolinite (KAY uh luh nite). Kaolinite clay is common in some soils. Clay is an end product of weathering.

✔ **Reading Check** *How does kaolinite clay form?*

SCIENCE Online

Research Visit the Glencoe Science Web site at **science.glencoe.com** for more information about chemical weathering. Communicate to your class what you learn.

Figure 6
Caves form when slightly acidic groundwater dissolves large amounts of limestone.

Carbon dioxide + Water = Carbonic acid
Carbonic acid dissolves limestone.

Chemical Weathering

Use an Analogy

Give two student volunteers each a piece of hard candy. Have one student chew the candy into pieces before allowing it to dissolve in the mouth. Have the other student let the candy dissolve without chewing it. Compare how long it takes for the candy to dissolve. Candy broken into pieces dissolves faster. The dissolving process is like chemical weathering, which occurs faster when more rock surface area is exposed.

Teacher FYI

Carlsbad Caverns in New Mexico is one of the world's largest caverns. Part of the caverns is a chamber called The Big Room. It measures 550 m long and 335 m wide. One part of the ceiling is 78 m high—more than the height of a 20-story building.

IDENTIFYING Misconceptions

Some students may believe that mechanical and chemical weathering occur at the same rate regardless of climate. Refer to page 182F for teaching strategies that address this misconception.

✔ **Reading Check**

Answer It forms when natural acids react with feldspar in granite and other rocks.

Chemical Weathering,
continued

TRY AT HOME

Mini LAB

Purpose Students compare rust formation to chemical weathering. [L2] [ELL] [IS] **Visual-Spatial**

Materials uncoated steel wool, shallow glass dish, water

Teaching Strategy Have students observe the steel wool each day.

Safety Precautions Use care when handling steel wool. Wash hands after handling it.

Analysis
1. Rust formed.
2. The steel wool oxidized in the presence of water.
3. Chemical changes break rock down, just as chemical changes in steel wool broke it down.

✓ Assessment

Performance Have students design experiments to see how length of exposure to an acid affects the chemical weathering of various metals such as an iron nail or a copper penny. Use **PASC**, p. 95.

Caption Answer
Figure 7 In both, iron oxidizes.

Effects of Climate

Discussion
What type of weathering would be more common in a desert? Explain. Mechanical; because it is dry.

TRY AT HOME

Mini LAB

Observing the Formation of Rust

Procedure 🌊 📏
1. Place some **steel wool** in a **glass petri dish** with 1 cm of **water.**
2. Observe for several days.

Analysis
1. What changes occurred?
2. What caused the changes?
3. How are these changes related to weathering?

Figure 7
Iron-containing minerals like the magnetite shown here can weather to form a rustlike mineral called limonite. *How is this similar to rust forming on your bicycle chain?*

188 **CHAPTER 7** Weathering and Soil

Plant Acids Some roots and decaying plants give off acids that also can dissolve minerals in rock. When these minerals are dissolved, the rock is weakened. Eventually, the rock will break into smaller pieces. Do you know how a plant can benefit by being able to dissolve rock?

Oxygen Oxygen helps cause chemical weathering. You've seen rusty swing sets, nails, and cars. Rust is caused by oxidation. **Oxidation** (ahk sih DAY shun) occurs when metallic materials are exposed to oxygen and water over prolonged periods of time. For example, when minerals containing iron are exposed to water and the oxygen in air, the iron in the mineral can form a new mineral that resembles rust. One common example of this type of weathering is alteration of the iron-bearing mineral magnetite to a rustlike mineral called limonite, as shown in **Figure 7.** Can you think of an example of a mineral, other than magnetite, that is weathered by oxidation?

Effects of Climate

Mechanical and chemical weathering occur everywhere. However, climate can affect the rate of weathering in different parts of the world. **Climate** is the pattern of weather that occurs in a particular area over many years. In cold climates, where freezing and thawing are frequent, mechanical weathering rapidly breaks down rocks through the process of ice wedging. Chemical weathering is more rapid in warm, wet climates. Thus, chemical weathering occurs quickly in tropical areas such as the Amazon River region of South America. Lack of moisture in deserts and low temperatures in polar regions slow down chemical weathering. Which type of weathering do you think is most rapid in the area where you live?

Curriculum Connection

History The Statue of Liberty has to be repaired periodically because of damage caused by weathering. Have students research the material of which the statue is made and the type of damage that weathering has caused to it over the years. Have them write reports on what has been done within the last few years to repair and protect the statue from weathering. [L2] [P]

Resource Manager 🦅

Chapter Resources Booklet
  MiniLAB, p. 3
  Reinforcement, p. 23

A

B

Figure 8
Different types of rock weather at different rates. **A** In humid climates, marble statues weather rapidly and become discolored. **B** Granite statues weather more slowly.

Effects of Rock Type Rock type also can affect the rate of weathering in a particular climate. In wet climates, for example, marble weathers more rapidly than granite, as shown in **Figure 8.**

Now you can understand how weathering affects rocks, caves, mountains, and even buildings and streets. Weathering is an important part of the rock cycle. When weathering breaks down rocks, it produces sediment that can form sedimentary rocks. Weathering also begins the process of forming soil from rock and sediment. This is discussed in the next section.

Section 1 Assessment

1. What is the difference between mechanical and chemical weathering?
2. Explain how tree roots can weather rock. How can prairie dogs weather rock?
3. What effect does carbonic acid have on limestone?
4. How does climate affect the rate of chemical weathering?
5. **Think Critically** Why does limestone often form cliffs in dry climates but not in wet climates?

Skill Builder Activities

6. **Concept Mapping** Make a network tree concept map about mechanical weathering. **For more help,** refer to the Science Skill Handbook.
7. **Using an Electronic Spreadsheet** Create a spreadsheet that identifies examples of weathering that you see around your neighborhood and school. Classify each example as the result of mechanical weathering, chemical weathering, or both. **For more help,** refer to the Technology Skill Handbook.

Discussion
How could you tell which of two limestone headstones in a cemetery is older without looking at the dates? The older headstone is likely to show more weathering.

3 Assess

Reteach
Have students make a bulletin board of local examples of weathering. Allow students to borrow an inexpensive camera (or use their own) to photograph chemical and mechanical weathering near their homes or in the schoolyard. After the pictures are posted, discuss what each shows. L1 ELL LS **Visual-Spatial**

Challenge
Allow students to choose a mountain peak or mountain range in the U.S. Have them use the library and Internet resources to research the geological history of the feature and write a report on how weathering has affected the way it looks today. L3 LS **Linguistic**

Assessment

Process Have students draw an events chain concept map that describes the process of mechanical weathering by ice or chemical weathering that results in rust. Use **Performance Assessment in the Science Classroom,** p. 163.

Answers to Section Assessment

1. Mechanical weathering breaks down rock without changing its chemical composition; chemical weathering changes a rock's composition as it breaks the rock down.
2. Roots grow into rocks and wedge them apart; prairie dogs loosen sediments and push them to the surface as they tunnel.
3. It dissolves the calcite in limestone.
4. Warm, wet climates have an increased rate of chemical weathering.
5. Limestone is more likely to dissolve in wet climates.
6. Students should include the agents of mechanical weathering and their effects. Check students' work.
7. Possible answer:
   Column 1:"Weathering Examples,"
   Column 2:"Mechanical Weathering,"
   Column 3:"Chemical Weathering,"
   students place an "X" in the column that applies.

SECTION

2

The Nature of Soil

Bellringer Transparency

Display the Section Focus Transparency for Section 2. Use the accompanying Transparency Activity Master. L2
ELL

Tie to Prior Knowledge

Ask students to describe different types of soil they have seen. Show photos or bring in different types of soil and have them describe the soils by color or particle size. Possible answers: coarse or fine sand, red soil, brown soil, black soil.

Caption Answer

Figure 9 Longer periods of time allow more weathering and the formation of smaller soil particles. Longer periods also allow more humus to form.

SECTION

2

The Nature of Soil

Formation of Soil

How often have you been told "Take off those dirty shoes before you come into this house"? Ever since you were a child, you've had experience with soil. Soil is found in many places—backyards, empty city lots, farm fields, gardens, and forests.

What is soil and where does it come from? A layer of rock and mineral fragments produced by weathering covers the surface of Earth. As you learned in Section 1, weathering gradually breaks rocks into smaller and smaller fragments. However, these fragments do not become soil until plants and animals live in them. Plants and animals add organic matter, the remains of once-living organisms, to the rock fragments. Organic matter can include leaves, twigs, roots, and dead worms and insects. After organic matter has been added, soil as you know it begins to develop. **Soil** is a mixture of weathered rock, decayed organic matter, mineral fragments, water, and air.

Soil can take thousands of years to form and ranges from 60 m thick in some areas to just a few centimeters thick in others. Climate, slope, types of rock, types of vegetation, and length of time that rock has been weathering all affect the formation of soil, as shown in **Figure 9.** For example, different kinds of soils develop in tropical regions than in polar regions. Soils that develop on steep slopes are different from soils that develop on flat land. **Figure 10** illustrates how soil develops from rock.

Figure 9
Five different factors affect soil formation. *How does time influence the development of soils?*

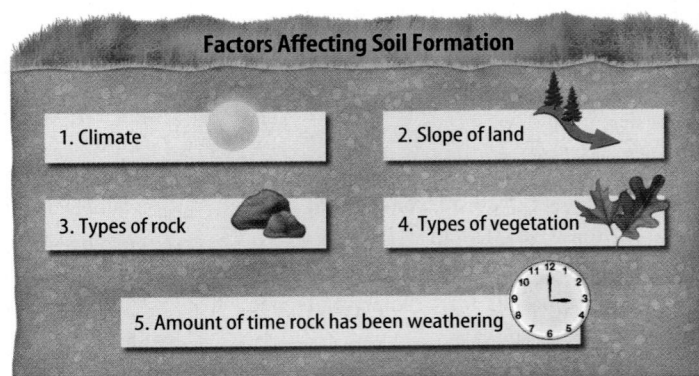

Factors Affecting Soil Formation

1. Climate
2. Slope of land
3. Types of rock
4. Types of vegetation
5. Amount of time rock has been weathering

Section ✓*Assessment* Planner

PORTFOLIO
Science Journal, p. 192
PERFORMANCE ASSESSMENT
MiniLAB, p. 192
Math Skills Activity, p. 194
Skill Builder Activities, p. 196
See page 208 for more options.

CONTENT ASSESSMENT
Section, p. 196
Challenge, p. 196
Chapter, pp. 208–209

Figure 10

It may take hundreds of years to form, but soil is constantly evolving from solid rock, as this series of illustrations shows. Soil is a mixture of weathered rock, mineral fragments, and organic material—the remains of dead plants and animals—along with water and air.

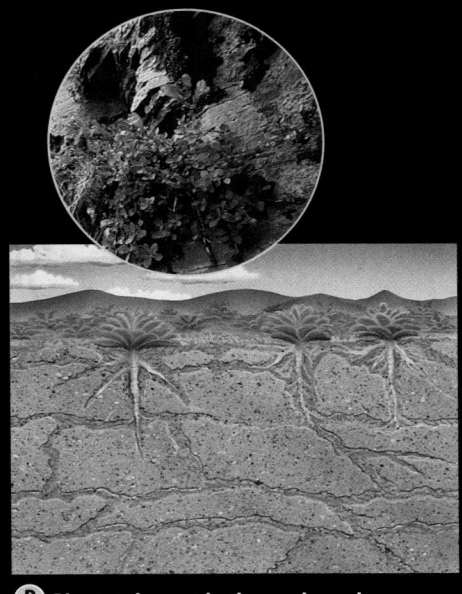

A Natural acids in rainwater weather the surface of exposed bedrock. Water can also freeze in cracks, causing rocks to fracture and break apart. The inset photo shows weathered rock in the Tien Shan Mountains of Central Asia.

B Plants take root in the cracks and among bits of weathered rock—shown in the inset photo above. As they grow, plants, along with other natural forces, continue the process of breaking down rocks, and a thin layer of soil begins to form.

C Like the sand hopper in the inset photo, insects, worms, and other living things take up residence among plant roots. Their wastes, along with dead plant material, add organic matter to the soil.

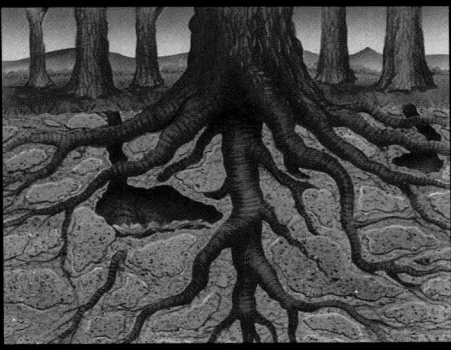

D As organic matter increases and underlying bedrock continues to break down, the soil layer thickens. Rich topsoil supports trees and other plants with large root systems.

191

Visualizing Soil Formation

Have students examine the pictures and read the captions. Then ask the following questions.

What role does water play in each stage of soil formation. It begins the process by weathering the bedrock, then nourishes the plants and animals that continue to break up the rock. Finally, it supports the trees and other organisms that contribute to the thick organic layer of mature soil.

Which type of climate would probably form soil the fastest? All of the processes described would occur fastest in a warm, wet climate, except water freezing in cracks. The easy, year-round growth of plants and animals in tropical climates allows for the quickest soil formation.

Activity

Have students make four pie charts showing their estimates of the relative composition of soil components—weathered rocks/minerals, organic matter, water and air—at each of the pictured stages of soil formation. Call on students to display their charts and discuss their reasoning with the class.

Extension

Challenge students to find out the composition of soils common in their state. Which regions have mature soil, and which regions have less mature soil? Have them speculate on the reasons for this and report their findings to the class.

Resource Manager

Chapter Resources Booklet
Transparency Activity, p. 41
Directed Reading for Content Mastery, p. 17

Performance Assessment in the Science Classroom, p. 44

Mini LAB

Purpose Students compare and contrast soil samples. [L2]

[ELL] [LS] **Interpersonal**

Materials soil samples (60 mL), magnifying glass

Teaching Strategy To ensure variety, have students bring soil samples from home.

Safety Precautions Have students wash their hands after handling soil.

Analysis
1. Students might find small pieces of rock as well as organic matter (pieces of leaves, bark, insect parts, feathers). Living organisms could also be present.
2. All samples should contain particles of weathered rock. Soils differ in particle size, color, and the amount and composition of organic matter.

Assessment

Performance Have students separate soils into three components: rock fragments, humus, and living organisms. Use **Performance Assessment in the Science Classroom,** p. 97.

Reading Check

Answer It serves as nutrients for plants.

Soil Profile

Caption Answer
Figure 11 It is darker because of large amounts of humus and it contains fewer mineral and rock fragments.

Mini LAB

Comparing Components of Soil

Procedure
1. Collect a sample of **soil**.
2. Observe it closely with a **magnifying glass.**

Analysis
1. Describe the different particles found in your sample. Did you find any remains of once-living organisms?
2. Compare and contrast your sample with those other students have collected.

Composition of Soil

As you have seen already, soil is made up of rock and mineral fragments, organic matter, air, and water. The rock and mineral fragments found in soils come from rocks that have been weathered. Most of these fragments are small particles of sediment such as clay, silt, and sand. However, some larger pieces of rock also might be present.

Most organic matter in soil comes from plants. Plant leaves, stems, and roots all contribute organic matter to soil. Animals and microorganisms provide additional organic matter when they die. After plant and animal material gets into soil, fungi and bacteria cause it to decay. The decayed organic matter turns into a dark-colored material called **humus** (HYEW mus). Humus serves as a source of nutrients for plants. As worms, insects, and rodents burrow throughout soil, they mix the humus with the fragments of rock. Good-quality surface soil has about as much humus as weathered rock material.

Reading Check *What does humus do for soil?*

Soil has many small spaces between individual soil particles that are filled with air or water. In swampy areas, water may fill the spaces year-round. In other areas, the spaces in soil are filled mostly with air.

Soil Profile

You have seen layers of soil if you've ever dug a deep hole or driven along a road that has been cut into a hillside. You probably observed that most plant roots grow in the top layer of soil. The top layer typically is darker than the soil layers below it. These different layers of soil are called **horizons.** All the horizons of a soil form a **soil profile.** Most soils have three horizons—labeled A, B, and C, as shown in **Figure 11.**

A Horizon

B Horizon

C Horizon

Figure 11
This soil, which developed beneath a grassy prairie, has three main horizons. *How is the A horizon different from the other two horizons?*

Teacher FYI

In tropical areas, nutrients are held largely in vegetation. When forests are cut, heavy rain quickly washes nutrients from the soil. In just a few years, the soil is often too poor to farm. To survive, people move, cut more forest, and continue the destructive cycle.

Science Journal

Prairie Soils In 1935, Laura Ingalls Wilder wrote *Little House on the Prairie.* In her book, she described life on the prairie in the late 1800s, when families were escaping from the crowded cities of the East by moving west. Ask students to research prairie topography and soil and write a paragraph on why settlers found it desirable. Fertile soils and flat lands were easy to farm. [P]

Horizon A The A horizon is the top layer of soil. In a forest or unplowed area, the A horizon might be covered with litter. **Litter** consists of leaves, twigs, and other organic material that eventually can be changed to humus by decomposing organisms. Litter helps prevent erosion and holds water. The A horizon also is known as topsoil. Topsoil has more humus and fewer rock and mineral particles than the other layers in a soil profile. The A horizon generally is dark and fertile. The dark color of soil is caused by organic material, which provides nutrients for plant growth and development.

Horizon B The layer below the A horizon is the B horizon. Because litter does not add organic matter to this horizon, it is lighter in color than the A horizon and contains less humus. As a result, the B horizon is less fertile. The B horizon contains material moved down from the A horizon by the process of leaching.

Leaching is the removal of minerals that have been dissolved in water. The process of leaching resembles making coffee in a drip coffeemaker. In a coffeemaker, water drips through ground coffee. In soil, water seeps through the A horizon. In a coffeemaker, water absorbs the flavor and color from the coffee and flows into a coffeepot below. In soil, water reacts with humus and carbon dioxide to form acid. The acid dissolves some of the minerals in the A horizon and carries the material into the B horizon, as shown in **Figure 12.**

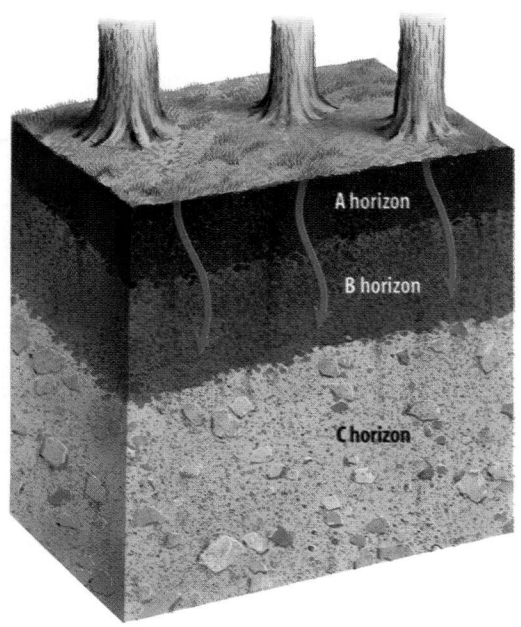

Figure 12
Leaching removes material from the upper layer of soil. Much of this material then is deposited in the B horizon.

☑ **Reading Check** *How does leaching transport material from the A horizon to the B horizon?*

Horizon C The C horizon consists of partially weathered rock and is the bottom horizon in a soil profile. It is often the thickest soil horizon. This horizon does not contain much organic matter and is not strongly affected by leaching. It usually is composed of coarser sediment than the soil horizons above it. What would you find if you dug to the bottom of the C horizon? As you might have guessed, you would find rock—the rock that gave rise to the soil horizons above it. This rock is called the parent material of the soil. The C horizon is the soil layer that is most like the parent material.

Life Science
INTEGRATION

Earthworms in the A horizon swallow sediment to obtain food. These worms then excrete waste into the soil. This material is fertile and helps produce high-quality soil. Do research to find out how other animals affect soil development.

Fun Fact

In 1 g of soil, there can be hundreds of millions of organisms.

Discussion

If you could remove soil from the C horizon, would it be useful for growing plants? Explain. No; it consists of rock that is only partially weathered and very little humus.

Quick Demo

Secure a coffee filter to the top of a beaker with a rubber band. Place soil into the filter and pour water through it. Have students examine the water that drips into the beaker and relate what they see to the leaching process in soil. ▥ **Visual-Spatial**

☑ **Reading Check**

Answer Acid carries minerals from the A horizon to the B horizon.

Life Science
INTEGRATION

Burrowing mammals such as ground squirrels and groundhogs mix soil and push loosened sediments to the surface, where the sediments are further exposed to weathering. Ants carry litter below ground as they dig tunnels. During tunneling, soil is mixed and air flow is increased. Ant excretions also become humus.

Resource Manager

Chapter Resources Booklet
  MiniLAB, p. 4
  Enrichment, p. 27
Life Science Critical Thinking/Problem Solving, p. 22

Teacher FYI

The concept of leaching is important in constructing landfills. Leaching of toxic materials in hazardous wastes must be controlled so that dangerous chemicals do not enter soil or water outside the landfill. Using leachate collection techniques or landfill liners usually prevents this problem.

Soil Profile, continued

Text Question Answer

The composition of soil in the A and possibly B horizons would be different from that of the parent material in the C horizon; it is material moved from elsewhere by the glacier.

Extension

Have interested students contact the local department of Sanitation or Public Works for information on what should be included in a compost pile. Encourage them to make a class compost pile, and to use the compost to enrich a school garden plot. L2 ELL COOP LEARN **LS Kinesthetic**

Math Skills Activity

National Math Standards

Correlation to Mathematics Objectives

1, 2, 5, 6, 9, 10

Answer to Practice Problem

- What you know: sand weight: 30g clay weight: 30g silt weight: 15g
- You need to find: total weight of sample percentage of silt
- Use equations on student page.
- 30 1 30 1 15 5 75g
- 15g/75g 5 0.2
- 20% silt

Glacial Deposits At many places on Earth, the land is covered by material that was deposited by glaciers. This unsorted mass of clay, silt, sand, and boulders covers much of the United States, creating, for example, the flat landscapes of the Midwest. The soils that developed on this glacial material are extremely fertile and are an important part of the Midwest's agricultural industry. How does this soil profile differ from the one described earlier? If you were to dig through the C horizon, you would find bedrock as before, but it would not be the rock the soil formed from. What material did this soil develop from?

Math Skills Activity

Calculating Percentages of Soil Particles

The properties of soil, such as the ability to hold water, are determined by the abundances of different types of particles. Therefore, it is important to determine particle percentages in soils.

Sample Problem

The circle graph represents a soil sample containing particles of clay, silt, and sand. Determine what percentage of the sample is clay.

(Circle graph labeled: 20 g Sand particles; 15 g Clay particles; 15 g Silt particles)

1 *This is what you know:*

sand weight: 20 g
clay weight: 15 g
silt weight: 15 g

2 *This is what you need to find:*

total weight of the sample
percentage of clay particles

3 *These are the equations you need to use:*

sand weight + clay weight + silt weight = total weight
decimal equivalent of percentage = clay weight/total weight
decimal equivalent of percentage $\times$ 100 = percentage of clay

4 *Solve for the total weight:* 20 g + 15 g + 15 g = 50 g

5 *Solve for the decimal equivalent of percentage:* 15 g/50 g = 0.3

6 *Solve for the percentage of particle type:* $0.3 \times 100 = 30\%$ clay particles

Practice Problem

A second soil sample is taken that contains 30 g of sand, 30 g of clay, and 15 g of silt. What percentage of the entire soil sample is silt? Draw a circle graph for this sample.

For more help, refer to the Math Skill Handbook.

194 CHAPTER 7 Weathering and Soil

LAB DEMONSTRATION

Purpose to make a soil profile model

Materials 250 mL beakers (4), coarse gravel, pea gravel, topsoil, mixture of light-colored sand and clay, large graduated cylinder

Preparation Fill each beaker with a different soil component.

Procedure Layer soil components into the cylinder to show the order of sediments from bottom to top in a normal soil profile: coarse gravel, pea gravel, sand and clay mixture, topsoil.

Expected Outcome Students will observe a soil profile.

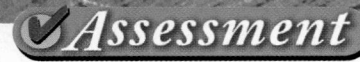
Assessment

What does each layer represent? coarse gravel: bedrock; pea gravel: C horizon; sand and clay: B horizon; topsoil: A horizon

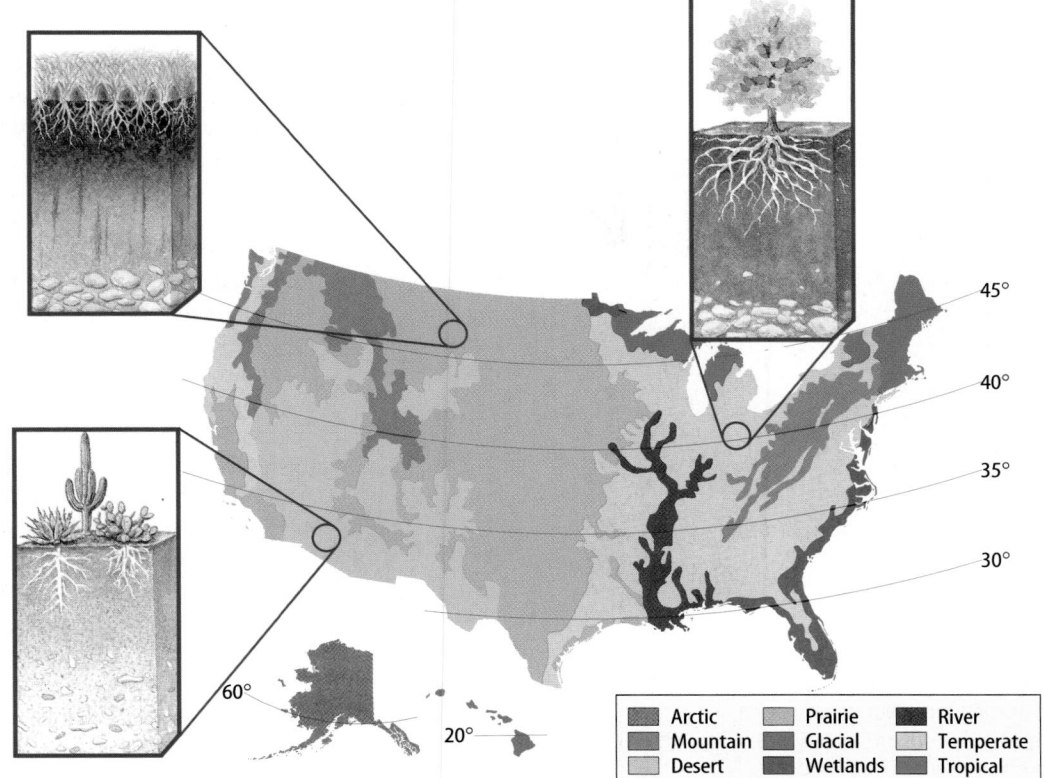

■ Arctic	■ Prairie	■ River
■ Mountain	■ Glacial	■ Temperate
■ Desert	■ Wetlands	■ Tropical

Soil Types

If you travel across the country and look at soils, you will notice that they are not all the same. Some soils are thick and red, some are brown with hard, rounded rock nodules, and some have thick, black A horizons. Many different types of soils exist, as shown in **Figure 13.**

Soil Types Reflect Climate Different regions on Earth have different climates. Deserts are dry, prairies are semidry, and temperate forests are mild and moist. These places also have different types of soils. Soils in deserts contain little organic material and also are thinner than soil horizons in wetter climates. Prairie soils have thick, dark A horizons because the grasses that grow there contribute lots of organic matter. Temperate forest soils have thinner A horizons and B horizons that have been enriched in many elements because of leaching. The abundant rainfall in forests promotes leaching. Other regions such as tundra and tropical areas also have distinct soils.

Figure 13
The United States has nine different soil types. They vary in color, depth, texture, and fertility.

SECTION 2 The Nature of Soil **195**

Section 2 The Nature of Soil **195**

Soil Types

Visual Learning

Figure 13 Have students use the map to identify the type of soil found in your region. Answers will vary.

Activity

Have students determine how soil type affects plant growth. Have them plant three identical plants in various soils, observe and record growth data, and present their findings as a bar graph. L2 IS **Naturalist**

IDENTIFYING Misconceptions

Students may think that the lack of water in dry environments would lead to fertile soils, since humus would not be washed away. Explain that dry climates have fewer organisms to add organic matter to the soil as they die. Also, organic matter decomposes more slowly in dry climates.

Resource Manager

Chapter Resources Booklet
  Reinforcement, p. 24
  Transparency Activity, pp. 43–45
Mathematics Skill Activities, p. 1

Inclusion Strategies

Gifted Have students collect soils from around your area to compare and contrast. Then have a farmer, soil analyst, or agriculture consultant come to class and talk about local soils. Have the person discuss how different soils affect crop or garden yields. L3 IS **Naturalist**

Caption Answer

Figure 14 Sediments move downhill and collect in valleys.

③ Assess

Reteach

Take students to an area near the school where they can examine an exposed soil profile. Badly eroded gullies, road cuts, and steep slopes are good places to observe soil horizons. Ask students to identify as many soil horizons as possible. L2
IS Visual-Spatial

Challenge

Why are sediments in the A horizon usually smaller than those in the B and C horizons? They usually have been exposed to more weathering. **What might cause weathering in the C horizon?** Tree roots, water, and dissolved acids leaching down from the A and B horizons, or anything else that might reach deep into the ground.

✔Assessment

Performance Have students make an events chain concept map to show how materials in the A horizon leach into the B horizon. Use **Performance Assessment in the Science Classroom,** p. 163.

Figure 14
The slope of the land affects soil development. Thin, poorly developed soils form on steep slopes, but valleys often have thick, well-developed soils. *Why is this so?*

Other Factors Parent rock has a strong effect on the soils that develop from it. Clay soils often develop on rocks like basalt, because minerals in the rock weather to clay. What type of soil do you think might develop on sandstone? Rock type also can affect the type of vegetation that grows in a region, because different rocks provide different nutrients for plant growth. Type of vegetation then affects soil formation.

Time also affects soil development. If weathering has been occurring for only a short time, the parent rock determines the soil characteristics. As weathering continues, the soil resembles the parent rock less and less.

Slope also is a factor affecting soil profiles as shown in **Figure 14.** On steep slopes, soil horizons often are poorly developed, because material moves downhill before it can be weathered much. In bottomlands, sediments and water are plentiful. Bottomland soils are often thick, dark, and full of organic material.

Section ② Assessment

1. List five factors that affect soil development.

2. Why do soil profiles contain layers or horizons?

3. How do organisms help soils develop dark A horizons?

4. How does horizon B differ from horizon A and horizon C?

5. **Think Critically** Why is the soil profile in a tropical rain forest different from one in a desert?

Skill Builder Activities

6. **Concept Mapping** Make an events chain concept map that explains how soil develops. **For more help, refer to the** Science Skill Handbook.

7. **Using Statistics** A farmer collected five soil samples from a field and tested their acidity or pH. His data were the following: 7.5, 8.2, 7.7, 8.1, and 8.0. Calculate the mean of these data. Also, determine the range and median. **For more help, refer to the** Math Skill Handbook.

Answers to Section Assessment

1. climate, slope, type of rock, type of vegetation, length of time for weathering
2. At different depths, sediments are exposed to different amounts of weathering and leaching, and accumulate different amounts of humus.
3. Decaying organisms add organic matter.

4. B is lighter in color, has larger particles, and contains less humus than A; B has smaller sediments and contains more leached minerals than C.
5. Deserts and rain forests have different types of vegetation and different climates, causing different amounts of humus to form and weathering to occur.

6. Rock is weathered. ➞ Plants grow. ➞ Worms and insects move in. ➞ Humus develops. ➞ Humus mixes with weathered rock. ➞ Soil is formed.
7. Mean = 7.9
Range = 8.2 − 7.5 = .7
Median = 8.0

Activity

Soil Characteristics

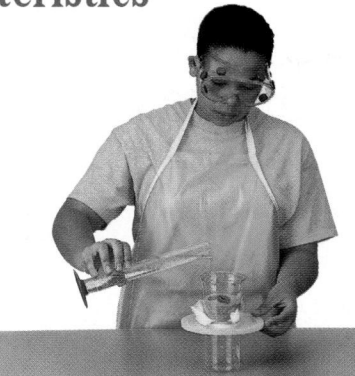

You've probably noticed a number of different types of soils. Collect samples of soil to compare from around your neighborhood and from designated areas of your school grounds.

What You'll Investigate
What are the characteristics of soils?

Materials
soil sample	water
cheesecloth squares	250-mL beakers (3)
sand	watch
100-mL graduated cylinder	large polystyrene or plastic cups (3)
gravel	pie pans
plastic coffee-can lids (3)	hand lens
clay	scissors
rubber bands (3)	thumbtack

Goals
- **Analyze** permeability of different soils.

Safety Precautions
🤚 🐾 🗑

WARNING: *Use care when punching holes in the bottom of the cups with the thumbtack.*

Procedure

1. Spread the soil sample in a pie pan.
2. **Describe** the color of the soil and examine the soil with a hand lens. Describe the different particles.
3. Rub a small amount of soil between your fingers. Describe how it feels. Also, press the soil sample together. Does it stick together? Wet the sample and try this again. Record all your observations.

4. **Test** the soil to see how water moves through it. Label the three cups A, B, and C. Using a thumbtack, punch ten holes in and around the bottom of each cup.
5. Cover the area of holes with a square of cheesecloth and secure with a rubber band.
6. To hold the cups over the beakers, cut the three coffee-can lids so that the cups will just fit inside the hole (see photo). Place a cup and lid over each beaker.
7. Fill cup A halfway with dry sand and cup B halfway with clay. Fill cup C halfway with a mixture of equal parts of sand, gravel, and clay.
8. Use the graduated cylinder to pour 100 mL of water into each cup. Record the time when the water is first poured into each cup and when the water first drips from each cup.
9. Allow the water to drip for 25 min, then measure and record the amount of water in each beaker.

Conclude and Apply

1. How does the addition of gravel and sand affect the permeability of clay?
2. **Describe** three characteristics of soil. Which characteristics affect permeability?

ACTIVITY 197

---

*C*ommunicating Your Data

Ask students to compare their data tables with one another. Discuss the different designs chosen by the students, as well as any differences in results of the investigation.

Activity

BENCH TESTED

Purpose Students compare and contrast different soils. [L2] [ELL] [COOP LEARN] [IS] **Kinesthetic**

Process Skills observing and inferring, comparing and contrasting, communicating, manipulating variables, interpreting data

Time Required two class periods

Safety Precautions Caution students to be careful when putting holes in the cups. Students should wash hands after handling soil.

Teaching Strategy Have students work in pairs. Encourage each student to do step 3.

Troubleshooting To control variables, students must punch the same number of holes in each cup. Cheesecloth must be tightly secured.

Answers to Questions
1. It increases permeability.
2. Possible answers: color, types of particles, type and amount of organic matter, texture, and permeability; size and type of particles and percentage of organic matter affect permeability.

✓ *Assessment*

Portfolio Have students design tables to display their data and add these tables to their portfolios. Use **Performance Assessment in the Science Classroom,** p. 109.

SECTION
3
Soil Erosion

1 Motivate

Bellringer Transparency

Display the Section Focus Transparency for Section 3. Use the accompanying Transparency Activity Master. L2

ELL

Tie to Prior Knowledge

Have students list ways humans use soil. Possible answers: grow food and other plants, make structures with materials such as adobe Inform students that they will learn about the importance of soil and the problems of preserving soil in this section.

SECTION
3
Soil Erosion

As You Read

What You'll Learn
- **Explain** why soil is important.
- **Identify** human activities that lead to soil loss.
- **Describe** ways to reduce soil loss.

Vocabulary
terracing

Why It's Important
If topsoil is eroded, soil becomes much less fertile.

Figure 15
Removing vegetation can lead to severe soil erosion. **A** Trees protect the soil from erosion in this forested region. **B** When forest is removed, soil erodes rapidly.

Soil—An Important Resource

While picnicking at a local park, a flash of lightning and a clap of thunder tell you that a storm is upon you. Watching the pounding rain from the park shelter, you notice that the water flowing off of the ball diamond is muddy, not clear. The flowing water is carrying away some of the soil that used to be on the field. This process is called soil erosion. Soil erosion is harmful because plants do not grow as well when topsoil has been lost.

Causes and Effects of Soil Erosion

Soil is eroded when it is moved from the place where it formed. Erosion occurs when water flows along Earth's surface or when wind picks up and transports sediments. Generally, erosion is more common on steep slopes than on gentle slopes. It's also more common in areas where there is little vegetation. Under normal conditions, a balance between soil production and soil erosion often is maintained. This means that soil forms at about the same rate as it is eroded. However, when vegetation is removed or slopes are steepened, soil erodes much faster than it can be produced. Many human activities result in the removal of vegetation and the steepening of slopes, as shown in **Figure 15.** Some of these activities are described in this section.

A

B

198 CHAPTER 7 Weathering and Soil

Section ✓Assessment Planner

PORTFOLIO
Extension, p. 200
PERFORMANCE ASSESSMENT
Skill Builder Activities, p. 201
See page 208 for more options.

CONTENT ASSESSMENT
Section, p. 201
Challenge, p. 201
Chapter, pp. 208–209

Figure 16
Tropical rain forests often are cleared by burning. *How can this increase soil erosion?*

Agricultural Cultivation Did you know that the population of Earth increases by nearly 95 million people every year? More people means that more food is needed. This has led to increased use of farmable land and to rapid soil erosion in many places. Plowing mechanically turns and loosens the soil, improving it for crops. However, this practice also removes the plant cover that holds soil particles in place, leaving soils vulnerable to wind and water erosion. Over time, this practice can reduce soil quality.

Forest Harvesting When forests are removed, soil is exposed and erosion increases. This creates severe problems in many parts of the world, but tropical regions are especially at risk. Each year, thousands of square kilometers of tropical rain forest are cleared for lumber, farming, and grazing, as shown in **Figure 16.** Soils in tropical rain forests appear rich in nutrients but are almost infertile below the first few centimeters. The soil is useful to farmers for only a few years before the nutrients are gone. Farmers then clear new land, repeating the process and increasing the damage to the soil.

Overgrazing In most places, land can be grazed with little damage to soil. However, overgrazing can increase soil erosion. In some arid regions of the world, sheep and cattle raised for food are grazed on grasses until almost no ground cover remains to protect the soil. When natural vegetation is removed from land that receives little rain, plants are slow to grow back. Without protection, soil is carried away by wind, and the moisture in the soil evaporates.

 **Reading Check** *How does overgrazing affect soil?*

 Physics INTEGRATION

Rain falling on farm fields can be an important agent of erosion. The erosive force of rain depends on how much rain falls and on how hard the rain falls. What type of rains do you think would have the most energy to erode soil?

Research Visit the Glencoe Science Web site at **science.glencoe.com** for information on soil erosion research and how this research can benefit the environment. Communicate to your class what you learn.

Causes and Effects of Soil Erosion

Reading Check

Answer It increases erosion.

Visual Learning

Figure 15 **Where is the soil that once covered this area?** It is now deposited elsewhere. Runoff carried it to streams and winds blew it to other locations.

Caption Answer
Figure 16 Burning removes the cover of vegetation, exposing the soil to erosion by wind and flowing water.

Physics INTEGRATION

Possible answer: torrential rain that falls for many hours

Activity
Take students to an area on the school grounds where soil is eroding. Have students write suggestions to the principal for solving the problem. With permission, organize students to carry out the plan. [L2]
Logical-Mathematical

Internet Addresses

_____
_____
_____
_____

Explore the Glencoe Science Web site at **science.glencoe.com** to find out more about topics in this section.

Resource Manager

Chapter Resources Booklet
Transparency Activity, p. 42
Directed Reading for Content Mastery, pp. 17, 18
Enrichment, p. 28

Active Reading

Quickwrites This strategy, sometimes called freewrites, lets students use spontaneous writing to discover what they already know. Have students write a list of ideas about a topic, then share these ideas with the class. Next, have students write their ideas freely in a paragraph without worrying about punctuation, spelling, and grammar. Have students use a Quickwrite to share ideas after learning about soil erosion.

**Causes and Effects
of Soil Erosion,**

continued

Caption Answer

Figure 17 It could cover stream-dwelling organisms and eggs, clog the stream, or reduce downstream water quality.

**Preventing Soil
Erosion**

Teacher FYI

Soil is eroding on cultivated land in the United States about 16 times faster than it can form. In fact, the amount of topsoil eroded each day in the U.S. would fill a row of dump trucks 9,000 kilometers (5,600 miles) long.

Extension

Have students research how soil farms could be used to make soils naturally and artificially. Have them write a brief report on their findings. L3 IS **Linguistic** P

✔ Reading Check

Answer They can plant shelter belts of trees, cover bare soils with decaying plants, graze animals on vegetation instead of plowing it under, or use no-till farming.

Figure 17
Erosion from exposed land can cause streams to fill with excessive amounts of sediment. *How could this damage streams?*

Figure 18
No-till farming helps prevent soil erosion because fields are not plowed before planting.

Urban Construction Each year in the United States, about 6,100 km^2 of land are developed for roadways and other structures. You've probably noticed that when construction takes place, land is cleared of vegetation and soil is moved. During the construction process, water and wind erode soils. Areas that have been strip mined also are susceptible to soil erosion. Eroded soil can enter streams, causing them to fill up with sediment, as shown in **Figure 17.**

Preventing Soil Erosion

Each year more than 4 billion metric tons of soil are eroded in the United States. Soil is a resource that must be managed and protected. People can do several things to conserve soil.

Manage Crops All over the world, farmers work to slow down soil erosion. They plant shelter belts of trees to break the force of the wind and cover bare soils with decaying plants to hold soil particles in place. In dry areas, instead of plowing under vegetation, many farmers graze animals on the vegetation. Proper grazing management can maintain vegetation and reduce soil erosion.

In recent years, many farmers have begun to practice no-till farming. Normally, farmers till or plow their fields one or more times each year. In no-till farming, seen in **Figure 18,** plant stalks are left in the field over the winter months. At the next planting, farmers seed crops without destroying these stalks and without plowing the soil. No-till farming provides cover for the soil year-round, which reduces water runoff and slows soil erosion. The leftover stalks also keep weeds from growing in the fields.

✔ Reading Check *How can farmers reduce soil erosion?*

Cultural Diversity

Managing with Stones In Burkina Faso, farmers line fields with stones to keep soil from blowing away. They also build centimeter-high rock dams that direct water into the ground instead of across it. As a result of these practices, crop yields have increased as much as 90 percent. Have students use an atlas to locate Burkina Faso. Burkina Faso is a landlocked state in western Africa.

Resource Manager

Chapter Resources Booklet
  Reinforcement, p. 25
  Activity Worksheet, pp. 7–8
Lab Management and Safety, p. 65

Reduce Erosion on Slopes On gentle slopes, planting along the natural contours of the land, as in **Figure 19,** helps reduce soil erosion. This practice, called contour farming, slows the flow of water down the slope and helps prevent the formation of gullies.

Where slopes are steep, terracing often is used. **Terracing** (TER uh sing) is a method in which steep-sided, level topped areas are built onto the sides of steep hills and mountains so that crops can be grown. These terraces reduce runoff by creating flat areas and shorter sections of slope. In the Philippines, Japan, China, and Peru, terraces have been used for centuries.

Figure 19
This orchard was planted along the natural contours of the land.
Why was this done?

Reduce Erosion at Construction Sites A variety of methods are used at construction sites to help reduce erosion. During the construction process, exposed ground sometimes is covered with mulch, mats, or plastic coverings. Water is sprayed onto bare soil to prevent erosion by wind. When construction is complete, topsoil is added in areas where it was removed and trees are planted. Some areas are sodded, but if an area is to be seeded, soil is reinforced using netting and straw. Netting and straw make the surface layer more stable, which allows plant seeds to germinate quickly and vegetation to uniformly cover any slopes. Along steeper slopes, retaining walls made of concrete, stones, or wood keep soil and rocks from sliding downhill.

Section 3 Assessment

1. Why is soil important?
2. Why does soil erosion increase when soil is plowed?
3. How can urban construction cause soil erosion?
4. What are two ways erosion can be reduced at construction sites?
5. **Think Critically** How can contour farming help water soak into the ground?

Skill Builder Activities

6. **Recognizing Cause and Effect** Explain how soil erosion contributes to pollution of streams and lakes. **For more help, refer to the** Science Skill Handbook.
7. **Communicating** In your Science Journal, write a poem about the causes and effects of soil erosion. **For more help, refer to the** Science Skill Handbook.

3 Assess

Reteach

Have students in small groups work together to sketch the school yard, noting the locations of all buildings, parking lots, sidewalks, paths, and athletic fields. Ask each group to estimate how the activities on one of these areas of land are affecting the soil. L2 COOP LEARN

Challenge

Have students research and report on the problem of soil erosion in your state. How much is occurring? How does it affect the state's economy? What is being done to combat the problem? L3

✔Assessment

Process Have students make a spider concept map showing the ways people can prevent soil erosion. Use **Performance Assessment in the Science Classroom,** p. 161.

Answers to Section Assessment

1. It is necessary for growing plants.
2. Plowing removes plants and loosens soil, making it easy for water and wind to erode it.
3. Land is cleared of vegetation, increasing erosion.
4. During construction: exposed land can be covered with mulch, mats, or plastic; water can be sprayed onto bare soil. After construction: topsoil can be added and sod and trees can be planted; retaining walls can be built.
5. Contour farming slows water flow, allowing the water time to soak into the ground.
6. Sediments that wash off the land and into streams choke organisms and clog streams and lakes.
7. Poems can also include information on how to reduce soil erosion.

Activity
Design Your Own Experiment

Recognize the Problem

Purpose
Students design and carry out an experiment to study variables that affect chemical weathering.

L2 ELL COOP LEARN

IS Interpersonal P

Process Skills
communicating, forming a hypothesis, designing an experiment to test a hypothesis, identifying and manipulating variables, observing and inferring, relating cause and effect, interpreting data, recording, using numbers, making and using graphs

Time Required
45 minutes to plan, 45 minutes to do the experiment

Materials
If materials are in short supply, place one or two sets of materials in a corner of the classroom. Have groups take turns completing the activity.

Alternate Materials
Two 8-ounce plastic cups can be substituted for the beakers.

Safety Precautions
Caution students to take care with the hot plate and heated vinegar. Tie back long hair.

Form a Hypothesis

Possible Hypotheses
Students will probably expect chalk to dissolve faster if exposed to vinegar and heat. They will probably also expect smaller pieces (more surface area) to dissolve faster than larger pieces.

Weathering Chalk

Chalk is a type of limestone made of the shells of microscopic organisms. The famous White Cliffs of Dover, England, are made up of chalk. This experiment will help you understand how chalk can be chemically weathered.

Recognize the Problem
How can you simulate chemical weathering of chalk? What variables affect the rate of chemical weathering?

Form a Hypothesis
How do you think acidity, surface area, and temperature affect the rate of chemical weathering of chalk? What happens to chalk in water or acid (vinegar)? How will the size of the chalk pieces affect the rate of weathering? What will happen if you heat the acid? Make hypotheses to support your ideas.

Possible Materials
equal-sized pieces of chalk (6)
small beakers or clear plastic cups (2)
metric ruler
water
white vinegar (100 mL)
hot plate
250-mL graduated cylinder
computer probe for temperature

Goals
- **Design** experiments to compare the effects of acidity, surface area, and temperature on the rate of chemical weathering of chalk.
- **Describe** factors that affect chemical weathering.
- **Explain** how the chemical weathering of chalk is similar to the chemical weathering of rocks.
- **Describe** how the factors used in this experiment apply to different parts of the world.

Safety Precautions
Wear safety goggles when pouring acids. Be careful when using a hot plate and heated solutions.
WARNING: *If mixing liquids, always add acid to water.*

Sample Data Table:

Test	Observations
Acid Test Chalk in Water	no reaction
Chalk in Vinegar	some reaction bubbles
Surface Area Test Whole Chalk	some reaction
Broken Chalk	more reaction than whole
Temperature Test Room Temperature Vinegar	some reaction
Warm Vinegar	more reaction than cooler

Test Your Hypothesis

Plan

1. **Develop** hypotheses about the effects of acidity, surface area, and temperature on the rate of chemical weathering.
2. **Decide** how to test your first hypothesis. List the steps needed to test the hypothesis.
3. Repeat step 2 for your other two hypotheses.
4. **Design** data tables in your Science Journal. Make one for acidity, one for surface area, and one for temperature.
5. **Identify** what remains constant in your experiment and what varies. Each test should have only one variable being tested. Determine the control for each experiment.

6. **Summarize** your data in a graph. Decide from reading the **Science Skill Handbook** which type of graph to use.

Do

1. Make sure your teacher approves your plan before you start.
2. Carry out the three experiments as planned.
3. While you are conducting the experiments, record your observations and complete the data tables in your Science Journal.
4. Graph your data to show how each variable affected the rate of weathering.

Analyze Your Data

1. **Analyze** your graph to find out which substance—water or acid—weathered the chalk more quickly. Was your hypothesis supported by your data?

2. **Infer** from your data whether the amount of surface area makes a difference in the rate of chemical weathering. Explain.

Draw Conclusions

1. **Explain** how the chalk was chemically weathered.
2. How does heat affect the rate of chemical weathering?
3. What does this imply about weathering in the tropics and in polar regions?

Communicating Your Data

Compare your results with those of your classmates. How were your data similar? How were they different? **For more help, refer to the** Science Skill Handbook.

ACTIVITY 203

Communicating Your Data

Exact data will vary, but all students should have similar results.

Test Your Hypotheses

Possible Procedures

Acidity test: Place equal-sized pieces of chalk into beakers of water and vinegar. Surface area test: Place a whole piece of chalk into a beaker and an equal-sized piece that is broken into pieces into a second beaker. Pour vinegar into both beakers. Temperature test: Place equal-sized pieces of chalk into room-temperature vinegar and heated vinegar.

Teaching Strategy

Explain that the settling of chalk flakes is not evidence of chemical weathering.

Expected Outcome

Water has no effect on chalk. Chalk bubbles and reacts with vinegar. Small chalk pieces react faster. Heated acid causes a faster reaction.

Analyze Your Data

1. Acid; answers will vary.
2. The greater the surface area, the faster the weathering because there is more contact with the acid.

Error Analysis

Age and concentration of vinegar can affect results, as can the number of pieces into which chalk is broken.

Draw Conclusions

1. Minerals in the chalk reacted with vinegar.
2. Heat increases the rate.
3. Chemical weathering is faster in the tropics and slower in polar regions.

Landscape, History, and the Pueblo Imagination
by Leslie Marmon Silko

In their science journals have students write their own observations about the Earth's soil. For example, if students have done gardening with parents or family members, ask them what they noticed to be distinguishing features about the Earth's soil. Some examples of questions to ask are: **What was the temperature of the soil? What was the soil composed of? Do you think the composition of the soil would have been different if you lived in a different part of the country? If so, why?**

Respond to the Reading

Active Reading Strategies

Visualize Keep the events and setting in your mind's eye as you read. Form pictures in your mind. Ask yourself questions as you read. For example, where do you picture the scene Silko is portraying? What part of the country do you visualize?

Review Review what you have read. By looking back over several paragraphs, you can see how the information fits together. Is the author using a particular writing style to make a point?

Answers to Questions
1. dust
2. Answers will vary but might suggest that repeating the word *dust* reminds the reader of how all living things return to the earth.

Respond to the Reading

1. What one word is repeated throughout this passage?
2. What effect does the repetition of this word have on the reader?

In this excerpt, Leslie Marmon Silko, a woman of Pueblo, Hispanic, and American heritage, explains what ancient Pueblo people believed about the circle of life on Earth.

You see that after a thing is dead, it dries up. It might take weeks or years, but eventually if you touch the thing, it crumbles under your fingers. It goes back to dust. The soul of the thing has long since departed. With the plants and wild game the soul may have already been borne back into bones and blood or thick green stalk and leaves. Nothing is wasted. What cannot be eaten by people or in some way used must then be left where other living creatures may benefit. What domestic animals or wild scavengers can't eat will be fed to the plants. The plants feed on the dust of these few remains.

. . . Corn cobs and husks, the rinds and stalks and animal bones were not regarded by the ancient people as filth or garbage. The remains were merely resting at a midpoint in their journey back to dust. . . .

The dead become dust . . . . The ancient Pueblo people called the earth the Mother Creator of all things in this world. Her sister, the Corn mother, occasionally merges with her because all . . . green life rises out of the depths of the earth.

Rocks and clay . . . become what they once were. Dust.

A rock shares this fate with us and with animals and plants as well.

Reading Further

Ceremony, by Leslie Marmon Silko, Viking Penguin, 1996.

Gardens in the Dunes, by Leslie Marmon Silko, Simon and Schuster, 2000.

Understanding Literature

Repetition Many authors use repetition as a literary tool. Repetition is the recurrence of sounds, words, or phrases in a piece of writing. Poets often use repetition to give their poems a particular rhythm. In Silko's passage above, she repeatedly uses the word *dust*. This repetition reminds the reader of the common link between rocks, clay, plants, and animals. Also, it gives this passage a storytelling quality that makes the reader feel like he or she is reading a myth or legend instead of a work of nonfiction.

Science Connection In this chapter, you learned how weathered rocks and mineral fragments combine with organic matter to make soil. Silko's writing explains how the ancient Pueblo people understood that all living matter returns to the earth, or becomes dust. Lines such as "green life rises out of the depths of the earth," show that the Pueblo people understood that the earth, or rocks and mineral fragments, must combine with living matter in order to make soil and support plant life. Are there other ways in which your scientific understanding of the formation of soil is similar to the ancient Pueblo beliefs outlined in Silko's writing?

Linking Science and Writing

Using Repetition Write a one-page, how-to paper for your classmates on a type of soil conservation practice. For instance, the subject can be no-till agriculture, strip-cropping, or contour plowing. Use repetition as a tool to remind your readers of important steps in the process.

Career Connection

Soil Scientist

Elvia Niebla works for the U.S. Environmental Protection Agency (EPA) studying soil and soil pollution. Soil scientists explain how people can use soil effectively. They develop plans that keep people from contaminating soil and that keep soil from eroding. Niebla's research has even helped keep hamburger safe to eat. How? In a report for the EPA, she explained how meat could be contaminated when cows graze on contaminated soil. She is now the National Coordinator of the Global Change Research Program.

SCIENCE *Online* To learn more about careers in soil science, visit the Glencoe Science Web site at **science.glencoe.com**.

SCIENCE AND LANGUAGE ARTS 205

Understanding Literature

Answer to Questions

Answers will vary but should include that one of the weathering factors of soil formation mentioned in the text was also referred to in the Silko passage.

Science Connection

Pedology is the scientific discipline concerned with all aspects of soils, including their physical and chemical properties, the role of organisms in soil production and in relation to soil character, the description and mapping of soil units, and the origin and formation of soils. Accordingly, pedology embraces several sub-disciplines, namely, soil chemistry, soil physics and soil microbiology.

Linking Science and Writing

Writing Strategies

Lead students in a brainstorming activity about what they might like to write about in using the technique of repetition as this activity suggests. Remind the students that a how-to paper should be about something they know very well. A goal for this activity would be to impart new knowledge about a subject.

Career Connection

Other professionals involved in the process of soil conservation include agronomists as well as agricultural engineers. Both careers involve the development of agriculture by using science in harmony with the environment and human activity.

Internet Addresses

_____
_____
_____

Explore the Glencoe Science Web site at **science.glencoe.com** to find out more about topics in this feature.

Reviewing Main Ideas

Preview

Students can answer the questions in their Science Journals. Discuss the answers as you go through the chapter. **IS Linguistic**

Review

Students can write their answers, then compare them with those of other students. **IS Interpersonal**

Reteach

Students can look at the illustrations and describe details that support the main ideas of the chapter. **IS Visual-Spatial**

Answers to Chapter Review

SECTION 1

1. As it burrows, it loosens sediments and pushes them to the surface where they are exposed to more weathering.

SECTION 2

2. They add organic matter to soil when they decompose.

SECTION 3

2. It holds soil in place so that erosion by wind and water is minimized.

Reviewing Main Ideas

Section 1 Weathering

1. Mechanical weathering breaks apart rock without changing its chemical composition. Plants, animals, and ice wedging are important agents of mechanical weathering. *How can this prairie dog weather rock?*

2. Chemical weathering changes the composition of rocks. Acidic water can dissolve rock or certain minerals within a rock. Some plants cause chemical weathering by secreting acids. Exposure to oxygen causes some rocks to weather, forming rustlike minerals.

Section 2 The Nature of Soil

1. Soil is a mixture of rock and mineral fragments, organic matter, air, and water.

2. Soil develops as rock is weathered and organic matter is added by organisms. Soil has horizons that differ in their color and composition. *How could the plants in the photo help soil develop?*

3. Climate, parent rock, slope of the land, type of vegetation, and the time that rock has been weathering affect the development of soil and cause different soils to have different characteristics.

Section 3 Soil Erosion

1. Soil is eroded when it is transported by wind and water. Erosion is more common on steep slopes and in areas where there is no ground cover.

2. Human activities like plowing, harvesting forests, overgrazing animals, and construction can increase soil erosion. *How does this netting help reduce soil erosion?*

3. Windbreaks, no-till farming, contour planting, and terracing help reduce soil erosion in farm fields. The best way to reduce soil erosion at construction sites is to replace vegetation quickly.

FOLDABLES Reading & Study Skills **After You Read**

To help you review the vocabulary words, use the Foldable you made at the beginning of the chapter.

FOLDABLES Reading & Study Skills **After You Read**

After students have read the chapter and completed the Foldable described in Before You Read, have them do the activity on the student page.

Dinah Zike

Visualizing Main Ideas

Complete the following concept map on weathering.

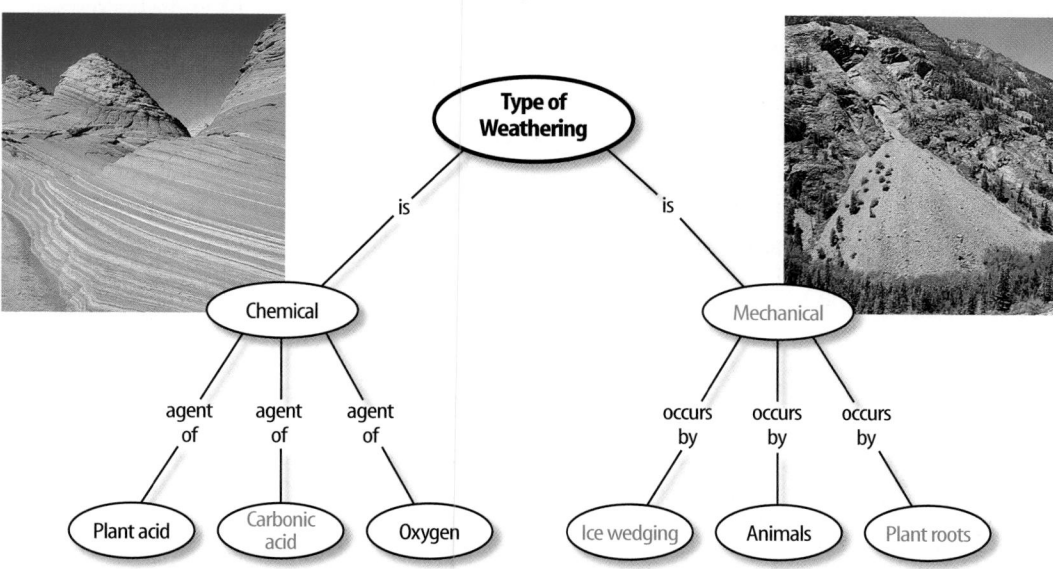

Visualizing Main Ideas

See student page.

Vocabulary Review

Using Vocabulary

1. <u>Chemical weathering</u> causes a change in a rock's composition.
2. <u>Humus</u> forms from organic matter such as leaves and roots.
3. The A, B, and C layers of a soil make up the <u>soil profile</u>.
4. <u>Leaching</u> transports materials to the B horizon.
5. <u>Oxidation</u> occurs when many materials containing iron are exposed to air and water.

Vocabulary Review

Vocabulary Words

a. chemical weathering
b. climate
c. horizon
d. humus
e. ice wedging
f. leaching
g. litter
h. mechanical weathering
i. oxidation
j. soil
k. soil profile
l. terracing
m. weathering

THE PRINCETON REVIEW

Study Tip

Make flashcards for new vocabulary words. Put the word on one side and the definition on the other. Use them to quiz yourself.

Using Vocabulary

The sentences below include vocabulary words that have been used incorrectly. Change the incorrect vocabulary words so that the sentence reads correctly. Underline your change.

1. Mechanical weathering causes a change in a rock's composition.

2. Leaching forms from organic matter such as leaves and roots.

3. The A, B, and C layers of a soil make up the soil horizon.

4. Ice wedging transports materials to the B horizon.

5. Litter occurs when many materials containing iron are exposed to oxygen and water.

CHAPTER STUDY GUIDE   207

⬦ IDENTIFYING ▷ Misconceptions

Assess

Use this assessment as follow-up to page 182F after students have completed the chapter.

Materials a copy of the National Climatic Data Center Climate Summary Regional Map for the United States (available online)

Procedure Organize the class into nine groups, one for each climate region as defined on the map. Have each group determine the type of climate in their region. From that information, have them determine the predominant weathering agents in their region.

Expected Outcome Students will recognize that climatic differences affect weathering rates. They will recognize that even one country may have a variety of climates.

Chapter 7 Assessment

Checking Concepts

1. D
2. A
3. A
4. A
5. C
6. A
7. B
8. A
9. D
10. C

Thinking Critically

11. Mechanical; chemical weathering would be slowed by lower temperatures.
12. They destroy plants and tear up soil, increasing erosion.
13. Increased population means more farming, cutting of forests, overgrazing, and urban construction, all of which increase soil erosion.
14. Topsoil forms very slowly.
15. Acidic groundwater can dissolve underground rock, forming caves.

Developing Skills

16. Control: 2 additional pans not subjected to water; constants: same amount and kind of soil, same pans, same slope, same amount of water, and same rate of pouring water; variable: amount of soil washed away
17. Chemical: rocks oxidize, acids from mosses, water seeping through cracks in limestone; mechanical: freezing/thawing, tree roots break rocks apart

---

Checking Concepts

Choose the word or phrase that best answers the question.

1. Which of the following is caused by acids produced by plants?
   A) soil erosion
   B) overgrazing
   C) mechanical weathering
   D) chemical weathering

2. What occurs when roots force rocks apart?
   A) mechanical weathering
   B) leaching
   C) ice wedging
   D) chemical weathering

3. What reacts with iron to form rust?
   A) oxygen   C) feldspar
   B) carbon dioxide D) paint

4. Which of the following is an agent of mechanical weathering?
   A) ice wedging   C) leaching
   B) oxidation   D) desert formation

5. In which region is chemical weathering most rapid?
   A) cold, dry   C) warm, moist
   B) cold, moist   D) warm, dry

6. What is a mixture of weathered rock, organic matter, air, and water called?
   A) soil   C) carbon dioxide
   B) limestone   D) clay

7. What is decayed organic matter called?
   A) leaching   C) soil
   B) humus   D) sediment

8. Where is most humus found?
   A) A horizon   C) C horizon
   B) B horizon   D) D horizon

9. What does no-till farming help prevent?
   A) leaching   C) overgrazing
   B) crop rotation   D) soil erosion

---

10. What is done to reduce erosion on steep slopes?
    A) weathering   C) terracing
    B) overgrazing   D) forest harvesting

Thinking Critically

11. Which type of weathering, mechanical or chemical, would you expect to have more effect in a polar region? Explain.

12. Explain how off-road vehicles affect soil erosion.

13. How does increasing human population affect soil erosion?

14. Why is it difficult to replace lost topsoil?

15. Describe how chemical weathering can form a cave.

Developing Skills

16. **Using Variables, Constants, and Controls** Juan wanted to know if planting grass on a slope would prevent soil from being washed away. To find out, he put the same amount and kind of soil in two identical pans. In one of the pans, he planted sod. To create equal slopes for his test, he placed identical wooden wedges under one end of each pan. He carefully poured the same amount of water at the same rate over the soil in the two pans. What is Juan's control? What factors in his activity are constants? What variable is he testing?

Chapter ✓ Assessment Planner

Portfolio Encourage students to place in their portfolios one or two items of what they consider to be their best work. Examples include:
- Science Journal, p. 185
- Curriculum Connection, p. 188
- Science Journal, p. 192
- Activity Assessment, p. 197

Performance Additional performance assessments, Performance Task Assessment Lists, and rubrics for evaluating these activities can be found in Glencoe's **Performance Assessment in the Science Classroom.**

17. Classifying Classify the following as examples of either chemical or mechanical weathering: rocks oxidize to form rustlike minerals, freezing and thawing of water causes a cliff face to break apart, acids from mosses discolor rocks, tree roots break rocks apart, and water seeping through cracks in limestone dissolves away some of the rock.

18. Concept Mapping Complete the events chain concept map that shows two ways in which acids can cause chemical weathering.

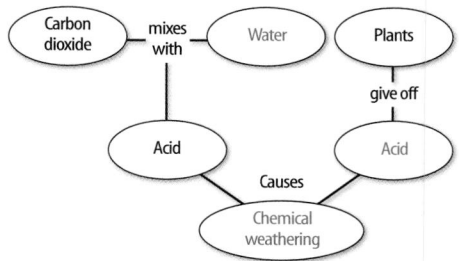

19. Forming a Hypothesis Over time, crop yields on a farm field diminish in spite of repeated applications of fertilizer. What hypothesis could be tested to explain this? How could an explanation benefit the farm owner?

Performance Assessment

20. Design a Landscape Find a slope in your area that might benefit from erosion maintenance. Design a landscape map showing the types of plants you would introduce and where you would put them.

TECHNOLOGY

Go to the Glencoe Science Web site at **science.glencoe.com** or use the **Glencoe Science CD-ROM** for additional chapter assessment.

THE PRINCETON REVIEW **Test Practice**

Scientists in North Dakota have recently analyzed a sample of soil for sand, silt, and clay. They placed their results in the following table.

Horizon	Percent		
	Sand	Silt	Clay
A	16.2	54.4	29.4
B	10.5	50.2	39.3
C	31.4	48.4	20.2
R (Bedrock)	31.7	50.1	18.2

Study the table and answer the following questions.

1. According to this information, which soil horizon has the lowest percentage of sand?
A) horizon A
B) horizon B
C) horizon C
D) horizon R

2. According to the table, horizon R refers to _____ .
F) topsoil
G) bedrock
H) humus
J) gravel

3. According to the information in the table, the best description of the soil in the table above would be _____ .
A) sandy
B) silty
C) clayey
D) organic

The Test-Taking Tip was written by The Princeton Review, the nation's leader in test preparation.
1. B
2. G
3. B

Developing Skills

18. See student page.
19. Possible answers: Over time, soil may become compacted. As a result, there is no longer a proper flow of air and water through the soil, and runoff increases. An explanation could benefit the farmer by providing a solution to the problems of loss of yield and loss of fertilizer.

Performance Assessment

20. Designs will vary. Grasses or other plants with fibrous roots will help hold soil. Students might choose to terrace the slope or install a retaining wall. Use **Performance Assessment in the Science Classroom**, p. 127.

✔Assessment Resources

📁 Reproducible Masters

Chapter Resources Booklet
    Chapter Review, pp. 33–34
    Chapter Tests, pp. 35–38
    Assessment Transparency Activity, p. 45

Glencoe Science Web site
    Interactive Tutor
    Chapter Quizzes

Glencoe Technology
    🖐 Assessment Transparency
    💿 Interactive CD-ROM Chapter Quizzes
    💿 ExamView Pro Test Bank
    💿 Vocabulary PuzzleMaker Software
    📼 MindJogger Videoquiz DVD/VHS

Section/Objectives	Standards		Activities/Features
Chapter Opener	**National**	**State/Local**	**Explore Activity:** Demonstrate sediment movement, p. 211 **Before You Read,** p. 211
	See p. 5T for a Key to Standards.		
Section 1 Erosion by Gravity 🕐 2 sessions 📦 1 block 1. **Explain** the differences between erosion and deposition. 2. **Compare and contrast** slumps, creep, rockfalls, rock slides, and mudflows. 3. **Explain** why building on steep slopes might not be wise.	National Content Standards: UCP2, A1, D1, E2, F3		**MiniLAB:** Modeling Slump, p. 213
Section 2 Glaciers 🕐 2 sessions 📦 1 block 1. **Explain** how glaciers move. 2. **Describe** evidence of glacial erosion and deposition. 3. **Compare and contrast** till and outwash.	National Content Standards: UCP2, A1, D1, D2		**Science Online,** p. 222 **Activity:** Glacial Grooving, p. 223
Section 3 Wind 🕐 2 sessions 📦 1 block 1. **Explain** how wind causes deflation and abrasion. 2. **Recognize** how loess and dunes form.	National Content Standards: UCP2, A1, D1, F4		**Problem-Solving Activity:** What factors affect wind erosion?, p. 225 **MiniLAB:** Observe How Soil Is Held in Place, p. 226 **Visualizing How Dunes Form and Move,** p. 228 **Activity:** Blowing in the Wind, pp. 230–231 **Science Stats:** Losing Against Erosion, pp. 232–233

NATIONAL GEOGRAPHIC   Teacher's Corner

PRODUCTS AVAILABLE FROM GLENCOE
To order call 1-800-334-7344:
CD-ROM
NGS PictureShow: Dynamic Earth
Curriculum Kit
GeoKit: Dynamic Earth

Transparency Set
NGS PicturePack: Dynamic Earth
PRODUCTS AVAILABLE FROM NATIONAL GEOGRAPHIC SOCIETY
To order call 1-800-368-2728:

Videos
Our Dynamic Earth
Glaciers: Ice on the Move

Activity Materials	Reproducible Resources	Section Assessment	Technology
Explore Activity: sand, gravel, shoe box lid	**Chapter Resources Booklet** Foldables Worksheet, p. 13 Directed Reading Overview, p. 15 Note-taking Worksheets, pp. 29–31	GLENCOE'S **ASSESSMENT** ADVANTAGE	
MiniLAB: baking pan; bricks (2); sink; gelatin powder; aquarium gravel; large, flat rock; watering can, water *Need materials?* Contact Science Kit at 1-800-828-7777 or www.sciencekit.com on the Internet.	**Chapter Resources Booklet** Transparency Activity, p. 40 MiniLAB, p. 3 Enrichment, p. 26 Reinforcement, p. 23 Directed Reading, p. 16 Lab Activity, pp. 9–10	**Portfolio** Extension, p. 215 **Performance** MiniLAB, p. 213 Skill Builder Activities, p. 216 **Content** Section Assessment, p. 216	Section Focus Transparency Interactive CD-ROM/DVD Guided Reading Audio Program
Activity: sand, large plastic or metal tray or stream table, ice block, books (2 or 3) or wood block, metric ruler, overhead light source with reflector	**Chapter Resources Booklet** Transparency Activity, p. 41 Enrichment, p. 27 Reinforcement, p. 24 Directed Reading, p. 16 Activity Worksheet, pp. 5–6 Lab Activity, pp. 11–12 Transparency Activity, pp. 43–44	**Portfolio** Curriculum Connection, p. 219 Challenge, p. 222 **Performance** Skill Builder Activities, p. 222 **Content** Section Assessment, p. 222	Section Focus Transparency Teaching Transparency Interactive CD-ROM/DVD Guided Reading Audio Program
MiniLAB: sod, hand lens **Activity:** flat pans (4), fine sand (400mL), gravel (400mL), hair drier, sprinkling can, water, 28 × 35–cm cardboard sheets (4), tape, mixing bowl, metric ruler	**Chapter Resources Booklet** Transparency Activity, p. 42 MiniLAB, p. 4 Enrichment, p. 28 Reinforcement, p. 25 Directed Reading, pp. 17, 18 Activity Worksheet, pp. 7–8 **Mathematics Skill Activities**, p. 9 **Lab Management and Safety,** p. 65	**Portfolio** Cultural Diversity, p. 227 **Performance** Problem-Solving Activity, p. 225 MiniLAB, p. 226 Skill Builder Activities, p. 229 **Content** Section Assessment, p. 229	Section Focus Transparency Interactive CD-ROM/DVD Guided Reading Audio Program

End of Chapter Assessment

GLENCOE'S **ASSESSMENT** ADVANTAGE

Blackline Masters	Technology	Professional Series
Chapter Resources Booklet Chapter Review, pp. 33–34 Chapter Tests, pp. 35–38 **Standardized Test Practice by The Princeton Review,** pp. 39–42	MindJogger Videoquiz CD-ROM Explorations and Quizzes Vocabulary Puzzle Makers ExamView Pro Test Bank Interactive Lesson Planner Interactive Teacher's Edition	Performance Assessment in the Science Classroom (PASC)

Transparencies

Section Focus

Section Focus Transparency Avalanche

Avalanches occur when snow on a mountain slope breaks loose and slides downhill. Because of avalanche danger, people in snowy, mountainous areas put a lot of effort into avalanche safety and control.

1. How is an avalanche like a landslide? How are they different?
2. What is the key force in avalanches and landslides?

L2

Section Focus Transparency I'll be back in 5,000 years.

Meet Ötzi, a human from the Stone Age who was preserved by a glacier about 5,000 years ago. He was somehow trapped in a rock depression and subsequently covered by the glacier. Ötzi was eventually discovered by hikers on a ridge that divides Austria from Italy.

1. Glaciers are powerful enough to carve valleys. How was a relatively fragile human preserved by a glacier?
2. Where can you see glaciers today?
3. How do you think glaciers move?

L2

Section Focus Transparency Rock on!

You may have noticed animal tracks in the sand, but have you ever seen boulder tracks? If you go to the Racetrack in Death Valley, this is exactly what you'll see. Rocks at the Racetrack seem to move without any help at all.

1. No one has ever seen a rock move at the Racetrack. What evidence do you have that these rocks are moving without human interference?
2. Pretend you are scientists studying Death Valley. Develop a scientific theory that explains the mysterious movements at the Racetrack.

L2

This is a representation of key blackline masters available in the Teacher Classroom Resources. See Resource Manager boxes within the chapter for additional information.

Assessment

Assessment Transparency Erosional Forces

Directions: Carefully review the graph and answer the following questions.

Shoreline Erosion on Beach Island

Distance of row of beach houses from ocean in 1980

Year

1. According to the information in the graph, the year that experienced the least amount of shoreline loss is ___.
   A 1980   B 1984   C 1988   D 1989
2. Based on this information, during which year did the ocean reach the first row of beach houses?
   F 1986   G 1987   H 1988   J 1989
3. If everything remains the same, how many meters of shoreline will be eroded by 1990?
   A 11 m   B 12m   C 14m   D 15m

L2

Teaching

Teaching Transparency Glacial Margin

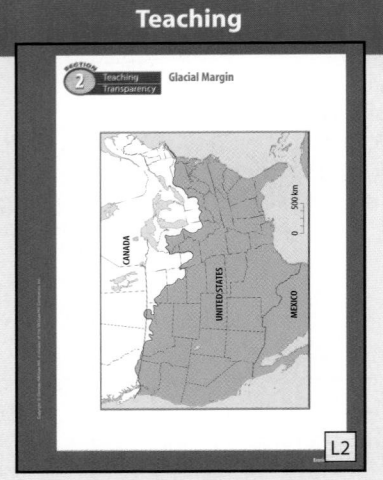

L2

Key to Teaching Strategies

The following designations will help you decide which activities are appropriate for your students.

L1 Level 1 activities should be appropriate for students with learning difficulties.

L2 Level 2 activities should be within the ability range of all students.

L3 Level 3 activities are designed for above-average students.

ELL ELL activities should be within the ability range of English Language Learners.

COOP LEARN Cooperative Learning activities are designed for small group work.

LS Multiple Learning Styles logos, as described on page 22T, are used throughout to indicate strategies that address different learning styles.

P These strategies represent student products that can be placed into a best-work portfolio.

Hands-on Activities

Activity Worksheets

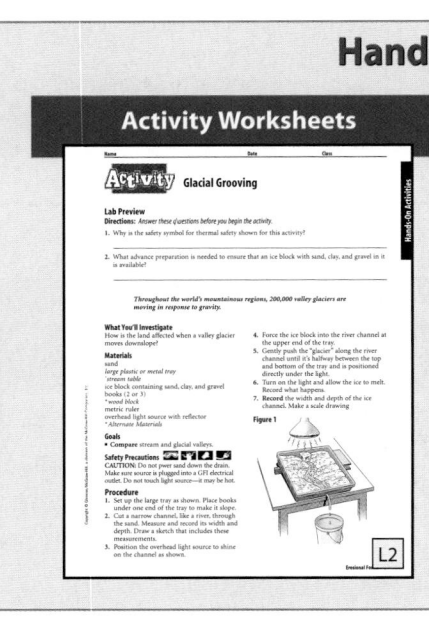

Activity Glacial Grooving

Lab Preview
Directions: Answer these questions before you begin the activity.

1. Why is the safety symbol for thermal safety shown for this activity?

2. What advance preparation is needed to ensure that an ice block with sand, clay, and gravel in it is available?

Throughout the world's mountainous regions, 200,000 valley glaciers are moving in response to gravity.

What You'll Investigate
How is the land affected when a valley glacier moves downslope?

Materials
sand
large plastic or metal tray
stream table
ice block containing sand, clay, and gravel
books (2 or 3)
*wood block
metric ruler
overhead light source with reflector
*Alternate Materials

Goals
• Compare stream and glacial valleys.

Safety Precautions
CAUTION: Do not pour sand down the drain. Make sure source is plugged into a GFI electrical outlet. Do not touch light source—it may be hot.

Procedure
1. Set up the large tray as shown. Place books under one end of the tray to make it slope.
2. Cut a narrow channel, like a river, through the sand. Measure and record its width and depth. Draw a sketch that includes these measurements.
3. Position the overhead light source to shine on the channel as shown.

4. Force the ice block into the river channel at the upper end of the tray.
5. Gently push the "glacier" along the river channel until it's halfway between the top and bottom of the tray and is positioned directly under the light.
6. Turn on the light and allow the ice to melt. Record what happens.
7. Record the width and depth of the ice channel. Make a scale drawing

Figure 1

L2

Laboratory Activities

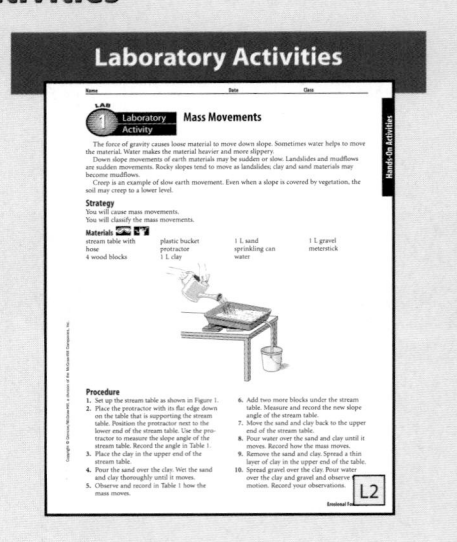

Laboratory Activity Mass Movements

The force of gravity causes loose material to move down slope. Sometimes water helps to move the material. Water makes the material heavier and more slippery.
Down slope movements of earth materials may be sudden or slow. Landslides and mudflows are sudden movements. Rocky slopes tend to move as landslides; clay and sand materials may become mudflows.
Creep is an example of slow earth movement. Even when a slope is covered by vegetation, the soil may creep to a lower level.

Strategy
You will cause mass movements.
You will classify the mass movements.

Materials
stream table with hose
4 wood blocks
plastic bucket
protractor
1 L sand
sprinkling can
water
1 L gravel
meterstick

Procedure
1. Set up the stream table as shown in Figure 1.
2. Place the protractor with its flat edge down on the table that is supporting the stream table. Position the protractor next to the lower end of the stream table. Use the protractor to measure the slope angle of the stream table. Record the angle in Table 1.
3. Place the clay in the upper end of the stream table.
4. Pour the sand over the clay. Wet the sand and clay thoroughly until it moves.
5. Observe and record in Table 1 how the mass moves.

6. Add two more blocks under the stream table. Measure and record the new slope angle of the stream table.
7. Move the sand and clay back to the upper end of the stream table.
8. Pour water over the sand and clay until it moves.
9. Remove the sand and clay. Spread a thin layer of clay in the upper end of the table.
10. Spread gravel over the clay. Pour water over the clay and gravel and observe motion. Record your observations.

L2

Meeting Different Ability Levels

Content Outline

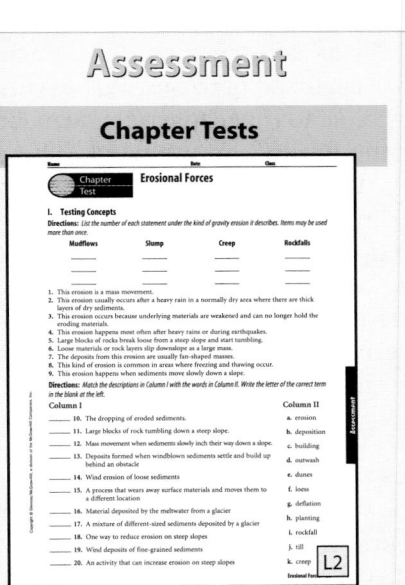

Note-taking Worksheet — **Erosional Forces**

Section 1   Erosion by Gravity
A. _____—wearing away and moving of surface materials by gravity, water, wind, or glaciers
B. Through the process of _____, sediments are dropped by erosion agents as they lose energy.
C. _____ occurs as gravity moves materials down a slope as one large mass.
  1. _____—material slips down a curved surface as one large mass
  2. Sediments slowly shift downhill in the process of _____.
  3. _____ and rock slides occur when rocks break off or slip suddenly down a hill.
  4. A _____ is a thick mixture of water and sediments flowing downhill.
D. _____ of erosion—Buildings on slopes eventually have problems due to erosion by gravity.
  a. Sometimes builders and residents make slopes more unstable by making them steeper or removing _____.
E. Steep slops can be made safer with vegetation, drainage pipes, and walls of _____ or railroad ties.

Section 2   Glaciers
A. _____—large mass of ice and snow slowly moving on land; an agent of erosion
B. As glaciers move, they pick up boulders, gravel, and sand in an erosion process called _____.
  1. Plucked rocks at the base of the glacier sand and _____ the soil and bedrock.
  2. Bedrock can be scarred in the process of _____—left from dragged rock fragments.
  3. _____ are shallower scars on bedrock.
  4. Grooves and erriations indicate the _____ a glacier moved.

L2

Reinforcement

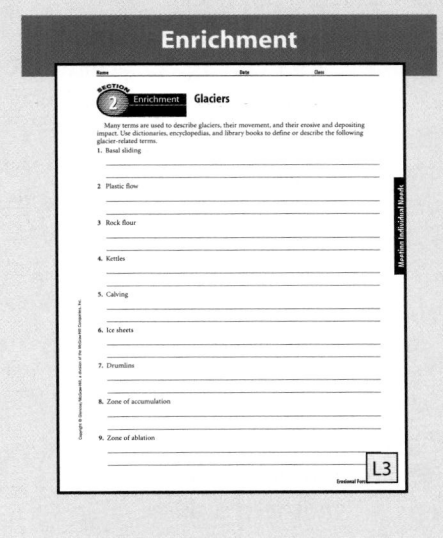

Reinforcement — **Erosion by Gravity**

Directions: *Complete the items on the lines provided.*
1. Identify the types of mass movement described below.
  _____ a. This happens when underlying material is weakened and can no longer support material on top of it. Loose material slips downward as a large mass.
  _____ b. These are common in mountainous areas. A sign that these have occurred is a pile of rocks at the bottom of a hill. They occur most often after heavy rains or during earthquakes.
  _____ c. These are likely to happen in relatively dry areas with thick layers of dry sediment. They occur after heavy rains fall. Sediment and water mix together to form a thick mixture that slides.
  _____ d. It causes sediments to slowly move downhill. It happens in areas where the ground freezes and thaws. As the ground freezes, expanding water in the soil pushes up sediments. When the ground thaws, the sediments fall downslope. This is a slow process.
2. What do the above four types of erosion have in common?

3. Identify the types of mass movement from the clues provided.
  _____ a. Leaning fenceposts
  _____ b. A curved scar where eroded material once was located
  _____ c. A fan-shaped deposit
  _____ d. "Beware of falling rock" signs
4. Answer the following questions in complete sentences.
  a. Hawaii consists of a chain of tropical islands. Would you expect to see evidence of creep there? Explain.

  b. In a usually dry area, homes were built on a hillside on thick layers of clay and dirt. Late one summer, a long drought was followed by heavy rain. What kind of mass movement might the area experience? Explain.

L2

Directed Reading

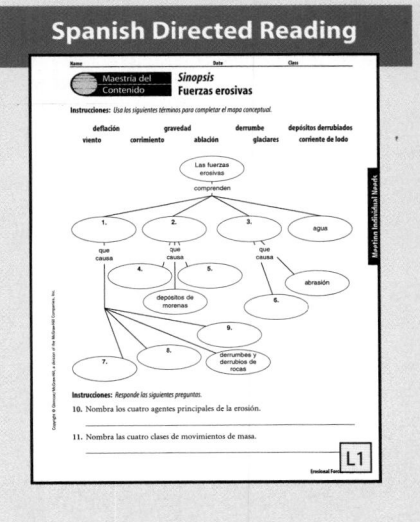

Directed Reading for Content Mastery — *Overview* **Erosional Forces**

Directions: *Use the following terms to complete the concept map below.*

deflation   gravity   slump   outwash deposits
wind   creep   plucking   glaciers   mudflow

Directions: *Answer the following questions on the lines provided.*
10. Name the four major agents of erosion.

11. Name four kinds of mass movement.

L1

Enrichment

Enrichment — **Glaciers**

Many terms are used to describe glaciers, their movement, and their erosive and depositing impact. Use dictionaries, encyclopedias, and library books to define or describe the following glacier-related terms.
1. Basal sliding

2. Plastic flow

3. Rock flour

4. Kettles

5. Calving

6. Ice sheets

7. Drumlins

8. Zone of accumulation

9. Zone of ablation

L3

Spanish Directed Reading

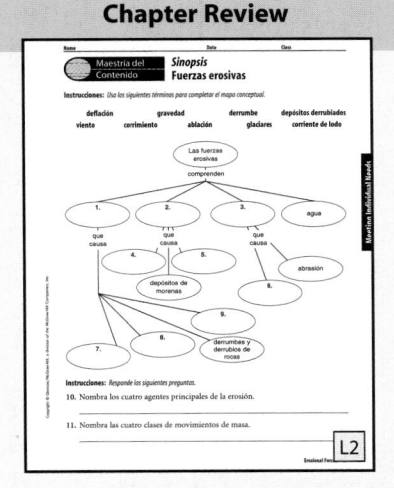

Maestría del Contenido — *Sinopsis* **Fuerzas erosivas**

Instrucciones: *Usa los siguientes términos para completar el mapa conceptual.*

deflación   gravedad   derrumbe   depósitos derrubiados
viento   corrimiento   ablación   glaciares   corriente de lodo

Instrucciones: *Responde las siguientes preguntas.*
10. Nombra los cuatro agentes principales de la erosión.

11. Nombra los cuatro clases de movimientos de masa.

L1

Assessment

Chapter Tests

Chapter Test — **Erosional Forces**

I.   Testing Concepts
Directions: *List the number of each statement under the kind of gravity erosion it describes. Items may be used more than once.*

Mudflows	Slump	Creep	Rockfalls

1. This erosion is a mass movement.
2. This erosion usually occurs after a heavy rain in a normally dry area where there are thick layers of dry sediments.
3. This erosion occurs because underlying materials are weakened and can no longer hold the eroding materials.
4. This erosion happens most often after heavy rains or during earthquakes.
5. Large blocks of rocks break loose from a steep slope and start tumbling.
6. Loose materials or rock layers slip downslope as a large mass.
7. The deposits from this erosion are usually fan-shaped masses.
8. This kind of erosion is common in areas where freezing and thawing occur.
9. This erosion happens when sediments move slowly down a slope.

Directions: *Match the descriptions in Column I with the words in Column II. Write the letter of the correct term in the blank at the left.*

Column I
_____ 10. The dropping of eroded sediments.
_____ 11. Large blocks of rock tumbling down a steep slope.
_____ 12. Mass movement when sediments slowly inch their way down a slope.
_____ 13. Deposits formed when windblown sediments settle and build up behind an obstacle
_____ 14. Wind erosion of loose sediments
_____ 15. A process that wears away surface materials and moves them to a different location
_____ 16. Material deposited by the meltwater from a glacier
_____ 17. A mixture of different-sized sediments deposited by a glacier
_____ 18. One way to reduce erosion on steep slopes
_____ 19. Wind deposits of fine-grained sediments
_____ 20. An activity that can increase erosion on steep slopes

Column II
a. erosion
b. deposition
c. building
d. outwash
e. dunes
f. loess
g. deflation
h. planting
i. rockfall
j. till
k. creep

L2

Test Practice Workbook

Standardized Test Practice
Teacher Edition

Glencoe Science
Earth Science

• Correlates to TEKS
• Prepares students for TAKS II
• Written by The Princeton Review

NATIONAL GEOGRAPHIC SOCIETY

L2

Chapter Review

Maestría del Contenido — *Sinopsis* **Fuerzas erosivas**

Instrucciones: *Usa los siguientes términos para completar el mapa conceptual.*

deflación   gravedad   derrumbe   depósitos derrubiados
viento   corrimiento   ablación   glaciares   corriente de lodo

Instrucciones: *Responde las siguientes preguntas.*
10. Nombra los cuatro agentes principales de la erosión.

11. Nombra las cuatro clases de movimientos de masa.

L2

Science Content Background

Erosion by Gravity
Erosion and Deposition

All mass movement requires energy, which comes from wind, water, or gravity. When energy of motion is reduced, deposition occurs. Energy is reduced when wind or water velocity slows or when the steepness of a slope is reduced. Mass movement occurs under all geological conditions. For example, it occurs on steep slopes of mountains, along riverbeds, on gently rolling plains, on cliffs by the sea, on slopes under the ocean, and even on other planets and the Moon.

Glaciers
Glacial Movement

Glaciers begin to move when the mass of the ice exerts enough pressure to cause the bottom of the ice to melt. This occurs when an ice sheet reaches a thickness of about 30 m. The glacier then flows slowly (less than 1 m per day) on a thin sheet of water. The most recent ice age began during the Pleistocene Epoch. During this epoch there were seven major ice advances followed by intervals of warmer climates called interglacial periods. Scientists hypothesize that we now are living in an interglacial period.

Glacial Erosion

Pleistocene glaciations formed many lakes. As ice scoured the landscape, depressions were left in bedrock. As the ice melted, these holes filled. Mountain peaks and sharp ridges also were formed by glacial ice. Meltwater froze around protruding rocks. The rocks then were plucked away as the ice advanced.

Tom Bean/DRK Photo

Student Misconception

Erosion is caused solely by wind.

Refer to the facing page for teaching strategies to address this misconception. Refer to page 214 for content related to this topic.

Wind
Abrasion

Abrasion by the wind depends on the availability of suspended particles that act as scouring tools. Gentle winds can move dust-sized particles. If the wind is strong enough, sand-sized particles can be bounced along the ground by the wind. These particles scour the ground over which they move in a series of intermittent leaps of varying lengths. During the 1930s dust bowl in the United States, a dust cloud near Wichita, Kansas, extended 3,650 m above the ground and was estimated to contain 50,000 metric tons of dust per cubic kilometer.

Sand Dunes and Wind Erosion

Wind erosion can be reduced by placing obstacles to divert the wind. As sand is blown into or around an obstacle, its energy of motion decreases, sand is dropped, and a dune forms. Once this process begins, the dune itself acts as a barrier to the wind. Dune migration occurs when wind blows sand up the windward side of a dune and drops it over the leeward side. When sand piles too high, a sheetlike mass of sand slips down the leeward side of the dune, and the dune moves forward.

SCIENCE *Online*

For additional content background on this topic, go to the Glencoe Science Web site at science.glencoe.com.

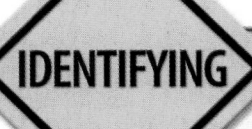

IDENTIFYING Misconceptions

Find Out What Students Think

Students may think that . . .

• Erosion is caused solely by the wind.

Students develop this misconception as they experience the wind blowing sand and soil across Earth's surface. Because the movement of these particles is readily observed, they may think that only the wind is responsible for the erosion of Earth's surface.

Discussion

Ask students to describe what happens before, during, and after a thunderstorm. Encourage them to describe the darkening of the sky, the increase of the wind, the pattern of rainfall, and the subsequent passing of the storm. List events on the board, placing them in sequential order, as students mention them.

When the list is complete, review the events with the class. Have students now describe how objects in the path of the storm move during each event. If necessary, prompt students with questions such as, "What happens to the trees as the wind speed increases?" "Are materials on the ground moved by the wind?" "How does the falling water affect materials on the ground?" Keep a list of all ideas offered by students.

Promote Understanding

Discussion

Show students a series of pictures of a town experiencing a flood. Include pictures of the river before, during, and immediately after the flood. Have students discuss how the river changes as the flood progresses.

• Point out that the river becomes more muddy and that larger materials are transported by the water as the flood grows stronger.

• As the flood wanes, the river carries smaller items and eventually runs clear again.

Activity

Organize students into small groups. Have each group use a stream table, a sprinkling can, and a hair drier to compare wind and water erosion.

• Direct students to compare the amount of erosion that occurs from wind and water when the sand is dry and when the sand is wet.

• Have each group present their observations of erosion by wind and water in dry and wet sand. Most should find that dry sand is

Tom Bean/DRK Photo

eroded strongly by wind, and somewhat by water. Wet sand is eroded much less by wind but is still eroded by water.

As an extension, have students debate whether wind or water is the most important erosional agent in a desert. Have students defend their ideas with data from this activity.

Assess

After completing the chapter, see *Identifying Misconceptions* in the Study Guide.

Chapter Vocabulary

erosion
deposition
mass movement
slump
creep
glacier
plucking
till
moraine
outwash
deflation
abrasion
loess
dune

What do you think?

Science Journal This photo shows a single palm tree and the remains of a house that was abandoned because of shifting desert sands near I-n-Salah Oasis in Algeria.

Erosional Forces

Loosened by years of wind, water, and ice, these displaced rocks came crashing down on the Karakoram Highway. Blocked by the boulders, travelers observe the aftermath of a powerful erosion force. As you can see, transport of rocks and sediment downslope can impact the lives of humans. In this chapter, you'll learn about some of the forces that cause erosion. You'll see how gravity, glaciers, and wind erode and deposit Earth materials—constantly changing landscapes.

What do you think?

Science Journal Look at the picture below with a classmate. Discuss what you think this might be or what is happening. Here's a hint: *Someone used to live here.* Write your answer or best guess in your Science Journal.

210

Theme Connection

Stability and Change Students learn that although landforms on Earth's surface are generally stable in the short term, in the long term (thousands or even millions of years) erosional forces make great changes in the landforms on Earth's surface.

Can you think of ways to move something without touching it? In nature, sediment is moved from one location to another by a variety of forces. What are some of these forces? In this activity, you will investigate to find out.

Demonstrate sediment movement

WARNING: *Do not pour sand or gravel down the drain.*

1. Place a small pile of a sand and gravel mixture in one end of a large shoe box lid.
2. Move the sediment pile to the other end of the lid without touching the particles with your hands. You may touch and manipulate the box lid.
3. Try to move the mixture in a number of different ways.

Observe

In your Science Journal, describe the methods you used to move the sediment. Which method was most effctive? Explain how your methods compare with forces of nature that move sediment.

FOLDABLES
Reading & Study Skills

Before You Read

Making an Organizational Study Fold
Make the following Foldable to help you organize your thoughts about erosion and deposition.

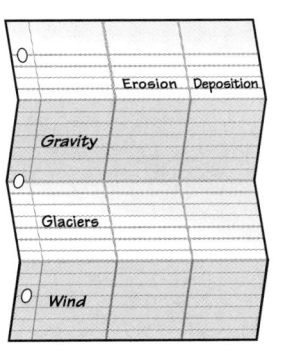

1. Place a sheet of paper in front of you so the short side is at the top.
2. Fold the paper in half from the top to bottom. Then fold it in half again. Unfold all the folds.
3. Trace over all the fold lines. Label the columns *Erosion* and *Deposition.* Label the rows *Gravity, Glaciers,* and *Wind* as shown.
4. As you read the chapter, record information including specific examples of erosion and deposition in the rows of your Foldable.

211

Purpose Use the Explore Activity to introduce students to the ways that sediments can be moved from place to place. L2 ELL COOP LEARN IS **Kinesthetic**

Preparation Make sure sand and gravel are dry.

Materials sand (250 g), gravel (250 g), shoebox lid, safety goggles

Teaching Strategy If students have trouble coming up with ideas for moving sediments, suggest the following: blowing, tilting the shoebox lid, flushing with water, or pushing with a piece of paper.

Safety Precautions Have all students wear safety goggles.

Observe

Possible answers: flushing with water is similar to rainfall and stream movement; blowing resembles wind; tilting the box lid creates a steep slope that allows gravity to pull sediments downhill; pushing resembles the scouring effects of glaciers.

Process Have students draw and label diagrams that explain the methods they used to move sediments in the activity. Use **Performance Assessment in the Science Classroom,** p. 165.

FOLDABLES
Reading & Study Skills

Before You Read

Dinah Zike Study Fold

Purpose Students make and use a Foldable table to collect information on erosion and deposition as they relate to gravity, glaciers, and wind. During reading, students compare and contrast the different types of erosion and resulting deposition.

For additional help, see Foldables Worksheet, p. 13 in **Chapter Resources Booklet,** or go to the Glencoe Science Web site at **science.glencoe.com.** See After You Read in the Study Guide at the end of this chapter.

SECTION

1 Erosion by Gravity

1 Motivate

Bellringer Transparency

Display the Section Focus Transparency for Section 1. Use the accompanying Transparency Activity Master. L2

ELL

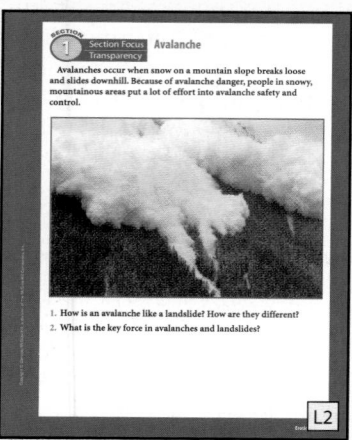

Tie to Prior Knowledge

Ask students to recall seeing rain wash away soil or wind blow it along the ground. Invite them to discuss whether these actions could have a great effect on changing the landscape. Explain that they will discover this answer as they read this section.

As You Read

What You'll Learn

- **Explain** the differences between erosion and deposition.
- **Compare and contrast** slumps, creep, rockfalls, rock slides, and mudflows.
- **Explain** why building on steep slopes might not be wise.

Vocabulary

erosion	slump
deposition	creep
mass movement	

Why It's Important

Many natural features throughout the world were shaped by erosion.

Figure 1
The jumbled sediment at the base of a landslide is material that once was located farther uphill. *What force moves materials toward the center of Earth?*

Erosion and Deposition

Do you live in an area where landslides occur? As **Figure 1** shows, large piles of sediment and rock can move downhill with devastating results. Such events often are triggered by heavy rainfall. The muddy debris at the lower end of the slide comes from material that once was further up the hillside. The displaced soil and rock debris is a product of erosion (ih ROH zhun). **Erosion** is a process that wears away surface materials and moves them from one place to another.

What wears away sediments? How were you able to move the pile of sediments in the Explore Activity? If you happened to tilt the box lid, you took advantage of an important erosional force—gravity. Gravity is the force of attraction that moves all objects toward Earth's center. Other causes of erosion, also called agents of erosion, are water, wind, and glaciers.

Water and wind erode materials only when they have enough energy of motion to do work. For example, air can't move much sediment on a calm day, but a strong wind can move dust and even larger particles. Glacial erosion works differently by slowly moving sediment that is trapped in solid ice. As the ice melts, sediment is deposited, or dropped. Sometimes sediment is carried farther by moving meltwater.

Section ✓Assessment Planner

PORTFOLIO
Extension, p. 215
PERFORMANCE ASSESSMENT
MiniLAB, p. 213
Skill Builder Activities, p. 216
See page 236 for more options.

CONTENT ASSESSMENT
Section, p. 216
Challenge, p. 216
Chapter, pp. 236–237

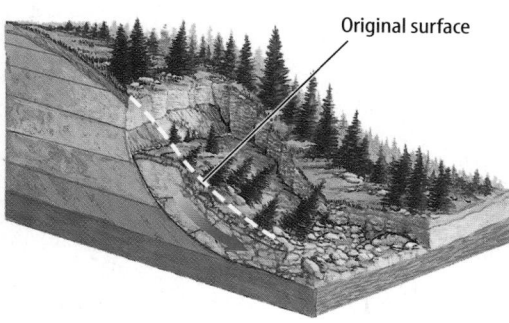
Original surface

Dropping Sediments Agents of erosion drop the sediments they are carrying as they lose energy. This is called **deposition.** When sediments are eroded, they are not lost from Earth—they are just relocated.

Mass Movement

The greater an object's mass is, the greater its gravitational force is. Earth has such a great mass that gravity is a major force of erosion and deposition. Rocks and other materials, especially on steep slopes, are pulled toward the center of Earth by gravity.

A **mass movement** is any type of erosion that happens as gravity moves materials downslope. Some mass movements are so slow that you hardly notice they're happening. Others happen quickly—possibly causing catastrophes. Common types of mass movement include slump, creep, rockfalls, rock slides, and mudflows. Landslides are mass movements that can be one of these types or a combination of these types of mass movement.

> ✔ **Reading Check** *What is a mass movement?*

Slump When a mass of material slips down along a curved surface, the mass movement is called **slump.** Often, when a slope becomes too steep, the base material no longer can support the rock and sediment above it. The soil and rock slips downslope as one large mass or breaks into several sections.

Sometimes a slump happens when water moves to the base of a slipping mass of sediment. This water weakens the slipping mass and can cause movement of material downhill. Or, if a strong rock layer lies on top of a weaker layer—commonly clay—the clay can weaken further under the weight of the rock. The clay no longer can support the strong rock on the hillside. As shown in **Figure 2,** a curved scar is left where the slumped materials originally rested.

Figure 2
Slump occurs when material slips downslope as one large mass. *What might have caused this slump to happen?*

Mini LAB

Modeling Slump
Procedure 🥽 👔 🧤 🚫
WARNING: *Do not pour lab materials down the drain.*
1. Place one end of a **baking pan** on **two bricks** and position the other end over a sink with a sealed drain.
2. Fill the bottom half of the pan with **gelatin powder,** and the top half of the pan with **aquarium gravel.** Place a large, **flat rock** on the gravel.
3. Using a **watering can,** sprinkle water on the materials in the pan for several minutes. Record your observations in your **Science Journal.**

Analysis
1. What happened to the different sediments in the pan?
2. Explain how your experiment models slump.

SECTION 1 Erosion by Gravity **213**

---

2 Teach

Erosion and Deposition

Caption Answers
- **Figure 1** gravity
- **Figure 2** Possible answer: The base was eroded away.

Mass Movement

✔ **Reading Check**

Answer any type of erosion that occurs as gravity moves materials downslope

Mini LAB

Purpose to model slump L2
ELL   COOP LEARN
IS Visual-Spatial
Materials baking pan; two bricks; gelatin powder; aquarium gravel; large, flat rock; watering can; water
Teaching Strategy If there is no slump evident in the model, suggest students gradually add a little more water.

Analysis
1. The gelatin powder washed away, causing the gravel and pebbles to slip down the pan.
2. The inclined pan models a steep slope and the water from the watering can models rain. Erosion of base sediments combined with gravity causes slump.

✔ Assessment

Performance Have students take before-and-after photos of their models to show the effects of slump. Use **Performance Assessment in the Science Classroom,** p. 149.

Teacher FYI

Slopes commonly become too steep when people remove materials near their bases. When this happens, a slope becomes unstable and gravity pulls the mass downward. Slopes also can be made too steep when overburden from a construction project is piled up.

Resource Manager

Chapter Resources Booklet
   Transparency Activity, p. 40
   MiniLAB, p. 3
   Directed Reading for Content Mastery, pp. 15, 16

Mass Movement,
continued

IDENTIFYING
Misconceptions

Students may think that erosion is caused solely by he wind. Refer to page 210F for teaching strategies that address this misconception.

Use Science Words

Word Meaning Have students use dictionaries to define *slump*. Ask volunteers to read aloud the definitions of slump that describe a person's physical appearance and the condition of economic activity. Then ask students what all meanings of the word have in common. *Slump describes a decline or collapse of something.* **IS Linguistic**

Discussion

Does creep occur in our area? Answers will depend on local climate and topography. **How does building on slopes increase erosion?** When people build on slopes, they often make the slopes steeper. Sometimes, they remove the vegetation that provides stability to the slope. Also, the weight of a structure on a slope puts stress on the supporting rocks.

Visual Learning

Figure 4 Have students use a dictionary to define the term *talus*. Then have them use the figure to explain what talus slopes are and how they form. Talus slopes are piles of loose material that often form at the bases of steep cliffs. They are composed of the materials that weathered and eroded from the cliff.

Figure 3
Over time, creep has deformed these railroad tracks.

Figure 4
Rockfalls and rockslides move solid materials rapidly downslope.

A Rockfalls, such as this one, occur as material free falls through the air.

Creep The next time you travel, look along the roadway or trail for slopes where trees and fence posts lean downhill. Leaning trees and human-built structures show another mass movement called creep. **Creep** occurs when sediments slowly shift their positions downhill, as **Figure 3** illustrates. Creep is common in areas of freezing and thawing.

Rockfalls and Rock Slides Signs along mountainous roadways warn of another type of mass movement called rockfalls. Rockfalls happen when blocks of rock break loose from a steep slope and tumble through the air. As they fall, these rocks crash into other rocks and knock them loose. More and more rocks break loose and tumble to the bottom. The fall of a single, large rock down a steep slope can cause serious damage to structures at the bottom. During the winter, when ice freezes in the cracks of rocks, the cracks expand and extend. In the spring, the pieces of rock break loose and fall down the mountainside, as shown in **Figure 4A.**

Rock slides occur when layers of rock—usually steep layers—slip downslope suddenly. Rock slides, like rockfalls, are fast and can be destructive in populated areas. They commonly occur in mountainous areas or in areas with steep cliffs, as shown in **Figure 4B.** Rock slides happen most often after heavy rains or during earthquakes, but they can happen on any rocky slope at any time without warning.

B Rock slides are common in regions where layers of rock are steep.

Original position of mass   Moving mass

214

Science Journal

Have students use **Figure 4** to explain in their journals how mass movement results in slopes that are less steep. Have them infer what the slope of the cliff looked like before weathering and erosion. **IS Visual-Spatial**

Mudflows What would happen if you took a long trip and forgot to turn off the sprinkler in your hillside garden before you left? If the soil is usually dry, the sprinkler water could change your yard into a muddy mass of material much like chocolate pudding. Part of your garden might slide downhill. You would have made a mudflow, a thick mixture of sediments and water flowing down a slope. The mudflow in **Figure 5** caused a lot of destruction.

Mudflows usually occur in areas that have thick layers of loose sediments. They often happen after vegetation has been removed by fire. When heavy rains fall on these areas, water mixes with sediment, causing it to become thick and pasty. Gravity causes this mass to flow downhill. When a mudflow finally reaches the bottom of a slope, it loses its energy of motion and deposits all the sediment and everything else it has been carrying. These deposits often form a mass that spreads out in a fan shape. Why might mudflows cause more damage than floodwaters?

 **Reading Check** *What conditions are favorable for triggering mudflows?*

Mudflows, rock slides, rockfalls, creep, and slump are similar in some ways. They all are most likely to occur on steep slopes, and they all depend on gravity to make them happen. Also, all types of mass movement occur more often after a heavy rain. The water adds mass and creates fluid pressure between grains and layers of sediment. This makes the sediment expand—possibly weakening it.

Consequences of Erosion

People like to have a great view and live in scenic areas away from noise and traffic. To live this way, they might build or move into houses and apartments on the sides of hills and mountains. When you consider gravity as an agent of erosion, do you think steep slopes are safe places to live?

Building on Steep Slopes When people build homes on steep slopes, they constantly must battle naturally occurring erosion. Sometimes builders or residents make a slope steeper or remove vegetation. This speeds up the erosion process and creates additional problems. Some steep slopes are prone to slumps because of weak sediment layers underneath.

Figure 5
Mudflows, such as these in the town of Sarno, Italy, have enough energy to move almost anything in their paths. *How do mudflows differ from slumps, creep, and rock slides?*

SECTION 1 Erosion by Gravity **215**

Section 1 Erosion by Gravity **215**

Text Question Answer
Because they carry large amounts of sediment, mudflows are denser and more destructive than floodwaters.

✔ **Reading Check**

Answer Normally dry area, with thick layers of dry sediments and vegetation removed by fire or other means, suddenly experiences a heavy rainfall.

Caption Answer
Figure 5 Mudslides are classified as mass movements of sediment that have the ability to move almost anything in their path. Slumps, creep, and rock slides are classified on a smaller scale even though they can cause damage as well.

Extension
Sediments involved in mass movement overcome friction when they move. Have students research friction and describe in a brief paragraph how it affects sediments on a slope. Friction is the force that resists motion between two touching surfaces. On a slope, this force tends to hold sediments in place. L2 P

Consequences of Erosion

Activity
Have students design and carry out an experiment to demonstrate how plant roots help hold soil and prevent erosion on slopes. Accept all reasonable designs. Students may notice that plants with fibrous roots spreading near the surface retain soil best. **Kinesthetic**

Inclusion Strategies

Gifted Have students use the new science words presented in this chapter to develop a crossword puzzle. They can use definitions from the chapter for clues.

Resource Manager

Chapter Resources Booklet
Reinforcement, p. 23
Enrichment, p. 26
Note-taking Worksheets, pp. 29–31
Lab Activity, pp. 9–10

Consequences of Erosion, continued

✓ **Reading Check**

Answer Place drainage pipes or tiles in slopes to drain water; put walls or railroad ties on hillsides or plant vegetation to hold soil in place.

3 Assess

Reteach

Have students examine each photograph in this section, identify the mass movement shown, and classify each type of movement as slow, fast, or very fast.

Challenge

How do climatic conditions affect mass movements? Mass movements are more likely to occur after a heavy rain because water adds mass to the sediments and also reduces the effects of friction that would otherwise slow down the mass movement.

✓Assessment

Process Instruct students to draw a concept map that compares and contrasts the types of mass movement covered in this section. Use **Performance Assessment in the Science Classroom,** p. 161.

Figure 6
Some slopes are stabilized by inserting tile that helps drain water from them.

Making Steep Slopes Safe Plants can be beautiful or weedlike—but they all have root structures that hold soil in place. One of the best ways to reduce erosion is to plant vegetation. The deeper the roots go, the more valuable the plant is for erosion control. Plants also absorb large amounts of water. Drainage pipes or tiles inserted into slopes, as shown in **Figure 6,** can prevent water from building up, too. These materials help increase the stability of a slope by allowing excess water to flow out of a hillside more easily.

Walls made of concrete or railroad ties also can reduce erosion by holding soil and rocks in place. However, preventing mass movements on a slope is difficult because rain or earthquakes can weaken all types of Earth materials, eventually causing them to move downhill.

 Reading Check *What can be done to slow erosion on steep slopes?*

People who live in areas with erosion problems spend a lot of time and money trying to preserve their land. Sometimes they're successful in slowing down erosion, but they never can eliminate erosion and the danger of mass movement. Eventually, gravity wins. Sediment moves from place to place, constantly reducing elevation and changing the shape of the land.

Section 1 Assessment

1. Define the term *erosion* and name the forces that cause it.
2. Explain how deposition changes the surface of Earth.
3. What characteristics do all types of mass movements have in common?
4. Describe ways to help slow erosion on steep slopes.
5. **Think Critically** When people build houses and roads, they often pile up dirt or cut into the sides of hills. Predict how this might affect sediment on a slope. Explain how to control the effects of such activities.

Skill Builder Activities

6. **Comparing and Contrasting** Compare and contrast rockfalls and rock slides. **For more help, refer to the** Science Skill Handbook.
7. **Using an Electronic Spreadsheet** Pretend that you live along a beach where the water is 500 m from your front door. Each year, slumping causes about 1.5 m of your beach to cave into the water. Design a spreadsheet that will predict how much property will be left each year for ten years. Type a formula that will compute the amount of land left the second year. **For more help, refer to the** Technology Skill Handbook.

216 CHAPTER 8 Erosional Forces

Answers to Section Assessment

1. Erosion: a process that wears away and moves surface materials; agents include gravity, glaciers, wind, and water.
2. Possible answer: Old surfaces are covered by sediments.
3. occur on slopes, depend on gravity, occur more often after heavy rain,

result in less steep slopes
4. plant vegetation; control runoff; build walls
5. These activities produce steep, unstable slopes, which are subject to mass movements.
6. Both involve rock moving quickly downhill; rockfall: rocks break free

from a steep slope and tumble through the air; rockslide: layers of rock slip downslope suddenly.
7. Students should use the formula $(x - 1.5)$, where x is the number of meters left the year before.

SECTION 2 Glaciers

How Glaciers Form and Move

If you've ever gone sledding, snowboarding, or skiing, you might have noticed that after awhile, the snow starts to pack down under your weight. A snowy hillside can become icy if it is well traveled. In much the same way, glaciers form in regions where snow accumulates. Some areas of the world, as shown in **Figure 7,** are so cold that snow remains on the ground year-round. When snow doesn't melt, it piles up. As it accumulates slowly, the increasing weight of the snow becomes great enough to compress the lower layers into ice. Eventually, there can be enough pressure on the ice so that it becomes plasticlike. The mass slowly begins to bend and flow in a thick plasticlike lower layer, and the glacier glides downhill. A large mass of ice and snow moving on land under its own weight is a **glacier.**

Ice Eroding Rock

Glaciers are agents of erosion. As glaciers pass over land, they erode it, changing features on the surface. Glaciers then carry eroded material along and deposit it somewhere else. Glacial erosion and deposition change large areas of Earth's surface. How is it possible that something as fragile as snow or ice can push aside trees, drag rocks along , and change the surface of Earth?

As You Read

What You'll Learn
- **Explain** how glaciers move.
- **Describe** evidence of glacial erosion and deposition.
- **Compare and contrast** till and outwash.

Vocabulary

glacier	moraine
plucking	outwash
till	

Why It's Important
Glacial erosion and deposition create many landforms on Earth.

Figure 7
The white regions on this map show areas that are glaciated today.

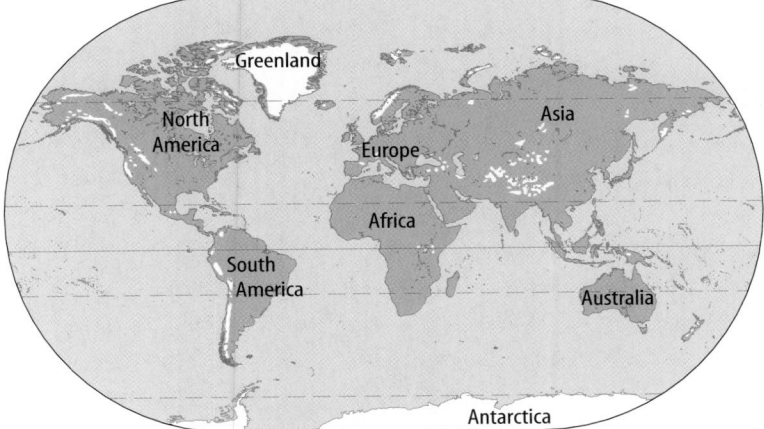

SECTION 2 Glaciers

1 Motivate

Bellringer Transparency

Display the Section Focus Transparency for Section 2. Use the accompanying Transparency Activity Master. L2
ELL

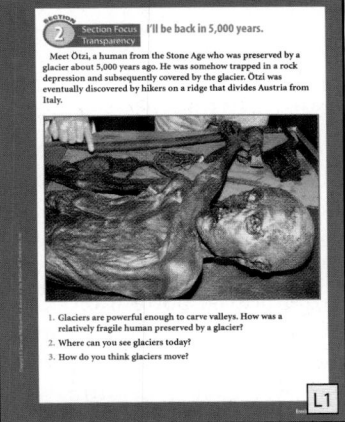

Tie to Prior Knowledge

Show pictures of glaciers and ask students to tell what they know about them. In this section, students will learn how glaciers can change Earth's surface.

Section ✔️ Assessment Planner

PORTFOLIO
Curriculum Connection, p. 219
Challenge, p. 222
PERFORMANCE ASSESSMENT
Skill Builder Activities, p. 222
See page 236 for more options.

CONTENT ASSESSMENT
Section, p. 222
Challenge, p. 222
Chapter, pp. 236–237

Resource Manager

Chapter Resources Booklet
Transparency Activity, p. 41
Directed Reading for Content Mastery, p. 16

How Glaciers Form and Move

Quick Demo

Mix cornstarch with water in a clear, plastic cup to make a thick paste. Have students observe the mixture. Then have a volunteer pick up a handful of the mixture and tilt his or her palm to deposit the mixture in a second plastic cup. **How is the cornstarch mixture like the ice at the base of a glacier?** They both appear to be solids, but they flow like liquids.

Ice Eroding Rock

Use an Analogy

Sandpaper is sand glued to paper. When sandpaper is pushed along a piece of wood, its sand particles leave small grooves in the wood. This is similar to rocks frozen in the bottom of glaciers. These rocks also leave grooves as they pass. Grooves from sandpaper and glaciers indicate the direction of movement.

✔ **Reading Check**

Answer removal of rock pieces by ice

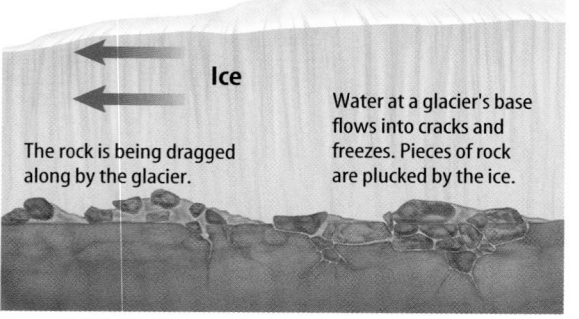

Ice

The rock is being dragged along by the glacier.

Water at a glacier's base flows into cracks and freezes. Pieces of rock are plucked by the ice.

Figure 8
Plucking is a process that picks up loosened rock particles over which a glacier is moving.

Figure 9
When glaciers melt, striations or grooves can be found on the rocks beneath. These glacial grooves on Kelley's Island, Ohio give evidence of past glacial erosion and movement.

Plucking Glaciers weather and erode solid rock. When glacial ice melts, water flows into cracks in rocks. Later, the water refreezes in these cracks, expands, and fractures the rock. Pieces of rock then are lifted out by the ice, as shown in **Figure 8.** This process, called **plucking,** results in boulders, gravel, and sand being added to the bottom and sides of a glacier.

✔ **Reading Check** *What is plucking?*

Transporting and Scouring As it moves forward over land, a glacier can transport huge volumes of sediment and rock. Plucked rock fragments and sand at its base scour and scrape the soil and bedrock like sandpaper against wood, eroding the ground below even more. When bedrock is gouged deeply by rock fragments being dragged along, marks such as those in **Figure 9** are left behind. These marks, called grooves, are deep, long, parallel scars on rocks. Shallower marks are called striations (stri AY shuns). Grooves and striations indicate the direction in which the glacier moved.

Ice Depositing Sediment

When glaciers begin to melt, they are unable to carry much sediment. The sediment drops, or is deposited, on the land. When a glacier melts and begins to shrink back, it is said to retreat. As it retreats, a jumble of boulders, sand, clay, and silt is left behind. This mixture of different-sized sediments is called **till.** Till deposits can cover huge areas of land. Thousands of years ago, huge ice sheets in the northern United States left enough till behind to fill valleys completely and make these areas appear flat. Till areas include the wide swath of what are now wheat farms running northwestward from Iowa to northern Montana. Some farmland in parts of Ohio, Indiana, and Illinois, and the rocky pastures of New England are also regions that contain till deposits.

 **LAB DEMONSTRATION**

Purpose to show the deposition of outwash sediments

Materials sand and gravel, rectangular loaf pan, large rectangular cake pan, hair dryer, book

Preparation Put a thin layer of sand and gravel in the loaf pan. Fill the pan with water and freeze it overnight.

Procedure Remove the ice-and-gravel-block and place it sediment-side down in the cake pan. Use a book to elevate the end of the pan under the ice. Use a hair dryer to slowly melt the ice.

Expected Outcome Students see outwash deposits form at the bottom of the slope.

✔ *Assessment*

How are the outwash materials deposited? Outwash is deposited from meltwater in layers—the heaviest sediments are closest to the "glacier," lighter sediments are carried farther away.

Moraine Deposits Till also is deposited at the end of a glacier when it stops moving forward, as shown in **Figure 10.** Unlike the till that is left behind as a sheet of sediment over the land, this type of deposit doesn't cover such a wide area. Rocks and soil are moved to the end of the glacier, much like items on a grocery store conveyor belt. Because of this, a big ridge of material piles up that looks as though it has been pushed along by a bulldozer. Such a ridge is called a **moraine.** Moraines deposited along the sides of a glacier are shown in **Figure 10.**

Outwash Deposits When glacial ice starts to melt, the meltwater can deposit sediment that is different from till. Material deposited by the meltwater from a glacier, most often beyond the end of the glacier, is called **outwash.** Meltwater carries sediments and deposits them in layers. Heavier sediments drop first, so bigger pieces of rock are deposited closer to the glacier. The outwash from a glacier also can form into a fan-shaped deposit when the stream of meltwater deposits sand and gravel in front of the glacier.

✔ Reading Check *What is outwash?*

Eskers Another type of outwash deposit looks like a long, winding ridge. This deposit forms in a melting glacier when meltwater forms a river within the ice, as shown in **Figure 11A.** This river carries sand and gravel and deposits them within its channel. When the glacier melts, a winding ridge of sand and gravel, called an esker (ES kur), is left behind. An esker is shown in **Figure 11B.**

Figure 10
Till is being deposited by this glacier.

Figure 11
Eskers are glacial deposits formed by meltwater.

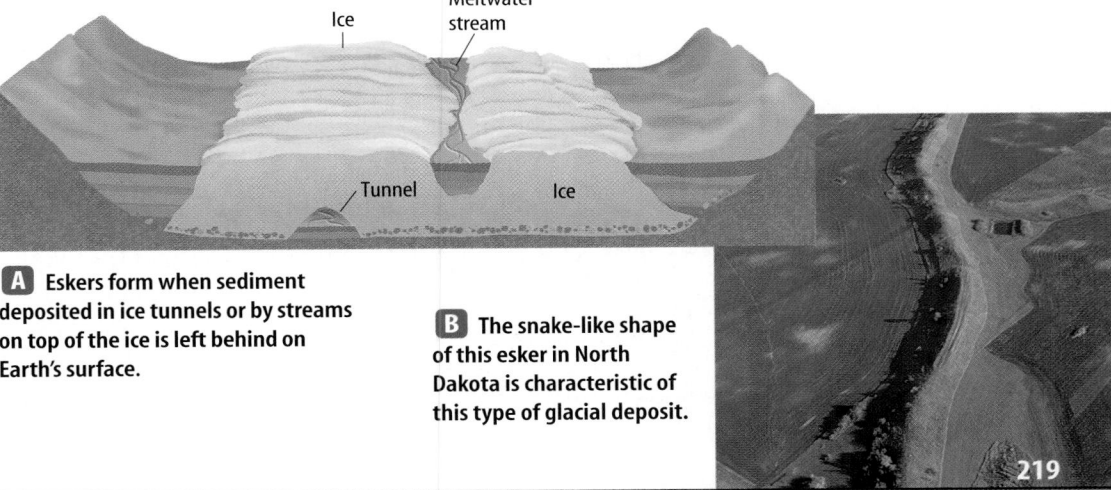

Ice

Meltwater stream

Tunnel   Ice

A Eskers form when sediment deposited in ice tunnels or by streams on top of the ice is left behind on Earth's surface.

B The snake-like shape of this esker in North Dakota is characteristic of this type of glacial deposit.

219

IDENTIFYING Misconceptions

Students may think that Earth's polar regions have always been covered with ice. In fact, for most of Earth's history, there have been no glaciers. The Antarctic ice sheet, for example, formed about 10 million years ago.

✔ Reading Check

Answer material deposited by the meltwater from a glacier

Extension

If you live in an area where glacial features can be seen, plan a field trip to allow students to observe these features.

Discussion

How might a geologist confirm that a ridge is an esker and not a ridge formed by some other means? Students should infer that geologists would have to dig into the ridge to discover its composition. If it is found to be made of deposits of sand and gravel, this is one clue that the ridge could be an esker.

Quick Demo

To reinforce how glacial plucking occurs, submerge a brick in water for one full day. Then, place the water-soaked brick in a freezer overnight. Show the frozen brick to students. They will observe that part of the brick has crumbled.

Curriculum Connection

Music Have students work in small groups to write lyrics that describe glacial erosion and deposition. Encourage interested students to perform their songs in class. COOP LEARN
IS Auditory-Musical P

Resource Manager

Chapter Resources Booklet
Enrichment, p. 27

Continental Glaciers

✓ **Reading Check**

Answer mostly near the poles

Extension

Have students research how much lower sea level was during the last ice age. Then instruct them to draw an outline of North America as it appears today alongside an outline of North America as it would have appeared during the last ice age. Post the drawings on a bulletin board. When the last ice age was at its peak, sea level was about 130 m lower than it is today. The coastline would have included many areas of continental shelf that are now below sea level. L2 **IS Visual-Spatial**

Discussion

Infer what happened to the average air temperature on Earth at the end of the last ice age. Average air temperature rose.

Caption Answer

Figure 13 If your area shows evidence of glaciation, have students look for landforms such as grooves in rocks, moraines, and outwash deposits such as alluvial fans and eskers.

Visual Learning

Figure 13 Would you expect to find landforms in Mexico that formed by glaciation during the last ice age? Explain. No; glaciers didn't extend that far south.

Figure 12
Continental glaciers and valley glaciers are agents of erosion and deposition. This continental glacier covers a large area in Antarctica.

Continental Glaciers

The two types of glaciers are continental glaciers and valley glaciers. Today, continental glaciers like the one in **Figure 12** cover only ten percent of Earth, mostly near the poles in Antarctica and Greenland. These continental glaciers are huge masses of ice and snow. Continental glaciers are thicker than some mountain ranges. Glaciers make it impossible to see most of the land features in Antarctica and Greenland.

✓ **Reading Check** *In what regions on Earth would you expect to find continental glaciers?*

Climate Changes In the past, continental glaciers covered as much as 28 percent of Earth. **Figure 13** shows how much of North America was covered by glaciers during the most recent ice advance. These periods of widespread glaciation are known as ice ages. Extensive glaciers have covered large portions of Earth many times over the last 2 million to 3 million years. During this time, glaciers advanced and retreated many times over much of North America. The average air temperature on Earth was about 5°C lower during these ice ages than it is today. The last major advance of ice reached its maximum extent about 18,000 years ago. After this last advance of glaciers, the ends of the ice sheets began to recede, or move back, by melting.

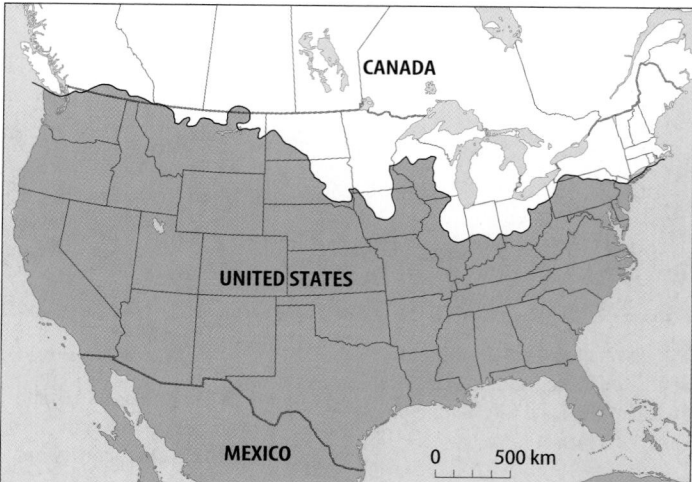

Figure 13
This map shows how far the continental glaciers spread in North America until about 18,000 years ago. *Was your location covered? If so, what evidence of glaciers does your area show?*

220 CHAPTER 8 Erosional Forces

Curriculum Connection

History During the last ice advance, people traveled from Asia to North America across a strip of land that connected the two continents. This Bering land bridge was located where the Bering Strait is today. Have students locate the Bering Strait on a map and explain why there was a land bridge during the last ice advance. Much of Earth's water was locked up in glaciers, so sea level was lower.

Valley Glaciers

Valley glaciers occur even in today's warmer global climate. In the high mountains where the average temperature is low enough to prevent snow from melting during the summer, valley glaciers grow and creep along. **Figure 14** shows a valley glacier in Africa.

Evidence of Valley Glaciers If you visit the mountains, you can tell whether valley glaciers ever existed there. You might look for striations, then search for evidence of plucking. Glacial plucking often occurs near the top of a mountain where a glacier is mainly in contact with solid rock. Valley glaciers erode bowl-shaped basins, called cirques (SURKS), into the sides of mountains. If two valley glaciers side by side erode a mountain peak, a long ridge called an arête (ah RAYT) forms between them. If valley glaciers erode a mountain from several directions, a sharpened peak called a horn might form. **Figure 15A** shows some features formed by valley glaciers.

Valley glaciers flow down mountain slopes and along valleys, eroding as they go. Valleys that have been eroded by glaciers have a different shape from those eroded by streams. Stream-eroded valleys are normally V-shaped. Glacially eroded valleys are U-shaped because a glacier plucks and scrapes soil and rock from the sides as well as from the bottom. A U-shaped valley is illustrated in **Figure 15B**.

Figure 14
Valley glaciers, like these on Mount Kilimanjaro in north Tanzania, Africa, form between mountain peaks that lie above the snow line, where snow lasts all year.

Figure 15
Valley glaciers transform the mountains over which they pass.

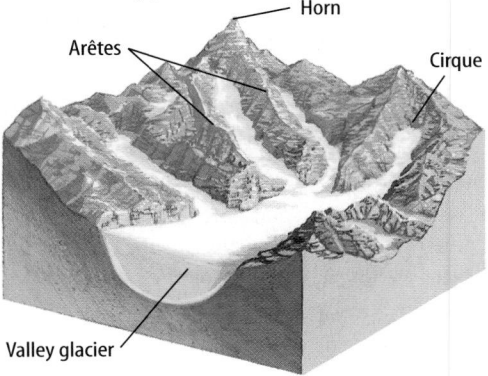

A Bowl-shaped basins called cirques form by erosion at the start of a valley glacier. Arêtes form where two adjacent valley glaciers meet and erode a long, sharp ridge. Horns are sharpened peaks formed by glacial action in three or more cirques.

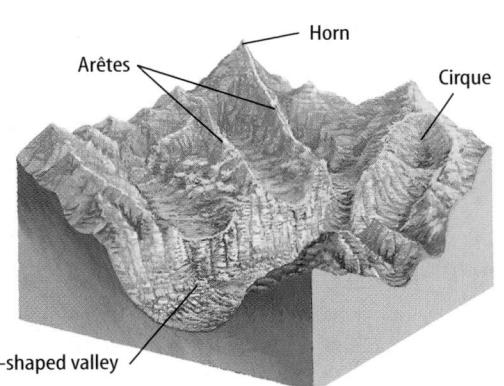

B U-shaped valleys result when valley glaciers move through regions once occupied by streams.

SECTION 2 Glaciers **221**

Importance of Glaciers

③ Assess

Reteach

What landforms might you see in an area once covered by glaciers? grooves gouged in rocks, till, moraines, eskers, cirques, arêtes, horns, U-shaped valleys

Challenge

Challenge students to write a story describing changes that might occur in daily living if a new ice age were to begin. [P]

✓Assessment

Content Have students compare and contrast the appearance of outwash and moraine deposits. Use **PASC,** p. 89.

Figure 16
Sand and gravel deposits left by glaciers are important starting materials for the construction of roadways and buildings.

Importance of Glaciers

Glaciers have had a profound effect on Earth's surface. They have eroded mountaintops and transformed valleys. Vast areas of the continents have sediments that were deposited by great ice sheets. Today, glaciers in polar regions and in mountains continue to change the surface features of Earth.

In addition to changing the appearance of Earth's surface, glaciers leave behind sediments that are economically important, as illustrated in **Figure 16.** The sand and gravel deposits from glacial outwash and eskers are important resources. These deposits are excellent starting materials for the construction of roads and buildings.

Section ② Assessment

1. How do glaciers move?
2. Describe two ways in which a glacier can cause erosion.
3. Till and outwash are glacial deposits. Explain how till and outwash are different.
4. How do moraines form? What are moraines made of?
5. **Think Critically** Rivers and lakes that receive water from glacial meltwater often appear milky blue in color. What do you think might cause the milky appearance of these waters?

Skill Builder Activities

6. **Recognizing Cause and Effect** Since 1900, the Alps have lost 50 percent of their ice caps, and New Zealand's glaciers have shrunk by 26 percent. Describe what you think the effects of glacial melting have been. **For more help, refer to the Science** Skill Handbook.

7. **Researching Information** The term *erratic* comes from the Latin word *errare,* meaning "to wander." Research how glaciers move erratics. Write a poem about the "life" of an erratic. **For more help, refer to the** Science Skill Handbook.

Answers to Section Assessment

1. Pressure from the weight the glacier causes ice near the bottom to become plasticlike, while gravity makes the glacier move downhill.
2. by scraping, scouring, and pushing sediments and big rocks beneath it; by water flowing from it
3. Till is a mixture of different-sized sediments dropped directly from the front, sides, and base of a glacier. Out-wash consists of sediments deposited by meltwater.
4. As a glacier melts and stops advancing, material drops out at the sides and front of the glacier. Moraines are made of sediments, called till.
5. sediments in the glacial meltwater
6. Possible answer: The melting of the glaciers could have adversely affected ski resorts that depend on snow and caused a rise in sea level.
7. Erratics freeze into the base of a glacier and move with it. They can be carried far from their source. When a glacier begins to melt, it drops its erratics. Poems should include some of these points.

Glacial Grooving

Throughout the world's mountainous regions, 200,000 valley glaciers are moving in response to gravity.

What You'll Investigate
How is the land affected when a valley glacier moves downslope?

Materials
sand
large plastic or
    metal tray
*stream table
ice block
books (2 or 3)

*wood block
metric ruler
overhead light source
    with reflector
*Alternate materials

Safety Precautions

WARNINGS: *Do not pour sand down the drain. Make sure source is plugged into a GFI electrical outlet. Do not touch light source—it may be hot.*

Goals
■ **Compare** stream and glacial valleys.

Procedure
1. Set up the large tray of sand as shown. Place books under one end of the tray to make a slope.
2. Cut a narrow channel, like a river, through the sand. Measure and record its width and depth. Draw a sketch that includes these measurements.
3. Position the overhead light source to shine on the channel as shown.
4. Force the ice block into the channel at the upper end of the tray.

5. Gently push the ice along the channel until it's halfway between the top and bottom of the tray, and directly under the light.
6. Turn on the light and allow the ice to melt. Record what happens.
7. **Record** the width and depth of the ice channel. Make a scale drawing.

Conclude and Apply
1. **Explain** how you can determine the direction that a glacier traveled from the location of deposits.
2. **Explain** how you can determine the direction of glacial movement from sediments deposited by meltwater.
3. How do valley glaciers affect the surface over which they move?

Glacier Data			
Sample Data	Width (cm)	Depth (cm)	Observations
Original Channel	1–2	3	Stream channel looked V-shaped
Glacier Channel	8	4	U-shaped channel
Meltwater Channel	1–2	3.5	V-shaped channel

ACTIVITY 223

BENCH TESTED

Purpose Students observe how valley glaciers affect the land.
L2 ELL COOP LEARN
LS **Visual-Spatial** P

Process Skills observing, recording and interpreting data, making models, comparing and contrasting, relating cause and effect, measuring in SI

Time Required 50 to 60 minutes

Safety Precautions Make sure light source is plugged into a GFI electrical outlet. Remind students not to touch the light source.

Teaching Strategy Prepare freezer trays of ice a day before students do this activity.

Troubleshooting Have students adjust the overhead light to provide enough heat to melt the ice.

Answers to Questions
1. Small hills of till mark the end position of a glacier.
2. Large outwash sediments are deposited closest to the glacial front. Smaller sediments are carried farther from the front.
3. Valley glaciers have a bulldozing effect that produces U-shaped valleys with steep sides and relatively flat bottoms.

✓ Assessment

Performance Have students design an experiment to test the effects of one of the following variables: slope, pressure applied to the ice block, mass of the ice block, amount of sediments in the ice block, or the width of the original channel. Use **PASC,** p. 95.

Resource Manager

Chapter Resources Booklet
Reinforcement, p. 24
Activity Worksheet, pp. 5–6
Lab Activity, pp. 11–12

Communicating Your Data
Students may design posters illustrating the different stages of glacial movement, width and depth of the ice channel at different points, or a chart depicting glacial deposits and how they are used as directional clues.

SECTION

3 Wind

1 Motivate

Bellringer Transparency

Display the Section Focus Transparency for Section 3. Use the accompanying Transparency Activity Master. L2

ELL

Tie to Prior Knowledge

Have students recall seeing dust carried by the wind. Ask students how wind speed affects the amount and type of material that the wind can transport. Stronger winds carry more and heavier materials. Tell students they will find out how wind can alter Earth's surface in this section.

As You Read

What You'll Learn

- **Explain** how wind causes deflation and abrasion.
- **Recognize** how loess and dunes form.

Vocabulary

deflation   loess
abrasion   dune

Why It's Important

Wind erosion and deposition change landscapes, especially in dry climates.

Figure 17
The odd shape of this boulder was produced by wind abrasion.

Wind Erosion

When air moves, it picks up loose material and transports it to other places. Air differs from other erosional forces because it usually cannot pick up heavy sediments. Unlike rivers that move in confined places like channels and valleys, wind carries and deposits sediments over large areas. For example, wind is capable of picking up and carrying dust particles from fields or volcanic ash high into the atmosphere and depositing them thousands of kilometers away.

Deflation Wind erodes Earth's surface by deflation (dih FLAY shun) and abrasion (uh BRAY zhun). When wind erodes by **deflation,** it blows across loose sediment, removing small particles such as silt and sand. The heavier, coarser material is left behind.

Abrasion When windblown sediments strike rock, the surface of the rock gets scraped and worn away by a process called abrasion. **Abrasion** shown in **Figure 17** is similar to sandblasting. Workers use machines that spray a mixture of sand and water under high pressure against a building. The friction wears away dirt from stone, concrete, or brick walls. It also polishes the walls of buildings by breaking away small pieces and leaving an even, smooth finish. Wind acts like a sandblasting machine, rolling and blowing sand grains along. These sand grains strike against rocks and break off small fragments. The rocks become pitted and are worn down.

✓ **Reading Check** *How is wind abrasion similar to sandblasting?*

Deflation and abrasion happen to all land surfaces but occur mostly in deserts, beaches, and plowed fields. These areas have fewer plants to hold the sediments in place. When winds blow over them, there is little to hold them down.

224 CHAPTER 8 Erosional Forces

Section ✓*Assessment* Planner

PORTFOLIO
Cultural Diversity, p. 227
PERFORMANCE ASSESSMENT
Problem-Solving Activity, p. 225
Try at Home MiniLAB, p. 226
Skill Builder Activities, p. 229
See page 236 for more options.

CONTENT ASSESSMENT
Section, p. 229
Challenge, p. 229
Chapter, pp. 236–237

Sandstorms Even when the wind blows strongly, it seldom carries sand grains higher than 0.5 m from the ground. However, sandstorms do occur. When the wind blows forcefully in the sandy parts of deserts, sand grains bounce along and hit other sand grains, causing more and more grains to rise into the air. These windblown sand grains form a low cloud just above the ground. Most sandstorms occur in deserts, but they can occur in other arid regions as shown in **Figure 18.**

Dust Storms When soil is moist, it stays packed on the ground, but when it dries out, it can be eroded by wind. Soil is composed largely of silt- and clay-sized particles. Because these small particles weigh less than sand-sized particles of the same material, wind can move them high into the air.

Silt and clay particles are small and closely packed. A faster wind is needed to lift these fine particles of soil than is needed to lift grains of sand. However, after they are airborne, the wind can carry them long distances. Where the land is dry, dust storms can cover hundreds of kilometers. These storms blow topsoil from open fields, overgrazed areas, and places where vegetation has disappeared. In the 1930s, silt and dust picked up in Kansas fell in New England and in the North Atlantic Ocean. Dust blown from the Sahara has been traced as far away as the West Indies—a distance of at least 6000 km.

Figure 18
Sandstorms can obscure visibility over large regions.

Problem-Solving Activity

What factors affect wind erosion?

There are many factors that compound the effects of wind erosion. But is there anything that can be done to minimize erosion?

Identifying the Problem
Wind velocity and duration, the size of sediment particles, the size of the area subjected to the wind, and the amount of vegetation present all affect how much soil is eroded by wind. The table shows different combinations of these factors. It also includes an erosion rating that depends upon what factors pertain to an area.

Factors Affecting Wind Erosion

Factor	Descriptions of Factors				
Wind velocity	high	high	low	low	low
Duration of wind	long	long	short	long	long
Particle size	coarse	fine	coarse	coarse	fine
Surface area	large	large	small	small	large
Amount of vegetation	high	low	high	high	high
Erosion rating	some	a lot	a little	some	?

Solving the Problem
1. Looking at the table, can you figure out which factors increase and which factors decrease the amount of erosion?
2. From what you've discovered , can you estimate the missing erosion rating?

SECTION 3 Wind **225**

Wind Erosion

✔ Reading Check

Answer The friction of the sand being thrown against the rocks wears the rocks down.

Discussion

How does over-farming and over-grazing make some lands vulnerable to wind erosion? Is the same land as easily harmed by rain as it is by wind? Over-farming and over-grazing exposes the soil. During dry periods, the soil can blow away. Likewise, heavy rain can wash exposed soil away.

Activity

On a map of the United States, have students locate dry areas that are most likely to be affected by sandstorms or dust storms. L3

Problem-Solving Activity

National Math Standards
Correlation to Mathematics Objectives
5–10

Answers

1. High wind velocity, long duration, and large surface area all increase wind erosion. Coarse particle size and a high amount of vegetation decrease erosion.
2. Students may say "a little" or "some." Low winds blowing over a large surface area for a long period of time would cause some erosion. However, the presence of a large amount of vegetation would reduce these effects.

Visual Learning
Figure 18 How is this sandstorm affecting the local area? Possible answers: Visibility is reduced; sand is removed from some places and deposited in others.

Resource Manager

Chapter Resources Booklet
Transparency Activity, p. 42
Directed Reading for Content Mastery, pp. 17, 18
Mathematics Skill Activities, p. 9

Reducing Wind Erosion

Fun Fact

A plant's root system may equal or exceed the size of the plant seen above the ground. For example, a tree that is 50 m tall might have a root system that covers an area the size of a football field.

TRY AT HOME
Mini LAB

Observing How Soil Is Held in Place

Procedure
1. Obtain a piece of **sod** (a chunk of soil about 5 cm thick with grass growing from it).
2. Carefully remove soil from the sod roots by hand. Examine the roots with a **magnifying glass or hand lens.**
3. Wash hands thoroughly with soap and water.

Analysis
1. Draw several of these roots in your **Science Journal.**
2. What characteristics of grass roots help hold soil in place and thus reduce erosion?

Figure 19
Rows of grasses and rocks were installed on these dunes in Qinghai, China to reduce wind erosion.

Reducing Wind Erosion

Life Science INTEGRATION

As you've learned, wind erosion is most common where there are no plants to protect the soil. Therefore, one of the best ways to slow or stop wind erosion is to plant vegetation. This practice helps conserve many natural reserves and farmland.

Windbreaks People in many countries plant vegetation to reduce wind erosion. For centuries, farmers have planted trees along their fields to act as windbreaks that prevent soil erosion. As the wind hits the trees, its energy of motion is reduced. It no longer is able to lift particles.

In one study, a thin belt of cottonwood trees reduced the effect of a 25-km/h wind to about 66 percent of its normal speed, or to about 16.5 km/h. Tree belts also trap snow and hold it on land. This increases the moisture level of the soil, which helps prevent further erosion.

Roots Along many seacoasts and deserts, vegetation is planted to reduce erosion. Plants with fibrous root systems, such as grasses, work best at stopping wind erosion. Grass roots are shallow and slender with many fibers. They twist and turn between particles in the soil and hold it in place.

Planting vegetation is a good way to reduce the effects of deflation and abrasion. Even so, if the wind is strong and the soil is dry, nothing can stop erosion completely. **Figure 19** shows a project designed to decrease wind erosion.

✔ Active Reading

Jigsaw In this collaborative learning technique, individuals become experts on a portion of a text and share their expertise with a small group, called their home group. Everyone shares responsibility for learning the assigned reading. Assign each person in each home group an expert number (1 through 5, for example). Have students gather into the expert groups that correspond to the number they were assigned. Have them read, discuss, and master chapter concepts and determine how best to teach them to their home groups. Have students return to their home groups and share the content they learned in their expert groups. Have students use the Jigsaw strategy to learn about ways to reduce wind erosion.

Deposition by Wind

Sediments blown away by wind eventually are deposited. Over time, these windblown deposits develop into landforms, such as accumulations of loess and dunes.

Loess Some examples of large deposits of windblown sediments are found near the Mississippi and Missouri Rivers. These wind deposits of fine-grained sediments known as **loess** (LOOS) are shown in **Figure 20.** Strong winds that blew across glacial outwash areas carried the sediments and deposited them. The sediments settled on hilltops and in valleys. Once there, the particles packed together, creating a thick, unlayered, yellowish-brown-colored deposit. Loess is as fine as talcum powder. Many farmlands of the midwestern United States have fertile soils that developed from loess deposits.

Dunes Do you notice what happens when wind blows sediments against an obstacle such as a rock or a clump of vegetation? The wind sweeps around or over the obstacle. Like a river, air drops sediment when its energy decreases. Sediment starts to build up behind the obstacle. The sediment itself then becomes an obstacle, trapping even more material. If the wind blows long enough, the mound will become a dune, as shown in **Figure 21.** A **dune** (DOON) is a mound of sediments drifted by the wind.

> ✔ **Reading Check** *What is a dune?*

Dunes are common in desert regions. You also can see sand dunes along the shores of oceans, seas, or lakes. If dry sediments exist in an area where prevailing winds or sea breezes blow daily, dunes build up. Sand or other sediment will continue to build up and form a dune until the sand runs out or the obstruction is removed. Some desert sand dunes can grow to 100 m high, but most are much shorter.

Moving Dunes A sand dune has two sides. The side facing the wind has a gentler slope. The side away from the wind is steeper. Examining the shape of a dune tells you the direction from which the wind usually blows.

Unless sand dunes are planted with grasses, most dunes move, or migrate away from the direction of the wind. This process is shown in **Figure 22.** Some dunes are known as traveling dunes because they move rapidly across desert areas. As they lose sand on one side, they build it up on the other.

Figure 20
This sediment deposit is composed partially of wind-blown loess.

Figure 21
Loose sediment of any type can form a dune if enough of it is present and an obstacle lies in the path of the wind.

Deposition by Wind

Discussion

Explain that along some beaches, people lay old Christmas trees in the sand to keep the sand from eroding. **Why do large dunes develop in these areas?** The trees act as barriers to the wind and trap the sand grains, which eventually form dunes.

> ✔ **Reading Check**

Answer a mound of sediments drifted by the wind

Make a Model

Have students wear goggles and use a large pan, cardboard, sand, and a hair dryer to create different sand dune shapes. Have students hold the cardboard against the far side of the pan to prevent sand from blowing out of the pan. By varying the amount of sand, the wind's velocity, and the direction of the wind, dune shapes will change. Have students match the dunes they make to the dunes shown in **Figure 23.**

Extension

The loess deposits in northern China originated in the Gobi Desert. This yellow sediment is responsible for the color of the Huang He (Yellow River) and Huang Hai (Yellow Sea). On a map, have students locate China, the Gobi and Ordos deserts, and the Huang He. Then have them determine the direction of the wind that forms the loess deposits in China. southeast. L2

Cultural Diversity

Wind Erosion In many areas of the world, deserts are spreading because of drought and the removal of native vegetation. To prevent wind erosion, women in Kenya are planting trees around cropland. Invite students to use the Internet to find out more about this project. Have students write short reports and share them in class. P

Resource Manager

Chapter Resources Booklet
   MiniLAB, p. 4
Home and Community Involvement, p. 41
Performance Assessment in the Science Classroom, p. 44

Visualizing How Dunes Form and Migrate

Have students examine the pictures and read the captions. Then ask the following questions.

What do you think dunes on Hawaii's volcanic islands would be made from? eroded materials from lava flows

Explain to students that the sloping side of the dune is the windward side, while the steep face is called leeward side of the dune. **Why do the sand grains stop blowing on the leeward side of a dune?** Because the dune itself shelters them from the wind.

Activity

Have small groups of students research the variety of shapes dunes form. Have use sand mixed with white glue as a bonding agent to make models of transverse, barchan, longitudinal, star, linear, and parabolic dunes. Models should be made on sturdy cardboard.

Extension

Have students research some of the methods people are using to stop the migration of dunes into populated areas. Students should present their research in brief oral or written reports.

NATIONAL GEOGRAPHIC VISUALIZING
HOW DUNES FORM AND MIGRATE

Figure 22

Sand blown loose from dry desert soil often builds up into dunes. A dune may begin to form when windblown sand is deposited in the sheltered area behind an obstacle, such as a rock outcrop. The sand pile grows as more grains accumulate. As shown in the diagram at right, dunes are mobile, gradually moved along by wind.

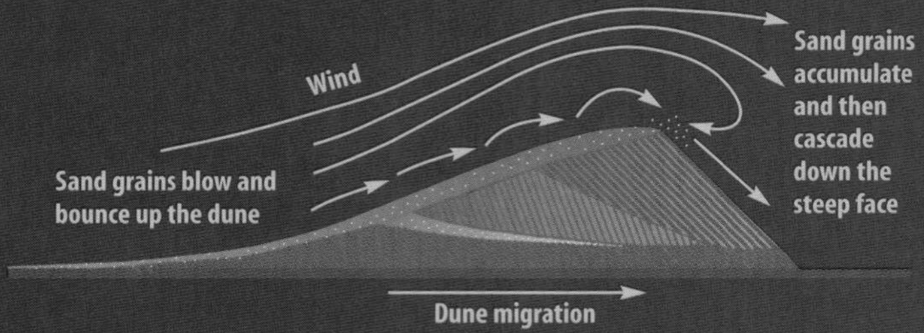

Wind

Sand grains blow and bounce up the dune

Sand grains accumulate and then cascade down the steep face

Dune migration

▲ A dune migrates as sand blows up its sloping side and then cascades down the steeper side. Gradually, a dune moves forward—in the same direction that the wind is blowing—as sand, lost from one side, piles up on the other side.

▲ Dunes are made of sediments eroded from local materials. Although many dunes are composed of quartz and feldspar, the brillant white dunes in White Sands National Park, New Mexico, are made of gypsum.

▲ Deserts may expand when humans move into the transition zone between habitable land and desert. Here, villagers in Mauritania in northwestern Africa shovel the sand that encroaches on their schoolhouse daily.

◄ The dunes at left are coastal dunes from the Laguna Madre region of South Texas on the Gulf of Mexico. Note the vegetation in the photo, which has served as an obstacle to trap sand.

Resource Manager

Chapter Resources Booklet
    Enrichment, p. 28
    Reinforcement, p. 25
Science Inquiry Labs, p. 5

Dune Shape The shape of a dune depends on the amount of sand or other sediment available, the wind speed and direction, and the amount of vegetation present. One common dune shape is a crescent-shaped dune known as a barchan (BAR kun) dune. The open side of a barchan dune faces the direction that the wind is blowing. When viewed from above, the points of the crescent are directed downwind. This type of dune forms on hard surfaces where the sand supply is limited.

Another common type of dune, called a transverse dune, forms where sand is abundant. Transverse dunes are so named because the long directions of these dunes are perpendicular to the general wind direction. In regions where the wind direction changes, star dunes, shown in **Figure 23,** form pointed structures. Other dune forms also exist, some of which show a combination of features.

Shifting Sediments When dunes and loess form, the landscape changes. Wind, like gravity, running water, and glaciers, shapes the land. New landforms created by these agents of erosion are themselves being eroded. Erosion and deposition are part of a cycle of change that constantly shapes and reshapes the land.

Figure 23
Star dunes form in areas where the wind blows from several different directions.

Section 3 Assessment

1. Compare and contrast abrasion and deflation. Describe how they affect the surface of Earth.

2. Explain the differences between dust storms and sandstorms. Describe how the energy of motion affects the deposition of sand and dust by these storms.

3. Explain what loess is made of and how a loess deposit forms.

4. Why do farmers plant trees along the edges of their fields?

5. **Think Critically** You notice that sand is piling up behind a fence outside your apartment building. Explain why this occurs.

Skill Builder Activities

6. **Predicting** Predict the sequence of the following events about dune formation. **For more help,** refer to the Science Skill Handbook.
   a. Grains collect to form a mound.
   b. Wind blows sand grains around an obstacle.
   c. Wind blows over an area and causes deflation.
   d. Vegetation grows on the dune.

7. **Solving One-Step Equations** Between 1972 and 1992, the Sahara Desert increased by nearly 700 km^2 in Mali and the Sudan. Calculate the average number of square kilometers the desert increased each year between 1972 and 1992. **For more help,** refer to the Math Skill Handbook.

Reteach
   Have students work in groups to determine the effect of clumps of grass on the development of sand dunes. Each team will need the following items: safety goggles, a flat pan filled with sand, a hair dryer, cardboard, and clumps of grass. L2
   ELL   COOP LEARN

Challenge
   Design an experiment using sticks to model how a fence affects wind erosion. Hypothesize what will happen. Student designs will vary. A fence acts as a windbreak, reducing the amount of erosion.

✔Assessment

Content Assess students' abilities to sequence by having them list the steps involved in the formation of loess deposits. Use **Performance Assessment in the Science Classroom,** p. 163.

Answers to Section Assessment

1. Both move sediment and change surface features; deflation: wind picks up and transports small particles, leaving behind larger particles; abrasion: blowing sand grains strike and break off small fragments of rock.

2. In sandstorms, sand remains close to the ground and doesn't blow very far. Dust storms pick up dust and carry it great distances. The greater the energy of motion, the greater the distance sediment is transported.

3. Loess is made of fine-grained, wind-blown sediments. Loess deposits form as winds that blow across glacial outwash areas pick up and later deposit fine sediments.

4. Trees decrease the speed of the wind and in this way reduce wind erosion.

5. Wind striking the fence loses some of its energy of motion and deposits the sand.

6. c, b, a, d

7. 700 km^2 ÷ 20 = 35 km^2 per year

Activity

Recognize the Problem

Purpose
Students observe how soil moisture and wind velocity affect wind erosion. L2 IS **Kinesthetic**

Process Skills
designing an experiment to test a hypothesis, identifying and manipulating variables, making models, observing and inferring, interpreting data, relating cause and effect, using numbers

Time Required
45 minutes for planning the experiment, 45 minutes for doing the experiment

Materials
Three-speed hair dryers are needed for this activity. Deep metal baking pans or paint trays will help contain the sediment.

Safety Precautions
Students should wear safety goggles when sediments are being blown. They should handle hot objects with care.

Form a Hypothesis

Possible Hypotheses
Students might hypothesize that the greater the velocity of the wind, the larger the sediments it can transport. Students might also suspect that moisture will add weight to the sediments, causing them to stick to one another and resulting in decreased erosion.

Test Your Hypothesis

Possible Procedures
- Put on safety goggles. Mix equal amounts of sediments. Place half of the mixture in

---

Activity Design Your Own Experiment

Blowing in the Wind

Have you ever played a sport outside and suddenly had the wind blow dust into your eyes? What did you do? Turn your back? Cover your eyes? How does wind pick up sediment? Why does wind pick up some sediments and leave others on the ground?

Recognize the Problem
What factors affect wind erosion?

Form a Hypothesis
How does moisture in sediment affect the ability of wind to erode sediments? Does the speed of the wind limit the size of sediments it can transport? Form a hypothesis about how sediment moisture affects wind erosion. Form another hypothesis about how wind speed affects the size of the sediment the wind can transport.

Goals
- **Observe** the effects of soil moisture and wind speed on wind erosion.
- **Design** and carry out experiments that test the effects of soil moisture and wind speed on wind erosion.

Possible Materials
flat pans (4)
fine sand (400 mL)
gravel (400 mL)
hairdryer
sprinkling can
water
28-cm × 35-cm cardboard sheets (4)
tape
mixing bowl
metric ruler
wind speed indicator

Safety Precautions

Wear your safety goggles at all times when using the hairdryer on sediments. Make sure the dryer is plugged into a GFI electrical outlet.

---

each of two pans. Tape a sheet of folded cardboard to one end of each pan. Sprinkle water onto the soil in one pan. Set the hair dryer at medium and blow the sediments toward the cardboard in each pan from the same angle and distance for two minutes.

Resource Manager

Chapter Resources Booklet
   Activity Worksheet, pp. 7–8
Lab Management and Safety, p. 65

Test Your Hypothesis

Plan

1. As a group, agree upon and write your hypothesis statements.

2. **List** the steps needed to test your first hypothesis. Plan specific steps and vary only one factor at a time. Then, list the steps needed to test your second hypothesis. Test only one factor at a time.

3. Mix the sediments in the pans. Plan how you will fold cardboard sheets and attach them to the pans to keep sediments contained.

4. **Design** data tables in your Science Journal. Use them as your group collects data.

5. **Identify** all constants, variables, and controls of the experiment. One example of a control is a pan of sediment not subjected to any wind.

Do

1. Make sure your teacher approves your plan before you start.

2. Carry out the experiments as planned.

3. While doing the experiments, write any observations that you or other members of your group make. Summarize your data in the data tables you designed in your Science Journal.

Sediment Movement		
Sediment	**Wind Speed**	**Sediment Moved**
Fine Sand (dry)	low	
	high	
Fine Sand (wet)	low	
	high	
Gravel (dry)	low	Answers
	high	will vary.
Gravel (wet)	low	
	high	
Fine Sand and Gravel (dry)	low	
	high	
Fine Sand and Gravel (wet)	low	
	high	

- To test the effect of wind velocity, begin as previously described. Sediments in both pans should be dry. Blow air over one pan for two minutes on low. Repeat with the other pan, with the dryer on high.

Teaching Strategy Emphasize that the angle at which the dryers are held and the distance of the dryers from the pans must be the same each time.

Expected Outcome

Soil moisture slows wind erosion. The greater the wind speed, the greater the size and amount of sediment transported.

Analyze Your Data

1. Results should be similar.
2. The greater the wind speed, the larger the sediments moved.

Error Analysis

If higher wind speeds did not result in the movement of larger particles, wind speeds or particle sizes may have been too similar.

Draw Conclusions

1. When energy of motion increases, erosion increases. When energy of motion decreases, deposition occurs.
2. Moist sediments are not easily eroded.

Analyze Your Data

1. **Compare** your results with those of other groups. Explain what might have caused any differences among the groups.

2. **Explain** the relationship that exists between the speed of the wind and the size of the sediments it transports.

Draw Conclusions

1. How does energy of motion of the wind influence sediment transport? What is the general relationship between wind speed and erosion?

2. **Explain** the relationship between the sediment moisture and the amount of sediment moved by the wind.

Communicating Your Data

Design a table on poster board or construction paper that summarizes the results of your experiment. Use your table to explain your interpretations to others in the class. **For more help, refer to the** Science Skill Handbook.

✓ Assessment

Performance To further assess students' understanding of wind erosion, have them design an experiment to collect data in order to graph the effects of different amounts of moisture on the amount of sediment that erodes. Use **Performance Assessment in the Science Classroom,** p. 95.

Communicating Your Data

Suggest that students use electronic spreadsheets for designing their tables.

Science Stats

Content Background

About 10 percent of Earth's land is covered with glaciers. Today, continental glaciers cover most of Antarctica and Greenland. Glaciers can be up to 1,800 m deep and sometimes cover entire mountains. Several of Iceland's glaciers cover active volcanoes, which occasionally erupt. When this happens. floods of water, ice, and rocks erode the lands.

Erosion also occurs beneath earth's surface where groundwater causes limestone to dissolve. Water then carries away the dissolved materials, sometimes forming caves.

If it were not for the shifting of Earth's plates, which builds mountains and raises the land's surface in other ways, the forces of weathering and erosion would eventually wear the surface of Earth into a smooth, low plain.

Discussion

Why might it be dangerous to build homes on the steep slopes of canyon? Mass movement, such as a landslide triggered by an earthquake could cause the homes to be destroyed with possible injury and loss of life to the people who live in them.

Activity

Have small groups of students research an area of the United States that has been sculpted by wind erosion or erosion by glaciers and prepare a travel brochure that would inform visitors to the area on how erosion affected the land.

Science Stats

Losing Against Erosion

Did you know...

...Some sand dunes migrate as much as 30 m per year. In a coastal region of France, traveling dunes have buried forests, farms, and villages. The dunes were halted by anti-erosion practices, such as planting grass in the sand and growing a barrier of trees between the dunes and farmland.

...Wind erosion never stops. Wind erosion robs rural areas in the United States of as much as 5,590 kg of soil per hectare per year. One hectare is equivalent to 10,000 m^2. This amounts to removing one small truckload of soil from an area about the size of a football field each year.

...Erosion can move mountains. Between 1982 and 1983, El Niño caused rockfalls along Highway 1 in California. The falling rock from the mountain alongside the road forced a section to close. The rocks stranded the residents of Half Moon Bay until the road was cleared.

SCIENCE
Online
Internet Addresses

_____
_____
_____
_____

Explore the Glencoe Science Web site at **science.glencoe.com** to find out more about topics in this feature.

...In 1959, an earthquake triggered a mass movement in Madison River Canyon, Montana. About 21 million km^3 of rock and soil slid down the canyon at an estimated 160 km/h. This type of mass movement of earth is called a rock slide.

...Glaciers, one of nature's most powerful erosional forces, can move more than 30 m per day. In one week, a fast-moving glacier can travel the length of almost two football fields. Glaciers such as these are unusual—most move less than 30 cm per day.

Homes in Danger from Shoreline Erosion by the Year 2060

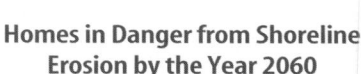
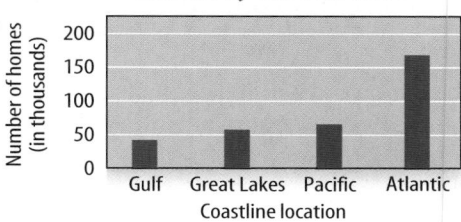

Do the Math

1. If you could devise a method to slow soil loss due to wind erosion by 25 percent, how much soil would be saved each year in the United States?
2. If erosion destroys 300 m of shoreline every 100 years, how long would it take to destroy 1 km of shoreline?
3. If a sand dune is traveling at 30 m per year, how many meters does it travel in one month?

Go Further

Go to **science.glencoe.com** to learn about landslides. When is a landslide called a mud slide? In which U.S. states are mud slides most likely to occur?

Do the Math

Teaching Strategies

- Have students calculate the mass of soil saved per hectare of land in the first question in Do the Math. Review with students how to convert percentages to decimals before multiplying.
- Review ratios with students to help them answer the second question in Do the Math. Also remind them to convert 1 km to m.

Answers

1. about 1,398 kg per hectare would be saved; 5,590 kg/hectare $\times$ 0.25 = 1,398 kg/hectare
2. about 333 years; 300 m $\div$ 100 years = 1,000 m $\div$ x years; 300x = 100,000; x = 100,000 $\div$ 300 = 333 years
3. 2.5 m; 30 m/year $\div$ 12 months/year = 2.5 m

Go Further

A land slide is called a mud slide when heavy rain soaks into loose soil on slopes, lubricating the soil and causing it to flow like a thick liquid. Mud slides often occur in California where homes have been built on steep slopes. During the wet season, heavy rains can quickly saturate the loose soil, resulting in mud slides.

Visual Learning

Homes in Danger from Shoreline Erosion by the Year 2060 Ask students how many homes each line of the x-axis of the graph represents. 50,000 Have students locate each coastline location on a U.S. map and ask them to compare the number of barrier islands along each coastline. Have them use an atlas or almanac to find the populations of states along each coast. Then ask why they think more homes along the Atlantic coastline are predicted to be in danger of shoreline erosion. Possible answer: More barrier islands on which homes are built occur along the Atlantic coastline. Hurricanes also affect this coastline more often. The states along this coastline have large populations.

Reviewing Main Ideas

Preview

Students can answer the questions in their Science Journals. Discuss the answers as you go through the chapter. **IS Linguistic**

Review

Students can write their answers, then compare them with those of other students. **IS Interpersonal**

Reteach

Students can look at the illustrations and describe details that support the main ideas of the chapter. **IS Visual-Spatial**

Answers to Chapter Review

SECTION 1

3. The sediments in mudflows are much smaller than those in rockslides. While both slip down a slope, mudflows are a thick mixture of sediments and water, while rockslides are layers of rock or rock fragments.

SECTION 2

2. till

SECTION 3

1. It doesn't have enough energy of motion.

Reviewing Main Ideas

Section 1 Erosion by Gravity

1. Erosion is the process that wears down and transports sediment.

2. Deposition occurs when an agent of erosion loses its energy and can no longer carry its load of sediment.

3. Slump, creep, rock slides, and mudflows are all mass movements caused by gravity. *Explain the differences between rock slides and mudflows.*

Section 2 Glaciers

1. Glaciers are powerful agents of erosion. As water freezes and thaws in cracks, it breaks off pieces of surrounding rock. These pieces then are incorporated into glacial ice by plucking.

2. As sediment embedded in the base of a glacier moves across the land, grooves and striations form. Glaciers deposit two kinds of material—till and outwash. *Which of these two sediments describes a jumbled pile of rocks and sediment?*

Section 3 Wind

1. Deflation occurs when wind erodes only fine-grained sediments, leaving coarse sediments behind. *Why doesn't wind normally pick up large-grained sediments?*

2. The pitting and polishing of rocks and grains of sediment by windblown sediment is called abrasion.

3. Wind deposits include loess and dunes. Loess consists of fine-grained particles that are tightly packed. Dunes form when windblown sediments accumulate behind an obstacle.

4. Dunes are common landforms in desert regions. The shapes and orientations of dunes can provide clues about the prevailing wind directions in an area.

FOLDABLES
Reading & Study Skills

After You Read

Use the Foldable you made at the beginning of the chapter to compare and contrast the forces causing erosion and deposition.

FOLDABLES
Reading & Study Skills

After You Read

After students have read the chapter and completed the Foldable described in Before You Read, have them do the activity on the student page.

Dinah Zike

Visualizing Main Ideas

Complete the following concept map on erosional forces. Use the following terms and phrases: abrasion, striations, leaning trees and structures, curved scar on slope, deflation, rockslides and rockfalls, *and* mudflows.

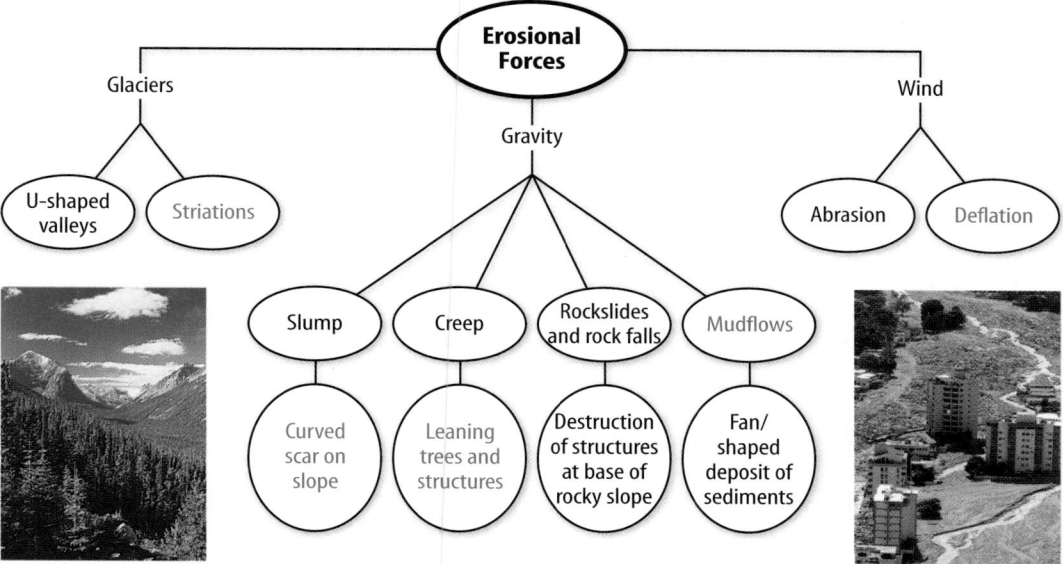

Erosional Forces

Glaciers — Gravity — Wind

U-shaped valleys — Striations

Abrasion — Deflation

Slump — Creep — Rockslides and rock falls — Mudflows

Curved scar on slope — Leaning trees and structures — Destruction of structures at base of rocky slope — Fan/shaped deposit of sediments

Vocabulary Review

Vocabulary Words

a. abrasion
b. creep
c. deflation
d. deposition
e. dune

f. erosion
g. glacier
h. loess
i. mass movement

j. moraine
k. outwash
l. plucking
m. slump
n. till

Using Vocabulary

Each phrase below describes a vocabulary word from the list. In your Science Journal, write the term that matches each description.

1. loess, dunes, and moraines are examples
2. slowest mass movement
3. freeze-thaw action at the base of a glacier
4. much like sandblasting
5. gravity transport of material downslope
6. sand and gravel deposited by meltwater
7. glacial deposit composed of sediment with many sizes and shapes

CHAPTER STUDY GUIDE 235

Visualizing Main Ideas

See student page.

Vocabulary Review

Using Vocabulary

1. deposition
2. creep
3. plucking
4. abrasion
5. mass movement (Note: creep and slump also are correct.)
6. outwash
7. till (Note: moraine also is correct.)

IDENTIFYING ► Misconceptions

Assess

Use the assessment as follow-up to page 210F after students have completed the chapter.

Materials stream table, sand, ice cubes

Procedure Organize students into groups and have them develop a procedure for investigating how an ice cube (representing a glacier) causes erosion. Ask each group to design a way to measure how the slope of the stream table affects the erosion by the ice cube glacier.

Expected Outcome Students should realize that in addition to wind, water and glacier are also agents of erosion. They will also discover that there is a direct correlation between the slope of the land and the amount of material that can be eroded.

Reinforcement Have students quantify their erosion activities and graph their results, that is, the direct correlation between the slope of the land (*x*-axis) and the amount of material eroded (*y*-axis).

Checking Concepts

1. B
2. C
3. D
4. B
5. B
6. C
7. D
8. A
9. A
10. D

Thinking Critically

11. Striations are generally parallel to glacial movement.
12. It only would prevent the movement of large particles.
13. Planting vegetation or erecting fences can reduce or prevent dune migration.
14. The mass of overlying snow and ice compresses underlying layers. Pressure causes the ice to become plastic and partially melt, causing movement at the bottom and within the glacier.
15. Warm weather at lower elevations causes the front end to melt and appear to retreat. Cold temperatures at higher elevations allow snow and ice to accumulate and make the glacier advance.

Chapter 8 Assessment

Checking Concepts

Choose the word or phrase that best answers the question.

1. Which of the following is suggested by leaning trees on a hillside?
   A) abrasion
   B) creep
   C) slump
   D) mudflow

2. The best plants for reducing wind erosion have what type of root system?
   A) taproot
   B) striated
   C) fibrous
   D) sheet

3. What does a valley glacier create at the point where it starts?
   A) esker
   B) moraine
   C) till
   D) cirque

4. Which is caused by glacial erosion?
   A) eskers
   B) arêtes
   C) moraines
   D) warmer climate

5. What term describes a mass of snow and ice in motion?
   A) loess deposit
   B) glacier
   C) outwash
   D) abrasion

6. What shape do glacier-created valleys have?
   A) V-shaped
   B) L-shaped
   C) U-shaped
   D) S-shaped

7. Which term is an example of a feature created by deposition?
   A) cirque
   B) abrasion
   C) striation
   D) dune

8. Which characteristic is common to all agents of erosion?
   A) They carry sediments when they have enough energy of motion.
   B) They are most likely to erode when sediments are moist.
   C) They create deposits called dunes.
   D) They erode large sediments before they erode small ones.

9. What type of wind erosion leaves pebbles and boulders behind?
   A) deflation
   B) loess
   C) abrasion
   D) sandblasting

10. What is a ridge formed by deposition of till called?
    A) striation
    B) esker
    C) cirque
    D) moraine

Thinking Critically

11. How can striations give information about the direction that a glacier moved?

12. How effective would a retaining wall made of fine wire mesh be against erosion?

13. Sand dunes often migrate. What can be done to prevent the migration of beach dunes?

14. A researcher finds evidence of movement of ice within a glacier. Explain how this could occur.

15. The end of a valley glacier is at a lower elevation than its point of origin is. How does this help explain melting at its end while snow and ice still are accumulating where it originated?

Developing Skills

16. **Making and Using Tables** Make a table to contrast continental and valley glaciers.

17. **Testing a Hypothesis** Explain how to test the effect of glacial thickness on a glacier's ability to erode.

18. **Forming Hypotheses** Hypothesize why silt in loess deposits is transported farther than sand in dune deposits.

Chapter ✓Assessment Planner

Portfolio Encourage students to place in their portfolios one or two items of what they consider to be their best work. Examples include:
- Extension, p. 215
- Curriculum Connection, p. 219
- Challenge, p. 222
- Cultural Diversity, p. 227

Performance Additional performance assessments, Performance Task Assessment Lists, and rubrics for evaluating these activities can be found in Glencoe's **Performance Assessment in the Science Classroom.**

19. Concept Mapping Copy and complete the events chain concept map below to show how a sand dune forms. Use the terms and phrases: *sand accumulates*, *dune*, *dry sand*, and *obstruction traps*.

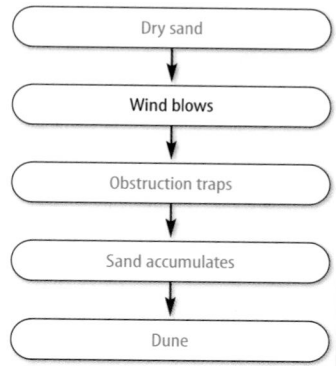

Dry sand
↓
Wind blows
↓
Obstruction traps
↓
Sand accumulates
↓
Dune

20. Classifying Classify the following as erosional or depositional features: loess, cirque, U-shaped valley, sand dune, abraded rock, striation, and moraine.

Performance Assessment

21. Poster Make a poster with magazine photos showing glacial features in North America. Add a map to locate each feature.

22. Design an Experiment Design an experiment to see how the amount of moisture added to sediments affects mass movement. Keep all variables constant except the amount of moisture in the sediment. Try your experiment.

TECHNOLOGY

Go to the Glencoe Science Web site at **science.glencoe.com** or use the **Glencoe Science CD-ROM** for additional chapter assessment.

Test Practice

Ms. Lee was reviewing examples of erosion caused by gravity for her science class.

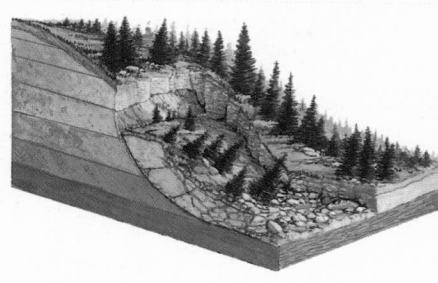

Examine the diagram above and answer the following questions.

1. This diagram shows the shape, in cross section, of one example of erosion by gravity. Which of the following choices best matches this type of erosion?

A) slump **C)** rock slide
B) creep **D)** mudflow

2. Select the most likely cause of this type of mass wasting from the choices below.

F) Pieces of rock became loosened and fell freely through the air.
G) Heavy rains caused a fluid mass of mud to form and flow rapidly downhill.
H) After a heavy rain, the underlying sediment was weakened and could no longer support the sediment and rock above it.
J) Sediments slowly shifted their positions downhill.

CHAPTER ASSESSMENT 237

Test Practice

The Test-Taking Tip was written by The Princeton Review, the nation's leader in test preparation.

1. A
2. H

Developing Skills

16. The table should contain two rows, headed "Continental Glacier" and "Valley Glacier." Possible elements in the table include: Continental: till, outwash, moraines, eskers; Valley: U-shaped valleys, cirques, aretes, horns
17. Two ice blocks, one thicker than the other, could be guided with the same amount of force over a pan containing sand.
18. Loess is made of smaller sediments that wind can carry farther.
19. See student page.
20. erosional: cirque, U-shaped valley, abraded rock, striation; depositional: loess, sand dune, moraine

Performance Assessment

21. Posters might show features such as eskers, moraines, U-shaped valleys, cirques, aretes, horns, and striations in rock. Use **PASC,** p. 145.
22. Student designs will vary. Remind students to vary only the amount of moisture, with all other conditions remaining constant. Use **PASC,** p. 95.

✓*Assessment* Resources

 Reproducible Masters

Chapter Resources Booklet
Chapter Review, pp. 33–34
Chapter Tests, pp. 35–38
Assessment Transparency Activity, p. 45

Glencoe Science Web site
Interactive Tutor
Chapter Quizzes

Glencoe Technology
Assessment Transparency
Interactive CD-ROM Chapter Quizzes
ExamView Pro Test Bank
Vocabulary PuzzleMaker Software
MindJogger Videoquiz DVD/VHS

Section/Objectives	Standards		Activities/Features
	National	State/Local	
Chapter Opener	See p. 5T for a Key to Standards.		**Explore Activity:** Model how erosion works, p. 239 **Before You Read,** p. 239
Section 1 Surface Water 🕐 2 sessions 📦 1 block 1. **Identify** the causes of runoff. 2. **Compare** rill, gully, sheet, and stream erosion. 3. **Identify** three different stages of stream development. 4. **Explain** how alluvial fans and deltas form.	National Content Standards: UCP1, A1, D1		**Physics Integration,** p. 241 **Science Online,** p. 244 **Visualizing Stream Development,** p. 246 **Science Online,** p. 248 **MiniLAB:** Observing Stream Erosion, p. 249
Section 2 Groundwater 🕐 2 sessions 📦 1 block 1. **Recognize** the importance of groundwater. 2. **Describe** the effect that soil and rock permeability have on groundwater movement. 3. **Explain** how groundwater dissolves and deposits minerals.	National Content Standards: UCP1, A1, D1, F1		**MiniLAB:** Measuring Pore Space, p. 252 **Math Skills Activity:** Calculating the Rate of Groundwater Flow, p. 253 **Chemistry Integration,** p. 255
Section 3 Ocean Shoreline 🕐 3 sessions 📦 1.5 blocks 1. **Identify** the different causes of shoreline erosion. 2. **Compare and contrast** different types of shorelines. 3. **Describe** some origins of sand.	National Content Standards: UCP1, A1, D1, F5		**Activity:** Classifying Types of Sand, p. 261 **Activity:** Water Speed and Erosion, pp. 262–263 **Science and Society:** Sands in Time, pp. 264–265

NATIONAL GEOGRAPHIC

Teacher's Corner

PRODUCTS AVAILABLE FROM GLENCOE
To order call 1-800-334-7344:
Transparency Set
NGS PicturePack: Water
Videodisc
STV: Water

PRODUCTS AVAILABLE FROM
NATIONAL GEOGRAPHIC SOCIETY
To order call 1-800-368-2728:
Videos
Can't Drown This Town
Water: Our Precious Resource

INDEX TO NATIONAL GEOGRAPHIC SOCIETY
The following articles may be used for research relating to this chapter: "Feeding the Planet," by T.R. Reid, October 1998; "Under New York," by Joel L. Swerdlow, February 1997.

Activity Materials	Reproducible Resources	Section Assessment	Technology
Explore Activity: aluminum pie pan, dry soil, dropper, water	**Chapter Resources Booklet** Foldables Worksheet, p. 13 Directed Reading Overview, p. 15 Note-taking Worksheets, pp. 29–31	GLENCOE'S **ASSESSMENT** ADVANTAGE	
MiniLAB: plastic rain gauge, drinking glass, sink, sprinkling can, water, funnel	**Chapter Resources Booklet** Transparency Activity, p. 40 MiniLAB, p. 3 Enrichment, p. 26 Reinforcement, p. 23 Directed Reading, p. 16 Transparency Activity, pp. 43–45 **Cultural Diversity,** p. 33	**Portfolio** Science Journal, p. 243 **Performance** MiniLAB, p. 249 Skill Builder Activities, p. 250 **Content** Section Assessment, p. 250	✎ Section Focus Transparency ✎ Teaching Transparency 💿 Interactive CD-ROM/DVD 🎧 Guided Reading Audio Program
MiniLAB: 2 identical clear plastic containers, metric ruler, sand, gravel, graduated beaker, water (200mL) *Need materials?* Contact Science Kit at 1-800-828-7777 or www.sciencekit.com on the Internet.	**Chapter Resources Booklet** Transparency Activity, p. 41 MiniLAB, p. 4 Enrichment, p. 27 Reinforcement, p. 24 Directed Reading, p. 17 Lab Activities, pp. 9–12 **Mathematics Skill Activities,** p. 11 **Physical Science Critical Thinking/ Problem Solving,** p. 12	**Portfolio** Science Journal, p. 253 **Performance** MiniLAB, p. 252 Math Skills Activity, p. 253 Skill Builder Activities, p. 256 **Content** Section Assessment, p. 256	✎ Section Focus Transparency 💿 Interactive CD-ROM/DVD 🎧 Guided Reading Audio Program
Activity: samples of different sands (3), hand lens, magnet **Activity:** paint roller pan, sand, 1-L beaker, rubber tubing (20 cm), metric ruler, water, stopwatch, screen, wood block, disposable wallpaper trays	**Chapter Resources Booklet** Transparency Activity, p. 42 Enrichment, p. 28 Reinforcement, p. 25 Directed Reading, pp. 17, 18 Activity Worksheet, pp. 5–6, 7–8 **Science Inquiry Labs,** p. 31 **Lab Management and Safety,** p. 74	**Portfolio** Extension, p. 258 **Performance** Skill Builder Activities, p. 260 **Content** Section Assessment, p. 260	✎ Section Focus Transparency 💿 Interactive CD-ROM/DVD 🎧 Guided Reading Audio Program

End of Chapter Assessment

GLENCOE'S **ASSESSMENT** ADVANTAGE

Blackline Masters	Technology	Professional Series
Chapter Resources Booklet Chapter Review, pp. 33–34 Chapter Tests, pp. 35–38 **Standardized Test Practice by The Princeton Review,** pp. 43–46	📺 MindJogger Videoquiz 💿 CD-ROM Explorations and Quizzes 💿 Vocabulary Puzzle Makers 💿 ExamView Pro Test Bank 💿 Interactive Lesson Planner 💿 Interactive Teacher's Edition	Performance Assessment in the Science Classroom (PASC)

Transparencies

Section Focus

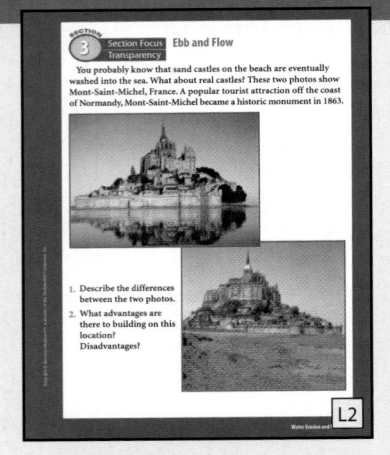

This is a representation of key blackline masters available in the Teacher Classroom Resources. See Resource Manager boxes within the chapter for additional information.

Assessment

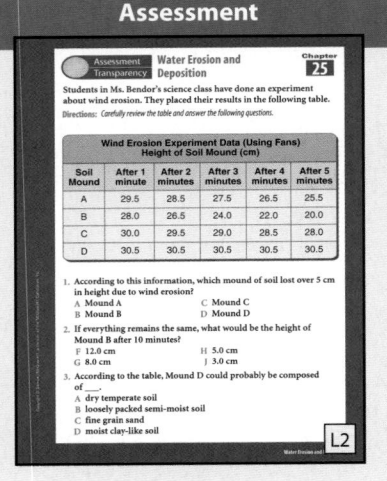

Teaching

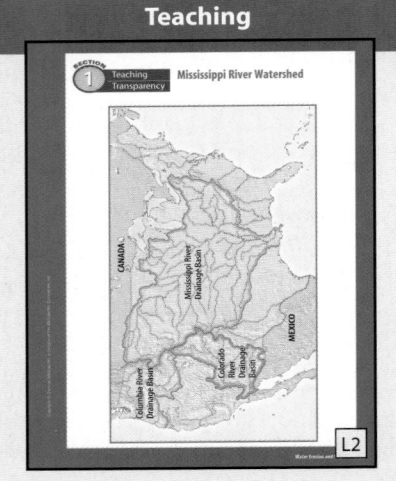

Key to Teaching Strategies

The following designations will help you decide which activities are appropriate for your students.

L1 Level 1 activities should be appropriate for students with learning difficulties.

L2 Level 2 activities should be within the ability range of all students.

L3 Level 3 activities are designed for above-average students.

ELL ELL activities should be within the ability range of English Language Learners.

COOP LEARN Cooperative Learning activities are designed for small group work.

LS Multiple Learning Styles logos, as described on page 22T, are used throughout to indicate strategies that address different learning styles.

P These strategies represent student products that can be placed into a best-work portfolio.

Hands-on Activities

Activity Worksheets

Laboratory Activities

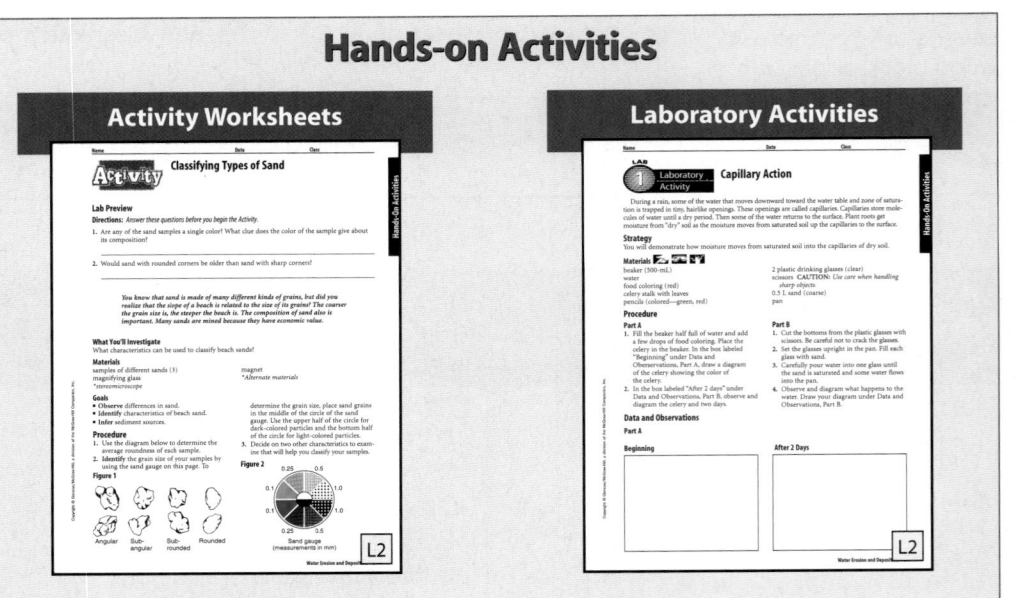

Meeting Different Ability Levels

Content Outline

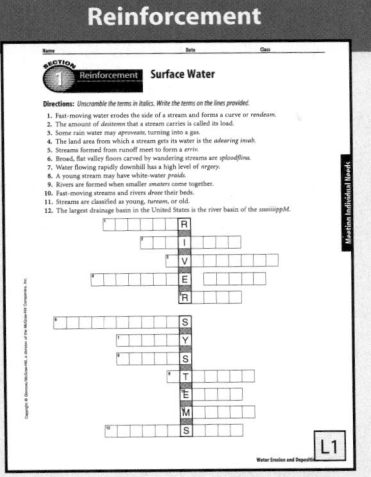

Reinforcement

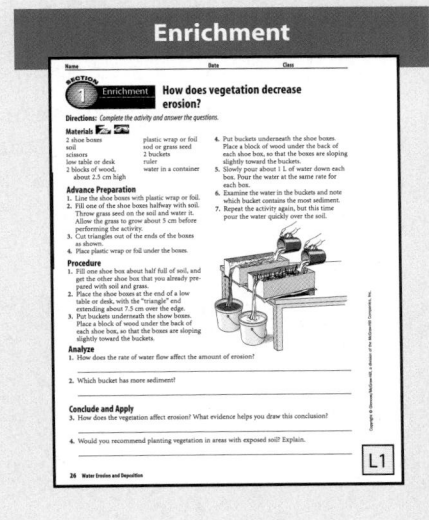

Directed Reading

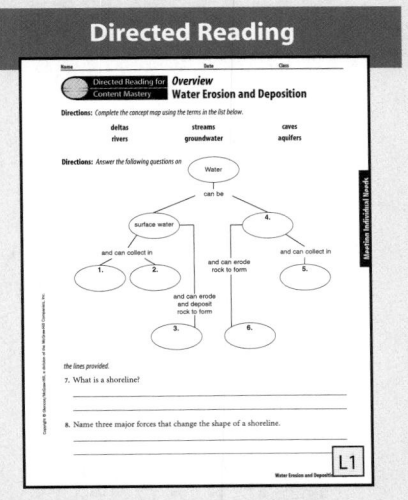

Assessment

Chapter Tests

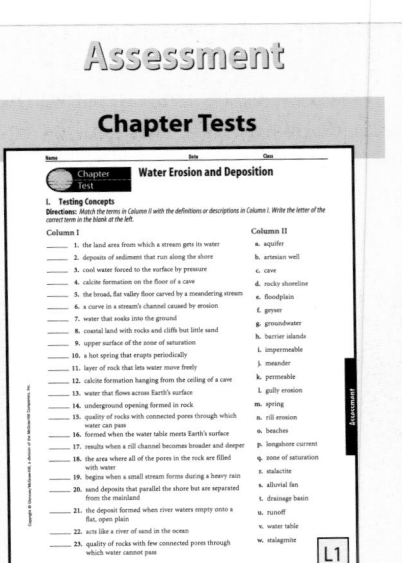

Enrichment

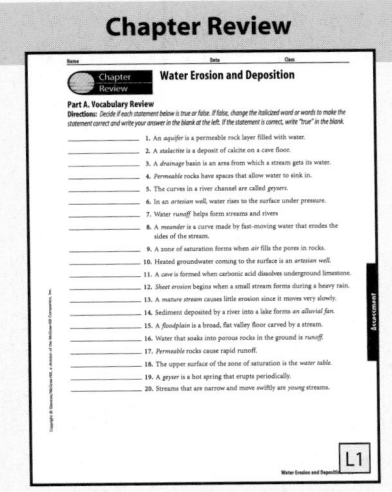

Spanish Directed Reading

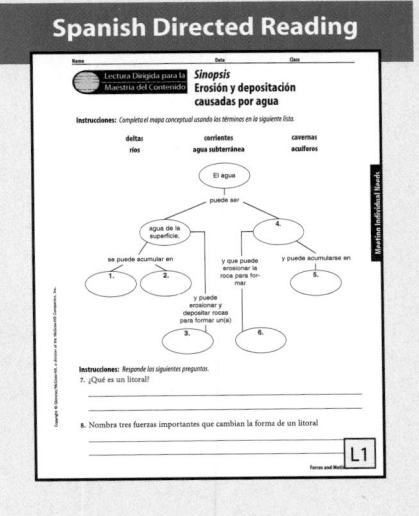

Test Practice Workbook

Chapter Review

Science Content Background

SECTION 1

Surface Water

Runoff

The average annual rainfall on the total land area of the United States is approximately 76 cm. Of this amount, 45 cm return to the atmosphere by evaporation and transpiration, 1 cm soaks into the ground, and 30 cm become runoff.

Fun Fact

There are approximately 265,000 L of water in an Olympic size swimming pool. An average family of 4 uses more than twice that amount of water in one year!

Effects of Gravity

Earth's gravity tries to pull everything on the planet toward its center. Every day, gravity pulls rocks, soil, and water down slopes. The weight of any object on Earth equals its mass times the acceleration of gravity, or $F^w = mg$.

Erosion

It generally takes between 80 and 400 years to form 1 cm of topsoil. In the United States, the amount of farmland soil lost to erosion each year exceeds the amount of newly formed soil by more than 2 billion tons. Worldwide, the estimated loss exceeds 25 billion tons a year. The world's most productive soils are being depleted at a rate of 7% each decade.

Drainage Basins

Drainage basins are separated from each other by high ground called divides. On a large scale, the Rocky Mountain and Appalachian Mountain divides separate the Mississippi River drainage basin. When a river system develops in a smaller drainage basin, rills and gullies can erode a divide. With time, the divide will become narrower.

Richard Price/FPG International

River systems develop specific drainage patterns. Dendritic drainage resembles a tree. Rectangular drainage forms when bedrock is fractured. Trellis drainage forms on areas covered with both hard and soft bedrock.

SECTION 2 Groundwater

Groundwater Systems

Urban growth and agriculture irrigation compete for water use. Water drawn from aquifers supports 21% of the United States' irrigated cropland. In the last decade, irrigation has been reduced because of depleted aquifers and increased urban use.

Cave Formation

Rainwater dissolves carbon dioxide from the air and decaying plants to form carbonic acid according to the equation $H_2O + CO_2 \rightarrow H_2CO_3$. When the resulting acidic groundwater comes in contact with limestone, the carbonic acid reacts with calcite in the rocks to form soluble calcium hydrogen carbonate that may be carried away with the water. Although limestone is commonly said to dissolve in groundwater, the actual process involves a chemical reaction, not a solution process.

SECTION 3 Ocean Shoreline

The Shore

During periods of calm weather, wave action is at a minimum. Waves have the most significant effect during a storm. Water is forced into cracks in cliffs and walls. This causes the air in these openings to become highly compressed. When the wave subsides, the air expands rapidly—in time, dislodging rock fragments and enlarging the preexisting fractures.

A sandy beach consists of four regions: dunes, berm, foreshore, and offshore. The offshore region is a zone with a gentle slope of fine sand. This region is exposed only when the tide is low. The foreshore is the zone of swash and backwash. The berm is a fairly flat area of beach that may be flooded during especially high tides or during storms. Dunes form on the dry sand behind the berm.

Bob Krist/Corbis

Barrier Islands

The origin of barrier islands is uncertain. Some may have originated as spits (small points of land) that were later severed from the mainland by wave erosion or by the general rise in sea level following the last episode of glaciation. Others may have been formed when turbulent water in the line of breakers heaped up sand that was scoured from the bottom. Still other barrier islands may be former sand dune ridges that developed along the shore when sea level was lower during the last glacial period. Sea level rose as the ice sheets melted and the area behind the beach-dune complex became flooded. Atlantic City, New Jersey; Galveston, Texas; and Kitty Hawk, North Carolina are built on barrier islands.

Fun Fact

Beach replenishment is costly. New Jersey is planning to spend $1.7 billion over the next 50 years to replenish its beaches, which have been eroded by waves and offshore currents. This project would cost $91 million dollars per mile!

SCIENCE *Online*

For additional content background on this topic, go to the Glencoe Science Web site at science.glencoe.com.

Water Erosion and Deposition

Chapter Vocabulary

runoff
channel
sheet erosion
drainage basin
meander
groundwater
permeable
impermeable
aquifer
water table
spring
geyser
cave
longshore current
beach

What do you think?

Science Journal This is a picture of the surface of Mars. The erosional patterns have led scientists to hypothesize that water once flowed across the Martian surface, just as it flows across Earth's surface.

Water Erosion and Deposition

B ryce Canyon National Park in Utah is home to the Hoodoo Formations. What carved these canyons and helped create these magnificent sculptures? They were made by one of the most powerful forces on Earth—water. Water, in the form of light rain or a great river, causes erosion. In this chapter, you will learn how rainwater runoff forms streams. You also will learn how water carries sediment and deposits it far from its source.

What do you think?

Science Journal Look at the picture below with a classmate. Discuss what you think this might be. Here's a hint: *It's something out of this world.* Write your answer in your Science Journal.

238

Theme Connection

Systems and Interactions Water forms a number of systems. Streams, rivers, and the ocean form surface systems, while groundwater forms a separate system. These systems interact with rocks and soil, producing erosion and deposition.

Moving water has great energy. Sometimes rainwater falls softly and soaks slowly into soil. Other times it rushes down a slope with tremendous force and carries away valuable topsoil. What determines whether rain soaks into the ground or runs off and wears away the surface?

Model how erosion works

1. Place an aluminum pie pan on your desktop.
2. Put a pile of dry soil about 7 cm high into the pan.
3. Slowly drip water from a dropper onto the pile and observe what happens next.
4. Drip the water faster and continue to observe what happens.
5. Repeat steps 1 through 4, but this time change the slope of the hill. Start again with dry soil.

Observe

Record in your Science Journal what effect the water had on the different slopes.

Before You Read

FOLDABLES
Reading & Study Skills

Making a Main Ideas Study Fold A main idea consists of the major concepts or topics talked about in a chapter. Before you read the chapter, make the following Foldable to help you identify the main ideas of this chapter.

1. Place a sheet of paper in front of you so the long side is at the top. Fold the left side and right side of the paper in to divide the paper into equal thirds.
2. Open the paper and label the three rows *Surface, Ground,* and *Shoreline,* as shown.
3. As you read the chapter, list characteristics of each type of water. Then, across the bottom of each fold, draw a picture of surface water, groundwater, and a shoreline.

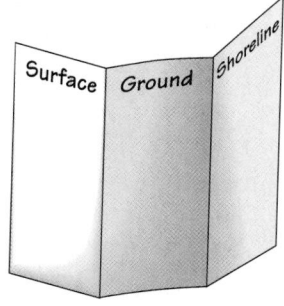

239

EXPLORE ACTIVITY

Purpose Students will model the soil erosion caused by running water.

Materials aluminum pie pan, dry soil, water, dropper

Safety Have students wear goggles and apron during this activity. Make provision for disposing of the sand.

Teaching Strategy To assist learning disabled students, substitute layers of colored sand for the mound of dry soil. As the trickle of water cuts a deeper groove into the sand, new colors will be eroded.

Observe

Students should observe more erosion when the "rain" fell faster, fell for longer periods, or fell on steeper slopes.

✓Assessment

Performance Ask students to infer how vegetation growing on the slope would affect their results. Use **Performance Assessment in the Science Classroom,** p. 89.

FOLDABLES
Reading & Study Skills

Before You Read

Dinah Zike Study Fold

Purpose Students make a Foldable in which they record information for comparing and contrasting erosion and deposition caused by surface water, groundwater, and shorelines.

For additional help, see Foldables Worksheet, p. 13 in **Chapter Resources Booklet,** or go to the Glencoe Science Web site at **science.glencoe.com.** See After You Read in the Study Guide at the end of this chapter.

1 Surface Water

As You Read

What You'll Learn
- **Identify** the causes of runoff.
- **Compare** rill, gully, sheet, and stream erosion.
- **Identify** three different stages of stream development.
- **Explain** how alluvial fans and deltas form.

Vocabulary
runoff   drainage basin
channel   meander
sheet erosion

Why It's Important
Runoff and streams shape Earth's surface.

Figure 1
A In areas with gentle slopes and vegetation, little runoff and erosion take place. **B** Lack of vegetation has led to severe soil erosion in some areas.

Runoff

Picture this. You pour a glass of milk, and it overflows, spilling onto the table. You grab a towel to clean up the mess, but the milk is already running through a crack in the table, over the edge, and onto the floor. This is similar to what happens to rainwater when it falls to Earth. Some rainwater soaks into the ground and some evaporates, turning into a gas. The rainwater that doesn't soak into the ground or evaporate runs over the ground. Eventually, it enters streams, lakes, or the ocean. Water that doesn't soak into the ground or evaporate but instead flows across Earth's surface is called **runoff.** If you've ever spilled milk while pouring it, you've experienced something similar to runoff.

Factors Affecting Runoff What determines whether rain soaks into the ground or runs off? The amount of rain and the length of time it falls are two factors that affect runoff. Light rain falling over several hours probably will have time to soak into the ground. Heavy rain falling in less than an hour or so will run off because it cannot soak in fast enough, or it can't soak in because the ground cannot hold any more water.

240   CHAPTER 9 Water Erosion and Deposition

Section ✓*Assessment* Planner

PORTFOLIO
Science Journal, p. 243
PERFORMANCE ASSESSMENT
MiniLAB, p. 249
Skill Builder Activities, p. 250
See page 268 for more options.

CONTENT ASSESSMENT
Section, p. 250
Challenge, p. 250
Chapter, pp. 268–269

Other Factors Another factor that affects the amount of runoff is the steepness, or slope, of the land. Gravity, the attractive force between all objects, causes water to move down slopes. Water moves rapidly down steep slopes so it has little chance to soak into the ground. Water moves more slowly down gentle slopes and across flat areas. Slower movement allows water more time to soak into the ground.

Vegetation, such as grass and trees, also affects the amount of runoff. Just like milk running off the table, water will run off smooth surfaces that have little or no vegetation. Imagine a tablecloth on the table. What would happen to the milk then? Runoff slows down when it flows around plants. Slower-moving water has a greater chance to sink into the ground. By slowing down runoff, plants and their roots help prevent soil from being carried away. Large amounts of soil may be carried away in areas that lack vegetation, as shown in **Figure 1.**

Physics INTEGRATION

Effects of Gravity When you lie on the ground and feel as if you are being held in place, you are experiencing the effects of gravity. Gravity is the attracting force all objects have for one another. The greater the mass of an object is, the greater its force of gravity is. Because Earth has a much greater mass than any of the objects on it, Earth's gravitational force pulls objects toward its center. Water runs downhill because of Earth's gravitational pull. When water begins to run down a slope, it picks up speed. As its speed increases, so does its energy. Fast-moving water, shown in **Figure 2,** carries more soil than slow-moving water does.

Physics INTEGRATION

The force that drives most types of erosion is gravity. Gravity gives water its potential, or stored, energy. When this energy is changed into kinetic energy, or energy of motion, water becomes a powerful force strong enough to move mountains. Find out how water has shaped the region in which you live.

Figure 2
During floods, the high volume of fast-moving water erodes large amounts of soil.

SECTION 1 Surface Water **241**

Water Erosion

Figure 3
Heavy rains can remove large amounts of sediment, forming deep gullies in the side of a slope.

Figure 4
When water accumulates, it can flow in sheets like the water seen flowing over the hood of this car.

Water Erosion

Suppose you and several friends walk the same way to school each day through a field or an empty lot. You always walk in the same footsteps as you did the day before. After a few weeks, you've worn a path through the field. When water travels down the same slope time after time, it also wears a path. The wearing away of soil and rock is called erosion.

Rill and Gully Erosion You may have noticed a groove or small ditch on the side of a slope that was left behind by running water. This is evidence of rill erosion. Rill erosion begins when a small stream forms during a heavy rain. As this stream flows along, it has enough energy to erode and carry away soil. Water moving down the same path creates a groove, called a **channel,** on the slope where the water eroded the soil. If water frequently flows in the same channel, rill erosion may change over time into another type of erosion called gully erosion.

During gully erosion, a rill channel becomes broader and deeper. **Figure 3** shows gullies that were formed when water carried away large amounts of soil.

Sheet Erosion Water often erodes without being in a channel. Rainwater that begins to run off during a rainstorm often flows as thin, broad sheets before forming rills and streams. For example, when it rains over an area, the rainwater accumulates until it eventually begins moving down a slope as a sheet, like the water flowing off the hood of the car in **Figure 4.** Water also can flow as sheets if it breaks out of its channel.

Floodwaters spilling out of a river can flow as sheets over the surrounding flatlands. Streams flowing out of mountains fan out and may flow as sheets away from the foot of the mountain. **Sheet erosion** occurs when water that is flowing as sheets picks up and carries away sediments.

Stream Erosion Sometimes water continues to flow along a low place it has formed. As the water in a stream moves along, it picks up sediments from the bottom and sides of its channel. By this process, a stream channel becomes deeper and wider.

The sediment that a stream carries is called its load. Water picks up and carries some of the lightweight sediments, called the suspended load. Larger, heavy particles called the bed load just roll along the bottom of the stream channel, as shown in **Figure 5.** Water can even dissolve some rocks and carry them away in solution. The different-sized sediments scrape against the bottom and sides of the channel like a piece of sandpaper. Gradually, these sediments can wear away the rock by a process called abrasion.

Figure 5
This cross section of a stream channel shows the location of the suspended load and the bed load. *How does the stream carry dissolved material?*

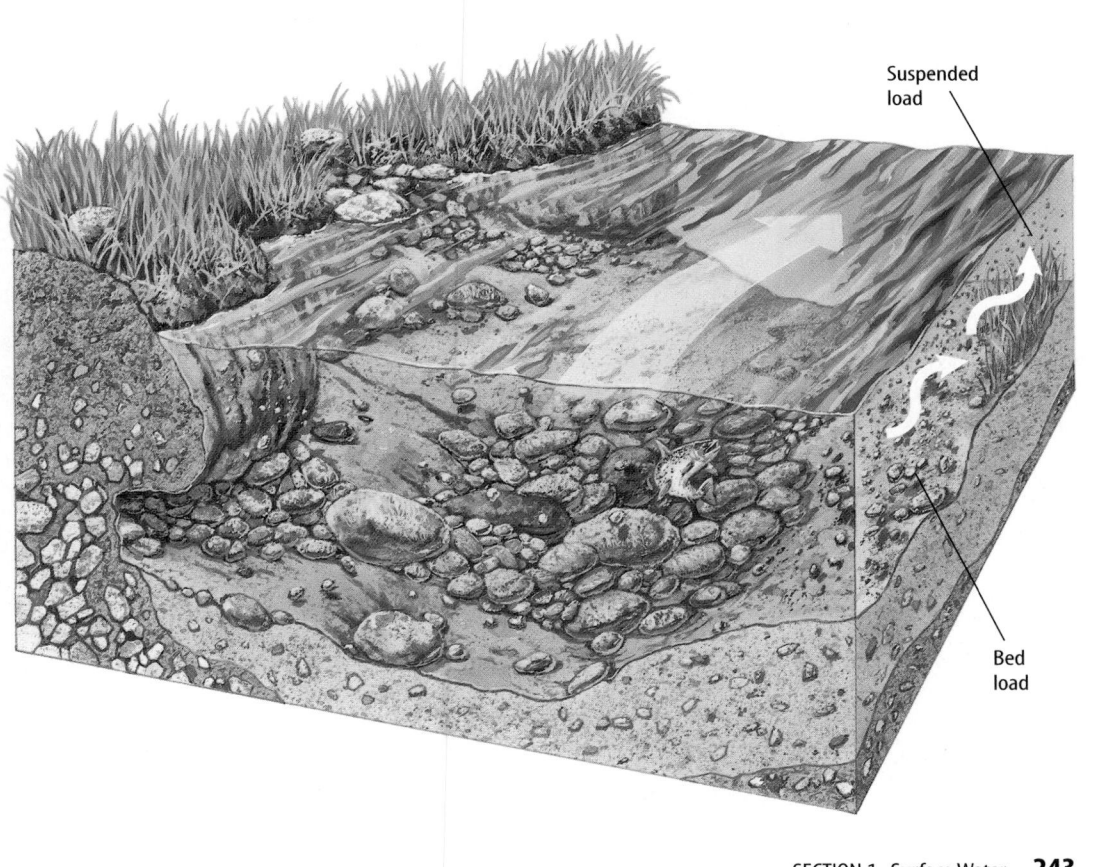

Suspended load

Bed load

Direct student groups to investigate how different surfaces affect runoff. Each team needs a paint tray half-filled with soil, a piece of cardboard, a clump of grass, and a beaker of water. Have groups design and carry out an experiment using the cardboard to simulate a paved street and the grass to simulate a grassy field. Students should find that paved surfaces have more runoff than grassy surfaces. L2 ELL COOP LEARN IS **Interpersonal**

Activity

Take students outside to look for evidence of water erosion around the school grounds. For example, they might find small channel scars on slopes or low, flat areas where fine sediments have collected. L2 ELL

Discussion

Have students compare and contrast the runoff from paved streets and grassy fields during a thunderstorm and a gentle rain. During a thunderstorm, paved streets have much more runoff than grassy fields. In a gentle rain, water will likely puddle slightly and evaporate from paved streets and be absorbed by grassy fields. There will be little runoff from either surface during a gentle rain.

Caption Answer
Figure 5 It carries them away in solution.

Resource Manager

Chapter Resources Booklet
Note-taking Worksheets, pp. 29–31
Earth Science Critical Thinking/Problem Solving, p. 7

Science Journal

Stream Erosion Have students write poems in their journals describing erosion in a stream channel like the one shown in **Figure 5**. Poems can describe lightweight particles carried in suspension and heavy particles rolled along the bottom of the channel. L2 IS **Auditory-Musical** P

Visual Learning

Figure 6 Have students trace this river's drainage system from source to mouth. Encourage them to use an atlas to name several of the major tributaries of the Mississippi. Some tributaries are the Ohio, Illinois, Cumberland, Missouri, Arkansas, and Tennessee Rivers. Have students discuss why the main river follows the path it does. The river flows through a lowland area or depression, which forms its bed.

SCIENCE Online

Internet Addresses

_____

_____

_____

_____

_____

Explore the Glencoe Science Web site at **science.glencoe.com** to find out more about topics in this section.

Caption Answer

Figure 6B the Mississippi River

Teacher FYI

The city of New Orleans is built on a part of the Mississippi River delta where sediments are consolidating. As a result, the city and surrounding area are sinking, and the city is actually below sea level. To protect it from flooding, levees have been built along the river's banks.

SCIENCE Online

Research Visit the Glencoe Science Web site at **science.glencoe.com** to learn more about drainage basins in your region. Make a poster that summarizes your findings, and share it with your class.

Figure 6
River systems can be compared with the structure of a tree.

A The system of twigs, branches, and the trunk that make up a tree is similar to the system of streams and rivers that make up a river system.

River System Development

Have you spent time near a river or stream in your community? Each day, probably millions of liters of water flow through that stream. Where does all the water come from? Where is it flowing to?

River Systems Streams are parts of river systems. The water comes from rills, gullies, and smaller streams located upstream. Just as the tree in **Figure 6A** is a system containing twigs, branches, and a trunk, a river system also has many parts. Runoff enters small streams, which join together to form larger streams. Larger streams come together to form rivers. Rivers grow and carry more water as more streams join.

Drainage Basins A **drainage basin** is the area of land from which a stream or river collects runoff. Compare a drainage basin to a bathtub. Water that collects in a bathtub flows toward one location—the drain. Likewise, all of the water in a river system eventually flows to one location—the main river, or trunk. The largest drainage basin in the United States is the Mississippi River drainage basin shown in **Figure 6B.**

✔ Reading Check *What is a drainage basin?*

CANADA

Columbia River
Drainage Basin

Mississippi River
Drainage Basin

Colorado
River
Drainage
Basin

MEXICO

B A large number of the streams and rivers in the United States are part of the Mississippi River drainage basin, or watershed. *What river represents the trunk of this system?*

Inclusion Strategies

Learning Disabled Have students look for and photograph places where water erosion has occurred in the community. Gather these photographs into a booklet that students can refer to when reviewing this material. L1

Curriculum Connection

Geography Have students use an atlas to explain how sediments on a Tennessee hillside might end up in the Mississippi delta. Local streams take sediments eroded from the hillside to the Mississippi River. When the river enters the Gulf of Mexico, it slows and deposits the sediments. L2 LS **Visual-Spatial**

Stages of Stream Development

Streams come in a variety of forms. Some are narrow and swift moving, and others are wide and slow moving. Streams differ because they are in different stages of development. These stages depend on the slope of the ground over which the stream flows. Streams are classified as young, mature, or old. **Figure 8** shows how the stages come together to form a river system.

The names of the stages of development aren't always related to the actual age of a river. The New River in West Virginia is one of the oldest rivers in North America. However, it has a steep valley and flows swiftly. As a result, it is classified as a young stream.

Young Streams A stream that flows swiftly through a steep valley is a young stream. A young stream may have whitewater rapids and waterfalls. Water flowing through a narrow channel with a rough bottom has a high level of energy and erodes the stream bottom faster than its sides.

Mature Streams The next stage in the development of a stream is the mature stage. A mature stream flows more smoothly through its valley. Over time, most of the rocks in the streambed that cause waterfalls and rapids are eroded by running water and the sediments it carries.

Erosion is no longer concentrated on the bottom in a mature stream. A mature stream starts to erode more along its sides, and curves develop. These curves form because the speed of the water changes throughout the width of the channel.

Water in a shallow area of a stream moves slower because it drags along the bottom. In the deeper part of the channel, the water flows faster. If the deep part of the channel is next to one side of the river, water will erode that side and form a slight curve. Over time, the curve grows to become a broad arc called a **meander** (mee AN dur), as shown in **Figure 7.**

The broad, flat valley floor formed by a meandering stream is called a floodplain. When a stream floods, it often will cover part or all of the floodplain.

Figure 7
A meander is a broad bend in a river or stream. As time passes, erosion of the outer bank increases the bend.

Stages of Stream Development

Activity

Explain to students that erosion is greatest where water speed is greatest. Then take students to a local stream. Have them determine the speed at the middle of the stream and at the edge of the stream by measuring 10 m along the bank and timing how long it takes a fishing bob to float that distance. Speed equals distance divided by time ($s = d/t$). Have them determine where in the stream erosion is greatest.

Extension

Have students research and write reports describing how erosion affects the land surrounding the Colorado or Mississippi River. [IS] **Linguistic** [P]

Make a Model

Have students work in groups to produce a 3-D model of a local riverbed. [L2] [ELL] [COOP LEARN]

Inclusion Strategies

Gifted Have students research what happens to local runoff and draw a map of the local drainage basin. [L3]

Visualizing Stream Development

Have students examine the pictures and read the captions. Then ask the following questions.

Which stage stream would be most likely to have a gravel streambed? Because older streams flow slowly, they are unable to carry suspended gravel and would be unlikely to have gravel beds. Fast flowing young streams can carry gravel and deposit gravel in their beds.

Why do old streams drop their loads of sediment near their mouths? Because when they reach the ocean, they stop flowing and the water no longer has the velocity to suspend sediments. Sediments drop to the bottom, building up deltas.

Where would the water flow fastest in a meander? The water on the outside of the curve must travel a greater distance than that on the inside; therefore, it flows faster.

Activity

Have students work in groups to create simple models using classroom materials that show the relationship between slope and velocity. Have them demonstrate their models to the class, and explain how they relate to stream development.

NATIONAL GEOGRAPHIC VISUALIZING STREAM DEVELOPMENT

Figure 8

Although no two streams are exactly alike, all go through three main stages—young, mature, and old—as they flow from higher to lower ground. A young stream, below, surging over steep terrain, moves rapidly. In a less steep landscape, right, a mature stream flows more smoothly. On nearly level ground, the stream—considered old—winds leisurely through its valley. The various stages of a stream's development are illustrated here.

Waterfall

Rapids

A A young stream begins at a source—here, a melting mountain glacier. From its source, the stream flows swiftly downhill, cutting a narrow valley.

B A mature stream flows smoothly through its valley. Mature streams often develop broad curves called meanders.

C Old streams flow through broad, flat floodplains. Near its mouth, the stream gradually drops its load of silt. This sediment forms a delta, an area of flat, fertile land extending into the ocean.

Oxbow lake

NATIONAL GEOGRAPHIC

Extension

About 12 percent of the population of the United States lives on land that periodically floods. Have students research the local area and find out whether floods occur and what effect they have on the local population.

Teacher FYI

Mature rivers are usually associated with a floodplain. On a floodplain where there are no levees, floodwaters spread over a wide area where the soil can absorb some of the water.

Discussion

Ask students why most whitewater rafting is done in young rivers. Young rivers flow downhill with enough energy to form rapids. Older rivers have already eroded away the rocks and irregularities of their beds and flow with less energy. Therefore, they cannot provide the thrilling rides that young rivers can.

Fun Fact

The oldest river in the United States is the New River in Virginia.

Resource Manager

Chapter Resources Booklet
Transparency Activity, pp. 43–45
Enrichment, p. 26

✔ **Reading Check**

Answer Old streams flow smoothly through flat, broad flood plains.

Too Much Water

SCIENCE *Online*

Research Visit the Glencoe Science Web site at **science.glencoe.com** to find out about major rivers in the United States. Classify two of these streams as young, mature, or old.

Figure 9
Flooding causes problems for people who live along major rivers. Floodwater broke through a levee during the Mississippi River flooding in 1993.

Old Streams The last stage in the development of a stream is the old stage. An old stream flows smoothly through a broad, flat floodplain that it has deposited. South of St. Louis, Missouri, the lower Mississippi River is in the old stage.

Major river systems, such as the Mississippi River, usually contain streams in all stages of development. In the upstream portion of a river system, you find whitewater streams moving swiftly down mountains and hills. At the bottom of mountains and hills, you find streams that start to meander and are in the mature stage of development. These streams meet at the trunk of the drainage basin and form a major river.

✔ **Reading Check** *How do old streams differ from young streams?*

Too Much Water

Sometimes heavy rains or a sudden melting of snow can cause large amounts of water to enter a river system. What happens when a river system has too much water in it? The water needs to go somewhere, and out and over the banks is the only choice. A river that overflows its banks can bring disaster by flooding homes or washing away bridges or crops.

Dams and levees are built in an attempt to prevent this type of flooding. A dam is built to control the water flow downstream. It may be built of soil, sand, or steel and concrete. Levees are mounds of earth that are built along the sides of a river. Dams and levees are built to prevent rivers from overflowing their banks. Unfortunately, they do not stop the water when flooding is great. This was the case in 1993 when heavy rains caused the Mississippi River to flood parts of nine midwestern states. Flooding resulted in billions of dollars in property damage. **Figure 9** shows some of the damage caused by this flood.

As you have seen, floods can cause great amounts of damage. But at certain times in Earth's past, great floods have completely changed the surface of Earth in a large region. Such floods are called catastrophic floods.

248 CHAPTER 9 Water Erosion and Deposition

LAB DEMONSTRATION

Purpose to show how levees help prevent flooding along rivers
Materials long paint tray, sand, water
Alternate Materials stream table
Preparation Fill the tray with sand, and make a shallow channel with flat banks in the sand.

Procedure Pour a stream of water through the channel. Slowly increase the volume until the stream overflows its banks. Rebuild the channel with levees and repeat.
Expected Outcome Students will see that with levees, overbank flooding will take much longer.

✔ *Assessment*

Why do some cities build levees along their rivers? Levees help prevent rivers from overflowing their banks. **Why don't levees work when flooding is great?** The water breaks through or flows over the levee.

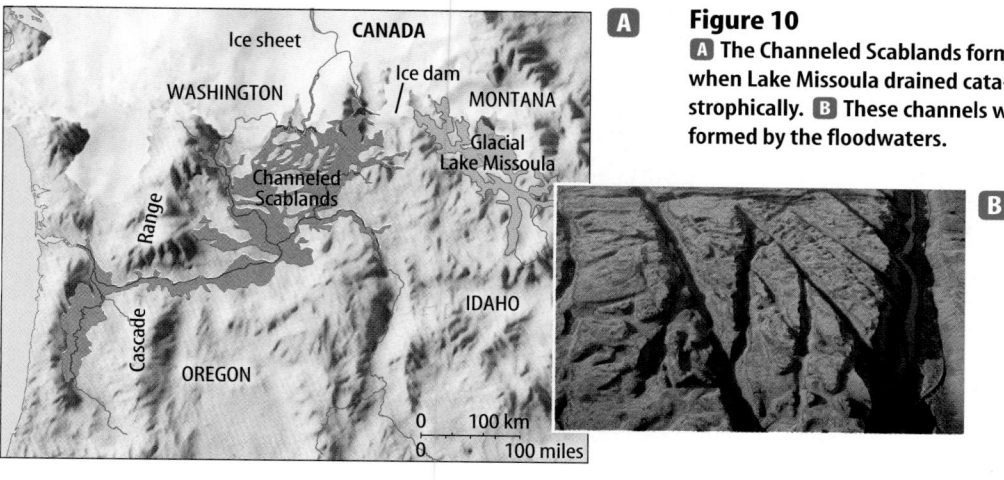

Figure 10
A The Channeled Scablands formed when Lake Missoula drained catastrophically. **B** These channels were formed by the floodwaters.

Catastrophic Floods During Earth's long history, many catastrophic floods have dramatically changed the face of the surrounding area. One catastrophic flood formed the Channeled Scablands in eastern Washington State, shown here in **Figure 10.** A vast lake named Lake Missoula covered much of western Montana. A natural dam of ice formed this lake. As the dam melted or was eroded away, tremendous amounts of water suddenly escaped through what is now the state of Idaho into Washington. In a short period of time, the floodwater removed overlying soil and carved channels into the underlying rock, some as deep as 50 m. Flooding occurred several more times as the lake refilled with water and the dam broke loose again. Scientists say the last such flood occurred about 13,000 years ago.

Deposition by Surface Water

You know how hard it is to carry a heavy object for a long time without putting it down. As water moves throughout a river system, it loses some of its energy of motion. The water can no longer carry some of its sediment. As a result, it drops, or is deposited, to the bottom of the stream.

Some stream sediment is carried only a short distance. In fact, sediment often is deposited within the stream channel itself. Other stream sediment is carried great distances before being deposited. Sediment picked up when rill and gully erosion occur are examples of this. Water usually has a lot of energy as it moves down a steep slope. When water begins flowing on a level surface, it slows, loses energy, and deposits its sediment. Water also loses energy and deposits sediment when it empties into an ocean or lake.

Mini LAB

Observing Runoff Collection

Procedure
1. Put a plastic **rain gauge** into a narrow **drinking glass** and place the glass in the sink.
2. Fill a plastic **sprinkling can** with **water.**
3. Hold the sprinkling can one-half meter above the sink for 30 s.
4. Record the amount of water in the rain gauge.
5. After emptying the rain gauge, place a **plastic funnel** into the rain gauge and sprinkle again for 30 s.
6. Record the amount of water in the gauge.

Analysis
Explain how a small amount of rain falling on a drainage basin can have a big effect on a river or stream.

SECTION 1 Surface Water **249**

Deposition by Surface Water

Extension
Have students research how the border between the United States and Mexico has changed over time because of changes in the channel of the Rio Grande. The Rio Grande forms part of the border between the United States and Mexico. Because the river meanders, Mexico has had to cede some land to the United States. L3

IDENTIFYING Misconceptions
Because students can see the effects of erosion more readily, they may not consider deposition to be of equal importance. Remind students of the rock cycle. In this cycle, erosion is followed by sedimentation to form sedimentary rocks.

Mini LAB

Purpose Students use a model to how infer how the effect of rain on a drainage basin affects a river or stream.

Materials plastic rain gauge, drinking glass, sink, sprinkling can, water, funnel

Teaching Strategy Use funnels with wide mouths for a more dramatic effect.

Analysis
The drainage basin funnels water from over a large area into a stream or river.

Cultural Diversity

Egypt's Nile No country depends on a river more than Egypt depends on the Nile. The Nile's floodplain provides fertile soil that has supported Egypt's agriculture and has been home to most of its people for thousands of years. Today, the Nile provides irrigation water, drinking water, transportation, and hydroelectric power for a nation which otherwise would be a desert wasteland.

Assessment

Oral Ask students to predict what would happen to the amount of water in the gauge if they used a funnel with a wider mouth. The amount of water would increase. Use **PASC,** p. 89.

Resource Manager

Chapter Resources Booklet
MiniLAB, p. 3
Reinforcement, p. 23

Use Science Words

Word Origin Have students find out how deltas got their name. Both the Greek letter *delta* (Δ), and the deposit have a triangular shape.

③ Assess

Reteach

Have students examine rivers shown on maps or in photographs. Ask students to classify these rivers as young, mature, or old and give reasons for their choices. L1 ℕ **Visual-Spatial**

Challenge

Challenge students to devise a way to collect and measure the amount of erosion that takes place on different slopes. One possible way is to lay plastic sheeting at the base of each slope. At the end of one week, determine the mass of the sediments that has collected on each piece of sheeting. L3 ℕ **Logical-Mathematical**

✓Assessment

Process Have students refer to **Figure 11** and then draw pictures of alluvial fans and deltas. Use **Performance Assessment in the Science Classroom,** p. 127.

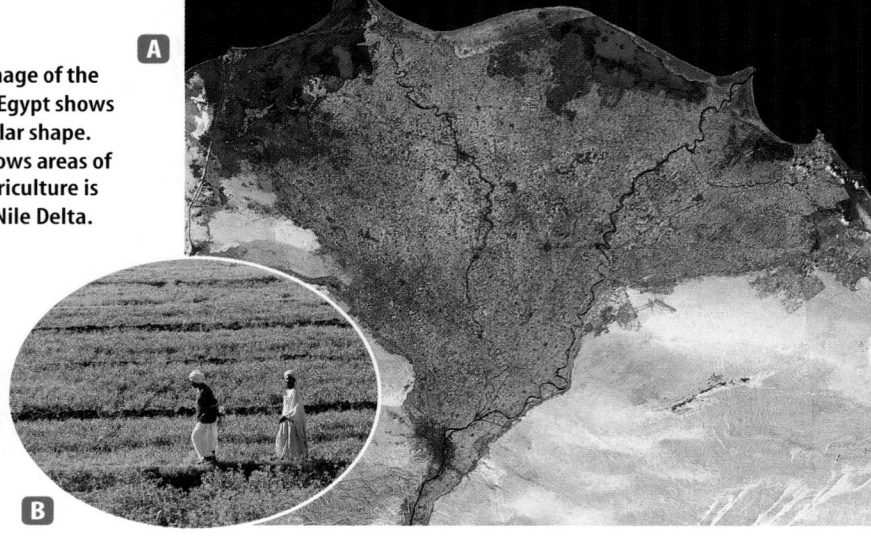

Figure 11
A This satellite image of the Nile River Delta in Egypt shows the typical triangular shape. The green color shows areas of vegetation. **B** Agriculture is important on the Nile Delta.

Deltas and Fans Sediment that is deposited as water empties into an ocean or lake forms a triangular, or fan-shaped, deposit called a delta, shown in **Figure 11.** When the river waters empty from a mountain valley onto an open plain, the deposit is called an alluvial (uh LEW vee ul) fan. The Mississippi River is an example of the topics presented in this section. Runoff causes rill and gully erosion. Sediment is picked up and carried into the larger streams that flow into the Mississippi River. As the Mississippi River flows, it cuts into its banks and picks up more sediment. Where the land is flat, the river deposits some of its sediment in its own channel. As the Mississippi enters the Gulf of Mexico, it slows, dropping much of its sediment and forming the Mississippi River delta.

Section 1 Assessment

1. How does the slope of an area affect runoff?
2. Compare rill and gully erosion.
3. Describe the three stages of stream development.
4. What is a delta?
5. **Think Critically** How is a stream's rate of flow related to the amount of erosion it causes? How is it related to the size of the sediments it deposits?

Skill Builder Activities

6. **Comparing and Contrasting** Compare and contrast the characteristics of rill, gully, sheet, and stream erosion. **For more help, refer to the Science Skill Handbook.**

7. **Using an Electronic Spreadsheet** Design a table to compare and contrast sheet, rill, gully, and stream erosion. **For more help, refer to the Technology Skill Handbook.**

250 CHAPTER 9 Water Erosion and Deposition

Answers to Section Assessment

1. the greater the slope, the greater the runoff
2. Both are types of erosion. Gully erosion is broader and deeper than rill erosion.
3. A youthful stream erodes its bottom more than its sides. A mature stream flows less swiftly, with erosion mostly along its sides. An old stream meanders slowly through a broad, flat floodplain.
4. a fan-shaped sediment deposit
5. The greater the rate of flow, the greater the erosion and the larger the sediment size a stream can carry.
6. Each type wears away rock and soil: rill—by a small stream that makes a channel during heavy rain; gully—by water that flows frequently through the path made by a rill; stream—by water that flows in a permanent channel; sheet—by water that flows over land in sheets with no channel.
7. Tables should include space for sediments transported, slope steepness, and type of erosion.

Groundwater

Groundwater Systems

What would have happened if the spilled milk in Section 1 ran off the table onto a carpeted floor? It probably would have quickly soaked into the carpet. Water that falls on Earth can soak into the ground just like the milk into the carpet.

Water that soaks into the ground becomes part of a system, just as water that stays above ground becomes part of a river system. Soil is made up of many small rock and mineral fragments. These fragments are all touching one another, as shown in **Figure 12,** but some empty space remains between them. Holes, cracks, and crevices exist in the rock underlying the soil. Water that soaks into the ground collects in these pores and empty spaces and becomes part of what is called **groundwater.**

How much of Earth's water do you think is held in the small openings in rock? Scientists estimate that 14 percent of all freshwater on Earth exists as groundwater. This is almost 30 times more water than is contained in all of Earth's lakes and rivers.

As You Read

What You'll Learn
- **Recognize** the importance of groundwater.
- **Describe** the effect that soil and rock permeability have on groundwater movement.
- **Explain** how groundwater dissolves and deposits minerals.

Vocabulary

groundwater	water table
permeable	spring
impermeable	geyser
aquifer	cave

Why It's Important
The groundwater system is an important source of your drinking water.

Figure 12
Soils have many small, connected pores through which water can move.

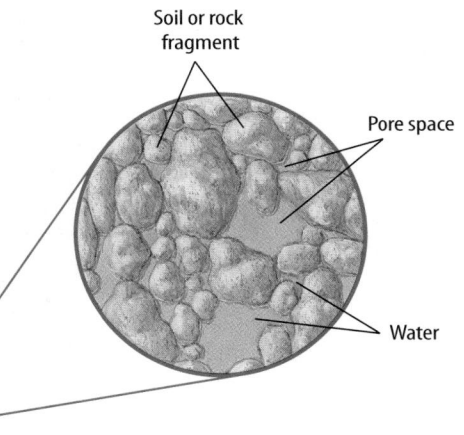

Soil or rock fragment

Pore space

Water

Section ✔*Assessment* Planner

PORTFOLIO
Science Journal, p. 253
PERFORMANCE ASSESSMENT
Try at Home MiniLAB, p. 252
Math Skills Activity, p. 253
Skill Builder Activities, p. 256
See page 268 for more options.

CONTENT ASSESSMENT
Section, p. 256
Challenge, p. 256
Chapter, pp. 268–269

SECTION

Groundwater

1 Motivate

Bellringer Transparency
Display the Section Focus Transparency for Section 2. Use the accompanying Transparency Activity Master. L2
ELL

Tie to Prior Knowledge

Have students recall watching a gentle rain fall onto and disappear into a field or lawn. Ask them where the water goes. It soaks into the soil to become a deposit of groundwater. If rainfall lasts long enough, the ground may become saturated and water will run off the lawn and possibly into a storm drain.

Resource Manager

Chapter Resources Booklet
Transparency Activity, p. 41
Directed Reading for Content Mastery, p. 17

Purpose Students measure and compare pore space. [L2] [ELL]
[IS] **Logical-Mathematical**

Materials 2 plastic cups, 250 g sand, 250 g gravel, metric measuring cups, 200 mL water

Teaching Strategies
• Have students predict which material will absorb more water before reaching capacity.
• Students must subtract the final volume reading on the measuring cup from 100 mL to find the volume of water used.

Troubleshooting The sand and the gravel mixtures should be of relatively uniform grain size and perfectly dry.

Analysis
Sand and gravel are about equal in total amount of pore space. Gravel has fewer but larger pore spaces when compared to the smaller but more numerous spaces among the sand grains. Average results should show that it takes about the same amount of water to fill both materials.

✔ Assessment

Content Have students draw a magnified image of the pore spaces and sediments in their two cups. Use **PASC**, p. 127.

✔ Reading Check

Answer Water flows through interconnected spaces in rock.

TRY AT HOME

Mini
LAB

Measuring Pore Space

Procedure
1. Use two identical, **clear-plastic containers.**
2. Put 3 cm of **sand** in one container and 3 cm of **gravel** in the other.
3. Pour **water** slowly into the containers and stop when the water just covers the top of the sediment.
4. Record the volume of water used in each.

Analysis
Which substance has more pore space—sand or gravel?

Figure 13
A stream's surface level is the water table. Below that is the zone of saturation.

Permeability A groundwater system is similar to a river system. However, instead of having channels that connect different parts of the drainage basin, the groundwater system has connecting pores. Soil and rock are **permeable** (PUR mee uh bul) if the pore spaces are connected and water can pass through them. Sandstone is an example of a permeable rock.

Soil or rock that has many large, connected pores is permeable. Water can pass through it easily. However, if a rock or sediment has few pore spaces or they are not well connected, then the flow of groundwater is blocked. These materials are **impermeable,** which means that water cannot pass through them. Granite has few or no pore spaces at all. Clay has many small pore spaces, but the spaces are not well connected.

✔ Reading Check
How does water move through permeable rock?

Groundwater Movement How deep into Earth's crust does groundwater go? **Figure 13** shows a model of a groundwater system. Groundwater keeps going deeper until it reaches a layer of impermeable rock. When this happens, the water stops moving down. As a result, water begins filling up the pores in the rocks above. A layer of permeable rock that lets water move freely is an **aquifer** (AK wuh fur). The area where all of the pores in the rock are filled with water is the zone of saturation. The upper surface of this zone is the **water table.**

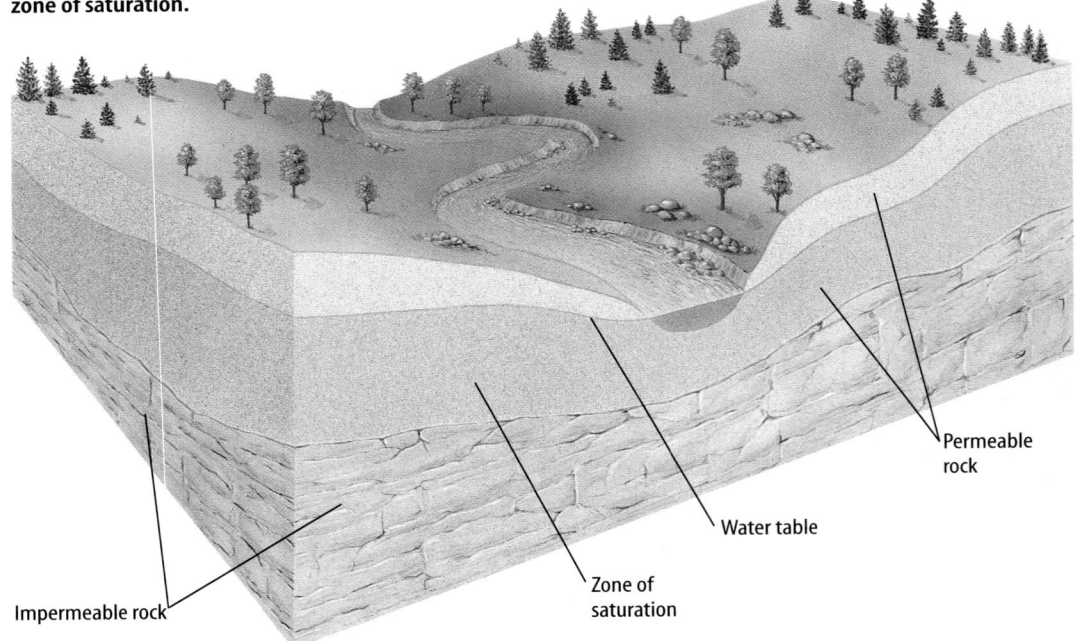

Permeable rock

Water table

Zone of saturation

Impermeable rock

Resource Manager

Chapter Resources Booklet
  MiniLAB, p. 4
Mathematics Skill Activities, p. 11

Water Table

Why are the zone of saturation and the water table so important? An average United States resident uses about 626 L of water per day. That's enough to fill nearly two thousand soft drink cans. Many people get their water from groundwater through wells that have been drilled into the zone of saturation. However, the supply of groundwater is limited. During a drought, the water table drops. This is why you should conserve water.

Math Skills Activity

Calculating the Rate of Groundwater Flow

You and your family are hiking and the temperature is hot. You feel as if you can't walk one step farther. Luckily, relief is in sight. On the side of a nearby hill you see a stream, and you rush to splash some water on your face. Although you probably feel that it's taking you forever to reach the stream, your pace is quick when compared to how long it takes groundwater to flow through the aquifer that feeds the stream. The following problem will give you some idea of just how slowly groundwater flows through an aquifer.

Example Problem

You've run 200 m to get some water from a stream. How long does it take the groundwater in the aquifer to travel the same distance? The groundwater flows at a rate of 0.6 m/day.

Solution

1 *This is what you know:*
the distance that the groundwater has to travel: $d = 200$ m
the rate that groundwater flows through the aquifer: $r = 0.6$ m/day

2 *This is what you want to find:* time = t

3 *This is the equation you use:* $r \times t = d$ (rate $\times$ time = distance)

4 *Solve the equation for* t *and then substitute known values:* $t = \dfrac{d}{r} = \dfrac{(200 \text{ m})}{(0.6 \text{ m/day})} = 333.33$ days

Practice Problem

The groundwater in an aquifer flows at a rate of 0.5 m/day. How far does the groundwater move in a year?

For more help, refer to the Math Skill Handbook.

Water Table

Discussion

Given the way groundwater collects in aquifers, how might pollution collect in aquifers? It can also seep into the ground and collect there. **Do you think pollution would be easier or harder to remove from groundwater or from surface water?** It would be harder to get pollution out of groundwater because the system is fairly closed.

Fun Fact

The United States is the world's largest user of both surface and groundwater. It loses about half of its potential supply through evaporation, leaks, and other means.

Math Skills Activity

National Math Standards

Correlation to Mathematics Objectives
1, 2, 6, 9

Answer to Practice Problem

Solve as originally given:
$d = (.5 \text{ m/day})(365 \text{ days}) = 182.5$ m

Science Journal

Groundwater Quality Have students research and describe in their journals ways pollutants from landfills, agriculture, and industry might affect groundwater quality and why this would be important. Pesticides, solvents, septic tank cleaners, and other wastes get into soil and permeable rocks from runoff. Some become dissolved in groundwater, which can cause harm to all organisms that use the water. P

Teacher FYI

In the United States, about half the drinking water and 40% of irrigation water comes from aquifers. But groundwater is being withdrawn at four times its replacement rate, with the greatest problems in the Plains from South Dakota to Texas, the Southwest, and California's Central Valley.

Water Table, continued

Figure 14
The years on the pole show how much the ground level dropped in the San Joaquin Valley, California, between 1925 and 1977.

Figure 15
The pressure of water in a sloping aquifer keeps an artesian well flowing. *What limits how high water can flow in an artesian well?*

Wells A good well extends deep into the zone of saturation, past the top of the water table. Groundwater flows into the well, and a pump brings it to the surface. Because the water table sometimes drops during very dry seasons, even a good well can go dry. Then time is needed for the water table to rise, either from rainfall or through groundwater flowing from other areas of the aquifer.

Where groundwater is the main source of drinking water, the number of wells and how much water is pumped out is important. If a large factory were built in such a town, the demand on the groundwater supply would be even greater. Even in times of normal rainfall, the wells could go dry if water were taken out at a rate greater than the rate at which it can be replaced.

In areas where too much water is pumped out, the land level can sink from the weight of the sediments above the now-empty pore spaces. **Figure 14** shows what occurred when too much groundwater was removed in a region of California.

One type of well doesn't need a pump to bring water to the surface. An artesian well is a well in which water rises to the surface under pressure. Artesian wells are less common than other types of wells because of the special conditions they require.

As shown in **Figure 15,** the aquifer for an artesian well needs to be located between two impermeable layers that are sloping. Water enters at the high part of the sloping aquifer. The weight of the water in the higher part of the aquifer puts pressure on the water in the lower part. If a well is drilled into the lower part of the aquifer, the pressurized water will flow to the surface. Sometimes, the pressure is great enough to force the water into the air, forming a fountain.

✔ Reading Check *Why does water flow from an artesian well?*

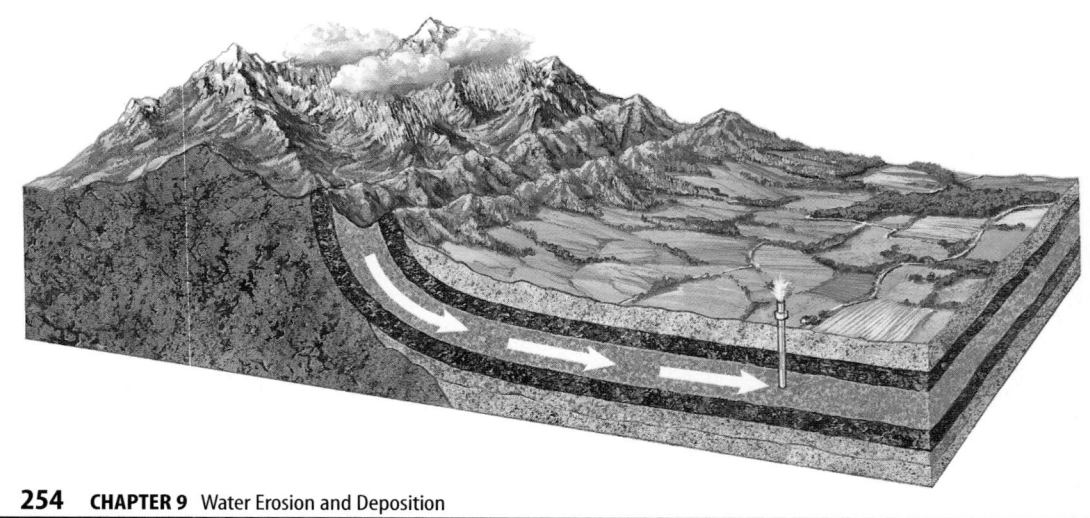

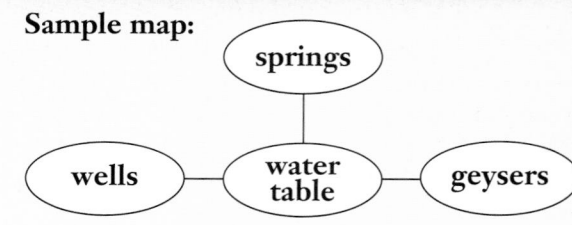

Springs In some places, the water table is so close to Earth's surface that water flows out and forms a **spring.** Springs are found on hillsides or other places where the water table meets a sloping surface. Springs often are used as a source of freshwater.

The water from most springs is a constant, cool temperature because soil and rock are good insulators and protect the groundwater from changes in temperature on Earth's surface. However, in some places, magma rises to within a few kilometers of Earth's surface and heats the surrounding rock. Groundwater that comes in contact with these hot rocks is heated and can come to the surface as a hot spring.

Geysers When water is put into a teakettle to boil, it heats slowly at first. Then some steam starts to come out of the cap on the spout, and suddenly the water starts boiling. The teakettle starts whistling as steam is forced through the cap. A similar process can occur with groundwater. One of the places where groundwater is heated is in Yellowstone National Park in Wyoming. Yellowstone has hot springs and geysers. A **geyser** is a hot spring that erupts periodically, shooting water and steam into the air. Groundwater is heated to high temperatures, causing it to expand underground. This expansion forces some of the water out of the ground, taking the pressure off of the remaining water. The remaining water boils quickly, with much of it turning to steam. The steam shoots out of the opening like steam out of a teakettle, forcing the remaining water out with it. Yellowstone's famous geyser, Old Faithful, pictured in **Figure 16,** shoots between 14,000 and 32,000 L of water and steam into the air about once every 80 min.

The Work of Groundwater

Although water is the most powerful agent of erosion on Earth's surface, it also can have a great effect underground. Water mixes with carbon dioxide gas to form a weak acid called carbonic acid. Some of this carbon dioxide is absorbed from the air by rainwater or surface water. Most carbon dioxide is absorbed by groundwater moving through soil. One type of rock that is dissolved easily by this acid is limestone. Acidic groundwater moves through natural cracks and pores in limestone, dissolving the rock. Gradually, the cracks in the limestone enlarge until an underground opening called a **cave** is formed.

Chemistry INTEGRATION

Acid rain occurs when gases released by burning oil and coal mix with water in the air. Infer what effect acid rain can have on a statue made of limestone.

Figure 16
Yellowstone's famous geyser, Old Faithful, used to erupt once about every 76 min. An earthquake on January 9, 1998, slowed Old Faithful's "clock" by 4 min to an average of one eruption about every 80 min. The average height of the geyser's water is 40.5 m.

Chemistry INTEGRATION

The acid in acid rain reacts chemically to erode the limestone in statues.

Extension

Have students research what has happened to the Ogallala Aquifer as a result of overpumping. Have students make posters and diagrams to illustrate their findings. A map showing the location of the Ogallala Aquifer should be included. It is estimated that 60% of this huge aquifer, which lies beneath the Great Plains from South Dakota to Texas, has been extracted, mostly for agricultural use. The rate of extraction has far exceeded the rate of recharging of the aquifer.

The Work of Groundwater

Quick Demo

Half-fill a large jar with limestone chips. Pour carbonated water over the chips and have students observe and describe what happens. Ask students to infer how what they observe relates to the action of groundwater on rock and soil. The carbonated water represents groundwater that dissolves underground limestone. **IS Visual-Spatial**

Resource Manager

Chapter Resources Booklet
Reinforcement, p. 27
Enrichment, p. 27
Physical Science Critical Thinking/Problem Solving, p. 12

Science Journal

Yellowstone Have students write short reports on geysers and other natural features in Yellowstone National Park. Have them include the mechanism that causes these eruptions. Geysers are produced by the heating of groundwater that come into contact with, or very close to, magma. L2
IS Linguistic

The Work of Groundwater, continued

Make a Model

After reading about cave formation and researching the topic in the library or on-line, have students make models of limestone caves that include labeled stalactites, stalagmites, and other dripstone features. Display completed models in the classroom.

L2 LS **Visual-Spatial**

3 Assess

Reteach

Direct students to **Figure 13**. Have students identify each component of the groundwater system and describe how all the components interact.

Challenge

Challenge students to design a way to compare the speeds at which different kinds of sediments or rocks dissolve in groundwater. Students must include a way to measure the rate at which the materials dissolve.

Assessment

Portfolio Have groups of students make models that show how the position of the water table affects the formation of a well, a geyser, a hillside spring, a stream, a lake, a hot spring, and an artesian well. Use **Performance Assessment in the Science Classroom,** p. 123.

Figure 17
Water dissolves rock to form caves and also deposits material to form spectacular formations, such as these in Carlsbad Caverns in New Mexico.

Cave Formation You've probably seen a picture of the inside of a cave, like the one shown in **Figure 17,** or perhaps you've visited one. Groundwater not only dissolves limestone to make caves, but it also can make deposits on the insides of caves.

Water often drips slowly from cracks in the cave walls and ceilings. This water contains calcium ions dissolved from the limestone. If the water evaporates while hanging from the ceiling of a cave, a deposit of calcium carbonate is left behind. Stalactites form when this happens over and over. Where drops of water fall to the floor of the cave, a stalagmite forms. The words *stalactite* and *stalagmite* come from Greek words that mean "to drip."

Sinkholes If underground rock is dissolved near the surface, a sinkhole may form. A sinkhole is a depression on the surface of the ground that forms when the roof of a cave collapses or when material near the surface dissolves. Sinkholes are common features in places like Florida and Kentucky that have lots of limestone and enough rainfall to keep the groundwater system supplied with water. Sinkholes can cause property damage if they form in a populated area.

In summary, when rain falls and becomes groundwater, it might dissolve limestone and form a cave, erupt from a geyser, or be pumped from a well to be used at your home.

Section 2 Assessment

1. Describe how water enters the groundwater system.
2. How does the permeability of soil and rocks affect the flow of groundwater?
3. Describe why a well might go dry.
4. Explain how caves form.
5. **Think Critically** Would you expect water in wells, geysers, and hot springs to contain dissolved materials? Why or why not?

Skill Builder Activities

6. **Comparing and Contrasting** Compare and contrast wells, geysers, and hot springs. **For more help, refer to the** Science Skill Handbook.
7. **Drawing Conclusions** Read an article about geothermal energy and draw a diagram in your Science Journal explaining how it works. Also, list the limitations of this energy source. **For more help, refer to the** Science Skill Handbook.

256   CHAPTER 9 Water Erosion and Deposition

Answers to Section Assessment

1. It soaks into the ground and collects in the pores in rocks.
2. The more permeable a soil or rock is, the better groundwater flows through it.
3. If water is removed from an aquifer faster than it can be replaced by nature, a well may go dry.
4. Caves form when water dissolves underground rock.
5. Yes; because groundwater dissolves materials as it flows through rock and soil.
6. All bring water to Earth's surface. In most wells, water must be pumped. Water is hot in geysers and hot

springs. A geyser is a hot spring that periodically erupts.
7. Geothermal energy comes from Earth's internal heat. It is a clean energy source used to produce heat and electricity. Limitations include restriction to certain locations.

Ocean Shoreline

The Shore

Picture yourself sitting on a beautiful, white-sand beach like the one shown in **Figure 18.** Nearby, palm trees sway in the breeze. Children play in the quiet waves lapping at the water's edge. It's hard to imagine a place more peaceful. Now, picture yourself sitting along another shore. You're on a high cliff watching waves crash onto boulders far below. Both of these places are shorelines. An ocean shoreline is where land meets the ocean.

The two shorelines just described are different even though both experience surface waves, tides, and currents. These actions cause shorelines to change constantly. Sometimes you can see these changes from hour to hour. Why are shorelines so different? You'll understand why they look different when you learn about the forces that shape shorelines.

As You Read

What You'll Learn

■ **Identify** the different causes of shoreline erosion.
■ **Compare and contrast** different types of shorelines.
■ **Describe** some origins of sand.

Vocabulary

longshore current
beach

Why It's Important

Constantly changing shorelines impact the people who live and work by them.

Figure 18

 **A** Waves, tides, and currents cause shorelines to change constantly. **B** Waves approaching the shoreline at an angle create a longshore current.

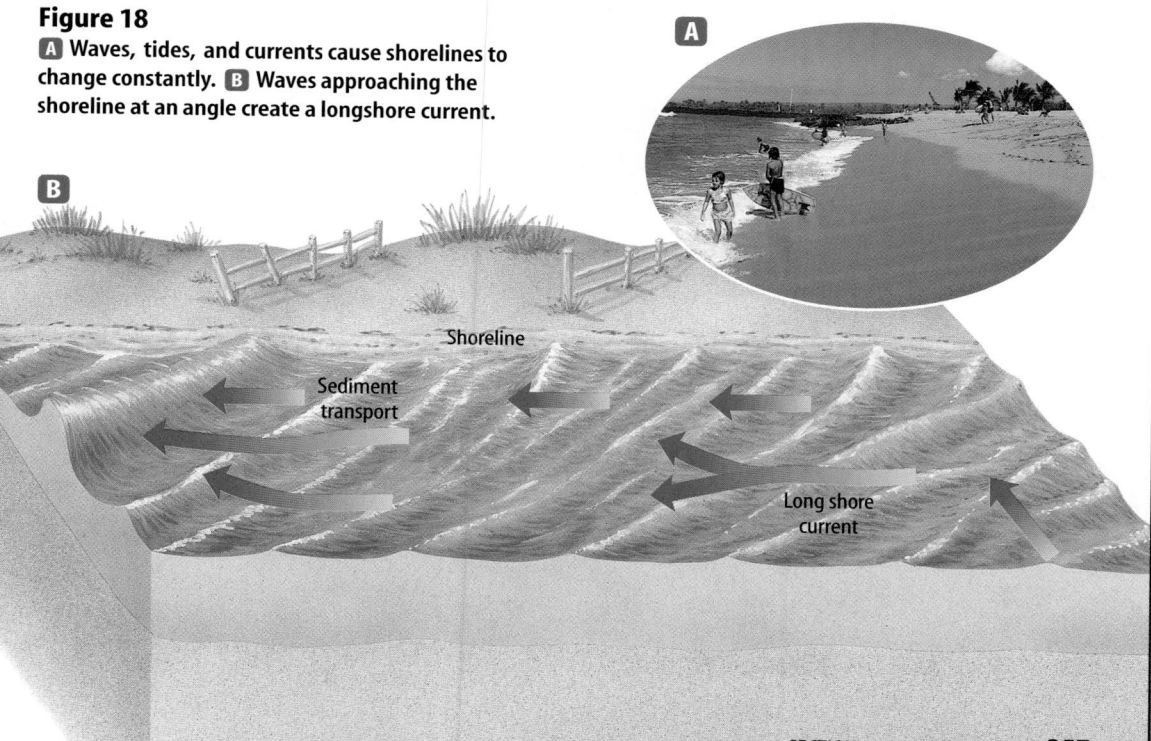

Shoreline

Sediment transport

Long shore current

Section ✔*Assessment* Planner

PORTFOLIO
Extension, p. 258
PERFORMANCE ASSESSMENT
Skill Builder Activities, p. 260
See page 268 for more options.

CONTENT ASSESSMENT
Section, p. 260
Challenge, p. 260
Chapter, pp. 268–269

1 Motivate

Bellringer Transparency

Display the Section Focus Transparency for Section 3. Use the accompanying Transparency Activity Master. [L2]
ELL

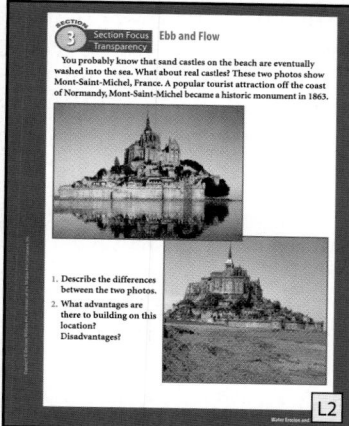

Tie to Prior Knowledge

Many students have visited shorelines. Those who have not have probably seen them on television. Have students recall the shoreline structures they have seen.

Resource Manager

Chapter Resources Booklet
Transparency Activity, p. 42
Directed Reading for Content Mastery, pp. 17, 18

Teacher FYI

Tides are the alternate rising and falling of the level of the ocean caused by the gravitational attraction of the Moon and Sun on Earth. In most places, there are two high tides and two low tides each day. Tidal range—the difference between high and low tide—varies. In some places, such as the shores of the Hawaiian and Caribbean Islands, the range is just 0.6 m. In Nova Scotia's Bay of Fundy, on the other hand, the tidal range is more than 15 m.

✔ Reading Check

Answer by waves colliding with shorelines at slight angles

Rocky Shorelines

Extension

The shape of coastal cliffs depends on the type of rock and the strength of waves battering the coast. Basalt, granite, and other hard rocks result in tall, straight cliffs, which sometimes rise 300 m or more over the sea's surface. Erosion of softer rock, such as chalk or conglomerate, usually forms a more sloping landscape where erosion occurs faster and undermines coastal forests and fields. Have students research a well-known coastal cliff, for example, the White Cliffs of Dover. Have them write a short report that includes a description of the type of rock in the cliff and the effects of ocean waves upon it.
L3 LS **Linguistic** P

What features would you find on the shoreline? To learn more about shoreline features, see the **Shoreline Field Guide** at the back of the book.

Figure 19
Along a rocky shoreline, the force of pounding waves breaks rock fragments loose, then grinds them into smaller and smaller pieces.

Shoreline Forces When waves constantly pound against the shore, they break rocks into ever-smaller pieces. Currents move many metric tons of sediment along the shoreline. The sediment grains grind against each other like sandpaper. The tide goes out carrying sediment to deeper water. When the tide returns, it brings new sediment with it. These forces are always at work, slowly changing the shape of the shoreline. Water is always in motion along the shore.

The three major forces at work on the shoreline are waves, currents, and tides. Winds blowing across the water make waves. Waves, crashing against a shoreline, are a powerful force. They can erode and move large amounts of material in a short time. Waves usually collide with a shore at slight angles. This creates a **longshore current** of water that runs parallel to the shoreline. Longshore currents, shown in **Figure 18B,** carry many metric tons of loose sediments and act like rivers of sand in the ocean.

✔ Reading Check *How does a longshore current form?*

Tides create currents that move at right angles to the shore. These are called tidal currents. Outgoing tides carry sediments away from the shore, and incoming tides bring new sediments toward the shore. Tides work with waves to shape shorelines. You've seen the forces that affect all shorelines. Now you will see the differences that make one shore a flat, sandy beach and another shore a steep, rocky cliff.

Rocky Shorelines

Rocks and cliffs are the most common features along rocky shorelines like the one in **Figure 19.** Waves crash against the rocks and cliffs. Sediments in the water grind against the cliffs, slowly wearing the rock away. Then rock fragments broken from the cliffs are ground up by the endless motion of waves. They are transported as sediment by longshore currents.

Softer rocks become eroded before harder rocks do, leaving islands of harder rocks. This takes thousands of years, but remember that the ocean never stops. In a single day, about 14,000 waves crash onto shore.

258   CHAPTER 9 Water Erosion and Deposition

Curriculum Connection

Music Suggest that students find music (tapes, CDs, videos, sheet music) about the coast or the beach. Have students play the music in class, or write the lyrics down and share them with classmates. Use the lyrics to spark a discussion of how people think about the shore and how it is used. L2 LS **Musical-Auditory**

A

B

Sandy Beaches

Smooth, gently sloping shorelines are different from steep, rocky shorelines. Beaches are the main feature here. **Beaches** are deposits of sediment that are parallel to the shore.

Beaches are made up of different materials. Some are made of rock fragments from the shoreline. Many sands are made of grains of quartz, and others are made of seashell fragments. These fragments range in size from stones larger than your hand to fine sand. Sand grains range in size from 0.06 mm to 2 mm in diameter. Why do many beaches have particles of this size? Waves break rocks and seashells down to sand-sized particles like those shown in **Figure 20.** The constant wave motion bumps sand grains together. This bumping not only breaks particles into smaller pieces but also smooths off their jagged corners making them more rounded.

Reading Check *How do waves affect beach particles?*

Sand in some places is made of other things. For example, Hawaii's black sands are made of basalt, and its green sands are made of the mineral olivine. Jamaica's white sands are made of coral and shell fragments.

Figure 20
Beach sand varies in size, color, and composition. **A** This quartz sand from a Texas beach is clear and glassy. **B** Some Hawaiian beaches are composed of black basalt sand.

Fun Fact

Some beach sands squeak, bark, and whistle. Grains of these sands are smooth, polished, and of similar size. These characteristics may allow them to slip over one another with little friction, producing sound.

Quick Demo

Use a glass of water and sand to demonstrate deposition. Students will see that moving water keeps materials suspended, but when movement stops, the sand settles out. **LS** **Visual-Spatial**

Extension

After performing library and on-line research, students can compare and contrast the ways organisms have adapted to life along rocky and sandy shorelines. Have students present their information by making colorful posters to display in the classroom. **L2** **LS** **Visual-Spatial**

Reading Check

Answer They break them down into sand-sized particles and make them more rounded.

Resource Manager

Chapter Resources Booklet
  Enrichment, p. 28
Science Inquiry Labs, p. 31
Home and Community Involvement, p. 19

Curriculum Connection

Economics Many coastal cities depend on tourism. When beaches disappear because of erosion, tourists do not visit. For this reason, many cities have spent a lot of money to preserve their beaches. Have students research costs involved in dredging and building seawalls. **Are these measures effective, or do they cause problems?** Sand migrates along beaches. Sand trapped by one city is "denied" to another.

Sand Erosion and Deposition

Visual Learning

Figure 21 How would buildings such as these be affected by hurricanes? They would be in danger from coastal flooding and storm surges. **Is development right along the coast a good idea?** Accept all opinions as a basis for class discussion.

3 Assess

Reteach

Obtain photographs or slides of various kinds of coastlines. Have students describe what caused the coastline features shown in each photograph. L1
Visual-Spatial

Challenge

Inform students that because sands have different compositions, their densities are also different. **How would the density of a sand grain affect its movement on a beach?** Less dense grains are transported farther by currents than are more dense grains.

✓ Assessment

Performance Have students make a sequence concept map that shows how an arch of rock can form along a rocky shoreline. Use **Performance Assessment in the Science Classroom**, p. 161.

Figure 21
Shorelines change constantly. Human development is often at risk from shoreline erosion.

Sand Erosion and Deposition

Longshore currents carry sand along beaches to form features such as barrier islands, spits, and sandbars. Storms and wind also move sand. Thus, beaches are fragile, short-term land features that are damaged easily by storms and human activities such as some types of construction. Communities in widely separated places such as Long Island, New York; Malibu, California; and Padre Island, Texas, have problems because of beach erosion.

Barrier Islands Barrier islands are sand deposits that lie parallel to the shore but are separated from the mainland. These islands start as underwater sand ridges formed by breaking waves. Hurricanes and storms add sediment to them, raising some to sea level. When a barrier island becomes large enough, the wind blows the loose sand into dunes, keeping the new island above sea level. As with all seashore features, barrier islands are short term, lasting from a few years to a few centuries.

The forces that build barrier islands also can erode them. Storms and waves carry sediments away. Beachfront development, as in **Figure 21,** can be affected by shoreline erosion.

Section 3 Assessment

1. What major forces cause shoreline erosion?
2. Contrast the features you would find along a steep, rocky shoreline with the features you would find along a gently sloping, sandy shoreline.
3. How could the type of shoreline affect the types of sediments you might find there?
4. List several materials that beach sand might be composed of. Where do these materials come from?
5. **Think Critically** How would erosion and deposition of sediment along a shoreline be affected if the longshore current was blocked by a wall built out into the water?

Skill Builder Activities

6. **Concept Mapping** Make an events chain concept map that shows how the sand from a barrier island can become a new barrier island 100 years from now. Use these terms: *barrier island, breaking waves, wind, longshore currents,* and *new barrier island.* **For more help, refer to the** Science Skill Handbook.
7. **Solving One-Step Equations** If 14,000 waves crash onto a shore daily, how many waves crash onto it in a year? Calculate how many have crashed onto it since you were born. Explain how you found your answer. **For more help, refer to the** Math Skill Handbook.

Answers to Section Assessment

1. waves and currents
2. rocky: boulders, cliffs, caves; sandy: flat beaches and barrier islands
3. Sediment size is larger along rocky shores than along gentle, sandy slopes.
4. Materials include quartz, seashell and coral fragments, olivine, and

basalt. They originate from rock fragments from the shoreline or from the shells of sea animals.
5. Sediments would be trapped by the wall instead of being deposited farther down the beach.
6. Concept map should be circular in shape and show arrows leading from

barrier island, to *wind,* to *breaking waves,* to *longshore current,* to *new barrier island,* and back to *barrier island.*
7. In one year, 14,000 × 365 = 5,110,000 waves. In the lifetime of a 13-year old student, 13 × 5,110,000 = 66,430,000 waves.

Activity

Classifying Types of Sand

You know that sand is made of many different kinds of grains, but did you realize that the slope of a beach is related to the size of its grains? The coarser the grain size is, the steeper the beach is. The composition of sand also is important. Many sands are mined because they have economic value.

What You'll Investigate
What characteristics can be used to classify different types of beach sand?

Materials
samples of different sands (3)
magnifying glass
*stereomicroscope
magnet
*Alternate materials

Goals
■ **Observe** differences in sand.
■ **Identify** characteristics of beach sand.
■ **Infer** sediment sources.

Procedure
1. **Design** a data table in which to record your data when you compare the three sand samples. You will need five columns in your table. One column will be for the samples and the others for the characteristics you will be examining.

Angular   Sub-Angular   Sub-Rounded   Rounded

Sand gauge
(measurements in mm)
0.25 0.5
0.1 1.0
0.1 1.0
0.25 0.5

2. Use the diagram to determine the average roundness of each sample.
3. **Identify** the grain size of your samples by using the sand gauge above. To determine the grain size, place sand grains in the middle of the circle of the sand gauge. Use the upper half of the circle for dark-colored particles and the bottom half for light-colored particles.
4. Decide on two other characteristics to examine that will help you classify your samples.

Conclude and Apply
1. **Compare and contrast** some characteristics of beach sand.
2. Why are there variations in the characteristics of different sand samples?
3. What do your observations tell you about the sources of the three samples?

Communicating Your Data
Compare your results with those of other students. **For more help, refer to the** Science Skill Handbook.

ACTIVITY 261

Resource Manager

Chapter Resources Booklet
  Activity Worksheets, pp. 5–6, 7–8
  Reinforcement, p. 25
Lab Management and Safety, p. 74

Communicating Your Data
Students should discuss why their conclusions did or did not agree with those of classmates. If possible, make overhead transparencies of several student's tables. Project them for the class to use while discussing and critiquing different classification systems.

Activity

BENCH TESTED

Purpose Students observe and classify beach sand. L2
IS Visual-Spatial
Process Skills classifying, observing and inferring, comparing and contrasting, interpreting data, making tables
Time Required 45 minutes
Alternate Materials stereomicroscope
Teaching Strategy Beach sands can be obtained from scientific supply distributors, hardware stores, and garden centers. Contact teachers in coastal areas for possible trading of sand samples.
Troubleshooting Advise students to avoid mixing the sand samples. They will need to examine only a small quantity of sand.

Answers to Questions
1. Possible characteristics: color, texture, shape, grain size, luster, magnetism, and composition
2. Samples will vary according to the length of time exposed to weathering and erosion, the type of erosion (wind or water), and the characteristics of parent material.
3. Answer depends on the characteristics of the samples. Possible answer: all three samples were from different sources.

✓ *Assessment*

Performance Show students pictures of different beaches. Have them use the results of this activity and the information that steeper beaches have coarser-sized sand grains to hypothesize as to the grain size likely to be found on each beach. Use **PASC**, p. 93.

Activity

What You'll Investigate

Purpose
Students will determine how water speed affects its ability to erode.

Process Skills
observing, collecting data, interpreting data, identifying and manipulating variables and controls, inferring, predicting

Time Required
one class period

Materials
Disposable paint trays are available at paint and hardware stores.

Alternate Materials
Disposable wallpaper trays can be substituted for paint roller pans.

Safety Precautions
Remind students to immediately clean up any water that spills on the floor.

Activity

Water Speed and Erosion

What would it be like to make a raft and use it to float on a river? Would it be easy? Would you feel like Tom Sawyer? Probably not. You'd be at the mercy of the current. Strong currents create fast rivers. But does fast moving water affect more than just floating rafts and other objects? How does the speed of a stream or river affect its ability to erode?

What You'll Investigate
How does the speed of water affect its ability to erode?

Materials
paint roller pan
sand
1-L beaker
rubber tubing (20 cm)
metric ruler
water
stopwatch
screen
wood block
disposable wallpaper trays

Goals
- Assemble an apparatus for measuring the effect of water speed on erosion.
- **Observe and measure** the ability of water traveling at different speeds to erode sand.

Safety Precautions

Wash your hands after you handle the sand. Immediately clean up any water that spills on the floor.

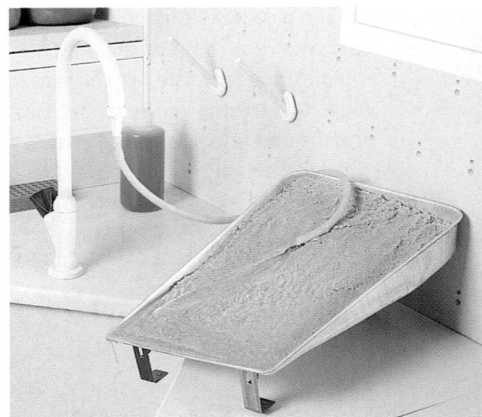

262 CHAPTER 9 Water Erosion and Deposition

Inclusion Strategies

Visually Impaired After other group members have measured the depth and length of the eroded channels, have these students feel the channels made by different water speeds so they can make a comparison.

Procedure

1. Copy the data table below.
2. Place the screen in the sink. Pour moist sand into your pan and smooth out the sand. Set one end of the pan on the wood block and hang the other end over the screen in the sink. Excess water will flow onto the screen in the sink.
3. Attach one end of the hose to the faucet and place the other end in the beaker. Turn on the water so that it trickles into the beaker. Time how long it takes for the trickle of water to fill the beaker to the 1-L mark. Divide 1 L by your time in seconds to calculate the water speed. Record the speed in your data table.

4. Without altering the water speed, hold the hose over the end of the pan that is resting on the wood block. Allow the water to flow into the sand for 2 min. At the end of 2 min, turn off the water.
5. **Measure** the depth and length of the eroded channel formed by the water. Count the number of branches formed on the channel. Record your measurements and observations in your data table.
6. Empty the excess water from the tray and smooth out the sand. Repeat steps 3 through 5 two more times increasing your water speed each time.

Water Speed and Erosion			
Water Speed (Liters per Second)	Depth of Channel	Length of Channel	Number of Channel Branches
	Answers will vary.		

Conclude and Apply

1. **Identify** the constants and variables in your experiment.
2. Which water speed created the deepest and longest channel?
3. Which water speed created the greatest number of branches?
4. **Infer** the effect that water speed has on erosion.
5. **Predict** how your results would have differed if one end of the pan had been raised higher.
6. **Infer** how streams and rivers can shape Earth's surface.

*C*ommunicating Your Data

Write a pamphlet for people buying homes near rivers or streams that outlines the different effects that water erosion could have on their property.

ACTIVITY   263

✓*Assessment*

Performance Have students design and carry out a procedure to test their prediction in question 5 of Conclude and Apply. Use **Performance Assessment in the Science Classroom,** p. 95.

*C*ommunicating Your Data

Students can use a word processing program and graphics program to prepare their pamphlets.

Procedure

Teaching Strategies
- Have students read through the procedure completely and prepare the data table before beginning.
- Set up stream tables in advance to save time.

Tie to Prior Knowledge
Most students have observed how gullies form when water runs down a bare slope so they are aware of what to expect.

Expected Outcome
Most results will reflect an increase in the amount of sand eroded as the water speed increased.

Conclude and Apply

1. constants: amount of sand, elevation of the slope, the amount of time water ran on the slope; variables: water speed, amount of water that ran on the slope, amount of sand eroded by water.
2. the fastest water speed
3. the fastest water speed
4. The faster the water moves, the greater the erosion that occurs.
5. The steeper the slope, the faster the water flows and the more it erodes.
6. When water flows through streams and rivers, it erodes soil and carries it to other areas. These processes change the shape of the land.

Error Analysis
Have each group compare their results with those of another group. If the data disagree, have students list possible reasons for the discrepancy.

Content Background

Explain that most of the erosion caused by the sea occurs where the breaking waves interact with the land. As waves approach the shore they are refracted. This means the bottom of each wave feels the shallow ocean bottom near the shore and is slowed down while the top of the wave continues unhindered and bends toward the shore. This results in an unequal distribution of the energy stored in the wave. As a consequence, the wave crests as it breaks onto the shore. The stored energy is concentrated on the headlands. Erosion occurs primarily by abrasion, the wearing away of a surface by friction. Sediments are carried out to sea by the retreating water and the shoreline retreats.

Coastal protection programs attempt to stabilize coastal areas by replenishing eroded shores or attempting to reduce the energy stored in waves, thereby reducing their potential to cause erosion.

Beach nourishment is one method commonly used to help stabilize eroded coastlines. Other methods include the construction of jetties (structures that extend perpendicular from the shore to trap sand), building of breakwaters (long dikes built off shore to slow waves down), and construction of armor protection (using concrete slabs to create erosion-resistant shores or embankments).

Two factors that should be considered when determining which method to use are natural features of the shoreline and cost.

Is there hope for America's coastlines or is beach erosion a "shore" thing?

Sands

Water levels are rising along the coastline of the United States. Serious storms and the building of homes and businesses along the shore are leading to the eroding of anywhere from 70 percent to 90 percent of the U.S. coastline. A report from the Federal Emergency Management Agency (FEMA) confirms this. The report says that one meter of United States beaches will be eaten away each year for the next 60 years. Since 1965, the federal government has spent millions of dollars replenishing more than 1,300 eroding sandy shores around the country. And still the tide continues to turn.

One meter of United States' beaches erode each year.

The slowly eroding beaches are upsetting to residents and officials of many communities who depend on their shore to earn money from visitors. Some city and state governments are turning to beach nourishment—a process in which sand is taken from the seafloor and dumped on beaches. The process is expensive, however. The state of Delaware, for example, is spending 7,000,000 dollars to bring in sand for its beaches.

Some geologists believe that beach nourishment does not work. They explain that the grains of the new sand are often smaller and finer than the original beach sand, so it erodes faster, carried back out to sea by waves.

264

Resources for Teachers and Students

Evaluation of Erosion Hazards Report, 2000. Federal Emergency Management Agency (FEMA), 500 C Street, Washington DC, 20472.

Beach Nourishment and Protection. Committee on Beach Nourishment and Protection, National Research Council, 1995.

Against the Tide: The Battle for America's Beaches. Cornelia Dean, Columbia University Press, 1999.

Dredged sand is pumped on to an eroded beach in Long Beach, North Carolina.

This beach house will collapse as its underpinnings are eroded.

Despite the odds, some people think beach nourishment is still the way to go even if it isn't a permanent solution. One person in favor of nourishing beaches answers those against beach nourishment this way: "That's like saying it's a losing battle to pave streets because some day grass is going to poke through."

Other methods of saving eroding beaches are being tried. In places along the Great Lakes shores and coastal shores, one company has installed fabrics underwater to slow currents. By slowing currents, sand is naturally deposited and kept in place.

Another shore-saving device is a synthetic barrier that is shaped like a plastic snowflake.

A string of these barriers are secured just off-shore. They absorb the energy of incoming waves. Reducing wave energy can prevent sand from being eroded from the beach. New sand also might accumulate because the barriers slow down the currents that flow along the shore.

Many people believe that communities along the shore must restrict the beachfront building of homes, hotels, and stores. Since some estimates claim that by the year 2025, nearly 75 percent of the U.S. population will live in coastal areas, it's a tough solution. Says one geologist, "We can retreat now and save our beaches or we can retreat later and probably ruin the beaches in the process."

CONNECTIONS **Debate** Using the facts in this article and other research you have done in your school media center or the Glencoe Science Web site, make a list of methods that could be used to save beaches. Debate the issue with your classmates.

SCIENCE *Online*
For more information, visit science.glencoe.com

CONNECTIONS Help students prepare their positions by constructing a table to compare the pros and cons (columns) of the methods (rows) used for saving beaches. Other factors that might be compared include natural shoreline features, land ownership (public vs. private), land use, erosion history, storm and flooding history, cost effectiveness, and environmental impacts.

SCIENCE *Online*

Internet Addresses

_____

_____

_____

_____

Explore the Glencoe Science Web site at **science.glencoe.com** to find out more about topics in this feature.

Discussion

What actions could be taken by local governments and landowners to reduce the environmental effects and financial costs of coastal erosion? Possible answers: restrict development along shorelines, relocating "at risk" homes and businesses, require landowners to have erosion insurance, use more than one method to save eroding beaches.

Activity

Have students search magazines to obtain pictures of different kinds of beach environments. Organize these pictures into three categories: shores resistant to erosion, shores easily eroded, and shores unaffected by erosion. Explain why each picture belongs in that category. The third category, shores unaffected by erosion, should be empty since all beaches are affected by erosion.

Investigate the Issue

Organize students into pairs. Have each pair choose two photographs, one from each category identified in the previous activity. For the photo of the shore resistant to erosion, have students identify the natural features responsible for the shore's resistance to erosion. For shores easily eroded, have students design a coastal protection plan. The coastal protection plan should include two or more methods for saving eroding beaches. Have students evaluate each design in terms of benefits, risks, and cost effectiveness.

Chapter **9** Study Guide

Preview

Students can answer the questions in their Science Journals. Discuss the answers as you go through the chapter. **Linguistic**

Review

Students can write their answers, then compare them with those of other students. **Interpersonal**

Reteach

Students can look at the illustrations and describe details that support the main ideas of the chapter. **Visual-Spatial**

Answers to Chapter Review

SECTION 1
2. gully

SECTION 2
2. It would decrease.

SECTION 3
1. In general, rocky coasts would erode more slowly than sandy beaches, because the rock is much more cohesive than loose sediment, which can be picked up by the waves. There are some sandy beaches where deposition may be occurring.

Reviewing Main Ideas

Section 1 Surface Water

1. Rainwater that does not soak into the ground is pulled down the slope by gravity. This water is called runoff.

2. Runoff has the ability to erode and carry sediment. Factors such as steepness of slope and number and type of plants affect the amount of erosion. Rill, gully, and sheet erosion are types of surface water erosion caused by runoff. *What type of erosion is occurring in this photograph?*

3. Runoff generally flows into streams that merge with larger and larger rivers until emptying into a lake or ocean. Major river systems usually contain several different types of streams.

4. In the mountains, young streams flow through steep valleys and have rapids and waterfalls. Mature streams flow through gentler terrain and have less energy. Old streams are often wide and snake back and forth across their floodplains.

Section 2 Groundwater

1. When water soaks into the ground, it becomes part of a vast groundwater system.

2. Although rock may seem solid, many types are filled with connected spaces called pores. Such rocks are permeable and can contain large amounts of groundwater. *What would happen to the permeability of this material if the pores filled with clay or some other material?*

Section 3 Ocean Shoreline

1. Ocean shorelines are always changing. *Would you expect the rocky coast, shown to the right, to erode slower or faster than a sandy coast? Why?*

2. Waves and currents have tremendous amounts of energy. Pounding waves break up rocks into tiny fragments called sediment. Over time, the waves and currents move this sediment and deposit it elsewhere constantly changing beaches, sandbars, and barrier islands.

FOLDABLES
Reading & Study
Skills

After You Read

Use the information in your Main Ideas Study Fold to review the different characteristics of surface water, groundwater, and ocean shorelines.

FOLDABLES
Reading & Study
Skills

After You Read

After students have read the chapter and completed the Foldable described in Before You Read, have them do the activity on the student page.

Dinah Zike

Visualizing Main Ideas

Complete the following concept map on caves.

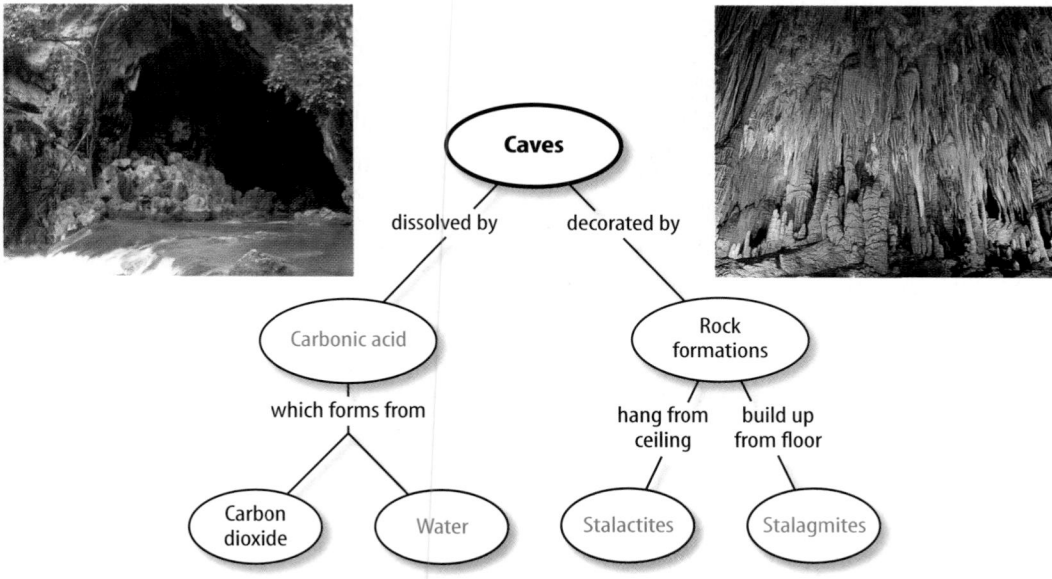

Caves

dissolved by → Carbonic acid

which forms from → Carbon dioxide, Water

decorated by → Rock formations

hang from ceiling → Stalactites

build up from floor → Stalagmites

Vocabulary Review

Vocabulary Words

a. aquifer
b. beach
c. cave
d. channel
e. drainage basin
f. geyser
g. groundwater
h. impermeable
i. longshore current
j. meander
k. permeable
l. runoff
m. sheet erosion
n. spring
o. water table

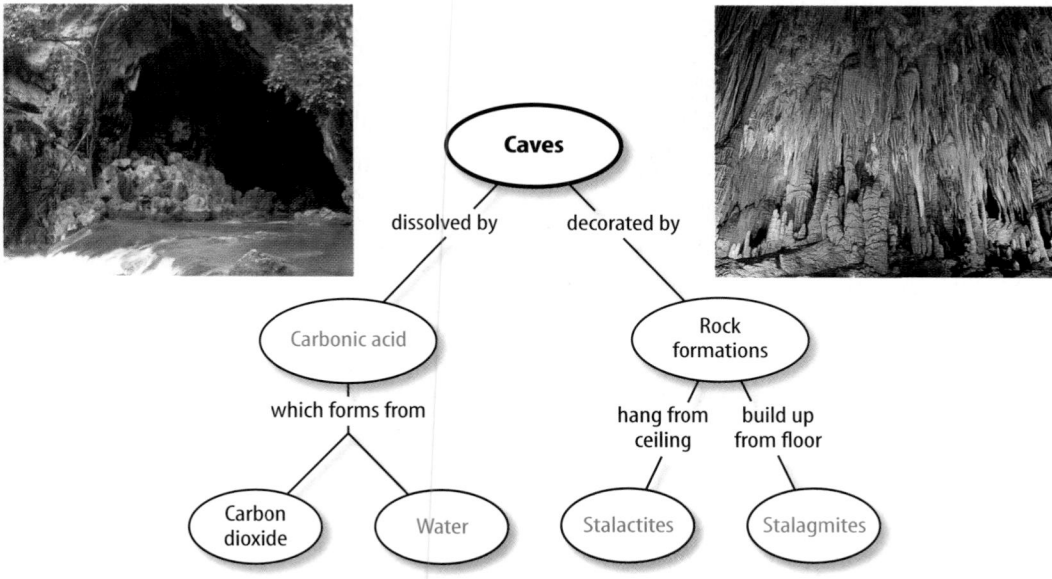

THE PRINCETON REVIEW

Study Tip

Don't just memorize definitions. Write complete sentences using new vocabulary words to be certain you understand what they mean.

Using Vocabulary

Explain the difference between the vocabulary words in each of the following sets.

1. runoff, sheet erosion
2. channel, drainage basin
3. aquifer, cave
4. spring, geyser
5. permeable, impermeable
6. sheet erosion, meander
7. groundwater, water table
8. permeable, aquifer
9. longshore current, beach
10. meander, channel

CHAPTER STUDY GUIDE 267

Visualizing Main Ideas

See student page.

Vocabulary Review

Using Vocabulary

1. Runoff is water that flows across Earth's surface. Sheet erosion is floodwater flowing as a sheet, picking up and carrying away sediments.
2. A channel is a groove made by flowing water. A drainage basin is the land area from which a stream collects runoff.
3. An aquifer is a layer of permeable rock that lets water move freely, albeit slowly, underground. A cave is an enlarged underground opening where the water has worn away or dissolved the rock.
4. A spring is where the water table intersects Earth's surface, allowing water to flow out. A geyser is a hot spring that erupts periodically.
5. Permeable materials let water pass through. Materials that are impermeable do not.
6. Sheet erosion moves sediments as water flows in sheets over flat land. A meander is a broad bend in a stream.
7. Groundwater is water that collects in underground pores in soil and rocks. The water table is the upper surface of the underground saturated zone.
8. Permeable substances allow water to pass through. An aquifer is a layer of permeable rock through which water moves slowly, but freely.
9. A longshore current runs along a shore. A beach is a deposit of sediments parallel to the shore.
10. A meander is a curve in a stream's channel. A channel is a groove where water flows.

CHAPTER STUDY GUIDE 267

Checking Concepts

1. A
2. B
3. A
4. C
5. D
6. A
7. B
8. D
9. B
10. D

Thinking Critically

11. The Mississippi River is in the old stage of development. Meanders are one characteristic of this stage.
12. The energy of the moving water, which is related to a stream's stage of development, determines erosion. Young streams erode downward; old streams erode their sides.
13. If a lot of water is drawn from the same aquifer, the supply could be depleted by overuse.
14. along flat, sandy shores where the islands start as underwater sand deposits
15. Sands vary according to their parent material and the length of time they have been exposed to weathering and erosion.

Checking Concepts

Choose the word or phrase that best answers the question.

1. Identify an example of a structure created by deposition.
   - A) beach
   - B) rill
   - C) cave
   - D) geyser

2. Name the deposit that forms when a mountain river runs onto a plain.
   - A) subsidence
   - B) an alluvial fan
   - C) infiltration
   - D) water diversion

3. What is a layer of permeable rock that water flows through?
   - A) an aquifer
   - B) a pore
   - C) a water table
   - D) impermeable

4. What is the network formed by a river and all the smaller streams that contribute to it?
   - A) groundwater system
   - B) zone of saturation
   - C) river system
   - D) water table

5. Which term describes rock through which fluids can flow easily?
   - A) impermeable
   - B) meanders
   - C) saturated
   - D) permeable

6. Which stage of development are mountain streams in?
   - A) young
   - B) mature
   - C) old
   - D) meandering

7. What forms as a result of the water table meeting Earth's surface?
   - A) meander
   - B) spring
   - C) aquifer
   - D) stalactite

8. What contains heated groundwater that reaches Earth's surface?
   - A) water table
   - B) cave
   - C) aquifer
   - D) hot spring

9. Where are beaches most common?
   - A) rocky shorelines
   - B) flat shorelines
   - C) aquifers
   - D) young streams

10. Why does water rise in an artesian well?
   - A) a pump
   - B) erosion
   - C) heat
   - D) pressure

Thinking Critically

11. Explain why the Mississippi River has meanders along its course.

12. What determines whether a stream erodes its bottom or its sides?

13. Why might you be concerned if developers of a new housing project started drilling wells near your well?

14. Along what kind of shoreline would you find barrier islands? Explain.

15. Explain why beach sands collected from different locations will differ.

Developing Skills

16. **Interpreting Data** The rate of water flowing out of the Brahmaputra River in India, the La Plata River in South America, and the Mississippi River in North America are given in the table below. Infer which river carries the most sediment.

River Flow Rates	
River	Flow, m^3/s
Brahmaputra River, India	19,800
La Plata River, South America	79,300
Mississippi River, North America	175,000

17. **Forming Hypotheses** Hypothesize why most of the silt in the Mississippi delta is found farther out to sea than the sand-sized particles are.

Chapter ✓Assessment Planner

Portfolio Encourage students to place in their portfolios one or two items of what they consider to be their best work. Examples include:
- Science Journal, p. 243
- Science Journal, p. 243
- Extension, p. 258

Performance Additional performance assessments, Performance Task Assessment Lists, and rubrics for evaluating these activities can be found in Glencoe's **Performance Assessment in the Science Classroom.**

18. Communicating Make an outline that explains the three stages of stream development. Share it with the class.

19. Concept Mapping Complete the concept map below using the following terms: *developed meanders, gentle curves, gentle gradient, old, rapids, steep gradient, wide floodplain,* and *young.*

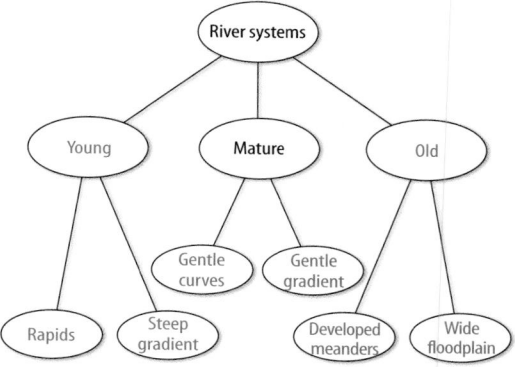

20. Using Variables, Constants, and Controls Explain how you could test the effect of slope on the amount of runoff produced.

Performance Assessment

21. Poster Do additional research about the distribution of water on Earth. Make a poster showing the different water reservoirs and what percentage of Earth's water is contained in each reservoir. Include processes such as erosion and deposition that are associated with each reservoir in your poster.

TECHNOLOGY

Go to the Glencoe Science Web site at **science.glencoe.com** or use the **Glencoe Science CD-ROM** for additional chapter assessment.

Test Practice

A scientist is gathering data and looking at trends in water erosion. The scientist's data are shown in the graph below.

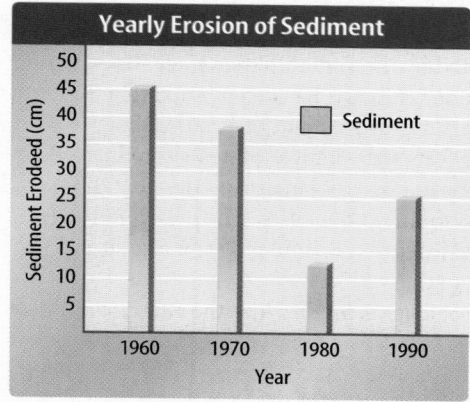

Study the graph and answer the following questions.

1. According to this information, which year had the most erosion?
A) 1960   **C)** 1980
B) 1970   **D)** 1990

2. According to the graph, between which years was erosion increasing?
F) 1960–1970   **H)** 1980–1990
G) 1970–1980   **J)** 1960–1980

3. According to the graph, which year had the least erosion?
A) 1960   **C)** 1980
B) 1970   **D)** 1990

4. According to the graph, how many centimeters of erosion were there in 1990?
F) 5   **H)** 15
G) 25   **J)** 20

Test Practice

The Test-Taking Tip was written by The Princeton Review, the nation's leader in test preparation.
1. A
2. H
3. C
4. G

Developing Skills

16. The Mississippi erodes more because it has more energy of motion. Its flow is much greater than the other two rivers.

17. Silt is smaller than sand. As water slows at the river's mouth, it drops larger sediments (sand) first.

18. Students' outlines should include details of the young, mature, and old stages.

19. See student page.

20. Answer should include (1) a way to allow a fixed amount of water to flow in the same way over the same type of soil surface, the difference being the angle of slope, and (2) a method to collect and measure the amount of runoff produced.

Performance Assessment

21. Use **PASC,** p. 145.

✓Assessment Resources

📁 Reproducible Masters

Chapter Resources Booklet
Chapter Review, pp. 33–34
Chapter Tests, pp. 35–38
Assessment Transparency Activity, p. 45

Glencoe Science Web site
Interactive Tutor
Chapter Quizzes

Glencoe Technology
🖐 Assessment Transparency
💿 Interactive CD-ROM Chapter Quizzes
💿 ExamView Pro Test Bank
💿 Vocabulary PuzzleMaker Software
📼 MindJogger Videoquiz DVD/VHS

Reading Comprehension

QUESTION 1: B

Students need to use the information in the passage in order to identify the most accurate conclusion. The passage states that *man-made structures that are within 500 feet of the United State's coastline and shorelines will be damaged.* Therefore the information in the passage supports choice B.

QUESTION 2: F

Students need to use the information in the passage, such as *many homes will be lost forever*, in order to identify the best-supported conclusion.

- **Choice F** Yes; the passage supports this.
- **Choice G** No; the passage does not support this.
- **Choice H** No; the passage does not support this.
- **Choice J** No; the passage does not support this.

Teaching Tip

Encourage students to underline key words found in questions.

Reading Comprehension

Read the passage carefully. Then read the questions that follow the passage. Decide which is the best answer to each question.

Shorelines

A recent study on shoreline erosion completed by the Federal Emergency Management Agency (FEMA) has determined that about one quarter of man-made structures that are within 500 feet of the United States' shorelines will be damaged by erosion during the next 60 years. If development of coasts continues and the level of the oceans continues to rise, the situation could be even worse.

Scientists predict that the Atlantic and Gulf of Mexico coastlines will experience the most erosion. The cost to homeowners is predicted to be about a half billion dollars per year. With yearly average erosion rates of 1m on the Atlantic Coast and 2m on the Gulf of Mexico coastlines, many homes will be lost forever. In fact, these areas will account for approximately 60 percent of nationwide losses.

The grain size of sediment is one factor that accounts for some of the difference in erosion rates between coasts. The sediment on the shores of the Gulf of Mexico generally is fine grained and easily picked up and carried away by wave action. On the Atlantic coast, the sediment generally is more coarse grained and therefore erodes at a slower rate. Along the Pacific Coast, rates of erosion vary from one area to another. Erosion rates of 2.4 m per year have been recorded along parts of the Alaskan coast, while the state of Washington's shoreline actually is growing in some places.

Test-Taking Tip After reading a passage, quickly glance over the questions and then skim the passage again, looking for important information.

1. Based on the passage, which of the following is most likely true?
   - **A)** Building a summer home along the Gulf of Mexico would be more secure than building one along the Atlantic Coast.
   - **B)** Erosion is a major threat to shorelines in many parts of the country.
   - **C)** All man-made structures within 500 feet of the Atlantic Coast will disappear.
   - **D)** Ocean water levels will decrease during the next 60 years.

2. The main purpose of the Federal Emergency Management Agency's study was most likely to _____.
   - **F)** discourage people from building homes near the coastline
   - **G)** explain how coastline erosion of various types of sediment occurs
   - **H)** help to limit erosion and protect property
   - **I)** figure out the costs of coastline erosion in the United States

Reasoning and Skills

Read each question and choose the best answer.

Group R

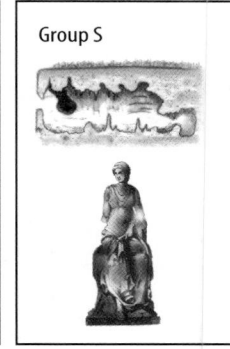
Group S

1. The weathering examples in Group R are different from weathering examples in Group S because only the weathering examples in Group R have been caused by _____.
   A) chemical weathering
   B) ice wedging
   C) mechanical weathering
   D) oxidation

Test-Taking Tip Think about the different kinds of weathering and how they affect Earth.

2. The rock slide pictured in the left column is most likely caused by the forces of _____.
   F) water
   G) gravity
   H) wind
   J) glacier movement

Test-Taking Tip Think about the forces that help cause erosion.

3. Which of the following is most responsible for the development of these landscapes?
   A) ice wedging
   B) the movement of wind
   C) the effects of acid rain
   D) the movement of water

Test-Taking Tip Consider what you know about erosion and specific examples of erosion, such as the Grand Canyon.

Consider this question carefully before writing your answer on a separate sheet of paper.

4. Earth's surface has been shaped by erosion. Discuss some of the different agents of erosion that affect Earth's surface. How do these agents of erosion reshape the landscape?

Reasoning and Skills

QUESTION 1: C

Students must use their knowledge of weathering and the information in the pictures to identify the correct choice.

- **Choice A** No; this describes the weathering examples in Group S.
- **Choice B** No; not all of the pictures in Group R are examples of ice wedging.
- **Choice C** Yes; Group R contains examples of mechanical weathering.
- **Choice D** No; one example of oxidation, a type of chemical weathering, is shown in Group S.

Teaching Tip

Encourage students to review the differences between mechanical and chemical weathering and how the two may work together.

QUESTION 2: G

Students must use what they have learned about forces to identify the cause of a rock slide. Although F, H, and J could lead to a rock slide, the primary force is choice G, *gravity*.

QUESTION 3: D

Students need to have an understanding of the landscaping forces and use the information in the pictures to identify the correct choice. All show an element of the movement of water, which is choice D.

QUESTION 4: Answers will vary.

Students should write a knowledgeable and well-researched response based upon the information from the text.

Unit Contents

☑ **Pre-Reading Activity**

Have students look for pictures of the effects of earthquakes and volcanoes and compare and contrast them.

How Are Volcanoes & Fish Connected?

It's hard to know exactly what happened four and a half billion years ago, when Earth was very young. But it's likely that Earth was much more volcanically active than it is today. Along with lava and ash, volcanoes emit gases—including water vapor. Some scientists think that ancient volcanoes spewed tremendous amounts of water vapor into the early atmosphere. When the water vapor cooled, it would have condensed to form liquid water. Then the water would have fallen to the surface and collected in low areas, creating the oceans. Scientists hypothesize that, roughly three and a half billion to four billion years ago, the first living things developed in the oceans. According to this hypothesis, these early life forms gradually gave rise to more and more complex organisms—including the multitudes of fish that swim through the world's waters.

272

Teacher to Teacher

"The geographic locations of volcanos is an important part of understanding plate tectonics. Have students plot the locations of volcanoes on a class map. This activity helps to either introduce or reinforce the concept of plates and plate boundaries."

Kevin Finnegan, Teacher
McCord Middle School
Worthington, OH

Introducing the Unit

How Are Volcanoes & Fish Connected?

The surface of Earth is constantly changing. New material is formed as older material is reincorporated into Earth's interior. The crust, the surface on which we live, is broken into sections called plates. These plates are constantly moving and interacting with each other, altering the shape of the planet. Convection of the material in Earth's interior provides the force to move these plates. The appearance of Earth is further changed by volcanic and earthquake activity caused largely by the motion of the plates.

The material making up the plates also undergoes changes due to weathering, heat, and pressure. Volcanoes form new rock as older rock is eroded away. Seas were once found far inland from today's ocean boundaries. This explains the existence of marine fossils in areas miles away from the ocean's shorelines. Examining these fossils gives scientists clues about what life was like earlier in Earth's history.

SCIENCE CONNECTION

VOLCANOES AND COMETS Not all scientists agree with the hypothesis that Earth's oceans were formed primarily by emissions from ancient volcanoes. For example, some researchers suggest that the water may have come largely from comets. Divide the class into two teams. Have one team investigate the volcano hypothesis, while the other team researches the comet hypothesis. Then hold a class debate, with each team presenting evidence in support of its hypothesis.

SCIENCE CONNECTION

Activity

Ask students to brainstorm about the environmental effects created by an asteroid impact on Earth. After listing their ideas, ask them to brainstorm about the effects of a large volcanic explosion. Include their ideas in a separate list. Ask students to compare the two lists and determine how the two events are similar and different.

SCIENCE Online
Internet Addresses

_____
_____
_____

Explore the Glencoe Science Web site at **science.glencoe.com** to find out more about topics in this unit.

Section/Objectives	Standards		Activities/Features
Chapter Opener	**National**	**State/Local**	**Explore Activity:** Reassemble an image, p. 275
	See p. 5T for a Key to Standards.		**Before You Read**, p. 275
Section 1 Continental Drift 🕐 2 sessions 📦 1 block 1. **Describe** the hypothesis of continental drift. 2. **Identify** evidence supporting continental drift.	National Content Standards: UCP2, UCP3, A1, A2, D1, D2, G1, G3		**Science Online**, p. 277 **MiniLAB:** Interpreting Fossil Data, p. 278
Section 2 Seafloor Spreading 🕐 2 sessions 📦 1 block 1. **Explain** seafloor spreading. 2. **Recognize** how age and magnetic clues support seafloor spreading.	National Content Standards: UCP2, UCP3, A1, D1, D2, G1, G3		**Chemistry Integration**, p. 281 **Activity:** Seafloor Spreading Rates, p. 283
Section 3 Theory of Plate Tectonics 🕐 4 sessions 📦 2 blocks 1. **Compare and contrast** different types of plate boundaries. 2. **Explain** how heat inside Earth causes plate tectonics. 3. **Recognize** features caused by plate tectonics.	National Content Standards: UCP2, UCP3, A1, A2, D1, D2, G1, G3		**Science Online**, p. 286 **Problem-Solving Activity:** How well do the continents fit together?, p. 286 **Visualizing Plate Boundaries**, p. 287 **MiniLAB:** Modeling Convection Currents, p. 289 **Physics Integration**, p. 292 **Activity:** Predicting Tectonic Activity, pp. 294–295 **Science and Language Arts:** Listening In, pp. 296–297

NATIONAL GEOGRAPHIC

Teacher's Corner

Activity Materials	Reproducible Resources	Section Assessment	Technology
Explore Activity: photographs from discarded magazines, scissors	**Chapter Resources Booklet** Foldables Worksheet, p. 17 Directed Reading Overview, p. 19 Note–taking Worksheets, pp. 33–35	GLENCOE'S **ASSESSMENT** ADVANTAGE	
MiniLAB: clay or modeling dough; objects for "fossils," such as paper clips, shells, and colored paper; plastic knife	**Chapter Resources Booklet** Transparency Activity, p. 44 MiniLAB, p. 3 Enrichment, p. 30 Reinforcement, p. 27 Directed Reading, p. 20 Lab Activity, pp. 9–11	**Portfolio** Challenge, p. 279 **Performance** MiniLAB, p. 278 Skill Builder Activities, p. 279 **Content** Section Assessment, p. 279	♪ Section Focus Transparency ◎ Interactive CD-ROM/DVD ∩ Guided Reading Audio Program
Activity: metric ruler, pencil *Need materials?* Contact Science Kit at 1-800-828-7777 or www.sciencekit.com on the Internet.	**Chapter Resources Booklet** Transparency Activity, p. 45 Enrichment, p. 31 Reinforcement, p. 28 Directed Reading, p. 20 Activity Worksheet, pp. 5–6 **Mathematics Skill Activities,** p. 5	**Portfolio** Chemistry Integration, p. 282 **Performance** Skill Builder Activities, p. 282 **Content** Section Assessment, p. 282	♪ Section Focus Transparency ◎ Interactive CD-ROM/DVD ∩ Guided Reading Audio Program
MiniLAB: water; clear, colorless casserole dish; hot plate; thermal mitts; food coloring **Activity:** Internet sites and other resources on earthquake and volcanic activity, world map	**Chapter Resources Booklet** Transparency Activity, p. 46 MiniLAB, p. 4 Enrichment, p. 32 Reinforcement, p. 29 Directed Reading, pp. 21, 22 Lab Activity, pp. 13–15 Activity Worksheet, pp. 7–8 Transparency Activity, pp. 47–48 **Lab Management and Safety,** p. 65 **Reading and Writing Skill Activities,** p. 27	**Portfolio** Science Journal, p. 285 Extension, p. 287 **Performance** MiniLAB, p. 289 Problem-Solving Activity, p. 286 Skill Builder Activities, p. 293 **Content** Section Assessment, p. 293	♪ Section Focus Transparency ♪ Teaching Transparency ◎ Interactive CD-ROM/DVD ∩ Guided Reading Audio Program

GLENCOE'S **ASSESSMENT** ADVANTAGE

End of Chapter Assessment

Blackline Masters	Technology	Professional Series
Chapter Resources Booklet Chapter Review, pp. 37–38 Chapter Tests, pp. 39–42 **Standardized Test Practice by The Princeton Review,** pp. 47–50	▭ MindJogger Videoquiz ◎ CD-ROM Explorations and Quizzes ◎ Vocabulary Puzzle Makers ◎ ExamView Pro Test Bank ◎ Interactive Lesson Planner ◎ Interactive Teacher's Edition	Performance Assessment in the Science Classroom (PASC)

Transparencies

Section Focus

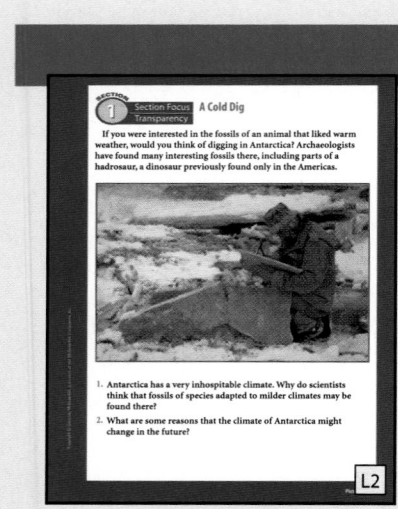

Section Focus Transparency A Cold Dig

If you were interested in the fossils of an animal that liked warm weather, would you think of digging in Antarctica? Archaeologists have found many interesting fossils there, including parts of a hadrosaur, a dinosaur previously found only in the Americas.

1. Antarctica has a very inhospitable climate. Why do scientists think that fossils of species adapted to milder climates may be found there?
2. What are some reasons that the climate of Antarctica might change in the future?

L2

Section Focus Transparency The Main Event

Until recently, the bottom of the sea was impossible to see. Now technology has improved the view, and we have a better idea of what is going on there. One ocean floor event, shown in this photograph, relates to plate tectonics.

1. What is occurring in the photograph?
2. Is this environment cold or warm? What is your evidence?
3. What is the connection between this picture and plate tectonics?

L2

Section Focus Transparency Valley of Ten Thousand Smokes

One of the most massive volcanic eruptions ever investigated occurred in a valley in southern Alaska in 1912. The eruption covered over forty square miles with ash as deep as 210 m and left thousands of vents (called fumaroles) in the valley spewing steam and gas. The valley was named the Valley of Ten Thousand Smokes after these fumaroles.

1. Why does Alaska experience volcanic activity?
2. What other areas of volcanic activity can you name?
3. Do these areas have anything in common?

L2

This is a representation of key blackline masters available in the Teacher Classroom Resources. See Resource Manager boxes within the chapter for additional information.

Key to Teaching Strategies

The following designations will help you decide which activities are appropriate for your students.

L1 Level 1 activities should be appropriate for students with learning difficulties.

L2 Level 2 activities should be within the ability range of all students.

L3 Level 3 activities are designed for above-average students.

ELL ELL activities should be within the ability range of English Language Learners.

COOP LEARN Cooperative Learning activities are designed for small group work.

LS Multiple Learning Styles logos, as described on page 22T, are used throughout to indicate strategies that address different learning styles.

P These strategies represent student products that can be placed into a best-work portfolio.

Assessment

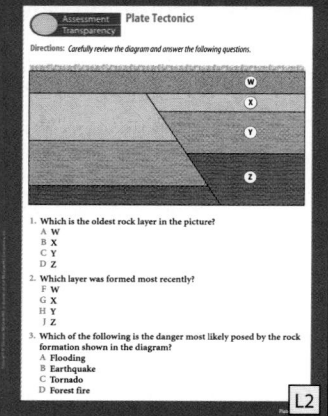

Assessment Transparency Plate Tectonics

Directions: *Carefully review the diagram and answer the following questions.*

1. Which is the oldest rock layer in the picture?
   A W
   B X
   C Y
   D Z
2. Which layer was formed most recently?
   F W
   G X
   H Y
   J Z
3. Which of the following is the danger most likely posed by the rock formation shown in the diagram?
   A Flooding
   B Earthquake
   C Tornado
   D Forest fire

L2

Teaching

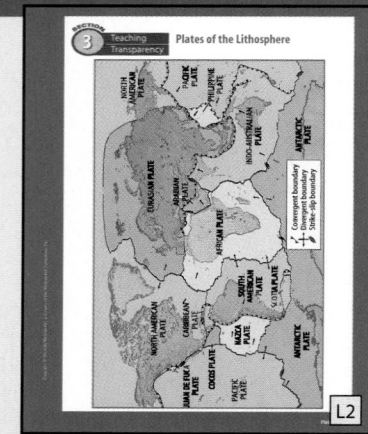

Teaching Transparency Plates of the Lithosphere

L2

Hands-on Activities

Activity Worksheets

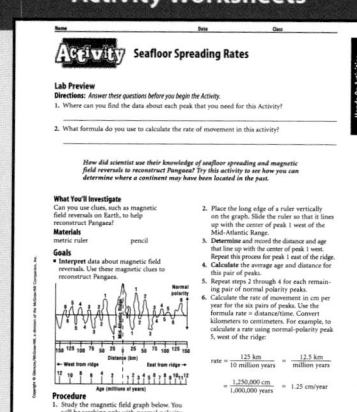

Activity Seafloor Spreading Rates

Lab Preview
Directions: *Answer these questions before you begin the Activity.*
1. Where can you find the data about each peak that you need for this Activity?

2. What formula do you use to calculate the rate of movement in this activity?

How did scientist use their knowledge of seafloor spreading and magnetic field reversals to reconstruct Pangaea? Try this activity to see how you can determine where a continent may have been located in the past.

What You'll Investigate
Can you use clues, such as magnetic field reversals on Earth, to help reconstruct Pangaea?

Materials
metric ruler   pencil

Goals
• **Interpret** data about magnetic field reversals. Use these magnetic clues to reconstruct Pangaea.

Procedure
1. Study the magnetic field graph below. You will be working only with normal polarity readings, which are the peaks above the baseline in the top half of the graph.

2. Place the long edge of a ruler vertically on the graph. Slide the ruler so that it lines up with the center of peak 1 west of the Mid-Atlantic Range.
3. **Determine** and record the distance and age that line up with the center of peak 1 west. Repeat this process for peak 1 east of the ridge.
4. **Calculate** the average age and distance for this pair of peaks.
5. Repeat steps 2 through 4 for each remaining pair of normal polarity peaks.
6. Calculate the rate of movement in cm per year for the six pairs of peaks. Use the formula rate = distance/time. Convert kilometers to centimeters. For example, to calculate a rate using normal-polarity peak 5, west of the ridge:

$$\text{rate} = \frac{125 \text{ km}}{10 \text{ million years}} = \frac{12.5 \text{ km}}{\text{million years}}$$

$$= \frac{1,250,000 \text{ cm}}{1,000,000 \text{ years}} = 1.25 \text{ cm/year}$$

L2

Laboratory Activities

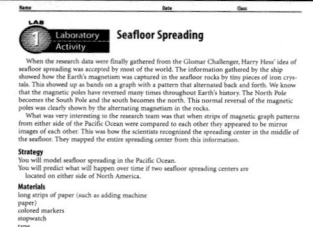

Laboratory Activity Seafloor Spreading

When the research data were finally gathered from the Glomar Challenger, Harry Hess' idea of seafloor spreading was accepted by most of the world. The information gathered by the ship showed how the Earth's magnetism was captured in the seafloor rocks by tiny pieces of iron crystals. This showed up as bands on a graph with a pattern that alternated back and forth. We know that the magnetic poles have reversed many times throughout Earth's history. The North Pole becomes the South Pole and the south becomes the north. This normal reversal of the magnetic poles was clearly shown by the alternating magnetism in the rocks.

What was very interesting to the research team was that when strips of magnetic graph patterns from either side of the Pacific Ocean were compared to each other they appeared to be mirror images of each other. This was how the scientists recognized the spreading center in the middle of the seafloor. They mapped the entire spreading center from this information.

Strategy
You will model seafloor spreading in the Pacific Ocean.
You will predict what will happen over time if two seafloor spreading centers are located on either side of North America.

Materials
long strips of paper (such as adding machine paper)
colored markers
stopwatch
tape

Procedure
1. Place students in groups of three or four. Assign two students to be responsible for making the straight line graph on the paper. Each should have two colored markers that are the same. Another student should be in charge of the stopwatch. The fourth student should monitor the speed of the graphers.
2. The student graphers will slowly draw a straight line down the center of the paper with one color. Their speed of drawing should be as close together as possible.
3. The student with the stopwatch will choose eight different time intervals for the graphers to draw. For example, 5, 8, 3, 15, 6, 18, 15, and 5 seconds. The timekeeper will tell the graphers when to begin and will call out at each predetermined time interval, signaling the graphers to change the colors of their markers.
4. Begin drawing. One grapher will draw from left to right. The other will draw from right to left.
5. When finished, compare the two graphs. Place them side by side and with one on top and the other on the bottom. Find the combination in which the similar pattern is revealed.
6. Now put the strips back in their original positions and tape them together.
7. Your instructor will collect all the graphing strips and place them one on top of another. Notice where the centers are on all the tapes.
8. Once you have identified the places where each group's center of spreading is, sketch this zig-zag line in the space in the Data and Observations section.

L2

Meeting Different Ability Levels

Content Outline

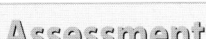

L2

Reinforcement

L2

Directed Reading

L1

Assessment

Chapter Tests

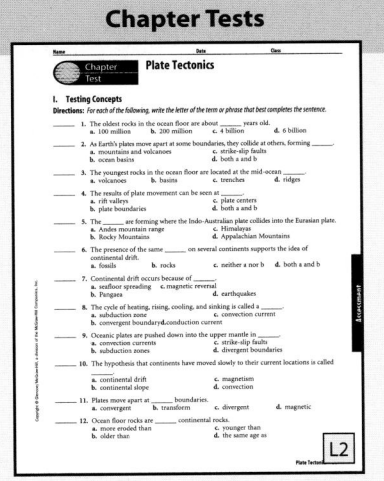

L2

Enrichment

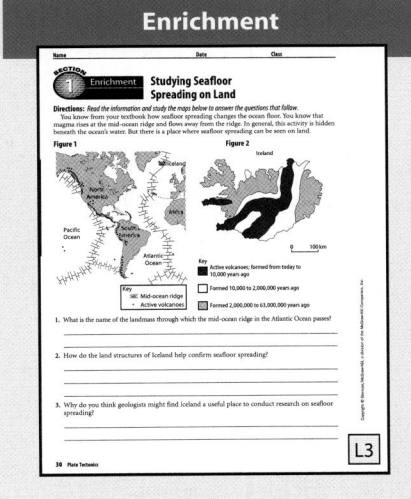

L3

Spanish Directed Reading

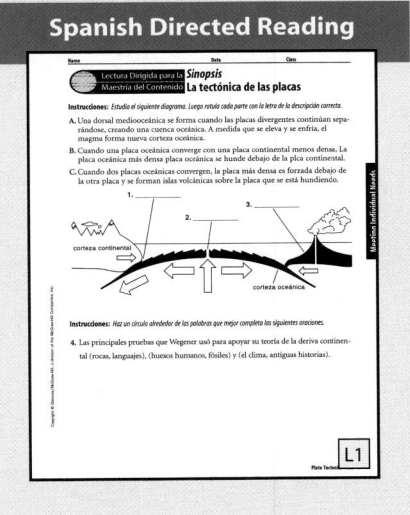

L1

Test Practice Workbook

L2

Chapter Review

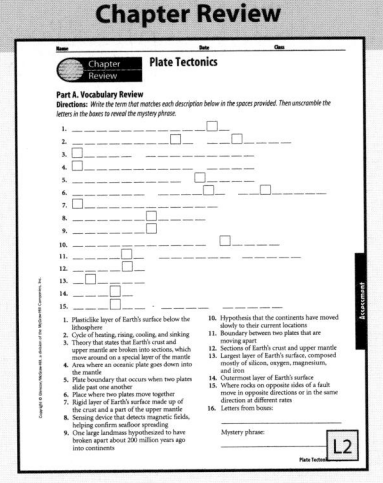

L2

Science Content Background

Continental Drift

Pangaea

About 200 million years ago, Pangaea covered around 40% of Earth's surface, while a large ocean, Panthalassa, covered the rest of the planet. Pangaea broke up to form Laurasia and Gondwana, which were separated by the Tethys Sea.

Climate Clues

The study of ancient climates is called paleoclimatology. Alfred Wegener, a meteorologist, collected data about ancient climates in hopes of finding supporting evidence for his hypothesis. During his study of paleoclimates, he noted that glaciers covered much of the southern hemisphere between 220 million and 300 million years ago.

Magnetic Time Scale

Paleomagnetism is the study of the magnetic properties of ancient rocks. When rock material is heated above the Curie point, magnetic minerals lose their magnetic properties. As they cool they align with the current magnetic field.

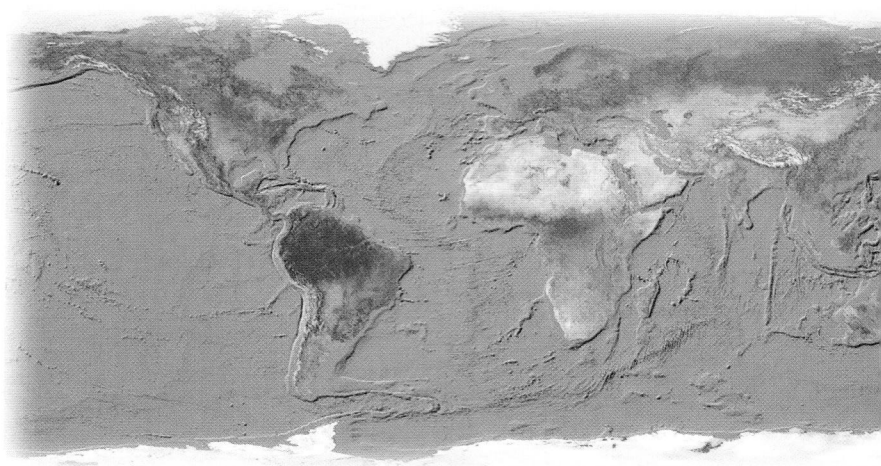

Tom Van Sant/Photo Researchers, Inc.

Thus the record of the reversals of Earth's magnetic field is recorded in the magnetic characteristics of rocks formed at that time.

SECTION 2

Seafloor Spreading

The Seafloor Moves

As the ocean floor slowly separates, new rocks form at a mid-ocean ridge. It is estimated that the Atlantic Ocean grows 4 to 5 cm wider every year as a result of new rock forming at the Mid-Atlantic Ridge. Around 200 million years ago, a rift began to form between Greenland and Scotland. This rift led to the formation of the North Atlantic, which appeared only 65 million years ago, and continued spreading to form the modern Atlantic Ocean.

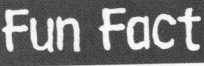

Fun Fact

Certain species of green turtles swim from South America to Ascension Island in the South Atlantic to lay their eggs. The turtles may have started this trip when these land masses were much closer. As the seafloor spread, the instinctive trip became longer.

SECTION 3

Theory of Plate Tectonics

Plate Boundaries

Motion of Earth's plates is accommodated at plate edges. Boundaries between lithospheric plates may be divergent, convergent, or transform. The intersection of any three plate boundaries is called a triple junction.

Divergent plate boundaries often begin as continental rifts such as the modern-day African Rift Valley. Tensional forces may stretch and thin the continental crust, forming a depression that fills with ocean water. Tensional forces continue to act on the area until a mid-ocean ridge develops. At this point, full-fledged seafloor spreading begins and the continental fragments begin to separate.

In order for Earth to maintain a constant size, lithosphere produced at mid-ocean ridges must be consumed elsewhere. This occurs at convergent boundaries. At these boundaries, older, cooler, and denser oceanic plates are forced beneath less-dense plates in subduction zones. The denser plate descends into the mantle along a plane that may dip at angles ranging from 30° to 90°. This plane is defined by the foci of earthquakes associated with the subducting slab.

Transform boundaries may occur on land or on the seafloor. These faults most commonly connect offset segments of mid-ocean ridges. These ridge-to-ridge transform faults are a conspicuous feature of any mid-ocean ridge system. Transform faults also may connect a ridge to a trench or a trench to another trench.

Mountains and Volcanoes

Most of the world's spectacular mountain ranges were formed at collision-type convergent plate boundaries. When two plates carrying continents collide, rocks are folded and faulted, which results in a thickened and uplifted continental crust. The Himalaya are a classic example of a collision-type mountain range. This range started to form about 50 million years ago when India began colliding with Tibet and the Eurasian plate. Even today, India is pushing northward into Tibet and the Himalaya continue to rise. To illustrate the magnitude of the uplift that has occurred during this collision, consider that marine fossils have been found in sandstone layers near Lhasa, Tibet, which has an altitude of 12,500 feet!

Mountains also can form along ocean–continent convergent boundaries. The Andes Mountains of South America have formed as a result of rock deformation and volcanism caused by the subduction of the Nazca plate under the South American plate. The ocean trench marking the subduction zone is named the Peru-Chile Trench after the two countries most strongly affected by their plate tectonic setting. When one oceanic plate descends beneath another at an ocean-ocean convergent plate boundary, a volcanic island arc forms behind the ocean trench. Volcanic arcs form as a result of partial melting of the subducting plate and possibly some mantle rock above the descending plate. The Japanese and Philippine Islands are examples of volcanic island arcs.

Fun Fact

The Indian plate, which collided with Asia to form the Himalaya, continues to move at a rate of almost 5 cm per year. This massive plate is moving twice as fast as your fingernails grow!

SCIENCE *Online*

For additional content background on this topic, go to the Glencoe Science Web site at science.glencoe.com.

Nicholas Parfitt/Stone

Plate Tectonics

Chapter Vocabulary

continental drift
Pangaea
seafloor spreading
plate tectonics
plate
lithosphere
asthenosphere
convection current

What do you think?

Science Journal This is an aerial photograph of a strike-slip fault. Its movement has formed a "dog leg" in the river that flows over it. A dog leg is a sharp angle or bend.

Plate Tectonics

Characterized by volcanoes and scenic vistas, the East African Rift Valley marks a place where Earth's crust is being pulled apart. If the pulling continues over millions of years, Africa will separate into two landmasses. In this chapter, you'll learn about Rift Valleys and other features explained by the theory of plate tectonics. You'll also learn about the fossil, climate, and rock clues that indicate that Earth's continents have drifted over time.

What do you think?

Science Journal Look at the picture below with a classmate. Discuss what you think this might be or what is happening. Here's a hint: *A river runs through this dog leg.* Write your answer or best guess in your Science Journal.

274

Theme Connection

Energy The transfer of energy in Earth's interior sets up massive convection currents in the mantle. These currents are thought to be the driving force that causes movement of Earth's plates.

Can you imagine a giant landmass that broke into many separate continents and Earth scientists working to reconstruct Earth's past? Do this activity to learn about clues that can be used to reassemble a supercontinent.

Reassemble an image

1. Collect interesting photographs from an old magazine.

2. You and a partner each select one photo, but don't show them to each other. Then each of you cut your photos into pieces no smaller than about 5 cm or 6 cm.

3. Trade your cut-up photo for your partner's.

4. Observe the pieces, and reassemble the photograph your partner has cut up.

Observe

In your Science Journal, describe the characteristics of the cut-up photograph that helped you put the image back together. Think of other examples in which characteristics of objects are used to match them up with other objects.

Before You Read

FOLDABLES
Reading & Study Skills

Making a Know-Want-Learn Study Fold It would be helpful to identify what you already know and what you want to know. Make the following Foldable to help you focus on reading about continental drift.

1. Place a sheet of paper in front of you so the short side is at the top. Fold the paper in half from top to bottom.

2. Fold both sides in to divide the paper into thirds. Unfold the paper so three sections show.

3. Through the top thickness of paper, cut along each of the fold lines to the topfold, forming three tabs. Label the tabs *Know, Want,* and *Learn,* as shown.

Know	Want	Learn

4. Before you read the chapter, write what you know about continental drift under the left tab and what you want to know under the middle tab.

5. As you read the chapter, write what you learn about continental drift under the right tab.

275

Continental Drift

Continental Drift

1 Motivate

Bellringer Transparency

Display the Section Focus Transparency for Section 1. Use the accompanying Transparency Activity Master. L2

ELL

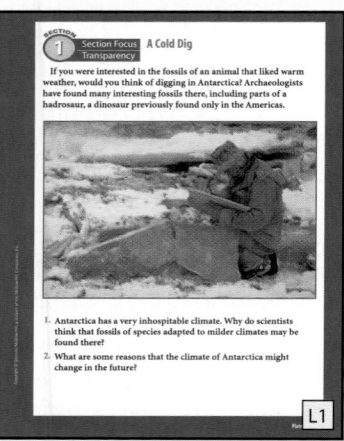

As You Read

What You'll Learn
- **Describe** the hypothesis of continental drift.
- **Identify** evidence supporting continental drift.

Vocabulary
continental drift
Pangaea

Why It's Important
The hypothesis of continental drift led to plate tectonics—a theory that explains many processes in Earth.

Figure 1
This illustration represents how the continents once were joined to form Pangaea. This fitting together of continents according to shape is not the only evidence supporting the past existence of Pangaea.

Evidence for Continental Drift

If you look at a map of Earth's surface, you can see that the edges of some continents look as though they could fit together like a puzzle. Other people also have noticed this fact. For example, Dutch mapmaker Abraham Ortelius noted the fit between the coastlines of South America and Africa more than 400 years ago.

Pangaea German meteorologist Alfred Wegener (VEG nur) thought that the fit of the continents wasn't just a coincidence. He suggested that all the continents were joined together at some time in the past. In a 1912 lecture, he proposed the hypothesis of continental drift. According to the hypothesis of **continental drift,** continents have moved slowly to their current locations. Wegener suggested that all continents once were connected as one large landmass, shown in **Figure 1,** that broke apart about 200 million years ago. He called this large landmass **Pangaea** (pan JEE uh), which means "all land."

✔ **Reading Check** *Who proposed continential drift?*

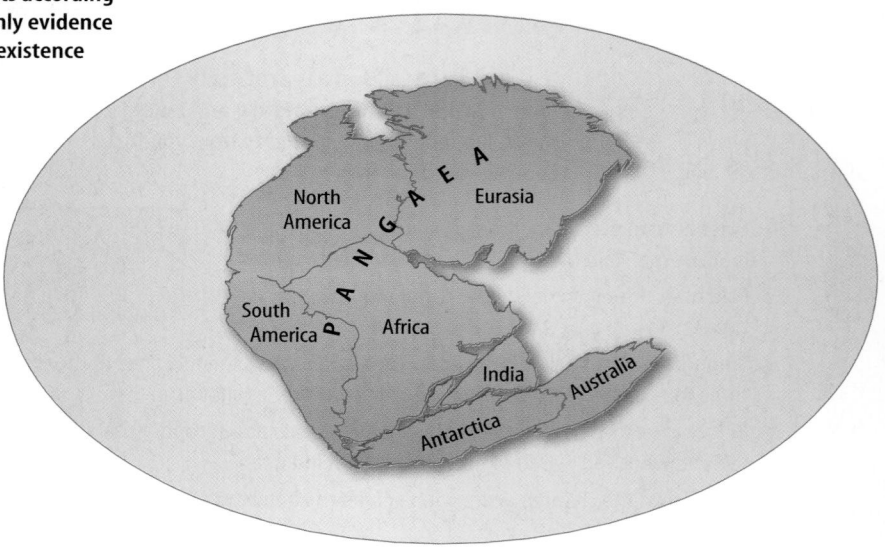

Tie to Prior Knowledge

Have students recall the general shapes of Africa and South America. Ask if they can recall how the eastern coast of South America seems to fit into the western coast of Africa. Display a world map, asking again if students can make the connection.

Reading Check

Answer Alfred Wegener

Section ✔ Assessment Planner

PORTFOLIO
Challenge, p. 279
PERFORMANCE ASSESSMENT
Try at Home MiniLAB, p. 278
Skill Builder Activities, p. 279
See page 300 for more options.

CONTENT ASSESSMENT
Section, p. 279
Challenge, p. 279
Chapter, pp. 300–301

A Controversial Idea Wegener's ideas about continental drift were controversial. It wasn't until long after Wegener's death in 1930 that his basic hypothesis was accepted. The evidence Wegener presented hadn't been enough to convince many people during his lifetime. He was unable to explain exactly how the continents drifted apart. He proposed that the continents plowed through the ocean floor, driven by the spin of Earth. Physicists and geologists of the time strongly disagreed with Wegener's explanation. They pointed out that continental drift would not be necessary to explain many of Wegener's observations. Other important observations that came later eventually supported Wegener's earlier evidence.

Fossil Clues Besides the puzzlelike fit of the continents, fossils provided support for continental drift. Fossils of the reptile *Mesosaurus* have been found in South America and Africa, as shown in **Figure 2.** This swimming reptile lived in freshwater and on land. How could fossils of *Mesosaurus* be found on land areas separated by a large ocean of salt water? It probably couldn't swim between the continents. Wegener hypothesized that this reptile lived on both continents when they were joined.

✔ **Reading Check** *How do* Mesosaurus *fossils support the past existence of Pangaea?*

SCIENCE *Online*

Research Visit the Glencoe Science Web site at **science.glencoe.com** for more information about the continental drift hypothesis. Communicate to your class what you learn.

Figure 2
Fossil remains of plants and animals that lived in Pangaea have been found on more than one continent. *How do the locations of* Glossopteris, Mesosaurus, Kannemeyerid, Labyrinthodont, *and other fossils support Wegener's hypothesis of continental drift?*

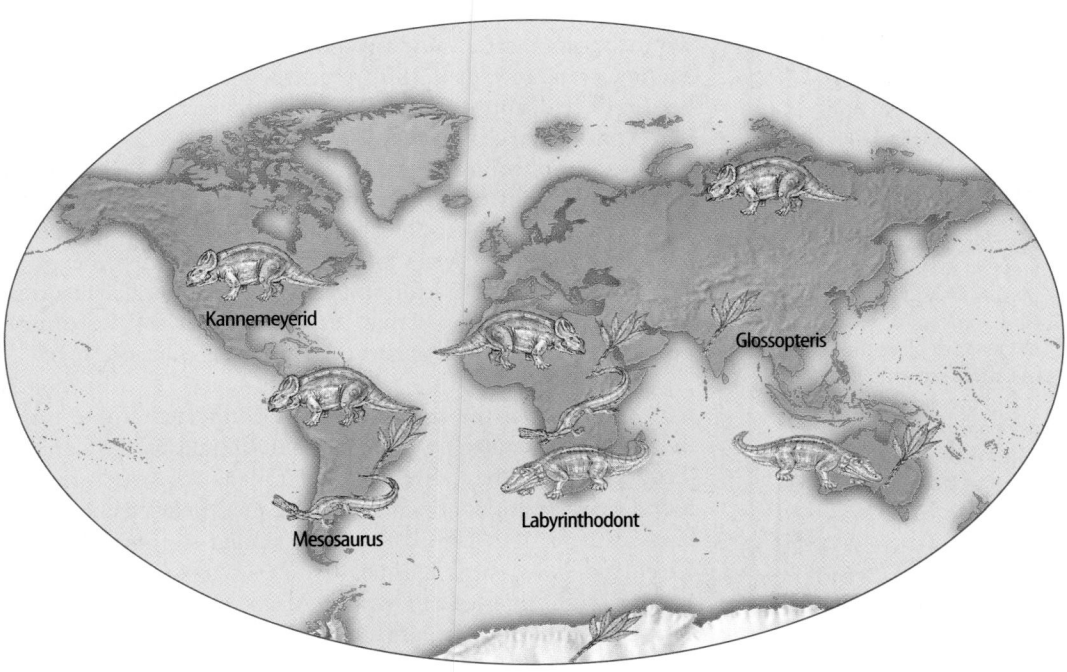

Kannemeyerid

Glossopteris

Mesosaurus

Labyrinthodont

② Teach

Evidence for Continental Drift

Use an Analogy

Have students recall that when putting together a jigsaw puzzle, they use the shapes of the puzzle pieces and the picture on the box as clues. When thinking about evidence of continental drift, the puzzle pieces are analogous to the shapes of the continents, and the picture clues are analogous to evidence found on each continent.

Discussion

Why was Wegener's idea of continental drift rejected? Scientists at the time thought Wegener's observations could be explained by something other than continental drift. Also, Wegener failed to provide a reasonable or believable mechanism to explain how continental drift might occur.

✔ **Reading Check**

Answer Fossils of Mesosaurus, a freshwater and land animal, have been found in widespread areas separated by oceans of salt water, through which they could not swim.

Caption Answer

Figure 2 Matching fossils on widely separated continents provide evidence that these land masses were once joined.

SCIENCE *Online*
Internet Addresses

_____

_____

_____

Explore the Glencoe Science Web site at **science.glencoe.com** to find out more about topics in this section.

Resource Manager

Chapter Resources Booklet

Transparency Activity, p. 44

Note-taking Worksheets, pp. 33–35

Directed Reading for Content Mastery, pp. 19, 20

Inclusion Strategies

Visually Impaired In order to help visually impaired students better understand how shapes that fit together can be used to help reconstruct Pangaea, make clay models of the continental masses that formed the supercontinent. Make sure the edges of the continents clearly match. Have students work with a partner to reconstruct the clay "Pangaea."

TRY AT HOME
Mini LAB

Purpose Students reaffirm that geologic clues can be used to show how continents that are now separate were once joined.

`L2` `ELL` `LS` **Kinesthetic**

Materials three colors of modeling clay or modeling dough; objects such as macaroni, small buttons, or peanuts to use as fossils; spatula for cutting landmasses apart

Teaching Strategy Review the procedure for making the landmasses with students in class before having them complete the activity at home.

Analysis
1. Possible answer: I looked for clues in the pattern of fossils and "mountain ranges."

✔Assessment

Oral Have students describe the characteristics they used to reconstruct the original landmass. Use **Performance Assessment in the Science Classroom,** p. 143.

Figure 3
This fossil plant, *Glossopteris,* grew in a warm, temperate climate.

TRY AT HOME
Mini LAB

Interpreting Fossil Data

Procedure 🔊 📋
1. Build a three-layer landmass using **clay or modeling dough.**
2. Mold the clay into mountain ranges.
3. Place similar **"fossils"** into the clay at various locations around the landmass.
4. Form five continents from the one landmass. Also, form two smaller landmasses out of different clay with different mountain ranges and fossils.
5. Place the five continents and two smaller landmasses around the room.
6. Have someone who did not make or place the landmasses make a model that shows how they once were positioned.
7. Return the clay to its container so it can be used again.

Analysis
What clues were useful in reconstructing the original landmass?

Resource Manager

Chapter Resources Booklet
MiniLAB, p. 3
Enrichment, p. 30
Reinforcement, p. 27
Lab Activity, pp. 9–11

A Widespread Plant Another fossil that supports the hypothesis of continental drift is *Glossopteris* (glahs AHP tur us). **Figure 3** shows this fossil plant, which has been found in Africa, Australia, India, South America, and Antarctica. The presence of *Glossopteris* in so many areas also supported Wegener's idea that all of these regions once were connected and had similar climates.

Climate Clues Wegener used continental drift to explain evidence of changing climates. For example, fossils of warm-weather plants were found on the island of Spitsbergen in the Arctic Ocean. To explain this, Wegener hypothesized that Spitsbergen drifted from tropical regions to the arctic. Wegener also used continental drift to explain evidence of glaciers found in temperate and tropical areas. Glacial deposits and rock surfaces scoured and polished by glaciers are found in South America, Africa, India, and Australia. This shows that these continents were covered with glaciers in the past. How could you explain why glacial deposits are found in areas where no glaciers exist today? Wegener thought that these continents all were connected and covered with ice near Earth's south pole long ago.

Rock Clues If the continents were connected at one time, then rocks that make up the continents should be the same in locations where they were joined. Similar rock structures are found on different continents. Parts of the Appalachian Mountains of the eastern United States are similar to those found in Greenland and western Europe. If you were to study rocks from eastern South America and western Africa, you would find other rock structures that also are similar. Rock clues like these support the idea that the continents were connected in the past.

Teacher FYI

About 200 million years ago, Pangaea covered about 40 percent of Earth's surface, while a large ocean, Panthalassa, covered the rest of the planet. Pangaea broke up to form Laurasia and Gondwana, which were separated by the Tethys Sea.

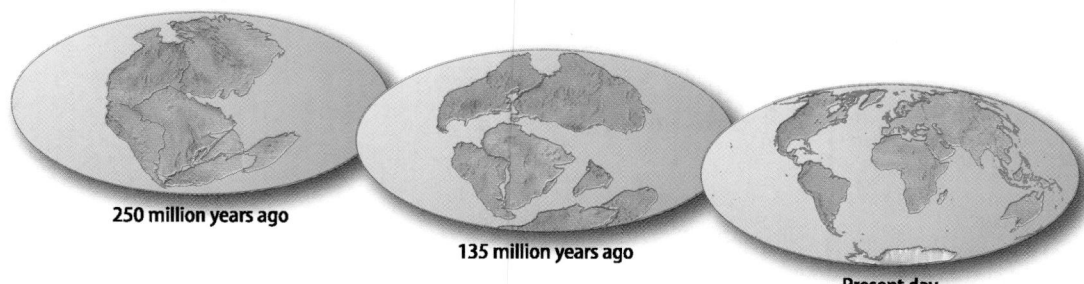

250 million years ago

135 million years ago

Present day

How could continents drift?

Although Wegener provided evidence to support his hypothesis of continental drift, he couldn't explain how, when, or why these changes, shown in **Figure 4,** took place. The idea suggested that lower-density, continental material somehow had to plow through higher-density, ocean-floor material. The force behind this plowing was thought to be the spin of Earth on its axis—a notion that was quickly rejected by physicists. Because other scientists could not provide explanations either, Wegener's idea of continental drift was initially rejected. The idea was so radically different at that time that most people closed their minds to it.

Rock, fossil, and climate clues were the main types of evidence for continental drift. After Wegener's death, more clues were found, largely because of advances in technology, and new ideas that related to continental drift were developed. You'll learn about one of these new ideas, seafloor spreading, in the next section. Seafloor spreading helped provide an explanation of how the continents could move.

Figure 4
These computer models show the probable course the continents have taken. On the far left is their position 250 million years ago. In the middle is their position 135 million years ago. At right is their current position.

Visual Learning

Figure 4 What is happening to eastern Africa? It is splitting apart.

3 Assess

Reteach
Have students outline the section, including all of the important points. Have pairs exchange outlines and then use the outlines to quiz one another. [L1]
IS Interpersonal

Challenge
New evidence suggests that mountains in southwest South America match up with the Appalachians. Have students research and write a report about how this came about. Possible answer: Before colliding with the African plate, the North American plate may have been positioned west of South America. [L3] [P]

✓ Assessment

Content Have groups of students write and perform skits in which one student plays Wegener introducing his theory, and others play scientists debunking it. Encourage students to use visual props. Use **Performance Assessment in the Science Classroom,** p. 147.

Section ① Assessment

1. Why were Wegener's ideas about continental drift initially rejected?
2. How did Wegener use climate clues to support his hypothesis of continental drift?
3. What rock clues did Wegener use to support his hypothesis of continental drift?
4. In what ways do fossils help support the hypothesis of continental drift?
5. **Think Critically** Why would you expect to see similar rocks and rock structures on two landmasses that were connected at one time?

Skill Builder Activities

6. **Comparing and Contrasting** Compare and contrast the locations of fossils of the temperate plant *Glossopteris,* as shown in **Figure 2,** with the climate that exists at each location today. **For more help, refer to the** Science Skill Handbook.

7. **Communicating** Imagine that you are Alfred Wegener in the year 1912. In your Science Journal, write a letter to another scientist explaining your idea about continental drift. Try to convince this scientist that your hypothesis is correct. **For more help, refer to the** Science Skill Handbook.

Answers to Section Assessment

1. Wegener could not explain how the continents drifted apart. There were also other ways to explain his observations.
2. Fossils of warm-weather plants found on islands in the Arctic Ocean and glacial features found in places such as South America supported the idea that continents drift.
3. Rock structures on different continents are similar.
4. Fossils of the same organism were found on widely separated continents.
5. The same rock structure they shared when attached would appear on both halves after the landmass split apart.
6. Possible answer: compare—all locations are on land masses; contrast—some locations are in temperate climates, others are in arid, semi-arid, or polar climates
7. Letters should include his evidence: continent shape and matching fossils and climate on widely separated continents.

Seafloor Spreading

Seafloor Spreading

1 Motivate

Bellringer Transparency

Display the Section Focus Transparency for Section 2. Use the accompanying Transparency Activity Master. L2

ELL

Tie to Prior Knowledge

Ask students if they ever have walked into an ocean, lake, or river. Have them describe how the floor of the body of water felt. Students may mention steep and gentle slopes, rocks, bars or ridges of sand, and depressions. Explain that the entire ocean floor has such features, and it took special tools to map it.

✔ **Reading Check**

Answer using sound waves

As You Read

What You'll Learn
- **Explain** seafloor spreading.
- **Recognize** how age and magnetic clues support seafloor spreading.

Vocabulary
seafloor spreading

Why It's Important
Seafloor spreading helps explain how continents moved apart.

Figure 5
As the seafloor spreads apart at a mid-ocean ridge, new seafloor is created. The older seafloor moves away from the ridge in opposite directions.

Mapping the Ocean Floor

If you were to lower a rope from a boat until it reached the seafloor, you could record the depth of the ocean at that particular point. In how many different locations would you have to do this to create an accurate map of the seafloor? This is exactly how it was done until World War I, when the use of sound waves was introduced to detect submarines. During the 1940s and 1950s, scientists began using sound waves on moving ships to map large areas of the ocean floor in detail. Sound waves echo off the ocean bottom—the longer the sound waves take to return to the ship, the deeper the water is.

Using sound waves, researchers discovered an underwater system of ridges, or mountains, and valleys like those found on the continents. In the Atlantic, the Pacific, and in other oceans around the world, a system of ridges, called the mid-ocean ridges, is present. These underwater mountain ranges, shown in **Figure 5,** stretch along the center of much of Earth's ocean floor. This discovery raised the curiosity of many scientists. What formed these mid-ocean ridges?

✔ **Reading Check** *How were mid-ocean ridges discovered?*

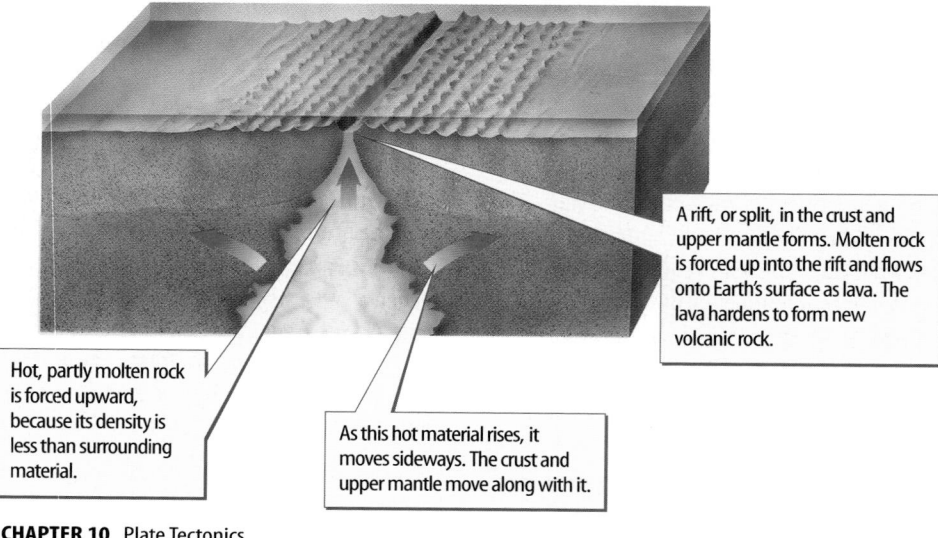

A rift, or split, in the crust and upper mantle forms. Molten rock is forced up into the rift and flows onto Earth's surface as lava. The lava hardens to form new volcanic rock.

Hot, partly molten rock is forced upward, because its density is less than surrounding material.

As this hot material rises, it moves sideways. The crust and upper mantle move along with it.

280 CHAPTER 10 Plate Tectonics

Section ✔ Assessment Planner

PORTFOLIO
Chemistry Integration, p. 281
PERFORMANCE ASSESSMENT
Skill Builder Activities, p. 282
See page 300 for more options.

CONTENT ASSESSMENT
Section, p. 282
Challenge, p. 282
Chapter, pp. 300–301

The Seafloor Moves In the early 1960s, Princeton University scientist Harry Hess suggested an explanation. His now-famous theory is known as **seafloor spreading.** Hess proposed that hot, less dense material below Earth's crust rises toward the surface at the mid-ocean ridges. Then, it flows sideways, carrying the seafloor away from the ridge in both directions, as seen in **Figure 5.**

As the seafloor spreads apart, magma moves upward and flows from the cracks. It becomes solid as it cools and forms new seafloor. As new seafloor moves away from the mid-ocean ridge, it cools, contracts, and becomes denser. This denser, colder seafloor sinks, helping to form the ridge. The theory of seafloor spreading was later supported by the following observations.

 **Reading Check** *How does new seafloor form at mid-ocean ridges?*

Evidence for Spreading In 1968, scientists aboard the research ship *Glomar Challenger* began gathering information about the rocks on the seafloor. *Glomar Challenger* was equipped with a drilling rig that allowed scientists to drill into the seafloor to obtain rock samples. They made a remarkable discovery as they studied the ages of the rocks. Scientists found that the youngest rocks are located at the mid-ocean ridges. The ages of the rocks become increasingly older in samples obtained farther from the ridges, adding to the evidence for seafloor spreading.

Using submersibles along mid-ocean ridges, new seafloor features and life-forms also were discovered there, as shown in **Figure 6.** As molten material rises along the ridges, it brings heat and chemicals that support exotic life-forms in deep, ocean water. Among these are giant clams, mussels, and tube worms.

 **Magnetic Clues** Earth's magnetic field has a north and a south pole. Magnetic lines, or directions, of force leave Earth near the south pole and enter Earth near the north pole. During a magnetic reversal, the lines of magnetic force run the opposite way. Scientists have determined that Earth's magnetic field has reversed itself many times in the past. These reversals occur over intervals of thousands or even millions of years. The reversals are recorded in rocks forming along mid-ocean ridges.

Figure 6
Many new discoveries have been made on the seafloor. These giant tube worms inhabit areas near hot water vents along mid-ocean ridges.

 **Chemistry INTEGRATION**

Find out what the Curie point is and describe in your Science Journal what happens to iron-bearing minerals when they are heated to the Curie point. Explain how this is important to studies of seafloor spreading.

Mapping the Ocean Floor

 **Reading Check**

Answer Magma moves upward and out of cracks in seafloor. As it solidifies on the surface, new seafloor forms. Older seafloor is pushed away from the ridge.

Chemistry INTEGRATION

The Curie point is the temperature above which iron-bearing minerals lose their magnetism. As lava cools into rock on the ocean floor, the rock acquires a magnetic field like that of Earth's. If these rocks are reheated beyond the Curie point, the magnetic signature they acquired at the time they formed is lost. **As an extension, have students research and write about the scientist for whom the Curie point is named.** French physicist Pierre Curie P

Teacher FYI

Harry Hess (1906–1969) was a geologist who collected important data about the seafloor during World War II, when he was captain of a navy transport vessel. His ship was fitted with a new device called a Fathometer, an echo sounder that showed ocean floor depth under the ship. The data was meant to allow troop ships to get close to shore, but Hess used it to map the floor of the Pacific Ocean.

Resource Manager

Chapter Resources Booklet
  Transparency Activity, p. 45
  Enrichment, p. 31
  Directed Reading for Content Mastery,
    p. 20

Mapping the Ocean Floor, continued

Caption Answer

Figure 7 It shows the rock continually formed and moved away from the ridge over time.

 **Assess**

Reteach

Have pairs of students construct three-dimensional models of the seafloor at a mid-ocean ridge. L1 ELL COOP LEARN  **Kinesthetic**

Challenge

Have students research the scientific and technological advances that led to the theory of seafloor spreading. Have students display their discoveries on a timeline. L3 **Logical-Mathematical**

✓ Assessment

Performance Assess students' understanding by challenging them to draw concept maps that contain the main ideas in this section. Use **Performance Assessment in the Science Classroom,** p. 161.

Resource Manager

Chapter Resources Booklet
Reinforcement, p. 28
Activity Worksheet, pp. 5–6
Mathematics Skill Activities, p. 5

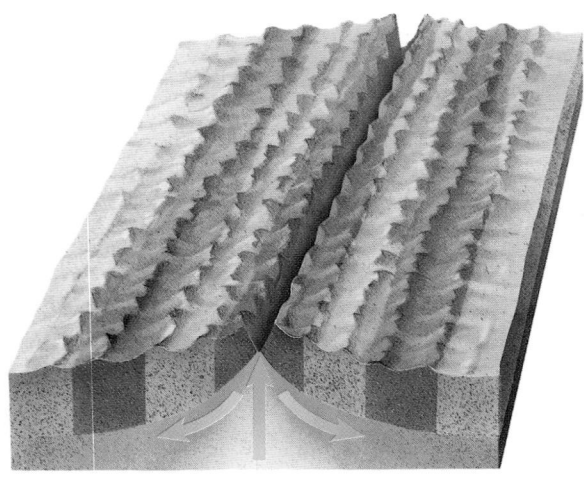

Figure 7
Changes in Earth's magnetic field are preserved in rock that forms on both sides of mid-ocean ridges. *Why is this considered to be evidence of seafloor spreading?*

Magnetic Time Scale

Iron-bearing minerals, such as magnetite, that are found in the rocks of the seafloor can record Earth's magnetic field direction when they form. Whenever Earth's magnetic field reverses, newly forming iron minerals will record the magnetic reversal.

Using a sensing device called a magnetometer (mag nuh TAH muh tur) to detect magnetic fields, scientists found that rocks on the ocean floor show many periods of magnetic reversal. The magnetic alignment in the rocks reverses back and forth over time in strips parallel to the mid-ocean ridges, as shown in **Figure 7.** A strong magnetic reading is recorded when the polarity of a rock is the same as the polarity of Earth's magnetic field today. Because of this, normal polarities in rocks show up as large peaks. This discovery provided strong support that seafloor spreading was indeed occurring. The magnetic reversals showed that new rock was being formed at the mid-ocean ridges. This helped explain how the crust could move—something that the continental drift hypothesis could not do.

Section Assessment

1. What properties of iron-bearing minerals on the seafloor support the theory of seafloor spreading?
2. How do the ages of the rocks on the ocean floor support the theory of seafloor spreading?
3. How did Harry Hess's hypothesis explain seafloor movement?
4. Why does some partly molten material rise toward Earth's surface?
5. **Think Critically** The ideas of Hess, Wegener, and others emphasize that Earth is a dynamic planet. How is seafloor spreading different from continental drift?

Skill Builder Activities

6. **Concept Mapping** Make a concept map that includes evidence for seafloor spreading using the following phrases: *ages increase away from ridge, pattern of magnetic field reversals, mid-ocean ridge, pattern of ages,* and *reverses back and forth.* **For more help, refer to the** Science Skill Handbook.
7. **Solving One-Step Equations** North America is moving about 1.25 cm per year away from a ridge in the middle of the Atlantic Ocean. Using this rate, how much farther apart will North America and the ridge be in 200 million years? **For more help, refer to the** Math Skill Handbook.

Answers to Section Assessment

1. Magnetic reversals recorded in iron-bearing minerals show that new rock was being formed at the ridges over time.
2. The rocks get older as you move farther from the mid-ocean ridge.
3. Hot, dense material is forced upward at mid-ocean ridges. It then moves sideways, carrying the seafloor away from the ridge in both directions.
4. The molten material is less dense than the surrounding rock. So it is forced upward toward the surface.
5. Continental drift hypothesis provided no mechanism for movement; seafloor spreading explained how continents have separated over time as ocean basins enlarged.
6. *Pattern of magnetic field reversals* and *pattern of ages around ridge* branch from *mid-ocean ridge. Reverses back and forth* branches from *pattern of magnetic field reversals,* and *ages increase away from ridges* branches from *pattern of ages around ridge.*
7. If the North American plate is moving away from the Mid-Atlantic Ridge at 1.25 cm/yr, and Africa is moving away from the ridge at an equal rate, North America and Africa separate by 2.5 cm more each year. After 200 million years, they will be 500,000,000 cm or 5,000 km farther apart.

Activity

Seafloor Spreading Rates

How did scientists use their knowledge of seafloor spreading and magnetic field reversals to reconstruct Pangaea? Try this activity to see how you can determine where a continent may have been located in the past.

What You'll Investigate
Can you use clues, such as magnetic field reversals on Earth, to help reconstruct Pangaea?

Materials
metric ruler
pencil

Goals
■ **Interpret** data about magnetic field reversals. Use these magnetic clues to reconstruct Pangaea.

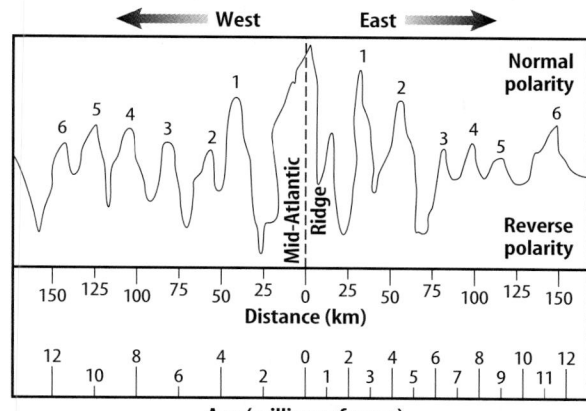

Procedure

1. Study the magnetic field graph above. You will be working only with normal polarity readings, which are the peaks above the baseline in the top half of the graph.

2. Place the long edge of a ruler vertically on the graph. Slide the ruler so that it lines up with the center of peak 1 west of the Mid-Atlantic Ridge.

3. **Determine** and record the distance and age that line up with the center of peak 1 west. Repeat this process for peak 1 east of the ridge.

4. **Calculate** the average age and distance for this pair of peaks.

5. Repeat steps 2 through 4 for the remaining pairs of normal-polarity peaks.

6. **Calculate** the rate of movement in cm per year for the six pairs of peaks. Use the formula rate = distance/time. Convert kilometers to centimeters. For example, to calculate a rate using normal-polarity peak 5, west of the ridge:

$$\text{rate} = \frac{125 \text{ km}}{10 \text{ million years}} = \frac{12.5 \text{ km}}{\text{million years}} = \frac{1,250,000 \text{ cm}}{1,000,000 \text{ years}} = 1.25 \text{ cm/year}$$

Conclude and Apply

1. **Compare** the age of igneous rock found near the mid-ocean ridge with that of igneous rock found farther away from the ridge.

2. If the distance from a point on the coast of Africa to the Mid-Atlantic Ridge is approximately 2,400 km, calculate how long ago that point in Africa was at or near the Mid-Atlantic Ridge.

3. How could you use this method to reconstruct Pangaea?

ACTIVITY 283

Purpose Students interpret magnetic field reversals in rock to determine the rate of seafloor spreading. L2

IS Logical-Mathematical

Process Skills making tables, using graphs, predicting, observing, inferring, using numbers, interpreting data

Time Required 50 to 60 minutes

Teaching Strategy Note that the rate of movement (half the spreading rate) is about 1.25 cm/yr.

Answers to Questions

1. The nearer rock is to the ridge, the younger it is.

2. About 192 million years ago, assuming a relatively constant rate of spreading

3. Students could determine when points on both coasts were at the ridge. This would mark when at least part of Pangaea was intact.

Performance Have students measure the distance between a point on the east coast of the United States and the Mid-Atlantic ridge. Have them determine when that point was near the mid-ocean ridge. Use **Performance Assessment in the Science Classroom**, p. 99.

Communicating Your Data

Students can use a table such as this to record data.

Sample Data Table:

Peak	1	2	3	4	5	6
Distance west normal polarity	40	60	75	100	120	140
Distance east normal polarity	36	60	80	100	118	145
Average distance	38	60	78	100	119	142
Age from scale (millions of years)	3.5	4.5	6.7	8.0	9.0	10.5
Rate of movement (cm/yr)	1.1	1.2	1.2	1.3	1.3	1.4

SECTION
3
Theory of Plate Tectonics

1 Motivate

Bellringer Transparency

Display the Section Focus Transparency for Section 3. Use the accompanying Transparency Activity Master. L2 ELL

Tie to Prior Knowledge

Ask if anyone has ever experienced an earthquake. If so, have these students explain what happened. If no one has, explain that earthquakes cause the ground to shake, often causing great damage. Tell students that earthquakes often happen because of the movement of plates.

As You Read

What You'll Learn

- **Compare and contrast** different types of plate boundaries.
- **Explain** how heat inside Earth causes plate tectonics.
- **Recognize** features caused by plate tectonics.

Vocabulary

plate tectonics
plate
lithosphere
asthenosphere
convection current

Why It's Important

Plate tectonics explains how many of Earth's features form.

Plate Tectonics

The idea of seafloor spreading showed that more than just continents were moving, as Wegener had thought. It was now clear to scientists that sections of the seafloor and continents move in relation to one another.

Plate Movements In the 1960s, scientists developed a new theory that combined continental drift and seafloor spreading. According to the theory of **plate tectonics,** Earth's crust and part of the upper mantle are broken into sections. These sections, called **plates,** move on a plasticlike layer of the mantle. The plates can be thought of as rafts that float and move on this layer.

Composition of Earth's Plates Plates are made of the crust and a part of the upper mantle, as shown in **Figure 8.** These two parts combined are the **lithosphere** (LIH thuh sfihr). This rigid layer is about 100 km thick and generally is less dense than material underneath. The plasticlike layer below the lithosphere is called the **asthenosphere** (as THE nuh sfihr). The rigid plates of the lithosphere float and move around on the asthenosphere.

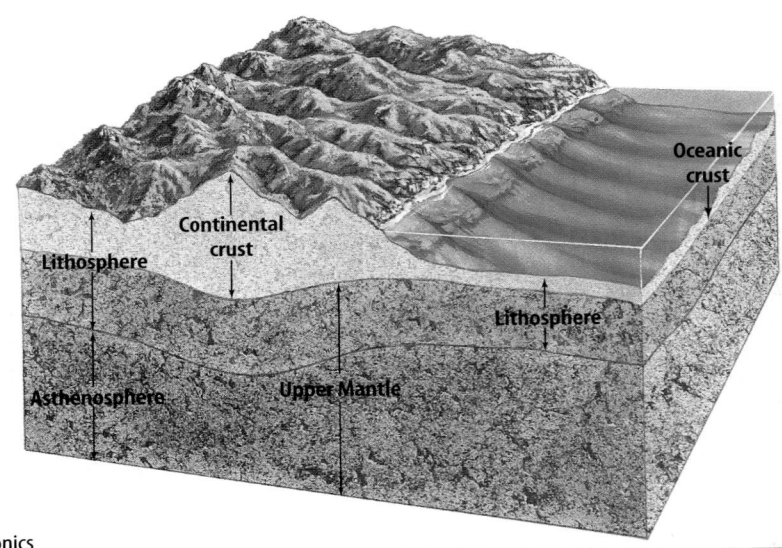

Figure 8
Plates of the lithosphere are composed of oceanic crust, continental crust, and rigid upper mantle.

Section ✓*Assessment* Planner

PORTFOLIO
Science Journal, p. 285
Extension, p. 287

PERFORMANCE ASSESSMENT
Problem-Solving Activity, p. 286
MiniLAB, p. 289

Skill Builder Activities, p. 293
See page 300 for more options.

CONTENT ASSESSMENT
Section, p. 293
Challenge, p. 293
Chapter, pp. 300–301

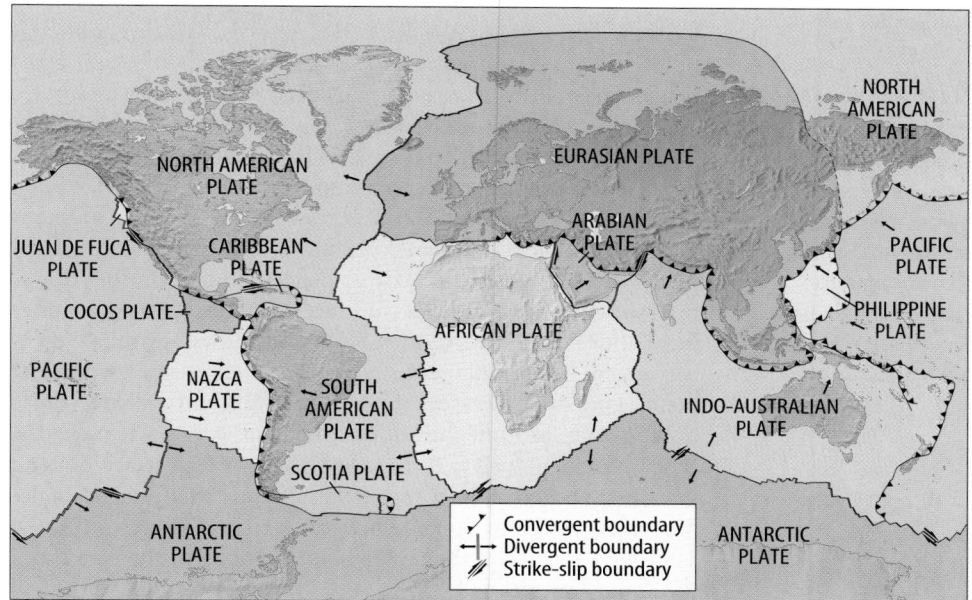

Convergent boundary
Divergent boundary
Strike-slip boundary

Plate Boundaries

When plates move, they can interact in several ways. They can move toward each other and converge, or collide. They also can pull apart or slide alongside one another. When the plates interact, the result of their movement is seen at the plate boundaries, as in **Figure 9.**

☑ **Reading Check** *What are the general ways that plates interact?*

Movement along any plate boundary means that changes must happen at other boundaries. What is happening to the Atlantic Ocean floor between the North American and African Plates? Compare this with what is happening along the western margin of South America.

Plates Moving Apart The boundary between two plates that are moving apart is called a divergent boundary. You learned about divergent boundaries when you read about seafloor spreading. In the Atlantic Ocean, the North American Plate is moving away from the Eurasian and the African Plates, as shown in **Figure 9.** That divergent boundary is called the Mid-Atlantic Ridge. The Great Rift Valley in eastern Africa is another example of a divergent plate boundary. There, a valley has formed where two continental plates are separating. **Figure 10** shows a side view of what a rift valley might look like and illustrates how the hot material rises up where plates separate.

Figure 9
This diagram shows the major plates of the lithosphere, their direction of movement, and the type of boundary between them. *Based on what is shown in this figure, what is happening where the Nazca Plate meets the Pacific Plate?*

Resource Manager

Chapter Resources Booklet
 Transparency Activity, p. 46
 Directed Reading for Content Mastery, pp. 21, 22
Cultural Diversity, p. 47

Science Journal

Theory Development Many scientists contributed ideas that led to plate tectonics theory. Have students select from A.L. Du Toit, S.K. Runcorn, Bruce Heezen, Arthur Holmes, J. Tuzo Wilson, Jack Oliver, Lynn R. Sykes, Fred Vine, D.H. Matthews, and L.W. Morley and write a one-page report in their Science Journals about his contributions. L2 P

2 Teach

Plate Tectonics

Quick Demo

Obtain a tectonic globe or make a map on which you can move continent pieces from a child's puzzle map. Use the globe or map to demonstrate continental movement.

Plate Boundaries

Caption Answer

Figure 9 These plates are moving away from each other.

☑ **Reading Check**

Answer Plates can collide, pull apart, or move past one another.

Extension

Have students research the geologic history of Iceland, concentrating on volcanic activity and its relationship to the Mid-Atlantic Ridge. Ask students to pinpoint on a map the location of the rift through the island and to indicate in which direction each section of the island is moving. L2 LS **Visual Spatial**

Plate Boundaries, continued

Activity

Show students a map with the location of volcanoes indicated. Have students use it to determine subduction areas. [L2]

[IS] **Visual-Spatial**

Use Science Words

Word Use Have students look up the words *diverge* and *converge* and use each word in a sentence. Then discuss how these meanings relate to plate boundaries. Possible answers: Two paths diverge at a fork in the road; traffic will converge in the center of the intersection. Plates converge, or come together, at some boundaries and diverge, or move apart, at others.

SCIENCE *Online*

Internet Addresses

Explore the Glencoe Science Web site at **science.glencoe.com** to find out more about topics in this section.

Problem-Solving Activity

National Math Standards

Correlation to Mathematics Objectives

6, 7, 8, 9

Answers

1. Yes, most fit together when continental shelves are included.
2. The continental shelves are the edges of continents. Present-day coastlines result from sea level changes.

SCIENCE *Online*

Research Visit the Glencoe Science Web site at **science.glencoe.com** for recent news or magazine articles about earthquakes and volcanic activity related to plate tectonics. Communicate to your class what you learned.

Plates Moving Together If new crust is being added at one location, why doesn't Earth's surface keep expanding? As new crust is added in one place, it disappears below the surface at another. The disappearance of crust can occur when seafloor cools, becomes denser, and sinks. This occurs where two plates move together at a convergent boundary.

When an oceanic plate converges with a less dense continental plate, the denser oceanic plate sinks under the continental plate. The area where an oceanic plate subducts, or goes down, into the mantle is called a subduction zone. Some volcanoes form above subduction zones. **Figure 10** shows how this type of convergent boundary creates a deep-sea trench where one plate bends and sinks beneath the other. High temperatures cause rock to melt around the subducting slab as it goes under the other plate. The newly formed magma is forced upward along these plate boundaries, forming volcanic mountains. The Andes mountain range of South America contains many volcanoes. They were formed at the convergent boundary of the Nazca and the South American Plates.

Problem-Solving Activity

How well do the continents fit together?

Recall the Explore Activity you performed at the beginning of this chapter. While you were trying to fit pieces of a cut-up photograph together, what clues did you use?

Identifying the Problem

Take a copy of a map of the world and cut out each continent. Lay them on a tabletop and try to fit them together, using techniques you used in the Explore Activity. You will find that the pieces of your Earth puzzle—the continents—do not fit together well. Yet, several of the areas on some continents fit together extremely well.

Take out another world map—one that shows the continental shelves as well as the continents. Copy it and cut out the continents, this time including the continental shelves.

Solving the Problem

1. Does including the continental shelves solve the problem of fitting the continents together?
2. Why should continental shelves be included with maps of the continents?

LAB DEMONSTRATION

Purpose to demonstrate compression forces that can form folded mountains

Materials two slabs of clay (5 cm thick and about 30 cm long), wax paper

Preparation Place the clay slabs on wax paper to make them easier to slide.

Procedure Lay the two clay pieces flat on a table. Have students predict what will happen when they are forced together. Push the two pieces together.

Expected Outcome Students will see folds and breaks form as the pieces of clay are pushed together.

✓ *Assessment*

What landforms are the folds in the clay analogous to on Earth's surface? folded mountains

Figure 10

By diverging at some boundaries and converging at others, Earth's plates are continually—but gradually—reshaping the landscape around you. The Mid-Atlantic Ridge, for example, was formed when the North and South American Plates pulled apart from the Eurasian and African Plates (see globe). Some features that occur along plate boundaries— rift valleys, volcanoes, and mountain ranges—are shown on the right and below.

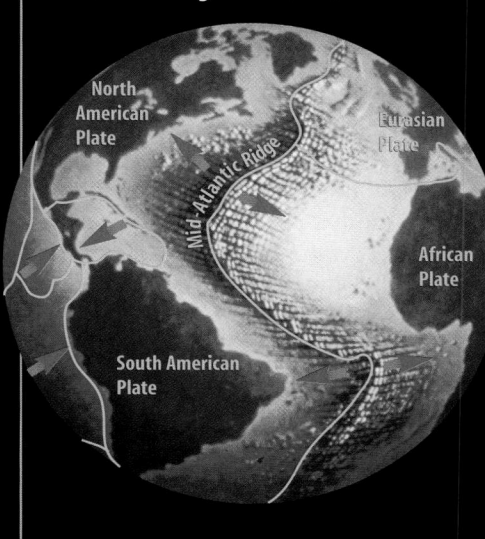

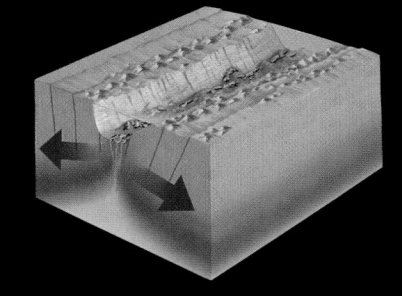

A RIFT VALLEY When continental plates pull apart, they can form rift valleys. The African continent is separating now along the East African Rift Valley.

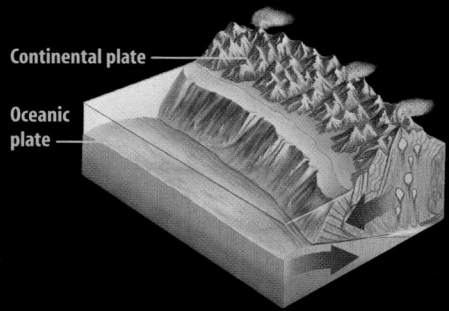

Continental plate

Oceanic plate

SUBDUCTION Where oceanic and continental plates collide, the oceanic plate plunges beneath the less dense continental plate. As the plate descends, molten rock (yellow) forms and rises toward the surface, creating volcanoes.

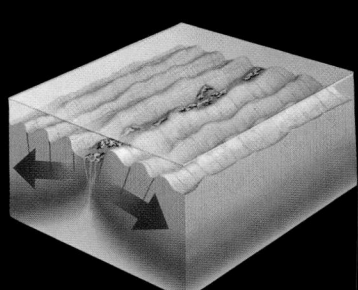

SEA-FLOOR SPREADING A mid-ocean ridge, like the Mid-Atlantic Ridge, forms where oceanic plates continue to separate. As rising magma (yellow) cools, it forms new oceanic crust.

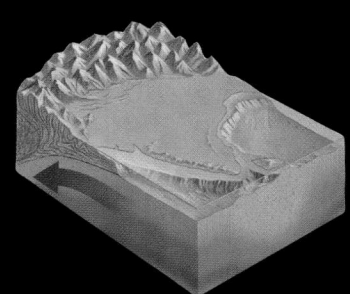

CONTINENTAL COLLISION Where two continental plates collide, they push up the crust to form mountain ranges such as the Himalaya.

287

Visualizing Plate Boundaries

Have students examine the pictures and read the captions. Then ask the following questions.

How would you predict the size of the Atlantic Ocean will change over the next 100 million years? Why? The Atlantic Ocean will become larger because seafloor spreading is occurring along the Mid-Atlantic Ridge.

The Andes Mountains are found along the west coast of South America. How did this mountain chain form? The plate boundary along the west coast of South America is a convergent boundary, which results in the formation of mountains and volcanoes.

Activity

Have small groups research the history of Surtsey, a small island in the North Atlantic Ocean. Ask them to draw a map of the island's location and write a summary of how the island formed, describing the type of plate boundary and the volcanic activity involved. [L2] ELL COOP LEARN
IS **Interpersonal**

Extension

Challenge students to research how lasers and other instruments are used to monitor plate movements. Have students report their findings in brief written reports. [L2] IS **Linguistic** P

Extension

Have students write reports in their Science Journals about the history of the study of the ocean floor. Reports should compare and contrast the work of crews aboard the *Glomar Challenger* and *JOIDES Resolution*. L3
LS **Linguistic**

IDENTIFYING
Misconceptions

Because students feel as though they are standing perfectly still on Earth's surface, they often forget that they are moving in several ways at the same time. Remind students that, as they sit in class, Earth is rotating at 464 m/s, speeding around the sun at 29.8 km/s, and the tectonic plate on which they sit is sliding around on Earth's plastic-like mantle.

Visual Learning

Figure 11B Have students study the photograph of the San Andreas fault and then describe evidence that shows the plates on either side of the fault are moving. Students should see that streams and other features that cross the fault are offset because of movement.

Caption Answer

Figure 11A The western side (Pacific Plate) of the fault is moving faster than the eastern side (North American Plate).

Where Plates Collide A subduction zone also can form where two oceanic plates converge. In this case, the colder, older, denser oceanic plate bends and sinks down into the mantle. The Mariana Islands in the western Pacific are a chain of volcanic islands formed where two oceanic plates collide.

Usually, no subduction occurs when two continental plates collide, as shown in **Figure 10.** Because both of these plates are less dense than the material in the asthenosphere, the two plates collide and crumple up, forming mountain ranges. Earthquakes are common at these convergent boundaries. However, volcanoes do not form because there is no, or little, subduction. The Himalaya in Asia are forming where the Indo-Australian Plate collides with the Eurasian Plate.

Where Plates Slide Past Each Other The third type of plate boundary is called a transform boundary. Transform boundaries occur where two plates slide past one another. They move in opposite directions or in the same direction at different rates. When one plate slips past another suddenly, earthquakes occur. The Pacific Plate is sliding past the North American Plate, forming the famous San Andreas Fault in California, as seen in **Figure 11.** The San Andreas Fault is part of a transform plate boundary. It has been the site of many earthquakes.

Figure 11
The San Andreas Fault in California occurs along the transform plate boundary where the Pacific Plate is sliding past the North American Plate.

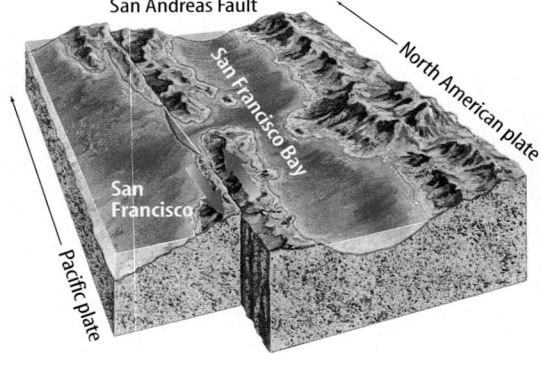

A Overall, the two plates are moving in roughly the same direction. *Why, then, do the red arrows show movement in opposite directions?*

San Andreas Fault
North American plate
San Francisco Bay
San Francisco
Pacific plate

B This photograph shows an aerial view of the San Andreas Fault.

288 CHAPTER 10 Plate Tectonics

Curriculum Connection

Mathematics The deepest point on Earth's surface is the bottom of the Mariana Trench, 11.2 km below sea level. Have students find Earth's highest point. Mt. Everest is 8.8 km above sea level. After students determine which is bigger, have them draw a scale diagram showing Mt. Everest in the trench. Their drawings should show how many kilometers Mt. Everest's top would be below sea level. 2.4 km

Resource Manager

Chapter Resources Booklet
  MiniLAB, p. 4

Earth Science Critical Thinking/Problem Solving, p. 8

Reading and Writing Skill Activities, p. 27

Causes of Plate Tectonics

Many new discoveries have been made about Earth's crust since Wegener's day, but one question still remains. What causes the plates to move? Scientists now think they have a good idea. They think that plates move by the same basic process that occurs when you heat soup.

Convection Inside Earth Soup that is cooking in a pan on the stove contains currents caused by an unequal distribution of heat in the pan. Hot, less dense soup is forced upward by the surrounding, cooler soup. As the hot soup reaches the surface, it cools and sinks back down into the pan. This entire cycle of heating, rising, cooling, and sinking is called a **convection current.** A version of this same process, occurring in the mantle, is thought to be the force behind plate tectonics. Scientists suggest that differences in density cause hot, plasticlike rock to be forced upward toward the surface.

Moving Mantle Material Wegener wasn't able to come up with an explanation for why plates move. Today, researchers who study the movement of heat in Earth's interior have proposed several possible explanations. All of the hypotheses use convection in one way or another. It is, therefore, the transfer of heat inside Earth that provides the energy to move plates and causes many of Earth's surface features. One hypothesis is shown in **Figure 12.** It relates plate motion directly to the movement of convection currents. According to this hypothesis, convection currents cause the movements of plates.

Mini LAB

Modeling Convection Currents

Procedure
1. Pour **water** into a **clear, colorless casserole dish** until it is 5 cm from the top.
2. Center the dish on a **hot plate** and heat it. **WARNING:** *Wear **thermal mitts** to protect your hands.*
3. Add a few drops of **food coloring** to the water above the center of the hot plate.
4. Looking from the side of the dish, observe what happens in the water.
5. Illustrate your observations in your **Science Journal.**

Analysis
1. Determine whether any currents form in the water.
2. Infer what causes the currents to form.

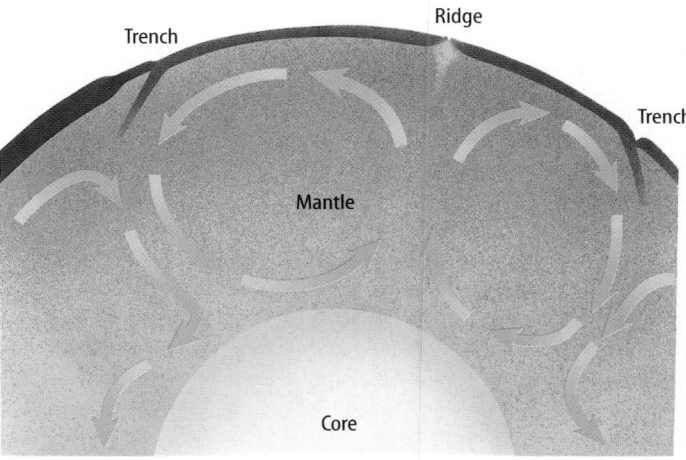

Figure 12
In one hypothesis, convection currents occur throughout the mantle. Such convection currents (see arrows) are the driving force of plate tectonics.

Trench
Ridge
Trench
Mantle
Core

Causes of Plate Tectonics

Mini LAB

Purpose Students model and observe currents. [L2] [ELL] **Visual-Spatial**

Materials clear glass casserole dish, water, hot plate, food coloring, thermal mitts

Teaching Strategy Have students note any movement in the water.

Safety Precautions Students must wear thermal mitts. Be sure the dish is stove-top safe.

Analysis
1. Some students will observe currents; others won't.
2. The transfer of thermal energy from the burner to the dish warms the water near the bottom of the dish. The cooler, denser water at the top of the dish sinks, displacing the warmer, less dense water, which then moves toward the top of the dish. As the warmer water cools, it becomes denser and sinks to start the cycle again.

✓ Assessment

Process Direct students to add informative labels to the drawings they made of their observations. The labels should be numbered and in sequence, explaining the steps in the formation and movement of convection currents. Use **PASC,** p. 127.

✔ Active Reading

Write-Draw-Discuss This strategy encourages students to actively participate in reading and lectures, assimilating content creatively. Have students write about an idea, clarify it, then make an illustration or drawing. Ask students to share responses with the class and display several examples. Have students Write-Draw-Discuss about the causes of plate tectonics.

Cultural Diversity

Hawaiian Terms The Hawaiian islands are volcanoes that formed as a result of magma rising through a "hot spot" in the middle of a plate. Some volcanic rocks have names that were made common in Hawaii. *Pahoehoe* (pa-hoe-ee-hoe-ee), from the Hawaiian word meaning "rope," forms in linear ridges. *Aa* (ah-ah) forms with sharp, jagged surfaces.

Features Caused by Plate Tectonics

Discussion

Why are earthquakes "associated" with plate boundaries? Plates do not move smoothly. Instead, they stick and catch on each other. When the plates are "stuck," strain, or potential energy, builds up in the rocks. When the plates move again, this energy is released as an earthquake.

Caption Answer

Figure 13 tension

Make a Model

Have students use paper to make a model of a divergent boundary with seafloor spreading. The model should be dynamic and show how spreading occurs. Students can draw parallel ridges on a long piece of paper and construct a mechanism for the paper to be drawn upward from both sides through a slot (the plate boundary), revealing "new" parallel ridges as it emerges. Accept any workable design. [L2] ELL

[IS] **Visual-Spatial**

Activity

Organize students into four groups and assign each group one of the following topics to master and present to the class: convergent boundaries, divergent boundaries, transform boundaries, and the driving mechanism of plate tectonics. [L2] COOP LEARN [IS] **Interpersonal**

✔ Reading Check

Answer earthquakes

Figure 13
Fault-block mountains can form when Earth's crust is stretched by tectonic forces. The arrows indicate the directions of moving blocks. *What type of force occurs when Earth's crust is pulled in opposite directions?*

Earth is a dynamic planet with a hot interior. This heat leads to convection, which powers the movement of plates. As the plates move, they interact. The interaction of plates produces forces that build mountains, create ocean basins, and cause volcanoes. When rocks in Earth's crust break and move, energy is released in the form of seismic waves. Humans feel this release as earthquakes. You can see some of the effects of plate tectonics in mountainous regions, where volcanoes erupt, or where landscapes have changed from past earthquake or volcanic activity.

✔ Reading Check

What happens when seismic energy is released as rocks in Earth's crust break and move?

Normal Faults and Rift Valleys Plates that are pulling apart cause tension forces that stretch Earth's crust. This causes large blocks of crust to break and tilt or slide down the broken surfaces of crust. When rocks break and move along surfaces, a fault forms. Faults interrupt rock layers by moving them out of place. Entire mountain ranges can form in the process, called fault-block mountains, as shown in **Figure 13.** Generally, the faults that form from pull-apart forces are normal faults—faults in which the rock layers above the fault move down when compared with rock layers below the fault.

Mid-ocean ridges and rift valleys can form when diverging plates separate Earth's crust. Examples of rift valleys are the Great Rift Valley in Africa, and the valleys that occur in the middle of mid-ocean ridges. Examples of mid-ocean ridges include the Mid-Atlantic Ridge and the East Pacific Rise.

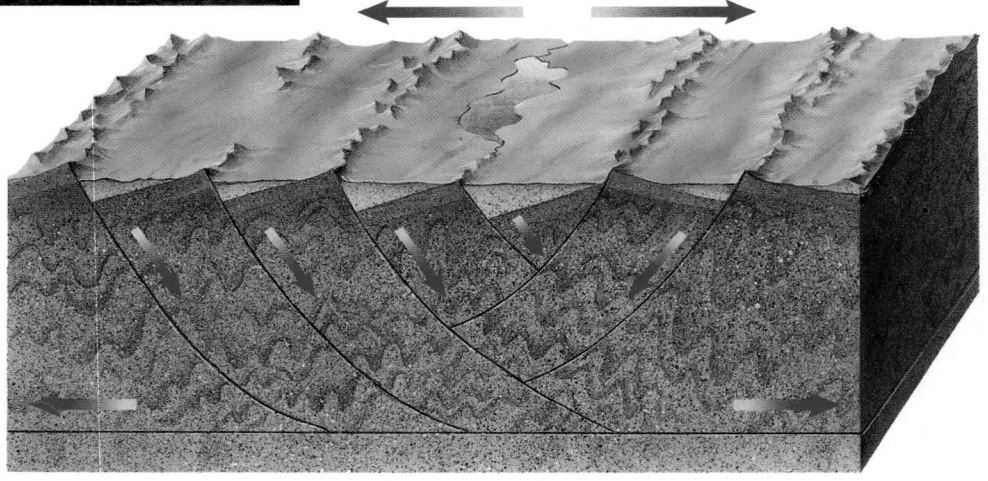

290 CHAPTER 10 Plate Tectonics

Inclusion Strategies

Gifted Have students place a piece of long, plastic tubing into the neck of a strong balloon and secure the tube so no air can escape from the balloon. Have them place the balloon at the bottom of an aquarium tank, with the tubing extending over the top of the tank. Then have students add alternating 2-mm layers of moist sand and dry sand to the bottom of the tank, covering the balloon. If they wish, students can build a small city on the top sand layer. Then have one student slowly blow up the balloon until the sand begins to crack to simulate an earthquake. Another student can videotape the "earthquake," and students can prepare a documentary showing how the quake affected the "city." [L3] COOP LEARN [IS] **Kinesthetic**

Mountains and Volcanoes Compression forces squeeze objects together. Where plates come together, compression forces produce several effects. As continental plates collide, the forces that are generated cause massive folding and faulting of rock layers into mountain ranges such as the Himalaya, shown in **Figure 14,** or the Appalachian Mountains. The type of faulting produced is generally reverse faulting. Along a reverse fault, the rock layers above the fault surface move up relative to the rock layers below the fault.

✔ **Reading Check** *What features occur where plates converge?*

As you learned earlier, when two oceanic plates converge, the denser plate is forced beneath the other plate. Curved chains of volcanic islands called island arcs form above the sinking plate. If an oceanic plate converges with a continental plate, the denser oceanic plate slides under the continental plate. Folding and faulting at the continental plate margin can thicken the continental crust to produce mountain ranges. Volcanoes also typically are formed at this type of convergent boundary.

Are there any features caused by plate tectonics in your area? To find out more about these features, see the **Field Guide to Faults and Folds** at the back of the book.

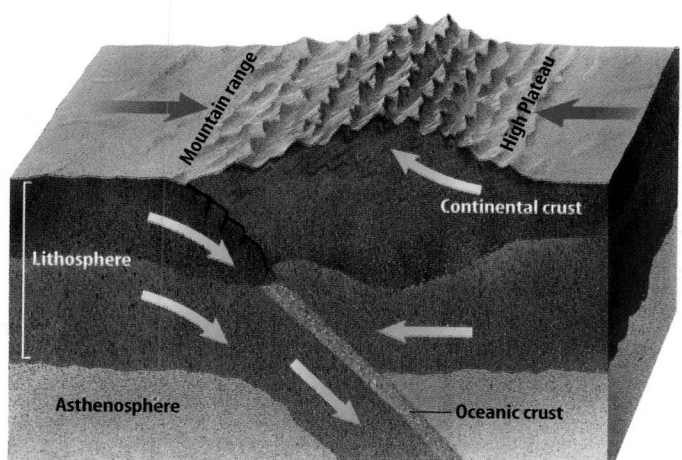

Figure 14
The Himalaya still are forming today as the Indo-Australian Plate collides with the Eurasian Plate.

✔ **Reading Check**

Answer continental–continental: high mountain ranges; oceanic–oceanic: island arcs; oceanic–continental: mountains and volcanoes

Teacher FYI

As the Indo-Australian plate continues to push into and under the European plate, the European plate is thrust up over it. India moves into Asia at a rate of 3.7 to 5.4 cm/yr, thrusting the Himalaya about 5 cm higher each year. But because forces of erosion wear down the mountains by about the same amount annually, they remain about the same height.

Make a Model

Provide clay with which students can make models to show the movement of plates at a strike-slip fault. Have them include surface features offset by the movement. L1 LS **Kinesthetic**

Resource Manager

Chapter Resources Booklet
 Enrichment, p. 32

Performance Assessment in the Science Classroom, p. 42

Curriculum Connection

Geography Have students search the Internet, newspapers, and magazines for stories about earthquakes and volcanic eruptions that have occurred as a result of plate movements along faults. Have students summarize their findings in written paragraphs to share in class. Have students make a bulletin board display that includes a map showing the location of these tectonic events. L2 LS **Visual-Spatial**

Features Caused by Plate Tectonics, continued

Discussion

Would you live or construct a building along a strike-slip fault? Explain. Most would not because of the danger of earthquakes and the likelihood of destruction. **Why might so many people live along the San Andreas fault?** Possible answers: Some people were there before the danger was known; some think the danger is minimal, some might be unable to relocate; some may think that other factors (climate, economic advantages) outweigh the negatives of earthquake danger.

Testing for Plate Tectonics

Physics
INTEGRATION

Convergent: toward each other; divergent: away from each other; transform: sliding past each other.

Teacher FYI

Creepmeters, lasers, and satellites are used to measure plate movements. They have shown that the Pacific Plate has been sliding past the North American plate along the San Andreas Fault at a rate of 1.2 to 3.3 cm/yr. If that continues, the Pacific Plate will continue to move north relative to the North American Plate, bringing Los Angeles up next to San Francisco in about 27 million years.

Figure 15
Most of the movement along a strike-slip fault is parallel to Earth's surface. When movement occurs, human-built structures along a strike-slip fault are offset, as shown here in this road.

Physics
INTEGRATION

In which directions do forces act at convergent, divergent, and transform boundaries? Demonstrate these forces using wooden blocks or your hands.

292 CHAPTER 10 Plate Tectonics

Strike-Slip Faults At transform boundaries, two plates slide past one another without converging or diverging. The plates stick and then slide, mostly in a horizontal direction, along large strike-slip faults. In a strike-slip fault, rocks on opposite sides of the fault move in opposite directions, or in the same direction at different rates. This type of fault movement is shown in **Figure 15.** One such example is the San Andreas Fault. When plates move suddenly, vibrations are generated inside Earth that are felt as an earthquake.

Earthquakes, volcanoes, and mountain ranges are evidence of plate motion. Plate tectonics explains how activity inside Earth can affect Earth's crust differently in different locations. You've seen how plates have moved since Pangaea separated. Is it possible to measure how far plates move each year?

Testing for Plate Tectonics

Until recently, the only tests scientists could use to check for plate movement were indirect. They could study the magnetic characteristics of rocks on the seafloor. They could study volcanoes and earthquakes. These methods supported the theory that the plates have moved and still are moving. However, they did not provide proof—only support—of the idea.

New methods had to be discovered to be able to measure the small amounts of movement of Earth's plates. One method, shown in **Figure 16,** uses lasers and a satellite. Now, scientists can measure exact movements of Earth's plates of as little as 1 cm per year.

Resource Manager

Chapter Resources Booklet
  Activity Worksheet, pp. 7–8
  Reinforcement, p. 29
Lab Management and Safety, p. 65

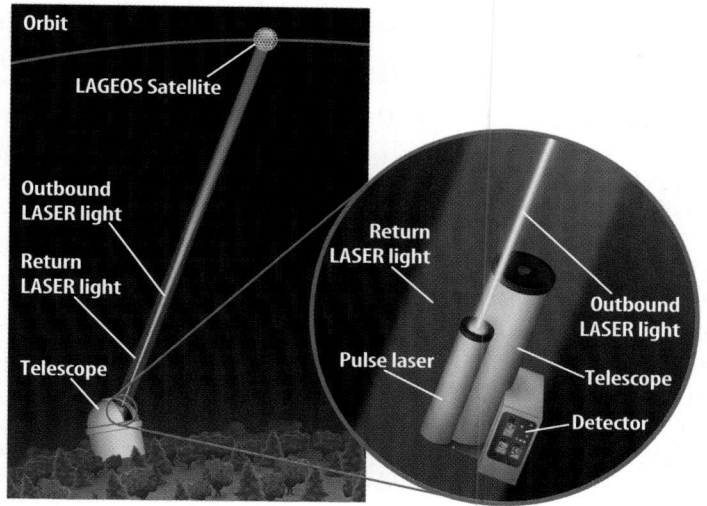

Orbit
LAGEOS Satellite
Outbound LASER light
Return LASER light
Telescope

Return LASER light
Pulse laser
Outbound LASER light
Telescope
Detector

Figure 16
When using the Satellite Laser Ranging System, scientists on the ground aim laser pulses at a satellite. The pulses reflect off the satellite and are used to determine a precise location on the ground.

Current Data Satellite data show that Hawaii is moving toward Japan at a rate of About 8.3 cm per year. Maryland is moving away from England at a rate of 1.7 cm per year. Using such methods, scientist have observed that the plates move at rates ranging from about 1 cm to 12 cm per year.

Section 3 Assessment

1. What happens to plates at a transform plate boundary?

2. What occurs at plate boundaries that are associated with seafloor spreading?

3. Describe three types of plate boundaries where volcanic eruptions can occur.

4. How are convection currents related to plate tectonics?

5. **Think Critically** Using **Figure 9** and a world map, determine what natural disasters might occur in Iceland. Also determine what disasters might occur in Tibet. Explain why some Icelandic disasters are not expected to occur in Tibet.

Skill Builder Activities

6. **Predicting** Plate tectonic activity causes many events that can be dangerous to humans. One of these events is a seismic sea wave, or tsunami. Learn how scientists predict the arrival time of a tsunami in a coastal area. **For more help, refer to the** Science Skill Handbook.

7. **Using an Electronic Spreadsheet** Make a spreadsheet with ten examples of plate-movement rates, such as how fast plates are moving apart at a specific location on the Mid-Atlantic Ridge. Make a bar graph that plots the rates on the y-axis in centimeters per year and the locations on the x-axis. **For more help, refer to the** Technology Skill Handbook.

SECTION 3 Theory of Plate Tectonics **293**

Activity
BENCH TESTED

Recognize the Problem

Internet Students will obtain the latitudes and longitudes of recent earthquakes and volcanic eruptions. Data can be accessed through the Glencoe Science Web site at **science.glencoe.com.** They will plot these locations on a map of the world. Once plotted, students will use the locations to determine tectonically active areas of Earth.

Non-Internet Sources Students will obtain maps of the world on which they will make their plots. They will use the plotted locations on the map to determine tectonically active areas of Earth.

Time Required

two 35- to 40-minute class periods or one block of 70 to 80 minutes

Preparation

Internet Access the Glencoe Science Web site at **science. glencoe.com** to run through the steps that students will follow.

Non-Internet Sources If the internet is not used, obtain tissue paper or sheets of plastic for students to use to draw copies of maps showing the locations of recent earthquakes and volcanic eruptions. The locations of earthquake epicenters and erupting volcanoes can be obtained from the U.S. Geological Survey or from local newspapers.

Activity *Use the Internet*

Predicting Tectonic Activity

The movement of plates on Earth causes forces that build up energy in rocks. The release of this energy can produce vibrations in Earth that you know as earthquakes. Earthquakes occur every day. Many of them are too small to be felt by humans, but each event tells scientists something more about the planet. Active volcanoes can do the same, and often form at plate boundaries.

Recognize the Problem

Can you predict tectonically active areas by plotting locations of earthquake epicenters and volcanic eruptions?

Form a Hypothesis

Think about where earthquakes and volcanoes have occurred in the past. Make a hypothesis about whether the locations of earthquake epicenters and active volcanoes can be used to predict tectonically active areas.

Goals

- **Research** the locations of earthquakes and volcanic eruptions from various locations around the world.
- **Plot** earthquake epicenters and the locations of volcanic eruptions obtained from the Glencoe Science Web site.
- **Predict** locations that are tectonically active based on a plot of the locations of earthquake epicenters and active volcanoes.

Data Sources

SCIENCE *Online* Go to the Glencoe Science Web site at **science.glencoe.com** for more information about earthquake and volcano sites, hints about earthquake and volcano sites, and data from other students.

Inclusion Strategies

Learning Disabled Pair learning disabled students with other students who can assist them with working on the computer. Encourage learning disabled students to take the lead in recording data, with the assistance of their partners.

SCIENCE *Online*
Internet Addresses
_____
_____
_____
_____

Explore the Glencoe Science Web site at **science.glencoe.com** to find out more about topics in this activity.

Test Your Hypothesis

Plan

1. Make a data table in your Science Journal like the one shown.
2. Collect data for earthquake epicenters and volcanic eruptions for at least the past two weeks. Your data should include the longitude and latitude for each location. For help, refer to the data sources given on the opposite page.

Do

1. Make sure your teacher approves your plan before you start.
2. **Plot** the locations of earthquake epicenters and volcanic eruptions on a map of the world. Use an overlay of tissue paper or plastic.

Locations of Epicenters and Eruptions		
Earthquake Epicenter/ Volcanic Eruption	Longitude	Latitude
Answers will vary.		

3. After you have collected the necessary data, predict where the tectonically active areas on Earth are.
4. **Compare and contrast** the areas that you predicted to be tectonically active with the plate boundary map shown in **Figure 9.**

Analyze Your Data

1. What areas on Earth do you predict to be the locations of tectonic activity?
2. How close did your prediction come to the actual location of tectonically active areas?

Draw Conclusions

1. How could you make your predictions closer to the locations of actual tectonic activity?
2. Would data from a longer period of time help? Explain.
3. What types of plate boundaries were close to your locations of earthquake epicenters? Volcanic eruptions?
4. **Explain** which types of plate boundaries produce volcanic eruptions. Be specific.

Communicating Your Data

SCIENCE Online Find this Internet activity on the Glencoe Science Web site at **science.glencoe.com.** **Post** your data in the table provided. **Compare** your data to those of other students. Combine your data with those of other students and **plot** these combined data on a map to **recognize** the relationship between tectonic activity, volcanic eruptions, and earthquake epicenters.

ACTIVITY 295

Form a Hypothesis

Possible Hypothesis

Most student hypotheses will reflect that earthquake and volcanic activity are good predictors of tectonically active areas.

Test Your Hypothesis

Teaching Strategy Encourage students to look for clusters of earthquake and volcanic activity, or for events that occur in a linear pattern.

Expected Outcome

Students should see patterns in the locations of earthquake and volcanic activity.

Analyze Your Data

1. Predictions will likely match the locations of plate boundaries.
2. Answers will depend on data collected. Most occur along plate boundaries. Hot spot eruptions may not coincide with plate boundaries.

Draw Conclusions

1. by collecting more data points
2. Yes; it would provide more data, which would help to more closely pinpoint these areas.
3. Earthquakes: near any type with many near convergent and transform boundaries; volcanoes: near divergent boundaries and subduction zones
4. Convergent-ocean and ocean-continental boundaries where one plate is subducted under the other produce magma that rises and forms volcanoes. Volcanoes also form along divergent boundaries where magma rises through cracks in the crust, either at mid-ocean ridges or on land in rift valleys.

✔Assessment

Oral Have pairs of students form a hypothesis that could explain the relationship between the locations of earthquake epicenters and active volcanoes and Earth's tectonic activity. Have each pair of students report to the class. Use **Performance Assessment in the Science Classroom,** p. 93.

Communicating Your Data

Plot all data from each student in the class on one large map. Lead students to the realization that as more and more data are placed on the map, the relationship of these data to the location of tectonically active areas on Earth becomes much more evident.

Science and Language Arts

Pre-Reading Activity

Ask students to think of a time when they listened to or overheard someone else's conversation. What happens when they can't hear everything that is being said? Tell students to keep this question in mind as they read the selection.

Respond to the Reading

Active Reading Strategies

Evaluate Titles are often important aspects of stories and poems. They help give the reader insight into the passage that he or she might not otherwise have. **What significance does this title have to the poem?**

Respond Consider the rhyme scheme of this poem. Ask yourself what affect the song-like quality of this poem has on you. **Does it remind you of other poems you've read?**

Question Reread the lines in the poem that discuss plate tectonics and other theories relating to the formation of volcanoes. Check these against relevant passages in this chapter to make sure you understand them.

Answers to Questions

1. a land, or continental, plate
2. Because the movement of continental, or land, plates is so slow.
3. an ocean plate.

Listening In
by Gordon Judge

Respond to the Reading

1. Who is narrating the poem?
2. Why might the narrator think he or she hasn't "moved for ages"?
3. Who or what is the narrator's "best mate"?

I'm just a bit of seafloor on this mighty solid sphere.
With no mind to be broadened, I'm quite content down here.
The mantle churns below me, and the sea's in turmoil, too;
But nothing much disturbs me, I'm rock solid through and
     through.

I do pick up occasional low-frequency vibrations –
(I think, although I can't be sure, they're sperm whales'
     conversations).
I know I shouldn't listen in, but what else can I do?
It seems they are all studying for degrees from the OU.

They've mentioned me in passing, as their minds begin improving:
I think I've heard them say "The theory says the sea-floor's
     moving…".
Well, that shook me, I can tell you; yes, it gave me quite a fright.
Yet I've not moved for ages, so I *know* it can't be right.

They call it "Plate Tectonics", this new theory in their noddle.
If they would only ask me, I could tell them it's all twaddle.
Apparently, I "oozed out from a mid-Atlantic split,
Solidified and cooled right down, then moved out bit by bit".

But, how can I be moving, when I know full well myself
That I'm quite firmly anchored to a continental shelf?
"Well, the continent is moving, too; you're *pushing* it, you see,"
I hear those OU whales intone, hydro-acoustically.

Now, my best mate's a sea floor in the mighty East Pacific.
He reckons life is balmy there: the summers are terrific!
He's heard the whale-talk, too, and found it pretty scary.
"Subduction" was the word he heard, which sounded rather hairy.

It was to be his fate, they claimed with undisguised great relish:
A hot and fiery end to things – it really would be hellish.
In fact, he'd end up underneath *my* continent, lengthwise,
So I would be the one to blame for my poor mate's demise.

Well, thank you very much, OU. You've upset my composure.
Next time you send your student whales to look at my exposure
I'll tell them it's a load of tosh: it's *they* who move, not me,
Those arty-smarty blobs of blubber, clogging up the sea!

Reading Further

Other sources on this topic include:

Volcano Cowboys: The Rocky Evolution of a Dangerous Science, by Dick Thompson, St. Martins Press, July 2000.

Encyclopedia of Volcanoes; by Haraldur Sigurdsson (Editor), Bruce Houghton, (Editor), Stephen R. McNutt (Editor), John Stix (Editor), Hazel Rymer (Editor); Academic Press; October 1999.

Melting the Earth: The History of Ideas on Volcanic Eruptions, by Haraldur Sigurdsson, Oxford University Press, June 1999.

Understanding Literature

Point of View Point of view refers to the perspective from which an author writes. This poem begins, "I'm just a bit of sea floor…." Right away, you know that the poem, or story, is being told from the point of view of the speaker, or the "first person." Not all first-person stories are told from the point of view of a person. The narrator in this poem is a geological feature, not a person. This point of view helps give the poem a fantastic or outlandish quality. It also gives a playful tone to the poem. What other effects does the first-person narration have on the story?

Science Connection Volcanoes can occur where two plates move toward each other. In the poem, the author gives several clues that a volcano will form. First, the narrator's "best mate" is a seafloor in the Pacific Ocean. When an oceanic plate and a continental plate collide, a volcano will form. The narrator also hears the word *subduction* spoken. Subduction zones occur when one plate sinks under another plate. Rocks melt in the zones where these plates converge, causing magma to move upward and form volcanic mountains. What other clues does the author give that a volcano will form?

Linking Science and Writing

Using Point of View Using the first-person point of view, write an account from the point of view of a living or nonliving thing. You could write an account of an object, such as a pencil, that you use or encounter every day. You also could write from the point of view of a living thing, such as a family pet. Be sure to use the personal pronoun "I" in your account.

Career Connection

Volcanologist

Ed Klimasauskas is a volcanologist at the Cascades Volcano Observatory in Washington State. His job is to study volcanoes in order to predict eruptions. Volcanologists' predictions can save lives: people can be evacuated from danger areas before an eruption occurs. Klimasauskas also educates the public about the hazards of volcanic eruptions and tells people who live near active volcanoes what they can do to be safe in case a volcano erupts. Volcanologists travel all over the world to study new sites.

SCIENCE *Online* To learn more about careers in volcanology, visit the Glencoe Science Web site at **science.glencoe.com.**

Career Connection

Because volcanoes are complex phenomena, it helps to get an early start if students are interested in the field. Students can take courses in high school such as biology, chemistry, physics, and earth sciences. Because of the specialized nature of volcanology, volcanologists usually have a Ph.D. degree in geology.

SCIENCE *Online*
Internet Addresses
_____
_____
_____
_____

Explore the Glencoe Science Web site at **science.glencoe.com** to find out more about topics in this feature.

Understanding Literature

Answers to Questions

Answers may vary but might include that the use of "I" gives a personal tone or human touch to otherwise technical or scientific material. Giving inanimate objects human traits personalizes science and gives it warmth.

Science Connection

There are approximately 1300 active volcanoes in the world. However, active volcanoes do not appear by chance. Most occur in belts, around mountain ranges that border the Pacific Ocean. In the poem, the narrator is "overhearing" a description of where the Pacific Plate is pushing beneath the adjacent continental plates—a process known as subduction. This is where Japan and the Aleutian Islands converge. Approximately 80 percent of the world's active volcanoes that have been recorded occur in these subduction zones.

Linking Science and Writing

Teaching Strategy

Warm-up the class to write from a point of view other than their own by playing a game. Think of a common household or classroom object, such as a hairbrush. Tell students that you spend your day living in rats' nests, trying to untangle things. Give students clues until they guess what you're thinking. Have other students do the same.

Reviewing Main Ideas

Preview

Students can answer the questions in their Science Journals. Discuss the answers as you go through the chapter. **IS** **Linguistic**

Review

Students can write their answers, then compare them with those of other students. **IS** **Interpersonal**

Reteach

Students can look at the illustrations and describe details that support the main ideas of the chapter. **IS** **Visual-Spatial**

Answers to Chapter Review

SECTION 1

2. Fossils of the same types of organisms on widely separated landmasses indicate that the landmasses were once joined.

SECTION 2

2. Seafloor basalt contains magnetic minerals that "lock in" Earth's magnetic field as they solidify.

SECTION 3

3. The crust on converging continental plates deforms into high mountains. At other converging boundaries, crust that sinks into the mantle melts and is forced upward to form volcanic mountains.

Chapter 10 Study Guide

Reviewing Main Ideas

Section 1 Continental Drift

1. Alfred Wegener suggested that the continents were joined together at some point in the past in a large landmass he called Pangaea. Wegener proposed that continents have moved slowly, over millions of years, to their current locations.

2. The puzzlelike fit of the continents, fossils, climatic evidence, and similar rock structures support Wegener's idea of continental drift. However, Wegener could not explain what process could cause the movement of the landmasses. *How do fossils support the hypothesis of continental drift?*

Section 2 Seafloor Spreading

1. Detailed mapping of the ocean floor in the 1950s showed underwater mountains and rift valleys.

2. In the 1960s, Harry Hess suggested seafloor spreading as an explanation for the formation of mid-ocean ridges. *How is magnetic evidence preserved in rocks forming along a mid-ocean ridge?*

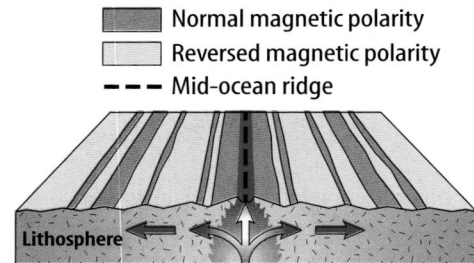

- ■ Normal magnetic polarity
- ▢ Reversed magnetic polarity
- – – – Mid-ocean ridge

Lithosphere

3. The theory of seafloor spreading is supported by magnetic evidence in rocks and in the ages of rocks on the ocean floor.

Section 3 Theory of Plate Tectonics

1. In the 1960s, scientists combined the ideas of continental drift and seafloor spreading to develop the theory of plate tectonics. The theory states that the surface of Earth is broken into sections called plates that move around on the asthenosphere.

2. Currents in Earth's mantle called convection currents transfer heat in Earth's interior. It is thought that this transfer of heat energy moves plates.

3. Earth is a dynamic planet. As the plates move, they interact, resulting in many of the features of Earth's surface. *How do converging plates form mountains?*

FOLDABLES
Reading & Study Skills

After You Read

To help you review what you learned about continental drift, use the Foldable you made at the beginning of the chapter.

FOLDABLES
Reading & Study Skills

After You Read

After students have read the chapter and completed the Foldable described in Before You Read, have them do the activity on the student page.

Dinah Zike

Visualizing Main Ideas

Complete the concept map below about continental drift, seafloor spreading, and plate tectonics.

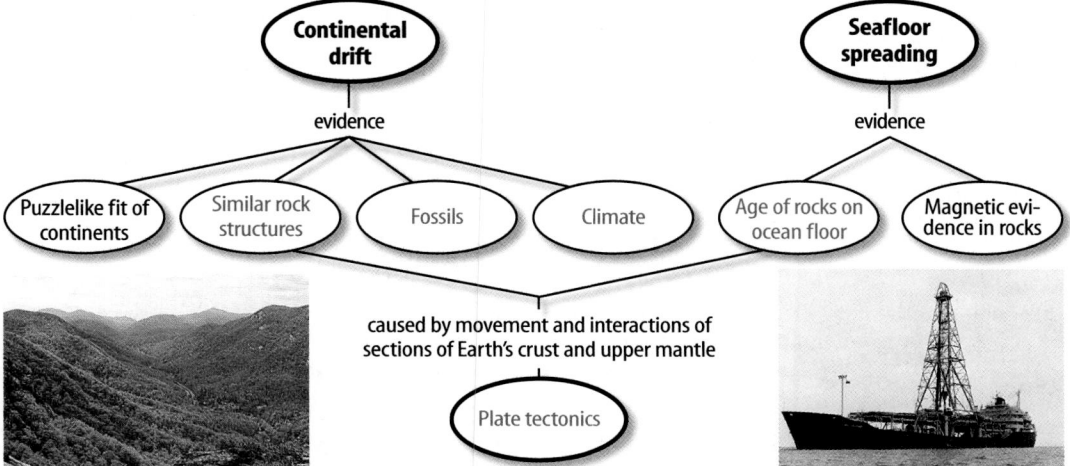

Continental drift — evidence: Puzzlelike fit of continents, Similar rock structures, Fossils, Climate

Seafloor spreading — evidence: Age of rocks on ocean floor, Magnetic evidence in rocks

caused by movement and interactions of sections of Earth's crust and upper mantle

Plate tectonics

Vocabulary Review

Vocabulary Words

a. asthenosphere
b. continental drift
c. convection current
d. lithosphere
e. Pangaea
f. plate
g. plate tectonics
h. seafloor spreading

Using Vocabulary

Each phrase below describes a vocabulary term from the list. Write the term that matches the phrase describing it.

1. plasticlike layer below the lithosphere

2. idea that continents move slowly across Earth's surface

3. large, ancient landmass that consisted of all the continents on Earth

4. process that forms new seafloor as hot material is forced upward

5. driving force for plate movement

6. composed of oceanic or continental crust and upper mantle

7. explains locations of mountains, trenches, and volcanoes

8. piece of the lithosphere that moves over a plasticlike layer

9. theory proposed by Harry Hess that includes processes along mid-ocean ridges

10. forms as warm material rises and cold material sinks

Visualizing Main Ideas

See student page.

Vocabulary Review

Vocabulary Words

1. asthenosphere
2. continental drift
3. Pangaea
4. seafloor spreading
5. convection current
6. lithosphere
7. plate tectonics
8. plate
9. seafloor spreading
10. convection current

Chapter 10 Assessment

Checking Concepts

1. B
2. D
3. C
4. D
5. A
6. B
7. B
8. D
9. A
10. B

Thinking Critically

11. The colliding continental plates cause earthquakes, but neither plate is forced deep into Earth, which would allow melting to occur and magma to rise through any cracks to form volcanoes.
12. Africa was located near the South Pole when all the continents were joined.
13. When molten material rises and cools at a ridge, magnetic rocks take on the orientation of Earth's magnetic field. Each time Earth's magnetic field reverses, new materials that form close to the ridge take on the new orientation.
14. It is a transform boundary. Without subduction no melting of plate edges occurs and no magma is produced.
15. The fish could have moved through the oceans between continents.

Checking Concepts

Choose the word or phrase that best answers the question.

1. Which layer of Earth contains the asthenosphere?
   A) crust C) outer core
   B) mantle D) inner core

2. What type of plate boundary is the San Andreas Fault part of?
   A) divergent C) convergent
   B) subduction D) transform

3. What hypothesis states that continents slowly moved to their present positions on Earth?
   A) subduction C) continental drift
   B) seafloor spreading D) erosion

4. Which plate is subducting beneath the South American Plate to form the Andes mountain range?
   A) North American C) Indo-Australian
   B) African D) Nazca

5. Which of the following features indicates that many continents were once near Earth's south pole?
   A) glacial deposits C) volcanoes
   B) mid-ocean ridges D) earthquakes

6. What evidence in rocks supports the theory of seafloor spreading?
   A) plate movement C) subduction
   B) magnetic reversals D) convergence

7. Which type of plate boundary is the Great Rift Valley a part of?
   A) convergent C) transform
   B) divergent D) lithosphere

8. What theory states that plates move around on the asthenosphere?
   A) continental drift C) subduction
   B) seafloor spreading D) plate tectonics

9. What forms when one plate slides past another plate?
   A) transform boundary
   B) divergent boundary
   C) subduction zone
   D) mid-ocean ridge

10. When oceanic plates collide, what volcanic landforms are made?
    A) folded mountains
    B) island arcs
    C) strike-slip faults
    D) mid-ocean ridges

Thinking Critically

11. Why are many earthquakes but few volcanoes found in the Himalaya?

12. Glacial deposits often form at high latitudes near the poles. Explain why glacial deposits have been found in Africa.

13. How is magnetism used to support the theory of seafloor spreading?

14. Explain why volcanoes do not form along the San Andreas Fault.

15. Explain why the fossil of an ocean fish found on two different continents would not be good evidence of continental drift.

Developing Skills

16. **Forming Hypotheses** Mount St. Helens in the Cascade Range is a volcano. Use **Figure 9** and a U.S. map to hypothesize how it might have formed.

17. **Measuring in SI** Movement along the African Rift Valley is about 2.1 cm per year. If plates continue to move apart at this rate, how much larger will the rift be (in meters) in 1,000 years? In 15,500 years?

300 CHAPTER ASSESSMENT

Chapter ✓Assessment Planner

Portfolio Encourage students to place in their portfolios one or two items of what they consider to be their best work. Examples include:
- Challenge, p. 279
- Chemistry Integration, p. 281
- Science Journal, p. 285
- Extension, p. 287

Performance Additional performance assessments, Performance Task Assessment Lists, and rubrics for evaluating these activities can be found in Glencoe's **Performance Assessment in the Science Classroom.**

18. Concept Mapping Make an events chain concept map that describes seafloor spreading along a divergent plate boundary. Choose from the following phrases: *magma cools to form new seafloor, magma rises to the seafloor, convection currents circulate hot material along divergent boundary,* and *older seafloor is forced apart.*

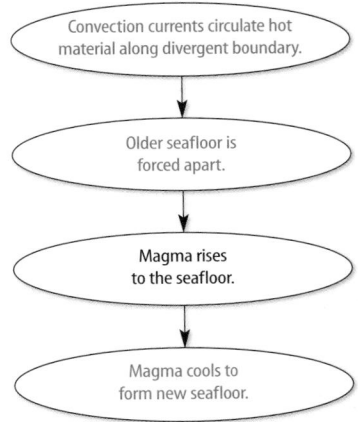

Convection currents circulate hot material along divergent boundary.

↓

Older seafloor is forced apart.

↓

Magma rises to the seafloor.

↓

Magma cools to form new seafloor.

=== Performance Assessment ===

19. Observe and Infer In the MiniLab Modeling Convection Currents, you observed convection currents produced in water as it was heated. Repeat the experiment, placing sequins, pieces of wood, or pieces of rubber bands into the water. How do their movements support your observations and inferences from the MiniLab?

=== TECHNOLOGY ===

Go to the Glencoe Science Web site at **science.glencoe.com** or use the **Glencoe Science CD-ROM** for additional chapter assessment.

THE PRINCETON REVIEW **Test Practice**

Ms. Fernandez was leading a class discussion on plate tectonics and Earth's interior.

Study the diagram below and then answer the following questions.

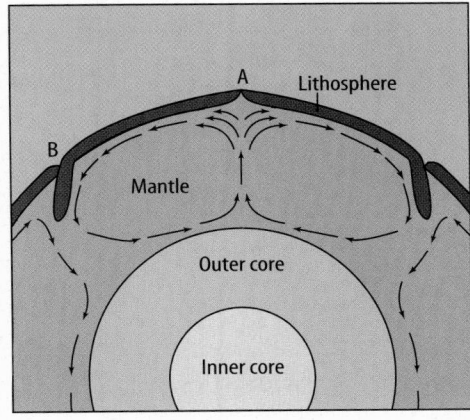

Lithosphere

A

B

Mantle

Outer core

Inner core

1. Suppose that the arrows in the diagram represent patterns of convection in Earth's mantle. Which type of plate boundary is most likely to form along the region labeled "A"?
A) transform
B) reverse
C) convergent
D) divergent

2. Which statement is true of the region marked "B" on the diagram?
F) Plates separate and slip past one another sideways.
G) Plates diverge and form volcanoes.
H) Plates converge and form volcanoes.
J) Plates collapse and form a strike-slip boundary.

CHAPTER ASSESSMENT   301

THE PRINCETON REVIEW **Test Practice**

The Test-Taking Tip was written by The Princeton Review, the nation's leader in test preparation.
1. D
2. H

=== Developing Skills ===

16. The volcanoes of the Cascade Range formed as the Juan de Fuca plate subducted beneath the North American Plate.
17. 21 m; 325.5 m
18. See student page.

=== Performance Assessment ===

19. The objects move around because of convection processes going on inside the water. Use **PASC**, p. 123.

✓*Assessment* **Resources**

📁 **Reproducible Masters**

Chapter Resources Booklet
Chapter Review, pp. 37–38
Chapter Tests, pp. 39–42
Assessment Transparency Activity, p. 49

Glencoe Science Web site
Interactive Tutor
Chapter Quizzes

Glencoe Technology
  🖑 Assessment Transparency
  💿 Interactive CD-ROM Chapter Quizzes
  💿 ExamView Pro Test Bank
  💿 Vocabulary PuzzleMaker Software
  📼 MindJogger Videoquiz DVD/VHS

Section/Objectives	Standards		Activities/Features
	National	State/Local	
Chapter Opener	See p. 5T for a Key to Standards.		**Explore Activity:** Model stress buildup along faults, p. 303 **Before You Read,** p. 303
Section 1 Forces Inside Earth ⏱ 2 sessions 📦 1 block 1. **Explain** how earthquakes result from the buildup of energy in rocks. 2. **Describe** how compression, tension, and shear forces make rocks move along faults. 3. **Distinguish** among normal, reverse, and strike-slip faults.	National Content Standards: UCP2, B2, B3, D1		**Physics Integration,** p. 306
Section 2 Features of Earthquakes ⏱ 2 sessions 📦 1 block 1. **Explain** how earthquake energy travels in seismic waves. 2. **Distinguish** among primary, secondary, and surface waves. 3. **Describe** the structure of Earth's interior.	National Content Standards: UCP2, A1, B2, B3, D1		**Physics Integration,** p. 309 **Visualizing Seismic Waves,** p. 310 **Science Online,** p. 311 **MiniLAB:** Interpreting Seismic Wave Data, p. 313 **Activity:** Epicenter Location, p. 316
Section 3 People and Earthquakes ⏱ 3 sessions 📦 1.5 blocks 1. **Explain** where most earthquakes in the United States occur. 2. **Describe** how scientists measure earthquakes. 3. **List** ways to make your classroom and home more earthquake-safe.	National Content Standards: UCP2, A1, B2, B3, D1, F1, F3, F5, G2		**Physics Integration,** p. 319 **Science Online,** p. 320 **Math Skills Activity:** Using Multiplication to Compare Earthquake Energy, p. 321 **MiniLAB:** Modeling Seismic-Safe Structures, p. 322 **Activity:** Earthquake Depths, pp. 324–325 **Science Stats:** Moving Earth!, pp. 326–327

Activity Materials	Reproducible Resources	Section Assessment	Technology
Explore Activity: medium-grain sandpaper (2 sheets); tape; textbook; large, thick rubber bands (2)	**Chapter Resources Booklet** Foldables Worksheet, p. 19 Directed Reading Overview, p. 21 Note-taking Worksheets, pp. 35–37	*GLENCOE'S* **ASSESSMENT** *ADVANTAGE*	
Need materials? Contact Science Kit at 1-800-828-7777 or www.sciencekit.com on the Internet.	**Chapter Resources Booklet** Transparency Activity, p. 46 Enrichment, p. 32 Reinforcement, p. 29 Directed Reading, p. 22 Transparency Activity, pp. 49–50	**Performance** Skill Builder Activities, p. 307 **Content** Section Assessment, p. 307	Section Focus Transparency Teaching Transparency Interactive CD-ROM/DVD Guided Reading Audio Program
MiniLAB: none **Activity:** string, metric ruler, globe, chalk	**Chapter Resources Booklet** Transparency Activity, p. 47 MiniLAB, p. 3 Lab Activity, pp. 9–13 Enrichment, p. 33 Reinforcement, p. 30 Directed Reading, p. 23 Activity Worksheet, pp. 5–6 **Home and Community Involvement,** p. 40	**Portfolio** Science Journal, p. 311 **Performance** MiniLAB, p. 313 Skill Builder Activities, p. 315 **Content** Section Assessment, p. 315	Section Focus Transparency Interactive CD-ROM/DVD Guided Reading Audio Program
MiniLAB: building blocks, rubber bands (medium and large sizes) **Activity:** graph paper, pencil	**Chapter Resources Booklet** Transparency Activity, p. 48 MiniLAB, p. 4 Lab Activity, pp. 15–18 Enrichment, p. 34 Reinforcement, p. 31 Directed Reading, pp. 23, 24 Activity Worksheet, pp. 7–8 **Lab Management and Safety,** p. 65	**Portfolio** Extension, p. 318 **Performance** Math Skills Activity, p. 321 MiniLAB, p. 322 Skill Builder Activities, p. 323 **Content** Section Assessment, p. 323	Section Focus Transparency Interactive CD-ROM/DVD Guided Reading Audio Program

GLENCOE'S **ASSESSMENT** *ADVANTAGE*

End of Chapter Assessment

Blackline Masters	Technology	Professional Series
Chapter Resources Booklet Chapter Review, pp. 39–40 Chapter Tests, pp. 41–44 **Standardized Test Practice by The Princeton Review,** pp. 51–54	MindJogger Videoquiz CD-ROM Explorations and Quizzes Vocabulary Puzzle Makers ExamView Pro Test Bank Interactive Lesson Planner Interactive Teacher's Edition	Performance Assessment in the Science Classroom (PASC)

Transparencies

Section Focus

Section Focus Transparency 1 — Nobody's Fault at All

In 1935, Charles F. Richter developed a method to analyze and display information about earthquakes. The Richter scale uses data from seismographs to rate earthquake strength. Though we know more about the causes of earthquakes and minimizing earthquake damage, predicting earthquakes remains tricky.

1. How does the Richter scale describe earthquakes?
2. What does a seismograph measure?
3. Why might predicting where earthquakes will strike be easier than predicting when they will strike?

L2

Section Focus Transparency 2 — Does the stork bring baby islands?

In November of 1963, the Atlantic Ocean got a new island. The island was named Surtsey after Sutur, a mythological fire god. The new island was the result of a volcanic eruption very near Iceland.

1. How do volcanoes reshape Earth?
2. What determines where volcanoes form?
3. What unique learning opportunities might scientists have on Surtsey?

L2

Section Focus Transparency 3 — Earth Shattering

The dots on this image show places where earthquakes have occurred. The line of dots in the middle of the Atlantic Ocean is the Mid-Atlantic Ridge. As you can see, the area is geologically very active!

1. What features do earthquakes generally follow?
2. What other geological activity is likely to follow a similar pattern?
3. Is all geological activity at plate boundaries? Defend your answer with examples.

L2

This is a representation of key blackline masters available in the Teacher Classroom Resources. See Resource Manager boxes within the chapter for additional information.

Key to Teaching Strategies

The following designations will help you decide which activities are appropriate for your students.

L1 Level 1 activities should be appropriate for students with learning difficulties.

L2 Level 2 activities should be within the ability range of all students.

L3 Level 3 activities are designed for above-average students.

ELL ELL activities should be within the ability range of English Language Learners.

COOP LEARN Cooperative Learning activities are designed for small group work.

LS Multiple Learning Styles logos, as described on page 22T, are used throughout to indicate strategies that address different learning styles.

P These strategies represent student products that can be placed into a best-work portfolio.

Assessment

Assessment Transparency — Earthquakes

Directions: *Carefully review the table and answer the following questions.*

Earthquake Activity

House	Location	Earthquakes in last 10 years	Average severity
A	Oregon	12	2.5
B	California	73	5.2
C	Illinois	0	0
D	Delaware	2	1.1

1. According to the table, which location has earthquakes with an average severity greater than 5.0?
   A A
   B B
   C C
   D D
2. The most likely cause of the earthquakes in California is ___.
   F collision of the ocean and land
   G vibrations from landslides
   H effects of the weather
   J faults in Earth's crust
3. According to the table, which house has had no earthquake damage in the last ten years?
   A A
   B B
   C C
   D D

L2

Teaching

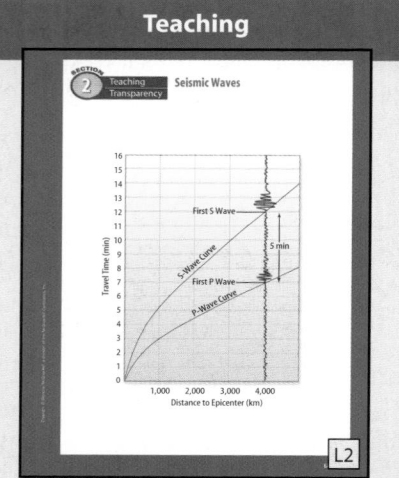

Teaching Transparency — Seismic Waves

L2

Hands-on Activities

Activity Worksheets

Activity — Disruptive Eruptions

Lab Preview
Directions: *Answer these questions before you begin the Activity.*
1. Why are safety goggles especially important when doing this activity?

2. Based on what you know about the activity from question 1, what can you expect to happen that might resemble a cinder-cone volcanic eruption? Explain.

A volcano's structure can influence how it erupts. Some volcanoes have only one central vent, while others have numerous fissures that allow lava to escape. Materials in magma influence its viscosity, or how it flows. If magma is a thin fluid—not viscous—gases can escape easily. But if magma is thick—viscous—gases cannot escape as easily. This builds up pressure within a volcano.

What You'll Investigate
What determines the explosiveness of a volcanic eruption?

Materials
plastic film canisters   baking soda (NaHCO₃)
vinegar (CH₃COOH)   teaspoon
50-mL graduated cylinder

Goals
• Infer how a volcano's opening contributes to how explosive an eruption might be.
• Hypothesize how the viscosity of magma can influence an eruption.

Safety Precautions
This activity should be done outdoors. Goggles must be worn at all times. The caps of the film canisters fly off due to the chemical reaction that occurs inside them. Never put anything in your mouth while doing the experiment.

Procedure
1. Watch your teacher demonstrate this activity.
2. Add 15 mL of vinegar to a film canister.
3. Place 1 teaspoon of baking soda in the film canister's lid, using it as a type of plate.
4. Place the lid on top of the film canister, but do not cap it. Just set it on top of the opening. Move a safe distance away. Record your observations in the Data and Observations section.
5. Carry out your second trial. This time cap the canister quickly and tightly. Record your observations.

L2

Laboratory Activities

Laboratory Activity 1 — Wave Detecting

Today, scientists use seismographs to observe and record seismic waves. Before the nineteenth century, however, scientists used other types of instruments to study earthquakes. These instruments did not record seismic waves. Instead, they indicated the magnitude or direction of an earthquake in a general way. In the 1600s in Italy, for example, scientists used a device that contained water to observe seismic waves. The amount of water spilling out during an earthquake indicated the amount of shaking. In this lab, you will make a simple earthquake-detecting device and determine how it is affected by seismic waves.

Strategy
You will model and observe seismic waves.
You will determine how the energy released by an earthquake affects the amplitude, or height, of seismic waves.

Materials
baking pan
large ceramic or stainless steel bowl
pitcher of tap water
dropper
meterstick
textbook
paper towels

Procedure
1. Work with a partner. Place the baking pan on a flat surface such as a desk or counter. Set the bowl inside the pan.
2. Pour water into the bowl from the pitcher. Fill the bowl to within 1 to 2 mm of the rim.
3. Using the dropper add water to the bowl until the surface of the water arches above the rim (Figure 1). This is your earthquake detector.
4. Model an earthquake by having a partner drop a book near the detector from a height of 2 cm. Observe what happens to the water in the bowl. Do waves appear? Does water spill over? Record your observation in the Data and Observations section. Add more water to the bowl with the dropper if any spills out. Then repeat this step, switching roles with your partner.
5. Repeat Step 4 several more times. Each time, you should increase the height at which you drop the book by several centimeters.
6. If any water spills outside the baking pan, be sure to wipe it up with the paper towels.

Figure 1

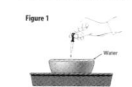

Water

L2

Meeting Different Ability Levels

Content Outline

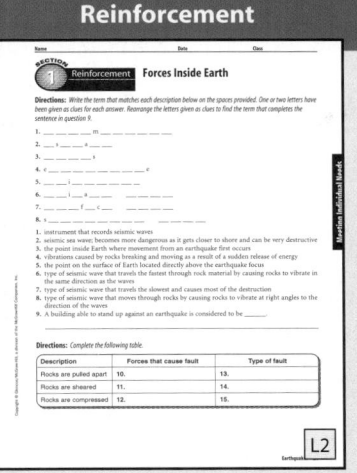

L2

Reinforcement

L2

Directed Reading

L1

Assessment

Chapter Tests

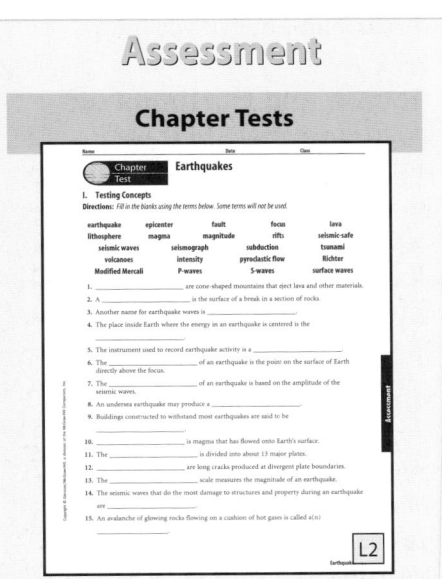

L2

Enrichment

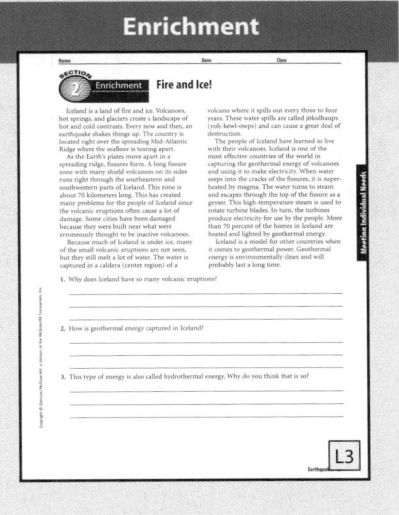

L3

Spanish Directed Reading

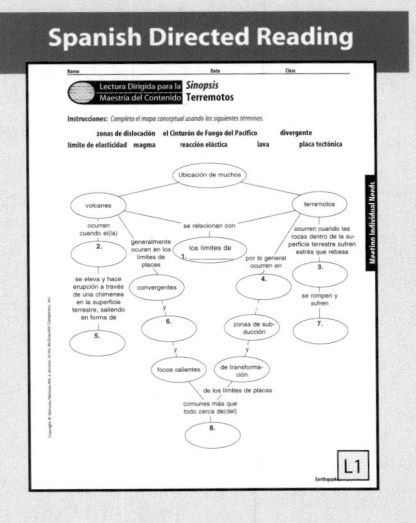

L1

Test Practice Workbook

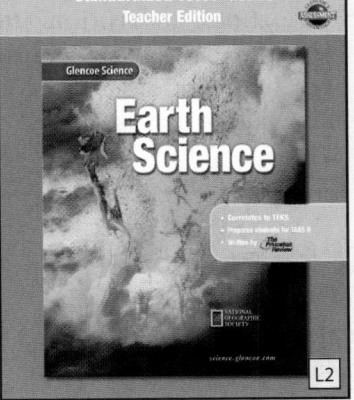

L2

Chapter Review

L2

Science Content Background

Forces Inside Earth

Types of Earthquakes

Shallow-focus earthquakes occur in two places: where two of Earth's plates are moving apart and near the edges of plates that are converging. Intermediate- and deep-focus earthquakes occur where one plate subducts under another. Subduction zone quakes account for about 75 percent of Earth's seismic energy and almost one-half of the destructive quakes.

Student Misconception

Earthquakes occur only in California.
Refer to the facing page for teaching strategies to address this misconception. Refer to pages 304–305 for content related to this topic.

Features of Earthquakes

Predicting Earthquakes

One method that is used in predicting earthquakes is the study of seismic gaps. Seismic gaps are areas of a fault zone that have not produced a major earthquake for more than 100 years. When a seismic gap area is located, researchers estimate how long it has been since the fault zone in question has experienced an earthquake. Using this information and knowledge of the average earthquake recurrence interval along the fault segment, scientists predict a time range over which the area could expect to experience a major earthquake.

Although much information is used in an attempt to predict earthquakes, success has been limited. Stress begins to build up in an area as soon as an earthquake has occurred. Without knowing how much stress can accumulate before rocks must shift, it is difficult to predict an earthquake with any amount of accuracy.

People and Earthquakes

Earthquake Magnitude

The extent of the damage caused by an earthquake depends on the distance to the epicenter, the type of bedrock in the area, the local soil or sediment types, and the number and type of structures subjected to the quake, among other factors.

Seismic-Safe Structures

Most loss of life in an earthquake occurs when people are trapped in and on crumbling structures, such as buildings, bridges, and highways. Making structures seismic-safe can reduce the loss of life in an earthquake. Seismic-safe structures are resistant to vibrations that occur during an earthquake.

The two main strategies for building seismic-safe structures are shock absorption and reinforcement. The goals of these building techniques are to prevent structures from collapsing and to minimize falling debris.

Gerald French/FPG International

SCIENCE Online

For additional content background on this topic, go to the Glencoe Science Web site at science.glencoe.com.

 **Misconceptions**

Find Out What Students Think

Students may think that . . .

- **Earthquakes occur only in California.**

Much of the publicity found in the media features California earthquakes. As a result, many students think that the major location for earthquakes in the world is in California. Actually, earthquakes occur throughout the world, including many areas of the United States. Thus, it is important to feature earthquakes from a variety of areas of the world as students learn about this topic.

Activity

Use the Internet to find information on recent earthquakes. One source is the National Earthquake Information Center World Data Center for Seismology: *http://wwwneic.cr.usgs.gov*. Have students plot on a world map earthquakes that have occurred over the last 30 days to begin to develop the idea that earthquakes occur worldwide.

Promote Understanding

Activity

After students understand that earthquakes are a world-wide phenomenon, reinforce the importance of having an "earthquake survival kit," especially if you live in an earthquake-prone areas. Tell students that they have been hired to design the ideal kit. Explain that the kit must meet several minimum requirements:

- It should provide supplies for a family of four.
- It should provide enough supplies for three days.
- It should be able to be stored for long periods of time without spoiling.

Have students work in small groups to discuss what they would put in their kits. Have each group prepare a list of items they would include, giving both the item name and a quantity. Remind students that after a major earthquake many of the things we take for granted would not be available.

When students have made their lists, have groups compare their ideas. Are all items the same? What were some of the issues that different families might face? Prompt students to think of families with small children or infants. Discuss the types of foods that might be stored safely for long periods of time. Remind students that obtaining safe drinking water can be a major problem after an earthquake.

After students finish designing their kits, suggest they compare their ideas to those of the Red Cross or other disaster-management groups. What have they overlooked? What might your students recommend to these groups?

Assess

After completing the chapter, see *Identifying Misconceptions* in the Study Guide.

Earthquakes

Chapter Vocabulary

fault
earthquake
normal fault
reverse fault
strike-slip fault
seismic wave
focus
primary wave
secondary wave
surface wave
epicenter
seismograph
magnitude
liquefaction
tsunami

What do you think?

Science Journal This is a record of vibrations produced by an earthquake. The record is a seismogram, produced by a seismograph.

Earthquakes

More than 14,000 deaths and at least 60,000 injuries resulted from a powerful earthquake in India on January 26, 2001. Collapse of structures, such as this building in Ahmedabad, India, is among the greatest dangers associated with earthquakes. What causes earthquakes? Why do some areas experience repeated earthquakes while other areas rarely do? In this chapter you'll learn the answers to these and other questions. You'll also learn how earthquake damage can be reduced.

What do you think?

Science Journal Look at the picture below with a classmate. Discuss what you think this might be. Here's a hint: *Something must have been shaking to make these waves.* Write your answer or best guess in your Science Journal.

302

Theme Connection

Energy The energy theme is highlighted as students learn how earthquakes unleash tremendous amounts of energy inside Earth's crust. That energy can change Earth's surface and affect both people and structures.

Why do earthquakes occur? The bedrock beneath the soil can break and form cracks known as faults. When blocks of rock move past each other along a fault, they cause the ground to shake. Why don't rocks move all the time, causing constant earthquakes? You'll find out during this activity.

Model stress buildup along faults

1. Tape a sheet of medium-grain sandpaper to the tabletop.

2. Tape a second sheet of sandpaper to the book cover on a textbook.

3. Place the book on the table so that both sheets of sandpaper meet.

4. Tie two large, thick rubber bands together and loop one of the rubber bands around the edge of the book so that it is not touching the sandpaper.

5. Pull on the free rubber band until the book moves and observe this movement.

Observe

Write a paragraph in your Science Journal describing how the book moved and explaining how this activity modeled the buildup of stress along a fault.

Before You Read

FOLDABLES
Reading & Study Skills

Making a Cause and Effect Study Fold Make the following Foldable to help you understand the cause and effect relationship of earthquakes and Earth's crust.

1. Place a sheet of paper in front of you so the long side is at the top. Fold the paper in half from the left side to the right side and then unfold.

2. Label the left side of the paper *Cause* and the right side *Effect*. Refold the paper.

3. Before you read the chapter, draw a cross section of Earth's crust showing what you think happens during an earthquake on the outside of your Foldable.

4. As you read the chapter, change your drawing and list causes of earthquakes on the inside of your Foldable.

Cause	Effect

303

EXPLORE ACTIVITY

Purpose Students explore the cause of earthquake activity at faults. **IS** **Kinesthetic**

Preparation Sandpaper can be bought at a hardware store.

Materials two sheets medium-grain sandpaper, textbook, two large rubber bands, tape

Teaching Strategy Have students work in pairs.

Safety Precautions Caution students to avoid scrapes or cuts when handling sandpaper.

Observe

The book moves with a quick jerk once the pulling force overcomes the friction between the two pieces of sandpaper. Rocks along fault lines build up stress in a similar manner until they rapidly slip past each other, causing an earthquake.

✓ *Assessment*

Process Have students create a labeled diagram that illustrates what happened in the activity. Use **Performance Assessment in the Science Classroom,** p. 163.

Before You Read

FOLDABLES
Reading & Study Skills

Dinah Zike Study Fold

Purpose Have students make and use a Foldable to diagram and explain what they think happens when an earthquake is taking place. As they read the chapter, have students collect information on the causes and effects of earthquakes and amend their initial diagram if necessary.

For additional help, see Foldables Worksheet, p. 19 in **Chapter Resources Booklet,** or go to the Glencoe Science Web site at **science.glencoe.com.** See After You Read in the Study Guide at the end of this chapter.

Forces Inside Earth

1 Motivate

Bellringer Transparency

Display the Section Focus Transparency for Section 1. Use the accompanying Transparency Activity Master. L2
ELL

As You Read

What You'll Learn

■ **Explain** how earthquakes result from the buildup of energy in rocks.
■ **Describe** how compression, tension, and shear forces make rocks move along faults.
■ **Distinguish** among normal, reverse, and strike-slip faults.

Vocabulary

fault   reverse fault
earthquake   strike-slip fault
normal fault

Why It's Important

Earthquakes are among the most dramatic of all natural disasters on Earth.

Earthquake Causes

Recall the last time you used a rubber band. Rubber bands stretch when you pull them. Because they are elastic, they return to their original shape once the force is released. However, if you stretch a rubber band too far, it will break. A wooden craft stick behaves in a similar way. When a force is first applied to the stick, it will bend and change shape, as shown in **Figure 1A.** The energy needed to bend the stick is stored inside the stick as potential energy. If the force keeping the stick bent is removed, the stick will return to its original shape, and the stored energy will be released as energy of motion.

Fault Formation There is a limit to how far a wooden craft stick can bend. This is called its elastic limit. Once its elastic limit is passed, the stick breaks, as shown in **Figure 1B.** Rocks behave in a similar way. Up to a point, applied forces cause rocks to bend and stretch, undergoing what is called elastic deformation. Once the elastic limit is passed, the rocks may break. When rocks break, they move along surfaces called **faults.** A tremendous amount of force is required to overcome the strength of rocks and to cause movement along a fault. Rock along one side of a fault can move up, down, or sideways in relation to rock along the other side of the fault.

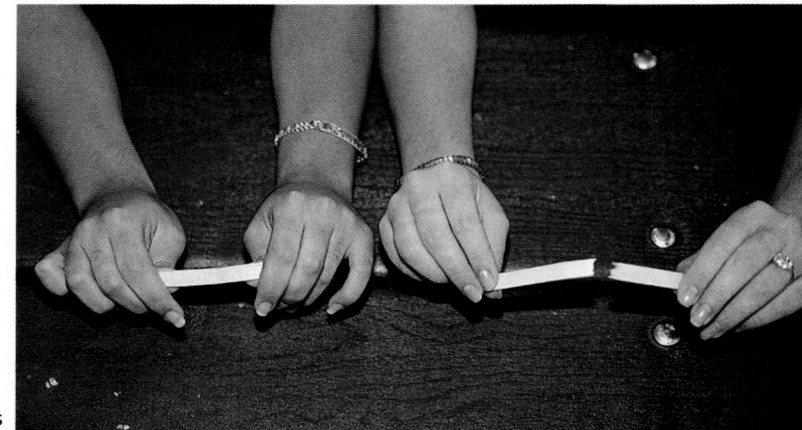

Figure 1
The 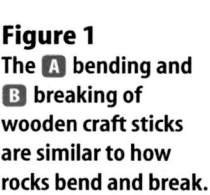 **A** bending and **B** breaking of wooden craft sticks are similar to how rocks bend and break.

304   CHAPTER 11 Earthquakes

Tie to Prior Knowledge

Ask students to recall any recent earthquakes they have heard about or experienced. Discuss with students where the earthquakes occurred and what happened as a result of them. Then tell students they will find out why earthquakes occur in this section.

Section ✓*Assessment* Planner

PORTFOLIO	**CONTENT ASSESSMENT**
Activity, p. 306	Section, p. 307
PERFORMANCE ASSESSMENT	Challenge, p. 307
Skill Builder Activities, p. 307	Chapter, pp. 330–331
See page 330 for more options.	

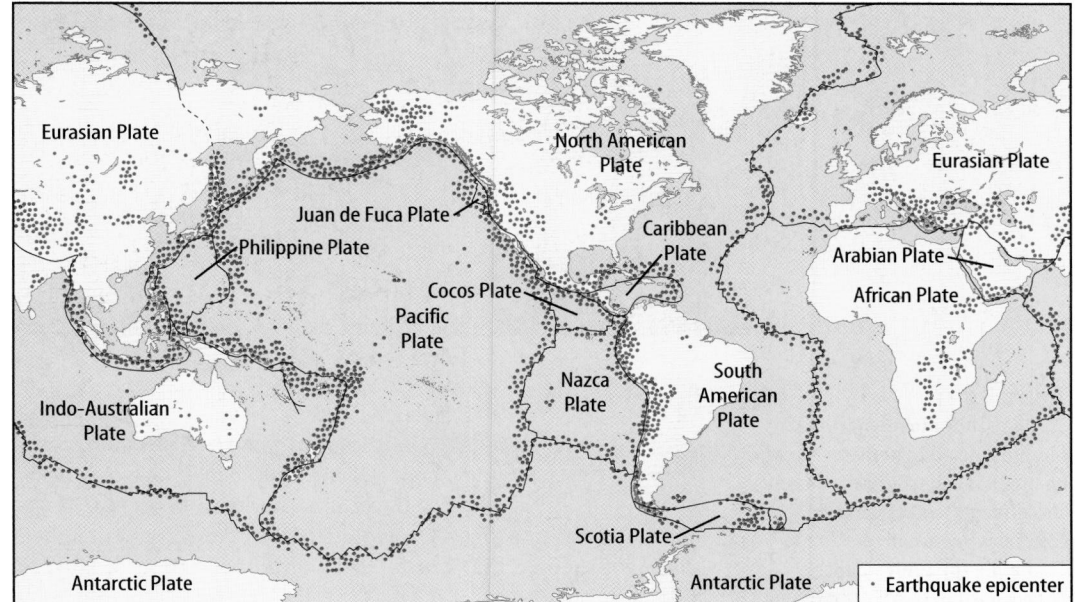

Eurasian Plate
North American Plate
Eurasian Plate
Juan de Fuca Plate
Philippine Plate
Caribbean Plate
Arabian Plate
Cocos Plate
African Plate
Pacific Plate
Indo-Australian Plate
Nazca Plate
South American Plate
Scotia Plate
Antarctic Plate
Antarctic Plate   · Earthquake epicenter

What causes faults? What produces the forces that cause rocks to break and faults to form? The surface of Earth is in constant motion because of forces inside the planet. These forces cause sections of Earth's surface, called plates, to move. This movement puts stress on the rocks near the plate edges. To relieve this stress, the rocks tend to bend, compress, or stretch. If the force is great enough, the rocks will break. An **earthquake** is the vibrations produced by the breaking of rock. **Figure 2** shows how the locations of earthquakes outline the plates that make up Earth's surface.

> ✔ **Reading Check** *Why do most earthquakes occur near plate boundaries?*

How Earthquakes Occur As rocks move past each other along a fault, their rough surfaces catch, temporarily halting movement along the fault. However, forces keep driving the rocks to move. This action builds up stress at the points where the rocks are stuck. The stress causes the rocks to bend and change shape. When the rocks are stressed beyond their elastic limit, they break, move along the fault, and return to their original shapes. An earthquake results. Earthquakes range from unnoticeable vibrations to devastating waves of energy. Regardless of their intensity, most earthquakes result from rocks moving over, under, or past each other along fault surfaces.

Figure 2
The dots represent the epicenters of major earthquakes over a ten-year period. Note that most earthquakes occur near plate boundaries. *Why do earthquakes rarely occur in the middle of plates?*

✔ **Active Reading**

Buddy Interviews This strategy helps students understand and clarify the reading. Have students interview one another to find out what helps them to understand what they are reading, how they find answers, and how they assimilate new vocabulary terms. Have students use Buddy Interviews to help them master the concept of what causes earthquakes.

Resource Manager

Chapter Resources Booklet
Transparency Activity, p. 46
Directed Reading for Content Mastery, pp. 21, 22
Enrichment, p. 32

---

② Teach

Earthquake Causes

Caption Answer
Figure 2 Because most of the stress on plates is at their edges, rock is more likely to break and cause quakes there than in central areas.

Activity
Different materials have different elastic limits. Have students bend the following materials to see what happens once the elastic limit is reached: a piece of cardboard; a plastic drinking straw; a wooden tongue depressor; a thin, steel wire; some silicon putty; a thin sheet of slate or shale. Have students wear goggles during this activity. L2 ELL IN **Kinesthetic**

✔ **Reading Check**

Answer Most stress and movement is at boundaries where plates meet.

Fun Fact

There is no spot on Earth that cannot experience an earthquake, but earthquakes are less likely to occur in Antarctica than in any other place.

IDENTIFYING Misconceptions

Some students think that earthquakes occur only in California. Refer to page 302F for teaching strategies that address this misconception.

Would it be possible to stand at a fault and not know it was there? Explain. Yes; the fault could be the site of hills or mountains, and the actual fault could have been covered by soil and rock as the result of erosion.

Activity

Have pairs of students apply compression, tension, and shear forces to bars of taffy. Tell students to make drawings that show what happens to the taffy in each instance. Have students write a paragraph relating this to what happens to rocks when forces are applied. Depending on the amount of force applied, students should see the taffy bend or break, which is what happens when force is applied to rock.

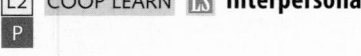 L2 COOP LEARN **Interpersonal** P

Quick Demo

Contrast the three types of faults by preparing a large, triple-decker peanut butter and jelly sandwich. Cut off the crusts so the individual layers can be seen. Construct a fault at about a 30° angle by cutting through the sandwich. Move the separate halves of the sandwich to demonstrate normal, reverse, and strike-slip faults.

 Visual-Spatial

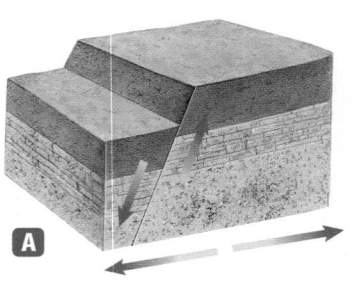

Figure 3
A When rock moves along a fracture caused by tension forces, the break is called a normal fault. Rock above the normal fault moves downward in relation to rock below the fault surface.
B This normal fault formed near Kanab, Utah.

Figure 4
A Compression forces in rocks form reverse faults. The rock above the reverse fault surface moves upward in relation to the rock below the fault surface.
B Rock layers have been offset along this reverse fault.

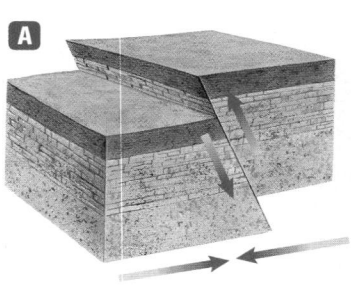

Types of Faults

Physics INTEGRATION

Three types of forces—tension, compression, and shear—act on rocks. Tension is the force that pulls rocks apart, and compression is the force that squeezes rocks together. Shear is the force that causes rocks on either side of a fault to slide past each other.

Normal Faults Tensional forces inside Earth cause rocks to be pulled apart. When rocks are stretched by these forces, a normal fault can form. Along a **normal fault,** rock above the fault surface moves downward in relation to rock below the fault surface. The motion along a normal fault is shown in **Figure 3A.** Notice the normal fault shown in the photograph in **Figure 3B.**

Reverse Faults Reverse faults result from compression forces that squeeze rock. **Figure 4A** shows the motion along a reverse fault. If rock breaks from forces pushing from opposite directions, rock above a **reverse fault** surface is forced up and over the rock below the fault surface. **Figure 4B** shows a large reverse fault in California.

306 CHAPTER 11 Earthquakes

Visual Learning

Figure 3 The arrows at the bottom of the figure illustrate how the tension forces are being applied. The arrows beside the fault line illustrate the relationship between the two blocks of rock. **Do the two pairs of arrows illustrate whether one block moved up or down?** No, the movement is relative. Either or both blocks could have moved.

Figure 5

A Shear forces push on rock in opposite—but not directly opposite—horizontal directions. When they are strong enough, these forces split rock and create strike-slip faults. Little vertical movement occurs along a strike-slip fault. **B** The North American Plate and the Pacific Plate slide past each other along the San Andreas Fault, a strike-slip fault, in California.

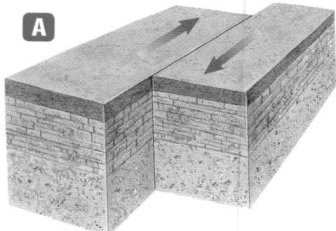

Strike-Slip Faults At a **strike-slip fault,** shown in **Figure 5A,** rocks on either side of the fault are moving past each other without much upward or downward movement. **Figure 5B** shows the largest fault in California—the San Andreas Fault— which stretches more than 1,100 km through the state. The San Andreas Fault is the boundary between two of Earth's plates that are moving sideways past each other because of shear forces.

 Reading Check *What is a strike-slip fault?*

Section ① Assessment

1. What is an earthquake?
2. The Himalaya in Tibet formed when two of Earth's plates collided. What type of faults would you expect to find in these mountains? Why?
3. In what direction do rocks above a normal fault surface move?
4. Why is California's San Andreas Fault a strike-slip fault?
5. **Think Critically** Why is it easier to predict where an earthquake will occur than it is to predict when it will occur?

Skill Builder Activities

6. **Forming Hypotheses** Hypothesize why the chances of an earthquake occurring along a fault increase rather than decrease as time since the last earthquake passes. **For more help, refer to the** Science Skill Handbook.
7. **Using Graphics Software** Use a graphics program to make models of the three types of faults—normal, reverse, and strike-slip. Add arrows to show the directions of movement along both sides of each type. **For more help, refer to the** Technology Skill Handbook.

Answers to Section Assessment

1. An earthquake is a vibration produced by the breaking of rock.
2. Reverse faults; they are the result of compression forces.
3. downward in relation to rocks below the fault
4. Rocks on either side of the fault move past each other.
5. Scientists know that most earthquakes occur near plate boundaries, but they cannot predict when rocks in the crust will break in response to the forces acting on them.
6. The longer the time between earthquakes, the more stress that builds up, and the more likely the chances of an earthquake.
7. Students' models should show appropriate crustal movement for each of the three fault types.

Types of Faults, continued

Discussion

Why is folding more likely with compression than with tension forces? Compression causes bending and therefore folding, while tension causes thinning and cracking.

✔ Reading Check

Answer a fault where rocks on either side are moving past each other in a horizontal direction

③ Assess

Reteach

Have students use their hands to demonstrate the movement that occurs along each of the three kinds of faults.

Challenge

Challenge students to do research on the Internet to find out what coastal California will look like in several million years because of the movement of plates along the San Andreas Fault. Instruct them to include diagrams to illustrate their answers. Because the Pacific Plate is moving northwest in relation to the North American Plate, a piece of crust containing Los Angeles will one day be adjacent to San Francisco. L2 IS **Visual-Spatial**

✔ Assessment

Content Have students write a brief paragraph to explain why streambeds are offset at the San Andreas Fault. Rocks on either side of the fault move past each other, causing the streambeds to be offset. Use **Performance Assessment in the Science Classroom,** p. 159.

Features of Earthquakes

 Motivate

Bellringer Transparency

Display the Section Focus Transparency for Section 2. Use the accompanying Transparency Activity Master. L2

ELL

L2

Tie to Prior Knowledge

Tell students that the energy of earthquakes travels in waves. Ask students to recall other types of energy that travel in waves. Possible answers: sound, electromagnetic radiation such as visible light, energy in ocean waves Tell students that in this section they will find out how earthquakes that happen inside Earth's crust can affect people and things on the surface.

Features of Earthquakes

As You Read

What You'll Learn

- **Explain** how earthquake energy travels in seismic waves.
- **Distinguish** among primary, secondary, and surface waves.
- **Describe** the structure of Earth's interior.

Vocabulary

seismic wave   surface wave
focus   epicenter
primary wave   seismograph
secondary wave

Why It's Important

Seismic waves are responsible for most damage caused by earthquakes.

Figure 6
Some seismic waves are similar to the wave that is traveling through the rope. Note that the rope moves perpendicular to the wave direction.

Seismic Waves

When two people hold opposite ends of a rope and shake one end, as shown in **Figure 6,** they send energy through the rope in the form of waves. Like the waves that travel through the rope, **seismic** (SIZE mihk) **waves** generated by an earthquake travel through Earth. During a strong earthquake, the ground moves forward and backward, heaves up and down, and shifts from side to side. The surface of the ground can ripple like waves do in water. Imagine trying to stand on ground that had waves traveling through it. This is what you might experience during a strong earthquake.

Origin of Seismic Waves You learned earlier that rocks move past each other along faults, creating stress at points where the rocks' irregular surfaces catch each other. The stress continues to build up until the elastic limit is exceeded and energy is released in the form of seismic waves. The point where this energy release occurs is the **focus** (plural, *foci*) of the earthquake. The foci of most earthquakes are within 65 km of Earth's surface. A few have been recorded as deep as 700 km. Seismic waves are produced and travel outward from the earthquake focus.

Section ✔Assessment Planner

PORTFOLIO
Science Journal, p. 311
PERFORMANCE ASSESSMENT
Try At Home MiniLAB, p. 313
Skill Builder Activities, p. 315
See page 330 for more options.

CONTENT ASSESSMENT
Section, p. 315
Challenge, p. 315
Chapter, pp. 330–331

Primary Waves When earthquakes occur, three different types of seismic waves are produced. All of the waves are generated at the same time, but each behaves differently within Earth. **Primary waves** (P-waves) cause particles in rocks to move back and forth in the same direction that the wave is traveling. If you squeeze one end of a coiled spring and then release it, you cause it to compress and then stretch as the wave travels through the spring, as shown in **Figure 7**. Particles in rocks also compress and then stretch apart, transmitting primary waves through the rock.

Secondary and Surface Waves **Secondary waves** (S-waves) move through Earth by causing particles in rocks to move at right angles to the direction of wave travel. The wave traveling through the rope shown in **Figure 6** is an example of a secondary wave.

Surface waves cause most of the destruction resulting from earthquakes. **Surface waves** move rock particles in a backward, rolling motion and a side-to-side, swaying motion, as shown in **Figure 8.** Many buildings are unable to withstand intense shaking because they are made with stiff materials. The buildings fall apart when surface waves cause different parts of the building to move in different directions.

✔ Reading Check *Why do surface waves damage buildings?*

Surface waves are produced when earthquake energy reaches the surface of Earth. Surface waves travel outward from the epicenter. The earthquake **epicenter** (EH pi sen tur) is the point on Earth's surface directly above the earthquake focus. Find the focus and epicenter in **Figure 9.**

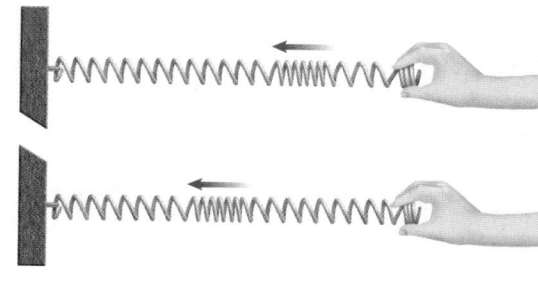

Figure 7
Primary waves move through Earth the same way that a wave travels through a coiled spring.

Physics
INTEGRATION

When sound is produced, waves move through air or some other material. Research sound waves to find out which type of seismic wave they are similar to.

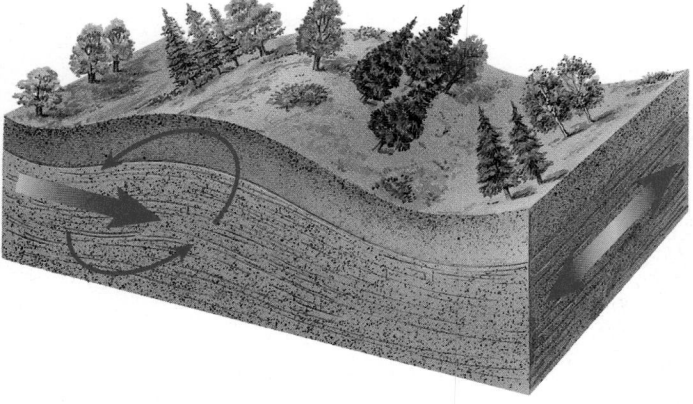

Figure 8
Surface waves move rock particles in a backward, rolling motion and a side-to-side, swaying motion. *How does this movement differ from rock movement caused by secondary waves?*

Visualizing Seismic Waves

Have students examine the pictures and read the captions. Then ask the following questions.

Which type of wave would a seismograph first record after an earthquake? A seismograph would first record a primary wave, then a secondary wave. Surface waves would be recorded last.

Why do some earthquakes cause more damage than others? Possible answers: Damage can be greater if the magnitude is higher or the focus is near Earth's surface. More damage also can occur if the epicenter is near populated areas or if buildings are not constructed to withstand earthquakes.

Activity

Have students demonstrate seismic waves using a coiled spring toy, stretched 1-2 meters on a table. Have a student hold one end of the spring firmly. Have another student demonstrate P-waves by quickly pushing the other end of the spring toward the first student. S-waves can be demonstrated by moving the spring up and down. Gently moving one end of the spring side to side while at the same time moving it in a rolling motion will demonstrates surface waves. Caution: Students should wear goggles when performing this activity.

Extension

Challenge your students to research the different types of surface waves and illustrate their movement.

Figure 9

As the plates that form Earth's lithosphere move, great stress is placed on rocks. They bend, stretch, and compress. Occasionally, rocks break, producing earthquakes that generate seismic waves. As shown here, different kinds of seismic waves—each with distinctive characteristics—move outward from the focus of the earthquake.

C The point on Earth's surface directly above an earthquake's focus is known as the epicenter. Surface waves spread out from the epicenter like ripples in a pond.

D The amplitudes, or heights, of surface waves are greater than those of primary and secondary waves. Surface waves cause the most damage during an earthquake.

B Primary waves and secondary waves originate at the focus and travel outward in all directions. Primary waves travel about twice as fast as secondary waves.

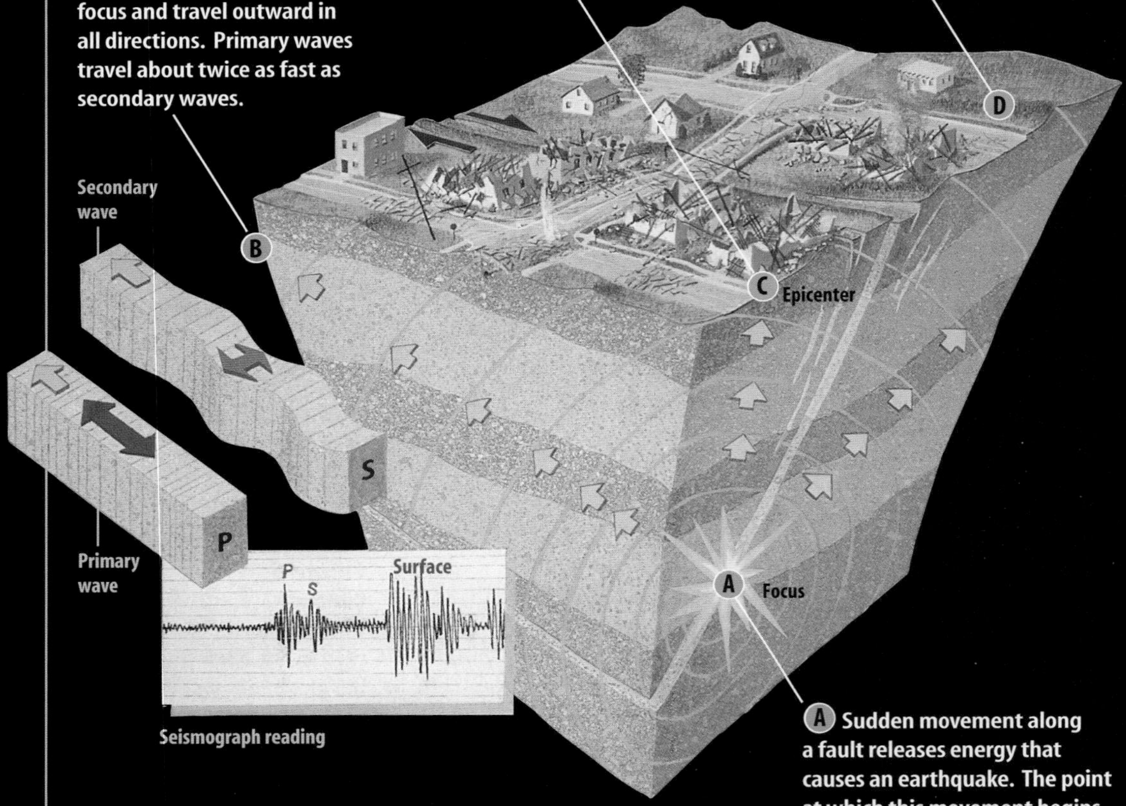

Secondary wave

Primary wave

Seismograph reading

Epicenter

Focus

A Sudden movement along a fault releases energy that causes an earthquake. The point at which this movement begins is called the earthquake's focus.

Resource Manager

Chapter Resources Booklet
Enrichment, p. 33
Lab Activity, pp. 9–13

Locating an Epicenter

Different seismic waves travel through Earth at different speeds. Primary waves are the fastest, secondary waves are slower, and surface waves are the slowest. Can you think of a way this information could be used to determine how far away an earthquake epicenter is? Think of the last time you saw two people running in a race. You probably noticed that the faster person got further ahead as the race continued. Like runners in a race, seismic waves travel at different speeds.

Scientists have learned how to use the different speeds of seismic waves to determine the distance to an earthquake epicenter. When an epicenter is far from a location, the primary wave has more time to put distance between it and the secondary and surface waves, just like the fastest runner in a race.

Measuring Seismic Waves Seismic waves from earthquakes are measured with an instrument known as a **seismograph.** Seismographs register the waves and record the time that each arrived. Seismographs consist of a rotating drum of paper and a pendulum with an attached pen. When seismic waves reach the seismograph, the drum vibrates but the pendulum remains at rest. The stationary pen traces a record of the vibrations on the moving drum of paper. The paper record of the seismic event is called a seismogram. **Figure 10** shows two types of seismographs that measure either vertical or horizontal ground movement, depending on the orientation of the drum.

SCIENCE *Online*

Research Visit the Glencoe Science Web site at **science.glencoe.com** to learn about the National Earthquake Information Center and the World Data Center for Seismology. Share what you learn with your class.

Figure 10
Seismographs differ according to whether they are intended to measure horizontal or vertical seismic motions. *Why can't one seismograph measure both horizontal and vertical motions?*

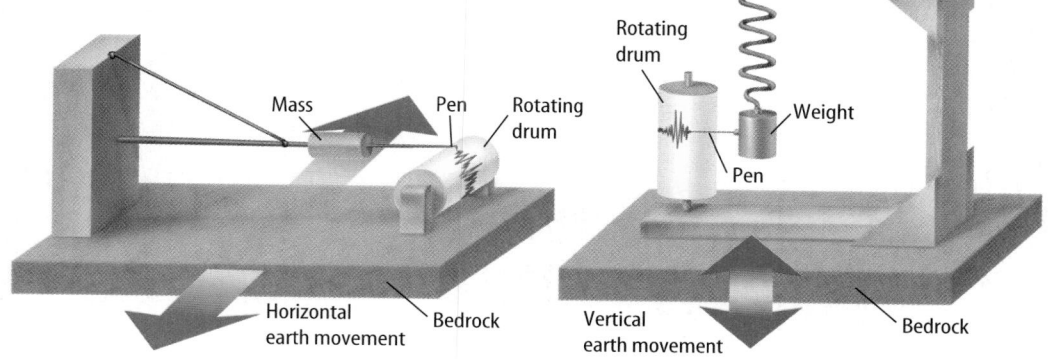

SECTION 2 Features of Earthquakes **311**

Locating an Epicenter

SCIENCE *Online*

Internet Addresses

_____

_____

_____

Explore the Glencoe Science Web site at **science.glencoe.com** to find out more about topics in this section.

Fun Fact

Primary waves travel at about 6.0 km/s, secondary waves at about 3.5 km/s, and surface waves at about 2.0 km/s through granite crust.

IDENTIFYING Misconceptions

Students may think that scientists can predict earthquakes. However, they can figure only the probability that an earthquake will happen in a certain place in the future based on scientific data. For example, geologists can't say for certain when the next major earthquake in San Francisco will happen. But they can estimate that the probability of a major earthquake there in the next 30 years is 67 percent.

Caption Answer

Figure 10 The drum on the seismograph can be oriented to measure either horizontal or vertical motion, but not both.

Science Journal

Landers Quake Have students write a summary in their Science Journals after researching the 1992 earthquake in Landers, California. Have them explain why this event is so important to the study of faults and earthquakes. Data obtained from the Landers quake may indicate that a new fault is being formed in that area of the desert. [P]

Teacher FYI

Primary waves generated at the focus of an earthquake travel outward through Earth's interior. Sometimes these waves enter Earth's atmosphere and cause the loud noises associated with earthquakes.

Locating an Epicenter, continued

Discussion

Would buildings on Earth's surface start to sway as soon as primary waves move out from the focus of a quake? Explain.
No; primary waves move more quickly than the surface waves that cause most of the damage during quakes.

Quick Demo

Place a large, flat pan of water in front of the class. Drop a small rock into the water. Have students observe the waves that are generated and write a paragraph in their Science Journals that explains how the wave movement in water is similar to the movement of certain types of earthquake waves at Earth's surface. L2 IS **Linguistic**

Caption Answer

Figure 11B The three stations are needed in order to pinpoint the exact location.

Figure 11
Primary waves arrive at a seismograph station before secondary waves do.

A This graph shows the distance that primary and secondary waves travel over time. By measuring the difference in arrival times, a seismologist can determine the distance to the epicenter.

Seismograph Stations Each type of seismic wave reaches a seismograph station at a different time based on its speed. Primary waves arrive first at seismograph stations, and secondary waves, which travel slower, arrive second, as shown in the graph in **Figure 11A.** Because surface waves travel slowest, they arrive at seismograph stations last.

If seismic waves reach three or more seismograph stations, the location of the epicenter can be determined. To locate an epicenter, scientists draw circles around each station on a map. The radius of each circle equals that station's distance from the earthquake epicenter. The point where all three circles intersect, shown in **Figure 11B,** is the location of the earthquake epicenter.

Seismologists usually describe earthquakes based on their distances from the seismograph. Local events occur less than 100 km away. Regional events occur 100 km to 1,400 km away. Teleseismic events are those that occur at distances greater than 1,400 km.

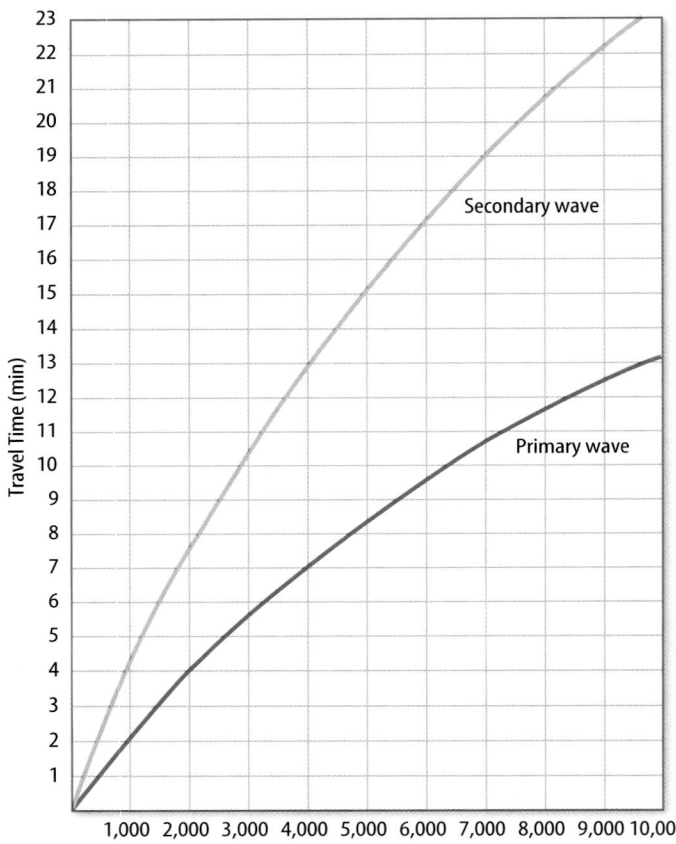

B The radius of each circle is equal to the distance from the epicenter to each seismograph station. The intersection of the three circles is the location of the epicenter. *Why is one seismograph station not enough?*

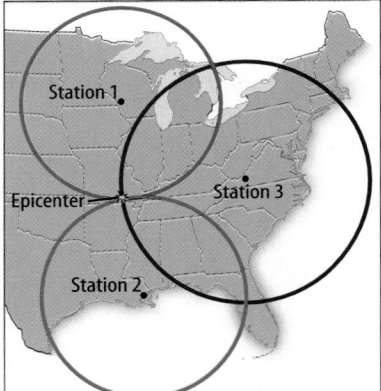

LAB DEMONSTRATION

Purpose to demonstrate each of the three types of seismic waves
Materials a coiled-spring toy
Preparation Tie pieces of string on the spring at five evenly spaced intervals.
Procedure Demonstrate primary waves by compressing about 20 coils together and releasing them, secondary waves by moving the spring from side to side, and a surface wave by moving the spring in an elliptical path while also moving it from side to side.
Expected Outcome Students will see that each wave causes a different type of movement in the material through which it is moving.

✓ *Assessment*

Ask students which type of wave would cause the most damage. Surface waves would cause the most damage because of the large amount of motion associated with them.

Basic Structure of Earth

Figure 12 shows Earth's internal structure. At the very center of Earth is a solid, dense inner core made mostly of iron with smaller amounts of nickel, oxygen, silicon, and sulfur. Pressure from the layers above causes the inner core to be solid. Above the solid inner core lies the liquid outer core, which also is made mainly of iron.

✓ Reading Check *How do the inner and outer cores differ?*

Earth's mantle is the largest layer, lying directly above the outer core. It is made mostly of silicon, oxygen, magnesium, and iron. The mantle often is divided into an upper part and a lower part based on changing seismic wave speeds. A portion of the upper mantle, called the asthenosphere (as THE nuh sfihr), consists of weak rock that can flow slowly.

Earth's Crust The outermost layer of Earth is the crust. Together, the crust and a part of the mantle just beneath it make up Earth's lithosphere (LIH thuh sfihr). The lithosphere is broken into a number of plates that move over the asthenosphere beneath it.

The thickness of Earth's crust varies. It is more than 60 km thick in some mountainous regions and less than 5 km thick under some parts of the oceans. Compared to the mantle, the crust contains more silicon and aluminum and less magnesium and iron. Earth's crust generally is less dense than the mantle beneath it.

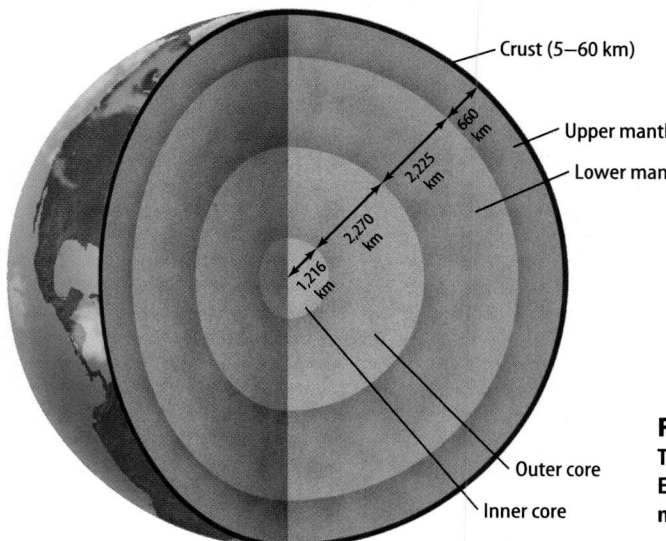
Crust (5–60 km)
660 km
2,225 km
2,270 km
1,216 km
Upper mantle
Lower mantle
Outer core
Inner core

Figure 12
The internal structure of Earth shows that it is made of different layers.

Mini LAB

Interpreting Seismic Wave Data

Procedure
1. Use the **graph** in **Figure 11** to determine the difference in arrival times for primary and secondary waves at the distances listed in the data table below. Two examples are provided for you.

Wave Data	
Distance (km)	**Difference in Arrival Time**
1,500	2 min, 45 s
2,250	
2,750	
3,000	
4,000	5 min, 55 s
7,000	
9,000	

2. Use the graph to determine the differences in arrival times for the other distances in the table.

Analysis
1. What happens to the difference in arrival times as the distance from the earthquake increases?
2. If the difference in arrival times at a seismograph station is 6 min, 30 s, how far away is the epicenter?

Basic Structure of Earth

Mini LAB

Purpose Students will use seismic wave data to determine the distance to an earthquake epicenter. [L2]
Logical-Mathematical [P]
Materials Figure 11 graph
Teaching Strategy Make sure students understand the graph before beginning.
Analysis
1. The difference in arrival times is a direct but not constant relationship. The difference in times increases with distance to the earthquake epicenter.
2. about 5,000 km

✓ Assessment

Performance Have students determine distances to earthquakes whose primary and secondary wave arrival times are separated by 5 minutes and 7 minutes. 5 min.—3,600 km; 7 min.—5,500 km Use **PASC,** p. 89.

✓ Reading Check

Answer The inner core is solid while the outer core is liquid.

Visual Learning

Figure 12 Which is the thinnest of Earth's layers? the crust

Basic Structure of Earth, continued

Make a Model

Have students make a model of Earth's interior using clay, cut paper, plaster of paris, or any other readily available materials. Have students share their models in a class presentation. L2

Kinesthetic

Using an Analogy

Explain to students that the internal structure of a peach is analogous to Earth's internal structure. The peach pit is like Earth's core. The meat of the peach, which is its thickest part, can be compared with the thickest part of Earth's interior, the mantle. The thin peach skin corresponds to Earth's crust, which is extremely thin compared with the planet's other layers.

> ✔ **Reading Check**

Answer They change speed as the density of rock inside Earth changes.

Mapping Earth's Internal Structure As shown in **Figure 13,** the speeds and paths of seismic waves change as they travel through materials with different densities. By studying seismic waves that have traveled through Earth, scientists have identified different layers with different densities. In general, the densities increase with depth as pressures increase. Studying seismic waves has allowed scientists to map Earth's internal structure without being there.

Early in the twentieth century, scientists discovered that large areas of Earth don't receive seismic waves from an earthquake. In the areas on Earth between 105° and 140° from the earthquake focus, no waves are detected. These areas, called shadow zones, also are shown in **Figure 13.** Secondary waves are not transmitted through a liquid, so they stop when they hit the liquid outer core. Primary waves are slowed and bent but not stopped by the liquid outer core. Because of this, scientists concluded that the outer core and mantle are made of different materials. Primary waves speed up again as they travel through the solid inner core. The bending of primary waves and the stopping of secondary waves create the shadow zones.

> ✔ **Reading Check** *Why do seismic waves change speed as they travel through Earth?*

Figure 13
Seismic waves bend and change speed as the density of rock changes. Primary waves bend when they contact the outer core, and secondary waves are stopped completely. This creates two shadow zones where no seismic waves are received.

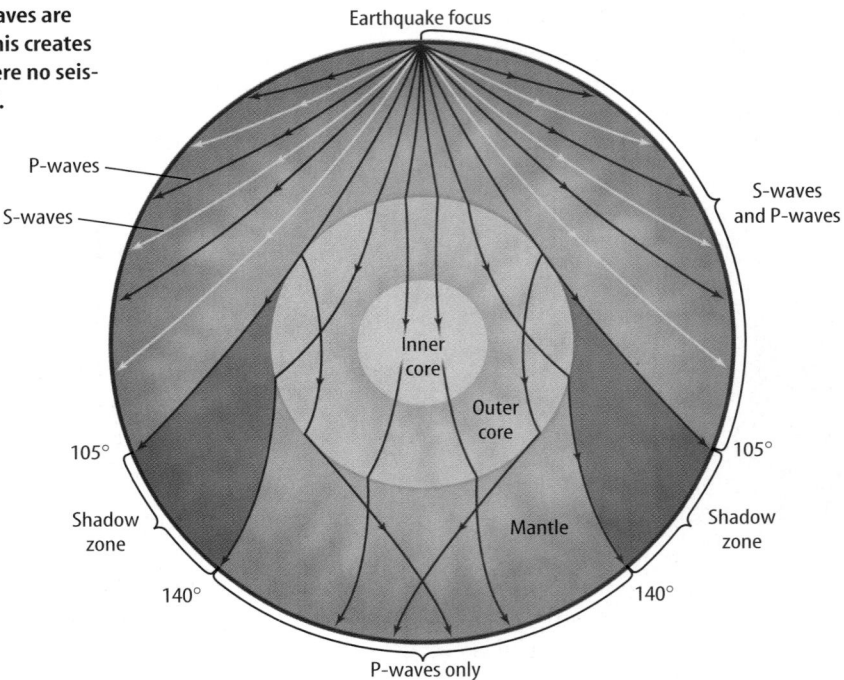

Resource Manager

Chapter Resources Booklet
Reinforcement, p. 30
Activity Worksheet, pp. 5–6

Inclusion Strategies

Learning Disabled To help these students, build a model of Earth's interior layers from modeling clay. First, make a ball of clay with a radius of 24 mm. Cut this ball in half and mold a 45-mm layer of different-colored clay around it. Around this second layer, mold a 58-mm-thick layer of a third color of clay. Mold a very thin layer of a fourth color around this third layer.

Layer Boundaries **Figure 14** shows how seismic waves change speed as they pass through layers of Earth. Seismic waves speed up when they pass through the bottom of the crust and enter the upper mantle, shown on the far left of the graph. This boundary between the crust and upper mantle is called the Mohorovicic discontinuity (moh huh ROH vuh chihch • dis kahn tuh NEW uh tee), or Moho.

The mantle is divided into layers based on changes in seismic wave speeds. For example, primary and secondary waves slow down again when they reach the asthenosphere. Then, they generally speed up as they move through a more solid region of the mantle below the asthenosphere.

The core is divided into two layers based on how seismic waves travel through it. Secondary waves do not travel through the liquid outer core, as you can see in the graph. Primary waves slow down when they reach the outer core, but they speed up again upon reaching the solid inner core.

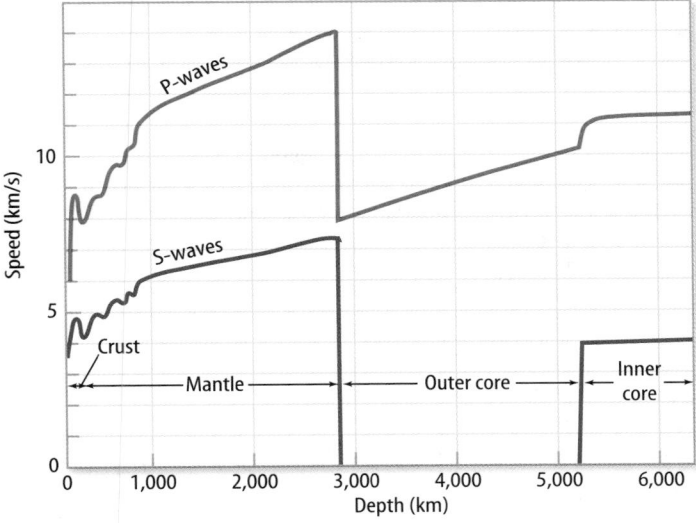

Seismic Wave Speeds

Figure 14
Changes in the speeds of seismic waves allowed scientists to detect boundaries between Earth's layers.

Section 2 Assessment

1. How many seismograph stations are needed to determine the location of an epicenter? Explain.

2. Name the layers of Earth's interior.

3. What makes up most of Earth's inner core?

4. What are the three types of seismic waves? Which one does the most damage to property?

5. **Think Critically** Why do some seismograph stations receive both primary and secondary waves from an earthquake but other stations don't?

Skill Builder Activities

6. **Predicting** What will happen to the distance between two opposite walls of a room as primary waves move through the room? **For more help, refer to the** Science Skill Handbook.

7. **Solving One-Step Equations** Primary waves travel about 6 km/s through Earth's crust. The distance from Los Angeles, California, to Phoenix, Arizona, is about 600 km. How long would it take primary waves to travel between the two cities? **For more help, refer to the** Math Skill Handbook.

Section 2 Features of Earthquakes **315**

Reteach
Work with students to devise a large chart on the bulletin board or chalkboard that lists the properties and effects of the different types of seismic waves covered in this section.

Challenge
Challenge students to write reports on the work of seismologists and other scientists who study earthquakes. Reports should include the types of places they work, what they do, and how their work is helpful to society. Encourage interested students to interview such a scientist about what he or she does. Have students share what they find in class. L2
LS **Linguistic**

✓ Assessment

Performance Assess students' abilities to make and use graphs. Ask students to use **Figure 11** and determine travel times for primary waves at a distance of 3,000 km, 4,000 km, and 6,000 km. 5 minutes, 30 s; 7 minutes, 10 s; 9 minutes, 30 s Use **Performance Assessment in the Science Classroom,** p. 89.

Answers to Section Assessment

1. Three; circles are drawn around each seismograph station representing the distance of the station from the earthquake epicenter. The point at which the circles around the three stations meet is the epicenter.

2. crust, mantle, outer core, inner core

3. iron

4. primary waves, secondary waves, surface waves; surface waves

5. Secondary waves do not pass through liquids; therefore, they are stopped by Earth's outer core. Seismograph stations within the outer core's secondary wave shadow zone, but beyond its primary wave shadow zone, will record only primary waves.

6. Particles within the walls will move back and forth in the direction that the wave is propagated. This would cause the walls to move toward and away from each other.

7. 100 seconds; 1 minute and 40 seconds

Epicenter Location

Purpose Students will interpret data on an earthquake wave distance-time graph to determine the locations of earthquake epicenters. L2 ELL COOP LEARN

LS **Logical-Mathematical** P

Process Skills using numbers, interpreting data, making and using tables, making and using graphs, comparing and contrasting

Time Required 45 minutes

Teaching Strategy Be sure students understand how to use **Figure 11** before beginning this activity.

Answers to Questions

1. The difference in arrival time between P- and S-waves increases as the distance of the seismograph station from the earthquake increases. This time interval can be used to calculate the distance between the seismograph and the earthquake.
2. A: Mexico City, Mexico; B: San Francisco, California
3. a minimum of three
4. Those seismograph stations were probably within the outer core's shadow zone.

I n this activity you can plot the distance of seismograph stations from the epicenters of earthquakes and determine the earthquake epicenters.

What You'll Investigate
Can plotting the distance of several seismograph stations from two earthquake epicenters allow you to determine the locations of the two epicenters?

Materials
string   globe
metric ruler   chalk

Goals
- **Plot** the distances of several seismograph stations based on primary and secondary wave arrival times.
- **Interpret** the location of earthquake epicenters from these plots.

Earthquake Data			
Location of Seismograph	Wave	Wave Arrival Times	
		Earthquake A	Earthquake B
New York, New York	P	2:24:05 P.M.	1:19:42 P.M.
	S	2:29:15 P.M.	1:25:27 P.M.
Seattle, Washington	P	2:24:40 P.M.	1:14:37 P.M.
	S	2:30:10 P.M.	1:16:57 P.M.
Rio de Janeiro, Brazil	P	2:29:10 P.M.	—
	S	2:37:50 P.M.	—
Paris, France	P	2:30:30 P.M.	1:24:57 P.M.
	S	2:40:10 P.M.	1:34:27 P.M.
Tokyo, Japan	P	—	1:24:27 P.M.
	S	—	1:33:27 P.M.

Procedure

1. Determine the difference in arrival time between the primary and secondary waves at each station for each earthquake listed in the table.
2. After you determine the arrival times of seismic waves for each seismograph station, use the graph in **Figure 11** to determine the distance in kilometers of each seismograph from the epicenter of each earthquake. Record these data in a data table. For example, the difference in arrival times in Paris for earthquake B is 9 min, 30 s. On the graph, the primary and secondary waves are separated along the vertical axis by 9 min, 30 s at a distance of 8,975 km.

3. Using the string, measure the circumference of the globe. Determine a scale of centimeters of string to kilometers on Earth's surface. (Earth's circumference is 40,000 km.)
4. For each earthquake, place one end of the string at each seismic station location on the globe. Use the chalk to draw a circle with a radius equal to the distance to the earthquake's epicenter.
5. **Identify** the epicenter for each earthquake.

Conclude and Apply

1. How is the distance of a seismograph from the earthquake related to the arrival times of the waves?
2. What is the location of the epicenter for each earthquake?
3. How many stations were needed to locate each epicenter accurately?
4. **Explain** why some seismographs didn't receive secondary waves from some quakes.

✓ Assessment

Performance Ask students to explain why data from two seismograph stations are not enough to locate an earthquake epicenter. Use **Performance Assessment in the Science Classroom**, p. 91.

Inclusion Strategies

Physically Challenged Help these students by assigning each one a partner who will provide support as he or she measures distances on the globe. Encourage helpers to provide each physically challenged student with just enough assistance to accomplish the task.

People and Earthquakes

Earthquake Activity

Imagine awakening in the middle of the night with your bed shaking, windows shattering, and furniture crashing together. That's what many people in Northridge, California, experienced at 4:30 A.M. on January 17, 1994. The ground beneath Northridge shook violently—it was an earthquake.

Although the earthquake lasted only 15 s, it killed 51 people, injured more than 9,000 people, and caused $44 billion in damage. More than 22,000 people were left homeless. **Figure 15A** shows some of the damage caused by the Northridge earthquake. **Figure 15B** shows the record of the Northridge earthquake on a seismogram.

Earthquakes are natural geological events that provide information about Earth. Unfortunately, they also cause billions of dollars in property damage and kill an average of 10,000 people every year. With so many lives lost and such destruction, it is important for scientists to learn as much as possible about earthquakes to try to reduce their impact on society.

As You Read

What You'll Learn
- **Explain** where most earthquakes in the United States occur.
- **Describe** how scientists measure earthquakes.
- **List** ways to make your classroom and home more earthquake-safe.

Vocabulary
magnitude
liquefaction
tsunami

Why It's Important
Earthquake preparation can save lives and reduce damage.

Figure 15
The 1994 Northridge, California, earthquake was a costly disaster. **A** Several major highways were damaged. **B** A seismograph made this record, called a seismogram, of the earthquake.

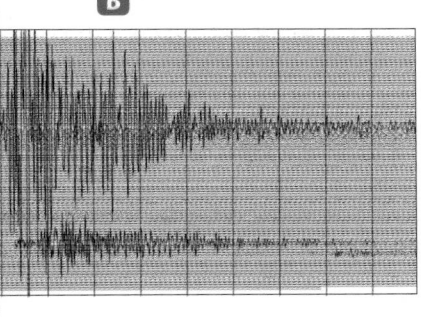

SECTION

People and Earthquakes

1 Motivate

Bellringer Transparency
Display the Section Focus Transparency for Section 3. Use the accompanying Transparency Activity Master. L2
ELL

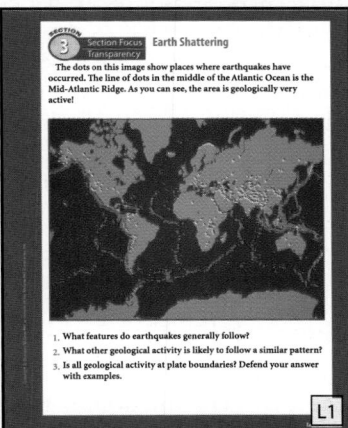

Tie to Prior Knowledge
Help students recall photographs of the destruction caused by earthquakes they may have seen in newspapers, in magazines, or on television.

Section ✓Assessment Planner

PORTFOLIO
Extension, p. 318

PERFORMANCE ASSESSMENT
Math Skills Activity, p. 321
MiniLAB, p. 322
Skill Builder Activities, p. 323
See page 330 for more options.

CONTENT ASSESSMENT
Section, p. 323
Challenge, p. 323
Chapter, pp. 330–331

Resource Manager

Chapter Resources Booklet
Transparency Activity, p. 48
Directed Reading for Content Mastery, pp. 23, 24

Earthquake Activity

Make a Model

Tape a stiff sheet of paper to the side of a closed shoe box. Have a volunteer slowly draw a straight line from the top of the sheet to the bottom. Then, have the volunteer attempt the same feat as another student bounces a small rubber ball on the top of the box. Use this model to explain how a seismograph works. **Ⓢ Visual-Spatial**

Extension

Have students write two or three paragraphs in their Science Journals about what it might be like at the epicenter of an earthquake. Encourage them to relate what might happen to buildings, bridges, and other structures. Have them address whether they would be able to feel any of the seismic waves they have learned about. L2 Ⓢ **Linguistic** P

Discussion

Instruct students to look at **Table 2. Why did some strong earthquakes cause so much loss of life while others caused little?** Possible answers: Some areas were more populous than others; the buildings in some areas were more able to withstand earthquake vibrations.

Visual Learning

Table 1 Ask students to identify the most powerful earthquake listed in the table. the 1960 earthquake in Chile Which earthquake resulted in the most deaths? the 1556 earthquake in China

Figure 16
The 1999 earthquake in Turkey released about 30 times more energy than the 1994 Northridge earthquake did.

Studying Earthquakes Scientists who study earthquakes and seismic waves are seismologists. As you learned earlier, the instrument that is used to record primary, secondary, and surface waves from earthquakes all over the world is called a seismograph. Seismologists can use records from seismographs, called seismograms, to learn more than just where the epicenter of an earthquake is located.

Measuring Earthquake Magnitude The height of the lines traced on the paper record of a seismograph is a measure of the energy that is released, or the **magnitude,** of the earthquake. The Richter scale is used most often to describe the strength of an earthquake and is based on the height of the lines on the seismogram. The Richter scale has no upper limit. However, scientists think that a value of about 9.5 would be the maximum strength an earthquake could register. For each increase of 1.0 on the Richter scale, the height of the line on a seismogram is ten times greater. However, about 30 times as much energy is released for every increase of 1.0 on the scale. For example, an earthquake with a magnitude of 8.5 releases about 30 times more energy than an earthquake with a magnitude of 7.5. **Figure 16** shows damage from the 7.8-magnitude earthquake in Turkey in 1999. **Table 1** is a list of some large-magnitude earthquakes that have occurred around the world and the damage they have caused.

Most of the earthquakes you hear about are large ones that cause great damage. However, of all the earthquakes detected throughout the world each year, most have magnitudes too low to be felt by humans. Scientists record thousands of earthquakes every day with magnitudes of less than 3.0. Each year, about 55,000 earthquakes are felt but cause little or no damage. These minor earthquakes have magnitudes that range from approximately 3.0 to 4.9 on the Richter scale.

Table 1 Large-Magnitude Earthquakes			
Year	Location	Magnitude	Deaths
1556	Shensi, China	?	830,000
1755	Lisbon, Portugal	8.8 (est.)	70,000
1811–12	New Madrid, MO	8.3 (est.)	few
1886	Charleston, SC	?	60
1906	San Francisco, CA	8.3	700 to 800
1923	Tokyo, Japan	9.2	143,000
1960	Chile	9.5	490 to 2,290
1964	Prince William Sound, AK	8.5	131
1976	Tangshan, China	8.2	242,000
1990	Iran	7.7	50,000
1995	Kobe, Japan	6.9	5,378
2000	Indonesia	7.9	90
2001	India	7.7	>15,000

318 CHAPTER 11 Earthquakes

Inclusion Strategies

Learning Disabled Have students use the information in **Table 1** to design and draw a time line of major earthquakes. Encourage students to illustrate the time line. Also encourage students to research other major earthquakes and add them to their timelines.

Describing Earthquake Intensity Earthquakes also can be described by the amount of damage they cause. The modified Mercalli intensity scale describes the intensity of an earthquake using the amount of structural and geologic damage in a specific location. The amount of damage done depends on the strength of the earthquake, the nature of surface material, the design of structures, and the distance from the epicenter. Under ideal conditions, only a few people would feel an intensity-I earthquake, and it would cause no damage. An intensity-IV earthquake would be felt by everyone indoors during the day but would be felt by only a few people outdoors. Pictures might fall off walls and books might fall from shelves. However, an intensity-IX earthquake would cause considerable damage to buildings and would cause cracks in the ground. An intensity-XII earthquake would cause total destruction of buildings, and objects such as cars would be thrown upward into the air. The 1994 6.8-magnitude earthquake in Northridge, California, was listed at an intensity of IX because of the damage it caused.

Liquefaction Have you ever tried to drink a thick milkshake from a cup? Sometimes the milkshake is so thick that it won't flow. How do you make the milkshake flow? You shake it. Something similar can happen to very wet soil during an earthquake. Wet soil can be strong most of the time, but the shaking from an earthquake can cause it to act more like a liquid. This is called **liquefaction.** When liquefaction occurs in soil under buildings, the buildings can sink into the soil and collapse, as shown in **Figure 17.** People living in earthquake regions should avoid building on loose soils.

Physics
INTEGRATION

In 1975, Chinese scientists successfully predicted an earthquake by measuring a slow tilt of Earth's surface and small changes in Earth's magnetism. Many lives were saved as a result of this prediction. Do research to find out why most earthquakes have not been predicted.

Physics
INTEGRATION

Many earthquakes occur with no prior warning. Seismologists can determine areas where earthquakes are likely to occur, but they can't determine exactly when.

Discussion

Why would the buildings in San Francisco's Marina district have been more susceptible to damage, having been built on a landfilled marsh? The soils of the filled-in marsh were probably not very compact and could be infiltrated with water, causing them to be susceptible to liquefaction.

Figure 17
San Francisco's Marina district suffered extensive damage from liquefaction in a 1989 earthquake because it is built on a landfilled marsh.

Teacher FYI

Moment Magnitude Moment magnitude, which is more precise than the Richter scale, is derived by multiplying the rigidity of the rock by the area of the fault rupture and then again by the amount of rock movement. This provides the seismic moment of the earthquake. Seismic moment is based on the concept of torque. The interaction of different segments of Earth on opposing sides of a fault set up internal torques that cause earthquakes. The magnitude usually first reported is Richter scale magnitude modified for modern equipment. After further study, the moment magnitude can be determined and is applied to the earthquake.

Earthquake Activity,
continued

SCIENCE *Online*
Internet Addresses

_____

_____

_____

Explore the Glencoe Science Web site at **science.glencoe.com** to find out more about topics in this section.

Extension

Have students research and report to the class on the Tsunami Warning System developed by the United States. The Tsunami Warning System was developed in 1948 after a tsunami hit the Aleutian and Hawaiian Islands two years earlier. After a 1964 Alaskan wave took 103 lives, an improved Regional TWS was developed. Now data from GOES (Geostationary Operational Environmental Satellite) satellites are able to help scientists issue tsunami warnings in as little as two minutes in some cases.

Caption Answer

Figure 18 Flooding could occur as the huge wave comes ashore. Buildings might be destroyed, boats and other objects on shore could be swept out to sea, and people could be killed.

SCIENCE *Online*

Research Visit the Glencoe Science Web site at **science.glencoe.com** for more information about tsunamis. Make a poster to illustrate what you learn.

Figure 18
A tsunami begins over the earthquake focus. *What might happen to towns located near the shore?*

Tsunamis Most earthquake damage occurs when surface waves cause buildings, bridges, and roads to collapse. People living near the seashore, however, have another problem. An earthquake under the ocean causes a sudden movement of the ocean floor. The movement pushes against the water, causing a powerful wave that can travel thousands of kilometers in all directions. Far from shore, a wave caused by an earthquake is so long that a large ship might ride over it without anyone noticing. But when one of these waves breaks on a shore, as shown in **Figure 18,** it forms a towering crest that can reach 30 m in height.

Ocean waves caused by earthquakes are called seismic sea waves, or **tsunamis** (soo NAH meez). Just before a tsunami crashes onto shore, the water along a shoreline might move rapidly toward the sea, exposing a large portion of land that normally is underwater. This should be taken as a warning sign that a tsunami could strike soon, and you should head for higher ground immediately.

Because of the number of earthquakes that occur around the Pacific Ocean, the threat of tsunamis is constant. To protect lives and property, a warning system has been set up in coastal areas and for the Pacific islands to alert people if a tsunami is likely to occur. The Pacific Tsunami Warning Center, located near Hilo, Hawaii, provides warning information including predicted tsunami arrival times at coastal areas.

However, even tsunami warnings can't prevent all loss of life. In the 1960 tsunami that struck Hawaii, 61 people died when they ignored the warning to move away from coastal areas.

320   CHAPTER 11 Earthquakes

Cultural **Diversity**

Tsunami! Tsunamis occur in many areas around the world and have been reported since ancient times. One of the earliest recorded tsunamis struck 1,400 km off the Chilean coast in 1562. Thera, one of the Cyclades Islands in the Mediterranean, may be the remnant of a volcano that erupted—causing tsunamis that ended the Minoan civilization on Crete. Tsunami is a Japanese word for "harbor wave."

Many have struck the Japanese shore. Because Japan is an island nation, the threat of tsunamis is a national safety concern. Today, by using expected tsunami characteristics, the Japan Meteorological Agency can forecast tsunami heights for the Japanese coastline. This provides residents with the knowledge necessary to move a safe distance away from the shore.

Earthquake Safety

You have learned that earthquakes can be destructive, but the damage and loss of life can be minimized. Although earthquakes cannot be predicted reliably, **Figure 19** shows where earthquakes are most likely to occur in the United States.

Knowing where large earthquakes are likely to occur helps in long-term planning. Cities in such regions can take action to prevent damage to buildings and loss of life. Many buildings withstood the 1989 San Francisco earthquake because they were built with the expectation that such an earthquake would occur someday.

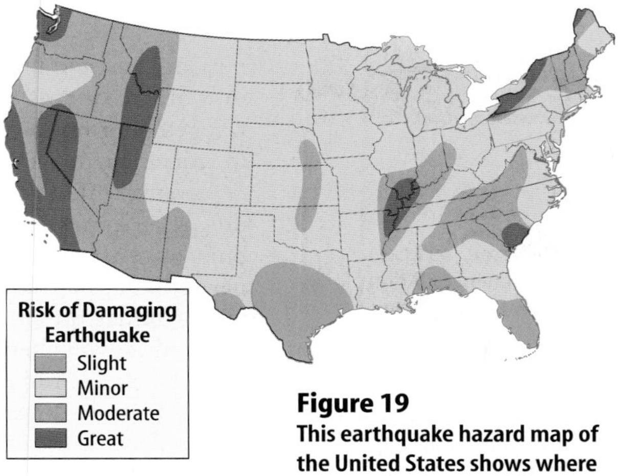

Risk of Damaging Earthquake
- Slight
- Minor
- Moderate
- Great

Figure 19
This earthquake hazard map of the United States shows where earthquakes are most likely to cause severe damage.

Math Skills Activity

Using Multiplication to Compare Earthquake Energy

Example Problem

The Richter scale is used to measure the magnitude of earthquakes. For each number increase on the Richter scale, 30 times more energy is released. How much more energy is released by a magnitude 6 earthquake than by a magnitude 3 earthquake?

Solution

1 *This is what you know:*   magnitude 6 earthquake, magnitude 3 earthquake energy increases 30 times per magnitude number

2 *This is what you need to find out:*   amount of additional energy released

3 *This is the procedure you need to use:*   Find the difference in magnitude numbers, then use that number of <u>multiples</u> of 30 to find the amount of additional energy released.

4 *Solve the equation:*   difference in magnitude = $6 - 3 = 3$
multiply 30 times itself 3 times: $30 \times 30 \times 30 = 27{,}000$
27,000 times more energy is released

Practice Problem

Calculate the difference in the amount of energy released between a magnitude 7 earthquake and a magnitude 2 earthquake.

For more help, refer to the Math Skill Handbook.

Earthquake Safety

Visual Learning

Figure 19 Have students determine whether your community has a high probability of having an earthquake. Answers will vary depending on your location.

Discussion

Of what use is a map that shows earthquake probability? It can alert people who live in certain areas of the country that there is a good chance they will experience an earthquake and that they should be prepared for one.

Math Skills Activity

National Math Standards
Correlation to Mathematics Objectives
1, 2, 9

Teaching Strategy

Follow the steps in the example problem. The difference in magnitude numbers is 5. Multiply 30 times itself 5 times.

Answer to Practice Problem

243,000,000 times more energy is released.

Science Journal

Tsunami at Papua New Guinea Have students search newspaper articles online to write brief descriptions in their Science Journals of the damage done when a tsunami hit the northern coast of Papua New Guinea, on July 17, 1998. Trees and houses were swept away by the tsunami and at least 2,000 people died.

Resource Manager

Chapter Resources Booklet
   Enrichment, p. 34
Mathematics Skill Activities, p. 9
Cultural Diversity, p. 47

Earthquake Safety,
continued

Text Question Answer
Buildings can be designed to withstand the shaking of earthquakes.

Mini LAB

Modeling Seismic-Safe Structures

Procedure
1. On a **tabletop,** build a structure out of **building blocks** by simply placing one block on top of another.
2. Build a second structure by wrapping sections of three blocks together with **rubber bands.** Then, wrap larger rubber bands around the entire completed structure.
3. Set the second structure on the tabletop next to the first one and pound on the side of the table with a slow, steady rhythm.

Analysis
1. Which of your two structures was better able to withstand the "earthquake" caused by pounding on the table?
2. How might the idea of wrapping the blocks with rubber bands be used in construction of supports for elevated highways?

Quake-Resistant Structures During earthquakes, buildings, bridges, and highways can be damaged or destroyed. Most loss of life during an earthquake occurs when people are trapped in or on these crumbling structures. What can be done to reduce loss of life?

Seismic-safe structures stand up to vibrations that occur during an earthquake. **Figure 20** shows how buildings can be built to resist earthquake damage. Today in California, some new buildings are held together by flexible, circular moorings placed under the buildings. The moorings are made of steel plates filled with alternating layers of rubber and steel. The rubber acts like a cushion to absorb earthquake waves. Tests have shown that buildings supported in this way should be able to withstand an earthquake measuring up to 8.3 on the Richter scale without major damage.

In older buildings, workers often install steel rods to reinforce building walls. Such measures protect buildings in areas that are likely to experience earthquakes.

✔ Reading Check *What are seismic-safe structures?*

Figure 20
The rubber portions of this building's moorings absorb most of the wave motion of an earthquake. The building itself only sways gently. *What purpose does the rubber serve?*

322   CHAPTER 11 Earthquakes

Curriculum Connection

Art Have students research what to do to keep safe during an earthquake. Then have them take one aspect of what they find and create a poster with one important "Earthquake Safety Tip." Hang the posters in class and use them as a foundation for a class discussion on earthquake safety.
IS Visual-Spatial

Before an Earthquake To make your home as earthquake-safe as possible, certain steps can be taken. To reduce the danger of injuries from falling objects, move heavy objects from high shelves and place them on lower shelves. Learn how to turn off the gas, water, and electricity in your home. To reduce the chance of fire from broken gas lines, make sure that hot-water heaters and other gas appliances are held securely in place, as shown in **Figure 21**. A newer method that is being used to minimize the danger of fire involves placing sensors on gas lines. The sensors automatically shut off the gas when earthquake vibrations are detected.

During an Earthquake If you're indoors, move away from windows and any objects that could fall on you. Seek shelter in a doorway or under a sturdy table or desk. If you're outdoors, stay in the open—away from power lines or anything that might fall. Stay away from buildings—chimneys or other parts of buildings could fall on you.

After an Earthquake Check water and gas lines for damage. If any are damaged, shut off the valves. If you smell gas, leave the building immediately and call authorities from a phone away from the leak area. Stay out of and away from damaged buildings. Be careful around broken glass and rubble that could contain sharp edges and wear boots or sturdy shoes to keep from cutting your feet. Finally, stay away from beaches. Tsunamis sometimes hit after the ground has stopped shaking.

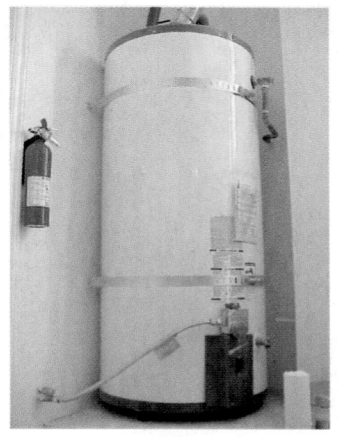

Figure 21
Securing gas water heaters to walls with sturdy straps helps reduce the danger of fires from broken gas lines.

Section ③ Assessment

1. How can you determine whether or not you live in an area where an earthquake is likely to occur?

2. What can you do to make your home more safe during an earthquake?

3. How is earthquake magnitude measured?

4. Name three ways that an earthquake can cause damage.

5. **Think Critically** How are shock absorbers on a car similar to the circular moorings used in modern earthquake-safe buildings? How do they absorb shock?

Skill Builder Activities

6. **Forming Hypotheses** Hypothesize why some earthquakes with smaller magnitudes result in more deaths than earthquakes with larger magnitudes. **For more help, refer to the** Science Skill Handbook.

7. **Solving One-Step Equations** What is the difference in energy released between an earthquake of Richter magnitude 8.5 and one of magnitude 4.5? Between one of magnitude 3.5 and one of magnitude 5.5? **For more help, refer to the** Math Skill Handbook.

SECTION 3 People and Earthquakes **323**

Activity

What You'll Investigate

Purpose

Students investigate whether there is a relationship between the depth of earthquake foci and epicenter locations and the movements of plates. [L2]

COOP LEARN

Ⓛⓢ Logical-Mathematical [P]

Process Skills

observing and inferring, communicating, using numbers, interpreting data, hypothesizing, using tables, making and using graphs, comparing and contrasting, separating and controlling variables

Time Required

45 minutes

Procedure

Teaching Strategies

- Review the definitions of focus and epicenter before starting the activity.
- Draw a blank version of the focus depth versus distance graph. Indicate the location of the coast on the graph. Help students begin by plotting the first two locations.

Expected Outcome

Students should find that earthquake foci occur deeper the farther they are from the shore.

Activity

Earthquake Depths

You learned earlier in this chapter that Earth's crust is broken into sections called plates. Stresses caused by movement of these plates generate energy within rocks that must be released. When this release of energy is sudden and rocks break, an earthquake occurs.

What You'll Investigate

Can a study of the foci of earthquakes tell you anything about plate movement in a particular region?

Goals

- **Observe** any connection between earthquake-focus depth and epicenter location using the data provided on the next page.
- **Describe** any observed relationship between earthquake-focus depth and the movement of plates at Earth's surface.

Materials

graph paper
pencil

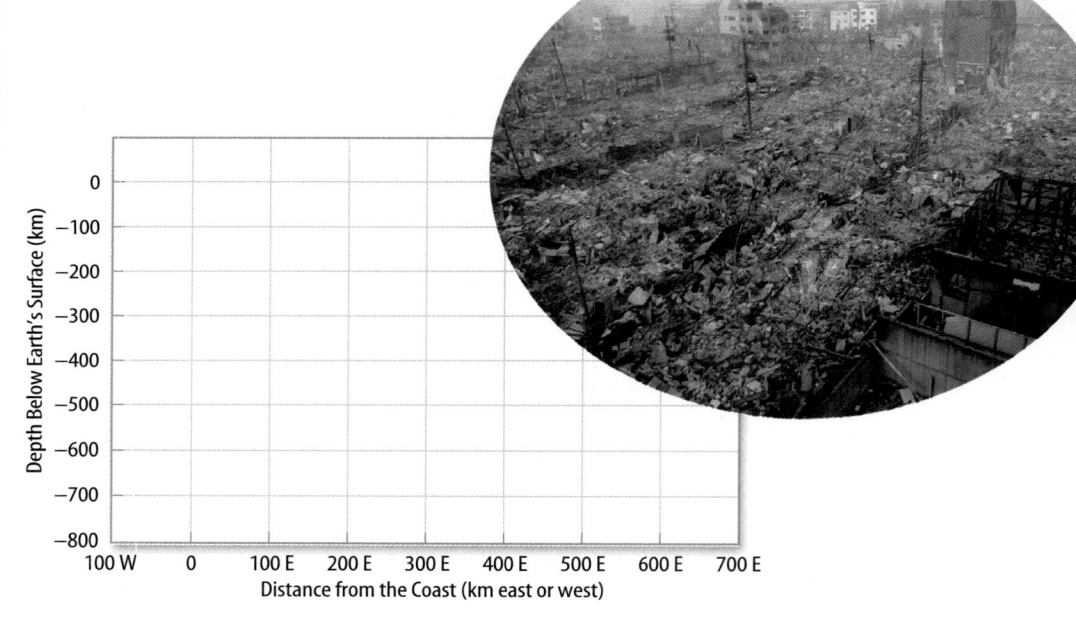

324 CHAPTER 11 Earthquakes

Curriculum Connection

Geography Have students research where on Earth the distribution of earthquake foci might be similar to that in this activity. Possible answer: the west coast of South America

Inclusion Strategies

Visually Impaired Ask some of your students to prepare copies of the maps and charts being used in this activity in a manner useful to those who are visually impaired. Outline the locations under study with thick lines, and identify earthquake foci by raised bumps on the maps. Students who are able could produce maps and charts using Braille.

Procedure

1. Use graph paper and the data table on the right to make a line graph plotting the depths of earthquake foci and the distances from the coast of a continent for each earthquake epicenter.

2. Use the graph on the previous page as a reference to draw your own graph. Place *Distance from the Coast* on the horizontal axis. Begin labeling at the far left with 100 km west. To the right of it should be 0 km, then 100 km east, 200 km east, 300 km east, and so on through 700 km east. What point on your graph represents the coast?

3. Label the vertical axis *Depth Below Earth's Surface.* Label the top of the graph 0 km to represent Earth's surface. Label the bottom of the vertical axis −800 km.

4. **Plot** the focus depths against the distance and direction from the coast for each earthquake in the table to the right.

Conclude and Apply

1. **Describe** any observed relationship between the location of earthquake epicenters and the depth of earthquake foci.

2. Based on the graph you have completed, hypothesize what is happening to the plates at Earth's surface in the vicinity of the plotted earthquake foci.

3. **Infer** what process is causing the earthquakes you plotted on your graph paper.

4. Hypothesize why none of the plotted earthquakes occurred below 700 km.

5. Based on what you have plotted, infer what continent these data could apply to. Explain what you based your answer on.

Focus and Epicenter Data

Earthquake	Focus Depth (km)	Distance of Epicenter from Coast (km)
A	−55	0
B	−295	100 east
C	−390	455 east
D	−60	75 east
E	−130	255 east
F	−195	65 east
G	−695	400 east
H	−20	40 west
I	−505	695 east
J	−520	390 east
K	−385	335 east
L	−45	95 east
M	−305	495 east
N	−480	285 east
O	−665	545 east
P	−85	90 west
Q	−525	205 east
R	−85	25 west
S	−445	595 east
T	−635	665 east
U	−55	95 west
V	−70	100 west

ommunicating
Your Data

Compare your graph with those of other members of your class. **For more help, refer to the** Science Skill Handbook.

ACTIVITY   325

Conclude and Apply

Answers to Questions

1. The earthquakes near the coast are shallow-focus earthquakes. Moving inland, the earthquake foci become progressively deeper.

2. Two plates are colliding, with one possibly being subducted beneath the other.

3. It's possible that an ocean plate is sliding beneath a land plate. As one plate slides under the other, earthquakes occur at increasing depth.

4. Generally, earthquakes occur because of the fracturing of solids. Because of the heat and pressure at a depth of 700 km, the consistency of rock material is like plastic, and stress is absorbed without fracturing.

5. South America, part of North America

Error Analysis

Students who do not get the correct outcome should check whether they have transferred data correctly from the table to the graph. Incorrect plotting of the graph itself also could introduce errors.

Assessment

Process Ask students to draw the plate boundary described by the data in this activity. Students should draw a convergent boundary where a sea plate meets a land plate and the sea plate is subducted. Use **Performance Assessment in the Science Classroom,** p. 127.

Resource Manager

Chapter Resources Booklet
    Activity Worksheet, pp. 7–8
Lab Management and Safety, p. 65

ommunicating
Your Data

Use a spreadsheet computer program to make a line graph to display the focus and epicenter data.

Science Stats

Science Stats

Moving Earth!

Did you know...

... The most powerful earthquake to hit the United States in recorded history shook Alaska in 1964. At 9.2 on the Richter scale, the quake shook all of Alaska for nearly 5 min, which is a long time for an earthquake. Nearly 320 km of roads near Anchorage suffered damage, and almost half of the 204 bridges had to be rebuilt.

... Snakes can sense the vibrations made by a small rodent up to 23 m away. Does this mean that they can detect vibrations prior to major earthquakes? Unusual animal behavior was observed just before a 1969 earthquake in China—an event that was successfully predicted.

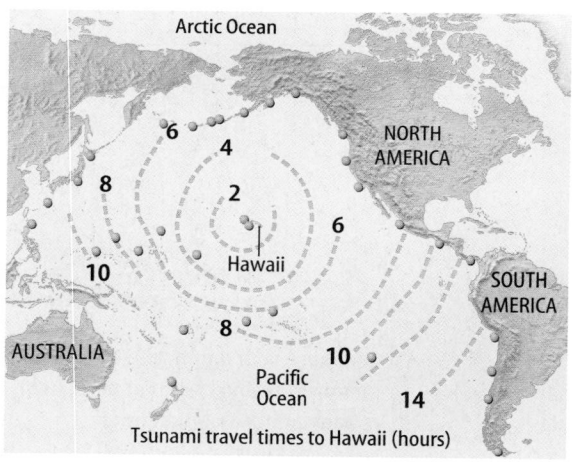

Tsunami travel times to Hawaii (hours)

... Earthquakes beneath the ocean floor can cause seismic sea waves, or tsunamis. Traveling at speeds of up to 950 km/h—as fast as a commercial jet—a tsunami can strike with little warning. Since 1945, more people have been killed by tsunamis than by the ground shaking from earthquakes.

326 **CHAPTER 11** Earthquakes

Content Background

Students might have heard tsunamis referred to as tidal waves. This term is incorrect, as tsunamis have nothing to do with tides. The word *tsunami* actually means "tidal wave" in Japanese, but has become the accepted term for waves generated by seismic activity. Sometimes a drop in sea level precedes the arrival of a tsunami. People have been killed after moving out to inspect exposed sea life, and then suddenly being faced with a fast-moving wall of water.

Discussion

• **What preparations for a tsunami could the people of Hawaii make if given several hours notice?** They could move ships out of harbors to the open sea and evacuate low-lying areas.

• **How might the duration of an earthquake contribute to its severity?** The longer the shaking, the more opportunity for damage. The psychological toll exacted by an earthquake on residents is greater the longer the shaking continues.

Activity

Have the class act out the nearly five minute duration of the Alaskan earthquake, imagining the panic and dangers involved. Use a stopwatch to give them accurate start and end times. Have them record their impressions in their science journals.

Kinesthetic and Linguistic

SCIENCE Online
Internet Addresses

Explore the Glencoe Science Web site at **science.glencoe.com** to find out more about topics in this section.

... Tsunamis can reach heights of 30 m. A wave that tall would knock over this lighthouse.

... On December 16, 1811 a strong earthquake occurred near New Madrid, Missouri. This earthquake was so strong that it changed the course of the Mississippi River. The earthquake also was reported to have rung the bell of St. Phillip's Steeple in Charleston, South Carolina.

Do the Math

1. On the Richter scale, a whole number increase means that the height of the largest recorded seismic wave increases by ten. How much higher is the largest wave from an 8.5 earthquake than the largest wave from a 3.5 earthquake?
2. Look at the tsunami warning system map on the previous page. About how long would a tsunami triggered near the Aleutian Islands take to reach Hawaii?

Go Further

Visit the Glencoe Science Web site at **science.glencoe.com.** Research the history and effects of earthquakes in the United States. Describe how the San Francisco earthquake of 1906 stimulated earthquake research.

SCIENCE STATS   327

Do the Math

Teaching Strategies

- Help students to identify what fact(s) they have been given and what they are asked to solve in the first Do the Math problem. Then have students determine which operation or operations they can use to solve the problem.
- To help students complete the second question in Do the Math, have them inspect the diagram showing tsunami travel times. Discuss what the dotted lines show.

Answers

1. 50 times higher
2. 6 hours

Go Further

Have students make charts to organize what they learn about various U.S. earthquakes. They can include columns to show the date, location, magnitude and effects of each earthquake.

Visual Learning

Earthquakes Beneath the Ocean Floor What is presumed to be occurring on each of the dotted lines shown in the diagram? earthquakes Use the times shown in the diagram to extrapolate: Predict how much time it would take a tsunami to reach Hawaii from an earthquake occurring near the southern tip of South America. About 16 hours **Approximately how distant is the epicenter of an earthquake if it takes 15 hours for the tsunami to reach Hawaii?** 15 hours times 950 km/h equals 14,250 km.

Chapter 11 Study Guide

Reviewing Main Ideas

Preview

Students can answer the questions in their Science Journals. Discuss the answers as you go through the chapter. **Linguistic**

Review

Students can write their answers, then compare them with those of other students. **Interpersonal**

Reteach

Students can look at the illustrations and describe details that support the main ideas of the chapter. **Visual-Spatial**

Answers to Chapter Review

SECTION 1

3. a normal fault

SECTION 2

1. surface waves

2. San Francisco

SECTION 3

1. a seismogram

Reviewing Main Ideas

Section 1 Forces Inside Earth

1. Plate movements put stress on rocks. To a certain point, the rocks bend and stretch. If the force is beyond the elastic limit, the rocks might break.

2. Earthquakes are vibrations that are created when rocks break along a fault.

3. Normal faults form when rocks undergo tension. Compression produces reverse faults. Strike-slip faults result from shearing forces. *What type of fault is shown here?*

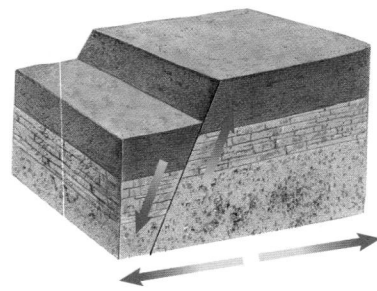

Section 2 Features of Earthquakes

1. Primary waves compress and stretch rock particles as the waves move. Secondary waves move by causing particles in rocks to move at right angles to the direction of the

waves. Surface waves move in a backward rolling motion and a side-to-side swaying motion. *Which kind of earthquake wave caused the damage shown here?*

2. Scientists can locate earthquake epicenters by recording seismic waves. *Where is the epicenter of the earthquake shown here?*

3. By observing the speeds and paths of seismic waves, scientists are able to determine the boundaries between Earth's internal layers.

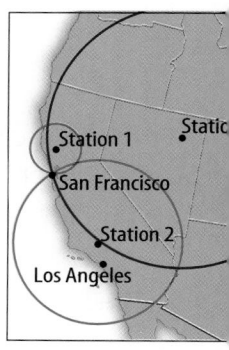

Section 3 People and Earthquakes

1. A seismograph is the instrument used to measure earthquake magnitude. *What is this record of an earthquake produced by a seismograph called?*

2. The magnitude of an earthquake is a measure of the energy released by the quake. The Richter scale describes how much energy an earthquake releases. The scale has no upper limit.

3. Earthquakes can cause liquefaction of wet soil and tsunamis, both of which increase the amount of structural damage produced by an earthquake.

FOLDABLES
Reading & Study Skills

After You Read

Using what you learned in this chapter, list and explain the effects of earthquakes on the inside of your Foldable.

FOLDABLES
Reading & Study Skills

After You Read

After students have read the chapter and completed the Foldable described in Before You Read, have them do the activity on the student page.

Dinah Zike

Visualizing Main Ideas

Complete the following concept map on earthquake damage.

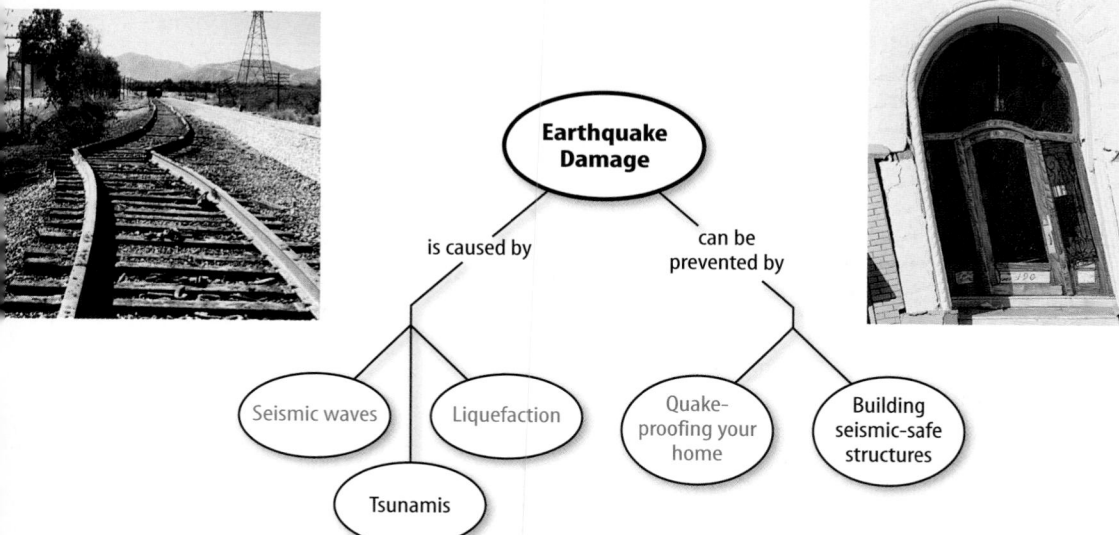

Visualizing Main Ideas

See student page.

Vocabulary Review

Using Vocabulary

1. surface waves
2. strike-slip fault
3. epicenter
4. magnitude
5. tsunami

Vocabulary Review

Vocabulary Words

a. earthquake
b. epicenter
c. fault
d. focus
e. liquefaction
f. magnitude
g. normal fault
h. primary wave
i. reverse fault
j. secondary wave
k. seismic wave
l. seismograph
m. strike-slip fault
n. surface wave
o. tsunami

THE PRINCETON REVIEW **Study Tip**

Be a teacher! Gather a group of friends and assign each one a section of the chapter to teach. Teaching helps you remember and understand information.

Using Vocabulary

Replace the underlined words with the correct vocabulary words.

1. Most earthquake damage results from <u>primary waves</u>.

2. At a <u>normal fault</u>, rocks move past each other without much upward or downward movement.

3. The point on Earth's surface directly above the earthquake focus is the <u>fault</u>.

4. The measure of the energy released during an earthquake is its <u>seismograph</u>.

5. An earthquake under the ocean can cause a <u>surface wave</u> that travels thousands of kilometers.

CHAPTER STUDY GUIDE 329

IDENTIFYING ▷ Misconceptions

Assess

Use the assessment as follow-up to page 305F after students have completed the chapter.

Activity Have students bring in newspaper articles describing earthquakes around the world. Have the class work together to make a bulletin board display showing the location of different earthquakes, and describing their intensity and the damage done. Have students compare their findings with the map in **Figure 2**. Have students explain why earthquakes are found where they are, and why everyone should know how to respond to an earthquake.

Checking Concepts

1. C
2. A
3. B
4. B
5. A
6. B
7. B
8. D
9. A
10. C

Thinking Critically

11. The earthquake generated tsunamis that caused the damage.
12. It is unlikely that anything will fall on him or her.
13. If the pendulum remains still, any movement recorded by the attached pen will be the result of seismic waves.
14. Tsunamis are caused by earthquakes on the ocean floor and have nothing to do with tides.
15. The single-story wood-frame house; the wood would probably give more with vibrations than would bricks, which are more likely to crumble and fall apart.

Chapter 11 Assessment

Checking Concepts

Choose the word or phrase that best answers the question.

1. Earthquakes can occur when which of the following is passed?
   A) tension limit
   B) seismic unit
   C) elastic limit
   D) shear limit

2. When the rock above the fault surface moves down relative to the rock below the fault surface, what kind of fault forms?
   A) normal
   B) strike-slip
   C) reverse
   D) shearing

3. From which of the following do primary and secondary waves move outward?
   A) epicenter
   B) focus
   C) Moho
   D) tsunami

4. What kind of earthquake waves stretch and compress rocks?
   A) surface
   B) primary
   C) secondary
   D) shear

5. What are the slowest seismic waves?
   A) surface
   B) primary
   C) secondary
   D) pressure

6. What is the fewest number of seismograph stations that are needed to locate the epicenter of an earthquake?
   A) two
   B) three
   C) four
   D) five

7. What happens to primary waves when they pass from liquids into solids?
   A) slow down
   B) speed up
   C) stay the same
   D) stop

8. What part of a seismograph does not move during an earthquake?
   A) sheet of paper
   B) fixed frame
   C) drum
   D) pendulum

9. How much more energy does an earthquake of magnitude 7.5 have than an earthquake of magnitude 6.5?
   A) 30 times more
   B) 30 times less
   C) twice as much
   D) about half as much

10. What are the recorded lines from an earthquake called?
    A) seismograph
    B) Mercalli scale
    C) seismogram
    D) Richter scale

Thinking Critically

11. The 1960 earthquake in the Pacific Ocean off the coast of Chile caused damage and loss of life in Chile and also in Hawaii, Japan, and other areas along the Pacific Ocean border. How could this earthquake do so much damage to areas thousands of kilometers from its epicenter?

12. Why is a person who is standing outside in an open field relatively safe during a strong earthquake?

13. Explain why the pendulum of a seismograph remains at rest.

14. Tsunamis often are called tidal waves. Explain why this is incorrect.

15. Which probably would be more stable during an earthquake—a single-story wood-frame house or a brick building? Explain.

Developing Skills

16. **Communicating** Imagine you are a science reporter assigned to interview the mayor about the earthquake safety of buildings in your city. What buildings would you be most concerned about? Make a list of questions about earthquake safety that you would ask the mayor.

Chapter ✓*Assessment* Planner

Portfolio Encourage students to place in their portfolios one or two items of what they consider to be their best work. Examples include:

- Activity, p. 306
- Science Journal, p. 311
- Extension, p. 318

Performance Additional performance assessments, Performance Task Assessment Lists, and rubrics for evaluating these activities can be found in Glencoe's **Performance Assessment in the Science Classroom.**

17. Measuring in SI Use an atlas and a metric ruler to answer the following question. Primary waves travel at about 6 km/s in continental crust. How long would it take a primary wave to travel from San Francisco, California, to Reno, Nevada?

18. Interpreting Data Use the data table below and a map of the United States to determine the location of the earthquake epicenter.

Seismograph Station Data			
Station	Latitude	Longitude	Distance from Earthquake
1	45° N	120° W	1,300 km
2	35° N	105° W	1,200 km
3	40° N	115° W	790 km

19. Forming Hypotheses Hypothesize how seismologists could assign Richter magnitudes to earthquakes that occurred before modern seismographs and the Richter scale were developed.

Performance Assessment

20. Model Use layers of different colors of clay to illustrate the three different kinds of faults. Label each model, explaining the forces involved and the rock movement.

21. Display Make a display showing why data from two seismograph stations are not enough to determine the location of an earthquake epicenter.

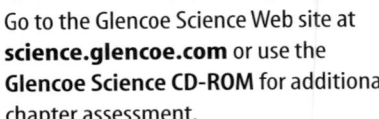

THE PRINCETON REVIEW — Test Practice

Seismologists used the modified Mercalli intensity scale to determine the intensity of the same earthquake from four different cities. They recorded their data in the following table.

Earthquake Intensity	
City	Intensity
A	VII
B	X
C	V
D	IX

Study the table and answer the following questions.

1. According to the table, which city probably was the closest to the epicenter of the earthquake?
  A) city B
  B) city D
  C) city A
  D) city C

2. Which of the following would be an accurate conclusion based on the intensity in city B?
  F) The earthquake was not felt by very many people.
  G) The earthquake destroyed well-built wooden and stone structures.
  H) Destruction was minimal. Dishes rattled in cabinets, and pictures fell off of walls.
  J) The earthquake was only felt indoors.

THE PRINCETON REVIEW — Test Practice

The Test-Taking Tip was written by The Princeton Review, the nation's leader in test preparation.
1. B
2. G

Developing Skills

16. Most concern: hospital, police and fire stations; Do you have an emergency plan in place in case of major earthquake damage? Have you educated the public about what to do? Are buildings earthquake resistant? Accept all reasonable answers.
17. about 61 seconds (d = 367 km)
18. The epicenter is near (just south of) Los Angeles, California.
19. It could be done by comparing the amount of damage done by early earthquakes to damage done by earthquakes today when the magnitude is known.

Performance Assessment

20. Models should show the relative movement of rock layers and the direction of forces acting at the fault. Use **Performance Assessment in the Science Classroom**, p. 123.
21. Answers will vary but students should conclude that the third location is needed to pinpoint the location of the epicenter.

Section/Objectives	Standards		Activities/Features
Chapter Opener	**National**	**State/Local**	**Explore Activity:** Map a volcano, p. 333
	See p. 5T for a Key to Standards.		**Before You Read,** p. 333
Section 1 Volcanoes and Earth's Moving Plates 🕐 2 sessions 📦 1 block 1. **Describe** how volcanoes can affect people. 2. **List** conditions that cause volcanoes to form. 3. **Identify** the relationship between volcanoes and Earth's moving plates.	National Content Standards: UCP3, A1, D1, F3		**Astronomy Integration,** p. 336 **MiniLAB:** Modeling Magma Movement, p. 338
Section 2 Types of Volcanoes 🕐 2 sessions 📦 1 block 1. **Explain** how the explosiveness of a volcanic eruption is related to the silica and water vapor content of its magma. 2. **List** three forms of volcanoes.	National Content Standards: UCP3, A1, B1, D1, F3		**Science Online,** p. 341 **Visualizing Lava,** p. 342 **MiniLAB:** Modeling Volcanic Cones, p. 344 **Activity:** Identifying Types of Volcanoes, p. 348
Section 3 Igneous Rock Features 🕐 3 sessions 📦 1.5 blocks 1. **Describe** intrusive igneous rock features and how they form. 2. **Explain** how a volcanic neck and a caldera form.	National Content Standards: UCP3, A1, B1, D1, G2		**Math Skill Activity:** Classifying Igneous Rock, p. 350 **Science Online,** p. 351 **Activity:** How do calderas form?, p. 354 **Oops! Accidents in Science:** Buried in Ash, p. 356

NATIONAL GEOGRAPHIC   Teacher's Corner

PRODUCTS AVAILABLE FROM GLENCOE
To order call 1-800-334-7344:
CD-ROM
NGS PictureShow: Dynamic Earth
Curriculum Kits
GeoKit: Dynamic Earth
GeoKit: Earth's Crust

Transparency Set
NGS PicturePack: Dynamic Earth
Videodisc
STV: Restless Earth

PRODUCTS AVAILABLE FROM
NATIONAL GEOGRAPHIC SOCIETY
To order call 1-800-368-2728:

Videos
Changing Earth: Forces That Create, Forces That Destroy
Living on Our Changing Planet
Our Dynamic Earth
Volcano!

Activity Materials	Reproducible Resources	Section Assessment	Technology
Explore Activity: one-half of a foam ball, metric ruler, permanent marker	**Chapter Resources Booklet** Foldables Worksheet, p. 15 Directed Reading Overview, p. 17 Note-taking Worksheets, pp. 31–33	GLENCOE'S **ASSESSMENT** ADVANTAGE	
MiniLAB: water, 2 transparent plastic cups, olive oil, dropper *Need materials?* Contact Science Kit at 1-800-828-7777 or www.sciencekit.com on the Internet.	**Chapter Resources Booklet** Transparency Activity, p. 42 MiniLAB, p. 3 Enrichment, p. 28 Reinforcement, p. 25 Directed Reading, p. 18 Transparency Activity, pp. 45–46 Lab Activity, pp. 9–10 **Cultural Diversity,** p. 47 **Science Inquiry Labs,** p. 35	**Portfolio** Science Journal, p. 337 Challenge, p. 339 **Performance** MiniLAB, p. 338 Skill Builder Activities, p. 339 **Content** Section Assessment, p. 339	Section Focus Transparency Teaching Transparency Interactive CD-ROM/DVD Guided Reading Audio Program
MiniLAB: dry sand or sugar, 2 paper plates, plaster of paris, protractor **Activity: Table 1,** paper, pencil	**Chapter Resources Booklet** Transparency Activity, p. 43 MiniLAB, p. 4 Enrichment, p. 29 Reinforcement, p. 26 Directed Reading, p. 18 Lab Activity, pp. 11–14 Activity Worksheet, pp. 5–6 **Reading and Writing Skill Activities,** p. 27	**Portfolio** Extension, p. 342 **Performance** MiniLAB, p. 344 Skill Builder Activities, p. 347 **Content** Section Assessment, p. 347	Section Focus Transparency Interactive CD-ROM/DVD Guided Reading Audio Program
MiniLAB: small box, small balloon, paper, newspaper, flour, plastic tubing, clamp for tubing, tape, scissors	**Chapter Resources Booklet** Transparency Activity, p. 44 Enrichment, p. 30 Reinforcement, p. 27 Directed Reading, pp. 19, 20 Activity Worksheet, pp. 7–8 **Mathematics Skill Activities,** p. 43 **Lab Management and Safety,** p. 38	**Portfolio** Extension, p. 352 **Performance** Math Skills Activity, p. 350 Skill Builder Activities, p. 353 **Content** Section Assessment, p. 353	Section Focus Transparency Interactive CD-ROM/DVD Guided Reading Audio Program

End of Chapter Assessment

GLENCOE'S **ASSESSMENT** ADVANTAGE

Blackline Masters	Technology	Professional Series
Chapter Resources Booklet Chapter Review, pp. 35–36 Chapter Tests, pp. 37–40 **Standardized Test Practice by The Princeton Review,** pp. 55–58	MindJogger Videoquiz CD-ROM Explorations and Quizzes Vocabulary Puzzle Makers ExamView Pro Test Bank Interactive Lesson Planner Interactive Teacher's Edition	Performance Assessment in the Science Classroom (PASC)

Transparencies

Section Focus

Section Focus Transparency **River Ablaze**

If you saw a black-and-white picture of this stream, it probably wouldn't impress you. But in living color, it's astonishing. The surface temperature is about 1000°C (1832°F).

1. What is this fiery, flowing substance?
2. Where did this glowing river originate?
3. What will become of this river of fire?

L2

Section Focus Transparency **An Island Escape**

Trapped gasses under pressure sometimes are released by volcanic eruptions, but there are other ways that Earth vents gases, too. One example is Dominica's Boiling Lake. Dominica is a volcanic island, but the volcanoes are not thought to be active. Instead, gases from inside Earth are released by vents beneath Boiling Lake.

1. Why is Boiling Lake shrouded in steam?
2. What might happen if the vents closed and gas continued to build up?

L2

Section Focus Transparency **Ancient Volcanic Rock**

Over many years, erosion by weather and water can create exotic landscapes from the layers of material deposited by volcanoes. The landscape you see below, for example, is in the Urgup Basin of Turkey. In this area, called Cappadocia, the volcanoes last erupted between seven and ten million years ago. Weathering and erosion continue to shape the land.

1. Where did the rock formations you see here come from?
2. Some of the rocks you see are relatively hard, and some are relatively soft. Why is this?
3. How is the action of weather and water on a landscape similar to the action of a sculptor working marble?

L2

This is a representation of key blackline masters available in the Teacher Classroom Resources. See Resource Manager boxes within the chapter for additional information.

Assessment

Assessment Transparency **Volcanoes**

Directions: *Carefully review the table and answer the following questions.*

Magnetic Eruptions at Mount St. Helens

Date	Explosive activity	Broken flows	Lava flows (dome)	Volume (million cubic yds)
6/12/80	x	x	x	54.5
7/22/80	x	x		13.1
10/16/80	x	x	x	3.6
12/27/80			x	2.1
6/18/81			x	5.4
10/30/81			x	4.7
3/19/82	x		x	4.4
8/18/82			x	6.0
2/7/83	x		x	29.3
3/29/84			x	1.4

1. According to the table, between which dates do you think Mount St. Helens experienced the most explosive activity?
   A 06/12/80–10/16/80   C 07/22/80–10/16/80
   B 06/18/81–10/30/81   D 08/18/82–03/29/84
2. According to the table, there was no explosive activity between ____.
   F 06/12/80–10/16/80   H 02/01/83–03/29/84
   G 10/17/80–05/14/82   J 12/27/80–03/18/82
3. All of the following days had lava flows from the dome EXCEPT ____.
   A December 27, 1980   C June 12, 1980
   B July 22, 1980   D August 18, 1982

L2

Teaching

Teaching Transparency **Volcanoes and Hot Spots**

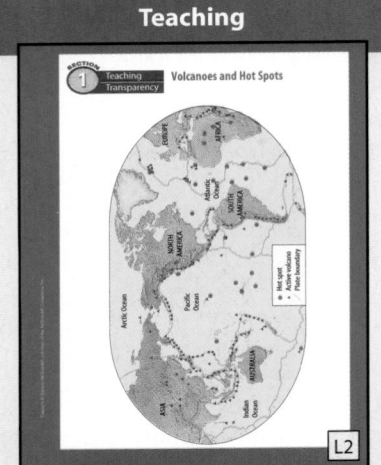

L2

Key to Teaching Strategies

The following designations will help you decide which activities are appropriate for your students.

L1 Level 1 activities should be appropriate for students with learning difficulties.

L2 Level 2 activities should be within the ability range of all students.

L3 Level 3 activities are designed for above-average students.

ELL ELL activities should be within the ability range of English Language Learners.

COOP LEARN Cooperative Learning activities are designed for small group work.

LS Multiple Learning Styles logos, as described on page 22T, are used throughout to indicate strategies that address different learning styles.

P These strategies represent student products that can be placed into a best-work portfolio.

Hands-on Activities

Activity Worksheets

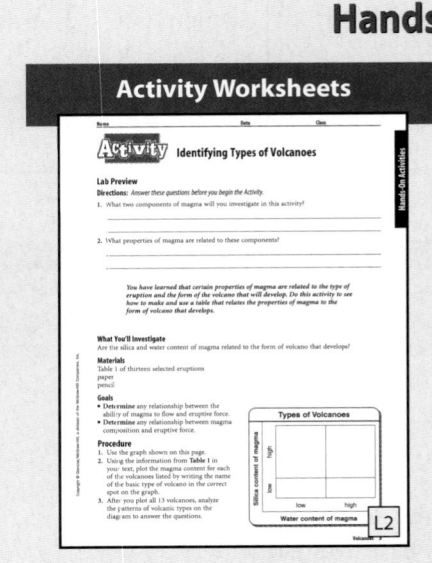

Activity **Identifying Types of Volcanoes**

Lab Preview
Directions: *Answer these questions before you begin the Activity.*
1. What two components of magma will you investigate in this activity?

2. What properties of magma are related to these components?

You have learned that certain properties of magma are related to the type of eruption and the form of the volcano that will develop. In this activity you will learn how to make and use a table that relates the properties of magma to the form of volcano that develops.

What You'll Investigate
Are the silica and water content of magma related to the form of volcano that develops?

Materials
Table 1 of thirteen selected eruptions
paper
pencil

Goals
• Determine any relationship between the ability of magma to flow and eruptive force.
• Determine any relationship between magma composition and eruptive force.

Procedure
1. Use the graph shown on this page.
2. Using the information from Table 1 in your text, plot the magma content for each of the volcanoes listed by writing the name of the basic type of volcano in the correct spot on the graph.
3. After you plot all 13 volcanoes, analyze the patterns of volcanic types on the diagram to answer the questions.

Types of Volcanoes

L2

Laboratory Activities

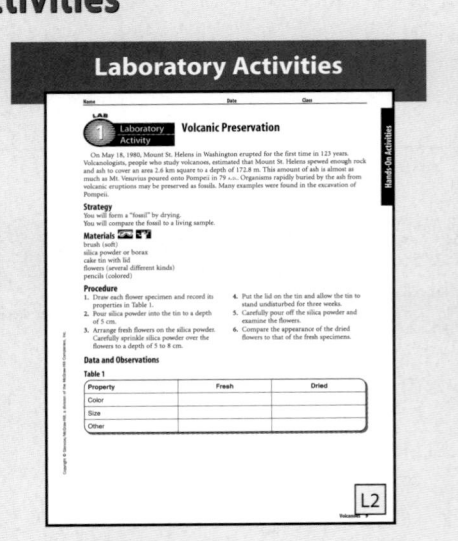

Laboratory Activity **Volcanic Preservation**

On May 18, 1980, Mount St. Helens in Washington erupted for the first time in 123 years. Volcanologists, people who study volcanoes, estimated that Mount St. Helens spewed enough rock and ash to cover an area 2.6 km square to a depth of 172.8 m. This amount of ash is almost as much as left. Mt. Vesuvius poured onto Pompeii in 79 A.D.. Organisms rapidly buried by the ash from volcanic eruptions may be preserved as fossils. Many individuals were found in the excavation of Pompeii.

Strategy
You will form a "fossil" by drying.
You will compare the fossil to a living sample.

Materials
brush (soft)
silica powder or borax
cake tin with lid
flowers (several different kinds)
pencils (colored)

Procedure
1. Draw each flower specimen and record its properties in Table 1.
2. Pour silica powder into the tin to a depth of 5 cm.
3. Arrange fresh flowers on the silica powder. Carefully sprinkle silica powder over the flowers to a depth of 5 to 8 cm.
4. Put the lid on the tin and allow the tin to stand undisturbed for three weeks.
5. Carefully pour off the silica powder and examine the flowers.
6. Compare the appearance of the dried flowers to that of the fresh specimens.

Data and Observations
Table 1

Property	Fresh	Dried
Color		
Size		
Other		

L2

Meeting Different Ability Levels

Content Outline

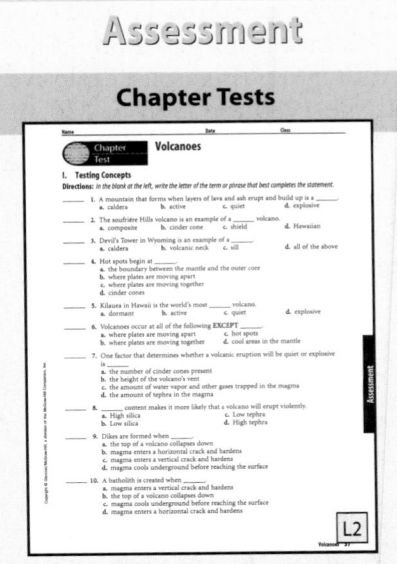

L2

Reinforcement

L2

Directed Reading

L1

Assessment

Chapter Tests

L2

Enrichment

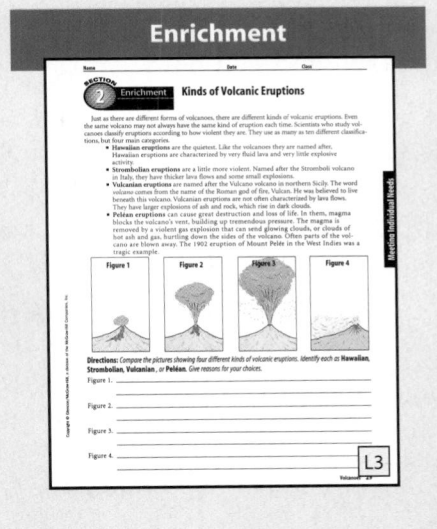

L3

Spanish Directed Reading

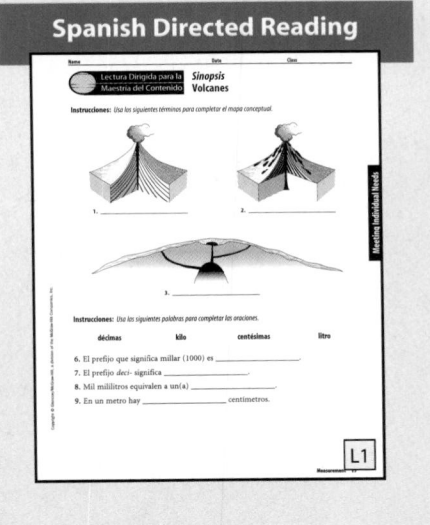

L1

Test Practice Workbook

Standardized Test Practice
Teacher Edition

Glencoe Science

Earth Science

L2

Chapter Review

L2

Science Content Background

SECTION 1

SECTION 1

Volcanoes and Earth's Moving Plates

How do volcanoes form?

Before scientists knew about plate movement, they thought volcanoes were caused by water reaching Earth's hot interior. Now we know that volcanoes are driven by the energy generated by the movement of Earth's tectonic plates.

Although few people in the United States are affected by volcanoes today, nearly every state has historical evidence of volcanic action ranging from direct lava flows to layers of volcanic ash. Over 80 percent of Earth's surface, including the portions under the oceans, is of volcanic origin.

Despite the damage they cause, volcanoes have positive effects. Extinct volcanoes are associated with many of our major veins of metallic minerals such as gold, silver, copper, lead and zinc. Diamonds also are found in deposits that are part of extinct volcanoes. Volcanic rock weathers into some of the most fertile soil on Earth. Volcanic eruptions early in Earth's history provided the atmosphere and water that make life on Earth possible.

> **Fun Fact**
>
> Jupiter's moon Io is the most volcanically active object in the solar system.

SECTION 2

Types of Volcanoes

Trapped Gases

Most of the gas released from volcanoes is water vapor. Gases make up between one and five percent of the total weight of most magmas.

Composition of Magma

Volcanic eruptions that form at divergent plate boundaries and hot spots tend to expel basaltic lava. This lava flows readily, releases gas easily, and is associated with nonexplosive eruptions, like most of those in Hawaii. Eruptions along convergent boundaries produce lava that is richer in silica. This lava traps gas more easily and is associated with more dangerous, explosive eruptions, such as the 1980 eruption of Mount St. Helens.

Mark Lewis/Stone

Forms of Volcanoes

Shield volcanoes form the largest cones. Mauna Loa measures 9 kilometers from top to base and about 200 kilometers from side to side. Next in size are composite volcanoes. Mount Rainer measures 3 kilometers from top to base and about 20 kilometers from side to side. Cinder cones form the smallest volcanoes. Sunset Crater measures about 0.3 kilometers from top to base and 1.8 kilometers from side to side.

Materials that comprise tephra are referred to as cinders when they are the size of peas and lapilli when they are the size of walnuts. Materials larger than lapilli are called blocks or bombs when ejected in a semi-molten state. Volcanic ash is tephra that is smaller than 4 millimeters.

Not all eruptions of lava come from volcanoes. Some lava is erupted through fissures, or cracks, in Earth's surface. The Columbia Plateau, located in the northwestern United States, formed from layer after layer of basaltic lava that extruded as fissure eruptions.

Viscous, or thick, lava does not flow easily. As this type of lava is extruded, it often produces a dome-shaped mass called a lava dome. Scientists study the growth of lava domes for signs of continued or renewed eruptions. Changes in growth rate of lava domes can indicate changes inside the volcano. Many lava domes form after explosive eruptions.

Darrell Gulin/DRK Photo

SECTION 3 Igneous Rock Features

Plutons

Another name for intrusive igneous rock bodies is plutons. Plutons are described by position, shape, and/or size. Plutons that are flat and shaped similar to a tabletop are called tabular. Examples are dikes and sills. Others, such as batholiths, are large and massive. Plutons, such as sills, are concordant. This means they form between layers of surrounding rock. Others, such as dikes, are discordant in that they cut across surrounding rock layers.

Crater Lake

Crater Lake, located in Oregon, formed about 7,000 years ago when a volcano spewed 40–50 cubic kilometers of volcanic material into the air. With the magma chamber then partly emptied, 1,500 meters of the original 3,600 meter cone collapsed. Rainwater filled the caldera to form a lake. Magma forced to the surface after the caldera formed built Wizard Island in the lake.

Fun Fact

Crater Lake, with a depth of 589 meters, is the deepest lake in the United States and the second deepest in North America.

SCIENCE *Online*

For additional content background on this topic, go to the Glencoe Science Web site at science.glencoe.com.

Volcanoes

Chapter Vocabulary

volcano
vent
crater
hot spot
shield volcano
tephra
cinder cone volcano
composite volcano
batholith
dike
sill
volcanic neck
caldera

What do you think?

Science Journal This photo shows underwater lava. Explain that there are volcanoes and cracks that release lava underwater. The lava can build up over thousands or millions of years, causing the volcano to grow higher and finally break through the surface of the ocean. This is how the islands of Hawaii formed. These islands are the tops of volcanoes whose bases are on the ocean floor.

CHAPTER 12
Volcanoes

Every few months, villagers in Bronte, Italy, watch as Mount Etna roars to life and oozes rivers of molten lava. The village, eleven kilometers from the mountain, was out of harm's way, and no one was injured in this October 29, 1999, eruption. In this chapter, you will learn about types of volcanoes and how they form. You will learn how volcanoes affect humans and the surrounding environment and you will see the rock features they leave behind.

What do you think?

Science Journal Look at the picture below with a classmate. Discuss what you think this might be or what is happening. Here's a hint: *Not all volcanoes occur where you can see them.* Write your answer or best guess in your Science Journal.

332

Theme Connection

Energy and Stability and Change The energy involved in the formation of magma, its movement up toward the surface, and its flow onto the surface as lava are focal points of the chapter. Stability and change is a secondary theme emphasized in the section on the eruption of volcanoes.

Y ou've seen pictures of volcanoes from the ground, but what would a volcano look like on a map? Volcanoes can be represented on maps that show the elevation of the land, as well as other important features. These maps are called topographic maps.

Map a volcano

1. Obtain half of a foam ball from your teacher and place it on the top of a table with the flat side down.

2. Using a metric ruler and a permanent marker, mark 1-cm intervals on the foam ball. Start at the base of the ball and mark up at equal points around the ball.

3. Connect the marks of equal elevation by drawing a line around the ball at the 1-cm mark, at the 2-cm mark, etc.

4. Look directly down on the top of the ball and make a drawing of what you see in your Science Journal.

Observe

In your Science Journal, write a paragraph that explains how your drawing shows the general shape of a volcano. What might the lines drawn around the foam ball represent?

Before You Read

FOLDABLES
Reading & Study
Skills

Making a Venn Diagram Study Fold As you prepare to read this chapter, make the following Foldable.

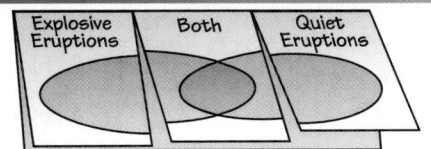

1. Place a sheet of paper in front of you so the short side is at the top. Fold the paper in half.

2. Label "Explosive Eruptions," "Quiet Eruptions," and "Both" across the front of the paper.

3. Fold both sides in to divide the paper into equal thirds. Unfold the paper so three columns show.

4. Through the top thickness of paper, cut along each of the fold lines to the top fold, forming three tabs.

5. As you read the chapter, collect information about each type of eruption under the left and right tabs. Under the middle tab, write what both types of eruptions have in common.

333

Purpose Students will create a model of a topographic map of a volcano.

Preparation Cut foam balls in half using a handheld jigsaw or sharp knife.

Materials half of a foam ball, metric ruler, permanent marker

Teaching Strategy As students perform the activity, remind them that real volcanoes have a variety of shapes and elevations. Ask them to think how their lines would look for different volcanoes.

Observe

Possible answer: The drawing shows how the volcano is wide at the base and narrow at the top. The lines connect similar elevations of the volcano.

Oral Ask students to explain how their drawings differ from the topographic maps of real volcanoes. For real volcanoes, the lines would be more jagged because the elevations around the volcano would not be uniform. Use **Performance Assessment in the Science Classroom,** p. 89.

Before You Read

FOLDABLES
Reading & Study
Skills

Dinah Zike Study Fold

Purpose Have students make a Foldable to determine what they know about volcanoes in general, and the similarities and differences between explosive and quiet eruptions.

For additional help, see Foldables Worksheet, p. 15 in **Chapter Resources Booklet,** or go to the Glencoe Science Web site at **science.glencoe.com.** See After You Read in the Study Guide at the end of this chapter.

SECTION

1

Volcanoes and Earth's Moving Plates

Volcanoes and Earth's Moving Plates

1 Motivate

Bellringer Transparency

Display the Section Focus Transparency for Section 1. Use the accompanying Transparency Activity Master. L2

ELL

L2

Tie to Prior Knowledge

Have students brainstorm words they associate with volcanoes. Record their ideas on the board. Possible answers: eruption, lava, ash, heat Discuss how the terms reveal what they think about volcanoes. Tell students that in this section they will learn why volcanoes form.

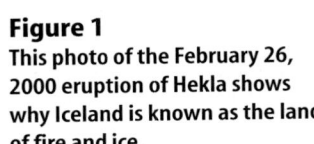

As You Read

What You'll Learn

■ **Describe** how volcanoes can affect people.
■ **List** conditions that cause volcanoes to form.
■ **Identify** the relationship between volcanoes and Earth's moving plates.

Vocabulary

volcano   crater
vent   hot spot

Why It's Important

Volcanoes can be dangerous to people and their communities.

Figure 1
This photo of the February 26, 2000 eruption of Hekla shows why Iceland is known as the land of fire and ice.

What are volcanoes?

A **volcano** is an opening in Earth that erupts gases, ash, and lava. Volcanic mountains form when layers of lava, ash, and other material build up around these openings. Can you name any volcanoes? Did you know that Earth has more than 600 active volcanoes?

Most Active Volcanoes Kilauea (kee low AY ah), located in Hawaii, is the world's most active volcano. For centuries, this volcano has been erupting, but not explosively. In May of 1990, most of the town of Kalapana Gardens was destroyed, but no one was hurt because the lava moved slowly and people could escape. The most recent series of eruptions from Kilauea began in January 1983 and still continues.

The island country of Iceland is also famous for its active volcanoes. It sits on an area where Earth's plates move apart and is known as the land of fire and ice. The February 26, 2000, eruption of Hekla, in Iceland, is shown in **Figure 1.**

334   **CHAPTER 12**   Volcanoes

Section ✓Assessment Planner

PORTFOLIO
Science Journal, p. 337
Challenge, p. 339
PERFORMANCE ASSESSMENT
Skill Builder Activities, p. 338
Try at Home MiniLab, p. 339
See page 360 for more options.

CONTENT ASSESSMENT
Section, p. 339
Challenge, p. 339
Chapter, pp. 360–361

2 Teach

What are volcanoes?

Quick Demo

Cut a small slit in the side of a tube of toothpaste. With the cap on, squeeze the tube. The toothpaste oozing out of the slit and down the side of the tube models a quiet eruption of a shield volcano. L1 ELL **Visual-Spatial**

Effects of Eruptions

When volcanoes erupt, they often have direct, dramatic effects on the lives of people and their property. Lava flows destroy everything in their path. Falling volcanic ash can collapse buildings, block roads, and in some cases cause lung disease in people and animals. Sometimes, volcanic ash and debris rush down the side of the volcano. This is called a pyroclastic flow. The temperatures inside the flow can be high enough to ignite wood. When big eruptions occur, people often are forced to abandon their land and homes. People who live farther away from volcanoes are more likely to survive, but cities, towns, crops, and buildings in the area can be damaged by falling debris.

Human and Environmental Impacts The eruption of Soufrière (sew free ER) Hills volcano in Montserrat, which began in July of 1995, was one of the largest recent volcanic eruptions near North America. Geologists knew it was about to erupt, and the people who lived near it were evacuated. On June 25, 1997, large pyroclastic flows swept down the volcano. As shown in **Figure 2,** they buried cities and towns that were in their path. The eruption killed 20 people who ignored the evacuation order.

Environmental Science
INTEGRATION

When sulfurous gases from volcanoes mix with water vapor in the atmosphere, acid rain forms. The vegetation, lakes, and streams around Soufrière Hills volcano were impacted significantly by acid rain. As the vegetation, shown in **Figure 3,** died the organisms that lived in the forest were forced to leave or died.

Effects of Eruptions

Discussion

Most people know that volcanoes erupt, sometimes with deadly results. Yet many people still choose to live near volcanoes. **Why do you think this is the case?** Possible answers: There haven't been recent eruptions, so the people living there are not afraid; people think that if there is a problem, they will be able to escape in time; some people are unable to move because of economic or other reasons.

Figure 3
The vegetation near the volcano on Chances Peak, on the island of Montserrat in the West Indies, was destroyed by acid rain, heat, and ash.

Teacher FYI

Pyroclastic flows of hot gases, ash, and rock can roll down the sides of a volcano at speeds of up to 200 km/h. Pyroclastic flows are responsible for most of the deaths and injuries caused by volcanic eruptions in the twentieth century. A pyroclastic flow caused almost all of the 29,000 deaths during Mount Pelée's eruption on the island of Martinique in 1902.

SECTION 1 Volcanoes and Earth's Moving Plates **335**

✔ Active Reading

Problem/Solution Journal Have students divide sheets of paper in half and label the left side *Problem* and the right side *Consequences of Not Resolving the Problem*. Through writing, have students identify a problem, brainstorm alternatives, choose a solution, anticipate stumbling blocks, and propose arguments. Have students apply this strategy to dealing with the effects of an eruption.

Resource Manager

Chapter Resources Booklet
  Transparency Activity, p. 42
  Directed Reading for Content Mastery,
    pp. 17, 18
  Note-taking Worksheets, pp. 31–33

How do volcanoes form?

The largest volcano in the solar system is Mons Olympus on Mars. This inactive volcano covers an area about the size of Ohio. Triton, a moon of Neptune, has volcanic-like eruptions of nitrogen and methane. Earth's Moon has ancient lava flows called maria.

Discussion

Why do you think magma cools quickly when it is forced out of a vent on Earth's surface? The temperature at Earth's surface is much lower than the temperature deep inside Earth, causing the rock to solidify.

Reading Check

Answer It is less dense than the surrounding rock.

Visual Learning

Figure 4 Do people who live near volcanoes have to be aware of areas other than the vent when protecting themselves against lava flows? Yes, lava can also flow from the branch pipes that lead to cracks in the volcano's sides.

Astronomy
INTEGRATION

Volcanoes are not unique to Earth. Io, a moon of Jupiter, has many active volcanoes. Research to find other planets or moons that have volcanoes. Do any planets show signs of past volcanic activity?

How do volcanoes form?

What happens inside Earth to create volcanoes? Why are some areas of Earth more likely to have volcanoes than others? Deep inside Earth, heat and pressure cause rock to melt, forming liquid rock or magma. Some deep rocks already are melted. Others are hot enough that a small rise in temperature or drop in pressure can cause them to melt and form magma. What makes magma come to the surface?

Magma Forced Upward Magma is less dense than the rock around it, so it is forced slowly toward Earth's surface. You can see this process if you turn a bottle of cold syrup upside down. Watch the dense syrup force the less dense air bubbles slowly toward the top.

✔ Reading Check *Why is magma forced toward Earth's surface?*

After many thousands or even millions of years, magma reaches Earth's surface and flows out through an opening called a **vent**. As lava flows out, it cools quickly and becomes solid, forming layers of igneous rock around the vent. The steep-walled depression around a volcano's vent is the **crater**. **Figure 4** shows magma being forced out of a volcano.

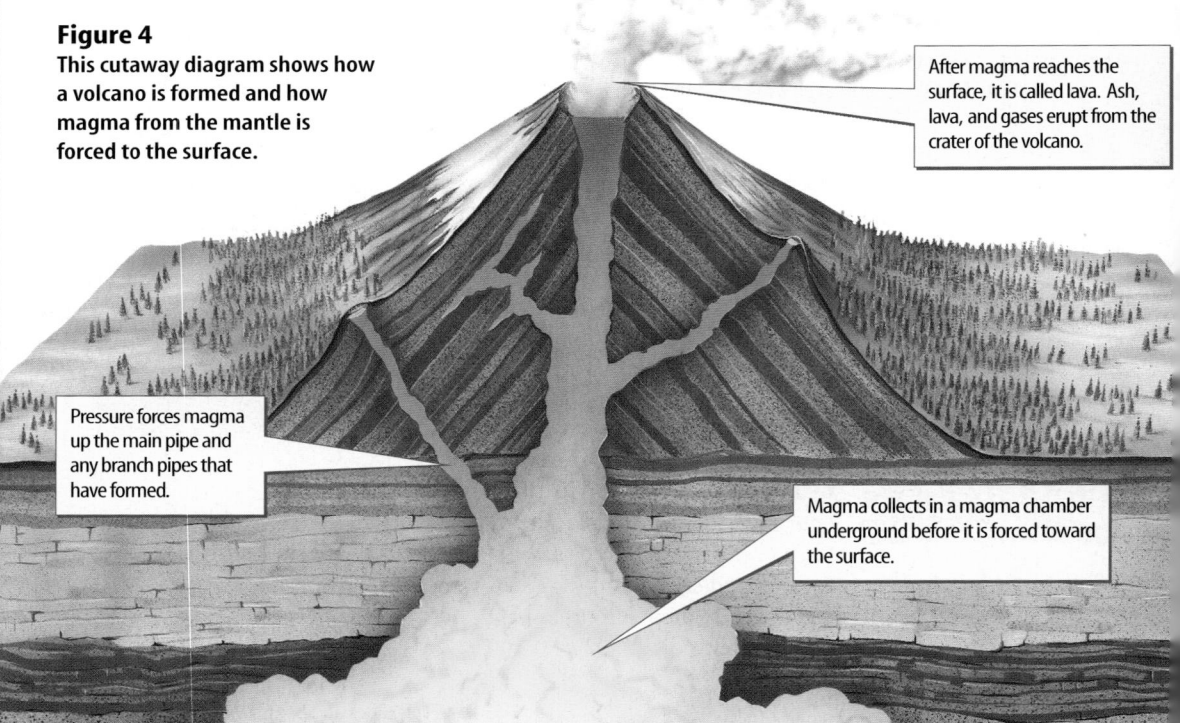

Figure 4
This cutaway diagram shows how a volcano is formed and how magma from the mantle is forced to the surface.

After magma reaches the surface, it is called lava. Ash, lava, and gases erupt from the crater of the volcano.

Pressure forces magma up the main pipe and any branch pipes that have formed.

Magma collects in a magma chamber underground before it is forced toward the surface.

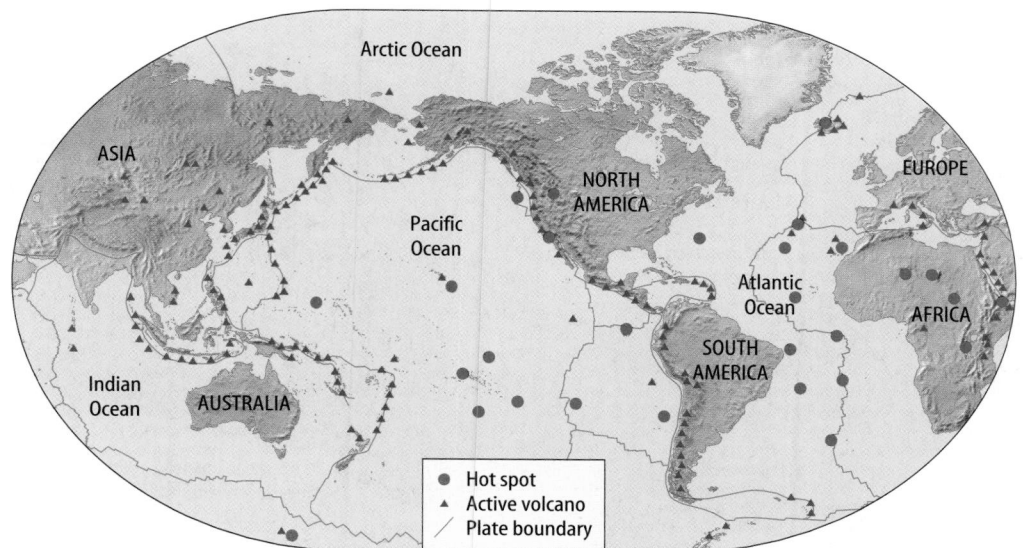

Where do volcanoes occur?

Volcanoes often form in places where plates are moving apart, where plates are moving together, and at locations called hot spots. You can find locations of active volcanoes at plate boundaries and at hot spots on the map in **Figure 5.** Many examples can be found of volcanoes around the world that form at these three different kinds of areas. You'll explore volcanoes in Iceland, on the island of Montserrat, and in Hawaii.

Divergent Plate Boundaries Iceland is a large island in the North Atlantic Ocean. It is near the Arctic Circle and therefore has some glaciers. Iceland has volcanic activity because it sits on top of the Mid-Atlantic Ridge.

The Mid-Atlantic Ridge is a divergent plate boundary, which is an area where Earth's plates are moving apart. When plates separate, they form long, deep cracks called rifts. Lava flows from these rifts and is cooled quickly by seawater. **Figure 6** shows how magma rises at rifts to form new volcanic rock. As more lava flows and hardens, it builds up on the seafloor. Sometimes, the volcanoes and rift eruptions rise above sea level, forming islands such as Iceland. In 1963, the new island Surtsey was formed during a volcanic eruption.

Figure 5
This map shows the locations of volcanoes, hot spots, and plate boundaries around the world. The Ring of Fire is a belt of active volcanoes that circles the Pacific Ocean.

Figure 6
This diagram shows how volcanic activity occurs where Earth's plates move apart.

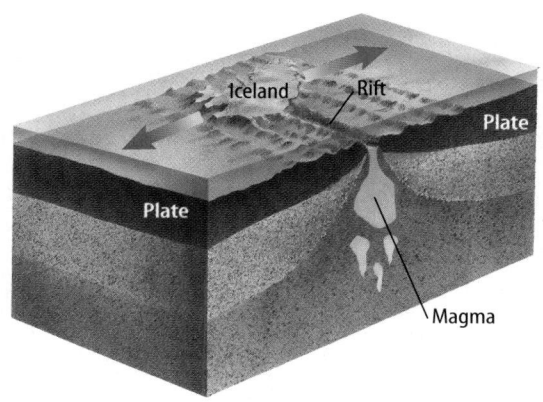

SECTION 1 Volcanoes and Earth's Moving Plates **337**

Visual Learning

Figure 5 **Where in the United States are you most likely to find volcanoes?** Along the Pacific coast and in Hawaii.

Quick Demo

Attach an air pump to a balloon neck and place the balloon under a large piece of cloth. As you inflate the balloon, explain that the bulge in the cloth represents magma that causes doming on a volcano. **What is likely to happen if this build-up of magma continues?** The volcano would eventually erupt. Inform students that bulging and earthquakes are often precursors to eruptions. L2
Visual-Spatial

Quick Demo

Show a lava lamp to the class and explain that the rising globs of material inside the lamp are warmer and less dense than the surrounding material. The globs are forced upward by the surrounding, denser material in much the same way as magma is forced up from below the surface. L1 **Visual-Spatial**

IDENTIFYING Misconceptions

Some students may think that an active volcano is one that is now erupting or has erupted very recently. Volcanologists consider an active volcano one that has erupted within recorded history. As a result, volcanoes that have been "quiet" for many decades are still considered active and could pose a danger to those nearby.

Science Journal

Energy From Volcanoes Scientists have discovered communities that include giant clams and worms living near mid-ocean ridges. Have students find out how these communities obtain energy from volcanic activity, and write a summary of their findings in their Science Journals. Bacteria oxidize the hydrogen sulfide deposited by plumes of hot water streaming from cracks along the ridge. L2 **Linguistic** P

Resource Manager

Chapter Resources Booklet
Enrichment, p. 28
Reinforcement, p. 25
Transparency Activity, pp. 45–46

TRY AT HOME
Mini LAB

Purpose Students will model the movement of magma toward Earth's surface.

Materials two small transparent plastic cups, small amount of olive oil, water, dropper

Teaching Strategy Students should squeeze the oil into the water as slowly as possible to avoid stirring the water.

Analysis
1. The oil rises to the surface of the water.
2. Oil is less dense than water, as magma is less dense than surrounding rock in Earth's crust.

Assessment

Oral Based on observations in this activity, ask students to explain why most volcanoes occur near plate boundaries. Magma can more easily rise through the crust at weak points along the plate boundaries. Use **PASC**, p. 89.

Text Question Answer

an unusually hot area that melts rock and causes it to be forced toward the surface

---

Figure 7
Volcanoes can form where plates collide and one plate slides below the other.

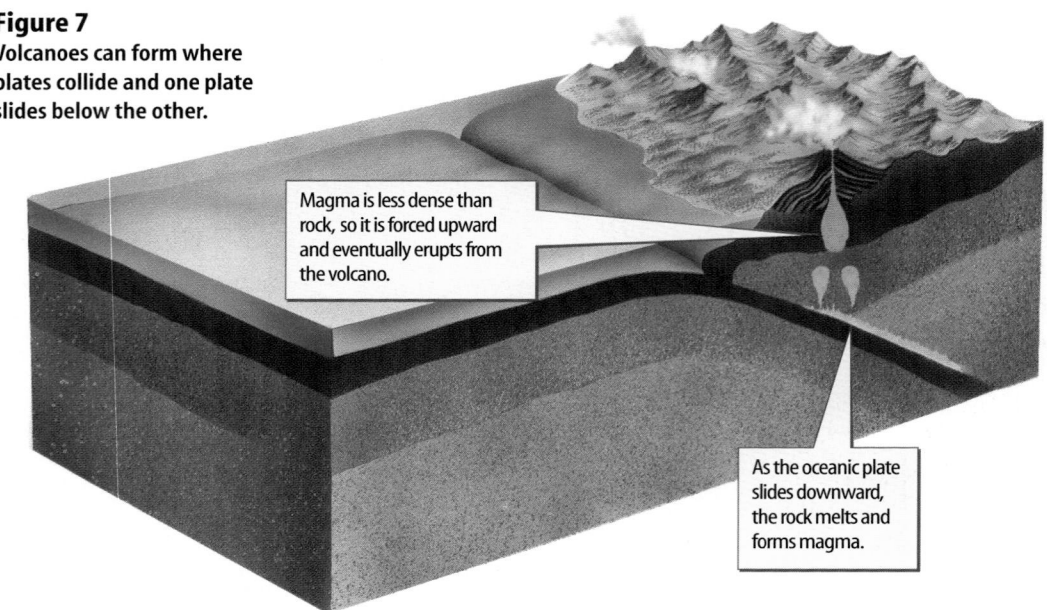

Magma is less dense than rock, so it is forced upward and eventually erupts from the volcano.

As the oceanic plate slides downward, the rock melts and forms magma.

TRY AT HOME
Mini LAB

Modeling Magma Movement

Procedure
1. Pour **water** into a **transparent, plastic cup.**
2. Pour a small amount of **olive oil** into a separate plastic cup.
3. Extract a small amount of oil with a **dropper.**
4. Submerge the dropper tip into the water cup and slowly squeeze oil drops into the water.

Analysis
1. Describe what happened to the oil.
2. How do your observations compare with the movement of magma within Earth's crust?

Convergent Plate Boundaries Places where Earth's plates move together are called convergent plate boundaries. They include areas where an oceanic plate slides below a continental plate as in **Figure 7,** and where one oceanic plate slides below another oceanic plate. The Andes in South America began forming when an oceanic plate started sliding below a continental plate. Volcanoes that form on convergent plate boundaries tend to erupt more violently than other volcanoes do.

Magma forms when one plate sliding below another plate gets deep enough and hot enough to melt partially. The magma then is forced upward to the surface, forming volcanoes like Soufrière Hills on the island of Montserrat.

Hot Spots The Hawaiian Islands are forming as a result of volcanic activity. However, unlike Iceland, they haven't formed at a plate boundary. The Hawaiian Islands are in the middle of the Pacific Plate, far from its edges. What process could be forming them?

It is thought that some areas at the boundary between Earth's mantle and core are unusually hot. Rock melts at these **hot spots** and then is forced toward the crust as magma. The Hawaiian Islands sit on top of a hot spot under the Pacific Plate. Magma from deep in Earth's mantle has broken through the crust to form several volcanoes. The volcanoes that rise above the water form the Hawaiian Islands, shown in **Figure 8A.**

Curriculum Connection

Geography Display a map of the world. Have each student locate one active volcano on the map and place a pin with the name of the volcano at the proper location. When the map is complete, ask students to list the countries that have the greatest number of active volcanoes. Have them note whether these countries are around the Ring of Fire. L2  **Visual-Spatial**

Resource Manager

Chapter Resources Booklet
  MiniLAB, p. 3
  Lab Activity, pp. 9–10

Figure 8
The Hawaiian Islands are actually volcanoes.

A This satellite photo shows the Hawaiian Islands. *Why are they in a relatively straight line?*

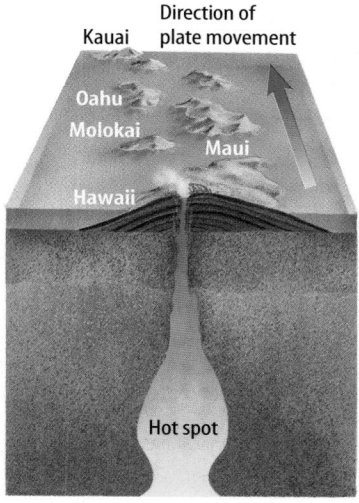

Direction of plate movement

Kauai

Oahu
Molokai
Maui
Hawaii

Hot spot

B This illustration shows how the Hawaiian Islands were formed over a hot spot.

The Hawaiian Islands As you can see in **Figure 8,** the Hawaiian Islands are all in a line. This is because the Pacific Plate is moving over a stationary hot spot. Kauai, the oldest Hawaiian island, was once located where the big island, Hawaii, is situated today. As the plate moved, Kauai moved away from the hot spot and became dormant. As the Pacific Plate continued to move, the islands of Oahu, Molokai, Maui, and Hawaii were formed. This process has been occurring over a period of about 5 million years.

Section 1 Assessment

1. How are volcanoes related to Earth's moving plates?

2. Hot lava is not the only danger associated with active volcanoes. What effects can pyroclastic flows have on people?

3. Why does lava cool rapidly along a mid-ocean ridge?

4. Describe processes that are occurring to cause Soufrière Hills volcano to erupt.

5. **Think Critically** If the Pacific Plate stopped moving, what might happen to the island of Hawaii?

Skill Builder Activities

6. **Concept Mapping** Make a concept map that shows how the Hawaiian Islands formed. Use the following phrases: *volcano forms, plate moves, volcano becomes dormant,* and *new volcano forms.* **For more help, refer to the** Science Skill Handbook.

7. **Communicating** Scientists were able to predict approximately when Mount Pinatubo in the Philippines would erupt in 1991. In your Science Journal, write a report on equipment used to predict volcanic eruptions. **For more help, refer to the** Science Skill Handbook.

Caption Answer
Figure 8A The plate moves over the hot spot in a straight line, leaving volcanoes in a straight line as it passes.

3 Assess

Reteach
Have students draw a cross section of an area of Earth's crust where one plate is forced under another. Have them label the diagram to indicate where volcanoes form. L2 ELL
Visual-Spatial

Challenge
Challenge students to find out what type of plate boundary exists along the northwest coast of the United States and what landforms have arisen as a result. Have students prepare short reports that include maps and diagrams of the plate boundary. Convergent continental-ocean boundary; mountains such as the Cascades formed here and include volcanoes such as Mount St. Helens. L2
Visual-Spatial P

✓ Assessment

Performance Have students draw concept maps that include the three main types of geological areas where volcanoes form. Convergent and divergent plate boundaries and hot spots Use **Performance Assessment in the Science Classroom,** p. 161.

Answers to Section Assessment

1. Volcanoes occur most often at plate boundaries where magma flows upward from the mantle toward the surface. They also occur where plates move over hot spots.

2. They can flow down the sides of volcanoes, burning most things and burying them under ash.

3. Lava flows from underwater cracks at mid-ocean ridges; the water cools lava quickly.

4. The North and South American plates are sinking under the converging Caribbean plate. The edges of the sinking plates melt, producing magma that rises to form volcanoes such as Soufriére Hills.

5. The island would grow larger as volcanoes on it would continue to produce lava.

6. Volcano forms → plate moves → volcano becomes dormant → new volcano forms.

7. Possible answers: tilt meters, creep meters, lasers, seismographs, instruments that measure and analyze gases released

SECTION

Types of Volcanoes

1 Motivate

Bellringer Transparency

Display the Section Focus Transparency for Section 2. Use the accompanying Transparency Activity Master. L2

ELL

Section Focus Transparency

2 Section Focus Transparency An Island Escape

Trapped gases under pressure sometimes are released by volcanic eruptions, but there are other ways that Earth vents gases, too. One example is Dominica's Boiling Lake. Dominica is a volcanic island, but the volcanoes are not thought to be active. Instead, gases from inside Earth are released by vents beneath Boiling Lake.

1. Why is Boiling Lake shrouded in steam?
2. What might happen if the vents closed and gas continued to build up?

L2

Tie to Prior Knowledge

Ask students to recall volcanic eruptions they have seen or heard about. **What did those eruptions do?** Some students will recall violent, destructive eruptions such as Mount St. Helens, while others will recall lava flows such as those that ooze over the landscape near Kilauea. Use this information to reinforce the idea that eruptions differ. Tell students they will find out why they differ in this section.

As You Read

What You'll Learn

■ **Explain** how the explosiveness of a volcanic eruption is related to the silica and water vapor content of its magma.
■ **List** three forms of volcanoes.

Vocabulary

shield volcano   cinder cone volcano
tephra   composite volcano

Why It's Important

If you know the type of volcano, you can predict how it will erupt.

Figure 9
A calm day in Washington state was shattered suddenly when Mount St. Helens erupted on May 18, 1980, as shown in this sequence of photographs.

What controls eruptions?

Some volcanic eruptions are explosive, like those from Soufrière Hills volcano, Mount Pinatubo, and Mount St. Helens. In others, the lava quietly flows from a vent, as in the Kilauea eruptions. What causes these differences?

Two important factors control whether an eruption will be explosive or quiet. One factor is the amount of water vapor and other gases that are trapped in the magma. The second factor is how much silica is present in the magma. Silica is a compound composed of the elements silicon and oxygen.

Trapped Gases When you shake a soft-drink container and then quickly open it, the pressure from the gas in the drink is released suddenly, spraying the drink all over. In the same way, gases such as water vapor and carbon dioxide are trapped in magma by the pressure of the surrounding magma and rock. As magma nears the surface, it is under less pressure. This allows the gas to escape from the magma. Gas escapes easily from some magma during quiet eruptions. However, gas that builds up to high pressures eventually causes explosive eruptions such as the one shown in **Figure 9.**

A 8:32 A.M.

B 38 seconds later

340 CHAPTER 12

Section ✔ *Assessment* Planner

PORTFOLIO
Extension, p. 342
PERFORMANCE ASSESSMENT
MiniLAB, p. 344
Skill Builder Activities, p. 347
See page 360 for more options.

CONTENT ASSESSMENT
Section, p. 347
Challenge, p. 347
Chapter, pp. 360–361

Water Vapor The magma at some convergent plate boundaries contains a lot of water vapor. This is because oceanic plate material and some of its water slide under other plate material at some convergent plate boundaries. The trapped water vapor in the magma can cause explosive eruptions.

Composition of Magma

The second major factor that affects the nature of the eruption is the composition of the magma. Magma can be divided into two major types—silica poor and silica rich.

Quiet Eruptions Magma that is relatively low in silica is called basaltic magma. It is fluid and produces quiet, nonexplosive eruptions such as those at Kilauea. This type of lava pours from volcanic vents and runs down the sides of a volcano. The lava is fluid. As this *pahoehoe* (pa-HOY-hoy) lava cools, it forms a ropelike structure. If the same lava flows at a lower temperature, a stiff, slowly moving *aa* (AH-ah) lava forms. In fact, you can walk right up to some aa lava flows on Kilauea.

Figure 10 shows some different types of lava. These quiet eruptions form volcanoes over hot spots such as the Hawaiian volcanoes. Basaltic magmas also flow from rift zones, which are long, deep cracks in Earth's surface. Many lava flows in Iceland are of this type. Because basaltic magma is fluid when it is forced upward in a vent, trapped gases can escape easily in a nonexplosive manner, sometimes forming lava fountains. Lavas that flow underwater form pillow lava formations. They are shaped like tubes, balloons, or pillows.

SCIENCE Online

Research Visit the Glencoe Science Web site at **science.glencoe.com** to learn more about Kilauea volcano in Hawaii. Draw a map of Hawaii that shows the location of Kilauea.

C 42 seconds later

D 53 seconds later

341

Curriculum Connection

History The eruption of Mount St. Helens in 1980 was a major event that made headlines all over the world. Assign groups of students to look for newspaper and magazine articles that discuss different aspects of the volcano either before, during, or in the aftermath of the eruption. Have groups work together to make a class report on the eruption **L2** COOP LEARN
 **Interpersonal and Naturalist**

2 Teach

What controls eruptions?

Visual Learning

Figure 9 Ask students to describe how Mount St. Helens changed as the volcano erupted. Accept any answer supported by the photos. In less than one minute a part of the top of the mountain was blown away.

Composition of Magma

SCIENCE Online

Internet Addresses

_____

_____

_____

Explore the Glencoe Science Web site at **science.glencoe.com** to find out more about topics in this section.

Visualizing Lava

Have students examine the pictures and read the captions. Then ask the following questions.

Which type of lava of the three shown probably cools most rapidly? Explain your answer. Pillow lava cools most rapidly because water conducts heat away more efficiently than does air.

Viscosity is a property of fluids. Viscous fluids resist flowing, while less viscous fluids flow easily. For example, a milkshake is more viscous than milk.

Which type of lava flow, an aa flow or a pahoehoe flow, is more viscous? an aa flow

Which kind of lava flow, an aa or a pahoehoe flow, do you think would present more of a danger to slow-moving animals? Why? Possible answer: A pahoehoe flow might present more of a danger because it is less viscous and so moves faster.

Activity

Pour dark-colored corn syrup into two containers. Refrigerate one and leave the other at room temperature. Have a student pour the chilled syrup onto a cookie sheet held at a 45° angle. Have another student time the syrup's transit down the cookie sheet. Then repeat the process for the other container of syrup. Ask students to describe the relationship between the temperature of a fluid and its viscosity. In general, the viscosity of a fluid increases as its temperature drops. L2

IS Kinesthetic

Extension

Have students research the effects of silica content on lava viscosity and the effect of lava viscosity on the explosiveness of a volcanic eruption. Have students make a poster showing an explosive and a nonexplosive eruption.

Figure 10

Lava rarely travels faster than a few kilometers an hour. Therefore, it poses little danger to people. However, homes and property can be damaged. On land, there are two main types of lava flows—aa (AH ah) and pahoehoe (pa HOY hoy). When lava comes out of cracks in the ocean floor, it is called pillow lava. The lava cooling here came from a volcanic eruption on the island of Hawaii.

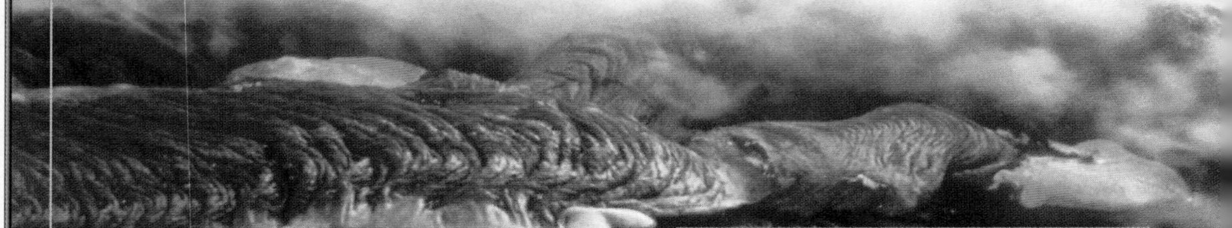

Aa flows, like this one on Mount Etna in Italy, carry sharp angular chunks of lava called scoria. Aa flows move slowly and are intensely hot.

Pillow lava occurs where lava oozes out of cracks in the ocean floor. It forms pillow-shaped lumps as it cools. Pillow lava is the most common type of lava on Earth.

Pahoehoe flows, like this one near Kilauea's Mauna Ulu Crater in Hawaii, are more fluid than aa flows. They develop a smooth skin and form rope-like patterns when they cool.

342 CHAPTER 12

Posters should indicate relative amounts of silica and dissolved gases in the lava. As silica content rises, lava usually becomes more viscous. Explosive eruptions tend to be associated with viscous, silica-rich lava having large amounts of dissolved gases. Nonexplosive eruptions tend to be associated with low-viscosity, silica-poor lava having small amounts of dissolved gases. L3 **IS Visual-Spatial** P

Resource Manager

Chapter Resources Booklet
Reinforcement, p. 26

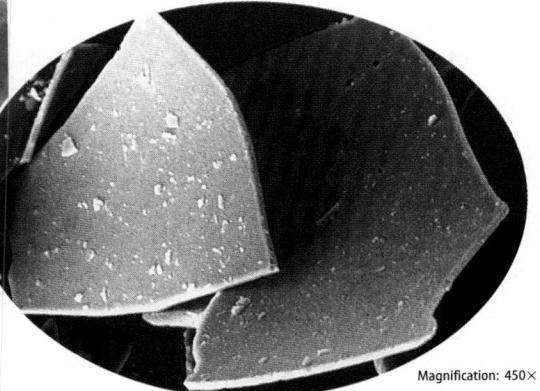

Figure 11
Magmas that are rich in silica produce violent eruptions, such as this one in Alaska. This color enhanced view of volcanic ash, from a 10 million year old volcano in Nebraska, shows the glass particles that make up ash.

Magnification: 450×

Explosive Magma Silica-rich, or granitic, magma on the other hand produces explosive eruptions such as those at Soufrière Hills volcano. This magma sometimes forms where Earth's plates are moving together and one plate slides under another. As the plate that is sliding under the other goes deeper and becomes heated, a portion of it is melted. The melted portion is forced upward by denser surrounding rock, comes in contact with the crust, and becomes enriched in silica. Silica-rich granitic magma is thick, and gas gets trapped in vents, causing pressure to build up. When an explosive eruption occurs, as shown in **Figure 11,** the gases expand rapidly, often carrying pieces of lava in the explosion.

✓ Reading Check *What type of magmas produce violent eruptions?*

Some magmas have an andesitic composition. Andesitic magma is more silica rich than basaltic magma is, but it is less silica rich than granitic magma. It often forms at convergent plate boundaries where one plate slides under the other. Because of their higher silica content, they also erupt more violently than basaltic magmas. One of the biggest eruptions in recorded history, Krakatau, was primarily andesitic in composition. The word *andesitic* comes from the Andes, which are mountains located along the western edge of South America, where andesite rock is common. Many of the volcanoes encircling the Pacific Ocean also are made of andesite.

Health
INTEGRATION

When volcanoes erupt, ash often is spread over a great distance. People who live near volcanoes must be careful not to inhale too much of the ash particles because the particles can cause respiratory problems. In your Science Journal, describe what people can do to prevent exposure to volcanic ash.

Composition of Magma, continued

Extension

Ask groups of students to research and role-play people in a community that is threatened with a volcanic eruption. Roles might include the mayor or other local government officials, doctors, farmers, firefighters, police officers, school officials, students, storekeepers, and volcanologists. Have students perform their role-playing skits in class. L2
COOP LEARN **IS** Interpersonal

Teacher FYI

When Soufriére Hills volcano erupted on Montserrat, many of the inhabitants were moved to the far side of the island. Others were removed from the island entirely. Many cities, including the capital, Plymouth, were covered by volcanic ash.

✓ Reading Check

Answer silica-rich, or granitic, magma

Health
INTEGRATION

People can wear over their noses and mouths masks made of a material that will not allow the ash to penetrate. People can also wear long sleeves and long pants and stay indoors.

Science Journal

Volcanoes and You Encourage students to use maps and other resources to determine whether or not volcanic activity might affect your geographic location. Have students write in their Science Journals what they discovered, and whether or not they were surprised by the information. L2 **IS** Intrapersonal

Curriculum Connection

Literature Have each student read a book or magazine article about a famous volcano, such as Mount St. Helens, Soufriére Hills, Vesuvius, or Kilauea. Have them examine how the eruptions of the volcano have affected or continues to affect nearby people. Have students write short stories describing what it would have been like to be near the volcano when it erupted. L2 **IS** Intrapersonal

Forms of Volcanoes

Mini LAB

Purpose Students will make models of cinder cone and shield volcanoes to learn about their shapes.

Materials sugar or sand, plaster of paris, paper plates, protractor

Teaching Strategies

- Mix the plaster of paris so that it flows but isn't runny.
- Students should pour the sand or sugar slowly.
- Review how to measure angles with a protractor.

Analysis

The model with steeper sides represents a cinder cone volcano.

✓Assessment

Performance Have students draw a cross-sectional diagram of their models in their Science Journals and identify the type of volcano each represents. The sand or sugar forms steeper sides and represents a cinder cone volcano. The plaster of paris model has gently sloping sides and represents a shield volcano. Use **PASC,** p. 127.

Visual Learning

Figure 12 Why is this type of volcano called a "shield" volcano? Its shape is broad and flat, like that of a shield.

Mini LAB

Modeling Volcanic Cones

Procedure

1. Pour **dry sand or sugar** onto one spot on a **paper plate. WARNING:** *Do not taste, eat, or drink any materials used in the lab.*
2. Mix a batch of **plaster of paris** and pour it onto one spot on another paper plate.
3. Allow the plaster of paris to dry. Use a **protractor** to measure the slope angles of the sides of the volcanoes.

Analysis

What form of volcano is represented by the model with steeper sides?

Figure 12
A shield volcano like Mauna Loa, shown here, is formed when lava flows from one or more vents without erupting violently.

Vent

Magma

Forms of Volcanoes

A volcano's form depends on whether it is the result of a quiet or an explosive eruption and the type of lava it is made of—basaltic, granitic, or andesitic (intermediate). The three basic types of volcanoes are shield volcanoes, cinder cone volcanoes, and composite volcanoes.

Shield Volcano Quiet eruptions of basaltic lava spread out in flat layers. The buildup of these layers forms a broad volcano with gently sloping sides called a **shield volcano,** as seen in **Figure 12.** The Hawaiian Islands are examples of shield volcanoes. Basaltic lava also can flow onto Earth's surface through large cracks called fissures. This type of eruption forms flood basalts, not volcanoes, and accounts for the greatest volume of erupted volcanic material. The basaltic lava flows over Earth's surface, covering large areas with thick deposits of basaltic igneous rock when it cools. The Columbia Plateau located in the northwestern United States was formed in this way. Much of the new seafloor that originates at mid-ocean ridges forms as underwater flood basalts.

Cinder Cone Volcano Explosive eruptions throw lava and rock high into the air. Bits of rock or solidified lava dropped from the air are called **tephra** (TEH fruh). Tephra varies in size from volcanic ash, to cinders, to larger rocks called bombs and blocks. When tephra falls to the ground, it forms a steep-sided, loosely packed **cinder cone volcano,** as seen in **Figure 13.**

LAB DEMONSTRATION

Purpose to observe properties of rocks formed from granitic and basaltic magma

Materials scoria, pumice, basalt, aquarium, water

Preparation Fill the aquarium with water.

Procedure Show students a light-colored rock (pumice) formed from silica-rich granitic lava and dark-colored rocks (scoria and basalt) formed from iron- and magnesium-rich basaltic lava. Point out the holes in pumice and scoria and explain that both form from lava with gas trapped inside. Place both the pumice and scoria in the aquarium as students observe.

Expected Outcome Pumice floats; scoria sinks.

✓Assessment

Why does the scoria sink and the pumice float? The material that makes up scoria is iron- and magnesium-rich. This makes the rock denser than water. The material that makes up pumice is silica-rich and thus is less dense than water. Also, air trapped in the holes in pumice add to its buoyancy. Note that not all pumice floats.

Igneous Rock Features

Intrusive Features

You can observe volcanic eruptions because they occur at Earth's surface. However, far more activity occurs underground. In fact, most magma never reaches Earth's surface to form volcanoes or to flow as flood basalts. This magma cools slowly underground and produces underground rock bodies that could become exposed later at Earth's surface by erosion. These rock bodies are called intrusive igneous rock features. There are several different types of intrusive features. Some of the most common are batholiths, sills, dikes, and volcanic necks. What do intrusive igneous rock bodies look like? You can see illustrations of these features in **Figure 16.**

As You Read

What You'll Learn

■ **Describe** intrusive igneous rock features and how they form.
■ **Explain** how a volcanic neck and a caldera form.

Vocabulary

batholith   volcanic neck
dike   caldera
sill

Why It's Important

Many features formed underground by igneous activity are exposed at Earth's surface by erosion.

Figure 16
This diagram shows intrusive and other features associated with volcanic activity. *Which features shown are formed above ground? Which are formed by intrusive activities?*

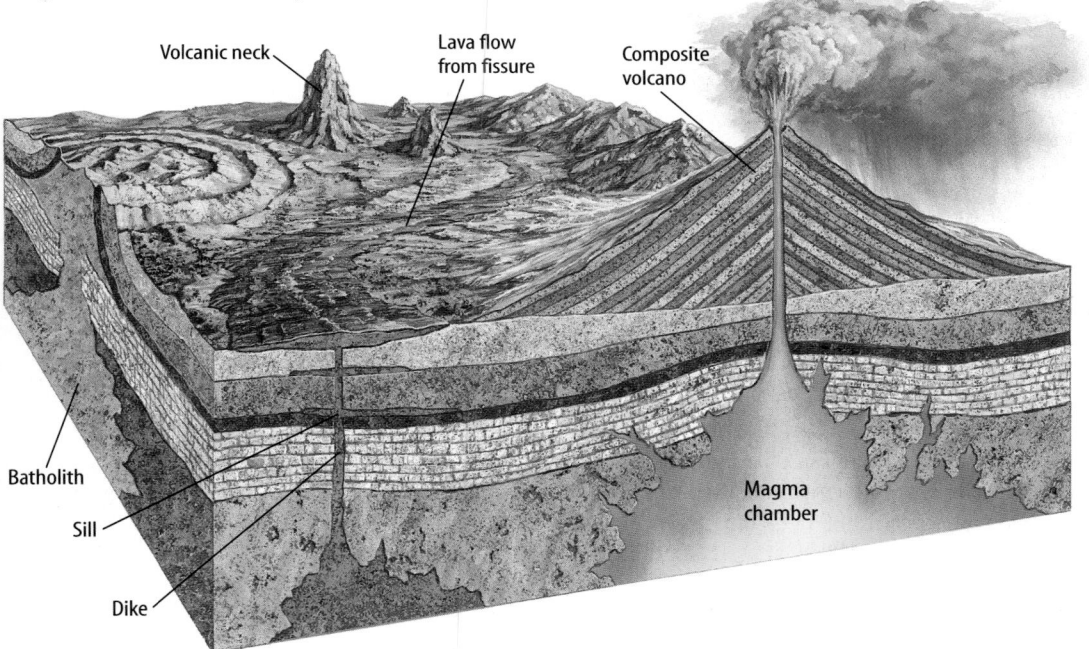

Volcanic neck
Lava flow from fissure
Composite volcano
Batholith
Sill
Dike
Magma chamber

SECTION 3 Igneous Rock Features **349**

Section ✓ *Assessment* Planner

PORTFOLIO
Extension, p. 352
PERFORMANCE ASSESSMENT
Math Skills Activity, p. 350
Skill Builder Activities, p. 353
See page 360 for more options.

CONTENT ASSESSMENT
Section, p. 353
Challenge, p. 353
Chapter, pp. 360–361

Igneous Rock Features

① Motivate

Bellringer Transparency

Display the Section Focus Transparency for Section 3. Use the accompanying Transparency Activity Master. [L2]
[ELL]

Tie to Prior Knowledge

Have students recall how a volcano looks in cross section. Explain that the magma in the central chamber leading to the vent can eventually cool and become rock. Show students a photo of Shiprock in New Mexico (available in encyclopedias and geology texts). Shiprock is the rocky central neck of a volcano that has been exposed by erosion. Students will learn in this section about many other volcanic features.

Caption Answer

Figure 16 above: lava flows; below: batholith, sill, dike, volcanic neck

Intrusive Features

Visual Learning

Figure 16 Ask students to hypothesize whether the igneous intrusions shown are younger or older than the rocks they cut through. They are younger. The rocks that they cut through had to be there first. **IS Logical-Mathematical**

Discussion

Remind students that batholiths are exposed on the surface by erosion. **Is the rock that forms these batholiths relatively hard or relatively soft rock? Explain.** It is relatively hard rock, or it would have been eroded in the same way as the material was that once surrounded it.

Activity

Have students collect several rocks in their neighborhood or on the way to school. Or, obtain rocks from a garden supply store or scientific supply company. Have groups of four students work together to identify any igneous rocks among the samples. Make available several rock and mineral guides that include color photos and descriptions. L2 COOP LEARN **IS Interpersonal and Naturalist**

Math Skills Activity

National Math Standards

Correlation to Mathematics Objectives
1, 2, 6–9

Answers to Practice Problems

1. dark
2. about 24 to 45 kg

Batholiths The largest intrusive igneous rock bodies are **batholiths.** They can be many hundreds of kilometers in width and length and several kilometers thick. Batholiths form when magma bodies that are being forced upward from inside Earth cool slowly and solidify before reaching the surface. However, not all of them remain hidden inside Earth. Some batholiths have been exposed at Earth's surface by many years of erosion. The granite domes of Yosemite National Park are the remains of a huge batholith that stretches across much of the length of California.

Math Skills Activity

Classifying Igneous Rocks

Igneous rocks are classified into three types depending on the amount of silica they contain. Basaltic rocks contain approximately 45 percent to 52 percent silica. Andesitic, or intermediate, rocks contain about 52 percent to 66 percent silica, and granitic rocks have more than 66 percent silica. The lighter the color is, the higher the silica content is.

Example Problem

A 900-kg block of igneous rock contains 630 kg of silica. Calculate the percent of silica in the rock to classify it.

Solution

1 *This is what you know:* rock = 900 kg
silica = 630 kg

2 *This is what you need to find:* The percentage of silica: x

3 *This is the equation you need to use:* Weight of silica / weight of rock = x / 100

4 *Solve the equation for x:* $x = (630 \text{ kg}) \times (100)/900 \text{ kg}$
$x = 70$ percent, therefore, the rock is granitic.

Check your answer by dividing it by 100, then multiplying by 900. Did you get the given amount of silica?

Practice Problems

1. A 250-kg sample of basalt contains 125 kg of silica. Use the classification system to determine whether basalt is light or dark.
2. Andesite is an intermediate, medium-colored rock with a silica content ranging from 52 percent to 66 percent. About how many kilograms of silica would you predict to be in a 68-kg sample of andesite?

For help with solving equations, refer to the Math Skill Handbook.

Teacher FYI

Intrusive structures such as dikes, sills, and batholiths are classified as plutons. The name comes from Pluto, the Roman god of the underworld. Some of the largest plutons are thought by geologists to be the remnants of magma reservoirs that fed the eruptions of volcanoes of the distant past.

Resource Manager

Chapter Resources Booklet
Transparency Activity, p. 44
Directed Reading for Content Mastery, pp. 19, 20

Dikes and Sills Magma sometimes squeezes into cracks in rock below the surface. This is like squeezing toothpaste into the spaces between your teeth. Magma that is forced into a crack that cuts across rock layers and hardens is called a **dike**. Magma that is forced into a crack parallel to rock layers and hardens is called a **sill**. These features are shown in **Figures 17A** and **17B**. Most dikes and sills run from a few meters to hundreds of meters long.

Other Features

When a volcano stops erupting, the magma hardens inside the vent. Erosion, usually by water and wind, begins to wear away the volcano. The cone is much softer than the solid igneous rock in the vent. Thus, the cone erodes first, leaving behind the solid igneous core as a **volcanic neck**. Devil's Tower in Wyoming, shown in **Figure 17C,** is an example of the many volcanic necks in the United States.

SCIENCE Online

Research Visit the Glencoe Science Web site at **science.glencoe.com** to learn more about igneous rock features. Share your research with your class.

A A sill is formed when magma is forced between rock layers.

C Devil's Tower in Wyoming is an example of a volcanic neck.

Figure 17
Igneous features can form in many different sizes and shapes.

B The vertical dikes shown here near Shiprock, New Mexico, were formed when magma squeezed into vertical cracks in the surrounding rock layers.

Use an Analogy

Use this analogy to help students remember the orientation of a sill. Point to the window sills. Have students note that these sills are horizontal in orientation, in the same way volcanic sills are. The threshold of a door is also called a sill. L2
Visual-Spatial

Other Features

Extension

Have students research when and how the Sierra Nevada batholith formed and how large it is thought to be. Tectonic plate convergence and the resulting melting of subducted rock material formed the Sierra Nevada over a 100- to 130-million year period ending about 80 million years ago. The batholith is thought to be over 60,000 km^2.

Use Science Words

Word Origin Have students find the origin of *-lith*. Greek lithos, meaning "stone" Have them find other words that contain *-lith* and explain their meanings. Possible answers: lithosphere—Earth's solid surface or rocky crust; lithography—printing on a flat surface, such as a rock; lithophyte—a plant that grows on rock L2 **Linguistic**

Visual Learning

Figure 17C Ask students to identify the type of climate area in which Devil's Tower is located. dry **How might this feature look if it were in a wet climate?** Water would have eroded the rock more severely. It is likely there would be few sharp edges.

SCIENCE Online
Internet Addresses
_____
_____
_____

Explore the Glencoe Science Web site at **science.glencoe.com** to find out more about topics in this section.

Other Features,
continued

Make a Model

Show students photographs and topographic maps of Crater Lake in Oregon. Have students use modeling clay to make a model of the caldera. Explain that Wizard Island formed after the caldera formed and should also be included in their model. L1
⟨LS⟩ Visual-Spatial

Discussion

Have students think back to the differences in the types of volcanoes they learned about in **Section 2. Is Mount Mazama, the volcano that exploded to form the Crater Lake caldera, more likely to have been a shield volcano or a composite volcano? Explain.** A composite volcano or a cinder cone volcano, because these volcanoes are most likely to erupt violently, as Mount Mazama did; shield volcanoes have fairly low eruptive force.

Extension

Invite a geologist from a local university or the United States Geological Survey to class to give a presentation on the geology of the local area. Encourage students to write questions they would like answered in their Science Journals before the presentation. Have them compose the answers using information from the presentation. L2
⟨LS⟩ Linguistic P

Figure 18
Calderas are formed when the top of a volcano collapses.

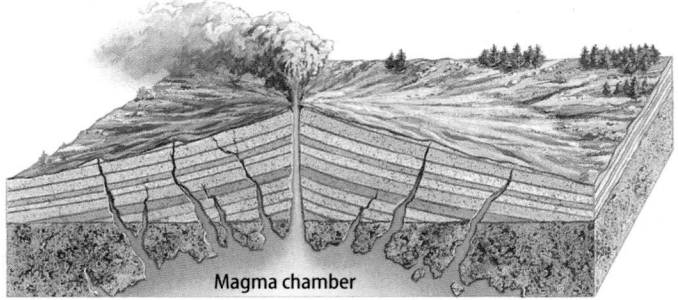

A Magma rises, causing volcanic activity to occur.

Calderas Sometimes after an eruption, the top of a volcano can collapse, as seen in **Figure 18.** This produces a large depression called a **caldera.** Crater Lake in Oregon, shown in **Figure 19,** is a caldera that filled with water and is now a lake. Crater Lake formed after the violent eruption and destruction of Mount Mazama about 7,000 years ago.

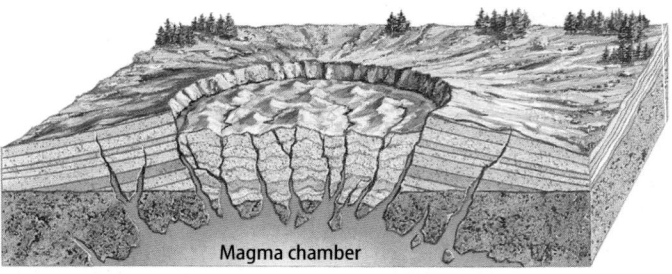

B The magma chamber partially empties, causing rock to collapse into the emptied chamber below the surface. This forms a circular-shaped caldera.

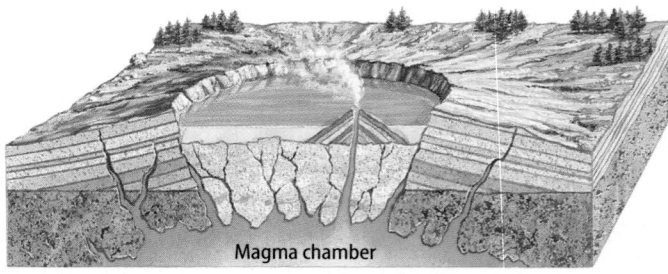

C Crater Lake in Oregon formed when water collected in the circular space left when surface material collapsed.

352 CHAPTER 12 Volcanoes

Inclusion Strategies

Visually Impaired Construct a hollow model of a volcano and associated volcanic features out of modeling clay. Allow students to become familiar with the model's shape. Then remove most of the upper portion of the volcano, leaving only the lower section of the mountain with a very large opening. Again, allow your students to study the model and discover caldera formation. L1 **⟨LS⟩ Kinesthetic**

Resource Manager

Chapter Resources Booklet
    Enrichment, p. 30
    Reinforcement, p. 27
    Activity Worksheet, pp. 7–8

Figure 19
Wizard Island in Crater Lake is a cinder cone volcano that erupted after the formation of the caldera. *What causes a caldera to form?*

Igneous Features Exposed You have learned in this chapter that Earth's surface is built up and worn down continually. The surface of Earth is built up by volcanoes. Also, igneous rock is formed when magma hardens below ground. Eventually, the processes of weathering and erosion wear down rock at the surface, exposing features like batholiths, dikes, and sills.

 Reading Check *What exposes igneous features that formed below the surface?*

Section 3 Assessment

1. What's the difference between a caldera and a crater?
2. Describe how a sill forms. How is it different from a dike?
3. What is a volcanic neck and how does it form?
4. Explain how a batholith forms.
5. **Think Critically** Why are the large, granite dome features of Yosemite National Park in California considered to be intrusive volcanic features when they are exposed at the surface?

Skill Builder Activities

6. **Comparing and Contrasting** Compare and contrast dikes, sills, batholiths, and volcanic necks. **For more help, refer to the** Science Skill Handbook.
7. **Using Graphics Software** Use the graphics software available on your computer to produce an illustration of igneous rock features based on **Figure 16.** Be sure to include intrusive features and features that form above ground. **For more help, refer to the** Technology Skill Handbook.

3 Assess

Reteach

Have students make and use flash cards of igneous rock features. They should draw each feature on one side of a card and place its name and a short description on the other. L1 ELL
Linguistic and Visual-Spatial

Challenge

Place an outline map of the United States on the wall. Challenge students to identify one example of an igneous feature covered in the section. Have students label the feature on the map. L2 **Visual-Spatial**

Assessment

Process Give each student an unlabeled diagram (such as **Figure 16**) that shows all of the igneous rock features covered in this section. Place arrows on the diagram pointing to each feature to be labeled. Have students label the features. Use **PASC,** p. 127.

Answers to Section Assessment

1. A caldera forms when the top of a volcano explodes and collapses. A crater is the steep-walled depression found around a volcano's vent.
2. A sill forms when magma squeezes between horizontal rock layers. Dikes form when magma squeezes into vertical cracks in rock.
3. It is the solid igneous core left behind when the softer material of the volcano's cone erodes around it.
4. It forms when magma bodies that are forced upward from inside Earth cool slowly and solidify before reaching the surface.
5. The features formed when magma cooled underground. Erosion later exposed them.
6. All are intrusive igneous features. Batholiths are large features hundreds of kilometers in width and length. Dikes and sills are smaller features that form in cracks, but

dikes form in vertical cracks while sills form in horizontal ones. Volcanic necks are the cores of extinct volcanoes that have been exposed by erosion.
7. Students can simplify the illustration, but should include all the major features.

Activity

Recognize the Problem

Purpose

Students experiment to discover how the sudden removal of magma would affect a volcano.

L2 COOP LEARN

Logical-Mathematical

Process Skills

experimenting, making a model, recording, analyzing, communicating, hypothesizing, observing

Time Required

30 minutes to design the experiment; 40 minutes to carry out the experiment, analyze data, and draw conclusions

Materials

Students might help supply the materials by contributing common items such as newspapers and balloons from home.

Safety Precautions

Caution students to use care with scissors.

Form a Hypothesis

Possible Hypothesis

Hypotheses should include the idea that suddenly removing magma would cause the volcano to collapse in on itself.

Test Your Hypothesis

Possible Procedure

1. Tape the end of a balloon around the plastic tubing.
2. Use the tubing to blow up the balloon, but not all the way, and then clamp the tubing to prevent the air from escaping.
3. Push the tubing through a pre-cut hole in the bottom of a small box until the balloon rests on the bottom.
4. Pour flour over the balloon to form a volcano.
5. Release the clamp on the tubing and let the air out of the balloon.
6. The result: The balloon deflates and the surface collapses to form a caldera.

Activity — *Design Your Own Experiment*

How do calderas form?

A caldera is a depression formed when the top of a volcano collapses after an eruption. What might cause the top of a volcano to collapse? What would happen if the magma inside the magma chamber suddenly were removed?

Recognize the Problem

How does the removal of magma from the magma chamber affect a volcano?

Form a Hypothesis

Based on your reading about volcanoes, state a hypothesis about what would happen if the magma inside the magma chamber of a volcano were suddenly removed.

Goals
- **Design** a volcano setup that will demonstrate how a caldera could form.
- **Observe** what happens during trials with your volcano setup.
- **Describe** what you observe.

Possible Materials
small box
small balloon
paper
newspaper
flour
plastic tubing
clamp for tubing
tape
scissors

Safety Precautions

Inclusion Strategies

Gifted Some students might want to work together to videotape the experiment setup and the quick extraction of material to collapse the volcano. Students can play the tapes, displaying what happens to the volcano for their classmates. L3 **Visual-Spatial and Interpersonal**

Test Your Hypothesis

Plan

1. As a group, agree upon the hypothesis and identify which results will support the hypothesis.

2. **Design** a volcano that allows you to test your hypothesis. What materials will you use to build your volcano?

3. What will you remove from inside your volcano to represent the loss of magma? How will you remove it?

4. Where will you place your volcano? What will you do to minimize messes?

5. **Identify** all constants, variables, and controls of the experiment.

Do

1. Make sure your teacher approves your plan before you start.

2. **Construct** your volcano with any features that will be required to test your hypothesis.

3. **Conduct** one or more appropriate trials to test your hypothesis. Record any observations that you make and any other data that are appropriate to test your hypothesis.

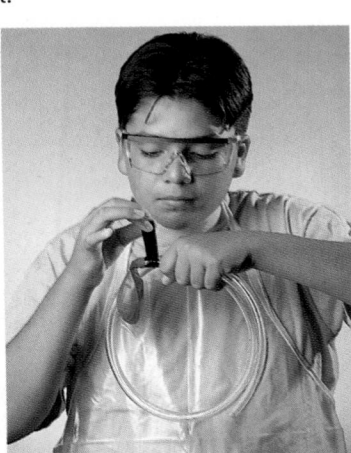

Analyze Your Data

1. **Describe** in words or with a drawing what your volcano looked like before you began.

2. What happened to your volcano during the experiment that you conducted? Did its appearance change?

3. **Describe** in words or with a drawing what your volcano looked like after the trial.

4. What other observations did you make?

5. **Describe** any other data that you recorded.

Draw Conclusions

1. Did your observations support your hypothesis? Explain.

2. How was your demonstration similar to what might happen to a real volcano? How was it different?

*C*ommunicating

Your Data

Make a poster with diagrams and descriptions of how a caldera forms. Use your visual aid to **describe** caldera formation to students in another class.

ACTIVITY 355

✓*Assessment*

Performance Have pairs of students write short critiques of each other's designs and procedures for carrying them out. Use **Performance Assessment in the Science Classroom**, p. 159.

*C*ommunicating
Your Data

Encourage students to use graphic art and word-processing programs to prepare their posters and diagrams.

Teaching Strategy

Encourage students to think in terms of something that will allow the volcano to hold its shape, but from which material can be removed quickly to make the volcano collapse.

Expected Outcome

Students will make a model volcano, then quickly withdraw material from its interior, causing the top of the volcano to collapse.

Analyze Your Data

1. Answers will vary but students should note shape and material used to make and fill the volcano.

2. Students should describe the process for quickly removing material from the interior and the collapse of the cone.

3. Students should describe a collapsed volcano.

4. Students should report any other observations.

5. Students should report additional recorded data.

Error Analysis

Errors may have occurred if air escaped from the balloon too soon, or was uncontrolled.

Draw Conclusions

1. Observations should support hypotheses. Possible answer: Yes; quickly emptying the magma chamber produces a caldera.

2. In a real volcano, the eruption removes material quickly from the volcano's interior, causing the top to collapse. In the experiment, removing material from the interior of the model volcano causes the model to collapse in on itself.

Oops! Accidents in SCIENCE

SOMETIMES GREAT DISCOVERIES HAPPEN BY ACCIDENT!

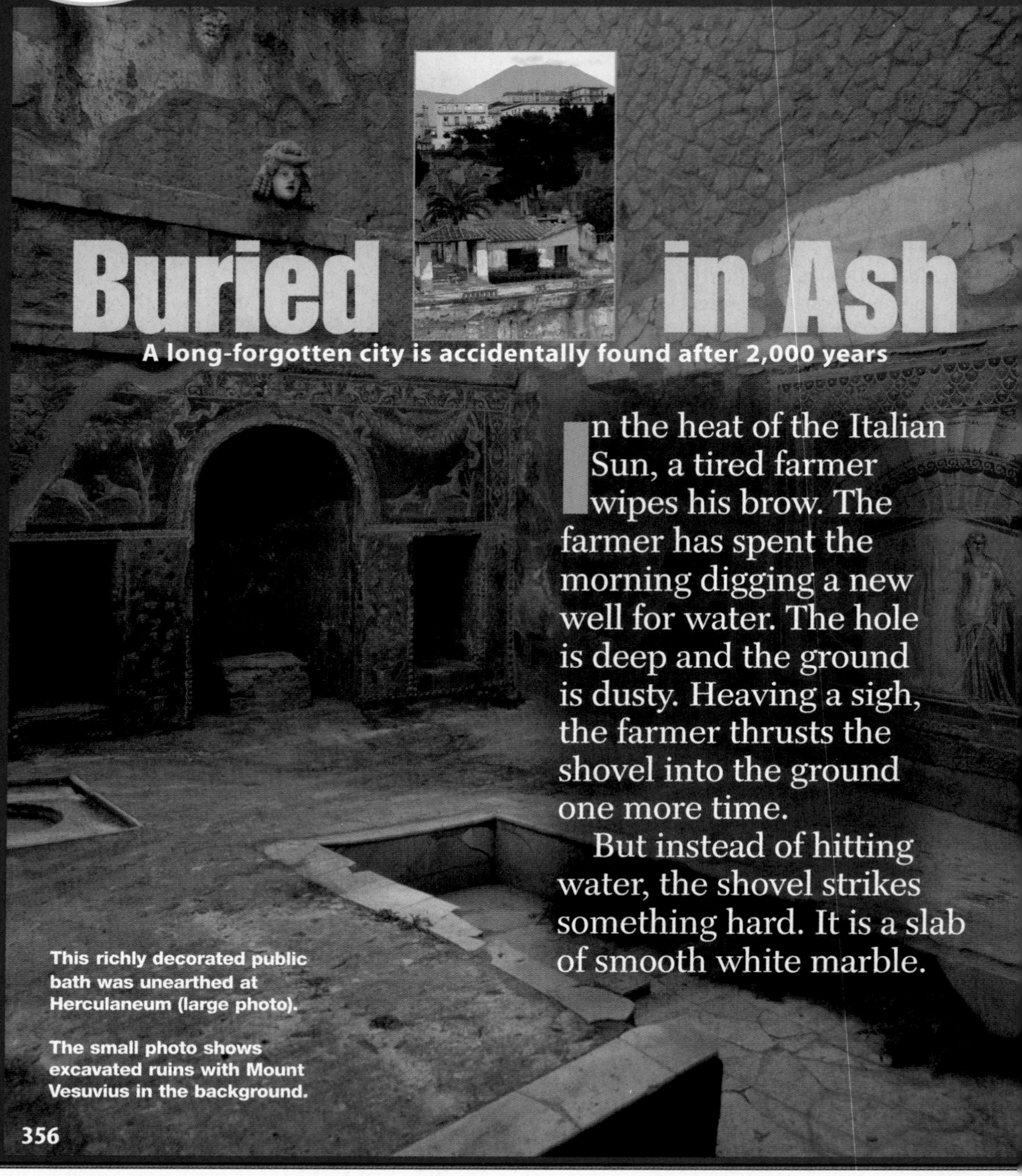

Content Background

Vesuvius is a 1,281-m-high, composite volcano. It is the only active volcano on the mainland of Europe. The volcano's crater is approximately 600 m in diameter and 300 m deep. Vesuvius lies within the remains of Monte Somma, a much larger volcano from the late Pleistocene.

Before the 79 A.D. eruption that buried Herculaneum, Pompeii, and Stabiae, Vesuvius was thought to be extinct. Ten smaller eruptions occurred between that time and 1631, when another major eruption occurred. Since 1631, Vesuvius has been continuously active and its activity is now closely monitored. After the 1906 eruption, forests were planted on the slopes in order to protect villages below from mud flows that often happen after large eruptions.

Despite the destruction that volcanoes cause, they also bring benefits. The fertile volcanic soil below the volcano supports many crops—vegetable gardens and orchards near the base and vineyards on the lower slopes.

Discussion

Explain to students that today more than 2 million people live near the base of Vesuvius. **Why would people still live so close to an active volcano?** Possible answers: Volcanic soil is very fertile so it is a good location for growing crops. Also, people whose families have lived there for generations may not want to leave the area.

Buried in Ash

A long-forgotten city is accidentally found after 2,000 years

In the heat of the Italian Sun, a tired farmer wipes his brow. The farmer has spent the morning digging a new well for water. The hole is deep and the ground is dusty. Heaving a sigh, the farmer thrusts the shovel into the ground one more time.

But instead of hitting water, the shovel strikes something hard. It is a slab of smooth white marble.

This richly decorated public bath was unearthed at Herculaneum (large photo).

The small photo shows excavated ruins with Mount Vesuvius in the background.

356

Resources for Teachers and Students

The Buried City of Pompeii: What It Was Like When Vesuvius Exploded, by Shelley Tanaka, Hyperion; Madison Press, 1997.

Lost City of Pompeii, by Dorothy Hinshaw Patent, Benchmark Press, 1999.

In Search of Pompeii: Uncovering a Buried Roman City, by Giovanni Caselli, P. Bedrick Books, 1999.

Mount Vesuvius: Europe's Mighty Volcano of Smoke and Ash, by Kathy Furgang, Powerkids Press, 2001.

The farmer didn't know it at the time (the early 1700s), but that marble was the first clue that something very big and very important lay beneath the farm fields. Under the ground people walked on every day, lay the ancient city of Herculaneum (her kew LAY nee um). The city, and its neighbor Pompeii (pom PAY) had been buried for more than 1,600 years. Why? Because on another summer day, August 24, 79 A.D., to be exact, Mount Vesuvius, a nearby volcano, erupted and buried both cities with pumice, rocks, mud, ash, and lava.

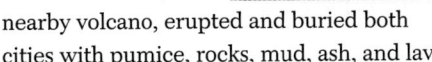
An archaeologist excavates a skeleton in Herculaneum.

Back in Time

The sun shone over the town of Herculaneum on that August morning almost 2,000 years ago. Nestled at the foot of the mountain, overlooking the Gulf of Naples, it was a peaceful place. But at about 1 P.M., that peace was shattered forever.

With massive force, the peak of Vesuvius exploded, sending six cubic kilometers of ash and pumice into the sky. Hours later, a fiery surge made its way from the volcano to the city. These pyroclastic flows continued as gray pumice fell from the sky. Buildings were crushed and buried by falling ash and pumice. Within six hours, much of Herculaneum was totally buried under the flow. After six surges and flows from Vesuvius, the deadly eruption ceased. But the city had disappeared under approximately 21 m of ash, rock, and mud.

A City Vanishes

More than 3,600 people were killed in the natural disaster. Scientists believe that most were killed by the pyroclastic surges. Many died trying to protect their faces from the air that was filled with hot ash. Those lucky enough to escape returned to find no trace of their city. Over hundreds of years, grass and fields covered Herculaneum erasing it from human memory. Eventually, a town called Resina was built on the site.

In the last couple of hundred years, archaeologists have unearthed colorful and perfectly preserved mosaics and an amazing library with ancient scrolls in excellent condition. In the 1980s, archaeologists found skeletons and the hardened remains, called casts, of people who died when Vesuvius erupted. Visitors to the site can see a Roman woman, a teen-aged girl, and a soldier with his sword still in his hand.

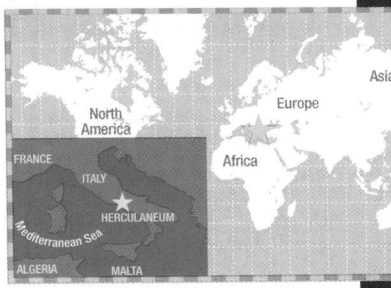

Much of Herculaneum still lies buried beneath thick layers of volcanic ash and archaeologists still are digging to expose more of the ruins. Their work is helping scientists better understand everyday life in an ancient Italian town. But if it weren't for a farmer's search for water, Herculaneum might not have been discovered at all!

Activity

Have students look up more information about the 79 A.D. eruption that destroyed Pompeii and Herculaneum and what life was like in those cities before the eruption. Have them write a story about a young person who survived the eruption. They should include descriptions of what the person was doing before the eruption and the events that he or she witnessed during the eruption. Students should be sure to incorporate scientific facts into their creative writing. L3 IS **Linguistic and Naturalist**

Analyze the Event

Ask students to speculate how they might have felt if they had been the farmer digging the well. Possible answer: curious or excited Ask what they might do if they were digging on their property and came across some trace of a buried city. Possible answers: Contact a local historical society, an archaeologist, or scientists at a nearby university to help them find out more.

CONNECTIONS Research the history of your town. Ask your local librarian to help "unearth" maps, drawings, or photos that let you travel back in time! Share your finds with your class.

SCIENCE *Online*
For more information, visit science.glencoe.com

CONNECTIONS What students find in their research will vary depending on your location. Many areas of the United States have artifacts and other evidence of cultures that inhabited the areas thousands of years ago. Suggest that students also ask local librarians to help them locate information on the prehistory of your area.

SCIENCE *Online*

Internet Addresses

_____

_____

_____

Explore the Glencoe Science Web site at **science.glencoe.com** to find out more about topics in this feature.

Reviewing Main Ideas

Preview

Students can answer the questions in their Science Journals. Discuss the answers as you go through the chapter. **Linguistic**

Review

Students can write their answers, then compare them with those of other students. **Interpersonal**

Reteach

Students can look at the illustrations and describe details that support the main ideas of the chapter. **Visual-Spatial**

Answers to Chapter Review

SECTION 1

2. It is flowing into the water where it vaporizes the water, forming steam, and quickly cools, forming new rock at the water's edge.

SECTION 2

1. a shield volcano

SECTION 3

2. sill

Reviewing Main Ideas

Section 1 Volcanoes and Earth's Moving Plates

1. Volcanoes can be dangerous to people because they can cause deaths and destroy property.

2. Rocks in the crust and mantle melt to form magma, which is forced toward Earth's surface. When the magma flows through vents, it's called lava and forms volcanoes. *What is happening to this lava?*

3. Volcanoes can form over hot spots when magma flows onto the seafloor. Sometimes the lava builds up from the seafloor to form an island. Volcanoes also form when Earth's plates pull apart or come together.

Section 2 Types of Volcanoes

1. The three types of volcanoes are shield volcanoes, cinder cone volcanoes, and composite volcanoes. *Which type of volcano is pictured below?*

2. Shield volcanoes produce quiet eruptions. Cinder cone and composite volcanoes can produce explosive eruptions.

3. Some lavas are thin and flow easily, producing quiet eruptions. Other lavas are thick and stiff, producing violent eruptions.

4. Water vapor and silica in magma add to its explosiveness.

Section 3 Igneous Rock Features

1. Intrusive igneous rock bodies such as batholiths, dikes, and sills form when magma solidifies underground.

2. Batholiths are the most massive igneous rock bodies. Dikes form when magma squeezes into cracks, cutting across rock layers. Sills form when magma squeezes in between rock layers. *Which rock feature is shown in this photo?*

3. A caldera forms when the top of a volcano collapses, forming a large depression. Crater Lake is a caldera in Oregon.

FOLDABLES
Reading & Study Skills

After You Read

Use your Foldable to help review the similarities and differences between quiet and explosive volcanic eruptions. Decide what type of volcano produces each style of eruption.

FOLDABLES
Reading & Study Skills

After You Read

After students have read the chapter and completed the Foldable described in Before You Read, have them do the activity on the student page.

Dinah Zike

Visualizing Main Ideas

Complete the following concept map on types of volcanic eruptions.

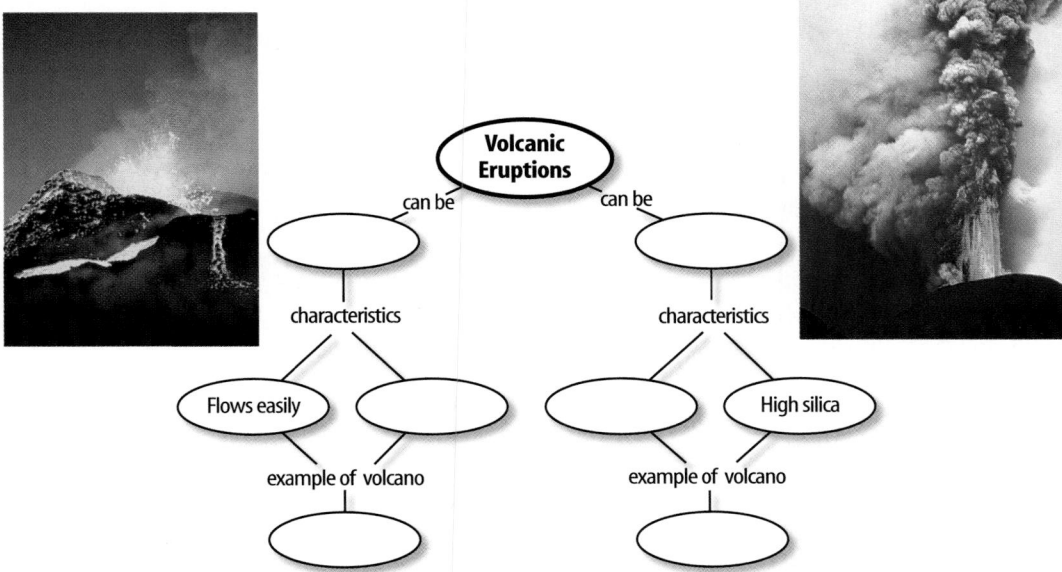

Vocabulary Review

Using Vocabulary
1. shield volcano
2. tephra
3. sill
4. crater
5. dike

Vocabulary Review

Vocabulary Words

a. batholith
b. caldera
c. cinder cone volcano
d. composite volcano
e. crater
f. dike
g. hot spot
h. shield volcano
i. sill
j. tephra
k. vent
l. volcanic neck
m. volcano

Study Tip

When you encounter new vocabulary, write it down in a sentence. This will help you understand, remember, and use new vocabulary words.

Using Vocabulary

Each of the following sentences is false. Make the sentence true by replacing each underlined word(s) with the correct vocabulary word(s).

1. A broad volcano with gently sloping sides is called a <u>composite volcano</u>.

2. <u>Sills</u> are bits of rock or solidified lava dropped from the air after a volcanic eruption.

3. Magma squeezed into a horizontal crack between rock layers is called a <u>caldera</u>.

4. The steep-walled depression around a volcano's vent is called a <u>tephra</u>.

5. Magma squeezed into a vertical crack across rock layers is called a <u>crater</u>.

Checking Concepts

1. C
2. B
3. A
4. C
5. C
6. A
7. B
8. D
9. C
10. D

Thinking Critically

11. Glaciers form because of Iceland's cold climate. Volcanoes also exist there because Iceland is located on the Mid-Atlantic Ridge, a divergent plate boundary.

12. The lava is very fluid. Because it flows easily, a relatively quiet eruption is produced.

13. They both occur at the boundaries between plates and are related to geological movements in Earth's crust.

14. Students should infer that the volcano formed as a result of one plate sliding under another.

15. A composite volcano is made up of alternating layers of tephra and lava. Tephra is deposited by violent, explosive eruptions. Lava is deposited by less-violent eruptions.

Chapter 12 Assessment

Checking Concepts

Choose the word or phrase that best answers the question.

1. What type of boundary is associated with composite volcanoes?
   A) plates moving apart
   B) plates sticking and slipping
   C) plates moving together
   D) plates sliding past each other

2. Why is Hawaii made of volcanoes?
   A) Plates are moving apart.
   B) A hot spot exists.
   C) Plates are moving together.
   D) Rift zones exist.

3. What kind of magmas produce violent volcanic eruptions?
   A) those rich in silica
   B) those that are fluid
   C) those forming shield volcanoes
   D) those rich in iron

4. Magma that is low in silica generally produces what kind of eruptions?
   A) thick   C) quiet
   B) caldera   D) explosive

5. What is made entirely of tephra?
   A) shield volcano   C) cinder cone volcano
   B) caldera   D) composite volcano

6. What kind of volcano is Kilauea?
   A) shield volcano   C) cinder cone volcano
   B) composite   D) caldera cone volcano

7. What is magma that hardens in a crack cutting across rock layers called?
   A) sill   C) volcanic neck
   B) dike   D) batholith

8. What is the largest intrusive igneous rock body?
   A) dike   C) sill
   B) volcanic neck   D) batholith

9. Which describes bits of material that fall to Earth after an eruption?
   A) dike   C) tephra
   B) sand   D) sill

10. What is the process that formed Soufrière Hills volcano on Montserrat?
    A) plates sticking and slipping
    B) caldera formation
    C) plates sliding sideways
    D) plates moving together

Thinking Critically

11. Explain how glaciers and volcanoes can exist on Iceland.

12. What kind of eruption is produced when basaltic lava that is low in silica flows from a volcano? Explain.

13. How are volcanoes related to earthquakes?

14. Misti is a volcano in Peru. Peru is on the western edge of South America. How might this volcano have formed?

15. Describe the layers of a composite volcano. Which layers represent violent eruptions?

Developing Skills

16. **Classifying** Classify Fuji, which has steep sides and is made of layers of silica-rich lava and ash.

17. **Measuring in SI** The base of the volcano Mauna Loa is about 5,000 m below sea level. The total height of the volcano is 9,170 m. What percentage of the volcano is above sea level? Below sea level?

18. **Comparing and Contrasting** Compare and contrast shield volcanoes, cinder cone volcanoes, and composite volcanoes.

Chapter ✓Assessment Planner

Portfolio Encourage students to place in their portfolios one or two items of what they consider to be their best work. Examples include:
- Science Journal, p. 337
- Challenge, p. 339
- Extension, p. 342
- Extension, p. 352

Performance Additional performance assessments, Performance Task Assessment Lists, and rubrics for evaluating these activities can be found in Glencoe's **Performance Assessment in the Science Classroom.**

19. Interpreting Scientific Illustrations Look at the map below. The Hawaiian Islands and Emperor Seamounts were formed when the Pacific Plate moved over a fixed hot spot. If the Emperor chain is northwest of the Hawaiian Islands, what can you infer about the Pacific Plate?

Map showing North America, Aleutian Islands, Emperor Seamounts, Hawaiian Ridge, and Pacific Ocean.

20. Concept Mapping Make a network tree concept map about where volcanoes can occur. Include the following words and phrases: *hot spots, divergent plate boundaries, convergent plate boundaries, volcanoes, can occur, examples, Iceland, Soufrière Hills,* and *Hawaiian Islands.*

Performance Assessment

21. Poster Make a poster of the three basic types of volcanoes. Label them and indicate what type of eruption occurs from each one.

TECHNOLOGY

Go to the Glencoe Science Web site at **science.glencoe.com** or use the **Glencoe Science CD-ROM** for additional chapter assessment.

Test Practice

A scientist who studies volcanoes brought the following information to a lecture he did at a middle school for the entire sixth grade.

Study the table and answer the following questions.

Data for Various Volcanoes

Volcano	Summit Before Eruption (meters)	Summit After Eruption (meters)	Silica Content in Magma	Trapped Gases in Magma
1	2,903	2,499	Medium to High	High
2	3,360	3,375	Low	Medium
3	2,617	2,493	Low to Medium	Medium
4	1,536	965	High	High
5	1,956	1,956	Low	Medium

1. According to this information, which volcano probably had the most violent eruption?
A) Volcano 1
B) Volcano 2
C) Volcano 4
D) Volcano 5

2. Based on this information, choose the most reasonable hypothesis.
F) The higher the silica content is, the stronger the eruption is.
G) The lower the trapped gas content is, the stronger the eruption is.
H) The lower the silica content is, the stronger the eruption is.
J) The higher the trapped gas content is, the weaker the eruption is.

Test Practice

The Test-Taking Tip was written by The Princeton Review, the nation's leader in test preparation.
1. C
2. F

Developing Skills

16. Fuji is a composite volcano.
17. 54.5 % below, 45.5 % above; (5,000 m / 9,170 m) × 100 % = 54.5 %
18. All three are types of volcanoes. Shield volcanoes are the largest and erupt relatively quietly. Cinder cone and composite volcanoes are smaller. Cinder cones erupt explosively with ash, gas, and rock. Composite volcanoes alternately erupt violently with ash, gas, and rock and less violently with lava flows.
19. The Pacific plate is moving in a northwesterly direction.
20. Check students' work.

Performance Assessment

21. Posters should show each type of volcano in cross section and labeled with the type of eruption it produces. Use **Performance Assessment in the Science Classroom**, p. 145.

✓Assessment Resources

📂 Reproducible Masters
Chapter Review, pp. 35–36
Assessment, pp. 37–40
Assessment Transparency Activity p. 47

Glencoe Science Web site
Interactive Tutor
Chapter Quizzes

Glencoe Technology
- Assessment Transparency
- Interactive CD-ROM Chapter Quizzes
- ExamView Pro Test Bank
- Vocabulary PuzzleMaker Software
- MindJogger Videoquiz DVD/VHS

QUESTION 1: B

Students need to use the information in the passage in order to correctly identify the best supported conclusion. Students can use such clues as *scientists can estimate how long, on average, time intervals are between earthquakes* in order to conclude that choice B is correct.

QUESTION 2: F

Students need to use the information in the passage in order to correctly identify the best supported conclusion.

- **Choice F** Yes; this is supported by the passage.
- **Choice G** No; this is not supported by information in the passage.
- **Choice H** No; this is not supported by information in the passage.
- **Choice J** No; this is not supported by information in the passage.

Standardized Test Practice

Read the passage carefully. Then read the questions that follow the passage. Decide which is the best answer to each question.

Earthquakes and Volcanoes

Earthquakes are destructive and potentially fatal natural disasters. Geologists have been working to learn what they can about earthquakes in order to better protect property and to save human lives.

Scientists know that many earthquakes occur because tectonic plates interact with one another at plate boundaries. They also know that many earthquakes occur every day all over the world. They forecast that major earthquakes will occur sometime in the future in certain regions, such as along the San Andreas Fault near Parkfield, California. But scientists cannot predict exactly when and where an earthquake will occur.

One approach to forecasting earthquakes is known as paleoseismology. Paleoseismology involves the study of past movement of rock and sediment along faults. Motion along a fault results in an earthquake, therefore, studying this movement is one way to study ancient earthquake occurrences.

This movement can be measured in the field by observing shifted rock and sediment along a fault. If this displaced sediment can be dated, the time at which the earthquake occurred also can be estimated. With information on several past earthquakes, scientists can estimate how long, on average, time intervals are between the earthquakes. This is one way to estimate how many earthquakes might occur along a fault over a period of time.

Although scientists are not yet able to predict earthquakes, the information gained from their research advances the field.

The San Andreas fault is the center of much tectonic activity, and many earthquakes occur along it.

1. Based on the information in this passage, what can the reader conclude?
  - **A)** Earthquakes always occur during heavy rainstorms.
  - **B)** Earthquakes can not be predicted reliably, but they can be forecasted over estimated periods of time.
  - **C)** Earthquakes are extremely rare natural occurrences.
  - **D)** Earthquakes do not affect property and human lives very much.

2. What does the information in this passage suggest?
  - **F)** Studies of displacement along faults can provide information for forecasting earthquakes.
  - **G)** Studying faults allows scientists to determine the time and date of the next earthquake.
  - **H)** Paleoseismology is the study of fossils along the San Andreas fault.
  - **J)** Scientists do not know what causes earthquakes.

Reasoning and Skills

Read each question and decide which is the best answer.

1. All of these statements are true about earthquakes EXCEPT _____.
   A) Earthquakes can range from unnoticeable vibrations to devastating waves of energy.
   B) Earthquakes occur along fault surfaces.
   C) When earthquakes occur, only primary waves and surface waves are produced.
   D) Surface waves are responsible for most of the damage caused by earthquakes.

Test-Taking Tip   Think about all that you know about how earthquakes form and what they are.

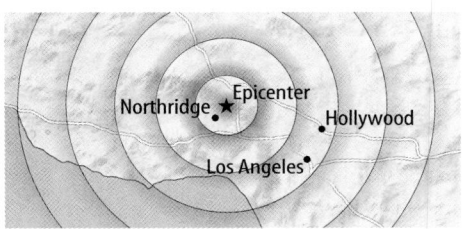

2. Refer to the diagram above. Which statement best describes the movement of surface waves after an earthquake?
   F) Surface waves move towards the epicenter just before an earthquake strikes.
   G) Surface waves travel throughout all layers of Earth.
   H) Surface waves travel faster than primary waves do.
   J) Surface waves travel outward from the epicenter of an earthquake.

Test-Taking Tip   Review what you know about wave movement and speed.

3. All of these statements are true about volcanoes EXCEPT ____.
   A) Three basic types of volcanoes are shield, cinder cone, and composite.
   B) The amount of water vapor, other gases, and silica in magma determine what kind of eruption will take place.
   C) The lower the silica content in magma, the more explosive an eruption will be.
   D) A volcano's form depends upon the type of eruption and the composition of erupted material.

Test-Taking Tip   Think about the different kinds of volcanoes, how they form, and what factors influence the type of eruption.

Consider this question carefully before writing your answer on a separate sheet of paper.

4. Volcanic eruptions transform the environment around them. Discuss some of the ways in which volcanoes change Earth's surface.

Test-Taking Tip   Consider the details of specific eruptions that you have learned about.

Reasoning and Skills

QUESTION 1: C
Students must understand earthquakes to identify which answer choice is the exception. Choices A, B, and D are all true statements about earthquakes. Only choice C is inaccurate.

QUESTION 2: J
Students must understand earthquakes and carefully consider all the information in the picture to identify the correct choice.
- **Choice F** No; surface waves do not move towards the epicenter and only occur after an earthquake has struck.
- **Choice G** No; surface waves decrease in intensity as they move away from the epicenter.
- **Choice H** No; primary waves travel faster than surface waves.
- **Choice J** Yes; surface waves travel outwards from the epicenter.

QUESTION 3: C
Students must understand volcanoes and carefully read the question to identify which answer is the exception. Answer choices A, B, and D are all true. Only choice C is an inaccurate statement about volcanoes.

QUESTION 4: Answers will vary.
Students should consider their knowledge of earthquakes and specific eruptions and write a thorough response.

Teaching Tip

Students should review volcanoes and earthquakes as well as understand how they can be related.

UNIT 4

Change and Earth's History

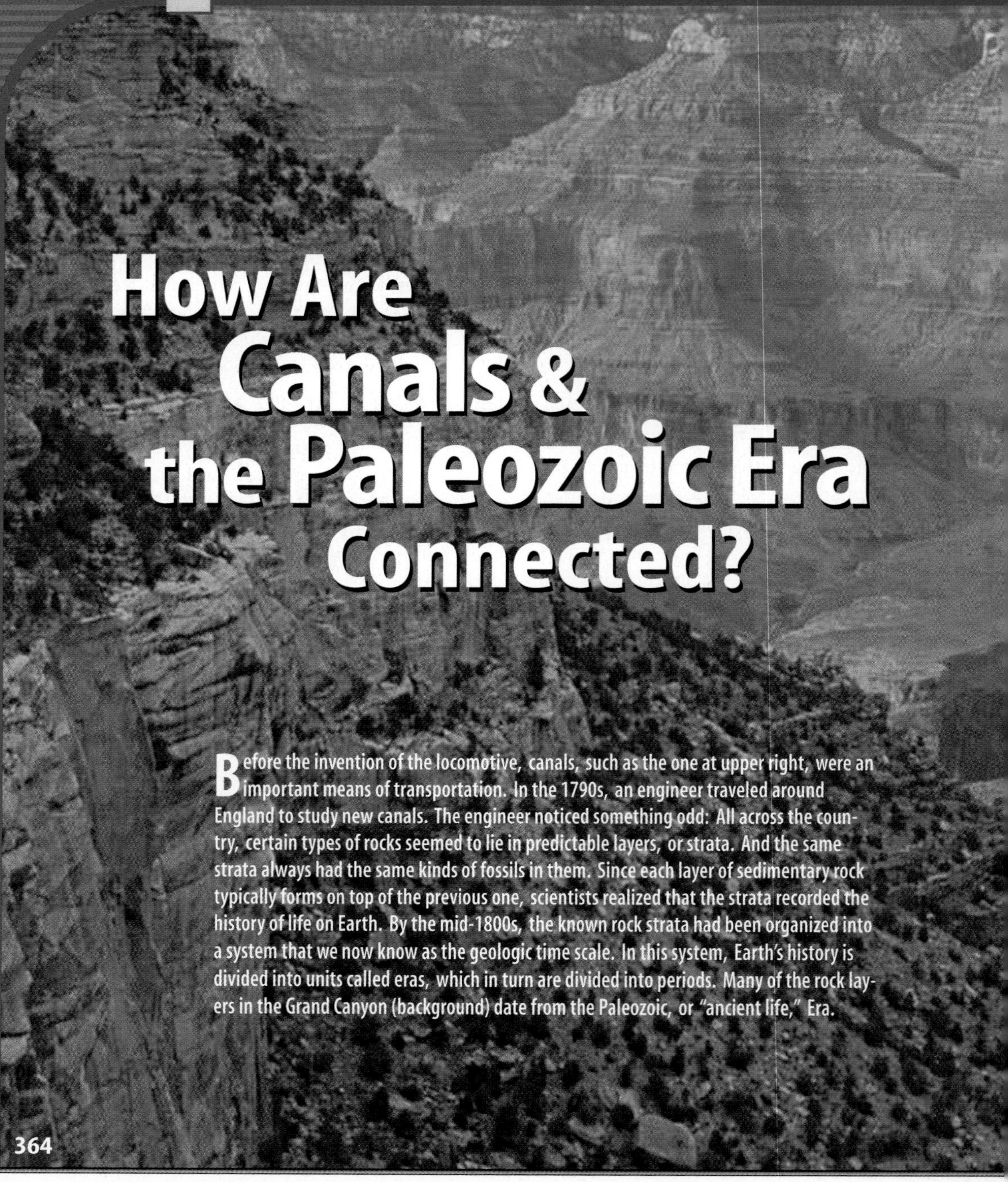

Unit Contents

✔ Pre-Reading Activity

Have students look at the illustrations in the unit, and discuss how the lifeforms pictured are similar to and different from modern organisms.

How Are Canals & the Paleozoic Era Connected?

Before the invention of the locomotive, canals, such as the one at upper right, were an important means of transportation. In the 1790s, an engineer traveled around England to study new canals. The engineer noticed something odd: All across the country, certain types of rocks seemed to lie in predictable layers, or strata. And the same strata always had the same kinds of fossils in them. Since each layer of sedimentary rock typically forms on top of the previous one, scientists realized that the strata recorded the history of life on Earth. By the mid-1800s, the known rock strata had been organized into a system that we now know as the geologic time scale. In this system, Earth's history is divided into units called eras, which in turn are divided into periods. Many of the rock layers in the Grand Canyon (background) date from the Paleozoic, or "ancient life," Era.

364

Teacher to Teacher

"Create a time line of the geologic time scale where 1 cm of yarn represents 1 million years. On index cards, have students write an event, the time it occurred in millions of years, and the distance on the yarn. Using paper clips, attach the cards to the yarn. Attach the time line to the ceiling, spiraling toward the center."

Rebecca Buckingham, Teacher
Lisbon Central School
Lisbon, NY

NATIONAL GEOGRAPHIC

NATIONAL GEOGRAPHIC

Introducing the Unit

How Are Canals & the Paleozoic Era Connected?

The excavation of land to build canals exposed previously unseen layers of rock and sediment. In other areas of the world, rivers have eroded rock and sediment creating deep canyons. The walls of the canyon contain exposed layers of rocks containing fossils. Some of these layers date back to the Paleozoic Era. By studying the age of the rock and the fossils contained in them, scientists have been able to construct a history of life on Earth. Fossils provide clues to the types of species inhabiting Earth during a particular era. Scientists also study the changing traits in fossils to determine how organisms may have adapted to changing environments.

SCIENCE CONNECTION

Activity

Choose a period on the geologic time scale. Make a list of possible Earth inhabitants. Possible categories include plants, fish, reptiles, mammals, and birds. **Have students determine which species may have been present during that time. Discuss whether the fossil record is complete. Are some species not represented? What types of creatures are missing from the fossil record? Why are they missing? Have students draw a plant or animal that may not have survived the fossil record.**

SCIENCE CONNECTION

FOSSIL RECORD Choose a period in the geologic time scale and find out what the fossil record tells us about the organisms that were alive during that time. Create a drawing or painting that shows what you think might have been a typical scene during that period in Earth's history, complete with appropriate plants and animals. What aspects of the scene are difficult or impossible to determine based on the fossil record?

SCIENCE Online
Internet Addresses

_____
_____
_____
_____

Explore the Glencoe Science Web site at **science.glencoe.com** to find out more about topics in this unit.

Section/Objectives	Standards		Activities/Features
	National	**State/Local**	
Chapter Opener	See p. 5T for a Key to Standards.		**Explore Activity:** Make a model of a fossil, p. 367 **Before You Read,** p. 367
Section 1 Fossils ⏱ 2 sessions 🗂 1 block 1. **List** the conditions necessary for fossils to form. 2. **Describe** several processes of fossil formation. 3. **Explain** how fossil correlation is used to determine rock ages.	National Content Standards: UCP2, A1, C5, D2		**MiniLAB:** Predicting Fossil Preservation, p. 369 **Chemistry Integration,** p. 371 **Life Science Integration,** p. 374
Section 2 Relative Ages of Rocks ⏱ 2 sessions 🗂 1 block 1. **Describe** methods used to assign relative ages to rock layers. 2. **Interpret** gaps in the rock record. 3. **Give an example** of how rock layers can be correlated with other rock layers.	National Content Standards: UCP2, A1, D2		**Science Online,** p. 377 **Visualizing Unconformities,** p. 379 **Science Online,** p. 380 **Activity: Relative Ages,** p. 382
Section 3 Absolute Ages of Rocks ⏱ 3 sessions 🗂 1.5 blocks 1. **Identify** how absolute age differs from relative age. 2. **Describe** how the half-lives of isotopes are used to determine a rock's age.	National Content Standards: UCP3, A1, B1, D2, G1, G2		**MiniLAB:** Jelly Bean Carbon-14 Dating, p. 384 **Problem-Solving Activity:** When did the Iceman die?, p. 386 **Activity:** Trace Fossils, pp. 388–389 **Oops! Accidents in Science:** The World's Oldest Fish Story, pp. 390–391

NATIONAL GEOGRAPHIC — Teacher's Corner

PRODUCTS AVAILABLE FROM GLENCOE
To order call 1-800-334-7344:
Curriculum Kit
GeoKit: Earth's History
PRODUCTS AVAILABLE FROM NATIONAL GEOGRAPHIC SOCIETY
To order call 1-800-368-2728:

Videos
Fossils: Clues to the Past

INDEX TO NATIONAL GEOGRAPHIC SOCIETY
The following articles may be used for research relating to this chapter:
"The Dawn of Humans: Redrawing Our Family Tree," by Lee Berger, Aug. 1998.

"Africa's Dinosaur Castaways," by Paul C. Sereno, June, 1996.
"The Great Dinosaur Egg Hunt," by Phillip J. Currie, May 1996.
"Fossils: Annals of Life Written in Rock," by David Jeffery, Aug. 1985.

Activity Materials	Reproducible Resources	Section Assessment	Technology
Explore Activity: 500-mL jar with lid, plaster of Paris, water, several small shells, paper or plastic bowl	**Chapter Resources Booklet** Foldables Worksheet, p. 17 Directed Reading Overview, p. 19 Note-taking Worksheets, pp. 33–35	GLENCOE'S **ASSESSMENT** ADVANTAGE	
MiniLAB: no materials needed *Need materials?* Contact Science Kit at 1-800-828-7777 or www.sciencekit.com on the Internet.	**Chapter Resources Booklet** Transparency Activity, p. 44 MiniLAB, p. 3 Enrichment, p. 30 Reinforcement, p. 27 Directed Reading, p. 20 Transparency Activity, pp. 47–48 Lab Activities, pp. 9–12 **Science Inquiry Labs,** p. 29	**Portfolio** Chemistry Integration, p. 371 **Performance** MiniLAB, p. 369 Skill Builder Activities, p. 375 **Content** Section Assessment, p. 375	Section Focus Transparency Teaching Transparency Interactive CD-ROM/DVD Guided Reading Audio Program
Activity: no materials needed	**Chapter Resources Booklet** Transparency Activity, p. 45 Enrichment, p. 31 Reinforcement, p. 28 Directed Reading, p. 21 Activity Worksheet, pp. 5–6 Lab Activities, pp. 13–15 **Reading and Writing Skill Activities,** p. 21	**Portfolio** Extension, p. 380 **Performance** Skill Builder Activities, p. 381 **Content** Section Assessment, p. 381	Section Focus Transparency Interactive CD-ROM/DVD Guided Reading Audio Program
MiniLAB: 80 red jelly beans, 80 green jelly beans **Activity:** construction paper, rigid plastic, plaster of Paris, sturdy cardboard, chenille stems, wire, scissors, toothpicks, clay, glue	**Chapter Resources Booklet** Transparency Activity, p. 46 MiniLAB, p. 4 Enrichment, p. 32 Reinforcement, p. 29 Directed Reading, pp. 21, 22 Activity Worksheet, pp. 7–8 **Lab Management and Safety,** p. 39	**Portfolio** Science Journal, p. 386 **Performance** MiniLAB, p. 384 Problem-Solving Activity, p. 386 Skill Builder Activities, p. 387 **Content** Section Assessment, p. 387	Section Focus Transparency Interactive CD-ROM/DVD Guided Reading Audio Program

End of Chapter Assessment

GLENCOE'S **ASSESSMENT** ADVANTAGE

Blackline Masters	Technology	Professional Series
Chapter Resources Booklet Chapter Review, pp. 37–38 Chapter Tests, pp. 39–42 **Standardized Test Practice by The Princeton Review,** pp. 59–62	MindJogger Videoquiz CD-ROM Explorations and Quizzes Vocabulary Puzzle Makers ExamView Pro Test Bank Interactive Lesson Planner Interactive Teacher's Edition	Performance Assessment in the Science Classroom (PASC)

Transparencies

Section Focus

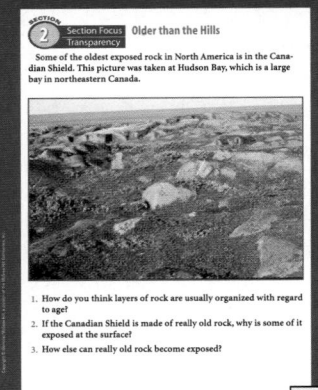

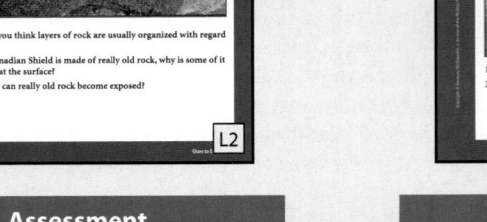

This is a representation of key blackline masters available in the Teacher Classroom Resources. See Resource Manager boxes within the chapter for additional information.

Assessment

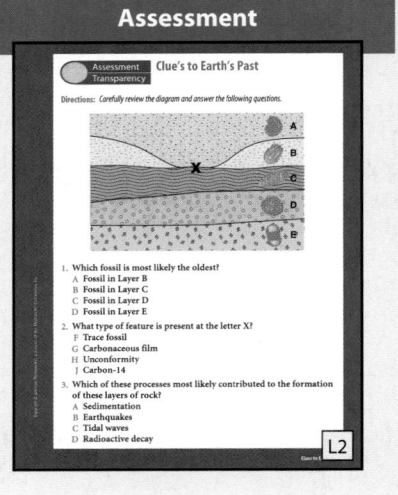

Teaching

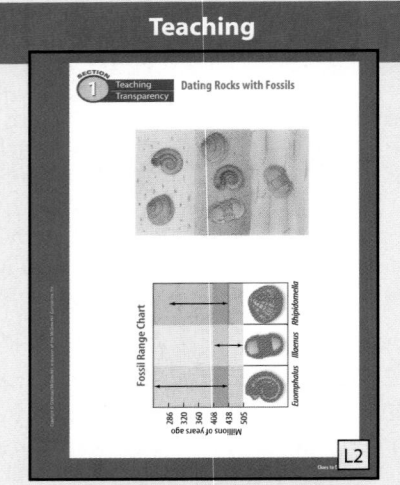

Key to Teaching Strategies

The following designations will help you decide which activities are appropriate for your students.

L1   Level 1 activities should be appropriate for students with learning difficulties.

L2   Level 2 activities should be within the ability range of all students.

L3   Level 3 activities are designed for above-average students.

ELL   ELL activities should be within the ability range of English Language Learners.

COOP LEARN   Cooperative Learning activities are designed for small group work.

LS   Multiple Learning Styles logos, as described on page 22T, are used throughout to indicate strategies that address different learning styles.

P   These strategies represent student products that can be placed into a best-work portfolio.

Hands-on Activities

Activity Worksheets

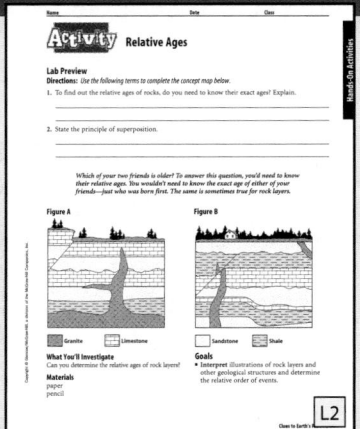

Laboratory Activities

Meeting Different Ability Levels

Content Outline

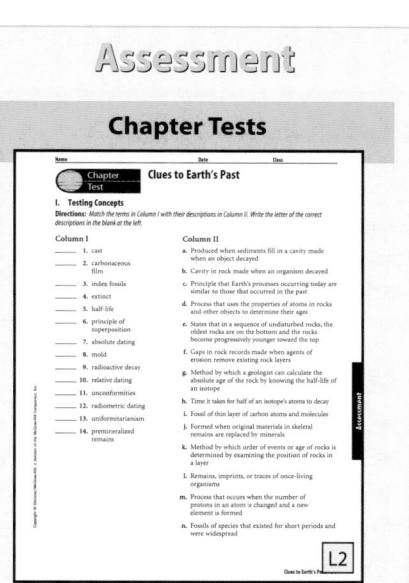

L2

Reinforcement

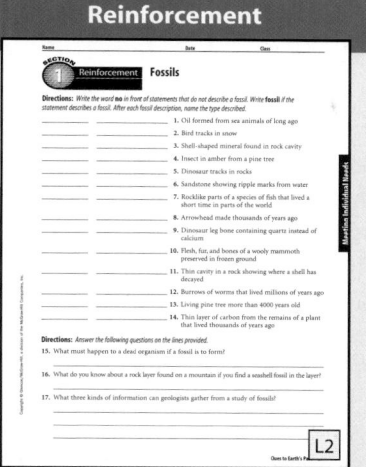

L2

Directed Reading

L1

Assessment

Chapter Tests

L2

Enrichment

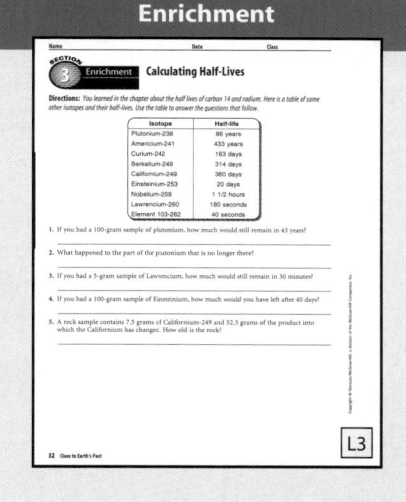

L3

Spanish Directed Reading

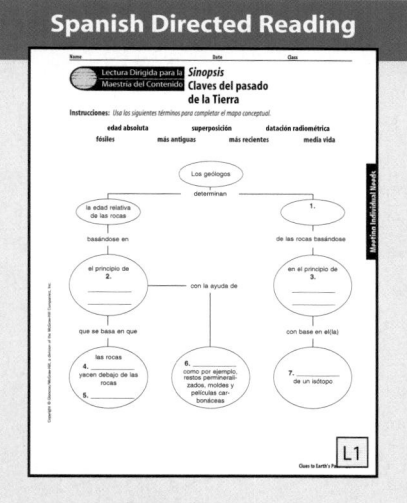

L1

Test Practice Workbook

L2

Chapter Review

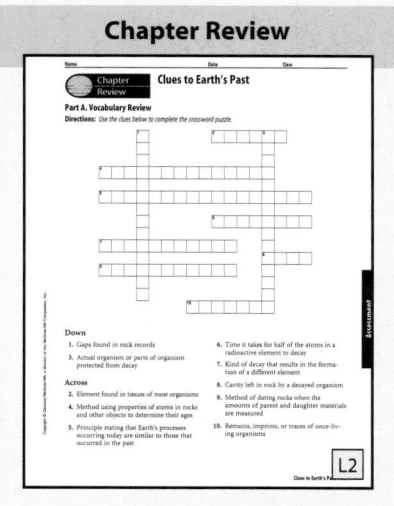

L2

Science Content Background

Fossils

Trace Fossils

Scientists hypothesize that certain reptiles swallowed stones to aid in digestion. When the organism died and decayed, the polished stones, called gastroliths, were left behind. Because gastroliths are traces of the original organism and not the organism itself, they are called trace fossils. Another trace fossil is a coprolite, or fossilized fecal material. Jewelry has been made from cut and polished coprolites.

Fossil Formation

Some fossils consist of the original parts of the organism. An insect trapped in amber and the skin and hair of some woolly mammoths have been found intact because they were protected from bacteria which would cause decay. Most fossils are formed as dead organisms are buried by layers of sediments that harden to form sedimentary rocks.

Tom Bean/DRK Photo

SECTION 2

Relative Ages of Rocks

Relative Dating

The principle of faunal succession states that fossil organisms occur in rocks in a definite and determinable order. Thus, rocks formed during a particular interval of geological time can be recognized by their fossils. A geological column is a composite diagram that shows the rocks of an area in the sequence in which they occur. Correlation of geological columns from many locations enables geologists to construct geologic maps. Geologic maps show the relative age, distribution, and structural features of surface rocks.

Student Misconception

The present is not the key to the past

Refer to the facing page for teaching strategies to address this misconception. Refer to page 386 for content related to this topic

SECTION 3

Absolute Ages of Rocks

Isotopes

When daughter isotopes are part of the original make-up of a rock, the calculated age of that rock can be wrong. However, for some isotopes, geologists are able to distinguish between original daughter isotopes and those that formed during radioactive decay. In order to cross-check their work in radiometric dating, geologists use several parent isotopes for the same age measurement. Because the different parent isotopes decay at different rates, using them for the same age measurement can ensure accuracy or expose errors.

SCIENCE Online

For additional content background on this topic, go to the Glencoe Science Web site at science.glencoe.com.

IDENTIFYING ❯ **Misconceptions**

Find Out What Students Think

Students may think that . . .

• **The present is *not* the key to the past.**

Students are often confused about uniformitarianism, which is one of the fundamental principles of geology. The principle of uniformitarianism states that Earth processes occurring today are similar to those that occurred in the past. Thus, our understanding of past Earth processes is based on those that are presently taking place.

Discussion

Have students imagine that they are geologists. During a field study, they observe that deposits of sediments in a mud flat contain cracks and ripple marks. Back in the lab, you observe several sedimentary rocks that also contain these features. Have students discuss what they can infer from these observations, and how observations such as these help scientists explain past events. Students should infer that the same processes that cause the ripple marks to form today also caused them to form in the past.

Tom Bean/Corbis

Promote Understanding

Activity

• Organize the class into small groups. Have groups examine samples of a layered sedimentary rock, such as shale. Ask each student to record his or her observations of the shale and then share these observations with their group members.

• Provide each group with a jar of water into which you have put sediment containing fine particles of clay. After students make sure that the lids are tightly sealed, have them gently shake the jar and observe the contents as they settle. Have students compare the rock sample and the layered sediments and determine how many of their original observations "fit" the sediments in the jar. Students should recognize that many of their observations are the same for both samples.

• Have each student group present their list of common characteristics to illustrate the principle of uniformitarianism.

Assess

After completing the chapter, see *Identifying Misconceptions* in the Study Guide.

Chapter Vocabulary

fossil
permineralized remains
carbonaceous film
mold
cast
index fossil
principle of superposition
relative age
unconformity
absolute age
radioactive decay
half-life
radiometric dating
uniformitarianism

What do you think?

Science Journal The photo shows a close-up of a fossil ammonite shell. Ammonites were invertebrate animals that lived in the oceans from the Devonian Period to the Cretaceous Period. They went extinct at about the same time as the dinosaurs. Ammonites belonged to the same class as the modern nautilus and appeared somewhat similar to this animal.

CHAPTER 13

Clues to Earth's Past

Studying the history of Earth is not as easy as studying the history of a country. This is because no people were around to record the events in Earth's past. Also, the long stretches of time between some events in geologic history are mind-boggling and difficult for humans to grasp. In a study of Earth's past, clues found in rocks and fossils of long-dead organisms take the place of words and pictures. In this chapter, you will encounter some of those long stretches of geologic time and learn how fossils form so that you can interpret some of Earth's past for yourself.

What do you think?

Science Journal Study the picture below. Discuss what you think this might be with a classmate. Here's a hint: *It lived in the ocean millions of years ago.* Write your answer or best guess in your Science Journal.

366

Theme Connection

Stability and Change The evolution of organisms throughout geologic time as shown by the fossil record is a major focus of the chapter. The changes in organisms on Earth can be used to obtain relative ages of rocks and to date geologic events.

The process of fossil formation begins when dead plants or animals are buried in sediment. In time, if conditions are right, the sediment hardens into sedimentary rock. Parts of the organism are preserved along with the impressions of parts that don't survive. Any evidence of once-living things contained in the rock record is a fossil.

Make a model of a fossil

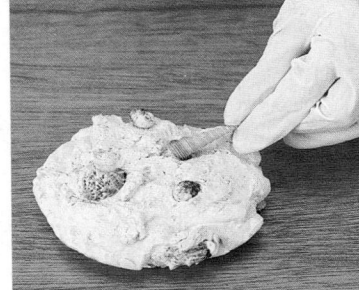

1. Fill a small jar (about 500 mL) one-third full of plaster of Paris. Add water until the jar is half full.
2. Drop in a few small shells.
3. To model a swift, muddy stream, cover the jar and shake it.
4. Now model the stream flowing into a lake by uncovering the jar and pouring the contents into a paper or plastic bowl. Let the mixture sit for an hour.
5. Crack open the hardened plaster to locate the model fossils.

Observe

Pick the shells out of the plaster and focus your attention on the impressions left by them. In your Science Journal, list what the impressions could tell you.

EXPLORE ACTIVITY

Purpose Use this Explore Activity to introduce students to fossil formation. L2 IS **Kinesthetic**

Preparation Put dry plaster of paris into jars before class starts.

Materials 500-mL jar with lid, plaster of paris, water, several small shells, paper or plastic bowl

Teaching Strategy Have students wear gloves when working with the plaster of paris. You may wish to do this activity as a demonstration.

Observe

Impressions can tell you the size and shape of an animal.

✓Assessment

Process Ask students to infer what would happen to the shells if the "stream" were carrying rocks. The shells would have been crushed. Use **Performance Assessment in the Science Classroom,** p. 89

Before You Read

FOLDABLES
Reading & Study Skills

Making a Question Study Fold Asking yourself questions helps you stay focused and better understand Earth's past when you are reading the chapter.

1. Place a sheet of paper in front of you so the long side is at the top. Fold the paper in half from the left side to the right side and then unfold.
2. Fold each side in to the centerfold line to divide the paper into fourths. Fold the paper in half from top to bottom and unfold.
3. Through the top thickness of paper, cut along both of the middle fold lines to form four tabs. Write these questions on the tabs: *What are fossils? How do fossils form? How is the relative age of rocks determined? How is the absolute age of rocks determined?*
4. As you read the chapter, write answers to the questions under the tabs.

> *What are fossils?*
> *How do fossils form?*
> *How is the relative age of rocks determined?*
> *How is the absolute age of rocks determined?*

367

Before You Read

FOLDABLES
Reading & Study Skills

Dinah Zike Study Fold

Purpose In this activity, you will pose four questions before reading the chapter to determine what students know about fossils as clues to Earth's past. Students will then make a Foldable for recording and organizing the answers to these questions as they read.

📁 For additional help, see Foldables Worksheet, p. 17 in **Chapter Resources Booklet,** or go to the Glencoe Science Web site at **science.glencoe.com.** See After You Read in the Study Guide at the end of this chapter.

SECTION

1 Fossils

1 Motivate

Bellringer Transparency

Display the Section Focus Transparency for Section 1. Use the accompanying Transparency Activity Master. L2

ELL

Section Focus Transparency — Guess Again

If you were asked to identify these objects, you'd probably say they were sections of tree trunks. Tree trunks are made of wood, right? Look again and you might come to a different conclusion.

1. What did you decide these trunks were made of? Why?
2. What usually happens to a tree after it dies?
3. Name some ways that ancient organisms might have been preserved.

L2

Tie to Prior Knowledge

Ask students to list things that can become fossils. In this section, they will learn that, under certain conditions, the remains of almost any organism or evidence of its activities can become a fossil.

As You Read

What You'll Learn

- **List** the conditions necessary for fossils to form.
- **Describe** several processes of fossil formation.
- **Explain** how fossil correlation is used to determine rock ages.

Vocabulary

fossil	mold
permineralized remains	cast
carbon film	index fossil

Why It's Important

Fossils help scientists find oil and other sources of energy necessary for society.

Figure 1
Scientists and artists can reconstruct what dinosaurs looked like in life using fossil remains.

A A paleontologist carefully examines a fossil skeleton and prepares a reconstruction of what the animal might have looked like when it was alive.

B The reconstruction is finished and ready for display.

Traces of the Distant Past

A giant crocodile lurks in the shallow water of a river. A herd of *Triceratops* emerges from the edge of the forest and cautiously moves toward the river. The dinosaurs are thirsty, but they know danger waits for them in the water. A large bull *Triceratops* moves into the river. The others follow.

Does this scene sound familiar to you? It's likely that you've read about dinosaurs and other past inhabitants of Earth. But how do you know that they really existed or what they were like? What evidence do humans have of past life on Earth? The answer is fossils. Paleontologists, scientists who study fossils, can reconstruct what an animal looked like from its fossil remains, as shown in **Figure 1.**

Section ✓Assessment Planner

PORTFOLIO
Chemistry Integration, p. 371

PERFORMANCE ASSESSMENT
Try At Home MiniLAB, p. 369
Skill Builder Activities, p. 375
See page 394 for more options.

CONTENT ASSESSMENT
Section, p. 375
Challenge, p. 375
Chapter, pp. 394–395

Formation of Fossils

Fossils are the remains, imprints, or traces of prehistoric organisms. Fossils have helped scientists determine approximately when life first appeared, when plants and animals first lived on land, and when organisms became extinct. Fossils are evidence of not only when and where organisms once lived, but also how they lived.

For the most part, the remains of dead plants and animals disappear quickly. Scavengers eat and scatter the remains of dead organisms. Fungi and bacteria invade, causing the remains to rot and disappear. If you've ever left a banana on the counter too long, you've seen this process begin. In time, compounds within the banana cause it to break down chemically and soften. Microorganisms, such as bacteria, cause it to decay. What keeps some plants and animals from disappearing before they become fossils? Which organisms are more likely to become fossils?

Conditions Needed for Fossil Formation Whether or not a dead organism becomes a fossil depends upon how well it is protected from scavengers and agents of physical destruction, such as waves and currents. One way a dead organism can be protected is for sediment to bury the body quickly. If a fish dies and sinks to the bottom of a lake, sediment carried into the lake by a stream can cover the fish rapidly. As a result, no waves or scavengers can get to it and tear it apart. The body parts then might be fossilized and included in a sedimentary rock like shale. However, quick burial alone isn't always enough to make a fossil.

Organisms have a better chance of becoming fossils if they have hard parts such as bones, shells, or teeth. One reason is that scavengers are less likely to eat these hard parts. Hard parts also decay more slowly than soft parts do. Most fossils are the hard parts of organisms, such as the fossil teeth in **Figure 2.**

Types of Preservation

Perhaps you've seen skeletal remains of *Tyrannosaurus rex* towering above you in a museum. You also have some idea of what this dinosaur looked like because you've seen illustrations. Artists who draw *Tyrannosaurus rex* and other dinosaurs base their illustrations on fossil bones. What preserves fossil bones?

Figure 2
These fossil shark teeth are hard parts. Soft parts of animals do not become fossilized as easily.

Mini LAB
TRY AT HOME

Predicting Fossil Preservation

Procedure
1. Take a brief walk outside and observe your neighborhood.
2. Look around and notice what kinds of plants and animals live nearby.

Analysis
1. Predict what remains from your time might be preserved far into the future.
2. Explain what conditions would need to exist for these remains to be fossilized.

---

2 Teach

Formation of Fossils

Mini LAB
TRY AT HOME

Purpose Students consider what conditions are necessary for living things to become fossils. L2

Logical-Mathematical Teaching Strategy Introduce this activity by asking students how we know about conditions that existed long ago on Earth's surface. Scientists study evidence of past life preserved in Earth's crust.

Analysis
1. The objects named must be the remains of living things or evidence of their activities, such as footprints or burrows. Possible answers: leaves, sticks, bones, shells
2. To best be preserved, the remains should have hard parts and be buried quickly.

Assessment

Oral Have students explain why shark teeth are often found as fossils but impressions of jellyfish are rarely found. Shark teeth are hard, and thus likely to be preserved. Jellyfish have no hard parts and thus are unlikely to be preserved. **Use Performance Assessment in the Science Classroom,** p. 89.

Resource Manager

Chapter Resources Booklet
Transparency Activity, p. 44
Note-taking Worksheets, pp. 33–35
MiniLAB, p. 3

Inclusion Strategies

Gifted Have students imagine that they are fossils. Have them write their autobiographies and describe what they have seen and experienced. The story should also include how the organism became a fossil and illustrations of the fossil. Encourage creativity but insist on scientific accuracy. L3 **Linguistic and Visual-Spatial**

Types of Preservation

IDENTIFYING
Misconceptions

Teacher FYI

Figure 3
Quartz and other minerals have replaced original materials and filled the hollow spaces in this permineralized dinosaur bone. *Why has this fossil retained the shape of the original bone?*

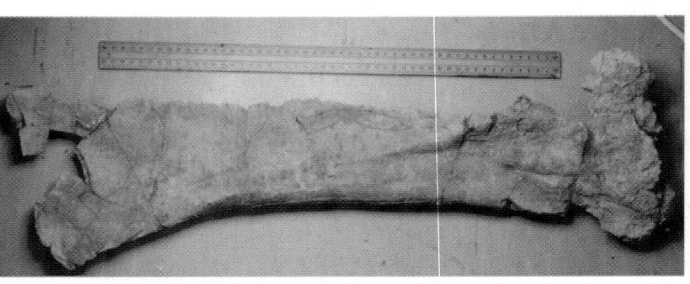

Mineral Replacment Most hard parts of organisms such as bones, teeth, and shells have tiny spaces within them. In life, these spaces can be filled with cells, blood vessels, nerves, or air. When the organism dies and the soft materials inside the hard parts decay, the tiny spaces become empty. If the hard part is buried, groundwater can seep in and deposit minerals in the spaces. **Permineralized remains** are fossils in which the spaces inside are filled with minerals from groundwater. In permineralized remains, some original material from the fossil organism's body might be preserved—encased within the minerals from groundwater. It is from these original materials that DNA, the chemical that contains an organism's genetic code, can sometimes be recovered.

Sometimes minerals replace the hard parts of fossil organisms. For example, a solution of water and dissolved silica (the compound SiO_2) might flow into and through the shell of a dead organism. If the water dissolves the shell and leaves silica in its place, the original shell is replaced.

Often people learn about past forms of life from bones, wood, and other remains that became permineralized or replaced with minerals from groundwater, as shown in **Figure 3**, but many other types of fossils can be found.

Figure 4
Graptolites lived hundreds of millions of years ago and drifted on currents in the oceans. These organisms often are preserved as carbon films.

Carbon Films The tissues of most organisms are made of compounds that contain carbon. Sometimes fossils contain only carbon. Fossils usually form when sediments bury a dead organism. As sediment piles up, the organism's remains are subjected to pressure and heat. These conditions force gases and liquids from the body. A thin film of carbon residue is left, forming a silhouette of the original organism called a **carbon film. Figure 4** shows the carbonized remains of graptolites, which are small marine animals. Graptolites have been found in rocks as old as 500 million years.

☑ Active Reading

Coal In swampy regions, large volumes of plant matter accumulate. Over millions of years, these deposits become completely carbonized, forming coal. Coal is more important as a source of fuel than as a fossil because the structure of the original plant often is lost when coal forms.

 **Reading Check** *In what sort of environment does coal form?*

Molds and Casts In nature, impressions form when seashells or other hard parts of organisms fall into a soft sediment such as mud. The object and sediment then are buried by more sediment. Compaction and cementation, the deposition of minerals from water into the pore spaces between sediment particles, turn the sediment into rock. Other open pores in the rock then let water and air reach the shell or hard part. The hard part might decay or dissolve, leaving behind a cavity in the rock called a **mold.** Later, mineral-rich water or other sediment might wash into the cavity, harden into rock, and produce a copy or **cast** of the original object, as shown in **Figure 5.**

Chemistry INTEGRATION

The bones of vertebrates contain calcium phosphate, and the shells of many invertebrates contain calcium carbonate. Calcium carbonate dissolves more easily in acid than calcium phosphate does. The ground water in some swampy environments is acidic. In your Science Journal, design an investigation to find out whether bones or shells would preserve best as fossils in a swamp.

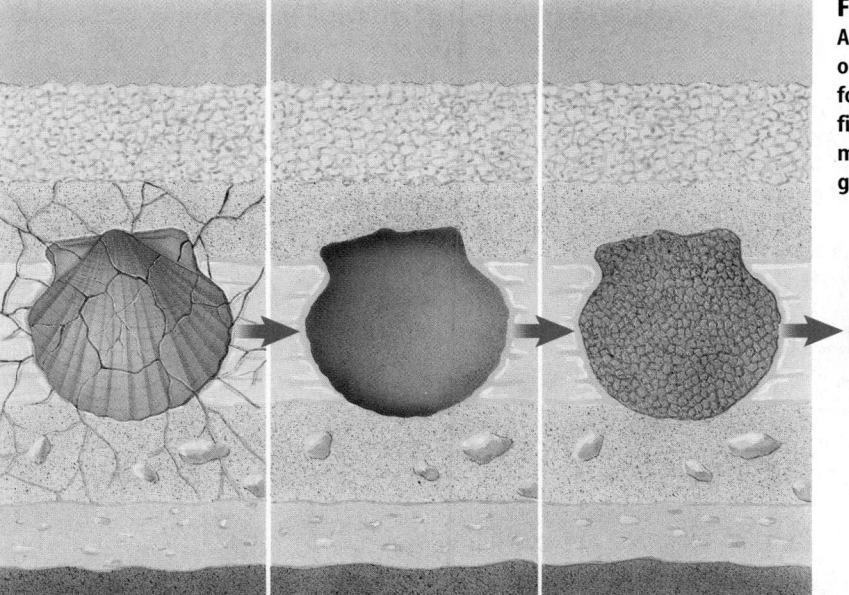

Figure 5
A cast resembling the original organism forms when a mold fills with sediment or minerals from groundwater.

A The fossil begins to dissolve as water moves through spaces in the rock layers.

B The fossil has been dissolved away. The harder rock once surrounding it forms a mold.

C Sediment washes into the mold and is deposited, or mineral crystals form.

D A cast forms.

Answer Coal forms in swampy regions.

Chemistry INTEGRATION

Possible Procedure: Obtain several different types of hard-parts, such as bone and teeth from vertebrates and shells from invertebrates. Place the hard parts in a flat pan and put several drops of dilute hydrochloric acid on each sample. Record the reaction of each part to the acid. Students should note that the invertebrate shells react to a greater extent than the bones and teeth. It therefore can be hypothesized that the shells would react to a greater extent with acidic water. [P]

Visual Learning

Figure 5 After students have studied the figure, provide them with a mold and cast of the same organism. **Which of your fossils is a mold and which is a cast?** The mold is the hollow or depression in the original rock, and the cast will be the bump that fits into the hollow.

Use an Analogy

Have students discuss an analogy between molds used in making ceramic statues and those formed in nature. Use modeling clay and a small statue to demonstrate why the internal structure of an organism is not preserved when casts are formed. [L2]

Resource Manager

Chapter Resources Booklet
Directed Reading for Content Mastery, pp. 19, 20
Transparency Activity, pp. 47–48

Earth Science Critical Thinking/Problem Solving, p. 12

Curriculum Connection

Geography Have students research and find on a map where replacement fossils have been found in the United States. As part of the task, have students explain what the name "Petrified Forest" refers to. This name refers to the Petrified Forest National Monument in Arizona, where there is wood in which much of the original matter has been replaced by minerals. [L2] [LS] **Visual-Spatial**

Types of Preservation,
continued

Extension

Ask students to bring in fossils they might have collected or received from others. Have the class determine the type of fossil and, if possible, the organism that produced each. Encourage students to research the time when the original organism lived and to illustrate a timeline showing all the fossils brought to class. L3 COOP LEARN

LS **Visual-Spatial and Interpersonal**

Use Science Words

Word Origin Trace fossils are not made of or from the original organism; they are just a trace of its activities. Ask students to find words that also use *trace* and explain their meanings. Possible answers: tracing—a graphic record; tracer—person who looks for clues of missing people; tracery—lacy, decorative openwork in a window

Discussion

What information about early organisms can be obtained from the depth and separation of tracks left in sediment? approximate size, mass, and speed of movement of the organism that left the tracks

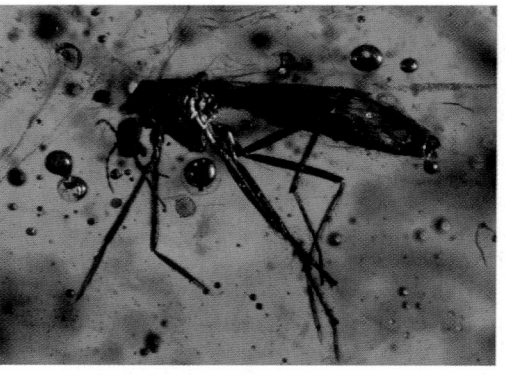

Figure 6
The original soft parts of this mosquito have been preserved in amber for millions of years.

Figure 7
Tracks made in soft mud, and now preserved in solid rock, can provide information about animal size, speed, and behavior.

A This dinosaur track is from the Glen Rose Formation in north-central Texas.

B These tracks are located on a Navajo Reservation in Arizona.

Original Remains Sometimes conditions allow original soft parts of organisms to be preserved for thousands or millions of years. For example, insects can be trapped in amber, a hardened form of sticky tree resin. The amber surrounds and protects the original material of the insect's exoskeleton from destruction, as shown in **Figure 6.** Some organisms, such as the mammoth, have been found preserved in frozen ground in Siberia. Original remains also have been found in natural tar deposits at Earth's surface, such as the La Brea tar pits in California.

Trace Fossils Do you have a handprint in plaster that you made when you were in kindergarten? If so, it's a record that tells something about you. From it, others can guess your size and maybe your weight at that age. Animals walking on Earth long ago left similar tracks, such as those in **Figure 7.** Trace fossils are fossilized tracks and other evidence of the activity of organisms. In some cases, tracks can tell you more about how an organism lived than any other type of fossil. For example, from a set of tracks at Davenport Ranch, Texas, you might be able to learn something about the social life of sauropods, which were large, plant-eating dinosaurs. The largest tracks of the herd are on the outer edges and the smallest are on the inside. These tracks cause some scientists to hypothesize that adult sauropods surrounded their young as they traveled—probably to protect them from predators. A nearby set of tracks might mean that another type of dinosaur, an allosaur, was stalking the herd.

Cultural Diversity

The Copper Man of the Alps On September 19, 1991, a German couple hiking in the Alps came across a 5,000-year-old traveler, naturally mummified in a small depression covered by glacial ice. The Iceman is now known to be one of the oldest and best-preserved mummified humans. Plant remains on his clothing suggest that he came from lowland South Tyrol. He wore finely stitched skin clothing, a woven grass cape, and boots. His deerskin quiver held two arrows tipped with flint and 12 unfinished arrows. He carried two antibiotic fungi, a backpack, a half-finished longbow, high-quality flint, and a flint dagger. One of his most intriguing possessions was an axe, originally thought to be bronze but now known to be copper. It is flanged in a style not found anywhere nearby until nearly 800 years later.

Trails and Burrows Other trace fossils include trails and burrows made by worms and other animals. These, too, tell something about how these animals lived. For example, by examining fossil burrows you can sometimes tell how firm the sediment the animals lived in was. As you can see, fossils can tell a great deal about the organisms that have inhabited Earth.

 **Reading Check** *How are trace fossils different from fossils that are the remains of an organism's body?*

Index Fossils

One thing you can learn by studying fossils is that species of organisms have changed over time. Some species of organisms inhabited Earth for long periods of time without changing. Other species changed a lot in comparatively short amounts of time. It is these organisms that became index fossils.

Index fossils are the remains of species that existed on Earth for relatively short periods of time, were abundant, and were widespread geographically. Because the organisms that became index fossils lived only during specific intervals of geologic time, geologists can estimate the ages of rock layers based on the particular index fossils they contain. However, not all rocks contain index fossils. Another way to approximate the age of a rock layer is to compare the spans of time, or ranges, over which more than one fossil lived. The estimated age is the time interval where fossil ranges overlap, as shown in **Figure 8.**

What types of fossils can be found in your part of the country? To find out, see the **Fossils Fieldguide** at the back of the book.

Figure 8
A The fossils in a sequence of sedimentary rock can be used to estimate the ages of each layer. **B** The chart shows when each organism inhabited Earth. *Why is it possible to say that the middle layer of rock was deposited between 438 million and 408 million years ago?*

Fossil Range Chart

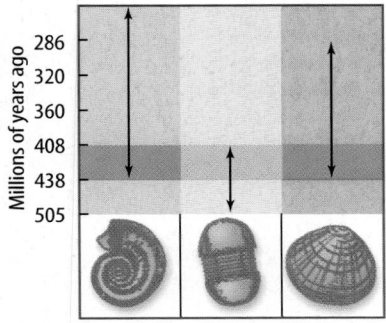

Millions of years ago
286
320
360
408
438
505

Euomphalus   Illaenus   Rhipidomella

Answer Trace fossils are fossilized tracks and other evidence of an organism's activity. They are not parts of the original organism.

Make a Model

Encourage pairs of students to produce a model of a fossil that depicts one of the five methods of formation. Display student models and actual samples in the classroom. L2 ELL COOP LEARN **Kinesthetic**

Index Fossils

Extension

Have students find out how index fossils are useful to Earth scientists. Possible answer: Because the organisms that formed them existed for relatively short periods of time over a wide area, the fossils are good indicators of the ages of the rocks in which they are found. L2 **Linguistic**

Caption Answer

Figure 8 The three fossils have ranges that overlap between 438 and 408 million years. The age of the layer cannot be dated more accurately than that.

Resource Manager

Chapter Resources Booklet
Enrichment, p. 30
Lab Activities, pp. 9–12
Science Inquiry Labs, p. 29

Science Journal

Traces of the Past Have students research and write a summary of what can be learned about extinct animals from studying gastroliths and coprolites. Possible answer: Gastroliths are stones swallowed to aid in digestion; coprolites are petrified feces. Both might provide clues about an organism's diet. L2 **Linguistic**

Fossils and Ancient Environments

Life Science
INTEGRATION

Possible answers: Study of fossils might indicate predator-prey relationships, migratory patterns, and climatic changes. Accept reasonable answers.

Visual Learning

Figure 9 How does the position of the North American plate explain the presence of fern fossils in shale beds of the Pennsylvanian Period?. The North American plate was closer to the equator during the Pennsylvanian Period. Much of the region was covered by swamps, in which ferns thrived. As ferns died, they fell into the swamp and were covered by sediments.

Text Question Answer

Because different organisms live at different depths, fossils can be general indicators of water depth in a region.

Life Science
INTEGRATION

Ecology is the study of how organisms interact with each other and with their environment. Some paleontologists study the ecology of ancient organisms. Hypothesize about the kinds of information you could use to determine how ancient organisms interacted with their environment.

Fossils and Ancient Environments

Scientists can use fossils to determine what the environment of an area was like long ago. Using fossils, you might be able to find out whether an area was land or whether it was covered by an ocean at a particular time. If the region was covered by ocean, it might even be possible to learn the depth of the water. What clues about the depth of water do you think fossils could provide?

Fossils also are used to determine the past climate of a region. For example, rocks in parts of the eastern United States contain fossils of tropical plants. The environment of this part of the United States today isn't tropical. However, because of the fossils, scientists know that it was tropical when these fossilized plants were living. **Figure 9** shows that North America was located near the equator when these fossils formed.

Figure 9
Because the continents on the surface of Earth slowly move, the climate of a given region changes through geologic time.

A The equator passed through North America 310 million years ago. At this time, warm shallow seas and coal swamps covered much of the continent.

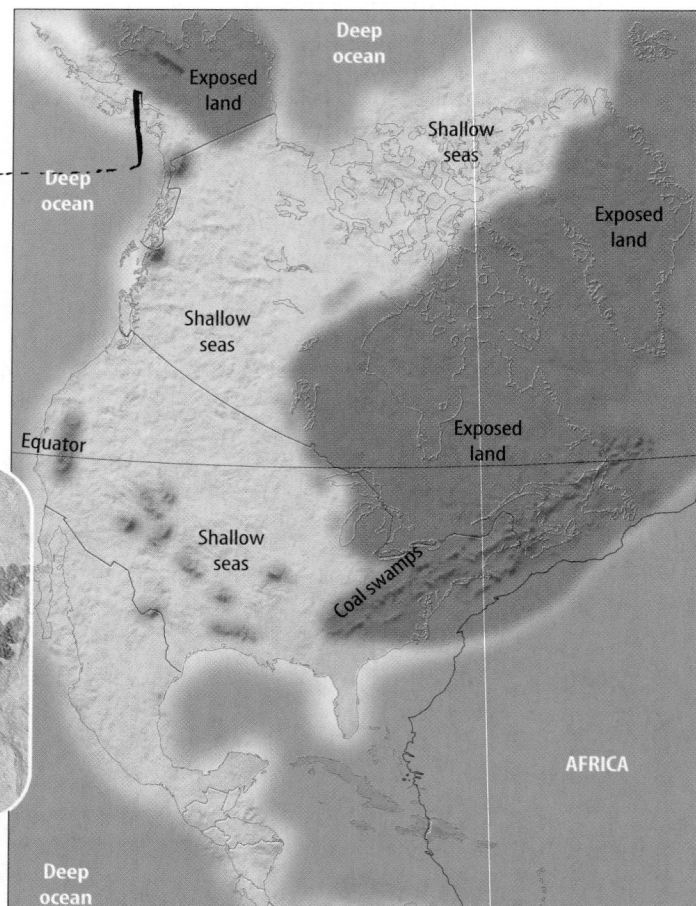

B *Neuropteris* was a common fern that grew in swamps during this time.

Inclusion Strategies

Learning Disabled To help students better understand how fossils can indicate ancient environments, show them samples of rocks that contain fossils of organisms that once lived in a shallow sea. Ask students to explain the environment that existed when the organisms were alive. L1 IS **Visual-Spatial**

Resource Manager

Chapter Resources Booklet
  Reinforcement, p. 27

Life Science Critical Thinking/Problem Solving, p. 3

Physical Science Critical Thinking/Problem Solving, p. 11

A

B

Shallow Seas How would you explain the presence of fossilized crinoids—animals that lived in shallow seas—in rocks just west of those containing the fern fossils? **Figure 10** shows a fossil crinoid and a living crinoid. When the fossil crinoids were alive, a shallow sea covered much of western and central North America. The crinoid hard parts were included in rocks that formed from the sediments at the bottom of this sea. Fossils provide information about past life on Earth and also about the history of the rock layers that contain them. Fossils can provide information about the ages of rocks and the climate and type of environment that existed when the rocks formed.

Figure 10
A This fossil crinoid lived in the warm, shallow seas that once covered part of North America.
B This crinoid lives in shallow water near Papua New Guinea.
How do the habitats of these crinoids compare?

Caption Answer
Figure 10 The habitats of the two crinoids are similar—warm, shallow marine water.

3 Assess

Reteach
Have students form groups of four. Have them press shells or bones into mixtures of sand and water, soft clay and water, and gravel and water. The recorder should report which sediment allowed the best imprint to be formed. soft clay and water L2 COOP LEARN
IS Kinesthetic and Interpersonal

Challenge
What could you conclude about an organism if you found small, fossilized tracks that were far apart? Possible answer: Small tracks indicate a small organism. Therefore, if tracks are far apart, the organism was probably running when the tracks were made. L1
IS Logical-Mathematical

✓Assessment

Performance Have students devise concept maps summarizing the major concepts of this section. Have pairs exchange maps and make suggestions as to ways to improve the maps. Use **Performance Assessment in the Science Classroom,** p. 161.

Section 1 Assessment

1. What conditions must exist for most fossils to form?

2. Describe how a fossil mold could form. Explain how a fossil mold is different from a fossil cast.

3. What characteristics do the organisms that become index fossils have? How are these characteristics useful to geologists?

4. How do carbon films form?

5. **Think Critically** What can you say about the ages of two widely separated layers of rock that contain the same type of fossil? What can you say about the environments of these widely separated layers?

Skill Builder Activities

6. **Concept Mapping** Make a concept map that compares and contrasts permineralized remains and original remains. Use the following phrases: *types of fossils, original remains, evidence of former life, permineralized remains, replaced by minerals,* and *parts of organisms.* **For more help, refer to the** Science Skill Handbook.

7. **Communicating** Visit a museum that has fossils on display. In your Science Journal, make an illustration of each fossil. Write a brief description, noting key facts about each. Also, write about how each fossil might have formed. **For more help, refer to the** Science Skill Handbook.

Answers to Section Assessment

1. hard parts that are quickly buried
2. A buried object decays, leaving a cavity, or mold. Later, sediments fill the cavity, harden, and produce a cast.
3. They lived for a relatively short period of time and were geographically widespread. Geologists can define the ages of rock layers based on the particular index fossils they contain.

4. Pressure and heat force out gases and liquids; only a film of carbon residue is left.
5. Both layers of rock formed when the fossil-producing organism lived; the rock layers may be similar in age if the organism existed for a short time; the climates of the areas were similar.

6. *Types of fossils* are *original remains* which are *parts of organisms* and are *evidence of former life* or *permineralized remains* in which hollow spaces are *filled in by minerals* and are *evidence of former life.*
7. Encourage students to set up their observations as a field notebook, which should include drawings

and important facts about each fossil observed.

SECTION

Relative Ages of Rocks

As You Read

What You'll Learn

- **Describe** methods used to assign relative ages to rock layers.
- **Interpret** gaps in the rock record.
- **Give** an example of how rock layers can be correlated with other rock layers.

Vocabulary

principle of superposition
relative age
unconformity

Why It's Important

Being able to determine the age of rock layers is important in trying to understand a history of Earth.

Superposition

Imagine that you are walking to your favorite store and you happen to notice an interesting car go by. You're not sure what kind it is, but you remember that you read an article about it. You decide to look it up. At home you have a stack of magazines from the past year, as seen in **Figure 11.**

You know that the article you're thinking of came out in the January edition, so it must be near the bottom of the pile. As you dig downward, you find magazines from March, then February. January must be next. How did you know that the January issue of the magazine would be on the bottom? To find the older edition under newer ones, you applied the principle of superposition.

Oldest Rocks on the Bottom According to the **principle of superposition,** in undisturbed layers of rock, the oldest rocks are on the bottom and the rocks become progressively younger toward the top. Why is this the case?

Figure 11
The pile of magazines illustrates the principle of superposition. According to this principle, the oldest rock layer (or magazine) is on the bottom.

Rock Layers Sediment accumulates in horizontal beds, forming layers of sedimentary rock. The first layer to form is on the bottom. The next layer forms on top of the previous one. Because of this, the oldest rocks are at the bottom. However, forces generated by mountain formation sometimes can turn layers over. When layers have been turned upside down, it's necessary to use other clues in the rock layers to determine their original positions and relative ages.

Relative Ages

Now you want to look for another magazine. You're not sure how old it is, but you know it arrived after the January issue. You can find it in the stack by using the principle of relative age.

The **relative age** of something is its age in comparison to other things. Geologists determine the relative ages of rocks and other structures by examining their places in a sequence. For example, if layers of sedimentary rock are offset by a fault, which is a break in Earth's surface, you know that the layers had to be there before a fault could cut through them. The relative age of the rocks is older than the relative age of the fault. Relative age determination doesn't tell you anything about the age of rock layers in actual years. You don't know if a layer is 100 million or 10,000 years old. You only know that it's younger than the layers below it and older than the fault cutting through it.

Other Clues Help Determination of relative age is easy if the rocks haven't been faulted or turned upside down. For example, look at **Figure 12A.** Which layer is the oldest? In cases where rock layers have been disturbed as in **Figure 12B,** you might have to look for fossils and other clues to date the rocks. If you find a fossil in the top layer that's older than a fossil in a lower layer, you can hypothesize that layers have been turned upside down by folding during mountain building.

SCIENCE
Online

Research Visit the Glencoe Science Web site at **science.glencoe.com** for more information about how geologists determine the relative ages of rocks. Communicate to your class what you learn.

Figure 12
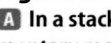 **A** In a stack of undisturbed sedimentary rocks, the oldest rocks are at the bottom. **B** This similar stack of rocks has been folded by forces within Earth. *How can you tell if an older rock is above a younger one?*

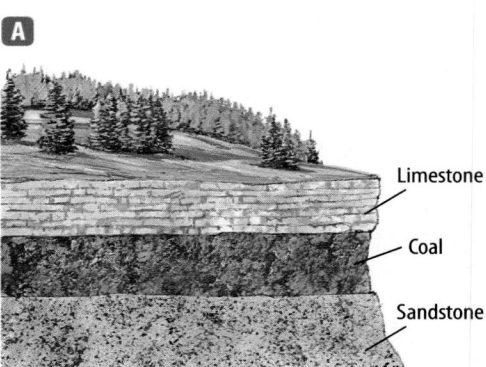

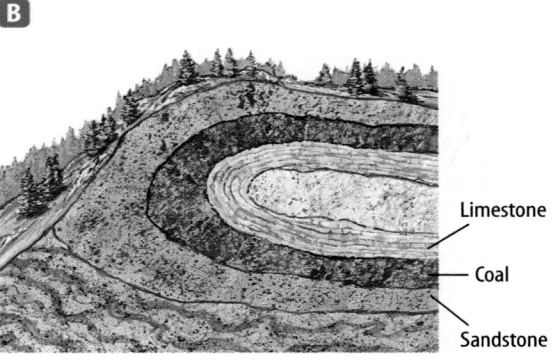

Limestone

Coal

Sandstone

Limestone

Coal

Sandstone

SECTION 2 Relative Ages of Rocks **377**

Unconformities

✔ Reading Check

Answer Unconformities form when rock is eroded, and new sediment is deposited on top of the erosion surface.

Visual Learning

Figure 13 Use several books from a set of encyclopedias to reinforce the appearance of an angular unconformity shown in **Figure B.** Place volumes 1, 2, 3, and 4 in numerical order, with volume 1 on the bottom. Tilt the books at an angle and then horizontally place volumes 7 and 8 on top of the tilted books.
LS **Visual-Spatial**

Quick Demo

Use books to demonstrate a disconformity. Stack volumes 1, 2, 3, and 4 in numerical order, with volume 1 on the bottom. Add volumes 7, 8, and 9 to the stack. Explain that the missing volumes indicate the disconformity.
LS **Visual-Spatial**

Discussion

What does an unconformity indicate about past geological processes of an area? At some point, erosion removed some rock, or time passed without any sediment deposition and rock formation, or both. Explain that Angular unconformities form when rock layers are uplifted, tilted, and eroded. Ask students to explain what causes the forces that produce angular unconformities. Plate tectonics generates compression, tension, and shear forces, which in turn cause rock layers to be folded, tilted, or faulted. The agents of erosion produce forces that wear away exposed rock. ⎣L2⎦
LS **Logical-Mathematical**

Figure 13
An angular unconformity results when horizontal layers cover tilted, eroded layers.

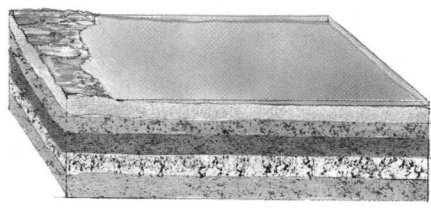

A Sedimentary rocks are deposited originally as horizontal layers.

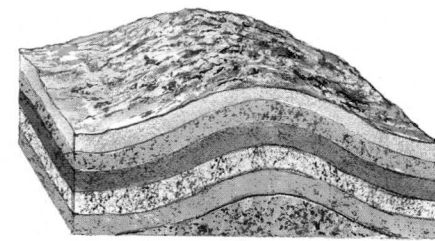

B The horizontal rock layers are tilted as forces within Earth deform them.

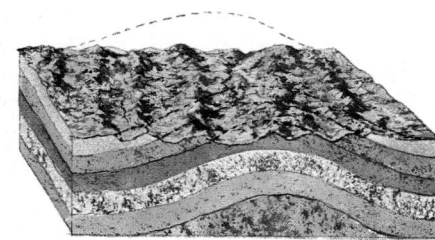

C The tilted layers erode.

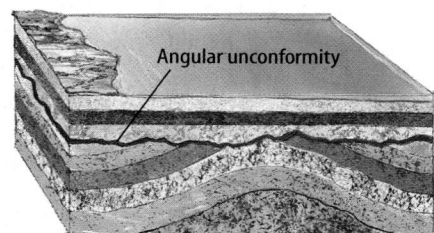

D An angular unconformity results when new layers form on the tilted layers as deposition resumes.

378 CHAPTER 13 Clues to Earth's Past

Unconformities

A sequence of rock is a record of past events. But most rock sequences are incomplete—layers are missing. These gaps in rock layers are called unconformities (un kun FOR mih teez). Unconformities develop when agents of erosion such as running water or glaciers remove existing rock layers by washing or scraping them away. They also form when a period of time passes without any new deposition occurring to form new layers of rock.

✔ Reading Check How do unconformities form?

Angular Unconformities Horizontal layers of sedimentary rock often are tilted and uplifted. Erosion and weathering then wear down these tilted rock layers. Eventually, younger sediment layers are deposited horizontally on top of the eroded and tilted layers. Geologists call such an unconformity an angular unconformity. **Figure 13** shows how angular unconformities develop.

Disconformity Suppose you're looking at a stack of sedimentary rock layers. They look complete, but layers are missing. If you look closely you might find an old surface of erosion. This records a time when the rocks were exposed and eroded. Later, younger rocks formed above the erosion surface when deposition of sediment began again. Even though all the layers are parallel, the rock record still has a gap. This type of unconformity is called a disconformity.

Nonconformity Another type of unconformity, called a nonconformity, occurs when metamorphic or igneous rocks are uplifted and eroded. Sedimentary rocks are then deposited on top of this erosion surface. The surface between the two rock types is a nonconformity. Sometimes rock fragments from below are incorporated into sediments deposited above the nonconformity. All types of unconformities are shown in **Figure 14.**

Inclusion Strategies

Visually Impaired To help students participate in the discussion of unconformities, mold models of each type of unconformity from clay. Allow students to handle the models and to remove each of the layers. ⎣L1⎦ ELL **LS** **Kinesthetic**

Figure 14

An unconformity is a gap in the rock record caused by erosion or a pause in deposition. There are three major kinds of unconformities—nonconformity, angular unconformity, and disconformity.

Nonconformity

▲ In a nonconformity, layers of sedimentary rock overlie older igneous or metamorphic rocks. A nonconformity in Big Bend National Park, Texas, is shown above.

Angular unconformity

▲ An angular unconformity develops when new horizontal layers of sedimentary rock form on top of older sedimentary rock layers that have been folded by compression. An example of an angular unconformity at Siccar Point in southeastern Scotland is shown above.

▼ A disconformity develops when horizontal rock layers are exposed and eroded, and new horizontal layers of rock are deposited on the eroded surface. The disconformity shown below is in the Grand Canyon.

Disconformity

SECTION 2 Relative Ages of Rocks **379**

Visualizing Unconformities

Have students examine the pictures and read the captions. Then ask the following questions.

How do geologists know there is a gap in the rock record in the disconformity shown at the Grand Canyon? The sequence of rock layers does not match the complete sequence found in surrounding areas. Some layers are missing and somewhere younger layers abut older layers. Fossils are often used to date the layers.

Could an unconformity occur that has metamorphic rock on top of sedimentary rock? Not likely. The forces of heat and pressure responsible for the metamorphism would likely occur throughout the rock layers, and not just on the surface.

Activity

Have students work in groups of three, with each student modeling one of the three types of unconformities shown in the feature. Have them use several colors of modeling clay so the models are vivid and obvious. Have students explain their models to each other.

Extension

Challenge students to go online to find where the nearest unconformities can be found. Have them fit the story of a nearby unconformity to the general story of the region's geology. Local universities would be a good starting point for research.

Resource Manager

Chapter Resources Booklet

Directed Reading for Content Mastery, p. 21

Lab Activities, pp. 13–15

Cultural Diversity, p. 13

Matching Up Rock Layers

Reading Check

Answer If the fossils are the same type or can be shown to be the same age, it is likely that the rocks are part of the same layer.

Extension

Obtain geologic maps of Colorado, Utah, Arizona, and New Mexico. Have students examine the maps and note that many of the rock units extend across state boundaries. Have students research the geologic history of this area during the Mesozoic and Cenozoic eras. Have them write a report on their findings. At one time, the area was a great coastal desert resulting in sandstone deposits.

Teacher FYI

The basic unit of layered rocks is the formation, a mappable unit of rock. A formation is named for basic characteristics such as rock type, color, and fossil content—all of which are readily observed. A group consists of more than one formation, stacked on top of one another. A member is a subdivision of a formation. It is designated by a specific characteristic within it, such as an abundance of fossils or a particular mineral.

SCIENCE Online

Research Visit the Glencoe Science Web site at **science.glencoe.com** for a link to more information about the process of correlation.

Figure 15
These rock layers, exposed at Hopi Point in Grand Canyon National Park, Arizona, can be correlated, or matched up, with rocks from across large areas of the western United States.

Matching Up Rock Layers

Suppose you're studying a layer of sandstone in Bryce Canyon in Utah. Later, when you visit Canyonlands National Park, Utah, you notice that a layer of sandstone there looks just like the sandstone in Bryce Canyon, 250 km away. Above the sandstone in the Canyonlands is a layer of limestone and then another sandstone layer. You return to Bryce Canyon and find the same sequence—sandstone, limestone, and sandstone. What do you infer? It's likely that you're looking at the same layers of rocks in two different locations. **Figure 15** shows that these rocks are parts of huge deposits that covered this whole area of the western United States. Geologists often can match up, or correlate, layers of rocks over great distances.

Evidence Used for Correlation It's not always easy to say that a rock layer exposed in one area is the same as a rock layer exposed in another area. Sometimes it's possible to walk along the layer for kilometers and prove that it's continuous. In other cases, such as at the Canyonlands area and Bryce Canyon as seen in **Figure 16,** the rock layers are exposed only where rivers have cut through overlying layers of rock and sediment. How can you show that the limestone sandwiched between the two layers of sandstone in Canyonlands is likely the same limestone as at Bryce Canyon? One way is to use fossil evidence. If the same types of fossils were found in the limestone layer in both places, it's a good indication that the limestone at each location is the same age, and, therefore, one continuous deposit.

Reading Check
How do fossils help show that rocks at different locations belong to the same rock layer?

Resource Manager

Chapter Resources Booklet
Enrichment, p. 31
Reinforcement, p. 28
Physical Science Critical Thinking/Problem Solving, p. 7

SCIENCE Online
Internet Addresses
_____
_____
_____
_____
Explore the Glencoe Science Web site at **science.glencoe.com** to find out more about topics in this section.

Canyonlands National Park

Bryce Canyon National Park

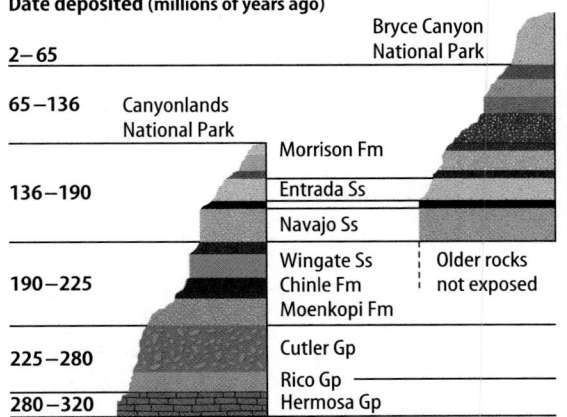

Date deposited (millions of years ago)

2–65	Bryce Canyon National Park / Wasatch Fm
65–136	Canyonlands National Park / Kaiparowits Fm / Straight Cliffs Ss
136–190	Morrison Fm / Entrada Ss / Navajo Ss / Dakota Ss / Winsor Fm / Entrada Ss / Navajo Ss
190–225	Wingate Ss / Chinle Fm / Moenkopi Fm / Older rocks not exposed
225–280	Cutler Gp
280–320	Rico Gp / Hermosa Gp

Figure 16
Geologists have named the many rock layers, or formations in Canyonlands and in Bryce Canyon, Utah. They also have correlated some formations between the two canyons.
Which layers are present at both canyons?

Can layers of rock be correlated in other ways? Sometimes determining relative ages isn't enough, and other dating methods must be used. In Section 3, you'll see how the numerical ages of rocks can be determined, and how geologists have used this information to estimate the age of Earth.

Section 2 Assessment

1. Suppose you haven't cleaned out your locker all year. Where would you expect to find papers from the beginning of the year? What principle of geology would you use to find these old papers?

2. Explain the concept of relative age.

3. What is a disconformity?

4. What is one way to correlate similar rock layers in two different areas?

5. **Think Critically** Explain the relationship between the concept of relative age and the principle of superposition.

Skill Builder Activities

6. **Interpreting Data** A sandstone contains a 400-million-year-old fossil. A shale contains fossils that are over 500 million years old. A limestone, underlying a sandstone, contains fossils that are between 400 million and 500 million years old. Which rock bed is oldest? Explain. **For more help, refer to the** Science Skill Handbook.

7. **Using an Electronic Spreadsheet** Use this section to prepare a table comparing and contrasting types of unconformities. **For more help, refer to the** Technology Skill Handbook.

SECTION 2 Relative Ages of Rocks **381**

 Assess

Reteach
Draw a geologic column on transparency acetate. Include layers of limestone, sandstone, shale, and metamorphic rock, a fault, a disconformity (indicated by a jagged line), and an igneous intrusion. Project the illustration, and have students explain the history of the area. L2 ELL
Visual-Spatial

Challenge
Obtain a geologic map and correlation chart for the area that includes your state. Invite students to examine the materials and describe the features used to correlate the rocks. Possible answers: rock type, presence of fossils, relative position in the geologic column

✓ *Assessment*

Performance Illustrate Question 6 of the Section Assessment on the board. Then have students interpret the relative ages of the rock layers. Assume that the rocks are undisturbed and that shale underlies the limestone. Use **PASC,** p. 89.

Answers to Section Assessment

1. Close to the bottom of the locker; applying the principle of superposition would help in finding the papers.
2. Relative age describes the age of one rock layer in relation to another; it does not describe age in actual years.
3. a stack of sedimentary rock layers in which one or more layers is missing
4. Possible answers: match rock types, look for presence of matching fossils, compare relative positions in the geologic column
5. The principle of superposition states that older rock is on the bottom; therefore, the relative age of the bottom layer is older.
6. The shale; its fossils are older than those found in the other layers.
7. See chart below.

Type	Similarities	Differences
Angular	All represent gaps in the rock record.	Horizontal layers over tilted layers
Disconformity	All indicate times of erosion and/or no deposition.	Horizontal layers over older horizontal layers; missing layers and erosional surface visible
Nonconformity	Sedimentary rock layers over eroded metamorphic or igneous rock layers	

Section 2 Relative Ages of Rocks **381**

Relative Ages

Purpose Students determine the relative order of events by interpreting geologic cross sections.

L2 ELL LS **Logical-Mathematical**

Process Skills inferring, interpreting data, formulating models, recognizing and using spatial relationships, sequencing, interpreting scientific illustrations

Time Required 40–45 minutes

Teaching Strategy If students are having trouble, reproduce the cross sections on an overhead. Then work as a class to identify the relative ages of the different layers.

Answers to Questions

1. Disconformity; yes, other rock layers could have been eroded.
2. The rocks moved upward.
3. as a result of a reverse fault
4. A fault cuts through the intrusion but stops at the unconformity. Thus the fault occurred after the intrusion but while erosion was occurring. Therefore, the intrusion is older.
5. The one on the left is older than the one on the right. The one on the right intrudes the sandstone and is therefore younger. The one offset by the fault is older than the sandstone.
6. The sandstone and shale may have been thicker. They exhibit erosional disconformities at their upper surfaces.

✔Assessment

Performance Based on what was learned about relative ages of rock layers, have students draw a block diagram similar to those in the Activity. Tell them to include all three rock types. Have students exchange and interpret their diagrams. Use **PASC**, p. 127.

W hich of your two friends is older? To answer this question, you'd need to know their relative ages. You wouldn't need to know the exact age of either of your friends—just who was born first. The same is sometimes true for rock layers.

What You'll Investigate
Can you determine the relative ages of rock layers?

Materials
paper   pencil

Goals
■ **Interpret** illustrations of rock layers and other geological structures and determine the relative order of events.

Procedure
1. **Analyze Figures A** and **B.**
2. Make a sketch of **Figure A.** On it, identify the relative age of each rock layer, igneous intrusion, fault, and unconformity. For example, the shale layer is the oldest, so mark it with a 1. Mark the next-oldest feature with a 2, and so on.
3. Repeat question 2 for **Figure B.**

Conclude and Apply

Figure A

1. **Identify** the type of unconformity shown. Is it possible that there were originally more layers of rock than are shown?
2. **Describe** how the rocks left of the fault moved in relation to rocks on the right.
3. **Hypothesize** how the hill on the left side of the figure formed.

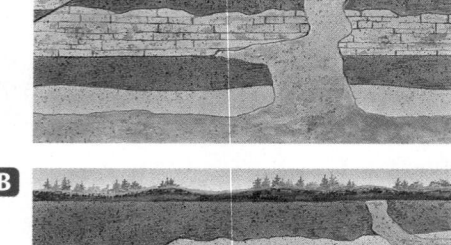

A

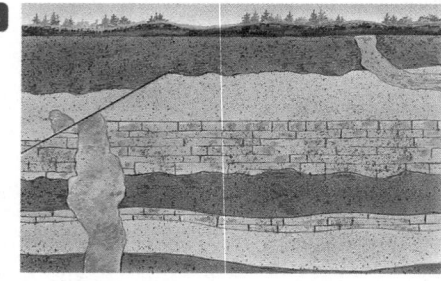

B

☐ Granite   ▦ Limestone
■ Sandstone   ☐ Shale

Figure B

4. Is it possible to conclude if the igneous intrusion on the left is older or younger than the unconformity nearest the surface?
5. **Describe** the relative ages of the two igneous intrusions. How did you know?
6. **Hypothesize** which two layers of rock might have been much thicker in the past.

Communicating Your Data

Compare your results with other students' results. **For more help, refer to the** Science Skill Handbook.

Resource Manager

Chapter Resources Booklet
Activity Worksheet, pp. 5–6

Earth Science Critical Thinking/Problem Solving, p. 11

Communicating Your Data

Oldest to youngest: A: shale, sandstone, limestone, disconformity, sandstone, limestone, fault, intrusion, fault; B: sandstone, shale, limestone, sandstone, disconformity, limestone, shale, intrusion (left), fault, disconformity, sandstone, intrusion (right)

Absolute Ages of Rocks

Absolute Ages

As you sort through your stack of magazines looking for that article about the car you saw, you decide that you need to restack them into a neat pile. By now, they're in a jumble and no longer in order of their relative age, as shown in **Figure 17.** How can you stack them so the oldest are on the bottom and the newest are on top? Fortunately, magazine dates are printed on the cover. Thus, stacking magazines in order is a simple process. Unfortunately, rocks don't have their ages stamped on them. Or do they? **Absolute age** is the age, in years, of a rock or other object. Geologists determine absolute ages by using properties of the atoms that make up materials.

Radioactive Decay

**Physics
INTEGRATION**

Atoms consist of a dense central region called the nucleus, which is surrounded by a cloud of negatively charged particles called electrons. The nucleus is made up of protons, which have a positive charge, and neutrons, which have no electric charge. The number of protons determines the identity of the element, and the number of neutrons determines the form of the element, or isotope. For example, every atom with a single proton is a hydrogen atom. Hydrogen atoms can have no neutrons, a single neutron, or two neutrons. This means that there are three isotopes of hydrogen.

✔ **Reading Check**   *What particles make up an atom's nucleus?*

Some isotopes are unstable and break down into other isotopes and particles. Sometimes a lot of energy is given off during this process. The process of breaking down is called **radioactive decay.** In the case of hydrogen, atoms with one proton and two neutrons are unstable and tend to break down. Many other elements have stable and unstable isotopes.

As You Read

What **You'll Learn**

■ **Identify** how absolute age differs from relative age.
■ **Describe** how the half-lives of isotopes are used to determine a rock's age.

Vocabulary
absolute age
radioactive decay
half-life
radiometric dating
uniformitarianism

Why **It's Important**
Events in Earth's history can be better understood if their absolute ages are known.

Figure 17
The magazines that have been shuffled through no longer illustrate the principle of superposition.

SECTION 3 Absolute Ages of Rocks   **383**

SECTION

3

Absolute Ages of Rocks

1 Motivate

Bellringer Transparency
Display the Section Focus Transparency for Section 3. Use the accompanying Transparency Activity Master. L2
ELL

Tie to Prior Knowledge

Have students recall the main parts of the atom and their positions within an atom. Proton and neutron—in nucleus; electrons—around nucleus

✔ **Reading Check**

Answer   protons and neutrons

Section ✔ *Assessment* Planner

PORTFOLIO
Science Journal, p. 386
PERFORMANCE ASSESSMENT
MiniLAB, p. 384
Problem-Solving Activity, p. 386
Skill Builder Activities, p. 387
See page 394 for more options.

CONTENT ASSESSMENT
Section, p. 387
Challenge, p. 387
Chapter, pp. 394–395

2 Teach

Radioactive Decay

Mini **LAB**

Purpose Students will model the principle of carbon-14 dating.

Materials red and green jelly beans

Teaching Strategy Advise students not to eat the jelly beans and to wash hands thoroughly after the activity.

Analysis
1. As in carbon-14, each half life resulted in half of the remaining jelly beans being removed.
2. 4
3. 22,920 years old

✓ Assessment

Performance Have students determine the relative and absolute ages of students in the classroom. Use **Performance Assessment in the Science Classroom,** p. 99. P

Mini **LAB**

Jelly Bean Carbon-14 Dating

Procedure:
1. Count out 80 **red jelly beans.**
2. Remove half the red jelly beans and replace them with **green jelly beans.**
3. Continue replacing half the red jelly beans with green jelly beans until only 5 red jelly beans remain. Count the number of times you replace half the red jelly beans.

Analysis
1. How did this activity model the decay of carbon-14 atoms?
2. How many half lives of carbon-14 did you model during this activity?
3. If the atoms in a bone experienced the same number of half lives as your jelly beans, how old would the bone be?

Figure 18

A In beta decay, a neutron changes into a proton by giving off an electron. This electron has a lot of energy and is called a beta particle.

B In the process of alpha decay, an unstable parent isotope nucleus gives off an alpha particle and changes into a new daughter product. Alpha particles contain two neutrons and two protons.

384   CHAPTER 13 Clues to Earth's Past

Alpha and Beta Decay In some isotopes, a neutron breaks down into a proton and an electron. This type of radioactive decay is called beta decay because the electron leaves the atom as a beta particle. The nucleus loses a neutron but gains a proton. When the number of protons in an atom is changed, a new element forms. Other isotopes give off two protons and two neutrons in the form of an alpha particle. Alpha and beta decay are shown in **Figure 18.**

Half-Life In radioactive decay, the parent isotope undergoes radioactive decay. The daughter product is produced by radioactive decay. Each radioactive parent isotope decays to its daughter product at a certain rate. Based on this decay rate, it takes a certain period of time for one half of the parent isotope to decay to its daughter product. The **half-life** of an isotope is the time it takes for half of the atoms in the isotope to decay. For example, the half-life of carbon-14 is 5,730 years. So it will take 5,730 years for half of the carbon-14 atoms in an object to change into nitrogen-14 atoms. You might guess that in another 5,730 years, all of the remaining carbon-14 atoms will decay to nitrogen-14. However, this is not the case. Only half of the atoms of carbon-14 remaining after the first 5,730 years will decay during the second 5,730 years. So, after two half-lives, one fourth of the original carbon-14 atoms still remain. Half of them will decay during another 5,730 years. After three half-lives, one eighth of the original carbon-14 atoms still remain. After many half-lives, such a small amount of the parent isotope remains that it might not be measurable.

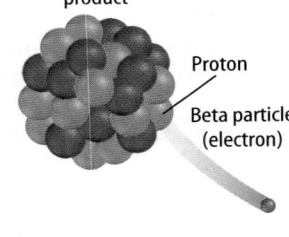

A Unstable parent isotope   **Beta decay**   Daughter product

Neutron   Proton

Beta particle (electron)

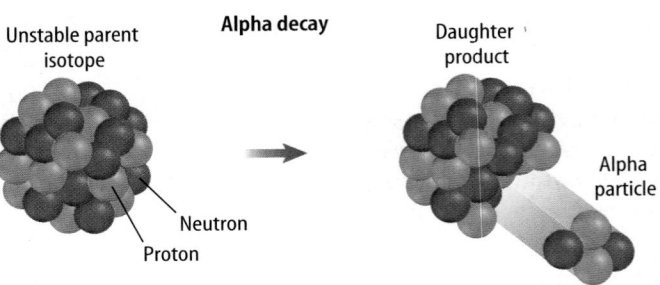

B Unstable parent isotope   **Alpha decay**   Daughter product

Neutron   Alpha particle

Proton

⚒ LAB DEMONSTRATION

Purpose to demonstrate how half-life works

Materials 100 pennies, 100 paper clips, box with lid

Preparation Place the pennies in the box, heads up.

Procedure Close the box and shake it twice. Show students that some pennies

have flipped (decayed). Record this number, remove the flipped pennies, and replace them with paper clips. Repeat until all pennies have been replaced.

Expected Outcome Each half-life (two shakes) is the same length of time. About half of the remaining pennies decay (flip over) during each half life.

✓ Assessment

What do the pennies represent? atoms of the parent isotope **What do the paper clips represent?** daughter products **What is each two shakes?** a half-life **Why do fewer isotopes decay in each successive half-life?** There are fewer atoms left to decay.

Radiometric Ages

Decay of radioactive isotopes is like a clock keeping track of time that has passed since rocks have formed. As time passes, the amount of parent isotope in a rock decreases as the amount of daughter product increases, as in **Figure 19.** By measuring the ratio of parent isotope to daughter product in a mineral and by knowing the half-life of the parent, in many cases you can calculate the absolute age of a rock. This process is called **radiometric dating.**

A scientist must decide which parent isotope to use when measuring the age of a rock. If the object to be dated seems old, then the geologist will use an isotope with a long half-life. The half-life for the decay of potassium-40 to argon-40 is 1.25 billion years. As a result, this isotope can be used to date rocks that are many millions of years old. To avoid error, conditions must be met for the ratios to give a correct indication of age. For example, the rock being studied must still retain all of the argon-40 that was produced by the decay of potassium-40. Also, it cannot contain any contamination of daughter product from other sources. Potassium-argon dating is good for rocks containing potassium, but what about other things?

Radiocarbon Dating Carbon-14 is useful for dating bones, wood, and charcoal up to 75,000 years old. Living things take in carbon from the environment to build their bodies. After the organism dies, the carbon-14 slowly decays and escapes as nitrogen-14 gas. If scientists can determine the amount of carbon-14 remaining in a sample, they can determine its age. For example, during much of human history, people built campfires. The wood from these fires often is preserved as charcoal. Scientists can determine the amount of carbon-14 remaining in a sample of charcoal by measuring the amount of radiation emitted by the carbon-14 isotope in labs like the one in **Figure 20.** Once they know the amount of carbon-14 in a charcoal sample, scientists can determine the age of the wood used to make the fire.

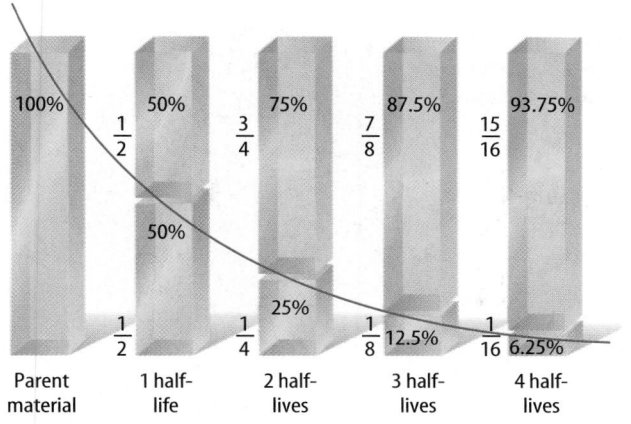

Figure 19
During each half-life, o[...] the parent material de[...] daughter product.

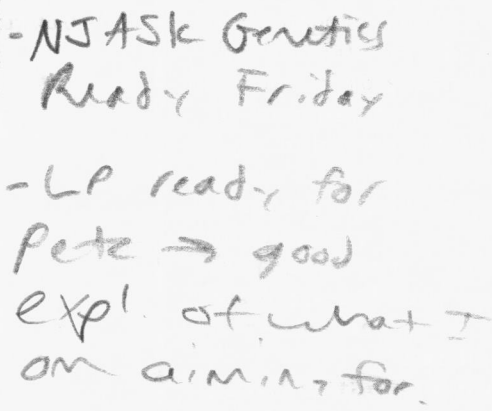

Figure 20
Radiometric ages are d[...] in labs like this one.

Resource Manager

Chapter Resources Booklet
Transparency Activity, p. 46
MiniLAB, p. 4
Enrichment, p. 32

Radiometric Ages

Activity

The half-life of potassium-40 is 1.3 billion years. An igneous rock is found with 25% potassium-40 and 75% daughter product. Calculate the absolute age of this rock. 2.6 billion years (two half-lives) L2

IS **Logical-Mathematical**

Quick Demo

Have students imagine that a sheet of paper is analogous to the amount of parent radioac-[...]

[handwritten note: NJASK Genetics Ready Friday — LP ready for Pete → good expl. of what I am aiming for.]

Figure 19 After students have studied the graph, discuss whether the overall amount of material changes after each half-life. Reinforce that the overall amount of material stays the same; it is the makeup of the material that changes.

Radiometric Ages, continued

✓ Reading Check

Answer Sedimentary rocks are made of particles eroded from older rocks. Dating these particles gives the age of the preexisting rock, not the newer sedimentary rock.

Problem-Solving Activity

National Math Standards

Correlation to Mathematics Objectives

1, 2, 6, 8, 9

Teaching Strategy

Explain that the age given by this method is an estimate. Radiometric dating does not give exact answers.

Answers to Questions

1. Since the Iceman is about 5,300 years old, students should estimate that about 55% of the original Carbon-14 still was present.
2. Using the chart, you can see that after 17,190 years, 12.5 percent of the carbon-14 would remain. $10 \times .125 = 1.25$ grams.

⬦ IDENTIFYING
Misconceptions

Students may think that the present is not the key to the past. Refer to page 366F for teaching strategies that address this misconception.

Figure 21
Meteorites like this one are thought to be as old as Earth.

Age Determinations Aside from carbon-14 dating, rocks that can be radiometrically dated are mostly igneous and metamorphic rocks. Most sedimentary rocks cannot be dated by this method. This is because many sedimentary rocks are made up of particles eroded from older rocks. Dating these pieces only gives the age of the preexisting rock from which it came.

The Oldest Known Rocks Radiometric dating has been used to date the oldest rocks on Earth. These rocks are about 3.96 billion years old. By dating meteorites like the one shown in **Figure 21** and using other evidence, scientists have estimated the age of Earth to be about 4.6 billion years. Earth rocks greater than 3.96 billion years old probably were eroded or changed by heat and pressure.

✓ **Reading Check** *Why can't most sedimentary rocks be dated radiometrically?*

Problem-Solving Activity

When did the Iceman die?

Carbon-14 dating has been used to date charcoal, wood, bones, mummies from Egypt and Peru, the Dead Sea Scrolls, and the Italian Iceman. The Iceman was found in 1991 in the Italian Alps, near the Austrian border. Based on carbon-14 analysis, scientists determined that the Iceman is 5,300 years old. In approximately what year did the Iceman die?

Half-Life of Carbon-14	
Percent Carbon-14	**Years Passed**
100	0
50	5,730
25	11,460
12.5	17,190
6.25	22,920
3.125	

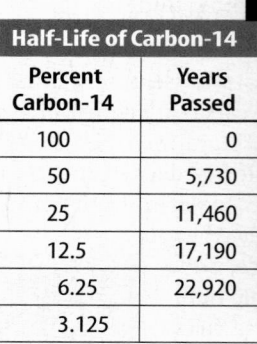

Reconstruction of Iceman

Identifying the Problem

The half-life chart shows the decay of carbon-14 over time. Half-life is the time it takes for half of a sample to decay. Fill in the years passed when only 3.125 percent of carbon-14 remain. Is there a point at which no carbon-14 would be present? Explain.

Solving the Problem

1. Estimate, using the data table, how much carbon-14 still was present in the Iceman's body that allowed scientists to determine his age.
2. If you had an artifact that contained 10.0 g of carbon-14, how many grams would remain after 17,190 years?

📖 *Science* Journal

Uniformitarianism Have students research and write a brief report in their Science Journals about uniformitarianism and the contributions of James Hutton, John Playfair, and Sir Charles Lyell. James Hutton thought Earth processes of today were similar to those of the past. John Playfair wrote about Hutton's ideas, but Sir Charles Lyell's written works were easier to read. [L2] [IS] **Linguistic** [P]

Resource Manager

Chapter Resources Booklet
  Reinforcement, p. 29
  Directed Reading for Content Mastery, pp. 21, 22
Mathematics Skill Activities, p. 3

Uniformitarianism

Can you imagine trying to determine the age of Earth without some of the information you know today? Before the discovery of radiometric dating, many people estimated that Earth is only a few thousand years old. But in the 1700s, Scottish scientist James Hutton estimated that Earth is much older. He used the principle of **uniformitarianism.** This principle states that Earth processes occurring today are similar to those that occurred in the past. Hutton's principle is often paraphrased as "the present is the key to the past."

Hutton observed that the processes that changed the landscape around him were slow, and he inferred that they were just as slow throughout Earth's history. Hutton hypothesized that it took much longer than a few thousand years to form the layers of rock around him and to erode mountains that once stood kilometers high. **Figure 22** shows Hutton's native Scotland, a region shaped by millions of years of geologic processes.

Today, scientists recognize that Earth has been shaped by two types of change: slow, everyday processes that take place over millions of years, and violent, unusual events such as the collision of a comet or asteroid about 65 million years ago that might have caused the extinction of the dinosaurs.

Figure 22
The rugged highlands of Scotland were shaped by erosion and uplift.

Section Assessment

1. You discover three rock layers that have not been turned upside down. The absolute age of the middle layer is 120 million years. What can you say about the ages of the layers above and below it?

2. How old would a fossil be if it had only one eighth of its original carbon-14 content remaining?

3. Explain the concept of uniformitarianism.

4. How do radioactive isotopes decay?

5. **Think Critically** Why can't scientists use carbon-14 to determine the age of an igneous rock?

Skill Builder Activities

6. **Making and Using Tables** Make a table that shows the amounts of parent and daughter material of a radioactive element that is left after four half-lives if the original parent material had a mass of 100 g. **For more help, refer to the** Science Skill Handbook.

7. **Using Fractions** You know that after every half-life, one half of the parent isotope changes to daughter product. In general, how would you determine how much parent isotope remains after any specified number of half-lives? **For more help, refer to the** Math Skill Handbook.

Visual Learning

Figure 22 Have students list some of the processes that helped shape this landscape.

3 Assess

Reteach

Have students determine the age of a rock containing 1/32 of the radium-226 originally in the rock. The half-life of radium-226 is 1,600 years. After five half-lives, or 8,000 years, 1/32 of the original isotope remains. L2

IS **Logical-Mathematical**

Challenge

Have students describe why all the remaining radioactive isotopes in a rock don't decay during its second half-life. Possible answer: There are fewer parent atoms remaining; therefore, there is a smaller number of decaying isotopes—only half of what remains decays each half-life.

✓ Assessment

Performance Have students plot the data from the tables they make in Question 6. Half-lives should appear on the horizontal axis, and the percentage of parent or daughter material should appear on the vertical axis. Use **Performance Assessment in the Science Classroom,** p. 109.

Answers to Section Assessment

1. The top layer is less than 120 million years old; the bottom layer is more than 120 million years old.

2. 17,190 years old

3. Earth processes occurring today are like those that have occurred in the past.

4. In some isotopes, a neutron breaks down into a proton and an electron (beta decay). In others, an isotope gives off two protons and two neutrons (alpha decay).

5. Carbon-14 dating works only for materials that were once alive. Volcanic rocks are nonliving materials.

6. See chart in side column.

7. Once you know the number of half-lives, you divide the original amount of parent material in half, once for each half-life.

Half-Life	Parent	Daughter
0	100 g	0 g
1	50 g	50 g
2	25 g	75 g
3	12.5 g	87.5 g
4	6.25 g	93.75 g

Activity

BENCH TESTED

Recognize the Problem

Purpose
Students will research information and create a model with trace fossils that show some behaviors of animals.

Process Skills
making a model, using reference materials, observing and inferring

Time Required
one or two class periods depending on the amount of research required

Thinking Critically

Discussion
Tell students to think about the types of animals with which they are familiar. **What types of food do these animals eat? Do they tend to stay in one area, or travel? What other behaviors could trace fossils show? What patterns of prints would indicate the behaviors you mentioned?** Provide reference materials or allow students to use library resources, including the Internet.

SCIENCE *Online*
Internet Addresses

_____

_____

_____

_____

Explore the Glencoe Science Web site at **science.glencoe.com** to find out more about topics in this activity.

Activity *Model and Invent*

Trace Fossils

Trace fossils can tell you a lot about the activities of organisms that left them. They can tell you how an organism fed or what kind of home it had. What else can you learn from trace fossils?

Recognize the Problem
How can you model trace fossils that can provide information about the behavior of organisms?

Thinking Critically
What can you use to model trace fossils? What types of behavior could you show with your trace fossil model?

Goals
■ **Construct** a model of trace fossils.
■ **Describe** the information that you can learn from looking at your model.

Possible Materials
construction paper	wire
plastic (a fairly rigid type)	scissors
plaster of Paris	toothpicks
sturdy cardboard	clay
pipe cleaners	glue

Data Source
SCIENCE *Online* Go to the Glencoe Science Web site at **science.glencoe.com** for more information about trace fossils and what can be learned from them.

Safety Precautions

Wash your hands after the activity.

388 CHAPTER 13 Clues to Earth's Past

Resource Manager

Chapter Resources Booklet
    Activity Worksheet, pp. 7–8
Cultural Diversity, p. 69
Lab Management and Safety, p. 39

Inclusion Strategies

Gifted Have these students create more involved models that include multiple species and multiple, or more complex, behaviors. L3

Planning the Model

1. **Decide** how you are going to make your model. What materials will you need?

2. **Decide** what types of activities you will demonstrate with your model. Were the organisms feeding? Resting? Traveling? Were they predators? Prey? How will your model indicate the activities you chose?

3. What is the setting of your model? Are you modeling the organism's home? Feeding areas? Is your model on land or water? How can the setting affect the way you build your model?

4. Will you only show trace fossils from a single species or multiple species? If you include more than one species, how will you provide evidence of any interaction between the species?

Check the Model Plans

1. Compare your plans with those of others in your class. Did other groups mention details that you had forgotten to think about? Are there any changes you would like to make to your plan before you continue?

2. Make sure your teacher approves your plan before you continue.

Making the Model

1. Following your plan, **construct** your model of trace fossils.

2. Have you included evidence of all the behaviors you intended to model?

Analyzing and Applying Results

1. Now that your model is complete, do you think that it adequately shows the behaviors you planned to demonstrate? Is there anything that you think you might want to do differently if you were going to make the model again?

2. Describe how using different kinds of materials might have affected your model. Can you think of other materials that would have allowed you to show more detail that you did?

3. Compare and contrast your model of trace fossils with trace fossils left by real organisms. Is one more easily interpreted than the other? Explain.

*C*ommunicating
Your Data

Ask other students in your class or another class to look at your model and describe what information they can learn from the trace fossils. Did their interpretations agree with what you intended to show?

ACTIVITY 389

Planning the Model

Teaching Strategies Have references available for students in class where they can look up information.

Troubleshooting Tell students to limit the number of specific behaviors that they are trying to show so that the model does not get too confusing.

Making the Model

Expected Outcome

Students will create a model that includes trace fossils that indicate certain behaviors of one or more species.

Analyzing and Applying Results

1. Answers will be individualized and based on the students' opinion of their research. Look for depth and quality of research performed.

2. Answers will vary depending on what materials students used. Clay would show three-dimensional fossils whereas paper or fabric would only be two-dimensional.

3. The models may be easier to interpret because they will not have any extraneous features and were not subject to weather or other factors that could damage them.

---

*A*ssessment

Process Have students use reference materials, such as textbooks or magazines to find photographs of trace fossils. Students should write a brief description of the type of animals and the behavior indicated. Then, groups of students can trade photographs and try to interpret those found by others. Use **Performance Assessment in the Science Classroom,** p. 159.

*C*ommunicating

Your Data

Students should discuss why their interpretations did or did not agree. They can cite their references to support their arguments.

Content Background

Coelacanths, or lobe-finned fishes, fall into the class of fish called Osteichthyes, the bony fishes. This class is further divided into three subclasses: the lungfishes, the ray-finned fish, and the lobe-finned fish. The lobe-finned fish, or Choanichthyes, has only one living species, the coelacanth *Latimeria chulumnae*, found in 1938.

The coelacanths are an ancient group, appearing in the fossil record about 395 million years ago. They are characterized by lobelike, fleshy fins, and live at great depths, where they are difficult to find. The limblike skeletal structure of the fleshy fins of coelacanths is thought to be an ancestral condition of all animals with four limbs. The earliest animal with four limbs discovered also had gills and therefore was still aquatic.

Discussion

Hypothesize how a fish could survive when many of the animals that evolved from it on land no longer exist. Conditions in the sea, such as temperature, salinity, and food sources are slow to change and are relatively constant, allowing marine species long periods to adjust to environmental changes.

The World's Oldest Fish Story

A catch-of-the-day set science on its ears

Second Dorsal Fin

Anal Fin

Pelvic Fin

On a December day in 1938, just before Christmas, Marjorie Courtenay-Latimer went to say hello to her friends on board a fishing boat that had just returned to port in South Africa. Courtenay-Latimer, who worked at a museum, often went aboard her friends' ship to check out the catch. On this visit, she received a surprise Christmas present—an odd-looking fish. As soon as the woman spotted its strange blue fins among the piles of sharks and rays, she knew it was special.

Courtenay-Latimer took the fish back to her museum to study it. "It was the most beautiful fish I had ever seen, five feet long, and a pale mauve blue with iridescent silver markings," she later wrote. Courtenay-Latimer sketched it and sent the drawing to a friend of hers, J. L. B. Smith.

Smith was a chemistry teacher who was passionate about fish. After a time, he realized it was a coelacanth (SEE luh kanth). Fish experts knew that coelacanths had first appeared on Earth 400 million years ago. But the experts thought the fish were extinct. People had found fossils of coelacanths, but no one had seen one alive. It was assumed that the last coelacanth species had died out 65 million years ago. They were wrong. The ship's crew had caught one by accident.

Smith figured there might be more living coelacanths. So he decided to offer a reward for anyone who could find a living specimen.

390

Resources for Teachers and Students

"An Ancient Fish in New Waters," *Time for Kids*, October 2, 1998.

"Dispute Over a Legendary Fish," by Constance Holden, *Science*, April 2, 1999.

A Fish Caught in Time, by Samantha Weinberg, Harper Collins Publishers, 2000.

First Dorsal Fin

Camouflage Marks

Marjorie Courtenay-Latimer poses with her fish (above).

Courtenay-Latimer's original sketch of the fish

Pectoral Fin

Some scientists call the coelacanth "Old Four Legs." It got its nickname because the fish has paired fins that look something like legs.

After 14 years of silence, a report came in that a coelacanth had been caught off the east coast of Africa.

Today, scientists know that there are at least several hundred coelacanths living in the Indian Ocean, just east of central Africa. Many of these fish live near the Comoros Islands. The coelacanths live in underwater caves during the day but move out at night to feed. The rare fish are now a protected species. With any luck, they will survive for another hundred million years.

CONNECTIONS Write Find out how people responded to the discovery of living coelacanths. Why do you think people were so fascinated by this fish? Use the Glencoe Science Web site to find out more about the coelacanth.

CONNECTIONS Students will find that at first, no one believed the story of the strange fish brought into East London, South Africa, in December 1938. Scientists believed that the coelacanth had died out during the Cretaceous Period. Ichthyologists who examined the fish and found it was indeed a coelacanth were astonished. These fish were believed to represent a group of fishes that eventually evolved into animals that could live on land.

Activity

Have students research species of fish in geologic history that lived at the time of the coelacanth. Have them write a story about a day in the life of the coelacanth, describing conditions on Earth 400 million years ago and the kinds of animals they lived with in the ocean. They should be careful to incorporate science facts into their creative writing.

Analyze the Event

Ask students to brainstorm the characteristics or circumstances that had to be present or occur for Courtenay-Latimer to have recognized the significance of her find. Possible answers: She was observant; she had friends who fished; she was curious; she knew to whom to send her sketch. Point out that she was not a scientist but had characteristics that are important for scientists, such as curiosity. Ask volunteers to describe their experiences of finding something by accident in the same way Courtenay-Latimer made her discovery.

Reviewing Main Ideas

Preview

Students can answer the questions in their Science Journals. Discuss the answers as you go through the chapter. **Linguistic**

Review

Students can write their answers, then compare them with those of other students. **Interpersonal**

Reteach

Students can look at the illustrations and describe details that support the main ideas of the chapter. **Visual-Spatial**

Answers to Chapter Review

SECTION 1

2. trace fossil

SECTION 2

1. the layer on the top

SECTION 3

2. carbon-14

Chapter 13 Study Guide

Reviewing Main Ideas

Section 1 Fossils

1. Fossils are more likely to form if hard parts of the dead organisms are buried quickly.

2. Some fossils form when original materials that made up the organisms are replaced with minerals. Other fossils form when remains are subjected to heat and pressure, leaving only a carbonaceous film behind. Some fossils are the tracks or traces left by ancient organisms. *What type of fossil is shown to the right?*

3. A rock layer can be no older than the age of the fossils embedded in it.

Section 2 Relative Ages of Rocks

1. The principle of superposition states that older rocks lie underneath younger rocks in areas where the rocks haven't been disturbed. Faults and igneous intrusions are always younger than the rocks they cut across. *Which of the rock layers shown below is youngest?*

2. Unconformities, or gaps in the rock record, are due to erosion or periods of time during which no deposition occurred.

3. Rock layers can be correlated using rock types and fossils.

Section 3 Absolute Ages of Rocks

1. Absolute dating of rocks and minerals, unlike relative age determination, provides an age in years for the rocks.

2. The half-life of a radioactive isotope is the time it takes for half of the atoms of the isotope to decay into another isotope. *Which isotope could be used to date the buried tree shown below?*

3. Because half-lives don't change, scientists can determine absolute ages of rocks and minerals containing radioactive elements.

FOLDABLES Reading & Study Skills

After You Read

To help review fossils and how to determine the age of rocks, use the Foldable you made at the beginning of the chapter.

FOLDABLES Reading & Study Skills

After You Read

After students have read the chapter and completed the Foldable described in Before You Read, have them do the activity on the student page.

Dinah Zike

Visualizing Main Ideas

Complete the following concept map on fossils.

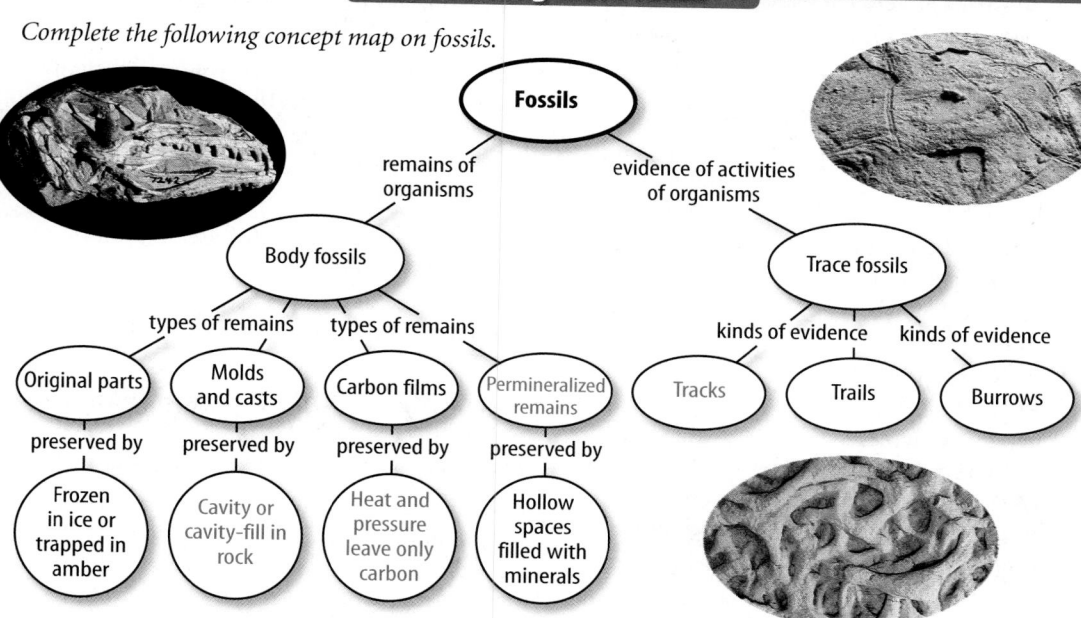

Vocabulary Review

Vocabulary Words

a. absolute age
b. carbon film
c. cast
d. fossil
e. half-life
f. index fossil
g. mold
h. permineralized remains
i. principle of superposition
j. radioactive decay
k. radiometric dating
l. relative age
m. unconformity
n. uniformitarianism

Study Tip

THE PRINCETON REVIEW

Reading material before your teacher explains it gives you a better understanding and provides you with an opportunity to ask questions.

Using Vocabulary

Write an original sentence using the vocabulary word to which each phrase refers.

1. thin film of carbon preserved as a fossil
2. older rocks lie under younger rocks
3. processes occur today as they did in the past
4. gap in the rock record
5. time needed for half the atoms to decay
6. fossil organism that lived for a short time
7. gives the age of rocks in years
8. minerals fill spaces inside fossil
9. a copy of a fossil produced by filling a mold with sediment or crystals
10. evidence of ancient life

Visualizing Main Ideas

See student page.

Vocabulary Review

Using Vocabulary

1. A carbon film is a thin film of carbon preserved as a fossil.
2. The principle of superposition states that older rocks lie under younger rocks in an undisturbed area.
3. According to uniformitarianism, processes occur today as they did in the past.
4. An unconformity is a gap in the rock record.
5. The time needed for half the atoms to decay is called half-life.
6. An index fossil is the fossil of an organism that lived for a short time but was widespread.
7. Absolute ages give the ages of rocks in years.
8. In permineralized remains, tiny spaces inside a fossil are filled with minerals.
9. A cast is a copy of a fossil produced inside a mold.
10. A fossil is evidence of ancient life.

◇IDENTIFYING◇ Misconceptions

Assess

Use the assessment as follow-up to page 366F after students have completed the chapter.

Procedure Set up a stream table with a meandering stream in it that flows into a lake. Have students observe the water flowing through the stream into the lake. After several minutes, ask the students to make a drawing of the feature created where the river flows into the lake. Show the students a photo of the Mississippi River delta. Ask them how they think the Mississippi River delta was formed.

Expected Outcome Students will recognize that the process of delta formation is a natural Earth process and that the process has been the same throughout Earth's history.

Chapter 13 Assessment

Checking Concepts

1. B
2. C
3. C
4. B
5. D
6. D
7. C
8. D
9. D
10. D

Thinking Critically

11. Relative age gives the age of an object in relation to the ages of other objects; absolute age gives an actual age in years.
12. three
13. Possible answers: Decay can destroy organic remains if they are not buried quickly; erosion destroys layers of rock; deeply buried materials are frequently destroyed by metamorphism.
14. Since the lava contains radioactive elements, an absolute age for the flow can be determined. This age can then be used to determine relative ages for the rocks above and below the flow.
15. It's likely that any layer of volcanic ash is part of the same deposit. The volcanic ash layer can act as a marker.

Checking Concepts

Choose the word or phrase that best answers the question.

1. What is any evidence of ancient life called?
   - **A)** half-life
   - **B)** a fossil
   - **C)** unconformity
   - **D)** disconformity

2. Which of the following conditions makes fossil formation more likely?
   - **A)** buried slowly
   - **B)** attacked by scavengers
   - **C)** made of hard parts
   - **D)** composed of soft parts

3. What are cavities left in rocks when a shell or bone dissolves called?
   - **A)** casts
   - **B)** original remains
   - **C)** molds
   - **D)** carbon films

4. When the tiny spaces inside a fossil are filled in with minerals, you have what kind of preservation?
   - **A)** original remains
   - **B)** permineralized remains
   - **C)** molds and casts
   - **D)** carbonaceous films

5. To say "the present is the key to the past" is a way to describe which of the following principles?
   - **A)** superposition
   - **B)** succession
   - **C)** radioactivity
   - **D)** uniformitarianism

6. A fault can be useful in determining which of the following for a group of rocks?
   - **A)** absolute age
   - **B)** radiometric age
   - **C)** index age
   - **D)** relative age

7. Which of the following is an unconformity between parallel rock layers?
   - **A)** angular unconformity
   - **B)** fault
   - **C)** disconformity
   - **D)** nonconformity

8. Which process forms new elements?
   - **A)** superposition
   - **B)** uniformitarianism
   - **C)** permineralization
   - **D)** radioactive decay

9. In one type of radioactive decay, which of the following breaks down, releasing an electron?
   - **A)** alpha particle
   - **B)** proton
   - **C)** beta particle
   - **D)** neutron

10. About how old is Earth, based on radiometric dating?
    - **A)** 2,000 years
    - **B)** 5,000 years
    - **C)** 3.5 billion years
    - **D)** 4.6 billion years

Thinking Critically

11. How do relative and absolute ages differ?

12. How many half-lives have passed in a rock containing one eighth of the original radioactive material and seven eighths of the daughter product?

13. The fossil record of life on Earth is incomplete. Give some reasons why.

14. Suppose a lava flow were found between two sedimentary rock layers. How could you use the lava flow to learn about the ages of the sedimentary rock layers? (Hint: Most lava contains radioactive isotopes.)

15. Suppose you're correlating rock layers in the western United States. You find a layer of volcanic ash deposits. How can this layer help you in your correlation over a large area?

Developing Skills

16. **Recognizing Cause and Effect** Explain how some woolly mammoths could have been preserved intact in frozen ground. What conditions must have persisted since the deaths of these animals?

Chapter ✔Assessment Planner

Portfolio Encourage students to place in their portfolios one or two items of what they consider to be their best work. Examples include:
- Chemistry Integration, p. 371
- Extension, p. 380
- Science Journal, p. 386

Performance Additional performance assessments, Performance Task Assessment Lists, and rubrics for evaluating these activities can be found in Glencoe's **Performance Assessment in the Science Classroom.**

17. Classifying Copy the table below, and place each of the following fossils in the correct category: *dinosaur footprint, worm burrow, dinosaur skull, insect in amber, fossil woodpecker hole,* and *fish tooth.*

Types of Fossils

Trace Fossils	Body Fossils
Dinosaur footprint	Dinosaur skull
Worm burrow	Insect in amber
Fossil woodpecker hole	Fish tooth

18. Concept Mapping Make a concept map using the following possible steps in the process of making a cast of a fossil: *organism dies, burial, protection from scavengers and bacteria, replacement by minerals, fossil erodes away,* and *mineral crystals form from solution.*

19. Communicating Make an outline of Section 1 that discusses the ways in which fossils form.

Performance Assessment

20. Write a Poem Write a poem explaining the principle of uniformitarianism.

21. Use a Classification System Start your own fossil collection. Label each find as to type, approximate age, and the place where it was found. Most state geological surveys can provide you with reference materials on local fossils.

TECHNOLOGY

Go to the Glencoe Science Web site at **science.glencoe.com** or use the **Glencoe Science CD-ROM** for additional chapter assessment.

THE PRINCETON REVIEW — Test Practice

A group of scientists found several different fossils. The scientists listed the different fossils in the table below.

Type of Fossils

Fossils A	Fossils B
Large footprint	Frozen mammoth
Trackway with small footprints	Dinosaur bones
Animal burrow	?

Study the table and answer the following questions.

1. Fossils A are different from Fossils B because only Fossils A are _____ .
   A) index fossils
   B) trace fossils
   C) permineralized fossils
   D) original remains

2. Which of these belongs with Fossils B?
   F) An imprint of a leaf in mud
   G) A footprint in cement
   H) An insect in amber
   J) A fossilized nest

3. All of the fossils in the table above are _____ .
   A) evidence of past life
   B) types of rocks
   C) softparts
   D) hardparts

THE PRINCETON REVIEW — Test Practice

The Test-Taking Tip was written by The Princeton Review, the nation's leader in test preparation.

1. B
2. H
3. A

Developing Skills

16. The cold temperatures preserved the entire animal, much like freezing helps preserve foods.
17. See student page.
18. The map should list concepts in the following order: organism dies, burial, protection from scavengers and bacteria, fossil eroded away, mineral crystals form from solution, replacement by minerals.
19. Possible answer:
   I. Conditions needed for fossil formation
      A. quick burial
      B. hard parts
   II. Types of preservation
      A. permineralized remains
      B. carbonaceous films
      C. molds and casts
      D. original remains
      E. trace fossils

Performance Assessment

20. Poems may be of any type as long as they indicate that Earth processes of today are similar to those of the past. Use **PASC,** p. 151.
21. Classification systems should indicate type of fossil formation, how old each is, and where each was found. Use **PASC,** p. 121.

Assessment Resources

Reproducible Masters

Chapter Resources Booklet
Chapter Review, pp. 37–38
Chapter Tests, pp. 39–42
Assessment Transparency Activity, p. 49

Glencoe Science Web site
Interactive Tutor
Chapter Quizzes

Glencoe Technology
- Assessment Transparency
- Interactive CD-ROM Chapter Quizzes
- ExamView Pro Test Bank
- Vocabulary PuzzleMaker Software
- MindJogger Videoquiz DVD/VHS

Section/Objectives	Standards		Activities/Features
Chapter Opener	**National**	**State/Local**	**Explore Activity:** Make a model environment, p. 397 **Before You Read,** p. 397
	See p. 5T for a Key to Standards.		
Section 1 Life and Geologic Time 🕐 2 sessions 🔲 1 block 1. **Explain** how geologic time can be divided into units. 2. **Relate** changes of Earth's organisms to division on the geologic time scale. 3. **Describe** how plate tectonics affects species.	National Content Standards: UCP2, UCP3, UCP4, A2, C5, D2, G3		
Section 2 Early Earth History 🕐 3 sessions 🔲 1 block 1. **Identify** characteristic Precambrian and Paleozoic life-forms. 2. **Draw conclusions** about how organisms adapted to changing environments in Precambrian time and the Paleozoic Era 3. **Describe** changes in Earth and its life-forms at the end of the Paleozoic Era.	National Content Standards: UCP2, UCP3, UCP4, A1, C5, D2		**Chemistry Integration,** p. 407 **MiniLAB:** Dating Rock Layers with Fossils, p. 408 **Visualizing Unusual Life Forms,** p. 409 **Science Online,** p. 410 **Activity:** Changing Species, p. 413
Section 3 Middle and Recent Earth 🕐 3 sessions 🔲 2 blocks 1. **Compare and contrast** characteristic life-forms in the Mesozoic and Cenozoic Eras 2. **Explain** how changes caused by plate tectonics affected organisms during the Mesozoic Era. 3. **Identify** when humans first appeared on Earth.	National Content Standards: UCP2, UCP3, UCP4, A1, C5, D2		**Science Online,** p. 415 **Math Skills Activity:** Calculating Extinction Using Percentages, p. 417 **MiniLAB:** Calculating the Age of the Atlantic Ocean, p. 418 **Activity:** Discovering the Past, pp. 420–421 **Science Stats:** Extinct!, pp. 422–423

▨ NATIONAL GEOGRAPHIC

Teacher's Corner

PRODUCTS AVAILABLE FROM GLENCOE
To order call 1-800-334-7344:
CD-ROM
NGS PictureShow: Age of Dinosaurs
Curriculum Kit
GeoKit: Earth's History

Transparency Set
NGS PicturePack: Age of Dinosaurs
PRODUCTS AVAILABLE FROM
NATIONAL GEOGRAPHIC SOCIETY
To order call 1-800-368-2728:
Videos
Dinosaurs: Then and Now

INDEX TO NATIONAL GEOGRAPHIC SOCIETY
The following articles may be used for research relating to this chapter:
"Dinosaur Embryos," by Luis Chiappe, December 1998.

Activity Materials	Reproducible Resources	Section Assessment	Technology
Explore Activity: green, orange, and blue yarn; scissors; green construction paper; tweezers	**Chapter Resources Booklet** Foldables Worksheet, p. 15 Directed Reading Overview, p. 17 Note-taking Worksheets, pp. 31–33	GLENCOE'S ASSESSMENT ADVANTAGE	
Need materials? Contact Science Kit at 1-800-828-7777 or www.sciencekit.com on the Internet.	**Chapter Resources Booklet** Transparency Activity, p. 42 Enrichment, p. 28 Reinforcement, p. 25 Directed Reading, p. 18 Lab Activity, pp. 9–10 Transparency Activity, pp. 45–46	Portfolio Science Journal, p. 400 Performance Skill Builder Activities, p. 405 Content Section Assessment, p. 405	Section Focus Transparency Teaching Transparency Interactive CD-ROM/DVD Guided Reading Audio Program
MiniLAB: paper, pencil **Activity:** deck of playing cards	**Chapter Resources Booklet** Transparency Activity, p. 43 MiniLAB, p. 3 Enrichment, p. 29 Reinforcement, p. 26 Directed Reading, p. 18 Activity Worksheet, pp. 5–6 **Reading and Writing Skill Activities,** p. 27 **Science Inquiry Labs,** p. 29 **Cultural Diversity,** p. 31	Portfolio Chemistry Integration, p. 407 Performance MiniLAB, p. 408 Skill Builder Activities, p. 412 Content Section Assessment, p. 412	Section Focus Transparency Interactive CD-ROM/DVD Guided Reading Audio Program
MiniLAB: world map or globe, metric ruler **Activity:** Internet and other resources on Earth's history	**Chapter Resources Booklet** Transparency Activity, p. 44 MiniLAB, p. 4 Enrichment, p. 30 Reinforcement, p. 27 Directed Reading, pp. 19, 20 Activity Worksheet, pp. 7–8 Lab Activity, pp. 11–14 **Mathematics Skill Activities,** p. 5 **Lab Management and Safety,** p. 73	Portfolio Extension, p. 415 Performance Math Skills Activity, p. 417 MiniLAB, p. 418 Skill Builder Activities , p. 419 Content Section Assessment, p. 419	Section Focus Transparency Interactive CD-ROM/DVD Guided Reading Audio Program

End of Chapter Assessment

GLENCOE'S ASSESSMENT ADVANTAGE

Blackline Masters	Technology	Professional Series
Chapter Resources Booklet Chapter Review, pp. 35–36 Chapter Tests, pp. 37–40 **Standardized Test Practice by The Princeton Review,** pp. 63–66	MindJogger Videoquiz CD-ROM Explorations and Quizzes Vocabulary Puzzle Makers ExamView Pro Test Bank Interactive Lesson Planner Interactive Teacher's Edition	Performance Assessment in the Science Classroom (PASC)

Transparencies

Section Focus

SECTION 1 Section Focus Transparency **Relatively Speaking . . .**

The spectacular bands of multicolored rock at sites like the Vermillion Cliffs are more than just beautiful. They are tools that help us learn about the history of Earth. As you examine the contours of this canyon, think about what these layers tell us.

1. Do you think all the rock in the picture was formed at the same time? Why or why not?
2. If you think the rock formed at different times, which layers are the oldest and which are the youngest? Why do you think so?
3. How could knowing which layers of rock two fossils came from tell you their relative ages?

L2

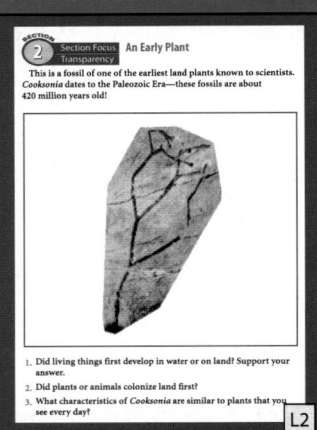

SECTION 2 Section Focus Transparency **An Early Plant**

This is a fossil of one of the earliest land plants known to scientists. *Cooksonia* dates to the Paleozoic Era—these fossils are about 420 million years old!

1. Did living things first develop in water or on land? Support your answer.
2. Did plants or animals colonize land first?
3. What characteristics of *Cooksonia* are similar to plants that you see every day?

L2

SECTION 3 Section Focus Transparency **Big Smile for the Camera**

While there are signs of the earliest sharks in the Middle Devonian period, modern sharks date to the Jurassic period of the Mesozoic Era. This is a great white shark, *Carcharodon carcharias*, and its family arose in the Upper Cretaceous.

1. What animals were dominant on land as sharks arose in the oceans?
2. How have the continents changed since the Mesozoic Era?
3. Why are sharks called living fossils?

L2

This is a representation of key blackline masters available in the Teacher Classroom Resources. See Resource Manager boxes within the chapter for additional information.

Key to Teaching Strategies

The following designations will help you decide which activities are appropriate for your students.

L1 **Level 1** activities should be appropriate for students with learning difficulties.

L2 **Level 2** activities should be within the ability range of all students.

L3 **Level 3** activities are designed for above-average students.

ELL **ELL** activities should be within the ability range of English Language Learners.

COOP LEARN **Cooperative Learning** activities are designed for small group work.

LS **Multiple Learning Styles** logos, as described on page 22T, are used throughout to indicate strategies that address different learning styles.

P These strategies represent student products that can be placed into a best-work portfolio.

Assessment

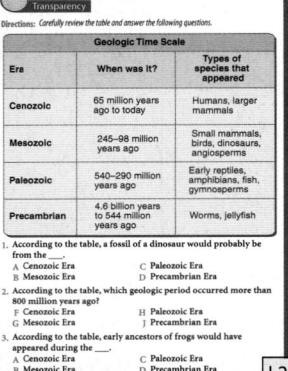

Assessment Transparency **Geologic Time**

Directions: *Carefully review the table and answer the following questions.*

Geologic Time Scale

Era	When was it?	Types of species that appeared
Cenozoic	65 million years ago to today	Humans, larger mammals
Mesozoic	245–98 million years ago	Small mammals, birds, dinosaurs, angiosperms
Paleozoic	540–290 million years ago	Early reptiles, amphibians, fish, gymnosperms
Precambrian	4.6 billion years to 544 million years ago	Worms, jellyfish

1. According to the table, a fossil of a dinosaur would probably be from the ___.
   A Cenozoic Era C Paleozoic Era
   B Mesozoic Era D Precambrian Era
2. According to the table, which geologic period occurred more than 800 million years ago?
   F Cenozoic Era H Paleozoic Era
   G Mesozoic Era J Precambrian Era
3. According to the table, early ancestors of frogs would have appeared during the ___.
   A Cenozoic Era C Paleozoic Era
   B Mesozoic Era D Precambrian Era

L2

Teaching

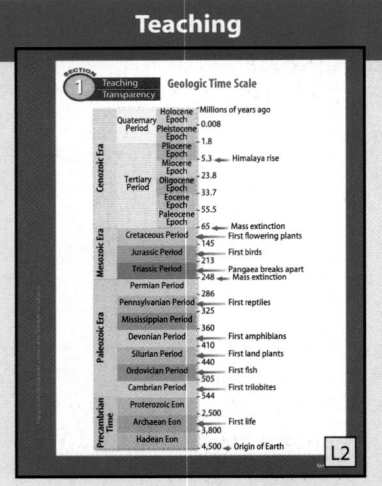

SECTION 1 Teaching Transparency **Geologic Time Scale**

Millions of years ago

Cenozoic Era	Quaternary Period	Holocene Epoch	0.008
		Pleistocene Epoch	1.8
		Pliocene Epoch	5.3 — Himalaya rise
	Tertiary Period	Miocene Epoch	23.8
		Oligocene Epoch	33.7
		Eocene Epoch	55.5
		Paleocene Epoch	65 — Mass extinction

Cretaceous Period 145 — First flowering plants
Jurassic Period 213 — First birds
Triassic Period 248 — Pangaea breaks apart / Mass extinction
Permian Period 286
Pennsylvanian Period 325 — First reptiles
Mississippian Period 360
Devonian Period 410 — First amphibians
Silurian Period 440 — First land plants
Ordovician Period 505 — First fish
Cambrian Period 544 — First trilobites
Proterozoic Eon 2,500
Archaean Eon 3,800 — First life
Hadean Eon 4,500 — Origin of Earth

L2

Hands-on Activities

Activity Worksheets

Activity Changing Species

Lab Preview
Directions: Answer the following questions before beginning the Activity.

1. How many times will you draw cards representing a pair of varimals that will mate and produce offspring?

2. Can you name another variable in your numbered playing cards and explain how that variable could model adaptation within a species?

In this activity, you will observe how adaptation within a species might cause the evolution of a particular trait, leading to the development of a new species.

What You'll Investigate
How might adaptation within a species cause the evolution of a particular trait?

Materials
Deck of playing cards

Goals
• **Model** adaptation within a species.

Procedure
1. **Remove** all of the kings, queens, jacks, and aces from a deck of playing cards.
2. Each remaining card represents an individual in a population of animals called "varimals." The number on each card represents the height of the varimal. For example, the 5 of diamonds is a varimal that's 5 units tall.
3. **Calculate** the average height of the population of varimals represented by your cards.
4. Suppose varimals eat grass, shrubs, and leaves from trees. A drought causes many of these plants to die. All that's left are a few tall trees. Only varimals at least 6 units high can reach the leaves on these trees.
5. All the varimals under 6 units leave the area to seek food elsewhere or die from

starvation. Discard all of the cards with a number value less than 6. 6. Calculate the new average height of the population of varimals.
7. Shuffle the deck of remaining cards.
8. Draw two cards at a time. Each pair represents a pair of varimals that will mate.
9. The offspring of each pair reaches a height equal to the average height of his or her parents. Calculate and record the height of each offspring.
10. Repeat by discarding all parents and offspring under 6 units tall. Now calculate the new average height of varimals. Include both the parents and offspring in your calculation.

L2

Laboratory Activities

LAB 1 Laboratory Activity **Differences in a Species**

To use fossil dating efficiently, paleontologists first separate fossils into groups. The most useful group is called a species. A species is a population of individuals that have similar characteristics. Small differences in individuals may result in the development of a new species by a series of gradual changes. These changes can be traced from one geologic time division to another, if the fossil record is good.

Strategy
You will describe the variations present within a species.
You will describe a species in terms of one characteristic.

Materials
meterstick   graph paper   pencils (colored)

Procedure
1. The species you will study is *Homo sapiens*, or yourself. You and your classmates are all members of this species. Remember that all living things grow at different rates. It is possible that you will find some big differences in your study, but everyone still belongs to the same species.
2. Record all characteristics of the species that you can. Record which of the characteristics

you could measure and compare for all members of the species.
3. Measure and record in Table 1 the height of yourself and each of your classmates. Round off the height to the nearest tenth of a meter (0.1 m).
4. Measure and record the heights of a class of younger students. Record in Table 2.

Data and Observations
Characteristics:

Table 1

Name	Height (m)	Name	Height (m)

L2

Meeting Different Ability Levels

Content Outline

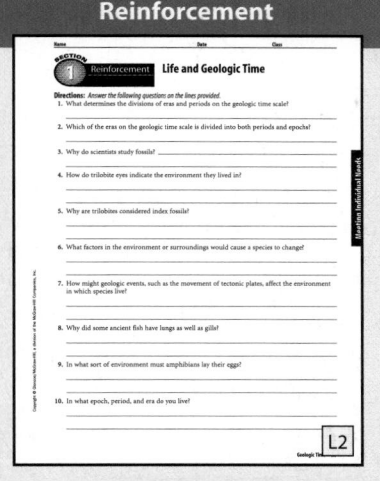

Note-taking Worksheet **Geologic Time**

Section 1 Life and Geologic Time

L2

Reinforcement

Reinforcement **Life and Geologic Time**

Directions: Answer the following question on the lines provided.

1. What determines the divisions of eras and periods on the geologic time scale?

2. Which of the eras on the geologic time scale is divided into both periods and epochs?

3. Why do scientists study fossils?

4. How do trilobite eyes indicate the environment they lived in?

5. Why are trilobites considered index fossils?

6. What factors in the environment or surroundings would cause a species to change?

7. How might geologic events, such as the movement of tectonic plates, affect the environment in which species live?

8. Why did some ancient fish have lungs as well as gills?

9. In what sort of environment must amphibians lay their eggs?

10. In what epoch, period, and era do you live?

L2

Directed Reading

Directed Reading for Content Mastery **Overview** **Geologic Time**

Directions: Study the diagram. Then complete the sentences below.

Era	Time Span	Period	Life-forms	Geologic Events
Mesozoic	245 to 66 MYBP	Triassic	The first small ___ appeared.	All continents joined as a single landmass called ___
		Jurassic	The first ___ appeared.	
		Cretaceous	New plants called ___ evolved.	
Cenozoic		Tertiary	Dinosaurs became extinct.	begin to rise. Ice Age began.
		Quaternary	___ sapiens appear.	

1. Ferns and reptiles appeared in the ___ Era.
2. In the ___ Era, humans and large mammals appeared.
3. Dinosaurs, birds, and flowering plants first appeared in the ___ Era.
4. During ___ time, the earliest life-forms appeared.
5. Small animals appeared in the ___ Era.
6. The earliest life-form shown above is ___.
7. Reptiles appeared during the same era as ferns, fish, and ___.
8. Worms and jellyfish first appeared in ___ time.

L1

Assessment

Chapter Tests

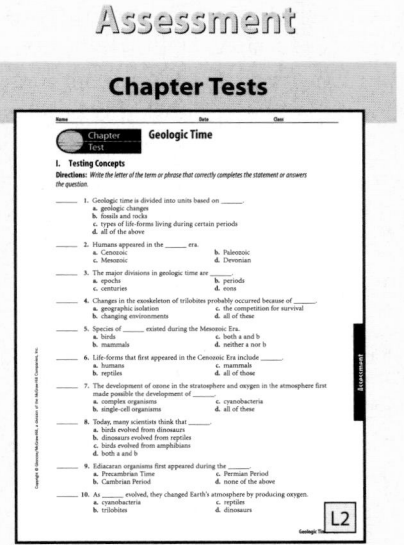

Chapter Test **Geologic Time**

I. Testing Concepts

Directions: Write the letter of the term or phrase that correctly completes the statement or answers the question.

1. Geologic time is divided into units based on ___.
   a. geologic changes
   b. fossils and rocks
   c. types of life-forms living during certain periods
   d. all of the above

2. Humans appeared in the ___ era.
   a. Cenozoic   c. Paleozoic
   b. Mesozoic   d. Devonian

3. The major divisions in geologic time are ___.
   a. epochs   b. periods
   c. centuries   d. eons

4. Changes in the exoskeleton of trilobites probably occurred because of ___.
   a. geographic isolation   c. the competition for survival
   b. changing environments   d. all of these

5. Species of ___ existed during the Mesozoic Era.
   a. birds   c. both a and b
   b. mammals   d. neither a nor b

6. Life-forms that first appeared in the Cenozoic Era include ___.
   a. humans   c. mammals
   b. reptiles   d. all of these

7. The development of ozone in the stratosphere and oxygen in the atmosphere first made possible the development of ___.
   a. complex organisms   c. cyanobacteria
   b. single-cell organisms   d. all of these

8. Today, many scientists think that ___.
   a. birds evolved from dinosaurs
   b. dinosaurs evolved from reptiles
   c. birds evolved from amphibians
   d. both a and b

9. Ediacaran organisms first appeared during the ___.
   a. Precambrian Time   c. Permian Period
   b. Cambrian Period   d. none of the above

10. As ___ evolved, they changed Earth's atmosphere by producing oxygen.
   a. cyanobacteria   c. reptiles
   b. trilobites   d. dinosaurs

L2

Enrichment

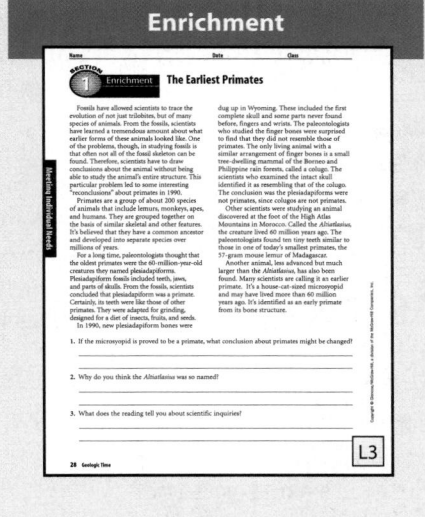

Enrichment **The Earliest Primates**

L3

Spanish Directed Reading

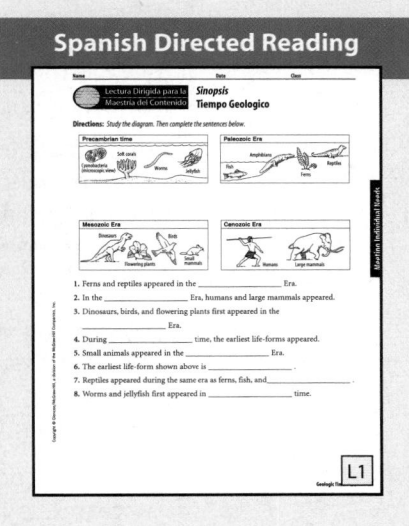

Lectura Dirigida para la Maestría del Contenido **Sinopsis** **Tiempo Geológico**

Directions: Study the diagram. Then complete the sentences below.

1. Ferns and reptiles appeared in the ___ Era.
2. In the ___ Era, humans and large mammals appeared.
3. Dinosaurs, birds, and flowering plants first appeared in the ___ Era.
4. During ___ time, the earliest life-forms appeared.
5. Small animals appeared in the ___ Era.
6. The earliest life-form shown above is ___.
7. Reptiles appeared during the same era as ferns, fish, and ___.
8. Worms and jellyfish first appeared in ___ time.

L1

Test Practice Workbook

Standardized Test Practice
Teacher Edition

Glencoe Science

Earth Science

L2

Chapter Review

Chapter Review **Geologic Time**

Part A. Vocabulary Review

Directions: Circle 11 terms in the puzzle and then write the terms in the blanks at the left of their description.

```
G E O L O G I C T I M E S C A L E V B
K D C Z B A J Y Q R E P T I L E S D M
V F M D K L T A M P H I B I A N S X I
T X K O R Y A N O C E P O L L T M O N
B X D G Y M N O S P E R M S X R D R D
I N V E R T E B R A T E S S Z J C K E
M B Y F M Y R A N G I O S P E R M S X
X D F L V P P C Q J D J Q E K Z M L F
C H X B I B A T K S A R D C F T K V O
J Y K D Q D V E V C F K F I Q B J C S
M V E R T E B R A T E S B E R A R T S
B K A B K X Z I P R B Z T S C S Z K I
A Z N A T U R A L S E L E C T I O N L
```

___ 1. animals evolved from a species of amphibians
___ 2. animals that live on land but return to water to reproduce
___ 3. animals without a backbone
___ 4. division of Earth's history into smaller units
___ 5. among the earliest life-forms on Earth
___ 6. group of organisms that normally reproduce only among themselves
___ 7. animals with a backbone
___ 8. flowering plants
___ 9. naked seed plants
___ 10. organism used to identify specific geologic time period
___ 11. process by which organisms with traits that are suited to a certain environment survive whereas others do not

L2

Science Content Background

SECTION 1
Life and Geologic Time
Understanding Earth's Past

Although the geologic time scale was originally based on relative dating, absolute methods such as radiometric dating have enabled geologists to determine absolute dates of many rocks and some geologic events. Some scientists believe that supercontinents such as Pangaea have existed multiple times during Earth's history.

Student Misconception

Time is measured only with a watch in minutes and seconds.

Refer to the facing page for teaching strategies to address this misconception. Refer to pages 398–399 for content related to this topic.

SECTION 2
Early Earth History
The End of the Paleozoic Era

The largest of all mass extinctions occurred at the end of the Paleozoic Era. Some evidence suggests that a huge volcanic eruption occurred in what is now Siberia. The eruption would have released large concentrations of poisonous gases. The release of these gases, along with global changes in climates associated with the volcanic eruptions, could have been the cause of the mass extinction. Other evidence suggests the cause may have been a global turnover of ocean water. The upwelling of deep ocean water would have brought large amounts of carbon dioxide to the surface, some of

Tom & Therisa Stack/ Tom Stack & Assoc.

which would have been released into the atmosphere. The blood of animals that inhale excess carbon dioxide can become acidified, which can lead to the animal's death. Carbon dioxide is also a greenhouse gas. Added to the atmosphere in sufficiently high quantities, the gas could have led to a global rise in temperatures and subsequent mass extinctions.

SECTION 3
Middle and Recent Earth History
Separating Middle and Recent Earth History

The KP (Cretaceous/Paleocene) boundary is the point in the geologic time scale that separates the Mesozoic Era from the Cenozoic Era. This boundary contains evidence of the factors that may have caused the extinction of the dinosaurs. An iridium-rich clay layer found at this boundary led to the hypothesis that a collision with an asteroid was the final blow to the already dying dinosaur population.

The Development of Humans

Geologic evidence indicates that humans and their direct ancestors make up a group of animals called hominids. The earliest hominids were of the genus *Australopithecus*. These hominids were bipedal and had rounded jaws. They lived in the open grasslands of what is now eastern and southern Africa. Australopithecines were smaller than modern humans. Standing less than 1.5 m tall, they weighed about 20 kg. Their brains were half the size of present-day humans' brains. Fossil evidence indicates that these early human ancestors used tools made of bone.

SCIENCE *Online*

For additional content background on this topic, go to the Glencoe Science Web site at science.glencoe.com.

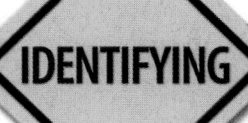

IDENTIFYING **Misconceptions**

Find Out What Students Think

Students may think that . . .

- **Time is measured only with a watch in minutes and seconds.**

Students probably have had few experiences with the concept of geologic time. The vast amount of time represented by the geologic time scale is beyond the grasp of many students and adults alike. To make the geologic time scale more manageable, it has been divided into eras based on major events in Earth's history.

Activity

Access the *Geological Time Scale Metaphor Calculator* through the Glencoe Science Web site at **science.glencoe.com**. Have small groups of students work together to develop their own metaphors for understanding geologic time. For example, one group of students might choose their average age to represent all of geologic time. They then could determine how old they would have been when dinosaurs lived on Earth or when human history started. Have students discuss with the class the different metaphors they develop.

Promote Understanding

Activity

Provide each group of three or four students with a meterstick, a calculator, several small self-stick notes, and a copy of the geologic time scale. If copies of time scales are not available, refer students to **Figure 2** in Section 1.

- Explain that each group will be making a geologic time scale on the meterstick. They should imagine that the meterstick represents all of geologic time.

- Review how to do percentages. Help students determine what percent of the meterstick should represent Precambrian Time using this formula: 4,056 million years ÷ 4,600 million years = x ÷ 1,000 mm; x = 882 mm. Direct students to place a self-stick note at this point on the meterstick and label it "Precambrian Time Ends."

- Have them repeat this process for each era.

- Direct students to estimate where major animal groups developed and when major geologic events, such as mass extinctions and changes in continental position or shape, occurred. Encourage each group to label at least three of these events on their metersticks.

- When groups have completed their tasks, have a representative from each group present their time scale to the class. As each group finishes its presentation, combine its data with those of others to make a class geologic time scale. Display this scale throughout the study of the chapter so that students have a concrete reference for understanding the vast length of Precambrian Time compared with the other eras and the relatively short amount of time life has been on Earth.

Assess

After completing the chapter, see *Identifying Misconceptions* in the Study Guide.

Chapter Vocabulary

trilobite
geologic time scale
eon
era
period
epoch
organic evolution
species
natural selection
Pangaea
Precambrian time
cyanobacteria
Paleozoic Era
Mesozoic Era
Cenozoic Era

What do you think?

Science Journal These are teeth from the fossil skeleton of a *Tyrannosaurus rex* that paleontologists have nicknamed Sue. The sharp, serrated teeth of the *T. Rex*, about 13 cm (5 in.) long, show that it was a meat eater.

Geologic Time

The discovery of a new fossil often changes scientists' ideas about how ancient organisms looked and lived. Pictured here is Sue, the most complete *Tyrannosaurus rex* fossil ever found. Discovered in 1990, Sue has provided evidence indicating that this type of dinosaur relied heavily on a very good sense of smell. In this chapter, you will learn how dinosaurs and other types of organisms changed over time. You also will come to appreciate the long span of geologic time.

What do you think?

Science Journal Look at the picture below with a classmate. Discuss what you think this might be or what is happening. Here's a hint: *Sue couldn't have survived without them.* Write your answer or best guess in your Science Journal.

396

Theme Connection

Stability and Change Overall, Earth's surface and the organisms that live on it may appear unchanging during the short period of time that makes up a human lifetime. However, over the millions or even billions of years that make up the divisions in the geologic time scale, major changes occur in the landscape and in species.

Environments include the living and nonliving things that surround and affect organisms. Whether or not an organism survives in its environment depends upon the characteristics that it has. Only if an organism survives until adulthood can it reproduce and pass on its characteristics to its offspring. In this activity, you will use a model to find out how one characteristic can determine whether individuals can compete and survive in an environment.

Make a model environment

1. Cut 15 pieces each of green, orange, and blue yarn into 3-cm lengths.

2. Scatter them on a sheet of green construction paper.

3. Have your partner use a pair of tweezers to pick up as many pieces as possible in 15 s.

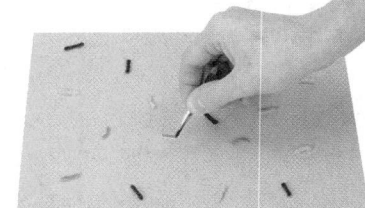

Observe

In your Science Journal, discuss which colors your partner selected. Which color was least selected? Suppose that the construction paper represents grass, the yarn pieces represent insects, and the tweezers represent an insect-eating bird. Which color of insect do you predict would survive to adulthood?

Before You Read

FOLDABLES
Reading & Study Skills

Making an Organizational Study Fold Make the following Foldable to help you organize your thoughts into clear categories about geological time.

1. Place a sheet of paper in front of you so the long side is at the top. Fold the paper in half from top to bottom.

2. Fold both sides in. Unfold the paper so three sections show.

3. Through the top thickness of paper, cut along each of the fold lines to the topfold, forming three tabs. Label the tabs *Paleozoic Era, Mesozoic Era,* and *Cenozoic Era*.

4. Before you read the chapter, find an example of an animal from each era and write it on the front of the tabs. As you read the chapter, write information about each era under the tabs.

Paleozoic Era   Mesozoic Era   Cenozoic Era

Purpose Use the Explore Activity to introduce students to the concept of natural selection. L1 ELL COOP LEARN IS **Kinesthetic**

Preparation To save time, cut the yarn into 3-cm lengths before class.

Materials 15 pieces each of green, orange, and blue yarn cut into 3-cm lengths; sheet of green construction paper; stopwatch; scissors; tweezers

Teaching Strategy For the activity to work well, match the color of the green yarn to the color of the green construction paper.

Safety Precautions Caution students to handle the scissors and tweezers with care.

Observe

Students will probably pick up more orange and blue pieces because they are more easily seen. Green was probably least selected. A green insect would blend in better with the background and have a better chance of going unnoticed by predators.

Assessment

Process Have students find photos or illustrations of animals whose coloration provides camouflage that helps them survive in their environment. Use **Performance Assessment in the Science Classroom,** p. 89.

Before You Read

FOLDABLES
Reading & Study Skills

Dinah Zike Study Fold
Purpose Use this activity to determine what students know about geologic time before they read the chapter. Have them use the Foldable for recording and organizing notes on the Paleozoic, Mesozoic, and Cenozoic eras as they read.

For additional help, see Foldables Worksheet, p. 15 in **Chapter Resources Booklet,** or go to the Glencoe Science Web site at **science.glencoe.com.** See After You Read in the Study Guide at the end of this chapter.

SECTION

Life and Geologic Time

1 Motivate

Bellringer Transparency

Display the Section Focus Transparency for Section 1. Use the accompanying Transparency Activity Master. L2 ELL

Section Focus Transparency 1 — Relatively Speaking . . .

The spectacular bands of multicolored rock at sites like the Vermillion Cliffs are more than just beautiful. They are tools that help us learn about the history of Earth. As you examine the contours of this canyon, think about what these layers tell us.

1. Do you think all the rock in the picture was formed at the same time? Why or why not?
2. If you think the rock formed at different times, which layers are the oldest and which are the youngest? Why do you think so?
3. How could knowing which layers of rock two fossils came from tell you their relative ages?

L2

Tie to Prior Knowledge

Are any dinosaurs living today? no **How long ago do you think dinosaurs disappeared?** Have students brainstorm answers, then explain that . . . they disappeared about 65 million years ago, long before there were any people on Earth. Note that although this is a long period of time, it is only a fraction of Earth's history. Tell students they will learn more about the major events in Earth's history in this section.

Text Question Answer

yes

As You Read

What You'll Learn

- **Explain** how geologic time can be divided into units.
- **Relate** changes of Earth's organisms to divisions on the geologic time scale.
- **Describe** how plate tectonics affects species.

Vocabulary

trilobite
geologic
  time scale
eon
era
period

epoch
organic evolution
species
natural selection
Pangaea

Why It's Important

The life and landscape around you are the products of change through geologic time.

Geologic Time

A group of students is searching for fossils. By looking in rocks that are hundreds of millions of years old, they hope to find many examples of **trilobites** (TRI loh bites) so that they can help piece together a puzzle. That puzzle is to find out what caused the extinction of these organisms. **Figure 1** shows some examples of what they are finding. The fossils are small, and their bodies are divided into segments. Some of them seem to have eyes. Could these be trilobites?

Trilobites are interesting fossils to search for. These small, hard-shelled organisms crawled on the seafloor and sometimes swam through the water. Most ranged in size from 2 cm to 7 cm in length and from 1 cm to 3 cm in width. They are considered to be index fossils because they lived over vast regions of the world during specific periods of geologic time.

The Geologic Time Scale The appearance or disappearance of types of organisms throughout Earth's history marks important occurrences in geologic time. Paleontologists have been able to divide Earth's history into time units based on the life-forms that lived only during certain periods. This division of Earth's history makes up the **geologic time scale.** However, sometimes fossils are not present, so certain divisions of the geologic time scale are based on other criteria.

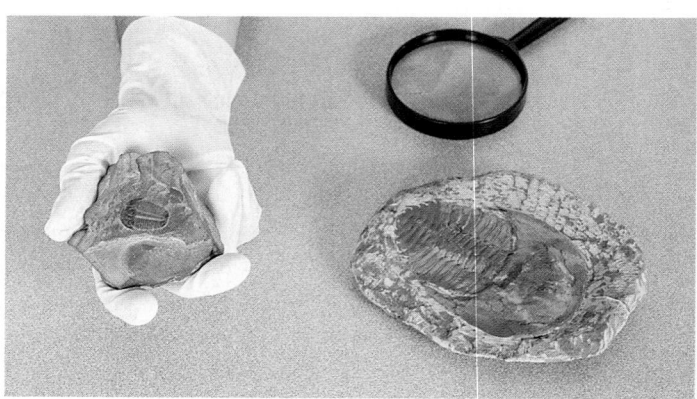

Figure 1
Many sedimentary rocks in the United States are rich in invertebrate fossils such as these trilobites.

Section ✓ *Assessment* Planner

PORTFOLIO
Science Journal, p. 400
PERFORMANCE ASSESSMENT
Skill Builder Activities, p. 405
See page 426 for more options.

CONTENT ASSESSMENT
Section, p. 405
Challenge, p. 405
Chapter, pp. 426–427

Major Subdivisions of Geologic Time The oldest rocks on Earth contain no fossils. Then, for many millions of years after the first appearance of fossils, the fossil record remained sparse. Later in Earth's history came an explosion in the abundance and diversity of fossil organisms. These organisms created a rich fossil record. As shown in **Figure 2,** four major subdivisions of geologic time are used—eons, eras, periods, and epochs. The longest subdivisions—**eons**—are based upon the abundance of fossils.

> **Reading Check** *What are the major subdivisions of geologic time?*

Next to eons, the longest subdivisions are the **eras,** which are marked by major, striking, and worldwide changes in the types of fossils present. For example, at the end of the Mesozoic Era, many kinds of invertebrates, birds, mammals, and reptiles became extinct.

Eras are subdivided into periods. **Periods** are units of geologic time characterized by the types of life existing worldwide at the time. Periods can be divided into smaller units of time called **epochs.** Epochs also are characterized by differences in life-forms, but some of these differences can vary regionally such as from continent to continent. Epochs of the Cenozoic Era have been given specific names. Epochs of other periods usually are referred to simply as early, middle, or late. Epochs are further subdivided into units of shorter duration.

Dividing Geologic Time There is a limit to how finely geologic time can be subdivided. It depends upon the kind of rock record that is being studied. Sometimes it is possible to distinguish layers of rock that formed during a single year or season. In other cases, thick stacks of rock that have no fossils provide little information that could help in subdividing geologic time.

Figure 2
Scientists have divided the geologic time scale into subunits based upon the appearance and disappearance of types of organisms.

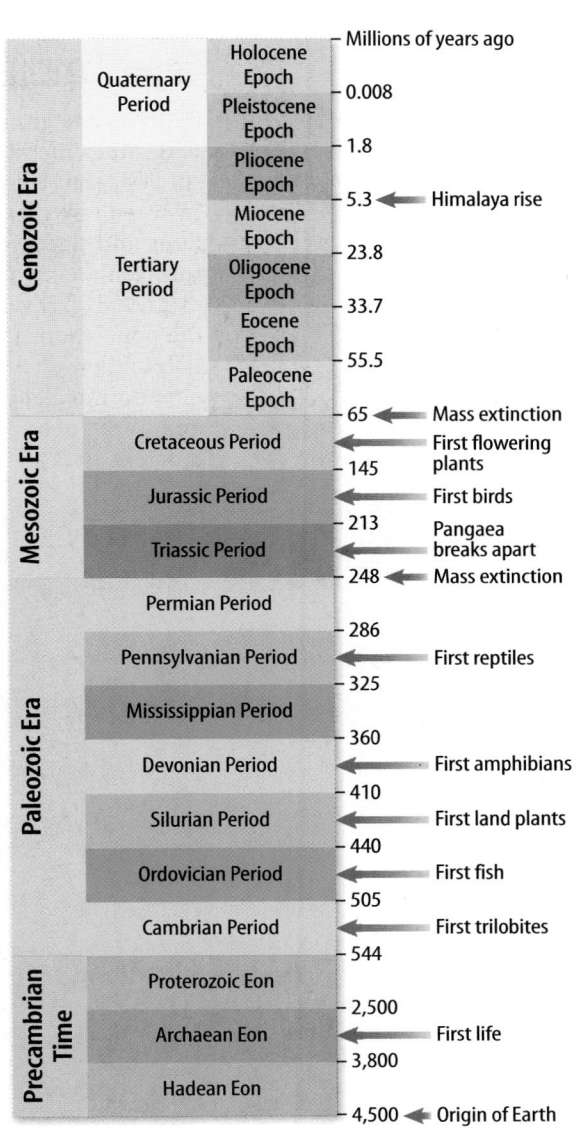

Section 1 Life and Geologic Time **399**

2 Teach

Geologic Time

Visual Learning

Figure 2 What major event in Earth's history happened in the era in which we now live? What is the name of that era?
Himalaya rise; Cenozoic Era

> **Reading Check**

Answer eons, eras, periods, epochs

Use an Analogy

Tell students that just as there are different periods in their lives, there are different periods in Earth's history. For example, eras in geologic time are marked by major worldwide changes in the kinds or abundance of organisms. Students might mark eras of their lives according to major events such as the birth of a sibling or changing schools. Have students discuss how they would divide their own lives into eras, periods, and epochs.

IDENTIFYING Misconceptions

Students may think that time is measured only with a watch in minutes and seconds. Refer to page 396F for teaching strategies that address this misconception.

Resource Manager

Chapter Resources Booklet
Transparency Activity, p. 42
Note-taking Worksheets, pp. 31–33
Directed Reading for Content Mastery, pp. 17, 18

Curriculum Connection

Geography Periods on the geologic time scale are often named for regions where the rocks of that age were first studied. Have students use inference to answer these questions. **Where were rocks of the Pennsylvanian Period first studied?** Pennsylvania **Which period represents rocks first studied in the Jura Mountains between France and Switzerland?** Jurassic Period

Organic Evolution

Extension

Have students research the work of early geologists who helped construct the geologic time scale. Scientists could include: Nicholas Steno (1638–1687), James Hutton (1726–1797), William "Strata" Smith (1769–1838), and Charles Lyell (1797–1875).

IDENTIFYING Misconceptions

Students may think that scientists have constructed a complete record of Earth's past from fossils contained in rocks. Explain that very little is known about a large part of Earth's history—the first 4 billion years—because much of the fossil record has been destroyed or never existed. Because of erosion or nondeposition, gaps also exist in the most recent part of the fossil record as well.

Use Science Words

Word Usage Reinforce the differences between the terms *hypothesis* and *theory*. Explain that a theory is more than a hypothesis; it is an accepted (by some) explanation based on a large number of tests. Have students use each word in a sentence. Possible answer: After a hypothesis is successfully tested over many years, it may become a theory.

Organic Evolution

The fossil record shows that species have changed over geologic time. This change through time is known as **organic evolution.** According to most theories about organic evolution, environmental changes can affect an organism's survival. Those organisms that are not adapted to changes are less likely to survive or reproduce. Over time, the elimination of individuals that are not adapted can cause changes to species of organisms.

Life Science INTEGRATION

Species Many ways of defining the term **species** (SPEE sheez) have been proposed. Life scientists often define a **species** as a group of organisms that normally reproduces only with other members of their group. For example, dogs are a species because dogs mate and reproduce only with other dogs. In some rare cases, members of two different species, such as lions and tigers, can mate and produce offspring. These offspring, however, are usually sterile and cannot produce offspring of their own. Even though two organisms look nearly alike, if the populations they each come from do not interbreed naturally and produce offspring that can reproduce, the two individuals do not belong to the same species. **Figure 3** shows an example of two species that look similar to each other but live in different areas and do not mate naturally with each other.

Figure 3
Just because two organisms look alike does not mean that they belong to the same species.

A The coast horned lizard lives along the coast of central and southern California.

B The desert horned lizard lives in arid regions of the southwestern United States.

Science Journal

Theories of Organic Evolution Have students compare and contrast *gradualism* and *punctuated equilibrium* in their Science Journals. Both are theories of organic evolution; gradualism refers to a gradual, slow change in species; punctuated equilibrium describes sudden bursts of evolution separated by times of little change. L2 LS **Linguistic** P

Inclusion Strategies

Gifted Ask students to invent their own species. Have them draw it, describe its habitat and diet, and give the species a history. They should describe the changes that may have occurred within the species over time, possibly making a timeline that shows the major physical changes and ecological events that coincided with them. L3 LS **Logical-Mathematical**

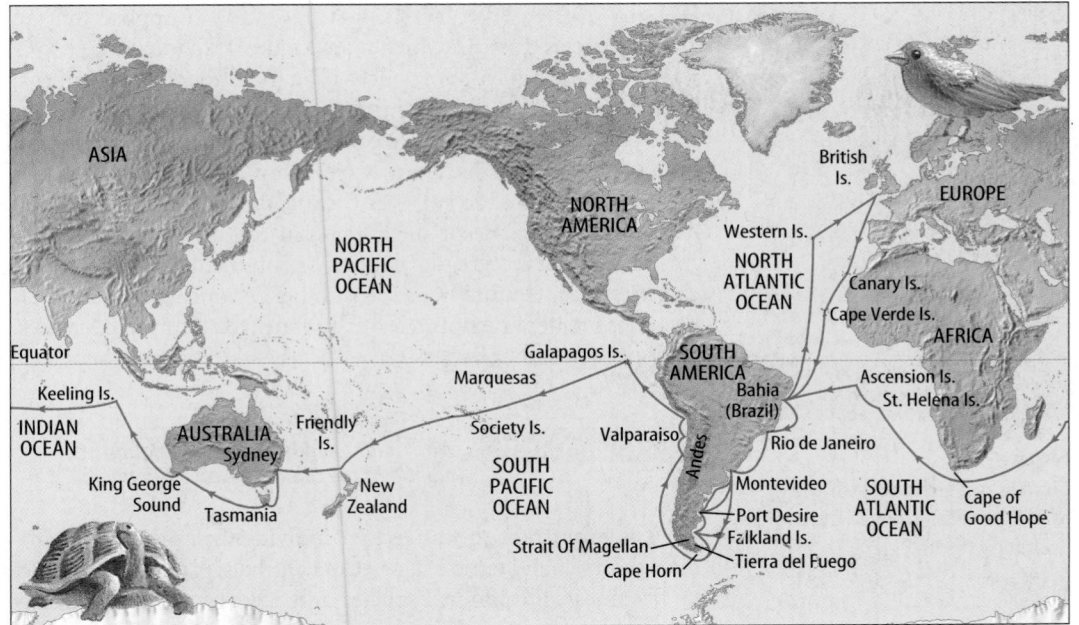

Make a Model

Have pairs of students make a model clay impression "fossil" of a common item, using plaster of paris. Then have sets of partners exchange their "fossils." Have the students imagine they are paleontologists as they identify the object that formed the fossil. L1 COOP LEARN

LS Kinesthetic

Discussion

According to Darwin's theory of natural selection, which type of animal species is more likely to survive in a polar climate: a cold-blooded animal with skin covered by scales or a warm-blooded animal with thick fur. Explain. A warm-blooded animal with thick fur. The thick fur serves to insulate, and warm-bloodedness means the internal temperature is higher than a cold-blooded animal's, so the warm-blooded animal is better suited to withstand cold temperatures.

Extension

Have students investigate Lamarck's ideas about acquired characteristics and describe how he explained change within a species. Then have students list the inadequacies of Lamarck's idea. Lamarck's hypothesis was that species evolve by keeping traits that their parents develop during their lives or losing traits that were not used. It's incorrect to think a trait acquired by a parent during its lifetime would be passed on. There is no identified mechanism by which an acquired trait can be passed on. There is also no evidence to back up Lamarck's assumption. For example, if a woman lifts weights, her children won't necessarily be stronger than children of women who do not lift weights.

Natural Selection Charles Darwin was a naturalist who sailed around the world from 1831 to 1836 to study biology and geology. **Figure 4** shows a map of his journey. With some of the information about the plants and animals he observed on this trip in mind, he later published a book about the theory of evolution by natural selection.

In his book, he proposed that **natural selection** is a process by which organisms with characteristics that are suited to a certain environment have a better chance of surviving and reproducing than organisms that do not have these characteristics. Darwin knew that many organisms are capable of producing more offspring than can survive. This means that organisms compete with each other for resources necessary for life, such as food and living space. He also knew that individual organisms within the same species could be different, or show variations, and that these differences could help or hurt the individual organism's chance of surviving.

Some organisms that were well suited to their environment lived longer and had a better chance of producing offspring. Organisms that were poorly adapted to their environment produced few or no offspring. Because many characteristics are inherited, the characteristics of organisms that are better adapted to the environment get passed on to offspring more often. According to Darwin, this can cause a species to change over time.

Figure 4
Charles Darwin sailed around the world between 1831 and 1836 aboard the HMS _Beagle_ as a naturalist. On his journey he saw an abundance of evidence for natural selection, especially on the Galápagos Islands off the western coast of South America.

Resource Manager

Chapter Resources Booklet
Enrichment, p. 28
Transparency Activity, pp. 45–46

Earth Science Critical Thinking/Problem Solving, p. 1

Teacher FYI

Charles Darwin was the grandson of Erasmus Darwin. Erasmus was a noted physician and naturalist in his own right and had proposed his own theory of evolution in the 1790s.

Organic Evolution, continued

Discussion

In a desert area where there is little moisture, what types of characteristics would be favored in animals? characteristics that would allow animals to live with little water, conserve water, or eat food, such as cacti, that contains water

Activity

Show students photographs of different organisms. Describe the type of environment in which each organism lives. Have students list the adaptations that are important for each organism's survival in its environment. L2 IS **Visual-Spatial**

✔ Reading Check

Answer Because short-necked and long-necked animals would have an equal opportunity for food, the number of short-necked members of the species might increase. Long-necked animals might also survive but would not necessarily continue in the majority.

Quick Demo

Place several "fossils", that vary slightly in appearance, into three different rock layers (potting soil, sand, coarse gravel) that you have set up in a clear plastic shoe box. **How is this model similar to evolution of trilobites?** Possible answer: These fossil organisms changed over time just like fossil trilobites changed.

Figure 5
Giraffes can eat leaves off the branches of tall trees because of their long necks.

Figure 6
Cat breeders have succeeded in producing a great variety of cats by using the principle of artificial selection.

Natural Selection Within a Species Suppose that an animal species exists in which a few of the individuals have long necks, but most have short necks. The main food for the animal is the leafy foliage on trees in the area. What happens if the climate changes and the area becomes dry? The lower branches of the trees might not have any leaves. Now which of the animals will be better suited to survive? Clearly, the long-necked animals have a better chance of surviving and reproducing. Their offspring will have a greater chance of inheriting the important characteristic. Gradually, as the number of long-necked animals becomes greater, the number of short-necked animals decreases. The species might change so that nearly all of its members have long necks as the giraffe in **Figure 5** does.

✔ Reading Check
What might happen to the population of animals if the climate became wet again?

It is important to notice that individual, short-necked animals didn't change into long-necked animals. A new characteristic becomes common in a species only if some members already possess that characteristic, and if the trait increases the animal's chance of survival. If no animal in the species possessed a long neck in the first place, a long-necked species could not have evolved by means of natural selection.

Artificial Selection Humans have long used the principle of selection when breeding domestic animals. By carefully choosing individuals with desired characteristics, animal breeders have created many breeds of cats, dogs, cattle, and chickens. **Figure 6** shows the great variety of cats produced by artificial selection.

The Evolution of New Species Natural selection explains how characteristics change and how new species arise. For example, if the short-necked animals migrated to a different location, they might have survived. They could have continued to reproduce in the new location, eventually developing enough different characteristics from the long-necked animals that they might not be able to breed with each other. At this point, at least one new species would have evolved.

402 CHAPTER 14 Geologic Time

Cultural Diversity

Domestication Domestication is the process of selectively breeding wild animals and plants into forms that better serve the needs of people. The first attempts at domestication were made as early as 9000 B.C. by tribes that engaged in hunting and in gathering wild edible plants. Dogs, goats, and possibly sheep were the first animals to be domesticated. Plants with tubers probably were domesticated before seed plants—cereals, legumes, and other vegetables. Some plants were domesticated for their fibrous stalks, which were used for making fishing nets. Suggest interested students research some of the earliest domesticated plants and animals, such as hemp, dogs, sheep, cattle, horses, and hens. Have them explain the different characteristics people were looking for as they bred these organisms.

Trilobites

Remember the trilobites? The term *trilobite* comes from the structure of the animal's hard outer skeleton or exoskeleton. The exoskeleton of a trilobite consists of three lobes that run the length of the body. As shown in **Figure 7,** the trilobite's body also has a head (cephalon), a segmented middle section (thorax), and a tail (pygidium).

Changing Characteristics of Trilobites
Trilobites inhabited Earth's oceans for more than 200 million years. Throughout the Paleozoic Era, some species of trilobites became extinct and other new species evolved. Species of trilobites that lived during one period of the Paleozoic Era showed different characteristics than species from other periods of this era. As **Figure 8** shows, paleontologists can use these different characteristics to demonstrate changes in trilobites through geologic time. These changes can tell you about how different trilobites from different periods lived and responded to changes in their environments.

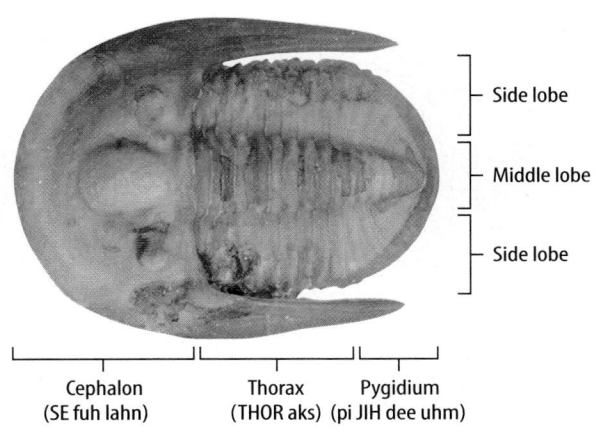

Cephalon (SE fuh lahn)   Thorax (THOR aks)   Pygidium (pi JIH dee uhm)

Figure 7
The trilobite's body was divided into three lobes that run the length of the body—two side lobes and one middle lobe.

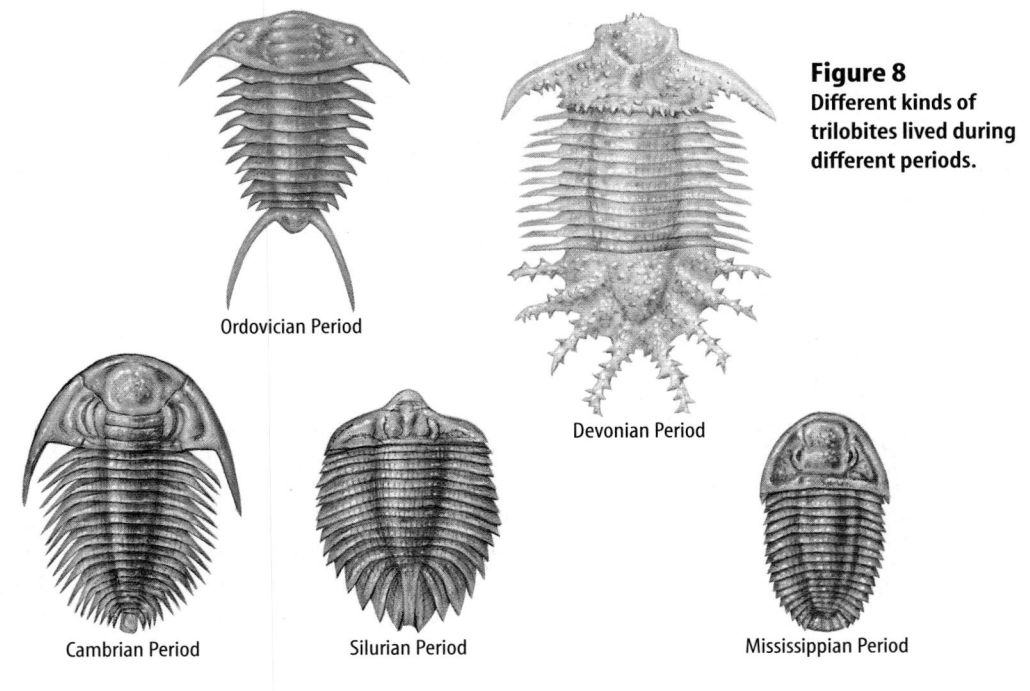

Ordovician Period

Cambrian Period   Silurian Period

Devonian Period

Mississippian Period

Figure 8
Different kinds of trilobites lived during different periods.

Teacher FYI
The exoskeletons of trilobites did not grow, so the animals had to molt as they increased in size. These shed skeletal remains were left behind to form many of the fossils we know today.

Discussion
Imagine that you find trilobites in a rock formation in a desert area. What does this tell you about how the environment of that area has changed? Because trilobites lived in oceans, it tells you that the area was once under the sea.

Visual Learning
Figure 8 Examine the diagram and describe how the appearance of trilobites changed through time. The trilobites' characteristics changed to suit its changing environment. Students may infer that during the Devonian Period, the environment became more hostile and the trilobite needed elaborate spines for defense.

Resource Manager

Chapter Resources Booklet
  Lab Activity, pp. 9–10

Life Science Critical Thinking/Problem Solving, p. 1

Earth Science Critical Thinking/Problem Solving, p. 18

✔ Active Reading

Flow Chart A flow chart helps students logically sequence events. Have students write the Geologic Eras in a series of large rectangles. As students read the chapter, have them write major events that occured in each era in smaller rectangles under the large rectangles.

Trilobites, continued

Discussion

Why were trilobites more likely to be preserved as fossils than many other animals that lived in Precambrian time? Trilobites had hard parts that could be preserved as body fossils. Trilobites also molted their exoskeletons. Therefore, one animal could produce many fossils.

Text Question Answer

Eyes on stalks would be useful to trilobites that burrowed into the sand.

Extension

Have students research, using the Internet, library books, or local experts in geology and paleontology, whether trilobite fossils have been found in your state. If so, have students explain where they were found and what this suggests about how the area has changed over time. If no trilobites have been found, have students hypothesize why this might be the case.

Text Question Answer

Possible answers: a sudden climate change such as that caused by a major volcanic eruption that placed a lot of ash and soot into the air, decreasing the solar energy reaching Earth; results of continental and oceanic movements caused by plate tectonics; asteroid impact

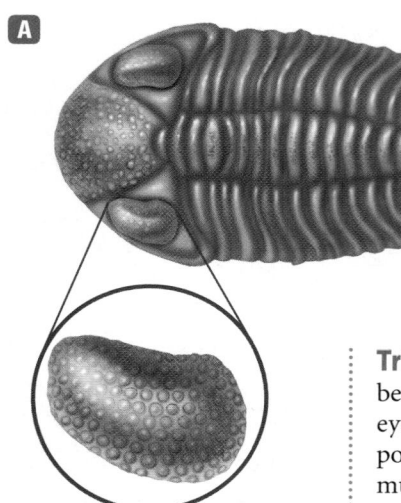

Figure 9
Trilobites had many different types of eyes. **A** Some had eyes that contained hundreds of small circular lenses, somewhat like an insect. **B** This blind trilobite had no eyes.

Figure 10
Olenellus is one of the most primitive trilobite species.

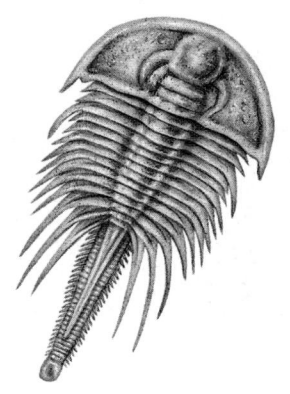

Trilobite Eyes Trilobites, shown in **Figure 9A,** might have been the first organisms that could view the world with complex eyes. Trilobite eyes show the result of natural selection. The position of the eyes on an organism gives clues about where it must have lived. Eyes that are located toward the front of the head indicate an organism that was adapted for active swimming. If the eyes are located toward the back of the head, the organism could have been a bottom dweller. In most species of trilobites, the eyes were located midway on the head—a compromise for an organism that was adapted for crawling on the seafloor and swimming in the water.

Over time, the eyes in trilobites changed. In many trilobite species, the eyes became progressively smaller until they completely disappeared. Blind trilobites, such as the one shown in **Figure 9B,** might have burrowed into sediments on the seafloor or lived deeper than light could penetrate. In other species, however, the eyes became more complex. One kind of trilobite, *Aeglina,* developed large compound eyes that had numerous individual lenses. Some trilobites developed stalks that held the eyes upward. Where would this be useful?

Trilobite Bodies The trilobite body and tail also underwent significant changes in form through time, as you can see in **Figure 8.** A special case is *Olenellus,* shown in **Figure 10.** This trilobite, which lived during the Early Cambrian Period, had an extremely segmented body—perhaps more so than any other known species of trilobite. It is thought that *Olenellus,* and other species that have so many body segments, are primitive trilobites.

Fossils Show Changes Trilobite exoskeletons changed as trilobites adapted to changing environments. Species that could not adapt became extinct. What processes on Earth caused environments to change so drastically that species adapted or became extinct?

Curriculum Connection

Math Have students construct a circle graph showing the 4.6 billion years of Earth's history divided into the four eras of geologic time. The Precambrian Era represents about 88.3%; the Paleozoic Era about 6.4%; the Mesozoic Era about 3.9%; and the Cenozoic Era about 1.4% of Earth's history. L2 **Logical-Mathematical**

Resource Manager

Chapter Resources Booklet
Reinforcement, p. 25
Earth Science Critical Thinking/Problem Solving, p. 14

Plate Tectonics and Earth History

Plate tectonics is one possible answer to the riddle of trilobite extinction. Earth's moving plates caused continents to collide and separate many times. Continental collisions formed mountains and closed seas. Continental separations created wider, deeper seas between continents. By the end of the Paleozoic Era, sea levels had dropped and the continents had come together to form one giant landmass, the supercontinent **Pangaea** (pan JEE uh). Because trilobites lived in the oceans, their environment was changed or destroyed. **Figure 11** shows the arrangement of continents at the end of the Paleozoic Era. What effect might these changes have had on the trilobite populations?

Not all scientists accept the above explanation for the extinctions at the end of the Paleozoic Era, and other possibilities—such as climate change—have been proposed. As in all scientific debates, you must consider the evidence carefully and come to conclusions based on the evidence.

Figure 11
The amount of shallow water environment was reduced when Pangaea formed. *How do you think this change affected organisms that lived along the coasts of continents?*

Section Assessment

1. Discuss how fossils relate to the geologic time scale.
2. How might plate tectonics affect species of organisms?
3. Relate trilobite eye type to lifestyle type.
4. Why can paleontologists use some trilobite fossils as index fossils for the Cambrian Period and other trilobite fossils as index fossils for other geologic time periods?
5. **Think Critically** Aside from moving continents, what other factors could cause an organism's environment to change? What effects could changing environments have on species?

Skill Builder Activities

6. **Recognizing Cause and Effect** Answer the questions below. **For more help, refer to the** Science Skill Handbook.
   a. How does natural selection cause evolutionary change to take place?
   b. How could the evolution of a characteristic within one species affect the evolution of a characteristic within another species? Give an example.
7. **Communicating** Write a short poem in your Science Journal that describes a day in the life of a trilobite. **For more help, refer to the** Science Skill Handbook.

Plate Tectonics and Earth History

Caption Answer
Figure 11 The habitats of such organisms would have changed greatly, and these organisms would have become extinct if they could not adapt.

3 Assess

Reteach
Reinforce how life forms change through geologic time by showing students illustrations of trilobites from the Cambrian Period and then from later periods in the Paleozoic Era. L1
Visual-Spatial

Challenge
List the three most recent eras of geologic time on the board. Challenge students to identify an organism that is thought to have become extinct in each era and give a possible reason for its extinction. L2 **Linguistic**

Assessment

Process Assess students' abilities to observe and infer by having them look at photographs of anteaters and infer why these animals have long snouts and tongues. Use **Performance Assessment in the Science Classroom,** p. 89.

Answers to Section Assessment

1. Appearance, disappearance, or change in abundance of fossil organism can be used to subdivide geologic time.
2. Changes in Earth's surface that altered habitats could have caused organisms with traits most suited to the new habitat to evolve.
3. no eyes: deep water, burrower; complex eyes: see in many directions;

stalked eyes: burrower; eyes toward front of head: swimmer; eyes toward back of head: bottom-dweller
4. Trilobites lived over a wide area and during different periods of geologic time.
5. Possible answer: Changes in climate; these changes could have caused organisms to evolve different

structures and eventually result in a new species.
6. a. Organisms best suited to survive pass traits to young. Over time, the species evolves.
   b. Possible answer: If a species evolves so that it eats one type of food instead of another, the species that it preys on would be

affected. The prey species would evolve so that traits that help it avoid capture would be emphasized.
7. Poems should include information on the animal's structure or the way it lived.

SECTION

② Early Earth History

① Motivate

Bellringer Transparency

Display the Section Focus Transparency for Section 2. Use the accompanying Transparency Activity Master. `L2`

`ELL`

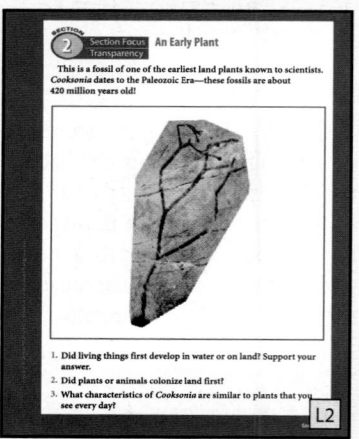

Tie to Prior Knowledge

Ask students to think of a place they have been or have seen in a photo that is barren rock with no plant or animal life. You may want to show some photographs. Explain that Earth may have looked like this after it formed more than 4 billion years ago.

As You Read

What You'll Learn

- **Identify** characteristic Precambrian and Paleozoic life-forms.
- **Draw conclusions** about how species adapted to changing environments in Precambrian time and the Paleozoic Era.
- **Describe** changes in Earth and its life-forms at the end of the Paleozoic Era.

Vocabulary

Precambrian time   Paleozoic Era
cyanobacteria

Why It's Important

The Precambrian includes most of Earth's history.

Figure 12
During the early Precambrian, Earth was a lifeless planet with many volcanoes.

Precambrian Time

Can you imagine a barren Earth with only rock and sea, as shown in **Figure 12?** This seems strange, but it's probably an accurate picture of Earth's first billion years. Over the next 3 billion years, simple life-forms began to colonize the oceans.

Look again at the geologic time scale shown in **Figure 2. Precambrian** (pree KAM bree un) **time** is the longest part of Earth's history and includes the Hadean, Archean, and Proterozoic Eons. Precambrian time lasted from about 4.5 billion years ago to about 544 million years ago. The oldest rocks that have been found on Earth are about 4 billion years old. However, rocks older than about 3.5 billion years are rare. This probably is due to remelting and erosion. Although the Precambrian was the longest interval of geologic time, relatively little is known about the organisms that lived during this time.

Why is the fossil record from Precambrian time so sparse? One reason is that many Precambrian rocks have been so deeply buried that they have been changed by heat and pressure. Many fossils can't withstand these conditions. In addition, most Precambrian organisms didn't have hard parts that otherwise would have increased their chances to be preserved as fossils.

Lava flow   Ash   Lava flow

Ash deposits

406   Ocean

Section ✓Assessment Planner

PORTFOLIO
Chemistry Integration, p. 407
PERFORMANCE ASSESSMENT
MiniLAB, p. 408
Skill Builder Activities, p. 412
See page 426 for more options.

CONTENT ASSESSMENT
Section, p. 412
Challenge, p. 412
Chapter, pp. 426–427

Resource Manager

Chapter Resources Booklet
Transparency Activity, p. 43
Directed Reading for Content Mastery, p. 18
Reading and Writing Skill Activities, p. 27

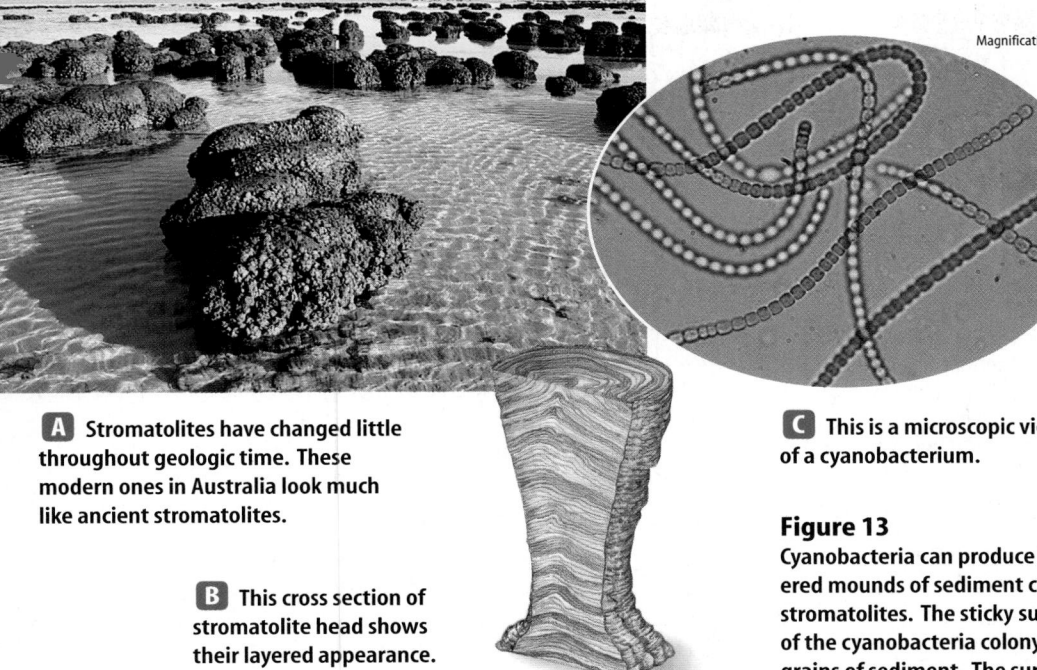

Magnification: 450×

A Stromatolites have changed little throughout geologic time. These modern ones in Australia look much like ancient stromatolites.

B This cross section of stromatolite head shows their layered appearance.

C This is a microscopic view of a cyanobacterium.

Figure 13
Cyanobacteria can produce layered mounds of sediment called stromatolites. The sticky surface of the cyanobacteria colony traps grains of sediment. The surface of the sediment then becomes colonized with cyanobacteria again, and the cycle repeats, producing the layers inside the stromatolite.

Early Life Many studies of the early history of life involve ancient stromatolites (stroh MAT oh lytes). **Figure 13** shows stromatolites, which are layered mats formed by cyanobacteria colonies. **Cyanobacteria** are blue-green algae thought to be one of the earliest forms of life on Earth. Cyanobacteria first appeared about 3.5 billion years ago. They contained chlorophyll and photosynthesized. This is important because during photosynthesis, they produced oxygen, which helped change Earth's atmosphere. For the few billion years following the appearance of cyanobacteria, oxygen became a major atmospheric gas. Also of importance was that the ozone layer in the atmosphere began to develop, shielding Earth from ultraviolet rays. It is hypothesized that these changes allowed species of single-celled organisms to evolve into more complex organisms.

Reading Check *What atmospheric gas is produced by photosynthesis?*

Animals without backbones, called invertebrates (in VURT uh brayts), appeared toward the end of Precambrian time. A few imprints of jellyfish and marine worms have been found in late Precambrian rocks, but because these early invertebrates were soft bodied, they weren't often preserved as fossils. Because of this, many Precambrian fossils are trace fossils.

Chemistry
INTEGRATION

Cyanobacteria are thought to have been one of the mechanisms by which Earth's early atmosphere became richer in oxygen. Research the composition of Earth's early atmosphere and where these gases probably came from. Record your findings in your Science Journal.

SECTION 2 Early Earth History **407**

2 Teach

Hadean and Precambrian Time

Discussion
How would life on Earth be different today if cyanobacteria had not produced oxygen for the planet's atmosphere? Animals as we know them might not have evolved, since they depend on oxygen to live. In addition, without the protection of the ozone layer it is likely that organisms as we know them would not have evolved.

Reading Check

Answer oxygen

Chemistry
INTEGRATION

Earth's early atmosphere was probably composed of water vapor, carbon dioxide, and nitrogen. These gases might have been in the original material that formed Earth and been given off into the atmosphere during volcanic eruptions. They might also have been brought to Earth by comets impacting. **P**

LAB DEMONSTRATION

Purpose to show the importance of hard parts to fossil preservation

Materials flat pan, gelatin dessert, small seashells, board that fits inside the pan, clay

Procedure Place a layer of clay in the bottom of a flat pan. Sprinkle pieces of the gelatin dessert and the shells on top of the clay. Cover with a second clay layer. Apply pressure to the top layer of clay with the board. Peel away the top clay layer to expose the shell layer.

Expected Outcome Students observe that hard parts (shells) retain their shape and leave an imprint, but the soft gelatin is smashed and leaves no recognizable trace

Assessment

Compare what you observed in this activity with the formation of fossils. Many fossils form from hard parts of living organisms. Most soft parts do not become fossilized.

Hadean and Precambrian Time, continued

✔ Reading Check

Answer Ediacaran organisms had shapes similar to modern jellyfish, worms, and soft corals.

The Paleozoic Era

Purpose Students use fossils to determine the age of rock layers. L2 IS **Visual-Spatial**

Teaching Strategy Suggest that students make a chart that lists the periods during which each rock layer could have formed.

Analysis
1. Layer 2; it contains fossils A and B. These fossil organisms lived together during the Ordovician Period.
2. There is only one fossil in each layer, and that fossil existed during two different periods.

✔ Assessment

Content Which rock layer is the oldest? Which is the youngest? Explain. Layer 1 is oldest; layer 3 is youngest; unless they have been disturbed, the oldest layer is always at the bottom and the youngest at the top. Use **Performance Assessment in the Science Classroom**, p. 89.

Mini LAB

Dating Rock Layers with Fossils

Procedure
1. Draw three rock layers.
2. Number the layers 1 to 3, bottom to top.
3. Layer 1 contains fossil A. Layer 2 contains fossils A and B. Layer 3 contains fossil C.
4. Fossil A lived from the Cambrian through the Ordovician. Fossil B lived from the Ordovician through the Silurian. Fossil C lived in the Silurian and Devonian.

Analysis
1. Which layers were you able to date to a specific period?
2. Why isn't it possible to determine during which specific period the other layers formed?

Figure 14
This giant predatory fish lived in North America during the Devonian Period. It grew to about 6 m in length.

Unusual Life-Forms Living late in Precambrian time was a group of animals with shapes similar to modern jellyfish, worms, and soft corals. Fossils of these organisms were first found in the Ediacara Hills in southern Australia. This group of organisms has become known as the Ediacaran (eed ee uh KAR un) fauna. **Figure 15** shows some of these organisms.

✔ Reading Check   *What modern organisms do some Ediacaran organisms resemble?*

Ediacaran animals were bottom dwellers and might have had tough outer coverings like air mattresses. Trilobites and other invertebrates might have outcompeted the Ediacarans and caused them to become extinct, but nobody knows for sure why these creatures disappeared.

The Paleozoic Era

As you have learned, fossils are unlikely to form if organisms have only soft parts. An abundance of organisms with hard parts, such as shells, marks the beginning of the Paleozoic (pay lee uh ZOH ihk) Era. The **Paleozoic Era,** or era of ancient life, began about 544 million years ago and ended about 248 million years ago. Traces of life are much easier to find in Paleozoic rocks than in Precambrian rocks.

Paleozoic Life Warm, shallow seas covered large parts of the continents during much of the Paleozoic Era, so many of the life-forms scientists know about were marine, meaning they lived in the ocean. Trilobites were common, especially early in the Paleozoic. Other organisms developed shells that were easily preserved as fossils. Therefore, the fossil record of this era contains abundant shells. However, invertebrates were not the only animals to live in the shallow, Paleozoic seas.

Vertebrates, or animals with backbones, also evolved during this era. The first vertebrates were fishlike creatures without jaws. Armoured fish with jaws such as the one shown in **Figure 14** lived during the Devonian Period. Some of these fish were so huge that they could eat large sharks with their powerful jaws. By the Devonian Period, forests had appeared, and vertebrates began to adapt to land environments, as well.

Inclusion Strategies

Learning Disabled and Visually Impaired Provide plastic, plaster, or clay models of important fossils of animals and plants that lived during the Paleozoic Period. Handling the fossils will help students picture these organisms' shapes, sizes, and external features.

Teacher FYI

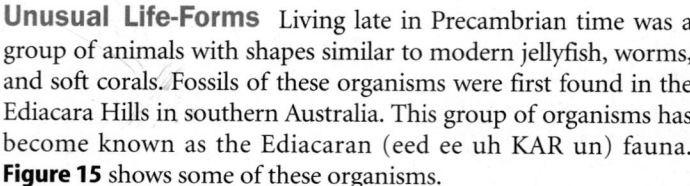

Fossils of Ediacaran organisms are so different from later organisms that the time when these organisms lived can be thought of as a distinct period, the Vendian Period. This period is the latest part of Precambrian time and occurred before the Cambrian Period of the Paleozoic Era.

Figure 15

A variety of 600-million-year-old fossils—known as Ediacaran (eed ee uh KAR un) fauna—have been found on every continent except Antarctica. These unusual organisms were originally thought to be descendants of early animals such as jellyfish, worms, and coral. Today, paleontologists debate whether these organisms were part of the animal kingdom or belonged to an entirely new kingdom whose members became extinct about 545 million years ago.

DICKENSONIA (dihk un suh NEE uh) Impressions of *Dickensonia,* a bottom-dwelling wormlike creature, have been discovered. Some are nearly one meter long.

RANGEA (rayn JEE uh) As it lay rooted in sea-bottom sediments, *Rangea* may have snagged tiny bits of food by filtering water through its body.

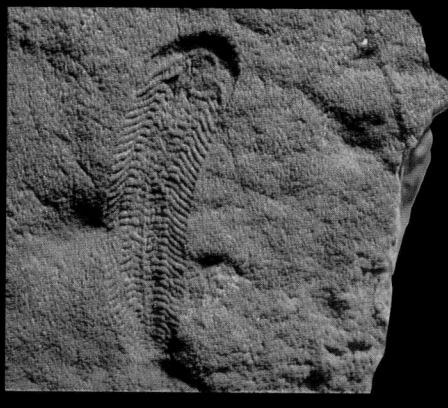

SPRIGGINA (sprih GIHN uh) Some scientists hypothesize that the four-centimeter-long *Spriggina* was a type of crawling, segmented organism. Others suggest that it sat upright while attached to the sea floor.

CYCLOMEDUSA (si kloh muh DEW suh) Although it looks a lot like a jellyfish, *Cyclomedusa* may have had more in common with modern sea anemones. Some paleontologists, however, hypothesize that it is unrelated to any living organism.

SECTION 2 Early Earth History **409**

Visualizing Unusual Life Forms

Have students examine the pictures and read the captions. Then ask the following questions.

If Ediacaran fauna belonged to a kingdom of organisms that became extinct about 545 million years ago, what does this tell you about the evolution of large and complex organisms? Large and complex organisms must have evolved two different times during evolutionary history.

If Ediacaran fauna were soft-bodied and did not have hard skeletons or shells, how might they have been fossilized? Their body shapes were probably preserved by quick burial by sand and/or sediments on the sea floor.

Activity

Have small groups of students research the locations around the world where Ediacaran fossils have been found and mark these locations on a world map. Ask each group to select one location and make an oral presentation about the fossils found there.

Extension

Have students locate a book or magazine article dealing with Ediacaran fauna and make a brief written report on what they learn. One article they might read is "When Life Was Odd," by Karen Wright in *Discover*, March 1997.

Resource Manager

Chapter Resources Booklet
  MiniLAB, p. 3
Science Inquiry Labs, p. 29
Cultural Diversity, p. 31

The Paleozoic Era, continued

Extension

Have students research the Pennsylvanian Period's swamps, where much of the coal used today was formed. Show students samples of peat, lignite, and bituminous and anthracite coal. Have students describe the process that must occur for plant remains to change into coal. Plant material must collect under water or be buried quickly in the absence of air so that the material's carbon content is not lost. Over time, the material increases in hardness, and carbon is concentrated as plant material changes from peat to lignite to bituminous coal and finally to anthracite coal.

✔ Reading Check

Answer lungs and leglike fins

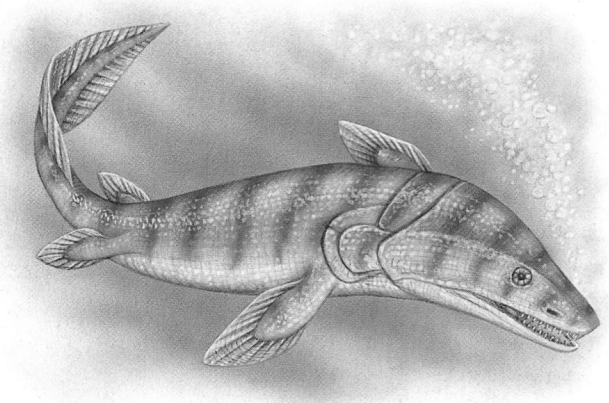

Figure 16
Amphibians probably evolved from fish like *Panderichthys* (pan dur IHK theez), which had leglike fins and lungs.

SCIENCE Online

Research Visit the Glencoe Science Web site at **science.glencoe.com** for more information about Paleozoic life. Communicate to your class what you learn.

Life on Land Based on their structure, paleontologists know that many ancient fish had lungs as well as gills. Lungs enabled these fish to live in water with low oxygen levels—when needed they could swim to the surface and breathe air. Today's lungfish also can get oxygen from the water through gills and from the air through lungs.

One kind of ancient fish had lungs and leglike fins, which were used to swim and crawl around on the bottom. Paleontologists hypothesize that amphibians might have evolved from this kind of fish, shown in **Figure 16.** The characteristics that helped animals survive in oxygen-poor waters also made living on land possible. Today, amphibians live in a variety of habitats in water and on land. They all have at least one thing in common, though. They must lay their eggs in water or moist places.

✔ Reading Check

What are some characteristics of the fish from which amphibians might have evolved?

By the Pennsylvanian Period, some amphibians evolved an egg with a membrane that protected it from drying out. Because of this, these animals, called reptiles, no longer needed to lay eggs in water. Reptiles also have skin with hard scales that prevent loss of body fluids. This adaptation enables them to survive farther from water and in relatively dry climates, as shown in **Figure 17,** where many amphibians cannot live.

Figure 17
Reptiles have scaly skins that allow them to live in dry places.

Visual Learning

Figure 17 Have students list another characteristics of reptiles that allow them to live on land. Students should cite eggs with a membrane that keeps it from drying out. This membrane allows eggs to be laid on land instead of in the water. L2 IS **Linguistic**

SCIENCE Online
Internet Addresses

Explore the Glencoe Science Web site at **science.glencoe.com** to find out more about topics in this section.

Figure 18
The Appalachian Mountains formed in several steps.

A More than 375 million years ago, volcanic island chains formed in the ocean and were pushed against the coast as Africa moved toward North America.

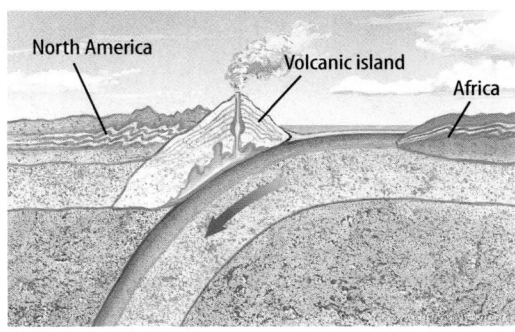

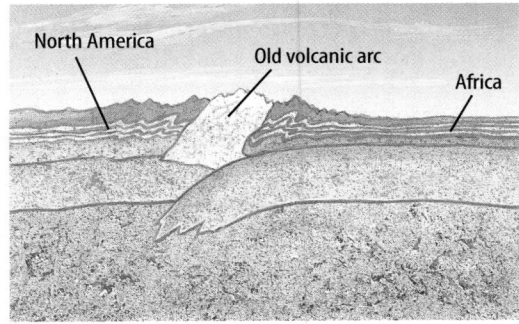

B About 375 million years ago, the African plate collided with the North American plate, forming mountains on both continents.

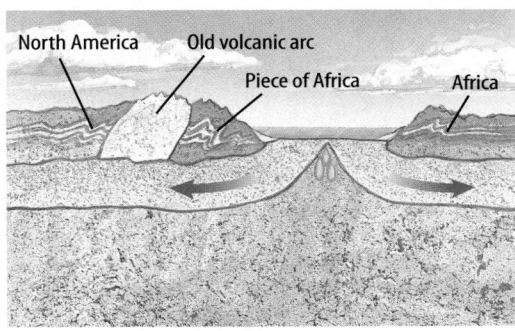

C About 200 million years ago, the Atlantic Ocean opened up, separating the two continents.

Mountain Building Several mountain-building episodes occurred during the Paleozoic Era. The Appalachian Mountains, for example, formed during this time. This happened in several stages, as shown in **Figure 18.** The first mountain-building episode occurred as the ocean separating North America from Europe and Africa closed. Several volcanic island chains that had formed in the ocean collided with the North American Plate, as shown in **Figure 18A.** The collision of the island chains generated high mountains.

The next mountain-building episode was a result of the African Plate colliding with the North American Plate, as shown in **Figure 18B.** When Africa and North America collided, rock layers were folded and faulted. Some rocks originally deposited near the eastern coast of the North American Plate were pushed along faults as much as 65 km westward by the collision. Sediments were uplifted to form an immense mountain belt, part of which still remains today.

Discussion

Show a physical features map of the U.S. to students. Remind students that they just read about the formation of the Appalachians along the east coast of North America. **If these mountains formed along the coast, why aren't they on the coast today?** Possible answers: erosion and deposition have extended land between the mountains and the coast; a drop in sea level has uncovered land that was once sea bottom.

Activity

Take students on a field trip to an exposure of Paleozoic Era rocks near your school. Show them how and where to look for fossils. Have students take photos or make sketches of the fossils. Back in the classroom, have students try to identify the fossils they found using a paleontology book. If no exposure exists, use fossils of Paleozoic age ordered from a science supply house. Display the labeled fossils in class. L2 **Visual-Spatial**

Science Journal

Extinctions Have students write reports on species that became extinct and causes of the extinctions that occurred at the ends of the Ordovician and Permian periods. Possible answers: Ordovician: graptolites, trilobites, brachiopods due to global cooling; Permian: 85% of marine species and 70% of land species due to several factors.

The Paleozoic Era, continued

Discussion

What would be the result of mass extinctions today? Possible answers: Depending on the plant or animal species, there could be widespread starvation or destruction of whole ecosystems. If the event that causes the mass extinction is catastrophic and of worldwide impact, the human population on Earth could be reduced or eliminated.

3 Assess

Reteach

Have small groups of students work together to outline the section, focusing on major topics contained in heads, subheads, captions, and Reading Check answers. L1 LS **Interpersonal**

Challenge

Instruct pairs of students to search discarded magazines for photographs that show the characteristics that make amphibians different from fish and reptiles different from amphibians. Have partners quiz each other on the differences. LS **Visual-Spatial**

✔Assessment

Oral Have students write questions on the material in the section, and then take turns quizzing each other. Use **Performance Assessment in the Science Classroom**, p. 91.

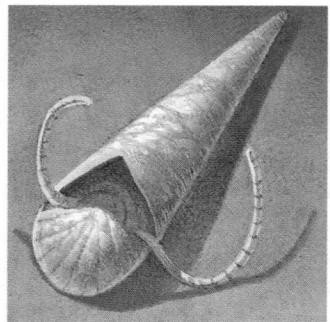

Figure 19
Hyoliths were organisms that became extinct at the end of the Paleozoic Era.

End of an Era At the end of the Paleozoic Era, as many as 85 percent of all marine species and 70 percent of all land species died off. **Figure 19** shows one such animal. The cause of these extinctions might have been changes in climate and a lowering of sea level.

Near the end of the Permian Period, all of the continental plates came together and formed Pangaea, and glaciers formed over most of its southern part. The slow, gradual collision of continental plates caused mountain building. Mountain-building processes caused seas to close and deserts to spread over North America and Europe. Many species, especially marine organisms, couldn't adapt to these changes, so they became extinct.

Other Hypotheses Other explanations also have been proposed for this mass extinction. During the late Paleozoic Era, volcanoes were extremely active. If the volcanic activity was great enough, it could have affected the entire globe. Another recent theory is similar to the one proposed to explain the extinction of dinosaurs. Perhaps a large asteroid or comet collided with Earth some 248 million years ago. This event could have caused widespread extinctions just as many paleontologists suggest happened at the end of the Mesozoic Era, 65 million years ago. Perhaps the extinction at the end of the Paleozoic Era was caused by several or all of these events happening at about the same time.

Section Assessment

1. What geologic events occurred at the end of the Paleozoic Era?

2. How might geologic events at the end of the Paleozoic Era have caused extinctions?

3. What advance allowed reptiles to reproduce away from water? Why was this an advantage?

4. What major change in life-forms occurred at the end of Precambrian time?

5. **Think Critically** How, and through what process, did cyanobacteria contribute to the evolution of complex life on land? Do you think cyanobacteria are as significant to this process today as they were during Precambrian time?

Skill Builder Activities

6. **Making and Using Tables** Use **Figure 2** to answer these questions. **For more help, refer to the** Science Skill Handbook.
   a. When did the Paleozoic Era begin?
   b. How long did the Silurian Period last?
   c. When did vertebrates invade dry land?

7. **Using a Database** Research trilobites in a geology book or computer database. Write a paragraph in your Science Journal describing these organisms and their habitat. Include hand-drawn illustrations and compare them with the illustrations in the computer database on geology. **For more help, refer to the** Technology Skill Handbook.

412   CHAPTER 14 Geologic Time

Answers to Section Assessment

1. mountain building, continental movement, drainage of seas, formation of deserts
2. Mountain building caused seas to close and deserts to spread over wide areas. Many species, especially marine organisms, could not adapt to these changes.
3. The development of a membrane-encased egg allowed reptiles to reproduce away from water. This allowed these animals to live in a greater variety of habitats than their amphibian ancestors.
4. The first invertebrates appeared in Earth's oceans.
5. They produced oxygen, which helped make Earth's atmosphere suitable for most animal life and helped develop Earth's protective ozone shield; no.
6. **a.** 544 m.y.a.
   b. 30 million years
   c. Devonian Period (over 360 m.y.a.)
7. Trilobites are marine invertebrates. Descriptions should provide basic information about the appearance, habitat, and habits of these animals.

Changing Species

In this activity, you will observe how adaptation within a species might cause the evolution of a particular trait, leading to the development of a new species.

What You'll Investigate
How might adaptation within a species cause the evolution of a particular trait?

Materials
Deck of playing cards

Goals
■ **Model** adaptation within a species.

Procedure

1. **Remove** all of the kings, queens, jacks, and aces from a deck of playing cards.
2. Each remaining card represents an individual in a population of animals called "varimals." The number on each card represents the height of the individual. For example, the 5 of diamonds is a varimal that's 5 units tall.
3. **Calculate** the average height of the population of varimals represented by your cards.
4. Suppose varimals eat grass, shrubs, and leaves from trees. A drought causes many of these plants to die. All that's left are a few tall trees. Only varimals at least 6 units tall can reach the leaves on these trees.
5. All the varimals under 6 units leave the area to seek food elsewhere or die from starvation. Discard all of the cards with a number value less than 6. Calculate the new average height of the population of varimals.
6. **Shuffle** the deck of remaining cards.
7. **Draw** two cards at a time. Each pair represents a pair of varimals that will mate.

8. The offspring of each pair reaches a height equal to the average height of his or her parents. Calculate and record the height of each offspring.
9. Repeat by discarding all parents and offspring under 8 units tall. Now calculate the new average height of varimals. Include both the parents and offspring in your calculation.

Conclude and Apply

1. How did the height of the population change?
2. If you hadn't discarded the shortest varimals, would the average height of the population have changed as much? **Explain.**
3. Why didn't every member of the original population reproduce?
4. If there had been no varimals over 6 units tall in step 5, what would have happened to the population?
5. If there had been no variation in height in the population before the droughts occurred, would the species have been able to evolve into a taller species? **Explain.**
6. How does this activity demonstrate that traits evolve in species?

ACTIVITY 413

Purpose Students will formulate a model showing the role of natural selection in creating variations within a species. L2
COOP LEARN IS **Visual-Spatial and Interpersonal**

Process Skills formulating models, using numbers, interpreting data, forming operational definitions, recognizing cause and effect, communicating

Time Required 30 minutes

Teaching Strategy To save time, before class remove the cards that will not be used in this activity. This will eliminate step 1 of the procedure.

Answers to Questions
1. It increased.
2. No; the average would remain at about 6. The shortest varminals would still have been part of the calculation for the average height.
3. Some of the original varminals weren't able to obtain enough food to survive and, therefore, weren't able to reproduce.
4. This particular population would have become extinct.
5. Probably not; if all the individuals would have been the same height, no group of individuals would have had an advantage in reaching high food. In that case, any evolution of the varimal population would likely have occurred from some variation of a trait other than height.
6. By creating the variation of a trait within the varminal population, in this case height, the model demonstrates how the species was able to evolve into one capable of reaching food high above the ground.

Resource Manager

Chapter Resources Booklet
Reinforcement, p. 26
Activity Worksheet, pp. 5–6

✓Assessment

Oral To further assess students' understanding of evolution, ask them whether any individual varimal increased in height because of natural selection. Encourage students to explain their answers. No; individuals do not evolve inheritable adaptations. Use **Performance Assessment in the Science Classroom**, p. 91.

SECTION

3

Middle and Recent Earth History

1 Motivate

Bellringer Transparency

Display the Section Focus Transparency for Section 3. Use the accompanying Transparency Activity Master. L2
ELL

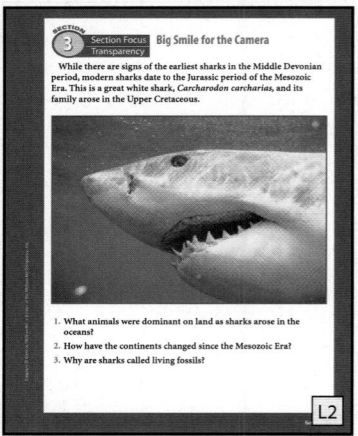

Tie to Prior Knowledge

Students are probably aware of the extinction of the dinosaurs, which is a major event of the Mesozoic Era. Have them list reasons they have heard for the extinction. Then tell students they will find out about this event and others in the most recent two eras of Earth's history in this section.

As You Read

What You'll Learn

- **Compare and contrast** characteristic life-forms in the Mesozoic and Cenozoic Eras.
- **Explain** how changes caused by plate tectonics affected organisms during the Mesozoic Era.
- **Identify** when humans first appeared on Earth.

Vocabulary
Mesozoic Era
Cenozoic Era

Why It's Important
Many important groups of animals, like birds and mammals, appeared during the Mesozoic Era.

Figure 20
The supercontinent Pangaea formed at the end of the Paleozoic Era. At the end of the Triassic Period, it began to break up into the northern supercontinent, Laurasia, and the southern supercontinent, Gondwanaland.

The Mesozoic Era

Dinosaurs have captured people's imaginations since their bones first were unearthed more than 150 years ago. Dinosaurs and other interesting animals lived during the Mesozoic Era, which was between 248 and 65 million years ago. The Mesozoic Era also was marked by rapid movement of Earth's continents.

The Breakup of Pangaea The **Mesozoic** (meh zuh ZOH ihk) **Era,** or era of middle life, was a time of many changes on Earth. At the beginning of the Mesozoic Era, all continents were joined as a single landmass called Pangaea, as shown in **Figure 11.**

Pangaea separated into two large landmasses during the Triassic Period, as shown in **Figure 20.** The northern mass was Laurasia (law RAY zhuh), and Gondwanaland (gahn DWAH nuh land) was the southern landmass. As the Mesozoic Era continued, Laurasia and Gondwanaland broke apart and eventually formed the present-day continents.

Species adapted to the new environments survived the mass extinction at the end of the Paleozoic Era. Recall that a reptile's skin helps it retain bodily fluids. This characteristic, along with their shelled eggs, enabled reptiles to adapt readily to the drier climate of the Mesozoic Era. Reptiles became the most conspicuous animals on land by the Triassic Period.

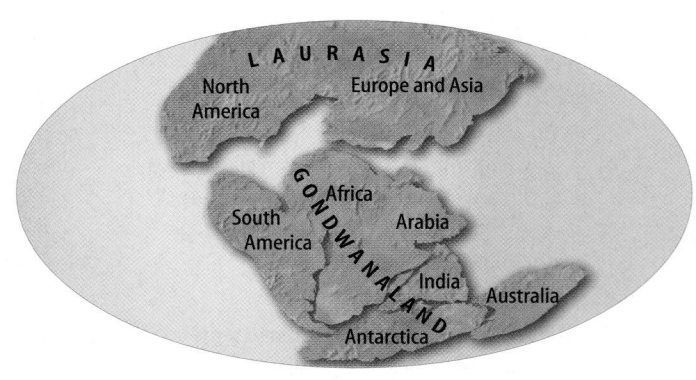

414 CHAPTER 14 Geologic Time

Section ✓*Assessment* Planner

PORTFOLIO
Extension, p. 415
PERFORMANCE ASSESSMENT
Math Skills Activity, p. 417
Try at Home MiniLAB, p. 418
Skill Builder Activities, p. 419
See page 426 for more options.

CONTENT ASSESSMENT
Section, p. 419
Challenge, p. 419
Chapter, pp. 426–427

Dinosaurs What were the dinosaurs like? Dinosaurs ranged in height from less than 1 m to enormous creatures like *Apatosaurus* and *Tyrannosaurus*. The first small dinosaurs appeared during the Triassic Period. Larger species appeared during the Jurassic and Cretaceous Periods. Throughout the Mesozoic Era, new species of dinosaurs evolved and other species became extinct.

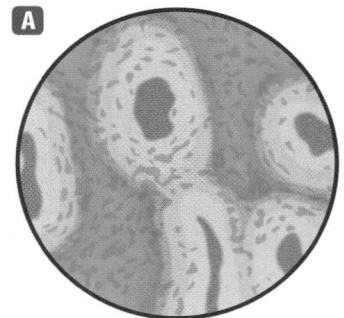 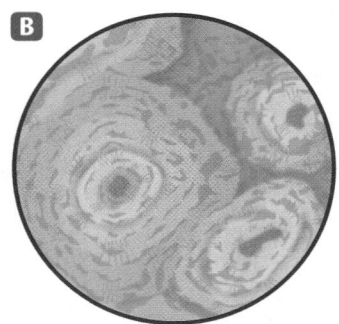

Dinosaurs Were Active Studying fossil footprints sometimes allows paleontologists to calculate how fast animals walked or ran. Some dinosaur tracks that have been found indicate that these animals were much faster runners than you might think. *Gallimimus* was 4 m long and could reach speeds of 65 km/h—as fast as a modern race horse.

Some studies also indicate that dinosaurs might have been warm blooded, not cold blooded like present-day reptiles. The evidence that leads to this conclusion has to do with their bone structure. Slices through some cold blooded animal bones show rings similar to growth rings in trees. The bones of some dinosaurs don't show this ring structure. Instead, they are similar to bones found in modern mammals, as you can see in **Figure 21.**

✔ Reading Check *Why do some paleontologists think that dinosaurs were warm blooded?*

These observations indicate that some dinosaurs might have been warm-blooded, fast-moving animals somewhat like present-day mammals and birds. They might have been quite different from present-day reptiles.

Good Mother Dinosaurs The fossil record also indicates that some dinosaurs nurtured their young and traveled in herds in which the adults surrounded their young.

One such dinosaur is *Maiasaura*. This dinosaur built nests in which it laid its eggs and raised its offspring. Nests have been found in relatively close clusters, indicating that more than one family of dinosaurs built in the same area. Some fossils of hatchlings have been found near adult animals, leading paleontologists to think that some dinosaurs nurtured their young. In fact, *Maiasaura* hatchlings might have stayed in the nest while they grew in length from about 35 cm to more than 1 m.

Figure 21
Some dinosaur bones show structural features that are like mammal bones, leading some paleontologists to think that dinosaurs were warm blooded like mammals. **A** This shows the structure of a dinosaur bone. **B** This shows the structure of a mammal bone.

SCIENCE Online
Research Visit the Glencoe Science Web site at **science.glencoe.com** for more information about dinosaurs. Communicate to your class what you learn.

---

② Teach

The Mesozoic Era

Visual Learning

Figure 20 How might the separation of Pangaea have affected organisms living there? Environments would have changed as the new oceans formed, (for example, the climates may have changed) so species would have had to adapt or become extinct. In addition, populations of the same species may have been separated by the growing oceans, forming subgroups from which different species could arise.

Extension

Have pairs of students read an article on dinosaurs and dinosaur extinction. Suggest these magazine issues: *Natural History*, June 1995; *The Planetary Report*, July/August 1996; "The Day the Dinosaurs Died," *Weatherwise*, July/August 1998. Have students discuss the key concepts of each article and then work together to write a summary of the article's main ideas. Have students compare and contrast in class discussions the theories on extinction presented by the articles. [L3] **LS Linguistic** P

✔ Reading Check

Answer Their bone structure is similar to that of bones found in mammals.

Resource Manager

Chapter Resources Booklet
Transparency Activity, p. 44
Directed Reading for Content Mastery, pp. 19, 20
Earth Science Critical Thinking/Problem Solving, p. 12

SCIENCE Online
Internet Addresses
_____
_____
_____
_____

Explore the Glencoe Science Web site at **science.glencoe.com** to find out more about topics in this section.

The Mesozoic Era, continued

Visual Learning

Figure 22A What about this dinosaur tells you that it was probably a meat eater? It has sharp teeth.

Use Science Words

Word Meaning The Triassic Period, the earliest period in the Mesozoic Era, is named for three related units of rock first studied in Germany. The Jurassic Period is named after the Jura Mountains between France and Switzerland, where rock from this period was first studied. Have students research the derivation of the most recent period of the Mesozoic Era, the Cretaceous Period. It is named for the white chalk cliffs of Dover, England. Cretaceous is derived from the Latin word for chalk, *creta*.

Figure 22
Birds might have evolved from dinosaurs.

A *Bambiraptor feinberger* is a 75-million-year-old member of a family of meat-eating dinosaurs thought by some paleontologists to be closely related to birds.

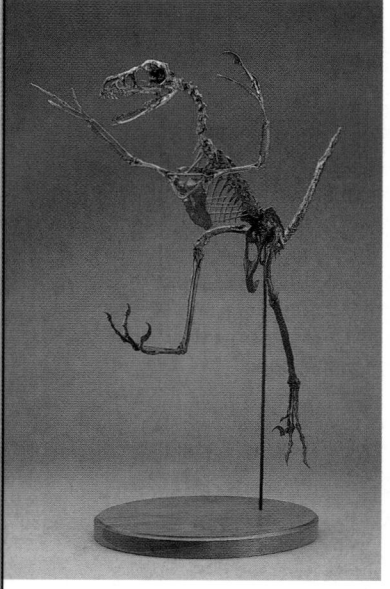

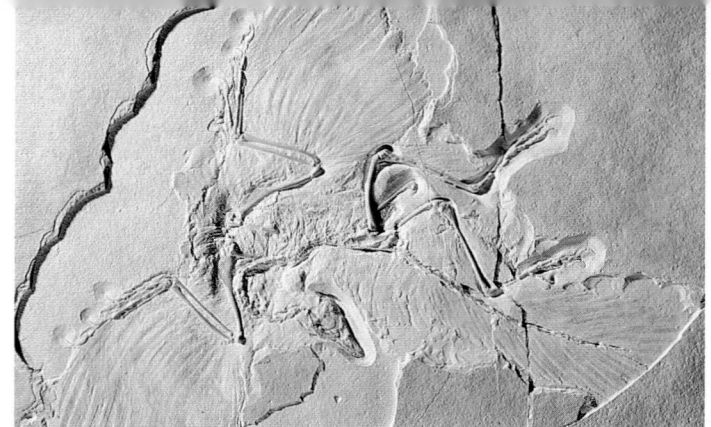

B Considered one of the world's most priceless fossils, *Archaeopteryx* was first found in a limestone quarry in Germany in 1861.

Birds Birds appeared during the Jurassic Period. Some paleontologists think that birds evolved from small, meat-eating dinosaurs much like *Bambiraptor feinberger* in **Figure 22A.** The earliest bird, *Archaeopteryx*, shown in **Figure 22B,** had wings and feathers. However, because *Archaeopteryx* had features not shared with modern birds, scientists know it was not a direct ancestor of today's birds.

Mammals Mammals first appeared in the Triassic Period. The earliest mammals were small, mouselike creatures, as shown in **Figure 23.** Mammals are warm-blooded vertebrates that have hair or fur covering their bodies. The females produce milk to feed their young. These two characteristics have enabled mammals to survive in many changing environments.

Gymnosperms During most of the Mesozoic Era, gymnosperms (JIHM nuh spurmz), which first appeared in the Paleozoic Era, dominated the land. Gymnosperms are plants that produce seeds but not flowers. Many gymnosperms are still around today. These include pines and ginkgo trees.

Figure 23
The earliest mammals were small creatures that resembled today's mice and shrews.

Angiosperms Angiosperms (AN jee uh spurmz), or flowering plants, first evolved during the Cretaceous Period. Angiosperms produce seeds with hard outer coverings.

Because their seeds are enclosed and protected, angiosperms can live in many environments. Angiosperms are the most diverse and abundant land plants today. Present-day angiosperms that evolved during the Mesozoic Era include magnolia and oak trees.

Inclusion Strategies

Learning Disabled Supply students with drawings or models of six different dinosaurs. Have them determine whether the dinosaurs were meat or plant eaters. Have students describe what characteristics were useful for their analysis. Possible answers: Different types of teeth will suggest the type of food they ate. Predators' eyes were in the front of the head for depth perception; plant-eaters' eyes were on the side of the head for a greater field of vision.

Science Journal

Dinosaur Questions Have students take a few minutes to think of a question about dinosaurs for which they still do not have an answer. Put the questions in a box, and have each student take a question, making sure it is not his or her own. Have students research the answers to the questions, writing the answers in their Science Journals.

End of an Era The Mesozoic Era ended about 65 million years ago with a major extinction of land and marine species. Many groups of animals, including the dinosaurs, disappeared suddenly at this time. Many paleontologists hypothesize that a comet or asteroid collided with Earth, causing a huge cloud of dust and smoke to rise into the atmosphere, blocking out the Sun. Without sunlight the plants died, and all the animals that depended on these plants also died. Not everything died, however. All the organisms that you see around you today are descendants of the survivors of the great extinction at the end of the Mesozoic Era.

Math Skills Activity

Calculating Extinction Using Percentages

Example Problem

At the end of the Cretaceous Period, large numbers of animals became extinct. Scientists still are trying to understand why some types of animals survived while others died. Looking at animals such as amphibians, reptiles, and mammals that lived during the Cretaceous Period, can you determine what percentage of amphibians died during the extinction?

Solution

1️⃣ *This is what you know:*

Animal Extinctions		
Animal Type	Groups Living Before Extinction Event (n)	Groups Left After Extinction Event (t)
Amphibians	12	4
Reptiles	63	30
Mammals	24	8

2️⃣ *This is what you need to find out:* p = the percentage of amphibian groups that died during the Cretaceous extinction

3️⃣ *This is the equation you need to use:* $p = t / n \times 100$
           Both t and n are shown on the above chart.

Check your answer by multiplying n *by the percentage you calculated, divide by 100, and you should get a number close to* t.

Practice Problem

Using the same equation, calculate the percentage of reptiles and then the percentage of mammals that died. Which group lost the greatest percentage of animals?

For more help, refer to the Math Skill Handbook.

SECTION 3 Middle and Recent Earth History **417**

Teacher FYI

One explanation of how the asteroid that may have killed off the dinosaurs caused such widespread damage concerns the angle at which it struck Earth. It is thought to have collided with Earth at a shallow angle on what is now the Yucatan Peninsula. This would have sent large amounts of hot debris over much of what is now North America.

Math Skills Activity

National Math Standards
Correlation to Mathematics Objectives
1, 2, 8, 9

Answer to Practice Problem

Reptiles:

p = percent of reptile groups that died during the Cretaceous extinction
$p = t/n; p = 30/63 = .476 = 48\%$

Mammals:

p = percent of mammal groups that died during the Cretaceous extinction
$p = t/n; p = 8/24 = .333 = 33\%$

Teacher FYI

The K-T boundary separates the Cretaceous Period (Mesozoic Era) from the Tertiary Period (Cenozoic Era). An iridium-rich clay layer found at this boundary led to the theory that a collision with an asteroid resulted in the demise of the dinosaurs. This is the boundary that might provide evidence about the extinction of the dinosaurs.

Resource Manager

Chapter Resources Booklet
  Enrichment, p. 30
Cultural Diversity, p. 13
Mathematics Skill Activities, p. 5

The Cenozoic Era

IDENTIFYING Misconceptions

Some students may think that humans were alive when dinosaurs lived on Earth. Explain that human ancestors *Australopithicians* appeared about 5 million years ago, long after dinosaurs became extinct about 65 million years ago.

TRY AT HOME

Mini LAB

Purpose Students use the rate of seafloor spreading to calculate the age of the Atlantic Ocean. IS **Logical-Mathematical**

Materials world map, metric ruler

Teaching Strategy The rate given is an average for several points along the Mid-Atlantic Ridge.

Analysis

1. Student answers will depend on the points they choose on each continent and their measurements. Separations of 6,000 to 7,000 km would take from 160 to 200 million years to achieve.

2. Values should be in the range of 160 to 200 million years.

TRY AT HOME

Mini LAB

Calculating the Age of the Atlantic Ocean

Procedure

1. On a **world map** or **globe**, measure the distance in kilometers between a point on the east coast of South America and a point on the west coast of Africa.

2. Measure in SI several times and take the average of your results.

3. Assuming that Africa has been moving away from South America at a rate of 3.5 cm per year, calculate how many years it took to create the Atlantic Ocean.

Analysis

1. Did the values used to obtain your average value vary much?

2. How close did your age come to the accepted estimate for the beginning of the breakup of Pangaea in the Triassic Period?

Figure 24

Ⓐ The Himalaya extend along the India-Tibet border and contain some of the world's tallest mountains. Ⓑ India drifted north and finally collided with Asia, forming the Himalaya.

418 CHAPTER 14 Geologic Time

The Cenozoic Era

The **Cenozoic** (sen uh ZOH ihk) **Era,** or era of recent life, began about 65 million years ago and continues today. Many mountain ranges in North and South America and Europe began to form in the Cenozoic Era. In the late Cenozoic, the climate became much cooler and ice ages occurred. The Cenozoic Era is subdivided into two periods. The first of these is the Tertiary Period. The present-day period is the Quaternary Period. It began about 1.8 million years ago.

✔ **Reading Check** *What happened to the climate during the late Cenozoic Era?*

Times of Mountain Building Many mountain ranges formed during the Cenozoic Era. These include the Alps in Europe and the Andes in South America. The Himalaya, shown in **Figure 24,** formed as India moved northward and collided with Asia. The collision crumpled and thickened Earth's crust, raising the highest mountains presently on Earth. Many people think the growth of these mountains has helped create cooler climates worldwide.

✔ Assessment

Portfolio Have students make sketches of something that may have happened on land, in the ocean, or to organisms during the time the Atlantic was forming. Use **Performance Assessment in the Science Classroom,** p. 127.

Resource Manager

Chapter Resources Booklet
Reinforcement, p. 27
MiniLAB, p. 4

Home and Community Involvement, p. 27

Further Evolution of Mammals

Throughout much of the Cenozoic Era, expanding grasslands favored grazing plant eaters like horses, camels, deer, and some elephants. Many kinds of mammals became larger. Horses evolved from small, multi-toed animals into the large, hoofed animals of today. However, not all mammals remained on land. Ancestors of the present-day whales and dolphins evolved to make their lives in the sea.

As Australia and South America separated from Antarctica during the continuing breakup of the continents, many species became isolated. They evolved separately from life-forms in other parts of the world. Evidence of this can be seen today in Australia's marsupials. Marsupials are mammals such as kangaroos, koalas, and wombats (shown in **Figure 25**) that carry their young in a pouch.

Your species, *Homo sapiens*, probably appeared about 140,000 years ago. Some people suggest that the appearance of humans could have led to the extinction of many other mammals. As their numbers grew, humans competed for food that other animals relied upon. Also, fossil bones and other evidence indicate that early humans were hunters.

Figure 25
The wombat is one of many Australian marsupials. As a result of human activities, the number and range of wombats have diminished.

Section 3 Assessment

1. In which era, period, and epoch did *Homo sapiens* first appear?

2. Did mammals become more or less abundant after the extinction of the dinosaurs? Explain why.

3. How did the development of seeds with a hard outer covering enable angiosperms to survive in a wide variety of climates?

4. Give two reasons why some paleontologists hypothesize that dinosaurs were warm-blooded animals.

5. **Think Critically** How could two species that evolved on separate continents have many similarities?

Skill Builder Activities

6. **Researching Information** Arrange these organisms in sequence according to when they first appeared on Earth: *mammals, reptiles, dinosaurs, fish, angiosperms, birds, insects, amphibians, land plants,* and *bacteria*. **For more help, refer to the** Science Skill Handbook.

7. **Converting Units** A fossil mosasaur, a giant marine reptile, measured 9 m in lenth and had a skull that measured 45 cm in length. What fraction of the mosasaur's total length did the skull account for? Compare your length with the mosasaur's length. **For more help, refer to the** Math Skill Handbook.

Answers to Section Assessment

1. Cenozoic Era, Quaternary Period, Pleistocene Epoch
2. More abundant; dinosaur extinction reduced the competition for food and habitat.
3. They survived better because their seeds are enclosed and protected.
4. Studies show they may have been fast moving and that some had bones similar in structure to those of mammals.
5. They could have evolved from a common ancestor, especially if the continents were once one land mass. (They also could have evolved in similar environments.)
6. bacteria, fish, land plants, insects, amphibians, reptiles, dinosaurs, mammals, birds, angiosperms
7. 9 m = 900 cm; 45 cm/900 cm = 0.05 = 5%; Students should use a similar formula, but substitute their height in centimeters for the length of mosasaur's skull.

Activity

Recognize the Problem

Purpose
Students will search for, gather, and analyze information on fossils from the Internet, library, and natural history museum. They will use this data to infer what North America looked like—especially in their local area—during the geologic past. They will present their results to the class. L2 COOP LEARN

LS **Visual-Spatial and Interpersonal**

Form a Hypothesis

Internet Students will gather data from Internet sites that can be accessed through the Glencoe Science Web site. Students can post their data on the site and get data from other schools around the country. Click on the geologic time period you are interested in. This will open a database of fossil and paleogeographic data for that time period. The site provides links to other sites where fossils and paleogeographic data are available. Maps and data tables are also provided on the Glencoe Science Web site. Students can print them out or use them as a guide.

Non-Internet Sources If you do not have Internet access, use historical geology references in a library or natural history museum. Use a map of North America with an overlay to reconstruct the environment during the chosen time period, paying special attention to your local region. Record your data in a table similar to the one shown.

Activity *Use the Internet*

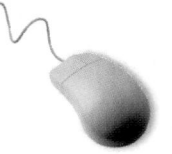

Discovering the Past

Imagine what your state was like millions of years ago. What animals might have been roaming around the spot where you now sit? Can you picture a Tyrannosaurus rex roaming the area that is now your school? The animals and plants that once inhabited your region might have left some clues to their identity—fossils. Scientists use fossils to piece together what Earth looked like in the geologic past. Fossils can help determine whether an area used to be dry land or was underwater. Fossils can help uncover clues about how plants and animals have evolved over the course of time. Using the resources of the Internet and by sharing data with your peers, you can start to discover how North America has changed through time.

Recognize the Problem
How has your area changed over geologic time?

Form a Hypothesis
How might the area where you are now living have looked thousands or millions of years ago? Do you think that the types of animals and plants have changed much over time? Form a hypothesis concerning the change in organisms and geography from long ago to the present day in your area.

Goals
- **Gather** information about fossils found in your area.
- **Communicate** details about fossils found in your area.
- **Synthesize** information from sources about the fossil record and the changes in your area over time.

SCIENCE*Online* Go to the Glencoe Science Web site at **science.glencoe.com** to get more information about fossils and changes over geologic time and for data collected by other students.

Fossils in Your Area					
Fossil Name	Plant or Animal Fossil	Age of Fossils	Details About Plant or Animal Fossil	Location of Fossil	Additional Information
			Answers will vary.		

420 CHAPTER 14 Geologic Time

SCIENCE *Online*
Internet Addresses
_____
_____
_____
_____

Explore the Glencoe Science Web site at **science.glencoe.com** to find out more about topics in this activity.

Test Your Hypothesis

Plan

1. **Determine** the age of the rocks that make up your area. Were they formed during Precambrian time, the Paleozoic Era, the Mesozoic Era, or the Cenozoic Era?

2. Gather information about the fossil plants and animals found in your area during one of the above geologic time intervals. Find specific information on when, where and how the fossil organisms lived. If no fossils are known from your area, find out information about the fossils found nearest your area.

Do

1. Make sure your teacher approves your plan before you start.

2. Go to the Glencoe Science Web site at **science.glencoe.com** to post your data in the table. Add any additional information you think is important to understanding the fossils found in your area.

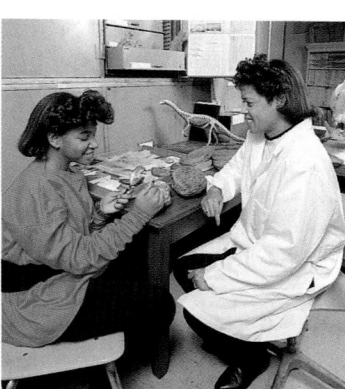

Analyze Your Data

1. What present-day relatives of prehistoric animals or plants exist in your area?

2. How have the organisms in your area changed over time? Is your hypothesis supported? Why or why not?

3. What other information did you discover about your area's climate or environment from the geologic time period you investigated?

Draw Conclusions

1. Find this *Use the Internet* activity on the Glencoe Science Web site at **science.glencoe.com.** Compare your data to those of other students. Study other students' data to compare information about the geologic time periods and fossils that you investigated. Review data that other students have entered about fossils they have researched.

2. **Describe** the plant and animal fossils that have been discovered in your area. What clues did you discover about the environment of your fossil organisms? How do these compare to the environment of your area today?

3. **Infer** from the fossil organisms found in your area what the geography and climate were like during the geologic time period you chose.

ACTIVITY 421

Time Required

one week for data collection, one week to interpret the data

Preparation

Internet Access the Glencoe Science Web site to run through the steps the students will follow.

Non-Internet Sources Obtain a larger map of North America and a thin paper or clear plastic overlay. Have some reference books about fossils available. Have students visit or write to a natural history museum.

Test Your Hypothesis

Teaching Strategies

• This activity will allow students to discover what their area and the rest of North America looked like in the past. The main goal is to use the fossil record to determine the paleoclimate and paleogeography of North America during the four selected geologic time periods.

• Make sure students research where the fossils they find lived—whether on land or in a freshwater or ocean environment.

Analyze Your Data

Answers will be subjective and based on student's individual research.

Draw Conclusions

Answers will be individualized and often based on the student's opinion of his or her research. Look for depth and quality of research performed.

Resource Manager

Chapter Resources Booklet
 Activity Worksheet, pp. 7–8
 Lab Activity, pp. 11–14
Lab Management and Safety, p. 73

✔Assessment

Performance Have students mount their data tables on poster board. Display them around the room. Provide time for each group to present their findings to the class. Use **Performance Assessment in the Science Classroom**, p. 143.

Content Background

Current estimates of the wild tiger population range from 5,000 to 7,200 individuals. That figure is only about 5 percent of the population in 1900. Tigers are the world's largest cat. They once roamed much of Asia. Their range is steadily shrinking and the Bali, Caspian, and Javan tiger subspecies have already become extinct. Demand for tiger pelts, body parts used for medicinal purposes, and continuing loss of habitat make the extinction of tigers in the wild likely by 2010.

Discussion

Which of these species could not have become extinct because of human activity? Explain. Humans could not have influenced the extinction of pterosaurs or Coelurosauravus because they lived long before humans appeared on Earth.

Activity

Have small groups of students use long sheets of butcher paper to make a timeline, showing the mass extinctions shown in the graph in this feature. Ask them to research some representative organisms that became extinct during each mass extinction and illustrate their time lines with drawings of those organisms. Display the groups' time lines in the classroom.

Science Stats

Extinct!

Did you know...

...In 1865, when Lewis Carroll wrote about the dodo in his famous book *Alice in Wonderland,* the bird had been gone for almost two hundred years from the island of Mauritius in the Indian Ocean. First seen by European settlers in 1598, the dodo was hunted for food. The birds were extinct by 1681.

...The earliest known gliding reptile had "wings" with a span of 30 cm that were wide flaps of flesh not attached to its limbs. From fossils found in Madagascar, scientists believe that the *Coelurosauravus* (see lor oh SOR uh vuhs) lived between 260 and 246 million years ago.

Coelurosauravus

Saber-toothed cat

...The saber-toothed cat lived in the Americas from about 1.6 million to 8,000 years ago. Smilodon, the best-known saber-toothed cat, was among the most ferocious carnivores. It had large canine teeth, about 15 cm long, which it used to pierce the flesh of its prey.

422   CHAPTER 14   Geologic Time

SCIENCE *Online*
Internet Addresses
_____
_____
_____
_____

Explore the Glencoe Science Web site at **science.glencoe.com** to find out more about topics in this feature.

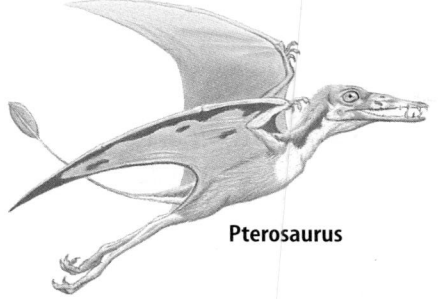

Pterosaurus

...The first vertebrates to fly were reptiles called pterosaurs (TER uh sawrz). The front limbs of these reptiles developed into wings during the Triassic Period. Their wingspans ranged from 1.8 m to more than 12 m. Some pterosaurs were fish eaters, flying low over water to catch fish with their narrow jaws.

Great Mass Extinctions of Species

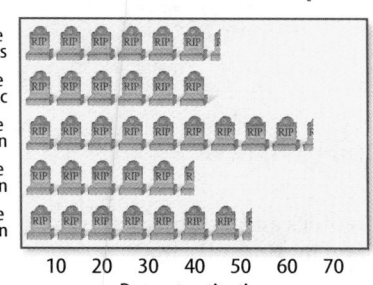

Periods

| Late Cretaceous |
| Late Triassic |
| Late Permian |
| Late Devonian |
| Late Ordovician |

10 20 30 40 50 60 70
Percent extinction

Woolly mammoth

...The woolly mammoth lived in the cold tundra regions during the Ice Age. It looked rather like an elephant with long hair, weighed between 5,300 kg and 7,300 kg, and was between 3 m and 4 m tall.

Do the Math

1. If 75 species of organisms become extinct each day, how many would become extinct during a leap year?
2. How many years did it take from the first sighting of the dodo bird by humans until it became extinct?
3. What is the range between the smallest and largest wingspans among pterosaurs?

Go Further

Use the Glencoe Science Web site at **science.glencoe.com** to research extinct animals, fish, birds, plants, and other life-forms. Trace the origins of each of the species and learn how long its kind existed on Earth.

SCIENCE STATS 423

Do the Math

Teaching Strategies

- Review with students how many days are in a leap year to help them answer the first question in Do the Math.
- Review subtracting decimal numbers to help students answer the third question in Do the Math.

Answers

1. During a leap year, 27,450 species would become extinct. (75 × 366 = 27,450)
2. 83 years (1681 − 1598 = 83)
3. 10.2 m (12 − 1.8 = 10.2)

Go Further

Students will find that some organisms existed on Earth for hundreds of millions of years, while others existed for much shorter periods of time. Have students select several different organisms and make a bar graph that compares the length of time the organisms existed on Earth. Discuss with students how to select a scale for the graph that will allow them to graph the organisms they have chosen.

Visual Learning

Graph of Mass Extinctions Which period had the largest percentage of extinctions? late Permian What percentage of organisms became extinct at that time? almost 70 percent Which period had the smallest percentage of extinctions? late Devonian What percentage of organisms became extinct at that time? about 40 percent

Reviewing Main Ideas

Preview

Students can answer the questions in their Science Journals. Discuss the answers as you go through the chapter. [LS] **Linguistic**

Review

Students can write their answers, then compare them with those of other students. [LS] **Interpersonal**

Reteach

Students can look at the illustrations and describe details that support the main ideas of the chapter. [LS] **Visual-Spatial**

Answers to Chapter Review

SECTION 1

3. Mountains can separate organisms of a single species. Adaptations can cause the separated populations to evolve differently, eventually causing separate species to form.

SECTION 2

4. trilobite

SECTION 3

3. Humans could have competed with these animals for food or could have hunted them as prey.

Reviewing Main Ideas

Section 1 Life and Geologic Time

1. Geologic time is divided into eons, eras, periods, and epochs.

2. Divisions within the geologic time scale are based largely on major evolutionary changes in organisms.

3. Plate movements cause changes that affect organic evolution. *How can the building of mountains like those shown here affect the evolution of species?*

Section 2 Early Earth History

1. Cyanobacteria were an early form of life that evolved during Precambrian time. Trilobites, fish, and corals were abundant during the Paleozoic Era.

2. Plants and animals began to move onto land during the middle of the Paleozoic Era. Land plants and animals then evolved rapidly and colonized the land.

3. The Paleozoic Era was a time of mountain building. The Appalachian Mountains formed when several islands and finally Africa collided with North America.

4. At the end of the Paleozoic Era, many marine invertebrates became extinct. *What kind of marine organism is shown here?*

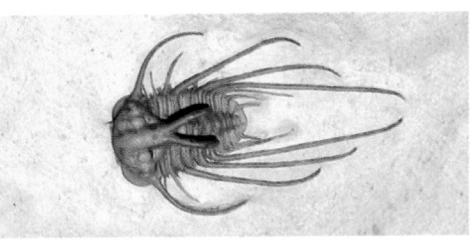

Section 3 Middle and Recent Earth History

1. Reptiles and gymnosperms were dominant land life-forms in the Mesozoic Era. Mammals and angiosperms began to dominate the land in the Cenozoic Era.

2. Pangaea broke apart during the Mesozoic Era. Many mountain ranges formed during the Cenozoic.

3. *Homo sapiens* appeared during the Pleistocene Epoch. *How might Homo sapiens have contributed to the extinction of animals like the one shown here?*

FOLDABLES Reading & Study Skills

After You Read

To help you review geological time, use the Organizational Study Fold you made at the beginning of the chapter.

FOLDABLES Reading & Study Skills

After You Read

After students have read the chapter and completed the Foldable described in Before You Read, have them do the activity on the student page.

Dinah Zike

Visualizing Main Ideas

Complete the concept map on geologic time using the following choices: Cenozoic, Trilobites in oceans, mammals common, Paleozoic, Dinosaurs roam Earth, and Abundant gymnosperms.

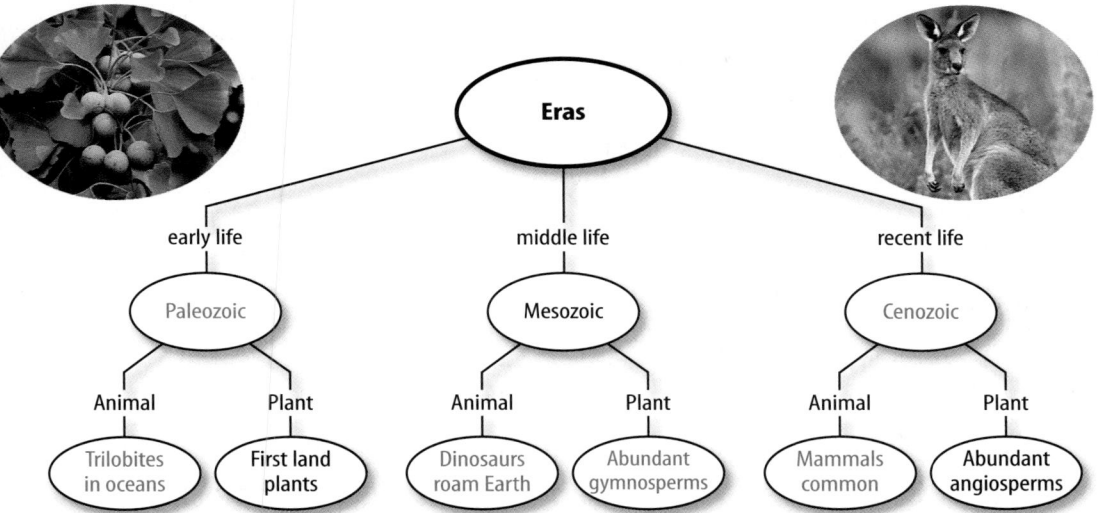

Eras

early life → Paleozoic
- Animal → Trilobites in oceans
- Plant → First land plants

middle life → Mesozoic
- Animal → Dinosaurs roam Earth
- Plant → Abundant gymnosperms

recent life → Cenozoic
- Animal → Mammals common
- Plant → Abundant angiosperms

Vocabulary Review

Vocabulary Words

a. Cenozoic Era
b. cyanobacteria
c. eon
d. epoch
e. era
f. geologic time scale
g. Mesozoic Era
h. natural selection
i. organic evolution
j. Paleozoic Era
k. Pangaea
l. period
m. Precambrian time
n. species
o. trilobite

Study Tip

THE PRINCETON REVIEW

Outline the chapters to make sure that you're understanding the key ideas. Writing down the main points of the chapter will help you remember important details and understand larger themes.

Using Vocabulary

The sentences below include vocabulary words that have been used incorrectly. Change the incorrect word so that the sentence reads correctly.

1. A change in the hereditary features of a species over a long period is extinction.

2. A record of events in Earth history is natural selection.

3. The largest subdivision of geologic time is the period.

4. The process by which the best-suited individuals survive in their environment is organic evolution.

5. A group of individuals that normally breed only among themselves is an epoch.

CHAPTER STUDY GUIDE   425

Visualizing Main Ideas

See student page.

Vocabulary Review

Using Vocabulary

1. A change in the hereditary features of a species over a long period of time is organic evolution.
2. A record of events in Earth history is the geologic time scale.
3. The largest subdivision of geologic time is the eon.
4. The process by which the best-suited individuals survive in their environment is natural selection.
5. A group of individuals that normally breed only among themselves is a species.

IDENTIFYING ⟩ Misconceptions

Assess

Use the assessment as follow-up to page 396F after students have completed the chapter.

Demonstration   Have students relate numerical and relative ages for the Geologic Time Scale by accessing the *Virtual Dating Simulation* through the Glencoe Science Web site.

Expected Outcome   Students will recognize that time is to be measured not only by a watch in minutes and seconds, but also in huge dimensions using both relative and numerical methods.

Reinforcement   Have a geologist visit the classroom to provide examples of how the geologic time scale is used in their work.

Checking Concepts

1. D
2. D
3. A
4. D
5. B
6. B
7. A
8. C
9. B
10. A

Thinking Critically

11. Too much harmful ultraviolet radiation from the Sun reached Earth's surface prior to the establishment of the ozone layer.
12. Trilobites were widespread and individual species existed for a limited amount of time before becoming extinct, so they can be used to date rocks in which their fossils are found.
13. Most organisms of Precambrian age lacked the hard parts that became common at the beginning of the Paleozoic Era.
14. Evolution occurs through natural selection, which is the process by which organisms with characteristics best suited to their environment survive and reproduce.
15. This idea suggests that evolution occurs because an organism acquires a trait for survival and passes that trait to its offspring. Acquired traits are not hereditary.

Chapter 14 Assessment

Checking Concepts

Choose the word or phrase that best completes the sentence.

1. How many millions of years ago did the era in which you live begin?
   A) 650   C) 1.6
   B) 245   D) 65

2. What is the process by which better-suited organisms survive and reproduce?
   A) endangerment   C) gymnosperm
   B) extinction   D) natural selection

3. What is the next smaller division of geologic time after the era?
   A) period   C) epoch
   B) stage   D) eon

4. When did the most recent ice age occur?
   A) Pennsylvanian   C) Tertiary
   B) Triassic   D) Quaternary

5. What was one of the earliest forms of life on Earth?
   A) gymnosperm   C) angiosperm
   B) cyanobacterium   D) dinosaur

6. Which group of organisms evolved from the same ancestors as amphibians?
   A) reptiles   C) angiosperms
   B) lungfish   D) gymnosperms

7. During which era did the dinosaurs live?
   A) Mesozoic   C) Miocene
   B) Paleozoic   D) Cenozoic

8. Which type of plant has seeds without protective coverings?
   A) angiosperms   C) gymnosperms
   B) flowering plants   D) magnolias

9. Which group of plants evolved during the Mesozoic Era and is the dominant plant group today?
   A) gymnosperms   C) ginkgoes
   B) angiosperms   D) algae

10. When did the Ediacaran animals live?
    A) Precambrian time   C) Mesozoic Era
    B) Paleozoic Era   D) Cenozoic Era

Thinking Critically

11. Why couldn't plants move onto land until an ozone layer formed?

12. Why are trilobites classified as index fossils?

13. What is the most significant difference between Precambrian life-forms and Paleozoic life-forms?

14. How is natural selection related to organic evolution?

15. In the early 1800s, a naturalist proposed that the giraffe species has a long neck as a result of years of stretching their necks to reach leaves in tall trees. Explain why this isn't true.

Developing Skills

16. **Interpreting Scientific Illustrations** The circle graph below represents geologic time. Determine which interval of geologic time is represented by each portion of the graph. Which interval was longest? Which do we know the least about?

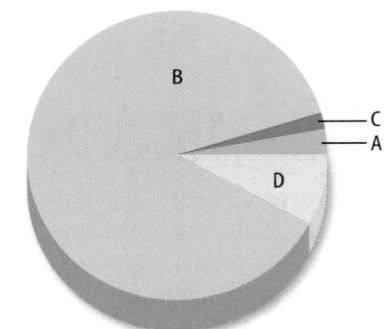

Chapter ✔Assessment Planner

Portfolio Encourage students to place in their portfolios one or two items of what they consider to be their best work. Examples include:
- Science Journal, p. 400
- Chemistry Integration, p. 407
- Extension, p. 415

Performance Additional performance assessments, Performance Task Assessment Lists, and rubrics for evaluating these activities can be found in Glencoe's **Performance Assessment in the Science Classroom.**

17. Interpreting Data The Cenozoic Era has lasted 65 million years. What percentage of Earth's 4.6-billion-year history is that?

18. Comparing and Contrasting Use the outlines of the present-day continents to make a sketch of Pangaea.

19. Forming Hypotheses Suggest some reasons why trilobites might have become extinct at the end of the Paleozoic Era?

20. Interpreting Data A student found what he thought was a piece of dinosaur bone in Pleistocene sediment. How likely is it that he is right? Explain.

Performance Assessment

21. Make a Model In the Activity, you learned how a particular characteristic might evolve within a species. Modify the experimental model by using color instead of height as a characteristic. Design your activity with the understanding that varimals live in a dark-colored forest environment.

TECHNOLOGY

Go to the Glencoe Science Web site at **science.glencoe.com** or use the **Glencoe Science CD-ROM** for additional chapter assessment.

THE PRINCETON REVIEW **Test Practice**

Many animals have inhabited Earth. Some of these animals have been divided into groups below.

Group A	Group B	Group C
Saber-toothed cat	*Apatosaurus*	Frog
Giant ground sloth	*Maiasaura*	Turtle
Woolly mammoth	*Tyrannosaurus*	Salamander

Study the table and answer the following questions.

1. The animals in Group A are different from the animals in Group B because only the animals in Group A are _____ .
   A) mammals   **C)** amphibians
   B) reptiles   **D)** birds

2. The animals in Group B are different from the animals in Group C because only the animals in Group B are _____ .
   F) dinosaurs   **H)** amphibians
   G) reptiles   **J)** herbivores

3. The animals in all three groups are similar because _____ .
   A) They make their own food.
   B) They have hair.
   C) They must eat other organisms.
   D) They are meat eaters.

THE PRINCETON REVIEW **Test Practice**

The Test-Taking Tip was written by The Princeton Review, the nation's leader in test preparation.
1. A
2. F
3. C

Developing Skills

16. A—Mesozoic Era, B—Precambrian time, C—Cenozoic Era, D—Paleozoic Era; Precambrian; Precambrian
17. The Cenozoic Era represents approximately 1.4% of Earth's history; 65,000,000/4,600,000,000 years = 0.014.
18. Students' illustrations should be similar to **Figure 11.**
19. Possible answers: plate tectonic processes that changed the configuration of land and seas, disappearance of shallow seas where they lived; climate changes
20. It is not likely that he is correct, because dinosaurs became extinct long before the Pleistocene Epoch.

Performance Assessment

21. Students should realize that black, as opposed to red, is an easier color to camouflage in a dark-colored forest environment. Use the **Performance Task Assessment List for Models** in **PASC,** p. 123.

Assessment Resources

📁 **Reproducible Masters**
Chapter Resources Booklet
  Chapter Review, pp. 35–36
  Chapter Tests, pp. 37–40
  Assessment Transparency Activity, p. 47
Glencoe Science Web site
  Interactive Tutor
  Chapter Quizzes

Glencoe Technology
🖌 Assessment Transparency
💿 Interactive CD-ROM Chapter Quizzes
💿 ExamView Pro Test Bank
💿 Vocabulary PuzzleMaker Software
📼 MindJogger Videoquiz DVD/VHS

QUESTION 1: C

Students should refer to the third paragraph of the reading passage to find the answer to this question.

QUESTION 2: H

Students must identify which sentence best summarizes the main idea of the passage.

- **Choice F** No; this is a detail from the passage.
- **Choice G** No; this is a detail from the passage.
- **Choice H** Yes; this is the best summary of the passage.
- **Choice J** No; this is a detail from the passage.

QUESTION 3: C

Students should reread the fourth paragraph to determine its main idea.

- **Choice A** No; this is a detail from the fourth paragraph.
- **Choice B** No; this is a detail from the fourth paragraph.
- **Choice C** Yes; this was the main point from the fourth paragraph.
- **Choice D** No; this is a detail from the fourth paragraph.

All questions written and validated by The Princeton Review.

Read the passage. Then read each question that follows the passage. Decide which is the best answer to each question.

Life on Earth

The oldest rocks found on Earth have been estimated to be about 4 billion years old. But these rocks do not contain any fossil remains. The oldest rocks that have been found with any evidence of life are about 3.5 billion years old. These rocks have fossils of single-celled organisms that once lived in the oceans.

No life could have survived on land at that time because there was so much ultraviolet radiation coming down to Earth's surface from the Sun. Early bacteria did something very important that made it possible for other species to inhabit Earth.

Scientists believe there was little oxygen in Earth's early atmosphere. Nearly 3 billion years ago, some early bacteria produced oxygen during photosynthesis. This oxygen bubbled into the oceans, and after millions of years, entered the atmosphere.

This oxygen from photosynthesis was very important. As it entered the atmosphere, some of it absorbed energy from the Sun's radiation. The radiation caused chemical reactions, which produced ozone gas. This ozone began acting as a protective shield, blocking Earth's surface from most of the incoming ultraviolet radiation. As a result, it became possible for life to survive on land without being damaged by ultraviolet radiation.

The fossil record provides clues about past life on Earth. The earliest multicellular organisms lived in the oceans during the late part of the Precambrian portion of Earth's history. Fossil evidence indicates that animals did not inhabit land until much later.

Test-Taking Tip Number the paragraphs in the passage to make sure that you are referring to the correct paragraph when answering a question.

1. According to the passage, what type of organism added oxygen to Earth's early atmosphere?
   - A) vertebrates
   - B) mammals
   - C) bacteria
   - D) fungi

2. Which of these is the best summary of this passage?
   - F) The earliest organisms lived in the ocean.
   - G) The oldest rocks that have been found with any evidence of life are about 3.5 billion years old.
   - H) The production of oxygen by bacteria, which began nearly 3 billion years ago, helped make life on land possible.
   - J) Oxygen can act like a protective shield, blocking Earth's surface from most of the incoming ultraviolet radiation.

3. What is the main idea of the fourth paragraph of this passage?
   - A) Oxygen entered the atmosphere.
   - B) Oxygen from photosynthesis was very important.
   - C) Oxygen absorbed radiation from the Sun to make ozone.
   - D) The oldest rocks on Earth do not have any fossils in them.

Reasoning and Skills

Read each question and choose the best answer.

1. Which of these facts best explains why the oldest fossils have been discovered in sediments that were deposited in ancient oceans?
   A) Only aquatic animals leave fossils.
   B) Fossils from land organisms have been destroyed.
   C) The first life on Earth began in the oceans.
   D) All living organisms need water.

Test-Taking Tip Some answer choices might be true statements but not the *best* explanation to a particular question.

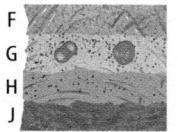
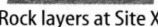
Rock layers at Site X

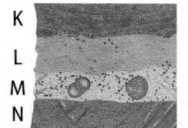
Rock layers at Site Z

2. The fossils found in layer G are considered index fossils by paleontologists. This means that _____.
   F) they are not as old as the fossils found in layer M
   G) layer G is most likely the same age as layer M
   H) they are the same age as the rock in layer L
   J) the fossils are the oldest types of fossils found on Earth

Test-Taking Tip Index fossils appeared during a specific block of time in Earth's history. They can be used to date layers of rock.

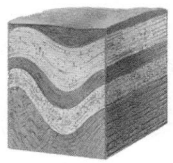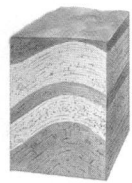

3. Which of the sequences below could fill the gap in the picture above?

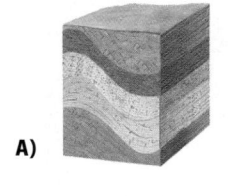
A)

B)

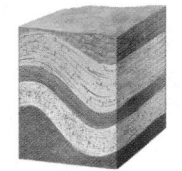
C)

D)

Test-Taking Tip Sedimentary rock layers can be distinguished from each other in pictures by using different patterns to represent each layer.

Consider this question carefully before writing your answer on a separate sheet of paper.

4. The Himalaya are found at the boundary between two large continental plates. These mountains were formed as the result of what geologic process?

Test-Taking Tip Think about what happens as the continental plates move slowly over Earth's plastic-like asthenosphere.

Reasoning and Skills

QUESTION 1: C
Students need to recognize which statement most directly explains why the oldest fossils are of aquatic species.
- **Choice A** No; this is not a correct statement.
- **Choice B** No; some land fossils might have been destroyed, as might have some aquatic fossils.
- **Choice C** Yes; this statement gives a good explanation for why the oldest fossils are aquatic.
- **Choice D** No; this statement is true but not an explanation of the described phenomenon.

QUESTION 2: G
Students must infer from the picture that the rock layers are drawn with the oldest at the bottom and youngest are at the top. They must know that an index fossil is a fossil found only during certain periods and can therefore be used to date a rock layer in which it is found.

QUESTION 3: D
Students must match the pattern of rock layers in the picture with the slices of rock layers in the answer choices. The layers in the correct slice match the layers in the picture both in type and in thickness.

Teaching Tip

Students should have a firm understanding of the theory of superposition in order to make valid inferences about rock layers in picture.

QUESTION 4: Answers will vary.
Students should write a thorough response based upon information from this unit.

Unit Contents

✔ Pre-Reading Activity

Have students read the objectives for each section and search for charts and pictures that relate to each objective.

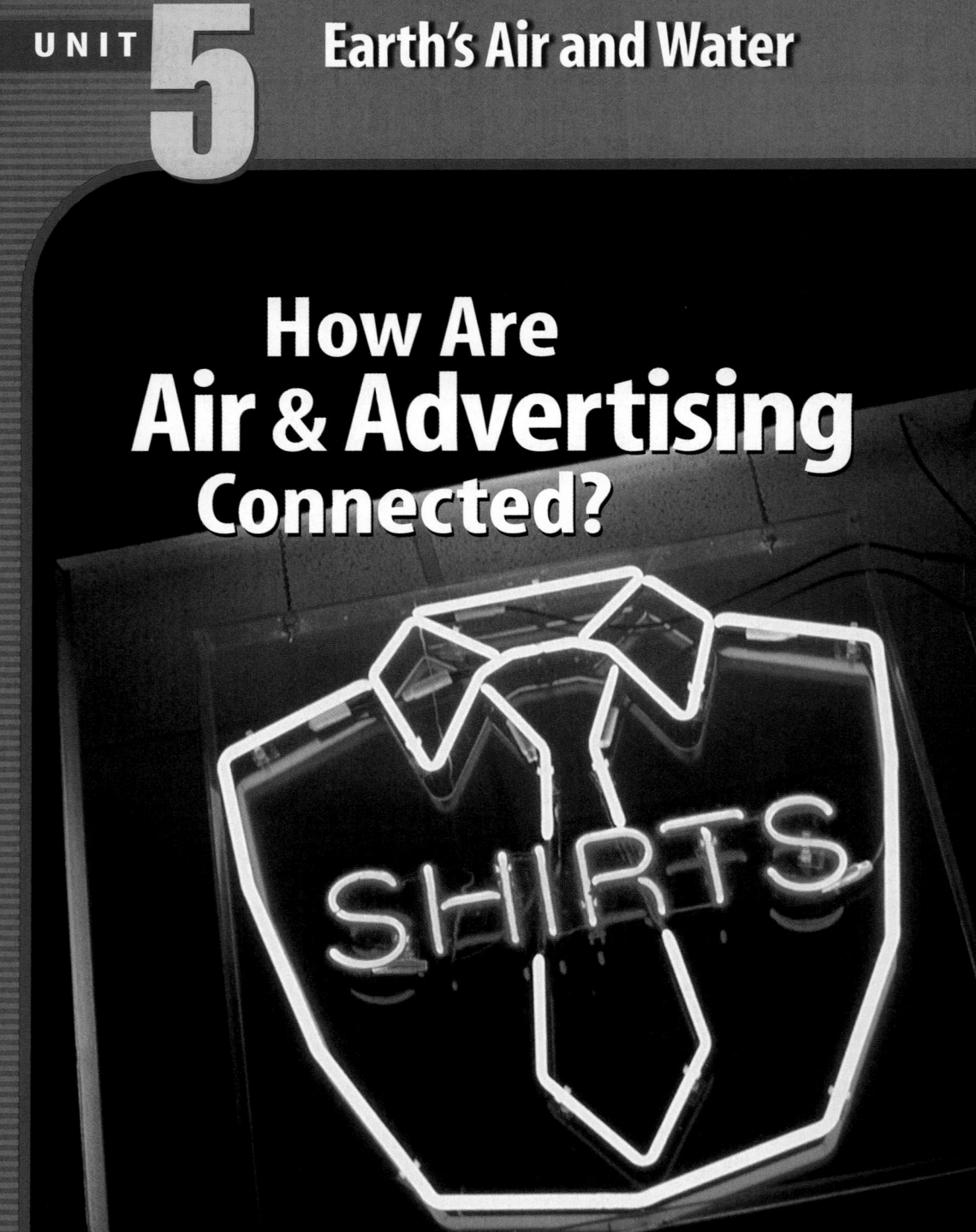

How Are Air & Advertising Connected?

430

Teacher to Teacher

"I have students do a semester-long project on tracking high/low temperatures in a major city of the United States. The finished product is a tri-fold advertisement brochure to attract tourism to the city. Data collection, graphing, reading, persuasive writing, and art are integrated in this project."

Leonard G. Rodríguez, Assistant Principal
First Avenue Middle School
Pasadena, CA

HAND LAUNDRY

In the late 1800s, two scientists were studying the composition of air when they discovered an element that hadn't been known before. They named it "neon," and soon this new element, represented by the chemical symbol Ne, had been assigned a spot in the periodic table (right). It took a few years for people to figure out something useful to do with neon! In 1910, a French engineer experimented with passing an electrical current through neon gas in a vacuum tube. The result was a spectacular orange-red light. Neon's advertising possibilities were quickly realized, and soon the first neon sign blazed on a boulevard in Paris. Today, neon signs in a wide range of colors advertise shops and services all over the world. The other colors are made by mixing neon with other gases and by using tinted tubes.

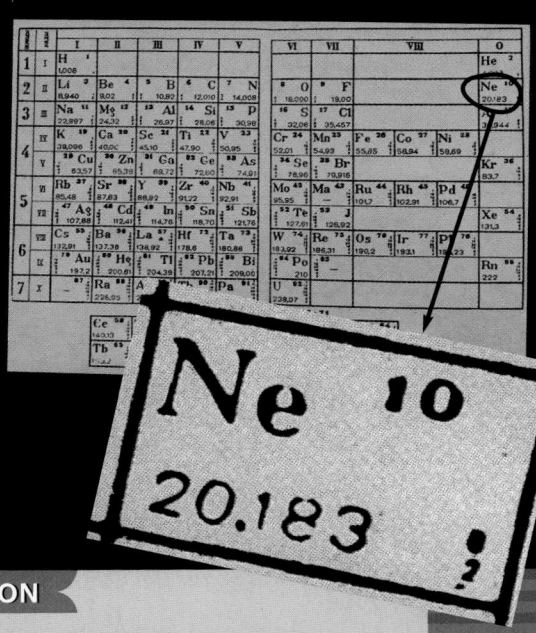

SCIENCE CONNECTION

NOBLE GASES Neon is one of six elements known as the noble gases. These gases make up a tiny fraction of the atmosphere. Conduct research to find out more about this group. What other gases belong to the group? What do they all have in common? Why are they called "noble"? Create a chart that shows when each of the noble gases was discovered and what distinctive characteristics and uses it has.

SCIENCE Online

Internet Addresses

_____
_____
_____

Explore the Glencoe Science Web site at **science.glencoe.com** to find out more about topics in this unit.

Introducing the Unit

How Are Air & Advertising Connected?

Although the noble gases make up only a small percentage of the atmosphere, the atmosphere as a whole is a unique feature that helps maintain the temperate conditions necessary for life.

Besides providing protection from harmful solar radiation, the atmosphere also drives the energy transfer between the oceans and large air masses.

Wind and clouds are created through differential heating of these air masses. The movement of these air masses produces global weather patterns.

These weather patterns, in combination with local geographical conditions, create the various climates found throughout the world.

Ask students to hypothesize why the atmosphere is 78% nitrogen and only 21% oxygen, despite the fact that oxygen is more important for life than nitrogen.

SCIENCE CONNECTION

Activity

Construct a chart with four columns and seven rows. In the top row list: name, discovered, characteristic, and use. In the first column, list the noble gases: helium, neon, argon, krypton, xenon, and radon. Divide the students into six groups; assign each group a noble gas to research. Have students complete their own chart as each group presents its findings to the class.

Section/Objectives	Standards		Activities/Features
Chapter Opener	**National**	**State/Local**	**Explore Activity:** Observe air pressure, p. 433
	See p. 5T for a Key to Standards.		**Before You Read,** p. 433
Section 1 Earth's Atmosphere ⏱ 2 sessions 📦 1 block 1. **Identify** the gases in Earth's atmosphere. 2. **Describe** the structures of Earth's atmosphere. 3. **Explain** what causes air pressure.	National Content Standards: UCP2, A1, D1, D3		**Science Online,** p. 436 **Problem-Solving Activity:** How does altitude affect air pressure?, p. 438 **MiniLAB:** Determining If Air Has Mass, p. 439 **Life Science Integration,** p. 440 **Activity:** Evaluating Sunscreens, p. 442
Section 2 Energy Transfer in the Atmosphere ⏱ 2 sessions 📦 1 block 1. **Describe** what happens to the energy Earth receives from the Sun. 2. **Compare and contrast** radiation, conduction, and convection. 3. **Explain** the water cycle.	National Content Standards: UCP3, A1, B3, D1		**Physics Integration,** p. 444 **MiniLAB:** Model Heat Transfer, p. 445
Section 3 Air Movement ⏱ 3 sessions 📦 1.5 blocks 1. **Explain** why different latitudes on Earth receive different amounts of solar energy. 2. **Describe** the Coriolis effect. 3. **Locate** doldrums, trade winds, prevailing westerlies, polar easterlies, and jet streams.	National Content Standards: UCP3, A1, B2, D1, G1		**Science Online,** p. 448 **Visualizing Global Winds,** p. 449 **Activity:** The Heat Is On, pp. 452–453 **Science and Language Arts:** Song of the Sky Loom, pp. 454–455

NATIONAL GEOGRAPHIC

Teacher's Corner

PRODUCTS AVAILABLE FROM GLENCOE
To order call 1-800-334-7344:
Curriculum Kit
GeoKit: Weather
Videodisc
STV: Atmosphere

PRODUCTS AVAILABLE FROM NATIONAL GEOGRAPHIC SOCIETY
To order call 1-800-368-2728:
Videos
Atmosphere: On the Air
The Sun: Earth's Star
Ozone: Protecting the Invisible Shield

INDEX TO NATIONAL GEOGRAPHIC SOCIETY
The following articles may be used for research relating to this chapter: "Antarctica: A Land of Isolation No More," by Bryan Hodgson, April 1990.

Activity Materials	Reproducible Resources	Section Assessment	Technology
Explore Activity: cardboard cereal box, glass, water	**Chapter Resources Booklet** Foldables Worksheet, p. 13 Directed Reading Overview, p. 15 Note-taking Worksheets, pp. 29–31	GLENCOE'S **ASSESSMENT** ADVANTAGE	
MiniLAB: pan balance, inflatable ball **Activity:** several different brands of sunscreen	**Chapter Resources Booklet** Transparency Activity, p. 40 MiniLAB, p. 3 Enrichment, p. 26 Reinforcement, p. 23 Directed Reading, p. 16 Activity Worksheet, pp. 5–6 Lab Activity, pp. 9–10	**Portfolio** Extension, p. 437 **Performance** Problem-Solving Activity, p. 438 MiniLAB, p. 439 Skill Builder Activities, p. 441 **Content** Section Assessment, p. 441	Section Focus Transparency Interactive CD-ROM/DVD Guided Reading Audio Program
MiniLAB: soup can, black construction paper, water *Need materials?* Contact Science Kit at 1-800-828-7777 or www.sciencekit.com on the Internet.	**Chapter Resources Booklet** Transparency Activity, p. 41 MiniLAB, p. 4 Enrichment, p. 27 Reinforcement, p. 24 Directed Reading, p. 16 Lab Activity, pp. 11–12 Transparency Activity, pp. 43–44	**Portfolio** Science Journal, p. 445 **Performance** MiniLAB, p. 445 Skill Builder Activities, p. 446 **Content** Section Assessment, p. 446	Section Focus Transparency Teaching Transparency Interactive CD-ROM/DVD Guided Reading Audio Program
Activity: ring stand, soil, metric ruler, water, masking tape, 2 clear-plastic boxes, overhead light with reflector, 4 thermometers, 4 colored pencils	**Chapter Resources Booklet** Transparency Activity, p. 42 Enrichment, p. 28 Reinforcement, p. 25 Directed Reading, pp. 17, 18 Activity Worksheet, pp. 7–8 **Lab Management and Safety,** p. 71	**Portfolio** Extension, p. 449 Assessment, p. 449 **Performance** Skill Builder Activities, p.451 **Content** Section Assessment, p. 451	Section Focus Transparency Interactive CD-ROM/DVD Guided Reading Audio Program

GLENCOE'S **ASSESSMENT** ADVANTAGE

End of Chapter Assessment

Blackline Masters	Technology	Professional Series
Chapter Resources Booklet Chapter Review, pp. 33–34 Chapter Tests, pp. 35–38 **Standardized Test Practice by** **The Princeton Review,** pp. 67–70	MindJogger Videoquiz CD-ROM Explorations and Quizzes Vocabulary Puzzle Makers ExamView Pro Test Bank Interactive Lesson Planner Interactive Teacher's Edition	Performance Assessment in the Science Classroom (PASC)

Transparencies

Section Focus

Section Focus Transparency 1 — Cosmic Impact

Impact craters on Earth are fairly rare, but they do exist. In comparison, impact craters on the Moon, especially the far side, are quite common. This impact crater is in Australia.

1. Why is the surface of the Moon struck by objects from space so much more frequently than the surface of Earth?
2. How does the atmosphere nurture life on Earth?
3. What usually happens to the temperature as you ascend to higher elevations on a mountain?

L2

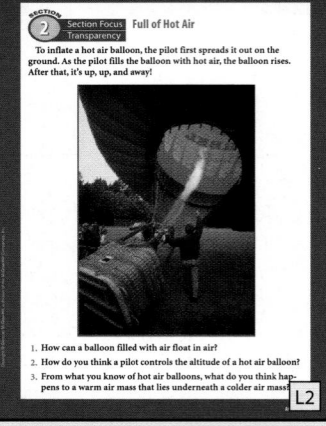

Section Focus Transparency 2 — Full of Hot Air

To inflate a hot air balloon, the pilot first spreads it out on the ground. As the pilot fills the balloon with hot air, the balloon rises. After that, it's up, up, and away!

1. How can a balloon filled with air float in air?
2. How do you think a pilot controls the altitude of a hot air balloon?
3. From what you know of hot air balloons, what do you think happens to a warm air mass that lies underneath a colder air mass?

L2

Section Focus Transparency 3 — The Growth of a Mountain

In 1999, the National Geographic Society sponsored an expedition to determine the height of Mount Everest using sophisticated satellite equipment. The researchers found the elevation to be 8,850 m (29,035 feet), which is two meters higher than the elevation of 8,848 m (29,028 feet) accepted since 1954.

1. What causes the plume coming off the summit of Mount Everest?
2. How do winds affect air travel?
3. Why does wind make you feel colder?

L2

This is a representation of key blackline masters available in the Teacher Classroom Resources. See Resource Manager boxes within the chapter for additional information.

Assessment

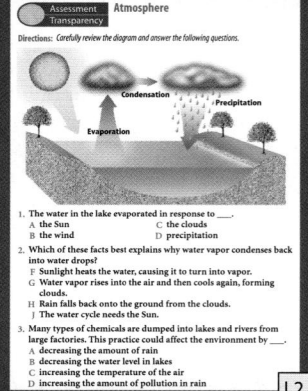

Assessment Transparency — Atmosphere

Directions: *Carefully review the diagram and answer the following questions.*

1. The water in the lake evaporated in response to ___.
   A the Sun   C the clouds
   B the wind   D precipitation
2. Which of these facts best explains why water vapor condenses back into water drops?
   F Sunlight heats the water, causing it to turn into vapor.
   G Water vapor rises into the air and then cools again, forming clouds.
   H Rain falls back onto the ground from the clouds.
   J The water cycle needs the Sun.
3. Many types of chemicals are dumped into lakes and rivers from large factories. This practice could affect the environment by ___.
   A decreasing the amount of rain
   B decreasing the water level in lakes
   C increasing the temperature of the air
   D increasing the amount of pollution in rain

L2

Teaching

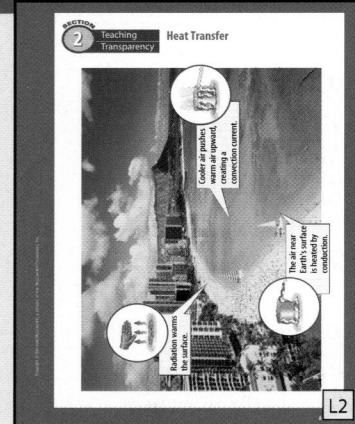

Teaching Transparency — Heat Transfer

L2

Key to Teaching Strategies

The following designations will help you decide which activities are appropriate for your students.

L1 Level 1 activities should be appropriate for students with learning difficulties.

L2 Level 2 activities should be within the ability range of all students.

L3 Level 3 activities are designed for above-average students.

ELL ELL activities should be within the ability range of English Language Learners.

COOP LEARN Cooperative Learning activities are designed for small group work.

LS Multiple Learning Styles logos, as described on page 22T, are used throughout to indicate strategies that address different learning styles.

P These strategies represent student products that can be placed into a best-work portfolio.

Hands-on Activities

Activity Worksheets

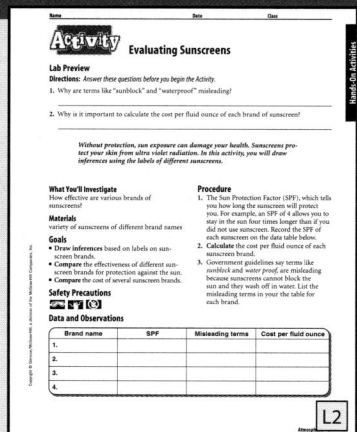

Activity — Evaluating Sunscreens

Lab Preview
Directions: *Answer these questions before you begin the Activity.*
1. Why are terms like "sunblock" and "waterproof" misleading?

2. Why is it important to calculate the cost per fluid ounce of each brand of sunscreen?

Without protection, sun exposure can damage your health. Sunscreens protect your skin from ultra violet radiation. In this activity, you will draw inferences using the labels of different sunscreens.

What You'll Investigate
How effective are various brands of sunscreens?
Materials
variety of sunscreens of different brand names
Goals
- **Draw inferences** based on labels on sunscreen brand.
- **Compare** the effectiveness of different sunscreen brands for protection against the sun.
- **Compare** the cost of several sunscreen brands.
Safety Precautions
Data and Observations

Procedure
1. The Sun Protection Factor (SPF), which tells you how long the sunscreen will protect you. For example, an SPF of 4 allows you to stay in the sun four times longer than if you did not use sunscreen. Record the SPF of each sunscreen on the data table below.
2. **Calculate** the cost per fluid ounce of each sunscreen brand.
3. Government guidelines say terms like *sunblock* and *water proof*, are misleading because sunscreens cannot block the sun and they wash off in water. List the misleading terms in your table for each brand.

Brand name	SPF	Misleading terms	Cost per fluid ounce
1.			
2.			
3.			
4.			

L2

Laboratory Activities

Laboratory Activity 1 — Air Volume and Pressure

You can't always see the air in Earth's atmosphere, but it is real! Like any other form of matter, air has definite physical properties. As you work through this activity, you will observe two of the properties of air—volume and pressure.
Strategy
You will demonstrate that air has volume (occupies space).
You will demonstrate that air exerts pressure.
Materials
water   bicycle pump   meterstick
beaker (500-ml)   air mattress
Procedure
1. Put 250 ml of water in the beaker.
2. Insert the hose of the bicycle pump so it is below the surface of the water.
3. To demonstrate that air occupies space, pump air into the water. Record your observations. Remove the pump hose.
4. To demonstrate that air exerts pressure, place the air mattress on the floor. Press the mattress flat to be sure it contains very little air. Feel the floor through the mattress.
5. Measure in centimeters the length, width, and thickness of the air mattress. Record your measurements in Table 1.
6. Inflate the mattress using the bicycle pump. Measure and record the dimensions of the mattress again.
7. Push down with your hand on one area of the inflated air mattress. Note how the dimensions of the area that you are pushing on change. How does the part of the mattress surrounding your hands change?

Data and Observations
Observations:
Air pumped into beaker:

Pushing down on mattress:

Table 1

Air mattress	Before pumping	After pumping
1. Length (cm)		
2. Width (cm)		
3. Thickness (cm)		

L2

Meeting Different Ability Levels

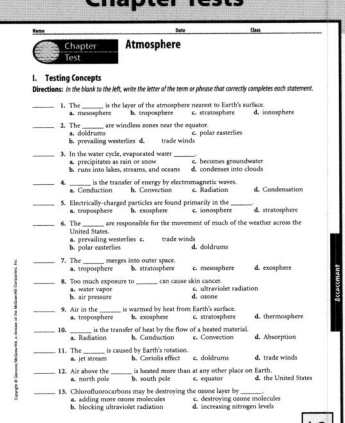

Assessment

Content Outline

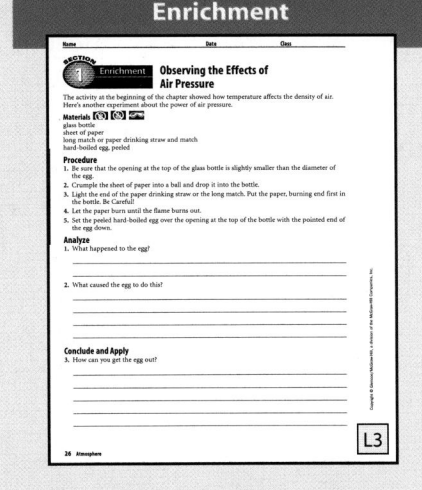

Reinforcement

Directed Reading

Chapter Tests

Enrichment

Spanish Directed Reading

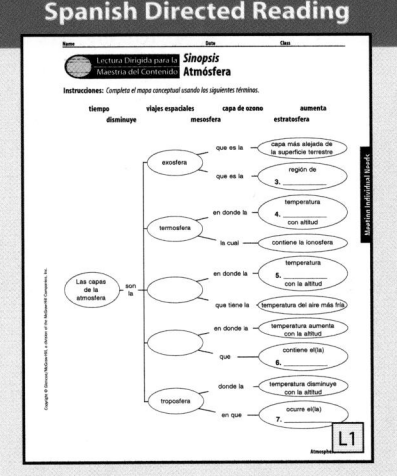

Test Practice Workbook

Chapter Review

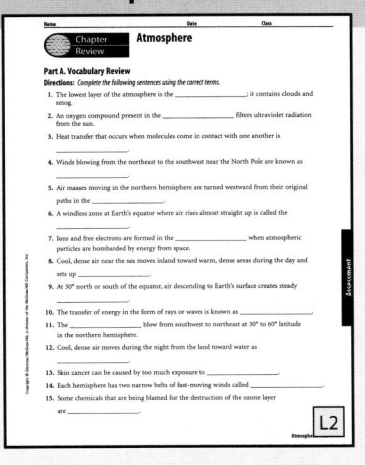

Science Content Background

SECTION 1

Earth's Atmosphere

Makeup of the Atmosphere

Earth's original atmosphere was probably composed mostly of methane and ammonia. This primitive atmosphere changed over geologic time as solar heating caused methane and ammonia to escape into space, and erupting volcanoes emitted gases such as water vapor, carbon dioxide, and nitrogen. As Earth continued to cool, the water vapor condensed and absorbed most of the carbon dioxide. Oxygen was probably formed from the dissociation of water molecules and by photosynthetic bacteria.

SECTION 2

Energy Transfer in the Atmosphere

Energy from the Sun

Transfer of energy by radiation does not involve matter. Convection currents distribute energy until equilibrium is reached. On Earth, however, equilibrium is never attained. The tropics always receive more radiant energy than the rest of Earth. Therefore, energy transfer is always occurring in the atmosphere.

About 90% of the water vapor in our atmosphere comes from the evaporation of ocean water. The greater the amount of solar energy, the greater the amount of water vapor that is evaporated. Solar energy also keeps water vapor molecules in constant motion. Our atmosphere is unique because its temperature range enables water to exist as liquid, gas (water vapor), and solid (ice).

SECTION 3

Air Movement

Forming Wind

The Sun heats the troposphere unevenly, activating a system of winds that move energy from one area of Earth to another. Whenever air pressure increases or decreases rapidly in relation to nearby areas, winds increase in velocity. Winds can be either horizontal or vertical in direction.

Student Misconception

Wind is caused by something in the sky, such as a cloud, that blows very hard.

Refer to the facing page for teaching strategies to address this misconception. Refer to page 448 for content related to this topic.

Global Winds

The doldrums are areas of permanent low pressure that occur in zones of maximum solar heating with a weak horizontal pressure gradient. The easterlies are relatively steady winds. Westerlies are more complex because their flows are impeded by mountains and valleys. Friction between land and air creates local eddies that slow wind movement.

E.R. Degginger/Photo Researchers, Inc.

SCIENCE *Online*

For additional content background on this topic, go to the Glencoe Science Web site at science.glencoe.com.

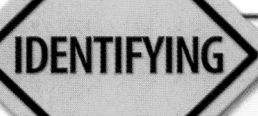 **Misconceptions**

Find Out What Students Think

Students may think that . . .

- **Wind is caused by something in the sky, such as a cloud, that blows very hard.**

Students often think that wind is caused by an external force. This has been reinforced by story books that picture winds as a cloud blowing air. Adding to this idea is the use of fans to move air. Taking these ideas together, some students have come to believe that some entity or device makes the wind. In fact, wind is caused by the uneven heating of Earth and its atmosphere.

Discussion
Bring a fan to class, plug it in, and turn it on.

- As students observe the fan, have them discuss what is causing the air to move. In this case electricity is running a motor that causes the fan blades to move. As the blades turn, they move the air.

Sunstar Photography/International Stock

- Organize the class into small groups. Ask each group to discuss how they think the outside air moves. Is there a "fan" that makes the wind blow? Have students write down their ideas, and then discuss them with the group. Have each group share their favorite ideas as well as the explanations they think are most correct.

Promote Understanding

Demonstration
Use this demonstration to develop the idea that air movements in nature are caused by uneven heating and cooling of Earth's surface.

- Use tape to attach a lunch bag, open end down, to each end of a meterstick. Balance the meterstick on the back of a chair.

- Carefully place an unshaded lamp under the open end of one of the bags. **CAUTION:** *Make sure the lightbulb does not touch the bag.* Have students observe what happens.

- Explain to students that what they have just observed happens in the atmosphere. The Sun (lightbulb) warms Earth's surface. This heat is transferred to the air directly above the surface. This warm air is less dense than the colder, surrounding air. It is pushed upward, which is what caused the bag to rise. As the warm air is pushed up, it is replaced with colder air. This trading places of warm and cold air in the atmosphere is what causes wind.

Assess
After completing the chapter, see *Identifying Misconceptions* in the Study Guide.

Atmosphere

Chapter Vocabulary

atmosphere
troposphere
ionosphere
ozone layer
ultraviolet radiation
chlorofluorocarbon
radiation
conduction
convection
hydrosphere
condensation
Coriolis effect
jet stream
sea breeze
land breeze

What do you think?

Science Journal The photo shows an eardrum. When there is a rapid change in air pressure outside the ear (as when a plane takes off), an air pressure difference develops between the middle and outer ear. The eardrum (between the middle and outer ear) bulges outward because the pressure in the middle ear is greater than the air pressure in the plane. Eventually, the pressures become equalized. As pressure changes, a person feels a popping sensation in the ear.

Atmosphere

Why is it difficult to breathe at high elevations? Why are some mountain peaks permanently covered with snow? These mountain climbers aren't supplementing oxygen just because the activity is physically demanding. At elevations like this, the amount of oxygen available in the air is so small that the climbers' bodily functions might not be supported. In this chapter, you'll learn about the composition and structure of the atmosphere. You also will learn how energy is transferred in the atmosphere. In addition, you'll examine the water cycle and major wind systems.

What do you think?

Science Journal Look at the picture below with a classmate. Discuss what this might be. Here's a hint: *It "pops" in thin air.* Write your answer or best guess in your Science Journal.

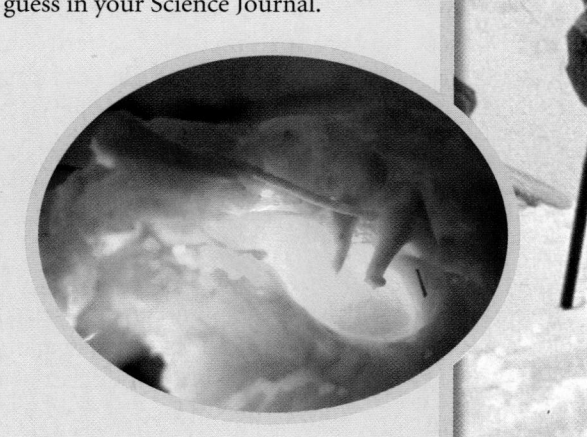

432

Theme Connection

Energy The Sun provides most of the energy that heats Earth's atmosphere, drives the water cycle, and (because of unequal heating) drives global wind systems.

EXPLORE ACTIVITY

The air around you is made of billions of molecules. These molecules are constantly moving in all directions and bouncing into every object in the room, including you. Air pressure is the result of the billions of collisions of molecules into these objects. Because you usually do not feel molecules in air hitting you, do the activity below to see the effect of air pressure.

Observe air pressure

1. Cut out a square of cardboard about 10 cm on a side from a cereal box.
2. Fill a glass to the brim with water.
3. Hold the cardboard firmly over the top of the glass covering the water and invert the glass.
4. Slowly remove your hand holding the cardboard in place and observe.

Observe

Write a paragraph in your Science Journal describing what happened to the cardboard when you inverted the glass and removed your hand. How does air pressure explain what happened?

Before You Read

FOLDABLES
Reading & Study Skills

Making a Sequence Study Fold Make the following Foldable to help you visualize the layers of Earth's atmosphere.

1. Stack three sheets of paper in front of you so the short sides are at the top.
2. Slide the top sheet up so that about four centimeters of the middle sheet show. Slide the middle sheet up so that about four centimeters of the bottom sheet show.
3. Fold the sheets top to bottom to form six tabs and staple along the topfold. Turn the Foldable so the staples are at the bottom.
4. Label each flap *Earth's Atmosphere, Troposphere, Stratosphere, Mesosphere, Thermosphere,* and *Exosphere,* as shown.
5. As you read the chapter, write information about each layer of Earth's atmosphere under the tabs.

> Exosphere
> Thermosphere
> Mesosphere
> Stratosphere
> Troposphere
> Earth's Atmosphere

433

EXPLORE ACTIVITY

Purpose Students will observe the force exerted by air pressure.

Preparation Collect cereal boxes and cut the sides from the boxes for students to use. Ask students to bring in cereal boxes from home to be certain you have enough.

Materials cereal box side, metric ruler, scissors, drinking glass, and water for each pair of students

Teaching Strategy Inspect the cardboard and glass of water of each pair before they turn the glass over. Be certain there is no gap between the water level and the cardboard. Have students turn their glasses upside down over a sink.

Observe

The cardboard will stick to the glass, trapping the water inside. Air pressure presses on the cardboard allowing it to adhere to the rim of the glass.

Assessment

Process Ask students to make a hypothesis about how their experiment would differ if they could conduct it in a vacuum. Without air to supply pressure on the cardboard, the cardboard square would fall and the water would spill out. Use **Performance Assessment in the Science Classroom,** p. 93

Before You Read

FOLDABLES
Reading & Study Skills

Dinah Zike Study Fold

Purpose Determine what students know about Earth's atmosphere before reading the chapter by providing a Foldable for recording and organizing notes on the layers of the atmosphere as they read.

For additional help, see Foldables Worksheet, p. 13 in **Chapter Resources Booklet,** or go to the Glencoe Science Web site at **science.glencoe.com.** See After You Read in the Study Guide at the end of this chapter.

Earth's Atmosphere

1 Motivate

Bellringer Transparency

Display the Section Focus Transparency for Section 1. Use the accompanying Transparency Activity Master. L2

ELL

Tie to Prior Knowledge

Ask students to name a major gas in Earth's atmosphere. Most students will name oxygen. Tell students oxygen is a major gas but not the most abundant gas in the air we breathe. In this section, they will learn what the most abundant gas is (nitrogen) and what other substances are in the atmosphere.

As You Read

What You'll Learn
- **Identify** the gases in Earth's atmosphere.
- **Describe** the structure of Earth's atmosphere.
- **Explain** what causes air pressure.

Vocabulary

atmosphere   ozone layer
troposphere   ultraviolet radiation
ionosphere   chlorofluorocarbon

Why It's Important
The atmosphere makes life on Earth possible.

Figure 1
Earth's atmosphere, as viewed from space, is a thin layer of gases. The atmosphere keeps Earth's temperature in a range that can support life.

Importance of the Atmosphere

Earth's **atmosphere,** shown in **Figure 1,** is a thin layer of air that forms a protective covering around the planet. If Earth had no atmosphere, days would be extremely hot and nights would be extremely cold. Earth's atmosphere maintains a balance between the amount of heat absorbed from the Sun and the amount of heat that escapes back into space. It also protects life-forms from some of the Sun's harmful rays.

Makeup of the Atmosphere

Earth's atmosphere is a mixture of gases, solids, and liquids that surround the planet. It extends from Earth's surface to outer space. The atmosphere is much different today from what it was when Earth was young.

Earth's early atmosphere, produced by erupting volcanoes, contained nitrogen and carbon dioxide, but little oxygen. Then, more than 2 billion years ago, Earth's early organisms released oxygen into the atmosphere as they made food with the aid of sunlight. These early organisms, however, were limited to layers of ocean water deep enough to be shielded from the Sun's harmful rays, yet close enough to the surface to receive sunlight. Eventually, a layer rich in ozone (O_3) that protects Earth from the Sun's harmful rays formed in the upper atmosphere. This protective layer allowed green plants eventually to flourish all over Earth, releasing even more oxygen. Today, a variety of life forms, including yours, depends on a certain amount of oxygen in Earth's atmosphere.

434   CHAPTER 15 Atmosphere

Section ✔Assessment Planner

PORTFOLIO
Extension, p. 437

PERFORMANCE ASSESSMENT
Problem-Solving Activity, p. 438
MiniLab, p. 439
Skill Builder Activities, p. 441
See page 458 for more options.

CONTENT ASSESSMENT
Section, p. 441
Challenge, p. 441
Chapter, pp. 458–459

Gases in the Atmosphere

Today's atmosphere is a mixture of the gases shown in **Figure 2**. Nitrogen is the most abundant gas, making up 78 percent of the atmosphere. Oxygen actually makes up only 21 percent of Earth's atmosphere. As much as four percent of the atmosphere is water vapor. Other gases that make up Earth's atmosphere include argon and carbon dioxide.

The composition of the atmosphere is changing in small but important ways. For example, car exhaust emits gases into the air. These pollutants mix with oxygen and other chemicals in the presence of sunlight and form a brown haze called smog. Humans burn fuel for energy. As fuel is burned, carbon dioxide is released as a by-product into Earth's atmosphere. Increasing energy use may increase the amount of carbon dioxide in the atmosphere.

Solids and Liquids in Earth's Atmosphere

In addition to gases, Earth's atmosphere contains small, solid particles such as dust, salt, and pollen. Dust particles get into the atmosphere when wind picks it up off the ground and carries it along. Salt is picked up from ocean spray. Plants give off pollen that becomes mixed throughout part of the atmosphere.

The atmosphere also contains small liquid droplets, other than water droplets in clouds. The atmosphere constantly moves these liquid droplets and solids from one region to another. For example, the atmosphere above you may contain liquid droplets and solids from an erupting volcano thousands of kilometers from your home, as illustrated in **Figure 3.**

Argon (0.93%)
Carbon dioxide (0.03%)
Neon
Helium
Methane
Krypton — Trace 1%
Xenon
Hydrogen
Ozone

21% Oxygen

78% Nitrogen

Figure 2
This graph shows the percentages of the gases, excluding water vapor, that make up Earth's atmosphere.

Figure 3
Solids and liquids can travel large distances in Earth's atmosphere, affecting regions far from their source.

A On June 12, 1991, Mount Pinatubo in the Philippines erupted, causing liquid droplets to form in Earth's atmosphere.

B Droplets of sulfuric acid from volcanoes can produce spectacular sunrises.

SECTION 1 Earth's Atmosphere **435**

② Teach

Makeup of the Atmosphere

Discussion

How does driving a car affect the composition of the atmosphere? Cars release exhaust that becomes pollution such as smog. Additional carbon dioxide is added to the air by the burning of fuel to produce energy.

Visual Learning

Figure 2 Ask students to compare the amount of nitrogen with the amount of oxygen in the atmosphere. There is more than three times more nitrogen than oxygen in the atmosphere.

Teacher FYI

The eruption of Mount Pinatubo released a large amount of sulfur dioxide into the atmosphere that became tiny droplets of sulfuric acid and particles of sulfate. These particles increased the amount of solar radiation reflected from Earth, which led to a decrease in mean global temperature that lasted from the time of the eruption in 1991 into 1992 and 1993.

✓ Active Reading

Reflective Journal Have students divide sheets of paper into several columns and record their thoughts under headings such as "What I did," "What I learned," "What questions do I have," "What surprises did I experience," and "Overall response." Have students write a Reflective Journal entry for the Explore activity.

Fun Fact

The thickness of the troposphere varies with latitude, being thickest over the equator. At other latitudes, it thickens in summer and thins in winter.

Discussion

Why do you think rain and clouds occur mostly in the troposphere? because most of the water vapor exists in that layer

Caption Answer

Figure 4 troposphere

IDENTIFYING
Misconceptions

Looking at **Figure 4,** students may infer that there is a thick concentration of ozone molecules. Inform students that the ozone layer in the stratosphere is a layer where there is a greater concentration of ozone molecules than elsewhere in the atmosphere.

SCIENCE Online

Research Visit the Glencoe Science Web site at **science.glencoe.com** for more information about layers of Earth's atmosphere. Communicate to your class what you learn.

Figure 4
Earth's atmosphere is divided into five layers. *Which layer of the atmosphere do you live in?*

436

Layers of the Atmosphere

What would happen if you left a glass of chocolate milk on the kitchen counter for a while? Eventually, you would see a lower layer with more chocolate separating from upper layers with less chocolate. Like a glass of chocolate milk, Earth's atmosphere has layers. There are five layers in Earth's atmosphere, each with its own properties, shown in **Figure 4.** The lower layers include the troposphere and stratosphere. The upper atmospheric layers are the mesosphere, thermosphere, and exosphere. The troposphere and stratosphere contain most of the air.

Lower Layers of the Atmosphere You study, eat, sleep, and play in the **troposphere,** which is the lowest of Earth's atmospheric layers. It contains 99 percent of the water vapor and 75 percent of the atmospheric gases. Rain, snow, and clouds occur in the troposphere, which extends up to about 10 km.

The stratosphere, the layer directly above the troposphere, extends from 10 km above Earth's surface to about 50 km. As **Figure 4** shows, a portion of the stratosphere contains higher levels of a gas called ozone. Each molecule of ozone is made up of three oxygen atoms bonded together. Later in this section you will learn how ozone protects Earth from the Sun's harmful rays.

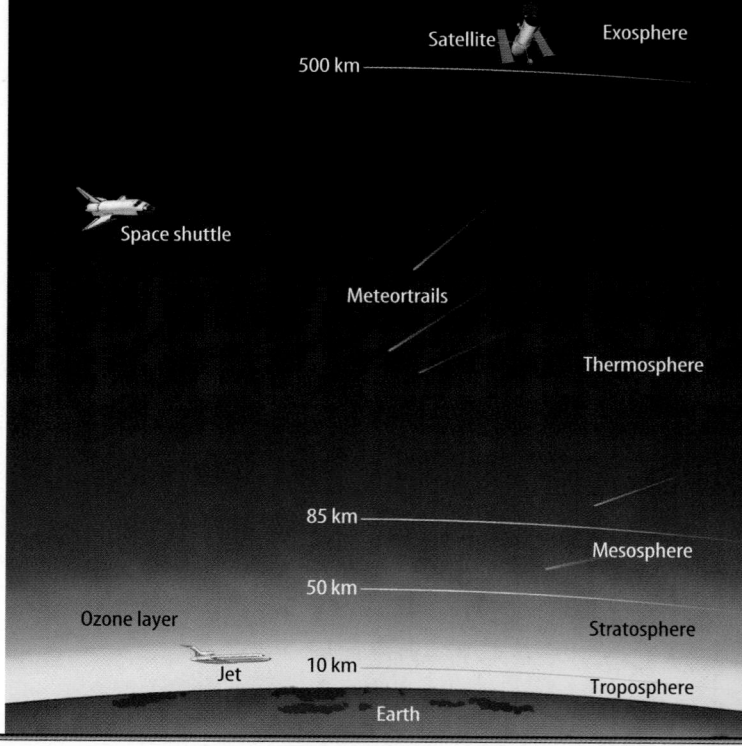

Inclusion Strategies

Gifted Scientists have been measuring the characteristics of Earth's atmosphere for centuries. Have students research the history of atmospheric study, finding out how people studied the upper atmosphere before there were airplanes and other sophisticated instruments. In the late 18th and early 19th centuries, some scientists took weather instruments up in hot air balloons to study the upper atmosphere.

SCIENCE Online

Internet Addresses

_____

_____

_____

Explore the Glencoe Science Web site at **science.glencoe.com** to find out more about topics in this section.

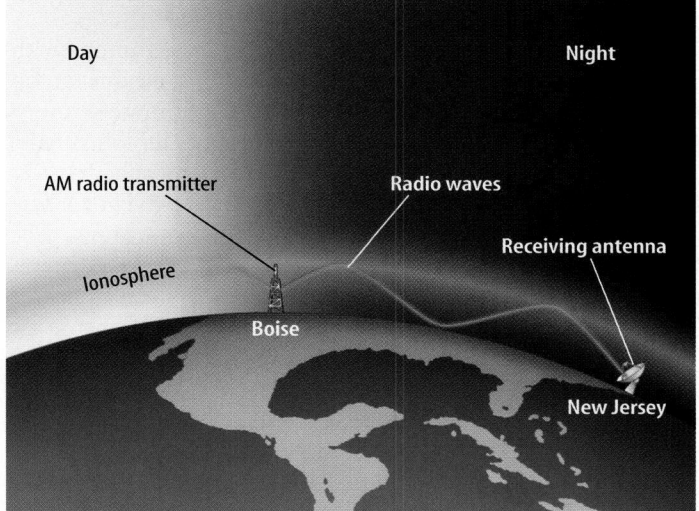

Day   Night

AM radio transmitter   Radio waves

Ionosphere

Boise

Receiving antenna

New Jersey

Figure 5
During the day, the ionosphere absorbs radio transmissions. This prevents you from hearing distant radio stations. At night, the ionosphere reflects radio waves. The reflected waves can travel to distant cities.

Upper Layers of the Atmosphere Beyond the stratosphere are the mesosphere, thermosphere, and exosphere. The mesosphere extends from the top of the stratosphere to about 85 km above Earth. If you've ever seen a shooting star, you have witnessed a meteor in the mesosphere.

The thermosphere is named for its high temperatures. This is the thickest atmospheric layer and is found between 85 km and 500 km above Earth's surface.

Within the thermosphere is a layer of electrically charged particles called the **ionosphere** (i AHN uh sfir). If you live in New Jersey and listen to the radio at night, you might pick up a station from Boise, Idaho. The ionosphere allows radio waves to travel across the country to another city, as shown in **Figure 5.** During the day, energy from the Sun interacts with the particles in the ionosphere, causing them to absorb AM radio frequencies. At night, without solar energy, AM radio transmissions reflect off the ionosphere, allowing radio transmissions to be received at greater distances.

The space shuttle in **Figure 6** orbits Earth in the exosphere. In contrast to the troposphere, the layer you live in, the exosphere has so few molecules that the wings of the shuttle are useless. In the exosphere, the spacecraft relies on bursts from small rocket thrusters to move around. Beyond the exosphere is outer space.

✓ **Reading Check** *How does the space shuttle maneuver in the exosphere?*

Figure 6
Wings help move aircraft in lower layers of the atmosphere. The space shuttle can't use its wings to maneuver in the exosphere because so few molecules are present.

Atmospheric Pressure

Text Question Answer
You feel the weight more.

Quick Demo
Display a barometer in the classroom. Demonstrate to students how to observe it each day to record pressure differences. Have students contrast pressure readings in fair and rainy weather. Readings will be lower during periods of precipitation. L2

LS **Visual-Spatial**

Extension
Have students write brief reports explaining how an aneroid barometer called an altimeter is used to determine an airplane's altitude. L3

LS **Linguistic**

✔ Reading Check

Answer in the troposphere

Figure 7
Air pressure decreases as you go higher in Earth's atmosphere.

Atmospheric Pressure

Imagine you're a football player running with the ball. Six players tackle you and pile one on top of the other. Who feels the weight more—you or the player on top? Like molecules anywhere else, atmospheric gases have mass. Atmospheric gases extend hundreds of kilometers above Earth's surface. As Earth's gravity pulls the gases toward its surface, the weight of these gases presses down on the air below. As a result, the molecules nearer Earth's surface are closer together. This dense air exerts more force than the less dense air near the top of the atmosphere. Force exerted on an area is known as pressure.

Like the pile of football players, air pressure is greater near Earth's surface and decreases higher in the atmosphere, as shown in **Figure 7**. People find it difficult to breathe in high mountains because fewer molecules of air exist there. Jets that fly in the stratosphere must maintain pressurized cabins so that people can breathe.

✔ Reading Check *Where is air pressure greater—in the exosphere or in the troposphere?*

Problem-Solving Activity

How does altitude affect air pressure?

Atmospheric gases extend hundreds of kilometers above Earth's surface, but the molecules that make up these gases are fewer and fewer in number as you go higher. This means that air pressure decreases with altitude.

Identifying the Problem
The graph on the right shows these changes in air pressure. Note that altitude on the graph goes up only to 50 km. The troposphere and the stratosphere are represented on the graph, but other layers of the atmosphere are not. By examining the graph, can you understand the relationship between altitude and pressure?

Air Pressure Changes with Altitude

[Graph: Pressure (millibars) on y-axis from 0 to 1000; Altitude (km) on x-axis from 0 to 50]

Solving the Problem
1. Estimate the air pressure at an altitude of 5 km.
2. Does air pressure change more quickly at higher altitudes or at lower altitudes?

LAB DEMONSTRATION

Purpose to observe the effects of temperature on air pressure

Materials aluminum soda can, water, hot plate, bucket of cold water, hot pad or tongs

Preparation Review the term *density* with students.

Procedure Pour a small amount of water into the can. Heat the can over the hot plate until the water boils. Using tongs or the hot pad, submerge the can upside down in the bucket of cold water.

Expected Outcome The can will collapse.

✓ Assessment

Why did the can collapse? When put into the cold water, air inside the can cooled. The molecules lost energy and exerted less outward pressure on the walls of the can. The greater air pressure outside the can caused it to collapse.

Temperature in Atmospheric Layers

The Sun is the source of most of the energy on Earth. Before it reaches Earth's surface, energy from the Sun must pass through the atmosphere. Because some layers contain gases that easily absorb the Sun's energy while other layers do not, the various layers have different temperatures, illustrated by the red line in **Figure 8.**

Molecules that make up air in the troposphere are warmed mostly by heat from Earth's surface. The Sun warms Earth's surface, which then warms the air above it. When you climb a mountain, the air at the top is usually cooler than the air at the bottom. Every kilometer you climb, the air temperature decreases about 6.5°C.

Molecules of ozone in the stratosphere absorb some of the Sun's energy. Energy absorbed by ozone molecules raises the temperature. Because more ozone molecules are in the upper portion of the stratosphere, the temperature in this layer rises with increasing altitude.

Like the troposphere, the temperature in the mesosphere decreases with altitude. The thermosphere and exosphere are the first layers to receive the Sun's rays. Few molecules are in these layers, but each molecule has a great deal of energy. Temperatures here are high.

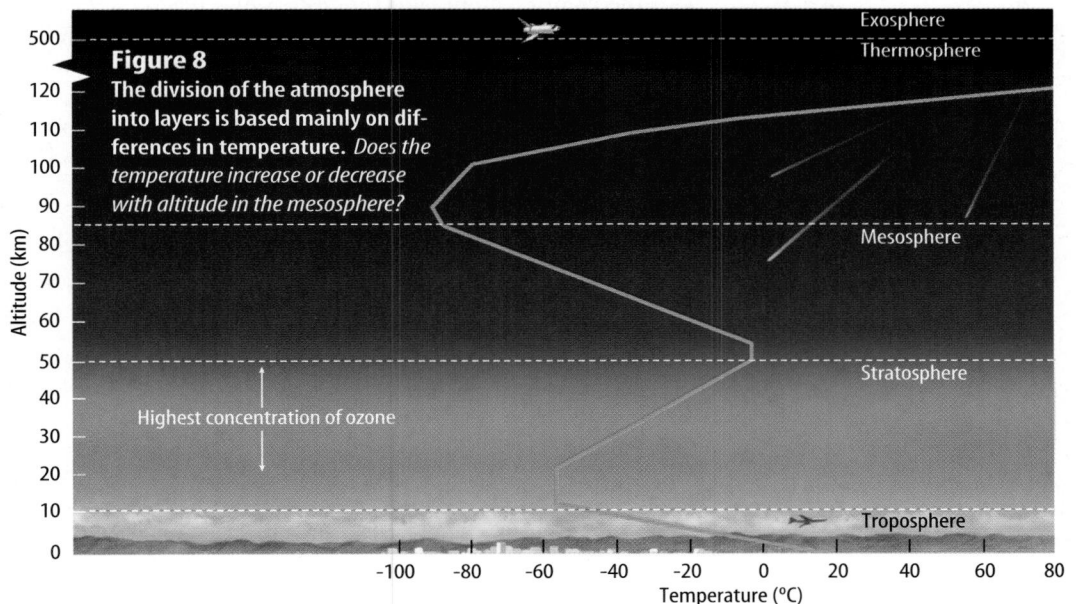

Temperature of the Atmosphere at Various Altitudes

Figure 8
The division of the atmosphere into layers is based mainly on differences in temperature. *Does the temperature increase or decrease with altitude in the mesosphere?*

Exosphere
Thermosphere
Mesosphere
Stratosphere
Highest concentration of ozone
 Troposphere

Altitude (km): 500, 120, 110, 100, 90, 80, 70, 60, 50, 40, 30, 20, 10, 0

Temperature (°C): -100, -80, -60, -40, -20, 0, 20, 40, 60, 80

SECTION 1 Earth's Atmosphere **439**

Temperature in Atmospheric Layers

Mini LAB

Purpose Students observe that air has mass. [L2] [ELL]
[IS] **Visual-Spatial**

Materials inflatable balls such as footballs or volleyballs; air pump with ball inflation needle; pressure gauge; pan balances

Teaching Strategy Review the use of the balance with students before starting the activity.

Safety Precautions Warn students to avoid overinflating the ball.

Troubleshooting Perform the activity in advance to make sure the ball is large enough to cause a detectable change in mass when air is added.

Analysis
1. The mass increases.
2. Air has mass.

✔ Assessment

Process Have students write a lab report describing the activity. The report should include a Purpose, Materials, Procedure, and Conclusion. Students with access to computers can write the report using a word processing program. Use **PASC,** p. 119

Caption Answer
Figure 8 Decrease

The Ozone Layer

Life Science
INTEGRATION

The level of oxygen might decrease.

Make a Model

Have students use small polystyrene balls and toothpicks to make models of ozone and chlorofluorocarbon molecules. Each polystyrene ball will represent an atom. The ozone molecule will have three oxygen atoms. The chlorofluorocarbon molecule will have one carbon atom, one fluorine atom, and three chlorine atoms. Have students use their models to demonstrate how a chlorine atom from the chlorofluorocarbon molecule destroys an ozone molecule as shown in **Figure 9**. L3 Ⓛ **Visual-Spatial**

Discussion

If chlorofluorocarbons harm the ozone layer, why were they produced at all? Students should infer that the harm CFCs do to the ozone layer wasn't known when they were originally produced. When the harm was discovered, it took time for bans to be put into place by some countries, and for companies that use CFCs to switch to ozone-friendly substitutes. Inform students that CFCs are still being used in some places and in some products.

Life Science
INTEGRATION

Algae are organisms that use sunlight to make their own food. This process releases oxygen to Earth's atmosphere. Some scientists suggest that growth is reduced when algae are exposed to ultraviolet radiation. Infer what might happen to the oxygen level of the atmosphere if increased ultraviolet radiation damages some algae.

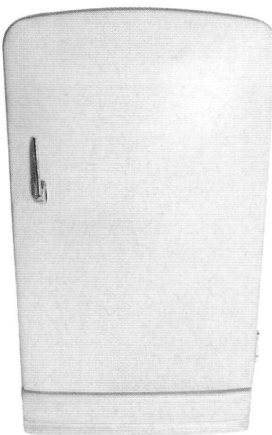

Figure 9
Chlorofluorocarbon (CFC) molecules were used in refrigerators and air conditioners. Each CFC molecule has three chlorine atoms. One atom of chlorine can destroy approximately 100,000 ozone molecules.

The Ozone Layer

Within the stratosphere, about 19 km to 48 km above your head, lies an atmospheric layer called the **ozone layer.** Ozone is made of oxygen. Although you cannot see the ozone layer, your life depends on it.

The oxygen you breathe has two atoms per molecule, but an ozone molecule is made up of three oxygen atoms bound together. The ozone layer contains a high concentration of ozone and shields you from the Sun's harmful energy. Ozone absorbs most of the ultraviolet radiation that enters the atmosphere. **Ultraviolet radiation** is one of the many types of energy that come to Earth from the Sun. Too much exposure to ultraviolet radiation can damage your skin and cause cancer.

CFCs Strong evidence exists that pollutants in the environment are destroying the ozone layer. Blame has fallen on **chlorofluorocarbons** (CFCs), a group of chemical compounds used in refrigerators, air conditioners, aerosol sprays, and foam packaging. If these products develop leaks or are manufactured improperly, chlorofluorocarbons can enter the atmosphere.

Recall that an ozone molecule is made of three oxygen atoms bonded together. Chlorofluorocarbon molecules, shown in **Figure 9,** destroy ozone. When a chlorine atom from a chlorofluorocarbon molecule comes near a molecule of ozone, the ozone molecule breaks apart. One of the oxygen atoms combines with the chlorine atom, and the rest form a regular, two-atom molecule. These compounds don't absorb ultraviolet radiation the way ozone can. In addition, the original chlorine atom can continue to break apart thousands of ozone molecules. The result is that more ultraviolet radiation reaches Earth's surface.

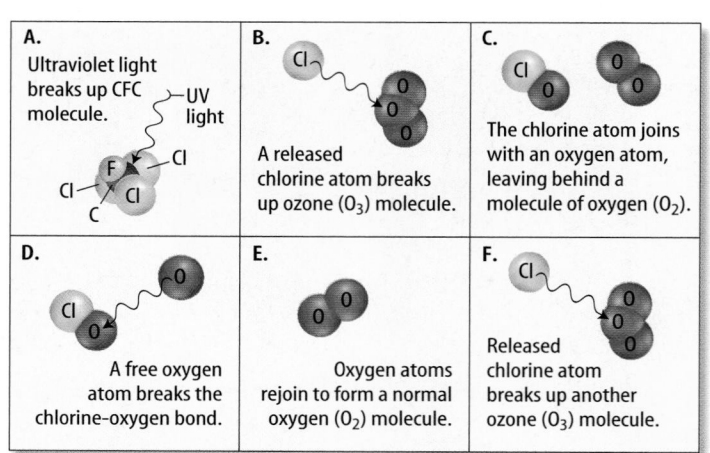

A.
Ultraviolet light breaks up CFC molecule.
UV light

B.
A released chlorine atom breaks up ozone (O_3) molecule.

C.
The chlorine atom joins with an oxygen atom, leaving behind a molecule of oxygen (O_2).

D.
A free oxygen atom breaks the chlorine-oxygen bond.

E.
Oxygen atoms rejoin to form a normal oxygen (O_2) molecule.

F.
Released chlorine atom breaks up another ozone (O_3) molecule.

Cultural Diversity

Changing Fashion Increased UV exposure because of thinning ozone has led to changing fashions in Australia. Baggy shorts, long sleeves, and hats are common on some beaches. Some cultures, such as those in northern Africa, traditionally wear clothing that protects them from the Sun. Have students research the traditional clothing of those cultures and explain why this style of clothing makes scientific sense.

Resource Manager

Chapter Resources Booklet
Lab Activity, pp. 9–10
Science Inquiry Labs, p. 25

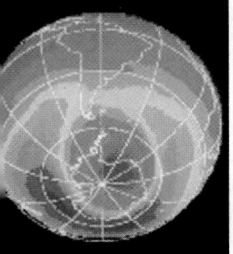
October 1980

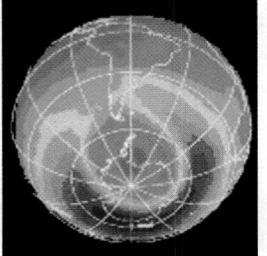
October 1988

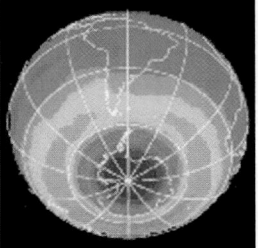
October 1990

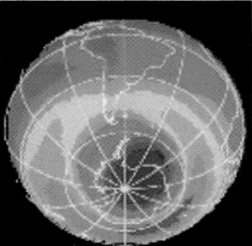
September 1999

Health
INTEGRATION

Ozone Holes Each year, more than 1.3 million Americans develop skin cancer, and more than 9,500 die from it. Exposure to ultraviolet radiation can cause skin cancer. If the ozone layer disappeared, skin cancer rates might increase. In 1986, scientists found areas in the stratosphere with extremely low amounts of ozone. One large hole was found over Antarctica. A smaller hole was discovered over the north pole. **Figure 10** shows how the ozone layer has thinned and developed holes.

In the mid 1990s, many governments banned the production and use of CFCs. Perhaps over time, the areas where the ozone layer is thinning will recover.

Figure 10
These images of Antarctica were produced using data from a NASA satellite. The purple color shows how the ozone hole has grown bigger over time.

Section ① Assessment

1. Earth's early atmosphere had little oxygen. How did oxygen come to make up 21 percent of Earth's present atmosphere?

2. List the layers of the atmosphere in order, beginning at Earth's surface.

3. While hiking in the mountains, you notice that it is harder to breathe as you climb higher. Explain why this is so.

4. What are some effects from a thinning ozone layer?

5. **Think Critically** During the day, the radio only receives AM stations from a city near you. At night, you are able to listen to an AM radio station from a distant city. Explain why this is possible.

Skill Builder Activities

6. **Interpreting Scientific Illustrations** Using **Figure 2,** determine the total percentage of nitrogen and oxygen in the atmosphere. What is the total percentage of argon and carbon dioxide? **For more help, refer to the** Science Skill Handbook.

7. **Communicating** The names of the atmospheric layers end with the suffix *-sphere,* a word that means "layer." Use a dictionary to find out what *tropo-, meso-, thermo-,* and *exo-* mean. In your Science Journal, write the meaning of these prefixes and explain if the layers are appropriately named. **For more help, refer to the** Science Skill Handbook.

Answers to Section Assessment

1. Early organisms released it into the air.
2. troposphere, stratosphere, mesosphere, thermosphere, exosphere
3. There are fewer molecules of oxygen per liter of air in the mountains.
4. Possible answers: Increased UV radiation reaches Earth, causing more cases of skin cancer; organisms such as algae could be damaged, resulting in the release of less oxygen into the atmosphere.
5. At night sunlight no longer interacts with particles in the ionosphere. This allows AM radio transmissions to be reflected back to Earth at greater distances.
6. 99 percent; 0.96 percent
7. The terms come from Greek and Latin. *Tropo-* means change, *strato-* comes from a word meaning to stretch out as in a layer, *meso-* means in the middle, *thermo-* means heat, and *exo-* means outside. Troposphere has some relevance, since temperature and pressure change with altitude and weather changes constantly. Stratosphere just means layer. Mesosphere and exosphere describe the positions of the layers. The thermosphere is named for its high temperature.

Activity

Purpose Students evaluate the effectiveness of various sunscreens. L2

IS Logical-Mathematical

Process Skills comparing and contrasting, observing, making and using tables, inferring, using numbers

Time Required about 45 minutes

Materials To get a large variety of sunscreens, ask students to bring in products from home.

Teaching Strategy In order to keep the time needed to one class period, have each student evaluate no more than three brands of sunscreen.

Answers to Questions

1. Sunscreen blocks harmful UV radiation from the Sun.
2. Answers will vary depending on SPF of brands chosen.
3. Sunscreens that cost the least per fluid ounce and provide adequate protection without misleading claims on the label should be considered the best buys.

✔Assessment

Process Have the class look at their results together to find the percentage of sunscreens evaluated that are considered good buys, as opposed to those that are overpriced or misleading in their claims. Use **Performance Assessment in the Science Classroom,** p. 115.

Activity

Evaluating Sunscreens

Without protection, sun exposure can damage your health. Sunscreens protect your skin from ultraviolet radiation. In this activity, you will draw inferences using the labels of different sunscreens.

What You'll Investigate
How effective are various brands of sunscreens?

Materials
variety of sunscreens of different brand names

Goals
- **Draw inferences** based on labels on sunscreen brands.
- **Compare** the effectiveness of different sunscreen brands for protection against the Sun.
- **Compare** the cost of several sunscreen brands.

Safety Precautions

Procedure

1. Make a data table in your Science Journal using the following terms: *brand name, SPF, misleading terms,* and *cost per fluid ounce.*

2. The Sun Protection Factor (SPF), tells you how long the sunscreen will protect you. For example, an SPF of 4 allows you to stay in the Sun four times longer than if you did not use sunscreen. Record the SPF of each sunscreen on your data table.

3. **Calculate** the cost per fluid ounce of each sunscreen brand.

4. Government guidelines say that terms like *sunblock* and *waterproof* are misleading because sunscreens cannot block the Sun, and they wash off in water. List the misleading terms in your data table for each brand.

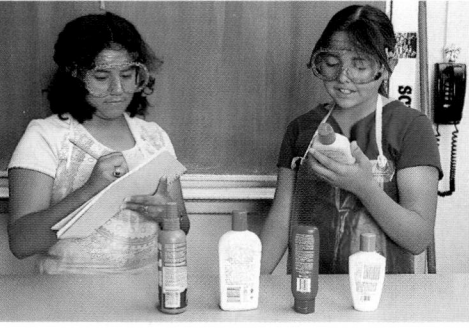

Sunsreen Assessment			
Brand Name			
SPF	Answers will vary.		
Misleading Terms			
Cost per Fluid Ounce			

Conclude and Apply

1. **Explain** why you need to use sunscreen.

2. A minimum of SPF 15 is considered adequate protection for a sunscreen. Sunscreens with an SPF greater than 30 are considered by government guidelines to be misleading because sunscreens will wash or wear off. Evaluate the SPF of each brand of sunscreen.

3. Considering the cost and effectiveness of all the sunscreen brands, discuss which brand you consider to be the best buy.

*C*ommunicating

Your Data

Create a poster on the proper use of sunscreens, and provide guidelines for selecting the safest product. **For more help, refer to the** Science Skill Handbook.

---

*C*ommunicating
Your Data

Direct students to choose one of the following subjects for the poster: (1) tips for the proper use of sunscreen; (2) what to look for when buying sunscreen; (3) why people should use sunscreen. P

Resource Manager

Chapter Resources Booklet
  Activity Worksheet, pp. 5, 6
  Reinforcement, p. 23
Reading and Writing Skill Activities, p. 27

Energy Transfer in the Atmosphere

Energy from the Sun

The Sun provides most of the energy on Earth. This energy drives winds and ocean currents and allows plants to grow and produce food, providing nutrition for many animals. When Earth receives energy from the Sun, three different things can happen to that energy, as shown in **Figure 11.** Some energy is reflected back into space by clouds, atmospheric particles, and Earth's surface. Some is absorbed by the atmosphere. The rest is absorbed by land and water on Earth's surface.

Heat

Heat is energy that flows from an object with a higher temperature to an object with a lower temperature. Energy from the Sun reaches Earth's surface and heats objects such as roads, rocks, and water. Heat then is transferred through the atmosphere in three ways—radiation, conduction, and convection, as shown in **Figure 12.**

As You Read

What **You'll Learn**
- **Describe** what happens to the energy Earth receives from the Sun.
- **Compare and contrast** radiation, conduction, and convection.
- **Explain** the water cycle.

Vocabulary

radiation	hydrosphere
conduction	condensation
convection	

Why **It's Important**
The Sun provides energy to Earth's atmosphere, allowing life to exist.

6% reflected by the atmosphere

25% reflected from clouds

4% reflected from Earth's surface

15% absorbed by the atmosphere

50% directly or indirectly absorbed by Earth's surface

Figure 11
The Sun is the source of energy for Earth's atmosphere. Thirty-five percent of incoming solar radiation is reflected back into space. *How much is absorbed by Earth's surface and atmosphere?*

443

---

1 Motivate

Bellringer Transparency

Display the Section Focus Transparency for Section 2. Use the accompanying Transparency Activity Master. L2
ELL

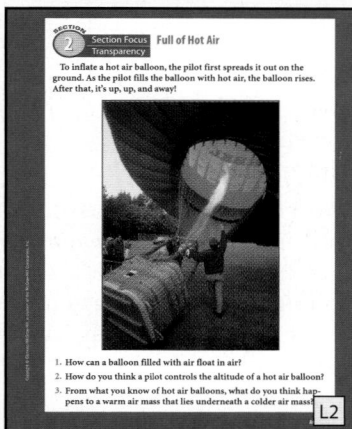

SECTION 2 | Section Focus Transparency | **Full of Hot Air**

To inflate a hot air balloon, the pilot first spreads it out on the ground. As the pilot fills the balloon with hot air, the balloon rises. After that, it's up, up and away!

1. How can a balloon filled with air float in air?
2. How do you think a pilot controls the altitude of a hot air balloon?
3. From what you know of hot air balloons, what do you think happens to a warm air mass that lies underneath a colder air mass?

L2

Tie to Prior Knowledge

Tell students that the air near the ground is heated mostly by Earth's surface, not directly by the Sun. Ask students to think of examples from their own experience that show Earth's surface absorbs the Sun's energy. Accept all reasonable answers, such as feeling hot road pavement or hot beach sand on a sunny day. Tell students that they will learn how the Sun heats the ground and the air in this section.

Caption Answer
Figure 11 65 percent

Section ✔*Assessment* Planner

PORTFOLIO
Science Journal, p. 445
PERFORMANCE ASSESSMENT
Try at Home MiniLAB, p. 445
Skill Builder Activities, p. 446
See page 458 for more options.

CONTENT ASSESSMENT
Section, p. 446
Challenge, p. 446
Chapter, pp. 458–459

Heat

Discussion

How can the Sun continue to heat the atmosphere at night? If the Sun has warmed the surface during the day, its heat can still warm the air in contact with the ground by conduction after sunset.

✔ Reading Check

Answer by radiation

Physics INTEGRATION

Water; it does not heat up as fast as land does.

Using Science Words

Word Meaning Have students look up the words *conduction*, *convection*, and *radiation* in the dictionary and write a sentence about how the meaning of each word reflects its root. The words come from the Latin roots *conducere* (to carry), *convehere* (to bring together), and *radius* (ray), respectively.

Use an Analogy

The behavior of air molecules in atmospheric convection currents is analogous to the principle used to control a hot air balloon. When air inside a hot air balloon is heated, the molecules spread apart and the air becomes less dense. The balloon then rises through the denser air around it. When air cools inside the balloon, the molecules cluster closer together, the air density increases, and the balloon descends.

Radiation warms the surface.

The air near Earth's surface is heated by conduction.

Cooler air pushes warm air upward, creating a convection current.

Figure 12
Heat is transferred within Earth's atmosphere by radiation, conduction, and convection.

Physics INTEGRATION

Specific heat is the amount of heat required to change the temperature of a substance one degree. Substances with high specific heat absorb a lot of heat for a small increase in temperature. Land heats up faster than water does. Infer whether soil or water has a higher specific heat value.

Radiation Sitting on the beach, you feel the Sun's warmth on your face. How can you feel the Sun's heat even though you aren't in direct contact with it? Energy from the Sun reaches Earth in the form of radiant energy, or radiation. **Radiation** is energy that is transferred in the form of rays or waves. Earth radiates some of the energy it absorbs from the Sun back toward space. Radiant energy from the Sun warms your face.

✔ Reading Check   *How does the Sun warm your skin?*

Conduction If you walk barefoot on a hot beach, your feet heat up because of conduction. **Conduction** is the transfer of energy that occurs when molecules bump into one another. Molecules are always in motion, but molecules in warmer objects move faster than molecules in cooler objects. When objects are in contact, energy is transferred from warmer objects to cooler objects.

Radiation from the Sun heated the beach sand, but direct contact with the sand warmed your feet. In a similar way, Earth's surface conducts energy directly to the atmosphere. As air moves over warm land or water, molecules in air are heated by direct contact.

Convection After the atmosphere is warmed by radiation or conduction, the heat is transferred by a third process called convection. **Convection** is the transfer of heat by the flow of material. Convection circulates heat throughout the atmosphere. How does this happen?

Teacher FYI
The Sun is the source of almost all energy on Earth. Some energy is generated by the radioactive decay of atoms contained in Earth's rocks and magma.

Resource Manager

Chapter Resources Booklet
Transparency Activities, pp. 41, 43–44
MiniLAB, p. 4
Enrichment, p. 27
Reinforcement, p. 24
Directed Reading, p. 16
Lab Activity, pp. 11–12

When air is warmed, the molecules in it move apart and the air becomes less dense. Air pressure decreases because fewer molecules are in the same space. In cold air, molecules move closer together. The air becomes more dense and air pressure increases. Cooler, denser air sinks while warmer, less dense air rises, forming a convection current. As **Figure 12** shows, radiation, conduction and convection together distribute the Sun's heat throughout Earth's atmosphere.

The Water Cycle

Hydrosphere is a term that describes all the water on Earth's surface. Water moves constantly between the atmosphere and the hydrosphere in the water cycle, shown in **Figure 13.**

If you watch a puddle in the Sun, you'll notice that over time the puddle gets smaller and smaller. Energy from the Sun causes the water in the puddle to change from a liquid to a gas by a process called evaporation. Water that evaporates from lakes, streams, and oceans enters Earth's atmosphere.

If water vapor in the atmosphere cools enough, it changes back into a liquid. This process of water vapor changing to a liquid is called **condensation.**

Clouds form when condensation occurs high in the atmosphere. Clouds are made up of tiny water droplets that can collide to form larger drops. As the drops grow, they fall to Earth as precipitation, which completes the cycle by returning water to the hydrosphere.

TRY AT HOME
Mini LAB

Modeling Heat Transfer

Procedure
1. Cover the outside of an empty **soup can** with **black construction paper.**
2. Fill the can with **cold water** and feel it with your fingers.
3. Cover the top of the can with black paper.
4. Place the can in the Sun for 1 h. Then pour the water over your fingers.

Analysis
1. Does the water in the can feel warmer or cooler after placing the can in the Sun?
2. What types of heat transfer did you model?

Figure 13
In the water cycle, water moves from Earth to the atmosphere and back to Earth again.

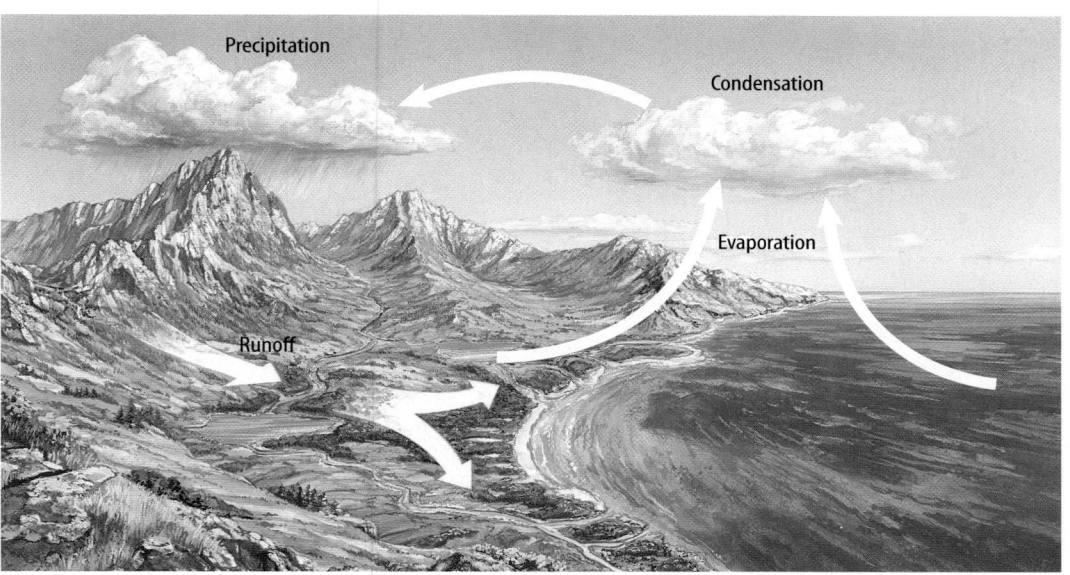

Precipitation

Condensation

Evaporation

Runoff

The Water Cycle

IDENTIFYING
Misconceptions

Some students may think that new water forms constantly. Explain that the water in the hydrosphere is continuously cycled between liquid water, water vapor, and ice.

TRY AT HOME
Mini LAB

Purpose Students model the transfer of heat.

Materials empty soup can, black construction paper, cold water

Teaching Strategy If the weather is cloudy, place the covered can under an incandescent light bulb.

Answers to Analysis
1. The water in the can felt warmer after placing it in the Sun.
2. The types of heat transfer modeled were radiation and conduction.

Science Journal

Water Cycle Have students write a poem that describes the water cycle. They should include all parts of the cycle in their poems. Challenge some students to write in Haiku, a Japanese poetic form consisting of 17 syllables arranged in three lines of 5, 7, and 5 syllables each. Have volunteers share their poems with the class. [L2] [LS] **Auditory-Musical** [P]

Assessment

Oral Ask students to use observations of their rain-making model to explain how rain is formed in clouds. When evaporated water hits a layer of cold air, the vapor condenses into water droplets, which fall as rain. Use **PASC,** p. 93.

Earth's Atmosphere Is Unique

Fun Fact

The temperature on Venus is hot enough to melt lead, about 470°C. Surface temperatures on Mars range from 35°C to −170°C.

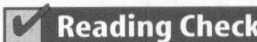

Reading Check

Answer Earth's atmosphere

3 Assess

Reteach

Have students draw an events cycle concept map that describes the steps in the water cycle. L1 **LS Visual-Spatial**

Challenge

Explain that worldwide, about 500,000 km^3 of water evaporates each year. About 110,000 km^3 of this falls as precipitation on land. **What probably happens to the rest of the water?** It falls into bodies of water, such as the ocean. **What happens to the water that falls on land?** Possible answers: Some is absorbed by plants, some seeps into soil, some becomes runoff that eventually flows to the ocean or evaporates into the atmosphere.

Assessment

Process Predict what would happen to the water cycle if Earth were covered by dense clouds that blocked the Sun's radiation. The cycle would not work; the Sun's energy is needed to drive the water cycle. Use **Performance Assessment in the Science Classroom,** p. 89.

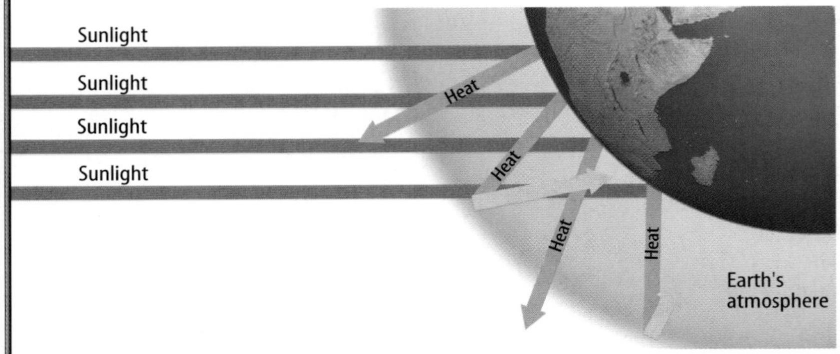

Sunlight
Sunlight
Sunlight
Sunlight
Heat
Heat
Heat
Heat
Earth's atmosphere

Figure 14
Earth's atmosphere creates a delicate balance between energy received and energy lost.

Earth's Atmosphere is Unique

On Earth, radiation from the Sun can be reflected into space, absorbed by the atmosphere, or absorbed by the surface and hydrosphere. Once it is absorbed, heat can be transferred by radiation, conduction, or convection. Earth's atmosphere, shown in **Figure 14,** helps control how much of the Sun's radiation is absorbed or lost.

Reading Check *What helps control how much of the Sun's radiation is absorbed on Earth?*

Why doesn't life exist on Mars or Venus? Mars is a cold, lifeless world because its atmosphere is too thin to support life or to hold much of the Sun's heat. Temperatuers on the surface of Mars range from 35° C to −170°C. On the other hand, Venus's atmosphere is so dense that almost no heat coming from the Sun can escape. The temperature on the surface of Venus is 470°C. Living things would burn instantly if they were placed on Venus's surface. Life on Earth exists because the atmosphere holds just the right amount of the Sun's energy.

Section 2 Assessment

1. How does the Sun transfer energy to Earth?
2. How is Earth's atmosphere different from the atmosphere on Mars?
3. How is heat transferred from the stove to the water when you boil a pot of water?
4. Briefly describe the steps included in the water cycle.
5. **Think Critically** What would happen to the temperature of Earth's surface if the Sun's heat were not distributed throughout the atmosphere?

Skill Builder Activities

6. **Concept Mapping** Make a concept map that explains what happens to radiant energy that reaches Earth. **For more help, refer to the Science Skill Handbook.**
7. **Solving One-Step Equations** Earth is about 150 million km from the Sun. The radiation coming from the Sun travels at 300,000 km/s. How long does it take for radiation from the Sun to reach Earth? **For more help, refer to the Math Skill Handbook.**

Answers to Section Assessment

1. radiation
2. Earth's atmosphere is denser, so it holds in more of the Sun's heat.
3. Conduction from the burner to the pot and from the pot to the water
4. Water evaporates from Earth's surface, condenses into clouds, and falls back to Earth as precipitation.
5. It would be much hotter right at the surface when the Sun was shining, and much colder at night when it was not. The atmosphere itself would also be much colder, even close to the surface.
6. Concept maps should summarize the information provided in **Figure 11.**
7. 150,000,000 km/300,000 km/s = 500 s or 8.3 minutes

Forming Wind

Uneven heating of Earth's surface by the Sun causes some areas to be warmer than others. Recall from Section 2 that warmer air expands, becoming less dense than colder air. This causes air pressure to be generally lower where air is heated. Wind is the movement of air from an area of higher pressure to an area of lower pressure.

Heated Air Areas of Earth receive different amounts of radiation from the Sun because Earth is curved. **Figure 15** illustrates why the equator receives more radiation than areas to the north or south. The heated air at the equator is less dense, so it is displaced by denser, colder air, creating convection currents.

This cold, denser air comes from the poles, which receive less radiation from the Sun, making air at the poles much cooler. The resulting dense, high-pressure air sinks and moves along Earth's surface. However, dense air sinking as less-dense air rises does not explain everything about wind.

As You Read

What You'll Learn
- **Explain** why different latitudes on Earth receive different amounts of solar energy.
- **Describe** the Coriolis effect.
- **Locate** doldrums, trade winds, prevailing westerlies, polar easterlies, and jet streams.

Vocabulary

Coriolis effect	sea breeze
jet stream	land breeze

Why It's Important
Wind systems determine major weather patterns on Earth.

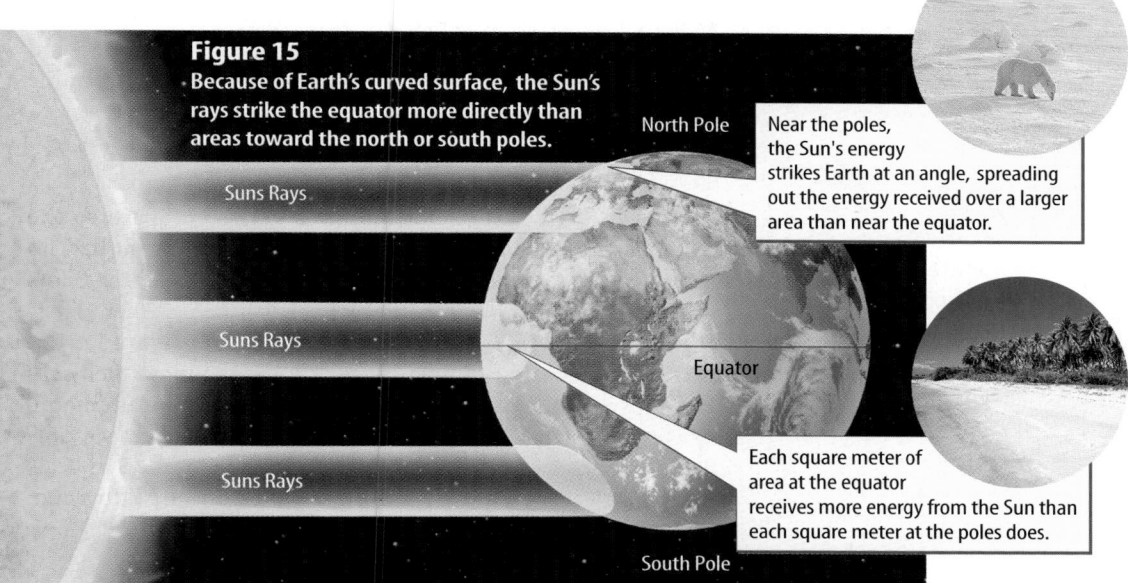

Figure 15
Because of Earth's curved surface, the Sun's rays strike the equator more directly than areas toward the north or south poles.

Suns Rays

Suns Rays

Suns Rays

North Pole

Near the poles, the Sun's energy strikes Earth at an angle, spreading out the energy received over a larger area than near the equator.

Equator

Each square meter of area at the equator receives more energy from the Sun than each square meter at the poles does.

South Pole

---

1 Motivate

Bellringer Transparency

Display the Section Focus Transparency for Section 3. Use the accompanying Transparency Activity Master. L2
ELL

Section Focus Transparency — The Growth of a Mountain

In 1999, the National Geographic Society sponsored an expedition to determine the height of Mount Everest using sophisticated satellite equipment. The researchers found the elevation to be 8,850 m (29,035 feet), which is two meters higher than the elevation of 8,848 m (29,028 feet) accepted since 1954.

1. What causes the plume coming off the summit of Mount Everest?
2. How do winds affect air travel?
3. Why does wind make you feel colder?

L2

Tie to Prior Knowledge

Ask for a show of hands for students who have experienced a windy day. Now ask students to speculate on why wind forms. List their responses on the board. Tell students they will learn the answer in this section. Return to the list later to check the accuracy of the responses.

Section ✔ Assessment Planner

PORTFOLIO
Extension, p. 449
Assessment, p. 451
PERFORMANCE ASSESSMENT
Skill Builder Activities, p. 451
See page 458 for more options.

CONTENT ASSESSMENT
Section, p. 451
Challenge, p. 451
Chapter, pp. 458–459

Resource Manager

Chapter Resources Booklet
Transparency Activity, p. 42
Enrichment, p. 28

Home and Community Involvement, p. 23

Forming Wind

Quick Demo

Use this activity to introduce the Coriolis effect. Tape a sheet of white paper to a phonograph turntable. On top of the paper, tape a sheet of carbon paper, carbon side down. Turn on the phonograph. While the turntable is rotating, roll a steel ball bearing straight across the carbon paper. Remove the carbon paper and have students observe the mark on the white paper. Have them compare it to what they observed. Although the ball bearing looks as though it rolls in a straight line, the spinning movement of the turntable actually deflects it. L2 ELL
IS **Visual-Spatial**

Global Winds

Use Science Words

Word Meaning Have students explain why the term *doldrums* is a good description of the air near the equator. Doldrums are a state of inactivity, stagnation, or slump. Air in the doldrums seems motionless.
L2 IS **Linguistic**

✔ Reading Check

Answer a windless, rainy zone near the equator

Figure 16
The Coriolis effect causes moving air to turn to the right in the northern hemisphere and to the left in the southern hemisphere.

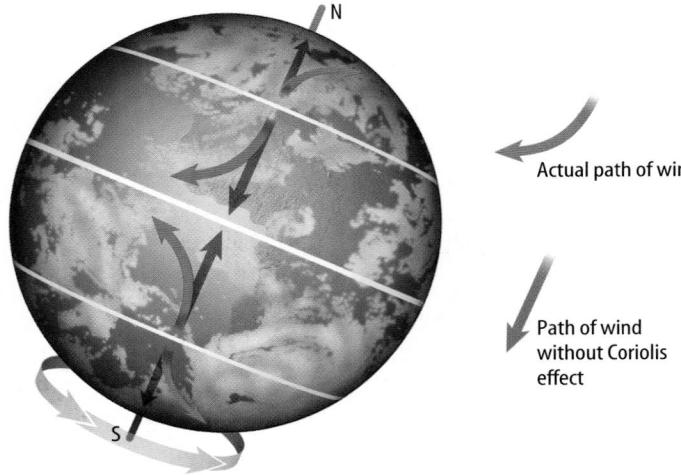

N

Actual path of wind

Path of wind without Coriolis effect

S

The Coriolis Effect What would happen if you threw a ball to someone sitting directly across from you on a moving merry-go-round? Would the ball go to your friend? By the time the ball got to the opposite side, your friend would have moved and the ball would appear to have curved.

Like the merry-go-round, the rotation of Earth causes moving air and water to appear to turn to the right north of the equator and to the left south of the equator. This is called the **Coriolis** (kohr ee OH lus) **effect,** and is illustrated in **Figure 16.** The flow of air caused by differences in the amount of solar radiation received on Earth's surface and by the Coriolis effect creates distinct wind patterns on Earth's surface. These wind systems not only influence the weather, they also determine when and where ships and planes travel most efficiently.

Global Winds

How did Christopher Columbus get from Spain to the Americas? The *Nina,* the *Pinta,* and the *Santa Maria* had no source of power other than the wind in their sails. Early sailors discovered that the wind patterns on Earth helped them navigate the oceans. These wind systems are shown in **Figure 17.**

Sometimes sailors found little or no wind to move their sailing ships near the equator. It also rained nearly every afternoon. This windless, rainy zone near the equator is called the doldrums. Look again at **Figure 17.** Near the equator, the Sun heats the air and causes it to rise, creating low pressure and little wind. The rising air then cools, causing rain.

✔ **Reading Check**   *What are the doldrums?*

SCIENCE *Online*

Data Update Visit the Glencoe Science Web site at **science.glencoe.com** to collect data on global winds. Communicate to your class what you've learned.

SCIENCE *Online*

Internet Addresses

_____

_____

_____

Explore the Glencoe Science Web site at **science.glencoe.com** to find out more about topics in this section.

Visual Learning

Figure 16 Have students trace the path of the curving winds. **How does the movement of the westerly trade winds affect northern Europe?** They bring warm, moist air from equatorial areas.

Figure 17

The Sun's uneven heating of Earth's surface forms giant loops, or cells, of moving air. The Coriolis effect deflects the surface winds to the west or east, setting up belts of prevailing winds that distribute heat and moisture around the globe.

A WESTERLIES Near 30° north and south latitude, Earth's rotation deflects air from west to east as air moves toward the polar regions. In the United States, the westerlies move weather systems, such as this one along the Oklahoma-Texas border, from west to east.

B DOLDRUMS Along the equator, heating causes air to expand, creating a zone of low pressure. Cloudy, rainy weather, as shown here, develops almost every afternoon.

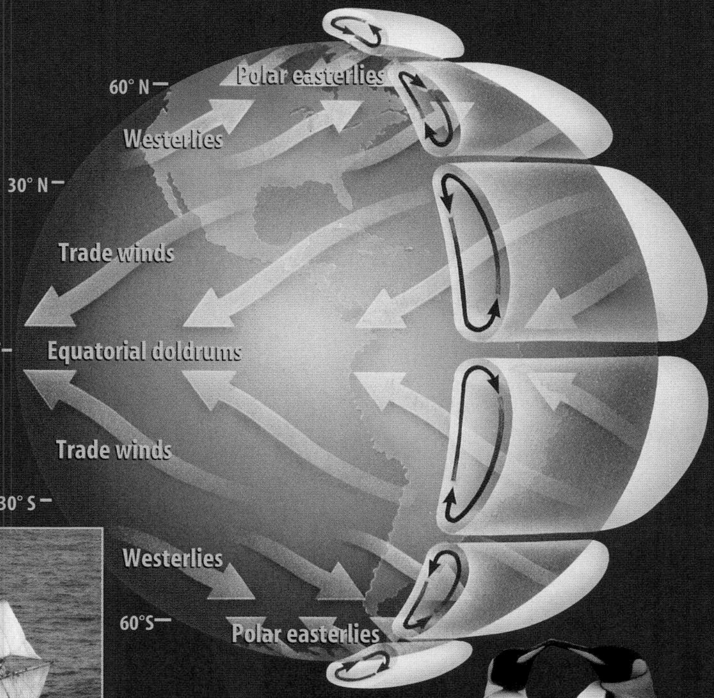

C TRADE WINDS Air warmed near the equator travels toward the Poles, but gradually cools and sinks. As the air flows back toward the low pressure of the doldrums, the Coriolis effect deflects the surface wind to the west. Early sailors, in ships like the one above, relied on these winds to navigate global trade routes.

D POLAR EASTERLIES In the polar regions, cold, dense air sinks and moves away from the Poles. Earth's rotation deflects this wind from east to west.

60° N — Polar easterlies
Westerlies
30° N —
Trade winds
0° — Equatorial doldrums
Trade winds
30° S —
Westerlies
60° S — Polar easterlies

Resource Manager

Chapter Resources Booklet
Directed Reading for Content Mastery, pp. 17, 18
Activity Worksheet, pp. 7, 8
Science Inquiry Labs, p. 41

Curriculum Connection

History The trade winds were used by ships to sail from Europe to the Americas. Have students draw maps showing the routes that early explorers took to cross the oceans. Then have them compare these routes with the wind systems shown in **Figure 16.** L2 ELL IS **Visual-Spatial** P

Visualizing Global Winds

Have students examine the pictures and read the captions. Then ask the following questions.

Why did sailors in past centuries sail kilometers away from a direct route to reach the trade winds? The strong winds with a regular path helped them sail faster.

Suppose Earth did not rotate. How would this affect the movement of global winds? Global winds would move in straight paths from areas of high pressure to areas of low pressure.

Activity

Have pairs of students draw a dot in the center of a piece of paper and label it *North Pole.* Have one student slowly turn the paper counterclockwise (the direction Earth rotates when viewed from above the North Pole) while the other student tries to draw a straight line away from the dot southward. Then have the other student start at the bottom edge of the paper and try to draw a straight line toward the dot as his or her partner turns the paper. Ask students to describe what happened in both cases. Relate this to how Earth's rotation deflects global winds.

Extension

Have students research the advantages of combining wind power and diesel power on fishing boats, cargo vessels, and oil tankers. Ask students to prepare posters illustrating one type of sail-assisted vessel and explaining how it operates. L2
IS **Visual-Spatial** P

Global Winds, continued

Local Wind Systems

Activity

Have students determine the wind direction near the school by using handmade wind vanes. Have groups of students submit designs, then make the wind vanes from easily-obtained materials. L1 ELL IS **Naturalist**

Extension

Have students research and describe other local winds, such as mountain breezes, foehn or chinook winds, and katabatic winds. L2 IS **Naturalist**

Surface Winds Between the equator and 30° latitude, air descending to Earth's surface creates steady winds. These are called trade winds because early sailors used their dependability to establish trade routes.

Between 30° and 60° latitude, winds called the prevailing westerlies blow in the opposite direction from the trade winds. Prevailing westerlies are responsible for much of the movement of weather across North America.

Polar easterlies are found near the poles. Near the north pole, easterlies blow from northeast to southwest. Near the south pole, polar easterlies blow from the southeast to the northwest.

Winds in the Upper Troposphere Narrow belts of strong winds, called **jet streams,** blow near the top of the troposphere. The polar jet stream forms at the boundary of cold, dry polar air to the north and warm, moist tropical air to the south, as shown in **Figure 18.** The jet stream moves faster in the winter because the difference between cold air and warm air is greater. The jet stream helps move storms across the country.

Jet pilots take advantage of the jet streams. When flying eastward, planes save time and fuel. Going west, planes fly at different altitudes to avoid the jet streams.

Local Wind Systems

Global wind systems determine the major weather patterns for the entire planet. Smaller wind systems affect local weather. If you live near a large body of water, you're familiar with two such wind systems—sea breezes and land breezes.

Figure 18
A strong current of air, called the jet stream, forms between cold, polar air and warm, tropical air.

A Flying from Boston to Seattle may take 1.5 h longer than flying from Seattle to Boston.

B The polar jet stream in North America usually is found between 10 km and 15 km above Earth's surface.

Cold air

Polar jet stream

Warm air

450   CHAPTER 15 Atmosphere

A

Warm air

Cool air

Sea breeze

B

Warm air is lifted

Cool air

Sea Breezes Convection currents over areas where the land meets the sea can cause wind. A **sea breeze,** shown in **Figure 19,** is created during the day because solar radiation warms the land more than the water. Air over the land is heated by conduction. This heated air is less dense and has lower pressure. Cooler, denser air over the water has higher pressure and flows toward the warmer, less dense air. A convection current results, and wind blows from the sea toward the land.

✔ **Reading Check** *How does a sea breeze form?*

Land Breezes At night, land cools much more rapidly than ocean water. Air over the land becomes cooler than air over the ocean. Cooler, denser air above the land moves over the water, as the warm air over the water rises. Movement of air toward the water from the land is called a **land breeze.**

Figure 19
These daily winds occur because land heats up and cools off faster than water does. **A** During the day, cool air from the water moves over the land, creating a sea breeze. **B** At night, cool air over the land moves toward the warmer air over the water, creating a land breeze.

Section 3 Assessment

1. Why do some parts of Earth's surface, such as the equator, receive more of the Sun's heat than other regions?

2. How does the Coriolis effect influence wind circulation on Earth?

3. Why does little wind and lots of afternoon rain occur in the doldrums?

4. Which wind system helped early sailors navigate Earth's oceans?

5. **Think Critically** How does the jet stream help move storms across North America?

Skill Builder Activities

6. **Comparing and Contrasting** Compare and contrast sea breezes and land breezes. **For more help, refer to the** Science Skill Handbook.

7. **Using Graphics Software** Use graphics software and **Figure 17** to draw the wind systems on Earth. Make separate graphics of major wind circulation cells shown by black arrows. On another graphic, show major surface winds. Print your graphics and share them with your class. **For more help, refer to the** Technology Skill Handbook.

Answers to Section Assessment

1. Earth's curved surface causes solar energy to strike Earth at different angles. The more direct the angle, the greater the energy received.

2. Air masses in the northern hemisphere are deflected to the right, while those in the southern hemisphere are deflected to the left.

3. As air at the equator is warmed it is lifted and cooled. This causes clouds and precipitation most afternoons.

4. trade winds

5. Storm systems are steered by the current of air in the polar jet stream.

6. Both occur near bodies of water. Sea breezes blow from the sea toward the land during the day when air over land is warmer than air over water.

Land breezes blow from the land toward the sea at night when conditions reverse.

7. Graphics should show three cells in each hemisphere where warm air rises and cooler air sinks. Major winds would be polar easterlies, westerlies, and trade winds. There should be two major jet streams in each hemisphere.

ACTIVITY
BENCH TESTED

Recognize the Problem

Purpose
Students observe how water and soil differ in their abilities to absorb and release heat. L2 ELL COOP LEARN Ⓝ **Visual-Spatial**

Process Skills
communicating, relating cause and effect, forming a hypothesis, using numbers, designing an experiment to test a hypothesis, identifying and manipulating variables, comparing and contrasting, interpreting data

Time Required
30 minutes to make and check the plan, 40 minutes to do the experiment, 30 minutes to analyze data and draw conclusions

Safety Precautions
Caution students to avoid touching the overhead light and to keep the electric cord away from the water.

Form a Hypothesis

Possible Hypothesis
Soil absorbs and releases heat faster than water.

Test Your Hypothesis

Possible Procedures
Tape one thermometer inside each box with the bulb 2 cm from the bottom. Tape another thermometer 8 cm from the bottom. Fill one box with 5 cm of water and the other with 5 cm of soil. Attach the light to the ring stand and suspend it above the boxes. Record the temperature of all thermometers

ACTIVITY *Design Your Own Experiment*

The Heat Is On

Sometimes, a plunge in a pool or lake on a hot summer day feels cool and refreshing. Why does the beach sand get so hot when the water remains cool? A few hours later, the water feels warmer than the land does. In this activity, you'll explore how water and land absorb heat.

Recognize the Problem
How do soil and water compare in their abilities to absorb and emit heat?

Form a Hypothesis
Form a hypothesis to explain how soil and water compare in their abilities to absorb and release heat. Write another hypothesis about how air temperatures above soil and above water differ during the day and night.

452

Safety Precautions
WARNING: *Be careful when handling the hot overhead light. Do not let the light or its cord make contact with water.*

Possible Materials
ring stand	clear plastic boxes (2)
soil	overhead light
metric ruler	with reflector
water	thermometers (4)
masking tape	*computer
colored pencils (4)	temperature probes
	*Alternate Materials

Goals
■ **Design** an experiment to compare the rates of heat absorption and release for soil and water.
■ **Observe** how these differing rates of heat absorption and release affect the air above soil and above water.

before turning on the light. After the light is turned on, record the temperature every minute for 14 minutes. When the light is turned off, record the temperature for an additional 14 minutes.

Sample Data Table:

Time (minutes)	Light on (temperature °C)			
	thermometer			
	in soil	above soil	in water	above water
0	25	25	24	25
2	27	27	25	27

Time (minutes)	Light off (temperature °C)			
0	34	33	32	33
2	31	30	32	30

Test Your Hypothesis

Plan

1. As a group, agree upon and write your hypothesis.
2. **List** the steps that you need to take to test your hypothesis. Include in your plan how you will use your equipment to compare the rates of heat absorption and release for water and soil.
3. **Design** a data table in your Science Journal for both parts of your experiment—when the light is on and energy can be absorbed and when the light is off and energy is released to the environment.

Do

1. Make sure your teacher approves your plan and your data table before you start.
2. Carry out the experiment as planned.
3. During the experiment, record your observations and complete the data table in your Science Journal.
4. Include in your measurements the temperatures of the soil and the water. Also compare the rate of release of heat for water and soil. Include the temperatures of the air immediately above both of the substances. Allow 15 min for each test.

Analyze Your Data

1. Use your colored pencils and the information in your data tables to make line graphs. Show the rate of temperature increase for soil and water. Graph the rate of temperature decrease for soil and water after you turn the light off.

2. **Analyze** your graphs. When the light was on, which heated up faster—the soil or the water?

3. **Compare** how fast the air temperatures over the water changed with how fast the temperatures over the land changed after the light was turned off.

Draw Conclusions

1. Was your hypothesis supported or not? Explain.
2. **Infer** from your graphs which lost heat faster—the water or the soil.
3. **Compare** the temperatures of the air above the water and above the soil 15 minutes after the light was turned off. How do water and soil compare in their abilities to absorb and release heat?

*C*ommunicating Your Data

Make a poster showing the steps you followed for your experiment. Include the graph of your data. **Display** your poster in the classroom. **For more help, refer to the Science Skill Handbook.**

ACTIVITY 453

Teaching Strategy

Have students graph data for each thermometer with a different colored pencil.

Expected Outcome

When the light is on, the soil and the air above it heats up faster than the water. When the light is turned off, soil loses heat faster than water.

Analyze Your Data

1. Graphs should show that energy absorption and release by soil is faster.
2. soil
3. Air above the land heated faster.

Error Analysis

If students do not get the expected outcome, they may have made an error in reading thermometers or may have skipped a temperature reading.

Draw Conclusions

1. Answers will vary depending on results.
2. soil
3. When the light was first turned off, the temperature above the soil was higher. After several minutes, the temperature above the water was higher. Soil absorbs and releases heat more quickly than water.

*A*ssessment

Oral Have students explain why in the summer a swimming pool can feel cool in the daytime and warm at night. More heat from the Sun is required to raise the temperature of water than of land. At night the land cools off faster. The water temperature doesn't change as fast as the land temperature does. Use **Performance Assessment in the Science Classroom**, p. 89.

*C*ommunicating Your Data

Suggest that students use word processing programs and electronic spreadsheets to make their posters.

Pre-Reading Activity

Have students research the craft of weaving. Have them write a definition of a term related to this craft with which they are unfamiliar.

Respond to the Reading

Active Reading Strategies

Respond Ask students to reread the poem out loud as a group. Ask them if reading it orally changes their understanding of it. **How was your understanding different the second time?**

Evaluate Tell students to consider the form the poem takes. **What might account for the way the poem broadens at the top, narrows in the center, and then broadens again at the bottom?**

Question Ask students to whom they think the poem is written.

Respond to the Reading

1. Student answers will vary but might include how Mother Earth and Father Sky appear to surround the song in the same way a mother and father shelter or take care of their children.

2. Student answers will vary but might suggest that a garment keeps you warm and protects you against harsh weather.

Science (and) Language Arts

Song of the Sky Loom[1]
Brian Swann, ed.

Respond to the Reading

1. Why do the words *Mother Earth* and *Father Sky* appear on either side and above and below the rest of the words?

2. Why does the song use the image of a garment to describe Earth's atmosphere?

This Native American prayer comes from the Tewa people who are part of the Pueblo tribe. The poem is actually a chanted prayer used in ceremonial rituals.

Mother Earth   Father Sky

we are your children

With tired backs we bring you gifts you love

Then weave for us a garment of brightness
its warp[2] the white light of morning,
weft[3] the red light of evening,
fringes the falling rain,
its border the standing rainbow.

Thus weave for us a garment of brightness
So we may walk fittingly where birds sing,
So we may walk fittingly where grass is green.

Mother Earth   Father Sky

[1] a machine or device from which cloth is produced

[2] threads that run lengthwise in a piece of cloth

[3] horizontal threads interlaced through the warp in a piece of cloth

---

Reading Further

Other sources on this topic include:

Weather Legends: Native American Lore and the Science of Weather by Carole Barbuny Vogel, September 2000.

Earthmaker's Tales (North American Indian Stories) by Gretchen Will Mayo, Walker & Co, reprint edition, February 1991.

Watching Weather (Accidental Scientist) by Tom Murphree, Mary K. Miller, Exploratorium, Owl Books, August 1998.

Understanding Literature

Metaphor A metaphor is a figure of speech that compares seemingly unlike things. Unlike a simile, a metaphor does not use the connecting words *like* or *as*. For instance, in the song you just read, Father Sky is a loom. A loom is a machine or device that weaves cloth. The song describes the relationship between Earth and sky as being a woven garment. Lines such as "weave for us a garment of brightness" serve as metaphors for how Mother Earth and Father Sky together create an atmosphere in which their "children," or humans, can thrive.

Science Connection In this chapter, you learned about the composition of Earth's atmosphere. The atmosphere maintains the balance between the amount of heat absorbed from the Sun and the amount of heat that escapes back into space. You also learned about the water cycle and how water evaporates from Earth's surface back into the atmosphere. Using metaphor instead of scientific facts, the Tewa song conveys to the reader how the relationship between Earth and its atmosphere are important to all living things.

Linking Science and Writing

Creating a Metaphor Write a four-line poem that uses a metaphor to describe rain. You can choose to write about a gentle spring rain or a thunderous rainstorm. Remember that a metaphor does not use the words *like* or *as*. Therefore, your poem should begin with something like "Rain is …" or "Heavy rain is …"

Career Connection

Meteorologist

Kim Perez is an on-air meteorologist for The Weather Channel, a national cable television network. She became interested in the weather when she was living in Cincinnati, Ohio. There, in 1974, she witnessed the largest tornado on record. Ms. Perez now broadcasts weather reports to millions of television viewers. Meteorologists study computer models of Earth's atmosphere. These models help them predict short-term and long-term weather conditions for the United States and the world.

SCIENCE *Online* To learn more about careers in meteorology, visit the Glencoe Science Web site at **science.glencoe.com.**

SCIENCE AND LANGUAGE ARTS 455

Career Connection

Atmospheric scientists are commonly called meteorologists. They study the characteristics, motions, and processes of Earth's atmosphere. Most predict the weather. However, other atmospheric scientists solve problems dealing with air-pollution control, air and sea transportation, global warming, droughts, or ozone depletion.

SCIENCE *Online*
Internet Addresses

_____
_____
_____

Explore the Glencoe Science Web site at **science.glencoe.com** to find out more about topics in this feature.

Understanding Literature

Science Connection

The atmosphere of the Earth has evolved over time and is constantly changing. It changes as human and organic activities change the ecosphere. For example, scientists believe that half-way through the history of Earth, oxygen was emitted into the atmosphere as a result of photo-synthesis from algae in the ocean. Today, oxygen is one of the atmosphere's primary elements.

The atmosphere continues to change based on human and organic activity. For example, human activities are having a potentially catastrophic effect on the stratosphere. Complex chemical reactions involving chlorofluorocarbons that have been released to the atmosphere have been blamed for causing temporary holes in the ozone layer.

Linking Science and Writing

Teaching Strategies

Tell students that they will do a prewriting activity to help write a poem using metaphor. On a sheet of paper have students make two columns. Tell students to write nouns in one column that are elements or objects found in nature, such as plants or animals. Tell students to write other nouns in the second column directly across from the nouns in the first column that remind them of those words. For example, if a student writes "weeping willow tree" in one column, he or she might write the words "crying man" in the second column.

Chapter 15 Study Guide

Reviewing Main Ideas

Preview

Students can answer the questions in their Science Journals. Discuss the answers as you go through the chapter. **Linguistic**

Review

Students can write their answers, then compare them with those of other students. **Interpersonal**

Reteach

Students can look at the illustrations and describe details that support the main ideas of the chapter. **Visual-Spatial**

Answers to Chapter Review

SECTION 1

3. Chlorine atoms from CFC molecules detach oxygen atoms from ozone molecules, destroying the ozone molecules.

SECTION 2

3. condensation

SECTION 3

4. Soil and water absorb and release heat at different rates. During the day, land heats more quickly than water, causing a sea breeze to move from water to land. During the night, land cools more quickly than water, causing a land breeze to move from land to water.

Reviewing Main Ideas

Section 1 Earth's Atmosphere

1. Earth's atmosphere is made up mostly of gases, with some suspended solids and liquids. The unique atmosphere allows life on Earth to exist.

2. The atmosphere is divided into five layers with different characteristics.

3. The ozone layer protects Earth from too much ultraviolet radiation, which can be harmful. *How do chlorofluorocarbon molecules destroy ozone?*

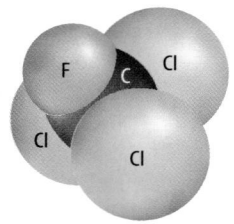

Section 2 Energy Transfer in the Atmosphere

1. Earth receives its energy from the Sun. Some of this energy is reflected back into space, and some is absorbed.

2. Heat is distributed in Earth's atmosphere by radiation, conduction, and convection.

3. Energy from the Sun powers the water cycle between the atmosphere and Earth's surface. *Clouds form during which part of the water cycle?*

4. Unlike the atmosphere on Mars or Venus, Earth's unique atmosphere maintains a balance between energy received and energy lost that keeps temperatures mild. This delicate balance allows life on Earth to exist.

Section 3 Air Movement

1. Because Earth's surface is curved, not all areas receive the same amount of solar radiation. This uneven heating causes temperature differences at Earth's surface.

2. Convection currents modified by the Coriolis effect produce Earth's global winds.

3. The polar jet stream is a strong current of wind found in the upper troposphere. It forms at the boundary between cold, polar air and warm, tropical air.

4. Land breezes and sea breezes occur near the ocean. *Why do winds change direction from day to night?*

FOLDABLES Reading & Study Skills
After You Read
Draw pictures on the front of your Foldable of things that you might find in each layer of Earth's atmosphere.

FOLDABLES Reading & Study Skills
After You Read
After students have read the chapter and completed the Foldable described in Before You Read, have them do the activity on the student page.

Dinah Zike

Visualizing Main Ideas

Complete the following cycle map on the water cycle.

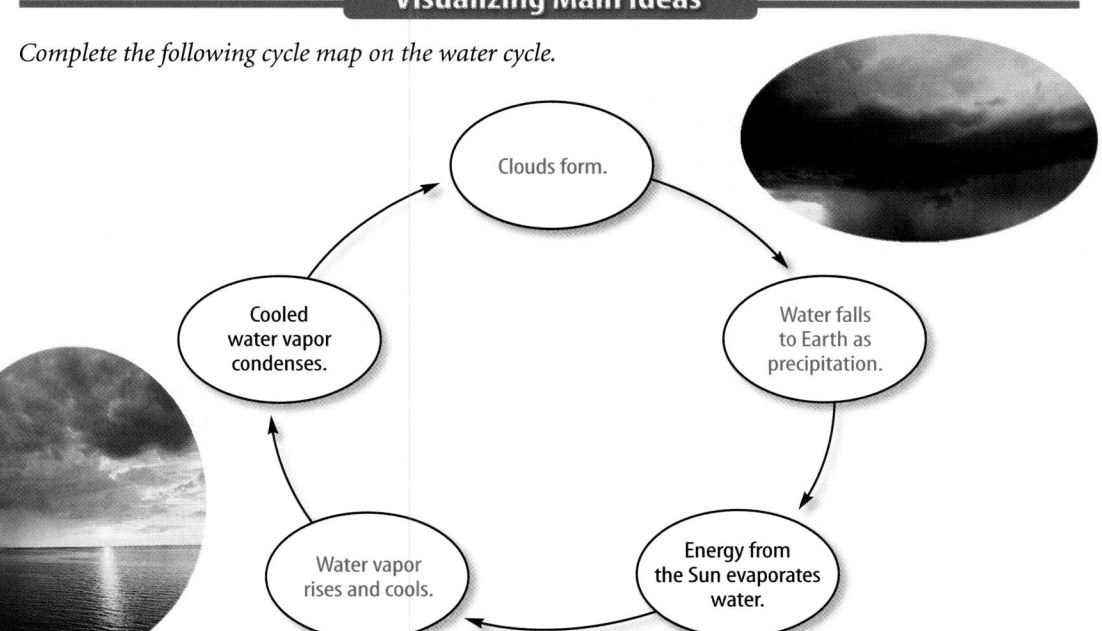

Clouds form.

Cooled water vapor condenses.

Water falls to Earth as precipitation.

Water vapor rises and cools.

Energy from the Sun evaporates water.

Vocabulary Review

Vocabulary Review

a. atmosphere
b. chlorofluorocarbon
c. condensation
d. conduction
e. convection
f. Coriolis effect
g. hydrosphere
h. ionosphere
i. jet stream
j. land breeze
k. ozone layer
l. radiation
m. sea breeze
n. troposphere
o. ultraviolet radiation

THE PRINCETON REVIEW **Study Tip**

Try to think of other ways that you might design an experiment to prove scientific principles.

Using Vocabulary

The sentences below include terms that have been used incorrectly. Change the incorrect terms so that the sentence reads correctly.

1. Chlorofluorocarbons are dangerous because they destroy the hydrosphere.

2. Narrow belts of strong winds called sea breezes blow near the top of the ionosphere.

3. The thin layer of air that surrounds Earth is called the troposphere.

4. Heat energy transferred in the form of waves is called condensation.

5. The ozone layer helps protect us from the Coriolis effect.

CHAPTER STUDY GUIDE 457

Vocabulary Review

Using Vocabulary

1. Chlorofluorocarbons are dangerous because they destroy the ozone layer.
2. Narrow belts of strong winds called the jet stream blow near the top of the ionosphere.
3. The thin layer of air that surrounds Earth is called the atmosphere.
4. Heat energy transferred in the form of waves is called radiation.
5. The ozone layer helps protect us from ultraviolet radiation.

IDENTIFYING Misconceptions

Assess

Use the assessment as follow-up to page 432F after students have completed the chapter.

Demonstration Take students outside to a large open area. Take a kite with you. Launch the kite and, while flying it, have students discuss what causes the kite to stay up in the sky.

Expected Outcome Students will begin to realize that the movement of air (wind) is caused by uneven heating of the Earth's surface.

Reinforcement Discuss with students what color clothes you would want to wear on a hot, sunny day compared to a cold, sunny day. Relate this to the uneven heating of the Earth's surface.

Chapter 15 Assessment

Checking Concepts

1. D
2. C
3. C
4. A
5. A
6. C
7. D
8. C
9. C
10. B

Thinking Critically

11. There is little or no water vapor available to form clouds.
12. The ozone layer prevents UV radiation, which is generally harmful to living organisms, from reaching Earth's surface. Early organisms living in the oceans were protected from UV by the water.
13. Sea breezes occur when the air over the water is cooler than the air over the land. This occurs during the day, when solar radiation is greatest.
14. It condenses. Students may also say it forms clouds.
15. With an increase in altitude, fewer and fewer molecules push against one another to cause air pressure.

Developing Skills

16. See student page.
17. During the afternoon, the ground warmed and heated the air above it through conduction. After sunset, the ground was no longer receiving solar energy and could no longer provide as much heat to the air above it.
18. Average global temperature might increase.

Checking Concepts

Choose the word or phrase that best answers the question.

1. What is the most abundant gas in the atmosphere?
   A) oxygen
   B) water vapor
   C) argon
   D) nitrogen

2. What causes a brown haze near cities?
   A) conduction
   B) mud
   C) car exhaust
   D) wind

3. Which is the uppermost layer of the atmosphere?
   A) troposphere
   B) stratosphere
   C) exosphere
   D) thermosphere

4. What layer of the atmosphere has the most water?
   A) troposphere
   B) stratosphere
   C) mesosphere
   D) exosphere

5. What protects living things from too much ultraviolet radiation?
   A) the ozone layer
   B) oxygen
   C) nitrogen
   D) argon

6. Where is air pressure least?
   A) troposphere
   B) stratosphere
   C) exosphere
   D) thermosphere

7. How is energy transferred when objects are in contact?
   A) trade winds
   B) convection
   C) radiation
   D) conduction

8. Which surface winds are responsible for most of the weather movement across the United States?
   A) polar easterlies
   B) doldrums
   C) prevailing westerlies
   D) trade winds

9. What type of wind is a movement of air toward water?
   A) sea breeze
   B) doldrum
   C) land breeze
   D) barometer

10. What are narrow belts of strong winds near the top of the troposphere called?
    A) doldrums
    B) jet streams
    C) polar easterlies
    D) trade winds

Thinking Critically

11. Why are there few or no clouds in the stratosphere?

12. It is thought that life could not have existed on land until the ozone layer formed about 2 billion years ago. Why does life on land require an ozone layer?

13. Why do sea breezes occur during the day, but not at night?

14. Describe what happens when water vapor rises and cools.

15. Why does air pressure decrease with an increase in altitude?

Developing Skills

16. **Concept Mapping** Complete the cycle concept map below using the following phrases to explain how air moves to form a convection current: *Cool air moves toward warm air, cool air is warmed by conduction, warm air is lifted and cools,* and *cool air sinks.*

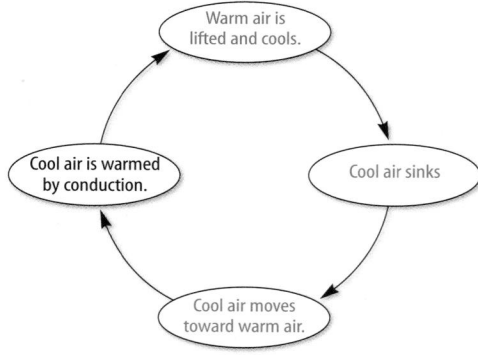

Warm air is lifted and cools.

Cool air is warmed by conduction.

Cool air sinks.

Cool air moves toward warm air.

Portfolio Encourage students to place in their portfolios one or two items of what they consider to be their best work. Examples include:

- Extension, p. 437
- Science Journal, p. 445
- Extension, p. 449
- Assessment, p. 451

Performance Additional performance assessments, Performance Task Assessment Lists, and rubrics for evaluating these activities can be found in Glencoe's **Performance Assessment in the Science Classroom.**

17. Drawing Conclusions In an experiment, a student measured the air temperature 1 m above the ground on a sunny afternoon and again in the same spot 1 h after sunset. The second reading was lower than the first. What can you infer from this?

18. Forming Hypotheses Carbon dioxide in the atmosphere prevents some radiation from Earth's surface from escaping to space. Hypothesize how the temperature on Earth might change if more carbon dioxide were released from burning fossil fuels.

19. Identifying and Manipulating Variables and Controls Design an experiment to find out how plants are affected by differing amounts of ultraviolet radiation. In the design, use filtering film made for car windows. What is the variable you are testing? What are your constants? Your controls?

20. Recognizing Cause and Effect Why is the inside of a car hotter than the outdoor temperature on a sunny summer day?

Performance Assessment

21. Poster Illustratate or find magazine photos of convection currents that occur in everyday life.

22. Experiment Design and conduct an experiment to find out how different surfaces such as asphalt, soil, sand, and grass absorb and reflect solar energy. Share the results with your class.

TECHNOLOGY

 Go to the Glencoe Science Web site at **science.glencoe.com** or use the **Glencoe Science CD-ROM** for additional chapter assessment.

 **THE PRINCETON REVIEW** Test Practice

Each layer of Earth's atmosphere has a unique composition and temperature. The four layers closest to Earth's surface are shown in the diagram below.

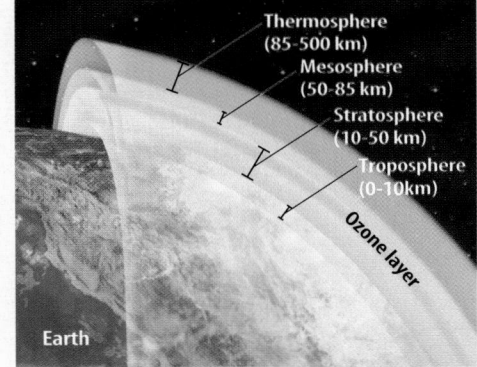

Thermosphere (85-500 km)
Mesosphere (50-85 km)
Stratosphere (10-50 km)
Troposphere (0-10km)
Ozone layer
Earth

Study the diagram and answer the following questions.

1. In which part of the atmosphere is ozone located?
- **A)** Thermosphere
- **C)** Stratosphere
- **B)** Troposphere
- **D)** Mesosphere

2. According to the diagram, how far does the mesosphere extend above Earth's surface?
- **F)** 10 km
- **H)** 50 km
- **G)** 85 km
- **J)** 60 km

3. What is the correct order of atmospheric layers that the space shuttle goes through when landing on Earth?
- **A)** Mesosphere Stratosphere Troposphere
- **C)** Stratosphere Troposphere Mesosphere
- **B)** Troposphere Stratosphere Mesosphere
- **D)** Mesosphere Troposphere Stratosphere

THE PRINCETON REVIEW Test Practice

The Test-Taking Tip was written by The Princeton Review, the nation's leader in test preparation.
1. C
2. G
3. A

Developing Skills

19. Accept all reasonable designs. The variable is the amount of ultraviolet light that the plants receive. The constants are identical plants, pots, watering, soil, and placement of the pots. The controls are the plants that receive ultraviolet radiation without filtering.

20. Solar energy passes through the glass windows, where it is absorbed by the car interior. The interior reradiates the energy as heat. The glass windows trap the heat, which builds up inside as long as the car sits in the Sun.

Performance Assessment

21. Possible visual: liquids such as soups or water cooking or boiling on a stove burner, or weather systems, since convection distributes heat. Have students mount their drawings or photos on poster board. Display the posters in the classroom. Use **PASC**, p. 145.

22. As part of the experiment setup, students might lay a thermometer on each surface and suspend another one above each surface to collect temperature readings. Thermometers should be suspended at the same height. Use **PASC**, p. 95.

✓Assessment Resources

📁 **Reproducible Masters**

Chapter Resources Booklet
Chapter Review, pp. 33–34
Chapter Tests, pp. 35–38
Assessment Transparency Activity, p. 45

Glencoe Science Web site
Interactive Tutor
Chapter Quizzes

Glencoe Technology
- Assessment Transparency
- Interactive CD-ROM Chapter Quizzes
- ExamView Pro Test Bank
- Vocabulary PuzzleMaker Software
- MindJogger Videoquiz DVD/VHS

Section/Objectives	Standards		Activities/Features
	National	State/Local	
Chapter Opener	See p. 5T for a Key to Standards.		**Explore Activity:** Demonstrate how rain forms, p. 461 **Before You Read,** p. 461
Section 1 What is weather? 🕐 2 sessions 📦 1 block 1. **Explain** how solar heating and water vapor in the atmosphere affect weather. 2. **Discuss** how clouds form and how they are classified. 3. **Describe** how rain, hail, sleet, and snow develop.	National Content Standards: UCP1, A1, D1, E2, F3		**Life Science Integration,** p. 463 **MiniLAB:** Determining Dew Point, p. 464 **Math Skills Activity,** p. 465
Section 2 Weather Patterns 🕐 2 sessions 📦 1 block 1. **Describe** how weather is associated with fronts and high- and low-pressure areas. 2. **Explain** how tornadoes develop from thunderstorms. 3. **Discuss** the dangers of severe weather.	National Content Standards: UCP1, UCP3, D1, F3		**Science Online,** p. 471 **Science Online,** p. 474 **Visualizing Tornadoes,** p. 475 **Environmental Science Integration,** p. 476
Section 3 Weather Forecasts 🕐 3 sessions 📦 1.5 blocks 1. **Explain** how data are collected for weather maps and forecasts. 2. **Identify** the symbols used in a weather station model.	National Content Standards: UCP1, UCP2, A1, A2, D1, E1, E2, F5, G1		**MiniLAB:** Measuring Rain, p. 479 **Activity:** Reading a Weather Map, p. 481 **Activity:** Measuring Wind Speed, pp. 482–483 **Science and Society:** Rainmakers, pp. 484–485

NATIONAL GEOGRAPHIC

Teacher's Corner

PRODUCTS AVAILABLE FROM GLENCOE
To order call 1-800-334-7344:
CD-ROM *NGS PictureShow: Introduction to Weather*
Curriculum Kit *GeoKit: Weather*
Transparency Set *NGS PicturePack: Introduction to Weather*

PRODUCTS AVAILABLE FROM NATIONAL GEOGRAPHIC SOCIETY
To order call 1-800-368-2728:
Videos
Telling the Weather
Weather: Come Rain, Come Shine

Activity Materials	Reproducible Resources	Section Assessment	Technology
Explore Activity: 2 metal pans, water, hot plate, ice	**Chapter Resources Booklet** Foldables Worksheet, p. 17 Directed Reading Overview, p. 19 Note-taking Worksheets, pp. 33–35	GLENCOE'S ASSESSMENT ADVANTAGE	
MiniLAB: metal can, paper towels, thermometer, stirring rod, crushed ice, water	**Chapter Resources Booklet** Transparency Activity, p. 44 MiniLAB, p. 3 Enrichment, p. 30 Reinforcement, p. 27 Directed Reading, p. 20 Lab Activities, pp. 9–12, 13–15 **Mathematics Skill Activities,** p. 7 **Physical Science Critical Thinking/Problem Solving,** p. 16	Portfolio Life Science Integration, p. 463 **Performance** MiniLAB, p. 464 Math Skills Activity, p. 465 Skill Builder Activities, p. 469 **Content** Section Assessment, p. 469	♪ Section Focus Transparency ◉ Interactive CD-ROM/DVD ⌒ Guided Reading Audio Program
Need materials? Contact Science Kit at 1-800-828-7777 or www.sciencekit.com on the Internet.	**Chapter Resources Booklet** Transparency Activity, p. 45 Enrichment, p. 31 Reinforcement, p. 28 Directed Reading, p. 21 **Reading and Writing Skill Activity,** pp. 3, 45 **Science Inquiry Labs,** p. 27	Portfolio Use Science Words, p. 471 **Performance** Skill Builder Activities, p. 477 **Content** Section Assessment, p. 477	♪ Section Focus Transparency ◉ Interactive CD-ROM/DVD ⌒ Guided Reading Audio Program
MiniLAB: soup or coffee can, tape, ruler **Activity:** hand lens **Activity:** paper, scissors, confetti, grass clippings, meterstick	**Chapter Resources Booklet** Transparency Activity, p. 46 MiniLAB, p. 4 Enrichment, p. 32 Reinforcement, p. 29 Directed Reading, pp. 21, 22 Activity Worksheet, pp. 5–6, 7–8 Transparency Activity, pp. 47–48 **Lab Management and Safety,** p. 4	Portfolio Challenge, p. 480 Assessment, p. 483 **Performance** MiniLAB, p. 479 Skill Builder Activities, p. 480 **Content** Section Assessment, p. 480	♪ Section Focus Transparency ♪ Teaching Transparency ◉ Interactive CD-ROM/DVD ⌒ Guided Reading Audio Program

End of Chapter Assessment

GLENCOE'S ASSESSMENT ADVANTAGE

Blackline Masters	Technology	Professional Series
Chapter Resources Booklet Chapter Review, pp. 37–38 Chapter Tests, pp. 39–42 **Standardized Test Practice by The Princeton Review,** pp. 71–74	▭ MindJogger Videoquiz ◉ CD-ROM Explorations and Quizzes ◉ Vocabulary Puzzle Makers ◉ ExamView Pro Test Bank ◉ Interactive Lesson Planner ◉ Interactive Teacher's Edition	Performance Assessment in the Science Classroom (PASC)

Transparencies

Section Focus

SECTION 1
Section Focus Transparency **Valley Mist**

This Chinese painting depicts a mountain and valley scene. When the artist drew the mountains, the empty space of the valley where the fog is hanging was also drawn. Valleys and fog are common in this style of painting.

1. What do you think the weather in this picture is like?
2. Describe how fog or mist feels.
3. How are fog and clouds similar?

L2

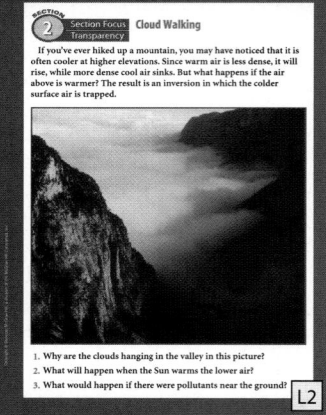

SECTION 2
Section Focus Transparency **Cloud Walking**

If you've ever hiked up a mountain, you may have noticed that it is often cooler at higher elevations. Since warm air is less dense, it will rise, while more dense cool air sinks. But what happens if the air above is warmer? The result is an inversion in which the colder surface air is trapped.

1. Why are the clouds hanging in the valley in this picture?
2. What will happen when the Sun warms the lower air?
3. What would happen if there were pollutants near the ground?

L2

SECTION 3
Section Focus Transparency **Whither wanders the weather?**

For many people, knowing what the weather will be like is important. People working on farms need to know when to plant, water, or harvest crops. Weather can alter travel schedules or even make travel unsafe. Many people like to know whether they should carry an umbrella.

1. Which of these items would you use if you wanted to know how much snow fell last night? Which item displays the path of a storm?
2. How has weather prediction changed in the last century?

L2

Assessment

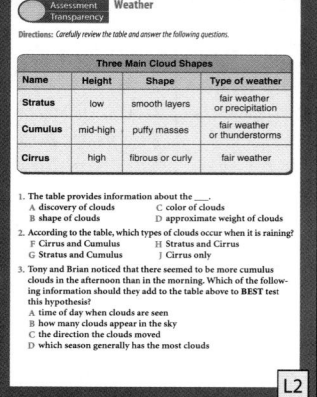

Assessment Transparency **Weather**

Directions: Carefully review the table and answer the following questions.

Three Main Cloud Shapes

Name	Height	Shape	Type of weather
Stratus	low	smooth layers	fair weather or precipitation
Cumulus	mid-high	puffy masses	fair weather or thunderstorms
Cirrus	high	fibrous or curly	fair weather

1. The table provides information about the ___.
   A discovery of clouds   C color of clouds
   B shape of clouds   D approximate weight of clouds
2. According to the table, which types of clouds occur when it is raining?
   F Cirrus and Cumulus   H Stratus and Cirrus
   G Stratus and Cumulus   J Cirrus only
3. Tony and Brian noticed that there seemed to be more cumulus clouds in the afternoon than in the morning. Which of the following information should they add to the table above to BEST test this hypothesis?
   A time of day when clouds are seen
   B how many clouds appear in the sky
   C the direction the clouds moved
   D which season generally has the most clouds

L2

Teaching

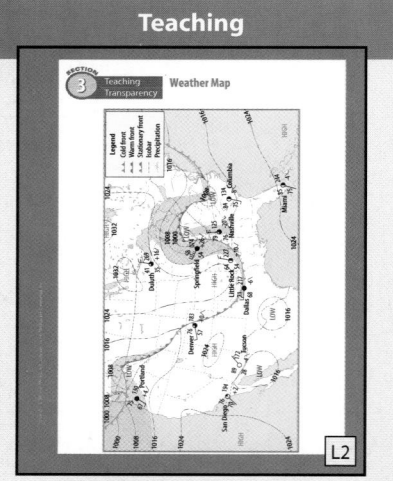

SECTION 3
Teaching Transparency **Weather Map**

L2

This is a representation of key blackline masters available in the Teacher Classroom Resources. See Resource Manager boxes within the chapter for additional information.

Key to Teaching Strategies

The following designations will help you decide which activities are appropriate for your students.

L1 Level 1 activities should be appropriate for students with learning difficulties.

L2 Level 2 activities should be within the ability range of all students.

L3 Level 3 activities are designed for above-average students.

ELL ELL activities should be within the ability range of English Language Learners.

COOP LEARN Cooperative Learning activities are designed for small group work.

LS Multiple Learning Styles logos, as described on page 22T, are used throughout to indicate strategies that address different learning styles.

P These strategies represent student products that can be placed into a best-work portfolio.

Hands-on Activities

Activity Worksheets

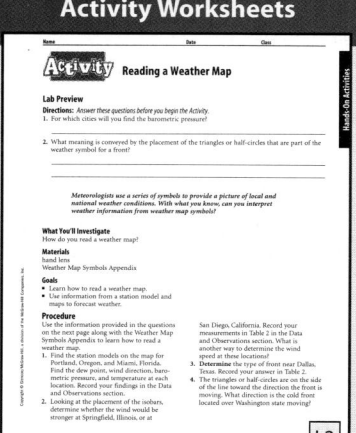

Activity **Reading a Weather Map**

Lab Preview
Directions: Answer these questions before you begin the Activity.
1. For which cities will you find the barometric pressure?

2. What meaning is conveyed by the placement of the triangles or half-circles that are part of the weather symbol for a front?

Meteorologists use a series of symbols to provide a picture of local and national weather conditions. With what you know, can you interpret weather information from weather map symbols?

What You'll Investigate
How do you read a weather map?

Materials
hand lens
Weather Map Symbols Appendix

Goals
• Learn how to read a weather map.
• Use information from a station model and maps to forecast weather.

Procedure
Use the information provided in the questions on the next page along with the Weather Map Symbols Appendix to learn how to read a weather map.
1. Find the station models on the map for Portland, Oregon, and Miami, Florida. Find the dew point, wind direction, barometric pressure, and temperature at each location. Record your findings in the Data and Observations section.
2. Looking at the placement of the isobars, determine whether the wind would be stronger at Springfield, Illinois, or at

San Diego, California. Record your measurements in Table 2 in the Data and Observations section.
3. Determine the type of front near Dallas, Texas. Record your answer in Table 2.
4. The triangles or half-circles are on the side of the line toward the direction the front is moving. What direction is the cold front located over Washington state moving?

L2

Laboratory Activities

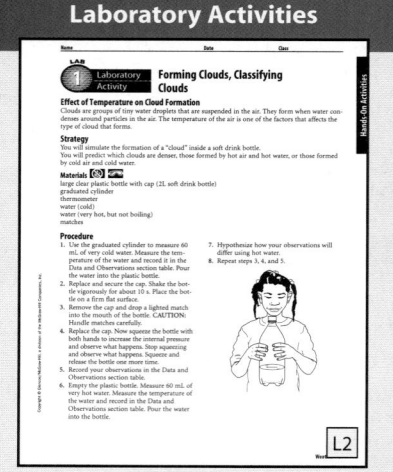

LAB 1
Laboratory Activity **Forming Clouds, Classifying Clouds**

Effect of Temperature on Cloud Formation
Clouds are groups of tiny water droplets that are suspended in the air. They form when water condenses around particles in the air. The temperature of the air is one of the factors that affect the type of cloud that forms.

Strategy
You will simulate the formation of a "cloud" inside a soft drink bottle.
You will predict which clouds are denser, those formed by hot air and hot water, or those formed by cold air and cold water.

Materials
large clear plastic bottle with cap (2L soft drink bottle)
graduated cylinder
thermometer
water (cold)
water (very hot, but not boiling)
matches

Procedure
1. Use the graduated cylinder to measure 60 mL of very cold water. Measure the temperature of the water and record it in the Data and Observations section table. Pour the water into the plastic bottle.
2. Replace and secure the cap. Shake the bottle vigorously for about 10 s. Place the bottle on a firm flat surface.
3. Remove the cap and drop a lighted match into the mouth of the bottle. CAUTION: Handle matches carefully.
4. Replace the cap. Now squeeze the bottle with both hands to increase the internal pressure and observe what happens. Stop squeezing and observe what happens. Squeeze and release the bottle one more time.
5. Record your observations in the Data and Observations section table.
6. Empty the plastic bottle. Measure 60 mL of very hot water. Measure the temperature of the water and record in the Data and Observations section table. Pour the water into the bottle.
7. Hypothesize how your observations will differ using hot water.
8. Repeat steps 3, 4, and 5.

L2

Meeting Different Ability Levels

Content Outline

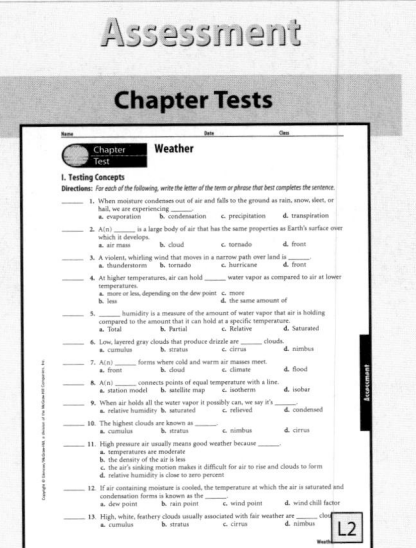

Note-taking Worksheet — Weather

Section 1 What is weather?

A. Weather is the state of the _____ at a specific time and place.

L2

Reinforcement

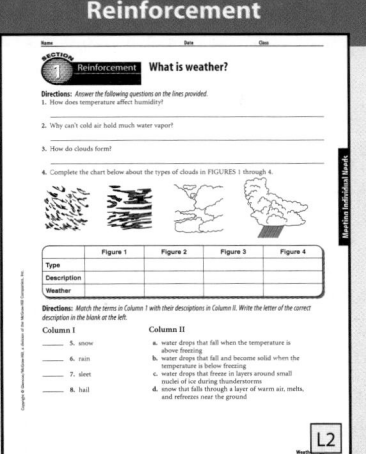

Reinforcement — What is weather?

Directions: Answer the following questions on the lines provided.

1. How does temperature affect humidity?

2. Why can't cold air hold much water vapor?

3. How do clouds form?

4. Complete the chart below about the types of clouds in FIGURES 1 through 4.

	Figure 1	Figure 2	Figure 3	Figure 4
Type				
Description				
Weather				

Directions: Match the terms in Column 1 with their descriptions in Column II. Write the letter of the correct description in the blank at the left.

Column I
___ 5. snow
___ 6. rain
___ 7. sleet
___ 8. hail

Column II
a. water drops that fall when the temperature is above freezing
b. water drops that fall and become solid when the temperature is below freezing
c. water drops that freeze in layers around small nuclei of ice during thunderstorms
d. snow that falls through a layer of warm air, melts, and refreezes near the ground

L2

Directed Reading

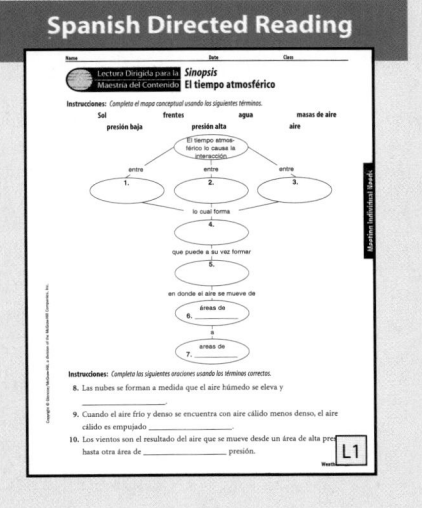

Directed Reading for Content Mastery — Overview — Weather

Directions: Complete the concept map using the terms in the list below.

sun   fronts   water   air masses
low pressure   high pressure   air

Directions: Complete the following sentences using the correct terms.

8. Clouds form as moist air rises and _____.
9. When dense, cold air meets less dense warmer air, the warm air is pushed _____.
10. Winds form because air moves from an area of high pressure to an area of _____ pressure.

L1

Assessment

Chapter Tests

Chapter Test — Weather

I. Testing Concepts

Directions: For each of the following, write the letter of the term or phrase that best completes the sentence.

1. When moisture comes out of air and falls to the ground as rain, snow, sleet, or hail, we are experiencing _____.
   a. evaporation   b. condensation   c. precipitation   d. transpiration

2. A(n) _____ is a large body of air that has the same properties as Earth's surface over which it develops.
   a. air mass   b. cloud   c. tornado   d. front

3. A violent, whirling wind that moves in a narrow path over land is _____.
   a. thunderstorm   b. tornado   c. hurricane   d. front

4. At higher temperatures, air can hold _____ water vapor as compared to air at lower temperatures.
   a. more or less, depending on the dew point   c. more
   b. less   d. the same amount of

5. _____ humidity is a measure of the amount of water vapor that air is holding compared to the amount that it can hold at a specific temperature.
   a. Total   b. Partial   c. Relative   d. Saturated

6. Low, layered gray clouds that produce drizzle are _____ clouds.
   a. cumulus   b. stratus   c. cirrus   d. nimbus

7. A(n) _____ forms where cold and warm air masses meet.
   a. front   b. cloud   c. climate   d. flood

8. A(n) _____ connects points of equal temperature with a line.
   a. station model   b. satellite map   c. isotherm   d. isobar

9. When air holds all the water vapor it possibly can, we say it's _____.
   a. relative humidity   b. saturated   c. relieved   d. condensed

10. The highest clouds are known as _____.
    a. cumulus   b. stratus   c. nimbus   d. cirrus

11. High pressure air usually means good weather because _____.
    a. temperatures are moderate
    b. the density of the air is less
    c. the air's sinking motion makes it difficult for air to rise and clouds to form
    d. relative humidity is close to zero percent

12. If air containing moisture is cooled, the temperature at which the air is saturated and condensation forms is known as the _____.
    a. dew point   b. rain point   c. wind point   d. wind chill factor

13. High, white, feathery clouds usually associated with fair weather are _____ clouds.
    a. cumulus   b. stratus   c. cirrus   d. nimbus

L2

Enrichment

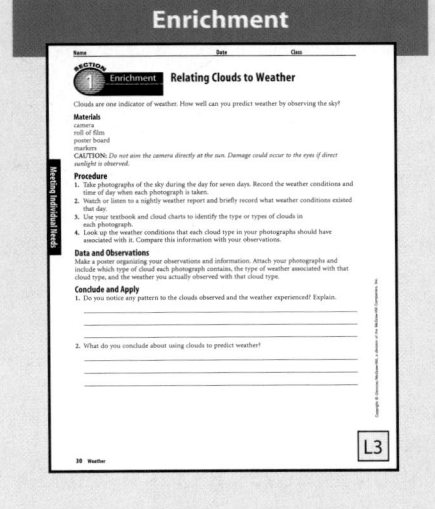

Enrichment — Relating Clouds to Weather

Clouds are one indicator of weather. How well can you predict weather by observing the sky?

Materials
camera
roll of film
poster board
markers
CAUTION: Do not aim the camera directly at the sun. Damage could occur to the eyes if direct sunlight is observed.

Procedure
1. Take photographs of the sky during the day for seven days. Record the weather conditions and time of day when each photograph is taken.
2. Watch or listen to a nightly weather report and briefly record what weather conditions existed that day.
3. Use your textbook and cloud charts to identify the type or types of clouds in each photograph.
4. Look up the weather conditions that each cloud type in your photographs should have associated with it. Compare this information with your observations.

Data and Observations
Make a poster organizing your observations and information. Attach your photographs and include which type of cloud each photograph contains, the type of weather associated with that cloud type, and the weather you actually observed with that cloud type.

Conclude and Apply
1. Do you notice any pattern to the clouds observed and the weather experienced? Explain.

2. What do you conclude about using clouds to predict weather?

L3

Spanish Directed Reading

Lectura Dirigida para la Maestría del Contenido — Sinopsis — El tiempo atmosférico

Instrucciones: Completa el mapa conceptual usando los siguientes términos.

Sol   frentes   presión alta   agua   masas de aire
presión baja   aire

Instrucciones: Completa las siguientes oraciones usando los términos correctos.

8. Las nubes se forman a medida que el aire húmedo se eleva y _____.
9. Cuando el aire frío y denso se encuentra con aire cálido menos denso, el aire cálido es empujado _____.
10. Los vientos son el resultado del aire que se mueve desde un área de alta presión hasta otra área de _____ presión.

L1

Test Practice Workbook

Standardized Test Practice — Teacher Edition

Glencoe Science

Earth Science

National Geographic Society

L2

Chapter Review

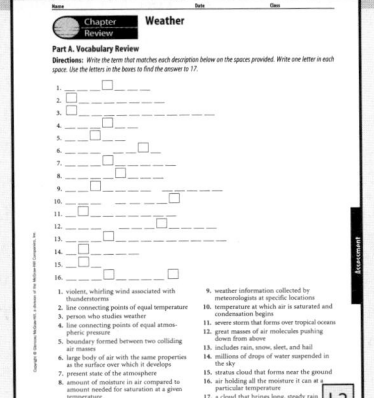

Chapter Review — Weather

Part A. Vocabulary Review

Directions: Write the term that matches each description below on the spaces provided. Write one letter in each space. Use the letters in the boxes to find the answer to 17.

1.
2.
3.
4.
5.
6.
7.
8.
9.
10.
11.
12.
13.
14.
15.
16.

1. violent, whirling wind associated with thunderstorms
2. line connecting points of equal temperature
3. person who studies weather
4. line connecting points of equal atmospheric pressure
5. boundary formed between two colliding air masses
6. large body of air with the same properties as the surface over which it develops
7. present state of the atmosphere
8. amount of moisture in the air compared to amount needed for saturation at a given temperature

9. weather information collected by meteorologists at specific locations
10. temperature at which air is saturated and condensation begins
11. severe storm that forms over tropical oceans
12. great masses of air molecules pushing down from above
13. includes rain, snow, sleet, and hail
14. millions of drops of water suspended in the sky
15. stratus cloud that forms near the ground
16. air holding all the moisture it can at a particular temperature
17. a cloud that brings long, steady rain

L2

Science Content Background

What is weather?

Weather Factors

Relative humidity is measured using a hygrometer or a psychrometer. An early hygrometer used paper disks that absorbed water vapor from the air. As the paper absorbed more water vapor, its weight caused a pointer to rise, indicating the humidity level on a scale. Today hygrometers use human hair. Hair is more flexible under humid conditions. The hair lengthens in high humidity and contracts when dry, causing a dial to move.

> ### Fun Fact
>
> The largest temperature change in a 24-hour period occurred in Browning, Montana, in 1916. The temperature dropped from 44°F on January 23 to −56°F on January 24. That's a change of 100°F in only 24 hours!

A psychrometer is made of a wet-bulb and a dry-bulb thermometer. The wet-bulb thermometer has its tip wrapped in gauze and dipped into water. Once removed from the water, if the relative humidity of the air is less than 100 percent, water evaporates from the gauze. As this happens, the temperature of the thermometer drops. The dry bulb measures the actual air temperature. By comparing the temperatures of the two thermometers and using a chart, the relative humidity is determined.

Forming Clouds

A cloud is made of hundreds of millions of tiny crystals and droplets of water that condense around solids suspended in the air. If the temperature is above 0°C, water vapor condenses to form a liquid. At temperatures below 0°C, water vapor may sublimate, or turn directly into ice crystals. Clouds that form at high

Corbis

altitudes contain ice crystals. At lower altitudes, clouds are made up mostly of water droplets. At middle altitudes, clouds contain a mixture of ice crystals, supercooled water droplets, and water droplets. The type of cloud that forms depends on the amount of air moisture, the uplift of the air, and the stability of the atmosphere.

Classifying Clouds

Luke Howard developed our current cloud classification system in 1803. This classification is based on the most common cloud shapes. Howard used Latin words to describe the shapes of the clouds. *Cumulus* means "heap"; *stratus*, "layer"; *cirrus*, "lock of hair"; and *nimbus*, "rain-bearing." His classification system allows for the combination of names to describe more specific cloud types.

SECTION 2 — Weather Patterns

Weather Changes

The stability of an air mass is one of the factors that determine the weather of an area. Warm, moist air masses are said to be unstable. Because the warm air at the surface is less dense than the cooler air above it, it will tend to be forced aloft, producing clouds, precipitation, and storms. Cold, dry air masses are stable because cold air is denser than warmer air and thus is not pushed aloft. In addition, cold air tends to evaporate less moisture than does warm air.

Thunderstorms

Hail is produced only in cumulonimbus clouds, where both strong updrafts and supercooled water exist. Rain freezes as it is tossed upward in the cloud. Each time an ice crystal is caught in an updraft and then falls, a new layer is added to the hailstone.

Tornadoes also form in cumulonimbus clouds. A tornado can develop in less than an hour and can destroy property and kill people within a matter of minutes. Although tornadic wind speed has been clocked at nearly 500 km/h, most tornadoes generate winds of less than 80 km/h.

Gene Moore/Phototake/Picturequest

Hurricanes

Hurricanes have been known to sustain winds of 250 km/h and gusts up to 300 km/h. A hurricane can last for weeks and cover thousands of kilometers. A well-developed hurricane has bands of cumulonimbus clouds spiraling around a calm eye. A hurricane can contain hundreds of cumulonimbus clouds and can measure 970 km in diameter.

Fun Fact

The average hurricane produces 3 trillion watts of energy per second. You would need to light 30 billion 100-watt light bulbs simultaneously to use that much energy!

SECTION 3 — Weather Forecasts

Weather Observations

Cameras on satellites take photographs of Earth's atmosphere and send the data to ground stations via microwave transmissions. At night, satellites photograph infrared waves to help determine the temperature differences between cloudy and clear areas. Satellite photos are important to weather forecasters because the data they provide about cloud movements enable forecasters to locate low-pressure areas and fronts.

Forecasting Weather

In addition to surface weather maps, meteorologists use upper-air charts that show the movement of air at various altitudes to help them make forecasts. Since the early 1950s, meteorologists around the world have exchanged information to help with forecasting. Today, computer technology provides a global network for the exchange of information to help make more accurate short-range and long-range forecasts.

SCIENCE *Online*

For additional content background on this topic, go to the Glencoe Science Web site at **science.glencoe.com.**

Weather

Chapter Vocabulary

weather
humidity
relative humidity
dew point
fog
precipitation
air mass
front
tornado
hurricane
blizzard
meteorologist
station model
isotherm
isobar

What do you think?

Science Journal The photograph shows a hurricane with a well-formed eye at its center. Although strong winds rage around the eye, the winds inside the eye are calm.

Weather

It's summer and you've gone to your aunt's house in the country. You're playing baseball with your cousins, getting ready to bat, when suddenly you feel a strange sensation. The hot, humid air has suddenly turned cooler, and a strong breeze has kicked up. To the west, tall, black clouds are rapidly advancing. You see a flash of lightning and hear a loud clap of thunder. In this chapter, you'll learn how to measure weather conditions, how to interpret weather information, and make predictions.

What do you think?

Science Journal Look at the picture below with a classmate. Discuss what this might be or what is happening. Here's a hint: *It's calm in the center and rough around the edges.* Write your answer or best guess in your Science Journal.

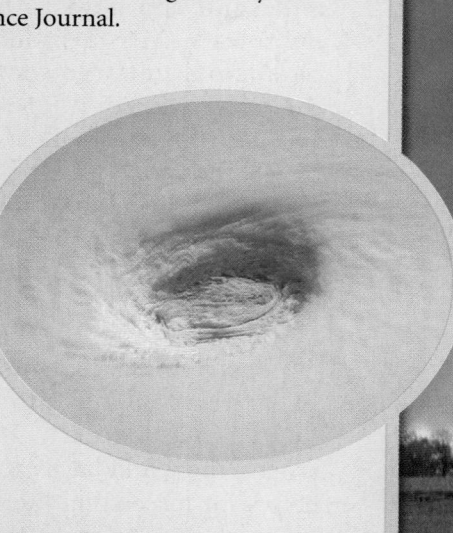

460

Theme Connection

Systems and Interactions In this chapter, students see how the interaction of solar energy, Earth's atmosphere, and Earth's waters form dynamic weather systems.

How can it rain one day and be sunny the next? Powered by heat from the Sun, the air that surrounds you stirs and swirls. This constant mixing produces storms, calm weather, and everything in between. What causes rain and where does the water come from? Do the activity below to find out.

Demonstrate how rain forms

WARNING: *Boiling water and steam can cause burns.*

1. Bring a pan of water to a boil on a hot plate.

2. Carefully hold another pan containing ice cubes about 20 cm above the boiling water. Be sure to keep your hands and face away from the steam.

3. Keep the pan with the ice cubes in place until you see drops of water dripping from the bottom.

Observe
In your Science Journal, describe how the droplets formed. Infer where the water on the bottom of the pan came from.

Before You Read

FOLDABLES
Reading & Study Skills

Making an Organizational Study Fold When information is grouped into clear categories, it is easier to make sense of what you are learning. Make the following Foldable to help you organize your thoughts about weather.

1. Stack two sheets of paper in front of you so the short side of both sheets is at the top.

2. Slide the top sheet up so that about 4 cm of the bottom sheet shows.

3. Fold both sheets top to bottom to form four tabs and staple along the top fold, as shown.

4. Label each flap *Weather, What is Weather, Weather Patterns,* and *Forecasting Weather,* as shown.

5. As you read the chapter, list what you learn under the appropriate flaps.

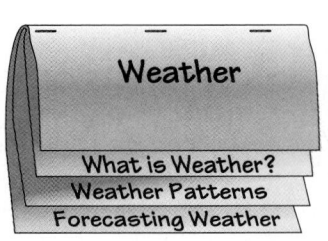

461

EXPLORE ACTIVITY

Purpose Use the Explore Activity to model parts of the water cycle. L2 ELL IS Kinesthetic

Preparation Bring in ice. Have students bring in aluminum pie pans.

Materials small pot, water, hot plate, aluminum pie pan, six ice cubes, oven mitts, goggles, apron

Teaching Strategy To save time, have students put the pots of water on to boil before starting the Activity.

Troubleshooting Make sure students hold the pan 20 cm above the boiling water. If it is held too far away, water droplets may not form.

Safety Precaution Students should use mitts and aprons and wear goggles when holding pans over hot water.

Observe
Water evaporated from the pot. It rose and condensed into droplets when it contacted the cold surface of the pan.

✓Assessment

Oral Have students explain why ice was used in the top pan. Ice cooled the pan and the air below it. As warm air containing water vapor rose under the pan, the water vapor cooled, causing it to condense and form water droplets on the pan's bottom surface. Use **Performance Assessment in the Science Classroom,** p. 89.

FOLDABLES
Reading & Study Skills

Before You Read

Dinah Zike Study Fold
Purpose Use this activity to determine what students know about weather before reading the chapter. Students can use the Foldable for recording and organizing notes from each of the three sections of the chapter as they read.

For additional help, see Foldables Worksheet, p. 17 in **Chapter Resources Booklet,** or go to the Glencoe Science Web site at **science.glencoe.com.** See After You Read in the Study Guide at the end of this chapter.

1 Motivate

Bellringer Transparency

Display the Section Focus Transparency for Section 1. Use the accompanying Transparency Activity Master. L2 ELL

SECTION

1 Section Focus Transparency

Valley Mist

This Chinese painting depicts a mountain and valley scene. When the artist drew the mountains, the empty space of the valley where the fog is hanging was also drawn. Valleys and fog are common in this style of painting.

1. What do you think the weather in this picture is like?
2. Describe how fog or mist feels.
3. How are fog and clouds similar?

L2

Tie to Prior Knowledge

Ask students what they think of when someone says "weather." Record their responses on the board. Return to the list after students have read this section. Discuss how accurate they were in their initial assessment of what constitutes weather.

Caption Answer

Figure 1 Students' answers will vary; encourage them to notice as many storms as possible.

1 What is weather?

As You Read

What You'll Learn

- **Explain** how solar heating and water vapor in the atmosphere affect weather.
- **Discuss** how clouds form and how they are classified.
- **Describe** how rain, hail, sleet, and snow develop.

Vocabulary

weather
humidity
relative humidity
dew point
fog
precipitation

Why It's Important

Weather changes affect your daily activities.

Weather Factors

It might seem like small talk to you, but for farmers, truck drivers, pilots, and construction workers, the weather can have a huge impact on their livelihoods. Even professional athletes, especially golfers, follow weather patterns closely. You can describe what happens in different kinds of weather, but can you explain how it happens?

Weather refers to the state of the atmosphere at a specific time and place. Weather describes conditions such as air pressure, wind, temperature, and the amount of moisture in the air.

The Sun provides almost all of Earth's energy. Energy from the Sun evaporates water into the atmosphere where it forms clouds. Eventually, the water falls back to Earth as rain or snow. However, the Sun does more than evaporate water. It is also a source of heat energy. Heat from the Sun is absorbed by Earth's surface, which then heats the air above it. Weather, as shown in **Figure 1,** is the result of heat and Earth's air and water.

Figure 1

The Sun provides the energy that drives Earth's weather.
Can you find any storms in this photograph?

Section ✓*Assessment* Planner

PORTFOLIO
Life Science Integration, p. 463
PERFORMANCE ASSESSMENT
MiniLAB, p. 464
Math Skills Activity, p. 465
Skill Builder Activities, p. 469
See page 488 for more options.

CONTENT ASSESSMENT
Section, p. 469
Challenge, p. 469
Chapter, pp. 488–489

A When air is heated, it expands and becomes less dense. This creates lower pressure.

B Molecules in air are closer together in cooler temperatures, creating high pressure. Wind blows from higher pressure toward lower pressure.

Air Temperature During the summer when the Sun is hot and the air is still, a swim can be refreshing. But would a swim seem refreshing on a cold winter day? The temperature of air influences your daily activities.

Air is made up of molecules that are always moving randomly, even when there's no wind. Temperature is a measure of the average amount of motion of molecules. When the temperature is high, molecules in air move rapidly and it feels warm. When the temperature is low, molecules in air move less rapidly, and it feels cold.

Wind Why can you fly a kite on some days but not others? Kites fly because air is moving. Air moving in a specific direction is called wind. As the Sun warms the air, the air expands and becomes less dense. Warm, expanding air has low atmospheric pressure. Cooler air is denser and tends to sink, bringing about high atmospheric pressure. Wind results because air moves from regions of high pressure to regions of low pressure. You may have experienced this on a small scale if you've ever spent time along a beach, as in **Figure 2.**

Many instruments are used to measure wind direction and speed. Wind direction can be measured using a wind vane. A wind vane has an arrow that points in the direction from which the wind is blowing. A wind sock has one open end that catches the wind, causing the sock to point in the direction toward which the wind is blowing. Wind speed can be measured using an anemometer (a nuh MAH muh tur). Anemometers have rotating cups that spin faster when the wind is strong.

Figure 2
The temperature of air can affect air pressure. Wind is air moving from high pressure to low pressure.

Life Science
INTEGRATION

Birds and mammals maintain a fairly constant internal temperature, even when the temperature outside their bodies changes. On the other hand, the internal temperature of fish and reptiles changes when the temperature around them changes. Infer from this which group is more likely to survive a quick change in the weather.

Weather Factors,
continued

Answer At warmer temperatures, water vapor molecules move too quickly to condense.

Purpose Students determine dew point. L2 ELL
IS **Kinesthetic**

Materials metal can, paper towels, thermometer, stirring rod, crushed ice, water

Teaching Strategy Have students start with 2/3 cup of water before adding ice.

Safety Precautions Caution students not to use the thermometers as stirring rods.

Troubleshooting Ice must be added to the water slowly.

Analysis
1. amount of moisture in the air at a given temperature
2. Yes; warm air has more water vapor than cool air because the molecules move too quickly in warm air for water vapor to condense.

✓ Assessment

Performance Have students determine the dew point at two different locations. Use **PASC**, p. 99.

Figure 3
Warmer air can have more water vapor than cooler air can because water vapor doesn't easily condense in warm air.

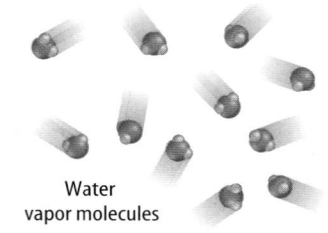
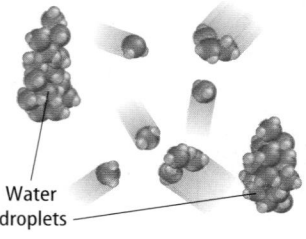

A Water vapor molecules in warm air move rapidly. The molecules can't easily come together and condense.

B As air cools, water molecules in air move closer together. Some of them collide, allowing condensation to take place.

Mini LAB

Determining Dew Point

Procedure
1. Partially fill a **metal can** with room-temperature **water.** Dry the outer surface of the can.
2. Place a **thermometer** in the water.
3. Slowly stir the water and add small amounts of **ice.**
4. On a data table in your **Science Journal,** note the exact water temperature at which a thin film of moisture first begins to form on the outside of the metal can.
5. Repeat steps 1 through 4 two more times.
6. The average of the three temperatures at which the moisture begins to appear is the dew point temperature of the air surrounding the metal container.

Analysis
1. What determines the dew point temperature?
2. Will the dew point change with increasing temperature if the amount of moisture in the air doesn't change? Explain.

Humidity Heat evaporates water into the atmosphere. Where does the water go? Water vapor molecules fit into spaces among the molecules that make up air. The amount of water vapor present in the air is called **humidity.**

Air doesn't always contain the same amount of water vapor. As you can see in **Figure 3,** more water vapor can be present when the air is warm than when it is cool. At warmer temperatures, the molecules of water vapor in air move quickly and don't easily come together. At cooler temperatures, molecules in air move more slowly. The slower movement allows water vapor molecules to collide with one another to form droplets of liquid water. Forming liquid water from water vapor is called condensation. When enough water vapor is present in air for condensation to take place, the air is saturated.

✓ **Reading Check** *Why can more water vapor be present in warm air than in cold air?*

Relative Humidity On a hot, sticky afternoon, the weather forecaster reports that the humidity is 50 percent. How can the humidity be low when it feels so humid? Weather forecasters report the amount of moisture in the air as relative humidity. **Relative humidity** is a measure of the amount of water vapor present in the air compared to the amount needed for saturation at a specific temperature.

If you hear a weather forecaster say that the relative humidity is 50 percent, it means that the air contains 50 percent of the water needed for the air to be saturated.

As shown in **Figure 4,** air at 25°C is saturated when it contains 22 g of water vapor per cubic meter of air. The relative humidity is 100 percent. If air at 25°C contains 11 g of water vapor per cubic meter, the relative humidity is 50 percent.

LAB DEMONSTRATION

Purpose to observe changes in relative humidity, using a chemical indicator

Materials beaker, spoon, concentrated solution of cobalt chloride, paintbrush, white paper, gloves

Preparation Add water to powdered cobalt chloride until the powder dissolves.

Procedure *Caution: Cobalt chloride is toxic; use gloves.* With a paintbrush, apply the solution to several sheets of paper. Let dry. Put the papers in different areas inside and outside. Have students record the color of the papers for several days.

Expected Outcome Colors change over time.

✓ Assessment

Pink indicates high relative humidity; blue indicates low relative humidity. **At which location was the relative humidity highest? Lowest?** Answers will vary with local weather and location of papers.

Dew Point

When the temperature drops, less water vapor can be present in air. The water vapor in air will condense to a liquid or form ice crystals. The temperature at which air is saturated and condensation forms is the **dew point.** The dew point changes with the amount of water vapor in the air.

You've probably seen water droplets form on the outside of a glass of cold milk. The cold glass cooled the air next to it to its dew point. The water vapor in the surrounding air condensed and formed water droplets on the glass. In a similar way, when air near the ground cools to its dew point, water vapor condenses and forms dew. Frost may form when temperatures are near 0°C.

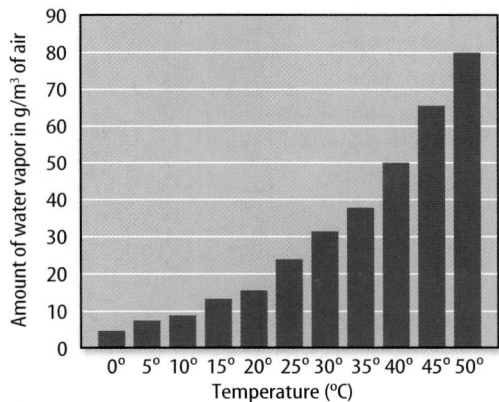

Figure 4
This graph shows that as the temperature of air increases, more water vapor can be present in the air.

Math Skills Activity

Calculating the Amount of Dew

Example Problem

One summer day, the relative humidity is 80 percent and the temperature is 35°C. Will the dew point be reached if the temperature falls to 25°C?

Solution

1 *This is what you know:*

From Figure 4

Air Temperature (°C)	Amount of Water Vapor Needed for Saturation (g)
35	37
25	24

2 *This is what you need to find:* x = amount of water vapor in 35°C air at 80 percent relative humidity. Is $x > 24$ g or is $x < 24$ g?

3 *This is how you solve the problem:* $x = .80\,(37\text{ g})$
$x = 29.6$ g of water vapor
29.6 g > 24 g, so the dew point is reached and dew will form

> ### Practice Problem
> If the relative humidity is 50 percent and the air temperature is 30°C, will the dew point be reached if the temperature falls to 20°C?

Discussion

Explain that a computer room and a science room are the same size and have the same humidity. The computer room is colder. **Which room has the higher relative humidity?** The colder air in the computer room is saturated at a lower temperature. The water vapor in the air of the computer room represents a greater percentage of the water vapor needed for saturation. Thus, the computer room has a greater relative humidity.

Math Skills Activity

National Math Standards

Correlation to Mathematics Objectives
1, 2, 6, 9

Teaching Strategy

Use **Figure 4** to help solve the problem.

Answer to Practice Problem

- What you know: at 30°C you need 30g of water vapor to reach saturation. At 20°C, you need 15g.
- You need to find: x = amount of water vapor in 30°C air at 50 percent relative humidity. Is $x > 15$g or is $x < 15$g?
- Solve the problem:
  $x = .50(37\text{g})$
  $x = 18.5$g of water vapor
  18.5g > 15g, so the dew point is reached and dew will form.

Curriculum Connection

Math Have students solve the following problem. At 20°C, 17 g of water vapor will saturate 1 m^3 of air. If only 4 g are present, what is the relative humidity? (4 g ÷ 17 g) × 100 = 23.5%
 ELL

Forming Clouds

Classifying Clouds

Extension

Have students use a video camera to take stop-frame pictures of clouds as they form. Have them take one picture every minute for thirty minutes. Then, have them show their tapes to the class at regular speed. Have students classify the clouds. `L2` `ELL` `IS` **Visual-Spatial**

Caption Answer

Figure 5C It condenses.

Visual Learning

Figure 5C Have students note that the leading edge of the clouds is high in the air, and well in front of most of the warm air mass. **Why do you think that high clouds can sometimes forecast a change in the weather?** These high clouds may be ahead of coming warm air, which will eventually replace the cool air near the ground.

What clouds are in the sky today? To find out more about clouds, see the **Cloud Field Guide** at the back of this book.

Forming Clouds

Why are there clouds in the sky? Clouds form as warm air is forced upward, expands, and cools. **Figure 5** shows several ways that warm, moist air forms clouds. As the air cools, the amount of water vapor needed for saturation decreases and the relative humidity increases. When the relative humidity reaches 100 percent, the air is saturated. Water vapor soon begins to condense in tiny droplets around small particles such as dust and salt. These droplets of water are so small that they remain suspended in the air. Billions of these droplets form a cloud.

Classifying Clouds

Clouds are classified mainly by shape and height. Some clouds extend high into the sky, and others are low and flat. Some dense clouds bring rain or snow, while thin, wispy clouds appear on mostly sunny days. The shape and height of clouds vary with temperature, pressure, and the amount of water vapor in the atmosphere.

Figure 5
Clouds form when moist air is lifted and cools. This occurs where air is heated, at mountain ranges, and where cold air meets warm air.

A Rays from the Sun heat the ground and the air next to it. The warm air rises and cools. If the air is moist, some water vapor condenses and forms clouds.

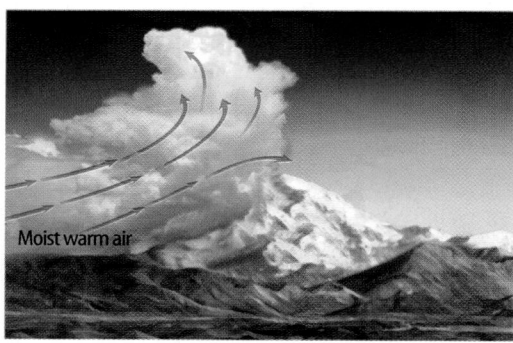

B As moist air moves over mountains, it is lifted and cools. Clouds formed in this way can cover mountains for long periods of time.

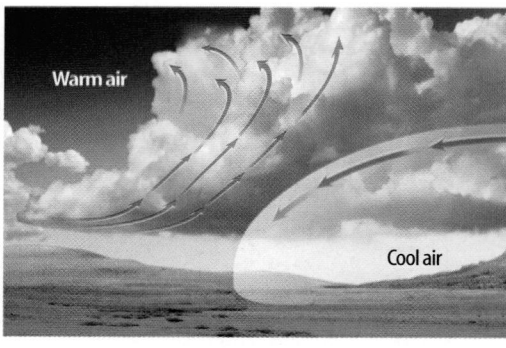

C When cool air meets warm, moist air, the warm air is lifted and cools. *What happens to the water vapor when the dew point is reached?*

✔ Active Reading

ReQuest To improve listening skills have students listen carefully as you read an interesting piece or story aloud. After the reading, have students construct discussion questions. Assign students to read the story and participate in the questioning with other students. Have students participate in a ReQuest with the chapter feature, "Rain," or another interesting piece related to weather.

Science Journal

Animal Behavior Some animals react to changes in air pressure and humidity. Before a storm, birds and bats fly lower and frogs croak more frequently. Have students research and write short reports on other ways that animals react to weather changes. `L2` `IS` **Linguistic**

Shape The three main cloud types are stratus, cumulus, and cirrus. Stratus clouds form layers, or smooth, even sheets in the sky. Stratus clouds usually form at low altitudes and may be associated with fair weather or rain or snow. When air is cooled to its dew point near the ground, it forms a stratus cloud called **fog,** as shown in **Figure 6.**

Cumulus (KYEW myuh lus) clouds are masses of puffy, white clouds, often with flat bases. They sometimes tower to great heights and can be associated with fair weather or thunderstorms.

Cirrus (SIHR us) clouds appear fibrous or curly. They are high, thin, white, feathery clouds made of ice crystals. Cirrus clouds are associated with fair weather, but they can indicate approaching storms.

Height Some prefixes of cloud names describe the height of the cloud base. The prefix *cirro-* describes high clouds, *alto-* describes middle-elevation clouds, and *strato-* refers to clouds at low elevations. Some clouds' names combine the altitude prefix with the term *stratus* or *cumulus*.

Cirrostratus clouds are high clouds, like those in **Figure 7.** Usually, cirrostratus clouds indicate fair weather, but they also can signal an approaching storm. Altostratus clouds form at middle levels. If the clouds are not too thick, sunlight can filter through them.

Figure 6
Fog surrounds the Golden Gate Bridge, San Francisco. Fog is a stratus cloud near the ground.

Figure 7
Cirrostratus clouds are made of ice crystals and form high in Earth's atmosphere.

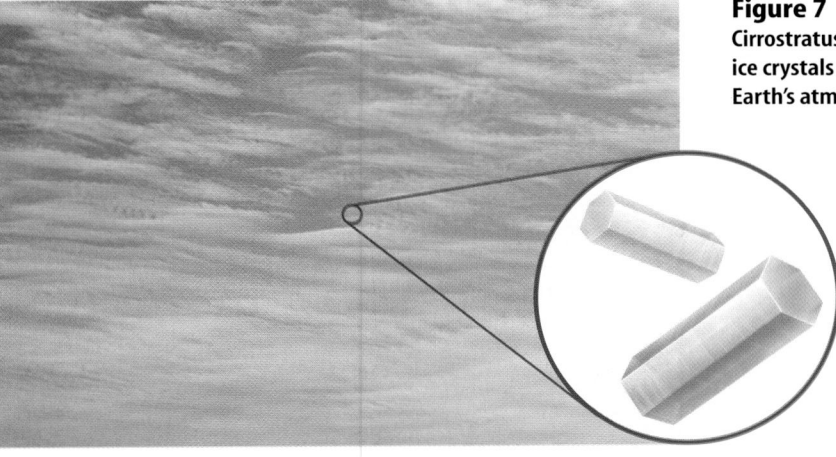

Use Science Words
Word Origins In 1802, Luke Howard classified clouds using the Latin terms *cirrus, cumulus, stratus,* and *nimbus.* Have students use a dictionary and other reference sources to find how the meanings of these words relate to cloud descriptions. *Cirrus* comes from a word meaning "hair"; *cumulus* from "heap"; *stratus* from "layer"; and *nimbus* from "rain."

IDENTIFYING Misconceptions
Students may wonder why clouds don't fall. Remind them that cloud droplets are tiny. They should infer that they are so small and light that that they stay suspended. Students might suggest that fog falls to the ground. But actually fog forms near the ground.

Discussion
What is the difference between an altocumulus and a stratocumulus cloud? The difference is cloud height. An altocumulus is a middle-elevation cumulus cloud; a stratocumulus is a low-elevation cumulus cloud.

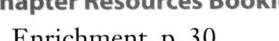

Resource Manager

Chapter Resources Booklet
Enrichment, p. 30
Physical Science Critical Thinking/Problem Solving, p. 16

Curriculum Connection

History Before satellites and radar, people used observations of nature to predict weather. They didn't know why things happened, but they noted patterns. For example, they knew rain often follows a halo around the moon. The reason? The ice crystals in cirrus clouds cause the halo, and cirrus clouds often mean coming rain. Have students research other weather folklore and make posters describing what they find.

Classifying Clouds

Precipitation

Discussion

Remind students that when the dew point is below 0° C, water vapor freezes on vegetation, forming frost. In some rural areas, frost is called "baby snow." **Is frost a type of precipitation? Explain.** No; it doesn't fall from clouds.

Figure 8
Water vapor in air collects on particles to form water droplets or ice crystals. The type of precipitation that is received on the ground depends on the temperature of the air.

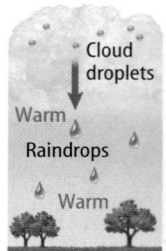   

A When the air is warm, water vapor forms raindrops that fall as rain.

B When the air is cold, water vapor forms snowflakes.

Rain- or Snow-Producing Clouds Clouds associated with rain or snow often have the word nimbus attached to them. The term *nimbus* is Latin for "dark rain cloud" and this is a good description, because the water content of these clouds is so high that little sunlight can pass through them. When a cumulus cloud grows into a thunderstorm, it is called a cumulonimbus (kyew myuh loh NIHM bus) cloud. These clouds can tower to nearly 18,000 km. Nimbostratus clouds are layered clouds that can bring long, steady rain or snowfall.

Precipitation

Water falling from clouds is called **precipitation.** Precipitation occurs when cloud droplets combine and grow large enough to fall to Earth. The cloud droplets form around small particles, such as salt and dust. These particles are so small that a puff of smoke can contain millions of them.

You might have noticed that raindrops are not all the same size. The size of raindrops depends on several factors. One factor is the strength of updrafts in a cloud. Strong updrafts can keep drops suspended in the air where they can combine with other drops and grow larger. The rate of evaporation as a drop falls to Earth also can affect its size. If the air is dry, the size of raindrops can be reduced or they can completely evaporate before reaching the ground.

Air temperature determines whether water forms rain, snow, sleet, or hail. **Figure 8** shows these main types of precipitation. Drops of water falling in temperatures above freezing fall as rain. Snow forms when the air temperature is so cold that water vapor changes directly to a solid. Sleet forms when raindrops pass through a layer of freezing air near Earth's surface, forming ice pellets.

✔ **Reading Check** *What are the four main types of precipitation?*

✔ **Reading Check**

Answer rain, snow, sleet, hail

Cultural Diversity

Changing the Weather For centuries, during periods of drought, people have tried to make it rain. In the Soyal festival, the Hopi Nation of the southwestern U.S. perform a dance for the purpose of bringing rain. Have students research other traditional customs for changing weather. Possible answer: The Hurocs of northern California hammer on a rain stone carved from soapstone to prevent excessive rain.

Resource Manager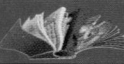

Chapter Resources Booklet
    Lab Activity, pp. 13–15
    Reinforcement, p. 27

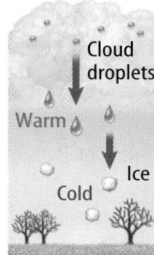

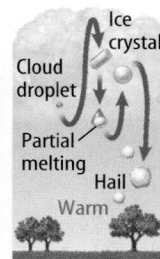

C When the air near the ground is cold, sleet, which is made up of many small ice pellets, falls.

D Hailstones are pellets of ice that form inside a cloud.

Hail Hail is precipitation in the form of lumps of ice. Hail forms in cumulonimbus clouds of a thunderstorm when water freezes in layers around a small nucleus of ice. Hailstones grow larger as they're tossed up and down by rising and falling air. Most hailstones are smaller than 2.5 cm but can grow larger than a softball. Of all forms of precipitation, hail produces the most damage immediately, especially if winds blow during a hailstorm. Falling hailstones can break windows and destroy crops.

If you understand the role of water vapor in the atmosphere, you can begin to understand weather. The relative humidity of the air helps determine whether a location will have a dry day or experience some form of precipitation. The temperature of the atmosphere determines the form of precipitation. Studying clouds can add to your ability to forecast weather.

3 Assess

Reteach

Collect a variety of cloud photographs. Identify each cloud type on the back of its picture. Have students work in pairs. Suggest that one student show the pictures, while the other identifies the clouds. Then have students switch roles. [L2]
COOP LEARN [IS] **Visual-Spatial**

Challenge

Have students observe and record the pattern of precipitation for several days. Have them also observe the cloud patterns that occur before and after precipitation. Challenge students to use this information to write a paragraph that describes how clouds can predict precipitation. [L3]

✓ Assessment

Content Have student pairs work together to write songs that explain how different types of precipitation form. Use **Performance Assessment in the Science Classroom**, p. 151.

SCIENCE
Online
Internet Addresses
_____
_____
_____

Explore the Glencoe Science Web site at **science.glencoe.com** to find out more about topics in this section.

Section 1 Assessment

1. When does water vapor in air condense?
2. What is the difference between humidity and relative humidity?
3. How do clouds form?
4. How does precipitation occur and what determines the type of precipitation that falls to Earth?
5. **Think Critically** Cumulonimbus clouds form when warm, moist air is suddenly lifted. How can the same cumulonimbus cloud produce rain and hail?

Skill Builder Activities

6. **Concept Mapping** Make a network-tree concept map that compares clouds and their descriptions. Use these terms: *cirrus, cumulus, stratus, feathery, fair weather, puffy, layered, precipitation, clouds, dark,* and *steady precipitation.* **For more help, refer to the** Science Skill Handbook.

7. **Making and Using Graphs** Use **Figure 4** to determine how much water vapor can be present in air when the temperature is 40°C. **For more help, refer to the** Science Skill Handbook.

SECTION 1 What is weather? **469**

Answers to Section Assessment

1. when it cools to the dew point
2. humidity: amount of water vapor in air; relative humidity: amount of water vapor present in air compared to the amount that is needed for saturation at a specific temperature
3. Moist, warm air is lifted and cools to its dew point; water vapor condenses

around dust particles and forms cloud drops.
4. cloud droplets combine and grow large enough to fall to Earth; the temperature of the atmosphere
5. Near the top of the cloud, water droplets freeze around small ice nuclei, forming ice crystals. Hailstones may grow as updrafts in the

cloud melt and refreeze ice crystals. Rain forms when precipitation does not melt and refreeze.

6.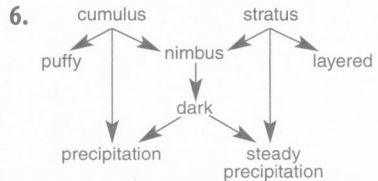

7. 80 g per m³ of air

SECTION
2
Weather Patterns

1 Motivate

Bellringer Transparency

Display the Section Focus Transparency for Section 2. Use the accompanying Transparency Activity Master. L2

ELL

Section Focus Transparency

2 Section Focus Transparency — **Cloud Walking**

If you've ever hiked up a mountain, you may have noticed that it is often cooler at higher elevations. Since warm air is less dense, it will rise, while more dense cool air sinks. But what happens if the air above is warmer? The result is an inversion in which the colder surface air is trapped.

1. Why are the clouds hanging in the valley in this picture?
2. What will happen when the Sun warms the lower air?
3. What would happen if there were pollutants near the ground?

L2

Tie to Prior Knowledge

Ask students if they have ever experienced a thunderstorm. Have students take turns describing what they saw, felt, and heard during such a storm. Tell students they will learn how thunderstorms form in the upcoming section.

SECTION
2 Weather Patterns

As You Read

What You'll Learn

- **Describe** how weather is associated with fronts and high- and low-pressure areas.
- **Explain** how tornadoes develop from thunderstorms.
- **Discuss** the dangers of severe weather.

Vocabulary

air mass   hurricane
front   blizzard
tornado

Why It's Important

Air masses, pressure systems, and fronts cause weather to change.

Figure 9
Six major air masses affect weather in the United States. Each air mass has the same characteristics of temperature and moisture content as the area over which it formed.

Weather Changes

When you leave for school in the morning, the weather might be different from what it is when you head home in the afternoon. Because of the movement of air and moisture in the atmosphere, weather constantly changes.

Air Masses An **air mass** is a large body of air that has properties similar to the part of Earth's surface over which it develops. For example, an air mass that develops over land is dry compared with one that develops over water. An air mass that develops in the tropics is warmer than one that develops over northern regions. An air mass can cover thousands of square kilometers. When you observe a change in the weather from one day to the next, it is due to the movement of air masses. **Figure 9** shows air masses that affect the United States.

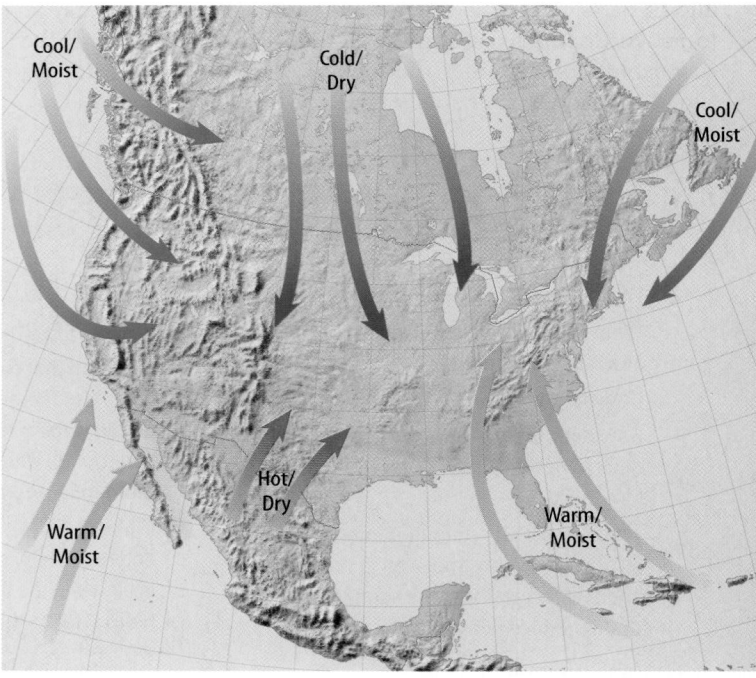

Cool/Moist

Cold/Dry

Cool/Moist

Hot/Dry

Warm/Moist

Warm/Moist

Section ✓Assessment Planner

PORTFOLIO
Use Science Words, p. 471
PERFORMANCE ASSESSMENT
Skill Builder Activities, p. 477
See page 488 for more options.

CONTENT ASSESSMENT
Section, p. 477
Challenge, p. 477
Chapter, pp. 488–489

Highs and Lows

Atmospheric pressure varies over Earth's surface. Anyone who has watched a weather report on television has heard about high- and low-pressure systems. Recall that winds blow from areas of high pressure to areas of low pressure. As winds blow into a low-pressure area in the northern hemisphere, Earth's rotation causes these winds to swirl in a counterclockwise direction. Large, swirling areas of low pressure are called cyclones and are associated with stormy weather.

Reading Check *How do winds move in a cyclone?*

Winds blow away from a center of high pressure. Earth's rotation causes these winds to spiral clockwise in the northern hemisphere. High-pressure areas are associated with fair weather and are called anticyclones. Air pressure is measured using a barometer, like the one shown in **Figure 10.**

Variation in atmospheric pressure affects the weather. Low pressure systems at Earth's surface are regions of rising air. In Section 1, you learned that clouds form when air is lifted and cools. Areas of low pressure usually have cloudy weather. Sinking motion in high-pressure air masses makes it difficult for air to rise and clouds to form. That's why high pressure usually means good weather.

Fronts

A boundary between two air masses of different density, moisture, or temperature is called a **front.** If you've seen a weather map in the newspaper or on the evening news, you've seen fronts represented by various types of curving lines.

Cloudiness, precipitation, and storms sometimes occur at frontal boundaries. Four types of fronts include cold, warm, occluded, and stationary.

Cold and Warm Fronts A cold front, shown on a map as a blue line with triangles, occurs when colder air advances toward warm air. The cold air wedges under the warm air like a plow. As the warm air is lifted, it cools and water vapor condenses, forming clouds. When the temperature difference between the cold and warm air is large, thunderstorms and even tornadoes may form.

Warm fronts form when lighter, warmer air advances over heavier, colder air. A warm front is drawn on weather maps as a red line with red semicircles.

Figure 10
A barometer measures atmospheric pressure. The red pointer points to the current pressure. *Watch how atmospheric pressure changes over time when you line up the white pointer to the one indicating the current pressure each day.*

Data Update Visit the Glencoe Science Web site at **science.glencoe.com** to find the current atmospheric pressure, temperature, and wind direction in your town or nearest city. Look up these weather conditons for a city west of your town. Forecast the weather for your town based on your research.

SECTION 2 Weather Patterns **471**

---

2 Teach

Weather Changes

Discussion
Why don't pressure systems always remain in one place? Because winds move them.

Reading Check

Answer counterclockwise in the northern hemisphere

Use Science Words
Word Meaning In the 1920s, the term *front* was used to describe the boundary between two air masses because this boundary was similar to the front along which opposing armies fought during a war. Norwegian meteorologists first used the term. Have students write a brief paragraph comparing military fronts with weather fronts. In both cases, there is a line between two opposing forces. Eventually, one side advances, often pushing the other out of the way. [L2] IS **Linguistic** P

SCIENCE Online
Internet Addresses
_____
_____
_____
_____
Explore the Glencoe Science Web site at **science.glencoe.com** to find out more about topics in this section.

Inclusion Strategies

Visually Impaired Have students listen to daily weather reports on the radio or TV and identify how meteorologists use the terms mentioned in the text. Students can use cassette recorders to make audio reports on what they find and share their reports with the class. Students should include terms such as precipitation, front, high, low, temperature, and relative humidity.

Fronts

Visual Learning

Figure 11 Why is it unlikely that towering clouds will form at a warm front? The slope of the front is too gentle—it doesn't allow for air to be pushed up steeply to form towering clouds.

Quick Demo

Use an aquarium with a glass lid, cold bags of sand or marbles, and a pan of very hot water to make a model of a cold front. Place the pan of hot water inside the aquarium next to the cold bags. Cover the aquarium with the glass lid. Have students observe what happens. They should notice that condensation occurs on the sides and top of the aquarium, and "clouds" appear above the cold bags. There is no "cloud" above the pan because the warm temperature of the air there prevents condensation. L2
IS Visual-Spatial

Teacher FYI

Atmospheric pressure drops before a front passes a region and rises after the front has passed. Also, as a front passes the wind changes direction. Winds usually shift from southwest to northwest after a cold front has passed and from southeast to southwest after a warm front has passed.

Figure 11
Cold, warm, occluded, and stationary fronts occur at the boundaries of air masses. Cloudiness and precipitation occur at front boundaries.

Occluded and Stationary Fronts An occluded front involves three air masses of different temperatures—colder air, cool air, and warm air. An occluded front may form when a cold air mass moves toward cooler air with warm air between the two. The colder air forces the warm air upward, closing off the warm air from the surface. Occluded fronts are shown on maps as purple lines with triangles and semicircles.

A stationary front occurs when a boundary between air masses stops advancing. Stationary fronts may remain in the same place for several days, producing light wind and precipitation. A stationary front is drawn on a weather map as an alternating red and blue line. Red semicircles point toward the cold air and blue triangles point toward the warm air. **Figure 11** summarizes the four types of fronts.

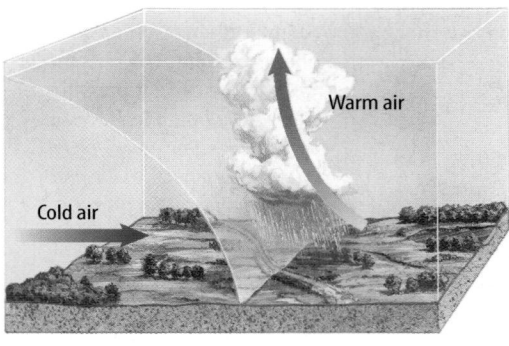

A A cold front can advance rapidly. Thunderstorms often form as warm air is suddenly lifted up over the cold air.

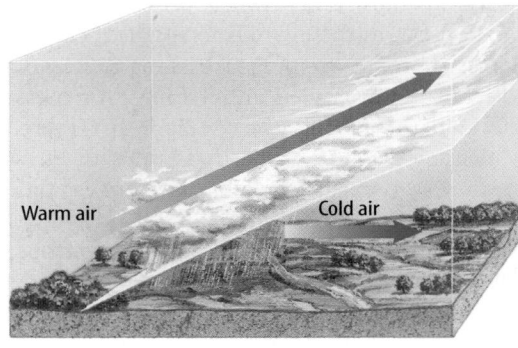

B Warm air slides over colder air along a warm front, forming a boundary with a gentle slope. This can lead to hours, if not days, of wet weather.

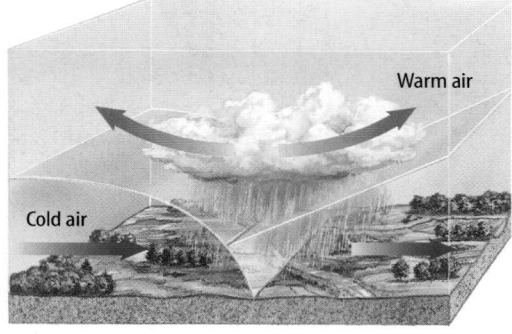

C The term *occlusion* means "closure." Colder air forces warm air upward, forming an occluded front that closes off the warm air from the surface.

D A stationary front results when neither cold air nor warm air advances.

472   CHAPTER 16 Weather

Inclusion Strategies

Learning Disabled Have students practice drawing symbols for fronts and describing the weather at each frontal boundary.

Curriculum Connection

Geography Obtain a simple weather map of the United States from a recent newspaper or access the Glencoe Science Web site. The map should show fronts. Display or copy the map for students. Have them use the fronts to describe the weather in at least two locations in the U.S. Several students can take turns using the map to present their weather forecasts to the class. L2
IS Visual-Spatial

Severe Weather

Despite the weather, you usually can do your daily activities. If it's raining, you still go to school. You can still get there even if it snows a little. However, some weather conditions, such as those caused by thunderstorms, tornadoes, and blizzards, prevent you from going about your normal routine. Severe weather poses danger to people, structures, and animals.

Thunderstorms In a thunderstorm, heavy rain falls, lightning flashes, thunder roars, and hail might fall. What forces cause such extreme weather conditions? Thunderstorms occur in warm, moist air masses and along fronts. Warm, moist air can be rapidly forced upward where it cools and condenses, forming cumulonimbus clouds that can reach heights of 18 km, like the one in **Figure 12.** When rising air cools, water vapor condenses into water droplets or ice crystals. Smaller droplets collide to form larger ones, and the droplets fall through the cloud toward Earth's surface. The falling droplets collide with still more droplets and grow larger. Raindrops cool the air around them. This cool, dense air then sinks and spreads over Earth's surface. Sinking rain-cooled air and strong updrafts of warmer air cause the strong winds associated with thunderstorms. Hail also may form as ice crystals alternately fall to warmer layers and are lifted into colder layers by the strong updrafts inside cumulonimbus clouds.

Thunderstorm damage Sometimes thunderstorms can stall over a region, causing rain to fall heavily for a period of time. When streams cannot contain all the water running into them, flash flooding can occur. Flash floods can be dangerous because they occur with little warning.

Strong winds generated by thunderstorms also can cause damage. If a thunderstorm is accompanied by winds traveling faster than 89 km/h, it is classified as a severe thunderstorm. Hail from a thunderstorm can dent cars and the aluminum siding on houses. Although rain from thunderstorms helps crops grow, hail has been known to flatten and destroy entire crops in a matter of minutes.

Figure 12
Tall cumulonimbus clouds may form quickly as warm, moist air rapidly rises.

SECTION 2 Weather Patterns **473**

Severe Weather

Extension

Have students research how the average annual damage from severe thunderstorms affects your local economy.

Teacher FYI

A thunderstorm has a three-stage life cycle. The initial stage, or cumulus stage, of strong updrafts lasts for about 15 minutes. The mature stage is the most intense period and begins as rain falls from the base of the clouds. Lightning, turbulence, and hail can be most severe during this stage. The falling rain produces downdrafts that spread outward along the ground. The downdrafts finally cut off the updrafts of warm air. This signals the beginning of the final stage. With the supply of warm air cut off by cooler air on the ground, cloud growth and precipitation cease and the storm ends.

Fun Fact

The largest officially measured hailstone in the United States fell on September 3, 1970, in Coffeyville, Kansas. Having a mass of 0.76 kg and a circumference of 45 cm, it was about the size of a cantaloupe. Larger stones have been reported, but they were never officially measured.

Resource Manager

Science Inquiry Labs, p. 27

Science Journal

Weather Effects Have students write in their Science Journals about the direct and indirect ways weather affects their lives. One indirect effect is paying more for fruits and vegetables when an agricultural region experiences an unusually wet or dry growing season. L2 LS **Intrapersonal and Linguistic**

IDENTIFYING Misconceptions

Students may think that lightning travels only from clouds to the ground. In less than 1/10 second, a single lightning discharge goes back and forth many times between a cloud and the ground. Although these discharges usually begin in clouds, sometimes they begin at Earth's surface.

Discussion

Why don't you see lightning and hear the thunder it causes at the same time? Light travels 903,614.5 times faster than sound in air. Only when lightning strikes nearby are thunder and lightning sensed at nearly the same time.

✔ Reading Check

Answer A wind shear can form a rotating column of air parallel to the ground. A thunderstorm's updraft can tilt the rotating column, forming a funnel cloud.

SCIENCE Online
Internet Addresses
_____
_____
_____
_____

Explore the Glencoe Science Web site at **science.glencoe.com** to find out more about topics in this section.

Figure 13
This time-elapsed photo shows a thunderstorm over Arizona.

SCIENCE Online

Research Visit the Glencoe Science Web site at **science.glencoe.com** to research the number of lightning strikes in your state during the last year. Compare your findings with previous years. Communicate to your class what you learn.

Lightning and Thunder

What are lightning and thunder? Inside a storm cloud, warm air is lifted rapidly as cooler air sinks. This movement of air can cause different parts of a cloud to become oppositely charged. When current flows between regions of opposite electrical charge, lightning flashes. Lightning, as shown in **Figure 13,** can occur within a cloud, between clouds, or between a cloud and the ground.

Thunder results from the rapid heating of air around a bolt of lightning. Lightning can reach temperatures of about 30,000°C, which is more than five times the temperature of the surface of the Sun. This extreme heat causes air around the lightning to expand rapidly. Then it cools quickly and contracts. The rapid movement of the molecules forms sound waves heard as thunder.

Tornadoes Some of the most severe thunderstorms produce tornadoes. A **tornado** is a violent, whirling wind that moves in a narrow path over land. In severe thunderstorms, wind at different heights blows in different directions and at different speeds. This difference in wind speed and direction, called wind shear, creates a rotating column parallel to the ground. A thunderstorm's updraft can tilt the rotating column upward into the thunderstorm creating a funnel cloud. If the funnel comes into contact with Earth's surface, it is called a tornado.

✔ Reading Check   *What causes a tornado to form?*

A tornado's destructive winds can rip apart buildings and uproot trees. High winds can blow through broken windows. When winds blow inside a house, they can lift off the roof and blow out the walls, making it look as though the building exploded. The updraft in the center of a powerful tornado can lift animals, cars, and even houses into the air. Although tornadoes rarely exceed 200 m in diameter and usually last only a few minutes, they often are extremely destructive. In May 1999, multiple thunderstorms produced more than 70 tornadoes in Kansas, Oklahoma, and Texas. This severe tornado outbreak caused 40 deaths, 100 injuries, and more than $1.2 billion in property damage.

Curriculum Connection

History In 1752, Benjamin Franklin proved that lightning is an electrical discharge. Later, he invented a lightning rod. Have students research his experiments. In his best-known experiment, he attached a key to a kite string and flew the kite early in a storm, before lightning had come near him. A spark jumped from the key to his hand, thereby showing that electricity was present. L2 Linguistic

Science Journal

Tornado Chasing Inform students that some scientists chase tornadoes to study them. They look for places where conditions are right for tornadoes to form. Then they go to these areas and try to place instruments in a storm's path. Have students write a short essay on why they would or would not want to do this type of research. Logical-Mathematical

NATIONAL GEOGRAPHIC **VISUALIZING TORNADOES**

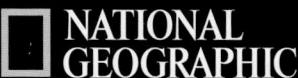

Figure 14

Tornadoes are extremely rapid, rotating winds that form at the base of cumulonimbus clouds. Smaller tornadoes may even form inside larger ones. Luckily, most tornadoes remain on the ground for just a few minutes. During that time, however, they can cause considerable—and sometimes strange—damage, such as driving a fork into a tree.

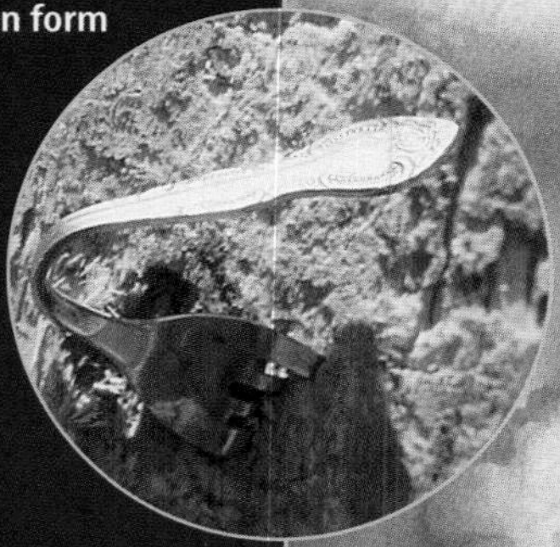

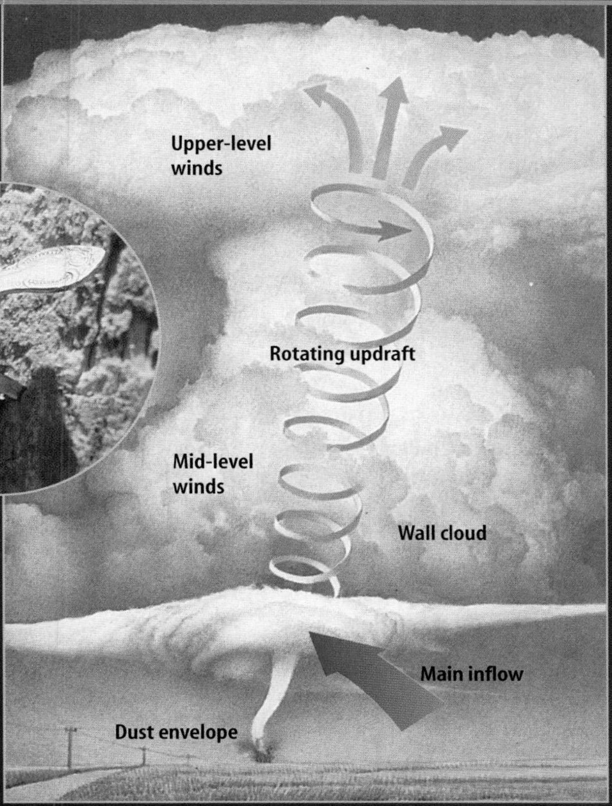

Upper-level winds
Rotating updraft
Mid-level winds
Wall cloud
Main inflow
Dust envelope

Tornadoes often form from a type of cumulonimbus cloud called a wall cloud. Strong, spiraling updrafts of warm, moist air may form in these clouds. As air spins upward, a low-pressure area forms, and the cloud descends to the ground in a funnel. The tornado sucks up debris as it moves along the ground, forming a dust envelope.

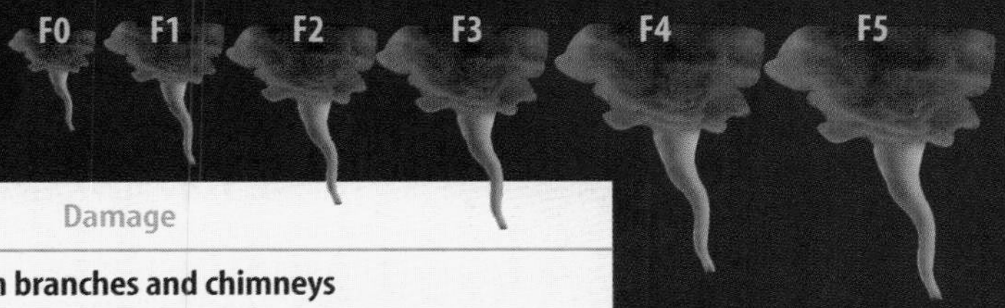

F0
F1
F2
F3
F4
F5

The Fujita Scale

	Wind speed (km/h)	Damage
F0	<116	Light: broken branches and chimneys
F1	116–180	Moderate: roofs damaged, mobile homes upturned
F2	181–253	Considerable: roofs torn off homes, large trees uprooted
F3	254–332	Severe: trains overturned, roofs and walls torn off
F4	333–419	Devastating: houses completely destroyed, cars picked up and carried elsewhere
F5	420–512	Incredible: total demolition

The Fujita scale, named after tornado expert Theodore Fujita, ranks tornadoes according to how much damage they cause. Fortunately, only one percent of tornadoes are classified as violent (F4 and F5).

475

Resource Manager

Reading and Writing Skill Activities, p. 45

NATIONAL GEOGRAPHIC

Visualizing Tornadoes

Have students examine the pictures and read the captions. Then ask the following questions.

What do you think causes most injuries and deaths during a tornado? Why do you think this is? Most are caused by flying objects that are blown around by the very strong winds of a tornado.

If a tornado were heading toward you, why would a car not be a safe place to stay? Cars can be overturned or even picked up and carried away by tornado winds.

Activity

Have small groups of students research the average number of tornadoes that occur each year in each state. Ask them to prepare an outline map of the United States with the data for each state on it. Then ask them to identify the area known as "tornado alley" and write an explanation of why so many tornadoes occur in this region. L2 COOP LEARN

LS **Linguistic and Visual-Spatial**

Extension

Challenge students to find out how Doppler radar works to allow meteorologists to detect and track possible tornadoes. Have them prepare a labeled diagram of their findings. L2

LS **Visual-Spatial**

Severe Weather,
continued

Activity

Have students work together to make mobiles showing different types of severe storms. L1

ELL COOP LEARN IS **Visual-Spatial**

Teacher FYI

- A storm is classified as a tropical depression if its winds are less than 63 km/h, a tropical storm if winds are 63–120 km/h, and a hurricane if winds exceed 120 km/h.

- The strongest hurricane winds are within 80 km of the eye.

- During El Niño years, there are usually fewer hurricanes. During the 1997 El Niño, there were 30% fewer tropical storms than normal. El Niño causes the tropical jet stream to curve eastward across the Atlantic Ocean, preventing tropical storms from moving west toward the Americas.

- The Saffir-Simpson Scale measures the intensity of hurricanes with numbers from 1 to 5. A Category 5 hurricane is the most intense, with sustained wind speed greater than 135 km/h. Category 1 hurricanes are the weakest, with sustained winds just past the hurricane threshold of 120 km/h.

Environmental Science

INTEGRATION

Some scientists hypothesize that Earth's ocean temperatures are increasing due to global warming. In your Science Journal, predict what might happen to the strength of hurricanes if Earth's oceans become warmer.

Figure 15
In this hurricane cross section, the small, red arrows indicate rising, warm, moist air. This air forms cumulus and cumulonimbus clouds in bands around the eye. The green arrows indicate cool, dry air sinking in the eye and between the cloud bands.

Hurricanes The most powerful storm is the hurricane. A **hurricane,** illustrated in **Figure 15,** is a large, swirling, low-pressure system that forms over the warm Atlantic ocean. It is like a machine that turns heat energy from the ocean into wind. A storm must have winds of at least 120 km/h to be called a hurricane. Similar storms are called typhoons in the Pacific Ocean and cyclones in the Indian Ocean.

Hurricanes are similar to low-pressure systems on land, but they are much stronger. In the Atlantic and Pacific Oceans, low pressure sometimes develops near the equator. In the northern hemisphere, winds around this low pressure begin rotating counterclockwise. The strongest hurricanes affecting North America usually begin as a low-pressure system east of Africa. Steered by surface winds, these storms can travel west, gaining strength from the heat and moisture of warm ocean water.

When a hurricane strikes land, high winds, tornadoes, heavy rains, and high waves can cause a lot of damage. Floods from the heavy rains can cause additional damage. Hurricane weather can destroy crops, demolish buildings, and kill people and other animals. As long as a hurricane is over water, the warm, moist air rises and provides energy for the storm. When a hurricane reaches land, however, its supply of energy disappears and the storm loses power.

Descending air

Warm moist air

Outflow

Eye

Spiral rain bands

Curriculum Connection

Math The locations of the five deadliest hurricanes to strike the U.S. since 1900 are: (1) Galveston, TX, 1900, 8,000 deaths; (2) Florida, 1928, 1,836 deaths; (3) Southern TX, 1919, 600 deaths; (4) New England, 1938, 600 deaths; and (5) Florida Keys, 1935, 498 deaths. Have students make bar graphs of these data, with location on the *x*-axis and number of deaths on the *y*-axis. Students should determine a scale.

Resource Manager

Chapter Resources Booklet
Reinforcement, p. 28
Enrichment, p. 31

Blizzards Severe storms also can occur in winter. If you live in the northern United States, you may have awakened from a winter night's sleep to a cold, howling wind and blowing snow, like the storm in **Figure 16**. The National Weather Service classifies a winter storm as a **blizzard** if the winds are 51 km/h, the temperature is −12°C or below, the visibility is less than 200 m in falling or blowing snow, and if these conditions persist for three hours or more.

Severe Weather Safety When severe weather threatens, the National Weather Service issues a watch or warning. Watches are issued when conditions are favorable for severe thunderstorms, tornadoes, floods, blizzards, and hurricanes. During a watch, stay tuned to a radio or television station reporting the weather. When a warning is issued, severe weather conditions already exist. You should take immediate action. During a severe thunderstorm or tornado warning, take shelter in the basement or a room in the middle of the house away from windows. When a hurricane or flood watch is issued, be prepared to leave your home and move farther inland.

Blizzards can be blinding and have dangerously low temperatures with high winds. During a blizzard, stay indoors. Spending too much time outside can result in severe frostbite.

Figure 16
Blizzards can be extremely dangerous because of their high winds, low temperatures, and poor visibility.

Section 2 Assessment

1. Why is fair weather common during periods of high pressure?
2. How does a cold front form? What effect does a cold front have on weather?
3. What causes lightning and thunder in a thunderstorm?
4. What is the difference between a watch and a warning? How can you keep safe during a hurricane warning?
5. **Think Critically** Explain why some fronts produce stronger storms than others.

Skill Builder Activities

6. **Recognizing Cause and Effect** Describe how an occluded front may form over your city and what effects it can have on the weather. **For more help, refer to the** Science Skill Handbook.
7. **Using an Electronic Spreadsheet** Make a spreadsheet comparing warm fronts, cold fronts, occluded fronts, and stationary fronts. Indicate what kind of clouds and weather systems form with each. **For more help, refer to the** Technology Skill Handbook.

Have students research specific hurricanes that have been especially destructive and present oral reports. Examples include Hurricanes Camille, Agnes, Gloria, Hugo, Andrew, Floyd, and Mitch.

3 Assess

Reteach

Have pairs of students make tables that compare and contrast tornadoes and hurricanes according to relative size, origin, type of pressure system, and damage. L2 COOP LEARN

Challenge

Have student pairs use the Internet to research severe weather safety. Encourage them to make posters that contain a list of safety tips with illustrations for hurricanes, tornadoes, thunderstorms, or blizzards. COOP LEARN

Assessment

Performance To assess students' abilities to describe the effects of weather systems, ask them to predict the resulting weather if a fast-moving cold air mass overtakes a slow-moving warm air mass over Texas in July. thunderstorms Use **Performance Assessment in the Science Classroom**, p. 89.

Answers to Section Assessment

1. Clouds can't form in the descending air of a high-pressure system.
2. Cold air moves into and pushes up warm air; thunderstorms are common.
3. Lightning is a current flow between areas of opposite electrical charge. Thunder results from rapid heating of air around the lightning bolt.
4. Watch: conditions are favorable for severe weather; warning: severe weather exists; hurricane warning: go inland and to higher ground.
5. The strongest storms form at the steepest frontal boundaries.
6. Possible answer: Cool air is over the city, with warmer air to the west. Fast-moving cold air comes from the west and forces the warm air up. Rain and wind may result.
7. Possible answer: warm: layers of clouds, light precipitation; cold: tall clouds, strong storms; stationary: light wind, precipitation; occluded: winds, heavy precipitation possible.

Weather Forecasts

Motivate

Bellringer Transparency

Display the Section Focus Transparency for Section 3. Use the accompanying Transparency Activity Master. L2

ELL

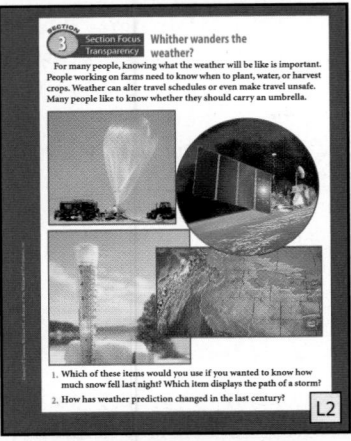

Tie to Prior Knowledge

Based on weather forecasts they have seen or heard, have students recall how far ahead weather forecasters predict the weather, and if forecasts are usually accurate. about five days; accuracy varies Explain that they will learn how the weather is predicted in this section.

Text Question Answer

Weather concerns might include hurricanes, tornadoes, blizzards, ice storms, or hail.

Weather Forecasts

As You Read

What You'll Learn
- **Explain** how data are collected for weather maps and forecasts.
- **Identify** the symbols used in a weather station model.

Vocabulary
meteorologist   isotherm
station model   isobar

Why It's Important
Weather observations help you predict future weather events.

Figure 17
A meteorologist uses Doppler radar to track a tornado. Since the nineteenth century, technology has greatly improved weather forecasting.

Weather Observations

You can determine current weather conditions by checking the thermometer and looking to see whether clouds are in the sky. You know when it's raining. You have a general idea of the weather because you are familiar with the typical weather where you live. If you live in Florida, you don't expect snow in the forecast. If you live in Maine, you assume it will snow every winter. What weather concerns do you have in your region?

A **meteorologist** (meet ee uh RAH luh jist) is a person who studies the weather. Meteorologists take measurements of temperature, air pressure, winds, humidity, and precipitation. Computers, weather satellites, Doppler radar shown in **Figure 17,** and instruments attached to balloons are used to gather data. Such instruments improve meteorologists' ability to predict the weather. Meteorologists use the information provided by weather instruments to make weather maps. These maps are used to make weather forecasts.

Forecasting Weather Meteorologists gather information about current weather and use computers to make predictions about future weather patterns. Because storms can be dangerous, you do not want to be unprepared for threatening weather. However, meteorologists cannot always predict the weather exactly because conditions can change rapidly.

The National Weather Service depends on two sources for its information—data collected from the upper atmosphere and data collected on Earth's surface. Meteorologists of the National Weather Service collect information recorded by satellites, instruments attached to weather balloons, and from radar. This information is used to describe weather conditions in the atmosphere above Earth's surface.

478 **CHAPTER 16** Weather

Section ✔*Assessment* Planner

PORTFOLIO
Challenge, p. 480
Assessment, p. 483
PERFORMANCE ASSESSMENT
Try at Home MiniLAB, p. 479
Skill Builder Activities, p. 480
See page 488 for more options.

CONTENT ASSESSMENT
Section, p. 480
Challenge, p. 480
Chapter, pp. 488–489

Station Models When meteorologists gather data from Earth's surface, it is recorded on a map using a combination of symbols, forming a **station model**. A station model, like the one in **Figure 18,** shows the weather conditions at a specific location on Earth's surface. Information provided by station models and instruments in the upper atmosphere is entered into computers and used to forecast weather.

Temperature and Pressure In addition to station models, weather maps have lines that connect locations of equal temperature or pressure. A line that connects points of equal temperature is called an **isotherm** (I suh thurm). *Iso* means "same" and *therm* means "temperature." You probably have seen isotherms on weather maps on TV or in the newspaper.

An **isobar** is a line drawn to connect points of equal atmospheric pressure. You can tell how fast wind is blowing in an area by noting how closely isobars are spaced. Isobars that are close together indicate a large pressure difference over a small area. A large pressure difference causes strong winds. Isobars that are spread apart indicate a smaller difference in pressure. Winds in this area are gentler. Isobars also indicate the locations of high- and low-pressure areas.

✓ Reading Check *How do isobars indicate wind speed?*

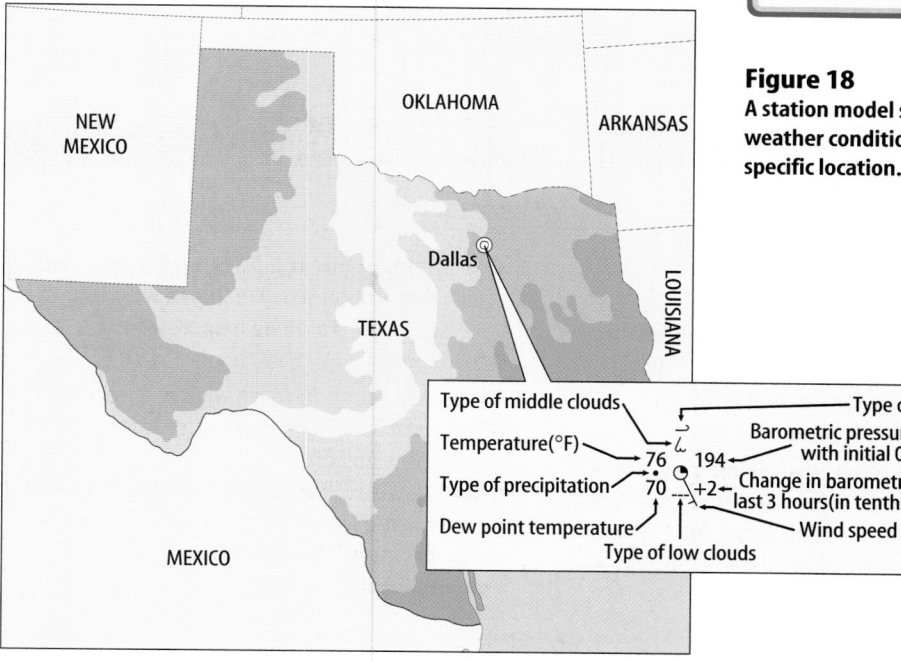

Figure 18
A station model shows the weather conditions at one specific location.

SECTION 3 Weather Forecasts **479**

3 Assess

Reteach
Have students examine daily weather maps and identify isotherms, the positions of high- and low-pressure areas, and fronts. L2 LS **Visual-Spatial**

Challenge
Have students research whether weather trends (climate) have changed over the years in your area. Direct them to write a report on what they find. Historical weather data are available from the National Weather Service, local meteorologists at universities or TV stations, or through searching local newspapers. If the trends have changed, encourage students to infer why they might have changed and to include this information in their reports. L3 LS **Linguistic** P

✓ Assessment

Process Assess students' abilities to interpret scientific illustrations. Have students locate your area in **Figure 19**. Tell them to locate and identify the closest front and pressure system. Answers will vary with location. Use **Performance Assessment in the Science Classroom,** p. 99.

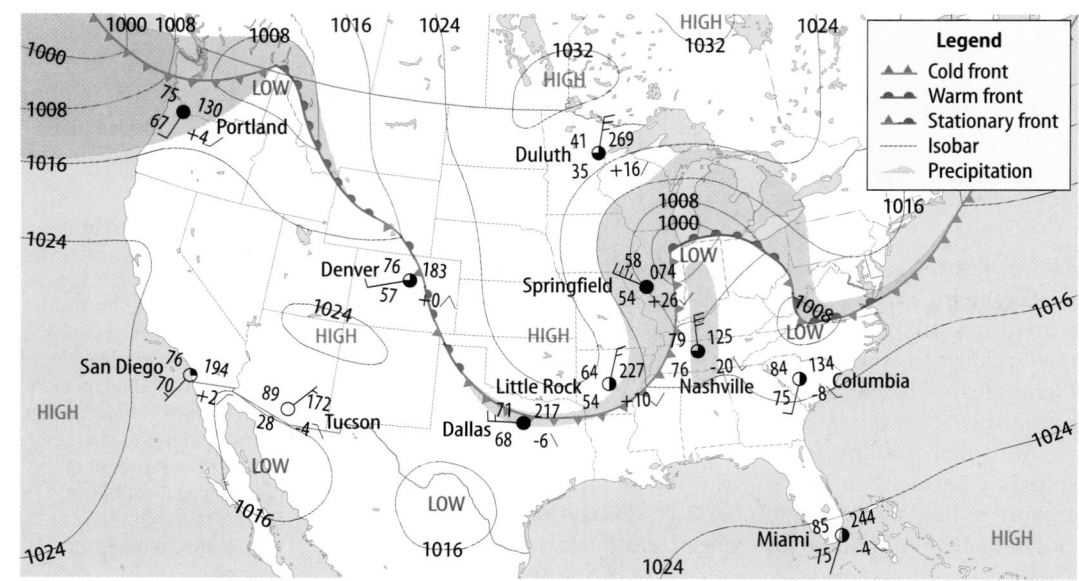

Figure 19
Highs, lows, isobars, and fronts on this weather map help meteorologists forecast the weather.

Weather Maps On a weather map like the one in **Figure 19,** pressure areas are drawn as circles with the word High or Low in the middle of the circle. Fronts are drawn as lines and symbols. When you watch weather forecasts on television, notice how weather fronts move from west to east. This is a pattern that meteorologists depend on to forecast weather.

Section 3 Assessment

1. What instruments do meteorologists use to collect weather data?
2. What is a station model?
3. Where does the National Weather Service get information to make weather maps?
4. What do closely spaced isobars on a weather map indicate?
5. **Think Critically** In the morning you hear a meteorologist forecast today's weather as sunny and warm. After school, it is raining. Why is the weather so hard to predict?

Skill Builder Activities

6. **Concept Mapping** Using a computer, make an events chain concept map for how a weather forecast is made. **For more help, refer to the** Science Skill Handbook.

7. **Communicating** Research what happened to American colonial troops at Valley Forge during the winter of 1777–1778. Imagine that you were a soldier during that winter. In your Science Journal, describe your experiences. **For more help, refer to the** Science Skill Handbook.

Answers to Section Assessment

1. Computers, weather satellites, Doppler radar, and instruments attached to balloons measure temperature, air pressure, wind, humidity, and precipitation.
2. symbols on a map that show weather conditions at one specific location
3. from meteorologists and satellites
4. strong winds
5. Atmospheric conditions can rapidly change, making forecasting difficult.
6. Data from Earth's surface and upper atmosphere are collected by National Weather Service meteorologists. Computers are used to make weather maps from data, meteorologists interpret maps, and forecasts are made.
7. Descriptions will vary. Strong winds, piercing cold, and snowfall took their toll on the many soldiers who were without proper clothing or shelter.

Activity

Reading a Weather Map

Meteorologists use a series of symbols to provide a picture of local and national weather conditions. With what you know, can you interpret weather information from weather map symbols?

What You'll Investigate
How do you read a weather map?

Materials
hand lens
Weather Map Symbols Appendix
Figure 19

Goals
- **Learn** how to read a weather map.
- **Use** information from a station model and maps to forecast weather.

Procedure
Use the information provided in the questions below and the Weather Map Symbols Appendix to learn how to read a weather map.

1. Find the station models on the map for Portland, Oregon, and Miami, Florida. Find the dew point, wind direction, barometric pressure, and temperature at each location.

2. Looking at the placement of the isobars, determine whether the wind would be stronger at Springfield, Illinois, or at San Diego, California. Record your answer. What is another way to determine the wind speed at these locations?

3. **Determine** the type of front near Dallas, Texas. Record your answer.

4. The triangles or half-circles are on the side of the line toward the direction the front is moving. What direction is the cold front located over Washington State moving?

Conclude and Apply

1. Locate the pressure system over southeast Kansas. Predict what will happen to the weather of Nashville, Tennessee, if this pressure system moves there.

2. Prevailing westerlies are winds responsible for the movement of much of the weather across the United States. Based on this, would you expect Columbia, South Carolina, to continue to have clear skies? Explain.

3. The direction line on the station model indicates the direction from which the wind blows. The wind is named for that direction. Infer from this the name of the wind blowing at Little Rock, Arkansas.

*C*ommunicating
Your Data

Pretend you are a meteorologist for a local TV news station. Make a poster of your weather data and present a weather forecast to your class. **For more help, refer to the** Science Skill Handbook.

ACTIVITY 481

*C*ommunicating
Your Data

Students may wish to use a word-processing program to make labels for their posters. Encourage students to be informative and creative in their presentations.

Resource Manager

Chapter Resources Booklet
Transparency Activity, p. 47–48
Activity Worksheet, pp. 5–6
Reinforcement, p. 29

Purpose Students read and interpret a weather map. L2
Visual-Spatial

Process Skills recording, observing, interpreting scientific illustrations, using numbers, predicting

Time Required 45 minutes

Teaching Strategy If an opaque projector is available, project the weather map onto a screen.

Troubleshooting Some students will need to review the location of the states and major U.S. cities before this activity. Post a U.S. map in the classroom.

Answers to Procedure Steps

1. Portland: dew point—67°F, wind direction—SSW, pressure—75°F; Miami: dew point—75°F, wind direction—SSW, pressure—244, temperature—85°F
2. Springfield; look at the station models
3. cold front
4. south southeast

Answers to Questions

1. Weather would be fair.
2. Yes; a high pressure system is moving in.
3. north wind

✓*Assessment*

Performance To assess students' abilities to interpret scientific illustrations, have them compare the weather shown on the map for Midland, Texas, and Birmingham, Alabama. Use **PASC**, p. 99.

Activity

Recognize the Problem

Purpose
Students will design and invent an instrument or system for measuring wind speed.

Process Skills
making models, observing, analyzing

Time Required
40 minutes/daily observations and measurements for one to two weeks

Thinking Critically

Discussion
Tell students to consider the effects of different speed winds on dead leaves, tree branches, and litter. Ask how they could create materials of different weights or shapes that would be influenced by different strength winds in observable patterns. What lightweight materials could they use that would travel small distances even in the slightest breeze? Have students evaluate their own designing skills to determine whether they should create an invention or a wind speed system. Provide Beaufort's scale of wind speeds as a reference source. Ask students to apply Beaufort's scale to determine the wind speed on different days so that they can see how a wind speed scale functions.

Possible Materials
Dried foods such as ground potato flakes or gelatin powder could be used instead of confetti or grass clippings. Students could also use paper of different weights, sizes or shapes.

Activity Model and Invent

Measuring Wind Speed

When you watch a gust of wind blow leaves down the street, do you wonder how fast the wind is moving? For centuries, people could only guess at wind speeds, but in 1805, Admiral Beaufort of the British navy invented a method for estimating wind speeds based on their effect on sails. Later, Beaufort's system was modified for use on land. Meteorologists use a simple instrument called an anemometer to measure wind speeds, and they still use Beaufort's system to estimate the speed of the wind. What type of instrument or system can you invent to measure wind speed?

Recognize the Problem

How could you use simple materials to invent an instrument or system for measuring wind speeds?

Thinking Critically

What observations do you use to estimate the speed of the wind?

Goals
- **Invent** an instrument or devise a system for measuring wind speeds using common materials.
- **Devise** a method for using your invention or system to compare different wind speeds.

Possible Materials
paper
scissors
confetti
grass clippings
meterstick
*measuring tape
*Alternate materials

Data Source
Refer to Section 1 for more information about anemometers and other wind speed instruments. Consult the data table for information about Beaufort's wind speed scale.

482 CHAPTER 16

SCIENCE *Online*
Internet Addresses

_____

_____

_____

Explore the Glencoe Science Web site at **science.glencoe.com** to find out more about topics in this activity.

Resource Manager

Chapter Resources Booklet
Activity Worksheet, pp. 7–8

Lab Management and Safety, p. 4

Planning the Model

1. Scan the list of possible materials and choose the materials you will need to devise your system.

2. **Devise** a system to measure different wind speeds. Be certain the materials you use are light enough to be moved by slight breezes.

Check the Model Plans

1. **Describe** your plan to your teacher. Provide a sketch of your instrument or system and ask your teacher how you might improve its design.

2. Present your idea for measuring wind speed to the class in the form of a diagram or poster. Ask your classmates to suggest improvements in your design that will make your system more accurate or easy to use.

Beaufort's Wind Speed Scale	
Description	**Wind Speed (km/h)**
calm—smoke drifts up	less than 1
light air— smoke drifts with wind	1–5
light breeze— leaves rustle	6–11
gentle breeze— leaves move constantly	12–19
moderate breeze— branches move	20–29
fresh breeze— small trees sway	30–39
strong breeze— large branches move	40–50
moderate gale— whole trees move	51–61
fresh gale—twigs break	62–74
strong gale— slight damage to houses	75–87
whole gale— much damage to houses	88–101
storm— extensive damage	102–120
hurricane— extreme damage	more than 120

Making the Model

1. Confetti or grass clippings that are all the same size can be used to measure wind speed by dropping them from a specific height. Measuring the distances they travel in different strength winds will provide data for devising a wind speed scale.

2. Different sizes and shapes of paper also could be dropped into the wind, and the strength of the wind would be determined by measuring the distances traveled by these different types of paper.

Analyzing and Applying Results

1. **Explain** why it is important for meteorologists to measure wind speeds.

2. **Compare** your results with Beaufort's wind speed scale.

3. **Develop** a scale for your method.

4. **Evaluate** how well your system worked in gentle breezes and strong winds.

5. **Analyze** what problems may exist in the design of your system and suggest steps you could take to improve your design.

Communicating
Your Data

Demonstrate your system for the class. **Compare** your results and measurements with the results of other classmates.

ACTIVITY 483

Planning the Model

Teaching Strategies

• Have the Beaufort scale of wind speeds posted in your room as a reference.

• Tell students to make a decision on creating an invention or a wind speed scale. Instruct them not to do both without first speaking to you.

• Ask students to make a checklist of items they will need to make their models.

Making the Model

Expected Outcome

Students should design and build an invention or create a system that accurately compares different wind speeds.

Analyzing and Applying Results

Answers

1. Aid in weather forecasts, warn of severe weather, warn air traffic of dangerous winds, and decide on locations for using wind power to generate electricity.
2. Answers will vary.
3. Answers will vary.
4. Answers will vary but students should discuss how their instruments or measuring systems would measure and compare increases in wind speed or wind gusts.
5. Answers will vary.

Assessment

Process Ask students to compare their methods for measuring wind speed with Beaufort's scale. Use **Performance Assessment in the Science Classroom**, p. 91.

Communicating
Your Data

Use an electric fan and a large painting tarp to test student inventions and systems inside the classroom.

Content Background

Before it can rain, water droplets in clouds have to grow large enough to reach the ground without evaporating.

Raindrops form by one of two processes, depending on the temperature of the clouds. In warm clouds, where temperatures are above freezing, small water droplets grow as they collide and merge with one another. Eventually, the drops are large enough to fall from the cloud as rain. Cold clouds, with temperatures at or below freezing, contain a mixture of ice crystals and supercooled water droplets. Supercooled water droplets are liquid water drops that exist below the freezing point. When a water droplet collides with an ice crystal, it freezes on impact, forming a larger ice crystal. When the crystal is large enough, it falls to the ground. Whether it falls as rain or snow depends on the air temperature below the cloud.

Cloud seeding attempts to promote rain by introducing condensation nuclei (particles intended to trigger condensation) into clouds. In warm clouds, large water drops are introduced. In cold clouds, cloud seeding attempts stimulate crystal growth by either chilling the air with dry ice or providing seed crystals. Silver iodide crystals are used as seeds because they form crystals similar to ice crystals.

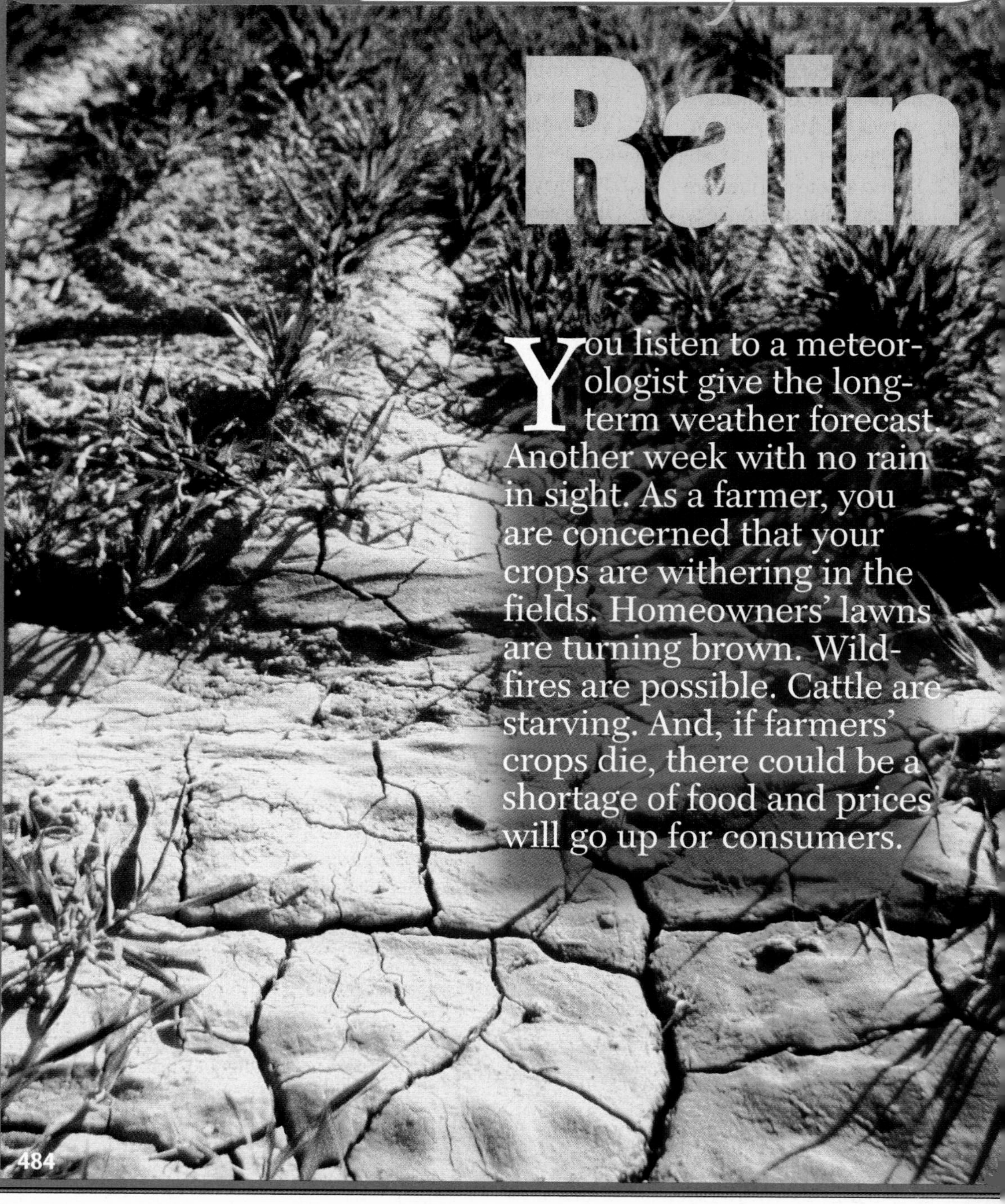

Rain

Y ou listen to a meteorologist give the long-term weather forecast. Another week with no rain in sight. As a farmer, you are concerned that your crops are withering in the fields. Homeowners' lawns are turning brown. Wildfires are possible. Cattle are starving. And, if farmers' crops die, there could be a shortage of food and prices will go up for consumers.

484

Resources for Teachers and Students

The Atmosphere: An Introduction to Meteorology. Frederick K. Lutgens and Edward J. Tarbuck, Prentice Hall, 1998.

Meteorology: The Atmosphere and the Science of Weather. Joseph M. Moran and Michael D. Morgan, Prentice Hall, 1997.

Human Impacts on Weather and Climate. W.R. Cotton and R.A. Pielke, Cambridge Univ. Press, 1995.

Cloud seeding is an inexact science makers

Flares contain chemicals which will seed clouds.

Meanwhile, several states away, another farmer is listening to the weather report calling for another week of rain. Her crops are getting so water-soaked that they are beginning to rot.

Weather. Can't scientists find a way to better control it? The answer is...not exactly. Scientists have been experimenting with methods to control our weather since the 1940s. And nothing really works.

Cloud seeding is one such attempt. It uses technology to enhance the natural rainfall process. The idea has been used to create rain where it is needed or to reduce hail damage. Government officials also use cloud seeding or weather modification to try to reduce the force of a severe storm.

Some people seed a cloud by flying a plane above it and releasing highway-type flares with chemicals, such as silver iodide. Another method is to fly beneath the cloud and spray a chemical that can be carried into the cloud by air currents.

Flares are lodged under a plane. The pilot will drop them into potential rain clouds.

Cloud seeding doesn't work with clouds that have little water vapor or are not near the dew point. Seeding chemicals must be released into potential rain clouds. The chemicals provide nuclei for water molecules to cluster around. Water then falls to Earth as precipitation.

Cloud seeding does have its critics. If you seed clouds and cause rain for your area, aren't you preventing rain from falling in another area? Would that be considered "rain theft" by people who live in places where the cloudburst would naturally occur? What about those cloud-seeding agents? Could the cloud-seeding chemicals, such as silver iodide and acetone, affect the environment in a harmful way? Are humans meddling with nature which might create problems in ways that haven't been determined?

Currently, Montana, Pennsylvania, and New Mexico are states that don't allow cloud seeding within their state boundaries. But, officials in Texas and California, the two states with the largest number of cloud-seeding programs, feel strongly that cloud seeding is an important technology when it comes to dealing with weather.

CONNECTIONS **Debate** Learn more about cloud seeding and other methods of changing weather. Then debate whether or not cloud seeding can be considered "rain theft."

SCIENCE
Online
For more information, visit
science.glencoe.com

SCIENCE
Online

Internet Addresses

_____

_____

_____

Explore the Glencoe Science Web site at **science.glencoe.com** to find out more about topics in this feature.

Chapter 16 Study Guide

Reviewing Main Ideas

Preview

Students can answer the questions in their Science Journals. Discuss the answers as you go through the chapter. **IS** **Linguistic**

Review

Students can write their answers, then compare them with those of other students. **IS** **Interpersonal**

Reteach

Students can look at the illustrations and describe details that support the main ideas of the chapter. **IS** **Visual-Spatial**

Answers to Chapter Review

SECTION 1

3. The hail formed high in a cumulonimbus cloud where the temperature was below freezing. Updrafts in the cumulonimbus cloud caused melting hail to refreeze.

SECTION 2

4. Its energy supply (warm, moist air over the ocean) is gone.

SECTION 3

2. 30°C

Reviewing Main Ideas

Section 1 What is weather?

1. Important factors that determine weather include air pressure, wind, temperature, and the amount of moisture in the air.

2. More water vapor can be present in warm air than in cold air. Water vapor condenses when the dew point is reached. Clouds are formed when warm, moist air rises and cools to its dew point.

3. Rain, hail, sleet, and snow are types of precipitation. *What causes hail to form during severe thunderstorms?*

Section 2 Weather Patterns

1. Fronts form when air masses with different characteristics, such as temperature, moisture, or density, meet. Types of fronts include cold fronts, warm fronts, occluded fronts, and stationary fronts.

2. High atmospheric pressure at Earth's surface usually means good weather. Cloudy and stormy weather usually have low pressure.

3. Tornadoes are intense, whirling windstorms that can result from wind shears inside a thunderstorm.

4. Hurricanes and blizzards are large, severe storms with strong winds. *Why does a hurricane, shown below, lose strength as it moves over land?*

Section 3 Weather Forecasts

1. Meteorologists use information from radar, satellites, computers, and other weather instruments to make weather maps and forecasts.

2. Symbols on a station model indicate the weather at a particular location. *What is the dew point temperature on the station model shown here?*

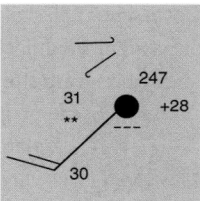

3. Weather maps include information about temperature and air pressure.

FOLDABLES
Reading & Study Skills

After You Read

To help you review facts about weather, use the Foldable you made at the beginning of the chapter.

FOLDABLES
Reading & Study Skills

After You Read

After students have read the chapter and completed the Foldable described in Before You Read, have them do the activity on the student page.

Dinah Zike

Visualizing Main Ideas

Complete the following concept map about air temperature, water vapor, and pressure.

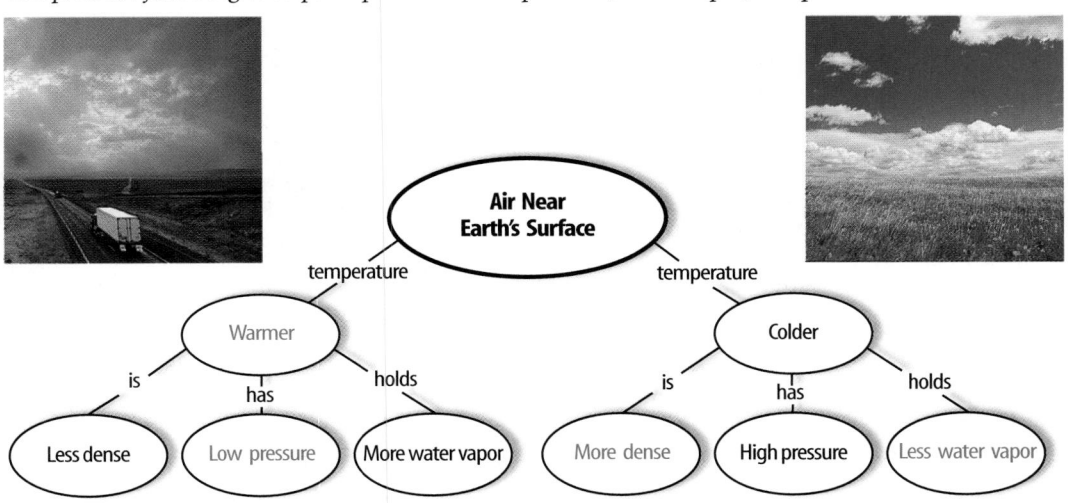

Vocabulary Review

Vocabulary Words

a. air mass
b. blizzard
c. dew point
d. fog
e. front
f. humidity
g. hurricane
h. isobar
i. isotherm
j. meteorologist
k. precipitation
l. relative humidity
m. station model
n. tornado
o. weather

THE PRINCETON REVIEW | **Study Tip**

After each day's lesson, make a practice quiz for yourself. Later, when you're studying for the test, take the practice quizzes that you created.

Using Vocabulary

Explain the differences between the vocabulary words in each of the following sets.

1. air mass, front
2. humidity, relative humidity
3. relative humidity, dew point
4. dew point, precipitation
5. thunderstorm, tornado
6. blizzard, hurricane
7. meteorologist, station model
8. precipitation, fog
9. isobar, isotherm
10. isobar, front

CHAPTER STUDY GUIDE 487

Visualizing Main Ideas

See student page.

Vocabulary Review

Using Vocabulary

1. air mass: large body of air of uniform temperature and moisture; front: boundary between air masses
2. humidity: amount of water vapor in air; relative humidity: ratio of humidity in air to the amount of water vapor needed for saturation at a specific temperature
3. relative humidity: ratio of humidity in air to the amount of water vapor needed for saturation; dew point: temperature at which condensation occurs
4. dew point: temperature at which condensation occurs; precipitation: water falling from clouds
5. thunderstorm: severe storm with heavy rain, lightning, and thunder; tornado: violent whirling wind produced by thunderstorms
6. blizzard: winter storm with high wind, freezing temperatures, and low visibility; hurricane: large, swirling tropical low-pressure system
7. meteorologist: scientist who studies weather; station model: symbols on a map that describe weather in one place
8. precipitation: water falling from clouds; fog: cloud that forms near the ground
9. isobar: line on map that connects points of equal air pressure; isotherm: line that connects points of equal temperature
10. isobar: line on map that connects points of equal air pressure; front: boundary between air masses

Checking Concepts

1. D
2. A
3. A
4. D
5. A
6. D
7. D
8. C
9. C
10. A

Thinking Critically

11. If humidity remains constant, relative humidity increases as temperature decreases.
12. Heat from the Sun causes water to evaporate, forming water vapor in the air. The water vapor rises and cools to form clouds, and then falls as precipitation.
13. The weather in Washington is influenced by air masses that form over water. The weather in Texas is influenced by air masses that form over arid land.
14. The air has 79% of the water vapor that is needed for saturation at that temperature.
15. Hurricanes derive energy from warm waters. The water in polar regions is too cold

---

Chapter 16 Assessment

Checking Concepts

Choose the word or phrase that best answers the question.

1. Which type of air has a relative humidity of 100 percent?
   A) humid
   B) temperate
   C) dry
   D) saturated

2. What is a large body of air that has the same properties as the area over which it formed called?
   A) air mass
   B) station model
   C) front
   D) isotherm

3. At what temperature does water vapor in air condense?
   A) dew point
   B) station model
   C) front
   D) isobar

4. Which type of precipitation forms when water vapor changes directly into a solid?
   A) rain
   B) hail
   C) sleet
   D) snow

5. Which type of the following clouds are high feathery clouds made of ice crystals?
   A) cirrus
   B) nimbus
   C) cumulus
   D) stratus

6. Which type of front may form when cool air, cold air and warm air meet?
   A) warm
   B) cold
   C) stationary
   D) occluded

7. Which is issued when severe weather conditions exist and immediate action should be taken?
   A) front
   B) watch
   C) station model
   D) warning

8. Which term means the amount of water vapor in the air?
   A) dew point
   B) precipitation
   C) humidity
   D) relative humidity

9. What does an anemometer measure?
   A) air pressure
   B) relative humidity
   C) wind speed
   D) precipitation

10. What is a large, swirling storm that forms over warm, tropical water called?
    A) hurricane
    B) tornado
    C) blizzard
    D) hailstorm

Thinking Critically

11. Explain the relationship between temperature and relative humidity.

12. Describe how air, water, and the Sun interact to cause weather.

13. Explain why northwest Washington often has rainy weather and southwest Texas is dry.

14. What does it mean if the relative humidity is 79 percent?

15. Why don't hurricanes form in Earth's polar regions?

Developing Skills

16. **Comparing and Contrasting** Compare and contrast the weather at a cold front to that at a warm front.

17. **Observing and Inferring** You take a hot shower. The mirror in the bathroom fogs up, like the one below. Infer from this information what has happened.

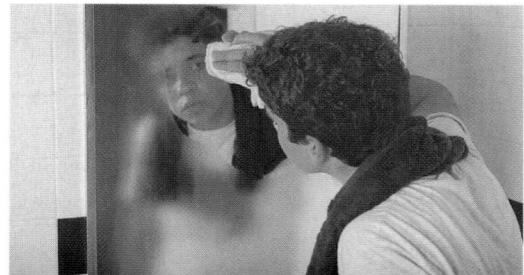

Chapter ✓Assessment Planner

Portfolio Encourage students to place in their portfolios one or two items of what they consider to be their best work. Examples include:
- Life Science Integration, p. 463
- Use Science Words, p. 471
- Challenge, p. 480
- Assessment, p. 483

Performance Additional performance assessments, Performance Task Assessment Lists, and rubrics for evaluating these activities can be found in Glencoe's **Performance Assessment in the Science Classroom.**

18. **Recording Observations** Use the cloud descriptions in Section 1 of this chapter to describe the weather at your location today. Then try to predict tomorrow's weather. Repeat for one week.

19. **Concept Mapping** Complete the sequence map below showing how precipitation forms.

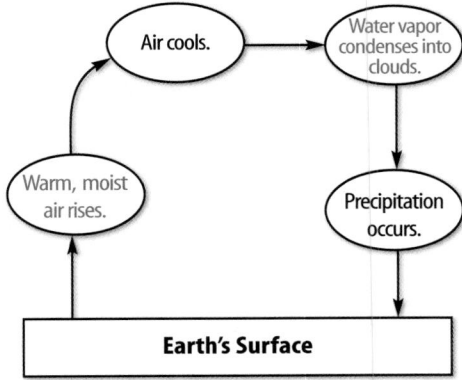

Air cools. → Water vapor condenses into clouds.

Warm, moist air rises.

Precipitation occurs.

Earth's Surface

20. **Comparing and Contrasting** Compare and contrast tornadoes and thunderstorms.

Performance Assessment

21. **Board Game** Make a board game using weather terms. You could make cards to advance or retreat a token.

22. **Design** your own weather station. Record temperature, precipitation, and wind speed for one week.

TECHNOLOGY

Go to the Glencoe Science Web site at **science.glencoe.com** or use the **Glencoe Science CD-ROM** for additional chapter assessment.

THE PRINCETON REVIEW — Test Practice

Hurricanes are rated on a scale based on their wind speed and barometric pressure. The table below lists the hurricane category by the wind speed and pressure of the storm.

Hurricane Rating Scale		
Category	**Wind Speed (km/h)**	**Barometric Pressure (millibars)**
1	120–154	>980
2	155–177	965–980
3	178–209	945–964
4	210–250	920–944
5	>250	<920

Study the table and answer the following questions.

1. In 1992, Hurricane Andrew, with winds of 233 km/hr and a pressure of 922 mb struck southeast Florida. What category was Hurricane Andrew?
   A) 1
   B) 2
   C) 3
   D) 4

2. Which of the following best describes the pressure and wind when categorizing a hurricane?
   F) Storm category increases as wind increases and pressure decreases.
   G) Storm category increases as wind decreases and pressure increases.
   H) Storm category increases as wind and pressure increase.
   J) Storm category decreases as wind and pressure decrease.

THE PRINCETON REVIEW — Test Practice

The Test-Taking Tip was written by The Princeton Review, the nation's leader in test preparation.
1. D
2. F

Developing Skills

16. Both bring clouds and precipitation; cold front: possible thunderstorms and tornadoes; warm front: long period of steady, light precipitation.
17. The bathroom air is warm and full of water vapor. The air cooled to its dew point when it hit the surface of the cooler mirror, causing water vapor in the air to condense into liquid water on the glass.
18. Students should correctly identify and predict cloudiness, precipitation, or sunshine based on cloud observations.
19. See student page.
20. Both can produce strong, damaging winds. Thunderstorms produce heavy bursts of rainfall as well as lightning, thunder, and possibly hail. Severe thunderstorms can also produce tornadoes, which are swirling funnels of wind that move along the ground, destroying things in their path

Performance Assessment

21. Encourage students to be creative, include detailed instructions for playing the game, and use accurate information. Have students play each other's games. Use **PASC**, p. 117.
22. Check students' work. Use **PASC**, p. 117.

✓ Assessment Resources

Reproducible Masters

Chapter Resources Booklet
Chapter Review, pp. 37–38
Chapter Tests, pp. 39–42
Assessment Transparency Activity, p. 49

Glencoe Science Web site
Interactive Tutor
Chapter Quizzes

Glencoe Technology
- Assessment Transparency
- Interactive CD-ROM Chapter Quizzes
- ExamView Pro Test Bank
- Vocabulary PuzzleMaker Software
- MindJogger Videoquiz DVD/VHS

Section/Objectives	Standards		Activities/Features
Chapter Opener	National	State/Local	**Explore Activity:** Track the climates of the world, p. 491 **Before You Read,** p. 491
	See p. 5T for a Key to Standards.		
Section 1 What is climate? 🕐 2 sessions 📦 1 block 1. **Describe** what determines climate. 2. **Explain** how latitude and other factors affect the climate of a region.	National Content Standards: UCP3, A1, D1		**MiniLAB:** Observing Solar Radiation, p. 493 **Physics Integration,** p. 494 **Problem-Solving Activity:** How do large cities influence temperature?, p. 494
Section 2 Climate Types 🕐 3 sessions 📦 1.5 blocks 1. **Describe** a climate classification system. 2. **Explain** how organisms adapt to particular climates.	National Content Standards: UCP4, C1, C4, C5, D1		
Section 3 Climatic Changes 🕐 4 sessions 📦 2 blocks 1. **Explain** what causes seasons. 2. **Describe** how El Niño affects climate. 3. **Explore** possible causes of climatic change.	National Content Standards: UCP1, UCP2, UCP3, A1, A2, D1		**MiniLAB:** Modeling El Niño, p. 501 **Visualizing El Niño and La Niña,** p. 502 **Health Integration,** p. 505 **Activity:** The Greenhouse Effect, p. 511 **Activity:** Microclimates, p. 512 **Science and History:** The Year There Was No Summer, p. 514

NATIONAL GEOGRAPHIC

Teacher's Corner

PRODUCTS AVAILABLE FROM GLENCOE
To order call 1-800-334-7344:
CD-ROM
NGS PictureShow: Earth's Climate
Curriculum Kit
GeoKit: Water

Transparency Set
NGS PicturePack: Earth's Climate

INDEX TO NATIONAL GEOGRAPHIC SOCIETY
The following articles may be used for research relating to this chapter:
"Unlocking the Climate Puzzle," by Curt Suplee, May 1996.

"Physical World," by Joel L. Swerdlow, May 1998.
"Exploring Antarctica Ice," by Jane Ellen Stevens, May 1996.
"Acid Rain: How Great a Menace?" by Anne LaBastille, November 1981.

Activity Materials	Reproducible Resources	Section Assessment	Technology
Explore Activity: world atlas, globe, or classroom map; sources for researching world temperatures	**Chapters Resources Booklet** Foldables Worksheet, p. 17 Directed Reading Overview, p. 19 Note-taking Worksheets, pp. 33–35	**GLENCOE'S ASSESSMENT ADVANTAGE**	
MiniLAB: flashlight, globe	**Chapter Resources Booklet** Transparency Activity, p. 44 MiniLAB, p. 3 Enrichment, p. 30 Reinforcement, p. 27 Directed Reading, p. 20 Lab Activity, pp. 9–11 **Mathematics Skill Activities,** p. 11	**Portfolio** Challenge, p. 495 **Performance** MiniLAB, p. 493 Problem-Solving Activity, p. 494 Skill Builder Activities, p. 495 **Content** Section Assessment, p. 495	Section Focus Transparency Interactive CD-ROM/DVD Guided Reading Audio Program
Need materials? Contact Science Kit at 1-800-828-7777 or www.sciencekit.com on the Internet.	**Chapter Resources Booklet** Transparency Activity, p. 45 Enrichment, p. 31 Reinforcement, p. 28 Directed Reading, p. 20 Transparency Activity, pp. 47–48 **Reading and Writing Skill Activities,** p. 3	**Portfolio** Make a Model, p. 498 **Performance** Skill Builder Activities, p. 499 **Content** Section Assessment, p. 499	Section Focus Transparency Teaching Transparency Interactive CD-ROM/DVD Guided Reading Audio Program
MiniLAB: baking pan (9 in. × 13 in.), warm water **Activity:** 2 identical large, glass jars, lid for one jar, 3 alcohol thermometers **Activity:** thermometers, psychrometer, paper strip or wind sock, 4–5 large cans, unlined paper	**Chapter Resources Booklet** Transparency Activity, p. 46 MiniLAB, p. 4 Enrichment, p. 32 Reinforcement, p. 29 Activity Worksheet, pp. 5–6, 7–8 Directed Reading, pp. 21, 22 Lab Activity, pp. 13–16 **Lab Management and Safety,** p. 37	**Portfolio** Curriculum Connection, p. 502 Science Journal, p. 504 **Performance** MiniLAB, p. 501 Skill Builder Activities, p. 510 **Content** Section Assessment, p. 510	Section Focus Transparency Interactive CD-ROM/DVD Guided Reading Audio Program

End of Chapter Assessment

GLENCOE'S ASSESSMENT ADVANTAGE

Blackline Masters	Technology	Professional Series
Chapter Resources Booklet Chapter Review, pp. 37–38 Chapter Tests, pp. 39–42 **Standardized Test Practice by The Princeton Review,** pp. 77–80	MindJogger Videoquiz CD-ROM Explorations and Quizzes Vocabulary Puzzle Makers ExamView Pro Test Bank Interactive Lesson Planner Interactive Teacher's Edition	Performance Assessment in the Science Classroom (PASC)

Transparencies

Section Focus

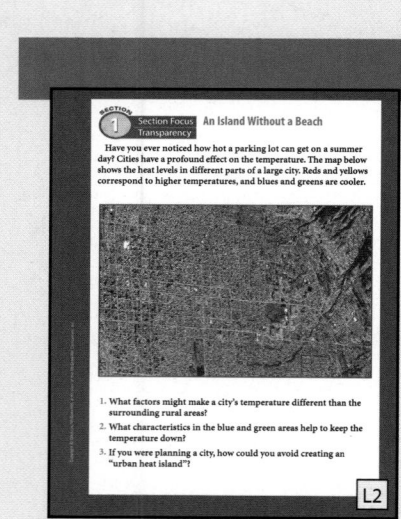

Section 1 · Section Focus Transparency · An Island Without a Beach

Have you ever noticed how hot a parking lot can get on a summer day? Cities have a profound effect on the temperature. The map below shows the heat levels in different parts of a large city. Reds and yellows correspond to higher temperatures, and blues and greens are cooler.

1. What factors might make a city's temperature different than the surrounding rural areas?
2. What characteristics in the blue and green areas help to keep the temperature down?
3. If you were planning a city, how could you avoid creating an "urban heat island"?

L2

Section 2 · Section Focus Transparency · Where are we?

You can drive around this place in just a few hours, but as you ride, you travel through many different climates. Cool mountains, dry deserts, tropical rainforests, and brilliant beaches are all just around the corner. So where are we?

1. Describe the climates you see in these four pictures.
2. How is it possible to have snow close to a desert?
3. What physical features affect the climate of an area?

L2

Section 3 · Section Focus Transparency · Informative Fruit

Paleoclimatologists are people who study Earth's past climate. You may have learned that ice cores, fossils, and sediments can reveal climatic information, but what about grapes? One study used the recorded dates of the French grape harvest to infer summer temperatures in Paris between 1370 and 1879!

1. How might temperature and harvest date be related?
2. What other factors might affect the climate and the harvest?

L2

This is a representation of key blackline masters available in the Teacher Classroom Resources. See Resource Manager boxes within the chapter for additional information.

Assessment

Assessment Transparency · Climate

Directions: Carefully review the picture and answer the following questions.

1. Which organism can probably most efficiently handle being exposed to the sunlight and heat?
   A cactus   B girl   C lizard   D snake
2. The most likely benefit of the adaptation of the snake shown in the picture is to ___.
   F keep it cool during the day
   G hide from predators
   H surprise attack its prey
   J get enough rest
3. When a human's body temperature rises too high, the body produces sweat. Which of these is most likely the main purpose of this adaptation?
   A To clean the body of dirt
   B To cure illness
   C To save energy
   D To cool the body

L2

Teaching

Section 2 · Teaching Transparency · Climate Classification System

L2

Key to Teaching Strategies

The following designations will help you decide which activities are appropriate for your students.

L1 Level 1 activities should be appropriate for students with learning difficulties.

L2 Level 2 activities should be within the ability range of all students.

L3 Level 3 activities are designed for above-average students.

ELL ELL activities should be within the ability range of English Language Learners.

COOP LEARN Cooperative Learning activities are designed for small group work.

LS Multiple Learning Styles logos, as described on page 22T, are used throughout to indicate strategies that address different learning styles.

P These strategies represent student products that can be placed into a best-work portfolio.

Hands-on Activities

Activity Worksheets

Activity · The Greenhouse Effect

Lab Preview
Directions: Answer the following questions before you begin the Activity.
1. What objects in this lab would be hazardous if broken?

2. You have just brought water to a boil in an uncovered pot and turned off the flame under the pot. Without turning the flame back on, how can you keep the water hot?

Do you remember climbing into the car on a warm, sunny day? Why was it so hot inside the car when it wasn't that hot outside? It was hotter in the car because the car functioned like a greenhouse. You experienced the greenhouse effect.

What You'll Investigate
How can you demonstrate the greenhouse effect?

Materials
identical large, empty glass jars (2)
lid for one jar
nonmercury thermometers (3)

Goals
• Model the greenhouse effect.
• Measure and graph temperature changes.

Safety Precautions
Be careful when you handle glass thermometers. If a thermometer breaks, do not touch it. Have your teacher dispose of the glass safely.

Data and Observations

Procedure
1. Lay a thermometer inside each jar.
2. Place the jars next to each other by a sunny window. Lay the third thermometer between the jars.
3. Record the temperatures of the three thermometers. They should be the same.
4. Place the lid on one jar.
5. Record the temperatures of all three thermometers at the end of 5, 10, and 15 min.
6. Make a line graph in the space in the Data and Observations section that shows the temperatures of the three thermometers for the 15 min of the experiment. Students will supply the temperature range for the graph.

Jar Temperature			
Time	Thermometer 1	Thermometer 2	Thermometer 3
5 min			
10 min			
15 min			

L2

Laboratory Activities

Lab 1 · Laboratory Activity · How do the oceans affect climate?

Meteorologists, people who study weather and climate, are always looking at what happens in the oceans. Most of the climate we experience on land is a result of winds and evaporated water at sea. One of the effects of the oceans is to keep the climate near their shores fairly constant. This happens because the water maintains a relatively even temperature. Molecules in water are closer together than molecules in the atmosphere. They are said to have a greater molecular density than molecules in the atmosphere. More energy is needed to get the relatively denser water molecules to move faster and produce heat, or to slow them down to freeze. Volume is also an important consideration in looking at the effects of the Sun's energy on water molecules. It is much easier for the Sun to heat or cool a small pond than it is for the Sun to heat or cool the ocean. In this laboratory exercise, you will compare the effect of the Sun's energy on water with its effect on the atmosphere. From your data, you will make conclusions about climate indifferent regions.

Strategy
You will model and observe the effect of energy from the Sun on water and on air. You will infer how oceans and energy from the Sun affect climate.

Materials
2 plastic soda bottles (labels removed)
2 cork or rubber stoppers with center holes
2 long, chemistry-type thermometers
water
paper towels
* 100-watt light source (if no sunlight is available)
* apparatus for holding light source stationary
* Alternate materials

Figure 1

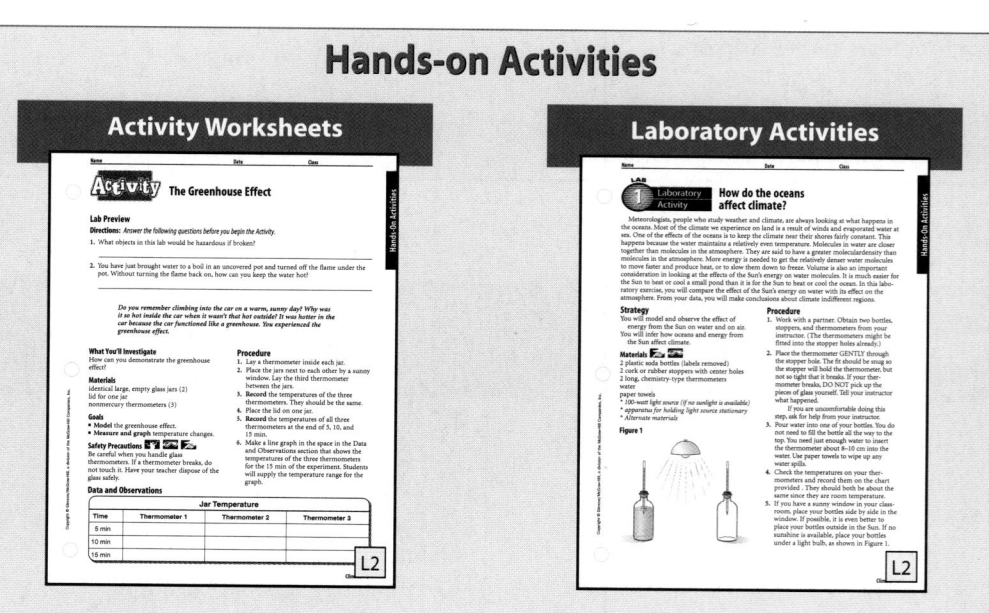

Procedure
1. Work with a partner. Obtain two bottles, stoppers, and thermometers from your instructor. (The thermometers might be fitted into the stopper holes already.)
2. Place the thermometer GENTLY through the stopper hole. The fit should be snug so the stopper will hold the thermometer, but not so tight that it breaks. If your thermometer breaks, DO NOT pick up the pieces of glass yourself. Tell your instructor what happened.
   If you are uncomfortable doing this step, ask for help from your instructor.
3. Pour water into one of your bottles. You do not need to fill the bottle all the way to the top. You need just enough water to insert the thermometer about 8–10 cm into the water. Use paper towels to wipe up any water spills.
4. Check the temperatures on your thermometers and record them on the chart provided. They should both be about the same since they are room temperature.
5. If you have a sunny window in your classroom, place your bottles side by side in the window. If possible, it is even better to place your bottles outside in the Sun. If no sunshine is available, place your bottles under a light bulb, as shown in Figure 1.

L2

Meeting Different Ability Levels

Content Outline
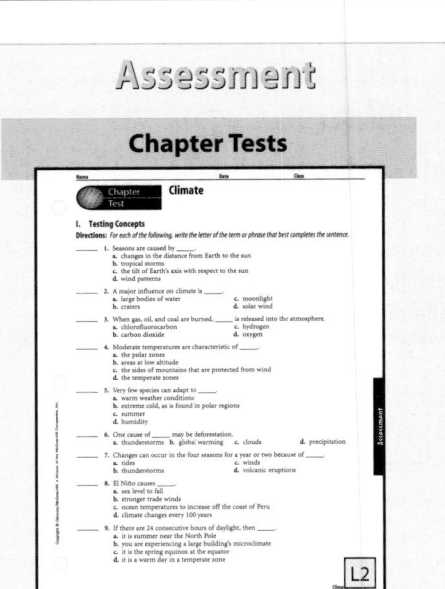
L2

Reinforcement
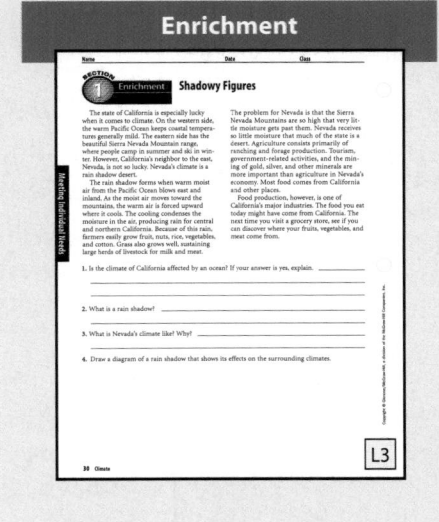
L2

Directed Reading
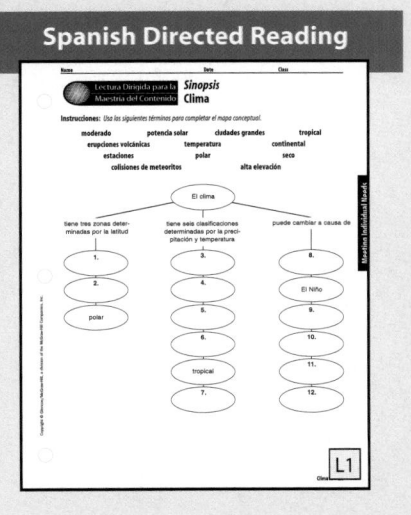
L1

Assessment

Chapter Tests
L2

Enrichment
L3

Spanish Directed Reading
L1

Test Practice Workbook

L2

Chapter Review
L2

Science Content Background

SECTION 1

What is climate?
Latitude and Climate

On a sunny day at 0° latitude, the amount of solar energy received is 300 W/m². At 60° latitude, it is 110 W/m², and at 90° only 60 W/m² of solar energy is received. At any latitude, the amount of energy received is lower when skies are cloudy.

Mountains

Mountains typically have higher precipitation and lower temperatures than surrounding lower elevations. Mountain slopes also affect climate. Orographic lifting occurs when an air mass encounters a mountain range and is forced upward. As the air rises, it cools and condenses, forming precipitation on the side of the mountain. When the air mass descends down the other side, it sinks and condensation stops. As a result, little precipitation occurs on the other side of the mountain. This phenomenon is known as a rain shadow. The eastern half of Washington State falls in the rain shadow of the Cascades, resulting in the near-arid climate of the Columbia basin.

SECTION 2

Climate Types
Classifying Climates

The early Greeks devised the first climate classification system. It was based on differences in temperature. Köppens's classification system is more biological in nature, based on the different types of flora found in a specific climate.

SECTION 3

Climatic Changes
Earth's Seasons

As a result of changes in temperature at different latitudes throughout the year, winds often shift direction, causing predictable changes in the climate of an area. The word *monsoon* comes from the Arabic word *mausim*, meaning "season." Monsoon season occurs in both India and Arizona when the winds shift, pulling in air from a very moist region. During this season the affected area experiences a significant increase in precipitation.

Student Misconception

Seasons are affected by the distance between Earth and the Sun.

Refer to the facing page for teaching strategies to address this misconception. Refer to page 500 for content related to this topic.

Climatic Change

The first great ice age occurred between 2.5 billion and 2 billion years ago. Evidence suggests that a period of warming followed that lasted until about 950 million years ago. A second ice age occurred between 950 and 650 million years ago, followed by another warming period that lasted until about 70 million years ago. Since that time, there have been several periods when glaciers have formed and then melted. The last ice age reached its peak about 18,000 years ago.

SCIENCE Online

For additional content background on this topic, go to the Glencoe Science Web site at science.glencoe.com.

IDENTIFYING > Misconceptions

Find Out What Students Think

Students may think that . . .

- **Seasons are affected by the distance between Earth and the Sun.**

Because Earth's orbit around the Sun is an ellipse and not a circle, Earth is not the same distance from the Sun throughout the year. However, summer and winter are not caused by Earth's changing distance from the Sun during its orbit. In fact, during winter in the Northern Hemisphere, Earth is actually closer to the Sun than it is during summer. The changing of the seasons is caused by Earth's tilt.

If Earth's axis were not tilted relative to its orbit around the Sun, each of Earth's hemispheres would receive the same amount of sunlight at all times throughout the year. The days would not grow longer during the summer and shorter in winter. Every day of the year would have 12 hours of daylight and 12 hours of night, and there would be no seasons.

Because of Earth's axial tilt, during most of its orbit around the Sun one or the other of Earth's hemispheres is tilted toward the Sun. The part of Earth that is tilted toward the sun experiences summer, and the part tilted away from the Sun experiences winter. As Earth orbits the Sun, this orientation constantly changes throughout the year. At two points in Earth's orbit, the first day of spring and the first day of autumn, neither hemisphere is tilted toward the sun. On those days, the Sun appears to us to be directly over the equator, and all points on Earth experience a 12-hour day and a 12-hour night.

Demonstration

Using a lightbulb to represent the Sun and a globe to represent Earth, have two students demonstrate the position of Earth and the Sun during the various seasons. Refer to **Figure 8.** Ask students to record which season they think will occur at various locations, first for the Northern Hemisphere and then for the Southern Hemisphere. Ask them what months these seasons would represent in each hemisphere, for example, Winter-Northern-December, or Winter-Southern-June. Be sure to reinforce the concept that seasons are not occurring relative to the distance between the Earth and the Sun but rather to the part of Earth that is tilted toward the Sun.

Promote Understanding

Activity

Reinforce that the greatest contributor to the change of seasons is the inclination of Earth's axis with respect to its orbital plane.

- Give each group a flashlight and a sheet of construction paper

- Have students shine the flashlight straight onto the paper. Instruct them to draw a circle around the light beam on the paper.

- Next, direct them to slowly tilt the paper so that the circle elongates into an ellipse. Again have students draw an outline around the ellipse, this time using a different color of pencil.

Students should infer that the same amount of light energy is spread over a greater area when the paper is tilted relative to the flashlight. Therefore, each point on the paper receives less energy from the light when the paper is tilted.

Assess

After completing the chapter, see *Identifying Misconceptions* in the Study Guide.

Climate

Chapter Vocabulary

climate
tropics
polar zone
temperate zone
adaptation
hibernation
season
El Niño
greenhouse effect
global warming
deforestation

What do you think?

Science Journal The photo shows ice crystals on a window that have formed a dendritic, or treelike, pattern.

CHAPTER 17

Climate

As summer fades, trees take on the beautiful colors of autumn. As the temperature continues to drop throughout the season, those beautiful leaves will fall, and the bare branches will signify winter. What causes the change in seasons? Why do some places have four distinct seasons, while others have only a wet and dry season? In this chapter, you will learn what climate is, and how climates are classified. You also will learn what causes climate changes and how humans and animals adapt to different climates.

What do you think?

Science Journal Look at the picture below with a classmate. Discuss what you think this might be or what is happening. Here's a hint: *These are frozen, but they aren't trees.* Write your best guess in your Science Journal.

490

Theme Connection

Stability and Change Although climate may appear to be constant, this chapter illustrates that Earth's climates undergo both short-term seasonal changes as well as long-term shifts, such as ice ages.

EXPLORE ACTIVITY

You wouldn't go to Alaska to swim or to Jamaica to snow ski. You know the climates in these places aren't suited for these sports. In this activity, you'll explore the climates in different parts of the world.

Track the climates of the world

1. Obtain a world atlas, globe, or large classroom map. Select several cities from as many different parts of the world as possible.

2. Record the longitude and latitude of your cities. Note if they are near mountains or an ocean.

3. Research the average temperature of your cities. In what months are they hottest? Coldest? What is the average yearly rainfall? What kinds of plants and animals live in the region? Record your findings.

4. Compare your findings with those of the rest of your class. Can you see any relationship between latitude and climate? Do cities near an ocean or a mountain range have different climatic characteristics?

Observe

As you read the chapter, keep track of the daily weather conditions in your cities. Are these representative of the kind of climates your cities are supposed to have? Suggest reasons why day-to-day weather conditions may vary.

FOLDABLES
Reading & Study Skills

Before You Read

Making a Classify Study Fold Make the following Foldable to help you organize objects or events into groups based on their common features.

1. Place a sheet of paper in front of you so the short side is at the top. Fold the paper in half from top to bottom. Then fold it in half again top to bottom two more times. Unfold all the folds.

2. Using the fold lines as a guide, refold the paper into a fan. Unfold all the folds again.

3. Title your Foldable *Climate Classifications* and label the sections *Tropical, Mild, Dry, Continental, Polar,* and *High Elevation.*

4. As you read the chapter, define each and write notes on weather patterns on the back of each fold.

Climate Classification
Tropical
Mild
Dry
Continental
Polar
High Elevation

491

EXPLORE ACTIVITY

Purpose Use the Explore Activity to introduce students to the relationship between location and climate. Inform them that in this chapter they will learn why climates vary around the world, how climates are classified, and why climates change.
L2 COOP LEARN Ⓘ **Visual-Spatial**
Preparation Obtain enough world globes, maps, or atlases to allow students to work in pairs.

Materials world globe, atlases, or maps, sources for researching world temperatures

Teaching Strategies Ask students to find cities in North America, Africa, Asia, or Europe.

Observe

Students may infer that mountains block precipitation, creating deserts, or that cities near the equator have warmer temperatures throughout the year.

✓ *Assessment*

Oral Many cities are near the ocean. Have students compare and contrast the locations of coastal cities they researched in the Explore Activity. Use **PASC**, p. 99.

FOLDABLES
Reading & Study Skills

Before You Read

Dinah Zike Study Fold

Purpose Students make a climate classification chart to introduce them to the six groups of the climate classification system before reading the chapter. Students use their Foldable to define terms and make notes on the weather patterns of each climate as they read the chapter.

📁 For additional help, see Foldables Worksheet, p. 17 in **Chapter Resources Booklet,** or go to the Glencoe Science Web site at **science.glencoe.com.** See After You Read in the Study Guide at the end of this chapter.

SECTION

1

Motivate

Bellringer Transparency

Display the Section Focus Transparency for Section 1. Use the accompanying Transparency Activity Master. L2

ELL

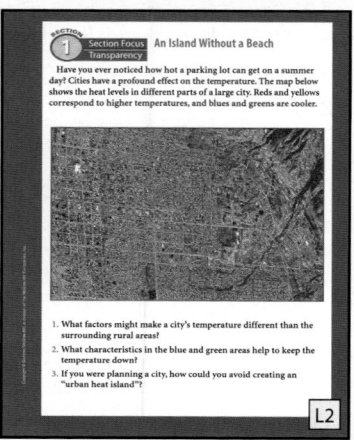

Tie to Prior Knowledge

Ask students to list the temperature and precipitation characteristics where they live, for both summer and winter. Write these characteristics on the board. Tell students they will later use these characteristics to determine their community's climate.

SECTION

1

What is climate?

As You Read

What You'll Learn
- **Describe** what determines climate.
- **Explain** how latitude and other factors affect the climate of a region.

Vocabulary
climate
tropics
polar zone
temperate zone

Why It's Important
Climate affects the way you live.

Figure 1
The tropics are warmer than the temperate zones and the polar zones because the tropics receive the most direct solar energy.

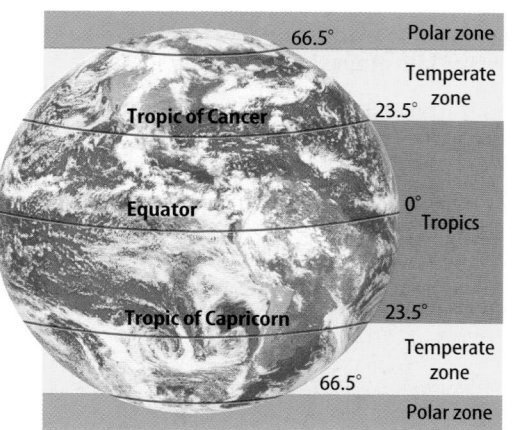

Climate

If you wandered through a tropical rain forest, you would see beautiful plants flowering in shades of pink and purple beneath a canopy of towering trees. A variety of exotic birds and other animals would dart among the tree branches and across the forest floor. The sounds of singing birds and croaking frogs would surround you. All of these organisms thrive in hot temperatures and abundant rainfall. Rain forests have a hot, wet climate. **Climate** is the pattern of weather that occurs in an area over many years. It determines the types of plants or animals that can survive, and it influences how people live.

Climate is determined by averaging the weather of a region over a long period of time, such as 30 years. Scientists average temperature, precipitation, air pressure, humidity, and number of days of sunshine to determine an area's climate. Some factors that affect the climate of a region include latitude, landforms, location of lakes and oceans, and ocean currents.

Latitude and Climate

As you can see in **Figure 1,** regions close to the equator receive the most solar radiation. Latitude, a measure of distance north or south of the equator, affects climate. **Figure 2** compares cities at different latitudes. The **tropics**—the region between latitudes 23°N and 23°S—receive the most solar radiation because the Sun shines almost directly over these areas. The tropics have temperatures that are always hot, except at high elevations. The **polar zones** extend from 66°N and 66°S latitude to the poles. Solar radiation hits these zones at a low angle, spreading energy over a large area. During winter, polar regions receive little or no solar radiation. Therefore, polar regions are never warm.

✔ **Reading Check** *How does latitude affect climate?*

Between the tropics and the polar zones are the **temperate zones.** Temperatures here are moderate. Most of the United States is in a temperate zone.

Section ✓*Assessment* Planner

PORTFOLIO
Challenge, p. 495
PERFORMANCE ASSESSMENT
MiniLAB, p. 493
Problem-Solving Activity, p. 494
Skill Builder Activities, p. 495
See page 518 for more options.

CONTENT ASSESSMENT
Section, p. 495
Challenge, p. 495
Chapter, pp. 518–519

Other Factors

In addition to the general climate divisions of polar, temperate, and tropical, natural features such as large bodies of water, ocean currents, and mountains affect climate within each zone. Large cities also change weather patterns and influence the local climate.

Large Bodies of Water If you live or have vacationed near an ocean, you may have noticed that water heats up and cools down more slowly than land does. This is because it takes a lot more heat to increase the temperature of water than it takes to increase the temperature of land. In addition, water must give up more heat than land does for it to cool. Large bodies of water can affect the climate of coastal areas by absorbing or giving off heat. This causes many coastal regions to be warmer in the winter and cooler in the summer than inland areas at similar latitude. Look at **Figure 2** again. You can see the effect of an ocean on climate by comparing the average temperatures in a coastal city and an inland city, both located at 37°N latitude.

Figure 2
This map shows average daily low temperatures in four cities during January and July. It also shows average yearly precipitation.

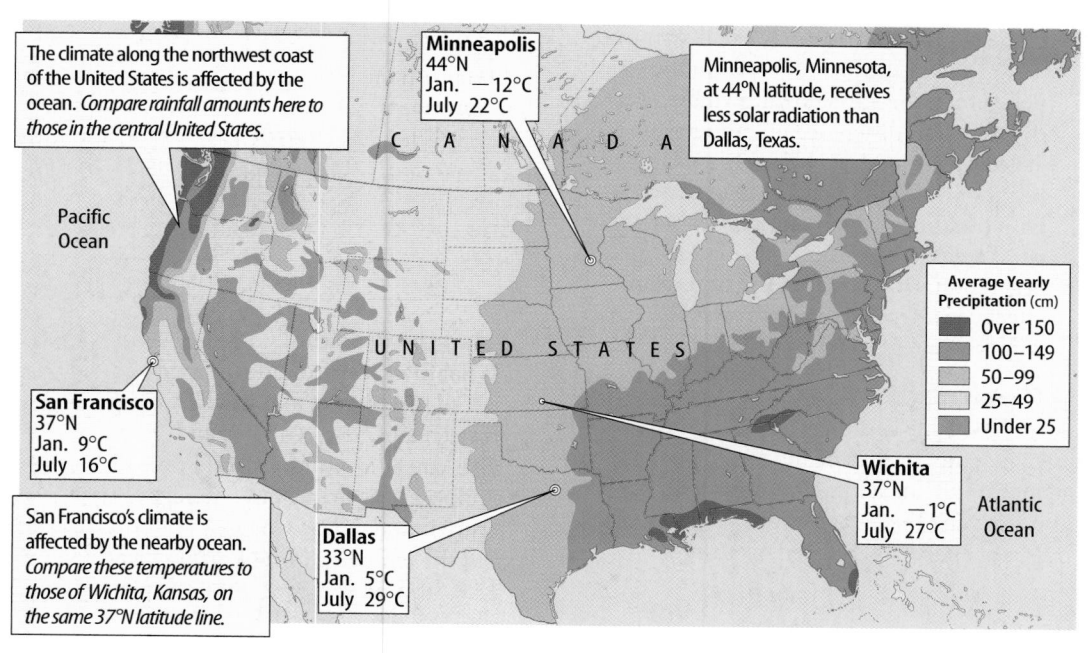

The climate along the northwest coast of the United States is affected by the ocean. *Compare rainfall amounts here to those in the central United States.*

Pacific Ocean

Minneapolis
44°N
Jan. −12°C
July 22°C

Minneapolis, Minnesota, at 44°N latitude, receives less solar radiation than Dallas, Texas.

C A N A D A

U N I T E D   S T A T E S

Average Yearly Precipitation (cm)
- Over 150
- 100–149
- 50–99
- 25–49
- Under 25

San Francisco
37°N
Jan. 9°C
July 16°C

San Francisco's climate is affected by the nearby ocean. *Compare these temperatures to those of Wichita, Kansas, on the same 37°N latitude line.*

Dallas
33°N
Jan. 5°C
July 29°C

Wichita
37°N
Jan. −1°C
July 27°C

Atlantic Ocean

Mini LAB

Observing Solar Radiation

Procedure
1. Darken the room.
2. Hold a **flashlight** about 30 cm from a **globe**. Shine the light directly on the equator. With your finger, trace around the light.
3. Now, tilt the flashlight to shine on 30°N latitude. The size of the lighted area should increase. Repeat at 60°N latitude.

Analysis
1. How did the size and shape of the light beam change as you directed the light toward higher latitudes?
2. How does Earth's tilt affect the solar radiation received by different latitudes?

Curriculum Connection

Geography Oceans and large lakes modify the nearby climate. Sandusky, Ohio, a town on Lake Erie, has more frost-free days and a smaller monthly temperature range than Bucyrus, Ohio, a city farther south and farther from the lake. As a result, the growing season is longer in Sandusky than in Bucyrus for crops such as peaches and grapes. Have students locate Lake Erie, Sandusky, and Bucyrus on a map. L1

---

2 Teach

Latitude and Climate

☑ **Reading Check**

Answer In general, the closer one is to the equator, the warmer the climate.

Mini LAB

Purpose Students observe how Earth's tilt affects the amount of solar radiation received at different latitudes. L2
LS Kinesthetic
Materials globe, flashlight
Teaching Strategy Have students use string and a ruler to measure the diameter of each lighted area.
Troubleshooting Instruct students to keep the light steady as they change its angle.

Analysis
1. The size of the area lit by the beam increases. The shape changes from fairly circular to more oval.
2. As latitude increases, light is more indirect and solar radiation is spread over a larger area. Thus, higher latitudes receive less concentrated solar radiation than lower latitudes.

✓ Assessment

Process Have students illustrate the different angles at which sunlight hits Earth's surface at the equator, 30°, and 60° latitude. Use **PASC**, p. 127.

Other Factors

Reading Check

Answer Warm currents warm nearby land; cool currents cool nearby land.

Fun Fact

The ocean-bordering forests of Washington's Olympic Peninsula are among the world's rainiest places. Moist winds moving over the area from the Pacific rise over the Olympic Mountains, dumping about 4 meters of rain each year on their eastern flank. The valleys of the Quinault, Queets, and Hoh rivers contain lush forests of spruce and hemlock, with trees reaching 90 meters tall.

Problem-Solving Activity

National Math Standards

Correlation to Mathematics Objectives
1, 5, 6, 8, 9

Answers to Practice Problems

1. 8 km had a change of 4° C; 24 km had a change of 2° C; The urbanized downtown area spread out to the 8 km mark in that period, but 24 km out, the temperature has only been mildly affected by urbanization.
2. No; the difference between downtown and 24 km out had been 5°C earlier, but now it would only be 3°. This might be caused by urban expansion.

Physics
INTEGRATION

When air rises over a mountain, the air expands and its temperature decreases, causing water vapor to condense and form rain. Temperature changes caused by air expanding or contracting also occur in some machines. Why does the air coming out of a bicycle pump feel cold?

Ocean Currents Ocean currents affect coastal climates. Warm currents begin near the equator and flow toward higher latitudes, warming the land regions they pass. When the currents cool off and flow back toward the equator, they cool the air and climates of nearby land.

Reading Check
How do ocean currents affect climate?

Winds blowing from the sea are often moister than those blowing from land. Therefore, some coastal areas have wetter climates than places farther inland. Look at the northwest coast of the United States shown in **Figure 2.** The large amounts of precipitation in Washington, Oregon, and northern California can be explained by this moist ocean air.

Mountains At the same latitude, the climate is colder in the mountains than at sea level. When radiation from the Sun is absorbed by Earth's surface, it heats the land. Heat from Earth then warms the atmosphere. In the mountains, the air has fewer molecules to absorb this heat. This is because Earth's atmosphere gets thinner at higher altitudes.

Problem-Solving Activity

How do large cities influence temperature?

The temperature of rural areas surrounding a large city can differ from the temperature in the city's downtown by several degrees. This difference in temperature is called the heat-island effect. It is partly a result of the land in cities being covered with buildings, roads, and pavement, while rural areas have far more open space and vegetation. Do you think the heat-island effect can change as a city grows? Use your ability to interpret data to find out.

Identifying the Problem

The table lists the average summer high temperatures in and around a large metropolitan city in 1978 and 1993. By examining the data, can you tell if the heat-island effect has changed over time?

Average Summer Temperatures		
Distance from Downtown (km)	Temperatures (ºC)	
	1978	1993
0	32.5	35
8	28.0	32.0
16	27.5	30.5
24	27.5	29.5

Solving the Problem

1. What distances from downtown experienced the greatest and smallest temperature change between 1978 and 1993? Can you account for the differences?
2. Suppose that in 1999 the average temperature in the downtown area was 36°C, but the temperature 24 km away was 33°C. Would you expect this? Explain.

Resource Manager

Chapter Resources Booklet
  Enrichment, p. 30
  Reinforcement, p. 27
  Lab Activity, pp. 9–11
Mathematics Skill Activities, p. 11

A The windward side of a large mountain range—the side facing the wind—often receives heavy precipitation.

B Deserts are common on the leeward side—the side away from the wind—of mountain ranges.

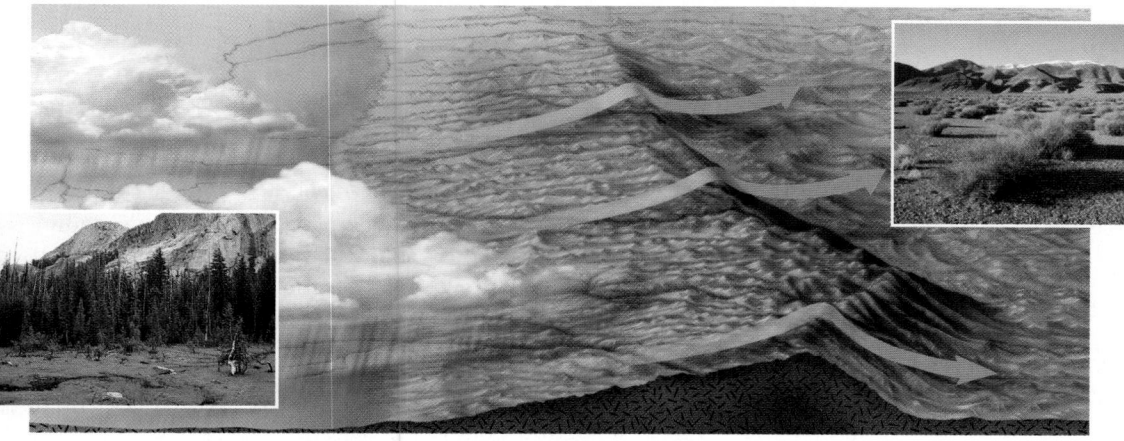

Rainshadows Mountains also affect regional climates, as shown in **Figure 3.** On the windward side of a mountain range, air rises, cools, and drops its moisture. On the leeward side of a mountain range air descends, heats up, and dries the land. Deserts are common behind mountains.

Cities Large cities affect local climates. Streets, parking lots, and buildings heat up, in turn heating the air. Air pollution traps this heat, creating what is known as the heat-island effect. Temperatures in a city can be 5°C higher than in surrounding rural areas.

Figure 3
Large mountain ranges can affect climate by forcing air to rise over the windward side and to descend on the leeward side. *How can this cause the two sides of the Sierra Nevada Mountain Range to be so different?*

Section 1 Assessment

1. What factors determine the climate of a region?
2. Explain how two cities located at the same latitude can have different climates.
3. How do mountains affect climate?
4. What is the heat island effect?
5. **Think Critically** Explain why types of plants and animals found at different elevations on a mountain range might differ. Would latitude affect the elevation at which some organisms are found?

Skill Builder Activities

6. **Comparing and Contrasting** Compare and contrast tropical and polar climates. **For more help, refer to the** Science Skill Handbook.
7. **Solving One-Step Equations** The coolest average summer temperature in the United States is 2°C at Barrow, Alaska, and the warmest is 37°C at Death Valley, California. Calculate the range of average summer temperatures in the United States. **For more help, refer to the** Math Skill Handbook.

Answers to Section Assessment

1. average temperature, precipitation, air pressure, humidity, and days of sunshine
2. If they are located at different altitudes, on different sides of mountains, or if only one is near a large water body, they will likely have different climates.
3. On the side facing the wind, air rises, cools, and precipitation occurs. On the other side, air descends, warms, and produces a dry climate.
4. Paved surfaces heat up and air pollution traps heat, producing higher temperatures in cities than in the surrounding countryside.
5. Because the climate would differ at different elevations and organisms adapt to their climates, Yes.
6. Both are affected by the angle of the Sun's rays. The tropics receive the most direct rays and are always hot. Polar zones get little solar energy, and are never warm.
7. $37° - 2° = 35° C$

Section 1 What is climate? **495**

Activity

Have students locate deserts next to mountain ranges on a world map. Have students infer the direction the winds blow across these mountain ranges. L2 IS **Visual-Spatial**

Caption Answer

Figure 3 windward side: air rises and cools, condensation occurs, and rain falls; leeward side: air descends, warms, and dries the land

Visual Learning

Figure 3 How would farming be different on each side of this mountain range? windward: wide range of crops that need plentiful rainfall; leeward: smaller range of crops, especially those that grow in dry areas or need irrigation

3 Assess

Reteach

Have students make a concept map that shows how latitude and topographic features affect climate. L2 IS **Visual-Spatial**

Challenge

Challenge students to look for newspaper or magazine articles on the American rain forests of the Pacific Northwest. Have them write a report on local plants and animals and the state of these forests. L3 P

Assessment

Process Ask students to infer what has the greatest effect on the climate where you live. Use **Performance Assessment in the Science Classroom,** p. 89.

SECTION

2 Climate Types

1 Motivate

Bellringer Transparency

Display the Section Focus Transparency for Section 2. Use the accompanying Transparency Activity Master. L2

ELL

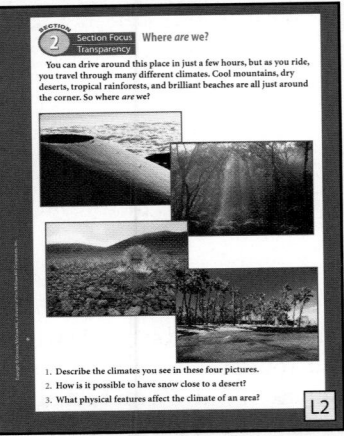

Tie to Prior Knowledge

Recall the climate characteristics that students listed at the start of Section 1. Have students use this list to determine the climate in which their community is located as they read this Section.

Caption Answer

Figure 4 that it's a desert

As You Read

What You'll Learn
- Describe a climate classification system.
- Explain how organisms adapt to particular climates.

Vocabulary
adaptation
hibernation

Why It's Important
Many organisms can survive only in climates to which they are adapted.

Figure 4
The type of vegetation in a region depends on the climate.
What do these plants tell you about the climate shown here?

496

Classifying Climates

What is the climate like where you live? Would you call it generally warm? Usually wet and cold? Or different depending on the time of year? How would you classify the climate in your region? Life is full of familiar classification systems—from musical categories to food groups. Classifications help to organize your thoughts and to make your life more efficient. That's why Earth's climates also are classified and are organized into the various types that exist. Climatologists—people who study climates—usually use a system developed in 1918 by Wladimir Köppen to classify climates. Köppen observed that the types of plants found in a region depended on the climate of the area. **Figure 4** shows one region Köppen might have observed. He classified climates by using the temperature and precipitation of regions that had different plant types.

The climate classification system shown in **Figure 5** separates climates into six groups—tropical, mild, dry, continental, polar, and high elevation. These groups are further separated into types. For example, the dry climate classification is separated into semiarid and arid.

Adaptations

Climates vary around the world, and as Köppen observed, the type of climate that exists in an area determines the vegetation found there. Fir trees aren't found in deserts, nor are cacti found in rain forests. In fact, all organisms are best suited for certain climates. Organisms are adapted to their environment. An **adaptation** is any structure or behavior that helps an organism survive in its environment. Adaptations are inherited. They develop in a population over a long period of time. Once adapted to a particular climate, organisms may not be able to survive in other climates.

Section ✓ *Assessment* Planner

PORTFOLIO
Make a Model, p. 498
PERFORMANCE ASSESSMENT
Skill Builder Activities, p. 499
See page 518 for more options.

CONTENT ASSESSMENT
Section, p. 499
Challenge, p. 499
Chapter, pp. 518–519

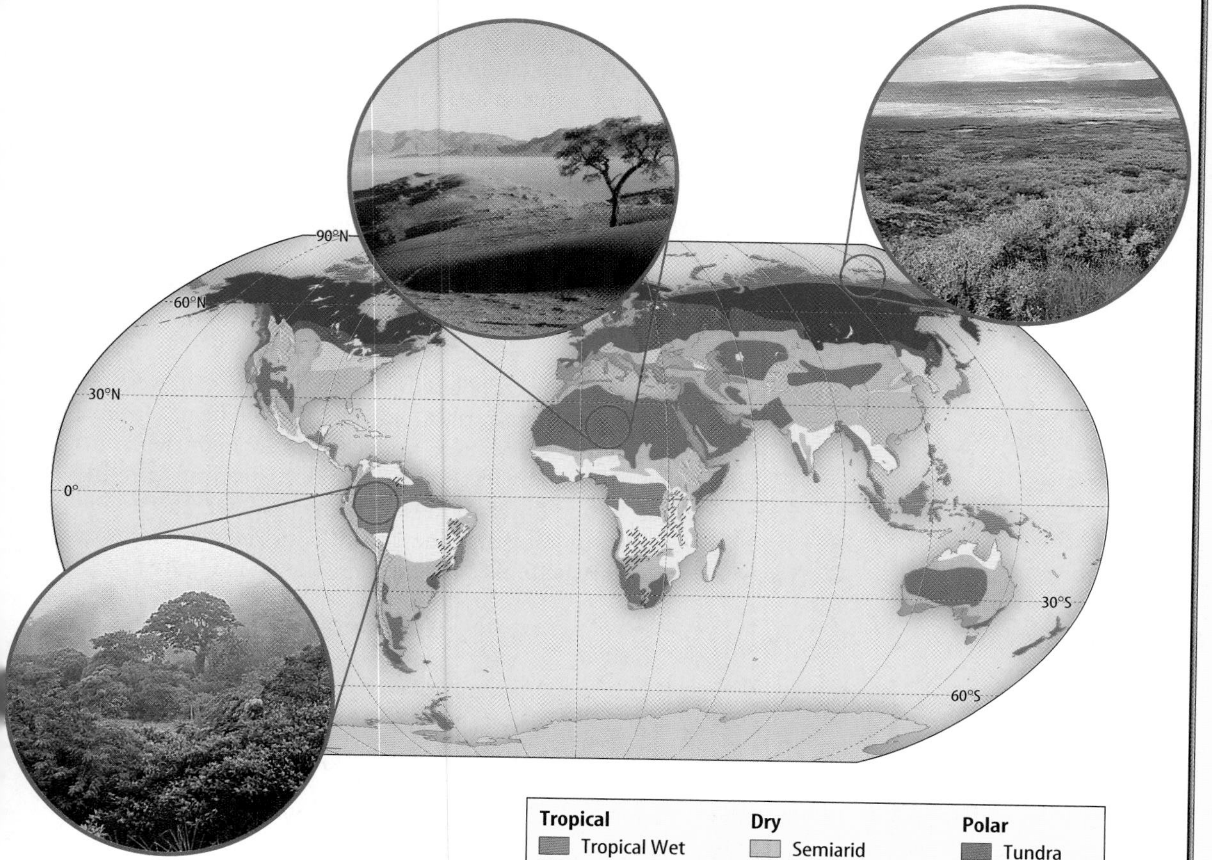

Tropical
- Tropical Wet
- Tropical Wet & Dry

Dry
- Semiarid
- Arid

Polar
- Tundra
- Icecap

Mild
- Marine West Coast
- Mediterranean
- Humid Subtropical

Continental
- Warm Summer
- Cool Summer
- Subarctic

High Elevation
- Highlands
- Uplands

Life Science INTEGRATION

Structural Adaptations Some organisms have body structures that help them survive in certain climates. The fur of mammals is really hair that insulates them from cold temperatures. A cactus has a thick, fleshy stem. This structural adaptation helps a cactus hold water. The waxy stem covering prevents water inside the cactus from evaporating. Instead of broad leaves, these plants have spiny leaves that further reduce water loss.

✔ Reading Check *How do cacti conserve water?*

Figure 5
This map shows a climate classification system similar to the one developed by Köppen. *What patterns can you see in the locations of certain climate types?*

SECTION 2 Climate Types **497**

2 Teach

Adaptations

Use an Analogy
Relate the insulating effect of a plastic foam cup to a mammal's fur. Normally, heat flows from a warm area to a cool area. Plastic foam contains many air bubbles, and air doesn't conduct heat well. That's why hot chocolate stays hot for a long time in a foam cup. Animal fur acts in this same way. Air trapped between hairs of a mammal's fur prevents heat loss. Have students think of other models that mimic the insulating ability of animal fur. Students may suggest a vacuum bottle.

Extension
Invite a wildlife specialist to class to talk about ways plants and animals are adapted to your climate.

Use Science Words
Word Meaning Tell students that "adaptation" comes from the Latin word *adaptare*, which means "to fit." Have students use this definition to explain the way the word is used on this page. Animals that live in different climates have body structures that help them fit those conditions.
L2 IN **Linguistic**

Caption Answer
Figure 5 Possible answer: Climates get cooler as you move away from the equator.

✔ Reading Check
Answer A thick, fleshy stem and spiney leaves help a cactus hold water.

Resource Manager

Chapter Resources Booklet
Transparency Activity, p. 45
Directed Reading for Content Mastery, p. 20
Enrichment, p. 31

Teacher FYI
Many adaptations occur because of DNA mutations in genes. Mutations can occur spontaneously or because of outside stimuli. While some mutations can be harmful, a trait resulting from a mutation may benefit an organism and be passed on to its offspring.

Section 2 Climate Types **497**

Adaptations, continued

Answer a period of greatly reduced activity in winter

Make a Model

After students have researched organisms that live in extreme climates such as hot springs or ocean vents on the seafloor, have them use pipe cleaners, gumdrops, straws, clay, and other items to make 3-D models of these organisms. Have each student write and present a brief report about his or her model. Students should explain in their reports how the organism is adapted to survival in its environment. L2 ELL 🤚 **Kinesthetic** P

Caption Answer

Figure 6B They reduce water loss.

Quick Demo

Use two thermometers to demonstrate that perspiration cools a person's body when water evaporates. Before you begin, be sure the temperature readings of both thermometers are identical. Wrap gauze around the tip of one thermometer. Dip the gauze into room temperature water. At the end of three minutes, read both thermometers. The gauze-covered thermometer will show a lower temperature than the one without gauze. As water evaporated from the gauze, heat was removed from the thermometer. L2 🤚 **Visual-Spatial**

Behavioral Adaptations Some organisms display behavioral adaptations that help them survive in a particular climate. For example, rodents and certain other mammals undergo a period of greatly reduced activity in winter called **hibernation**. During hibernation, body temperature drops and body processes are reduced to a minimum. Some of the factors thought to trigger hibernation include cooler temperatures, shorter days, and lack of adequate food. The length of time that an animal hibernates varies depending on the particular species of animal and the environmental conditions.

✔ **Reading Check** *What is hibernation?*

Other animals have adapted differently. During cold weather, bees cluster together in a tight ball to conserve heat. On hot, sunny days, desert snakes hide under rocks. At night when it's cooler, they slither out in search of food. Instead of drinking water as turtles and lizards do in wet climates, desert turtles and lizards obtain the moisture they need from their food. Some behavioral and structural adaptations are shown in **Figure 6**.

Figure 6
Organisms have structural and behavioral adaptations that help them survive in particular climates.

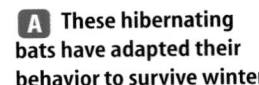 **A** These hibernating bats have adapted their behavior to survive winter.

B The needles and the waxy skin of a cactus are structural adaptations to a desert climate. *How do these adaptations help cacti conserve water?*

C Polar bears have structural adaptations to keep them warm. The hairs of their fur trap air and heat.

498 CHAPTER 17 Climate

Resource Manager

Chapter Resources Booklet
  Transparency Activity, pp. 47–48
  Reinforcement, p. 28
Reading and Writing Skill Activities, p. 3

Visual Learning

Figure 6A How can you tell that the bat is not adapted to live in a polar climate? Students should infer the bat would need thick fur or long hair to keep it warm in frigid polar temperatures. This bat has neither of these structural adaptations.

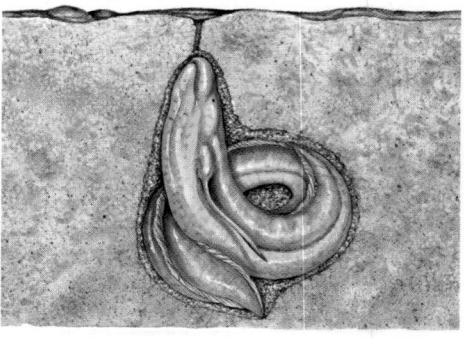

A

B

Figure 7
Lungfish survive periods of intense heat and drought by going into an inactive state called estivation. **A** During the dry season when water evaporates, lungfish dig into the mud and curl up in a small chamber they make at the lake's bottom. **B** During the wet season, lungfish reemerge to live in small lakes and pools.

Estivation Lungfish, shown in **Figure 7,** survive periods of intense heat by entering an inactive state called estivation (es tuh VAY shun). As the weather gets hot and water evaporates, the fish burrows into mud and covers itself in a leathery mixture of mud and mucus. It lives this way until the warm, dry months pass.

Like other organisms, you have adaptations that help you adjust to climate. In hot weather, your sweat glands release water onto your skin. The water evaporates, taking some heat with it. As a result, you become cooler. In cold weather, you may shiver to help your body stay warm. When you shiver, the rapid muscle movements produce some heat. What other adaptations to climate do people have?

Section 2 Assessment

1. How can climates be classified? What type of climate do you live in?
2. Use **Figure 5** and a world map to identify the climate type for each of the following locations: Cuba, North Korea, Egypt, and Uruguay.
3. What are some behavioral adaptations that allow animals to stay warm? What structural adaptations help keep animals warm?
4. How is hibernation different from estivation? How is it similar?
5. **Think Critically** What adaptations help dogs keep cool during hot weather?

Skill Builder Activities

6. **Forming Hypotheses** Some scientists have suggested that Earth's climate is getting warmer. What effects might this have on vegetation and animal life in various parts of the United States? **For more help, refer to the** Science Skill Handbook.
7. **Communicating** Research the types of vegetation found in the six climate regions shown in **Figure 5.** Write a paragraph in your Science Journal describing why vegetation can be used to help define climate boundaries. **For more help, refer to the** Science Skill Handbook.

SECTION 2 Climate Types **499**

Answers to Section Assessment

1. They are classified using temperature, precipitation, and vegetation. Answers will vary.
2. Cuba: tropical wet and dry; North Korea: warm summer; Egypt: arid; Uruguay: Mediterranean
3. Behavioral: bees cluster, snakes bask in sunlight, some mammals hibernate, desert animals get moisture

from food; structural: mammals have fur, desert plants have structures that reduce water loss.
4. Estivation is an inactive state; hibernation is a period in which body temperature drops and life processes slow. Both help animals survive extreme climate conditions.

5. They pant and sweat to reduce body heat, sit in shade, and drink water.
6. Those species adapted to live in warm climates will survive, others may not. Accept any reasonable answers.
7. Sample answer: Vegetation varies with temperature and light conditions. Thus, it can define climatic regions.

SECTION

3

Climatic Changes

1 Motivate

Bellringer Transparency

Display the Section Focus Transparency for Section 3. Use the accompanying Transparency Activity Master. L2

ELL

Tie to Prior Knowledge

Tell students that seasons are short-term climate changes. Ask them to write a brief paragraph contrasting any two seasons where you live. Then have students share their ideas.

Caption Answer

Figure 8 winter

✔ Reading Check

Answer Tropics have dry and rainy seasons.

As You Read

What You'll Learn

- **Explain** what causes seasons.
- **Describe** how El Niño affects climate.
- **Explore** possible causes of climatic change.

Vocabulary

season
El Niño
greenhouse effect
global warming
deforestation

Why It's Important

Changing climates could affect sea level and life on Earth.

Earth's Seasons

In temperate zones, you can play softball under the summer Sun and in the winter go sledding with friends. Weather changes with the season. **Seasons** are short periods of climatic change caused by changes in the amount of solar radiation an area receives. **Figure 8** shows Earth revolving around the Sun. Because Earth is tilted, different areas of Earth receive changing amounts of solar radiation throughout the year.

Seasonal Changes Because of fairly constant solar radiation near the equator, the tropics do not have much seasonal temperature change. However, they do experience dry and rainy seasons. The middle latitudes, or temperate zones, have warm summers and cool winters. Spring and fall are usually mild.

✔ **Reading Check** *What are seasons like in the tropics?*

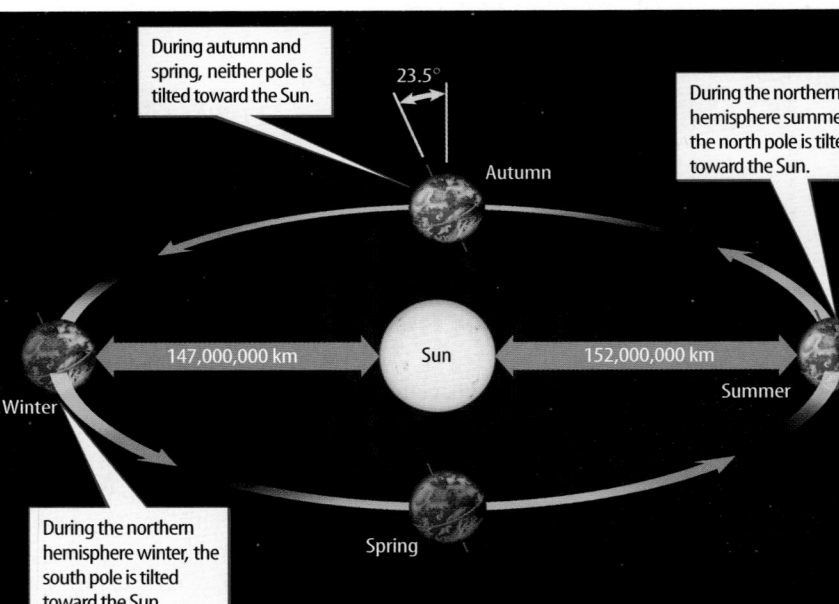

Figure 8
As Earth revolves around the Sun, different areas of Earth are tilted toward the Sun, which causes different seasons. *During which northern hemisphere season is Earth closer to the Sun?*

During autumn and spring, neither pole is tilted toward the Sun.

23.5°

Autumn

During the northern hemisphere summer the north pole is tilted toward the Sun.

147,000,000 km — Sun — 152,000,000 km

Winter

Summer

During the northern hemisphere winter, the south pole is tilted toward the Sun.

Spring

Section ✔Assessment Planner

PORTFOLIO
Curriculum Connection, p. 502
Science Journal, p. 504
PERFORMANCE ASSESSMENT
Try at Home MiniLAB, p. 501
Skill Builder Activities, p. 510
See page 518 for more options.

CONTENT ASSESSMENT
Section, p. 510
Challenge, p. 510
Chapter, pp. 518–519

Figure 9
A strong El Niño, like the one that occurred in 1998, can affect weather patterns around the world.

A A severe drought struck Indonesia, contributing to forest fires.

B California was plagued by large storms that produced pounding surf and shoreline erosion.

High Latitudes During the year, the high latitudes near the poles have great differences in temperature and number of daylight hours. As shown in **Figure 8,** during summer in the northern hemisphere, the north pole is tilted toward the Sun. During summer at the north pole, the Sun doesn't set for nearly six months. During that same time, the Sun never rises at the south pole. At the equator days are about the same length all year long.

El Niño and La Niña

El Niño (el NEEN yoh) is a climatic event that involves the tropical Pacific Ocean and the atmosphere. During normal years, strong trade winds that blow east to west along the equator push warm surface water toward the western Pacific Ocean. Cold, deep water then is forced up from below along the coast of South America. During El Niño years, these winds weaken and sometimes reverse. The change in the winds allows warm, tropical water in the upper layers of the Pacific to flow back eastward to South America. Cold, deep water is no longer forced up from below. Ocean temperatures increase by 1°C to 7°C off the coast of Peru.

El Niño can affect weather patterns. It can alter the position and strength of one of the jet streams. This changes the atmospheric pressure off California and wind and precipitation patterns around the world. This can cause drought in Australia and Africa. This also affects monsoon rains in Indonesia and causes storms in California, as shown in **Figure 9.**

The opposite of El Niño is La Niña, shown in **Figure 10.** During La Niña, the winds blowing across the Pacific are stronger than normal, causing warm water to accumulate in the western Pacific. The water in the eastern Pacific near Peru is cooler than normal. La Niña may cause droughts in the southern United States and excess rainfall in the northwestern United States.

TRY AT HOME Mini LAB

Modeling El Niño

Procedure

1. During El Niño, trade winds blowing across the Pacific Ocean from east to west slacken or even reverse. Surface waters move back toward the coast of Peru.
2. Add **warm water** to a **9 in by 13 in baking pan** until it is two-thirds full. Place the pan on a smooth countertop.
3. Blow as hard as you can across the surface of the water along the length of the pan. Next, blow with less force. Then, blow in the opposite direction.

Analysis

1. What happened to the water as you blew across its surface? What was different when you blew with less force and when you blew from the opposite direction?
2. Explain how this is similar to what happens during an El Niño event.

Resource Manager

Chapter Resources Booklet
Transparency Activity, p. 46
MiniLAB, p. 4
Directed Reading for Content Mastery, pp. 21, 22

Cultural Diversity

Peru El Niño is Spanish for "the Christ child," so named because it usually appears near Christmas. Because fish become less abundant during El Niño, fishers use this time to repair equipment and spend time with their families. Have students infer why there are fewer fish during El Niño. Cold water fish usually found along the coast of Peru cannot survive in the warm water caused by El Niño.

2 Teach

Earth's Seasons

IDENTIFYING Misconceptions

Many students think summer occurs when Earth is closest to the Sun. Refer to page 490F for teaching strategies that address this misconception.

El Niño and La Niña

TRY AT HOME Mini LAB

Purpose Students model winds that blow during El Niño. L1
Kinesthetic
Materials warm water, baking pan (9 in. x 13 in.)
Teaching Strategy Have students concentrate their breath by blowing through a straw.
Analysis
1. Water moved in ripples toward the opposite end of the pan; the water moved in the same direction with less force; water moved in the opposite direction.
2. Winds weaken and can reverse, causing surface currents to switch direction.

✓Assessment

Oral Ask students to explain what blowing across the water and ripples on the water modeled. wind; surface currents Use **PASC,** p. 143.

Visualizing El Niño and La Niña

Have students examine the pictures and read the captions. Then ask the following questions.

How does El Niño affect the weather in your area? Students should use the map on page 501 to determine their answer.

What effect can La Niña have on farming? Possible answer: In areas that are affected by La Niña, the drought conditions can ruin an entire season or year's worth of crops.

Activity

The two most extreme El Niño events in recent history were in 1982–83 and 1997–98. Have students research how these events affected different areas worldwide. Students can make a simple world map and symbolically represent the effects of the events in the appropriate area. Possible answer: In February 1998 the southeastern U.S. experienced a rash of tornadoes, while in Peru heavy rains caused flooding and mudslides.

Extension

Have students investigate how El Niño events may be responsible for coral bleaching. Have students make a poster showing their results. Possible answer: Under the stress of a change in water temperature, the corals expel the algae that live symbiotically in their tissues. It is these algae that give corals their brilliant colors. When the algae are no longer present, the corals' own transparent tissues allow the white calcium carbonate skeleton to show through.

Figure 10

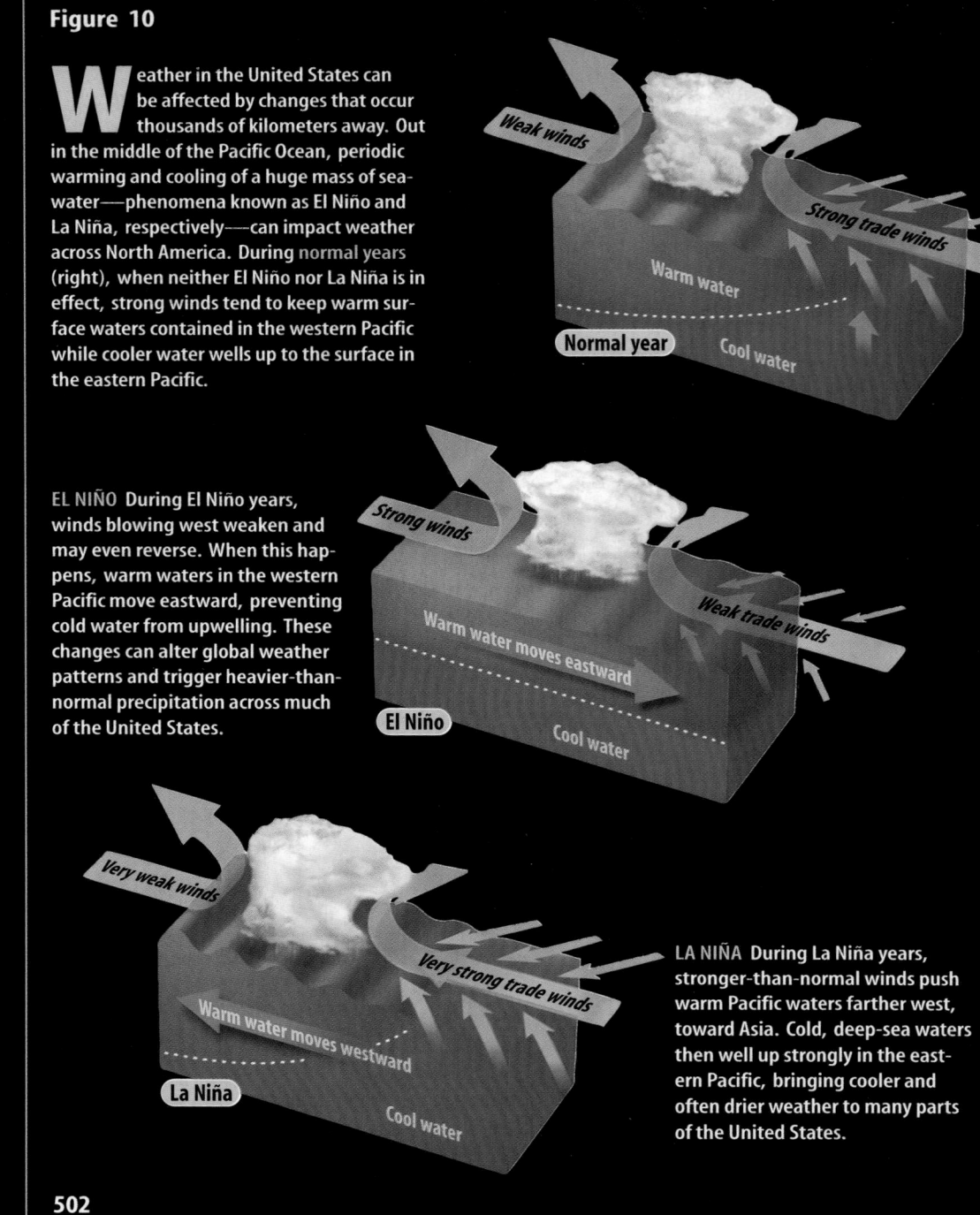

Weather in the United States can be affected by changes that occur thousands of kilometers away. Out in the middle of the Pacific Ocean, periodic warming and cooling of a huge mass of seawater—phenomena known as El Niño and La Niña, respectively—can impact weather across North America. During normal years (right), when neither El Niño nor La Niña is in effect, strong winds tend to keep warm surface waters contained in the western Pacific while cooler water wells up to the surface in the eastern Pacific.

Weak winds
Strong trade winds
Warm water
Normal year   Cool water

EL NIÑO During El Niño years, winds blowing west weaken and may even reverse. When this happens, warm waters in the western Pacific move eastward, preventing cold water from upwelling. These changes can alter global weather patterns and trigger heavier-than-normal precipitation across much of the United States.

Strong winds
Weak trade winds
Warm water moves eastward
El Niño   Cool water

Very weak winds
Very strong trade winds
Warm water moves westward
La Niña   Cool water

LA NIÑA During La Niña years, stronger-than-normal winds push warm Pacific waters farther west, toward Asia. Cold, deep-sea waters then well up strongly in the eastern Pacific, bringing cooler and often drier weather to many parts of the United States.

502

Curriculum Connection

Social Studies In 1982–1983 and 1998, two powerful El Niños caused billions of dollars worth of damage and thousands of deaths. Have students research and write a report about the reasons for El Niño's destructiveness. Floods destroyed crops and drowned people; drought resulted in fires and crop destruction; crop loss lead to starvation. [L2]
LS Linguistic

El Niño

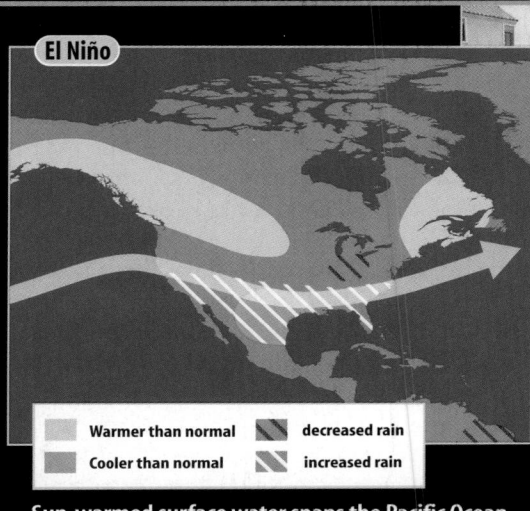

| Warmer than normal | decreased rain |
| Cooler than normal | increased rain |

Sun-warmed surface water spans the Pacific Ocean during El Niño years. Clouds form above the warm ocean, carrying moisture aloft. The jet stream, shown by the white arrow above, helps bring some of this warm, moist air to the United States.

▲ LANDSLIDE Heavy rains in California resulting from El Niño can lead to landslides. This upended house in Laguna Niguel, California, took a ride downhill during the El Niño storms of 1998.

La Niña

| Warmer than normal | decreased rain |
| Cooler than normal | increased rain |

During a typical La Niña year, warm ocean waters, clouds, and moisture are pushed away from North America. A weaker jet stream often brings cooler weather to the northern parts of the continent and hot, dry weather to southern areas.

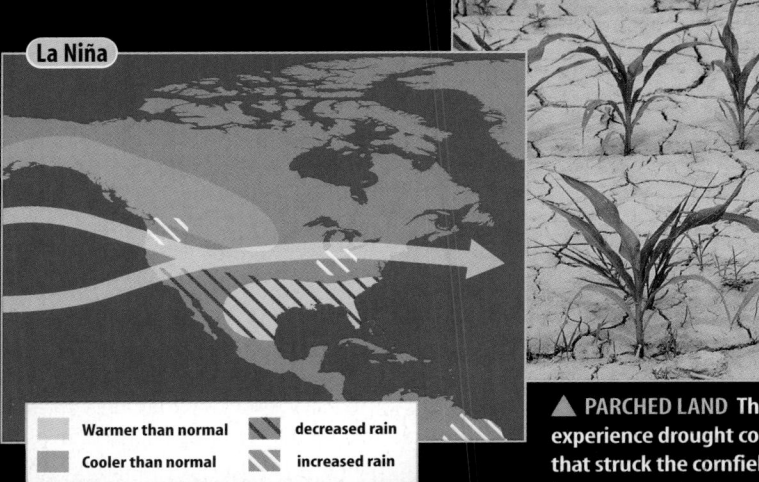

▲ PARCHED LAND The Southeast may experience drought conditions, like those that struck the cornfields of Montgomery County, Maryland, during the La Niña summer of 1988.

503

Resource Manager

Chapter Resources Booklet
  Enrichment, p. 32
Earth Science Critical Thinking/Problem Solving, p. 13

Content Background

Scientists are still not sure what causes an El Niño Southern Oscillation (ENSO) event to occur. Careful study of data from recent ENSO events has provided scientists with information about the change in conditions that occurs at the onset of an ENSO. However, the trigger for these changes remains a mystery. Under normal conditions, a high-pressure system sits over the eastern Pacific and a low-pressure system over the western Pacific. The position of these pressure systems drives the trade winds, which blow from east to west across the Pacific.

The onset of an ENSO is marked by a reversal in the position of these pressure systems. This reversal causes the trade winds to weaken and sometimes even to reverse in direction. The change in atmospheric pressure across the Pacific is referred to as the Southern Oscillation. Aside from the extreme weather conditions, often created worldwide as a result of an ENSO, these events can also cause problems for organisms living in the waters of the eastern Pacific. The cold water that is normally upwelled brings large amounts of nutrients to the surface. Primary producers that live on these nutrients thrive in this area, providing a large base for the food web. Thus, fish, birds, and marine mammals such as sea lions depend on these primary producers. When the upwelling either stops, or the warm water that surfaces during an ENSO event does not provide the necessary nutrients, the number of producers decreases and greater numbers of consumers face starvation.

Fun Fact

Major ice ages occurred 2 billion, 600 million, 250 million, and 2.5 million to 10,000 years ago. In the most recent ice age, the ice sheet in some places was 3,000 meters thick.

What causes climatic change?

Discussion

Is it possible to prepare for long-term climatic changes caused by catastrophic events like meteorite collisions or volcanic eruptions? Accept all reasonable answers, such as no, because we can't predict when these events will happen; or yes, we can prepare for the possible effects if they do occur.

Figure 11
Each layer of ice in a core records detailed climate information for a single year. Some cores cover 300,000 years.

Climatic Change

If you were exploring in Antarctica near Earth's south pole and found a 3-million-year-old fossil of a warm-weather plant or animal, what would it tell you? You might conclude that the climate of that region changed because Antarctica is much too cold for similar plants and animals to survive today. Some warm-weather fossils found in polar regions indicate that at times in Earth's past, worldwide climate was much warmer than at present. At other times Earth's climate has been much colder than it is today.

Sediments in many parts of the world show that at several different times in the past 2 million years, glaciers covered large parts of Earth's surface. These times are called ice ages. During the past 2 million years, ice ages have alternated with warm periods called interglacial intervals. Ice ages seem to last 60,000 to 100,000 years. Most interglacial periods are shorter, lasting 10,000 to 15,000 years. We are now in an interglacial interval that began about 11,500 years ago. Additional evidence suggests that climate can change even more quickly. Ice cores record climate in a way similar to tree rings. Cores drilled in Greenland show that during the last ice age, colder times lasting 1,000 to 2,000 years changed quickly to warmer spells that lasted about as long. **Figure 11** shows a scientist working with ice cores.

What causes climatic change?

Climatic change has many varied causes. These causes of climatic change can operate over short periods of time or very long periods of time. Catastrophic events, including meteorite collisions and large volcanic eruptions, can affect climate over short periods of time, such as a year or several years. These events add solid particles and liquid droplets to the upper atmosphere, which can change climate. Another factor that can alter Earth's climate is short- or long-term changes in solar output, which is the amount of energy given off by the Sun. Changes in Earth's movements in space affect climate over many thousands of years, and movement of Earth's crustal plates can change climate over millions of years. All of these things can work separately or together to alter Earth's climate.

504 CHAPTER 17 Climate

Science Journal

Glacial Living Have students imagine that they are living near the edge of a thick sheet of glacial ice during an ice age. Have them write a story describing the difficulties of daily survival, including where they would live, how they would keep warm, and how they would get food. Have students share their stories. [L2]

[LS] Linguistic [P]

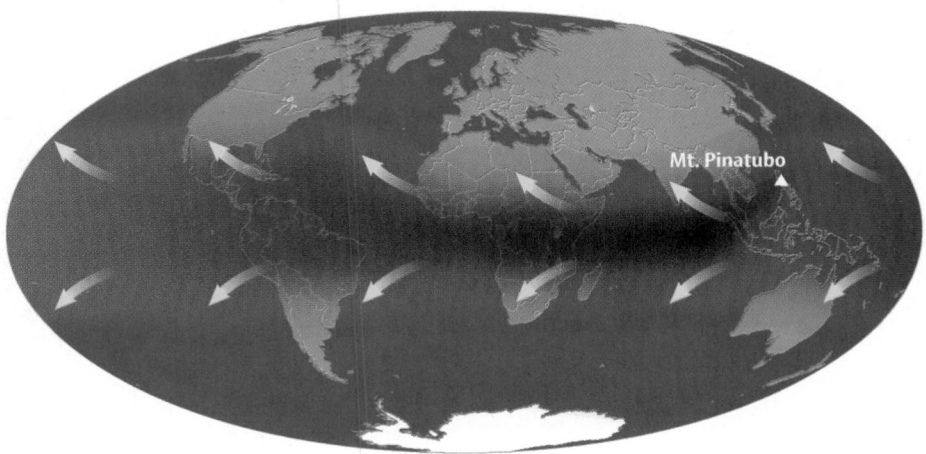

Mt. Pinatubo

Atmospheric Solids and Liquids Small solid and liquid particles always are present in Earth's atmosphere. These particles can enter the atmosphere naturally or be added to the atmosphere by humans as pollution. Some ways that particles enter the atmosphere naturally include volcanic eruptions, soot from fires, and wind erosion of soil particles. Humans add particles to the atmosphere through automobile exhaust and smokestack emissions. These small particles can affect climate.

Catastrophic events such as meteorite collisions and volcanic eruptions put enormous volumes of dust, ash, and other particles into the atmosphere. These particles block so much solar radiation that they can cool the planet. **Figure 12** shows how a major volcanic eruption affected Earth's atmosphere.

In cities, particles put into the atmosphere as pollution can change the local climate. These particles can increase the amount of cloud cover downwind from the city. Some studies have even suggested that rainfall amounts can be reduced in these areas. This may happen because many small cloud droplets form rather than larger droplets that could produce rain.

Energy from the Sun Solar radiation provides Earth's energy. If the output of radiation from the Sun varies, Earth's climate could change. Some changes in the amount of energy given off by the Sun seem to be related to the presence of sunspots. Sunspots are dark spots on the surface of the Sun. **WARNING:** *Never look directly at the Sun.* Evidence supporting the link between sunspots and climate includes an extremely cold period in Europe between 1645 and 1715. During this time, very few sunspots appeared on the Sun.

Figure 12
Mount Pinatubo in the Philippines erupted in 1991. During the eruption, particles were spread high into the atmosphere and circled the globe. Over time, particles spread around the world, blocking some of the Sun's energy from reaching Earth. The gray areas show how particles from the eruption moved around the world.

Health
INTEGRATION

Atmospheric particles produced as pollution can affect human health as well as climate. These small particles, often called particulates, can enter the lungs and cause tissue damage. People who have existing lung or heart problems are affected most seriously. Do research to find out what types of laws have been written to reduce particulate pollution.

Health
INTEGRATION

One purpose of the 1990 Clean Air Act Amendments was to reduce particulates, or soot. As a result, better emission control devices and cleaner-burning gasoline were developed for cars. Scrubbers were mandated to remove particulates from power-plant emissions.

Fun Fact

The cold period in Europe between 1645 and 1715 is called the Little Ice Age.
• Alpine glaciers grew.
• Some winters were so harsh that London's Thames River froze.
• Some summers were so wet and cold that crops could not be grown.

SECTION 3 Climatic Changes **505**

✔ **Active Reading**

Cause-and-Effect Chart This strategy is used to focus on cause-and-effect reasoning. In the center, have students write the topic that they are trying to understand. To the left of center, write the apparent causes of the topic. On the right side, write the apparent effects of the topic. Have students design a Cause-and-Effect Chart for a concept about climate. A sample is shown here.

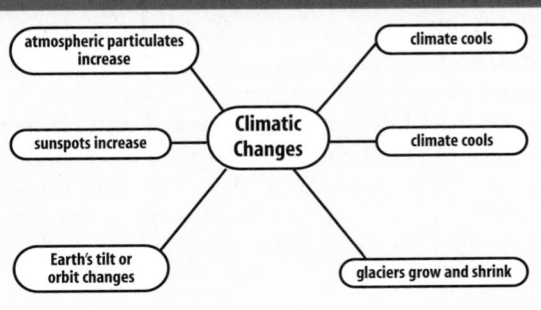

atmospheric particulates increase — climate cools
sunspots increase — **Climatic Changes** — climate cools
Earth's tilt or orbit changes — glaciers grow and shrink

Caption Answer
Figure 13: Low; during the middle of the last ice age—the solar energy reaching Earth was lower than normal.

Quick Demo
Use a top to demonstrate the wobble of a spinning object on its axis. Remind students that Earth's wobbling is so slow that one complete wobble takes thousands of years.

Extension
Have student groups research the answers to the following questions: What crustal plate do you live on? Where was this plate at the beginning of the Triassic Period? What kind of organisms lived in your area during the Triassic Period? What was the climate of your area at that time? Students should write reports about their research and document their sources. Most students live on the North American Plate; the region was part of Pangaea, located near the equator; organisms and climates vary. COOP LEARN [IS] **Interpersonal**

Use Science Words
Word Origin Paleoclimatology is the study of ancient climates. Have students find the meaning of the word part *paleo*. Have them list other words that include this word part and explain their meanings. Paleo means dealing with or involved with ancient forms or conditions. Possible examples: Paleobotany is the study of fossil plants. Paleontology is the study of ancient life forms. L3 [IS] **Linguistic**

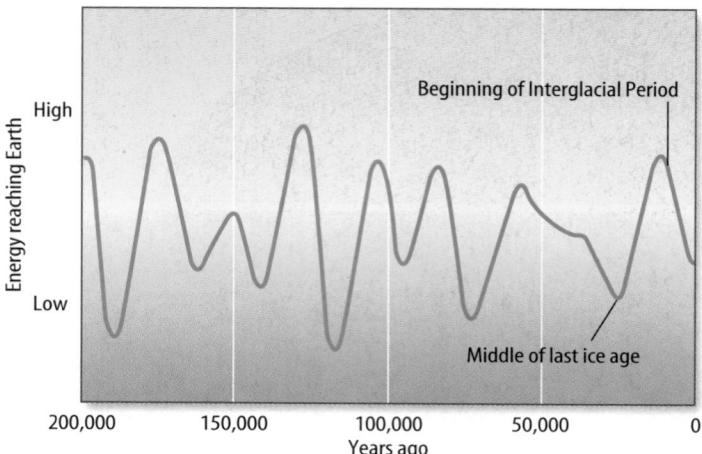

Energy From the Sun

Beginning of Interglacial Period

Middle of last ice age

High

Low

Energy reaching Earth

200,000   150,000   100,000   50,000   0
Years ago

Figure 13
The curving line shows how the amount of the Sun's energy that strikes the northern hemisphere changed over the last 200,000 years. *Describe the amount of energy that reached the northern hemisphere during the last ice age.*

Earth Movements Another explanation for some climatic changes involves Earth's movements in space. Earth's axis currently is tilted 23.5° from perpendicular to the plane of its orbit around the Sun. In the past, this tilt has increased to 24.5° and has decreased to 21.5°. When this tilt is at its maximum, the change between summer and winter is probably greater. Earth's tilt changes about every 41,000 years. Some scientists hypothesize that the change in tilt affects climate.

Two additional Earth movements also cause climatic change. Earth's axis wobbles in space just like the axis of a top wobbles when it begins to spin more slowly. This can affect the amount of solar energy received by different parts of Earth. Also, the shape of Earth's orbit changes. Sometimes it is more circular than at present and sometimes it is more flattened. The shape of Earth's orbit changes over a 100,000-year cycle.

Amount of Solar Energy These movements of Earth cause the amount of solar energy reaching different parts of Earth to vary over time, as shown in **Figure 13.** These changes might have caused glaciers to grow and shrink over the last few million years. However, they do not explain why glaciers have occurred so rarely over long spans of geologic time.

Crustal Plate Movement Another explanation for major climatic change over tens or hundreds of millions of years concerns the movement of Earth's crustal plates. The movement of continents and oceans affects the transfer of heat on Earth, which in turn affects wind and precipitation patterns. Through time, these altered patterns can change climate. One example of this is when movement of Earth's plates created the Himalaya about 40 million years ago. The growth of these mountains changed climate over much of Earth.

As you've learned, many theories attempt to answer questions about why Earth's climate has changed through the ages. Probably all of these things play some role in changing climates. More study needs to be done before all the factors that affect climate will be understood.

506   CHAPTER 17 Climate

Curriculum Connection

Geography A new ocean is forming where crustal plates are moving apart in Africa's Great Rift Valley. As this ocean grows, it will affect the transfer of heat on Earth's surface and change wind and precipitation patterns. Have students locate the Great Rift Valley on a map. Have them also locate photographs that show evidence of the growing rift.

Teacher FYI

When Earth's orbit is nearly circular, its axis is tilted the least, and summers in the northern hemisphere are cooler. This situation encourages the growth of ice sheets in the middle latitudes, possibly triggering ice ages.

Climatic Changes Today

Beginning in 1994, representatives from many countries have met to discuss the greenhouse effect and global warming. These subjects also have appeared frequently in the headlines of newspapers and magazines. Some people are concerned that the greenhouse effect could be responsible for some present-day warming of Earth's atmosphere and oceans.

The **greenhouse effect** is a natural heating that occurs when certain gases in Earth's atmosphere trap heat. Radiation from the Sun strikes Earth's surface and causes it to warm. Some of this heat then is radiated back toward space. Greenhouse gases in the atmosphere absorb a portion of this heat. This keeps Earth warmer than it would be otherwise. The greenhouse effect is illustrated in **Figure 14.**

There are many natural greenhouse gases in Earth's atmosphere. Water vapor, carbon dioxide, and methane are some of the most important ones. Without these greenhouse gases, life would not be possible on Earth. Like Mars, Earth would be too cold. However, if the greenhouse effect is too strong, Earth could get too warm. High levels of carbon dioxide in its atmosphere indicate that this has happened on the planet Venus.

SCIENCE Online

Research Visit the Glencoe Science Web site at **science.glencoe.com** for more information about the greenhouse effect.

Figure 14
The Sun's radiation travels through Earth's atmosphere and heats the surface. Greenhouse gases in our atmosphere trap the heat. *How is this similar to the way a greenhouse works?*

Climatic Changes Today

SCIENCE Online

Internet Addresses

_____

_____

_____

_____

Explore the Glencoe Science Web site at **science.glencoe.com** to find out more about topics in this section.

Discussion

Tell students that scientists recently pumped iron into a patch of seawater. The number of phytoplankton in their test patch increased significantly as the iron fertilized the water. **Infer what happened to the concentration of CO_2 in the nearby air. How might this process reduce the concentration of CO_2 in the atmosphere?** CO_2 decreased because it was used by the phytoplankton during photosynthesis. Since CO_2 is a greenhouse gas, removing it from the air might slow global warming. Inform students that testing must be done to find out if this process has negative effects.

Caption Answer

Figure 14 Glass in a greenhouse lets in solar radiation and traps heat.

Resource Manager

Reading and Writing Skill Activities, p. 19

Science Inquiry Labs, p. 29

Teacher FYI

An extreme example of the greenhouse effect at work has been observed on Venus. Boiling-hot temperatures are common on the planet's surface both at night and during the day. Venus' atmosphere is dense with carbon dioxide, a greenhouse gas that traps heat around the planet.

Global Warming

✔ **Reading Check**

Answer They increase the greenhouse effect, making climate warmer.

Text Question Answer

Sometimes organisms can adjust, but if not, they die out.

Make a Model

Have students make a model to show how a rise in sea level could affect coastal cities. Give each team a large, unlined index card. Have them draw a line and a scale along the length of the card. Let each centimeter on the line represent 2 m in elevation. Have them write the names of the following cities on the card according to elevation: New York City (4 m), Washington, D.C. (3 m), Boston (4.6 m), Miami (2 m), Los Angeles (29.6 m). Tape the card around a large glass jar so it can be read through the glass. Sea level should be at the bottom. Pour water to the 5-m line and observe which cities are submerged. New York City, Washington, D.C., Boston, Miami Pour water to represent a sea level rise of 30 m, the rise predicted if the ice caps melt. Which cities would be underwater? all cities on the card

L2 ELL IS **Visual-Spatial**

Global Warming

Global warming means that the average global temperature of Earth is rising. One likely reason for global warming is the increase of greenhouse gases in our atmosphere. An increase in greenhouse gases increases the greenhouse effect. In the last 100 years, the surface temperature on Earth has increased 0.5°C. This might be a result of more greenhouse gases.

✔ **Reading Check** *How can greenhouse gases affect Earth's climate?*

If Earth's average temperature continues to rise, many glaciers could melt. When glaciers melt, the extra water causes sea levels to rise. Low-lying coastal areas would experience increased flooding. Already some ice caps and small glaciers are beginning to melt and recede, as shown in **Figure 15.** Sea level is rising in some places. Some scientific studies show that these events are related to Earth's increased temperature.

You learned in the previous section that organisms are adapted to their environments. When environments change, can organisms cope? In some tropical waters around the world, corals are dying. Many people think these deaths are caused by warmer water to which the corals are not adapted.

Some climate models show that in the future, Earth's temperatures will increase faster than they have in the last 100 years. Next, you will learn how human activity might contribute to global warming, and you will find out what you can do to help reduce the amount of greenhouse gases entering the atmosphere.

Figure 15
This glacier in Greenland might have receded from its previous position because of global warming. The pile of rock in front shows how far the glacier once reached.

LAB DEMONSTRATION

Purpose to show that burning hydrocarbons produces CO_2

Materials phenol red; candle; match; two petri dishes; tall, narrow jar; clay

Preparation Explain that coal, oil, natural gas, trees, and candles are hydrocarbons; phenol red is an indicator for carbon dioxide.

Procedure Secure the candle to the bottom of one petri dish with clay. Cover the bottoms of each dish with phenol red. Light the candle. Invert the jar over the candle. Observe.

Expected Outcome The phenol red turns yellow in the dish with the candle; it stays red in the other petri dish.

✔ *Assessment*

What caused the color change? presence of carbon dioxide **What was the source of the carbon dioxide?** Carbon from the burning candle combined with oxygen to produce CO_2. **Why was the second petri dish used?** It was a control.

Figure 16
When forests are cleared or burned, carbon dioxide levels increase in the atmosphere. *What can people do to help reduce CO_2 levels in the atmosphere?*

Human Activities

Human activities affect the air in Earth's atmosphere. Burning fossil fuels and removing vegetation increase the amount of carbon dioxide (CO_2) in the atmosphere. Each year, the amount of carbon dioxide in the atmosphere continues to increase. Because carbon dioxide is a greenhouse gas, it might cause Earth's temperature to increase.

Burning Fossil Fuels When natural gas, oil, and coal are burned for energy, the carbon in these fossil fuels combines with atmospheric oxygen to form carbon dioxide. This increases the amount of carbon dioxide in Earth's atmosphere. Studies indicate that humans have increased carbon dioxide levels in the atmosphere by about 25 percent over the last 150 years.

Deforestation Destroying and cutting down forests, called **deforestation,** also affects the amount of carbon dioxide in the atmosphere. Forests, such as the one shown in **Figure 16,** are cleared for mining, roads, buildings, and grazing cattle. Large tracts of forest have been cleared in every country on Earth. Tropical forests have been decreasing at a rate of about one percent each year for the past two decades.

As trees grow, they take in carbon dioxide from the atmosphere. Trees use this carbon dioxide to produce wood and leaves. When trees are cut down, the carbon dioxide they could have removed from the atmosphere remains. Cut-down trees often are burned for fuel or to clear the land. Burning trees produces even more carbon dioxide.

Research Visit the Glencoe Science Web site at **science.glencoe.com** for more information about deforestation. Communicate to your class what you learn.

Human Activities

Caption Answer

Figure 16 Possible answers: recycle paper, stop burning wood, plant trees, conserve electricity, use different energy sources to meet energy needs

Teacher FYI

The idea that burning coal increases carbon dioxide and leads to an increase in Earth's temperature is not new. It was first suggested in 1896 by Svante Arrhenius, a Swedish chemist.

Discussion

The preindustrial concentration of CO_2 in the atmosphere was 280 parts per million (ppm). The concentration in 2000 was nearly 370 ppm. Some scientists expect the concentration by 2100 to be around 700 ppm. **Why is CO_2 concentration increasing so rapidly?** Human population is increasing. With more energy needs more fossil fuels are being burned, and more forests are being cleared for mining, roads, buildings, and agriculture.

Resource Manager

Chapter Resources Booklet
   Lab Activity, pp. 13–16
Earth Science Critical Thinking/Problem Solving, p. 18

Internet Addresses

_____

_____

_____

Explore the Glencoe Science Web site at **science.glencoe.com** to find out more about topics in this section.

Visual Learning

Figure 17B Emphasize the positive aspects of solar energy (free fuel, no pollution). **Could there be a problem with placing large areas of solar panels in urban areas? If so, how would you solve the problem?** Yes; they require a lot of space. One solution would be to place the panels on buildings. Accept reasonable answers.

3 Assess

Reteach

Have students explain why scientists cannot agree on their forecasts for Earth's climate. Students should discuss the many variables that must be considered in making such predictions. L2
LS Logical-Mathematical

Challenge

Challenge students to access the Glencoe Science Web site to find out about the role of the ocean in absorbing atmospheric CO₂. Instruct students to report on their findings. L3 **LS** Linguistic

Oral Have students contrast the effects of volcanic ash and CO₂ on atmospheric temperature. Volcanic ash reflects heat, making Earth cooler. CO₂ traps heat, making Earth warmer. Use **Performance Assessment in the Science Classroom,** p. 99.

Figure 17
Solar energy is beginning to fill some human energy needs.
A These solar panels in California generate electricity without adding CO₂ to the atmosphere.
B Solar-powered cars may be common in the future.

How to Reduce CO₂

What can you do to help reduce the amount of CO₂ in the atmosphere? Conserving electricity is one answer. When you conserve electricity, you reduce the amount of fossil fuel that is burned. One way to save fuel is to change daily activities that rely on energy from burning fossil fuels. Turn off the TV, for instance, when no one is watching it. Walk or ride a bike to the store, if possible, instead of using a car. People also can use different energy sources to meet their energy needs, as shown in **Figure 17.**

Another way to reduce CO₂ is to plant vegetation. As you've learned, plants remove carbon dioxide from the atmosphere. Correctly planted vegetation also can shelter homes from cold winds or the blazing Sun and reduce the use of electricity.

Section 3 Assessment

1. How is Earth's tilted axis responsible for seasons?
2. In what way does El Niño change the climate? What climate changes are caused by La Niña?
3. What factors can cause Earth's climate to change?
4. How are people adding carbon dioxide to the atmosphere?
5. **Think Critically** If Earth's climate continues to warm, how might your community be affected?

Skill Builder Activities

6. **Recognizing Cause and Effect** Using a globe, model the three movements of Earth in space that can cause climatic change. **For more help, refer to the** Science Skill Handbook.
7. **Using a Word Processor** Use word processing software to design a pamphlet to inform people why Earth's climate changes. What are your predictions for the future? On what evidence do you base these predictions? Include this evidence in your pamphlet. **For more help, refer to the** Technology Skill Handbook.

Answers to Section Assessment

1. It causes areas to receive changing amounts of solar radiation throughout the year.
2. El Niño: drought in Australia and Africa, less dependable monsoons in Indonesia, storms in California; La Niña: droughts in southern U.S., excess rainfall in northwestern U.S.
3. Factors include: seasons, El Niño/La

Niña, Earth's tilt, Earth's wobble, changes in the shape of Earth's orbit, volcanic eruptions, meteorite impacts, excess CO₂.
4. by burning fossil fuels, deforestation
5. Answers could include a need for more energy for air conditioning and possibility of flooding as sea level rises.

6. Students should model Earth's changing orbit, tilt, and wobble.
7. Students should include several of the reasons for climate change discussed in this section. Predictions will vary, but students should cite the evidence on which their predictions are based.

Activity

The Greenhouse Effect

Do you remember climbing into the car on a warm, sunny day? Why was it so hot inside the car when it wasn't that hot outside? It was hotter in the car because the car functioned like a greenhouse. You experienced the greenhouse effect.

What You'll Investigate
How can you demonstrate the greenhouse effect?

Materials
identical large, empty glass jars (2)
lid for one jar
nonmercury thermometers (3)

Goals
■ **Model** the greenhouse effect.
■ **Measure and graph** temperature changes.

Safety Precautions 🥽 🧤 ♨
Be careful when you handle glass thermometers. If a thermometer breaks, do not touch it. Have your teacher dispose of the glass safely.

Procedure

1. Lay a thermometer inside each jar.
2. Place the jars next to each other by a sunny window. Lay the third thermometer between the jars.
3. **Record** the temperatures of the three thermometers. They should be the same.
4. Place the lid on one jar.
5. **Record** the temperatures of all three thermometers at the end of 5, 10, and 15 min.
6. Make a line graph that shows the temperatures of the three thermometers for the 15 min of the experiment.

Conclude and Apply

1. **Explain** why you placed a thermometer between the two jars.
2. What were the constants in this experiment? What was the variable?
3. Which thermometer experienced the greatest temperature change during your experiment?
4. **Analyze** what occurred in this experiment. How was the lid in this experiment like the greenhouse gases in the atmosphere?
5. **Infer** from this experiment why you should never leave a pet inside a closed car in warm weather.

Communicating Your Data

Give a brief speech describing your conclusions to your class. **For more help, refer to the** Science Skill Handbook.

ACTIVITY **511**

Communicating Your Data
Students should support their conclusions with data.

Resource Manager

Chapter Resources Booklet
Activity Worksheet, pp. 5–6
Reinforcement, p. 29

Science Inquiry Labs, p. 39

BENCH TESTED

Purpose Students model the greenhouse effect. [L2] ELL
IS Kinesthetic
Process Skills communicating, identifying and manipulating variables, interpreting data, using numbers, making models, measuring in SI, recording, relating cause and effect, making graphs
Time Required 45 minutes
Safety Precautions Students should handle thermometers carefully.
Teaching Strategy Before the activity, keep the thermometers in the same area and away from direct sunlight or heating and cooling vents.
Troubleshooting Temperatures on the three thermometers should be the same.

Answers to Questions

1. It is the control.
2. constants: identical jars and thermometers, exposure to Sun's radiation; variable: presence of jars and a glass lid on one jar
3. the one inside the jar with the lid; Heat could not escape as easily.
4. Similar to greenhouse gases in the atmosphere, the glass let radiation in, but heat could not escape due to the lid.
5. Trapped heat can sicken or kill pets.

✓ *Assessment*

Process Have students infer how global warming might affect the water cycle. Possible answer: because warmer air holds more moisture, evaporation could increase and precipitation patterns could change. Use **PASC,** p. 89.

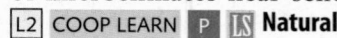

Activity

What You'll Investigate

Purpose

Students observe characteristics of microclimates near school.

L2 COOP LEARN **P** **LS** **Naturalist**

Process Skills

measuring in SI, using numbers, observing and inferring, recording, interpreting data, relating cause and effect, analyzing, communicating, comparing and contrasting

Time Required

40 minutes to set up testing sites, 20 minutes twice each day for a week to observe and record measurements, 40 minutes to do Procedure #5 and the Conclude and Apply questions

Materials

Make a thermometer and rain gauge available for each test site. Have a psychrometer and windsock available for each group.

Alternate Materials

If psychrometers need to be assembled, have students do this prior to the activity. To make a wet bulb thermometer, have students wrap the tip of a thermometer with gauze, as was done in the Quick Demo earlier in this chapter.

Safety Precautions

Students should handle thermometers with care.

Activity

Microclimates

A microclimate is a localized climate that differs from the main climate of a region. Buildings in a city, for instance, can affect the climate of the surrounding area. Large buildings can create microclimates by blocking the Sun or changing wind patterns.

What You'll Investigate

Does your school create microclimates?

Materials

thermometers
psychrometer
paper strip or wind sock
large cans (4 or 5)
* beakers or rain gauges (4 or 5)
unlined paper
*Alternate materials

Goals

■ **Observe** temperature, wind speed, relative humidity, and precipitation in areas outside your school.
■ **Identify** local microclimates.

Safety Precautions

WARNING: *If a thermometer breaks, do not touch it. Have your teacher dispose of the glass safely.*

Relative Humidity										
Dry Bulb Temperature (°C)	Dry Bulb Temperature Minus Wet Bulb Temperature (°C)									
	1	2	3	4	5	6	7	8	9	10
14	90	79	70	60	51	42	34	26	18	10
15	90	80	71	61	53	44	36	27	20	13
16	90	81	71	63	54	46	38	30	23	15
17	90	81	72	64	55	47	40	32	25	18
18	91	82	73	65	57	49	41	34	27	20
19	91	82	74	65	58	50	43	36	29	22
20	91	83	74	66	59	51	44	37	31	24
21	91	83	75	67	60	53	46	39	32	26
22	92	83	76	68	61	54	47	40	34	28
23	92	84	76	69	62	55	48	42	36	30
24	92	84	77	69	62	56	49	43	37	31
25	92	84	77	70	63	57	50	44	39	33

512 CHAPTER 17 Climate

Resource Manager

Chapter Resources Booklet
  Activity Worksheet, pp. 7–8
Lab Management and Safety, p. 37

Sample Student Data Table :
Test Site 1

Day	Time	Temp.	Precip.	Wind
1	AM PM			
2	AM PM			
3	AM PM			
4	AM PM			
5	AM PM			

Procedure

1. Select four or five sites around your school building. Also, select a control site well away from the school.

2. Attach a thermometer to an object near each of the locations you selected. Set up a rain gauge, beaker, or can to collect precipitation.

3. Visit each site at two predetermined times, one in the morning and one in the afternoon, each day for a week. Record the temperature and measure any precipitation that might have fallen. Use a wind sock or paper strip to determine wind direction.

4. To find relative humidity, you'll need to use a psychrometer. A psychrometer is an instrument with two thermometers—one wet and one dry. As moisture from the wet thermometer evaporates, it takes heat energy from its environment, and the environment immediately around the wet thermometer cools. The thermometer records a lower temperature. Relative humidity can be found by finding the difference between the wet thermometer and the dry thermometer and by using the chart on the previous page. Record all of your weather data.

5. **Analyze** your data to find patterns. Make separate line graphs for temperature, relative humidity, and precipitation for your morning and afternoon data. Make a table showing wind direction data.

Conclude and Apply

1. Why did you take weather data at a control site away from the school building? How did the control help you analyze and interpret your data?

2. **Compare and contrast** weather data for each of your sites. What microclimates did you identify around your school building? How did these climates differ from the control site? How did they differ from each other?

3. **Infer** what conditions could have caused the microclimates that you identified. Are your microclimates similar to those that might exist in a large city? Explain.

*C*ommunicating
Your Data

Use your graphs to make a large poster explaining your conclusions. Display your posters in the school building. **For more help, refer to the** Science Skill Handbook.

ACTIVITY 513

Procedure

Teaching Strategies

- Students should dip the wet bulb thermometer in water at each site and wait several minutes before reading both thermometers.
- Students can find relative humidity at the intersection of the "dry bulb" temperature and the "dry bulb minus wet bulb" temperature on the Relative Humidity table.

Expected Outcome

Students should find that microclimate varies with location.

Conclude and Apply

1. To see what the climate was like when not influenced by the building; when test sites were compared to the control, climatic effects caused by the building could be determined.

2. Answers will be subjective and based on the student's individual research.

3. Possible answers: shaded areas, walls blocking wind or rainfall. Students may infer that a large city would have similar microclimates because of the effects of the buildings.

Error Analysis

If students did not find differences, they may not have read the thermometers correctly.

*A*ssessment

Performance Have students hypothesize how microclimates change throughout a 24-hour period around the school building. Use **Performance Assessment in the Science Classroom,** p. 93.

*C*ommunicating
Your Data

Students may wish to use electronic spreadsheets to make their graphs.

Content Background

Volcanoes are found throughout the world. However, not all volcanoes erupt in the same way. Kilauea, on the island of Hawaii, erupts quietly, pouring lava out slowly. Others, such as Mount St. Helens, spew out hot ash and debris in violent explosions. The type of eruption that occurs largely depends on the location of the volcano with respect to the boundaries of tectonic plates.

Volcanoes similar to Mount St. Helens occur where an oceanic plate converges with a continental plate. A large trench is formed as the oceanic plate is dragged below the continental plate. Water trapped in the trench is also pulled along with the plate. As the plate material is heated it melts. The water vaporizes and forms large pockets of gas. Because the melting plate material is sticky, it forms plugs that trap these gases underground. Over time, pressure increases beneath the surface, creating a time bomb. Sooner or later, these pressures are released through a weakness in the continental plate, forming a volcano. As the gases are released, they rapidly expand, causing powerful explosions. The hot materials blasted out of the volcano contain a mixture of molten rock and pieces of the volcano itself.

The Year There Was

Mount St. Helens in Washington state erupted in May 1980. Its ash cloud temporarily darkened the sky and was carried thousands of kilometers away by upper-air currents.

You've seen pictures of erupting volcanoes. One kind of volcano sends smoke, rock, and ash high into the air above the crater. Another kind of volcano erupts with fiery, red-hot rivers of lava snaking down its sides. Erupting volcanoes are nature's forces at their mightiest, causing destruction and death. But not everyone realizes how far-reaching the destruction can be.

Large volcanic eruptions can affect people thousands of kilometers away. In fact, major volcanic eruptions can have effects that reach around the globe.

An erupting volcano can temporarily change Earth's climate. The ash a volcano ejects into the atmosphere can create day after day without sunshine. Other particles move high into the atmosphere and are carried all the way around Earth, sometimes causing global temperatures to drop for several months.

The Summer That Never Came

An example of a volcanic eruption with wide-ranging effects occurred in 1783 in Iceland, an island nation in the North Atlantic Ocean. Winds carried a black cloud of ash from an erupting volcano in Iceland westward across northern Canada, Alaska, and across the Pacific Ocean to Japan. The summer turned bitterly cold in these places. Water froze, and heavy snowstorms pelted the land. Sulfurous gases from the erupting volcano combined with water to form particles of acid that reflected solar energy back into space. This "blanket" in the atmosphere kept the Sun's rays from heating up part of Earth.

The most tragic result of this eruption was the death of many Kauwerak people, who lived in western Alaska. Only a handful of Kauwerak survived the summer that never came. They had no opportunity to catch needed foods to keep them alive through the following winter.

514

Resources for Teachers and Students

In the Path of a Killer Volcano, by NOVA, WGBH Boston Video, Boston, MA. 1993.

Earth Science, by Ralph Feather, Jr. and Susan Leach Snyder. Glencoe/McGraw-Hill. 1999.

Volcano Cowboys: the Rocky Evolution of a Dangerous Science, by Dick Thompson. St. Martin's Press, New York. 2000.

No Summer

Erupting volcanoes can cause unusual changes in climate

A truck is dwarfed by clouds of volcanic ash during the eruption of Mt. Pinatubo in the Philippines. The volcano had been dormant for 611 years.

Another Year Without a Summer

In 1815, the eruption of Tambora, on the island of Sumbawa in Indonesia, is blamed for North America and Europe having "the year without a summer" in 1816. Once again, the blanket of acid particles, pushed by upper-level winds, caused areas far removed from the volcanic activity to face a drastic change in weather patterns. In New England in 1816, frosts occurred and snow fell well into June. Massive crop failures occurred in North America and Europe.

Only volcanoes that throw debris above the troposphere cause this kind of climatic change. Melissa Free, a researcher for the National Oceanographic and Atmospheric Administration, says, "If [debris] is in the troposphere, it is taken out and dissipated more rapidly by rainfall." But, Free says, to cause climatic change, "...the eruption has to be strong enough to push material above the troposphere and into the stratosphere." And that's what happened when Tambora erupted, leading to a very unusual summer.

Discussion

What are some of the other unfavorable effects that may result from debris blown into the upper atmosphere during a volcanic eruption? Possible answers: Aircraft flying through it might suffer broken windows or experience engine trouble; as the ash settles to the ground, breathing problems and long-term lung damage may result from inhaling ash; engines in motor vehicles could clog up; and rivers could become rivers of mud jeopardizing aquatic life and human populations downstream.

Historical Significance

The eruption of Mount St. Helens in 1980 provided volcanologists with a rare opportunity to study an explosive volcanic eruption. From the information they gathered on seismic activity, gases emitted, temperatures, and deformation of the crater and surrounding area, scientists were able to improve their understanding of the events that lead up to an explosive eruption. This, in turn, has enabled them to refine their ability to predict future eruptions. In 1991, their ability to predict eruptions was successfully tested when Mt. Pinatubo in the Philippines awoke from its long sleep.

CONNECTIONS Locate Using an atlas, locate Indonesia and Iceland. Using reference materials, find five facts about each place. Make a map of each nation and illustrate the map with your five facts.

SCIENCE *Online*

For more information, visit science.glencoe.com

CONNECTIONS Collect books from your school library and local public library for students to use while researching facts on Iceland and Indonesia. Encourage the students to look for unique details. Have students share their maps in small groups. Let each group select five facts from their collection to share with the class.

SCIENCE *Online*

Internet Addresses

_____

_____

_____

Explore the Glencoe Science Web site at **science.glencoe.com** to find out more about topics in this feature.

Reviewing Main Ideas

Preview

Students can answer the questions in their Science Journals. Discuss the answers as you go through the chapter. **LS** **Linguistic**

Review

Students can write their answers, then compare them with those of other students. **LS** **Interpersonal**

Reteach

Students can look at the illustrations and describe details that support the main ideas of the chapter. **LS** **Visual-Spatial**

Answers to Chapter Review

SECTION 1

3. On the windward side, it will be moist because as air rises and cools, moisture condenses and falls as precipitation. On the leeward side, air descends, warms, and dries the land.

SECTION 3

2. The water from El Niño's heavy rains mixes with loose sediments, which then move downhill.

5. Trees remove carbon dioxide, a greenhouse gas, as they photosynthesize.

Reviewing Main Ideas

Section 1   What is climate?

1. An area's climate is the average weather over a long period of time, such as 30 years.

2. The three main climate zones are tropical, polar, and temperate.

3. Features such as oceans, mountains, and even large cities affect climate. *What differences might you find in the climates on the opposite sides of this mountain range?*

Section 2   Climate Types

1. Climates can be classified by various characteristics, such as temperature, precipitation, and vegetation. World climates commonly are separated into six major groups.

2. Organisms have structural and behavioral adaptations that help them survive in particular climates. Many organisms can survive only in the climate they are adapted to.

3. Adaptations develop in a population over a long period of time.

Section 3   Climatic Changes

1. Seasons are caused by the tilt of Earth's axis as Earth revolves around the Sun.

2. El Niño disrupts normal temperature and precipitation patterns around the world. *How could El Niño help cause California mudflows like this one?*

3. Geological records show that over the past few million years, Earth's climate has alternated between ice ages and warmer periods called interglacials.

4. The greenhouse effect occurs when certain gases trap heat in Earth's atmosphere.

5. Humans might be contributing to global warming by producing greenhouse gases. Carbon dioxide enters the atmosphere when fossil fuels such as oil and coal are burned. *How can planting vegetation like the tree shown here help decrease greenhouse gases in the atmosphere?*

FOLDABLES
Reading & Study Skills

After You Read

To help you review the various aspects of the climate classification system, use the Classify Study Fold you made at the beginning of the chapter.

FOLDABLES
Reading & Study Skills

After You Read

After students have read the chapter and completed the Foldable described in Before You Read, have them do the activity on the student page.

Dinah Zike

Visualizing Main Ideas

Complete the following concept map on climate.

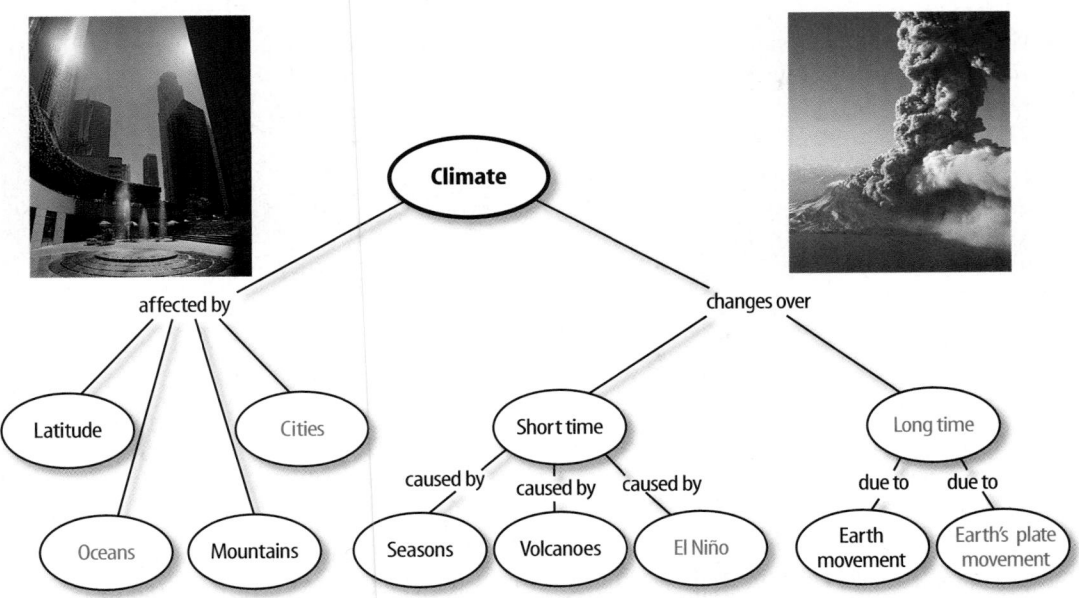

Vocabulary Review

Vocabulary Words

a. adaptation
b. climate
c. deforestation
d. El Niño
e. global warming
f. greenhouse effect
g. hibernation
h. polar zone
i. season
j. temperate zone
k. tropics

Study Tip

Use tables and graphs to help you organize written material. For example, put the levels of biological organization in a table. Show what each level contains. Referring to the table may help you revise concepts quickly.

Using Vocabulary

The sentences below include vocabulary words that have been used incorrectly. Change the incorrect words so that the sentence reads correctly. Underline your change.

1. Earth's north pole is in the temperate zone.

2. Deforestation causes the Pacific Ocean to become warmer off the coast of Peru.

3. During adaptation, an animal's body temperature drops.

4. Season is the pattern of weather that occurs over many years.

5. Greenhouse effect means global temperatures are rising.

Visualizing Main Ideas

See student page.

Vocabulary Review

Using Vocabulary

1. Earth's north pole is in the <u>polar zone.</u>
2. <u>El Niño</u> causes the Pacific Ocean to become warmer off the coast of Peru.
3. During <u>hibernation</u>, an animal's body temperature drops.
4. <u>Climate</u> is the pattern of weather that occurs over many years.
5. <u>Global warming</u> means global temperatures are rising.

IDENTIFYING ▷ Misconceptions

Assess

Use this assessment as follow-up to Page 490F after students have completed the chapter.

Materials (for each group) globe, light source

Procedure Using **Figure 8**, have each group determine on location of Earth and the axis tilts that illustrate the four seasons in the Northern Hemisphere. Repeat the activity to illustrate the four seasons in the Southern Hemisphere.

Expected Outcome Students will recognize that the major contributor to the cause of seasons is the tilt of the Earth on its axis at about 23.5° and that the distance between the Earth and the Sun is not a major factor in causing seasons.

Chapter ⑰ Assessment

Checking Concepts

1. C
2. A
3. B
4. D
5. A
6. D
7. B
8. A
9. C
10. A

Thinking Critically

11. Some organisms are not adapted for warmer temperatures.
12. The region was wetter and possibly warmer in the past.
13. Air near water is often cooler than air inland.
14. Earth's temperature would increase.
15. Temperature decreases with altitude.

Checking Concepts

Choose the word or phrase that best answers the question.

1. What is commonly found in places where warm air crosses a mountain and descends?
   A) lakes   C) deserts
   B) rain forests   D) glaciers

2. During which of the following is the eastern Pacific warmer than normal?
   A) El Niño   C) summer
   B) La Niña   D) spring

3. Which of the following is a greenhouse gas in Earth's atmosphere?
   A) helium   C) hydrogen
   B) carbon dioxide D) oxygen

4. Which latitude receives the most direct rays of the Sun year-round?
   A) 60°N   C) 30°S
   B) 90°N   D) 0°

5. What happens as you climb a mountain?
   A) temperature decreases
   B) temperature increases
   C) air pressure increases
   D) air pressure remains constant

6. Which of the following is true of El Niño?
   A) It cools the Pacific Ocean near Peru.
   B) It causes flooding in Australia.
   C) It cools the waters off Alaska.
   D) It may occur when the trade winds slacken or reverse.

7. What do changes in Earth's orbit affect?
   A) Earth's shape   C) Earth's rotation
   B) Earth's climate D) Earth's tilt

8. The Köppen climate classification system includes categories based on precipitation and what other factor?
   A) temperature   C) winds
   B) air pressure D) latitude

9. Which of the following is an example of structural adaptation?
   A) hibernation   C) fur
   B) migration   D) estivation

10. Which of these can people do in order to help reduce global warming?
    A) conserve energy C) produce methane
    B) burn coal   D) remove trees

Thinking Critically

11. Why might global warming lead to the extinction of some organisms?

12. What might you infer if you find fossils of tropical plants in a desert?

13. On a summer day, why would a Florida beach be cooler than an orange grove that is 2 km inland?

14. What would happen to global climates if the Sun emitted more energy?

15. Why will it be cooler if you climb to a higher elevation in a desert?

Developing Skills

16. **Making and Using Graphs** The following table gives average precipitation amounts for Phoenix, Arizona. Make a bar graph of these data. Which climate type do you think Phoenix represents?

Precipitation in Phoenix, Arizona	
Season	Precipitation (cm)
Winter	5.7
Spring	1.2
Summer	6.7
Autumn	5.9
Total	19.5

Chapter ✓*Assessment* Planner

Portfolio Encourage students to place in their portfolios one or two items of what they consider to be their best work. Examples include:
- Challenge, p. 495
- Make a Model, p. 498
- Curriculum Connection, p. 502
- Science Journal, p. 504

Performance Additional performance assessments, Performance Task Assessment Lists, and rubrics for evaluating these activities can be found in Glencoe's **Performance Assessment in the Science Classroom.**

17. Communicating Explain how atmospheric pressure over the Pacific Ocean might affect the direction that the trade winds blow.

18. Predicting Make a chain-of-events chart to explain the effect of a major volcanic eruption on climate.

19. Forming Hypotheses A mountain glacier in South America has been getting smaller over several decades. What hypotheses should a scientist consider to explain why this is occurring?

20. Concept Mapping Complete the concept map using the following: *tropics, 0°–23° latitude, polar, temperature zones, temperate, 23°–66° latitude, 66° latitude to poles.*

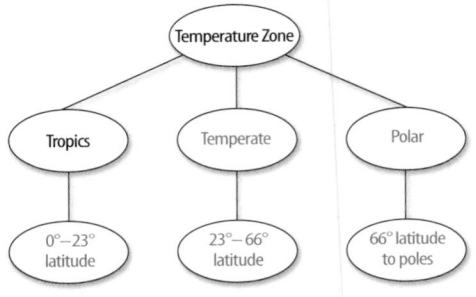

Performance Assessment

21. Science Display Make a display illustrating different factors that can affect climate. Be sure to include detailed diagrams and descriptions for each factor in your display. Present your display to the class.

TECHNOLOGY

 Go to the Glencoe Science Web site at **science.glencoe.com** or use the **Glencoe Science CD-ROM** for additional chapter assessment.

 **Test Practice**

The graph below shows long-term variations in atmospheric carbon dioxide levels and global temperature.

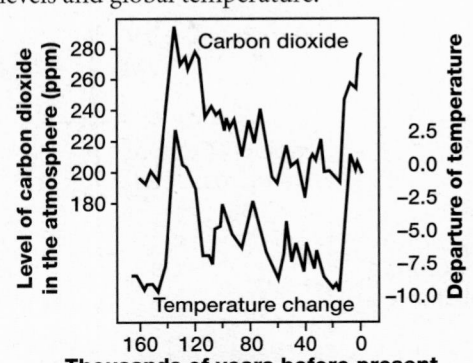

Study the graph and answer the following questions.

1. Which of these statements is TRUE according to the graph?
 A) Earth's mean temperature has never been hotter than it is today.
 B) The level of CO_2 has never been higher than today.
 C) The mean global temperature 60,000 years ago was less than today.
 D) The level of CO_2 in the atmosphere 80,000 years ago was 280 parts per million.

2. Which of the following statements BEST describes this graph?
 F) As CO_2 levels have increased, so has global temperature.
 G) As CO_2 levels have increased, global temperature has decreased.
 H) As global temperature has increased, CO_2 levels have decreased.
 J) No relationship exists between CO_2 and global temperatures.

CHAPTER ASSESSMENT 519

Test Practice

The Test-Taking Tip was written by The Princeton Review, the nation's leader in test preparation.
1. C
2. F

Developing Skills

16. Check students' graphs against data in table; desert
17. When air pressure is high, air molecules move toward low pressure and produce wind. If air pressure is high in the eastern Pacific, winds blow west; if air pressure is high in the western Pacific, winds blow east.
18. Charts may include the following steps: volcano erupts, ash rises into air, ash spreads around world, ash blocks solar radiation, world climate cools.
19. Climate is getting warmer; perhaps precipitation is less. Accept reasonable responses.
20. See student page.

Performance Assessment

21. Displays should include data about seasons; El Niño; volcanic eruptions; meteorite impacts; changes in Earth's tilt, wobble, and orbit shape; and the effect of greenhouse gases. Use the **Performance Task Assessment List for Science Displays** in PASC, p. 135.

✓Assessment Resources

📁 Reproducible Masters

Chapter Resources Booklet
 Chapter Review, pp. 37–38
 Chapter Tests, pp. 39–42
 Assessment Transparency Activity, p. 49

Glencoe Science Web site
 Interactive Tutor
 Chapter Quizzes

Glencoe Technology
 🖌 Assessment Transparency
 💿 Interactive CD-ROM Chapter Quizzes
 💿 ExamView Pro Test Bank
 💿 Vocabulary PuzzleMaker Software
 📼 MindJogger Videoquiz DVD/VHS

Section/Objectives	Standards		Activities/Features
Chapter Opener	**National**	**State/Local**	**Explore Activity:** Explore how currents work, p. 521
	See p. 5T for a Key to Standards.		**Before You Read,** p. 521
Section 1 Ocean Water 🕐 2 sessions 📦 1 block 1. **Identify** the origin of the water in Earth's oceans. 2. **Explain** how dissolved salts and other substances get into seawater. 3. **Describe** the composition of seawater.	National Content Standards: UCP4, D1, D2		
Section 2 Ocean Currents 🕐 2 sessions 📦 1 block 1. **Explain** how winds and the Coriollis effect influence surface currents. 2. **Discuss** the temperatures of coastal waters. 3. **Describe** density currents.	National Content Standards: UCP2, A1, B1, B3, D1		**Science Online,** p. 527 **MiniLAB:** Modeling a Density Current, p. 529 **Math Skills Activity:** Calculating Density, p. 530
Section 3 Ocean Waves and Tides 🕐 3 sessions 📦 1.5 blocks 1. **Describe** wave formation. 2. **Distinguish** between the movement of water particles in a wave and the movement of the wave. 3. **Explain** how ocean tides form.	National Content Standards: UCP3, B1, B3, D1, D3, E2, G1, G2		**MiniLAB:** Modeling Water Particle Movement, p. 533 **Visualizing Wave Movement,** p. 534 **Science Online,** p. 535 **Life Science Integration,** p. 537 **Activity:** Making Waves, p. 539 **Activity:** Sink or Float, pp. 540–541 **Science and Language Arts:** The Jungle of Ceylon, pp. 542–543

▣ NATIONAL GEOGRAPHIC

Teacher's Corner

PRODUCTS AVAILABLE FROM GLENCOE
To order call 1-800-334-7344:
CD-ROM
NGS PictureShow: Oceans
Curriculum Kit
GeoKit: Oceans

Transparency Set
NGS PicturePack: Oceans

PRODUCTS AVAILABLE FROM NATIONAL GEOGRAPHIC SOCIETY
To order call 1-800-368-2728:
Videos
Living Ocean
Oceans in Motion
Water: A Precious Resource

Activity Materials	Reproducible Resources	Section Assessment	Technology
Explore Activity: 2 beakers, ice, warm water, dropper, food coloring	**Chapter Resources Booklet** Foldables Worksheet, p. 13 Directed Reading Overview, p. 15 Note-taking Worksheets, pp. 29–31	GLENCOE'S **ASSESSMENT** ADVANTAGE	
Need materials? Contact Science Kit at 1-800-828-7777 or www.sciencekit.com on the Internet.	**Chapter Resources Booklet** Transparency Activity, p. 40 Lab Activity, pp. 9–10 Enrichment, p. 26 Reinforcement, p. 23 Directed Reading, p. 16 **Cultural Diversity,** p. 65	Portfolio Assessment, p. 525 Performance Skill Builder Activities, p. 525 Content Section Assessment, p. 525	Section Focus Transparency Interactive CD-ROM/DVD Guided Reading Audio Program
MiniLAB: clear plastic storage box, water, salt, glass, food coloring, spoon	**Chapter Resources Booklet** Transparency Activity, p. 41 MiniLAB, p. 3 Lab Activity, pp. 11–12 Enrichment, p. 27 Reinforcement, p. 24 Directed Reading, p. 16 **Mathematics Skill Activities,** p. 9 **Science Inquiry Labs,** p. 31	Portfolio Curriculum Connection, p. 528 Performance MiniLAB, p. 529 Math Skills Activity, p. 530 Skill Builder Activities, p. 531 Content Section Assessment, p. 532	Section Focus Transparency Interactive CD-ROM/DVD Guided Reading Audio Program
MiniLAB: plastic storage box, tape, water, cork, spoon **Activity:** 11" x 14" white paper, 3-speed electric fan, gooseneck lamp, clock or watch, clear-plastic storage box, water, metric ruler **Activity:** small, uncooked potato; teaspoon; salt; large glass bowl; water; balance; large graduated cylinder; metric ruler	**Chapter Resources Booklet** Transparency Activity, p. 42 MiniLAB, p. 4 Enrichment, p. 28 Reinforcement, p. 25 Directed Reading, pp. 17, 18 Transparency Activity, pp. 43–44 Activity Worksheet, pp. 5–6, 7–8 **Lab Management and Safety,** p. 65	Portfolio Extension, p. 534 Performance MiniLAB, p. 533 Skill Builder Activities, p. 538 Content Section Assessment, p. 538	Section Focus Transparency Teaching Transparency Interactive CD-ROM/DVD Guided Reading Audio Program

End of Chapter Assessment

Blackline Masters	Technology	Professional Series
Chapter Resources Booklet Chapter Review, pp. 33–34 Chapter Tests, pp. 35–38 **Standardized Test Practice by The Princeton Review,** pp. 79–82	MindJogger Videoquiz CD-ROM Explorations and Quizzes Vocabulary Puzzle Makers ExamView Pro Test Bank Interactive Lesson Planner Interactive Teacher's Edition	Performance Assessment in the Science Classroom (PASC)

Transparencies

Section Focus

Section Focus Transparency 1 — Livin' Life Large

What's the biggest animal that ever lived? You might be surprised to learn that it's not a dinosaur, but the blue whale. The biggest blue whales are roughly 30 meters (100 feet) long and weigh about 136,000 kilograms (150 tons).

1. How does water help support the blue whale's massive size?
2. How is life on land tied to life in the oceans?

L2

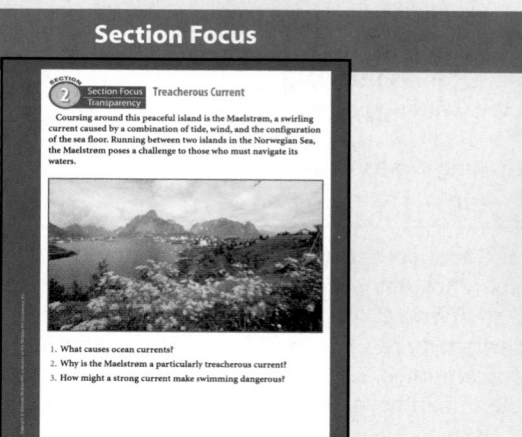

Section Focus Transparency 2 — Treacherous Current

Coursing around this peaceful island is the Maelstrom, a swirling current caused by a combination of tide, wind, and the configuration of the sea floor. Running between two islands in the Norwegian Sea, the Maelstrom poses a challenge to those who must navigate its waters.

1. What causes ocean currents?
2. Why is the Maelstrom a particularly treacherous current?
3. How might a strong current make swimming dangerous?

L2

Section Focus Transparency 3 — Deadly Wave

Giant waves called tsunamis are created in the oceans by earthquakes or volcanoes. Tsunamis, or tidal waves, can be over 30 m (100 feet) high and are capable of traveling long distances over water. This photo shows a tidal wave that struck Hilo, Hawaii, in 1946.

1. What happens when you drop a rock in water?
2. What causes ocean waves?
3. What effects do waves have on the shoreline?

L2

This is a representation of key blackline masters available in the Teacher Classroom Resources. See Resource Manager boxes within the chapter for additional information.

Key to Teaching Strategies

The following designations will help you decide which activities are appropriate for your students.

L1 Level 1 activities should be appropriate for students with learning difficulties.

L2 Level 2 activities should be within the ability range of all students.

L3 Level 3 activities are designed for above-average students.

ELL ELL activities should be within the ability range of English Language Learners.

COOP LEARN Cooperative Learning activities are designed for small group work.

LS Multiple Learning Styles logos, as described on page 22T, are used throughout to indicate strategies that address different learning styles.

P These strategies represent student products that can be placed into a best-work portfolio.

Assessment

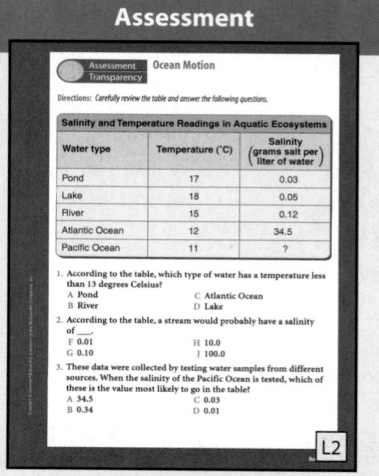

Assessment Transparency — Ocean Motion

Directions: *Carefully review the table and answer the following questions.*

Salinity and Temperature Readings in Aquatic Ecosystems		
Water type	Temperature (°C)	Salinity (grams salt per liter of water)
Pond	17	0.03
Lake	18	0.05
River	15	0.12
Atlantic Ocean	12	34.5
Pacific Ocean	11	?

1. According to the table, which type of water has a temperature less than 13 degrees Celsius?
   A Pond   C Atlantic Ocean
   B River   D Lake
2. According to the table, a stream would probably have a salinity of ___.
   F 0.01   H 10.0
   G 0.10   J 100.0
3. These data were collected by testing water samples from different sources. When the salinity of the Pacific Ocean is tested, which of these is the value most likely to go in the table?
   A 34.5   C 0.03
   B 0.34   D 0.01

L2

Teaching

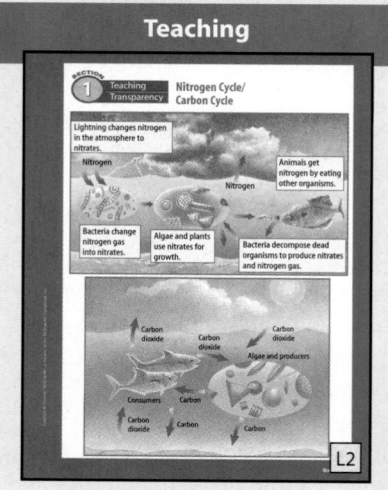

Teaching Transparency 1 — Nitrogen Cycle/Carbon Cycle

L2

Hands-on Activities

Activity Worksheets

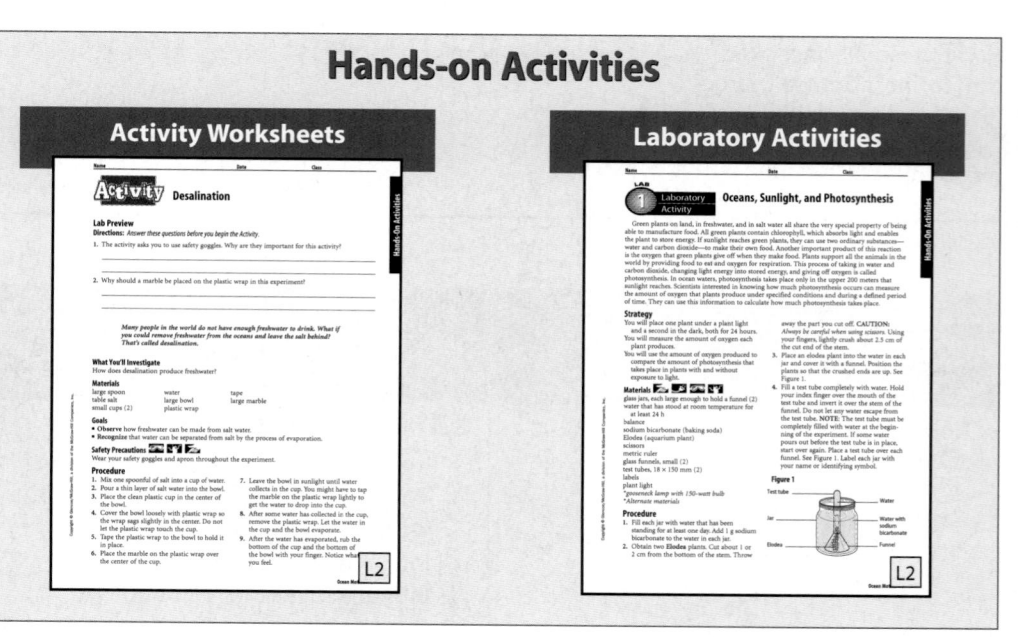

Activity — Desalination

L2

Laboratory Activities

Laboratory Activity 1 — Oceans, Sunlight, and Photosynthesis

L2

RESOURCE MANAGER

Meeting Different Ability Levels

Content Outline

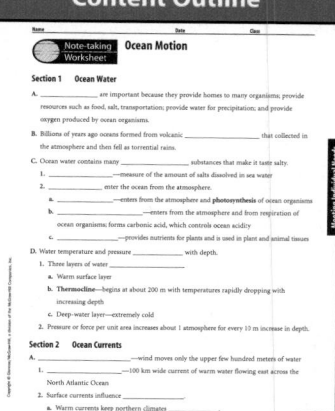

L2

Reinforcement

L2

Directed Reading

L1

Assessment

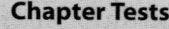

Chapter Tests

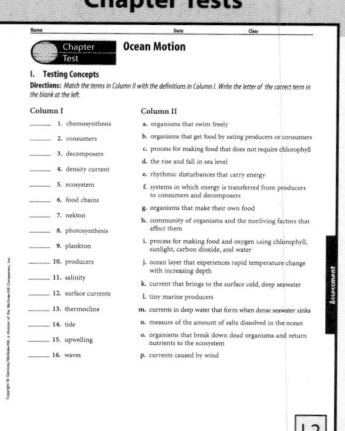

L2

Enrichment

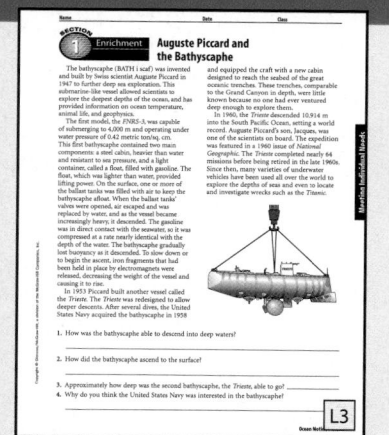

L3

Spanish Directed Reading

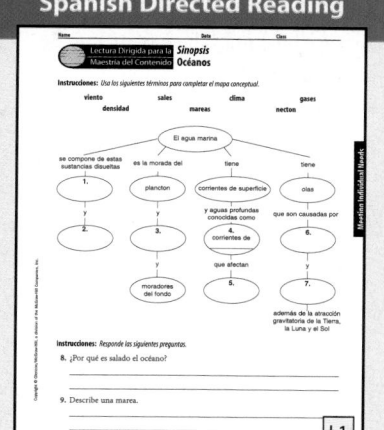

L1

Test Practice Workbook

L2

Chapter Review

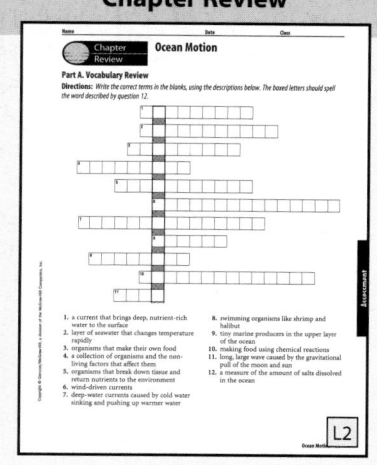

L2

Science Content Background

SECTION 1

Ocean Water

Importance of Oceans

Oceans cover 71 percent of Earth's surface—61 percent of the northern hemisphere and 81 percent of the southern hemisphere. Photosynthetic marine organisms produce 70 percent of the worlds' oxygen, and the oceans play a major role in determining weather and climate patterns. Physical oceanography concerns energy transmission through ocean water. It deals with wave formation and movement, currents, and tides.

Although oceans are important to life on Earth, they make up only a thin skin on its surface. Isaac Asimov made the following analogy: If Earth were the size of a billiard ball, the oceans would be an unnoticeable film of dampness.

Origin of Oceans

The locations of the ocean basins have changed throughout geologic time. Presently, all oceans connect. Geographers have given them names according to where they are divided by continents. The average depth of the oceans is 3.8 kilometers; the volume of the oceans is 1.35 billion cubic kilometers.

Composition of Oceans

Chemical oceanography is the study of the chemical properties of seawater and the causes, effects, and changes in ocean chemistry. Salinity is measured with a conductivity indicator. This instrument detects ions in a seawater sample. Because the ions in seawater are in nearly constant proportions, the indicator is used to measure only one kind of ion, chloride. Total salinity can be determined from this one measurement.

Scientists once thought that oceans increased in salinity over time. As our understanding of oceanic processes has increased, that idea has been revised. Current models show that the overall salinity of the oceans has been roughly constant for the last several hundred million years and probably hasn't changed much since the oceans formed.

On average each cubic kilometer of ocean water contains about 50 kilograms (roughly 100 pounds) of gold. At $300 an ounce, that much gold would be worth approximately half a million dollars. Unfortunately, at present technology levels, to extract that much gold would cost much more than it's worth because of equipment and energy expenses.

Oceans can be divided into three layers based on temperature. Thermal energy in the surface layer is evenly distributed because waves mix the water and because of the turbulence caused by currents. The depth of this layer averages 200 m to 300 m. Below the surface layer is the thermocline, where the temperature drops rapidly to about $5°$ C. Below the thermocline, temperature decreases slightly to about $1°$ C.

SECTION 2

Ocean Currents

Upwelling

Most upwellings occur along the eastern shores of oceans where winds blow surface water away from the shore. From space, satellites can detect upwellings. Because the water in an upwelling is cold compared to the surrounding water, infrared cameras can spot the difference. This information is useful to fishers.

Fun Fact

England has a much warmer climate than Scandinavia and Labrador, which are at similar latitudes, because heat from the warm North Atlantic Drift current warms the country.

Fun Fact

The typical residence time in the ocean for a sodium ion is 260 million years.

Density Currents

Most dense water on the ocean floor is thought to originate in the Norwegian Sea near the north pole and the Ross and Weddell Seas off the coast of Antarctica. The water at these locations is very dense because of the cold temperatures. The dense water sinks and is pushed along the ocean bottom toward the equator. Here the water warms, expands, and rises toward the surface forming an upwelling. The rising water causes a bulge about 5 cm high. Water flows down off the bulge toward the poles. Deep water rises to replace the surface water. As it rises, it is heated by the Sun. A density current is really a large convection cell. Density currents are also known as thermohaline currents, because temperature and salinity determine density.

SECTION 3 Ocean Waves and Tides

Waves

The longer winds blows, the higher the waves mount until they reach a maximum height for a given wind velocity. For a given wind velocity, waves tend to be higher on large, deep bodies of water than on shallower bodies of water. Waves on the larger, deeper bodies develop without the interference of drag on the ocean bottom.

Storm waves have longer wavelengths than normal waves. Their erosional effects on the basin bottom extend relatively far from shore.

SCIENCE Online

For additional content background on this topic, go to the Glencoe Science Web site at science.glencoe.com.

Tides

The wave crest closes to the Moon is called direct tide; the crest on the opposite side of Earth is called opposite tide. Although the high and low tides in the Atlantic Ocean are generally about the same height, in other bodies of water the tidal heights vary greatly.

Dale E. Boyer/Photo Researchers, Inc.

CHAPTER 18

Ocean Motion

Chapter Vocabulary

basin
salinity
surface current
Coriolis effect
upwelling
density current
wave
crest
trough
breaker
tide
tidal range

What do you think?

Science Journal The photo shows houses built on stilts along the Bay of Fundy, between Nova Scotia and New Brunswick, Canada. The bay has the world's highest high tides, about 15 meters above low tide. To keep houses along parts of its shore from being swamped by water at high tide, some are built on stilts. This photo shows the houses at low tide.

CHAPTER 18

Ocean Motion

Surfers in Hawaii experience firsthand the enormous power of moving water. It surprises people to learn that wind causes most waves, from small ripples to the giant waves of hurricanes, some more than 30 m high. Wind also creates surface currents. Other types of currents move through the ocean, too. In this chapter, you'll learn about the composition of ocean water, the interaction between the atmosphere and the oceans, and how waves, currents, and tides are created.

What do you think?

Science Journal Look at the picture below with a classmate. Discuss what you think this might be or what is happening. Here's a hint: *Daily fluctuations make this happen.* Write your answer or best guess in your Science Journal.

520

Theme Connection

Energy Students will learn that wind provides the energy for surface currents and most ocean waves, that temperature and density power deep-ocean circulation, and that the gravitational attraction of the Sun and the Moon supply the force that sets tides in motion.

EXPLORE ACTIVITY

Surface currents are caused by wind, but wind cannot cause currents deep in the ocean. Instead, deep-water currents are created by differences in the density of ocean water. Several factors affect water density. One is temperature. Do the activity below to see how temperature differences create these kinds of currents.

Explore how currents work

1. In a beaker, melt ice to make ice water.
2. Fill another beaker with warm water.
3. Add a few drops of food coloring to the ice water.
4. Use a dropper to place some of this ice water on top of the warm water. Repeat the experiment, placing warm water on top of the ice water.

Observe

In your Science Journal, describe what happened each time. Did adding warm or cold water on top produce a current? Look up the word *convection* in a dictionary. Infer why the current you created is called a convection current.

Before You Read

FOLDABLES
Reading & Study Skills

Making a Cause and Effect Study Fold **Make the following Foldable to help you understand the cause and effect relationship of ocean motion.**

1. Place a sheet of paper in front of you so the long side is at the top. Fold the paper in half from the left side to the right side. Fold top to bottom and crease. Then unfold.

2. Through the top thickness of paper, cut along the middle fold line to form two tabs. Label the tabs *Causes of Ocean Motion* and *Effects of Ocean Motion*.

3. As you read the chapter, write what you learn about why the ocean moves and the types of ocean motion under the top tab.

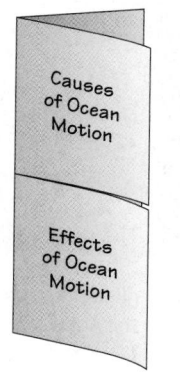

Causes of Ocean Motion

Effects of Ocean Motion

521

EXPLORE ACTIVITY

Purpose Use the Explore Activity to introduce students to the way deep-ocean currents work. L2 ELL COOP LEARN
IS Visual-Spatial
Preparation Prepare ice ahead of time.
Materials ice cubes, warm water, two beakers, food coloring, dropper
Teaching Strategy Be sure that students understand the term *density*.

Observe

When ice water was placed on top of warm water, a current formed as the denser cold water sank through the warmer water, displacing and forcing the warmer water upward. Convection is defined as the movement of fluid between areas that have unequal densities caused by unequal temperatures. It's called a convection current because the difference in density and temperature drives the movement of water.

Assessment

Oral Ask students why a current did not form when warm water was placed on top of ice water. Warm water is less dense than cold water, so it stays on top and there is no movement. Use **Performance Assessment in the Science Classroom,** p. 89.

Before You Read

FOLDABLES
Reading & Study Skills

Dinah Zike Study Fold
Purpose Students make and use a Foldable to collect information on the motion of the ocean and then use what they have learned to investigate its cause and effect.

For additional help, see Foldables Worksheet, p. 13 in **Chapter Resources Booklet,** or go to the Glencoe Science Web site at **science.glencoe.com.** See After You Read in the Study Guide at the end of this chapter.

SECTION
1
Ocean Water

Ocean Water

1 Motivate

Bellringer Transparency

Display the Section Focus Transparency for Section 1. Use the accompanying Transparency Activity Master. L2

ELL

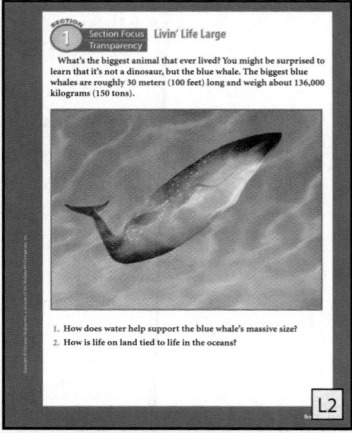

As You Read

What You'll Learn
- **Identify** the origin of the water in Earth's oceans.
- **Explain** how dissolved salts and other substances get into seawater.
- **Describe** the composition of seawater.

Vocabulary
basin
salinity

Why It's Important
Oceans affect weather and provide food and natural resources.

Importance of Oceans

Imagine yourself lying on a beach and listening to the waves gently roll onto shore. A warm breeze blows off the water, making it seem as if you're in a tropical paradise. It's easy to appreciate the oceans under these circumstances, but the oceans affect your life in other ways, too.

Varied Resources   Oceans are important for food, minerals, transportation, and weather. Today, as shown in **Figure 1,** a huge variety of different resources comes from the oceans of the world. Oceans also allow efficient transportation. Can you think of a product you own that was transported by a ship? Energy and mineral resources also are found in oceans. Oil wells often are drilled in shallow ocean water. Oceans affect weather and climate. Hurricanes develop in some tropical waters, and moist air masses move onto land from oceans. Ocean currents keep some places warm while creating cool, foggy days elsewhere.

✔ **Reading Check**   *What resources come from oceans?*

Tie to Prior Knowledge

Have students quickly list three things they know about the ocean. **How many listed that the water is salty? Where did the salt come from?** Most enters the water from surrounding land. Tell students they will discover many things about the ocean in this section, including the reason its water salty.

Figure 1
People depend on the oceans for many resources.

A Krill are tiny, shrimplike animals that live in the Antarctic Ocean. Some cultures use krill in noodles and rice cakes.

B Kelp is a fast-growing seaweed that is a source of algin, used in making ice cream, salad dressing, medicines, and cosmetics.

522   CHAPTER 18 Ocean Motion

Section ✔*Assessment* Planner

PORTFOLIO
Assessment, p. 525
PERFORMANCE ASSESSMENT
Skill Builder Activities, p. 525
See page 546 for more options.

CONTENT ASSESSMENT
Section, p. 525
Challenge, p. 525
Chapter, pp. 546–547

Origin of Oceans

During Earth's first billion years, its surface, shown in **Figure 2A,** was much more volcanically active than it is today. When volcanoes erupt, they spew lava and ash, and they give off water vapor, carbon dioxide, and other gases. Scientists hypothesize that about 4 billion years ago, this water vapor began to be stored in Earth's early atmosphere. Over millions of years, it cooled enough to condense into storm clouds. Torrential rains began to fall. Shown in **Figure 2B,** oceans were formed as this water filled low areas on Earth called **basins.** Today, 70 percent of Earth's surface is covered by ocean water.

Composition of Oceans

Ocean water contains dissolved gases such as oxygen, carbon dioxide, and nitrogen. Oxygen is the gas that almost all organisms need for respiration. It enters the oceans in two ways—directly from the atmosphere and from organisms that photosynthesize. Carbon dioxide enters the ocean from the atmosphere and from organisms when they respire. The atmosphere is the only important source of nitrogen gas. Bacteria combine nitrogen and oxygen to create nitrates, which are important nutrients for plants.

If you've ever tasted ocean water, you know that it is salty. Ocean water contains many dissolved salts. Chloride, sodium, sulfate, magnesium, calcium, and potassium are some of the ions in seawater. An ion is a charged atom or group of atoms. Some of these ions come from rocks that are dissolved slowly by rivers and groundwater. These include calcium, magnesium, and sodium. Rivers carry these chemicals to the oceans. Erupting volcanoes add other ions, such as sulfate and chloride.

✔ Reading Check *How do sodium and chloride ions get into seawater?*

Figure 2
Earth's oceans formed from water vapor.

A Water vapor was released into the atmosphere by volcanoes that also gave off other gases, such as carbon dioxide and nitrogen.

B Condensed water vapor formed storm clouds. Oceans formed when basins filled with water from torrential rains.

SECTION 1 Ocean Water **523**

Resource Manager

Chapter Resources Booklet
Transparency Activity, p. 40
Note-taking Worksheets, pp. 29–31
Directed Reading for Content Mastery, pp. 15, 16

Inclusion Strategies

Learning Disabled Have groups of students make puzzles of Earth's oceans and landmasses. They can transfer a map of the world onto cardboard and cut it into pieces. Ocean names should be included on the puzzle pieces. Groups should then exchange puzzles and compete to see which group puts the puzzle together fastest. L2
ELL  **Kinesthetic**

Importance of Oceans

✔ Reading Check

Answer substances that are used in foods, medicines, and cosmetics; fuels such as oil; minerals such as manganese

Origin of Oceans

Make a Model

Have students model how salt gets into oceans. Make a mixture of half salt and half soil. Have pairs of students put a couple of tablespoons of the mixture into a coffee filter and place the filter inside a paper cup with five small holes punched into the bottom. Have students pour three tablespoons of water into the cup and hold it 2 cm above a sheet of black construction paper as the water drips onto the paper. When all the water has dripped out, put the paper in the Sun to dry. Students will find a dried salt residue on the paper. Have them explain their results. As water was poured through the soil, salt dissolved in it and was deposited on the paper. In the same way, runoff picks up and deposits dissolved salts from the land in the ocean.

Composition of Oceans

✔ Reading Check

Answer Rivers and groundwater slowly dissolve rocks and carry sodium and chloride ions to oceans. Volcanoes also release chloride.

Composition of Oceans, continued

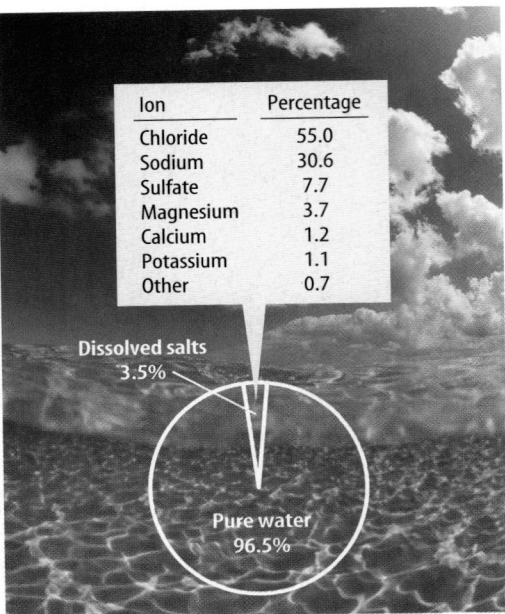

Ion	Percentage
Chloride	55.0
Sodium	30.6
Sulfate	7.7
Magnesium	3.7
Calcium	1.2
Potassium	1.1
Other	0.7

Dissolved salts 3.5%

Pure water 96.5%

Figure 3
Ocean water contains about 3.5 percent dissolved salts. *If you evaporated 1,000 g of seawater, how many grams of salt would be left?*

Salts The most abundant elements in seawater are the hydrogen and oxygen that make up water. Ions of many other elements are found dissolved in seawater. When seawater is evaporated, these ions combine to form materials called salts. Sodium and chloride make up most of the ions in seawater. If seawater evaporates, the sodium and chloride ions combine to form a salt called halite. Halite is the common table salt you use to season food. It is this dissolved salt and similar ones that give ocean water its salty taste.

Salinity (say LIH nuh tee) is a measure of the amount of salts dissolved in seawater. It usually is measured in grams of dissolved salt per kilogram of seawater. One kilogram of ocean water contains about 35 g of dissolved salts, or 3.5 percent. The chart in **Figure 3** shows the most abundant ions in ocean water. The proportion and amount of dissolved salts in seawater remain nearly constant and have stayed about the same for hundreds of millions of years. This tells you that the composition of the oceans is in balance. Evidence that scientists have gathered indicates that Earth's oceans are not growing saltier.

Life Science INTEGRATION

Removal of Elements Although rivers, volcanoes, and the atmosphere constantly add material to the oceans, the oceans are considered to be in a steady state. This means that elements are added to the oceans at about the same rate that they are removed. They are removed when ocean water evaporates, leaving salt behind, and when organisms use the dissolved salts to make shells. Some marine animals remove calcium ions from the water to form bones. Other animals, such as oysters and clams, use the dissolved calcium to form shells. Some algae, called diatoms, have silica shells. Because many organisms use calcium and silicon, these elements are removed more quickly from seawater than elements such as chlorine or sodium.

Desalination Salt can be removed from ocean water by a process called desalination (dee sa luh NAY shun). If you have ever swum in the ocean, you know what happens when your skin dries. The white, flaky substance on your skin is salt. As seawater evaporates, salt is left behind. As demand for freshwater increases throughout the world, scientists are working on technology to remove salt to make seawater drinkable.

524 CHAPTER 18 Ocean Motion

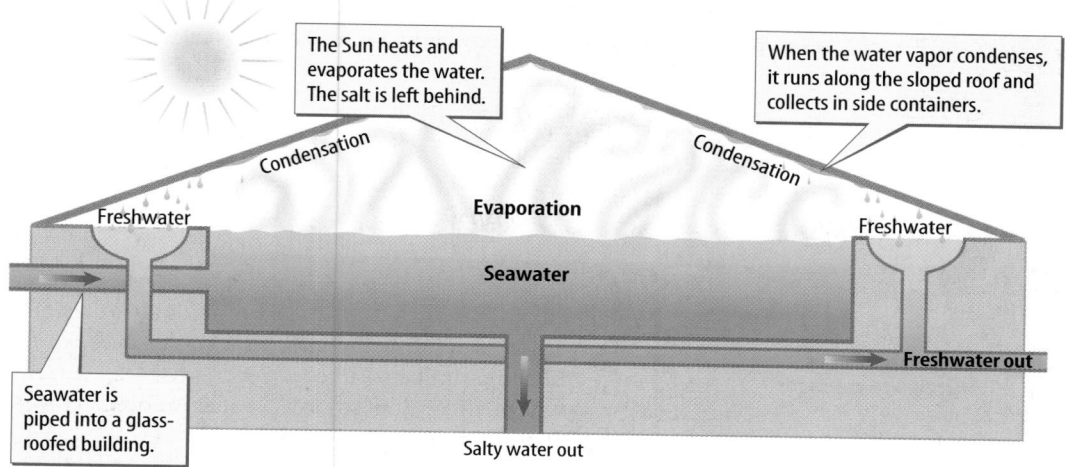

The Sun heats and evaporates the water. The salt is left behind.

When the water vapor condenses, it runs along the sloped roof and collects in side containers.

Condensation

Condensation

Evaporation

Freshwater

Freshwater

Seawater

Freshwater out

Seawater is piped into a glass-roofed building.

Salty water out

Desalination Plants Some methods of desalination include evaporating seawater and collecting the freshwater as it condenses on a glass roof. **Figure 4** shows how a desalination plant that uses solar energy works. Other plants desalinate water by passing it through a membrane that removes the dissolved salts. Freshwater also can be obtained by melting frozen seawater. When seawater freezes, only about one third of the dissolved salts are frozen into the ice. The rest remain behind in the unfrozen water. The smaller amounts of salt crystals can be separated from the ice, leaving freshwater.

Figure 4
This desalination plant uses solar energy to produce freshwater.

Section 1 Assessment

1. Describe at least five ways that Earth's oceans affect your life.

2. According to scientific hypothesis, how were Earth's oceans formed? When do scientists hypothesize they formed?

3. Where do the dissolved salts in ocean water come from?

4. How does oxygen get into oceans?

5. **Think Critically** Some people have proposed towing sea ice from polar oceans to use as a source of freshwater. Why would the water in sea ice be a good source of drinking water?

Skill Builder Activities

6. **Concept Mapping** Make a concept map that shows how sodium and chloride become dissolved in ocean water and what happens when the seawater evaporates. Use the terms *rivers, volcanoes, halite, source of, sodium, chloride,* and *combine to form*. **For more help, refer to the** Science Skill Handbook.

7. **Using Proportions** If the average salinity of seawater is 35 parts per thousand, how many grams of dissolved salts will 500 g of seawater contain? **For more help, refer to the** Math Skill Handbook.

Answers to Section Assessment

1. Possible answers: source of food, oxygen, minerals, medicines, and energy; means of transportation; effects on weather and climate; recreation

2. Volcanoes released water vapor that accumulated, cooled, and condensed to fall as rain that filled the basins about 4 billion years ago.

3. River water and groundwater carry dissolved salts from soil and rock on land into the ocean. Volcanoes also provide chlorine.

4. Some oxygen comes directly from the atmosphere, and other oxygen is produced when organisms photosynthesize.

5. When seawater freezes, only about one third of the salts are frozen into the ice. The salt crystals can be separated from the ice, leaving freshwater.

6. See concept map in side column.

7. 17.5 g (1/2 × 35)

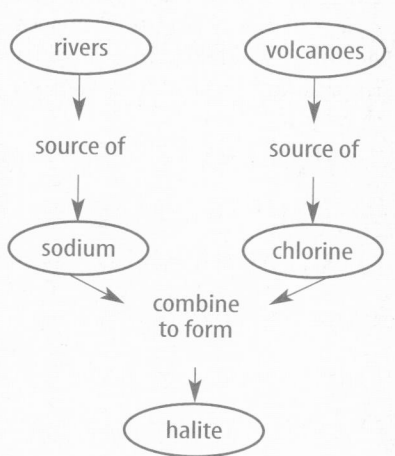

Ocean Currents

① Motivate

Bellringer Transparency

Display the Section Focus Transparency for Section 2. Use the accompanying Transparency Activity Master. L2

ELL

Tie to Prior Knowledge

Ask students whether they have ever gone swimming or wading in a river, a large lake, or the ocean. Have they ever felt tugged or pulled by water moving under the surface? Tell students these were currents. Also tell them that in this section they will learn how currents in the ocean form and how they move.

As You Read

What You'll Learn

- **Explain** how winds and the Coriolis effect influence surface currents.
- **Discuss** the temperatures of coastal waters.
- **Describe** density currents.

Vocabulary

surface current   upwelling
Coriolis effect   density current

Why It's Important

Ocean currents and the atmosphere transfer heat that creates the climate you live in.

Figure 5
These are the major surface currents of Earth's oceans.

Surface Currents

When you stir chocolate into a glass of milk, do you notice the milk swirling around in the glass in a circle? If so, you've observed something similar to an ocean current. Ocean currents are a mass movement, or flow, of ocean water. An ocean current is like a river within the ocean.

Surface currents move water horizontally—parallel to Earth's surface. These currents are powered by wind. The wind forces the ocean to move in huge, circular patterns. **Figure 5** shows these major surface currents. Notice that some currents are shown with red arrows and some are shown with blue arrows. Red arrows indicate warm currents. Blue arrows indicate cold currents. The currents on the ocean's surface are related to the general circulation of winds on Earth.

Surface currents move only the upper few hundred meters of seawater. Some seeds and plants are carried between continents by surface currents. Sailors take advantage of these currents along with winds to sail more efficiently from place to place.

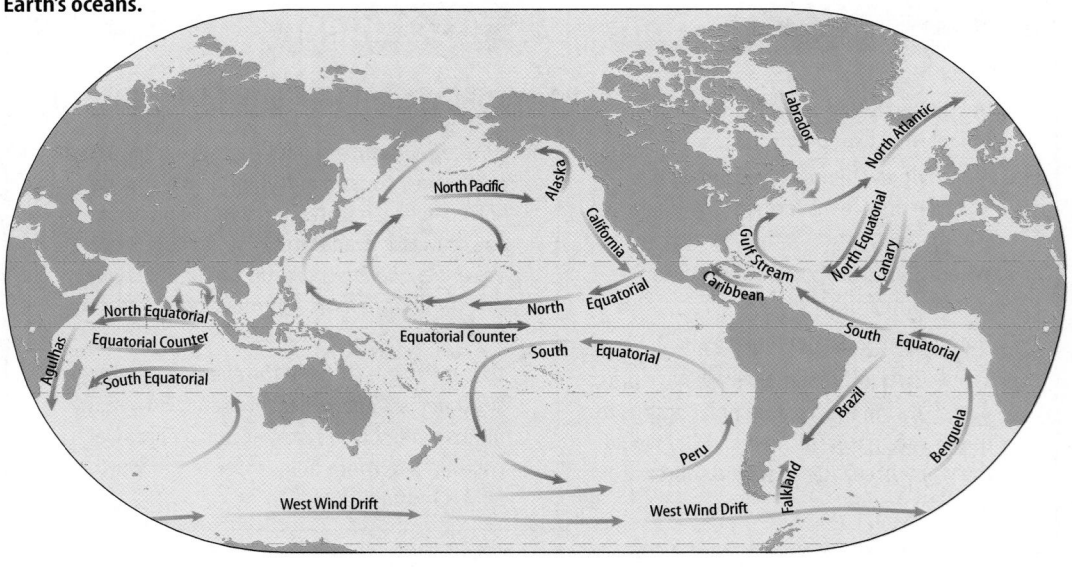

Section ✓Assessment Planner

PORTFOLIO
Curriculum Connection, p. 528
PERFORMANCE ASSESSMENT
Try at Home MiniLAB, p. 529
Math Skills Activity, p. 530
Skill Builder Activities, p. 531
See page 546 for more options.

CONTENT ASSESSMENT
Section, p. 531
Challenge, p. 531
Chapter, pp. 546–547

How Surface Currents
Form Surface ocean currents and surface winds are affected by the Coriolis (kor ee OH lus) effect. The **Coriolis effect** is the shifting of winds and surface currents from their expected paths that is caused by Earth's rotation. Imagine that you try to draw a line straight out from the center of a disk to the edge of the disk. You probably could do that with no problem. But what would happen if the disk were slowly spinning like the one in **Figure 6A?** As the student tried to draw a straight line, the disk rotated and, as shown in **Figure 6B,** the line curved.

A similar thing happens to wind and surface currents. Because Earth rotates toward the east, winds appear to curve to the right in the northern hemisphere and to the left in the southern hemisphere. These surface winds can cause water to pile up in certain parts of the ocean. When gravity pulls water off the pile, the Coriolis effect turns the water. This causes surface water in the oceans to spiral around the piles of water. The Coriolis effect causes currents north of the equator to turn to the right. Currents south of the equator are turned to the left. Look again at the map of surface currents in **Figure 5** to see the results of the Coriolis effect.

The Gulf Stream
Although satellites provide new information about ocean movements, much of what is known about surface currents comes from records that were kept by sailors of the nineteenth century. Sailors always have used surface currents to help them travel quickly. Sailing ships depend on some surface currents to carry them to the west and others to carry them east. During the American colonial era, ships floated on the 100-km-wide Gulf Stream current to go quickly from North America to England. Find the Gulf Stream current in the Atlantic Ocean on the map in **Figure 5.**

In the late 1700s, Deputy Postmaster General Benjamin Franklin received complaints about why it took longer to receive a letter from England than it did to send one there. Upon investigation, Franklin found that a Nantucket whaling captain's map furnished the answer. Going against the Gulf Stream delayed ships sailing west from England by up to 110 km per day.

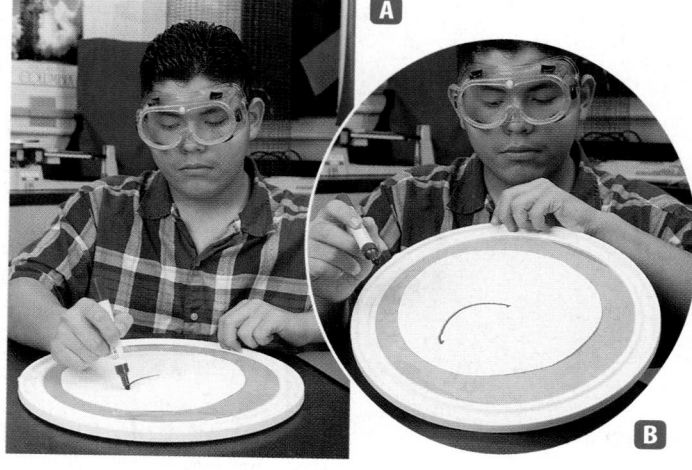

Figure 6
A The student draws a line straight out from the center of the disk. **B** Because the disk was spinning, the line is curved.

SCIENCE *Online*

Research Visit the Glencoe Science Web site at **science.glencoe.com** for more information about ocean currents. Communicate to your class what you learn.

Surface Currents, continued

IDENTIFYING Misconceptions

Students may think that the Gulf Stream is located in the Gulf of Mexico. The current begins there, but then sweeps northeastward along the east coast of the United States and eventually turns east toward Europe.

Discussion

Although the climate in the area is warm in summer, the waters of San Francisco Bay never get very warm. Ask students to use what they know about currents to give a possible explanation. Cold currents along the coast of California could influence the temperature of the bay.

Teacher FYI

Oceanographers track ocean currents with neutrally buoyant floats, swallow floats, and satellites. Neutrally buoyant floats sink to a desired depth and move with the current. Swallow floats drift on the surface and emit "pings" that are picked up by equipment on ships. Satellites are equipped with devices that detect surface-current velocities using infrared, color, and microwave emissions from the sea's surface.

Figure 7
Bottles and other floating objects that enter the ocean are used to gain information about surface currents.

Figure 8
Data about ocean temperature collected by a satellite were used to make this surface-temperature image of the Atlantic Ocean.

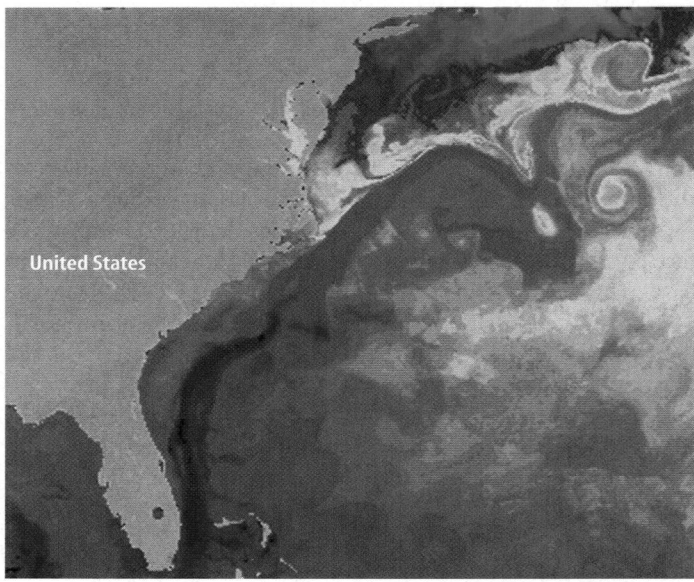

United States

Tracking Surface Currents Items that wash up on beaches, such as the bottle shown in **Figure 7,** provide information about ocean currents. Drift bottles containing messages and numbered cards are released from a variety of coastal locations. The bottles are carried by surface currents and might end up on a beach. The person who finds a bottle writes down the date and the location where the bottle was found. Then the card is sent back to the institution that launched the bottle. By doing this, valuable information is provided about the current that carried the bottle.

Warm and Cold Surface Currents Notice in **Figure 5** that currents on the west coasts of continents begin near the poles where the water is colder. The California Current that flows along the west coast of the United States is a cold surface current. East-coast currents originate near the equator where the water is warmer. Warm surface currents, such as the Gulf Stream, distribute heat from equatorial regions to other areas of Earth. **Figure 8** shows the warm water of the Gulf Stream in red and orange. Cooler water appears in blue and green.

As warm water flows away from the equator, heat is released to the atmosphere. The atmosphere is warmed. This transfer of heat influences climate.

Curriculum Connection

History Have students research either the way the positions of currents affected ancient trade routes, or Benjamin Franklin's study of the Gulf Stream. Have them write brief reports on what they find. L2 IS **Linguistic** P

Fun Fact

Surface currents generally affect only the upper 100 to 200 meters of ocean water.

Figure 9
Winds push surface water away from the coast of Peru, causing upwelling. This process brings colder water to the surface.

Water movement

Southerly wind

Upwelling

Upwelling

Upwelling is a circulation in the ocean that brings deep, cold water to the ocean surface. Along some coasts of continents, wind blowing parallel to the coast carries water away from the land because of the Coriolis effect, as shown in **Figure 9.** Cold, deep ocean water rises to the surface and replaces water that has moved away from shore. This water contains high concentrations of nutrients from organisms that died, sank to the bottom, and decayed. Nutrients promote plankton growth, which attracts fish. Areas of upwelling occur along the coasts of Oregon, Washington, and Peru and create important fishing grounds.

Density Currents

Deep in the ocean, waters circulate not because of wind but because of density differences. A **density current** forms when a mass of seawater becomes more dense than the surrounding water. Gravity causes more dense seawater to sink beneath less dense seawater. This deep, dense water then slowly spreads to the rest of the ocean.

The density of seawater can be increased if salinity increases, as you can see if you perform the MiniLAB on this page. It also can be increased by a decrease in temperature. In the Explore Activity, the cold water was more dense than the warm water in the beaker. The cold water sank to the bottom. This created a density current that moved the food coloring.

Changes in temperature and salinity work together to create density currents. Density currents circulate ocean water slowly— moving as little as a few meters per month.

TRY AT HOME
Mini LAB

Modeling a Density Current

Procedure 🔥 👓
1. Fill a **clear plastic storage box** (shoe-box size) with room-temperature **water.**
2. Mix several spoonfuls of table **salt** into a **glass** of water at room temperature.
3. Add a few drops of **food coloring** to the saltwater solution. Pour the solution slowly into the freshwater in the large container.

Analysis
1. Describe what happened when you added salt water to freshwater.
2. How does this lab relate to density currents?

Density Currents

TRY AT HOME
Mini LAB

Purpose Students model a density current. L1 ELL COOP LEARN 🅺 **Kinesthetic**

Materials clear plastic storage box, water, 8-ounce glass or beaker, 55 g table salt, food coloring, teaspoon

Teaching Strategy Review density with students before assigning the MiniLAB.

Safety Precautions Caution students not to taste, eat, or drink any lab materials.

Troubleshooting To see the current, have students look into the box from the side, not the top.

Analysis
1. The salt water sank to the bottom and spread out toward the sides of the container.
2. Denser ocean water sinks to the bottom of the ocean basin, displacing warmer water and causing the movement of density currents.

✓Assessment

Process Have students draw and label a diagram based on this MiniLAB that shows how density currents in the ocean work. Use **PASC,** p. 161.

Resource Manager

Chapter Resources Booklet
MiniLAB, p. 3
Lab Activity, pp. 11–12

Cultural Diversity

Fishing Upwelling of cold water off the coast of Peru brings large numbers of anchovies to the coast. Peruvians eat these fish and make them into fish meal, which is used to make tortillas and bread and to feed chickens. Have students research what happens during an El Niño. Wind patterns reverse, blocking the upwelling cold water, and stopping the movement of anchovies to the Peruvian coast.

Density Currents, continued

Chemistry INTEGRATION

Because of its salt concentration, ocean water has a much lower freezing point than freshwater.

Math Skills Activity

National Math Standards

Correlation to Mathematics Objectives

1, 2, 4, 6, 9

Answers to Practice Problems

1. You know the density and the mass of the sample and the equation $d = m/v$. Substituting these values into this equation gives $d = 79,000\ g/78,000\ cm^3$. This equals a density of $1.01\ g/cm^3$.

2. In this problem you know the density and the mass, so you must rearrange the equation $d = m/v$ to solve for v. This is $v = m/d$. Then substituting the given values gives $v = 50,000\ g/1.03\ g/cm3$. Solving this gives a volume of $48,544\ cm^3$ or $48,500\ cm^3$ in significant digits.

Resource Manager

Chapter Resources Booklet
Enrichment, p. 27
Reinforcement, p. 24

Chemistry INTEGRATION

When salt dissolves in water, the freezing point of the mixture is lowered. The greater the number of particles dissolved in the water is, the more the freezing point is lowered. How does this help ocean water near the poles get colder than freshwater could?

Deep Waters An important density current begins in Antarctica where the most dense ocean water forms during the winter. As ice forms, seawater freezes, but the salt is left behind in the unfrozen water. This extra salt increases the salinity and, therefore, the density of the ocean water until it is very dense. This dense water sinks and slowly spreads along the ocean bottom toward the equator, forming a density current. In the Pacific Ocean, this water could take 1,000 years to reach the equator.

In the North Atlantic Ocean, cold, dense water forms around Norway, Greenland, and Labrador. These waters sink forming North Atlantic Deep Water. In about the northern one-third to one-half of the Atlantic Ocean, North Atlantic Deep Water forms the bottom layer of ocean water. In the southern part of the Atlantic Ocean, it flows at depths of about 3,000 m, just above the denser water formed near Antarctica. The dense waters circulate more quickly in the Atlantic Ocean than in the Pacific Ocean. In the Atlantic, a density current could circulate in 275 years.

Math Skills Activity

Calculating Density

Example Problem

You have an aquarium full of freshwater in which you have dissolved salt. If the mass of the salt water is 123,000 g and its volume is 120,000 cm³, what is the density of the salt water?

Solution

1 *This is what you know:*   volume: $v = 120,000\ cm^3$
mass of salt water: $m = 123,000\ g$

2 *This is what you need to find:*   density of water: d

3 *This is the equation you need to use:* $d = m/v$

4 *Substitute the known values:* $d = 123,000g\ /120,000cm^3 = 1.025\ g/cm^3$

Check your answer by multiplying your answer by the volume.
Do you calculate the same mass of saltwater that was given?

Practice Problems

1. Calculate the density of 78,000 cm³ of salt water with a mass of 79,000 g.
2. If a sample of ocean water has a density of 1.03 g/cm³, and a mass of 50,000 g, how much volume does the water take?

For more help, refer to the Math Skill Handbook.

LAB DEMONSTRATION

Purpose to model a density current

Materials four Erlenmeyer flasks, two 2-hole stoppers, four glass tubes, water, salt, food coloring

Preparation Insert the glass tubes into the stoppers.

Procedure Fill the four flasks with water. Add food coloring to two flasks. Add 35 g of salt to the water in a third flask. Insert stoppers into the two flasks without colored water. Invert each stoppered flask over a flask of colored water. Observe.

Expected Outcome Colored water moves up into the flask with salt water, but does not move into the flask with fresh water.

✓Assessment

What caused the density current in one set of flasks? Salty, dense water sank, forcing less dense water up. **What was the purpose of the other set of flasks?** That set was the control.

Intermediate Waters A density current also occurs in the Mediterranean Sea, a nearly enclosed body of water. The warm temperatures and dry air in the region cause large amounts of water to evaporate from the surface of the sea. This evaporation increases the salinity and density of the water. This dense water from the Mediterranean flows through the narrow Straits of Gibraltar into the Atlantic Ocean at a depth of about 320 m. When it reaches the Atlantic, it flows to depths of 1,000 m to 2,000 m because it is more dense than the water in the upper parts of the North Atlantic Ocean. However, the water from the Mediterranean is less dense than the very cold, salty water flowing from the North Atlantic Ocean around Greenland, Norway, and Labrador. Therefore, as shown in **Figure 10,** the Mediterranean water forms a middle layer of water—the Mediterranean Intermediate Water.

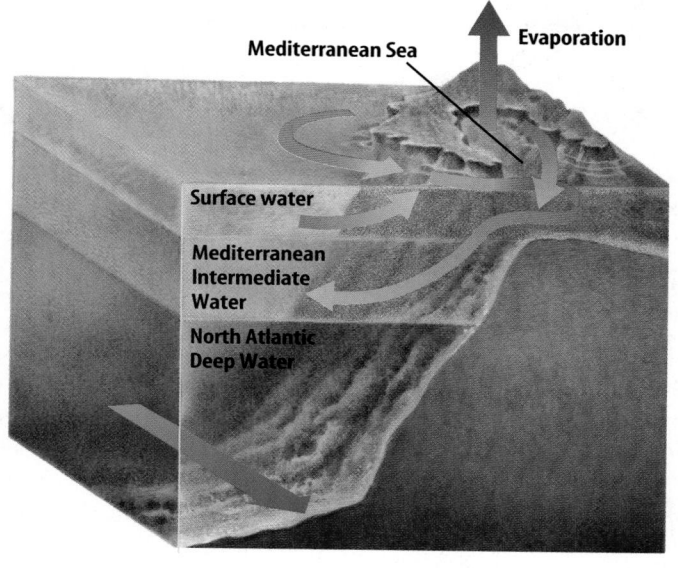

Figure 10
Dense layers of North Atlantic Deep Water form in the Greenland, Labrador, and Norwegian Seas. This water flows southward along the North Atlantic seafloor. Less dense water from the Mediterranean Sea forms Mediterranean Intermediate Water.

 Reading Check *What causes the Mediterranean Intermediate Water to form?*

Answer Less dense water from the Mediterranean Sea flows over denser North Atlantic water from around Greenland, Norway, and Labrador.

③ Assess

Reteach
Obtain a map that shows wind circulation patterns. Have students discuss how major wind patterns influence major surface currents as shown in **Figure 5.**

Challenge
Challenge students to research how the Gulf Stream affects the climate in land areas it passes close to on its trip from the Gulf of Mexico to northwestern Europe. In general, because of prevailing wind patterns, the Gulf Stream has more of an effect on the climate in northwestern Europe, making it warmer than the climate of eastern North America.

✓ Assessment

Process Assess students' abilities to interpret scientific illustrations by having them use **Figure 5** to determine which surface currents are deflected by continents. Possible answer: Currents moving west in the Atlantic Ocean are deflected north and south by North and South America. The Coriolis effect moves the currents eastward until Africa deflects them. Use **PASC,** p. 89.

Section ② Assessment

1. What factors create surface currents?
2. What is the Coriolis effect?
3. How do density currents circulate water?
4. What is upwelling?
5. **Think Critically** The latitudes of San Diego, California, and Charleston, South Carolina, are exactly the same. However, the average yearly water temperature in the ocean off Charleston is much higher than the water temperature off San Diego. Explain why.

Skill Builder Activities

6. **Predicting** A river flows into the ocean. Predict what will happen to this layer of freshwater. Explain your prediction. **For more help, refer to the** Science Skill Handbook.

7. **Using an Electronic Spreadsheet** Make a spreadsheet that compares surface and density currents. Focus on characteristics such as wind, horizontal and vertical movement, temperature, and density. **For more help, refer to the** Technology Skill Handbook.

Answers to Section Assessment

1. wind and the Coriolis effect
2. the shifting of winds and surface currents from their expected paths that is caused by Earth's rotation
3. Cold or very salty water is denser than warm or less salty water and sinks in the ocean. This displaces warmer or less salty water, which moves upward. This movement drives density currents.
4. It is a circulation in the ocean that brings deep, cold water to the ocean surface.
5. Ocean water off Charleston is influenced by the warm water of the Gulf Stream current, while ocean water off San Diego is influenced by the cold water of the California current.
6. It will flow along the surface because it is less dense than salty seawater.
7. Spreadsheets should include that surface currents are caused by winds, move horizontally on the surface, are warm or cold, and have an average density. Density currents are caused by differences in temperature and salinity, move both vertically and horizontally under the surface, have cold and warm sections, and have varying densities.

Bellringer Transparency

Display the Section Focus Transparency for Section 3. Use the accompanying Transparency Activity Master. L2

ELL

Tie to Prior Knowledge

Ask students whether they have ever seen waves on a lake, a river, or the ocean. Then ask whether they know how waves form. Write students' responses on the board and allow the class to discuss them. Then tell students they will find out in this section how waves form.

Ocean Waves and Tides

As You Read

What **You'll Learn**

■ **Describe** wave formation.
■ **Distinguish** between the movement of water particles in a wave and the movement of the wave.
■ **Explain** how ocean tides form.

Vocabulary

wave	breaker
crest	tide
trough	tidal range

Why **It's Important**

Waves and tides affect life and property in coastal areas.

Figure 11
Ocean waves carry energy through seawater.

A Identify the crests and troughs in this picture.

Waves

If you've been to the seashore or seen a beach on TV, you've watched waves roll in. There is something hypnotic about ocean waves. They keep coming and coming, one after another. But what is an ocean wave? A **wave** is a rhythmic movement that carries energy through matter or space. In the ocean, waves like those in **Figure 11A** move through seawater.

Describing Waves Several terms are used to describe waves, as shown in **Figure 11B.** Notice that waves look like hills and valleys. The **crest** is the highest point of the wave. The **trough** (TRAWF) is the lowest point of the wave. Wavelength is the horizontal distance between the crests or between the troughs of two adjacent waves. Wave height is the vertical distance between crest and trough.

Half the distance of the wave height is called the amplitude (AM pluh tewd) of the wave. The amplitude squared is proportional to the amount of energy the wave carries. For example, a wave with twice the amplitude of the wave in **Figure 11** carries four times ($2 \times 2 = 4$) the energy. On a calm day, the amplitude of ocean waves is small. But during a storm, wave amplitude increases and the waves carry a lot more energy. Large waves can damage ships and coastal property.

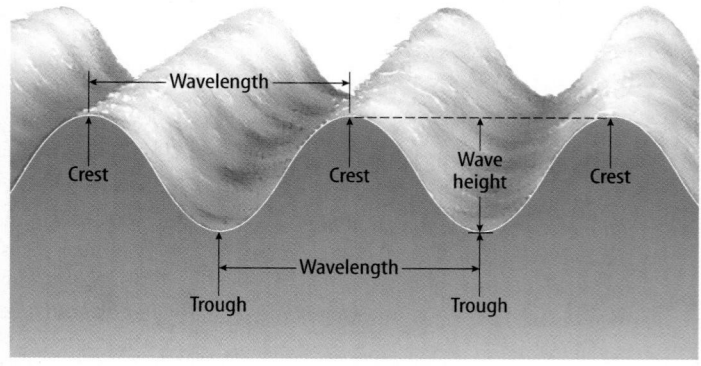

B The crest, trough, wavelength, and wave height describe a wave.

Section ✓ *Assessment* Planner

PORTFOLIO
Extension, p. 534
PERFORMANCE ASSESSMENT
MiniLAB, p. 533
Skill Builder Activities, p. 538
See page 546 for more options.

CONTENT ASSESSMENT
Section, p. 538
Challenge, p. 538
Chapter, pp. 546–547

Figure 12
As a wave passes, only energy moves forward. The water particles and the bobber remain in place.

Wave Movement You might have noticed that if you throw a pebble into a pond, a circular wave moves outward from where the pebble entered the water, as shown in **Figure 12.** A bobber on a fishing line floating in the water will bob up and down as the wave passes, but it will not move outward with the wave. Notice that the bobber's position doesn't change.

When you watch an ocean wave, it looks as though the water is moving forward. But unless the wave is breaking onto shore, the water does not move forward. Each molecule of water stays in about the same place as the wave passes. **Figure 13** shows this. Water in a wave moves around in circles. Only the energy moves forward while the water remains in about the same place. Below a depth equal to about half the wavelength, water movement stops. Below that depth, water is not affected by waves. Submarines that travel below this level usually are not affected by surface storms.

Breakers A wave changes shape in the shallow area near shore. Near the shoreline, friction with the ocean bottom slows water at the bottom of the wave. As the wave slows, its crest and trough come closer together. The wave height increases. The top of a wave, not slowed by friction, moves faster than the bottom. Eventually, the top of the wave outruns the bottom and it collapses. The wave crest falls as water tumbles over on itself. The wave breaks onto the shore. **Figure 13** also shows this process. This collapsing wave is a **breaker.** It is the collapse of this wave that propels a surfer and surfboard onto shore. After a wave breaks onto shore, gravity pulls the water back into the sea.

✓ **Reading Check** *What causes an ocean wave to slow down?*

Mini LAB

Modeling Water Particle Movement

Procedure
1. Put a piece of **tape** on the outside bottom of a clear, rectangular **plastic storage box.** Fill the box with **water.**
2. Float a **cork** in the container above the piece of tape.
3. Use a **spoon** to make gentle waves in the container.
4. Observe the movement of the waves and the cork.

Analysis
1. Describe the movement of the waves and the motion of the cork.
2. Compare the movement of the cork in the water with the movement of water particles in a wave.

2 Teach

Waves

Mini LAB

Purpose Students make a wave model that shows water particle movement. L2 ELL COOP LEARN IS **Kinesthetic**

Materials masking tape, clear plastic storage box, water, cork, spoon

Teaching Strategy Students need to make waves, not currents. Thus they must gently tap the bowl of the spoon in one spot on the water.

Analysis
1. The wave moves across the box from the point where the spoon is generating them. The cork bobs up and down as waves pass under it.
2. The cork and the water particles move in small circles as a wave passes. They stay in about the same place, rather than moving across the body of water.

Performance Have students devise other ways of creating waves in the box and have them observe the motion of the cork. Use **PASC,** p. 123.

✓ **Reading Check**

Answer friction with the ocean bottom

Resource Manager

Chapter Resources Booklet
Transparency Activity, p. 42
MiniLAB, p. 4

Curriculum Connection

Language Arts Explain to students that onomatopoeia is a poetry technique that uses words with sounds that make you think about their meanings. Examples include words like buzz, hiss, plop, flop, gunk, gushy, swish, splash, zigzag, zing, and zip. Have students write poems using onomatopoeia to describe waves and wave motion. L2 IS **Linguistic**

Visualizing Wave Movement

Have students examine the pictures and read the captions. Then ask the following questions.

How does the movement of the dominoes differ from the movement of water particles in waves? The dominoes simply fall down, while the water particles move around in circles. Both the dominoes and the water particles transfer energy in their movements. (The source of a wave's energy is usually wind.)

How does the degree of slope of the ocean floor near the beach affect the height of waves breaking on the beach? The steeper the slope, the taller the breaking waves; more gradually sloping ocean floor produces shorter waves.

Activity

Have students make diagrams of wave movement and include in their diagrams evidence that energy, not water particles, is moving forward. Offer them the example of a floating seagull bobbing up and down in the waves but not moving closer to the beach. Encourage them to brainstorm as many examples as they can.

Extension

Challenge students to find out the location of the world's most popular surfing sites and the reasons for the big waves at those sites. Have them write a report on their findings. L2

LS **Linguistic** P

Figure 13

As ocean waves roar toward the shore, they seem to be traveling in from a great distance, hurrying toward land. Actually, the water in waves moves relatively little, as shown here. It's the energy in the waves that moves across the ocean surface. Eventually that energy is transferred—in a crash of foam and spray—to the land.

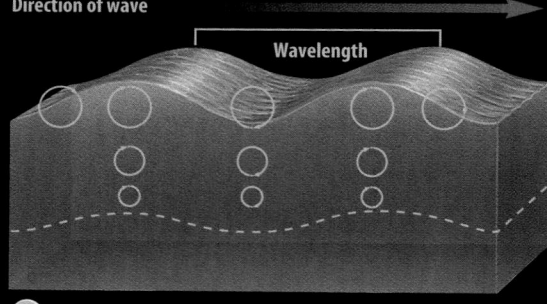

Direction of wave

Wavelength

A Particles of water move around in circles rather than forward. Near the water's surface, the circles are relatively large. Below the surface, the circles become progressively smaller. Little water movement occurs below a depth equal to about one-half of a wave's length.

B The energy in waves, however, does move forward. One way to visualize this energy movement is to imagine a line of dominoes. Knock over the first domino, and the others fall in seqence. As they fall, individual dominoes—like water particles in waves—remain close to where they started. But each transfers its energy to the next one down the line.

Wavelengths are constant

Wavelengths decrease as bottom drag increases

Waves break

C As waves approach shore, wavelength decreases and wave height increases. This causes breakers to form. Where ocean floor rises steeply to beach, incoming waves break quickly at a great height, forming huge arching waves.

Resource Manager

Chapter Resources Booklet
Transparency Activity, pp. 43–44
Directed Reading for Content Mastery, pp. 17, 18

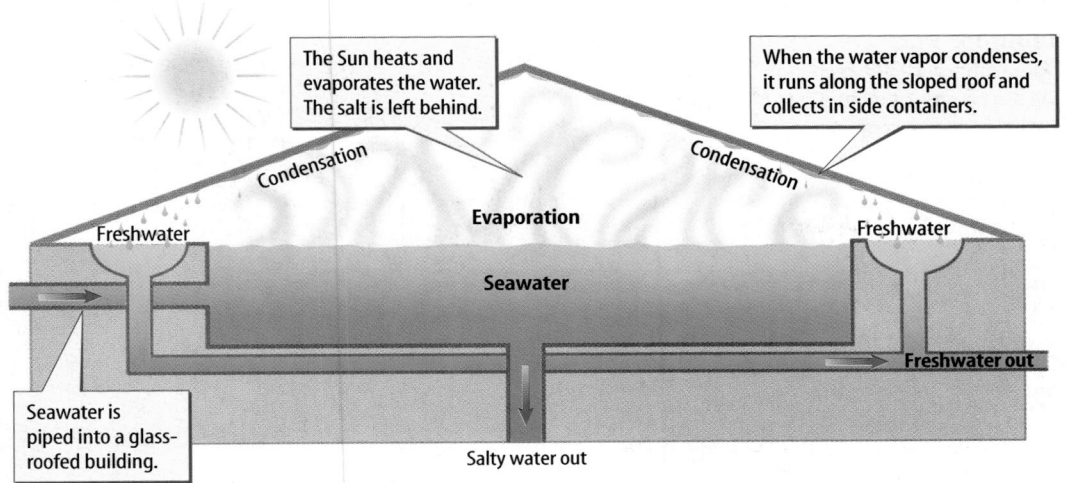

The Sun heats and evaporates the water. The salt is left behind.

When the water vapor condenses, it runs along the sloped roof and collects in side containers.

Condensation

Condensation

Evaporation

Freshwater

Freshwater

Seawater

Freshwater out

Seawater is piped into a glass-roofed building.

Salty water out

Desalination Plants Some methods of desalination include evaporating seawater and collecting the freshwater as it condenses on a glass roof. **Figure 4** shows how a desalination plant that uses solar energy works. Other plants desalinate water by passing it through a membrane that removes the dissolved salts. Freshwater also can be obtained by melting frozen seawater. When seawater freezes, only about one third of the dissolved salts are frozen into the ice. The rest remain behind in the unfrozen water. The smaller amounts of salt crystals can be separated from the ice, leaving freshwater.

Figure 4
This desalination plant uses solar energy to produce freshwater.

Section 1 Assessment

1. Describe at least five ways that Earth's oceans affect your life.

2. According to scientific hypothesis, how were Earth's oceans formed? When do scientists hypothesize they formed?

3. Where do the dissolved salts in ocean water come from?

4. How does oxygen get into oceans?

5. **Think Critically** Some people have proposed towing sea ice from polar oceans to use as a source of freshwater. Why would the water in sea ice be a good source of drinking water?

Skill Builder Activities

6. **Concept Mapping** Make a concept map that shows how sodium and chloride become dissolved in ocean water and what happens when the seawater evaporates. Use the terms *rivers, volcanoes, halite, source of, sodium, chloride,* and *combine to form*. **For more help, refer to the** Science Skill Handbook.

7. **Using Proportions** If the average salinity of seawater is 35 parts per thousand, how many grams of dissolved salts will 500 g of seawater contain? **For more help, refer to the** Math Skill Handbook.

Waves, continued

Use an Analogy

Arrange chairs in a long row. Have a group of students sit in the chairs and quickly stand up and sit down in succession to make a human wave while other students watch. Have students compare the movement of each person in the wave to the movement of water molecules in an ocean wave. L2 ELL COOP LEARN IS **Interpersonal**

Fun Fact

The height of an average wave is 3.7 m. The largest waves occur in the West Wind Drift beneath the continuous strong winds surrounding Antarctica.

✔ Reading Check

Answer speed of wind, distance over which wind blows, length of time wind blows

Tides

Quick Demo

Use a model of the Sun, the Moon, and Earth to show students how all three bodies interact to produce tides in Earth's oceans. Show the arrangement of all three bodies during a new moon and full moon, when the gravity of the Moon and the Sun pull together to generate the greatest tidal range.

Teacher **FYI**

For a given wind velocity, waves tend to be higher on large, deep bodies of water than on shallower water bodies. Waves on the larger, deeper bodies develop without the interference of drag on the ocean bottom.

SCIENCE *Online*

Internet Addresses

_____

_____

_____

Explore the Glencoe Science Web site at **science.glencoe.com** to find out more about topics in this section.

Visual Learning

Figure 15 Would there be any problem with walking from the mainland to Mont-Saint-Michel at low tide, without using the causeway? Explain. Yes; although it would depend on the time of the walk, the fact that the tide returns quickly would mean someone walking on the tidal flats could become trapped or be drowned by the waters as they return at high tide.

Activity

If your school is located near an ocean, have students determine the times of today's low and high tides and the phase of the Moon. Have them relate the Moon's phase to the tides. If you do not live near a seacoast, tidal information can be obtained from coastal weather stations.
L2

Caption Answer

Figure 16 low tide Have students note the difference between the height of the wharf and sea level. Point out the ladders that allow sailors to access the wharf during low tide.

Figure 15
A large difference between high tide and low tide can be seen at Mont-Saint-Michel off the northwestern coast of France.

A Mont-Saint-Michel lies about 1.6 km offshore and is connected to the mainland at low tide.

B Incoming tides move very quickly, making Mont-Saint-Michel an island at high tide.

Figure 16
The Bay of Fundy has the greatest tidal range in the world. *Was this picture taken at high tide or low tide?*

Tidal Range As Earth rotates, different locations on Earth's surface pass through the high and low positions. Many coastal locations, such as the Atlantic and Pacific coasts of the United States, experience two high tides and two low tides each day. One low-tide/high-tide cycle takes 12 h, 25 min. A daily cycle of two high tides and two low tides takes 24 h, 50 min—slightly more than a day. But because ocean basins vary in size and shape, some coastal locations, such as many along the Gulf of Mexico, have only one high and one low tide each day. The **tidal range** is the difference between the level of the ocean at high tide and low tide. Notice the tidal range in the photos in **Figure 15.**

Extreme Tidal Ranges The shape of the seacoast and the shape of the ocean floor affect the ranges of tides. Along a smooth, wide beach, the incoming water can spread over a large area. There the water level might rise only a few centimeters at high tide. In a narrow gulf or bay, however, the water might rise many meters at high tide.

Most shorelines have tidal ranges between 1 m and 2 m. Some places, such as those on the Mediterranean Sea, have tidal ranges of only about 30 cm. Other places have large tidal ranges. Mont-Saint-Michel, shown in **Figure 15,** lies in the Gulf of Saint-Malo off the northwestern coast of France. There the tidal range reaches about 13.5 m.

The dock shown in **Figure 16** is in Digby, Nova Scotia in the Bay of Fundy. This bay is extremely narrow, which contributes to large tidal ranges. The difference between water levels at high tide and low tide can be as much as 15 m.

Science Journal

Grunion In the waters off southern California, the reproductive cycle of the grunion fish follows the tidal schedule. Have students research the egg-laying habits of the grunion and write about them in their Science Journals. On several nights after the full moon in spring and summer spawning season, grunion swim onto beaches. Females deposit their eggs in the sand and males spread their milt on top of the eggs. About ten nights later, as the tides are again increasing in height, the eggs are washed out of the sand and hatch.

Tidal Bores In some areas when a rising tide enters a shallow, narrow river from a wide area of the sea, a wave called a tidal bore forms. A tidal bore can have a breaking crest or it can be a smooth wave. Tidal bores tend to be found in places with large tidal ranges. The Amazon River in Brazil, the Tsientang River in China, and rivers that empty into the Bay of Fundy in Nova Scotia have tidal bores.

When a tidal bore enters a river, it causes surface water to reverse its flow. In the Amazon River, the tidal bore rushes 650 km upstream at speeds of 65 km/h, causing a wave more than 5 m in height. Four rivers that empty into the Bay of Fundy have tidal bores. In those rivers, bore rafting is a popular sport.

The Gravitational Effect of the Moon For the most part, tides are caused by the interaction of gravity in the Earth-Moon system. The Moon's gravity exerts a strong pull on Earth. Earth and the water in Earth's oceans responds to this pull. The water bulges outward as Earth and the Moon revolve around a common center of mass. These events are explained in **Figure 17.**

Two bulges of water form, one on the side of Earth closest to the Moon and one on the opposite side of Earth. The reason two bulges form is because the Moon's gravity pulls harder on parts of Earth closer to the Moon than on parts farther away. You can imagine this if you think about pulling a large ball of dough in the same direction but harder on one side than the other side. The ball of dough will stretch and form two bulges. Earth does the same thing. The ocean bulges are the high tides, and the areas of Earth's oceans that are not toward or away from the Moon are the low tides. As Earth rotates, different locations on its surface pass through high and low tide.

Extension

Have students write research reports about using tides and ocean waves to generate electricity.

Teacher FYI

The action of the tides is slowing down Earth's rotation by about 0.002 second per century. Eventually, billions of years from now, Earth's rotation will be so slow that Earth will be "gravitationally locked" with the Moon. Just as the Moon keeps the same face always toward Earth, Earth will keep one face always toward the Moon.

Figure 17
The Moon and Earth revolve around a common center of mass. Because the Moon's gravity pulls harder on parts of Earth closer to the Moon, a bulge of water forms on the side of Earth facing the Moon and the side of Earth opposite the Moon.

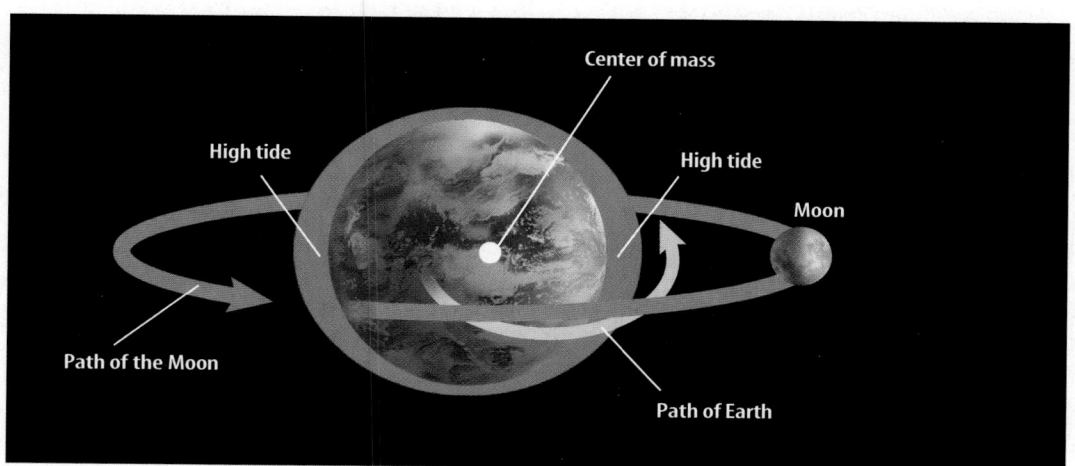

Center of mass
High tide
High tide
Moon
Path of the Moon
Path of Earth

SECTION 3 Ocean Waves and Tides **537**

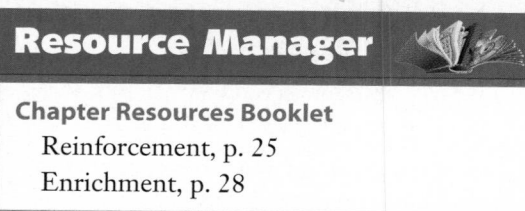

Resource Manager

Chapter Resources Booklet
   Reinforcement, p. 25
   Enrichment, p. 28

Tides, continued

Visual Learning

Figure 18 What phase of the Moon would you expect to see during a neap tide and during a spring tide? first or third quarter; full or new Moon

3 Assess

Reteach

Use a wave demonstration spring or coiled-spring toy to show how energy is transferred through a wave. Tie a piece of ribbon to the middle of the spring. Have two students create a wave while another student holds the ribbon. Have the class note that the ribbon does not move forward with the wave as energy moves through the ribbon. **IS Interpersonal**

Challenge

Why does the Moon have a greater gravitational effect on Earth's tides than the Sun, although the Sun is much larger? The Sun is much farther from Earth than the Moon is.

Assessment

Oral Have students write questions on the content of the chapter and quiz each other aloud. Use **Performance Assessment in the Science Classroom,** p. 91.

Figure 18
The gravitational attraction of the Sun causes spring tides and neap tides.

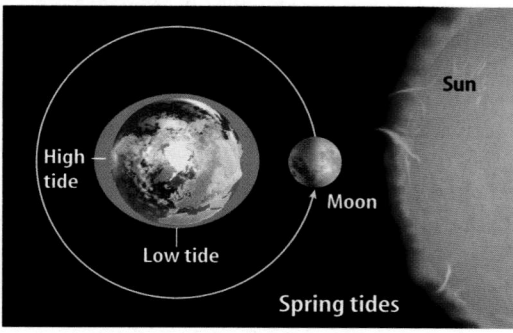

A When the Sun, the Moon, and Earth are aligned, spring tides occur.

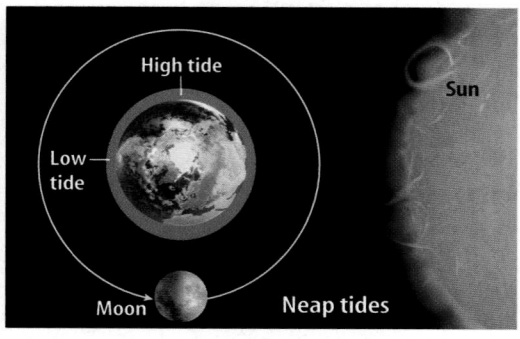

B When the Sun, the Moon, and Earth form a right angle, neap tides occur.

The Gravitational Effect of the Sun The Sun also affects tides. The Sun can strengthen or weaken the Moon's effects. When the Moon, Earth, and the Sun are lined up together, the combined pull of the Sun and the Moon causes spring tides, shown in **Figure 18A.** During spring tides, high tides are higher and low tides are lower than normal. The name *spring tide* has nothing to do with the season of spring. It comes from the German word *springen,* which means "to jump." When the Sun, Earth, and the Moon form a right angle, as shown in **Figure 18B,** high tides are lower and low tides are higher than normal. These are called neap tides.

Section 3 Assessment

1. Describe the parts of an ocean wave.
2. How does wind create water waves?
3. What causes high tides? Spring tides?
4. Compare water and wave movement.
5. **Think Critically** At the ocean, you spot a wave about 200 m from shore. A few seconds later, the wave breaks on the beach. Explain why the water in the breaker is not the same water that was in the wave 200 m away.

Skill Builder Activities

6. **Comparing and Contrasting** Compare and contrast the effects of the Sun and the Moon on Earth's tides. **For more help,** refer to the Science Skill Handbook.
7. **Communicating** Many planets have more than one moon. In your Science Journal, write a description of what tides might be like if Earth had two moons. **For more help,** refer to the Science Skill Handbook.

Answers to Section Assessment

1. crest: highest point, trough: lowest point, wave height: vertical distance between crest and trough, wavelength: horizontal distance between crests or troughs of two successive waves, amplitude: half of wave height
2. Friction pulls water along with wind.
3. Tides are caused by a giant wave that forms as the result of the gravitational pull of the Sun and the Moon. As the wave's crest approaches the shore, the water level appears to rise in a high tide. Spring tides are caused by the combined gravitational effect when the Moon, Earth, and the Sun are in line
4. As the wave moves horizontally through the water, particles of water are moved up, forward, down, and back.
5. Although the energy in waves moves, the water particles themselves do not.
6. Both affect tides because of gravitational attraction, but the effect of the Moon is greater because it's so much closer.
7. Answers will vary, but both moons would exert gravitational attraction that would result in tides. If both moons and the Sun lined up with Earth, the tidal range would be greater. If the two moons were at right angles to one another, tidal range would be smaller.

Activity

Making Waves

Wind generates some waves. The energy of motion is transferred from the wind to the surface water of the ocean. What factors influence the generation of waves?

What You'll Investigate
How do the speed of the wind and the length of time the wind blows affect the height of a wave?

Materials
11" × 14" white paper   water
3-speed electric fan   metric ruler
gooseneck lamp
clock or watch
rectangular, clear-plastic storage box

Goals
■ **Observe** how wind speed and duration affect wave height.

Safety Precautions
Do not allow any part of the light or cord to come in contact with the water.

Procedure

1. Position the box on white paper beside the lamp.
2. Fill the plastic box with water to within 3 cm of the top. Direct light from the lamp onto the box.
3. Place the fan at one end of the box to create waves. Start the fan on its slowest speed. Keep the fan on during measuring.
4. After 3 min, measure the height of the waves caused by the fan. Record your observations in a table similar to the one shown. Through the plastic box, observe the shadows of the waves on the white paper.

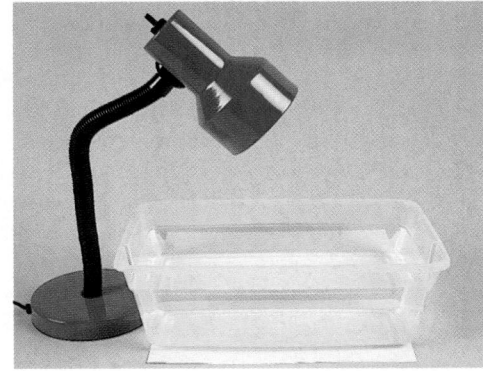

5. After 5 min, measure the wave height and record your observations.
6. Repeat steps 3 to 5 with the fan on medium, then on high.
7. Turn off the fan. Unplug it. Observe what happens.

Wave Data			
Fan Speed	Time (min)	Wave Height (mm)	Observations
Low	3	2	
Low	5	3	
Medium	3	3.5	
Medium	5	4.5	
High	3	5	
High	5	5.5	

Conclude and Apply

1. **Analyze** your data to determine whether the wave height is affected by the length of time that the wind blows. Explain.
2. **Analyze** your data to determine whether the height of the waves is affected by the speed of the wind. Explain.

ACTIVITY 539

Communicating
Your Data

Use a computer graphics program to plot the data obtained from this activity. Compare your plot with those of other students in the class. Graphs should show how the length of time the wind blows and wind speed affects wave height.

Activity

BENCH TESTED

Purpose Students observe and describe the factors that affect the height of waves. L2 ELL COOP LEARN **Visual-Spatial**

Process Skills making models, observing and inferring, relating cause and effect, interpreting data, predicting, analyzing

Time Required 35 minutes

Alternate Materials If enough table-model, three-speed fans cannot be obtained, the activity can be done by placing three or four student setups on the floor in front of a large floor fan that operates at several speeds. An overhead or filmstrip projector works well in place of the recommended light source and ring stand setup.

Safety Precautions Caution students to keep electrical cords and appliances away from water, to use care when handling the hot light source, and to keep objects away from moving fan blades.

Teaching Strategy If necessary, have students review Recognizing Cause and Effect in the Skill Handbook.

Answers to Questions
1. It is; the longer the wind blows, the higher the wave.
2. It is; the stronger the wind, the higher the wave.

Assessment

Performance To further assess students' ability to understand factors that affect the height of waves, have them design an experiment to see how the fetch (the distance over which the wind blows) affects wave height. Use **Performance Assessment in the Science Classroom**, p. 95.

Activity

BENCH TESTED

Recognize the Problem

Purpose

Students will design an experiment and data table to chart how increasing salinity affects the ability of a potato to float in water.

Process Skills

designing an experiment, forming a hypothesis, comparing, observing and inferring, communicating, interpreting data, recording data, analyzing results, making and using tables

Time Required

one class period

Form a Hypothesis

Possible Hypothesis

Students may hypothesize that with increasing salinity, the potato rises or the opposite, that it sinks with increasing salinity.

Test Your Hypothesis

Possible Procedures

Fill a large glass bowl with approximately 960 mL of water. Weigh a small potato and drop it into the bowl. Use the metric ruler to record the displacement of the water. Remove the potato and add 1 teaspoon of salt to the water. Stir the water until the salt dissolves. Drop the potato into the water and record the results. Use a metric ruler to measure the amount of water that is displaced each time. Repeat the above steps until you notice a change in the potato's ability to float. For help figuring density, refer to the Math Skills Activity in this chapter.

Activity *Design Your Own Experiment*

Sink or Float

As you know, ocean water contains many dissolved salts. How does this affect objects within the oceans? Why do certain objects float on top of the ocean's waves, while others sink directly to the bottom? Density is a measurement of mass per volume. You can use density to determine whether an object will float within a certain volume of water of a specific salinity. In this activity you will investigate the effect of salinity on whether an object floats or sinks.

Recognizing the Problem

How does salinity affect whether a potato will float or sink?

Form a Hypothesis

Based on what you know so far about salinity, why things float or sink, and the density of a potato, plus what it looks and feels like, formulate a hypothesis. Do you think the salinity of water has any effect on objects that are floating in water? What kind of effect? Will they float or sink? How would a dense object like a potato be different from a less dense object like a cork?

Goals

- **Design** an experiment to identify how increasing salinity affects the ability of a potato to float in water.

Possible Materials

small, uncooked potato
teaspoon
salt
large glass bowl
water
balance
large graduated cylinder
metric ruler

Safety

Resource Manager

Chapter Resources Booklet
   Activity Worksheet, pp. 7–8
Lab Management and Safety, p. 65

Test Your Hypothesis

Plan

1. As a group, agree upon and write your hypothesis statement.

2. Devise a method to test how salinity affects whether a potato floats in water.

3. **List** the steps you need to take to test your hypothesis. Be specific, describing exactly what you will do at each step.

4. Read over your plan for testing your hypothesis.

5. How will you determine the densities of the potato and the different water samples? How you will measure the salinity of the water? How will you change the salinity of the water? Will you add teaspoons of salt one at a time?

6. How you will measure the ability of an object to float? Could you somehow measure the displacement of the water? Perhaps you could draw a line somewhere on your bowl and see how the position of the potato changes.

7. **Design** a data table where you can record your results. Include columns/rows for the salinity and float/sink measurements. What else should you include?

Do

1. Make sure your teacher approves your plan before you start.

2. Carry out the experiment.

3. While conducting the experiment, record your data and any observations that you or other group members make in your Science Journal.

Analyze Your Data

1. **Compare** how the potato floated in water with different salinities.

2. How does the ability of an object to float change with changing salinity?

Draw Conclusions

1. Did your experiment support the hypothesis you made?

2. A heavily loaded ship barely floats in the Gulf of Mexico. Based on what you learned, infer what might happen to the ship if it travels into the freshwater of the Mississippi River.

Prepare a chart showing the results of your experiment. Share the chart with members of your class. **For more help, refer to the** Science Skill Handbook.

ACTIVITY 541

Teaching Strategy

Before students create their own hypothesis, show three different beakers with different salt concentrations and float an object in each.

Expected Outcome

The potato will float better in higher salt concentrations. It will take approximately 12-14 teaspoons of salt to float a 100 g potato.

Analyze Your Data

1. As the salinity of the water increased, the potato became more buoyant.

2. If the salinity is lowered, denser objects will not float as well. The density of the object affects whether or not it will float. For example, a bobber will float in freshwater or salt water.

Error Analysis

If students are unable to get their potato to float in the time allowed, have them review the procedure steps. How much water did they use? How much salt?

Draw Conclusions

1. Answers will vary.

2. Students might indicate that the ship will sink if it travels into freshwater.

✔ *Assessment*

Process Have students evaluate the data from other classmates. If their data is significantly different, have them discuss why it might be different. Use **Performance Assessment in the Science Classroom,** p. 99.

Student charts should show how much salt was added each time and whether or not the potato changed position with the addition of salt.

Science and Language Arts

"The Jungle of Ceylon"
from Passions and Impressions
by Pablo Neruda

Respond to the Reading

Active Reading Strategies

Visualize The author skillfully describes the coast of the island of Ceylon. Ask students to try to visualize all of the features of the island he depicts, including the reef, the birds, the tides, the trees and the boats.

Question The author describes the jungle as having "a silence like that of libraries: abstract and humid." **Why does he compare the jungle to a library?**

Listen Read the passage aloud. Have students notice how the author uses words that have the same first letter or consonant sound. This is called alliteration.

Question Ask students whether they think the author's use of alliteration helps them visualize the scene he is describing?

Answers to Questions

1. It was a gentle and happy place; he describes it as *felicitous.*
2. rippling ruff of feathers and foam
3. tropical

Respond to the Reading

1. What were his impressions of the island on arrival?
2. What words does the author choose to describe waves?
3. How would you describe the climate of Ceylon?

The following passage is part of a travel chronicle describing the Chilean poet Pablo Neruda's visit to the island of Ceylon, now called Sri Lanka, which is located southeast of India. The author considered himself so connected to Earth that he wrote in green ink.

Felicitous[1] shore! A coral reef stretches parallel to the beach; there the ocean interposes in its blues the perpetual white of a rippling ruff[2] of feathers and foam; the triangular red sails of sampans[3]; the unmarred line of the coast on which the straight trunks of the coconut palms rise like explosions, their brilliant green Spanish combs nearly touching the sky.

… In the deep jungle, there is a silence like that of libraries: abstract and humid.

1 Happy
2 round collar made of layers of lace
3 East Asian boats

Reading Further

Other works by this author include:

Residence on Earth, by Pablo Neruda, New Directions, March 1973.

The Book of Questions, by Pablo Neruda, Copper Canyon Press, September 1991.

Other sources on this topic include:

Currents of Change: Impacts of El Nino and La Nina on Climate and Society, Cambridge University Press, February 2001.

Understanding Literature

Imagery Imagery is a series of words that evoke pictures to the reader. Poets use imagery to connect images to abstract concepts. The poet, here, wants to capture a particular feature of the reef and does so by describing it as a "ruff of feathers and foam", invoking the image of a gentle place, without the author saying so. Imagery also gives the reader more information about the story or chronicle. The poet further describes the shore as "happy", which helps us learn that the poet is arriving on the island on a clear, calm day.

Where else in the poem does the poet use imagery to convey a mood or feeling?

Science Connection In the poem there are several indicators that the wind, which causes waves and currents, is light and the waves are small, using imagery as discussed above.

Sri Lanka, however, often is plagued by monsoons, which affect ocean conditions and local climate. Monsoons are seasonal reversals of the regional winds. During the wet season, moist winds blow in from the sea causing storms and producing waves. During the dry season, winds blow from the land and sunny days are common.

Career Connection

Oceanographer

Oceanographer Dr. Robert D. Ballard is an American oceanographer who introduced deep-sea archaeology. He developed several high-tech vessels that can explore ocean bottoms previously out of reach. Dr. Ballard discovered the location of the wreckage of the *Titanic, Lusitania,* and *Bismark.* He also discovered the wreckage of eight ancient ships in the Mediterranean Sea. Dr. Ballard has degrees in chemistry and geology as well as doctorate degrees in marine geology and geophysics.

SCIENCE *Online*   To learn more about careers in oceanography, visit the Glencoe Science Web site at **science.glencoe.com.**

Linking Science and Writing

Weather Report Write a weather report for fishers and others who work at sea. Pick a geographic location to focus on. If possible, do research on wave conditions in this area. Include the times for low and high tides in your report. Add any additional weather information that you think might be important to people who work at or around the sea.

Understanding Literature

Answers to Questions

Answers may vary but might include that the author uses the word "explosion" when referring to the tops of palm trees to convey a contrast between the trees and the gentle sea. He also compares the silence of the jungle to that of a library as a way of emphasizing the jungle's stillness and solitude.

Science Connection

Atlantic and Pacific Ocean currents circulate clockwise north of the Equator. However in the northern Indian Ocean, surface currents change with the seasonal monsoon. This is called the Monsoon Drift or Current. During the northeast monsoons of Sri Lanka, the Northeast Monsoon Drift flows southwest and west, crossing the Equator. From April to October, the southwest monsoon sets in, reversing the flow of the current and pushing the Southwest Monsoon Drift eastward.

Linking Science and Writing

Teaching Strategies

Tell students to bring to class maps from the newspaper that describe area weather patterns. Have students do brief oral presentations describing the weather patterns on the map.

SCIENCE AND LANGUAGE ARTS   543

Career Connection

Students interested in a career in marine science should enroll in as many chemistry, Earth science, biology, physics, computer science, and mathematics classes as possible, in high school and in college. Oceanographers do not specialize until later in their education.

With a high school education or a two-year degree, students can be technicians in marine science. In order analyze the data they collect, however, students will need to go to a 4-year college as well as get an advanced degree. About 30 U.S. schools offer specialized technical training in marine-related fields.

Reviewing Main Ideas

Preview

Students can answer the questions in their Science Journals. Discuss the answers as you go through the chapter. **IS** **Linguistic**

Review

Students can write their answers, then compare them with those of other students. **IS** **Interpersonal**

Reteach

Students can look at the illustrations and describe details that support the main ideas of the chapter. **IS** **Visual-Spatial**

Answers to Chapter Review

SECTION 1

3. halite

SECTION 2

4. The warm temperature and dry air cause large amounts of water to evaporate from the sea's surface. The remaining water contains an increased salt concentration and is more dense than the water around it. The denser water sinks and flows out of the Mediterranean Sea at the Straits of Gibraltar. Less dense water from the Atlantic Ocean flows in to replace it.

SECTION 3

3. They result when the gravitational effect of the Moon and the Sun causes a bulge, or wave, in Earth's oceans that spreads around the planet. When the crest of the wave approaches a shore, the water appears to rise on the shore as high tide. Low tide occurs when the trough of the wave approaches the shore.

Chapter 18 Study Guide

Reviewing Main Ideas

Section 1 Ocean Water

1. Earth's ocean water might have originated from water vapor released from volcanoes. Over millions of years, the water condensed and rain fell, filling basins.

2. The oceans are a mixture of water, dissolved salts, and dissolved gases that are in constant motion.

3. Groundwater and rivers weather rock and dissolve some minerals to form ions. The ions are carried to the oceans. When they reach the oceans, these ions give seawater its salty taste. *What kind of salt, shown here, makes up most of the salt left when seawater is evaporated?*

Section 2 Ocean Currents

1. Wind causes surface currents. Surface currents are affected by the Coriolis effect. The Coriolis effect turns currents north of the equator clockwise and turns currents south of the equator counterclockwise.

2. Surface currents can greatly affect climate and economic activity such as fishing. Upwelling brings deep, cold water to the ocean's surface.

3. Cool currents off western coasts originate far from the equator. Warmer currents along eastern coasts begin near the equator.

4. Differences in temperature and salinity between water masses in the oceans set up circulation patterns called density currents. *How do density currents originate in the Mediterranean Sea, shown here?*

Section 3 Ocean Waves and Tides

1. A wave is a rhythmic movement that carries energy. The crest is the highest point of a wave. The trough is the lowest point.

2. In a wave, energy moves forward while water particles move around in small circles.

3. Wind causes water to pile up and form most water waves. Tides are not caused by wind. *What causes the high and low tides shown here?*

FOLDABLES
Reading & Study Skills

After You Read

Write the effects of ocean motion on climate, world economics, and the ocean water under the bottom tab of your Foldable.

FOLDABLES
Reading & Study Skills

After You Read

After students have read the chapter and completed the Foldable described in Before You Read, have them do the activity on the student page.

Dinah Zike

Visualizing Main Ideas

Complete the following concept map on ocean motions.

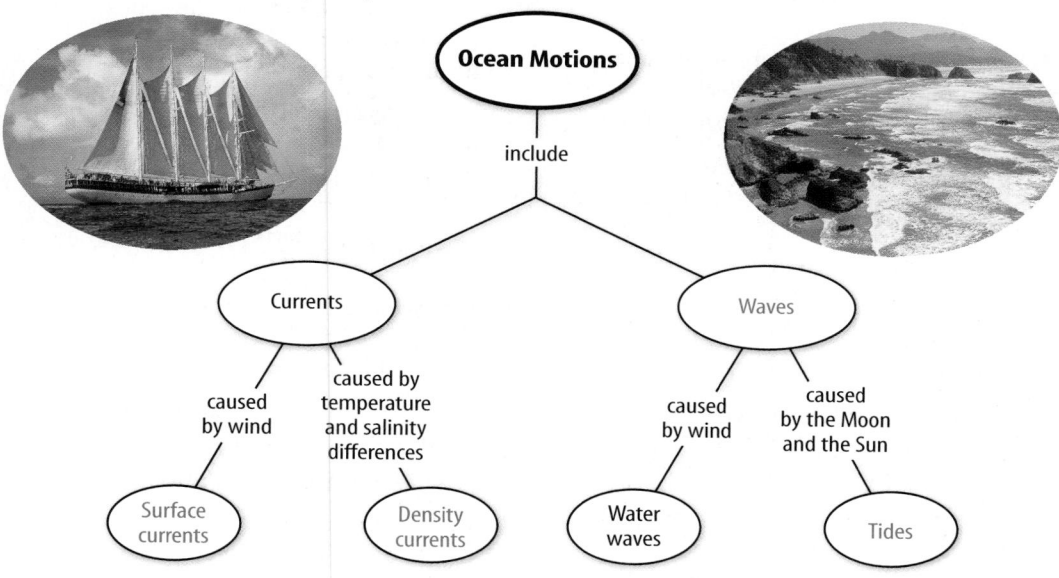

Ocean Motions

include

Currents — caused by wind → **Surface currents**

Currents — caused by temperature and salinity differences → **Density currents**

Waves — caused by wind → **Water waves**

Waves — caused by the Moon and the Sun → **Tides**

Vocabulary Review

Vocabulary Words

a. basin
b. breaker
c. Coriolis effect
d. crest
e. density current
f. salinity
g. surface current
h. tidal range
i. tide
j. trough
k. upwelling
l. wave

THE PRINCETON REVIEW — Study Tip

After you've read a chapter, go back to the beginning and speed-read through what you've just read. This will help you better remember what you have read.

Using Vocabulary

Replace the underlined words with the vocabulary words that have the same meaning.

1. The <u>amount of dissolved salts</u> in seawater has stayed about the same for hundreds of millions of years.

2. An <u>area where nutrient-rich water comes to the surface</u> is a good place to catch fish.

3. Wind creates a <u>horizontal current at the top of the ocean</u>.

4. Along most ocean beaches, a <u>rise and fall of the ocean related to gravitational pull</u> is easy to see.

5. Wind pushes on water to make a <u>movement of energy through the water</u>.

CHAPTER STUDY GUIDE   545

Visualizing Main Ideas

See student page.

Vocabulary Review

Using Vocabulary

1. The *salinity* in seawater has stayed about the same for hundreds of millions of years.
2. An *upwelling* is a good place to catch fish.
3. Wind creates a *surface current*.
4. Along most ocean beaches, a *tide* is easy to see.
5. Wind pushes on water to make a *wave*.

Checking Concepts

1. B
2. A
3. A
4. D
5. C
6. B
7. A
8. D
9. B
10. C

Thinking Critically

11. It could wash up onto a beach on the coast of western or northwestern Europe because the Gulf Stream travels there from Florida.
12. Many marine organisms use these elements in their life processes, thus removing them from the ocean.
13. It forms when salt is left over as ice forms from salt water at the South Pole. The salt increases the density of the cold water, causing it to sink beneath less-dense water.
14. At the mouth of the Mississippi River the water is fresh, while it is very salty at the entrance to the Mediterranean Sea. The water is therefore denser at the entrance to the Mediterranean.
15. highest high tide, day 4; lowest high tide, day 23; highest low tide, day 24; lowest low tide, day 4; spring tide, day 4; neap tide, days 23 and 24

Chapter 18 Assessment

Checking Concepts

Choose the word or phrase that best answers the question.

1. Where might ocean water have originated?
   - A) salt marshes
   - B) volcanoes
   - C) basins
   - D) surface currents

2. How does chlorine enter the oceans?
   - A) volcanoes
   - B) rivers
   - C) density currents
   - D) groundwater

3. What is the most common ion found in ocean water?
   - A) chloride
   - B) calcium
   - C) boron
   - D) sulfate

4. What causes most surface currents?
   - A) density differences
   - B) the Gulf Stream
   - C) salinity
   - D) wind

5. What is the highest point on a wave called?
   - A) wave height
   - B) trough
   - C) crest
   - D) wavelength

6. In the ocean, what is the rhythmic movement that carries energy through seawater?
   - A) current
   - B) wave
   - C) crest
   - D) upwelling

7. Which of the following causes the density of seawater to increase?
   - A) a decrease in temperature
   - B) a decrease in salinity
   - C) an increase in temperature
   - D) a decrease in pressure

8. In which direction does the Coriolis effect cause currents in the northern hemisphere to turn?
   - A) east
   - B) south
   - C) counterclockwise
   - D) clockwise

9. Tides are affected by the positions of which celestial bodies?
   - A) Earth and the Moon
   - B) Earth, the Moon, and the Sun
   - C) Venus, Earth, and Mars
   - D) the Sun, Earth, and Mars

10. What affects surface currents?
    - A) crests
    - B) upwellings
    - C) the Coriolis effect
    - D) tides

Thinking Critically

11. If a sealed bottle is dropped into the ocean off the coast of Florida, where do you think it might wash up? Explain.

12. Why do silicon and calcium remain in seawater for a shorter time than sodium?

13. Describe the Antarctic density current.

14. How would the density of seawater at the mouth of the Mississippi River and in the Mediterranean Sea compare? Explain.

15. Refer to the graph below. On which day is the high tide highest? Lowest? On which day(s) is the low tide lowest? Highest? On which day(s) would Earth, the Moon, and the Sun be lined up? On which day(s) would the Moon, Earth, and the Sun form a right angle?

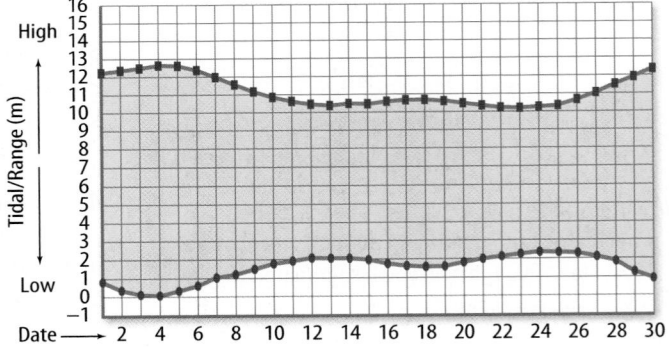

Chapter ✓Assessment Planner

Portfolio Encourage students to place in their portfolios one or two items of what they consider to be their best work. Examples include:
- Assessment, p. 525
- Curriculum Connection, p. 528
- Extension, p. 534

Performance Additional performance assessments, Performance Task Assessment Lists, and rubrics for evaluating these activities can be found in Glencoe's **Performance Assessment in the Science Classroom.**

Developing Skills

16. Recognizing Cause and Effect What causes upwelling? What effect does it have? What can happen when upwelling stops?

17. Comparing and Contrasting Compare and contrast ocean waves and ocean currents.

18. Predicting Predict how drift bottles that are dropped into the ocean at points A and B will move. Explain.

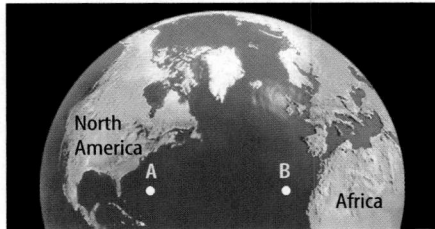

19. Recognizing Cause and Effect In the Mediterranean Sea, a density current forms because of the high rate of evaporation of water from the surface. How can evaporation cause a density current?

Performance Assessment

20. Invention Design a method for desalinating water that does not use solar energy. Draw it, and display it for your class.

21. Design and Perform an Experiment Create an experiment to test the density of water at different temperatures.

TECHNOLOGY

 Go to the Glencoe Science Web site at **science.glencoe.com** or use the **Glencoe Science CD-ROM** for additional chapter assessment.

 **THE PRINCETON REVIEW** **Test Practice**

A marine scientist used the following graphic to support a lecture about ocean currents.

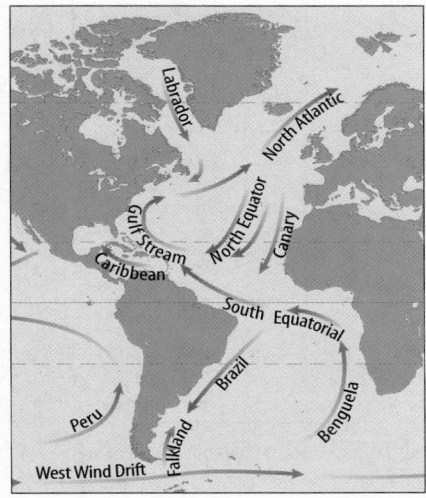

Study the graphic and answer the following questions.

1. The direction of ocean currents in the northern hemisphere is _____.
A) counter-clockwise
B) north to south only
C) clockwise
D) east to west only

2. A reasonable conclusion based on the information in the graphic is that _____.
F) the ocean's currents only flow in one direction
G) the ocean's waters are constantly in motion
H) the Gulf Stream flows east to west
J) the Atlantic Ocean is deep

CHAPTER ASSESSMENT 547

 **THE PRINCETON REVIEW** **Test Practice**

The Test-Taking Tip was written by The Princeton Review, the nation's leader in test preparation.
1. C
2. G

Developing Skills

16. Surface water is pushed away from an area by wind, allowing underlying cold water to rise to the surface, and sometimes fish rise as well. If upwelling stops, good fishing areas can become barren.

17. Wind causes surface currents and waves. But surface currents move water from one place to another. Energy moves laterally in waves, but the water does not.

18. North from A, following shorelines around in clockwise pattern, moving south toward B. Movement would be caused by surface currents.

19. When salt water evaporates, the water left behind has a higher concentration of salt, making it denser. The denser water sinks and flows out of the Mediterranean Sea into the Atlantic Ocean. Less dense surface water from the Atlantic flows in to replace it.

Performance Assessment

20. Students can use some artificial source, such as a hot plate, to heat and evaporate water. Use **PASC**, p. 117.

21. Designs should include procedures for heating and cooling the water; ways to measure the temperature, volume, and mass of the water samples; and a method for calculating density. Hydrometers can be used to determine actual densities of samples. They can be made by students or purchased from aquarium supply stores. Use **PASC**, p. 95.

Section/Objectives	Standards		Activities/Features
Chapter Opener	**National**	**State/Local**	**Explore Activity:** Model Sonar, p. 549 **Before You Read,** p. 549
	See p. 5T for a Key to Standards.		
Section 1 The Seafloor 🕐 2 sessions 📦 1 block 1. **Differentiate** between a continental shelf and a continental slope. 2. **Describe** a mid-ocean ridge, an abyssal plain, and an ocean trench. 3. **Identify** the mineral resources found on the continental shelf and in the deep ocean.	National Content Standards: UCP1, A1, D1, F2		**Science Online,** p. 551 **Math Skills Activity:** Calculating a Feature's Slope, p. 552 **MiniLAB:** Modeling the Mid-Atlantic Ridge, p. 553 **Activity:** Mapping the Ocean Floor, p. 556
Section 2 Life in the Ocean 🕐 2 sessions 📦 1 block 1. **Describe** photosynthesis and chemosynthesis in the oceans. 2. **List** the key characteristics of plankton, nekton, and benthos. 3. **Compare and contrast** ocean margin habitats.	National Content Standards: UCP2, A1, C1, C3, C4, C5		**Life Science Integration,** p. 558 **Chemistry Integration,** p. 560 **MiniLAB:** Observing Plankton, p. 561 **Science Online,** p. 562 **Visualizing the Rocky Shore Habitat,** p. 563
Section 3 Ocean Pollution 🕐 4 sessions 📦 2 blocks 1. **List** five types of ocean pollution. 2. **Explain** how ocean pollution affects the entire world. 3. **Describe** how ocean pollution can be controlled.	National Content Standards: UCP1, A1, C4, D1, F2, F4, F5, G1, G2		**Activity:** Resources from the Ocean, pp. 570–571 **Oops! Accidents in Science:** Strange Creatures from the Ocean Floor, pp. 572–573

▣ NATIONAL GEOGRAPHIC

Teacher's Corner

PRODUCTS AVAILABLE FROM GLENCOE
To order call 1-800-334-7344:
CD-ROMs
NGS PictureShow: Oceans
Curriculum Kit
GeoKits: Oceans

Transparency Set
NGS PicturePack: Oceans

PRODUCTS AVAILABLE FROM NATIONAL GEOGRAPHIC SOCIETY
To order call 1-800-368-2728:
Videos
Oceans in Motion

INDEX TO NATIONAL GEOGRAPHIC SOCIETY
The following articles may be used for research relating to this chapter: "Blue Refuges: U.S. National Marine Sanctuaries," by Douglas H. Chadwick, March 1998.

Activity Materials	Reproducible Resources	Section Assessment	Technology
Explore Activity: spring, meterstick, stopwatch	**Chapter Resources Booklet** Foldables Worksheet, p. 17 Directed Reading Overview, p. 19 Note-taking Worksheets, pp. 33–35	GLENCOE'S ASSESSMENT ADVANTAGE	
MiniLAB: 2 tray tables, 10 paper towels **Activity:** Graph Paper	**Chapter Resources Booklet** Transparency Activity, p. 44 MiniLAB, p. 3 Lab Activity, pp. 9–11 Enrichment, p. 30 Reinforcement, p. 27 Directed Reading, p. 20 Transparency Activity, pp. 47–48 Activity Worksheet, pp. 5–6 **Cultural Diversity,** p. 27 **Science Inquiry Labs,** p. 31	**Portfolio** Science Journal, p. 554 **Performance** Math Skills Activity, p. 552 MiniLAB, p. 553 Skill Builder Activities, p. 555 **Content** Section Assessment, p. 555	Section Focus Transparency Teaching Transparency Interactive CD-ROM/DVD Guided Reading Audio Program
MiniLAB: pond, lake, or ocean water; dropper; microscope slide; light microscope *Need materials?* Contact Science Kit at 1-800-828-7777 or www.sciencekit.com on the Internet.	**Chapter Resources Booklet** Transparency Activity, p. 45 MiniLAB, p. 4 Enrichment, p. 31 Reinforcement, p. 28 Directed Reading, p. 21 **Reading and Writing Skill Activities,** p. 7 **Home and Community Involvement,** p. 30	**Portfolio** Curriculum Connection, p. 559 **Performance** MiniLAB, p. 561 Skill Builder Activities, p. 564 **Content** Section Assessment, p. 564	Section Focus Transparency Interactive CD-ROM/DVD Guided Reading Audio Program
Activity: Internet or other resources describing products from the ocean	**Chapter Resources Booklet** Transparency Activity, p. 46 Lab Activity, pp. 13–16 Enrichment, p. 32 Reinforcement, p. 29 Directed Reading, pp. 21, 22 Activity Worksheet, pp. 7–8 **Lab Management and Safety,** p. 73 **Life Science Critical Thinking/ Problem Solving,** p. 10	**Portfolio** Curriculum Connection, p. 568 **Performance** Skill Builder Activities, p. 569 **Content** Section Assessment, p. 569	Section Focus Transparency Interactive CD-ROM/DVD Guided Reading Audio Program

End of Chapter Assessment

GLENCOE'S ASSESSMENT ADVANTAGE

Blackline Masters	Technology	Professional Series
Chapter Resources Booklet Chapter Review, pp. 37–38 Chapter Tests, pp. 39–42 **Standardized Test Practice by The Princeton Review,** pp. 83–86	MindJogger Videoquiz CD-ROM Explorations and Quizzes Vocabulary Puzzle Makers ExamView Pro Test Bank Interactive Lesson Planner Interactive Teacher's Edition	Performance Assessment in the Science Classroom (PASC)

Transparencies

Section Focus

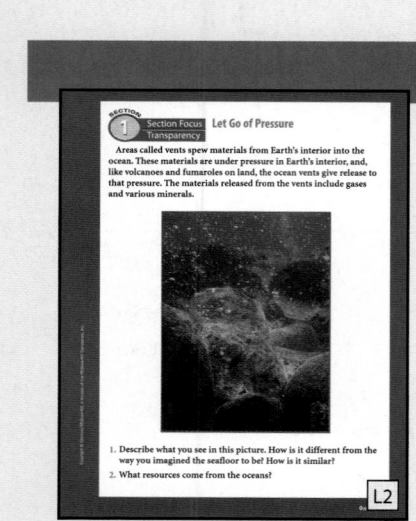

Section Focus Transparency 1 — Let Go of Pressure

Areas called vents spew materials from Earth's interior into the ocean. These materials are under pressure in Earth's interior, and, like volcanoes and fumaroles on land, the ocean vents give release to that pressure. The materials released from the vents include gases and various minerals.

1. Describe what you see in this picture. How is it different from the way you imagined the seafloor to be? How is it similar?
2. What resources come from the oceans?

L2

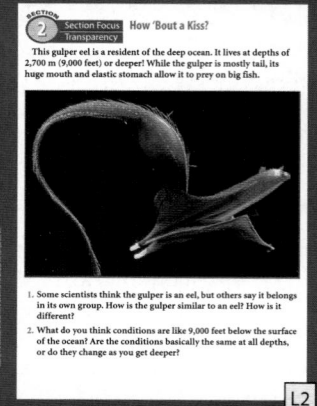

Section Focus Transparency 2 — How 'Bout a Kiss?

This gulper eel is a resident of the deep ocean. It lives at depths of 2,700 m (9,000 feet) or deeper! While the gulper is mostly tail, its huge mouth and elastic stomach allow it to prey on big fish.

1. Some scientists think the gulper is an eel, but others say it belongs in its own group. How is the gulper similar to an eel? How is it different?
2. What do you think conditions are like 9,000 feet below the surface of the ocean? Are the conditions basically the same at all depths, or do they change as you get deeper?

L2

Section Focus Transparency 3 — The "Dead Zone"

Due to sewage and fertilizer run-off from the Mississippi River, massive algal blooms have created an 18,100 km2 (7000 square mile) "dead zone" in the Gulf of Mexico. The algae not only make it unsafe to eat seafood caught on the fringes of this area, but they severely deplete oxygen supplies in the water, making it almost impossible for plants and animals to exist in these areas. Below are photographs of a healthy marine environment and the "dead zone."

1. Describe the differences in the images.
2. How does pollution contribute to algal blooms?
3. Give some examples of ocean pollution.

L2

Assessment

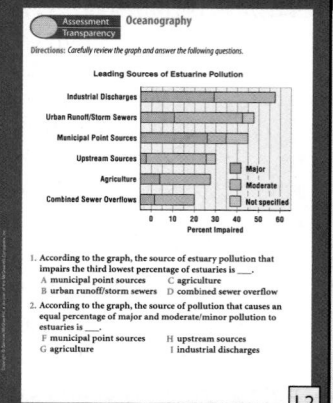

Assessment Transparency — Oceanography

Directions: *Carefully review the graph and answer the following questions.*

Leading Sources of Estuarine Pollution

- Industrial Discharges
- Urban Runoff/Storm Sewers
- Manicipal Point Sources
- Upstream Sources
- Agriculture
- Combined Sewer Overflows

Percent Impaired: 0 10 20 30 40 50 60

Legend: Major / Moderate / Not specified

1. According to the graph, the source of estuary pollution that impairs the third lowest percentage of estuaries is ___.
   A municipal point sources   C agriculture
   B urban runoff/storm sewers   D combined sewer overflow
2. According to the graph, the source of pollution that causes an equal percentage of major and moderate/minor pollution to estuaries is ___.
   F municipal point sources   H upstream sources
   G agriculture   I industrial discharges

L2

Teaching

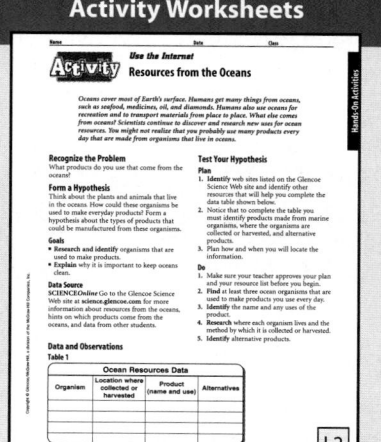

Teaching Transparency 1 — Ocean Basin

L2

Key to Teaching Strategies

This is a representation of key blackline masters available in the Teacher Classroom Resources. See Resource Manager boxes within the chapter for additional information.

Key to Teaching Strategies

The following designations will help you decide which activities are appropriate for your students.

L1 Level 1 activities should be appropriate for students with learning difficulties.

L2 Level 2 activities should be within the ability range of all students.

L3 Level 3 activities are designed for above-average students.

ELL ELL activities should be within the ability range of English Language Learners.

COOP LEARN Cooperative Learning activities are designed for small group work.

LS Multiple Learning Styles logos, as described on page 22T, are used throughout to indicate strategies that address different learning styles.

P These strategies represent student products that can be placed into a best-work portfolio.

Hands-on Activities

Activity Worksheets

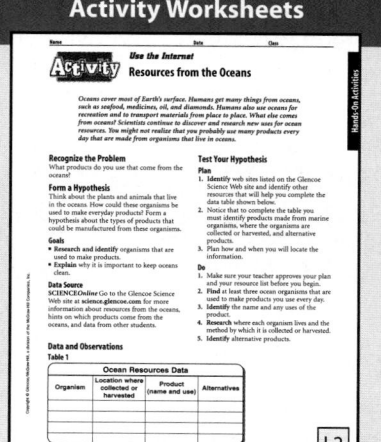

Activity — *Use the Internet*
Resources from the Oceans

Oceans cover most of Earth's surface. Humans get many things from oceans, such as seafood, medicines, oil, and diamonds. Humans also use oceans for recreation and to transport materials from place to place. What else comes from oceans? Scientists continue to discover and research new uses for ocean resources. You might not realize that you probably use many products every day that are made from organisms that live in oceans.

Recognize the Problem
What products do you use that come from the oceans?

Form a Hypothesis
Think about the plants and animals that live in the oceans. How could these organisms be used to make everyday products? Form a hypothesis about the types of products that could be manufactured from these organisms.

Goals
- **Research and identify** organisms that are used to make products.
- **Explain** why it is important to keep oceans clean.

Data Source
SCIENCEOnline Go to the Glencoe Science Web site at science.glencoe.com for more information about resources from the oceans, hints on which products come from the oceans, and data from other students.

Data and Observations
Table 1

Ocean Resources Data

Organism	Location where collected or harvested	Product (name and use)	Alternatives

Test Your Hypothesis
Plan
1. **Identify** web sites listed on the Glencoe Science Web site and identify other resources that will help you complete the data table shown below.
2. Notice that to complete the table you must identify products made from marine organisms, where the organisms are collected or harvested, and alternative products.
3. Plan how and when you will locate the information.

Do
1. Make sure your teacher approves your plan and your resource list before you begin.
2. **Find** at least three ocean organisms that are used to make products you use every day.
3. **Identify** the name and any uses of the product.
4. **Research** where each organism lives and the method by which it is collected or harvested.
5. **Identify** alternative products.

L2

Laboratory Activities

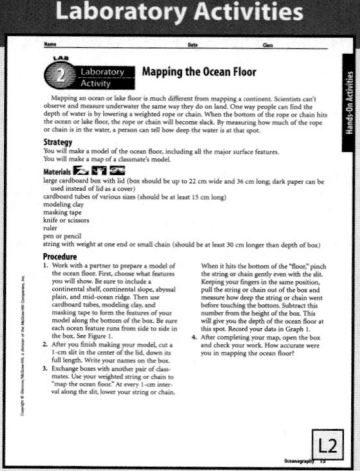

Laboratory Activity 2 — Mapping the Ocean Floor

Mapping an ocean or lake floor is much different from mapping a continent. Scientists can't observe and measure underwater the same way they do on land. One way people can find the depth of water is by lowering a weighted rope or chain. When the bottom of the rope or chain hits the ocean or lake floor, the rope or chain will become slack. By measuring how much of the rope or chain is in the water, a person can tell how deep the water is at that spot.

Strategy
You will make a model of the ocean floor, including all the major surface features.
You will make a map of a classmate's model.

Materials
large cardboard box with lid (box should be up to 22 cm wide and 36 cm long; dark paper can be used instead of lid as a cover)
cardboard tubes of various sizes (should be at least 15 cm long)
modeling clay
masking tape
knife or scissors
ruler
pen or pencil
string with weight at one end or small chain (should be at least 30 cm longer than depth of box)

Procedure
1. Work with a partner to prepare a model of the ocean floor. First, choose what features you will show. Be sure to include a continental shelf, continental slope, abyssal plain, and mid-ocean ridge. Then use cardboard tubes, modeling clay, and masking tape to form the features of your model along the bottom of the box. Be sure each ocean feature runs from side to side in the box. See Figure 1.
2. After you finish making your model, cut a 1-cm slit in the center of the lid, down its full length. Write your names on the box.
3. Exchange boxes with another pair of classmates. Use your weighted string or chain to "map the ocean floor." At every 1-cm interval along the slit, lower your string or chain.

When it hits the bottom of the "floor," pinch the string or chain gently even with the slit. Keeping your fingers in the same position, pull the string or chain out of the box and measure how deep the string or chain went before touching the bottom. Subtract this number from the height of the box. This will give you the depth of the ocean floor at this spot. Record your data in Graph 1.
4. After completing your map, open the box and check your work. How accurate were you in mapping the ocean floor?

L2

Meeting Different Ability Levels

Content Outline

Reinforcement

Directed Reading

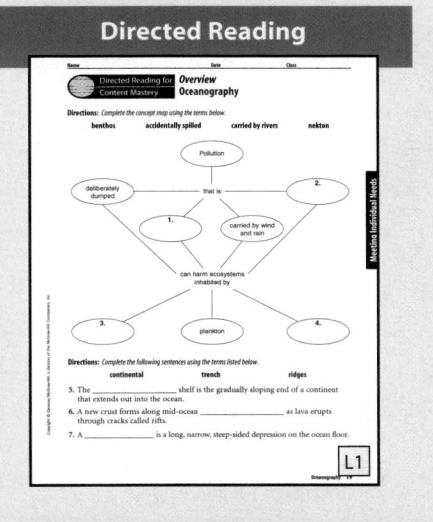

Enrichment

Spanish Directed Reading

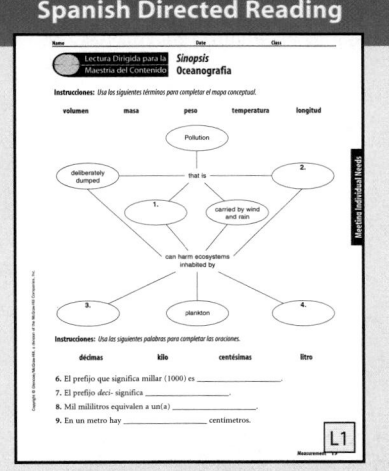

Assessment

Chapter Tests

Test Practice Workbook

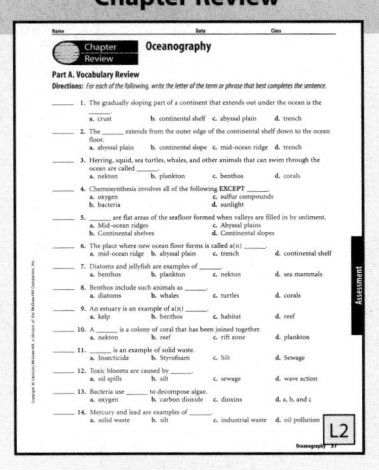

Chapter Review

Science Content Background

SECTION **1**

The Seafloor
The Ocean Basins

When the last ice age was at its peak, sea level was approximately 110 m lower than it is today. Many of the structures on the continental shelf were at or above sea level. This may explain why some seamounts have flattened tops. Perhaps they were at or above sea level during that time and the tops were eroded away. These flat-topped seamounts are called guyots.

Today about three percent of the water-covered Earth is continental shelf. At the base of the continental slope, coarse sediments fall down the slope and are deposited into a mound called the continental rise. Fine-grained sediments are carried farther out onto the ocean floor and deposited as thin layers over existing structures. These layers form the flat abyssal plains.

Fun Fact

Many of the rocks that form the mountains of the world were formed underwater. Evidence of this comes from fossils of marine life found within rocks on mountain slopes and peaks.

Convection currents of molten magma within Earth are thought to be the driving force behind the moving plates. Where two convection currents are moving toward each other, the plates above them converge. If both plates are of the same density, mountains are folded upward, but if a more dense plate (basalt) collides with a less dense continental plate (granite), the ocean plate will slip below the continental plate and melt.

Mineral Resources from the Seafloor

Nations disagree about mining rights to mineral deposits. Since 1958, nations have met to decide international policy at the United Nations Law of the Sea Conferences. Many countries claim mining rights to 322 km of seafloor that borders them. These regions are called their economic zones.

Water beyond the economic zones of all countries is considered to be international water, and many countries have agreed that it cannot be mined. Some countries do not border oceans, but want the right to mine them. Other countries bordering the ocean can mine their own economic zones but want to be able to mine international waters as well.

SECTION **2**

Life in the Ocean
Life Processes

Photosynthetic marine organisms need minerals and sunlight to survive. Water above continental shelves is shallow enough for sunlight to penetrate and is rich in nutrients and minerals because of runoff from the land. Factors such as temperature, light, nutrients, oxygen, substrate, and pollution limit where particular marine organisms can live. These are called limiting factors.

Chuck Davis/Stone

Fun Fact

Sharks are highly adapted fish with few natural enemies. They can lose up to 30,000 teeth in a lifetime.

Ocean Life

Many ocean creatures are bizarre in appearance and behavior, but these adaptations help them survive.

- Lanternfish, which are small deep-water fish, have photophores (light organs) on the sides of their bodies. By flashing their lights in a certain pattern, they can attract mates.

- When a flounder or flatfish is young, it swims like a normal fish and has one eye on either side of its head. As it matures, one of its eyes migrates to the other side of its head. The fish begins swimming along the ocean bottom on its side with both eyes on the top side, looking up.

- Camouflage helps keep many organisms from becoming a meal. For example, a decorator crab attaches sponges to the top of its shell so that it appears to be part of the ocean bottom.

Drugs from the Sea

Special adaptations of some organisms have attracted the attention of pharmaceutical companies. Because some organisms appear to have no natural enemies, scientists are interested in their chemical makeup.

When looking at developing new drugs from the sea, many different disciplines of scientists work together. Biologists and ecologists collect and separate the species. Chemists extract substances from the organisms. Biologists and pharmaceutical specialists test and purify the substances. Finally, researchers perform clinical trials to see whether these substances are effective in the treatment of certain diseases.

Art Brewer/International Stock

SECTION 3

Ocean Pollution

Sources of Pollution

The Environmental Protection Agency conducted a survey in conjunction with the coastal states in 1996 to determine the pollutants in their estuaries. The most common pollutants were excessive nutrients, which were found in 22 percent of the estuaries surveyed. Bacteria such as *E. coli* were the second most prevalent pollutants, indicating the presence of sewage. Bacteria were found to pollute 16 percent of the estuaries surveyed. Organic chemicals (15 percent), oxygen-depleting chemicals (12 percent), and petroleum products (8 percent) were the other major pollutants.

SCIENCE Online

For additional content background on this topic, go to the Glencoe Science Web site at science.glencoe.com.

Oceanography

Chapter Vocabulary

continental shelf
continental slope
abyssal plain
mid-ocean ridge
trench
photosynthesis
chemosynthesis
plankton
nekton
benthos
estuary
reef
pollution

What do you think?

Science Journal This jellyfish lives in the deep ocean. The glow you see is bioluminescence, a process that produces light in an organism's body. Most bioluminescence occurs in the deep oceans where sunlight cannot penetrate. Organisms living there use their own light to attract prey, find mates, and perform other functions needed for survival.

Oceanography

What would it be like to live in the ocean? Imagine all the different organisms you might see. What would the ocean floor look like? In this chapter, you will learn about ocean basin features and the structures located along ocean plate boundaries. You'll learn about the mineral resources found in the ocean. You also will read about many different kinds of ocean inhabitants. Finally, you'll learn how the oceans are being polluted, the effects of this pollution, and what you can do to help clean up the oceans.

What do you think?

Science Journal Examine the photo below with a classmate. Discuss what this might be or what is happening. Here's a hint: *It lives in the dark depths.* Write your answer or best guess in your Science Journal.

548

Theme Connection

Scale and Structure The scale and structure of ocean floor topography are presented.

Scientists use sonar to map the sea bottom. Using the speed of sound waves and the time it takes them to travel, scientists can calculate the depth of the ocean bottom. You will model sonar in this activity.

Model sonar

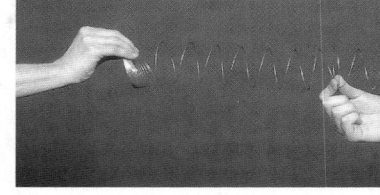

1. With one person holding each end, stretch a spring until it is taut. Measure the distance between the ends.
2. Pinch two coils together. When the spring is steady, release the coils to create a wave.
3. Record the time it takes the wave to travel back and forth five times. Divide this number by five to calculate the time of one round trip.
4. Calculate the speed of the wave by multiplying the distance by two and dividing this number by the time.
5. Move closer to your partner. Take in coils to keep the spring at the same tension. Repeat step three.
6. Calculate the new distance by multiplying the new time by the speed from step four, and then dividing this number by two.

Observe

Write in your Science Journal about how this activity models sonar.

Before You Read

FOLDABLES
Reading & Study Skills

Making a Main Ideas Study Fold
Make the following Foldable to help you identify the major topics about oceanography.

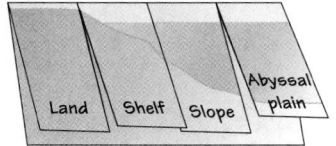

1. Place a sheet of paper in front of you so the long side is at the top. Fold the paper in half from top to bottom.
2. Now fold the paper in half from the left side to the right side two times. Unfold the last two folds.
3. Through the top thickness of paper, cut along each of the fold lines to form four tabs. Label the tabs *Land, Shelf, Slope*, and *Abyssal Plain*.
4. Before you read the chapter, draw the regions of the ocean on the front of the tabs. As you read the chapter, write information about each region under the tabs.

549

EXPLORE ACTIVITY

Purpose Students will model sonar by observing waves traveling on a spring.
Preparation Before beginning the activity, remind students that distance can be calculated from the travel time multiplied by the speed.
Materials large spring, timer

Teaching Strategy

Troubleshooting Keeping the spring at the same tension in step 5 is important for obtaining accurate measurements. Before moving closer together, have students notice the distance between the coils and try to maintain that distance when they move.

✔ *Assessment*

Oral Ask students to compare and contrast the measurements in this activity with real sonar. In both this activity and in real sonar, the speed of compressional wave travel is used to calculate distance. In this activity, the waves travel along a spring. In real sonar, the waves are sound waves. Use **Performance Assessment in the Science Classroom,** p. 89.

Before You Read

FOLDABLES
Reading & Study Skills

Dinah Zike Study Fold
Purpose Students make and use a Foldable diagram. They use it to label the parts of and collect information about the regions of the ocean.

📂 For additional help, see Foldables Worksheet, p. 17 in **Chapter Resources Booklet,** or go to the Glencoe Science Web site at **science.glencoe.com.** See After You Read in the Study Guide at the end of this chapter.

Bellringer Transparency

Display the Section Focus Transparency for Section 1. Use the accompanying Transparency Activity Master. [L2]

ELL

Tie to Prior Knowledge

Have students list landforms with which they are familiar. Explain that throughout their lives, students have observed geological features of Earth's surface. In this section, they will learn about similar structures on the ocean floor.

Caption Answer

Figure 1 Most trenches are in the Pacific basin; the mid-ocean ridge in the mid-Atlantic basin is easy to see.

1 The Seafloor

As You Read

What You'll Learn

- **Differentiate** between a continental shelf and a continental slope.
- **Describe** a mid-ocean ridge, an abyssal plain, and an ocean trench.
- **Identify** the mineral resources found on the continental shelf and in the deep ocean.

Vocabulary

continental shelf   mid-ocean ridge
continental slope   trench
abyssal plain

Why It's Important

Oceans cover nearly three fourths of Earth's surface.

Figure 1
This map shows features of the ocean basins. Locate a trench and a mid-ocean ridge.

The Ocean Basins

Imagine yourself driving a deep-sea submersible along the ocean floor. Surrounded by cold, black water, the lights of your vessel reflect off of what looks like a mountain range ahead. As you continue, you find a huge opening in the seafloor—so deep you can't even see the bottom. What other ocean floor features can you find in **Figure 1?**

Ocean basins, which are low areas of Earth that are filled with water, have many different features. Beginning at the ocean shoreline is the continental shelf. The **continental shelf** is the gradually sloping end of a continent that extends under the ocean. On some coasts, the continental shelf extends a long distance. For instance, on North America's Atlantic and Gulf coasts, it extends 100 km to 350 km into the sea. On the Pacific Coast, where the coastal range mountains are close to the shore, the shelf is only 10 km to 30 km wide. The ocean covering the continental shelf can be as deep as 150 m.

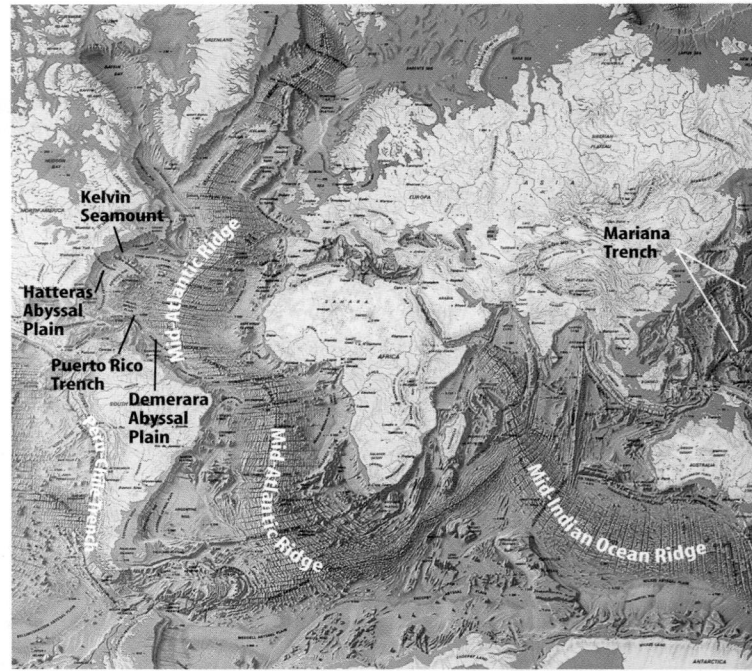

Section ✓Assessment Planner

PORTFOLIO
Science Journal, p. 554
PERFORMANCE ASSESSMENT
Problem-Solving Activity, p. 552
Try at Home MiniLAB, p. 553
Skill Builder Activities, p. 555
See page 576 for more options.

CONTENT ASSESSMENT
Section, p. 555
Challenge, p. 555
Chapter, pp. 576–577

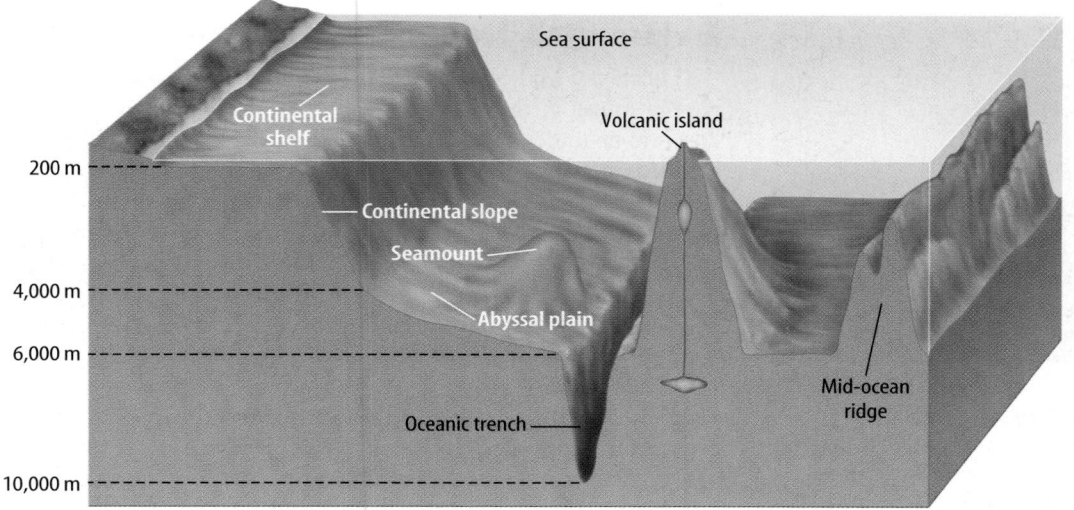

Sea surface

Continental
shelf

200 m

Continental slope

Volcanic island

Seamount

4,000 m

Abyssal plain

6,000 m

Mid-ocean
ridge

Oceanic trench

10,000 m

Figure 2 shows that beyond the shelf, the ocean floor drops more steeply, forming the continental slope. The **continental slope** extends from the outer edge of the continental shelf down to the ocean floor. Beyond the continental slope lie the trenches, valleys, plains, mountains, and ridges of the ocean basin.

In the ocean, currents flow along the continental shelves and down the slopes, depositing sediment on the seafloor. These deposits fill in valleys and create flat seafloor areas called **abyssal** (uh BIH sul) **plains.** Abyssal plains are from 4,000 m to 6,000 m below the ocean surface. Can you locate the abyssal plains shown in **Figure 2?**

In the Atlantic Ocean, areas of completely flat abyssal plains can be large. One example is the Canary Abyssal Plain, which has an area of approximately 900,000 km^2. Other abyssal plains found in the Atlantic Ocean include the Hatteras and Demerara Abyssal Plains, both shown in **Figure 1.** Some areas of abyssal plains have small hills and seamounts. Seamounts are underwater, inactive volcanic peaks. They most commonly are found in the Pacific Ocean. Can you locate a seamount in **Figure 1?**

 **Reading Check** *What are seamounts?*

Figure 2
Ocean basin features are continuous from shore to shore. (Features in this diagram are not to scale.) *Where does the continental shelf end and the continental slope begin?*

SCIENCE
Online

Research Visit the Glencoe Science Web site at **science.glencoe.com** for more information about ocean basins. Communicate to your class what you learn.

SECTION 1 The Seafloor **551**

Aleutian
Abyssal Plain

East Pacific Rise

Peru-Chile Trench

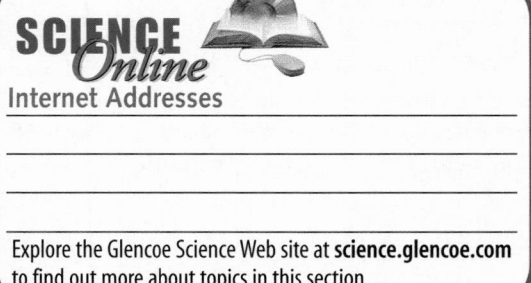

Resource Manager

Chapter Resources Booklet
Transparency Activity, p. 44
Directed Reading for Content Mastery,
pp. 19, 20
Note-taking Worksheets, pp. 33–35

SCIENCE
Online
Internet Addresses

Explore the Glencoe Science Web site at **science.glencoe.com** to find out more about topics in this section.

2 Teach

The Ocean Basins

Activity
Obtain bathymetric maps (topographic maps of the bottom of the ocean). Refer to the maps frequently throughout this section. Have students contrast the width of the continental shelf off the east coast of the United States with that off the west coast. The shelf off the east coast is much wider. L2 **IS Visual-Spatial**

Caption Answer
Figure 2 The shelf ends and the slope begins where the elevation drops steeply.

Visual Learning

Figure 2 Have students describe the structure of trenches and islands. Trenches are like very deep valleys. Islands look like the tops of mountains. L2 **IS Linguistic**

Use Science Words
Word Meaning Have students find out why plains from 4,000 to 6,000 m below the ocean's surface are called *abyssal plains. Abyssal* relates to bottom waters in the ocean. L2 **IS Linguistic**

✔ Reading Check

Answer submerged, inactive volcanic peaks

Ridges and Trenches

Discussion

Where is the oldest crust on the Atlantic Ocean bottom? Where is the youngest crust? The oldest is at its margins; the youngest is in its middle.

✔ Reading Check

Answer Lava erupting from mid-ocean ridges forms new ocean floor.

Math Skills Activity

National Math Standards

Correlation to Mathematics Objectives

1, 2, 5, 9

Answer to Practice Problem

- What you know: width = 40 km increase in depth = 2,000 m
- What you need to find: slope s
- Equation to use: s = 2,000 m ÷ 40 km = 50 m/km
- Answer: 50 m/km

Figure 3
New seafloor forms at mid-ocean ridges. A type of lava called pillow lava lies newly formed at this ridge on the ocean floor.

Ridges and Trenches

Locate the Mid-Atlantic Ridge in **Figure 1**. Mid-ocean ridges can be found at the bottom of all ocean basins. They form a continuous underwater ridge approximately 65,000 km long. A **mid-ocean ridge** is the area in an ocean basin where new ocean floor is formed. Crustal plates, which are large sections of Earth's uppermost mantle and crust, are moving constantly. As they move, the ocean floor changes. When ocean plates separate, hot magma from Earth's interior forms new ocean crust. This is the process of seafloor spreading. New ocean floor is being formed at a rate of approximately 2.5 cm per year along the Mid-Atlantic Ridge.

New ocean floor forms along mid-ocean ridges as lava erupts through cracks in Earth's crust. **Figure 3** shows newly erupted lava on the seafloor. When the lava hits the water, it cools quickly into solid rock, forming new seafloor. While seafloor is being formed in some parts of the oceans, it is being destroyed in others. Areas where old ocean floor slides beneath another plate and descends into Earth's mantle are called subduction zones.

✔ Reading Check *How does new ocean floor form?*

Math Skills Activity

Calculating a Feature's Slope

Example Problem

If the width of a continental shelf is 320 km and it increases in depth a total of 500 m in that distance, what is its slope?

Solution

1 *This is what you know:* width = 320 km
increase in depth = 500 m

2 *This is what you need to find:* slope: s

3 *This is the equation you need to use:* s = increase in depth ÷ width

4 *Solve the equation by substituting in known values:* s = 500 m ÷ 320 km = 1.56 m/km

Practice Problem

The width of a continental slope is 40 km. It increases in depth by 2,000 m. What is the slope of the continental slope?

For more help, refer to the Math Skill Handbook.

Science Journal

Ocean Features Ask each student to write a paragraph that begins, "Many landforms were revealed the day the oceans suddenly disappeared. I saw. . ." L2 IN **Linguistic**

Teacher FYI

Four general ocean depths are recognized. The neritic depth is 0–200 m below the surface, and the bathyal depth is 200–2,000 m. The abyssal depth is 2,000–6,000 m below the surface. Eighty-five percent of the ocean floor is at abyssal depth. The hadal depth is anything deeper than 6,000 m.

Figure 4
Located at convergent boundaries, trenches are important ocean basin features.

A In 1960 the world's deepest dive was made in the Mariana Trench. The *Trieste* carried Jacque Piccard and Donald Walsh to a depth of almost 11 km.

Height of Mt. Everest

11,000 m

Depth of trench

B If Earth's tallest mountain, Mount Everest, were set in the bottom of the Mariana Trench of the Pacific Basin, it would be covered with more than 2,000 m of water.

Subduction Zones On the ocean floor, subduction zones are marked by deep ocean trenches. A **trench** is a long, narrow, steep-sided depression where one crustal plate sinks beneath another. Most trenches are found in the Pacific Basin. Ocean trenches are usually longer and deeper than any valley on any continent. One trench, famous for its depth, is the Mariana Trench. It is located to the south and east of Japan in the Pacific Basin. This trench reaches 11 km below the surface of the water, and it is the deepest place in the Pacific. **Figure 4A** shows the deep-sea vessel, the *Trieste,* that descended into the trench in 1960. **Figure 4B** shows that the Mariana Trench is so deep that Mount Everest could easily fit into it.

Mineral Resources from the Seafloor

Resources can be found in many places in the ocean. Some deposits on the continental shelf are relatively easy to extract. Others can be found only in the deep abyssal regions on the ocean floor. People still are trying to figure out how to get these valuable resources to the surface. As you read, suggest some methods that could be used to retrieve hard-to-reach resources.

SECTION 1 The Seafloor **553**

Use an Analogy

Relate what happens at trenches and rifts to recycling. At trenches, crustal material disappears into the mantle. At rifts, material from the mantle emerges to form new crust. In this way, Earth's crust is recycled.

Curriculum Connection

History In 1960, Auguste Piccard's bathyscaphe submersible, the *Trieste,* descended to the deepest point a person has ever been, the Mariana Trench (–10,912 meters). Have students research to find out more about the *Trieste* expedition.  **Linguistic**

Mineral Resources from the Seafloor

Caption Answer

Figure 5 phosphorite: Pacific coast of North America; diamonds: Southern Africa, Eastern India, Southeast Asia, Northern Australia

Quick Demo

To demonstrate the settling rates of sediments where rivers flow into oceans, pour a mixture of gravel, sand, and powdered clay into a jar of water. Put a lid on the jar and slowly swirl the contents until they are well mixed. Allow the sediments to settle. Students will observe that the gravel will settle to the bottom first, followed by the sand, and then the clay. **Why does the gravel settle first?** It has the largest particle size and is the heaviest of the three sediments.

IS **Visual-Spatial**

Extension

Have students write research reports about how placer deposits are mined. Reports should describe panning and sluicing. L2 **IS** **Linguistic**

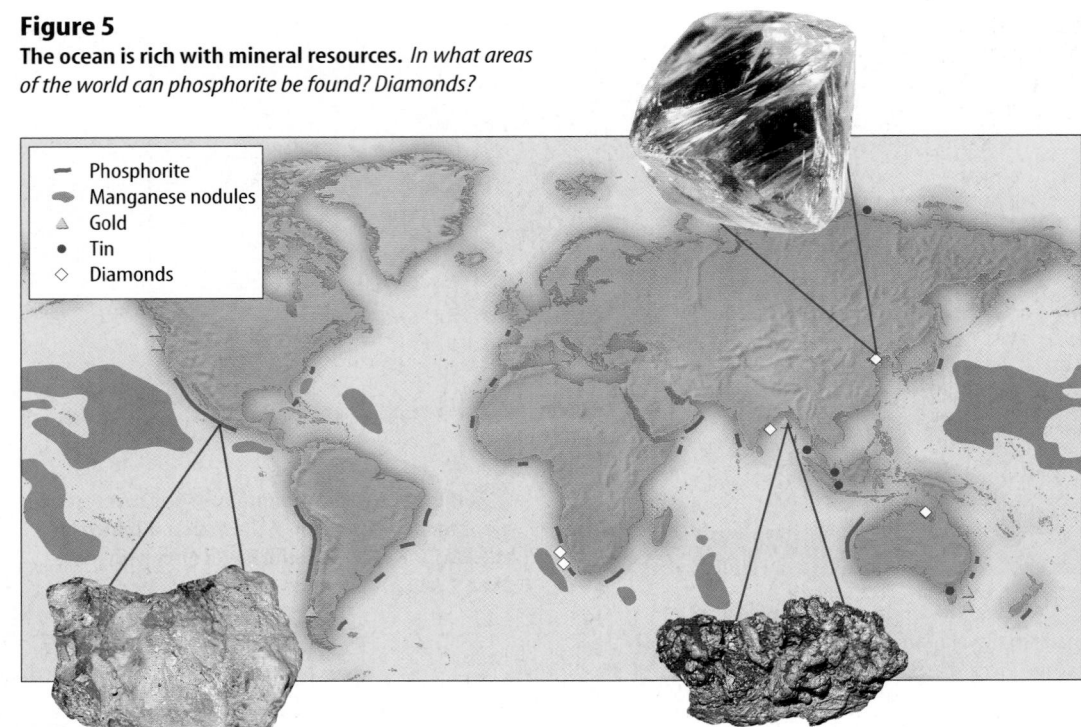

Figure 5
The ocean is rich with mineral resources. *In what areas of the world can phosphorite be found? Diamonds?*

- — Phosphorite
- Manganese nodules
- △ Gold
- • Tin
- ◇ Diamonds

Continental Shelf Deposits A high amount of organic activity occurs in the waters above the continental shelf, and sediment accumulates to great thickness on the ocean floor. This is why many different kinds of resources can be found there, such as petroleum and natural gas deposits. Approximately 20 percent of the world's oil comes from under the seabed. To extract these substances, wells are drilled into the seafloor from floating vessels and fixed platforms.

Other deposits on the continental shelf include phosphorite, which is used to make fertilizer, and limestone, which is used to make cement. Sand and gravel, both economically important, also can be dredged from the continental shelf.

Rivers that flow into oceans transport important minerals to the continental shelf from land. Sometimes the energy of ocean waves and currents can cause denser mineral grains that have been brought in by rivers to concentrate in one place. These deposits, called placer (PLAHS ur) deposits, can occur in coastal regions where rivers entering the ocean suddenly lose energy, slow down, and drop their sediment. Metals such as gold and titanium and gemstones such as diamonds are mined from placer deposits in some coastal regions. **Figure 5** shows where some resources in the ocean can be found.

Resource Manager

Chapter Resources Booklet
  Enrichment, p. 30
  Reinforcement, p. 27
Earth Science Critical Thinking/Problem Solving, p. 1

Science Journal

Law of the Sea Many nations disagree about mining rights to mineral deposits on the ocean floor. Ask students to research United Nations Law of the Sea Conferences, find out why nations disagree, and summarize the information in a brief report. Students may find nations disagree on definition of international waters. There are also environmental questions. L3 **IS** **Linguistic** P

Deep-Water Deposits Through the holes and cracks along mid-ocean ridges, chimneys of hot water billow out into surrounding seawater. As the superheated water cools, mineral deposits sometimes form. As a result, elements such as sulfur and metals like iron, copper, zinc, and silver can be concentrated in these areas. Today, no one is mining these valuable materials from the depths because it would be too expensive to recover them. However, in the future, these deposits could become important.

Other mineral deposits can precipitate from seawater. In this process, minerals that are dissolved in ocean water come out of solution and form solids on the ocean floor. Manganese nodules are small, black lumps strewn across 20 percent to 50 percent of the Pacific Basin. **Figure 6** shows these nodules. Manganese nodules form by a chemical process that is not fully understood. They form around nuclei such as discarded shark's teeth, growing slowly, perhaps as little as 1 mm to 10 mm per million years. These nodules are rich in manganese, copper, iron, nickel, and cobalt, all of which are used in the manufacture of steel, paint, and batteries. Most of the nodules lie thousands of meters deep in the ocean and are not currently being mined, although suction devices similar to huge vacuum cleaners have been tested to collect them.

Figure 6
These manganese nodules were found on the floor of the Pacific Ocean. *Can you think of an efficient way to gather them from a depth of 4 km?*

3 Assess

Reteach
Organize the class into groups of five. Have each student in the group write one of the terms learned in this section on one side of a note card and its meaning on the opposite side. Then, have students quiz one another on the terms. L1 COOP LEARN
Interpersonal

Challenge
Have the ocean basins always been in the same locations as they are today? Explain. No; locations have changed throughout geologic time because of moving plates, formation of new ocean floor, destruction of old ocean crust, and climatic change. L3
Logical Mathematical

Assessment
Oral Which ocean basins are getting larger? Which is getting smaller? How do you know? The Atlantic and Indian Basins are getting larger; the plates are diverging at the mid-ocean ridges. The Pacific Basin is getting smaller; crust is sinking into its trenches as plates converge. Use **Performance Assessment in the Science Classroom,** p. 89.

Section 1 Assessment

1. Compare and contrast continental shelves and continental slopes.
2. Contrast mid-ocean ridges and trenches.
3. Describe what an abyssal plain looks like and how it forms.
4. How do placer deposits form? Name two examples of placer deposits that are mined. How do manganese nodules form?
5. **Think Critically** The depth soundings taken as a ship moves across an ocean are consistently between 4,000 m and 4,500 m. Infer over which area of seafloor the ship is passing.

Skill Builder Activities

6. **Comparing and Contrasting** Compare and contrast the Atlantic Ocean Basin with the Pacific Ocean Basin. Which basin contains many deep-sea trenches? Which basin is getting larger with time? **For more help, refer to the** Science Skill Handbook.
7. **Using Statistics** Each year for three years, the distance between two locations across an ocean basin increases by 1.8 cm, 4.1 cm, and 3.2 cm respectively. What is the average rate of separation of these locations during this time? **For more help, refer to the** Math Skill Handbook.

Answers to Section Assessment

1. They are adjacent to each other. Shelves are relatively flat; slopes are steep.
2. Both are on the ocean basin floor. Mid-ocean ridges are mountains formed where plates diverge. Trenches are valleys formed where plates converge and one plate moves under the other.
3. An abyssal plain is very flat, and it forms where deposits fill in valleys on the ocean basin floor.
4. Placers form where rivers enter the ocean, lose their energy of motion, and drop sediments; examples: metals, diamonds. Manganese nodules form in deep water by a chemical process.
5. the abyssal plain
6. They are both large oceans that touch the American Continents; The Pacific Ocean Basin has the most trenches, where crustal plates slide under one other; the Atlantic Ocean Basin's plates are separating, which means the basin is getting larger.
7. 3.03 cm per year

ACTIVITY

Purpose Students make and analyze a profile map of the ocean floor. [L3] COOP LEARN [P]

IS Visual-Spatial and Kinesthetic

Process Skills using numbers, observing and inferring, interpreting data, forming operational definitions, interpreting scientific illustrations, making models, measuring in SI

Time Required 30 to 40 minutes

Teaching Strategy Be sure that students realize that the graph is set up in a form that is different from what they may be used to. Usually, zero is at the bottom of the vertical axis. However, on this graph, it is at the top of the vertical axis because the data represent depths below sea level. Students may become confused and reverse the data as they begin to plot the points.

Answers to Questions

1. A continental slope occurs between 160 and 1,050 km. The Mid-Atlantic Ridge occurs between 2,000 and 4,500 km from New Jersey. A continental slope lies between 5,300 and 5,600 km from New Jersey.

2. No; the profile has extensive vertical exaggeration. To make an accurate profile, the vertical and horizontal scales must be the same.

ACTIVITY

Mapping the Ocean Floor

How do people know what the ocean floor looks like? Scientists use sonar and radar to identify structures on the ocean floor. Data from these instruments are used to calculate the distance to the bottom. You will use data collected in the Atlantic Ocean to make a bottom profile.

What You'll Investigate
What does the ocean floor look like?

Materials
graph paper

Goals
- **Make** a profile of the ocean floor.
- **Identify** seafloor structures.

Procedure

1. Set up a graph as shown.

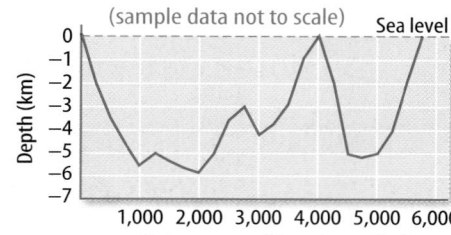

2. **Plot** each data point and connect the points with a smooth line.

3. **Color** water blue and the seafloor brown.

Conclude and Apply

1. What ocean floor structures occur between 160 km and 1,050 km east of New Jersey? Between 2,000 km and 4,500 km? Between 5,300 km and 5,650 km?

Ocean Floor Data		
Station Number	Distance from New Jersey (km)	Depth to Ocean Floor (m)
1	0	0
2	160	165
3	200	1,800
4	500	3,500
5	1,050	5,450
6	1,450	5,100
7	1,800	5,300
8	2,000	5,600
9	2,300	4,750
10	2,400	3,500
11	2,600	3,100
12	3,000	4,300
13	3,200	3,900
14	3,450	3,400
15	3,550	2,100
16	3,700	1,275
17	3,950	1,000
18	4,000	0
19	4,100	1,800
20	4,350	3,650
21	4,500	5,100
22	5,000	5,000
23	5,300	4,200
24	5,450	1,800
25	5,500	920
26	5,650	0

2. When a profile of a feature is drawn to scale, the horizontal and vertical scales must be the same. Does your profile give an accurate picture of the ocean floor? Explain.

Performance To further assess students' understanding of the ocean floor profile, have them draw a profile of an abyssal plain and a seamount. Use **Performance Assessment in the Science Classroom,** p. 127.

Resource Manager

Chapter Resources Booklet
Activity Worksheet, pp. 5–6
Lab Activity, pp. 9–11

Life in the Ocean

Life Processes

Life processes such as breathing oxygen, eating and digesting food, making new cells, and growing take place in your body every day. It takes energy to do this plus walk from one classroom to another or play soccer. Organisms that live in the ocean also carry out life processes every day. The octopus shown in **Figure 7** will get the oxygen it needs from the water. It will have to eat, and it will use energy to capture prey and to escape predators. It will make new cells and eventually reproduce. Like other marine organisms, it is adapted to accomplish these processes in the salty water of the ocean.

One of the most important processes in the ocean, as it is on land, is that organisms obtain food to use for energy. Obtaining the food necessary to survive can be done in several ways.

Life Science
INTEGRATION

Photosynthesis Nearly all of the energy used by organisms in the ocean ultimately comes from the Sun. Radiant energy from the Sun penetrates seawater to an average depth of 100 m. Marine organisms such as plants and algae use energy from the Sun to build their tissues and produce their own food. This process of making food is called **photosynthesis**. During photosynthesis, carbon dioxide and water are changed to sugar and oxygen in the presence of sunlight. Organisms that undergo photosynthesis are called producers. Marine producers include sea grasses, seaweeds, and microscopic algae. Although they might seem unimportant because they are small, microscopic algae are responsible for approximately 90 percent of all marine production. Seaweeds account for only about two percent to five percent of total marine production. Organisms that feed on producers are called consumers. Consumers in the marine environment include shrimp, fish, dolphins, whales, and sharks.

As You Read

What You'll Learn

- **Describe** photosynthesis and chemosynthesis in the oceans.
- **List** the key characteristics of plankton, nekton, and benthos.
- **Compare and contrast** ocean margin habitats.

Vocabulary

photosynthesis	benthos
chemosynthesis	estuary
plankton	reef
nekton	

Why It's Important

The ocean environment is fragile, and many organisms, including humans, depend on it for their survival.

Figure 7
Hunting at night, this Pacific octopus feeds on snails and crabs. It uses camouflage, ink, and speed to avoid predators.

SECTION 2 Life in the Ocean **557**

SECTION

2

Life in the Ocean

1 Motivate

Bellringer Transparency

Display the Section Focus Transparency for Section 2. Use the accompanying Transparency Activity Master. L2
ELL

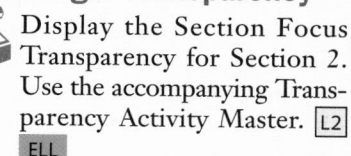

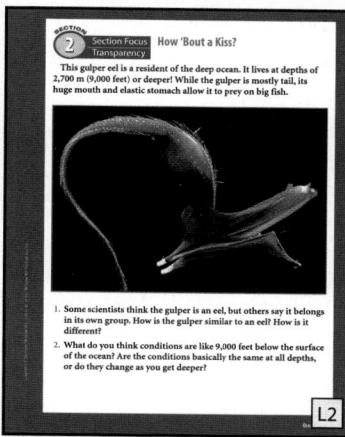

Tie to Prior Knowledge

Review the structure of a simple food chain, such as Sun ➡ grass ➡ cow ➡ humans. Remind students that they have observed different kinds of organisms interacting with one another. In this section, they will learn about life processes in the ocean, including the transfer of energy through food webs.

Section ✓Assessment Planner

PORTFOLIO
Curriculum Connection, p. 559

PERFORMANCE ASSESSMENT
MiniLAB, p. 561
Skill Builder Activities, p. 564
See page 576 for more options.

CONTENT ASSESSMENT
Section, p. 564
Challenge, p. 564
Chapter, pp. 576–577

Life Processes

Life Science INTEGRATION

Have students sketch an energy pyramid, showing how energy is lost as it is passed up a food chain.

Discussion

What happens to the wastes of organisms that live in the oceans? The wastes dissolve in seawater and decay. They are then used as nutrients by other organisms.

✔ Reading Check

Answer energy

Make a Model

Have student teams make mobiles of food chains that exist in the ocean. Hang the mobiles from the classroom ceiling. L2 ELL COOP LEARN
IS Kinesthetic

Visual Learning

Figure 8 Have a student volunteer compare and contrast the food chains that include great white sharks and whale sharks. L2

Life Science INTEGRATION

As energy is passed through the food chain, only about 10 percent of the total energy available is stored by a consumer at each level of the food chain. Most of the energy is lost as an organism carries out daily life processes.

Figure 8
Numerous food chains exist in the ocean. Some food chains are simple and some are complex.

Energy Relationships Energy from the Sun is transferred through food chains. Although the organisms of the ocean capture only a small part of the Sun's energy, this energy is passed from producer to consumer, then to other consumers. In **Figure 8,** notice that in one food chain, a large whale shark consumes small, shrimplike organisms as its basic food. In the other chain, microscopic algae found in water are eaten by microscopic animals called copepods (KOH pah pahdz). The copepods are, in turn, eaten by herring. Cod eat the herring, seals eat the cod, and eventually great white sharks eat the seals. At each stage in the food chain, energy obtained by one organism is used by other organisms to move, grow, repair cells, reproduce, and eliminate waste.

✔ Reading Check   *What is passed on at each stage in a food chain?*

In an ecosystem—a community of organisms and their environment—many complex feeding relationships exist. Most organisms depend on more than one species for food. For example, herring eat more than copepods, cod eat more than herring, seals eat more than cod, and white sharks eat more than seals. In an ecosystem, food chains overlap and are connected much like the threads of a spider's web. These highly complex systems are called food webs.

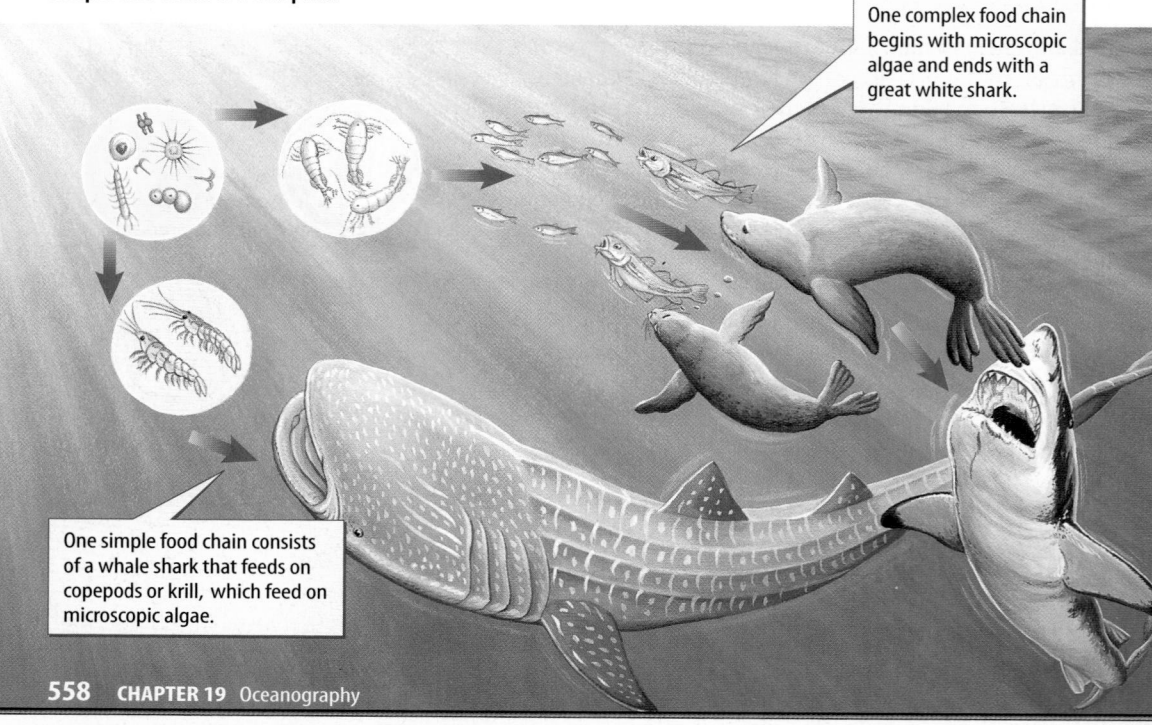

One complex food chain begins with microscopic algae and ends with a great white shark.

One simple food chain consists of a whale shark that feeds on copepods or krill, which feed on microscopic algae.

558   CHAPTER 19 Oceanography

✔ Active Reading

Learning Journal Have students draw a vertical line down each page of the Learning Journal. Have them enter research notes, lecture notes, or vocabulary terms on the left. On the right, have them respond to, interpret, question, or analyze left column entries. Suggest students write a Learning Journal about energy relationships in the ocean.

Curriculum Connection

Math Blue whales can consume 8 metric tons of krill daily. Adults average 26 m in length and have a mass of 137 metric tons. Have students calculate the number of grams of krill a blue whale consumes each day and the length in centimeters and mass in kilograms of an average adult blue whale. 8 million g of krill each day, 2,600 cm long, mass of 137,000 kg IS **Logical-Mathematical**

Chemosynthesis Other types of food webs do not depend on the Sun and photosynthesis. These food webs depend on bacteria that perform chemosynthesis. **Chemosynthesis** (kee moh SIHN thuh sus) involves using sulfur or nitrogen compounds as an energy source, instead of light from the Sun, to produce food. Bacteria that perform chemosynthesis using sulfur compounds live along mid-ocean ridges near hydrothermal vents where no light is available. Recall that superheated water from the crust contains high amounts of sulfur. The bacteria found here form the base of a food chain and support a host of highly specialized organisms such as giant tube worms, clams, crabs, and shrimp.

Other Life Processes Reproduction also is a vital life process. Some organisms, such as corals and sponges, depend on ocean currents for successful reproduction. Shown in **Figure 9,** these organisms release reproductive cells into the water where they unite to form more organisms of the same type. Other organisms, such as salmon and the Atlantic eel, travel long distances across the ocean in order to reproduce in a specific location. One important aspect of successful reproduction is finding a safe place for eggs and newly hatched larvae to develop. You will learn later in this section that some places in the ocean are used by marine organisms for this purpose.

Ocean Life

Many varieties of plants and animals live in the ocean. Although some organisms live in the open ocean or on the deep ocean floor, most marine organisms live in the waters above or on the floor of the continental shelf. In this relatively shallow water, the Sun penetrates to the bottom, allowing for photosynthesis. Because light is available for photosynthesis, large numbers of producers live in the waters above the continental shelf. These waters also contain many nutrients that producers use to carry out life processes. As a result, the greatest source of food is located in the waters of the continental shelf.

Figure 9
Because sponges live attached to the ocean bottom, they depend on currents to carry their reproductive cells to nearby sponges. *What would happen if a sponge settled in an area without strong currents?*

Resource Manager

Chapter Resources Booklet
Transparency Activity, p. 45
Directed Reading for Content Mastery, p. 21

Curriculum Connection

Literature Suggest that students read a poem about the ocean. Ask them to write a paragraph on how the ocean and ocean life were used in the poem. Paragraphs may say fish from the ocean were used for food, or products were made from ocean life. L2

 **Linguistic** P

Discussion
Compare and contrast photosynthesis and chemosynthesis. Both result in the production of food and oxygen. During photosynthesis, producers use sunlight as the energy source. During chemosynthesis, bacteria use sulfur and nitrogen compounds as energy sources.

Caption Answer
Figure 9 Their reproductive cells could not be widely dispersed. Some students may also suggest that the sponge would starve, as these organisms rely on currents to bring nutrients to their bodies.

SCIENCE Online
Internet Addresses

_____
_____
_____
_____

Explore the Glencoe Science Web site at **science.glencoe.com** to find out more about topics in this section.

Ocean Life

IDENTIFYING Misconceptions

Students may think that only animals respire. Plants and algae produce food through photosynthesis. They also break down complex organic molecules and obtain energy from them in the process of respiration.

Ocean Life, continued

Activity

For every 10 m in depth, water pressure increases 1 kg/cm². Have students calculate the pressure that a deep-sea fish experiences. Multiply 1,000 × 4 to find the depth in meters. To complete the calculation, divide 4,000 m by 10 m. Then, multiply that number by 1 kg/cm², and add 1 kg/cm² (the pressure of the air at sea level). The answer is 401 kg/cm². Challenge students to calculate the pressure on organisms living at the bottom of the Mariana Trench (10,912 m). 1,092.2 kg/cm² [L3]

 **Logical-Mathematical**

Chemistry INTEGRATION

Students may be familiar with the bioluminence of fireflies. Fireflies produce light by the oxidation of luciferin. In fireflies, the flashing is probably a mating response. In marine organisms, flashing is used to attract food or a mate or to temporarily blind predators.

✔ Reading Check

Answer animals that actively swim rather than drift with the current

Figure 10
A Diatoms are phytoplankton that live in freshwater and ocean water. **B** The zooplankton shown here is a copepod. Although it has reached its adult size, it is still microscopic.

Chemistry INTEGRATION

Some marine organisms, including types of bacteria, one-celled algae, and fish can make their own light through a process called bioluminescence. The main molecule involved in producing light is luciferin. During a chemical reaction involving salt and water, the luciferin changes structure. In the process, a burst of light is given off.

Plankton Marine organisms that drift with the currents are called **plankton.** Plankton range from microscopic algae and animals to organisms as large as jellyfish. Most phytoplankton—plankton that are producers—are one-celled organisms that float in the upper layers of the ocean where light needed for photosynthesis is available. One abundant form of phytoplankton is a one-celled organism called a diatom. Diatoms are shown in **Figure 10A.** Diatoms and other phytoplankton are the source of food for zooplankton, animals that drift with ocean currents.

Examples of zooplankton include newly hatched fish and crabs, jellyfish, and tiny adults of some organisms like the one shown in **Figure 10B.** These organisms feed on phytoplankton and are usually the second step in ocean food chains. Most animal plankton depend on surface currents to move them, but some can swim short distances.

Nekton Animals that actively swim, rather than drift with the currents in the ocean, are called **nekton.** Nekton include all swimming forms of fish and other animals, from tiny herring to huge whales. Nekton can be found from polar regions to the tropics and from shallow water to the deepest parts of the ocean. In **Figure 11,** the Greenland shark, the manatee, and the deep-ocean fish are all nekton. As nekton move throughout the oceans, it is important that they are able to control their buoyancy, or how easily they float or sink. What happens when you hold your breath underwater then let all of the air out of your lungs at once? The air provides buoyancy and helps you float. As the air is released, you sink. Many fish have a special organ filled with gas that helps them control their buoyancy. By changing their buoyancy, organisms can change their depth in the ocean. The ability to move between different depths allows animals to search more areas for food.

✔ Reading Check *What are nekton?*

Some deep-dwelling nekton are adapted with special light-generating organs. The light has several uses for these organisms. The deep-sea fish, shown in **Figure 11C,** dangles a luminous lure from beneath its jaw. When prey attracted by the lure are close enough, they are swallowed quickly. Some deep-sea organisms use this light to momentarily blind predators so they can escape. Others use it to attract mates.

LAB DEMONSTRATION

Purpose to demonstrate buoyancy
Materials 2-L plastic bottle with cap, dropper, water, 1,000-mL beaker
Preparation Fill the beaker with water. Fill the bottle three-quarters full with water.
Procedure Draw water into the dropper from the beaker, allowing the dropper to float. Adjust the amount of water in the dropper until the bottom of its bulb is level with the water in the beaker. Place the dropper in the bottle. Cap the bottle. Then squeeze and release the bottle.
Expected Outcome The dropper sank when the bottle was squeezed and rose when pressure was released.

✔ Assessment

Why did the dropper move up and down? When water was pushed into the dropper, it gained mass, became less buoyant, and sank. When pressure was released, air in the dropper expanded and pushed water out, mass was lost, buoyancy increased, and the dropper rose.

Figure 11
Nekton are found living in all areas of the ocean, warm or cold, shallow or deep.

A This Greenland shark lives in the cold waters of the North Atlantic.

B Manatees are found in tropical regions around the world.

C This deep-sea fish deals with living under pressure at a depth of 4 km.

Bottom Dwellers The plants and animals living on or in the seafloor are the **benthos** (BEN thohs). Benthic animals include crabs, snails, sea urchins, and bottom-dwelling fish such as flounder. These organisms move or swim across the bottom to find food. Other benthic animals that live permanently attached to the bottom, such as sea anemones and sponges, filter out food particles from seawater. Certain types of worms live burrowed in the sediment of the ocean floor. Bottom-dwelling animals can be found living from the shallow water of the continental shelf to the deepest areas of the ocean. Benthic plants and algae, however, are limited to the shallow areas of the ocean where enough sunlight penetrates the water to allow for photosynthesis. One example of a benthic algae is kelp, which is anchored to the bottom and grows toward the surface from depths of up to 30 m.

Ocean Margin Habitats

The area of the environment where a plant or animal normally lives is called a habitat. Along the near-shore areas of the continental shelf, called ocean margins, a variety of habitats exist. Beaches, rocky shores, estuaries, and coral reefs are some examples of the different habitats found along ocean margins.

Ocean Margin Habitats

Activity

Explain that some scientists predict future human societies will live in underwater cities. Have students design such a city. Have them plan their cities so that waves and currents will not threaten the city; the rough terrain and tremendous water pressure will not be problems; and people will have air, food, and drinking water. L2 ELL COOP LEARN
IS **Kinesthetic and Interpersonal**

Extension

Make a list of various kinds of seafood. Have each student select one organism from the list and write a brief profile describing its appearance, habitat, source of food or nutrients, and importance in marine food webs. L2 IS **Linguistic**

Caption Answer

Figure 12 Encourage students to completely describe the habitat in which they would like to live.

SCIENCE *Online*
Internet Addresses

_____

_____

_____

_____

Explore the Glencoe Science Web site at **science.glencoe.com** to find out more about topics in this section.

SCIENCE *Online*

Research Visit the Glencoe Science Web site at **science.glencoe.com** for more information about beach erosion. Communicate to your class what you learn.

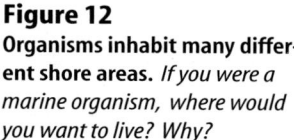

Figure 12
Organisms inhabit many different shore areas. *If you were a marine organism, where would you want to live? Why?*

Beaches At the edge of a sandy beach where the waves splash, you can find some microscopic organisms and worms that spend their entire lives between moist grains of sand. Burrowing animals such as small clams and mole crabs make holes in the sand. When water covers the holes, these animals rise to the surface to filter food from the water. Where sand is covered constantly by water, larger animals like horseshoe crabs, snails, fish, turtles, and sand dollars reside. **Figure 12** shows some of the organisms that are found living on sandy beaches.

Although the beach is great fun for people, it is a very stressful environment for the plants and animals that live there. They constantly deal with waves, changing tides, and storms, all of which redistribute large amounts of sand. Large waves produced by storms, such as hurricanes, can cause damage to beaches as they crash onto shore. These organisms must adapt to natural change as well as changes created by humans. Damming rivers, building harbors, and constructing homes and hotels near the shoreline disrupts natural processes on the beach.

Rocky Shore Areas In some regions the shoreline is rocky, as shown in **Figure 13.** Algae, sea anemones, mussels, and barnacles encrust submerged rocks. Sea stars, sea urchins, octopuses, and hermit crabs crawl along the rock surfaces, looking for food.

Tide pools are formed when water remains onshore, trapped by the rocks during low tide. Tide pools are an important habitat for many marine organisms. They serve as protected areas where many animals such as octopus and fish can develop safely from juveniles to adults. Tide pools contain an abundance of food and offer protection from larger predators.

Inclusion Strategies

Gifted Have students research different symbiotic relationships in the oceans, including competition, predation, parasitism, and mutualism. Students can use pictures or their own drawings to present their findings to the class.
L3 IS **Linguistic and Visual-Spatial**

Curriculum Connection

Art Have students make a mural showing a cross section of the ocean from the shore to the deep ocean. The mural should show the diversity of life that occurs from the ocean floor to the surface and from the shore to the deep ocean. L2 ELL COOP LEARN IS **Visual-Spatial**

Figure 13

Life is tough in the intertidal zone—the coastal area between the highest high tide and the lowest low tide. Organisms here are pounded by waves and alternately covered and uncovered by water as tides rise and fall. These organisms tend to cluster into three general zones along the shore. Where they live depends on how well they tolerate being washed by waves, submerged at high tide, or exposed to air and sunlight when the tide is low.

Upper intertidal zone

Mid-intertidal zone

Lower intertidal zone

UPPER INTERTIDAL ZONE This part of the intertidal zone is splashed by high waves and is usually covered by water only during the highest tides each month. It is home to crabs that scuttle among periwinkle snails, limpets, and a few kinds of algae that can withstand long periods of dryness.

Wavy turban snail

Stone crab

Periwinkle

Algae

MID-INTERTIDAL ZONE Submerged at most high tides and exposed at most low tides, this zone is populated by brown algae, sponges, barnacles, mussels, chitons, snails, and sea stars. These creatures are resistant to drying out and good at clinging to slippery surfaces.

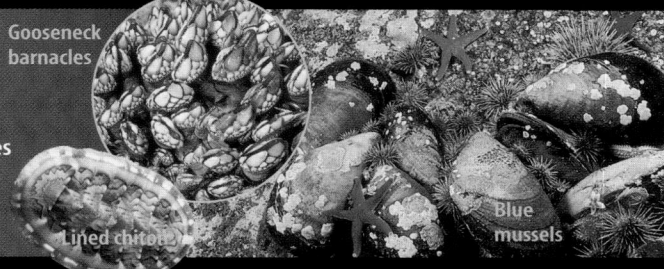

Gooseneck barnacles

Lined chiton

Blue mussels

LOWER INTERTIDAL ZONE This section of the intertidal zone is exposed only during the lowest tides each month. It contains the most diverse collection of living things. Here you find sea urchins, large sea stars, brittle stars, nudibranchs, sea cucumbers, anemones, and many kinds of fish.

Sea lemon nudibranch

African sea star

Sea urchins

SECTION 2 Life in the Ocean **563**

Resarce Manager

Chapter Resources Booklet
Enrichment, p. 31
Reinforcement, p. 28

Earth Science Critical Thinking/Problem Solving, p. 16

Visualizing the Rocky Shore Habitat

Have students examine the pictures and read the captions. Then ask the following questions.

Mussels feed by straining tiny bits of food from ocean water. Why do they live in the mid-intertidal zone rather than the upper intertidal zone? In the upper intertidal zone, they would be covered by water only during the highest tides each month and would not be able to get enough food, but in the mid-intertidal zone, they are submerged a most high tides so they are able to get enough food.

How would life in the intertidal zone be affected if sea levels rose by several meters? Organisms that live in the intertidal zone would have to be able to move higher if sea levels rose. Those that were not able to do so might not survive.

Activity

Organize the class into three groups. Assign each group one of the three intertidal zones. Have them research. information about how the organisms that live there are specifically adapted to life in that zone. Have each group make a multimedia presentation of its information to the class. L2 COOP LEARN
IS Naturalist and Linguistic

Extension

Have students locate an area where people could visit to experience a rocky shore habitat. Have students prepare a travel brochure on the area. L2
IS Linguistic

Ocean Margin Habitats, continued

Discussion

Why might nekton choose to live within a reef? Reefs provide shelter from predators and readily available sources of food.

③ Assess

Reteach

Have each student write the names of three marine organisms on separate index cards. Collect and mix the cards. Organize the class into teams. Each team will try to identify the organisms as producers or consumers, and then as plankton, nekton, or benthos. For example, kelp can be classified as producer and benthos. L2 COOP LEARN

Challenge

Why is a fish considered plankton at one stage of its life and nekton at another stage? When a fish is still inside an egg or is a young hatchling, it drifts with the surface currents and can be considered plankton. When it matures, a fish can move from one depth and place to another and is considered nekton. L3

✓Assessment

Performance To assess students' abilities to use variables, constants, and controls, have them describe how they could test the effects of temperature on marine organisms. Use **Performance Assessment in the Science Classroom,** p. 95.

Figure 14
Estuaries are called the nurseries of the oceans because many creatures spend their early lives there.

Estuaries An **estuary** is an area where the mouth of a river opens into an ocean. Because estuaries receive freshwater from rivers, they are not as salty as the ocean. Rivers also bring nutrients to estuaries. Areas with many nutrients usually have many phytoplankton, which form the base of the food chain. Shown in **Figure 14,** estuaries are full of life from salt-tolerant grasses to oysters, clams, shrimps, fish, and even manatees.

Estuaries are an important habitat to many marine organisms. Newly hatched fish, shrimps, crabs, and other animals enter estuaries as microscopic organisms and remain there until adulthood. For these vulnerable animals, less predators and more food are found in estuaries.

Coral Reefs Corals thrive in clear, warm water that receives a lot of sunlight. This means that they generally live in warm latitudes, between 30°N and 30°S, and in water that is no deeper than 30 m. Each coral animal builds a hard capsule around its body from the calcium it removes from seawater. Each capsule is cemented to others to form a large colony called a reef. A **reef** is a rigid, wave-resistant structure built by corals from skeletal material. As a coral reef forms, other benthos such as sea stars and sponges and nekton such as fish and turtles begin living on it.

In all ocean margin habitats, nutrients, food, and energy are cycled among organisms in complex food webs. Plankton, nekton, and benthos depend on each other for survival.

Section ② Assessment

1. Describe the processes of photosynthesis and chemosynthesis.
2. Give an example of a marine producer and a marine consumer.
3. List the key characteristics of plankton, nekton, and benthos.
4. Compare and contrast the characteristics of coral reef and estuary habitats.
5. **Think Critically** The amount of nutrients in the water decreases as the distance from the continental shelf increases. What effect does this have on open-ocean food chains?

Skill Builder Activities

6. **Identifying and Manipulating Variables and Controls** Describe how you could set up an experiment to test the effects of different amounts of light on marine producers. **For more help, refer to the** Science Skill Handbook.
7. **Using Graphics Software** Design a creative poster that shows energy relationships in a food chain. Begin with photosynthesis. Use clip art, scanned photographs, or computer graphics. **For more help, refer to the** Technology Skill Handbook.

Answers to Section Assessment

1. Producers use CO_2, water, and sunlight to make food by photosynthesis, and sulfur or nitrogen to make food by chemosynthesis.
2. Possible answers: algae, krill
3. Plankton drift in surface currents. Nekton move from one depth to another. Benthos live on or near the bottom.
4. Both are important habitats to many shallow-water organisms. Coral reefs: clear, warm, salt water; estuary: freshwater and salt water are mixed.
5. There aren't many organisms in open ocean food chains.
6. Test several of the same type of marine algae with three different light levels. The control has natural sunlight. Salinity and temperature are kept constant.
7. Posters should be colorful, describe photosynthesis, and explain how energy moves through a food chain.

Ocean Pollution

Sources of Pollution

How would you feel if someone came into your bedroom; spilled oil on your carpet; littered your room with plastic bags, cans, bottles, and newspapers; then sprayed insect killer and scattered sand all over? Organisms in the ocean experience these things when people pollute seawater.

Pollution is the introduction of harmful waste products, chemicals, and other substances not native to an environment. A pollutant is a substance that causes damage to organisms by interfering with life processes.

Pollutants from land eventually will reach the ocean in one of four main ways. They can be dumped deliberately and directly into the ocean. Material can be lost overboard accidentally during storms or shipwrecks. Some pollutants begin in the air and enter the ocean through rain. Other pollutants will reach the ocean by being carried in rivers that empty into the ocean. **Figure 15** illustrates how pollutants from land enter the oceans.

✔ Reading Check   *How do pollutants reach the ocean?*

As You Read

What You'll Learn
- **List** five types of ocean pollution.
- **Explain** how ocean pollution affects the entire world.
- **Describe** how ocean pollution can be controlled.

Vocabulary
pollution

Why It's Important
Earth's health depends on the oceans being unpolluted.

Figure 15
Ocean pollution comes from many sources.

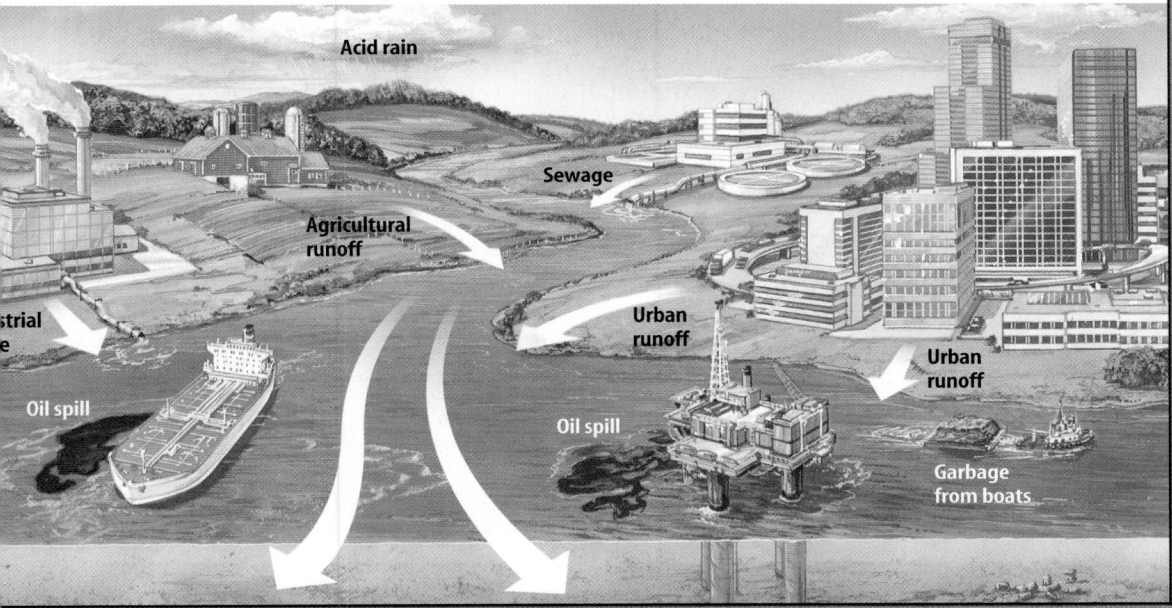

Acid rain
Sewage
Agricultural runoff
Urban runoff
Urban runoff
Oil spill
Oil spill
...strial ...e
Garbage from boats

Section ✔Assessment Planner

PORTFOLIO
Curriculum Connection, p. 568
PERFORMANCE ASSESSMENT
Skill Builder Activities, p. 569
See page 576 for more options.

CONTENT ASSESSMENT
Section, p. 569
Challenge, p. 569
Chapter, pp. 576–577

Ocean Pollution

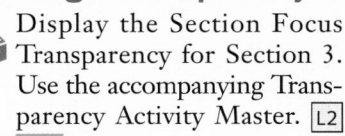
1 Motivate

Bellringer Transparency

Display the Section Focus Transparency for Section 3. Use the accompanying Transparency Activity Master. [L2] ELL

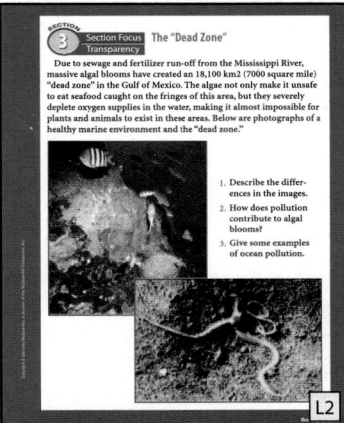

Tie to Prior Knowledge

Ask volunteers to tell the class about one thing they have learned about life in the ocean. Explain that they will learn how marine life is affected by pollution. In this section they will learn how pollution affects these processes.

✔ Reading Check

Answer deliberate dumping, in air, in river water

Resource Manager

Chapter Resources Booklet
Transparency Activity, p. 46

2 Teach

Sources of Pollution

✔ Reading Check

Answer rapid reproduction of algae

Caption Answer

Figure 16 The organisms that feed on the fish no longer have food. Also, the decomposition of many fish at one time may cause chemical changes in the water.

Discussion

Stress that ocean pollution is an international problem. Have student teams discuss who should pay for the cleanup of ocean pollution. [L1]

[LS] **Interpersonal**

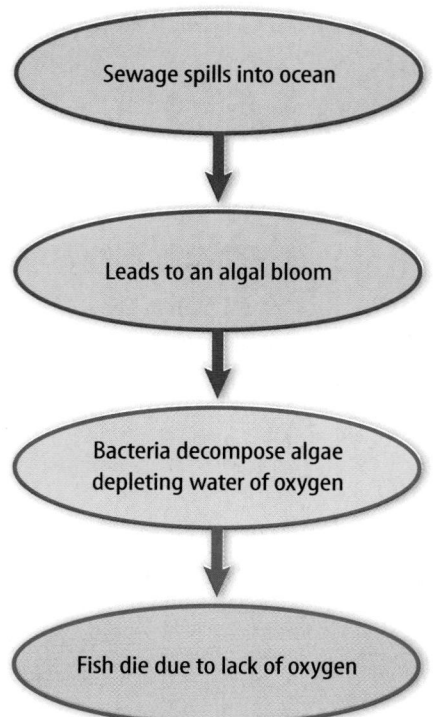

Sewage spills into ocean

↓

Leads to an algal bloom

↓

Bacteria decompose algae depleting water of oxygen

↓

Fish die due to lack of oxygen

Figure 16
Fish kills occur when oxygen supply is low. *How does a fish kill affect the food web?*

Sewage In some regions, human sewage leaks from septic tanks or is pumped directly into oceans or into rivers leading to an ocean. The introduction of sewage to an area of the ocean can cause immediate changes in the ecosystem, as shown by the following example. Sewage is a pollutant that acts like fertilizer. It is rich in nutrients that cause some types of algae to reproduce rapidly, creating what is called a bloom. The problem occurs when the algae die. As huge numbers of bacteria reproduce and decompose the algae, much of the oxygen in the water is used up. Other organisms, such as fish, cannot get enough oxygen. As a result, fish die in a phenomenon called a fish kill, as shown in **Figure 16.**

✔ Reading Check *What is an algal bloom?*

When sewage is dumped routinely into the same area year after year, changes take place. Entire ecosystems have been altered drastically as a result of long-term, repeated exposure to sewage and fertilizer runoff. In some areas of the world, sewage is dumped directly onto coral reefs. When this happens algae can outgrow the coral because the sewage acts like a fertilizer. Eventually, the coral organisms die, along with many of the other animals, like fish and crabs, that depend on the reef for food and shelter.

Chemical Pollution Industrial wastes from land can harm marine organisms. When it rains, the herbicides (weed killers) and insecticides (insect killers) used in farming and on lawns, are carried to streams. Eventually, they can reach the ocean and kill other organisms far from where they were applied originally. Sometimes industrial wastes are released directly into streams that eventually empty into oceans. Other chemicals are released into the air, where they later settle into the ocean. Industrial chemicals include metals like mercury and lead and chemicals like polychlorinated biphenyls (PCBs). In a process called biological amplification (am plah fah KAY shun), harmful chemicals can build up in the tissues of organisms that are at the top of the food chain. Higher consumers like dolphins and seabirds accumulate greater amounts of a toxin as they continue to feed on smaller organisms. At high concentrations, some chemicals can damage an organism's immune and reproductive systems. Explosives and nuclear wastes also have been dumped, by accident and on purpose, into some regions of the oceans.

566   CHAPTER 19 Oceanography

Cultural **Diversity**

Reef Destruction In Belize, the 180-mile-long barrier reef is dying. Possible causes include agricultural pollutants, overfishing, and abuse by scuba divers and snorkelers. Fertilizers, pesticides, and sediments wash into the ocean, killing the coral animals. Overfishing disrupts the food web. Scuba divers and snorkelers step on the coral and take away pieces of the reef for souvenirs. To protect the Belize reef, a Coastal Zone Management Project has recently designated certain areas of the reef as commercial and recreational zones. Other areas have been designated as marine preserves and wilderness areas. This project also regulates fishing and recreational use. Ask students what effect they think the Coastal Zone Management Project will have on the health of the reef.

Oil Pollution Although oil spills from tankers that have collided or are leaking are usually highly publicized, they are not the biggest source of oil pollution in the ocean. As much as 44 percent of oil that reaches the ocean comes from land. Oil that washes from cars and streets, or that is poured down drains or into soil, flows into streams. Eventually, this oil reaches the ocean. Other sources of oil pollution are leaks at offshore oil wells and oil mixed with wastewater that is pumped out of ships. **Figure 17** shows the percentage of different sources of oil entering the oceans each year.

Ocean dumping 10%

Offshore mining, oil and gas drilling 1%

Shipping and accidental spills 12%

Runoff and discharges from land 44%

Airborne emissions from land 33%

Figure 17
Although oil spills are highly publicized and tragic, the same harmful oil enters the ocean every day from many other sources. *What can be done to reduce the amount of oil entering the oceans?*

Solid-Waste Pollution Even in the most remote areas of the world, such as uninhabited islands that are thousands of miles from any major city, large amounts of trash wash up on the beach. **Figure 18** shows the amount of debris collected by a scientist on an island in the Pacific Ocean, 8,000 km east of Australia. The presence of trash ruins a beautiful beach, and solid wastes, such as plastic bags and fishing line, can entangle animals. Animals such as sea turtles mistakenly eat plastic bags, because they look so much like their normal prey, floating jellyfish. Illegally dumped medical waste such as needles, plastic tubing, and bags also are a threat to humans and other animals.

6 Lightbulbs

7 Aerosol cans

25 Shoes

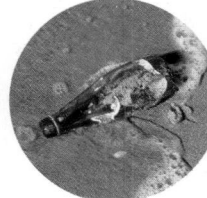
71 Plastic bottles

171 Glass bottles

268 Plastic pieces

Figure 18
These items are like the ones found washed ashore on one of the Pitcairn Islands in the South Pacific. The number of each item found is shown below the figure. Also among the rubble were broken toys, a pair of gloves, and an asthma inhaler.

Resource Manager

Chapter Resources Booklet
  Enrichment, p. 32
  Directed Reading for Content Mastery, pp. 21, 22

Visual Learning

Figure 17 What is the greatest source of oil pollution? Runoff from the land.

Extension

Have students research oil spills that have occurred over the last ten years. On a world map, have them pinpoint the location of these spills. L2
IS Linguistic and Visual-Spatial

Caption Answer

Figure 17 Possible answers: reduce the likelihood of tanker collisions and oil spills, fix leaky cars, treat runoff from roadways before water enters rivers and oceans

Activity

Have students use olive oil, a pan, gravel, water, toothpicks, a sponge, paper towels, cotton balls, feathers, string, liquid soap, a sheet of cardboard, and a dropper to make a model of an oil spill along a beach. Then have students clean up the spill. Students should analyze which materials were the most effective in cleaning up the oil from the water's surface and from the rocks. At the conclusion of the activity, ask students why oil spills are difficult to clean up. The oil spreads over both the water and the beach. Different techniques must be used to clean up these different areas.
L2 **IS Kinesthetic**

Fun Fact

In one survey, 86 percent of the solid waste observed floating in the northern Pacific Ocean was plastic.

Sources of Pollution,
continued

Discussion

How does cutting down forests increase the amount of sediment in the oceans? When trees are removed, soil erosion increases. Runoff carries the soil to streams and eventually to an ocean. **Why is sediment pollution a special problem for benthos that are attached to the bottom?** If they are covered by sediments, they cannot crawl or swim away. They can be crushed by the weight of the sediments. Also, their gills and filter-feeding mechanisms clog with sediments and they cannot obtain oxygen or food.

Effects of Pollution

Figure 19
When silt gets into seawater, it clogs the filter-feeding systems of animals such as corals, oysters, and clams.

Figure 20
Some scientists hypothesize that a relationship exists between increased pollution in the ocean and the number of harmful algal blooms in the last 30 years.

Sediment Silt also pollutes the ocean. Human activities such as agriculture, deforestation, and construction tear up the soil. Rain washes soil into streams and eventually into an ocean nearby, as shown in **Figure 19.** This causes huge amounts of silt to accumulate in many coastal areas. Coral reefs and saltwater marshes are safe, protected places where young marine organisms grow to adults. When large amounts of silt cover coral reefs and fill marshes, these habitats are destroyed. Without a safe place to grow larger, many organisms will not survive.

Effects of Pollution

You already have learned some examples of how pollution affects the ocean and the organisms that live there. Today, there is not a single area of the ocean that is not polluted in some way. As pollution from land continues to reach the ocean, scientists are recording dramatic changes in this environment

Estuaries and the rivers that feed into them from Delaware to North Carolina have suffered from toxic blooms of *Pfiesteria* since the late 1980s. These blooms have killed billions of fish. *Pfiesteria*, a type of plankton, also has caused rashes, nausea, memory loss, and the weakening of the immune system in humans. The cause of these blooms is thought to be runoff contaminated by fertilizers and other waste materials. In Florida, toxic red tides kill fish and manatees. Some people also blame these red tides on sewage releases and fertilizer runoff. **Figure 20** shows an increase in the number of harmful algal blooms since the early 1970s.

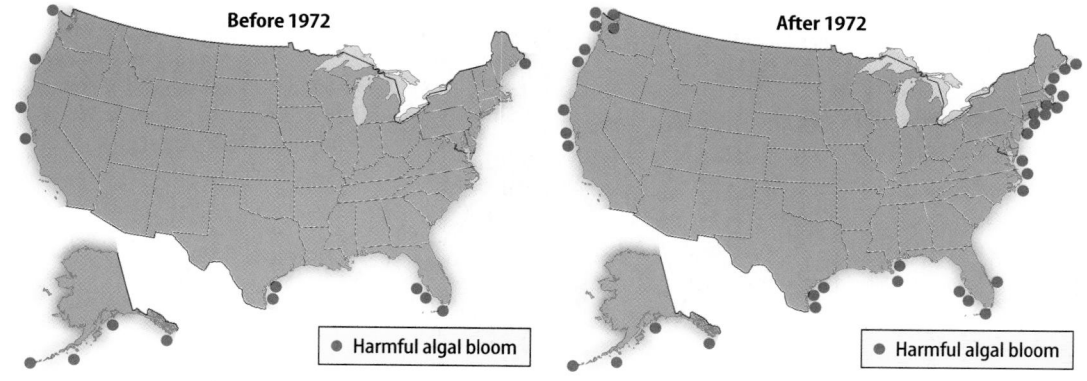

Before 1972   After 1972

• Harmful algal bloom   • Harmful algal bloom

568 CHAPTER 19 Oceanography

Resource Manager

Chapter Resources Booklet
  Reinforcement, p. 29
Cultural Diversity, p. 7
Reading and Writing Skill Activities, p. 29

Curriculum Connection

Health From 1953 to 1960, mercury had been discharged into Minamata Bay, Japan. When people ingested seafood caught in the bay, they became very ill. Have students research the health effects on these people and write a report on their findings. Some effects were cerebral palsy and mental retardation in children; deformities in newborns; tremors, slurred speech, delirium, convulsions, and coma in people of all ages. Some people died. L3 P

Controlling Pollution

Some people believe that oceans take care of themselves because they are large. However, other people view ocean pollution as a serious problem. Many international organizations have met to develop ways of reducing ocean pollution. Treaties prohibit the dumping of some kinds of hazardous wastes from vessels, aircraft, and platforms. One treaty requires that some ships and operators of offshore platforms have oil pollution emergency plans. This includes having the proper equipment to combat oil spills and practicing what to do if a spill takes place. Recall that a large amount of pollution enters the ocean from land. Although the idea of reducing land pollution to better protect the ocean has been discussed, no international agreement exists to prevent and control land-based activities that affect the oceans.

 Reading Check *What has been done to help control ocean pollution?*

What You Can Do Current international and U.S. laws aren't effective enough. Further cooperation is needed to reduce ocean pollution. You can help by disposing wastes properly and volunteering for beach or community cleanups, like the one shown in **Figure 21.** You can recycle materials such as newspapers, glass, and plastics and never dump chemicals like oil or paint onto soil or into water. One of the best things you can do is continue to learn about marine pollution and how people affect the oceans. What other things will help reduce ocean pollution?

Figure 21
Picking up trash is an easy way to help reduce ocean pollution.

Controlling Pollution

✔ **Reading Check**

Answer Treaties prohibit dumping of some types of wastes into the ocean.

③ Assess

Reteach

Have students discuss why locating the exact source of an ocean pollutant is sometimes difficult. Students should include the fact that there are many sources of pollution. Rivers, air, and ocean currents also move pollutants from place to place. L2
🅻🅢 **Linguistic**

Challenge

Why is ocean pollution an international problem? Earth's oceans are interconnected, making pollution a worldwide problem. Pollution disrupts food chains and oxygen supplies.

✔ *Assessment*

Process Assess students' ability to relate cause and effect by asking them to explain why the health of our planet depends on the oceans being unpolluted. Use **Performance Assessment in the Science Classroom,** p. 89.

Section ③ Assessment

1. List five human activities that pollute the oceans. Suggest a solution to each.
2. How does pollution of the oceans affect the entire world?
3. In what ways have international treaties helped reduce pollution?
4. What can you do to help prevent ocean pollution?
5. **Think Critically** To widen beaches, some cities pump offshore sediment onto them. How might this affect organisms that live in coastal waters?

Skill Builder Activities

6. **Concept Mapping** Make an events-chain concept map that describes how runoff from land can reach the ocean. Include examples of pollution that could be in the runoff. **For more help, refer to the** Science Skill Handbook.
7. **Communicating** Submit a letter to the editor of a newspaper. In your letter, explain why ocean pollution is a problem that people can help prevent. List examples of things people can do to help. **For more help, refer to the** Science Skill Handbook.

Answers to Section Assessment

1. dumping untreated sewage—build treatment plants; using herbicides on lawns—use fewer chemicals; oil leaks from car—check and repair leaks; leaving trash on beach—provide trash cans/take waste home; construction—plant grass over bare soil
2. affects food chains and oxygen supply
3. They prohibit hazardous waste

   dumping from vessels, aircraft, and platforms, and they require merchant fleets and operators of platforms to have pollution emergency plans.
4. Possible answers: Properly dispose of wastes, clean up trash, recycle, don't dump chemicals into soil, educate yourself about marine pollution.
5. Habitats are destroyed; organisms

   are covered by sediments and sucked into pumps.
6. Runoff flows into stream, stream water flows into river, river flows into ocean. Examples include fertilizer, oil and gasoline, and solid wastes such as litter.
7. Letters should include some of the ideas listed in answer #4 above.

Activity

Recognize the Problem

Students will study ways that people make use of the oceans and products from the oceans. Students will search for, gather, and analyze information from the Internet and various other sources to piece together the intricate reliance that humans have upon the ocean.

Internet Students will gather data from the Internet sites that can be accessed through the Glencoe Science Web site at **science.glencoe.com.** Students can post their findings on the Web site and get information from other schools around the country.

Non-Internet Sources If you do not have access to the Internet, then the school and local libraries are a good place to start. Science television programs and video tapes dealing with the ocean are also reliable sources of information.

Time Required

one to two weeks

Preparation

Internet Access the Glencoe Science Web site at **science. glencoe.com** to run through the steps that the students will follow.

Non-Internet Sources Obtain books and magazines that have information on ocean resources.

Form a Hypothesis

Possible Hypothesis

Food and drug products come from marine organisms, and petroleum and natural gas deposits began as deposits of marine organisms.

Activity *Use the Internet*

Resources from the Oceans

Oceans cover most of Earth's surface. Humans get many things from oceans such as seafood, medicines, oil, and diamonds. Humans also use oceans for recreation and to transport materials from place to place. What else comes from oceans? Scientists continue to discover and research new uses for ocean resources. You might not realize that you probably use many products every day that are made from organisms that live in oceans.

Recognize the Problem

What products do you use that come from the oceans?

Form a Hypothesis

Think about the plants and animals that live in the oceans. How could these organisms be used to make everyday products? Form a hypothesis about the types of products that could be manufactured from these organisms.

Goals
- **Research and identify** organisms that are used to make products.
- **Explain** why it is important to keep oceans clean.

Data Source
SCIENCE *Online* Go to the Glencoe Science Web site at **science.glencoe.com** for more information about resources from the oceans, hints on which products come from the oceans, and data from other students.

570 CHAPTER 19 Oceanography

Resource Manager

Chapter Resources Booklet
    Activity Worksheet, pp. 7–8
    Lab Activity, pp. 13–16
Lab Management and Safety, p. 73

SCIENCE *Online*
Internet Addresses

_____

_____

_____

Explore the Glencoe Science Web site at **science.glencoe.com** to find out more about topics in this activity.

Test Your Hypothesis

Plan

1. **Identify** web sites listed on the Glencoe Science Web site and identify other resources that will help you complete the data table shown on the right.

2. Notice that to complete the table you must identify products made from marine organisms, where the organisms are collected or harvested, and alternative products.

3. Plan how and when you will locate the information.

Do

1. Make sure your teacher approves your plan and your resource list before you begin.

Ocean Resources Data			
Organism	Location Where Collected or Harvested	Product (name and use)	Alternatives

2. Find at least three ocean organisms that are used to make products you use every day.

3. **Identify** the name and any uses of the product.

4. **Research** where each organism lives and the method by which it is collected or harvested.

5. **Identify** alternative products.

Analyze Your Data

1. **Describe** the different ways in which ocean organisms are useful to humans.

2. Are there any substitutes or alternatives available for the ocean organisms in the products?

Draw Conclusions

1. How might the activities of humans affect any of the ocean organisms you researched?

2. Are the substitute or alternative products more or less expensive?

3. Can you tell whether the ocean-made product is better than the substitute product? Explain.

4. Why is it important to conserve ocean resources and keep oceans clean?

Communicating Your Data

SCIENCE Online Find this *Use the Internet* activity on the Glencoe Science Web site at **science.glencoe.com.** Post your data in the table provided. Compare your data to that of other students.

ACTIVITY 571

Test Your Hypothesis

Teaching Strategies

- Motivate students by bringing in unusual products from the sea. For example, have students taste Japanese nori (dried red algae).

- Present the idea of overharvesting ocean resources and the use of substitute products. Recount the story of whale oil in the late nineteenth century and the eventual substitution of petroleum products.

Analyze Your Data

1. They can be used for food and as a raw material for products and medicines. For example, seaweeds are a source of iodine; algin from kelp is used in making ice cream, pudding, and paint; diatomaceous earth is used to make toothpaste and car polish; horseshoe crab blood is used to detect dangerous bacteria in human blood.

2. Answer depends on products chosen. Possible answers: using synthetic sponges instead of sponges, using plastic or glass instead of pearls.

Draw Conclusions

1. Activities that pollute the oceans kill organisms.

2. Answers will vary depending on the product chosen. Alternative products may be more expensive.

3. Answers will vary.

4. Marine organisms are a good source of many essential products, such as foods and medicines. Polluting the oceans may endanger these organisms.

Assessment

Performance Have students form large groups to design and produce skits that demonstrate the key concepts they have learned in their investigation. Suggest that their presentation target an audience of upper elementary school students. Use **Performance Assessment in the Science Classroom,** p. 147.

Communicating Your Data

Have students use a computer program to prepare a display of the products they find that are made from marine organisms. Students should present their displays to the class.

Content Background

Just as photosynthetic organisms use the Sun's radiant energy to produce food and oxygen, chemosynthetic bacteria produce food and oxygen from sulphur compounds blasted from ocean vents. These bacteria form the base of the food chain. The bacteria can be found growing freely in large mats covering the hot rocks near the vents.

Some organisms feed directly on the bacteria. Many of the other organisms at the vents, such as the giant tube worms and the large white clams that are found scattered throughout the area around the vents, have a mutualistic relationship with the bacteria. They house the bacteria in their tissues and absorb hydrogen sulfide for the bacteria to use. In return they live off of the carbohydrates produced by the bacteria.

Filter feeding tubeworm

Strange Creatures from the

In 1977, the *Alvin*, a small submersible craft specially designed to explore the ocean depths, took three geologists down about 2,200 m below the sea surface. They wanted to be the first to observe and study the formations of the Galápagos Rift deep in the Pacific Ocean. What they saw was totally unexpected. Instead of barren rock, the geologists found life—a lot of life. And they had never even considered having a life scientist as part of the research team!

The crew of the *Alvin* discovered hydrothermal vents—underwater openings where hot water (400°C) spurts from cracks in the rocks on the ocean floor. Some organisms thrive there because of the hydrogen sulfide that exists at the vents. Many of these organisms are like nothing humans had ever seen before. They are organisms that live in extremely hot temperatures and use hydrogen sulfide as their food supply.

Some of these organisms begin as nothing more than a mouth and grow into long, tube-like shapes. These organisms don't need sunlight to live but thrive in total darkness and can withstand pressure hundreds of times greater than at sea level.

The worm, *Alvinella pompejana*, can tolerate very high temperatures.

The discovery and study of hydrothermal vents almost has been overshadowed by the amazing variety of life that was found there. But scientists think these openings on the ocean floor (many located along the Mid-Atlantic Ridge) control the temperature and movement of nearby ocean waters, as well as have a significant effect on the ocean's chemical content. These vents also act as outlets for Earth's inner heat.

572

Resources for Teachers and Students

Eternal Darkness, A Personal History of Deep-Sea Exploration, by Robert Ballard, Princeton University Press, 2000.

"Deep Sea Vents, Science at the Extreme," by Richard Lutz, *National Geographic*, October 2000.

Life Without Light: A Journey to Earth's Dark Ecosystems, by Melissa Stewart, Franklin Watts, 1999.

"Explosive Earth," videotape, National Geographic and Salmon City Productions, 1996.

The *Alvin* enters the water.

Scientists also have discovered that the vent communities are temporary. Each vent eventually shuts down and the organisms somehow disperse to other vents. Exactly how this happens is an area of ongoing research. One idea is that "whale falls" provide stepping stones from one vent to another. A whale fall is the remains of a whale that has died and sunk to the seafloor. The offspring of vent creatures might take refuge and grow to adulthood at a whale fall, releasing their own young to seek out a new vent community.

Ocean Floor

Blood-red tube worms live deep beneath the sea.

CONNECTIONS Creative Writing Imagine you were a passenger on the *Alvin*. Write about your adventure as you came upon the hydrothermal communities. Describe in detail some of the things you saw. Draw pictures of some of the unique creatures that live there.

SCIENCE *Online*

For more information, visit science.glencoe.com

CONNECTIONS
Making Connections
Student's answers will vary. The scientists who were in the Alvin at the time, all geologists, had no idea what they were looking at. What they described as a field of dandelions turned out to be a new species of jellyfish.

SCIENCE *Online*

Internet Addresses

_____

_____

_____

Explore the Glencoe Science Web site at **science.glencoe.com** to find out more about topics in this feature.

Discussion
Ask students to think about why a vent would "shut down" and why the organisms would either die or move to another vent. Possible answers: In the short term, vents may shut down as a result of the magma beneath the rift moving and no longer providing a heat source. In the long term, vents shut down as the section of crust they are on moves further from the area of spreading and its source of heat. Either way, the organisms can no longer survive if there is not a source of hydrogen sulfide from the black smoker. With no hydrogen sulfide, the bacteria can no longer fulfill their role as the primary producer in the food chain.

Activity
Have students find more information on the organisms of hydrothermal vent communities and make a food chain or food web, if possible, using what they find. They should begin with the chemosynthetic bacteria. Have students make a poster showing their results.
LS Visual-Spatial

Analyze the Event
Have students discuss the importance of the discovery of hydrothermal vents in science, particularly the fields of biology and oceanography. The discovery of a new species is always fascinating. In this case an entirely new habitat, along with all of the organisms that lived there, was found. The environment is like no other on Earth, and these organisms are highly specialized to be able to live under such conditions. For oceanographers, the mineral-rich water coming from the vents helped answer questions about the chemical composition of seawater and the source of many salts in the ocean.

Reviewing Main Ideas

Preview

Students can answer the questions in their Science Journals. Discuss the answers as you go through the chapter. **Linguistic**

Review

Students can write their answers, then compare them with those of other students. **Interpersonal**

Reteach

Students can look at the illustrations and describe details that support the main ideas of the chapter. **Visual-Spatial**

Answers to Chapter Review

SECTION 1

1. Most students will be able to recognize the continental shelf and slope in the figure. The shelf is near the coast. The slope is the steep area at the edge of the shelf.

SECTION 2

3. benthos

SECTION 3

1. sewage

Reviewing Main Ideas

Section 1   The Seafloor

1. The continental shelf is a gently sloping part of the continent that extends into the oceans. The continental slope extends beyond the continental shelf to the ocean floor. The abyssal plain is a flat area of the ocean floor. *Can you identify the continental shelf and slope in the figure below?*

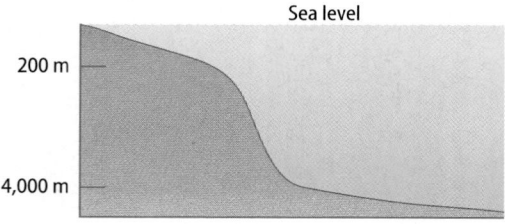

Sea level
200 m
4,000 m

2. Cracks form where the seafloor is spreading apart. Along mid-ocean ridges, new seafloor forms. Seafloor slips beneath another crustal plate at a trench.

3. Petroleum, natural gas, and placer deposits are mined from continental shelves. In the future, perhaps manganese nodules and other deep-water deposits will be mined.

Section 2   Life in the Ocean

1. Marine organisms are specially adapted to live in salt water. These organisms consume food, produce energy, and reproduce in the oceans.

2. Photosynthesis is the basis of most of the food chains in the ocean. Chemosynthesis is a special process of making food near thermal vents. Energy is transferred through food webs. Organisms that can make their own food are called producers. Organisms that feed on producers are called consumers.

3. Organisms that drift in ocean currents are called plankton. Nekton are marine organisms that swim. Benthos are plants and animals that live on or near the ocean floor. *Is this sponge classified as plankton, nekton, or benthos?*

4. Ocean margin habitats, found along the continental shelf, include sandy beaches, rocky shores, estuaries, and coral reefs.

Section 3   Ocean Pollution

1. Sources of pollution include sewage, chemical pollution, oil spills, solid waste pollution, and sediment. *Can you name the source of pollution shown here?*

2. Ocean pollution can disrupt food webs and threaten marine organisms.

3. International treaties and U.S. laws have been made to help reduce ocean pollution. Everyone can help reduce ocean pollution.

FOLDABLES Reading & Study Skills

After You Read

Using the information in your Foldable, explain the effects of ocean pollution. Predict whether pollution will increase or decrease.

FOLDABLES Reading & Study Skills

After You Read

After students have read the chapter and completed the Foldable described in Before You Read, have them do the activity on the student page.

Dinah Zike

Visualizing Main Ideas

Complete the following chart on ocean-margin organisms.

Ocean Margin Organisms

Organism	Ocean-Margin Environments			
	Sandy Beach	Rocky Shore	Estuary	Coral Reef
Plankton	phytoplankton zooplankton	phytoplankton zooplankton	phytoplankton, zooplankton	phytoplankton zooplankton
Nekton	fish,	octopuses, fish	shrimps, fish	fish, turtles
Benthos	worms, horseshoe crabs	algae, sponges, mussels, sea urchins	grasses, snails, clams	corals, sea stars, sponges

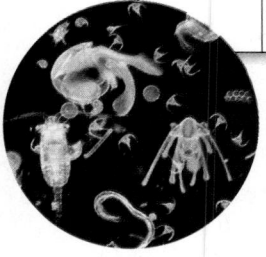

Visualizing Main Ideas

See student page.

Vocabulary Review

Using Vocabulary

1. nekton
2. Chemosynthesis
3. continental slope
4. mid-ocean ridges
5. estuary

Vocabulary Review

Vocabulary Words

a. abyssal plain
b. benthos
c. chemosynthesis
d. continental shelf
e. continental slope
f. estuary
g. mid-ocean ridge
h. nekton
i. photosynthesis
j. plankton
k. pollution
l. reef
m. trench

THE PRINCETON REVIEW **Study Tip**

Copy your notes from class. As you do, explaining each concept in detail, will help you understand it completely.

Using Vocabulary

Replace the underlined word(s) with the correct vocabulary word(s).

1. Animals such as whales, sea turtles and fish are examples of <u>plankton</u>.

2. <u>Photosynthesis</u> occurs in areas where there is no light and organisms use sulfur as energy to produce their own food.

3. The <u>continental shelf</u> drops from the edge of a continent out to the deep abyssal plains of the ocean floor.

4. New ocean floor is formed at <u>trenches</u>.

5. An area where the mouth of a river opens into an ocean is a <u>reef</u>.

Checking Concepts

1. D
2. D
3. C
4. D
5. B
6. C
7. C
8. B
9. B
10. A

Thinking Critically

11. They are rich in manganese, copper, iron, nickel, and cobalt. These metals are used to manufacture steel, paint, and batteries.
12. Ocean pollution knows no boundaries. Currents carry pollution from one region to another.
13. Herbicides, pesticides, and fertilizers are carried in runoff to streams. From streams, they go to rivers, and then to the ocean. Herbicides and pesticides kill marine organisms. Fertilizers cause algal blooms and fish kills.
14. No; the waters in the region are too cold for corals, which need warm, tropical waters. But there may be reef structures there from the past.
15. Ocean pollution kills many organisms. As a result, we would have fewer organisms to analyze as possible drug sources.

Chapter 19 Assessment

Checking Concepts

Choose the word or phrase that best answers the question.

1. What is the flattest feature of the ocean floor?
   A) rift valley   C) seamount
   B) continental slope   D) abyssal plain

2. What might be found in areas where rivers enter oceans?
   A) rift valleys
   B) manganese nodules
   C) abyssal plains
   D) placer deposits

3. What are formed along subduction zones?
   A) mid-ocean ridges   C) trenches
   B) continental slopes   D) density currents

4. What are ocean organisms that drift in ocean currents called?
   A) nekton   C) benthos
   B) pollutants   D) plankton

5. How do some deep-water bacteria in the ocean make food?
   A) photosynthesis   C) respiration
   B) chemosynthesis   D) rifting

6. Which organisms reproduce rapidly, resulting eventually in a lack of oxygen?
   A) fish   C) algae
   B) animal plankton   D) corals

7. In which area of the ocean is the greatest source of food found?
   A) on abyssal plains
   B) in trenches
   C) along continental shelves
   D) along the mid-ocean ridge

8. Where does most oil pollution originate?
   A) tanker collisions
   B) runoff from land
   C) leaks at offshore wells
   D) in wastewater pumped from ships

9. Where does seafloor spreading occur?
   A) trenches   C) abyssal plains
   B) mid-ocean ridges   D) continental shelves

10. What do organisms do to produce their own food?
   A) photosynthesize   C) consume
   B) excrete wastes   D) respire

Thinking Critically

11. Why might some industries be interested in mining manganese nodules?

12. Explain why ocean pollution is considered to be a serious international problem.

13. Discuss how agricultural chemicals can kill marine organisms.

14. Would you expect to find coral reefs growing around the bases of underwater volcanoes off the coast of Alaska? Explain.

15. Scientists currently are researching the use of chemicals produced by marine organisms to help fight diseases that affect humans including viruses and certain types of cancer. How would ocean pollution affect the ability to discover and research new drugs?

Developing Skills

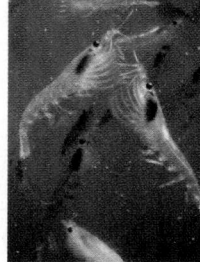

16. **Using Scientific Illustrations** Use **Figure 8** to determine which organisms would starve if phytoplankton became extinct.

17. **Classifying** Classify each of these sea creatures as plankton, nekton, or benthos: shrimps, dolphins, sea stars, krill, coral, manatees, and algae.

Chapter ✓ *Assessment* Planner

Portfolio Encourage students to place in their portfolios one or two items of what they consider to be their best work. Examples include:
- Science Journal, p. 554
- Curriculum Connection, p. 559
- Curriculum Connection, p. 568

Performance Additional performance assessments, Performance Task Assessment Lists, and rubrics for evaluating these activities can be found in Glencoe's **Performance Assessment in the Science Classroom.**

18. Drawing Conclusions At point A an echo, a sound wave bounced off the ocean floor, took 2 s to reach the ship. It took 2.4 s at point B. Which point is deeper?

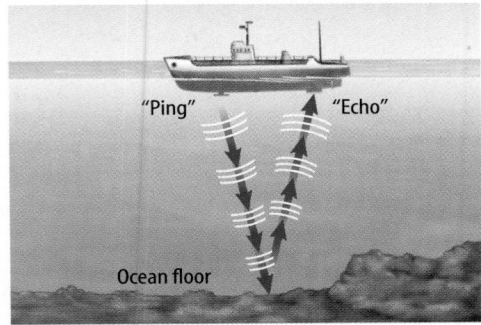

"Ping" "Echo"

Ocean floor

19. Measuring in SI If kelp grows at a steady rate of 30 cm per day, how long would it take to reach a length of 25 m?

20. Comparing and Contrasting Compare and contrast estuary and coral reef habitats.

Performance Assessment

21. Graph a Profile Previously, you made a profile of the ocean bottom along the 38° N latitude line, but it was not drawn to scale. Make a scale profile of the area between 3,600 km and 4,100 km from New Jersey. Use the scale 1 mm = 1,000 m.

22. Poster Choose a sea animal and research its life processes. Classify it as plankton, nekton, or benthos. Design a poster that includes all of this information.

TECHNOLOGY

Go to the Glencoe Science Web site at **science.glencoe.com** or use the **Glencoe Science CD-ROM** for additional chapter assessment.

THE PRINCETON REVIEW — Test Practice

The table shows the year and location of oil being spilled into the ocean as a result of fire, ships running aground, or leakage.

Oil Spills Around the World		
Year	Location	Spill Size (millions of liters)
1967	Land's End, England	144.7
1972	Gulf of Oman, Oman	143.5
1978	Brittany, France	260.2
1979	Bay of Campeche, Mexico	530.3
1983	South Africa	297.3
1988	Newfoundland, Canada	163.2
1991	Persian Gulf	909.0
2001	Galapagos Islands	0.6

Use the information given in the table to answer the following questions.

1. At which location was the largest spill?
A) Brittany, France
B) South Africa
C) Persian Gulf
D) Lands End, England

2. Oil entering the ocean is a major concern because:
F) the presence of oil can reduce water quality
G) the presence of oil in the water can be harmful to marine life
H) large oils spills can be difficult to clean up
J) all of the above

THE PRINCETON REVIEW — Test Practice

The Test-Taking Tip was written by The Princeton Review, the nation's leader in test preparation.
1. C
2. J

Developing Skills

16. krill, small and medium fish, whale sharks, seals
17. Shrimp can be benthos, nekton, or plankton. Dolphins are nekton. Sea stars and corals are plankton as larvae and benthos as adults. Krill and some algae are plankton.
18. The ocean is deeper at point B because the echo took longer to reach the ship from point B.
19. 25 m/0.3 m/d = 83 days
20. Both are important habitats to many shallow-water organisms, Coral reefs are clear and warm and have salt water. Estuaries are fresh and salt water mixed.

Performance Assessment

21. Using the scale 1 mm = 1 km, the horizontal axis will be 5 m long; the vertical axis will be 7 mm high. Use **PASC**, p. 111.
22. Posters will vary but should be colorful and informative. Use **PASC**, p. 145.

✓ *Assessment* Resources

📁 Reproducible Masters

Chapter Resources Booklet
Chapter Review, pp. 37–38
Chapter Tests, pp. 39–42
Assessment Transparency Activity, p. 49

Glencoe Science Web site
Interactive Tutor
Chapter Quizzes

Glencoe Technology
Assessment Transparency
Interactive CD-ROM Chapter Quizzes
ExamView Pro Test Bank
Vocabulary PuzzleMaker Software
MindJogger Videoquiz DVD/VHS

Standardized Test Practice

Reading Comprehension

QUESTION 1: B

Students must refer back to the reading passage in order to recall the chronology of events.

- **Choice A** No; this occurred second in the passage.
- **Choice B** Yes; this occurred first in the passage.
- **Choice C** No; this occurred last in the passage.
- **Choice D** No; this did not occur in the passage.

QUESTION 2: H

Students must refer to the information in the reading passage to identify the correct answer, choice H, *119 km/h*.

QUESTION 3: B

Students should identify in the question key words such as *energy source* in order to find the important information, which is located in the last paragraph of the passage. Only answer choice B, *warm ocean water*, is supported by information in the passage.

THE PRINCETON REVIEW — All questions written and validated by The Princeton Review.

Reading Comprehension

Read the passage. Then read each question that follows the passage. Decide which is the best answer to each question.

Hurricanes: An Exchange Between Ocean and Atmosphere

Hurricanes are among the most feared of all weather storms in the Atlantic region. In the western Pacific they are known as typhoons, and in Australia and the Indian Ocean they are called cyclones. Hurricane season in the United States and Caribbean occurs each year between June and November.

Hurricanes over the Atlantic Ocean begin as low-pressure systems, usually in the tropical seas west of Africa. The trade winds blow these storms westward. Heat from the warm ocean water gives the system energy. Once the water temperature rises to 27°C, a hurricane can form.

To be classified as a hurricane, the wind speed of the storm must exceed 119 km/h. Hurricanes can last for several days and can reach heights up to 16 km above the water.

The Atlantic has about ten tropical storms each year. Of these, six of them might develop into full-blown hurricanes.

Hurricanes can cause severe damage to anything near them on the water. After a hurricane reaches land, it loses its source of energy—warm ocean water—and begins to weaken. Even though the strength of these storms fades as they reach shore, hurricanes frequently are responsible for bllions of dollars of damage and loss of lives.

Test-Taking Tip Take your time and read the passage carefully.

1. Which of the following was described first in the passage?
   - **A)** Hurricanes can reach heights up to 16 km above the surface of the water.
   - **B)** Hurricane season in the Atlantic region occurs between June and November.
   - **C)** Hurricanes start to lose energy upon reaching land.
   - **D)** Hurricanes can be suppressed by the high, strong winds of El Niño.

2. To classify as a hurricane, the wind speed of the storm must be more than _____.
   - **F)** 27 km/h
   - **G)** 16 km/h
   - **H)** 119 km/h
   - **J)** 140 km/h

3. What is the energy source of hurricanes?
   - **A)** high winds
   - **B)** warm ocean water
   - **C)** trade winds
   - **D)** cold air from land

Reasoning and Skills

Read each question and choose the best answer.

1. During El Niño years, upwelling of ocean water off the coast of Peru is greatly reduced, the water warms, and the number of fish decreases. Which of the following best explains why this occurs?
   A) The Coriolis effect shifts currents toward land.
   B) High concentrations of nutrients in the surface water increase its density.
   C) Winds blowing water from the coast slacken.
   D) The Eastern Pacific warms, thus changing the direction of currents off Peru.

Test-Taking Tip Think about what causes upwelling, then choose the answer that offers the most reasonable explanation for why it might stop.

Characteristics of Earth's Atmosphere

Layer	Characteristic
Troposphere	Contains most of the water vapor
Stratosphere	Includes ozone layer
Mesosphere	Falling temperatures
Thermosphere	Very high temperatures

2. According to the information in the table, rain would most likely originate in the _____.
   F) troposphere
   H) mesosphere
   G) stratosphere
   J) thermosphere

Test-Taking Tip Examine the table carefully. Find the words you would most closely associate with rain and follow the row back to the correct answer.

Tornado Damage

Type of Tornado	Damage
F0	Light: Broken branches and chimneys
F1	Moderate: Roof damage
F2	Considerable: Roofs torn off, trees uprooted
F3	Severe: Heavy roofs and walls torn off
F4	Devastating: Houses leveled
F5	Incredible: Houses picked up
F6	Total demolition

3. What type of tornado occurred near this home?
   A) light
   C) considerable
   B) moderate
   D) severe

Test-Taking Tip Obtain a copy of the photograph above and circle all of the things damaged in the picture. Compare what you found to the information given in the table.

Standardized Test Practice

Reasoning and Skills

QUESTION 1: D

Students must understand that uncharacteristically warm water in the Eastern Pacific diminishes upwelling.

QUESTION 2: F

Students must use the information in the chart and make the connection between rain and water vapor in order to identify choice F, *troposphere*, as the layer of Earth's atmosphere in which rain originates.

QUESTION 3: C

Students must relate the damage shown in the picture to the information given in the table.

Teaching Tip

When questions ask about a table or chart, instruct students to read the chart carefully to determine the relationships between columns.

Unit Contents

✔ Pre-Reading Activity

Have students look through the unit for photographs and illustrations that show relationships between humans and the environment.

How Are Cotton & Cookies Connected?

580

Teacher to Teacher

"On the left-hand page of their open Science Journals, I have students take 'home notes' and write questions about what they read. In class the following day, they take 'class notes' on the right-hand page of their journals. This arrangement can be used for review of chapter content."

Dennis L. Stockdale, Teacher
Asheville High School
Asheville, NC

In the 1800s, the economy of the South depended heavily on cotton and tobacco—two crops that rob the soil of nutrients, especially nitrogen. By the late 1800s, the soil was in poor shape. A scientist named George Washington Carver set out to change that. He promoted the technique of crop rotation—alternating soil-depleting crops such as cotton with soil-enriching crops such as peanuts. Many farmers listened to Carver and began planting peanuts. However, there was little market for the crop. So Carver poured his energy into developing uses for peanuts. Ultimately, he came up with more than 300 products made from peanuts—everything from soap to axle grease. He also created the first recipe for peanut butter cookies, which have become an American favorite.

SCIENCE CONNECTION

NITROGEN FIXATION Plants need nitrogen to grow well. Peanuts are legumes, plants that—with the help of certain bacteria—take nitrogen from the air and convert it into a form that plants can use. Conduct research to identify some other legumes and to discover how they "fix" nitrogen. In a one-page report, describe nitrogen fixation. If you were a farmer, what crops would you choose and how would you plant them to make your farm more productive?

Introducing the Unit

How Are Cotton & Cookies Connected?

The human body requires water, air, and energy derived from food in order to function properly. Air quality, water, and appropriate land have an impact on the health of human populations.

George Washington Carver recognized the impact of human activity on soil quality when he observed the nitrogen depleting effects of cotton plants on soil. To remedy this situation he suggested planting peanuts, which could use nitrogen directly from the air. By rotating crops, soil could be productive again.

It is important to recognize the impact of human activities on the environment. Creative solutions, such as Carver's 300 uses for peanuts, are necessary for clean water, air, and land to sustain an ever-increasing human population.

SCIENCE CONNECTION

Activity

Borrow books from the school library on plants and nitrogen fixation and place in a classroom reference center. Give students a list of legumes. Have students determine which legumes fix nitrogen from soil and which fix nitrogen from air. Have students develop flow charts of both types of nitrogen fixation.

SCIENCE Online
Internet Addresses

_____
_____
_____

Explore the Glencoe Science Web site at **science.glencoe.com** to find out more about topics in this unit.

Section/Objectives	Standards		Activities/Features
Chapter Opener	**National**	**State/Local**	**Explore Activity:** Model human population growth, p. 583 **Before You Read,** p. 583
	See p. 5T for a Key to Standards.		
Section 1 Population Impact on the Environment ⏱ 2 sessions ▱ 1 block 1. **Describe** how fast the human population is increasing. 2. **Identify** reasons for Earth's rapid increase in human population. 3. **List** several ways each person can affect the environment.	National Content Standards: UCP3, C4, F2		**Science Online,** p. 585 **Life Science Integration,** p. 586
Section 2 Using Land ⏱ 2 sessions ▱ 1 block 1. **Identify** ways that land is used. 2. **Explain** how land use creates environmental problems. 3. **Identify** things you can do to help protect the environment.	National Content Standards: UCP3, A1, C4, F2		**MiniLAB:** Modeling Earth's Farmland, p. 589 **Problem Solving Activity:** How does land use affect stream discharge?, p. 591 **Physics Integration,** p. 592 **Activity:** What to Wear?, p. 595
Section 3 Conserving Resources ⏱ 3 sessions ▱ 1.5 blocks 1. **Identify** three ways to conserve resources. 2. **Explain** the advantages of recycling.	National Content Standards: UCP3, A1, C4, F2, F5		**MiniLAB,** Classifying Your Trash for One Day, p. 597 **Visualizing Trash Disposal,** p. 598 **Activity:** A World Full of People, pp. 600–601 **Science and Society:** Hazardous Waste, pp. 602–603

NATIONAL GEOGRAPHIC

Teacher's Corner

PRODUCTS AVAILABLE FROM GLENCOE
To order call 1-800-334-7344:
Videodisc
GTV: Planetary Manager
PRODUCTS AVAILABLE FROM NATIONAL GEOGRAPHIC SOCIETY
To order call 1-800-368-2728:

Videos
Healing the Earth
The Living Earth
Recycling: It's Everybody's Job
Recycling: The Endless Cycle

INDEX TO NATIONAL GEOGRAPHIC SOCIETY
The following articles may be used for research relating to this chapter: "Feeding the Planet" by T.R. Reid, Oct. 1998; "Population," by Joel L. Swerdlow, Oct. 1998; "Women and Population," by Erla Zwingle, Oct. 1998.

Activity Materials	Reproducible Resources	Section Assessment	Technology
Explore Activity: paper, pencil, metric ruler	**Chapter Resources Booklet** Foldables Worksheet, p. 15 Directed Reading Overview, p. 17 Note-taking Worksheets, pp. 31–33	GLENCOE'S **ASSESSMENT** ADVANTAGE	
Need materials? Contact Science Kit at 1-800-828-7777 or www.sciencekit.com on the Internet.	**Chapter Resources Booklet** Transparency Activity, p. 42 Enrichment, p. 28 Reinforcement, p. 25 Directed Reading, p. 18 Lab Activity, pp. 9–12	Portfolio Science Journal, p. 586 Performance Skill Builder Activities, p. 587 Content Section Assessment, p. 587	Section Focus Transparency Interactive CD-ROM/DVD Guided Reading Audio Program
MiniLAB: apple, knife **Activity:** 2 identical baking trays, garden soil, clothing made of natural fibers, clothing made of artificial materials, toothpicks, transparent tape, scissors, spray bottle, water	**Chapter Resources Booklet** Transparency Activity, p. 43 MiniLAB, p. 3 Enrichment, p. 29 Reinforcement, p. 26 Directed Reading, p. 18 Activity Worksheet, pp. 5–6 Transparency Activity, pp. 45–46 Lab Activity, pp. 13–14 **Reading and Writing Skill Activities,** p. 1	Portfolio Extension, p. 590 Performance MiniLAB, p. 589 Problem-Solving Activity, p. 591 Skill Builder Activities, p. 594 Content Section Assessment, p. 594	Section Focus Transparency Teaching Transparency Interactive CD-ROM/DVD Guided Reading Audio Program
Activity: 1,000 small objects such as popcorn kernels or dried beans, large map that shows the countries of the world, clock or watch, calculator	**Chapter Resources Booklet** Transparency Activity, p. 44 MiniLAB, p. 4 Enrichment, p. 30 Reinforcement, p. 27 Directed Reading, pp. 19, 20 Activity Worksheet, pp. 7–8 **Lab Management and Safety,** p. 71	Portfolio Activity, p. 598 Performance MiniLAB, p. 597 Skill Builder Activities, p. 599 Content Section Assessment, p. 599	Section Focus Transparency Interactive CD-ROM/DVD Guided Reading Audio Program

End of Chapter Assessment

GLENCOE'S **ASSESSMENT** ADVANTAGE

Blackline Masters	Technology	Professional Series
Chapter Resources Booklet Chapter Review, pp. 35–36 Chapter Tests, pp. 37–40 **Standardized Test Practice by The Princeton Review,** pp. 87–90	MindJogger Videoquiz CD-ROM Explorations and Quizzes Vocabulary Puzzle Makers ExamView Pro Test Bank Interactive Lesson Planner Interactive Teacher's Edition	Performance Assessment in the Science Classroom (PASC)

Transparencies

Section Focus

Assessment

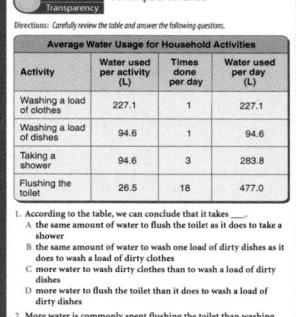

Teaching

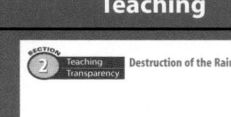
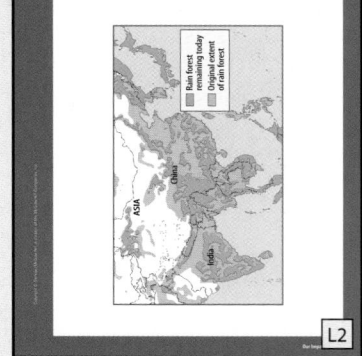

This is a representation of key blackline masters available in the Teacher Classroom Resources. See Resource Manager boxes within the chapter for additional information.

Key to Teaching Strategies

The following designations will help you decide which activities are appropriate for your students.

L1 Level 1 activities should be appropriate for students with learning difficulties.

L2 Level 2 activities should be within the ability range of all students.

L3 Level 3 activities are designed for above-average students.

ELL ELL activities should be within the ability range of English Language Learners.

COOP LEARN Cooperative Learning activities are designed for small group work.

LS Multiple Learning Styles logos, as described on page 22T, are used throughout to indicate strategies that address different learning styles.

P These strategies represent student products that can be placed into a best-work portfolio.

Hands-on Activities

Activity Worksheets

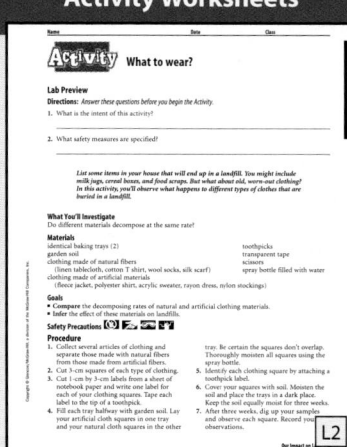

Laboratory Activities

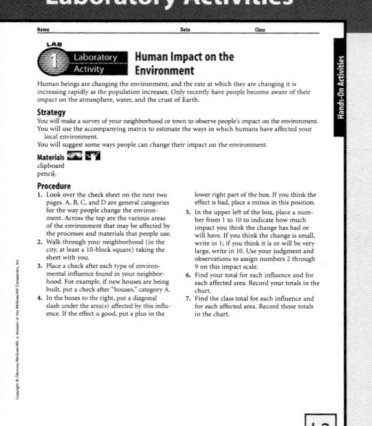

Meeting Different Ability Levels

Content Outline

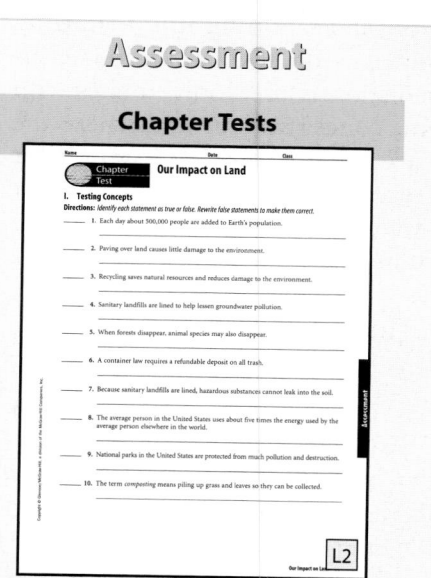

Note-taking Worksheet — Our Impact on Land

Section 1   Population Impact on the Environment

A. _____—all of the individuals of one species living in the same area at the same time
  1. Population explosion—Earth's population is _____ rapidly.
    a. Medicine, clean water, and _____ have lowered the death rate.
    b. Number of _____ has increased because more people live to child-bearing age.
  2. By 2100, Earth's population is predicted to reach _____ billion.
B. Earth has a _____—the largest number of individuals of a particular species the environment will support
C. People affect the environment by:
  1. Using _____, which is sometimes produced by burning _____.
    a. The environment changes when fossil fuels are _____.
    b. The environment changes again when fossil fuels are _____.
  2. Eating food
    a. It takes _____ to grow food.
    b. Farmers use _____ to grow food, which can get into water supplies and threaten other species.
  3. Using _____
    a. Made from _____.
    b. Refining oil produces _____—substances that contaminate the environment.
  4. Using _____
    a. _____ are cut down.
    b. Water and _____ are given off in the papermaking process.
  5. Producing _____, which must be disposed of somewhere

L2

Reinforcement

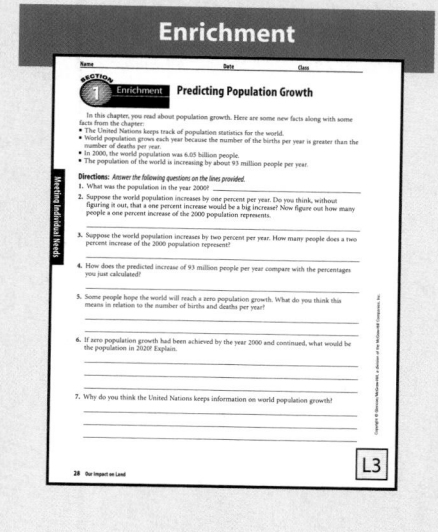

Reinforcement — Conserving Resources

Directions: Answer the following questions on the lines provided.
1. What is a recyclable object?

2. What are three reasons that paper should be recycled?

3. Why should aluminum be recycled?

4. How do container laws encourage recycling?

5. How much does recycling reduce the amount of trash a person generates in a lifetime?

6. List two ways governments encourage recycling.

7. List three ways you can reduce your consumption of materials at school and at home.

8. Do you think governments should require recycling? Why or why not?

L2

Directed Reading

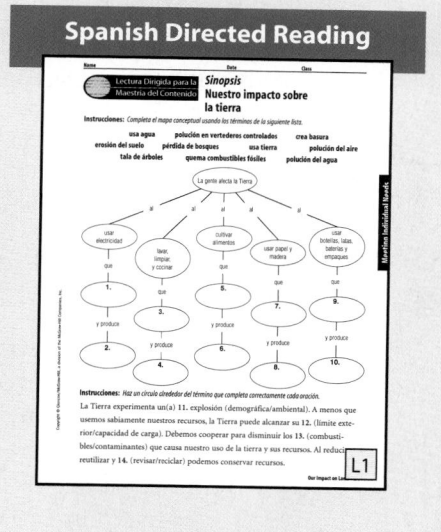

Directed Reading for Content Mastery — Overview: Our Impact on Land

Directions: Complete the concept map using the terms in the list below.

uses water   creates garbage   pollution from landfills
soil erosion   loss of forests   uses land   burns fossil fuels
cuts trees   air pollution   water pollution

Directions: Circle the term that correctly completes the sentences below.
Earth is now experiencing a(n) 11. (population/environment) explosion. Unless we use our resources wisely, Earth may reach its 12. (outer limits/carrying capacity). All of us can work together to decrease the 13. (fuels/pollutants) that are caused by our use of the land and its resources. We can conserve resources by reducing, reusing, and 14. (revising/recycling).

L1

Assessment

Chapter Tests

Chapter Test — Our Impact on Land

I.   Testing Concepts
Directions: Identify each statement as true or false. Rewrite false statements to make them correct.

_____ 1. Each day about 500,000 people are added to Earth's population.

_____ 2. Paving over land causes little damage to the environment.

_____ 3. Recycling saves natural resources and reduces damage to the environment.

_____ 4. Sanitary landfills are lined to help lessen groundwater pollution.

_____ 5. When forests disappear, animal species may also disappear.

_____ 6. A container law requires a refundable deposit on all trash.

_____ 7. Because sanitary landfills are lined, hazardous substances cannot leak into the soil.

_____ 8. The average person in the United States uses about five times the energy used by the average person elsewhere in the world.

_____ 9. National parks in the United States are protected from much pollution and destruction.

_____ 10. The term composting means piling up grass and leaves so they can be collected.

L2

Enrichment

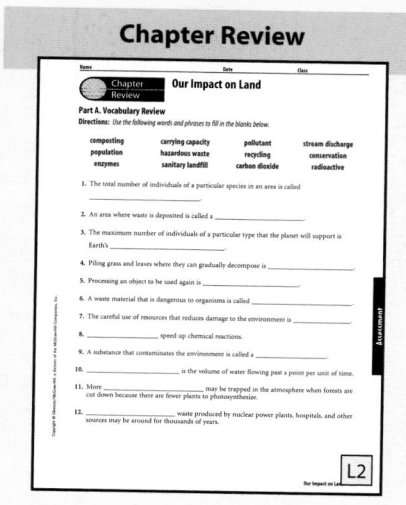

Enrichment — Predicting Population Growth

In this chapter, you read about population growth. Here are some new facts along with some facts from the chapter:
• The United Nations keeps track of population statistics for the world.
• World population grows each year because the number of the births per year is greater than the number of deaths per year.
• In 2000, the world population was 6.05 billion people.
• The population of the world is increasing by about 93 million people per year.

Directions: Answer the following questions on the lines provided.
1. What was the population in the year 2000?
2. Suppose the world population increases by one percent per year. Do you think, without figuring it out, that a one percent increase would be a big increase? Now figure out how many people a one percent increase of the 2000 population represents.

3. Suppose the world population increases by two percent per year. How many people does a two percent increase of the 2000 population represent?

4. How does the predicted increase of 93 million people per year compare with the percentages you just calculated?

5. Some people hope the world will reach a zero population growth. What do you think this means in relation to the number of births and deaths per year?

6. If zero population growth had been achieved by the year 2000 and continued, what would be the population in 2020? Explain.

7. Why do you think the United Nations keeps information on world population growth?

L3

Spanish Directed Reading

Lectura Dirigida para la Maestría del Contenido — Sinopsis: Nuestro impacto sobre la tierra

Instrucciones: Completa el mapa conceptual usando los términos de la siguiente lista.

usa agua   polución en vertederos controlados   crea basura
erosión del suelo   pérdida de bosques   usa tierra   polución del aire
tala de árboles   quema combustibles fósiles   polución del agua

Instrucciones: Haz un círculo alrededor del término que complete correctamente cada oración.
La Tierra experimenta un(a) 11. explosión (demográfica/ambiental). A menos que usemos sabiamente nuestros recursos, la Tierra puede alcanzar su 12. (límite exterior/capacidad de carga). Debemos cooperar para disminuir los 13. (combustibles/contaminantes) que causa nuestro uso de la tierra y sus recursos. Al reducir, reutilizar y 14. (revisar/reciclar) podemos conservar recursos.

L1

Test Practice Workbook

Standardized Test Practice
Teacher Edition

Glencoe Science

Earth Science

• Correlates to TEKS
• Prepares students for TAKS II
• Written by The Princeton Review

NATIONAL GEOGRAPHIC SOCIETY

L2

Chapter Review

Chapter Review — Our Impact on Land

Part A. Vocabulary Review
Directions: Use the following words and phrases to fill in the blanks below.

composting   carrying capacity   pollutant   stream discharge
population   hazardous waste   recycling   conservation
enzymes   sanitary landfill   carbon dioxide   radioactive

1. The total number of individuals of a particular species in an area is called _____.

2. An area where waste is deposited is called a _____.

3. The maximum number of individuals of a particular type that the planet will support is Earth's _____.

4. Piling grass and leaves where they can gradually decompose is _____.

5. Processing an object to be used again is _____.

6. A waste material that is dangerous to organisms is called _____.

7. The careful use of resources that reduces damage to the environment is _____.

8. _____ speed up chemical reactions.

9. A substance that contaminates the environment is called a _____.

10. _____ is the volume of water flowing past a point per unit of time.

11. More _____ may be trapped in the atmosphere when forests are cut down because there are fewer plants to photosynthesize.

12. _____ waste produced by nuclear power plants, hospitals, and other sources may be around for thousands of years.

L2

Science Content Background

SECTION
1
Population Impact on the Environment
Population and Carrying Capacity

Approximately 3 billion people, or half the world's population, are under the age of 25. With such a large portion of the population at or near childbearing age, the current population explosion is likely to continue and may even gain momentum.

Fun Fact

Italy is experiencing a significant decline in population. Couples now marry later in life and have an average of only 1.2 children. In order to reverse this trend, the government offers to pay $100 a month to couples who are willing to have a third child.

Daily Activities

There are few parts of the environment that are not affected in some way by human activities. People change the environment by moving soil, altering vegetation, adding chemicals, and removing minerals. People use, divert, and pollute water resources. People pollute the atmosphere and deplete the ozone layer. Humans are the only species on Earth that affect the environment in so many different ways. With this much power, it is important that people become aware of the consequences of misusing Earth's resources. Such an awareness would help ensure that proper choices are made regarding the future of our planet.

SECTION
2
Using Land
Land Usage

Because of population growth, the world's farmers have to feed 95 million more people each year. The farmland that produces the crops to feed this growing population loses trillions of kilograms of topsoil each year. The erosion of topsoil results not only from farming practices but also from the construction of homes and roads.

Development

In the contiguous 48 states, close to half of the land area in most cities is used for roads, highways, and parking lots. This equals two percent of the total land surface, or an area the size of the state of Georgia.

Phytoremediation

There are several methods of phytoremediation. The process of breaking down (degrading) organic pollutants is called phytodegradation. Filtering metal contaminants from water is rhizofiltration, trapping metal contaminates in soil is phytoextraction, and capturing and volatilizing water contaminates is photovolatilization. Usually, phytoremediation is used only at sites with low contaminant concentrations and where the contaminants are in areas shallow enough for plant roots to reach. In the case of groundwater pollution, the water can be treated by pumping it out of the ground and using it to irrigate trees.

SECTION
3
Conserving Resources
A Disposable Lifestyle

Waste deposited in sanitary landfills or open dumps is sometimes called "urban ore" because it contains many materials that could be recycled and used again to provide energy or useful products.

Resources include energy sources, such as oil and natural gas, as well as water, air, biological diversity, soil, and forests. Human activities threaten many of these resources. The management of these resources depends directly on the economy of a region and the value the human population places on these resources.

Precycling is one way to conserve resources. Precycling reduces waste before an item is even bought. For example, shoppers precycle by buying food in bulk, thus reducing the amount of packaging they use. Precycling also means buying products in environmentally friendly packaging or in packaging made from recycled materials.

Recycling Materials

People in the United States produce enough garbage annually to completely fill 5 million large truck trailers. If these trailers were placed end-to-end along the equator, they would extend twice around the world. Many items in this garbage could be recycled.

Recyclable materials can be used in many ways. Some plastics are melted down and spun into polyester fiber that is used to make sleeping bags, insulation, and fishing line. Also, plastics can be made into rot-resistant materials for picnic tables, waterfront decks, boat hulls, and bathtubs. Old tires, properly shredded, can be used to make new rubber, fuel, and plastic products, and can be substituted for concrete and asphalt in road pavement.

Fun Fact

Producing a quarter-pound of hamburger
- requires 100 gallons of water, 1.2 pounds of grain, and energy equal to a cup of gasoline.
- causes the loss of 1.25 pounds of topsoil.
- produces greenhouse gas emissions equal to a 6-mile drive in a typical U.S. automobile.

Telegraph Colour Library/FPG International

Our Impact on Land

Chapter Vocabulary

population
carrying capacity
pollutant
stream discharge
sanitary landfill
hazardous waste
enzyme
conservation
composting
recycling

What do you think?

Science Journal This photograph shows an apple that has been partially decayed. Inspite of the fact that fruits and vegetables can be decayed by fungi and bacteria, many foods, including the apple, can remain undecayed in a landfill because not enough oxygen reaches them. The oxygen is needed by organisms that bring about the decay. Some carrots, buried in landfills for up to 10 years have been dug up practically pristine.

Our Impact on Land

People are everywhere. You see people while at school, while waiting in traffic, or while shopping at the mall. There are a lot of people on Earth and more are added every second. How do you think the human population affects natural resources on Earth? In this chapter, you'll learn about the impact that human population has on land. You also will read about ways humans use the land and how recycling helps conserve energy and materials.

What do you think?

Science Journal Look at the picture below with a classmate. Discuss what you think this might be. Here's a hint: *It will be here for a very long time.* Write your answer or best guess in your Science Journal.

582

Theme Connection

Systems and Interactions This chapter highlights human interactions with the natural environment and the way these interactions can change natural systems.

You're the first one on the school bus in the morning. After a few more stops, you notice that the bus is rather noisy. By the time you get to school, every seat is taken. It's loud, and it's hot. Like the school bus, space on Earth is limited. Do the activity below to see what happens when the number of people on Earth increases over time.

Model human population growth

1. On a piece of paper, draw a square that is 10 cm on each side. This square represents 1 km^2 of land.

2. In 1965, an average of 21 people lived on 1 km^2 of land. Draw 21 small circles inside your square to represent this.

3. In 1990, the average was 35. Add 14 circles to illustrate this increase.

4. In 2025, the estimated number of people will be 58. Add enough circles to represent this increase.

5. Prepare a bar graph that shows population density for these years.

Observe

In your Science Journal, use the bar graph you made to explain how Earth's human population has changed over time.

Before You Read

FOLDABLES
Reading & Study
Skills

Making a Know-Want-Learn Study Fold **Make the following Foldable to help you identify what you already know and what you want to know about how human activities impact land.**

1. Place a sheet of paper in front of you so the long side is at the top. Fold the paper in half from top to bottom.

2. Fold both sides in. Unfold the paper so three sections show.

3. Through the top thickness of paper, cut along each of the fold lines to the topfold, forming three tabs. Label each tab *Know*, *Want*, and *Learned*, as shown and then, *How humans impact land* across the front of the paper.

4. Before you read the chapter, write what you know and what you want to know about how humans impact land under the first two tabs.

5. As you read the chapter, add to or correct what you have written under the tabs.

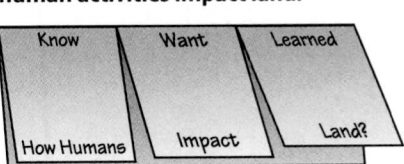

583

Purpose Use the Explore Activity to introduce students to human population growth.
L2 ELL COOP LEARN
IS Logical-Mathematical

Preparation You may want to discuss the concept of scale drawings with students before they perform this activity. The scale of the drawing in this activity is 1:10,000.

Materials metric ruler, pencil, paper

Teaching Strategy Review the setup of the bar graph with students: Put years on the x-axis, and the density of people in the square (km^2) on the y-axis.

Observe

Possible answer: Population is increasing more rapidly, as more people live to maturity and reproduce.

✓ Assessment

Performance Draw a square to represent the 1990 average population density in the United States (25 people/km^2) and compare it with the world average used in the activity. Hypothesize how the U.S. population density might differ from the world average in 2025. Students will likely say that U.S. population density will remain lower than the world average. Use **PASC,** p. 93.

FOLDABLES
Reading & Study
Skills

Before You Read

Dinah Zike Study Fold

Purpose Use this activity to help students identify what they already know and what they want to know about how human activities impact land. The resulting Foldable can be used for recording information as students read.

📁 For additional help, see Foldables Worksheet, p. 15 in **Chapter Resources Booklet,** or go to the Glencoe Science Web site at **science.glencoe.com.** See After You Read in the Study Guide at the end of this chapter.

1 Motivate

Bellringer Transparency

Display the Section Focus Transparency for Section 1. Use the accompanying Transparency Activity Master. L2 ELL

Section Focus Transparency **All Tied Up**

More and more we are seeing traffic situations like this one all across the country. Our ever increasing population means even more drivers—and vehicles—on the roads.

1. Do you think this road has reached its capacity to carry traffic?
2. Is building bigger roads a good solution to this problem? Why or why not?
3. How might it be possible to have more people, but less traffic? L2

Tie to Prior Knowledge

Have students brainstorm a list of resources that people need each day. Then discuss how these needs change when population increases greatly and how this might affect the environment. Possible answers: clean air and water, food, energy for electricity, heat, or cooling; the need for more energy, food, and other products strains resources and causes more pollution.

✔ Reading Check

Answer because the population has increased so rapidly

Population Impact on the Environment

1 Population Impact on the Environment

As You Read

What **You'll Learn**
- **Describe** how fast the human population is increasing.
- **Identify** reasons for Earth's rapid increase in human population.
- **List** several ways each person can affect the environment.

Vocabulary
population
carrying capacity
pollutant

Why **It's Important**
As the human population grows, resources are depleted and more waste is produced.

Population and Carrying Capacity

Look around and identify the kinds of living things you see. You might see students, fish in an aquarium, or squirrels in the trees. Perhaps plants are on the windowsill. These are examples of populations. A **population** is all of the individuals of one species occupying a particular area. As you can see in **Figure 1,** the area can be small or large. For example, a human population can be of one community, such as Los Angeles, or the entire planet.

Earth's Increasing Population Do you ever wonder how many people live on Earth? The global population in 2000 was 6.05 billion. Each day, the number of humans increases by approximately 260,000. Earth is now experiencing a population explosion. The word *explosion* is used because the rate at which the population is growing has increased rapidly in recent history.

✔ Reading Check *Why is the increasing number of humans on Earth called a population explosion?*

Figure 1
A population is the number of individuals occupying an area. **A** The population of this classroom is 24. **B** The population of Cranford includes the population of the classroom.

CRANFORD
POP. 10,290

Section ✔*Assessment* Planner

PORTFOLIO
Science Journal, p. 586
PERFORMANCE ASSESSMENT
Skill Builder Activities, p. 587
See page 606 for more options.

CONTENT ASSESSMENT
Section, p. 587
Challenge, p. 587
Chapter, pp. 606–607

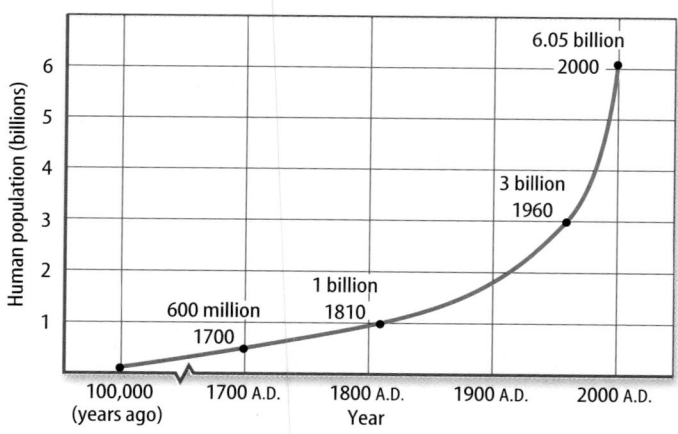

Population Growth of Modern Humans

Human population (billions)

- 6.05 billion 2000
- 3 billion 1960
- 1 billion 1810
- 600 million 1700

Year: 100,000 (years ago), 1700 A.D., 1800 A.D., 1900 A.D., 2000 A.D.

Figure 2
Human population remained relatively steady until the beginning of the nineteeth century. *Why has the human population experienced such a sharp increase in growth rate since about 1800?*

Population Growth Many years ago, few people lived on Earth. You can see in **Figure 2** that it took thousands of years for the population to reach one billion people. After that, the population increased much faster. The human population has increased because modern medicine, clean water, and better nutrition have decreased the death rate. This means that more people are living longer. In addition, the number of births has increased because more people survive to the age at which they can have children.

By 2100, the population is predicted to be about 11 billion—nearly twice what it is now. Imagine the effect such a large human population will have on the environment. Will the things that have helped the population grow, such as improved health care and clean water, be maintainable? Will Earth have enough natural resources to support such a large population?

Population Limits Each person uses space and resources. Population size depends on the amount of available resources and how members of the population use them. If resources become scarce or if the environment is damaged, members of the population can suffer and population size could decrease.

People once thought that Earth had an endless supply of resources such as fossil fuels, metals, and rich soils. It's now known that this isn't true. Earth's resources are limited. The planet has a carrying capacity. **Carrying capacity** is the largest number of individuals of a particular species that the environment can support. Unless Earth's resources are treated with care, they could disappear and the human population might reach its carrying capacity.

SCIENCE Online

Data Update For an online population update, visit the Glencoe Science Web site at **science.glencoe.com.** Communicate to your class what you've learned.

Section 1 Population Impact on the Environment **585**

---

2 Teach

Population and Carrying Capacity

Caption Answer

Figure 2 The death rate slowed because of better medicines, sanitation, and nutrition; birthrate increased because more people survive to child-bearing age.

Text Question Answers

No one knows; eventually if population continues to grow, it will not.

Discussion

Explain to students that in nature, individuals within any population compete for resources. When population density is low, resources are abundant, and population increases. **What happens as the population approaches the carrying capacity?** Resources become scarce, and the rate of population increase declines.

Fun Fact

The current annual population growth rate of about 1.4% increases world population by about 85 million people each year. This is equivalent to adding a city the size of Los Angeles every two and a half weeks.

SCIENCE Online

Internet Addresses

_____

_____

_____

_____

Explore the Glencoe Science Web site at **science.glencoe.com** to find out more about topics in this section.

Resource Manager

Chapter Resources Booklet

Transparency Activity, p. 42

Directed Reading for Content Mastery, pp. 17, 18

Note-taking Worksheets, pp. 31–33

Inclusion Strategies

Gifted Have students make population graphs that compare the population changes in Europe, Asia, Africa, North America, and South America during the past 100 years. If data are hard to find, tell students to use data from the last few decades only.  **Logical-Mathematical**

People and the Environment

Life Science
INTEGRATION

Pesticides get into streams through runoff. Streams carry water to lakes. Pesticides enter eagles' bodies when they eat contaminated fish.

Text Question Answers

Possible answers: by using resources and causing pollution; by making wastes that go to landfills or pollute land or water; using mineral resources that require destructive mining

✔ Reading Check

Answer Students should include information on using resources and causing pollution.

Caption Answer

Figure 3 oil, trees, water

Discussion

How do you change Earth each day? by using natural resources and creating wastes **What can you do to strike a balance between people and the environment?** conserve energy, recycle

Life Science
INTEGRATION

Bald eagles are fish-eating birds whose population in the Unites States declined rapidly during the 1950s and early 1960s. One of the reasons this occurred was the use of pesticides, which affected reproduction. Research how pesticides applied to land can end up in an eagle's body.

Figure 3
You use many resources every day. *What resources were consumed to produce items you use, such as those you see here?*

People and the Environment

How will you affect the environment over your lifetime? By the time you're 75 years old, you will have produced enough garbage to equal the mass of seven African elephants (53,000 kg). You will have consumed enough water to fill 75,000 bathtubs (19 million L). If you live in the United States, you will have used five times as much energy as an average person living elsewhere in the world.

Daily Activities Every day you affect the environment. The electricty you use is generated by burning fossil fuels. The environment changes when fuels are mined, and again later when they are burned. The water that you use must be treated to make it as clean as possible before being returned to the environment. You eat food, which needs soil to grow. Much of the food you eat is grown using chemical substances, such as pesticides and herbicides, to kill insects and weeds. These chemicals can get into water supplies and threaten the health of living things if the chemicals become too concentrated. How else do you and other people affect the environment?

As you can see in **Figure 3,** many of the products you use are made of plastic and paper. Plastic begins as oil. The process of refining oil can produce **pollutants**—substances that contaminate the environment. In the process of changing trees to paper, several things happen that impact the environment. Trees are cut down. Oil is used to transport the trees to the paper mill, and water and air pollutants are given off in the papermaking process.

✔ Reading Check

How do the products you use affect the environment?

Science Journal

The Future Have students imagine Earth in 200 years. Ask them to write several paragraphs answering the following questions: **Where will most people live? What will Earth's environment be like?** Possible answers: People will live in high-rises, on the Moon, on other planets, or under the sea; Earth will be more polluted and have less diversity of life. L2 LS **Intrapersonal** P

Resource Manager

Chapter Resources Booklet
Reinforcement, p. 25
Enrichment, p. 28
Lab Activity, pp. 9–12

Packaging Produces Waste

The land is changed when resources are removed from it. The environment is further impacted when those resources are shaped into usable products. After the products are produced and consumed, they must be discarded. Look at **Figure 4.** Unnecessary packaging is only one of the problems associated with waste disposal.

The Future As the population continues to grow, more resources are used and more waste is created. Traffic-choked highways, overflowing garbage dumps, shrinking forests, and vanishing wildlife are possible. What can be done to prevent these problems? As you learn more about how you affect the environment, you'll discover what you can do to help make the future world one that everyone can live in and enjoy. An important step that you can take is to think carefully about your use of natural resources. If you conserve resources, you can lessen the impact on the environment.

Figure 4
Packaging foods for single servings uses more paper and plastic than buying food in bulk does.

Visual Learning

Figure 4 Repeat that the new packaging uses less material than the old. **Might there be problems with the new packaging as well?** It is a type of plastic that is not easily recycled, and it is made using petroleum, a limited resource.

3 Assess

Reteach
Have students keep a diary for one week of everything they use, and then have them analyze how this affects the environment. L1 IS **Linguistic**

Challenge
Tell students that all the humans on Earth would cover a small portion of Earth's surface. **If this is so, why is population growth a problem?** Although people's bodies do not take up much space, things people build, use, and throw away occupy and impact the land. People also need space to grow food and for shelter.

✓Assessment

Performance Have students graph the population growth of their community for the last few decades. Does it mirror world or national trends? Use **PASC,** p. 111.

Section ① Assessment

1. Using **Figure 2,** estimate the human population increase from 1800 to 1960. How many people were added to the population from 1960 to 2000?

2. List three reasons why the human population is increasing rapidly.

3. What might happen if the human population reaches its carrying capacity?

4. How do your daily activities affect Earth's available resources?

5. **Think Critically** In some areas of the world, individuals have less negative impact on the environment than citizens in the United States do. In your Science Journal, explain why this is so.

Skill Builder Activities

6. **Researching Information** Some areas of the world are experiencing a decrease in population. Find out where this is happening and some reasons for the decrease. **For more help,** refer to the Science Skill Handbook.

7. **Making and Using Graphs** Make a line graph of the data shown below. Plot years on the *x*-axis and population on the *y*-axis. Use your graph to infer the population of humans in the year 2040. **For more help, refer to the** Science Skill Handbook.

Human Population (billions)
1998 — 5.86
2010 — 6.97
2025 — 8.66

Answers to Section Assessment

1. about 2 billion; about 3.5 billion
2. The death rate slowed because of better medicines, sanitation, and nutrition; birthrate increased because more people now reach childbearing age.
3. Resources will be more limited; population might level off or decrease.

4. Activities reduce available resources; production of food, plastic, and paper destroy habitats and pollute water, air, and soil resources.
5. Possible answer: People in the U.S. use more water, energy, and food and generate more wastes per person than do people in developing countries.

6. Answers will vary depending on the student's individual research.
7. approximately 11.6 billion

Using Land

1 Motivate

Bellringer Transparency

Display the Section Focus Transparency for Section 2. Use the accompanying Transparency Activity Master. L2

ELL

Tie to Prior Knowledge

Ask students what signs they have seen around them that population is increasing. Possible answers: more homes and shopping centers being built; open spaces such as forests disappearing; more traffic

As You Read

What You'll Learn

- **Identify** ways that land is used.
- **Explain** how land use creates environmental problems.
- **Identify** things you can do to help protect the environment.

Vocabulary

stream discharge
sanitary landfill
hazardous waste
enzyme

Why It's Important

Land is a resource to use responsibly.

Land Usage

You may not think of land as a natural resource. Yet it is as important to people as oil, clean air, and clean water. Through agriculture, logging, garbage disposal, and urban development, we use land—and sometimes abuse it.

Agriculture About 16 million km^2 of Earth's total land surface is used as farmland. To feed the growing world population, some farmers use higher-yielding seeds and chemical fertilizers. These methods help increase the amount of food grown on each km^2 of land. Herbicides and pesticides also are used to reduce weeds, insects, and other pests that can damage crops.

Organic farming techniques, as shown in **Figure 5,** use natural fertilizers, crop rotation, and biological pest controls. These methods help crops thrive without using chemicals. You can buy organically grown fruits and vegetables in many places today.

Whenever vegetation is removed from an area, such as a construction site or tilled farmland, soil is exposed. Without plant roots to hold soil in place, nothing prevents the soil from being carried away by running water and wind. Several centimeters of topsoil may be lost in one year. In some places, it can take more than 1,000 years for new topsoil to develop.

Figure 5
Organic farms such as this one reduce the environmental impact of chemicals on land. *How does organic farming differ from other techniques?*

Section ✓Assessment Planner

PORTFOLIO
Extension, p. 590
PERFORMANCE ASSESSMENT
MiniLAB, p. 589
Problem-Solving Activity, p. 591
Skill Builder Activities, p. 594
See page 606 for more options.

CONTENT ASSESSMENT
Section, p. 594
Challenge, p. 594
Chapter, pp. 606–607

Reducing Erosion Some farmers practice no-till farming. They don't plow the soil from harvest until planting. Instead, farmers plant seed between the stubble left from the previous year.

Another way to reduce soil loss is by contour plowing. The rows are tilled across hills and valleys. When it rains, water and soil are captured by the plowed rows, reducing erosion.

Feeding Livestock Land also is used for feeding livestock. Animals such as cattle eat vegetation and then are used as food for humans. In the United States, the majority of land used for grazing is unsuitable for crops. However, about 20 percent of the total cropland in our country is used to grow feed for livestock.

Look at **Figure 6.** A square kilometer of vegetable crops can feed many more people than a square kilometer of land used to raise livestock. Some people argue that a more efficient use of the land would be to grow crops directly for human consumption, rather than for consumption by livestock. However, many consider meat and dairy products an important part of their diet. They argue that these foods are important sources of protein.

Figure 6
Land is used for feeding livestock. **A** About half the corn raised in the United States, such as the corn grown on this Iowa farm, is used to feed livestock. **B** Land is used more efficiently when vegetable crops are grown directly for human consumption.

Amount of Food Grown on 1 km² of Land

5.6 million kg of Tomatoes

4.5 million kg of Potatoes

28,000 kg of Beef

Mini LAB

Modeling Earth's Farmland

Procedure
1. Cut an **apple** into four quarters and set aside three.
2. Slice the remaining quarter in half and set one of the halves aside—1/8 of Earth's surface is uninhabitable.
3. Cut the remaining piece into four sections. Keep only one piece because the others represent developed land or land that can't be farmed.
4. Carefully peel the 1/32 piece that's left. This represents the thin layer of Earth that is used to grow food for the entire human population.

Analysis
1. What may happen if available farmland is converted to other uses?

2 Teach

Land Usage

Caption Answer

Figure 5 It reduces chemical use and it rebuilds topsoil.

Mini LAB

Purpose Students observe how little of Earth's surface is available for farming. L2
IS Visual-Spatial
Materials apple, plastic knife
Teaching Strategy Discuss with students why three parts of the apple are set aside in Step 1. Remind them that water covers three-fourths of Earth's surface.
Safety Precaution Have students use knives with care.
Analysis
1. Too little land might be available for food production.

✓ Assessment

Oral Why will the amount of farmland decrease in your lifetime? How can we grow more food on less land? Some land will be converted to homes and roads because of increased population. Possible answers: Use hydroponics in high-rise buildings or high-yield crops to grow more on less land. Use **PASC**, p. 143.

Visual Learning

Figure 6B If only mass, and not nutritional value, is considered, it is obvious that 1 km² of land can produce many more kilograms of potatoes than of beef. **What percent of the potato yield in kilograms per km² does the beef yield represent?** $28,000 \div 4,500,000 = .006$, or .6%, or less than 1%

Land Usage, continued

Make a Model

To model the way organic farmers grow food, have students design and build a school compost pile. Then have them add the compost to plantings on school property. L2 ELL COOP LEARN

Use an Analogy

Large areas of forest, such as Earth's tropical rain forests, are often called CO_2 sinks. Plants remove CO_2 from the air and incorporate it in their tissues. In the same way, sinks remove water that flows from a tap.

✔ Reading Check

Answer Levels could increase.

Extension

Have students research and write reports about the connection between CO_2 concentration in the air and global temperature increase, called global warming. Have them include the causes of CO_2 rise, its effects, and efforts internationally to stop it. P

Discussion

Remind students that the harm caused by destruction of tropical rain forests is well known. **Why might people continue to cut the tropical forests, even though they know it is harmful?** Accept all reasonable answers as a basis for discussion. Possible answers: People who use tropical wood products may not realize the harm their individual purchases cause; some indigenous people may need the wood for fuel or the land for farming.

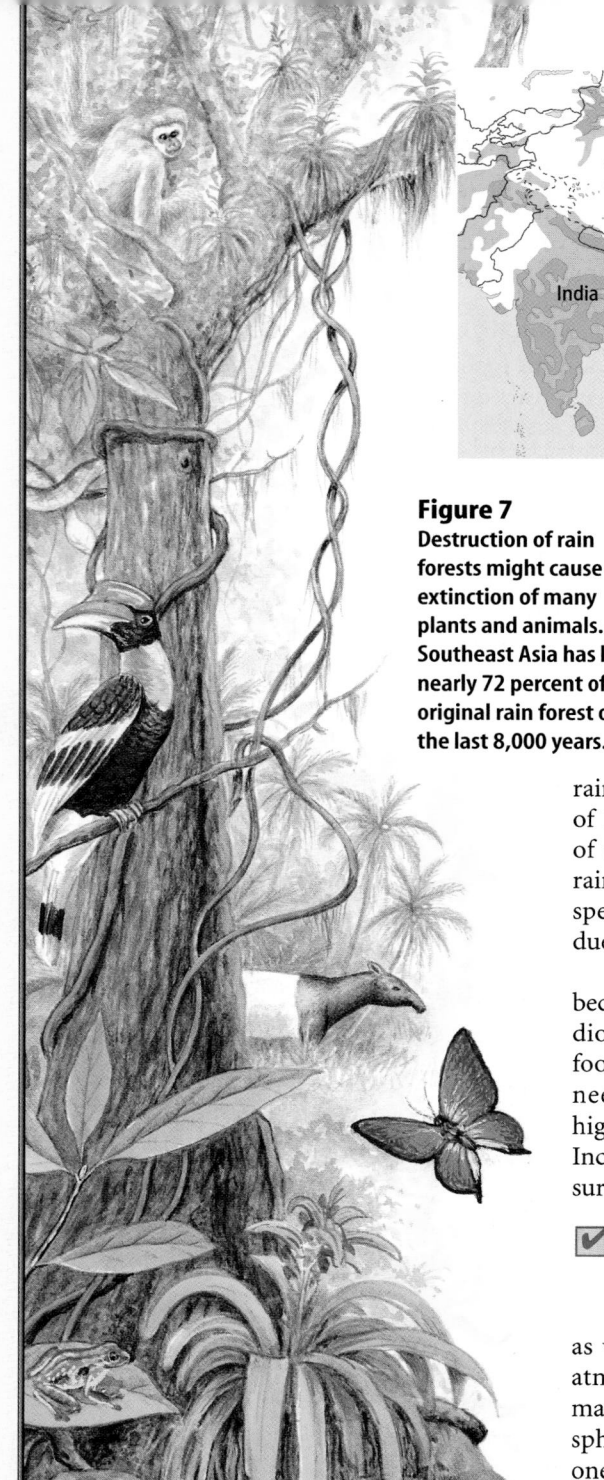

Figure 7
Destruction of rain forests might cause the extinction of many plants and animals. Southeast Asia has lost nearly 72 percent of its original rain forest over the last 8,000 years.

Forest Resources Are a lot of houses being built in or around your community? Trees are cut down and used in the United States and elsewhere for lumber, fuel, and paper. Often, new trees are planted to take their places. But in some cases, as in tropical regions shown in **Figure 7,** forests are cut down without being replaced. Each year, 310,000 km^2 of rain forest are destroyed on Earth—an area the size of Poland. Ecologists estimate that 30 to 50 percent of all species depend on habitats found in tropical rain forests. Evidence also suggests that up to 25,000 species worldwide might become extinct each year due to the loss of rain forests.

Organisms living outside of the tropics also suffer because of the lost vegetation. Plants remove carbon dioxide from the air as they use sunlight to make food. This process produces oxygen that organisms need to breathe. Less vegetation could result in higher levels of carbon dioxide in the atmosphere. Increased levels of carbon dioxide may cause Earth's surface temperature to rise.

✔ Reading Check

What can happen to carbon dioxide levels in air if trees are cut down?

Cutting trees can have a regional effect on climate as well. Water from tree leaves evaporates into the atmosphere where it can condense to form rain. If many trees are cut down, less water enters the atmosphere and the region receives less rainfall. This is one way humans can affect the water cycle.

590 CHAPTER 20

Cultural Diversity

Making Land-Smart Decisions Allan Savory worked as a wildlife biologist and tracker in Zimbabwe for 40 years before moving to Albuquerque, New Mexico, and beginning a program of holistic land management. Savory has established the Center for Holistic Management, which works with individuals, businesses, ranchers, community planners, and resource managers. At the center, people learn a decision-making process that helps them attain their goals and sustain the environment. Important aspects of this decision making include assessing effects of choices on the water cycle, mineral use, solar energy flow, and biological communities. Have students hypothesize how these elements might affect their local community and the decisions of local community planners.

Development Since 1960, nearly 640,000 km of highway pavement have been added in the United States. Highway building often leads to more paving as office buildings, stores, and parking lots are constructed.

Paving land prevents water from soaking into the soil. Instead, it runs off into sewers or streams. A stream's discharge increases when more water enters its channel. **Stream discharge** is the volume of water flowing past a point per unit of time. During heavy rainstorms in paved areas, rainwater flows directly into streams, increasing stream discharge and the risk of flooding.

Many communities use underground water supplies for drinking. Covering land with roads, sidewalks, and parking lots reduces the amount of rainwater that soaks into the ground to refill underground water supplies.

Some communities preserve areas that cannot be paved. Land is set aside for environmental protection, as shown in **Figure 8.** Preserving space beautifies the environment, increases the area into which water can soak, and provides space for recreation and other outdoor activities.

Figure 8
Some communities set aside land that cannot be developed, such as this area near Portland, Oregon. *How does preserving green space near cities protect the environment?*

Problem-Solving Activity

How does land use affect stream discharge?

It's not unusual for streams and rivers to flood after heavy rain. The amount of water flowing quickly into waterways may be more than streams and rivers can carry. Land use can affect how much runoff enters a waterway. Would changing the landscape increase flooding? Use your ability to interpret a data table to find out.

Land Use	Runoff to Streams (%)
Commercial (offices and stores)	75
Residential (houses)	40
Natural areas (forest and grassland)	29

Identifying the Problem
The table at the right lists the percentage of rainfall that runs off land. Compare the amount of runoff for each of the land uses listed. Assume that all of the regions are the same size and have the same slope. Looking at the table, do you see a relationship between what is on the land and how much water runs off of it?

Solving the Problem
1. Two years after construction of a commercial development near a stream, houses downstream flooded after a heavy rain. What contributed to the flooding?
2. What are some ways that developers can help reduce the risk of flooding?

SECTION 2 Using Land **591**

Curriculum Connection

Math Remind students that 4,000 km² (988,422 acres) of farmland are converted to other uses each year. In 1998, the average farm in the United States was 435 acres. Have students use this data to describe farmland lost in terms of number of farms lost. 988,422 acres ÷ 435 acres / farm = 2,272.23 farms lost each year As an extension, have students determine the number of farms lost per state. about 45

Caption Answer

Figure 9A Landfill space is scarce, some materials in landfills decompose slowly, and some hazardous wastes leak into surrounding soil and groundwater.

Teacher FYI

Biodegradable materials make up about 65% of the waste in landfills, by volume. Paper and cardboard alone make up more than 50% of the volume of landfill waste.

Hazardous Wastes

Physics INTEGRATION

When unstable elements, such as uranium-238, decay, they emit particles. This property of emitting particles is called radioactivity. The particles these elements emit can damage living tissue.

Extension

Have students work with adults to conduct home hazardous waste audits. Suggest they look for hazardous waste items under kitchen and bathroom sinks and in basements and garages. Have students share their findings. Encourage them to get information on safe hazardous waste disposal from the local sanitation, public works, or health department to share with their families.

A

Figure 9

A The majority of garbage is deposited in sanitary landfills. *What are some problems associated with landfill disposal?*

B Sanitary landfills are designed to contain garbage and prevent contamination of the surrounding land and water.

Physics INTEGRATION

Wastes from nuclear power plants must be stored safely because radioactivity is dangerous. The U.S. government is currently studying a site in Nevada for nuclear waste disposal because the area is remote, little rain falls, and the underground water supply is far below the proposed storage facility. What is radioactivity and how can it harm the environment?

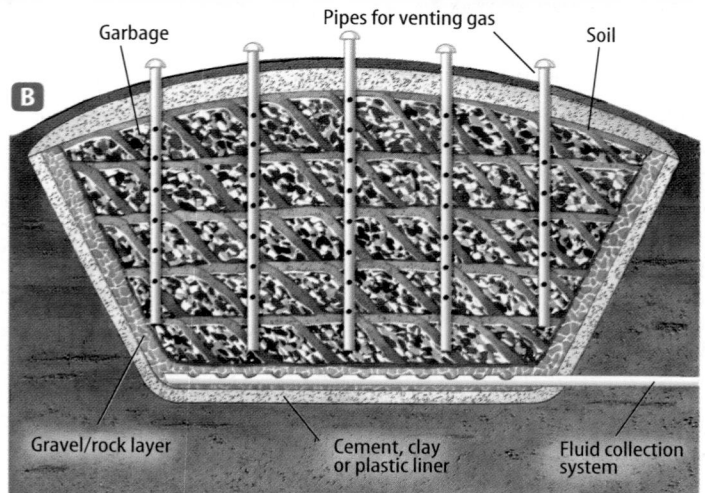

B

Garbage — Pipes for venting gas — Soil

Gravel/rock layer — Cement, clay or plastic liner — Fluid collection system

Sanitary Landfills

Land also is used when consumed products are thrown away. About 60 percent of our garbage goes into sanitary landfills. A **sanitary landfill,** like the one illustrated in **Figure 9,** is an area where each day's garbage is deposited and covered with soil. The soil prevents the deposit from blowing away, helps decompose some materials, and reduces the odor produced by the decaying waste.

Sanitary landfills also are designed to prevent liquid wastes from draining into the soil and groundwater below. New sanitary landfills are lined with plastic, concrete, or clay-rich soils that trap the liquid waste. Because of these linings, sanitary landfills greatly reduce the chance that pollutants will leak into the surrounding soil and groundwater.

Since many materials do not decompose in landfills, or they decompose slowly, landfills fill with garbage, and new ones must be built. Locating an acceptable area to build a landfill can be difficult. Type of soil, the depth to groundwater, and neighborhood concerns must be considered.

Hazardous Wastes

Some of the wastes that are thrown away are dangerous to organisms. Wastes that are poisonous, that cause cancer, or that can catch fire are called **hazardous wastes.** Previously, everyone—industries and individuals alike—put hazardous wastes into landfills, along with household garbage. In the 1980s, many states passed environmental laws that prohibit industries from disposing of hazardous wastes in sanitary landfills. New technologies which help recycle hazardous wastes have decreased the need to dispose of them.

592 CHAPTER 20 Our Impact on Land

LAB DEMONSTRATION

Purpose to show the effectiveness of sanitary landfill liners

Materials scissors, 3 beakers (1,000 mL), plastic bag, modeling clay, dry sand (1,200 mL), water (600 mL) with food coloring

Preparation Cut a 20-cm diameter circle from a plastic bag. Pour 400 mL of sand into each beaker.

Procedure Place the plastic circle on top of the sand in one beaker and a layer of clay on the sand in a second beaker. Pour 200 mL of water into each beaker. Have students describe what they see.

Expected Outcome Water remains above the plastic and clay, but moves into the exposed sand.

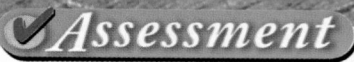

Assessment

Did the plastic and clay stop water from getting to the sand? Yes. **Why do landfills use liners?** They stop pollutants from leaking into soil and groundwater.

Household Hazardous Waste Unlike most industries, individuals discard hazardous wastes such as insect sprays, batteries, drain cleaners, bleaches, medicines, and paints in the trash. It may seem that when you throw something in the garbage, it's gone and you don't need to be concerned with it anymore. Unfortunately, some garbage can remain unchanged in a landfill for hundreds of years. You can help by disposing of hazardous wastes at special hazardous waste-collection sites. Contact your local government to find out about collections in your area.

Phytoremediation Hazardous substances can contaminate soil. These contaminants may come from nearby industries or leaking landfills. Water contaminated from such a source can filter into the ground and leave the toxic substances in the soil. Some plants can help fix this problem in a method called phytoremediation (FITE uh rem ee dee AY shun). *Phyto* means "plant" and *remediation* means "to fix or remedy a problem."

During phytoremediation, roots of certain plants such as alfalfa, grasses, and pine trees can absorb metals, including copper, lead, and zinc from contaminated soil just as they absorb other nutrients. **Figure 10** shows how metals are absorbed from the soil and taken into plant tissue.

What happens to these plants after they absorb metals? If livestock were to eat contaminated alfalfa, the harmful metals could end up in your milk or meat. Plants that become concentrated with metals from soil eventually must be harvested and either composted to recycle the metals or burned. If these plants are destroyed by burning, the ash residue contains the hazardous waste that was in the plant tissue and must be disposed of at a hazardous waste site.

Chemistry INTEGRATION

Breaking Down Organic Pollutants Living things also can clean up pollutants other than metals. Substances that contain carbon and other elements like hydrogen, oxygen, and nitrogen, are called organic compounds. Examples of organic pollutants are gasoline, oil, and solvents.

Organic pollutants can be broken down into simpler, harmless substances, some of which plants use for growth. Some plant roots release enzymes (EN zimez) into the soil. **Enzymes** are substances that make chemical reactions go faster. Enzymes from plant roots increase the rate at which organic pollutants are broken down into simpler substances. Plants use these substances for growth.

 **Reading Check** *What is the role of enzymes in the breakdown of organic pollutants?*

Figure 10
Metals such as copper can be removed from soil and be absorbed by plant tissues. *Why can't this vegetation be fed to livestock?*

Metal absorbed

Composting   Burning

Metal recovery

Ash disposal

Caption Answer
Figure 10 Livestock tissue would become contaminated, making it unfit to eat.

Extension
Have students research and write reports about human health problems caused by toxic metals. Students will find that toxic metals affect many of the body's systems and can cause cancer and birth defects.

Fun Fact

Bioremediation is the use of microorganisms (bacteria, fungi) to treat hazardous wastes and change them into harmless substances. Bioremediation works on certain organic wastes, but doesn't work as well for toxic metals or chemical wastes that are very concentrated.

Use Science Words
Word Meaning Have students infer the meanings of *phytohormone* and *phytoplankton*. Then have them check their definitions in a dictionary. Phytohormone is a plant hormone; phytoplankton is plantlike plankton.

Reading Check

Answer They speed up the reactions that break down organic pollutants.

Resource Manager

Chapter Resources Booklet
    Enrichment, p. 29
    Lab Activity, pp. 13–14

Teacher **FYI**

When plants used in phytoremediation are incinerated, the volume of ash is only about ten percent of the volume of the soil that was contaminated. Therefore, much less waste landfill space is required for disposal of these plant residues than would be necessary if all the soil had to be removed and placed into this type of landfill.

Natural Preserves

③ Assess

Reteach

Review with students the ways that humans have changed Earth over the past century. List on the board students' suggestions of ways to better balance our need to use land with our need for a quality environment. Take a poll: How many students would be willing to adopt each change? L2 COOP LEARN
LS **Interpersonal**

Challenge

Encourage students to research natural preserves in your own state. Where are they? How are they used by the public? Is there adequate funding to maintain them? If one of these preserves is nearby, organize a visit to the preserve that includes a presentation by a park ranger. L3

✔Assessment

Content Have each student write a fictitious newspaper article, dateline 2100. The article should report on either a major environmental problem of the time, or a major victory in solving such a problem. Have students share their articles. Use **Performance Assessment in the Science Classroom,** p. 141.

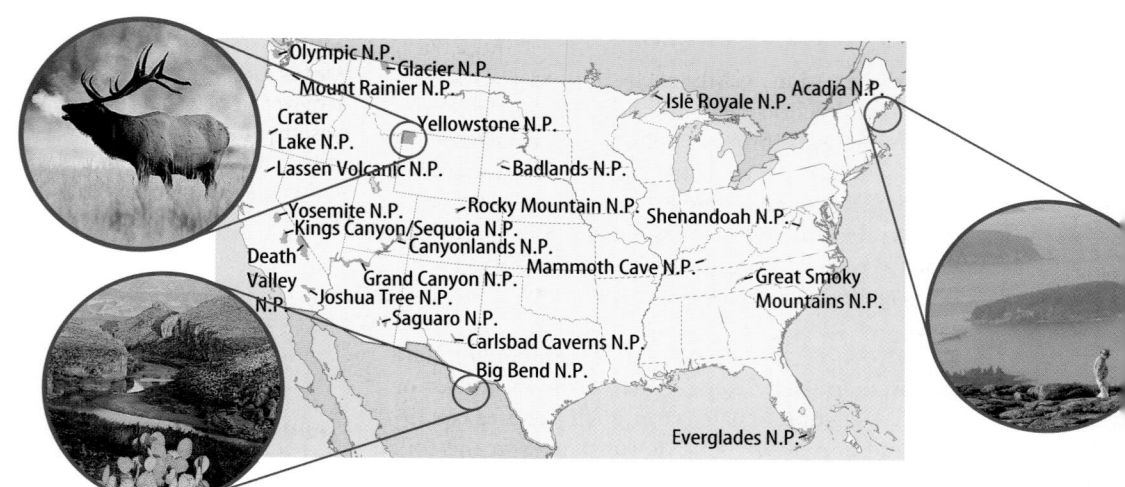

Figure 11
Many countries set aside land in the form of national parks as natural preserves. *How do these natural preserves benefit humans and other living things?*

Natural Preserves

Not all land on Earth is being utilized to produce usable materials or for storing waste. As shown in **Figure 11,** some land remains mostly uninhabited by people. National forestlands, grasslands, and national parks in the United States are protected from many problems that you've read about in this section. In many other countries throughout the world, land also is set aside for natural preserves. As the world population continues to rise, the strain on the environment is likely to worsen. Preserving some land in its natural state will benefit future generations.

Section ② Assessment

1. In your Science Journal, list six ways that people use land.
2. Discuss environmental problems that can be created by agriculture and trash disposal.
3. What can you do that would benefit the environment?
4. How can development increase flooding?
5. **Think Critically** Preserving land beautifies the environment, provides recreational space, and benefits future generations. Are there any disadvantages to setting aside large areas of land as natural preserves?

Skill Builder Activities

6. **Forming a Hypothesis** Develop a hypothesis about how migrating birds might be affected by cutting down forests. **For more help, refer to the** Science Skill Handbook.
7. **Using a Word Processor** Suppose that a new landfill is needed in your community. Where do you think it should be located? Try to convince people that you've selected the best place for the landfill. Write a letter to the editor of the local newspaper listing reasons for your choice. Map the location of your choice. **For more help, refer to the** Technology Skill Handbook.

Answers to Section Assessment

1. farming, grazing, lumber, landfills, development, preserves
2. agriculture: soil erosion, pesticide pollution; trash disposal: leakage into soil and water, use of space
3. Possible answers: dispose of hazardous waste at special collection sites, conserve water and energy, recycle

4. Development prevents water from soaking into the ground, resulting in more runoff and flooding.
5. As population increases, the land could be used for homes, farms, or other needs.
6. Migrating birds who nest in the forests would lose their habitat. Without proper nesting sites, the

birds may eventually become extinct.
7. Letters should address the community's need for a landfill, lack of other options, and concerns about environmental impacts.

Activity

What to wear?

List some items in your house that will end up in a landfill. You might include milk jugs, cereal boxes, and food scraps. But what about old worn-out clothing? In this activity, you'll observe what happens to different types of clothes that are buried in a landfill.

What You'll Investigate
Do different materials decompose at the same rate?

Materials
identical baking trays (2)
garden soil
clothing made of natural fibers (linen tablecloth, cotton shirt, wool socks, silk scarf)
clothing made of artificial materials (fleece jacket, polyester shirt, acrylic sweater, rayon dress, nylon stockings)
toothpicks
transparent tape
scissors
spray bottle filled with water

Goals
- **Compare** the decomposing rates of natural and artificial clothing materials.
- **Infer** the effect of these materials on landfills.

Procedure
1. Collect several articles of clothing and separate those made with natural fibers from those made from artificial materials.
2. Cut 3-cm squares of each type of clothing.
3. Cut 1-cm by 3-cm labels from a sheet of notebook paper, and write one label for each of your clothing squares. Tape each label to the tip of a toothpick.
4. Fill each tray halfway with garden soil. Lay your artificial cloth squares in one tray and your natural cloth squares in the other tray. Be certain the squares don't overlap. Thoroughly moisten all squares using the spray bottle.
5. Identify each clothing square by attaching a toothpick label.
6. Cover your squares with soil. Moisten the soil and place the trays in a dark place. Keep the soil equally moist for three weeks.
7. After three weeks, dig up your samples and observe each square. Record your observations in your Science Journal.

Conclude and Apply:
1. **Compare** the amount of decomposition of the two types of materials.
2. **Infer** the effects of clothing made with natural materials on landfills.
3. **Infer** the effects of clothing made with artificial materials on landfills.
4. **Research** materials used to manufacture clothing. Determine if the material is made from recycled products such as plastic bottles.

Communicating Your Data
Compare the types of clothing worn by your classmates with the types you used in your experiment. Contrast the results of their experiments with your observations. **For more help, refer to the** Science Skill Handbook.

ACTIVITY **595**

Resource Manager

Communicating Your Data
Ask students to bring in sample clothing from their own wardrobes to be evaluated. Students' results should be similar.

1 Motivate

Bellringer Transparency

Display the Section Focus Transparency for Section 3. Use the accompanying Transparency Activity Master. L2

ELL

Tie to Prior Knowledge

Ask students if any of them reuse or recycle materials at home or at school. If so, have them describe how. Encourage them to think creatively—do they give clothing they have outgrown to a charitable group? Do they sell items at a yard sale instead of throwing them away? Explain that recycling is one way to conserve resources, and that they will learn about other ways in this section.

Conserving Resources

As You Read

What You'll Learn
■ **Identify** three ways to conserve resources.
■ **Explain** the advantages of recycling.

Vocabulary
conservation
composting
recycling

Why It's Important
Conserving resources helps reduce solid waste.

Field GUIDE

What happens to the material you recycle? To find out how your trash is reused, see the **Waste Management Field Guide** at the back of the book.

Figure 12
A person in the United States consumes more resources than the average consumption per person elsewhere.

A Disposable Lifestyle

In the United States and other industrialized countries, people have a throwaway lifestyle. When they are done with something, they throw it away. This means more products must be made to replace what's been thrown away, more land is used, and landfills become filled. You can help by conserving resources. **Conservation** is the careful use of Earth materials to reduce damage to the environment.

Reduce, Reuse, Recycle

The United States makes up only five percent of the world's human population, yet it consumes 30 percent of the world's natural resources, as shown in **Figure 12.** Ways to conserve resources include reducing the use of materials, and reusing and recycling materials. You can reduce the consumption of materials in simple ways, such as using both sides of notebook paper or carrying lunch to school in a nondisposable container. Reusing an item means finding another use for it instead of throwing it away. You can reuse old clothes by giving them to someone else or by cutting them into rags. The rags can be used in place of paper towels for cleaning jobs around your home.

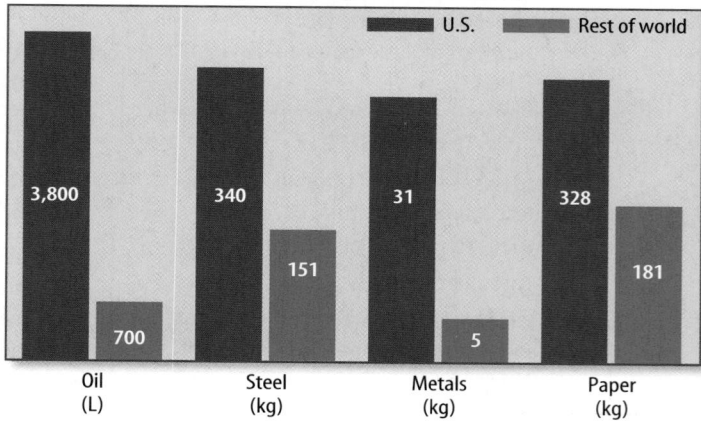

Yearly Consumption Per Person

■ U.S. ■ Rest of world

	Oil (L)	Steel (kg)	Metals (kg)	Paper (kg)
U.S.	3,800	340	31	328
Rest of world	700	151	5	181

596 CHAPTER 20 Our Impact on Land

Section ✓Assessment Planner

PORTFOLIO
Activity, p. 598

PERFORMANCE ASSESSMENT
Try at Home MiniLAB, p. 597
Skill Builder Activities, p. 599
See page 606 for more options.

CONTENT ASSESSMENT
Section, p. 599
Challenge, p. 599
Chapter, pp. 606–607

Reusing Yard Waste Outdoors, you can do helpful things, too. If you cut grass or rake leaves, you can compost these items instead of putting them into the trash. **Composting** means piling yard wastes where they can decompose gradually. Decomposed material provides needed nutrients for your garden or flower bed. Some cities no longer pick up yard waste to take to landfills. In these places, composting is common. If everyone in the United States composted, it would reduce the trash put into landfills by 20 percent.

Recycling Materials **Recycling** means using materials again. When you recycle wastes such as glass, paper, plastic, steel, or tires, you help conserve Earth's resources, energy, and landfill space.

Paper makes up about 40 percent of the mass of trash. As shown in **Figure 13,** Americans throw away a large amount of paper each year. Recycling this paper would use 58 percent less water and generate 74 percent less air pollution than producing new paper from trees. The paper shown in the figure doesn't even include newspapers. More than 500,000 trees are cut every week just to print newspapers.

How much energy do you think is saved when you recycle aluminum cans? Twenty aluminum cans can be recycled with the energy that is needed to produce a single new can from aluminum ore. If you recycle, you will reduce the trash you generate in your lifetime by 60 percent. If you don't recycle, you'll generate trash equal to at least 600 times your mass.

Figure 14 shows that the amount of material deposited in landfills has decreased since 1980. In addition to saving landfill space, reducing, reusing and recycling can reduce energy use and minimize the need to extract raw materials from Earth.

Mini LAB

Classifying Your Trash for One Day

Procedure
1. Label a table with the following columns: Paper, Plastic, Glass, Metal, and Food Waste.
2. Record items you throw out in one day. At the end of the day, count the number of **trash items** in each column.
3. Rank each column by number from the fewest trash items to the most trash items.

Analysis
1. Compare your rankings with those of others in your household.
2. What activities can you change to decrease the amount of trash you produce?

SECTION 3 Conserving Resources **597**

Teacher FYI

Recycling aluminum uses one-twentieth of the energy required for extracting new aluminum from bauxite. Other metals that are recycled include platinum, gold, silver, copper, lead, and iron.

② Teach

Reduce, Reuse, Recycle

Visual Learning

Figure 12 As more countries become industrialized, how would you expect this graph to change? Possible answer: the rest of the world will be using more resources.

Activity

Organize a field trip to a recycling plant. Then have students set up a recycling center at school. [L2] [ELL] [COOP LEARN] [IS] **Interpersonal**

Mini LAB

Purpose Students classify what they throw away. [L2] [IS] **Interpersonal**

Teaching Strategy Suggest that students leave their tables and a pencil near the trash cans at home. Encourage them to assign a different letter or symbol to each family member, and to ask family members to mark their symbol in the correct column each time they throw something away.

Analysis
1. Answers will vary; most households discard more paper than anything else.
2. Possible answers: buying materials with less packaging, reusing certain items.

✔Assessment

Performance Have each student find the percentage of their trash that is recyclable. Use **PASC,** p. 101.

Visualizing Trash Disposal

Have students examine the pictures and read the captions. Then ask the following questions.

How might the graph change over the next ten years if people become lazy about recycling and composting? The bottom line would start to rise, showing less difference between the amount of trash generated and the amount deposited in landfills.

What factors might explain why the amount of trash that is recycled has increased since 1980? Possible answers: Legislation and citizen awareness have increased; more recycling companies exist; more manufacturing companies are willing to use recycled materials.

Activity

Have students research how waste-to-energy plants work and how many such plants exist. What are the benefits and drawbacks associated with waste-to-energy plants? Have students create informational posters based on their research and present them to the class. [L2]

🔲 **Visual-Spatial** [P]

Extension

Challenge students to consider ways that new technology might change the amount of trash generated in the United States. Have students apply their conclusions to the graph, extending it to the year 2030.

NATIONAL GEOGRAPHIC VISUALIZING TRASH DISPOSAL

Figure 14

Although trash production in the United States is increasing, the amount of trash deposited in landfills is decreasing. In 1980, 82 percent of discarded trash ended up in a landfill. Today, only 55 percent is taken to the dump—thanks to the use of waste-reducing methods such as those shown below.

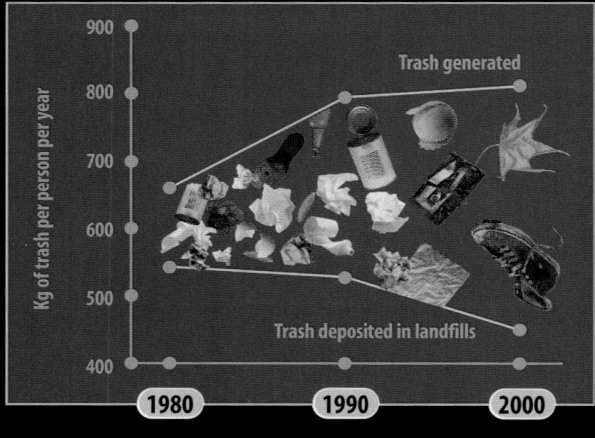

Landfill Use in the United States

Trash generated

Kg of trash per person per year

Trash deposited in landfills

1980   1990   2000

 **RECYCLING** In 1980, about nine percent of trash was recycled. Now nearly 30 percent of America's trash is reused.

◀ **COMPOSTING** Yard trimmings placed in a pile will decompose and form a substance called compost. Compost then can be used on flowers and vegetables to help them grow.

▶ **WASTE TO ENERGY** Some waste material can be burned to produce electricity. This plant in Rochester, Massachusetts, burns trash to generate electricity for a local paper company.

598 **CHAPTER 20** Our Impact on Land

Resource Manager

Chapter Resources Booklet
   Enrichment, p. 30
   Reinforcement, p. 27
   Activity Worksheet, pp. 7–8
Lab Management and Safety, p. 71

✔ Active Reading

Speculation About Effects/Prediction Journal This strategy allows students to examine events and speculate about their possible long-term effects. Have students divide their papers in half. On the left side record "What happened." On the right side, write "What might/should happen as a result of this." Have students write a Speculation About Effects/Prediction Journal about consumption of natural resources.

Recycling Methods What types of recycling programs does your state have? Many states or cities have some form of recycling laws. For example, in some places people who recycle pay lower trash-collection fees. In other places a refundable deposit is made on all beverage containers. This means paying extra money at the store for a drink, but you get your money back if you return the container to the store for recycling.

 Reading Check *How have states and cities encouraged people to recycle?*

There are several disadvantages to recycling. More people and trucks are needed to haul materials separately from your trash. The materials then must be separated at special facilities like the one shown in **Figure 15.** In addition, demand for things made from recycled materials must exist, and items made from recycled materials often cost more.

The Population Outlook The human population explosion already has had an effect on the environment and the organisms that inhabit Earth. It's unlikely that the population will begin to decline in the near future. To make up for this, resources must be used wisely. Conserving resources by reducing, reusing, and recycling is an important way that you can make a difference.

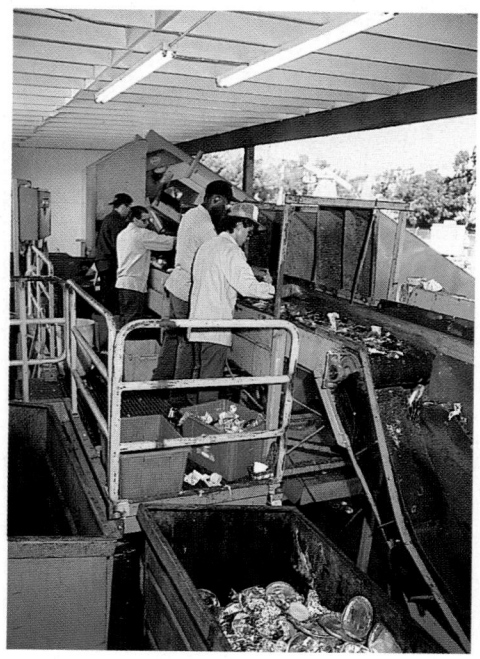

Figure 15
In recycling facilities like this one, materials must be separated before they can be reused.

Section 3 Assessment

1. List four advantages and two disadvantages of recycling.

2. What is the difference between reducing and reusing materials?

3. How does compost benefit your garden or flower bed?

4. List two simple ways that you and your classmates can reduce your consumption of Earth materials.

5. **Think Critically** Why is it more important to conserve resources as the human population increases?

Skill Builder Activities

6. **Collecting and Organizing Data** Contact a local sanitary landfill. Find out how long it will take for your community's landfill to be full. How will waste be disposed of after the landfill is full? **For more help, refer to the** Science Skill Handbook.

7. **Using a Word Processor** Find out the email address of your local chamber of commerce. Compose a letter suggesting ways to encourage businesses to recycle. **For more help, refer to the** Technology Skill Handbook.

 Reading Check

Answer Recyclers pay a lower trash collection fee; refundable deposits are made on beverage containers.

3 Assess

Reteach
Have students respond to the following: **Suppose your friend has a business making jewelry from scrap metal. You start a metal recycling business and sell scraps to her. What will happen if people stop buying her jewelry?** You will have one less place to sell your recycled scrap and will have to find a new market. L2

Challenge
Interested students can report on recycling programs in their own or a nearby community. What is collected? How often? Where does it go? How would they change the program to make it better?

✓ Assessment

Process Have students draw a concept map that describes the process of using and recycling paper or metal items, starting with the raw materials (trees, ore) from which the items are made. Use **Performance Assessment in the Science Classroom,** p. 161.

Answers to Section Assessment

1. Possible answers: advantages—saves landfill space, energy, and resources; reduces damage from mining, logging, and manufacturing; disadvantages—less convenient; takes up space in home; extra trash pickups; extra labor costs for separating materials, removing contaminants, and processing

2. Reducing means using fewer materials. Reusing means finding other uses instead of throwing materials away.

3. It is a natural fertilizer. It also increases the ability of soil to hold water.

4. Possible answers: carry lunch to school in reusable container, reuse old clothing as cleaning rags, use both sides of notebook paper.

5. With more people, more materials will be needed. Conservation would provide adequate supplies for a longer period of time.

6. Answers will vary. Have students suggest alternatives to landfills.

7. Students might suggest creative new recycling programs or incentives for business owners to recycle.

Activity

What You'll Investigate

Purpose

Students model population growth over a 10-minute period.

L2 ELL COOP LEARN

LS Logical-Mathematical

Process Skills

making models, using numbers, communicating, recording, interpreting data, comparing and contrasting, making tables, making graphs

Time Required

40 minutes

Alternate Materials

Beans can be substituted for popcorn. A 1-lb (484-g) bag of black-eyed peas contains approximately 2,100 beans.

Safety Precautions

Remind students not to eat or taste materials used in the lab.

Time (years)	Total Population Increase (millions)
1	94
2	188
3	282
4	376
5	470
6	564
7	658
8	752
9	846
10	940

Activity

A World Full of People

Every second, five people are born on Earth and two people die. As a result, there is a net increase of three people in the world every second of every day. That amounts to about 95 million new people every year. This is nearly equal to the population of Central Africa. What effects will this rapid increase in human population have on Earth? How crowded will Earth become in your lifetime?

What You'll Investigate

How crowded will different regions of Earth become in the next ten years?

Materials

small objects such as popcorn kernels or dried beans (1,000)

large map of the world (the map must show the countries of the world)

clock or watch

calculator

Goals

- **Demonstrate** the world's human population increase in the next decade.
- **Predict** the world's population in 50 years.
- **Record, graph,** and **interpret** population data.

Safety Precautions

Never eat or taste anything from a lab, even if you are confident that you know what it is.

Inclusion Strategies

Behaviorally Disordered Have behaviorally disordered students use the clock or watch to keep track of the time intervals for their partners in this activity.

Procedure

1. Copy the data table below in your Science Journal.

2. Lay the map out on a table. The map represents Earth and the 6 billion people already living here.

3. Each minute of time will represent one year. During your first minute, place 95 popcorn kernels on the continents of your map. Each kernel represents 1 million new people.

4. Place nine of your kernels inside the borders of developed countries such as the United States, Canada, Japan, Australia, and countries in Europe. Place 86 kernels inside the borders of developing nations located in South America, Africa, and Asia.

5. Continue adding 95 kernels to your map in the same fashion each minute for 10 min. Record the total population increase for each year (each minute of the lab) in your data table.

Population Data	
Time (years)	Total Population Increase
1	95 million
2	190 million
3	285 million
4	380 million
5	425 million
6	570 million
7	665 million
8	760 million
9	855 million
10	950 million

Conclude and Apply

1. Make a graph of your data showing the time in years on the horizontal axis and the world population on the vertical axis.

2. How many new people will be added to Earth in the next 10 years? Determine the world's population in 10 years.

3. At the current rate of population growth, calculate the world's population in 50 years.

4. **Determine** world population in ten years if only 4.5 million people are added each year.

5. **Compare** the population growth in developed countries to the growth of developing countries.

6. **Discuss** ways the increase in the human population will affect Earth's resources in the future.

Communicating Your Data

Draw your graph on a computer and present your findings to the class. **For more help, refer to the** Science Skill Handbook.

ACTIVITY 601

Procedure

Teaching Strategy

Have students count in advance 94 kernels into each of ten small paper cups. They can then add each cup's contents to the map during the experiment without stopping to count.

Expected Outcome

Over time, some areas of the map become more crowded than others.

Conclude and Apply

1. Students' graphs should show a steady increase in population over the 10 years.

2. 950,000,000 people added; world population: 6,950,000,000

3. (95,000,000/year × 50 years) + 6,000,000,000 = 10,750,000,000 people in 50 years

4. 4,500,000 × 50 + 6,000,000,000 = 6,225,000,000

5. Both show population growth. However, population growth is much slower in industrialized nations than in developing countries.

6. Possible answers: People will use more fuel and mineral resources. Land use will increase, resulting in habitat destruction and increased soil erosion. Air and water pollution may increase.

Error Analysis

Students who do not have the expected number of "people" at the end may have miscounted when placing kernels on the map.

Communicating Your Data

Encourage students to make their graphs using spreadsheet software.

TIME
SCIENCE AND Society

SCIENCE ISSUES THAT AFFECT YOU!

Content Background

Chemical, thermal, biological, and physical methods can treat hazardous waste. Chemical methods include ion exchange, precipitation, oxidation and reduction, and neutralization. Among thermal methods is high-temperature incineration, which can not only detoxify certain organic wastes but also destroy them. Special types of thermal equipment are used for burning waste in either a solid, liquid, or sludge form. As debated in the SE, one problem posed by hazardous-waste incineration is the potential for air pollution.

Biological treatment of certain organic wastes, such as those from the petroleum industry, is an option as well. One method used to treat hazardous waste biologically is called landfarming. In this technique the waste is mixed with topsoil on a suitable tract of land. Microbes that can metabolize the waste may be added, along with nutrients.

In some instances, a genetically engineered species of bacteria is used. Food or forage crops are not grown on the same site. Microbes can also be used for stabilizing hazardous wastes on previously contaminated sites. In that case the process is called bioremediation. Physical treatment, on the other hand, concentrates, solidifies, or reduces the volume of the waste instead of changing the molecular form of the waste material, as is the case with the other types of disposal methods.

Hazardous

Danger: Hazardous Waste Area. Unauthorized Persons Keep Out.

During much of the 1980s, this sign greeted visitors to Love Canal, a housing project in Niagara Falls, New York. The housing project was closed because it had been built on a hazardous waste dump and people were getting sick. Hazardous wastes are substances that are poisonous, that cause cancer, or that can catch fire. Some human health effects of exposure to hazardous waste include nerve damage, birth defects, and lowered resistance to disease.

Many types of manufacturing companies produce hazardous waste. In addition, some common household items, such as paints and oven cleaners, contain hazardous wastes.

The Environmental Protection Agency (EPA) estimates that U.S. industries produce about 265 million metric tons of hazardous wastes each year. Much of this waste is handled by the industries themselves—they recycle the waste or convert it to harmless substances. About 60 million tons of hazardous waste, however, must be disposed of in a safe manner. Incineration, or burning, is one way to dispose of hazardous wastes. However, the safety of this method is hotly debated.

For Incineration

People in favor of incineration note that the EPA has strict rules that govern the effectiveness of incinerators. Done correctly, it destroys 99.99 percent of toxic materials.

602

Resources for Teachers and Students

A Hazardous Inquiry: The Rashomon Effect at Love Canal, by Allan Mazur, Harvard University Press, 1997.

Road to Love Canal: Managing Industrial Waste Before EPA, by Carig E. Colton and Peter N. Skinner, University of Texas Press, 1996.

A danger sign in a garbage dump alerts visitors to the presence of hazardous waste.

The Love Canal housing development was closed because of toxic waste.

Waste

It causes health risks, but how to safely get rid of it?

Although the remaining ash must still be disposed of, it is often less hazardous than the original waste material. Supporters also note that incineration is safer than simply storing the hazardous wastes or dumping them in landfills.

Against Incineration

Other people say that incinerators fail to destroy all hazardous wastes and that some toxins are released in the process. They also note that new substances are generated during incineration, and that scientists don't yet know how these new substances will impact the environment or human health.

Lastly, they say that incineration may reduce efforts to reuse or recycle hazardous wastes.

While the debate goes on, scientists continue to develop better methods for dealing with hazardous wastes. As Roberta Crowell Barbalace, an environmental scientist, wrote in an article, "In an ideal environment there would be no hazardous waste facilities. The problem is that we don't live in an ideal environment ... Until some new technology is found for dealing with or eliminating hazardous waste, disposal facilities will be necessary to protect both humans and the environment."

CONNECTIONS Research Find out more about incineration. Then use this feature and your research to conduct a class debate about the advantages and disadvantages of incineration.

SCIENCE *Online*
For more information, visit science.glencoe.com

SCIENCE *Online*

Internet Addresses
_____
_____
_____

Explore the Glencoe Science Web site at **science.glencoe.com** to find out more about topics in this feature.

Reviewing Main Ideas

Preview

Students can answer the questions in their Science Journals. Discuss the answers as you go through the chapter. **IS Linguistic**

Review

Students can write their answers, then compare them with those of other students. **IS Interpersonal**

Reteach

Students can look at the illustrations and describe details that support the main ideas of the chapter. **IS Visual-Spatial**

Answers to Chapter Review

SECTION 1

3. Possible answers: wood, petroleum, metals

SECTION 2

2. Reduced amounts of water reach underground water supplies, resulting in runoff, stream discharge, and flooding. Runoff also occurs more rapidly, contributing to flooding problems.

SECTION 3

1. Compost the clippings.

Reviewing Main Ideas

Section 1 Population Impact on the Environment

1. Modern medicine, clean water, and better nutrition have contributed to the human population explosion on Earth.

2. Earth's resources are limited.

3. Our daily activities use resources and produce waste. *What resources were consumed to produce the items shown here?*

Section 2 Using Land

1. Land is used for farming, grazing livestock, lumber, development, and disposal.

2. Farming and development are ways that using land can impact the environment. Chemicals are used in farming. *What are some of the impacts caused by paving land?*

3. Using forest resources can impact organisms and Earth's climate.

4. Plants are sometimes used to break down and absorb pollutants from contaminated land.

5. New technologies have reduced greatly the need for hazardous waste disposal.

6. One way to preserve our land is to set aside natural areas.

Section 3 Conserving Resources

1. Recycling, reducing, and reusing materials are important ways to conserve natural resources. *How can you recycle yard waste, such as these grass clippings?*

2. Recycling saves energy and much-needed space in landfills.

3. Different methods can be used to encourage recycling.

4. Reducing, reusing, and recycling consumed items has decreased the annual deposits of trash in landfills since 1980.

FOLDABLES
Reading & Study Skills

After You Read

Write what you learned about how human activities impact land under the right tab of your Foldable. Explain the importance of human activities on land.

FOLDABLES
Reading & Study Skills

After You Read

After students have read the chapter and completed the Foldable described in Before You Read, have them do the activity on the student page.

Dinah Zike

Visualizing Main Ideas

Complete the concept map about using land.

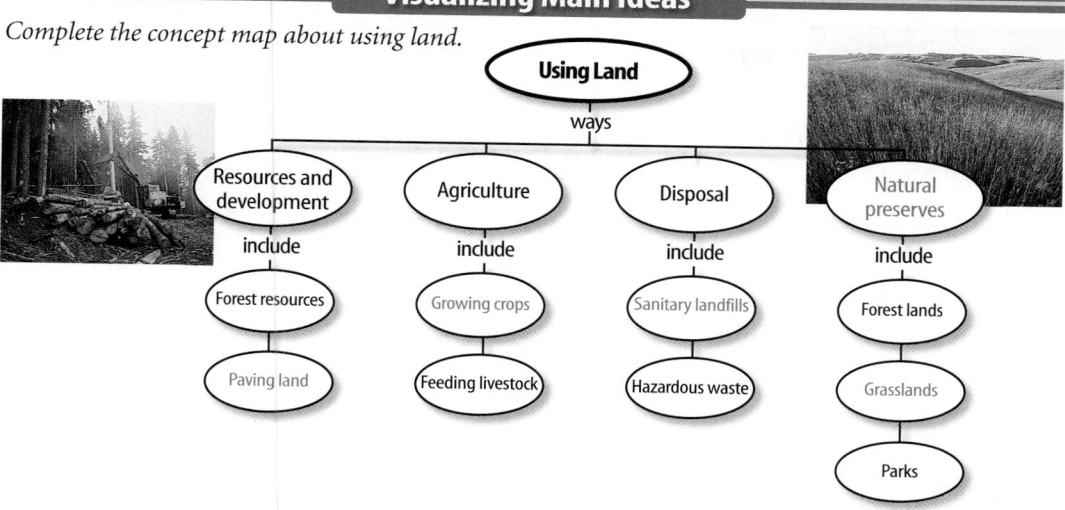

Using Land

ways

- Resources and development — include — Forest resources — Paving land
- Agriculture — include — Growing crops — Feeding livestock
- Disposal — include — Sanitary landfills — Hazardous waste
- Natural preserves — include — Forest lands — Grasslands — Parks

Visualizing Main Ideas

See student page.

Vocabulary Review

Vocabulary Words

a. carrying capacity
b. composting
c. conservation
d. enzyme
e. hazardous waste
f. pollutant
g. population
h. recycling
i. sanitary landfill
j. stream discharge

Using Vocabulary

Using the vocabulary list above, replace the underlined word or phrase with the correct vocabulary word.

1. The total number of individuals of a particular species in an area is called the <u>carrying capacity</u>.

THE PRINCETON REVIEW **Study Tip**

Get together with a friend. Quiz each other from your textbook and class material.

2. <u>Composting</u> means using resources carefully to reduce damage to the environment.

3. Substances that can make chemical reactions go faster are called <u>pollutants</u>.

4. <u>Hazardous wastes</u> means using materials again.

5. A <u>population</u> is the maximum number of individuals of a particular type that the planet will support.

6. An area where waste is deposited is called <u>stream discharge</u>.

7. Poisonous, cancer-causing, or ignitable wastes are called <u>enzymes</u>.

8. <u>Conservation</u> means piling yard wastes where they can decompose gradually.

9. A <u>sanitary landfill</u> is a substance that contaminates the environment.

10. The volume of river water flowing past a point per unit of time is called <u>recycling</u>.

Using Vocabulary

1. population
2. Conservation
3. enzymes
4. Recycling
5. carrying capacity
6. a sanitary landfill
7. hazardous wastes
8. Composting
9. pollutant
10. stream discharge

Checking Concepts

1. B
2. D
3. C
4. D
5. B
6. D
7. B
8. C
9. B
10. A

Thinking Critically

11. With less packaging, there is less need for waste disposal space.
12. Green spaces near buildings and highways can provide places where water soaks into the ground. Storm sewers can collect water from pavement areas and divert it.
13. Farmers often can't afford machinery, improved strains of seed, pesticides, or fertilizers. Insects often destroy crops. A lack of fertilizers causes soil nutrients to become depleted.
14. The decrease in plants causes an increase in soil erosion. Species of plants and animals that depend on the forest habitat may become extinct if they are unable to adapt to the changes produced by the dying trees.
15. Answers will vary but might include providing collection bins in a convenient place or going door to door to collect the cans. People might be given a monetary incentive.

Checking Concepts

Choose the word or phrase that best answers the question.

1. Where is most of the trash in the United States disposed of?
   A) recycling centers
   B) landfills
   C) hazardous waste sites
   D) compost piles

2. Between 1960 and 2000, world population increased by how many billions of people?
   A) 5.9   C) 1.0
   B) 3.2   D) 3.0

3. What percentage of Earth's resources does the United States use?
   A) 5   C) 30
   B) 10   D) 50

4. About what percentage of U.S. cropland is used to grow feed for livestock?
   A) 100   C) 50
   B) 1   D) 20

5. What do we call an object that can be processed in some way so that it can be used again?
   A) trash   C) disposable
   B) recyclable   D) hazardous

6. What is about 40 percent of the mass of our trash made up of?
   A) glass   C) yard waste
   B) aluminum   D) paper

7. What term is used to describe using plants to clean up contaminated soil?
   A) recycling   C) sanitary landfill
   B) phytoremediation   D) composting

8. Which of the following increases a stream's discharge?
   A) planting trees   C) paving land
   B) preserving land D) organic farming

9. How many thousand square kilometers of rain forest disappear each year?
   A) 3   C) 31
   B) 310   D) 150

10. What is used to cover daily deposits of trash in a landfill?
    A) soil   C) gravel
    B) plastic   D) hazardous waste

Thinking Critically

11. How would reducing materials used for packaging products affect our disposal of solid wastes?

12. Developing land can change stream discharge. What are some ways that land can be developed without this impact?

13. Although land is farmable in several developing countries, hunger is a major problem in many of these places. Give some reasons why this might be so.

14. Forests in Germany are dying due to acid rain. What effects might this loss of trees have on the environment?

15. Describe how you could encourage your neighbors to recycle their aluminum cans.

Developing Skills

16. **Classifying** Group the following materials as hazardous or non-hazardous: gasoline, newspaper, leaves, lead, can of paint, glass.

17. **Interpreting Scientific Illustrations** One hectare, shown here, is a square of land measuring 100 meters by 100 meters. How many hectares are in one km² of land?

100 m

100 m

1 hectare
or
10,000 m²

Chapter ✓Assessment Planner

Portfolio Encourage students to place in their portfolios one or two items of what they consider to be their best work. Examples include:
• Science Journal, p. 586
• Extension, p. 590
• Activity, p. 598

Performance Additional performance assessments, Performance Task Assessment Lists, and rubrics for evaluating these activities can be found in Glencoe's **Performance Assessment in the Science Classroom.**

18. Concept Mapping Complete this concept map about phytoremediation.

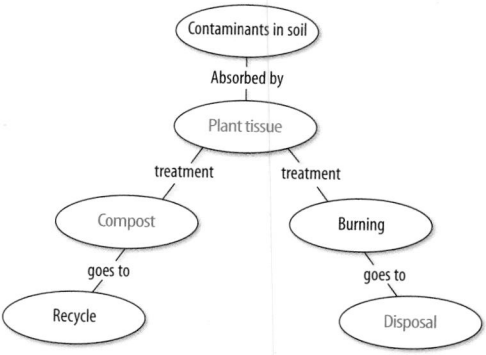

19. Comparing and Contrasting Compare and contrast farming and developing land. How do these activities affect stream discharge?

20. Researching Find out whether your community excludes yard waste from landfills.

Performance Assessment

21. Using Math in Science Collect your family's junk mail for one week and weigh it. Divide this weight by the number of people in your home. Multiply this number by 300 million (the U.S. population). If 17 trees are cut to make each metric ton of paper, calculate how many trees are cut each year to make junk mail for the entire U.S. population.

22. Evaluating a Hypothesis Design an experiment to determine factors that decrease the time it takes for newspapers or yard wastes to decompose.

TECHNOLOGY

 Go to the Glencoe Science Web site at **science.glencoe.com** or use the **Glencoe Science CD-ROM** for additional chapter assessment.

 **Test Practice**

In 1782, when the Bald Eagle was named the national symbol of the U.S., there were about 75,000 pairs in the lower 48 states. By 1963, there were only 450 pairs. Alarmed, Americans supported laws banning the use of pesticides, such as DDT, which had been determined to be harmful to the eagle.

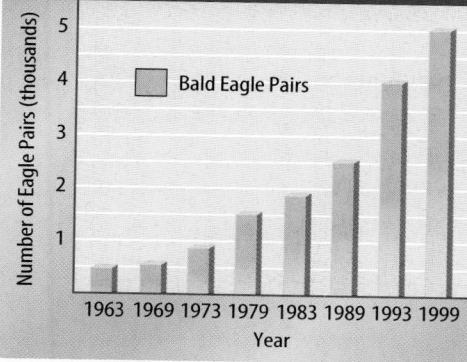

Bald Eagle Pairs in the Lower 48 States

Study the graph and answer the following questions.

1. According to the graph, the number of pairs of eagles in 1973 was _____.
A) fewer than 500
B) fewer than 1,000
C) greater than 1,000
D) greater than 2,000

2. How many more pairs of bald eagles were in the lower 48 states in 1999 than in 1973?
F) just over 4,000
G) just over 3,000
H) about 5,000
J) about 2,000

CHAPTER ASSESSMENT 607

Test Practice

The Test-Taking Tip was written by The Princeton Review, the nation's leader in test preparation.
1. B
2. F

Developing Skills

16. hazardous: gasoline, lead, can of paint; nonhazardous: newspaper, leaves, glass
17. 100
18. See student page.
19. Farmland has vegetation and water soaks into the soil. There is less stream discharge. Developed land has less vegetation and more pavement, preventing water from soaking into soil. This increases stream runoff and discharge.
20. Answers will vary with location.

Performance Assessment

21. Answers will vary, but the steps are: (a) find weight of mail, (b) divide by number of family members, (c) multiply by 300 million, (d) multiply by 52, (e) convert to metric tons, (f) divide by 17. Use **PASC**, p. 101.
22. Designs will vary. Variables that might be tested are temperature, moisture, and degree of compaction. Use **PASC**, p. 95.

Assessment Resources

Reproducible Masters
Chapter Resources Booklet
Chapter Review, pp. 35–36
Chapter Tests, pp. 37–40
Assessment Transparency Activity, p. 47

Glencoe Science Web site
Interactive Tutor
Chapter Quizzes

Glencoe Technology
Assessment Transparency
Interactive CD-ROM Chapter Quizzes
ExamView Pro Test Bank
Vocabulary PuzzleMaker Software
MindJogger Videoquiz DVD/VHS

Section/Objectives	Standards		Activities/Features
	National	**State/Local**	
Chapter Opener	See p. 5T for a Key to Standards.		**Explore Activity:** Model water pollution, p. 609 **Before You Read,** p. 609
Section 1 Water Pollution 🕐 3 sessions 📦 1.5 blocks 1. **Identify** types of water pollutants and their effects. 2. **Discuss** ways to reduce water pollution. 3. **List** ways that you can help reduce water pollution.	National Content Standards: UCP3, A1, F2, F4, F5		**Math Skills Activity:** Calculating with Percentages, p. 612 **Visualizing Sewage Treatment,** p. 613 **Physics Integration,** p. 614 **Health Integration,** p. 616 **Science Online,** p. 616 **Activity:** Elements in Water, p. 618
Section 2 Air Pollution 🕐 4 sessions 📦 2 blocks 1. **List** the different sources of air pollutants. 2. **Describe** how air pollution affects people and the environment. 3. **Discuss** how air pollution can be reduced.	National Content Standards: UCP3, A1, F1, F2, F3, F4, F5, G1, G3		**MiniLAB:** Identifying Acid Rain, p. 621 **Science Online,** p. 622 **MiniLAB:** Examining the Content of Air, p. 623 **Activity:** What's in the air?, p. 626–627 **Science and History:** Meet Rachel Carson, pp. 628–629

Teacher's Corner

PRODUCTS AVAILABLE FROM GLENCOE
To order call 1-800-334-7344:
Curriculum Kit
GeoKit: Pollution
Poster
Pollution

Videodisc
GTV: Planetary Manager

PRODUCTS AVAILABLE FROM NATIONAL GEOGRAPHIC SOCIETY
To order call 1-800-368-2728:
Videos
The Living Earth
Pollution: World at Risk
"Recycling," by Noel Grove, July 1994

Activity Materials	Reproducible Resources	Section Assessment	Technology
Explore Activity: water, large jar, food coloring, dropper	**Chapter Resources Booklet** Foldables Worksheet, p. 13 Directed Reading Overview, p. 15 Note-taking Worksheets, pp. 27–29	GLENCOE'S **ASSESSMENT** ADVANTAGE	
Activity: 2 beakers, tap water, plant fertilizer, spoon or other stirrer *Need materials?* Contact Science Kit at 1-800-828-7777 or www.sciencekit.com on the Internet.	**Chapter Resources Booklet** Transparency Activity, p. 38 Enrichment, p. 25 Reinforcement, p. 23 Directed Reading, p. 16 Activity Worksheet, pp. 5–6 Lab Activity, pp. 9–10 **Reading and Writing Skill Activities,** p. 29 **Math Skill Activities,** p. 29	**Portfolio** Extension, p. 615 Challenge, p. 617 **Performance** Math Skills Activity, p. 612 Skill Builder Activities, p. 617 **Content** Section Assessment, p. 617	Section Focus Transparency Interactive CD-ROM/DVD Guided Reading Audio Program
MiniLAB: glass or plastic container, sample of precipitation (rain or snow), pH paper or pH computer probe **MiniLAB:** high shelf or the top of a tall cabinet, white cloth, hand lens **Activity:** small box of plain gelatin, hot plate, pan or pot, water, marker, refrigerator, 4 plastic lids, microscope	**Chapter Resources Booklet** Transparency Activity, p. 39 MiniLAB, pp. 3, 4 Enrichment, p. 26 Reinforcement, p. 24 Directed Reading, pp. 17, 18 Activity Worksheet, pp. 7–8 Lab Activity, pp. 11–12 Transparency Activity, pp. 41–42 **Home and Community Involvement,** p. 46 **Lab Management and Safety,** p. 76	**Portfolio** Science Journal, p. 621 **Performance** MiniLAB, p. 621 MiniLAB, p. 623 Skill Builder Activities, p. 625 **Content** Section Assessment, p. 625	Section Focus Transparency Teaching Transparency Interactive CD-ROM/DVD Guided Reading Audio Program

End of Chapter Assessment

GLENCOE'S **ASSESSMENT** ADVANTAGE

Blackline Masters	Technology	Professional Series
Chapter Resources Booklet Chapter Review, pp. 33–36 Chapter Tests, pp. 31–32 **Standardized Test Practice by The Princeton Review,** pp. 91–94	MindJogger Videoquiz CD-ROM Explorations and Quizzes Vocabulary Puzzle Makers ExamView Pro Test Bank Interactive Lesson Planner Interactive Teacher's Edition	Performance Assessment in the Science Classroom (PASC)

Transparencies

Section Focus

Section Focus Transparency 1 — Oil Disaster

Water pollution can have a devastating impact on animals. For example, this oil spill off the coast of South Africa affected forty-four percent of the world's African penguins (*Spheniscus demersus*). The oil spilled when the freighter *Treasure* sank about six miles out from Cape Town, South Africa.

1. How do oil spills endanger wildlife?
2. What other kinds of water pollution can you name?
3. How can you help prevent water pollution?

L2

Section Focus Transparency 2 — Mountain of Ash

A lot of pollution comes from people, but there are other sources. This is a photo of the eruption of Mount St. Helens in Washington. Mount St. Helens erupted on May 18, 1980. The force of the eruption sent ash kilometers into the sky. Wind carried some of the ash all the way to Oklahoma.

1. How is the eruption of Mount St. Helens similar to pollution generated by people?
2. How is it different?
3. What can people do to reduce air pollution?

L2

This is a representation of key blackline masters available in the Teacher Classroom Resources. See Resource Manager boxes within the chapter for additional information.

Assessment

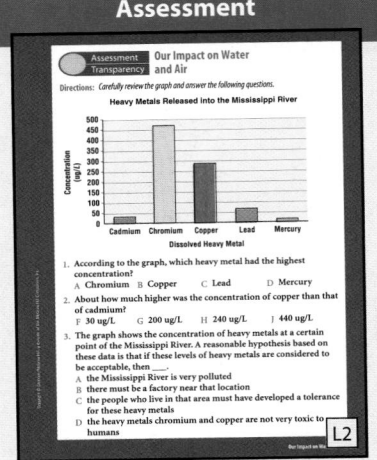

Assessment Transparency — Our Impact on Water and Air

Directions: *Carefully review the graph and answer the following questions.*

Heavy Metals Released into the Mississippi River

1. According to the graph, which heavy metal had the highest concentration?
   A Chromium   B Copper   C Lead   D Mercury
2. About how much higher was the concentration of copper than that of cadmium?
   F 30 ug/L   G 200 ug/L   H 240 ug/L   J 440 ug/L
3. The graph shows the concentration of heavy metals at a certain point of the Mississippi River. A reasonable hypothesis based on these data is that if these levels of heavy metals are considered to be acceptable, then ___.
   A the Mississippi River is very polluted
   B there must be a factory near that location
   C the people who live in that area must have developed a tolerance for these heavy metals
   D the heavy metals chromium and copper are not very toxic to humans

L2

Teaching

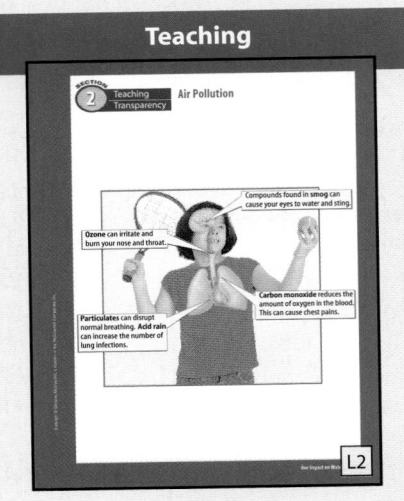

Teaching Transparency 2 — Air Pollution

Compounds found in smog can cause your eyes to water and sting.

Ozone can irritate and burn your nose and throat.

Carbon monoxide reduces the amount of oxygen in the blood. This can cause chest pains.

Particulates can disrupt normal breathing. Acid rain can increase the number of lung infections.

L2

Key to Teaching Strategies

The following designations will help you decide which activities are appropriate for your students.

L1 Level 1 activities should be appropriate for students with learning difficulties.

L2 Level 2 activities should be within the ability range of all students.

L3 Level 3 activities are designed for above-average students.

ELL ELL activities should be within the ability range of English Language Learners.

COOP LEARN Cooperative Learning activities are designed for small group work.

LS Multiple Learning Styles logos, as described on page 22T, are used throughout to indicate strategies that address different learning styles.

P These strategies represent student products that can be placed into a best-work portfolio.

Hands-on Activities

Activity Worksheets

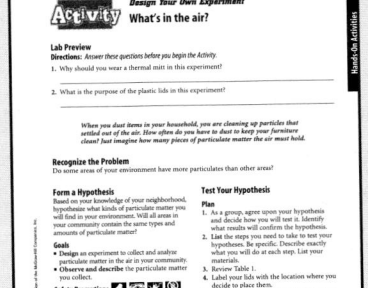

Activity — *Design Your Own Experiment*
What's in the air?

Lab Preview
Directions: Answer these questions before you begin the Activity.
1. Why should you wear a thermal mitt in this experiment?

2. What is the purpose of the plastic lids in this experiment?

When you dust items in your household, you are cleaning up particles that settled out of the air. How often do you have to dust to keep your furniture clean? Just imagine how many pieces of particulate matter the air must hold.

Recognize the Problem
Do some areas of your environment have more particulates than others?

Form a Hypothesis
Based on your knowledge of your neighborhood, hypothesize what kinds of particulate matter you will find in your environment. Will all areas in your community contain the same types and amounts of particulate matter?

Goals
• **Design** an experiment to collect and analyze particulate matter in the air in your community.
• **Observe and describe** the particulate matter you collect.

Safety Precautions
Wear a thermal mitt, safety goggles, and an apron while working with a hot pan and while pouring the gelatin from the pan or pot into the lids. Don't eat anything in the lab.

Possible Materials
small box of plain gelatin
hot plate
pan or pot
water
marker
refrigerator
plastic lids (4)
microscope
*hand lens
Alternate Materials*

Test Your Hypothesis
Plan
1. As a group, agree upon your hypothesis and decide how you will test it. Identify what results will confirm the hypothesis.
2. List the steps you need to take to test your hypothesis. Be specific. Describe exactly what you will do at each step. List your materials.
3. Review Table 1.
4. Label your lids with the location where you decide to place them.
5. Mix the gelatin according to the directions on the box. Carefully pour a thin layer of gelatin into each lid. Use this to collect air particulate matter.
6. Read over your entire experiment to make sure that all steps are in a logical order.
7. Identify any constants, variables, and controls of the experiment.

L2

Laboratory Activities

Laboratory Activity 1 — Water Purification

Pure water is essential to all life forms. But what about a situation in which you do not have pure water available? Life rafts on boats are equipped with an apparatus that can be used to distill water from salt water. Desert safety survival rules provide another means to distill water.

Strategy
You will purify water by using a simple distillation process.
You will discuss how this process could be used in an emergency situation.

Materials
2 coat hangers, or bendable wire
sand (fine) or soil
water
cereal bowl
pen (felt-tip)
pan (larger than the circumference of the bag)
plastic bag (clear)
sunlamp or bright sunshine

Procedure
1. Bend the coat hangers into a frame (see Figure 1).
2. Mix the sand or soil into water in the cereal bowl. Mark the water level on the inside with the pen.
3. Place the cereal bowl in the pan and place the wire frame over it.
4. Pull the plastic bag over the frame until it touches the pen. Record the appearance of the water.
5. Set the apparatus in direct sun or under a sunlamp.
6. Allow the apparatus to stand undisturbed. Observe and record your observations after about 10 min and again after 30 min in Table 1.

Figure 1

Water mark

L2

Meeting Different Ability Levels

Content Outline

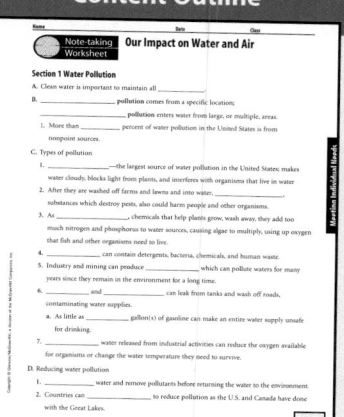

Reinforcement

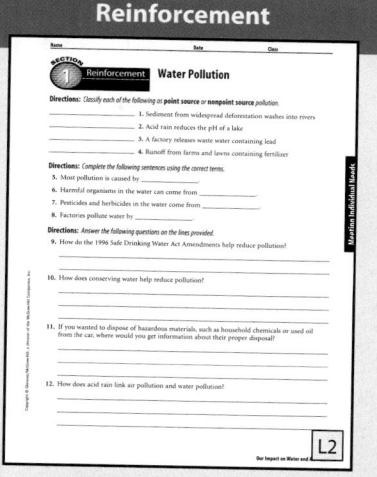

Directed Reading

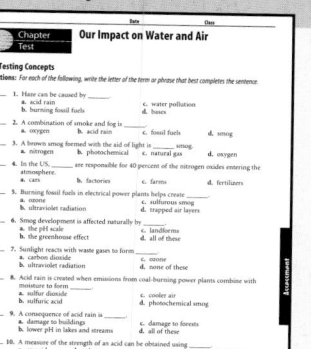

Assessment

Chapter Tests

Enrichment

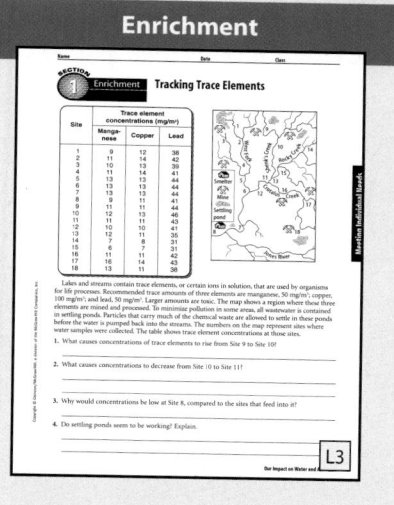

Spanish Directed Reading

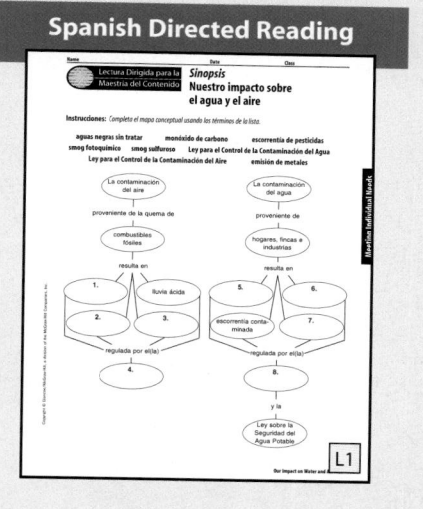

Test Practice Workbook

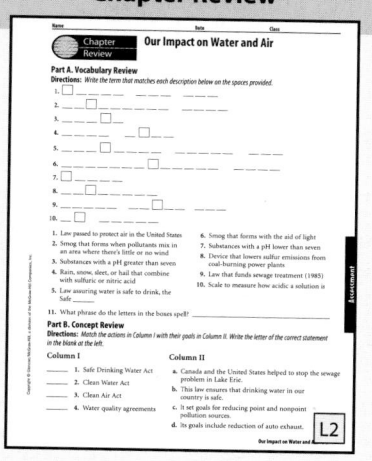

Chapter Review

Science Content Background

Water Pollution

Sources of Water Pollution

Substantial amounts of pesticides have percolated into groundwater in at least 34 states. More than 100 million people in the United States rely on underground wells for their drinking water. Some of the toxins in Lake Erie originate from as far away as Central America. The toxins are carried to Lake Erie by wind.

Student Misconception

Dumping material into the ocean causes no pollution problems because the ocean is so huge.

Refer to the facing page for teaching strategies to address this misconception. Refer to pages 610–617 for content related to this topic.

Keren Su/FPG International

Reducing Water Pollution

In the United States, 40 percent of water sources do not presently meet basic water-quality standards. The Clean Water Act requires states to identify these water sources and to establish Total Daily Maximum Loads, or TDMLs, for pollutants. States must prioritize cleanup based on the severity of the pollution problem and the intended use of a water source. For the cleanup to be successful, it is essential that all possible pollution sources be identified.

Air Pollution

Causes of Air Pollution

Common indoor pollutants include copying-machine fluids, cleaning fluids, cigarette smoke, paint, and items that contain formaldehyde. Another indoor pollutant is radon-222, radioactive gas produced by the decay of uranium-238. In urban areas carbon monoxide, nitrogen oxides, hydrocarbons, and particulate matter are the primary outdoor air pollutants. The carbon dioxide content in Earth's atmosphere has increased greatly since the 1850s. Much of this increase has been attributed to the burning of fossil fuels.

Acid Rain

If soil has a low pH, acid rain falling onto it will be damaging, but if acid rain falls onto soil that has a high pH, the acid is neutralized. Soils in the midwestern states have a high pH. However, northeastern states and eastern Canada are acidic. When acid rain falls in these areas, it is harmful to plants and fish. Water with a pH of 5 or less is considered unlikely to be able to support most forms of life. Around the world, acid rain causes billions of dollars in economic damage each year.

Reducing Air Pollution

Despite the Clean Air Act, more than 150 million people in the United States live in metropolitan areas in which ozone or carbon monoxide levels exceed federal health standards. In U.S. cities where smog is a serious problem, systems have been installed to warn people when pollution reaches unsafe levels. Technology exists that enables pollution to be traced to its source when the pollutant is present in as little as one part per trillion parts of air.

SCIENCE *Online*

For additional content background on this topic, go to the Glencoe Science Web site at science.glencoe.com.

IDENTIFYING

Misconceptions

Find Out What Students Think

Students may think that . . .

• **Using fossil fuels only affects air quality.**

Fossil fuels, such as oil, must be transported from its drilling location to a refinery. Often, transportation routes include Earth's oceans.

Demonstration

Discuss the problem of oil spills, and then share with students the data provided in Table 1. Discuss trends as represented by the data and the possible reasons for the trends. For example, because of the increased used of double-hulled oil tankers, the average number of oil spills per year has dropped since 1970.

Table 1: Number of Spills over 7 Tonnes and Total Quantity of Oil Spilled*

Year	7-700 tonnes	over 700 tonnes	Quantity ('000 tonnes)
1970	6	29	301
1973	25	32	166
1976	67	25	369
1979	59	34	608
1982	44	3	11
1985	29	8	88
1988	11	10	198
1991	27	8	435
1994	27	7	105
1997	27	10	67
1999	19	5	24

*****Source:** International Tanker Owners Pollution Federation Limited Web site*

Promote Understanding

Discussion

Share with students the data in Table 2. Have students determine the location of each spill on a world map. Discuss the impact of these spills on the ocean environment. Inform students that the impact from an oil slick depend on the type of oil. Light oils, such as Kerosene, tend to evaporate and dissipate quickly. Most crude oils, used for gasoline and home heating, are persistent and usually require a clean-up response.

Table 2: Selected Oil Spills

Ship Name	Year	Location	Oil lost (tonnes)
Atlantic Empress	1979	off Tobago, West Indies	287,000
ABT Summer	1991	700 naut. miles off Angola	260,000
Castillo de Bellver	1983	off Saldanha Bay, South Africa	252,000
Amoco Cadiz	1978	off Brittany, France	223,000
Haven	1991	Genoa, Italy	144,000
Odyssey	1988	700 naut. miles off Nova Scotia	132,000
Braer	1993	Shetland Islands, UK	85,000
Khark 5	1989	120 naut. miles off Atlantic coast of Morocco	80,000
Aegean Sea	1992	La Coruna, Spain	74,000
Sea Empress	1996	Milford Haven, UK	72,000
Katina P.	1992	off Maputo, Mozambique	72,000
Assimi	1983	55 naut. miles off Muscat, Oman	53,000
Exxon Valdez	1989	Prince William Sound, Alaska	37,000

*****Source:** International Tanker Owners Pollution Federation Limited Web site*

Assess

After completing the chapter, see *Identifying Misconceptions* in the Study Guide.

Our Impact on Water and Air

Chapter Vocabulary

point source pollution
nonpoint source pollution
pesticide
fertilizer
sewage
photochemical smog
acid rain
pH scale
acid
base
carbon monoxide
particulate matter
scrubber

What do you think?

Science Journal The photograph shows *Cryptosporidium parvium*, a protozoan that is difficult to detect and control. This parasite is protected by an outer shell that makes it resistant to treatment by water. People who become infected with "crypto," as it is commonly called, suffer from diarrhea and vomiting. A healthy human immune system will eventually eliminate the parasite.

Our Impact on Water and Air

The canoe glides peacefully through the water. A gentle breeze invites you to breathe deeply, almost tasting the fresh air. You look down as your paddle pulls through the clear water and see fish swimming. Once upon a time all the water on Earth was like this. In this chapter, you'll investigate water and air pollution sources, ways of reducing water and air pollution, and the importance of clean water and air.

What do you think?

Science Journal Look at the picture below with a classmate and discuss what this might be. Here's a hint: *They're small and difficult to detect in water.* Write your answer or best guess in your Science Journal.

608

Theme Connection

Systems and Interactions Water and air pollution are harmful to humans, yet human activities contribute to the pollution of these Earth systems. Interactions between humans and these systems are the focus of the chapter.

Some water pollution is easy to see. Where pollutants have directly entered a stream, the water can be discolored, have an odor, or contain dead fish. Suppose the water appears to be clean. Does that mean it's free of pollution? Do the activity below to find out.

Model water pollution

1. Pour 125 mL of water into a large jar.
2. Add one drop (0.05 ml) of food coloring to the water and stir.
3. Add an additional 125 mL of water to the jar and stir.
4. Repeat step 3 until you cannot see the food coloring.

Observe

In your Science Journal, calculate the concentration of food coloring in your jar with each 125-mL addition of water. Will the concentration of food coloring ever become zero by diluting the solution?

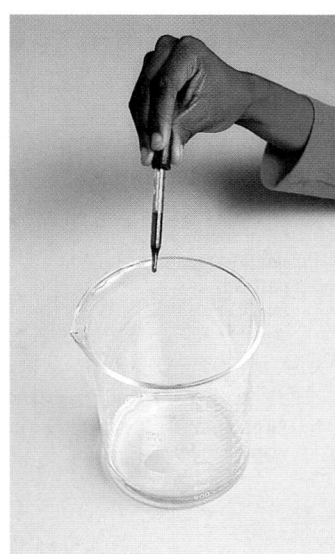

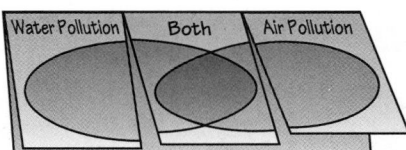

Before You Read

FOLDABLES
Reading & Study Skills

Making a Venn Diagram Study Fold Make the following Foldable to compare and contrast the characteristics of water pollution and air pollution.

1. Place a sheet of paper in front of you so the short side is at the top. Fold the paper in half from top to bottom.
2. Fold both sides in. Unfold the paper so three sections show.
3. Through the top thickness of paper, cut along each of the fold lines to the top fold, forming three tabs. Label the tabs *Water Pollution, Both,* and *Air Pollution* and draw ovals on the front of the foldable as shown.
4. As you read the chapter, write information about each type of pollution under the tabs.

609

Purpose Use the Explore Activity to model water pollution. [L1]
ELL COOP LEARN **Kinesthetic**

Materials large jar; graduated cylinder or metric measuring cup; food coloring; water; stirring rod; dropper

Teaching Strategy Placing a piece of white paper behind the jar will help students observe variations in the water's color.

Observe

In Step 2, the concentration is 1 drop per 125 mL, or 0.04%. In Step 3, the concentration is 1 drop per 250 mL, or 0.02%. Each time water is added, the amount of food coloring remains the same but the amount of water increases by 125 mL. The concentration will never become zero. Although dilution can reduce the concentration of pollutants, it will not make them disappear.

Assessment

Oral If water and air appear to be clean, does that mean they are free of pollution? Not necessarily; pollution can exist without being seen. Use **Performance Assessment in the Science Classroom,** p. 103.

FOLDABLES
Reading & Study Skills

Before You Read

Dinah Zike Study Fold
Purpose To determine what students know about pollution in general and to focus their attention on air and water pollution, students will use a Venn diagram Foldable to identify similarities and differences between the two types of pollution.

For additional help, see Foldables Worksheet, p. 13 in **Chapter Resources Booklet,** or go to the Glencoe Science Web site at **science.glencoe.com.** See After You Read in the Study Guide at the end of this chapter.

1
Water Pollution

Bellringer Transparency

Display the Section Focus Transparency for Section 1. Use the accompanying Transparency Activity Master. **L2**

ELL

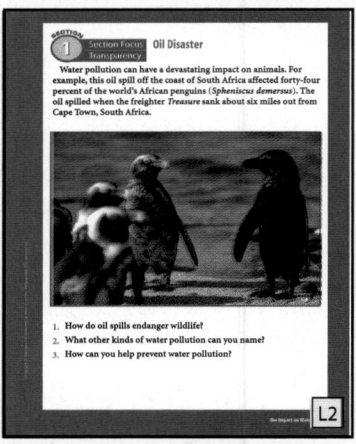

Tie to Prior Knowledge

Ask students if they have ever been restricted from swimming or fishing because of polluted water. Have volunteers explain how such a ban affected their plans.

SECTION

1 Water Pollution

As You Read

***What* You'll Learn**
- **Identify** types of water pollutants and their effects.
- **Discuss** ways to reduce water pollution.
- **List** ways that you can help reduce water pollution.

Vocabulary
point source pollution
nonpoint source pollution
pesticide
fertilizer
sewage

***Why* It's Important**
All organisms on Earth depend on water for life.

Figure 1
A Point sources include industrial wastes. **B** Nonpoint sources cannot be traced to a single location.

Importance of Clean Water

All organisms need water. Plants need water to make food from sunlight. Some animals such as fish, frogs, and whales live in water. What about you? You cannot live without drinking water. What happens if water isn't clean? Polluted water contains chemicals and organisms that can cause disease or bring death to many living things. Water also can be polluted with sediments, such as silt and clay.

Sources of Water Pollution

If you were hiking along a stream or lake and became thirsty, would it be safe to drink the stream water? Many streams and lakes in the United States are polluted in some way. Even streams that look clear and sparkling might not be safe for drinking.

Point source pollution is pollution that enters water from a specific location, such as drainpipes or ditches, as shown in **Figure 1.** Pollution from point sources can be controlled or treated before the water is released to a body of water.

However, many times bodies of water become polluted and no one knows exactly where the pollution comes from. Pollution that enters a body of water from a large area, such as lawns, construction sites, and roads, is called **nonpoint source pollution.** Nonpoint sources also include pollutants in rain or snow. More than 75 percent of water pollution in the United States comes from nonpoint sources.

A **B**

Section ✔ *Assessment* Planner

PORTFOLIO
Extension, p. 615
Challenge, p. 617
PERFORMANCE ASSESSMENT
Math Skills Activity, p. 612
Skill Builder Activities, p. 617
See page 632 for more options.

CONTENT ASSESSMENT
Section, p. 617
Challenge, p. 617
Chapter, pp. 632–633

Sediment The largest source of water pollution in the United States is sediment. Sediment is loose material, such as rock fragments and mineral grains, that is moved by erosion. Rivers always have carried sediment to oceans, but human activities can increase the amount of sediment in rivers, lakes, and oceans. Each year, about 25 billion metric tons of sediment are carried from farm fields to bodies of water on Earth. At least 50 billion additional tons run off of construction sites, cleared forests, and land used to graze livestock. Sediment makes water cloudy by blocking sunlight that underwater plants need to make food. Sediment also covers the eggs of organisms that live in water, preventing organisms from receiving the oxygen they need to develop.

Agriculture and Lawn Care Farmers and home owners apply **pesticides,** which are substances that destroy pests, to keep insects and weeds from destroying their crops and lawns. When farmers and home owners apply pesticides to their crops and lawns, some of the chemicals may run off into water. These chemicals might be harmful to people and other organisms, such as the frog in **Figure 2.**

Fertilizers are chemicals that help plants grow. However, rain washes away as much as 25 percent of the fertilizers applied to farms and yards into ponds, streams, and rivers. Fertilizers contain nitrogen and phosphorus that algae, living in water, use to grow and multiply. Lakes or ponds with high nitrogen and phosphorous levels, such as the one shown in **Figure 3,** can be choked with algae. When algae die and decompose, oxygen in the lake is used up more rapidly. This can cause fish and other organisms to die. Earth's nitrogen cycle is modified when fertilizers enter the water system.

✔ Reading Check *How do fertilizers cause water pollution?*

Figure 2
Research suggests that some pesticides in the environment could lead to deformities in frogs, such as missing legs.

Figure 3
Nitrogen and phosphorus in fertilizer cause algae to grow and multiply. Fish can die when decomposing algae use up oxygen in the water.

A Fertilizer applied to lawns or farms runs off.
B Algae grow and multiply.
C Algae die and decay, using up oxygen.
D Without enough oxygen, fish may die.

2 Teach

Importance of Clean Water

Discussion

Why do humans need water to live? About 60% of your body's mass is water. The body continually uses and eliminates water. This water must be replenished.

Sources of Water Pollution

Activity

Using small clear jars, have students collect surface water samples from nearby lakes and streams after a heavy rain. Let the samples stand undisturbed for several days. Then, have students compare the volume of sediment in each sample. Ask students to infer the source of the sediment. Possible answers: runoff from land, erosion of the banks
L1 ELL LS **Visual-Spatial**

Discussion

All over the world, the amphibian population is declining. **What types of pollution might affect amphibians?** They are susceptible to air, water, and land pollution.

✔ Reading Check

Answer Algae use fertilizer to grow and reproduce; when they die and decompose, oxygen is depleted. This kills the other organisms in the water.

Resource Manager

Chapter Resources Booklet
Transparency Activity, p. 38
Note-taking Worksheets, pp. 27–29
Reading and Writing Skill Activities, p. 29

Inclusion Strategies

Gifted More than half of the nation's 2,000 watersheds are facing water-quality problems. Have students research the health of their local water supply by visiting the Glencoe Science Web site. Invite volunteers to report their findings to the class. L3 LS **Linguistic**

Sources of Water Pollution, continued

Extension

Invite a worker from a local sewage treatment plant to talk to your class about the operation of the plant. If possible, organize a field trip to have students visit the plant.

Discussion

Why shouldn't people throw wastes into storm sewers? Water goes directly into water bodies untreated.

Problem-Solving Activity

National Math Standards

Correlation to Mathematics Objectives

1, 2, 5, 6, 9

Answers to Practice Problems

1. Total number of stations with decrease = 41
   Total number of stations examined = 313
   percent = 41/313 = 13%
2. Total number of stations with increase = 6
   Total number of stations examined = 324
   percent = 6/324 = 2%

IDENTIFYING Misconceptions

Some students may think that using fossil fuels only affects air quality. Refer to page 608F for teaching strategies that address this misconception.

Human Waste Another source of water pollution is human waste. When you flush a toilet or take a shower, the water that goes into drains, called **sewage,** contains human waste, household detergents, and other chemicals. Human waste contains harmful organisms that can make people sick.

In most cities and towns in the United States, underground pipes take the water you use from your home to a sewage treatment plant. Sewage treatment plants, such as the one in **Figure 4,** remove pollution using several steps. These steps purify the water by removing solid materials from the sewage, killing harmful bacteria, and reducing the amount of nitrogen and phosphorus in the water before it is returned to the environment.

Math Skills Activity

Calculating with Percentages

The following table lists surface water pollutants in rivers and streams. It shows the number of sampling stations that have an increased or a decreased level of pollution in a 10-year period.

Trends in River and Stream Water Quality 1980–1989

Measured Pollutant	Total No. of Stations Examined	No. of Stations With Decrease in Pollutant Level	No. of Stations With Increase in Pollutant Level	No Change
Sediments	324	36	6	282
Bacteria From Sewage	313	41	9	263
Total Phosphorus	410	90	21	299
Nitrogen	344	27	21	296

Example Problem

What percent of stations has shown an increase in nitrogen over a 10-year period?

Solution

1 *This is what you know:*   Nitrogen: number of stations with an increase = 21
   total number of stations examined = 344

2 *This is what you need to find:*   percentage: _____%

3 *This is the equation you need to use:*   % = (stations with increase)/(total stations) $\times$ 100

4 *Substitute the known values:*   (21)/(344) $\times$ 100 = 6.1%

Check your answer by multiplying the total stations by the percent in decimal form to obtain the number of stations with an increase.

Practice Problems

1. What percent of stations has shown a decrease in bacteria?

2. What percent of stations has shown an increase in sediment?

For more help, refer to the Math Skill Handbook.

612   CHAPTER 21 Our Impact on Water and Air

Science Journal

Report on Planet Earth Have students take the role of a traveler from the 1600s who visits the future. Ask them to write an entry in their Science Journal describing their first glimpse of industrially polluted water. L2
[S] **Linguistic**

Curriculum Connection

Math The water used during a shower must be treated in a sewage treatment plant before it can be reused. An average shower uses 19 L of water per minute. **If you take a five-minute shower daily, how much water must be treated in one year as a result?**
19 L/min $\times$ 5 min/day $\times$ 365 days/year = 34,675 L/yr

Figure 4

Sewage from most towns and cities is treated at municipal sewage treatment plants. Wastewater entering a sewage plant contains organic matter, paper, grease, bacteria, nitrogen, and phosphorus. As shown below, the wastewater from homes and businesses is purified in three stages—primary, secondary, and tertiary—before it is pumped back into a stream or river.

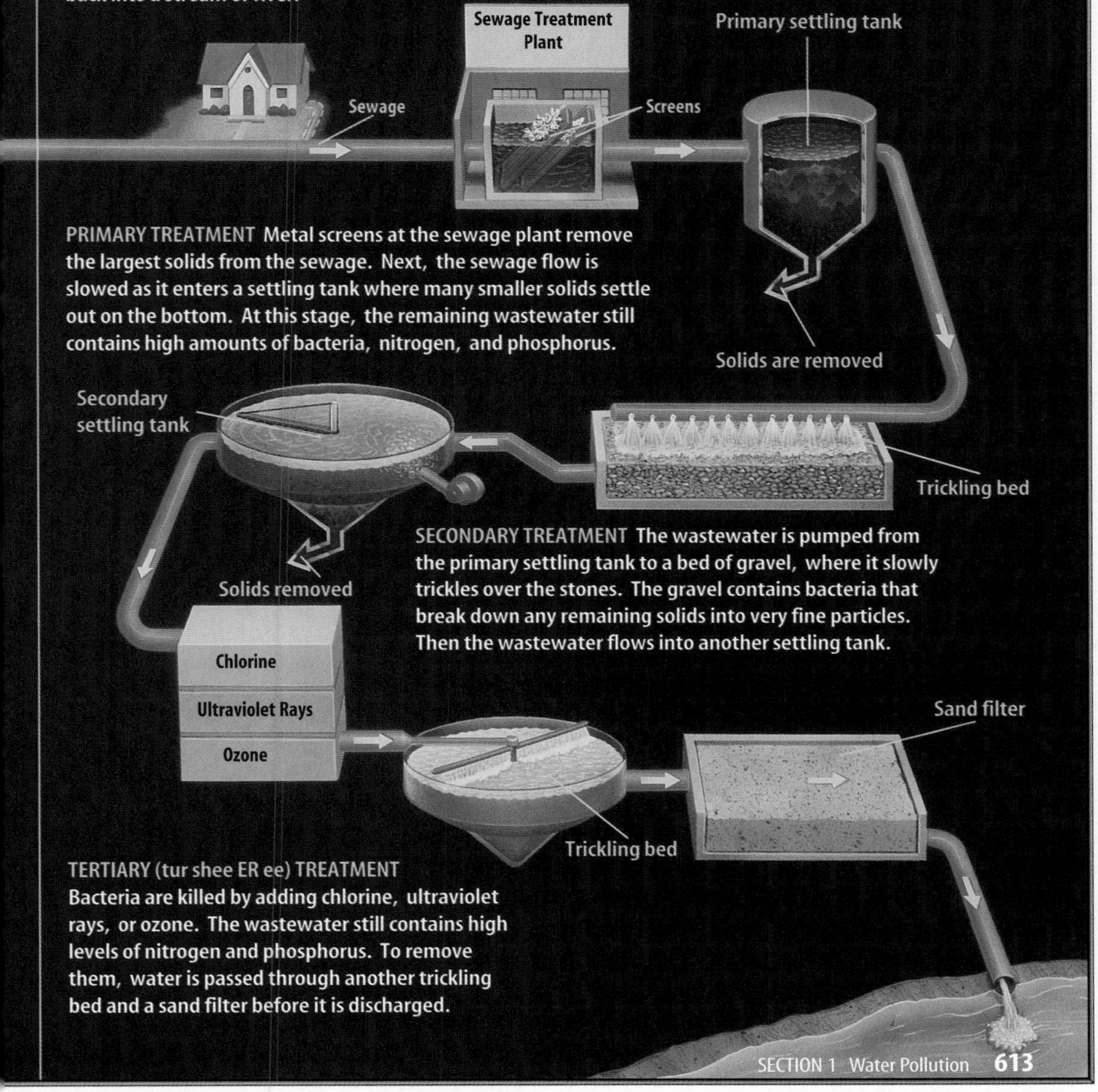

Sewage Treatment Plant

Primary settling tank

Sewage

Screens

PRIMARY TREATMENT Metal screens at the sewage plant remove the largest solids from the sewage. Next, the sewage flow is slowed as it enters a settling tank where many smaller solids settle out on the bottom. At this stage, the remaining wastewater still contains high amounts of bacteria, nitrogen, and phosphorus.

Solids are removed

Secondary settling tank

Trickling bed

SECONDARY TREATMENT The wastewater is pumped from the primary settling tank to a bed of gravel, where it slowly trickles over the stones. The gravel contains bacteria that break down any remaining solids into very fine particles. Then the wastewater flows into another settling tank.

Solids removed

Chlorine

Ultraviolet Rays

Ozone

Sand filter

Trickling bed

TERTIARY (tur shee ER ee) TREATMENT Bacteria are killed by adding chlorine, ultraviolet rays, or ozone. The wastewater still contains high levels of nitrogen and phosphorus. To remove them, water is passed through another trickling bed and a sand filter before it is discharged.

Visualizing Sewage Treatment

Have students examine the pictures and read the captions. Then ask the following questions.

Which stage of treatment is most important for removing paper and grease? These items are removed in the initial screening and settling that happens during the primary treatment process.

What would be released into streams and rivers if sewage treatment stopped after the secondary stage? Bacteria, nitrogen and phosphorous.

What might be the effects on the local environment if the tertiary treatment stage malfunctioned? Beach closings and water supply problems caused by bacterial contamination. Algae blooms from over-fertilization with nitrogen and phosphorous.

Activity

Have students work in groups to make up songs that describe the entire process of treating sewage. Make sure the songs include the function of each stage in the treatment process. Have each group perform its song in class. L2 COOP LEARN
IS **Auditory-Musical**

Extension

Challenge students to find out what can occur to sewage treatment plants when they are overwhelmed by stormwater runoff. Have them create informational posters describing their findings and display them in class. L2 ELL
IS **Linguistic and Visual-Spatial**

Resource Manager

Chapter Resources Booklet
Enrichment, p. 25
Mathematics Skill Activities, p. 1

Sources of Water Pollution, continued

Figure 5
During the manufacture of many products, such as electricity from this power plant, water is needed for cooling the machinery. Heated water remains in large towers and ponds until it has cooled to a temperature that is safe for fish and other organisms.

614   CHAPTER 21   Our Impact on Water and Air

Metals Many metals such as mercury, lead, nickel, and cadmium can be poisonous, even in small amounts. For example, lead and mercury in drinking water can damage the nervous system. However, metals such as these are valuable in making items you use such as paper, paints, and stereos. Before environmental laws were written, a large amount of metal was released with wastewater from factories. Today, laws control how much metal can be released. Because metals remain in the environment for a long time, metals released many years ago still are polluting bodies of water today.

Mining also releases metals into water. For example, in the state of Tennessee, more than 43 percent of all streams and lakes contain metals from mining activities. In the mid 1980s, gold was found near the Amazon River in South America. Miners use mercury to trap the gold and separate it from sediments. Each year, more than 130 tons of mercury end up in the Amazon River.

Oil and Gasoline Oil and gasoline run off roads and parking lots and into streams and rivers when it rains. These compounds contain pollutants that might cause cancer. Gasoline is stored at gas stations in tanks below the ground. In the past, the tanks were made of steel. Some of these tanks rusted and leaked gasoline and oil into the surrounding soil and groundwater. As little as one gallon of gasoline can make an entire water supply unsafe for drinking.

Federal laws passed in 1988 require all new gasoline tanks to have a double layer of steel or fiberglass. In addition, by 1998, all new and old underground tanks must have had special equipment installed that detects spills and must be made of materials that will not develop holes. These laws help protect soil and groundwater from gasoline and oil stored in underground tanks.

Heat When a factory makes a product, heat often is released. Sometimes, cool water from a nearby ocean, river, lake, or underground supply is used to cool factory machines. The heated water then is released. This water can pollute because it contains less oxygen than cool water does. In addition, organisms that live in water are sensitive to changes in temperature. A sudden release of heated water can kill a large number of fish in a short time. Water can be cooled before it is released into a river by using a cooling tower or pond, as shown in **Figure 5.**

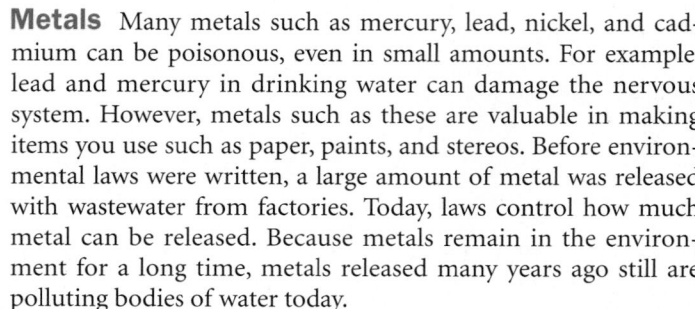

Cultural Diversity

Polluted Water The Vistula River, the largest river in Poland, is so polluted that its water cannot even be used by industries because it would corrode machinery. Cost estimates for cleaning up this river have ranged from $100 million to $15 billion. Sweden has contributed $60 million to the cause because the Vistula River contributes about 40% of the total nitrogen runoff into the Baltic Sea, which borders Sweden. The United States has also contributed money for environmental aid to Poland. **Why should all countries work together to control pollution?** Pollution doesn't stop at political boundaries.

Reducing Water Pollution

One way to reduce water pollution is by treating water before it enters a stream, lake, or river. In 1972, the United States Congress passed the Water Pollution Control Act. This law provided funds to build sewage-treatment facilities. It required industries to remove or treat pollution in water discharged to a lake or stream. The Clean Water Act of 1987 made additional money available for sewage treatment and set goals for reducing point source and nonpoint source pollution.

Another law, the Safe Drinking Water Act of 1996, strengthens health standards for drinking water. This legislation also protects rivers, lakes, and streams that are sources of drinking water.

International Cooperation Several countries have worked together to reduce water pollution. Lake Erie is on the border between the United States and Canada. Prior to the 1970s, phosphorus and nitrogen from sewage, soaps, and fertilizers entered Lake Erie from homes, yards, and farms, causing algae to grow and reproduce. The lake became a green, soupy mess. In the summer, the algae died and sank to the lake bottom. As the dead algae decayed, large areas of the lake bottom no longer had oxygen and, therefore, no life.

Pollutants also were discharged from many steel, automobile, and other factories along Lake Erie. **Figure 6** shows how on June 29, 1969, greasy debris on a large river flowing through Cleveland, Ohio, caught fire. This event was a wake-up call for everyone concerned about the quality of water in the United States and around the world.

In the 1970s, the United States and Canada made two water-quality agreements. These agreements set goals for reducing pollution in the Great Lakes. As a result of these agreements, limits were placed on the amount of phosphorus and other pollutants allowed into Lake Erie.

Reading Check *Which countries worked together to control water pollution in Lake Erie?*

Today, the green slime is gone and the fish are back. However, more than 300 human-made chemicals still can be found in Lake Erie, and some of them are hazardous. The United States and Canada are studying ways to remove them from the lake.

Figure 6
Because of laws passed since 1972, Lake Erie's water has improved.

A Firefighters battled debris burning on the Cuyahoga River in Cleveland, Ohio. This alerted people in the United States to water pollution problems.

B Today, millions of people enjoy this natural resource.

SECTION 1 Water Pollution **615**

How can you help?

Carcinogenic means that a substance can produce cancer. If people drink water containing hazardous wastes, they can develop cancers and other diseases and disorders.

Activity

Have students read their home water meters and determine the amount of water used in a week. Encourage students to talk with their families about the importance of water conservation. Have them read the meters after a second week to determine the effect water conservation practices had on water use. L1 IS **Logical-Mathematical**

Caption Answer

Figure 7 about 35%

SCIENCE
Online
Internet Addresses

_____

_____

_____

_____

Explore the Glencoe Science Web site at **science.glencoe.com** to find out more about topics in this section.

Visual Learning

Figure 7 Have students compare the data shown. Discuss the laws that helped reduce pollution in Lake Erie.

Health
INTEGRATION

Some wastes are called hazardous because they are carcinogenic (kar sun uh JEH nik). What does carcinogenic mean? What may happen if hazardous wastes seeped into a drinking water supply?

SCIENCE
Online

Research Visit the Glencoe Science Web site at **science.glencoe.com** for more information about water conservation. Communicate to your class what you learn.

Figure 7
This graph shows that water pollution is still a problem in the United States. *What is the percentage of rivers listed as polluted?*

How can you help?

Through laws and regulations, the quality of many streams, rivers, and lakes in the United States has improved. However, as **Figure 7** shows, much remains to be done. Individuals and industries alike need to continue to work to reduce water pollution. You easily can help by keeping contaminants out of Earth's water supply and by conserving water.

Dispose of Wastes Safely When you dispose of household chemicals such as paint and motor oil, don't pour them onto the ground or down the drain. Hazardous wastes that are poured directly onto the ground move through the soil and eventually reach the groundwater below. Pouring them down the drain is no better because they flow through the sewer, through the wastewater-treatment plant, and into a stream or river where they can harm the organisms living there.

What should you do with these wastes? First, read the label on the container for instructions on disposal. Don't throw the container into the trash if the label tells you not to. Store chemical wastes so that they can't leak. Call your local government officials and ask how to dispose of these wastes in your area safely. Many communities have specific times each year when they collect hazardous wastes. These wastes then are disposed of at special hazardous waste sites.

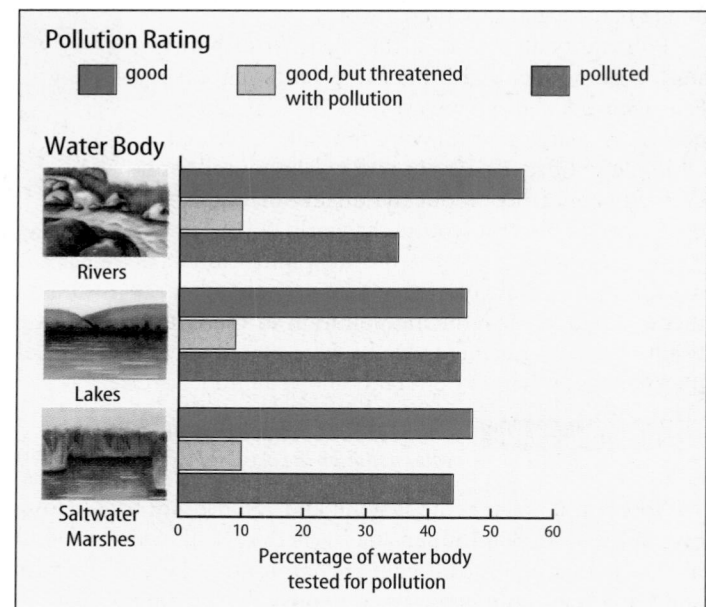

Pollution Rating
good | good, but threatened with pollution | polluted

Water Body
Rivers
Lakes
Saltwater Marshes

Percentage of water body tested for pollution

Inclusion Strategies

Behaviorally Disordered Encourage students to get permission to "adopt" a section of a river, lake, or stream. Ask them to work with an adult to keep this area clean by picking up trash and posting waterproof signs urging others to help keep the location pollution-free. L1 IS **Kinesthetic**

Resource Manager

Chapter Resources Booklet
Reinforcement, p. 23
Activity Worksheet, pp. 5–6
Lab Activity, pp. 9–10

Figure 8
Water pollution can be reduced if less water is used.

B One drip every 5s from a leaky faucet will waste nearly 2,400 L of water per year.

A Toilets made before 1994 use nearly 76 L of water per person per day. Replacing your old toilet with a new one can save your family up to 82,000 L of water per year.

C Turning off the water while brushing your teeth will save more than 19 L per day.

Conserve Water How much water do you use every day? You use water every time you flush a toilet, take a bath, clean your clothes, wash dishes, wash a car, or use a hose or lawn sprinkler. A typical U.S. citizen uses an average of 692 L of water per day. Unless it comes from a home well, this water must be purified before it reaches your home. After you use it, it must be treated again. **Figure 8** shows how using simple conservation methods can save water. Conserving water reduces the need for water treatment and reduces water pollution.

Section ① Assessment

1. Name six sources of water pollution.
2. What is the difference between point source and nonpoint source pollution?
3. How have U.S. laws helped reduce water pollution?
4. What are two things you can do to help reduce water pollution?
5. **Think Critically** Southern Florida has many dairy farms and sugar cane fields. It also contains Everglades National Park—a shallow river system with polluted waters. What kinds of pollutants are in the Everglades? How did they get there?

Skill Builder Activities

6. **Testing a Hypothesis** A stream near your home is polluted. You hypothesize that a large factory is responsible. Test your hypothesis by designing an experiment that will help you identify whether the factory is the pollution source. **For more help, refer to the** Science Skill Handbook.

7. **Using Graphics Software** Use graphics software to design a pamphlet that informs people how to reduce the amount of water they use. Be creative and include graphics in your pamphlet. **For more help, refer to the** Technology Skill Handbook.

Answers to Section Assessment

Activity

Purpose Students will observe the nitrate and phosphate levels in various samples of water.

Process collecting data, recording observations, analyzing results, comparing and contrasting, recognizing cause and effect

Time Required 40 minutes

Safety Precautions

Caution students not to drink from lab glassware. Use gloves while handling fertilizer.

Teaching Strategy Have two groups share a phosphate and nitrate test kit. One can test the phosphate while the other tests the nitrate.

Answers to Questions

1. Answers will vary
2. Answers will vary
3. Answers will vary
4. Possible answer: Runoff from fertilized land can raise the phosphate and nitrate level in lakes and streams.

✓Assessment

Oral Ask students what additional chemicals are used that end up in lakes and streams. pesticides and herbicides Use **Performance Assessment in the Science Classroom**, p. 91.

Activity

Elements in Water

When you look at water, it is often clear and looks as if there is not much in it. However, there are many compounds, microscopic organisms, and other substances that can be in the water, but aren't easily visible. How can you find out what else might be in the water? Can you also find out how much of it is in the water?

What You'll Investigate
What is the nitrate and phosphate content of water?

Materials
beakers (2)   nitrate test kit
tap water   phosphate test kit
plant fertilizer
spoon or other
  stirrer

Goals
- **Determine** the nitrate and phosphate content of two samples of water.
- **Compare** the levels and explain any differences you find.

Safety Precautions
Never eat or drink anything in the lab. Use gloves and goggles when handling fertilizer.

Procedure

1. Half-fill two large beakers with tap water.
2. Add a teaspoon of plant fertilizer to one of the beakers and stir well.
3. **Predict** which beaker might have a greater level of nitrate.
4. Using an appropriate kit, measure the nitrate content of each beaker of water.

5. Clean the test kit between measurements. Record your measurements.
6. **Predict** which beaker might have a greater level of phosphates.
7. Using an appropriate kit, measure the phosphate content of each beaker of water. Be sure to clean the kit between measurements. Record your measurements.

Conclude and Apply

1. **Describe** your results. Were the levels of each compound you measured the same in both samples?
2. Were your predictions correct?
3. **Explain** any differences that you found.
4. **Explain** how the use of fertilizers can cause problems in lakes and streams.

Communicating Your Data

Compare your results with those of others in your class. Discuss any differences found in your measurements.

Science Journal

Water Contamination Write a paragraph in your science journal describing the fertilizer, pesticide, and other chemicals that are used on your lawn or around your home that may cause water contamination.

Communicating Your Data

Results should compare favorably. Some possible sources of error are variation in the amount of fertilizer added to water sample and error in reading tester.

SECTION 2 Air Pollution

Causes of Air Pollution

Cities can be exciting because they are centers of business, culture, and entertainment. Unfortunately, cities also have many cars, buses, and trucks that burn fuel for energy. The brown haze you sometimes see forms from the exhaust of these vehicles. Air pollution comes from burning fuels in factories, generating electricity, and burning trash. Dust from plowed fields, construction sites, and mines also contributes to air pollution.

Natural sources add pollutants to the air, too. For example, radon is a naturally occurring gas given off by certain kinds of rock. This gas can seep into basements of homes built on these rocks. Exposure to radon can increase the risk of lung cancer. Natural sources of pollution also include particles and gases emitted into air from erupting volcanoes and fires.

What is smog?

One type of air pollution found in urban areas is called smog, a term originally used to describe the combination of smoke and fog. Major sources of smog, shown in **Figure 9,** include cars, factories, and power plants.

As You Read

What You'll Learn
- **List** the different sources of air pollutants.
- **Describe** how air pollution affects people and the environment.
- **Discuss** how air pollution can be reduced.

Vocabulary
photochemical smog
acid rain
pH scale
acid
base
carbon monoxide
particulate matter
scrubber

Why It's Important
Air pollution can adversely affect your health and the health of others.

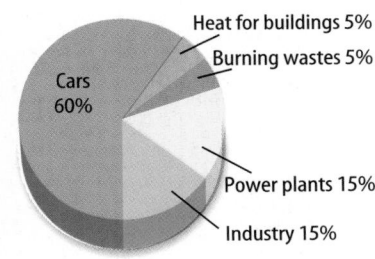

Sources of Smog

- Heat for buildings 5%
- Burning wastes 5%
- Cars 60%
- Power plants 15%
- Industry 15%

Figure 9
Cars are one of the main sources of air pollution in the United States. *What percentage of smog comes from power plants and industry combined?*

SECTION 2

Air Pollution

1 Motivate

Bellringer Transparency

Display the Section Focus Transparency for Section 2. Use the accompanying Transparency Activity Master. L2
ELL

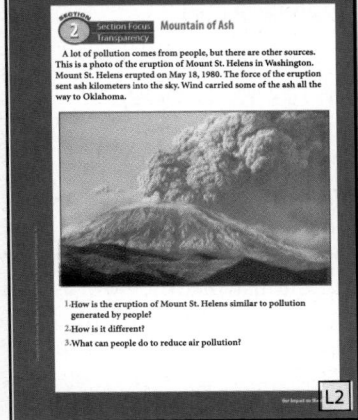

SECTION 2 Section Focus Transparency — **Mountain of Ash**

A lot of pollution comes from people, but there are other sources. This is a photo of the eruption of Mount St. Helens in Washington. Mount St. Helens erupted on May 18, 1980. The force of the eruption sent ash kilometers into the sky. Wind carried some of the ash all the way to Oklahoma.

1. How is the eruption of Mount St. Helens similar to pollution generated by people?
2. How is it different?
3. What can people do to reduce air pollution?

L2

Tie to Prior Knowledge

Ask students if they ever heard or read a news report on air quality levels. Discuss reasons why such information is shared with the public.

Caption Answer

Figure 9 30%

Section ✓ *Assessment* Planner

PORTFOLIO
Science Journal, p. 621

PERFORMANCE ASSESSMENT
MiniLAB, p. 621
Try at Home MiniLAB, p. 623
Skill Builder Activities, p. 625
See page 632 for more options.

CONTENT ASSESSMENT
Section, p. 625
Challenge, p. 625
Chapter, pp. 632–633

Resource Manager

Chapter Resources Booklet
Transparency Activity, p. 39
Enrichment, p. 26
Activity Worksheet, pp. 7–8

Causes of Air Pollution

Quick Demo

Using clay, secure several birthday candles to the bottom of a glass aquarium. Light the candles and let them burn for a few seconds so that the smoke is easy to see. Tell students the smoke represents car exhaust. Cover the top of the aquarium with plastic wrap. The wrap traps the smoke in the same way that smog is trapped when there is no wind to disperse it.
LS Visual-Spatial

What is smog?

Use Science Words

Word Origin Have students determine the meaning of the prefix *photo* in the word *photochemical*, make a list of other words containing this prefix, and define each term. Photo means "light." Other words: photocopy (copy using light); photography (using light to make images on film)

Discussion

Why might cities have more smog during the week than on the weekend? There are more cars on the road on weekdays when people are going to and from work.

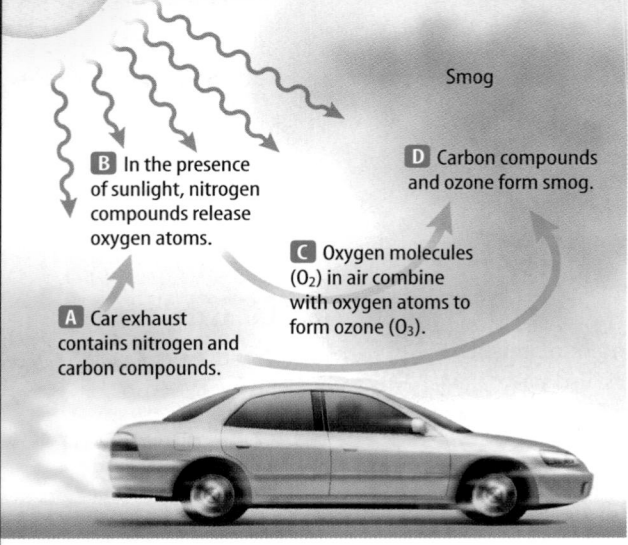

B In the presence of sunlight, nitrogen compounds release oxygen atoms.

A Car exhaust contains nitrogen and carbon compounds.

C Oxygen molecules (O_2) in air combine with oxygen atoms to form ozone (O_3).

D Carbon compounds and ozone form smog.

Smog

Figure 10
In the presence of sunlight, car exhaust can form smog.

Figure 11
Temperatures in the atmosphere can worsen air pollution.

How Smog Forms The hazy, yellowish brown blanket of smog that is sometimes found over cities is called **photochemical smog** because it forms with the help of sunlight. Pollutants get into the air when gasoline is burned, releasing nitrogen, oxygen, and carbon compounds. These compounds, as shown in **Figure 10,** react in the presence of sunlight to produce other substances. One of the substances produced is ozone. Ozone high in the atmosphere protects you from the Sun's ultraviolet radiation. However, ozone near Earth's surface is a major component of smog. Smog can damage sensitive tissues, like plants or your lungs.

Nature and Smog Certain natural conditions contribute to smoggy air. For example, in many places, smog is not a problem because winds disperse the pollutants that cause smog to form. In other areas, landforms add to smog development. The mountains surrounding Los Angeles, for example, can prevent smog from being carried away by winds.

Figure 11 shows how the atmosphere also can influence the formation of smog. Normally, warmer air is found near Earth's surface. However, sometimes warm air traps cool air near the ground. This is called a temperature inversion, and it reduces the amount of mixing in the atmosphere, causing pollutants to accumulate near Earth's surface.

Normal Conditions

Cooler air

Cool air

Warm air

A Usually, air temperature decreases with distance above Earth's surface. Air pollutants can be carried far away from their source.

Temperature Inversion

Cooler air

Warm air

Cool air

B During a temperature inversion, warm air overlies cool air. Air pollutants can't be dispersed and can accumulate to unhealthy levels.

620 CHAPTER 21 Our Impact on Water and Air

LAB DEMONSTRATION

Purpose to demonstrate the effect of acid rain on buildings and statues
Materials 2 pieces of chalk, cup of vinegar, cup of tap water, 2 small glass jars
Preparation Explain that some buildings and statues are made of limestone or marble, which, like chalk, are made of calcite and small bits of sea shells.

Procedure Place one piece of chalk in a jar with the vinegar. Place the other piece of chalk in a jar with the water. Wait 5 minutes.

Expected Outcome The chalk dissolves in the vinegar, but not in the water. Bubbles are produced.

Assessment

What caused the chalk to dissolve? It reacted with the vinegar (acetic acid). **What was the purpose of putting a piece of chalk in the jar of water?** It was a control. **How does acid rain affect some statues and buildings?** It slowly dissolves them.

Acid Rain

When sulfur oxides from coal-burning power plants and nitrogen oxides from cars combine with moisture in the air, they form acids. When acidic moisture falls to Earth as rain or snow, it is called **acid rain.** Acid rain can corrode structures, damage forests, and harm organisms. The amount of acid is measured using the **pH scale,** shown in **Figure 12.** A lower number means greater acidity. Substances with a pH lower than 7 are **acids.** Substances with a pH above 7 are **bases.**

Natural lakes and streams have a pH between 6 and 8. When rain is acidic, the pH of streams and lakes may decrease. As **Figure 12** shows, certain organisms, like snails and clams, can't live in acidic water.

CFCs

In the atmosphere, a concentrated layer of ozone molecules protects Earth from some of the Sun's harmful rays. Chlorofluorocarbons (CFCs) from air conditioners and refrigerators might be destroying this ozone layer. Even though the use of CFCs is declining worldwide, these compounds can remain in the upper atmosphere for decades.

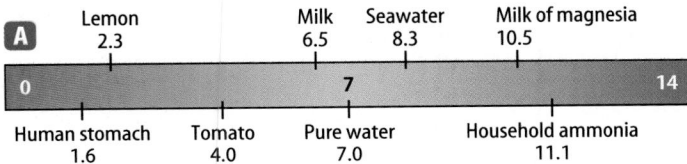

A

Lemon 2.3			Milk 6.5	Seawater 8.3		Milk of magnesia 10.5	
0				7			14

Human stomach 1.6   Tomato 4.0   Pure water 7.0   Household ammonia 11.1

B

pH Tolerance of Various Organisms

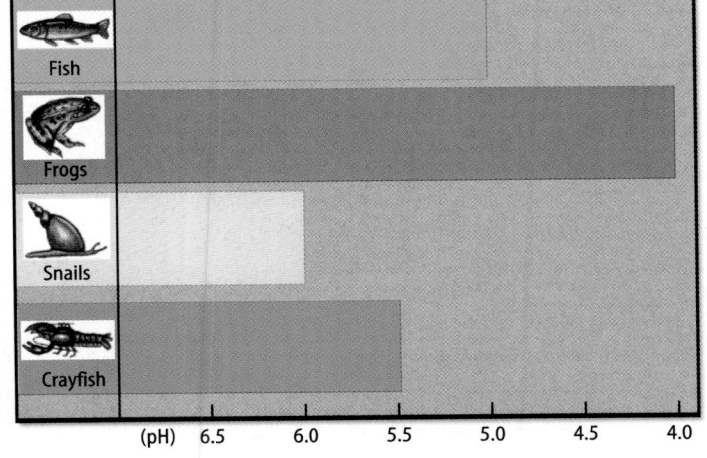

Fish

Frogs

Snails

Crayfish

(pH)   6.5   6.0   5.5   5.0   4.5   4.0

Mini LAB

Identifying Acid Rain

Procedure

1. Use a clean **glass or plastic container** to collect a sample of precipitation.
2. Use **pH paper** or a **pH computer probe** to determine the acidity level of your sample. If you have collected snow, allow it to melt before measuring its pH.
3. Record the indicated pH of your sample and compare it with the results of other classmates who have followed the same procedure.

Analysis

1. What is the average pH of the samples obtained from this precipitation?
2. Compare and contrast the pH of your samples with those of the substances shown on the pH scale in **Figure 12.**

Figure 12

A The natural pH of rainwater is about 5.6. Acid rain is precipitation with a pH below 5.6.

B This chart shows the different levels of acidity in water that certain organisms can live in. *Which types of organisms might you find in a pond with a pH of 5.5 or greater? Which organisms would be in the pond if the pH dropped to 4.5?*

Acid Rain

Mini LAB

Purpose Students determine whether their community has acid rain. [L2] [ELL]

[IS] **Interpersonal**

Materials pH paper, glass or plastic containers

Teaching Strategy Have students collect their samples at about the same time of day and from the same source of precipitation.

Analysis

1. Samples should have reasonably similar pH levels. The acidity of the precipitation will depend on location and the prevailing wind direction.
2. Have students use the pH scale (Fig. 12) to determine which substance has a pH closest to local precipitation.

✔ Assessment

Performance Have students collect and test water samples from the same location over a period of time to determine whether the pH varies daily. Use **PASC,** p. 97.

Caption Answer

Figure 12 fish, frogs, crayfish, snails (at pH 6.0 or greater); frogs

---

Resource Manager

Chapter Resources Booklet
   MiniLAB, p. 3
   Directed Reading for Content Mastery, pp. 17, 18
Reading and Writing Skill Activities, p. 9

Science Journal

Acid Rain Have students write an essay describing the effects of acid rain. Acid rain removes essential nutrients from soil. It lowers a plant's resistance to diseases, insects, and bad weather. Acid rain can kill organisms living in lakes. It damages the surfaces of buildings and other structures. [L2] [IS] **Linguistic** [P]

Extension

Encourage students to research the causes and symptoms of asthma, pneumonia, and lung cancer. After students share their findings with the class, invite the school nurse or other health care professional to speak to the class about ways to avoid getting certain respiratory diseases. Encourage the speaker to also discuss treatment of various respiratory diseases. L2

Make a Model

Have student pairs simulate acid rain by adding a few drops of lemon juice to a sample of tap water. Ask them to determine the pH of the lemon water with pH paper and a pH color chart. Then have students slowly add just enough baking soda to neutralize the acid. L2 ELL COOP LEARN [N] **Linguistic**

Teacher FYI

From 1980 to 1998, the number of people with asthma in the United States rose from 6.8 million to 15 million. More than 7.4 percent of children between the ages of 5 and 14 have asthma.

Figure 13
Air pollution can be a health hazard. Compounds in the air can affect your body.

Air Pollution and Your Health

Suppose you're an athlete in a large city training for a competition. You might have to get up at 4:30 A.M. to exercise. Later in the day, the smog levels might be so high that it wouldn't be safe for you to exercise outdoors. In some large cities, athletes adjust their training schedules to avoid exposure to ozone and other pollutants. Schools schedule football games for Saturday afternoons when smog levels are lower. Parents are warned to keep their children indoors when smog exceeds certain levels.

Health Disorders How hazardous is dirty air? Approximately 250,000 people in the United States suffer from pollution-related breathing disorders. About 60,000 deaths each year in the United States are blamed on air pollution. **Figure 13** illustrates some of the health problems caused by air pollution. Ozone damages lung tissue, making people more susceptible to diseases such as pneumonia and asthma. Less severe symptoms of ozone include burning eyes, dry throat, and headache.

How do you know if ozone levels in your community are safe? You may have seen the Air Quality Index reported in your newspaper. **Table 1** shows the index along with ways to protect your health when ozone levels are high.

Carbon monoxide, a colorless, odorless gas found in car exhaust, also contributes to air pollution. This gas can make people ill, even in small concentrations because it replaces oxygen in your blood.

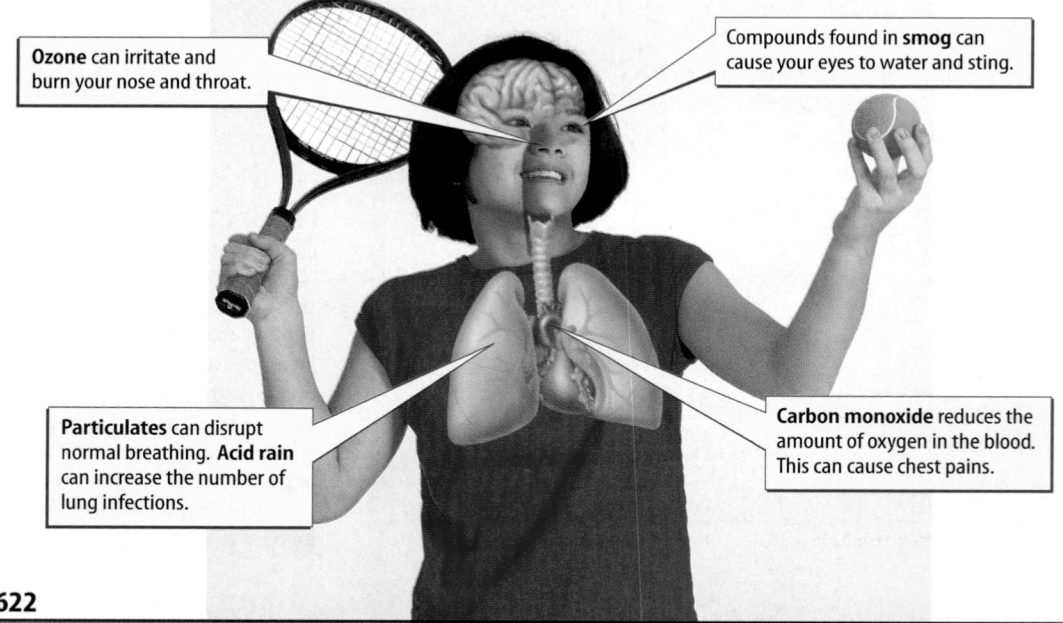

Ozone can irritate and burn your nose and throat.

Compounds found in **smog** can cause your eyes to water and sting.

Particulates can disrupt normal breathing. **Acid rain** can increase the number of lung infections.

Carbon monoxide reduces the amount of oxygen in the blood. This can cause chest pains.

622

✔ Active Reading

Think-Pair-Share Have students respond to a question by writing a response. After thinking for a few minutes, have partners share responses to the question. Finally, ask students to share responses with the class. Have students do a Think-Pair-Share after reading about air pollution and health.

Curriculum Connection

Health The EPA has determined that toxic chemicals found inside American homes are more likely to cause some types of cancer than outdoor air pollutants. Have students use reference materials to identify sources of indoor air pollution such as asbestos, cleaning agents, formaldehyde, radon, and cigarette smoke. Have students make visual displays of their findings. L2 P

Acid Rain What do you suppose happens when you inhale the humid air from acid rain? Acid is breathed deep inside your lungs. This may cause irritation and reduce your ability to fight respiratory infections. When you breathe, oxygen travels from the air to your lungs. Lungs damaged by acid rain cannot move oxygen to the blood easily. This puts stress on your heart.

Particulates Thick, black smoke from a forest fire, exhaust from school buses and large trucks, smoke billowing from a factory, and dust picked up by the wind all contain **particulate** (par TIH kyuh luht) **matter.** Particulate matter consists of fine solids and liquid droplets such as dust, pollen, mold, ash, and soot that are in the air.

Particulate matter ranges in size from large, visible solids like dust and soil particles to microscopic particles that form when substances are burned. Smaller particles are more dangerous, because they can travel deeper into the lungs. When particulate matter is breathed in, it can irritate and damage the lungs, causing breathing problems.

☑ Reading Check *Why are small particles dangerous to your health?*

Reducing Air Pollution

Pollutants moving through the atmosphere don't stop when they reach the borders between states and countries. They go wherever the wind carries them. This makes them difficult to control. Even if one state or country reduces its air pollution levels, pollutants from another state or country can blow across the border. For example, burning coal in midwestern states might cause acid rain in the northeast and Canada.

When states and nations cooperate, pollution problems can be reduced. People from around the world have met on several occasions to try to eliminate some kinds of air pollution. At one meeting in Montreal, Canada, an agreement called the Montreal Protocol was written to phase out the manufacture and use of CFCs by 2000. In 1989, 29 countries that consumed 82 percent of CFCs signed the agreement. By 1999, 184 countries signed it.

Table 1 Air-Quality Guide for Ozone

Air Quality	Air Quality Index	Protect Your Health
Good	0–50	No health impacts occur.
Moderate	51–100	People with breathing problems should limit outdoor exercise.
Unhealthy for Certain People	101–150	Everyone, especially children and elderly, should not exercise outside for long periods of time.
Unhealthy	151–200	All people should limit outdoor activities.

TRY AT HOME
Mini LAB

Examining the Content of Air

Use caution when reaching high places. Students with dust allergies should not perform this activity.

Procedure
1. Find a **high shelf or the top of a tall cabinet** in your home—someplace that hasn't been cleaned for a while.
2. Using a **white cloth,** thoroughly dust the surface.
3. Observe the cloth under a **magnifying lens.**

Analysis
1. What did you see on your cloth? Where did these particles come from?
2. Explain what you think happens when you breathe in these particles.

Answer Small particles cans travel deep into the lungs, causing irritation and damage, and may eventually cause breathing problems.

TRY AT HOME
Mini LAB

Purpose Students collect and examine particulate matter.
L1 ELL IS **Visual-Spatial**

Materials clean white rag, dusty shelf, magnifying lens

Teaching Strategy Students with dust allergies should wear a mask while collecting and examining their samples.

Analysis
1. Students should see dust particles. They came from sources inside and outside the home and were carried through the air to the shelf.
2. They move into the lungs, where they may cause irritation.

☑ Assessment

Performance Have students compare and contrast the different particles that they observed. Use **PASC,** p. 99.

Visual Learning

Table 1 Why is air quality reported to a community? Possible answer: so that people can know when they should take precautions because of poor air quality **Suppose the air quality index number rises from one week to the next. What does this indicate about air quality?** The air is becoming more unhealthful.

Reducing Air Pollution

Discussion

How is local air quality affected by weather changes and other variables? When an air mass is stationary, factories are operating, and traffic is congested, air quality is poor. When factories are shut down and traffic is less congested, air quality improves. Rain tends to wash dust and pollutants from the atmosphere, improving air quality.

Activity

Have students work in small groups to compose a list of logos that promote clean air by conservation and recycling. Then have each group make posters or banners that illustrate their logos. L2 COOP LEARN **Linguistic**

Extension

Ask students to search newspapers and magazines for articles about air pollution in the United States and relate each article to section content. L2 **Visual Spatial**

Caption Answer

Figure 14 about 30,000

Table 2 Clean Air Regulations

Urban Air Pollution	All cars manufactured since 1996 must reduce nitrogen oxide emissions by 60 percent and hydrocarbons by 35 percent from their 1990 levels.
Acid Rain	Sulfur dioxide emissions must be reduced by 14 million tons from 1990 levels by the year 2000.
Airborne Toxins	Industries must limit the emission of 200 compounds that cause cancer and birth defects.
Ozone-Depleting Chemicals	Industries were required to immediately cease production of many ozone-depleting substances in 1996.

Air Pollution in the United States The United States Congress passed several laws to protect the air. The Clean Air Act of 1990, summarized in **Table 2,** addressed some air pollution problems by regulating emissions from cars, energy production, and other industries. In 1997, new levels for ozone and particulate matter were proposed.

Since the passage of the Clean Air Act, the amount of some pollutants released into the air has decreased, as shown in **Figure 14.** However, one out of four people in the United States still breathes unhealthy air.

Reducing Emissions More than 80 percent of sulfur dioxide emissions comes from coal-burning power plants. Coal from some parts of the United States contains a lot of sulfur. When this coal is burned, sulfur combines with moisture in the air to form sulfuric acid, causing acid rain. Sulfur dioxide can be removed by passing the smoke through a scrubber. A **scrubber** lets the gases in the smoke dissolve in water, removing some of the sulfur. Another way to decrease the amount of sulfur dioxide is by burning low-sulfur coal.

Electric power plants that burn fossil fuels emit particulates into the atmosphere. **Figure 15** shows how nearly 99 percent of particulates can be removed using an electrostatic separator.

Figure 14
This graph shows that some air pollutants have decreased since the passage of the Clean Air Act.
How many tons of particulates were release to the air in 1994?

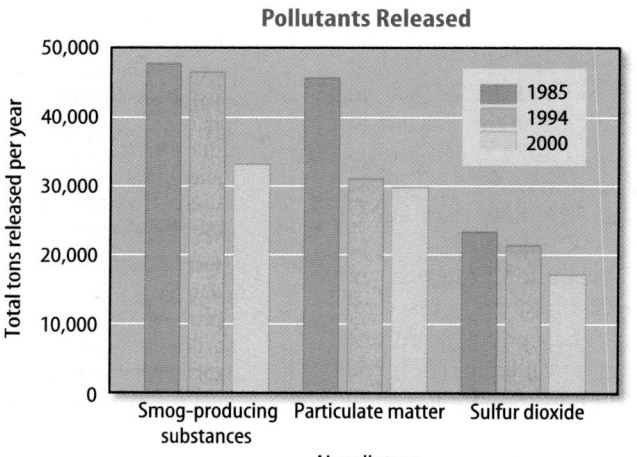

 **Cultural Diversity**

Stove Pollution A major environmental problem in Latin America, Asia, and Africa is indoor air pollution caused by burning biomass in stoves. Inefficient burning of fuels produces substances that cause health problems such as pneumonia in children. Ask students to research the meaning of *biomass*. Biomass is plant and animal matter used as fuel. L2

Resource Manager

Chapter Resources Booklet
 Reinforcement, p. 24
 Lab Activity, pp. 11–12
Lab Management and Safety, p. 76

Getting Around Cars produce more than 80 percent of the carbon monoxide and 40 percent of the nitrogen oxides that enter the atmosphere in the United States. Better emission-control devices on cars will help, but will that be enough to solve smog problems? Today, Americans drive an average of 16,000 kilometers more per year than they did 15 years ago. More time spent driving also leads to more traffic congestion. Cars produce even more pollutants when they are stopped in traffic.

The Clean Air Act can work only if we all cooperate. Cleaning the air takes money, time, and effort. How might you take part in this clean up? You can change your lifestyle. For example, you can walk, ride a bike, or use public transportation to get to a friend's house instead of asking for a ride. You also can set the thermostat in your house lower in the winter and higher in the summer.

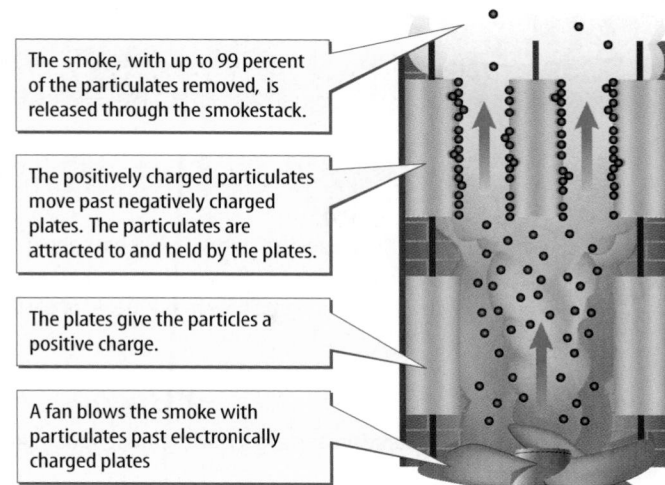

The smoke, with up to 99 percent of the particulates removed, is released through the smokestack.

The positively charged particulates move past negatively charged plates. The particulates are attracted to and held by the plates.

The plates give the particles a positive charge.

A fan blows the smoke with particulates past electronically charged plates

Figure 15
Electrostatic separators can remove almost all of the particulates in industrial smoke.

 Reading Check *What can you do to prevent air pollution?*

Section 2 Assessment

1. Name four sources of air pollution.
2. What are three pollutants released into the air when fuels are burned?
3. Name several ways air pollution can affect your health.
4. How can people reduce air pollution?
5. **Think Critically** Laws were passed in 1970 requiring coal-burning power plants to use tall smokestacks to disperse pollutants. Power plants in the midwestern states complied with that law, and people in eastern Canada began complaining about acid rain. Explain the connection.

Skill Builder Activities

6. **Classifying** Use the information in **Table 1** to classify the following air quality indices: 43, 152, 7, 52, 147, and 98. What category of air quality would you like to have in your neighborhood? Why is it important to have limits on pollutants from cars and factories as the U.S. population grows and people drive more? **For more help, refer to the** Science Skill Handbook.
7. **Communicating** In your Science Journal, create a crossword puzzle using at least 12 important terms found in this section. **For more help, refer to the** Science Skill Handbook.

---

3 Assess

Reteach

Have pairs of students review what they know about conserving resources, recycling, and air pollution. Then have the pairs make lists of at least 15 ways they can help reduce air pollution. [L2]
COOP LEARN **Interpersonal**

Challenge

Have students identify and explain the tradeoffs involved when a person changes his or her lifestyle in order to help reduce air pollution. Conserving energy may involve giving up some conveniences. For example, walking instead of driving to the store will reduce air pollution, but will take more time and effort. [L3]

Assessment

Oral Ask students who they think should be responsible for protecting Earth's air and water for future generations. Use **Performance Assessment in the Science Classroom,** p. 89.

Answers to Section Assessment

1. Possible answers: cars, factories, power plants, volcanoes, fires
2. carbon monoxide, nitrogen oxide, sulfur dioxide
3. It burns eyes, causes dry throat and headaches, damages lung tissue, makes people more susceptible to pneumonia and asthma, and puts stress on the heart.
4. by reducing fossil fuel consumption and emissions of other chemicals
5. Sulfur dioxide from these plants mixed with water vapor in the air to form sulfuric acid. Clouds drifted northeast and released acid rain onto Canada.
6. Good: 7, 43; moderate: 52, 98; unhealthy for some: 147;
   unhealthy: 152; most will want high quality air; increasing population can lead to higher pollution levels unless stricter limits are imposed.
7. Students should spell words correctly and provide Across and Down clues.

Activity

Recognize the Problem

Purpose

Students design and carry out an experiment to collect particulate matter that is carried by air. [L2]

ELL **[IS] Logical-Mathematical**

Process Skills

designing an experiment to test a hypothesis, communicating, forming a hypothesis, observing, inferring, classifying, interpreting data

Time Required

15 to 20 minutes for planning, 25 to 30 minutes to prepare lids, 40 minutes one week later to analyze the data and draw conclusions

Materials

The lids with gelatin can be prepared in advance to save time.

Alternate Materials

If gelatin is not available, petroleum jelly can be rubbed onto lids, petri dishes, or microscope slides.

Safety Precautions

Caution students to use thermal mitts and safety goggles while working with the hot plate and hot gelatin.

Form a Hypothesis

Possible Hypotheses

Students might hypothesize that they will find soot, dust particles, and pieces of plants and insects, and that different areas of the community will contain different types and amounts of particulate matter.

Activity — Design Your Own Experiment

What's in the air?

When you dust items in your household, you are cleaning up particles that settled out of the air. How often do you have to dust to keep your furniture clean? Just imagine how many pieces of particulate matter the air must hold.

Recognize the Problem

Do some areas of your environment have more particulates than other areas?

Form a Hypothesis

Based on your knowledge of your neighborhood, hypothesize what kinds of particulate matter you will find in your environment. Will all areas in your community contain the same types and amounts of particulate matter?

Goals
- **Design** an experiment to collect and analyze particulate matter in the air in your community.
- **Observe and describe** the particulate matter you collect.

Safety Precautions

Wear a thermal mitt, safety goggles, and an apron while working with a hot plate and while pouring the gelatin from the pan or pot into the lids. Never eat anything in the lab.

Possible Materials
small box of plain gelatin
hot plate
pan or pot
water
marker
refrigerator
plastic lids (4)
microscope
*Hand lens
*Alternate materials

Sample data table:

Lid number	Lid location	Number of particles	Types of particles
1	next to school	15	plant fragments, tree droppings, insects
2	parking lot	14	soot, dust
3	near factory	18	mostly soot
4	grassy field	20	dust, insects, plant fragments

Test Your Hypothesis

Possible Procedures

Empty a box of plain gelatin into a pot. Stir in the appropriate amount of water. Heat the mixture on a hot plate. Pour the mixture onto plastic lids. Place the lids into a refrigerator overnight. The next day, place the lids at various outdoor locations. At the end of one week, examine the lids with a stereomicroscope.

Test Your Hypothesis

Plan

1. As a group, agree upon your hypothesis and decide how you will test it. Identify which results will confirm or refute the hypothesis.

2. **List** the steps you need to take to test your hypothesis. Be specific. Describe exactly what you will do at each step. List your materials.

3. Prepare a data table in your Science Journal to record your observations.

4. Label your lids with the location where you decide to place them.

5. Mix the gelatin according to the directions on the box. Carefully pour a thin layer of gelatin into each lid. Use this to collect air particulate matter.

6. Read over your entire experiment to make sure that all steps are in a logical order.

7. Identify any constants, variables, and controls of the experiment.

Do

1. Make sure your teacher approves your plan.

2. Carry out the experiment as planned.

3. While the experiment is going on, record any observations that you make and complete the data table in your Science Journal.

Analyze Your Data

1. **Describe** the types of materials you collected in each lid.

2. **Calculate** the number of particles on each lid.

3. What did you use as a control in this experiment?

4. What were your variables?

5. **Graph** your results using a bar graph. Place the number of particulates on the *y*-axis and the test site location on the *x*-axis.

Draw Conclusions

1. Did the results support your hypothesis? Explain.

2. **Explain** why different sizes of particulate matter may be found at different locations.

3. **Infer** why some test-site locations showed more particulates than other sites did.

Communicating Your Data

Give an oral presentation to another class on air pollution in your community. Demonstrate your experiment and graphically display the results.

ACTIVITY 627

Teaching Strategies

- Have students discuss how their bodies filter solid particles from the air they breathe. The hairs and mucus in the nose filter particulate matter.

- Have students study maps that show the locations of nearby industries and weather maps that show local wind patterns. Ask them to establish a correlation to their test results.

Expected Outcome

Students will observe that particulate matter is stuck to the gelatin.

Analyze Your Data

1. Possible materials: dust particles, soot, paint chips, plant seeds, pieces of leaves and twigs, small insects

2. Answers will vary depending on actual number of particles collected.

3. plastic lids with gelatin covered with clear wrap and set out with the exposed experimental lids

4. Possible answers: direction of the wind; proximity to factories, trees, and other particulate sources

5. Graphs will vary depending on materials collected.

Error Analysis

Have students compare their results and their hypotheses and explain any differences identified.

Draw Conclusions

1. Answers will vary and are based on the students' individual research.

2. The size of the particles will depend on their source.

3. Some locations were closer to sources of particulates.

Communicating Your Data

Presentations should incorporate the results of this activity. Visual aids should include the tables and graphs that were made from data obtained.

TIME
SCIENCE AND HISTORY

SCIENCE CAN CHANGE THE COURSE OF HISTORY!

Content Background

DDT's toxicity, its persistence in the environment, and its ability to accumulate in living tissue made the eventual banning of the chemical necessary. The problem with DDT was not apparent immediately. Over time, the regular spraying of the insecticide caused the DDT residue to seep into the groundwater, rivers, lakes and oceans. Microbes ingested it. Insects, worms and small fish ate the microbes. Larger fish, birds and mammals in turn fed off the smaller prey. This chain of feeding resulted in the chemical being passed along in higher, more toxic levels.

The eagle in particular was affected. DDT hurt its reproductive process by chemically blocking the eagle's ability to create a strong coating on the outside of the egg. Lacking this protective shell, even the weight of the incubating female was enough to destroy the egg. As a result, fewer chicks were raised. This exposure to pesticide as well as other environmental factors, such as habitat loss and hunting, nearly caused the eagle to become extinct by the early 1970s.

After DDT was banned and the Endangered Species Act was passed, the eagle population began to recover. Reintroduction programs and the eagle's ability to adapt by nesting near people have helped the eagle population to grow to an estimated 6,000 breeding pairs.

MEET

In 1958, retired biologist Rachel Carson (1907–1964) received a letter from a worried friend. Several songbirds had died immediately after the pesticide DDT was sprayed over an area of woods. In the 1940s and 1950s, DDT was sprayed over large areas of land to kill insects that caused crop damage and to eliminate diseases such as malaria. DDT was considered to be a scientific miracle. The letter Carson received, however, indicated something she had long suspected—there was a downside to the miracle.

Her friend's letter troubled Carson so much that she launched an investigation into the possible harmful effects of pesticides—a study that took four years of research, interviews, and analysis. The result was Carson's famous book, *Silent Spring*. In it, she stated her findings that pesticide use was destroying the food supply of many animals, killing birds and fish, and poisoning human food supplies. She wrote that unless action was taken, an eerie stillness would settle over the world, a world without songbirds—a silent spring.

628

Resources for Teachers and Students

Just Eagles, by Alan Hutchison and Bill Silliker (photographer), Willow Creek Press, 2000.

"Eagles Remain on List," editor-in-chief of *Birder's World*, 2000 v14 i5 p16.

Silent Spring, by Rachel Carson, Houghton Mifflin Company, 1962.

Silent Spring Revisited, edited by Gino J. Marco, Robert M. Hollingworth and William Durham, American Chemical Society, 1987

A **biologist** and **writer** who made people aware of the fragility of **nature**

RACHEL CARSON

Historical Significance

Silent Spring launched the environmental movement and also spurred revolutionary changes in government policy. Rachel Carson's warning nearly 40 years ago that chemicals were poisoning the earth not only opened the public's eyes to the dangers of pesticides, but also forced a debate that led to the involvement of citizens, scientists, and environmental groups in affecting policy.

The Environmental Defense Fund took these concerns to court. Using scientific evidence, conservationists and other activists made their case that the government needed laws to protect the environment. For example, the Endangered Species Act allows for the protection of certain animals. The eagle, which has benefited from being on the list for two decades, was scheduled to be removed in 2000. Concerns regarding habitat protection forced the government to reconsider doing so.

Hold a brainstorming session about what criteria students think should be used to determine whether or not an animal should be put on the endangered species list. You can start the session by asking: What human activities disturb animal habitats?

The publication of *Silent Spring* led to a heated debate in the United States over the use of pesticides. But it also led to a change in how people thought about the natural world. Before Carson's book, few people thought about nature and how human activities might affect Earth's organisms. Thanks to *Silent Spring*, many people began to realize that Earth and the organisms living on Earth are closely connected.

"The more clearly we can focus our attention on the wonders and realities of the universe about us, the less taste we have for its destruction," Carson wrote.

Carson's findings were verified and DDT was banned. Many species of birds owe their continuing existence to her efforts. The most famous example is the national symbol of the United States—the bald eagle. DDT caused the bald eagles' eggs to weaken and break, bringing the species close to extinction. Since the ban on DDT, bald eagles have been making a slow comeback. Their recovery was affirmed in 1999, when the U.S. Fish & Wildlife Service proposed to remove the bald eagle from the endangered species list.

CONNECTIONS Make Posters **Research an environmental issue you are concerned about. Make posters to educate others in your school or community about the issue. Look for quotes you'd like to use to help illustrate your poster. You might find some in Carson's book.**

SCIENCE *Online*

For more information, visit science.glencoe.com

SCIENCE *Online*

Internet Addresses

Explore the Glencoe Science Web site at **science.glencoe.com** to find out more about topics in this section.

Chapter 21 Study Guide

Reviewing Main Ideas

Preview

Students can answer the questions in their Science Journals. Discuss the answers as you go through the chapter. **LS Linguistic**

Review

Students can write their answers, then compare them with those of other students. **LS Interpersonal**

Reteach

Students can look at the illustrations and describe details that support the main ideas of the chapter. **LS Visual-Spatial**

Answers to Chapter Review

SECTION 1

1. When it rains, runoff can carry the oil into streams.
3. By washing full loads of laundry, less water is needed than would be necessary to wash several smaller loads.

SECTION 2

4. acid rain

Section 1 Water Pollution

1. Water pollution comes from industrial discharge; runoff of pesticides, herbicides, and fertilizers from lawns and farms; and water from your home. *How can oil dripping onto pavement eventually pollute a stream?*

2. National and international cooperation is necessary if water pollution is to be reduced. In the United States, the 1990 Clean Water Act set up standards for sewage and wastewater-treatment facilities and for runoff from roadways and farms.

3. Conserving water in your daily activities can help reduce water pollution. *How can doing laundry conserve water and electricity if only full loads are washed?*

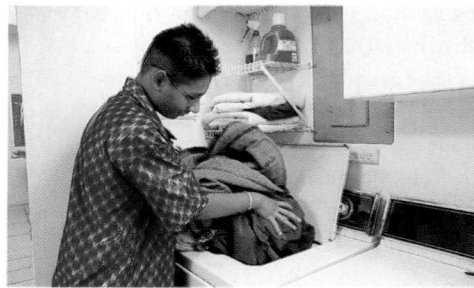

4. The water quality of many lakes and rivers in the United States is improving.

Section 2 Air Pollution

1. Exhaust from vehicles pollutes the air. Other sources of air pollution include power plants, fires and volcanoes.

2. Natural conditions, such as landforms and temperature inversions can affect air quality.

3. Polluted air can affect human health. Breathing particles, ozone, and acid rain can damage your lungs.

4. Air pollutants don't have boundaries. They drift between states and countries. National and international cooperation is necessary to reduce the problem. *Which type of air pollution can damage structures like the statue below?*

FOLDABLES Reading & Study Skills

After You Read

Compare and contrast characteristics of water and air pollution. List things in common under the middle tab of your Foldable.

FOLDABLES Reading & Study Skills

After You Read

After students have read the chapter and completed the Foldable described in Before You Read, have them do the activity on the student page.

Visualizing Main Ideas

Complete the following concept map on types of pollution.

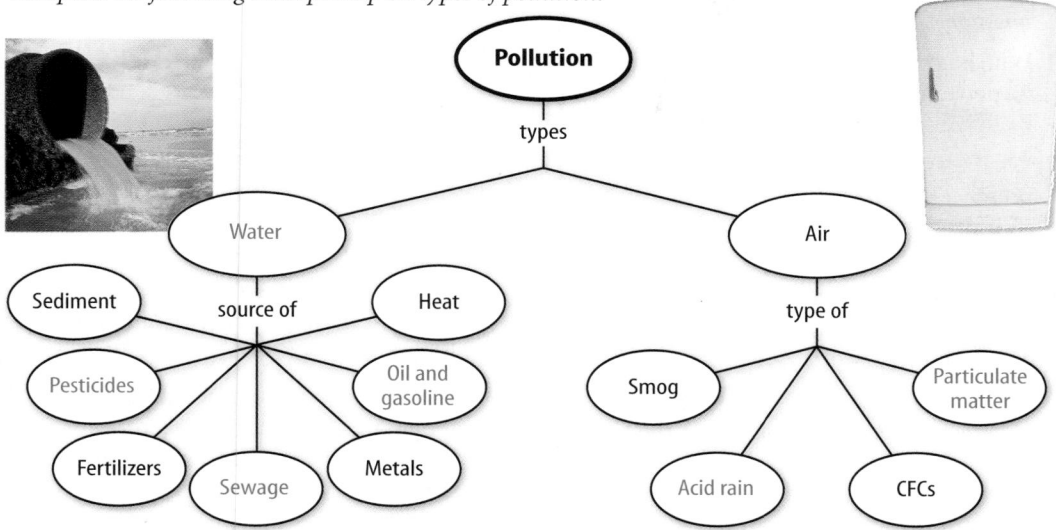

Visualizing Main Ideas

See student page.

Vocabulary Review

Using Vocabulary
1. Photochemical smog
2. Point source pollution
3. Fertilizers
4. A scrubber
5. particulates

Vocabulary Review

Vocabulary words

a. acid
b. acid rain
c. base
d. carbon monoxide
e. fertilizer
f. nonpoint source pollution
g. particulate matter
h. pesticide
i. pH scale
j. photochemical smog
k. point source pollution
l. scrubber
m. sewage

Using Vocabulary

Replace the underlined phrase with the correct vocabulary words.

1. <u>Smog that forms with the aid of sunlight</u> contains ozone near Earth's surface.

2. <u>Pollution that enters water from a specific location</u> can be controlled or treated before it enters a body of water.

3. <u>Chemicals that help plants and other organisms grow</u> can reduce the amount of oxygen in lakes.

4. <u>A device that lowers sulfur emissions from coal-burning power plants</u> can help reduce acid rain.

5. When <u>fine solids such as dust, ash, and soot that are in the air</u> are inhaled, they can irritate and damage the lungs.

THE PRINCETON REVIEW Study Tip

Write the questions as well as the answers to end-of-chapter quizzes. This will help you form complete responses to important questions.

IDENTIFYING Misconceptions

Assess

Use the assessment as follow-up to page 608F after students have completed the chapter.

Materials plastic shoe box, water, cooking oil, blue food coloring, measuring cup, paper towels, fabric, coffee filters, string, sponges, construction paper, detergent

Procedure Have student teams clean up an oil spill. Fill the shoebox about 1/3 full of water. Add one drop of blue food coloring. Add a half cup of cooking oil. Have student teams develop a hypothesis regarding what they can use to clean up the oil spill, test their hypothesis, and record their results.

Expected Outcome Students should see how difficult it is to clean up an oil spill. They should realize this is a time-consuming and costly task. And, they will realize that pollution affects our oceans.

Reinforcement Have students discuss cost-effective ways to clean up an oil spill. Have them discuss what each of them might do to protect Earth's oceans.

Checking Concepts

1. D
2. B
3. B
4. B
5. A
6. A
7. A
8. C
9. D
10. A

Thinking Critically

11. Cities can publish the Air Quality Index for ozone and alert the public about other air quality problems. At these times, factories that contribute to the pollution could be closed or driving could be restricted.

12. Possible answers: planting vegetation to keep sediments from eroding; spraying water at construction sites to keep dust from blowing

13. More people driving more miles adds to air pollution. Stricter limits must be enforced if air quality is to remain the same or is to improve.

14. Heat kills some organisms because they cannot tolerate high temperatures. Heat also reduces the amount of available oxygen in the water.

15. They could pump groundwater or pipe in surface water. The water would need to be stored in covered containers to reduce evaporation. Conservation would be extremely important in such communities.

Checking Concepts

Choose the word or phrase that best answers the question.

1. Which is most responsible for city smog?
   A) power plants   C) industries
   B) burning wastes   D) cars

2. What forms when pollutants react in the presence of sunlight?
   A) pH   C) particulates
   B) photochemical smog   D) acid rain

3. Which of the following describes substances with a low pH?
   A) neutral   C) dense
   B) acidic   D) basic

4. What combines with moisture in the air to form acid rain?
   A) ozone   C) lead
   B) sulfur oxides D) oxygen

5. Which of the following is a nonpoint source?
   A) runoff from a golf course
   B) sewage
   C) wastewater from industry
   D) discharge from a ditch into a river

6. What is the largest source of water pollution in the United States?
   A) sediment   C) heat
   B) metals   D) gasoline

7. What is the pH of acid rain?
   A) less than 5.6   C) greater than 7.0
   B) between 5.6 and 7.0 D) greater than 9.5

8. What kind of pollution are airborne solids that range in size from large grains to microscopic?
   A) pH   C) particulate
   B) ozone D) acid rain

9. Which of the following causes algae to grow?
   A) pesticides   C) metals
   B) sediment   D) fertilizers

10. Which act gives money to local governments to treat wastewater?
    A) Water Pollution Control Act
    B) Clean Air Act
    C) Montreal Protocol
    D) Safe Drinking Water Act

Thinking Critically

11. How might cities with smog problems lessen the dangers to people who live and work in the cities?

12. What are some ways to control nonpoint pollution sources?

13. Why is it important to place stricter limits on pollutants from cars and factories as the U.S. population grows and people drive more?

14. Pollution occurs when heated water is released into a nearby body of water. What effects does this type of pollution have on organisms living in the water?

15. How might a community living near a desert cope with water-supply problems?

Developing Skills

16. **Making and Using Graphs** This table lists the total phosphorus entering Lake Erie for the listed year. Make a line graph of these data.

17. **Recognizing Cause and Effect** What effect will an increase in the human population have on the need for freshwater?

Phosphorus Entering Lake Erie	
Year	Metric Tons
1976	15,000
1982	12,000
1988	8,000
1995	7,000

Chapter ✓Assessment Planner

Portfolio Encourage students to place in their portfolios one or two items of what they consider to be their best work. Examples include:
- Extension, p. 615
- Challenge, p. 617
- Science Journal, p. 621

Performance Additional performance assessments, Performance Task Assessment Lists, and rubrics for evaluating these activities can be found in Glencoe's **Performance Assessment in the Science Classroom.**

18. Concept Mapping Complete this concept map about sewage treatment.

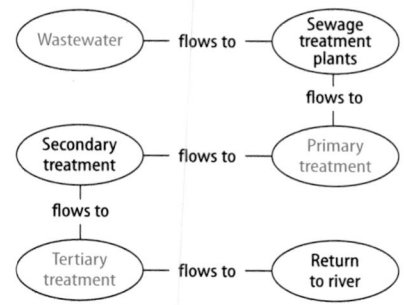

19. Relating Cause and Effect Explain how air and water are polluted when automobiles are used for transportation.

20. Communicating Explain what you personally can do to reduce air pollution.

Performance Assessment

21. Design and Perform an Experiment Design and perform an experiment to test the effects of acid rain on different kinds of vegetation. You might choose to use different types of vegetation as your variables and use acidity level as your control, or you might want to vary the pH of the solution.

22. Letter to the Editor Survey your town for evidence of air and water pollution. Write a letter to the editor of your local newspaper communicating what you have observed. Include suggestions for reducing pollution.

TECHNOLOGY

Go to the Glencoe Science Web site at **science.glencoe.com** or use the **Glencoe Science CD-ROM** for additional chapter assessment.

Test Practice

Rafael went to the library to do some research on acid rain. One of the pages he photocopied was the pH scale shown in the diagram below.

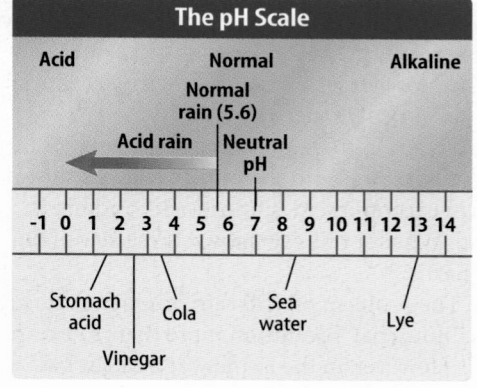

Study the diagram and answer the following questions.

1. According to the diagram, which substance has a pH greater than 10?
A) cola   C) sea water
B) lye   D) vinegar

2. Which of the following statements is correct?
F) Stomach acid has a higher pH than sea water.
G) Normal rain has a neutral pH.
H) Vinegar has a lower pH than cola.
J) Sea water has a higher pH than lye.

3. Which of the following best describes normal rain?
A) strongly alkaline
B) slightly alkaline
C) strongly acid
D) slightly acid

Test Practice

The Test-Taking Tip was written by The Princeton Review, the nation's leader in test preparation.
1. B
2. H
3. D

Developing Skills

16. Check students' work.
17. It will increase the demand for freshwater.
18. See student page.
19. Possible answers: Air is polluted by particulates and gases in car emissions. Water is polluted when nitrogen oxide from emissions forms acid rain, or when oil and gasoline dripping onto pavement are carried with runoff to streams.
20. Answers might include walking or cycling to destinations, recycling, planting trees, reducing wastes, and conserving resources.

Performance Assessment

21. If testing effect of acid rain on different types of plants, students could set up two trays of different plant species and give them both water of the same pH. If testing pH, trays would contain identical plants that are exposed to water with different pH's. In both cases, students could observe the color and growth of the plants. Use **PASC**, p. 95.
22. Information should be accurate and the letter should be in proper business form. Use **PASC**, p. 139.

⚫Assessment Resources

 Reproducible Masters
Chapter Resources Booklet
Chapter Review, pp. 31–32
Chapter Tests, pp. 33–36
Assessment Transparency Activity, p. 43

Glencoe Science Web site
Interactive Tutor
Chapter Quizzes

Glencoe Technology
🔊 Assessment Transparency
💿 Interactive CD-ROM Chapter Quizzes
💿 ExamView Pro Test Bank
💿 Vocabulary PuzzleMaker Software
📼 MindJogger Videoquiz DVD/VHS

Reading Comprehension

QUESTION 1: D

Students should read the sentences surrounding the underlined word and use context clues in order to identify the correct answer choice. Only choice D, *serious*, is the correct meaning for the usage of *severe* in the passage.

QUESTION 2: F

Students must use the information in the passage to identify which choice is the best supported conclusion.

- **Choice F** Yes; this is supported by the information in the passage.
- **Choice G** No; this is not supported by the information in the passage.
- **Choice H** No; this is not supported by the information in the passage.
- **Choice J** No; this is not supported by the information in the passage.

QUESTION 3: B

Only choice B illustrates a means of increasing air pollution. Students should refer to the statement in the passage, *Power plants are permitted to burn only low-sulfur coal.* Students should therefore recognize that high-sulfur coal might be harmful to the air.

Reading Comprehension

Read the passage. Then read each question that follows the passage. Decide which is the best answer to each question.

Acid Rain

The United States has become increasingly dependent on fossil fuels as sources of energy. When fossil fuels such as coal, oil, and natural gas are burned, they emit oxides of carbon, sulfur, and nitrogen into the air. These pollutants combine with the moisture in the air to form carbonic acid, sulfuric acid, and nitric acid. When it rains or snows, these acids fall to Earth.

The problem of acid rain originated during the Industrial Revolution more than 150 years ago. However, in the last few decades, it has become more <u>severe</u>. Recent increases are due mainly to industrial coal and oil combustion and automobile exhaust emissions.

Acid rain upsets the delicate balance of the ecosystems in streams, rivers, and lakes. It also increases soil acidity, reducing crop production and forest growth. Acid rain also contributes to the destruction of buildings and monuments made of stone.

The problem of acid rain is not limited to industrial and urban areas. Winds can carry polluted clouds hundreds of miles before they release their acidic moisture. Consequently, it has become a global problem requiring a global solution.

Efforts to reduce the production of acid rain have concentrated on removing dangerous emissions at their source. Power plants are permitted to burn only low-sulfur coal. Anti-pollution devices called "scrubbers" are used to trap gases emitted from smokestacks before they can enter the atmosphere. Cars must pass strict emissions tests before they can be sold.

The average citizen can help by conserving energy at home and by buying more fuel-efficient automobiles. Nevertheless, the only long-range solution to the problems of air pollution in general and acid rain in particular is the development of alternative sources of energy other than fossil fuels.

Test-Taking Tip Try drawing a picture or making a concept map to help you organize the main ideas in this passage.

1. In this passage, the word <u>severe</u> means _____.
   A) apparent
   B) complicated
   C) obvious
   D) serious

2. Which conclusion is best supported by information given in the passage?
   F) The problem of acid rain has no quick solution.
   G) The problem of acid rain appeared only recently.
   H) Scientists do not know what chemicals make up acid rain.
   J) There is little the average citizen can do to help reduce the incidence of acid rain.

3. Which of the following would NOT help reduce air pollution?
   A) conserving more energy at home
   B) burning high-sulfur coal
   C) requiring cars to pass stricter emissions tests
   D) removing more of the dangerous emissions at their source

Teaching Tip

Students should always choose answer choices that are supported by information in a passage.

Standardized Test Practice

Reasoning and Skills

Read each question and choose the best answer.

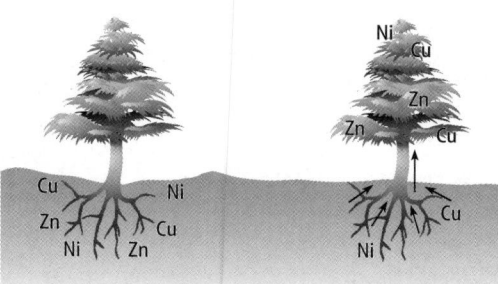

1. Phytoremediation occurs when certain types of plants remove harmful metals from soil. According to the picture, all of the following metals were removed from the soil EXCEPT _____.
   A) copper
   B) zirconium
   C) nickel
   D) zinc

Test-Taking Tip Review the chemical element symbols for different metals. Refer to the periodic table at the back of the book.

2. A scientist is going to study the effects of phytoremediation. She wants to measure the rates at which certain types of trees remove different metals. When chosing an area to study, which would be the best choice?
   F) along the banks of a stream
   G) a closed auto factory
   H) a new housing development
   J) along a sea coastline

3. Information about enzymes would most likely be found under which heading in a table of contents?
   A) Carrying Capacity
   B) Yard Waste and You
   C) Breaking Down Pollutants
   D) Lining Our Landfills

Test-Taking Tip Review the characteristics and uses of enzymes.

> **PESTICIDES**
> **SEDIMENT**
> **FERTILIZERS**

4. Which if these belongs with the group above?
   F) smog
   G) carbon monoxide
   H) human waste
   J) particulates

Test-Taking Tip Review the different types of water and air pollution.

Consider this question carefully before writing your answer on a separate sheet of paper.

5. There are different types of smog. Explain the causes and characteristics of each different type of smog.

Test-Taking Tip Review the causes and characteristics of photochemical smog and sulfurous smog.

Reasoning and Skills

QUESTION 1: B
Students need to use their understanding of phytoremediation and the information in the picture. Students also need to carefully read the question in order to identify which answer choice is an exception. Only answer choice B, *zirconium*, is an exception.

QUESTION 2: G
Students must understand the meaning of phytoremediation and that the most likely location containing many harmful metals would be choice G, *a closed auto factory*.

QUESTION 3: C
Students must use their knowledge of enzymes in order to identify choice C, *breaking down pollutants*, as the correct answer.

QUESTION 4: H
Students need to use their understanding of air and water pollution in order to identify the correct answer choice. Students should identify that all the words in the group are concerned with water pollution. Answer choices F, G, and J are air pollutants. Only answer choice H, *human wastes*, is a water pollutant.

QUESTION 5: Answers will vary.
Students should consider what they know about photochemical and sulfurous smog and write a thorough response.

Teaching Tip

Students should always choose the answer choice supported by their own knowledge and the information presented in illustrations.

UNIT 7 Astronomy

Unit Contents

✔ Pre-Reading Activity

Have students search for a figure that shows the relative sizes of all the planets.

How Are Thunderstorms & Neutron Stars Connected?

636

Teacher to Teacher

"While studying the stars, my students build a planetarium from a 50-foot square of plastic film. The final product will be 30 feet in diameter and 16 feet tall. Plans are available in *The Science Teacher*, vol. 64, no. 7, October 1997."

Dennis L. Stockdale, Teacher
Asheville High School
Asheville, NC

In 1931, an engineer built an antenna to study thunderstorm static that was interfering with radio communication. The antenna did detect static from storms, but it also picked up something else: radio signals coming from beyond our solar system. That discovery marked the birth of radio astronomy. By the 1960s, radio astronomy was thriving. In 1967, astronomer Jocelyn Bell Burnell detected a peculiar series of radio pulses coming from far out in space. At first, she and her colleagues theorized that the signals might be a message from a distant civilization. Soon, however, scientists determined that the signals must be coming from something called a neutron star (below)—a rapidly spinning star that gives off a radio beam from its magnetic pole.

Axis

Direction of spin

Radio beam

SCIENCE CONNECTION

NEUTRON STARS Find out more about what neutron stars are and how they form. You might begin your research by visiting the Glencoe Science Web site at **science.glencoe.com** or by consulting an encyclopedia or astronomy textbook. Then work with a partner to design a demonstration that uses a flashlight to show how a spinning neutron star emits a radio signal that sweeps past Earth like the rotating beam of a lighthouse.

Introducing the Unit

How Are Thunderstorms & Neutron Stars Connected?

Much of what we know today about the objects in our galaxy is based upon observations. Ancient astronomers watched the night sky, and they formed hypotheses about how our solar system works. The invention of the telescope led to more accurate models of our solar system and galaxy.

The advent of space flight has offered even greater tools for the exploration of the planets and moons closest to us, as well as discoveries of objects more distant than our own galaxy. Explorer spacecraft, like those used in the *Voyager* and *Mariner* missions, have collected information as they moved past the outer planets. The Apollo missions to our own Moon allowed humans to directly explore the surface and collect soil and rock samples.

As the Hubble Telescope orbits Earth, it continues to capture amazing photographs of objects beyond our galaxy. Radio astronomy provides a way to look even further past the limitations of our vision. Astronomers use these and other tools to collect information and to propose theories about the nature of our universe, and to hypothesize about its future.

SCIENCE Online
Internet Addresses

_____

_____

_____

_____

Explore the Glencoe Science Web site at **science.glencoe.com** to find out more about topics in this unit.

SCIENCE CONNECTION
Activity

Ask students to research a discovered neutron star and summarize their findings. They should report on who discovered the star, where the discovery was made, what tools were used to discover the star, the distance of the star from Earth, and the star's age.

Section/Objectives	Standards		Activities/Features
Chapter Opener	**National**	**State/Local**	**Explore Activity:** Model visible light seen through nebulae, p. 639 **Before You Read,** p. 639
	See p. 5T for a Key to Standards.		
Section 1 Radiation from Space ⏱ 2 sessions 📦 1 block 1. **Explain** the electromagnetic spectrum. 2. **Identify** the differences between refracting and reflecting telescopes. 3. **Recognize** the differences between optical and radio telescopes.	National Content Standards: UCP2, A1, D3		**Health Integration,** p. 641 **MiniLAB:** Observing the Effects of Light Pollution, p. 644 **Activity:** Building a Reflecting Telescope, p. 646
Section 2 Early Space Missions ⏱ 1 session 📦 0.5 block 1. **Compare and contrast** natural and artificial satellites. 2. **Identify** the differences between artificial satellites and space probes. 3. **Explain** the history of the race to the Moon.	National Content Standards: UCP2, A1, D3, F5, G1		**Math Skills Activity:** Using a Grid to Draw, p. 648 **Chemistry Integration,** p. 650 **Visualizing Space Probes,** p. 651 **Science Online,** p. 652 **MiniLAB:** Modeling a Satellite, p. 653
Section 3 Current and Future Space Missions ⏱ 4 sessions 📦 2 blocks 1. **Explain** the benefits of the space shuttle. 2. **Identify** the usefulness of orbital space stations. 3. **Explore** future space missions.	National Content Standards: UCP2, A1, D3, F5		**Science Online,** p. 657 **Science Online,** p. 659 **Activity:** Star Sightings, p. 662 **Science and Society:** Cities in Space, p. 664

NATIONAL GEOGRAPHIC

Teacher's Corner

PRODUCTS AVAILABLE FROM NATIONAL GEOGRAPHIC SOCIETY
To order call 1-800-368-2728:
Books
Discover Mars
Mars: Uncovering the Secrets of the Red Planet
National Geographic Satellite Atlas of

the World
Waves: The Electromagnetic Universe
Video
What We Learn About Earth from Space

INDEX TO NATIONAL GEOGRAPHIC SOCIETY
The following articles may be used for research relating to this chapter:

"Return to Mars," by William R. Newcott, August 1998.
"New Eyes on the Universe," by Bradford A. Smith, January 1994.
"Satellite Rescue," by Thomas Y. Canby, November 1991.
"Mission to Mars," by Michael Collins, November 1988.

Activity Materials	Reproducible Resources	Section Assessment	Technology
Explore Activity: lightbulb; sheet of dark plastic; sheets of plastic in different colors; yellow, red, blue, purple, and green balloons	**Chapter Resources Booklet** Foldables Worksheet, p. 13 Directed Reading Overview, p. 15 Note-taking Worksheets, pp. 29–31	*GLENCOE'S* **ASSESSMENT** *ADVANTAGE*	
MiniLAB: cardboard tube **Activity:** flat mirror, curved mirror, magnifying lenses	**Chapter Resources Booklet** Transparency Activity, p. 638 MiniLAB, p. 3 Enrichment, p. 26 Reinforcement, p. 23 Directed Reading, p. 16 Activity Worksheet, pp. 5–6 Transparency Activity, pp. 43–44 Lab Activity, pp. 9–12 **Science Inquiry Labs,** p. 59 **Cultural Diversity,** p. 51	**Portfolio** Science Journal, p. 643 **Performance** MiniLAB, p. 644 Skill Builder Activities, p. 645 **Content** Section Assessment, p. 645	♦ Section Focus Transparency ♦ Teaching Transparency ◉ Interactive CD-ROM/DVD ∩ Guided Reading Audio Program
MiniLAB: string, rubber stopper, hose, steel nuts *Need materials?* Contact Science Kit at 1-800-828-7777 or www.sciencekit.com on the Internet.	**Chapter Resources Booklet** Transparency Activity, p. 41 MiniLAB, p. 4 Enrichment, p. 27 Reinforcement, p. 24 Directed Reading, p. 17 **Mathematics Skill Activities,** p. 15 **Reading and Writing Skill Activities,** p. 11	**Portfolio** Chemistry Integration, p. 650 **Performance** Math Skills Activity, p. 648 MiniLAB, p. 653 Skill Builder Activities, p. 654 **Content** Section Assessment, p. 654	♦ Section Focus Transparency ◉ Interactive CD-ROM/DVD ∩ Guided Reading Audio Program
Activity: computer, Internet and other resources on space technology	**Chapter Resources Booklet** Transparency Activity, p. 42 Enrichment, p. 28 Reinforcement, p. 25 Directed Reading, pp. 17, 18 Activity Worksheet, pp. 7–8 **Home and Community Involvement,** p. 31 **Lab Management and Safety,** p. 73 **Physical Science Critical Thinking/ Problem Solving,** p. 5 **Cultural Diversity,** p. 25	**Portfolio** Curriculum Connection, p. 657 **Performance** Skill Builder Activities, p. 661 Activity, p. 662 **Content** Section Assessment, p. 661	♦ Section Focus Transparency ◉ Interactive CD-ROM/DVD ∩ Guided Reading Audio Program

End of Chapter Assessment

GLENCOE'S **ASSESSMENT** *ADVANTAGE*

Blackline Masters	Technology	Professional Series
Chapter Resources Booklet Chapter Review, pp. 33–34 Chapter Tests, pp. 35–38 **Standardized Test Practice by The Princeton Review,** pp. 95–98	▭ MindJogger Videoquiz ◉ CD-ROM Explorations and Quizzes ◉ Vocabulary Puzzle Makers ◉ ExamView Pro Test Bank ◉ Interactive Lesson Planner ◉ Interactive Teacher's Edition	Performance Assessment in the Science Classroom (PASC)

Transparencies

Section Focus

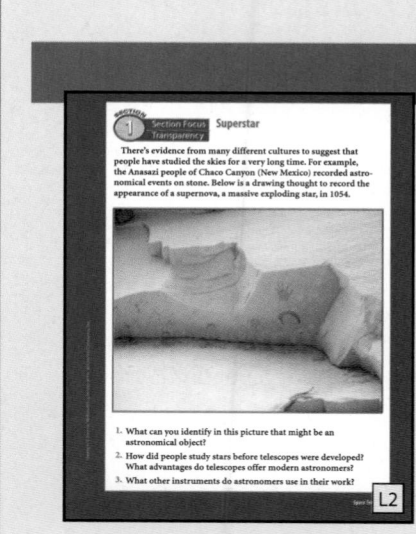

Section Focus Transparency 1 — Superstar

There's evidence from many different cultures to suggest that people have studied the skies for a very long time. For example, the Anasazi people of Chaco Canyon (New Mexico) recorded astronomical events on stone. Below is a drawing thought to record the appearance of a supernova, a massive exploding star, in 1054.

1. What can you identify in this picture that might be an astronomical object?
2. How did people study stars before telescopes were developed? What advantages do telescopes offer modern astronomers?
3. What other instruments do astronomers use in their work?

L2

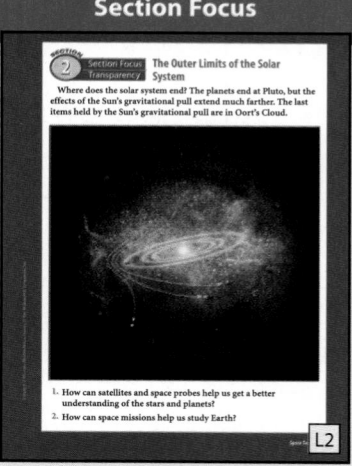

Section Focus Transparency 2 — The Outer Limits of the Solar System

Where does the solar system end? The planets end at Pluto, but the effects of the Sun's gravitational pull extend much farther. The last items held by the Sun's gravitational pull are in Oort's Cloud.

1. How can satellites and space probes help us get a better understanding of the stars and planets?
2. How can space missions help us study Earth?

L2

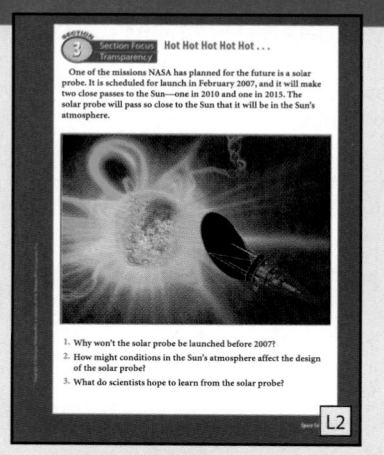

Section Focus Transparency 3 — Hot Hot Hot Hot Hot . . .

One of the missions NASA has planned for the future is a solar probe. It is scheduled for launch in February 2007, and it will make two close passes to the Sun—one in 2010 and one in 2015. The solar probe will pass so close to the Sun that it will be in the Sun's atmosphere.

1. Why won't the solar probe be launched before 2007?
2. How might conditions in the Sun's atmosphere affect the design of the solar probe?
3. What do scientists hope to learn from the solar probe?

L2

This is a representation of key blackline masters available in the Teacher Classroom Resources. See Resource Manager boxes within the chapter for additional information.

Assessment

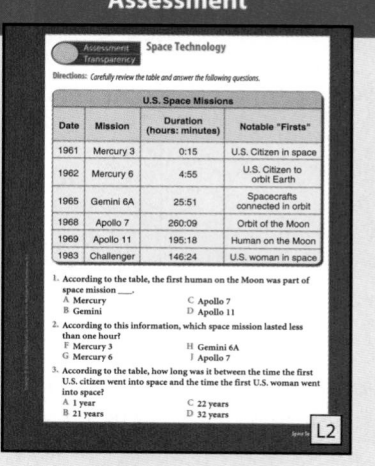

Assessment Transparency — Space Technology

Directions: Carefully review the table and answer the following questions.

U.S. Space Missions

Date	Mission	Duration (hours: minutes)	Notable "Firsts"
1961	Mercury 3	0:15	U.S. Citizen in space
1962	Mercury 6	4:55	U.S. Citizen to orbit Earth
1965	Gemini 6A	25:51	Spacecrafts connected in orbit
1968	Apollo 7	260:09	Orbit of the Moon
1969	Apollo 11	195:18	Human on the Moon
1983	Challenger	146:24	U.S. woman in space

1. According to the table, the first human on the Moon was part of space mission ___.
   A Mercury   C Apollo 7
   B Gemini   D Apollo 11
2. According to this information, which space mission lasted less than one hour?
   F Mercury 3   H Gemini 6A
   G Mercury 6   J Apollo 7
3. According to the table, how long was it between the time the first U.S. citizen went into space and the time the first U.S. woman went into space?
   A 1 year   C 22 years
   B 21 years   D 32 years

L2

Teaching

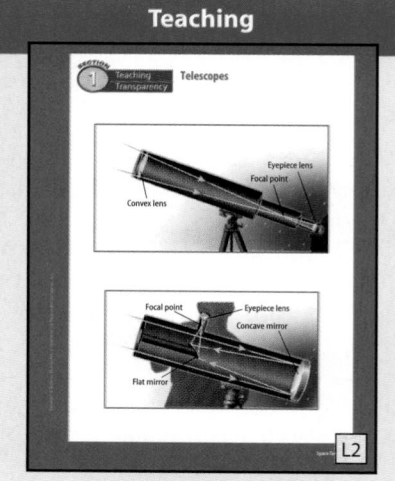

Teaching Transparency 1 — Telescopes

L2

Key to Teaching Strategies

The following designations will help you decide which activities are appropriate for your students.

L1 Level 1 activities should be appropriate for students with learning difficulties.

L2 Level 2 activities should be within the ability range of all students.

L3 Level 3 activities are designed for above-average students.

ELL ELL activities should be within the ability range of English Language Learners.

COOP LEARN Cooperative Learning activities are designed for small group work.

LS Multiple Learning Styles logos, as described on page 22T, are used throughout to indicate strategies that address different learning styles.

P These strategies represent student products that can be placed into a best-work portfolio.

Hands-on Activities

Activity Worksheets

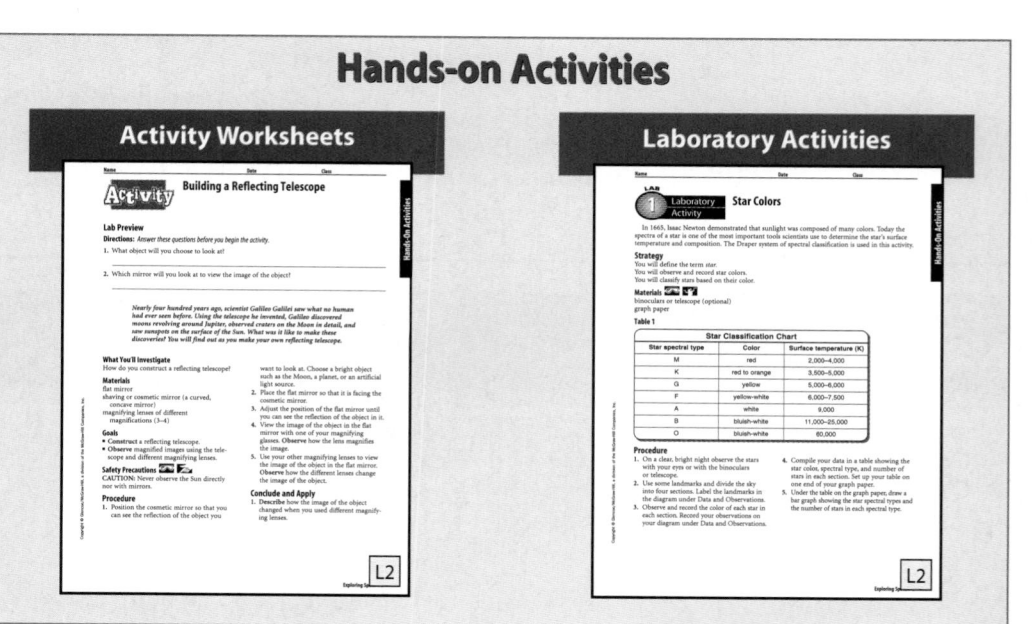

Activity — Building a Reflecting Telescope

L2

Laboratory Activities

Laboratory Activity 1 — Star Colors

L2

Meeting Different Ability Levels

Content Outline

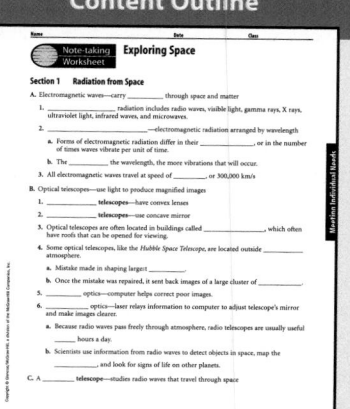

L2

Reinforcement

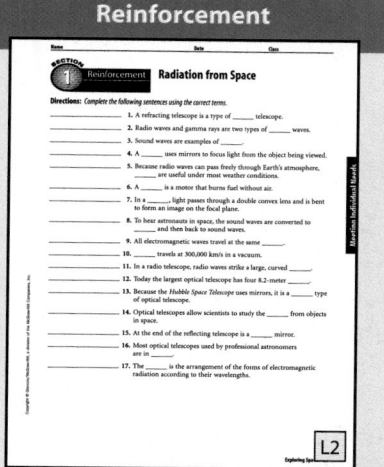

L2

Directed Reading

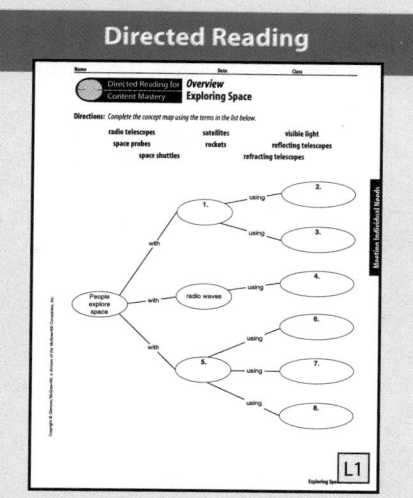

L1

Assessment

Chapter Tests

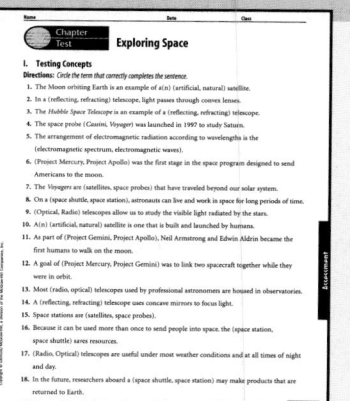

L2

Enrichment

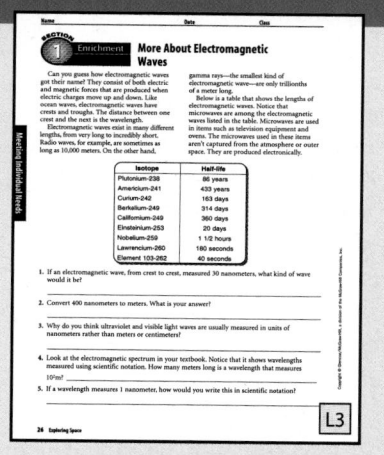

L3

Spanish Directed Reading

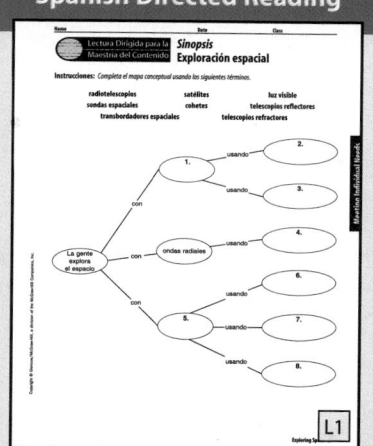

L1

Test Practice Workbook

L2

Chapter Review

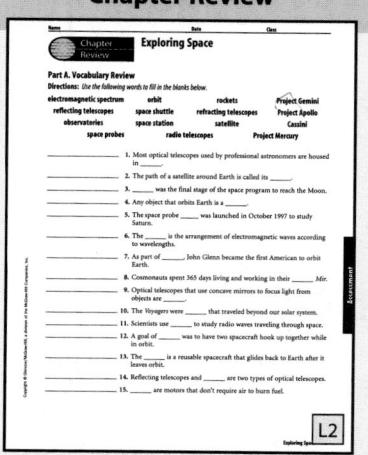

L2

Science Content Background

Exploring Space
Large Telescopes

On April 21, 1998, the largest telescope on Earth captured light from its first star. The European Southern Observatory's Very Large Telescope (VLT) is composed of four identical 8.2-m individual telescopes and several movable 1.8-m telescopes.

Other large telescopes include the twin 10-m Keck reflecting telescopes on Mauna Kea in Hawaii. The primary mirror of each telescope has been constructed from 36 hexagonal glass segments, each 1.8 m in diameter.

The NASA Orbital Debris Observatory (NODO) uses a liquid mirror telescope. The objective mirror is made of a shallow container of the liquid element mercury. It is 3 m in diameter and is constantly spinning at one revolution every 6.02315 seconds. This spinning forces the liquid mercury to form a parabolic reflector. The telescope is kept level; thus, it observes only the sky's zenith. Its main mission is to locate and count orbital debris (space junk) as small as 1 cm in diameter.

The Very Large Array (VLA) of telescopes near Socorro, New Mexico, is composed of 27 radio telescopes. All 27 telescopes can be used at once to operate as one large telescope.

Light Pollution

Light pollution is a glow in the sky caused by city lights. The glow makes it difficult to see dim stars.

In several United States cities, work has begun to reduce light pollution. Tucson, Arizona, located only 80 km from the Kitt Peak National Observatory, has replaced its street lighting with low-pressure sodium lamps. These lamps shine at wavelengths that can be filtered out by astronomers. Other cities have put hoods on billboards, parking-lot lights, and floodlights so they illuminate the object or the ground rather than the sky.

Early Space Missions
The First Missions into Space

The first mission into space was conducted by the Soviet Union, which launched the uncrewed *Sputnik 1*. It was designed to prove that human-made satellites could orbit Earth in the manner of a natural satellite, such as the moon. Within a year of that launch, the United States had built its own satellite and sent it into space. Known as *Explorer 1*, it was followed by three more attempts, all unsuccessful, to send probes into an orbit similar to that of Earth's Moon.

In 1959 the Soviet Union did what the United States hadn't been able to do. Their probe, *Luna 1*, became the first human-made satellite to travel past the Moon. Two months later, American attempts at a lunar

> **Fun Fact**
>
> The first U.S. weather satellite, *Vanguard 2*, was launched in February 1959. Its mission was to take photographs of Earth's cloud patterns.

Harold Sund/The Image Bank

flyby, or voyage past the Moon, became successful with *Pioneer 4*. The United States followed this successful effort with a series of probes known as *Ranger 1* and *2*. Both were failures. Finally, with *7*, *8*, and *9*, the United States was able to capture detailed pictures of the Moon's surface. This led into the Apollo program, which placed astronauts on the Moon itself.

David Ducros/Photo Researchers, Inc.

SECTION 3 Current and Future Space Missions

Water on Other Planets

Jupiter's moon Europa may contain water. Recent preliminary studies of Europa by the *Galileo* spacecraft indicate an ocean of water or ice under the moon's crustal layer of ice.

The *Cassini* mission to Saturn will have similar goals to the Galileo mission to Jupiter. The science goals of the Cassini mission involve studying and collecting data on Saturn, its magnetosphere, rings, icy moons, and Titan.

The International Space Station

The *International Space Station* will be a permanently crewed platform in which teams of astronauts from many nations will work cooperatively in space. Launch of materials and modules that are part of the *International Space Station* assembly began with the launch of the space shuttle *Endeavor*. Work continues on this international undertaking.

Everyday Space Technology

Much of the technology developed by NASA to achieve its goals in space is now being used by people throughout the world. These technologies are called spin-offs. For example, NASA developed lightweight, compact breathing systems for astronauts to carry as they ventured out of their spacecraft and onto the Moon. Today, firefighters use these breathing systems as well as fire-resistant uniforms originally designed as flight suits for NASA pilots. The lightweight material in the suits won't burn or crack. A material designed for boots worn by astronauts on the Moon is now found in some athletic shoes. Other materials have been incorporated into ski goggles, blankets, and bicycle seats.

People who are visually impaired also have benefited from spin-offs. One device vibrates ink on a printed page, enabling them to read materials that are not printed in Braille. Another device determines the denomination of currency and generates an audible signal. Other spin-offs include pens that write without the help of gravity and sunglasses that adjust to various light levels.

Fun Fact

At our present level of technology, a space probe sent to the nearest star would take lifetimes to reach its destination. Scientists currently are working to overcome the problems in designing and building such a multigenerational mission.

SCIENCE Online

For additional content background on this topic, go to the Glencoe Science Web site at science.glencoe.com.

Exploring Space

Chapter Vocabulary

electromagnetic spectrum
refracting telescope
reflecting telescope
observatory
radio telescope
rocket
satellite
orbit
space probe
Project Mercury
Project Gemini
Project Apollo
space shuttle
space station

What do you think?

Science Journal This is a photograph of a footprint being left on the moon by an Apollo astronaut. Because there is no wind or rain on the surface of the Moon, this footprint will remain as it is for eons until it is weathered away by the slow and gradual action of micrometeorite bombardment.

Exploring Space

Stars and planets have always fascinated humans. We admire their beauty, and our nearest star—the Sun—provides energy that enables life to exist on Earth. For centuries, people have studied space from the ground. But, in the last few decades, space travel has allowed us to get a closer look. In this chapter, you'll learn how space is explored with telescopes, rockets, probes, satellites, and space shuttles. You'll see how astronauts like Shannon Lucid, shown here, now can spend months living and working aboard space stations.

What do you think?

Science Journal Look at the picture below with a classmate. Discuss what you think this might be or what might be happening. Here's a hint: *It's part of a dusty trail that's far, far away.* Write your answer or best guess in your Science Journal.

638

Theme Connection

Energy Students are introduced to the way astronomers use various types of electromagnetic radiation (energy) to explore the solar system and the rest of the universe.

 You might think exploring space with a telescope is easy because the visible light coming from stars is so bright and space is dark. But space contains massive clouds of gases, dust, and other debris called nebulae that block part of the starlight traveling to Earth making it more difficult for astronomers to observe deep space. What does visible light look like when viewed through clouds of dust or gas?

Model visible light seen through nebulae

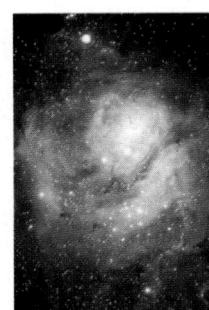

1. Turn on a light bulb and darken the room.
2. View the light bulb through a sheet of dark plastic.
3. View the light bulb through different colored plastic sheets.
4. View the light through a variety of different colored balloons such as yellow, blue, red, and purple. Observe how the light changes when you slowly let the air out of each balloon.

Observe

Write a paragraph in your Science Journal describing how this activity modeled the difficulty astronomers have when viewing stars through a thick nebulae?

Before You Read

Making a Sequence Study Fold Identifying a sequence helps you understand what you are experiencing and predict what might occur next. Before you read this chapter, make the following Foldable to prepare you to learn about the sequence of space exploration.

1. Place a sheet of paper in front of you so the short side is at the top. Fold the paper in half from the left side to the right side.
2. Fold the top and bottom in to divide the paper into thirds. Unfold the paper so three columns show.
3. Through the top thickness of paper, cut along each of the fold lines to the left fold, forming three tabs. Label the tabs "Past", "Present", and "Future", as shown.
4. As you read the chapter, write what you learn under the tabs.

639

EXPLORE ACTIVITY

Purpose Use this Explore Activity to introduce students to how a nebula obscures and dims starlight.

Preparation Collect or purchase different colored plastic sheets. Arrange your room so that the light bulb will be at its center.

Materials several different colored plastic sheets and several different colored balloons for each pair of students, one light bulb for the class

Teaching Strategy Arrange student pairs in a circle around the light bulb to make certain each pair has an unobstructed view of the light. For larger classes, two light bulbs at opposite ends of the room can be used.

Observe

Dark colored balloons and plastic sheets will block out more light than light colored balloons just as a dark nebula blocks out more starlight than a lighter colored one. When a balloon is deflated, less light can penetrate it, just as less starlight penetrates denser nebulae. A dense nebula dramatically dims and reddens visible light coming from stars, and at times, astronomers cannot clearly view the stars and galaxies behind it.

✓ Assessment

Process Have students infer from their results why astronomical observatories are built on high mountains. Like a nebulae, the atmosphere dims starlight. On high mountains, starlight passes through less air and celestial objects can be seen more clearly. Use **Performance Assessment in the Science Classroom**, p. 89

Before You Read

Dinah Zike Study Fold

Purpose Use this activity to provide a Foldable in which students record what they know about space exploration in the past and the present, and predict its future based on information obtained while reading the chapter.

For additional help, see Foldables Worksheet, p. 13 in **Chapter Resources Booklet,** or go to the Glencoe Science Web site at **science.glencoe.com.** See After You Read in the Study Guide at the end of this chapter.

Radiation from Space

Bellringer Transparency

Display the Section Focus Transparency for Section 1. Use the accompanying Transparency Activity Master. L2

ELL

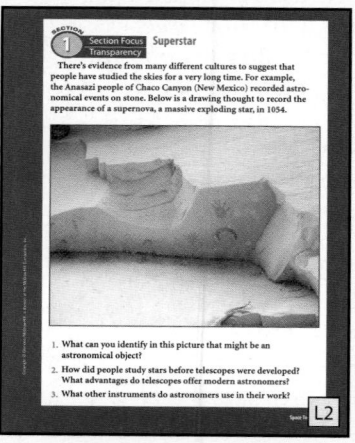

Tie to Prior Knowledge

Ask for a show of hands for each of these questions: **Have you ever used electromagnetic radiation? How many have had an X ray? Used a microwave? Listened to the radio? Seen sunshine or felt the Sun's heat?** Explain that anyone who has raised his or her hand has experienced electromagnetic radiation.

As You Read

What You'll Learn

- **Explain** the electromagnetic spectrum.
- **Identify** the differences between refracting and reflecting telescopes.
- **Recognize** the differences between optical and radio telescopes.

Vocabulary

electromagnetic spectrum
refracting telescope
reflecting telescope
observatory
radio telescope

Why It's Important

You can learn much about space without traveling there.

Electromagnetic Waves

As you just read, living in space soon will be possible. The same can't be said, though, for space travel to distant galaxies. If you've dreamed about racing toward distant parts of the universe—think again. Even at the speed of light, it would take years and years to reach even the nearest stars.

Light from the Past When you look at a star, the light that you see left the star many years ago. Although light travels fast, distances between objects in space are so great that it sometimes takes millions of years for the light to reach Earth.

The light and other energy leaving a star are forms of radiation. Radiation is energy that is transmitted from one place to another by electromagnetic waves. Because of the electric and magnetic properties of this radiation, it's called electromagnetic radiation. Electromagnetic waves carry energy through empty space and through matter.

Electromagnetic radiation is everywhere around you. When you turn on the radio, peer down a microscope, or have an X ray taken—you're using various forms of electromagnetic radiation.

Figure 1
The electromagnetic spectrum ranges from gamma rays with wavelengths of less than 0.000 000 0000 1 m to radio waves more than 100,000 m long. *How does frequency change as wavelength shortens?*

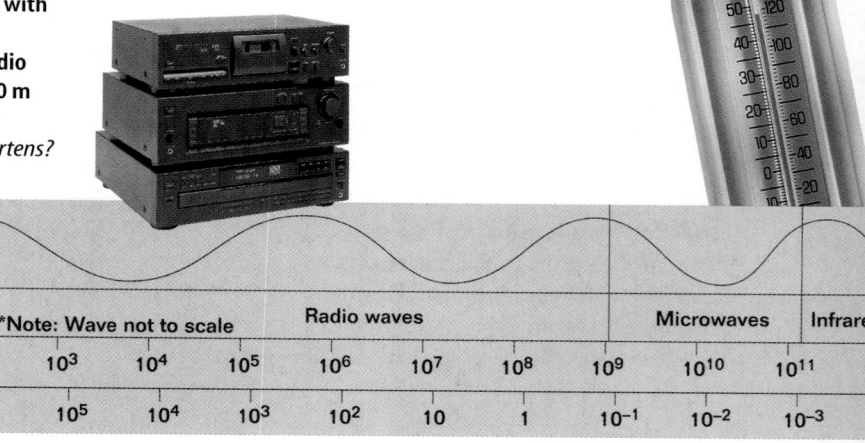

*Note: Wave not to scale	Radio waves						Microwaves		Infrare
10^3	10^4	10^5	10^6	10^7	10^8	10^9	10^{10}	10^{11}	
10^5	10^4	10^3	10^2	10	1	10^{-1}	10^{-2}	10^{-3}	

Section ✓*Assessment* Planner

PORTFOLIO
Science Journal, p. 643
PERFORMANCE ASSESSMENT
Try at Home MiniLAB, p. 644
Skill Builder Activities, p. 645
See page 668 for more options.

CONTENT ASSESSMENT
Section, p. 645
Challenge, p. 645
Chapter, pp. 668–669

Electromagnetic Radiation Sound waves, which are a type of mechanical wave, can't travel through empty space. How, then, do we hear the voices of the astronauts while they're in space? When astronauts speak into a microphone, the sound waves are converted into electromagnetic waves called radio waves. The radio waves travel through space and through Earth's atmosphere. They're then converted back into sound waves by electronic equipment and audio speakers.

Radio waves and visible light from the Sun are just two types of electromagnetic radiation. Other types include gamma rays, X rays, ultraviolet waves, infrared waves, and microwaves. **Figure 1** shows these forms of electromagnetic radiation arranged according to their wavelengths. This arrangement of electromagnetic radiation is called the **electromagnetic spectrum.** Forms of electromagnetic radiation also differ in their frequencies. Frequency is the number of times a wave vibrates per unit of time. The shorter the wavelength is, the more vibrations will occur, as shown in **Figure 1.**

Speed of Light Although the various electromagnetic waves differ in their wavelengths, they all travel at 300,000 km/s in a vacuum. This is called the speed of light. Visible light and other forms of electromagnetic radiation travel at this incredible speed, but the universe is so large that it takes millions of years for the light from some stars to reach Earth.

When electromagnetic radiation from stars and other objects reaches Earth, scientists use it to learn about its source. One tool for studying electromagnetic radiation from distant sources is a telescope.

Health
INTEGRATION

Many newspapers include an ultraviolet (UV) index to urge people to minimize their exposure to the Sun. Compare the wavelengths and frequencies of red and violet light, shown below in **Figure 1.** Infer what properties of UV light cause damage to tissues of organisms.

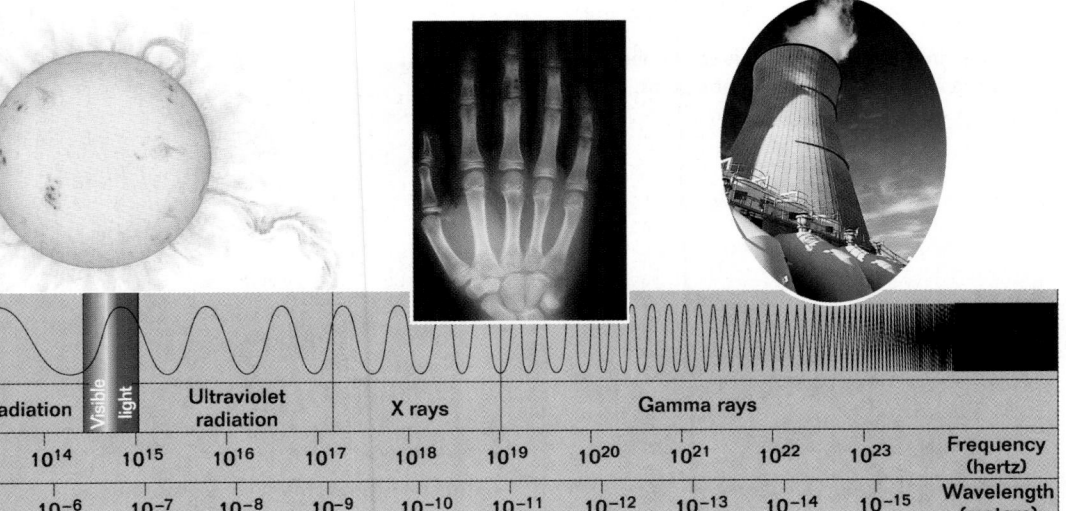

radiation	Visible light	Ultraviolet radiation	X rays		Gamma rays						
10^{14}	10^{15}	10^{16}	10^{17}	10^{18}	10^{19}	10^{20}	10^{21}	10^{22}	10^{23}		Frequency (hertz)
10^{-6}	10^{-7}	10^{-8}	10^{-9}	10^{-10}	10^{-11}	10^{-12}	10^{-13}	10^{-14}	10^{-15}		Wavelength (meters)

---

2 Teach

Electromagnetic Waves

Caption Answer
Figure 1 Frequency increases.

Health
INTEGRATION

Violet light has a shorter wavelength and therefore a higher frequency than red light. Since UV light has an even shorter wavelength, it also has an even higher frequency and more energy. The added energy in UV light is damaging to living tissues.

Discussion

Do you think electromagnetic waves can travel through a vacuum? Explain. Yes; solar energy is electromagnetic radiation. It travels to Earth through the vacuum of space.

Resource Manager

Chapter Resources Booklet
Note-taking Worksheets, pp. 29–31
Transparency Activity, p. 40
Directed Reading for Content Mastery, pp. 15, 16

Inclusion Strategies

Learning Disabled Have each student investigate a different type of electromagnetic radiation, noting its characteristics, what natural or artificial objects generate it, and how (if this is the case) it is used by people. Have students work together to make an informative bulletin board that includes diagrams and labels explaining their findings. L2 ELL COOP LEARN IS **Interpersonal**

Optical Telescopes

Quick Demo

Use one double-convex lens to demonstrate how a lens collects light to form an image. Hold a 15-cm focal length lens in one hand and a sheet of blank white paper in the other. With lights off, hold the lens so that light coming in a window passes through the lens and falls on the sheet of paper. Students will see an inverted image of the window and whatever can be seen outside the window. L2
🄸🄽 **Visual-Spatial**

Visual Learning

Figure 2 Have students compare the two types of light telescopes. **Which one seems as though it would be easier to construct? Why?** The refracting telescope; it has a simpler design.

Optical Telescopes

Optical telescopes use light, which is a form of electromagnetic radiation, to produce magnified images of objects. Light is collected by an objective lens or mirror, which then forms an image at the focal plane of the telescope. The focal point is where light that is bent by the lens or reflected by the mirror comes together to form a point on the focal plane. The eyepiece lens then magnifies the image. The two types of optical telescopes are shown in **Figure 2.**

A **refracting telescope** uses convex lenses, which are curved outward like the surface of a ball. Light from an object passes through a double convex objective lens and is bent to form an image on the focal plane. The eyepiece magnifies the image.

A **reflecting telescope** uses a curved mirror to direct light. Light from the object being viewed passes through the open end of a reflecting telescope. This light strikes a concave mirror, which is curved inward like a bowl and located at the base of the telescope. The light is reflected off the interior surface of the bowl to the focal plane where it forms an image. A smaller mirror often is used to reflect light into the eyepiece lens, where it is magnified for viewing.

Using Optical Telescopes Most optical telescopes used by professional astronomers are housed in buildings called **observatories.** Observatories often have dome-shaped roofs that can be opened up for viewing. However, not all telescopes are located in observatories. The *Hubble Space Telescope* is an example.

Figure 2
These diagrams show how each type of optical telescope collects light and forms an image.

Eyepiece lens
Focal point
Convex lens

A In a refracting telescope, a double convex lens focuses light to form an image at the focal point.

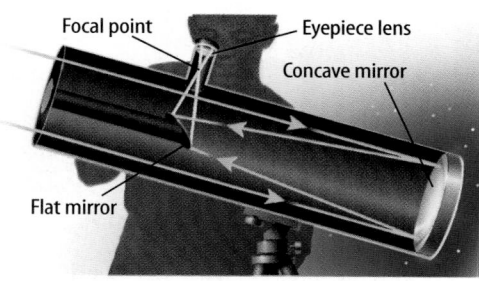

Focal point
Eyepiece lens
Concave mirror
Flat mirror

B In a reflecting telescope, a concave mirror focuses light to form an image at the focal point.

C Optical telescopes are widely available for use by individuals.

642 CHAPTER 22 Exploring Space

Hubble Space Telescope The *Hubble Space Telescope* was launched in 1990 by the space shuttle *Discovery*. Because *Hubble* is located outside Earth's atmosphere, which absorbs and distorts some of the energy received from space, it should have produced clear images. However, when the largest mirror of this reflecting telescope was shaped, a mistake was made. As a result, images obtained by the telescope were not as clear as expected. In December 1993, a team of astronauts repaired the *Hubble Space Telescope* by installing a set of small mirrors designed to correct images obtained by the faulty mirror. Two more missions to service *Hubble* were carried out in 1997 and 1999, shown in **Figure 3**. Among the objects viewed by *Hubble* after it was repaired in 1999 was a large cluster of galaxies known as Abell 2218.

✔ **Reading Check** *Why is* Hubble *located outside Earth's atmosphere?*

Figure 3
The *Hubble Space Telescope* was serviced at the end of 1999. Astronauts replaced devices on *Hubble* that are used to stabilize the telescope.

Teacher **FYI**

The *Hubble Space Telescope* is a reflecting telescope with a light-gathering mirror 240 cm in diameter. It is in orbit 610 km above Earth's surface. NASA controls the telescope with radio commands beamed to it from the ground. The images obtained by *Hubble* are sent to the ground as radio signals as well.

✔ **Reading Check**

Answer to avoid the interference caused by Earth's atmosphere

Discussion
Tell students that NASA built the *Hubble Space Telescope* and put it in orbit. Now astronomers from all over the world share the use of the telescope and the images it provides. **Do you think the United States should share resources like the *Hubble* with other nations? Explain.** Possible answers: Yes; everyone should share any tool that advances scientific discovery. No; the United States built it and U.S. scientists should have the benefit of sole use of the telescope.

Resource Manager

Chapter Resources Booklet
Enrichment, p. 26
Reinforcement, p. 23
Transparency Activity, pp. 43–44

Science **Journal**

Hubble Space Telescope Have students research and write about some of the discoveries made by astronomers using the Hubble Space Telescope. Discoveries should include galaxies at the edge of the known universe and galaxies colliding and tearing each other apart. L2 IN **Linguistic** P

Optical Telescopes, continued

TRY AT HOME Mini LAB

Purpose Students contrast the number of stars visible from each of their homes and determine whether light pollution accounts for the difference. L2 IS **Visual-Spatial**

Materials cardboard tube

Teaching Strategy Explain that light pollution is a glow in the sky caused by city lights. The glow makes it difficult to see dim stars. Remind them to record light conditions at their viewing spot.

Analysis
1. Students in areas away from street lights will see more stars than students in urban areas or on main streets.
2. More stars are visible in areas with less background light.

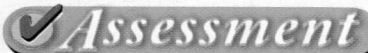

Process Have students observe and record common sources of light pollution. Possible answers: street lights, lights from homes, apartment buildings, and shopping centers Use **PASC,** p. 97.

TRY AT HOME Mini LAB

Observing Effects of Light Pollution

Procedure
1. Obtain a **cardboard tube** from an empty roll of paper towels.
2. Go outside on a clear night about two hours after sunset. Look through the cardboard tube at a specific constellation decided upon ahead of time.
3. Count the number of stars you can see without moving the observing tube. Repeat this three times.
4. Calculate the average number of observable stars at your location.

Analysis
1. Compare and contrast the number of stars visible from other students' homes.
2. Explain the causes and effects of your observations.

Figure 4
The twin Keck telescopes on Mauna Kea in Hawaii can be used together, more than doubling their ability to distinguish objects. A Keck reflector is shown in the inset photo. Currently, plans include using these telescopes, along with four others to obtain images that will help answer questions about the origin of planetary systems.

Large Reflecting Telescopes Since the early 1600s, when the Italian scientist Galileo Galilei first turned a telescope toward the stars, people have been searching for better ways to study what lies beyond Earth's atmosphere. For example, the twin Keck reflecting telescopes, shown in **Figure 4,** have segmented mirrors 10 m wide. Until 2000, these mirrors were the largest reflectors ever used. To cope with the difficulty of building such huge mirrors, the Keck telescope mirrors are built out of many small mirrors that are pieced together. In 2000, the European Southern Observatory's telescope, in Chile, consisted of four 8.2-m reflectors, making it the largest optical telescope in use.

✔ **Reading Check** *About how long have people been using telescopes?*

Active and Adaptive Optics The most recent innovations in optical telescopes involve active and adaptive optics. With active optics, a computer corrects for changes in temperature, mirror distortions, and bad viewing conditions. Adaptive optics is even more ambitious. Adaptive optics uses a laser to probe the atmosphere and relay information to a computer about air turbulence. The computer then adjusts the telescope's mirror thousands of times per second, which lessens the effects of atmospheric turbulence. Telescope images are clearer when corrections for air turbulence, temperature changes, and mirror-shape changes are made.

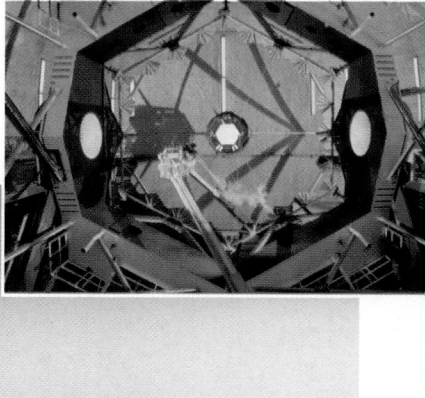

Teacher FYI

Each of the Keck's mirrors actually consists of 36 hexagonal mirrors mounted extremely close together to form one reflecting surface 10 m across. An electronic sensing system keeps each of the mirrors in place and adjusts each automatically if it becomes misaligned.

Resource Manager

Chapter Resources Booklet
   MiniLAB, p. 3

Cultural Diversity, p. 51

Science Inquiry Labs, p. 59

Radio Telescopes

As shown in the spectrum illustrated in **Figure 1,** stars and other objects radiate electromagnetic energy of various types. Radio waves are an example of long-wavelength energy in the electromagnetic spectrum. A **radio telescope,** such as the one shown in **Figure 5,** is used to study radio waves traveling through space. Unlike visible light, radio waves pass freely through Earth's atmosphere. Because of this, radio telescopes are useful 24 hours per day under most weather conditions.

Radio waves reaching Earth's surface strike the large, concave dish of a radio telescope. This dish reflects the waves to a focal point where a receiver is located. The information allows scientists to detect objects in space, to map the universe, and to search for signs of intelligent life on other planets.

Later in this chapter, you'll learn about the instruments that travel into space and send back information that telescopes on Earth's surface cannot obtain.

Figure 5
This radio telescope is used to study radio waves traveling through space.

Fun Fact

The Very Large Array (VLA) in New Mexico consists of 27 movable dishes, each 25 m wide. The dishes operate as one telescope, making the VLA one of the world's most powerful radio telescopes.

③ Assess

Reteach

Give students a photocopy containing a labeled cross section of both a refracting and a reflecting telescope. Have them identify and label the telescopes and indicate what is used to focus light in each type.

Challenge

Have students research solutions to the problem of light pollution, and then moderate a class discussion on the topic. Possible answers: hoods or covers over lights, lights not directed skyward, turning lights off at specific times

✓ Assessment

Process Have students make a table describing the types of telescopes covered in this section and the type of electromagnetic radiation examined by each. Use **Performance Assessment in the Science Classroom,** p. 109.

Section ① Assessment

1. What is the difference between radio telescopes and optical telescopes?
2. If red light has a longer wavelength than blue light, which has a greater frequency?
3. Compare and contrast refracting and reflecting telescopes.
4. How does adaptive optics in a telescope help solve problems caused by atmospheric turbulence?
5. **Think Critically** It takes light from the closest star to Earth (other than the Sun) about four years to reach Earth. If intelligent life were on a planet circling that star, how long would it take for scientists on Earth to send them a radio transmission and for the scientists to receive their reply?

Skill Builder Activities

6. **Comparing and Contrasting** Compare and contrast these electromagnetic waves from longest wavelength to shortest wavelength: *gamma rays, visible light, X rays, radio waves, infrared waves, ultraviolet waves,* and *microwaves.* **For more help,** refer to the Science Skill Handbook.

7. **Solving One-Step Equations** The magnifying power (*Mp*) of a telescope is determined by dividing the focal length of the objective lens (FL_{obj}) by the focal length of the eyepiece lens (FL_{eye}) using the following equation:

$$Mp = Fl_{obj}/Fl_{eye}$$

If $FL_{obj} = 1{,}200$ mm and $FL_{eye} = 6$ mm, what is the telescope's magnifying power? **For more help,** refer to the Math Skill Handbook.

SECTION 1   Radiation from Space   **645**

Answers to Section Assessment

1. Radio telescopes use a dish antenna to collect and focus radio waves, whereas optical telescopes use lenses or mirrors to collect and focus visible light.
2. blue light
3. Both are optical telescopes. Refracting telescopes use a glass lens to collect light; reflecting telescopes use a mirror to collect light.
4. Adaptive optics uses a computer to adjust the telescope's objective mirror to decrease the effects of air turbulence.
5. about 8 years
6. radio waves, microwaves, infrared waves, visible light, ultraviolet waves, X rays, gamma rays
7. 200 (Mp) = $FL_{obj} \div FL_{eye}$ = 1200 mm ÷ 6 mm = 200)

Activity

Purpose Students will construct a working reflecting telescope.

L2 COOP LEARN LS **Visual-Spatial**

Process Skills observing, constructing, designing

Time Requirement 25 minutes

Safety precautions Caution students to never touch broken glass.

Teaching Strategy Collect photographs of the moon or other celestial objects for students to use as their viewing objects.

Troubleshooting Be certain each pair of students has both a flat mirror and curved mirror. Label the two types of mirrors for easy reference.

Answers to Questions

1. The object's image will appear larger or smaller depending upon the level of magnification of each lens.
2. The cosmetic mirror reflects the light onto the flat mirror. The flat mirror reflects the light onto the magnifying lens.
3. Magnifying lenses.
4. The curved mirror gathered the light reflecting from the object and focused the light on the flat mirror. The flat mirror reflected the light onto the magnifying lens, and each lens magnified the image.
5. Concave lenses would have been used instead of mirrors.

Assessment

Portfolio Ask students to construct a permanent reflecting scope with a housing of their design. Use **Performance** in the **Science** ...

Activity

Building a Reflecting Telescope

Nearly four hundred years ago, scientist Galileo Galilei saw what no human had ever seen before. Using the telescope he invented, Galileo discovered moons revolving around Jupiter, observed craters on the Moon in detail, and saw sunspots on the surface of the Sun. What was it like to make these discoveries? You will find out as you make your own reflecting telescope.

What You'll Investigate
How do you construct a reflecting telescope?

Materials
flat mirror
shaving or cosmetic mirror (a curved, concave mirror)
magnifying lenses of different magnifications (3–4)

Goals
- **Construct** a reflecting telescope.
- **Observe** magnified images using the telescope and different magnifying lenses.

Safety Precautions
WARNING: *Never observe the Sun directly nor with mirrors.*

Procedure

1. Position the cosmetic mirror so that you can see the reflection of the object you want to look at. Choose a bright object such as the Moon, a planet, or an artificial light source.
2. Place the flat mirror so that it is facing the cosmetic mirror.
3. Adjust the position of the flat mirror until you can see the reflection of the object in it.

4. View the image of the object in the flat mirror with one of your magnifying glasses. Observe how the lens magnifies the image.
5. Use your other magnifying lenses to view the image of the object in the flat mirror. Observe how the different lenses change the image of the object.

Conclude and Apply

1. **Describe** how the image of the object changed when you used different magnifying lenses.
2. **Identify** the part or parts of your telescope that reflected the light of the image.
3. **Identify** the part or parts of your telescope that magnified the image of the object.
4. **Explain** how the three parts of your telescope worked to reflect and magnify the light of the object.
5. **Infer** how the materials you used would have differed if you had constructed a refracting telescope instead of a reflecting telescope.

Communicating Your Data

Write an instructional pamphlet for amateur astronomers about how to construct a reflecting telescope. **For more help, refer to the Science Skill Handbook.**

646 CHAPTER 22 Exploring Space

Communicating Your Data

Students may want to include a labeled diagram with their pamphlets.

Resource Manager

Chapter Resources Booklet
Activity Worksheet, pp. 5–6
Lab Activities, pp. 9–12

Early Space Missions

The First Missions into Space

You're offered a choice—front-row-center seats for this weekend's rock concert, or a copy of the video when it's released. Wouldn't you rather be right next to the action? Astronomers feel the same way about space. Even though telescopes have taught them a great deal about the Moon and planets, they want to learn more by going to those places or by sending spacecraft where humans can't go.

Rockets The space program would not have gotten far off the ground using ordinary airplane engines. To break free of gravity and enter Earth's orbit, spacecraft must travel at speeds greater than 11 km/s. The space shuttle and several other spacecrafts are equipped with special engines that carry their own fuel. **Rockets,** like the one in **Figure 6,** are engines that have everything they need for the burning of fuel. They don't even require air to carry out the process. Therefore, they can work in space, which has no air. The simplest rocket engine is made of a burning chamber and a nozzle. More complex rockets have more than one burning chamber.

Rockets Types Two types of rockets are distinguished by the type of fuel they use. One type is the liquid-propellant rocket and the other is the solid-propellant rocket. Solid-propellant rockets are generally simpler but they can't be shut down after they are ignited. Liquid-propellant rockets can be shut down after they are ignited and can be restarted. The space shuttle uses liquid-propellant rockets and solid-propellant rockets.

As You Read

What You'll Learn

- **Compare and contrast** natural and artificial satellites.
- **Identify** the differences between artificial satellites and space probes.
- **Explain** the history of the race to the Moon.

Vocabulary
rocket
satellite
orbit
space probe

Project Mercury
Project Gemini
Project Apollo

Why It's Important

Early missions that sent objects and people into space began a new era of human exploration.

Figure 6
Rockets differ according to the types of fuel used to launch them. This rocket uses liquid oxygen for fuel.

SECTION 2 Early Space Missions **647**

1 Motivate

Bellringer Transparency
Display the Section Focus Transparency for Section 2. Use the accompanying Transparency Activity Master. [L2] [ELL]

Tie to Prior Knowledge
Ask students if astronauts have ever traveled to the moon. Write responses on the board as students brainstorm facts they know about the moon landings. Possible answers: First one occurred in 1969; first person to step on moon was Neil Armstrong. Have students review this list after reading the section to see how many "facts" were correct.

Section ✓*Assessment* Planner

PORTFOLIO
Chemistry Integration, p. 650

PERFORMANCE ASSESSMENT
Math Skills Activity, p. 648
Skill Builder Activities, p. 654
See page 668 for more options.

CONTENT ASSESSMENT
Section, p. 654
Challenge, p. 654
Chapter, pp. 668–669

The First Missions into Space

Discussion

Remind students that solid propellant rockets are simpler than liquid propellant rockets. **What advantage might a liquid propellant rocket have over a solid propellant rocket?** Possible answer: the ability to start and stop the rocket makes it easier to control the rocket's velocity.

Quick Demo

Demonstrate how rockets move. Inflate a long balloon and hold the end closed. Have students run a long string through a drinking straw and then tape the straw to one side of the balloon. Have two students hold the string tight. Release the balloon. Students should see that gases escaping from behind the balloon push it forward along the string.

Math Skills Activity

National Math Standards

Correlation to Mathematics Objectives
3, 9, 10

Answer to Practice Problem

Students' graphs should look like a line drawing of the space shuttle on the launch pad.

Figure 7
In this view of the shuttle, the red-colored liquid rocket booster is behind a white solid rocket booster.

Rocket Launching Solid-propellant rockets use a powdery or rubberlike fuel and a liquid such as liquid oxygen. The burning chamber of a rocket is a tube that has a nozzle at one end. As the solid propellant burns, hot gases exert pressure on all inner surfaces of the tube. The tube pushes back on the inside surfaces except at the nozzle where hot gases escape. Thrust builds up and pushes the rocket forward.

Liquid propellant rockets use a liquid fuel and, commonly, liquid oxygen, stored in separate tanks. To ignite the rocket, the liquid oxygen is mixed with the liquid fuel in the burning chamber. As the mixture burns, forces are exerted and the rocket is propelled forward. **Figure 7** shows the space shuttle, with both types of rockets being launched.

Math Skills Activity

Using a Grid to Draw

Points are defined by two coordinates, called an ordered pair. To plot an ordered pair, find the first number on the horizontal x-axis and the second on the vertical y-axis. The point is placed where these two coordinates intersect. Line segments are drawn to connect points.

Example Problem
Using an x-y grid and point coordinates, draw a symmetrical house.

Solution

1 On a piece of graph paper, label and number the x-axis 0 to 6 and the y-axis 0 to 6, as shown here.

2 Plot the following points and connect them with straight line segments, as shown here. (1,1), (5,1), (5,4), (3,6), (1,4)

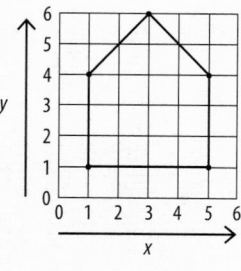

Section	Points
1	(13,1) (13,4) (6,5) (7,8) (12,16) (13,25) (14,28),(15,29) (16,28) (17,25) (18,16) (23,8) (24,5) (17,4) (17,1) (13,1)
2	(10,13) (10,32) (11,34) (12,32)
3	(12,16) (12,34) (15,39) (18,34) (18,16)
4	(18,32) (19,34) (20,32) (20,13)
5	(15,25) (14,24) (14,25) (15,26) (16,25) (16,24) (15,25)
6	(11,10) (11,8) (13,8) (13,10)
7	(16,10) (14,10) (14,9) (16,9) (16,8) (14,8)
8	(17,9) (19,9)
9	(17,8) (17,9) (18,10) (19,9) (19,8)
10	(12,4) (12,1) (13,0) (9,0) (10,1) (10,4)
11	(18,4) (18,1) (17,0) (21,0) (20,1) (20,4)

Practice Problem

Label and number the x-axis 0 to 30 and the y-axis 0 to 40. Draw a space shuttle by plotting and connecting the points in each section. Do not draw segments to connect points in different sections.

For more help, refer to the Math Skill Handbook.

Curriculum Connection

History In 1926, American scientist Robert Goddard tested the first liquid-fueled rocket. The small rocket rose 12.3 m before crashing. It was the forerunner of the rockets we send into space today. Have students research that first rocket launch and do a report on videotape or audiotape as if they were journalists reporting from the scene. Have students play the tapes in class. L2 ELL LS **Musical-Auditory**

Cultural Diversity

Chinese Rockets Historians and scientists generally agree that the Chinese invented the rocket centuries ago. During the 1200s, Chinese soldiers fired small rockets (called "fire arrows" by some) as weapons in battle. Have students research these early rockets and write reports on what they were like as well as how they contrast with rockets today. L2 LS **Logical-Mathematical**

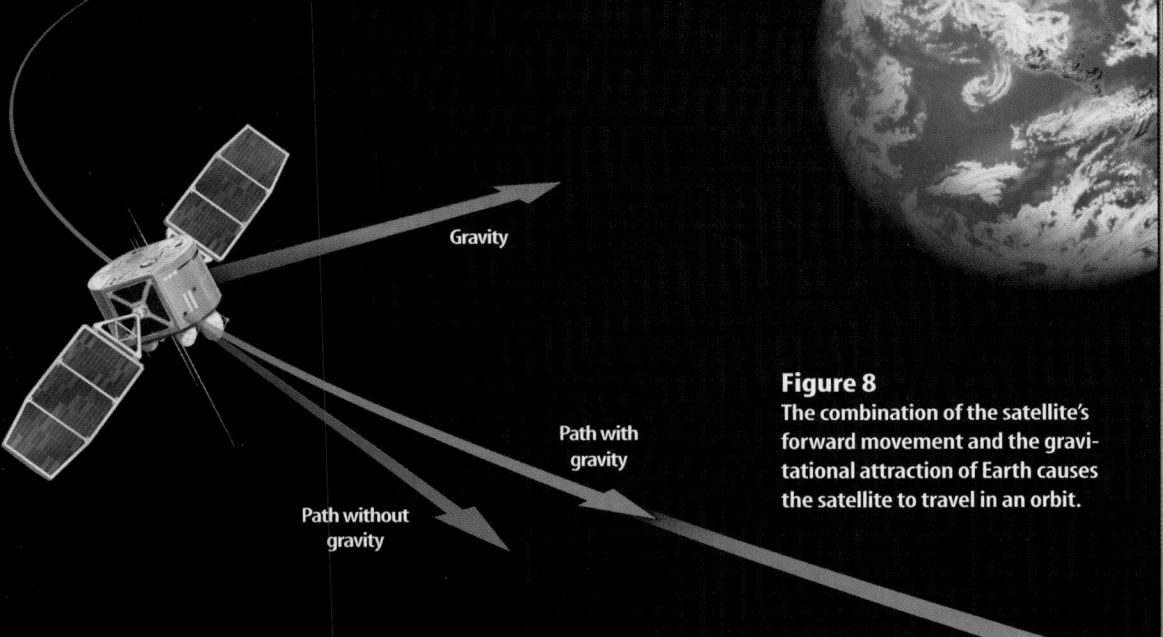

Gravity

Path with gravity

Path without gravity

Figure 8
The combination of the satellite's forward movement and the gravitational attraction of Earth causes the satellite to travel in an orbit.

Extension

Have pairs of students collaborate on a written report that answers the following questions. **What type of information could be obtained about Earth by artificial satellites in orbit?** weather, military information, communication, scientific **How could people on Earth use this information?** better predict the weather, keep track of military movements in other parts of the globe, communicate with others, study landforms from space Conduct a class discussion dealing with these questions. L2 COOP LEARN
Ⓘ Interpersonal

Satellites   The space age began in 1957 when the former Soviet Union used a rocket to send *Sputnik I* into space. *Sputnik I* was the first artificial satellite. A **satellite** is any object that revolves around another object. When an object enters space, it travels in a straight line unless a force, such as gravity, makes it turn. Earth's gravity pulls a satellite toward Earth. The result of the satellite traveling forward while at the same time being pulled toward Earth is a curved path, called an **orbit,** around Earth. This is shown in **Figure 8.** *Sputnik I* orbited Earth for 57 days before gravity pulled it back into the atmosphere, where it burned up.

Satellite Uses   *Sputnik I* was an experiment to show that artificial satellites could be made and placed into orbit around Earth.

Today, thousands of artificial satellites orbit Earth. Communication satellites transmit radio and television programs to locations around the world. Other satellites, like those shown in **Figure 9,** gather scientific data which can't be obtained from Earth, and weather satellites constantly monitor Earth's global weather patterns.

Figure 9
Data obtained from the satellite *Terra,* launched in 1999, illustrates the use of space technology to study Earth. This false-color image includes data on spring growth, sea-surface temperature, carbon monoxide concentrations, and reflected sunlight, among others.

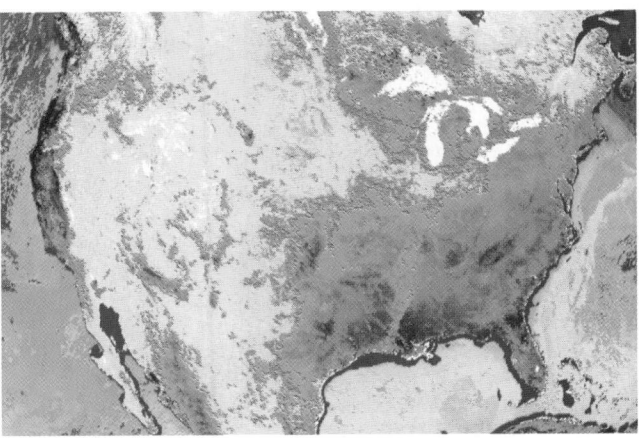

Teacher FYI

Although not as successful as the American effort, the Soviet Union (today's Russia) also had a space program that sent several probes to other planets. The Soviet Union's *Venera* probes made several voyages to Venus between the late 1960s and the 1980s. The probes sent back data on Venus's atmosphere, beamed back pictures from Venus's surface, and analyzed rocks from the planet's surface.

SECTION 2 Early Space Missions   **649**

☑ **Active Reading**

Think-Pair-Share Ask students to respond to a question by writing a response. After thinking for a few minutes, have partners share responses to the question. Finally, ask the students to share responses with the class. Have students become involved in a Think-Pair-Share about the importance of exploring space. L1 COOP LEARN
Ⓘ Interpersonal

Resource Manager

Chapter Resources Booklet
   Transparency Activity, p. 41
Mathematics Skill Activities, p. 15

Space Probes

Chemistry
INTEGRATION

Oxygen in Mars's early atmosphere, or water that may have existed on the planet, combined with iron in surface rocks to form iron oxide or rust. Iron oxide is deep red and causes the Martian surface to look red. P

Use Science Words

Word Usage Have students use the term *space probe* in a sentence. Have pairs take turns reading their sentences and critiquing one another on whether the term was used correctly.

Visual Learning

Table 1 Direct students to look carefully at the names of the space probes in the table. Ask them to determine what the names have in common. They all concern adventure and exploration. Mariners are seafarers. Pioneers are people who are among the first to travel to a place. Vikings were ancient Scandinavian explorers. Magellan commanded the first expedition to sail around the world in the early 1500s. IS **Linguistic**

Chemistry
INTEGRATION

The *Viking* landers collected samples of the soil on Mars. Tests concluded that the soil on Mars contains iron. Based on this information, write a paragraph in your Science Journal about why Mars is called the red planet.

Space Probes

Not all objects carried into space by rockets become satellites. Rockets also can be used to send instruments into space to collect data. A **space probe** is an instrument that gathers information and sends it back to Earth. Unlike satellites that orbit Earth, space probes travel far into the solar system as illustrated in **Figure 10.** Some even have traveled out of the solar system. Space probes, like many satellites, carry cameras and other data-gathering equipment, as well as radio transmitters and receivers that allow them to communicate with scientists on Earth. **Table 1** shows some of the early space probes launched by the National Aeronautics and Space Administration (NASA).

Table 1 Some Early Space Missions

Mission Name		Date Launched	Destination	Data Obtained
Mariner 2		August 1962	Venus	verified high temperatures in Venus's atmosphere
Pioneer 10		March 1972	Jupiter	sent back photos of Jupiter—first probe to encounter an outer planet
Viking 1		August 1975	Mars	orbiter mapped the surface of Mars; lander searched for life on Mars
Magellan		May 1989	Venus	mapped Venus's surface and returned data on the composition of Venus's atmosphere

Curriculum Connection

Social Studies Have students speculate why so many developments occurred in the space program during the 1960s. Possible answer: Students should realize that the United States and the former Soviet Union were participating in a "race for space." L2
IS **Logical-Mathematical**

Inclusion Strategies

Gifted Have students research space junk—unused and nonfunctional materials orbiting Earth. It ranges from sand-grain-sized paint chips to large satellites. Students can search the Glencoe Science Web site for information. Students should write papers discussing the growing threat space junk might pose to the safety of future space flights. L3

Figure 10

Probes have taught us much about the solar system. As they travel through space, these car-size craft gather data with their onboard instruments and send results back to Earth via radio waves. Some data collected during these missions are made into pictures, a selection of which is shown here.

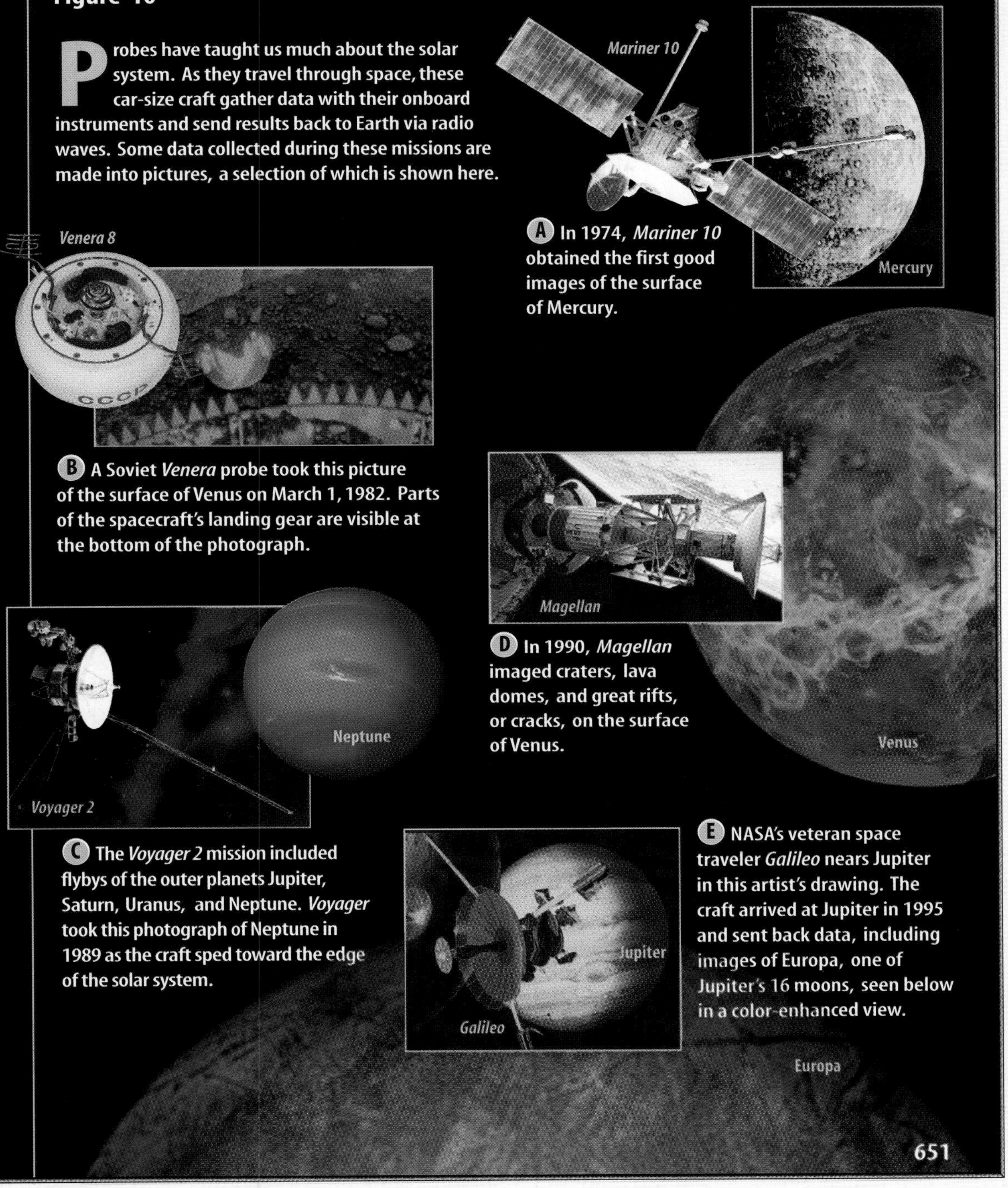

Mariner 10

A In 1974, *Mariner 10* obtained the first good images of the surface of Mercury.

Mercury

Venera 8

B A Soviet *Venera* probe took this picture of the surface of Venus on March 1, 1982. Parts of the spacecraft's landing gear are visible at the bottom of the photograph.

Magellan

D In 1990, *Magellan* imaged craters, lava domes, and great rifts, or cracks, on the surface of Venus.

Venus

Neptune

Voyager 2

C The *Voyager 2* mission included flybys of the outer planets Jupiter, Saturn, Uranus, and Neptune. *Voyager* took this photograph of Neptune in 1989 as the craft sped toward the edge of the solar system.

E NASA's veteran space traveler *Galileo* nears Jupiter in this artist's drawing. The craft arrived at Jupiter in 1995 and sent back data, including images of Europa, one of Jupiter's 16 moons, seen below in a color-enhanced view.

Jupiter

Galileo

Europa

651

Visualizing Space Probes

Have students examine the pictures and read the captions. Then ask the following questions.

What features on the pictured space probes might have helped them communicate with Earth? All have some type of antennae. Mariner, Magellan, Voyager 2, and Galileo, for example, have "dish" antennae for receiving signals from Earth. Solar panels on Mariner and Magellan might have helped power communication equipment.

In what manner is the scale of the planets and moon pictured incorrectly? Possible answer: The smallest planet pictured, Mercury, appears larger than Jupiter, the largest. Venus, while larger than Mercury, would be dwarfed by Neptune and Jupiter and appears far larger than true scale. Europa is the smallest body shown here and is vastly inflated in scale.

Activity

Have students make space probe flash cards. On one side of each card have them draw a picture of a probe and write its name. On the other side have them write facts about the mission of each probe, including the planets or moons that were visited. Have students quiz each other using the cards.

Extension

Challenge students to find out about more recent and future space missions. Have them present their findings to the class, and give details as to the objectives and itineraries of each mission.

Space Probes,
continued

Activity

Have students explore the Glencoe Science Web site to find photographs of Saturn, Jupiter, Uranus, or Neptune sent back to Earth by the *Voyager* probes. Have each student print out a photo and describe what it shows about the planet. Make a bulletin board with the photos and student captions.

✔ Reading Check

Answer Cracks in Europa's outer layer of ice might indicate geological activity that could heat Europa's ice, forming liquid water under the surface.

SCIENCE *Online*
Internet Addresses

Explore the Glencoe Science Web site at **science.glencoe.com** to find out more about topics in this section.

SCIENCE *Online*

Collect Data Visit the Glencoe Science Web site at **science.glencoe.com** to get the latest information on Galileo's discoveries. Record your information in your Science Journal.

Figure 11
Future missions will be needed to determine whether life exists on Europa.

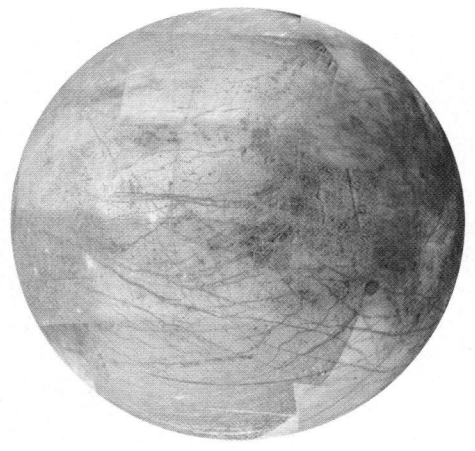

Voyager and Pioneer Probes Space probes *Voyager 1* and *Voyager 2* were launched in 1977 and now are heading toward deep space. *Voyager 1* flew past Jupiter and Saturn. *Voyager 2* flew past Jupiter, Saturn, Uranus, and Neptune. These probes now are exploring beyond the solar system as part of the Voyager Interstellar Mission. Scientists expect these probes to continue to transmit data to Earth for at least 20 more years.

Pioneer 10, launched in 1972, was the first probe to survive a trip through the asteroid belt and encounter an outer planet, Jupiter. As of 2000, *Pioneer 10* is more than 11 billion km from Earth, and will continue beyond the solar system. The probe carries a gold medallion with an engraving of a man, a woman, and Earth's position in the galaxy.

Galileo Launched in 1989, *Galileo* reached Jupiter in 1995. In July 1995, *Galileo* released a smaller probe that began a five-month approach to Jupiter. The small probe took a parachute ride through Jupiter's violent atmosphere in December 1995. Before being crushed by the atmospheric pressure, it transmitted information about Jupiter's composition, temperature, and pressure to the ship orbiting above. *Galileo* studied Jupiter's moons, rings, and magnetic fields and then relayed this information to scientists who were waiting eagerly for it on Earth.

 **Life Science INTEGRATION** Studies of Jupiter's moon Europa by *Galileo* indicate that an ocean of water may exist under the surface of Europa. An outer layer of ice covers Europa's cracked surface, shown in **Figure 11.** The cracks in the surface may be caused by geologic activity that heats the ocean underneath the surface. Sunlight penetrates these cracks, further heating the ocean and setting the stage for the possible existence of life on Europa. *Galileo* ended its study of Europa in 2000. More advanced probes will be needed to determine whether life exists on this icy moon.

✔ Reading Check
What features on Europa suggest the possibility of life existing on this moon?

In October and November of 1999, *Galileo* approached Io, another one of Jupiter's moons. It came within 300 km and took photographs of a volcanic vent named Loki, which emits more energy than all of Earth's volcanoes combined. *Galileo* discovered a lava fountain that shoots lava made of a compound of sulfur and oxygen.

652 CHAPTER 22 Exploring Space

Cultural **Diversity**

History Early standards for astronauts limited which Americans could participate. For example, the earliest astronauts had to be test pilots, but women were not allowed to train as test pilots until 1970. Astronaut candidate selection broadened in the late 1970s. The 1978 astronaut group included six women, three African Americans, and an Asian American.

Teacher **FYI**

The most distant human-made object as of August 2000 was the *Voyager 1* space probe. At that time, it was 11.7 billion km (78 AU) from Earth. *Voyager 1* is expected to continue sending information back to Earth until it runs out of electrical power, around 2020. *Voyager 1*, along with *Voyager 2*, is now part of the Voyager Interstellar Mission (VIM).

Moon Quest

Throughout the world, people were shocked when they turned on their radios and television sets in 1957 and heard the radio transmissions from *Sputnik I* as it orbited Earth. All that *Sputnik I* transmitted was a sort of beeping sound, but people quickly realized that launching a human into space wasn't far off.

In 1961, Soviet cosmonaut Yuri A. Gagarin became the first human in space. He orbited Earth and returned safely. Soon, President John F. Kennedy called for the United States to send humans to the Moon and return them safely to Earth. His goal was to achieve this by the end of the 1960s. The race for space was underway.

The U.S. program to reach the Moon began with **Project Mercury.** The goals of Project Mercury were to orbit a piloted spacecraft around Earth and to bring it back safely. The program provided data and experience in the basics of space flight. On May 5, 1961, Alan B. Shepard became the first U.S. citizen in space. In 1962, *Mercury* astronaut John Glenn became the first U.S. citizen to orbit Earth. **Figure 12** shows Glenn preparing for liftoff.

 **Reading Check** *What were the goals of Project Mercury?*

Project Gemini The next step in reaching the Moon was called **Project Gemini.** Teams of two astronauts in the same *Gemini* spacecraft orbited Earth. One *Gemini* team met and connected with another spacecraft in orbit—a skill that would be needed on a voyage to the Moon.

The *Gemini* spacecraft was much like the *Mercury* spacecraft, except it was larger and easier for the astronauts to maintain. It was launched by a rocket known as a *Titan II,* which was a liquid fuel rocket.

In addition to connecting spacecraft in orbit, another goal of Project *Gemini* was to investigate the effects of space travel on the human body.

Along with the Mercury and Gemini programs, a series of robotic probes was sent to the Moon. *Ranger* proved that a spacecraft could be sent to the Moon. In 1966, *Surveyor* landed gently on the Moon's surface, indicating that the Moon's surface could support spacecraft and humans. The mission of *Lunar Orbiter* was to take pictures of the Moon's surface that would help determine the best future lunar landing sites.

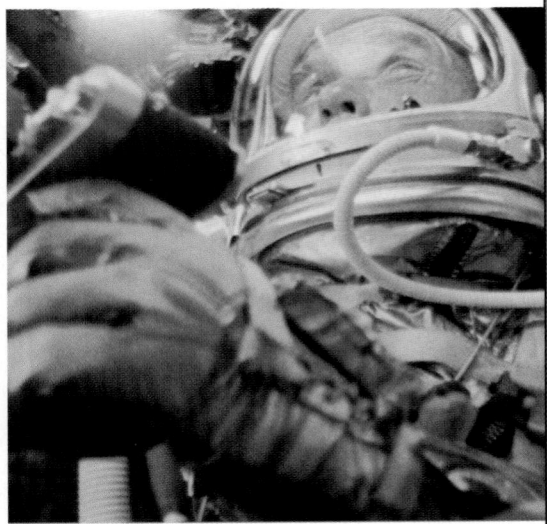

Figure 12
An important step in the attempt to reach the Moon was John Glenn's first orbit around Earth.

Modeling a Satellite

WARNING: *Stand a safe distance away from classmates. Use heavyweight string.*

Procedure
1. Tie one end of a 2-m-long **string** to a **rubber stopper.**
2. Thread the string through a 15-cm piece of **hose.**
3. Tie the other end of the string to several large **steel nuts.**
4. Swing the rubber stopper in a circle above your head. Swing the stopper at different speeds.

Analysis
Based upon your observations, explain how a satellite stays in orbit above Earth.

Resource Manager

Chapter Resources Booklet
MiniLAB, p. 4
Reinforcement, p. 24

Science Journal

Project Apollo Have students write a paragraph in their Science Journals why they do or do not think it was important for the United States to win the race to the moon. Encourage students to fully explain the reasons for their point of view. Use these paragraphs as a springboard for a class debate. L2 IS **Linguistic**

Moon Quest

Extension

Have different pairs of students use the school library to research one of the seven original Project Mercury astronauts. Pairs should collaborate on written reports about the missions each astronaut performed in the *Mercury* and other space missions, and what these astronauts are doing now. The Project Mercury astronauts were Carpenter, Cooper, Glenn, Grissom, Schirra, Shepard, and Slayton. L2 COOP LEARN IS **Linguistic**

Answer to orbit a piloted spacecraft around Earth and bring it back safely

Mini LAB

Purpose Students will model how satellites stay in orbit. IS **Kinesthetic**

Materials string (2m), rubber stopper

Teaching Strategy Discuss gravity—the attractive force between objects.

Safety Precautions Make sure students stand a safe distance from one another. Suggest students wear safety glasses.

Analysis
The force of gravity pulls the satellite toward Earth; the satellite's inertia keeps it moving in a straight line. Together, these forces keep a satellite in orbit.

✓ Assessment

Process Infer what would happen to a satellite whose **forward motion was very slow.** It would fall to Earth. Use **Performance Assessment in the Science Classroom,** p. 89

Reteach

Have pairs of students make flash cards of the artificial satellites and space probes presented in this section. Have them write the spacecraft name on one side and its mission and discoveries on the other. Have partners quiz each other to review the material. L1 COOP LEARN

IS Interpersonal

Challenge

Ask students to research how the space program has directly affected their lives. Students will discover that many items in everyday use came about through the space program, such as quartz watches, hand-held calculators, computers, battery-powered hand tools, portable breathing units for firefighters, and new materials for athletic shoes.

✓Assessment

Portfolio Ask each student to write a poem about one of the American missions to space or a famous figure from the United States space program. Encourage students to read their poems in class. Use **Performance Assessment in the Science Classroom,** p. 151.

Figure 13
The Lunar Rover vehicle was first used during the *Apollo 15* mission. Riding in the moon buggy, *Apollo 15, 16,* and *17* astronauts explored large areas of the lunar surface.

Project Apollo The final stage of the U.S. program to reach the Moon was **Project Apollo.** On July 20, 1969, *Apollo 11* landed on the Moon's surface. Neil Armstrong was the first human to set foot on the Moon. His first words as he stepped onto its surface were, "That's one small step for man, one giant leap for mankind." Edwin Aldrin, the second of the three *Apollo 11* astronauts, joined Armstrong on the Moon, and they explored its surface for two hours. While they were exploring, Michael Collins remained in the Command Module; Armstrong and Aldrin then returned to the Command Module before beginning the journey home. A total of six lunar landings brought back more than 2,000 samples of moon rock and soil for study before the program ended in 1972. **Figure 13** shows an astronaut exploring the Moon's surface from the Lunar Rover vehicle.

Sharing Knowledge During the past three decades, most missions in space have been carried out by individual countries, often competing to be the first or the best. Today, countries of the world cooperate more and work together, sharing what each has learned. Projects are being planned for cooperative missions to Mars and elsewhere. As you read the next section, you'll see how the U.S. program has progressed since the days of Project Apollo and what may be planned for the future.

Section 2 Assessment

1. Explain why human-made objects currently are not orbiting Neptune, yet Neptune has eight satellites.
2. *Galileo* was considered a space probe as it traveled to Jupiter. Once there, however, it became an artificial satellite. Explain.
3. List several discoveries made by the *Voyager 1* and *Voyager 2* space probes.
4. Draw a time line beginning with *Sputnik* and ending with Project Apollo. Include descriptions of important missions.
5. **Think Critically** Is Earth a satellite of any other body in space? Explain.

Skill Builder Activities

6. **Using an Electronic Spreadsheet** Use a spreadsheet program to generate a table of recent successful satellites and space probes launched by the United States. Include a description of the craft, the date it was launched, and its mission. **For more help, refer to the** Technology Skill Handbook.
7. **Solving One-Step Equations** Suppose a spacecraft were launched at a speed of 40,200 km/h. Express this speed in kilometers per second. **For more help, refer to the** Math Skill Handbook.

654   CHAPTER 22 Exploring Space

Answers to Section Assessment

1. They are all natural satellites of Neptune.
2. Once *Galileo* arrived at Jupiter, it went into orbit around that planet.
3. Discoveries include: ring around Jupiter; additional moons of Jupiter, Saturn, Uranus, and Neptune; erupting volcanoes on Io; complexity of

Saturn's rings; geysers on Triton; storms on Neptune
4. Timeline should begin in 1957 with *Sputnik.* Timeline should include Project Mercury, 1961–1962; Project Gemini, 1965–1966; Project Apollo, 1967–1972, especially *Apollo 11,* 1969.

5. Yes; Earth is a natural satellite of the Sun because Earth revolves around the Sun.
6. Students can find this data on the Glencoe Science Web site.
7. Because there are 3,600 seconds in one hour, 40,200 km/hr ÷ 3,600 sec/hr = 11.17 km/s.

Current and Future Space Missions

The Space Shuttle

Imagine spending millions of dollars to build a machine, sending it off into space, and watching its 3,000 metric tons of metal and other materials burn up after only a few minutes of work. That's exactly what NASA did with the rocket portions of spacecraft for many years. The early rockets were used only to launch a small capsule holding astronauts into orbit. Then sections of the rocket separated from the rest and burned when reentering the atmosphere.

A Reusable Spacecraft NASA administrators, like many others, realized that it would be less expensive and less wasteful to reuse resources. The reusable spacecraft that transports astronauts, satellites, and other materials to and from space is called the **space shuttle,** shown in **Figure 14,** as it is landing.

At launch, the space shuttle stands on end and is connected to an external liquid-fuel tank and two solid-fuel booster rockets. When the shuttle reaches an altitude of about 45 km, the emptied, solid-fuel booster rockets drop off and parachutes back to Earth. These are recovered and used again. The external liquid-fuel tank separates and falls back to Earth, but it isn't recovered.

Work on the Shuttle After the space shuttle reaches space, it begins to orbit Earth. There, astronauts perform many different tasks. In the cargo bay, astronauts can conduct scientific experiments and determine the effects of spaceflight on the human body. When the cargo bay isn't used as a laboratory, the shuttle can launch, repair, and retrieve satellites. Then the satellites can be returned to Earth or repaired onboard and returned to space. After a mission, the shuttle glides back to Earth and lands like an airplane. A large landing field is needed as the gliding speed of the shuttle is 335 km/h.

As You Read

What You'll Learn
- **Explain** the benefits of the space shuttle.
- **Identify** the usefulness of orbital space stations.
- **Explore** future space missions.

Vocabulary
space shuttle
space station

Why It's Important
Many future space missions have planned experiments that may benefit you.

Figure 14
The space shuttle is designed to make many trips into space.

Section ✓ Assessment Planner

PORTFOLIO
Curriculum Connection, p. 657

PERFORMANCE ASSESSMENT
Skill Builder Activities, p. 661
See page 668 for more options.

CONTENT ASSESSMENT
Section, p. 661
Challenge, p. 661
Chapter, pp. 668–669

---

1 Motivate

Bellringer Transparency

Display the Section Focus Transparency for Section 3. Use the accompanying Transparency Activity Master. L2
ELL

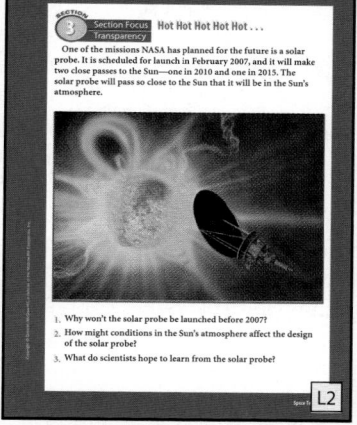

Tie to Prior Knowledge

Have students recall watching the launch or landing of a space shuttle. Have each student try to contribute one fact about the shuttle. Make a list of the facts on the board. Review the list with students after reading this section.

Resource Manager

Chapter Resources Booklet
Transparency Activity, p. 42
Cultural Diversity, p. 25

The Space Shuttle

Quick Demo

Obtain a model of a space shuttle. Use the model to demonstrate how the cargo bay is used to carry artificial satellites to and from Earth and how the mobile arm is used to place satellites into orbit and to bring them back into the cargo bay for repairs. If possible, use photos or a video of a recent mission to show the use of the cargo bay and mobile arm.

Cooperation in Space

IDENTIFYING
Misconceptions

Students may think that people on the *International Space Station* will walk around, work, and play normally, much as they see in science fiction TV shows. Remind students that astronauts in orbit around Earth experience microgravity, or weightlessness, which will affect their movements.

Discussion

Should the United States cooperate with other nations to build a space station, or should the United States build it alone? Accept all answers as a basis for discussion. Some students might think cooperation would cut costs and bring nations together. Other students might think the United States should not share space technology with other nations.

Figure 15
Astronauts performed a variety of tasks while living and working in space on board *Skylab*.

Figure 16
Russian and American scientists have worked together to maintain the *Mir* space station.

656 **CHAPTER 22** Exploring Space

Space Stations

Astronauts can spend only a short time living in the space shuttle. Its living area is small, and the crew needs more room to live, exercise, and work. A **space station** has living quarters, work and exercise areas, and all the equipment and support systems needed for humans to live and work in space.

In 1973, the United States launched the space station *Skylab*, shown in **Figure 15.** Crews of astronauts spent up to 84 days there performing experiments, and collecting data on the effects on humans of living in space. In 1979, the abandoned *Skylab* fell out of orbit and burned up as it entered Earth's atmosphere.

Crews from the former Soviet Union have spent more time onboard the space station *Mir* than crews from any other country. Cosmonaut Dr. Valery Polyakov returned to Earth after 438 days in space studying the long-term effects of weightlessness.

Cooperation in Space

In 1995, the United States and Russia began an era of cooperation and trust in exploring space. Early in the year, American Dr. Norman Thagard was launched into orbit aboard the Russian *Soyuz* spacecraft, along with two Russian cosmonaut crewmates. Dr. Thagard was the first U.S. astronaut launched into space by a Russian booster and the first American resident of the Russian space station *Mir*.

In June 1995, Russian cosmonauts rode into orbit onboard the space shuttle *Atlantis,* America's 100th crewed launch. The mission of *Atlantis* involved, among other studies, a rendezvous and docking with the space station *Mir*. The cooperation that existed on this mission, as shown in **Figure 16,** continued through eight more space shuttle-*Mir* docking missions. Each of the eight missions was an important step toward building and operating the *International Space Station*. Cooperation continued as the *International Space Station* began to take form. Astronauts from several nations were involved in key space shuttle flights that were designed for station preparation and maintenance.

Inclusion Strategies

Hearing Impaired and Learning Disabled Provide illustrations and photos of the spacecraft discussed. Have students do research to write extended captions for the images. Students can also work on the Internet to find and print out photos of various probes and satellites to make a bulletin board of United States space travel.
Visual-Spatial

Teacher FYI

When first launched in 1973, *Skylab* lost part of its protective covering and one of its solar panels. The other panel didn't fully open and malfunctioned. At first, the station had limited power and temperatures inside rose. Astronauts heading to the station first had to repair it. Once repaired, *Skylab* went on to complete its mission.

The International Space Station The *International Space Station (ISS)* will be a permanent laboratory designed for long-term research projects. Diverse topics will be studied, including research on the growth of protein crystals. This particular project will help scientists determine protein structure and function, which is expected to enhance work on drug design and the treatment of many diseases.

The *ISS* will draw on the resources of 16 nations. These nations will build units for the space station, which then will be transported into space onboard the space shuttle and Russian launch rockets. The station will be constructed in space. **Figure 17** shows what the completed station will look like.

 **Reading Check** *What is the purpose of the* **International Space Station?**

Phases of *ISS* NASA is planning the *ISS* program in phases. Phase One, now concluded, involved the space shuttle-*Mir* docking missions. Phase Two began in 1998 with the launch of the Russian-built *Zarya Module*, also known as the Functional Cargo Block, and will end with the delivery of a U.S. laboratory onboard the space shuttle. The first assembly of *ISS* occurred in December of 1998 when a space shuttle mission attached the Unity module to *Zarya*. During Phase Two, a crew of three people will be delivered to the space station.

Living in Space The project will continue with Phase Three when the Japanese Experiment Module, the European Columbus Orbiting Facility, and another Russian lab will be delivered.

The United States hopes to deliver its Habitation Module in 2005. The delivery will end Phase Three and make the *ISS* fully operational and ready for its permanent six- or seven-person crew. A total of 47 separate launches will be required to take all the components of the *ISS* into space and prepare it for permanent habitation. NASA plans for crews of astronauts to stay onboard the station for several months at a time. NASA already has conducted numerous tests to prepare crews of astronauts for extended space missions. One day, the station could be a construction site for ships that will travel to the Moon and Mars.

Figure 17
This is a picture of what the proposed *International Space Station* will look like when it is completed in 2006.

SCIENCE *Online*

Research Visit the Glencoe Science Web site at **science.glencoe.com** for more information on the *International Space Station.* Share your information with the class.

SECTION 3 Current and Future Space Missions **657**

Visual Learning

Figure 17 What do you think the flat panels do? They are solar panels that provide electricity for the space station.

✔ **Reading Check**

Answer It is a laboratory that will be used for long-term research projects.

Make a Model

Have pairs of students construct models of the *International Space Station*, using the photos in the text or images from other sources. Have each pair design and add one new feature to the station. Each group should make a presentation, explaining what the new feature would do. Display the models in class. L2 COOP LEARN
IS **Interpersonal**

SCIENCE *Online*
Internet Addresses
_____
_____
_____
_____
Explore the Glencoe Science Web site at **science.glencoe.com** to find out more about topics in this section.

Resource Manager

Chapter Resources Booklet
Enrichment, p. 28
Home and Community Involvement, p. 31

Curriculum Connection

Health The space program has been used to benefit humans in many fields, including health and medicine. Have students write a report in their Science Journals about advancements in health and medicine that have occurred as a direct result of the space program.

Exploring Mars

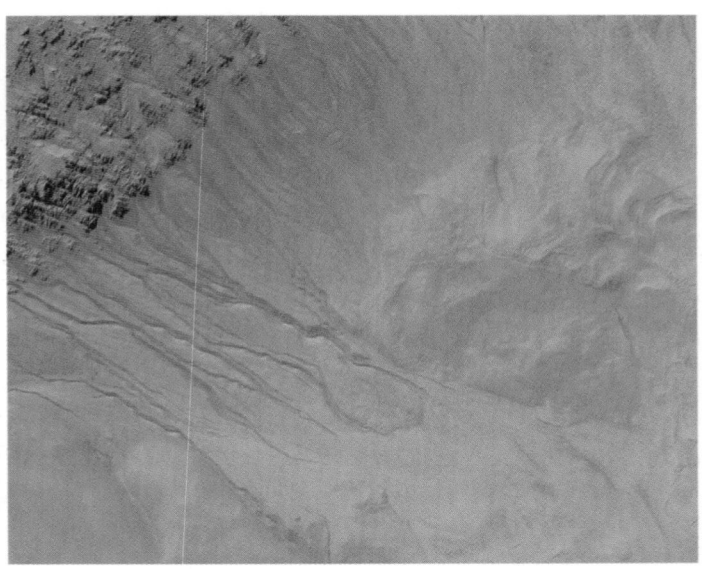

Figure 18
Gulleys, channels, and aprons of sediment imaged by the *Mars Global Surveyor* are similar to features on Earth known to be caused by flowing water. This water is thought to seep out from beneath the surface of Mars.

Exploring Mars

Two of the most successful missions in recent years were the 1996 launchings of the *Mars Global Surveyor* and the *Mars Pathfinder*. *Surveyor* orbited Mars, taking high-quality photos of the planet's surface as shown in **Figure 18.** *Pathfinder* descended to the Martian surface, using rockets and a parachute system to slow its descent. Large balloons absorbed the shock of landing. *Pathfinder* carried technology to study the surface of the planet, including a remote-controlled robot rover called Sojourner. Using information gathered by the rover and photographs taken by *Surveyor,* scientists determined that areas of the planet's surface were covered with water in the recent past.

✔ Reading Check *What type of data were obtained by the* Mars Global Surveyor?

Although the *Mars Global Surveyor* and the *Mars Pathfinder* missions were successful, not all the missions to Mars have met with the same success. The *Mars Climate Orbiter,* launched in 1998, was lost in September of 1999. An incorrect calculation of the force that the thrusters were to exert caused the spacecraft to be lost. Engineers had used English units instead of metric units. Then, in December of 1999, the *Mars Polar Lander* was lost just as it was making its descent to the planet. This time, it is believed that the spacecraft thought it had landed and shut off its thrusters too soon. NASA tried to make contact with the lander but never had any success.

658 **CHAPTER 22** Exploring Space

 LAB DEMONSTRATION

Purpose to demonstrate simulated gravity
Materials turntable, LP record, scissors, construction paper, tape, marbles
Preparation Fold 8-cm wide strips of construction paper in half lengthwise, then unfold.
Procedure Wrap the strips along the fold around the circumference of the record so

there is a 4-cm wall. Securely tape the remainder underneath. Place the record on the turntable, place three marbles at its center, and switch it on.
Expected Outcome The marbles are accelerated outward; the paper exerts a force and stops them.

✔ Assessment

How could this procedure generate artificial gravity in a space station? If the space station were spinning, inertia would cause objects to accelerate toward the outer edge, producing a feeling of gravity.

New Millennium Program

To continue space missions into the future, NASA has created the New Millennium Program (NMP). The goal of the NMP is to develop advanced technology that will let NASA send smart spacecraft into the solar system. This will reduce the amount of ground control needed. They also hope to reduce the size of future spacecraft to keep the cost of launching them under control. NASA's challenge is to prove that certain cutting-edge technologies, as well as mission concepts, work in space.

Exploring the Moon

Does water exist in the craters of the Moon's poles? This is one question NASA intends to explore with data gathered from the *Lunar Prospector* spacecraft shown in **Figure 19.** Launched in 1998, the *Lunar Prospector's* one-year mission was to orbit the Moon, taking photographs of its surface for mapping purposes. Early data obtained from the spacecraft indicate that hydrogen might be present in the rocks of the Moon's poles. Hydrogen is one of the elements found in water. Scientists now hypothesize that ice on the floors of the Moon's polar craters may be the source of this hydrogen. Ice might survive indefinitely at the bottom of these craters because it would always be shaded from the Sun.

Other things could account for the presence of hydrogen. It could be from solar wind or minerals that contain water. The *Lunar Prospector* was directed to crash into a crater at the Moon's south pole when its mission ended in July 1999. Scientists hoped that material would be thrown up by the collision and then recovered for analysis. However, it didn't work. Further studies are needed to determine if water exists on the Moon.

SCIENCE Online

Data Update For an online update on the New Millenium Program, visit the Glencoe Science Web site at **science.glencoe.com**

Figure 19
The *Lunar Prospector* took pictures of the Moon's surface during its one-year mission.

SCIENCE Online
Internet Addresses

Explore the Glencoe Science Web site at **science.glencoe.com** to find out more about topics in this section.

New Millennium Program

Activity

Ask students: What do other students in your school think about the future of the space program? Do they want it to continue? If so, what do they think NASA should explore? Should uncrewed probes be sent or should there be many more crewed missions to space? Have groups of students design a poll to find the answers to these questions. They should finalize the questions, decide how many students they will survey, carry out the poll, and report the results. Have different student groups share their results in class.

Exploring the Moon

Discussion

Why is it important for scientists to determine if there is water on the moon? Possible answer: Having water on the moon would make it easier to set up a moon base. Water would be available for drinking, and also could be used to produce oxygen.

Extension

The 1994 probe *Clementine* sent back the initial data that led scientists to speculate that water might be on the moon. *Lunar Prospector* followed up on what radar signals bounced off the lunar surface by *Clementine* seemed to show—possible water under the surface. Have students search 1994 newspapers for an article on *Clementine's* exciting discovery. Have them report on what the probe found, and how it led to the present search for water on the moon.

Cassini

Use an Analogy

To help students understand the vast distances space probes travel, tell them that the *Cassini* probe, headed toward Saturn, must travel roughly 1.3 billion km one way. That's nearly equivalent to walking around Earth along the equator more than 100,000 times.

Extension

Have interested students research NASA's Origins Program. Ask them to find out when the program began, what stages are involved, and where the program is heading. Possible answer: The program began in 1990 with precursor missions including the *Hubble Space Telescope*. The first generation missions will be ST3, SIM, and NGST. The program will continue with the second generation mission, Terrestrial Planet Finder. Third generation missions include Life Finder and Planet Imager.

Figure 20
Cassini is currently on its way to Saturn. After it arrives, it will spend four years studying Saturn and its surrounding area.

Cassini

In October 1997, NASA launched the space probe *Cassini*. This probe's destination is Saturn. *Cassini*, shown in **Figure 20,** will not reach its goal until 2004. At that time, the space probe will explore Saturn and surrounding areas for four years. One part of its mission is to deliver the European Space Agency's *Huygens* probe to Saturn's largest moon, Titan. Some scientists theorize that Titan's atmosphere may be similar to the atmosphere of early Earth.

The Next Generation Space Telescope Not all space missions involve sending astronauts or probes into space. Plans are being made to launch a new space telescope that is capable of observing the first stars and galaxies in the universe. The *Next Generation Space Telescope*, shown in **Figure 21,** will be the successor to the *Hubble Space Telescope*. As part of the Origins project, it will provide scientists with the opportunity to study the evolution of galaxies, the production of elements by stars, and the process of star and planet formation. To accomplish these tasks, the telescope will have to be able to see objects 400 times fainter than those currently studied with ground-based telescopes such as the twin Keck telescopes. NASA hopes to launch the *Next Generation Space Telescope* as early as 2009.

Figure 21
The *Next Generation Space Telescope* will attempt to observe stars and galaxies that formed early in the history of the universe.

Inclusion Strategies

Learning Disabled Help your students better understand the *Cassini* mission by showing them photos of the Saturn system with its many rings and moons. These will be the objects that *Cassini* will study. Point out Titan and explain to students that *Cassini* will deliver the probe *Huygens* to study this large moon.
LS Visual-Spatial

Resource Manager

Chapter Resources Booklet
    Activity Worksheet, pp. 7–8
    Reinforcement, p. 25
Lab Management and Safety, p. 73

Everyday Space Technology Items developed for space exploration don't always stay in space. In fact, many of today's cutting-edge technologies are modifications of research or technology used in the space program. For example, NASA space suit technology, shown in **Figure 22,** was used to give a child with a skin disorder the opportunity to play outside. Without the suit, the child could have been seriously hurt by the Sun's rays.

Space technology also has been used to understand, diagnose, and treat heart disease. Programmable pacemakers, developed through space technology, have given doctors more programming possibilities and more detailed information about their patients' health.

Other advances include ribbed swimsuits that reduce water resistance. Also, badges have been designed that warn workers of toxic chemicals in the air by turning color when the wearer is exposed to a particular chemical. Jet engines capable of much higher speeds than current jet engines are being developed as well.

A new technology that may prevent many accidents also has been developed. Equipment on emergency vehicles causes traffic lights to turn yellow and then red for other vehicles approaching the same intersections. The equipment activates the traffic lights when fast-moving emergency vehicles come close to such an intersection, preventing crashes.

Figure 22
Space technology has helped children go places and do things that they otherwise wouldn't be able to do.

Section Assessment

1. What is the main advantage of the space shuttle?

2. Why were the space shuttle-*Mir* docking missions so important?

3. What is the *International Space Station* used for? Describe how the *ISS* could help future space missions.

4. Describe Phase Three of the *International Space Station* program.

5. **Think Critically** What makes the space shuttle more versatile than earlier spacecraft?

Skill Builder Activities

6. **Making and Using Tables** Make a table of the discoveries from missions to the Moon and Mars. **For more help, refer to the** Science Skill Handbook.

7. **Communicating** Suppose you're in charge of assembling a crew for a new space station. Select 50 people to do a variety of jobs, such as farming, maintenance, scientific experimentation, and so on. In your Science Journal, list and explain your choices. **For more help, refer to the** Science Skill Handbook.

Reteach

Have students compare and contrast the space shuttle and the *International Space Station.* Possible answers: Both orbit Earth and are used for research; astronauts can live longer on the *ISS*, and the *ISS* has more room; shuttle returns to Earth while ISS does not; shuttle is an American ship while ISS is international. L1

Challenge

Challenge students to make a chart that summarizes the NASA missions on the drawing board for the next ten years, and what each one intends to accomplish. Have the class pool the information they find to make one large chart on poster board. If the next mission will happen in the near future, have students compare the goals of the mission to what it actually accomplishes. L2

Assessment

Oral Have each student make up a question and answer on information in this section for a brief oral quiz. Arrange students in a circle, then have each student address his or her question to the person on his or her left. Use **Performance Assessment in the Science Classroom,** p. 91.

Answers to Section Assessment

1. It is a reusable spacecraft.
2. They allowed astronauts to practice a maneuver that would be needed to build the ISS.
3. It will be used for long-term research projects. It could one day be a construction site for ships that go to the moon or Mars.
4. It includes delivery of the Japanese

Experiment Module, the European Columbus Orbiting Facility, a Russian lab, and the United States Habitation Module.

5. It's reusable and can carry cargo into orbit, including satellites. It can also retrieve objects from orbit and take astronauts into orbit to repair satellites.

6. Students can use the information in the text as well as additional sources such as encyclopedias and the Internet.

7. Lists should include a range of people needed to grow food, make repairs, treat medical emergencies, pilot spacecraft, and do experiments. Accept reasonable answers.

Activity

Recognize the Problem

Internet Students will gather data from Internet sites that can be accessed through the Glencoe Science Web site to obtain directions for making an astrolabe. The astrolabe will be used for star sightings that can help students determine Earth's circumference.

Non-Internet Sources Students can check their calculations by using an encyclopedia to look up Earth's circumference.

Time Required

one week

Preparation

Internet Access the Glencoe Science Web site to run through the steps students will follow.

Non-Internet Have books on astronomy and the history of astronomy as well as an encyclopedia available in class for students to use. Also provide atlases that students can use to determine the distance between cities.

Form a Hypothesis

Possible Hypotheses

- The fact that Polaris appears at different altitudes in the sky depending on latitude suggests that Earth's surface is curved.
- An estimate of the circumference of Earth can be determined by comparing astrolabe readings.

Activity *Use the Internet*

Star Sightings

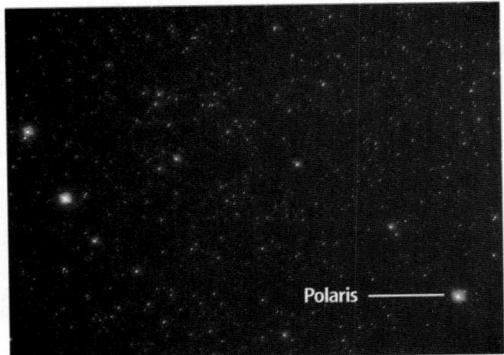

Polaris

For thousands of years, humans have used the stars to learn about Earth. From star sightings, you can map the change of seasons, navigate the oceans, and even determine the size of Earth.

Polaris, or the North Star, has occupied an important place in human history. The location of Polaris is not affected by Earth's rotation. At any given observation point, it always appears at the same angle above the horizon. At Earth's north pole, Polaris appears directly overhead. At the equator, it is just above the northern horizon. Polaris provides a standard from which other locations can be measured. Such star sightings can be made using the astrolabe, an instrument used to measure the height of a star above the horizon.

Recognize the Problem

How can you determine the size of Earth?

Form a Hypothesis

Think about what you have learned about sightings of Polaris. How does this tell you that Earth is round? Knowing that Earth is round, form a hypothesis about how you can estimate the circumference of Earth based on star sightings.

Goals
- ■ **Record** your sightings of Polaris.
- ■ **Share** the data with other students to calculate the circumference of Earth.

Safety Precautions
WARNING: *Do not use the astrolabe during the daytime to observe the Sun.*

Data Sources
SCIENCE *Online* Go to the Glencoe Science Web site at **science.glencoe.com** to obtain instructions on how to make an astrolabe. Also visit the Web site for more information about the location of Polaris, and for data from other students.

662 CHAPTER 22 Exploring Space

SCIENCE *Online*
Internet Addresses
_____
_____
_____

Explore the Glencoe Science Web site at **science.glencoe.com** to find out more about topics in this activity.

Test Your Hypothesis

Plan

1. Obtain an astrolabe or construct one using the instructions posted on the Glencoe Science Web site.

2. **Design** a data table in your Science Journal similar to the one below.

Polaris Observations

Your Location:		
Date	Time	Astrolabe Reading
Readings will vary with school's location.		

3. Decide as a group how you will make your observations. Does it take more than one person to make each observation? When will it be easiest to see Polaris?

Do

1. Make sure your teacher approves your plan before you start.

2. Carry out your observations.

3. **Record** your observations in your data table.

4. Average your readings and post them in the table provided on the Glencoe Science Web site.

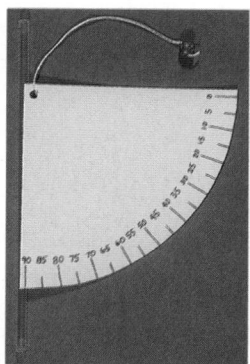

Analyze Your Data

1. **Research** the names of cities that are at approximately the same longitude as your hometown. Gather astrolabe readings at the Glencoe Science Web site from students in one of those cities.

2. **Compare** your astrolabe readings. Subtract the smaller reading from the larger one.

3. Determine the distance between your star sighting location and the other city.

4. **Calculate** the circumference of Earth using the following relationship.

Circumference = (360°) × (distance between locations)/ difference between readings

Draw Conclusions

1. How does the circumference of Earth that you calculated compare with the accepted value of 40,079 km?

2. What are some possible sources of error in this method of determining the size of Earth? What improvements would you suggest?

*C*ommunicating Your Data

SCIENCE Online Find this *Use the Internet* activity on the Glencoe Science Web site at **science.glencoe.com** Create a poster that includes a table of your data and data from students in other cities. Perform a sample circumference calculation for your class.

ACTIVITY 663

Test Your Hypothesis

Teaching Strategies

- Have students make repeated star sightings of Polaris and other stars over a few nights and at different times.

- After students have made a few observations, explain the circumference equation. Have them practice explaining the logic behind the circumference equation to a partner.

Analyze Your Data

1. Students can use an atlas to locate cities at approximately the same longitude as your hometown.
2. Answers will vary depending on readings.
3. Answers will vary on cities chosen.
4. Earth's circumference at the equator is 24,901 mi. (40,079 km).

Draw Conclusions

1. Values should be close.
2. Possible answers: making errors in calculations, choosing a city not on your longitude, misreading the astrolabe. Students might suggest being more careful or repeating calculations several times.

Assessment

Process Have students draw an events chain concept map that shows the steps used in completing this activity. Use **Performance Assessment in the Science Classroom**, p. 163.

*C*ommunicating Your Data

Have students use a computer spreadsheet program to record data on star sightings at their location and at various other cities on the same line of longitude.

Content Background

The idea of space travel and colonization has been around since the beginning of the Industrial Revolution. The advent of modern electronics, synthetic materials and medical advances has convinced many people that extraterrestrial habitation will be feasible, if not necessary, in the near future.

The critics of space travel claim that the effort and money spent on space colonization would be better spent on programs to solve current problems. The advocates see space as a new frontier equal or greater in potential to the Americas in the 1600s. Advocates also point out that, if the materials and systems required for the construction of self-sufficient space colonies can be developed, these same technologies can be applied to similar problems on planet Earth.

The current economic model also demands that the enterprise or its spin-off technologies must eventually become profitable. The existing state of production and propulsion technology do not permit large-scale space travel, but that may change rapidly. Nanotechnology and biotechnology are producing materials and plants for off-Earth environments. For now, however, space travel for the general public is not feasible.

Cities in Space

Should the U.S. spend money to colonize space?

Humans have landed on the Moon, and a spacecraft has landed on Mars. But these space missions are just small steps that may lead to a giant new space program. As technology improves, humans may be able to visit and even live on other planets. The twenty-first century may turn science fiction into science fact. But is it worth the time and money involved?

Those in favor of living in space point to the *International Space Station* that already is orbiting Earth. It's an early step toward establishing floating cities where astronauts can live and work. The 94 billion dollar station may pave the way for "ordinary people" to live in space, too. As Earth's population continues to increase and there is less room on this planet, why not create ideal cities on another planet or a floating city in space? That reason, combined with the fact that there is little pollution in space, makes the idea appealing to many.

Critics of colonizing space think we should spend the hundreds of billions of dollars that it would cost to colonize space on projects to help improve people's lives here on Earth. Building better housing, developing ways to feed the hungry, finding cures for diseases, and increasing funds for education should come first, these people say. And, critics continue, if people want to explore, why not explore right here on Earth? "The ocean floor is Earth's last frontier," says one person. "Why not explore that?"

If humans were to move permanently to space, the two most likely destinations would be Mars and the Moon, both bleak places.

Resources for Teachers and Students

"Home Sweet Home," by Alan Hall, Explorations, *Scientific American*, March 16, 1998.

The Case for Mars: The Plan to Settle the Red Planet and Why We Must, Robert Zubrin with Richard Wagner, NY, NY: The Free Press, 1996

But those in favor of moving to these places say humans could find a way to make them livable. They argue that humans have made homes in harsh climates and in rugged areas, and people can meet the challenges of living in space.

Choosing Mars

Mars may be the best place to live. Photos suggest that the planet once had liquid water on its surface. If that water is now frozen underground, humans may someday be able to tap into it.

NASA is studying whether it makes sense to send astronauts and scientists to explore Mars. An international team would live there for about 500 days, collecting and studying soil and rock samples for clues as to whether Mars is a planet that could be settled. NASA says this journey could begin as early as 2009.

But a longer-range dream to transform Mars into an Earthlike place with breathable air and usable water is just that—a dream. Some small steps are being taken to make that dream more realistic. Experimental plants are being developed that could absorb Mars' excess carbon dioxide and release oxygen. Solar mirrors, already available, could warm Mars' surface.

Those for and against colonizing space agree on one thing—setting up colonies on Mars or the Moon will take large amounts of of money, research, and planning. It also will take the same spirit of adventure that has led history's pioneers into so many bold frontiers—deserts, the Poles, and the sky.

Is the International Space Station a small step toward colonizing space?

An early Mars colony might look something like this. Settlers would live in air-filled domes and even grow crops.

CONNECTIONS **Debate** Research further information about colonizing space. Make a list of the pros and cons for colonizing space. Do you think the United States should spend the money to create space cities or should use the money now to improve lives of people on Earth? Debate with your class.

SCIENCE *Online*

For more information, visit science.glencoe.com

Discussion

Why have long term missions such as Skylab, Mir, and the International Space Station been very small compared to the size a space colony would be? Possible answer: The expense and small carrying capacity of current lift vehicles (rockets) prevents the transport of large amounts of material and supplies into space and are confined to a relatively low orbit.

Activity

Organize the class into teams to look into these aspects of space habitation: breathable air, energy (for all purposes), water, building materials, sustainable food supplies, protection from cosmic radiation, gravity, and transportation. Instruct the teams to prepare charts indicating the technology required compared with available technology. They can then pool their research and try to determine when they feel space colonization will be feasible.

Investigate the Issue

The settling of Mars and the Moon has been compared to inhabiting harsh climates on the Earth. Have students compare the conditions on Mars with those found in a desert, the Arctic, and underwater. Which are most similar? Most different? What problems are unique to each place?

SCIENCE *Online*

Internet Addresses

_____

_____

_____

Explore the Glencoe Science Web site at **science.glencoe.com** to find out more about topics in this feature.

CONNECTIONS **Debate**

Students will have gathered enough information from their research activity to form some idea of the requirements for living for an indefinite length of time outside Earth's atmosphere. Lead students in a debate about the reasonableness of pursuing this goal considering the cost, possible benefits, and time frame involved. The cost will be enormous in terms of finances and scientific resources and might be viewed in light possible returns on the investment. A possible frame for the discussion of benefits might be the steadily dropping cost of high-tech products that were unavailable only a few years ago.

Chapter 22 Study Guide

Preview

Students can answer the questions in their Science Journals. Discuss the answers as you go through the chapter. **LS Linguistic**

Review

Students can write their answers, then compare them with those of other students. **LS Interpersonal**

Reteach

Students can look at the illustrations and describe details that support the main ideas of the chapter. **LS Visual-Spatial**

Answers to Chapter Review

SECTION 1
2. mirrors

SECTION 2
2. Space probes have traveled to the edge of the solar system and beyond.

SECTION 3
2. Possible answers: microgravity; close quarters; having to exercise to prevent muscle deterioration; having to bring food, water, and air with them into space

---

Reviewing Main Ideas

Section 1 Radiation from Space

1. The arrangement of electromagnetic waves according to their wavelengths is the electromagnetic spectrum.

2. Optical telescopes produce magnified images of objects. *What does this reflecting telescope use to focus light that produces an image?*

3. Radio telescopes collect and record radio waves given off by some space objects.

Section 2 Early Space Missions

1. A satellite is an object that revolves around another object. The moons of planets are natural satellites. Artificial satellites are those made by people.

2. A space probe travels into the solar system, gathers data, and sends them back to Earth. *How far can space probes, like the one pictured here, travel?*

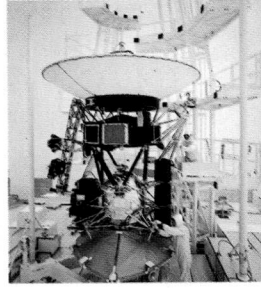

3. Early American piloted space programs included the Gemini and Apollo Projects.

Section 3 Recent and Future Space Missions

1. Space stations provide the opportunity to conduct research not possible on Earth. The *International Space Station* will be constructed in space with the cooperation of more than a dozen nations.

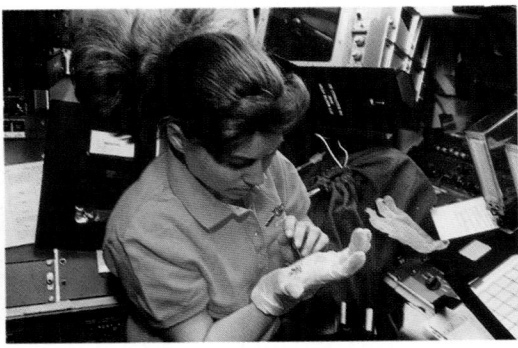

2. The space shuttle is a reusable spacecraft that carries astronauts, satellites, and other cargo to and from space. *What special obstacles must astronauts overcome when they conduct research in space?*

3. Space technology is used to solve problems on Earth not related to space travel. Advances in engineering related to space travel have led to problem solving in medicine and environmental sciences, among other fields.

FOLDABLES
Reading & Study Skills

After You Read

Use what you've learned to predict the future of space exploration. Record your predictions under the Future tab of your Foldable.

FOLDABLES
Reading & Study Skills

After You Read

After students have read the chapter and completed the Foldable described in Before You Read, have them do the activity on the student page.

Dinah Zike

Visualizing Main Ideas

Complete the following concept map about the race to the Moon. Use the following phrases: first human on the Moon, *Sputnik I,* orbited Earth safely, first satellite, Project Gemini, Project Mercury, team of 2 astronauts orbits Earth, Project Apollo.

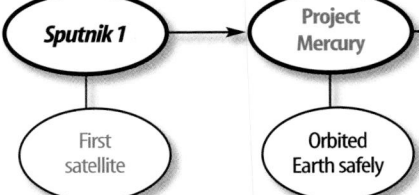
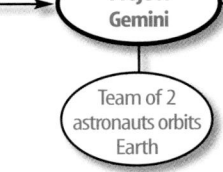
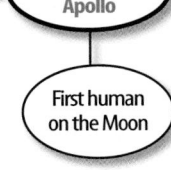

Sputnik 1 → **Project Mercury** → **Project Gemini** → **Project Apollo**

- First satellite
- Orbited Earth safely
- Team of 2 astronauts orbits Earth
- First human on the Moon

Vocabulary Review

Vocabulary Words

a. electromagnetic spectrum
b. observatory
c. orbit
d. Project Apollo
e. Project Gemini
f. Project Mercury
g. radio telescope
h. reflecting telescope
i. refracting telescope
j. rocket
k. satellite
l. space probe
m. space shuttle
n. space station

THE PRINCETON REVIEW   Study Tip

Without looking back at your textbook, write a summary of each section of a chapter after you've read it. If you write it in your own words, you will remember it better.

Using Vocabulary

Each of the following sentences is false. Make each sentence true by replacing the underlined word(s) with the correct vocabulary word(s).

1. A <u>radio</u> telescope uses lenses to bend light.

2. A <u>space probe</u> is an object that revolves around another object in space.

3. <u>Project Apollo</u> was the first piloted U.S. space program.

4. A <u>satellite</u> carries people and tools to and from space.

5. In the <u>space station</u>, electromagnetic waves are arranged according to their wavelengths.

CHAPTER STUDY GUIDE   667

Visualizing Main Ideas

See student page.

Vocabulary Review

Using Vocabulary

1. refracting
2. satellite
3. Project Mercury
4. space shuttle
5. electromagnetic spectrum

Chapter 22 Assessment

Checking Concepts

1. D
2. D
3. B
4. A
5. B
6. A
7. D
8. C
9. B
10. C

Thinking Critically

11. Because the Moon has no atmosphere, light and other forms of energy can reach its surface without distortion.
12. No; the high surface temperature of the Sun would destroy any probes sent to study it.
13. Possible answers: Robotic space probes are cheaper and can go on one-way deep space missions that people cannot. Crewed flights provide information about living in space, and astronauts can use judgment to deal with unforeseen circumstances.
14. No; sound must travel through matter. Space is a vacuum, so sound will not travel across it.
15. When the probes crossed Pluto's orbit, Pluto was at another point in its orbit.

Checking Concepts

Choose the word or phrase that best answers the question.

1. Which spacecraft has sent images of Venus to scientists on Earth?
   A) *Voyager*   C) *Apollo 11*
   B) *Viking*   D) *Magellan*

2. Which kind of telescope uses mirrors to collect light?
   A) radio   C) refracting
   B) electromagnetic   D) reflecting

3. What was *Sputnik I?*
   A) the first telescope
   B) the first artificial satellite
   C) the first observatory
   D) the first U.S. space probe

4. Which kind of telescope can be used during the day or night and during bad weather?
   A) radio   C) refracting
   B) electromagnetic   D) reflecting

5. When fully operational, what is the maximum number of people who will crew the *International Space Station?*
   A) 3   C) 15
   B) 7   D) 50

6. Which space mission's goal was to put a spacecraft into orbit and bring it back safely?
   A) Project Mercury   C) Project Gemini
   B) Project Apollo   D) *Viking I*

7. Which of the following is a natural satellite of Earth?
   A) *Skylab*   C) the Sun
   B) the space shuttle   D) the Moon

8. What does the space shuttle use to place a satellite into space?
   A) liquid-fuel tank   C) mechanical arm
   B) booster rocket   D) cargo bay

9. What was *Skylab?*
   A) a space probe   C) a space shuttle
   B) a space station   D) an optical telescope

10. What part of the space shuttle is reused?
    A) liquid-fuel tanks   C) booster engines
    B) *Gemini* rockets   D) Saturn rockets

Thinking Critically

11. Describe any advantages that a Moon-based telescope would have over an Earth-based telescope?

12. Would a space probe to the Sun's surface be useful? Explain.

13. Which do you think is a wiser method of exploration—space missions with people onboard or robotic space probes? Why?

14. Suppose two astronauts are outside the space shuttle orbiting Earth. The audio speaker in the helmet of one astronaut quits working. The other astronaut is 1 m away and shouts a message. Can the first astronaut hear the message? Explain.

15. Space probes have crossed Pluto's orbit, but never have visited the planet. Explain.

Developing Skills

16. **Making and Using Tables** Copy and complete the table below. Use information from several resources.

United States Space Probes		
Probe	Launch Date(s)	Planets or Objects Visited
Vikings 1 and *2*		
Galileo		
Lunar Prospector		
Pathfinder		

Chapter ✓Assessment Planner

Portfolio Encourage students to place in their portfolios one or two items of what they consider to be their best work. Examples include:
- Science Journal, p. 643
- Chemistry Integration, p. 650
- Curriculum Connection, p. 657

Performance Additional performance assessments, Performance Task Assessment Lists, and rubrics for evaluating these activities can be found in Glencoe's **Performance Assessment in the Science Classroom.**

17. Concept Mapping Use the following phrases to complete the concept map about rocket launching: *thrust pushes rocket forward, rocket breaks free of Earth's gravity, propellant is ignited,* and *hot gases exert pressure on walls of burning chamber.*

propellant ignited

hot gases exert pressure on walls of burning chamber

thrust pushes rocket forward

rocket breaks free of Earth's gravity

18. Classifying Classify the following as a satellite or a space probe: *Cassini, Sputnik I, Hubble Space Telescope,* space shuttle, and *Voyager 2.*

19. Comparing and Contrasting Compare and contrast space probes and satellites.

Performance Assessment

20. Poem Research a space probe launched within the last five years. Write a poem that includes its destination, the goals for its mission and something about the individuals who crewed the flight.

TECHNOLOGY

Go to the Glencoe Science Web site at **science.glencoe.com** or use the **Glencoe Science CD-ROM** for additional chapter assessment.

THE PRINCETON REVIEW — Test Practice

Scientists use several different kinds of telescopes to make observations about space. Information about some types of telescopes is listed in the table below.

1. According to the table, a refracting telescope focuses light using a—
  A) convex lens
  B) mirror
  C) dish
  D) receiver

Types of Telescopes

Telescope	Use	How it Works
Optical Refracting Telescope	Produces magnified images of distant objects	Uses a convex lens to bend and focus light
Optical Reflecting Telescope	Produces magnified images of distant objects	Uses mirrors to reflect and focus light
Radio Telescope	Collects radio waves from space	Large dish reflects and focuses waves to receiver

2. While in space, the *Hubble Space Telescope* needed its largest mirror repaired in 1993. While costly, the repair mission was a huge success. According to the chart, the *Hubble Space Telescope* is—
  F) an optical refracting telescope
  G) an optical reflecting telescope
  H) a radio telescope
  J) an optical radio receiver

CHAPTER ASSESSMENT 669

THE PRINCETON REVIEW — Test Practice

The Test-Taking Tip was written by The Princeton Review, the nation's leader in test preparation.
1. A
2. G

Developing Skills

16.

United States Space Probes

Probe	Launch Date	Planets or Objects Visited
Vikings 1 and 2	1975	Mars
Galileo	1989	Venus, Europa, Jupiter
Lunar Prospector	1998	Earth's Moon
Pathfinder	1996	Mars

17. See student page.
18. *Sputnik,* the shuttle, and *Hubble* all orbit Earth like satellites. *Voyager 2* and *Cassini* are space probes.
19. Both are sent into space to collect data and send it back to Earth. Space probes travel into space to collect data as they fly by other bodies, whereas satellites are placed in orbit around Earth or other bodies.

Performance Assessment

20. Students can find detailed information for their poems in encyclopedias under "Space Exploration" and at the NASA Web site. Use **Performance Assessment in the Science Classroom,** p. 151.

✓Assessment Resources

📁 Reproducible Masters

Chapter Resources Booklet
Chapter Review, pp. 33–34
Chapter Tests, pp. 35–38
Assessment Transparency Activity, p. 45

Glencoe Science Web site
Interactive Tutor
Chapter Quizzes

Glencoe Technology
🔬 Assessment Transparency
💿 Interactive CD-ROM Chapter Quizzes
💿 ExamView Pro Test Bank
💿 Vocabulary PuzzleMaker Software
📼 MindJogger Videoquiz DVD/VHS

Section/Objectives	Standards		Activities/Features
Chapter Opener	**National**	**State/Local**	**Explore Activity:** Model rotation and revolution, p. 671 **Before You Read,** p. 671
	See p. 5T for a Key to Standards.		
Section 1 Earth ⏱ 2 sessions 📦 1 block 1. **Examine** Earth's physical characteristics. 2. **Differentiate** between rotation and revolution. 3. **Discuss** what causes seasons to change.	National Content Standards: UCP2, A1, D3		**Life Science Integration,** p. 675 **MiniLAB:** Making Your Own Compass, p. 674 **Science Online,** p. 675 **Science Online,** p. 677
Section 2 The Moon–Earth's Satellite ⏱ 2 sessions 📦 1 block 1. **Identify** phases of the Moon and their cause. 2. **Explain** why solar and lunar eclipses occur. 3. **Infer** what the Moon's surface features may reveal about its history.	National Content Standards: UCP2, A1, D3		**MiniLAB:** Comparing the Sun and the Moon, p. 679 **Science Online,** p. 681 **Physics Integration,** p. 683 **Visualizing the Moon's Surface,** p. 684 **Problem-Solving Activity:** What will you use to survive on the Moon?, p. 685 **Activity:** Moon Phases and Eclipses, p. 687
Section 3 Exploring Earth's Moon ⏱ 4 sessions 📦 2 blocks 1. **Describe** recent discoveries about the Moon. 2. **Examine** facts about the Moon that might influence future space travel.	National Content Standards: UCP2, A1, D3, E1, G1, G3		**MiniLAB:** Modeling a shaded impact basin, p. 689 **Activity:** Tilt and Temperature, p. 692 **Science and History:** The Mayan Calendar, p. 694

NATIONAL GEOGRAPHIC

Teacher's Corner

PRODUCTS AVAILABLE FROM GLENCOE
To order call 1-800-368-2728:
Poster
The Earth's Moon
Videodisc
Sun, Earth, Moon

INDEX TO NATIONAL GEOGRAPHIC MAGAZINE
"Physical World," by Joel L. Swerdlow, May 1998.
"Orbit: The Astronauts' View of Home," by Jay Apt, November 1996.
"The Darkness that Enlighten," by Jay M. Pasachoff, May 1992.

"The Moon's Racing Shadow," by Roger, August 1985.
"Our Restless Planet Earth," by Rick Gore, August 1985.

Activity Materials	Reproducible Resources	Section Assessment	Technology
Explore Activity: basketball	**Chapter Resources Booklet** Foldables Worksheet, p. 15 Directed Reading Overview, p. 17 Note-taking Worksheets, pp. 31–34	GLENCOE'S ASSESSMENT ADVANTAGE	
MiniLAB: plastic foam cup, sewing needle, tape, plate, water	**Chapter Resources Booklet** Transparency Activity, p. 44 MiniLAB, p. 3 Enrichment, p. 28 Reinforcement, p. 25 Directed Reading, p. 18 Lab Activity, pp. 11–12, 13–14 Transparency Activity, pp. 47–48	**Portfolio** Life Science Integration, p. 673 **Performance** MiniLAB, p. 674 Skill Builder Activities, p. 677 **Content** Section Assessment, p. 677	♪ Section Focus Transparency ♪ Teaching Transparency ◎ Interactive CD-ROM/DVD ∩ Guided Reading Audio Program
MiniLAB: chalk, pavement, string, meterstick **Activity:** unshaded light source, polystyrene ball, globe, pencil *Need materials?* Contact Science Kit at 1-800-828-7777 or www.sciencekit.com on the Internet.	**Chapter Resources Booklet** Transparency Activity, p. 45 MiniLAB, p. 4 Enrichment, p. 29 Reinforcement, p. 26 Directed Reading, p. 19 Activity Worksheet, pp. 7–8 **Cultural Diversity**, pp. 29, 71	**Portfolio** Life Science Integration, p. 673 Activity, p. 682 **Performance** MiniLAB, p. 679 Problem-Solving Activity, p. 685 Skill Builder Activities, p. 677 **Content** Section Assessment, p. 686	♪ Section Focus Transparency ◎ Interactive CD-ROM/DVD ∩ Guided Reading Audio Program
MiniLAB: modeling clay, metric ruler, flashlight **Activity:** tape, black construction paper, gooseneck lamp with 75-W bulb, celsius thermometer, watch, protractor	**Chapter Resources Booklet** Transparency Activity, p. 46 MiniLAB, p. 5 Enrichment, p. 30 Reinforcement, p. 27 Directed Reading, pp. 19, 20 Activity Worksheet, pp. 9–10 **Lab Management and Safety**, p. 61	**Portfolio** Extension, p. 690 **Performance** MiniLAB, p. 689 Skill Builder Activities, p. 691 **Content** Section Assessment, p. 691	♪ Section Focus Transparency ◎ Interactive CD-ROM/DVD ∩ Guided Reading Audio Program

End of Chapter Assessment

GLENCOE'S ASSESSMENT ADVANTAGE

Blackline Masters	Technology	Professional Series
Chapter Resources Booklet Chapter Review, pp. 37–38 Chapter Tests, pp. 39–42 **Standardized Test Practice by The Princeton Review**, pp. 99–102	▭ MindJogger Videoquiz ◉ CD-ROM Explorations and Quizzes ◉ Vocabulary Puzzle Makers ◉ ExamView Pro Test Bank ◉ Interactive Lesson Planner ◉ Interactive Teacher's Edition	Performance Assessment in the Science Classroom (PASC)

Transparencies

Section Focus

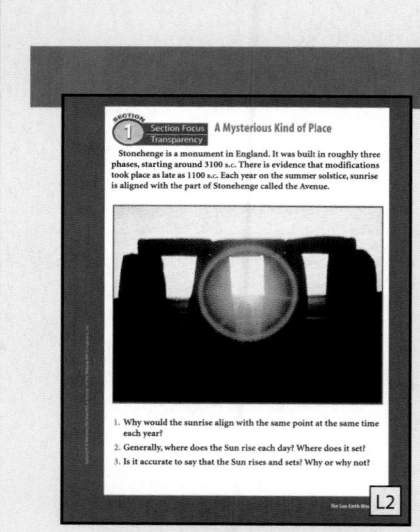

Section Focus Transparency 1 — A Mysterious Kind of Place

Stonehenge is a monument in England. It was built in roughly three phases, starting around 3100 B.C. There is evidence that modifications took place as late as 1100 B.C. Each year on the summer solstice, sunrise is aligned with the part of Stonehenge called the Avenue.

1. Why would the sunrise align with the same point at the same time each year?
2. Generally, where does the Sun rise each day? Where does it set?
3. Is it accurate to say that the Sun rises and sets? Why or why not?

L2

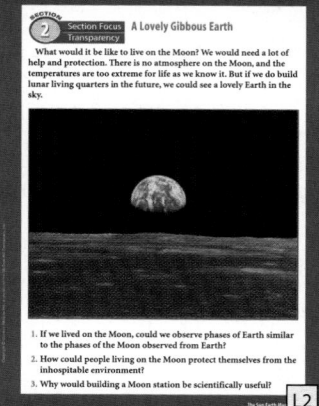

Section Focus Transparency 2 — A Lovely Gibbous Earth

What would it be like to live on the Moon? We would need a lot of help and protection. There is no atmosphere on the Moon, and the temperatures are too extreme for life as we know it. But if we build lunar living quarters in the future, we could see a lovely Earth in the sky.

1. If we lived on the Moon, could we observe phases of Earth similar to the phases of the Moon observed from Earth?
2. How could people living on the Moon protect themselves from the inhospitable environment?
3. Why would building a Moon station be scientifically useful?

L2

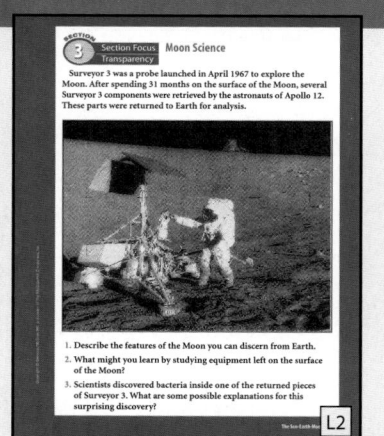

Section Focus Transparency 3 — Moon Science

Surveyor 3 was a probe launched in April 1967 to explore the Moon. After spending 31 months on the surface of the Moon, several Surveyor 3 components were retrieved by the astronauts of Apollo 12. These parts were returned to Earth for analysis.

1. Describe the features of the Moon you can discern from Earth.
2. What might you learn by studying equipment left on the surface of the Moon?
3. Scientists discovered bacteria inside one of the returned pieces of Surveyor 3. What are some possible explanations for this surprising discovery?

L2

This is a representation of key blackline masters available in the Teacher Classroom Resources. See Resource Manager boxes within the chapter for additional information.

Key to Teaching Strategies

The following designations will help you decide which activities are appropriate for your students.

L1 Level 1 activities should be appropriate for students with learning difficulties.

L2 Level 2 activities should be within the ability range of all students.

L3 Level 3 activities are designed for above-average students.

ELL ELL activities should be within the ability range of English Language Learners.

COOP LEARN Cooperative Learning activities are designed for small group work.

LS Multiple Learning Styles logos, as described on page 22T, are used throughout to indicate strategies that address different learning styles.

P These strategies represent student products that can be placed into a best-work portfolio.

Assessment

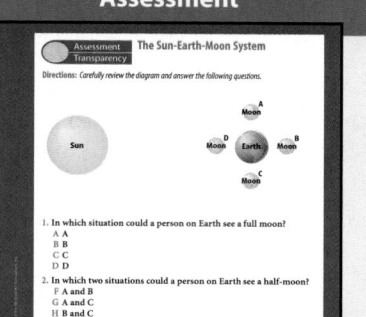

Assessment Transparency — The Sun-Earth-Moon System

Directions: Carefully review the diagram and answer the following questions.

1. In which situation could a person on Earth see a full moon?
   A A
   B B
   C C
   D D
2. In which two situations could a person on Earth see a half-moon?
   F A and B
   G A and C
   H B and C
   J B and D
3. In which situation could a solar eclipse be occurring?
   A A
   B B
   C C
   D D

L2

Teaching

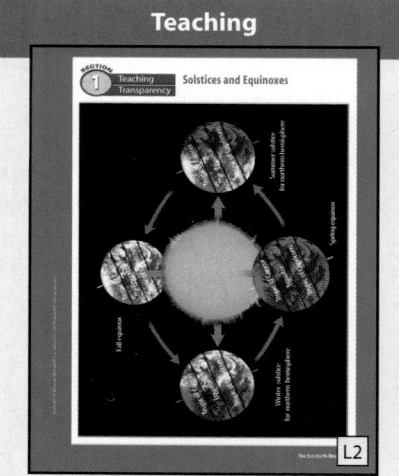

Teaching Transparency 1 — Solstices and Equinoxes

L2

Hands-on Activities

Activity Worksheets

Activity — Moon Phases and Eclipses

Lab Preview
Directions: Answer these questions before you begin the Activity.

1. What safety symbols are used in this activity?

2. What precautions should you take with this activity?

You have learned that Moon phases and eclipses result from the relative positions of the Sun, the Moon, and Earth. In this activity, you will demonstrate the positions of these bodies during certain phases and eclipses. You also will see why only a small portion of the people on Earth witness a total solar eclipse during a particular eclipse event.

What You'll Investigate
Can a model be devised to show the positions of the Sun, the Moon, and Earth during various phases and eclipses?

Materials
light source (unshaded)   globe
polystyrene ball

Goals
- Model Moon phases.
- Model solar and lunar eclipses.

Safety Precaution
Do not touch the light source. It will be hot.

Procedure
1. Review the illustrations of Moon phases and eclipses shown in Section 2.
2. Use the light source as a Sun model and a polystyrene ball on a pencil as a Moon model. Move the Moon around the globe to duplicate the exact position that would have to occur for a lunar eclipse to take place.
3. Move the Moon to the position that would cause a solar.
4. Place the Moon at each of the following phases: first quarter, full moon, third

quarter, and new moon. Identify which, if any, type of eclipse could occur during each phase. Record your data in the table on the next page.
5. Place the Moon at the location where a lunar eclipse could occur. Move it slightly toward Earth, then away from Earth. Note the amount of change in the size of the shadow.
6. Repeat step 5 with the Moon in a position where a solar eclipse could occur.

L2

Laboratory Activities

Laboratory Activity 1 — Earth's Spin

The speed at which Earth turns on its axis can be described in two ways. The velocity of rotation refers to the rate at which Earth turns on its axis. Velocity of rotation refers to Earth as a whole. For any point on Earth's surface, the speed of Earth's rotation can be described as its instantaneous linear velocity. This velocity is the speed of the point as it follows a circular path around Earth.

Strategy
You will determine the instantaneous linear velocity of some points on Earth.
You will compare the linear velocities of points at different locations on Earth.

Materials
globe (mounted on axis)   meterstick
tape (adhesive)   stopwatch
string

Procedure
Part A
1. Place small pieces of adhesive tape on the globe at the Prime Meridian at the equator, at 30° N latitude, at 60° N latitude, and at the north pole.
2. Line up the tape with the metal circle above the globe, see Figure 1.
3. With your finger on the globe, move it west to east for one second; see Figure 2.
4. For each location marked by tape, measure the distance from the Prime Meridian to the metal circle. Use the string and the meterstick to get accurate distances. Record the distances in Table 1.

5. Realign the metal circle with the pieces of tape. Move the globe west to east for 2 s. Record the distances from the tapes to the metal circle in Table 1.
6. Repeat step 5, moving the globe for 3 s. Record your results in Table 1.

Part B
Calculate the speed of each point for each trial. Record the speeds in Table 2. Use the formula:
$$velocity\ (cm/s) = distance\ (cm)/time\ (s)$$

Figure 1   **Figure 2**

L2

Meeting Different Ability Levels

Content Outline

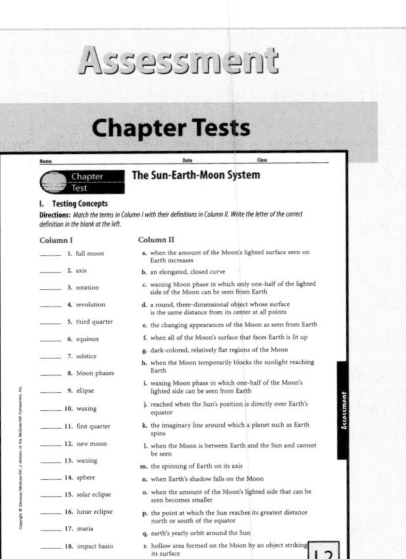

L2

Reinforcement

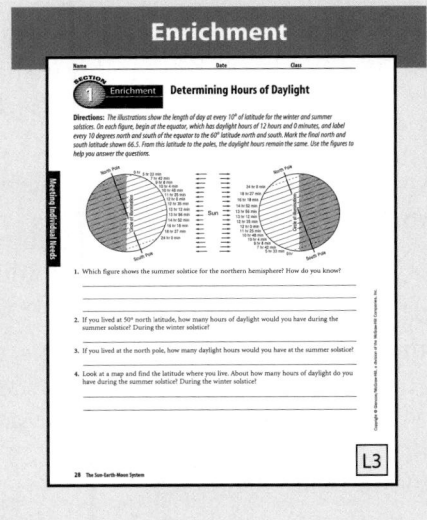

L2

Directed Reading

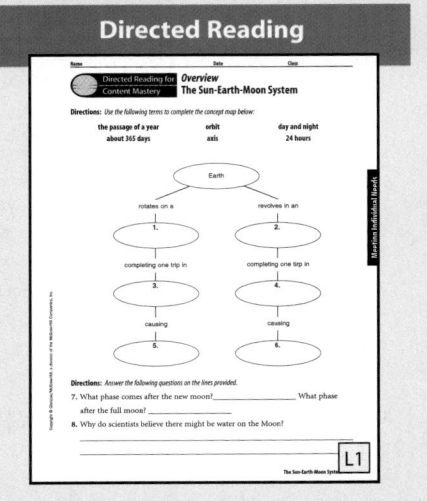

L1

Assessment

Chapter Tests

L2

Enrichment

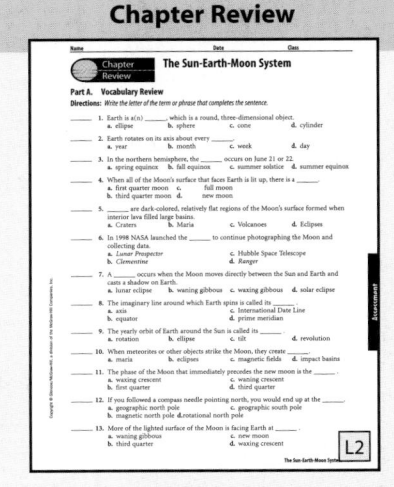

L3

Spanish Directed Reading

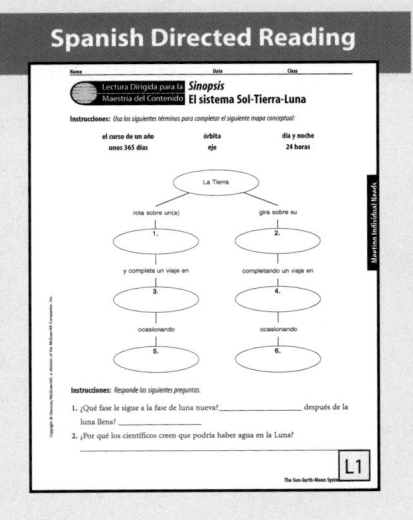

L1

Test Practice Workbook

Standardized Test Practice
Teacher Edition

Glencoe Science

Earth Science

L2

Chapter Review

L2

Science Content Background

Earth

Earth's Rotation

Scientists hypothesize that the gravitational attraction of the Moon is dragging on Earth, causing the length of a day to increase. Evidence from atomic clocks and ancient corals support the hypothesis that Earth's rotation is slowing. Atomic clocks measure time by recording the frequency of electromagnetic waves given off by atoms. They gain or lose less than one second in 200,000 years. Using these clocks, scientists have found that each successive day on Earth is getting longer. Corals deposit monthly growth lines on their shells in much the same way trees develop yearly growth rings. By studying growth lines on 375-million-year-old corals, scientists have determined that one year had 440 shorter days at the time these corals were growing.

Earth's Magnetic Field

The direction of Earth's magnetic field changes periodically over time. Minerals in rocks such as basalt align themselves according to the magnetic field orientation at the time they form. When Earth's magnetic field is reversed, new iron minerals being formed reflect that magnetic reversal. Charged particles from the Sun, called the solar wind, can be captured by Earth's magnetic field near Earth's poles. When these particles interact with the atmosphere, they form the northern lights.

SECTION 2

The Moon—Earth's Satellite

The Moon's Surface

About 4 billion years ago, large meteorites formed huge impact basins on the Moon's surface. By 3.3 billion years ago, lava flows had filled in the basins, forming the large, relatively flat maria seen today.

Student Misconception

Moon phases are caused by the Sun lighting up different parts of the Moon as the Sun moves through the sky.

Refer to the facing page for teaching strategies to address this misconception. Refer to pages 679–680 for content related to this topic.

SECTION 3

Exploring the Moon

Learning from Moon Explorations

Deviations in the lunar orbits of spacecraft led to the discovery of mascons, which are areas of high concentrations of mass. The presence of mascons indicates that the entire interior of the Moon cannot be liquid. Enough crust must be present to support mascons.

NASA/Photo Researchers, Inc.

SCIENCE Online

For additional content background on this topic, go to the Glencoe Science Web site at science.glencoe.com.

IDENTIFYING ▷ Misconceptions

Find Out What Students Think

Students may think that . . .

• **The Sun lights up different parts of the Moon as the Sun moves through the sky.**

Students' experiences are with a large Sun and a small Moon, thus some students develop the idea that the Sun moves through the sky and shines on different parts of the Moon. In reality, the Moon shines because light is reflected from the surface facing the Sun. Because half of the Moon is always facing the Sun, half of its surface is always lit. As the Moon revolves around Earth, we see different amounts of this lighted half. The shape seen at any one time depends on the relative positions of the Moon, Earth, and Sun.

Discussion

Organize the class into groups, and have them work together to draw the cycle of phases of the Moon from memory. Then have each student write a paragraph explaining how he or she thinks these changing shapes are produced. Review the paragraphs to help you identify which students harbor misconceptions about this process.

Promote Understanding

Activity

Have students observe and record the appearance of the Moon one night each week for four weeks.

• Have students compare their drawings with those they completed as a group. Point out that as the cycle starts, the Moon is completely dark. Then the lighted side of the Moon is revealed, starting on the right and working toward the left. After the full Moon, the lighted side of the Moon that we can see gets smaller, and darkness progresses over the face of the Moon from right to left.

• Have students explain where the lighted side of the Moon "goes." If necessary, reinforce how the Sun lights the face of the Moon, using a light source and two balls— one representing the Moon, and the other representing Earth. Underscore that half of the Moon's surface is always lit; we just can't see it from Earth.

Telegraph Colour Library/FPG International

Assess

After completing the chapter, see *Identifying Misconceptions* in the Study Guide.

The Sun-Earth-Moon System

Chapter Vocabulary

sphere
axis
rotation
revolution
ellipse
solstice
equinox
moon phase
new moon
waxing
full moon
waning
solar eclipse
lunar eclipse
maria
impact basin

What do you think?

Science Journal The photo shows the heavily cratered lunar surface. Most objects that fall toward Earth from space burn up in the atmosphere before reaching Earth's surface. Because the Moon has no atmosphere, craters made by the impact of thousands of rocky objects from space mark the Moon's surface.

The Sun-Earth-Moon System

Can you say with certainty that Earth is round? Why do you feel coldest when Earth is closest to the Sun? In this chapter, you will find the answers to these questions. You'll learn why the lengths of day and night change and why seasons occur. You'll also learn why the Moon's appearance changes throughout the month and why scientists think its surface might be a home for humans one day.

What do you think?

Science Journal Look at the picture below with a classmate. Discuss what this might be. Here's a hint: *It's behind the man in the Moon.* Write your best guess in your Science Journal.

670

Theme Connection

Systems and Interactions Earth's rotation and revolution in the Earth-Sun system are responsible for the day-night cycle and the seasons. Phases of the Moon and solar and lunar eclipses are caused by interactions among the Sun, the Moon, and Earth.

The Sun rises in the morning. This occurs because Earth is moving through space. The movements of Earth cause day and night, as well as the seasons. In this activity, you will explore Earth's movements.

Model rotation and revolution

1. Hold a basketball with one finger at the top and one at the bottom. Have a classmate gently spin the ball.

2. Explain how this models rotation.

3. Continue to hold the basketball and walk one complete circle around another student in your class.

4. How does this model revolution?

Observe
In your Science Journal, compare and contrast rotation and revolution.

Before You Read

FOLDABLES
Reading & Study Skills

Making a Question Study Fold **Make the following Foldable to organize and answer questions as you read this chapter.**

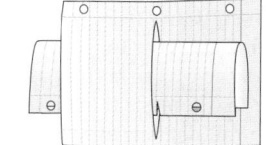

1. Stack two sheets of notebook paper so the long side of both sheets is at the top. Fold both sheets in half from the left side to the right side. Unfold and separate the sheets of paper.

2. Take one sheet of paper and cut along the fold line, starting in the center of the fold and stopping at both margin lines as shown.

3. Place the second sheet in front so the long side is at the top. Cut along the fold line from the bottom and from the top, stopping at the margin lines.

4. Insert the second sheet into the cut of the first sheet. Unfold the inserted sheet; align the cuts along the fold of the other.

Sun
Earth
Moon

5. Fold both sheets in half to make a book as shown. On the first two pages, record questions you have about the Sun, on the middle two pages, questions about Earth, and on the last two pages, questions about the Moon. As you read the chapter, answer your questions.

1 Earth

1 Motivate

Bellringer Transparency

Display the Section Focus Transparency for Section 1. Use the accompanying Transparency Activity Master. L2

ELL

Tie to Prior Knowledge

Tell students that every planet has unique physical properties. Ask students to brainstorm physical properties of Earth. Start them out by writing "Earth is nearly spherical" on the board. Accept other student responses. Review responses after finishing the section.

SECTION

1 Earth

As You Read

What You'll Learn
- **Examine** Earth's physical characteristics.
- **Differentiate** between rotation and revolution.
- **Discuss** what causes seasons to change.

Vocabulary

sphere   ellipse
axis   solstice
rotation   equinox
revolution

Why It's Important
Earth's movements cause night and day and the changing of seasons.

Figure 1
For many years, sailors have observed that the tops of ships coming across the horizon appear first. This suggests that Earth is spherical, not flat, as was once widely believed.

Properties of Earth

You awaken at daybreak to catch the Sun "rising" from the dark horizon. Then it begins its daily "journey" from east to west across the sky. Finally the Sun "sinks" out of view as night falls. Is the Sun moving—or are you?

It wasn't long ago that people thought Earth was the center of the universe. It was widely believed that the Sun revolved around Earth, which stood still. It is now common knowledge that the Sun only appears to be moving around Earth. Because Earth spins as it revolves around the Sun, it creates the illusion that the Sun is moving across the sky.

Another mistaken idea about Earth concerned its shape. Even as recently as the days of Christopher Columbus, many uneducated people believed Earth to be flat. Because of this, they were afraid that if they sailed far enough out to sea, they would fall off the edge of the world. How do you know this isn't true? How have scientists determined the true shape of Earth?

Spherical Shape A round, three-dimensional object is called a **sphere** (SFIHR). Its surface is the same distance from its center at all points. Some common examples of spheres are basketballs and tennis balls.

In the late twentieth century, artificial satellites and space probes sent back pictures showing that Earth is spherical. Much earlier, Aristotle, a Greek astronomer and philosopher who lived around 350 B.C., suspected that Earth was spherical. He observed that Earth cast a curved shadow on the Moon during an eclipse.

In addition to Aristotle, other individuals made observations that indicated Earth's spherical shape. Early sailors, for example, noticed that approaching ships came into view a little at a time, as shown in **Figure 1.**

672 CHAPTER 23 The Sun-Earth-Moon System

Section ✓Assessment Planner

PORTFOLIO
Life Science Integration, p. 673
PERFORMANCE ASSESSMENT
Try at Home MiniLAB, p. 674
Skill Builder Activities, p. 677
See page 698 for more options.

CONTENT ASSESSMENT
Section, p. 678
Challenge, p. 677
Chapter, pp. 698–699

Additional Evidence Sailors also noticed changes in how the night sky looked. As they sailed north or south, the North Star moved higher or lower in the sky. The best explanation was a spherical Earth.

Today, most people know that Earth is spherical. They also know all objects are attracted by gravity to the center of a spherical Earth. Astronauts have clearly seen the spherical shape of Earth. However, it bulges slightly at the equator and is somewhat flattened at the poles, so it is not a perfect sphere.

Rotation Earth's **axis** is the imaginary vertical line around which Earth spins. This line cuts directly through the center of Earth, as shown in the illustration accompanying **Table 1.** The poles are located at the north and south ends of Earth's axis. The spinning of Earth on its axis, called **rotation,** causes day and night to occur. Here is how it works. As Earth rotates, you can see the Sun come into view at daybreak. Earth continues to spin, making it seem as if the Sun moves across the sky until it sets at night. During night, your area of Earth has rotated so that it is on the opposite side as the Sun. Because of this, the Sun is no longer visible to you. Earth continues to rotate steadily, and eventually the Sun comes into view again the next morning. One complete rotation takes about 24 h, or one day. How many rotations does Earth complete during one year? As you can infer from **Table 1,** it completes about 365 rotations during its one-year journey around the Sun.

> ✓ **Reading Check**   *Why does the Sun seem to rise and set?*

Life Science
INTEGRATION

Suppose that Earth's rotation took twice as long as it does now. In your Science Journal, predict how conditions such as global temperatures, work schedules, plant growth, and other factors might change under these circumstances.

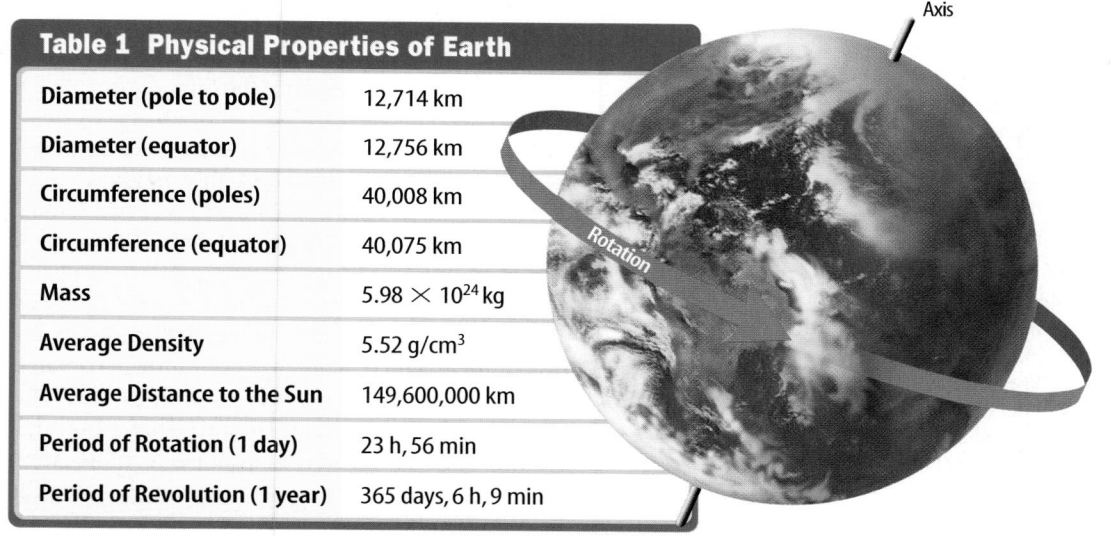

Axis

Rotation

Table 1 Physical Properties of Earth	
Diameter (pole to pole)	12,714 km
Diameter (equator)	12,756 km
Circumference (poles)	40,008 km
Circumference (equator)	40,075 km
Mass	5.98×10^{24} kg
Average Density	5.52 g/cm³
Average Distance to the Sun	149,600,000 km
Period of Rotation (1 day)	23 h, 56 min
Period of Revolution (1 year)	365 days, 6 h, 9 min

2 Teach

Properties of Earth

Life Science
INTEGRATION

Students should infer that global daytime temperatures would be higher as a result of longer hours of sunlight, and nighttime temperatures would be cooler because of more continuous hours of darkness. Students might also suggest that people would have different daily habits, perhaps taking naps during the longer day, and having periods of activity in the longer night. In Alaska, the growing season is short, but the long hours of summer sunlight are good for the production of oats, barley, potatoes, hay, and cool-climate vegetables. Many people in Alaska try to maintain a "normal" 24-hour cycle, even during periods of extended light or darkness. This necessitates adding additional lighting during the dark periods and having black-out shades to provide artificial night during the light periods.

> ✓ **Reading Check**

Answer because Earth spins

Visual Learning

Table 1 Challenge students to use the information in **Table 1** to prove that Earth is not a perfect sphere. If Earth were a perfect sphere, the diameter would be the same at the equator and from pole to pole. Earth's diameter at the equator is slightly larger than its diameter at the poles. Likewise, Earth's circumference is not the same all around. It is slightly larger at the equator than at the poles.

Resource Manager

Chapter Resources Booklet
   Transparency Activity, p. 44
   Directed Reading for Content Mastery, pp. 17, 18
   Note-taking Worksheets, pp. 31–34

Cultural Diversity

Babylonian Astronomers Babylonian records of solar eclipses have been used to document the slowing of Earth's rotation. The eclipses could have occurred on those dates only if Earth were rotating slightly faster in the past than it is now. Have students research other areas of interest of these early astronomers. dates of appearance of the new Moon (when each month began), lunar and solar calendars, weather forecasting

Properties of Earth,
continued

Quick Demo

Make a sketch of Earth on an overhead transparency. Label the geographic poles. Place the transparency over a bar magnet on an overhead projector. Rotate the transparency so that Earth's makes an 11.5° angle with the magnet. Sprinkle iron filings over the transparency and tap it lightly. Ask students how this model is similar to Earth and its magnetic field.

TRY AT HOME
Mini LAB

Purpose Students make simple compasses. L1 ELL

Kinesthetic

Materials plastic foam cup, scissors, bar magnet, sewing needle, tape, plate, water

Teaching Strategy Have students use a compass to locate north before beginning.

Safety Precautions Warn students to use sharp objects carefully. Collect and count needles before the end of class.

Analysis
1. The needle lines up with Earth's magnetic field, with the needle oriented roughly north-south.
2. There are no landmarks on the open ocean. Simple compasses could have helped sailors navigate by indicating north.

Assessment

Process Ask students to write an operational definition of a compass. The needle of a compass helps you determine direction by pointing toward the north pole in the northern hemisphere. Use **PASC**, p. 159.

TRY AT HOME
Mini LAB

Making Your Own Compass

Procedure
WARNING: *Use care when handling sharp objects.*
1. Cut off the bottom of a **plastic foam cup** to make a polystyrene disk.
2. Magnetize a **sewing needle** by continuously stroking the needle in the same direction with a **magnet** for 1 min.
3. **Tape** the needle to the center of the foam disk.
4. Fill a **plate** with **water** and float the disk, needle side up, in the water.

Analysis
1. What happened to the needle and disk when you placed them in the water? Why did this happen?
2. Infer how ancient sailors might have used magnets to help them navigate on the open seas.

Text Question Answer
People using the map for navigation would need to adjust for the movement of the magnetic pole.

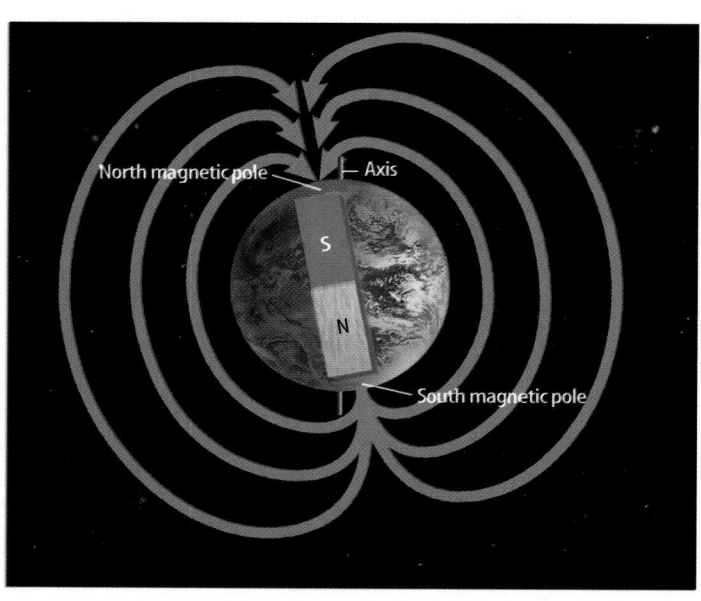

Figure 2
Earth's magnetic field is similar to that of a bar magnet, almost as if Earth contained a giant magnet. Earth's magnetic axis is angled 11.5 degrees from its rotational axis.

Magnetic Field Scientists hypothesize that the movement of material inside Earth's core, along with Earth's rotation, generates a magnetic field. This magnetic field is much like that of a bar magnet. Earth has a north and a south magnetic pole, just as a bar magnet has opposite magnetic poles at each of its ends. When you sprinkle iron shavings over a bar magnet, the shavings align with the magnetic field of the magnet. As you can see in **Figure 2**, Earth's magnetic field is similar—almost as if Earth contained a giant bar magnet. Earth's magnetic field protects you from harmful solar radiation by trapping many charged particles from the Sun.

Magnetic Axis When you observe a compass needle pointing north, you are seeing evidence of Earth's magnetic field. Earth's magnetic axis, the line joining its north and south magnetic poles, does not align with its rotational axis. The magnetic axis is inclined at an angle of 11.5° to the rotational axis. If you followed a compass needle, you would end up at the magnetic north pole rather than the rotational north pole.

The location of the magnetic poles has been shown to change slowly over time. The magnetic poles move around the rotational (geographic) poles in an irregular way. This movement can be significant over decades. Many maps include information about the position of the magnetic north pole at the time the map was made. Why would this information be important?

Curriculum Connection

Geography Challenge students to draw a map showing the location of both the geographic and magnetic north poles. The geographic north pole is in the Arctic Ocean, about 725 km (450 mi.) north of Greenland. The magnetic north pole, to which magnetic compasses point, is in the Queen Elizabeth Islands of northern Canada, at about 78°27′ N, 104°24′ W. L3

Logical-Mathematical

What causes changing seasons?

Flowers bloom as the days get warmer. The Sun appears higher in the sky, and daylight lasts longer. Spring seems like a fresh, new beginning. What causes these wonderful changes?

Orbiting the Sun You learned earlier that Earth's rotation causes day and night. Another important motion is **revolution,** which is Earth's yearly orbit around the Sun. Just as the Moon is Earth's satellite, Earth is a satellite of the Sun. If Earth's orbit were a circle with the Sun at the center, Earth would maintain a constant distance from the Sun. However, this is not the case. Earth's orbit is an **ellipse** (ee LIHPS)—an elongated, closed curve. The Sun is not at the center of the ellipse but is a little toward one end. Because of this, the distance between Earth and the Sun changes during Earth's yearlong orbit. Earth gets closest to the Sun—about 147 million km away—around January 3. The farthest Earth gets from the Sun is about 152 million km away. This happens around July 4 each year.

> ✔ **Reading Check** *What is an ellipse?*

Does this elliptical orbit cause seasonal temperatures on Earth? If it did, you would expect the warmest days to be in January. You know this isn't the case in the northern hemisphere, something else must cause the change.

Even though Earth is closest to the Sun in January, the change in distance is small. Earth is exposed to almost the same amount of Sun all year. But the amount of solar energy any one place on Earth receives varies greatly during the year. Next, you will learn why.

A Tilted Axis Earth's axis is tilted 23.5° from a line drawn perpendicular to the plane of its orbit. It is this tilt that causes seasons. Daylight hours are longer for the hemisphere, or half of Earth, that is tilted toward the Sun. Think of how early it gets dark in the winter compared to the summer. As shown in **Figure 3,** the hemisphere that is tilted toward the Sun receives more hours of sunlight each day than the hemisphere that is tilted away from the Sun. The longer period of sunlight is one reason summer is warmer than winter, but it is not the only reason.

Figure 3
In summer, the northern hemisphere is tilted toward the Sun. Notice that the north pole is always lit during the summer. *Why are daylight hours longer in the summer than in the winter?*

North Pole

What causes changing seasons?

✔ **Reading Check**

Answer An elongated, closed curve

Visual Learning

Figure 3 How long do daylight hours last at the South Pole when the northern hemisphere experiences summer? The South Pole is always in darkness.

Caption Answer
Figure 3 Because the hemisphere experiencing summer is tilted toward the Sun

Fun Fact

Earth's orientation in space changes with time. Its axis now points toward Polaris, the North Star. In about 13,000 years, it will point toward Vega. This change is the result of Earth's slow "wobble" on its axis.

Resource Manager

Chapter Resources Booklet
MiniLAB, p. 3
Lab Activity, pp. 11–12
Enrichment, p. 28

Inclusion Strategies

Learning Disabled Have students draw a picture or write a short paragraph describing their favorite season of the year. Encourage students to include science-connected observations, such as weather conditions, the condition of plant and animal life, and the look of the sky. Display their work in the classroom. L1 ELL
LS Visual-Spatial

What causes changing seasons?, continued

Quick Demo

Have students observe the light from an overhead projector as it strikes a wall straight on. Then slant the lens so that the light hits the wall at an angle. **How is this similar to the way sunlight strikes areas of Earth during different seasons?** When light hits straight on, it covers a smaller area and is stronger. When it hits at an angle, it covers a larger area but is less intense. On Earth, sunlight hits more directly in summer and more at an angle in winter.

Solstices

Discussion

Remind students that seasons are reversed in the southern hemisphere. **How would your life be different if midsummer came in January and midwinter came in July?** Students might mention the change in how holidays are celebrated, when school is in session, or when vacations are taken. L2

IS Interpersonal

Figure 4
During the summer solstice in the northern hemisphere, the Sun is directly over the tropic of Cancer, the latitude line at 23.5° N latitude. During the winter solstice, the Sun is directly over the tropic of Capricorn, the latitude line at 23.5° S latitude. At fall and spring equinoxes, the Sun is directly over the equator.

Radiation from the Sun Earth's tilt also causes the Sun's radiation to strike the hemispheres at different angles. The hemisphere tilted toward the Sun receives more direct rays, thus more total solar radiation than the hemisphere tilted away from the Sun. In the hemisphere tilted away from the Sun, the Sun appears low in the sky, and its rays are slanted.

Summer occurs in the hemisphere tilted toward the Sun, where the Sun appears high in the sky. Its radiation strikes Earth at a higher angle and for longer periods of time. The hemisphere receiving less radiation experiences winter.

Solstices

The **solstice** is the day when the Sun reaches its greatest distance north or south of the equator. In the northern hemisphere, the summer solstice occurs on June 21 or 22, and the winter solstice occurs on December 21 or 22. Both solstices are illustrated in **Figure 4.** In the southern hemisphere, the winter solstice is in June and the summer solstice is in December. The summer solstice has more daylight hours than any other day of the year. After the summer solstice, days begin to get shorter. The winter solstice is the shortest day of the year, but after the winter solstice, the period of sunlight grows longer each day.

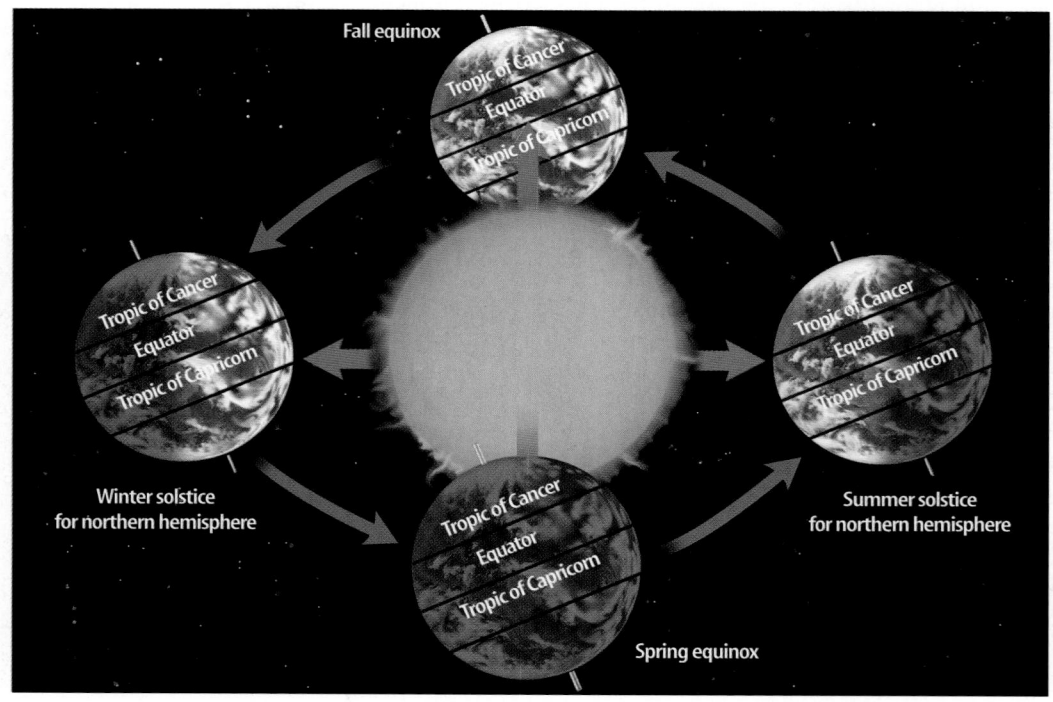

Fall equinox
Tropic of Cancer
Equator
Tropic of Capricorn

Winter solstice for northern hemisphere
Tropic of Cancer
Equator
Tropic of Capricorn

Summer solstice for northern hemisphere
Tropic of Cancer
Equator
Tropic of Capricorn

Spring equinox
Tropic of Cancer
Equator
Tropic of Capricorn

Curriculum Connection

History Discuss with students why we do certain things during certain seasons. For example, ask students if they know why school in the United States usually lasts from fall through spring and is (in most areas) closed in summer. This custom dates back to when the United States was an agrarian society and children were needed to help with farm work in late spring and summer. Have students research the historical ties of other seasonal activities.

Resource Manager

Chapter Resources Booklet
Transparency Activity, pp. 47–48
Lab Activity, pp. 13–14
Reinforcement, p. 25

Equinoxes

An **equinox** (EE kwuh nahks) occurs when the Sun is directly above Earth's equator. Because of the tilt of Earth's axis, the Sun's position relative to the equator changes constantly. Most of the time, the Sun is either north or south of the equator, but two times each year it is directly over it, resulting in the spring and fall equinoxes. As you can see in **Figure 4,** on the equinox the Sun's most direct rays shine on the equator.

During an equinox, the number of daylight hours and nighttime hours is equal all over the world. Also at this time, neither the northern hemisphere nor the southern hemisphere is tilted toward the Sun.

In the northern hemisphere, the Sun reaches the spring equinox on March 20 or 21, and the fall equinox occurs on September 22 or 23. In the southern hemisphere, the equinoxes are reversed. Spring occurs in September and fall occurs in March.

Earth Data Review As you have learned, Earth is a sphere that rotates on a tilted axis. This rotation causes day and night. Earth's tilted axis and its revolution around the Sun cause the seasons. One Earth revolution takes one year. In the next section, you will read how the Moon rotates on its axis and revolves around Earth.

SCIENCE *Online*

Collect Data Visit the Glencoe Science Web site at **science.glencoe.com** for data about seasons. How are seasons different in other parts of the world? Make a poster summarizing what you learn.

Section 1 Assessment

1. Why did Aristotle think Earth was spherical?
2. Compare and contrast rotation and revolution.
3. Describe how Earth's distance from the Sun changes throughout the year. When is Earth closest to the Sun?
4. Why is it summer in Earth's northern hemisphere at the same time it is winter in the southern hemisphere?
5. **Think Critically** Table 1 lists Earth's distance from the Sun as an average. Why isn't an exact measurement available for this distance?

Skill Builder Activities

6. **Recognizing Cause and Effect** Answer these questions about the Sun-Earth-Moon relationship. **For more help, refer to the** Science Skill Handbook.
   a. What causes seasons on Earth?
   b. Why is the number of daylight and nighttime hours equal during an equinox?
7. **Using an Electronic Spreadsheet** Create a table of Earth's physical properties. Show the following: *diameter, mass, period of rotation,* and *other data*. Then, write a description of Earth based on your table. **For more help, refer to the** Technology Skill Handbook.

SECTION 1 Earth **677**

Answers to Section Assessment

1. Aristotle noted that Earth always cast a round shadow on the Moon during an eclipse.
2. Both are movements. Rotation is a spinning motion, whereas revolution is movement of one body around another.
3. Earth's orbit is elliptical. It is farthest from the Sun around July 4 and closest to the Sun around January 3.
4. The hemisphere tilted toward the Sun has summer; the hemisphere tilted away has winter.
5. Because Earth's orbit is elliptical, Earth's distance from the Sun changes as the planet revolves around it.
6. a. The tilt of Earth's axis and Earth's revolution around the Sun. b. The Sun is directly over the equator; neither hemisphere is tilted toward or away from the Sun.
7. Tables should include the data in Table 1.

Equinoxes

SCIENCE *Online*
Internet Addresses
_____
_____
_____
_____

Explore the Glencoe Science Web site at **science.glencoe.com** to find out more about topics in this section.

3 Assess

Reteach

Darken the room and place a globe next to a light source. Tilt the globe 23.5°. Hold the globe so that its axis points toward and then away from the light. Slowly spin the globe to demonstrate how the amount of light striking each hemisphere changes with the globe's tilt. Reinforce that days are shorter in the northern hemisphere when it is tilted away from the Sun, and longer when it is tilted toward the Sun.
IS Visual-Spatial

Challenge

Have students work in small groups to form explanations for why the hottest day of the year is usually not the longest day. Possible answer: The hottest day usually occurs in mid- to late summer, when the surface has had a chance to retain enough solar energy to produce high temperatures.
IS Logical-Mathematical

✓Assessment

Oral Have each student write a question on the section content. Pair students and have each student ask his or her partner their question. One pair can exchange questions with another pair to extend the activity. Use **PASC,** p. 91.

SECTION

The Moon—
Earth's Satellite

1 Motivate

Bellringer Transparency

Display the Section Focus Transparency for Section 2. Use the accompanying Transparency Activity Master. L2

ELL

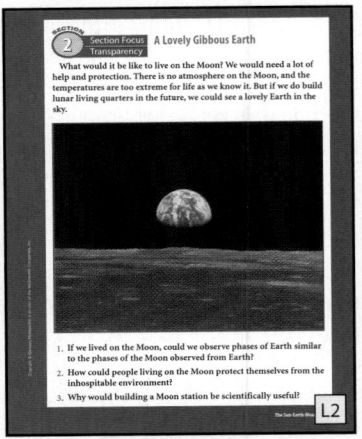

Tie to Prior Knowledge

Ask students to describe a full Moon. round disk in the night sky Have volunteers describe other moon shapes they have seen and draw these shapes on the board. Explain that they will find out why the moon seems to change shape in this section.

Text Question Answer

The Moon's revolution causes different portions of its lighted side to be visible to viewers on Earth.

Caption Answer

Figure 5 Yes; the same side always faces Earth.

The Moon—
Earth's Satellite

As You Read

What You'll Learn
- **Identify** phases of the Moon and their cause.
- **Explain** why solar and lunar eclipses occur.
- **Infer** what the Moon's surface features may reveal about its history.

Vocabulary
moon phase	waning
new moon	solar eclipse
waxing	lunar eclipse
full moon	maria

Why It's Important
Learning about the Moon can teach you about Earth.

Motions of the Moon

Doesn't it seem as if the Moon's shape changes night after night? Sometimes, just after sunset, you can see a full, round Moon low in the sky. Other times, only half of the Moon is visible, and it's high in the sky at sunset. At times, the Moon is even visible during the day. What causes the Moon to change in appearance and position in the sky?

Rotation and Revolution Just as Earth rotates on its axis and revolves around the Sun, the Moon rotates on its axis and revolves around Earth. The Moon's revolution around Earth is responsible for the changes in its appearance. If the Moon rotates on its axis, why can't you see it spin around in space? The reason is that the Moon's rotation takes 27.3 days—the same amount of time it takes to revolve once around Earth. Because these two motions take the same amount of time, the same side of the Moon always faces Earth, as shown in **Figure 5.**

You can demonstrate this by having a friend hold a ball in front of you. Direct your friend to move the ball in a circle around you while keeping the same side of it facing you. Everyone else in the room will see all sides of the ball. You will see only one side.

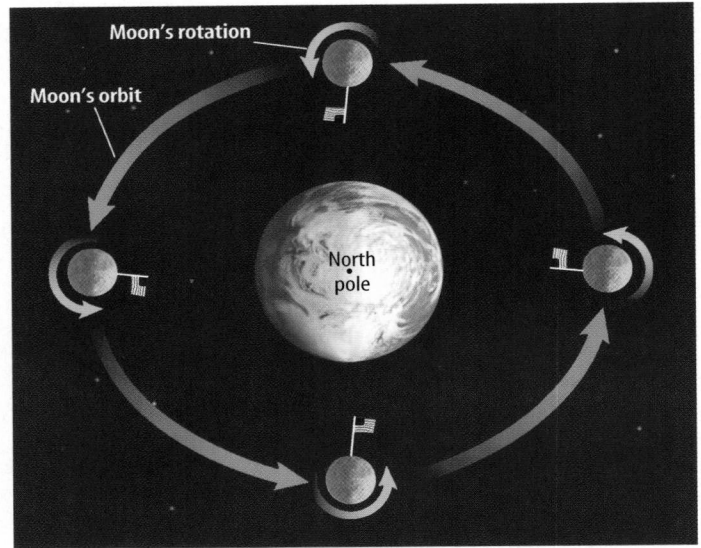

Figure 5
In about one month, the Moon orbits Earth. It also completes one rotation on its axis during the same period. *Does this affect which side of the Moon faces Earth? Explain.*

678 CHAPTER 23 The Sun-Earth-Moon System

Section ✓ *Assessment* Planner

PORTFOLIO	See page 698 for more options.
Science Journal, p. 679	**CONTENT ASSESSMENT**
Activity, p. 682	Section, p. 686
PERFORMANCE ASSESSMENT	Challenge, p. 686
MiniLAB, p. 680	Chapter, pp. 698–699
Problem-Solving Activity, p. 685	
Skill Builder Activities, p. 686	

Reflection of the Sun The Moon seems to shine because its surface reflects sunlight. Just as half of Earth experiences day as the other half experiences night, half of the Moon is lighted while the other half is dark. As the Moon revolves around Earth, you see different portions of its lighted side, causing the Moon's appearance to change.

Phases of the Moon

Moon phases are the different forms that the Moon takes in its appearance from Earth. The phase depends on the relative positions of the Moon, Earth, and the Sun, as seen in **Figure 6** on the next page. A **new moon** occurs when the Moon is between Earth and the Sun. During a new moon, the lighted half of the Moon is facing the Sun and the dark side faces Earth. The Moon is in the sky, but it cannot be seen. The new moon rises and sets with the Sun.

✔ **Reading Check** *Why can't you see a new moon?*

Waxing Phases After a new moon, the phases begin waxing. **Waxing** means that more of the illuminated half of the Moon can be seen each night. About 24 h after a new moon, you can see a thin slice of the Moon. This phase is called the waxing crescent. About a week after a new moon, you can see half of the lighted side of the Moon, or one quarter of the Moon's surface. This is the first quarter phase.

The phases continue to wax. When more than one quarter is visible, it is called waxing *gibbous* after the Latin word for "humpbacked." A **full moon** occurs when all of the Moon's surface facing Earth reflects light.

Waning Phases After a full moon, the phases are said to be waning. When the Moon's phases are **waning,** you see less of its illuminated half each night. Waning gibbous begins just after a full moon. When you can see only half of the lighted side, it is the third-quarter phase. The Moon continues to appear to shrink. Waning crescent occurs just before another new moon. Once again, you can see only a small slice of the Moon.

It takes about 29.5 days for the Moon to complete its cycle of phases. Recall that it takes about 27.3 days for the Moon to revolve around Earth. The discrepancy between these two numbers is due to Earth's revolution. The roughly two extra days are what it takes for the Moon to keep up constantly with Earth as it orbits around the Sun.

Mini LAB

Comparing the Sun and the Moon

Procedure
1. Find an area where you can make a chalk mark on **pavement or another surface.**
2. Tie a piece of **chalk** to one end of a 400-cm-long **string.**
3. Hold the other end of the string to the pavement.
4. Have a friend pull the string tight and walk around you, leaving a mark (the Sun) on the pavement.
5. Draw a 1-cm-diameter circle in the middle of the larger circle (the Moon).

Analysis
1. How big is the Sun compared to the Moon?
2. The diameter of the Sun is 1.39 million km. The diameter of Earth is 12,756 km. Draw two new circles modeling the sizes of the Sun and Earth. What scale did you use?

Resource Manager

Chapter Resources Booklet
Transparency Activity, p. 45
MiniLAB, p. 4
Directed Reading for Content Mastery, p. 19

Science Journal

Phases of the Moon Invite students to write an essay in their Science Journals about the way the Moon looks in the night sky. Essays can include science facts about the Moon as well as students' thoughts on the way the Moon makes them feel. Invite volunteers to share their essays in class. L2  **Intrapersonal** P

Motions of the Moon

Mini LAB

Purpose Students compare the sizes of the Sun, the Moon, and Earth. L2 ELL
LS Logical-Mathematical
Materials meter stick, chalk, string (400 cm)
Teaching Strategy Conduct this activity on a large, paved playground or parking lot.
Analysis
1. The Sun's diameter is about 400 times that of the Moon.
2. The Sun's diameter is about 109 times greater than that of Earth. Scales will vary. The diameters of new circles could be 109 cm (Sun) and 1 cm (Earth).

✔ Assessment

Performance Tell students that the Moon's diameter is 3,476 km, and Earth's is 12,756 km. Have them draw new circles representing the relative sizes of Earth and the Moon. Use **Performance Assessment in the Science Classroom,** p. 127.

Phases of the Moon

✔ **Reading Check**

Answer because the Moon's lighted side is facing away from Earth

Figure 6 **What phase follows full moon?** waning gibbous **New moon?** waxing crescent **During which phase do you think a total solar eclipse could happen?** new moon

Use Science Words

Word Usage Have students write sentences about the Moon's phases using the words wax and wane. Possible answer: Phases wax after a new moon. Once full moon occurs, the phases begin to wane.

IDENTIFYING Misconceptions

Students may think that the Sun lights up different parts of the Moon as the Sun moves through the sky. Refer to page 670F for teaching strategies that address this misconception.

Eclipses

Text Question Answer

The Moon passes directly between the Sun and Earth, blocking the light from the Sun.

✔ Reading Check

Answer The shadow of the Moon falls on a small portion of Earth's surface; the Moon completely blocks the Sun.

Figure 6
The phases of the Moon change during a cycle that lasts about 29.5 days.

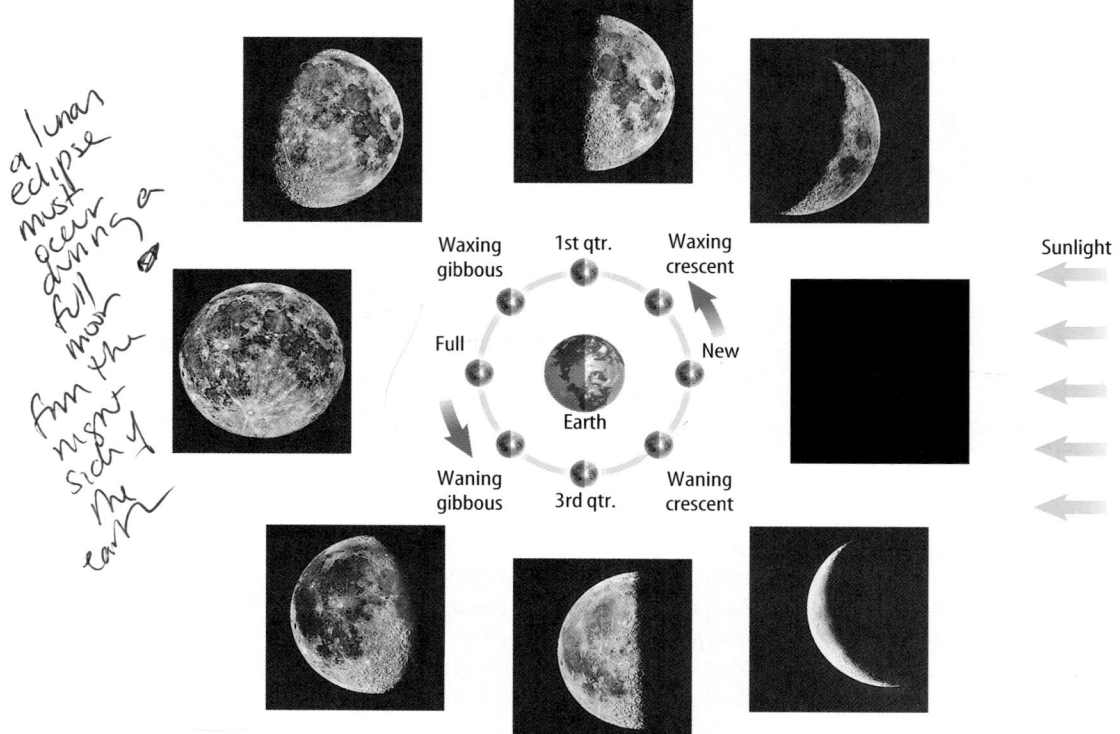

Figure 7
Only the outer portion of the Sun's atmosphere is visible during a total solar eclipse. It looks like a halo around the Moon.

Eclipses

Imagine living 10,000 years ago. You are foraging for nuts and fruit when unexpectedly the Sun disappears from the sky. The darkness lasts only a short time, and the Sun soon returns to full brightness. You know something strange has happened, but you don't know why. It will be almost 8,000 years before anyone can explain what you just experienced.

The event just described was a total solar eclipse (ih KLIPS), shown in **Figure 7.** Today, most people know what causes such eclipses, but without this knowledge, they would have been terrifying events. During a solar eclipse, many animals act as if it is nighttime. Cows return to their barns and chickens go to sleep. What causes the day to become night and then change back into day?

✔ Reading Check   *What happens during a total solar eclipse?*

✔ Guided Reading

Write-Draw-Discuss This strategy encourages students to actively participate in reading and lectures, assimilating content creatively. Have students write about an idea, clarify it, then make an illustration or drawing. Ask students to share responses with the class and display several examples. Have students Write-Draw-Discuss about a concept in this section.

Resource Manager

Cultural Diversity, p. 29

What causes an eclipse? The revolution of the Moon causes eclipses. Eclipses occur when Earth or the Moon temporarily blocks the sunlight from reaching the other. Sometimes, during a new moon, the Moon's shadow falls on Earth and causes a solar eclipse. During a full moon, Earth's shadow can be cast on the Moon, resulting in a lunar eclipse.

An eclipse can occur only when the Sun, the Moon, and Earth are lined up perfectly. Because the Moon's orbit is not in the same plane as Earth's orbit around the Sun, eclipses occur only a few times each year.

Eclipses of the Sun A **solar eclipse** occurs when the Moon moves directly between the Sun and Earth and casts its shadow over part of Earth, as seen in **Figure 8.** Depending on where you are on Earth, you may experience a total eclipse or a partial eclipse. The darkest portion of the Moon's shadow is called the umbra (UM bruh). A person standing within the umbra experiences a total solar eclipse. During a total solar eclipse, the only visible portion of the Sun is a pearly white glow around the edge of the eclipsing Moon.

Surrounding the umbra is a lighter shadow on Earth's surface called the penumbra (puh NUM bruh). Persons standing in the penumbra experience a partial solar eclipse. **WARNING:** *Regardless of where you stand, never look directly at the Sun during an eclipse. The light can permanently damage your eyes.*

SCIENCE *Online*

Collect Data Visit the Glencoe Science Web site at **science.glencoe.com** for more information about solar and lunar eclipses due to occur over the next several years. Make a chart showing when and where they will occur.

Figure 8
Only a small area of Earth experiences a total solar eclipse during the eclipse event.

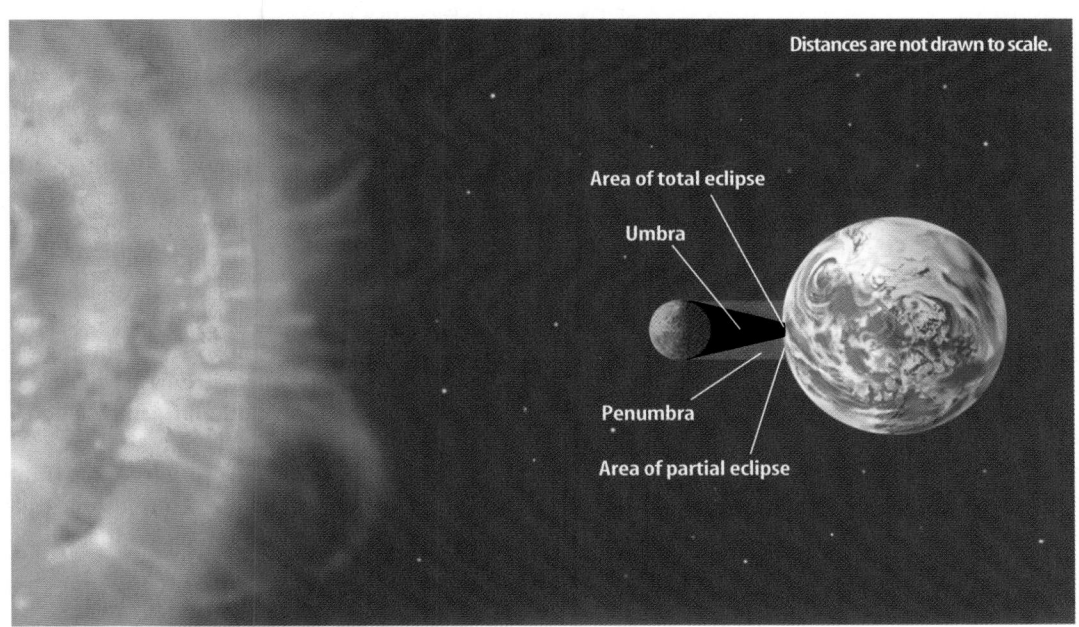

Distances are not drawn to scale.

Area of total eclipse
Umbra
Penumbra
Area of partial eclipse

SECTION 2 The Moon—Earth's Satellite **681**

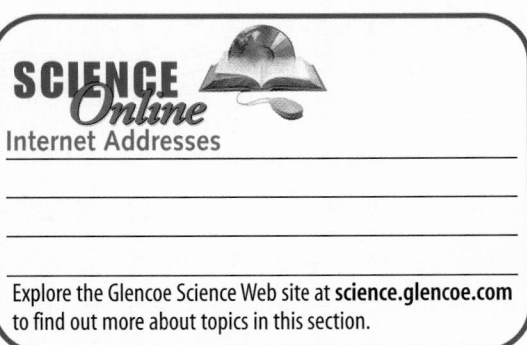

Eclipses, continued

Some students may think that having one or more moons is a feature of *all* planets. Explain that not all planets have moons. In our solar system, neither Mercury nor Venus has a moon.

Discussion

Why can a lunar eclipse only be seen on the night side of Earth? A lunar eclipse occurs when the Moon moves into Earth's shadow. Earth's shadow is cast on the night side of the planet, opposite the side facing the Sun. Thus, a lunar eclipse is only visible on the night side of Earth. (Also, it must occur during a full moon, when the moon is on the opposite side of Earth from the Sun.)

Activity

Have students sketch and label the positions of the Sun, the Moon, and Earth during a solar and a lunar eclipse. L1
Visual-Spatial P

Figure 9
These photographs show the Moon moving from right to left into Earth's umbra, then out again.

Figure 10
During a total lunar eclipse, Earth's shadow blocks light coming from the Sun.

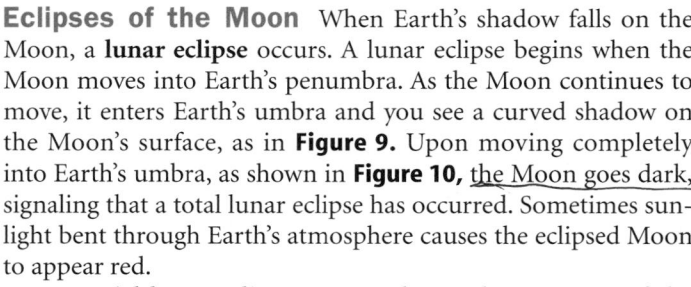
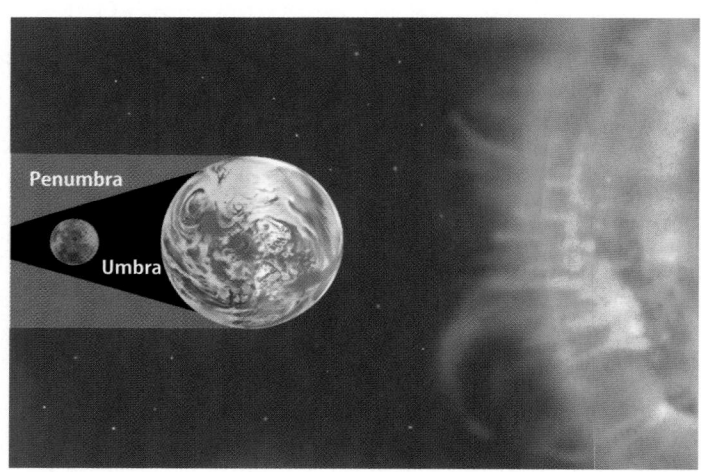

Penumbra

Umbra

Eclipses of the Moon When Earth's shadow falls on the Moon, a **lunar eclipse** occurs. A lunar eclipse begins when the Moon moves into Earth's penumbra. As the Moon continues to move, it enters Earth's umbra and you see a curved shadow on the Moon's surface, as in **Figure 9.** Upon moving completely into Earth's umbra, as shown in **Figure 10,** the Moon goes dark, signaling that a total lunar eclipse has occurred. Sometimes sunlight bent through Earth's atmosphere causes the eclipsed Moon to appear red.

A partial lunar eclipse occurs when only a portion of the Moon moves into Earth's umbra. The remainder of the Moon is in Earth's penumbra and, therefore, receives some direct sunlight. A partial lunar eclipse also occurs when the Moon is totally within Earth's penumbra. However, it is difficult to tell when a partial lunar eclipse occurs because some direct sunlight is falling on the side of the Moon facing Earth.

A total lunar eclipse can be seen by anyone on the nighttime side of Earth where the Moon is not hidden by clouds. In contrast, only a lucky few people get to witness a total solar eclipse. Only those people in the small region where the Moon's umbra strikes Earth can witness one.

682   CHAPTER 23 The Sun-Earth-Moon System

LAB DEMONSTRATION

Purpose to reinforce how solar eclipses occur
Materials marble, tennis ball
Preparation Obtain marbles and tennis balls.
Procedure Hold the tennis ball at arm's length, and hold the marble in front of the ball. Close one eye, and slowly move the marble toward your open eye. Observe what happens.

Expected Outcome As the marble nears the face. Less and less of the ball is visible until it is no longer seen.

Assessment

What do the marble, the tennis ball, and your open eye represent?
Marble—Moon; ball—Sun; open eye—observer on Earth **Why did the "Sun" disappear?** The moon is closer to Earth than the Sun. It is able to block the Sun when it passes directly between it and Earth.

The Moon's Surface

When you look at the Moon, as shown in **Figure 12** on the next page, you can see many depressions called craters. Meteorites, asteroids, and comets striking the Moon's surface created most of these craters, which formed early in the Moon's history. Upon impact, cracks may have formed in the Moon's crust, allowing lava to reach the surface and fill up the large craters. The resulting dark, flat regions are called **maria** (MAHR ee uh). The igneous rocks of the maria are 3 billion to 4 billion years old. So far, they are the youngest rocks to be found on the Moon. This indicates that craters formed after the Moon's surface originally cooled. The maria formed early enough in the Moon's history that molten material still remained in the Moon's interior. The Moon once must have been as geologically active as Earth is today. Before the Moon cooled to the current condition, the interior separated into distinct layers.

Inside the Moon

Earthquakes allow scientists to learn about Earth's interior. In a similar way, scientists use instruments such as the one in **Figure 11A** to study moonquakes. The data they have received have led to the construction of several models of the Moon's interior. One such model, shown in **Figure 11B,** suggests that the Moon's crust is about 60 km thick on the side facing Earth. On the far side, it is thought to be about 150 km thick. Under the crust, a solid mantle may extend to a depth of 1,000 km. A partly molten zone of the mantle may extend even farther down. Below this mantle may lie a solid, iron-rich core.

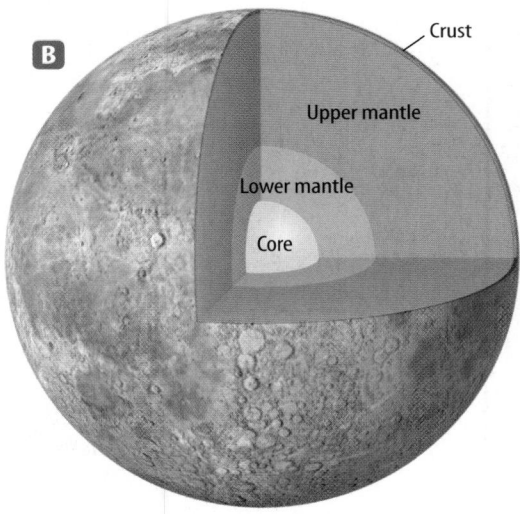

Crust
Upper mantle
Lower mantle
Core

B

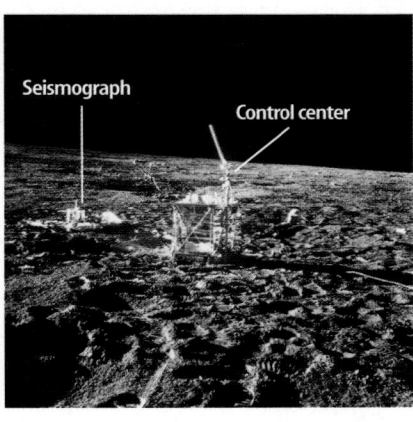

A

Seismograph

Control center

Figure 11
A Equipment, such as the seismograph left on the Moon by the *Apollo 12* mission, helps scientists study moonquakes.
B Models of the Moon's interior were created from data obtained by scientists studying moonquakes.

The Moon's Surface

Activity

Provide each group of four students a map of the Moon's surface. Have students identify and describe key surface features and explain how each might have formed. L2 COOP LEARN

Use Science Words

Word Origin Ask students to research the origin of the word *month* and write a short paragraph summarizing their findings. The word *month* comes from the same root as *Moon*. It is a period of time that can be measured by the movement of the Moon.

Inside the Moon

**Physics
INTEGRATION**

The speed and direction of waves are affected by where and how they are generated and the density of the materials they move through. Some waves will not travel through liquid. If scientists know the speed at which quake waves move through various materials, they might be able to tell what type of material waves on another body, such as the Moon, are moving through by measuring their speed. If certain waves appear to stop in their tracks, it's an indication they have hit liquid rock.

Discussion

What might cause quakes on the Moon? Possible answers: objects hitting the Moon's surface; geological processes, such as the movement of magma, inside the Moon

---

Cultural Diversity

Lunar Calendars The Nuer, a group of seminomadic people in East Africa, base their calendar on full Moons, each of which has a name that corresponds to an activity. For example, in *Kur*, the year's first cattle camps are made. In *Dwat*, the Nuer break camp and return home. Challenge students to discover other cultures that use lunar calendars. Chinese, Islamic, and Hebrew calendars are lunar calendars.

NATIONAL GEOGRAPHIC

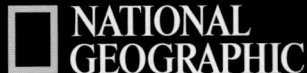

Visualizing the Moon's Surface

Have students examine the pictures and read the captions. Then ask the following questions.

How does the landing site chosen for Apollo 16 appear different from the other Apollo landing sites? Apollo 16 is the only one with a landing site obviously outside of the "seas." It is clearly placed in a mountainous region. However, Apollo 14 also landed in highlands.

Which do you think formed first: the craters or the "seas"? Because there are few craters in the "sea" regions, they must have formed after the asteroid bombardments that formed the craters.

What do the crater names seem to reflect? They are named for great scientists and philosophers.

Activity

Have groups of students write poems about the Apollo missions. Each poem should convey information about the missions, such as where they landed and what they did. Have students read the poems aloud in class.
L2 COOP LEARN LS **Linguistic**

Extension

Challenge students to research the names of moon craters not shown in this image. Have them choose five people for whom craters are named and research their contributions to modern thinking. Have them make and present an informational poster.
L2 ELL LS **Visual-Spatial**

NATIONAL GEOGRAPHIC **VISUALIZING THE MOON'S SURFACE**

Figure 12

By looking through binoculars, you can see many of the features on the surface of the Moon. These include craters that are hundreds of kilometers wide, light-colored mountains, and darker patches that early astronomers called maria (Latin for "seas"). However, as the NASA Apollo missions discovered, these so-called seas do not contain water. In fact, maria (singular, mare) are flat, dry areas formed by ancient lava flows. Some of the Moon's geographic features are shown below, along with the landing sites of Apollo missions sent to investigate Earth's closest neighbor in space.

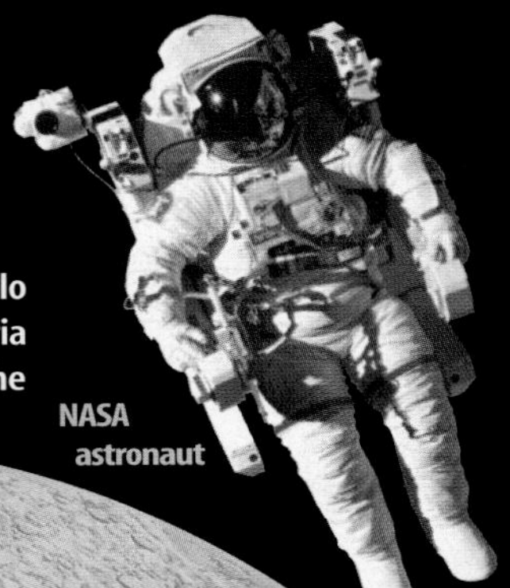
NASA astronaut

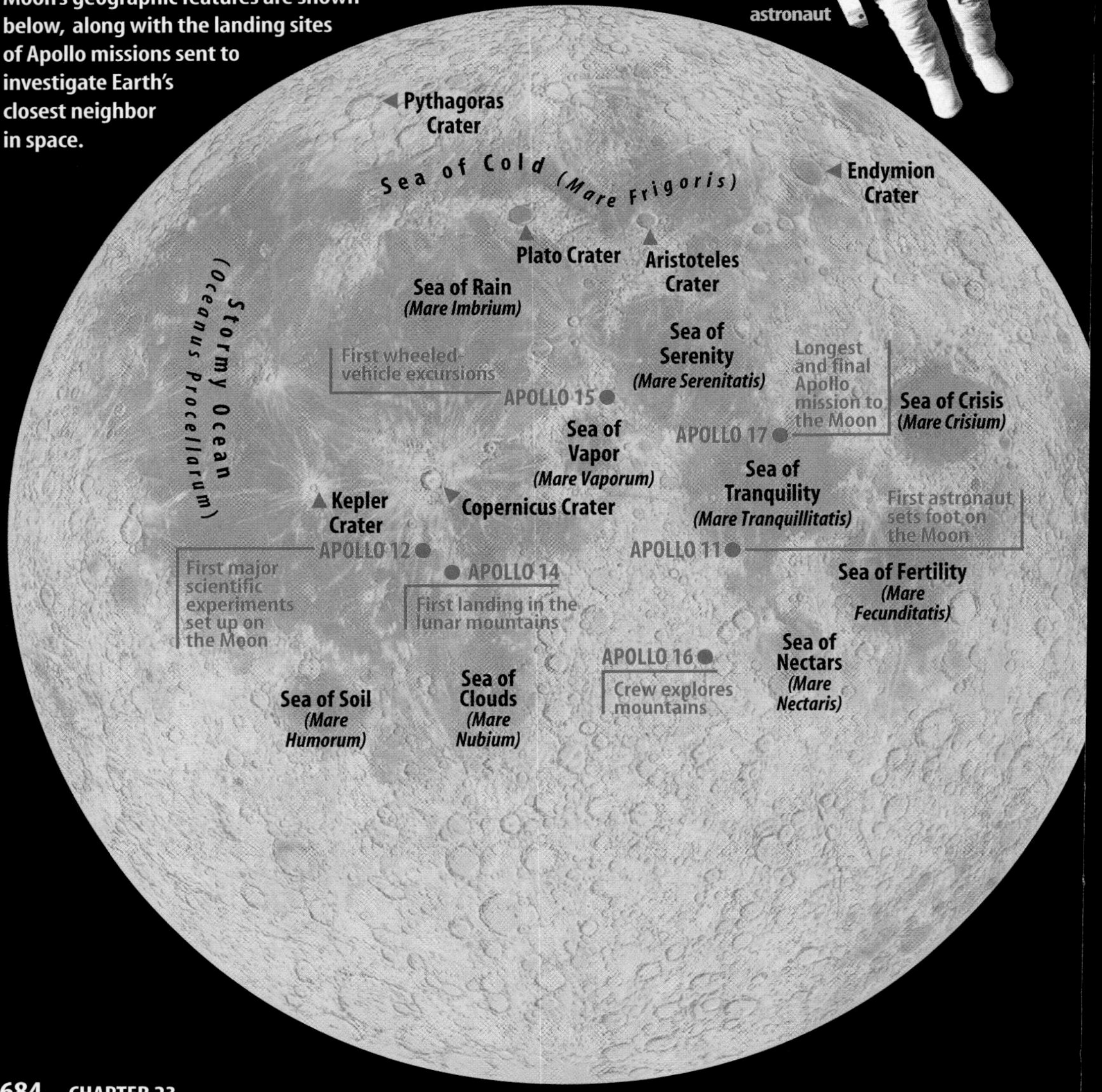
Pythagoras Crater
Sea of Cold (Mare Frigoris)
Endymion Crater
Plato Crater
Aristoteles Crater
Sea of Rain (Mare Imbrium)
Stormy Ocean (Oceanus Procellarum)
First wheeled vehicle excursions
APOLLO 15
Sea of Serenity (Mare Serenitatis)
Longest and final Apollo mission to the Moon
APOLLO 17
Sea of Crisis (Mare Crisium)
Sea of Vapor (Mare Vaporum)
Sea of Tranquility (Mare Tranquillitatis)
First astronaut sets foot on the Moon
Kepler Crater
Copernicus Crater
APOLLO 12
APOLLO 11
APOLLO 14
First major scientific experiments set up on the Moon
First landing in the lunar mountains
Sea of Fertility (Mare Fecunditatis)
APOLLO 16
Crew explores mountains
Sea of Nectars (Mare Nectaris)
Sea of Soil (Mare Humorum)
Sea of Clouds (Mare Nubium)

684 CHAPTER 23

Resource Manager

Cultural Diversity, p. 71

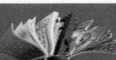

A A Mars-sized object collided with Earth.

B The blast ejected material from both objects into space.

C A ring of gas and debris formed around Earth.

D Particles in the ring joined together to form the Moon.

The Moon's Origin

Before the *Apollo* space missions in the 1960s and 1970s, there were three leading theories about the Moon's origin. According to one theory, the Moon was captured by Earth's gravity. Another held that material surrounding Earth condensed to produce the Moon. An alternative theory proposed that Earth ejected molten material that became the Moon.

The Impact Theory The data gathered by the *Apollo* missions have led many scientists to support a new theory, known as the impact theory. It states that the Moon formed billions of years ago from condensing gas and debris thrown off when Earth collided with a Mars-sized object as shown in **Figure 13.**

Figure 13
According to the impact theory, a Mars-sized object collided with Earth around 4.6 billion years ago. Vaporized materials ejected by the collision began orbiting Earth and quickly consolidated into the Moon.

Problem-Solving Activity

What will you use to survive on the Moon?

You have crash-landed on the Moon. It will take one day to reach a moon colony on foot. The side of the Moon that you are on will be facing away from the Sun during your entire trip. You manage to salvage the following items from your wrecked ship: food, rope, solar-powered heating unit, battery-operated heating unit, oxygen tanks, map of the constellations, compass, matches, water, solar-powered radio transmitter, three flashlights, signal mirror, and binoculars.

Identifying the Problem

The Moon lacks a magnetic field and has no atmosphere. How do the Moon's physical properties and the lack of sunlight affect your decisions?

Solving the Problem
1. Which items will be of no use to you? Which items will you take with you?
2. Describe why each of the salvaged items is useful or not useful.

SECTION 2   The Moon—Earth's Satellite   **685**

The Moon's Origin,
continued

✔ **Reading Check**

Answer These studies have helped scientists draw conclusions about Earth's shape, the movement of Earth and the Moon around the Sun, and the presence of surface features on bodies other than Earth.

③ Assess

Reteach

Have groups of three students use a globe, a tennis ball, and a large beach ball to model solar and lunar eclipses. L1 ELL
 Kinesthetic

Challenge

Have students research why early theories about the origin of the Moon are not supported by *Apollo* mission data. Possible answer: Mineral composition and density of Moon rocks were different than expected for each proposed theory.

✔Assessment

Process Assess students' abilities to recall and organize information about the Moon by having them draw a spider concept map. "The Moon" should be at the center of the concept map, with related topics radiating around it. Subtopics should branch off the main topics. See the Science Skill Handbook. Use **PASC,** p. 161. P

Figure 14
Moon rocks collected by astronauts provide scientists with information about the Moon and Earth.

The Moon in History Regardless of how the Moon formed, it has played an important role. Studying the Moon's phases and eclipses led to the conclusion that both Earth and the Moon were in motion around the Sun. The curved shadow Earth casts on the Moon indicated to early scientists that Earth was spherical. When Galileo first turned his telescope toward the Moon, he found a surface scarred by craters and maria. Before that time, many people believed that all planetary bodies were perfectly smooth and lacking surface features.

 **Reading Check** *How has observing the Moon been important to science?*

More recently, actual Moon rocks became available for scientists to study, as seen in **Figure 14.** By doing so, they hope to learn more about Earth. The Moon was important in the past and promises to be important in the future, as well.

Section ② Assessment

1. How are the Sun, the Moon, and Earth positioned relative to each other during a new moon?
2. What do maria look like? How did they form?
3. What are the umbra and penumbra? How do they relate to eclipses?
4. What is the difference between a solar and a lunar eclipse? Explain what causes each and why more people see a lunar eclipse.
5. **Think Critically** What do the surface features of the Moon tell you about its history?

Skill Builder Activities

6. **Predicting** Look at a calendar or almanac to find out when the next new moon will occur. Using this information, predict when the first-quarter phase will begin. **For more help,** refer to the Science Skill Handbook.
7. **Communicating** Research the various theories about the Moon's origin in astronomy books and magazines. In your Science Journal, report on and make a diagram of each, including the impact theory. Evaluate the strengths and weaknesses of each theory. **For more help,** refer to the Science Skill Handbook.

Answers to Section Assessment

1. The Moon is between the Sun and Earth.
2. Maria are large, flat areas on the Moon that were probably formed as lava flowing through cracks reached the Moon's surface.
3. The umbra is the dark central shadow; the penumbra is the light shadow around the umbra. Both are

cast by one object onto another during an eclipse.
4. Solar eclipses occur when the Moon's shadow falls on Earth. Lunar eclipses occur when Earth's shadow falls on the Moon. Because Earth's shadow is large compared with that of the Moon, everyone on the night side of Earth can see a lunar eclipse. The

Moon's shadow on Earth is relatively small, so only those people inside the shadow can see a solar eclipse.
5. Possible answers: There have been many impacts on its surface, the Moon may have been geologically active at one time, as it has features that include cooled lava flows.

6. The first-quarter phase should occur one week after new Moon.
7. Answers should relate to the theories of capture, condensation, fission, and impact.

Activity

Moon Phases and Eclipses

You have learned that Moon phases and eclipses result from the relative positions of the Sun, the Moon, and Earth. In this activity, you will demonstrate the positions of these bodies during certain phases and eclipses. You also will see why only a small portion of the people on Earth witness a total solar eclipse during a particular eclipse event.

What You'll Investigate
Can a model be devised to show the positions of the Sun, the Moon, and Earth during various phases and eclipses?

Materials
light source (unshaded)   globe
polystyrene ball   pencil

Goals
- **Model** moon phases.
- **Model** solar and lunar eclipses.

Procedure

1. Review the illustrations of Moon phases and eclipses shown in Section 2.
2. Use the light source as a Sun model and a polystyrene ball on a pencil as a Moon model. Move the Moon around the globe to duplicate the exact position that would have to occur for a lunar eclipse to take place.
3. Move the Moon to the position that would cause a solar eclipse.
4. Place the Moon at each of the following phases: first quarter, full moon, third quarter, and new moon. Identify which, if any, type of eclipse could occur during each phase. Record your data.

Moon Phase Observations

Moon Phase	Observations
first quarter	no eclipse
full moon	lunar eclipse
third quarter	no eclipse
new moon	solar eclipse

5. Place the Moon at the location where a lunar eclipse could occur. Move it slightly toward Earth, then away from Earth. Note the amount of change in the size of the shadow.
6. Repeat step 5 with the Moon in a position where a solar eclipse could occur.

Conclude and Apply

1. During which phase(s) of the Moon is it possible for an eclipse to occur?
2. **Describe** the effect of a small change in distance between Earth and the Moon on the size of the umbra and penumbra.
3. **Infer** why a lunar and a solar eclipse do not occur every month.
4. Why have only a few people experienced a total solar eclipse?
5. **Diagram** the positions of the Sun, Earth, and the Moon during a first quarter moon.
6. Why might it be better to call a full moon a half moon?

Communicating Your Data

Communicate your answers to other students. **For more help, refer to the** Science Skill Handbook.

Resource Manager

Chapter Resources Booklet
Reinforcement, p. 26
Activity Worksheet, pp. 7–8

Communicating Your Data

Instruct students to write short lab reports that describe their goal during this experiment, the procedure they used, and what they concluded.

Activity

Purpose Students model the positions of Earth, the Moon, and the Sun during lunar phases and eclipses. L2 ELL COOP LEARN IS Kinesthetic

Process Skills sequencing, communicating, observing and inferring, comparing and contrasting, recognizing and using spatial relationships, recognizing cause and effect

Time Required 45 minutes

Safety Precautions Caution students to avoid touching the bulb.

Answers to Questions
1. lunar eclipse: full moon; solar eclipse: new moon
2. During solar eclipses, the closer the two bodies, the larger the Moon's umbra and penumbra.
3. The Sun, the Moon, and Earth must be lined up perfectly, with the Moon in Earth's orbital plane. Most months, the Moon is above or below Earth's orbital plane.
4. When the umbra falls on Earth, it covers only a small area.
5. Sun, Earth, and Moon form a right angle.
6. We see a round Moon that looks full, but only half of the surface is lit.

Assessment

Performance Assign each student a phase of the Moon. Have them draw what the Moon looks like from Earth, as well as a diagram of the positions of the Sun, Earth, and Moon during that phase. Use **PASC**, p. 127.

SECTION

3

Exploring Earth's Moon

① Motivate

Bellringer Transparency

Display the Section Focus Transparency for Section 3. Use the accompanying Transparency Activity Master. L2
ELL

Tie to Prior Knowledge

Ask students to recall the latest "news" they have heard about the Moon. Possible answers: There may be water on the Moon; a space probe was sent to the Moon in recent years; astronauts might visit the Moon again. Tell students they will learn in this section about the first trip to the Moon and the possibility of future lunar missions.

▶As You Read

𝘞𝘩𝘢𝘵 You'll Learn
■ **Describe** recent discoveries about the Moon.
■ **Examine** facts about the Moon that might influence future space travel.

Vocabulary
impact basin

𝘞𝘩𝘺 It's Important
Continuing Moon missions may result in discoveries about Earth's origin.

Figure 15
This time line illustrates some of the most important events in the history of Moon exploration.

Missions to the Moon

The Moon has always fascinated humanity. People have made up stories about how it formed. Children's stories even suggested it was made of cheese. Of course, for centuries astronomers also have studied the Moon for clues to its makeup and origin. In 1958, the former Soviet Union launched the first *Luna* spacecraft, enabling up-close study of the Moon. Three years later, the United States began a similar program with the first *Ranger* spacecraft. Following the uncrewed *Ranger* missions, the United States launched a series of *Lunar Orbiters.* The spacecraft in these early missions took detailed photographs of the Moon. There also were seven *Surveyor* spacecraft designed to land on the Moon. Five of these spacecraft successfully touched down on the lunar surface. The *Surveyor* probes took detailed photographs and performed the first analysis of lunar soil. The goal of the program was to prepare for landing astronauts on the Moon. This goal was achieved in 1969 by the astronauts of *Apollo 11.* By 1972, when the *Apollo* missions ended, 12 U.S. astronauts had walked on the Moon. A time line of these important moon missions can be seen in **Figure 15.**

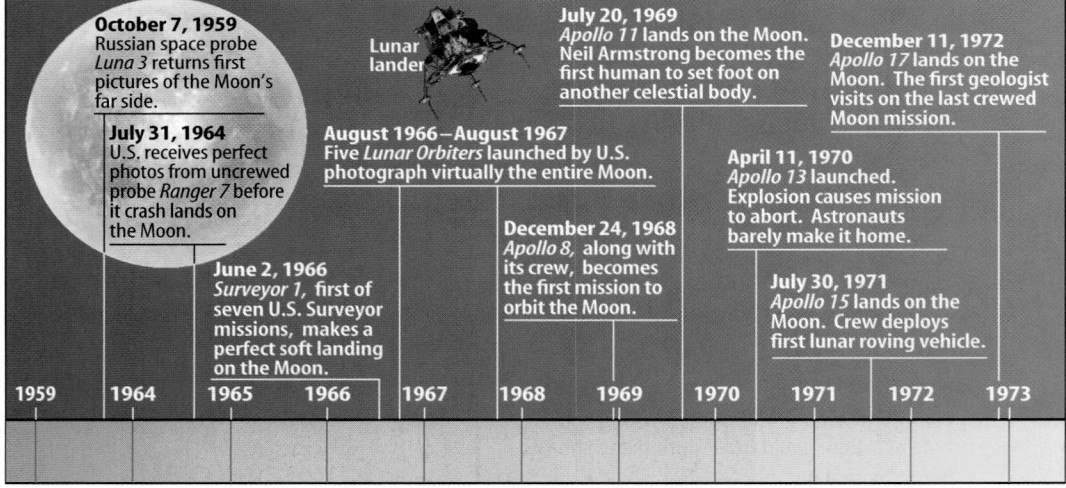

Section ✔*Assessment* Planner

PORTFOLIO
Extension, p. 690
PERFORMANCE ASSESSMENT
MiniLAB, p. 689
Skill Builder Activities, p. 691
See page 698 for more options.

CONTENT ASSESSMENT
Section, p. 691
Challenge, p. 691
Chapter, pp. 698–699

Surveying the Moon More than 20 years passed before the United States resumed its studies of the Moon from space. In 1994, the *Clementine* was placed into lunar orbit. Its goal was to conduct a two-month survey of the Moon's surface. An important aspect of this study was collecting data on the mineral content of Moon rocks. In fact, this part of its mission was instrumental in naming the spacecraft. Clementine was the daughter of a miner in the ballad *My Darlin' Clementine.* While in orbit, *Clementine* also mapped features on the Moon's surface, including huge impact basins.

✔ **Reading Check** *Why was* Clementine *placed in lunar orbit?*

Impact Basins When meteorites and other objects strike the Moon, they leave behind depressions in the Moon's surface. The depression left behind by an object striking the Moon is known as an **impact basin,** or impact crater. The South Pole-Aitken Basin is the oldest identifiable impact feature on the Moon's surface. At 12 km in depth and 2,500 km in diameter, it is also the largest and deepest impact basin in the solar system. Data returned by *Clementine* gave scientists the first set of high-resolution photographs of this area of the Moon. Because much of this basin stays in shadow throughout the Moon's rotation, a cold area has formed where ice deposits from impacting comets might have collected, as shown in **Figure 16.** A large plateau that is always in sunlight also was discovered in this area. If ice truly is near this plateau, as indicated by radio signals that *Clementine* reflected off the Moon to Earth, it would be the ideal location to build a moon colony powered by solar energy.

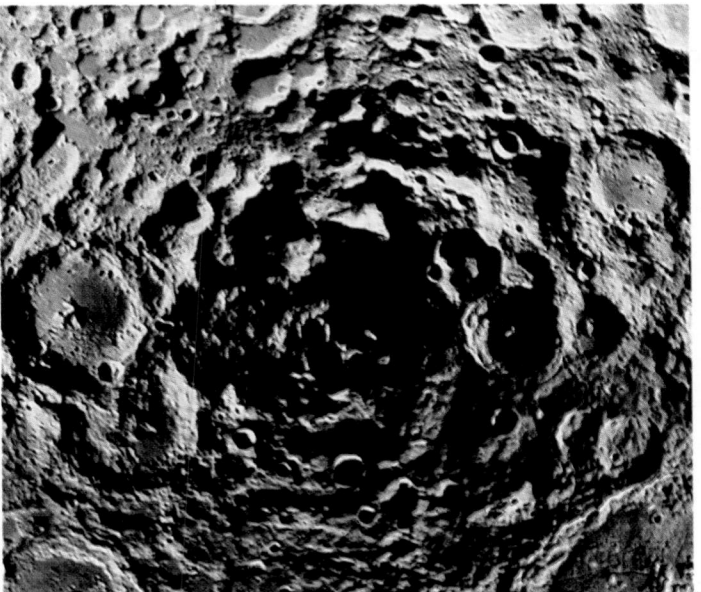

Figure 16
The South Pole-Aitken Basin is the largest of its kind found anywhere in the solar system. The deepest craters in the basin stay in shadow throughout the Moon's rotation. Ice deposits from impacting comets are thought to have collected at the bottom of these craters. This image shows the possible location of such ice.

689

Mini LAB

Modeling a shaded impact basin

Procedure
1. Roll some **modeling clay** into a sphere about 20 cm in diameter.
2. Add a craterlike depression about 2 cm wide and 0.5 cm deep by sinking your thumb into the clay. Be sure to form a lip around your crater.
3. Hold your model so that the crater is at one pole, then rotate it before the beam of a **flashlight**. Observe the inside of your crater.

Analysis
1. Did light from the flashlight reach the bottom of your polar impact crater? In your **Science Journal** describe what you observed.
2. Infer how water could remain forever frozen in a polar impact basin on the Moon.

2 Teach

Missions to the Moon

Mini LAB

Purpose Students model a shaded impact basin. L1 ELL
IS **Kinesthetic**

Materials modeling clay, flashlight

Teaching Strategy Instruct students to hold the flashlight to one side of the model Moon.

Analysis
1. Light might reach the upper edges of the crater, but should not reach its bottom.
2. Water at the bottom of the crater where sunlight does not reach would stay forever frozen.

✔ *Assessment*

Process Have students draw a diagram that shows what they observed during the activity. Use **Performance Assessment in the Science Classroom,** p. 127.

✔ **Reading Check**

Answer to conduct a two-month survey of the Moon's surface, including collecting data on the mineral content of lunar rocks

---

VisualLearning

Figure 16 Have students contrast the appearance of the Moon's south pole, shown here, with that of Earth's north pole. Earth's north pole is covered with an ice sheet and snow. The Moon's south pole is bare rock.

Mapping the Moon

Activity

Have students observe the Moon's surface during the next full Moon. Assign some students make their observations with the unaided eye, some to use binoculars, and others to use telescopes. Direct students to draw the Moon's surface as they see it, sketching any features they observe. Have students compare and contrast the drawings in class. Discuss which features are prominent, even without instruments, and which features can only be seen using binoculars or telescopes. L2  **Visual-Spatial**

Extension

Have students research the mission of the *Lunar Prospector*. Then have them write a press release on the mission's successes and failures that could have been released by NASA when the mission ended in July 1999. L2  **Linguistic** P

Figure 17
This computer-enhanced map based on *Clementine* data indicates the thickness of the Moon's crust. The crust of the side of the Moon facing Earth, shown mostly in red, is thinner than the crust on the far side of the Moon.

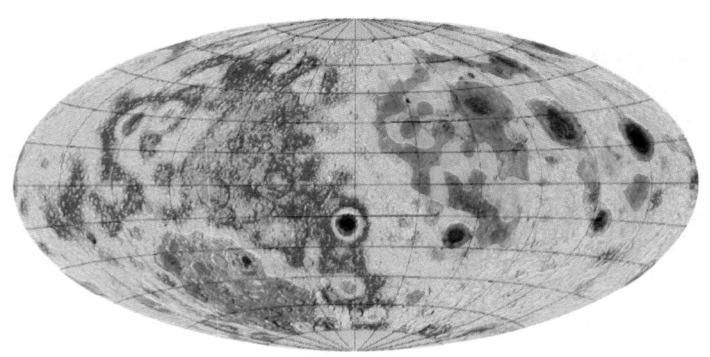

Mapping the Moon

A large part of *Clementine's* mission included taking high-resolution photographs so a detailed map of the Moon's surface could be compiled. Because the five cameras mounted on *Clementine* were able to resolve features as small as 200 m across, human knowledge of the Moon's surface increased immensely. One image resulting from other *Clementine* data is shown in **Figure 17.** It shows that the crust on the side of the Moon that faces Earth is much thinner than the crust on the far side. Additional information shows that the Moon's crust is thinnest under impact basins. Based on analysis of the light data received from *Clementine,* a global map of the Moon also was created that shows its composition, as seen in **Figure 18.**

✔ Reading Check *What information about the Moon did scientists learn from* Clementine?

The Lunar Prospector The success of *Clementine* at a relatively low cost opened the door for further Moon missions. In 1998, NASA launched the desk-sized *Lunar Prospector* into orbit to collect more information about the lunar surface. The spacecraft spent a year orbiting the Moon from pole to pole, once every two hours. The resulting maps confirmed the *Clementine* data. The *Lunar Prospector* was scheduled to conduct a detailed study of the Moon from 100 km above the surface and to look for clues about its origin and makeup.

Figure 18
One of *Clementine's* main missions was to map the Moon. The different colors in this map represent the different types of lunar surface material, because not all parts of the Moon are made up of the same materials. This is the side of the Moon that faces Earth.

Resource Manager

Chapter Resources Booklet
 Enrichment, p. 30
 Reinforcement, p. 27
Home and Community Involvement, p. 24

Teacher FYI

Although both the United States and the former Soviet Union have sent spacecraft to the Moon, no nation owns the Moon. More than 90 nations signed a treaty in 1967 stating that neither the Moon nor any other body in space could be claimed by one nation or used for military purposes.

Icy Poles Early data from the *Lunar Prospector*, shown in **Figure 19**, indicate hydrogen is present in crater rocks at the Moon's poles. Hydrogen is one of the two elements in water. This information, combined with data from *Clementine*, has led scientists to hypothesize that ice may exist in the floors of craters at both Moon poles. These deep craters are cold because sunlight never reaches their floors. Temperatures are as low as −233°C. They are definitely cold enough to have preserved any ice that may have collected from colliding comets. Scientists estimate that 6 billion tons of ice might lie buried under 40 cm of crushed rock at the Moon's poles.

When the *Lunar Prospector* mission ended in July of 1999, it still was unknown whether the hydrogen was from water on the Moon or some other source, such as solar wind. NASA decided to crash the spacecraft into a crater at the Moon's south pole that might contain ice. The scientists hoped that the crash would release large quantities of water vapor that might be detected with telescopes on Earth. The chance of this experiment working was considered slight, and the results were inconclusive. Water might exist on the Moon, but additional research will be needed before definite conclusions can be drawn. However, data from the *Lunar Prospector* have enabled scientists to confirm that the Moon has a small, iron-rich core about 600 km in diameter. The fact that the Moon has such a small core supports the impact theory of its origin because only small amounts of iron would have been blasted off the primitive Earth. Most of Earth's iron would have remained deep in the planet's interior.

Figure 19
The *Lunar Prospector* provided data indicating that ice might exist at the Moon's poles. Further investigation will reveal whether or not this is true.

Discussion

Should the United States continue to explore the Moon? Possible answers: Yes; exploration advances science; the Moon might be a base for further study of space or for staging space missions one day. No; studying the Moon has no relevance to everyday life; the money could be better used elsewhere.

③ Assess

Reteach

Have pairs of students make a concept map that describes all of the lunar missions mentioned in this section and their accomplishments. L2 ELL COOP LEARN IS Visual-Spatial

Challenge

Challenge students to research news concerning the possible existence of water on the Moon, and missions dedicated to answering that question planned for the future. Have students write reports on their findings.

✔ Assessment

Content Have students make a two-column chart categorizing the missions that landed on the Moon and those that orbited the Moon. Landed: *Surveyor, Apollo;* orbited: *Lunar Orbiter, Clementine, Lunar Prospector* Use **Performance Assessment in the Science Classroom**, p. 109.

Section ③ Assessment

1. List two discoveries about the Moon made by *Clementine*.

2. What was the main mission of the *Lunar Prospector*?

3. How did studies of the Moon change after the 1950s?

4. What was the goal of the *Surveyor* and *Apollo* missions? How did these missions further scientists' studies of the Moon?

5. **Think Critically** Why would the discovery of ice at the Moon's poles be important to future space flights?

Skill Builder Activities

6. **Concept Mapping** Sequence the following Moon missions in the order they occurred: *Lunar Prospector, Apollo, Lunar Orbiter, Ranger,* and *Clementine*. **For more help, refer to the Science Skill Handbook.**

7. **Using Fractions** The Moon's orbit is tilted at an angle of 5° to Earth's orbit around the Sun. Using a protractor draw the Moon's orbit around Earth. What fraction of a full circle (360°) is 5°? **For more help, refer to the Math Skill Handbook.**

SECTION 3 Exploring Earth's Moon **691**

Answers to Section Assessment

1. Possible answers: detailed data on surface features; ice at the Moon's poles; sunlit plateau near the Moon's south pole; thin crust under impact basins; new data on mineral content of Moon rocks

2. to orbit the Moon, take photos of its surface, search for clues to its origin and makeup

3. Countries began to study the Moon from orbiting spacecraft and from lunar landers.

4. *Surveyor:* to prepare for a Moon landing; *Apollo:* to land astronauts on the Moon; they enabled scientists to make more detailed studies of the lunar surface, including the study of lunar rocks.

5. Future astronauts who might spend time on the Moon would have a source of water.

6. *Ranger, Lunar Orbiter, Surveyor, Apollo, Clementine, Lunar Prospector*

7. Students should show the moon approximately 5° above or below Earth.

Activity

What You'll Investigate

Purpose

Students design and carry out an experiment to show how the angle at which sunlight strikes an area of Earth's surface determines the amount of heat received by that area. L2 ELL

IS Logical-Mathematical

Process Skills

Communicating, making and using tables, observing, inferring, comparing and contrasting, recognizing cause and effect, designing an experiment, measuring, hypothesizing, separating and controlling variables, interpreting data, formulating models

Time Required

one class period

Alternate Materials

A desk lamp held at the proper angle can be used instead of a gooseneck lamp.

Safety Precautions

The light bulb and shade may be hot for some time after the lamp has been turned off.

Procedure

Teaching Strategies

Remind students to allow the thermometer to return to room temperature before each use.

Activity

Tilt and Temperature

If you walk barefeet on blacktop pavement at noon, you can feel the effect of solar energy. The Sun's rays hit most directly at midday. Now consider the fact that Earth is tilted on its axis. How does this tilt affect how directly light rays strike an area on Earth? How is the angle of the light rays related to the amount of heat energy and the changing seasons?

What You'll Investigate

How does the angle at which light strikes Earth affect the amount of heat energy received by any area on Earth?

Materials

tape
black construction paper (one sheet)
gooseneck lamp with 75-watt bulb
celsius thermometer
watch
protractor

Goals

■ **Measure** the temperature change in a surface after light strikes it at different angles.
■ **Describe** how the angle of light relates to seasons on Earth.

Safety Precautions

Do not touch the lamp without safety gloves. The lightbulb and shade can be hot even when the lamp has been turned off. Handle the thermometer carefully. If it breaks, do not touch anything. Inform your teacher immediately.

Procedure

1. Choose three angles that you will use to aim the light at the paper.

2. **Determine** how long you will shine the light at each angle before you measure the temperature. Measure the temperature at two times for each angle. Use the same time periods for each angle.

3. Copy the following data table into your Science Journal and fill in the temperature the paper reached at each angle and time.

4. Tape a sheet of black construction paper to a desk or the floor.

5. Using the protractor, set the gooseneck lamp so that it will shine on the paper at one of the angles you chose.

6. Turn on the lamp. Use the thermometer to measure the temperature of the paper at the end of the first time period. Continue shining the lamp on the paper until the second time period has passed. Measure the temperature again. Record your data in your data table.

7. Turn off the lamp until the paper cools to room temperature. Repeat steps 5 and 6 using your other two angles.

Temperature Data

Angle of Lamp	Initial Temperature	Temperature at ____ Minutes/Seconds	Temperature at ____ Minutes/Seconds
First angle			
Second angle			
Third angle			

Conclude and Apply

1. **Describe** your experiment. Identify the variables in your experiment. Which were your independent and dependent variables?

2. **Graph** your data using a line graph. Describe what your graph tells you about the data.

3. What happened to the temperature of the paper as you changed the angle of light?

4. **Predict** how your results might have been different if you used white paper. Explain why.

5. **Describe** how the results of this experiment apply to seasons on Earth.

Communicating Your Data

Compare your results with those of other students in your class. **Discuss** how the different angles and time periods affected the temperatures.

ACTIVITY   693

Resource Manager

Chapter Resources Booklet
   Activity Worksheet, pp. 9–10

Reading and Writing Skill Activities, p. 11

Lab Management and Safety, p. 61

Communicating Your Data

Compile data from all students in the class and display it on a class graph.

Expected Outcome

The surface area heats up more quickly when light hits it from a more direct angle.

Conclude and Apply

1. Students should mention that they varied the angle at which light struck the thermometer. The independent variable was the angle of the light. The dependent variable was the increase in temperature of the sheet of paper.

2. Graphs should have time on the y axis and temperature on the x axis.

3. Temperature increased more as the angle of the light became more direct, i.e. closer to 90°.

4. If you used white paper, direct light would still produce the greatest temperature change, but temperature would not rise as high as with black paper.

5. During the summer, the Sun's rays strike the Northern Hemisphere most directly, causing the high summer temperature. During the winter, the Sun's ray strike the Northern Hemisphere least directly, causing the winter's low temperatures.

Error Analysis

Possible causes of error include mismeasuring angles and changing the distance between the light and the paper, and not monitoring time correctly.

Assessment

Process Ask students to explain in writing why temperatures rise faster when light hits a surface area at a more direct angle. Use **Performance Assessment in the Science Classroom,** p. 159.

TIME ⟩ SCIENCE AND HISTORY

Content Background

The Mayan civilization flourished for centuries. As agriculturalists, wealth and power depended entirely on what the Mayan people could produce from the land. Studying the passage of time and the cycle of the seasons was crucial to their culture. It was imperative, for example, that they be able to predict the onset of floods or periods of drought. This was the impetus behind the development of their calendars. The *Tzolkin* was based on cycles of 20 days, similar to our months. This, in turn, was based on Mayan mathematics, which used 20 digits, 0 through 19. Important dates for planting and harvesting, along with religious celebrations, were recorded in this calendar.

The 365-day calendar, the *Haab*, was based on the Mayan's skillful observations of Earth's orbit, the phases of the Moon, and the movements of the visible planets and constellations. Each of these celestial bodies was given a mythological personality and religious significance. The good fortune or bad luck of each day was interpreted from the mythological stories that were read into various planets and stars.

A third calendar, called the Long Count, measured the number of days that had passed since the year Zero. For the Mayans this was around August 2 in the year 3114 B.C.

An ancient people used many calendars to track time and to help them in everyday life

THE Mayan Calendar

Most people don't give the set up of calendars a second thought. They take for granted that a week is seven days, and that a year is 12 months. But this wasn't always the case. Roughly 1,750 years ago, in what is now south Mexico and Central America, the Mayan people invented a sophisticated calendar system. Their system used observations of Sun and Moon cycles to help them figure out time. They also developed a sophisticated mathematical system where single units are written with dots, and bars are used to represent five single units.

The Mayans had several calendars that they used at the same time. Two were most important. One was based on 260 days, the other on 365 days. The calendars were so accurate and useful that later civilizations, including the Aztecs, adopted them.

694

Resources for Teachers and Students

The Atlas of World Archaeology, edited by Paul G. Bahn, Checkmark Books, 2000.

Ancient Mexico, The History and Culture of the Maya, Aztec and Other Pre-Columbian Peoples, by Longchena, Stewart, Tabori, and Chang, 1998.

Atlas of Ancient America, by Coe, Snow, and Benson, Andromeda Oxford, Ltd., 1996.

"Ancient Mesoamerica", Map Supplement, *National Geographic Magazine*, December 1997.

These glyphs represent four different days of the *Tzolkin* calendar.

The 260-Day Calendar

One calendar, called the *Tzolkin* (tz uhl KIN), was based on the planting, harvesting, drying, and storing of corn—the main crop of the Mayans. Each day of the *Tzolkin* had one of 20 names, as well as a number from 1 to 13. Each day also had a Mayan god associated with it.

Mayan priests used this calendar to determine the dates of religious festivals. The priests also used it to help decide when to go to war and what to name children. Just as important, the Mayans used the *Tzolkin* for timing their planting and harvesting.

The 365-Day Calendar

Another Mayan calendar was called the *Haab* (HAHB) and was based on the orbit of Earth around the Sun. It was divided into 18 months with 20 days each, plus five extra days at the end of each year. The 260-day *Tzolkin* calendar fit into the 365-day *Haab* year, so the Mayans used both calendars at once.

Used together, these calendars made the Mayans the most accurate reckoners of time before the modern period. In fact, they were only one day off every 6,000 years. Their idea of measuring time by Earth moving around the Sun is the basis for our calendar today.

This calendar was carved more than 1,000 years ago by an unknown Mayan.

Kukulkan (*left*), built around the year 1050, was used by the Mayans as a calendar. It had four stairways, each with 91 steps. Including the platform on top, the total number of steps is 365, the number of days in a year. You can see this pyramid if you visit Chichén Itzá in Mexico.

CONNECTIONS Drawing Symbols The Mayans created picture symbols for each day of their week. Historians call these symbols glyphs. Collaborate with another student to invent seven glyphs—one for each day of the week. Compare them with other glyphs on the Glencoe Science Web site.

SCIENCE Online For more information, visit science.glencoe.com

CONNECTIONS The Mayan pyramid shown was built as a temple for rituals and ceremonies associated with the god *Kukulkan*. The Mayans' sense of time and history was so important to them that they incorporated the structure of their calendar into the temple's construction. Ask students to look for ways in which we do this in our culture. Perhaps your school is named after someone from history. What events and people are commemorated in statues or plaques found in courthouses, libraries, churches and temples?

SCIENCE Online

Internet Addresses

_____

_____

_____

_____

Explore the Glencoe Science Web site at **science.glencoe.com** to find out more about topics in this feature.

Discussion

The 260- and 365-day calendars coincided once every 52 years. The interval of 52 years is another unit of time for the Mayans. What units do we use to mark time? Possible answer: We mark time not only in years, but also in decades, centuries, and millennia.

What are some examples of how we associate important cultural events with particular time periods? Possible answers: Crewed exploration of space begins in the 1960s; World War II in the 1940s; Civil War in the 1860s, and so on.

Historic Significance

Measuring the passage of time is common to many, perhaps all, human societies. The Mayan "Long Count" measured the time since year Zero. Historical dates were calculated in days using the following units: a *baktun* =144,000 days, a *katun* = 72,000 days, a *tun* = 360 days, a *uinal* = 20 days and a *kin* = 1 day. A date recorded as 2.1.1.1.6 (2 *baktun*, 1 *katun*, etc.) would equal 360,386 days since year Zero. Ask students to explain how this is similar to our own method of recording dates, using, for example, 07/04/2001. This date is seven months, four days, and 2001 years after the year Zero.

Chapter 23 Study Guide

Reviewing Main Ideas

Preview

Students can answer the questions in their Science Journals. Discuss the answers as you go through the chapter. **Linguistic**

Review

Students can write their answers, then compare them with those of other students. **Interpersonal**

Reteach

Students can look at the illustrations and describe details that support the main ideas of the chapter. **Visual-Spatial**

Answers to Chapter Review

SECTION 2

1. The Sun, the Moon, and Earth are lined up with the Moon between the Sun and Earth.

3. The Moon's surface is covered with craters, circular-shaped relatively flat plains, and mountains.

SECTION 3

2. Possible answer: They could drink it, wash with it, use it for growing and preparing food.

Reviewing Main Ideas

Section 1 Earth

1. Earth is a sphere that bulges slightly at its equator.

2. Earth rotates once per day and completes its orbit around the Sun in a little more than 365 days.

3. Earth has a magnetic field like that of a bar magnet.

4. Seasons on Earth are caused by the tilt of Earth's axis and its revolution around the Sun. Because Earth's axis is tilted, the amount of solar energy each hemisphere receives varies throughout the year, causing the seasons.

Section 2 The Moon—Earth's Satellite

1. Earth's Moon goes through phases that depend on the relative positions of the Sun, the Moon, and Earth. *What are the relative positions of the Sun, Earth, and the Moon during a new moon?*

Moon's orbit

Earth's orbit

2. Eclipses occur when Earth or the Moon temporarily blocks sunlight from reaching the other. A solar eclipse occurs when the Moon moves directly between the Sun and Earth. A lunar eclipse occurs when Earth's shadow falls on the Moon.

3. The Moon's maria are the result of ancient lava flows. Craters on the Moon's surface formed from impacts with meteorites, asteroids, and comets. *What is the Moon's surface like?*

Section 3 Exploring Earth's Moon

1. The *Clementine* spacecraft took detailed, high-resolution photographs of the Moon's surface.

2. Data from *Clementine* indicate that the Moon's South Pole-Aitken Basin may contain ice deposits that could supply water for a Moon colony. *What could people living on the Moon do with water?*

3. NASA has resumed exploring the Moon with its latest spacecraft, the *Lunar Prospector*. Data from *Lunar Prospector* lends support to the ice theory.

FOLDABLES Reading & Study Skills — **After You Read**

Exchange Foldables with a classmate and quiz each other. Ask questions that can be answered with the information in your classmate's Foldable.

FOLDABLES Reading & Study Skills — **After You Read**

After students have read the chapter and completed the Foldable described in Before You Read, have them do the activity on the student page.

Dinah Zike

Visualizing Main Ideas

Complete the following concept map on Moon formation.

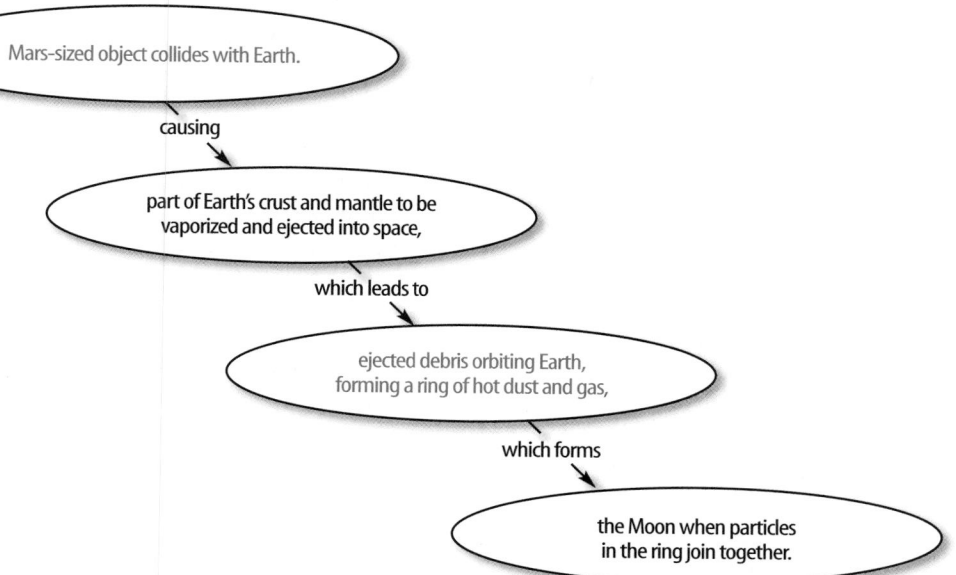

Visualizing Main Ideas

See student page.

Vocabulary Review

Using Vocabulary

1. rotation
2. solstice
3. waning
4. impact basin
5. ellipse

Vocabulary Review

Vocabulary Words

a. axis
b. ellipse
c. equinox
d. full moon
e. impact basin
f. lunar eclipse
g. maria
h. moon phase
i. new moon
j. revolution
k. rotation
l. solar eclipse
m. solstice
n. sphere
o. waning
p. waxing

> **THE PRINCETON REVIEW** **Study Tip**
>
> Practice reading graphs and charts. Make a table that contains the same information that a graph does.

Using Vocabulary

Replace each underlined word with the correct vocabulary word.

1. The spinning of Earth around its axis is called <u>revolution</u>.

2. The <u>equinox</u> is the point at which the Sun reaches its greatest distance north or south of the equator.

3. The Moon is said to be <u>waxing</u> when the portion of the lighted side that can be seen becomes smaller.

4. The depression left behind by an object striking the Moon is called an <u>ellipse</u>.

5. Earth's orbit is an <u>eclipse</u>.

◇ IDENTIFYING ◇ **Misconceptions**

Assess

Use the assessment as follow-up to page 670F after students have completed the chapter.

Demonstration Have students demonstrate the phases of the Moon using a light source and two balls.

Expected Outcome Students will realize that the relative motions of the Sun-Earth-Moon model cause the phases of the Moon.

Reinforcement Have students locate information about lunar phases. Then have them mark the upcoming phases of the Moon on a calendar.

Chapter ㉓ Assessment

Checking Concepts

Checking Concepts

1. D
2. A
3. C
4. C
5. D
6. B
7. A
8. B
9. D
10. B

Choose the word or phrase that best answers the question.

1. How long does it take for the Moon to rotate once?
A) 24 hours **C)** 27.3 hours
B) 365 days **D)** 27.3 days

2. Where is Earth's circumference greatest?
A) equator **C)** poles
B) mantle **D)** axis

3. During an equinox, the Sun is directly over what part of Earth?
A) southern hemisphere
B) northern hemisphere
C) equator
D) pole

4. What causes the Sun to appear to rise and set?
A) Earth's revolution
B) the Sun's revolution
C) Earth's rotation
D) Earth's elliptical orbit

5. How long does it take for the Moon to revolve once around Earth?
A) 24 hours **C)** 27.3 hours
B) 365 days **D)** 27.3 days

6. What is it called when the lighted portion of the Moon appears to get larger?
A) waning **C)** rotating
B) waxing **D)** crescent shaped

7. What kind of eclipse occurs when the Moon blocks sunlight from reaching Earth?
A) solar **C)** full
B) new **D)** lunar

8. What is the darkest part of the shadow during an eclipse?
A) waxing gibbous **C)** waning gibbous
B) umbra **D)** penumbra

9. What is the name for a depression on the Moon caused by an object striking its surface?
A) eclipse **C)** phase
B) moonquake **D)** impact basin

10. What fact does data gathered from the *Clementine* spacecraft support?
A) The Moon rotates once in 29.5 days.
B) The Moon has a thinner crust on the side facing Earth.
C) The Moon revolves once in 29.5 days.
D) The Moon has no crust.

Thinking Critically

11. How would the Moon appear to an observer in space during its revolution? Would phases be observable? Explain.

12. What would be the effect on Earth's seasons if the axis were tilted at 28.5° instead of 23.5°?

13. Seasons in the southern hemisphere are reversed. Explain how this supports the statement that seasons are NOT caused by Earth's changing distance from the Sun.

14. How would solar eclipses be different if the Moon were twice as far from Earth? Explain.

15. Which observed motions of the Moon are real? Which are apparent? Explain.

Thinking Critically

Thinking Critically

11. If the Moon were between the observer and the Sun, phases would be observed. The specific phases would depend on the relative positions of the observer, the Moon, and the Sun.

12. The seasons would probably be more extreme, with warmer summers and colder winters.

13. If Earth being closer to the Sun caused summer, winter could not occur at the same time in the other hemisphere.

14. If the Moon were farther away, its shadow would fall over a smaller area of Earth, or might not reach Earth at all. Thus, solar eclipses would occur less frequently or not at all.

15. The changing position of the Moon from night to night is a real motion caused by the Moon orbiting Earth. Movement across Earth's sky each day or night is an apparent motion caused by Earth's rotation. The lack of rotation of the Moon as seen from Earth is an apparent motion caused by the Moon having a period of rotation equal to its period of revolution.

Developing Skills

16. Predicting Predict how the information gathered by Moon missions could be helpful in the future for people wanting to establish a colony on the Moon.

17. Using Variables, Constants, and Controls Describe a simple activity to show how the Moon's rotation and revolution work to keep the same side facing Earth at all times.

Chapter ✓*Assessment* Planner

Portfolio Encourage students to place in their portfolios one or two items of what they consider to be their best work. Examples include:
- Life Science Integration, p. 673
- Science Journal, p. 679
- Activity, p. 682
- Extension, p. 690

Performance Additional performance assessments, Performance Task Assessment Lists, and rubrics for evaluating these activities can be found in Glencoe's **Performance Assessment in the Science Classroom.**

18. Comparing and Contrasting Compare and contrast a waning moon and a waxing moon.

19. Concept Mapping Copy and complete the cycle concept map shown on this page. Show the sequences of the Moon's phases.

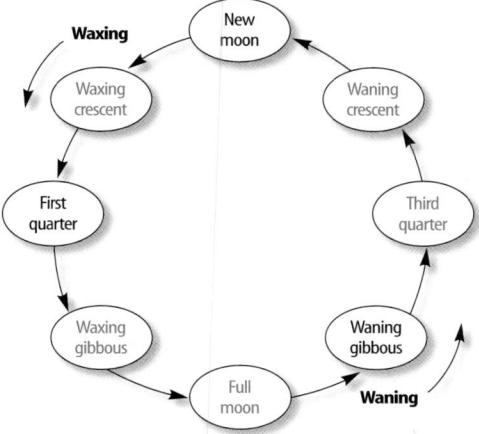

20. Hypothesizing Gravity is weaker on the Moon than it is on Earth. Use this fact to help you form a hypothesis as to why more craters are present on the far side of the Moon than on the side facing Earth.

Performance Assessment

21. Poem Write a poem in which you describe the various surface features of the Moon. Be sure to include information on how these features formed. Share your poem with others.

TECHNOLOGY

 Go to the Glencoe Science Web site at **science.glencoe.com** or use the **Glencoe Science CD-ROM** for additional chapter assessment.

 **Test Practice**

The diagram below shows one complete lunar cycle.

1 **2** **3** **4** **5**

Study the picture and answer the following questions.

1. About how long does it take the Moon to complete the cycle shown above?
A) one hour
B) one day
C) one month
D) one year

2. Which phase of the Moon shown above does not reflect any sunlight toward Earth?
A) 1
B) 2
C) 3
D) 4

3. At which phase could a solar eclipse occur?
A) 1
B) 2
C) 3
D) 4

4. Which of the above phases is first quarter?
A) 1
B) 2
C) 3
D) 4

 **Test Practice**

The Test-Taking Tip was written by The Princeton Review, the nation's leader in test preparation.
1. C
2. C
3. C
4. D

Developing Skills

16. Possible answers: Scientists will be able to choose a colony location that is relatively flat and near a water supply.
17. Possible answer: Place an X on a basketball. As you walk around a classmate, turn the ball to keep the X facing him or her. As the ball revolves once, it rotates once.
18. At both times, the Moon's apparent size is changing. A waxing Moon appears to get larger each night; a waning Moon appears to get smaller.
19. See student page.
20. Meteoroids traveling between the Moon and Earth are more likely to be pulled toward Earth than toward the Moon because of Earth's greater gravity.

Performance Assessment

21. Use the **Performance Task Assessment List for Poems** in **Performance Assessment in the Science Classroom**, p. 151.

✓*Assessment* Resources

📁 **Reproducible Masters**

Chapter Resources Booklet
Chapter Review, pp. 37–38
Chapter Tests, pp. 39–42
Assessment Transparency Activity, p. 49

Glencoe Science Web site
Interactive Tutor
Chapter Quizzes

Glencoe Technology
🖌 Assessment Transparency
💿 Interactive CD-ROM Chapter Quizzes
💿 ExamView Pro Test Bank
💿 Vocabulary PuzzleMaker Software
📼 MindJogger Videoquiz DVD/VHS

Section/Objectives	Standards		Activities/Features
Chapter Opener	National	State/Local	**Explore Activity:** Model crater formation, p. 701 **Before You Read,** p. 701
	See p. 5T for a Key to Standards.		
Section 1 The Solar System 🕐 2 sessions 📦 1 block 1. **Compare** the the sun-centered and Earth-centered models of the solar system. 2. **Describe** current models of the formation of the solar system.	National Content Standards: UCP2, A1, D3, G3		**Science Online,** p. 703 **Physics Integration,** p. 704 **Visualizing the Solar System's Formation,** p. 705 **Activity:** Planetary Orbits, p. 707
Section 2 The Inner Planets 🕐 2 sessions 📦 1 block 1. **List** the inner planets in their relative order from the Sun. 2. **Describe** important characteristics of each inner planet. 3. **Compare and contrast** Venus and Earth.	National Content Standards: UCP1, A1, B2, D3		**MiniLAB:** Inferring Effects of Gravity, p. 711 **Science Online,** p. 712 **Math Skills Activity:** Calculating with Percentages, p. 712
Section 3 The Outer Planets 🕐 2 sessions 📦 1 block 1. **Describe** the major characteristics of Jupiter, Saturn, Uranus, and Neptune. 2. **Explain** how Pluto differs from the other outer planets.	National Content Standards: UCP1, A1, D3,		**MiniLAB:** Modeling Planets, p. 716 **Physics Integration,** p. 718
Section 4 Other Objects in the Solar System 🕐 3 sessions 📦 1.5 blocks 1. **Describe** where comets come from and how a comet develops as it approaches the Sun. 2. **Distinguish** among comets, meteoroids, and asteroids.	National Content Standards: UCP1, A1, D3, G2		**Activity:** Solar System Distance Model, p. 726 **Oops! Accidents in Science:** It Came from Outer Space, p. 728

NATIONAL GEOGRAPHIC

Teacher's Corner

PRODUCTS AVAILABLE FROM GLENCOE
To order call 1-800-334-7344:
CD-ROM: *NGS PictureShow: Solar System*
Transparency Set: *NGS PicturePack: Solar System*
Videodisc; *STV: Solar System*

PRODUCTS AVAILABLE FROM NATIONAL GEOGRAPHIC SOCIETY
To order call 1-800-368-2728:
Poster: *Solar System/Celestial Family*
Videos: *Comets and Asteroids*
INDEX TO NATIONAL GEOGRAPHIC SOCIETY
The following articles may be used

for research relating to this chapter:
"The Age of Comets," by William R. Newcott, Dec. 1997; "Venus Revealed," by William R. Newcott, Feb. 1993 "Neptune: Voyager's Last Picture Show," by Rick Gore, Dec. 1990 "Halley's Comet 1986," by Rick Gore, December 1986

Activity Materials	Reproducible Resources	Section Assessment	Technology
Explore Activity: white flour, metal cake pan, colored powdered drink mix, marbles, bolts, nuts, metric ruler	**Chapter Resources Booklet** Foldables Worksheet, p. 17 Directed Reading Overview, p. 19 Note-taking Worksheets, pp. 35–38	*GLENCOE'S ASSESSMENT ADVANTAGE*	
Activity: 2 thumbtacks or pins, cardboard, paper, metric ruler, string, pencil	**Chapter Resources Booklet** Transparency Activity, p. 48 Activity Worksheet, pp. 5–6 Enrichment, p. 31 Reinforcement, p. 27 Directed Reading, p. 20 **Cultural Diversity,** p. 29	Portfolio Science Journal, p. 704 Performance Skill Builder Activities, p. 706 Content Section Assessment, p. 706	Section Focus Transparency Interactive CD-ROM/DVD Guided Reading Audio Program
MiniLAB: calculator *Need materials? Contact Science Kit at 1-800-828-7777 or www.sciencekit.com on the Internet.*	**Chapter Resources Booklet** Transparency Activity, p. 49 MiniLAB, p. 3 Enrichment, p. 32 Reinforcement, p. 28 Directed Reading, p. 20 **Mathematics Skill Activities,** p. 1	Portfolio Activity, p. 709 Performance MiniLAB, p. 711 Math Skills Activity, p. 712 Skill Builder Activities, p. 713 Content Section Assessment, p. 713	Section Focus Transparency Interactive CD-ROM/DVD Guided Reading Audio Programs
MiniLAB: metric ruler, paper	**Chapter Resources Booklet** Transparency Activity, p. 50 MiniLAB, p. 4 Enrichment, p. 33 Reinforcement, p. 29 Directed Reading, p. 21	Portfolio Science Journal, p. 718 Performance MiniLAB, p. 716 Skill Builder Activities, p. 719 Content Section Assessment, p. 719	Section Focus Transparency Interactive CD-ROM/DVD Guided Reading Audio Programs
Activity: meterstick, scissors, pencil, string, several sheets of notebook paper	**Chapter Resources Booklet** Transparency Activity, p. 51 Activity Worksheet, pp. 7–8 Transparency Activity, pp. 53–54 Enrichment, p. 34 Reinforcement, p. 30 Directed Reading, pp. 21, 22 **Lab Management and Safety,** p. 69	Portfolio Challenge, p. 725 Performance Skill Builder Activities, p. 725 Content Section Assessment, p. 725	Section Focus Transparency Teaching Transparency Interactive CD-ROM/DVD Guided Reading Audio Program

End of Chapter Assessment

GLENCOE'S ASSESSMENT ADVANTAGE

Blackline Masters	Technology	Professional Series
Chapter Resources Booklet Chapter Review, pp. 41–42 Chapter Tests, pp. 43–46 **Standardized Test Practice by The Princeton Review,** pp. 21–24	MindJogger Videoquiz CD-ROM Explorations and Quizzes Vocabulary Puzzle Makers ExamView Pro Test Bank Interactive Lesson Planner Interactive Teacher's Edition	Performance Assessment in the Science Classroom (PASC)

Transparencies

Section Focus

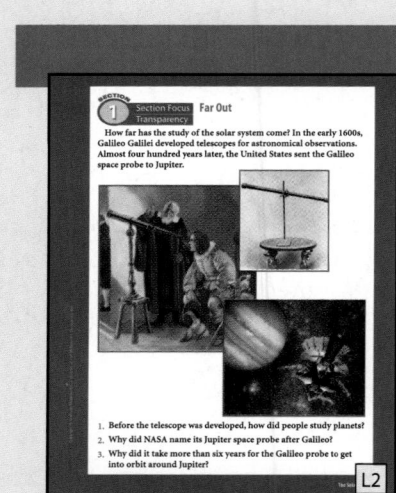

1 Section Focus Transparency **Far Out**

How far has the study of the solar system come? In the early 1600s, Galileo Galilei developed telescopes for astronomical observations. Almost four hundred years later, the United States sent the Galileo space probe to Jupiter.

1. Before the telescope was developed, how did people study planets?
2. Why did NASA name its Jupiter space probe after Galileo?
3. Why did it take more than six years for the Galileo probe to get into orbit around Jupiter?

L2

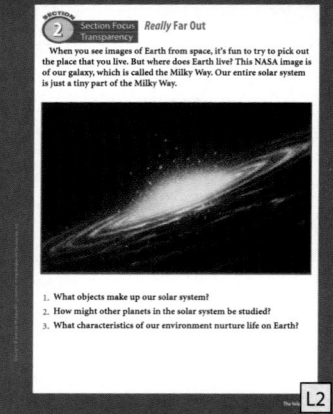

2 Section Focus Transparency **Really Far Out**

When you see images of Earth from space, it's fun to try to pick out the place that you live. But where does Earth live? This NASA image is of our galaxy, which is called the Milky Way. Our entire solar system is just a tiny part of the Milky Way.

1. What objects make up our solar system?
2. How might other planets in the system be studied?
3. What characteristics of our environment nurture life on Earth?

L2

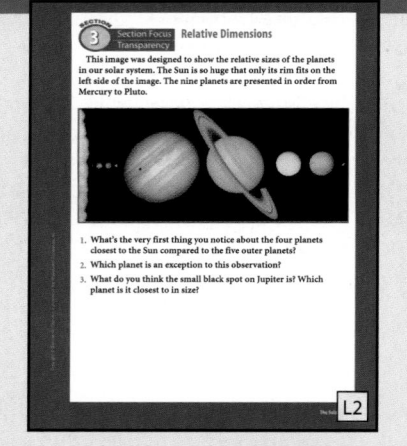

3 Section Focus Transparency **Relative Dimensions**

This image was designed to show the relative sizes of the planets in our solar system. The Sun is so huge that only its rim fits on the left side of the image. The nine planets are presented in order from Mercury to Pluto.

1. What's the very first thing you notice about the four planets closest to the Sun compared to the five outer planets?
2. Which planet is an exception to this observation?
3. What do you think the small black spot on Jupiter is? Which planet is it closest to in size?

L2

Assessment

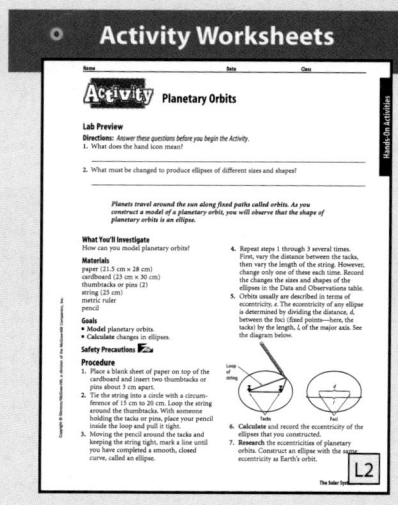

Assessment Transparency **The Solar System**

Directions: *Carefully review the graph and answer the following questions.*

Rotation of the Planets

1. Which two planets have the same period of rotation?
   A Earth and Saturn
   B Mars and Jupiter
   C Earth and Jupiter
   D Jupiter and Saturn
2. Which of the following is caused by the rotation of Earth on its axis?
   F The change between day and night
   G The changing of the seasons
   H The changing of the phases of the moon
   J The movement of water downhill
3. The period of rotation of a planet is the time it takes to ____.
   A travel around the Sun
   B spin once on its axis
   C travel around Earth
   D complete one change of season

L2

Teaching

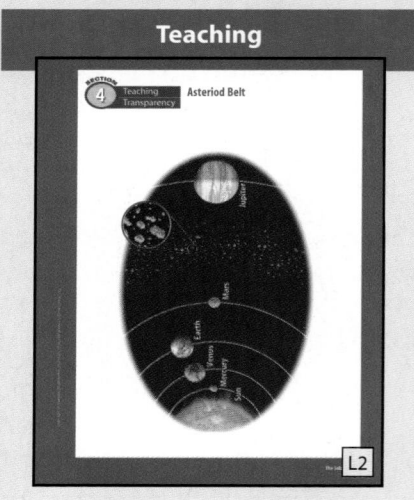

4 Teaching Transparency **Asteroid Belt**

L2

This is a representation of key blackline masters available in the Teacher Classroom Resources. See Resource Manager boxes within the chapter for additional information.

Key to Teaching Strategies

The following designations will help you decide which activities are appropriate for your students.

L1 Level 1 activities should be appropriate for students with learning difficulties.

L2 Level 2 activities should be within the ability range of all students.

L3 Level 3 activities are designed for above-average students.

ELL ELL activities should be within the ability range of English Language Learners.

COOP LEARN Cooperative Learning activities are designed for small group work.

LS Multiple Learning Styles logos, as described on page 22T, are used throughout to indicate strategies that address different learning styles.

P These strategies represent student products that can be placed into a best-work portfolio.

Hands-on Activities

Activity Worksheets

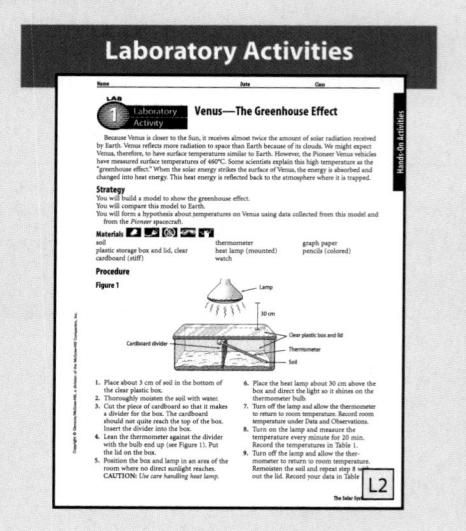

Activity **Planetary Orbits**

Lab Preview
Directions: *Answer these questions before you begin the Activity.*
1. What does the hand icon mean?

2. What must be changed to produce ellipses of different sizes and shapes?

Planets travel around the sun along fixed paths called orbits. As you construct a model of a planetary orbit, you will observe that the shape of planetary orbits is an ellipse.

What You'll Investigate
How can you model planetary orbits?

Materials
paper (21.5 cm × 28 cm)
cardboard (23 cm × 30 cm)
thumbtacks or pins (2)
string (25 cm)
metric ruler
pencil

Goals
• Model planetary orbits.
• Calculate changes in ellipses.

Safety Precautions

Procedure
1. Place a blank sheet of paper on top of the cardboard and insert two thumbtacks or pins about 3 cm apart.
2. Tie the string into a circle with a circumference of 15 cm to 20 cm. Loop the string around the thumbtacks. With someone holding the tacks or pins, place your pencil inside the loop and pull it tight.
3. Moving the pencil around the tacks and keeping the string tight, mark a line until you have completed a smooth, closed curve, called an ellipse.

4. Repeat steps 1 through 3 several times. First, vary the distance between the tacks, then vary the length of the string. However, change only one of these each time. Record the changes the sizes and shapes of the ellipses in the Data and Observations table.
5. Orbits usually are described in terms of eccentricity, e. The eccentricity of any ellipse is determined by dividing the distance, d, between the foci (fixed points—here, the tacks) by the length, l, of the major axis. See the diagram below.

6. Calculate and record the eccentricity of the ellipses that you constructed.
7. Research the eccentricities of planetary orbits. Construct an ellipse with the same eccentricity as Earth's orbit.

L2

Laboratory Activities

1 Laboratory Activity **Venus—The Greenhouse Effect**

Because Venus is closer to the Sun, it receives almost twice the amount of solar radiation received by Earth. Venus reflects more radiation to space than Earth because of its clouds. We might expect Venus, therefore, to have surface temperatures similar to Earth. However, the Pioneer Venus vehicles have measured surface temperatures of 460°C. Some scientists explain this high temperature as the "greenhouse effect." When the solar energy strikes the surface of Venus, the energy is absorbed and changed into heat energy. This heat energy is reflected back to the atmosphere where it is trapped.

Strategy
You will build a model to show the greenhouse effect.
You will compare this model to Earth.
You will form a hypothesis about temperatures on Venus using data collected from this model and from the *Pioneer* spacecraft.

Materials
soil
plastic storage box and lid, clear
cardboard (stiff)
thermometer
heat lamp (mounted)
watch
graph paper
pencils (colored)

Procedure
Figure 1

1. Place about 3 cm of soil in the bottom of the clear plastic box.
2. Thoroughly moisten the soil with water.
3. Cut the piece of cardboard so that it makes a divider for the box. The cardboard should not quite reach the top of the box. Insert the divider into the box.
4. Lean the thermometer against the divider with the bulb end up (see Figure 1). Put the lid on the box.
5. Position the box and lamp in an area of the room where no direct sunlight reaches.
   CAUTION: *Use care handling heat lamp.*

6. Place the heat lamp about 30 cm above the box and direct the light so it shines on the thermometer bulb.
7. Turn off the lamp and allow the thermometer to return to room temperature. Record room temperature under Data and Observations.
8. Turn on the lamp and measure the temperature every minute for 20 min. Record the temperatures in Table 1.
9. Turn off the lamp and allow the thermometer to return to room temperature. Remoisten the soil and repeat step 8 with the lid off. Record your data in Table.

L2

Meeting Different Ability Levels

Content Outline

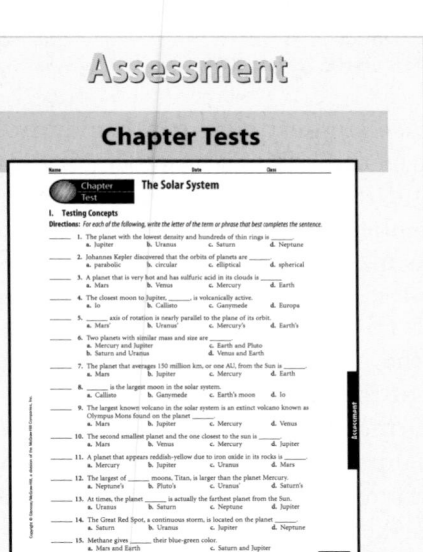

Note-taking Worksheet — **The Solar System**

Section 1   The Solar System

A. Ideas about the night sky have _____ over time.
  1. _____-centered model—early Greeks thought planets, Sun, Moon, and stars rotated around Earth.
  2. _____-centered model—Nicholas Copernicus and Galileo Galilei observed that the Moon revolved around Earth and that Earth and the other planets revolved around the Sun.
  3. _____ view—_____ includes Sun, nine planets, many small objects, and a huge volume of space.
  4. Sun is the _____ of the solar system
  5. All other objects in the solar system _____ around the Sun.

B. How the _____ system formed
  1. A _____ of gas, ice, and dust slowly formed
  2. A cloud of material in the nebula slowly _____ in space.
  3. Shock waves might have caused the cloud to _____, and the matter was squeezed into less space.
  4. The cloud became more _____, rotated faster, heated up, and flattened to form a disk
  5. As the cloud contracted, it grew warmer, triggering a _____ fusion reaction that created the Sun.
  6. The leftover _____ became the planets and asteroids.
    a. First four _____ planets—small and rocky with iron cores
    b. Last five _____ planets—larger and lightweight except for Pluto

C. Planet
  1. Copernicus—planets had _____ orbits around the Sun.
  2. Johannes Kepler—German mathematician
    a. Discovered that the planet orbits were _____ and that the Sun was not directly in the center of the orbits
    b. Determined that planets do not orbit the Sun at the same _____

L2

Reinforcement

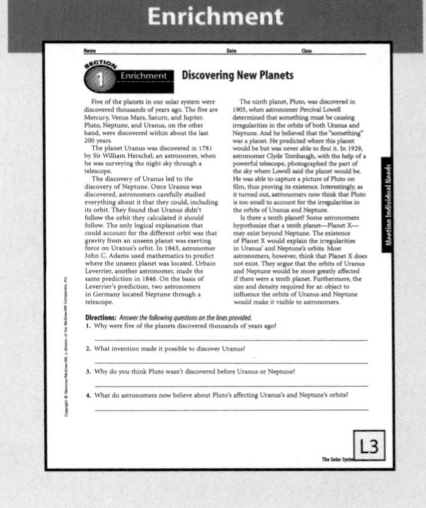

Reinforcement — **The Solar System**

Directions: *Answer the following questions on the lines provided.*
1. Name the two models of the solar system and explain the difference between them.

2. State what scientists hypothesize regarding the formation of the Sun and the planets.

3. Name the inner and outer planets and contrast the two groups of planets.

Directions: *In the chart below, list the discoveries about the solar system made by each scientist.*

1. Copernicus	
2. Galileo	
3. Kepler	

L2

Directed Reading

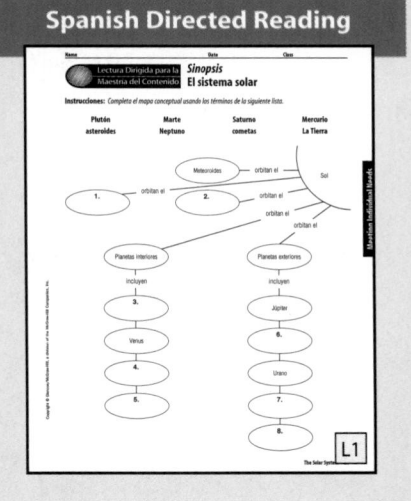

Directed Reading for Content Mastery — *Overview* **The Solar System**

Directions: *Complete the concept map using the terms in the list below.*

Pluto   Mars   Saturn   Mercury
asteroids   Neptune   comets   Earth

L1

Assessment

Chapter Tests

Chapter Test — **The Solar System**

I.   Testing Concepts

Directions: *For each of the following, write the letter of the term or phrase that best completes the sentence.*

_____ 1. The planet with the lowest density and hundreds of thin rings is _____.
  a. Jupiter   b. Uranus   c. Saturn   d. Neptune

_____ 2. Johannes Kepler discovered that the orbits of planets are _____.
  a. parabolic   b. circular   c. elliptical   d. spherical

_____ 3. A planet that is very hot and has sulfuric acid in its clouds is _____.
  a. Mars   b. Venus   c. Mercury   d. Earth

_____ 4. The closest moon to Jupiter, _____, is volcanically active.
  a. Io   b. Callisto   c. Ganymede   d. Europa

_____ 5. _____ axis of rotation is nearly parallel to the plane of its orbit.
  a. Mars'   b. Venus'   c. Mercury's   d. Earth's

_____ 6. Two planets with similar mass and size are _____.
  a. Mercury and Jupiter   c. Earth and Pluto
  b. Saturn and Uranus   d. Venus and Earth

_____ 7. The planet that averages 150 million km, or one AU, from the Sun is _____.
  a. Mars   b. Venus   c. Mercury   d. Earth

_____ 8. _____ is the largest moon in the solar system.
  a. Callisto   b. Ganymede   c. Earth's moon   d. Io

_____ 9. The largest known volcano in the solar system is an extinct volcano known as Olympus Mons found on the planet _____.
  a. Mars   b. Jupiter   c. Mercury   d. Venus

_____ 10. The second smallest planet and the one closest to the sun is _____.
  a. Mars   b. Venus   c. Mercury   d. Jupiter

_____ 11. A planet that appears reddish-yellow due to iron oxide in its rocks is _____.
  a. Mercury   b. Jupiter   c. Uranus   d. Mars

_____ 12. The largest of _____ moons, Titan, is larger than the planet Mercury.
  a. Neptune's   b. Pluto's   c. Uranus'   d. Saturn's

_____ 13. At times, the planet _____ is actually the farthest planet from the Sun.
  a. Uranus   b. Saturn   c. Neptune   d. Jupiter

_____ 14. The Great Red Spot, a continuous storm, is located on the planet _____.
  a. Saturn   b. Uranus   c. Jupiter   d. Neptune

_____ 15. Methane gives _____ their blue-green color.
  a. Mars and Earth   c. Saturn and Jupiter
  b. Uranus and Neptune   d. Neptune and Venus

L2

Enrichment

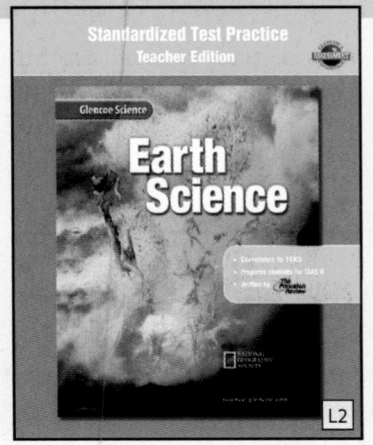

Enrichment — **Discovering New Planets**

Five of the planets in our solar system were discovered thousands of years ago. The five are Mercury, Venus, Mars, Saturn, and Jupiter. Pluto, Neptune, and Uranus, on the other hand, were discovered within about the last 200 years.

The planet Uranus was discovered in 1781 by Sir William Herschel, an astronomer, when he was surveying the night sky through a telescope.

The discovery of Uranus led to the discovery of Neptune. Once Uranus was discovered, astronomers carefully studied everything about it that they could, including its orbit. They found that Uranus didn't follow the orbit they calculated it should follow. The only logical explanation that could account for the different orbit was that gravity from an unseen planet was exerting force on Uranus's orbit. In 1843, astronomer John C. Adams used mathematics to predict where the unseen planet was located. Urbain Leverrier, another astronomer, made the same prediction in 1846. On the basis of Leverrier's prediction, two astronomers in Germany located Neptune through a telescope.

The ninth planet, Pluto, was discovered in 1905, when astronomer Percival Lowell determined that something must be causing irregularities in the orbits of both Uranus and Neptune. And he believed that the "something" was a planet. He predicted where this planet would be but was never able to find it. In 1929, astronomer Clyde Tombaugh, with the help of a powerful telescope, photographed the part of the sky where Lowell said the planet would be. He was able to capture a picture of Pluto on film, thus proving its existence. Interestingly, as it turned out, astronomers now think that Pluto is too small to account for the irregularities in the orbits of Uranus and Neptune.

Is there a tenth planet? Some astronomers hypothesize that a tenth planet—Planet X—may exist beyond Neptune. The existence of Planet X would explain the irregularities in Uranus' and Neptune's orbits. Most astronomers, however, think that Planet X does not exist. They argue that the orbits of Uranus and Neptune would be more greatly affected if there were a tenth planet. Furthermore, the size and density required for an object to influence the orbits of Uranus and Neptune would make it visible to astronomers.

Directions: *Answer the following questions on the lines provided.*
1. Why were five of the planets discovered thousands of years ago?

2. What invention made it possible to discover Uranus?

3. Why do you think Pluto wasn't discovered before Uranus or Neptune?

4. What do astronomers now believe about Pluto's affecting Uranus' and Neptune's orbits?

L3

Spanish Directed Reading

Lectura Dirigida para la Maestría del Contenido — *Sinopsis* **El sistema solar**

Instrucciones: *Completa el mapa conceptual usando los términos de la siguiente lista.*

Plutón   Marte   Saturno   Mercurio
asteroides   Neptuno   cometas   La Tierra

L1

Test Practice Workbook

Standardized Test Practice
Teacher Edition

Glencoe Science
Earth Science

L2

Chapter Review

Chapter Review — **The Solar System**

Part A. Vocabulary Review

Directions: *If a statement is true, write "true" in the blank. If a statement is false, change the italicized term to make the statement true, and write the new term in the blank.*

_____ 1. A *meteor* is a meteoroid that burns up in Earth's atmosphere.
_____ 2. A *meteoroid* is composed of dust, rock particles, and frozen gases and has a nucleus, coma, and tail.
_____ 3. The heavily cratered planet closest to the Sun is *Pluto*.
_____ 4. On the third planet from the Sun, *Mars*, water exists as a solid, liquid, and gas.
_____ 5. The Martian atmosphere is much *thinner* than Earth's.
_____ 6. The largest gaseous planet, *Saturn*, has at least 16 moons.
_____ 7. A belt of *meteoroids* (small, planetlike fragments) lies between the inner planets and outer planets.
_____ 8. A gaseous planet with thin, dark rings and 18 satellites is *Neptune*.
_____ 9. *Meteorites* are small pieces of rock moving in space.
_____ 10. The Sun and all objects orbiting it make up the *solar system*.
_____ 11. A large, gaseous planet with the lowest density and 18 moons is *Saturn*.
_____ 12. The second planet from the Sun, which has moonlike phases and a surface heat of over 450°C caused by the greenhouse effect, is *Mercury*.
_____ 13. An *astronomical unit* is 150 million kilometers.
_____ 14. A *comet* is a meteoroid that strikes Earth.
_____ 15. The reddish-yellow planet that has polar ice caps and is the fourth planet from the Sun is *Jupiter*.
_____ 16. A large, blue-green, gaseous planet similar to Uranus is *Neptune*.
_____ 17. A large, swirling gas storm on Jupiter is the *Io*.
_____ 18. The *outer* planets are Mars, Earth, Venus, and Mercury.
_____ 19. Usually the outermost planet of the solar system is *Neptune*.
_____ 20. The *inner planets* are Pluto, Uranus, Neptune, Saturn, and Jupiter.

L2

Science Content Background

SECTION 1 The Solar System
Sun-Centered Model

Most objects in the solar system rotate and revolve toward the east. Motion different from eastward motion is called retrograde motion. The retrograde motion of Mars was one piece of evidence used by Copernicus to support his Sun-centered model of the solar system.

Student Misconception

The Sun is not a star.

Refer to the facing page for teaching strategies to address this misconception. Refer to pages 704–705 for content related to this topic.

SECTION 2 The Inner Planets
Inner Planets

Radar observations indicate that Mercury may have polar ice caps that exist inside craters where the Sun's light does not reach. The Caloris Basin, the result of an asteroid impact early in the formation of the solar system, is 1,300 km (800 mi) in diameter.

Venus is typically the brightest planet in the night sky, because its dense, cloud-covered atmosphere reflects most of the Sun's light back into space. The Sun's heat, however, is absorbed and trapped by the dense atmosphere. As a result, Venus has an average surface temperature of 450°C (842°F), hot enough to melt lead!

Mars today is a dry planet. Evidence of dried-up riverbeds and surface erosion indicate that Mars once supported water. There is no evidence that the planet does, or ever has, contained life.

Science Photo Library/Photo Researchers, Inc.

SECTION 3 The Outer Planets
Outer Planets

The atmospheres of Jupiter and Saturn contain three layers. The upper layer is composed of ammonia ice, the second layer is made of ammonium hydrosulfide ice, and the lowest layer is mainly frozen water. Uranus is cold. Scientists believe a collision with another object may have turned Uranus on its side and destroyed its heat source.

Hypotheses suggest that Pluto may not have formed in the orbit it now occupies or that Pluto and its moon, Charon, are large cometary members of the Kuiper belt. Pluto and Neptune's moon Triton are the most similar objects in the solar system. The retrograde revolution of Triton may indicate that it was captured by the gravity of Neptune and once was a planet of the Sun, like Pluto. This supports the idea that Pluto, and perhaps Triton, are two of many dwarf planets that may have formed far from the Sun. Discovery of the Kuiper belt further supports this idea.

SECTION 4 Other Objects in the Solar System
Comets

Comets appear to orbit the Sun in the Oort Cloud some 50,000 AU from the Sun. Some comets take more than a million years to complete one orbit.

For additional content background on this topic, go to the Glencoe Science Web site at science.glencoe.com.

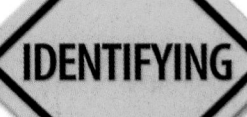

IDENTIFYING > Misconceptions

Students may think that . . .

• **The Sun is not a star.**

Students have learned about stars and about the Sun. But some students do not make the connection that the Sun is the closest star to Earth. The Sun is a main sequence star that is the source of all energy for our solar system.

Demonstration

The Sun can be observed by using an index card and a thin, stiff piece of white cardboard. **CAUTION:** *Warn students not to look directly at the Sun! Permanent eye damage can result.*

• Place the cardboard, which acts as a viewing screen, on the ground. Prop up one side of the screen so that it is perpendicular to incoming sunlight.

• Next, use a pin to poke a small hole in the index card. Hold the index card about 60 cm above the screen with the hole pointing toward the Sun. The Sun's image should appear on the screen.

After students have viewed the Sun's image, discuss what they have seen. Show pictures of the Sun, and emphasize that this body provides heat and light for our solar system.

Discussion

Have the class brainstorm a list what they know about the Sun, including what they observed using the pin-hole viewer. Record students' ideas on the board. Next to this list, draw a diagram similar to that shown here. Then have students identify features of the star shown the diagram and compare them to the features of the Sun. For example, they could state that stars have a core and the Sun has a core, stars have a photosphere and the Sun has a photosphere, and so on. After the comparison, have students draw conclusions as to whether the Sun is a star.

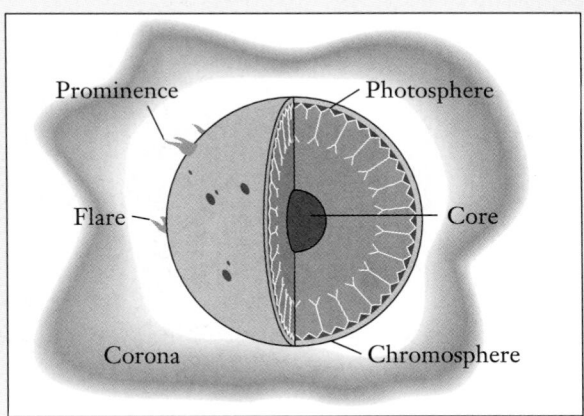

After completing the chapter, see *Identifying Misconceptions* in the Study Guide.

CHAPTER 24

The Solar System

Chapter Vocabulary

solar system
Mercury
Venus
Earth
Mars
Jupiter
Great Red Spot
Saturn
Uranus
Neptune
Pluto
comet
meteor
meteorite
asteroid

What do you think?

Science Journal This photo shows the remnants of a supernova explosion that happened many years ago. The ring is the outer portion of the star that was blown out into space. The bright object in the center is the stellar core that was left behind. New stars may form from the matter that is ejected into space by a supernova. Supernova nebulas contribute significantly more material to space than planetary nebulas do.

CHAPTER 24 The Solar System

Did you know that some of the brightest objects in the night sky are not stars at all but other planets in the solar system? A planetarium, such as New York's Hayden Planetarium pictured here, is a place where people can go to learn about objects in space. In this chapter, you will learn about the solar system's planets and how they are being explored. You also will learn about other objects such as comets, meteoroids, and asteroids.

What do you think?

Science Journal Look at the picture below with a classmate. Discuss what you think this might be or what is happening. Here's a hint: *Death sometimes can foster new birth*. Write down your answer or best guess in your Science Journal.

700

Theme Connection

Scale and Structure The solar system is composed of many objects of different sizes and structures. This theme is emphasized in the contrast between inner planets, which are small and rocky, and outer planets, most of which are large and composed of gases.

The planets of the solar system are like neighbors in space, but to humans on Earth, they look like tiny points of light among the thousands of others visible on a clear night. With the help of telescopes and space probes, the points of light become giant spheres, some with rings and moons and others pitted with countless craters. In this activity, you'll explore how craters are formed on the surfaces of planets and moons.

Model crater formation

1. Place white flour into a metal cake pan to a depth of 3 cm, completely covering the bottom of the pan.
2. Cover the flour with 1 cm of colored powdered drink mix or different colors of gelatin powder.
3. From different heights ranging from 10 cm to 25 cm, drop various-sized objects into the pan. Use marbles, bolts, and nuts.

Observe

In your Science Journal, make a drawing that shows what happened to the surface of the powder in the pan when each object was dropped from different heights.

Before You Read

FOLDABLES
Reading & Study Skills

Making a Compare and Contrast Study Fold As you study this chapter, use this Foldable to compare and contrast inner planets and outer planets. When you compare two things, you say how they are similar. When you contrast two things, you say how they are different.

| INNER PLANETS | OUTER PLANETS |

1. Place a sheet of paper in front of you so the long side is at the top. Fold the paper in half from the left side to the right side and then unfold.
2. Fold each side in to the centerfold line to divide the paper into fourths.
3. Write "Inner Planets" on one flap and "Outer Planets" on the other.
4. On the back of each flap, contrast inner planets and outer planets.
5. Under the flaps in the center section, compare inner planets and outer planets.

701

Purpose Use the Explore Activity to introduce students to the effects of impacts on planetary surfaces. L2 ELL COOP LEARN IS **Kinesthetic**

Materials cake pan, white flour, powdered drink mix or gelatin powder, marbles, bolts, nuts

Teaching Strategy Have students work in pairs or, if materials are in short supply, in groups of four.

Safety Precautions Students should wear safety goggles while dropping objects. Students with wheat allergies should not participate in this activity.

Troubleshooting Have students place the pans on large sheets of newspaper for easier clean-up.

Observe

A crater forms as the object impacts the powder. White flour splashes outward over the dark powder surface.

Performance Ask students to determine which craters were caused by the biggest objects. For craters that overlap, have them determine which ones were formed first. Use **Performance Assessment in the Science Classroom,** p. 89.

Before You Read

FOLDABLES
Reading & Study Skills

Dinah Zike Study Fold

Purpose Students use this Foldable to identify, illustrate, and collect information on the inner and outer planets. Then they can use what they have learned to compare and contrast the planets.

For additional help, see Foldables Worksheet, p. 17 in **Chapter Resources Booklet,** or go to the Glencoe Science Web site at **science.glencoe.com.** See After You Read in the Study Guide at the end of this chapter.

The Solar System

The Solar System

1 Motivate

Bellringer Transparency

Display the Section Focus Transparency for Section 1. Use the accompanying Transparency Activity Master. L2

ELL

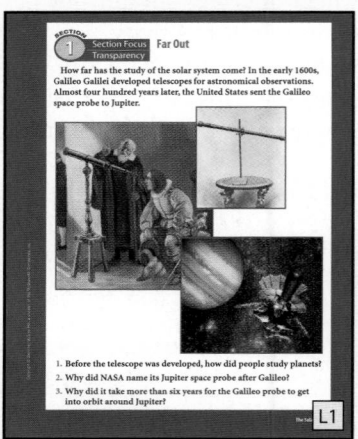

Tie to Prior Knowledge

Have students think about the apparent movement of the Sun in the sky each day. They should remember that it appears to rise in the east, move across the sky, and set in the west. Discuss with students why this apparent movement of the Sun once led people to think that Earth was the center of the universe. It seemed as though everything moved around Earth.

As You Read

What You'll Learn

■ **Compare** the Sun-centered and Earth-centered models of the solar system.
■ **Describe** current models of the formation of the solar system.

Vocabulary
solar system

Why It's Important
The solar system is your neighborhood in space.

Ideas About the Solar System

On a clear night, gazing at the sky can be an awe-inspiring experience. Early observers who noted the changing positions of the planets presented differing ideas about the solar system based on their observations and beliefs. Today, people know that the Sun and the stars only appear to move through the sky because Earth is moving. This wasn't always an accepted fact.

Earth-Centered Model Many early Greek scientists thought the planets, the Sun, and the Moon were fixed in separate spheres that rotated around Earth. The stars were thought to be fixed in another sphere that also rotated around Earth.

This is called the Earth-centered model of the solar system. It included Earth, the Moon, the Sun, five planets—Mercury, Venus, Mars, Jupiter, and Saturn—and the sphere of stars.

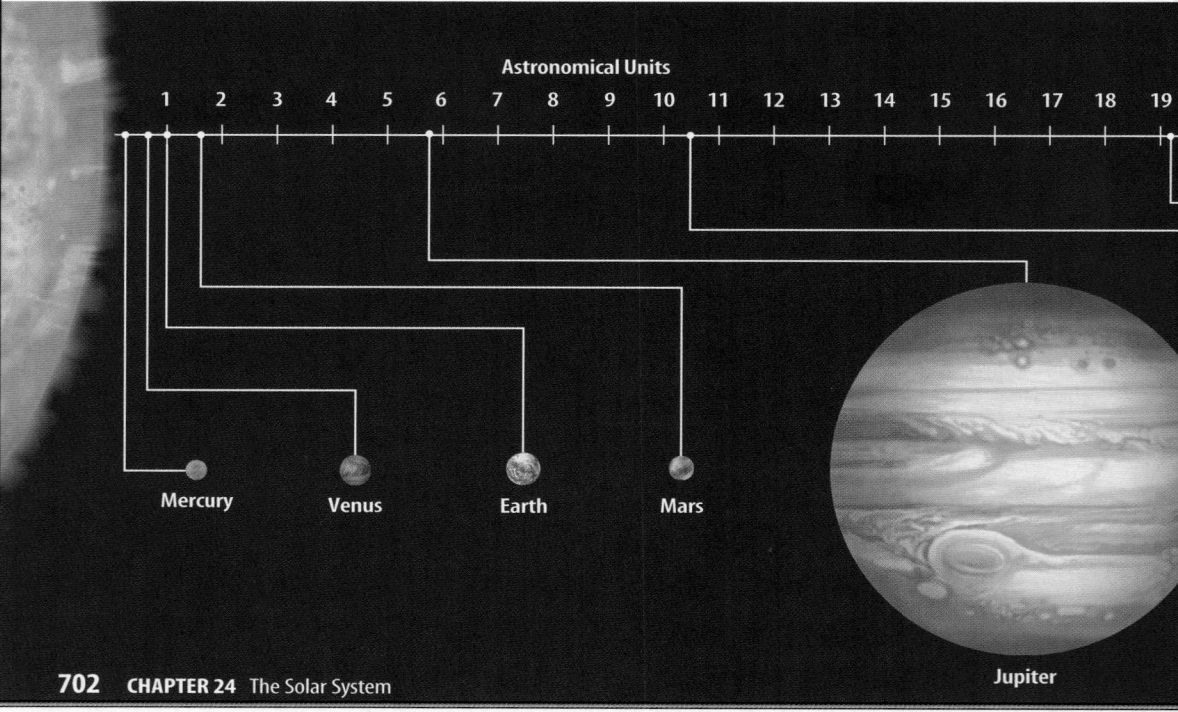

Astronomical Units

Mercury   Venus   Earth   Mars   Jupiter

702   CHAPTER 24 The Solar System

Section ✓ *Assessment* Planner

PORTFOLIO
Science Journal, p. 704
PERFORMANCE ASSESSMENT
Skill Builder Activities, p. 706
See page 732 for more options.

CONTENT ASSESSMENT
Section, p. 706
Challenge, p. 706
Chapter, pp. 732–733

Sun-Centered Model People believed the idea of an Earth-centered solar system for centuries. Then in 1543, Polish astronomer Nicholas Copernicus published a different view.

Copernicus stated that the Moon revolved around Earth and that Earth and the other planets revolved around the Sun. He also stated that the daily movement of the planets and the stars was due to Earth's rotation. This is the Sun-centered model of the solar system.

Using his telescope, Italian astronomer Galileo Galilei observed that Venus went through a full cycle of phases like the Moon's, which could be explained only if Venus were orbiting the Sun. From this, he concluded that Venus revolves around the Sun and that the Sun is the center of the solar system.

Modern View of the Solar System We now know that the **solar system** is made up of nine planets, including Earth, and many smaller objects that orbit the Sun. The nine planets and the Sun are shown in **Figure 1**. Notice how small Earth is compared with some of the other planets and the Sun.

The solar system includes a huge volume of space that stretches in all directions from the Sun. The Sun contains 99.86 percent of the mass of the solar system. Because of its gravitational pull, the Sun is the central object in the solar system. All other objects in the solar system revolve around the Sun.

SCIENCE *Online*

Research Visit the Glencoe Science Web site at **science.glencoe.com** for more information about the Solar System. Communicate to your class what you learn.

Figure 1
Each of the nine planets in the solar system is unique. The sizes of the planets are drawn to scale. The distances between the planets and the Sun are shown on a separate scale. One astronomical unit (AU) is the average distance between Earth and the Sun.

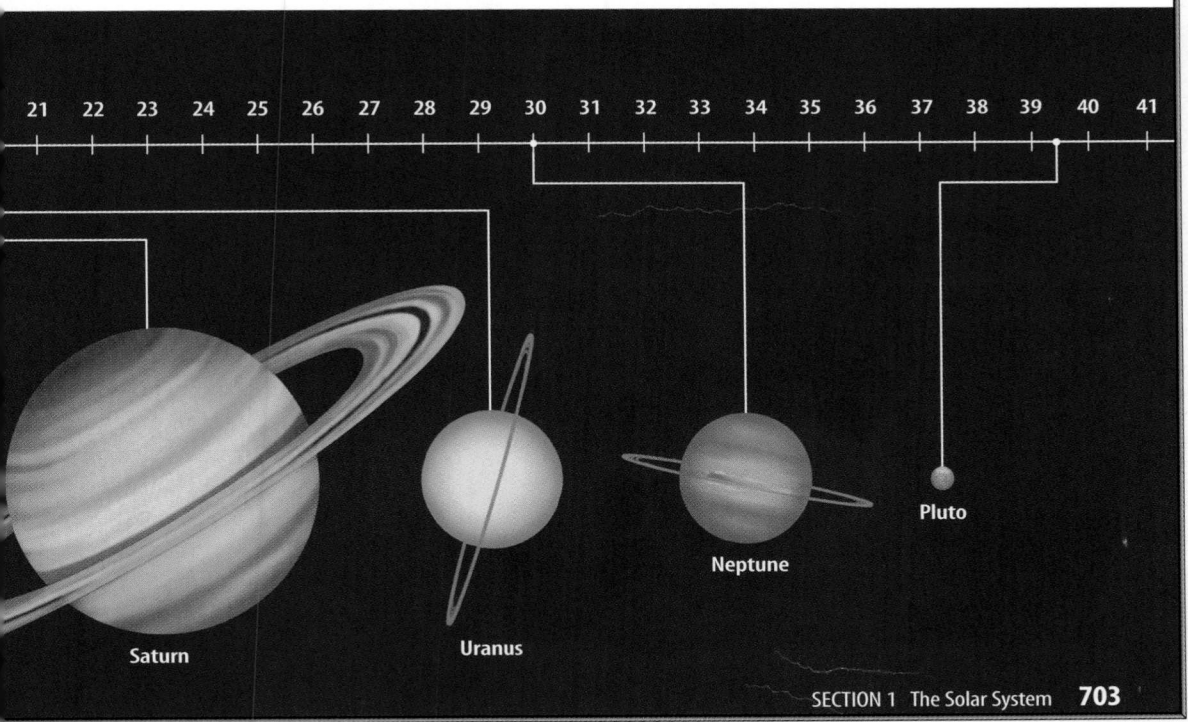

21 22 23 24 25 26 27 28 29 30 31 32 33 34 35 36 37 38 39 40 41

Pluto

Neptune

Saturn

Uranus

SECTION 1 The Solar System **703**

Ideas About the Solar System

Make a Model

Have students use common objects to make three-dimensional models of Earth-centered and Sun-centered solar systems. Display the models in class. L2
COOP LEARN **Visual-Spatial**

Discussion

Remind students that we now know the solar system has nine planets. **Is it possible that there could be other planets beyond Pluto?** Accept reasonable answers. Some may say no, that telescopes would have spotted other planets by now. Others may say that it is hard to detect objects at the outer reaches of the solar system, making the existence of undiscovered bodies possible. Explain that astronomers have studied the movements of Pluto to determine whether the gravity of an object farther out is affecting the tiny planet.

Visual Learning

Figure 1 **Why couldn't the same scale be used to show all the planets and relative distances between them?** If the same scale were used, the sizes of the planets would be too small to recognize or the overall size of the art would extend well beyond the room.

SCIENCE *Online*
Internet Addresses

_____

_____

_____

Explore the Glencoe Science Web site at **science.glencoe.com** to find out more about topics in this section.

Resource Manager

Chapter Resources Booklet
Transparency Activity, p. 48
Note-taking Worksheets, pp. 35–38
Directed Reading for Content Mastery, pp. 19, 20

How the Solar System Formed

☑ Reading Check

Answer at about 10 million degrees Celsius

Use Science Words

Word Origin Have students find the origin of the word *solar* (from the Latin *sol* meaning "Sun"). Have them list and define terms other than "solar system" that use solar. Possible answers: solar cell (device that converts sunlight into electricity), solar battery (system connecting many solar cells), solar flare (eruption of solar gases from the Sun's surface)

Use an Analogy

Ask students to visualize spinning ice skaters. Remind them of the way that skaters pull in their arms toward their bodies as they spin to increase rotational speed. This is analogous to the increase in rotational speed of the cloud from which the solar system formed. This cloud spun faster as more material was pulled toward its center.

Figure 2
Systems of planets such as the solar system form in areas of space like this, called a nebula.

How the Solar System Formed

Scientists hypothesize that the solar system formed from part of a nebula of gas, ice, and dust, like the one shown in **Figure 2,** about 4.6 billion years ago. Follow the steps shown in **Figures 3A** through **3D,** which illustrate how this might have happened. A cloud of material in this nebula was rotating slowly in space. A nearby star might have exploded, and the shock waves from this event could have caused the cloud to start contracting. As it contracted, the matter in the cloud was squeezed into less space. The cloud's density became greater, and the attraction of gravity pulled more gas and dust toward the cloud center. This caused the cloud to rotate faster, which in turn caused it to flatten into a disk with a dense center.

As the cloud contracted, its temperature began to increase. Eventually, the temperature in the core of the cloud reached about 10 million degrees Celsius and nuclear fusion began. A star was born—the beginning of the Sun.

Nuclear fusion occurs when atoms with low mass, such as hydrogen, combine to form heavier elements, such as helium. The new, heavier element contains slightly less mass than the sum of the lighter atoms that formed it. The "lost" mass is converted into energy.

☑ Reading Check *At what temperature does nuclear fusion begin?*

Planet Formation Not all of the nearby gas, ice, and dust was drawn into the core of the cloud. The matter that did not get pulled into the cloud's center collided and stuck together to form the planets and asteroids. Close to the Sun, the temperature was hot, and the easily vaporized elements could not condense into solids. This is why lighter elements are scarcer in the planets near the Sun than in planets farther out in the solar system.

The inner planets of the solar system—Mercury, Venus, Earth, and Mars—are small, rocky planets with iron cores. The outer planets are Jupiter, Saturn, Uranus, Neptune, and Pluto. Pluto, a small planet, is the only outer planet made mostly of rock and ice. The other outer planets are much larger and are made mostly of lighter substances such as hydrogen, helium, methane, and ammonia.

Science Journal

Solar System Models Have students write one-page reports in their Science Journals that describe what evidence led Copernicus to propose the Sun-centered model of the solar system. Some planets experience retrograde motion. Ask students to explain how this evidence refuted the Earth-centered model. Retrograde motion is difficult to explain with the Earth-centered model. L3 P

Inclusion Strategies

Learning Disabled Have students work in small groups to make mobiles of the solar system to display in class. Place learning disabled students in groups where they can contribute their ideas and knowledge. On the back side of each planet model, students should include facts such as temperature extremes, atmospheric conditions, length of orbit, and number of moons. L2
COOP LEARN Ⓝ **Visual-Spatial**

Figure 3

Through careful observations, astronomers have found clues that help explain how the solar system may have formed. A About 4.6 billion years ago, the solar system was a vast, swirling cloud of gas, ice, and dust. B Gradually, part of the nebula contracted into a large, tightly packed, spinning disk. The disk's center was so hot and dense that nuclear fusion reactions began to occur, and the Sun was born. C Eventually, the rest of the material in the disk cooled enough to clump into scattered solids. D Finally, these clumps collided and combined to become the nine planets that make up the solar system today.

Resource Manager

Chapter Resources Booklet
   Enrichment, p. 31
Home and Community Involvement, p. 48
Reading and Writing Skill Activities, p. 47

NATIONAL GEOGRAPHIC

Visualizing the Solar System's Formation

Have students examine the pictures and read the captions. Then ask the following questions.

How may gravity have affected the formation of the solar system? Gravity pulled the cloud of gas, ice, and dust together, causing it to spin faster and then form the Sun and planets.

How would the solar system have been different if the disk's center had been as hot and as dense as it was? Nuclear fusion reactions might not have occurred in the body that might have formed there, and the Sun would not have given off light and heat energy. Life would not have been possible anywhere in the solar system.

Activity

Have small groups of students use materials of their choice to make three-dimensional models of the different stages in the solar system's formation. Ask each group to present its model to the class. L2 COOP LEARN
Visual-Spatial and Interpersonal

Extension

Challenge students to research other solar systems that have been discovered in recent years and how they differ from our solar system. Ask students to present oral reports on their findings. L2 **Linguistic**

IDENTIFYING Misconceptions

Students may think the Sun is not a star. Refer to page 700F for teaching strategies that address this misconception.

Reteach

Have students refer to **Figure 3** and make a series of cards, each of which lists one step in the formation of the solar system. Pass the set of cards around and have students take turns putting the steps in order.

Challenge

Instruct students to write a mathematical formula that can be used to answer **Question 7.** Student answers should follow this pattern, although they may not use the same symbols: Where S₁ is the greater speed, S₂ is the lesser speed, and F is how much faster one planet moves, $F = S_1 - S_2$. L2

LS Logical-Mathematical

✓ *Assessment*

Process Have students use **Figure 1** to classify the planets in two groups based on size alone. In each group, have them order the planets from largest to smallest, determine how Earth compares in size to the other planets, and where Pluto fits into this classification. Four planets are larger and four are smaller than Earth; Pluto is the smallest planet. Use **Performance Assessment in the Science Classroom,** p. 99.

Table 1 Average Orbital Speed	
Planet	**Average Orbital Speed (km/s)**
Mercury	48
Venus	35
Earth	30
Mars	24
Jupiter	13
Saturn	9.7
Uranus	6.8
Neptune	5.4
Pluto	4.7

Johannes Kepler

Motions of the Planets

Physics INTEGRATION

When Nicholas Copernicus developed his Sun-centered model of the solar system, he thought that the planets orbited the Sun in circles. In the early 1600s, German mathematician Johannes Kepler began studying the orbits of the planets. He discovered that the shapes of the orbits are not circular. They are oval shaped, or elliptical. His calculations further showed that the Sun is not at the center of the orbits but is slightly offset.

Kepler also discovered that the planets travel at different speeds in their orbits around the Sun, as shown in **Table 1.** By studying these speeds, you can see that the planets closer to the Sun travel faster than planets farther away from the Sun. Because of their slower speeds and the longer distance they must travel, the outer planets take much longer to orbit the Sun than the inner planets do.

Copernicus's ideas, considered radical at the time, led to the birth of modern astronomy. Early scientists didn't have technology such as computers and space probes to perform rapid calculations and learn about the planets. Nevertheless, they developed theories about the solar system that still are used today.

Section 1 Assessment

1. Describe the Sun-centered model of the solar system.
2. How do most scientists hypothesize that the solar system formed?
3. The outer planets are rich in water, methane, and ammonia—the materials needed for life. Yet life is unlikely on these planets. Explain.
4. Why do the outer planets take longer to orbit the Sun than the inner planets do?
5. **Think Critically** Would a year on the planet Neptune be longer or shorter than an Earth year? Explain.

Skill Builder Activities

6. **Concept Mapping** Make a concept map that compares and contrasts the Earth-centered model with the Sun-centered model of the solar system. **For more help, refer to the** Science Skill Handbook.
7. **Solving One-Step Equations** Use the average-orbital-speed data in **Table 1** to determine how much faster Mercury travels in its orbit than Earth travels in its orbit. How much faster does Mars travel than Neptune? How much faster does Earth travel than Pluto? **For more help, refer to the** Science Skill Handbook.

706 **CHAPTER 24** The Solar System

Resource Manager

Chapter Resources Booklet
Reinforcement, p. 27
Activity Worksheets, pp. 5–6
Cultural Diversity, p. 29

Answers to Section Assessment

1. All objects in the solar system orbit the Sun.
2. About 4.6 billion years ago, a large cloud of gas, ice, and dust began to condense. The center of the cloud formed the Sun. The planets and other objects formed from the outer portions of the cloud.
3. Because the outer planets are very cold, these materials are frozen or are in the gaseous state.
4. Outer planets travel at a slower speed and have larger orbits.
5. Longer; Neptune's orbit is much larger, and it travels more slowly.
6. Concept maps should include information on the central body of each

model, and the reason objects in the night sky are observed to move as they do.
7. Mercury travels 18 km/s faster than Earth (48 km/s − 30 km/s). Mars travels 18.6 km/sec faster than Neptune (24 km/s − 5.4 km/s). Earth travels 25.3 km/s faster than Pluto (30 km/s − 4.7 km/s).

Planetary Orbits

Planets travel around the Sun along fixed paths called orbits. As you construct a model of a planetary orbit, you will observe that the shape of planetary orbits is an ellipse.

What You'll Investigate
How can you model planetary orbits?

Materials
thumbtacks or pins (2)   metric ruler
cardboard (23 cm × 30 cm)   string (25 cm)
paper (21.5 cm × 28 cm)   pencil

Goals
■ **Model** planetary orbits.
■ **Calculate** changes in ellipses.

Safety Precautions

Procedure

1. Place a blank sheet of paper on top of the cardboard and insert two thumbtacks or pins about 3 cm apart.

2. Tie the string into a circle with a circumference of 15 cm to 20 cm. Loop the string around the thumbtacks. With someone holding the tacks or pins, place your pencil inside the loop and pull it tight.

3. Moving the pencil around the tacks and keeping the string tight, mark a line until you have completed a smooth, closed curve, called an ellipse.

4. Repeat steps 1 through 3 several times. First, vary the distance between the tacks, then vary the length of the string. However, change only one of these each time. Make a data table to record the changes in the sizes and shapes of the ellipses.

5. Orbits usually are described in terms of eccentricity, *e.* The eccentricity of any ellipse is determined by dividing the distance, *d,* between the foci (fixed points—here, the tacks) by the length, *l,* of the major axis. See the diagram below.

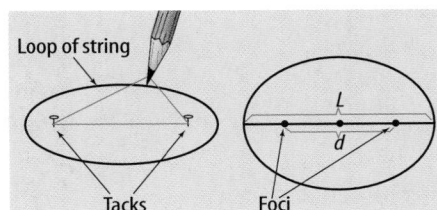

Loop of string / Tacks / Foci / l / d

6. **Calculate** and record the eccentricity of the ellipses that you constructed.

7. **Research** the eccentricities of planetary orbits. Construct an ellipse with the same eccentricity as Earth's orbit.

Conclude and Apply

1. **Analyze** the effect that a change in the length of the string or the distance between the tacks has on the shape of the ellipse.

2. **Hypothesize** what must be done to the string or placement of tacks to decrease the eccentricity of a constructed ellipse.

3. **Describe** the shape of Earth's orbit. Where is the Sun located within the orbit?

*C*ommunicating
Your Data

Compare your results with those of other students. **For more help, refer to the** Science Skill Handbook.

Sample data:

Ellipse	d (cm)	l (cm)	e (d/l)
#1	3	15.6	0.19
#2	5	13.5	0.37
#3	5	8.7	0.57
Earth	0.48	28	0.017

*C*ommunicating
Your Data

Students' results should be similar. Have them identify which ellipse produced the most circular orbit. The one with foci closest together.

BENCH TESTED

Purpose Students model planetary orbits and calculate the eccentricity of ellipses. ⌊L2⌋ ⌊ELL⌋
⌊IS⌋ **Logical-Mathematical**
Process Skills observing, using numbers, comparing and contrasting, forming a hypothesis, making and using tables, communicating
Time Required 40 minutes
Teaching Strategy Provide students with several values for *d* and *l* for imaginary ellipses and allow them to practice solving for *e* using the equation $e = d/l$.

Answers to Questions

1. Increasing the length of the string or decreasing the distance between the tacks makes the shape more circular. Decreasing the string's length or increasing the distance between the foci makes the shape more elliptical.

2. Lengthen the string or move the tacks closer to each other.

3. Earth's orbit is an ellipse with the Sun at one of the foci.

✓ *Assessment*

Process Have students compare and contrast drawing ellipses and circles. A circle is drawn in the same way as an ellipse, but both foci are at the same point. Use **PASC,** p. 127.

SECTION

2

The Inner Planets

1 Motivate

Bellringer Transparency

Display the Section Focus Transparency for Section 2. Use the accompanying Transparency Activity Master. L2
ELL

Tie to Prior Knowledge

Make four columns on the board, with the name of one of the four inner planets at the top of each column. Have students brainstorm things they know about each planet. Add each item to the list. Save the list and review it with the class after reading this section.

SECTION

2 The Inner Planets

As You Read

What You'll Learn

- **List** the inner planets in their relative order from the Sun.
- **Describe** important characteristics of each inner planet.
- **Compare and contrast** Venus and Earth.

Vocabulary

Mercury   Earth
Venus   Mars

Why It's Important

The planet you live on is uniquely capable of sustaining life.

Figure 4
Large cliffs on Mercury might have formed when the crust of the planet broke as the planet contracted.

Inner Planets

Today, people know more about the solar system than ever before. Better telescopes allow astronomers to observe the planets from Earth and space. In addition, space probes have explored much of the solar system. Prepare to take a tour of the solar system through the eyes of some space probes.

Mercury The closest planet to the Sun is **Mercury.** It is also the second-smallest planet. The first American spacecraft mission to Mercury was in 1974–1975 by *Mariner 10.* The spacecraft flew by the planet and sent pictures back to Earth. *Mariner 10* photographed only 45 percent of Mercury's surface, so scientists don't know what the other 55 percent looks like. What they do know is that the surface of Mercury has many craters and looks much like Earth's Moon. It also has cliffs as high as 3 km on its surface. These cliffs may have formed at a time when Mercury apparently shrank in diameter, as seen in **Figure 4.**

Why would Mercury have shrunk? *Mariner 10* detected a weak magnetic field around Mercury. This indicates that the planet has an iron core. Some scientists hypothesize that the crust of Mercury solidified while the iron core was still hot and molten.

As the core cooled and solidified, it contracted. The cliffs might have resulted from breaks in the crust caused by this contraction.

B Cliffs on the surface provide evidence that Mercury shrank.

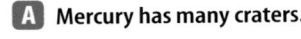

A Mercury has many craters.

708   CHAPTER 24 The Solar System

Section ✓*Assessment* Planner

PORTFOLIO
Activity, p. 709
PERFORMANCE ASSESSMENT
MiniLab, p. 711
Math Skills Integration, p. 712
Skill Building Activities, p. 713
See page 732 for more options.

CONTENT ASSESSMENT
Section, p. 713
Challenge, p. 713
Chapter, pp. 732–733

Does Mercury have an atmosphere? Because of Mercury's small size and low gravitational pull, most gases that could form an atmosphere escape into space. *Mariner 10* found traces of gases that were first thought to be an atmosphere. However, these gases are now known to be temporarily trapped hydrogen and helium from the solar wind. Mercury traps these gases and holds them for just a few weeks.

Earth-based observations have also found traces of sodium and potassium around Mercury. Scientists think that these atoms come from rocks in the planet's crust. Therefore, Mercury has no true atmosphere. This lack of atmosphere and the nearness of Mercury to the Sun cause this planet to have great extremes in temperature. Mercury's surface temperature can reach 425°C during the day and it can drop to −170°C at night.

Venus The second planet from the Sun is **Venus.** Venus is sometimes called Earth's twin because its size and mass are similar to Earth's. In 1962, *Mariner 2* flew within 34,400 km of Venus and sent back information about Venus's atmosphere and rotation. The former Soviet Union landed the first probe on the surface of Venus in 1970. *Venera 7,* however, stopped working in less than an hour because of the high temperature and pressure. Additional *Venera* probes photographed and mapped the surface of Venus using cameras and radar. Between 1990 and 1994, the U.S. *Magellan* probe used its radar to make the most detailed maps yet of Venus's surface. It collected radar images of 98 percent of Venus's surface. Notice the huge volcano with visible lava flows shown in **Figure 5.**

Clouds on Venus are so dense that only a small percentage of the sunlight that strikes the top of the clouds reaches the planet's surface. The solar energy that does reach the surface is trapped by the carbon dioxide gas. This causes a greenhouse effect similar to, but more intense than, Earth's greenhouse effect. Due to this intense greenhouse effect, the temperature on the surface of Venus is between 450°C and 475°C.

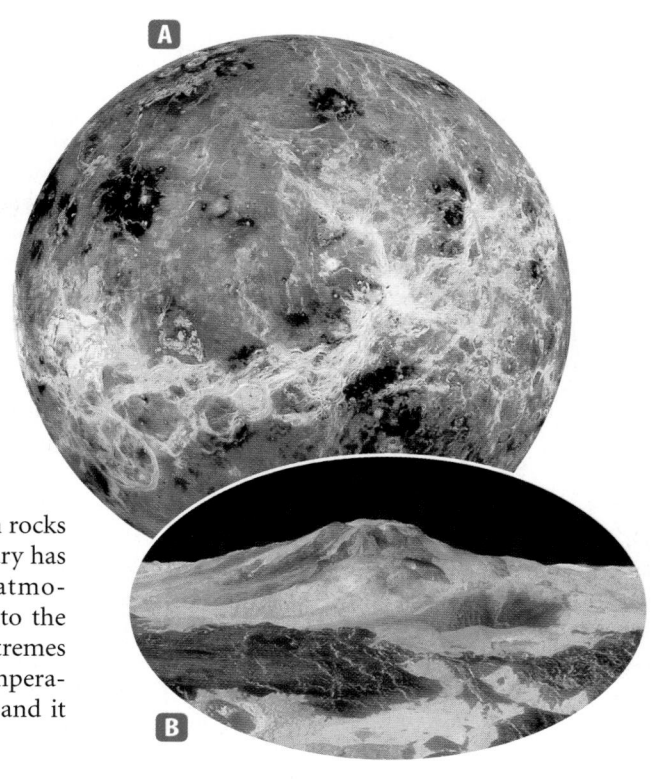

Figure 5
A Although Venus is similar to Earth, important differences exist. *What are some of these differences?* **B** Maat Mons is the highest volcano on Venus. Lava flows extend for hundreds of kilometers across the plains.

2 Teach

Inner Planets

Extension
Direct interested students to research the *Mariner 10* mission to Mercury. Students can access the Glencoe Science Web site for more information. Have these students work together to organize their findings and present them to the class. L2 COOP LEARN IS **Linguistic**

Caption Answer
Figure 5 It's much hotter, its air pressure is much higher, it is completely covered with clouds.

Activity
Have students research the sizes and surface conditions of the inner planets and then draw each planet to scale in their Science Journals. Challenge them to illustrate at least one important characteristic of each planet's surface. L2 ELL IS **Visual-Spatial** P

Teacher FYI
The composition of the atmosphere or the surface of a planet produces its apparent color. Venus's yellow color is due to its clouds of sulfuric acid. Earth's oceans of liquid water help give it a distinctive blue color. Mars, the red planet, gets its color from iron oxide or rust in weathered rocks on its surface.

Resource Manager

Chapter Resources Booklet
Transparency Activity, p. 49
Directed Reading for Content Mastery, p. 20
Enrichment, p. 32

Discussion

The two closest planets to Earth are Venus and Mars. But when astronauts from Earth visit another planet, it will be Mars rather than Venus. **Why is Mars a more likely candidate for a visit than Venus?** Venus has very high temperature and air pressure, which have caused space probes to malfunction. Students should infer that surface conditions on Mars are less hostile for humans.

Caption Answer

Figure 6 Earth's surface temperatures allow water to exist as a solid, a liquid, and a gas.

Quick Demo

Demonstrate the general difference in size between inner and outer planets by cutting circles out of poster board that represent Jupiter and Earth. The radius of the circle representing Jupiter should be 11.2 times the radius of the circle representing Earth. Pass the two circles around the class.

Visual Learning

Figure 7C How might the discovery of this deep valley help support the idea that Mars once had surface water? What does this valley resemble on Earth? The valley may have been cut by flowing water; it resembles valleys and canyons on Earth that have been cut by rivers.

Figure 6
More than 70 percent of Earth's surface is covered by liquid water. *What is unique about surface temperatures on Earth?*

Figure 7
Many features on Mars are similar to those on Earth.

Earth **Figure 6** shows **Earth,** the third planet from the Sun. The average distance from Earth to the Sun is 150 million km, or one astronomical unit (AU). Unlike other planets, surface temperatures on Earth allow water to exist as a solid, liquid, and gas. Earth's atmosphere causes most meteors to burn up before they reach the surface, and it protects life-forms from the effects of the Sun's intense radiation.

Mars Look at **Figure 7A.** Can you guess why **Mars,** the fourth planet from the Sun, has been called the red planet? Iron oxide in the weathered rocks on its surface gives it a reddish-yellow color. Other features of Mars visible from Earth are its polar ice caps and changes in the coloring of the planet's surface. The ice caps are made mostly of frozen carbon dioxide and frozen water.

Most of the information scientists have about Mars came from *Mariner 9,* the *Viking* probes, *Mars Global Surveyor,* and *Mars Pathfinder. Mariner 9* orbited Mars in 1971 and 1972. It revealed long channels on the planet that might have been carved by flowing water. *Mariner 9* also discovered the largest volcano in the solar system, Olympus Mons, shown in **Figure 7B.** Olympus Mons is probably extinct. Large rift valleys that formed in the Martian crust also were discovered. One such valley, Valles Marineris, is shown in **Figure 7C.**

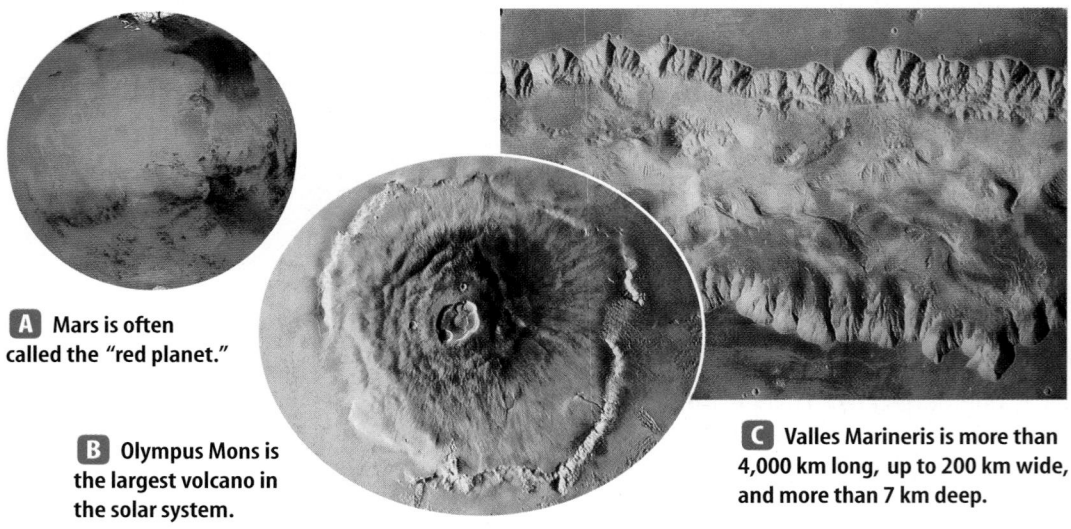

A Mars is often called the "red planet."

B Olympus Mons is the largest volcano in the solar system.

C Valles Marineris is more than 4,000 km long, up to 200 km wide, and more than 7 km deep.

Curriculum Connection

Literature Invite students to read a classic work of fiction that deals with Martians, such as *War of the Worlds* by H.G. Wells, originally published in 1898. Encourage students to discuss in class what they've read, concentrating on the differences between what the authors thought Mars was like and what we know of it today. L2
Linguistic

✓ Active Reading

Pair of Pairs This strategy encourages students as partners to respond to a question. They brainstorm together, writing down their ideas. After a few minutes, they combine with another pair and share responses. Finally, the teacher asks the groups of four to share any responses. Have students use the Pair of Pairs strategy on a Think Critically question in a Section Assessment in this chapter.

The Viking Probes The *Viking 1* and *2* probes arrived at Mars in 1976. Each spacecraft consisted of an orbiter and a lander. The *Viking 1* and *2* orbiters photographed the entire surface of Mars from their orbits, while the *Viking 1* and *2* landers touched down on the planet's surface. The landers carried equipment to detect possible life on Mars. Some of this equipment was designed to analyze gases in Martian soil. These experiments found no evidence of gaseous life by-products in the soil. The *Viking* landers also sent back pictures of a reddish-colored, barren, rocky, windswept surface.

Global Surveyor and Pathfinder The *Mars Pathfinder* carried a robot rover named Sojourner with equipment that allowed it to analyze samples of Martian rock and soil. Data from these tests indicated that iron in Mars's crust might have been leached out by groundwater. *Mars Pathfinder* also gathered data on Mars's weather. In addition, cameras onboard *Global Surveyor* showed features that looked like gullies formed by flowing water and deposits of soil and rock carried by water flows. The features, shown in **Figure 8,** are young enough that scientists are considering the idea that liquid groundwater may exist on Mars and that it sometimes reaches the surface. It is also possible that recent volcanic activity could have melted frost beneath the Martian surface. The features compare to those left by flash floods on Earth, such as on Mount St. Helens. Scientists also believe that water is frozen into Mars's crust at the poles.

✔ Reading Check *What evidence indicates that Mars has water?*

 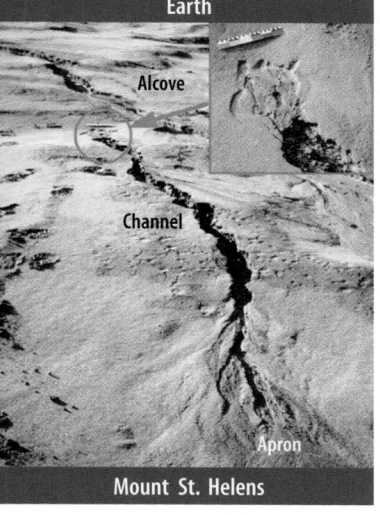 

Mars — Alcove — Channels — Aprons — Crater Wall

Earth — Alcove — Channel — Apron — Mount St. Helens

Figure 8
Compare the features found on Mars with those found on an area of Mount St. Helens in Washington state that experienced a flash flood.

Mini LAB

Inferring Effects of Gravity

Procedure
1. Suppose you are a crane operator who is sent to Mars to help build a Mars colony.
2. You know that your crane can lift 44,500 N on Earth, but the gravity on Mars is only 40 percent of Earth's gravity.
3. Determine how much mass your crane could lift on Mars.

Analysis
1. How can what you have discovered be an advantage over construction on Earth?
2. How might construction advantages change the overall design of the Mars colony?

Mini LAB

Purpose Students compare the mass of objects on Earth and Mars. ☐L2
IS Logical-Mathematical

Teaching Strategy Help students determine how much mass the crane will lift on Mars.

44,500 N + .6(44,500 N) =
44,500 N + 26,700 = 71,200 N

Analysis
1. Because Mars's gravity is weaker, the same crane could lift more massive objects on Mars than on Earth.
2. Possible answer: Designers would be able to use construction materials with greater mass.

✔ Assessment

Process Have students infer how construction would be affected on a planet with greater gravity than Earth's. Only items less massive than those used on Earth could be lifted. Use **PASC,** p. 89.

✔ Reading Check

Answer Mars has surface features that could have been formed by flowing water. Rock and soil analysis shows that iron in Mars's crust might have been leached by groundwater.

Resource Manager

Chapter Resources Booklet
    MiniLAB, p. 3
Mathematics Skill Activities, p. 1
Reading and Writing Skill Activities, p. 11

Inner Planets, continued

SCIENCE *Online*

Internet Addresses

_____

_____

_____

Explore the Glencoe Science Web site at **science.glencoe.com** to find out more about topics in this section.

Math Skills Activity

National Math Standards

Correlation to Mathematics Objectives

1, 2, 9

Answer to Practice Problem

1. (12,756 km) × (0.96) = 12,246 km

Teacher FYI

Biological tests conducted on Mars by the *Viking 1* and *Viking 2* landers did not show evidence of life, but did not rule it out. One test in particular gave a reading that could have indicated a biological reaction, but the same reading could have been achieved by chemical reactions.

SCIENCE *Online*

Research Visit the Glencoe Science Web site at **science.glencoe.com** for information about NASA space exploration. Communicate to your class what you learn.

Mars's Atmosphere The *Viking* and *Global Surveyor* probes analyzed gases in the Martian atmosphere and determined atmospheric pressure and temperature. They found that Mars's atmosphere is much thinner than Earth's. It is composed mostly of carbon dioxide, with some nitrogen and argon. Surface temperatures range from −125°C to 35°C. The temperature difference between day and night results in strong winds on the planet, which can cause global dust storms during certain seasons. This information will help in planning possible human exploration of Mars in the future.

Martian Seasons Mars is tilted on its axis by 24°, which is close to Earth's tilt of 23.5°. Because of this, Mars goes through seasons as it orbits the Sun, just like Earth does. The polar ice caps get larger during the Martian winter as ice collects on their surface. The ice caps shrink during the summer. As one ice cap shrinks, the other expands, and both their surfaces change color during different seasons. Wind causes this seasonal change in the coloration of the Martian surface. When the seasons change, winds blow the dust around on the planet's surface. As dust blows off one area, it might look darker.

Math Skills Activity

Calculating with Percentages

Example Problem

The diameter of Earth is 12,756 km. The diameter of Mars is 53.2 percent of the diameter of Earth. Calculate the diameter of Mars.

Solution

1 *This is what you know:*

diameter of Earth: 12,756 km
percent of Earth's diameter: 53.2%
decimal equivalent: 0.532 (53.2% ÷ 100%)

2 *This is what you need to find:* diameter of Mars

3 *This is the equation you need to use:* (diameter of Earth) × (decimal equivalent) = diameter of Mars

4 *Solve the equation for the diameter of Mars:* (12,756 km) × (0.532) = 6,786 km

> **Practice Problem**
>
> Use the same procedure to calculate the diameter of Venus. Its diameter is 96.0 percent of the diameter of Earth.

For more help, refer to the Math Skill Handbook.

Inclusion Strategies

Gifted Have students research famous astronomers from different eras. Students can work in groups of five or six to write plays in which these astronomers are brought together to discuss their ideas. Encourage students to perform their plays for the class. L3 COOP LEARN

Resource Manager

Chapter Resources Booklet
Reinforcement, p. 28

Earth Science Critical Thinking/Problem Solving, p. 8

Performance Assessment in the Science Classroom, p. 46

Martian Moons Mars has two small, irregularly shaped moons that are heavily cratered. Phobos, shown in **Figure 9,** is about 25 km in length, and Deimos is about 13 km in length. Deimos orbits Mars once every 31 h, while Phobos speeds around Mars once every 7 h.

Phobos has grooves on its surface that seem to radiate out in all directions from the giant Stickney Crater. Some of the grooves are 700 m across and 90 m deep. Phobos's orbit is spiraling slowly inward toward Mars. It is expected to crash into the Martian surface in about 50 million years.

Deimos is the outer of Mars's two moons. It is among the smallest known moons in the solar system. Its surface is smoother in appearance than that of Phobos because some of its craters have partially filled with soil and rock.

As you toured the inner planets through the eyes of the space probes, you saw how each planet is unique. Refer to **Table 3** following Section 3 for a summary of the planets. Mercury, Venus, Earth, and Mars are different from the outer planets, which you'll explore in the next section.

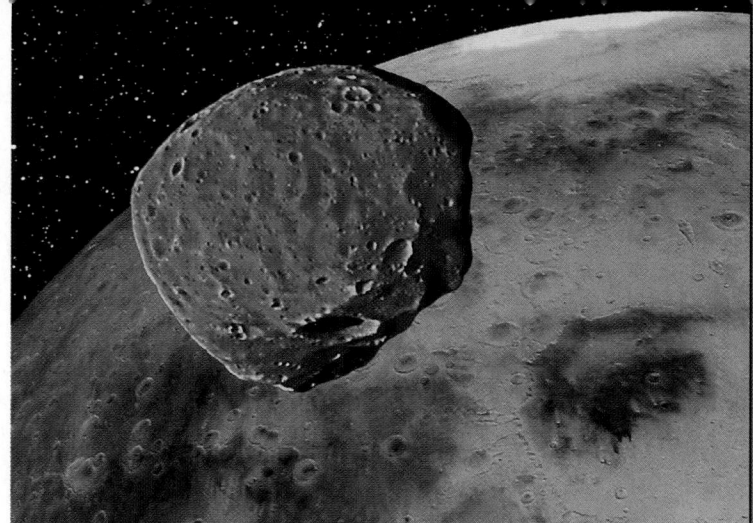

Figure 9
Phobos orbits Mars once every 7 h. *Why does Phobos have so many craters?*

Section Assessment

1. How are Mercury and Earth's Moon similar?

2. List one important characteristic of each inner planet.

3. Although Venus often is called Earth's twin, why would life as you know it be unlikely on Venus?

4. Name the inner planets in order from the Sun.

5. **Think Critically** Do the closest planets to the Sun always have the hottest surface temperatures? Explain.

Skill Builder Activities

6. **Interpreting Data** Using the information in this section, explain how Mars is like Earth. How are they different? **For more help, refer to the** Science Skill Handbook.

7. **Communicating** Use textbooks and NASA materials to investigate NASA's missions to Mars. In your Science Journal, report on the possibility of life on Mars and the tests that have been conducted to see whether life-forms exist. **For more help, refer to the** Science Skill Handbook.

Answers to Section Assessment

1. Both are heavily cratered.
2. Possible answer: Mercury: many craters; Venus: dense cloud cover; Earth: water exists in three states; Mars: appears red because of iron oxide
3. because of very high surface temperatures and pressure

4. Mercury, Venus, Earth, Mars
5. No; Venus is hotter than Mercury because of dense clouds that trap heat.
6. Alike: inner planets, rocky, polar ice caps, volcanoes, features made by flowing water, seasons; different: Mars has red surface, no known liquid water or life, Mars has thinner

atmosphere of mostly CO_2, Mars is colder than Earth, Mars has two moons while Earth has one.
7. Students can find detailed information on past, present, and future Mars missions by accessing the Glencoe Science Web site.

---

3 Assess

Reteach
Review the information on the inner planets that students gave at the beginning of this section. Ask if they would like to change or add to this information. [L1]

Challenge
Earth's sky is basically blue, while Mars's is basically pink. Challenge students to find out why. Have them write a two-paragraph explanation. Earth's sky is blue because blue light is scattered by the atmosphere more than colors with shorter wavelengths. Mars's sky is pink for two reasons: its surface is red, and its thin atmosphere contains reddish dust particles from the surface; the red-colored dust makes the scattered light look pinkish. [L3]

Assessment

Performance Ask students to write a list of the equipment they would need to live on the surface of Mars. As students call out items, have them explain why each was included. Use **Performance Assessment in the Science Classroom,** p. 173.

SECTION

3

The Outer Planets

1 Motivate

Bellringer Transparency

Display the Section Focus Transparency for Section 3. Use the accompanying Transparency Activity Master. L2

ELL

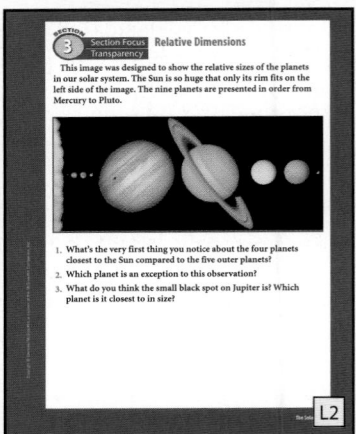

Section Focus Transparency — Relative Dimensions

This image was designed to show the relative sizes of the planets in our solar system. The Sun is so huge that only its rim fits on the left side of the image. The nine planets are presented in order from Mercury to Pluto.

1. What's the very first thing you notice about the four planets closest to the Sun compared to the five outer planets?
2. Which planet is an exception to this observation?
3. What do you think the small black spot on Jupiter is? Which planet is it closest to in size?

L2

Tie to Prior Knowledge

Ask students to recall an important characteristic of one of the outer planets. Students might recall Saturn's rings or Jupiter's Great Red Spot. Explain that some of these characteristics, such as Saturn's rings, are visible from Earth.

SECTION

3

The Outer Planets

As You Read

What You'll Learn

- **Describe** the major characteristics of Jupiter, Saturn, Uranus, and Neptune.
- **Explain** how Pluto differs from the other outer planets.

Vocabulary

Jupiter — Uranus
Great Red Spot — Neptune
Saturn — Pluto

Why It's Important

Studying the outer planets might help scientists better understand Earth.

Figure 10

A Jupiter is the largest planet in the solar system, containing more mass than all of the other planets combined. **B** The Great Red Spot is a giant storm about 12,000 km in size from east to west.

Outer Planets

You may have heard about the *Voyager* and *Galileo* spacecrafts. They were not the first probes to the outer planets, but they gathered a lot of new information about them. Follow the spacecrafts as you read about their journeys to the outer planets.

Jupiter In 1979, *Voyager 1* and *Voyager 2* flew past **Jupiter,** the largest planet and the fifth planet from the Sun. *Galileo* reached Jupiter in 1995. The spacecrafts gathered new information about Jupiter's atmosphere and discovered three new moons. *Voyager* probes also revealed that Jupiter has faint dust rings around it and that one of its moons has volcanoes on it.

Jupiter's Atmosphere Jupiter is composed mostly of hydrogen and helium, with some ammonia, methane, and water vapor. Scientists hypothesize that the atmosphere of hydrogen and helium gradually changes to a planetwide ocean of liquid hydrogen and helium toward the middle of the planet. Below this liquid layer might be a solid rocky core. The extreme pressure and temperature, however, would make the core different from any rock on Earth.

You've probably seen pictures from the probes of Jupiter's colorful clouds. In **Figure 10,** you can see bands of white, red, tan, and brown clouds in its atmosphere. Continuous storms of swirling, high-pressure gas have been observed on Jupiter. The **Great Red Spot** is the most spectacular of these storms. Lightning also has been observed within Jupiter's clouds.

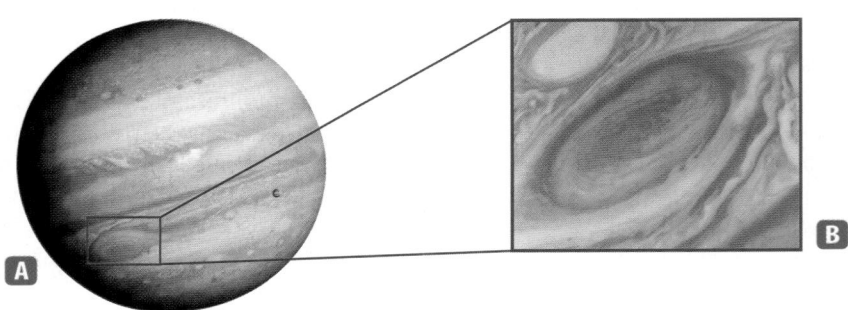

Section ✓ *Assessment* Planner

PORTFOLIO
Science Journal, p. 718

PERFORMANCE ASSESSMENT
Try at Home MiniLAB, p. 716
Skill Builder Activities, p. 719
See page 732 for more options.

CONTENT ASSESSMENT
Section, p. 719
Challenge, p. 719
Chapter, pp. 732–733

Table 2 Large Moons of Jupiter

Io The most volcanically active object in the solar system; sulfur lava gives it its distinctive reddish and orange colors; has a thin oxygen, sulfur, and sulfur dioxide atmosphere.

Europa Rocky interior is covered by a 100-km-thick crust of ice, which has a network of cracks, indicating tectonic activity; an ocean might exist under the ice crust; has a thin oxygen atmosphere.

Ganymede Has a crust of ice about 100 km thick, covered with grooves; crust might surround a mantle of water or slushy ice; has a rocky core and a thin hydrogen atmosphere.

Callisto Has a heavily cratered crust of ice and rock several hundred kilometers thick; crust might surround a salty ocean around a rock core; has a thin atmosphere of hydrogen, oxygen, and carbon dioxide.

Moons of Jupiter At least 16 moons orbit Jupiter. In 1610, the astronomer Galileo Galilei was the first person to see Jupiter's four largest moons, shown in **Table 2.** Io (I oh) is the closest large moon to Jupiter. Jupiter's tremendous gravitational force and the gravity of Europa, Jupiter's next large moon, pull on Io. This force heats up Io, causing it to be the most volcanically active object in the solar system. You can see a volcano erupting on Io in **Figure 11.** Europa is composed mostly of rock with a thick, smooth crust of ice. Under the ice might be an ocean as deep as 50 km. If this ocean of water exists, it will be the only place in the solar system, other than Earth and possibly Callisto, where liquid water exists in large quantities. Next is Ganymede, the largest moon in the solar system—larger even than the planet Mercury. Callisto, the last of Jupiter's large moons, is composed of ice and rock. Studying these moons adds to knowledge about the origin of Earth and the rest of the solar system.

Figure 11
Voyager 2 **photographed the eruption of this volcano on Io in July 1979.**

Outer Planets

Activity

Have pairs of students make flash cards of the planets in the solar system. They can draw the planet on one side of the card and write anything they know about it on the other side. Students should keep their flash cards handy so they can correct or update their information as they continue to read this chapter. L2
COOP LEARN ⚠ **Interpersonal**

Visual Learning

Table 2 Have students compare and contrast the large moons of Jupiter.

Activity

Form teams of four students to play "Planet Jeopardy." Have a student read statements from this section and the previous section and then call on a team to form the correct question. Award points for correct questions. L2
COOP LEARN ⚠ **Linguistic**

Resource Manager

Chapter Resources Booklet
Transparency Activity, p. 50
Directed Reading for Content Mastery, p. 21

Teacher FYI

In 1994, astronomers witnessed comet fragments crash into Jupiter's atmosphere. The impact left huge holes in Jupiter's clouds that lasted for weeks. No one knows what the fragments encountered under the clouds because no one has ever seen beneath Jupiter's cloud tops.

Outer Planets,
continued

TRY AT HOME
Mini LAB

Purpose Students design and draw a scale model that compares the planets. [L1] [ELL]

[IS] Logical-Mathematical

Materials metric ruler, drawing compass, pencil, paper

Teaching Strategy Have students use Earth's diameter as a basis for the scale. If Earth's diameter equals 1 unit, dividing the other planets' diameters by Earth's diameter yields the units for each planet.

Analysis
1. Answers should equal the distance from Sun to Earth in each model.
2. At 1 AU = 2 m, the Sun would be 19 mm in diameter. The model Earth would be considerably smaller—0.18 mm, or 0.018 cm.

✓ Assessment

Performance To further assess students' understanding of scale models, have them make planet models out of balls of clay. Use **PASC**, p. 123.

Figure 12
Saturn's rings are composed of pieces of rock and ice.

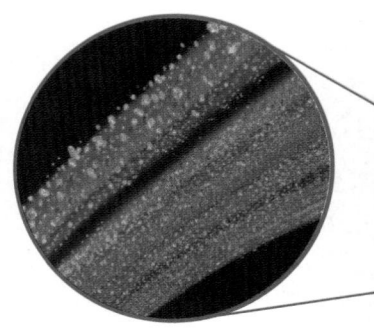

TRY AT HOME
Mini LAB

Modeling Planets

Procedure
1. Research the planets to determine how the sizes of the planets in the solar system compare with each other.
2. Select a scale for the diameter of Earth.
3. Make a model by drawing a circle with this diameter on **paper.**
4. Using Earth's diameter as 1.0 unit, draw each of the other planets to scale.

Analysis
1. What would 1 AU be equal to in this model?
2. Using a scale of 1 AU = 2 m, how large would the models have to be to remain in scale?

716 CHAPTER 24 The Solar System

Saturn The *Voyager* probes next surveyed Saturn in 1980 and 1981. **Saturn** is the sixth planet from the Sun. It is the second-largest planet in the solar system, but it has the lowest density. Its density is so low that the planet would float in water.

Saturn's Atmosphere Similar to Jupiter, Saturn is a large, gaseous planet. It has a thick outer atmosphere composed mostly of hydrogen and helium. Saturn's atmosphere also contains ammonia, methane, and water vapor. As you go deeper into Saturn's atmosphere, the gases gradually change to liquid hydrogen and helium. Below its atmosphere and liquid layer, Saturn might have a small, rocky core.

Rings and Moons The *Voyager* probes gathered new information about Saturn's ring system and its moons. The probes showed that Saturn has several broad rings. Each large ring is composed of thousands of thin ringlets. **Figure 12** shows that they are composed of countless ice and rock particles. These particles range in size from a speck of dust to tens of meters across. This makes Saturn's ring system the most complex of all the outer gaseous planets.

At least 18 moons orbit Saturn. More have been reported, but many, if not all, of these might have been temporary clumps of ring matter and not true satellites. This mystery might be answered when other spacecrafts study Saturn. The largest of Saturn's moons, Titan, is larger than the planet Mercury. It has an atmosphere of nitrogen, argon, and methane. Thick clouds prevent scientists from seeing the surface of Titan.

Cultural Diversity

Sumerian Calendar The ancient Sumerians, whose civilization in Mesopotamia reached its height about 3500 B.C., were among the earliest astronomers. They observed movement of the Sun and Moon and made a 28-day lunar calendar. This calendar allowed the Sumerians to predict the cycle of seasons. It also alerted farmers when it was time to plant and harvest crops. Invite students to research astronomy in places such as ancient China, Egypt, and Central America. Have them design a classroom bulletin board summarizing the accomplishments of ancient astronomers.

Uranus Beyond Saturn, *Voyager 2* flew by Uranus in 1986. **Uranus** (YOOR uh nus) is the seventh planet from the Sun and was discovered in 1781. It is a large, gaseous planet with 18 satellites and a system of thin, dark rings. Three additional satellites were tentatively discovered in 1999 from Earth-based observations. If these objects are confirmed to be true satellites, Uranus will have more moons than any other planet in the solar system.

Uranus's Characteristics The atmosphere of Uranus is composed of hydrogen, helium, and some methane. Methane gives the planet the bluish-green color that you see in **Figure 13.** Methane absorbs the red and yellow light, and the clouds reflect the green and blue. Few cloud bands and storm systems can be seen on Uranus. Evidence suggests that under its atmosphere, Uranus has a mantle of liquid and solid water, methane, and ammonia surrounding a rocky core.

Figure 14 shows one of the most unusual features of Uranus. Its axis of rotation is tilted on its side compared with the other planets. The axes of rotation of the other planets, except Pluto, are nearly perpendicular to the planes of their orbits. However, Uranus's axis of rotation is nearly parallel to the plane of its orbit. Some scientists believe a collision with another object tipped Uranus on its side.

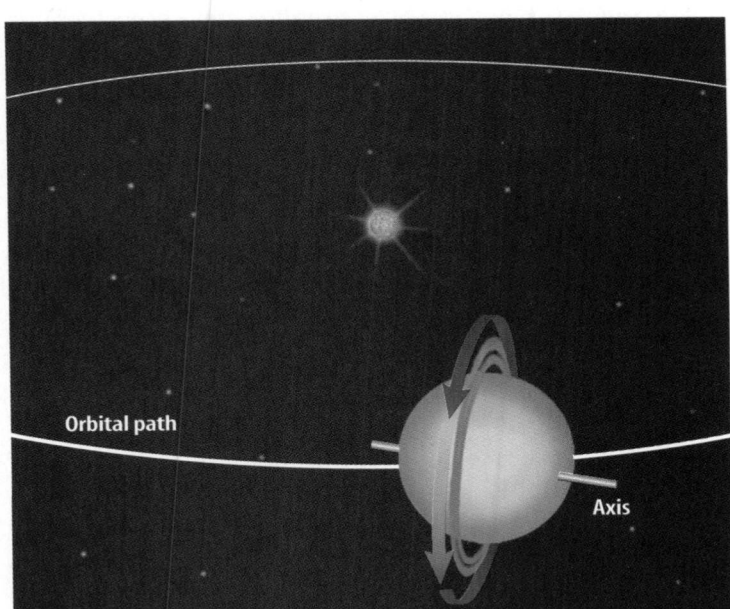

Figure 13
The atmosphere of Uranus gives the planet its distinct bluish-green color.

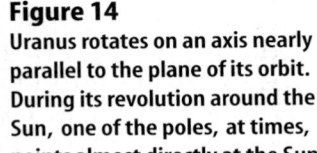

Figure 14
Uranus rotates on an axis nearly parallel to the plane of its orbit. During its revolution around the Sun, one of the poles, at times, points almost directly at the Sun.

Orbital path

Axis

SECTION 3 The Outer Planets **717**

Discussion

Remind students that new moons continue to be discovered around the outer planets. **Why might astronomers continue to find moons they have not seen before?** Students should infer that continued exploration with more powerful telescopes, in addition to images sent back by new probes, allow astronomers to identify small bodies that were previously unseen.

Fun Fact

William Herschel discovered a new planet in 1781. Herschel originally named the new planet *Georgium Sidus. Sidus* is Latin for "star," and *Georgium* refers to England's King George III. Another astronomer, Johann Bode, suggested it be named after Greek and Roman gods. Uranus, god of the sky and father of Saturn, was chosen as its name.

IDENTIFYING Misconceptions

Some students may think that the solar system is composed of the Sun, the nine planets, the asteroids, and a few comets. Inform them that scientists hypothesize that Pluto, Charon, and perhaps Triton, are what is left of many icy dwarf planets that once formed far from the Sun. They think that the area of the solar system located between 30 and 50 AUs from the Sun is littered with icy dwarf planets, comets, and other debris.

Resource Manager

Chapter Resources Booklet
MiniLAB, p. 4
Enrichment, p. 33

Curriculum Connection

Math Using a scale of 1 mm = 100 km, have students draw the listed moons to scale. Have them use the following diameters: Earth's Moon (3,476 km), Io (3,630 km), Europa (3,138 km), Ganymede (5,262 km), Callisto (4,800 km), Titan (5,150 km), and Triton (2,760 km). **How does Earth's Moon compare to the others?** It is one of the smaller moons in the group.

Fun Fact

Pluto and Neptune's moon Triton are more similar to each other than any other two objects in the solar system. Some scientists think that Triton was captured by the gravity of Neptune and could once have been a planet.

✔ Reading Check

Answer methane in its atmosphere

Discussion

Is it likely that astronauts will ever visit Neptune? Explain. It isn't likely; Neptune is a gaseous planet, meaning it doesn't have a solid surface like Earth does. It is also very distant and has a hostile environment.

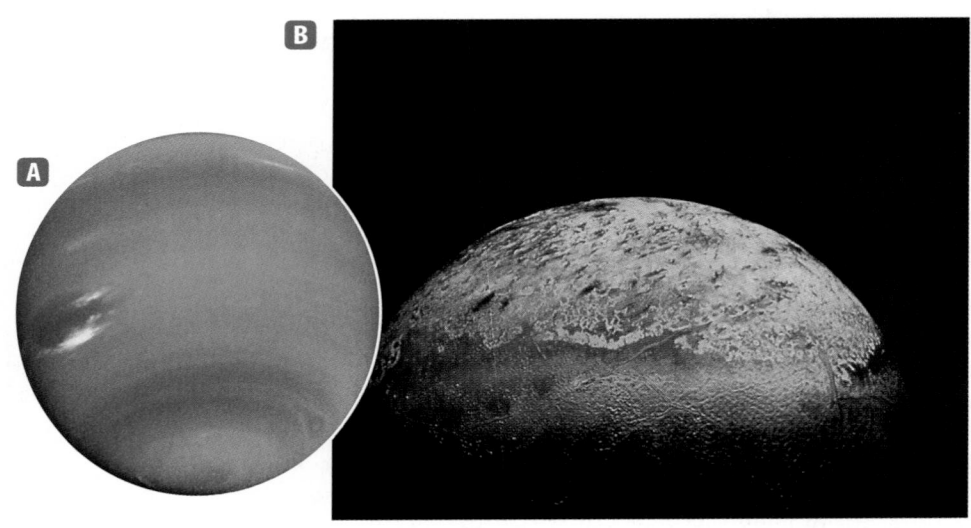

Figure 15
A Neptune has a distinctive bluish-green color. **B** The pinkish hue of Neptune's largest moon, Triton, is thought to come from an evaporating layer of nitrogen ice.

Physics
INTEGRATION

All change requires energy. On Earth energy from the Sun powers hurricanes. However, hurricanes on Neptune probably get most of their energy from Neptune's interior. Do research and write a short paragraph comparing and contrasting hurricanes on Earth and storms on Neptune.

Neptune Passing Uranus, *Voyager 2* traveled to Neptune, another large, gaseous planet. Discovered in 1846, **Neptune** is usually the eighth planet from the Sun. However, Pluto's orbit crosses inside Neptune's during part of its voyage around the Sun. Between 1979 and 1999, Pluto was closer to the Sun than was Neptune. Early in 1999, Pluto once again became the farthest planet from the Sun.

Neptune's Characteristics Neptune's atmosphere is similar to Uranus's atmosphere. The methane content gives Neptune, shown in **Figure 15A,** its distinctive bluish-green color, just as it does for Uranus.

✔ Reading Check   *What gives Neptune its bluish-green color?*

Neptune has dark-colored storms in its atmosphere that are similar to the Great Red Spot on Jupiter. One discovered by *Voyager 2* in 1989 was called the Great Dark Spot. It was about the size of Earth. However, observations by the *Hubble Space Telescope* in 1994 showed that the Great Dark Spot had disappeared. Bright clouds also form, then disappear in several hours. This shows that Neptune's atmosphere is active and changes rapidly.

Under its atmosphere, Neptune is thought to have a layer of liquid water, methane, and ammonia that might change to solid ice. Neptune probably has a rocky core.

Voyager 2 detected six new moons, so the total number of Neptune's known moons is now eight. Triton, shown in **Figure 15B,** is the largest. It has a thin atmosphere composed mostly of nitrogen.

Science Journal

Galileo Probe Have students write reports in their Science Journals about the information the probe *Galileo* gathered about Jupiter, its moons, and its rings. Ask them to include how the probe was launched on its mission and how NASA used gravity assists to power the space probe during its long flight to Jupiter. L2 **Linguistic** P

Resource Manager

Physical Science Critical Thinking/Problem Solving, p. 4

Pluto The smallest planet in the solar system, and the one scientists know the least about, is Pluto. For 20 years of its 249-year orbit, Pluto is closer to the Sun than Neptune. However, because **Pluto** is farther from the Sun than Neptune during most of its orbit, it is considered to be the ninth planet from the Sun. From Pluto's surface, the Sun would appear as only a bright star. Pluto is vastly different from the other outer planets. It's surrounded by only a thin atmosphere, and it's the only outer planet with a solid, icy-rock surface.

Figure 16
The *Hubble Space Telescope* gave astronomers their first clear view of Pluto and Charon as distinct objects.

Pluto's Moon Pluto's single moon, Charon, has a diameter about half the size of Pluto's. It was discovered in 1978 when a bulge was noticed on a photograph of the planet. Later photographs, taken with improved telescopes, showed that the bulge was a moon. Pluto and Charon are shown in **Figure 16.** Because of their close size and orbit, some scientists consider them to be a double planet.

Data from the *Hubble Space Telescope* indicate the presence of a vast disk of icy comets called the Kuiper Belt near Neptune's orbit. Some of the comets are hundreds of kilometers in diameter. Are Pluto and Charon members of this belt? Or did they simply form at the distance where they are? Scientists might not find out until a probe is sent to Pluto.

Section 3 Assessment

1. Describe the main differences between the outer planets and the inner planets.
2. Are any moons in the solar system larger than any planets? If so, which ones?
3. How does Pluto differ from the other outer planets? How is it similar to the inner planets?
4. Why are Pluto and Charon sometimes considered a double planet?
5. **Think Critically** Some scientists think life could exist on one of Jupiter's moons. On which moons would you look for life? Why?

Skill Builder Activities

6. **Recognizing Cause and Effect** Answer the following questions about Jupiter. **For more help, refer to the** Science Skill Handbook.
   a. How is the Great Red Spot affected by Jupiter's atmosphere?
   b. How does Jupiter's mass affect its gravitational force?
7. **Using Graphics Software** Use graphing software to plot each planet's average speed against its distance from the Sun. Describe the type of curve that is produced. **For more help, refer to the** Technology Skill Handbook.

Answers to Section Assessment

1. outer: large and gaseous, except Pluto; inner: small, solid, rocky bodies
2. Yes; Ganymede and Titan are larger than Mercury and Pluto.
3. The other outer planets are gaseous giants. Pluto is small and rocky like the inner planets.

4. because of their close size and orbit
5. Possible answer: Europa; it might have liquid water under its icy crust. This would be the only place in the solar system other than Earth with a large supply of the liquid water needed for life.

6. a. Areas of swirling high-pressure gases in the atmosphere formed it.
   b. Jupiter's large mass produces a very strong gravitational force.
7. If distance from the Sun is on the x-axis and speed is on the y-axis, the line graph will trend downward.

Section 3 The Outer Planets **719**

---

(3) Assess

Reteach
Have each student write down a question about one of the outer planets and then exchange questions with a partner, who will find the answer. Students can then read the questions and answers in class. L1 COOP LEARN **IS** Interpersonal

Challenge
Challenge students to find out when and by whom each planet was discovered. Have them hypothesize about the events that led up to the different discoveries. Students might mention the development of telescopes, which would have made the discovery of faraway planets more likely. L3

Assessment

Content Tell students to imagine themselves as NASA scientists who are planning the mission of a new space probe. Direct them to choose which outer planet the probe will visit and write a paragraph that defends the choice. Use **Performance Assessment in the Science Classroom,** p. 89. P

Table 3 Planets

Make a Model

Have students choose one planet in this table. Have them make an illustration or a model of an organism that might be able to survive on their chosen planet. In addition, have them describe the conditions to which the organism would have to be adapted. `L2` `ELL` `IS` **Kinesthetic**

Activity

Have students make a table that contains the following information for each planet: name, relative distance from Sun, relative size, type of atmosphere, and number of moons. `L2` `IS` **Logical-Mathematical**

Table 3 Planets

Mercury

- closest to the Sun
- second-smallest planet
- surface has many craters and high cliffs
- no atmosphere
- temperatures range from 425°C during the day to −170°C at night
- has no moons

Venus

- similar to Earth in size and mass
- thick atmosphere made mostly of carbon dioxide
- droplets of sulfuric acid in atmosphere give clouds a yellowish colo
- surface has craters, faultlike cracks, and volcanoes
- greenhouse effect causes surface temperatures of 450°C to 475°C
- has no moons

Earth

- atmosphere protects life
- surface temperatures allow water to exist as solid, liquid, and gas
- only planet where life is known to exist
- has one large moon

Mars

- surface appears reddish-yellow because of iron oxide in rocks
- ice caps are made of frozen carbon dioxide and water
- channels indicate that water has flowed on the surface; has large volcanoes and valleys
- has a thin atmosphere composed mostly of carbon dioxide
- surface temperatures range from −125°C to 35°C
- huge dust storms often blanket the planet
- has two small moons

LAB DEMONSTRATION

Purpose to show why the planets are not perfect spheres

Materials construction paper, scissors, hole punch, metric ruler, glue, pencil

Preparation Cut two 3 × 40 cm strips of paper. Cross strips in their centers and glue. Bring the four ends together, overlap, and glue to form a sphere. Allow glue to dry.

Procedure Punch a hole through the center of the overlapped ends. Push 5 cm of the pencil through the hole. Hold the pencil between your palms, and move your hands back and forth, spinning the sphere.

Expected Outcome The spinning sphere flattens, causing the middle to bulge.

Assessment

What causes the flattening of the sphere? Forces exerted on the spinning sphere cause it to flatten. **Why is this bulge hard to observe?** Planets don't bulge very much. For example, the difference between Earth's equatorial and pole-to-pole circumference is 27.5 km.

Jupiter		- largest planet - has faint rings - atmosphere is mostly hydrogen and helium; continuous storms swirl on the planet—the largest is the Great Red Spot - has four large moons and at least 12 smaller moons; one of its moons, Io, has active volcanoes
Saturn		- second-largest planet - thick atmosphere is mostly hydrogen and helium - has a complex ring system - has at least 18 moons—the largest, Titan, is larger than Mercury
Uranus	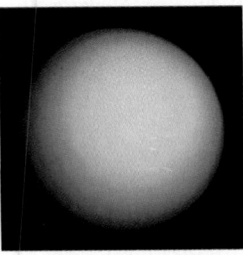	- large, gaseous planet with thin, dark rings - atmosphere is hydrogen, helium, and methane - axis of rotation is parallel to plane of orbit - might have more moons than any other planet
Neptune	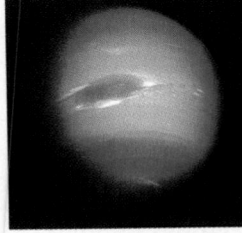	- large, gaseous planet with rings that vary in thickness - is sometimes farther from the Sun than Pluto is - methane in atmosphere causes its bluish-green color - has dark-colored storms in atmosphere - has eight moons
Pluto	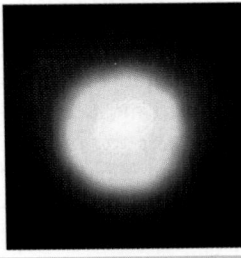	- small, icy-rock planet with thin atmosphere - single moon, Charon, is half the diameter of the planet

SECTION 3 The Outer Planets **721**

Teacher FYI

The main assignment of the *Galileo* spacecraft ended in December 1997. At that time, NASA extended its mission for two years and renamed it the *Galileo Europa Mission*. During this mission, *Galileo* conducted several fly-bys of Europa. *Galileo* was then repurposed for a third mission, called the *Galileo Millennium Mission*.

Extension

Studies by the *Galileo* spacecraft indicate that two of Jupiter's moons, Europa and Callisto, may have oceans under their crusts. Saturn's moon, Titan, has an atmosphere made mostly of nitrogen, as is Earth's. Have students research NASA's plans to study these and other moons of the outer planets.

Resource Manager

Chapter Resources Booklet
Reinforcement, p. 29

Inclusion Strategies

Visually Impaired Help your visually impaired students use this table of planet data by having larger versions of the table produced. Also, try pairing your visually impaired students with mentors who could read aloud the information on the table as it is presented in class.

SECTION

4

Other Objects in the Solar System

Other Objects in the Solar System

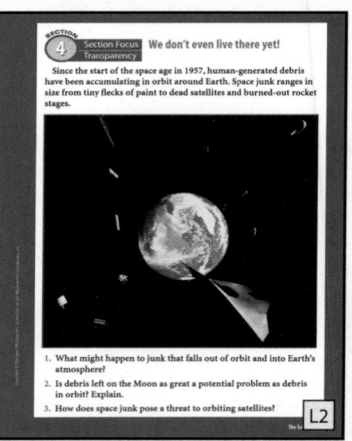
As You Read

What You'll Learn

- **Describe** where comets come from and how a comet develops as it approaches the Sun.
- **Distinguish** among comets, meteoroids, and asteroids.

Vocabulary

comet   meteorite
meteor   asteroid

Why It's Important

Comets, meteoroids, and asteroids might be composed of material that formed early in the history of the solar system.

Figure 17
Comet Hale-Bopp was most visible in March and April 1997.

Comets

The planets and their moons are the most noticeable members of the Sun's family, but many other objects also orbit the Sun. Comets, meteoroids, and asteroids are important other objects in the solar system.

You might have heard of Halley's comet. A **comet** is composed of dust and rock particles mixed with frozen water, methane, and ammonia. Halley's comet was last seen from Earth in 1986. English astronomer Edmund Halley realized that comet sightings that had taken place about every 76 years were really sightings of the same comet. This comet, which takes about 76 years to orbit the Sun, was named after him. Halley's comet is just one example of the many other objects in the solar system besides the planets.

Oort Cloud Dutch astronomer Jan Oort proposed the idea that a large collection of comets lies in a cloud that completely surrounds the solar system. This cloud, called the Oort Cloud, is located beyond the orbit of Pluto. Oort suggested that the gravities of the Sun and nearby stars interact with comets in the Oort Cloud. Comets either escape from the solar system or get captured into smaller orbits.

Comet Hale-Bopp On July 23, 1995, two amateur astronomers made an exciting discovery. A new comet, Comet Hale-Bopp, was headed toward the Sun. Larger than most that approach the Sun, it was the brightest comet visible from Earth in 20 years. Shown in **Figure 17,** Comet Hale-Bopp was at its brightest in March and April 1997.

722 CHAPTER 24 The Solar System

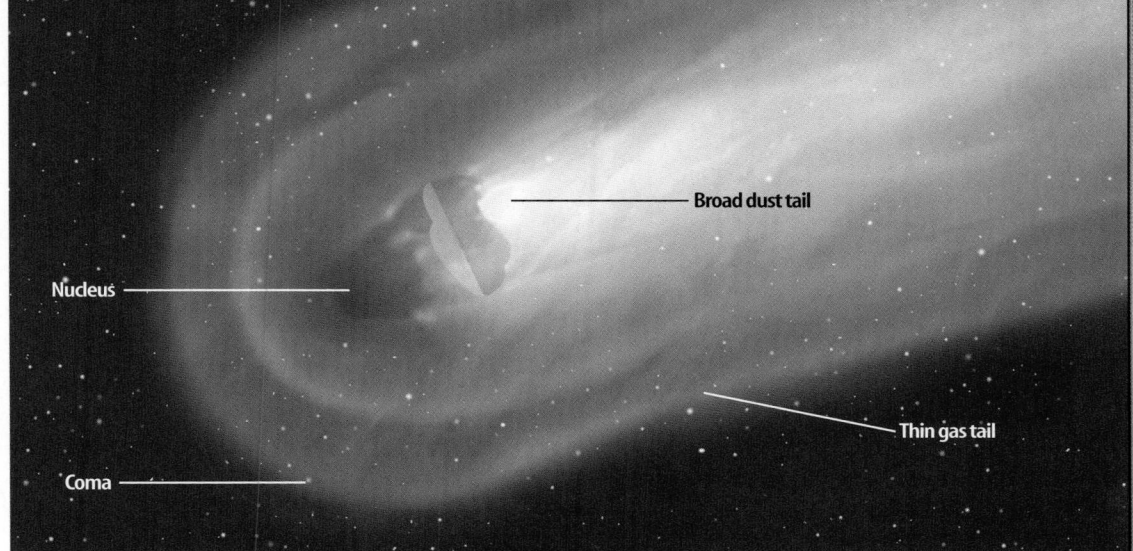

Broad dust tail

Nucleus

Thin gas tail

Coma

Structure of Comets

The *Hubble Space Telescope*, satellites orbiting Earth, and spacecrafts such as the *International Cometary Explorer* have all gathered information about comets. Notice the structure of a comet shown in **Figure 18.** It is like a large, dirty snowball or a mass of frozen ice and rock.

As the comet approaches the Sun, it starts to change. Ices of water, methane, and ammonia begin to vaporize because of the heat from the Sun, releasing dust and bits of rock. The vaporized gases and released dust form a bright cloud called a coma around the nucleus, or solid part, of the comet. The solar wind pushes on the gases and released dust in the coma, causing the particles to form a tail that always points away from the Sun.

After many trips around the Sun, most of the frozen ice in a comet's nucleus has vaporized. All that's left are the small particles, which are spread throughout the orbit of the original comet.

Meteoroids, Meteors, and Meteorites

You learned that comets tend to vaporize and break up after they have passed close to the Sun many times. The small pieces of the comet's nucleus spread out into a loose group within the original orbit of the comet. These smaller pieces of rock moving through space are then called meteoroids.

Sometimes the path of a meteoroid crosses the position of Earth, and it enters Earth's atmosphere at speeds of 15 km/s to 70 km/s. Most meteoroids are so small that they completely burn up in Earth's atmosphere. A meteoroid that burns up in Earth's atmosphere is called a **meteor.** People often see meteors like the one in **Figure 19** and call them shooting stars.

Figure 18
A comet consists of a nucleus, a coma, and a tail.

Figure 19
A meteoroid that burns up in Earth's atmosphere is called a meteor.

SECTION 4 Other Objects in the Solar System **723**

2 Teach

Comets

Discussion

Remind students that comets have large orbits that bring them periodically near Earth. Halley's comet returns every 76 years, and it was last visible in 1986. **When will Halley's comet again be visible?** 2062 **Will this pattern of reappearance repeat indefinitely? Explain.** No; the frozen ice in a comet's nucleus will eventually be totally vaporized, leaving only debris in its orbit. This will happen to Halley's comet one day.

Meteoroids, Meteors, and Meteorites

IDENTIFYING Misconceptions

Many people refer to meteors as "shooting stars." They were named this long ago when people thought they were bright stars shooting across the sky. Today we know they are chunks of rock that glow as they streak through Earth's atmosphere.

Activity

Alert students to the occurrence of the next meteor shower, using magazines or accessing the Glencoe Science Web site for tips on how and when to look. Have students observe the meteor shower and report on the number of meteors they were able to see during a half hour.

Resource Manager

Chapter Resources Booklet
  Transparency Activity, p. 51
  Directed Reading for Content Mastery, pp. 21, 22
  Transparency Activity, pp. 53–54

Science Journal

Comet Studies Have students with Internet access research the mission of one of the five space probes sent by the former Soviet Union, Japan, and Europe to study the last approach of Halley's comet in 1986. They were the Soviet *Vega 1* and *Vega 2*, the Japanese *Suisei* and *Sakigake*, and the European Space Agency's *Giotto*.

Figure 20
Meteorites occasionally strike Earth's surface. A large meteorite struck Arizona forming a crater 1.3 km in diameter and 175 m deep.

Figure 21
The asteroid belt lies between the orbits of Mars and Jupiter.

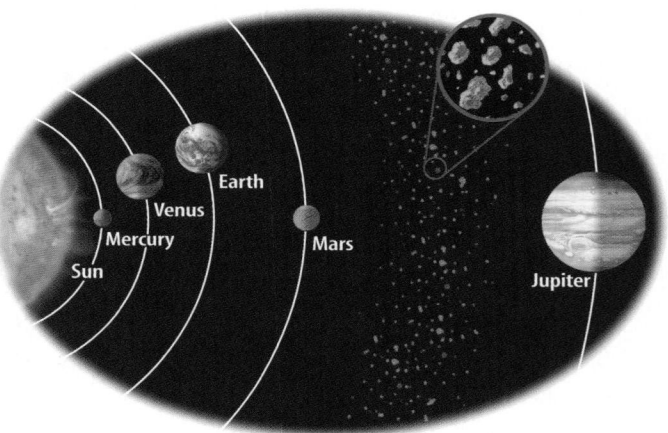

Meteor Showers Each time Earth passes through the loose group of particles within the old orbit of a comet, many small particles of rock and dust enter the atmosphere. Because more meteors than usual are seen, the event is called a meteor shower.

When a meteoroid is large enough, it might not burn up completely in the atmosphere. If it strikes Earth, it is called a **meteorite.** Barringer Crater in Arizona, shown in **Figure 20,** was formed when a large meteorite struck Earth about 50,000 years ago. Most meteorites are probably debris from asteroid collisions or broken-up comets, but some originate from the Moon and Mars.

✔ Reading Check   *What is a meteorite?*

Asteroids

An **asteroid** is a piece of rock similar to the material that formed into the planets. Most asteroids are located in an area between the orbits of Mars and Jupiter called the asteroid belt. Find the asteroid belt in **Figure 21.** Why are they located there? The gravity of Jupiter might have kept a planet from forming in the area where the asteroid belt is located now.

Other asteroids are scattered throughout the solar system. They might have been thrown out of the belt by Jupiter's gravity. Some may have since been captured as moons around other planets. Some scientists think that Mars's moons are captured asteroids.

724   CHAPTER 24 The Solar System

SCIENCE *Online*
Internet Addresses

_____

_____

_____

_____

Explore the Glencoe Science Web site at **science.glencoe.com** to find out more about topics in this section.

Exploring Asteroids The sizes of the asteroids in the asteroid belt range from tiny particles to objects 940 km in diameter. Ceres is the largest and the first one discovered. The next three in order of size are Pallas (580 km), Vesta (540 km), and Juno (244 km). Two asteroids, Ida and Gaspra, shown in **Figure 22,** were photographed by *Galileo* on its way to Jupiter.

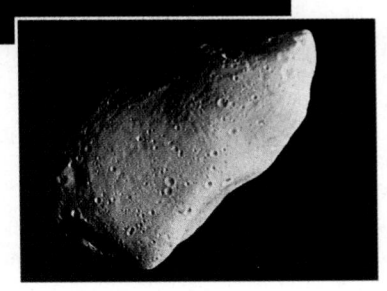

NEAR On February 14, 2000, the *Near Earth Asteroid Rendezvous (NEAR)* spacecraft went into orbit around the asteroid 433 Eros and successfully began its one-year mission. Data from the spacecraft show that Eros's surface has a large number of craters. This tells scientists that asteroid 433 Eros has been exposed to collisions over a long period of time. Other data indicate that Eros might be similar to the most common type of meteorite that strikes Earth.

Comets, meteoroids, and asteroids probably are composed of material that formed early in the history of the solar system. Scientists study the structure and composition of these space objects in order to learn what the solar system might have been like long ago. Understanding this could help scientists better understand how Earth formed.

Figure 22
A The asteroid Ida is about 56 km long. **B** Gaspra is about 20 km long.

Section 4 Assessment

1. Why does a comet's tail form as it approaches the Sun?
2. What type of feature might be formed on Earth if a large meteorite reached its surface?
3. Describe differences among comets, meteoroids, and asteroids.
4. What is the mission of the *NEAR* spacecraft?
5. **Think Critically** What is the chemical composition of comets? Are comets more similar to the inner or the outer planets?

Skill Builder Activities

6. **Forming Hypotheses** A meteorite found in Antarctica in 1979 is thought to have originated on Mars about 16 million years ago. Write a hypothesis to explain how a piece of Mars might have ended up on Earth. **For more help, refer to the** Science Skill Handbook.

7. **Communicating** The asteroid belt contains many objects—from tiny particles to objects 940 km in diameter. In your Science Journal, describe how mining the asteroids for valuable minerals might be accomplished. **For more help, refer to the** Science Skill Handbook.

---

3 Assess

Reteach
Have students write three sentences, each containing one of the following terms: *Oort Cloud, Kuiper Belt,* and *asteroid belt between Mars and Jupiter.* Instruct students to take turns reading their sentences aloud. Write a few on the board as you discuss with students whether or not the terms were used correctly. L2 IS **Linguistic**

Challenge
Have students research the nickel mines of Sudbury Basin in Ontario, Canada. Ask them to write reports telling why so much nickel is found there. It is thought that about 2 billion years ago, an asteroid 6 km in diameter collided with Earth at this location. The collision caused the formation of rich deposits of nickel, cobalt, and platinum. L2 IS **Linguistic** P

✔Assessment

Content Have students draw a picture of a comet at several points in its orbit. The comet's tail should point away from the Sun, no matter where in its orbit the comet is. Use **Performance Assessment in the Science Classroom,** p. 127. P

Answers to Section Assessment

1. Heat causes ice in its head to vaporize and glow; solar wind pushes it away from the Sun.
2. a crater
3. Comets: chunks of rock, dust, ice in large orbits around the Sun; many are in the Oort Cloud or Kuiper Belt; meteoroids: small pieces of rock that are remnants of old comets;

asteroids: large chunks of rock, most of which orbit the Sun between Mars and Jupiter
4. to orbit and study asteroid 433 Eros
5. dust and rock particles mixed with ice, methane, and ammonia; outer planets

6. Possible answer: An asteroid collided with Mars 16 million years ago, knocking pieces of rock into space. These pieces of rock then collided with Earth.
7. Encourage creativity and scientific reasoning. Possible answers: Collect smaller asteroids and return them to Earth; mine larger asteroids in space.

Activity

Recognize the Problem

Purpose

Students design a model that shows the distances between the Sun and the planets. `L2` `ELL`
`COOP LEARN`
`IS` **Logical-Mathematical** `P`

Process Skills

measuring in SI, using numbers, sequencing, researching, forming a hypothesis, separating and controlling variables, interpreting data, making models

Time Required

one class period

Materials

Photocopy one copy of the Planetary Distances table for each group. Enlarge it slightly if possible.

Safety Precautions

Caution students to handle scissors with care.

Thinking Critically

Discussion

- If the model is to be a reasonable size, then the scale that represents 1 AU must remain fairly small.
- If the model is to be a reasonable size, then different scales must be used for the inner and outer planets.

Activity Model and Invent

Solar System Distance Model

Distances between the planets of the solar system are large. Can you design a model that will demonstrate these large distances?

Recognize the Problem

Can a model be designed to show relative distances in the solar system?

Thinking Critically

How can you design a model of a reasonable size that will demonstrate the distances between and among the Sun and planets of the solar system?

Possible Materials

meterstick   string (several meters)
scissors   notebook paper
pencil   (several sheets)

Safety Precautions

Use care when handling scissors.

Data Source

SCIENCE *Online* Go to the Glencoe Science Web site at **science.glencoe.com** to find information about distances in the solar system.

Goals

■ **Design** a table of scale distances and model the distances between and among the Sun and the planets.

Planetary Distances				
Planet	Distance to Sun (km)	Distance to Sun (AU)	Scale Distance (1 AU = 10 cm)	Scale Distance (1 AU = 2 m)
Mercury	5.80×10^7	0.39	3.9 cm	78.00 cm
Venus	1.08×10^8	0.72	7.2 cm	1.44 m
Earth	1.50×10^8	1.00	10.0 cm	2.00 m
Mars	2.28×10^8	1.52	15.2 cm	3.04 m
Jupiter	7.80×10^8	5.20	52.0 cm	10.40 m
Saturn	1.43×10^9	9.53	95.3 cm	19.06 m
Uranus	2.88×10^9	19.20	192.0 cm	38.40 m
Neptune	4.51×10^9	30.07	300.7 cm	60.14 m
Pluto	5.92×10^9	39.47	394.7 cm	78.94 m

726 CHAPTER 24 The Solar System

Resource Manager

Chapter Resources Booklet
    Activity Worksheet, pp. 7–8
Lab Management and Safety, p. 69

Inclusion Strategies

Gifted Have interested students use a computer spreadsheet program to do the calculations for the scale. `L3` `IS` **Logical-Mathematical**

Test Your Hypothesis

Planning the Model

1. **List** the steps that you need to take in making your model. Be specific, describing exactly what you will do at each step.

2. **List** the materials that you will need to complete your model.

3. **Make a table** of scale distances you will use in your model.

4. **Write** a description of how you will build your model, explaining how it will demonstrate relative distances between and among the Sun and planets of the solar system.

Check the Model Plans

1. **Compare** your scale distances with those of other students. Discuss why each of you chose the scale you did.

2. Make sure your teacher approves your plan before you start.

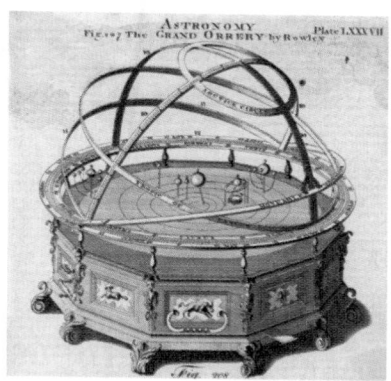

Making the Model

1. **Construct** the model using your scale distances.

2. While constructing the model, write any observations that you or other members of your group make, and complete the data table in your Science Journal. Calculate the scale distance that would be used in your model if 1 AU = 2 m.

Analyzing and Applying Results

1. **Explain** how a scale distance is determined.

2. Was it possible to work with your scale? Explain why or why not.

3. How much string would be required to construct a model with a scale distance of 1 AU = 2 m?

4. Proxima Centauri, the closest star to the Sun, is about 270,000 AU from the Sun. Based on your scale, how much string would you need to place this star on your model?

Compare your scale models with those of other students. Discuss any differences. **For more help,** refer to the Science Skill Handbook.

Test Your Hypothesis

Possible Procedures

Determine a scale for making a solar system model from string. Design a method for placing the planets in proper positions on the model.

Teaching Strategy

Have students test their scales by first seeing how far Pluto would be from the Sun. If this distance is too large, they should change the scale.

Expected Outcome

Students will make models that show the distances between bodies in the solar system to scale.

Analyzing and Applying Results

1. by multiplying the AU distance of planets by the scale selected
2. Answers will be subjective and based on the student's individual choices.
3. 78.9 m or nearly 80 m
4. Possible answer: For a scale of 1 AU = 10 cm, Proxima Centauri would be about 27 km away from the model Sun.

Error Analysis

Have students determine whether the distance to Pluto is too large with this scale. Are the distances between the inner planets and the Sun too small? If so, change the scale.

Assessment

Performance Using the same scales selected for planet distances on their solar system models, have students place the asteroid Ceres in their models. The orbit of Ceres lies 2.77 AU from the Sun. Use **Performance Assessment in the Science Classroom,** p. 123.

Have students compare and contrast their scales and models with representations of the solar system in books and encyclopedias. Did these sources handle the problem of scale in the same way? Ask students to evaluate what they did well and what they could have done better.

Content Background

A large number of meteoroids enter Earth's atmosphere every day. The total mass of this daily onslaught amounts to more than 100 tons of material. However, most of these objects are very small, only a few milligrams each. Only the largest ones ever reach Earth's surface to become meteorites. The largest single meteorite found is the 60–ton Hoba Meteorite, discovered in 1920 in Namibia, in southwestern Africa.

The average meteoroid enters Earth's atmosphere at between 10 km/s and 70 km/s, but most are quickly slowed to a few hundred km/h by friction with the atmosphere. These strike Earth with little force. However, meteoroids larger than a few hundred tons are slowed very little, and these large, but rare, ones form craters.

Discussion

Explain to students that, of all the meteorites found on Earth, about a third were witnessed "falls," which means the meteorite was seen by someone as it fell from the sky. The rest are classified as "finds," which means they were found on the ground, but no one witnessed their falling. **Would you classify the Burnwell meteorite a fall or a find? Why?** It was a fall. Even thought the Peggs did not see it fall, they heard the noise of its fall and its impact when it occurred.

Oops! Oops! Accidents in SCIENCE

SOMETIMES GREAT DISCOVERIES HAPPEN BY ACCIDENT!

IT CAME FROM OUTER

An unexpected visitor crashes into "Old Kentucky Home"

On September 4, 1990, Frances Pegg had just returned from grocery shopping and was unloading bags of groceries in her kitchen in Burnwell, Kentucky. Suddenly and unexpectedly, she heard a loud crashing sound. Her husband, Arthur, had heard the same sound. Before it, however, he had heard another sound—one that was similar to a noise a helicopter makes. The sound frightened the couple's goat and horse. The noise had come from an object that had crashed through the Peggs' roof, their ceiling, and the floor of their porch. They couldn't see what the object was, but the noise sounded like a gunshot, and pieces of wood from their home flew everywhere.

The Burnwell meteorite crashed into the Peggs' home and landed in their basement on the right.

Frances and Arthur Pegg were not hurt, but they certainly were puzzled. They thought that perhaps a part of an airplane had fallen off as it flew overhead. The next day the couple looked under their front porch and found the culprit—a chunk of rock from outer space. It was a meteorite!

Resources for Teachers and Students

Comets, Asteroids and Meteorites by Cynthia Pratt Nicolson, Kids Can Press, 1999.

Meteorites by Paul P. Sipiera, Childrens Press, 1994.

Rocks from Space by O. Richard Norton, Mountain Press Publishers, 1998.

Collision Earth!: The Threat from Outerspace by Peter Grego, Sterling Publishing, 1998.

SPACE!

Actual size

When the Burnwell meteorite entered Earth's atmosphere, it became covered in a shiny black crust. Its mass is about 2 kilograms.

For seven years, the Peggs kept their "space rock" at home, making them local celebrities. The rock appeared on TV, and the couple were interviewed by newspaper reporters. In 1997, the Peggs sold the meteorite to the National Museum of Natural History in Washington, D.C., which has a collection of over 9,000 meteorites. Scientists there study meteorites to learn more about space and the beginnings of the solar system. One astronomer explained, "Meteorites were formed at about the same time as the solar system, about 4.6 billion years ago, though some are younger."

Scientists especially are interested in the Burnwell meteorite because its chemical make up is different from other meteorites previously studied. Meteorites are made of various amounts of minerals and metals, including iron, cobalt, and nickel. The Burnwell meteorite is richer in metallic iron and nickel than other known meteorites and is less rich in some metals such as cobalt. Scientists are comparing the rare Burnwell rock with data from NASA space probes to find out if there are more meteorites like the one that fell on the Peggs' roof. But so far, it seems the Peggs' visitor from outer space is one-of-a-kind.

Activity

Students can research the discoveries of some meteorites. Ask each student to select three meteorites to research. Ask each student to make a poster that shows the location where the meteorites were found, the sizes of the meteorites, how they were discovered, the type of meteorite each is, and any other interesting facts about each one. Have each student present his of her poster to the class. L2

LS Visual-Spatial and Naturalist

Analyze the Event

Discuss with students how the discovery of the Burnwell meteorite might have been affected if the Peggs had not been home at the time. Possible answer: They might not have realized what caused the damage to their home or realized that it was something that came from outer space. If so, scientists might not have become involved in investigating the incident, and the rare characteristics of the meteorite might never have been discovered.

CONNECTIONS Research the latest information on meteorites. How do they give clues to how our solar system was formed? Visit the Glencoe Science Web site. Report to the class.

SCIENCE *Online*

For more information, visit science.glencoe.com

CONNECTIONS

Have students discuss why they think it is important for scientists to learn more about how the solar system was formed.

SCIENCE *Online*

Internet Addresses

_____

_____

_____

Explore the Glencoe Science Web site at **science.glencoe.com** to find out more about topics in this feature.

Reviewing Main Ideas

Preview

Students can answer the questions in their Science Journals. Discuss the answers as you go through the chapter. **[LS] Linguistic**

Review

Students can write their answers, then compare them with those of other students. **[LS] Interpersonal**

Reteach

Students can look at the illustrations and describe details that support the main ideas of the chapter. **[LS] Visual-Spatial**

Answers to Chapter Review

SECTION 2
4. Seasonal changes cause one ice cap to shrink while the other expands.

SECTION 3
2. ice and rock particles

SECTION 4
1. The solar wind pushes the tail away from the Sun.

Reviewing Main Ideas

Section 1 The Solar System

1. Early astronomers thought that the planets, the Moon, the Sun, and the stars were fixed in separate spheres that rotated around Earth.

2. The Sun-centered model of the solar system states that the Sun is the center of the solar system. Earth and the other planets revolve around the Sun.

3. Scientists think the solar system formed from a cloud of gas, ice, and dust about 4.6 billion years ago.

4. Johannes Kepler discovered that the planets orbit the Sun in elliptical, not circular, orbits.

Section 2 The Inner Planets

1. The moonlike planet Mercury has craters and cliffs on its surface.

2. Venus and Earth are similar in size and mass. Venus has a dense atmosphere.

3. On Earth, surface temperatures allow water to exist as a solid, liquid, and gas. Earth's atmosphere protects life-forms from the Sun's radiation.

4. Mars appears to be reddish-yellow due to the iron oxide content of its weathered rocks. Recent studies by *Global Surveyor* indicate that Mars's surface once had large amounts of water flowing over it. *Why do the polar ice caps of Mars, shown here, change size?*

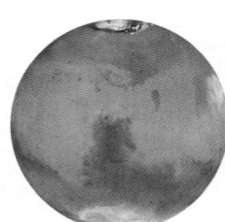

Section 3 The Outer Planets

1. Faint rings and at least 16 moons orbit the gaseous planet Jupiter.

2. Saturn has pronounced rings. *What are Saturn's rings, shown here, made of?*

3. Uranus is a large, gaseous planet with many moons and several rings. Neptune is similar to Uranus in size, composition, and storm-like features.

4. Pluto has a surface of icy rock.

Section 4 Other Objects in the Solar System

1. As a comet approaches the Sun, a bright coma forms. *Why does the tail of a comet, shown here, always point away from the Sun?*

2. Meteoroids and asteroids are relatively small objects within the solar system. Meteroids form when asteroids collide, when comets break up, or when meteorites collide with the Moon or planets.

FOLDABLES Reading & Study Skills — **After You Read**

To help you review the similarities and differences among inner planets and outer planets, use the Foldable you made at the beginning of the chapter.

FOLDABLES Reading & Study Skills — **After You Read**

After students have read the chapter and completed the Foldable described in Before You Read, have them do the activity on the student page.

Dinah Zike

Visualizing Main Ideas

Complete the following concept map on planets.

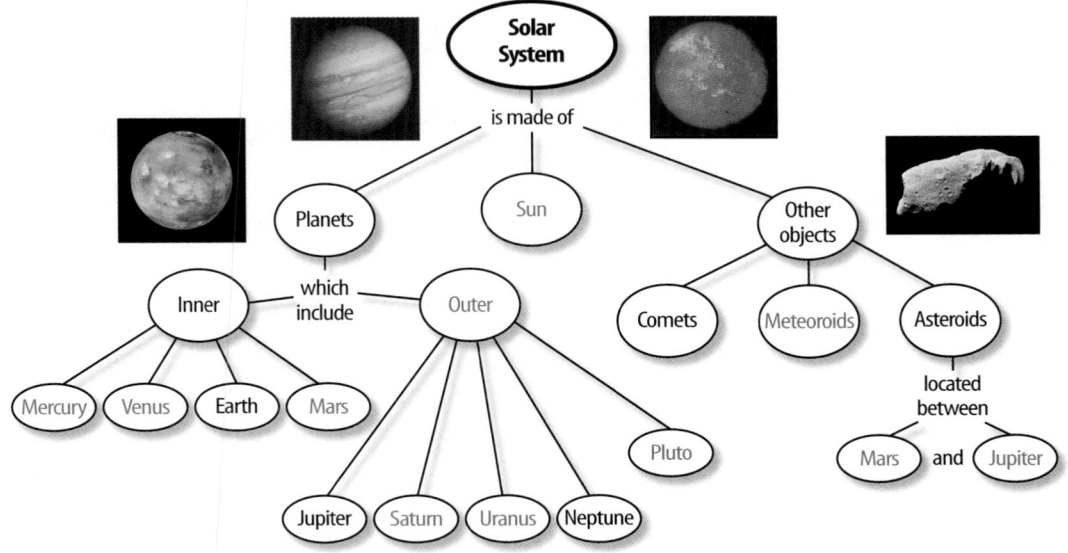

Vocabulary Review

Vocabulary Words

a. asteroid
b. comet
c. Earth
d. Great Red Spot
e. Jupiter
f. Mars
g. Mercury
h. meteor
i. meteorite
j. Neptune
k. Pluto
l. Saturn
m. solar system
n. Uranus
o. Venus

Study Tip

Practice reading tables. See if you can devise a graph that shows the same information that a table does.

Using Vocabulary

Replace the underlined words with the correct vocabulary words.

1. A meteoroid that burns up in Earth's atmosphere is called a <u>meteorite</u>.

2. The axis of rotation of <u>Neptune</u> is tilted on its side compared with the other planets.

3. <u>Uranus</u> is the second-largest planet in the solar system, but it has the lowest density.

4. The *Viking 1* and *2* orbiters photographed the entire surface of <u>Venus</u> from orbit.

5. One of the moons of <u>Mars</u> has volcanoes on it.

CHAPTER STUDY GUIDE 731

Visualizing Main Ideas

See student page.

Vocabulary Review

Using Vocabulary

1. A meteoroid that burns up in Earth's atmosphere is called a <u>meteor</u>.
2. The axis of rotation of <u>Uranus</u> is tilted on its side compared with the other planets.
3. <u>Saturn</u> is the second largest planet in the solar system, but it has the lowest density.
4. The *Viking 1* and *2* orbiters photographed the entire surface of <u>Mars</u> from orbit.
5. One of the moons of <u>Jupiter</u> has volcanoes on it.

IDENTIFYING Misconceptions

Assess

Use the assessment as follow-up to page 700F after students have completed the chapter.

Discussion Use the following table to discuss three of the four types of stars. Include the radius, density, and mass of the Sun. Which type of star is the Sun?

Star	Class	Radius (solar radii)	Density (solar density)	Mass (solar mass)
Rigel	Supergiant	78	0.00004	20
Deneb	Supergiant	96	0.00002	20
Sirius	Main Sequence	1.9	0.335	2.3
61 Cygni A	Main Sequence	0.7	1.69	0.58
Sun	Main Sequence	1	1	1
40 Erdani B	White Dwarf	0.018	71,000	0.41
Von Maanen's Star	White Dwarf	0.007	47,000	0.14

Expected Outcome This discussion will assist students in recognizing that the Sun is a star just like other stars in our galaxy.

Chapter 24 Assessment

Checking Concepts

1. B
2. C
3. B
4. D
5. D
6. C
7. C
8. B
9. C
10. B

Thinking Critically

11. Clouds on Venus are very dense, and the amount of carbon dioxide in the air is greater. The CO_2 retains the heat.
12. More massive planets have more satellites.
13. They don't have solid surfaces. Extreme heat and dense, gaseous atmospheres would probably destroy probes.
14. Some surface features appear to have been formed by flowing water; surface iron oxide could have been formed by water.
15. As Venus orbits the Sun, different parts of its lighted side can be seen from Earth.

Developing Skills

16. The farther a planet is from the Sun, the longer its period of revolution.

Checking Concepts

Choose the word or phrase that best answers the question.

1. Who proposed a Sun-centered solar system?
   A) Ptolemy   C) Galileo
   B) Copernicus   D) Oort

2. How does the Sun produce energy?
   A) magnetism
   B) nuclear fission
   C) nuclear fusion
   D) the greenhouse effect

3. What is the shape of planetary orbits?
   A) circles   C) squares
   B) ellipses   D) rectangles

4. Which planet has extreme temperatures because it has no atmosphere?
   A) Earth   C) Saturn
   B) Jupiter   D) Mercury

5. Water is a solid, liquid, and gas on which planet?
   A) Pluto   C) Saturn
   B) Uranus   D) Earth

6. Where is the largest known volcano in the solar system?
   A) Earth   C) Mars
   B) Jupiter   D) Uranus

7. What do scientists call a rock that strikes Earth's surface?
   A) asteroid   C) meteorite
   B) comet   D) meteoroid

8. Which planet has a complex ring system made of thousands of ringlets?
   A) Pluto   C) Uranus
   B) Saturn   D) Mars

9. Which planet has a Great Red Spot?
   A) Uranus   C) Jupiter
   B) Earth   D) Pluto

10. In what direction does the tail of a comet always point?
    A) toward the Sun
    B) away from the Sun
    C) toward Earth
    D) away from the Oort Cloud

Thinking Critically

11. Why is the surface temperature on Venus so much higher than that on Earth?

12. Describe a relationship between a planet's mass and the number of satellites it has.

13. Why are probe landings on Jupiter or Saturn unlikely events?

14. What evidence suggests that water is or once was present on Mars?

15. An observer on Earth can watch Venus go through phases much like Earth's Moon does. Explain.

Developing Skills

16. **Making and Using Graphs** Use the graph below to explain how the time of a planet's revolution is related to its distance from the Sun.

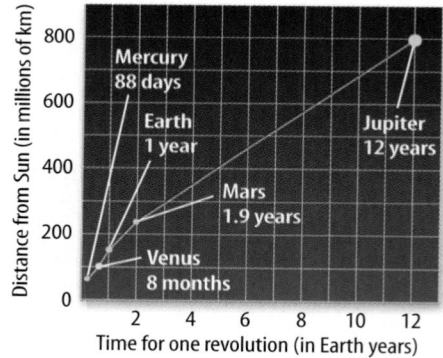

Chapter ✓Assessment Planner

Portfolio Encourage students to place in their portfolios one or two items of what they consider to be their best work. Examples include:
- Science Journal, p. 704
- Activity, p. 709
- Science Journal, p. 718
- Challenge, p. 725

Performance Additional performance assessments, Performance Task Assessment Lists, and rubrics for evaluating these activities can be found in Glencoe's **Performance Assessment in the Science Classroom.**

17. Forming a Hypothesis Mercury is the closest planet to the Sun, yet it does not reflect much of the Sun's light. What can you say about Mercury's color?

18. Concept Mapping Complete the concept map on this page to show how a comet changes as it travels through space.

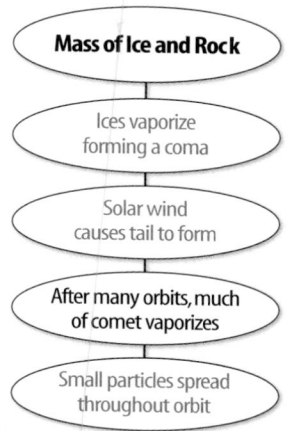

Mass of Ice and Rock

Ices vaporize forming a coma

Solar wind causes tail to form

After many orbits, much of comet vaporizes

Small particles spread throughout orbit

Performance Assessment

19. Display Mercury, Venus, Mars, Jupiter, and Saturn can be observed with the unaided eye. Research where in the sky these planets can be observed in the next year. Construct a display with your findings. Include time of day, day of the year, and locations with respect to known landmarks in your area on your display.

TECHNOLOGY

Go to the Glencoe Science Web site at **science.glencoe.com** or use the **Glencoe Science CD-ROM** for additional chapter assessment.

Test Practice

The table below presents data about the four inner planets of the solar system.

The Inner Planets			
Planet	Diameter (km)	Distance from the Sun (millions of km)	Period of Revolution (days)
Mercury	4,880	69	88
Venus	12,104	109	225
Earth	12,756	150	365
Mars	6,794	249	687

Study the table and answer the following questions.

1. How many millions of kilometers farther from the Sun is Venus than Mercury?
- **A)** 150
- **B)** 108
- **C)** 58
- **D)** 40

2. The best conclusion to be made from these data is that:
- **F)** Mercury is a larger planet than Mars.
- **G)** the period of a planet's revolution increases with increasing distance from the Sun.
- **H)** over time, the planets are gradually moving farther and farther away from the Sun.
- **J)** the size of a planet increases with increasing period of revolution.

CHAPTER ASSESSMENT 733

Test Practice

The Test-Taking Tip was written by The Princeton Review, the nation's leader in test preparation.
1. D
2. G

Developing Skills

17. Mercury is dark in color.
18. See student page.

Performance Assessment

19. Students can use magazines such as *Astronomy* and planetarium Web sites to get this information. Planetarium sites also offer other useful links. Use **Performance Assessment in the Science Classroom**, p. 135.

✓Assessment Resources

Reproducible Masters

Chapter Resources Booklet
Chapter Review, pp. 41–42
Chapter Tests, pp. 43–46
Assessment Transparency Activity, p. 55

Glencoe Science Web site
Interactive Tutor
Chapter Quizzes

Glencoe Technology
- Assessment Transparency
- Interactive CD-ROM Chapter Quizzes
- ExamView Pro Test Bank
- Vocabulary PuzzleMaker Software
- MindJogger Videoquiz DVD/VHS

Section/Objectives	Standards		Activities/Features
	National	**State/Local**	
Chapter Opener	See p. 5T for a Key to Standards.		**Explore Activity:** Model the universe, p. 735 **Before You Read,** p. 735
Section 1 Stars ⏱ 1 session 📦 .5 block 1. **Explain** why the positions of constellations change throughout the year. 2. **Distinguish** between absolute magnitude and apparent magnitude. 3. **Describe** how parallax is used to determine distance.	National Content Standards: UCP2, A1, D3		**MiniLAB:** Observing Star Patterns, p. 737 **Problem-Solving Activity:** Are distance and brightness related?, p. 738
Section 2 The Sun ⏱ 2 sessions 📦 1 block 1. **Describe** the structure of the Sun. 2. **Explain** how sunspots, prominences, and solar flares are related. 3. **Explain** why the Sun is considered an average star and how it differs from stars in binary systems.	National Content Standards: UCP5, A1, B3, D3		**Science Online,** p. 743 **Activity:** Sunspots, p. 745
Section 3 Evolution of Stars ⏱ 2 sessions 📦 1 block 1. **Describe** how stars are classified. 2. **Explain** how the temperature of a star relates to its color. 3. **Describe** how a star evolves.	National Content Standards: UCP1, UCP4, B1, D3		**Physics Integration,** p. 747 **Science Online,** p. 748 **Physics Integration,** p. 750
Section 4 Galaxies and the Universe ⏱ 4 sessions 📦 2 blocks 1. **Identify** the three main types of galaxies. 2. **List** several characteristics of the Milky Way Galaxy. 3. **Describe** evidence that supports the Big Bang theory.	National Content Standards: UCP2, A1, D3		**MiniLAB:** Measuring Distance in Space, p. 754 **Visualizing the Big Bang Theory,** p. 756 **Activity:** Measuring Parallax, pp. 758–759 **Science Stats:** Stars and Galaxies, pp. 760–761

NATIONAL GEOGRAPHIC

Teacher's Corner

PRODUCTS AVAILABLE FROM GLENCOE
To order call 1-800-334-7344:
CD-ROM
NGS PictureShow: Stars and Galaxies
Transparency Set
NGS PicturePack: Stars and Galaxies

PRODUCTS AVAILABLE FROM NATIONAL GEOGRAPHIC SOCIETY
To order call 1-800-368-2728:
Videos
Stars and Constellations
Sun: Earth's Star

INDEX TO NATIONAL GEOGRAPHIC SOCIETY
The following articles may be used for research relating to this chapter:
"New Eyes on the Universe," by Bradford A. Smith, January 1994.
"Orion: Where Stars Are Born," by James Reston, Jr., December 1995.

Activity Materials	Reproducible Resources	Section Assessment	Technology
Explore Activity: balloon, clothespin, felt-tip marker, string, metric ruler	**Chapter Resources Booklet** Foldables Worksheet, p. 17 Directed Reading Overview, p. 19 Note-taking Worksheets, pp. 35–38	GLENCOE'S **ASSESSMENT** ADVANTAGE	
MiniLAB: no materials needed	**Chapter Resources Booklet** Transparency Activity, p. 48 MiniLAB, p. 3 Enrichment, p. 31 Reinforcement, p. 27 Directed Reading, p. 20 Lab Activity, pp. 9–12, 13–15 Transparency Activity, pp. 53–54	Portfolio Science Journal, p. 737 Performance MiniLAB, p. 737 Problem-Solving Activity, p. 738 Skill Builder Activities, p. 740 Content Section Assessment, p. 740	♪ Section Focus Transparency ♪ Teaching Transparency 💿 Interactive CD-ROM/DVD 🎧 Guided Reading Audio Program
Activity: several books, piece of cardboard, drawing paper, refracting telescope, clipboard, small tripod, scissors	**Chapter Resources Booklet** Transparency Activity, p. 49 Activity Worksheet, pp. 5–6 Enrichment, p. 32 Reinforcement, p. 28 Directed Reading, p. 20 **Cultural Diversity,** p. 29 **Science Inquiry Labs,** p.43	Portfolio Challenge, p. 744 Performance Skill Builder Activities, p. 744 Content Section Assessment, p. 744	♪ Section Focus Transparency 💿 Interactive CD-ROM/DVD 🎧 Guided Reading Audio Program
Need materials? Contact Science Kit at 1-800-828-7777 or www.sciencekit.com on the Internet.	**Chapter Resources Booklet** Transparency Activity, p. 50 Enrichment, p. 33 Reinforcement, p. 29 Directed Reading, p. 21	Portfolio Extension, p. 747 Performance Skill Builder Activities, p. 751 Content Section Assessment, p. 751	♪ Section Focus Transparency 💿 Interactive CD-ROM/DVD 🎧 Guided Reading Audio Program
MiniLAB: large sheet of paper, metric ruler or meterstick **Activity:** meterstick, metric ruler, masking tape, pencil	**Chapter Resources Booklet** Transparency Activity, p. 51 Activity Worksheet, pp. 7–8 MiniLAB, p. 4 Enrichment, p. 34 Reinforcement, p. 30 Directed Reading, pp. 21, 22 **Lab Management and Safety,** p. 65 **Cultural Diversity,** p. 31	Portfolio Extension, p. 756 Performance MiniLAB, p. 754 Skill Builder Activities, p. 757 Content Section Assessment, p. 757	♪ Section Focus Transparency 💿 Interactive CD-ROM/DVD 🎧 Guided Reading Audio Program

End of Chapter Assessment

GLENCOE'S **ASSESSMENT** ADVANTAGE

Blackline Masters	Technology	Professional Series
Chapter Resources Booklet Chapter Review, pp. 41–42 Chapter Tests, pp. 43–46 **Standardized Test Practice by The Princeton Review,** pp. 107–110	📺 MindJogger Videoquiz 💿 CD-ROM Explorations and Quizzes 💿 Vocabulary Puzzle Makers 💿 ExamView Pro Test Bank 💿 Interactive Lesson Planner 💿 Interactive Teacher's Edition	Performance Assessment in the Science Classroom (PASC)

Transparencies

Section Focus

Section Focus Transparency

1 A Starry Night

On a clear night, if you are far away from city lights, you can see hundreds of stars.

1. What constellations can you identify where you live?
2. Make up your own constellations using the stars in this photograph. Name each constellation and explain what it represents.
3. Give several reasons some stars look brighter than others.

L2

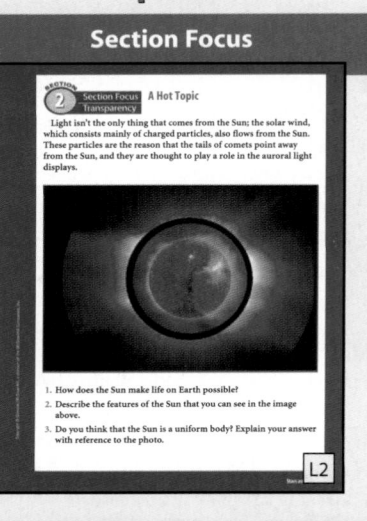

Section Focus Transparency

2 A Hot Topic

Light isn't the only thing that comes from the Sun; the solar wind, which consists mainly of charged particles, also flows from the Sun. These particles are the reason that the tails of comets point away from the Sun, and they are thought to play a role in the auroral light displays.

1. How does the Sun make life on Earth possible?
2. Describe the features of the Sun that you can see in the image above.
3. Do you think that the Sun is a uniform body? Explain your answer with reference to the photo.

L2

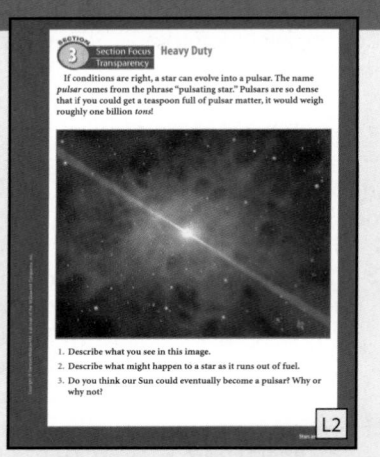

Section Focus Transparency

3 Heavy Duty

If conditions are right, a star can evolve into a pulsar. The name *pulsar* comes from the phrase "pulsating star." Pulsars are so dense that if you could get a teaspoon full of pulsar matter, it would weigh roughly one billion *tons*!

1. Describe what you see in this image.
2. Describe what might happen to a star as it runs out of fuel.
3. Do you think our Sun could eventually become a pulsar? Why or why not!

L2

This is a representation of key blackline masters available in the Teacher Classroom Resources. See Resource Manager boxes within the chapter for additional information.

Key to Teaching Strategies

The following designations will help you decide which activities are appropriate for your students.

L1 Level 1 activities should be appropriate for students with learning difficulties.

L2 Level 2 activities should be within the ability range of all students.

L3 Level 3 activities are designed for above-average students.

ELL ELL activities should be within the ability range of English Language Learners.

COOP LEARN Cooperative Learning activities are designed for small group work.

LS Multiple Learning Styles logos, as described on page 22T, are used throughout to indicate strategies that address different learning styles.

P These strategies represent student products that can be placed into a best-work portfolio.

Assessment

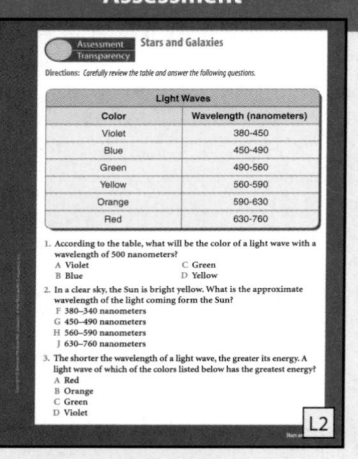

Assessment Transparency

Stars and Galaxies

Directions: Carefully review the table and answer the following questions.

Light Waves	
Color	Wavelength (nanometers)
Violet	380-450
Blue	450-490
Green	490-560
Yellow	560-590
Orange	590-630
Red	630-760

1. According to the table, what will be the color of a light wave with a wavelength of 500 nanometers?
   A Violet   C Green
   B Blue   D Yellow
2. In a clear sky, the Sun is bright yellow. What is the approximate wavelength of the light coming form the Sun?
   F 380–340 nanometers
   G 450–490 nanometers
   H 560–590 nanometers
   J 630–760 nanometers
3. The shorter the wavelength of a light wave, the greater its energy. A light wave of which of the colors listed below has the greatest energy?
   A Red
   B Orange
   C Green
   D Violet

L2

Teaching

Teaching Transparency

1 Circumpolar Constellations

L2

Hands-on Activities

Activity Worksheets

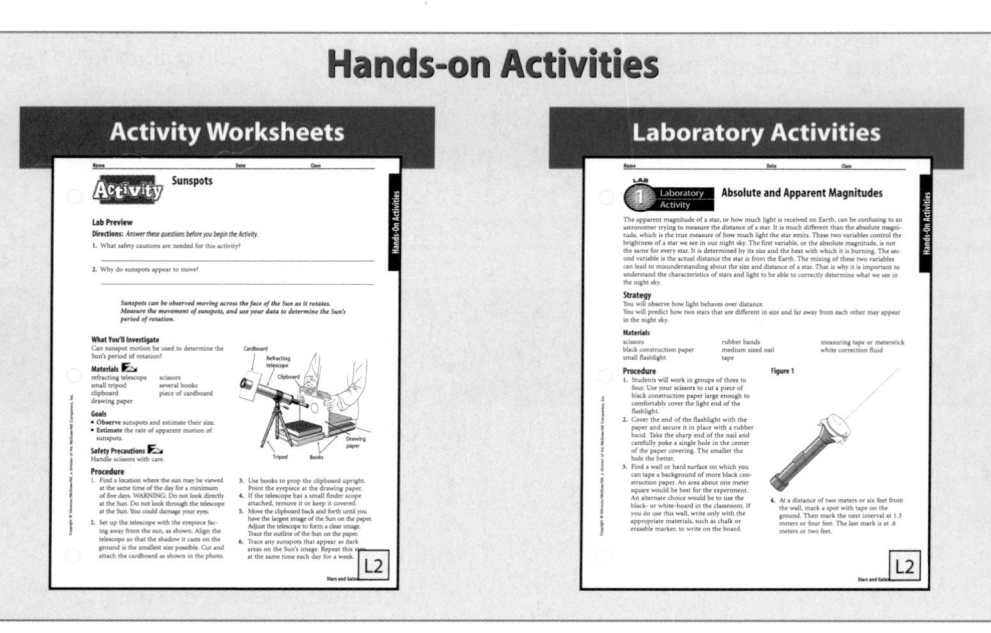

Activity

Sunspots

Lab Preview

Directions: Answer these questions before you begin the Activity.

1. What safety cautions are needed for this activity?

2. Why do sunspots appear to move?

Sunspots can be observed moving across the face of the Sun as it rotates. Measure the movement of sunspots, and use your data to determine the Sun's period of rotation.

What You'll Investigate
Can sunspot motion be used to determine the Sun's period of rotation?

Materials
refracting telescope   scissors
small tripod   several books
clipboard   piece of cardboard
drawing paper

Goals
• **Observe** sunspots and estimate their size.
• **Estimate** the rate of apparent motion of sunspots.

Safety Precautions
Handle scissors with care.

Procedure
1. Find a location where the sun may be viewed at the same time of the day for a minimum of five days. WARNING: Do not look directly at the Sun. Do not look through the telescope at the Sun. You could damage your eyes.
2. Set up the telescope with the eyepiece facing away from the sun, as shown. Align the telescope so that the shadow it casts on the ground is the smallest size possible. Cut and attach the cardboard as shown in the photo.
3. Use books to prop the clipboard upright. Point the eyepiece at the drawing paper.
4. If the telescope has a small finder scope attached, remove it or keep it covered.
5. Move the clipboard back and forth until you have the largest image of the Sun on the paper. Adjust the telescope to form a clear image. Trace the outline of the Sun on the paper.
6. Trace any sunspots that appear as dark areas on the Sun's image. Repeat this at the same time each day for a week.

L2

Laboratory Activities

Laboratory Activity

1 Absolute and Apparent Magnitudes

The apparent magnitude of a star, or how much light is received on Earth, can be confusing to an astronomer trying to measure the distance of a star. It is much different than the absolute magnitude, which is the true measure of how much light the star emits. These two variables control the brightness of a star we see in our night sky. The first variable, or the absolute magnitude, is not the same for every star. It is determined by its size and the heat with which it is burning. The second variable is the actual distance the star is from the Earth. The mixing of these two variables can lead to misunderstanding about the size and distance of a star. That is why it is important to understand the characteristics of stars and light to be able to correctly determine what we see in the night sky.

Strategy
You will observe how light behaves over distance.
You will predict how two stars are different in size and far away from each other may appear in the night sky.

Materials
scissors   rubber bands   measuring tape or meterstick
black construction paper   medium sized nail   white correction fluid
small flashlight   tape

Procedure
1. Students will work in groups of three to four. Use your scissors to cut a piece of black construction paper large enough to comfortably cover the light end of the flashlight.
2. Cover the end of the flashlight with the paper and secure it in place with a rubber band. Take the sharp end of the nail and carefully poke a single hole in the center of the paper covering. The smaller the hole the better.
3. Find a wall or hard surface on which you can tape a background of more black construction paper. An area about one meter square would be best for the experiment. An alternate choice would be to use the black- or white-board in the classroom. If you do use this wall, write only with the appropriate materials, such as chalk or erasable marker, to write on the board.

Figure 1

4. At a distance of two meters or six feet from the wall, mark a spot with tape on the ground. Then mark the next interval at 1.3 meters or four feet. The last mark is at 8 meters or two feet.

L2

Meeting Different Ability Levels

Content Outline

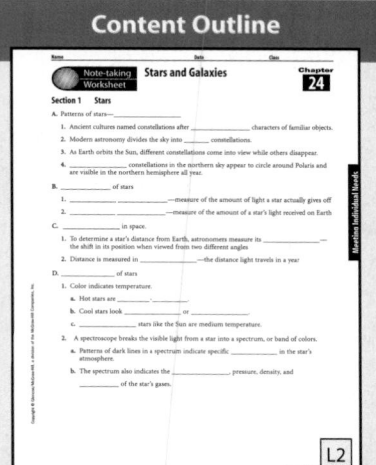

Reinforcement

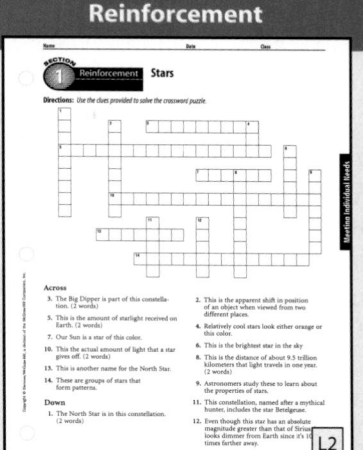

Directed Reading

Assessment

Chapter Tests

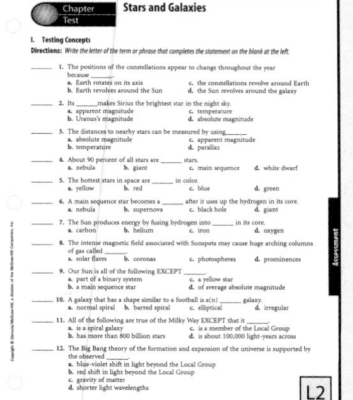

Enrichment

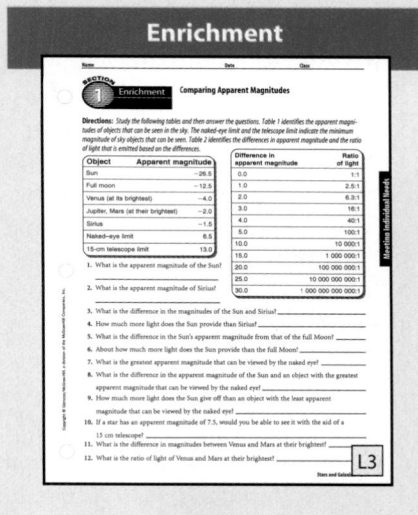

Spanish Directed Reading

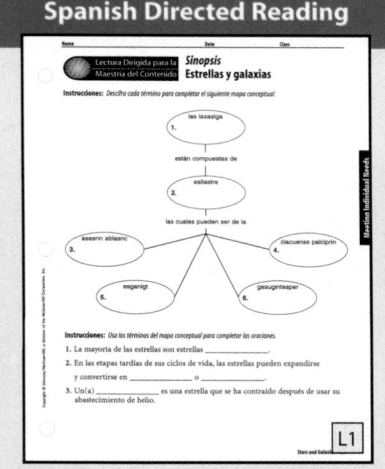

Test Practice Workbook

Chapter Review

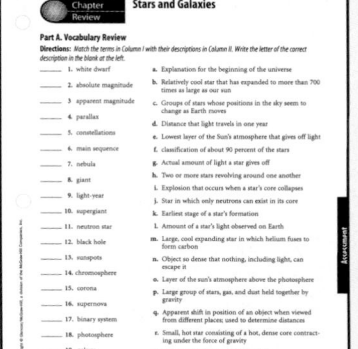

Science Content Background

SECTION 1 Stars

Absolute and Apparent Magnitudes

The size and temperature of a star affect its absolute magnitude. The size and temperature of a star, along with its distance from Earth, affect its apparent magnitude. If the absolute and apparent magnitudes of a star are known, the distance from the star to Earth can be determined.

Clouds of gas and dust in space, called nebulas, can obscure starlight, thus reducing a star's apparent magnitude. Interstellar nebulas reduce the apparent magnitude of stars in many parts of our galaxy to the point where they cannot be seen. The gas and dust from these interstellar nebulas can also make a star appear red in color. Interstellar material tends to be opaque to light of shorter wavelengths, allowing longer wavelengths of red light to pass through.

AFP/Corbis

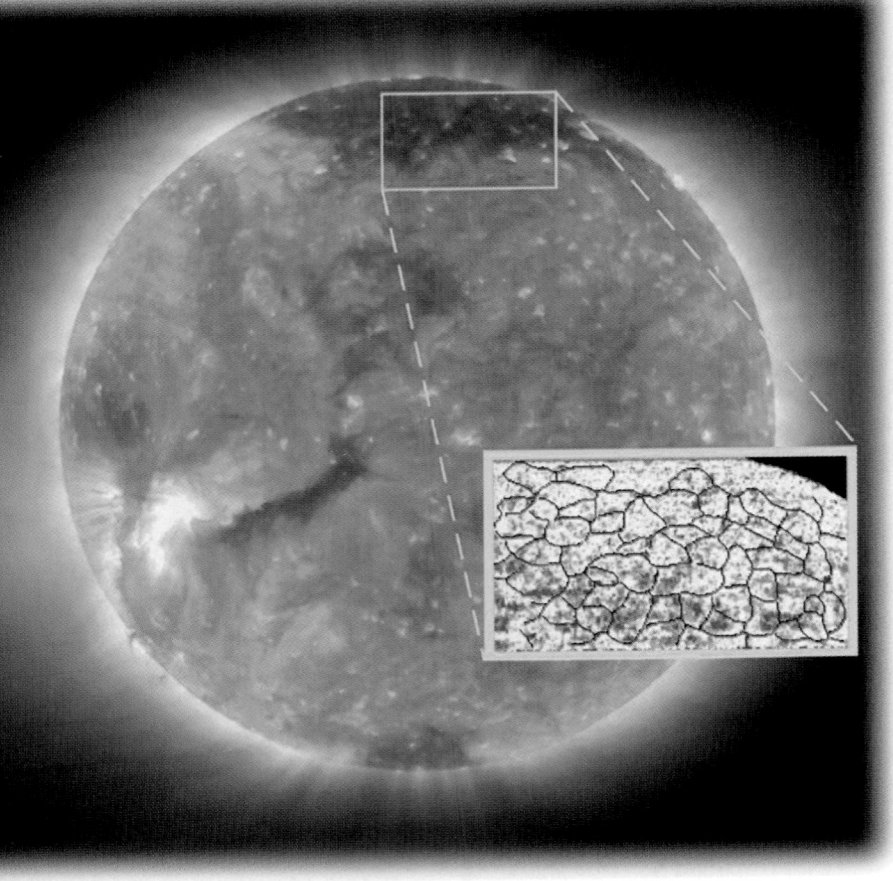

> **Fun Fact**
>
> Matter flows outward from the South Pole of the Sun at a rate of one million tons per second.

SECTION 2 The Sun

Surface Features

The phenomenon called granulation seen on the surface of the Sun was first observed by Galileo. He thought the patterns he observed resembled grains of wheat and thus called the features granules. Granules on the Sun's surface are the tops of large convection cells that extend deep into the center of the Sun. Their presence is evidence that convection currents do exist inside the Sun, just under the photosphere. These granules form when hot gases are forced upward by surrounding denser gases. The hot gases flow toward the surface, emit energy, cool, and sink back toward the Sun's interior. Each granule measures about 1,000 km across.

Sunspots

Sunspots occur in a periodic pattern. Magnetic reversals occur every 11 years; therefore, a sunspot cycle is complete after 22 years. Solar activity affects circulation within Earth's atmosphere. Thus, there appears to be a correlation between the Sun's 22-year activity cycle and droughts on Earth. Solar activity can affect Earth's climate over a long period of time. The Little Ice Age that occurred in northern Europe during the late 1600s occurred during the Maunder minimum, a time when sunspot occurrences were very low.

SECTION 3

Evolution of Stars

Classifying Stars

Not all stars shine with a steady light. Stars that change brightness are called variable stars. Stars may vary because the outer layers of the star expand and contract, causing a change in the temperature and the absolute magnitude of the star.

One class of variable stars, the Cepheid variable, provides important information related to the study of the universe. These stars vary regularly, and their period of variation is an indication of their absolute magnitudes. Because of this, they can be used to determine distances to faraway clusters and galaxies. If two Cepheid variables have the same period of pulsation, they are the same average size and have the same average absolute magnitude. Any difference noted in the apparent magnitudes of the two stars is caused by a difference in the distance to each of the stars. Polaris is an example of a Cepheid variable.

> ### Fun Fact
>
> Our Sun may be very important to us, but it is not a major feature of our galaxy. There are 5 billion stars larger than the Sun contained in the Milky Way.

Black Holes

New infrared studies of the center of the Milky Way provide more evidence for a super-massive black hole at the core of our galaxy. The total output of energy from this object at the Milky Way's core is more than 1 million times that of

SCIENCE *Online*

For additional content background on this topic, go to the Glencoe Science Web site at science.glencoe.com.

Luke Dodd/Science Library/Photo Researchers, Inc.

the Sun, and it appears to contain between 1 and 2 million solar masses (1 solar mass = mass of the Sun = $2 \times 1{,}030$ kg).

SECTION 4

Galaxies and the Universe

Galaxies

The Milky Way and Andromeda Galaxies both have a number of companion dwarf spheroidal galaxies. A new dwarf spheroidal galaxy has been found just 50,000 light-years from the nucleus of the Milky Way. It lies on the opposite side of the Milky Way from Earth. Researchers hypothesize that within another 100 million years, the stars from this small galaxy will be incorporated into our own. This corresponds to a theory that large galaxies, such as the Milky Way, are formed, in part, by the incorporation of smaller galaxies. Larger galaxies therefore, are thought to have been built up over time from smaller galaxies.

CHAPTER 25
Stars and Galaxies

Chapter Vocabulary

constellation
absolute magnitude
apparent magnitude
light-year
photosphere
chromosphere
corona
sunspot
nebula
giant
white dwarf
supergiant
neutron star
black hole
galaxy
Big Bang theory

What do you think?

Science Journal This is a binary star system in which two stars are orbiting each other. This is different from our Sun, which is a single star with orbiting planets.

CHAPTER 25
Stars and Galaxies

When you look at stars, do you ever wonder why some stars appear brighter than others do? How do you know how far stars are from Earth and what they are made of? How does the Sun compare to the other stars you see? In this chapter, you will find the answers to these questions. You'll also learn how stars are classified and about the different kinds of galaxies that stars are grouped into. In addition, you'll learn about the Big Bang theory, which most astronomers believe is the most likely way that the universe began.

What do you think?

Science Journal Look at the picture below with a classmate. Discuss what this might be or what is happening. Here's a hint: *When it comes to space, two is sometimes better than one.* Write down your answer or best guess in your Science Journal.

734

Theme Connection

Scale and Structure and **Stability and Change** The major themes of this chapter deal with the vast scale and structure of the universe and how the universe and the matter that makes it up changes.

This photo may look like a scene from the latest science fiction movie, but it shows a real event—two galaxies colliding. However, don't be worried. Most clusters of galaxies are not moving toward each other. They are moving apart, and astronomers have concluded that the universe is expanding in all directions. In the following activity, model how the universe might be expanding.

Model the universe

1. Partially inflate a balloon. Clip the neck shut with a clothespin.
2. Draw six evenly spaced dots on the balloon with a felt-tip marker. Label the dots A through F.
3. Use a string and ruler to measure the distance, in millimeters, from dot A to each of the other dots.
4. Inflate the balloon some more.
5. Measure the distances from dot A again.
6. Inflate the balloon again and take new measurements.

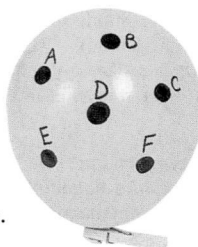

Observe
If each dot represents a cluster of galaxies and the balloon represents the universe, describe in your Science Journal the motion of the clusters relative to one another.

Before You Read

FOLDABLES
Reading & Study Skills

Making a Concept Map Study Fold
A concept map is a diagram that shows how concepts or ideas are related and organizes information. Make this Foldable to show what you already know about stars, galaxies, and the universe.

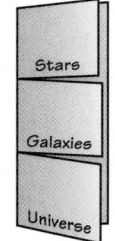
Stars
Galaxies
Universe

1. Place a sheet of paper in front of you so the short side is at the top. Fold the paper in half from the left side to the right side.
2. Fold the top and bottom in to divide the paper into thirds. Unfold the paper so three columns show.
3. Through the top thickness of paper, cut along each of the fold lines to the left fold, forming three tabs. Label the tabs "Stars," "Galaxies," and "Universe," as shown.
4. Before you read the chapter, write what you already know about stars, galaxies, and the Universe under the tabs.
5. As you read the chapter, add to or correct what you have written under the tabs.

735

EXPLORE ACTIVITY

Purpose Use the Explore Activity to introduce the concept of an expanding universe. L1 ELL COOP LEARN IN Kinesthetic

Materials balloon, clothespin, felt-tip marker, string, metric ruler

Teaching Strategies

• Divide the class into groups of four students. Assign roles to students. One student should blow up the balloon and clip it shut. Another should draw the dots on the balloon. The remaining students should measure the distance between the dots.

• Have students compare their results with those of classmates. Discuss differences and similarities.

Safety Precautions Caution students not to blow up the balloons to the breaking point.

Observe
The galaxies are moving away from each other. This type of motion implies that the universe is expanding.

Assessment

Process Have students make illustrations that depict the motion of galaxies. Drawings should indicate that galaxies are moving away from each other. Use **PASC**, p. 123.

FOLDABLES
Reading & Study Skills

Before You Read

Dinah Zike Study Fold
Purpose Students will develop and use a Foldable concept map to diagram the relationships between stars, galaxies, and the universe. The Foldable will also serve as a study guide for recording information about chapter concepts.

For additional help, see Foldables Worksheet, p. 17 in **Chapter Resources Booklet,** or go to the Glencoe Science Web site at **science.glencoe.com.** See After You Read in the Study Guide at the end of this chapter.

SECTION

Stars

1 Motivate

Bellringer Transparency

Display the Section Focus Transparency for Section 1. Use the accompanying Transparency Activity Master. L2

ELL

Tie to Prior Knowledge

Ask students if they have observed the Big Dipper, part of the constellation known as Ursa Major. Invite a volunteer to draw the stars of the Big Dipper on the chalkboard to illustrate why it's called a dipper.

SECTION

Stars

As You Read

What You'll Learn

- **Explain** why the positions of constellations change throughout the year.
- **Distinguish** between absolute magnitude and apparent magnitude.
- **Describe** how parallax is used to determine distance.

Vocabulary

constellation
absolute magnitude
apparent magnitude
light-year

Why It's Important

Each of the thousands of stars you see in the night sky is a sun.

Constellations

It's fun to look at cloud formations and find ones that remind you of animals, people, or objects that you recognize. It takes much more imagination to play this game with celestial bodies. Ancient Greeks, Romans, and other early cultures observed patterns of stars in the sky called **constellations** and imagined that they represented mythological characters, animals, or familiar objects.

From Earth, a constellation looks like spots of light arranged in a particular shape against the dark night sky. **Figure 1** shows how the constellation of the mythological Greek hunter Orion appears from Earth. It also shows how stars in the constellation have no relationship to each other in space.

Stars in the sky can be found at specific locations within a constellation. For example, you can find the star Betelgeuse (BEE tul jooz) in the shoulder of the mighty hunter Orion. Orion's faithful companion is his dog, Canis Major. The brightest star in the northern sky, Sirius, is in the constellation Canis Major.

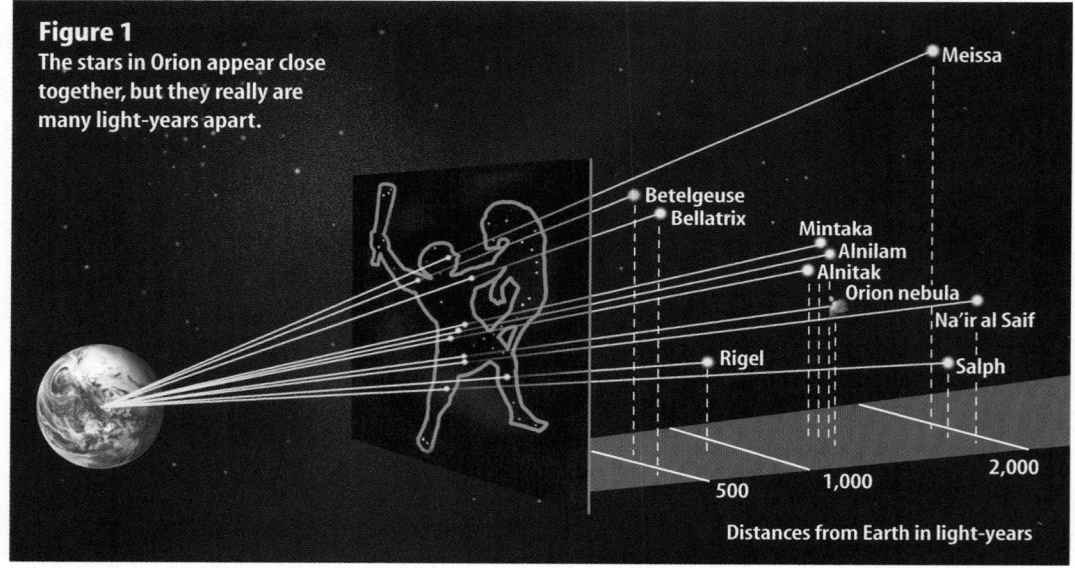

Figure 1
The stars in Orion appear close together, but they really are many light-years apart.

Meissa
Betelgeuse
Bellatrix
Mintaka
Alnilam
Alnitak
Orion nebula
Na'ir al Saif
Rigel
Salph

500   1,000   2,000

Distances from Earth in light-years

736 **CHAPTER 25** Stars and Galaxies

Section ✓*Assessment* Planner

PORTFOLIO
Science Journal, p. 737
PERFORMANCE ASSESSMENT
Try at Home MiniLAB, p. 737
Problem-Solving Activity, p. 738
Skill Builder Activities, p. 740
See page 764 for more options.

CONTENT ASSESSMENT
Section, p. 740
Challenge, p. 740
Chapter, pp. 764–765

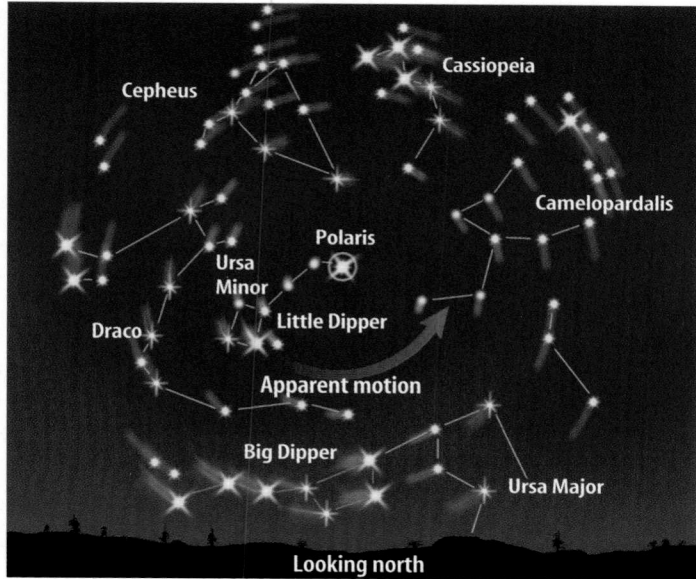

Figure 2
The Big Dipper, in red, is part of the constellation Ursa Major. It is visible year-round in the northern hemisphere. Constellations close to Polaris rotate around Polaris, which is almost directly over the north pole.

Labels in figure: Cepheus, Cassiopeia, Camelopardalis, Polaris, Ursa Minor, Little Dipper, Draco, Apparent motion, Big Dipper, Ursa Major, Looking north

Modern Constellations

Modern astronomy divides the sky into 88 constellations, many of which were named by early astronomers. You probably know some of them. Can you recognize the Big Dipper? It's part of the constellation Ursa Major, shown in **Figure 2.** Notice how the front two stars of the Big Dipper point almost directly at the North Star, Polaris, which is located at the end of the Little Dipper in the constellation Ursa Minor. Polaris is positioned almost directly over Earth's north pole.

Circumpolar Constellations

As Earth rotates, Ursa Major, Ursa Minor, and other constellations in the northern sky circle around Polaris. Because of this, they are called circumpolar constellations. The constellations appear to move, as shown in **Figure 2,** because Earth is in motion. The stars appear to complete one full circle in the sky in less than 24 h as Earth rotates on its axis. One circumpolar constellation that's easy to find is Cassiopeia (kas ee uh PEE uh). You can look for five bright stars that form a big W or a big M in the northern sky, depending on the season. In spring and summer, Cassiopeia forms an M, and in fall and winter, it forms a W.

As Earth orbits the Sun, different constellations come into view while others disappear. Because of their unique position, circumpolar constellations are visible all year long. Other constellations are not. Orion, which is visible in the winter in the northern hemisphere, can't be seen there in the summer because the daytime side of Earth is facing it.

TRY AT HOME

Mini LAB

Observing Star Patterns

Procedure
1. On a clear night, go outside after dark and study the stars. Take an adult with you and help each other find some common constellations.
2. Let your imagination flow to find patterns of stars that look like something familiar.
3. Draw the stars you see, note their positions, and include a drawing of what you think each star pattern resembles.

Analysis
1. Which of your constellations match those observed by your classmates?
2. How can recognizing star patterns be useful?

Constellations

TRY AT HOME

Mini LAB

Purpose Students identify common constellations. L2
ELL LS **Visual-Spatial**
Materials paper, pencil
Teaching Strategy Provide star charts for students to refer to.
Analysis
1. Many students will likely include familiar constellations (Big Dipper, Orion); other constellations included will be unique.
2. Possible answer: Constellations can be used to identify directions.

✓Assessment

Performance Have students write a myth about one of the drawings they made. Use **PASC,** p. 159.

IDENTIFYING Misconceptions

Students may think that stars within a constellation are close to one another in space. Explain that two stars that appear to be side by side may be separated by hundreds of light-years.

Resource Manager

Chapter Resources Booklet
Transparency Activity, p. 48
MiniLAB, p. 3
Directed Reading for Content Mastery, pp. 19, 20
Note-taking Worksheets, pp. 35–38

Science Journal

Constellations from Mythology Have students research a constellation of their choice and write a report in their Science Journals that identifies the stars in the constellation and describes the mythological character or story for which the constellation is named.
L2 LS **Linguistic** P

Quick Demo

Move students into a hallway. Give two volunteers identical flashlights, have them walk to different locations, and have them shine the flashlights toward the class. **Which has a brighter apparent magnitude?** the closer flashlight **Which has the brighter absolute magnitude?** Neither; they have equal absolute magnitudes. L2 [IS] **Visual-Spatial**

Text Question Answer

The brighter star may be bigger or hotter.

✔ Reading Check

Answer absolute—a measure of the light given off by a star; apparent—a measure of the amount of light received from a star

Fun Fact

Luminosity, *L*, measures how many times brighter or dimmer a star is compared with the Sun.

Problem-Solving Activity

National Math Standards
Correlation to Mathematics Objectives
1, 5, 6, 8–10

Answers

1. As distance is doubled (20 cm to 40 cm), light intensity is cut to 1/4. As distance is tripled (20 cm to 60 cm), light intensity is cut to 1/9.
2. The relationship can be expressed as 1 divided by the square of how many times distance is increased. At 100 cm, the light intensity will be decreased to 1/25 of its original intensity.

Which constellations are visible during different seasons? To find out, see the **Backyard Astronomy Field Guide** at the back of the book.

Absolute and Apparent Magnitudes

When you look at constellations, you'll notice that some stars are brighter than others. For example, Sirius looks much brighter than Rigel. Is Sirius a brighter star, or is it just closer to Earth, making it appear to be brighter? As it turns out, Sirius is 100 times closer to Earth than Rigel is. If Sirius and Rigel were the same distance from Earth, Rigel would appear much brighter in the night sky than Sirius would.

When you refer to the brightness of a star, you can refer to its absolute magnitude or its apparent magnitude. The **absolute magnitude** of a star is a measure of the amount of light it gives off. A measure of the amount of light received on Earth is called the **apparent magnitude.** A star that's rather dim can appear bright in the sky if it's close to Earth, and a star that's bright can appear dim if it's far away. If two stars are the same distance away, what might cause one of them to be brighter than the other?

✔ Reading Check
What is the difference between absolute and apparent magnitude?

Problem-Solving Activity

Are distance and brightness related?

The apparent magnitude of a star is affected by its distance from Earth. This activity will help you determine the relationship between distance and brightness.

Identifying the Problem

Luisa conducted an experiment to determine the relationship between distance and the brightness of stars. She used a meterstick, a light meter, and a lightbulb. She placed the bulb at the zero end of the meterstick, then placed the light meter at the 20-cm mark and recorded the distance and the light-meter reading in her data table. Readings are in luxes, which are units for measuring light intensity. Luisa then increased the distance from the bulb to the light meter and took more readings. By examining the data in the table, can you see a relationship between the two variables?

Effect of Distance on Light	
Distance (cm)	**Meter Reading (luxes)**
20	4150.0
40	1037.5
60	461.1
80	259.4

Solving the Problem

1. What happened to the amount of light recorded when the distance was increased from 20 cm to 40 cm? When the distance was increased from 20 cm to 60 cm?
2. What does this indicate about the relationship between light intensity and distance? What would the light intensity be at 100 cm? Would making a graph help you visualize the relationship?

Teacher FYI

A recognizable pattern of stars within a constellation or among stars in different constellations is called an asterism. The Big Dipper and Little Dipper are asterisms in the constellations of Ursa Major and Ursa Minor.

Inclusion Strategies

Learning Disabled Pair each learning disabled student with another student. Have pairs cut a 4-cm square from black construction paper and punch pinholes in the square to show a constellation's outline. Then have students put the square at one end of a cardboard tube and point the tube toward a light source to view the constellation. L2 ELL [IS] **Visual-Spatial**

Measurement in Space

How do scientists determine distance to stars from the solar system that Earth is part of? One way is to measure its parallax—the apparent shift in the position of an object when viewed from two different positions. Extend your arm and look at your thumb first with your left eye closed and then with your right eye closed, as the girl in **Figure 3A** is doing. Your thumb appears to change position with respect to the background. Now do the same experiment with your thumb closer to your face, as shown in **Figure 3B.** What do you observe? The nearer an object is to the observer, the greater its parallax is.

Astronomers can measure the parallax of relatively close stars to determine their distances from Earth. **Figure 4** shows how a close star's position appears to change. Knowing the angle that the star's position changes and the size of Earth's orbit, astronomers can calculate the distance of the star from Earth.

Because space is so vast, a special unit of measure is needed to record distances. Distances between stars and galaxies are measured in light-years. A **light-year** is the distance that light travels in one year. Light travels at 300,000 km/s, or about 9.5 trillion km in one year. The nearest star to Earth, other than the Sun, is Proxima Centauri. Proxima Centauri is a mere 4.3 light-years away, or about 40 trillion km.

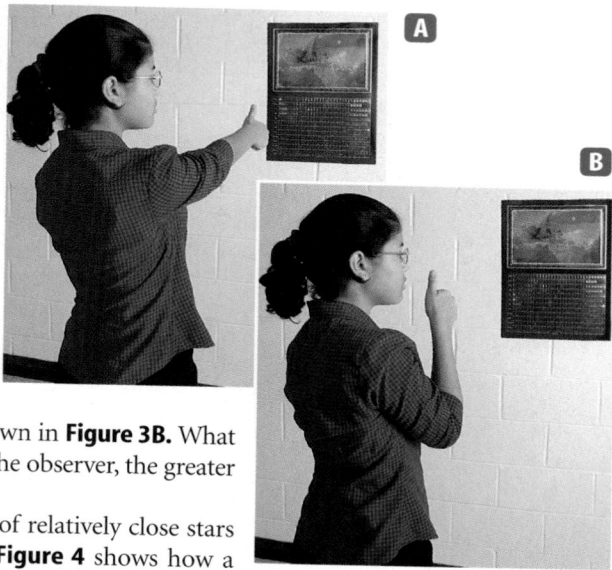

Figure 3
A Your thumb appears to move less against the background when it is farther away.
B It appears to move more when it is closer.

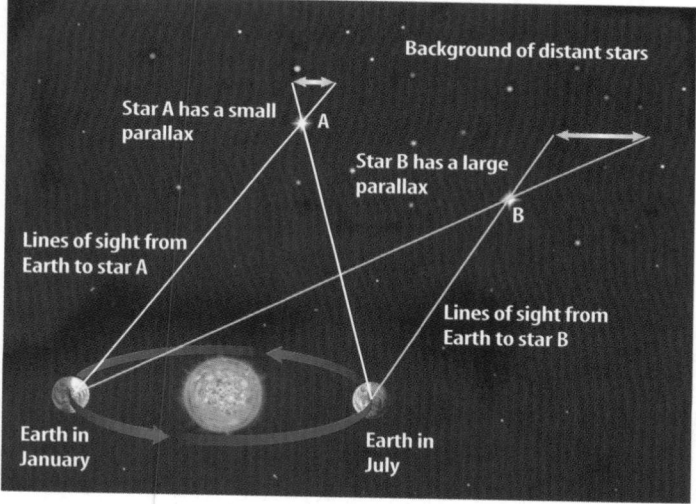

Background of distant stars

Star A has a small parallax

Star B has a large parallax

Lines of sight from Earth to star A

Lines of sight from Earth to star B

Earth in January

Earth in July

Figure 4
Parallax can be seen if you observe the same star when Earth is at two different points during its orbit around the Sun. The star's position relative to more distant background stars will appear to change. *Is star* **A** *or* **B** *farther from Earth?*

SECTION 1 Stars **739**

Measurement in Space

Activity

Arrange a numbered scale in the front of the room. Place two objects at different distances from the scale. Have students observe the objects relative to the scale from three different classroom locations. Ask them to explain differences in their observations. Students should note that as the distance to the viewed object decreases, the shift in the position of the object in relation to the scale increases. This occurs because the parallax angle of the closer object is greater than that of the farther object. **LS** **Visual-Spatial**

Visual Learning

Figure 3 Have students repeat the activity shown in the figure. They should notice that the closer their thumb is to their face, the more the position of the thumb appears to shift and the greater the parallax.

Caption Answer
Figure 4 Star A is more distant

Curriculum Connection

Math Use the following equation to calculate the distance in light-years to two stars:
$d = 3.26/p$

In this equation, d represents light-years and p represents parallax angle. Star 1 has a parallax angle of 0.77″, and Star 2 has a parallax angle of 0.04″. Star 1 = 4.23 light-years; Star 2 = 81.5 light-years

Properties of Stars

Extension

Have students investigate what a star's color and spectrum indicate. surface temperature, atmosphere composition, and movement toward or away from Earth

3 Assess

Reteach

Take students to an open area to demonstrate parallax. Have two volunteers stand approximately 50 m apart. Give one student a compass with a sighting mirror. Have the student determine the exact compass heading to the other student. Now have the student holding the compass move sideways 20 m, and determine the new compass heading to the other student. Repeat this activity, varying the distances between students. L2 ELL COOP LEARN

 **Kinesthetic**

Challenge

Provide students with unlabeled star charts and have them make and explain their own constellations. L2 ELL

Visual-Spatial

✓Assessment

Performance Have students write paragraphs explaining why Deneb appears so bright and yet is more than 1,400 light-years away. Deneb is either very large, very hot, or both. Use **PASC**, p. 99.

Figure 5
These star spectra were made by placing a diffraction grating over a telescope's objective lens. *What causes the lines in spectra?*

Properties of Stars

The color of a star indicates its temperature. For example, hot stars are a blue-white color. A relatively cool star looks orange or red. Stars that have the same temperature as the Sun have a yellow color.

Astronomers study the composition of stars by observing their spectra. When fitted into a telescope, a spectroscope acts like a prism. It spreads light out in the rainbow band called a spectrum. When light from a star passes through a spectroscope, it breaks into its component colors. Look at the spectrum of a star in **Figure 5.** Notice the dark lines caused by elements in the star's atmosphere. Light radiated from a star passes through the star's atmosphere. As it does, elements in the atmosphere absorb some of this light. The wavelengths of visible light that are absorbed appear as dark lines in the spectrum. Each element absorbs certain wavelengths, producing a certain pattern of dark lines. Every chemical element produces a unique pattern of dark lines. Like a fingerprint, the patterns of lines can be used to identify which elements are in a star's atmosphere.

Section 1 Assessment

1. What is a constellation?
2. How does Earth's revolution affect the viewing of constellations throughout the year?
3. If two stars give off equal amounts of light, why might one look brighter?
4. If the spectrum of a star shows the same absorption lines as the Sun, what can be said about the star's composition?
5. **Think Critically** Several thousand stars have large enough parallaxes that their distances can be studied using parallax. Most of these stars are invisible to the naked eye. What does this indicate about their absolute magnitudes?

Skill Builder Activities

6. **Recognizing Cause and Effect** Suppose you viewed Proxima Centauri through a telescope today. How old were you when the light that you see left Proxima Centauri? Why might Proxima Centauri look dimmer than Betelgeuse, a large star that is 489 light-years away? **For more help, refer to the** Science Skill Handbook.
7. **Using Graphics Software** Use graphics software on a computer to make a star chart of major constellations visible from where you live during the current season. Include several reference points to help others find the charted constellations. **For more help, refer to the** Technology Skill Handbook.

Answers to Section Assessment

1. a pattern of stars
2. As Earth revolves, its nighttime side faces different directions. As a result, different constellations are visible during the year.
3. Both stars have the same absolute magnitude. The star that appears brighter is probably closer to Earth.
4. Its composition is similar to that of the Sun's.
5. Because the nearest stars are mostly invisible when viewed from Earth, their absolute magnitudes are low.
6. Answers should equal the students' ages minus 4.2 years. Proxima Centauri is smaller than Betelgeuse and doesn't give off as much light. Both the absolute and apparent magnitudes of Betelgeuse are brighter than those of Proxima Centauri.
7. Charts will vary depending on the season. Reference points and the time of observation should be included.

The Sun

The Sun's Layers

Within the universe, the Sun is an ordinary star—not too spectacular. However, to you it's important. The Sun is the center of the solar system, and it makes life possible on Earth. More than 99 percent of all the matter in the solar system is in the Sun.

Notice the different layers of the Sun, shown in **Figure 6,** as you read about them. Like other stars, the Sun is an enormous ball of gas that produces energy by fusing hydrogen into helium in its core. This energy travels outward through the radiation zone and the convection zone. In the convection zone, gases circulate in giant swirls. Finally, energy passes into the Sun's atmosphere.

The Sun's Atmosphere

The lowest layer of the Sun's atmosphere and the layer from which light is given off is the **photosphere.** The photosphere often is called the surface of the Sun, although the surface is not a smooth feature. Temperatures there are about 6,000 K. Above the photosphere is the **chromosphere.** This layer extends upward about 2,000 km above the photosphere. A transition zone occurs between 2,000 km and 10,000 km above the photosphere. Above the transition zone is the **corona.** This is the largest layer of the Sun's atmosphere and extends millions of kilometers into space. Temperatures in the corona are as high as 2 million K. Charged particles continually escape from the corona and move through space as solar wind.

Figure 6
Energy produced by fusion in the Sun's core travels outward by radiation and convection. The Sun's atmosphere—the photosphere, chromosphere, and corona—shines by the energy produced in the core.

As You Read

What You'll Learn

- **Describe** the strucure of the Sun.
- **Explain** how sunspots, prominences, and solar flares are related.
- **Explain** why the Sun is considered an average star and how it differs from stars in binary systems.

Vocabulary

photosphere   corona
chromosphere   sunspot

Why It's Important

The Sun is the source of most energy on Earth.

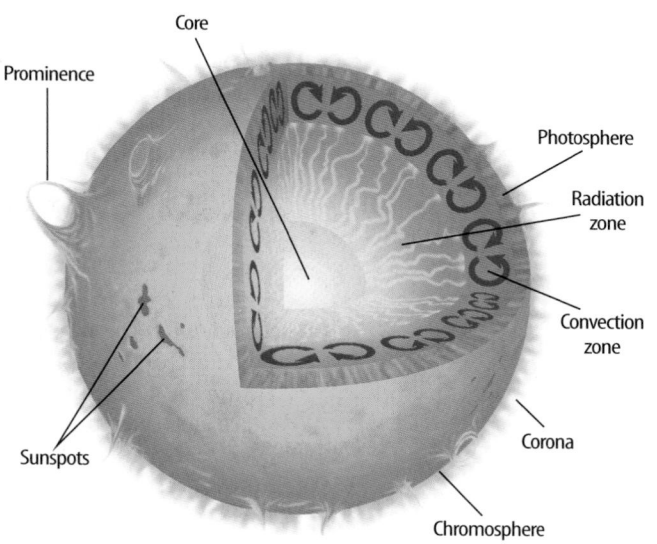

Core
Prominence
Photosphere
Radiation zone
Convection zone
Sunspots
Corona
Chromosphere

SECTION 2

The Sun

1 Motivate

Bellringer Transparency

Display the Section Focus Transparency for Section 2. Use the accompanying Transparency Activity Master. L2
ELL

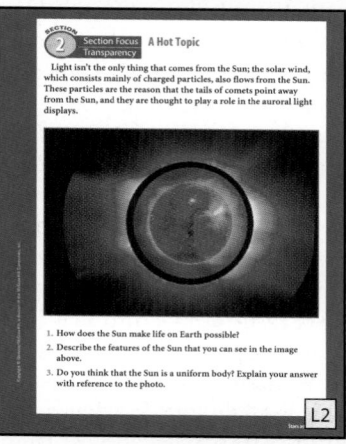

A Hot Topic

Light isn't the only thing that comes from the Sun; the solar wind, which consists mainly of charged particles, also flows from the Sun. These particles are the reason that the tails of comets point away from the Sun, and they are thought to play a role in the auroral light displays.

1. How does the Sun make life on Earth possible?
2. Describe the features of the Sun that you can see in the image above.
3. Do you think that the Sun is a uniform body? Explain your answer with reference to the photo.

L2

Tie to Prior Knowledge

Have students recall the warmth of a sunny summer day. Remind them that interactions of air, water, and energy from the Sun cause Earth's weather.

Section ✔Assessment Planner

PORTFOLIO
Challenge, p. 744
PERFORMANCE ASSESSMENT
Skill Builder Activities, p. 744
See page 764 for more options.

CONTENT ASSESSMENT
Section, p. 744
Challenge, p. 744
Chapter, pp. 764–765

Resource Manager

Chapter Resources Booklet
Transparency Activity, p. 49
Directed Reading for
Content Mastery, p. 20

The Sun's Atmosphere

Fun Fact

Temperatures rise from 6,000 K to more than 1,000,000 K in a transition zone between the chromosphere and corona.

Surface Features

Quick Demo

Use this demo to help students understand why sunspots look dark even though they are quite bright. Turn on an overhead projector, and have students observe the light that falls on the screen. Then partially cover the surface of the projector with a blank transparency. Have students compare both sides of the screen. They should note a difference in brightness. This is analogous to what occurs on the Sun's surface. Next to the brighter surrounding areas of the Sun's surface, the sunspots look dark.

✔ Reading Check

Answer the regular pattern of increasing and decreasing sunspot activity on the Sun

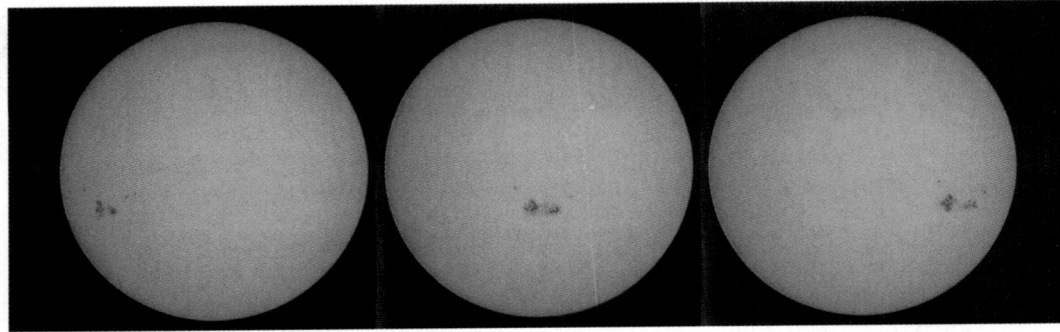

A Notice how these sunspots appear to move as the Sun rotates.

Figure 7
Sunspots are bright, but when viewed against the rest of the photosphere, they appear dark.

B This is a close-up photo of a large sunspot.

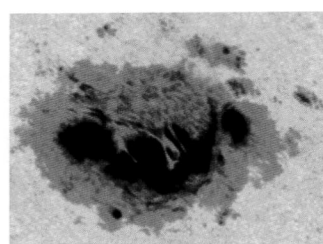

Surface Features

From the viewpoint that you observe the Sun, its surface appears to be a smooth layer. But the Sun's surface has many features, including sunspots, prominences, flares, and CMEs.

Sunspots Areas of the Sun's surface that appear dark because they are cooler than surrounding areas are called **sunspots**. Ever since Galileo Galilei viewed sunspots with a telescope, scientists have been studying them. Because scientists could observe the movement of individual sunspots, shown in **Figure 7**, they concluded that the Sun rotates. However, the Sun doesn't rotate as a solid body, as Earth does. It rotates faster at its equator than at its poles. Sunspots near the equator take about 27 days to complete one rotation. Near the poles, they take 31 days.

Sunspots aren't permanent features on the Sun. They appear and disappear over a period of several days, weeks, or months. The number of sunspots increases and decreases in a fairly regular pattern called the sunspot, or solar activity, cycle. Times when many large sunspots occur are called sunspot maximums. Sunspot maximums occur about every 10 to 11 years. Periods of sunspot minimum occur in between.

✔ Reading Check *What is a sunspot cycle?*

Prominences and Flares Sunspots are related to several features on the Sun's surface. The intense magnetic field associated with sunspots might cause prominences, which are huge, arching columns of gas. Notice the huge prominence in **Figure 8A.** Some prominences blast material from the Sun into space at speeds ranging from 600 km/s to more than 1,000 km/s.

Gases near a sunspot sometimes brighten suddenly, shooting outward at high speed. These violent eruptions are called solar flares. You can see a solar flare in **Figure 8B.**

742 **CHAPTER 25** Stars and Galaxies

Resource Manager

Chapter Resources Booklet
  Enrichment, p. 32
Cultural Diversity, p. 29

Teacher FYI
Sunspots are caused by intense magnetic storms on the Sun. As the Sun rotates, lines of magnetic force wrap around it. These lines dip into the Sun's interior and then back out, forming sunspots. This explains why many sunspots occur in pairs and why the members of the pair have opposite magnetic poles.

CMEs During a sunspot maximum, like the one that occurred in 2000, brilliant coronal mass ejections (CMEs) are emitted from the Sun. When a CME is released in the direction of Earth, it appears as a halo around the Sun, as shown in **Figure 8C.**

CMEs present little danger to life on Earth, but the highly charged solar wind material, along with ultraviolet light and X rays from solar flares, can reach Earth and cause disruption of radio signals. High-energy particles contained in CMEs and emitted by solar flares are captured by Earth's magnetic field, disrupting power distribution and communication equipment. These particles also interact with Earth's atmosphere near the polar regions and create light. This light is called an aurora, as shown in **Figure 8D.**

SCIENCE *Online*

Research Visit the Glencoe Science Web site at **science.glencoe.com** for more information about sunspots, solar flares, and prominences. Communicate to your class what you learned.

SCIENCE *Online*
Internet Addresses
_____
_____
_____
_____

Explore the Glencoe Science Web site at **science.glencoe.com** to find out more about topics in this section.

Figure 8
Features such as solar prominences and solar flares can reach hundreds of thousands of kilometers into space. CMEs are generated as magnetic fields above sunspot groups rearrange. Particles from solar flares interact with Earth's atmosphere to create auroras.

A Solar prominence

B Solar flare

D Aurora

C CME

Visual Learning

Figure 8 Explain that CMEs can send as much as ten billion tons of plasma away from the Sun at speeds up to 2,000 km/s. It takes from 2 to 4 days for the shock wave caused by a CME to reach Earth. If a CME is observed, additional sightings of auroras can be expected within a few days as the shock wave passes Earth. Additional geomagnetic activity lasts for 1 to 2 days after the shock wave passes. Have students make an events chain using the information from **Figure 8** and the text detailing the events from the production of a solar flare on the Sun to the sighting of auroras on Earth.

Use Science Words

Word Meaning Have students find out why a study of sunspots, solar flares, CMEs, and magnetic disturbances such as auroras on Earth are part of a study called *space weather*. Space weather deals with any factors affecting the environment of space in the vicinity of Earth and the Sun.

Curriculum Connection

Math Using the data provided, have student groups graph sunspot activity. Have each group describe any observed trends. Sunspot activity seems to increase and decrease in a cycle. [L2] COOP LEARN [P]

Year	Sunspots	Year	Sunspots	Year	Sunspots	Year	Sunspots
1985	18	1989	159	1993	54	1997	22
1986	14	1990	147	1994	31	1998	65
1987	29	1991	145	1995	18	1999	94
1988	100	1992	94	1996	9	2000	127

Figure 9
Most stars were formed originally in large clusters containing hundreds, or even thousands, of stars.

The Sun—An Average Star

The Sun is a middle-aged star. Its absolute magnitude is typical, and it shines with a yellow light. Although the Sun is an average star, it is somewhat unusual in one way. Most stars are part of a system in which two or more stars orbit each other. When two stars orbit each other, they make up a binary system.

In some cases, astronomers can detect binary systems because one star occasionally eclipses the other. Algol, in the constellation Perseus, is an example of this. The total amount of light from the star system becomes dim and then bright again on a regular cycle. In other cases, three stars orbit around each other, forming a triple star system. The closest star system to the Sun—the Alpha Centauri system, including Proxima Centauri—is a triple star.

Stars also can move through space together as a cluster. In a star cluster, many stars are relatively close to one another, so their gravitational attraction to each other is strong. Most star clusters are far from the solar system, and each appears as a fuzzy patch in the night sky. The double cluster in the northern part of the constellation Perseus is shown in **Figure 9.** On a dark night in autumn, you can see the double cluster with binoculars, but you can't see its individual stars. The Pleiades star cluster can be seen in the constellation of Taurus in the winter sky. On a clear, dark night, you might be able to see seven of the stars in this cluster.

Section Assessment

1. What are the different layers that make up the Sun?

2. Describe the characteristics of sunspots.

3. How are sunspots, prominences, solar flares, and CMEs related? How does each affect Earth?

4. What characteristics does the Sun have in common with other stars? What characteristic makes it different from most other stars?

5. **Think Critically** Because most stars are found in multiple-star systems, what might explain why the Sun is a single star?

Skill Builder Activities

6. **Interpreting Scientific Illustrations** Use **Figure 6** to answer the questions below. **For more help, refer to the** Science Skill Handbook.
   a. Which layers make up the Sun's atmosphere?
   b. What process circulates gas in the Sun's convection zone?

7. **Communicating** Explain how the Sun generates energy. In your Science Journal, write a short paragraph hypothesizing what might happen to the Sun when it exhausts its supply of hydrogen. **For more help, refer to the** Science Skill Handbook.

744 **CHAPTER 25** Stars and Galaxies

Answers to Section Assessment

1. core, radiation zone, convection zone, photosphere, chromosphere, corona
2. Sunspots are darker and cooler than surrounding areas of the Sun.
3. Magnetic fields near a sunspot can cause prominences. CMEs are emitted during sunspot maximums. Gases near sunspots can shoot outward as a solar flare, which may cause disruption of

communication by radio and television and can produce auroras.
4. The Sun's size, temperature, and absolute magnitude are similar to those of other yellow stars on the main sequence. The Sun is not part of a binary system.
5. Possible answer: The Sun might have been part of a multiple-star system

that spread out.
6. Photosphere, chromosphere, corona; gases heated at the bottom of the convection zone are forced upward where they release energy, cool, and sink.
7. Possible answer: Fusion reactions in the core change hydrogen into helium. When hydrogen is exhausted, it will fuse helium in its core.

Activity

Sunspots

Sunspots can be observed moving across the face of the Sun as it rotates. Measure the movement of sunspots, and use your data to determine the Sun's period of rotation.

What You'll Investigate
Can sunspot motion be used to determine the Sun's period of rotation?

Materials
several books	clipboard
piece of cardboard	small tripod
drawing paper	scissors
refracting telescope	

Goals
- **Observe** sunspots and estimate their size.
- **Estimate** the rate of apparent motion of sunspots.

Safety Precautions
Handle scissors with care.

Procedure

1. Find a location where the Sun can be viewed at the same time of day for a minimum of five days. **WARNING:** *Do not look directly at the Sun. Do not look through the telescope at the Sun. You could damage your eyes.*

2. Set up the telescope with the eyepiece facing away from the Sun, as shown. Align the telescope so that the shadow it casts on the ground is the smallest size possible. Cut and attach the cardboard as shown in the photo.

3. Use books to prop the clipboard upright. Point the eyepiece at the drawing paper.

4. If the telescope has a small finder scope attached, remove it or keep it covered.

5. Move the clipboard back and forth until you have the largest image of the Sun on the paper. Adjust the telescope to form a clear image. Trace the outline of the Sun on the paper.

6. Trace any sunspots that appear as dark areas on the Sun's image. Repeat this step at the same time each day for a week.

7. Using the Sun's diameter (approximately 1,390,000 km), estimate the size of the largest sunspots that you observed.

8. **Calculate** how many kilometers the sunspots appear to move each day.

9. **Predict** how many days it will take for the same group of sunspots to return to the same position in which they appeared on day 1.

Conclude and Apply

1. What was the estimated size and rate of apparent motion of the largest sunspots?

2. **Infer** how sunspots can be used to determine that the Sun's surface is not solid like Earth's.

*C*ommunicating Your Data

Compare your conclusions with those of other students in your class. **For more help, refer to the** Science Skill Handbook.

---

*C*ommunicating Your Data

Use a computer to produce a table to record sunspot data. Explain possible causes of differences in observations. Possible answer: Students observed sunspots at different times.

Activity

BENCH TESTED

Purpose Students estimate the size and rate of movement of sunspots. L2 ELL

Visual-Spatial

Process Skills observing and inferring, interpreting data, using numbers

Time Required 10 minutes each day for five days

Alternate Materials binoculars

Safety Precautions Caution students not to look directly at the Sun. Do not allow them to look at the Sun through the telescope.

Teaching Strategies If no sunspots are visible, check to see whether it is currently a sunspot minimum.

Answers to Questions

1. Answers will vary. Possible answer: size—3 to 4 times the size of Earth; rate of motion—about 16 days to cross the Sun's face

2. Sunspots near the Sun's equator move at different rates than those near the poles.

*✔*Assessment

Content To further assess students' understanding of sunspots, ask them to hypothesize about sunspot movement on the hemisphere they did not observe. **How might sunspots on the opposite hemisphere (north or south) move compared to those plotted in this activity?** Possible answer: Sunspots in the opposite hemisphere should move in a similar manner. Use **PASC,** p. 93.

SECTION

Evolution of Stars

1 Motivate

Bellringer Transparency

Display the Section Focus Transparency for Section 3. Use the accompanying Transparency Activity Master. L2

ELL

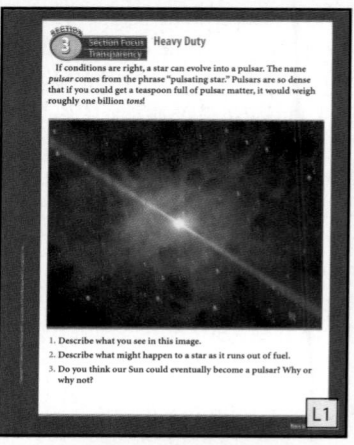

Tie to Prior Knowledge

Have students recall the four states of matter: solid, liquid, gas, and plasma. Explain that stars are composed of matter in the plasma state. Ask students to describe traits of matter in this state. Plasma is the state of matter in which there are roughly equal numbers of positively and negatively charged particles. It is produced when the atoms in a gas become ionized.

Caption Answer

Figure 10 red supergiant

SECTION

Evolution of Stars

As You Read

What You'll Learn

- **Describe** how stars are classified.
- **Explain** how the temperature of a star relates to its color.
- **Describe** how a star evolves.

Vocabulary

nebula	supergiant
giant	neutron star
white dwarf	black hole

Why It's Important

Like humans, stars are born, mature, grow old, and die.

Classifying Stars

When you look at the night sky, all stars might appear to be similar, but they are quite different. Like people, they vary in age and size, but stars also vary in temperature.

In the early 1900s, Ejnar Hertzsprung and Henry Russell made some important observations. They noticed that in general, stars with higher temperatures also have brighter absolute magnitudes.

Hertzsprung and Russell developed a graph, shown in **Figure 10,** to show this relationship. They placed temperatures across the bottom and absolute magnitudes up one side. A graph that shows the relationship of a star's temperature to its absolute magnitude is called a Hertzsprung-Russell (H-R) diagram.

The Main Sequence As you can see, stars seem to fit into specific areas of the graph. Most stars fit into a diagonal band that runs from the upper left to the lower right of the chart. This band, called the main sequence, contains hot, blue, bright stars in the upper left and cool, red, dim stars in the lower right. Yellow, main sequence stars, like the Sun, fall in between.

Figure 10
The relationships among a star's color, temperature, and brightness are shown in this Hertzsprung-Russell diagram. Main sequence stars run from the upper-left corner to the lower-right corner. Stars in the upper left are hot, bright stars, and stars in the lower right are cool, faint stars. *What type of star shown in the diagram is the coolest, brightest star?*

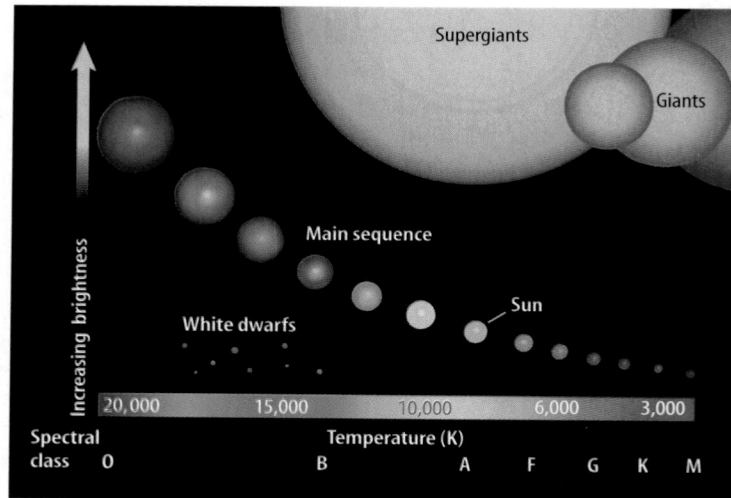

746 **CHAPTER 25** Stars and Galaxies

Section ✓*Assessment* Planner

PORTFOLIO
Extension, p. 747

PERFORMANCE ASSESSMENT
Skill Builder Activities, p. 751
See page 764 for more options.

CONTENT ASSESSMENT
Section, p. 751
Challenge, p. 751
Chapter, pp. 764–765

Dwarfs and Giants About 90 percent of all stars are main sequence stars. Most of these are small, red stars found in the lower right of the H-R diagram. Among main sequence stars, the hottest stars generate the most light and the coolest ones generate the least. What about the ten percent of stars that are not part of the main sequence? Some of these stars are hot but not bright. These small stars are located on the lower left of the H-R diagram and are called white dwarfs. Other stars are extremely bright but not hot. These large stars on the upper right of the H-R diagram are called giants, or red giants because they are usually red in color. The largest giants are called super-giants. **Figure 11** shows the red giant, Antares—a star 300 times the Sun's diameter—in the constellation Scorpius. It is 5,600 times as bright as the Sun.

> ✓ **Reading Check** *What kinds of stars are on the main sequence?*

How do stars shine?

When the H-R diagram was developed, scientists didn't know what caused stars to shine. Hertzsprung and Russell developed their diagram without knowing what produced the light and heat of stars.

For centuries, people were puzzled by the questions of what stars were made of and how they produced light. Many people had estimated that Earth was only a few thousand years old. The Sun could have been made of coal and shined for that long. However, when people realized that Earth was much older, they wondered what material possibly could burn for so many years. Early in the twentieth century, scientists began to understand the process that keeps stars shining for billions of years.

Generating Energy In the 1930s, scientists discovered reactions between the nuclei of atoms. They hypothesized that temperatures in the center of the Sun must be high enough to cause hydrogen to fuse to make helium. That reaction would release tremendous amounts of energy. In this reaction, four hydrogen nuclei combine to create one helium nucleus. The mass of one helium nucleus is less than the mass of four hydrogen nuclei, so some mass is lost in the reaction.

Years earlier, in 1905, Albert Einstein had proposed a theory stating that mass can be converted into energy. This was stated as the famous equation $E = mc^2$. In this equation, E is the energy produced, m is the mass, and c is the speed of light. The small amount of mass "lost" when hydrogen atoms fuse to form a helium atom is converted to a large amount of energy.

Figure 11
Antares is a bright, red giant located 400 light-years from Earth. Although its temperature is only about 3,500 K, it is the 16th brightest star in the sky.

Physics INTEGRATION

Fusion in stars produces more than just visible light. It also produces radiation that you cannot see. Do research to find out about the different types of radiation emitted by stars.

② Teach

Classifying Stars

✓ **Reading Check**

Answer Most of the stars on the main sequence are small, red stars. Hot, blue, bright stars and medium-sized, medium-temperature yellow stars also are on the main sequence.

Extension

Have students research the work of A. S. Eddington, Robert Atkinson, and Hans Bethe, the scientists whose discoveries in the 1920s and 1930s led to an understanding of energy production in stars like our Sun and hotter stars. Have them write a brief report on their findings. Eddington hypothesized that temperatures in the center of the Sun must be high, Robert Atkinson suggested that with these high temperatures, hydrogen could fuse into helium. Bethe hypothesized that carbon could be a catalyst in fusion reactions, which explained energy production in hotter stars. L2 Linguistics P

How do stars shine?

Physics INTEGRATION

Stars, including the Sun, emit photons, extremely high-energy photons (called gamma rays), electrons, X rays, and protons (called cosmic rays). Students may find additional information in their research. Check students' sources.

Resource Manager

Chapter Resources Booklet
 Transparency Activity, p. 50
 Directed Reading for Content Mastery, p. 21

Inclusion Strategies

Learning Disabled Have students prepare a bulletin board display illustrating the Hertzsprung-Russell (H-R) diagram. Encourage them to use **Figure 10** as a guide. L2
COOP LEARN Kinesthetic

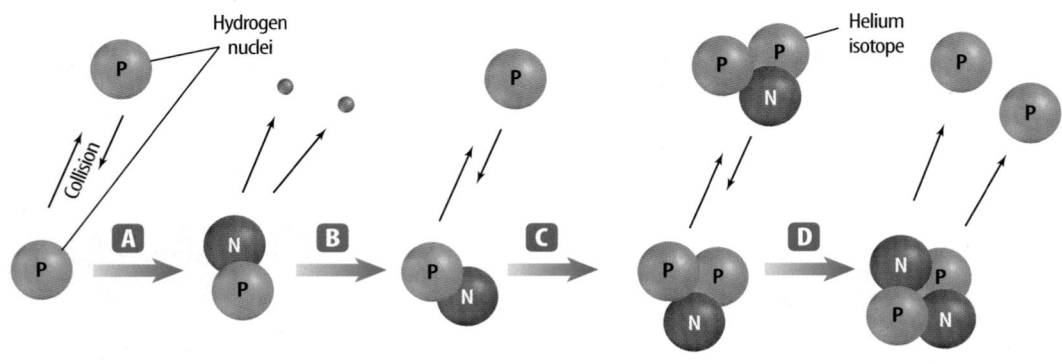

A One proton decays to a neutron, releasing subatomic particles and some energy.

B Another proton fuses with a proton and neutron to form an isotope of helium. Energy is given off again.

C Two helium isotopes fuse.

D A helium nucleus (two protons and two neutrons) forms as two protons break away. In the process, still more energy is released.

How do stars shine?, continued

Caption Answer

Figure 12 It is converted into energy; $E = mc^2$.

Evolution of Stars

Make a Model

Ask students to make a model of the fusion of hydrogen into helium. Have them use medium-sized and small polystyrene balls to represent neutrons, protons, neutrinos, and positrons. Ask students to use the model to demonstrate how the fusion reaction progresses. Two protons fuse to form hydrogen-2 and release a positron and a neutrino. Hydrogen-2 fuses with a proton to produce helium-3. Two helium-3 nuclei fuse to form helium-4 and two protons. L3

LS Visual-Spatial

Use Science Words

Word Meaning Have students compare and contrast the words *fusion* and *fission*. Both are nuclear processes. Fusion is the combining of nuclei. Fission is the splitting apart of nuclei.

Figure 12
Fusion begins in a star's core as protons (hydrogen nuclei) collide. *What happens to the "lost" mass during this process?*

Research Visit the Glencoe Science Web site at **science.glencoe.com** to find out more about the evolution of stars. Record this information in your Science Journal.

Fusion Shown in **Figure 12,** fusion occurs in the cores of stars. Only in the core are temperatures and pressures high enough to cause atoms to fuse. Normally, they would repel each other, but in the core of a star where the gravitational force is tremendous, atoms are pulled close enough that their nuclei fuse.

Evolution of Stars

Physics INTEGRATION

The H-R diagram explained a lot about stars. However, it also led to more questions. Many wondered why some stars didn't fit in the main sequence group and what happened when a star exhausted its supply of hydrogen fuel. Today, scientists have theories of how stars evolve, what makes them different from one another, and what happens when they die. **Figure 13** illustrates the lives of different types of stars.

When hydrogen fuel is used up, a star loses its main sequence status. This can take less than 1 million years for the brightest stars to many billions of years for the faintest stars. The Sun has a main sequence life span of about 10 billion years. Half of its life span is still in the future.

Nebula Stars begin as a large cloud of gas and dust called a **nebula.** As the particles of gas and dust exert a gravitational force on each other, the nebula begins to contract. Gravitational forces cause instability within the nebula. The nebula can break apart into smaller pieces. Each piece eventually will collapse to form a star.

748 CHAPTER 25 Stars and Galaxies

LAB DEMONSTRATION

Purpose To demonstrate how color changes as a material is heated
Materials Bunsen burner, wire, tongs, insulated pad
Preparation Set up Bunsen burner and obtain safety goggles and gloves.
Procedure Using tongs, hold a wire over a burner flame until it begins to glow. Have students record the color of the glowing wire. Continue heating the wire as students record changes and summarize their observations.
Expected Outcome The wire changed from reddish-orange to yellowish-white as it became hotter.

✔Assessment

How do the color changes you observed relate to star colors? Blue-white and yellow stars are hotter than red stars.

A Star Is Born As the particles in the smaller clouds move closer together, the temperatures in each nebula increase. When the temperature inside a nebula reaches 10 million K, fusion begins. The energy released radiates outward through the condensing ball of gas. As the energy radiates into space, stars are born.

✔ **Reading Check** *How are stars born?*

Main Sequence to Giant Stars In the newly formed star, the heat from fusion causes pressure that balances the attraction due to gravity. The star becomes a main sequence star. It continues to use up its hydrogen fuel.

When hydrogen in the core of the star is exhausted, a balance no longer exists between pressure and gravity. The core contracts, and temperatures inside the star increase. This causes the outer layers of the star to expand and cool. In this late stage of its life cycle, a star is called a **giant.**

After the core temperature reaches 100 million K, helium nuclei fuse to form carbon in the giant's core. By this time, the star has expanded to an enormous size, and its outer layers are much cooler than they were when it was a main sequence star. In about 5 billion years, the Sun will become a giant.

White Dwarfs After the star's core uses up its helium, it contracts even more and its outer layers escape into space. This leaves behind the hot, dense core. The core contracts under the force of gravity. At this stage in a star's evolution, it becomes a **white dwarf.** A white dwarf is about the size of Earth.

Chemistry
INTEGRATION

The spectrum of a star shows dark absorption lines of helium and hydrogen and is bright in the blue end. Describe as much as you can about the star's composition and surface temperature.

Figure 13
The life of a star depends greatly on its mass. Massive stars eventually become neutron stars or possibly black holes. *What happens to stars that are the size of the Sun?*

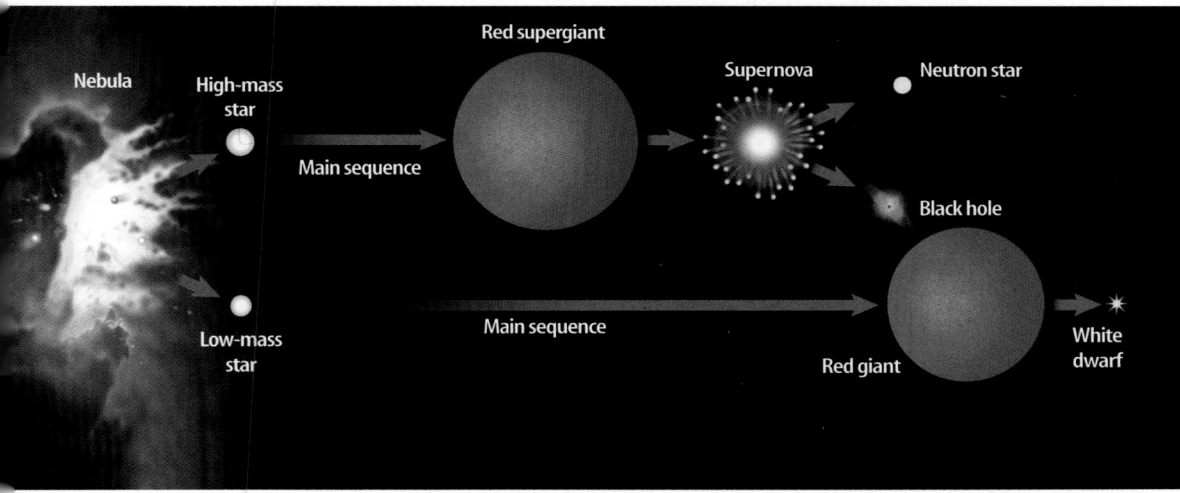

Nebula — High-mass star — Main sequence — Red supergiant — Supernova — Neutron star / Black hole
Low-mass star — Main sequence — Red giant — White dwarf

Chemistry
INTEGRATION

The star's atmosphere contains helium and hydrogen. Its surface has a high temperature.

✔ **Reading Check**

Answer temperatures in nebula increase, fusion begins; energy radiates

Extension

Have students research the Horsehead and Orion nebulas, located in the constellation of Orion. Ask them to determine the composition of each type of nebula. The Horsehead Nebula is composed of cool gases that block light from behind, whereas the Orion Nebula is composed of hot, glowing gases. L3
IS Linguistic

Caption Answer

Figure 13 Stars the size of the Sun will become giants, white dwarfs, and finally black cinders.

Visual Learning

Figure 13 Have students construct sequence diagrams showing the evolution of a massive star. After students read about black holes, ask the following questions: **After a supernova, what type of object forms if the remaining dense core collapses?** a black hole **If no light is given off, how are black holes located?** X rays are emitted by matter as it is pulled into the black hole.

SCIENCE *Online*
Internet Addresses
_____
_____
_____
_____
Explore the Glencoe Science Web site at **science.glencoe.com** to find out more about topics in this section.

Teacher FYI

A nebula may produce a steady stream of stars over a given period. In the Orion Nebula (M42), a star nursery located 1,500 light-years away, hundreds of stars have already formed and many more will follow. The brightest star that has been seen in the Orion Nebula by the *Hubble Space Telescope* is the Becklin-Neugebauer object.

Resource Manager

Chapter Resources Booklet
Enrichment, p. 33

Evolution of Stars,
continued

Fun Fact

In a star with a mass similar to that of the Sun, outer layers become unstable and begin escaping into space when the core runs out of hydrogen fuel. The escaping gases form a shell around the star, producing a nebula. The Ring Nebula in the constellation Lyra is a result of this process.

Extension

Have students explain the relationship between the brightness of a nebula and the star-formation processes occurring within it. Dark nebulas contain cool gases. Bright nebulas, such as the Orion Nebula and the Eagle Nebula, contain hot, glowing gases that are forming into stars.

Teacher FYI

Brown dwarfs are stars that never generated fusion in their cores. These dim stars are found by observing the movement of a companion star. A single star's path through space is a nearly straight line. The path of a star orbited by a brown dwarf has a distinct wobble. This wobble is used to locate brown dwarfs as well as planets beyond the solar system.

Supergiants and Supernovas In stars that are more than ten times more massive than the Sun, the stages of evolution occur more quickly and more violently. Look back at **Figure 13.** In massive stars, the core heats up to much higher temperatures. Heavier and heavier elements form by fusion, and the star expands into a **supergiant.** Eventually, iron forms in the core. Because fusion no longer releases energy after iron forms, the core collapses violently, sending a shock wave outward through the star. The outer portion of the star explodes, producing a supernova. A supernova can be millions of times brighter than the original star was.

Neutron Stars If the collapsed core of a supernova is about twice as massive as the Sun, it may shrink to approximately 20 km in diameter. Only neutrons can exist in the dense core, and it becomes a **neutron star.** Neutron stars are so dense that a teaspoonful would weigh about 100 million metric tons in Earth's gravity. As dense as neutron stars are, they can contract only so far because the neutrons resist the inward pull of gravity.

Black Holes If the remaining dense core from a supernova is more than three times more massive than the Sun, probably nothing can stop the core's collapse. Under these conditions, all of the core's mass collapses to a point that has no volume. The gravity from this mass is so strong that nothing can escape from it, not even light. Because light cannot escape, the region is called a **black hole.** If you could shine a flashlight on a black hole, the light simply would disappear into it.

Figure 14
The black hole at the center of galaxy M87 pulls matter into it at extremely high velocities. This matter interacts to produce a jet of particles that stream away from the center of the galaxy at nearly light speed.

✔ **Reading Check** *What is a black hole?*

Black holes, however, are not like giant vacuum cleaners, sucking in distant objects. A black hole has an event horizon, which is a region inside of which nothing can escape. If something—including light—crosses the event horizon, it will be pulled into the black hole. Beyond the event horizon, the black hole's gravity pulls on objects just as it would if the mass had not collapsed. Stars and planets can orbit around a black hole.

The photograph in **Figure 14** was taken by the *Hubble Space Telescope.* It shows a jet of particles streaming out of the center of galaxy M87, 50 million light-years from Earth. These particles are formed because matter is being pulled into a black hole.

✔ Active Reading

Learning Journal Students should draw a vertical line down each page of their Learning Journals. The left-column entries can be research notes, lecture notes, or vocabulary terms. The right-column entries are the student's response to, interpretation of, questions about, or analysis of the left-column entries. Have students write a Learning Journal related to stars and galaxies.

Resource Manager

Chapter Resources Booklet
  Reinforcement, p. 29

Recycling Matter A star begins its life as a nebula, such as the one shown in **Figure 15.** Where does the matter in a nebula come from? Nebulas form partly from the matter that was once in other stars. A star ejects enormous amounts of matter during its lifetime. Some of this matter is incorporated into nebulas, which can evolve to form new stars. The matter in stars is recycled many times.

What about the matter created in the cores of stars? Are elements such as carbon and iron also recycled? These elements can become parts of new stars. In fact, spectrographs have shown that the Sun contains some carbon, iron, and other such elements. Because the Sun is an average, main sequence star, it is too young and its mass is too small to have formed these elements itself. The Sun condensed from material that was created in stars that died many billions of years ago.

Some elements condense to form planets and other bodies rather than stars. In fact, your body contains many atoms that were fused in the cores of ancient stars. Evidence suggests that the first stars formed from hydrogen and helium and that all the other elements have formed in the cores of stars or as stars explode.

Figure 15
Stars are forming in the Orion Nebula and other similar nebulae.

Discussion
What is the origin of the carbon and iron found in the Sun? These and other elements that did not form in the Sun were in the nebula from which the Sun formed. The nebula obtained its carbon and iron from stars that evolved earlier.

③ Assess

Reteach
Refer students to **Figure 10** and ask why the stars located in the upper-left portion of the H-R diagram have such a high absolute magnitude. These stars are massive, fairly large, and have high temperatures. **Visual-Spatial**

Challenge
Refer students to **Figure 10. Why do supergiant stars have such a high absolute magnitude even though they have such a relatively low temperature?** Supergiant stars are very large compared with other stars. **Why do supergiant stars have such low temperatures?** Supergiant stars form because their outer shells have expanded. This expansion causes the outer layers to cool.
 **Logical-Mathematical**

✓ Assessment

Content Have students explain where elements in their bodies, such as carbon, may have come from. They were most likely produced in a supernova explosion. Use **Performance Assessment in the Science Classroom,** p. 93.

Section ③ Assessment

1. Explain why giants are not in the main sequence on the H-R diagram. How do their temperatures and absolute magnitudes compare with those of main sequence stars?

2. What can be said about the absolute magnitudes of two equal-sized stars whose colors are blue and yellow?

3. How do stars produce energy?

4. Outline the history and probable future of the Sun.

5. **Think Critically** Why doesn't the helium currently in the Sun's core undergo fusion?

Skill Builder Activities

6. **Comparing and Contrasting** Sequence the following in order of most evolved to least evolved: *main sequence star, supergiant, neutron star,* and *nebula.* **For more help, refer to the** Science Skill Handbook.

7. **Solving One-Step Equations** Assume that a star's core has shrunk to a diameter of 12 km. What would be the circumference of the shrunken stellar core? Use the equation $C = \pi d$. How does this compare with the circumference of Earth with a diameter of 12,756 km? **For more help, refer to the** Math Skill Handbook.

Answers to Section Assessment

1. Giants are large, relatively cool stars. Their temperatures compare with small main sequence stars, but their absolute magnitudes compare with the larger, more massive main sequence stars.

2. The blue star has a greater absolute magnitude.

3. Stars produce energy by fusion.

4. Nebula—fusion in cloud center; main sequence star—fusion balances gravity; giant—fuses helium; white dwarf—core contracts

5. The Sun still has a supply of hydrogen for fusion. Currently, the Sun's core is not hot enough to fuse helium.

6. neutron star, supergiant, main sequence star, nebula

7. $C = \pi d = (3.14)(12\text{ km}) = 37.7\text{ km}$; $C = (3.14)(12,756\text{ km}) = 40,054\text{ km}$; Earth's circumference is 1,062 times larger than the shrunken stellar core.

SECTION

4

Galaxies and the Universe

1 Motivate

Bellringer Transparency

Display the Section Focus Transparency for Section 4. Use the accompanying Transparency Activity Master. [L2] [ELL]

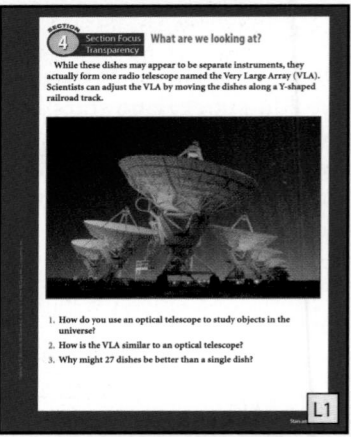

Tie to Prior Knowledge

Ask students if they have ever observed the night sky far from city lights. If so, they may have seen the band of stars that stretches across the sky—the Milky Way, our home galaxy.

SECTION

4 Galaxies and the Universe

As You Read

What You'll Learn
- **Identify** the three main types of galaxies.
- **List** several characteristics of the Milky Way Galaxy.
- **Describe** evidence that supports the Big Bang theory.

Vocabulary
galaxy
Big Bang theory

Why It's Important
Studying the universe could help scientists determine whether life is possible elsewhere.

Galaxies

Long ago, people believed that Earth was the center of the universe. Today you know that the Sun is the center of the solar system. But where is the solar system in relation to the galaxy? Where is the galaxy located in the universe?

You are on Earth, and Earth orbits the Sun. Does the Sun orbit anything? How does it interact with other objects in the universe? The Sun is one star among many in a **galaxy**—a large group of stars, gas, and dust held together by gravity. The galaxy in which Earth is found is called the Milky Way. It contains about 200 billion stars, including the Sun. Galaxies are separated by huge distances—often millions of light-years.

In the same way that stars are grouped together within galaxies, galaxies are grouped into clusters. The cluster that the Milky Way belongs to is called the Local Group. It contains about 20 galaxies of various sizes and types. The three major types of galaxies are spiral, elliptical, and irregular.

Spiral Galaxies The Milky Way is a spiral galaxy, as shown in **Figure 16.** Notice that spiral galaxies have spiral arms that wind outward from inner regions. These arms are made up of bright stars and dust. The fuzzy patch seen in the constellation of Andromeda is a spiral galaxy. It's so far away that you can't see its individual stars. Instead, its combined light appears as a hazy spot in the sky. The Andromeda Galaxy is about 2 million light-years away and is a member of the Local Group.

Arms in a normal spiral start close to the center of the galaxy. Barred spirals have spiral arms extending from a large bar of stars and gas that passes through the center of the galaxy.

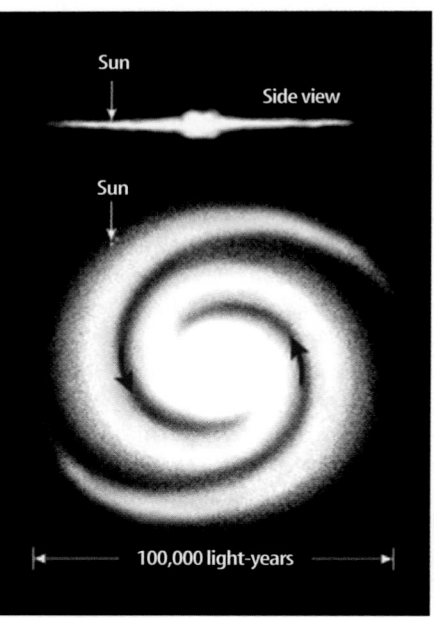

Figure 16
This illustration shows a side view and an overhead view of the Milky Way. *What group of galaxies is the Milky Way part of?*

Section ✓*Assessment* Planner

PORTFOLIO
Extension, p. 756
PERFORMANCE ASSESSMENT
MiniLAB, p. 754
Skill Builder Activities, p. 757
See page 764 for more options.

CONTENT ASSESSMENT
Section, p. 757
Challenge, p. 757
Chapter, pp. 764–765

Elliptical Galaxies Probably the most common type of galaxy is the elliptical galaxy. **Figure 17** shows an elliptical galaxy in the constellation Andromeda. These galaxies are shaped like large, three-dimensional ellipses. Many are football shaped, but others are round. Some elliptical galaxies are small, while others are so large that the entire Local Group of galaxies would fit inside one of them.

Irregular Galaxies The third type—an irregular galaxy—includes most of those galaxies that don't fit into the other classifications. Irregular galaxies have many different shapes. They are smaller and less common than the other types. Two irregular galaxies called the Clouds of Magellan orbit the Milky Way. The Large Magellanic Cloud is shown in **Figure 18.**

✔ **Reading Check** *How do the three different types of galaxies differ?*

The Milky Way Galaxy

The Milky Way contains more than 200 billion stars. The visible disk of stars shown in **Figure 16** is about 100,000 light-years across. Find the location of the Sun. Notice that it is located about 30,000 light-years from the galaxy's center in one of the spiral arms. In the galaxy, all stars orbit around a central region, or core. Based on a distance of 30,000 light-years and a speed of 235 km/s, the Sun orbits the center of the Milky Way once every 240 million years.

The Milky Way usually is classified as a normal spiral galaxy. However, some evidence suggests that it might be a barred spiral. It is difficult to know for sure because astronomers have limited data about how the galaxy looks from the outside.

You can't see the normal spiral or barred shape of the Milky Way because you are located within one of its spiral arms. You can, however, see the Milky Way stretching across the sky as a misty band of faint light. You can see the brightest part of the Milky Way if you look low in the southern sky on a moonless summer night. All the stars you can see in the night sky belong to the Milky Way.

Figure 17
This photo shows an example of an elliptical galaxy. *What are the two other types of galaxies?*

Figure 18
The Large Magellanic Cloud is an irregular galaxy. It's a member of the Local Group, and it orbits the Milky Way.

SECTION 4 Galaxies and the Universe **753**

Origin of the Universe

Mini LAB

Purpose Students develop a scale illustrating the vastness of space. `L2` `ELL`

`LS` **Logical-Mathematical**

Materials large sheet of paper, metric ruler or meterstick

Teaching Strategies Help students conceptualize the vast scale of their model. If our Sun were represented by a dot, the circle representing the distance to Proxima Centauri would be nearly within that same dot.

Analysis

1. Answers will vary depending on the scale chosen.
2. The distance to the Andromeda Galaxy should be 29 times the diameter of the student's Milky Way model. This can be determined by dividing the distance to the Andromeda Galaxy (2.9 million light-years) by the diameter of the Milky Way (100,000 light-years).

✓ Assessment

Content Have students determine the scale distance to the Large Magellanic Cloud. Its true distance is about 169,000 light-years. The distance to the Large Magellanic Cloud should be about 1.69 times the diameter of the student's Milky Way model. Use **Performance Assessment in the Science Classroom,** p. 123.

Mini LAB

Measuring Distance in Space

Procedure

1. On a large sheet of **paper,** draw an overhead view of the Milky Way. If necessary, refer to **Figure 16.** Choose a scale to show distance in light-years.
2. Mark the approximate location of the solar system, which is about two thirds of the way out on one of the spiral arms.
3. Draw a small circle around the Sun indicating the 4.2 light-year distance of the next-closet star to Earth, Proxima Centauri.

Analysis

1. What scale did you use to represent distance on your model of the Milky Way?
2. At this scale, interpret how far away the next-closest spiral galaxy—the Andromeda Galaxy—would be.

Origin of the Universe

People have long wondered how the universe formed. Several models of its origin have been proposed. One model was the steady state theory. It proposed that the universe always has been the same as it is now. The universe always has existed and always will. As matter in the universe expands outward, new matter is created to keep the overall density of the universe the same or in a steady state. However, evidence indicates that the universe was much different in the past from what it is today.

A second idea is called the oscillating model. In this model, the universe began with expansion occurring in all areas of the universe. Over time, the expansion slowed and the matter in the universe contracted. Then the process began again—repeating over and over, oscillating back and forth.

Neither of these theories can be proven or disproven, but evidence suggests that a third idea is more likely to be correct. The universe started with a big bang and has been expanding ever since. This theory will be described later.

Expansion of the Universe

What does it sound like when a train is blowing its whistle while it travels past you? The whistle has a higher pitch as the train approaches you. Then the whistle seems to drop in pitch as the train moves away. This effect is called the Doppler shift. The Doppler shift occurs with light as well as with sound. **Figure 19** shows how the Doppler shift causes changes in the light coming from distant stars and galaxies. If a star is moving toward Earth, its wavelengths of light are compressed. If a star is moving away from Earth, its wavelengths of light are stretched.

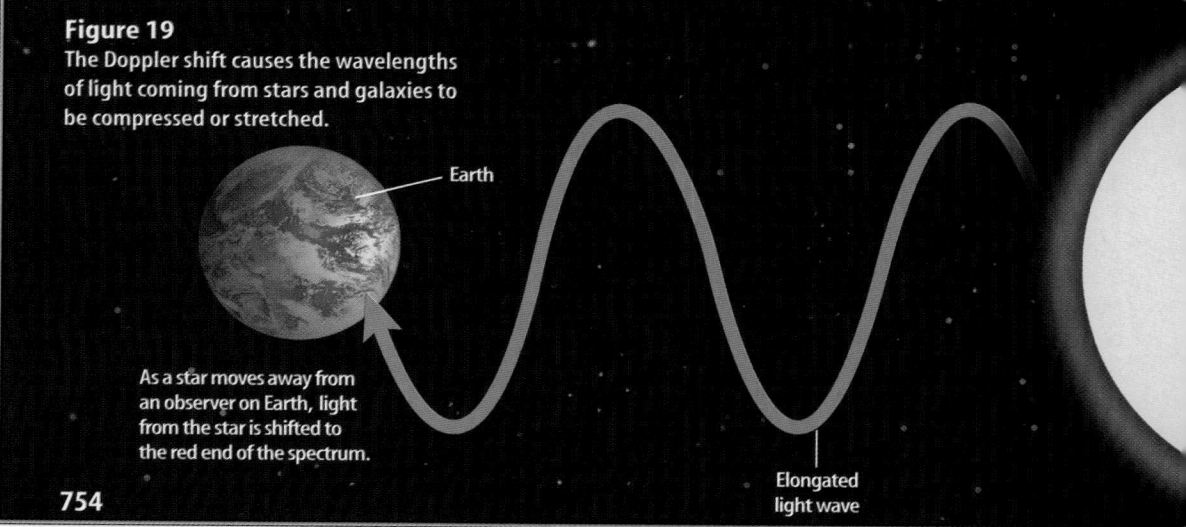

Figure 19
The Doppler shift causes the wavelengths of light coming from stars and galaxies to be compressed or stretched.

Earth

As a star moves away from an observer on Earth, light from the star is shifted to the red end of the spectrum.

Elongated light wave

754

Curriculum Connection

Art Suggest that a group of students research and draw a diagram of the *Hubble Space Telescope*, which is used to gather data about the origin of the universe. When they present their diagram, have students explain the advantage of having a telescope in space. Images are clearer because there is no interference from the atmosphere. `L2` COOP LEARN

`LS` **Visual-Spatial**

Inclusion Strategies

Learning Disabled Use a balloon to demonstrate the oscillating model of the origin of the universe. Blow up the balloon, and explain that this is like the expansion phase of this model. Then slowly let the air out of the balloon, and explain that this is like the contraction phase of this model. Have students describe what would happen next. The balloon (universe) would again begin to expand. `L1` `ELL` `LS` **Visual-Spatial**

The Doppler Shift

Look at the spectrum of a star in **Figure 20A.** Note the position of the dark lines. How do they compare with the lines in **Figures 20B** and **20C?** They have shifted in position. What caused this shift? As you just read, when a star is moving toward Earth, its wavelengths of light are compressed, just as the sound waves from the train's whistle are. This causes the dark lines in the spectrum to shift toward the blue-violet end of the spectrum. A red shift in the spectrum occurs when a star is moving away from Earth. In a red shift, the dark lines shift toward the red end of the spectrum.

Red Shift

In 1924, Edwin Hubble used an interesting fact about the light coming from most galaxies. When a spectrograph is used to study light from galaxies beyond the Local Group, a red shift occurs in the light. What does this red shift tell you about the universe?

Because all galaxies beyond the Local Group show a red shift in their spectra, they must be moving away from Earth. If all galaxies outside the Local Group are moving away from Earth, then the entire universe must be expanding. Remember the Explore Activity at the beginning of the chapter? The dots on the balloon moved apart as the model universe expanded. Regardless of which dot you picked, all the other dots moved away from it. In a similar way, galaxies beyond the Local Group are moving away from Earth.

Figure 20
A This spectrum shows dark absorption lines. **B** The dark lines shift toward the blue-violet end for a star moving toward Earth. **C** The lines shift toward the red end for a star moving away from Earth.

Expansion of the Universe

Text Question Answer
The universe is expanding.

Quick Demo
Illustrate the Doppler shift of sound waves by securely tying a cord to an alarm clock and gently swinging the ringing clock. Students will observe a change in pitch as the clock approaches them and then recedes. **Ⓢ Auditory-Musical**

Extension
Have students learn about mapping the universe by researching the work of Margaret Geller and John Huchra of the Harvard-Smithsonian Center for Astrophysics. Invite volunteers to share their findings in an oral report to the class. Reports should note that great voids and large concentrations of galaxies, such as the Local Group, alternate throughout the universe. L3 **Ⓢ Linguistic**

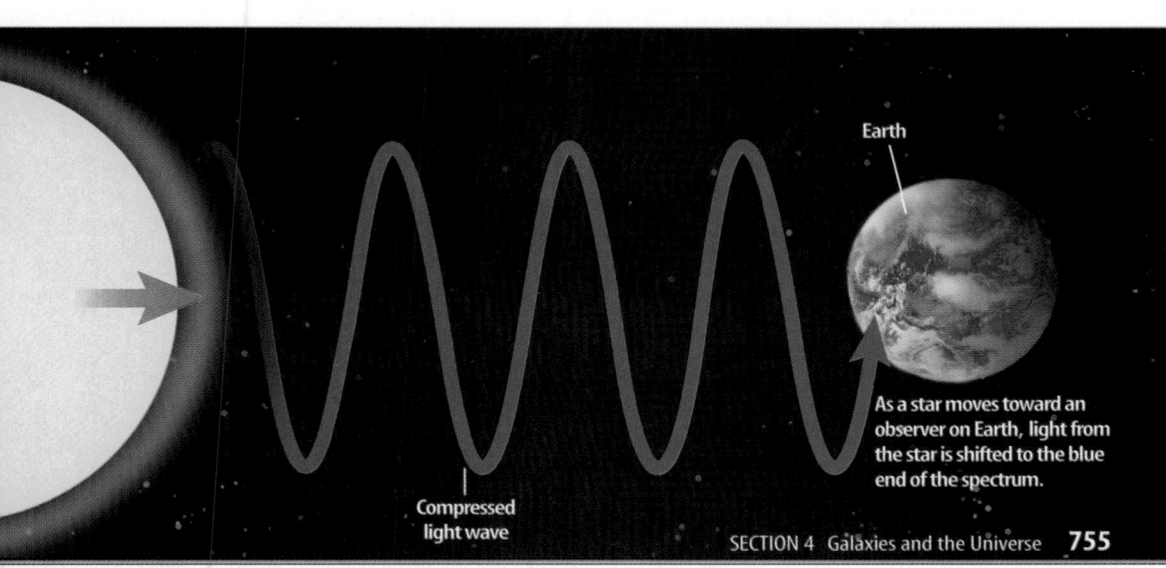

Earth

As a star moves toward an observer on Earth, light from the star is shifted to the blue end of the spectrum.

Compressed light wave

SECTION 4 Galaxies and the Universe **755**

Resource Manager

Chapter Resources Booklet
MiniLAB, p. 4
Enrichment, p. 34
Reading and Writing Skill Activities, p. 47

Visualizing the Big Bang Theory

Have students examine the pictures and read the captions. Then ask the following questions.

If a galaxy were discovered at a distance of 24 billion light years from Earth, how would this change the estimated age of the universe? According to the Big Bang theory, it would mean that the universe had been expanding for at least 24 billion years, making it much older that its present estimated age.

When you look at distant galaxies, why can you say that you are looking back in time? Because light that is now reaching Earth left those galaxies millions or even billions of years ago.

Activity

Have small groups of students research the work of Arno A. Penzias and Robert W. Wilson that resulted in their winning a Nobel Prize. Ask each group to make a comic book that illustrates the story of their work and explains how it relates to the Big Bang theory. L2
COOP LEARN ⎍ **Visual-Spatial and Linguistic**

Extension

Challenge students to find out about research carried on at the Lawrence Berkeley Lab in California and at the Harvard University Center for Astrophysics. Ask students to write a brief report on this research and the inflation theory of the universe. L3 ⎍ **Logical-Mathematical and Linguistic** P

Figure 21

The Big Bang theory states that the universe probably began 12 billion to 15 billion years ago with an enormous explosion. Even today, galaxies are rushing apart from this explosion.

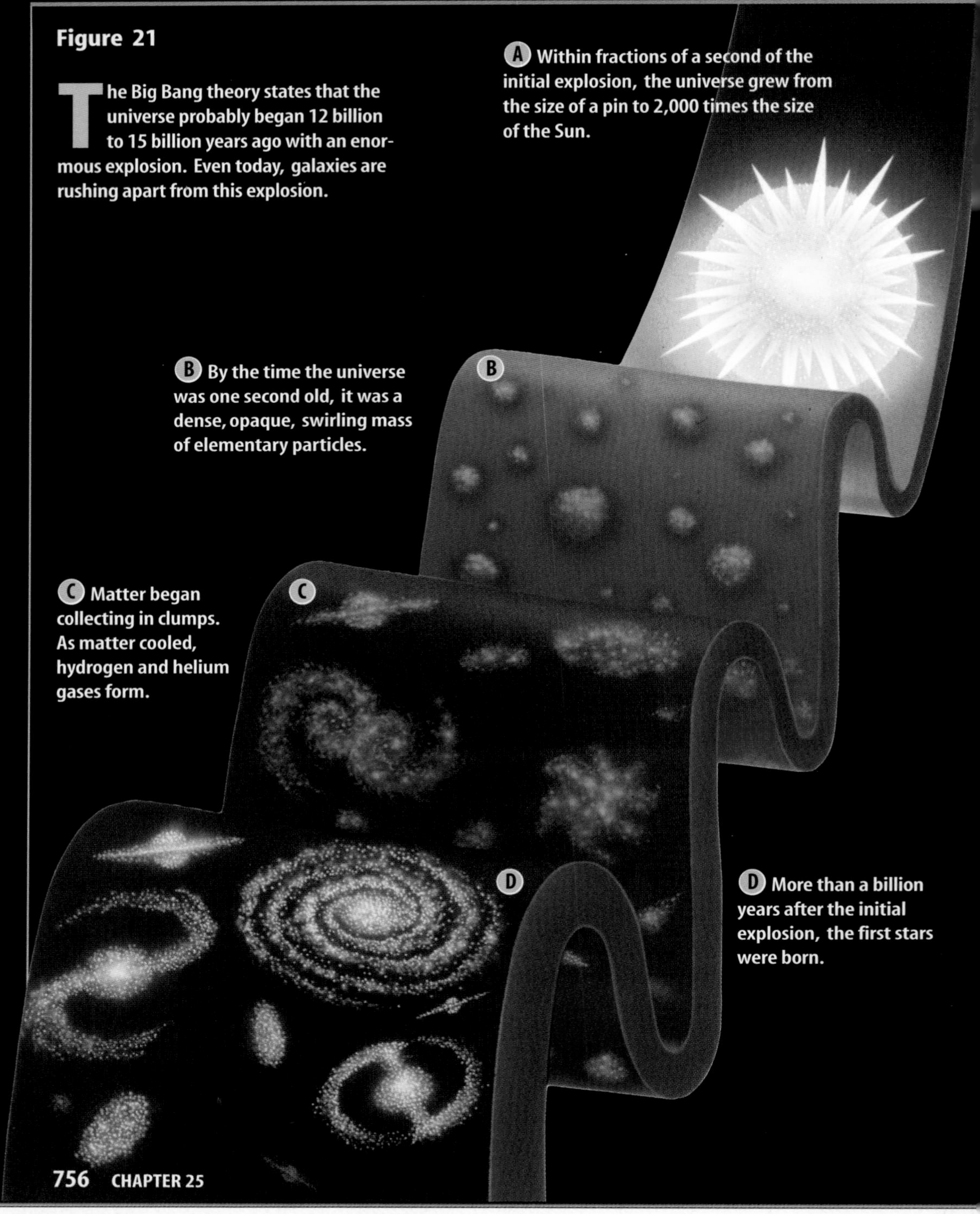

A Within fractions of a second of the initial explosion, the universe grew from the size of a pin to 2,000 times the size of the Sun.

B By the time the universe was one second old, it was a dense, opaque, swirling mass of elementary particles.

C Matter began collecting in clumps. As matter cooled, hydrogen and helium gases form.

D More than a billion years after the initial explosion, the first stars were born.

756 CHAPTER 25

Resource Manager

Chapter Resources Booklet
  Reinforcement, p. 30
  Activity Worksheet, pp. 7–8
Lab Management and Safety, p. 65

The Big Bang Theory

When scientists determined that the universe was expanding, they realized that galaxy clusters must have been closer together in the past. The leading theory about the formation of the universe, called the **Big Bang theory,** is based on this explanation. **Figure 21** illustrates the Big Bang theory. According to this theory, approximately 12 billion to 15 billion years ago, the universe began with an enormous explosion. The entire universe began to expand everywhere at the same time.

Looking Back in Time The time-exposure photograph shown in **Figure 22** was taken by the *Hubble Space Telescope.* It shows more than 1,500 galaxies at distances of more than 10 billion light-years. These galaxies could date back to when the universe was no more than 1 billion years old and are in various stages of development. One astronomer says humans might be looking back to a time when the Milky Way was forming. Studies like this eventually will allow astronomers to determine the approximate age of the universe.

Whether the universe expands forever or stops depends on how much matter is in the universe. If enough matter exists, gravity will halt the expansion, and the universe will contract until everything comes to a single point. Recent studies of dark matter in the universe indicate that enough matter exists for the universe eventually to stop expanding and then to begin contracting.

Figure 22
The light from the galaxies in this photo mosaic took billions of years to reach Earth.

Section 4 Assessment

1. List the three major types of galaxies. What do they have in common?
2. What is the name of the galaxy that you live in? What motion do its stars exhibit?
3. What is the Doppler shift?
4. How far away are the most distant galaxies?
5. **Think Critically** All galaxies outside the Local Group show a red shift. Within the Local Group, some galaxies show a red shift and some show a blue shift. What does this tell you about the galaxies in the Local Group?

Skill Builder Activities

6. **Comparing and Contrasting** Compare and contrast the three models of the origin of the universe. **For more help, refer to the** Science Skill Handbook.
7. **Communicating** Research and write a report in your Science Journal about the most recent evidence supporting or disputing the Big Bang theory. Describe how the Big Bang theory explains observations of galaxies made with spectrometers. **For more help, refer to the** Science Skill Handbook.

The Big Bang Theory

Use an Analogy

Ask students to think of a loaf of raisin bread. When the bread is unbaked, the raisins are relatively close together. As the bread bakes, all the raisins move apart from one another. Have students compare this to the way scientists hypothesize galaxies are moving in the universe.

3 Assess

Reteach

Have a student use a spring toy to demonstrate the compression and expansion of light waves described by the Doppler shift. L1 IS **Visual-Spatial**

Challenge

Have students write brief paragraphs in their Science Journals explaining why the spiral shape of the Milky Way Galaxy is not visible from Earth. To see the spiral shape, an observer would have to be above or below the plane of the galaxy. Earth is located in one of the spiral arms.
IS **Logical-Mathematical**

✓ Assessment

Content Have students write a paragraph that summarizes the Big Bang theory. Encourage them to illustrate their summaries. Use **Performance Assessment in the Science Classroom,** p. 159.

Answers to Section Assessment

1. Elliptical, spiral, irregular; all are groups of stars, gas, and dust held together by gravity and grouped in clusters.
2. Milky Way Galaxy; stars orbit its nucleus.
3. shift in wavelength caused by movement
4. more than 10 billion light-years

5. All galaxies of the Local Group travel through space together. However, some within the group are moving toward the Milky Way and others are moving away from it.
6. All are based on observed data. Big bang theory—universe began with a huge explosion and continues to expand; oscillation theory—the

same, except that the universe eventually will stop expanding, contract back together, and then the process will repeat; steady state theory—universe has always been here, always will be, and new matter is created as the universe expands.
7. Students should include the latest information obtained by the *Hubble*

Space Telescope. The red shift observed by spectrometers indicates that galaxies are moving away from us, which supports the big bang theory.

Activity
BENCH TESTED

Recognize the Problem

Purpose
Students conduct an experiment that shows how distance from an object affects the object's parallax shift. L2 ELL COOP LEARN

LS Logical-Mathematical

Process Skills
communicating, comparing and contrasting, forming operational definitions, recognizing cause and effect, separating and controlling variables, measuring in SI, using numbers, formulating models, observing and inferring, and hypothesizing

Time Required
one class period

Materials
meterstick, metric ruler, masking tape, pencil

Safety Precautions
Caution students to wear goggles during the experiment.

Form a Hypothesis

Possible Hypothesis
Students may hypothesize that the amount of observed parallax increases as an object is moved closer.

Activity — *Design Your Own Experiment*

Measuring Parallax

Parallax is the apparent shift in the position of an object when viewed from two locations. The nearer an object is to the observer, the greater its parallax is. Do this activity to design a model and use it in an experiment that will show how distance affects the amount of observed parallax.

Recognizing the Problem
How can you build a model to show the relationship between distance and parallax?

Form a Hypothesis
State a hypothesis about how a model must be built in order for it to be used to show how distance affects the amount of observed parallax.

Possible Materials

meterstick	masking tape
metric ruler	pencil

Goals
- **Design** a model to show how the distance from an observer to an object affects the object's parallax shift.
- **Design** an experiment that shows how distance affects the amount of observed parallax.

Safety Precautions

WARNING: *Be sure to wear goggles to protect your eyes.*

Test Your Hypothesis

Possible Procedures
Choose and mark three different positions on the meterstick (20 cm, 40 cm, and 60 cm). Attach a metric ruler to one end, forming a T shape, and place it on a table. Hold a pencil upright at one of the marked positions. Observe the pencil's apparent movement against the meterstick with one eye closed and then the other. Repeat for all positions.

Teaching Strategies
Pair students and have one act as recorder while the other student carries out the experiment. Students should then switch roles.

Test Your Hypothesis

Plan

1. As a group, agree upon and write your hypothesis statement.

2. **List** the steps you need to take to build your model. Be specific, describing exactly what you will do at each step.

3. Devise a method to test how distance from an observer to an object, such as a pencil, affects the relative position of the object.

4. **List** the steps you will take to test your hypothesis. Be specific, describing exactly what you will do at each step.

5. Read over your plan for the model to be used in this experiment.

6. How will you determine changes in observed parallax? Remember, these changes should occur when the distance from the observer to the object is changed.

7. You should measure shifts in parallax from several different positions. How will these positions differ?

8. How will you measure distances accurately and compare relative position shift?

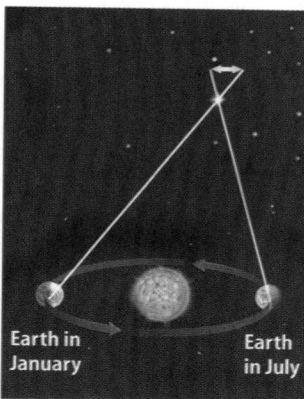

Earth in January   Earth in July

Do

1. Make sure your teacher approves your plan before you start.

2. **Construct** the model your team has planned.

3. Carry out the experiment as planned.

4. While conducting the experiment, record any observations that you or other members of your group make in your Science Journal.

Analyze Your Data

1. **Compare** what happened to the object when it was viewed with one eye closed, then the other.

2. At what distance from the observer did the object appear to shift the most?

Draw Conclusions

1. **Infer** what happened to the apparent shift of the object's location as the distance from the observer was increased or decreased.

2. **Describe** how astronomers might use parallax to study stars.

*C*ommunicating
Your Data

Prepare a chart showing the results of your experiment. **Share** the chart with members of your class. **For more help, refer to the** Science Skill Handbook.

ACTIVITY   759

*C*ommunicating
Your Data

Have students use a computer to prepare a table on which they can enter the data from their experiment.

✓Assessment

Oral How can astronomers use parallax to determine distances to stars relatively close to Earth? Parallax angle decreases with distance from observer. Very distant stars will show no parallax. Use **Performance Assessment in the Science Classroom,** p. 89.

Tie to Prior Knowledge Ask students if they have ever noticed that the speedometer reading in a car appears different to a front-seat passenger than to the driver. Explain that the passenger is viewing the speedometer from an angle. Relate this to parallax.

Expected Outcome
If students position themselves so that the meterstick is lined up with their noses and distances of 20 cm, 40 cm, and 60 cm are used, the following results can be expected: Observed parallax is about 20 cm at the 20-cm mark, 8.5 cm at the 40-cm mark, and 4.9 cm at the 60-cm mark.

Analyze Your Data

1. The position of the pencil seemed to shift, but this motion was only apparent.

2. the closest distance used

Error Analysis

Ask students how the pencil's apparent motion changed as it was placed at progressively farther distances. The pencil appeared to move less.

Draw Conclusions

1. As distance from the observer increased, the pencil's apparent shift decreased. As the distance from the observer decreased, the pencil's apparent shift increased.

2. Astronomers use parallax angles or shifts in the apparent position of astronomical objects to determine distances to the objects.

Content Background

American astronomer Edwin Hubble (1889-1953) showed that other galaxies beside the Milky Way do exist and that the universe is expanding. The Hubble Space Telescope (HST) was named in his honor.

The HST was placed into low-Earth orbit (600 km) in April 1990 by the crew of the space shuttle *Discovery*. After the HST was launched, scientists discovered a manufacturing error in its mirror. A service mission in December 1993 corrected the problem and vastly improved images were received. Space shuttle crews carried out other servicing missions in 1997 and 1999.

Discussion

Tell students that Betelgeuse is 300 light-years from Earth. **If Betelgeuse is so much larger than the Sun, why isn't it brighter than the Sun?** It is much farther away from Earth, so it looks much smaller and dimmer than the Sun.

Activity

Have students select a scale to use and make scale models that compare the diameters of the Sun and Betelgeuse. Then have students research the sizes of other stars and make additional scale models showing how their diameters compare to those of the Sun and Betelgeuse.

Science Stats

Stars and Galaxies

Did you know...

...The 11,000-kg Hubble Space Telescope orbits Earth every 95 minutes—that's a speed of about 27,250 km/h. The heavy telescope moves more than 750 times faster than the fastest human does on Earth.

...A star in Earth's galaxy explodes as a supernova about once a century. The most famous supernova of this galaxy occurred in 1054 and was recorded by the ancient Chinese and Koreans. The explosion was so powerful that it could be seen during the day, and its brightness lasted for weeks. Other major supernovas in the Milky Way that were observed from Earth occurred in 185, 393, 1006, 1181, 1572, and 1604.

Supernova

...The large loops of material called solar prominences can extend more than 320,000 km above the Sun's surface. This is so high that two Jupiters and three Earths could fit under the arch.

760   CHAPTER 25 Stars and Galaxies

SCIENCE *Online*
Internet Addresses _____
_____
_____
_____

Explore the Glencoe Science Web site at **science.glencoe.com** to find out more about topics in this feature.

. . . Some of the most famous stars on Earth can be found on the Hollywood Walk of Fame. The walk contains more than 2,000 stars in honor of various Hollywood film actors and actresses and is located in Hollywood, California.

. . . The red giant star Betelgeuse has a diameter larger than that of Earth's Sun. This gigantic star measures 450,520,000 km in diameter, while the Sun's diameter is a mere 1,390,176 km.

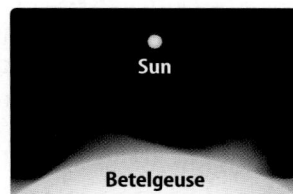

Sun

Betelgeuse

Distance from Earth to the Brightest Stars in the Northern Sky in January (in light-years)

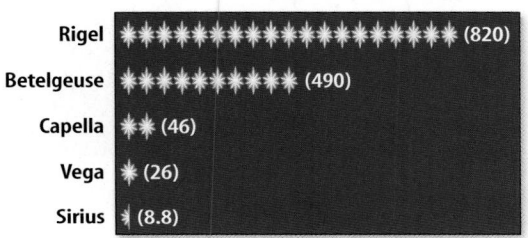

Rigel ★★★★★★★★★★★★★★★★★★★★ (820)
Betelgeuse ★★★★★★★★★ (490)
Capella ★★ (46)
Vega ★ (26)
Sirius ★ (8.8)

. . . Just as Earth goes around the Sun, the whole solar system is going around the center of the Milky Way. It takes Earth one year to go around the Sun, but it takes the solar system about 240 million years to go around the center of the Milky Way.

Do the Math

1. Compare the diameter of Betelgeuse to that of the Sun.
2. The Sun orbits the Milky Way once every 240 million years. About how many revolutions of the galaxy has it made since its formation?
3. How many kilometers does the *Hubble Space Telescope* travel in one minute? About how long would it take the fastest human to travel that distance?

Go Further

Is it possible for Earth astronauts to travel to the nearest stars? For more information go to the Glencoe Science Web site at **science.glencoe.com.** How long would such a trip take? What problems would have to be overcome? Write a brief report on what you find.

SCIENCE STATS   761

Do the Math

Teaching Strategies

In the second part of question 3, students first need to calculate the speed at which the fastest human runs. They then need to use the formula time = distance ÷ rate to calculate how long it would take a human to run 454 km. Finally you might want them to convert their answer in minutes to hours and minutes.

Answers

1. The diameter of Betelgeuse is about 324 times the diameter of the Sun.
2. The sun is about 5 billion years old. 5,000,000,000 ÷ 240,000,000 = 24.83, or about 25 times.
3. 27,250 km/h ÷ 60 min/h = 454 km/min; 27,250 km/h ÷ 750 = 36 km/h (human speed), 36 km/h ÷ 60 min/h = 0.6 km/min; 454 km ÷ 0.6 km/min = 757 min, 757 min ÷ 60 min/h = 12 hours, 37 min.

Go Further

Students will need to find out how fast a space craft travels, the distance to the nearest stars, and how many kilometers are in a light year in order to calculate how long a trip to the nearest stars would take. Based on their calculations, students can infer some of problems faced by astronauts traveling in space for such long periods of time.

Visual Learning

Distance from Earth to the Brightest Star in the Northern Sky in January (in light-years) Ask students to calculate how many times farther from Earth Rigel is than Capella almost 18 times, how many times farther from Earth Betelgeuse is than Vega almost 19 times, and how many times farther from Earth Capella is than Sirius a little more than 5 times.

Chapter 25 Study Guide

Reviewing Main Ideas

Preview

Students can answer the questions in their Science Journals. Discuss the answers as you go through the chapter. **IS Linguistic**

Review

Students can write their answers, then compare them with those of other students. **IS Interpersonal**

Reteach

Students can look at the illustrations and describe details that support the main ideas of the chapter. **IS Visual-Spatial**

Answers to Chapter Review

SECTION 2

3. Its absolute magnitude is about average, and it shines with a yellow light, which is in the middle range of visible star colors.

SECTION 3

3. 10,000,000 K

Reviewing Main Ideas

Section 1 Stars

1. Constellations are groups of stars that change positions throughout the year because Earth moves. The constellations seem to move because Earth rotates on its axis and revolves around the Sun.

2. The magnitude of a star is a measure of the star's brightness. Absolute magnitude is a measure of the light actually given off by a star. Apparent magnitude is a measure of the amount of light received on Earth.

3. Parallax is the apparent shift in the position of an object when viewed from two different positions. The closer to Earth a star is, the greater its shift in parallax is.

4. A star's composition can be determined from the star's spectrum.

Section 2 The Sun

1. The Sun produces energy by fusing hydrogen into helium in its core. Light is given off from the photosphere, which is the lowest layer of the Sun's atmosphere.

2. Sunspots are areas of the Sun that are cooler and less bright than surrounding areas.

3. Sunspots, prominences, flares, and CMEs are caused by the intense magnetic field of the Sun, which is a main sequence star. *Why is the Sun, shown here, considered an average star?*

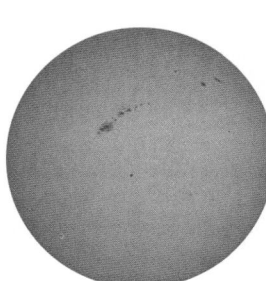

Section 3 Evolution of Stars

1. Stars are classified by their positions on the H-R diagram. Most stars are main sequence stars.

2. When hydrogen is used up in a main sequence star, the star's core collapses and its temperature increases. The star becomes a giant or a supergiant. As the star evolves, it becomes a white dwarf.

3. Stars with large masses can explode to form a supernova. The outer layers are blown away and the core evolves into a neutron star or black hole. *At what temperature does fusion begin inside a nebula like the one shown here?*

Section 4 Galaxies and the Universe

1. A galaxy is a large group of stars, gas, and dust held together by gravity. Galaxies can be spiral, elliptical, or irregular in shape.

2. The Milky Way is a spiral galaxy containing about 200 billion stars.

3. The most accepted theory about the origin of the universe is the Big Bang theory.

FOLDABLES Reading & Study Skills

After You Read

To help you review what you have read in this chapter, use your Foldable to explain the relationship among stars, galaxies, and the universe.

FOLDABLES Reading & Study Skills

After You Read

After students have read the chapter and completed the Foldable described in Before You Read, have them do the activity on the student page.

Dinah Zike

Visualizing Main Ideas

Complete the following concept map that shows the evolution of a main sequence star with a mass similar to that of the Sun.

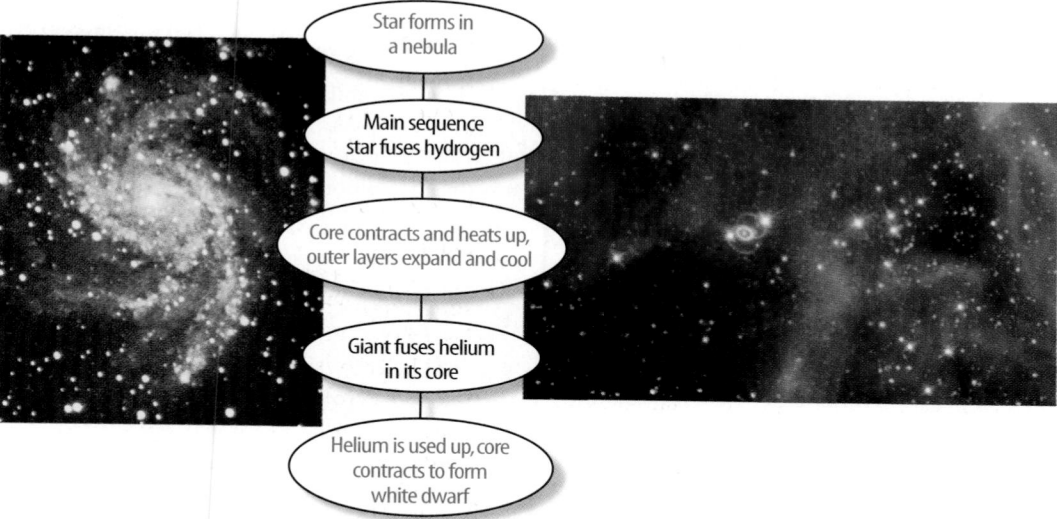

- Star forms in a nebula
- Main sequence star fuses hydrogen
- Core contracts and heats up, outer layers expand and cool
- Giant fuses helium in its core
- Helium is used up, core contracts to form white dwarf

Vocabulary Review

Vocabulary Review

a. absolute magnitude
b. apparent magnitude
c. Big Bang theory
d. black hole
e. chromosphere
f. constellation
g. corona
h. galaxy
i. giant
j. light-year
k. nebula
l. neutron star
m. photosphere
n. sunspot
o. supergiant
p. white dwarf

Study Tip

As you read, look up the definition of any prefixes you do not recognize. Once you know the meaning of a prefix, you'll be able to figure out the definitions of many new words.

Using Vocabulary

Explain the difference between the terms in each of the following sets.

1. absolute magnitude, apparent magnitude
2. black hole, neutron star
3. chromosphere, photosphere
4. galaxy, constellation
5. light-year, galaxy
6. giant, white dwarf
7. corona, sunspot
8. giant, supergiant
9. apparent magnitude, light-year
10. galaxy, Big Bang theory

Visualizing Main Ideas

See student page.

Vocabulary Review

Using Vocabulary

1. Absolute magnitude measures light given off, apparent magnitude measures light received on Earth; both measure light.
2. A black hole is so dense that no light can escape; a neutron star is composed of neutrons and is the stage prior to black hole; both are stages in star evolution.
3. The photosphere is the lowest layer of the Sun's atmosphere; the chromosphere is directly above it; both are part of the Sun's atmosphere.
4. A constellation is a pattern of stars; a galaxy is a large family of stars; both contain stars.
5. A galaxy is a large family of stars; a light-year is a unit of distance; both are involved in the study of stars.
6. A white dwarf is a small, dense, hot star; a giant is a large, less dense, cool star; both are stars on the H-R diagram.
7. The corona is the Sun's outer atmosphere; a sunspot is a cool, dark spot on the Sun's surface; both are features of the Sun.
8. A giant is the late stage of a main sequence star; a supergiant is the late stage of a very massive star; both are large, cool stars.
9. Apparent magnitude measures light received on Earth; a light-year is a unit of distance; both measure star properties.
10. Big bang theory explains how the universe began; a galaxy is a large family of stars; formation of galaxies occurred after the big bang.

Chapter 25 Assessment

Checking Concepts

1. D
2. B
3. C or D
4. C
5. D
6. D
7. D
8. A
9. B
10. A

Thinking Critically

11. Astronomers are looking at galaxies that may have formed when the universe was only 1 billion years old. Studies of this nature help determine the true age of the universe.

12. Astronomers are able to use instruments to detect the X rays surrounding black holes. X rays are thought to be emitted by material as it is pulled into a black hole.

13. Parallax angles are too small to be accurately measured for objects that are far from our solar system.

14. The temperature of the Sun's core is not high enough to fuse helium.

15. A star's apparent magnitude is affected by distance, temperature, and size. Cool, distant Betelgeuse must be very large.

Checking Concepts

Choose the word or phrase that best answers the question.

1. What are constellations?
   - **A)** clusters
   - **B)** giants
   - **C)** black holes
   - **D)** patterns

2. What is a measure of the amount of a star's light received on Earth?
   - **A)** absolute magnitude
   - **B)** apparent magnitude
   - **C)** fusion
   - **D)** parallax

3. What increases as an object comes closer to an observer?
   - **A)** absolute magnitude
   - **B)** red shift
   - **C)** parallax
   - **D)** blue shift

4. What happens after a nebula contracts and temperatures increase to 10 million K?
   - **A)** a black hole forms
   - **B)** a supernova forms
   - **C)** fusion begins
   - **D)** white dwarfs form

5. What is about 20 km in size?
   - **A)** giant
   - **B)** white dwarf
   - **C)** black hole
   - **D)** neutron star

6. What does the Sun fuse hydrogen into?
   - **A)** carbon
   - **B)** oxygen
   - **C)** iron
   - **D)** helium

7. What are loops of matter flowing from the Sun called?
   - **A)** sunspots
   - **B)** auroras
   - **C)** coronas
   - **D)** prominences

8. What are groups of galaxies called?
   - **A)** clusters
   - **B)** supergiants
   - **C)** giants
   - **D)** binary systems

9. Which galaxies are sometimes shaped like footballs?
   - **A)** spiral
   - **B)** elliptical
   - **C)** barred
   - **D)** irregular

---

10. What do scientists study to determine shifts in wavelengths of light?
    - **A)** spectrum
    - **B)** surface
    - **C)** corona
    - **D)** chromosphere

Thinking Critically

11. What is significant about the 1995 discovery by the *Hubble Space Telescope* of more than 1,500 galaxies, some at distances of more than 10 billion light-years?

12. How do scientists know that black holes exist if these objects don't emit any visible light?

13. Why can parallax be used only to measure distances to stars that are relatively close to the solar system?

14. Why doesn't the helium currently in the Sun's core undergo fusion?

15. Betelgeuse is the brightest star in the constellation Orion. However, Betelgeuse is a cool, red star that is 400 light-years from Earth. How can Betelgeuse look so bright if it is far away and has a cool surface?

Developing Skills

16. **Concept Mapping** Make a concept map that shows the relationship of temperature, color, and brightness of stars and their positions on the H-R diagram.

17. **Comparing and Contrasting** Compare and contrast the Sun with other stars on the H-R diagram.

18. **Measuring in SI** The Milky Way is 100,000 light-years in diameter. What scale would you use if you were to construct a model of the Milky Way with a diameter of 20 cm? What scale would you use to construct a model with a diameter of 5 m?

Chapter ✓Assessment Planner

Portfolio Encourage students to place in their portfolios one or two items of what they consider to be their best work. Examples include:
- Science Journal, p. 737
- Challenge, p. 744
- Extension, p. 747
- Extension, p. 756

Performance Additional performance assessments, Performance Task Assessment Lists, and rubrics for evaluating these activities can be found in Glencoe's **Performance Assessment in the Science Classroom.**

19. Interpreting Data Use the chart below to answer the following questions.

Magnitude and Distance of Stars

Star	Apparent Magnitude	Absolute Magnitude	Distance in Light-Years
A	−26	4.8	0.00002
B	−1.5	1.4	8.7
C	0.1	4.4	4.3
D	0.1	−7.0	815
E	0.4	−5.9	520
F	1.0	−0.6	45

a. Which star appears brightest from Earth? Which star appears dimmest from Earth?

b. Which star would appear brightest from a distance of 10 light-years? Which star would appear dimmest from this distance?

20. Making a Model Design and construct scale models of a spiral and a barred spiral Milky Way. Show the approximate position of the Sun in each.

Performance Assessment

21. Story Write a short science-fiction story about an astronaut traveling through the universe. In your story, tell what the astronaut observes. Use as many of the vocabulary terms from this chapter as you can.

TECHNOLOGY

Go to the Glencoe Science Web site at **science.glencoe.com** or use the **Glencoe Science CD-ROM** for additional chapter assessment.

 **Test Practice**

The diagram below shows the distance from Earth to Proxima Centauri.

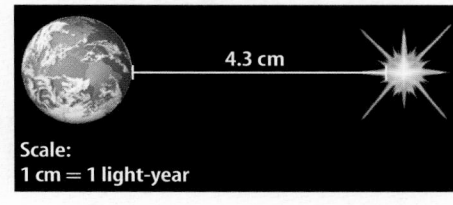

4.3 cm

Scale:
1 cm = 1 light-year

Study the picture and answer the following questions.

1. Which of these instruments should you use to view Proxima Centauri?
A) binoculars
B) magnifying glass
C) telescope
D) microscope

2. What is the approximate distance of Proxima Centauri from Earth?
F) 3.2 light-years
G) 4.3 light-years
H) 5.2 light-years
J) 6.2 light-years

3. If astronomers shined a beam of laser light from Earth, how long would it take to reach Proxima Centauri?
A) 3.2 years
B) 4.3 years
C) 5.2 years
D) 6.2 years

4. At this scale, how far from Earth would you draw a star that is 100 light-years away?
F) 50 cm **H)** 100 cm
G) 75 cm **J)** 200 cm

Test Practice

The Test-Taking Tip was written by The Princeton Review, the nation's leader in test preparation.
1. C
2. G
3. B
4. H

Developing Skills

16. Students should refer to **Figure 10** as they construct their maps.
17. The Sun is a yellow star that is classified as a main sequence star. Compared to other stars in the H-R diagram, the Sun is about average in terms of temperature and brightness.
18. 1 cm = 5,000 light-years, 1 m = 20,000 light-years
19. a. A, F; b. D, A
20. Student models should correspond to descriptions of spiral and barred spiral galaxies given in the student text. Possible answer: The Sun should be positioned about two-thirds of the way outward from the nucleus of the galaxy.

Performance Assessment

21. Stories should discuss traveling through the universe and describe what the traveler observes. Use **Performance Assessment in the Science Classroom**, p. 159.

Assessment Resources

Reproducible Masters
Chapter Resources Booklet
   Chapter Review, pp. 41–42
   Chapter Tests, pp. 43–46
   Assessment Transparency Activity, p. 55
Glencoe Science Web site
   Interactive Tutor
   Chapter Quizzes

Glencoe Technology
   Assessment Transparency
   Interactive CD-ROM Chapter Quizzes
   ExamView Pro Test Bank
   Vocabulary PuzzleMaker Software
   MindJogger Videoquiz DVD/VHS

QUESTION 1: C

This question requires students to demonstrate that they understand the chronology of the events in the passage.

- **Choice A** No; this event occurred second in the passage.
- **Choice B** No; this event occurred fourth in the passage.
- **Choice C** Yes; this event occurred first in the passage.
- **Choice D** No; this event occurred third in the passage.

QUESTION 2: B

Students need to identify the answer choice that *most fully* describes the main idea of the story. Choices A, C, and D contain information that is true, but that is not the main idea.

Teaching Tip

As students work through the questions, encourage them to use the answer choices whenever possible. Often, students will be able to use the answer choices to locate information in the passage quickly.

Standardized Test Practice

Read the passage. Then read each question following the passage. Determine the best answer.

Miss Mitchell's Comet

Maria Mitchell, born in 1818, grew up on the island of Nantucket, off the coast of Massachusetts. Maria Mitchell's father believed girls should aspire to high academic goals. An astronomer himself, he encouraged his daughter's interest in the stars and planets. Mr. Mitchell built a small observatory including a telescope on the roof of the family home.

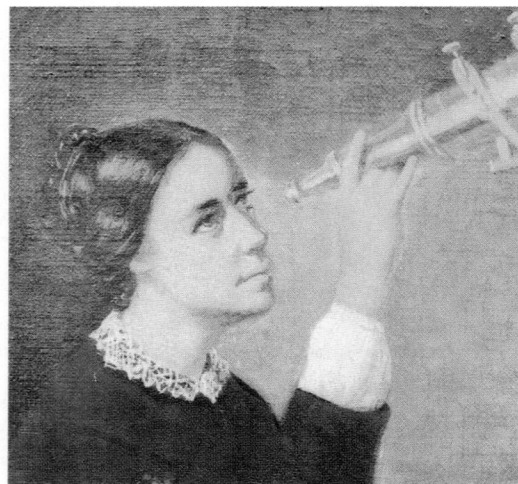

One night in 1847, Maria spotted a star that she had never noticed before. It was five degrees above the North Star. The next night, Maria looked for the star, and it had moved. Maria realized that what she saw was not a star but a comet. Maria told her father the news. Mr. Mitchell wrote a letter to Professor William Bond of the Harvard University Observatory. Professor Bond sent Maria's name to the King of Denmark, who had offered a prize to the first person who discovered a comet using a telescope instead of binoculars or the naked eye. Maria became acknowledged as a scholar, and in 1848 she became the first woman admitted to the American Academy of Arts and Sciences. After studying, Maria traveled the world. She lectured about astronomy and encouraged girls to get involved in science. She was Professor of Astronomy at Vassar College in Poughkeepsie, New York from 1865 until a year before her death in 1889.

Today, the Maria Mitchell Association continues her work. Every year, it awards a prize to a group or person who encourages the advancement of females in science. The association is at Maria's house on Nantucket where there is a large observatory.

Test-Taking Tip When asked the order of events in a story, find each answer choice in the passage and number them 1 to 4, from first to last.

1. Which of these happened first in Maria Mitchell's life?
   A) Maria joined the American Academy of Arts and Sciences.
   B) Maria began teaching at Vassar College.
   C) Maria discovered a comet while looking through a telescope.
   D) Maria traveled the world, lecturing about astronomy.

2. The main idea of this passage is that Maria _____.
   A) was not sure if she saw a star or a comet
   B) used her success to encourage others
   C) grew up on Nantucket Island
   D) received credit for her comet because of her father's help

Reasoning and Skills

Read each question and choose the best answer.

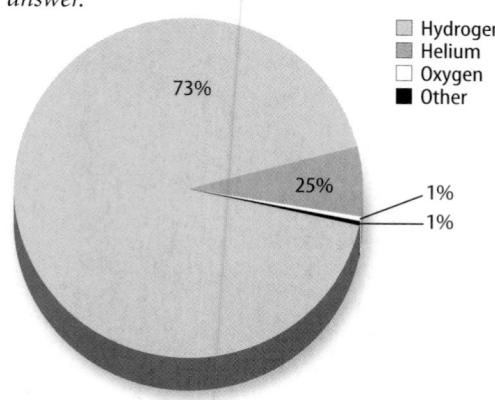

- Hydrogen
- Helium
- Oxygen
- Other

73%

25%

1%

1%

1. The circle graph shows the percentages of elements found in the Sun. What element is most abundant in the Sun?

A) Helium **C)** Hydrogen
B) Other **D)** Oxygen

Test-Taking Tip The key next to the graph is shaded to represent the elements found in the Sun.

2. The Sun produces energy by a process called fusion. During fusion, hydrogen nuclei combine to form helium. How would the circle graph shown above change as the Sun ages?

F) The helium slice would get larger.
G) The hydrogen slice would get larger.
H) The helium slice would get smaller.
J) The circle graph would not change.

Test-Taking Tip Think about what happens during fusion. Then examine the circle graph and select the best answer.

Consider this question carefully before writing your answer on a separate sheet of paper.

3. Astronomers indicate the brightness of a star in two ways—actual brightness and apparent brightness. What do these terms mean, and why is it helpful to talk about the stars in two different ways?

Test-Taking Tip After defining each term on a separate sheet of paper, decide what the major difference between the two is. Then decide why this difference is important and carefully write out your answer.

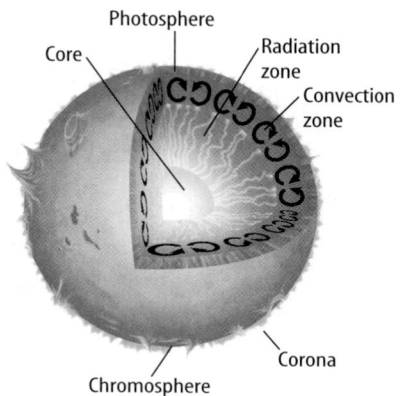

Photosphere
Core
Radiation zone
Convection zone
Corona
Chromosphere

4. The figure above represents a cross-section of _____.

A) Earth **C)** the Sun
B) the Moon **D)** Saturn

Test-Taking Tip Use key words from the graphic, such as Photosphere, to identify the correct answer.

QUESTION 4: C

This question tests students' ability to recognize the defining physical characteristics of the Sun.

Standardized Test Practice

Reasoning and Skills

QUESTION 1: C

Students must identify which gas has the largest percentage on the circle graph.

- **Choice A** No; helium only makes up 25 percent of the total elements found in the Sun.
- **Choice B** No; other elements account for 19 percent of total elements in the Sun.
- **Choice C** Yes; hydrogen is the most abundant element found in the Sun.
- **Choice D** No; oxygen only accounts for 19 percent of the total elements in the Sun.

Teaching Tip

Students are sometimes tempted to rush through questions that require them to retrieve information from a graph. Remind students that all questions are worth the same amount.

QUESTION 2: A

Students must infer that as the Sun ages, hydrogen is converted to helium. As the hydrogen combines to form helium, the percentage of helium increases while the percentage of hydrogen decreases.

QUESTION 3: Answers will vary.

The "actual brightness" of a star refers to the true, calculable amount of light a star produces. The "apparent brightness" of a star refers to how bright that star appears from Earth. Referring to stars by their apparent brightness allows us to identify them more easily in the night sky. Referring to stars by their actual brightness allows us to compare stars to one another more accurately.

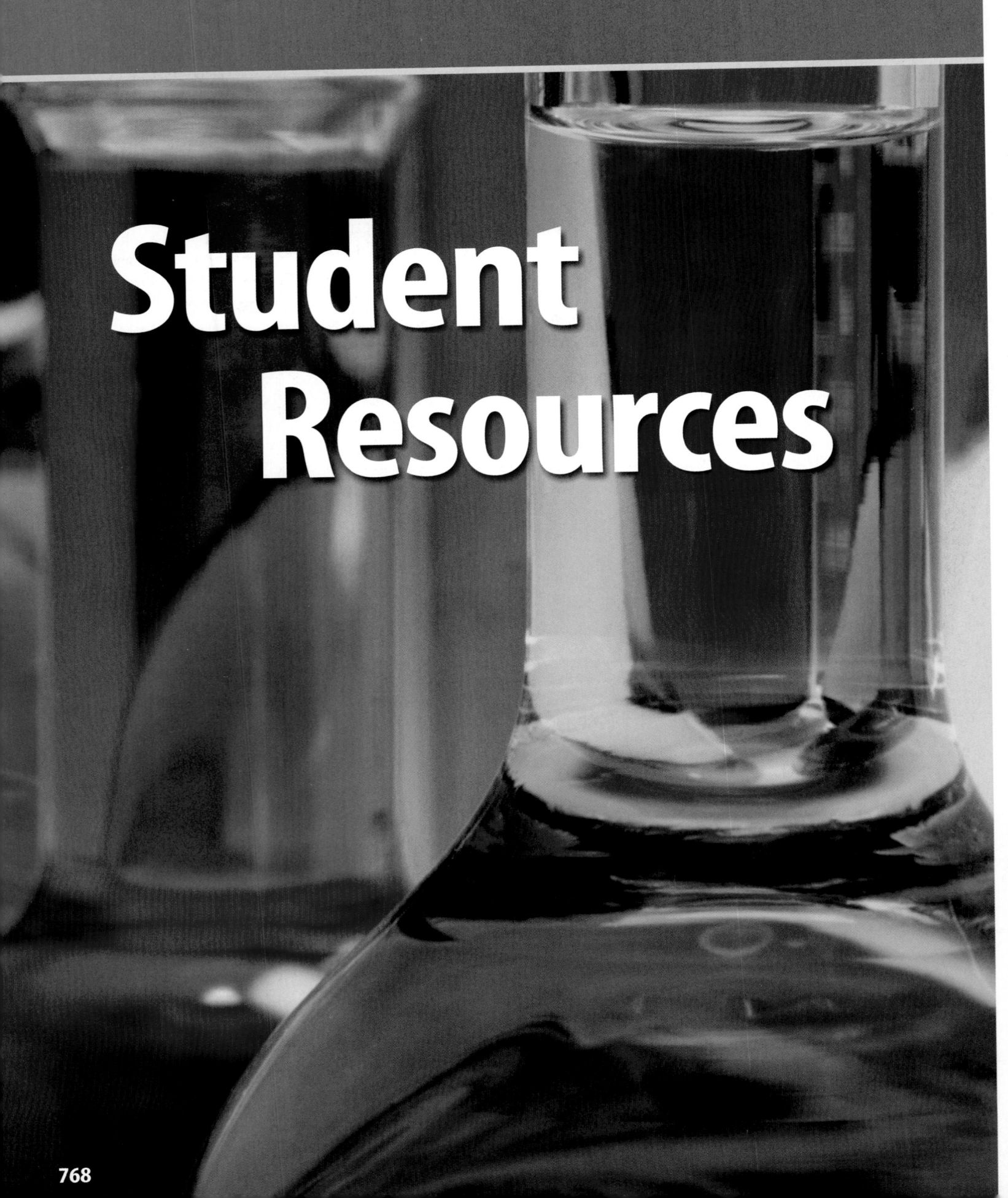

Student Resources

CONTENTS

Field GUIDE

About the Field Guide

- This field guide contains descriptions and photos of monuments and other uses of building stones.

- A field guide contains a key that enables the user to classify or identify an item or concept.

- In using a field guide, students will apply steps of a scientific method as they observe, investigate, and draw conclusions.

- Encourage students to use the field guide outside the classroom.

Tie to Prior Knowledge

Have students name buildings or monuments they know of that are constructed of stone. List the places they name on the chalkboard. Then ask if anyone knows what kind of stone was used in each building or monument.

Field Activity

If possible, take the class on a field trip to look at stone buildings or monuments in your community. Have students work in small groups to identify the stone used in each building or monument.

Field GUIDE

Since ancient times, people have used naturally available materials such as stone and wood to construct their homes, places of worship, palaces, and other buildings and monuments. As early as 2500 B.C., the Egyptians had learned how to cut and transport large blocks of limestone from mountainsides for use in the construction of the pyramids. The Maya also used stone to construct their magnificent cities. Since those times, stone has remained a popular building material not only for its beauty but also for its durability and strength.

Types of Building Stone and Some Famous Stone Monuments

The choice of stone used in construction depends on the purpose, availability, cost, and properties of the particular stone. On the following pages are some of the most common building stones, one or more of which was used in the construction of many of the famous buildings in the world. By using this Field Guide, you can learn which stones were used to build these structures. You also can learn to identify the stones used to construct other monuments, buildings, and structures in your neighborhood or town.

Building Stones

Granite

Granite's mineral composition determines its color. For example, some granites are pink because they contain the mineral potassium feldspar. The minerals in granite resist wear and tear caused by wind and precipitation.

The pink color of granite in Enchanted Rock is caused by the presence of microcline, a variety of potassium feldspar.

Marischal College

Built in the late 1890s in Aberdeen, Scotland, Marischal College is one of the largest granite buildings in the world. Constructed in a gothic style, the building has an ornate façade and represents unusually intricate sculpture work for granite.

Field Activity

Take a walk around your town and find a public building or structure made of stone. Then use this field guide to identify the stones used to construct that building. Record your findings in your Science Journal. Visit the Glencoe Science Web site at **science.glencoe.com** to find out which stones were used to build other famous buildings.

Resources for Teachers and Students

"Romancing the Stone," by Aries Keck, *Earth*, November, 1998, pp. 22–23.

Eyewitness Books: Building, by Philip Wilkinson, Alfred A. Knopf, 1995.

Eyewitness Books: Rocks and Minerals, by R.F. Symes, Alfred A. Knopf, 1988.

My First Pocket Guide: Rocks and Minerals, by Paul M. A. Willis, National Geographic Society, 1997.

Stone, Clay, Glass: How Building Materials are Found and Used, by Robert L. Bates, Enslow Publishers, 1987.

The Rock Quarry Book, by Michael Kehoe, Carolrhoda Books, 1981.

Limestone

Limestone commonly ranges in color from white to gray, but other colors are possible. Compared to other stones, limestone is not resistant when exposed to air and water in humid climates. However, it still is used as a building stone, especially where it is available locally.

Indiana limestone

Marble

In its purest form marble is white, but impurities produce other colors. The impurities often weave throughout marble, producing a beautiful mosaic appearance. Many marbles are composed mainly of calcite or dolomite. The softness of these minerals allows marble to be carved easily.

Italian marble

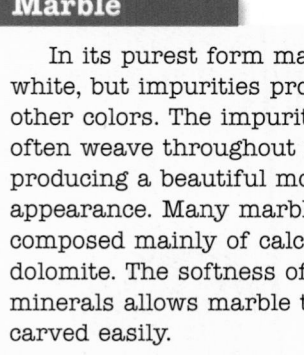

Lincoln Memorial

The Lincoln Memorial in Washington, D.C., was built to honor Abraham Lincoln. The exterior of the building, which is constructed in the Greek style, is made of marble quarried from Colorado and Tennessee. The walls and columns inside are made of Indiana limestone, and the ceiling, floor, and platform are made of marble from Tennessee and Alabama. Lincoln's statue was carved using white marble from Georgia.

FIELD GUIDE 771

SCIENCE Online
Internet Addresses

_____
_____
_____
_____

Explore the Glencoe Science Web site at **science.glencoe.com** to find out more about topics in this field guide.

Curriculum Connection

Art Have students research the sculptures of Michelangelo, the material he used to make his sculptures, and where that material came from. Have them write a brief report on what they learn. The world's most famous marble, which Michelangelo used for his sculptures, comes from the Carrara quarry in Tuscany, Italy.

Visual Learning

Lincoln Memorial Have students locate each kind of stone described in the picture and tell where it came from. Then have them use a map of the United States to locate the states mentioned.

Quick Demo

Allow students to examine samples of marble and limestone with magnifying lenses. Marble chips and limestone chips are available at most landscaping supply stores. Ask students to compare and contrast the characteristics of both kinds of rock. Limestone may contain interlocking shells, while marble has large interlocking crystals. Both tend to be light-colored rocks, although the color of marble may vary. Demonstrate for students a common property that both rocks share. Place a few drops of dilute hydrochloric acid on a sample of each. Allow students to observe that both rocks fizz and begin to dissolve when exposed to acid. Point out that sometimes rain is acidic enough to damage buildings or monuments made from limestone or marble. Explain that in some cemeteries old marble or limestone grave markers have been so damaged that they are illegible.

Teacher FYI

In addition to its geological classification, building stone is classified as cut (dimension) stone or rubble. Rubble walls can be composed of stones as they are collected (field stones) or of unfinished stone as it comes from a quarry. Rubble stones are often set in a random pattern, as often seen in fireplaces. Ashlar walls are built of cut and squared dimension stone. They can consist of stones of the same size or stones of various sizes.

FIELD GUIDE 771

Content Background

Each stone quarry provides rock unique enough that scientists can identify the quarry from which the stone used in a particular building or monument came. Jim Harrel of the University of Toledo in Ohio has used such technology as thin-section petrography and X-ray fluorescence spectroscopy to come up with chemical fingerprints from over 100 different quarries. Using his techniques, he was able to identify that the lid of an Egyptian sarcophagus in London's British Museum had been carved from stone from the Wadi Hammamat quarry in Egypt's Eastern Desert.

Activity

Ask students to imagine that they are going to build a house and want to use several different building stones in the construction. Have students work in small groups to make sketches showing where and how they would use each type of building stone in the house. Have each group present their plans to the class, explaining why they chose the building stones they did.

Field GUIDE

Sandstone

The sand grains in sandstone give it a coarse, rustic appearance. Although sandstone often is white or tan, mineral cements can color the rock vivid shades of orange or red. When sand grains are well-cemented and composed mainly of resistant minerals such as quartz, sandstones can be excellent building materials.

Uluru (yew LEW rew), often called Ayers Rock in Australia, is the world's largest outcropping of sandstone.

Piece of sandstone

The Red Fort

Built by the Shah Jahan in the seventeenth century, the Red Fort in Delhi, India, is made of red sandstone. The octagonal, or eight-sided, fort contains palaces, gardens, army barracks, and other buildings, including a stable for the king's horses and elephants. The entire fort is surrounded by a large wall.

772   STUDENT RESOURCES

Curriculum Connection

History Have students research the ancient Nabataean city of Petra in present-day Jordan. Students should prepare a multi-media presentation on the location of the city, the unique building technique, when it was built, and the rock involved. Petra was carved into a sandstone formation about 2,000 years age.

Field GUIDE

Gloddfa Ganol Slate Mine
...ales is the world's largest
...mine.

Slate

The color of slate varies, but it is usually gray, black, green, or red. The color is determined by the stones' organic and mineral content. Slate contains fine-grained, well-compacted clay minerals and mica which make it water-tight and easy to separate into layers. These properties make slate ideal to use for roofing and paving.

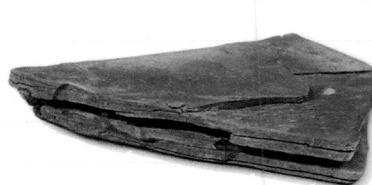

Mud Island Park

The flat and compact nature of slate make it a natural choice for this River Walk in Mud Island Park, Memphis, Tennessee. A street map of Memphis was etched into the surface of the slate.

Mud Island Park River Walk

FIELD GUIDE 773

Use Science Words

Word Meaning Have students use a dictionary to look up all the meanings of the word *slate*. Ask them to identify the three meanings that are related to one another and how they are related. Slate is the grayish metamorphic rock. Slate also refers to a thin piece of this rock that school children used to use to write on. Slate is also a bluish-gray color that resembles the color of the rock.

Extension

Have students contact your state Geological Survey for information about the types of building stones that are found in your state. Have them research any locations where quarries are located, find out what kind of stone is quarried there, and how most of it is used. Students could make a poster with a state map showing locations of quarries, illustrations of the types of stones, and any other interesting information they find.

Fun Fact

People are now able to manufacture building stone substitutes such as brick, tiles, and concrete. In many parts of the world, roofing tiles are molded and fired from clay.

Inclusion Strategies

Visually Impaired Allow students to handle samples of the building stones described in this field guide. Ask them to describe and compare the textures of the samples.

About the Field Guide

- A field guide contains a key that enables the user to classify or identify an item or concept.
- In using a field guide, students will apply steps of a scientific method as they observe, investigate, and draw conclusions.
- This field guide applies nationally; local and regional field guides are usually available for more specific local use.
- Encourage students to use the field guide outside the classroom.

Tie to Prior Knowledge

Some students may never have been to the ocean shoreline, but almost all will have seen shorelines in movies or on television. Have students describe some of the things they've noticed about shorelines. Have them identify some of the ways shorelines in different areas vary.

Field Activity

Individual student responses will vary depending on the location of the shoreline chosen. Have students discuss the relationships between the geographic location and the shoreline features found there.

Fun Fact

The land on Earth has approximately 504,000 km of shorelines.

If you've ever built a sandcastle on a beach, you know that shoreline features are often temporary. Shorelines are constantly changing. As the tide comes in, waves wash higher and higher onto the beach, getting closer to your sandcastle. Finally, your sandcastle disappears as the waves rush over it. However, the ocean water that carried away the sand in your castle simply deposited it somewhere else.

Earth's Shorelines

Every landmass on Earth has a shoreline—an area where the ocean meets the land. The United States has approximately 153,000 km of shoreline. Natural forces, such as wind, waves, and currents constantly shape and sculpt these shoreline regions. Along rocky shores, rock-laden waves batter the land away. The chemical action of seawater in waves slowly dissolves some of the minerals coastal rock contains. Yet, along gently sloping shores, fragments that were eroded elsewhere are deposited to form beaches and barrier islands. Along shorelines, the ocean both erodes and builds the land.

Shorelines vary in shape and they have different features. This field guide offers a look at some features you might see along various shorelines.

Shorelines

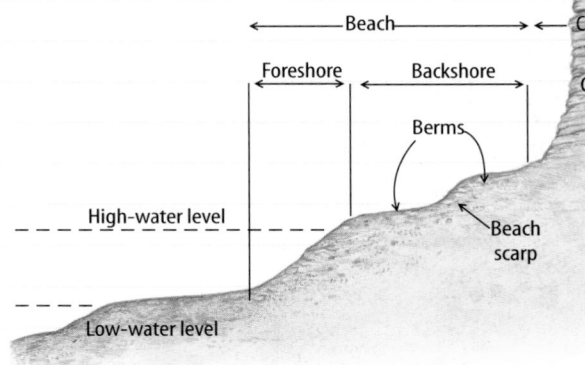

General Shoreline Features

Along a shoreline is an area of loose materials that extends from the low-water line landward to the place where permanent vegetation occurs. This area is called the beach or shore. The beach includes the **foreshore**—the part which lies between high-water and low-water marks at ordinary tide—and the **backshore**—the part of the beach that is usually dry. **Berms** are nearly horizontal parts of the backshore formed by materials deposited by wave action. Some beaches have no berms, but others might have several. On beaches with more than one berm, the berms are separated by **scarps**, which are steep slopes. Some beaches also have cliffs—areas where the land rises sharply a large distance above the water or surrounding land.

Field Activity

Research a location along the shoreline of the United States. Identify the shoreline features in that location. In your Science Journal, describe the features and the patterns of erosion and deposition that created them.

Resources for Teachers and Students

Where Land Meets Sea, by Allan Fowler, Children's Press, 1997.

Along the Seashore, by Rod Theodorou, Heinemann Library, 2000.

Coasts, by David Cumming, Raintree Steck-Vaughn, 1997.

The Everglades and the Gulf Coast, by Daniel Blaustein, Benchmark Books, 2000.

The Seacoast Reader, edited by John Murphy, Lyons Press, 1999.

Rocky Shores: Cliffs

Where cliffs or rocks line the shore, the land is probably retreating. Cliffs are sometimes made of layers of different kinds of rock. You often can see these layers in the face of a cliff. The steepness of a cliff varies with the rock hardness and the angle of rock layers. Usually, the harder the rock is, the steeper the cliff is. Sometimes, when lower layers of rock are eroded, an overhanging cliff can form. If the overhang becomes too great, it can collapse and send rocks tumbling down, leaving a pile of rubble at the base of the cliff.

Rocky Shores: Sea Caves, Arches, and Stacks

As waves pound against a sea cliff, the rock near the base of a cliff gradually wears down to form sea caves. Sometimes waves enlarge a cave so much that a crack appears in the roof. During rough weather, water can be seen spraying out of the opening, forming what is called a blowhole.

Sometimes headlands extend into the water like the prow of a boat. If waves erode both sides of a headland, arches will form. Eventually, arches collapse, leaving isolated rock columns called stacks.

Blowhole

Stack

Arch

Sea cave

Rocky Shores: Boulder and Bay-head Beaches

The ocean transports loose rock that it wears away from shorelines. Waves grind the rock into smaller particles and deposit them onto the shore, forming beaches. Boulder beaches are narrow areas of rocks, stones, and gravel, called shingle, at the base of sea cliffs. Bay-head beaches are small, sandy, crescent-shaped beaches that form in coves between two rocky headlands.

FIELD GUIDE   775

Use Science Words
Word Meaning Have students find out why the part of a beach between high-water and low-water marks at ordinary tide is called the foreshore. *Fore-* is a prefix meaning "front" and the foreshore is the front of the shoreline, closest to the ocean.

Activity
Have small groups of students use clay and a variety of other materials, such as toothpicks, tissue paper, and tempera paints, to construct three-dimensional models of several different shoreline features. When groups have completed their models, have each group present its models to the class. Have them explain how the features formed and where they might be found.

Use an Analogy
Compare the way waves erode the cliffs along a rocky shoreline to the way an electric sander erodes a tall block of wood. Ask students what would happen if you kept sanding the lower part of the wood block. You would eventually wear away enough of the lower part that the top part might collapse. Then ask them what the sawdust produced from the sanding process is analogous to in the erosion of a rocky shoreline. The sand, gravel, and stones that are eroded from the cliffs.

Fun Fact

The highest sea cliffs are at Molokai, Hawaii. They descend 1,010 m to the sea.

Content Background

Dunes closest to the beach proper are called primary dunes. The dunes behind the primary dunes are secondary dunes. Sea oats are one of the few plants that will grow on primary dunes. The roots of sea oats help hold the sand in place and keep the dunes from blowing away. Although barrier islands are found from New England to the Gulf coast of Texas, most of the barrier islands in the United States are found off the coasts of North Carolina, South Carolina, and Florida. The most dramatic changes in barrier islands are caused by storms, particularly hurricanes. Storm waves may move sediments to the secondary dunes by breaking through or over primary dunes.

Fun Fact

Extension

Have students research the Coastal Barrier Resources Act of 1982 and the Coastal Barrier Improvement Act of 1990. Ask them to find out the purposes of the federal acts, what areas are covered by the acts, and the impact these acts have had on shoreline protection in the United States. Ask them also to find out why some people are opposed to this federal legislation. Have students write a position paper explaining what they learned and where they stand on the issue.

Field GUIDE

Sandy Beaches

Lowland beaches are broad, gently sloping sandy beaches, usually with a strip of stones and gravel along the upper part. They often have dunes of sand blown inland by onshore winds.

The **beach proper** is the exposed, sandy area of the shoreline. Waves breaking at an angle to the land produce longshore drift. As a wave approaches, it slides up the beach at an angle, then drains straight back into the ocean. This process shifts sand along the beach, moving it from one area to another, often forming cusps that give the beach a scalloped look.

Sandy Beaches: Swash Zone

The **swash zone,** which separates the exposed beach from the ocean, is where waves lap onto the shore. The upper limit of the beach is the swash line, which is the highest level that the sea reaches during large storms. On a gently sloping shore, the ocean erodes beach sediment on the lower part of the swash zone and deposits it on the upper part. On a steeply sloping shore, the opposite occurs.

Sandy Beaches: Dunes

Dunes are large mounds of sand behind ocean beaches. Dunes form as wind carries dry sand farther inland away from the beach proper. A dune begins when an obstruction, such as a rock, a shell, or a piece of driftwood, breaks the wind stream and causes sand to drop on the side of the object that is facing away from the wind direction.

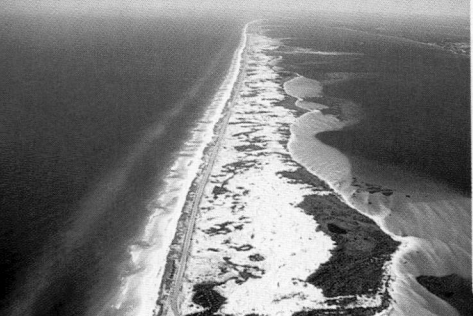

Barrier Islands

Barrier islands are elongated islands of sediments—usually sand—that typically form parallel to the shore. They are separated from the mainland by bodies of water that vary in size. Barrier islands are found along the Atlantic Coast and the Gulf of Mexico. For barrier islands to form, a large supply of sand and moderate wave energy are needed. Barrier islands are constantly changing and moving. Winds, waves, currents, and tides build and erode island shorelines in a never-ending process.

776 STUDENT RESOURCES

Science Journal

Building on Barrier Islands Tell students that for many years homes have been built on many of the barrier islands along the Atlantic and Gulf Coasts. Have them describe in their Science Journals why they think many scientists have been opposed to this practice.

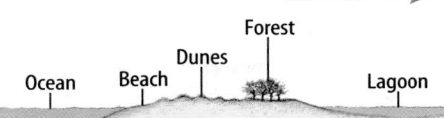
Barrier Islands: Structure

Barrier islands have several distinct zones. Beaches on barrier islands are usually sandy, but some are composed of gravel. Behind the beaches are dunes that help protect the islands from winds, waves, and storms. Sea oats and beach grass growing on the dunes help stabilize the island. On some islands, maritime forests grow behind the dunes. Trees and bushes that are salt tolerant grow in this region. Some islands also have inland ponds that serve as nurseries for young fish, crabs, and shrimp.

Ocean — Beach — Dunes — Forest — Mainland → — Lagoon

Deltas

Some rivers build up huge deposits of soil or silt where they empty into the ocean, forming coastal lands called deltas. The Mississippi River flows south and empties into the Gulf of Mexico. As the river meets the Gulf, it loses speed and dumps its sediments in an expanding fan-shaped zone. The sediments dropped at the river's mouth tend to build rapidly, causing the river's mouth to grow outward toward the open waters of the Gulf.

Estuaries

Estuaries are partially enclosed bodies of water where freshwater from rivers and streams runs into and mixes with salty ocean water. Water flowing from the land carries

sediments, nutrients, and pollutants. As water flows through freshwater and saltwater marshes in estuaries, much of the sediment and pollution is filtered out. Wetland plants and soils also protect the areas further inland by absorbing floodwaters and lessening storm surges. Saltwater marsh grasses and other plants help prevent erosion and stabilize the shoreline. Over long periods of time, unless sea levels rise, estuaries tend to fill with sediment and become much smaller.

FIELD GUIDE 777

Visual Learning

Barrier Island Structure Have students identify the zones of the barrier island. Point out the location of the maritime forest. Ask students why they think only salt-tolerant trees and bushes can grow on this part of the barrier island. Ocean water is salty and sometimes washes over the island. Also, water that is taken in by the plant roots will normally be somewhat salty because the island is surrounded by saltwater. **Ask students what the water is called that separates a barrier island from the mainland.** Lagoon Explain that sediment is washed into these areas by tides or rivers and forms a sandy or muddy floor. Ask if they think the water level in the lagoon is always the same. No, water flows in or drains out with the tides. Point out that with this changing water level, areas called tidal flats form along the edges of the lagoon.

Extension

Have students gather information about the Mississippi Delta. Ask them to find out how large it is, whether its land area is increasing or decreasing, and how the changes in the delta affect the city of New Orleans. Have students present oral reports on what they learn.

Fun Fact

Estuaries go by many names. Galveston Bay, Boston Harbor, Cook Inlet, Indian River Lagoon, and Puget Sound are all estuaries.

Inclusion Strategies

Learning Disabled Have students examine a map of the United States. Have them identify and list the states that have ocean shorelines. Then have them locate examples of several shoreline features, such as a barrier island, a delta, and an estuary. Ask them to compare the number of states with ocean shorelines to those without shorelines. Ask them whether your state has ocean shorelines.

About the Field Guide

- A field guide enables the user to classify or identify a feature or concept.
- In using a field guide, students will apply steps of a scientific method as they observe, investigate, and draw conclusions.
- This Faults and Folds field guide applies nationally; local and regional field guides are available for more specific local use. Two sources of regional information are listed at the bottom of this page.
- Encourage students to use this field guide outside.

Tie to Prior Knowledge

Students have seen many of the Earth structures discussed here as backdrops to movies and SUV commercials set in the West. Tell them they will appreciate these settings more after studying this field guide.

Field Activity

Have students work in small groups to compare their notes and classify the formations they documented. They should be able to distinguish between folds and faults and to further determine the types. Ask students if they can identify the forces at work to form the structures they saw. For example, compression from plate collisions could form an anticline.

Earth's crust is squeezed and pulled as tectonic plates move. Energy builds up in rocks and when it is released, it can dramatically and visibly change the structure of the land surface. Faults are fractures in Earth produced when sections of Earth's crust move past each other and release energy, sometimes during earthquakes. Small faults can be nearly invisible on the surface. Large faults, caused by intense, long-time crustal movement, can be huge cracks in the ground that extend for hundreds of miles. Types of faults include normal; reverse, or thrust; and strike-slip.

When tectonic plates collide, great mountain chains can be uplifted out of Earth. When rocks are subjected to stress, they do not always break and form faults—under some conditions, rocks will bend and fold. These folded rocks can reach Earth's surface. Upward-arching folds are known as anticlines. Downward-sagging folds are known as synclines. Folds can be large enough to form mountains or small enough to hold in your hand.

Earth's tectonic plates have been moving for hundreds of millions of years. Although they move very slowly—about 10 cm per year—they have moved across great distances over time.

778 STUDENT RESOURCES

Faults and Folds

Normal Fault: The Rio Grand Rift

Extending across a distance of more than 1,200 km, the Rio Grande Rift stretches from Colorado to Northern Mexico and separates the Colorado Plateau from the Great Plains. The Rio Grande Rift is an example of how normal faults can affect Earth's surface. It is the result of fractures in Earth's crust that are formed as the crust is pulled apart. The Rio Grande Rift is active and the faults in the rift release their built-up energy in the form of frequent, small tremors rather than as large earthquakes. The region also contains many volcanoes.

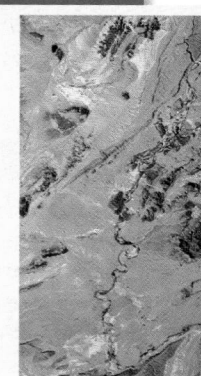

The Rio Grande Rift

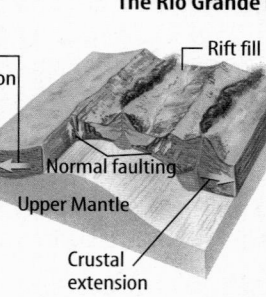

Crustal extension — Rift fill — Normal faulting — Upper Mantle — Crustal extension

Formation of rift

Field Activity

Go to **science.glencoe.com** to take an online geology field trip. Click on the links provided to view different rock formations throughout the United States. In your Science Journal, write or draw the overall structure and attitude, or positioning, of the rock formations.

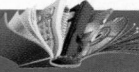

Resources for Teachers and Students

The Roadside Geology series, Mountain Press Publishing Company, Missoula, Montana

The Geological Highway Map series, The American Association of Petroleum Geologists, Tulsa, Oklahoma

Thrust Fault: The Appalachian Mountains

The Appalachian Mountains were uplifted more than 300 million years ago during a plate collision. As the African and North American Plates collided, huge slices of Earth's crust were moved great distances along thrust faults. These slices of crust make up Earth's surface in some parts of the Appalachian Mountains today.

Fault Surface

Thrust fault

Hayward Fault

Tectonic Plate collision

Location of Hayward Fault

Make a Model

Have student groups use different-colored modeling clay to make three identical stacks of horizontal rock layers. Then, have students use a spatula to cut a normal fault in one clay stack, a thrust fault in another, and a strike-slip fault in the third, moving the blocks appropriately. Ask the students to use their spatulas to model the effects of erosion on their faulted terrains and then to observe the surface morphology and the arrangement of different rock layer for each terrain.

Activity

Obtain interesting geologic maps from a university library or from your state geologic survey. Have students work in groups around each map, locating and identifying by symbol any normal, thrust, and strike-slip faults on the maps. Have them also examine other features on the maps.

Fun Fact

Estes Park, Colorado, and Park City, Utah, probably offer plenty of recreation, but that's beside the point. Their names refer instead to their geology—a *park* is a down-dropped piece of crust, as in a rift.

Strike-Slip Fault: The Hayward Fault

This strike-slip fault—part of the 900-km San Andreas Fault system—extends about 120 km and is considered to be the state's second-strongest fault. It is a fracture in Earth's crust: the Pacific Plate to the west is moving northwest in relation to the North American Plate. Energy from this movement continues to build until it is released in the form of an earthquake. In 1868, an earthquake occurred along the Hayward Fault, damaging San Francisco.

FIELD GUIDE   779

Visual Learning

Have students look at the picture of the Appalachians and ask them to explain how a plate collision could result in uplift. Then demonstrate by holding a meter stick at both ends and compressing until it bows upward.

Quick Demo

Lay a tablecloth over a smooth classroom desk. Have two students stand on opposite sides of the desk and push the tablecloth toward the center. This should create upward and downward folds similar to anticlines and synclines in folded rock. Ask students which folds resemble anticlines and which resemble synclines. **What force did the students who applied force represent?** Students pushing cloth toward the center acted as compressional forces do on plates.

Teacher FYI

Folding and faulting are different versions of crust deformation caused by crustal movement. Geologists believe the ultimate force behind such crustal movement is convection occurring in the asthenosphere portion of the upper mantle. Diverging convection currents produce tension; converging currents produce compression.

Extension

Challenge students to research the parts of anticlines and synclines, and the different types classified by geologists. The sides are called limbs; the angle of dip is called the axis. Folds can be classified as asymmetrical, overturned, recumbent, and plunging. Have students create informational posters displaying what they learned.

Field GUIDE

Fold: Anticline at Hartland Quay

Layers of sedimentary rock are folded in this spectacular anticline at Hartland Quay in Devon, England. The anticline has been eroded in the foreground exposing the ends of the tilted rock layers.

Anticline at Hartland Quay

Anticlines and synclines in sequence

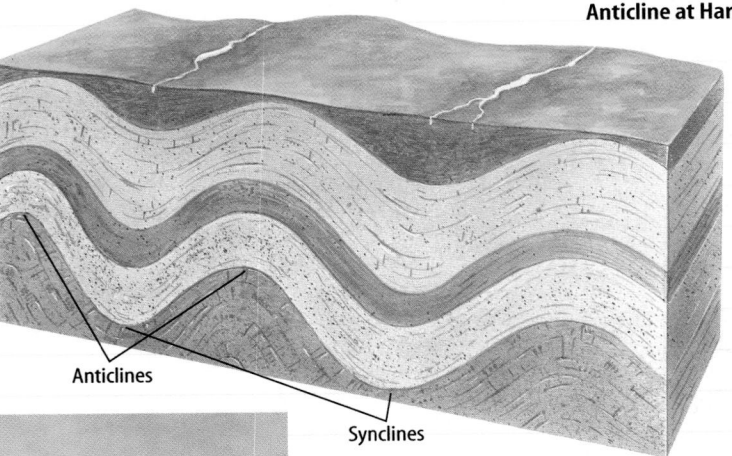

Anticlines

Synclines

Fold: Syncline on Mount Kidd

This syncline is part of Mount Kidd in Alberta, Canada, in the Kananaskis Valley of the Canadian Rockies. Unlike the American Rockies, which were originally large chunks of granite, the Canadian Rockies began as piles of sediment that were compressed when plates collided.

The syncline on Mount Kidd

780 STUDENT RESOURCES

Visual Learning

Direct students to inspect the pictures of anticlines and synclines. Ask them to identify the locations of the youngest and the oldest rock in each structure. The oldest rock rises up from the center in an anticline; it dips downward in a syncline. Should either structure be eroded, these locations become important. At the surface in an eroded anticline, older rock will be surrounded by younger rock. An eroded syncline features the youngest rock at its center. Make a diagram on the board to illustrate this idea.

Fold: The Alps

Location of the Alps

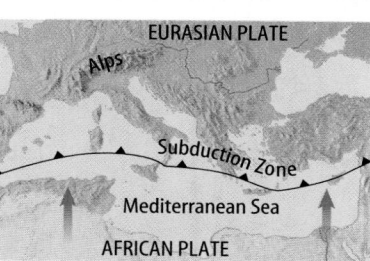

EURASIAN PLATE

Alps

Subduction Zone

Mediterranean Sea

AFRICAN PLATE

The Alps, which are a beautiful example of folded mountains, were formed as the African Plate began to move closer to the Eurasian Plate. The pressure exerted by this movement caused the land to fold, creating these peaks more than 15 million years ago.

The folded Alps

Erosion of the Blue Ridge Mountains

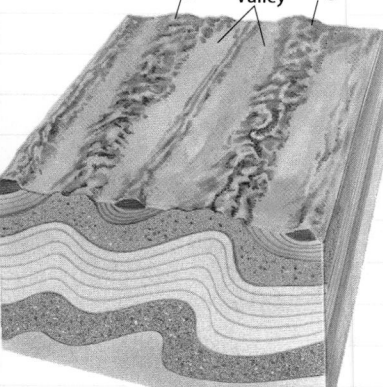

Ridge   Valley   Ridge

Erosion of folds

Fold: The Blue Ridge Mountains

Folded mountains derive their name from the abundance of folds in the rocks. The Blue Ridge Mountains in the Valley and Ridge region of the Appalachians are an excellent example of mountains formed by rocks that folded, then began to erode. The harder rocks formed ridges, and the softer rocks eroded to form valleys.

FIELD GUIDE   781

Use Science Words

Word Meaning Have students investigate the meaning of the word *anticline* and the word *syncline*. After they have finished investigating these two words, ask them to speculate about the meaning of the word *monocline*. The word *anticline* means, "opposite inclined" and reflects the fact that the limbs of an anticline dip in opposite directions. The word *syncline* means, "together inclined" and reflects the fact that the limbs of a syncline dip toward each other. A *monocline* is a fold with only one limb.

Discussion

Folding occurs when plates are subject to compression, usually because they are colliding with other plates. What might happen if the situation changed, and plates that had been compressed began to be pulled apart? Students might answer that the plate would "unfold." In fact, the likely result would be normal faulting.

Curriculum Connection

Geography The Valley and Ridge Province of the Appalachian Mountains consists of sedimentary rock layers deformed into a series of plunging anticlines and synclines. The ridges and valleys are sculpted by erosion. Resistant sandstone layers in the limbs of folds stand up to form ridges, and soft-shale layers are eroded into valleys. Explain to students how the Valley and Ridge Province formed, and have each student draw a plausible cross section of such a province in their Science Journal.

About the Field Guide

- A field guide contains a key that enables the user to classify or identify an item or concept.
- In using a field guide, students will apply steps of a scientific method as they observe, investigate, and draw conclusions.
- This Fossils field guide applies nationally; local and regional field guides to fossils are usually available for more specific local use.
- Encourage students to use the field guide outside the classroom.

Tie to Prior Knowledge

Ask students to name kinds of organisms that they have seen as fossils. Write their responses on the board or overhead transparency. Ask if any have seen fossils of small animals or plants on display at museums. Encourage students to share their fossil-viewing experiences with the class.

 **Field Activity**

Have students work in small groups to find fossils of interest to them. Remind them to make their sketches as accurate as possible.

Suppose you live hundreds of miles from the ocean. One day, you find a rock with a clear imprint of a seashell on its surface. What might this imprint, or fossil, tell you about the area in which you live?

Fossils are the traces or remains of organisms that lived long ago. Fossils provide a record of the vast array of life-forms that have lived on Earth, and they show how these life-forms have changed over time. Fossils also can give clues about how the rock formed over millions of years.

Common Fossils

The most easily found fossils are shells, or casts of shells, from the sea animals that once lived in them. Some fossils might have been well preserved, but most are only fragments of the ancient organism. Fossils of soft-bodied animals and plants are not so easily found because they decay more quickly. However, some rare fossils of soft-bodied organisms have been found and have provided a wealth of information about the organisms.

This field guide shows examples of common fossils belonging to some of the major fossil groups. When you find a fossil, you can use this guide to help identify the group to which the fossil belongs.

Fossils

Fossil Groups

Coral fossil

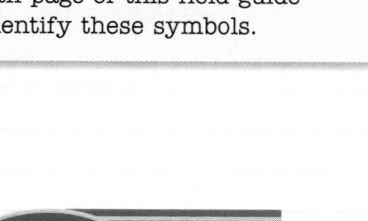

Coral

Corals are small sea creatures that live attached to the ocean floor in warm, shallow waters. The animals build structures that have a honeycomb-like appearance. These structures commonly are found as fossils. The first corals appeared during the Paleozoic Era of geologic time. Use the key on the fourth page of this field guide to identify these symbols.

Field Activity

Go on an Internet fossil hunt at **science.glencoe.com**. Find five different fossils and make a sketch of each in your Science Journal. Then, below each illustration, write a description of the fossil and explain what kind of organism the fossil came from.

Resources for Teachers and Students

Fossils, by Douglas Palmer, DK Publishing, 1996.

Cambridge Guide to Minerals, Rocks, and Fossils, by A.C. Bishop, Cambridge University Press, 1999.

The Nature and Science of Fossils, by Jane Burton, Gareth Stevens Publisher, 1999.

Fossils, by Melissa Gish, Creative Education, 1999.

Fossils and Bones, by Saviour Pirotta, Raintree Steck-Vaughn, 1997.

Field GUIDE

Trilobite

Trilobites (TRI loh bites) are now extinct, but they once were common in ancient seas. Their bodies were divided into three parts—one slightly raised center lobe flanked by two flatter lobes. Trilobites measured from less than 1 cm long to more than 20 cm long.

Trilobite fossil

Gastropod or Snail

Gastropods (GAS troh pahdz), or snails, have a head with eyes and mouth, one flat foot for crawling, and a spiral shell. They can be found in oceans, in freshwater ponds and lakes, and on land.

Snail fossil

Crinoid or Sea Lily

In spite of its name, the sea lily is an animal. Most crinoids (KRI noydz) attach themselves to the soft, muddy floor of the ocean and then use their long arms to catch prey.

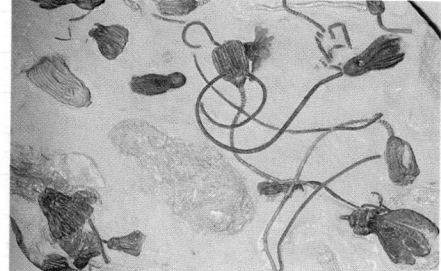

Multiple Sea lily fossils

Ammonoid

Ammonoids (A muh noydz) were free-swimming shellfish, related to squid. Ammonites appeared during the Devonian Era, long before dinosaurs roamed Earth. They became extinct when dinosaurs did.

Ammonite fossil

FIELD GUIDE   783

Content Background

Only a small fraction of organisms are preserved as fossils—usually only organisms that have a solid skeleton or a shell. The shells of clams or brachiopods are relatively common in sedimentary rocks. The great majority of fossils are preserved in a water environment because remains on land are more easily destroyed. Anaerobic conditions at the bottom of bodies of water are much more likely to preserve fine details since only anaerobic bacteria are present to destroy the remains. Generally, two conditions are needed for an organism to be preserved—rapid burial that slows or stops decay and excludes scavengers, and the organism's possession of hard parts capable of being fossilized.

Fun Fact

One of the most spectacular fossil coral sites is an outcrop of Devonian (375 to 380 million years ago) coral-bearing limestone located in and around the Ohio River near Louisville, Kentucky.

Extension

Have students research the coal deposits that formed during the Carboniferous Period and the types of fossils that are found in these deposits. Students should make a booklet that includes labeled drawings of the fossil types as well as a written summary of what they learn. Crinoids, club mosses, horsetails, ferns, and gastropods are commonly found in coal.

Curriculum Connection

Art Provide small groups of students with several plain oval-shaped cookies, some small round candies, and one or two tubes of icing, paper plates, plastic knives, and paper towels for cleanup. Have students use the materials to make models of trilobites. They can refer to picture in the field guide or find other examples of trilobites in books or on websites to model. Tell them to model the three parts of the trilobite's body using the icing and use the candies to represent the eyes. Have members of each group present their completed models to the class.

Activity

Have small groups of students use modeling clay to make casts of several objects in the room. Have them flatten the clay on a sheet of newspaper, then press an object or part of an object into the clay and remove it to form a cast. Encourage them to use creativity in their selection of objects. After all the groups have made several casts, have each group exchange its casts with another group. Ask each group to write a description of each cast and infer the identity what object made the cast. Discuss how scientists who study fossils must make inferences about what they find.

Fun Fact

Charcarodon, a shark that lived about 65 million years ago, may have grown to lengths of more than 15 m. Its fossilized teeth can be up to 15 cm long.

Use Science Words

Word Origin The prefix *petro-* or *petri-* comes from the Greek word for rock or stone. Ask students to find words with this prefix and explain their meaning. petrify: to convert into stone or a stony substance; petroglyph: drawing or carving made on rock by ancient cultures; petrography: the scientific description and classification of rocks; petrology: the scientific study of rocks

Echinoid

Echinoids (ih KI noydz)—sea urchins and sand dollars—can be ball shaped, cone shaped, or flat. The sea urchin that left this fossil was cone shaped. It used its mouth, located on the flat bottom side, to swallow sand from which it took its nourishment.

Echinoid fossil

Shark

The soft cartilage of a shark's body decays rapidly, so shark fossils are usually teeth or scales. Sharks are abundant in today's oceans.

Shark's tooth fossils

Plant (Leaves)

Some plant fossils show leaves, fronds, or stems. Fern trees thrived during the Carboniferous Period (360 million to 286 million years ago). Seed ferns can be identified by their fronds, or branches, which are divided into smaller leaflets.

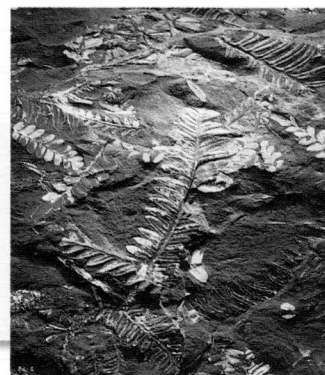

Seed fern fossils

Plant (Wood)

Some plant fossils are pieces of wood. This petrified wood fossil is from the Petrified Forest in Arizona. Growth rings in wood indicate changing growth rates during each year. Growth rings often are clear enough to be counted.

Petrified wood fossil

Curriculum Connection

Literature Have students read a book about Mary Anning and her fossil discoveries. Possible books include: *The Fossil Girl: Mary Anning's Dinosaur Discovery,* by Catherine Brighton, Milbrook Press, 1999; *Rare Treasure: Mary Anning and Her Remarkable Discoveries,* by Don Brown, Houghton Mifflin, 1999; and *Stone Girl, Bone Girl,* by Laurence Anholt, Orchard Books, 1999. Have students present oral reports on the books they read.

FOSSIL MAP OF THE UNITED STATES

The key below provides a symbol for each fossil group shown in this guide. Use the key to find out which fossils can be found in your region.

Key

Coral	Crinoid	Shark
Trilobite	Ammonoid	Plant (leaves)
Gastropod	Echinoid	Plant (wood)

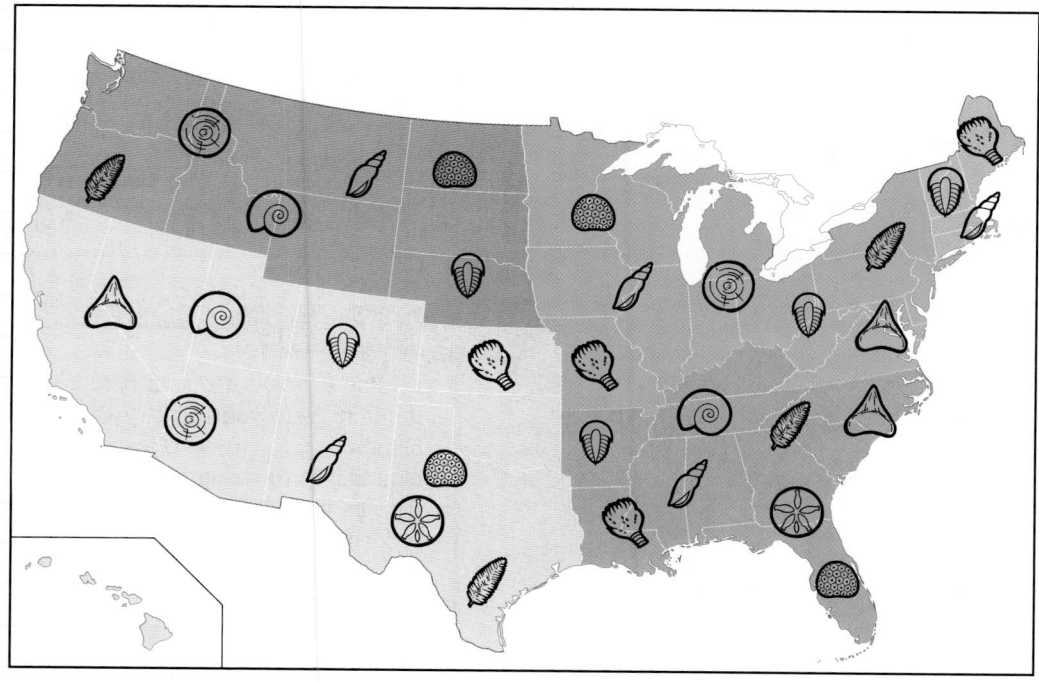

FIELD GUIDE 785

Visual Learning

Have students look at the symbols on the key of the fossil map. Point out that the key shows symbols for the fossils pictured on the first three pages of the field guide. Have students locate your area on the map and identify the types of fossils found there. Fossil types will depend on your geographic location. Then have them refer back to the photographs in the field guide of these fossils. Ask them to identify where most of the fossil organisms shown on this map lived. Most lived in oceans. Ask students what inference might be made from this information. Students might infer that much of the United States was covered by oceans at one point in time.

Extension

Have students use magazines, such as *Geotimes*, or the internet to research rules governing the removal of fossils from different locations—federal lands, state lands, and private lands. Ask them to also find out about problems encountered trying to enforce these various regulations. Have students make oral reports on what they find.

Fun Fact

Because shale is such a fine-grained rock, many of the detailed, well-preserved fossils of plants and animals are found in shale.

Inclusion Strategies

Visually Impaired Provide fossils or models of fossils for these students to handle. Ask them to describe the features of the fossil organisms.

Field Guides

About the Field Guide

- This field guide contains representative descriptions and photos of different types of clouds that enable the user to classify clouds based on shape and height.
- In using a field guide, students will apply steps of a scientific method as they observe, investigate, and draw conclusions.
- This field guide applies internationally—clouds are similar around the world.
- Encourage students to use the field guide outside the classroom.

Tie to Prior Knowledge

All students are familiar with clouds, but many may not have noticed that clouds are of certain identifiable types. Have students describe different types of clouds that they have noticed. Have them attempt to recall what the weather was like when each of the clouds was present.

Field Activity

Have students observe and identify clouds several times each day, looking for patterns. They may find that puffy clouds often develop in the afternoons, as warm air is pushed aloft. They may also find that clouds change height and shape as weather fronts approach and pass. Encourage students to discuss the relationships between the weather and the types of clouds observed and come to a consensus.

Clouds are like people—they come in many different sizes and shapes. Some tower thousands of meters in the sky. Others are like fragile wisps of cotton candy floating in the air. All clouds are formed by atmospheric conditions that in turn form Earth's weather. Using this field guide, you can learn to identify different types of clouds and try your hand at weather forecasting.

How Clouds Are Classified

Clouds are classified based on their shape and height. The height of a cloud is represented by the prefix used in its name. For example, a cirrocumulus (*cirro + cumulus*) cloud is a high cloud with a puffy shape.

Clouds

Key to Cloud Classification

The following symbols are used in this field guide to represent the height and shape of common clouds.

Key to Cloud Classification			
Height		**Shape**	
symbol	prefix	symbol	prefix
	Cirro Describes high clouds with bases starting above 6000 m.		**Cirrus** Latin meaning: hair Describes wispy, stringy clouds
	Alto Describes middle clouds with bases between 2000 m to 6000 m.		**Cumulus** Latin meaning: pile or heap. Describes puffy, lumpy-looking clouds
			Stratus Latin meaning: layer Describes featureless sheets of clouds
	Strato Refers to low clouds below 2000 m.		**Nimbus** Latin meaning: cloud Describes low, gray rain clouds

Field Activity

For a week, use this field guide to help you identify the clouds in your area. Observe the clouds two to three times each day. In your Science Journal, record the date, time, types of clouds observed, and the general weather conditions. What relationships can you infer between the weather and types of clouds that are present?

Resources for Teachers and Students

The National Audubon Society Pocket Guide: Clouds and Storms, by Ron Holle and Richard A. Keen, Alfred A. Knopf, Inc., 1995.

Clouds, by Gail Saunders-Smith, Pebble Books, 1998.

Weather for Dummies, by John D. Cox, IDG Books Worldwide, 2000.

Watching Weather, by Tom Murphree, Henry Holt & Company, 1998.

The Weather Wizard's Cloud Book: How You Can Forecast the Weather Accurately and Easily by Reading the Clouds, by Louis D. Rubin, Jim Duncan, and Hiram J. Herbert; Algonquin Books of Chapel Hill, 1988.

Quick Demo

Use an aquarium with a glass or clear-plastic lid, bags of cold sand or marbles, and a pan of hot water to demonstrate cloud formation at a cold front. Place the pan of hot water inside the aquarium next to the cold bags. Cover the aquarium with the lid. Have students observe what happens. They will notice that condensation occurs on the sides and top of the aquarium, and clouds appear above the cold bags. No cloud forms above the pan because the temperature of the air prevents condensation.
LS Visual-Spatial

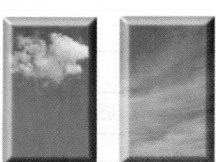

Cirrus

Feathery cirrus clouds are the highest clouds. They are formed of ice crystals. They usually signal fair weather, but they also can be a sign of changing weather.

Visual Learning

Have students compare and contrast the altitudes and shapes of the different stratus clouds shown on this page and the next. Cirrostratus are high clouds, altostratus are middle clouds, and nimbostratus are low clouds. All three types are layered sheets of clouds.

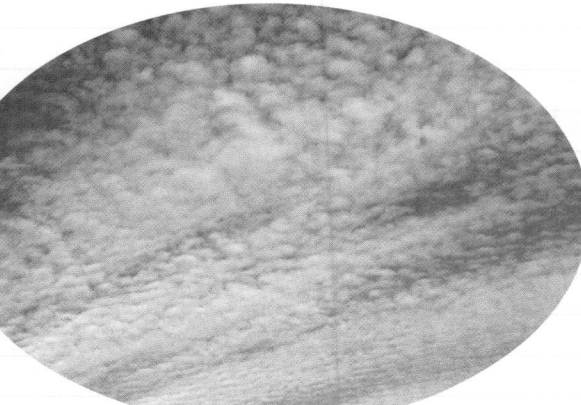

Cirrostratus

These thin, sheetlike clouds often form ahead of advancing storms, particularly if they're followed by middle clouds.

Fun Fact

In the 1800s sailors described the cloud sequence of a warm front as "cat tails" (cirrus) giving way to "flocks of sheep" (altocumulus) before developing into "cotton bales" (cumulus).

Cirrocumulus

Cirrocumulus clouds are small, rounded, white puffs. They appear individually or in long rows. Their rippled pattern resembles the scales of fish. Hence, a sky full of cirrocumulus clouds is called a mackerel sky.

SCIENCE *Online*
Internet Addresses

_____

_____

_____

Explore the Glencoe Science Web site at **science.glencoe.com** to find out more about topics in this field guide.

Teacher FYI

Because high-level clouds form at very cold elevation, they contain mainly ice crystals. Midlevel clouds contain mainly water droplets, but also may contain ice crystals. Lowlevel clouds contain ice crystals only when temperatures are cold enough.

Content Background

Luke Howard, an English pharmacist and amateur meteorologist, was the first to publish a classification system for clouds in 1803. The clouds were classified by shape. Howard used the Latin words for hair (cirrus), heap (cumulus), layer (stratus), and rain (nimbus) to describe the clouds in the sky. This new classification system caught on quickly because every type of cloud was self-descriptive. Howard's three primary classifications are still used; however, ten major cloud types are described in modern meteorology.

Use Science Words

Word Origins Have students use a dictionary to define the words *stratum* and *stratus* and identify the root word of both. Then have them compare the usage of these terms in biology, meteorology, and geology. Both words come from the Latin *sternere* meaning "to spread." In biology, stratum is a layer of tissue. In geology, strata are parallel layers of rocks. In meteorology, stratus clouds are layered clouds. L2 IS **Linguistic**

Extension

Challenge students to write a mnemonic device for remembering cloud types, cloud names, or cloud shapes. L1 IS **Linguistic**

Altostratus

Gray or blue-gray altostratus clouds—they're never white—often cover the entire sky. They are a sign of widespread, steady rain ahead.

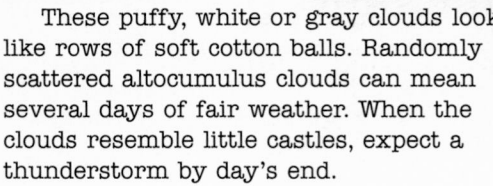
Altocumulus

These puffy, white or gray clouds look like rows of soft cotton balls. Randomly scattered altocumulus clouds can mean several days of fair weather. When the clouds resemble little castles, expect a thunderstorm by day's end.

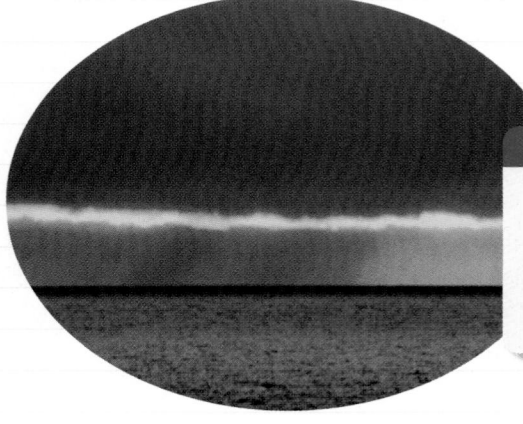

Nimbostratus

Dark-gray nimbostratus clouds are associated with steady rain or snow. This precipitation is light to moderate—rarely heavy. Nimbostratus clouds often have streaks that extend to the ground.

Inclusion Strategies

Learning Disabled Have students write descriptive sentences or poems about the shape, color, and movement of the clouds. Encourage students to illustrate their sentences or poems, and display the descriptions in class. L1 IS **Linguistic and Visual-Spatial**

Fun Fact

In parts of Alaska, Canada, and Siberia, air near the ground can be cold enough for water vapor to change directly to tiny ice crystals, forming ice fog. Herds of caribou sometimes become hidden in ice fog caused by their own breathing.

Stratus

Low-lying stratus clouds cover the sky in a blanket of gray. Light rain or drizzle usually accompanies these clouds.

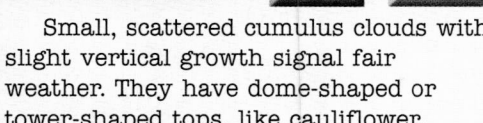

Stratocumulus

Low, lumpy stratocumulus clouds are often a sign of fair weather. To distinguish them from altocumulus clouds, extend your arm toward the cloud. An altocumulus cloud will be roughly the size of your thumbnail. A stratocumulus cloud will be about the size of your fist.

Cumulus

Small, scattered cumulus clouds with slight vertical growth signal fair weather. They have dome-shaped or tower-shaped tops, like cauliflower.

Cumulonimbus

These are thunderstorm clouds. They form near Earth's surface and grow to nearly 18,000 m. Lightning, thunder, and strong winds are associated with cumulonimbus clouds.

FIELD GUIDE 789

Discussion

Write the following folk-lore sayings about the clouds on the board: *A round-topped cloud with flattened base carries rainfall in its face. If the clouds be bright, t'will clear tonight. If the clouds be dark, t'will rain, you hark.* Ask students to infer what types of clouds are referred to in each saying. cumulonimbus; nimbostratus Then have them discuss whether the saying is accurate.

Extension

Have students investigate other, less common cloud types. Some suggested types are listed here.

- Contrails: a cirruslike trail of condensed water vapor produced by jet aircraft at high altitudes
- Kelvin-Helmholtz clouds: wavelike clouds that form as a result of a strong wind speed change between two adjoining layers of air
- mammatus clouds: pouchlike clouds normally seen on the underside of cumulonimbus clouds
- orographic clouds: clouds formed by air being forced up by topographical features such as mountains
- pileus clouds: clouds attached to either a growing cumulus tower or the top of a high topographical feature

Curriculum Connection

Art Have students make a bulletin-board sky, showing and labeling each of the major types of clouds. For the next two weeks, have them attach a "Today's Clouds" sign to the type of cloud present at class time. The sign can be moved throughout the day as the types of clouds change. **IS Visual-Spatial**

GUIDE

About the Field Guide
- A field guide enables the user to classify or identify an item or concept.
- In using a field guide, students apply steps of a scientific method as they observe, investigate, and draw conclusions.
- This Waste Management field guide applies nationally; local and regional fields guides are usually available for more specific local use.
- Encourage students to use the field guide outside.

Tie to Prior Knowledge
Have students recall items they have used so far today that are made of recyclable plastics. Have them bring in empty, plastic soft-drink bottles, milk jugs and other plastic items and show the recycling code that is imprinted on each item.

Field Activity

Numbers are placed on plastic products by recyclers to indicate the type of plastic resin used in their manufacture. The Plastics Code System is presented in **Table 1**. It is the basis for sorting plastics sent for recycling, but does not necessarily mean they are recyclable. The largest percentage should be Code 4; the smallest, Code 7. Have students research to find out what, if any, uses there are for each code of reclaimed plastic.

GUIDE

Managing waste properly can reduce the use of resources and prevent pollution. To cut down on waste production and reduce harm to the environment, people can follow the three Rs of waste management: reduce, reuse, and recycle. For example, a 450-g, family-sized box of cereal uses a lot less cardboard than 18 25-g single-serving boxes use. Finding other functions for used items could include donating magazines that you already have read to local hospitals, nursing homes, or even your doctor's office. You can use many products every day that are recyclable. Also, you can help complete the cycle by purchasing items that are made from recycled materials.

Types of Recyclables
Recycled items are either pre- or post-consumer. Pre-consumer items are made of pieces that were left over during manufacturing. Pre-consumer items have never been used by a consumer. Post-consumer items are made of products that have been used, recycled, and made into something new. Cereal boxes, plastic bottles, writing paper, paper towels, and tissues often include post-consumer recycled materials.

Waste Management

Paper

White paper, newspaper, magazines, and telephone books are common paper goods that can be recycled. New products made from these items include newsprint, cardboard, egg cartons, and building materials. Not all glossy and colored papers are recyclable at all recycling centers. As with any recycled material, you should check with your local recycling center for specific instructions about properly sorting your paper goods.

Field Activity

Collect recyclable plastics in your school for one week. Using the Plastics Code System Table, organize the plastic products by code number so that they can be recycled. In your Science Journal, make a bar graph showing the amount and types of plastic you collected.

Resources for Teachers and Students

Use Less Stuff: Environmental Solutions for Who We Really Are, by Robert M. Lilienfeld and William L. Rathje, Fawcett Rook Group, 1998.

The McGraw-Hill Recycling Handbook, by Herbert F. Lund, McGraw-Hill Professional Book Group, 2000.

The Toilet Papers: Recycling Waste and Conserving Water, by Sim Van der Ryn, Chelsea Green Publishing, 2000.

Plastics

Plastics are difficult products to recycle. Most plastics are composed of complex molecules that tend not to break down easily. Many types of plastics exist, and they often cannot be recycled together. **Table 1** lists the codes that are used to sort plastic items for recycling. Plastic is recycled into lumber, containers, carpet, and other products.

Table 1	The Plastics Code System	
Code	**Material**	
1	PETE	Polyethylene terephthalate
2	HDPE	High-density polyethylene
3	PVC	Polyvinyl chloride
4	LDPE	Low-density polyethylene
5	PP	Polypropylene
6	PS	Polystyrene
7	Other	All others and mixed

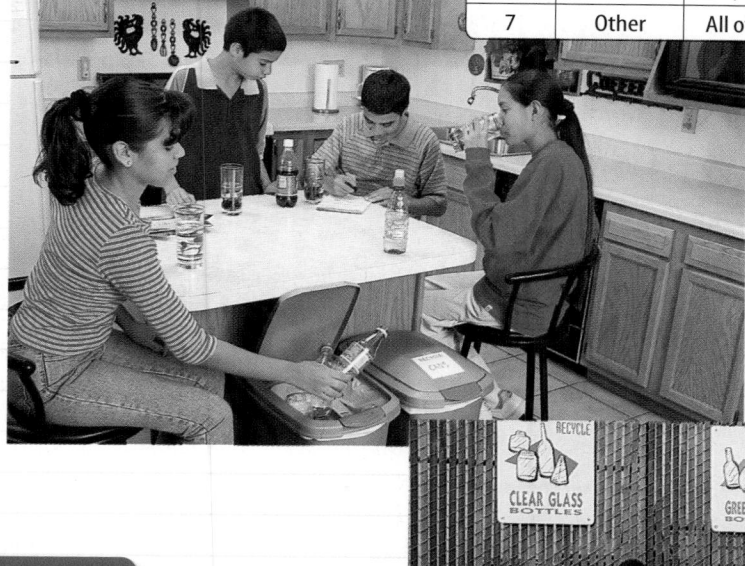

Glass

Glass often is separated by color before recycling. Most glass bottles are recyclable, but some glassware such as lightbulbs is too thin to be recycled. New products made from recycled glass include food and beverage containers.

FIELD GUIDE 791

Activity

Have students work in groups to hunt for classroom items that could be recycled. Eventually, call a halt to the search and ask a member from each group to write the results on the board. Have the class compare and discuss the results. Additionally, discuss with them the fate of any hazardous wastes that might be generated in their science classroom.

Extension

Challenge students to find out what recycling programs are actually in place in their school. Of the items the class found that could be recycled, which ones will be recycled? Have students present their findings to the class.

Content Background

Code 2 plastic, also known as HDPE (high density polyethylene) is the most useful kind for recycling. Among other things, it is used to make translucent, milk jugs. Because of its neutral color, it can be changed into various colors during recycling. During recycling, bales of HDPE are broken and ground into small flakes about 1 cm in diameter. The small flakes are washed and floated in a solution to remove heavy impurities. The clean, plastic pieces are then dried by hot air and packaged to be used for the production of plastic pipes, traffic cones, plastic lumbers, combs, trash cans, and bottles for holding materials other than food.

Use Science Words

Word Meaning The first six code numbers of plastic are also referred to by what type of plastic they contain. Some terms used to describe recyclable plastics are common. For example, plastic code 6 is also called PS (polystyrene). This type of plastic may be familiar to students. It is commonly used in Styrofoam cups, food trays, and other packaging.

Content Background

The billions of microbes in a compost pile digest yard and kitchen wastes and create productive soil. Sometimes worms and insects help them. It is important to note that some organic wastes must never go into a compost pile. Chemically treated wood products can contain toxic levels of arsenic, chromium and copper. Diseased plants can infect a garden. Human and pet wastes can transmit diseases. Pernicious weeds can multiply in a new garden. Meat, bones, and fatty food wastes are slow to break down and will attract pests, including rodents.

Visual Learning

Ask students to examine the cans shown on this page. Have them try to identify the type of metal each is made of, and make a list of items in their homes made of this type of metal. Discuss whether any of the items at home might be further recycled.

Field Guide

Field Guide

Metals

A variety of metals are recyclable. Steel is the most common material recycled in the United States. Steel is recycled into any item new steel would be used for such as food cans, structural beams for buildings, and parts for automobiles. Aluminum is a commonly recycled material. It is recycled into new beverage cans, lawn chair frames, siding, and cookware. Even precious metals that are used in laboratories or in jewelry such as gold, silver, and platinum are recyclable. Recycling steel saves enough energy to supply one-fifth of the households in the United States (18 million homes) electricity for one year. A recycled aluminum beverage can uses 95 percent less energy to produce than a can made from new aluminum, which is enough energy to burn a 100W light bulb for three and a half ($3\frac{1}{2}$) hours.

Organic Waste

Organic waste such as yard trimmings, food waste, paper, and wood make up a large percentage of solid waste in the United States. Composting is one way to recycle organic wastes. Food and yard wastes can be placed in compost bins and converted into nutrient rich soil. Mulching is another way to recycle yard waste and wood. In some communities grass clippings, leaves, sticks, and other yard waste can be shredded at local recycling centers to make mulch. Mulch is used to reduce water loss from soil and to keep weeds from growing. As the mulch decays it enriches the soil.

792 STUDENT RESOURCES

Inclusion Strategies

Learning Disabled Have students visit several restaurants near their homes or their school. Have them meet with the restaurant manager or staff and determine what glass or metallic materials are used. Have students collect samples of the recyclable products used by the restaurants and determine how they should be separated for recycling.

Household Hazardous Wastes

Household Hazardous Wastes (HHWs) include household and car batteries, bleach, household cleaners, paint, paint thinner, motor oil, gasoline, herbicides, pesticides, solvents, and automotive fluids. They contain chemicals that can cause injury or are harmful if used, stored, or discarded improperly. HHWs are marked with a skull and crossbones, caution words or special handling directions. HHWs should not be sent with other garbage to landfills or to incinerators. Water seeps into landfill areas and the toxins could end up in the water supply. Burning may send toxins into the air you breathe. Garbage companies and recycling agencies have free HHW drop-off days or locations.

Follow These Steps to Reduce HHWs:

1. Whenever possible, buy nontoxic alternatives to hazardous products.
2. If you buy a hazardous product, buy only what you need to do the job.
3. Before you store leftover products on the shelf, try to find someone who can use them.

FIELD GUIDE   793

Curriculum Connection

Health Mercury is a hazardous waste that can make its way into water supplies and has caused serious health problems in humans who depend on local water. Research to find a significant episode of mercury pollution in terms of human health. Report on your findings to the class.

Quick Demo

Place a number of common household products that are HHWs on a table. Lift each one and ask those who have the product in their homes to raise their hands. Read the special handling instructions on the packaging and ask students what precautions they take in handling each product. Include items like flashlight batteries, a bottle of bleach, drain cleaner, a medical thermometer, and an aerosol can of insect killer.

Use Science Words

Word Meaning Have students use the word *toxin* in a sentence describing its characteristics. Possible answer: A poisonous substance harmful to living things is a toxin.

Discussion

Finding nontoxic alternatives to hazardous products is often easier than you might think. For example, baking soda and hydrogen peroxide can perform a similar function to chlorine-based scouring powder. **What other alternatives to hazardous household products can you think of?** Possible answers might include: using rechargeable batteries, using a plumber's "snake" to clear a clogged drain instead of using drain cleaner, buying citronella candles to ward off mosquitoes, buying a digital, non-mercury thermometer.

Field GUIDE

About the Field Guide

- This field guide contains star charts for the northern hemisphere for autumn, winter, and spring.
- A field guide contains a key that enables the user to classify or identity and item or concept.
- Encourage students to use this Backyard Astronomy field guide outside the classroom.

Tie to Prior Knowledge

What far away things do you see when you look up at the sky at night? Possible answers: stars, constellations, planets **Name some constellations.** Possible answers: Orion, Hercules; answers might include asterisms, such as the Big Dipper, which are not constellations.

Field Activity

Review with students how to orient the star map. Direct students to view the night sky with an adult. Suggest that students who live within cities or near other bright lights go to a darker area for their observations, if possible. Student drawings will vary depending on the constellations chosen.

Field GUIDE

For thousands of years, people have looked at the night sky and wondered about what they saw. To early Greek and Roman astronomers, groups of stars seemed to form pictures of animals, heroes, and other characters in myths. These star groups are called **constellations.** Constellations have guided travelers and have been an important part of some religions for a long time.

The Stars of the Zodiac

Are you a Leo, a Libra, a Capricorn, or a Virgo? The sign you were born under represents the constellation that the Sun was in at the moment of your first breath. What are the Zodiac signs, and why are they represented as constellations in the sky?

The Ancient Greeks noticed that the planets moved along a path in the sky. They also noticed star groups behind the revolving planets. They divided this path in the sky into 12 equal sectors, or divisions, and named them according to the star group that is found there. For example, Leo is a constellation resembling a lion; Aries is a ram. Ancient people referred to these star groups as the *Zodiac,* which means "little zoo" in Greek.

794 STUDENT RESOURCES

Backyard Astronomy

Big Dipper

Ursa Major

You've probably heard of the Big Dipper and even found it in the night sky. The Big Dipper is not a constellation. It's one part of a large constellation named Ursa Major, which is Latin for "Great Bear." The next time you look at 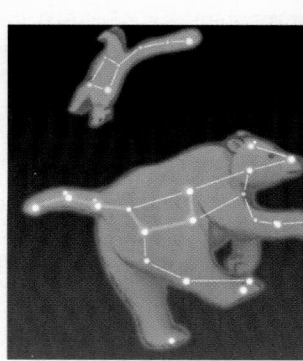 the night sky, find the Big Dipper. Then try to find the rest of the stars that form the Great Bear.

The Great Bear is just one of 88 identified constellations. You can't see all 88 constellations from the northern hemisphere, which is where you live. Some constellations are visible only in the northern hemisphere, and others are visible only in the southern hemisphere.

Field Activity

Observe the sky each night at the same time for a week. Use the appropriate star map and the instructions on the third page of this Field Guide to find the Big Dipper, Little Dipper, and Polaris. Then find at least three constellations. Draw the constellations in your Science Journal and label them with their names.

Resources for Teachers and Students

Your Guide to the Sky, by Rick Shaffer, RGA Publishing Group, 1994.

My First Pocket Guide: Constellations, by Patricia Daniels, National Geographic Society, 2000.

Constellations, by Diane M. Sipiera and Paul P. Sipiera, Children's Press, 1997.

See the Stars: Your First Guide to the Night Sky, by Ken Croswell, Boyds Mill Press, 2000.

Walk Through the Heavens: A Guide to Stars and Constellations, by Milton D. Heifetz, Cambridge University Press, 1997.

Constellations

The constellations always are in the same part of the sky, but they appear to move over time. As Earth rotates on its polar axis, the constellations appear to move from east to west across the sky each night. As Earth revolves around the Sun and the seasons change, some constellations come into view and others move out of view. For example, in the northern hemisphere, you can see Orion in winter and spring but not during summer and autumn. Pegasus is visible in autumn and winter but not in spring and summer. Other constellations, including Cassiopeia (ka see uh PEE uh) and the Great Bear, are visible to you all year.

In the northern hemisphere, all of the constellations rotate in a big circle around a bright star called Polaris, the North Star, which lies at the tail end of a group of stars called the Little Dipper. The Little Dipper is part of a constellation called Ursa Minor, which is Latin for "Little Bear." Ancient sailors used the North Star to navigate the oceans and find their way home.

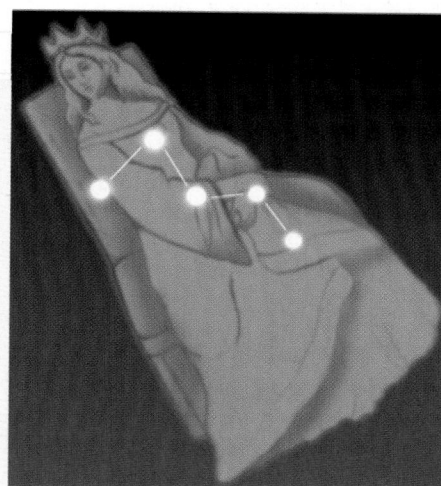

To find Cassiopeia, look for five bright stars that form a large *W* or a large *M*.

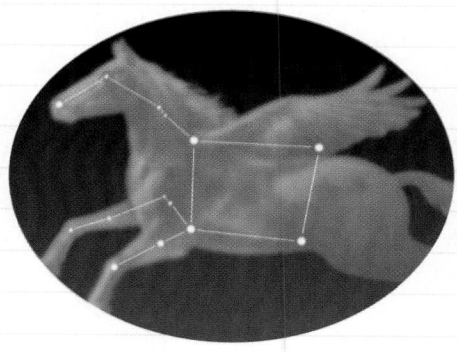

To find Pegasus, look for four bright stars that form a large square.

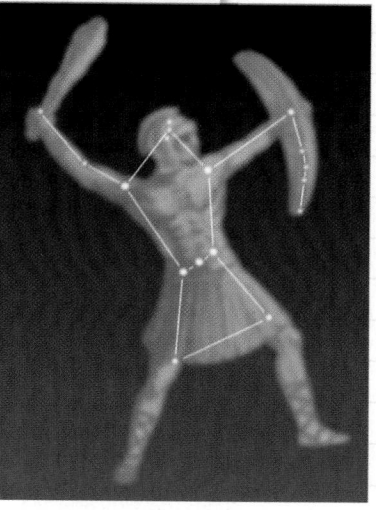

To find Orion, look for three bright stars close together in a straight line. These stars form Orion's belt.

FIELD GUIDE 795

Content Background

In modern astronomy, a constellation includes not only the stars of its shape but also other stars and galaxies. Astronomers have mapped the sky so that every visible object belongs to one of 88 constellations, 54 of which are visible from the northern hemisphere. Some constellations include a distinct star group that is recognizable and named. These star groups are called asterisms. The Big Dipper is an asterism within the constellation Ursa Major. The Little Dipper, in the constellation Ursa Minor, is another asterism.

Quick Demo

On a globe, point out your exact latitude. Explain that latitude can be used to find Polaris. For example, if you live at latitude 40°N, then Polaris will be positioned 40° above your northern horizon. Polaris, in turn, can be used to locate northern circumpolar constellations. Show students how to make several approximate angular measurements using a hand held at arm's length:

    2° = width of thumb
    5° = length of thumb
   10° = length of closed fist
   15° = length of closed fist with
         thumb extended

LS Visual-Spatial

Curriculum Connection

Social Studies Have students research cultural myths about some of the constellations. They might consider Greek, Hawaiian, Native American, Chinese, Babylonian, or other cultures. Have each student make a booklet that includes favorite myths along with drawings that illustrate them. Ask volunteers to make oral presentations of their myths. [L2] **LS Visual-Spatial and Linguistic**

Content Background

The celestial sphere is the imaginary dome on which the stars appear in the night sky. Each person's zenith is the imaginary point on the celestial sphere located directly above his or her head. An imaginary line drawn from the northern horizon up through the zenith, then down to the southern horizon, traces the celestial median. The celestial median is used to locate the constellations of each season.

Visual Learning

Seasonal Star Charts Direct students to locate Ursa Major in each of the three seasonal charts. Have them describe the apparent path of the constellation from autumn through spring. It appears to move southeastward. Stress that the apparent change in position is the result of Earth's movement in space, not the actual movement of the stars.

Fun Fact

Pegasus is named for a flying horse owned by the Greek hero Perseus. The constellation Perseus can be found next to Andromeda, the maiden he rescued from a sea monster.

How to Find Constellations

Use these instructions to find constellations in the sky. The only time you'll be able to see the stars well is on a clear night without bright moonlight or light from buildings.

1. Choose the star map that shows the night sky for the season it is now. Take this book and a compass outside with you.
2. Use the compass to determine which direction is north and stand facing that way. Turn the star map so the word *North* is right-side up. Compare the star patterns on the map with the stars you see in the northern sky. Find the Big Dipper. Use the picture on the first page of the field guide to help you.
3. Find the two stars that form the outer side of the Big Dipper's bowl. Imagine a line that connects those two stars and extends straight up from the dipper's bowl. Follow that line until you find a bright star. That star is Polaris, the North Star.
4. Starting from Polaris, find the stars that form the Little Bear. Find the stars that form the Great Bear.
5. Use the star map to find other constellations in the northern sky.
6. Turn around to face south. Turn the star map so the word *South* is right-side up. Use the map to find constellations in the southern sky.
7. Repeat step 6 facing west, then east.
8. As you search, try to find Cassiopeia. Look for Orion and/or Pegasus depending on the season. Use the star map and the pictures on the second page of the field guide to help you.

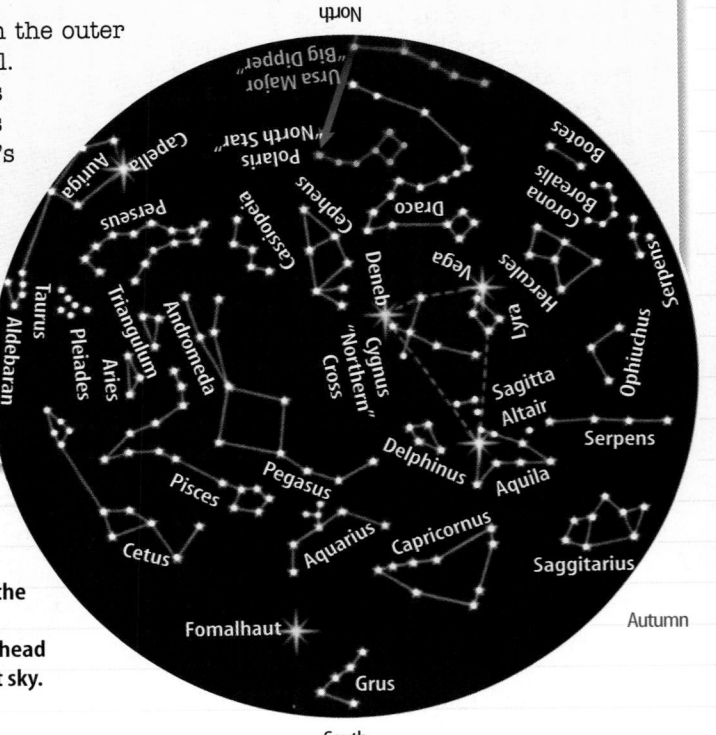

Cygnus (SIHG nus), the "northern cross," is almost directly overhead in the autumn night sky.

796   STUDENT RESOURCES

Explore the Glencoe Science Web site at **science.glencoe.com** to find out more about topics in this field guide.

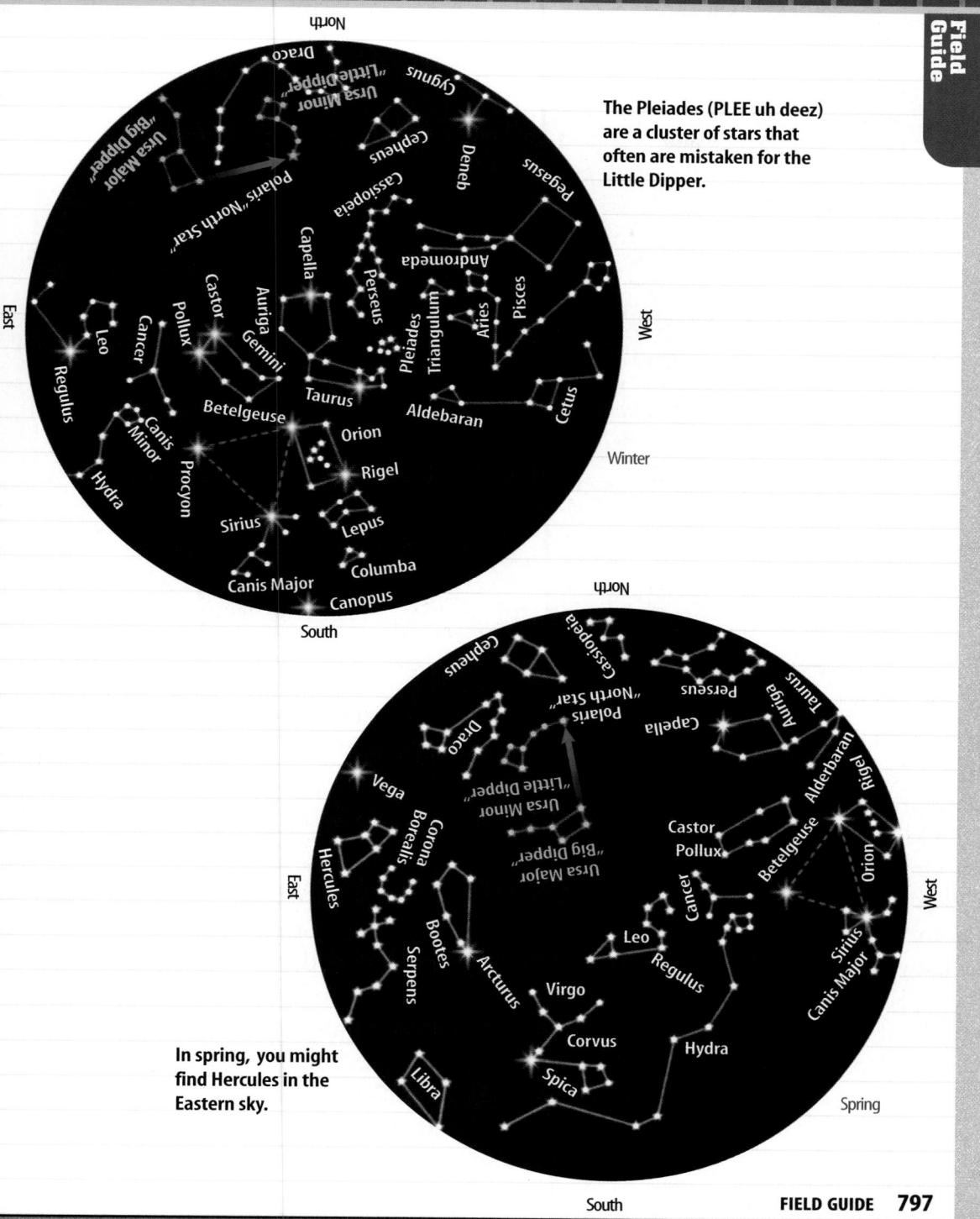

The Pleiades (PLEE uh deez) are a cluster of stars that often are mistaken for the Little Dipper.

Winter

In spring, you might find Hercules in the Eastern sky.

Spring

Activity

Obtain a circumpolar star chart showing constellations of the southern hemisphere. Have students compare and contrast the locations of circumpolar constellations in the northern and southern hemispheres. L2 IS **Visual-Spatial**

Fun Fact

The most famous constellation in the southern hemisphere is Crux, commonly known as the Southern Cross. Its four main stars form a distinct cross or diamond shape. Crux is on the flag of Australia, as well as on flags of many other countries in the southern hemisphere.

Activity

Have small groups of students use sheets of black construction paper and chalk to mark the positions of stars in various constellations. Then have them use a sharpened pencil to make a large hole at the position of each star. In a darkened room, allow each group to shine the light from a projector through the holes in each sheet of paper, so that the image of the constellation is projected on the board. Challenge members of other groups to identify each constellation as it is being projected. L1 IS **Visual-Spatial**

Inclusion Strategies

Learning Disabled Draw the stars of various constellations on the board. Use lines to connect the stars within each constellation. Have students draw around the connecting lines pictures of the objects each constellation represents. IS **Visual-Spatial**

Skill Handbooks

Organizing Information

As you study science, you will make many observations and conduct investigations and experiments. You will also research information that is available from many sources. These activities will involve organizing and recording data. The quality of the data you collect and the way you organize it will determine how well others can understand and use it. In **Figure 1,** the student is obtaining and recording information using a thermometer.

Putting your observations in writing is an important way of communicating to others the information you have found and the results of your investigations and experiments.

Researching Information

Scientists work to build on and add to human knowledge of the world. Before moving in a new direction, it is important to gather the information that already is known about a subject. You will look for such information in various reference sources. Follow these steps to research information on a scientific subject:

Step 1 Determine exactly what you need to know about the subject. For instance, you might want to find out what happened when Mount St. Helens erupted in 1980.

Step 2 Make a list of questions, such as: When did the eruption begin? How long did it last? What kind of material was expelled and how much?

Step 3 Use multiple sources such as textbooks, encyclopedias, government documents, professional journals, science magazines, and the Internet.

Step 4 List where you found the sources. Make sure the sources you use are reliable and the most current available.

Figure 1
Collecting data is one way to gather information directly.

Evaluating Print and Nonprint Sources

Not all sources of information are reliable. Evaluate the sources you use for information, and use only those you know to be dependable. For example, suppose you live in an area where earthquakes are common and you want to know what to do to keep safe. You might find two Web sites on earthquake safety. One Web site contains "Earthquake Tips" written by a company that sells metal scrapings to help secure your hot-water tank to the wall. The other is a Web page on "Earthquake Safety" written by the U.S. Geological Survey. You would choose the second Web site as the more reliable source of information.

In science, information can change rapidly. Always consult the most current sources. A 1985 source about the Moon would not reflect the most recent research and findings.

Interpreting Scientific Illustrations

As you research a science topic, you will see drawings, diagrams, and photographs. Illustrations help you understand what you read. Some illustrations are included to help you understand an idea that you can't see easily by yourself. For instance, you can't see the layers of Earth, but you can look at a diagram of Earth's layers, as labeled in **Figure 2,** that helps you understand what the layers are and where they are located. Visualizing a drawing helps many people remember details more easily. Illustrations also provide examples that clarify difficult concepts or give additional information about the topic you are studying.

Most illustrations have a label or caption. A label or caption identifies the illustration or provides additional information to better explain it. Can you find the caption or labels in **Figure 2?**

Figure 2
This cross section shows a slice through Earth's interior and the positions of its layers.

Concept Mapping

If you were taking a car trip, you might take some sort of road map. By using a map, you begin to learn where you are in relation to other places on the map.

A concept map is similar to a road map, but a concept map shows relationships among ideas (or concepts) rather than places. It is a diagram that visually shows how concepts are related. Because a concept map shows relationships among ideas, it can make the meanings of ideas and terms clear and help you understand what you are studying.

Overall, concept maps are useful for breaking large concepts down into smaller parts, making learning easier.

Venn Diagram

Although it is not a concept map, a Venn diagram illustrates how two subjects compare and contrast. In other words, you can see the characteristics that the subjects have in common and those that they do not.

The Venn diagram in **Figure 3** shows the relationship between two types of rocks made from the same basic chemical. Both rocks share the chemical calcium carbonate. However, due to the way they are formed, one rock is the sedimentary rock limestone, and the other is the metamorphic rock marble.

Figure 3
A Venn diagram shows how objects or concepts are alike and how they are different.

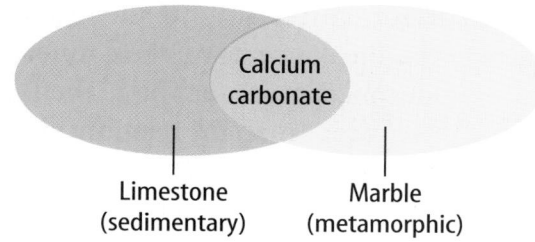

Calcium carbonate

Limestone (sedimentary)   Marble (metamorphic)

Skill Handbooks

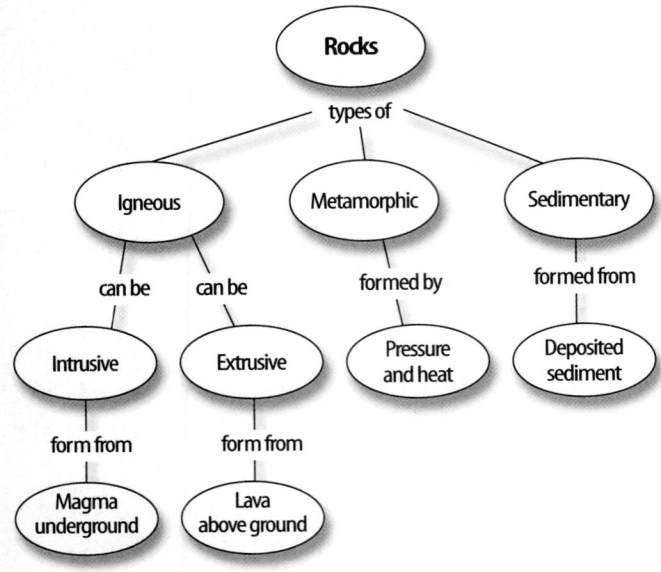

Figure 4
A network tree shows how concepts or objects are related.

Network Tree Look at the concept map in **Figure 4,** that shows the three main types of rock. This is called a network tree concept map. Notice how some words are in ovals while others are written across connecting lines. The words inside the ovals are science terms or concepts. The words written on the connecting lines describe the relationships between the concepts.

When constructing a network tree, write the topic on a note card or piece of paper. Write the major concepts related to that topic on separate note cards or pieces of paper. Then arrange them in order from general to specific. Branch the related concepts from the major concept and describe the relationships on the connecting lines. Continue branching to more specific concepts. Write the relationships between the concepts on the connecting lines until all concepts are mapped. Then examine the concept map for relationships that cross branches, and add them to the concept map.

Events Chain An events chain is another type of concept map. It models the order of items or their sequence. In science, an events chain can be used to describe a sequence of events, the steps in a procedure, or the stages of a process.

When making an events chain, first find the one event that starts the chain. This event is called the *initiating event.* Then, find the next event in the chain and continue until you reach an outcome. Suppose you are asked to describe why and how a sound might make an echo. You might draw an events chain such as the one in **Figure 5.** Notice that connecting words are not necessary in an events chain.

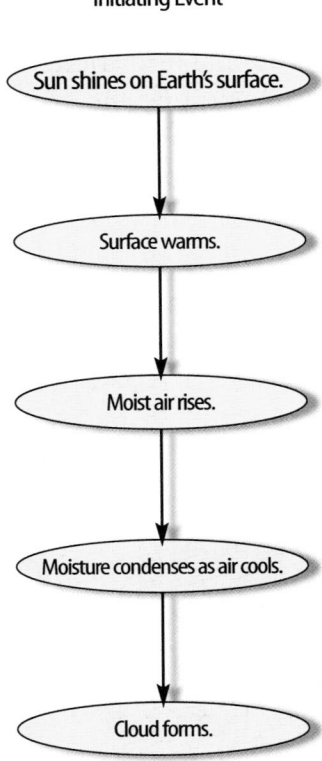

Figure 5
Events chains show the order of steps in a process or event.

Cycle Map A cycle concept map is a specific type of events chain map. In a cycle concept map, the series of events does not produce a final outcome. Instead, the last event in the chain relates back to the beginning event.

You first decide what event will be used as the beginning event. Once that is decided, you list events in order that occur after it. Words are written between events that describe what happens from one event to the next. The last event in a cycle concept map relates back to the beginning event. The number of events in a cycle concept varies, but is usually three or more. Look at the cycle map, as shown in **Figure 6.**

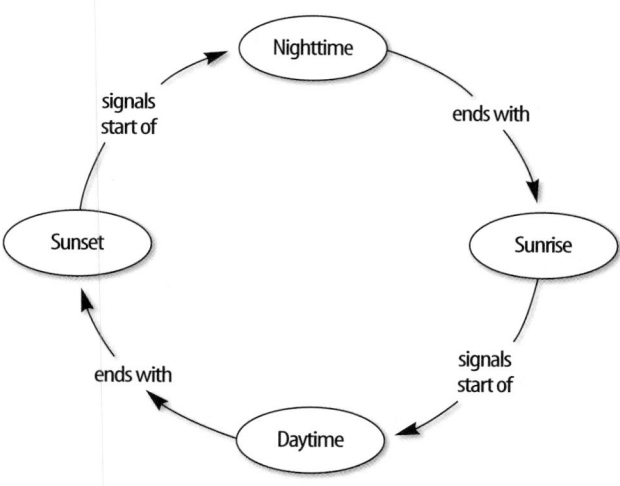

Figure 6
A cycle map shows events that occur in a cycle.

Spider Map A type of concept map that you can use for brainstorming is the spider map. When you have a central idea, you might find you have a jumble of ideas that relate to it but are not necessarily clearly related to each other. The spider map on sound in **Figure 7** shows that if you write these ideas outside the main concept, then you can begin to separate and group un-related terms so they become more useful.

Figure 7
A spider map allows you to list ideas that relate to a central topic but not necessarily to one another.

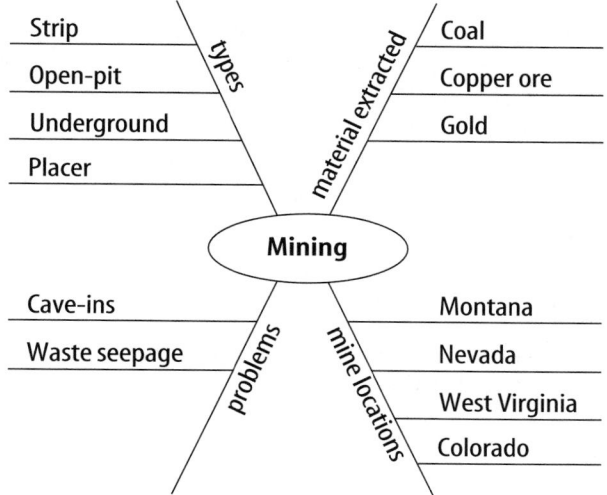

Writing a Paper

You will write papers often when researching science topics or reporting the results of investigations or experiments. Scientists frequently write papers to share their data and conclusions with other scientists and the public. When writing a paper, use these steps.

Step 1 Assemble your data by using graphs, tables, or a concept map. Create an outline.

Step 2 Start with an introduction that contains a clear statement of purpose and what you intend to discuss or prove.

Step 3 Organize the body into paragraphs. Each paragraph should start with a topic sentence, and the remaining sentences in that paragraph should support your point.

Step 4 Position data to help support your points.

Step 5 Summarize the main points and finish with a conclusion statement.

Step 6 Use tables, graphs, charts, and illustrations whenever possible.

Skill Handbooks

You might say the work of a scientist is to solve problems. When you decide to find out why one corner of your yard is always soggy, you are problem solving, too. You might observe the corner is lower than the surrounding area and has less vegetation growing in it. You might decide to see whether planting some grass will keep the corner drier.

Scientists use orderly approaches to solve problems. The methods scientists use include identifying a question, making observations, forming a hypothesis, testing a hypothesis, analyzing results, and drawing conclusions.

Scientific investigations involve careful observation under controlled conditions. Such observation of an object or a process can suggest new and interesting questions about it. These questions sometimes lead to the formation of a hypothesis. Scientific investigations are designed to test a hypothesis.

Identifying a Question

The first step in a scientific investigation or experiment is to identify a question to be answered or a problem to be solved. You might be interested in knowing why a rock like the one in **Figure 8** looks the way it does.

Figure 8
When you find a rock, you might ask yourself, "How did this rock form?"

Forming Hypotheses

Hypotheses are based on observations that have been made. A hypothesis is a possible explanation based on previous knowledge and observations.

Perhaps a scientist has observed that thunderstorms happen more often on hot days than on cooler days. Based on these observations, the scientist can make a statement that he or she can test. The statement is a hypothesis. The hypothesis could be: *Warm temperatures cause thunderstorms.* A hypothesis has to be something you can test by using an investigation. A testable hypothesis is a valid hypothesis.

Predicting

When you apply a hypothesis, or general explanation, to a specific situation, you predict something about that situation. First, you must identify which hypothesis fits the situation you are considering. People use predictions to make everyday decisions. Based on previous observations and experiences, you might form a prediction that if warm temperatures cause thunderstorms, then more thunderstorms will occur in summer months than in spring months. Someone could use these predictions to plan when to take a camping trip or when to schedule an outdoor activity.

Testing a Hypothesis

To test a hypothesis, you need a procedure. A procedure is the plan you follow in your experiment. A procedure tells you what materials to use, as well as how and in what order to use them. When you follow a procedure, data are generated that support or do not support the original hypothesis statement.

For example, premium gasoline costs more than regular gasoline. Does premium gasoline increase the efficiency or fuel mileage of your family car? You decide to test the hypothesis: "If premium gasoline is more efficient, then it should increase the fuel mileage of my family's car." Then you write the procedure shown in **Figure 9** for your experiment and generate the data presented in the table below.

Figure 9
A procedure tells you what to do step by step.

> **Procedure**
> 1. Use regular gasoline for two weeks.
> 2. Record the number of kilometers between fill-ups and the amount of gasoline used.
> 3. Switch to premium gasoline for two weeks.
> 4. Record the number of kilometers between fill-ups and the amount of gasoline used.

Gasoline Data			
Type of Gasoline	Kilometers Traveled	Liters Used	Liters per Kilometer
Regular	762	45.34	0.059
Premium	661	42.30	0.064

These data show that premium gasoline is less efficient than regular gasoline in one particular car. It took more gasoline to travel 1 km (0.064) using premium gasoline than it did to travel 1 km using regular gasoline (0.059). This conclusion does not support the hypothesis.

Are all investigations alike? Keep in mind as you perform investigations in science that a hypothesis can be tested in many ways. Not every investigation makes use of all the ways that are described on these pages, and not all hypotheses are tested by investigations. Scientists encounter many variations in the methods that are used when they perform experiments. The skills in this handbook are here for you to use and practice.

Identifying and Manipulating Variables and Controls

In any experiment, it is important to keep everything the same except for the item you are testing. The one factor you change is called the independent variable. The factor that changes as a result of the independent variable is called the dependent variable. Always make sure you have only one independent variable. If you allow more than one, you will not know what causes the changes you observe in the dependent variable. Many experiments also have controls—individual instances or experimental subjects for which the independent variable is not changed. You can then compare the test results to the control results.

For example, in the fuel-mileage experiment, you made everything the same except the type of gasoline that was used. The driver, the type of automobile, and the type of driving were the same throughout. In this way, you could be sure that any mileage differences were caused by the type of fuel—the independent variable. The fuel mileage was the dependent variable.

If you could repeat the experiment using several automobiles of the same type on a standard driving track with the same driver, you could make one automobile a control by using regular gasoline over the four-week period.

Collecting Data

Whether you are carrying out an investigation or a short observational experiment, you will collect data, or information. Scientists collect data accurately as numbers and descriptions and organize it in specific ways.

Observing Scientists observe items and events, then record what they see. When they use only words to describe an observation, it is called qualitative data. For example, a scientist might describe the color, texture, or odor of a substance produced in a chemical reaction. Scientists' observations also can describe how much there is of something. These observations use numbers, as well as words, in the description and are called quantitative data. For example, if a sample of the element gold is described as being "shiny and very dense," the data are clearly qualitative. Quantitative data on this sample of gold might include "a mass of 30 g and a density of 19.3 g/cm^3." Quantitative data often are organized into tables. Then, from information in the table, a graph can be drawn. Graphs can reveal relationships that exist in experimental data.

When you make observations in science, you should examine the entire object or situation first, then look carefully for details. If you're looking at a rock sample, for instance, check the general color and pattern of the rock before using a hand lens to examine the small mineral grains that make up its underlying structure. Remember to record accurately everything you see.

Scientists try to make careful and accurate observations. When possible, they use instruments such as microscopes, metric rulers, graduated cylinders, thermometers, and balances. Measurements provide numerical data that can be repeated and checked.

Sampling When working with large numbers of objects or a large population, scientists usually cannot observe or study every one of them. Instead, they use a sample or a portion of the total number. To *sample* is to take a small, representative portion of the objects or organisms of a population for research. By making careful observations or manipulating variables within a portion of a group, information is discovered and conclusions are drawn that might apply to the whole population.

Estimating Scientific work also involves estimating. To *estimate* is to make a judgment about the amount or the number of something without measuring every part of an object or counting every member of a population. Scientists first measure or count the amount or number in a small sample. A chemist, for example, might remove a 10-g piece of a large rock that is rich in copper ore, such as the one shown in **Figure 10.** Then the chemist can determine the percentage of copper by mass and multiply that percentage by the mass of the rock to get an estimate of the total mass of copper in the rock.

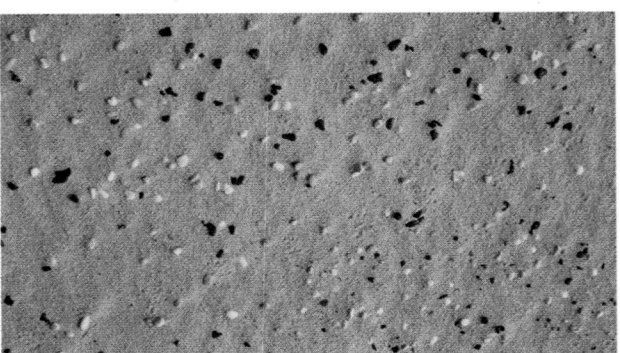

Figure 10
In a 1-meter frame positioned on a beach, count the pebbles that are longer than 2.5 cm. Multiply this number by the area of the beach. This will give you an estimate for the total number of pebbles on the beach.

Measuring in SI

The metric system of measurement was developed in 1795. A modern form of the metric system, called the International System, or SI, was adopted in 1960. SI provides standard measurements that all scientists around the world can understand.

The metric system is convenient because unit sizes vary by multiples of 10. When changing from smaller units to larger units, divide by a multiple of 10. When changing from larger units to smaller, multiply by a multiple of 10. To convert millimeters to centimeters, divide the millimeters by 10. To convert 30 mm to centimeters, divide 30 by 10 (30 mm equal 3 cm).

Prefixes are used to name units. Look at the table below for some common metric prefixes and their meanings. Do you see how the prefix *kilo-* attached to the unit *gram* is *kilogram*, or 1,000 g?

Metric Prefixes			
Prefix	**Symbol**	**Meaning**	
kilo-	k	1,000	thousand
hecto-	h	100	hundred
deka-	da	10	ten
deci-	d	0.1	tenth
centi-	c	0.01	hundredth
milli-	m	0.001	thousandth

Now look at the metric ruler shown in **Figure 11.** The centimeter lines are the long, numbered lines, and the shorter lines are millimeter lines.

When using a metric ruler, line up the 0-cm mark with the end of the object being measured, and read the number of the unit where the object ends, in this instance it would be 4.5 cm.

Figure 11
This metric ruler shows centimeters and millimeter divisions.

Liquid Volume In some science activities, you will measure liquids. The unit that is used to measure liquids is the liter. A liter has the volume of 1,000 cm³. The prefix *milli-* means "thousandth (0.001)." A milliliter is one thousandth of 1 L, and 1 L has the volume of 1,000 mL. One milliliter of liquid completely fills a cube measuring 1 cm on each side. Therefore, 1 mL equals 1 cm³.

You will use beakers and graduated cylinders to measure liquid volume. A graduated cylinder, as illustrated in **Figure 12,** is marked from bottom to top in milliliters. This one contains 79 mL of a liquid.

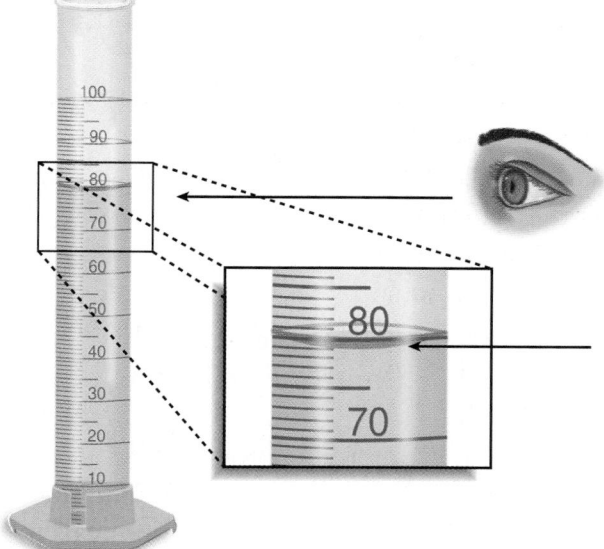

Figure 12
Graduated cylinders measure liquid volume.

Mass Scientists measure mass in grams. You might use a beam balance similar to the one shown in **Figure 13.** The balance has a pan on one side and a set of beams on the other side. Each beam has a rider that slides on the beam.

Before you find the mass of an object, slide all the riders back to the zero point. Check the pointer on the right to make sure it swings an equal distance above and below the zero point. If the swing is unequal, find and turn the adjusting screw until you have an equal swing.

Place an object on the pan. Slide the largest rider along its beam until the pointer drops below zero. Then move it back one notch. Repeat the process on each beam until the pointer swings an equal distance above and below the zero point. Sum the masses on each beam to find the mass of the object. Move all riders back to zero when finished.

Figure 13
A triple beam balance is used to determine the mass of an object.

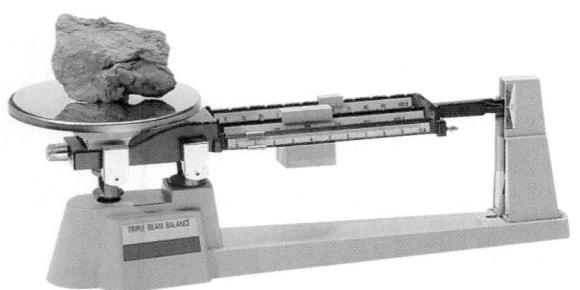

You should never place a hot object on the pan or pour chemicals directly onto the pan. Instead, find the mass of a clean container. Remove the container from the pan, then place the chemicals in the container. Find the mass of the container with the chemicals in it. To find the mass of the chemicals, subtract the mass of the empty container from the mass of the filled container.

Making and Using Tables

Browse through your textbook and you will see tables in the text and in the activities. In a table, data, or information, are arranged so that they are easier to understand. Activity tables help organize the data you collect during an activity so results can be interpreted.

Making Tables To make a table, list the items to be compared in the first column and the characteristics to be compared in the first row. The title should clearly indicate the content of the table, and the column or row heads should tell the reader what information is found in there. The table below lists materials collected for recycling on three weekly pick-up days. The inclusion of kilograms in parentheses also identifies for the reader that the figures are mass units.

Recyclable Materials Collected During Week			
Day of Week	Paper (kg)	Aluminum (kg)	Glass (kg)
Monday	5.0	4.0	12.0
Wednesday	4.0	1.0	10.0
Friday	2.5	2.0	10.0

Using Tables How much paper, in kilograms, is being recycled on Wednesday? Locate the column labeled "Paper (kg)" and the row "Wednesday." The information in the box where the column and row intersect is the answer. Did you answer "4.0"? How much aluminum, in kilograms, is being recycled on Friday? If you answered "2.0," you understand how to read the table. How much glass is collected for recycling each week? Locate the column labeled "Glass (kg)" and add the figures for all three rows. If you answered "32.0," then you know how to locate and use the data provided in the table.

Recording Data

To be useful, the data you collect must be recorded carefully. Accuracy is key. A well-thought-out experiment includes a way to record procedures, observations, and results accurately. Data tables are one way to organize and record results. Set up the tables you will need ahead of time so you can record the data right away.

Record information properly and neatly. Never put unidentified data on scraps of paper. Instead, data should be written in a notebook like the one in **Figure 14.** Write in pencil so information isn't lost if your data gets wet. At each point in the experiment, record your data and label it. That way, your information will be accurate and you will not have to determine what the figures mean when you look at your notes later.

Figure 14
Record data neatly and clearly so it is easy to understand.

Recording Observations

It is important to record observations accurately and completely. That is why you always should record observations in your notes immediately as you make them. It is easy to miss details or make mistakes when recording results from memory. Do not include your personal thoughts when you record your data. Record only what you observe to eliminate bias. For example, when you record the time required for five students to climb the same set of stairs, you would note which student took the longest time. However, you would not refer to that student's time as "the worst time of all the students in the group."

Making Models

You can organize the observations and other data you collect and record in many ways. Making models is one way to help you better understand the parts of a structure you have been observing or the way a process for which you have been taking various measurements works.

Models often show things that are too large or too small for normal viewing. For example, you normally won't see the inside of an atom. However, you can understand the structure of the atom better by making a three-dimensional model of an atom. The relative sizes, the positions, and the movements of protons, neutrons, and electrons can be explained in words. An atomic model made of a plastic-ball nucleus and pipe-cleaner electron shells can help you visualize how the parts of the atom relate to each other.

Other models can be devised on a computer. Some models, such as those that illustrate the chemical combinations of different elements, are mathematical and are represented by equations.

Science Skill Handbook

Making and Using Graphs

After scientists organize data in tables, they might display the data in a graph that shows the relationship of one variable to another. A graph makes interpretation and analysis of data easier. Three types of graphs are the line graph, the bar graph, and the circle graph.

Line Graphs A line graph like in **Figure 15** is used to show the relationship between two variables. The variables being compared go on two axes of the graph. For data from an experiment, the independent variable always goes on the horizontal axis, called the *x*-axis. The dependent variable always goes on the vertical axis, called the *y*-axis. After drawing your axes, label each with a scale. Next, plot the data points.

A data point is the intersection of the recorded value of the dependent variable for each tested value of the independent variable. After all the points are plotted, connect them.

Bar Graphs Bar graphs compare data that do not change continuously. Vertical bars show the relationships among data.

To make a bar graph, set up the *y*-axis as you did for the line graph. Draw vertical bars of equal size from the *x*-axis up to the point on the *y*-axis that represents value of *x*.

Figure 16
The amount of aluminum collected for recycling during one week can be shown as a bar graph or circle graph.

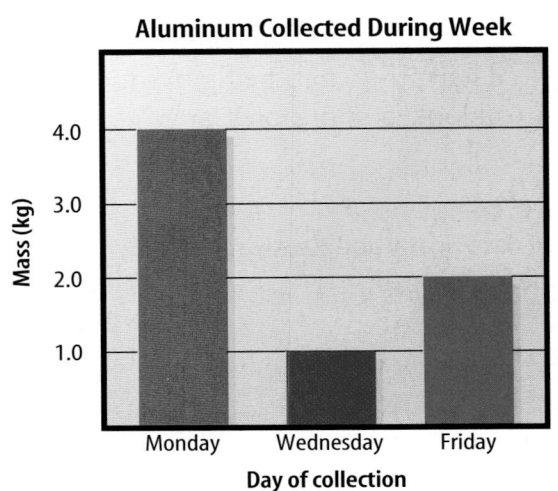

Circle Graphs A circle graph uses a circle divided into sections to display data as parts (fractions or percentages) of a whole. The size of each section corresponds to the fraction or percentage of the data that the section represents. So, the entire circle represents 100 percent, one-half represents 50 percent, one-fifth represents 20 percent, and so on.

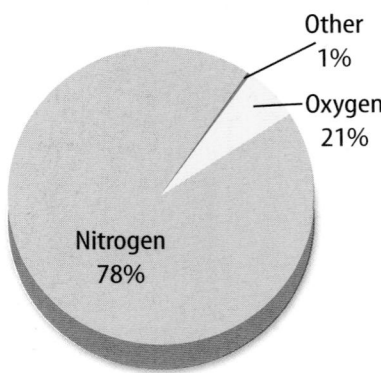

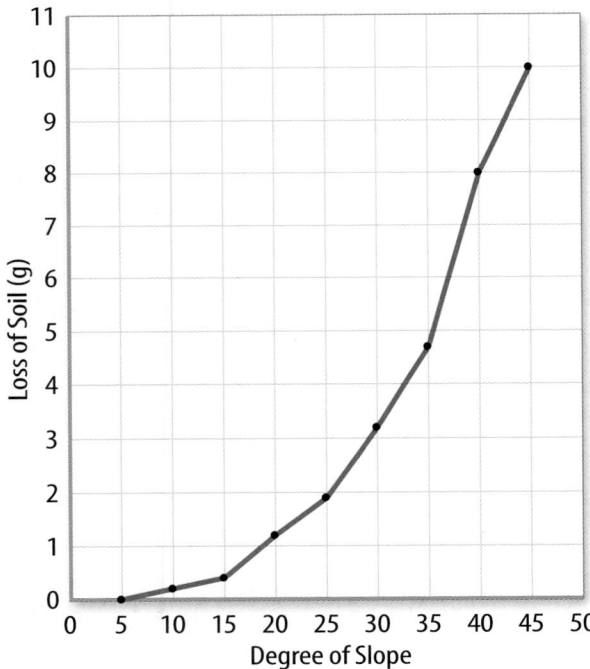

Figure 15
This line graph shows the relationship between degree of slope and the loss of soil in grams from a container during an experiment.

Analyzing Results

To determine the meaning of your observations and investigation results, you will need to look for patterns in the data. You can organize your information in several of the ways that are discussed in this handbook. Then you must think critically to determine what the data mean. Scientists use several approaches when they analyze the data they have collected and recorded. Each approach is useful for identifying specific patterns in the data.

Forming Operational Definitions

An operational definition defines an object by showing how it functions, works, or behaves. Such definitions are written in terms of how an object works or how it can be used; that is, they describe its job or purpose.

For example, a ruler can be defined as a tool that measures the length of an object (how it can be used). A ruler also can be defined as something that contains a series of marks that can be used as a standard when measuring (how it works).

Classifying

Classifying is the process of sorting objects or events into groups based on common features. When classifying, first observe the objects or events to be classified. Then select one feature that is shared by some members in the group but not by all. Place those members that share that feature into a subgroup. You can classify members into smaller and smaller subgroups based on characteristics.

How might you classify a group of rocks? You might first classify them by color, putting all of the black, white, and red rocks into separate groups. Within each group, you could then look for another common feature to classify further, such as size or whether the rocks have sharp or smooth edges.

Remember that when you classify, you are grouping objects or events for a purpose. For example, classifying rocks can be the first step in identifying them. You might know that obsidian is a black, shiny rock with sharp edges. To find it in a large group of rocks, you might start with the classification scheme mentioned. You'll locate obsidian within the group of black, sharp-edged rocks that you separate from the rest. Pumice could be located by its white color and by the fact that it contains many small holes called vesicles. Keep your purpose in mind as you select the features to form groups and subgroups.

Figure 17
Color is one of many characteristics that are used to classify rocks.

Comparing and Contrasting

Observations can be analyzed by noting the similarities and differences between two or more objects or events that you observe. When you look at objects or events to see how they are similar, you are comparing them. Contrasting is looking for differences in objects or events. The table below compares and contrasts the characteristics of two minerals.

Mineral Characteristics		
Mineral	Graphite	Gold
Color	black	bright yellow
Hardness	1–2	2.5–3
Luster	metallic	metallic
Uses	pencil "lead"	jewelry, electronics

Recognizing Cause and Effect

Have you ever heard a loud pop right before the power went out and then suggested that an electric transformer probably blew out? If so, you have observed an effect and inferred a cause. The event is the effect, and the reason for the event is the cause.

When scientists are unsure of the cause of a certain event, they design controlled experiments to determine what caused it.

Interpreting Data

The word *interpret* means "to explain the meaning of something." Look at the problem originally being explored in an experiment and figure out what the data show. Identify the control group and the test group so you can see whether or not changes in the independent variable have had an effect. Look for differences in the dependent variable between the control and test groups.

These differences you observe can be qualitative or quantitative. You would be able to describe a qualitative difference using only words, whereas you would measure a quantitative difference and describe it using numbers. If there are differences, the independent variable that is being tested could have had an effect. If no differences are found between the control and test groups, the variable that is being tested apparently had no effect.

For example, suppose that three beakers each contain 100 mL of water. The beakers are placed on hot plates, and two of the hot plates are turned on, but the third is left off for a period of 5 min. Suppose you are then asked to describe any differences in the water in the three beakers. A qualitative difference might be the appearance of bubbles rising to the top in the water that is being heated but no rising bubbles in the unheated water. A quantitative difference might be a difference in the amount of water that is present in the beakers.

Inferring Scientists often make inferences based on their observations. An inference is an attempt to explain, or interpret, observations or to indicate what caused what you observed. An inference is a type of conclusion.

When making an inference, be certain to use accurate data and accurately described observations. Analyze all of the data that you've collected. Then, based on everything you know, explain or interpret what you've observed.

Drawing Conclusions

When scientists have analyzed the data they collected, they proceed to draw conclusions about what the data mean. These conclusions are sometimes stated using words similar to those found in the hypothesis formed earlier in the process.

Conclusions To analyze your data, you must review all of the observations and measurements that you made and recorded. Recheck all data for accuracy. After your data are rechecked and organized, you are almost ready to draw a conclusion such as "salt water boils at a higher temperature than freshwater."

Before you can draw a conclusion, however, you must determine whether the data allow you to come to a conclusion that supports a hypothesis. Sometimes that will be the case, other times it will not.

If your data do not support a hypothesis, it does not mean that the hypothesis is wrong. It means only that the results of the investigation did not support the hypothesis. Maybe the experiment needs to be redesigned, but very likely, some of the initial observations on which the hypothesis was based were incomplete or biased. Perhaps more observation or research is needed to refine the hypothesis.

Avoiding Bias Sometimes drawing a conclusion involves making judgments. When you make a judgment, you form an opinion about what your data mean. It is important to be honest and to avoid reaching a conclusion if there were no supporting evidence for it or if it were based on a small sample. It also is important not to allow any expectations of results to bias your judgments. If possible, it is a good idea to collect additional data. Scientists do this all the time.

For example, the *Hubble Space Telescope* was sent into space in April, 1990, to provide scientists with clearer views of the universe. The *Hubble* is the size of a school bus and has a 2.4-m-diameter mirror. The *Hubble* helped scientists answer questions about the planet Pluto.

For many years, scientists had only been able to hypothesize about the surface of the planet Pluto. The *Hubble* has now provided pictures of Pluto's surface that show a rough texture with light and dark regions on it. This might be the best information about Pluto scientists will have until they are able to send a space probe to it.

Evaluating Others' Data and Conclusions

Sometimes scientists have to use data that they did not collect themselves, or they have to rely on observations and conclusions drawn by other researchers. In cases such as these, the data must be evaluated carefully.

How were the data obtained? How was the investigation done? Was it carried out properly? Has it been duplicated by other researchers? Were they able to follow the exact procedure? Did they come up with the same results? Look at the conclusion, as well. Would you reach the same conclusion from these results? Only when you have confidence in the data of others can you believe it is true and feel comfortable using it.

Communicating

The communication of ideas is an important part of the work of scientists. A discovery that is not reported will not advance the scientific community's understanding or knowledge. Communication among scientists also is important as a way of improving their investigations.

Scientists communicate in many ways, from writing articles in journals and magazines that explain their investigations and experiments, to announcing important discoveries on television and radio, to sharing ideas with colleagues on the Internet or presenting them as lectures.

Computer Skills

People who study science rely on computers to record and store data and to analyze results from investigations. Whether you work in a laboratory or just need to write a lab report with tables, good computer skills are a necessity.

Using a Word Processor

Suppose your teacher has assigned a written report. After you've completed your research and decided how you want to write the information, you need to put all that information on paper. The easiest way to do this is with a word processing application on a computer.

A computer application that allows you to type your information, change it as many times as you need to, and then print it out so that it looks neat and clean is called a word processing application. You also can use this type of application to create tables and columns, add bullets or cartoon art to your page, include page numbers, and check your spelling.

Helpful Hints

- If you aren't sure how to do something using your word processing program, look in the help menu. You will find a list of topics there to click on for help. After you locate the help topic you need, just follow the step-by-step instructions you see on your screen.
- Just because you've spell checked your report doesn't mean that the spelling is perfect. The spell check feature can't catch misspelled words that look like other words. If you've accidentally typed *mind* instead of *mine*, the spell checker won't know the difference. Always reread your report to make sure you didn't miss any mistakes.

Figure 18
You can use computer programs to make graphs and tables.

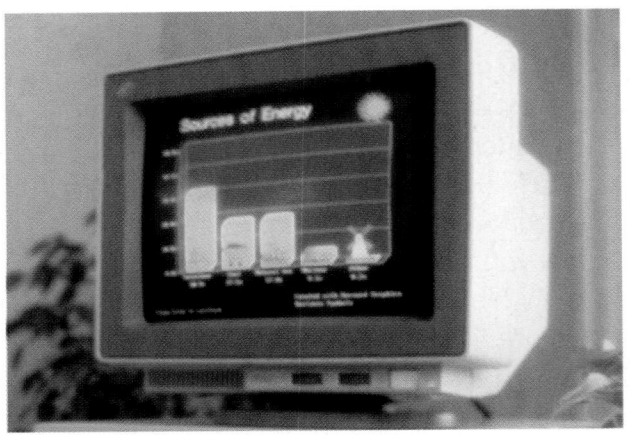

Using a Database

Imagine you're in the middle of a research project, busily gathering facts and information. You soon realize that it's becoming more difficult to organize and keep track of all the information. The tool to use to solve information overload is a database. Just as a file cabinet organizes paper records, a database organizes computer records. However, a database is more powerful than a simple file cabinet because at the click of a mouse, the contents can be reshuffled and reorganized. At computer-quick speeds, databases can sort information by any characteristics and filter data into multiple categories.

Helpful Hints

- Before setting up a database, take some time to learn the features of your database software by practicing with established database software.
- Periodically save your database as you enter data. That way, if something happens such as your computer malfunctions or the power goes off, you won't lose all of your work.

Doing a Database Search

When searching for information in a database, use the following search strategies to get the best results. These are the same search methods used for searching internet databases.

- Place the word *and* between two words in your search if you want the database to look for any entries that have both the words. For example, "Earth *and* Mars" would give you information that mentions both Earth and Mars.
- Place the word *or* between two words if you want the database to show entries that have at least one of the words. For example "Earth *or* Mars" would show you information that mentions either Earth or Mars.
- Place the word *not* between two words if you want the database to look for entries that have the first word but do not have the second word. For example, "Moon *not* phases" would show you information that mentions the Moon but does not mention its phases.

In summary, databases can be used to store large amounts of information about a particular subject. Databases allow biologists, Earth scientists, and physical scientists to search for information quickly and accurately.

Using an Electronic Spreadsheet

Your science fair experiment has produced lots of numbers. How do you keep track of all the data, and how can you easily work out all the calculations needed? You can use a computer program called a spreadsheet to record data that involve numbers. A spreadsheet is an electronic mathematical worksheet.

Type your data in rows and columns, just as they would look in a data table on a sheet of paper. A spreadsheet uses simple math to do data calculations. For example, you could add, subtract, divide, or multiply any of the values in the spreadsheet by another number. You also could set up a series of math steps you want to apply to the data. If you want to add 12 to all the numbers and then multiply all the numbers by 10, the computer does all the calculations for you in the spreadsheet. Below is an example of a spreadsheet that records weather data.

Helpful Hints

- Before you set up the spreadsheet, identify how you want to organize the data. Include any formulas you will need to use.
- Make sure you have entered the correct data into the correct rows and columns.
- You also can display your results in a graph. Pick the style of graph that best represents the data with which you are working.

Figure 19
A spreadsheet allows you to display large amounts of data and do calculations automatically.

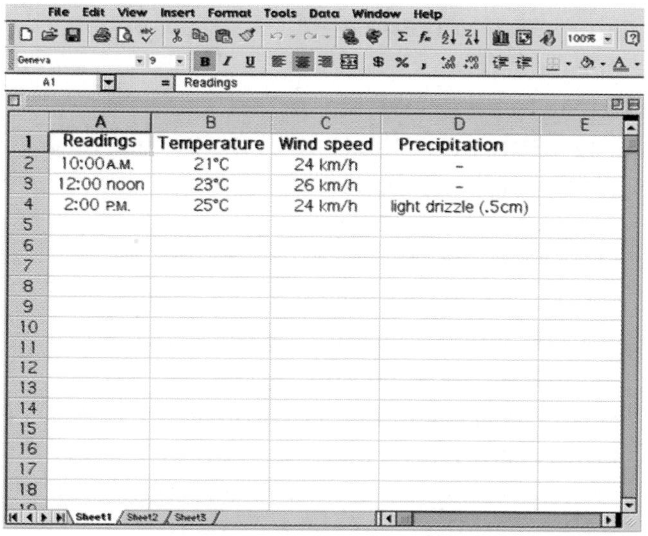

Readings	Temperature	Wind speed	Precipitation
10:00 A.M.	21°C	24 km/h	–
12:00 noon	23°C	26 km/h	–
2:00 P.M.	25°C	24 km/h	light drizzle (.5cm)

Using a Computerized Card Catalog

When you have a report or paper to research, you probably go to the library. To find the information you need in the library, you might have to use a computerized card catalog. This type of card catalog allows you to search for information by subject, by title, or by author. The computer then will display all the holdings the library has on the subject, title, or author requested.

A library's holdings can include books, magazines, databases, videos, and audio materials. When you have chosen something from this list, the computer will show whether an item is available and where in the library to find it.

Helpful Hints

- Remember that you can use the computer to search by subject, author, or title. If you know a book's author but not the title, you can search for all the books the library has by that author.
- When searching by subject, it's often most helpful to narrow your search by using specific search terms, such as *and, or,* and *not.* If you don't find enough sources, you can broaden your search.
- Pay attention to the type of materials found in your search. If you need a book, you can eliminate any videos or other resources that come up in your search.
- Knowing how your library is arranged can save you a lot of time. If you need help, the librarian will show you where certain types of materials are kept and how to find specific items.

Using Graphics Software

Are you having trouble finding that exact piece of art you're looking for? Do you have a picture in your mind of what you want but can't seem to find the right graphic to represent your ideas? To solve these problems, you can use graphics software. Graphics software allows you to create and change images and diagrams in almost unlimited ways. Typical uses for graphics software include arranging clip art, changing scanned images, and constructing pictures from scratch. Most graphics software applications work in similar ways. They use the same basic tools and functions. Once you master one graphics application, you can use other graphics applications.

Figure 20
Graphics software can use your data to draw bar graphs.

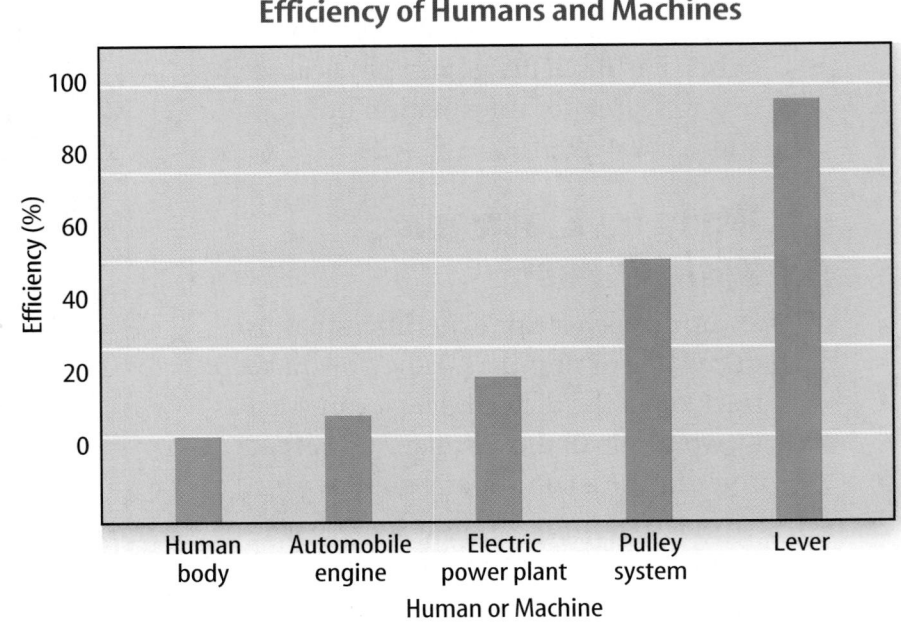

Figure 21
You can use this circle graph to find the names of the major gases that make up Earth's atmosphere.

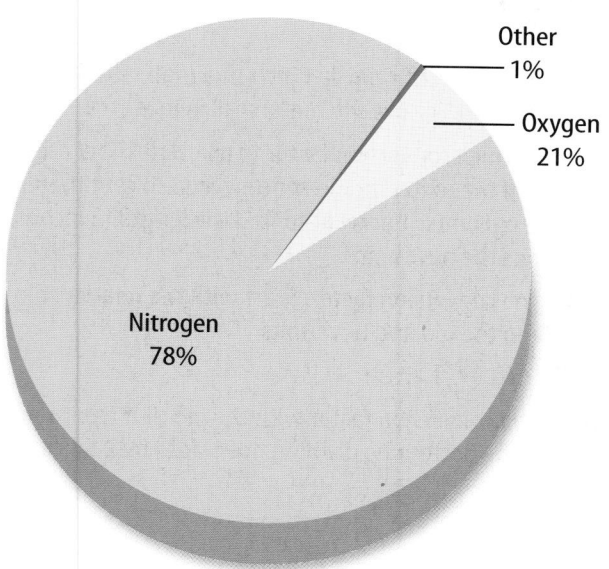

Other
1%

Oxygen
21%

Nitrogen
78%

Helpful Hints

■ As with any method of drawing, the more you practice using the graphics software the better your results will be.

■ Start by using the software to manipulate existing drawings. Once you master this, making your own illustrations will be easier.

■ Clip art is available on CD-ROMs and the Internet. With these resources, finding a piece of clip art to suit your purposes is simple.

■ As you work on a drawing, save it often.

Developing Multimedia Presentations

It's your turn—you have to present your science report to the entire class. How do you do it? You can use many different sources of information to get the class excited about your presentation. Posters, videos, photographs, sound, computers, and the Internet can help show your ideas.

First, determine what important points you want to make in your presentation. Then, write an outline of what materials and types of media would best illustrate those points. Maybe you could start with an outline on an overhead projector, then show a video, followed by something from the Internet or a slide show accompanied by music or recorded voices. You might choose to use a presentation builder computer application that can combine all these elements into one presentation. Make sure the presentation is well constructed to make the most impact on the audience.

Figure 21
Multimedia presentations use many types of print and electronic materials.

Helpful Hints

■ Carefully consider what media will best communicate the point you are trying to make.

■ Make sure you know how to use any equipment you will be using in your presentation.

■ Practice the presentation several times.

■ If possible, set up all of the equipment ahead of time. Make sure everything is working correctly.

Use this Math Skill Handbook to help solve problems you are given in this text. You might find it useful to review topics in this Math Skill Handbook first.

In science, quantities such as length, mass, and time sometimes are measured using different units. Suppose you want to know how many miles are in 12.7 km?

Conversion factors are used to change from one unit of measure to another. A conversion factor is a ratio that is equal to one. For example, there are 1,000 mL in 1 L, so 1,000 mL equals 1 L, or:

$$1{,}000 \text{ mL} = 1 \text{ L}$$

If both sides are divided by 1 L, this equation becomes:

$$\frac{1{,}000 \text{ mL}}{1 \text{ L}} = 1$$

The **ratio** on the left side of this equation is equal to one and is a conversion factor. You can make another conversion factor by dividing both sides of the top equation by 1,000 mL:

$$1 = \frac{1 \text{ L}}{1{,}000 \text{ mL}}$$

To **convert units,** you multiply by the appropriate conversion factor. For example, how many milliliters are in 1.255 L? To convert 1.255 L to milliliters, multiply 1.255 L by a conversion factor.

Use the **conversion factor** with new units (mL) in the numerator and the old units (L) in the denominator.

$$1.255 \text{ L} \times \frac{1{,}000 \text{ mL}}{1 \text{ L}} = 1{,}255 \text{ mL}$$

The unit L divides in this equation, just as if it were a number.

Example 1 There are 2.54 cm in 1 inch. If a meterstick has a length of 100 cm, how long is the meterstick in inches?

Step 1 Decide which conversion factor to use. You know the length of the meterstick in centimeters, so centimeters are the old units. You want to find the length in inches, so inch is the new unit.

Step 2 Form the conversion factor. Start with the relationship between the old and new units.

$$2.54 \text{ cm} = 1 \text{ inch}$$

Step 3 Form the conversion factor with the old unit (centimeter) on the bottom by dividing both sides by 2.54 cm.

$$1 = \frac{2.54 \text{ cm}}{2.54 \text{ cm}} = \frac{1 \text{ inch}}{2.54 \text{ cm}}$$

Step 4 Multiply the old measurement by the conversion factor.

$$100 \text{ cm} \times \frac{1 \text{ inch}}{2.54 \text{ cm}} = 39.37 \text{ inches}$$

The meter stick is 39.37 inches long.

Example 2 There are 365 days in one year. If a person is 14 years old, what is his or her age in days? (Ignore leap years)

Step 1 Decide which conversion factor to use. You want to convert years to days.

Step 2 Form the conversion factor. Start with the relation between the old and new units.

$$1 \text{ year} = 365 \text{ days}$$

Step 3 Form the conversion factor with the old unit (year) on the bottom by dividing both sides by 1 year.

$$1 = \frac{1 \text{ year}}{1 \text{ year}} = \frac{365 \text{ days}}{1 \text{ year}}$$

Step 4 Multiply the old measurement by the conversion factor:

$$14 \text{ years} \times \frac{365 \text{ days}}{1 \text{ year}} = 5{,}110 \text{ days}$$

The person's age is 5,110 days.

Practice Problem A book has a mass of 2.31 kg. If there are 1,000 g in 1 kg, what is the mass of the book in grams?

Using Fractions

A **fraction** is a number that compares a part to the whole. For example, in the fraction $\frac{2}{3}$, the 2 represents the part and the 3 represents the whole. In the fraction $\frac{2}{3}$, the top number, 2, is called the numerator. The bottom number, 3, is called the denominator.

Sometimes fractions are not written in their simplest form. To determine a fraction's **simplest form,** you must find the greatest common factor (GCF) of the numerator and denominator. The greatest common factor is the largest common factor of all the factors the two numbers have in common.

For example, because the number 3 divides into 12 and 30 evenly, it is a common factor of 12 and 30. However, because the number 6 is the largest number that evenly divides into 12 and 30, it is the **greatest common factor.**

After you find the greatest common factor, you can write a fraction in its simplest form. Divide both the numerator and the denominator by the greatest common factor. The number that results is the fraction in its **simplest form.**

Example   Twelve of the 20 peaks in a mountain range have elevations over 10,000 m. What fraction of the peaks in the mountain range are over 10,000 m? Write the fraction in simplest form.

Step 1   Write the fraction.

$$\frac{\text{part}}{\text{whole}} = \frac{12}{20}$$

Step 2   To find the GCF of the numerator and denominator, list all of the factors of each number.

Factors of 12: 1, 2, 3, 4, 6, 12 (the numbers that divide evenly into 12)

Factors of 20: 1, 2, 4, 5, 10, 20 (the numbers that divide evenly into 20)

Step 3   List the common factors.

1, 2, 4.

Step 4   Choose the greatest factor in the list of common factors.

The GCF of 12 and 20 is 4.

Step 5   Divide the numerator and denominator by the GCF.

$$\frac{12 \div 4}{20 \div 4} = \frac{3}{5}$$

In the mountain range, $\frac{3}{5}$ of the peaks are over 10,000 m.

Practice Problem   There are 90 rides at an amusement park. Of those rides, 66 have a height restriction. What fraction of the rides has a height restriction? Write the fraction in simplest form. $\frac{11}{15}$

Math Skill Handbook

Calculating Ratios

A **ratio** is a comparison of two numbers by division.

Ratios can be written 3 to 5 or 3:5. Ratios also can be written as fractions, such as $\frac{3}{5}$. Ratios, like fractions, can be written in simplest form. Recall that a fraction is in **simplest form** when the greatest common factor (GCF) of the numerator and denominator is 1.

Example A particular geologic sample contains 40 kg of shale and 64 kg of granite. What is the ratio of shale to granite as a fraction in simplest form?

Step 1 Write the ratio as a fraction. $\dfrac{\text{shale}}{\text{granite}} = \dfrac{40}{64}$

Step 2 Express the fraction in simplest form. The GCF of 40 and 64 is 8.

$$\frac{40}{64} = \frac{40 \div 8}{64 \div 8} = \frac{5}{8}$$

The ratio of shale to granite in the sample is $\frac{5}{8}$.

Practice Problem Two metal rods measure 100 cm and 144 cm in length. What is the ratio of their lengths in simplest fraction form? $\frac{5}{6}$

Using Decimals

A **decimal** is a fraction with a denominator of 10, 100, 1,000, or another power of 10. For example, 0.854 is the same as the fraction $\frac{854}{1,000}$.

In a decimal, the decimal point separates the ones place and the tenths place. For example, 0.27 means twenty-seven hundredths, or $\frac{27}{100}$, where 27 is the **number of units** out of 100 units. Any fraction can be written as a decimal using division.

Example Write $\frac{5}{8}$ as a decimal.

Step 1 Write a division problem with the numerator, 5, as the dividend and the denominator, 8, as the divisor. Write 5 as 5.000.

Step 2 Solve the problem.

```
     0.625
 8)5.000
   48
   20
   16
    40
    40
     0
```

Therefore, $\frac{5}{8} = 0.625$.

Practice Problem Write $\frac{19}{25}$ as a decimal. 0.76

Using Percentages

The word *percent* means "out of one hundred." A **percent** is a ratio that compares a number to 100. Suppose you read that 77 percent of Earth's surface is covered by water. That is the same as reading that the fraction of Earth's surface covered by water is $\frac{77}{100}$. To express a fraction as a percent, first find an equivalent decimal for the fraction. Then, multiply the decimal by 100 and add the percent symbol. For example, $\frac{1}{2} = 1 \div 2 = 0.5$. Then $0.5 = 0.50 = 50\%$.

Example Express $\frac{13}{20}$ as a percent.

Step 1 Find the equivalent decimal for the fraction.

$$20)\overline{13.00} = 0.65$$
$$\underline{120}$$
$$100$$
$$\underline{100}$$
$$0$$

Step 2 Rewrite the fraction $\frac{13}{20}$ as 0.65.

Step 3 Multiply 0.65 by 100 and add the % sign.

$$0.65 \cdot 100 = 65 = 65\%$$

So, $\frac{13}{20} = 65\%$.

Practice Problem In one year, 73 of 365 days were rainy in one city. What percent of the days in that city were rainy? 20%

Using Precision and Significant Digits

When you make a **measurement,** the value you record depends on the precision of the measuring instrument. When adding or subtracting numbers with different precision, the answer is rounded to the smallest number of decimal places of any number in the sum or difference. When multiplying or dividing, the answer is rounded to the smallest number of significant figures of any number being multiplied or divided. When counting the number of **significant figures,** all digits are counted except zeros at the end of a number with no decimal such as 2,500, and zeros at the beginning of a decimal such as 0.03020.

Example The lengths 5.28 and 5.2 are measured in meters. Find the sum of these lengths and report the sum using the least precise measurement.

Step 1 Find the sum.

5.28 m	2 digits after the decimal
+ 5.2 m	1 digit after the decimal
10.48 m	

Step 2 Round to one digit after the decimal because the least number of digits after the decimal of the numbers being added is 1.

The sum is 10.5 m.

Practice Problem Multiply the numbers in the example using the rule for multiplying and dividing. Report the answer with the correct number of significant figures. 27.5 m²

Skill Handbooks

Math Skill Handbook

An **equation** is a statement that two things are equal. For example, $A = B$ is an equation that states that A is equal to B.

Sometimes one side of the equation will contain a **variable** whose value is not known. In the equation $3x = 12$, the variable is x.

The equation is solved when the variable is replaced with a value that makes both sides of the equation equal to each other. For example, the solution of the equation $3x = 12$ is $x = 4$. If the x is replaced with 4, then the equation becomes $3 \cdot 4 = 12$, or $12 = 12$.

To solve an equation such as $8x = 40$, divide both sides of the equation by the number that multiplies the variable.

$$8x = 40$$
$$\frac{8x}{8} = \frac{40}{8}$$
$$x = 5$$

You can check your answer by replacing the variable with your solution and seeing if both sides of the equation are the same.

$$8x = 8 \cdot 5 = 40$$

The left and right sides of the equation are the same, so $x = 5$ is the solution.

Sometimes an equation is written in this way: $a = bc$. This also is called a **formula.** The letters can be replaced by numbers, but the numbers must still make both sides of the equation the same.

Example 1 Solve the equation $10x = 35$.

Step 1 Find the solution by dividing each side of the equation by 10.

$$10x = 35 \qquad \frac{10x}{10} = \frac{35}{10} \qquad x = 3.5$$

Step 2 Check the solution.

$$10x = 35 \qquad 10 \times 3.5 = 35 \qquad 35 = 35$$

Both sides of the equation are equal, so $x = 3.5$ is the solution to the equation.

Example 2 In the formula $a = bc$, find the value of c if $a = 20$ and $b = 2$.

Step 1 Rearrange the formula so the unknown value is by itself on one side of the equation by dividing both sides by b.

$$a = bc$$
$$\frac{a}{b} = \frac{bc}{b}$$
$$\frac{a}{b} = c$$

Step 2 Replace the variables a and b with the values that are given.

$$\frac{a}{b} = c$$
$$\frac{20}{2} = c$$
$$10 = c$$

Step 3 Check the solution.

$$a = bc$$
$$20 = 2 \times 10$$
$$20 = 20$$

Both sides of the equation are equal, so $c = 10$ is the solution when $a = 20$ and $b = 2$.

Practice Problem In the formula $h = gd$, find the value of d if $g = 12.3$ and $h = 17.4$. $d = 1.4$

Using Proportions

A **proportion** is an equation that shows that two ratios are equivalent. The ratios $\frac{2}{4}$ and $\frac{5}{10}$ are equivalent, so they can be written as $\frac{2}{4} = \frac{5}{10}$. This equation is an example of a proportion.

When two ratios form a proportion, the **cross products** are equal. To find the cross products in the proportion $\frac{2}{4} = \frac{5}{10}$, multiply the 2 and the 10, and the 4 and the 5. Therefore $2 \cdot 10 = 4 \cdot 5$, or $20 = 20$.

Because you know that both proportions are equal, you can use cross products to find a missing term in a proportion. This is known as **solving the proportion.** Solving a proportion is similar to solving an equation.

Example The heights of a tree and a pole are proportional to the lengths of their shadows. The tree casts a shadow of 24 m at the same time that a 6-m pole casts a shadow of 4 m. What is the height of the tree?

Step 1 Write a proportion.

$$\frac{\text{height of tree}}{\text{height of pole}} = \frac{\text{length of tree's shadow}}{\text{length of pole's shadow}}$$

Step 2 Substitute the known values into the proportion. Let h represent the unknown value, the height of the tree.

$$\frac{h}{6} = \frac{24}{4}$$

Step 3 Find the cross products.

$$h \cdot 4 = 6 \cdot 24$$

Step 4 Simplify the equation.

$$4h = 144$$

Step 5 Divide each side by 4.

$$\frac{4h}{4} = \frac{144}{4}$$
$$h = 36$$

The height of the tree is 36 m.

Practice Problem The ratios of the weights of two objects on the Moon and on Earth are in proportion. A rock weighing 3 N on the Moon weighs 18 N on Earth. How much would a rock that weighs 5 N on the Moon weigh on Earth? 30 N

Math Skill Handbook

Statistics is the branch of mathematics that deals with collecting, analyzing, and presenting data. In statistics, there are three common ways to summarize the data with a single number—the mean, the median, and the mode.

The **mean** of a set of data is the arithmetic average. It is found by adding the numbers in the data set and dividing by the number of items in the set.

The **median** is the middle number in a set of data when the data are arranged in numerical order. If there were an even number of data points, the median would be the mean of the two middle numbers.

The **mode** of a set of data is the number or item that appears most often.

Another number that often is used to describe a set of data is the range. The **range** is the difference between the largest number and the smallest number in a set of data.

A **frequency table** shows how many times each piece of data occurs, usually in a survey. The frequency table below shows the results of a student survey on favorite color.

Color	Tally	Frequency
red	||||	4
blue	⊞⊞	5
black	||	2
green	|||	3
purple	⊞⊞ ||	7
yellow	⊞⊞ |	6

Based on the frequency table data, which color is the favorite?

Example The high temperatures (in °C) on five consecutive days at a desert observation station are 39°, 37°, 44°, 36°, and 44°. Find the mean, median, mode, and range of this set.

To find the mean:
Step 1 Find the sum of the numbers.

$$39 + 37 + 44 + 36 + 44 = 200$$

Step 2 Divide the sum by the number of items, which is 5.

$$200 \div 5 = 40$$

The mean high temperature is 40°C.

To find the median:
Step 1 Arrange the temperatures from least to greatest.

$$36, \ 37, \ \underline{39}, \ 44, \ 44$$

Step 2 Determine the middle temperature.

The median high temperature is 39°C.

To find the mode:
Step 1 Group the numbers that are the same together.

$$44, 44, 36, 37, 39$$

Step 2 Determine the number that occurs most in the set.

$$\underline{44, 44}, 36, 37, 39$$

The mode measure is 44°C.

To find the range:
Step 1 Arrange the temperatures from largest to smallest.

$$44, 44, 39, 37, 36$$

Step 2 Determine the largest and smallest temperature in the set.

$$\underline{44}, 44, 39, 37, \underline{36}$$

Step 3 Find the difference between the largest and smallest temperatures.

$$44 - 36 = 8$$

The range is 8°C.

Practice Problem Find the mean, median, mode, and range for the data set 8, 4, 12, 8, 11, 14, 16.

Safety in the Science Classroom

1. Always obtain your teacher's permission to begin an investigation.

2. Study the procedure. If you have questions, ask your teacher. Be sure you understand any safety symbols shown on the page.

3. Use the safety equipment provided for you. Goggles and a safety apron should be worn during most investigations.

4. Always slant test tubes away from yourself and others when heating them or adding substances to them.

5. Never eat or drink in the lab, and never use lab glassware as food or drink containers. Never inhale chemicals. Do not taste any substances or draw any material into a tube with your mouth.

6. Report any spill, accident, or injury, no matter how small, immediately to your teacher, then follow his or her instructions.

7. Know the location and proper use of the fire extinguisher, safety shower, fire blanket, first aid kit, and fire alarm.

8. Keep all materials away from open flames. Tie back long hair and tie down loose clothing.

9. If your clothing should catch fire, smother it with the fire blanket, or get under a safety shower. NEVER RUN.

10. If a fire should occur, turn off the gas then leave the room according to established procedures.

Follow these procedures as you clean up your work area

1. Turn off the water and gas. Disconnect electrical devices.

2. Clean all pieces of equipment and return all materials to their proper places.

3. Dispose of chemicals and other materials as directed by your teacher. Place broken glass and solid substances in the proper containers. Make sure never to discard materials in the sink.

4. Clean your work area. Wash your hands thoroughly after working in the laboratory.

First Aid	
Injury	Safe Response ALWAYS NOTIFY YOUR TEACHER IMMEDIATELY
Burns	Apply cold water.
Cuts and Bruises	Stop any bleeding by applying direct pressure. Cover cuts with a clean dressing. Apply ice packs or cold compresses to bruises.
Fainting	Leave the person lying down. Loosen any tight clothing and keep crowds away.
Foreign Matter in Eye	Flush with plenty of water. Use eyewash bottle or fountain.
Poisoning	Note the suspected poisoning agent.
Any Spills on Skin	Flush with large amounts of water or use safety shower.

SI—Metric/English, English/Metric Conversions

	When you want to convert:	To:	Multiply by:
Length	inches	centimeters	2.54
	centimeters	inches	0.39
	yards	meters	0.91
	meters	yards	1.09
	miles	kilometers	1.61
	kilometers	miles	0.62
Mass and Weight*	ounces	grams	28.35
	grams	ounces	0.04
	pounds	kilograms	0.45
	kilograms	pounds	2.2
	tons (short)	tonnes (metric tons)	0.91
	tonnes (metric tons)	tons (short)	1.10
	pounds	newtons	4.45
	newtons	pounds	0.22
Volume	cubic inches	cubic centimeters	16.39
	cubic centimeters	cubic inches	0.06
	liters	quarts	1.06
	quarts	liters	0.95
	gallons	liters	3.78
Area	square inches	square centimeters	6.45
	square centimeters	square inches	0.16
	square yards	square meters	0.83
	square meters	square yards	1.19
	square miles	square kilometers	2.59
	square kilometers	square miles	0.39
	hectares	acres	2.47
	acres	hectares	0.40
Temperature	To convert °Celsius to °Fahrenheit		$°C \times 9/5 + 32$
	To convert °Fahrenheit to °Celsius		$5/9 \ (°F - 32)$

*Weight is measured in standard Earth gravity.

REFERENCE HANDBOOK C

Weather Map Symbols

Sample Station Model

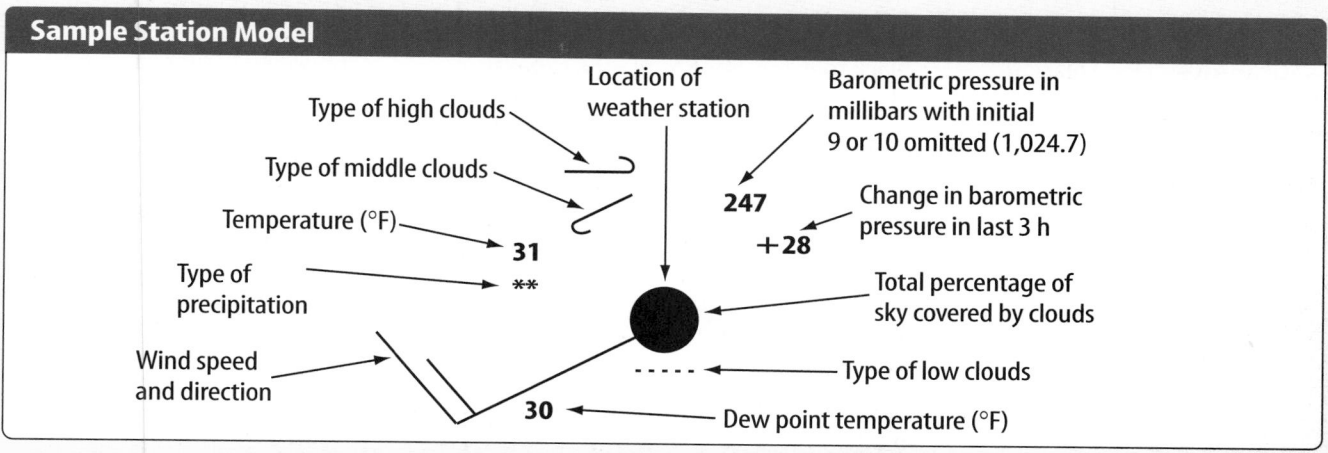

Location of weather station

Type of high clouds

Type of middle clouds

Temperature (°F) — **31**

Type of precipitation — **＊＊**

Wind speed and direction

Barometric pressure in millibars with initial 9 or 10 omitted (1,024.7)

247

Change in barometric pressure in last 3 h

+28

Total percentage of sky covered by clouds

Type of low clouds

Dew point temperature (°F) — **30**

Sample Plotted Report at Each Station

Precipitation		Wind Speed and Direction		Sky Coverage		Some Types of High Clouds	
≡	Fog	◯	0 calm	◯	No cover	⟶	Scattered cirrus
★	Snow	╱	1–2 knots	◍	1/10 or less	⟹	Dense cirrus in patches
●	Rain	⤙	3–7 knots	◑	2/10 to 3/10	⟿	Veil of cirrus covering entire sky
⊼	Thunderstorm	⤛	8–12 knots	◗	4/10	⟼	Cirrus not covering entire sky
,	Drizzle	⤜	13–17 knots	◐	–		
▽	Showers	⤝	18–22 knots	◕	6/10		
		⤞	23–27 knots	◔	7/10		
		⤟	48–52 knots	◖	Overcast with openings		
		1 knot = 1.852 km/h		●	Completely overcast		

Some Types of Middle Clouds		Some Types of Low Clouds		Fronts and Pressure Systems	
∠	Thin altostratus layer	⌒	Cumulus of fair weather	(H) or High (L) or Low	Center of high- or low-pressure system
⫽	Thick altostratus layer	⌣	Stratocumulus	▲▲▲▲	Cold front
⟋	Thin altostratus in patches	-----	Fractocumulus of bad weather	●●●●	Warm front
⟋	Thin altostratus in bands	—	Stratus of fair weather	▲●▲●▲	Occluded front
				▲⌒▲⌒▼	Stationary front

Reference Handbook

Minerals

Mineral (formula)	Color	Streak	Hardness	Breakage Pattern	Uses and Other Properties
Graphite (C)	black to gray	black to gray	1–1.5	basal cleavage (scales)	pencil lead, lubricants for locks, rods to control some small nuclear reactions, battery poles
Galena (PbS)	gray	gray to black	2.5	cubic cleavage perfect	source of lead, used for pipes, shields for X rays, fishing equipment sinkers
Hematite (Fe_2O_3)	black or reddish-brown	reddish-brown	5.5–6.5	irregular fracture	source of iron; converted to pig iron, made into steel
Magnetite (Fe_3O_4)	black	black	6	conchoidal fracture	source of iron, attracts a magnet
Pyrite (FeS_2)	light, brassy, yellow	greenish-black	6–6.5	uneven fracture	fool's gold
Talc ($Mg_3 Si_4O_{10}(OH)_2$)	white, greenish	white	1	cleavage in one direction	used for talcum powder, sculptures, paper, and tabletops
Gypsum ($CaSO_4 \cdot 2H_2O$)	colorless, gray, white, brown	white	2	basal cleavage	used in plaster of paris and dry wall for building construction
Sphalerite (ZnS)	brown, reddish-brown, greenish	light to dark brown	3.5–4	cleavage in six directions	main ore of zinc; used in paints, dyes, and medicine
Muscovite ($KAl_3Si_3O_{10}(OH)_2$)	white, light gray, yellow, rose, green	colorless	2–2.5	basal cleavage	occurs in large, flexible plates; used as an insulator in electrical equipment, lubricant
Biotite ($K(Mg,Fe)_3(AlSi_3O_{10})(OH)_2$)	black to dark brown	colorless	2.5–3	basal cleavage	occurs in large, flexible plates
Halite (NaCl)	colorless, red, white, blue	colorless	2.5	cubic cleavage	salt; soluble in water; a preservative

Minerals

Mineral (formula)	Color	Streak	Hardness	Breakage Pattern	Uses and Other Properties
Calcite ($CaCO_3$)	colorless, white, pale blue	colorless, white	3	cleavage in three directions	fizzes when HCl is added; used in cements and other building materials
Dolomite ($CaMg(CO_3)_2$)	colorless, white, pink, green, gray, black	white	3.5–4	cleavage in three directions	concrete and cement; used as an ornamental building stone
Fluorite (CaF_2)	colorless, white, blue, green, red, yellow, purple	colorless	4	cleavage in four directions	used in the manufacture of optical equipment; glows under ultraviolet light
Hornblende ($(CaNa)_{2-3}(Mg,Al,Fe)_5-(Al,Si)_2 Si_6O_{22}(OH)_2$)	green to black	gray to white	5–6	cleavage in two directions	will transmit light on thin edges; 6-sided cross section
Feldspar ($KAlSi_3O_8$) ($NaAlSi_3O_8$), ($CaAl_2Si_2O_8$)	colorless, white to gray, green	colorless	6	two cleavage planes meet at 90° angle	used in the manufacture of ceramics
Augite ($(Ca,Na)(Mg,Fe,Al)(Al,Si)_2 O_6$)	black	colorless	6	cleavage in two directions	square or 8-sided cross section
Olivine ($(Mg,Fe)_2 SiO_4$)	olive, green	none	6.5–7	conchoidal fracture	gemstones, refractory sand
Quartz (SiO_2)	colorless, various colors	none	7	conchoidal fracture	used in glass manufacture, electronic equipment, radios, computers, watches, gemstones

Rocks

Rock Type	Rock Name	Characteristics
Igneous (intrusive)	Granite	Large mineral grains of quartz, feldspar, hornblende, and mica. Usually light in color.
	Diorite	Large mineral grains of feldspar, hornblende, and mica. Less quartz than granite. Intermediate in color.
	Gabbro	Large mineral grains of feldspar, augite, and olivine. No quartz. Dark in color.
Igneous (extrusive)	Rhyolite	Small mineral grains of quartz, feldspar, hornblende, and mica, or no visible grains. Light in color.
	Andesite	Small mineral grains of feldspar, hornblende, and mica or no visible grains. Intermediate in color.
	Basalt	Small mineral grains of feldspar, augite, and olivine or no visible grains. No quartz. Dark in color.
	Obsidian	Glassy texture. No visible grains. Volcanic glass. Fracture looks like broken glass.
	Pumice	Frothy texture. Floats in water. Usually light in color.
Sedimentary (detrital)	Conglomerate	Coarse grained. Gravel or pebble size grains.
	Sandstone	Sand-sized grains 1/16 to 2 mm.
	Siltstone	Grains are smaller than sand but larger than clay.
	Shale	Smallest grains. Often dark in color. Usually platy.
Sedimentary (chemical or organic)	Limestone	Major mineral is calcite. Usually forms in oceans, lakes, and caves. Often contains fossils.
	Coal	Occurs in swampy areas. Compacted layers of organic material, mainly plant remains.
Sedimentary (chemical)	Rock Salt	Commonly forms by the evaporation of seawater.
Metamorphic (foliated)	Gneiss	Banding due to alternate layers of different minerals, of different colors. Parent rock often is granite.
	Schist	Parallel arrangement of sheetlike minerals, mainly micas. Forms from different parent rocks.
	Phyllite	Shiny or silky appearance. May look wrinkled. Common parent rocks are shale and slate.
	Slate	Harder, denser, and shinier than shale. Common parent rock is shale.
Metamorphic (non-foliated)	Marble	Calcite or dolomite. Common parent rock is limestone.
	Soapstone	Mainly of talc. Soft with greasy feel.
	Quartzite	Hard with interlocking quartz crystals. Common parent rock is sandstone.

Topographic Map Symbols

▬▬▬	Primary highway, hard surface	～～	Index contour
▬▬▬	Secondary highway, hard surface	··········	Supplementary contour
═══	Light-duty road, hard or improved surface	～～	Intermediate contour
=========	Unimproved road	⬭	Depression contours
┼┼┼┼	Railroad: single track		
╪╪╪	Railroad: multiple track	▬ ▬ ▬	Boundaries: national
╫╫╫	Railroads in juxtaposition	▬ ▬ ▬	State
		▬ ▬ ·	County, parish, municipal
▪▫■🏴	Buildings	▬ ▬ ▬	Civil township, precinct, town, barrio
⚐ ✚ cem	Schools, church, and cemetery	▬ · ▬ ·	Incorporated city, village, town, hamlet
▪▭▨	Buildings (barn, warehouse, etc)	· ▬ · ▬ ·	Reservation, national or state
○　○	Wells other than water (labeled as to type)	- - - - -	Small park, cemetery, airport, etc.
●●●◍	Tanks: oil, water, etc. (labeled only if water)	▬ ·· ▬ ···	Land grant
⊙　⚐	Located or landmark object; windmill	▬▬	Township or range line, U.S. land survey
✕　✕	Open pit, mine, or quarry; prospect	- - - - -	Township or range line, approximate location
⬚	Marsh (swamp)		
⬚	Wooded marsh	～～	Perennial streams
⬚	Woods or brushwood	→←←	Elevated aqueduct
⬚	Vineyard	○　～	Water well and spring
⬚	Land subject to controlled inundation	～⤙	Small rapids
⬚	Submerged marsh	～	Large rapids
⬚	Mangrove	▨	Intermittent lake
⬚	Orchard	～	Intermittent stream
⬚	Scrub	→=====←	Aqueduct tunnel
⬚	Urban area	▨	Glacier
		～✕	Small falls
x7369	Spot elevation	▨	Large falls
670	Water elevation	▨	Dry lake bed

PERIODIC TABLE OF THE ELEMENTS

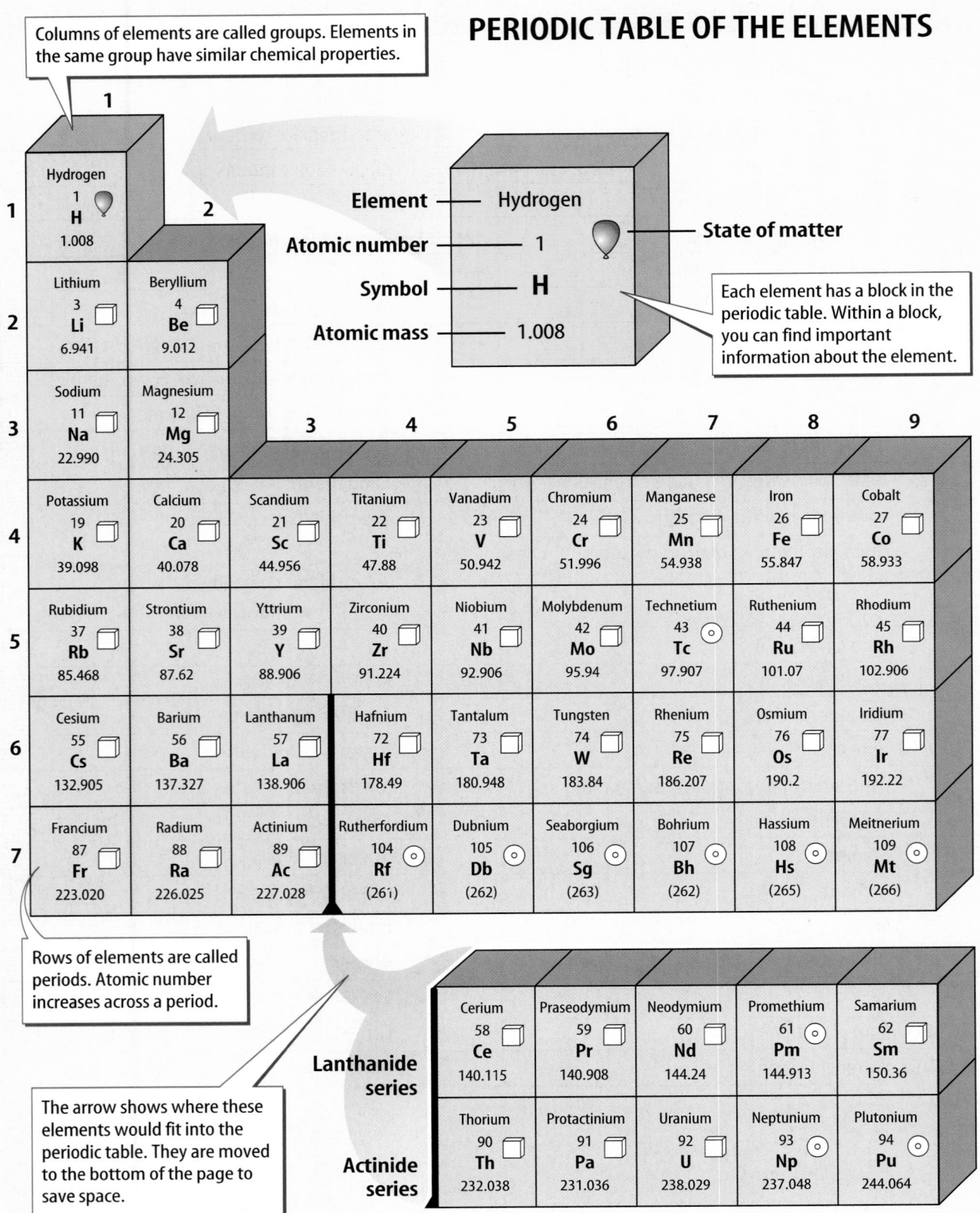

Columns of elements are called groups. Elements in the same group have similar chemical properties.

Element —— Hydrogen

Atomic number —— 1

Symbol —— H

Atomic mass —— 1.008

State of matter

Each element has a block in the periodic table. Within a block, you can find important information about the element.

1

1
Hydrogen
1
H
1.008

2

Lithium
3
Li
6.941

Beryllium
4
Be
9.012

2
Sodium
11
Na
22.990

Magnesium
12
Mg
24.305

3 | **4** | **5** | **6** | **7** | **8** | **9**

4
Potassium
19
K
39.098

Calcium
20
Ca
40.078

Scandium
21
Sc
44.956

Titanium
22
Ti
47.88

Vanadium
23
V
50.942

Chromium
24
Cr
51.996

Manganese
25
Mn
54.938

Iron
26
Fe
55.847

Cobalt
27
Co
58.933

5
Rubidium
37
Rb
85.468

Strontium
38
Sr
87.62

Yttrium
39
Y
88.906

Zirconium
40
Zr
91.224

Niobium
41
Nb
92.906

Molybdenum
42
Mo
95.94

Technetium
43
Tc
97.907

Ruthenium
44
Ru
101.07

Rhodium
45
Rh
102.906

6
Cesium
55
Cs
132.905

Barium
56
Ba
137.327

Lanthanum
57
La
138.906

Hafnium
72
Hf
178.49

Tantalum
73
Ta
180.948

Tungsten
74
W
183.84

Rhenium
75
Re
186.207

Osmium
76
Os
190.2

Iridium
77
Ir
192.22

7
Francium
87
Fr
223.020

Radium
88
Ra
226.025

Actinium
89
Ac
227.028

Rutherfordium
104
Rf
(261)

Dubnium
105
Db
(262)

Seaborgium
106
Sg
(263)

Bohrium
107
Bh
(262)

Hassium
108
Hs
(265)

Meitnerium
109
Mt
(266)

Rows of elements are called periods. Atomic number increases across a period.

The arrow shows where these elements would fit into the periodic table. They are moved to the bottom of the page to save space.

Lanthanide series

Cerium
58
Ce
140.115

Praseodymium
59
Pr
140.908

Neodymium
60
Nd
144.24

Promethium
61
Pm
144.913

Samarium
62
Sm
150.36

Actinide series

Thorium
90
Th
232.038

Protactinium
91
Pa
231.036

Uranium
92
U
238.029

Neptunium
93
Np
237.048

Plutonium
94
Pu
244.064

Reference Handbook

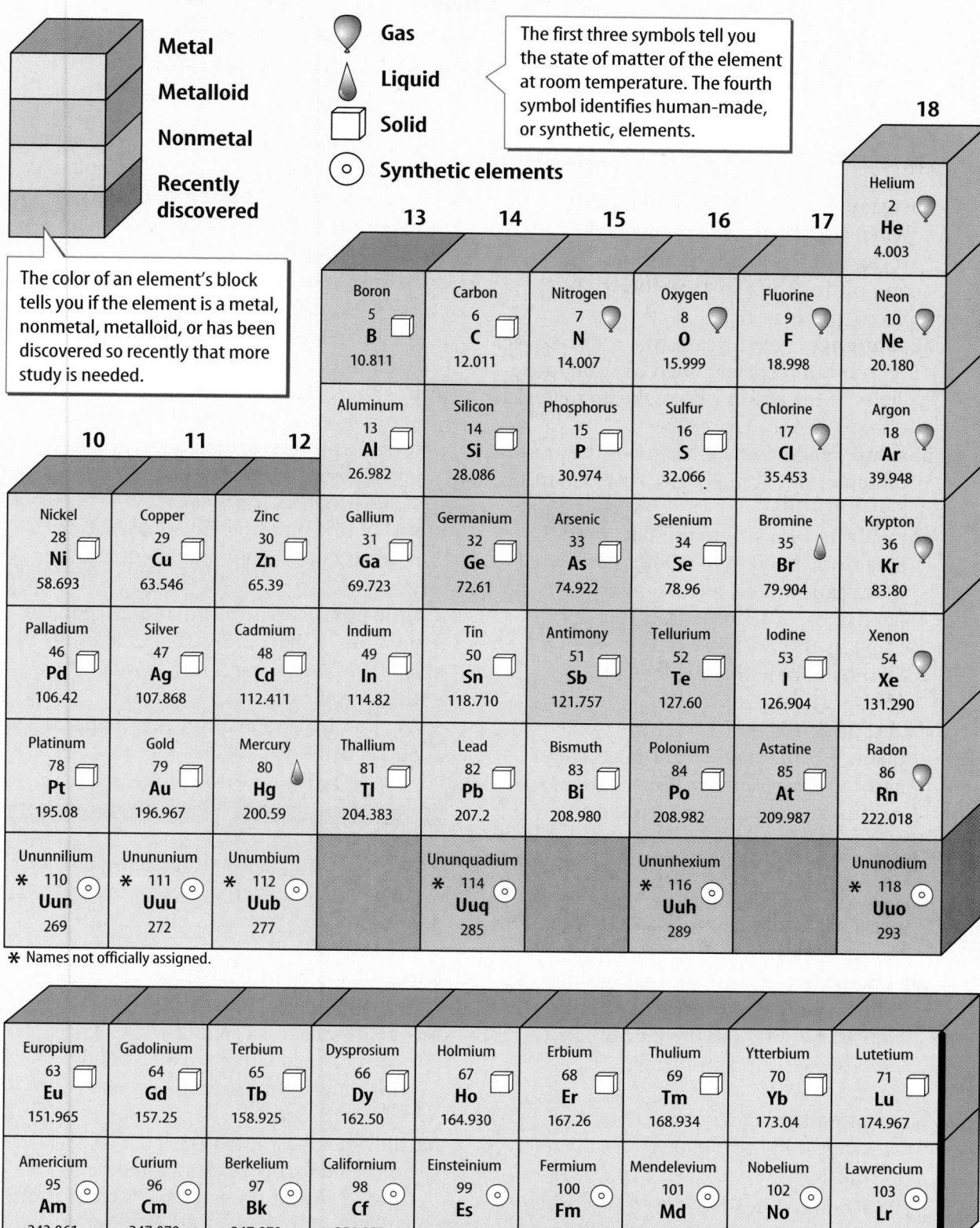

Metal

Metalloid

Nonmetal

Recently discovered

Gas

Liquid

Solid

Synthetic elements

The first three symbols tell you the state of matter of the element at room temperature. The fourth symbol identifies human-made, or synthetic, elements.

The color of an element's block tells you if the element is a metal, nonmetal, metalloid, or has been discovered so recently that more study is needed.

18

Helium
2
He
4.003

13 **14** **15** **16** **17**

Boron	Carbon	Nitrogen	Oxygen	Fluorine	Neon
5	6	7	8	9	10
B	**C**	**N**	**O**	**F**	**Ne**
10.811	12.011	14.007	15.999	18.998	20.180

10 **11** **12**

Aluminum	Silicon	Phosphorus	Sulfur	Chlorine	Argon
13	14	15	16	17	18
Al	**Si**	**P**	**S**	**Cl**	**Ar**
26.982	28.086	30.974	32.066	35.453	39.948

Nickel	Copper	Zinc	Gallium	Germanium	Arsenic	Selenium	Bromine	Krypton
28	29	30	31	32	33	34	35	36
Ni	**Cu**	**Zn**	**Ga**	**Ge**	**As**	**Se**	**Br**	**Kr**
58.693	63.546	65.39	69.723	72.61	74.922	78.96	79.904	83.80

Palladium	Silver	Cadmium	Indium	Tin	Antimony	Tellurium	Iodine	Xenon
46	47	48	49	50	51	52	53	54
Pd	**Ag**	**Cd**	**In**	**Sn**	**Sb**	**Te**	**I**	**Xe**
106.42	107.868	112.411	114.82	118.710	121.757	127.60	126.904	131.290

Platinum	Gold	Mercury	Thallium	Lead	Bismuth	Polonium	Astatine	Radon
78	79	80	81	82	83	84	85	86
Pt	**Au**	**Hg**	**Tl**	**Pb**	**Bi**	**Po**	**At**	**Rn**
195.08	196.967	200.59	204.383	207.2	208.980	208.982	209.987	222.018

Ununnilium	Unununium	Ununbium		Ununquadium		Ununhexium		Ununodium
✱ 110	✱ 111	✱ 112		✱ 114		✱ 116		✱ 118
Uun	**Uuu**	**Uub**		**Uuq**		**Uuh**		**Uuo**
269	272	277		285		289		293

✱ Names not officially assigned.

Europium	Gadolinium	Terbium	Dysprosium	Holmium	Erbium	Thulium	Ytterbium	Lutetium
63	64	65	66	67	68	69	70	71
Eu	**Gd**	**Tb**	**Dy**	**Ho**	**Er**	**Tm**	**Yb**	**Lu**
151.965	157.25	158.925	162.50	164.930	167.26	168.934	173.04	174.967

Americium	Curium	Berkelium	Californium	Einsteinium	Fermium	Mendelevium	Nobelium	Lawrencium
95	96	97	98	99	100	101	102	103
Am	**Cm**	**Bk**	**Cf**	**Es**	**Fm**	**Md**	**No**	**Lr**
243.061	247.070	247.070	251.080	252.083	257.095	258.099	259.101	260.105

English Glossary

This glossary defines each key term that appears in bold type in the text. It also shows the chapter, section, and page number where you can find the word(s) used.

A

abrasion: a type of erosion that occurs when windblown sediments strike rocks and sediments, polishing and pitting their surface. (Chap. 8, Sec. 3, p. 224)

absolute age: age, in years, of a rock or other object; can be determined by using properties of the atoms that make up materials. (Chap. 13, Sec. 3, p. 383)

absolute magnitude: measure of the amount of light a star actually gives off. (Chap. 25, Sec. 1, p. 738)

abyssal (uh BIH sul) **plain:** flat seafloor area from 4,000 m to 6,000 m below the ocean surface, formed by the deposition of sediments. (Chap. 19, Sec. 1, p. 551)

acid: substance with a pH lower than 7. (Chap. 21, Sec. 2, p. 620)

acid rain: acidic moisture, with a pH below 5.6, that falls to Earth as rain or snow and can damage forests, harm organisms, and corrode structures. (Chap. 21, Sec. 2, p. 620)

adaptation: any structural or behavioral change that helps an organism survive in its particular environment. (Chap. 17, Sec. 2, p. 496)

air mass: large body of air that has the same characteristics of temperature and moisture content as the part of Earth's surface over which it formed. (Chap. 16, Sec. 2, p. 470)

apparent magnitude: measure of the amount of light from a star that is received on Earth. (Chap. 25, Sec. 1, p. 738)

aquifer (AK wuh fur): layer of permeable rock that allows water to flow through. (Chap. 9, Sec. 2, p. 252)

asteroid: a piece of rock made up of material similar to that which formed the planets; mostly found in the asteroid belt between the orbits of Mars and Jupiter. (Chap. 24, Sec. 4, p. 724)

asthenosphere (as THE nuh sfihr): plastic-like layer of Earth on which the lithospheric plates float and move around. (Chap. 10, Sec. 3, p. 284)

atmosphere: Earth's air, which is made up of a thin layer of gases, solids, and liquids; forms a protective layer around the planet and is divided into five distinct layers. (Chap. 15, Sec. 1, p. 434)

atom(s): tiny building blocks of matter, made up of protons, neutrons, and electrons. (Chap. 2, Sec. 1, p. 34)

atomic number: the number of protons in an atom. (Chap. 2, Sec. 1, p. 37)

axis: imaginary vertical line that cuts through the center of Earth and around which Earth spins. (Chap. 23, Sec. 1, p. 673)

B

basaltic: dense, dark-colored igneous rock formed from magma; rich in magnesium and iron and poor in silica. (Chap. 4, Sec. 2, p. 97)

base: substance with a pH above 7. (Chap. 21, Sec. 2, p. 620)

basin: low area on Earth in which an ocean formed when the area filled with water from torrential rains. (Chap. 18, Sec. 1, p. 523)

batholith: largest intrusive igneous rock body that forms when magma being forced upward toward Earth's crust cools slowly and solidifies underground. (Chap. 12, Sec. 3, p. 350)

beach: deposit of sediment whose materials vary in size, color, and composition and is most commonly found on a smooth, gently sloped shoreline. (Chap. 9, Sec. 3, p. 259)

benthos: marine plants and animals that live on or in the ocean floor. (Chap. 19, Sec. 2, p. 561)

bias: personal opinion. (Chap. 1, Sec. 2, p. 21)

big bang theory: states that about 12 to 15 billion years ago, the universe began with a huge, fiery explosion. (Chap. 25, Sec. 4, p. 757)

biomass energy: renewable energy derived from burning organic materials such as wood and alcohol. (Chap. 5, Sec. 2, p. 133)

black hole: final stage in the evolution of a supernova, where the core's mass collapses to a point that it has no volume and whose gravity is so strong that not even light can escape. (Chap. 25, Sec. 3, p. 16)

blizzard: winter storm that lasts at least three hours with temperatures of −12°C or below, poor visibility, and winds of at least 51 km/h. (Chap. 16, Sec. 2, p. 477)

breaker: collapsing ocean wave that forms in shallow water and breaks onto the shore. (Chap. 18, Sec. 3, p. 533)

C

caldera: large, circular-shaped opening formed when the top of a volcano collapses. (Chap. 12, Sec. 3, p. 352)

carbon film: thin film of carbon residue preserved as a fossil. (Chap. 13, Sec. 1, p. 370)

carbon monoxide: colorless, odorless gas that reduces the oxygen content in the blood, is found in car exhaust, and contributes to air pollution. (Chap. 21, Sec. 2, p. 621)

carrying capacity: maximum number of individuals of a given species that the environment will support. (Chap. 20, Sec. 1, p. 585)

cast: a type of body fossil that forms when crystals fill a mold or sediments wash into a mold and harden into rock. (Chap. 13, Sec. 1, p. 371)

cave: underground opening that can form when acidic groundwater dissolves limestone. (Chap. 9, Sec. 2, p. 255)

cementation: sedimentary rock-forming process in which large sediments are held together by natural cements that are produced when water soaks through rock and soil. (Chap. 4, Sec. 4, p. 105)

Cenozoic (sen uh ZOH ihk) **Era:** era of recent life that began about 66 million years ago and continues today; includes the first appearance of *Homo sapiens* about 400,000 years ago. (Chap. 14, Sec. 3, p. 418)

channel: groove created by water moving down the same path. (Chap. 9, Sec. 1, p. 242)

chemical weathering: occurs when chemical reactions dissolve the minerals in rocks or change them into different minerals. (Chap. 7, Sec. 1, p. 187)

chemosynthesis (kee moh SIHN thuh sihs): food-making process using sulfur or nitrogen compounds, rather than light energy from the Sun, that is used by bacteria living near thermal vents. (Chap. 19, Sec. 2, p. 559)

chlorofluorocarbons (CFCs): group of chemical compounds used in refrigerators, air conditioners, foam packaging, and aerosol sprays that may enter the atmosphere and destroy ozone. (Chap. 15, Sec. 1, p. 440)

chromosphere: layer of the Sun's atmosphere above the photosphere. (Chap. 25, Sec. 2, p. 143)

cinder cone volcano: steep-sided, loosely packed volcano formed when tephra falls to the ground. (Chap. 12, Sec. 2, p. 344)

cleavage: physical property of some minerals that causes them to break along smooth, flat surfaces. (Chap. 3, Sec. 2, p. 71)

climate: average weather pattern in an area over a long period of time; can be classified by temperature, humidity, precipitation, and vegetation. (Chap. 7, Sec. 1, p. 188) (Chap. 17, Sec. 1, p. 492)

coal: sedimentary rock formed from decayed plant material; the world's most abundant fossil fuel. (Chap. 5, Sec. 1, p. 121)

comet: space object formed from dust and rock particles mixed with frozen water, methane, and ammonia that forms a bright coma as it approaches the Sun. (Chap. 24, Sec. 4, p. 722)

compaction: process that forms sedimentary rocks when layers of small sediments are compressed by the weight of the layers above them. (Chap. 4, Sec. 4, p. 104)

composite volcano: volcano built by alternating explosive and quiet eruptions that produce layers of tephra and lava; found mostly where Earth's plates come together and one plate sinks below the other. (Chap. 12, Sec. 2, p. 345)

composting: conservation method in which yard wastes such as cut grass, pulled weeds, and raked leaves are piled and left to decompose gradually. (Chap. 20, Sec. 3, p. 597)

compound: matter that is made of two of more elements and has physical and chemical properties different from each of the elements that make it up. (Chap. 2, Sec. 2, p. 40)

condensation: process in which water vapor changes to a liquid. (Chap. 15, Sec. 2, p. 445)

conduction: transfer of energy that occurs when molecules bump into each other. (Chap. 15, Sec. 2, p. 444)

conic projection: map made by projecting points and lines from a globe onto a cone. (Chap. 6, Sec. 3, p. 167)

conservation: careful use of resources to reduce damage to the environment through such methods as composting and recycling materials. (Chap. 20, Sec. 3, p. 596)

constant: variable that does not change in an experiment. (Chap. 1, Sec. 1, p. 10)

constellation: group of stars that forms a pattern in the sky that looks like a familiar object (Big Dipper), animal (Pegasus), or character (Orion). (Chap. 25, Sec. 1, p. 736)

continental drift: Wegener's hypothesis that all continents were once connected in a single, large landmass that broke apart about 200 million years ago and drifted slowly to their current positions. (Chap. 910 Sec. 1, p. 276)

continental shelf: gradually sloping end of a continent that extends beneath the ocean and provides a home for most marine organisms. (Chap. 19, Sec. 1, p. 550)

continental slope: ocean basin feature that dips steeply down from the continental shelf. (Chap. 19, Sec. 1, p. 551)

contour line: line on a map that connects points of equal elevation. (Chap. 6, Sec. 3, p. 168)

control: standard for comparison in an experiment. (Chap. 1, Sec. 1, p. 10)

convection: transfer of heat by the flow of material. (Chap. 15, Sec. 2, p. 444)

convection current: current in Earth's mantle that transfers heat in Earth's interior and is the driving force for plate tectonics. (Chap. 10, Sec. 3, p. 289)

Coriolis (kor ee OH lus) **effect:** causes moving air and water to turn left in the southern hemisphere and turn right in the northern hemisphere due to Earth's rotation. (Chap. 15, Sec. 3, p. 448)

Coriolis effect: shifting of winds and surface currents caused by Earth's rotation that turns currents north of the equator clockwise and south of the equator counterclockwise. (Chap. 18, Sec. 2, p. 527)

corona: outermost, largest layer of the Sun's atmosphere; extends millions of kilometers into space and has temperatures up to 2 million K. (Chap. 25, Sec. 2, p. 741)

crater: steep-walled depression around a volcano's vent. (Chap. 12, Sec. 1, p. 336)

creep: a type of mass movement in which sediments move downslope very slowly; is common in areas of freezing and thawing, and can cause walls, trees, and fences to lean downhill. (Chap. 8, Sec. 1, p. 214)

crest: highest point of a wave. (Chap. 18, Sec. 3, p. 532)

crystal: solid in which the atoms are arranged in an orderly, repeating pattern. (Chap. 3, Sec. 1, p. 63)

cyanobacteria: chlorophyll-containing, photosynthetic bacteria thought to be one of Earth's earliest life-forms. (Chap. 14, Sec. 2, p. 407)

D

deflation: a type of erosion that occurs when wind blows over loose sediments, removes small particles, and leaves coarser sediments behind. (Chap. 8, Sec. 3, p. 224)

deforestation: destruction and cutting down of forests—often to clear land for mining, roads, and grazing of cattle—resulting in increased atmospheric CO_2 levels. (Chap. 17, Sec. 3, p. 509)

density: a physical property of matter that can be determined by dividing the mass of an object by its volume. (Chap. 2, Sec. 3, p. 46)

density current: circulation pattern in the ocean that forms when a mass of more dense seawater sinks beneath less dense seawater. (Chap. 18, Sec. 2, p. 529)

dependent variable: factor being measured in an experiment. (Chap. 1, Sec. 1, p. 10)

deposition: dropping of sediments that occurs when an agent of erosion, such as gravity, a glacier, wind, or water, loses its energy and can no longer carry its load. (Chap. 8, Sec. 1, p. 213)

dew point: temperature at which air is saturated and condensation forms. (Chap. 16, Sec. 1, p. 465)

dike: igneous rock feature formed when magma is squeezed into a vertical crack that cuts across rock layers and hardens underground. (Chap. 12, Sec. 3, p. 351)

drainage basin: land area from which a river or stream collects runoff. (Chap. 9, Sec. 1, p. 244)

dune (DOON): mound formed when wind-blown sediments pile up behind an obstacle; common landform in desert areas. (Chap. 8, Sec. 3, p. 227)

E

Earth: third planet from the Sun; has an atmosphere that protects life and surface temperatures that allow water to exist as a solid, liquid, and gas. (Chap. 24, Sec. 2, p. 710)

earthquake: vibrations produced when rocks break along a fault. (Chap. 11, Sec. 1, p. 305)

Earth science: study of Earth and space, including rocks, fossils, climate, volcanoes, land use, ocean water, earthquakes, and objects in space. (Chap. 1, Sec. 1, p. 9)

electromagnetic spectrum: arrangement of electromagnetic waves according to their wavelengths. (Chap. 22, Sec. 1, p. 641)

electrons: negatively charged particles that move around the nucleus of an atom and form an electron cloud. (Chap. 2, Sec. 1, p. 36)

element: substance that contains only one type of atom—for example, oxygen, aluminum, and iron. (Chap. 2, Sec. 1, p. 35)

ellipse (ee LIHPS): elongated, closed curve that describes Earth's yearlong orbit around the Sun. (Chap. 23, Sec. 1, p. 675)

El Niño (el NEEN yoh): climatic event that begins in the tropical Pacific Ocean; may occur when trade winds weaken or reverse, and can disrupt normal temperature and precipitation patterns around the world. (Chap. 17, Sec. 3, p. 501)

enzyme: substance that causes chemical reactions to happen more quickly. (Chap. 20, Sec. 2, p. 593)

eon: longest subdivision in the geologic time scale that is based on the abundance of certain types of fossils and is subdivided into eras, periods, and epochs. (Chap. 14, Sec. 1, p. 399)

epicenter (EP ih sent ur): point on Earth's surface directly above an earthquake's focus. (Chap. 11, Sec. 2, p. 309)

epoch: next-smaller division of geologic time after the period; is characterized by differences in life-forms that may vary regionally. (Chap. 14, Sec. 1, p. 399)

equator: imaginary line that wraps around Earth at 0° latitude, halfway between the north and south poles. (Chap. 6, Sec. 2, p. 162)

equinox (EE kwuh nahks): twice-yearly time—each spring and fall—when the Sun is directly over the equator and the number of daylight and nighttime hours are equal worldwide. (Chap. 23, Sec. 1, p. 677)

era: second-longest division of geologic time; is subdivided into periods and is based on major worldwide changes in types of fossils. (Chap. 14, Sec. 1, p. 399)

erosion: process in which surface materials are worn away and transported from one place to another by agents such as gravity, water, wind, and glaciers. (Chap. 8, Sec. 1, p. 212)

estuary: area where a river meets the ocean that contains a mixture of freshwater and ocean water and provides an important habitat to many marine organisms. (Chap. 19, Sec. 2, p. 564)

ethics: study of moral values about what is good or bad. (Chap. 1, Sec. 2, p. 20)

extrusive: fine-grained igneous rock that forms when magma cools quickly at or near Earth's surface. (Chap. 4, Sec. 2, p. 95)

F

fault: surface along which rocks move when they pass their elastic limit and break. (Chap. 11, Sec. 1, p. 304)

fault-block mountains: mountains formed from huge, tilted blocks of rock that are separated from surrounding rocks by faults. (Chap. 6, Sec. 1, p. 160)

fertilizer: chemical that helps plants and other organisms grow. (Chap. 21, Sec. 1, p. 611)

focus: in an earthquake, the point below Earth's surface where energy is released in the form of seismic waves. (Chap. 11, Sec. 2, p. 308)

fog: a stratus cloud that forms when air is cooled to its dew point near the ground. (Chap. 16, Sec. 1, p. 467)

folded mountains: mountains formed when horizontal rock layers are squeezed from opposite sides, causing them to buckle and fold. (Chap. 6, Sec. 1, p. 159)

foliated: metamorphic rock, such as slate and gneiss, whose mineral grains flatten and line up in parallel layers. (Chap. 4, Sec. 3, p. 101)

fossil fuel: nonrenewable energy resource, such as oil and coal, formed over millions of years from the remains of dead plants and other organisms. (Chap. 5, Sec. 1, p. 120)

fossils: remains, imprints, or traces of prehistoric organisms that can tell when and where organisms once lived and how they lived. (Chap. 13, Sec. 1, p. 369)

fracture: physical property of some minerals that causes them to break with uneven, rough, or jagged surfaces. (Chap. 3, Sec. 2, p. 71)

front: boundary between two air masses with different temperatures, density, or moisture; can be cold, warm, occluded, and stationary. (Chap. 16, Sec. 2, p. 471)

full moon: phase that occurs when all of the Moon's surface facing Earth reflects light. (Chap. 23, Sec. 2, p. 679)

G

galaxy: large group of stars, dust, and gas held together by gravity; can be elliptical, spiral, or irregular. (Chap. 25, Sec. 4, p. 752)

gem: beautiful, rare, highly prized mineral that can be worn in jewelry. (Chap. 3, Sec. 3, p. 73)

geologic time scale: division of Earth's history into time units based largely on the types of life-forms that lived only during certain periods. (Chap. 14, Sec. 1, p. 398)

geothermal energy: inexhaustible energy resource that uses hot magma or hot, dry rocks from below Earth's surface to generate electricity. (Chap. 5, Sec. 2, p. 132)

geyser: hot spring that erupts periodically and shoots water and steam into the air—for example, Old Faithful in Yellowstone National Park. (Chap. 9, Sec. 2, p. 255)

giant: late stage in the life of a main sequence star when hydrogen in the core is used up, the core contracts and temperatures inside the star increase, causing its outer layers to expand and cool. (Chap. 25, Sec. 3, p. 749)

glaciers: large, moving masses of ice and snow that change large areas of Earth's surface through erosion and deposition. (Chap. 8, Sec. 2, p. 217)

global warming: increase in the average global temperature of Earth. (Chap. 17, Sec. 3, p. 508)

granitic: light-colored, silica-rich igneous rock that is less dense than basaltic rock. (Chap. 4, Sec. 2, p. 97)

Great Red Spot: giant, high-pressure gas storm on Jupiter. (Chap. 24, Sec. 3, p. 714)

greenhouse effect: natural heating that occurs when certain gases in Earth's atmosphere, such as methane, CO_2, and water vapor, trap heat. (Chap. 17, Sec. 3, p. 507)

groundwater: water that soaks into the ground and collects in pores and empty spaces and is an important source of drinking water. (Chap. 9, Sec. 2, p. 251)

H

half-life: time it takes for half the atoms of an isotope to decay. (Chap. 13, Sec. 3, p. 384)

hardness: measure of how easily a mineral can be scratched; is determined by the arrangement of the mineral's atoms. (Chap. 3, Sec. 2, p. 69)

hazardous waste: poisonous, ignitable, or cancer-causing waste. (Chap. 20, Sec. 2, p. 592)

heterogeneous mixture: a mixture which is not mixed evenly and each component retains its own properties. (Chap. 2, Sec. 2, p. 43)

hibernation: behavioral adaptation for winter survival in which an animal's activity is greatly reduced, its body temperature drops, and body processes slow down. (Chap. 17, Sec. 2, p. 498)

homogeneous mixture: a mixture which is evenly mixed throughout. (Chap. 2, Sec. 2, p. 43)

horizon: each layer in a soil profile—horizon A (top layer of soil), horizon B (middle layer), and horizon C (bottom layer). (Chap. 7, Sec. 2, p. 192)

hot spot: unusually hot area at the boundary between Earth's mantle and core that forms volcanoes when melted rock is forced upward and breaks through the crust. (Chap. 12, Sec. 1, p. 338)

humidity: amount of water vapor held in the air. (Chap. 16, Sec. 1, p. 464)

humus (HYEW mus): dark-colored, decayed organic matter that supplies nutrients to plants and is found mainly in topsoil. (Chap. 7, Sec. 2, p. 192)

hurricane: large, severe storm that forms over tropical oceans, has winds of at least 120 km/h, and loses power when it reaches land. (Chap. 16, Sec. 2, p. 476)

hydroelectric energy: electricity produced by waterpower using large dams in a river. (Chap. 5, Sec. 2, p. 132)

hydrosphere: all the water on Earth's surface. (Chap. 15, Sec. 2, p. 13)

hypothesis: an educated guess. (Chap. 1, Sec. 1, p. 7)

I

ice wedging: mechanical weathering process that occurs when water freezes in the cracks of rocks and expands, causing the rock to break apart. (Chap. 7, Sec. 1, p. 186)

igneous rock: intrusive or extrusive rock formed when hot magma cools and hardens. (Chap. 4, Sec. 2, p. 94)

impact basin: a hollow left on the surface of the Moon caused by an object striking its surface. (Chap. 23, Sec. 3, p. 689)

impermeable: describes materials that water cannot pass through. (Chap. 9, Sec. 2, p. 252)

independent variable: factor that changes in an experiment. (Chap. 1, Sec. 1, p. 10)

index fossils: remains of species that existed on Earth for a relatively short period of time, were abundant and widespread geographically, and can be used by geologists to assign the ages of rock layers. (Chap. 13, Sec. 1, p. 373)

intrusive: a type of igneous rock that generally contains large crystals and forms when magma cools slowly beneath Earth's surface. (Chap. 4, Sec. 2, p. 95)

ion: electrically charged atom whose charge results from an atom losing or gaining electrons. (Chap. 2, Sec. 2, p. 41)

ionosphere: layer of electrically charged particles in the thermosphere that absorbs AM radio waves during the day and reflects them back at night. (Chap. 15, Sec. 1, p. 437)

isobars: lines drawn on a weather map that connect points having equal atmospheric pressure; also indicate the location of high- and low-pressure areas and can show wind speed. (Chap. 16, Sec. 3, p. 479)

isotherm (I suh thurm): line drawn on a weather map that connects points having equal temperature. (Chap. 16, Sec. 3, p. 479)

isotopes: atoms of the same element that have different numbers of neutrons. (Chap. 2, Sec. 1, p. 37)

J

jet stream: narrow belt of strong winds that blows near the top of the troposphere. (Chap. 15, Sec. 3, p. 450)

Jupiter: largest and fifth planet from the Sun; contains more mass than all the other planets combined, has continuous storms of high-pressure gas, and an atmosphere mostly of hydrogen and helium. (Chap. 24, Sec. 3, p. 714)

L

land breeze: movement of air from land to sea at night, created when cooler, denser air from the land forces warmer air up over the sea. (Chap. 15, Sec. 3, p. 451)

latitude: distance in degrees north or south of the equator. (Chap. 6, Sec. 2, p. 162)

lava: thick, gooey, molten rock material flowing from volcanoes onto Earth's surface. (Chap. 4, Sec. 2, p. 94)

leaching: removal of minerals that have been dissolved in water. (Chap. 7, Sec. 2, p. 193)

light-year: distance light travels in one year—about 9.5 trillion km—which is used to record distances between stars and galaxies. (Chap. 25, Sec. 1, p. 739)

liquefaction: occurs when wet soil acts more like a liquid during an earthquake. (Chap. 11, Sec. 3, p. 319)

lithosphere (LIH thuh sfihr): rigid layer of Earth about 100 km thick, made of the crust and a part of the upper mantle. (Chap. 10, Sec. 3, p. 284)

litter: twigs, leaves, and other organic matter that help prevent erosion, hold water and eventually might be changed into humus by decomposing organisms. (Chap. 7, Sec. 2, p. 193)

loess (LOOS): windblown deposit of tightly packed, fine-grained sediments. (Chap. 8, Sec. 3, p. 227)

longitude: distance in degrees east or west of the prime meridian. (Chap. 6, Sec. 2, p. 163)

longshore current: current that runs parallel to the shoreline, is caused by waves colliding with the shore at slight angles, and moves tons of loose sediment. (Chap. 9, Sec. 3, p. 258)

lunar eclipse: occurs when Earth's shadow falls on the Moon. (Chap. 23, Sec. 2, p. 682)

luster: describes the way a mineral reflects light from its surface; can be either metallic or nonmetallic. (Chap. 3, Sec. 2, p. 70)

M

magma: hot, melted rock material beneath Earth's surface. (Chap. 3, Sec. 1, p. 65)

magnitude: measure of the energy released during an earthquake. (Chap. 11, Sec. 3, p. 318)

map legend: explains the meaning of symbols used on a map. (Chap. 6, Sec. 3, p. 170)

map scale: relationship between distances on a map and distances on Earth's surface that can be represented as a ratio or as a small bar divided into sections. (Chap. 6, Sec. 3, p. 170)

maria (MAHR ee uh): dark-colored, relatively flat regions of the Moon formed when ancient lava reached the surface and filled craters on the Moon's surface. (Chap. 23, Sec. 2, p. 683)

Mars: fourth planet from the Sun; has polar ice caps, a thin atmosphere, and a reddish appearance from iron oxide in weathered rocks. (Chap. 24, Sec. 2, p. 710)

mass movement: any type of erosion that occurs as gravity moves materials downslope. (Chap. 8, Sec. 1, p. 213)

mass number: the number of protons plus the number of neutrons in an atom. (Chap. 2, Sec. 1, p. 37)

matter: anything that has mass and takes up space; matter's properties are determined by the structure of its atoms and how they are joined. (Chap. 2, Sec. 1, p. 34)

meander (mee AN dur): broad, c-shaped curve in a river or stream, formed by erosion of its outer bank. (Chap. 9, Sec. 1, p. 245)

mechanical weathering: physical process that breaks rocks apart without changing their chemical makeup; can be caused by ice wedging, animals, and plant roots. (Chap. 7, Sec. 1, p. 185)

Mercury: smallest planet, closest to the Sun; has a thin atmosphere and a surface with many craters and high cliffs. (Chap. 24, Sec. 2, p. 708)

Mesozoic (mez uh ZOH ihk) **Era:** middle era of Earth's history, during which Pangaea broke apart, dinosaurs appeared, and reptiles and gymnosperms were the dominant land life-forms. (Chap. 14, Sec. 3, p. 414)

metamorphic rock: forms when heat, pressure, or fluids act on igneous, sedimentary, or other metamorphic rock and affect its form or composition, or both. (Chap. 4, Sec. 3, p. 99)

meteor: a meteoroid that burns up in Earth's atmosphere. (Chap. 24, Sec. 4, p. 723)

meteorite: a meteoroid that strikes the surface of a moon or planet. (Chap. 24, Sec. 4, p. 724)

meteorologist (meet ee uh RAHL uh just): studies weather and uses information from Doppler radar, weather satellites, computers and other instruments to make weather maps and provide forecasts. (Chap. 16, Sec. 3, p. 478)

mid-ocean ridge: area where new ocean floor is formed when lava erupts through cracks in Earth's crust. (Chap. 19, Sec. 1, p. 552)

mineral: naturally occurring inorganic solid that has a definite chemical composition and an orderly internal atomic structure. (Chap. 3, Sec. 1, p. 62)

mineral resources: resources from which metals are obtained. (Chap. 5, Sec. 3, p. 137)

mixture: describes two or more substances that retain their own properties even when they are combined and that can be separated from one another by physical means. (Chap. 2, Sec. 2, p. 43)

mold: a type of body fossil that forms in rock when an organism with hard parts is buried, decays or dissolves, and leaves a cavity in the rock. (Chap. 13, Sec. 1, p. 371)

moon phase: change in appearance of the Moon as viewed from the Earth, due to the relative positions of the Moon, Earth, and Sun. (Chap. 23, Sec. 2, p. 679)

moraine: large ridge of rocks and soil deposited by a glacier when it stops moving forward. (Chap. 8, Sec. 2, p. 219)

N

natural gas: fossil fuel formed from marine organisms that is often found in tilted or folded rock layers and is used for heating and cooking. (Chap. 5, Sec. 1, p. 123)

natural selection: process by which organisms that are suited to a particular environment are better able to survive and reproduce than organisms that are not. (Chap. 14, Sec. 1, p. 401)

nebula: large cloud of gas and dust that contracts under gravitational force and breaks apart into smaller pieces, each of which will collapse to form a star. (Chap. 25, Sec. 3, p. 748)

nekton: marine organisms that actively swim in the ocean. (Chap. 19, Sec. 2, p. 560)

Neptune: usually the eighth planet from the Sun; is large and gaseous, has rings that vary in thickness, and is bluish-green in color. (Chap. 24, Sec. 3, p. 718)

neutron: particle without an electric charge that is located in the nucleus of an atom. (Chap. 2, Sec. 1, p. 36)

neutron star: collapsed core of a supernova that can shrink to about 20 km in diameter and contains only neutrons in the dense core. (Chap. 25, Sec. 3, p. 750)

new moon: moon phase that occurs when the Moon is between Earth and the Sun, at which point the Moon cannot be seen because its lighted half is facing the Sun and its dark side faces Earth. (Chap. 23, Sec. 2, p. 679)

non-foliated: metamorphic rock, such as quartzite and marble, whose mineral grains grow and rearrange but do not form layers. (Chap. 4, Sec. 3, p. 102)

nonpoint source pollution: pollution that enters water from a large area and cannot be traced to a single location. (Chap. 21, Sec. 1, p. 610)

normal fault: break in rock caused by tension forces, where rock above the fault surface moves down relative to the rock below the fault surface. (Chap. 11, Sec. 1, p. 306)

nuclear energy: alternative energy source that is based on atomic fission. (Chap. 5, Sec. 1, p. 127)

O

observatory: building that can house an optical telescope; often has a dome-shaped roof that can be opened for viewing. (Chap. 22, Sec. 1, p. 642)

oil: liquid fossil fuel formed from marine organisms that is burned to obtain energy and used in the manufacture of plastics. (Chap. 5, Sec. 1, p. 123)

orbit: curved path followed by a satellite as it revolves around an object. (Chap. 22, Sec. 2, p. 649)

ore: deposit in which a mineral exists in large enough amounts to be mined at a profit. (Chap. 5, Sec. 3, p. 137)

organic evolution: change of organisms over geologic time. (Chap. 14, Sec. 1, p. 400)

outwash: material deposited by meltwater from a glacier. (Chap. 8, Sec. 2, p. 219)

oxidation (ahk sih DAY shun): chemical weathering process that occurs when metallic material is exposed to oxygen and water over time. (Chap. 7, Sec. 1, p. 188)

ozone layer: layer of the stratosphere with a high concentration of ozone; absorbs most of the Sun's harmful ultraviolet radiation. (Chap. 15, Sec. 1, p. 440)

P

Paleozoic Era: era of ancient life, which began about 544 million years ago, when organisms developed hard parts, and ended with mass extinctions about 245 million years ago. (Chap. 14, Sec. 2, p. 408)

Pangaea (pan JEE uh): large, ancient landmass that was composed of all the continents joined together. (Chap. 10, Sec. 1, p. 276) (Chap. 14, Sec. 1, p. 405)

particulate (par TIHK yuh layt) **matter:** fine solids such as pollen, dust, mold, ash and soot as well as liquid droplets in the air that can irritate and damage lungs when breathed in. (Chap. 21, Sec. 2, p. 622)

period: third-longest division of geologic time; is subdivided into epochs and is characterized by the types of life that existed worldwide. (Chap. 14, Sec. 1, p. 399)

permeable (PUR mee uh bul): describes soil and rock with connecting pores through which water can flow. (Chap. 9, Sec. 2, p. 252)

permineralized remains: fossils in which the spaces inside are filled with minerals from groundwater. (Chap. 13, Sec. 1, p. 370)

pesticide: substance used to keep insects and weeds from destroying crops and lawns. (Chap. 21, Sec. 1, p. 611)

photochemical smog: hazy, yellow-brown blanket of smog found over cities that is formed with the help of sunlight, contains ozone near Earth's surface, and can damage lungs and plants. (Chap. 21, Sec. 2, p. 619)

photosphere: lowest layer of the Sun's atmosphere; gives off light and has temperatures of about 6,000 K. (Chap. 25, Sec. 2, p. 741)

photosynthesis: food-making process using light energy from the Sun, carbon dioxide, and water. (Chap. 19, Sec. 2, p. 557)

English Glossary

pH scale: scale used to measure how acidic or basic something is. (Chap. 21, Sec. 2, p. 620)

plain: large, flat landform that often has thick, fertile soil and is usually found in the interior region of a continent. (Chap. 6, Sec. 1, p. 156)

plankton: marine plants and animals that drift in ocean currents. (Chap. 19, Sec. 2, p. 560)

plate: a large section of Earth's oceanic or continental crust and rigid upper mantle that moves around on the asthenosphere. (Chap. 10, Sec. 3, p. 284)

plateau (pla TOH): flat, raised landform made up of nearly horizontal rocks that have been uplifted. (Chap. 6, Sec. 1, p. 158)

plate tectonics: theory that Earth's crust and upper mantle are broken into plates that float and move around on a plastic-like layer of the mantle. (Chap. 10, Sec. 3, p. 284)

plucking: process that adds gravel, sand, and boulders to a glacier's bottom and sides as water freezes and thaws, breaking off pieces of surrounding rock. (Chap. 8, Sec. 2, p. 218)

Pluto: considered to be the ninth planet from the Sun; has a solid icy-rock surface and a single moon. (Chap. 24, Sec. 3, p. 719)

point source pollution: pollution that enters water from a specific location and can be controlled or treated before it enters a body of water. (Chap. 21, Sec. 1, p. 610)

polar zones: climate zones that receive solar radiation at a low angle, extend from 66°N and S latitude to the poles, and are never warm. (Chap. 17, Sec. 1, p. 492)

pollutant: any substance that contaminates the environment. (Chap. 20, Sec. 1, p. 586)

pollution: introduction of wastes to an environment, such as sewage and chemicals, that can damage organisms. (Chap. 19, Sec. 3, p. 565)

population: total number of individuals of one species occupying the same area. (Chap. 20, Sec. 1, p. 584)

Precambrian (pree KAM bree un) **time:** longest part of Earth's history, lasting from 4 billion to about 544 million years ago. (Chap. 14, Sec. 2, p. 406)

precipitation: water falling from clouds—including rain, snow, sleet, and hail—whose form is determined by air temperature. (Chap. 16, Sec. 1, p. 468)

primary wave: seismic wave that moves rock particles back-and-forth in the same direction that the wave travels. (Chap. 11, Sec. 2, p. 309)

prime meridian: imaginary line that represents 0° longitude and runs from the north pole through Greenwich, England, to the south pole. (Chap. 6, Sec. 2, p. 163)

principle of superposition: states that in undisturbed rock layers, the oldest rocks are on the bottom and the rocks become progressively younger toward the top. (Chap. 13, Sec. 2, p. 376)

Project Apollo: final stage in the U.S. program to reach the Moon in which Neil Armstrong was the first human to step onto the Moon's surface. (Chap. 22, Sec. 2, p. 654)

Project Gemini: second stage in the U.S. program to reach the Moon in which an astronaut team connected with another spacecraft in orbit. (Chap. 22, Sec. 2, p. 653)

Project Mercury: first step in the U.S. program to reach the Moon that orbited a piloted spacecraft around Earth and brought it back safely. (Chap. 22, Sec. 2, p. 653)

proton: positively charged particle that is located in the nucleus of an atom. (Chap. 2, Sec. 1, p. 36)

R

radiation: energy transferred by waves or rays. (Chap. 15, Sec. 2, p. 444)

radioactive decay: process in which some isotopes break down into other isotopes and particles. (Chap. 13, Sec. 3, p. 383)

radiometric dating: process used to calculate the absolute age of rock by measuring the ratio of parent isotope to daughter product in a mineral and knowing the half-life of the parent. (Chap. 13, Sec. 3, p. 385)

radio telescope: collects and records radio waves traveling through space; can be used day or night under most weather conditions. (Chap. 22, Sec. 1, p. 645)

recycling: conservation method in which old materials are processed to make new ones. (Chap. 5, Sec. 3, p. 141) (Chap. 20, Sec. 3, p. 597)

reef: rigid, wave-resistant, ocean margin habitat built by corals from skeletal materials and calcium. (Chap. 19, Sec. 2, p. 564)

reflecting telescope: optical telescope that uses a concave mirror to focus light and form an image at the focal point. (Chap. 22, Sec. 1, p. 642)

refracting telescope: optical telescope that uses a double convex lens to bend light and form an image at the focal point. (Chap. 22, Sec. 1, p. 642)

relative age: the age of something compared with other things. (Chap. 13, Sec. 2, p. 377)

relative humidity: measure of the amount of moisture held in the air compared with the amount it can hold at a given temperature; can range from 0 percent to 100 percent. (Chap. 16, Sec. 1, p. 464)

reserve: amount of a fossil fuel that can be extracted from Earth at a profit using current technology. (Chap. 5, Sec. 1, p. 125)

reverse fault: break in rock caused by compressive forces, where rock above the fault surface moves upward relative to the rock below the fault surface. (Chap. 11, Sec. 1, p. 306)

revolution: Earth's yearlong elliptical orbit around the Sun. (Chap. 23, Sec. 1, p. 675)

rock: mixture of one or more minerals, volcanic glass, organic matter, or other materials; can be igneous, metamorphic, or sedimentary. (Chap. 4, Sec. 1, p. 90)

rock cycle: model that describes how rocks slowly change from one form to another through time. (Chap. 4, Sec. 1, p. 91)

rocket: special motor that can work in space and burns liquid or solid fuel. (Chap. 22, Sec. 2, p. 647)

rotation: spinning of Earth on its imaginary axis, which takes about 24 hours to complete, and causes day and night to occur. (Chap 23, Sec. 1, p. 673)

runoff: any rainwater that does not soak into the ground or evaporate but flows over Earth's surface; generally flows into streams and has the ability to erode and carry sediments. (Chap. 9, Sec. 1, p. 240)

S

salinity (say LIHN ut ee): a measure of the amount of salts dissolved in seawater. (Chap. 18, Sec. 1, p. 524)

sanitary landfill: area where garbage is deposited and covered with soil and that is designed to prevent contamination of land and water. (Chap. 20, Sec. 2, p. 592)

satellite: any natural or artificial object that revolves around another object. (Chap. 22, Sec. 2, p. 649)

Saturn: second-largest and sixth planet from the Sun; has a complex ring system, at least 18 moons, and a thick atmosphere made mostly of hydrogen and helium. (Chap. 24, Sec. 3, p. 716)

English Glossary

science: process of looking at and studying things in the world in order to gain knowledge. (Chap. 1, Sec. 1, p. 24)

scientific law: rule that describes the behavior of something in nature; usually describes what will happen in a situation but not why it happens. (Chap. 1, Sec. 2, p. 19)

scientific methods: problem-solving procedures that can include identifying the problem or question, gathering information, developing a hypothesis, testing the hypothesis, analyzing the results, and drawing conclusions. (Chap. 1, Sec. 1, p. 8)

scientific theory: explanation that is supported by results from repeated experimentation or testing. (Chap. 1, Sec. 2, p. 18)

scrubber: device that lowers sulfur emissions from coal-burning power plants. (Chap. 21, Sec. 2, p. 623)

sea breeze: movement of air from sea to land during the day when cooler air from above the water moves over the land, forcing the heated, less dense air above the land to rise. (Chap. 15, Sec. 3, p. 451)

seafloor spreading: Hess's theory that new seafloor is formed when magma is forced upward toward the surface at a mid-ocean ridge. (Chap. 10, Sec. 2, p. 281)

season: short period of climate change in an area caused by the tilt of Earth's axis as Earth revolves around the Sun. (Chap. 17, Sec. 3, p. 500)

secondary wave: seismic wave that moves rock particles at right angles to the direction of the wave. (Chap. 11, Sec. 2, p. 309)

sedimentary rock: forms when sediments are compacted and cemented together or when minerals come out of solution or are left behind by evaporation. (Chap. 4, Sec. 4, p. 103)

sediments: loose materials, such as rock fragments, mineral grains, and the remains of once-living plants and animals, that have been moved by wind, water, ice, or gravity. (Chap. 4, Sec. 4, p. 103)

seismic (SIZE mihk) **wave:** wave generated by an earthquake. (Chap. 11, Sec. 2, p. 308)

seismograph: instrument used to register earthquake waves and record the time that each arrived. (Chap. 11, Sec. 2, p. 311)

sewage: water that goes into drains and contains human waste, household detergents, and soaps. (Chap. 21, Sec. 1, p. 612)

sheet erosion: a type of surface water erosion caused by runoff that occurs when water flowing as sheets picks up sediments and carries them away. (Chap. 9, Sec. 1, p. 243)

shield volcano: broad, gently sloping volcano formed by quiet eruptions of basaltic lava. (Chap. 12, Sec. 2, p. 344)

silicate: mineral that contains silicon and oxygen and usually one or more other elements. (Chap. 3, Sec. 1, p. 66)

sill: igneous rock feature formed when magma is squeezed into a horizontal crack between layers of rock and hardens underground. (Chap. 12, Sec. 3, p. 351)

slump: a type of mass movement that occurs when a mass of material moves down a curved slope. (Chap. 8, Sec. 1, p. 213)

soil: mixture of weathered rock, decayed organic matter, mineral fragments, water, and air that can take thousands of years to develop. (Chap. 7, Sec. 2, p. 190)

soil profile: vertical section of soil layers, each of which is a horizon. (Chap. 7, Sec. 2, p. 192)

solar eclipse: occurs when the Moon passes directly between the Sun and Earth and casts a shadow over part of Earth. (Chap. 23, Sec. 2, p. 681)

solar energy: energy from the Sun that is clean, inexhaustible, and can be transformed into electricity by solar cells. (Chap. 5, Sec. 2, p. 130)

solar system: system of nine planets, including Earth, and other objects that revolve around the Sun. (Chap. 24, Sec. 1, p. 703)

solstice: twice-yearly point at which the Sun reaches its greatest distance north or south of the equator. (Chap. 23, Sec. 1, p. 675)

solution: a kind of mixture in which one substance is completely and evenly mixed in another substance and is the same throughout. (Chap. 2, Sec. 2, p. 43)

space probe: instrument that travels far into the solar system, gathers data, and sends them back to Earth. (Chap. 22, Sec. 2, p. 650)

space shuttle: reusable spacecraft that can carry cargo, astronauts, and satellites to and from space. (Chap. 22, Sec. 3, p. 655)

space station: large facility with living quarters, work and exercise areas, and equipment and support systems for humans to live and work in space and conduct research not possible on Earth. (Chap. 22, Sec. 3, p. 656)

species: group of organisms that reproduces only with other members of their own group. (Chap. 14, Sec. 1, p. 400)

specific gravity: ratio of a mineral's weight compared with the weight of an equal volume of water. (Chap. 3, Sec. 2, p. 70)

sphere (SFIHR): a round, three-dimensional object whose surface is the same distance from its center at all points; Earth is a sphere that bulges somewhat at the equator and is slightly flattened at the poles. (Chap. 23, Sec. 1, p. 672)

spring: forms when the water table meets Earth's surface; often found on hillsides and used as a freshwater source. (Chap. 9, Sec. 2, p. 255)

station model: indicates weather conditions at a specific location, using a combination of symbols on a map. (Chap. 16, Sec. 3, p. 479)

streak: color of a mineral when it is in powdered form. (Chap. 3, Sec. 2, p. 71)

stream discharge: volume of water that flows past a specific point per unit of time. (Chap. 20, Sec. 2, p. 591)

strike-slip fault: break in rock caused by shear forces, where rocks move past each other without much vertical movement. (Chap. 11, Sec. 1, p. 307)

sunspots: areas of the Sun that are cooler and less bright than surrounding areas, are caused by the Sun's magnetic field, and occur in cycles. (Chap. 25, Sec. 2, p. 742)

supergiant: late stage in the life cycle of a massive star in which the core heats up, heavy elements form by fusion, and the star expands; can eventually explode to form a supernova. (Chap. 25, Sec. 3, p. 750)

surface current: wind-powered ocean current that moves water horizontally—parallel to Earth's surface—and moves only the upper few hundred meters of seawater. (Chap. 18, Sec. 2, p. 526)

surface wave: seismic wave that moves rock particles up-and-down in a backward rolling motion and side-to-side in a swaying motion. (Chap. 11, Sec. 2, p. 309)

T

technology: use of scientific discoveries for practical purposes, making people's lives easier and better. (Chap. 1, Sec. 1, p. 12)

temperate zones: climate zones with moderate temperatures that are located between the tropics and the polar zones. (Chap. 17, Sec. 1, p. 492)

tephra (TEFF ruh): bits of rock or solidified lava dropped from the air during an explosive volcanic eruption; ranges in size from volcanic ash to volcanic bombs and blocks. (Chap. 12, Sec. 2, p. 344)

terracing: farming method used to reduce erosion on steep slopes. (Chap. 7, Sec. 3, p. 201)

tidal range: the difference between the level of the ocean at high tide and the level at low tide. (Chap. 18, Sec. 3, p. 536)

English Glossary

tide: daily rise and fall in sea level caused, for the most part, by the interaction of gravity in the Earth-Moon system. (Chap. 18, Sec. 3, p. 535)

till: mixture of different-sized sediments that is dropped from the base of a retreating glacier and can cover huge areas of land. (Chap. 8, Sec. 2, p. 218)

topographic map: map that shows the changes in elevation of Earth's surface and indicates such features as roads and cities. (Chap. 6, Sec. 3, p. 168)

tornado: violent, whirling windstorm that crosses land in a narrow path and can result from wind shears inside a thunderhead. (Chap. 16, Sec. 2, p. 474)

trench: long, narrow, steep-sided depression in the seafloor formed where one crustal plate sinks beneath another. (Chap. 19, Sec. 1, p. 553)

trilobite (TRI luh bite): organism with a three-lobed exoskeleton that was abundant in Paleozoic oceans and is considered to be an index fossil. (Chap. 14, Sec. 1, p. 398)

tropics: climate zone that receives the most solar radiation, is located between latitudes 23° N and 23° S, and is always hot, except at high elevations. (Chap. 17, Sec. 1, p. 492)

troposphere: layer of Earth's atmosphere that is closest to the ground, contains 99 percent of the water vapor and 75 percent of the atmospheric gases; where clouds and weather occur. (Chap. 15, Sec. 1, p. 436)

trough: lowest point of a wave. (Chap. 18, Sec. 3, p. 532)

tsunami (soo NAHM ee): seismic sea wave that begins over an earthquake focus and can be highly destructive when it crashes on shore. (Chap. 11, Sec. 3, p. 320)

U

ultraviolet radiation: a type of energy that comes to Earth from the Sun, can damage skin and cause cancer, and is mostly absorbed by the ozone layer. (Chap. 15, Sec. 1, p. 440)

unconformity (un kun FOR mih tee): gap in the rock layer that is due to erosion or periods without any deposition. (Chap. 13, Sec. 2, p. 377)

uniformitarianism: principle stating that Earth processes occurring today are similar to those that occurred in the past. (Chap. 13, Sec. 3, p. 387)

upwarped mountains: mountains formed when blocks of Earth's crust are pushed up by forces inside Earth. (Chap. 6, Sec. 1, p. 160)

upwelling: circulation in the ocean that brings deep, cold water to the ocean surface. (Chap. 18, Sec. 2, p. 529)

Uranus (YOOR uh nus): seventh planet from the Sun, is large and gaseous, has a distinct bluish-green color, and rotates on an axis nearly parallel to the plane of its orbit. (Chap. 24, Sec. 3, p. 717)

V

variables: different factors that can be changed in an experiment. (Chap. 1, Sec. 1, p. 10)

vent: opening where magma is forced up and flows out onto Earth's surface as lava, forming a volcano. (Chap. 12, Sec. 1, p. 336)

Venus: second planet from the Sun; similar to Earth in mass and size; has a thick atmosphere and a surface with craters, faultlike cracks, and volcanoes. (Chap. 24, Sec. 2, p. 709)

volcanic mountains: mountains formed when molten material reaches Earth's surface through a weak crustal area and piles up into a cone-shaped structure. (Chap. 6, Sec. 1, p. 161)

volcanic neck: solid igneous core of a volcano left behind after the softer cone has been eroded. (Chap. 12, Sec. 3, p. 351)

volcano: opening in Earth's surface that erupts sulfurous gases, ash, and lava; can form at Earth's plate boundaries, where plates move apart or together, and at hot spots. (Chap. 12, Sec. 1, p. 334)

W

waning: describes phases that occur after a full moon, as the visible lighted side of the Moon grows smaller. (Chap. 23, Sec. 2, p. 679)

water table: upper surface of the zone of saturation; drops during a drought. (Chap. 9, Sec. 2, p. 252)

wave: rhythmic movement that carries energy through matter or space; can be described by its crest, trough, wavelength, and wave height. (Chap. 18, Sec. 3, p. 532)

waxing: describes phases following a new moon, as more of the Moon's lighted side becomes visible. (Chap. 23, Sec. 2, p. 679)

weather: state of the atmosphere at a specific time and place, determined by factors including air pressure, amount of moisture in the air, temperature, and wind. (Chap. 16, Sec. 1, p. 462)

weathering: mechanical or chemical surface processes that break rocks into smaller and smaller pieces. (Chap. 7, Sec. 1, p. 184)

white dwarf: late stage in the life cycle of a main sequence star in which its core uses up its helium and its outer layers escape into space, leaving behind a hot, dense core. (Chap. 25, Sec. 3, p. 749)

wind farm: area where many windmills use wind to generate electricity. (Chap. 5, Sec. 2, p. 131)

Spanish Glossary

Este glossario define cada término clave que aparece en negrillas en el texto. También muestra el capítulo, sección y el número de página en donde se usa dicho término.

A

abrasion / abrasión: tipo de erosión que ocurre cuando los sedimentos soplados por el viento golpean rocas y sedimentos, puliendo y dejando huecos en su superficie. (Cap. 8, Sec. 3, pág. 224)

absolute age / edad absoluta: edad, expresada en años, de una roca u otro material; se puede determinar usando las propiedades de los átomos que componen tales materiales. (Cap. 13, Sec. 3, pág. 383)

absolute magnitude / magnitud absoluta: medida de la cantidad de luz que en realidad emite una estrella. (Cap. 25, Sec. 1, pág. 738)

abyssal plain / planicie abisal: área plana de suelo marino que desciende de 4,000 a 6,000 m debajo de la superficie del océano y que se forma de la depositación de sedimentos. (Cap. 19, Sec. 1, pág. 551)

acid / ácido: sustancia cuyo pH es inferior a 7. (Cap. 21, Sec. 2, pág. 620)

acid rain / lluvia ácida: humedad ácida, cuyo pH es inferior a 5.6, que cae a la Tierra como lluvia o nieve y puede causar daños a bosques, perjudicar organismos y corroer las estructuras. (Cap. 21, Sec. 2, pág. 620)

adaptation / adaptación: todo cambio estructural o de comportamiento que le ayuda a un organismo a sobrevivir en un ambiente en particular. (Cap. 17, Sec. 2, pág. 496)

air mass / masa de aire: flujo enorme de aire que tiene las mismas características de temperatura y contenido de humedad que la superficie terrestre sobre la cual se formó. (Cap. 16, Sec. 2, pág. 470)

apparent magnitude / magnitud aparente: medida de la cantidad de luz proveniente de una estrella que recibe la Tierra. (Cap. 25, Sec. 1, pág. 738)

aquifer / acuífero: capa de roca permeable que permite la infiltración del agua. (Cap. 9, Sec. 2, pág. 253)

asteroid / asteroide: fragmento rocoso formado por material semejante a aquel que formó los planetas; se encuentra principalmente en el cinturón de asteroides entre las órbitas de Marte y Júpiter. (Cap. 24, Sec. 4, pág. 724)

asthenosphere / astenosfera: capa de la Tierra tipo plástico en la cual las placas litosféricas flotan y se mueven. (Cap. 10, Sec. 3, pág. 284)

atmosphere / atmósfera: el aire de la Tierra, el cual está compuesto por una capa tenue de gases, sólidos y líquidos; forma una capa protectora alrededor del planeta y está dividida en cinco capas distintivas. (Cap. 15, Sec. 1, pág. 434)

atomic number / número atómico: el número de protones en un átomo. (Cap. 2, Sec. 1, pág. 34)

atoms / átomos: partículas diminutas de materia compuestas de protones, neutrones y electrones. (Cap. 2, Sec. 1, pág. 34)

axis / eje: línea vertical imaginaria que pasa a través del centro de la Tierra y alrededor de la cual gira nuestro planeta. (Cap. 23, Sec. 1, pág. 673)

B

basaltic / basáltica: roca ígnea densa y oscura que se forma del magma rico en magnesio y hierro y deficiente en silicio. (Cap. 4, Sec. 2, pág. 97)

base / base: sustancia cuyo pH es superior a 7. (Cap. 21, Sec. 2, pág. 620)

basin / cuenca: depresión en la Tierra en la

cual se formó un océano cuando el área se llenó de agua debido a lluvias torrenciales. (Cap. 18, Sec. 1, pág. 523)

batholith / batolito: cuerpo rocoso ígneo e intrusivo más grande que se forma cuando el magma que es forzado a ascender hacia la corteza terrestre se enfría lentamente y se solidifica bajo tierra. (Cap. 12, Sec. 3, pág. 350)

beach / playa: depósito de sedimentos cuyos materiales varían en tamaño, color y composición y que se halla comúnmente en un litoral liso y levemente inclinado. (Cap. 9, Sec. 3, pág. 259)

benthos / bentos: plantas y animales marinos que viven en el suelo oceánico o sobre él. (Cap. 19, Sec. 2, pág. 561)

bias / sesgo: opinión personal. (Cap. 1, Sec. 2, pág. 21)

big bang theory / teoría de la gran explosión: afirma que el universo comenzó hace unos 12 a 15 billones de años con una inmensa y ardiente explosión. (Cap. 25, Sec. 4, pág. 757)

biomass energy / energía de biomasa: energía renovable proveniente de la quema de materiales orgánicos, como la leña y el alcohol. (Cap. 5, Sec. 2, pág. 133)

black hole / agujero negro: etapa final en la evolución de una supernova, cuando la masa del núcleo colapsa hasta el punto de que no existe volumen y cuya gravedad es tan poderosa que ni siquiera la luz puede escapar. (Cap. 25, Sec. 3, pág. 750)

blizzard / ventisca: tormenta invernal que dura por lo menos tres horas, con temperaturas de −12°C o más bajas, poca visibilidad y vientos de por lo menos 51 km/h. (Cap. 16, Sec. 2, pág. 477)

breaker / cachón: ola oceánica que se forma en aguas poco profundas y que rompe en la playa. (Cap. 18, Sec. 3, pág. 533)

C

caldera / caldera: extensa abertura circular que se forma cuando colapsa la parte superior de un volcán. (Cap. 12, Sec. 3, pág. 352)

carbon film / película carbonácea: fina película de residuo carbonoso preservada como fósil. (Cap. 13, Sec. 1, pág. 370)

carbon monoxide / monóxido de carbono: gas incoloro e inodoro que reduce el contenido de oxígeno en la sangre, se encuentra en los gases de escape de los vehículos y contribuye a la contaminación del aire. (Cap. 21, Sec. 2, pág. 621)

carrying capacity / capacidad de carga: número máximo de individuos de una especie dada que el ambiente puede mantener. (Cap. 20, Sec. 1, pág. 585)

cast / impresión fósil: tipo de fósil corporal que se forma cuando los cristales llenan un molde o cuando los sedimentos se asientan en un molde y se endurecen convirtiéndose en roca. (Cap. 13, Sec. 1, pág. 371)

cave / caverna: abertura subterránea que se puede formar cuando las aguas subterráneas ácidas disuelven la piedra caliza. (Cap. 9, Sec. 2, pág. 255)

cementation / cementación: proceso formador de rocas sedimentarias en el cual los cementos naturales que se producen cuando el agua se filtra por la roca y el suelo mantienen unidos los sedimentos grandes. (Cap. 4, Sec. 4, pág. 105)

Cenozoic Era / Era Cenozoica: era de vida reciente que comenzó hace 66 millones de años aproximadamente y que continúa hoy en día; incluye la primera aparición del *Homo sapiens* hace unos 400,000 años. (Cap. 14, Sec. 3, pág. 418)

channel / cauce: surco creado por agua que corre hacia abajo del mismo sendero. (Cap. 9, Sec. 1, pág. 242)

chemical weathering / meteorización química: se presenta cuando las reacciones químicas disuelven los minerales de las rocas o los transforman en minerales diferentes. (Cap. 7, Sec. 1, pág. 187)

chemosynthesis / quimiosíntesis: proceso mediante el cual las bacterias que viven cerca de respiraderos térmicos elaboran el

Spanish Glossary

alimento a partir de compuestos de azufre o nitrógeno, en lugar de la energía luminosa proveniente del Sol. (Cap. 19, Sec. 2, pág. 559)

chlorofluorocarbons (CFCs) / clorofluoro-carbonos: grupo de compuestos químicos que se utilizan en refrigeradores, acondicionadores de aire, empaques de espuma y rociadores de aerosol; estos compuestos químicos pueden penetrar en la atmósfera y destruir el ozono. (Cap. 15, Sec. 1, pág. 440)

chromosphere / cromosfera: capa de la atmósfera del Sol ubicada encima de la fotosfera. (Cap. 25, Sec. 2, pág. 741)

cinder cone volcano / volcán de cono de carbonilla: volcán de laderas abruptas y vagamente compreso que se forma cuando la tefrita cae al suelo. (Cap. 12, Sec. 2, pág. 344)

cleavage / crucero: propiedad física de algunos minerales de poder romperse a lo largo de superficies suaves y planas. (Cap. 3, Sec. 2, pág. 71)

climate / clima: patrón de tiempo promedio en una área a lo largo de un período largo de tiempo; puede clasificarse según la temperatura, la humedad, la precipitación y la vegetación. (Cap. 7, Sec. 1, pág. 188; Cap. 17, Sec. 1, pág. 492)

coal / carbón: roca sedimentaria formada de material vegetal en descomposición; el combustible fósil más abundante en el mundo. (Cap. 5, Sec. 1, pág. 121)

comet / cometa: astro formado por polvo y partículas rocosas mezcladas con agua congelada, metano y amoníaco, que forma una cola brillante a medida que se acerca al Sol. (Cap. 24, Sec. 4, pág. 722)

compaction / compactación: proceso que forma rocas sedimentarias cuando las capas de sedimentos pequeños se comprimen debido al peso de las capas superiores. (Cap. 4, Sec. 4, pág. 104)

composite volcano / volcán compuesto: volcán que se ha formado por la alter-nación de erupciones explosivas y silenciosas que producen capas de tefrita y lava; se halla principalmente donde se juntan las placas terrestres y una placa se hunde debajo de otra. (Cap. 12, Sec. 2, pág. 345)

composting / abono orgánico: método de conservación en que los desperdicios del jardín, como el pasto, la maleza y las hojas rastrilladas, se amontonan y se dejan descomponer gradualmente. (Cap. 20, Sec. 3, pág. 597)

compound / compuesto: materia que está hecha de dos o más elementos y que tiene propiedades físicas y químicas diferentes a las de los elementos que la formaron. (Cap. 2, Sec. 2, pág. 40)

condensation / condensación: proceso en el cual el vapor de agua se transforma en un líquido. (Cap. 15, Sec. 2, pág. 445)

conduction / conducción: transferencia de energía que ocurre cuando las moléculas chocan entre sí. (Cap. 15, Sec. 2, pág. 444)

conic projection / proyección cónica: mapa que se hace proyectando puntos y líneas de un globo terráqueo a un cono. (Cap. 6, Sec. 3, pág. 167)

conservation / conservación: uso cuidadoso de los recursos para disminuir el daño al ambiente a través de métodos como el abono orgánico y el reciclaje de los materiales. (Cap. 20, Sec. 3, pág. 596)

constant / constante: variable que no cambia en un experimento. (Cap. 1, Sec. 1, pág. 10)

constellation / constelación: grupo de estrellas que forma un patrón en el cielo que se ve como un objeto conocido (el Carro Mayor), un animal (Pegaso) o un personaje (Orión). (Cap. 25, Sec. 1, pág. 736)

continental drift / deriva continental: hipótesis de Wegener que afirmaba que todos los continentes estuvieron unidos en algún momento formando una sola masa continental, la cual se separó hace unos 200 millones de años, haciendo que los continentes derivaran lentamente a sus posiciones actuales. (Cap. 10, Sec. 1, pág. 276)

continental shelf / plataforma continental: extremo gradualmente inclinado de un continente que se extiende debajo del océano y que provee morada a la mayoría de los organismos marinos. (Cap. 19, Sec. 1, pág. 550)

continental slope / talud continental: relieve de la cuenca oceánica que desciende abruptamente a partir de la plataforma continental. (Cap. 19, Sec. 1, pág. 551)

contour line / curva de nivel: línea en un mapa que conecta puntos con igual elevación. (Cap. 6, Sec. 3, pág. 168)

control / control: estándar de comparación en un experimento. (Cap. 1, Sec. 1, pág. 10)

convection / convección: transferencia de calor a través del flujo de un material. (Cap. 15, Sec. 2, pág. 444)

convection current / corriente de convección: corriente en el manto terrestre que transfiere energía en el interior de la Tierra y que provee la potencia de la tectónica de placas. (Cap. 10, Sec. 3, pág. 289)

Coriolis effect / efecto de Coriolis: cambio de vientos y corrientes superficiales provocados por la rotación de la Tierra; hace que las corrientes al norte del ecuador fluyan en dirección de las manecillas del reloj y las corrientes al sur del ecuador en dirección contraria. (Cap. 18, Sec. 2, pág. 527)

Coriolis effect / efecto de Coriolis: es la causa de que el aire y el agua en movimiento giren a la izquierda en el hemisferio sur y a la derecha en el hemisferio norte, debido a la rotación de la Tierra. (Cap. 15, Sec. 3, pág. 448)

corona / corona: la capa más externa y grande de la atmósfera del Sol; se extiende millones de kilómetros y soporta temperaturas de hasta 2 millones K. (Cap. 25, Sec. 2, pág. 741)

crater / cráter: depresión de murallas escarpadas alrededor de la chimenea de un volcán. (Cap. 12, Sec. 1, pág. 336)

creep / corrimiento: tipo de movimiento de masas en el cual los sedimentos se mueven cuesta abajo paulatinamente; es común en áreas de congelamiento y derretimiento; puede hacer que las paredes, los árboles y las cercas se inclinen. (Cap. 8, Sec. 1, pág. 214)

crest / cresta: punto más alto de una onda. (Cap. 18, Sec. 3, pág. 532)

crystal / cristal: sólido cuyos átomos están arreglados en un patrón ordenado y repetitivo. (Cap. 3, Sec. 1, pág. 63)

cyanobacteria / cianobacterias: bacterias fotosintéticas que contienen clorofila y que se piensa son unas de las primeras formas de vida terrestre. (Cap. 14, Sec. 2, pág. 407)

D

deflation / deflacción: tipo de erosión que se presenta cuando el viento sopla sobre sedimentos sueltos, extrae micropartículas y deja atrás sedimentos más gruesos. (Cap. 8, Sec. 3, pág. 224)

deforestation / deforestación: destrucción y tala de bosques en que a menudo se despeja la tierra para la minería, la construcción de caminos y el pastoreo del ganado y la cual resulta en aumentos en los niveles atmosféricos de CO_2. (Cap. 17, Sec. 3, pág. 509)

density / densidad: cambio físico de la materia que puede calcularse dividiendo la masa de un cuerpo entre su volumen. (Cap. 2, Sec. 3, pág. 46)

density current / corriente de densidad: patrón de circulación en el océano que se forma cuando una masa de agua salada más densa se hunde debajo de agua salada menos densa. (Cap. 18, Sec. 2, pág. 529)

dependent variable / variable dependiente: factor que se mide en un experimento. (Cap. 1, Sec. 1, pág. 10)

deposition / depositación: acción de dejar caer los sedimentos, la cual ocurre cuando un agente erosivo, como la gravedad, un glaciar, el viento o el agua, pierde su energía y no puede seguir transportando su carga. (Cap. 8, Sec. 1, pág. 213)

dew point / punto de condensación: temperatura a la cual el aire se satura y se forma la condensación. (Cap. 16, Sec. 1, pág. 465)

dike / dique: filón de roca ígnea que se forma cuando el magma es inyectado en una fisura vertical que atraviesa capas rocosas y se endurece bajo tierra. (Cap. 12, Sec. 3, pág. 351)

drainage basin / cuenca hidrográfica: terreno del cual un río u otra corriente de agua recoge las aguas de escorrentía. (Cap. 9, Sec. 1, pág. 244)

dune / duna: montículo que se forma cuando los sedimentos arrastrados por el viento se acumulan detrás de una barrera; relieve común en las regiones desérticas. (Cap. 8, Sec. 3, pág. 227)

E

Earth / la Tierra: tercer planeta más cercano al Sol; posee una atmósfera que protege la vida y las temperaturas de su superficie permiten la existencia de agua como sólido, líquido y gas. (Cap. 24, Sec. 2, pág. 710)

earthquake / terremoto: vibraciones producidas cuando las rocas se rompen a lo largo de una falla. (Cap. 11, Sec. 1, pág. 305)

Earth science / ciencias terrestres: estudio de la Tierra y del espacio, incluye el estudio de rocas, fósiles, clima, volcanes, uso del terreno, agua marina, terremotos y astros en el espacio. (Cap. 1, Sec. 1, pág. 9)

electromagnetic spectrum / espectro electromagnético: arreglo de ondas electromagnéticas según sus longitudes de onda. (Cap. 22, Sec. 1, pág. 641)

electrons / electrones: partículas con carga negativa que se mueven alrededor del núcleo de un átomo y forman la nube electrónica. (Cap. 2, Sec. 1, pág. 36)

element / elemento: sustancia que sólo contiene un tipo de átomo; por ejemplo, el oxígeno, el aluminio y el hierro. (Cap. 2, Sec. 1, pág. 35)

ellipse / elipse: trayectoria curva cerrada y alargada que describe la órbita anual alrededor del Sol que efectúa la Tierra. (Cap. 23, Sec. 1, pág. 675)

El Niño / El Niño: fenómeno climático que comienza en el océano Pacífico tropical; puede ocurrir debido al debilitamiento o inversión de los vientos alisios, y puede interrumpir los patrones normales de temperatura y precipitación por todo el mundo. (Cap. 17, Sec. 3, pág. 501)

enzyme / enzima: sustancia que acelera las reacciones químicas. (Cap. 20, Sec. 2, pág. 593)

eon / eón: la subdivisión más larga de la escala del tiempo geológico, basada en la abundancia de ciertos tipos de fósiles; se subdivide en eras, períodos y épocas. (Cap. 14, Sec. 1, pág. 399)

epicenter / epicentro: punto sobre la superficie terrestre directamente sobre el foco de un terremoto. (Cap. 11, Sec. 2, pág. 309)

epoch / época: la siguiente subdivisión de tiempo geológico que le sigue al período; se caracteriza por diferencias en formas de vida que pueden variar regionalmente. (Cap. 14, Sec. 1, pág. 399)

equator / ecuador: línea imaginaria que rodea la Tierra alrededor de 0° de latitud, equidistante del polo norte y el polo sur. (Cap. 6, Sec. 2, pág. 162)

equinox / equinoccio: ocurre dos veces al año, en la primavera y en el verano, cuando el Sol está directamente sobre el ecuador, ocasionando que la noche y el día tengan la misma duración en todo el mundo. (Cap. 23, Sec. 1, pág. 677)

Spanish Glossary

era / era: segunda división mayor del tiempo geológico; se subdivide en períodos y se basa en cambios importantes a nivel mundial en los tipos de fósiles. (Cap. 14, Sec. 1, pág. 399)

erosion / erosión: proceso en el cual los materiales superficiales se desgastan y son transportados de un lugar a otro por agentes como la gravedad, el agua, el viento y los glaciares. (Cap. 8, Sec. 1, pág. 212)

estuary / estuario: área donde un río desemboca en el océano, la cual contiene una mezcla de agua dulce y agua marina y provee un hábitat importante para muchos organismos marinos. (Cap. 19, Sec. 2, pág. 564)

ethics / ética: estudio de los valores morales sobre el bien y el mal. (Cap. 1, Sec. 2, pág. 20)

extrusive / extrusiva: roca ígnea de grano fino que se forma cuando el magma se enfría rápidamente sobre o cerca de la superficie terrestre. (Cap. 4, Sec. 2, pág. 95)

F
---

fault / falla: superficie a lo largo de la cual se mueven y se rompen las rocas cuando exceden su límite de elasticidad. (Cap. 11, Sec. 1, pág. 304)

fault-block mountains / montañas de bloques de falla: montañas que se forman de enormes bloques rocosos inclinados, pero separados de las rocas circundantes por fallas. (Cap. 6, Sec. 1, pág. 160)

fertilizer / fertilizante: sustancia química que ayuda en el crecimiento de plantas y otros organismos. (Cap. 21, Sec. 1, pág. 611)

focus / foco: en un terremoto, es el punto sobre la superficie terrestre donde se libera la energía en forma de ondas sísmicas. (Cap. 11, Sec. 2, pág. 308)

fog / neblina: una nube estrato que se forma cuando el aire se enfría hasta su punto de rocío, cerca de la superficie terrestre. (Cap. 16, Sec. 1, pág. 467)

folded mountains / montañas plegadas: montañas que se forman cuando las capas rocosas horizontales son comprimidas desde lados opuestos, lo cual hace que se encorven y se doblen. (Cap. 6, Sec. 1, pág. 159)

foliated / foliada: roca metamórfica, como la pizarra y el gneiss, cuyos granos minerales se aplanan y se alinean en capas paralelas. (Cap. 4, Sec. 3, pág. 101)

fossil fuel / combustible fósil: recurso energético no renovable, como el petróleo y el carbón, que se formó hace millones de años a partir de los restos de plantas y otros organismos muertos. (Cap. 5, Sec. 1, pág. 120)

fossils / fósiles: restos, impresiones o trazas de organismos prehistóricos que pueden indicar cuándo y dónde los organismos vivieron y cómo vivieron. (Cap. 13, Sec. 1, pág. 369)

fracture / fractura: propiedad física de algunos minerales de romperse a lo largo de superficies disparejas, ásperas o dentadas. (Cap. 3, Sec. 2, pág. 71)

front / frente: límite entre dos masas de aire que poseen diferentes temperaturas, densidad o humedad; puede ser frío, cálido, ocluido y estacionario. (Cap. 16, Sec. 2, pág. 471)

full moon / luna llena: fase lunar que ocurre cuando toda la superficie lunar que da la cara a la Tierra refleja luz. (Cap. 23, Sec. 2, pág. 679)

G
---

galaxy / galaxia: extenso grupo de estrellas, polvo y gas que se mantiene unido gracias a la gravedad; puede ser elíptica, espiral o irregular. (Cap. 25, Sec. 4, pág. 752)

gem / gema: mineral precioso, muy valioso que se puede usar en joyería. (Cap. 3, Sec. 3, pág. 73)

geologic time scale / escala del tiempo geológico: división de la historia de la

Tierra en unidades cronológicas basadas en gran parte en los tipos de formas de vida que existieron solamente en ciertos períodos. (Cap. 14, Sec. 1, pág. 398)

geothermal energy / energía geotérmica: recurso energético interminable que hace uso del magma caliente o del calor de las rocas calientes y secas debajo de la superficie terrestre para generar electricidad. (Cap. 5, Sec. 2, pág. 132)

geyser / géiser: manantial de agua caliente que brota periódicamente y lanza agua y vapor al aire. Un ejemplo es el Old Faithful en el parque nacional de Yellowstone. (Cap. 9, Sec. 2, pág. 255)

giant / gigante: etapa avanzada en la vida de una estrella de la secuencia principal en la cual el hidrógeno del núcleo se agota, el núcleo se contrae y las temperaturas en el interior de la estrella aumentan, haciendo que sus capas externas se expandan y enfríen. (Cap. 25, Sec. 3, pág. 749)

glaciers / glaciares: extensas masas de hielo y nieve en movimiento que cambian grandes regiones de la superficie terrestre, a través de la erosión y la depositación. (Cap. 8, Sec. 2, pág. 217)

global warming / calentamiento global: aumento en el promedio de la temperatura global de la Tierra. (Cap. 17, Sec. 3, pág. 508)

granitic / granítica: roca ígnea de color claro y rica en sílice que es menos densa que la roca basáltica. (Cap. 4, Sec. 2, pág. 97)

Great Red Spot / Gran Mancha Roja: gigantesca tormenta de gases de altas presiones en Júpiter. (Cap. 24, Sec. 3, pág. 714)

greenhouse effect / efecto de invernadero: calentamiento natural que ocurre cuando ciertos gases en la atmósfera de la Tierra, por ejemplo, el metano, el CO_2 y el vapor de agua, atrapan el calor. (Cap. 17, Sec. 3, pág. 507)

groundwater / agua subterránea: agua que se filtra en el suelo y se junta en poros y espacios vacíos y la cual es una fuente importante de agua potable. (Cap. 9, Sec. 2, pág. 251)

H

half-life / media vida: tiempo que se demora en desintegrarse la mitad de los átomos de un isótopo. (Cap. 13, Sec. 3, pág. 384)

hardness / dureza: medida del grado de facilidad con que se puede rayar un mineral; se determina según el arreglo de los átomos del mineral. (Cap. 3, Sec. 2, pág. 69)

hazardous waste / desechos peligrosos: desechos venenosos, inflamables o carcinógenos. (Cap. 20, Sec. 2, pág. 592)

heterogeneous mixture / mezcla heterogénea: mezcla que no está distribuida uniformemente y en la cual cada componente retiene sus propiedades. (Cap. 2, Sec. 2, pág. 43)

hibernation / hibernación: adaptación del comportamiento para sobrevivir el invierno en que un animal disminuye considerablemente sus actividades corporales, la temperatura de su cuerpo baja y los procesos corporales se vuelven más lentos. (Cap. 17, Sec. 2, pág. 498)

homogeneous mixture / mezcla homogénea: mezcla que está distribuida uniformemente. (Cap. 2, Sec. 2, pág. 43)

horizon / horizonte: cada capa del perfil del suelo: horizonte A (capa superior del suelo), horizonte B (capa intermedia) y horizonte C (capa inferior). (Cap. 7, Sec. 2, pág. 192)

hot spot / foco caliente: zona de intenso calor ubicada en el límite entre el manto y el núcleo de la Tierra que forma volcanes cuando la roca derretida es forzada a ascender y atraviesa la corteza. (Cap. 12, Sec. 1, pág. 338)

humidity / humedad: cantidad de vapor de agua que sostiene el aire. (Cap. 16, Sec. 1, pág. 464)

humus / humus: materia orgánica negruzca

y descompuesta que suministra nutrientes a las plantas y que se halla principalmente en la capa de suelo arable. (Cap. 7, Sec. 2, pág. 192)

hurricane / huracán: tormenta extensa y severa que se forma sobre los océanos tropicales, con vientos de por lo menos 120 km/h y que pierde fuerza al llegar a tierra firme. (Cap. 16, Sec. 2, pág. 476)

hydroelectric energy / energía hidroeléctrica: electricidad que produce la potencia del agua al hacer grandes represas en un río. (Cap. 5, Sec. 2, pág. 132)

hydrosphere / hidrosfera: toda el agua de la superficie terrestre. (Cap. 15, Sec. 2, pág. 13)

hypothesis / hipótesis: una conjetura informada. (Cap. 1, Sec. 1, pág. 7)

I

---

ice wedging / grietas debido al hielo: proceso de meteorización mecánica que ocurre cuando el agua se congela en las grietas de las rocas y se expande, haciendo que la roca se fragmente. (Cap. 7, Sec. 1, pág. 186)

igneous rock / roca ígnea: roca intrusiva o extrusiva que se forma cuando el magma caliente se enfría y se endurece. (Cap. 4, Sec. 2, pág. 94)

impact basin / cuenca de impacto: cavidad formada sobre la superficie de la Luna por el impacto de un objeto. (Cap. 23, Sec. 3, pág. 689)

impermeable / impermeable: describe los materiales por los cuales el agua no puede filtrarse. (Cap. 9, Sec. 2, pág. 252)

independent variable / variable independiente: factor que cambia en un experimento. (Cap. 1, Sec. 1, pág. 10)

index fossils / fósiles guía: restos de especies que existieron en la Tierra durante un período relativamente corto de tiempo, fueron abundantes y se extendieron geográficamente ; los geólogos pueden usar estos fósiles para determinar las edades de las capas rocosas. (Cap. 13, Sec. 1, pág. 373)

intrusive / intrusiva: tipo de roca ígnea que, por lo general, contiene cristales de gran tamaño y que se forma cuando el magma se enfría lentamente debajo de la superficie terrestre. (Cap. 4, Sec. 2, pág. 95)

ion / ion: átomo con carga eléctrica cuya carga resulta cuando un átomo pierde o gana electrones. (Cap. 2, Sec. 2, pág. 41)

ionosphere / ionosfera: capa de partículas cargadas eléctricamente en la termosfera que absorbe las ondas radiales AM durante el día y las vuelve a reflejar durante la noche. (Cap. 15, Sec. 1, pág. 437)

isobars / isobaras: líneas que se trazan en un mapa meteorológico conectando puntos que tienen la misma presión atmosférica; también indican la ubicación de las áreas de alta y de baja presión y pueden mostrar la velocidad del viento. (Cap. 16, Sec. 3, pág. 479)

isotherm / isoterma: línea que se traza en un mapa meteorológico conectando puntos que tienen la misma temperatura. (Cap. 16, Sec. 3, pág. 479)

isotopes / isótopos: átomos del mismo elemento con distintos números de neutrones. (Cap. 2, Sec. 1, pág. 37)

J

---

jet stream / corriente de chorro: franja estrecha de vientos fuertes que sopla cerca de la troposfera. (Cap. 15, Sec. 3, pág. 450)

Jupiter / Júpiter: el planeta más grande de nuestro sistema solar y el quinto más cercano al Sol; contiene más masa que todos los otros planetas juntos, tiene tormentas continuas de gases a altas presiones y una atmósfera compuesta en su mayor parte de hidrógeno y helio. (Cap. 24, Sec. 3, pág. 714)

L

land breeze / brisa terrestre: movimiento de aire nocturno desde la tierra hacia el mar y que se forma cuando el aire más frío y denso proveniente de la tierra fuerza el aire más cálido a ascender sobre el mar. (Cap. 15, Sec. 3, pág. 451)

latitude / latitud: distancia en grados al norte o al sur del ecuador. (Cap. 6, Sec. 2, pág. 162)

lava / lava: materia rocosa derretida, espesa y viscosa, que fluye de los volcanes hacia la superficie terrestre. (Cap. 4, Sec. 2, pág. 94)

leaching / lixiviación: extracción de minerales que se han disuelto en agua. (Cap. 7, Sec. 2, pág. 193)

light-year / año-luz: la distancia que viaja la luz en un año (cerca de 9.5 trillones de km), la cual se usa para registrar distancias entre estrellas y galaxias. (Cap. 25, Sec. 1, pág. 739)

liquefaction / liquefacción: ocurre cuando el suelo mojado actúa como un líquido durante un terremoto. (Cap. 11, Sec. 3, pág. 319)

lithosphere / litosfera: capa rígida de la Tierra de unos 100 km de grosor formada por la corteza y parte del manto superior. (Cap. 10, Sec. 3, pág. 284)

litter / desechos orgánicos: ramitas, hojas y otras materias orgánicas que ayudan a evitar la erosión y que retienen agua y pueden, a la larga, convertirse en humus gracias a la acción de organismos descomponedores. (Cap. 7, Sec. 2, pág. 193)

loess / loess: depósito de sedimentos firmemente compactados y de granos finos que es arrastrado por el viento. (Cap. 8, Sec. 3, pág. 227)

longitude / longitud: distancia en grados al este o al oeste del primer meridiano. (Cap. 6, Sec. 2, pág. 163)

longshore current / corriente costera: corriente que corre paralela a la costa, producto de olas que chocan contra la costa haciendo ángulos leves y que mueven toneladas de sedimento suelto. (Cap. 9, Sec. 3, pág. 258)

lunar eclipse / eclipse lunar: ocurre cuando la sombra de la Tierra cubre la Luna. (Cap. 23, Sec. 2, pág. 682)

luster / lustre: describe la manera en que un mineral refleja la luz desde su superficie; puede ser metálico o no metálico. (Cap. 3, Sec. 2, pág. 70)

M

magma / magma: material rocoso caliente y fundido que se halla debajo de la superficie terrestre. (Cap. 3, Sec. 1, pág. 65)

magnitude / magnitud: medida de la energía liberada durante un movimiento sísmico. (Cap. 11, Sec. 3, pág. 318)

map legend / leyenda de mapa: explica los símbolos que se usan en un mapa. (Cap. 6, Sec. 3, pág. 170)

map scale / escala de un mapa: relación entre la distancia en un mapa y la distancia real sobre la superficie terrestre, la cual se puede representar como una razón o como una pequeña barra dividida en secciones. (Cap. 6, Sec. 3, pág. 170)

maria / mares: regiones de la Luna relativamente planas y de color oscuro que se formaron cuando la lava alcanzó la superficie y llenó los cráteres en la superficie lunar. (Cap. 23, Sec. 2, pág. 683)

Mars / Marte: cuarto planeta más cercano al Sol; tiene casquetes polares de hielo, una atmósfera tenue y una apariencia rojiza que proviene del óxido de hierro de rocas desgastadas. (Cap. 24, Sec. 2, pág. 710)

mass movement / movimiento de masas: cualquier tipo de erosión que ocurre a medida que la gravedad mueve materiales cuesta abajo. (Cap. 8, Sec. 1, pág. 213)

mass number / número de masa: el número de protones más el número de electrones en un átomo. (Cap. 2, Sec. 1, pág. 37)

matter / materia: cualquier cosa que tiene masa y ocupa espacio; las propiedades de la materia están determinadas según la estructura y enlace de sus átomos. (Cap. 2, Sec. 1, pág. 34)

meander / meandro: curva ancha y en forma de c en un río u otra corriente de agua, formada por la erosión de su ribera externa. (Cap. 9, Sec. 1, pág. 245)

mechanical weathering / meteorización mecánica: proceso físico que fragmenta rocas sin alterar su composición química; puede ser el resultado de las grietas debido al hielo, a la acción de los animales y a las raíces vegetales. (Cap. 7, Sec. 1, pág. 185)

Mercury / Mercurio: el planeta más pequeño y el más cercano al Sol; posee una atmósfera tenue y una superficie con muchos cráteres y altos acantilados. (Cap. 24, Sec. 2, pág. 708)

Mesozoic Era / Era Mesozoica: era intermedia de la historia de la Tierra, durante la cual se separó Pangaea, aparecieron los dinosaurios y los reptiles y las gimnospermas eran las formas de vida dominantes en tierra. (Cap. 14, Sec. 3, pág. 414)

metamorphic rock / roca metamórfica: se forma cuando el calor, la presión o los líquidos actúan sobre rocas ígneas, sedimentarias u otras rocas metamórficas y les afectan la forma o composición o ambas. (Cap. 4, Sec. 3, pág. 99)

meteor / meteoro: meteoroide que se incendia en la atmósfera terrestre. (Cap. 24, Sec. 4, pág. 723)

meteorite / meteorito: meteoroide que choca contra la superficie de una luna o planeta. (Cap. 24, Sec. 4, pág. 724)

meteorologist / meteorólogo: persona que estudia el tiempo y usa información del radar Doppler, de los satélites meteorológicos, computadoras y otros instrumentos para hacer mapas meteorológicos y pronósticos del tiempo. (Cap. 16, Sec. 3, pág. 478)

mid-ocean ridge / dorsal mediooceánica: área donde se forma el nuevo suelo oceánico cuando la lava sale a través de las grietas en la corteza terrestre. (Cap. 19, Sec. 1, pág. 552)

mineral / mineral: sólido inorgánico que ocurre en forma natural y que posee una composición química definida y una estructura atómica interna ordenada. (Cap. 3, Sec. 1, pág. 62)

mineral resources / recursos minerales: recursos a partir de los cuales se obtienen metales. (Cap. 5, Sec. 3, pág. 137)

mixture / mezcla: describe dos o más sustancias que retienen sus propiedades a pesar de estar combinadas y la cual se puede separar mediante medios físicos. (Cap. 2, Sec. 2, pág. 43)

mold / molde: tipo de fósil corporal que se forma en la roca cuando un organismo con partes duras se entierra, se descompone o se disuelve y deja una cavidad en la roca. (Cap. 13, Sec. 1, pág. 371)

moon phase / fase lunar: cambio en la apariencia de la Luna, vista desde la Tierra, debido a las posiciones relativas de la Luna, la Tierra y el Sol. (Cap. 23, Sec. 2, pág. 679)

moraine / morrena: extenso banco de rocas y suelo que un glaciar deposita cuando se detiene su movimiento. (Cap. 8, Sec. 2, pág. 219)

N

natural gas / gas natural: combustible fósil que se formó de organismos marinos y que con frecuencia se encuentra en capas rocosas inclinadas o plegadas y que se usa en calefacción y cocción. (Cap. 5, Sec. 1, pág. 123)

natural selection / selección natural: proceso por el cual los organismos que están adaptados a un entorno en particular son más capaces de sobrevivir y reproducirse que organismos que no lo están. (Cap. 14, Sec. 1, pág. 401)

nebula / nebulosa: extensa nube de gas y polvo que se contrae bajo la fuerza gravitatoria y se separa en fragmentos más pequeños, cada uno de los cuales colapsará para formar una estrella. (Cap. 25, Sec. 3, pág. 748)

nekton / necton: organismos marinos que nadan activamente en el océano. (Cap. 19, Sec. 2, pág. 560)

Neptune / Neptuno: por lo general el octavo planeta más alejado del Sol; es grande y gaseoso, posee anillos que varían en grosor y es de color verde-azulado. (Cap. 24, Sec. 3, pág. 718)

neutron / neutrón: partícula sin carga eléctrica ubicada en el núcleo del átomo. (Cap. 2, Sec. 1, pág. 36)

neutron star / estrella de neutrones: núcleo colapsado de una supernova que se puede compactar hasta alcanzar unos 20 km de diámetro y que contiene solamente neutrones en el núcleo denso. (Cap. 25, Sec. 3, pág. 750)

new moon / luna nueva: fase lunar que ocurre cuando la Luna está entre el Sol y la Tierra. En esta fase no se puede ver la Luna porque su mitad iluminada mira hacia el Sol mientras que su mitad oscura mira hacia la Tierra. (Cap. 23, Sec. 2, pág. 679)

non-foliated / no foliada: roca metamórfica, como la cuarcita y el mármol, cuyos granos minerales crecen y se reordenan, pero sin formar capas. (Cap. 4, Sec. 3, pág. 102)

nonpoint source pollution / contaminación de fuente no puntual: contaminación proveniente de un área extensa que penetra en el agua y que no puede rastrearse a una sola localidad. (Cap. 21, Sec. 1, pág. 610)

normal fault / falla normal: ruptura en la roca causada por las fuerzas de tensión, en donde la roca sobre la superficie de la falla se mueve hacia abajo en relación con la roca debajo de la falla. (Cap. 11, Sec. 1, pág. 306)

nuclear energy / energía nuclear: fuente energética alterna que se basa en la fisión del átomo. (Cap. 5, Sec. 1, pág. 127)

O

observatory / observatorio: centro que puede albergar un telescopio óptico; tiene a menudo un techo en forma de domo que se puede abrir para observar el espacio. (Cap. 22, Sec. 1, pág. 642)

oil / petróleo: combustible fósil líquido formado a partir de organismos marinos que se quema para obtener energía y el cual se utiliza en la manufactura de plásticos. (Cap. 5, Sec. 1, pág. 123)

orbit / órbita: trayectoria curva que sigue un satélite a medida que gira alrededor de un objeto. (Cap. 22, Sec. 2, pág. 649)

ore / mena: depósito en que un mineral existe en cantidades lo suficientemente grandes para ser minado con fines de lucro. (Cap. 5, Sec. 3, pág. 137)

organic evolution / evolución orgánica: cambio de organismos a través del tiempo geológico. (Cap. 14, Sec. 1, pág. 400)

outwash / derrubio: material depositado por el agua derretida de un glaciar. (Cap. 8, Sec. 2, pág. 219)

oxidation / oxidación: proceso de meteorización química que ocurre cuando el material metálico se expone al oxígeno y al agua durante un período de tiempo. (Cap. 7, Sec. 1, pág. 188)

ozone layer / capa de ozono: capa de la estratosfera con una alta concentración de ozono; absorbe la mayor parte de la radiación ultravioleta dañina proveniente del Sol. (Cap. 15, Sec. 1, pág. 440)

P

Paleozoic Era / Era Paleozoica: era de vida antigua, la cual comenzó hace unos 544 millones de años, cuando los organismos desarrollaron partes duras y terminó con extinciones en masa hace unos 245 millones de años. (Cap. 14, Sec. 2, pág. 408)

Pangaea / Pangaea: masa de tierra extensa y antigua que una vez estuvo formada por

Spanish Glossary

el conjunto de todos los continentes. (Cap. 10, Sec. 1, pág. 276; Cap. 14, Sec. 1, pág. 405)

particulate matter / materia particulada: sólidos finos como el polen, el polvo, el moho, la ceniza y el hollín como también las gotitas líquidas del aire que pueden irritar y dañar los pulmones cuando se aspiran. (Cap. 21, Sec. 2, pág. 622)

period / período: tercera división mayor del tiempo geológico; se subdivide en épocas y se caracteriza por los tipos de vida que existieron por todo el planeta. (Cap. 14, Sec. 1, pág. 399)

permeable / permeable: describe el suelo y la roca con poros que se conectan y a través de los cuales puede correr el agua. (Cap. 9, Sec. 2, pág. 252)

permineralized remains / restos permineralizados: fósiles cuyos espacios interiores están llenos de minerales provenientes de aguas subterráneas. (Cap. 13, Sec. 1, pág. 370)

pesticide / pesticida: sustancia que se utiliza para evitar que los insectos y la maleza destruyan las cosechas y los céspedes. (Cap. 21, Sec. 1, pág. 611)

photochemical smog / smog fotoquímico: capa de smog brumoso y de color café amarillento que se presenta sobre las ciudades; se forma con la ayuda de la luz solar, contiene ozono cerca de la superficie terrestre y puede dañar los pulmones y las plantas. (Cap. 21, Sec. 2, pág. 619)

photosphere / fotosfera: la capa más baja de la atmósfera del Sol; emite luz y tiene temperaturas de hasta 6,000 K. (Cap. 25, Sec. 2, pág. 741)

photosynthesis / fotosíntesis: proceso de elaboración de alimentos que usa energía luminosa proveniente del Sol, dióxido de carbono y agua. (Cap. 19, Sec. 2, pág. 557)

pH scale / escala del pH: escala utilizada para medir el grado de acidez o basicidad de algo. (Cap. 21, Sec. 2, pág. 620)

plain / llanura: relieve enorme y plano que con frecuencia posee suelos gruesos y fértiles; por lo general se encuentra en las regiones interiores de un continente. (Cap. 6, Sec. 1, pág. 156)

plankton / plancton: plantas y animales marinos que nadan a la deriva en las corrientes oceánicas. (Cap. 19, Sec. 2, pág. 560)

plate / placa: región extensa del manto superior rígido y de la corteza oceánica o continental de la Tierra que se mueve sobre la astenosfera. (Cap. 10, Sec. 3, pág. 284)

plateau / meseta: relieve levantado formado principalmente de rocas casi horizontales que han sido levantadas. (Cap. 6, Sec. 1, pág. 158)

plate tectonics / tectónica de placas: teoría que afirma que la corteza y el manto superior terrestres se separan en placas que flotan y se mueven sobre una capa viscosa del manto. (Cap. 10, Sec. 3, pág. 284)

plucking / ablación: proceso mediante el cual se agrega grava, arena y piedras a las partes inferior y lateral de un glaciar conforme el agua se congela y derrite, rompiendo fragmentos de la roca circundante. (Cap. 8, Sec. 2, pág. 218)

Pluto / Plutón: se le considera el noveno planeta más alejado del Sol; posee una superficie sólida, rocosa y glacial, y una sola luna. (Cap. 24, Sec. 3, pág. 719)

point source pollution / contaminación de fuente puntual: contaminación proveniente de una fuente específica que penetra en el agua y que puede controlarse o tratarse antes de que entre a una masa de agua. (Cap. 21, Sec. 1, pág. 610)

polar zones / zonas polares: zona climática que recibe la radiación solar a un ángulo bajo; se extiende desde la latitud 66°N y S hasta los polos y en donde nunca hace calor. (Cap. 17, Sec. 1, pág. 492)

pollutant / contaminante: cualquier sustancia que contamina el ambiente. (Cap. 20, Sec. 1, pág. 586)

pollution / contaminación: introducción de

desperdicios en el ambiente; por ejemplo, aguas negras y sustancias químicas, las cuales pueden causar daños a los organismos. (Cap. 19, Sec. 3, pág. 565)

population / población: número total de individuos de una especie que ocupan la misma área. (Cap. 20, Sec. 1, pág. 584)

Precambrian time / Era Precámbrica: la parte más larga de la historia de la Tierra, la cual duró de 4 billones de años hasta hace cerca de 544 millones de años. (Cap. 14, Sec. 2, pág. 406)

precipitation / precipitación: agua que cae de las nubes, incluye la lluvia, la nieve, la cellisca y el granizo, y cuya forma la determina la temperatura del aire. (Cap. 16, Sec. 1, pág. 468)

primary wave / onda primaria: onda sísmica que mueve las partículas rocosas en un movimiento oscilatorio en la misma dirección en que viaja la onda. (Cap. 11, Sec. 2, pág. 309)

prime meridian / primer meridiano: línea imaginaria que representa 0° de longitud y corre desde el polo norte, atravesando Greenwich, Inglaterra, hasta el polo sur. (Cap. 6, Sec. 2, pág. 163)

principle of superposition / principio de sobreposición: establece que en capas rocosas inalteradas, las rocas más antiguas se encuentran en el fondo y las rocas más recientes se hallan en la parte superior. (Cap. 13, Sec. 2, pág. 376)

Project Apollo / Proyecto Apolo: etapa final del programa espacial de EE.UU. para llegar a la Luna, en la cual el astronauta Neil Armstrong fue el primer ser humano en poner pie sobre la superficie lunar. (Cap. 22, Sec. 2, pág. 654)

Project Gemini / Proyecto Géminis: segunda etapa del programa espacial de EE.UU. para llegar a la Luna, en la cual un equipo de astronautas se conectó con otra astronave en órbita. (Cap. 22, Sec. 2, pág. 653)

Project Mercury / Proyecto Mercurio: primer paso en el programa espacial de EE.UU. para llegar a la Luna que orbitó una astronave piloteada alrededor de la Tierra, la cual regresó a salvo. (Cap. 22, Sec. 2, pág. 653)

proton / protón: partícula con carga positiva ubicada en el núcleo de un átomo. (Cap. 2, Sec. 1, pág. 36)

R

radiation / radiación: energía que transmiten las ondas o los rayos. (Cap. 15, Sec. 2, pág. 444)

radioactive decay / desintegración radiactiva: proceso en el cual algunos isótopos se desintegran en otros isótopos y partículas. (Cap. 13, Sec. 3, pág. 383)

radiometric dating / datación radiométrica: proceso que se usa para calcular la edad absoluta de las rocas midiendo la razón del isótopo original al producto descendiente en un mineral y conociendo la vida media del isótopo original. (Cap. 13, Sec. 3, pág. 385)

radio telescope / radiotelescopio: tipo de telescopio que recopila y registra ondas radiales que viajan por el espacio; se puede usar de día o de noche bajo casi cualquier condición meteorológica. (Cap. 22, Sec. 1, pág. 645)

recycling / reciclaje: método de conservación en que los materiales usados se procesan para hacer materiales nuevos. (Cap. 5, Sec. 3, pág. 141; Cap. 20, Sec. 3, pág. 597)

reef / arrecife: hábitat oceánico resistente a las olas y rígido construido por corales a partir de esqueletos y calcio. (Cap. 19, Sec. 2, pág. 564)

reflecting telescope / telescopio reflector: telescopio óptico que usa un espejo cóncavo para enfocar la luz y formar una imagen en el punto focal. (Cap. 22, Sec. 1, pág. 642)

refracting telescope / telescopio refractor: telescopio óptico que usa una lente convexa doble para doblar la luz y formar una imagen en el punto focal. (Cap. 22, Sec. 1, pág. 642)

relative age / edad relativa: la edad de algo comparada con otras cosas. (Cap. 13, Sec. 2, pág. 377)

relative humidity / humedad relativa: medida de la cantidad de humedad que sostiene el aire, comparada con la cantidad de humedad que el aire puede sostener a una temperatura dada; puede variar de 0 por ciento a 100 por ciento. (Cap. 16, Sec. 1, pág. 464)

reserve / reserva: cantidad de combustible fósil que se puede extraer de la Tierra con fines de lucro, usando tecnología contemporánea. (Cap. 5, Sec. 1, pág. 125)

reverse fault / falla invertida: ruptura en la roca causada por las fuerzas de compresión, en que la roca sobre la superficie de la falla se mueve hacia arriba en relación con la roca debajo de la falla. (Cap. 11, Sec. 1, pág. 306)

revolution / traslación: órbita elíptica de la Tierra alrededor del Sol, la cual dura todo un año. (Cap. 23, Sec. 1, pág. 675)

rock / roca: mezcla de uno o más minerales, vidrio volcánico, materia orgánica u otros materiales; las rocas pueden ser ígneas, metamórficas o sedimentarias. (Cap. 4, Sec. 1, pág. 90)

rock cycle / ciclo de las rocas: modelo que describe el cambio lento de las rocas de una forma a otra a través del tiempo. (Cap. 4, Sec. 1, pág. 91)

rocket / cohete: motor especial que puede funcionar en el espacio y que quema combustible líquido o sólido. (Cap. 22, Sec. 2, pág. 647)

rotation / rotación: giro de la Tierra, alrededor de su eje imaginario, que dura 24 horas y que ocasiona el día y la noche. (Cap. 23, Sec. 1, pág. 673)

runoff / escorrentía: cualquier agua lluvia que no se filtra en el suelo o que no se evapora pero que corre por la superficie terrestre: por lo general, corre hacia corrientes de agua y tiene la capacidad de erosionar y transportar sedimentos. (Cap. 9, Sec. 1, pág. 240)

S

salinity / salinidad: medida de la cantidad de sales disueltas en el agua marina. (Cap. 18, Sec. 1, pág. 524)

sanitary landfill / vertedero controlado: área en donde la basura es depositada y cubierta con tierra; está diseñado para prevenir la contaminación del terreno y del agua. (Cap. 20, Sec. 2, pág. 592)

satellite / satélite: cualquier cuerpo natural o artificial que gira alrededor de otro objeto. (Cap. 22, Sec. 2, pág. 649)

Saturn / Saturno: es el segundo planeta más grande del sistema solar y el sexto más alejado del Sol; posee un complejo sistema de anillos, por lo menos 18 lunas y una atmósfera densa compuesta principalmente de hidrógeno y helio. (Cap. 24, Sec. 3, pág. 716)

science / ciencia: proceso de observación y estudio de la naturaleza con el propósito de adquirir conocimientos. (Cap. 1, Sec. 1, pág. 24)

scientific law / ley científica: regla que describe el comportamiento de algo en la naturaleza; por lo general describe lo que ocurrirá en cierta situación, pero no por qué ocurrirá ese fenómeno. (Cap. 1, Sec. Z2, pág. 19)

scientific methods / métodos científicos: procedimientos para resolver problemas que pueden incluir: identificar el problema o pregunta, recoger información, desarrollar una hipótesis, probar la hipótesis, analizar los resultados y sacar conclusiones. (Cap. 1, Sec. 1, pág. 8)

scientific theory / teoría científica: explicación que es apoyada por los resultados de experimentos o pruebas repetidas. (Cap. 1, Sec. 2, pág. 18)

scrubber / depurador: dispositivo que reduce las emisiones sulfúricas de las plantas que queman carbón. (Cap. 21, Sec. 2, pág. 623)

sea breeze / brisa marina: movimiento de aire diurno desde el mar hacia la tierra; se forma cuando el aire más frío sobre el agua se mueve hacia el interior forzando el ascenso del aire calentado y menos denso sobre la tierra. (Cap. 15, Sec. 3, pág. 451)

seafloor spreading / expansión del suelo marino: teoría de Hess que afirma que el nuevo suelo marino se forma cuando el magma es forzado a subir a la superficie en una dorsal medieoceánica. (Cap. 10, Sec. 2, pág. 281)

season / estación: período corto de cambio climático en un área causado por la inclinación de eje terrestre a medida que la Tierra gira alrededor del Sol. (Cap. 17, Sec. 3, pág. 500)

secondary wave / onda secundaria: onda sísmica que al moverse hace que las partículas rocosas vibren formando un ángulo recto a la dirección de la onda. (Cap. 11, Sec. 2, pág. 309)

sedimentary rock / roca sedimentaria: se forma cuando los sedimentos se compactan y se cementan o cuando los minerales salen de una solución o cuando la evaporación los deja atrás. (Cap. 4, Sec. 4, pág. 103)

sediments / sedimentos: materiales sueltos, como fragmentos rocosos, granos minerales y restos de plantas y animales, dejados por el viento, el agua, el hielo o la gravedad. (Cap. 4, Sec. 4, pág. 103)

seismic wave / onda sísmica: onda generada por un movimiento sísmico. (Cap. 11, Sec. 2, pág. 308)

seismograph / sismógrafo: instrumento que registra las ondas sísmicas y anota el momento de llegada de cada onda. (Cap. 11, Sec. 2, pág. 311)

sewage / aguas negras: agua que se va por las alcantarillas y que contiene residuos humanos, detergentes caseros y jabones. (Cap. 21, Sec. 1, pág. 612)

sheet erosion / erosión laminar: tipo de erosión hídrica de superficie causada por el agua de escorrentía que ocurre cuando el agua que fluye sobre capas extensas recoge sedimentos y los transporta. (Cap. 9, Sec. 1, pág. 243)

shield volcano / volcán de escudo: volcán ancho y de laderas levemente inclinadas que se forma gracias a erupciones silenciosas de lava basáltica. (Cap. 12, Sec. 2, pág. 344)

silicate / silicato: mineral que contiene sílice y oxígeno y, por lo general, uno o más elementos. (Cap. 3, Sec. 1, pág. 66)

sill / intrusión: rasgo rocoso ígneo que se forma cuando el magma es inyectado en una grieta horizontal entre capas de roca y se endurece bajo tierra. (Cap. 12, Sec. 3, pág. 351)

slump / desprendimiento: tipo de movimiento de masas que se presenta cuando una masa de material se mueve cuesta abajo por una pendiente curva. (Cap. 8, Sec. 1, pág. 213)

soil / suelo: mezcla de roca meteorizada, materia orgánica descompuesta, fragmentos minerales y aire; su formación puede tomar miles de años. (Cap. 7, Sec. 2, pág. 190)

soil profile / perfil del suelo: corte vertical de las capas del suelo, cada una de las cuales constituye un horizonte. (Cap. 7, Sec. 2, pág. 192)

solar eclipse / eclipse solar: ocurre cuando la Luna se atraviesa entre el Sol y la Tierra y proyecta su sombra sobre una parte de la Tierra. (Cap. 23, Sec. 2, pág. 681)

solar energy / energía solar: energía proveniente del sol que es limpia, inagotable y que se puede transformar en electricidad por medio de células solares. (Cap. 5, Sec. 2, pág. 130)

solar system / sistema solar: sistema de

nueve planetas, entre ellos, la Tierra, y otros cuerpos sólidos que giran alrededor del Sol. (Cap. 24, Sec. 1, pág. 703)

solstice / solsticio: ocurre dos veces al año y es el punto en que el Sol se aleja más del ecuador, hacia el norte o hacia el sur. (Cap. 23, Sec. 1, pág. 675)

solution / solución: tipo de mezcla en que una sustancia se mezcla completa y uniformemente en otra y que es idéntica en toda su extensión. (Cap. 2, Sec. 2, pág. 43)

space probe / sonda espacial: instrumento que viaja a gran distancia en el sistema solar, recopila datos y los envía a la Tierra. (Cap. 22, Sec. 2, pág. 650)

space shuttle / transbordador espacial: astronave reutilizable que puede transportar cargamento, astronautas y satélites hacia y desde el espacio. (Cap. 22, Sec. 3, pág. 655)

space station / estación espacial: instalaciones con zonas de habitación, de trabajo y de ejercicio y equipo y sistemas de apoyo para que los seres humanos vivan y trabajen en el espacio y efectúen investigación que no es posible llevar a cabo en la Tierra. (Cap. 22, Sec. 3, pág. 656)

species / especie: grupo de organismos que se reproduce sólo con otros miembros de su propio grupo. (Cap. 14, Sec. 1, pág. 400)

specific gravity / gravedad específica: razón del peso de un mineral comparada con el peso de un volumen igual de agua. (Cap. 3, Sec. 2, pág. 70)

sphere / esfera: objeto tridimensional redondo en que cualquier punto sobre su superficie está equidistante del centro. La Tierra es una esfera un poco alargada en el ecuador y ligeramente achatada en los polos. (Cap. 23, Sec. 1, pág. 672)

spring / manantial: se forma cuando el nivel hidrostático se junta con la superficie terrestre; a menudo se halla en las laderas de las colinas y se utiliza como una fuente de agua dulce. (Cap. 9, Sec. 2, pág. 255)

station model / código meteorológico: indica las condiciones del tiempo en un lugar específico, mediante el uso de símbolos en un mapa. (Cap. 16, Sec. 3, pág. 479)

streak / veta: color de un mineral cuando se encuentra en forma de polvo. (Cap. 3, Sec. 2, pág. 71)

stream discharge / descarga de corriente: volumen de agua que fluye por un punto específico por unidad de tiempo. (Cap. 20, Sec. 2, pág. 591)

strike-slip fault / falla transformante: lugar donde las fuerzas de cizalleamiento han ocasionado el rompimiento de las rocas, las cuales se deslizan una al lado de la otra en direcciones opuestas, pero sin mucho movimiento vertical. (Cap. 11, Sec. 1, pág. 307)

sunspots / manchas solares: áreas del Sol que son menos calientes y brillantes que las áreas circundantes, son causadas por el campo magnético del Sol y ocurren en ciclos. (Cap. 25, Sec. 2, pág. 742)

supergiant / supergigante: etapa avanzada en el ciclo de vida de una estrella masiva en la cual el núcleo se calienta, se forman elementos pesados por fusión y la estrella se expande; con el tiempo, puede explotar para formar una supernova. (Cap. 25, Sec. 3, pág. 750)

surface current / corriente de superficie: corriente oceánica accionada por el viento; se mueve horizontalmente, paralela a la superficie de la Tierra y solamente mueve unos pocos cientos de metros superiores de agua marina. (Cap. 18, Sec. 2, pág. 526)

surface wave / onda de superficie: onda sísmica que mueve las partículas rocosas de arriba hacia abajo en un movimiento rotatorio y de lado a lado en un movimiento de vaivén. (Cap. 11, Sec. 2, pág. 309)

T

technology / tecnología: usa los descubrimientos científicos para propósitos prácticos y para facilitar y mejorar la vida de las personas. (Cap. 1, Sec. 1, pág. 12)

temperate zones / zonas templadas: zonas climáticas con temperaturas moderadas, las cuales se encuentran entre los trópicos y las zonas polares. (Cap. 17, Sec. 1, pág. 492)

tephra / tefrita: fragmentos pequeños de roca o lava solidificada que caen del aire durante una erupción volcánica explosiva; varía en tamaño desde cenizas volcánicas a bombas y bloques volcánicos. (Cap. 12, Sec. 2, pág. 344)

terracing / cultivo en terrazas: método de cultivo que se utiliza para reducir la erosión en laderas inclinadas. (Cap. 7, Sec. 3, pág. 201)

tidal range / amplitud de la marea: la diferencia entre el nivel del océano en pleamar y su nivel en bajamar. (Cap. 18, Sec. 3, pág. 536)

tide / marea: ascenso y descenso del nivel del mar provocado, en su mayor parte, por la interacción de la gravedad en el sistema Tierra-Luna. (Cap. 18, Sec. 3, pág. 535)

till / tilita: mezcla de sedimentos de diferentes tamaños que un glaciar en retirada deja caer de la base y que puede cubrir inmensas áreas de terreno. (Cap. 8, Sec. 2, pág. 218)

topographic map / mapa topográfico: mapa que muestra los cambios en elevación en la superficie terrestre e indica rasgos como caminos y ciudades. (Cap. 6, Sec. 3, pág. 168)

tornado / tornado: tormenta de viento violento y arremolinado que se mueve sobre una estrecha trayectoria sobre la tierra y que puede ser resultado de los vientos laterales dentro de una tormenta eléctrica. (Cap. 16, Sec. 2, pág. 474)

trench / fosa: depresión de lados empinados angosta y larga en el suelo marino que se forma cuando una placa se hunde debajo de otra placa. (Cap. 19, Sec. 1, pág. 553)

trilobite / trilobites: organismo con un exoesqueleto dividido en tres partes; existía en abundancia en los océanos del Paleozoico; se le considera un fósil guía. (Cap. 14, Sec. 1, pág. 398)

tropics / trópicos: zona climática que recibe la mayor cantidad de radiación solar; está ubicada entre los 23°N y los 23°S y en donde siempre hace calor, con excepción de las altas elevaciones. (Cap. 17, Sec. 1, pág. 492)

troposphere / troposfera: capa de la atmósfera terrestre más próxima a la tierra, contiene un 99 por ciento de vapor de agua y un 75 por ciento de los gases atmosféricos; es la región donde se forman las nubes y ocurre el estado del tiempo. (Cap. 15, Sec. 1, pág. 436)

trough / seno: punto más bajo de una onda. (Cap. 18, Sec. 3, pág. 532)

tsunami / tsunami: onda marina sísmica que comienza sobre el foco de un terremoto y la cual puede ser muy destructiva cuando llega al litoral. (Cap. 11, Sec. 3, pág. 320)

U

ultraviolet radiation / radiación ultravioleta: tipo de energía que llega a la Tierra proveniente del Sol; puede causar daños a la piel y ocasionar cáncer; gran parte de esta radiación es absorbida por la capa de ozono. (Cap. 15, Sec. 1, pág. 440)

unconformity / discordancia: brecha en una capa rocosa provocada por la erosión o por períodos cuando no hubo depositación. (Cap. 13, Sec. 2, pág. 377)

uniformitarianism / uniformitarianismo: principio que establece que los procesos terrestres que suceden en la actualidad son semejantes a aquéllos que ocurrieron en el pasado. (Cap. 13, Sec. 3, pág. 387)

upwarped mountains / montañas plegadas anticlinales: montañas que se forman cuando los bloques de corteza terrestre son forzados a ascender por fuerzas internas de la Tierra. (Cap. 6, Sec. 1, pág. 160)

upwelling / corriente resurgente: circulación del océano que lleva agua fría y profunda a la superficie oceánica. (Cap. 18, Sec. 2, pág. 529)

Uranus / Urano: séptimo planeta más alejado del Sol; es grande y gaseoso, posee un marcado color verde-azulado y gira en un eje casi paralelo al plano de su órbita. (Cap. 24, Sec. 3, pág. 717)

V

variables / variables: diferentes factores que pueden cambiarse en un experimento. (Cap. 1, Sec. 1, pág. 10)

vent / chimenea: abertura por donde sube el magma y sale a la superficie terrestre como lava, formando un volcán. (Cap. 12, Sec. 1, pág. 336)

Venus / Venus: segundo planeta más cercano al Sol; semejante a la Tierra en masa y tamaño; posee una atmósfera densa y una superficie con cráteres, grietas que parecen fallas y volcanes. (Cap. 24, Sec. 2, pág. 709)

volcanic mountains / montañas volcánicas: montañas que se forman cuando el material fundido llega a la superficie terrestre a través de partes debilitadas de la corteza y se amontona en una estructura que tiene forma de cono. (Cap. 6, Sec. 1, pág. 161)

volcanic neck / chimenea volcánica: núcleo ígneo sólido de un volcán que queda atrás después de la erosión del cono más suave. (Cap. 12, Sec. 3, pág. 351)

volcano / volcán: abertura en la superficie terrestre que arroja gases sulfurosos, cenizas y lava; se puede formar en el límite de las placas terrestres, donde éstas se separan o se juntan y también en los focos calientes. (Cap. 12, Sec. 1, pág. 334)

W

waning / octante menguante: describe la fase que ocurre después de la luna nueva, cuando el lado visible de la Luna que vemos desde la Tierra empieza a decrecer. (Cap. 23, Sec. 2, pág. 679)

water table / nivel hidrostático o capa freática: nivel superior de la zona de saturación; disminuye durante una sequía. (Cap. 9, Sec. 2, pág. 252)

wave / onda: movimiento rítmico que transporta energía a través de la materia o el espacio; se puede describir por su cresta, seno, longitud y altura. (Cap. 18, Sec. 3, pág. 532)

waxing / octante creciente: describe la fase después de la luna nueva, cuando la parte iluminada de la Luna que vemos desde la Tierra empieza a ser más visible. (Cap. 23, Sec. 2, pág. 679)

weather / tiempo atmosférico: estado de la atmósfera en un momento y lugar específicos, determinado por factores que incluyen la presión atmosférica, la cantidad de humedad en el aire, la temperatura y el viento. (Cap. 16, Sec. 1, pág. 462)

weathering / meteorización: procesos superficiales mecánicos o químicos que rompen las rocas en fragmentos cada vez más pequeños. (Cap. 7, Sec. 1, pág. 184)

white dwarf / enana blanca: etapa avanzada en el ciclo de vida de una estrella de la secuencia principal en la cual su núcleo agota todo su helio y sus capas externas escapan hacia el espacio, dejando atrás un núcleo caliente y denso. (Cap. 25, Sec. 3, pág. 749)

wind farm / fincas de energía eólica: área en que muchos molinos de viento usan el viento para generar electricidad. (Cap. 5, Sec. 2, pág. 131)

Index

The index for *Glencoe Earth Science* will help you locate major topics in the book quickly and easily. Each entry in the index is followed by the number of the pages on which the entry is discussed. A page number given in boldfaced type indicates the page on which that entry is defined. A page number given in italic type indicates a page on which the entry is used in an illustration or photograph. The abbreviation *act.* indicates a page on which the entry is used in an activity.

Index

Index

Index

Index

Index

Index

Index

Index

Index

X

Z

Index

Art Credits

Glencoe would like to acknowledge the artists and agencies who participated in illustrating this program: Absolute Science Illustration; Andrew Evansen; Argosy; Articulate Graphics; Craig Attebery represented by Frank & Jeff Lavaty; CHK America; Gagliano Graphics; Pedro Julio Gonzalez represented by Melissa Turk & The Artist Network; Robert Hynes represented by Mendola Ltd.; Morgan Cain & Associates; JTH Illustration; Laurie O'Keefe; Matthew Pippin represented by Beranbaum Artist's Representative; Precision Graphics; Publisher's Art; Rolin Graphics, Inc.; Wendy Smith represented by Melissa Turk & The Artist Network; Kevin Torline represented by Berendsen and Associates, Inc.; WILDlife ART; Phil Wilson represented by Cliff Knecht Artist Representative; Zoo Botanica.

Photo Credits

Abbreviation key: AA=Animals Animals; AH=Aaron Haupt; AMP=Amanita Pictures; BC=Bruce Coleman, Inc.; CB=CORBIS; DM=Doug Martin; DRK=DRK Photo; ES=Earth Scenes; FP=Fundamental Photographs; GH=Grant Heilman Photography; IC=Icon Images; KS=KS Studios; LA=Liaison Agency; MB=Mark Burnett; MM=Matt Meadows; PE=PhotoEdit; PD=PhotoDisc; PQ=PictureQuest; PR=Photo Researchers; SB=Stock Boston; TSA=Tom Stack & Associates; TSM=The Stock Market; VU=Visuals Unlimited.

Cover PD; **viii** Mark A. Schneider/VU; **ix** Hans Strand/Stone; **x** Dr. Russ Utgard; **xi** Burhan Ozbilici/AP/Wide World Photos; **xii** Stone; **xiii** Peter Miller/Science Source/PR; **xv** SuperStock; **xvi** NASA/Science Source/PR; **xviii** Ken Whitmore/Stone; **xix** Wyman P. Meinzer; **xx** Emory Kristof/National Geographic; **xxi** (l)Jose Manuel Sanchis/CB, (r)DM; **xxii** Fred Bavendam/Minden Pictures; **xxiii** Sigurjon Sindrason; **xxiv** Paul Rocheleau/Index Stock; **xxv** Geoff Butler; **1** Roine Magnusson/Stone; **2-3** Mike Zens/CB; **3** Mark A. Schneider/VU; **4** Ken Lucas/VU, **4-5** Jim Page/North Carolina Museum of Natural Sciences; **5** Richard Hutchings; **7** (t)Michael Habicht/ES, (b)Michael Wilhelm/ENP Images; **8** Richard Cummins/CB; **9** John Heseltine/Science Photo Library/PR; **10 11** AH; **12** (l)Michael Dwyer/SB, (c)Carolas, (r)Mark Segal/SB; **13** (t)Science Museum/Science & Society Picture Library, (cl)reprinted by permission of Parks Canada and Newfoundland Museum, (c cr)Dorling Kindersley, (b)NASA; **14** Russ Underwood/Lockheed Martin Space Systems; **15** Todd Gustafson/Danita Delimont; **16** Smithsonian Institution; **18** NASA/MSFC; **19** European Space Agency/Science Photo Library/PR; **20** (l)Frans Lanting/Minden Pictures, (c)Ted Levin/AA, (r)Al, Linda Bristor/VU; **21** MM; **22** Bates Littlehales/National Geographic Image Collection; **23** AH; **24** MB; **25** Timothy Fuller; **26** AP Photo; **27** Dan Mauersberg/DMH Photography; **28** (l)Krafft/PR, (r)D.A. Calvert, Royal Greenwich Observatory/Science Photo Library/PR; **29** (l)CABISCO/VU, (r)Jan Hinsch/Science Photo Libray/PR; **32** IBMRL/VU; **32-33** Roine Magnusson/Stone; **33** MM;

35 (t, l to r)Mark Schneider/Peter Arnold, Inc, Dane S. Johnson/VU, Ken Lucas/VU, Mark A. Schneider/PR, (b, l to r) AH, AMP, Charles D. Winters/PR, AH; **36** John Evans; **39** (l)Herbert Kehrer/OKAPIA/PR, (c)DM, (r)Bruce Hands/Stone; **40** Kenji Kerins; **42** Ken Whitmore/Stone; **43** AMP; **44** Stuart Westmorland; **46** John S. Lough/VU; **48** CB; **49** (t)Storm Pirate Productions/Artville/PQ, (c)Breck P. Kent/ES, (b)CB/PQ; A**50** (t)Paul Chesley/Stone, (b)David Muench/CB; **51** NASA/JPL/Malin Space Science Systems; **52** (t)StudiOhio, (b)MM; **53** (t)Tim Courlas, (b)AH; **54** (t)Geoff Butler, (bl)KS, (br)StudiOhio; **56** (tl)MM, (tr)Keith Kent/Science Photo Library, (b)John Evans; **57** (l)DM, (r)MM; **58** MM; **60** Mark A. Schneider/PR; **60-61** D. Boone/CB; **61** (t)MM, (c)DM, (b)José Manuel Sanchis Calvete/CB; **62** MM; **63** (t)John R. Foster/PR, (b)Mark A. Schneider/VU; **64** (t)Mark A. Schneider/VU, (cl)Albert J. Copley/VU, (cr)Harry Taylor/DK Images, (bl)Harry Taylor/DK Images, (bc)First Image, (br)Mark A. Schneider/VU; **65** (l)Patricia K. Armstrong/VU, (r)Dennis Flaherty Photography/PR; **67** KS; **68** (l)MB/PR, (c)Dan Suzio/PR, (r)Breck P. Kent/ES; **69** (t)Bud Roberts/VU, (c)Charles D. Winters/PR, (b)IC; **70** (l)Andrew McClenaghan/Science Photo Library/PR, (r)Charles D. Winters/PR; **71** (t)Geoff Butler, (bl)DM, (br)PR; **72** MM; **73** Reuters NewMedia Inc./CB; **74** (tl)Biophoto Associates/PR, (tr)H. Stern/PR, (cl)Biophoto Associates/PR, (cr)A.J. Copley/VU, (b, l to r)Mark A. Schneider/VU, VU, A.J. Copley/VU, H. Stern/PR; **75** (tl)University of Houston, (tr)Charles D. Winters/PR; (cl)Arthur R. Hill/VU, (cr)David Lees/CB, (b, l to r)DM, DM, A.J. Copley/VU, Vaughan Fleming/Science Photo Library/PR; **76** (l)Francis G. Mayer/CB, (r)Smithsonian Institution; **77** (l)Randolph King/PR, (r)DM; **78** (t)Maurice Nimmo/Frank Lane Picture Agency/CB, (bl)Paul Silverman/FP, (br)Biophoto Associates/PR; **79** Jim Cummins/FPG; **80** (t)DM, (c)Jose Manuel Sanchis/CB, (b)MM; **81** (l)Charles D. Winter/PR, (r)Andrew J. Martinez/PR; **82** SPL/Custom Medical Stock Photo; **83** Bettmann/CB; **84** (tl)Mark A. Schneider/PR, (tr)Charles R. Belinky/PR, (c)Phillip Hayson/PR, (b)Mark A. Schneider/PR; **88** John D. Cunningham/VU; **88-89** Cliff Leight; **89** Geoff Butler; **90** (l)CB, (r)DM; **91** (tl)Steve Hoffman, (tr)Breck P. Kent/ES, (bl)Brent Turner/BLT Productions, (br)Breck P. Kent/ES; **92** (bkgd) CB/PQ, (t)CB, (bl)Martin Miller, (bc)Jeff Gnass, (br)Doug Sokell/TSA; **93** Russ Clark; **94** USGS/HVO; **95** (t)Breck P. Kent/ES, (b)DM; **96** (tl tc tr)Breck P. Kent/ES, (c, l to r) Mark Steinmetz, Breck P. Kent/ES, Breck P. Kent/ES, DM, (bl)DM, (br)Tim Courlas; **98** (l)Breck P. Kent/ES, (r)DM/PR; **99** (tc)courtesy Kent Ratajeski & Dr. Allen Glazner, University of NC, (b)Alfred Pasieka/PR, (others) Breck P. Kent/ES; **101** (l)John Evans, (r)Robert Estall/CB; **102** Paul Rocheleau/Index Stock; **103** (l)Timothy Fuller, (r)Steve McCutcheon/VU; **105** (l)IC, (lc)DM, (rc) Andrew Martinez/PR, (r)John R. Foster/PR; **106** (l) Breck P. Kent/ES, (r)AH; **107** (t)Georg Gerster/PR, (b)IC; **109** Beth Davidow/VU; **110** (t)Breck P. Kent/ES, (c)IC, (bl)Jack Sekowski, (br)Tim Courlas; **112-113** Y. Kawasaki/Photonica; **113** Matt Turner/LA; **114** (t)Mark Segal/Index Stock, (c)Albert J. Copley/VU, (b)DM; **116** Jeremy Woodhouse/DRK; **118** Lowell Georgia/CB; **118-119** Bill Ross/CB; **119** MM; **121** VU;

Credits

124 (l)George Lepp/CB, (r)Carson Baldwin Jr./ES; 125 Paul A. Souders/CB; 126 (tl)Emory Kristof, (tr)National Energy Technology Laboratory, (b)Ian R. MacDonald/Texas A&M University; 127 Hal Beral/VU; 129 Roger Ressmeyer/CB; 130 Spencer Grant/PE; 131 Inga Spence/VU; 132 Robert Cameron/Stone; 133 Vince Streano/CB; 134 (t)David Young-Wolff, (b)Earl Young/Archive Photos; 135 Peter Holden/VU; 137 AH; 138 Joseph Nettis/PR; 139 (t)Mark Joseph/Stone, (bl)AH, (br)Wyoming Mining Association; 142 (t)Joel W. Rogers/CB, (b)AH; 143 AH; 144 Brown Brothers; 145 (l)Ed Clark, (r)Shell Oil Co.; 146 (t)Betty Sederquist/VU, (c)Bob Rowan/CB, (b)C. Osborne/PR; 147 (tl)Michael Mancuso/Omni-Photo Communications, (tr)file photo, (bl)Andrew J. Martinez/PR, (br)Coco McCoy/Rainbow; 148 David Frazier; 150 Mickey Gibson/ES; 150-151 Francois Gohier/PR; 151 Mary Kate Denny/PE; 152 MB; 152-153 Thierry Borredon/Stone; 153 (tl)Studiohio, (tr)Tom Bean/DRK, (b)Robert Caputo/Aurora/PQ; 154 David Weintraub/SB; 154-155 GSFC/NASA; 155 Dominic Oldershaw; 157 (t)Carr Clifton/Minden Pictures, (c)Alan Maichrowicz/Peter Arnold, Inc., (b)Stephen G. Maka/DRK; 158 (t)Tom Bean/DRK, (b)Liz Hymans/Stone; 159 John Lemker/ES; 160 (t)John Kieffer/Peter Arnold, Inc., (b)Carr Clifton/Minden Pictures; 161 David Muench/CB; 164 Dominic Oldershaw; 169 (t)Rob & Ann Simpson, (c)Robert E. Pratt, (b)courtesy Maps a la Carte, Inc. and TopoZone.com; 174 John Evans; 175 Layne Kennedy/CB; 176 (l)Culver Pictures, (r)PD; 176-177 Pictor; 177 (t)PD, (bl)William Manning/The Stock Market, (br)Kunio Owaki/The Stock Market; 178 (l)William J. Weber, (r)AH; 179 (l)Tom Bean/DRK, (r)Marc Muench; 182 Mickey Gibson/ES; 182-183 Francois Gohier/PR; 183 Mary Kate Denny/PE; 184 MB; 185 (l)Studiohio, (r)Tom Bean/DRK; 186 W. Perry Conway/CB; 187 Hans Strand/Stone; 188 (tl)Craig Kramer, (tr)A.J. Copley/VU, (bl br)John Evans; 189 (l)Runk/Schoenberger from GH, (r)William Johnson/SB; 191 (bkgd)Stephen R. Wagner, (t)James D. Balog, (c)Martin Miller, (b)Steven C. Wilson/Entheos; 192 (l)Bonnie Heidel/VU, (r)John Bova/PR; 197 MM; 198 (l)Gary Braasch/CB, (r)Donna Ikenberry/ES; 199 Chip & Jill Isenhart/TSA; 200 (t)Dr. Russ Utgard, (b)Denny Eilers from GH; 201 Georg Custer/PR; 202 (t)George H. Harrison from GH, (b)Bob Daemmrich; 203 KS; 204 Larry Hamill; 205 Courtesy Elvia Niebla; 206 (t)Adam Jones/Masterfile, (c)Berry L. Runk from GH, (b)Tom Bean/DRK; 207 (l)Tom Bean/DRK, (r)David M. Dennis/ES; 208 MB; 210 Victor Englebert; 210-211 Robert Holmes/CB; 211 MM; 212 Robert L. Schuster/USGS; 213 Martin G. Miller/VU; 214 (t)Atwood/USGS, (bl) Sylvester Allred/VU, (br)Tom Uhlman/VU; 215 AP/Wide World Photos; 216 D. Newman/VU; 218 James N. Westwater; 219 (t)Michael Marten/Science Photo Library/PR, (b)Tom Bean/CB; 220 John Gerlach/VU; 221 Gregory G. Dimijian/PR; 222 Mark E. Gibson/VU; 223 Timothy Fuller; 224 Galen Rowell/CB; 225 Jerry Howard/SB; 226 Fletcher & Baylis/PR; 227 (t)John D. Cunningham/VU, (b)file photo; 228 (bkgd) Breck P. Kent/ES, (tl)Stephen J. Krasemann/PR, (tr)Steve McCurry, (b)Wyman P. Meinzer; 229 Georg Gerster/PR; 230 (t)Greg Vaughn/TSA, (b)MM; 232 (t)Yann Arthus-Bertrand/CB, (b)Curt Schieber; 233 (t)Wide World Photos, (b)World Class Images;

234 (t)David Cavagnaro/VU, (c)MB/PR, (b)David Weintraub/PR; 235 (l)David Hosking/PR, (r)Wide World Photos; 238 NASA; 238-239 William Manning/TSM; 239 AH; 240 (l)Michael Busselle/Stone, (r)David Woodfall/DRK; 241 Tim Davis/Stone; 242 (t)GH, (b)KS; 244 Panoramic Images; 246 CB/PQ; 246 (bkgd)Stephen R. Wagner; 247 (l)Harald Sund/The Image Bank, (r)Loren McIntyre; 248 C. Davidson/Comstock; 249 James L. Amos/CB; 250 First Image; 250 (l)Wolfgang Kaehler, (r)Nigel Press/Stone; 253 CB; 254 file photo; 255 Barbara Filet/Stone; 256 Chad Ehlers/Stone; 257 Steve Lissau; 258 Macduff Everton/The Image Bank; 259 (tl)Steve Bentsen, (tr)SuperStock, (bl)Runk/Schoenberger from GH, (br)Breck P. Kent/ES; 260 Bruce Roberts/PR; 262 263 KS; 264 Jack Dermid/BC; 265 (l)David Alan Harvey/National Geographic, (r)Gary Bogdon/CB Sygma; 266 (l)Tom Bean/DRK, (r)David W. Hamilton/The Image Bank; 267 (l)Todd Powell/Index Stock, (r)J. Wengle/DRK; 272 (t)Ken Lucas/TCL/Masterfile, (b)Patrice Ceisel/SB/PQ; 272-273 Index Stock; 273 (t)Hal Beral/Photo Network/PQ, (b)Archive Photos/PQ; 274 Francois Gohier/PR; 274-275 Stone; 275 MB; 278 Martin Land/Science Source/PR; 281 Ralph White/CB; 287 Davis Meltzer; 288 Craig Aurness/CB; 290 Craig Brown/Index Stock; 291 Ric Ergenbright/CB; 292 Roger Ressmeyer/CB; 294 Burhan Ozbilici/AP/Wide World Photos; 296 L. Lauber/ES; 297 Courtesy Ed Klimasauskas; 298 Galen Rowell/CB; 299 (l)Tim Barnwen/SB, (r)Bettmann/CB; 302 Bettmann/CB; 302-303 Paras Shah/AP/Wide World Photo; 303 MB; 304 Tom & Therisa Stack/TSA; 306 (t)Tom Bean/DRK, (b)Lysbeth Corsi/VU; 307 David Parker/PR; 308 Tom & Therisa Stack/TSA; 310 Robert W. Tope/Natural Science Illustrations; 317 (l)Steven D. Starr/SB, (r)Berkeley Seismological Laboratory; 318 AP Photo/HURRIYET; 319 David J. Cross/Peter Arnold, Inc.; 322 James L. Stanfield/National Geographic Society; 323 Courtesy of Safe-T-Proof; 324 (l)Ben Simmons/TSM, (r)Reuters NewMedia Inc./CB; 326 (l)Bettmann/CB, (r)RO-MA Stock/Index Stock; 327 Richard Cummins/CB; 328 (l)Reuters/STR/Archive Photos, (r)Russell D. Curtis/PR; 329 (l)Science VU/VU, (r)Peter Menzel/SB; 330 Vince Streano/CB; 332 Roger Ressmeyer/CB; 332-333 Fabrizio Villa/AP/Wide World; 333 KS; 334 Sigurjon Sindrason; 335 (t)John Cancalosi/DRK, (b)Deborah Brosnan, Sustainable Ecosystems Institute; 339 NASA/CB; 340 341 Gary Rosenquist; 342 (bkgd)API/Explorer/PR, (t)G. Brad Lewis/Photo Resource Hawaii, (bl)Robert Hessler/Planet Earth Pictures, (br)Paul Chesley; 343 (l)Steve Kaufman/DRK, (r)Dee Breger/PR; 344 James L. Amos/CB; 345 (t)Krafft/Explorer/Science Source/PR, (b)Darrell Gulin/DRK; 347 Bernard Edmaier/PR; 350 (t)Joyce Photo/PR, (bl)Brent Turner, (br)DM; 351 (tl)Dick Canby, (tr)Tom Bean/DRK, (b)Jeff Foott/TSA; 353 Larry Ulrich/DRK; 354 AMP; 355 Spencer Grant/PE; 356 (bkgd)Mimmo Jodice/CB, (inset)Roger Ressmeyer/CB; 357 Jonathan Blair/CB; 358 (tl)Dave B. Fleetham/TSA, (b)Tom Bean/DRK; 359 (l)Soames Summerhays/PR, (r)Photri/TSM; 364-365 Coco McCoy from Rainbow/PQ; 365 Mary Evans Picture Library; 366 James L. Amos/PR; 366-367 Larry Ulrich/DRK; 367 MM; 368 (t)Mark E. Gibson/VU, (b)A.J. Copley/VU; 369 Jeffrey Rotman/CB; 370 (t)Dr. John A. Long, (b)Martin Land/PR;

884 CREDITS

372 (t)PhotoTake NYC/PQ, (bl br)Louis Psihoyos/Matrix; 374 David M. Dennis; 375 (l)Gary Retherford/PR, (r)Fred McConnaughey/PR; 376 AH; 379 (tl)IPR/12-18 T. Bain, British Geological Survey/NERC. All rights reserved, (tr)Tom Bean/CB, (b)Lyle Rosbotham; 380 Jim Hughes/ PhotoVenture/VU; 381 (l)Michael T. Sedam/CB, (r)Pat O'Hara/CB; 383 AH; 385 James King-Holmes/Science Photo Library/PR; 386 (t)Breck P. Kent/ES, (b)Kenneth Garrett; 387 WildCountry/CB; 388 (t)A.J. Copley/VU, (b)MM; 389 Lawson Wood/CB; 390-391 Jacques Bredy; 391 (t)CMN Archives/Dinofish, (c)CMN Archives/Dinofish, (b)Norbert Wu; 392 (t)Francois Gohier/PR, (c)From Journal of Ecology 2000, 88, p. 45-53. Photo courtesy Michigan Technological University, (b)Tom Bean/DRK; 393 (tl)Francois Gohier/PR, (tr)Mark E. Gibson/DRK, (b)Sinclair Stammers/PR; 396 CB; 396-397 Reuters New Media Inc./CB; 397 KS; 398 Tom & Therisa Stack/TSA; 400 (l)Gerald & Buff Corsi/VU, (r)John Gerlach/AA; 402 (t)Mark Boulron/PR, (others)Walter Chandoha; 403 Jeff Lepore/PR; 407 (l)Mitsuaki Iwago/Minden Pictures, (r)R. Calentine/VU; 409 J.G. Gehling/Discover Magazine; 410 Gerry Ellis/ENP Images; 413 MM; 416 (l)David Burnham/Fossilworks, Inc., (r)Francois Gohier/PR; 418 Michael Andrews/ES; 419 Tom J. Ulrich/VU; 420 David M. Dennis; 421 MB; 422 The Bridgeman Art Library; 424 (l)Adam Jones/PR, (r)Ken Lucas/VU; 425 (l)E. Webber/VU, (r)Len Rue, Jr./AA; 427 John Cancalosi/SB; 430-431 Angela Wyant/Stone; 431 (t)Henry Diltz/CB, (c b)Granger Collection, NY; 432 Lester V. Bergman/CB; 432-433 David Keaton/TSM; 433 First Image; 434 NASA; 435 (t)David S. Addison/VU, (bl)Frank Rossotto/TSM, (br)Larry Lee/CB; 438 Laurence Fordyce/ CB; 440 DM; 441 NASA/GSFC; 442 Michael Newman/PE; 444 Larry Fisher/Masterfile; 447 (t)Dan Guravich/PR, (b)Bill Brooks/Masterfile; 449 (t)Gene Moore/PhotoTake NYC/PQ, (cl)Phil Schermeister/CB, (cr)Stephen R. Wagner, (bl)Joel W. Rogers, (br)Kevin Schafer/CB; 450 Bill Brooks/ Masterfile; 452 453 David Young-Wolff/PE; 454 Bob Rowan/ CB; 455 (l)J.A. Kraulis/Masterfile, (r)CB; 457 (l)Tom Bean/ DRK, (r)Keith Kent/Science Photo Library/PR; 460 NASA; 460-461 Michael S. Yamashita/CB; 461 KS; 462 Kevin Horgan/Stone; 463 Fabio Colombini/ES; 467 (t)Charles O'Rear/CB, (b)Joyce Photographics/PR; 468 (l)Roy Morsch/TSM, (r)Mark McDermott/Stone; 469 (l)Mark E. Gibson/VU, (r)EPI Nancy Adams/TSA; 471 Van Bucher/Science Source/PR; 473 Jeffrey Howe/VU; 474 (t)Warren Faidley/Weatherstock, (b)Robert Hynes; 476 NASA/Science Photo Library/PR; 477 Fritz Pölking/Peter Arnold, Inc; 478 Howard Bluestein/Science Source/PR; 481 MB; 482 (t)Marc Epstein/DRK, (b)Timothy Fuller; 484 Erik Rank/Photonica; 485 Courtesy Weather Modification Inc.; 486 (l)Peter Miller/Science Source/PR, Inc, (r)Gary Williams/LA; 487 (l)George D. Lepp/PR, (r)Janet Foster/Masterfile; 488 Bob Daemmrich; 490 Pekka Parviainen/PR; 490-491 Rod Planck/PR; 491 AH; 492 CB; 495 (l)William Leonard/DRK, (r)Bob Rowan, Progressive Image/CB; 496 John Shaw/TSA; 497 (tl)David Hosking/ CB, (tr)Yva Momatiuk & John Eastcott/PR, (b)Michael Melford/The Image Bank; 498 (t)S.R. Maglione/PR, (bl)Fritz Pölking/VU, (br)Jack Grove/TSA; 499 Zig Zeszczynski/AA; 500 SuperStock; 501 (l)Jonathan Head/AP/Wide World Photos, (r)Jim Corwin/Index Stock; 503 (t)A. Ramey/PE,

(b)Peter Beck/Pictor; 504 Galen Rowell/Mountain Light; 508 John Bolzan; 509 Chip & Jill Isenhart/TSA; 510 (l)Jim Sugar Photography/CB, (r)AFP/CB; 511 MM; 513 DM; 514 (b)Gary Rosenquist; 514-515 Alberto Garcia/Saba; 516 (t)Paul Sakuma/Associated Press, (c)Galen Rowell/ Mountain Light, (b)Michael Melford/The Image Bank; 517 (l)Spencer Grant/PE, (r)Steve Kaufman/DRK; 520 Judy Griesedieck/CB; 520-521 Warren Bolster/Stone; 521 Raven/Explorer/PR; 522 (l)Norbert Wu/Peter Arnold, Inc., (r)Darryl Torckler/Stone; 525 Cathy Church/Picturesque/PQ; 527 Bob Daemmrich; 528 (t)Darryl Torckler/Stone, (b)Raven/Explorer/PR; 532 Jack Fields/PR; 533 Tom & Therisa Stack; 534 (bkgd)Stephen R. Wagner, (l)Spike Mafford/PD, (r)Douglas Peebles/CB; 535 Arnulf Husmo/Stone; 536 (tl)Groenendyk/PR, (tr)Patrick Ingrand/Stone, (b)Kent Knudson/SB; 539 AH; 540 (t)Mark E. Gibson/VU, (b)Timothy Fuller; 541 Timothy Fuller; 543 Seth Resnick/SB/PQ; 544 (t)Worldsat Productions/ NRSC/Science Photo Library, (cl)Phillippe Diederich/Contact Press Images/PQ, (b)S.J. Krasemann/Peter Arnold, Inc.; 545 (l)Carl R. Sams II/Peter Arnold, Inc., (r)Edna Douthat; 548 L.P. Madin/Woods Hole Oceanographic Institution, Woods Hole, MA; 548-549 Stuart Westmorland/Stone; 549 MB; 550-551 "The Floor of the Oceans" by Bruce C. Heezen and Marie Tharp, ©1980 by Marie Tharp. Reproduced by permission of Marie Tharp; 552 Woods Hole Oceanographic Institution; 553 Thomas J. Abercrombie/ National Geographic Society; 554 (t)J. & L. Weber/Peter Arnold, Inc., (bl)Arthur Hill/VU, (br)John Cancalosi/Peter Arnold, Inc.; 555 (t)Instutute of Oceanographic Sciences/ NERC/Science Photo Library/PR, (b)Biophoto Associates/ PR; 557 Fred Bavendam/Minden Pictures; 559 Nanct Sefton/PR; 560 (l)Manfred Kage/Peter Arnold, Inc., (r)M.I. Walker/Science Source/PR; 561 (l)Nick Caloyianis/National Geographic Society, (c)Herb Segars/AA, (r)Norbert Wu; 562 Fred Bavendam/Peter Arnold, Inc.; 563 (clockwise from top)Lloyd K. Townsend, Michael Abbey/PR, Andrew J. Martinez/PR, Peter Skinner/PR, Gregory Ochocki/PR, Zig Leszczynski/AA, Gerald & Buff Corsi/VU, Anne W. Rosenfeld/AA, AA, Andrew J. Martinez/PR, Andrew J. Martinez/PR, Hal Beral/VU; 564 James H. Robinson/PR; 567 (tl)C.C. Lockwood/ES, (bl)C.C. Lockwood/DRK, (others)David Young-Wolff/Photo Edit; 568 NASA; 569 David Young-Wolff/Photo Edit; 570 (t)Jim Nilsen/ Stone, (bl)Jeff Rotman/Peter Arnold, Inc., (br)Fred Bavendam/Minden Pictures; 571 Fred Bavendam/Minden Pictures; 572 Rick Price/CB; 572-573 Emory Kristof/National Geographic; 573 (t)Ralph White/CB, (b)Emory Kristof/ National Geographic; 574 (t)Hal Beral/VU, (b)AP Photo/ Dolores Ochoa; 575 (l)D.P. Wilson/Science Source/PR, (r)Fred Bavendam/Minden Pictures; 576 Peter Johnson/CB; 580-581 Joseph Sohm/ChromoSohm Inc./CB; 581 Andrew A. Wagner; 582 Astrid & Hans-Frieder Michler/Science Photo Library/PR; 582-583 George D. Lepp/PR; 583 AH; 584 (l)Bob Daemmrich/SB, (r)TK/CB; 586 Timothy Fuller; 587 AH; 588 Paul Bousquet; 589 Andy Sacks/Stone; 591 Rich Iwasaki; 592 Simon Fraser/Northumbrian Environmental Management Ltd./Science Photo Library/ Photo Researchers; 594 (t)Gloria H. Chomica/Masterfile, (c)Raymond Gehman/CB, (b)David Muench/Stone; 595 John Evans; 598 (tl)Philip James Corwin/CB, (cl)Bill

Gallery/SB/PQ, (cr)Skiold/PE/PQ, (b)Aerials Only, (tooth-paste, egg shell, shoe, tin can, baseball, cassette, sneaker, leaf, tin can lid)Image Ideas, (olive oil)Digital Stock, (others)PD; **599** David Young-Wolff/Photo Edit; **600** MM; **602-603** VCG/FPG; **603** Andy Levin/PR; **604** (t)Timothy Fuller, (c)KS, (b)Eric Neurath/SB; **605** (l)Stacy Pick/SB, (r)Tom Bean/Stone; **608** Michael Abbey/PR; **608-609** Art Wolfe/Stone; **609** MB; **610** (l)Michael J. Pettypool/Pictor, (r)VU; **611** (t)Bob Child/AP/Wide World Photos, (b)David Hoffman/Stone; **613** Stephen R. Wagner; **614** Colin Raw/Stone; **615** (t)Cleveland Public Library, (b)Jim Baron/The Image Finders; **617** (l)C. Squared Studios/PD, (c)Larry Lefever from GH, (r)Dominic Oldershaw; **618** MB; **619** Alan Pitcairn from GH; **622** John Evans; **626** (t)Dr. Ryder/Jason Burns/Photo-Take NYC, (b)Dominic Oldershaw; **627** file photo; **628** Jeff Vanuga/CB; **629** Eric Hartmann/Magnum Photos; **630** (t)Alan Pitcairn from GH, (c)John D. Cunningham/VU; **631** (l)David Woodfall/Stone, (r)DM; **636-637** Steve Murray/PQ; **637** Davis Meltzer; **638** NASA; **638-639** NASA/Roger Ressmeyer/CB; **639** CB; **640** (l)Weinberg-Clark/The Image Bank, (r)Stephen Marks/The Image Bank; **641** (l)PE, (r)Wernher Krutein/LA; **642** Chuck Place/SB; **643** NASA; **644** (t)Roger Ressmeyer/CB, (b)Simon Fraser/Science Photo Library/PR; **645** Raphael Gaillarde/LA; **646** (t)IC, (b)Diane Graham-Henry & Kathleen Culbert-Aguilar; **647** NASA; **648** NASA/Science Photo Library/PR; **649** NASA; **650** (tl tr) NASA/Science Source/PR, (bl)Julian Baum/Science Photo Library/PR, (br)M. Salaber/LA; **651** (t, l to r)Dorling Kindersley Images, TASS from Sovfoto, NASA, NASA/JPL, (c, l to r)NASA/JPL/Caltech, NASA/JPL/Caltech, NASA, NASA/JPL, (bl br)NASA; **652** AFP/CB; **653** NASA/CB; **654** NASA/Science Source/PR; **655** NASA/LA; **656** (t)NASA, (b)NASA/LA; **657** NASA/Science Source/PR; **658** NASA/JPL/Malin Space Science Systems; **659** NASA/JPL/LA; **660** (t)David Ducros/Science Photo Library/PR, (b)NASA; **661** HED Foundation/NASA; **662** Roger Ressmeyer/CB; **663** DM; **664-665** Robert McCall; **665** NASA/Science Photo Library/PR; **666** (tl)David Parker/Science Photo Library/PR, (tr)NASA/Science Photo Library/PR, (b)NASA; **667** (l)Novosti/Science Photo Library/PR, (c)Roger K. Burnard, (r)NASA; **670** NASA; **670-671** Chad Ehlers/Stone; **671** Bob Daemmrich; **680** (t)Lick Observatory, (b)Richard J. Wainscoat/Peter Arnold, Inc.; **682** Dr. Fred Espenak/Science Photo Library/PR; **683** Bettmann/CB; **684** NASA; **686** Roger Ressmeyer/CB; **689** BMDO/NRL/LLNL/Science Photo Library/PR; **690** (t)Zuber et al/Johns Hopkins University /NASA/PR, (b)NASA; **691** NASA; **692** MM; **694-695** Cosmo Condina/Stone; **695** Brown Brothers; **696** (t)NASA/Peter Arnold, Inc., (b)NASA; **700** PD; **700-701** Ted Thai/TimePix; **701** MM; **704** John R. Foster/PR; **705** Davis Meltzer; **706** Bettmann/CB; **708** USGS/Science Photo Library/PR; **709** (t)NASA/PR, (b)JPL/TSADO/TSA; **710** (t)Science Photo Library/PR, (bl)USGS/TSADO/TSA, (bc br) USGS/TSA; **711** NASA/JPL/Malin Space Science Systems; **713** Science Photo Library/PR; **714** (l)NASA/Science Photo Library/PR, (r)CB; **715** (t)USGS/TSADO/TSA, (tr)NASA/

JPL/PR, (bl)JPL, (bc)TSADO/NASA/TSA, (br)NASA; **716** JPL; **717** Heidi Hammel/NASA; **718** (l)NASA/Science Source/PR, (r)JPL/NASA/TSADO/TSA; **719** CB; **720** (tl)NASA/JPL/TSADO/TSA, (tr)NASA/Science Source/PR, (bl)USGS/NASA/TSADO/TSA, (br)CB; **721** (tl)NASA/Science Photo Library/PR, (tr)NASA/Science Source/PR, (c)ASP/Science Source/PR, (bl)CB, (br)W. Kaufmann/JPL/Sscience Source/PR; **722 723** Pekka Parviainen/Science Photo Library/PR; **724** Georg Gerster/PR; **725** JPL/TSADO/TSA; **727** Bettmann/CB; **728 729** Smithsonian National Museum of Natural History; **730** (t)NASA, (c)John Thomas/Science Photo Library/PR, (b)NASA/JPL; **731** (l)NASA; **731** (lc)JPL/NASA; **731** (l)NASA, (lc)JPL/NASA, (rc)file photo; **731** (r)NASA; **734** Science Photo Library/PR; **734-735** Space Telescope Science Institute/NASA/Science Photo Library/PR; **735** First Image; **739** Bob Daemmrich; **742** (t)Carnegie Institution of Washington, (b)NSO/SEL/Roger Ressmeyer/CB; **743** (tl)NASA, (tr)Picture Press/CB, (bl)AFP/CB, (br)Bryan & Cherry Alexander/PR; **744** Celestial Image Co./Science Photo Library/PR; **745** Tim Courlas; **747** Luke Dodd/Science Photo Library/PR; **750** AFP/CB; **751** NASA; **753** (t)Kitt Peak National Observatory, (b)CB; **756** Stephen R. Wagner; **757** AFP/CB; **758** MM; **760** Dennis Di Cicco/Peter Arnold, Inc.; **761** Bill Ross/CB; **762** (t)CB, (b)file photo; **763** (l)CB, (r)AURA/STScl/NASA; **768-769** PD; **770** Garry D. McMichael/PR; **770-771** Harvey Wood/The Still Moving Picture Co.; **771** (t c)AH, (b)Daniel Chester French/CB; **772** (t)SuperStock, (bl)Lindsay Hebberd/CB, (br)PhotoTake NYC/PQ; **773** (t)Ric Ergenbright/CB, (bl)IC, (br)Raymond Gehman/CB; **775** (t)Fred Habegger from GH, (b)Larry Lefever from GH; **776** (t)Murray & Associates, Inc./Picturesque/PQ, (c)Digital Vision/PQ, (b)Frank M. Hanna/VU; **777** (t)NASA/GH, (b)Yann Arthus-Bertrand/CB; **778** CNES/PR; **779** (t)Neil E. Johnson, (b)Lloyd Cluff/CB; **780** (t)Tom Bean/DRK, (b)Buddy Mays/CB; **781** (t)Joe Cornish/Stone, (b)SuperStock; **782** Townsend P. Dickinson/The Image Works; **783** (tl)A.J. Copley/VU, (tr)Townsend P. Dickinson/The Image Works, (bl)Stephen J. Krasemann/DRK, (br)Ken Lucas/VU; **784** (tl)Townsend P. Dickinson/The ImageWorks, (tr)Sinclair Stammers/Science Photo Library/PR, (bl)John Elk III/SB, (br)James L. Amos/PR; **787** (t)Ruth Dixon, (c)Bryan Pickering: Eye Ubiquitous/CB, (b)Rod Currie/Stone; **788** (t)Warren Faidley/Weatherstock, (c)James N. Westwater: Papilio/CB, (b)Steve Austin: Papilio/CB; **789** (tl)MB, (tr)Chinch Gryniewicz: Ecoscene/CB, (bl)Annie Griffiths Belt/CB, (br)James N. Westwater; **790** Tony Freeman/PE/PQ; **791** (t)Dominic Oldershaw, (b)Mary Kate Denny/PE; **792** (t)file photo, (b)John Evans; **793** (t)KS, (b)Ken Lax; **798** Michell D. Bridwell/PE; **802** David Young-Wolff/PE; **804** Kaz Chiba/PD; **805** Dominic Oldershaw; **806** StudiOhio; **807** MM; **809** (bl)Elaine Shay, (br)Brent Turner/BLT Productions, (others)Mark Steinmetz; **812** Paul Barton/TSM; **815** Davis Barber/PE.

PERIODIC TABLE OF THE ELEMENTS

Columns of elements are called groups. Elements in the same group have similar chemical properties.

Element — Hydrogen

Atomic number — 1

Symbol — H

Atomic mass — 1.008

State of matter

Each element has a block in the periodic table. Within a block, you can find important information about the element.

Rows of elements are called periods. Atomic number increases across a period.

The arrow shows where these elements would fit into the periodic table. They are moved to the bottom of the page to save space.

	1	2	3	4	5	6	7	8	9
1	Hydrogen 1 **H** 1.008								
2	Lithium 3 **Li** 6.941	Beryllium 4 **Be** 9.012							
3	Sodium 11 **Na** 22.990	Magnesium 12 **Mg** 24.305							
4	Potassium 19 **K** 39.098	Calcium 20 **Ca** 40.078	Scandium 21 **Sc** 44.956	Titanium 22 **Ti** 47.88	Vanadium 23 **V** 50.942	Chromium 24 **Cr** 51.996	Manganese 25 **Mn** 54.938	Iron 26 **Fe** 55.847	Cobalt 27 **Co** 58.933
5	Rubidium 37 **Rb** 85.468	Strontium 38 **Sr** 87.62	Yttrium 39 **Y** 88.906	Zirconium 40 **Zr** 91.224	Niobium 41 **Nb** 92.906	Molybdenum 42 **Mo** 95.94	Technetium 43 **Tc** 97.907	Ruthenium 44 **Ru** 101.07	Rhodium 45 **Rh** 102.906
6	Cesium 55 **Cs** 132.905	Barium 56 **Ba** 137.327	Lanthanum 57 **La** 138.906	Hafnium 72 **Hf** 178.49	Tantalum 73 **Ta** 180.948	Tungsten 74 **W** 183.84	Rhenium 75 **Re** 186.207	Osmium 76 **Os** 190.2	Iridium 77 **Ir** 192.22
7	Francium 87 **Fr** 223.020	Radium 88 **Ra** 226.025	Actinium 89 **Ac** 227.028	Rutherfordium 104 **Rf** (261)	Dubnium 105 **Db** (262)	Seaborgium 106 **Sg** (263)	Bohrium 107 **Bh** (262)	Hassium 108 **Hs** (265)	Meitnerium 109 **Mt** (266)

Lanthanide series

Cerium 58 **Ce** 140.115	Praseodymium 59 **Pr** 140.908	Neodymium 60 **Nd** 144.24	Promethium 61 **Pm** 144.913	Samarium 62 **Sm** 150.36

Actinide series

Thorium 90 **Th** 232.038	Protactinium 91 **Pa** 231.036	Uranium 92 **U** 238.029	Neptunium 93 **Np** 237.048	Plutonium 94 **Pu** 244.064